A NEW
DICTIONARY OF QUOTATIONS

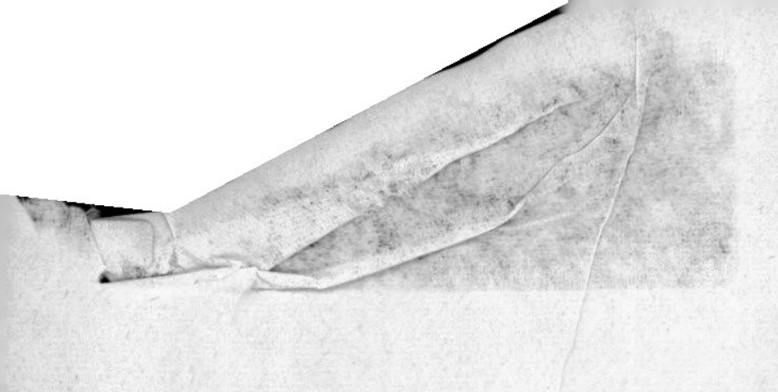

A New DICTIONARY OF QUOTATIONS

ON *HISTORICAL* PRINCIPLES

FROM

ANCIENT AND MODERN SOURCES

Selected and Edited by

H. L. MENCKEN

NEW YORK : ALFRED A. KNOPF : 1962

This is a Borzoi Book, published by Alfred A. Knopf, Inc.

 Manufactured in the United States of America and distributed by Random House, Inc. Published in Canada by Random House of Canada, Limited.

Published April 20, 1942
Reprinted five times
Seventh printing, August 1962

Preface

THIS book is based upon a collection of quotations begun in 1918 or thereabout for my own use. Its purpose was to keep track of sayings that, for one reason or another, interested me and seemed worth remembering, but that, also for one reason or another, were not in the existing quotation-books. The collection grew steadily, helped by the contributions of friends who knew of it, and there arose inevitably the notion that it might be worth printing. To that end, of course, it would be necessary to conduct a more systematic search for material than I had ever undertaken, and to admit some of the common stock of other such works. In March, 1933, I suggested to Charles Angoff, then my assistant on the *American Mercury,* that he join me in this enterprise, and for a couple of years thereafter the two of us proceeded with it. But in 1935 Mr. Angoff found himself unable to give it the time it needed, and so withdrew. Thereafter I continued it on my own, and have since dealt with it unaided. Mr. Angoff's researches were very valuable to the work, and without his diligent collaboration it would have come to nothing, but he is not responsible for its present contents, which represent my own undivided choice.

There are already a number of large and useful dictionaries of quotations in English, and some of them have wide and deserved reputations — for example, John Bartlett's (first published in 1855, and revised and augmented in 1937, for its eleventh edition, by Christopher Morley and Louella D. Everett), Jehiel Keeler Hoyt's (first published in 1881, and revised and enlarged in 1927 by Kate Louise Roberts), and Burton Stevenson's monumental Home Book of Quotations, first brought out in 1934. All these are valuable works, and in my literary scavenging I use them almost every day, but I have nevertheless found room beside them for this collection of my own, and it is now published in the hope that it may be useful also to others. It differs from the three excellent works I have just mentioned, and from all others of their kind, in the following particulars:

1. It is planned on strictly historical principles, with the quotations dated whenever possible. In all cases I have sought to ascer-

tain the first utterer of a saying or an idea, and, save where it has undergone significant changes, have disregarded those who have merely echoed it.

2. It is arranged under many more rubrics than any other such work can show, and that fact, I hope, will facilitate navigation of its contents.

3. Save in a few cases, it gives all authors' names and all titles of works in full, or nearly in full. This practice, I trust, will appeal to students, for it avoids the drudgery of consulting other books.

4. It omits, as much as possible, all mere platitudes, and confines itself to authors who really had something to say, and said it to some effect. The immemorial tags and scraps of wisdom, real and false, have been included, and most of the purple passages that everyone knows, but I have tried to leaven them with better and less hackneyed stuff.

5. Special attention has been given to the proverbs of all peoples, for in them some of the soundest thinking of the human race is embodied, and also some of the most pungent wit.

6. The Biblical quotations are newly chosen, and include many that are not as familiar as they ought to be.

7. In the case of quotations from foreign languages an effort has been made to procure better translations than those commonly encountered, and in every case where it has seemed useful the original text has been given in parentheses.

8. Proper names are included in the general alphabet, with quotations showing the ebb and flow of opinion about men of mark in all fields of serious endeavor.

An effort has been made to attain to the highest possible degree of accuracy in the dating of quotations. In not a few cases, unhappily, exactness has been impossible. In others it has even been impossible to establish authorship. I am in hopes that many of these gaps will be filled in later editions, either by myself (aided by friendly volunteers) or by my successors.

Whenever a foreign work is familiar in English translation, I have used the usual English title; in other cases I have given the original titles. In the case of plays, I have given the date of first performance or the date of first publication, whichever happened to be the earlier. Whenever month and day seemed to be significant I have added them to the year — for example, in extracts from memorable speeches. Sometimes this has been impossible, for the written records are often incomplete, and even Boswell does not always give the precise date of Johnson's sayings. In the case of posthumous publications I have tried to ascertain, as accurately as possible, the date of actual composition, and in all cases of doubt I have followed the opinion of the most trustworthy authorities. In my effort to sort out my quotations as finely as possible, always with the aim of facilitating reference, I have not hesitated to make nice distinctions, *e.g.*, between Ascetic and Asceticism, Thinking and Thoughts. Nor have I hesitated to set up separate rubrics for words virtually identical in meaning, *e.g.*, Doctor–Physician, Freedom–Liberty, if ready reference could be promoted thereby. I assume that persons seeking the author and date of "Who shall decide when doctors disagree?" will look under Doctor, and that those seeking "Physician, heal thyself" will look under Physician. And I have granted the right of every author to choose between, say, Freedom and Liberty, and contented myself with bringing the two schools together by means of cross-references.

I am in hopes that, despite certain obvious inconveniences, this scheme of cross-references will prove to be more workable than the huge indexes which now burden nearly all other such books.[1] In general, they refer to merely auxiliary quotations; the main entries are always under the most obvious rubric. That rubric, whenever possible, is the principal noun or gerund, the thing about which something is said, and I have avoided generalizations as much as possible. "Hindsight is better than foresight" is not indexed under Retrospection or Experience, but under Hindsight, with a cross-reference from Foresight. Adjectives and verbs appear as rubrics very seldom, but in certain cases they have been necessary, and I have not hesitated to indicate by separate rubrics the difference in meaning between such pairs as Wisdom and [the] Wise. In a few cases the accumulation of cross-references at the end of a rubric is unquestionably formidable, and even forbidding — for example, after Devil, Love and Woman. But that is only proof that such themes have been constantly in the thought of mankind since its earliest days, and frequently color its thinking

[1] Stevenson's fills 202 pages of fine print and runs to almost 50,000 entries. Champion, in his "Racial Proverbs," prints *two* indexes on different plans, and speaks in his introduction of the difficulties encountered in making them.

on other subjects. Each entry gathers in all the really important sayings on its subject, and only the curious who enjoy browsing down the byways of thought need go further.

In the case of sayings embodying two or more main themes I have entered them under both or all. For the accommodation of the more familiar antitheses, *e.g.*, Body and Soul, Man and Woman, Husband and Wife, Pleasure and Pain, Truth and Error, I have set up separate rubrics, but the cross-references keep their material in contact with its parts. Such pairs have been common in poetry for many centuries, as readers of the Book of Proverbs well know, and some of the most familiar of all examples of traditional wisdom embody them.

The uses of such a collection as this are obviously not the same for all readers. There are, first, those who seek to determine the precise text of a quotation heard or read, often in garbled form. There are, second, those who want to run down authorship, or date, or both. Third, there are those who desire authority for their arguments, or ornaments for their discourse. Finally, there are those who like to explore the flowery meads of wit and wisdom merely voluptuously, nibbling here and lingering there. I am in hopes that my book will meet in some measure the demands of all four classes. It is aimed, frankly, at readers whose general tastes and ideas approximate my own, and I have proceeded on the assumption that such readers are reasonably numerous, and deserve some service. The Congressman hunting for platitudes to embellish his eulogy upon a fallen colleague will find relatively little to his purpose, and the suburban clergyman in search of fresh texts had better stick to Cruden's Concordance, but the less conventional seeker, I trust, will find plenty to amuse him, and maybe also a certain amount of edification. I have included many authors and books that have been strangers, hitherto, to such collections, and I have made new searches of those already familiar. Some immemorial imbecilities have been added deliberately, on the ground that it is just as interesting to note how foolish men have been as to note how wise they have been. These last, at worst, help toward one end that I have always had in mind — to make the book readable, to give the reader who seeks only entertainment something to content him. There is no reason why a book of quotations should be dull; it has its uses in idleness as well as in study.

IX

A casual glance through the following pages will show how two books dominate the thinking of all persons of English speech. They are, of course, the King James Bible and the plays of Shakespeare. There are more quotations from Shakespeare in this collection than from any other single author, and that will probably be true of all quotation books for centuries to come. I have made no attempt to count the lines, but my guess is that at least ten per cent. of " Hamlet " is here included. There are, again, many, many quotations from such old favorites as Samuel Johnson, Joseph Addison, Alexander Pope, and, to turn from authors to a political sage, Thomas Jefferson — some of them familiar, but a large number of them presented for the first time. I make no apology for leaning heavily on such standbys, for they really had something to say, and said it with vast effect. Relatively few living authors are included, for not many of them save the politicians have said anything worth remembering, but I have given full representation to such exceptions as George Bernard Shaw, and plenty of space to the non-Euclidian sages of the generations preceding our own, *e.g.*, Nietzsche, Huxley, Wilde, W. G. Sumner, and, not least among them, E. W. Howe, and, to go back a bit, G. C. Lichtenberg, Thomas Paine, Leigh Hunt, C. C. Colton and Alexander Smith.

My debt to my predecessors is large and obvious. I have accumulated, in the course of the years, a great many books of quotations, most in English but many in other languages, some of general scope and the others restricted to special fields, and I have made steady use of them. It would be an affectation, in a work so large, to pretend that all of my quotations come direct from the sources, but that is certainly true of the overwhelming majority of them, and the rest have been checked whenever possible. I have depended for my dates upon the best authorities available, and particularly upon the bibliographies in the Cambridge Histories of English and American Literature, the collections of English proverbs by G. L. Apperson and William George Smith, the Annals of English Literature, 1475–1925, published by the Clarendon Press, the Chronological Outlines of American Literature by Selden L. Whitcomb, the Oxford Companion to English Literature by Sir Paul Harvey, and Georg Büchmann's Geflügelte Worte. The admirable Apperson and Smith collections, the first published in 1929 and the second in 1935, have put the study of English proverbs on a new and more scientific basis, and they have since got reinforcement from Selwyn Gurney Champion's large and valuable work on all the world's proverbs, published in 1938. Unhappily, every such study shows a defect that is also visible in the greatest of dictionaries, the colossal Oxford: they must depend principally upon printed sources. Most proverbs, like most words, are much older than their first (detected) appearance in print: all we can do is to trace the record back as far as possible. In many cases that quest reveals the unexpected fact that what has become a proverb originated with a definite author, though sometimes it has undergone verbal changes.

To many private friends I owe long encouragement and much practical aid. Judge Eugene O'Dunne of Baltimore, a diligent collector of literary curiosities, has called my attention to a number of sayings that I would have missed otherwise; Dr. Ola E. Winslow, author of the standard Life of Jonathan Edwards, has gone to great trouble to enrich my collection of early American Theologica; Mr. Bernard De Voto has done the same to help me solve a difficult problem; and the late Dr. Raymond Pearl, of the Johns Hopkins, was generous over twenty years with suggestions from his immensely wide reading. Above all, I am indebted to another friend now dead, Herman Schapiro. He was a linguist of wide scope, and if the translations in this book are measurably better than those commonly encountered the fact is mainly due to his constant interest and unfailing help. My debt to my secretary, Mrs. Rosalind C. Lohrfinck, is endless. The amount of hard work she has put into this volume is almost incredible, and, like "The American Language," it owes more to her, in some ways, than to the compiler.

I am uneasily aware, as I close the intermittent labor of nearly twenty-five years, that there must be many gaps in my collection, and, what is worse, many errors, including false ascriptions and inadvertent invasions of copyright. I rely upon friendly readers and publishers to rectify these blunders. Corrections, suggestions and remonstrances sent to me at 1524 Hollins street, Baltimore, will be received in a properly humble and grateful spirit.

H. L. Mencken

Baltimore, 1942

Acknowledgments

I AM indebted to the kindness of the following for permission to print copyrighted quotations from the authors and books listed after their names:

Allen and Unwin, George — " Zones of the Spirit," by August Strindberg.
American Jewish Committee, The — " The Jews in Nazi Germany."
Armstrong, Joseph — Letters by W. S. Landor.
Aronson, Moses J. — " Everyday Life and the Law," by Gerhart Husserl.
Ballantine, W. G. — " The Logic of Science," by himself.
Bierce, Helen — Ambrose Bierce.
Blackburn, W. H. — A magazine interview.
Boni, Albert and Charles — " The Devil's Dictionary," by Ambrose Bierce; " Studies in Classic American Literature," by D. H. Lawrence.
Brentano's — George Bernard Shaw.
Cabell, James Branch — " Jurgen," by himself.
Cassell & Company — " My Own Way," by Sir Edward Parry.
Clark, Kenneth S. — " Bottoms Up," edited by himself.
Cleghorn, Sarah N. — A quatrain by herself.
Clendening, Logan — " Modern Methods of Treatment," by himself.
Cohen, Felix S. — " Transcendental Nonsense and the Functional Approach," by himself.
Collins, Frank — " Pepigrams and Jingles in Pure Jinglish," by himself.
Columbia University Press, The — " The Pastures of Wonder," by Cassius J. Keyser.
Crowell Company, The Thomas Y. — " The Logic of Science," by W. G. Ballantine.
Day Company, The John — " Poetry and Mathematics," by Scott Buchanan.
DeCasseres, Benjamin — His own works.
Dorrance & Company — Mary Pettibone Poole.
Doubleday, Doran & Company — Joseph Conrad, Rudyard Kipling, Walt Whitman.
Dreiser, Theodore — His own works.
Dutton, E. P. & Company — " Letters and Leadership," " The Literary Life in America," and " America's Coming of Age," by Van Wyck Brooks, all now republished in " Three Essays on America," 1934; " Note-Books," by Samuel Butler.
Ellis, Colin — " Mournful Numbers," by himself.
Empire State Book Company — " Notebooks," by Leonardo da Vinci.
Fabing, Howard — Notes of lectures by Martin Fischer.
Gillilan, Strickland — " The Antiquity of Microbes," by himself.
Haldeman-Julius, E. — " Preaching From the Audience," " Notes for My Biographer," " Sinner Sermons," and " Indignations," by E. W. Howe.

Harper & Brothers — Samuel L. Clemens (Mark Twain); "The Riddle of the Universe," by Ernst Haeckel.

Holt & Company, Henry — "Psychology, Briefer Course," by William James; "Chicago Poems," by Carl Sandburg; "Contemporary Literature," by S. P. Sherman.

Houghton Mifflin Company, The — The Journals of Ralph Waldo Emerson and H. D. Thoreau; the Autobiography of Havelock Ellis; "Rousseau and Romanticism," by Irving Babbitt; "Science and Immortality," by William Osler.

Howe, E. W. — His own works.

Howells, Mildred — "Criticism and Fiction," by William Dean Howells.

Hubbard II, Elbert — "The Roycroft Book of Epigrams," by Elbert Hubbard.

Husserl, Gerhart — "Everyday Life and the Law," by himself.

Jeans, Sir James — "The Mysterious Universe," by himself.

Jones, Edgar DeWitt — Addresses by himself.

Levy, Oscar — F. W. Nietzsche.

Liveright Publishing Corporation — "The Confessions of a Young Man," by George Moore; "The Conquest of Happiness," by Bertram Russell.

Longmans, Green & Company — "The Foundations of Belief," by Arthur James Balfour; "Varieties of Religious Experience," by William James.

Macaulay Company, The — "Sin and Sex," by Robert Briffault.

Macmillan Company, The — "Time and Free Will," by Henri Bergson; "The Intelligent Individual and Society," by P. W. Bridgman; "The Mysterious Universe," by Sir James Jeans; "A Preface to Morals," by Walter Lippmann.

Macmillan Company of Canada, The — Rudyard Kipling.

McBride & Company, Robert M. — James Branch Cabell.

McClurg & Company, A. C. — "Talks of Napoleon at St. Helena," by General Gaspard Gouraud.

McEvoy, J. P. — His own works.

Methodist Book Concern, The — The Methodist Book of Discipline.

Metro Music Company — "L'Internationale," by Eugene Pottier.

Miller, Vaughn — "There Aint Gonna Be No Whiskey," by himself.

Minton, Balch & Company — "The Quest for Certainty," by John Dewey.

Morley, J. Kenfield — "Some Things I Believe," by himself.

Mosby Company, The C. V. — "Modern Methods of Treatment," by Logan Clendening.

Mulligan, Kathleen — "In Kentucky," by James H. Mulligan.

Murphy Company, The John — "The Faith of Our Fathers," by James Cardinal Gibbons.

Neale, Walter — Ambrose Bierce.

Neilson, W. A. — His own works.

Norton, W. W. & Company — "Where is Science Going?" by Max Planck.

Odum, Howard W. — "Rainbow Round My Shoulder" and "Wings on My Feet," by himself.

Oxford University Press, The — "Pages From an Oxford Diary," by Paul

Elmer More; " The Apocryphal New Testament," by Montague Rhodes James.

Paull-Pioneer Music Corporation — " Bottoms Up," edited by Kenneth S. Clark.

Poole, Mary Pettibone — Her own works.

Presser Company, The Theodore — " Old Fogy," by James Huneker.

Ryan, Oswald — A letter by Mr. Justice O. W. Holmes.

Sacher, A. L. — " History of the Jews," by himself.

Schaff, Harrison Hale — " Riders to the Sea," by J. M. Synge; Oscar Wilde.

Scribner's Sons, Charles — W. C. Brownell; " The Love Affairs of a Bibliomaniac," by Eugene Field; " The Life of Reason " and " The Genteel Tradition," by George Santayana.

Shaw, George Bernard — His own works.

Shaw, James Byrnie — " The Unity of Mathematics," by himself.

Townsend, Terry M. — " The Doctor Looks at the Citizen," by himself.

Trustees under the will of Mary Baker Eddy — " Science and Health," by Mary Baker Eddy.

Tucker, Benjamin R. — " Instead of a Book," by himself.

University of Chicago Press, The — " The Origin and History of Hebrew Law," by J. M. P. Smith; the Code of Hammurabi, translated by Daniel D. Luckenbill and Arnold Walther.

Viking Press, The — " The Letters of Sacco and Vanzetti," by Marion Denman Frankfurter and Gardner Jackson; " Absentee Ownership " and " The Nature of Peace," by Thornstein Veblen; " Love and Ethics," by Ellen Key.

Warne & Company, Frederick — " The Talmud," by Dr. Polano.

Watts & Son, A. P. — Rudyard Kipling.

Wood, Ray — " Mother Goose in the Ozarks," by himself.

Yale University Press, The — W. G. Sumner; " The Universe and Life," by H. S. Jennings.

Oxford University Press — "The Apocryphal New Testament," by Montague Rhodes James.

Schall, Harrison Hale — "Tributes to the [illegible]," [illegible] Oscar Wilde.

A NEW
DICTIONARY OF QUOTATIONS

A Dictionary of Quotations

A

Abbot

When anyone receives the name of abbot he ought to rule over his disciples with a double teaching: that is, let him show forth all good and holy things by deeds more than by words.
THE RULE OF ST. BENEDICT, II, *c.* 529

He swears like an abbot, *viz.*, extremely.
RANDLE COTGRAVE: *French-English Dictionary,* 1611

Such as the abbot is, such is the monk.
GIOVANNI TORRIANO: *Italian Proverbs,* 1666

Happy convents, bosom'd deep in vines,
Where slumber abbots purple as their wines.
ALEXANDER POPE: *The Dunciad,* IV, 1742

A spiritual father in enjoyment of a temporal income, attached to an abbey on condition that he read his breviary daily and torment the monks.
VOLTAIRE: *Philosophical Dictionary,* 1764

The abbot hath donn'd his mitre and ring,
His rich dalmatic, and maniple fine;
And the choristers sing, as the lay-brothers bring
To the board a magnificent turkey and chine.
R. H. BARHAM: *The Ingoldsby Legends,* I, 1840 (*Chine*=backbone of meat)

When the abbot has dice in his pocket the convent will play.
J. L. MOTLEY: *The Rise of the Dutch Republic,* I, 1861 (Cited as a Dutch proverb)

The abbot of misrule — in medieval history, the master of the revels; called in Scotland the abbot of unreason.
H. PERCY SMITH: *Glossary of Terms and Phrases,* 1883 (Fr. abbé de liesse)

The husband or fancy man of an abbess.
JOHN S. FARMER: *Slang and Its Analogues,* I, 1890 (*Abbess*=" the keeper of a house of ill-fame ")

There is no worse abbot than one who has been a monk.
SPANISH PROVERB

Abdication

I give this heavy weight from off my head,
And this unwieldy sceptre from my hand,
The pride of kingly sway from out my heart;
With mine own tears I wash away my balm,
With mine own hands I give away my crown,
With mine own tongue deny my sacred state,
With mine own breath release all duteous oaths.
SHAKESPEARE: *Richard II,* IV, *c.* 1596

The Allied Powers having declared that the Emperor Napoleon is the only obstacle to the restoration of peace in Europe, he, faithful to his oath, announces that he is ready to relinquish the throne, leave France, and even to surrender his life, for the good of his country.
NAPOLEON I: *Act of Abdication,* April 4, 1814

To address an abdicated monarch is a nice point of breeding. To give him his lost titles is to mock him; to withhold 'em is to wound him.
CHARLES LAMB: *Letter to Edward Moxon,* Oct. 24, 1831

An act whereby a sovereign attests his sense of the high temperature of the throne.
AMBROSE BIERCE: *The Devil's Dictionary,* 1906

At long last I am able to say a few words of my own. I have never wanted to withhold anything, but until now it has not been constitutionally possible for me to speak. A few hours ago I discharged my last duty as king and emperor, and now that I have been succeeded by my brother, the Duke of York, my first words must be to declare my allegiance to him . . . I now quit altogether public affairs and I lay down my burden . . . God bless you all! God save the king!
EDWARD VIII: Radio broadcast, Dec. 11, 1936

Abide

Abide with me! Fast falls the eventide;
The darkness deepens; Lord, with me abide!
When other helpers fail, and comforts flee,
Help of the helpless, oh, abide with me!
H. F. LYTE: *Abide With Me,* 1820 (The tune is by W. H. MONK, 1861)

Ability

They are able because they think they are able.
VIRGIL: *Aeneid,* V, 19 B.C.

Unto one he gave five talents, to another two, and to another one; to every man according to his several ability.
MATTHEW XXV, 15, *c.* 75

It is a great ability to be able to conceal one's ability.
LA ROCHEFOUCAULD: *Maxims,* 1665

Gentility without ability is worse than plain beggary.
JOHN RAY: *English Proverbs,* 1670

One man is more nimble and strong, and more patient of labor than another.
WILLIAM PETTY: *Political Arithmetic,* I, *c.* 1677

The heart to conceive, the understanding to direct, or the hand to execute.

LETTERS OF JUNIUS, March 19, 1770 (*Cf.* EDWARD GIBBON: *The Decline and Fall of the Roman Empire,* VI, 1788: "In every deed of mischief [Andronicus Comnenus] had a heart to resolve, a head to contrive, and a hand to execute")

The winds and waves are always on the side of the ablest navigators.
EDWARD GIBBON: *The Decline and Fall of the Roman Empire,* IV, 1788

Men of great abilities are generally of a large and vigorous animal nature.
HENRY TAYLOR: *The Statesman,* 1836

Every man who can be a first-rate something — as every man can be who is a man at all — has no right to be a fifth-rate something; for a fifth-rate something is no better than a first-rate nothing.
J. G. HOLLAND: *Plain Talks on Familiar Subjects,* I, 1865

In the last analysis ability is commonly found to consist mainly in a high degree of solemnity.
AMBROSE BIERCE: *The Devil's Dictionary,* 1906

Behind an able man there are always other able men. CHINESE PROVERB

[*See also* Capacity, Expert, Health, Instinct, Modesty, Skill, Talent.

Abolition

Abolitionism proposes to destroy the right and extinguish the principle of self-government for which our forefathers waged a seven years' bloody war, and upon which our whole system of free government is founded.
STEPHEN A. DOUGLAS: Speech in the Senate, March 3, 1854

[*See also* Emancipation, Institution, Slavery, States' Rights.

Abolitionist

I hear you have Abolitionists here. We have a few in Illinois, but we shot one the other day.
ABRAHAM LINCOLN: Speech at Worcester, Mass., 1848

The Abolitionist . . . must see that he has neither the right or power of operating except by moral means and suasion, and . . . that the reasons he gives for interference in what he has no concern holds good for every kind of interference with our neighbors when we disapprove their conduct.
ROBERT E. LEE: *Letter to his wife,* Dec. 27, 1856

Abolitionists . . . have for long years been sowing dragons' teeth, and have finally got a crop of armed men.
ROBERT TOOMBS: Speech in the Senate, Jan. 7, 1861

[*See also* Emancipation, Slavery.

Abomination

These six things doth the Lord hate: yea, seven are an abomination unto him: A proud look, a lying tongue, and hands that shed innocent blood. An heart that deviseth wicked imaginations, feet that be swift in running to mischief, a false witness that speaketh lies, and he that soweth discord among brethren.
PROVERBS VI, 16–19, *c.* 350 B.C.

The abomination that maketh desolate.
DANIEL XI, 31, *c.* 165 B.C. (*Cf.* XII, 11; also MARK XIII, 14, *post, c.* 70)

The abomination of desolation.
MARK XIII, 14, *c.* 70 (Quoted from DANIEL XI, 31, *ante, c.* 165 B.C.; cf. also MATTHEW XXIV, 15, *c.* 75)

I find seven abominations in my heart: (1) Inclinings to unbelief. (2) Suddenly to forget the love and mercy that Christ manifesteth. (3) A leaning to the works of the law. (4) Wanderings and coldness in prayer. (5) To forget to watch for that I pray for. (6) Apt to murmur because I have no more, and yet ready to abuse what I have. (7) I can do none of those things which God commands me, but my corruptions will thrust in themselves. "When I would do good, evil is present with me."
JOHN BUNYAN: *Grace Abounding to the Chief of Sinners,* 1666

[*See also* Lying.

Aborigine

[*See* Indian.

Abortion

If a woman of her own accord drops that which is in her, they shall crucify her and not bury her. THE ASSYRIAN CODE, *c.* 2000 B.C.

If a maid with child says to her lover, "I have conceived by thee," and he says, "Go, then, to the old woman and ask her for a drug, that thou mayest miscarry," and the old woman gives her some *banga* or *shaeta,* that kills in the womb, then the sin is on the head of all three.
THE ZEND-AVESTA (*The Vendidad,* XV), *c.* 550 B.C.

I will not give to a woman an instrument to procure abortion.
The Hippocratic Oath, taken by medical students on receiving their degrees, and supposed to have been drawn by Hippocrates, *c.* 400 B.C.

Prevention of birth is a precipitation of murder. He also is a man who is about to be one.
TERTULLIAN: *Apologeticus,* 197

Witches . . . make women abortive.
ROBERT BURTON: *The Anatomy of Melancholy,* I, 1621

[Abortion] was probably regarded by the average Roman of the later days of paganism

much as an Englishman of the last century regarded convivial excesses, as certainly wrong, but so venial as scarcely to deserve censure.
W. E. H. LECKY: *History of European Morals*, II, 1869

It cannot be taught safely in Catholic schools that it is lawful to perform any operation which directly destroys either the unborn child or the mother.
Decree of the Tribunal of the Holy Office, May 28, 1884

However we may pity the mother whose health and even life is imperiled by the performance of her natural duty, there yet remains no sufficient reason for condoning the direct murder of the innocent.
POPE PIUS XI: *Casti connubii*, Dec. 31, 1930

[*See also* Birth-control.

Abraham (c. 1550 B.C.?)

These are the days of the years of Abraham's life which he lived, a hundred threescore and fifteen years.
GENESIS XXV, 7, *c.* 700 B.C.

Abraham is dead. JOHN VIII, 52, *c.* 115

Abraham was a giant of giants; his height was that of seventy-four men. His food, his drink, his strength were in proportion.
THE TALMUD (*Bechoroth*), *c.* 200

Abraham was neither a Jew nor a Christian, but he was of the true religion, one resigned unto God, and was not of the number of the idolaters. THE KORAN, III, *c.* 625

[*See also* Bosom.

Absence

Achilles absent was still Achilles.
HOMER: *The Iliad*, XXII, *c.* 800 B.C.

The Lord watch between me and thee when we are absent from one another.
GENESIS XXXI, 49, *c.* 700 B.C.

Speak no evil of an absent friend. (Non male loquare absenti amico.)
PLAUTUS: *Trinummus*, IV, *c.* 190 B.C.

A short absence is safest.
OVID: *Ars amatoria*, II, *c.* 2 B.C.

Absent in body, but present in spirit.
I CORINTHIANS V, 3, *c.* 55

The absent have a ringing in the ears when they are talked about.
PLINY THE ELDER: *Natural History*, XXVIII, *c.* 79

Out of sight, out of mind.
ENGLISH PROVERB, traced by Apperson to *c.* 1270

Far from eye, far from heart.
THE PROVERBS OF HENDYNG, *c.* 1300

The absent are always in the wrong.
ENGLISH PROVERB, traced by Smith to the XV century

Seldom seen, soon forgotten.
RICHARD HILLES: *Commonplace book*, *c.* 1535

The farther off, the more desired; thus lovers tie their knot.
HENRY HOWARD (EARL OF SURREY): *The Faithful Lover*, 1557

Absence is death, or worse, to them that love.
PHILIP SIDNEY: *A Country Song*, *c.* 1580

Absence doth nurse the fire,
Which starves and feeds desire
With sweet delays.
FULKE GREVILLE (LORD BROOKE): *Absence and Presence*, *c.* 1586

I dote on his very absence.
SHAKESPEARE: *The Merchant of Venice*, I, *c.* 1597

Though absent, present in desires they be;
Our soul much further than our eyes can see.
MICHAEL DRAYTON: *The Barons' Wars*, 1603

How like a Winter hath my absence been
From thee, the pleasure of the fleeting year!
What freezings have I felt, what dark days seen!
What old December bareness everywhere!
SHAKESPEARE: *Sonnets*, XCVII, 1609

I do perceive that the old proverb be not always true, for I do find that the absence of my Nath. doth breed in me the most continual remembrance of him.
ANNE, LADY BACON: *Letter to Jane Cornwallis*, 1613

Absence, not long enough to root out quite
All love, increases love at second sight.
THOMAS MAY: *Henry II*, III, 1633

When what is lov'd is present, love doth spring;
But being absent, love lies languishing.
ROBERT HERRICK: *Hesperides*, 1648

Absence diminishes moderate passions and increases great ones, as the wind extinguishes tapers and adds fury to fire.
LA ROCHEFOUCAULD: *Maxims*, 1665

It was not kind
To leave me, like a turtle, here alone,
To droop and mourn the absence of my mate.
THOMAS OTWAY: *The Orphan*, II, 1680

Our hours in love have wings; in absence, crutches. COLLEY CIBBER: *Xerxes*, IV, 1699

They are aye good that are away.
JAMES KELLY: *Complete Collection of Scottish Proverbs*, 1721

Absence sharpens love; presence strengthens it.
THOMAS FULLER: *Gnomologia*, 1732

He that fears you present will hate you absent.
IBID.

Every degree of separation is a degree of alienation. BENJAMIN WHICHCOTE: *Moral and Religious Aphorisms,* 1753

I seek for one as fair and gay,
But find none to remind me;
How blest the hours pass'd away
With the girl I left behind me.
Anon.: *The Girl I Left Behind Me,* 1759

The attraction of love, I find, is in an inverse proportion to the attraction of the Newtonian philosophy. In the system of Sir Isaac, the nearer objects were to one another, the stronger was the attractive force.
ROBERT BURNS: *Letter to Mrs. McLehose,* Feb., 1788

Absence and salt water wash away love.
ENGLISH PROVERB, not recorded before the XIX century

Wives in their husbands' absences grow subtler,
And daughters sometimes run off with the butler. BYRON: *Don Juan,* III, 1821

The pain without the peace of death.
THOMAS CAMPBELL: *Absence,* 1824

Only two months since you stood here!
Two shortest months! Then tell me why
Voices are harsher than they were,
And tears are longer ere they dry.
W. S. LANDOR: *Absence,* 1846

Absence makes the heart grow fonder.
T. H. BAYLY: *Isle of Beauty,* 1850

Conspicuous by its absence.
LORD JOHN RUSSELL: Address to the electors of London, April 6, 1859

Absence and death are the same — only that in death there is no suffering.
W. S. LANDOR: *Letter to Robert Browning,* c. 1862

A woman absent is a woman dead.
AMBROSE BIERCE: *The Devil's Dictionary,* 1906

Absence is the dark-room in which lovers develop negatives. Author unidentified

He who praises in *præsentia*
And abuses in *absentia,*
May he have the *pestilentia!*
GERMAN RHYME

The absent one will not be the heir.
IRISH PROVERB

Absence is the enemy of love.
ITALIAN PROVERB

The absent are further away every day.
JAPANESE PROVERB

The absent are as good as dead.
LATIN PROVERB

His absence is gude company.
SCOTTISH SAYING

The absent and the dead have no friends.
SPANISH PROVERB

The cure for love is absence. IBID.

[*See also* Desire, Love, Parting.

Absent-minded

I was like the countryman who looked for his donkey while mounted on its back.
CERVANTES: *Don Quixote,* II, 1615

I distinguish a man who is absent because he thinks of something else from one who is absent because he thinks of nothing at all.
EUSTACE BUDGELL: *The Spectator,* May 29, 1711

You gazed at the moon and fell in the gutter.
THOMAS FULLER: *Gnomologia,* 1732

I would rather be in company with a dead man than with an absent one; for if the dead man gives me no pleasure, at least he shows me no contempt; whereas the absent man, silently indeed, but very plainly, tells me that he does not think me worth his attention.
LORD CHESTERFIELD: *Letter to his son,* Sept. 22, 1749

The absent-minded beggar.
RUDYARD KIPLING: Title of a poem, 1899

Absolute

Objection, evasion, distrust and irony are signs of health. Everything absolute belongs to pathology.
F. W. NIETZSCHE: *Beyond Good and Evil,* 1886

Absolution

Though your sins be as scarlet, they shall be as white as snow; though they be red like crimson, they shall be as wool.
ISAIAH I, 18, *c.* 700 B.C.

Wash me, and I shall be whiter than snow.
PSALMS LI, 7, *c.* 150 B.C.

I will give unto thee the keys of the kingdom of heaven: and whatsoever thou shalt bind on earth shall be bound in heaven; and whatsoever thou shalt loose on earth shall be loosed in heaven.
MATTHEW XVI, 19, *c.* 75

Whosesoever sins ye remit, they are remitted unto them; and whosesoever sins ye retain, they are retained. JOHN XX, 23, *c.* 115

He who confesses his sins freely receives pardon from the priest by virtue of the grace of Christ.
ST. ATHANASIUS: *Contra Novatiani, c.* 350

Christ has given to his priests a power he would not give to his angels, for has he not said to them, Whatsoever thou shalt bind on earth . . .
ST. JOHN CHRYSOSTOM: *De sacerdotio, c.* 390 (The quotation is from MATTHEW XVI, 19, *ante, c.* 75)

I absolve you from your sins in the name of the Father, and of the Son, and of the Holy Ghost. (Ego te absolvo a peccatis tuis in nomine Patris, et Filii, et Spiritus Sancti.)
Formula of absolution in the Roman Catholic Church, probably dating in its present form from the XIV century (The Latin is always used)

He who swears a rash or trifling oath, if he repents, and perceives his grief will be very great should he keep his oath; or anything should happen which he did not think of when he swore, which will occasion his repentance of it, let him consult one learned man, or three of the vulgar, and they may free him from his oath.
MAIMONIDES: *The Guide of the Perplexed,* 1190

The Lord instituted the Sacrament of Penance when, on being raised from the dead, He breathed upon His disciples, saying, Whose-soever sins ye remit . . .
DECREES OF THE COUNCIL OF TRENT, XIV, 1564 (The quotation is from JOHN XX, 23, *ante, c.* 115)

Absolution is not to be refused to such as continue in the proximate occasions of sin, if they are so situated that they cannot give them up without becoming the common talk of the world, or subjecting themselves to personal inconvenience.
ANTONIO ESCOBAR: *Summula casuum conscientiae,* I, 1627

Haste, holy friar,
Haste, ere the sinner shall expire!
Of all this guilt let him be shriven,
And smooth his path from earth to Heaven!
WALTER SCOTT: *The Lay of the Last Minstrel,* V, 1805

Sin undetected is sin absolved.
Author unidentified

[*See also* Confession, Penance, Sin.

Absolutism

[*See* Autocracy, Despotism, King, Government, Monarchy, Morality, Sovereignty, Tyranny, Tyrant.

Abstemiousness

He wrongs not an old man that steals his supper from him.
GEORGE HERBERT: *Outlandish Proverbs,* 1640

To lengthen thy life, lessen thy meals.
BENJAMIN FRANKLIN: *Poor Richard's Almanac,* 1733

Who eats of but one dish never needs a physician.
ITALIAN PROVERB

Short supper; long life.
SERBIAN PROVERB

[*See also* Abstinence, Ascetic, Diet, Eating, Temperance.

Abstinence

On the Day of Atonement it is forbidden to eat or to drink, to wash, to anoint one's self, or to fasten the shoes. Whoever eats food to the size of a large date, or drinks as much as a mouthful, is guilty.
THE TALMUD (*Yomah,* VIII), *c.* 200

Total abstinence is easier than perfect moderation.
ST. AUGUSTINE: *On the Good of Marriage, c.* 401

Abstinence is whereby a man refraineth from anything which he may lawfully take.
THOMAS ELYOT: *The Governour,* III, 1531

Against diseases here the strongest fence
Is the defensive virtue, abstinence.
ROBERT HERRICK: *Hesperides,* 1648

Constantly practise abstinence and temperance, so that you may be as wakeful after eating as before.
E. L. GRUBER: *Rules for the Examination of Our Daily Lives,* 1715

I have noticed, walking about the country, that the children seem to eat much less than they require: it is hard to imagine so immoderate a passion for abstinence.
VOLTAIRE: *Letter to M. de Bastide,* 1760

[*See also* Abstemiousness, Breakfast, Capital, Diet, Eating, Fasting, Teetotaler, Temperance.

Absurd

[*See* Belief, Jest, Joke, Philosopher, Ridiculous.

Abundance

Abundance kills more than hunger.
GERMAN PROVERB

Abuse [= berate]

Thine is an oyster knife that hacks and hews —
The rage but not the talent to abuse.
MARY WORTLEY MONTAGU: *Verses Addressed to an Imitator of Horace, c.* 1720

The difference between coarse and refined abuse is as the difference between being bruised by a club, and wounded by a poisoned arrow.
SAMUEL JOHNSON: *Boswell's Life,* June 11, 1784

When certain persons abuse us, let us ask ourselves what description of character it is that they admire; we shall often find this is a very consolatory question.
C. C. COLTON: *Lacon,* 1820

What you can't have, abuse.
ITALIAN PROVERB

[*See also* Criticism, Friend, Objurgation.

Abuse [=misuse]

There is nothing but through the malice of man may be abused.
JOHN LYLY: *Euphues,* 1579

The abuse of a thing is no argument against the use of it.

JEREMY COLLIER: *A Short View of the Immorality and Profaneness of the English Stage,* intro., 1698

Accent

The accent of a man's native country dwells in his mind and in his heart as well as in his speech.

LA ROCHEFOUCAULD: *Maxims,* 1665

Accent is the soul of talk: it gives it feeling and verity. J.-J. ROUSSEAU: *Émile,* I, 1762

Accent is a kind of chanting; all men have accent of their own, — though they only notice that of others.

THOMAS CARLYLE: *Heroes and Hero-Worship,* III, 1840 (Lecture in London, May 12)

[*See also* Actor, Language, Speech.

Accessory

We may be accessory to another's sin by counsel, by command, by consent, by concealment, by provoking, by praise, by partaking, by silence, by defence.

JOHN MCCAFFREY: *A Catechism of Christian Doctrine for General Use,* 1866

An accessory follows the nature of his principal. (Accesorius sequitur naturam sui principalis.) LEGAL MAXIM

[*See also* Accomplice.

Accident

I spake of most disastrous chances,
Of moving accidents by flood and field.

SHAKESPEARE: *Othello,* I, *c.* 1604

Nothing under the sun is ever accidental.

G. E. LESSING: *Emilia Galotti,* IV, 1772

The accident of an accident.

LORD THURLOW: Speech in the House of Lords, 1769 (Thurlow used the phrase to designate noble birth)

A happy accident.

THOMAS MIDDLETON: *No Wit, No Help, Like a Woman's,* II, *c.* 1625 (The most familiar embodiment of the phrase is in OLIVER GOLDSMITH: *The Vicar of Wakefield,* XIX, 1766: "To what happy accident is it that we owe so unexpected a visit?")

A chapter of accidents.

LORD CHESTERFIELD: *Letter to his son,* Feb. 16, 1753

Accidents will occur in the best regulated families.

CHARLES DICKENS: *David Copperfield,* XXVIII, 1849

An accident is an event happening unexpectedly and without fault; if there is any fault, there is liability.

T. M. COOLEY: *The Law of Torts,* 1879

An inevitable occurrence due to the action of immutable natural laws.

AMBROSE BIERCE: *The Devil's Dictionary,* 1906

[*See also* Cause and Effect, Chance, Danger, War.

Accomplice

One associated with another in a crime, having guilty knowledge and complicity, as an attorney who defends a criminal, knowing him guilty.

AMBROSE BIERCE: *The Devil's Dictionary,* 1906

[*See also* Accessory.

Accounts

Keeping accounts is of no use when a man is spending his own money. You won't eat less beef today because you have written down what it cost yesterday.

SAMUEL JOHNSON: *Boswell's Life,* 1783

Accursed

[*See* Hanging.

Accusation

Let your accusations be few in number, even if they be just.

POPE XYSTUS I: *The Ring, c.* 120

In all criminal proceedings, the accused shall enjoy the right . . . to be informed of the nature and cause of the accusations, [and] to be confronted with the witnesses against him.

CONSTITUTION OF THE UNITED STATES, Amendment VI, Dec. 15, 1791

The breath
Of accusation kills an innocent name,
And leaves for lame acquittal the poor life,
Which is a mask without it.

P. B. SHELLEY: *The Cenci,* IV, 1819

I accuse. (J'accuse.)

ÉMILE ZOLA: Open letter to President Félix Faure, on the Dreyfus case, Jan. 13, 1898 (Each paragraph began with these words)

[*See also* Excuse, Guilt, Scandal, Slander.

Ache

[*See* Void.

Achievement

Report followeth not all goodness, except difficult and rarity be joined thereto.

MICHEL DE MONTAIGNE: *Essays,* III, 1588

How my achievements mock me!

SHAKESPEARE: *Troilus and Cressida,* IV, *c.* 1601

So much one man can do that does both act and know.
ANDREW MARVELL: *Horatian Ode Upon Cromwell's Return From Ireland,* 1650

The death of endeavor and the birth of disgust.
AMBROSE BIERCE: *The Devil's Dictionary,* 1906

No man has lived to much purpose unless he has built a house, begotten a son, or written a book. ITALIAN PROVERB

[*See also* Action, Doing, Success.

Achilles

[*See* Absence, Agamemnon, Siren.

Acorn

[*See* Bread, Oak.

Acquaintance

People never know each other until they have eaten a certain amount of salt together.
ARISTOTLE: *The Nicomachean Ethics,* VIII, *c.* 340 B.C. (Cited as a proverb)

What makes us like new acquaintances is not so much any weariness of our old ones, or the pleasure of change, as disgust at not being sufficiently admired by those who know us too well, and the hope of being more so by those who do not know so much of us.
LA ROCHEFOUCAULD: *Maxims,* 1665

Have but few friends, though much acquaintance.
JOHN RAY: *English Proverbs,* 1670

'Tis a lamentable thing that one has not the liberty of choosing one's acquaintance as one does one's clothes.
WILLIAM CONGREVE: *The Way of the World,* III, 1700

Sudden acquaintance brings repentance.
THOMAS FULLER: *Gnomologia,* 1732

Should auld acquaintance be forgot,
And never brought to min'?
Should auld acquaintance be forgot,
And days o' lang syne?
ROBERT BURNS: *Auld Lang Syne,* 1788 (Based on an old Scotch song, and first found in a letter to Mrs. Dunlop, Dec. 17)

If a man is worth knowing at all, he is worth knowing well.
ALEXANDER SMITH: *Dreamthorp,* 1863

A person whom we know well enough to borrow from, but not well enough to lend to.
AMBROSE BIERCE: *The Devil's Dictionary,* 1906

A wise man knows everything; a shrewd one, everybody. Author unidentified

[*See also* Friend, Friendship.

Acrobat

A good acrobat is always graceful, though grace is never his object; he is graceful because he does what he has to do in the best way in which it can be done — graceful because he is natural.
OSCAR WILDE: *London Models,* 1889 (English Illustrated Magazine, Jan.)

Act

[*See* Intention.

Acting

Speak the speech, I pray you, as I pronounced it to you, trippingly on the tongue; but if you mouth it, as many of your players do, I had as lief the town-crier spoke my lines. Nor do not saw the air too much with your hand, but use all gently; for in the very torrent, tempest, and, as I may say, the whirlwind of passion, you must acquire and beget a temperance that may give it smoothness. SHAKESPEARE: *Hamlet,* III, *c.* 1601

The most difficult character in comedy is that of a fool, and he must be no simpleton who plays the part.
CERVANTES: *Don Quixote,* I, 1605

The glory of the scenic art is to personate passion, and the turns of passion; and the more coarse and palpable the passion is, the more hold upon the eyes and ears of the spectators the performer obviously possesses. For this reason, scolding scenes, scenes where two persons talk themselves into a fit of fury, and then in a surprising manner talk themselves out of it again, have always been the most popular upon our stage.
CHARLES LAMB: *On the Tragedies of Shakespeare,* 1811 (The Reflector, IV)

It would create a kind of loathing to see me act Hamlet.
CHARLES LAMB: *Letter to William Ayrton,* May 17, 1817

The market for this kind of talent must always be understocked, because very few of those who are really qualified to gain theatrical fame will condescend to start for it.
C. C. COLTON: *Lacon,* 1820

[*See also* Actor, Actress, Stage, Theatre.

Action

We must not stint
Our necessary actions in the fear
To cope malicious censurers.
SHAKESPEARE and JOHN FLETCHER: *Henry VIII,* I, 1613

However brilliant an action, it should not be esteemed great unless the result of a great motive.
LA ROCHEFOUCAULD: *Maxims,* 1665

Every action done in company ought to be with some sign of respect to those that are present.
GEORGE WASHINGTON: *Early copy-book,* before 1748

I plow, but I do not write about plowing.

VOLTAIRE: *Letter to an unknown correspondent*, Jan. 5, 1759

It seems to me that man is made to act rather than to know: the principles of things escape our most persevering researches.

FREDERICK THE GREAT: *Letter to J. L. D'Alembert*, Sept. 30, 1783

Action is transitory, a step, a blow,
The motion of a muscle — this way or that.

WILLIAM WORDSWORTH: *The Borderers*, III, 1796

We do not act because we know, but we know because we are called upon to act: the practical reason is the root of all reason.

J. G. FICHTE: *Die Bestimmung des Menschen*, III, 1800

Actions are our epochs.

BYRON: *Manfred*, I, 1817

Every natural action is graceful.

R. W. EMERSON: *Nature*, 1836

Trust no future, howe'er pleasant;
Let the dead past bury its dead;
Act — act in the living present,
Heart within, the God o'erhead.

H. W. LONGFELLOW: *A Psalm of Life*, 1839

Action is only coarsened thought — thought become concrete, obscure, and unconscious.

H. F. AMIEL: *Journal*, Dec. 30, 1850

Action may not always bring happiness; but there is no happiness without action.

BENJAMIN DISRAELI: *Lothair*, III, 1870

All the beautiful sentiments in the world weigh less than a single lovely action.

J. R. LOWELL: *Among My Books*, 1870

[*See also* Achievement, Cause and Effect, Chance, Doing, Done, Emotion, Law, Morality, Motive, Talk.

Activity

[*See* Joy.

Act of God

An act of God does injury to no one. (Actus Dei nemini facit injuriam.) LEGAL MAXIM

Actor

Beggars, actors, buffoons, and all that sort. (Mendici, mimæ, balatrones, hoc genus omne.) HORACE: *Satires*, I, *c.* 25 B.C.

No man, being forbidden to do so, shall converse with the wife of another man. But this shall not apply to the wives of actors.

THE CODE OF MANU, VIII, *c.* 100

Even those magistrates who abet the stage discountenance the players. They stigmatize their characters and cramp their freedom. The whole tribe of them is thrown out of all honor and privilege.

TERTULLIAN: *De spectaculis*, *c.* 200

It shall not be lawful for any woman who is either in full communion or a probationer for baptism to marry or entertain any comedians or actors; whoever takes this liberty shall be excommunicated.

Decree of the Council of Illiberis in Spain, 305

What shall I say of the mimes who make a public profession of corruption? They teach men the tricks of adultery by representing them on the stage, and by pretence train to reality. LACTANTIUS: *Divinæ institutiones*, VI, *c.* 310

Concerning players, we have thought fit to excommunicate them so long as they continue to act. Decree of the First Council of Arles, 314

A native of Curubis, who had been an actor, was made whole in his baptism, not only from paralysis, but also from a deformity of his privy parts; and came up from the fountain of regeneration free of both troubles.

ST. AUGUSTINE: *The City of God*, XXII, 427

All bearwards, common players of interludes, counterfeit Egyptians, etc., shall be taken, adjudged and deemed rogues, vagabonds and sturdy beggars.

ACT OF PARLIAMENT, 1597

Oh! it offends me to the soul to see a robustious periwigpated fellow tear a passion to tatters, to very rags, to split the ears of the groundlings.

SHAKESPEARE: *Hamlet*, III, *c.* 1601

There be players that I have seen play, and heard others praise, and that highly, not to speak it profanely, that neither have the accent of Christian, pagan, nor man, have so strutted and bellowed, that I have thought some of nature's journeymen had made men, and not made them well, they imitated humanity so abominably. IBID.

A strutting player whose conceit lies in his hamstring.

SHAKESPEARE: *Troilus and Cressida*, I, *c.* 1601

All stage-players and players of interludes and common plays are hereby declared to be, and are, and shall be taken to be rogues, . . . whether they be wanderers or no, and notwithstanding any license whatsoever from the king or any person or persons to that purpose.

ORDINANCE OF PARLIAMENT, Feb. 9, 1647

The whole world acts the actor. (Totus mundus agit histrionem.)

MOTTO ON THE PROSCENIUM ARCH OF DRURY LANE THEATRE, LONDON, *c.* 1674

As for the case of players both men and women, we expressly forbid all our rectors, pastors and confessors to admit them to the sacraments unless they shall repent them of their crime, make proof of their reformation, renounce their business, and retrieve the scandal they have given.
GUY DE SEVE DE ROCHE CHOUART, BISHOP OF ARRAS: *Pastoral Letter,* Dec. 4, 1695

The players should be generally discouraged. They have no relish of modesty, nor any scruples upon the quality of the treat. The grossest dish, when 'twill down, is as ready as the best. To say money is their business and they must live is the plea of pickpockets and highwaymen.
JEREMY COLLIER: *A Short View of the Immorality and Profaneness of the English Stage,* intro., 1698

Peel'd, patch'd, and piebald, linsey-woolsey brothers,
Grave mummers! sleeveless some and shirtless others.
ALEXANDER POPE: *The Dunciad,* III, 1728

If he excels on the stage, and is irreproachable in his personal morals and behavior, his profession is so far from being an impediment that it will be oftener a just reason for his being receiv'd among people of condition with favor, and sometimes with a more social distinction than the best, though more profitable, trade he might have follow'd could have recommended him to.
COLLEY CIBBER: *Apology For His Life,* III, 1740

He speaks all his words distinctly, half as loud again as the other. Anybody may see he is an actor.
HENRY FIELDING: *Tom Jones,* XVI, 1749

Be a little upon your guard: remember, he is an actor.
HORACE WALPOLE: *Letter to Horace Mann,* Sept. 1, 1763 (Referring to David Garrick)

On the stage he was natural, simple, affecting;
'Twas only that when he was off he was acting.
OLIVER GOLDSMITH: *Retaliation,* 1774 (Referring to Garrick)

Players, sir! I look upon them as no better than creatures set upon tables and joint stools to make faces and produce laughter, like dancing dogs.
SAMUEL JOHNSON: *Boswell's Life,* 1775

The exorbitant rewards of players, opera-singers, opera-dancers, &c. are founded upon two principles: the rarity and beauty of the talents, and the discredit of employing them in this manner.
ADAM SMITH: *The Wealth of Nations,* I, 1776

When the actor sinks to rest,
And the turf lies upon his breast,
A poor traditionary fame
Is all that's left to grace his name.
WILLIAM COMBE: *Dr. Syntax in Search of the Picturesque,* XXIV, 1809

Sad happy race! soon raised and soon depressed,
Your days all pass'd in jeopardy and jest;
Poor without prudence, with afflictions vain,
Not warn'd by misery, not enrich'd by gain;
Whom justice, pitying, chides from place to place,
A wandering, careless, wretched, merry race.
GEORGE CRABBE: *The Borough,* XI, 1810

There is no class of society whom so many persons regard with affection as actors.
WILLIAM HAZLITT: *The Round Table,* II, 1817

Actors are a nuisance in the earth, the very offal of society.
TIMOTHY DWIGHT: *An Essay on the Stage,* 1824

I have seen no men in life loving their profession so much as painters, except, perhaps, actors, who, when not engaged themselves, always go to the play.
W. M. THACKERAY: *The Adventures of Philip,* I, 1862

People generally overrate a fine actor's genius, and underrate his trained skill. They are apt to credit him with a power of intellectual conception and poetic creation to which he has really a very slight claim, and fail to recognize all the difficulties which his artistic training has enabled him to master.
G. H. LEWES: *On Actors and the Art of Acting,* 1875

An actor is a sculptor who carves in snow.
Ascribed variously to LAWRENCE BARRETT (1838–91) and EDWIN BOOTH (1833–93)

[*See also* Acting, Actress, Drama, Opera, Physician, Play (=drama), Player, Stage, Theatre.

Actress

The life of youth and beauty is too short for the bringing an actress to her perfection.
COLLEY CIBBER: *Apology For His Life,* XVI, 1740

To play Rosalind a woman must have had more than one lover, and if she has been made to wait in the rain and has been beaten she will have done a great deal to qualify herself for the part.
GEORGE MOORE: *Confessions of a Young Man,* IX, 1888

Adage

Boned wisdom for weak teeth.
AMBROSE BIERCE: *The Devil's Dictionary,* 1906

[*See also* Aphorism, Maxim, Proverb.

Adam (c. 4004 B.C.?)

God, in the beginning, created one man only in order to prevent heretics saying that there are other gods in Heaven.
THE TALMUD (*Sanhedrin*), *c.* 200

Divine educator; first inventor of science and literature. (Adam, divinitus edoctus, primus scientiarum et literarum inventor.)
INSCRIPTION UPON A PORTRAIT OF ADAM IN THE VATICAN, *c.* 1550

In what eternal, unstirring paralysis, and deadly, hopeless trance, yet lies antique Adam who died sixty round centuries ago?
HERMAN MELVILLE: *Moby Dick,* VII, 1851

Adam ate the apple, and our teeth still ache.
HUNGARIAN PROVERB

[*See also* Death, Microbe.

Adam and Eve (c. 4004 B.C.?)

For contemplation he and valor form'd,
For softness she and sweet attractive grace;
He for God only, she for God in him.
JOHN MILTON: *Paradise Lost,* IV, 1667

All other men, being born of woman, have a navel, by reason of the umbilical vessels inserted into it, which from the placenta carry nourishment to children in the womb of their mothers; but it could not be so with our first parents. It cannot be believed that God gave them navels which would have been altogether useless.
RICHARD CUMBERLAND: *De legibus naturae,* I, 1672

When Eve upon the first of men
The apple pressed with specious cant,
Oh! what a thousand pities then
That Adam was not adamant.
THOMAS HOOD: *Adam and Eve, c.* 1840

Adam and Eve had many advantages, but the principal one was that they escaped teething.
S. L. CLEMENS (MARK TWAIN): *Pudd'nhead Wilson,* IV, 1894

Madam, I'm Adam.
Author unidentified (A palindrome which reads the same backward as forward)

Whilst Adam slept, Eve from his side arose:
Strange his first sleep would be his last repose.
Author unidentified

Eve always seems nearer to us than Adam.
CROATIAN PROVERB

What could Adam have done to God that made Him put Eve in the garden?
POLISH PROVERB

[*See also* Gentleman, Persian Language.

Adamant

They made their hearts as an adamant stone.
ZECHARIAH VII, 12, *c.* 520 B.C.

Adam, Old

O Merciful God, grant that the old Adam in these persons may be so buried that the new man may be raised up in them. Amen.
THE BOOK OF COMMON PRAYER (*Baptism to Such As Are of Riper Years*), 1662

When shall concupiscence and pride
No more my tortured heart divide?
When shall this agony be o'er,
And the old Adam rage no more?
CHARLES WESLEY: *On Galatians,* III, 22, 1739

[*See also* Sin (Original).

Adams, Abigail (1744–1818)

There is not a virtue that can abide in the female heart but it was the ornament of hers. She had been fifty-four years the delight of my father's heart, the sweetener of all his toils, the comforter of all his sorrows, the sharer and heightener of all his joys.
JOHN QUINCY ADAMS: *Diary,* Nov. 2, 1818

Adams, John (1735–1826)

He is vain, irritable, and a bad calculator of the force and probable effect of the motives which govern men. This is all the ill which can possibly be said of him. He is as disinterested as the Being who made him.
THOMAS JEFFERSON: *Letter to James Madison,* 1787

It has been the political career of this man to begin with hypocrisy, proceed with arrogance, and finish in contempt.
THOMAS PAINE: *Open Letter to the Citizens of the United States,* Nov. 22, 1802

Could I have obtained a troop of horse or a company of foot, I should infallibly have been a soldier.
JOHN ADAMS: *Letter to Thomas Cushing,* March 13, 1817

Mrs. Clark said to him that it was the 4th of July, the fiftieth anniversary of independence. He answered, "It is a great day. It is a good day." About one in the afternoon he said, "Thomas Jefferson survives," but the last word was indistinctly and imperfectly spoken. He spoke no more.
JOHN QUINCY ADAMS: *Diary,* July 21, 1826

Adams, John Quincy (1767–1848)

I am a man of reserved, cold, austere, and forbidding manners: my political adversaries say, a gloomy misanthropist, and my personal enemies, an unsocial savage.
JOHN QUINCY ADAMS: *Diary,* June 4, 1819

My whole life has been a succession of disappointments. I can scarcely recollect a single instance of success to anything that I ever undertook. Yet, with fervent gratitude to God, I confess that my life has been equally

marked by great and signal successes which I neither aimed at nor anticipated.
JOHN QUINCY ADAMS: *Diary*, Aug. 9, 1833

[*See also* Ambition.

Adder

An adder in the path.
ZECHARIAH XLIX, 17, *c.* 700 B.C.

Addison, Joseph (1672–1719)

Nor e'er was to the bowers of bliss convey'd
A fairer spirit or more welcome shade.
THOMAS TICKELL: *On the Death of Mr. Addison*, 1719

Alike reserved to blame or to commend,
A tim'rous foe, and a suspicious friend;
Dreading ev'n fools; by flatterers besieged,
And so obliging that he ne'er obliged.
ALEXANDER POPE: *Epistle to Dr. Arbuthnot*, 1735

Whoever wishes to attain an English style, familiar but not coarse, and elegant but not ostentatious, must give his days and nights to the volumes of Addison.
SAMUEL JOHNSON: *Lives of the Poets* (Addison), I, 1778

[*See also* Spectator.

Ad Infinitum

[*See* Flea.

Adjective

Though the adjective may agree with the noun in gender, number and case, nevertheless the adjective and the noun may not agree.
Ascribed to VOLTAIRE (1694–1778)

As to the adjective, when in doubt strike it out.
S. L. CLEMENS (MARK TWAIN): *Pudd'nhead Wilson*, XI, 1894

The adjective is the enemy of the noun.
Author unidentified

Admiral

An admiral has to be put to death now and then to encourage the others.
VOLTAIRE: *Candide*, XXIII, 1759

Admirals extoll'd for standing still
Or doing nothing with a deal of skill.
WILLIAM COWPER: *Table Talk*, 1782

That part of a war-ship which does the talking while the figure-head does the thinking.
AMBROSE BIERCE: *The Devil's Dictionary*, 1906

Admiralty

If blood be the price of admiralty,
Lord God, we ha' paid in full!
RUDYARD KIPLING: *The Song of the Dead*, II, 1893

[*See also* Sea-power.

Admiration

I saw the woman drunken with the blood of the saints, and with the blood of the martyrs of Jesus: and when I saw her I wondered with great admiration.
REVELATION XVII, 6, *c.* 95

We always love those who admire us, but we do not always love those whom we admire.
LA ROCHEFOUCAULD: *Maxims*, 1665

He who affects or loves a man for the sake of something which is reputed honorable, but which is in reality vicious, is himself vicious and ill.
ANTHONY A. COOPER (EARL OF SHAFTESBURY): *An Inquiry Concerning Virtue or Merit*, I, 1699

Admiration is a very short-lived passion, that immediately decays upon growing familiar with its object.
JOSEPH ADDISON: *The Spectator*, Dec. 24, 1711

Fools admire, but men of sense approve.
ALEXANDER POPE: *An Essay on Criticism*, II, 1711

Admiration [is] one of the most bewitching, enthusiastic passions of the mind; and every common moralist knows that it arises from novelty and surprise, the inseparable attendants of imposture.
WILLIAM WARBURTON (BISHOP OF GLOUCESTER): *The Causes of Prodigies and Miracles*, I, 1727

Things not understood are admired.
THOMAS FULLER: *Gnomologia*, 1732

Admiration is the daughter of ignorance.
BENJAMIN FRANKLIN: *Poor Richard's Almanac*, 1736

Approbation, heightened by wonder and surprise, constitutes the sentiment which is properly called admiration, and of which applause is the natural expression. The decision of the man who judges that exquisite beauty is preferable to the grossest deformity, or that twice two are equal to four, must certainly be approved of by all the world, but will not, surely, be much admired.
ADAM SMITH: *The Theory of Moral Sentiments*, I, 1759

We live by admiration, hope and love.
WILLIAM WORDSWORTH: *The Excursion*, IV, 1814

To admire on principle is the only way to imitate without loss of originality.
S. T. COLERIDGE: *Biographia Literaria*, IV, 1817

Let a man admire himself, and he will infallibly find plenty of simpletons to admire him.
WILLIAM HAZLITT: *Butts of Different Sorts*, 1829 (The Atlas, Feb. 8)

Biographers, translators, editors, all, in short, who employ themselves in illustrating the lives or the writings of others, are peculiarly exposed to the *lues Boswelliana*, or disease of admiration.

T. B. MACAULAY: *William Pitt*, 1834 (Edinburgh Review, Jan.)

No nobler feeling than this of admiration for one higher than himself dwells in the breast of man.

THOMAS CARLYLE: *Heroes and Hero-Worship*, I, 1841 (Lecture in London, May 5)

Our polite recognition of another's resemblance to ourselves.

AMBROSE BIERCE: *The Devil's Dictionary*, 1906

The mean admiration of mean things.

Author unidentified

[*See also* Abuse, Approbation, Approval, Fame, Ignorance, Superiority.

Admonition

Admonish your friends in private; praise them in public.

PUBLILIUS SYRUS: *Sententiae*, *c.* 50 B.C.

Ado

Why make ye this ado? MARK V, 39, *c.* 70

Great cry and little wool.

ENGLISH PHRASE, traced by SMITH to *c.* 1475

Much ado about nothing.

SHAKESPEARE: *Title of play*, *c.* 1599 (The phrase seems to be much older)

Adolescence

Not yet old enough for a man, nor young enough for a boy; as a squash is before 'tis a peas-cod, or a codling when 'tis almost an apple.

SHAKESPEARE: *Twelfth Night*, I, *c.* 1601

My salad days;
When I was green in judgment, cold in blood.

SHAKESPEARE: *Antony and Cleopatra*, I, *c.* 1606

Just at the age 'twixt boy and youth,
When thought is speech, and speech is truth.

WALTER SCOTT: *Marmion*, II, 1808

A stage between infancy and adultery.

Author unidentified

[*See also* Youth.

Adornment

A ship and a woman are never sufficiently adorned, or too much.

PLAUTUS: *Poenulus*, I, *c.* 200 B.C.

She seems most hideous when adorned the most.

LUDOVICO ARIOSTO: *Orlando Furioso*, XX, 1532

He adorned whatever he touched. (Il embellit tout qu'il touche.)

FRANÇOIS FENELON: *Lettre sur les occupations de l'Académie Française*, IV, *c.* 1705

Loveliness
Needs not the foreign aid of ornament,
But is, when unadorn'd, adorned the most.

JAMES THOMSON: *The Seasons*, IV, 1730

[*See also* Dress, Finery, Ornament, Loveliness.

Adulation

The wicked wind of adulation.

ROBERT HENRYSON: *Moral Fables of Aesop*, 1570

You want to stifle me with roses. (Vous voulez m'étouffer sous les roses.)

Ascribed to VOLTAIRE, *c.* 1778, then very popular

Adult

When I was a child, I spake as a child, I understood as a child, I thought as a child: but when I became a man, I put away childish things. I CORINTHIANS XIII, 10, *c.* 55

I believe our souls are as adult at twenty as they are ever like to be, and as capable then as ever.

MICHEL DE MONTAIGNE: *Essays*, I, 1580

An adult is one who has ceased to grow vertically but not horizontally.

Author unidentified

Adulteration

Thy silver is become dross, thy wine mixed with water. ISAIAH I, 22, *c.* 700 B.C.

Adulterer

They are all adulterers, as an oven heated by the baker. HOSEA VII, 4, *c.* 740 B.C.

The adulterer and the adulteress shall surely be put to death.

LEVITICUS XX, 10, *c.* 700 B.C.

The eye also of the adulterer waiteth for the twilight, saying, No eye shall see me: and disguiseth his face.

JOB XXIV, 15, *c.* 325 B.C.

Whoremongers and adulterers God will judge.

HEBREWS XIII, 4, *c.* 65

The adulterer is a more grievous offender than the thief.

ST. JOHN CHRYSOSTOM: *Homily X*, *c.* 388

The way of the adulterer is hedged with thorns; full of fears and jealousies, burning desires and impatient waitings, tediousness of delay and suffrance of affronts, and amazements of discovery.

JEREMY TAYLOR: *The Rule and Exercises of Holy Living*, II, 1650

[*See also* Adulteress, Adultery, Judge.

Adulteress

Such is the way of an adulterous woman; she eateth, and wipeth her mouth, and saith, I have done no wickedness.
PROVERBS XXX, 20, *c.* 350 B.C.

Whenever a woman commits adultery with a man of a caste inferior to her husband's she shall be torn to pieces by dogs, and in some public place.
THE MAHABHARATA, XII, *c.* 200 B.C.

If, while her husband liveth, she be married to another man, she shall be called an adulteress. ROMANS VII, 2, *c.* 55

Th' adultress! What a theme for angry verse!
WILLIAM COWPER: *The Task,* III, 1785

[*See also* Adulterer, Adultery.

Adultery

If a married woman shall be caught lying with another man, both shall be bound and thrown into the river.
THE CODE OF HAMMURABI, *c.* 2250 B.C.

If a man lie with the wife of another man at her wish there shall be no penalty for him. As for the woman, her husband shall punish her as he pleases.
THE ASSYRIAN CODE, *c.* 2000 B.C.

Thou shalt not commit adultery.
EXODUS XX, 14, *c.* 700 B.C. (*Cf.* DEUTERONOMY V, 18, *c.* 650 B.C.; ROMANS XIII, 9, *c.* 55; JAMES II, 11, *c.* 60; MARK X, 19, *c.* 70; LUKE XVIII, 20, *c.* 75)

Old in adulteries.
EZEKIEL XXIII, 43, *c.* 600 B.C.

Whoso committeth adultery with a woman lacketh understanding: he that doeth it destroyeth his own soul.
PROVERBS VI, 32, *c.* 350 B.C.

Come, let us take our fill of love until the morning; let us solace ourselves with love. For the good man is not at home, he is gone a long journey. PROVERBS VII, 18–19

A man may commit adultery with a woman knowing well who she is, but not of free choice, because he is under the influence of passion. In that case he is not an unjust man, though he has done an injustice.
ARISTOTLE: *The Nicomachean Ethics,* V, *c.* 340 B.C.

Eyes full of adultery. II PETER II, 14, *c.* 60

Whosoever looketh on a woman to lust after her hath committed adultery with her already in his heart. MATTHEW V, 28, *c.* 75

It shall be considered adultery to offer presents to a married woman, to romp with her, to touch her dress or ornaments, or to sit with her on a bed.
THE CODE OF MANU, VIII, *c.* 100

(The story of the woman taken in adultery is in JOHN VIII, 3–11, *c.* 115.)

The mind is guilty of adultery even if it merely pictures to itself a vision of carnal pleasure.
LACTANTIUS: *Divinæ institutiones,* VI, *c.* 310

Die for adultery? No;
The wren goes to 't, and the small gilded fly
Does lecher in my sight.
SHAKESPEARE: *King Lear,* IV, 1606

A wanton and lascivious eye
Betrays the heart's adultery.
ROBERT HERRICK: *Hesperides,* 1648

It is ordered that Miss Batcheller for her adultery shall be branded with the letter A.
RECORDS OF MAINE PROVINCE, 1651

God that commanded us to forgive our enemies left it in our choice, and hath not commanded us to forgive an adulterous husband or a wife.
JEREMY TAYLOR: *The Mysteriousness of Marriage,* 1651

A husband may murder his adulterous wife.
Doctrine condemned by POPE ALEXANDER VII, Sept. 24, 1665

I heard, when I was young, of one or two that for adultery stood in a white sheet in the church.
RICHARD BAXTER: *In Answer to Henry Dodwell,* 1677 (Baxter was born in 1615)

As they were committing adultery in London, they were immediately struck dead with fire from Heaven, in the very act. Their bodies were so found, half burned up, and sending out a most loathsome savor.
JOHN BUNYAN: *The Life and Death of Mr. Badman,* 1680

Your acquaintance, D. Rodrigue, has had a small accident befallen him. Mr. Annesley found him in bed with his wife, prosecuted, and brought a bill of divorce into Parliament. Those things grow more fashionable every day.
MARY WORTLEY MONTAGU: *Letter to the Countess of Mar,* 1725

When the angels hear adultery mentioned they turn themselves away.
EMANUEL SWEDENBORG: *Heaven and Hell,* 1758

I look with horror upon adultery. But my amiable mistress is no longer bound to him who was her husband. He has used her shockingly ill. He has deserted her. He lives with another. Is she not then free? She is.
JAMES BOSWELL: *Letter to William Temple,* Feb. 1, 1767

Private news I know none. The bishops are trying to put a stop to one staple commodity of that kind, adultery. I do not suppose that they expect to lessen it.

HORACE WALPOLE: *Letter to Horace Mann,* March 22, 1779

Between a man and his wife a husband's infidelity is nothing. The man imposes no bastards on his wife.

SAMUEL JOHNSON: *Boswell's Life,* Oct. 10, 1779

Jesus was sitting in Moses' chair;
They brought the trembling woman there.
Moses commands she be stoned to death:
What was the sound of Jesus' breath?
He laid his hand on Moses' law;
The ancient heavens, in silent awe,
Writ with curses from pole to pole,
All away began to roll.

WILLIAM BLAKE: *The Everlasting Gospel,* *c.* 1810

What men call gallantry, and gods adultery,
Is much more common where the climate's sultry.

BYRON: *Don Juan,* I, 1819

There's nothing in the world like the devotion of a married woman. It's a thing no married man knows anything about.

OSCAR WILDE: *Lady Windermere's Fan,* III, 1892

Is not the sin of adultery much easier than that of murder? and yet can one man say to another: "Go and commit adultery. I shall bear your sin, because I am your commander"?

LYOF N. TOLSTOY: *Notes For Soldiers,* 1901

The psychology of adultery has been falsified by conventional morals, which assume, in monogamous countries, that attraction to one person cannot coexist with a serious affection for another. Everybody knows that this is untrue.

BERTRAND RUSSELL: *Marriage and Morals,* XVI, 1929

Adultery, sometimes necessary plot material, must not be explicitly treated, or justified, or presented attractively.

A CODE TO GOVERN THE MAKING OF MOTION AND TALKING PICTURES BY THE MOTION PICTURE PRODUCERS AND DISTRIBUTORS OF AMERICA, INC., II, March 31, 1930

They are foes of mutual fidelity who teach that the ideas prevailing at the present time concerning false and harmful relations with a third party can be tolerated, and that a greater freedom of feeling and action should be permitted to man or wife.

POPE PIUS XI: *Casti connubii,* Dec. 31, 1930

Adultery is usually an act done under cover of darkness and secrecy, and in which the parties are seldom surprised.

DECISION OF THE MARYLAND COURT OF APPEALS, 1931

Adultery brings on early old age.

HEBREW PROVERB

The husband's sin remains on the threshold; the wife's enters the house.

RUSSIAN PROVERB

[*See also* Actor, Christian, Clergy, Divorce, Evidence, Flesh, Husband and Wife, Law, Mistress, Sin, Stage.

Adventure

He who has no adventure has neither horse nor mule.

RABELAIS: *Gargantua,* I, 1535

The fruit of my tree of knowledge is plucked, and it is this: "Adventures are to the adventurous."

BENJAMIN DISRAELI: *Ixion in Heaven,* II, 1833

[*See also* Piracy.

Adverb

God loveth adverbs.

JOSEPH HALL (BISHOP OF NORWICH): *Holy Observations,* XIV, 1607

The adverb is the enemy of the verb.

Author unidentified

Adversary

Oh, that . . . mine adversary had written a book.

JOB XXXI, 35, *c.* 325 B.C.

Agree with thine adversary quickly, whiles thou art in the way with him.

MATTHEW V, 25, *c.* 75

Do as adversaries do in law, —
Strive mightily, but eat and drink as friends.

SHAKESPEARE: *The Taming of the Shrew,* I, 1594

Treating your adversary with respect is giving him an advantage to which he is not entitled.

SAMUEL JOHNSON: *Boswell's Life,* 1779

[*See also* Books, Devil, Foe, Friend, Friendship.

Adversity

The bread of adversity.

ISAIAH XXX, 20, *c.* 700 B.C.

A friend loveth at all times, and a brother is born for adversity.

PROVERBS XVII, 17, *c.* 350 B.C.

If thou faint in the day of adversity, thy strength is small.

PROVERBS XXIV, 10

In the day of prosperity be joyful, but in the day of adversity consider.

ECCLESIASTES VIII, 14, *c.* 200 B.C.

Gold is tried in fire, and acceptable men in the furnace of adversity.

ECCLESIASTICUS II, 5, *c.* 180 B.C. (Apparently an ancient proverb. It is also found in SENECA: *De providentia,* V, *c.* 64)

Adversity reminds men of religion.
LIVY: *History of Rome*, V, *c.* 10

Adversity always finds at last the man she has passed by. SENECA: *Hercules Furens*, *c.* 50

To rejoice in adversity is to joy in the cross of Christ.
THOMAS À KEMPIS: *Imitation of Christ*, II, *c.* 1420

Prosperity getteth friends, but adversity trieth them. NICHOLAS LING: *Politeuphuia*, 1597

Sweet are the uses of adversity,
Which, like the toad, ugly and venomous,
Wears yet a precious jewel in his head.
SHAKESPEARE: *As You Like It*, II, *c.* 1600

The virtue of prosperity is temperance; the virtue of adversity is fortitude, which in morals is the more heroical virtue.
FRANCIS BACON: *Essays*, V, 1625

A man hath many enemies when his back is to the wall.
JOHN CLARKE: *Paroemiologia Anglo-Latina*, 1639

In time of prosperity friends will be plenty;
In time of adversity not one in twenty.
JAMES HOWELL: *Proverbs*, 1659

In the adversity of our best friends we often find something that is not wholly displeasing to us.
LA ROCHEFOUCAULD: *Maxims*, 1665

Adversity makes a man wise, not rich.
JOHN RAY: *English Proverbs*, 1670

Friendship, of itself a holy tie,
Is made more sacred by adversity.
JOHN DRYDEN: *The Hind and the Panther*, III, 1687

Human life is a state of probation, and adversity is the post of honor in it.
JOHN HUGHES: *The Spectator*, Dec. 1, 1711

Daughter of Jove, relentless power,
Thou tamer of the human breast,
Whose iron scourge and torturing hour
The bad affright, afflict the best.
THOMAS GRAY: *Hymn to Adversity*, 1753

The greatest object in the universe, says a certain philosopher, is a good man struggling with adversity; yet there is a still greater, which is the good man that comes to relieve it.
OLIVER GOLDSMITH: *The Vicar of Wakefield*, XXX, 1766

If adversity purifies men, why not nations?
JEAN PAUL RICHTER: *Levana*, II, 1807

In prosperous times I have sometimes felt my fancy and powers of language flag, but adversity is to me at least a tonic and bracer.
WALTER SCOTT: *Journal*, Jan. 22, 1826

Adversity is sometimes hard upon a man; but for one man who can stand prosperity, there are a hundred that will stand adversity.
THOMAS CARLYLE: *Heroes and Hero-Worship*, V, 1840 (Lecture in London, May 19)

Adversity is easier borne than prosperity forgot.
H. G. BOHN: *Handbook of Proverbs*, 1855

Adversity introduces a man to himself.
Author unidentified

In prosperity, caution; in adversity, patience.
DUTCH PROVERB

Adversity makes men; prosperity, monsters.
FRENCH PROVERB

Adversity comes with instruction in his hand.
WELSH PROVERB

[*See also* Affliction, Calamity, Contempt, English, General, Greatness, Humiliation, Love, Misfortune, Philosophy, Prosperity.

Advertisement

Advertisements contain the only truths to be relied on in a newspaper.
THOMAS JEFFERSON: *Letter to Nathaniel Macon*, 1819

Blow your own horn — even if you don't sell a clam. AMERICAN PROVERB

It pays to advertise. IBID.

When business is good it pays to advertise; when business is bad you've got to advertise. Author unidentified

[*See also* Newspaper.

Advice

Blessed be thy advice, and blessed be thou.
I SAMUEL XXV, 33, *c.* 500 B.C.

All of us, when well, give good advice to the sick. TERENCE: *Andria*, II, *c.* 160 B.C.

When the life of a counsellor is known to be in accord with his words, it is impossible that his advice should not have great weight.
POLYBIUS: *Histories*, XI, *c.* 125 B.C.

Even the best pilots are willing to take advice from their passengers in bad weather.
CICERO: *Orationes Philippicæ*, VII, *c.* 60 B.C.

No one can give you better advice than yourself. CICERO: *Ad Atticum*, II, *c.* 50 B.C.

It is bad advice that cannot be changed.
PUBLILIUS SYRUS: *Sententiae*, *c.* 50 B.C.

No matter how harsh advice may be, it injures no one. IBID.

Whatever your advice, make it brief.
HORACE: *De arte poetica*, *c.* 8 B.C.

It is better to advise than upbraid, for the one corrects the erring; the other only convicts them. EPICTETUS: *Encheiridion, c.* 110

He who doth not wish another's ruin should, even unasked, speak to him for his good. This is a supreme duty, and the contrary is the opinion of bad men.
THE HITOPADESA, II, *c.* 500

Advice is less necessary to the wise than to fools, but the wise derive most advantage from it.
FRANCESCO GUICCIARDINI: *Storia d'Italia,* 1564

To take advice of friends is ever honorable: for lookers on many times see more than gamesters, and the vale best discovereth the hill.
FRANCIS BACON: *Essays,* IV, 1597

Advice is least heeded when most needed.
ENGLISH PROVERB, familiar since the XVII century

A woman's advice is not worth much, but he who doesn't heed it is a fool.
PEDRO CALDERÓN: *El médico de su honra,* I, *c.* 1630

Know when to speak; for many times it brings
Danger to give the best advice to kings.
ROBERT HERRICK: *Hesperides,* 1648

Sometimes it takes as much ability to profit by good advice as to arrive at a correct opinion ourselves.
LA ROCHEFOUCAULD: *Maxims,* 1665

Advice comes too late when a thing is done.
JOHN RAY: *English Proverbs,* 1670

In vain he craves advice who will not follow it.
IBID.

Sometimes a fool makes a good suggestion.
NICOLAS BOILEAU: *L'Art poétique,* IV, 1674

How is it possible to expect that mankind will take advice, when they will not so much as take warning?
JONATHAN SWIFT: *Thoughts on Various Subjects,* 1706

I give myself sometimes admirable advice, but I am incapable of taking it.
MARY WORTLEY MONTAGU: *Letter to the Countess of Mar,* 1725

You may give him good advice, but who can give him wit to take it?
THOMAS FULLER: *Gnomologia,* 1732

Advice is seldom welcome; and those who want it the most always like it the least.
LORD CHESTERFIELD: *Letter to his son,* Jan. 29, 1748

Advice, as it always gives a temporary appearance of superiority, can never be very grateful, even when it is most necessary or most judicious.
SAMUEL JOHNSON: *The Rambler,* Jan. 15, 1751

If ever I one thought bestow
On what such fools advise,
May I be dull enough to grow
Most miserably wise.
MARY WORTLEY MONTAGU: *Letter to James Steuart,* July 19, 1759

It is comfortable to give advice from a safe harbor.
J. C. F. SCHILLER: *Wilhelm Tell,* I, 1804

We ask advice, but we mean approbation.
C. C. COLTON: *Lacon,* 1820

Advice is not disliked because it is advice; but because so few people know how to give it.
LEIGH HUNT: *The Indicator,* LI, 1821

Good but rarely came from good advice.
BYRON: *Don Juan,* XIV, 1823

Good advice is one of those injuries which a good man ought, if possible, to forgive.
HORACE SMITH: *Gaieties and Gravities,* 1826

One should never ask anybody if one means to write anything. If Schiller had asked me about his "Wallenstein" before he had written it, I should surely have advised him against it; for I could never have dreamed that, from such a subject, so excellent a drama could be made.
J. W. GOETHE: *Conversations with Eckermann,* Jan. 18, 1827

The worst men often give the best advice.
P. J. BAILEY: *Festus,* 1839

It is always a silly thing to give advice, but to give good advice is absolutely fatal.
OSCAR WILDE: *The Portrait of Mr. W. H.,* 1889

The only thing to do with good advice is to pass it on. It is never of any use to oneself.
OSCAR WILDE: *An Ideal Husband,* II, 1895

"The man was in such deep distress,"
Said Tom, "that I could do no less
Than give him good advice." Said Jim:
"If less could have been done for him
I know you well enough, my son,
To know that's what you would have done."
AMBROSE BIERCE: *The Devil's Dictionary,* 1906

A good scare is worth more to a man than good advice.
E. W. HOWE: *Country Town Sayings,* 1911

Never give advice in a crowd.
ARAB PROVERB

Advice after an evil is done is like medicine after death. DANISH PROVERB

Ask advice only of your equals. IBID.

Good advice is no better than bad — unless it comes at the right time. IBID.

The best advice is to be found on the pillow.
IBID.

Advisers are not givers. DUTCH PROVERB

Good advice is as good as an eye in the hand. FRENCH PROVERB

He who pays has the right to advise. IBID.

Take the first advice of a woman; not the second. IBID.

Never give advice unless asked. GERMAN PROVERB

Advice bought is worth twice as much as advice gratis. IRISH PROVERB

Women's advice is either too cheap or too dear. ITALIAN PROVERB

Advice is always wanting when most needed. MEDIEVAL LATIN PROVERB

Beware the advice of a poor man. SPANISH PROVERB

Never advise anyone to go to war or to marry. IBID.

[*See also* Age (Old), Counsel, Fool, Judge, Prince.

Advocate

[*See* Lawyer.

Aesthete

He's stuffed with the sublime and beautiful. You'd think he'd been bit by a poet's mad dog. DOUGLAS JERROLD: *Bubbles of the Day,* I, 1842

[*See also* Artist.

Aesthetics

[*See* Beauty.

Affectation

Affectation gives a vulgar flavor to everything. BALTASAR GRACIÁN: *The Art of Worldly Wisdom,* 1647

The qualities we have do not make us so ridiculous as those we affect to have. LA ROCHEFOUCAULD: *Maxims,* 1665

Affectation is an awkward and forced imitation of what should be genuine and easy, wanting the beauty that accompanies what is natural. JOHN LOCKE: *Some Thoughts of Education,* 1693

Affectation is a more terrible enemy to fine faces than the smallpox. RICHARD STEELE: *The Spectator,* April 7, 1711

Any affectation whatsoever in dress implies, in my mind, a flaw in the understanding. LORD CHESTERFIELD: *Letter to his son,* Dec. 30, 1748

Affectation is always to be distinguished from hypocrisy, as being the art of counterfeiting those qualities which we might with innocence and safety be known to want. SAMUEL JOHNSON: *The Rambler,* May 26, 1750

An affected man cannot be a moral man. The whole study of his life is to cheat you. Ascribed to J. HORNE TOOKE (1736–1812) in G. H. POWELL: *Reminiscences and Table-Talk of Samuel Rogers*

There is a pleasure in *affecting* affectation. CHARLES LAMB: *Detached Thoughts on Books and Reading,* 1822 (London Magazine, July)

[*See also* Agreeable, Character, Hypocrisy, Merit, Pretense, Simplicity.

Affection

Be kindly affectioned one to another with brotherly love. ROMANS XII, 10, *c.* 55

Set your affection on things above, not on things on the earth. COLOSSIANS III, 2, *c.* 60

Affection bends the judgment to her uses. DANTE: *Inferno,* XIII, *c.* 1320

Affection is a coal that must be cooled;
Else, suffered, it will set the heart on fire.
SHAKESPEARE: *Venus and Adonis,* 1593

My affection hath an unknown bottom, like the Bay of Portugal. SHAKESPEARE: *As You Like It,* IV, *c.* 1600

True affection is a body of enigmas, mysteries and riddles, wherein two so become one that they both become two. THOMAS BROWNE: *Religio Medici,* II, 1642

When affection speaks
Truth is not always there.
THOMAS MIDDLETON, PHILIP MASSINGER and WILLIAM ROWLEY: *The Old Law,* IV, 1656

'Tis sweet to feel by what fine-spun threads our affections are drawn together. LAURENCE STERNE: *A Sentimental Journey,* 1768

All men, even the most surly, are influenced by affection, even when little fitted to excite it. I could have been happy with a servant girl had she only in sincerity of heart responded to my affection. S. T. COLERIDGE: *To Thomas Allsop,* *c.* 1823

The effect of the indulgence of human affection is a certain cordial exhilaration. R. W. EMERSON: *Friendship,* 1841

Talk not of wasted affection; affection never was wasted. H. W. LONGFELLOW: *Evangeline,* II, 1847

Affection magnifies trifles.
LEIGH HUNT: *Table-Talk,* 1851

Affection is a bad adviser. GERMAN PROVERB

[*See also* German Language, Happiness, Love, Pleasure.

Affirmative

[*See* Negative.

Afflatus, Divine

[*See* Inspiration.

Affliction

I have chosen thee in the furnace of affliction.
ISAIAH XLVIII, 10, *c.* 700 B.C.

The bread of affliction.
DEUTERONOMY XVI, 3, *c.* 650 B.C. (The phrase is also in I KINGS XXII, 27, *c.* 500 B.C., and II CHRONICLES XVIII, 26, *c.* 300 B.C., along with "the water of affliction")

No one could be more unhappy than a man who has never known affliction.
Ascribed to DEMETRIUS PHALERENS (*c.* 345–283 B.C.)

The gods spare the afflicted.
OVID: *Epistolae ex Ponto, c.* 5

Whom the Lord loveth he chasteneth.
HEBREWS XII, 6, *c.* 65

God measures out affliction to our need.
ST. JOHN CHRYSOSTOM: *Homily* IV, *c.* 388

One and the same violence of affliction proves, purifies, and melts the good, and condemns, wastes and casts out the bad.
ST. AUGUSTINE: *The City of God,* I, 427

Affliction is enamour'd of thy parts,
And thou art wedded to calamity.
SHAKESPEARE: *Romeo and Juliet,* III, *c.* 1596

God n'ere afflicts us more than our desert,
Though He may seem to over-act His part:
Sometimes He strikes us more than flesh can bear;
But yet still less than grace can suffer here.
ROBERT HERRICK: *Noble Numbers,* 1647

Afflictions induce callosities.
THOMAS BROWNE: *Urn Burial,* V, 1658

The afflicted have no consolation for the afflicted. ARAB PROVERB

[*See also* Adversity, Calamity, Consolation, Jew, Misfortune.

Affront

Young men soon give, and soon forget, affronts;
Old age is slow in both.
JOSEPH ADDISON: *Cato,* II, 1713

A moral, sensible, and well-bred man
Will not affront me, and no other can.
WILLIAM COWPER: *Conversation,* 1782

[*See also* Insult.

Africa

I hold thee fast, Africa. (Teneo te, Africa.)
JULIUS CAESAR: *As he fell on landing in Africa,* 47 B.C.

There is always something new from Africa.
PLINY THE ELDER: *Natural History,* VIII, 77 (A Greek proverb)

Where Afric's sunny fountains
Roll down their golden strand.
REGINALD HEBER: *From Greenland's Icy Mountains,* 1827

He who has drunk of African waters will drink again. ARAB PROVERB

African

Among the Gentiles in Heaven, the Africans are the most loved, for they receive the goods and truths of Heaven more readily than others.
EMANUEL SWEDENBORG: *Heaven and Hell,* 1758

[*See also* Negro.

Afternoon

The posteriors of this day, which the rude multitude call the afternoon.
SHAKESPEARE: *Love's Labor's Lost,* V, *c.* 1595

The day becomes more solemn and serene
When noon is past.
P. B. SHELLEY: *Hymn to Intellectual Beauty,* VII, 1816

In the afternoon they came unto a land
In which it seemed always afternoon.
ALFRED TENNYSON: *The Lotus-Eaters,* 1833

Time has fallen asleep in the afternoon sunshine.
ALEXANDER SMITH: *Dreamthorp,* I, 1863

The afternoon knows what the morning never suspected. SWEDISH PROVERB

[*See also* Siesta, Weather.

Agamemnon

Many brave men lived before Agamemnon. (Vivere fortes ante Agamemnona multi.)
HORACE: *Carmina,* IV, *c.* 13 B.C.

It is by writings that you know about Agamemnon, and those who fought against him or with him.
OVID: *Epistolae ex Ponto, c.* 5

The Iliad would never have come down to these times if Agamemnon had given Achilles a box on the ear.
SYDNEY SMITH: *In the Edinburgh Review,* 1826

Agamogenesis

I never knew more than one individual who believed in agamogenesis; she was unmarried, a lovely character, was suffering from incipient insanity, and a Christian Scientist cured her.

MARY BAKER G. EDDY: *Science and Health,* III, 1908 (*Agamogenesis*=the production of offspring by one sex only)

Agate

[*See* June.

Age

As thy days, so shall thy strength be.

DEUTERONOMY XXXIII, 25, *c.* 650 B.C.

The flower of their age.

I SAMUEL II, 33, *c.* 500 B.C.

Age cannot wither her, nor custom stale
Her infinite variety.

SHAKESPEARE: *Antony and Cleopatra,* II, *c.* 1606

Discern of the coming on of years, and think not to do the same things still, for age will not be defied.

FRANCIS BACON: *Essays,* XXX, 1625

They need not look in your mouth to know your age.

JAMES KELLY: *Complete Collection of Scottish Proverbs,* 1721

Oh, sir, I must not tell you my age; they say women and music should never be dated.

OLIVER GOLDSMITH: *She Stoops to Conquer,* III, 1773

The more we live, more brief appear
Our life's succeeding stages;
A day to childhood seems a year,
And years like passing ages.

THOMAS CAMPBELL: *A Thought Suggested by the New Year, c.* 1824

Age is the most terrible misfortune that can happen to any man; other evils will mend, but this is every day getting worse.

G. P. R. JAMES: *Richelieu,* XIV, 1829

One should never trust a woman who tells one her real age. A woman who would tell that would tell anything.

OSCAR WILDE: *A Woman of No Importance,* II, 1893

[*See also* Age (Middle), Age (Old), Ages, Artery, Face, Man and Woman, Old, Travel, Youth and Age.

Age, Middle

Your lordship, though not clean past your youth, hath yet some smack of age in you, some relish of the saltness of time.

SHAKESPEARE: *II Henry IV,* I, *c.* 1598

With steady foot and even pace
I tread the Milky Way;
I've youth without its levity
And age without decay.

DANIEL DEFOE: *A Review of the Affairs of France and of All Europe,* VIII, 1712

When all the fiercer passions cease
(The glory and disgrace of youth);
When the deluded soul, in peace,
Can listen to the voice of truth;
When we are taught in whom to trust,
And how to spare, to spend, to give,
(Our prudence kind, our pity just,)
'Tis then we rightly learn to live.

GEORGE CRABBE: *Reflections,* 1807

On his bold visage middle age
Had slightly press'd its signet sage,
Yet had not quenched the open truth
And fiery vehemence of youth;
Forward and frolic glee was there,
The will to do, the soul to dare.

WALTER SCOTT: *The Lady of the Lake,* I, 1810

Though her years were waning
Her climacteric teased her like her teens.

BYRON: *Don Juan,* X, 1823

Of all the barbarous middle ages, that
Which is most barbarous is the middle age
Of man.

BYRON: *Don Juan,* XII, 1823

Sweet is the infant's waking smile,
And sweet the old man's rest —
But middle age by no fond wile,
No soothing calm is blest.

JOHN KEBLE: *The Christian Year,* 1827

Our judgment ripens; our imagination decays. We cannot at once enjoy the flowers of the Spring of life and the fruits of its Autumn, the pleasures of close investigation and those of agreeable error. We cannot sit at once in the front of the stage and behind the scenes.

T. B. MACAULAY: *John Dryden,* 1828 (Edinburgh Review, Jan.)

[*See also* Forty, Fifty.

Agent

He who does a thing through an agent does it himself. (Qui facit per alium facit per se.)

LEGAL MAXIM

Age, Old

Thou shalt go to thy fathers in peace; thou shalt be buried in a good old age.

GENESIS XV, 15, *c.* 700 B.C.

They all shall wax old as a garment; the moth shall eat them up.

ISAIAH L, 9, *c.* 700 B.C.

When death comes near the old find that age is no longer burdensome.

EURIPIDES: *Alcestis,* 438 B.C.

The pegs fall out, the tone is gone, the harmony becomes dissonance.

ARISTOPHANES: *The Knights,* 424 B.C.

Now that I have reached old age, how I hate it!

EURIPIDES: *The Suppliant Woman, c.* 421 B.C.

Happy is he who has finished the labors of life.
EURIPIDES: *The Bacchae*, c. 410 B.C.

Old people have fewer diseases than the young, but their diseases never leave them.
HIPPOCRATES: *Aphorisms*, c. 400 B.C.

It gives me great pleasure to converse with the aged. They have been over the road that all of us must travel, and know where it is rough and difficult and where it is level and easy. PLATO: *The Republic*, I, c. 370 B.C.

Old age has a great sense of calm and freedom. When the passions have relaxed their hold you have escaped, not from one master, but from many. IBID.

Old age is a dreary solitude.
PLATO: *Laws*, V, c. 360 B.C.

In old age no one ever speaks well of thee, but only ill – if he speaks with wisdom.
ANTIPHANES: *Fragment*, c. 350 B.C.

Old age is, so to speak, the sanctuary of ills: they all take refuge in it. IBID.

He . . . taketh away the understanding of the aged. JOB XII, 20, c. 325 B.C.

He died in a good old age, full of days, riches, and honor.
I CHRONICLES XXIX, 28, c. 300 B.C.

Old age is itself a disease. (Senectus ipsa est morbus.)
TERENCE: *Phormio*, IV, c. 160 B.C.

Now when I am old and gray-headed, O God, forsake me not.
PSALMS LXXI, 18, c. 150 B.C.

The days of our years are threescore and ten; and if by reason of strength they be fourscore years, yet is their strength labor and sorrow; for it is soon cut off, and we fly away. PSALMS XC, 10, c. 150 B.C.

Alas! Posthumus, Posthumus, the years fly fast, nor can piety ward off wrinkles, or advancing age invincible death. (Eheu! fugaces, Posthume, Posthume, labuntur anni; nec pietas moram rugis et instanti senectae afferet, indomitæque morti.)
HORACE: *Carmina*, II, c. 20 B.C.

Waning years steal from us our pleasures one by one; they have already snatched away my jokes, my loves, my revellings, and my play. HORACE: *Epistles*, II, c. 5 B.C.

Old age is an incurable disease. (Senectus insanibilis morbus est.)
SENECA: *Epistulæ morales ad Lucilium*, CVII, c. 63 (*Cf.* Terence, *ante*, c. 160 B.C.)

When thou shalt be old, thou shalt stretch forth thy hands, and another shall gird thee, and carry thee whither thou wouldest not.
JOHN XXI, 18, c. 115

When men wish for old age for themselves, what else do they wish for but lengthened infirmity?
ST. AUGUSTINE: *Of the Catechizing of the Unlearned*, c. 400

He that lives the longest life
Shall find but sorrow, care and strife.
Anon.: *The Life of Man*, c. 1550

Age, with stealing steps, hath clawed me.
THOMAS VAUX: *The Aged Lover Renounceth Love*, c. 1550

One of his feet is already in the grave.
ENGLISH SAYING, traced by Smith to 1566

It were a goodly thing to be old, if we did only march toward amendment. But it is the motion of a drunkard, stumbling, reeling, giddy-brained, formless, or of reeds, which the air doth casually wave to and fro, what way it bloweth.
MICHEL DE MONTAIGNE: *Essays*, III, 1588

When thou art old there's grief enough for thee.
ROBERT GREENE: *Sephestra's Lullaby*, 1589

I have not that alacrity of spirit,
Nor cheer of mind, that I was wont to have.
SHAKESPEARE: *Richard III*, V, c. 1592

Age pulls down the pride of every man.
RICHARD BARNFIELD: *The Affectionate Shepherd*, 1594

Age breeds aches.
JOHN HARINGTON: *The Metamorphosis of Ajax*, 1596

When the age is in, the wit is out.
SHAKESPEARE: *Much Ado About Nothing*, III, c. 1599

Age is like love: it cannot be hid.
THOMAS DEKKER: *Old Fortunatus*, II, 1600

My age is as a lusty Winter,
Frosty, but kindly.
SHAKESPEARE: *As You Like It*, II, 1600

The sixth age shifts
Into the lean and slipper'd pantaloon,
With spectacles on nose and pouch on side,
His youthful hose, well saved, a world too wide
For his shrunk shank; and his big manly voice,
Turning again toward childish treble, pipes
And whistles in his sound. Last scene of all,
That ends this strange eventful history,
Is second childishness and mere oblivion,
Sans teeth, sans eyes, sans taste, sans every thing. IBID.

Let me not live,
After my flame lacks oil, to be the snuff
Of younger spirits.
SHAKESPEARE: *All's Well that Ends Well*, I, c. 1602

Their limbs faint,
Their senses dull, their seeing, hearing, going,

All dead before them; yea, their very teeth,
Their instruments of eating, failing them.
BEN JONSON: *Volpone*, I, 1603

I am declined into the vale of years.
SHAKESPEARE: *Othello*, III, 1604

It is hard to teach an old dog new tricks.
ENGLISH PROVERB, traced by Apperson to 1605

I have lived long enough: my way of life
Is fallen into the sere, the yellow leaf.
SHAKESPEARE: *Macbeth*, V, *c.* 1605

What should we speak of
When we are old as you? When we shall hear
The rain and wind beat dark December?
SHAKESPEARE: *Cymbeline*, III, *c.* 1609

Old folks talk of nothing but defects
Because they grow so full of 'em themselves.
THOMAS MIDDLETON: *Women Beware Women*, I, *c.* 1625

When age is jocund it makes sport for death.
GEORGE HERBERT: *Outlandish Proverbs*, 1640

The stones and trees, insensible to time,
Nor age nor wrinkle on their front are seen;
If Winter come, and greenness then do fade,
A Spring returns, and they more youthful made;
But man grows old, lies down, remains where once he's laid.
ANNE BRADSTREET: *Contemplations*, 1650

Man is a Summer's day, whose youth and fire
Cool to a glorious evening and expire.
HENRY VAUGHAN: *Silex scintillans*, I, 1650

Old age consoles itself by giving good precepts for being unable to give bad examples.
LA ROCHEFOUCAULD: *Maxims*, 1665

Old age is a tyrant who forbids, on penalty of death, all the pleasures of youth. IBID.

The blemishes of the mind, like those of the face, increase with age. IBID.

The most dangerous weakness of old people who have been amiable is to forget that they are no longer so. IBID.

When our vices quit us we flatter ourselves with the belief that it is we who quit them.
IBID.

So mays't thou live till, like ripe fruit, thou drop
Into thy mother's lap, or be with ease
Gather'd, not harshly pluck'd, for death mature:
This is old age.
JOHN MILTON: *Paradise Lost*, XI, 1667

Old age makes us wiser and more foolish.
JOHN RAY: *English Proverbs*, 1760

Age . . . brings along with him
A terrible artillery.
THOMAS FLATMAN: *Poems and Songs*, 1674

A green old age.
JOHN DRYDEN and NATHANIEL LEE: *Oedipus*, III, 1679

We hope to grow old, and yet we dread old age.
JEAN DE LA BRUYÈRE: *Caractères*, XI, 1688

Already I am worn with cares and age;
And just abandoning th' ungrateful stage;
Unprofitably kept at Heav'ns expense,
I live a rent-charge on His Providence.
JOHN DRYDEN: *To Mr. Congreve*, 1694

One is past being lucky at our age.
LOUIS XIV OF FRANCE: To Marshall Villeroi after the Battle of Ramillies, May 23, 1706 (Louis was then 68 and Villeroi 62)

Let time that makes you homely make you sage;
The sphere of wisdom is the sphere of age.
THOMAS PARNELL: *To an Old Beauty*, 1722

Life protracted is protracted woe.
SAMUEL JOHNSON: *The Vanity of Human Wishes*, 1749

Superfluous lags the veteran on the stage.
IBID.

The heart never grows better by age; I fear rather worse; always harder. A young liar will be an old one; and a young knave will only be a greater knave as he grows older.
LORD CHESTERFIELD: *Letter to his son*, May 17, 1750

Age is rarely despised but when it is contemptible. SAMUEL JOHNSON: *The Rambler*, Sept. 8, 1750

In the decline of life, shame and grief are of short duration.
SAMUEL JOHNSON: *Rasselas*, IV, 1759

Old age, a second child, by Nature curst,
With more and greater evils than the first:
Weak, sickly, full of pains, in every breath
Railing at life and yet afraid of death.
CHARLES CHURCHILL: *Gotham*, I, 1763

How foolish was my hope and vain
That age would conquer sin.
CHARLES WESLEY: *In Advancing Age*, 1772

Old age is no such uncomfortable thing, if one gives oneself up to it with a good grace.
HORACE WALPOLE: *Letter to the Countess of Ailesbury*, Nov. 7, 1774

The fears all, the tears all,
Of dim declining age.
ROBERT BURNS: *Despondency*, 1786

By my rambling digressions I perceive myself to be growing old.
BENJAMIN FRANKLIN: *Autobiography*, 1798

How do we spend our old age? In defending opinions, not because we believe them to be true, but simply because we once said that we thought they were.

G. C. LICHTENBERG: *Reflections,* 1799

My only fear is that I may live too long. This would be a subject of dread to me.

THOMAS JEFFERSON: *Letter to Philip Mazzei,* March, 1801

It is not the end of joy that makes old age so sad, but the end of hope.

JEAN PAUL RICHTER: *Titan,* XXXIV, 1803

What is the worst of woes that wait on age?
What stamps the wrinkle deeper on the brow?
To view each loved one blotted from life's page,
And be alone on earth as I am now.

BYRON: *Childe Harold,* II, 1812

The monumental pomp of age.

WILLIAM WORDSWORTH: *The White Doe of Rylstone,* III, 1817

Tranquility is the *summum bonum* of old age.

THOMAS JEFFERSON: *Letter to Mark L. Hill,* 1820

Just as old age is creeping on apace,
And clouds come o'er the sunset of our day,
They kindly leave us, though not quite alone,
But in good company – the gout or stone.

BYRON: *Don Juan,* III, 1821

The worst old age is that of the mind.

WILLIAM HAZLITT: *The Prose Album,* 1829 (Monthly Magazine, July)

I am as one who is left alone at a banquet, the lights dead and the flowers faded.

E. G. BULWER-LYTTON: *The Last Days of Pompeii,* V, 1834

One evil in old age is that, as your time is come, you think every little illness is the beginning of the end. When a man expects to be arrested, every knock at the door is an alarm.

SYDNEY SMITH: *Letter to Wilmot Horton,* Feb. 8, 1836

Father Time is not always a hard parent, and, though he tarries for none of his children, often lays his hand lightly on those who have used him well.

CHARLES DICKENS: *Barnaby Rudge,* II, 1840

Nature abhors the old, and old age seems the only disease; all others run into this one.

R. W. EMERSON: *Circles,* 1841

The days darken round me, and the years,
Among new men, strange faces, other minds.

ALFRED TENNYSON: *Morte d'Arthur,* 1842

Every man wants to reach old age – which is to say, a state of life wherein he may say "It is bad today, and it will be worse tomorrow, and so on until the worst of all."

ARTHUR SCHOPENHAUER: *Parerga und Paralipomena,* I, 1851

The closing years of life are like the end of a mask-ball, when the masks are dropped.

IBID.

How earthly old people become – mouldy as the grave . . . They remind me of earthworms.

H. D. THOREAU: *Journal,* Aug. 16, 1853

Old age, calm, expanded, broad with the haughty breadth of the universe,
Old age, flowing free with the delicious near-by freedom of death.

WALT WHITMAN: *Song of the Open Road,* 1856

I'm growing fonder of my staff;
  I'm growing dimmer in the eyes;
I'm growing fainter in my laugh;
  I'm growing deeper in my sighs;
I'm growing careless of my dress;
  I'm growing frugal of my gold;
I'm growing wise; I'm growing – yes –
    I'm growing old.

J. G. SAXE: *I'm Growing Old,* 1860

The grandeur and exquisiteness of old age.

WALT WHITMAN: *Song at Sunset,* 1860

I see in you the estuary that enlarges and spreads itself grandly as it pours in the grave sea.

WALT WHITMAN: *To Old Age,* 1860

Living with old people, however good, is not good for a man.

JOHN RUSKIN: *Letter to Rawdon Brown,* May 10, 1862

When all the world is old, lad,
  And all the trees are brown;
And all the sport is stale, lad,
  And all the wheels run down:
Creep home, and take your place there,
  The spent and maimed among:
God grant you find one face there
  You loved when all was young.

CHARLES KINGSLEY: *The Water-Babies,* II, 1863

Grow old along with me!
The best is yet to be,
The last of life, for which the first was made.

ROBERT BROWNING: *Rabbi Ben Ezra,* 1864

I am nearly blind and totally deaf. My son Charles undresses me, and I do not give any trouble. I dine on soup.

W. S. LANDOR: *Letter to Robert Browning,* Aug. 22, 1864 (Landor died on Sept. 17, aged 89)

How strange it seems, with so much gone
Of life and love, to still live on.

J. G. WHITTIER: *Snow-Bound,* 1866

It is time to be old,
To take in sail.

R. W. EMERSON: *Terminus,* 1867 (Atlantic Monthly, Jan.)

A man over ninety is a great comfort to all his elderly neighbors: he is a picket-guard at the extreme outpost; and the young folks of sixty and seventy feel that the enemy must get by him before he can come near their camp.

O. W. HOLMES: *The Guardian Angel,* II, 1867

We are but older children, dear,
Who fret to find our bedtime near.

C. L. DODGSON (LEWIS CARROLL): *Through the Looking-Glass,* 1871

I stay a little longer, as one stays
To cover up the embers that still burn.

H. W. LONGFELLOW: *Three Friends of Mine,* IV, 1874

Age is opportunity no less
Than youth itself, though in another dress,
And as the evening twilight fades away
The sky is filled with stars, invisible by day.

H. W. LONGFELLOW: *Morituri Salutamus,* 1875

There is beauty in extreme old age —
Do you fancy you are elderly enough?

W. S. GILBERT: *The Mikado,* II, 1885

As life runs on, the road grows strange
With faces new, — and near the end
The milestones into headstones change: —
'Neath every one a friend.

J. R. LOWELL: On his 68th birthday, 1887

The tragedy of old age is not that one is old, but that one is young.

OSCAR WILDE: *The Picture of Dorian Grey,* 1891

My experience is that as soon as people are old enough to know better, they don't know anything at all.

OSCAR WILDE: *Lady Windermere's Fan,* II, 1892

Old age is an infectious chronic disease, characterized by the degeneration or enfeebling of the noble elements and by the excessive activity of the phagocytes.

ELIÉ METCHNIKOFF: *La Vieillesse,* 1904

My wife is going blind; and on the whole she is glad of it; there is nothing worth seeing. She says she hopes she will also become deaf; for there is nothing worth hearing. The best thing about being old is that you are near the goal.

AUGUST STRINDBERG: *Heat Lightning,* 1905

I am in the prime of senility.

Ascribed to JOEL CHANDLER HARRIS (*c.* 1906) in *Julia Collier Harris: Life and Letters,* 1918

As you become older, gradually accustom yourself to neglect.

E. W. HOWE: *Sinner Sermons,* 1926

When they gets old, old an' gray,
White folks looks like monkeys.

American Negro song, quoted by HOWARD W. ODUM: *Rainbow Round My Shoulder,* XXI, 1928

The riders in a race do not stop short when they reach the goal. There is a little finishing canter before coming to a standstill. There is time to hear the kind voice of friends and to say to one's self: "The work is done."

O. W. HOLMES II: Speech on his 91st birthday, Washington, March 8, 1932

King Solomon and King David
Led very merry lives,
With very many concubines
And very many wives,
Until old age came creeping,
With very many qualms,
Then Solomon wrote the Proverbs,
And David wrote the Psalms.

Author unidentified

Ve get too soon old, and too late smart.

IBID.

Respect for the aged is respect for God.

BULGARIAN PROVERB

Age lacks kindness as dry weather lacks dew.

CHINESE PROVERB

Old trees have withered tops. IBID.

Old age makes a sorry traveling companion.

DANISH PROVERB

Age does not increase sense; it only makes one go slower. FINNISH PROVERB

Children sometimes flatter old people, but they never love them. FRENCH PROVERB

Old age is a curse that never comes alone.

GREEK PROVERB

To the old cat give a tender mouse.

ITALIAN PROVERB

[*See also* Abstemiousness, Affront, Age, Ages, Alliteration, Avarice, Beer, Building, Care, Cheerfulness, City, Drinking, Eighty, Friend, Happiness, Kindness, Life, Loneliness, Lying, Man and Woman, Man (Old), Senility, Seventy, Sixty, Slovenliness, Superannuation, Tranquility, Woman (Old), Youth and Age.

Ages

Childhood is ignorant, boyhood is lightheaded, youth is rash, and old age is ill-humored.

LUIS DE GRANADA: *Guia de Peccadores,* *c.* 1555

He that is not handsome at 20, nor strong at 30, nor rich at 40, nor wise at 50, will never be handsome, strong, rich or wise.

GEORGE HERBERT: *Outlandish Proverbs*, 1640

At 20 a man is a peacock, at 30 a lion, at 40 a camel, at 50 a serpent, at 60 a dog, at 70 an ape, and at 80 nothing.

BALTASAR GRACIÁN: *The Art of Worldly Wisdom*, 1647

Although the whole of life is allowed by everyone to be short, the several divisions of it appear long and tedious.

JOSEPH ADDISON: *The Spectator*, June 16, 1711

At 20 years of age the will reigns; at 30 the wit; at 40 the judgment.

BENJAMIN FRANKLIN: *Poor Richard's Almanac*, 1741

Youth is confident, manhood wary, and old age confident again.

M. F. TUPPER: *Proverbial Philosophy*, 1838

Youth is a blunder; manhood a struggle; old age a regret.

BENJAMIN DISRAELI: *Coningsby*, III, 1844

The first forty years of life give us the text; the next thirty supply the commentary on it.

ARTHUR SCHOPENHAUER: *Parerga und Paralipomena*, I, 1851

A man is still young so long as women can make him happy or unhappy. He reaches middle age when they can no longer make him unhappy. He is old when they cease to make him either happy or unhappy.

Author unidentified

At ten, a child; at twenty, wild;
At thirty, tame if ever;
At forty, wise; at fifty, rich;
At sixty, good, or never.

IBID.

For twenty years man grows; for twenty he blooms; for twenty he stands still; and for twenty he fades away.

FLEMISH PROVERB

Childhood ends at 12, youth at 18, love at 20, faith at 30, hope at 40, and desire at 50.

GERMAN PROVERB

In the morning of life, work; in the midday, give counsel; in the evening, pray.

GREEK PROVERB

When a man is young he writes songs; grown up, he speaks in proverbs; in old age he preaches pessimism.

HEBREW PROVERB

[*See also* Age (Old), Ague, Body and Mind, Enjoyment, Experience, Folly, Idleness, Longevity, Man (Old), Marriage, Pedagogue, Woman (Old), Youth and Age.

Ages, Dark

The Dark Ages were nothing but a brief eclipse of the sun.

JEAN PAUL RICHTER: *Hesperus*, XXIV, 1795

Perhaps in time the so-called Dark Ages will be thought of as including our own.

G. C. LICHTENBERG: *Reflections*, 1799

In the long night of the Dark Ages we look upon the earth, and only the convent and the castle appear to be alive. . . . The convent prays and the castle sings; the cottage hungers and groans and dies.

W. WINWOOD READE: *The Martyrdom of Man*, III, 1872

Ages, Middle

The Middle Ages had their wars and agonies, but also intense delights. Their gold was dashed with blood; but ours is sprinkled with dust.

JOHN RUSKIN: *Modern Painters*, IV, 1856

Agitation

[*See* Bloodshed, Republic.

Agitator

Agitators are like those who fish for eels. When the water is tranquil they catch nothing, but if they stir up the mud they make a haul.

ARISTOPHANES: *The Knights*, 424 B.C.

A man who is sure to cause injuries to be done to him wherever he goes is almost as great an evil and inconvenience as if he were himself the wrong-doer.

HENRY TAYLOR: *The Statesman*, 1836

[*See also* Demagogue, Labor.

Agnostic

Stranger
Beneath this cone, in unconsecrated ground,
A friend to the liberties of mankind
Directed his body to be inurned.
May the example contribute to emancipate thy mind from the fears of superstition, and the wicked arts of priestcraft.

JOHN BASKERVILLE: *Epitaph for himself*, c. 1775

I do not see much difference between avowing that there is no God, and implying that nothing definite can for certain be known about Him.

J. H. NEWMAN: *On the Scope and Nature of University Education*, I, 1852

Alas, for him who never sees
The stars shine through the cypress trees!
Who, hopeless, lays his dead away,
Nor looks to see the breaking day
Across the mournful marbles play!

J. G. WHITTIER: *Snow-Bound*, 1866

Every person, upon objecting to being sworn, and stating as the ground of such objection to being sworn that he has no religious belief, or that the taking of an oath is contrary to his religious belief, shall be permitted to make this solemn affirmation instead of taking an oath.

The English Oaths Act, 1888

It is wrong for a man to say that he is certain of the objective truth of any proposition unless he can produce evidence which logically justifies that certainty. This is what agnosticism asserts.

T. H. HUXLEY: *Agnosticism and Christianity,* 1889

There never was on this earth a body of educated and cultured men so thoroughly agnostic and atheistic as the mass of Confucian scholars.

ARTHUR H. SMITH: *Chinese Characteristics,* 1892

I do not consider it an insult, but rather a compliment to be called an agnostic. I do not pretend to know where many ignorant men are sure — that is all that agnosticism means.

CLARENCE DARROW: At the Scopes trial, Dayton, Tenn., July 13, 1925

[*See also* Annihilation, Antichrist, Atheism, Atheist, Education, Infidel, Skeptic, Skepticism.

Agreeable

What we call an agreeable man is he who is endowed with the natural bent to do acceptable things, from a delight he takes in them merely as such; the affectation of that character is what constitutes a fop.

RICHARD STEELE: *The Spectator,* Jan. 21, 1712

My business in the social system is to be agreeable; I take it that everybody's business in the social system is to be agreeable.

CHARLES DICKENS: *Bleak House,* XVIII, 1853

My idea of an agreeable person is a person who agrees with me.

BENJAMIN DISRAELI: *Lothair,* XII, 1870

The greatest mistake is the trying to be more agreeable than you can be.

WALTER BAGEHOT: *Biographical Studies,* 1880

[*See also* Applause.

Agreement

Men keep their agreements when it is to the advantage of neither to break them.

Ascribed to SOLON (*c.* 638–558 B.C.)

They two agreed like two cats in a gutter.

JOHN HEYWOOD: *Proverbs,* 1546

To agree like cats and dogs.

ENGLISH PHRASE, traced by Smith to 1579

Agree, for the law is costly.

WILLIAM CAMDEN: *Remains Concerning Britain* (*4th ed.*), 1636

An ill agreement is better than a good judgment.

GEORGE HERBERT: *Outlandish Proverbs,* 1640

They agree like bells; they want nothing but hanging.

JOHN RAY: *English Proverbs,* 1670

An agreement will break a custom.

WELSH PROVERB

[*See also* Coöperation, Lawyer.

Agriculture

There seem to be but three ways for a nation to acquire wealth. The first is by war, as the Romans did, in plundering their conquered neighbors. This is robbery. The second by commerce, which is generally cheating. The third by agriculture, the only honest way, wherein man receives a real increase of the seed thrown into the ground, in a kind of continual miracle, wrought by the hand of God in his favor, as a reward for his innocent life and his virtuous industry.

BENJAMIN FRANKLIN: *Positions to be Examined Concerning National Wealth,* April 4, 1769

I know of no pursuit in which more real and important services can be rendered to any country than by improving its agriculture, its breed of useful animals, and other branches of a husbandman's cares.

GEORGE WASHINGTON: *Letter to John Sinclair,* July 20, 1794

The first and most precious of all the arts.

THOMAS JEFFERSON: *Letter to Robert R. Livingston,* 1800

With the introduction of agriculture mankind entered upon a long period of meanness, misery, and madness, from which they are only now being freed by the beneficent operation of the machine.

BERTRAND RUSSELL: *The Conquest of Happiness,* x, 1930

[*See also* Farm, Farmer, Farming, Laissez-faire.

Ague

The burning ague.

LEVITICUS XXVI, 16, *c.* 700 B.C.

A quartan ague kills old men, and heals young.

JOHN RAY: *English Proverbs,* 1670

An ague in Spring is physic for a king.

H. G. BOHN: *Handbook of Proverbs,* 1855

[*See also* Joy.

Air

Sooner slays ill air than sword.

Anon.: *Ratis Raving, c.* 1450

Air coming in at the window is as bad as a cross-bow shot.

THOMAS FULLER: *Gnomologia,* 1732 (An Italian proverb, recorded a century earlier)

A nutritive substance supplied by a bountiful Providence for the fattening of the poor.
AMBROSE BIERCE: *The Devil's Dictionary,* 1906

Fresh air keeps the doctor poor.
DANISH PROVERB

[*See also* Chameleon, City, Language.

Airship

[*See* Aviation.

Airy

Airy, fairy Lilian,
Flitting, fairy Lilian,
When I ask her if she love me,
Clasps her tiny hands above me,
Laughing all she can.
ALFRED TENNYSON: *Lilian,* 1830

Alabaster

[*See* Smooth.

Alamo

Remember the Alamo!
Battle-cry of the Texans at the Battle of San Jacinto, April 21, 1836 (The Alamo at San Antonio was stormed by the Mexicans on March 6, 1836, and its whole garrison, including David Crockett and James Bowie, killed)

Alarm

Hear the loud alarum bells —
Brazen bells!
What a tale of terror, now, their turbulency tells!
In the startled ear of night
How they scream out their affright!
E. A. POE: *The Bells,* 1849 (Sartain's Union Magazine, Nov.)

[*See also* Soldier, Trumpet.

Alarmist

You could spy trouble if your eyes were out.
THOMAS FULLER: *Gnomologia,* 1732

Albatross

"God save thee, ancient mariner!
From the fiends that plague thee thus! —
Why look'st thou so?" — "With my cross-bow
I shot the albatross."
S. T. COLERIDGE: *The Ancient Mariner,* I, 1798

Alchemy

The science of alchemy I like very well. I like it not only for the profits it brings in melting metals, in decocting, preparing, extracting, and distilling herbs, roots; I like it also for the sake of the allegory and secret signification, which is exceedingly fine, touching the resurrection of the dead at the last day.
MARTIN LUTHER: *Table-Talk,* DCCCV, 1569

Alcibiades (c. 450–404 B.C.)

[*See* Flute.

Alcott, A. Bronson (1799–1888)

He soared into the infinite and dived into the unfathomable, but never paid cash.
Author unidentified

Ale

Ale will make a cat speak.
ENGLISH PROVERB, familiar since the XVI century

Nor frost, nor snow, nor wind I trow,
Can hurt me if it would,
I am so wrapped within and lapped
With jolly good ale and old.
Anon.: *A Song of Ale, c.* 1500

When ale is in, wit is out.
JOHN HEYWOOD: *Proverbs,* 1546

Back and side go bare, go bare,
Both foot and hand go cold;
But belly, God send thee good ale enough,
Whether it be new or old.
JOHN STILL (BISHOP OF BATH AND WELLS) (?): *Gammer Gurton's Needle,* II, 1566

I would give all my fame for a pot of ale and safety.
SHAKESPEARE: *Henry V,* III, *c.* 1599

In . . . ale is all included: meat, drink and cloth.
BEAUMONT and FLETCHER: *The Scornful Lady,* IV, 1610

It is worse to be drunk with ale or beer than with wine; for the drunkenness endureth longer to the utter ruin of the brain and understanding, by reason that the fumes and vapors of ale or beer that ascend to the head are more gross, and therefore cannot be so soon resolved as those that rise up of wine.
TOBIAS VENNER: *Via recta,* 1620

He that buys land buys many stones;
He that buys flesh buys many bones;
He that buys eggs buys many shells;
But he that buys good ale buys nothing else.
JOHN RAY: *English Proverbs,* 1670

I have fed purely upon ale; I have ate my ale, drank my ale, and I always sleep upon ale.
GEORGE FARQUHAR: *The Beaux' Stratagem,* I, 1707

All-powerful ale! whose sorrow-soothing sweets
Oft I repeat in vacant afternoons.
THOMAS WARTON: *The Oxford Sausage,* 1764

Merry swains who quaff the nut-brown ale,
And sing enamour'd of the nut-brown maid.
JAMES BEATTIE: *The Minstrel,* I, 1771

Genial and gladdening is the power of good ale, the true and proper drink of Englishmen. He

is not deserving of the name of Englishman who speaketh against ale.
GEORGE BORROW: *Lavengro,* LXVIII, 1851

[*See also* Beer, Christian, Drinker, Drinking.

Ale-house

Everyone has a penny to spend at a new ale-house. JOHN RAY: *English Proverbs,* 1670

The third generation is never seen in an ale-house. IRISH PROVERB

[*See also* Character (National), Church (house).

Alexander of Macedon (365–323 B.C.)

Alexander fought many battles, and took of the strongholds of all, and slew the kings of the earth. And he went through even to the ends of the earth, and took the spoils of many nations: and the earth was quiet before him. And he gathered a power, and a very strong army; and his heart was exalted and lifted up. And he subdued countries of nations, and princes; and they became tributary to him. And after these things he fell down upon his bed, and knew that he should die.
I MACCABEES, I, 2–6, *c.* 75 B.C.

Alexandrine

A needless Alexandrine ends the song,
That, like a wounded snake, drags its slow length along.
ALEXANDER POPE: *An Essay on Criticism,* II, 1711

Algebra

Nothing proves more clearly that the mind seeks truth, and nothing reflects more glory upon it, than the delight it takes, sometimes in spite of itself, in the driest and thorniest researches of algebra.
BERNARD DE FONTENELLE: *Histoire du renouvellement de l'Académie des Sciences,* pref., 1708

Alibi

Oh, Sammy, Sammy, vy worn't there a alleybi!
CHARLES DICKENS: *The Pickwick Papers,* II, 1837

Alice

Don't you remember sweet Alice, Ben Bolt?
Sweet Alice, whose hair was so brown?
Who wept with delight when you gave her a smile
And trembled with fear at your frown?
T. D. ENGLISH: *Ben Bolt,* 1843 (New York Mirror, Sept. 2)

Alien

The sons of the alien shall be your plowmen and your vinedressers.
ISAIAH LXI, 5, *c.* 700 B.C.

An alien ought to attend to nothing but his own business, never meddle with the affairs of others, and least of all pry into the concerns of state. CICERO: *De officiis,* I, 78 B.C.

Aliens within the jurisdiction of the United States are not entitled of right to liberty of agitation directed against the government or American institutions.
Republican National Platform, 1920

On the strength of the solidarity of the workers of all nations the U.S.S.R. grants all political rights to foreigners domiciled in its territory as useful members of the working class.
CONSTITUTION OF THE U.S.S.R., I, Jan. 31, 1924

[*See also* Foreigner, Polygamy, Stranger.

Alimony

She is as implacable an adversary as a wife suing for alimony.
WILLIAM WYCHERLEY: *The Plain Dealer,* I, *c.* 1674

The cash surrender value of a husband.
Author unidentified

Alive

All live things look bigger than dead ones.
ADRIAN JONES: *Thoughts of an Old Sculptor,* 1935

Allegiance

I (A.B.) being by God's Providence an inhabitant and freeman within the jurisdiction of this commonwealth, do freely acknowledge myself to be subject to the government thereof, and therefore do here swear by the great and dreadful Name of the Ever-living God, that I will be true and faithful to the same, and will accordingly yield assistance and support thereunto with my person and estate, as in equity I am bound.
STEPHEN DAYE: *The Oath of a Free Man,* 1639

Allegory

Allegories, when well chosen, are like so many tracts of light in a discourse, that make everything about them clear and beautiful.
JOSEPH ADDISON: *The Spectator,* July 3, 1712

However agreeable long allegories may at first be by their novelty, they never afford any lasting pleasure: witness "The Faerie Queene," which, with great power of expression, variety of images, and melody of versification, is scarce ever read a second time.
H. H. KAMES: *Elements of Criticism,* 1762

Allegory lives in a transparent palace.
A. M. LEMIERRE: *Peinture, c.* 1775

Headstrong as an allegory on the banks of the Nile.
R. B. SHERIDAN: *The Rivals,* III, 1775

A man's life of any worth is a continual allegory.
JOHN KEATS: *Letter,* Feb. 18, 1819

No human ingenuity could produce such a centipede as a long allegory in which the correspondence between the outward sign and the thing signified should be exactly preserved.

T. B. MACAULAY: *John Bunyan*, 1830 (Edinburgh Review, Dec.)

Allergy

Some men have strange antipathies in their natures against that sort of food which others love and live upon. I have read of one that could not endure to eat either bread or flesh; of another that fell swoondling into a fit at the smell of a rose. . . . There are some who, if a cat accidentally come into the room, though they neither see it, nor are told of it, will presently be in a sweat, and ready to die.

INCREASE MATHER: *Remarkable Providences*, IV, 1684

[*See also* Cheese, Pork.

Alley

He despises me, I suppose, because I live in an alley: tell him his soul lives in an alley.

Ascribed to BEN JONSON: Said of James I, *c.* 1620

There is no lady in the land
Is half so sweet as Sally;
She is the darling of my heart,
And she lives in our alley.

HENRY CAREY: *Sally in Our Alley*, 1729

All-Fools' Day

The first day of April,
You may send a fool whither you will.

THOMAS FULLER: *Gnomologia*, 1732

The first of April, some do say,
Is set apart for All-Fools' Day;
But why the people call it so
Nor I nor they themselves do know.

Anon.: *Poor Robin's Almanac*, 1760

Alliance

Close alliances with despots are never safe for free states.

DEMOSTHENES: *Second Philippic*, *c.* 345 B.C.

[The Utopians] never enter into any alliance with any other state. They think leagues are useless things, and reckon that if the common ties of human nature do not knit men together the faith of promises will have no great effect on them.

THOMAS MORE: *Utopia*, 1516

How can tyrants safely govern home
Unless abroad they purchase great alliance?

SHAKESPEARE: *III Henry VI*, III, *c.* 1591

'Tis our true policy to steer clear of permanent alliances with any portion of the foreign world.

GEORGE WASHINGTON: Farewell Address, Sept. 17, 1796

Peace, commerce and honest friendship with all nations — entangling alliances with none.

THOMAS JEFFERSON: Inaugural Address, March 4, 1801

The nature of the English government forbids, of itself, reliance on her engagements; and it is well known she has been the least faithful to her alliances of any nation of Europe.

THOMAS JEFFERSON: *Letter to John Langdon*, 1810

Any alliance whose purpose is not the intention to wage war is senseless and useless.

ADOLF HITLER: *Mein Kampf*, I, 1925

After the war is over, make alliances.

GREEK PROVERB

[*See also* Foreign Relations, Treaty.

Alligator

[*See* Insult.

Alliteration

O *T*ite *t*ute, *T*ati, *t*ibi *t*anta, *t*yranne, *t*ulisti.

Ascribed by Cicero to QUINTUS ENNIUS (239–169 B.C.)

In a Summer *s*eason, when *s*oft was the *s*un.

WILLIAM LANGLAND: *Piers Plowman*, 1377

The *p*reyful *p*rincess *p*ierced and *p*ricked a *p*retty *p*leasing *p*ricket.

SHAKESPEARE: *Love's Labor's Lost*, IV, *c.* 1595

Apt *a*lliteration's *a*rtful *a*id.

CHARLES CHURCHILL: *The Prophecy of Famine*, 1763

*A*n *A*ustri*a*n *a*rmy, *a*wfully *a*rr*a*yed,
*B*oldly *b*y *b*attery *b*esieged *B*elgrade;
*C*ossa*c*k *c*ommanders *c*annonading *c*ome,
*D*ealing *d*estruction's *d*evastating *d*oom . . .

Author unidentified (The poem is an acrostic on the alphabet, and every line is alliterative. It has been traced to 1817)

The *m*oan of doves in im*m*e*m*orial el*m*s,
The *m*ur*m*uring of innu*m*erable bees.

ALFRED TENNYSON: *The Princess*, VII, 1847

Wha*t* a *t*ale of *t*error now *t*heir *t*urbulency *t*ells.

E. A. POE: *The Bells*, 1849 (Sartain's Union Magazine, Nov.)

Alliteration tickles the ear, and is a very popular form of language among savages.

BENJAMIN DISRAELI: Speech in the House of Commons, March 19, 1860

*A*s *a*ge *a*dvances, *a*ils *a*nd *a*ches *a*ttend,
*B*acks *b*uilded *b*roadest *b*urdensomely *b*end;
*C*uttingly *c*ruel *c*omes *c*onsuming *c*are,
*D*ealing *d*elusions, *d*rivelry, *d*espair.

R. H. NEWELL (ORPHEUS C. KERR): *Age Bluntly Considered*, 1864

*M*ute in the *m*idst, the whole *m*an one a*m*aze.

ROBERT BROWNING: *The Ring and the Book*, II, 1869

Almanac

The almanac is part of the Common Law.

MR. CHIEF JUSTICE HOLT: *Judgment in Brough* vs. *Parkings*, 1703

Almost

Almost and well nigh
Saves many a lie.
JOHN CLARKE: *Paroemiologia Anglo-Latina,* 1639

Almost was never hanged. IBID.

Almost never killed a fly.
GERMAN PROVERB

Alms

Almsgiving will make atonement for sin.
ECCLESIASTICUS III, 33, *c.* 180 B.C.

Take heed that ye do not your alms before men, to be seen of them: otherwise ye have no reward of your Father which is in heaven.
MATTHEW VI, 1, *c.* 75

When thou doest alms, let not thy left hand know what thy right hand doeth.
MATTHEW VI, 3

Sell that ye have, and give alms.
LUKE XII, 33, *c.* 75

A householder, by giving alms, gains the same reward in Heaven as a student who presents a cow to his teacher.
THE CODE OF MANU, III, *c.* 100

Be constant in prayer and give alms, and what good ye have sent before for your souls ye shall find it with God.
THE KORAN, II, *c.* 625

Alms never make poor.
GEORGE HERBERT: *Outlandish Proverbs,* 1640

Steal the hog, and give the feet for alms.
GEORGE HERBERT: *Jacula Prudentum,* 1651

He that hath a good memory giveth few alms.
THOMAS FULLER: *Worthies of England,* 1662 (Cited as a Welsh proverb)

Steal the goose and give the giblets in alms.
JOHN RAY: *English Proverbs,* 1670

I must be dunned for alms, and do not scramble over hedges and ditches in searching for opportunities of flinging away my money on good works.
HORACE WALPOLE: *Letter to Hannah More,* Feb. 20, 1790

His alms were money put to interest
In the other world.
ROBERT SOUTHEY: *The Alderman's Funeral, c.* 1820

The greatest of almsgivers is cowardice.
F. W. NIETZSCHE: *Human All-too-Human,* II, 1878

I do not give alms: I am not poor enough for that.
F. W. NIETZSCHE: *Thus Spake Zarathustra,* intro., 1885

The little alms are the best alms.
FRENCH PROVERB

[*See also* Benevolence, Charity, Generosity, Philanthropy, Poor.

Alone

It is not good that man should be alone.
GENESIS II, 18, *c.* 700 B.C.

Woe to him that is alone when he falleth, for he hath not another to help him up.
ECCLESIASTES IV, 10, *c.* 200 B.C.

I am as a sparrow alone upon the housetop.
PSALMS CII, 7, *c.* 150 B.C.

It is better to be alone than in ill company.
GEORGE PETTIE: *Civil Conversations of Stefano Guazzo,* 1581 (Quoted as a proverb)

Eagles commonly fly alone; they are crows, daws and starlings that flock together.
JOHN WEBSTER: *The Duchess of Malfi,* V, *c.* 1614

By all means use sometimes to be alone:
Salute thyself; see what thy soul doth wear.
GEORGE HERBERT: *The Temple,* 1633

Who eats his cock alone must saddle his horse alone.
GEORGE HERBERT: *Outlandish Proverbs,* 1640

A man is never alone, not only because he is with himself and his own thoughts, but because he is with the Devil, who ever consorts with our solitude.
THOMAS BROWNE: *Religio Medici,* II, 1642

Two Paradises 'twere in one
To live in Paradise alone.
ANDREW MARVELL: *Thoughts in a Garden, c.* 1650

Who can enjoy alone?
JOHN MILTON: *Paradise Lost,* VIII, 1667

At the beginning of love and at its end the lovers are embarrassed to be left alone.
JEAN DE LA BRUYÈRE: *Caractères,* IV, 1688

Oh! lost to virtue, lost to manly thought,
Lost to the noble sallies of the soul,
Who think it solitude to be alone.
EDWARD YOUNG: *Night Thoughts,* III, 1742

I was never less alone than while by myself.
EDWARD GIBBON: *Memoirs,* I, *c.* 1793

Alone, alone, all all alone,
Alone on a wide wide sea!
And never a saint took pity on
My soul in agony.
S. T. COLERIDGE: *The Ancient Mariner,* IV, 1798

Oh, the pleasure of eating alone! — eating my dinner alone!
CHARLES LAMB: *Letter to Mrs. Wordsworth,* Feb. 18, 1818

Why should we faint and fear to live alone,
Since all alone, so Heaven has willed, we die?
JOHN KEBLE: *The Christian Year,* 1827

We walk alone in the world. Friends, such as we desire, are dreams and fables.
R. W. EMERSON: *Friendship,* 1841

When is man strong until he feels alone?
ROBERT BROWNING: *Colombe's Birthday,* 1844

Myson the misanthropist was once surprised as he was laughing to himself. "Why do you laugh?" he was asked; "there is no one with you." "That," he replied, "is just why I do."
ARTHUR SCHOPENHAUER: *Parerga und Paralipomena,* I, 1851

All we ask is to be let alone.
JEFFERSON DAVIS: Message to the Confederate Congress, April 29, 1861

Woe unto him that is never alone, and cannot bear to be alone.
P. G. HAMERTON: *The Intellectual Life,* IX, 1873

The strongest man is the one who stands most alone.
HENRIK IBSEN: *An Enemy of the People,* V, 1882

When a man is alone he is safe.
ARAB PROVERB

He who eats alone chokes alone. IBID.

A man alone is either a god or a devil. (Homo solus aut deus, aut daemon.)
LATIN PROVERB

Never less alone than when alone. (Nunquam minus solus, quam quum solus.) IBID.

It is unpleasant to go alone, even to be drowned. RUSSIAN PROVERB

[*See also* Age (Old), Dinner, Enjoyment, Forsaken, Liberty, Loneliness, Love, Marriage, Retirement, Sin, Solitude, Travel, Widowed, Wisdom.

Alpha and Omega

I am Alpha and Omega, the beginning and the end, the first and the last.
REVELATION XXII, 13, *c.* 95

Alphabet

What a stupid thing is an old man learning an alphabet.
MICHEL DE MONTAIGNE: *Essays,* II, 1580

Thou must learn the alphabet, to wit, the order of the letters as they stand, perfectly without book, and where every letter standeth: as (*b*) near the beginning, (*n*) about the middest, and (*t*) toward the end.
ROBERT CAWDREY: *Table Alphabetical,* 1604

[*See also* Anger.

Alps

[*See* Hill, Italy.

Altar

Noah builded an altar unto the Lord; and took of every clean beast, and of every clean fowl, and offered burnt offerings on the altar.
GENESIS VIII, 20, *c.* 700 B.C.

I found an altar with this inscription: To the Unknown God. ACTS XVII, 23, *c.* 75

He that serves at the altar ought to live by the altar. THOMAS FULLER: *Gnomologia,* 1732

So shall they build me altars in their zeal
Where knaves shall minister, and fools shall kneel. THOMAS MOORE: *Lalla Rookh,* 1817

Strike — for your altars and your fires.
FITZ-GREENE HALLECK: *Marco Bozzaris,* 1825 (Borrowed from a Latin phrase: *pro aris et focis*)

Altruism

Man is not so wedded to his own interest but that he can make the common good the mark of his aim.
JOHN WISE: *A Vindication of the Government of New England Churches,* II, 1717

There is no merit in saving an innocent babe ready to drop into the fire; the action is neither good nor bad, and what benefit soever the infant received, we only obliged ourselves, for to have seen it fall, and not striven to have hindered it, would have caused a pain which self-preservation compelled us to prevent.
BERNARD DE MANDEVILLE: *An Inquiry Into the Origin of Moral Virtue,* 1723

It is the freeman who must win freedom for the slave; it is the wise man who must think for the fool; it is the happy who must serve the unhappy.
JEAN PAUL RICHTER: *Hesperus,* I, 1795

A race of altruists is necessarily a race of slaves. A race of free men is necessarily a race of egoists.
MAX STIRNER: *The Ego and His Own,* 1845

I have tried to do good in the world, not harm, as my enemies would have the world believe. I have helped men, and have attempted in my humble way to be of some service to my country.
Ascribed to J. PIERPONT MORGAN I (1837–1913)

Nobody does good to men with impunity.
AUGUSTE RODIN (1840–1917)

The art of doing unselfish things for selfish reasons. Author unidentified

[*See also* Benevolence, Charity, Philanthropy, Self-sacrifice, Unselfishness.

Ambassador

The ambassadors of peace shall weep bitterly.
ISAIAH XXXIII, 7, *c.* 700 B.C.

An ambassador is sent unto the heathen.
JEREMIAH XLIX, 14, *c.* 625 B.C.

A man who is base at home will not acquit himself with honor when he is sent to represent his country abroad: the place will be changed, but not the man.
AESCHINES: *Ctesiphontem,* 337 B.C.

An ambassador should be versed in all the sciences; he should understand hints, gestures and expressions of the face; he should be honest, skillful and of good family.
THE CODE OF MANU, VII, *c.* 100

A sovereign should always regard an ambassador as a spy.
THE HITOPADESA, III, *c.* 500

Ambassadors are the eyes and ears of states.
FRANCESCO GUICCIARDINI: *Storia d'Italia,* 1564

An ambassador is an honest man sent to lie abroad for the commonwealth.
HENRY WOTTON: Written in the autograph album of Christopher Fleckamore, 1604

Above all, do not fail to give good dinners, and to pay attention to the women.
NAPOLEON I: To the Archbishop of Malines, on appointing him ambassador to London, 1802

There are a large number of well-meaning ambassadors . . . who belong to what I call the pink-tea type, who merely reside in the service instead of working in the service.
THEODORE ROOSEVELT: *Letter to R. H. Davis,* Jan. 3, 1905

A politician who is given a job abroad in order to get him out of the country.
Author unidentified

[*See also* Diplomat.

Amber

We see how flies, and spiders, and the like, get a sepulchre in amber, more durable than the monument and embalming of the body of any king.
FRANCIS BACON: *Sylva Sylvarum,* 1627

I saw a fly within a bead
Of amber cleanly buried:
The urn was little, but the room
More rich than Cleopatra's tomb.
ROBERT HERRICK: *Hesperides,* 1648

Pretty, in amber, to observe the forms
Of hairs, or straws, or dirt, or grubs, or worms;
The things, we know, are neither rich nor rare,
But wonder how the devil they got there.
ALEXANDER POPE: *An Epistle to Dr. Arbuthnot,* 1735

Ambition

In men of the highest character and noblest genius there is to be found an insatiable desire for honor, command, power, and glory.
CICERO: *De officiis,* I, 78 B.C.

Ambition is a vice, but it may be the father of virtue.
QUINTILIAN: *De institutione oratoria,* II, *c.* 90

The noble Brutus
Hath told you Caesar was ambitious;
If it were so, it was a grievous fault;
And grievously hath Caesar answered it.
SHAKESPEARE: *Julius Caesar,* III, 1599

When that the poor have cried, Caesar hath wept:
Ambition should be made of sterner stuff.
IBID.

Ambition, like a torrent, ne'er looks back;
And is a swelling, and the last affection
A high mind can put off.
BEN JONSON: *Catiline,* III, 1611

Vain the ambition of kings
Who seek by trophies and dead things
To leave a living name behind,
And weave but nets to catch the wind.
JOHN WEBSTER: *Vanitas Vanitatum,* 1612

I charge thee, fling away ambition.
By that sin fell the angels; how can man then,
The image of his Maker, hope to win by it?
SHAKESPEARE and JOHN FLETCHER: *Henry VIII,* III, 1613

The ambitious climbs up high and perilous stairs, and never cares how to come down; the desire of rising hath swallowed up his fear of a fall.
THOMAS ADAMS: *Diseases of the Soul,* 1616

Ambition is like choler, which is a humor that maketh man active, earnest, full of alacrity and stirring, if it be not stopped. But if it be stopped, and cannot have its way, it becometh a dust, and thereby malign and venomous.
FRANCIS BACON: *Essays,* XXXVI, 1625

Ambition, having reached the summit, longs to descend.
PIERRE CORNEILLE: *Cinna,* II, 1639

Ambition is most aroused by the trumpet-clang of another's fame.
BALTASAR GRACIÁN: *The Art of Worldly Wisdom,* 1647

We are so presumptuous that we would be known by the whole world, and even by those who shall come when we shall be no more; and we are so vain that the esteem of five or six persons who surround us amuses and contents us.
BLAISE PASCAL: *Pensées,* III, 1670

Wild ambition loves to slide, not stand,
And fortune's ice prefers to virtue's land.
JOHN DRYDEN: *Absalom and Achitophel,* I, 1682

The slave has but one master; the man of ambition has as many as there are people useful to his fortune.
JEAN DE LA BRUYÈRE: *Caractères,* VIII, 1688

Ambition often puts men upon doing the meanest offices: so climbing is performed in the same posture with creeping.
JONATHAN SWIFT: *Thoughts on Various Subjects,* 1706

Ambition raises a secret tumult in the soul; it inflames the mind, and puts it into a violent hurry of thought.
JOSEPH ADDISON: *The Spectator,* Dec. 24, 1711

What are men who grasp at praise sublime,
But bubbles on the rapid stream of time,
That rise, and fall, that swell, and are no more,
Born, and forgot, ten thousand in an hour?
EDWARD YOUNG: *Love of Fame,* II, 1728

The same ambition can destroy or save,
And makes a patriot as it makes a knave.
ALEXANDER POPE: *An Essay on Man,* II, 1732

The same sun which gilds all nature, and exhilarates the whole creation, does not shine upon disappointed ambition.
EDMUND BURKE: *Observations on a Late State of the Nation,* 1769

I want the voice of honest praise
To follow me behind,
And to be thought, in future days,
The friend of humankind;
That after-ages, as they rise,
Exulting may proclaim,
In choral union to the skies,
Their blessings on my name.
JOHN QUINCY ADAMS: *The Wants of Man,* c. 1787

The little spice of ambition which I had in my younger days has long since evaporated, and I set still less store by a posthumous than a present name.
THOMAS JEFFERSON: *Letter to James Madison,* April, 1795

Ambition and suspicion always go together.
G. C. LICHTENBERG: *Reflections,* 1799

Ambition does not see the earth she treads on: the rock and the herbage are of one substance to her.
W. S. LANDOR: *Imaginary Conversations,* II, 1824

Hitch your wagon to a star. Let us not fag in paltry works which serve our pot and bag alone.
R. W. EMERSON: *Society and Solitude,* 1870

Rather than die,
And glide a lonely, nameless, shivering ghost
Down the dark tide of utter nothingness,
I'd write a name in blood and orphans' tears.
CINCINNATUS HEINE (JOAQUIN MILLER): *Ida,* II, 1871

Ambition is the last refuge of the failure.
OSCAR WILDE: *Phrases and Philosophies for the Use of the Young,* 1894

An overmastering desire to be vilified by enemies while living and made ridiculous by friends when dead.
AMBROSE BIERCE: *The Devil's Dictionary,* 1906

The ass went seeking for horns and lost its ears.
ARAB PROVERB

Ambition and the belly are the two worst counsellors. GERMAN PROVERB

Every eel hopes to become a whale. IBID.

Where ambition ends happiness begins.
HUNGARIAN PROVERB

[*See also* Aspiration, Avarice, Charity, Devil, Eminence, Fame, Generosity, Poe (E. A.), Power, Soldier, Wealth.

Amen

All the people shall answer and say, Amen.
DEUTERONOMY XXVII, 15, *c.* 650 B.C.

And the four beasts said Amen.
REVELATION V, 14, *c.* 95

Amendment

[*See* Late.

America

The next Augustan age will dawn on the other side of the Atlantic. There will, perhaps, be a Thucydides at Boston, a Xenophon at New York, in time a Virgil at Mexico, and a Newton at Peru. At last some curious traveler from Lima will visit England, and give a description of the ruins of St. Paul's, like the editions of Baalbec and Palmyra.
HORACE WALPOLE: *Letter to Horace Mann,* Nov. 24, 1774

Torn from a world of tyrants,
Beneath this western sky,
We formed a new dominion,
A land of liberty:
The world shall own we're masters here;
Then hasten on the day:
Huzza, huzza, huzza, huzza,
For free America.
JOSEPH WARREN: *Free America,* 1774

You cannot conquer America.
WILLIAM PITT: Speech in the House of Commons, Nov. 18, 1777

That land is like an eagle whose young gaze
Feeds on the noontide beam, whose golden plume

Floats moveless on the storm, and in the blaze
Of sunrise gleams when earth is wrapped in gloom;
An epitaph of glory for the tomb
Of murdered Europe.

P. B. SHELLEY: *The Revolt of Islam*, XI, 1818

In America the geography is sublime, but the men are not: the inventions are excellent, but the inventors one is sometimes ashamed of.

R. W. EMERSON: *The Conduct of Life*, VII, 1860

It was wonderful to find America, but it would have been more wonderful to miss it.

S. L. CLEMENS (MARK TWAIN): *Pudd'nhead Wilson*, conclusion, 1894

America is not a mere body of traders; it is a body of free men. Our greatness is built upon our freedom — is moral, not material. We have a great ardor for gain; but we have a deep passion for the rights of man.

WOODROW WILSON: Speech in New York City, Dec. 6, 1911

See America first.

Slogan invented by some unidentified railway advertising agent when the World War cut off travel to Europe, 1914

Our whole duty, for the present at any rate, is summed up in the motto: America first.

WOODROW WILSON: Speech in New York, April 20, 1915

Just what is it that America stands for? If she stands for one thing more than another it is for the sovereignty of self-governing people.

WOODROW WILSON: Speech at Pittsburgh, Jan. 29, 1916

Don't sell America short.

American saying, popular from 1925 to 1929, and attributed, in the form of "Do not sell a bear on the United States," to Junius S. Morgan (1813–1890)

In America an hour is forty minutes.

GERMAN PROVERB

[*See also* Columbus (Christopher), Idealist, United States.

American

Put none but Americans on guard tonight.

Ascribed to GEORGE WASHINGTON (It seems to be based on an order he issued April 30, 1777: "You will send me none but natives," *i.e.*, for his bodyguard)

The Americans equally detest the pageantry of a king and the superstitious hypocrisy of a bishop. *Letters of Junius*, Dec. 19, 1769

I am not a Virginian but an American.

PATRICK HENRY: Speech in the Continental Congress, Sept. 5, 1774

They are a race of convicts, and ought to be thankful for anything we allow them short of hanging.

SAMUEL JOHNSON: *Boswell's Life*, March 21, 1775

If I were an American, as I am an Englishman, while a foreign troop was landed in my country, I never would lay down my arms — never, never, never!

WILLIAM PITT: Speech in the House of Commons, Nov. 18, 1777

I am willing to love all mankind, except an American.

SAMUEL JOHNSON: *Boswell's Life*, April 15, 1778

I cannot conclude without mentioning how sensibly I feel the dismemberment of America from this empire, and that I should be miserable indeed if I did not feel that no blame on that account can be laid at my door, and did I not also know that knavery seems to be so much the striking feature of its inhabitants that it may not in the end be an evil that they will become aliens to this kingdom.

GEORGE III OF ENGLAND: *Letter to the Earl of Shelburne*, Nov. 10, 1782

What then is the American, this new man? He is either an European, or the descendant of an European, hence that strange mixture of blood, which you will find in no other country. I could point out to you a family whose grandfather was an Englishman, whose wife was Dutch, whose son married a French woman, and whose present four sons have now four wives of different nations.

ST. JOHN DE CRÈVECOEUR: *Letters From an American Farmer*, III, 1782

The name of American, which belongs to you in your national capacity, must always exalt the just pride of patriotism more than appellatives derived from local discriminations.

GEORGE WASHINGTON: Farewell Address, Sept. 19, 1796

All the men in America make money their pursuit.

RICHARD PARKINSON: *A Tour of America*, 1805

See what it is to have a nation to take its place among civilized states before it has either gentlemen or scholars. They have in the course of twenty years acquired a distinct national character for low, lying knavery.

ROBERT SOUTHEY: *Letter to W. S. Landor*, 1812

I detest the American character as much as you do.

W. S. LANDOR: *Letter to Robert Southey*, 1812

I have traveled more than four thousand miles about this country; and I never met with one single insolent or rude native American.

THOMAS HOLME: *Journal of a Year's Residence in America*, 1818

In the four quarters of the globe, who reads an American book? or goes to an American play? or looks at an American picture or statue? What does the world yet owe to American physicians or surgeons? What new substances have their chemists discovered? or what old ones have they analyzed? What new constellations have been discovered by the telescopes of Americans? What have they done in mathematics? Who drinks out of American glasses? or eats from American plates? or wears American coats or gowns? or sleeps in American blankets? Finally, under which of the old tyrannical governments of Europe is every sixth man a slave, whom his fellow-creatures may buy, and sell, and torture?

SYDNEY SMITH: In the Edinburgh Review, Jan.–May, 1820

Two selfish gods, pleasure and gain, enslave the Americans.

WILLIAM FAUX: *Memorable Days in America,* 1823

That singular people who know a little, and but a little, of everything.

JOHN NEAL: *Brother Jonathan,* I, 1825

One of the most amiable features in the character of American society is this: that men never boast of their riches, and never disguise their poverty.

WILLIAM COBBETT: *Advice to Young Men,* II, 1829

Thank God! I — I also — am an American.

DANIEL WEBSTER: Address on the completion of the Bunker Hill Monument, June 17, 1843

The American is horn-handed, and pig-headed, hard, persevering, unscrupulous, carnivorous, . . . with an incredible genius for lying.

Anon.: In the Foreign Quarterly (London), Jan., 1844

We are a puny and a fickle folk. Avarice, hesitation, and following are our diseases.

R. W. EMERSON: *The Method of Nature,* 1849

I was born an American; I will live an American; I shall die an American.

DANIEL WEBSTER: Speech in the Senate, July 17, 1850

The American is only the continuation of the English genius into new conditions, more or less propitious.

R. W. EMERSON: *English Traits,* III, 1856

The Americans, like the English, probably make love worse than any other race.

WALT WHITMAN: *An American Primer,* c. 1856

An Anglo-Saxon relapsed into semi-barbarism.

BAYARD TAYLOR: *At Home and Abroad,* 1859

I do not like the Americans of the lower orders. I am not comfortable among them. They tread on my corns and offend me. They make my daily life unpleasant. But I do respect them. I acknowledge their intelligence and personal dignity. I know that they are men and women worthy to be so called.

ANTHONY TROLLOPE: *North America,* I, 1862

Look at those phrases which so amuse us in their speech and books; at their reckless exaggeration and contempt for congruity; and then compare the sense of moral obligation and duty to man; its open disregard of conventional right where aggrandisement is to be obtained; and I may now say, its reckless and fruitless maintenance of the most cruel and unprincipled war in the history of the world.

HENRY ALFORD: *A Plea for the Queen's English,* 1863

The American is nomadic in religion, in ideas, in morals.

J. R. LOWELL: *Fireside Travels,* 1864

Good Americans, when they die, go to Paris.

Ascribed to THOMAS G. APPLETON (1812–84)

When good Americans die they go to Paris; when bad Americans die they go to America.

OSCAR WILDE: *A Woman of No Importance,* III, 1893

Enslaved, illogical, elate,
He greets the embarrassed gods, nor fears
To shake the iron hand of fate
Or match with destiny for beers.

RUDYARD KIPLING: *An American,* 1894

Great has been the Greek, the Latin, the Slav, the Celt, the Teuton, and the Anglo-Saxon, but greater than any of these is the American, in whom are blended the virtues of them all.

W. J. BRYAN: Speech in Washington, Feb. 22, 1899

From the very beginning our people have markedly combined practical capacity for affairs with power of devotion to an ideal. The lack of either quality would have rendered the possession of the other of small value.

THEODORE ROOSEVELT: Speech in Philadelphia, Nov. 22, 1902

The American people from the first had been less phlegmatic, less conservative than the English. There were climatic influences, it may be; there was surely a spirit of intensity everywhere that made for short effort.

FRED LEWIS PATTEE: *A History of American Literature Since 1870,* 1915

The American mind has long been honeycombed with moral impulse; it is very much what the German mind was up to the middle of the Nineteenth Century.

W. L. GEORGE: *The Intelligence of Woman,* 1916

God will save the good American, and seat him at His right hand on the Golden Throne.
THEODORE DREISER: *Life, Art, and America,* 1917

It is impossible for a stranger traveling through the United States to tell from the appearance of the people or the country whether he is in Toledo, O., or Portland, Ore. Ninety million Americans cut their hair in the same way, eat each morning exactly the same breakfast, tie up the small girls' curls with precisely the same kind of ribbon fashioned into bows exactly alike; and in every way all try to look and act as much like all the others as they can — just as the Chinese do.
LORD NORTHCLIFFE: In W. E. CARSON: *Northcliffe,* 1918

Ours is not only a fortunate people but a very commonsensical people, with vision high but their feet on the earth, with belief in themselves and faith in God.
W. G. HARDING: Speech of Acceptance, Marion, O., July 22, 1920

I am a one hundred per cent. American!
I am, God damn, I am!
W. W. WOOLLCOTT: *I Am a One Hundred Per Cent. American,* 1920

An American has no sense of privacy. He does not know what it means. There is no such thing in the country.
GEORGE BERNARD SHAW: Address in New York, April 11, 1933

God looks after drunks, children, and Americans.
Quoted as an " old saying " by JAMES TRUSLOW ADAMS in the Virginia Quarterly, July, 1934

We hear about constitutional rights, free speech and the free press. Every time I hear those words I say to myself, " That man is a Red, that man is a Communist." You never heard a real American talk in that manner.
FRANK HAGUE: Speech before the Jersey City Chamber of Commerce, Jan. 12, 1938

Americans generally are an arrogant, self-centered, dogmatic and unreflecting lot. What they call frankness is merely the result of prejudice.
Editorial in the Tokyo Yomiuri, Oct. 23, 1939

I am an American citizen. (Civis Americanus sum.) Borrowed from the Latin: " Civis Romanus sum."

[*See also* Americanism, Anglomania, Art, Ballad, Cant, Character (National), Hyphen, Idealist, Music, Woman (American), Yankee.

American Civil War

[*See* War (American Civil).

American Creed

I believe in the United States of America as a government of the people, by the people, for the people, whose just powers are derived from the consent of the governed; a democracy in a republic; a sovereign nation of many sovereign states; a perfect union, one and inseparable; established upon those principles of freedom, equality, justice and humanity for which American patriots sacrificed their lives and their fortunes. I therefore believe it is my duty to my country to love it, to support its constitution, to obey its laws, to respect its flag, and to defend it against all enemies.
WILLIAM TYLER PAGE: *The American's Creed* (Adopted by House of Representatives, April 3, 1918)

American, Hyphenated

[*See* Hyphen.

Americanism

We join ourselves to no party that does not carry the American flag, and keep step to the music of the Union.
RUFUS CHOATE: *Letter to the Whig Convention at Worcester Mass.,* Oct. 1, 1855

Anglo-Saxon civilization has taught the individual to protect his own rights; American civilization will teach him to respect the rights of others.
W. J. BRYAN: Speech in Washington, Feb. 22, 1899

There can be no fifty-fifty Americanism in this country. There is room here for only 100% Americanism, only for those who are Americans and nothing else.
THEODORE ROOSEVELT: Speech at the State Republican Convention, Saratoga, N. Y., July 19, 1918

The American system of private enterprise and economic democracy.
F. D. ROOSEVELT: Speech in Chicago, Oct. 14, 1936

American Language

I have heard in this country, in the senate, at the bar, and from the pulpit, and see daily in dissertations from the press, errors in grammar, improprieties and vulgarisms which hardly any person of the same class in point of rank and literature would have fallen into in Great Britain.
JOHN WITHERSPOON: *The Druid,* v, 1781 (Pennsylvania Journal and Weekly Advertiser, Phila., May 9)

Numerous local causes, such as a new country, new associations of people, new combinations of ideas in arts and sciences, and some intercourse with tribes wholly unknown in Europe, will introduce new words into the American tongue. These causes will produce, in a course of time, a language in North

America as different from the future language of England as the modern Dutch, Danish and Swedish are from the German, or from one another.

NOAH WEBSTER: *Dissertations on the English Language,* 1789

The common speech of the United States has departed very considerably from the standard adopted in England.

Anon.: In a review of JOHN MARSHALL: *Life of Washington,* in the British Critic, April, 1808

The new circumstances under which we are placed call for new words, new phrases, and for the transfer of old words to new objects. An American dialect will therefore be formed.

THOMAS JEFFERSON: *Letter to John Waldo,* Aug. 16, 1813

I very seldom, during my whole stay in the country, heard a sentence elegantly turned and correctly pronounced from the lips of an American.

FRANCES TROLLOPE: *Domestic Manners of the Americans,* V, 1832

The common faults of American language are an ambition of effect, a want of simplicity, and a turgid abuse of terms.

J. FENIMORE COOPER: *The American Democrat,* XXIV, 1838

It is remarkable how very debased the language has become in a short period in America.

FREDERICK MARRYAT: *A Diary in America,* II, 1839

The Americans are going to be the most fluent and melodious-voiced people in the world — and the most perfect users of words. The new world, the new times, the new people, the new vistas need a new tongue according — yes, what is more, they will have such a new tongue — will not be satisfied until it is evolved.

WALT WHITMAN: *An American Primer,* c. 1856

In point of naked syntactical accuracy, the English of America is not at all inferior to that of England; but we do not discriminate so precisely in the meaning of words.

G. P. MARSH: *Lectures on the English Language,* XXX, 1861

A tendency to slang, to colloquial inelegancies, and even vulgarities, is the besetting sin against which we, as Americans, have especially to guard and to struggle.

W. D. WHITNEY: *Language and the Study of Language,* 1867

When I speak my native tongue in its utmost purity in England, an Englishman can't understand me at all.

S. L. CLEMENS (MARK TWAIN): *The Stolen White Elephant,* 1882

The speech of the United States is quite unlike that of Great Britain in the important particular that here we have no dialects.

GILBERT M. TUCKER: *American English,* 1883

We have really everything in common with America nowadays, except, of course, language.

OSCAR WILDE: *The Canterville Ghost,* 1888

The official language of the State of Illinois shall be known hereafter as the American language, and not as the English language.

Acts of the Legislature of Illinois, ch. 127, sec. 178, 1923

American Revolution

[*See* Revolution (American).

America, South

I called the New World into existence to redress the balance of the Old.

GEORGE CANNING: Speech in the House of Commons, 1826 (Explaining his recognition, as Prime Minister, of the independence of the revolting Spanish colonies)

Amethyst

[*See* February.

Amiability

Be amiable if you would be loved. (Ut ameris, amabilis esto.)

OVID: *Ars amatoria,* II, *c.* 2 B.C.

[*See also* Age (Old), Character, Happiness.

Amnesty

Amnesty is a noble word. What it stands for is the true dictate of wisdom.

AESCHINES: *Ctesiphontem,* 337 B.C.

Amnesty is the most beautiful word in all human speech.

VICTOR HUGO: *Ninety-Three,* 1879

Amulet

Just Judge and divine Son of the Virgin Maria, who wast born in Bethlehem, a Nazarene, and wast crucified in the midst of all Jewry, I beseech thee, O Lord, by thy sixth day, that the body of me be not caught, nor put to death by the hands of justice at all; peace be with you, the peace of Christ, may I receive peace, may you receive peace, said God to his disciples.

GEORGE BORROW: *The Bible in Spain,* II, 1843 (Inscription in amulet worn by Don Geronimo Azveto)

[*See also* Exorcism.

Amusement

Money and time are the heaviest burdens of life, and the unhappiest of all mortals are those who have more of either than they

know how to use. To set himself free from these incumbrances, one hurries to Newmarket; another travels over Europe; one pulls down his house and calls architects about him; another buys a seat in the country, and follows his hounds over hedges and through rivers; one makes collections of shells; and another searches the world for tulips and carnations.
SAMUEL JOHNSON: *The Idler,* Nov. 11, 1758

Nothing is so perfectly amusement as a total change of ideas.
LAURENCE STERNE: *Tristram Shandy,* IX, 1767

I am a great friend to public amusements, for they keep people from vice.
SAMUEL JOHNSON: *Boswell's Life,* 1772

The inhabitants have a right to take their amusements in a lawful way.
MR. JUSTICE HEATH: *Judgment in Fitch* vs. *Fitch,* 1797

The Queen is not amused.
Ascribed to QUEEN VICTORIA (1819–1901) on various occasions when she sought to rebuke indecorum

[*See also* Criticism, Entertainment, Sport.

Amusing

An amoozin little cuss.
C. F. BROWNE (ARTEMUS WARD): *Artemus Ward: His Book,* 1862 (Said of his kangaroo)

There are amusing people who do not interest, and interesting people who do not amuse.
BENJAMIN DISRAELI: *Lothair,* XLI, 1870

Ananias (flourished c. 50)

[*See* Lying.

Anarchism

Anarchism stands for the liberation of the human mind from the dominion of religion; the liberation of the human body from the dominion of property; liberation from the shackles and restraints of government.
EMMA GOLDMAN: *Anarchism,* 1917

Anarchist

The anarchist denies the right of any government to trench on his individual freedom.
HERBERT SPENCER: *First Principles,* I, 1862

The anarchist and the Christian have the same ancestry.
F. W. NIETZSCHE: *The Antichrist,* LVII, 1888

The following classes of aliens shall be excluded from admission into the United States: . . . anarchists, or persons who believe in or advocate the overthrow by force or violence of the government of the United States, or of all government, or of all forms of law, or the assassination of public officials.
Act of Congress, Feb. 20, 1907

The ordinary man is an anarchist. He wants to do as he likes. He may want his neighbor to be governed, but he himself doesn't want to be governed. He is mortally afraid of government officials and policemen.
GEORGE BERNARD SHAW: Address in New York, April 11, 1933

Anarchy

The instant formal government is abolished, society begins to act. A general association takes place, and common interest produces common security.
THOMAS PAINE: *The Rights of Man,* II, 1791

Anarchy is a horrible calamity, but it is less horrible than despotism. Where anarchy has slain its hundreds, despotism has sacrificed millions upon millions, with this only effect, to perpetuate the ignorance, the vices and the misery of mankind.
WILLIAM GODWIN: *An Enquiry Concerning Political Justice,* 1793

No evil is greater than anarchy. (Nullum anarchia majus est malum.) LATIN PROVERB

[*See also* Democracy, Government, State.

Anathema

If any man love not the Lord Jesus Christ, let him be anathema maranatha.
I CORINTHIANS XVI, 22, *c.* 55

Anathema, which ought to be very rarely resorted to, or never, precludes all pardon, execrates a person, and consigns him to eternal damnation.
JOHN CALVIN: *Institutes of the Christian Religion,* IV, 1536

Anatomist

Anatomists see no beautiful woman in all their lives, but only a ghastly sack of bones with Latin names to them, and a network of nerves and muscles and tissues inflamed by disease.
S. L. CLEMENS (MARK TWAIN): *Letter from New York to the Alta Californian (San Francisco),* May 28, 1867

Ancestry

Such is the stock I spring from. (Eo sum genere gnatus.)
PLAUTUS: *Pseudolus,* II, *c.* 190 B.C.

He who boasts of his descent praises another.
SENECA: *Hercules Furens, c.* 50

I cannot think but I am come of the race of some rich king or prince in former times; for never yet saw you any man that had a greater desire to be a king, and to be rich, than I have. RABELAIS: *Gargantua,* I, 1535

Brag of thy father's faults: they are thine own;
Brag of his lands, if those be not forgone;
Brag of thine own good deeds, for they are thine,
More than his life, or lands, or golden line.

JOSEPH HALL (BISHOP OF NORWICH): *Virgidemiae*, IV, 1598

There's legion now of beggars on the earth
That their original did spring from kings:
And many monarchs now whose fathers were
The riff-raff of their age.

Anon.: *The Chronicle History of Thomas Cromwell*, I, 1602

The man who has not anything to boast of but his illustrious ancestors is like a potato, – the only good belonging to him is underground.

THOMAS OVERBURY: *Characters*, 1614

Almost in every kingdom the most ancient families have been at first princes' bastards.

ROBERT BURTON: *The Anatomy of Melancholy*, II, 1621

There are few families in the world that do not reach at one end of the line to the highest prince, and at the other end to simple plebeians.

JEAN DE LA BRUYÈRE: *Caractères*, XIV, 1688

Heralds and statesman, by your leave,
There lies what once was Matthew Prior;
The son of Adam and of Eve;
Can Bourbon or Nassau go higher?

MATTHEW PRIOR: *Epitaph for himself*, *c.* 1700

He who serves his country well has no need of ancestors. VOLTAIRE: *Mérope*, I, 1743

Our ancestors are very good kind of folks; but they are the last people I should choose to have a visiting acquaintance with.

R. B. SHERIDAN: *The Rivals*, IV, 1775

Happy the man who thinks of his ancestors with pride, who likes to tell of their deeds and greatness, and rejoices to feel himself linked to the end of their goodly chain.

J. W. GOETHE: *Iphigenia auf Tauris*, I, 1787

People will not look forward to posterity who never look backward to their ancestors.

EDMUND BURKE: *Reflections on the Revolution in France*, III, 1790

I have ever had pleasure in obtaining any little anecdotes of my ancestors.

BENJAMIN FRANKLIN: *Autobiography*, 1798

I am my own ancestor.

ANDOCHE JUNOT: *On being made Duc d'Abrantes*, 1807

Our ancestors, up to the Conquest, were children in arms; chubby boys in the time of Edward the First; striplings under Elizabeth; men in the reign of Queen Anne.

SYDNEY SMITH: In the Edinburgh Review, Aug., 1825

There is no pride like the pride of ancestry, for it is a blending of all emotions. How immeasurably superior to the herd is the man whose father only is famous! Imagine then the feelings of one who can trace his line through a thousand years of heroes and of princes.

BENJAMIN DISRAELI: *The Young Duke*, VI, 1831

If I am to live only with my equals, then I must go down into the tomb of my ancestors, and stay there forever.

FRANCES II OF AUSTRIA (1768–1835)

The Heaven-inspired melodious singer; loftiest Serene Highness; nay, thy own amber-locked, snow-and-rosebloom maiden, worthy to glide sylphlike almost on air, whom thou lovest, worshippest as a divine Presence, which indeed, symbolically taken, she is, – has descended, like thyself, from the same hair-mantled, flint-hurling aboriginal Anthropopophagus.

THOMAS CARLYLE: *Sartor Resartus*, I, 1836

A man's ancestry is a positive property to him. How much, not only of acres, but of his constitution, his temper, his conduct, character and nature he may inherit from some progenitor ten times removed!

E. G. BULWER-LYTTON: *The Caxtons*, XI, 1849

How shall a man escape from his ancestors, or draw off from his veins the black drop which he drew from his father's or his mother's life?

R. W. EMERSON: *The Conduct of Life*, VII, 1860

Man is descended from a hairy, tailed quadruped, probably arboreal in its habits.

CHARLES DARWIN: *The Descent of Man*, XXI, 1871

My father was a creole, his father a Negro, and his father a monkey; my family, it seems begins where yours left off.

Ascribed to ALEXANDER DUMAS, *père*, in J. C. YOUNG: *A Memoir of Charles Mayne Young*, 1871 (On being asked "Who was your father?")

From my Gaulish ancestors I inherit light blue eyes, a narrow head, and clumsiness in fighting. My clothes are as barbarous as theirs. But I do not rub butter in my hair.

ARTHUR RIMBAUD: *Une saison en enfer*, 1873

I am, in point of fact, a particularly haughty and exclusive person, of pre-Adamite ancestral descent. You will understand this when I tell you that I can trace my ancestry back to a protoplasmal primordial atomic globule.

W. S. GILBERT: *The Mikado*, I, 1885

A man is the sum of his ancestors; to reform him you must begin with a dead ape and work downward through a million graves.

He is like the lower end of a suspended chain; you can sway him slightly to the right or the left, but remove your hand and he falls into line with the other links.
AMBROSE BIERCE: *Collected Works,* VIII, 1911

They brag most of their ancestors who are unworthy of them. DANISH PROVERB

A mule always boasts that its ancestors were horses. GERMAN PROVERB

Noble ancestry makes a poor dish at table.
ITALIAN PROVERB

[*See also* Aristocracy, Birth (High), Family, Genealogy, Gentleman, Heredity, Heritage, Nobility, Patriot, Peasant, Pedigree, Peerage, Posterity, Rank.

Anchor

Good riding at two anchors, men have told,
For if the one fail the other may hold.
JOHN HEYWOOD: *Proverbs,* 1546

Like the Dutchman's anchor: he keeps it at home. SPANISH SAYING

Ancient

The ancient and honorable, he is the head.
ISAIAH IX, 15, *c.* 700 B.C.

Ancient things are always extolled.
TACITUS: *History,* II, *c.* 100

Speak of the moderns without contempt and of the ancients without idolatry; judge them all by their merits and not by their age.
LORD CHESTERFIELD: *Letter to his son,* Feb. 22, 1748

[*See also* Antique, Antiquity, Old.

Anecdotage

The disgusting perversions of their anile anecdotage.
Anon.: In Blackwood's Magazine, 1835 (The invention of the term is ascribed to JOHN WILKES, 1727–97. *Anile*=old-womanish)

Anesthetic

The three natural anesthetics . . . are . . . sleep, fainting, death.
O. W. HOLMES: *The Medical Profession in Massachusetts,* 1869 (Lecture in Boston, Jan. 29)

Angel

God spared not the angels that sinned, but cast them down to hell, and delivered them into chains of darkness. II PETER II, 4, *c.* 60

Be not forgetful to entertain strangers, for thereby some have entertained angels unawares. HEBREWS XIII, 2, *c.* 65

Every angel and demon is winged. Consequently, they are everywhere in a moment; to them the whole world is one place.
TERTULLIAN: *The Christian's Defence,* *c.* 215

Beauty is not necessary to God's angels.
TERTULLIAN: *Women's Dress, c.* 220

Angels may become men or demons, and again from the latter they may rise to be men or angels. ORIGEN: *De principiis, c.* 254

We should pray to the angels, for they are given to us as guardians.
ST. AMBROSE: *On Bereavement, c.* 380

There are nine orders of angels, to wit, angels, archangels, virtues, powers, principalities, dominations, thrones, cherubim and seraphim.
POPE GREGORY THE GREAT: *Homilies,* XXXIV, *c.* 600

Not Angles, but angels. (Non Angli, sed angeli.)
POPE GREGORY THE GREAT: On observing the blond British captives offered for sale in Rome, *c.* 600

Praise be to Allah, the creator of the heavens and earth, who maketh the angels his messengers, and giveth them two, three or four pairs of wings. THE KORAN, XXXV, *c.* 625

How many angels can dance upon the point of a needle?
Quodlibet ascribed to various medieval theologians, *c.* 1400

The angels are the dispensers and administrators of the Divine beneficence toward us; they regard our safety, undertake our defense, direct our ways, and exercise a constant solicitude that no evil befall us.
JOHN CALVIN: *Institutes of the Christian Religion,* I, 1536

An angel is a spiritual creature created by God without a body, for the service of Christendom and of the Church.
MARTIN LUTHER: *Table-Talk,* DLXIX, 1569

Angels and ministers of grace, defend us!
SHAKESPEARE: *Hamlet,* I, *c.* 1601

A ministering angel.
SHAKESPEARE: *Hamlet,* V

Make yourself familiar with the angels, and behold them frequently in spirit; for, without being seen, they are present with you.
ST. FRANCIS DE SALES: *Introduction to the Devout Life,* XVI, 1609

Thou hast the sweetest face I ever looked on;
Sir, as I have a soul, she is an angel.
SHAKESPEARE and JOHN FLETCHER: *Henry VIII,* IV, 1613

Every man hath a good and a bad angel attending on him in particular all his life long.
ROBERT BURTON: *The Anatomy of Melancholy,* I, 1621

Look homeward, angel.
JOHN MILTON: *Lycidas,* 1638 (THOMAS C. WOLFE: Title of a novel, 1929)

Between creatures of mere existence and things of life there is a large disproportion of nature: between plants and animals, or creatures of sense, a wider difference: between them and man a far greater: and if the proportion hold on, between man and angels there should be yet a greater.

THOMAS BROWNE: *Religio Medici*, I, 1642

What's impossible to all humanity may be possible to the metaphysics and physiology of angels.

JOSEPH GLANVILL: *The Vanity of Dogmatizing*, XX, 1661

Like angel visits, short and bright.

JOHN NORRIS: *Miscellanies*, 1687

While shepherds watched their flocks by night,
All seated on the ground,
The angel of the Lord came down,
And glory shone around.

NAHUM TATE: *While Shepherds Watched*, *c.* 1700

Who does the best his circumstance allows
Does well, acts nobly; angels could do no more.

EDWARD YOUNG: *Night Thoughts*, II, 1732 (This seems to be the original of Mark Twain's " He done his level damndest; angels could do no more ")

Visits
Like those of angels, short and far between.

ROBERT BLAIR: *The Grave*, II, 1743 (Cf. JOHN NORRIS, *ante*, 1687)

I have seen a thousand times that angels are human forms, or men, for I have conversed with them as man to man, sometimes with one alone, sometimes with many in company.

EMANUEL SWEDENBORG: *Arcana Coelestia*, 1756

That there are angels and spirits good and bad . . . is so clear from Scripture that no believer, unless he be first of all spoiled by philosophy and vain deceit, can possibly entertain a doubt of it.

RICHARD HURD (BISHOP OF WORCESTER): *Sermon on James V, 7*, *c.* 1782

I have always found that angels have the vanity to speak of themselves as the only wise; this they do with a confident insolence sprouting from systematic reasoning.

WILLIAM BLAKE: *The Marriage of Heaven and Hell*, 1790

Whether God loves a lying angel better than a true man.

CHARLES LAMB: Proposition submitted (satirically) to S. T. Coleridge for debate " at Leipsic or Göttingen," 1798

Like angels' visits, few and far between.

THOMAS CAMPBELL: *The Pleasures of Hope*, II, 1799 (Cf. ROBERT BLAIR, *ante*, 1743)

The angels were all singing out of tune,
And hoarse with having little else to do,
Excepting to wind up the sun and moon
Or curb a runaway young star or two.

BYRON: *The Vision of Judgment*, 1823

God hath chosen her as a pattern for the other angels.

Epitaph in West Moulsey churchyard, England, 1832

Like outcast spirits who wait,
And see, through Heaven's gate,
Angels within it.

W. M. THACKERAY: *The Church Porch*, 1849

I want to be an angel,
And with the angels stand,
A crown upon my forehead,
A harp within my hand.

URANIA BAILEY: *I Want to be an Angel*, *c.* 1850

Miss Eva is gone to Heaven; she is an angel.

HARRIET BEECHER STOWE: *Uncle Tom's Cabin*, XXVII, 1852

If some people really see angels where others see only empty space, let them paint the angels; only let not anybody else think *they* can paint an angel too, on any calculated principles of the angelic.

JOHN RUSKIN: *Modern Painters*, I, 1856

We not only live among men, but there are airy hosts, blessed spectators, sympathetic lookers-on, that see and know and appreciate our thoughts and feelings and acts.

H. W. BEECHER: *Royal Truths*, 1862

I am on the side of the angels.

BENJAMIN DISRAELI: Speech at Oxford, Nov. 25, 1864

Leonainie — angels named her,
And they took the light
Of the laughing star and framed her
In a smile of white,
And they made her hair of gloomy
Midnight, and her eyes of bloomy
Moonshine, and they brought her to me
In the solemn night.

J. W. RILEY: *Leonainie*, 1877 (Kokomo, Ind., Dispatch, Aug. 2. The poem was printed as a lost one by E. A. Poe)

The more materialistic science becomes, the more angels shall I paint: their wings are my protest in favor of the immortality of the soul.

E. C. BURNE-JONES: *To Oscar Wilde*, *c.* 1880

In Heaven an angel is nobody in particular.

GEORGE BERNARD SHAW: *Maxims for Revolutionists*, 1903

Look over yonder: whut do I see?
Big white angel comin' after me.
Dry bones gonna rise again.

American Negro song, quoted by HOWARD W. ODUM: *Wings On My Feet*, XIII, 1929

A young angel, an old devil.
FRENCH PROVERB

In these days you must go to Heaven to find an angel.
POLISH PROVERB

[*See also* Adultery, Aspiration, Chastity, Children, Darwinism, Death, Evolution, Foible, Fool, Heart, Heaven, Jesus Christ, Judgment Day, Ladder, Language, Man, Naked, Paul (St.), Power, Pride, Priest, Virgin.

Anger

Cursed be their anger, for it was fierce; and their wrath, for it was cruel.
GENESIS XLIX, 7, *c.* 700 B.C.

Be master of thy anger.
Ascribed to PERIANDER OF CORINTH, *c.* 600 B.C.

He that is slow to anger is better than the mighty: and he that ruleth his spirit than he that taketh a city.
PROVERBS XVI, 32, *c.* 350 B.C.

Make no friendships with an angry man.
PROVERBS XXII, 24

We praise a man who is angry on the right grounds, against the right persons, in the right manner, at the right moment, and for the right length of time.
ARISTOTLE: *The Nicomachean Ethics,* IV, *c.* 340 B.C.

Anger, even violent anger, against one person will cease if vengeance is taken on another.
ARISTOTLE: *Rhetoric,* II, *c.* 322 B.C.

We are all crazy when we are angry.
PHILEMON: *Fragment, c.* 300 B.C.

Be not hasty in thy spirit to be angry: for anger resteth in the bosom of fools.
ECCLESIASTES VII, 9, *c.* 200 B.C.

Anger is a brief lunacy.
HORACE: *Epistles,* I, *c.* 5 B.C. (Cf. PHILEMON, *ante, c.* 300 B.C.)

When you are angry say nothing and do nothing until you have recited the alphabet.
Ascribed to ATHENODORUS CANANITES (*c.* 74 B.C.–8 A.D.)

Anger is like those ruins which smash themselves on what they fall.
SENECA: *De Ira,* I, *c.* 43

The best cure for anger is delay.
SENECA: *De Ira,* II

If you would cure anger, do not feed it. Say to yourself: "I used to be angry every day; then every other day; now only every third or fourth day." When you reach thirty days offer a sacrifice of thanksgiving to the gods.
EPICTETUS: *Discourses,* II, *c.* 110

How much more grievous are the consequences of anger than the causes of it.
MARCUS AURELIUS: *Meditations,* XI, *c.* 170

As angry as a pissmire.
GEOFFREY CHAUCER: *The Canterbury Tales* (*The Summoner's Tale*), *c.* 1386
(*Pissmire*=an ant)

As angry as a wasp.
JOHN HEYWOOD: *Proverbs,* 1546

When I am angry I can write, pray, and preach well, for then my whole temperament is quickened, my understanding sharpened, and all mundane vexations and temptations depart.
MARTIN LUTHER: *Table-Talk,* CCCXIX, 1569

He that cannot be angry is no man.
THOMAS DEKKER: *I The Honest Whore, I,* 1604

Touch me with noble anger.
SHAKESPEARE: *King Lear,* II, 1606

Anger's my meat: I sup upon myself.
SHAKESPEARE: *Coriolanus,* IV, *c.* 1607

As angry as an ass with a squib in his breech.
RANDLE COTGRAVE: *French-English Dictionary,* 1611

Anger is like
A full-hot horse; who being allowed his way,
Self-mettle tires him.
SHAKESPEARE and JOHN FLETCHER: *Henry VIII,* I, 1613

Women are like wasps in their anger.
NICHOLAS BRETON: *Crossing of Proverbs,* 1616

The angry man never wanted woe.
THOMAS DRAXE: *Bibliotheca scholastica instructissima,* 1633

Anger edgeth valor.
JOHN CLARKE: *Parœmiologia Anglo-Latina,* 1639

Two things a man should never be angry at: what he can help, and what he cannot help.
THOMAS FULLER: *Historie of the Holy Warre,* III, 1639

He hath wit at will that with an angry heart can hold him still.
DAVID FERGUSSON: *Scottish Proverbs,* 1641

He that is angry without a cause shall be pleased without amends.
JOHN RAY: *English Proverbs,* 1670

He that strives not to stem his anger's tide
Does a wild horse without a bridle ride.
COLLEY CIBBER: *Love's Last Shift,* III, 1696

There is a holy anger, excited by zeal, which moves us to reprove with warmth those whom our mildness failed to correct.
ST. JEAN BAPTISTE DE LA SALLE: *Les devoirs du chrétien,* XIV, 1703

Anger makes a rich man hated, and a poor man scorned.
THOMAS FULLER: *Gnomologia,* 1732

As fire is kindled by bellows, so is anger by words. IBID.

Two to one in all things against the angry man. IBID.

Whate'er's begun in anger ends in shame.
BENJAMIN FRANKLIN: *Poor Richard's Almanac*, 1734

Anger and folly walk cheek by jowl; repentance treads on both their heels. IBID.

Angry men make themselves beds of nettles.
SAMUEL RICHARDSON: *Clarissa*, VII, 1748

Anger is never without a reason, but seldom with a good one.
BENJAMIN FRANKLIN: *Poor Richard's Almanac*, 1753

Anger is excited principally by pride.
SAMUEL JOHNSON: *Boswell's Life*, May 1, 1773

I was angry with my friend:
I told my wrath, my wrath did end.
I was angry with my foe:
I told it not, my wrath did grow.
WILLIAM BLAKE: *A Poison Tree*, *c.* 1792

Anger wishes that all mankind had only one neck.
JEAN PAUL RICHTER: *Flower, Fruit, and Thorn Pieces*, VI, 1796

When angry, count ten before you speak; if very angry, an hundred.
THOMAS JEFFERSON: *Letter to Thomas Jefferson Smith*, 1825

Anger is a vulgar passion directed to vulgar ends, and it always sinks to the level of its object.
ERNST VON FEUCHTERSLEBEN: *Zur Diätetik der Seele*, VI, 1838

Anger begins with folly, and ends with repentance.
H. G. BOHN: *Handbook of Proverbs*, 1855

Never forget what a man has said to you when he was angry. If he has charged you with any thing, you had better look it up.
H. W. BEECHER: *Life Thoughts*, 1858

A man deep-wounded may feel too much pain
To feel much anger.
MARIAN EVANS (GEORGE ELIOT): *The Spanish Gypsy*, I, 1868

When angry, count four; when very angry, swear.
S. L. CLEMENS (MARK TWAIN): *Pudd'nhead Wilson*, X, 1894. (Cf. THOMAS JEFFERSON, *ante*, 1825)

The size of a man can be measured by the size of the thing that makes him angry.
J. KENFIELD MORLEY: *Some Things I Believe*, 1937

Never answer a letter while you are angry.
CHINESE PROVERB

So long as a man is angry he can't be in the right. IBID.

Beware the anger of the dove. IBID.

The best answer to anger is silence.
GERMAN PROVERB

He who is slow to anger is longer getting over it. HUNGARIAN PROVERB

Anger increases love. ITALIAN PROVERB

Laughter cannot bring back what anger has driven away. JAPANESE PROVERB

He who restrains his anger overcomes his greatest enemy. LATIN PROVERB

The anger of a good man lasts an instant; that of a meddler two hours; that of a base man a day and a night; and that of a great sinner until death. SANSKRIT PROVERB

He that will be angry for onything will be angry for naething.
SCOTTISH PROVERB

Little folk are soon angry. IBID.

In a fight anger is as good as courage.
WELSH PROVERB

[*See also* Age (Old), Crime, Danger, Envy, Evil, Fault, Fury, Goat, Haste, Hatred, Hunger, Judge, Passion, Perplexity, Rage, Self-Command, Short, Sin, Sorrow, Temper, Wrath.

Angler

[*See* Fisherman.

Angling

[*See* Fishing.

Anglomania

There is not a more disgusting spectacle under the sun than our subserviency to British criticism. It is disgusting, first, because it is truckling, servile, pusillanimous — secondly, because of its gross irrationality. We know the British to bear us little but ill will — we know this, and yet, day after day, submit our necks to the degrading yoke of the crudest opinion that emanates from the fatherland.
E. A. POE: *Marginalia*, 1844–49

An American, whether he be embarked in politics, in literature, or in commerce, desires English admiration, English appreciation of his energy, and English encouragement.
ANTHONY TROLLOPE: *North America*, I, 1862

We are worth nothing except so far as we have disinfected ourselves of Anglicism.
J. R. LOWELL: *On a Certain Condescension in Foreigners*, 1869

[*See also* Bostonian.

Anglo-Saxon

The great qualities of the Anglo-Saxon race are industry, intelligence, and self-confidence.
ANTHONY TROLLOPE: *North America*, I, 1862

The Anglo-Saxon carries self-government and self-development with him wherever he goes.
H. W. BEECHER: Address at Liverpool, Oct. 16, 1863

To no race are we more indebted for the virtues which constitute a great people than to the Anglo-Saxon.
ROBERT E. LEE: *Letter to W. H. Nettleton*, May 21, 1866

We of the Anglo-Saxon race do not know how to enjoy ourselves; we do not know how to get the most out of this life that flies so rapidly.
HENRY GEORGE: In the San Francisco State, April 12, 1879

Only Anglo-Saxons can govern themselves.
W. A. WHITE: In the Emporia (Kansas) Gazette, March 20, 1899

[*See also* American, Angel, Englishman, Pantomime.

Animal

A righteous man regardeth the life of his beast.
PROVERBS XII, 10, *c.* 350 B.C.

Ask now the beasts, and they shall teach thee; and the fowls of the air, and they shall tell thee.
JOB XII, 7, *c.* 325 B.C.

The beasts that perish.
PSALMS XLIX, 12, *c.* 150 B.C.

All wild animals live in fear and quaking; they have all black flesh by reason of their fear; but tame animals have white flesh, for they live securely with mankind.
MARTIN LUTHER: *Table-Talk*, CXXVII, 1569

Nature teaches beasts to know their friends.
SHAKESPEARE: *Coriolanus*, II, *c.* 1607

There be beasts that, at a year old, observe more, and pursue that which is for their good more prudently, than a child can do at ten.
THOMAS HOBBES: *Leviathan*, III, 1651

Animals, in their generation, are wiser than the sons of men; but their wisdom is confined to a few particulars, and lies in a very narrow compass.
JOSEPH ADDISON: *The Spectator*, July 18, 1711

Learn from the birds what food the thickets yield;
Learn from the beasts the physic of the field;
The arts of building from the bee receive;
Learn of the mole to plow, the worm to weave.
ALEXANDER POPE: *An Essay on Man*, III, 1733

No truth appears to me more evident than that the beasts are endowed with thought and reason as well as men. The arguments are in this case so obvious that they never escape the most stupid and ignorant.
DAVID HUME: *A Treatise of Human Nature*, IV, 1739

The animals glory in being cynics. Having no education, they are devoid of prejudices.
J. O. DE LA METTRIE: *L'Homme machine*, 1748

The lower animals have not the high advantages which we have, but they have some which we lack. They know nothing of our hopes, but they also know nothing of our fears; they are subject to death as we are, but they are not aware of it; most of them are better able to take care of themselves than we are, and they make a less evil use of their passions.
C. L. DE MONTESQUIEU: *The Spirit of the Laws*, I, 1748

There is something in animals beside the power of motion. They are not machines: they feel.
E. B. DE CONDILLAC: *Traité des animaux*, I, 1755

Every man has a wild animal within him.
FREDERICK THE GREAT: *Letter to Voltaire*, 1759

Animals have these advantages over man: they never hear the clock strike, they die without any idea of death, they have no theologians to instruct them, their last moments are not disturbed by unwelcome and unpleasant ceremonies, their funerals cost them nothing, and no one starts lawsuits over their wills.
VOLTAIRE: *Letter to Count de Schomberg*, Aug. 31, 1769

The question is not, Can they reason? nor, Can they talk? but, Can they suffer?
JEREMY BENTHAM: *The Principles of Morals and Legislation*, XVII, 1789

It is only in our eyes that animals grow old.
G. C. LICHTENBERG: *Reflections*, 1799

Animals hear about death for the first time when they die.
ARTHUR SCHOPENHAUER: *The World as Will and Idea*, I, 1819

Who can guess how much industry and providence and affection we have caught from the pantomime of brutes?
R. W. EMERSON: *Nature*, V, 1836

The behavior of men to the lower animals, and their behavior to each other, bear a constant relationship.
HERBERT SPENCER: *Social Statics*, IV, 1851

I think I could turn and live with animals, they are so placid and self-contain'd;
I stand and look at them long and long.
They do not sweat and whine about their condition;

They do not lie awake in the dark and weep for their sins;
They do not make me sick discussing their duty to God.

WALT WHITMAN: *Walt Whitman,* 1855

Animals are such agreeable friends — they ask no questions, they pass no criticisms.

MARIAN EVANS (GEORGE ELIOT): *Mr. Gilfil's Love-Story,* VII, 1857

Honor your parents; worship the gods; be kind to animals.

Ascribed to TRIPTOLEMUS, a minor god of the Greeks

God himself is the soul of brutes. (Deus est anima brutorum.) Author unidentified

The kind man first feeds his beast before sitting down to table. HEBREW PROVERB

Of a wild nature. (Ferae naturae.)

LEGAL PHRASE

Men show their superiority inside; animals, outside. RUSSIAN PROVERB

[*See also* Camel, Cat, Death, Dog, Elephant, Evil, Fierceness, Hog, Horse, Language, Lawyer, Liberty, Lion, Mammal, Man, Mind, Morality, Nature.

Animosity

The animosities of sovereigns are temporary, and may be allayed; but those which seize the whole body of a people, and of a people, too, who dictate their own measures, produce calamities of long duration.

THOMAS JEFFERSON: *Letter to C. W. F. Dumas,* 1786

Animosity is not a policy.

H. C. LODGE: Speech in the Senate, Jan. 6, 1915

Anne of England (1665–1714)

The Church's wet-nurse, Goody Anne.

HORACE WALPOLE: *Letter to William Mason,* 1778

Annihilation

He shall perish for ever like his own dung: they which have seen him shall say, Where is he? JOB XX, 7, *c.* 325 B.C.

Nature abhors annihilation.

CICERO: *De finibus,* V, *c.* 50 B.C.

After death there is nothing.

SENECA: *Troades, c.* 60

Death restores man to the state he was in before he was born; neither soul nor body has any feeling more.

PLINY THE ELDER: *Natural History, c.* 79

The cloud-capp'd towers, the gorgeous palaces,
The solemn temples, the great globe itself,
Yea, all which it inherit, shall dissolve
And, like this insubstantial pageant faded,
Leave not a rack behind.

SHAKESPEARE: *The Tempest,* IV, 1611

How can he exalt his thought to anything great and noble who only believes that, after a short turn on the stage of this world, he is to sink into oblivion, and to lose his consciousness forever?

JOHN HUGHES: *The Spectator,* Oct. 31, 1711

Alas! that all we loved of him should be,
But for our grief, as if it had not been,
And grief itself be mortal!

P. B. SHELLEY: *Adonais,* XXI, 1821

Oh, threats of Hell and hopes of Paradise!
One thing at least is certain — this life flies;
One thing is certain and the rest is lies:
The flower that once has blown forever dies.

EDWARD FITZGERALD: Tr. of OMAR KHAYYÁM: *Rubáiyát* (*c.* 1100), 1857

Only the sleep eternal
In an eternal night.

A. C. SWINBURNE: *The Garden of Proserpine,* 1866

We fall asleep and never wake again.

JAMES THOMSON: *The City of Dreadful Night,* 1874

[*See also* Dead, Judaism, Nihilism.

Anniversary

The secret anniversaries of the heart.

H. W. LONGFELLOW: *Holidays,* 1876

Anonymity

Whoever stabs a reputation in the dark, without setting his name, is a cowardly, malignant, and scandalous scoundrel.

SAMUEL MARTIN: Speech in the House of Commons, Nov. 16, 1763

I have preserved through life a resolution, set in a very early part of it, never to write in a public paper without subscribing my name.

THOMAS JEFFERSON: *Letter to Edmund Randolph,* 1792

Answer

A soft answer turneth away wrath.

PROVERBS XV, 1, *c.* 350 B.C.

Answer me in one word.

SHAKESPEARE: *As You Like It,* III, *c.* 1600

The poor man's answer (i.e., a flat denial).

JAMES KELLY: *Complete Collection of Scottish Proverbs,* 1721

When that question is made to me in a proper time, in a proper place, under proper qualifications, and with proper motives, I will hesitate long before I will refuse to take it into consideration.

ROBERT PEEL: Speech in the House of Commons, *c.* 1828

No answer is also an answer.

GERMAN PROVERB

It is a good answer which knows when to stop.
ITALIAN PROVERB

[*See also* Fool.

Ant

Go to the ant, thou sluggard; consider her ways, and be wise. PROVERBS VI, 6, *c.* 350 B.C.

Ants are never found in empty barns.
OVID: *Tristia,* I, *c.* 10

Ants have bile and flies have spleen.
LATIN PROVERB, quoted by THOMAS BROWNE: *Pseudodoxia Epidemica,* 1646

Who can observe the careful ant
And not provide for future want?
JOHN GAY: *Fables,* intro., 1727

None preaches better than the ant, and she says nothing.
BENJAMIN FRANKLIN: *Poor Richard's Almanac,* 1736

As a thinker and planner the ant is the equal of any savage race of men; as a self-educated specialist in several arts she is the superior of any savage race of men; and in one or two high mental qualities she is above the reach of any man, savage or civilized.
S. L. CLEMENS (MARK TWAIN): *What Is Man?,* VI, 1906

He has ants in his pants.
AMERICAN SAYING, popularized by Hugh S. Johnson, 1939. (In the form of " He has a breeze in his breech " it goes back to the XVII century; *breeze*=horsefly= *Tabanus atratus*)

Even an ant casts a shadow.
BULGARIAN PROVERB

[*See also* Anger.

Antagonist

He that wrestles with us strengthens our nerves, and sharpens our skill. Our antagonist is our helper.
EDMUND BURKE: *Reflections on the Revolution in France,* 1790

[*See also* Combat, Fight, Foe, Opponent.

Anthem

Through the long-drawn aisle and fretted vault
The pealing anthem swells the note of praise.
THOMAS GRAY: *Elegy Written in a Country Churchyard,* 1750

[*See also* Hymn.

Anthropomorphism

Why may not a goose say: " I have an interest in all parts of the universe. The earth serves me to walk upon; the sun to light me; the stars influence me; I get advantage from the winds and the waters; the roof of Heaven looks down upon nothing more favorably than on me. I am the darling of nature. Man himself keeps, lodges and serves me."
MICHEL DE MONTAIGNE: *Essays,* II, 1580

Antichrist

Even now there are many antichrists.
I JOHN II, 18, *c.* 115

He is antichrist that denieth the Father and the Son. I JOHN II, 22

Whoever refuses to confess that Jesus Christ is come in the flesh is Antichrist.
POLYCARP: *Epistle to the Philippians,* *c.* 115

Antichrist is the pope and the Turk together. A beast full of life must have a body and soul. The spirit or soul of Antichrist is the pope, his flesh or body the Turk.
MARTIN LUTHER: *Table-Talk,* CCCXXIX, 1569

If the pope be not Antichrist, he is in bad luck to be so like him.
Author unidentified (The gibe appears often in the Lutheran literature of the Reformation period)

The Antichrist. (Der Antichrist.)
F. W. NIETZSCHE: Title of a book, 1888

[*See also* Christianity, Nietzsche (F. W.).

Anticipation

There is nothing more miserable and foolish than anticipation.
SENECA: *Epistulae morales ad Lucilium,* XCVIII, *c.* 63

Don't count your chickens before they are hatched.
ENGLISH PROVERB, borrowed from the Greek and traced by Apperson to 1577

The man that once did sell the lion's skin
While the beast lived, was killed with hunting him. SHAKESPEARE: *Henry V,* IV, *c.* 1599

A man's delight in looking forward to and hoping for some particular satisfaction is a part of the pleasure flowing out of it, enjoyed in advance. But this is afterward deducted, for the more we look forward to anything the less we enjoy it when it comes.
ARTHUR SCHOPENHAUER: *Parerga und Paralipomena,* 1851

[*See also* Expectation, Fear

Antidote

Antidotes are poison.
SHAKESPEARE: *Timon of Athens,* IV, *c.* 1607

Never take the antidote before the poison. (Ne prius antidotum quam venenum.)
LATIN PROVERB

Antinomianism

Shall we sin because we are not under the law, but under grace? God forbid.
ROMANS VI, 15, *c.* 55

Antipathy

The horse does abominate the camel; the mighty elephant is afraid of a mouse; and they say that the lion, which scorneth to turn his back upon the stoutest animal, will tremble at the crowing of a cock.
INCREASE MATHER: *Remarkable Providences*, IV, 1684

Violent antipathies are always suspicious, and betray a secret affinity.
WILLIAM HAZLITT: *Table-Talk*, I, 1824

Antique

Antiquities are remnants of history which have casually escaped the shipwrecks of time.
FRANCIS BACON: *The Advancement of Learning*, II, 1605

With sharpen'd sight pale antiquaries pore,
Th' inscription value, but the rust adore.
This the blue varnish, that the green endears,
The sacred rust of twice ten hundred years.
ALEXANDER POPE: *Moral Essays*, V (To Mr. Addison), 1720

Rare are the buttons of a Roman's breeches,
In antiquarian eyes surpassing riches:
Rare is each crack'd, black, rotten earthen dish,
That held, of ancient Rome, the flesh and fish.
JOHN WOLCOT: *The Lousiad*, II, 1785

Antiquity

The nearer antiquity was to its divine origin, the more clearly it perceived what was true.
CICERO: *Tusculanae disputationes*, I, 45 B.C.

Let others praise ancient times; I am glad that I was born in these.
OVID: *Ars amatoria*, III, *c.* 2 B.C.

A little skill in antiquity inclines a man to popery; but depth in that study brings him about again to our religion.
THOMAS FULLER: *The Holy State and the Profane State*, 1642

In ancient times all things were cheap.
MARTIN PARKER: *Ballad*, *c.* 1650

To antiquity itself I think nothing due. For if we will reverence the age, the present is the oldest.
THOMAS HOBBES: *Leviathan*, conclusion, 1651

Damn the age; I will write for antiquity.
Ascribed to CHARLES LAMB (1775–1834)

In the morning of the world,
When earth was nigher Heaven than now.
ROBERT BROWNING: *Pippa Passes*, III, 1841

Man's life was spacious in the early world:
It paused, like some slow ship with sail unfurled
Waiting in seas by scarce a wavelet curled.
MARIAN EVANS (GEORGE ELIOT): *The Legend of Jubal*, 1872

[*See also* Ancient, Old, Past, Present, Time.

Anti-Semitism

[*See* Jew.

Antisocial

The antisocial or asocial man is either a beast or a god.
ARISTOTLE: *Politics*, *c.* 322 B.C.

Antwerp

Antwerp is a pistol pointed at the heart of England.
Ascribed to NAPOLEON I, *c.* 1810

Anvil

The anvil fears no blows.
THOMAS FULLER: *Gnomologia*, 1732

[*See also* Church, Hammer and Anvil, Measure.

Anxiety

Thoughtful without anxiety.
DANIEL DEFOE: *A Review of the Affairs of France and of All Europe*, VIII, 1712

Life is too short for mean anxieties.
CHARLES KINGSLEY: *The Saint's Tragedy*, II, 1848

A hundred cartloads of anxiety will not pay an ounce of debt.
ITALIAN PROVERB

[*See also* Pleasure, Worry.

Ape

Once in three years came the navy of Tharshish, bringing gold, and silver, and apes, and peacocks.
I KINGS X, 22, *c.* 500 B.C.; (Cf. II CHRONICLES IX, 21, *c.* 300 B.C.)

How like to us is that filthy beast the ape.
CICERO: *De natura deorum*, I, 45 B.C.

An ape is an ape, though clad in purple.
DESIDERIUS ERASMUS: *The Praise of Folly*, 1509

Apes . . . kill by culling.
JOHN LYLY: *Love's Metamorphosis*, 1601
(*Culling*=fondling)

Man is God's ape, and an ape is zany to a man, doing over those tricks (especially if they be knavish) which he sees done before him.
THOMAS DEKKER: *The Seven Deadly Sins of London*, V, 1606

Men laugh at apes, they men contemn;
For what are we but apes to them?
JOHN GAY: *Fables*, I, 1727

Of beasts, it is confess'd, the ape
Comes nearest us in human shape;
Like man he imitates each fashion,
And malice is his ruling passion.
JONATHAN SWIFT: *The Logicians Refuted*, 1731

An ape is ne'er so like an ape
As when he wears a doctor's cape.
THOMAS FULLER: *Gnomologia*, 1732

The higher an ape mounts, the more he shows his breech. IBID.

What is the ape to man? A laughingstock, a thing of shame.
F. W. NIETZSCHE: *Thus Spake Zarathustra,* prologue, 1885

I have played the sedulous ape to Hazlitt, to Lamb, to Wordsworth, to Sir Thomas Browne, to Defoe, to Hawthorne, to Montaigne, to Baudelaire and to Obermann.
R. L. STEVENSON: *Memories and Portraits,* IV, 1887

[*See also* Clothes, Darwinism, Dress, Evolution, Invective, Man, Monkey, Priest, Spinster.

Aphorism

The excellence of aphorisms consists not so much in the expression of some rare or abstruse sentiment, as in the comprehension of some obvious and useful truth in a few words. SAMUEL JOHNSON: *The Rambler,* Nov. 19, 1751

Exclusively of the abstract sciences, the largest and worthiest portion of our knowledge consists of aphorisms: and the greatest and best of men is but an aphorism.
S. T. COLERIDGE: *Aids to Reflection,* 1825

It is my ambition to say in ten sentences what other men say in whole books — what other men do *not* say in whole books.
F. W. NIETZSCHE: *The Twilight of the Idols,* 1889

[*See also* Adage, Maxim, Proverb.

Apollo

[*See* Gods.

Apology

Apology is only egotism wrong side out. Nine times out of ten, the first thing a man's companion knows of his shortcomings is from his apology.
O. W. HOLMES: *The Professor at the Breakfast-Table,* VI, 1859

Apologies only account for that which they do not alter.
BENJAMIN DISRAELI: Speech in the House Commons, July 28, 1871

[*See also* Excuse, Explanation.

Apoplexy

This apoplexy is, as I take it, a kind of lethargy, an't please your lordship; a kind of sleeping in the blood, a whoreson tingling.
SHAKESPEARE: *II Henry IV,* I, *c.* 1598

Apostacy

If I am asked, Shall I utter the formula of Islam or submit to death? I answer, Utter the formula and live.
MAIMONIDES: *Maamar Kiddush Hashem,* *c.* 1160

[*See also* Heresy, Jew, Wordsworth (William).

Apostle

We are made a spectacle unto the world, and to angels, and to men.
I CORINTHIANS IV, 9, *c.* 55

We are fools for Christ's sake.
I CORINTHIANS IV, 10

The names of the twelve apostles are these: The first Simon, who is called Peter, and Andrew his brother; James the son of Zebedee, and John his brother; Philip, and Bartholomew; Thomas, and Matthew the publican; James the son of Alpheus, and Lebbeus, whose surname was Thaddeus; Simon the Canaanite, and Judas Iscariot, who also betrayed him.
MATTHEW X, 2–4, *c.* 75

[*See also* Christian, Disciple.

Apothecary

I do remember an apothecary, —
And hereabouts he dwells, — whom late I noted
In tatter'd weeds, with overwhelming brows,
Culling of simples; meagre were his looks,
Sharp misery had worn him to the bones:
And in his needy shop a tortoise hung,
An alligator stuff'd, and other skins
Of ill-shaped fishes; and about his shelves
A beggarly account of empty boxes,
Green earthen pots, bladders and musty seeds,
Remnants of packthread and old cakes of roses,
Were thinly scatter'd to make up a show.
SHAKESPEARE: *Romeo and Juliet,* V, *c.* 1596

It appears to me that apothecaries bear the same relation to physicians that priests do to philosophers; the ignorance of the former makes them positive, and dogmatical, and assuming, and enterprising, and pretending, and consequently much more taking with people.
DAVID HUME: *Letter to John Clephane,* Feb. 18, 1751

[*See also* Keats (John).

Apparel

Costly thy habit as thy purse can buy,
But not express'd in fancy; rich, not gaudy;
For the apparel oft proclaims the man.
SHAKESPEARE: *Hamlet,* I, *c.* 1601

See, where she comes, apparelled like the Spring. SHAKESPEARE: *Pericles,* I, *c.* 1608

[*See also* Clothes, Dress, Finery.

Apparition

[*See* Ghost.

Appeal

I appeal unto Caesar. ACTS XXV, 2, *c.* 75

Appearance

A good exterior is a silent recommendation.
PUBLILIUS SYRUS: *Sententiae,* *c.* 50 B.C.

Abstain from all appearance of evil.
I THESSALONIANS V, 22, *c.* 51

Ye are like unto whited sepulchres, which indeed appear beautiful outward, but are within full of dead men's bones.
MATTHEW XXIII, 27, *c.* 75

Judge not according to the appearance.
JOHN VII, 24, *c.* 115

All is not gold that shines like gold. (Non teneas aurum totum quod splendet ut aurum.)
ALANUS DE INSULIS: *Parabolae,* III, *c.* 1270

It is not all gold that glareth.
GEOFFREY CHAUCER: *The House of Fame,* I, *c.* 1384

Never judge by appearances.
ENGLISH PROVERB, traced by Smith to 1526

It is not all gold that gloweth.
RICHARD HILLES: *Commonplace book, c.* 1535

All is not gold which glisteneth.
GEORGE PETTIE: *Petite Palace of Pettie His Pleasure,* 1576

What, is the jay more precious than the lark,
Because his feathers are more beautiful?
Or is the adder better than the eel,
Because his painted skin contents the eye?
SHAKESPEARE: *The Taming of the Shrew,* IV, 1594

All that glisters is not gold.
SHAKESPEARE: *The Merchant of Venice,* II, *c.* 1597

All hoods make not monks.
SHAKESPEARE and JOHN FLETCHER: *Henry VIII,* III, 1613

Only in unimportant things do we dare not trust to appearance.
LA ROCHEFOUCAULD: *Maxims,* 1665

Appearances are very deceitful.
TOBIAS SMOLLETT: *Gil Blas,* III, 1750

All is not gold that glitters.
DAVID GARRICK: Prologue to OLIVER GOLDSMITH: *She Stoops to Conquer,* 1773 (Apparently the first appearance of the saying in the form now most familiar)

There is no trusting to appearances.
R. B. SHERIDAN: *The School for Scandal,* V, 1777

Oh, wad some power the giftie gie us
To see oursel's as ithers see us.
ROBERT BURNS: *To a Louse,* 1786

People who are much older than they look seldom have much intelligence.
G. C. LICHTENBERG: *Reflections,* 1799

Men are valued, not for what they are, but for what they seem to be.
E. G. BULWER-LYTTON: *Money,* I, 1840

Always scorn appearances, and you always may.
R. W. EMERSON: *Self-Reliance,* 1841

Things are seldom what they seem.
Skim milk masquerades as cream.
W. S. GILBERT: *H. M. S. Pinafore,* II, 1878

It is only shallow people who do not judge by appearances.
OSCAR WILDE: *The Picture of Dorian Gray,* 1891

Three-tenths of a good appearance are due to nature; seven-tenths to dress.
CHINESE PROVERB

If the beard were all, goats could preach.
DANISH PROVERB

All that is white is not milk. HINDU PROVERB

That which is not apparent does not exist. (Quod non apparet non est.)
LEGAL MAXIM

[*See also* Apparel, Clothes, Dress, Evil, Gold, Judgment.

Appetite

Put a knife to thy throat if thou be a man given to appetite.
PROVERBS XXIII, 2, *c.* 350 B.C.

All the labor of man is for his mouth, and yet the appetite is not filled.
ECCLESIASTES VI, 7, *c.* 200 B.C.

Let appetite obey reason.
CICERO: *De officiis,* I, 78 B.C.

The appetites of the belly and the palate, far from diminishing as men grow older, go on increasing.
CICERO: *Ad Caelium, c.* 50 B.C.

Let the first satisfaction of appetite be always the measure to you of eating and drinking; and appetite itself the sauce and the pleasure. EPICTETUS: *Encheiridion, c.* 110

Appetite comes by eating.
RABELAIS: *Gargantua,* I, 1535

Leave with an appetite.
WILLIAM BULLEIN: *The Government of Health,* 1558

Who riseth from a feast
With that keen appetite that he sits down?
SHAKESPEARE: *The Merchant of Venice,* II, *c.* 1597

Doth not the appetite alter? A man loves the meat in his youth that he cannot endure in his age.
SHAKESPEARE: *Much Ado About Nothing,* II, *c.* 1599

Now good digestion wait on appetite,
And health on both!
SHAKESPEARE: *Macbeth,* III, *c.* 1605

Eating and drinking take away appetite.
ENGLISH PROVERB, traced by Smith to 1611 (*Stomach* often appears in place of *appetite*)

That which is not good is not delicious
To a well-governed and wise appetite.
JOHN MILTON: *Comus,* 1637

All things require skill but an appetite.
GEORGE HERBERT: *Outlandish Proverbs,* 1640

New meat begets a new appetite.
JOHN RAY: *English Proverbs,* 1670

If thou rise with an appetite thou art sure never to sit down without one.
WILLIAM PENN: *Fruits of Solitude,* 1693

The most violent appetites in all creatures are lust and hunger; the first is a perpetual call upon them to propagate their kind, the latter to preserve themselves.
JOSEPH ADDISON: *The Spectator,* July 18, 1711

Now to the meal
Of silence, grandeur, and excess, he drags
His palled unwilling appetite.
P. B. SHELLEY: *Queen Mab,* III, 1813

Subdue your appetites, and you've conquered human nature.
CHARLES DICKENS: *Nicholas Nickleby,* V, 1839

Appetite is the best sauce.
FRENCH PROVERB

Sharp stomachs make short graces.
SCOTCH PROVERB

[*See also* Boy, Eating, Eating and Drinking, English, Good, Hope, Hunger, Lean, Newspaper, Stomach.

Applause

To gain the applause of all, what is useful must be mixed with the agreeable, and they must never be separated.
HORACE: *Ars poetica, c.* 8 B.C.

Dost thou wish to be applauded? Applaud another.
ST. JOHN CHRYSOSTOM: *Homily* XIII, *c.* 388

I would applaud thee to the very echo.
SHAKESPEARE: *Macbeth,* V, *c.* 1605

They threw their caps
As they would hang them on the horn o' the moon,
Shouting their emulation.
SHAKESPEARE: *Coriolanus,* I, *c.* 1607

Such a noise arose
As the shrouds make at sea in a stiff tempest.
SHAKESPEARE and JOHN FLETCHER: *Henry VIII,* IV, 1613

Do not trust to the cheering, for those very persons would shout as much if you and I were going to be hanged.
OLIVER CROMWELL: To John Lambert, on their march to the North, 1651

The applause of the crowd makes the head giddy, but the attestation of a reasonable man makes the heart glad.
RICHARD STEELE: *The Spectator,* Oct. 5, 1712

When most the world applauds you, most beware:
'Tis often less a blessing than a snare.
EDWARD YOUNG: *Love of Fame,* VI, 1728

The applause of listening senates to command.
THOMAS GRAY: *Elegy Written in a Country Churchyard,* 1750

Applause abates diligence.
SAMUEL JOHNSON: *The Rambler:* April 9, 1751

The applause of a single human being is of great consequence.
SAMUEL JOHNSON: *Boswell's Life,* 1780

O popular applause! what heart of man
Is proof against thy sweet, seducing charms?
WILLIAM COWPER: *The Task,* II, 1785

Go on deserving applause, and you will be sure to meet with it; and the way to deserve it is to be good, and to be industrious.
THOMAS JEFFERSON: *Letter to J. W. Eppes,* 1787

I am not reconciled to the idea of a chief magistrate parading himself through the several states as an object of public gaze, and in quest of applause which, to be valuable, should be purely voluntary. I had rather acquire silent goodwill by a faithful discharge of my duties than owe expressions of it to my putting myself in the way of receiving them.
THOMAS JEFFERSON: *Letter to James Sullivan,* 1807

Applause is the spur of noble minds, the end and aim of weak ones.
C. C. COLTON: *Lacon,* 1820

When the million applaud, you ask yourself what harm you have done; when they censure you, what good. IBID.

The silence that accepts merit as the most natural thing in the world is the highest applause.
R. W. EMERSON: Address at the Divinity College, Cambridge, Mass., July 15, 1838

The echo of a platitude.
AMBROSE BIERCE: *The Devil's Dictionary,* 1906

Applause is the beginning of abuse.
JAPANESE PROVERB

[*See also* Admiration, Approbation, Author, Hiss.

Apple

The apple of his eye.
DEUTERONOMY XXXII, 10, *c.* 650 B.C.

Comfort me with apples: for I am sick of love.
SOLOMON'S SONG, II, 5, *c.* 200

From the eggs to the apples. (Ab ovo usque ad mala.)
JUVENAL: *Satires*, I, *c.* 110 (A Latin saying corresponding to our "from soup to nuts")

One rotten apple in the barrel is enough to spoil all the rest.
ENGLISH PROVERB, borrowed from the Latin, and familiar in various forms since the XIV century

He that will not a wife wed
Must eat an apple on going to bed.
ENGLISH RHYME, traced to the XVI century

There's small choice in rotten apples.
SHAKESPEARE: *The Taming of the Shrew*, I, 1594

He pares his apple that will cleanly feed.
GEORGE HERBERT: *The Temple*, 1633

The apples on the other side of the wall are the sweetest.
GEORGE HERBERT: *Jacula Prudentum*, 1651

The fruit
Of that forbidden tree, whose mortal taste
Brought death into the world, and all our woe.
JOHN MILTON: *Paradise Lost*, I, 1667

An apple, an egg and a nut
You may eat after a slut.
JOHN RAY: *English Proverbs*, 1670 (i.e., after a dirty cook)

What is more melancholy than the old apple-trees that linger about the spot where once stood a homestead, but where there is now only a ruined chimney rising out of a grassy and weed-grown cellar? They offer their fruit to every wayfarer – apples that bear bitter-sweet with the moral of time's vicissitude.
NATHANIEL HAWTHORNE: *Mosses from an Old Manse*, 1846

An apple a day keeps the doctor away.
ENGLISH PROVERB, not recorded before the XIX century

All the evil in the world was brought into it by an apple. (Mala mali malo mala contulit omnia mundo.)
MEDIEVAL LATIN PROVERB

Worms eat even a sour apple.
POLISH PROVERB

Don't pluck a green apple; when it is ripe it will fall itself.
RUSSIAN PROVERB

[*See also* Adam, Rotten, Voice.

Apple-dumpling

C—— holds that a man cannot have a pure mind who refuses apple-dumplings.
CHARLES LAMB: *Grace Before Meat*, 1821 (London Magazine, Nov.; C—— was S. T. Coleridge)

Apple-pie

[*See* Cheese.

Apple-tree

An apple-tree puts to shame all the men and women that have attempted to dress since the world began.
H. W. BEECHER: *Royal Truths*, 1862

In the shade of the old apple-tree.
HARRY WILLIAMS: Title of a popular song, 1905

[*See also* Appomattox.

Application

The bearings of this observation lays in the application on it.
CHARLES DICKENS: *Dombey and Son*, XXIII, 1848

Appomattox

When asked what state he hails from,
Our sole reply shall be,
He comes from Appomattox
And its famous apple tree.
C. G. HALPIN (MILES O'REILLY): *Appomattox*, 1865

Up every flagstaff sprang the Stars and Stripes –
Out rushed the extras wild with mammoth types –
Down went the laborer's hod, the schoolboy's book –
"Hooraw!" he cried, – "the rebel army's took!"
O. W. HOLMES: *Rip Van Windle, M.D.*, II, 1870

Approbation

Approbation from Sir Hubert Stanley is praise indeed.
THOMAS MORTON: *A Cure for the Heartache*, V, 1797

We thirst for approbation, yet cannot forgive the approver.
R. W. EMERSON: *Circles*, 1841

[*See also* Admiration, Advice, Applause.

Approximation

All goes by approximation in this world; with any not insupportable approximation we must be patient.
THOMAS CARLYLE: *Past and Present*, I, 1843

April

April showers do bring May flowers.
THOMAS TUSSER: *Five Hundred Points of Good Husbandry*, 1580

The uncertain glory of an April day.
SHAKESPEARE: *Two Gentlemen of Verona,* I, *c.* 1595

Well-apparel'd April on the heel
Of limping Winter treads.
SHAKESPEARE: *Romeo and Juliet,* I, *c.* 1596

April's in her eyes; it is love's Spring.
SHAKESPEARE: *Antony and Cleopatra,* III, *c.* 1606

I shine in tears, like the sun in April.
CYRIL TOURNEUR: *The Revenger's Tragedy,* V, 1607

Proud-pied April dressed in all his trim
Hath put a spirit of youth in everything.
SHAKESPEARE: *Sonnets,* XCVIII, 1609

Spongy April.
SHAKESPEARE: *The Tempest,* IV, 1611

When April blows his horn it's good for both hay and corn.
JOHN RAY: *English Proverbs,* 1670 (*Blows his horn*=thunders)

A cold April
The barn will fill.
THOMAS FULLER: *Gnomologia,* 1732

April brings the primrose sweet,
Scatters daisies at our feet.
SARA COLERIDGE: *Pretty Lessons in Verse,* 1834

Oh, to be in England
Now that April's there.
ROBERT BROWNING: *Home Thoughts from Abroad,* 1847

April, April,
Laugh thy girlish laughter;
Then, the moment after,
Weep thy girlish tears!
WILLIAM WATSON: *April,* 1885

She who from April dates her years,
Diamonds should wear, lest bitter tears
For vain repentance flow; this stone,
Emblem of innocence is known.
Author unidentified

April and May are the keys to the whole year.
GERMAN PROVERB

You can have all the rest of the year if you will give me April and May.
SPANISH PROVERB

[*See also* All-Fools' Day, Months.

April First

[*See* All-Fools' Day.

Aquinas, Thomas (c. 1225–74)

The teaching of Blessed Thomas is the true and Catholic doctrine.
POPE URBAN V: *Letter to the University of Toulouse,* Aug. 4, 1368

Thomas is but Aristotle sainted.
JOSEPH GLANVILL: *The Vanity of Dogmatizing,* XVI, 1661

Reason, as borne on the wings of Thomas, can scarcely rise higher.
POPE LEO XIII: *Aeterni patris,* Aug. 4, 1879

Arab

We will call the Arabs oriental Italians. A gifted, noble people; a people of wild, strong feelings, and of iron restraint over these; the characteristic of noblemindedness, of genius.
THOMAS CARLYLE: *Heroes and Hero-Worship,* II, 1840 (Lecture in London, May 8)

The Arabs of today are the Arabs of Pharaoh.
R. W. EMERSON: *English Traits,* IV, 1856

Arabia is the cradle of the Arabs, and Mesopotamia is their grave.
ARAB PROVERB

Better the oppression of Turks than the justice of Arabs.
IBID.

Arabic Language

[*See* Language.

Ararat

The ark rested in the seventh month, on the seventeenth day of the month, upon the mountains of Ararat.
GENESIS VIII, 4, *c.* 700 B.C.

Arcadia

I too was born in Arcadia.
Origin unknown (The phrase began to appear as a motto on paintings in the XVI century, and was used by Goethe as a motto for his *Travels in Italy,* 1816)

Arch

An arch never sleeps.
HINDU SAYING

Archangel

[*See* Angel.

Archbishop

A tree or a brute stone is more respectable as such than a mortal called an archbishop.
HORACE WALPOLE: *Letter to William Cole,* July 12, 1778

I was much inclined to congratulate a writer who, in defiance of prejudice and fashion, made the archbishop a good man.
SAMUEL JOHNSON: *Letter to Mrs. Chapone,* Nov. 28, 1783

If I were a jolly archbishop
On Fridays I'd eat all the fish up —
Salmon and flounders and smelts;
On other days everything else.
AMBROSE BIERCE: *The Devil's Dictionary,* 1906

Scanavius relates that he knew an archbishop who was so old that he could remember a time when he did not deserve hanging.

IBID.

[*See also* Bishop, Hypocrisy, Prelate.

Architect

Under this stone, reader, survey
Dead Sir John Vanbrugh's house of clay.
Lie heavy on him, earth! for he
Laid many heavy loads on thee.

ABEL EVANS: *On Sir John Vanbrugh,* 1699 (Vanbrugh (1664–1726) was the architect of many public buildings)

A man who could build a church, as one may say, by squinting at a sheet of paper.

CHARLES DICKENS: *Martin Chuzzlewit,* II, 1844

No profession in England has done its duty until it has furnished a victim; even our boasted navy never achieved a great victory until we shot an admiral. Suppose an architect were hanged. Terror has its inspiration, as well as competition.

BENJAMIN DISRAELI: *Tancred,* XXI, 1847

An architect should live as little in cities as a painter. Send him to our hills, and let him study there what nature understands by a buttress, and what by a dome.

JOHN RUSKIN: *The Seven Lamps of Architecture,* III, 1849

One who drafts a plan of your house, and plans a draft of your money.

AMBROSE BIERCE: *The Devil's Dictionary,* 1906

[*See also* Brick.

Architecture

The ancient Romans built their greatest masterpieces of architecture, the ampitheatres, for wild beasts to fight in.

VOLTAIRE: *Letter to the Commissioner of Police of Paris,* June 20, 1733

In buildings, when the highest degree of the sublime is intended, the materials and ornaments ought neither to be white, nor green, nor yellow, nor blue, nor of a pale red, nor violet, nor spotted, but of sad or fuscous colors, as black, or brown, or deep purple, and the like.

EDMUND BURKE: *The Sublime and Beautiful,* II, 1756 (*Fuscous*=dark)

Architecture is the basis and groundwork of all other imitative arts, and no revival of art can take place until a grand improvement is seen in architectural design.

FRIEDRICH VON SCHLEGEL: *Principles of Gothic Architecture,* 1805

I have found a paper of mine in which I call architecture frozen music [erstarrte Musik]. Really there is something in this; the tone of mind produced by architecture approaches the effect of music.

J. W. GOETHE: *Conversations with Eckermann,* March 23, 1829

If cities were built by the sound of music, then some edifices would appear to be constructed by grave, solemn tones; others to have danced forth to light, fantastic airs.

NATHANIEL HAWTHORNE: American Note-Books, Jan. 4, 1839

Architecture concerns itself only with those characters of an edifice which are above and beyond its common use.

JOHN RUSKIN: *The Seven Lamps of Architecture,* I, 1849

We may live without architecture, and worship without her, but we cannot remember without her.

JOHN RUSKIN: *The Seven Lamps of Architecture,* VI

We require from buildings, as from men, two kinds of goodness: first, doing their practical duty well; then that they be graceful and pleasing in doing it.

JOHN RUSKIN: *Stones of Venice,* I, 1851

All good architecture rises out of good and simple domestic work; and therefore, before you attempt to build great churches and palaces, you must build good house doors and garret windows.

JOHN RUSKIN: *Lectures on Architecture and Painting,* I, 1853

In architecture the pride of man, his triumph over gravitation, his will to power, assume a visible form. Architecture is a sort of oratory of power.

F. W. NIETZSCHE: *The Twilight of the Idols,* 1889

[*See also* Architect, Art, Brick, Chimney.

Architecture, Gothic

The principle of the Gothic architecture is infinity made imaginable.

S. T. COLERIDGE: *Table-Talk,* June 29, 1833

The Gothic cathedral is a blossoming in stone subdued by the insatiable demand of harmony in man.

R. W. EMERSON: *History,* 1841

In one point of view Gothic is not only the best, but the only rational architecture, as being that which can fit itself most easily to all services, vulgar or noble.

JOHN RUSKIN: *Stones of Venice,* II, 1853

Arctic

This gloomy region, where the year is divided into one day and one night, lies entirely outside the stream of history.

W. WINWOOD READE: *The Martyrdom of Man,* III, 1872

Argument

The first the retort courteous; the second the quip modest; the third the reply churlish; the fourth the reproof valiant; the fifth the countercheck quarrelsome; the sixth the lie with circumstance; the seventh the lie direct.
SHAKESPEARE: *As You Like It*, V, *c.* 1600

If he takes you in hand, sir, with an argument,
He'll bray you in a mortar.
BEN JONSON: *The Alchemist*, II, 1612

Strong affections give credit to weak arguments.
JOHN CLARKE: *Parœmiologia Anglo-Latina*, 1639

When we desire to be informed 'tis good to contest with men above ourselves; but to confirm and establish our opinions 'tis best to argue with judgments below our own, that the frequent spoils and victories over their reasons may settle in ourselves an esteem and confirmed opinion of our own.
THOMAS BROWNE: *Religio Medici*, I, 1642

When we wish to reprove with profit, and show another that he is mistaken, we must observe on what side he looks at the thing, for it is usually true on that side, and to admit to him that truth, but to discover to him the side whereon it is false. He is pleased with this, for he perceives that he was not mistaken, and that he only failed to look on all sides.
BLAISE PASCAL: *Pensées*, VIII, 1670

A knock-down argument: 'tis but a word and a blow.
JOHN DRYDEN: *Amphitryon*, I, 1690

Socrates introduced a catechetical method of arguing. Aristotle changed this method of attack, and invented a great variety of little weapons called syllogisms. Socrates conquers you by strategy; Aristotle by force. The one takes the town by sap; the other sword in hand.
JOSEPH ADDISON: *The Spectator*, Dec. 4, 1711

Strive not with your superiors in argument, but always submit your judgment to others with modesty.
GEORGE WASHINGTON: *Early copy-book*, before 1748

Even though vanquished he could argue still.
OLIVER GOLDSMITH: *The Deserted Village*, 1770

It is not necessary to understand things in order to argue about them.
CARON DE BEAUMARCHAIS: *Le barbier de Séville*, IV, 1775

To attempt to argue any great question upon facts only is absurd; you cannot state any fact before a mixed audience which an opponent as clever as yourself cannot with ease twist towards another bearing, or at least meet by a contrary fact, as it is called.
S. T. COLERIDGE: *Table-Talk*, Dec. 27, 1831

Use soft words and hard arguments.
H. G. BOHN: *Handbook of Proverbs*, 1855

A *tu quoque* argument should always be good-humored, for it has nothing else to recommend it.
BENJAMIN DISRAELI: Speech in the House of Commons, May 24, 1855

Myself when young did eagerly frequent
Doctor and saint, and heard great argument
About it and about: but evermore
Came out by the same door wherein I went.
EDWARD FITZGERALD: Tr. of OMAR KHAYYÁM: *Rubáiyát* (*c.* 1100), 1857

The one thet fust gits mad's most ollers wrong.
J. R. LOWELL: *The Biglow Papers*, II, 1862

There is no greater mistake than the hasty conclusion that opinions are worthless because they are badly argued.
T. H. HUXLEY: *Natural Rights and Political Rights*, 1890

It is only the intellectually lost who ever argue.
OSCAR WILDE: *The Picture of Dorian Gray*, 1891

Arguments are to be avoided; they are always vulgar and often convincing.
OSCAR WILDE: *The Importance of Being Earnest*, II, 1895

The stronger the man the more weighty his argument.
FRENCH PROVERB

An argument based on ignorance (argumentum ad ignorantiam); to ignorance or prejudice (ad captandum); to the judgment (ad judiciam); to the man himself (ad hominem); to the purse (ad crumenam); to the sense of decency (ad verecundiam); with a stick (ad baculinum).
LATIN PHRASES

One does not argue against the sun (i.e., against what is self-evident). (Adversus solem ne loquitor.)
LATIN PROVERB

Every time a man engages in argument he loses a drop of blood from his liver.
PERSIAN PROVERB

[*See also* Casuist, Casuistry, Controversy, Dispute, Education, Fighting, Haste, Lawyer, Oratory, Shibboleth.

Aristocracy

Aristocracy is that form of government in which education and discipline are qualifications for suffrage or office-holding.
ARISTOTLE: *Rhetoric*, I, *c.* 322 B.C.

High people are the best. Take a hundred ladies of quality, you'll find them better wives, better mothers, more willing to sac-

rifice their own pleasures to their children, than a hundred other women.
SAMUEL JOHNSON: *Boswell's Life,* May 14, 1778

There is a natural aristocracy among men. The grounds for this are virtue and talents.
THOMAS JEFFERSON: *Letter to John Adams,* Oct. 28, 1813

The aristocracy of feudal parchment has passed away with a mighty rushing, and now, by a natural course, we arrive at aristocracy of the money-bag.
THOMAS CARLYLE: *The French Revolution,* VII, 1837

An aristocracy is a combination of many powerful men, for the purpose of maintaining and advancing their own particular interests. It is consequently a concentration of all the most effective parts of a community for a given end; hence its energy, efficiency and success.
J. FENIMORE COOPER: *The American Democrat,* x, 1838

It is well said, " Land is the right basis of an aristocracy "; whoever possesses the land, he, more emphatically than any other, is the governor, vice-king of the people of the land.
THOMAS CARLYLE: *Past and Present,* III, 1843

English history is aristocracy with the doors open. Who has courage and faculty, let him come in.
R. W. EMERSON: *English Traits,* XI, 1856

The aristocracy is the immediate power between tyranny and democracy. It saves the people from violating the law, and the king from oppressing the people. If ever aristocracy be destroyed in England, the crown and the people will come into inevitable collision, and destroy each other.
B. R. HAYDON: *Table-Talk,* 1876

The aristocracy of labor.
WALTER BESANT: *The Alabaster Box,* 1900

There is something to be said for government by a great aristocracy which has furnished leaders to the nation in peace and war for generations; even a democrat like myself must admit this.
THEODORE ROOSEVELT: *Letter to Edward Grey,* Nov. 15, 1913

The cardinal virtue of an aristocracy is to know when to surrender.
CLAUD SUTTON: *Farewell to Rousseau,* IV, 1936

[*See also* Ancestry, Aristocrat, Birth (High), Civilization, Government, Heredity, Jew, Nobility, Party, Peerage, Rank.

Aristocrat

The aristocrat is the democrat ripe and gone to seed.
R. W. EMERSON: *Representative Men,* VI, 1850

A demokrat with hiz pockets filled.
H. W. SHAW: *Josh Billings' Comical Lexicon,* 1877

[*See also* Aristocracy, Ruler.

Aristotle (384–322 B.C.)

He was a man of excellent genius, though inferior in eloquence to Plato.
ST. AUGUSTINE: *The City of God,* VIII, 427

He did not consult experience, as he should have done, in the framing of his decisions and axioms; but, having first determined the question according to his will, he then resorted to experience, and, bending her into conformity with his placets, led her about like a captive in a procession.
FRANCIS BACON: *Novum Organum,* I, 1620

His intellect was piercing and comprehensive; his attainments surpassed those of every known philosopher; his influence has only been exceeded by the great founders of religions; nevertheless, if we now estimate the product of his labors in the discovery of positive truths, it appears insignificant, when not erroneous. None of the great germinal discoveries in science are due to him, or to his disciples.
G. H. LEWES: *A Biographical History of Philosophy,* 1845

Aristotle displayed what we should consider some of the worst attributes of a modern physical investigator — indistinctness of ideas, confusion of mind, and a confident use of language which led to the delusive notion that he had really mastered his subject, while he had as yet failed to grasp even the elements of it. He put words in the place of things, subject in the place of object.
JOHN TYNDALL: Address to the British Association, Belfast, 1874

Aristotle hesitates and suggests; proposes first one formula and then another; rejects both, gives a multitude of reasons, and ends at last with an expression which he admits to be incorrect and an apologetic " let it make no difference." There are whole passages in his writings in which he appears like a schoolboy who knows the answer to a sum, but cannot get the figures to come to it.
WALTER BAGEHOT: *Literary Studies,* II, 1879

[*See also* Argument, Plato.

Aristotelian

[*See* Philosophy.

Arithmetic

Multiplication is vexation,
Division is as bad,
The rule of three doth puzzle me,
And fractions drive me mad.
Author unidentified

[*See also* Art.

Arizona

Come to Arizona, where Summer spends the Winter.
Slogan of Arizona boosters, *c.* 1935

And Hell spends the Summer.
Addendum of local cynics

Ark

(The story of Noah and his ark runs from GENESIS VI, 7 to IX, 29, *c.* 700 B.C.)

Arkansas

Biggest fool I ever saw
Come from state of Arkansaw;
Put his shirt on over his coat,
Button his britches up round his throat.
American Negro song, quoted by HOWARD W. ODUM: *Wings On My Feet,* I, 1929

If I die in Arkansaw
Jes' ship my body to my mother-in-law.
American Negro song

Armageddon

And he gathered them together in a place called in the Hebrew tongue Armageddon.
REVELATION XVI, 16, *c.* 95

We seemed to see our flag unfurled,
Our champion waiting in his place
For the last battle of the world,
The Armageddon of the race.
J. G. WHITTIER: *Rantoul, c.* 1870

We stand at Armageddon and we battle for the Lord.
THEODORE ROOSEVELT: Speech at Chicago, Aug. 5, 1912

Armenian

If you can make a good bargain with an Armenian you can make a good bargain with the Devil. PERSIAN PROVERB

[*See also* Cheating.

Arms

The blade itself incites to violence.
HOMER: *Odyssey,* XVI, *c.* 800 B.C.

Arms and the man I sing. (Arma virumque cano.) VIRGIL: *Aeneid,* I, 19 B.C.

All the armed prophets conquered; all the unarmed ones perished.
NICCOLO MACHIAVELLI: *The Prince,* VI, 1513

The principal foundations of all states are good laws and good arms; and there cannot be good laws where there are not good arms.
NICCOLO MACHIAVELLI: *The Prince,* XII

The subjects which are Protestants may have arms for their defense suitable to their conditions, and as allowed by law.
THE ENGLISH BILL OF RIGHTS, VII, Dec. 1689

I do not wish to see guns in the hands of all the world, for there are other *ferae naturae* besides hares and partridges.
HORACE WALPOLE: *Letter to the Countess Ossory,* Sept. 26, 1789

A well-regulated militia being necessary to the security of a free state, the right of the people to keep and bear arms shall not be infringed.
CONSTITUTION OF THE UNITED STATES, Amendment II, Dec. 15, 1791

Arms, women, and books need to be looked at every day. DUTCH PROVERB

Arms are the props of peace. (Arma pacis fulcra.) LATIN PROVERB

A horseman unarmed is like a bird without wings. MOROCCAN PROVERB

[*See also* Cannon, Gun, Weapon.

Army

A large army is always disorderly.
EURIPIDES: *Hecuba, c.* 426 B.C.

The strength of an army lies in strict discipline and undeviating obedience to its officers.
THUCYDIDES: *History,* II, *c.* 410 B.C.

Regular troops lose their courage when they confront dangers greater than they looked for, and find themselves surpassed in numbers and arms. They are the first to turn their backs. But militiamen die in their places.
ARISTOTLE: *The Nicomachean Ethics,* III, *c.* 340 B.C.

An army of stags led by a lion is more to be feared than an army of lions led by a stag.
Ascribed to CHABRIAS (*c.* 410–357 B.C.)

Terrible as an army with banners.
SOLOMON'S SONG VI, 4, *c.* 200 B.C. (Cf. VI, 10)

A small army consisting of chosen troops is far better than a vast body chiefly composed of rabble; for when the bad give way, the good are inevitably broken in consequence.
THE HITOPADESA, III, *c.* 500

Walled towns, stored arsenals and armories, goodly races of horse, chariots of war, elephants, ordnance, artillery, and the like; all this is but a sheep in a lion's skin except the breed and disposition of the people be stout and warlike.
FRANCIS BACON: *Essays,* XXIX, 1625

Pay well, command well, hang well.
RALPH HOPTON (LORD HOPTON OF STRATTON): Maxims for the management of an army, 1643 (Hopton was a Royalist commander in the English Civil War; he died in exile at Bruges, 1652)

The raising or keeping a standing army within the kingdom in time of peace, unless it be with consent of Parliament, is against law.
THE ENGLISH BILL OF RIGHTS, VI, Dec. 1689

Mouths without hands; maintained at vast expense,
In peace a charge, in war a weak defense.
JOHN DRYDEN: *Cymon and Iphigenia,* 1699

When men are irritated and their passions inflamed they fly hastily and cheerfully to arms, but after the first emotions are over, to expect among such people as compose the bulk of an army that they are influenced by any other principles than those of interest is to look for what never did and I fear never will happen.
GEORGE WASHINGTON: *Letter to the president of Congress,* Sept., 1776

Standing armies can never consist of resolute robust men; they may be well-disciplined machines, but they will seldom contain men under the influence of strong passions, or with very vigorous faculties.
MARY WOLLSTONECRAFT: *A Vindication of the Rights of Women,* II, 1792

The Greeks by their laws, and the Romans by the spirit of their people, took care to put into the hands of their rulers no such engine of oppression as a standing army. Their system was to make every man a soldier, and oblige him to repair to the standard of his country whenever that was reared. This made them invincible; and the same remedy will make us so.
THOMAS JEFFERSON: *Letter to Thomas Cooper,* 1814

The German army is the German people in arms.
PRINCE REGENT WILHELM OF PRUSSIA: Speech at the opening of the Prussian Diet, Jan. 12, 1860

We are coming, Father Abraham, three hundred thousand more.
J. S. GIBBONS: *We Are Coming, Father Abraham,* 1862

Back to the army again, sergeant,
Back to the army again.
RUDYARD KIPLING: *Back to the Army Again,* 1892

Governments need armies to protect them against their enslaved and oppressed subjects.
LYOF N. TOLSTOY: *The Kingdom of God Is Within You,* 1893

The army has always been the basis of power, and it is so today. Power is always in the hands of those who command it. IBID.

You're in the army now,
You're not behind the plow;
You'll never get rich, you son of a bitch,
You're in the army now.
Anon.: American soldiers' song

An army marches on its belly.
Author unidentified; often ascribed to NAPOLEON I, apparently without ground

[*See also* Alliteration, Army and Navy, Conscription, Horse, Infantry, Leadership, Mercenary, Militia, Officer, Soldier, War.

Army and Navy

A naval force can never endanger our liberties, nor occasion bloodshed; a land force would do both.
THOMAS JEFFERSON: *Letter to James Monroe,* 1786

The President shall be the commander in chief of the army and navy of the United States, and of the militia of the several states when called into the actual service of the United States.
CONSTITUTION OF THE UNITED STATES, II, 1789

The services in war time are fit only for desperadoes, but in peace are fit only for fools.
BENJAMIN DISRAELI: *Vivian Grey,* IV, 1827

The whole present system of the officering and personnel of the army and navy of These States, and the spirit and letter of their trebly-aristocratic rules and regulations, is a monstrous exotic, a nuisance and revolt, and belongs here just as much as orders of nobility or the pope's council of cardinals. I say if the present theory of our army and navy is sensible and true, then the rest of America is an unmitigated fraud.
WALT WHITMAN: *Democratic Vistas,* 1870

Army, Confederate

The rebels now have in their ranks their last man. The little boys and old men are guarding prisoners and railroad bridges, and forming a good part of their forces, manning forts and positions, and any man lost by them cannot be replaced. They have robbed the cradle and the grave.
U. S. GRANT: *Letter for publication,* Aug. 16, 1864

Arnold, Matthew (1822–88)

Poor Matt, he's gone to Heaven, no doubt — but he won't like God.
R. L. STEVENSON: On hearing of Arnold's death, 1888

Arnold is a dandy Isaiah, a poet without passion, whose verse, written in a surplice, is for freshmen and for gentle maidens who will be wooed to the arms of these future rectors.
GEORGE MEREDITH: To Edward Clodd (Fortnightly Review, July, 1909), *c.* 1900

Arrogance

Arrogance and boldness belong to those that are accursed of God.
ST. CLEMENT: *First Epistle to the Corinthians, c.* 100

Undertake not to teach your equal in the art himself professes; it savors arrogancy.
GEORGE WASHINGTON: *Early copy-book,* before 1748

[*See also* Prosperity.

Arrow

I shot an arrow into the air,
It fell to earth, I knew not where;
For, so swiftly it flew, the sight
Could not follow it in its flight.
H. W. LONGFELLOW: *The Arrow and the Song,* 1841

Arson

If a free man set a house ablaze, he shall build the house again.
HITTITE CODE, *c.* 1350 B.C.

Art

Life is short, art long, opportunity fleeting, experience treacherous, judgment difficult.
HIPPOCRATES: *Aphorisms, c.* 400 B.C. (The saying is most familiar in the shortened Latin form: "Ars longa, vita brevis" — Art is long, and life short)

If arithmetic, mensuration and the weighing of things be taken away from any art, that which remains will not be much.
PLATO: *Philebus, c.* 375 B.C.

All art consists in bringing something into existence.
ARISTOTLE: *The Nicomachean Ethics,* VI, *c.* 340 B.C.

Art is a higher type of knowledge than experience.
ARISTOTLE: *Metaphysics, c.* 322 B.C.

Art has no regard to the individual case.
ARISTOTLE: *Rhetoric,* I, *c.* 322 B.C.

In part, art completes what nature cannot elaborate; and in part, it imitates nature.
ARISTOTLE: *Physics, c.* 320 B.C.

All the arts have a certain common bond of union, and are connected by blood relationship with one another.
CICERO: *Pro archia poeta,* 62 B.C.

To what point cannot art reach? Some learn even to weep with grace.
OVID: *Ars amatoria,* III, *c.* 2 B.C.

Nothing is more useful to man than those arts which have no utility.
OVID: *Epistulae ex Ponto,* I, *c.* 5

The height of art is to conceal art.
QUINTILIAN: *De institutione oratoria,* I, *c.* 90

Art may be called complete and perfect when it seems to be nature.
LONGINUS: *On the Sublime,* XXII, *c.* 250

Art is simply a right method of doing things. The test of the artist does not lie in the will with which he goes to work, but in the excellence of the work he produces.
THOMAS AQUINAS: *Summa theologiae,* LVII, *c.* 1265

Art imitates nature as well as it can, as a pupil follows his master; thus it is a sort of grandchild of God.
DANTE: *Inferno,* XI, *c.* 1320

Art hath an enemy called ignorance.
BEN JONSON: *Every Man Out of His Humor,* I, 1600

Art made tongue-tied by authority.
SHAKESPEARE: *Sonnets,* LXVI, 1609

The shows of things are better than themselves.
Anon.: *Nero,* III, 1624

In every art it is good to have a master.
GEORGE HERBERT: *Outlandish Proverbs,* 1640

Art is the perfection of nature.
THOMAS BROWNE: *Religio Medici,* XVI, 1642

A man who has a taste in music, painting or architecture is like one that has another sense when compared with such as have no relish of those arts.
JOSEPH ADDISON: *The Spectator,* June 16, 1711

Art is only a prudent steward that lives on managing the riches of nature.
ALEXANDER POPE: Tr. of HOMER: *Iliad,* pref., 1715

Art helps nature, and experience art.
THOMAS FULLER: *Gnomologia,* 1732

No work of art can be great but as it deceives; to be otherwise is the prerogative of nature only.
EDMUND BURKE: *The Sublime and Beautiful,* II, 1756

Art in its perfection is not ostentatious; it lies hid and works its effect, itself unseen.
JOSHUA REYNOLDS: *Discourses,* VI, 1774 (Lecture at the Royal Academy, London, Dec. 10)

Art is the right hand of nature. The latter has only given us being; the former has made us men.
J. C. F. SCHILLER: *Fiesco,* II, 1784

The arts, in general, have need of a king. They glow only under the influence of the scepter. In free states they never shine save when liberty is declining.
JOSEPH DE MAISTRE: *Étude sur la souveraineté,* 1794

Art alone supplies an enjoyment which requires no appreciable effort, which costs no sacrifice, and which we need not repay with repentance.
J. C. F. SCHILLER: *Essays, Æsthetical and Philosophical,* 1796

Art is difficult, and its reward is transient.
J. C. F. SCHILLER: *Wallenstein's Camp*, prologue, 1799

Art! Who comprehends her? With whom can one consult concerning this great goddess?
LUDWIG VAN BEETHOVEN: *Letter to Bettina von Arnim*, August 11, 1810

Art for art's sake. (L'art pour l'art.)
VICTOR COUSIN: *Lecture at the Sorbonne*, 1818

The mother of the practical arts is need; that of the fine arts is luxury. The father of the former is intelligence and of the latter genius, which is itself a kind of luxury.
ARTHUR SCHOPENHAUER: *The World as Will and Idea*, II, 1819

The world is a king, and, like a king, desires flattery in return for favor; but true art is selfish and perverse—it will not submit to the mold of flattery.
LUDWIG VAN BEETHOVEN: *Conversation-Book*, March, 1820

What makes a regiment of soldiers a more noble object of view than the same mass of mob? Their arms, their dresses, their banners, and the *art* and artificial symmetry of their position and movements.
BYRON: *Letter to John Murray*, Feb. 7, 1821

The perfection of an art consists in the employment of a comprehensive system of laws, commensurate to every purpose within its scope, but concealed from the eye of the spectator.
J. M. GOOD: *The Book of Nature*, I, 1826

Art is long, and time is fleeting.
H. W. LONGFELLOW: *A Psalm of Life*, 1839
(Cf. HIPPOCRATES, *ante*, *c.* 499 B.C.)

Our arts are happy hits. We are like the musician on the lake, whose melody is sweeter than he knows; or like a traveler, surprised by a mountain echo, whose trivial word returns to him in romantic thunders.
R. W. EMERSON: *Art*, 1841

Art, in any but its infant stage, presupposes scientific knowledge; and if every art does not bear the name of a science it is only because several sciences are often necessary to form the groundwork of a single art.
J. S. MILL: *System of Logic*, 1843

All works of art should begin . . . at the end.
E. A. POE: *The Rationale of Verse*, 1843
(The Pioneer, March)

The highest art, being based on sensations of peculiar minds, sensations occurring to *them* only at particular times, and to a plurality of mankind perhaps never, and being expressive of thoughts which could only rise out of a mass of the most extended knowledge, and of dispositions modified in a thousand ways by peculiarity of intellect—can only be met and understood by persons having some sort of sympathy with the high and solitary minds which produce it—sympathy only to be felt by minds in some degree high and solitary themselves.
JOHN RUSKIN: *Modern Painters*, II, 1846

Were I called on to define, very briefly, the term *art*, I should call it "the reproduction of what the senses perceive in nature through the veil of the soul."
E. A. POE: *Marginalia*, 1844–49

Perpetual modernness is the measure of merit in every work of art.
R. W. EMERSON: *Representative Men*, II, 1850

You must treat a work of art like a great man: stand before it and wait patiently till it deigns to speak.
ARTHUR SCHOPENHAUER: *Note-Books*, *c.* 1850

If your work of art is good, if it is true, it will find its echo and make its place—in six months, in six years, or after you are gone. What is the difference?
GUSTAVE FLAUBERT: *Letter to Maxime du Camp*, June 26, 1852

Nature I loved, and next to nature, art.
W. S. LANDOR: *The Last Fruit of an Old Tree*, 1853

The first universal characteristic of all great art is tenderness, as the second is truth.
JOHN RUSKIN: *The Two Paths*, I, 1859

The period in which any given people reach their highest power in art is precisely that in which they appear to sign the warrant of their own ruin.
IBID.

No one can explain how the notes of a Mozart melody, or the folds of a piece of Titian's drapery, produce their essential effects. If you do not feel it, no one can by reasoning make you feel it.
JOHN RUSKIN: *Modern Painters*, V, 1860

Great art is of no real use to anybody but the next great artist; . . . it is wholly invisible to people in general.
JOHN RUSKIN: *Letter to E. B. Browning*, Nov. 5, 1860

Art reveals nature by interpreting its intentions and formulating its desires. The great artist is the simplifier.
H. F. AMIEL: *Journal*, Nov. 25, 1861

Art is I; science is we.
CLAUDE BERNARD: *Introduction à la médecine expérimentale*, 1865

No great art ever yet rose on earth but among a nation of soldiers.
JOHN RUSKIN: *The Crown of Wild Olive*, III, 1866

A work of art is a corner of creation seen through a temperament.
ÉMILE ZOLA: *Mes haines*, 1866

It is a gratification to me to know that I am ignorant of art.
S. L. CLEMENS (MARK TWAIN): *Letter from New York to the Alta Californian* (*San Francisco*), May 28, 1867

It is the glory and good of art
That art remains the one way possible
Of speaking truth, — to mouths like mine, at least.
ROBERT BROWNING: *The Ring and the Book*, I, 1868

No good art is unbeautiful, but much able and effective work may be and is.
A. C. SWINBURNE: *Notes on Some Pictures of 1868*, 1869

It is the treating of the commonplace with the feeling of the sublime that gives to art its true power.
JEAN-FRANÇOIS MILLET: MS. note, *c.* 1870

Art has no independent powers of its own: art is but the employment of the powers of nature for an end.
J. S. MILL: *Three Essays on Religion*, I, 1874

All passes, art alone
Enduring stays to us;
The bust outlasts the throne, —
The coin, Tiberius.
AUSTIN DOBSON: Tr. of THÉOPHILE GAUTIER: *Ars Victrix*, *c.* 1875

The arts were intended to be the handmaids of religion.
JAMES CARDINAL GIBBONS: *The Faith of Our Fathers*, XV, 1876

Art is not an end in itself, but a means of addressing humanity.
M. P. MUSSORGSKY: Autobiographical fragment, 1880

Art precedes philosophy and even science. People must have noticed things and interested themselves in them before they begin to debate upon their causes or influence.
R. L. STEVENSON: *Familiar Studies of Men and Books*, I, 1882

Art never harms itself by keeping aloof from the social problems of the day; rather, by so doing, it more completely realizes for us that which we desire.
OSCAR WILDE: *The English Renaissance of Art*, 1882 (Lecture in New York, Jan. 9)

He who does not love art in all things does not love it at all, and he who does not need art in all things does not need it at all. IBID.

All human art is the increment of the power of the hand.
JOHN FISKE: *The Destiny of Man*, VI, 1884

Art is not nature. Art is nature digested. Art is a sublime excrement.
GEORGE MOORE: *Confessions of a Young Man*, VII, 1888

The struggle against a purpose in art is always a struggle against the moral tendency in art — against its subordination to morality. *L'art pour l'art* means, Let morality go to the Devil.
F. W. NIETZSCHE: *The Twilight of the Idols*, 1889

Art reveals nature's lack of design, her curious crudities, her absolutely unfinished condition. Nature has good intentions, but she cannot carry them out. Art is our gallant attempt to teach nature her proper place.
OSCAR WILDE: *The Decay of Lying*, 1889

To art's subject-matter we should be more or less indifferent. We should, at any rate, have no preferences, no prejudices, no partisan feeling of any kind. It is exactly because Hecuba is nothing to us that her sorrows are such an admirable motive for a tragedy.
IBID.

It's pretty, but is it art?
RUDYARD KIPLING: *The Conundrum of the Workshops*, 1890

Art should be independent of all clap-trap — should stand alone, and appeal to the artistic sense of eye and ear, without confounding this with emotions entirely foreign to it, as devotion, pity, love, patriotism, and the like.
J. MCN. WHISTLER: *The Gentle Art of Making Enemies*, 1890

If one loves art at all, one must love it beyond all other things in the world, and against such love the reason, if one listened to it, would cry out.
OSCAR WILDE: *The Critic as Artist*, 1891

Lying, the telling of beautiful untrue things, is the proper aim of art. IBID.

All art is quite useless.
OSCAR WILDE: *The Picture of Dorian Gray*, 1891

To reveal art and conceal the artist is art's aim.
IBID.

A work of art is the unique result of a unique temperament. Its beauty comes from the fact that its author is what he is.
OSCAR WILDE: *The Soul of Man Under Socialism*, 1891

When art is understood by everybody it will cease to be art.
ARSÈNE HOUSSAYE (1815–96)

Art is a human activity consisting in this, that one man consciously, by means of certain external signs, hands on to others feelings he has lived through, and that other people are

infected by these feelings, and also experience them.
LYOF N. TOLSTOY: *What Is Art?*, 1898

The principle underlying all art is of a purely religious nature.
VINCENT D'INDY: *Cours de composition musicale*, I, 1902

Nothing is so poor and melancholy as an art that is interested in itself and not in its subject.
GEORGE SANTAYANA: *The Life of Reason*, IV, 1905

I don't know anything about art, but I know what I like.
AMERICAN PROVERB, apparently first recorded by GELLETT BURGESS: *Are You a Bromide?* 1907 (The following variation was suggested by JAMES THURBER in the New Yorker, Nov. 4, 1939: " He knows all about art, but he doesn't know what he likes")

No kind of good art exists unless it grows out of the ideas of the average man.
G. K. CHESTERTON: Evidence before the Joint Select Committee on the Stage Plays, Sept. 24, 1909

Conscience, who said conscience? Is there such a thing in art any more?
JAMES HUNEKER: *Old Fogy*, XVI, 1913

Art is the stored honey of the human soul, gathered on wings of misery and travail.
THEODORE DREISER: *Life, Art and America*, 1917

To let one's self go — that is what art is always aiming at. All art is lyrical.
J. E. SPINGARN: *Creative Criticism*, 1917.

Art in the native American mind enjoys the dubious importance attached to the Devil in the medieval mind.
ALEXANDER HARVEY: *William Dean Howells*, 1917

In art I pull no highbrow stuff;
I know what I like, and that's enough.
W. W. WOOLLCOTT: *I Am a 100% American*, 1918 (Cf. GELETT BURGESS, *ante*, 1907)

Art is a weapon in the class struggle.
MOTTO OF THE JOHN REED CLUB, *c.* 1921

Art is a kind of illness.
GIACOMO PUCCINI (1858–1924)

Good art weathers the ages because once in so often a man of intelligence commands the mass to adore it.
EZRA POUND: *Imaginary Letters*, 1930

Democracy and liberty are not the only orthodoxies within the limits of which art may express itself. The ideals of Communism or Fascism may capture the genius of men, and their powers may find adequate expression within those systems.
HUNTINGTON CAIRNS: *Freedom of Expression in Literature*, 1938

In the field of art there is not — there should not be — any rivalry among nations. The only combat worthy of us is that which is waged, in every country and at every hour, between culture and ignorance, between light and chaos. Let us save all the light that can be saved!
ROMAIN ROLLAND: *Letter to the congress of the American Musicological Society*, New York, Sept., 1939

There are but two boons in life: the love of art and the art of love. Author unidentified

[*See also* Artist, Beauty, Business, Capital, Christian, Criticism, Eloquence, Freedom, Imitation, Life, Literature, Medicine, Nature, Poetry, Standard, Supply and Demand.

Art, Christian

The idea of a Christian art is a contradiction in terms.
ERNST HAECKEL: *The Riddle of the Universe*, XVIII, 1899

Artery

A man is as old as his arteries.
THOMAS SYDENHAM (1624–89) (This was a favorite saying of Rudolf Virchow, 1821–1902)

Artificiality

Nothing artificial is really pleasing.
ST. AMBROSE: *A Clergyman's Duties*, I, *c.* 390

The first duty in life is to be as artificial as possible. What the second duty is no one has yet discovered.
OSCAR WILDE: *Phrases and Philosophies for the Use of the Young*, 1891

Artillery

Then shook the hills with thunder riven;
Then rush'd the steed, to battle driven;
And louder than the bolts of Heaven,
Far flash'd the red artillery.
THOMAS CAMPBELL: *Hohenlinden*, 1803

Over hill, over dale, we have hit the dusty trail,
And our caissons go rolling along.
In and out, hear them shout " Countermarch and right-about,"
And the caissons go rolling along.
E. L. GRUBER: *Field Artillery Song*, *c.* 1909

[*See also* Cannon, Firearms, General, Infantry, War.

Artilleryman

[*See* Engineer.

Artisan

[*See* Profession, Trade (=calling).

Artist

The gods that first taught artists their craft laid a great curse on mankind.
ANTIPHANES: *Fragments, c.* 350 B.C.

A man may be an artist though he have not his tools about him.
THOMAS FULLER: *Gnomologia,* 1732

Only a part of art can be taught, but the artist needs the whole.
J. W. GOETHE: *Wilhelm Meisters Lehrjahre,* VII, 1795

It is harder for an artist to be a Stoic than for anybody else.
LUDWIG VAN BEETHOVEN: *The Testament of Heiligenstadt,* Oct. 6, 1802

Only the artist, or the free scholar, carries his happiness within him.
LUDWIG VAN BEETHOVEN: *To Karl von Bursy,* 1816

Horace, Virgil, Hortensius, Varro, and Livy were more occupied in writing what deserved to be read than in doing anything that deserved to be written.
C. C. COLTON: *Lacon,* 1820

No one should drive a hard bargain with an artist.
LUDWIG VAN BEETHOVEN: *Letter to Peters & Company,* June 5, 1822

The artist has a twofold relation to nature; he is at once her master and her slave. He is her slave, inasmuch as he must work with earthly things, in order to be understood; but he is her master, inasmuch as he subjects these earthly means to his higher intentions, and renders them subservient.
J. W. GOETHE: *Conversations with Eckermann,* April 18, 1827

Artists are always young.
MARGARET FULLER OSSOLI: *Letter to W. H. Channing,* Aug., 1842

I prefer fiddles and tambourines to the bell of the president of the Chamber. I would sell my breeches for a ring, and my bread for marmalade.
THEOPHILE GAUTIER: *Caprices et zigzags,* 1845

One who has some artistical ability may know how to do a thing, and even show how to do it, and yet fail in doing it after all; but the artist and the man of some artistic ability must not be confounded. He only is the former who can carry his most shadowy precepts into successful application.
E. A. POE: *Marginalia,* 1844–49

Does he paint? he fain would write a poem;
Does he write? he fain would paint a picture.
ROBERT BROWNING: *One Word More,* 1855

Artists will always be sufficiently jealous of one another.
JOHN RUSKIN: *The Political Economy of Art,* 1857

The one thing that marks the true artist is a clear perception and a firm, bold hand, in distinction from that imperfect mental vision and uncertain touch which give us the feeble pictures and the lumpy statues of the mere artisans on canvas or in stone.
O. W. HOLMES: *The Professor at the Breakfast-Table,* IX, 1859

The torpid artist seeks inspiration at any cost — by virtue or by vice, by friend or by fiend, by prayer or by wine.
E. W. EMERSON: *The Conduct of Life,* II, 1860

If a man have a genius for painting, poetry, music, architecture, or philosophy, he makes a bad husband, and an ill provider.
E. W. EMERSON: *The Conduct of Life,* III

He is the greatest artist who has embodied, in the sum of his works, the greatest number of the greatest ideas.
JOHN RUSKIN: *Modern Painters,* I, 1860

The great artist is the simplifier.
H. F. AMIEL: Nov. 25, 1861

None of the best head work in art, literature, or science, is ever paid for. How much do you think Homer got for his Iliad? or Dante for his Paradise? Only bitter bread and salt, and going up and down other people's stairs.
JOHN RUSKIN: *The Crown of Wild Olive,* I, 1866

Artistic genius is an expansion of monkey imitativeness.
W. WINWOOD READE: *The Martyrdom of Man,* III, 1872

You cannot put an artist's day into the life of any one but an artist.
P. G. HAMERTON: *The Intellectual Life,* X, 1873

There is no such thing as a dumb poet or a handless painter. The essence of an artist is that he should be articulate.
A. C. SWINBURNE: *Essays and Studies,* 1875

If you are an artist at all, you will be not the mouthpiece of a century, but the master of eternity.
OSCAR WILDE: Lecture to art students, Royal Academy, London, June 30, 1883

In even a mediocre artist one sometimes finds a remarkable man.
F. W. NIETZSCHE: *Beyond Good and Evil,* 1886

The artist shows what he is going to do the moment he puts pen to paper, or brush to canvas; he improves on his first attempts, that is all.
GEORGE MOORE: *Confessions of a Young Man,* X, 1888

Good artists give everything to their art and consequently are perfectly uninteresting themselves.
OSCAR WILDE: *The Picture of Dorian Gray,* 1891

No artist desires to prove anything. IBID.

A true artist takes no notice whatever of the public. The public are to him nonexistent.
OSCAR WILDE: *The Critic as Artist,* 1891

No great artist ever sees things as they really are. If he did, he would cease to be an artist.
OSCAR WILDE: *The Decay of Lying,* 1891

But each for the joy of working, and each in his separate star
Shall draw the Thing as he sees it for the God of Things as They are.
RUDYARD KIPLING: *When Earth's Last Picture Is Painted,* 1892

The true artist will let his wife starve, his children go barefoot, his mother drudge for his living at seventy, sooner than work at anything but his art.
GEORGE BERNARD SHAW: *Man and Superman,* I, 1903

An artist is a dreamer consenting to dream of the actual world.
GEORGE SANTAYANA: *The Life of Reason,* III, 1905

True artists are almost the only men who do their work with pleasure.
AUGUSTE RODIN (1840–1917)

Artists are on the average less happy than men of science.
BERTRAND RUSSELL: *The Conquest of Happiness,* X, 1930

The artist doesn't see things as they are, but as he is. Author unidentified

An artist lives everywhere. GREEK PROVERB

[*See also* Art, Dress, Fame, Painter, Standard.

Aryan

A man who is not an Aryan is betrayed by behavior unworthy of an Aryan: harshness, cruelty, and neglect of duty.
THE CODE OF MANU, X, *c.* 100

To me an ethnologist who speaks of Aryan race, Aryan blood, Aryan eyes and hair, is as great a sinner as a linguist who speaks of a dolichocephalic dictionary or a brachycephalic grammar.
F. MAX MÜLLER: *Biographies of Words,* 1888

[*See also* Race.

Ascension

While they beheld, he was taken up, and a cloud received him out of their sight.
ACTS I, 9, *c.* 75

In the theological faculty of the University of Paris, the leading medieval university, it was seriously discussed whether Jesus at His ascension had His clothes on or not. If He had not, did He appear before His apostles naked? If He had, what became of the clothes?
MATTHEW ARNOLD: *Literature and Dogma,* IX, 1873

Ascetic

He shall separate himself from wine and strong drink, and shall drink no vinegar of wine, or vinegar of strong drink, neither shall he drink any liquor of grapes, nor eat moist grapes, or dried.
NUMBERS VI, 3, *c.* 700 B.C.

Holding his head, body and neck even and immovable, firmly seated, regarding only the tip of his nose and not looking in different directions, he should remain quiet with passionless soul, free from anxiety and intent on Krishna.
THE BHAGAVAD-GITA, *c.* 150 B.C.

Let an ascetic eat no honey, no flesh, no mushrooms, nor anything grown on plowed ground. THE CODE OF MANU, VI, *c.* 100

The ascetic, rejoicing in his heart because he has been liberated from desire, lives as peacefully and happily as if he were ruler of the universe. The earth is his bed, the vines are his pillow, the sky is his roof, the winds are his fan, and the moon is his lamp.
BHARTRIHARI: *The Vairagya Sataka, c.* 625

The true ascetic counts nothing his own save his harp. JOACHIM OF FLORA: *Expositio in Apocalipsim, c.* 1175

The ascetic makes a necessity of virtue.
F. W. NIETZSCHE: *Human All-too-Human,* I, 1878

Asceticism

The sacrifice most acceptable to God is complete renunciation of the body and its passions. This is the only real piety.
CLEMENT OF ALEXANDRIA: *Stromateis,* V, *c.* 193

What greater pleasure can there be than to scorn being pleased, to contemn the world?
TERTULLIAN: *De spectaculis, c.* 200

Man was created to praise, honor and serve God. We therefore no more prefer health to sickness, riches to poverty, honor to disdain, long life to short, but desire and choose only that which more surely conduces toward the end for which we were created.
IGNATIUS LOYOLA: *Exercitia spiritualia,* 1541

There is no virtue in penance and fasting, which waste the body; they are only fanatical and monkish.
IMMANUEL KANT: *Lecture at Königsberg,* 1775

The principle of asceticism never was, nor ever can be, consistently pursued by any living creature. Let but one tenth part of the inhabitants of the earth pursue it consistently, and in a day's time they will have turned it into a Hell.
JEREMY BENTHAM: *The Principles of Morals and Legislation,* II, 1780

It is not until lately that mankind have admitted that happiness is the sole end of the science of ethics, as of all other sciences; and that the fanatical idea of mortifying the flesh for the love of God has been discarded.
P. B. SHELLEY: *Queen Mab,* notes, 1813

A dominant religion is never ascetic.
T. B. MACAULAY: *John Dryden,* 1828 (Edinburgh Review, Jan.)

I believe all manner of asceticism to be the vilest blasphemy — blasphemy towards the whole of the human race.
RICHARD JEFFERIES: *The Story of My Heart,* 1883

What is meant by ascetic ideals? . . . In women, at best, an additional implement of seduction, a little *morbidezza* on a fine piece of flesh, the angelhood of a plump, pretty animal.
F. W. NIETZSCHE: *The Genealogy of Morals,* III, 1887

Asceticism may be a mere expression of organic hardihood, disgusted with too much ease.
WILLIAM JAMES: *The Varieties of Religious Experience,* XI, 1902

[*See also* Ascetic, Monk, Nun.

Ashes

[*See* Dirt.

Asia

Asia was civilized when Europe was a forest and a swamp. Asia taught Europe its ABC; Asia taught Europe to cipher and to draw; Asia taught Europe . . . how to philosophize with abstract ideas.
W. WINWOOD READE: *The Martyrdom of Man,* III, 1872

[*See also* Religion.

Asking

Ask, and it shall be given you.
MATTHEW VII, 7, *c.* 75

He that cannot ask cannot live.
THOMAS DRAXE: *Bibliotheca scholastica instructissima,* 1633

Ask much to have little.
GEORGE HERBERT: *Jacula Prudentum,* 1651

He that asketh faintly beggeth a denial.
THOMAS FULLER: *Gnomologia,* 1732

The Devil made askers.
JONATHAN SWIFT: *Polite Conversation,* 1738

The man who is afraid of asking is ashamed of learning.
DANISH PROVERB

Asking costs more than buying.
GERMAN PROVERB

The vice of asking is balanced by the virtue of saying no.
SWEDISH PROVERB

Aspiration

If you aspire to the highest place it is no disgrace to stop at the second, or even the third.
CICERO: *De oratore,* I, *c.* 80 B.C.

Thy destiny is only that of man, but thy aspirations may be those of a god.
OVID: *Metamorphoses,* II, *c.* 5

Let us not flutter too high, but remain by the manger and the swaddling clothes of Christ.
MARTIN LUTHER: *Table-Talk,* CXV, 1569

Who shoots at the midday sun, though he be sure he shall never hit the mark: yet as sure he is, he shall shoot higher than he who aims at a bush.
PHILIP SIDNEY: *Arcadia,* II, 1590

'Tis immortality to die aspiring.
GEORGE CHAPMAN: *The Conspiracy of Byron,* I, 1608

If I could only fill my coffers with money, and then learn Hebrew, the sciences, history!
JEAN DE LA FONTAINE: *Fables,* VIII, 1671

Tell me, ye pow'rs that rule our fate,
Why are frail men so vain,
With so much zeal to wish for that
They never can attain?
ROBERT GOULD: *The Hopeless Comfort,* 1689

Men would be angels, angels would be gods.
ALEXANDER POPE: *An Essay on Man,* I, 1732

The high-born soul
Disdains to rest her heaven-aspiring wing
Beneath its native quarry. Tired of earth
And this diurnal scene, she springs aloft
Through fields of air; pursues the flying storm;
Rides on the vollied lightning through the heavens;
Or, yoked with whirlwinds and the northern blast,
Sweeps the long tract of day.
MARK AKENSIDE: *The Pleasure of Imagination,* I, 1744

To love the beautiful, to desire the good, to do the best.
MOTTO OF MOSES MENDELSSOHN (1729–86)

Look to a gown of gold, and you will at least get a sleeve of it.
WALTER SCOTT: *Redgauntlet,* II, 1824 (Quoted as a proverb)

I held it truth, with him who sings
To one clear harp in divers tones,
That men may rise on stepping-stones
Of their dead selves to higher things.

ALFRED TENNYSON: *In Memoriam*, I, 1850

Ah, but a man's reach should exceed his grasp,
Or what's Heaven for?

ROBERT BROWNING: *Andrea del Sarto*, 1855

The aim, if reached or not, makes great the life:
Try to be Shakespeare, leave the rest to fate.

ROBERT BROWNING: *Bishop Blougram's Apology*, 1855

My business is to teach my aspirations to conform themselves to fact, not to try and make facts harmonize with my aspirations.

T. H. HUXLEY: *Letter to Charles Kingsley*, Sept. 23, 1860

What I aspired to be,
And was not, comforts me.

ROBERT BROWNING: *Rabbi Ben Ezra*, 1864

Hitch your wagon to a star.

R. W. EMERSON: *Society and Solitude*, 1870

We are all in the gutter, but some of us are looking at the stars.

OSCAR WILDE: *Lady Windermere's Fan*, I, 1892

[*See also* Ambition, Eminence, Power.

Ass

(The story of Balaam and his ass is in NUMBERS XII, 21–35, *c.* 700 B.C.)

[Samson] found a new jawbone of an ass, and put forth his hand, and took it, and slew a thousand men therewith.

JUDGES XV, 15, *c.* 500 B.C.

Imitate the ass in his love for his master.

ST. JOHN CHRYSOSTOM: *Homily XII*, *c.* 388

Who washeth an ass's head loseth both labor and soap.

JOHN FLORIO: *First Fruites*, 1578

Oh, that he were here to write me down an ass! But, masters, remember, that I am an ass; though it be not written down, yet forget not that I am an ass.

SHAKESPEARE: *Much Ado About Nothing*, IV, *c.* 1599

Hood an ass with rev'rend purple,
So you can hide his too ambitious ears,
And he shall pass for a cathedral doctor.

BEN JONSON: *Volpone*, I, 1607

Better ride an ass that carries me than a horse that throws me.

THOMAS DRAXE: *Bibliotheca scholastica instructissima*, 1633

Every ass thinks himself worthy to stand with the king's horses.

JOHN CLARKE: *Parœmiologia Anglo-Latina*, 1639

Asses die, and wolves bury them.

THOMAS FULLER: *Gnomologia*, 1732

Every ass loves to hear himself bray. IBID.

What good can it do an ass to be called a lion? IBID.

An ass should like an ass be treated.

JOHN GAY: *Fables*, II, *c.* 1732

An ass is but an ass, though laden with gold.

H. G. BOHN: *Handbook of Proverbs*, 1855

Even an ass will not fall twice in the same quicksand. IBID.

The ass that carrieth wine drinketh water. IBID.

Asses carry the oats and horses eat them.

DUTCH PROVERB

A living ass is better than a dead doctor.

ITALIAN PROVERB

The bridge of asses. (Pons asinorum.)

Latin term applied to the fifth proposition in the first book of Euclid

It's better to be killed by a robber than by the kick of an ass. PORTUGUESE PROVERB

If three people say you are an ass, put on a bridle. SPANISH PROVERB

[*See also* Braggart, Dancing, Devil, Donkey, Fool, Gold, Gravity, Invective, Obstinacy, Prince, Solemnity, Travel.

Assassin

Are assassins unworthy of sanctuary in churches? Yes, by the bull of Gregory XIV, they are. But by the word assassins we understand those that have received money to murder one; and accordingly, such as kill without taking any reward for the deed, but merely to oblige their friends, do not come under the category of assassins.

ANTONIO ESCOBAR: *Summula casuum conscientiae*, I, 1627

Rebellion must be managed with many swords; treason to his prince's person may be with one knife.

THOMAS FULLER: *The Holy State and the Profane State*, 1642

Is there a crime
Beneath the roof of Heaven that stains the soul
Of man with more infernal hue than damn'd
Assassination?

COLLEY CIBBER: *Caesar in Egypt*, I, *c.* 1710

I am too much of a fatalist to take any precautions against assassination.

NAPOLEON I: To Barry E. O'Meara at St. Helena, Sept. 20, 1817

Assassination has never changed the history of the world.

BENJAMIN DISRAELI: Speech in the House of Commons on the assassination of Lincoln, May 10, 1865

It is one of the incidents of my trade.
HUMBERT I of Italy: On being shot at near Rome, 1897 (He was killed by Bresci, July 29, 1900)

The bullet that pierced Goebel's breast
Cannot be found in all the West;
Good reason: it is speeding here
To stretch McKinley on his bier.
AMBROSE BIERCE: In the New York Journal, Feb. 4, 1901 (William Goebel was shot at Frankfort, Ky., Jan. 30, 1900, and died on Feb. 3; William McKinley was shot at Buffalo, Sept. 6, 1901, and died on Sept. 14. Bierce and the owner of the Journal, W. R. Hearst, were accused of instigating McKinley's assassination by printing this quatrain, but nothing ever came of the charge)

I do not believe there is any danger of . . . any assault upon my life . . . and if there were it would be simple nonsense to try to prevent it, for, as Lincoln said, though it would be safer for a President to live in a cage, it would interfere with his business.
THEODORE ROOSEVELT: *Letter to H. C. Lodge,* Aug. 6, 1906

[*See also* Caesar (Julius), Communism.

Assembly

The resolutions of a monarch are subject to no other inconstancy than that of human nature, but in assemblies, beside that of nature, there ariseth an inconstancy from the number. The absence of a few . . . undoes today all that was concluded yesterday.
THOMAS HOBBES: *Leviathan,* I, 1651

The more numerous an assembly may be, of whatever characters composed, the greater is known to be the ascendancy of passion over reason.
ALEXANDER HAMILTON: *The Federalist,* 1788

[*See also* Board, Committee, Council, Legislature, Mob, Parliament.

Assent

Such is our good pleasure. (Tel est notre bon plaisir.)
Form of assent of Francis I of France (1494–1547)

Assistance

[*See* Help.

Association

I am always longing to be with men more excellent than myself.
CHARLES LAMB: *Letter to* S. T. *Coleridge,* Jan. 10, 1797

There are many objects of great value to man which cannot be attained by unconnected individuals, but must be attained, if attained at all, by association.
DANIEL WEBSTER: Speech at Pittsburgh, July, 1833

A wise man who associates with the vicious becomes an idiot; a dog long in the company of good men becomes a rational creature.
ARAB PROVERB

When a dove begins to associate with crows its feathers remain white but its heart grows black.
GERMAN PROVERB

[*See also* Combination, Company.

Assurance

I'll make assurance double sure.
SHAKESPEARE: *Macbeth,* IV, *c.* 1605

Assyrian

The Assyrian came down like the wolf on the fold,
And his cohorts were gleaming in purple and gold;
And the sheen of their spears was like stars on the sea,
When the blue wave rolls nightly on deep Galilee.
BYRON: *The Destruction of Sennacherib,* 1815

Astonishment

Be astonished, O ye heavens, at this, and be horribly afraid.
JEREMIAH II, 12, *c.* 625 B.C.

Astrology

Canst thou bind the sweet influences of Pleiades, or loose the bands of Orion?
JOB XXXVIII, 31, *c.* 325 B.C.

God did not create the planets and stars with the intention that they should dominate man, but that they, like other creatures, should obey and serve him.
THEOPHRASTUS BOMBAST VON HOHENHEIM (PARACELSUS): *Concerning the Nature of Things,* IX, *c.* 1541

Astrology is framed by the Devil to the end that the people may be scared from entering into the state of matrimony, and from every divine and human office and calling.
MARTIN LUTHER: *Table-Talk,* DCCCXLIII, 1569

Nature has given us astrology as an adjunct and ally to astronomy.
JOHANN KEPLER: *De fundamentis astrologiae certioribus,* 1602

This is the excellent foppery of the world, that, when we are sick in fortune (often the surfeit of our own behavior) we make guilty of our disasters the sun, the moon, and the stars; as if we were villains by necessity; fools by heavenly compulsion; knaves, thieves, and teachers by spherical predominance; drunkards, liars, and adulterers by an enforced obedience of planetary influence.
SHAKESPEARE: *King Lear,* I, 1606

The stars above us govern our conditions.
SHAKESPEARE: *King Lear*, IV, 1606

The stars do sometimes foreshow such things as happen, but they are not the enforcing causes of such things as happen.
ROBERT GRAY: *An Alarum to England*, 1609

[*See also* Magician, Star, Superstition.

Astronomer

Astronomers, painters and poets may lie by authority.
JOHN HARINGTON: *An Apologie of Poetrie*, 1591

These earthly godfathers of Heaven's lights
That give a name to every fixed star
Have no more profit of their shining nights
Than those that walk and wot not what they are.
SHAKESPEARE: *Love's Labor Lost*, I, *c.* 1595

When I, sitting, heard the astronomer, where he lectured with such applause in the lecture-room,
How soon, unaccountable, I became tired and sick;
Till rising and gliding out, I wander'd off by myself,
In the mystical moist night-air, and from time to time,
Look'd up in perfect silence at the stars.
WALT WHITMAN: *When I Heard the Learn'd Astronomer*, 1865

[*See also* Poet.

Astronomy

Astronomy was the daughter of idleness.
BERNARD DE FONTENELLE: *Entretiens sur la pluralite des mondes*, I, 1686

[*See also* Cosmology.

Asylum

[*See* Immigrant.

At

Where are we at?
Ascribed to various members of the Senate and House of Representatives, *c.* 1885

Athanasius, St. (c. 293–373)

Athanasius against the world. (Athanasius contra mundum.)
MEDIEVAL LATIN PHRASE (A reference to Athanasius's long war on Arianism, which had formidable support but was finally overthrown)

Atheism

The fool hath said in his heart, There is no God.
PSALMS XIV, 1, *c.* 150 B.C. (Cf. LIII, 1)

That the New Testament and Gospel of Christ is but foolishness, a mere fable; that Christ is not God or the Saviour of the world, but a mere man, a shameful man, and an abominable idol; that He did not rise again from death or ascend unto Heaven; that the Holy Ghost is not God; and that baptism is not necessary, nor the sacrament of the body and blood of Christ.
MATTHEW HAMOUNT: Propositions maintained at Norwich, England, 1579 (He was burned at the stake May 20)

God sleeps! God sleeps! God is an idle tale! There cannot be a god!
Ascribed to ANTONIO PEREZ (1539–1611)

It is atheism and blasphemy to dispute what God can do: good Christians content themselves with His will revealed in His Word.
JAMES I: Speech in the Star Chamber, June 20, 1616

A little philosophy inclineth man's mind to atheism; but depth in philosophy bringeth man's mind about to religion.
FRANCIS BACON: *Essays*, XVI, 1625

The Devil divides the world between atheism and superstition.
GEORGE HERBERT: *Jacula Prudentum*, 1651

Atheism indicates force of mind, but to a certain degree only.
BLAISE PASCAL: *Pensées*, XXIV, 1670

That I may be preserved from atheism and infidelity, impiety, and profaneness, and, in my addresses to Thee, carefully avoid irreverence and ostentation, formality and odious hypocrisy, — help me, O Father!
BENJAMIN FRANKLIN: *Articles of Belief and Acts of Religion*, Nov. 20, 1728

Belief in the existence of God is as groundless as it is useless. The world will never be happy until atheism is universal.
J. O. LA METTRIE: *L'Homme machine*, 1748

I believe that there is no God, but that matter is God and God is matter; and that it is no matter whether there is any God or no.
Anon.: *The Unbeliever's Creed*, 1754

Atheism is the vice of a few intelligent people.
VOLTAIRE: *Philosophical Dictionary*, 1764

Atheism is aristocratic.
M. M. I. ROBESPIERRE: Speech at the Jacobin Club, Paris, Nov. 1, 1793

There is a need of multiplying books a hundredfold in this philosophical age to *prevent* converts to atheism, for they seem too tough disputants to meddle with afterwards.
CHARLES LAMB: *Letter to S. T. Coleridge*, May 27, 1796

Forth from his dark and lonely hiding-place,
(Portentous sight!) the owlet atheism,
Sailing on obscene wings athwart the noon,
Drops his blue-fringed lids, and holds them close,
And hooting at the glorious sun in Heaven,
Cries out, "Where is it?"

S. T. COLERIDGE: *Fears in Solitude,* 1798

The three great apostles of practical atheism, that make converts without persecuting, and retain them without preaching, are wealth, health, and power.

C. C. COLTON: *Lacon,* 1820

Practical atheism, seeing no guidance for human affairs but its own limited foresight, endeavors itself to play the god, and decide what will be good for mankind and what bad.

HERBERT SPENCER: *Social Statics,* IV, 1851

I do not believe there is such a thing as a God.

G. J. HOLYOAKE: Lecture in London, 1868
(For this utterance Holyoake was sentenced to six months in prison)

Once dethrone humanity, regard it as a mere local incident in an endless and aimless series of cosmical changes, and you arrive at a doctrine which, under whatever specious name it may be veiled, is at bottom neither more or less than atheism.

JOHN FISKE: *The Destiny of Man,* I, 1884

Atheism thrives where religion is most debated.

WELSH PROVERB

[*See also* Agnostic, Atheist, Christianity, Fanaticism, Fool, Infidel, Philosophy, Skepticism, Toleration, Unitarianism.

Atheist

No one has ever died an atheist.

PLATO: *Laws,* X, *c.* 360 B.C.

The kingdom that is infested by atheists is beset by famine and disease and soon perishes.

THE CODE OF MANU, VIII, *c.* 100

These things shall by good and honest witness be approved to be his opinions and common speeches and that this Marlowe doth not only hold them himself but almost into every company he cometh he persuades men to atheism, willing them not to be afeard of bugbearers and hobgoblins . . . I think all men in Christianity ought to endeavor that the mouth of so dangerous a member may be stopped.

Charges filed with the Privy Council against Christopher Marlowe, 1593

I should like to hear a sober, moderate, chaste and just man say that there is no God. He would at least speak disinterestedly. But such a man is not to be found.

JEAN DE LA BRUYÈRE: *Caractères,* XVI, 1688

All revolutions run into extremes: the bigot makes the boldest atheist.

JOHN VANBRUGH: *The Provok'd Wife,* V, 1697

A solemn judicial death is too great an honor for an atheist.

EUSTACE BLUDGELL: *The Spectator,* May 27, 1712

An atheist is got one point beyond the Devil.

THOMAS FULLER: *Gnomologia,* 1732

Some are atheists only in fair weather. IBID.

By night an atheist half believes a God.

EDWARD YOUNG: *Night Thoughts,* V, 1742

Some are atheists by neglect; others are so by affectation; they that think there is no God at some times do not think so at all times.

BENJAMIN WHICHCOTE: *Moral and Religious Aphorisms,* 1753

The atheists are for the most part impudent and misguided scholars who reason badly, and who, not being able to understand the Creation, the origin of evil, and other difficulties, have recourse to the hypothesis of the eternity of things and of inevitability.

VOLTAIRE: *Philosophical Dictionary,* 1764

An atheist is a man who destroys the chimeras which afflict the human race, and so leads men back to nature, to experience and to reason.

P. H. D. D'HOLBACH: *Le système de la nature,* XXVI, 1770

An atheist laugh's a poor exchange
For Deity offended!

ROBERT BURNS: *Epistle to a Young Friend,* 1786

I was an infant when my mother went
To see an atheist burned. She took me there:
The dark-robed priests were met around the pile;
The multitude was gazing silently.

P. B. SHELLEY: *Queen Mab,* VII, 1813

Not one man in ten thousand has goodness of heart or strength of mind to be an atheist.

S. T. COLERIDGE: To Thomas Allsop, *c.* 1820

An atheist . . . I can never be.

THOMAS JEFFERSON: *Letter to John Adams,* 1823

He only is a true atheist to whom the predicates of the Divine Being — for example, love, wisdom and justice — are nothing.

L. A. FEUERBACH: *Das Wesen des Christentums,* 1841

The atheist does not say, "There is no God," but he says, "I know not what you mean by God; the word God is to me a sound conveying no clear or distinct affirmation."

CHARLES BRADLAUGH: *A Plea for Atheism,* 1864

Nearly all atheists on record have been men of extremely debauched and vile conduct.
J. P. SMITH: *Instructions on Christian Theology*, c. 1865

The man who has the hardihood to avow that he does not believe in God shows a restlessness of moral character and utter want of moral responsibility such as very little entitles him either to be heard or believed in a court of justice sitting in a country designated as Christian.
Decision of the Supreme Court of Tennessee in Odell *vs.* Koppel, 1871

All atheists are rascals, and all rascals are atheists.
AUGUST STRINDBERG: *Zones of the Spirit*, 1913

I'm an atheist, thank God.
WILBUR G. GAFFNEY, 1927

I don't believe in God because I don't believe in Mother Goose.
CLARENCE DARROW: Speech at Toronto, 1930

[*See also* Agnostic, Antichrist, Atheism, Carlyle (Thomas), Chinese, Education, Heathen, Infidel, Jefferson (Thomas), Methodist, Miracle, Physician, Skeptic, War (Civil).

Athenian

The Athenians, and strangers which were there, spent their time in nothing else, but either to tell or to hear some new thing.
ACTS XVII, 21, *c.* 75

[*See also* News, Public Affairs.

Athens

Athens, the eye of Greece, mother of arts
And eloquence.
JOHN MILTON: *Paradise Regained*, IV, 1671

Ancient of days! august Athena! where,
Where are thy men of might? thy grand in soul?
Gone — glimmering through the dream of things that were.
BYRON: *Childe Harold*, II, 1812

Wherever literature consoles sorrow or assuages pain; wherever it brings gladness to eyes which fail with wakefulness and tears, and ache for the dark house and the long sleep, — there is exhibited in its noblest form the immortal influence of Athens.
T. B. MACAULAY: *Milford's History of Greece*, 1824

Athens, that home of all learning.
POPE LEO XIII: *Aeterni patris*, Aug. 4, 1879

To carry owls to Athens.
GREEK PHRASE, signifying futility, familiar in English since the XVI century

Athlete

Th' athletic fool, to whom what Heaven denied
Of soul, is well compensated in limbs.
JOHN ARMSTRONG: *The Art of Preserving Health*, III, 1744

Atonement

The blood of Jesus Christ His Son cleanseth us from all sin.
I JOHN I, 7, *c.* 115

By Thine agony and bloody sweat; by Thy cross and passion; by Thy precious death and burial; by Thy glorious resurrection and ascension; and by the coming of the Holy Ghost, good Lord, deliver us.
THE BOOK OF COMMON PRAYER (*The Litany*), 1662

He left His Father's throne above,
(So free, so infinite His grace!)
Emptied Himself of all but love,
And bled for Adam's helpless race.
CHARLES WESLEY: *Free Grace*, 1739

What can be more immoral than that awful theology according to which God is cruel and revengeful, punishes all men for the sin of Adam, and to save them sends His Son to the earth knowing beforehand that men will kill Him and will be cursed for doing so?
LYOF N. TOLSTOY: *What Is Religion?*, 1902

[*See also* Baptism.

Atonement, Day of

On the tenth day of this seventh month there shall be a day of atonement: it shall be an holy convocation unto you; and ye shall afflict your souls, and offer an offering made by fire unto the Lord.
LEVITICUS XXIII, 27, *c.* 700 B.C.

[*See also* Abstinence.

Attachment

We never attach ourselves lastingly to anything that has not cost us care, labor and longing.
BALZAC: *The Physiology of Marriage*, 1830

Attack

I am your king. You are a Frenchman. There is the enemy. Charge!
HENRY IV of France: At the battle of Ivry, March 14, 1590

Attack is the reaction; I never think I have hit hard unless it rebounds.
SAMUEL JOHNSON: *Boswell's Life*, April 2, 1775

Don't fire until you can see the whites of their eyes.
WILLIAM PRESCOTT: Order to the American troops at the Battle of Bunker Hill, June 17, 1775

The enemy is there, General Longstreet, and I am going to strike him.
R. E. LEE: To James Longstreet, at Gettysburg, July 3, 1863

My center gives way; my right recedes; the situation is excellent; I shall attack.
FERDINAND FOCH: Telegram to French G.H.Q. during the first battle of the Marne, Sept. 9, 1914

[*See also* Timidity, War.

Attention

[*See* Genius.

Attila

[*See* Greatness.

Attorney

[*See* Lawsuit, Lawyer.

Auction

My wish is that my drawings, my prints, my curiosities, my books — in a word, those things of art which have been the joy of my life — shall not be consigned to the cold tomb of a museum, and subjected to the stupid glance of the careless passer-by; but I require that they shall all be dispersed under the hammer of the auctioneer, so that the pleasure which the acquiring of each one of them has given me shall be given again, in each case, to some inheritor of my own tastes.

WILL OF EDMOND DE GONCOURT, 1896

Auctioneer

The man who is stationed at the door does not pick people's pockets; that is done within, by the auctioneer.

SAMUEL JOHNSON: *Boswell's Life,* May 8, 1775

The man who proclaims with a hammer that he has picked a pocket with his tongue.

AMBROSE BIERCE: *The Devil's Dictionary,* 1906

[*See also* Taste.

Audacity

Oh, the impudent audacity of man! (O hominis impudentem audaciam!)

TERENCE: *Heautontimorumenos,* *c.* 160 B.C.

Fortune favors the audacious.

DESIDERIUS ERASMUS: *Adagia,* 1508

Audacity, again audacity, and always audacity! (De l'audace, encore de l'audace, et toujours de l'audace!)

G. J. DANTON: Speech in the French Legislative Assembly, Sept. 2, 1792

Success is the child of audacity.

BENJAMIN DISRAELI: *The Rise of Iskander,* 1834

[*See also* Bold.

Audience

Where none admire, 'tis useless to excel;
Where none are beaux, 'tis vain to be a belle.

GEORGE, BARON LYTTELTON: *Soliloquy on a Beauty in the Country, c.* 1760

August

If the twenty-fourth of August be fair and clear,
Then hope for a prosperous Autumn that year.

JOHN RAY: *English Proverbs,* 1670

Wear a sardonyx or for thee
No conjugal felicity.
The August-born without this stone
'Tis said must live unloved and lone.

Author unidentified

[*See also* Harvest, Months.

Augustine, St. (354–430)

Augustine was the ablest and purest of all the doctors.

MARTIN LUTHER: *Table-Talk,* DXXXV, 1569

Augustine's Saviour is not the Saviour of the world. He is only the Saviour of the Church, and even in the Church itself the Saviour only of a mere handful of the elect, whom he saves only under strictly ecclesiastical conditions.

F. W. FARRAR: *Lives of the Fathers,* II, 1889

There's no pot without bacon in it, and no sermon without St. Augustine.

SPANISH PROVERB

Aunt

As cold as an aunt's kiss.

Author unidentified

[*See also* If.

Austen, Jane (1775–1817)

Shakespeare has had neither equal nor second. But among the writers who have approached nearest to the manner of the great master, we have no hesitation in placing Jane Austen.

T. B. MACAULAY: *Madame D'Arblay,* 1843

Jane Austen was the first and the last of the English novelists to treat material with entire truthfulness.

W. D. HOWELLS: *Criticism and Fiction,* 1892

Austerity

Austerity is a disease. I would a thousand times rather be stricken with fever . . . than think gloomily.

VOLTAIRE: *Letter to Frederick the Great,* July, 1737

He never unbuttons himself.

Said of Robert Peel (1788–1850)

Australia

The land where the second-rate are on top.

Author unidentified (Quoted in P. R. STEPHENSON: *The Foundations of Culture in Australia,* II, 1936)

Australian

What do they do when they an't stealing?

CHARLES LAMB: *Letter to Barron Field,* Aug. 13, 1817

Austria

It is for Austria to rule the whole earth. (Austriæ est imperare orbi universo.)

MOTTO OF FREDERICK III, Holy Roman Emperor from 1440 to 1493 (The initials are commonly used, viz.: A. E. I. O. U. The German form is " Alles Erdreich ist Oesterreich untertan." The same initials are sometimes used to stand for " Austria erit in orbe ultima " — Austria will be the last thing in the world)

If Austria did not exist it would have to be invented. FRANTISEK PALACKY, *c.* 1845

I hold that the maintenance of the Austrian Empire is necessary to the independence, and, if necessary to the independence, necessary to the civilization and even to the liberties of Europe.
BENJAMIN DISRAELI: Speech in the House of Commons, July 25, 1856

Poor Austria! Two things made her a nation: she was German and she was Catholic, and now she is neither.
BENJAMIN DISRAELI: *Lothair,* IX, 1870

Austrian

So long as the Austrian has his beer and sausages he will not revolt.
LUDWIG VAN BEETHOVEN: *Letter to Nikolaus Simrock,* Aug. 2, 1794

No Italian can hate an Austrian more than I do; unless it be the English, the Austrians seem to me the most obnoxious race under the sky.
BYRON: *Letter to John Murray,* April 16, 1820

Author

An author is always pleased with his own work. (Auctor opus laudat.)
OVID: *Epistulae ex Ponto,* III, *c.* 5

There are men that will make you books, and turn 'em loose into the world, with as much dispatch as they would do a dish of fritters.
CERVANTES: *Don Quixote,* II, 1615

Like author, like book.
JOHN RAY: *English Proverbs,* 1670

Choose an author as you choose a friend.
WENTWORTH DILLON (EARL OF ROSCOMMON): *Essay on Translated Verse,* 1864

Making a book is quite as much a trade as making a clock. It takes much more than genius to be an author.
JEAN DE LA BRUYÈRE: *Caractères,* I, 1688

The circumstance which gives authors an advantage above [painters] is this, that they can multiply their originals; or rather, can make copies of their works, to what number they please, which shall be as valuable as the originals themselves.
JOSEPH ADDISON: *The Spectator,* Sept. 10, 1711

Of all artificial relations formed between mankind, the most capricious and variable is that of author and reader.
ANTHONY A. COOPER (EARL OF SHAFTESBURY): *Characteristics of Men, Manners, Opinions, Times,* III, *c.* 1713

From the moment one sets up for an author one must be treated as ceremoniously, that is as unfaithfully, " as a king's favorite, or as a king." This proceeding, joined to that natural vanity which first makes a man an author, is certainly enough to render him a coxcomb for life.
ALEXANDER POPE: *Letter to William Trumbull,* March 12, 1713

Authors are judged by strange capricious rules,
The great ones are thought mad, the small ones fools.
ALEXANDER POPE: *Prologue for Three Hours After Marriage,* 1717 (The play has been ascribed to John Gay, John Arbuthnot, and Pope himself)

A fool who, not content with having bored those who have lived with him, insists on tormenting the generations to come.
C. L. DE MONTESQUIEU: *Persian Letters,* LXVI, 1721

No author ever spared a brother;
Wits are gamecocks to one another.
JOHN GAY: *Fables,* I, 1727

A successful author is equally in danger of the diminution of his fame, whether he continues or ceases to write.
SAMUEL JOHNSON: *The Rambler,* May 29, 1750

The chief glory of every people arises from its authors.
SAMUEL JOHNSON: *Dictionary,* pref., 1755

A man, when he is once an author, is an author for life.
DAVID HUME: *Letter to John Clephane,* Sept. 3, 1757

The best part of every author is in general to be found in his book, I assure you.
SAMUEL JOHNSON: *Boswell's Life,* July 21, 1763

The greatest misfortune of a man of letters is not perhaps being the object of his confrères' jealousy, the victim of the cabal, the despised of the men of power; but of being judged by fools.
VOLTAIRE: *Philosophical Dictionary,* 1764

While an author is yet living we estimate his powers by his worst performance, and when he is dead we rate them by his best.
SAMUEL JOHNSON: *The Plays of Shakespeare,* pref., 1765

None but an author knows an author's cares.
WILLIAM COWPER: *The Progress of Error,* 1782

I have been so foolish as to be an author (of which I most heartily repent). It is not only exposing oneself, but giving others an opportunity to expose one.
HORACE WALPOLE: *Letter to Earl Harcourt,* Sept. 1, 1787

One hates an author that's all author.
BYRON: *Beppo,* 1818

The conversation of authors is not so good as might be imagined: but, such as it is (and with rare exceptions) it is better than any other.
WILLIAM HAZLITT: *The Conversation of Authors,* 1821

An author is like a baker; it is for him to make the sweets, and others to buy and enjoy them.
LEIGH HUNT: *The Indicator,* XLI, 1821

If you once understand an author's character, the comprehension of his writings becomes easy.
H. W. LONGFELLOW: *Hyperion,* I, 1839

The most "popular," the most "successful" writers among us (for a brief period, at least) are, ninety-nine times out of a hundred, persons of mere address, perseverance, effrontery — in a word, busy-bodies, toadies, quacks.
E. A. POE: *Of Criticism,* 1846

All people have their enemies, especially authors.
GEORGE BORROW: *Lavengro,* LXVI, 1851

Authors may be divided into three classes — shooting stars, planets, and fixed stars.
ARTHUR SCHOPENHAUER: *Parerga und Paralipomena,* II, 1851

We male authors write for or against something, for or against an idea, for or against a party; but women always write for or against one particular man, or, to be more precise, on account of one particular man.
HEINRICH HEINE: *Confessions,* 1854

Of all animals, authors are the vainest. No eulogies of their works can be too gross or too often repeated.
Ascribed to AARON BURR in JAMES PARTON: *The Life and Times of Aaron Burr,* 1858 (*c.* 1835)

I never saw an author in my life, saving perhaps one, that did not purr as audibly as a full-grown domestic cat on having his fur smoothed the right way by a skilful hand.
O. W. HOLMES: *The Autocrat of the Breakfast-Table,* III, 1858

The author is of peculiar organization. He is a being born with a predisposition which with him is irresistible, the bent of which he cannot in any way avoid.
BENJAMIN DISRAELI: Speech in London, May 6, 1868

Our fundamental want today in the United States is of a class, and the clear idea of a class, of native authors, literatuses, far different, far higher in grade, than any yet known, sacerdotal, modern, fit to cope with our occasions, lands, permeating the whole mass of American mentality, taste, belief, breathing into it a new breath of life, giving it decision.
WALT WHITMAN: *Democratic Vistas,* 1870

The author who speaks about his own books is almost as bad as a mother who talks about her own children.
BENJAMIN DISRAELI: Speech at Glasgow, Nov. 19, 1870

A good author possesses not only his own intellect, but also that of his friends.
F. W. NIETZSCHE: *Human All-too-Human,* I, 1878

There is no form of lead-poisoning which more rapidly and thoroughly pervades the blood and bones and marrow than that which reaches the young author through mental contact with type-metal.
O. W. HOLMES: *Some of My Early Teachers,* 1882 (Farewell lecture at the Harvard Medical School, Nov. 28)

How these authors magnify that office. One dishonest plumber does more harm than 100 poetasters.
AUGUSTINE BIRRELL: Written in the margin of his copy of GEORGE BRANDES: *Main Currents in Nineteenth Century Literature,* 1918

A writing man is something of a black sheep, like the village fiddler. Occasionally a fiddler becomes a violinist, and is a credit to his family, but as a rule he would have done better had his tendency been toward industry and saving.
E. W. HOWE: *The Blessing of Business,* 1918

A refusal to imitate obscenity or to load a book with it is an author's professional chastity.
JUDGE M. T. MANTON: *Dissenting opinion in United States* vs. *One Book Entitled "Ulysses,"* 1934

No one is more to be feared than an enraged author. FRENCH PROVERB

[*See also* Authorship, Books, Classic, Fame, Letters, Literature, Pen, Poet, Style, Writer, Writing.

Authority

The man whose authority is recent is always stern.
AESCHYLUS: *Prometheus Bound, c.* 490 B.C.

I am a man under authority, having soldiers under me: and I say to this man, Go, and he goeth; and to another, Come, and he cometh.
MATTHEW VIII, 9, *c.* 75

Authority to teach. (Potestas magisterii.) Authority to govern. (Potestas regiminis.)
Rights exercised by Roman Catholic bishops, probably going back to the v century

Man, proud man,
Drest in a little brief authority,
Most ignorant of what he's most assur'd,
His glassy essence, like an angry ape,
Plays such fantastic tricks before high Heaven,
As make the angels weep.

SHAKESPEARE: *Measure for Measure,* II, 1604

Thou hast seen a farmer's dog bark at a beggar,
And the creature run from the cur:
There, thou might'st behold the great image of authority;
A dog's obeyed in office.

SHAKESPEARE: *King Lear,* IV, 1606

Though authority be a stubborn bear, yet he is oft led by the nose with gold.

SHAKESPEARE: *The Winter's Tale,* IV, *c.* 1611

Words are wise men's counters, they do but reckon by them; but they are the money of fools, that value them by the authority of an Aristotle, a Cicero, or a Thomas, or any other doctor whatsoever, if but a man.

THOMAS HOBBES: *Leviathan,* IV, 1651

Authority can make leather as current as gold.

JOSEPH GLANVILLE: *The Vanity of Dogmatizing,* XIX, 1661

Authority without wisdom is like a heavy ax without an edge, fitter to bruise than polish.

ANNE BRADSTREET: *Meditations Divine and Moral, c.* 1670

The general story of mankind will evince that lawful and settled authority is very seldom resisted when it is well employed.

SAMUEL JOHNSON: *The Rambler,* Sept. 8, 1750

A country is in a bad state which is governed only by laws, because a thousand things occur for which laws cannot provide where authority ought to interpose.

SAMUEL JOHNSON: *Boswell's Tour to the Hebrides,* Sept. 11, 1773

In the name of the great Jehovah and the Continental Congress.

ETHAN ALLEN: Reply to Captain Delaplace of the British Army, on being asked by whose authority he demanded the surrender of Ticonderoga, May 10, 1775

The Deity has not given any order or family of men authority over others, and if any men have given it they only could give it for themselves.

SAMUEL ADAMS: Speech on American Independence, July 4, 1776

All authority belongs to the people.

THOMAS JEFFERSON: *Letter to Spencer Roane,* 1821

In any given society the authority of man over man runs in inverse proportion to the intellectual development of that society.

P. J. PROUDHON: *Qu'est-ce que la propriété?,* 1840

Authority, not majority. (Autorität, nicht Majorität.)

J. F. STAHL: Speech in the German Parliament at Erfurt, April 11, 1850

Able men who have given their time to special subjects, are authorities upon it to be listened to with deference, and the ultimate authority at any given time is the collective general sense of the wisest men living in the department to which they belong.

J. A. FROUDE: *A Plea for the Free Discussion of Theological Difficulties,* 1863 (Frazer's Magazine)

Every great advance in natural knowledge has involved the absolute rejection of authority.

T. H. HUXLEY: *Lay Sermons,* 1870

It's not because I hate Casey that I bate him; it's to show me authority.

Ascribed to an Irish policeman, *c.* 1880

To despise legitimate authority, no matter in whom it is invested, is unlawful; it is a rebellion against God's will.

POPE LEO XIII: *Immortale Dei,* Nov. 1, 1885

The highest duty is to respect authority.

POPE LEO XIII: *Libertas praestantissimum,* June 20, 1888

The power of authority is never more subtle and effective than when it produces a psychological " atmosphere " or " climate " favorable to the life of certain modes of belief, unfavorable, and even, fatal, to the life of others.

A. J. BALFOUR: *The Foundations of Belief,* III, 1895

When the rulers of the people disdain the authority of God, the people in turn despise the authority of men.

POPE BENEDICT XV: *Ad beatissimi,* Nov. 1, 1914

The best test of a man is authority.

MONTENEGRAN PROVERB

[*See also* Classes, Democracy, Government, Inequality, Judge, Law, Liberty, People, Theology.

Authorship

I have protracted my work till most of those whom I wished to please have sunk into the grave, and success and miscarriage are empty sounds. I therefore dismiss it with frigid tranquility, having little to fear or hope from censure or from praise.

SAMUEL JOHNSON: *Dictionary,* pref., 1755

No man but a blockhead ever wrote except for money.

SAMUEL JOHNSON: *Boswell's Life,* 1776

There are three difficulties in authorship: to write anything worth the publishing — to find honest men to publish it — and to get sensible men to read it.

C. C. COLTON: *Lacon,* 1820

If a man have no heroism in his soul, no animating purpose beyond living easily and faring sumptuously, I can imagine no greater mistake on his part than that of resorting to authorship as a vocation.

HORACE GREELEY: *Letter to Robert Dale Owen,* March 5, 1860

[*See also* Author, Writer, Writing.

Autobiography

You may reasonably ask me, of what importance can the history of my private life be to the public? To this I can only make you a ludicrous answer, which is, that the public very well knows my life has not been a private one.

COLLEY CIBBER: *Apology for His Life,* I, 1740

It is a hard and a nice subject for a man to write of himself. It pains his own heart to say any thing of disparagement, and the reader's ears to hear any thing of praise from him.

ABRAHAM CROWLEY: *Of Myself,* 1665

Let the trumpet of the day of judgment sound when it will, I shall appear with this book in my hand before the Sovereign Judge, and cry with a loud voice, This is my work, there were my thoughts, and thus was I. I have freely told both the good and the bad, have hid nothing wicked, added nothing good.

J.-J. ROUSSEAU: *Confessions,* I, 1766

The next thing like living one's life over again seems to be a recollection of that life, and to make that recollection as durable as possible by putting it down in writing.

BENJAMIN FRANKLIN: *Autobiography,* 1798

We should read the lives of great men, if written by themselves, for two reasons: to find out what others really were, and what they themselves would appear to be.

C. C. COLTON: *Lacon,* 1820

You have sent no autobiographies. Nor do I want any. They are of the books which I give away.

CHARLES LAMB: *Letter to Cowden Clarke,* Feb. 2, 1829

Old men love to dwell upon their recollections; and that, I suppose, is one reason for the many volumes published under that name — recollections of gentlemen who tell us what they please, and amuse us, in their old age, with the follies of their youth.

GEORGE CRABBE: *Letter to Henchman Crowfoot,* Jan. 19, 1831

If any ambitious man have a fancy to revolutionize, at one effort, the universal world of human thought, human opinion, and human sentiment, the opportunity is his own — the road to immortal renown lies straight, open, and unencumbered before him. All that he has to do is to write and publish a very little book. Its title should be simple — a few plain words — " My Heart Laid Bare." But — this little book must be true to its title.

E. A. POE: *Marginalia,* 1844–49

To write a criticism of one's self would be an embarrassing, even an impossible task. I should be a coxcomb to obtrude the good I might be able to say of myself, and I should be a fool to proclaim to the world the defects of which I am conscious.

HEINRICH HEINE: *Confessions,* 1854

To set about writing my own life would be no less than horrible to me; and shall of a certainty never be done. The common impious vulgar of this earth, what has it to do with my life or me?

THOMAS CARLYLE: *Letter to R. W. Emerson,* Jan. 27, 1867

[*See also* Biography.

Autocracy

[*See* Democracy, Despot, Despotism, Government, Monarchy, Tyranny.

Automobile

Carriage without horses shall go,
And accidents fill the world with woe.

Anon.: *The Prophecies of Mother Shipton,* 1862 (The doggerel of which these lines form a part is commonly ascribed to a mysterious Mother Shipton of 1641, or, by some accounts, of 1448. Actually, it was concocted in 1862 by Charles Hindley, a London bookseller)

Autopsy

Osler went into the post-mortem room with the joyous demeanor of the youthful Sophocles leading the chorus of victory after the Battle of Salamis.

H. A. HARE (1862–): Quoted in GARRISON: *An Introduction to the History of Medicine,* XI, 1921

Autumn

The teeming Autumn.

SHAKESPEARE: *Sonnets,* XCVII, 1609

Thick as autumnal leaves that strow the brooks
In Vallombrosa.

JOHN MILTON: *Paradise Lost,* I, 1667

Autumn is marching on: even the scarecrows are wearing dead leaves.

OTSUYU NAKAGAWA: *Scarecrows, c.* 1730

There is a harmony
In Autumn, and a lustre in its sky,
Which thro' the Summer is not heard or seen.

P. B. SHELLEY: *Hymn to Intellectual Beauty,* 1816

I saw old Autumn in the misty morn
Stand shadowless like silence.

THOMAS HOOD: *Autumn,* 1823

The melancholy days are come, the saddest of the year,
Of wailing winds, and naked woods, and meadows brown and sear.

W. C. BRYANT: *The Death of the Flowers,* 1825

Earth's crammed with Heaven,
And every common bush afire with God.

E. B. BROWNING: *Aurora Leigh,* VII, 1857

[*See also* Beautiful, Seasons.

Avarice

Avarice and luxury have been the ruin of every great state.

LIVY: *History of Rome,* XXXIV, *c.* 10

Avarice has so seized upon mankind that their wealth seems rather to possess them than they to possess their wealth.

PLINY THE YOUNGER: *Letters,* IX, *c.* 110

He would have flayed a louse to save the skin of it. JOHN FLORIO: *Second Fruites,* 1591

Let me tell you, Cassius, you yourself
Are much condemn'd to have an itching palm.

SHAKESPEARE: *Julius Caesar,* IV, 1599

Avarice is more opposed to economy than liberality.

LA ROCHEFAUCAULD: *Maxims,* 1665

If avarice be thy vice, yet make it not thy punishment. Let the fruition of things bless the possession of them, and think it more satisfaction to live richly than die rich.

THOMAS BROWNE: *Christian Morals,* I, *c.* 1680

No vice like avarice.

THOMAS FULLER: *Gnomologia,* 1732

The sphincter of the heart.

MATTHEW GREEN: *The Spleen,* 1737

Avarice, or the desire of gain, is a universal passion, which operates at all times, at all places, and upon all persons.

DAVID HUME: *Essays,* XIII, 1741

The lust of gold, unfeeling and remorseless,
The last corruption of degenerate man.

SAMUEL JOHNSON: *Irene,* I, 1749

Avarice is generally the last passion of those lives of which the first part has been squandered in pleasure, and the second devoted to ambition.

SAMUEL JOHNSON: *The Rambler,* Aug. 27, 1751

Some men are called sagacious, merely on account of their avarice: whereas a child can clench its fist the moment it is born.

WILLIAM SHENSTONE: *Of Men and Manners,* 1764

So for a good old-gentlemanly vice
I think I must take up with avarice.

BYRON: *Don Juan,* I, 1819

Avarice begets more vices than Priam did children, and like Priam survives them all. It starves its keeper to surfeit those who wish him dead.

C. C. COLTON: *Lacon,* 1820

Long after all other sins are old, avarice remains young. FRENCH PROVERB

More wealth, more avarice.

ITALIAN PROVERB

Avarice is the mother of cruelty. (Crudelitatis mater avaritia est.) LATIN PROVERB

[*See also* Ages, American, Brewery, Covetousness, Envy, Gambling, King, Luxury, Miser, Pride.

Aversion

Some men there are love not a gaping pig;
Some that are mad if they behold a cat;
And others, when the bag-pipe sings i' the nose,
Cannot contain their urine.

SHAKESPEARE: *The Merchant of Venice,* I, *c.* 1597

Aversion we have for things, not only which we know have hurt us, but also that we do not know whether they will hurt us or not.

THOMAS HOBBES: *Leviathan,* VI, 1651

I do not love thee, Doctor Fell;
The reason why I cannot tell.
But this I'm sure I know full well,
I do not love thee, Doctor Fell.

THOMAS BROWN (1663–1704) (John Fell was dean of Christ Church, Oxford. The epigram, which is a paraphrase of one by Martial, was written when Fell threatened to send Brown down from Oxford, *c.* 1680. Fell died as Bishop of Oxford in 1686)

Man can start with aversion and end with love, but if he begins with love and comes round to aversion he will never get back to love.

BALZAC: *The Physiology of Marriage,* 1830

[*See also* Antipathy, Marriage.

Aviation

He rode upon a cherub, and did fly: yea, he did fly upon the wings of the wind.

PSALMS XVIII, 10, *c.* 150 B.C.

If the heavens be penetrable, and no lets, it were not amiss to make wings and fly up, and some new-fangled wits should some time or other find out.

ROBERT BURTON: *The Anatomy of Melancholy,* II, 1621

The volant or flying automata are such mechanical contrivances as have self-motion, whereby they are carried aloft in the air, like the flight of birds. Such was the wooden dove made by Archytas, a citizen of Tarentum, and one of Plato's acquaintances, and that wooden eagle framed by Regiomontanus

Noremberg, which by way of triumph did fly out of the city to meet Charles V.

JOHN WILKINS (BISHOP OF CHESTER): *Mechanical Magick,* 1680

Flying would give such occasions for intrigues as people cannot meet with who have nothing but legs to carry them. You should have a couple of lovers make a midnight assignation upon the top of the monument, and see the cupola of St. Paul's covered with both sexes like the outside of a pigeon-house. Nothing would be more frequent than to see a beau flying in at a garret window, or a gallant giving chase to his mistress, like a hawk after a lark. The poor husband could not dream what was doing over his head. If he were jealous, indeed, he might clip his wife's wings, but what would this avail when there were flocks of whore-masters perpetually hovering over his house?

JOSEPH ADDISON: *The Guardian,* July 20, 1713

What can you conceive more silly and extravagant than to suppose a man racking his brains, and studying night and day how to fly?

WILLIAM LAW: *A Serious Call to a Devout and Holy Life,* XI, 1728

The English, a haughty nation, arrogate to themselves the empire of the sea; the French, a buoyant nation, make themselves masters of the air.

(Les Anglais, nation trop fière,
S'arrogent l'empire des mers;
Les Français, nation légère,
S'emparent de celui des airs.)

THE COUNT OF PROVENCE (afterward Louis XVIII of France): Impromptu on the first successful balloon ascension by the brothers Montgolfier, 1783

At sea let the British their neighbors defy —
The French shall have frigates to traverse the sky.

PHILIP FRENEAU: *The Progress of Balloons,* 1784

How posterity will laugh at us, one way or other! If half a dozen break their necks, and balloonism is exploded, we shall be called fools for having imagined it could be brought to use: if it should be turned to account, we shall be ridiculed for having doubted.

HORACE WALPOLE: *Letter to Horace Mann,* June 24, 1785

Soon shall thy arm, unconquer'd steam! afar
Drag the slow barge, or drive the rapid car;
Or on wide-waving wings extended bear
The flying chariot through the field of air.

ERASMUS DARWIN: *The Botanic Garden,* I, 1791

Bishop Wilkins prophesied that the time would come when gentlemen, when they were to go a journey, would call for their wings as regularly as they call for their boots.

MARIA EDGEWORTH: *Essay on Irish Bulls,* II, 1802

Are there no foolish projects in Great Britain? Did not good Bishop Wilkins project a scheme to fly?

TIMOTHY DWIGHT: *Remarks on the Review of Inchiquin's Letters,* 1815

Providence has given to the French the empire of the land, to the English that of the sea, and to the Germans that of the air.

JEAN PAUL RICHTER: Quoted by Thomas Carlyle, in the Edinburgh Review, 1827

I dipt into the future far as human eye could see,
Saw the vision of the world, and all the wonder that would be;
Saw the heavens fill with commerce, argosies of magic sails,
Pilots of the purple twilight, dropping down with costly bales;
Heard the heavens fill with shouting, and there rain'd a ghastly dew
From the nations' airy navies grappling in the central blue.

ALFRED TENNYSON: *Locksley Hall,* 1842

In the air men shall be seen
In white, in black and in green.

Anon.: *The Prophecie of Mother Shipton,* 1862 (See the explanation under Automobile)

The birds can fly,
An' why can't I?

J. T. TROWBRIDGE: *Darius Green and His Flying Machine,* 1869

The example of the bird does not prove that man can fly. Imagine the proud possessor of the aeroplane darting through the air at a speed of several hundred feet per second. It is the speed alone that sustains him. How is he ever going to stop?

SIMON NEWCOMB: In the Independent, Oct. 22, 1903

Bombardment from the air is legitimate only when directed at a military objective, the destruction or injury of which would constitute a distinct military disadvantage to the belligerent.

The Hague Convention of Jurists, 1923

[*See also* Balloon.

Awkwardness

Men lose more conquests by their own awkwardness than by any virtue in the woman.

NINON DE ENCLOS (1616–1706)

Awkward, embarrassed, stiff, without the skill
Of moving gracefully or standing still,
One leg, as if suspicious of his brother,
Desirous seems to run away from t'other.

CHARLES CHURCHILL: *The Rosciad,* 1761

Awkwardness has no forgiveness in Heaven or earth.

R. W. EMERSON: *Society and Solitude,* 1870

Axiom

[*See* Belief.

B

Baboon

[*See* Lincoln (Abraham).

Baby

Behold, the babe wept.
EXODUS II, 6, *c.* 700 B.C.

Out of the mouths of babes and sucklings hast thou ordained strength.
PSALMS VIII, 2, *c.* 150 B.C.

Out of the mouths of babes and sucklings thou hast perfected praise.
MATTHEW XXI, 16, *c.* 75 (Cf. PSALMS VIII, 2, *ante, c.* 150 B.C.)

A man deposits seed in a womb and goes away, and then another cause takes it, and labors on it, and makes a baby. What a consummation from such a beginning!
MARCUS AURELIUS: *Meditations,* X, *c.* 170

Who would not tremble and rather choose to die than to be a baby again, if he were given such a choice?
ST. AUGUSTINE: *The City of God,* XVII, 427

At first the infant,
Mewling and puking in the nurse's arms.
SHAKESPEARE: *As You Like It,* II, *c.* 1600

Some, admiring what motives to mirth infants meet with in their silent and solitary smiles, have resolved . . . that then they converse with angels.
THOMAS FULLER: *A Pisgah-Sight of Palestine,* 1650

Happy those early days, when I
Shined in my angel-infancy.
HENRY VAUGHAN: *The Retreat,* 1650

The babe
In the dim newness of its being feels
The impulses of sublunary things.
P. B. SHELLEY: *Queen Mab,* VI, 1813

An infant . . . is all gut and squall.
CHARLES BROWN: *Letter to John Keats,* Dec. 21, 1820

Every baby born into the world is a finer one than the last.
CHARLES DICKENS: *Nicholas Nickleby,* XXXVI, 1839

An infant crying in the night:
An infant crying for the light:
And with no language but a cry.
ALFRED TENNYSON: *In Memoriam,* LIV, 1850

Where did you come from baby dear?
Out of the everywhere into the here.
GEORGE MACDONALD: *At the Back of the North Wind,* 1871

Coiled within the dark womb he sits, the image of an ape; a caricature and a prophecy of the man that is to be.
W. WINWOOD READE: *The Martyrdom of Man,* III, 1872

A soiled baby, with a neglected nose, cannot be conscientiously regarded as a thing of beauty.
S. L. CLEMENS (MARK TWAIN): *Answers to Correspondents,* 1875

Here we have a baby. It is composed of a bald head and a pair of lungs.
EUGENE FIELD: *The Tribune Primer,* 1882

Rock-a-bye baby on the tree top,
When the wind blows the cradle will rock,
When the bough breaks the cradle will fall,
And down will come baby, cradle and all.
Author unidentified

Beneath this stone three infants lie;
Say, are they lost or saved?
If death's by sin, they sinned, for they are here;
If Heaven's by words, in Heaven they can't appear.
Reverse the sacred page, — the knot's untied:
They die, for Adam sinned; they live, for Jesus died.
Epitaph in the churchyard of Dunse, near Berwick, England

[*See also* Child, Damnation (Infant), Epitaph, Midwife.

Babylon

Babylon is fallen, is fallen; and all the graven images of her gods he hath broken unto the ground. ISAIAH XXI, 9, *c.* 700 B.C.

How is Babylon become a desolation among the nations! JEREMIAH I, 23, *c.* 625 B.C.

Babylon the great, the mother of harlots and abominations of the earth.
REVELATION XVII, 5, *c.* 95

The way to Babylon will never bring you to Jerusalem.
THOMAS FULLER: *Gnomologia,* 1732

Bach, Johann Sebastian (1685–1750)

My heart beats wholly for the majestic art of this father of harmony.
LUDWIG VAN BEETHOVEN: *Letter to Franz Hofmeister,* Jan. 15, 1801

Bach is the musical type of Protestantism.
FELIX MENDELSSOHN-BARTHOLDY (1809–47)

In Bach there is too much crude Christianity, crude Germanism, crude scholasticism. He stands at the threshold of modern European music, but he is always looking back toward the Middle Ages.
F. W. NIETZSCHE: *Human All-too-Human,* II, 1878

With my prying nose I dipped into all composers, and found that the houses they erected were stable in the exact proportion that Bach was used in the foundation.
JAMES HUNEKER: *Old Fogy*, x, 1913

Bachelor

Happy am I who have no wife.
MENANDER: *Adelphoi*, *c.* 300 B.C.

Cock's bones! now again I stand
The jolliest bachelor i' th' land.
Ascribed to HENRY VIII of England: On the beheading of Anne Boleyn, 1536

The world must be peopled. When I said I would die a bachelor I did not think I should live till I were married.
SHAKESPEARE: *Much Ado About Nothing*, II, *c.* 1599

The best works, and of greatest merit for the public have proceeded from the unmarried or childless men.
FRANCIS BACON: *Essays*, VIII, 1625

We bachelors laugh and show our teeth, but you married men laugh until your hearts ache.
GEORGE HERBERT: *Jacula Prudentum*, 1651

Let sinful bachelors their woes deplore;
Full well they merit all they feel, and more;
Unaw'd by precepts, human or divine,
Like birds and beasts, promiscuously they join.
ALEXANDER POPE: *January and May*, 1709

Bachelor's fare: bread and cheese and kisses.
JONATHAN SWIFT: *Polite Conversation*, I, 1738

A single man has not nearly the value he would have in [a] state of union. He is an incomplete animal. He resembles the odd half of a pair of scissors.
BENJAMIN FRANKLIN: *Letter to a young man*, June 25, 1745

My gen'rous heart disdains
The slave of love to be,
I scorn his servile chains
And boast my liberty.
FRANCIS HOPKINSON: *Song*, 1788

A lewd bachelor makes a jealous husband.
H. G. BOHN: *Handbook of Proverbs*, 1855

An old bachelor is a poor critter.
C. F. BROWNE (ARTEMUS WARD): *Artemus Ward: His Book*, 1862

By persistently remaining single a man converts himself into a permanent public temptation.
OSCAR WILDE: *The Importance of Being Earnest*, II, 1895

There's a funny smell in a bachelor's house.
AMERICAN NEGRO SAYING

A bachelor is a souvenir of some woman who found a better one at the last minute.
Author unidentified

A bachelor is one who enjoys the chase but does not eat the game.
IBID.

Praise all wives, but remain a bachelor.
ITALIAN PROVERB

A bachelor is like a man in Winter without a fur cap.
RUSSIAN PROVERB

So long as a man is without a wife he is only half a man.
SANSKRIT PROVERB

[*See also* Celibacy, Happiness, Husband, Jealousy, Marriage.

Back-Seat

He that rides behind another must not think to guide.
THOMAS FULLER: *Gnomologia*, 1732

Backside

The place where honor's lodg'd,
As wise philosophers have judg'd;
Because a kick in that part more
Hurts honor than deep wounds before.
SAMUEL BUTLER: *Hudibras*, II, 1664

We all have something to fall back on, and I never knew a phony who didn't land on it eventually.
WILSON MIZNER (1876–1933)

Backsliding

When Pharaoh saw that the rain and the hail and the thunders were ceased, he sinned yet more.
EXODUS IX, 34, *c.* 700 B.C.

Our backslidings are many; we have sinned against thee.
JEREMIAH XIV, 7, *c.* 625 B.C.

Bacon, Francis (1561–1626)

My conceit of his person was never increased toward him by his place or honors, but I have and do reverence him for the greatness that was only proper to himself, in that he seemed to me ever, by his work, one of the greatest men, and most worthy of admiration, that had been in many ages.
BEN JONSON: *Discoveries*, *c.* 1635

He had the sound, distinct, comprehensive knowledge of Aristotle, with all the beautiful lights, graces and embellishments of Cicero.
JOSEPH ADDISON: *The Tatler*, Dec. 23, 1710

The wisest, brightest, meanest of mankind.
ALEXANDER POPE: *An Essay on Man*, IV, 1734

The art which Bacon taught was the art of inventing arts. The knowledge in which Bacon excelled all men was a knowledge of the mutual relations of all departments of knowledge.
T. B. MACAULAY: *Lord Bacon*, 1837

Bacon always seems to write with his ermine on.
ALEXANDER SMITH: *Dreamthorp*, II, 1863

[*See also* Burke (Edmund), Dryden (John), Greatness.

Bad

No man becomes bad all at once.
JUVENAL: *Satires*, II, *c.* 110

A bold bad man.
EDMUND SPENSER: *The Faerie Queene*, I, *c.* 1589

Nothing so bad but it might be worse.
ENGLISH PROVERB, not recorded before the XIX century

Preëminently bad among the worst.
ROBERT SOUTHEY: *The Poet's Pilgrimage to Waterloo*, IV, 1822

A man once bad is assumed to be always bad. (Semel malus, semper presumitur esse malus.) LEGAL MAXIM

No one is presumed to be bad. (Nemo praesumitur malus.) IBID.

[*See also* Best, Cat, Good and Bad, Hell, Worse.

Baggage

Bag and baggage.
SHAKESPEARE: *As You Like It*, III, *c.* 1600

Bagpipe

What trifles make for happiness! The sound of a bagpipe!
F. W. NIETZSCHE: *The Twilight of the Idols*, 1889

A bagpipe never makes a sound until its belly is full. IRISH PROVERB

[*See also* Aversion.

Bail

[*See* Jail, Punishment.

Bait

You must lose a fly to catch a trout.
GEORGE HERBERT: *Jacula Prudentum*, 1651

Fish, or cut bait. AMERICAN PROVERB

[*See also* Frog.

Baker

He hanged the chief baker.
GENESIS XL, 22, *c.* 700 B.C.

Balance

[*See* Weights and Measures.

Balance of Power

[*See* Power (Balance of)

Bald

He is bald, yet he is clean.
LEVITICUS XIII, 40, *c.* 700 B.C.

As he was going up by the way, there came forth little children out of the city, and mocked him, and said unto him, Go up, thou bald head; go up, thou bald head.
II KINGS II, 23, *c.* 500 B.C.

There is nothing more contemptible than a bald man who pretends to have hair.
MARTIAL: *Epigrams*, X, *c.* 95

He was ballid as a coot.
JOHN LYDGATE: *Troy-Book*, II, *c.* 1415
(*Coot*=a bird with a white plate on the forehead, giving it the appearance of being bald)

Time himself is bald.
SHAKESPEARE: *The Comedy of Errors*, II, 1593

A bald head is soon shaven.
ENGLISH PROVERB, traced by Smith to the XVII century

For ointment juice of onions is a sign
To heads whose hair falls faster than it grows.
JOHN HARINGTON: *The Englishman's Doctor*, 1608

How ugly is a bald pate! It looks like a face wanting a nose.
THOMAS DEKKER: *The Gull's Hornbook*, III, 1609

Of ten bald men nine are deceitful and the tenth is stupid. CHINESE PROVERB

A good man grows gray, but a rascal grows bald. CZECH PROVERB

Honest men grow gray; others grow bald.
HUNGARIAN PROVERB

[*See also* Incredulity.

Ballad

I love a ballad but even too well; if it be doleful matter, merrily set down, or a very pleasant thing indeed, and sung lamentably.
SHAKESPEARE: *The Winter's Tale*, IV, *c.* 1611

Does any tune become
A gentleman so well as a ballad?
JAMES SHIRLEY: *Hyde Park*, IV, 1632

More solid things do not show the complexion of the time so well as ballads.
JOHN SELDEN: *Table-Talk*, 1689

I knew a very wise man that believed if a man were permitted to make all the ballads, he need not care who should make the laws of a nation.
ANDREW FLETCHER: *An Account of a Conversation Concerning a Right to Regulation of Governments*, 1703

Ballads . . . are the gypsy children of song, born under green hedgerows in the leafy lanes and by-paths of literature, — in the genial Summertime.
H. W. LONGFELLOW: *Hyperion,* II, 1839

The Scotch have their born ballads, subtly expressing their past and present, and expressing character. The Irish have theirs. England, Italy, France, Spain, theirs. What has America?
WALT WHITMAN: *Democratic Vistas,* 1870

The farmer's daughter hath soft brown hair
(*Butter and eggs and a pound of cheese*)
And I met with a ballad, I can't say where,
That wholly consisted of lines like these.
C. S. CALVERLEY: *Ballad,* 1872

[*See also* Poet.

Balloon

Five thousand balloons, capable of raising two men each, could not cost more than five ships of the line; and where is the prince who can afford so to cover his country with troops for its defense as that 10,000 men descending from the clouds might not in many places do an infinite deal of mischief before a force could be brought together to repel them?
BENJAMIN FRANKLIN: *Letter to Jan Ingenhousz,* Jan. 16, 1784

[*See also* Aviation.

Ballot

A weapon that comes down as still
As snowflakes fall upon the sod,
But executes a freeman's will
As lightning does the will of God,
And from its force nor doors nor locks
Can shield you — 'tis the ballot-box.
JOHN PIERPONT: *A Word from a Petitioner,* c. 1830

Ballots are the rightful and peaceful successors of bullets.
ABRAHAM LINCOLN: Message to Congress, July 4, 1861

Among free men there can be no successful appeal from the ballot to the bullet.
ABRAHAM LINCOLN: *Letter to James C. Conkling,* Aug. 26, 1863

What is the ballot? It is neither more nor less than a paper representative of the bayonet, the billy, and the bullet. It is a labor-saving device for ascertaining on which side force lies and bowing to the inevitable. The voice of the majority saves bloodshed, but it is no less the arbitrament of force than is the decree of the most absolute of despots backed by the most powerful of armies.
BENJAMIN R. TUCKER: *Instead of a Book,* 1893

[*See also* Election, Franchise, Majority, Suffrage, Vote.

Balm

Is there no balm in Gilead?
JEREMIAH VIII, 22, *c.* 625 B.C.

Balzac, Honore de (1799–1850)

The spiritual analysis of Balzac equals the triumphant imagination of Shakespeare, and by different roads they reach the same height of tragic awe.
GEORGE MOORE: *Confessions of a Young Man,* X, 1888

Balzac is no more a realist than Holbein was. He created life, he did not copy it.
OSCAR WILDE: *The Decay of Lying,* 1891

Banana

Animals of all kinds, including even cats, are fond of this fruit.
J. B. LABAT: *Nouveau voyage aux îles de l'Amérique,* 1722

Where the banana grows man is sensual and cruel.
R. W. EMERSON: *Society and Solitude,* 1870

Yes, we have no bananas.
FRANK SILVER: Title of a popular song, 1923

Bandit

[*See* Manchuria.

Banishment

The bitter bread of banishment.
SHAKESPEARE: *Richard II,* III, *c.* 1596

Banjo

The wild banshaw's melancholy sound.
JAMES GRAINGER: *The Sugar Cane,* 1764
(*Banjo* is not recorded before 1800; earlier it was *banjer, banjore* or *banshaw*)

O, Susanna! O, don't you cry for me;
I've come from Alabama wid my banjo on my knee.
S. C. FOSTER: *O, Susanna,* 1848

Never was a man yit what plucked a banjo that was worth a goddam.
AMERICAN NEGRO PROVERB

Bank

Banking establishments are more dangerous than standing armies.
THOMAS JEFFERSON: *Letter to Elbridge Gerry,* Jan. 26, 1799

A power has risen up in the government greater than the people themselves, consisting of many and various and powerful interests combined in one mass, and held together by the cohesive power of the vast surplus in the banks.
JOHN C. CALHOUN: Speech in the Senate, May 28, 1836

Should all the banks of Europe crash,
The Bank of England smash,

Bring all your notes to Zion's bank,
You're sure to get your cash.
HENRY HOYT: *Zion's Bank*, 1857

If you owe a bank enough money you own it.
Author unidentified

Banker

A banker is a man who lends you an umbrella when the weather is fair, and takes it away from you when it rains. IBID.

[*See also* Financier.

Bank of England

The old Lady in Threadneedle street.
Title of a cartoon by JAMES GILROY, 1797

Bankruptcy

A beggar can never be bankrupt.
JOHN CLARKE: *Parœmiologia Anglo-Latina*, 1639

Bankruptcy in my opinion ever was and yet is considered as a crime, whatever tradesmen may now think of it. It was anciently punished with corporal punishment.
MR. JUSTICE ABNEY: *Judgment in Tribe* vs. *Webber*, 1744

It has been long my deliberate judgment that all bankrupts, of whatsoever denomination, civil or religious, ought to be hanged.
CHARLES LAMB: *Letter to Bernard Barton*, Dec. 8, 1829

If the nation is living within its income its credit is good. If in some crisis it lives beyond its income for a year or two it can usually borrow temporarily on reasonable terms. But if, like the spendthrift, it throws discretion to the winds, is willing to make no sacrifice at all in spending, extends its taxing up to the limit of the people's power to pay, and continues to pile up deficits, it is on the road to bankruptcy.
F. D. ROOSEVELT: Speech at Pittsburgh, Oct. 19, 1932

He who desires to sleep soundly, let him buy the bed of a bankrupt. SPANISH PROVERB

Banquet

Lasciviousness, lusts, excess of wine, revellings, banquetings. I PETER IV, 3, *c.* 60

We have a trifling foolish banquet towards.
SHAKESPEARE: *Romeo and Juliet*, I, *c.* 1596

There is no great banquet but some fares ill.
GEORGE HERBERT: *Outlandish Proverbs*, 1640

Baptism

One Lord, one faith, one baptism.
EPHESIANS IV, 5, *c.* 60

Go ye therefore, and teach all nations, baptizing them in the name of the Father, and of the Son, and of the Holy Ghost.
MATTHEW XXVIII, 19, *c.* 75

Repent, and be baptized every one of you in the name of Jesus Christ for the remission of sins, and ye shall receive the gift of the Holy Ghost. ACTS II, 38, *c.* 75

The infants of papists are not to be baptized.
EDWIN SANDYS (BISHOP OF LONDON): *Letter to Henry Bullinger of Zürich, setting forth the principles of the Puritans*, 1573

The strength of baptism, that's within;
It saves the soul by drowning sin.
ROBERT HERRICK: *Noble Numbers*, 1647

Being by nature born in sin, and the children of wrath, we are hereby made the children of grace.
THE BOOK OF COMMON PRAYER (*The Catechism*), 1662

The baptism of the Christians is an emblem of our Moslem ablutions. Their only error consists in ascribing to one ablution an efficacy which permits them to omit all others.
C. L. DE MONTESQUIEU: *Persian Letters*, XXXV, 1721

Baptismal water . . . has the virtue of cleansing an infant of an enormous sin expiated by the Son of God, and committed thousands of years before the parents of the child dreamed of making him.
VOLTAIRE: *Philosophical Dictionary*, 1764

I think the baptismal service almost perfect. I never could attend a christening without tears bursting forth at the sight of the helpless innocent in a pious clergyman's arms.
S. T. COLERIDGE: *Table-Talk*, Aug. 9, 1832

[*See also* Christening, Jew.

Baptist

Baptist, Baptist is my belief;
I'm a Baptist till I die;
I've been baptized in a Baptist church,
And I've eaten of the Baptist pie.
Anon.: *Denominational Pie*, *c.* 1880

Barbarian

[*See* Conquest.

Barbarism

[*See* Fanaticism.

Barber

As common as a barber's chair.
STEPHEN GOSSON: *The School of Abuse*, 1579

The barber's chair is the very Royal Exchange of news.
GABRIEL HARVEY: *The Trimming of Thomas Nashe*, 1597

A barber's chair . . . fits all buttocks.
SHAKESPEARE: *All's Well that Ends Well*, II, *c.* 1602

Barbers learn to shave by shaving fools.
RANDLE COTGRAVE: *French-English Dictionary,* 1611

No barber shaves so close but another finds work.
GEORGE HERBERT: *Outlandish Proverbs,* 1640

Has a minaret fallen down? Then hang the barber. ARAB PROVERB

One barber shaves another free.
FRENCH PROVERB

A bad barber needs a great many razors.
HINDU PROVERB

Barbers learn their trade on the heads of orphans. MOROCCAN PROVERB

[*See also* Common, Physician, Shaving, Vocation.

Bard

A bard may chant too often and too long.
BYRON: *English Bards and Scotch Reviewers,* 1809

[*See also* Poet.

Barefoot

Blessings on thee, little man,
Barefoot boy, with cheek of tan.
J. G. WHITTIER: *The Barefoot Boy,* 1855

A barefoot boy among the buttercups.
CINCINNATUS HEINE (JOAQUIN MILLER): *Ida,* II, 1871

Barère, Bertrand (1755–1841)

Barère approaches nearer than any person mentioned in history or fiction, whether man or devil, to the idea of consummate and universal depravity. In him the qualities which are the proper objects of hatred, and the qualities which are the proper objects of contempt, preserved an exquisite and absolute harmony.
T. B. MACAULAY: *Memoires de Bertrand Barère,* 1843

[*See also* Lying.

Bargain

It takes two to make a bargain.
ENGLISH PROVERB, familiar since the XVI century

A bargain is a bargain.
THOMAS WILSON: *The Arte of Rhetorique,* 1553

Bargains made in speed are commonly repented at leisure.
GEORGE PETTIE: *Petite Palace of Pettie His Pleasure,* 1576

It's a bad bargain where nobody gains.
ENGLISH PROVERB, traced by Apperson to *c.* 1597

My true love hath my heart, and I have his
By just exchange one for another given:
I hold his dear, and mine he cannot miss,
There never was a better bargain driven.
PHILIP SIDNEY: *The Bargain,* 1598

Some bargain's dear bought.
JOHN DAVIES: *The Scourge of Folly,* 1611

Bare words are no good bargain.
JOHN CLARKE: *Parœmiologia Anglo-Latina,* 1639

A good bargain is a pick-purse.
GEORGE HERBERT: *Outlandish Proverbs,* 1640

On a good bargain think twice. IBID.

The best of a bad bargain.
SAMUEL PEPYS: *Diary,* Aug. 14, 1663

At a good pennyworth pause a little while.
GIOVANNI TORRIANO: *Italian Proverbs,* 1666

Make every bargain clear and plain,
That none may afterward complain.
JOHN RAY: *English Proverbs,* 1670

If you buy the cow take the tail into the bargain.
THOMAS FULLER: *Gnomologia,* 1732

My old father used to have a saying: If you make a bad bargain, hug it all the tighter.
ABRAHAM LINCOLN: *Letter to Joshua Speed,* Feb. 25, 1842

No bargain without wine. LATIN SAYING

[*See also* Exchange, Golden Rule, Necessity.

Bargaining

In the way of a bargain, mark ye me, I'l cavil on the ninth part of a hair.
SHAKESPEARE: *I Henry IV,* III, *c.* 1598

He that blames would buy.
GEORGE HERBERT: *Outlandish Proverbs,* 1640

He'll ne'er get a pennyworth that is afraid to ask a price.
THOMAS FULLER: *Gnomologia,* 1732

Do other men, for they would do you.
CHARLES DICKENS: *Martin Chuzzlewit,* XI, 1844

Bargain like a gipsy, but pay like a gentleman.
HUNGARIAN PROVERB

[*See also* Bargain, Buying and Selling, Cheap.

Baritone

Hark to the red-faced beeritone —
Gargling, gorgling, gurgling.
Author unidentified

Barometer

When the glass falls low
Prepare for a blow;

When it rises high
Let all your kites fly.
SAILORS' RHYME

Baron

[*See* Thief.

Baronet

All baronets are bad.
W. S. GILBERT: *Ruddigore*, I, 1887

Barrel

[*See* Change, Empty.

Barren

A barren sow was never good to pigs.
JOHN RAY: *English Proverbs*, 1670

Barroom

'Twas a balmy Summer even, and a goodly crowd was there,
Which well-nigh filled Joe's barroom on the corner of the square:
And as songs and witty stories came through the open door
A vagabond crept slowly in and posed upon the floor.
H. A. D'ARCY: *The Face on the Barroom Floor*, 1912

Bartender

Oh, give us a drink, bartender,
For we love you, as you know;
Will you be so good as to oblige us
With another drink or so?
AMERICAN POPULAR SONG, *c.* 1875

[*See also* Drinking.

Baseball

The ball once struck off,
Away flies the boy
To the next destined post,
And then home with joy.
Anon.: *A Little Pretty Pocketbook*, 1744 (The quatrain is headed *Base Ball*. This is said to be the first mention of baseball in print)

[*See also* Calamity.

Bashfulness

To get thine ends, lay bashfulness aside;
Who fears to ask doth teach to be deny'd.
ROBERT HERRICK: *Hesperides*, 1648

Though modesty be a virtue, yet bashfulness is a vice.
THOMAS FULLER: *Gnomologia*, 1732

He had that sort of bashfulness which makes a man surly and obstinate in his taciturnity; which makes him turn upon all who approach him as if they were going to assault him; which makes him answer a question as if it were an injury, and repel a compliment as if it were an insult.
MARIA EDGEWORTH: *Tales of Fashionable Life* (*Ennui*), 1812

The bashful always lose. FRENCH PROVERB

Bashfulness is useless to a man in want. (Verecundia inutilis viro egenti.)
LATIN PROVERB

True love is aye blate.
SCOTTISH PROVERB (*Blate*=bashful)

A maid's best dress is bashfulness.
WELSH PROVERB

[*See also* Blush, Irish.

Basilisk

A land of trouble and distress, from whence come the lioness, and the lion, the viper, and the flying basilisk.
ISAIAH XXX, 6, *c.* 700 B.C. (Douay Version; in the Authorized Version *basilisk* is made *fiery serpent*)

Basque Language

The Basques say they understand one another, but they lie. J. J. SCALIGER, *c.* 1590

When the Devil himself tried to study Basque, he learned only three words in seven years.
BASQUE PROVERB

Bass (singer)

As for the bass, the beast can only bellow.
BYRON: *Don Juan*, IV, 1821

Gentlemen, you are hanging the best bass singer in Tennessee.
Dying speech ascribed to a Negro hanged in Tennessee

[*See also* Beer, Choir, Singing, Tenor.

Bassoon

The wedding guest here beat his breast,
For he heard the loud bassoon.
S. T. COLERIDGE: *The Ancient Mariner*, I, 1798

[*See also* Dancing.

Bastard

A bastard shall not enter into the congregation of the Lord; even to his tenth generation shall he not enter into the congregation of the Lord.
DEUTERONOMY XXIII, 2, *c.* 650 B.C.

From whatever source men be born, if they follow not the vices of their parents, and worship God aright, they shall be honest and safe. ST. AUGUSTINE: *On the Good of Marriage*, *c.* 401

He lives to build, not boast, a generous race;
No tenth transmitter of a foolish face.
RICHARD SAVAGE: *The Bastard*, 1728

A bastard brood is always proud.
ENGLISH PROVERB, first recorded in 1736

Keep as far away as possible from a bastard.
HINDU PROVERB

A bastard is the son of no one, or rather the son of all. (Bastardus nullius est filius, aut filius populi.) LEGAL MAXIM

Those born of sinful intercourse are not counted as children. (Qui ex damnato coitu nascuntur, inter liberos non computantur.) IBID.

[*See also* Adultery, Ancestry, Envy, Money.

Bath

A man likes to hear his own voice in the bath. SENECA: *Epistulae morales ad Lucilium*, *c.* 63

The use of baths shall be offered to the sick as often as it is necessary; to the healthy, and especially to youths, it shall not be so readily conceded. THE RULE OF ST. BENEDICT, *c.* 529

Thy baths shall be the juice of July-flowers,
Spirit of roses, and of violets,
The milk of unicorns, and panthers' breath
Gathered in bags, and mixed with Cretan wines. BEN JONSON: *Volpone*, III, 1603

Wash your hands often, your feet seldom, and your head never.
JOHN RAY: *English Proverbs*, 1670

They who bathe in May will soon be laid in clay. WILLIAM HONE: *Table-Talk*, 1827 (Quoted as "an old saying")

Wash me in the water
That you washed the colonel's daughter,
And I shall be whiter
Than the whitewash on the wall.
Song popular among the British troops in France, 1914–18

The father of liars took the first cold [or shower] bath. Author unidentified

He who bathes in May will soon be laid in clay;
He who bathes in June will sing a merry tune;
He who bathes in July will dance like a fly.
OLD ENGLISH RHYME

[*See also* Washing.

Bathing-Suit

A bathing suit is a device to help people from bathing. It lets the water in, but it doesn't let the dirt out. Author unidentified

Baton

Every French soldier carries a marshal's baton in his knapsack.
Ascribed to LOUIS XVIII of France (1755–1824)

Battle

The horseman lifteth up both the bright sword and the glittering spear: and there is a multitude of slain, and a great number of carcasses; and there is none end of their corpses; they stumble upon their corpses.
NAHUM III, 3, *c.* 625 B.C.

He smote them hip and thigh with a great slaughter. JUDGES XV, 8, *c.* 500 B.C.

He saith among the trumpets, Ha, ha; and he smelleth the battle afar off.
JOB XXXIX, 25, *c.* 325 B.C.

The race is not to the swift, nor the battle to the strong. ECCLESIASTES IX, *c.* 200 B.C.

In battle those who are most afraid are always in most danger.
CATILINE: Address to his army in the field near Pistoria, 63 B.C.

Paradise is under the shadow of our swords. Forward!
Ascribed to the CALIPH OMAR IBN AL-KHATTAB: At the battle of Kadisiya, 637

This battle began in Cheviot
An hour before the noon,
And when even-song bell was rang,
The battle was not half done.
Anon.: *Chevy Chase*, *c.* 1400

It is better to be on hand with ten men than to be absent with ten thousand.
Ascribed to TAMERLANE (1336–1405)

Fight, gentlemen of England! fight, bold yeomen!
Draw, archers, draw your arrows to the head!
Spur your proud horses hard, and ride in blood;
Amaze the welkin with your broken staves!
SHAKESPEARE: *Richard III*, V, *c.* 1592

There are few die well that die in a battle.
SHAKESPEARE: *Henry V*, IV, *c.* 1599

Fire low.
OLIVER CROMWELL: Order to his troops at the Battle of Preston, Aug. 17–19, 1648

It is an ill battle where the Devil carries the colors. JOHN RAY: *English Proverbs*, 1670

'Tis a hard battle where none escapes.
JEREMY COLLIER: *A Short View of the Immorality and Profaneness of the English Stage*, intro., 1698

The battle was a very pretty battle as one should desire to see, but we were all so intent upon victory that we never minded the battle.
GEORGE FARQUHAR: *The Recruiting Officer*, II, 1706

There are six or seven thousand of the human species less than there were a month ago, and that seems to me to be all.
LORD CHESTERFIELD: *Letter to his son*, Nov. 20, 1757

The first blow is half the battle.
OLIVER GOLDSMITH: *She Stoops to Conquer*, II, 1773

The battle is not to the strong alone; it is to the vigilant, the active, the brave.
PATRICK HENRY: Speech in the Virginia Convention, March 23, 1775 (Cf. ECCLESIASTES IX, *ante*, *c.* 200 B.C.)

Don't fire until you can see the whites of their eyes.

WILLIAM PRESCOTT: Order to the American troops at the battle of Bunker Hill, June 17, 1775

When we enter the lists of battle we quit the sure domain of truth and leave the decision to the caprice of chance.

WILLIAM GODWIN: *An Enquiry Concerning Political Justice,* 1793

The battle rages loud and long,
And the stormy winds do blow.

THOMAS CAMPBELL: *Ye Mariners of England,* 1801

Old, unhappy, far-off things,
And battles long ago.

WILLIAM WORDSWORTH: *The Solitary Reaper,* 1807

Tell the men to fire faster and not to give up the ship. Fight her till she sinks.

JAMES LAWRENCE: Order during the battle between the Chesapeake and the Shannon, off Boston, June 1, 1813 (The Chesapeake was captured and Lawrence was taken to Halifax, where he died on June 5)

Nothing except a battle lost can be half so melancholy as a battle won.

THE DUKE OF WELLINGTON: Despatch from the field of Waterloo, June, 1815

Battle's magnificently stern array.

BYRON: *Childe Harold,* III, 1816

A battle sometimes decides everything; and sometimes the most trifling thing decides the fate of a battle.

NAPOLEON I: To Barry E. O'Meara at St. Helena, Nov. 9, 1816

Strike — for your altars and your fires;
Strike — for the green graves of your sires;
God — and your native land!

FITZ-GREENE HALLECK: *Marco Bozzaris,* 1825

Battles, in these ages, are transacted by mechanism; men now even die, and kill one another, in an artificial manner.

THOMAS CARLYLE: *The French Revolution,* VII, 1837

So all day long the noise of battle roll'd
Among the mountains by the Winter sea,
Until King Arthur's table, man by man,
Had fallen in Lyonness about their lord.

ALFRED TENNYSON: *Morte d'Arthur,* 1842

To men of a sedate and mature spirit, in whom is any knowledge or mental activity, the detail of battle becomes insupportably tedious and revolting.

R. W. EMERSON: *War,* 1849

I have seen battles, too, —
Have waded foremost in their bloody waves,
And heard their hollow roar of dying men.

MATTHEW ARNOLD: *Sohrab and Rustum,* 1853

In enterprise of martial kind,
When there was any fighting,
He led his regiment from behind,
He found it less exciting.

W. S. GILBERT: *The Gondoliers,* I, 1889

If your bayonet breaks, strike with the stock; if the stock gives way, hit with your fists; if your fists are hurt, bite with your teeth.

M. I. DRAGOMIROFF: *Notes for Soldiers,* *c.* 1890

A method of untying with the teeth a political knot that would not yield to the tongue.

AMBROSE BIERCE: *The Devil's Dictionary,* 1906

Soldiers of the Western Front, your hour has come. The fight which begins today will determine Germany's destiny for a thousand years.

ADOLF HITLER: Order to the German Army, May 10, 1940

That was a hard-fought battle from which no man returned to tell the tale.

IRISH PROVERB

[*See also* Army, Artillery, Attack, Cannon, Cause and Effect, Cavalry, Fierce, Fighting, Forefront, General, Infantry, Soldier, Victory, War.

Battlefield

They caught every one his fellow by the head, and thrust his sword in his fellow's side; so they fell down together: wherefore that place was called Helkath-hazzurim.

II SAMUEL II, 16, *c.* 500 B.C.

They say it was a shocking sight
After the field was won;
For many thousand bodies here
Lay rotting in the sun;
But things like that, you know, must be
After a famous victory.

ROBERT SOUTHEY: *After Blenheim,* 1798

A battlefield is at once the playroom of all the gods and the dancehall of all the furies.

JEAN PAUL RICHTER: *Titan,* CV, 1803

They there may dig each other's graves,
And call the sad work glory.

P. B. SHELLEY: *Queen Mab,* VI, 1813

On fame's eternal camping-ground
Their silent tents are spread,
And glory guards with solemn round
The bivouac of the dead.

THEODORE O'HARA: *The Bivouac of the Dead,* 1847

Well, well, General, bury these poor men, and let us say no more about it.

R. E. LEE: To General A. P. Hill after the battle of Bristoe Station, Oct. 14, 1863

In a large sense we cannot dedicate, we cannot hallow this ground. The brave men, living and dead, who struggled here, have con-

secrated it far above our poor power to add or detract.
ABRAHAM LINCOLN: *Gettysburg Address,* Nov. 19, 1863

Baudelaire, Charles (1821–67)

All that is worst in Mr. Swinburne belongs to Baudelaire. The offensive choice of subject, the obtrusion of unnatural passion, the blasphemy, the wretched animalism, are all taken intact out of the Fleurs de Mal. Pitiful! that any sane man, least of all any English poet, should think this dunghill worthy of importation.
ROBERT BUCHANAN: *The Fleshly School of Poetry,* 1872

[*See also* Ape.

Bawd

[*See* Opportunity.

Bawdiness

[*See* Walpole (Robert).

Bawdy-house

He who sets one foot in a bawdy-house claps t'other in an hospital.
THOMAS FULLER: *Gnomologia,* 1732

Bayonet

A bayonet is a weapon with a worker at each end.
Slogan of English pacifists, 1940

[*See also* Ballot, Battle.

Bay-tree

I have seen the wicked . . . spreading himself like a green bay tree.
PSALMS XXXVII, 35, *c.* 150 B.C.

Be-all

The be-all and the end-all.
SHAKESPEARE: *Macbeth,* I, *c.* 1605

Bear

When a bear catches a cow he kills her in the following manner: he bites a hole into the hide and blows with all his power into it, till the animal swells excessively and dies; for the air expands greatly between the flesh and the hide.
PEHR KALM: *En resa til Norra Amerika,* I, 1753

[*See also* Fighting, Honey, King, Puritan, Ugliness.

Beard

Ye shall not round the corners of your heads, neither shall thou mar the corners of thy beard. LEVITICUS XIX, 27, *c.* 700 B.C.

I caught him by his beard, and smote him, and slew him. I SAMUEL XVII, 35, *c.* 500 B.C.

Stay, friend, until I put aside my beard, for that never committed treason.
THOMAS MORE: On the scaffold, to the headman, July 7, 1535

What a beard hast thou got! thou hast got more hair on thy chin than Dobbin my fill-horse has on his tail.
SHAKESPEARE: *The Merchant of Venice,* II, *c.* 1597

His chin new reap'd,
Show'd like a stubble-land at harvest-home.
SHAKESPEARE: *I Henry IV,* I, *c.* 1598

He that hath a beard is more than a youth, and he that hath no beard is less than a man.
SHAKESPEARE: *Much Ado About Nothing,* II, *c.* 1599

I could not endure a husband with a beard on his face; I had rather lie in the woolen.
IBID.

The properness of a man lives altogether in the fashion of his beard.
Anon.: *Humor Out of Breath,* III, 1608

That ornamental excrement which groweth beneath the chin.
THOMAS FULLER: *Worthies of England,* 1662

Look on this beard, and tell me whether
Eunuchs were such or geldings either.
SAMUEL BUTLER: *Hudibras,* I, 1663

If Providence did beards devise
To prove the wearers of them wise,
A fulsome goat would then by nature
Excel each other human creature.
THOMAS D'URFEY: *Colin's Walk,* 1690

He is false by nature that has a black head and a red beard.
THOMAS FULLER: *Gnomologia,* 1732

It is not the beard that makes the philosopher.
IBID.

There was an old man with a beard,
Who said: " It is just as I feared —
Two owls and a hen,
Four larks and a wren
Have all built their nests in my beard."
EDWARD LEAR: *The Book of Nonsense,* 1846

The beards of the young men glisten'd with wet, it ran from their long hair:
Little streams pass'd all over their bodies.
WALT WHITMAN: *Walt Whitman,* 1855

Come out o' that bunch o' ha'r! I know you're in thar! I see your ears a-workin'!
Derisive shout to heavily-bearded men, in vogue in Lee's army, 1862–63

A foul mouth is ill-matched with a white beard.
A. C. SWINBURNE: *Letter to R. W. Emerson,* Jan. 30, 1874

Beware of women with beards and men without them. BASQUE PROVERB

A red-bearded man was never any good.
GERMAN PROVERB

No beard, no understanding. IBID.

[*See also* Age (Old), Appearance, Whiskers.

Beard, v.

And darest thou then
To beard the lion in his den,
The Douglas in his hall?
WALTER SCOTT: *Marmion,* VI, 1808

Bearing

The bearings of this observation lays in the application on it.
CHARLES DICKENS: *Dombey and Son,* XXIII, 1848

Beast

[*See* Animal.

Beating

A woman, an ass, and a walnut tree,
Bring the more fruit, the more beaten they be.
GEORGE PETTIE: *Civil Conversations of Stefano Guazzo,* 1581

A spaniel, a woman and a walnut tree,
The more they're beaten the better they be.
JOHN RAY: *English Proverbs,* 1670

[*See also* Dog, Wife.

Beatitudes

(They are in MATTHEW V, 3–12, *c.* 75. *See also* LUKE VI, 20–22)

Beaumarchais, Caron de (1732–99)

That man will be hanged, but the rope will break.
SOPHIE ARNOULD: Said of Beaumarchais, *c.* 1785

Beauty

What is beautiful is good, and who is good will soon be beautiful.
SAPPHO: *Fragment, c.* 610 B.C.

Nature gave horns to bulls, hooves to horses, speed to hares, the power of swimming to fishes, that of flying to birds, and understanding to men. She had nothing left to give to women save beauty. Beauty is proof against spears and shields. She who is beautiful is more formidable than fire and iron.
ANACREON: *Fragment, c.* 500 B.C.

When a man loves the beautiful, what does he desire? That the beautiful may be his.
PLATO: *Symposium, c.* 360 B.C.

Beauty is vain.
PROVERBS XXXI, 30, *c.* 350 B.C.

Beauty depends on size as well as symmetry. No very small animal can be beautiful, for looking at it takes so small a portion of time that the impression of it will be confused. Nor can any very large one, for a whole view of it cannot be had at once, and so there will be no unity and completeness.
ARISTOTLE: *Poetics,* VII, *c.* 322 B.C.

Behold, thou art fair, my love; behold, thou art fair; thou hast doves' eyes within thy locks: thy hair is as a flock of goats, that appear from mount Gilead.
SOLOMON'S SONG IV, I, *c.* 200 B.C.

Gaze not upon a maiden, lest her beauty be a stumbling-block to thee.
ECCLESIASTICUS IX, 5, *c.* 180 B.C.

There are two kinds of beauty — loveliness and dignity. We ought to regard loveliness as the quality of woman, dignity that of man.
CICERO: *De officiis,* I, 78 B.C.

Nothing can be beautiful in all parts.
HORACE: *Carmina,* II, *c.* 20 B.C.

Beautiful! good! perfect! (Pulchre! bene! recte!) HORACE: *De arte poetica, c.* 8 B.C.

Beauty is a frail good. (Forma bonum fragile est.) OVID: *Ara amatoria,* II, *c.* 2 B.C.

Beauty and wisdom are seldom found together.
PETRONIUS ARBITER: *Satyricon,* XCIV, *c.* 50

If the wife hath beauty the whole house is bright, but if she lack it all will appear dismal. THE CODE OF MANU, III, *c.* 100

Does beauty need anything more? Nay, no more than law, or truth, or kindness, or modesty. Which of them owes its virtue to being praised or loses it by being blamed?
MARCUS AURELIUS: *Meditations,* IV, *c.* 170

A holy woman may be beautiful by the gift of nature, but she must not give occasion to lust. If beauty be hers, so far from setting it off she ought rather to obscure it.
TERTULLIAN: *Women's Dress, c.* 220

Beauty is rather a light that plays over the symmetry of things than that symmetry itself.
PLOTINUS: *Enneads,* V, *c.* 250

People are all the more enamored of beauty when it is talked of but not seen, for there are then two incentives to passion, the craving for love and the craving for knowledge.
ST. AMBROSE: *On Virgins,* II, *c.* 390

The beauty of women deserves no praise.
BHARTRIHARI: *The Vairagya Sataka, c.* 625

In life beauty perishes, but not in art.
LEONARDO DA VINCI: *Notebook, c.* 1500

How rare a thing it is to match virginity with beauty.
JOHN LYLY: *Euphues and His England,* 1580

She's beautiful and therefore to be woo'd.
SHAKESPEARE: *I Henry VI*, v, 1592

Had she deigned to remove her veil, God Himself would have fallen in love with her.
TORQUATO TASSO: *Gerusalemme*, IV, 1592

All orators are dumb where beauty pleadeth.
SHAKESPEARE: *The Rape of Lucrece*, 1594

What, is the jay more precious than the lark,
Because his feathers are more beautiful?
Or is the adder better than the eel,
Because his painted skin contents the eye?
SHAKESPEARE: *The Taming of the Shrew*, IV, 1594

Beauty too rich for use, for earth too dear.
SHAKESPEARE: *Romeo and Juliet*, I, *c.* 1596

Oh, she doth teach the torches to burn bright;
It seems she hangs upon the cheek of night
Like a rich jewel in an Ethiop's ear. IBID.

Beauty is but a vain and doubtful good;
A shining gloss that fadeth suddenly;
A flower that dies when first it 'gins to bud;
A brittle glass that's broken presently.
SHAKESPEARE: *The Passionate Pilgrim*, 1599

Beauty provoketh thieves sooner than gold.
SHAKESPEARE: *As You Like It*, I, *c.* 1600

Beauty is but a flower
Which wrinkles will devour;
Brightness falls from the air,
Queens have died young and fair,
Dust hath closed Helen's eye.
THOMAS NASHE: *In Plague Time*, *c.* 1600

Oh, thou art fairer than the evening air,
Clad in the beauty of a thousand stars.
CHRISTOPHER MARLOWE: *Dr. Faustus*, XIV, 1604

Beauty is but skin-deep.
ENGLISH PROVERB, traced by Apperson to 1606

Beauty in a good woman is like fire at a distance or a sharp sword: the one does not burn, or the other wound, those who come not too close.
CERVANTES: *Don Quixote*, II, 1615

Beauty is as Summer fruits, which are easy to corrupt, and cannot last.
FRANCIS BACON: *Essays*, XLIII, 1625

There is no excellent beauty that hath not some strangeness in the proportion. IBID.

A poor beauty finds more lovers than husbands.
GEORGE HERBERT: *Outlandish Proverbs*, 1640

Beauty and folly are generally companions.
BALTASAR GRACIÁN: *The Art of Worldly Wisdom*, CCLXXIII, 1647

Beauty draws more than oxen.
GEORGE HERBERT: *Jacula Prudentum*, 1651

An ass is beautiful to an ass, and a pig to a pig.
JOHN RAY: *English Proverbs*, 1670

Beauty stands
In the admiration only of weak minds
Led captive.
JOHN MILTON: *Paradise Regained*, II, 1671

Beauty's a coward still without the help of art, and may have the fortune of a conquest, but cannot keep it. Beauty and art can no more be asunder than love and honor.
WILLIAM WYCHERLEY: *Love in a Wood*, III, 1671

If the motion which objects we see communicate to our nerves be conducive to health, the objects causing it are styled beautiful; if a contrary motion be excited, they are styled ugly.
BARUCH SPINOZA: *Ethica*, I, 1677

A beautiful face is of all spectacles the most beautiful.
JEAN DE LA BRUYÈRE: *Caractères*, 1688

There is in true beauty, as in courage, somewhat which narrow souls cannot dare to admire.
WILLIAM CONGREVE: *The Old Bachelor*, IV, 1693

Old as I am, for ladies' love unfit,
The power of beauty I remember yet.
JOHN DRYDEN: *Cymon and Iphigenia*, 1699

'Tis not a lip, or eye, we beauty call,
But the joint force and full result of all.
ALEXANDER POPE: *An Essay on Criticism*, II, 1711

Beauties in vain their pretty eyes may roll;
Charms strike the sight, but merit wins the soul.
ALEXANDER POPE: *The Rape of the Lock*, v, 1712

Beauty soon grows familiar to the lover,
Fades in his eye, and palls upon the sense.
JOSEPH ADDISON: *Cato*, I, 1713

Beauty should be kind, as well as charm.
GEORGE GRANVILLE (LORD LANSDOWNE): *To Myra*, *c.* 1725

Tell a woman she's a beauty and the Devil will tell her so ten times.
THOMAS FULLER: *Gnomologia*, 1732

Beautiful as sweet!
And young as beautiful! and soft as young!
And gay as soft! and innocent as gay!
EDWARD YOUNG: *Night Thoughts*, III, 1742

I never remember that anything beautiful, whether a man, a beast, a bird, or a plant, was ever shown, though it were to a hundred people, that they did not all immediately agree that it was beautiful.
EDMUND BURKE: *The Sublime and Beautiful*, intro., 1756

The passion excited by beauty is nearer to a species of melancholy than to jollity and mirth. IBID.

Beauty in distress is much the most affecting beauty. IBID.

Whenever, at a party, I have been in the mood to study fools, I have always looked for a great beauty: they always gather round her like flies around a fruit-stall.
JEAN PAUL RICHTER: *Hesperus,* XXI, 1795

Beauty's tears are lovelier than her smile.
THOMAS CAMPBELL: *The Pleasures of Hope,* I, 1799

I, too, was beautiful, and that was my undoing. (Schön war ich auch, und das war mein Verderben.)
J. W. GOETHE: *I Faust,* I, 1808

The fatal gift of beauty.
BYRON: *Childe Harold,* IV, 1818

A thing of beauty is a joy forever;
Its loveliness increases; it will never
Pass into nothingness; but still will keep
A bower quiet for us, and a sleep
Full of sweet dreams, and health, and quiet breathing.
JOHN KEATS: *Endymion,* I, 1818

There was a woman beautiful as morning.
P. B. SHELLEY: *The Revolt of Islam,* I, 1818

Beauty is truth, truth beauty.
JOHN KEATS: *Ode on a Grecian Urn,* *c.* 1819

She walks in beauty like the night
Of cloudless climes and starry skies;
And all that's best of dark and bright
Meet in her aspect and her eyes.
BYRON: *She Walks in Beauty,* 1820

A beautiful woman, if poor, should use a double circumspection; for her beauty will tempt others, her poverty herself.
C. C. COLTON: *Lacon,* 1820

A marriageable girl, whose natural destiny is to bear and suckle children, will not be beautiful without the proper breadth of the pelvis and the necessary fullness of the breasts.
J. W. GOETHE: *Conversations with Eckermann,* April 18, 1827

The great use of female beauty, the great practical advantage of it is, that it naturally and unavoidably tends to keep the husband in good humor with himself.
WILLIAM COBBETT: *Advice to Young Men,* III, 1829

Helen, thy beauty is to me
Like those Nicæan barks of yore,
That gently, o'er a perfumed sea,
The weary, wayworn wanderer bore.
E. A. POE: *To Helen,* 1831

Beauty is its own excuse for being.
R. W. EMERSON: *The Rhodora,* 1839 (Western Messenger, July)

Beauty will not come at the call of a legislature, nor will it repeat in England or America its history in Greece.
R. W. EMERSON: *Art,* 1841

Beauty of whatever kind, in its supreme development, invariably excites the sensitive soul to tears.
E. A. POE: *The Rationale of Verse,* 1843 (The Pioneer, March)

Virginal Lilian, rigidly, humblily dutiful;
Saintlily, lowlily,
Thrillingly, holily
Beautiful. IBID.

Too bright, too beautiful to last.
W. C. BRYANT: *The Rivulet, c.* 1845

Nature covers all her works with a varnish of beauty.
ARTHUR SCHOPENHAUER: *Parerga und Paralipomena,* 1851

If you get simple beauty, and nought else.
You get about the best thing God invents.
ROBERT BROWNING: *Fra Lippo Lippi,* 1855

Beauty and sadness always go together.
GEORGE MACDONALD: *Within and Without,* IV, 1855

Beauty is the index of a larger fact than wisdom.
O. W. HOLMES: *The Professor at the Breakfast-Table,* II, 1859

We ascribe beauty to that which is simple; which has no superfluous parts; which exactly answers its end; which stands related to all things; which is the mean of many extremes.
R. W. EMERSON: *The Conduct of Life,* VII, 1860

The utmost possible sense of beauty is conveyed by a feebly translucent, smooth, but not lustrous surface of white, and pale warm red, subdued by the most pure and delicate greys, as in the finer portions of the human frame, in wreaths of snow, and in white plumage under rose light.
JOHN RUSKIN: *Modern Painters,* IV, 1860

There is hardly a human life which would not have been different if the idea of beauty in the mind of the man who had lived it had been different.
WALTER BAGEHOT: *Literary Studies,* II, 1879

Beauty is the only thing that time cannot harm. Philosophies fall away like sand, and creeds follow one another like the withered leaves of Autumn; but what is beautiful is a joy for all seasons and a possession for all eternity.
OSCAR WILDE: *The English Renaissance of Art,* 1882 (Lecture in New York, Jan. 9)

There is beauty in the bellow of the blast.
W. S. GILBERT: *The Mikado,* II, 1885

Physical science may, and probably will, some day, enable our posterity to set forth the exact physical concomitants and conditions of the strange rapture called beauty. But if ever that day arrives the rapture will remain, just as it is now, outside and beyond the physical world.
T. H. HUXLEY: *Science and Morals,* 1886

Beauty-in-itself is simply a word; it is not even a concept. In his view of the beautiful, man postulates himself as the standard of perfection. A species has no alternative to saying yea to itself in this way.
F. W. NIETZSCHE: *The Twilight of the Idols,* 1889

It is better to be beautiful than to be good, but it is better to be good than to be ugly.
OSCAR WILDE: *The Picture of Dorian Grey,* 1891

She is a woman so beautiful that to expect sense from her would be hoggish.
WILLIAM II OF GERMANY: On the Countess Goertz, *c.* 1900

The beautiful should be defined as that of which the admiring contemplation is good in itself.
G. E. MOORE: *Principia Ethica,* VI, 1903

Beauty aims at neither morals nor truth.
J. E. SPINGARN: *Creative Criticism,* 1917

Beauty is an immense predilection, a perfect conviction of the desirability of a certain thing.
WYNDHAM LEWIS: *Inferior Religions,* 1920

White hen mighty pretty, but de black chicken is de luckiest when de hawk come sailin' ovah de chicken yard.
AMERICAN NEGRO PROVERB

Beauty is but skin deep,
Ugly lies the bone;
Beauty dies and fades away,
But ugly holds its own.
Author unidentified

To marry a woman for her beauty is like buying a house for its paint. IBID.

It is the beautiful bird which gets caged.
CHINESE PROVERB

Beauty is silent eloquence.
FRENCH PROVERB

Beauty is a good letter of introduction.
GERMAN PROVERB

If the housewife is beautiful, the wine is good.
IBID.

These three soon pass away: the echo, the rainbow, and the beauty of woman. IBID.

Those who are beautiful die easily. IBID.

What worth has beauty if it be not seen?
ITALIAN PROVERB

Beautiful enough if good enough. (Sat pulchra si sat bona.) LATIN PROVERB

Everything that is beautiful is lovable. (Omne pulchrum amabile.) IBID.

The Autumn of the beautiful is beautiful. (Pulchrorum autumnus pulcher.) IBID.

Beauty may die, but it leaves traces behind it.
MOROCCAN PROVERB

Beauty will not season soup.
POLISH PROVERB

Beauty and chastity are always quarreling.
SPANISH PROVERB

[*See also* Angel, Clothes, Comeliness, Complexion, Coquetry, Cosmetics, Darkness, Dead, Delicacy, Desire, Devil, Face, Fair, Freedom, Graceful, Hair, Handsome, Harmony, Health, Husband and Wife, Indian, Italy, Lady, Love, Lover, Mask, Money, Nature, Poetry, Poor, Pretty, Stature, Truth, Ugliness, Utility.

Because

I think him so because I think him so.
SHAKESPEARE: *Two Gentlemen of Verona,* I, *c.* 1595

Because is a woman's reason.
JAMES KELLY: *Complete Collection of Scottish Proverbs,* 1721

I sent a message to the fish:
I told them "This is what I wish."
The little fishes of the sea,
They sent an answer back to me.
The little fishes' answer was
"We cannot do it, sir, because —"
C. L. DODGSON (LEWIS CARROLL): *Through the Looking-Glass,* 1871

Bed

They howled upon their beds.
HOSEA VII, 14, *c.* 740 B.C.

Woe to them that . . . work evil upon their beds. MICAH II, 1, *c.* 700 B.C.

Og king of Bashan remained of the remnant of giants; behold, his bedstead was a bedstead of iron. DEUTERONOMY III, 11, *c.* 650 B.C.

I have decked my bed with coverings of tapestry, with carved works, with fine linen of Egypt. I have perfumed my bed with myrrh, aloes, and cinnamon.
PROVERBS VII, 16–17, *c.* 350 B.C.

My bed shall comfort me.
JOB VII, 13, *c.* 325 B.C.

Arise, and take up thy bed, and walk.
MARK II, 9, *c.* 70 (Cf. MATTHEW IX, 6, *c.* 75; JOHN V, 11, *c.* 115)

As you make your bed you must lie in it.
ENGLISH PROVERB, borrowed from the Latin, and current since the XVI century

Thou shalt lie in a bed stuff'd with turtles' feathers; swoon in perfumed linen, like the fellow was smothered in roses.

JOHN WEBSTER: *The White Devil,* I, *c.* 1608

Loath to bed, and loath to rise.

JOHN CLARKE: *Parœmiologia Anglo-Latina,* 1639

And so to bed.

SAMUEL PEPYS: *Diary,* July 22, 1660 (Frequently repeated later)

If the bed could tell all it knows it would put many to the blush.

JOHN RAY: *English Proverbs,* 1670

A bed smoothly laid, and soft, that is, where the resistance is every way inconsiderable, is a great luxury, disposing to an universal relaxation, and inducing beyond anything else that species of it called sleep.

EDMUND BURKE: *The Sublime and Beautiful,* IV, 1756

When one begins to turn in bed it is time to turn out.

Ascribed to the DUKE OF WELLINGTON (1769–1852)

In Winter I get up at night
And dress by yellow candle-light;
In Summer, quite the other way,
I have to go to bed by day.

R. L. STEVENSON: *Bed in Summer,* 1885

No bed is big enough to hold three.

GERMAN PROVERB

The patient's bed is his best medicine.

ITALIAN PROVERB

Matthew, Mark, Luke, and John,
Bless the bed that I lay on;
Four corners to my bed,
Four angels round my head,
One to watch and one to pray,
And two to bear my soul away.

OLD ENGLISH RHYME

[*See also* Insomnia, Kiss, Marriage, Rising (Early), Rising (Late), Sleep.

Bedfellow

[*See* Misery, Politics, Poverty.

Bedroom

A husband and wife who have separate bedrooms have either drifted apart – or found happiness.

BALZAC: *The Physiology of Marriage,* 1830

Bee

The bee is small among flying things, but her fruit hath the chiefest sweetness.

ECCLESIASTICUS XI, 3, *c.* 180 B.C.

The bee is more honored than other animals, not because she labors, but because she labors for others.

ST. JOHN CHRYSOSTOM: *Homily XII, c.* 388

Where the bee sucketh honey the spider sucketh poison.

THOMAS DRAXE: *Bibliotheca scholastica instructissima,* 1633 (The idea is traced by Smith to 1573)

The bee that hath honey in her mouth hath a sting in her tail.

JOHN LYLY: *Euphues,* 1579

He has a bee in his bonnet.

ENGLISH SAYING, traced by Smith to 1681

The bee goes out, and honey home doth bring,
And some who seek that honey find a sting;
And wouldst thou have the honey, and be free
From stinging, in the first place kill the bee.

JOHN BUNYAN: *A Book for Boys and Girls,* 1686

How doth the little busy bee
Improve each shining hour.

ISAAC WATTS: *Divine Songs for Children,* pref., 1715

The bee . . . does the whole business of life at once, and at the same time feeds, and works, and diverts itself.

JONATHAN SWIFT: *A Letter of Advice to a Young Poet,* Dec. 1, 1720

Wiser far than human seer,
Yellow-breeched philosopher!
Seeing only what is fair,
Sipping only what is sweet,
Thou dost mock at fate and care,
Leave the chaff, and take the wheat.

R. W. EMERSON: *The Humble-Bee,* 1839

The moan of doves in immemorial elms,
And murmuring of innumerable bees.

ALFRED TENNYSON: *The Princess,* VII, 1847

[*See also* Busy, Dead, Honey, Morality, Old.

Beecher, H. W. (1813–87)

Mr. Beecher is a remarkably handsome man when he is in the full tide of sermonizing, and his face is lit up with animation, but he is as homely as a singed cat when he isn't doing anything.

S. L. CLEMENS (MARK TWAIN): *Letter from New York to the Alta Californian* (San Francisco), Feb. 18, 1867

Beef

What say you to a piece of beef and mustard?

SHAKESPEARE: *The Taming of the Shrew,* IV, 1594

Pudding and beef make Britons fight.

MATTHEW PRIOR: *Alma,* III, *c.* 1716

When mighty roast beef was the Englishman's food
It ennobled our hearts and enriched our blood –
Our soldiers were brave and our courtiers were good.
Oh, the roast beef of England.

HENRY FIELDING: *The Grub Street Opera,* III, 1731

Beefsteaks and porter are gude belly mortar.
SCOTTISH PROVERB

[*See also* England, Pork.

Beer

They had beer to drink, very strong when not mixed with water, but agreeable to those accustomed to it.
XENOPHON: *Anabasis*, IV, *c.* 398 B.C.

Beer is chiefly to be desired in the Summer, and it is a drink (believe me) for all constitutions, but especially for the cholerick and melancholick most wholesome.
TOBIAS VENNER: *Via recta*, 1620

If smirking wine be wanting here,
There's that which drowns all care, stout beer.
ROBERT HERRICK: *Hesperides*, 1648

He that drinks strong beer,
And goes to bed mellow,
Lives as he ought to live,
And dies a hearty fellow.
Anon.: *Come, Landlord, Fill a Flowing Bowl*, *c.* 1650

Here sleeps in peace a Hampshire grenadier,
Who caught his death by drinking cold small beer.
Soldiers! take heed from his untimely fall,
And when you're hot, drink strong, or none at all.
Epitaph on THOMAS THETCHER at Winchester, England, 1764

They who drink beer will think beer.
Attributed to WILLIAM WARBURTON, BISHOP OF GLOUCESTER (1698–1779)

I wish to see this beverage become common instead of the whisky which kills one-third of our citizens, and ruins their families.
THOMAS JEFFERSON: *Letter to Charles Yancey*, 1815

I wish I were a brewer's horse
Five quarters of a year;
I'd place my head where was my tail,
And drink up all the beer.
CATHERINE SINCLAIR: *Holiday House*, 1839

Here
With my beer
I sit,
While golden moments flit:
Alas!
They pass
Unheeded by:
And as they fly,
I,
Being dry,
Sit, idly sipping here
My beer.
GEORGE ARNOLD: *Beer*, *c.* 1855

Beer that is not drunk has missed its vocation.
MEYER BRESLAU: Speech in the Reichstag, Jan. 21, 1880

Beer here! Beer here! Or I'll fall down. Shall the beer lie in the cellar — and I fall in a swoon here? (Bier her! Bier her! Oder ich fall' um. Soll das Bier im Keller liegen — und ich hier die Ohnmacht kriegen?)
Anon.: *Bier Her* (A German students' song of unknown date)

Here's to the girl I love —
I wish that she were nigh;
If drinking beer would bring her here,
I'd drink the damn place dry.
Author unidentified

Who has money can buy himself beer; who has none can swill water. (Wer a Geld hat, kann Bier sich kaufen; wer keins hat, kann a Wasser saufen.) BAVARIAN PROVERB

Man lives but once, and then it's all over; so draw me another, but it must be Bavarian. (De Mensch lebt nur einmal und dann ist's vorbei; drum schenkt nochmal ei, aber Bayrisch muss sei.) BAVARIAN SAYING

Beer makes the hero. CZECH PROVERB

When beer goes in wit comes out.
DANISH PROVERB

Beer-bass (Bierbass). Beer-paunch (Bierbauch). Beer-brother (Bierbruder). Beer-zeal (Biereifer). Beer-idea (Bieridee). Beer-speech (Bierrede).
GERMAN PHRASES

Beer and bread make the cheeks red.
GERMAN PROVERB

Beer on wine: let it alone. (Bier auf Wein, das lass' sein.) IBID.

Beer on wine: that tastes good. (Bier auf Wein, das schmeckt fein.) IBID.

Clear wine in the morning; beer at midday. (Des Morgens bei dem klaren Wein; des Mittags bei dem Bier.) IBID.

There is no bad beer: some kinds are better than others. IBID.

What is one keg of beer among one man?
GERMAN-AMERICAN SAYING

Bread is the staff of life, but beer is life itself.
OXFORDSHIRE PROVERB

The best beer is where priests go to drink.
POLISH PROVERB

Milk for children; meat for men; beer for the old. WELSH PROVERB

[*See also* Ale, Brewery, Drinking, Friar, Good, Hops, Irishman, One, Wine.

Beethoven, Ludwig van (1770–1827)

Keep your eyes on him; he'll make the world talk of him some day.
W. A. MOZART: *Letter to his father*, 1787

Beethoven can write music, thank God — but he can do nothing else on earth.
LUDWIG VAN BEETHOVEN: *Letter to Ferdinand Ries,* Dec. 22, 1822

Beethoven's music is music about music.
F. W. NIETZSCHE: *Human All-too-Human,* II, 1878

Before the name of Beethoven we must all bow in reverence.
GIUSEPPE VERDI: *Letter to Joseph Joachim,* May, 7, 1889

Beethoven is not beautiful. He is dramatic, powerful, a maker of storms, a subduer of tempests; but his speech is the speech of a self-centered egotist. He is the father of all the modern melomaniacs, who, looking into their own souls, write what they see therein — misery, corruption, slighting selfishness, and ugliness.
JAMES HUNEKER: *Old Fogy,* IV, 1913

There can no more be a new Beethoven than there can be a new Christopher Columbus.
RENÉ LEONORMAND: *Etude sur l'harmonie moderne,* 1913

[*See also* Generosity.

Beetle

The poor beetle that we tread upon,
In corporal sufferance finds a pang as great
As when a giant dies.
SHAKESPEARE: *Measure for Measure,* III, 1604

At eve the beetle boometh
Athwart the thicket lone.
ALFRED TENNYSON: *Claribel,* 1830

Beggar

He raiseth up the poor out of the dust, and lifteth up the beggar from the dunghill.
I SAMUEL II, 8, *c.* 500 B.C.

The beggar died, and was carried by the angels into Abraham's bosom.
LUKE XVI, 22, *c.* 75

A beggar may sing before a thief.
JUVENAL: *Satires,* X, 118

The beggar fears no reverse of fortune.
BHARTRIHARI: *The Vairagya Sataka, c.* 625

Set a beggar on horseback and he'll ride to the Devil.
ENGLISH PROVERB, familiar since the XVI century

Beggars should be no choosers.
JOHN HEYWARD: *Proverbs,* 1546

A beggar wisheth he might be a monarch while he lives, and the greatest potentate wisheth he had lived a beggar when he comes to die.
JOSEPH HALL: *Meditations and Vows,* III, 1606

He makes a beggar first that first relieves him.
THOMAS HEYWOOD: *The Royal King and the Loyal Subject,* 1637

One beggar is enough at a door.
JOHN CLARKE: *Parœmiologia Anglo-Latina,* 1639

A beggar payeth a benefit with a louse.
JOHN RAY: *English Proverbs,* 1670

Beggars breed and rich men feed. IBID.

With the ready trick and fable
Round we wander all the day,
And at night, in barn or stable,
Hug our doxies on the hay.
ROBERT BURNS: *The Jolly Beggars,* 1785

The true beggar is the true king.
G. E. LESSING: *Nathan der Weise,* II, 1779

He is not expected to become bail or surety for any one. No man troubleth him with questioning his religion or politics. He is the only free man in the universe.
CHARLES LAMB: *A Complaint of the Decay of Beggars in the Metropolis,* 1822 (London Magazine, June)

The beggar is taxed for a corner to die in.
JAMES R. LOWELL: *The Vision of Sir Launfal,* 1848

Enormous populations, if they be beggars, are disgusting, like moving cheese, like hills of ants, or of fleas, — the more, the worse.
R. W. EMERSON: *Representative Men,* I, 1850

Beggars should be abolished. It annoys one to give to them, and it annoys one not to give to them.
F. W. NIETZSCHE: *Thus Spake Zarathustra,* II, 1885

One who has relied on the assistance of his friends.
AMBROSE BIERCE: *The Devil's Dictionary,* 1906

If begging is your lot, knock only at the larger gates. ARAB PROVERB

A beggar's estate lies in all lands.
DUTCH PROVERB

It is a beggar's pride that he is not a thief.
JAPANESE PROVERB

Not even his parents are friendly to a beggar.
LATIN PROVERB

[*See also* Actor, Ancestry, Bankruptcy, Begging, Dead, Enough, Family, Futility, Heaven and Hell, Lawsuit, Modesty, Patience, Poverty, Soldier, Wish.

Begging

The horseleech hath two daughters, crying, Give, give. PROVERBS XXX, 15, *c.* 350 B.C.

To beg I am ashamed. LUKE XVI, 3, *c.* 75

What we are told about the great sums got by begging is not true: the trade is overstocked.
SAMUEL JOHNSON: *Boswell's Life,* Oct. 10, 1779

He who beggeth for others is contriving for himself.
H. G. BOHN: *Handbook of Proverbs,* 1855

As for begging, it is safer to beg than to take, but it is finer to take than to beg.
OSCAR WILDE: *The Soul of Man Under Socialism,* 1891

Better stretch your hand than your neck.
DUTCH PROVERB

What is got by begging is always dear.
ITALIAN PROVERB

Never beg of him who has been a beggar, and never serve him who has been a servant.
SPANISH PROVERB

[*See also* Beggar, Borrowing, Pride.

Beginner

A good man is always a beginner.
MARTIAL: *Epigrams,* I, 86

Beginning

The beginning is half of the whole.
PLATO: *Laws,* V, *c.* 360 B.C. (Cited as a proverb)

The beginnings of all things are small.
CICERO: *De finibus,* V, *c.* 50 B.C.

Well begun is half done.
HORACE: *Epistles,* I, *c.* 5 B.C.

Good beginning maketh good ending.
Anon.: *The Proverbs of Hending, c.* 1300

A hard beginning maketh a good ending.
JOHN HEYWOOD: *Proverbs,* 1546

The beginnings of all things are weak and tender. We must therefore be clear-sighted in beginnings, for, as in their budding we discern not the danger, so in their full growth we perceive not the remedy.
MICHEL DE MONTAIGNE: *Essays,* III, 1588

All things in their beginning are good for something.
GEORGE HERBERT: *Outlandish Proverbs,* 1640

Every beginning is cheerful.
J. W. GOETHE: *Wilhelm Meisters Lehrjahre,* VII, 1795

He that climbs a ladder must begin at the first round.
WALTER SCOTT: *Kenilworth,* VII, 1821

That which the fool does in the end the wise man does in the beginning.
R. C. TRENCH (ARCHBISHOP OF DUBLIN): *Lessons in Proverbs,* 1853

Setting out well is a quarter of the journey.
H. G. BOHN: *Handbook of Proverbs,* 1855

The first hundred years are the hardest.
Saying of the American soldiers in France, 1917–20

All beginnings are hard, said the thief, and began by stealing an anvil.
DUTCH PROVERB

Beginning and end shake hands with each other.
GERMAN PROVERB

Beginning hot, middle lukewarm, end cold.
IBID.

Every beginning is hard. (Aller Anfang ist schwer.)
IBID.

From the beginning. (Ab initio.)
LATIN PHRASE

[*See also* End, Fool.

Behavior

Men's behavior should be like their apparel, not too strait, or point device, but free for exercise or motion.
FRANCIS BACON: *Essays,* LII, 1597

In no case may we interpret an action as the outcome of the exercise of a higher psychical faculty if it can be interpreted as the outcome of the exercise of one which stands lower in the psychological scale.
C. L. MORGAN: *Introduction to Comparative Psychology,* 1894 (Lloyd Morgan's canon)

Behaviorism.
Psychological theory introduced by J. B. WATSON: *Psychology from the Standpoint of the Behaviorist,* 1919

During good behavior. (Quando se bene gesserit.)
LEGAL PHRASE

[*See also* Judge.

Behemoth

[*See* Elephant.

Being

To be, or not to be: that is the question.
SHAKESPEARE: *Hamlet,* III, *c.* 1601

That, that is, is; that, that is not, is not; but that, that is not, is not that that is; nor is that, that is, that that is not.
Author unidentified

Belgian

Patience is the virtue of the Belgian.
BALTASAR GRACIÁN: *The Art of Worldly Wisdom,* CCXLIII, 1647

Belgium

[*See* Netherlands.

Belgrade

[*See* Alliteration.

Belief

We believe whatever we want to believe.
DEMOSTHENES: *Third Olynthiac*, 348 B.C.

He that believeth not shall be damned.
MARK XVI, 16, *c.* 70

I believe it because it is absurd. (Credo, quia absurdum.)
Commonly ascribed to TERTULLIAN; what he actually said (*De Carne Christi*, *c.* 210) was "Et mortuus est Dei Filius; prorsus credibile, quia ineptum est," — And dead is the Son of God: that can be believed only because it is absurd; the saying appears in various forms, e.g., "Credible est, quia ineptum est," and "Certum est, quia impossible est."

If the thing believed is incredible, it is also incredible that the incredible should have been so believed.
ST. AUGUSTINE: *The City of God*, XXII, 427

We believe nothing so firmly as what we least know.
MICHEL DE MONTAIGNE: *Essays*, I, 1580

He that believes all, misseth; he that believes nothing, hits not.
GEORGE HERBERT: *Outlandish Proverbs*, 1640

A man may be a heretic to the truth if he believes things only because his pastor says so, or the assembly so determines, without knowing other reason; though his belief be true, yet the very truth he holds becomes his heresy.
JOHN MILTON: *Areopagitica*, 1644

Confidence in uncertainties is the greatest enemy of what is certain.
JOSEPH GLANVILL: *The Vanity of Dogmatizing*, dedication, 1661

Everyone believes very easily whatever he fears or desires.
JEAN DE LA FONTAINE: *Fables*, XI, 1671

He does not believe that does not live according to his belief.
THOMAS FULLER: *Gnomologia*, 1732

Believe things, rather than man.
BENJAMIN WHICHCOTE: *Moral and Religious Aphorisms*, 1753

Every man who attacks my belief diminishes in some degree my confidence in it, and therefore makes me uneasy, and I am angry with him who makes me uneasy.
SAMUEL JOHNSON: *Boswell's Life*, April 3, 1776

There is a great difference between believing a thing and not being able to believe the contrary. I often come to believe in things without being able to prove them, and to disbelieve in others without being able to disprove them.
G. C. LICHTENBERG: *Reflections*, 1799

I believe because I do believe.
P. B. SHELLEY: *Letter to T. J. Hogg*, Jan. 11, 1811 (Described as his father's "equine argument")

Belief is a passion, or involuntary operation of the mind, and like other passions, its intensity is precisely proportionate to the degrees of excitement.
P. B. SHELLEY: *Queen Mab*, notes, 1813

We do everything by custom, even believe by it; our very axioms, let us boast of freethinking as we may, are oftenest simply such beliefs as we have never heard questioned.
THOMAS CARLYLE: *Sartor Resartus*, III, 1836

A man lives by believing something; not by debating and arguing about many things.
THOMAS CARLYLE: *Heroes and Hero-Worship*, V, 1840 (Lecture in London, May 19)

Believe only half of what you see and nothing that you hear.
DINAH MULOCK CRAIK: *A Woman's Thoughts*, 1858 (Quoted as "a cynical saying")

We are born believing. A man bears beliefs as a tree bears apples.
R. W. EMERSON: *The Conduct of Life*, VI, 1860

All ages of belief have been great; all of unbelief have been mean.
R. W. EMERSON: *The Sovereignty of Ethics*, 1878

What we call rational grounds for our beliefs are often extremely irrational attempts to justify our instincts.
T. H. HUXLEY: *On the Natural Inequality of Man*, 1890

Man can believe the impossible, but man can never believe the improbable.
OSCAR WILDE: *The Decay of Lying*, 1891

No one finds any serious difficulty in attributing the origin of other people's beliefs, especially if he disagree with them, to causes which are not reasons.
A. J. BALFOUR: *The Foundations of Belief*, III, 1895

Whatever one likes to see one likes to believe.
GERMAN PROVERB

Universal belief. (Consensus gentium.)
LATIN PHRASE

Believe you have it, and you have it. (Crede quod habes, et habes.) LATIN PROVERB

The belief of the faithful. (Sensus fidelium.)
MEDIEVAL LATIN PHRASE

[What has been believed] always, everywhere, and by all. (Quod semper, quod ubique, et quod ab omnibus.) IBID.

Believe that you may understand. (Crede ut intelligas.) MEDIEVAL LATIN SAYING

Never tell all that you know, or do all that you can, or believe all that you hear.
PORTUGUESE PROVERB

Only the deaf and the blind have to believe.
RUMANIAN PROVERB

[*See also* Cause and Effect, Credulity, Doubt, Faith, Inconsistency, Lying, Motive, Opinion (Public), Skeptic, Skepticism.

Believer

One in whom persuasion and belief
Had ripened into faith, and faith become
A passionate intuition.
WILLIAM WORDSWORTH: *The Excursion,* IV, 1814

A believer is a songless bird in a cage.
R. G. INGERSOLL: Speech in Chicago, Dec. 21, 1873

The believer is happy; the doubter is wise.
HUNGARIAN PROVERB

[*See also* Classes.

Bell

Like sweet bells jangled, out of tune and harsh.
SHAKESPEARE: *Hamlet,* III, *c.* 1601

How soft the music of those village bells,
Falling at intervals upon the ear
In cadence sweet; now dying all away,
Now pealing loud again, and louder still.
WILLIAM COWPER: *The Task,* VI, 1785

The tocsin of the soul — the dinner bell.
BYRON: *Don Juan,* V, 1821

Those evening bells! those evening bells!
How many a tale their music tells!
THOMAS MOORE: *Those Evening Bells,* *c.* 1825

The bells of Shandon
That sound so grand on
The pleasant waters
Of the river Lee.
F. S. MAHONY (FATHER PROUT): *The Bells of Shandon,* *c.* 1830

Bells are music's laughter.
THOMAS HOOD: *Miss Kilmansegg,* 1840

How they tinkle, tinkle, tinkle,
In the icy air of night,
While the stars that oversprinkle
All the heavens seem to twinkle
With a crystalline delight.
Keeping time, time, time,
In a sort of Runic rhyme
To the tintinnabulation that so musically wells
From the bells, bells, bells, bells,
Bells, bells, bells —
From the jingling and the tingling of the bells.
E. A. POE: *The Bells,* 1849 (Sartain's Union Magazine, Nov.)

Ring out, wild bells, to the wild sky.
ALFRED TENNYSON: *In Memoriam,* CVI, 1850

All the church-bells made a solemn din —
A fire-alarm to those who lived in sin.
AMBROSE BIERCE: *The Devil's Dictionary,* 1906

I mourn death, I disperse the lightning, I announce the Sabbath, I rouse the lazy, I scatter the winds, I appease the bloodthirsty. (Funera plango, fulmina frango, Sabbata pango, Excito lentos, dissipo ventos, paco cruentos.)
Inscription for a bell; date undetermined

[*See also* Alarm, Alliteration, Dinner, Hell.

Belly

Behold, my belly is as wine which hath no vent; it is ready to burst like new bottles.
JOB XXXII, 19, *c.* 325 B.C.

His belly is as bright ivory overlaid with sapphires. SOLOMON'S SONG, V, 14, *c.* 200 B.C.

Meats for the belly, and the belly for meats.
I CORINTHIANS VI, 13, *c.* 55

Whose God is their belly.
PHILLIPPIANS III, 19, *c.* 60

When the belly is full the bones would have rest. ENGLISH PROVERB, traced by Smith to *c.* 1530

A full belly doth not engender a subtle wit.
GEORGE PETTIE: *Civil Conversations of Stefano Guazzo,* 1581

The belly carries the legs, and not the legs the belly.
THOMAS SHELTON: Tr. of CERVANTES: *Don Quixote,* II (1615), 1620

A full belly neither fights nor flies well.
GEORGE HERBERT: *Outlandish Proverbs,* 1640

The eye is bigger than the belly. IBID.

Better belly burst than good liquor be lost.
JAMES HOWELL: *Proverbs,* 1659

The belly robs the back. IBID.

The belly is not filled with fair words.
JOHN RAY: *English Proverbs,* 1670

If it were not for the belly the back might wear gold.
THOMAS FULLER: *Gnomologia,* 1732

He who does not mind his belly will hardly mind anything else.
SAMUEL JOHNSON: *Boswell's Life,* August 5, 1763

Full bellies make empty skulls.
H. G. BOHN: *Handbook of Proverbs,* 1855

The belly is the reason why man does not mistake himself for a god.
F. W. NIETZSCHE: *Beyond Good and Evil,* 1886

The belly gives no credit. DANISH PROVERB

A full belly never studies willingly. (Impletus venter non vult studere libenter.)
LATIN PROVERB

When the belly is full the mind is amongst the maids. SCOTTISH PROVERB

[*See also* Eating, Gluttony, Hunger, Stomach.

Bench

Wooden seats upon which theologians rest their pious posteriors, and often throw at one another's heads in their friendly discussions of theology.
VOLTAIRE: *Philosophical Dictionary,* 1764

Bend

Better bend than break.
H. G. BOHN: *Handbook of Proverbs,* 1855

Benediction

The Lord bless thee, and keep thee; the Lord make His face shine upon thee, and be gracious unto thee; the Lord lift up His countenance upon thee, and give thee peace.
NUMBERS VI, 24–26, *c.* 700 B.C.

Grace be to you, and peace, from God the Father, and from our Lord Jesus Christ.
GALATIANS I, 3, *c.* 50 (Cf. I THESSALONIANS I, 1, *c.* 51; II THESSALONIANS I, 2, *c.* 51; ROMANS I, 7, *c.* 55; I CORINTHIANS I, 3, *c.* 55; II CORINTHIANS I, 2, *c.* 55; EPHESIANS I, 2, *c.* 60; PHILIPPIANS I, 2, *c.* 60; COLOSSIANS I, 2, *c.* 60; PHILEMON 3, *c.* 60)

The grace of our Lord Jesus Christ be with you. Amen.
I THESSALONIANS V, 28, *c.* 51 (Cf. II THESSALONIANS III, 18, *c.* 51; ROMANS XVI, 20, *c.* 55; I CORINTHIANS XVI, 23; *c.* 55; PHILIPPIANS IV, 23, *c.* 60; REVELATION XX, 21, *c.* 95)

The grace of the Lord Jesus Christ, and the love of God, and the communion of the Holy Ghost, be with you all. Amen.
II CORINTHIANS XIII, 14, *c.* 55

Grace be with you.
COLOSSIANS IV, 18, *c.* 60 (Cf. I TIMOTHY VI, 21, *c.* 60; TITUS III, 15, *c.* 60; II TIMOTHY IV, 22, *c.* 65; HEBREWS XIII, 25, *c.* 65)

Grace, mercy and peace, from God our Father, and Jesus Christ our Lord.
I TIMOTHY I, 2, *c.* 60 (Cf. TITUS I, 4, *c.* 60; II TIMOTHY II, 2, *c.* 65; II JOHN 3, *c.* 115)

The gentleness of all the gods go with thee.
SHAKESPEARE: *Twelfth Night,* II, *c.* 1601

[*See also* Benedictus.

Benedictus, The

Blessed be the Lord God of Israel; for he hath visited and redeemed his people.
LUKE I, 68, *c.* 75 (The text runs to v. 79)

Benefit

The high-minded man is fond of conferring benefits, but it shames him to receive them.
ARISTOTLE: *The Nicomachean Ethics,* IV, *c.* 340 B.C.

Let him who bestows the benefit conceal it; let him who receives it reveal it.
SENECA: *De beneficiis,* II, *c.* 63

No one wearies of benefits received.
MARCUS AURELIUS: *Meditations,* VII, *c.* 170

New benefits cannot obliterate old injuries.
NICCOLO MACHIAVELLI: *The Prince,* V, 1513

There is a hook in every benefit, that sticks in his jaws that takes that benefit, and draws him whither the benefactor will.
JOHN DONNE: *LXXX Sermons,* 1640

Benefits please, like flowers, while they are fresh.
GEORGE HERBERT: *Jacula Prudentum,* 1651

One should honor the tree which gives one shade. DUTCH PROVERB

A benefit cannot be conferred upon an unwilling person. (Beneficium invito non datur.)
LEGAL MAXIM

[*See also* Alms, Charity, Giving, Intention, Injury.

Benefit of Clergy

[*See* Clergy, Benefit of

Benevolence

Benevolence is one of the distinguishing characters of man. It is the path of duty.
MENCIUS: *Discourses,* VII, *c.* 300 B.C.

To act from pure benevolence is not possible for finite beings. Human benevolence is mingled with vanity, interest, or some other motive. SAMUEL JOHNSON: *Boswell's Life,* April 26, 1776

I believe . . . that every human mind feels pleasure in doing good to another.
THOMAS JEFFERSON: *Letter to John Adams,* 1816

The most melancholy of human reflections, perhaps, is that, on the whole, it is a question whether the benevolence of mankind does more harm or good.
WALTER BAGEHOT: *Physics and Politics,* 1869

When a man has been highly honored, and has eaten a little, he is most benevolent.
F. W. NIETZSCHE: *Human All-too-Human,* II, 1878

The time-honored thesis of physiotheology, that the sentient world is, on the whole, regulated by principles of benevolence, does but ill

stand the test of impartial confrontation with the facts of the case.
T. H. HUXLEY: *The Struggle for Existence in Human Society*, 1888

[*See also* Alms, Altruism, Charity, Giving, Philanthropy, Politeness.

Bentham, Jeremy (1748–1832)

Jeremy Bentham's skeleton, which is preserved in the library of one of his executors, correctly conveys the idea of a burly-browed utilitarian old gentleman.
HERMAN MELVILLE: *Moby Dick*, LIV, 1851

The arch-philistine Jeremy Bentham was the insipid, pedantic, leather-tongued oracle of the bourgeois intelligence of the Nineteenth Century.
KARL MARX: *Das Kapital*, I, 1867

Bequest

No man should be allowed to bequeath his property to any descendant unborn. What affection can he feel for such an heir? What relationship is there between a man and his grandson?
Ascribed to J. HORNE TOOKE (1736–1812) in G. H. POWELL: *Reminiscences and Table-Talk of Samuel Rogers*, 1903

[*See also* Heir, Testament.

Berlioz, Hector (1803–69)

In Berlioz's music there is something primeval, not to say antidiluvian. It makes me think of gigantic extinct animals, of fabulous empires full of fabulous sins, of heaped-up impossibilities. He is a colossal nightingale, a lark built like an eagle.
HEINRICH HEINE: *Lutezia*, 1854

He says nothing in his music, but says it magnificently.
JAMES HUNEKER: *Old Fogy*, I, 1913

Bermuda

The still-vexed Bermoothes.
SHAKESPEARE: *The Tempest*, I, 1611

Bernard, St. (1091–1153)

St. Bernard was the best monk that ever was, and I love him beyond all the rest put together.
MARTIN LUTHER: *Table-Talk*, CCCCXC, 1569

Best

The best cart may be overthrown.
JOHN HEYWOOD: *Proverbs*, 1546

An egg of one hour old, bread of one day, a goat of one month, wine of six months, flesh of a year, fish of ten years, a wife of twenty years, a friend among a hundred, are the best of all number.
JOHN WODROEPHE: *Spared Hours*, 1623

The best things are worst to come by.
JOHN CLARKE: *Parœmiologia Anglo-Latina*, 1639

The best smell is bread, the best savor salt, the best love that of children.
GEORGE HERBERT: *Outlandish Proverbs*, 1640

All is for the best in the best of possible worlds. (Tout est pour le meiux dans le meilleur des mondes possibles.)
VOLTAIRE: *Candide*, XXX, 1759

The best is good enough. (Das Beste ist gut genug.)
GERMAN PROVERB, apparently derived from a letter dated Naples, March 3, 1787, in J. W. GOETHE's *Italienischer Reise;* but Goethe qualifies it thus: "*In der Kunst* ist das Beste gut genug" — *In the arts* the best is good enough

The best is the enemy of the good.
ENGLISH PROVERB, not recorded before the XIX century

The best go first; the bad remain to men.
H. G. BOHN: *Handbook of Proverbs*, 1855

If he'd a reg'lar task to do,
He never took no rest;
Or if 'twas off-and-on — the same —
He done his level best.
S. L. CLEMENS (MARK TWAIN): *He Done His Level Best*, 1875 (Ascribed to a mythical SIMON WHEELER)

The best is aye the cheapest.
SCOTTISH PROVERB

[*See also* Better, Good, Honey, Hope.

Bethlehem

But thou, Beth-lehem Ephratah, though thou be little among the thousands of Judah, yet out of thee shall come forth unto me that is to be ruler in Israel.
MICAH V, 2, *c.* 700 B.C.

Jesus was born in Bethlehem in the days of Herod the king. MATTHEW II, 1, *c.* 75

O little town of Bethlehem!
How still we see thee lie;
Above thy deep and dreamless sleep
The silent stars go by;
Yet in thy dark streets shineth
The everlasting Light;
The hopes and fears of all the years
Are met in thee tonight.
PHILLIPS BROOKS: *O Little Town of Bethlehem*, 1868

Betrayal

[*See* Traitor.

Better

Good is good, but better carrieth it.
H. G. BOHN: *Handbook of Proverbs*, 1855

Every day, and in every way, I am growing better and better. (Tous les jours, à tous points de vue, je vais de mieux en mieux.)
ÉMILE COUÉ: Healing formula first announced *c.* 1910

The better is the enemy of the good.
FRENCH PROVERB

[*See also* Best.

Betters

[*See* Bold.

Betting

I've heard old cunning stagers
Say fools for arguments use wagers.
SAMUEL BUTLER: *Hudibras*, II, 1664

Most men (till by losing rendered sager)
Will back their own opinions by a wager.
BYRON: *Beppo*, 1818

Put up or shut up. AMERICAN SAYING

The race is not always to the swift nor the battle to the strong — but that's the way to bet.
Author unidentified

[*See also* Gambling.

Bible

Thy word is a lamp unto my feet, and a light unto my path.
PSALMS CXIX, 105, *c.* 150 B.C.

What saith the Scripture?
GALATIANS IV, 30, *c.* 50 (Also in ROMANS IV, 3, *c.* 55)

Wot ye not what the Scripture saith?
ROMANS XI, 2, *c.* 55

No prophecy of the Scripture is of any private interpretation. For the prophecy came not in old time by the will of man: but holy men of God spake as they were moved by the Holy Ghost. II PETER I, 20–21, *c.* 60

All Scripture is given by inspiration of God, and is profitable for doctrine, for reproof, for correction, for instruction in righteousness. II TIMOTHY III, 16, *c.* 65

Search the Scriptures. JOHN V, 39, *c.* 115

The Scriptures of God, whether belonging to Christian or Jew, are much more ancient than any secular literature.
TERTULLIAN: *The Testimony of the Christian Soul*, *c.* 210

The Bible is a stream wherein the elephant may swim and the lamb may wade.
POPE GREGORY THE GREAT (*c.* 540–604)

There can be no falsehood anywhere in the literal sense of Holy Scripture.
ST. THOMAS AQUINAS: *Summa theologicæ*, I, *c.* 1265

Christ is the Master; the Scriptures are only the servant. The true way to test all the Books is to see whether they work the will of Christ or not. No Book which does not preach Christ can be apostolic, though Peter or Paul were its author. And no Book which does preach Christ can fail to be apostolic, though Judas, Ananias, Pilate or Herod were its author.
MARTIN LUTHER: Intro. to his German tr. of the New Testament, 1522

Oh, that pestilent book! Never on it more look —
I wish I could sing it out louder — ;
It has done men more harm, I dare boldly affirm,
Than th' invention of guns and of powder.
Anon.: *The Catholick Ballad*, *c.* 1550

If anyone receive not, as sacred and canonical, the said books entire with all their parts as they have been read in the Catholic Church, and as they are contained in the Vulgate, let him be anathema.
DECREES OF THE COUNCIL OF TRENT, III, 1564

I have always had a Bible in my parlor these many years, and ofttimes when the weather hath been foul, and that I have had no other book to read on, and have wanted company to play at cards or at tables with me, I have read in those books.
JOHN HARINGTON: *The Metamorphosis of Ajax*, 1596

Brown bread and the Gospels is good fare.
ENGLISH PURITAN SAYING, *c.* 1600

The Bible only is the religion of Protestants.
WILLIAM CHILLINGWORTH: *The Religion of Protestants a Safe Way to Salvation*, 1637

Jest not with the two-edged sword of God's word.
THOMAS FULLER: *The Holy State and the Profane State*, 1642

This is a work too hard for the teeth of time, and cannot perish but in the general flames, when all things shall confess their ashes.
THOMAS BROWNE: *Religio Medici*, I, 1642

I have sometimes seen more in a line of the Bible than I could well tell how to stand under, and yet at another time the whole Bible hath been to me as dry as a stick.
JOHN BUNYAN: *Grace Abounding to the Chief of Sinners*, 1666

Objection: The Bible is full of matters that were plainly not dictated by the Holy Spirit. *Answer:* Then they do no harm to faith. *Objection:* But the Church has decided that the whole Bible is of the Holy Spirit. *Answer:* First, the Church has not so decided; second, if it should so decide, it could be maintained. BLAISE PASCAL: *Pensées*, IV, 1670

The only objection against the Bible is a bad life.
THE EARL OF ROCHESTER: *Last words*, 1680

How glad the heathen would have been,
  That worship idols, wood and stone,
If they the book of God had seen,
  Or Jesus and His Gospel know.

ISAAC WATTS: *Hymns and Spiritual Songs,* 1707

The Scriptures are undoubtedly a fund of wit, and a subject for wit. You may, according to the modern practise, be witty upon them, or out of them.

JONATHAN SWIFT: *A Letter of Advice to a Young Poet,* Dec. 1, 1720

Sir, if the Bible be not true, I am as very a fool and madman as you can conceive; but if it be of God I am sober-minded.

JOHN WESLEY: To a friend, on sailing for Georgia, 1735

Fear is the denomination of the Old Testament; belief is the denomination of the New.

BENJAMIN WHICHCOTE: *Moral and Religious Aphorisms,* 1753

Nothing is of faith that is not in Scripture.

IBID.

I am a Bible-bigot. I follow it in all things, both great and small.

JOHN WESLEY: *Journal,* June 2, 1766

I believe that the time will come when the Old and New Testaments will be no longer necessary, and though human progress is slow, nevertheless I expect it to come every day.

G. H. LESSING: *Die Erziehung des Menschengeschlechts,* 1780

Whenever we read the obscene stories, the voluptuous debaucheries, the cruel and tortuous executions, the unrelenting vindictiveness, with which more than half the Bible is filled, it would be more consistent that we called it the word of a demon than the word of God. It is a history of wickedness that has served to corrupt and brutalize mankind.

THOMAS PAINE: *The Age of Reason,* I, 1794

I have made it a practice for several years to read the Bible through in the course of every year. I usually devote to this reading the first hour after I rise every morning.

JOHN QUINCY ADAMS: *Diary,* Sept. 26, 1810

A book is put into our hands when children, called the Bible, the purport of whose history is briefly this: That God made the earth in six days, and there planted a delightful garden, in which He placed the first pair of human beings. In the midst of the garden He planted a tree, whose fruit, although within their reach, they were forbidden to touch. That the Devil, in the shape of a snake, persuaded them to eat of this fruit; in consequence of which God condemned both them and their posterity yet unborn to satisfy His justice by their eternal misery. That, four thousand years after these events (the human race in the meantime having gone unredeemed to perdition), God engendered with the betrothed wife of a carpenter in Judea (whose virginity was nevertheless uninjured), and begat a son, whose name was Jesus Christ; and who was crucified and died, in order that no more men might be devoted to hell-fire, He bearing the burthen of His Father's displeasure by proxy. The book states, in addition, that the soul of whoever disbelieves this sacrifice will be burned with everlasting fire.

P. B. SHELLEY: *Queen Mab,* notes, 1813

Within this awful volume lies
The mystery of mysteries!
Happiest they of human race,
To whom God has granted grace
To read, to fear, to hope, to pray,
To lift the latch, and force the way:
And better had they ne'er been born,
Who read to doubt, or read to scorn.

WALTER SCOTT: *The Monastery,* XII, 1820

In gay countries the Bible is little read, and there is gallantry.

M. H. BEYLE (STENDHAL): *De l'amour,* 1822

The English Bible [is] a book which, if everything else in our language should perish, would alone suffice to show the whole extent of its beauty and power.

T. B. MACAULAY: *John Dryden,* 1828 (Edinburgh Review, Jan.)

Because that ye have a Bible ye need not suppose that it contains all my words; neither need ye suppose that I have not caused more to be written.

The Book of Mormon (II NEPHI XXIX, 10), 1830

Intense study of the Bible will keep any writer from being vulgar in point of style.

S. T. COLERIDGE: *Table-Talk,* June 14, 1830

A person who professes to be a critic in the delicacies of the English language ought to have the Bible at his fingers' ends.

T. B. MACAULAY: *Letter to his sister,* May 30, 1831

I believe in it first, because I am Bishop of Autun; and, secondly, because I know nothing about it at all.

Ascribed to C. M. TALLEYRAND (1754–1838)

The Bible is a book of faith, and a book of doctrine, and a book of morals, and a book of religion, of especial revelation from God.

DANIEL WEBSTER: Address on the completion of the Bunker Hill Monument, June 17, 1843

Foul shame and scorn be on ye all
  Who turn the good to evil,
And steal the Bible from the Lord
  And give it to the Devil.

J. G. WHITTIER: *A Sabbath Scene,* 1850

The Bible is a respectable book, but I should hardly call it one whose philosophy is of the soundest. All truth, especially historic truth, requires cool, dispassionate investigation, for which the Jews do not appear to have ever been famous.

GEORGE BORROW: *Lavengro*, XXIII, 1851

The Bible is the most betrashed book in the world. Coming to it through commentaries is much like looking at a landscape through garret windows, over which generations of unmolested spiders have spun their webs.

H. W. BEECHER: *Life Thoughts*, 1858

Jesus loves me — this I know,
For the Bible tells me so.

SUSAN WARNER: *The Love of Jesus*, 1860

This great book . . . is the best gift God has given to man . . . But for it we could not know right from wrong.

ABRAHAM LINCOLN: To a colored delegation come to give him a Bible, Aug., 1864

We, the undersigned presbyters and deacons in holy orders in the Church of England and Ireland, feel it to be our bounden duty to the Church and to the souls of men to declare our firm belief that the Church, in common with the whole Catholic Church, maintains without reserve or qualification the inspiration and authority of the whole of the canonical Scriptures as not only containing, but being the word of God.

Manifesto drawn up by E. B. PUSEY in answer to *Essays and Reviews*, by FREDERICK TEMPLE, ROWLAND WILLIAMS, H. B. WILSON, BENJAMIN JOWETT and others (1860), and signed by 11,000 clergymen, 1864

We anathematize all who do not receive as sacred and canonical the books of Holy Scripture in their integrity, with all their parts, as enumerated by the Holy Council of Trent, or who may deny that they are divinely inspired.

DECREE OF THE VATICAN COUNCIL, 1870

The language of the Bible is literary, not scientific language; language thrown out at an object of consciousness not fully grasped, which inspired emotion.

MATTHEW ARNOLD: *Literature and Dogma*, I, 1873

The Bible is like an old Cremona; it has been played upon by the devotion of thousands of years until every word and particle is public and tunable.

R. W. EMERSON: *Letters and Social Aims*, 1876

A competent religious guide must be clear and intelligible to all, so that every one may fully understand the true meaning of the instructions it contains. Is the Bible a book intelligible to all? Far from it; it is full of obscurities and difficulties not only for the illiterate, but even for the learned.

JAMES CARDINAL GIBBONS: *The Faith of Our Fathers*, VIII, 1876

The B–I–B–L–E,
That's the book for me;
The B–I–B,
Oh, the B–I–B;
Oh, the B–I–B–L–E!

Methodist hymn, *c.* 1880

The inspiration of the Bible depends upon the ignorance of the gentleman who reads it.

R. G. INGERSOLL: Speech in New York, April 25, 1881

The dogma of the infallibility of the Bible is no more self-evident than is that of the infallibility of the popes.

T. H. HUXLEY: *Controverted Questions*, 1892

It will never be lawful to restrict inspiration merely to certain portions of the Holy Scriptures, or to grant that the sacred writers could have made mistakes . . . They render in exact language, with infallible truth, all that God commanded, and nothing else.

POPE LEO XIII: *Providentissumus Deus*, 1893

We gratefully receive the Holy Scriptures, given by inspiration, to be the faithful record of God's gracious revelations and the sure witness to Christ, as the Word of God, the only infallible rule of faith and life.

Statement of the Reformed Faith by the General Assembly of the Presbyterian Church in the U. S. A., May 22, 1902

I believe the Bible as it is.

W. J. BRYAN: At the Scopes trial, Dayton, Tenn., July 21, 1925

It takes a long tall yaller brown
To make a preacher lay his Bible down.

American Negro song, quoted by HOWARD W. ODUM: *Wings On My Feet*, I, 1929

The common assumption, hardly disputed even now, that the moral influence of the Bible has been wholly good, and that all that is needed to improve our society is to "spread the gospel," is not borne out by a candid study of history.

PRESERVED SMITH: *A History of Modern Culture*, I, 1930

The Holy Scriptures contain all things necessary to salvation; so that whatsoever is not read therein, nor may be proved thereby, is not to be required requisite or necessary to salvation.

The Doctrines and Discipline of the Methodist Episcopal Church, I, 1932

The German people need no Bible. The Edda and the Sagas, Master Ekkehart and Frederick the Great, Goethe and Schiller, Hoelderlin and Nietzsche and many other great Germans were no Christians; they believed in life, in Nature and in the power of the German soul.

BUSSO LOEWE: *Creed of the German Pagan Movement*, 1936

The whole of the Bible is inspired, but we cannot venture to describe the mode or method of this inspiration, but accept it as a fact of which faith assures us.
Declaration of the United Lutheran Church in America, Oct. 11, 1938

The Bible and a stone do well together: if one misses the other hits. WELSH PROVERB

[*See also* Books, Deism, Devil, Evolution, Gentleman, Gospel, Hell, Heretic, Language, Library, Missionary, Novel, People, War.

Bibliography

[*See* Books.

Bibliomania

To desire to have many books, and never use them, is like the child that will have a candle burning by him all the while he is sleeping.
HENRY PEACHAM: *The Compleat Gentleman,* 1622

Bibliomania, or the collecting an enormous heap of books without intelligent curiosity, has, since libraries have existed, infected weak minds.
ISAAC D'ISRAELI: *Curiosities of Literature,* I, 1793

[*See also* Books, Collector, Library.

Bibliophile

[*See* Bibliomania, Collector.

Bigot

Whenever you find a little interested bustling bigot, do not hate him, do not imitate him; pity him if you can.
JOHN PHILPOT CURRAN: Speech at Newry, Ireland, 1812

[*See also* Atheist.

Bigotry

All bigotries hang to one another.
THOMAS JEFFERSON: *Letter to John Adams,* 1814

Bigotry murders religion, to frighten fools with her ghost. C. C. COLTON: *Lacon,* 1820

I am not fond of bigots myself, because they are not fond of me. But what is meant by bigotry, that we should regard it as a blemish in a priest?
R. L. STEVENSON: *Letter to the Rev. C. M. Hyde,* Feb. 25, 1890

Big Stick

[*See* Stick.

Bile

[*See* Liver.

Billiards

Let's to billiards.
SHAKESPEARE: *Antony and Cleopatra,* II, *c.* 1606

To play billiards well is a sign of a misspent youth. Author unidentified

Billion

This is a billion dollar country.
Ascribed variously to THOMAS B. REED and to CHARLES FOSTER (It was a reply to complaints that the Fifty-first was a billion-dollar Congress)

Bimetallism

The Republican party is in favor of the use of both gold and silver as money, and condemns the policy of the Democratic administration in its efforts to demonetize silver.
Republican National Platform, 1888

We hold to the use of both gold and silver as the standard money of the country.
Democratic National Platform, 1892

We demand the free and unlimited coinage of both silver and gold at the present legal ratio of 16 to 1, without waiting for the aid or consent of any other nation.
Democratic National Platform, 1896

We are unalterably opposed to every measure calculated to debase our currency or impair the credit of our country. We are, therefore, opposed to the free coinage of silver except by international agreement with the leading commercial nations of the world, which we pledge ourselves to promote, and until such agreement can be obtained, the existing gold standard must be preserved.
Republican National Platform, 1896

Bind and Loose

[*See* Absolution.

Biographer

[*See* Admiration, Boswell (James).

Biography

There has rarely passed a life of which a judicious and faithful narrative would not be useful.
SAMUEL JOHNSON: *The Rambler,* Oct. 13, 1750

They only who live with a man can write his life with any genuine exactness and discrimination; and few people who have lived with a man know what to remark about him.
SAMUEL JOHNSON: *Boswell's Life,* March 20, 1776

A well-written life is almost as rare as a well-spent one.
THOMAS CARLYLE: *J. P. F. Richter,* 1827

Biography is the only true history.
THOMAS CARLYLE: *Journal,* Jan. 13, 1832

There is no heroic poem in the world but is at bottom a biography, the life of a man; also, it may be said, there is no life of a man, faithfully recorded, but is a heroic poem of its sort, rhymed or unrhymed.
THOMAS CARLYLE: *Sir Walter Scott,* 1838

Let there be nothing of this when I am gone.
W. M. THACKERAY: On reading *Memorials of Thomas Hood,* by his daughter, 1860

There are few less exhilarating books than the biographies of men of letters, and of artists generally; and this arises from the pictures of comparative defeat which, in almost every instance, such books contain.
ALEXANDER SMITH: *Dreamthorp,* VII, 1863

In a biography this and that is displayed; the hero is seen at home, playing the flute; the different tendencies of his work come, one after another, into notice; and then something like a true, general impression of the subject may at last be struck.
R. L. STEVENSON: *Familiar Studies of Men and Books,* pref., 1882

Every great man nowadays has his disciples, and it is always Judas who writes the biography.
OSCAR WILDE: *The Critic as Artist,* 1891

There are now three projects on foot to serve me up and help people to breast or dark meat, with or without stuffing.
GROVER CLEVELAND: *Letter to R. W. Gilder,* Nov. 20, 1896

Biographies should be a man's conversation, not his deeds.
GEORGE MOORE: *To Philip Gosse,* 1932

[*See also* Autobiography.

Biped

[*See* Man.

Bird

In vain the net is spread in the sight of any bird. PROVERBS I, 17, *c.* 350 B.C.

A bird of the air shall carry the voice, and that which hath wings shall tell the matter.
ECCLESIASTES X, 20, *c.* 200 B.C.

A rare bird. (Rara avis.)
JUVENAL: *Satires,* VI, 116

Dost thou not perceive that all creatures both in Heaven and earth prize God, and the birds also, extending their wings?
THE KORAN, XXIV, *c.* 625

A bird in the hand is worth two in the bush.
ENGLISH PROVERB, borrowed from the Greek, and familiar since the XV century (Sometimes *wood* was substituted for *bush* and the number was set at three or ten)

Birds of a feather flock together.
ENGLISH PROVERB, borrowed from the Greek and traced by Apperson to 1578

I had a little bird that brought me news of it.
BRIAN MELBANCKE: *Philotimus,* 1583

There are no birds of this year in last year's nests.
THOMAS SHELTON: Tr. of CERVANTES: *Don Quixote,* II (1615), 1620

Behold the merry minstrels of the morn,
The swarming songsters of the careless grove,
Ten thousand throats that, from the flowering thorn,
Hymn their good God and carol sweet of love.
JAMES THOMSON: *The Castle of Indolence,* II, 1748

Even when a bird walks we see that it has wings. A. M. LEMIERRE: *Fastes, c.* 1775

Birds act by instinct, and ne'er can
Attain the rectitude of man.
MARY LAMB: *The Rook and the Sparrows,* 1809

All the little birds had laid their heads
Under their wings — sleeping in feather beds.
THOMAS HOOD: *Blanca's Dream,* 1827

A bird knows nothing of gladness,
Is only a song machine.
GEORGE MACDONALD: *A Book of Dreams,* II, *c.* 1860

The little birds in the forest, they sing, sing, sing so wondrously beautifully. (Die Vöglein im Walde, die sang', sang', sang' so wunder, wunderschön.)
Anon.: *Die Vöglein im Walde* (The song was popular among the German soldiers at the beginning of the War of 1914–18. Its date is unknown)

If birds knew how poor they are they wouldn't sing so sweetly. DANISH PROVERB

God gives to every bird its proper food, but they must all fly for it. DUTCH PROVERB

Birds of prey do not sing. GERMAN PROVERB

Bonny birds are aye the warst singers.
SCOTTISH PROVERB

Every bird knows its mate.
WELSH PROVERB

[*See also* Birth, Blind, Cat, Home, Like, Old, Possession, Worth.

Birth

Behold, I was shapen in iniquity; and in sin did my mother conceive me.
PSALMS LI, 5, *c.* 150 B.C.

When I was born I drew in the common air, and fell upon the earth, which is of like nature, and the first voice which I uttered was crying, as all others do.
WISDOM OF SOLOMON VII, 3, *c.* 100 B.C.

Man alone, at the moment of his birth, is cast naked upon the naked earth.
PLINY THE ELDER: *Natural History,* VII, 77

My mother cried; but then there was a star danced, and under that I was born.
SHAKESPEARE: *Much Ado About Nothing,* II, *c.* 1599

When we are born we cry that we are come
To this great stage of fools.
SHAKESPEARE: *King Lear,* IV, 1606

Great births are hard in the labor, and many glorious men have been cut out of the womb.
JOHN HALL: *The Dissolution of the Late Parliament,* 1653

My mother groan'd, my father wept;
Into the dangerous world I leapt,
Helpless, naked, piping loud,
Like a fiend hid in a cloud.
WILLIAM BLAKE: *Infant Sorrow, c.* 1793

Our birth is but a sleep and a forgetting;
The soul that rises with us, our life's star,
Hath had elsewhere its setting,
And cometh from afar:
Not in entire forgetfulness,
And not in utter nakedness,
But trailing clouds of glory do we come
From God, who is our home.
WILLIAM WORDSWORTH: *Intimations of Immortality,* 1807

Death we can face, but knowing, as some of us do, what is human life, which of us is it that, without shuddering, should (if consciously we were summoned) face the hour of birth?
THOMAS DE QUINCEY: *Suspiria de Profundis,* II, 1845

The he-birds carol mornings and evenings, while the she-birds sit on their nests,
The young of poultry break through the hatch'd eggs,
The new-born of animals appear — the calf is dropt from the cow, the colt from the mare,
Out of its little hill faithfully rise the potato's dark leaves.
WALT WHITMAN: *This Compost,* 1856

[*See also* Accident, Childbirth, Day, Life, Naked, Sunday.

Birth and Death

We begin to die at birth; the end flows from the beginning.
MARCUS MANILIUS: *Astronomica,* IV, *c.* 40 B.C.

If thou grievest for the dead, mourn also for those who are born into the world; for as the one thing is of nature, so is the other too of nature.
ST. JOHN CHRYSOSTOM: *Homily* VI, *c.* 388

It is natural to die as to be born, and to a little infant perhaps the one is as painful as the other.
FRANCIS BACON: *Essays,* II, 1625

The first breath is the beginning of death.
THOMAS FULLER: *Gnomologia,* 1732

We are born crying, live complaining, and die disappointed.
IBID.

The coffin is the cradle's brother.
GERMAN PROVERB

[*See also* Birth, Death.

Birth-Control

Prevention of birth is premature murder, and it makes no difference whether it is a life already born that one snatches away or a life that is coming to birth.
TERTULLIAN: *The Christian's Defence, c.* 215

Everyone should remember that the union of the two sexes is meant only for the purpose of procreation.
LACTANTIUS: *Divinae institutiones,* VI, *c.* 310

Intercourse with even a lawful wife is unlawful and wicked if the conception of offspring be prevented.
ST. AUGUSTINE: *Conjugal Adultery,* II, *c.* 400

Nuptial commerce, which is so holy, just, and commendable in itself, and so profitable to the commonwealth, is, nevertheless, in certain cases dangerous to those that exercise it, as when the order appointed for the procreation of children is violated and perverted; in which case, according as one departs more or less from it, the sins are more or less abominable, but always mortal.
ST. FRANCIS DE SALES: *Introduction to the Devout Life,* XXXIX, 1609

If government knew how, I should like to see it check, not multiply the population. When it reaches its true law of action, every man that is born will be hailed as essential.
R. W. EMERSON: *The Conduct of Life,* VII, 1860

The most revolutionary invention of the Nineteenth Century was the artificial sterilization of marriage.
GEORGE BERNARD SHAW: *Maxims for Revolutionists,* 1903

Wilful sterility is, from the standpoint of the human race, the one sin for which the penalty is national death, race death; a sin for which there is no atonement.
THEODORE ROOSEVELT: Message to Congress, Dec. 3, 1906

Since the conjugal act is designed primarily by nature for the begetting of children, those who in exercising it deliberately frustrate its natural power and purpose sin against nature and commit a deed which is shameful and intrinsically vicious.
POPE PIUS XI: *Casti connubii,* 1930

Those are not considered as acting against nature who, in the married state, use their right in the proper manner, even though, on account of natural reasons, either of time or of defect, new life cannot be brought forth.

IBID.

The state must distinguish between the right to live and the right to give life.

H. F. K. GÜNTHER: *Volk und Staat,* 1933

[*See also* Abortion, Malthusianism.

Birthday

Our birthdays are feathers in the broad wing of time.

JEAN PAUL RICHTER: *Titan,* XLVII, 1803

Disapproving of transferring the honors and veneration for the great birthday of our Republic to any individual, or of dividing them with individuals, I have declined letting my own birthday be known, and have engaged my family not to communicate it.

THOMAS JEFFERSON: *Letter to Levi Lincoln,* Aug., 1803

Monday's child is fair in face,
Tuesday's child is full of grace,
Wednesday's child is full of woe,
Thursday's child has far to go,
Friday's child is loving and giving,
Saturday's child works hard for its living;
And a child that's born on Christmas Day,
Is fair and wise, and good and gay.

J. O. HALLIWELL-PHILLIPS: *Nursery Rhymes and Nursery Tales of England,* 1845

Born on Monday, fair in the face;
Born on Tuesday, full of God's grace;
Born on Wednesday, sour and sad;
Born on Thursday, merry and glad;
Born on Friday, worthily given;
Born on Saturday, work hard for your living;
Born on Sunday, you will never know want.

Another version

Sunday's child is full of grace,
Monday's child is fair in the face,
Tuesday's child is solemn and sad,
Wednesday's child is merry and glad,
Thursday's child is inclined to thieving,
Friday's child is free in giving,
Saturday's child works hard for his living.

IBID.

[*See also* Days.

Birth, Gentle

[*See* Manners.

Birth, High

The nearer high birth approaches royalty, the more grandeur enslaves the man.

PIERRE CORNEILLE: *Rodogune,* III, 1646

Men do not choose among navigators the one who is of highest birth to command a ship.

BLAISE PASCAL: *Pensées,* VI, 1670

Prodigious actions may as well be done
By weaver's issue, as by prince's son.

JOHN DRYDEN: *Absalom and Achitophel,* I, 1682

It is fortunate to be of high birth, but it is no less so to be of such character that people do not care to know whether you are or are not.

JEAN DE LA BRUYÈRE: *Caractères,* II, 1688

Were the genealogy of every family preserved there would probably be no man valued or despised on account of his birth. There is scarce a beggar in the streets who would not find himself lineally descended from some great man.

Author unidentified: *The Spectator,* Oct. 27, 1714

The noblest mortal, in his entrance on to the stage of life, is not distinguished by any pomp or of passage from the lowest of mankind.

JOHN WISE: *A Vindication of the Government of New England Churches,* II, 1717

High birth is mere accident, and not virtue; for if reason had controlled birth, and given empire only to the worthy, perhaps Arabaces would have been Xerxes, and Xerxes Arabaces.

PIETRO METASTASIO: *Artaserse,* I, 1730

The noble lord cannot look before him, behind him, or on either side of him without seeing some noble peer who owes his seat in this House to his successful exertions in the profession to which I belong. Does he not feel that it is as honorable to owe it to these as to being the accident of an accident?

LORD THURLOW: Speech in the House of Lords in reply to the Duke of Grafton, 1769

Some decent regulated preëminence, some preference (not exclusive appropriation) given to birth, is neither unnatural, nor unjust, nor impolitic.

EDMUND BURKE: *Reflections on the Revolution in France,* III, 1790

The son imbibes a portion of the intelligence, refinement and habits of the father, and he shares in his associations. These must be enumerated as the legitimate advantages of birth, and without invading the private arrangements of families and individuals, and establishing a perfect community of education, they are unavoidable.

J. FENIMORE COOPER: *The American Democrat,* XVI, 1838

[*See also* Ancestry, Aristocracy, Blood, Breeding, Generosity, Heredity, Heritage, Nobility, Pride, Rank, Wealth.

Birthplace

I remember, I remember,
The house where I was born,

The little window where the sun
Came peeping in at morn.

THOMAS HOOD: *I Remember*, 1826

Birthright

Jacob said, Sell me this day thy birthright: . . . and [Esau] sold his birthright unto Jacob. Then Jacob gave Esau bread and pottage of lentiles; and he did eat and drink, and rose up, and went his way.

GENESIS XXV, 31–34, *c.* 700 B.C. (The phrase, "a mess of pottage," does not occur in the text. It appeared as a chapter heading in Thomas Matthew's English Bible of 1537 and in the Geneva Bible of 1560, but was not taken into the Authorized Version of 1611)

Bishop

And I said, Let them set a fair mitre upon his head. So they set a fair mitre upon his head, and clothed him with garments. And the angel of the Lord stood by.

ZECHARIAH III, 5, *c.* 520 B.C.

A bishop . . . must be blameless, the husband of one wife, vigilant, sober, of good behavior, given to hospitality, apt to teach; not given to wine, no striker, not greedy of filthy lucre; but patient, not a brawler, not covetous; one that ruleth well his own house, having his children in subjection with all gravity.

I TIMOTHY III, 2–4, *c.* 60

A bishop must be blameless, as the steward of God; not self-willed, not soon angry, not given to wine, no striker, not given to filthy lucre; but a lover of hospitality, a lover of good men, sober, just, holy, temperate.

TITUS I, 7–8, *c.* 60

Bishops burn who they list, and whosoever displeaseth them.

WILLIAM TYNDALE: *Obedience of a Christian Man*, 1528

When a thing speedeth not well we borrow speech and say "the bishop hath blessed it," because that nothing speedeth well that they meddle withal.

IBID.

Bishops shall not preach upon subtle and difficult questions which do not tend to edification, and the discussion of which cannot augment piety and devotion.

DECREE OF THE COUNCIL OF TRENT, XXV, 1564

A bishop should die preaching.

JOHN JEWEL (BISHOP OF SALISBURY): On his deathbed, 1571

They been clad in purple and pall,
So hath their God them blest;
They reign and rulen over all
And lord it as they list.

EDMUND SPENSER: *The Shepherd's Calendar*, VII, 1579

A bishop ought to die on his legs.

JOHN WOOLTON (BISHOP OF EXETER): On his deathbed, 1594

No bishop, no king.

Ascribed to JAMES I of England (1566–1625)

Weals him and woes him that has a bishop among his kin.

DAVID FERGUSSON: *Scottish Proverbs*, 1641

Were the punishment and misery of being a prelate bishop terminated only in the person, and did not extend to the affliction of the whole diocese, if I would wish anything in the bitterness of soul to mine enemy, I would wish him the biggest and fattest bishopric.

JOHN MILTON: *An Apology for Smectymunus*, 1642

The bishop is in the nature of an ecclesiastical sheriff.

MR. CHIEF JUSTICE NORTH: *Judgment in Walwyn* vs. *Awberry*, 1678

For a bishop to preach, 'tis to do other folks' office, as if the steward of the house should execute the porter's or the cook's place. 'Tis his business to see that they and all other about the house perform their duties.

JOHN SELDON: *Table-Talk*, 1689

People may go to church together, and be all of one mind as much as they please, I am apt to believe that when they pray for their daily bread, the bishop includes several things in that petition which the sexton does not think on.

BERNARD MANDEVILLE: *The Fable of the Bees*, I, 1714

In their corporate capacity the bishops, like the pope, have the right to articles of faith. But individually, their sole duty is to dispense with the observation of those articles.

C. L. DE MONTESQUIEU: *Persian Letters*, XXIX, 1721

Old Latimer preaching did fairly describe
A bishop, who rul'd all the rest of his tribe:
And who is this bishop? and where does he dwell?
Why truly 'tis Satan, archbishop of Hell.
And he was a primate and he wore a mitre
Surrounded with jewels of sulphur and nitre.

JONATHAN SWIFT: *On the Irish Bishops*, 1731

The power and authority of a bishop . . . consist principally in inspecting the manners of the people and clergy, and punishing them in order to reformation, by ecclesiastical censures.

WILLIAM BLACKSTONE: *Commentaries on the Laws of England*, I, 1765

If improper bishops be made that is not the fault of the bishops, but of those who make them.

SAMUEL JOHNSON: *Boswell's Life*, March 31, 1772

A bishop should not go to a house where he may meet a young fellow leading out a wench.

SAMUEL JOHNSON: *Boswell's Life*, March 19, 1781

If the bishops are driven from their palaces they will take refuge in the hovels of the poor that they have fed. If their crosses of gold are taken from them, they will take up crosses of wood. It was a cross of wood that saved the world.
Ascribed to BISHOP MONTLOSIER (The occasion was the threat of the French Revolutionary Tribunal to seize all the property of the Church, 1793)

How can a bishop marry? How can he flirt? The most he can say is, " I will see you in the vestry after service."
Ascribed to SYDNEY SMITH in *A Memoir of the Rev. Sydney Smith* by his daughter, Lady Holland, 1855

The Bishop of —— is so like Judas that I now firmly believe in the apostolical succession.
IBID.

[An English] bishop is only a surpliced merchant. Through his lawn I can see the bright buttons of the shopman's coat.
R. W. EMERSON: *English Traits*, XIII, 1856

On the decease of a bishop, whatever may be the general advantages of simony, do we (yet) offer his diocese to the clergyman who will take the episcopacy at the lowest contract?
JOHN RUSKIN: *Unto This Last*, I, 1862

Nearly all the evils in the church have arisen from bishops desiring power more than light; they want authority, not outlook.
JOHN RUSKIN: *Sesame and Lilies*, 1865

It was a bishop bold,
And London was his see,
He was short and stout and round about,
And zealous as could be.
W. S. GILBERT: *Bab Ballads*, 1869

Making a man a bishop really does not in the smallest degree augment such title to respect as his opinions may intrinsically possess.
T. H. HUXLEY: *On the Hypothesis that Animals Are Automata*, 1874

And bishops in their shovel hats
Were plentiful as tabby cats —
In point of fact, too many.
W. S. GILBERT: *The Gondoliers*, II, 1889

So she came up to the city
For to hide her bloody shame,
But she met a bloated bishop
And again she lost her name.
Anon.: *She Was Poor but She Was Honest* (Sung by British soldiers, 1914–18)

I am the president of a firm dealing in spiritual life, whose days are spent auditing books and hiring and firing the personnel.
An unidentified Roman Catholic bishop, quoted in the *Commonweal*, Aug. 16, 1935

Everything suffers by translation except a bishop.
Author unidentified

Bishop of gold, staff of wood; staff of gold, bishop of wood.
FRENCH PROVERB

[*See also* Adultery, American, Archbishop, Celibacy, Clergy, Clergyman, Democracy, Dog, Monk, Patient, Prelate, Priest, Temptation.

Bite

[*See* Dog, Poison.

Black

Black and blue.
ENGLISH PHRASE, in common use since the XIV century

As black as a crow.
ENGLISH PHRASE, traced by Smith to *c.* 1320

Black will take no other hue.
JOHN HEYWOOD: *Proverbs*, 1546

All the water in the ocean
Can never turn the swan's black legs to white.
SHAKESPEARE: *Titus Adronicus*, IV, 1594

Though I am black, I am not the Devil.
ROBERT GREENE: *Quips for an Upstart Courtier*, 1592

A black man is a jewel in a fair woman's eye.
JOHN RAY: *English Proverbs*, 1670

Two blacks make no white.
JAMES KELLY: *Complete Collection of Scottish Proverbs*, 1721

[*See also* African, Color, Hell, Negro, Recrimination.

Blackbird

[*See* Pie.

Blackguard

[*See* English, Keats (John).

Black Sea

There's not a sea the passenger e'er pukes in,
Turns up more dangerous breakers than the Euxine.
BYRON: *Don Juan*, V, 1821

Blacksmith

And he sang: " Hurra for my handiwork! "
And the red sparks lit the air;
Not alone for the blade was the bright steel made;
And he fashioned the first plough-share.
CHARLES MACKAY: *Tubal Cain*, *c.* 1840

Under a spreading chestnut tree
The village smithy stands;
The smith, a mighty man is he,
With large and sinewy hands;
And the muscles of his brawny arms
Are strong as iron bands.
H. W. LONGFELLOW: *The Village Blacksmith*, 1841

Blackstone, William (1723–80)

Blackstone and Hume have made Tories of all England, and are making Tories of those young Americans whose native feelings of independence do not place them above the wily sophistries of a Hume or a Blackstone.
THOMAS JEFFERSON: *Letter to Horatio G. Spafford,* 1814

Judge Blackstone composed his Commentaries (he was a poet too in his youth) with a bottle of port before him.
BYRON: *Letter to John Murray,* Feb. 7, 1821

Blade

[*See* Pliancy.

Blaine, James G. (1830–93)

Like an armed warrior, like a plumed knight, James G. Blaine marched down the halls of the American Congress and threw his shining lance full and fair against the brazen foreheads of the defamers of his country, and the maligners of his honor.
R. G. INGERSOLL: Speech placing Blaine in nomination for President at the Republican National Convention, Cincinnati, June 15, 1876

Blaine, Blaine, James G. Blaine,
Continental liar from the State of Maine.
Democratic slogan in the Presidential campaign of 1884

Blake, William (1757–1827)

An unfortunate lunatic whose personal inoffensiveness secures him from confinement.
THE LONDON EXAMINER: *Editorial,* Sept. 17, 1809

I must look on him as one of the most extraordinary persons of the age.
CHARLES LAMB: *Letter to Bernard Barton,* May 15, 1824

Blame

Blame is safer than praise.
R. W. EMERSON: *Compensation,* 1841

Blame is the lazy man's wages.
DANISH PROVERB

The greater the name, the greater the blame.
WELSH PROVERB

[*See also* Dead, Praise.

Blank Verse

[*See* Verse (Blank).

Blasphemy

Thou shalt not take the name of the Lord thy God in vain; for the Lord will not hold him guiltless that taketh his name in vain.
EXODUS XX, 7, *c.* 700 B.C. (Cf. DEUTERONOMY V, 11, *c.* 650 B.C.)

He that blasphemeth the name of the Lord, he shall surely be put to death, and all the congregation shall certainly stone him.
LEVITICUS XXIV, 16, *c.* 700 B.C.

He that shall blaspheme against the Holy Ghost hath never forgiveness, but is in danger of eternal damnation.
MARK III, 29, *c.* 70 (Cf. MATTHEW XII, 31, *c.* 75)

I stood upon the sand of the sea, and saw a beast rise up out of the sea, having seven heads and ten horns, and upon his horns ten crowns, and upon his head the name of blasphemy.
REVELATION XIII, 1, *c.* 95

There is nothing worse than blasphemy.
ST. JOHN CHRYSOSTOM: *Homily* I, *c.* 388

That in the captain's but a choleric word
Which in the soldier is flat blasphemy.
SHAKESPEARE: *Measure for Measure,* II, 1604

[Blasphemy is] denying the being or providence of God, contumelious reproaches of our Saviour Christ, profane scoffing at the Holy Scripture, or exposing it to contempt or ridicule.
WILLIAM BLACKSTONE: *Commentaries on the Laws of England,* IV, 1765

Shrink not from blasphemy — 'twill pass for wit.
BYRON: *English Bards and Scotch Reviewers,* 1809

[*See also* Calvinism, Hail, Injustice, Swearing.

Bleeding

In malignant fevers, with the blood vessels so gorged with blood that they are about to burst, and the blood about to rush to the brain, and the body filled with bile and various other fermenting substances, all of them poisonous to the organism, it is plain to common sense that bleeding is necessary.
VOLTAIRE: *Letter to Baron de Bretuil,* Dec., 1723

[*See also* Bloodshed, Wound.

Blessing

The five blessings are long life, riches, serenity, the love of virtue, and the attainment of ambition.
THE HUNG-FAN, *c.* 1100 B.C. (Chinese)

He that blesseth his friend with a loud voice, rising early in the morning, it shall be counted a curse to him.
PROVERBS XXVII, 14, *c.* 350 B.C.

No blessing lasts for ever.
PLAUTUS: *Curculio,* I, *c.* 200 B.C.

Judge none blessed before his death.
ECCLESIASTICUS XI, 28, *c.* 180 B.C.

Bless the Lord, O my soul: and all that is within me, bless His holy name.
PSALMS CIII, 1, *c.* 150 B.C.

Blessed are the dead which die in the Lord.
REVELATION XIV, 13, *c.* 95

Will God's blessing make my pot boil?
JAMES KELLY: *Complete Collection of Scottish Proverbs,* 1721

Good when He gives, supremely good,
Nor less when He denies,
E'en crosses from His sovereign hand
Are blessings in disguise.
Anon.: *Hymn, c.* 1750

My God! how little do my countrymen know what precious blessings they are in possession of, and which no other people on earth enjoy.
THOMAS JEFFERSON: *Letter to James Monroe,* 1785

There is in man a higher than love of happiness: he can do without happiness, and instead thereof seek blessedness.
THOMAS CARLYLE: *Sartor Resartus,* II, 1836

"God bless us every one," said Tiny Tim.
CHARLES DICKENS: *A Christmas Carol,* III, 1843

Experience teaches us that we do not always receive the blessings we ask for in prayer.
MARY BAKER G. EDDY: *Science and Health,* I, 1908

God bless me and my son John
Me and my wife, him and his wife,
Us four, and no more. Author unidentified

Blessings never come in pairs; misfortunes never come alone. CHINESE PROVERB

A father's blessing cannot be destroyed by fire or water. RUSSIAN PROVERB

[*See also* Beatitudes, Bishop, Damn, Death, Expectation.

Blind

If the blind lead the blind, both shall fall into the ditch. MATTHEW XV, 14, *c.* 75

The blind eat many a fly.
JOHN LYDGATE: *Ballad, c.* 1430

In the country of the blind the one-eyed man is king.
DESIDERIUS ERASMUS: *Adagia,* 1508

Who is blinder than he that will not see?
ANDREW BOORDE: *Breviary of Health,* 1547

Better to be blind than to see ill.
GEORGE HERBERT: *Outlandish Proverbs,* 1640

Why should I not submit with complacency to this loss of sight, which seems only withdrawn from the body without to increase the sight of the mind within?
JOHN MILTON: *Letter to Emeric Bigot,* March 24, 1658

The blind man's wife needs no painting.
JAMES HOWELL: *Proverbs,* 1659

Thus with the year
Seasons return, but not to me returns
Day, or the sweet approach of even or morn,
Or sight of vernal bloom, or Summer's rose,
Or flocks, or herds, or human face divine;
But cloud instead, and ever-during dark
Surrounds me, from the cheerful ways of men
Cut off, and for the book of knowledge fair
Presented with a universal blank.
JOHN MILTON: *Paradise Lost,* III, 1667

He is blind enough who sees not through the holes of a sieve.
JOHN RAY: *English Proverbs,* 1670

What matters it to a blind man that his father could see?
H. G. BOHN: *Handbook of Proverbs,* 1855

A blind man, leaning against a wall, said: "This is the end of the world."
GREEK PROVERB

Nothing so bold as a blind horse. IBID.

God watches over the blind man's wife.
HINDU PROVERB

God builds the nest of the blind bird.
TURKISH PROVERB

[*See also* Age (Old), Belief, Charity, Cosmetics, Deaf, Elephant, Hunger, Lame, Marriage, Master, Nest, Priest.

Bliss

The sum of earthly bliss.
JOHN MILTON: *Paradise Lost,* VIII, 1667

Condition, circumstance, is not the thing;
Bliss is the same in subject or in king.
ALEXANDER POPE: *An Essay on Man,* IV, 1734

The bliss e'en of a moment still is bliss.
JOANNA BAILLIE: *The Beacon,* I, 1830

Happiness biling over and running down both sides of the pot.
H. W. SHAW (JOSH BILLINGS): *Josh Billings' Comical Lexicon,* 1877

Blockhead

There is a secret propensity in nature, from generation to generation, in the blockheads of one age to admire those of another.
RICHARD STEELE: *The Tatler,* July 13, 1710

The bookful blockhead, ignorantly read,
With loads of learned lumber in his head.
ALEXANDER POPE: *An Essay on Criticism,* III, 1711

A blockhead rubs his thoughtless skull,
And thanks his stars he was not born a fool.
ALEXANDER POPE: *Epilogue for* NICHOLAS ROWE: *Jane Shore,* 1714

[*See also* Insult, Mystery.

Blonde

Gentlemen prefer blondes.
ANITA LOOS: Title of a book, 1925

Blood

Ye shall eat no manner of blood, whether it be of fowl or of beast.
LEVITICUS VII, 26, *c.* 700 B.C.

Your blood be upon your own heads.
ACTS XVIII, 6, *c.* 75

The blood of the martyrs is the seed of the church.
An adaptation of TERTULLIAN's "Semen est sanguis Christianorum" — Christian blood is seed: *Apologeticus,* 197

You can't get blood out of a turnip [or a stone].
ENGLISH PROVERB, borrowed from the Latin and traced by Apperson to 1599

Will all great Neptune's ocean wash this blood
Clean from my hands? No; this my hand will rather
The multitudinous seas incarnadine.
SHAKESPEARE: *Macbeth,* II, *c.* 1605

All blood is alike ancient.
THOMAS FULLER: *Gnomologia,* 1732

There is a fountain fill'd with blood
Drawn from Emmanuel's veins;
And sinners, plung'd beneath that flood,
Lose all their guilty stains.
WILLIAM COWPER: *Olney Hymns,* 1779

Blood is a very special kind of sap. (Blut ist ein ganz besondrer Saft.)
J. W. GOETHE: *I Faust,* I, 1808

Blood is thicker than water.
JOSIAH TATTNALL: On going to the aid of an English squadron in the Peiho river, China, 1859 (Tattnall was flag officer on the American Asiatic station, and was aboard a small steamer, the Toeywan. The saying was not original with him, but he made it popular)

Blood, as all men know, than water's thicker,
But water's wider, thank the Lord, than blood.
ALDOUS HUXLEY: *Ninth Philosopher's Song,* 1920

Blood is warmer than water.
ESTONIAN PROVERB

Good blood cannot lie. (Bon sang ne peut mentir.)
FRENCH PROVERB

Send your noble blood to market and see what it will buy.
ITALIAN PROVERB

[*See also* Ancestry, Atonement, Birth (High), Bloodshed, Church (Christian), Disease, Drink, Hard, Impossible, Law, Martyrdom, Nobility, Nose, Redemption, Salvation.

Blood and Iron

Not by speechifying and counting majorities are the great questions of the time to be solved — that was the error of 1848 and 1849 —, but by iron and blood (Eisen und Blut.)
OTTO VON BISMARCK: Speech in the Prussian Diet, Sept. 30, 1862

Blood, Corruption of

[*See* Treason.

Bloodshed

Whoso sheddeth man's blood, by man shall his blood be shed.
GENESIS IX, 6, *c.* 700 B.C.

The land cannot be cleansed of the blood that is shed therein, but by the blood of him that shed it.
NUMBERS XXXV, 33, *c.* 700 B.C.

Almost all things are by the law purged with blood; and without shedding of blood is no remission.
HEBREWS IX, 22, *c.* 65

The Church abhors bloodshed. (Ecclesia abhorret a sanguine.)
DECREE OF THE COUNCIL OF TOURS, 1163 (In compliance with this decree the Inquisition in Spain resorted to the burning of heretics, which could be accomplished without hemorrhage. The sentence usually included the admonition, "ut quam clementissime et ultra sanguinis effusionem puniretur" — as humanely as possible, and without any shedding of blood)

The blood of man should never be shed but to redeem the blood of man. It is well shed for our family, for our friends, for our God, for our country, for our kind. The rest is vanity; the rest is crime.
EDMUND BURKE: *Letters on a Regicide Peace,* I, 1797

Bloodshed and persecution form no part of the creed of the Catholic Church. So much does she abhor the shedding of blood that a man becomes disqualified to serve as a minister at her altars who, by act or counsel, voluntarily sheds the blood of another.
JAMES CARDINAL GIBBONS: *The Faith of Our Fathers,* XVIII, 1876

When we must have freedom of agitation, and nothing but bloodshed will secure it, then bloodshed is wise.
BENJAMIN R. TUCKER: *Instead of a Book,* 1893

Bloodstone

[*See* March.

Blot

The fairer the paper the fouler the blot.
THOMAS FULLER: *Gnomologia,* 1732

Blow

The first blow is as much as two.
GEORGE HERBERT: *Outlandish Proverbs,* 1640

[*See also* Battle, Child.

Blue

Blue is not merely a color; it is a mystery.
Ascribed to ISRALL BEN MOSES NAJARA, *c.* 1590

Blueness doth express trueness.
BEN JONSON: *Cynthia's Revels,* V, 1601

True blue will never stain.
JAMES HOWELL: *Proverbs,* 1659

Presbyterian true blue.
SAMUEL BUTLER: *Hudibras,* I, 1663

The blues (or blue devils).
ENGLISH PHRASE, not recorded before the XVIII century

Deep, dismal blue
Becomes alone the melancholy crew;
Emblem of plagues, the worst which Heaven hath sent,
Of cankered care, and gloomy discontent.
CHARLES STEARNS: *The Ladies' Philosophy of Love,* 1797

A bolt from the blue.
ENGLISH PHRASE, not recorded before the XIX century

Blue, darkly, deeply, beautifully blue.
ROBERT SOUTHEY: *Modoc in Wales,* V, 1805

Blue! Gentle cousin of the forest-green,
Married to green in all the sweetest flowers, —
Forget-me-not — the blue bell.
JOHN KEATS: *Written in Answer to a Sonnet,* 1818

The blue of distance, however intense, is not the blue of a bright blue flower.
JOHN RUSKIN: *Modern Painters,* I, 1843

Blue is love true. SCOTTISH PROVERB

[*See also* Black, Color, Moon, Sky.

Blue and the Gray, The

[*See* Judgment Day.

Bluestocking

Tho' Artemisia talks by fits
Of councils, classics, fathers, wits,
Reads Malebranche, Boyle, and Locke,
Yet in some things methinks she fails:
'Twere well if she would pare her nails,
And wear a cleaner smock.
ALEXANDER POPE: *Artemisia,* 1727 (Imitation of the Earl of Dorset)

I have always (at least from fifteen) thought the reputation of learning a misfortune to a woman.
MARY WORTLEY MONTAGU: *Letter to James Steuart,* July 19, 1759

A *femme bel-espirit* is a scourge to her husband, her children, her friends, her servants, and the whole world.
J.-J. ROUSSEAU: *Émile,* I, 1762

Historic, critic and poetic dames.
JOHN WOLCOT (PETER PINDAR): *To Apollo,* 1790

But, oh ye lords of ladies intellectual,
Inform us truly, — have they not henpecked you all?
BYRON: *Don Juan,* I, 1819

I have an utter aversion to bluestockings. I do not care a fig for any woman that knows even what an author means.
WILLIAM HAZLITT: *Table-Talk,* II, 1824

When we think very ill of a woman, and wish to blacken her character, we merely call her a bluestocking.
E. A. POE: *Fifty Suggestions,* 1845 (Graham's Magazine, May–June)

Erudita. Latin name for a learned woman.

Blunder

It is more than a crime; it is a blunder. (C'est plus qu'un crime; c'est une faute.)
JOSEPH FOUCHÉ: *On the execution of the Duc d'Enghien,* March 21, 1804

Bluntness

I am no orator, as Brutus is;
But, as you know me all, a plain blunt man.
SHAKESPEARE: *Julius Caesar,* III, 1599

Blush

O my God, I am ashamed and blush to lift up my face to thee, my God.
EZRA IX, 6, *c.* 300 B.C.

I will go wash;
And when my face is fair, you shall perceive
Whether I blush or no.
SHAKESPEARE: *Coriolanus,* I, *c.* 1607

Blushing is virtue's color.
JOHN RAY: *English Proverbs,* 1670

Blushes are badges of imperfection. Saints have no shame.
WILLIAM WYCHERLEY: *Love in a Wood,* I, 1673

Men blush for their crimes much less than for their weaknesses and vanity.
JEAN DE LA BRUYÈRE: *Caractères,* II, 1688

From every blush that kindles in thy cheeks,
Ten thousand little loves and graces spring
To revel in the roses.
NICHOLAS ROWE: *Tamerlane,* I, 1702

The man that blushes is not quite a brute.
EDWARD YOUNG: *Night Thoughts,* VII, 1745

No man blushes in the dark.
BENJAMIN WHICHCOTE: *Moral and Religious Aphorisms,* 1753

A blush is beautiful, but sometimes inconvenient.
CARLO GOLDONI: *Pamela nubile,* I, 1757

Whoever blushes is already guilty; true innocence is ashamed of nothing.
J.-J. ROUSSEAU: *Émile,* I, 1762

Do people ever blush in the dark? That they grow pale with fright in the dark is probable — but not red with shame. For they get pale on their own account, whereas they blush on account of others.
G. C. LICHTENBERG: *Reflections,* 1799

So sweet the blush of bashfulness,
E'en pity scarce can wish it less.
BYRON: *The Bride of Abydos,* I, 1813

There's a blush for won't, and a blush for shan't,
And a blush for having done it:
There's a blush for thought and a blush for nought,
And a blush for just begun it.
JOHN KEATS: *Letter to J. H. Reynolds,* Jan. 13, 1818 (Quoted as "the old song")

When you blush, it is notice to be careful.
E. W. HOWE: *Sinner Sermons,* 1926

[*See also* Bashfulness, Cosmetics, Fear, Kiss, Prudery.

Boar

[*See* Bull.

Board

All boards are bad.
T. B. MACAULAY: *Diary,* Nov. 25, 1848

I have always noticed that a board is long, narrow and wooden.
GEORGE W. GOETHALS (1858–1928)

[*See also* Assembly, Committee, Council.

Boarding-house

An odor for which there is no name, and which should be called *odeur de pension.*
HONORÉ DE BALZAC: *Père Goriot,* XVI, 1834 (*Pension*=Fr. boarding-house)

Boarding-school

Methodist parents, who would send your girls headlong to Hell, send them to a fashionable boarding-school.
JOHN WESLEY: *Journal,* April 6, 1772

Boasting

Great boast, small roast.
JOHN HEYWOOD: *Proverbs,* 1546

Every other enjoyment malice may destroy; every other panegyric envy may withhold; but no human power can deprive the boaster of his own encomiums.
SAMUEL JOHNSON: *The Rambler,* Jan. 21, 1752

It is harder to be poor without complaining than to be rich without boasting.
CHINESE PROVERB

A boaster and a liar are first cousins.
GERMAN PROVERB

As with feathers, so with big words: it takes many to the pound.
IBID.

Braggin river never drown somebody.
JAMAICAN PROVERB

[*See also* Braggart, Lying, Valor.

Body

We are bound to our bodies like an oyster to its shell.
PLATO: *Phaedrus, c.* 360 B.C.

Your body is the temple of the Holy Ghost.
I CORINTHIANS VI, 19, *c.* 55

I keep under my body and bring it into subjection.
I CORINTHIANS IX, 27

The body of a man is not a home but an inn — and that only briefly.
SENECA: *Epistulae morales ad Lucilium,* CXX, *c.* 63

All the orifices of the body above the navel are pure, and all below are impure, save in a maiden, in whom the whole body is pure.
THE CODE OF MANU, *c.* 100

It is shameful to have one's body praised.
POPE XYSTUS I: *The Ring, c.* 120

This body of ours consists of four elements; viz., of what is warm, that is, of blood; of what is dry, that is, of yellow bile; of what is moist, that is, of phlegm; of what is cold, that is, of black bile.
ST. JOHN CHRYSOSTOM: *Homily* X, *c.* 388

A human body is composed of a large number of different entities, and each of them is itself a composite.
BARUCH SPINOZA: *Ethica,* 1677

The tenement of clay.
JOHN DRYDEN: *Absalom and Achitophel,* I, 1682

The body of man is a machine which winds its own springs.
J. O. DE LA METTRIE: *L'Homme machine,* 1748

The [body], for a time the unwilling sport
Of circumstance and passion, struggles on;
Fleets through its sad duration rapidly:
Then like an useless and worn-out machine,
Rots, perishes, and passes.
P. B. SHELLEY: *Queen Mab,* I, 1813

No knowledge can be more satisfactory to a man than that of his own frame, its parts, their functions and actions.
THOMAS JEFFERSON: *Letter to Thomas Cooper,* 1814

This house of clay not built with hands.
S. T. COLERIDGE: *Youth and Age,* 1817 (In the first version "this house of clay" was "this breathing house." Cf. DRYDEN, *ante,* 1682)

If any thing is sacred, the human body is sacred,
And the glory and sweet of a man is the token of manhood untainted;
And in man or woman a clean, strong, firm-fibred body is beautiful as the most beautiful face.

WALT WHITMAN: *I Sing the Body Electric*, 1855

A cell state in which every cell is a citizen.

RUDOLF VIRCHOW: *Cellular-Pathologie*, 1858

The utmost glory of the human body is a mean subject of contemplation compared to the emotion, exertion and character of that which animates it.

JOHN RUSKIN: *Modern Painters*, I, 1860

The human body is the magazine of inventions, the patent office, where are the models from which every hint is taken. All the tools and engines on earth are only extensions of its limbs and senses.

R. W. EMERSON: *Society and Solitude*, 1870

The body is but a pair of pincers set over a bellows and a stewpan and the whole fixed upon stilts.

SAMUEL BUTLER: *Note-Books*, *c.* 1890

[*See also* Body and Soul, Clothes, Darwinism, Death, Education, Energy, Flesh and Blood, Health, Imprisonment, Laughter, Mind and Body, Physician, Purity.

Body and Mind

[*See* Mind and Body.

Body and Soul

The body is the tomb of the soul.

PLATO: *Cratylus*, XVII, *c.* 360 B.C.

They have mighty souls in tiny bodies.

VIRGIL: *Georgics*, IV, 30 B.C.

A healthy body is a guest-chamber for the soul; a sick body is a prison.

FRANCIS BACON: *The Advancement of Learning*, II, 1605

The body is sooner dressed than the soul.

GEORGE HERBERT: *Jacula Prudentum*, 1651

The body is the socket of the soul.

JOHN RAY: *English Proverbs*, 1670

I consider the body as a system of tubes and glands, or to use a more rustic phrase, a bundle of pipes and strainers, fitted to one another after so wonderful a manner as to make a proper engine for the soul to work with.

JOSEPH ADDISON: *The Spectator*, July 12, 1711

There are no souls without bodies. God alone is wholly without body.

G. W. LEIBNIZ: *The Monadology*, LXXII, 1714

If our bodies were to cost no more than our souls, we might board cheap.

THOMAS FULLER: *Gnomologia*, 1732

The soul is a mere spectator of the movements of its body.

CHARLES BONNET: *Essai de psychologie*, XXVII, 1754

Man has no body distinct from his soul; for that called body is a portion of soul discern'd by the five senses, the chief inlets of soul in this age.

WILLIAM BLAKE: *The Marriage of Heaven and Hell*, 1790

The body is the workhouse of the soul.

H. G. BOHN: *Handbook of Proverbs*, 1855

There is nothing the body suffers that the soul may not profit by.

GEORGE MEREDITH: *Diana of the Crossways*, I, 1885

The soul is born old, but it grows young; that is the comedy of life. The body is born young and grows old; that is life's tragedy.

OSCAR WILDE: *A Woman of No Importance*, III, 1893

Those who see any difference between soul and body have neither.

OSCAR WILDE: *Phrases and Philosophies for the Use of the Young*, 1894

Coddle the body and you harm the soul.

POLISH PROVERB

[*See also* Brown (John).

Body-snatcher

One who supplies the young physicians with that with which the old physicians have supplied the undertaker.

AMBROSE BIERCE: *The Devil's Dictionary*, 1906

Bohemia

What is now called Bohemia [is] a pleasant land, not fenced with drab stucco, like Tyburnia or Belgravia.

W. M. THACKERAY: *The Adventures of Philip*, V, 1862

The coast of Bohemia.

W. D. HOWELLS: Title of a novel, 1893

[*See also* Czecho-Slovakia.

Bohemian

She was of a wild, roving nature, inherited from father and mother, who were both Bohemians.

W. M. THACKERAY: *Vanity Fair*, LXIV, 1848

A Bohemian is an educated hoss-thief.

C. F. BROWNE (ARTEMUS WARD): *Artemus Ward: His Book*, 1862

A person open to the suspicion of irregular and immoral living.

R. W. EMERSON: *Letters and Social Aims*, 1875

[*See also* Czech, Jesus Christ.

Bohemian Language

[*See* Czech Language.

Bold

Only the bold get to the top.
PUBLILIUS SYRUS: *Sententiae, c.* 50 B.C.

Every man is bold when his whole fortune is at stake.
DIONYSIUS OF HALICARNASSUS: *Antiquities of Rome,* VIII, *c.* 20 B.C.

Fortune helps the bold. (Audentes fortuna juvat.) VIRGIL: *Æneid,* X, 19 B.C.

Both fortune and love befriend the bold.
OVID: *Ars amatoria,* I, *c.* 2 B.C.

The gods favor the bold.
OVID: *Metamorphoses,* X, *c.* 5

A bold bad man.
EDMUND SPENSER: *The Faerie Queene,* I, *c.* 1589

Be bold, be bold, and everywhere be bold.
EDMUND SPENSER: *The Faerie Queene,* III

Boldness is a child of ignorance and baseness, far inferior to other parts. But, nevertheless, it doth fascinate, and bind hand and foot those that are either shallow in judgment or weak in courage, which are the greatest part, yea, and prevaileth with wise men at weak times. FRANCIS BACON: *Essays,* XII, 1625

A wight man wanted never a weapon.
DAVID FERGUSSON: *Scottish Proverbs,* 1641 (*Wight*=bold)

Put a grain of boldness into everything you do.
BALTASAR GRACIÁN: *The Art of Worldly Wisdom,* CLXXXII, 1647

Be not too bold with your betters.
JAMES HOWELL: *Proverbs,* 1659

I cowhearted? I'm as bold as a lion.
Anon.: *Terence Made English,* 1694

A bad, bold, blustering, bloody, blundering booby.
Anon.: *Epigram on the first Earl Cadogan* (1670–1726)

He had read the inscription on the gates of Busyrane — "Be bold"; and on the second gate — "Be bold, be bold, and evermore be bold"; and then again had paused well at the third gate — "But not too bold."
R. W. EMERSON: *Representative Men,* II, 1850

The bold are always lucky.
DANISH PROVERB

They that are bold with women are never bold with men. SPANISH PROVERB

[*See also* Audacity, Bravery, Business, Courage, Daring, Luck.

Boleyn, Anne (c. 1507–36)

I have seen many men and also women executed, and they all have been in great sorrow, and to my knowledge this lady has much joy and pleasure in death.
WILLIAM KINGSTON, governor of the Tower of London: After the execution of Anne Boleyn, 1536

[*See also* Bachelor.

Bologna

Bologna is celebrated for producing popes, painters, and sausages.
BYRON: *Letter to John Murray,* June 4, 1817

Boloney

I am for gold dollars as against bolony dollars.
ALFRED E. SMITH: Press interview in New York, Nov. 24, 1933 (First appearance of the phrase)

Bolshevist

[*See* Child, Communist, Jew.

Bombast

Such damned bombast no age that's past
Will show, or time to come.
ROBERT BURNS: Reply to a poetaster named Symon Gray, who had sent Burns some bad verses, 1787

Bonaparte, Napoleon

[*See* Napoleon I.

Bond

[*See* Promise, Trust.

Bone

The nearer the bone, the sweeter the meat.
ENGLISH PROVERB, found in the Percy Ballads, 1559 (Cf. KELLY, *post,* 1721)

The broken bone, once set together, is stronger than ever. JOHN LYLY: *Euphues,* 1579

He that gives thee a bone would not have thee die.
GEORGE HERBERT: *Outlandish Proverbs,* 1640

Bones bring meat to town.
THOMAS FULLER: *The Holy State and the Profane State,* V, 1642 (Cited as a proverb)

The flesh is aye fairest that is farthest from the bone.
JAMES KELLY: *Complete Collection of Scottish Proverbs,* 1721 (Cf. ENGLISH PROVERB, *ante,* 1559)

He who eats the meat, let him pick the bone.
H. G. BOHN: *Handbook of Proverbs,* 1855

[*See also* Breeding, Dog, Meat, Skeleton, Skin.

Books

Oh, that mine adversary had written a book.
JOB XXXI, 35, *c.* 325 B.C.

Of making many books there is no end; and much study is a weariness of the flesh.
ECCLESIASTES XII, 12, *c.* 200 B.C.

My books are always at leisure for me; they are never engaged.
CICERO: *De republica,* I, *c.* 50 B.C.

These are the masters who instruct us without rods and ferules, without hard words and anger, without clothes or money. If you approach them, they are not asleep; if, investigating, you interrogate them, they conceal nothing; if you mistake them, they never grumble; if you are ignorant, they cannot laugh at you.
RICHARD DE BURY (BISHOP OF DURHAM): *Philobiblon,* 1473

The multitude of books is a great evil. There is no limit to this fever for writing; every one must be an author; some out of vanity, to acquire celebrity and raise up a name; others for the sake of mere gain.
MARTIN LUTHER: *Table-Talk,* DCCCCXI, 1569

There are more books upon books than upon all other subjects.
MICHEL DE MONTAIGNE: *Essays,* III, 1588

He hath never fed of the dainties that are bred of a book; he hath not eat paper, as it were; he hath not drunk ink: his intellect is not replenished; he is only an animal, only sensible in the duller parts.
SHAKESPEARE: *Love's Labor's Lost,* IV, *c.* 1595

Some books are to be tasted, others to be swallowed, and some few to be chewed and digested. FRANCIS BACON: *Essays,* II, 1597

The wise are above books.
SAMUEL DANIEL: *A Defense of Rhyme,* 1602

The images of men's wits and knowledges remain in books, exempted from the wrong of time, and capable of perpetual renovation.
FRANCIS BACON: *The Advancement of Learning,* I, 1605

Ignorant asses visiting stationers' shops, their use is not to inquire for good books, but new books.
JOHN WEBSTER: *The White Devil,* pref., *c.* 1608

There's no book so bad that something good may not be found in it.
CERVANTES: *Don Quixote,* II, 1615

Books treating of light subjects are nurseries of wantonness; they instruct the loose reader to become naught, whereas, before touching naughtiness, he knew naught.
RICHARD BRATHWAITE: *The English Gentlewoman,* 1631

Years know more than books.
GEORGE HERBERT: *Outlandish Proverbs,* 1640

Learning hath gained most by those books by which the printers have lost.
THOMAS FULLER: *The Holy State and the Profane State,* 1642

As good almost kill a man as kill a good book: who kills a man kills a reasonable creature, God's image; but he who destroys a good book, kills reason itself, kills the image of God, as it were, in the eye. Many a man lives a burden to the earth; but a good book is the precious life-blood of a master-spirit, embalmed and treasured up on purpose to a life beyond life.
JOHN MILTON: *Areopagitica,* 1644

Books should to one of these four ends conduce,
For wisdom, piety, delight, or use.
JOHN DENHAM: *Of Prudence,* 1650

They are for company the best friends, in doubts counsellors, in damps comforters, time's perspective, the home-traveler's ship or horse, the busy man's best recreation, the opiate of idle weariness, the mind's best ordinary, nature's garden, and the seed-plot of immortality.
RICHARD WHITELOCK: *Zoötomia,* 1654

It is more necessary to study men than books.
LA ROCHEFOUCAULD: *Maxims,* 1665

Some said, John, print it; others said, Not so:
Some said, It might do good; others said, No.
JOHN BUNYAN: *Pilgrim's Progress,* I, 1678

Books, like proverbs, receive their chief value from the stamp and esteem of ages through which they have passed.
WILLIAM TEMPLE: *Of Ancient and Modern Learning,* 1692

Sometimes I read a book with pleasure, and detest the author.
JONATHAN SWIFT: *Thoughts on Various Subjects,* 1706

A great book is a great evil.
JOSEPH ADDISON: *The Spectator,* July 23, 1711 (Quoted as "the famous Greek proverb." The context shows that *great* is intended to mean large, not meritorious)

Books are the legacies that a great genius leaves to mankind.
JOSEPH ADDISON: *The Spectator,* Sept. 10

A wicked book is the wickeder because it cannot repent.
THOMAS FULLER: *Gnomologia,* 1732

Books have always a secret influence on the understanding; we cannot at pleasure obliterate ideas: he that reads books of science, though without any desire fixed of improvement, will grow more knowing; he that entertains himself with moral or religious treatises will imperceptibly advance in goodness.

SAMUEL JOHNSON: *The Adventurer,* Feb. 26, 1753

Books teach us very little of the world.

OLIVER GOLDSMITH: *Letter to Henry Goldsmith,* Feb., 1759

I keep to old books, for they teach me something; from the new I learn very little.

VOLTAIRE: *Letter to an unknown correspondent,* Jan. 5, 1759

The sums laid out on books one should, at first sight, think an indication of encouragement to letters; but booksellers only are encouraged, not books.

HORACE WALPOLE: *Letter to Henry Zonch,* Jan. 3, 1761

The first time I read an excellent book, it is to me just as if I had gained a new friend. When I read over a book I have perused before, it resembles the meeting with an old one.

OLIVER GOLDSMITH: *The Citizen of the World,* LXXXIII, 1762

I hate books, for they only teach people to talk about what they do not understand.

J.-J. ROUSSEAU: *Émile,* I, 1762

I showed her that books were sweet unreproaching companions to the miserable, and that if they could not bring us to enjoy life, they would at least teach us to endure it.

OLIVER GOLDSMITH: *The Vicar of Wakefield,* XXII, 1766

Any fool may write a most valuable book by chance, if he will only tell us what he heard and saw, with veracity.

THOMAS GRAY: *Letter to Horace Walpole,* Feb. 25, 1768

There are but very few who are capable of comparing and digesting what passes before their eyes at different times and occasions, so as to form the whole into a distinct system. But in books everything is settled for them, without the exertion of any considerable diligence or sagacity.

EDMUND BURKE: *Thoughts on the Cause of the Present Discontents,* 1770

Food of the spirit. (Nutrimentum spiritus.)

INSCRIPTION ON THE BERLIN ROYAL LIBRARY, 1780

But what strange art, what magic can dispose
The troubled mind to change its native woes?
Or lead us willing from ourselves, to see
Others more wretched, more undone than we?
This, books can do: — nor this alone; they give
New views to life, and teach us how to live.

GEORGE CRABBE: *The Library,* 1781

What! Another of those damned, fat, square, thick books! Always scribble, scribble, scribble, eh, Mr. Gibbon?

THE DUKE OF GLOUCESTER, brother to George III: To Edward Gibbon on being presented a copy of Vol. III of *The Decline and Fall of the Roman Empire,* 1781

Books tell me so much that they inform me of nothing.

ST. JOHN DE CRÈVECOEUR: *Letters from an American Farmer,* XII, 1782

Some books are lies frae end to end.

ROBERT BURNS: *Death and Dr. Hornbook,* 1785

Books, nowadays, are printed by people who do not understand them, sold by people who do not understand them, read and reviewed by people who do not understand them, and even written by people who do not understand them.

G. C. LICHTENBERG: *Reflections,* 1799

Books with striking and ingenious titles are seldom worth reading. IBID.

The one fault of really good books is that they almost always produce a great prodigy of bad ones. IBID.

This book has had the effect which good books usually have: it has made the fools more foolish, the intelligent more intelligent, and left the majority as they were. IBID.

A book's a book, although there's nothing in it.

BYRON: *English Bards and Scotch Reviewers,* 1809

I cannot live without books.

THOMAS JEFFERSON: *Letter to John Adams,* 1815

My books are friends that never fail me.

THOMAS CARLYLE: *Letter to his mother,* March 17, 1817

May blessings be upon the head of Cadmus, or the Phoenicians, or whoever invented books.

THOMAS CARLYLE: *Letter to R. Mitchell,* 1820

Many books require no thought from those who read them, and for a very simple reason; — they made no such demand upon those who wrote them.

C. C. COLTON: *Lacon,* 1820

That an author's work is the mirror of his mind is a position that has led to very false conclusions. If Satan were to write a book it would be in praise of virtue, because the good would purchase it for use, and the bad for ostentation. IBID.

Books are less often made use of as spectacles to look at nature with than as blinds to keep out its strong light and shifting scenery from weak eyes and indolent dispositions.

WILLIAM HAZLITT: *The Ignorance of the Learned,* 1821

Books constitute capital. A library book lasts as long as a house, for hundreds of years. It is not, then, an article of mere consumption but fairly of capital, and often in the case of professional men, setting out in life, it is their only capital.

THOMAS JEFFERSON: *Letter to James Madison*, Sept., 1821

Books are the best things, well used; abused, among the worst.

R. W. EMERSON: *The American Scholar*, 1837

Books are the true levellers. They give to all, who will faithfully use them, the society, the spiritual presence, of the best and greatest of our race.

W. E. CHANNING: *Self-Culture*, 1838

Books are a triviality. Life alone is great.

THOMAS CARLYLE: *Journal*, May 29, 1839

All that mankind has done, thought, gained or been: it is lying as in magic preservation in the pages of books.

THOMAS CARLYLE: *Heroes and Hero-Worship*, v, 1840 (Lecture in London, May 19)

The true university of these days is a collection of books. IBID.

Iron-jointed, supple-sinew'd, they shall dive, and they shall run,
Catch the wild goat by the hair, and hurl their lances in the sun;
Whistle back the parrot's call, and leap the rainbows of the brooks,
Not with blinded eyesight pouring over miserable books.

ALFRED TENNYSON: *Locksley Hall*, 1842

The intellect is a diœcious plant, and books are the bees which carry the quickening pollen from one to another mind.

J. R. LOWELL: *Nationality in Literature*, 1849

The enormous multiplication of books in every branch of knowledge is one of the greatest evils of this age; since it presents one of the most serious obstacles to the acquisition of correct information, by throwing in the reader's way piles of lumber in which he must painfully grope for the scraps of useful matter, peradventure interspersed.

E. A. POE: *Marginalia*, 1844–49

Books, not which afford us a cowering enjoyment, but in which each thought is of unusual daring; such as an idle man cannot read, and a timid one would not be entertained by, which even make us dangerous to existing institutions — such call I good books.

H. D. THOREAU: *A Week on the Concord and Merrimack Rivers*, 1849

A book ought to be like a man or a woman, with some individual character in it, though eccentric, yet its own; with some blood in its veins and speculation in its eyes and a way and a will of its own.

JOHN MITCHEL: *Jail Journal*, 1854

Books are a finer world within the world.

ALEXANDER SMITH: *Dreamthorp*, VII, 1863

I go into my library, and all history unrolls before me. I breathe the morning air of the world while the scent of Eden's roses yet lingered in it, while it vibrated only to the world's first brood of nightingales, and to the laugh of Eve. I see the pyramids building; I hear the shoutings of the armies of Alexander.

ALEXANDER SMITH: *Dreamthorp*, XI

How long most people would look at the best book before they would give the price of a large turbot for it!

JOHN RUSKIN: *Sesame and Lilies*, I, 1865

It is those books which a man possesses but does not read which constitute the most suspicious evidence against him.

VICTOR HUGO: *Toilers of the Sea*, I, 1866

I conceive that books are like men's souls, divided into sheep and goats. Some few are going up, and carrying us up, heavenward; calculated, I mean, to be of priceless advantage in teaching, in forwarding the teaching of all generations. Others, a frightful multitude, are going down, down; doing ever the more and the wider and the wilder mischief.

THOMAS CARLYLE: Address at Edinburgh, April 2, 1866

Books are sepulchres of thought.

H. W. LONGFELLOW: *The Wind Over the Chimney*, 1867

A good book is fruitful of other books; it perpetuates its fame from age to age, and makes eras in the lives of its readers.

A. BRONSON ALCOTT: *Tablets*, I, 1868

Books are fatal: they are the curse of the human race. Nine-tenths of existing books are nonsense, and the clever books are the refutation of that nonsense. The greatest misfortune that ever befell man was the invention of printing.

BENJAMIN DISRAELI: *Lothair*, XXIV, 1870

Books are to be call'd for, and supplied, on the assumption that the process of reading is not a half sleep, but, in the highest sense, an exercise, a gymnast's struggle; that the reader is to do something for himself.

WALT WHITMAN: *Democratic Vistas*, 1870

The foolishest book is a kind of leaky boat on a sea of wisdom; some of the wisdom will get in anyhow.

O. W. HOLMES: *The Poet at the Breakfast-Table*, XI, 1872

That is a good book which is opened with expectation, and closed with profit.

A. BRONSON ALCOTT: *Table-Talk*, I, 1877

A man says: "Judging by its effect on me, this book is harmful." Let him wait, and maybe he will confess some day that it did him a great service by bringing to light a hidden disease of his soul.

F. W. NIETZSCHE: *Human All-too-Human,* II, 1878

Books are good enough in their own way, but they are a mighty bloodless substitute for life.

R. L. STEVENSON: *Virginibus Puerisque,* 1881

Books for general reading always smell badly; the odor of common people hangs about them.

F. W. NIETZSCHE: *Beyond Good and Evil,* II, 1886

Books are like individuals; you know at once if they are going to create a sense within the sense, to fever, to madden you in blood and brain, or if they will merely leave you indifferent, or irritable, having unpleasantly disturbed sweet intimate musings as might a draught from an open window.

GEORGE MOORE: *Confessions of a Young Man,* IV, 1888

Books should be tried by a judge and jury as though they were crimes, and counsel should be heard on both sides.

SAMUEL BUTLER: *Note-Books, c.* 1890

Those books are condemned which are derogatory to God, or the Virgin Mary, or the saints, or the Catholic Church and her worship, or to the Sacraments, or to the Holy See. So also are condemned those books in which the idea of the inspiration of Holy Scripture is perverted. So also are condemned those books which revile the ecclesiastical hierarchy, or the clerical or religious state.

POPE LEO XIII: *General Decrees Concerning the Prohibition and Censorship of Books,* Jan. 25, 1897

I would never read a book if it were possible for me to talk half an hour with the man who wrote it.

WOODROW WILSON: To his students at Princeton, *c.* 1900

A book is like a garden carried in the pocket.

ARAB PROVERB

A book you haven't read is a new book.

Author unidentified

There's no thief like a bad book.

ITALIAN PROVERB

Beware of the man of one book. (Cave ab homine unius libri.) LATIN PROVERB

Books and friends, few and good.

SPANISH PROVERB

[*See also* Achievement, Adversary, Adversity, Arms, Author, Bibliomania, Bibliophile, Censorship, Cook, Criticism, Drinking, Friend, Happiness, Index, Library, Margin, Old, Pedant, Printing, Publisher, Reader, Reading, Style, Talk, Teacher, Translation, Writer, Writing.

Bookseller

Here lies a bookseller, the leaf of his life being finished, awaiting a new edition, augmented and corrected.

Epitaph on the grave of Jacob Tonson, St. Margaret's Church, Westminster, 1735

What should we when booksellers break?
We should rejoice.
Da Capo.

CHARLES LAMB: *Letter to Thomas Allsop,* Jan. 7, 1825

[*See also* Author, Books, Publisher.

Boor

The boor is of no use in conversation. He contributes nothing worth hearing, and takes offense at everything.

ARISTOTLE: *The Nicomachean Ethics,* IV, *c.* 340 B.C.

Boost

[*See* Knock, Opposition.

Bore

Oh, he's as tedious
As is a tir'd horse, a railing wife;
Worse than a smoky house; I have rather live
With cheese and garlic in a windmill, far,
Than feed on cates, and have him talk to me,
In any Summer-house in Christendom.

SHAKESPEARE: *I Henry IV,* I, *c.* 1598 (*Cate*=delicacy)

The secret of being a bore is to tell everything.

VOLTAIRE: *L'Enfant prodique,* 1736

A person who talks when you wish him to listen.

AMBROSE BIERCE: *The Devil's Dictionary,* 1906

A bore is one who, when you ask him "How are you?", tells you.

Author unidentified

[*See also* Philistine, Polygamy.

Boredom

The tedium of life. (Taedium vitae.)

AURUS GELLIUS: *Noctes Atticae,* VI, *c.* 150

We often pardon those who weary us, but we cannot pardon those whom we weary.

LA ROCHEFOUCAULD: *Maxims,* 1665

There is nothing so insupportable to man as complete repose, without passion, occupation, amusement, care. Then it is that he feels his nothingness, his isolation, his insufficiency, his dependence, his impotence, his emptiness.

BLAISE PASCAL: *Pensées,* XXV, 1670

Pleasures never can be so multiplied or continued as not to leave much of life unemployed.
SAMUEL JOHNSON: *Rasselas,* 1759

If need is the standing scourge of the lower classes, then boredom is that of the upper. In the middle classes the latter is represented by Sunday, and the former by the six weekdays.
ARTHUR SCHOPENHAUER: *The World as Will and Idea,* I, 1819

Boredom is an evil that is not to be estimated lightly. It can come in the end to real despair. The public authority takes precautions against it everywhere, as against other universal calamities.
ARTHUR SCHOPENHAUER: *The World as Will and Idea,* IV

Ennui has made more gamblers than avarice, more drunkards than thirst, and perhaps as many suicides as despair.
C. C. COLTON: *Lacon,* 1820

Our dearly beloved countrymen have only discovered that they are tired, and not that they are tiresome.
BYRON: *Letter to the Earl of Blessington,* April 5, 1823

Men and women can endure to be ruined, to be torn from their friends, to be overwhelmed with avalanches of misfortune, better than they can endure to be dull.
ANTHONY TROLLOPE: *North America,* I, 1862

I have had enough of sights and shows, and noise and bustle, and confusion, and now I want to disperse. I am ready to go.
S. L. CLEMENS (MARK TWAIN): *Letter from New York to the Alta Californian* (San Francisco), June 6, 1867

Boredom is a vital problem for the moralist, since at least half the sins of mankind are caused by the fear of it.
BERTRAND RUSSELL: *The Conquest of Happiness,* IV, 1930

One must know how to be bored. (Il faut savoir s'ennuyer.) FRENCH PROVERB

[*See also* Education, Happiness, Learning, Mind, Monotony, Polygamy, Society (fashionable).

Borrowing

Every woman shall borrow of her neighbor.
EXODUS III, 22, *c.* 700 B.C.

Be not made a beggar by banqueting upon borrowing.
ECCLESIASTICUS XVIII, 33, *c.* 180 B.C.

Neither borrow money of a friend; but of a mere stranger; where, paying for it, thou shalt hear of it no more: otherwise thou shalt eclipse thy credit, lose thy friend, and yet pay as dear as to another.
WILLIAM CECIL (LORD BURLEIGH): *Advice to his son, c.* 1555

Who goeth a borrowing
Goeth a sorrowing.
THOMAS TUSSER: *Five Hundred Points of Good Husbandry,* 1580

I had rather ask of my fire brown bread than borrow of my neighbor white.
GEORGE HERBERT: *Outlandish Proverbs,* 1640

Would you know what money is, go borrow some. IBID.

Better buy than borrow.
DAVID FERGUSSON: *Scottish Proverb,* 1641

Have a horse of thy own, thou mayest borrow another.
JAMES HOWELL: *Proverbs,* 1659

Borrowed garments never fit well.
THOMAS FULLER: *Gnomologia,* 1732

Thou canst not fly high with borrowed wings.
IBID.

He that would have a short Lent, let him borrow money to be repaid at Easter.
BENJAMIN FRANKLIN: *Poor Richard's Almanac,* 1738

Borrowing is not much better than begging.
G. E. LESSING: *Nathan der Weise,* II, 1779

What a careless, even deportment hath your borrower! what rosy gills! what a beautiful reliance on Providence doth he manifest,— taking no more thought than lilies. What contempt for money.
CHARLES LAMB: *The Two Races of Men,* 1820 (London Magazine, Dec.)

Who would borrow when he hath not let him borrow when he hath.
H. G. BOHN: *Handbook of Proverbs,* 1855

Let us have the courage to stop borrowing to meet continuing deficits. Stop the deficits.
F. D. ROOSEVELT: Speech in Pittsburgh, July 30, 1932

He who borrows sells his freedom.
GERMAN PROVERB

It is better to wash an old kimono than to borrow a new one. JAPANESE PROVERB

[*See also* Acquaintance, Building, Friend.

Borrowing and Lending

The borrower is servant to the lender.
PROVERBS XXII, 7, *c.* 350 B.C.

Neither a borrower nor a lender be;
For loan oft loses both itself and friend,
And borrowing dulls the edge of husbandry.
SHAKESPEARE: *Hamlet,* I, *c.* 1601

The world still he keeps at his stave's end
That need not to borrow and never will lend.
JOHN DAVIES: *The Scourge of Folly,* 1611

The human species is composed of two distinct races, the men who borrow, and the men who lend. To these two original diversities may be reduced all those impertinent classifications of Gothic and Celtic tribes, white men, black men, red men.
CHARLES LAMB: *The Two Races of Men,* 1820 (London Magazine, Dec.)

Don't lend or borrow salt or pepper; it will break friendship. If you must borrow it, don't pay it back.
AMERICAN NEGRO PROVERB

The borrower does not care who the lender is.
FRENCH PROVERB

[*See also* Borrowing, Lending.

Bosom

The beggar died, and was carried by the angels into Abraham's bosom.
LUKE XVI, 22, *c.* 75

[*See also* Breast.

Boss

People ask the difference between a leader and a boss . . . The leader works in the open, and the boss in covert. The leader leads, and the boss drives.
THEODORE ROOSEVELT: Speech at Binghamton, N. Y., Oct. 24, 1910

Boston

Tarring and feathering: a punishment lately inflicted by the good people of Boston on any person convicted, or suspected, of loyalty.
FRANCIS GROSE: *A Classical Dictionary of the Vulgar Tongue,* 1785

Boston state-house is the hub of the solar system. You couldn't pry that out of a Boston man if you had the tire of all creation straightened out for a crow-bar.
O. W. HOLMES: *The Autocrat of the Breakfast-Table,* VI, 1858

What she was is Boston still.
J. G. WHITTIER: *The Landmarks,* 1879

There is a good deal of the Hellenic in B., and the people are getting handsomer too — padded out, with freer motions, and with color in their faces.
WALT WHITMAN: *Specimen Days,* May 1, 1881

And this is good old Boston,
The home of the bean and the cod,
Where the Cabots speak only to Lowells,
And the Lowells speak only to God.
JOHN C. BOSSIDY, *c.* 1891

There are not ten men in Boston equal to Shakespeare.
Ascribed to an unnamed Bostonian by W. E. GLADSTONE in a conversation with Lionel A. Tollemache, Dec. 23, 1891

It will be a cold day when Boston gets left. (Dies erit praegelida sinistra quum Bostonia.)
J. J. ROCHE: *The V–A–S–E,* 1900

If you hear an owl hoot: " To whom " instead of " To who," you can make up your mind he was born and educated in Boston.
Author unidentified

[*See also* America, Faneuil Hall, Puritan.

Bostonian

Gouge: to squeeze out a man's eye with the thumb, a cruel practice used by the Bostonians in America.
FRANCIS GROSE: *A Classical Dictionary of the Vulgar Tongue,* 1785

The Bostonians are really, as a race, far inferior in point of anything beyond mere talent to any other set upon the continent of North America. They are decidedly the most servile imitators of the English it is possible to conceive.
E. A. POE: *Letter to —— Thomas,* Feb. 4, 1849

A solid man of Boston;
A comfortable man with dividends.
H. W. LONGFELLOW: *New England Tragedies,* 1868

Your grave Bostonian, stately of pace,
With second-hand English writ in his face.
Anon.: *Nebulae,* 1871 (Galaxy, Aug.: ascribed to a " poetaster of A.D. 1851 ")

A Boston man is the East wind made flesh.
THOMAS G. APPLETON (1812–1884)

[*See also* Boston.

Boswell, James (1740–95)

I love you as a kind man, I value you as a worthy man, and hope in time to reverence you as a man of exemplary piety.
SAMUEL JOHNSON: *Letter to Boswell,* Aug. 27, 1775

I have heard you mentioned as a man whom everybody likes. I think life has little more to give.
SAMUEL JOHNSON: *Letter to Boswell,* July 3, 1778

Jemmy had a sycophantish, but a sincere admiration of the genius, erudition and virtue of Ursa-Major, and in recording the noble growlings of the Great Bear, thought not of his own Scotch snivel.
JOHN WILSON: *Noctes Ambrosianæ,* I, 1822

The Life of Johnson is assuredly a great, a very great work. Homer is not more decidedly the first of heroic poets, Shakespeare is not more decidedly the first of dramatists, Demosthenes is not more decidedly the first of orators, than Boswell is the first of biographers. He has no second.

T. B. MACAULAY: *Samuel Johnson,* 1831 (Edinburgh Review, Sept.)

Lues Boswelliana, or the disease of admiration.

T. B. MACAULAY: *William Pitt,* 1834 (Edinburgh Review, Jan.)

Bottle

Neither do men put new wine into old bottles; else the bottles break, and the wine runneth out, and the bottles perish: but they put new wine into new bottles, and both are preserved. MATTHEW IX, 17, *c.* 75

Bottom

[*See* Independence.

Bouillabaisse

This bouillabaisse a noble dish is —
A sort of soup or broth, or brew,
Or hotchpotch of all sorts of fishes,
That Greenwich never could outdo;
Green herbs, red peppers, mussels, saffron,
Soles, onions, garlic, roach, and dace;
All these you eat at Terre's tavern,
In that one dish of bouillabaisse.

W. M. THACKERAY: *Ballad of Bouillabaisse, c.* 1850

Bourbon

They have learned nothing and forgotten nothing.

Ascribed to various Frenchmen, including C. M. TALLEYRAND, *c.* 1800

The Bourbons are a set of imbeciles.

NAPOLEON I: To Barry E. O'Meara at St. Helena, March 10, 1817

Bourgeoisie

The bourgeoisie is unfit to rule because it is incompetent to assure an existence to its slave within his slavery, because it cannot help letting him sink into such a state that it has to feed him instead of being fed by him.

KARL MARX and FRIEDRICH ENGELS: *The Communist Manifesto,* 1848

Bourgeois rule is bourgeois rule; national peculiarities do not affect it.

NIKOLAI LENIN: *In Pravda,* June 14, 1917

[*See also* Capital, Classes, Communism, English, Family, Jew, Proletariat, State.

Bow

At her feet he bowed, he fell, he lay down: at her feet be bowed, he fell: where he bowed, there he fell down dead.

JUDGES V, 27, *c.* 500 B.C.

Rather let my head
Stoop to the block than those knees bow to any
Save to the God of Heaven and to my king.

SHAKESPEARE: *II Henry VI,* IV, *c.* 1591

[*See also* Politeness.

Bow-wows

He has gone to the demnition bow-wows.

CHARLES DICKENS: *Nicholas Nickleby,* LXIV, 1839

Boy

The boys grew. GENESIS XXV, 27, *c.* 700 B.C.

A boy is, of all wild beasts, the most difficult to manage. PLATO: *Laws,* VII, *c.* 360 B.C.

He that is manned with boys and horsed with colts shall have his meat eaten and his work undone.

WILLIAM CAMDEN: *Remains Concerning Britain* (4th ed.), 1636

Boys will be men.

THOMAS FULLER: *Gnomologia,* 1732

Boys are, at best, but pretty buds unblown,
Whose scent and hues are rather guess'd than known.

WILLIAM COWPER: *Tirocinium,* 1785

Boys will be boys.

ENGLISH PROVERB, apparently not recorded in its present form before the XIX century; in the form of "Children will do like children" Apperson traces it to 1681, and in that of "Young fellows will be young fellows" it is to be found in ISAAC BICKERSTAFF: *Love in a Village,* II, 1762

One boy is more trouble than a dozen girls.

ENGLISH PROVERB, not recorded before the XIX century

Boys are capital fellows in their own way, among their mates; but they are unwholesome companions for grown people.

CHARLES LAMB: *The Old and the New Schoolmaster,* 1821 (London Magazine, May)

"Sir — sir, it is a boy!" "A boy," said my father, looking up from his book, and evidently much puzzled; "what is a boy?"

E. G. BULWER-LYTTON: *The Caxtons,* I, 1849

A boy's will is the wind's will,
And the thoughts of youth are long, long thoughts.

H. W. LONGFELLOW: *My Lost Youth,* 1855 (Credited to "a Lapland song")

[Boys] know truth from counterfeit as quick as the chemist does. They detect weakness in your eye and behavior a week before you open your mouth, and have given you the benefit of their opinion quick as a wink.

R. W. EMERSON: *Education,* 1865

The fact that boys are allowed to exist at all is evidence of a remarkable Christian forbearance among men.

AMBROSE BIERCE: *In the San Francisco News Letter,* 1869

Speak roughly to your little boy,
And beat him when he sneezes.

C. L. DODGSON (LEWIS CARROLL): *Through the Looking-Glass,* 1871

I devise to boys, jointly, all the idle fields and commons, where ball may be played, all pleasant waters where one may swim, all snow-clad hills where one may coast, and all streams and ponds where one may fish, or where, when Winter comes, one may skate, to have and to hold the same for the period of their boyhood. And all the meadows, with the clover-blossoms and butterflies thereof, the woods with their appurtenances, the birds and squirrels and echoes and strange noises, and all distant places which may be visited, together with the adventures there to be found.

CHARLES LOUNSBURY: Last will and testament, *c.* 1875

About the ugliest creature on earth is a tall, slim boy wearing spectacles.

E. W. HOWE: *Country Town Sayings,* 1911

A boy is a cross between a god and a goat.

Author unidentified

A boy is an appetite with a skin pulled over it.

IBID.

A growing boy has a wolf in his belly.

GERMAN PROVERB

A boy's love is water in a basket.

SPANISH PROVERB

[*See also* Boy and Girl, Boyhood, Brandy, Child, Children, Education, Girl.

Boy and Girl

The streets of the city shall be full of boys and girls playing.

ZECHARIAH VIII, 5, *c.* 520 B.C.

They . . . have given a boy for a harlot, and sold a girl for wine.

JOEL III, 3, *c.* 350 B.C.

You may chisel a boy into shape, as you would a rock, or hammer him into it if he be of a better kind, as you would a piece of bronze. But you cannot hammer a girl into anything. She grows as a flower does.

JOHN RUSKIN: *Sesame and Lilies,* II, 1865

A girl is worth only a tenth of a boy.

CHINESE PROVERB

One boy is better than three girls.

GERMAN PROVERB

[*See also* Boy, Child, Children, Girl.

Boyhood

Boyhood is a Summer sun.

E. A. POE: *Tamerlane,* 1827

Oh, for boyhood's painless play,
Sleep that wakes in laughing day,
Health that mocks the doctor's rules,
Knowledge never learned of schools.

J. G. WHITTIER: *The Barefoot Boy,* 1855

[*See also* Ages, Boy.

Braggart

Brag is a good dog, but Holdfast is better.

ENGLISH PROVERB, traced by Apperson to 1598

Every braggart shall be found an ass.

SHAKESPEARE: *All's Well that Ends Well,* IV, *c.* 1602

[*See also* Boasting.

Brahma

If the red slayer think he slays,
Or if the slain think he is slain,
They know not well the subtle ways
I keep, and pass, and turn again.

R. W. EMERSON: *Brahma,* 1867

Brahmin

No worse crime is known on earth than killing a Brahmin. Even a king must not commit it, nor even imagine it.

THE CODE OF MANU, VIII, *c.* 100

The man who despises a Brahmin will endure many hells, and then be reborn into the world as a cow.

TULSĪ DĀS: *Rāmāyan,* 1574

It is better a Brahmin should be respected than that nobody should be respected.

SYDNEY SMITH: In the Edinburgh Review, 1808

[*See also* Ferry.

Brahms, Johannes (1833–97)

There would, there must, come one who would claim mastership by no gradual development, but would burst upon us fully grown, as Minerva sprang from the head of Jupiter. He has come, this chosen youth, over whose cradle the graces and heroes seem to have kept watch. His name is Johannes Brahms.

ROBERT SCHUMANN: *Neue Bahnen,* 1854 (*Neue Zeitschrift für Musick,* Oct. 28)

It irritates me to see this self-conscious mediocrity hailed as a genius. Compared to him, Raff was a giant, not to mention Rubinstein — a much greater man.

P. I. TSCHAIKOVSKY: *Diary,* Oct., 1886

Exit in case of Brahms.

PHILIP HALE: Inscription proposed for the doors of Symphony Hall, Boston, *c.* 1895

Brain

There are three kinds of brains: one understands of itself, another can be taught to understand, and the third can neither understand of itself or be taught to understand.

NICCOLÒ MACHIAVELLI: *The Prince,* XXII, 1513

Cudgel thy brains.

SHAKESPEARE: *Hamlet,* V, *c.* 1601

'Tis not good manners to offer brains.

JONATHAN SWIFT: *Polite Conversation,* II, 1738

The brain has muscles for thinking as the legs have muscles for walking.
J. O. DE LA METTRIE: *L'Homme machine,* 1748

The white medullary substance of the brain is the immediate instrument by which ideas are presented to the mind; or, in other words, whatever changes are made in this substance, corresponding changes are made in our ideas, and vice versa.
DAVID HARTLEY: *Observations on Man,* I, 1749

Our brains are seventy-year clocks. The angel of life winds them up once for all, then closes the case, and gives the key into the hands of the angel of the resurrection.
O. W. HOLMES: *The Autocrat of the Breakfast-Table,* VIII, 1858

The brain is only one condition out of many on which intellectual manifestations depend; the others being, chiefly, the organs of the senses and the motor apparatuses, especially those which are concerned in prehension and in the production of articulate speech.
T. H. HUXLEY: *Evidence as to Man's Place in Nature,* II, 1863

An apparatus with which we think that we think.
AMBROSE BIERCE: *The Devil's Dictionary,* 1906

The brain is not an organ to be relied upon. It is developing monstrously. It is swelling like a goitre.
ALEXANDER BLOK: *The Scythians,* 1918

We use our brains very little, and when we do, it is only to make excuses for our reflexes and our instincts — only to make our acts appear more studied.
MARTIN H. FISCHER (1879–)

There's brains enough ootside his head.
SCOTTISH PROVERB

[*See also* Head, Mind, Mind and Body, Money, Soul, Thinking, Understanding.

Brandy

Man can die
Much bolder with brandy.
JOHN GAY: *The Beggar's Opera,* III, 1728

Claret is the liquor for boys; port for men; but he who aspires to be a hero must drink brandy.
SAMUEL JOHNSON: *Boswell's Life,* April 7, 1779

A dose of brandy, by stimulating the circulation, produces Dutch courage.
HERBERT SPENCER: *The Study of Sociology,* VIII, 1873

Red wine for children, champagne for men, and brandy for soldiers.
OTTO VON BISMARCK (1815–1898)

Brandy is lead in the morning, silver at noon, gold at night.
GERMAN PROVERB

[*See also* Teetotaler.

Bravery

Fortune favors the brave. (Fortes fortuna adjuvat.)
TERENCE: *Phormio,* I, *c.* 160 B.C.

Only the brave enjoy noble and glorious deaths.
DIONYSIUS OF HALICARNASSUS: *Antiquities of Rome,* VI, *c.* 20 B.C.

God himself helps the brave. (Audentes Deus ipse juvat.)
OVID: *Metamorphoses, c.* 5

What man dare, I dare:
Approach thou like the rugged Russian bear,
The arm'd rhinoceros, or the Hyrcan tiger,
Take any shape but that, and my firm nerves
Shall never tremble.
SHAKESPEARE: *Macbeth,* III, *c.* 1605

What's brave, what's noble,
Let's do it after the high Roman fashion,
And make death proud to take us.
SHAKESPEARE: *Antony and Cleopatra,* IV, *c.* 1606

I have done one braver thing
Than all the worthies did;
And yet a braver thing doth spring,
Which is, to keep that hid.
JOHN DONNE: *The Undertaking, c.* 1610

Brave men are brave from the first blow.
PIERRE CORNEILLE: *The Cid,* II, 1636

None but the brave deserve the fair.
JOHN DRYDEN: *Alexander's Feast,* 1697

Women are partial to the brave, and they think every man handsome who is going to the camp or the gallows.
JOHN GAY: *The Beggar's Opera,* I, 1728

Some have been thought brave because they were afraid to run away.
THOMAS FULLER: *Gnomologia,* 1732

How sleep the brave who sink to rest
By all their country's wishes bless'd!
WILLIAM COLLINS: *Ode Written in the Year* 1746

That man is not truly brave who is afraid either to seem or to be, when it suits him, a coward.
E. A. POE: *Marginalia,* 1844–49

Bravery never goes out of fashion.
W. M. THACKERAY: *The Four Georges,* II, 1860

The bravest are the tenderest,
The loving are the daring.
BAYARD TAYLOR: *The Song of the Camp,* 1864

A brave man, were he seven times king,
Is but a brave man's peer.
A. C. SWINBURNE: *Marino Faliero,* II, 1885

Bravery is not an individual, a racial, a national quality, in which some excel others *per se.* It is an accident of circumstances.
MICHAEL J. DEE: *Conclusions,* VI, 1917

The world belongs to the brave.
GERMAN PROVERB

A brave man may fall but he cannot yield. (Fortis cadere, cedere non potest.)
LATIN PROVERB

The brave are in prison, and the stupid are priests.
RUSSIAN PROVERB

It is easy to be brave behind a castle wall.
WELSH PROVERB

[*See also* Agamemnon, Audacity, Bold, Courage, Mercy, Peace, Soldier, Sword, Valor, War.

Braying

[*See* Ass.

Bread

Man doth not live by bread only.
DEUTERONOMY VIII, 4, *c.* 650 B.C. (In MATTHEW IV, 4, *c.* 75, and LUKE IV, 4, *c.* 75, *doth* is changed to *shall,* and *only* to *alone*)

Cast thy bread upon the waters: for thou shalt find it after many days.
ECCLESIASTES XI, 1, *c.* 200 B.C.

Bread . . . strengtheneth man's heart.
PSALMS CIV, 15, *c.* 150 B.C.

Give us this day our daily bread.
MATTHEW VI, 11, *c.* 75 (Cf. LUKE XI, 3, *c.* 75)

What man is there of you, whom if his son ask bread, will he give him a stone?
MATTHEW VII, 9, *c.* 75 (Cf. LUKE XI, 11, *c.* 75)

Bread and circuses. (Panem et circenses.)
LATIN PHRASE, indicating the bribes held out to the populace by wealthy politicians; probably first recorded in JUVENAL: *Satires,* X, 125

Acorns were good enough until bread was invented.
JUVENAL: *Satires,* XIV, 128

He hath enough that hath bread enough.
WILLIAM LANGLAND: *Piers Plowman,* 1377 (Borrowed from the Latin)

Better is half a loaf than no bread.
JOHN HEYWOOD: *Proverbs,* 1546

Bread made only of the branny part of the meal, which the poorest sort of people use, especially in time of dearth and necessity, giveth a very bad and excremental nourishment to the body: it is well called *panis canicarius,* because it is more fit for dogs than for men.
TOBIAS VENNER: *Via recta,* 1620

Bread is the staff of life.
ENGLISH SAYING, traced by Smith to 1638, but probably much older

Bread is the staff of life; in which is contained, inclusive, the quintessence of beef, mutton, veal, venison, partridge, plum-pudding, and custard: and to render all complete, there is intermingled a due quantity of water, whose crudities are also corrected by yeast or barm, through which means it becomes a wholesome fermented liquor, diffused through the mass of the bread.
JONATHAN SWIFT: *A Tale of a Tub,* IV, 1704

Bread . . . strengthens man's heart, and [is] therefore called the staff of life.
MATTHEW HENRY: *Exposition of Psalm CIV,* 1705 (Cf. PSALMS CIV, 15, *ante, c.* 150 B.C.)

If the people have no bread, let them eat cake. (Si le peuple n'a pas de pain, qu'il mange la brioche.)
Commonly ascribed to MARIE ANTOINETTE (1755–93), but Latham shows that the saying is to be found in J.-J. ROUSSEAU: *Confessions,* written in 1737–41; it is there credited to an unnamed *grande princesse*

The second side of the bread takes less time to toast.
ENGLISH PROVERB, not recorded before the XIX century

Oh, God! that bread should be so dear,
And flesh and blood so cheap!
THOMAS HOOD: *The Song of the Shirt,* 1846

God gave us teeth; let us trust to him for bread.
CZECH PROVERB

Bread and salt make the cheeks red.
GERMAN PROVERB

[*See also* Beer, Best, Bible, Good, Home, Hunger, Labor, Olive.

Bread and Butter

I know on which side my bread is buttered.
JOHN HEYWOOD: *Proverbs,* 1546

They that have no other meat
Bread and butter are glad to eat.
JOHN CLARKE: *Parœmiologia Anglo-Latina,* 1639

I won't quarrel with my bread and butter.
JONATHAN SWIFT: *Polite Conversation,* I, 1738

Bread always falls on its buttered side.
ENGLISH PROVERB, not recorded before the XIX century

Bread, milk, and butter are of venerable antiquity. They taste of the morning of the world.
LEIGH HUNT: *The Seer,* XI, 1840

[*See also* Prudence.

Bread and Cheese

Bread and cheese is medicine for the well.
FRENCH PROVERB

Bread and cheese is gude to eat when folk can get nae ither meat. SCOTTISH PROVERB

[*See also* Bachelor.

Bread and Wine

[*See* Transubstantiation.

Bread of Life

Jesus said unto them, I am the bread of life: he that cometh to me shall never hunger; and he that believeth on me shall never thirst. JOHN VI, 35, *c.* 115

Breakfast

I advertise all such as have plethorick and full bodies, especially living at rest, and which are of a phlegmatick temperament, that they not only eschew the use of breakfasts, but also oftentimes content themselves with one meal in a day.
TOBIAS VENNER: *Via recta,* 1620

A good, honest, wholesome, hungry breakfast.
IZAAK WALTON: *The Compleat Angler,* V, 1653

If I were to fast for my life I would eat a good breakfast in the morning.
JOHN RAY: *English Proverbs,* 1670

An honest Yorkshire gentleman used to invite his acquaintances at Paris to break their fast with him on cold roast beef and mum.
RICHARD STEELE: *The Guardian,* April 20, 1713 (*Mum*=a German beer)

Few things bought with money are more delightful than a French breakfast . . . [It] costs about one-third as much as the beefsteaks and coffee in America.
N. P. WILLIS: *Pencillings by the Way,* IV, 1835

Before breakfast a man feels but queasily,
And a sinking at the lower abdomen
Begins the day with indifferent omen.
ROBERT BROWNING: *The Flight of the Duchess,* 1844

The average American's simplest and commonest form of breakfast consists of coffee and beefsteak.
S. L. CLEMENS (MARK TWAIN): *A Tramp Abroad,* XLIX, 1879

Only dull people are brilliant at breakfast.
OSCAR WILDE: *An Ideal Husband,* II, 1895

[*See also* Kiss.

Breast

Thy two breasts are like two young roes that are twins, which feed among the lilies.
SOLOMON'S SONG IV, 5, *c.* 200 B.C. (The heading of the chapter in the King James Bible reads "Christ setteth forth the graces of the church." Cf. VII, 3)

Her paps are centers of delight,
Her breasts are orbs of heavenly frame.
THOMAS LODGE: *Rosalynde,* 1590

Show me no more those snowy breasts
With azure riverets branched
Where, whilst mine eye with plenty feasts
Yet is my thirst not staunched;
O Tantalus, thy pains ne'er tell
By me thou are prevented
'Tis nothing to be plagued in Hell,
But thus in Heaven tormented.
MICHAEL DRAYTON: *To His Coy Love,* 1631

The yielding marble of her snowy breast.
EDMUND WALLER: *On a Lady Passing through a Crowd of People, c.* 1680

The reason why the bosom of a beautiful woman is an object of such peculiar delight arises from hence: that all our first pleasurable sensations of warmth, sustenance, and repose are derived from this interesting source.
C. C. COLTON: *Lacon,* 1820

Under its loosened vest
Fluttered her little breast,
Like birds within their nest
By the hawk frighted.
H. W. LONGFELLOW: *The Skeleton in Armor,* 1841

A woman without breasts is like a bed without pillows.
JACQUES THIBAULT (ANATOLE FRANCE): *La rôtisserie de la Reine Pédauque,* XVI, 1893

Breath

The breath of life. GENESIS II, 7, *c.* 700 B.C.

Save your breath to cool your porridge.
ENGLISH PROVERB, traced by Smith to 1599, and probably much older (*Broth* sometimes appears in place of *porridge*)

Sh'as a breath stinks worse than fifty polecats.
THOMAS DEKKAR: *II The Honest Whore,* IV, 1630

The first breath is the beginning of death.
THOMAS FULLER: *Gnomologia,* 1732

Breeches

Thou shalt make them linen breeches to cover their nakedness; from the loins even unto the thighs they shall reach.
EXODUS XXVIII, 42, *c.* 700 B.C.

They sewed fig tree leaves together and make themselves breeches.
GENESIS III, 7 in the Geneva Bible, 1560 (In the Authorized Version of 1611 the passage reads: "They sewed fig leaves to-

gether and made themselves aprons." The Geneva Bible is often called the Breeches Bible)

[*See also* Pantaloons, Trout.

Breeding

What's bred in the bone will not out of the flesh.
ENGLISH PROVERB, borrowed from the Latin and traced to *c.* 1290

Breed is stronger than pasture.
CHESHIRE PROVERB

Birth's gude but breeding's better.
SCOTTISH PROVERB

[*See also* Ancestry, Birth (High), Heredity, Heritage, Marriage, Well-bred.

Breton

[*See* Pasteur (Louis).

Brevity

Let thy speech be short, comprehending much in few words.
ECCLESIASTICUS XXXII, 8, *c.* 180 B.C.

Let your communication be, Yea, yea; Nay, nay: for whatsoever is more than these cometh of evil.
MATTHEW V, 37, *c.* 75

Do you wish to instruct? Be brief, that the mind may catch thy precepts and the more easily retain them.
HORACE: *De arte poetica, c.* 8 B.C.

Brevity is the soul of wit.
SHAKESPEARE: *Hamlet,* II, *c.* 1601

In order to speak short upon any subject, think long.
H. H. BRACKENRIDGE: *Modern Chivalry,* 1792

All intelligent people incline to express themselves briefly — to say at once whatever is to be said.
G. C. LICHTENBERG: *Reflections,* 1799

That which is brief, if it be good, is good twice over.
SPANISH PROVERB

[*See also* Advice, Epigram.

Brewery

We are not here to sell a parcel of boilers and vats, but the potentiality of growing rich beyond the dreams of avarice.
SAMUEL JOHNSON: On the sale of Thrale's brewery, April 4, 1781

I have no pain, dear mother, now,
But oh! I am so dry.
Connect me to a brewery
And leave me there to die.
Anon.: British soldiers' song, 1914–18
(Sung to the regimental marching tune of the Loyal North Lancashires)

The brewery is the best drug-store.
GERMAN PROVERB

Bribery

[Samuel's] sons . . . took bribes and perverted judgment.
I SAMUEL VIII, 3, *c.* 500 B.C.

Fire shall consume the tabernacles of bribery.
JOB XV, 34, *c.* 325 B.C.

A bribe will enter without knocking.
JOHN CLARKE: *Parœmiologia Anglo-Latina,* 1639

[*See also* Chinese, Impeachment, Treaty.

Brick

Let us make brick.
GENESIS XI, 3, *c.* 700 B.C.

The best academy for architects would be the brick-field; for of this they may rest assured, that till they know how to use clay, they will never know how to use marble.
JOHN RUSKIN: *The Stones of Venice,* II, 1853

Bricklayer

He was an honest man and a good bricklayer.
SHAKESPEARE: *II Henry VI,* IV, *c.* 1591

Bride

Can a maid forget her ornaments, or a bride her attire?
JEREMIAH II, 32, *c.* 625 B.C.

He took the bride about the neck
And kiss'd her lips with such a clamorous smack
That at the parting, all the church did echo.
SHAKESPEARE: *The Taming of the Shrew,* III, 1594

The newly married wife dreams that, rid of her young husband, she hugs her old love, and likes her dream well enough, too.
Anon.: *Humor Out of Breath,* I, 1608

A bonny bride is soon buskit.
DAVID FERGUSSON: *Scottish Proverbs,* 1641
(*Buskit*=dressed)

Blest is the bride on whom the sun doth shine.
ROBERT HERRICK: *Hesperides,* 1648

A woman with a fine prospect of happiness behind her.
AMBROSE BIERCE: *The Devil's Dictionary,* 1906

When the men meet a bride, they look at her face; the women look at her clothes.
E. W. HOWE: *Country Town Sayings,* 1911

Weeping bride, laughing wife; laughing bride, weeping wife.
GERMAN PROVERB

When the bride is hungry she recalls the seven days of her marriage feast.
HEBREW PROVERB

The father gives the dowry and God gives the bride.
SPANISH PROVERB

[*See also* Bridegroom, Kiss, Niagara Falls, Wedding.

Bridegroom

When a man hath taken a new wife, he shall not go out to war, neither shall he be charged with any business; but he shall be free at home one year, and shall cheer up his wife which he hath taken.
DEUTERONOMY XXIV, 5, *c.* 650 B.C.

Behold, the bridegroom cometh; go ye out to meet him. MATTHEW XXV, 6, *c.* 75

As neatly sponged as if he had been a bridegroom.
ROBERT GREENE: *A Quip for an Upstart Courtier*, 1592

When the bride is in the cradle the bridegroom ought to be old enough to ride a horse.
RUSSIAN PROVERB

[*See also* Bride.

Bridge

Let every man praise the bridge that carries him over.
ENGLISH PROVERB, traced by Smith to 1678

Don't cross the bridge until you get to it.
ENGLISH PROVERB, not recorded before the XIX century

Brief

[*See* Brevity.

Brimstone

[*See* Hell.

Britain

Hail, happy Britain! highly favored isle,
And Heaven's peculiar care!
WILLIAM SOMERVILLE: *The Chase*, I, 1735

When Britain first, at Heaven's command,
Arose from out the azure main,
This was the charter of the land,
And guardian angels sung this strain —
" Rule, Britannia, rule the waves;
Britons never will be slaves."
JAMES THOMSON: *Rule, Britannia*, 1740

[*See also* England, Great Britain, Peace.

British

I consider the British as our natural enemies, and as the only nation on earth who wish us ill from the bottom of their souls. And I am satisfied that, were our continent to be swallowed up by the ocean, Great Britain would be in a bonfire from one end to the other.
THOMAS JEFFERSON: *Letter to William Carmichael*, 1787

I never yet found any other general rule for foretelling what the British will do but that of examining what they ought not to do.
THOMAS JEFFERSON: *Letter to John Adams*, 1787

Of all nations on earth, the British require to be treated with the most *hauteur*. They require to be kicked into common manners.
THOMAS JEFFERSON: *Letter to Colonel W. S. Smith*, 1787

We know no spectacle so ridiculous as the British public in one of its periodical fits of morality.
T. B. MACAULAY: *Moore's Life of Lord Byron*, 1831 (Edinburgh Review, June)

[*See also* Briton, Clergy, English, Englishman.

Briton

But we, brave Britons, foreign laws despised,
And kept unconquer'd and uncivilized.
ALEXANDER POPE: *An Essay on Criticism*, III, 1711

Born and educated in this country, I glory in the name of Briton.
GEORGE III of England: Speech from the throne, 1760

[*See* also Britain, Englishman.

Bromide

Are you a bromide?
GELETT BURGESS: Title of an article in the Smart Set, April, 1906

Brook

A noise like a hidden brook
In the leafy month of June,
That to the sleeping woods all night
Singeth a quiet tune.
S. T. COLERIDGE: *The Ancient Mariner*, V, 1798

I chatter, chatter, as I flow,
To join the brimming river,
For men may come and men may go,
But I go on forever.
ALFRED TENNYSON: *The Brook*, 1887

Broom

The green new broom sweepeth clean.
JOHN HEYWOOD: *Proverbs*, 1546

A bad broom leaves a dirty room.
CHESHIRE PROVERB

Brothel

[*See* Bawdy-house, Monasticism, Nunnery, Prison.

Brother

Am I my brother's keeper?
GENESIS IV, 9, *c.* 700 B.C.

A brother offended is harder to be won than a strong city. PROVERBS XVIII, 19, *c.* 350 B.C.

Why dost thou judge thy brother?
ROMANS XIV, 10, *c.* 55

If a man die, having no children, his brother shall marry his wife, and raise up seed unto his brother. MATTHEW XXII, 24, *c.* 75

Some account [the younger brother] the better gentleman of the two, because son to the more ancient gentleman.
THOMAS FULLER: *The Holy State and the Profane State*, xv, 1642

The younger brother hath the more wit.
JOHN RAY: *English Proverbs*, 1670

The wrath of brothers is fierce and devilish.
THOMAS FULLER: *Gnomologia*, 1732

We tell the ladies that good wives make good husbands; I believe it is a more certain position that good brothers make good sisters.
SAMUEL JOHNSON: *Letter to Bennet Langton*, Jan. 9, 1759

Where'er I roam, whatever realms to see,
My heart untravell'd fondly turns to thee;
Still to my brother turns with ceaseless pain,
And drags at each remove a lengthening chain.
OLIVER GOLDSMITH: *The Traveler*, 1764

I think, am sure, a brother's love exceeds
All the world's loves in its unworldliness.
ROBERT BROWNING: *A Blot on the 'Scutcheon*, II, 1843

Brothers quarrel like thieves inside a house, but outside their swords leap out in each other's defense. JAPANESE PROVERB

He that hath no brother hath weak legs.
PERSIAN PROVERB

[*See also* Fratricide, Friend, Kiss, Man and Woman, Sister, Twins.

Brotherhood

Be kindly affectioned one to another with brotherly love; in honor preferring one another. ROMANS XII, 10, *c.* 55

A new commandment I give unto you, That ye love one another; as I have loved you, that ye also love one another.
JOHN XIII, 34, *c.* 115

Let us be brothers – or I'll cut your throat.
ECOUCHARD LEBRUN-PINDARE: *Sur la fraternité ou la mort*, *c.* 1800

Write me as one that loves his fellowmen.
LEIGH HUNT: *Abou Ben Adhem*, 1834

Grant stood by me when I was crazy, and I stood by him when he was drunk, and now we stand by each other.
W. T. SHERMAN, *c.* 1870

Lo, soul! seest thou not God's purpose from the first?
The earth to be spann'd, connected by network,
The people to become brothers and sisters,
The races, neighbors, to marry and be given in marriage,
The oceans to be cross'd, the distant brought near,
The lands to be welded together.
WALT WHITMAN: *Passage to India*, 1870

The virtues which must be practised by rude men, so that they may associate in a body, . . . are practised almost exclusively in relation to the men of the same tribe; and their opposites are not regarded as crimes in relation to men of other tribes.
CHARLES DARWIN: *The Descent of Man*, IV, 1871

[*See also* Coöperation, Fellow-feeling.

Brow

Her glossy hair was cluster'd o'er a brow
Bright with intelligence, and fair, and smooth.
BYRON: *Don Juan*, I, 1819

Whose was the hand that slanted back this brow?
EDWIN MARKHAM: *The Man With the Hoe*, 1899

[*See also* Character.

Brown, John (1800–59)

Old Brown
Osawatomie Brown,
May trouble you worse than ever, when you've nailed his coffin down.
E. C. STEDMAN: *How Old Brown Took Harper's Ferry*, 1859

John Brown's body lies a-mouldering in the grave,
But his soul goes marching on.
C. S. HALL: *John Brown's Body*, 1860

Browne, Thomas (1605–82)

[*See* Ape.

Browning, Elizabeth Barrett (1806–61)

Mrs. Browning's death was rather a relief to me, I must say; no more "Aurora Leighs," thank God!
EDWARD FITZGERALD: *Letter*, July 15, 1861

Browning, Robert (1812–89)

To charge him with obscurity is about as accurate as to call Lynceus purblind, or complain of the sluggish action of the telegraph wire. He is something too much the reverse of obscure; he is too brilliant and subtle for the ready reader to follow with any certainty the track of an intelligence which moves with such incessant rapidity.
A. C. SWINBURNE: *George Chapman*, 1875

Brownstone

Nothing could be more beautiful, more refined, more elegant, than the brownstone used in facing buildings here.
S. L. CLEMENS (MARK TWAIN): *Letter from New York to the Alta Californian* (San Francisco), May 28, 1867

Brute

[*See* Animal.

Bryan, W. J. (1860–1925)

Bryan is a personally honest and rather attractive man, a real orator and a born demagogue, who has every crank, fool and putative criminal in the country behind him, and a large proportion of the ignorant honest class.

THEODORE ROOSEVELT: *Letter to Anna Roosevelt Cowles,* July 19, 1896

Buddhism

They have their belief, these poor Tibet people, that Providence sends down always an Incarnation of Himself into every generation. At bottom some belief in a kind of pope! At bottom still better, belief that there is a *Greatest* Man; that *he* is discoverable; that, once discovered, we ought to treat him with an obedience which knows no bounds. This is the truth of Grand Lamaism; the "discoverability" is the only error here.

THOMAS CARLYLE: *Heroes and Hero-Worship,* I, 1840 (Lecture in London, May 5)

A religion so cheerless, a philosophy so sorrowful, could never have succeeded with the masses of mankind if presented only as a system of metaphysics. Buddhism owed its success to its catholic spirit and its beautiful morality.

W. WINWOOD READE: *The Martyrdom of Man,* III, 1872

Buddhism is a hundred times as realistic as Christianity. It is part of its living heritage that it is able to face problems objectively and coolly. It is the product of long centuries of philosophical speculation.

F. W. NIETZSCHE: *The Antichrist.* XX, 1888

The things necessary to Buddhism are a very mild climate, customs of great gentleness and liberality, and no militarism.

F. W. NIETZSCHE: *The Antichrist,* XXI

The Buddhist doctrine [is] that real riches consist not in the abundance of goods but in the paucity of wants.

ALFRED MARSHALL: *Principles of Economics,* I, 1890

Buffalo

[*See* Prairie.

Buffoon

[*See* Actor.

Bug

[*See* Insect.

Bugbear

[*See* English.

Bugle

One blast upon his bugle horn
Were worth a thousand men.

WALTER SCOTT: *The Lady of the Lake,* VI, 1810

Blow, bugle, blow; set the wild echoes flying.
Blow, bugle; answer, echoes, dying, dying, dying.

ALFRED TENNYSON: *The Princess,* 1850

Bring the good old bugle, boys! we'll sing another song —
Sing it with a spirit that will start the world along —
Sing it as we used to sing it, fifty thousand strong,
While we were marching through Georgia.

HENRY CLAY WORK: *Marching Through Georgia,* 1865

Builder

If a builder erect a house for a man and do not make its construction firm, and the house which he built collapse and cause the death of the owner of the house, that builder shall be put to death.

THE CODE OF HAMMURABI, *c.* 2250 B.C.

Building

The easiest road to poverty is to build many houses.

THE GREEK ANTHOLOGY, X, *c.* 80 B.C.

Building and marrying of children are great wasters.

GEORGE HERBERT: *Outlandish Proverbs,* 1640

Building is the general weakness of old people, and as sure a proof of dotage as pink-colored ribands or even matrimony.

MARY WORTLEY MONTAGU: *Letter to the Countess of Bute,* May 22, 1759

To build is to be robbed.

SAMUEL JOHNSON: *The Idler,* June 23, 1759

Build and borrow,
A sackful of sorrow.
(Bauen und Borgen,
Ein Sack voll Sorgen.)

GERMAN PROVERB

One may not build upon one's own land what may do injury to another. (Ædificare in tuo proprio solo non licet quod alteri noceat.)

LEGAL MAXIM

[*See also* Marble.

Bull

Strong bulls of Bashan have beset me round.

PSALMS XXII, 12, *c.* 150 B.C.

He that cometh before [a bull] will not wear . . . red.

JOHN LYLY: *Euphues and His England,* 1580

Why dost thou, bull and boar, so sillily
Dissemble weakness, and by one man's stroke die,
Whose whole kind you might swallow and feed upon?

JOHN DONNE: *Holy Sonnets,* XII, *c.* 1617

The masters of bulls keep from them all garments of blood and scarlet, as knowing that

they will be impatient of civil usages and disciplines when their natures are provoked by their proper antipathies.
JEREMY TAYLOR: *The Mysteriousness of Marriage*, 1651

A mad bull is not to be tied up with a pack-thread.
THOMAS FULLER: *Gnomologia*, 1732

To take the bull by the horns.
ENGLISH PHRASE, not recorded before the XIX century

I'm like a bull in a china-shop.
FREDERICK MARRYAT: *Jacob Faithful*, XV, 1834 (This seems to be the earliest recorded use of the phrase)

You may play with a bull till you get his horn in your eye. CHESHIRE PROVERB

[*See also* Heredity, Monk.

Bull Moose

I wish in this campaign to do . . . whatever is likely to produce the best results for the Republican ticket. I am as strong as a bull moose and you can use me to the limit.
THEODORE ROOSEVELT: *Letter to Mark Hanna*, June 27, 1900 (Origin of the popular name of the Progressive party, 1912)

Bullet

Every bullet hath its billet.
JOHN WESLEY: *Journal*, June 6, 1765 (Cited as "the odd saying of King William")

[*See also* Ballot.

Bulletin

"False as a bulletin" became a proverb in Napoleon's time.
THOMAS CARLYLE: *Heroes and Hero-Worship*, VI, 1840 (Lecture in London, May 22)

Bull, John

[*See* John Bull.

Bully

A bully is always a coward.
ENGLISH PROVERB, not recorded before the XIX century

There are only two parts in the interlude of life, the bully and the coward — whoever has the spirit to assume the one will find his neighbor sitting down quietly under the other.
WILLIAM HAZLITT: *Butts of Different Sorts*, 1829 (The Atlas, Feb. 8)

Burden

Bear ye one another's burdens.
GALATIANS VI, 2, *c.* 50

[We] have borne the burden and heat of the day. MATTHEW XX, 12, *c.* 75

Light burdens, long borne, grow heavy.
GEORGE HERBERT: *Outlandish Proverbs*, 1640

None knows the weight of another's burden.
IBID.

The greatest burdens are not the gainfullest.
JOHN RAY: *English Proverbs*, 1670

God has made the back to the burden.
WILLIAM COBBETT: *Rural Rides*, 1822 (Quoted as a proverb)

The white man's burden.
RUDYARD KIPLING: Title of a poem, 1899

It is not the burden but the overburden that kills the beast. SPANISH PROVERB

Bureaucracy

If public officers will infringe men's rights, they ought to pay greater damages than other men, to deter and hinder other officers from the like offences.
LORD HOLT: *Judgment in Ashby* vs. *Aylesbury*, 1702

The functionaries of every government have propensities to command at will the liberty and property of their constituents.
THOMAS JEFFERSON: *Letter to Charles Yancey*, 1816

I think we have more machinery of government than is necessary, too many parasites living on the labor of the industrious.
THOMAS JEFFERSON: *Letter to William Ludlow*, 1824

The only governments, not representative, in which high political skill and ability have been other than exceptional, whether under monarchical or aristocratic forms, have been essentially bureaucracies. The work of government has been in the hands of governors by profession; which is the essence and meaning of bureaucracy.
J. S. MILL: *Representative Government*, V, 1861

I know of no duty of the court which it is more important to observe, and no powers of the court which it is more important to enforce, than its power of keeping public bodies within their rights. The moment public bodies exceed their rights, they do so to the injury and oppression of private individuals, and those persons are entitled to be protected from injury arising from such operations of public bodies.
MR. JUSTICE LINDLEY: *Judgment in Roberts* vs. *Gwyrfai District Council*, 1899

If we do not halt this steady process of building commissions and regulatory bodies and special legislation like huge inverted pyramids over every one of the simple constitutional provisions, we shall soon be spending many billions of dollars more.
F. D. ROOSEVELT: Radio address, March 2, 1930

Burglar

When the enterprising burglar isn't burgling,
  When the cut-throat isn't occupied in crime,
He loves to hear the little brook a-gurgling,
  And to listen to the merry village chime.

W. S. GILBERT: *The Pirates of Penzance,* II, 1880

Burglary

Burglary fascinates some men as sailoring fascinates some boys.

GEORGE BERNARD SHAW: *Androcles and the Lion,* pref., 1912

Burgundy

[*See* Wine (Burgundy).

Burial

He shall be buried with the burial of an ass, drawn and cast forth beyond the gates of Jerusalem. JEREMIAH XXII, 19, *c.* 625 B.C.

As for the burying of the body, whatever is bestowed on that is no aid of salvation, but an office of humanity.

ST. AUGUSTINE: *On the Care to be Had for the Dead, c.* 405

When a man dies, no gold or silver, no silk brocades, and no dyed stuffs are to be buried with him.

THE LAWS OF KOTOKU (JAPAN), *c.* 650

  Lay her i' the earth;
And from her fair and unpolluted flesh
May violets spring.

SHAKESPEARE: *Hamlet,* V, *c.* 1601

Earth to earth, ashes to ashes, dust to dust; in sure and certain hope of the Resurrection.

THE BOOK OF COMMON PRAYER (*The Burial Service*), 1662

All I desire for my own burial is not to be buried alive.

LORD CHESTERFIELD: *Letter to his daughter-in-law,* March 16, 1769

Not a drum was heard, not a funeral note,
  As his corse to the rampart we hurried;
Not a soldier discharged his farewell shot
  O'er the grave where our hero we buried.

CHARLES WOLFE: *The Burial of Sir John Moore,* 1817

Strew on her roses, roses,
  And never a spray of yew!
In quiet she reposes;
  Ah, would that I did too!

MATTHEW ARNOLD: *Requiescat,* 1853

Steady the trot to the cemetery, duly rattles the death-bell, the gate is pass'd, the new-dug grave is halted at, the living alight, the hearse uncloses,
The coffin is pass'd out, lower'd and settled, the whip is laid on the coffin, the earth is swiftly shovel'd,
The mound above is flatted with the spades — silence.

WALT WHITMAN: *To Think of Time,* 1855

[*See also* Coffin, Dead, Funeral.

Burke, Edmund (1729–97)

Though free from all little vanity, high above envy, and glowing with zeal to exalt talents and merit in others, he had a consciousness of his own greatness that shut out those occasional and useful self-doubts which keep our judgment in order by calling our motives and our passions to account.

FRANCES BURNEY: *Letter to her father,* July 27, 1797

When posterity read the speeches of Burke, they will hardly be able to believe that, during his lifetime, he was not considered as a first-rate speaker, not even as a second-rate one.

R. B. SHERIDAN: *To Samuel Rogers, c.* 1800

Burke referred habitually to principles. He was a scientific statesman; and therefore a seer.

S. T. COLERIDGE: *Biographia Literaria,* X, 1817

Burke is the fourth Englishman — Shakespeare, Bacon, Milton, Burke. Out of Burke might be cut fifty Macintoshes, one hundred and seventy-five Macaulays, forty Jeffreys, and two hundred and fifty Sir Robert Peels, and leave him greater than Pitt and Fox together.

RUFUS CHOATE: *Letter to Charles Sumner, c.* 1845

This celebrated sophist and sycophant who, . . . in the pay of the English oligarchy, played the romantic *laudator temporis acti* against the French Revolution, just as, in the pay of the North American colonies, . . . he had played the Liberal against the English oligarchy, was an out-and-out vulgar bourgeois.

KARL MARX: *Das Kapital,* I, 1867

Burlesque

[*See* Comedy.

Burns, Robert (1759–96)

I don't well know what is the reason of it, but somehow or other, though I am, when I have a mind, pretty generally loved, yet I never could get the art of commanding respect.

ROBERT BURNS: *Commonplace-Book,* May 8, 1784 (?)

Compeared Robert Burns, with Jean Armour, his alleged spouse. They both acknowledge their irregular marriage, and their sorrow for that irregularity, and desiring that the Session will take such steps as may seem to them proper, in order to the solemn confirmation of the said marriage. The Session, taking this affair under their consideration, agree that they both be rebuked for this acknowledged irregularity, and that they be solemnly engaged to adhere faithfully to one another as man and wife all the days of their life. Mr. Burns gave a guinea-note for behoof of the poor.

Entry in the Session-Book of Manchline, Aug. 5, 1788

Burns, the Ayreshire Bard, is now enjoying the sweets of retirement on his farm. Burns, in thus retiring, has acted wisely.

THE EDINBURGH ADVERTISER: *Editorial,* Nov. 28, 1788

The lark of Scotia's morning sky!
Whose voice may sing his praises?
With Heaven's own sunlight in his eye,
He walked among the daisies,
Till through the cloud of fortune's wrong
He soared to fields of glory;
But left his land her sweetest song
And earth her saddest story.

O. W. HOLMES: *For a Meeting of the Burns Club,* 1856

He had no genteel timidities in the conduct of his life. He loved to force his personality upon the world. He would please himself, and shine.

R. L. STEVENSON: *Familiar Studies of Men and Books,* II, 1882

Lord, send a man like Robbie Burns to sing the song o' steam.

RUDYARD KIPLING: *M'Andrew's Hymn,* 1893

[*See also* Fame.

Burnt

[*See* Experience.

Burr, Aaron (1756–1836)

I never thought him an honest, frank-dealing man, but considered him as a crooked gun, or other perverted machine, whose aim or shot you could never be sure of.

THOMAS JEFFERSON: *Letter to William B. Giles,* April, 1807

Business

Wist ye not that I must be about my Father's business? LUKE II, 49, *c.* 75

An honest man is not accountable for the vice and folly of his trade, and therefore ought not to refuse the exercise of it. It is the custom of his country, and there is profit in it. We must live by the world, and such as we find it, so make use of it.

MICHEL DE MONTAIGNE: *Essays,* III, 1588

Mind your own business.

ENGLISH PROVERB, borrowed from CERVANTES: *Don Quixote,* I, 1605; often called, in the United States, the Eleventh Commandment

To business that we love we rise betime,
And go to't with delight.

SHAKESPEARE: *Antony and Cleopatra,* IV, *c.* 1606

Everybody's business is nobody's business.

ENGLISH PROVERB, traced by Apperson to 1611

Great businesses turn on a little pin.

GEORGE HERBERT: *Outlandish Proverbs,* 1640

It is a great art to know how to sell wind.

BALTASAR GRACIÁN: *The Art of Worldly Wisdom,* CCLXVII, 1647

He that stays does the business.

GEORGE HERBERT: *Jacula Prudentum,* 1651

Business is the salt of life.

THOMAS FULLER: *Gnomologia,* 1732

Men of business must not break their word twice. IBID.

Let your discourse with men of business be short and comprehensive.

GEORGE WASHINGTON: *Early copy-book,* before 1748

Few people do business well who do nothing else.

LORD CHESTERFIELD: *Letter to his son,* Aug. 7, 1749

Business is business.

GEORGE COLMAN THE YOUNGER: *The Heir-at-Law,* III, 1797

The most sensible people to be met with in society are men of business and of the world, who argue from what they see and know, instead of spinning cobweb distinctions of what things ought to be.

WILLIAM HAZLITT: *The Ignorance of the Learned,* 1821

Every man to his own business.

J. S. KNOWLES: *The Love-Chase,* V, 1837

There are geniuses in trade as well as in war, or the state, or letters; and the reason why this or that man is fortunate is not to be told. It lies in the man: that is all anybody can tell you about it.

R. W. EMERSON: *Character,* 1841

Boldness, in business, is the first, second, and third thing.

H. G. BOHN: *Handbook of Proverbs,* 1855

Business is really more agreeable than pleasure; it interests the whole mind, the aggregate nature of man more continuously, and more deeply. But it does not look as if it did.

WALTER BAGEHOT: *The English Constitution,* 1867

Who likes not his business, his business likes not him.

W. C. HAZLITT: *English Proverbs,* 1869

The nature of business is swindling.

AUGUST BEBEL: Speech in Zürich, Dec., 1892

My own business always bores me to death; I prefer other people's.

OSCAR WILDE: *Lady Windermere's Fan,* II, 1892

Whatever is not nailed down is mine. Whatever I can pry loose is not nailed down.

Ascribed to COLLIS P. HUNTINGTON (1821–1900)

The fundamental principles which govern the handling of postage stamps and of millions of dollars are exactly the same. They are the common law of business, and the whole practice of commerce is founded on them. They are so simple that a fool can't learn them; so hard that a lazy man won't.
PHILIP D. ARMOUR (1832–1901)

The gambling known as business looks with austere disfavor upon the business known as gambling.
AMBROSE BIERCE: *The Devil's Dictionary,* 1906

We have witnessed in modern business the submergence of the individual within the organization, and yet the increase to an extraordinary degree of the power of the individual, of the individual who happens to control the organization. Most men are individuals no longer so far as their business, its activities, or its moralities are concerned. They are not units but fractions.
WOODROW WILSON: Speech at Chattanooga, Tenn., Aug. 31, 1910

I hold it to be our duty to see that the wage-worker, the small producer, the ordinary consumer, shall get their fair share of the benefit of business prosperity. But it either is or ought to be evident to everyone that business has to prosper before anybody can get any benefit from it.
THEODORE ROOSEVELT: Address to the Ohio Constitutional Convention, Feb. 1, 1912

Business underlies everything in our national life, including our spiritual life. Witness the fact that in the Lord's Prayer, the first petition is for daily bread. No one can worship God or love his neighbor on an empty stomach.
WOODROW WILSON: Speech in New York, May 23, 1912

The maxim of the British people is "Business as usual."
WINSTON CHURCHILL: Speech at the Guildhall, London, Nov. 9, 1914

In thousands of years there has been no advance in public morals, in philosophy, in religion or in politics, but the advance in business has been the greatest miracle the world has ever known.
E. W. HOWE: *The Blessing of Business,* 1918

All business sagacity reduces itself in the last analysis to a judicious use of sabotage.
THORSTEIN VEBLEN: *The Nature of Peace,* 1919

The business of America is business.
CALVIN COOLIDGE: Speech before the Society of American Newspaper Editors, Washington, Jan. 17, 1925

Subject to compensation when compensation is due, the legislature may forbid or restrict any business when it has a sufficient force of public opinion behind it.
MR. JUSTICE O. W. HOLMES: *Dissenting opinion in Tyson* vs. *Banton,* 1926

Call upon a man of business during hours of business only to transact your business. Then go about your business and give him time to attend to his business.
Author unidentified

I was figuring on starting some kind of a business, but most every business is already engaged in more than's necessary; and then I ain't got no business ability. What I want is something that don't call for no kind of ability whatsoever and no kind of exertion to speak of, and ain't out of town, and pays good, and has a future. IBID.

When I hear artists or authors making fun of business men I think of a regiment in which the band makes fun of the cooks. IBID.

Business is always business. (Geschäft ist immer Geschäft.) GERMAN PROVERB

No one fouls his hands in his own business.
ITALIAN PROVERB

Secrecy is the soul of business.
SPANISH PROVERB

[*See also* Age (Old), Bargain, Buyer and Seller, Commerce, Communism, Dispatch, Golden Rule, Haste, Modesty, Money, Punctuality, Trade (=commerce), Wages.

Busy

As busy as bees.
GEOFFREY CHAUCER: *The Canterbury Tales* (The Merchant's Tale), *c.* 1386 (*Bee* is usually singular)

It has been a proverb: as busy as a hen with one chicken.
JAMES SHIRLEY: *The Witty Fair One,* II, 1628

Who is more busy than he that hath least to do?
JOHN CLARKE: *Parœmiologia Anglo-Latina,* 1639

To be too busy gets contempt.
GEORGE HERBERT: *Outlandish Proverbs,* 1640

None are so busy as the fool and knave.
JOHN DRYDEN: *The Medal,* 1682

Ever busy, ever bare.
JAMES KELLY: *Complete Collection of Scottish Proverbs,* 1721

He that is busy is tempted by but one devil; he that is idle, by a legion.
THOMAS FULLER: *Gnomologia,* 1732

The busy man has few idle visitors; to the boiling pot the flies come not.
BENJAMIN FRANKLIN: *Poor Richard's Almanac,* 1752

The busier we are, the more acutely we feel that we live, the more conscious we are of life.
IMMANUEL KANT: Lecture at Königsberg, 1775

The busiest men have the most leisure.
ENGLISH PROVERB, not recorded before the XIX century

The busy have no time for tears.
BYRON: *The Two Foscari,* IV, 1821

Those who have most to do, and are willing to work, will find the most time.
SAMUEL SMILES: *Self-Help,* I, 1859 (Quoted as "the saying")

A man who is very busy seldom changes his opinions.
F. W. NIETZSCHE: *Human All-too-Human,* I, 1878

As busy as a one-armed paperhanger with the itch. AMERICAN SAYING

Busybody

Withal they learn to be idle, wandering about from house to house, and not only idle, but tattlers also and busybodies, speaking things which they ought not.
I TIMOTHY V, 13, *c.* 60

The veriest nobodies are the greatest busybodies.
BENJAMIN WHICHCOTE: *Moral and Religious Aphorisms,* 1753

Those who are fond of setting things to rights have no great objection to seeing them wrong.
WILLIAM HAZLITT: *Characteristics,* CXLVIII, 1823

The danger of minding other people's business is twofold. First, there is the danger that a man may leave his own business unattended to; and, second, there is the danger of an impertinent interference with another's affairs. The "friends of humanity" almost always run into both dangers.
W. G. SUMNER: *What Social Classes Owe to Each Other,* 1883

[*See also* Gossip.

But

But me no buts.
HENRY FIELDING: *Rape Upon Rape,* II, 1730

All would be well if there were no buts.
GERMAN PROVERB

The case has a but in it. (Die Sache hat ein Aber.) GERMAN SAYING

Butcher

One butcher does not fear many sheep.
Ascribed to ALEXANDER THE GREAT (365–323 B.C.)

Brave, bold, battering, beef-braining butchers.
JOHN TAYLOR: *Jack-a-Lent,* 1630

Your butcher breathes an atmosphere of good living. The beef mingles kindly with his animal nature. He grows fat with the best of it, perhaps with inhaling its very essence; and has no time to grow spare, theoretical, and hypochondriacal.
LEIGH HUNT: *The Seer,* XXI, 1840

Whoever has never seen a tiger, let him look at a cat; whoever has never seen a thief, let him look at a butcher. HINDU PROVERB

[*See also* Odds.

Butler

[*See* Cook, Cookery.

Butler, Samuel (1612–80)

While Butler, needy wretch, was yet alive,
No gen'rous patron would a dinner give:
See him, when starv'd to death, and turn'd to dust,
Presented with a monumental bust.
The poet's fate is here in emblem shown,
He ask'd for bread, and he receiv'd a stone.
SAMUEL WESLEY: Lines written on the setting up of a monument to Butler in Westminster Abbey, 1681

[*See also* Poet.

Butter

She brought forth butter in a lordly dish.
JUDGES V, 25, *c.* 500 B.C.

Butter is gold in the morning, silver at noon, and lead at night.
ENGLISH PROVERB, traced by Apperson to 1588

Butter is life. SANSKRIT PROVERB

[*See also* Bread and Butter, Demure.

Buttercup

Buttercups and daisies,
  Oh, the pretty flowers;
Coming ere the Springtime,
  To tell of sunny hours.
MARY HOWITT: *Buttercups and Daisies,* 1823

I'm called little Buttercup,
Dear little Buttercup,
Though I could never tell why.
W. S. GILBERT: *H.M.S. Pinafore,* I, 1878

Butterfly

And what's a butterfly? At best,
He's but a caterpillar, drest.
JOHN GAY: *Fables,* I, 1727

First grubs obscene, then wriggling worms,
Then painted butterflies.
ALEXANDER POPE: *Phryne,* 1727 (Imitation of the Earl of Dorset)

Button

You press the button, and we'll do the rest.
Advertisement of the first Kodak cameras, *c.* 1888

Buyer

It is naught, it is naught, saith the buyer: but when he is gone his way, then he boasteth.
PROVERBS XX, 14, *c.* 350 B.C.

The buyer always depreciates.
ITALIAN PROVERB

Let the buyer beware. (Caveat emptor.)
LEGAL MAXIM

[*See also* Buying and Selling, Cheap, Price, Value.

Buying

When you go to buy use your eyes, not your ears. CZECH PROVERB

Buying is cheaper than asking.
GERMAN PROVERB

Buying and Selling

Buy cheap, sell dear.
THOMAS LODGE: *A Fig for Momus,* 1595

Whatever may be the case in the court of morals, there is no legal obligation on the vendor to inform the purchaser that he is under a mistake, not induced by the act of the vendor.
MR. JUSTICE BLACKBURN: *Judgment in Smith* vs. *Hughes,* 1871

There are more fools among buyers than among sellers. FRENCH PROVERB

The buyer needs a hundred eyes; the seller but one. ITALIAN PROVERB

The buyer buys for as little as possible; the seller sells for as much as possible. (Emptor emit quam minimo potest, venditor vendit quam maximo potest.) LEGAL MAXIM

[*See also* Bargain, Bargaining, Cheap.

Buzz-saw

[*See* Caution.

By-and-bye

[*See* Procrastination.

Bygones

Let bygones be bygones.
ENGLISH PROVERB, borrowed from the Greek and traced by Apperson to 1546

Byron, Lord (1788–1824)

Lord Byron is an exceedingly interesting person, and as such is it not to be regretted that he is a slave to the vilest and most vulgar prejudices, and as mad as the winds?
P. B. SHELLEY: *Letter to T. L. Peacock,* Aug. 2, 1816

A denaturalized being who, having exhausted every species of sensual gratification, and drained the cup of sin to its bitterest dregs, is resolved to show that he is no longer human, even in his frailities, but a cool, unconcerned fiend.
JOHN STYLES: *Lord Byron's Works, Viewed in Connection with Christianity and the Obligations of Social Life,* 1821 (Sermon in Holland Chapel, London)

I really am the meekest and mildest of men since Moses.
BYRON: *Letter to Thomas Moore,* March 8, 1822 (Cf. NUMBERS XII, 3)

Lord Byron is only great as a poet; as soon as he reflects, he is a child.
J. W. GOETHE: *Conversations with Eckermann,* Jan. 18, 1825

I have a thorough aversion to his character, and a very moderate admiration of his genius; he is great in so little a way.
CHARLES LAMB: *Letter to Joseph Cottle,* May 26, 1829

He had a head which statuaries loved to copy, and a foot the deformity of which the beggars in the streets mimicked.
T. B. MACAULAY: *Moore's Life of Lord Byron,* 1831 (Edinburgh Review, June)

I never heard a single expression of fondness for him fall from the lips of any of those who knew him well.
T. B. MACAULAY: *Letter to Hannah and Margaret Macaulay,* June 7, 1831

A coxcomb who would have gone into hysterics if a tailor had laughed at him.
EBENEZER ELLIOTT: *The Village Patriarch,* note, 1840

Foreigners have erred in taking Byron too seriously. We have erred in not taking him seriously enough.
AUGUSTINE BIRRELL: Written in the margin of his copy of GEORGE BRANDES: *Main Currents in Nineteenth Century Literature,* 1918

[*See also* Tschaikovsky (P. I.).

C

Cabbage

In our precious cabbage patches the holometabolous insecta are the hosts of parasitic polyembryonic hymenoptera, upon the prevalence of which rests the psychic and somatic stamina of our fellow-countrymen.
WILLIAM OSLER: Address before the Classical Association at Oxford, May 16, 1919

A familiar kitchen-garden vegetable about as large and wise as a man's head.
AMBROSE BIERCE: *The Devil's Dictionary,* 1906

The gardener's dog neither eats cabbage himself nor lets anyone else eat it.
FRENCH PROVERB

Cabbage twice cooked is death.
GREEK PROVERB

[*See also* Cauliflower.

Cadmus

[*See* Books.

Caesar

Either Caesar or nothing. (Aut Caesar, aut nihil.)
MOTTO OF CAESAR BORGIA (1476–1507)

[*See also* Church and State, Duty (Public), Dying, Flower, German, Grammar, Grave, Name.

Caesar, Julius (102–44 B.C.)

The gods in past times have been reported as possessing some unworthy children, but no one could deem this man unworthy to have had gods for his ancestors.
MARK ANTONY: Oration over the body of Caesar, 44 B.C.

Why risk the world's great empire for a punk?
Caesar perhaps might answer he was drunk.
ALEXANDER POPE: *Moral Essays,* I (Of the Knowledge and Characters of Men), 1733

All the world allows that the emperor was the greatest genius that ever was, and the greatest judge of mankind.
DAVID HUME: *Letter to Mrs. Dysart,* March 19, 1751

Caesar was a failure. Otherwise he would not have been assassinated.
NAPOLEON I: To Gaspard Gourgaud at St. Helena, Sept. 10, 1817

The complete and perfect man.
THEODOR MOMMSEN: *Römische Geschichte,* I, 1854

[*See also* Ambition, Dead, Fall, Fat, History, Pen.

Cain

As the inventor of murder, and the father of the art, Cain must have been a man of first-rate genius.
THOMAS DE QUINCEY: *On Murder Considered as One of the Fine Arts,* 1827

[*See also* Garden.

Cake

You can't eat your cake and have it.
ENGLISH PROVERB, traced by Smith to the XVI century

[*See also* Bread.

Calamity

He that is glad at calamities shall not be unpunished.
PROVERBS XVII, 5, *c.* 350 B.C.

I am poured out like water, and all my bones are out of the joint: my heart is like wax; it is melted in the midst of my bowels.
PSALMS XXII, 14, *c.* 150 B.C.

Calamity is virtue's opportunity. (Calamitas virtutis occasio est.)
SENECA: *De providentia, c.* 64

Thou art wedded to calamity.
SHAKESPEARE: *Romeo and Juliet,* III, *c.* 1596

To have been happy adds to calamity.
JOHN FLETCHER: *The Fair Maid of the Inn,* I, 1647

When we have lost everything, including hope, life becomes a disgrace and death a duty.
VOLTAIRE: *Mérope,* II, 1743

Public calamity is a mighty leveller.
EDMUND BURKE: Speech on Conciliation with America, March 22, 1775

Who hath expounded the law that rendereth calamities gregarious,
Pressing down with yet more woes the heavy-laden mourner?
MARTIN F. TUPPER: *Proverbial Philosophy,* I, 1838

Ah, somewhere in this favored land the sun is shining bright,
The band is playing somewhere, and somewhere hearts are light.
And somewhere men are laughing, and somewhere children shout:
But there is no joy in Mudville — mighty Casey has struck out.
ERNEST L. THAYER: *Casey at the Bat,* 1888 (San Francisco Examiner, June 3)

Calamities are of two kinds: misfortune to ourselves, and good fortune to others.
AMBROSE BIERCE: *The Devil's Dictionary,* 1906

A calamity that affects everyone is only half a calamity.
ITALIAN PROVERB

[*See also* Affliction, God, Misfortune.

Calf

[*See* Heredity, Veal.

Calhoun, John C. (1782–1850)

Mr. Calhoun's friendships and enmities are regulated exclusively by his interests. His opinions are the sport of every popular blast, and his career as a statesman has been marked by a series of the most flagrant inconsistencies.
JOHN QUINCY ADAMS: *Diary,* March 2, 1831

Mr. Calhoun, the cast-iron man, looks as if he had never been born and could not be extinguished.
HARRIET MARTINEAU: *A Retrospect of Western Travel,* XII, 1838

California

We cultivate and irrigate, but it is God who exaggerates.
Ascribed to an unidentified Californian, bragging about the fertility of the state

In Southern California the vegetables have no flavor, and the flowers have no smell.
HOLLYWOOD PROVERB

The California climate makes the sick well and the well sick, the old young and the young old. IBID.

[*See also* Hollywood.

Calling

[*See* Profession, Trade (=craft), Vocation.

Calm

After a calm cometh a storm.
THOMAS DRAXE: *Bibliotheca scholastica instructissima,* 1633

It is the first duty of the citizen to be calm. (Ruhe ist die erste Bürgerpflicht.)
F. W. COUNT VON DER SCHULENBURG-KEHNERT: Proclamation to the people of Berlin, Oct. 17, 1806, three days after the Battle of Jena

[*See also* Serenity.

Calumny

A man calumniated is doubly injured — first by him who utters the calumny, and then by him who believes it.
HERODOTUS: *Histories,* VII, *c.* 430 B.C.

Calumny disregarded is soon forgotten by the world, but if you get into a passion about it, it seems to have a foundation of truth.
TACITUS: *History,* IV, *c.* 100

Be thou as chaste as ice, as pure as snow, thou shalt not escape calumny.
SHAKESPEARE: *Hamlet,* II, *c.* 1601

Back-wounding calumny
The whitest virtue strikes.
SHAKESPEARE: *Measure for Measure,* III, 1604

Calumniate! Calumniate! Some of it will always stick.
CARON DE BEAUMARCHAIS: *Le barbier de Séville,* III, 1775

I laid it down as a law to myself, to take no notice of the thousand calumnies issued against me, but to trust my character to my own conduct, and the good sense and candor of my fellow citizens.
THOMAS JEFFERSON: *Letter to Wilson C. Nicholas,* 1809

The upright, if he suffer calumny to move him, fears the tongue of man more than the eye of God. C. C. COLTON: *Lacon,* 1820

We resent calumny, hypocrisy, and treachery, because they harm us, not because they are untrue.
JOHN RUSKIN: *The Seven Lamps of Architecture,* II, 1849

Sticks and stones
Will break your bones,
But names will never hurt you.
CHILDREN'S RHYME, *c.* 1850

Sticks and stones are thrown only at fruit-bearing trees. PERSIAN PROVERB

You may escape a snake, but not a calumny.
RUSSIAN PROVERB

As there is no mountain without mist, so there is no man of merit without calumniators.
TURKISH PROVERB

[*See also* Gossip, Greatness, Prince, Slander.

Calvary

[*See* Crucifixion.

Calvin, John (1509–64)

Calvin and Wesley had just the same views as the popes; power and wealth their objects. I abhor both.
HORACE WALPOLE: *Letter to William Cole,* July 12, 1778

I should prefer the worst man in Greek or Roman history to John Calvin.
R. G. INGERSOLL: Interview in the Chicago Times, Nov. 14, 1879

[*See also* Gentleman.

Calvinism

You can and you can't,
You will and you won't;
You'll be damn'd if you do,
You'll be damn'd if you don't.
LORENZO DOW: *Polemical Works,* 1814

Calvinism, or the belief in election, is not simply blasphemy, but the superfetation of blasphemy.
S. T. COLERIDGE: *To Thomas Allsop, c.* 1820

What is Calvinism? It is the doctrine that an infinite God made millions of people, knowing that they would be damned. No God has a right to make a mistake, and then damn the mistake.
R. G. INGERSOLL: Speech in Chicago, Nov. 26, 1882

The Protestant movement was saved from being sunk in the quicksands of doctrinal dispute chiefly by the new moral direction given it at Geneva . . . Sparta against Persia was not such odds as Geneva against Spain. Calvinism saved Europe.
MARK PATTISON: Quoted by John Morley, in the Nineteenth Century, Feb. 1892

[*See also* Predestination, Presbyterian, Unitarianism.

Calvinist

I knew a witty physician who found the creed in the biliary duct, and used to affirm that if there was disease in the liver the man became a Calvinist.

R. W. EMERSON: *Experience,* 1841

[*See also* Materialist, Presbyterian.

Camel

Ye blind guides, which strain at a gnat, and swallow a camel.

MATTHEW XXIII, 24, *c.* 74

The ship of the desert.

ENGLISH PHRASE, not recorded before the XVIII century

[*See also* Last.

Camomile

The camomile, the more it is trodden and pressed down, the more it spreadeth.

JOHN LYLY: *Euphues,* 1579

Campaign Fund

It shall be unlawful for any national bank, or any corporation organized by authority of any laws of Congress, to make a money contribution in connection with any election to any political office. It shall also be unlawful for any corporation whatever to make a money contribution in connection with any election at which Presidential and Vice-Presidential electors or a representative in Congress is to be voted for or any election of a United States senator.

ACT OF CONGRESS approved Jan. 26, 1907

Canada

Canada, acceding to this confederation, and joining in the measures of the United States, shall be admitted into, and entitled to all the advantages of this Union: but no other colony shall be admitted into the same unless such admission be agreed to by nine states.

ARTICLES OF CONFEDERATION, XI, Nov. 15, 1777

England would be better off without Canada; it keeps her in a prepared state for war at a great expense and constant irritation.

NAPOLEON I: *Diary of Pulteney Malcolm at St. Helena,* Jan. 11, 1817

In going from the [United] States into Canada an Englishman is struck by the feeling that he is going from a richer country into one that is poorer, and from a greater country into one that is less.

ANTHONY TROLLOPE: *North America,* I, 1862

Candle

Is a candle brought to be put under a bushel, or under a bed?

MARK IV, 21, *c.* 70 (Cf. MATTHEW V, 15, *c.* 75; LUKE VIII, 16; XI, 33, *c.* 75)

To burn the candle at both ends.

ENGLISH PHRASE, familiar since the XVII century

Candlelight

Choose not a woman nor linen cloth by the candle.

JAMES SANDFORD: *Hours of Recreation,* 1572

How far that little candle throws his beams!
So shines a good deed in a naughty world.

SHAKESPEARE: *The Merchant of Venice,* V, *c.* 1597

By candlelight nobody would have taken you for above five-and-twenty.

ISAAC BICKERSTAFF: *The Maid of the Mill,* I, 1765

By candlelight a goat and a lady look alike.

FRENCH PROVERB

[*See also* Color.

Candor

Always be ready to speak your mind, and a base man will avoid you.

WILLIAM BLAKE: *The Marriage of Heaven and Hell,* 1790

I wish that not only no act but no thought of mine should be unknown.

THOMAS JEFFERSON: *Letter to James Main,* Oct., 1808

There is a candor near akin to folly, and a meekness looking like shame.

MARTIN F. TUPPER: *Proverbial Philosophy,* I, 1837

Candor is a proof of both a just frame of mind, and of a good tone of breeding. It is a quality that belongs equally to the honest man and to the gentleman.

J. FENIMORE COOPER: *The American Democrat,* XXIII, 1838

Whenever one has anything unpleasant to say one should always be quite candid.

OSCAR WILDE: *The Importance of Being Earnest,* II, 1895

[*See also* Frankness, Plain-speaking, Truth.

Cannibal

Cannibals have the same notions of right and wrong that we have. They make war in the same anger and passion that move us, and the same crimes are committed everywhere. Eating fallen enemies is only an extra ceremonial. The wrong does not consist in roasting them, but in killing them.

VOLTAIRE: *Letter to Frederick the Great,* Oct., 1737

Oh, I am a cook and a captain bold,
  And the mate of the Nancy brig,
And a bo'sun tight, and a midshipmite,
  And the crew of the captain's gig.

W. S. GILBERT: *The Bab Ballads,* 1869

A gastronome of the old school.

AMBROSE BIERCE: *The Devil's Dictionary,* 1906

[*See also* Gods.

Cannibalism

I have been assured by a very knowing American of my acquaintance in London that a young healthy child, well nursed, is at a year old a most delicious, nourishing and wholesome food, whether stewed, roasted, baked or boiled; and I make no doubt that it will equally serve in a fricassee or a ragout.

JONATHAN SWIFT: *A Modest Proposal For Preventing the Children of Poor People in Ireland From Being a Burden to Their Parents or Country,* 1729

The most unblest
Survived — sad sepulchre of all the rest.

W. C. WENTWORTH: *Australasia,* 1823

[*See also* Siege, Slander.

Cannon

Cannons and fire-arms are cruel and damnable machines; I believe them to have been the direct suggestion of the Devil. If Adam had seen in a vision the horrible instruments his children were to invent, he would have died of grief.

MARTIN LUTHER: *Table-Talk,* DCCCXX, 1569

The cannons have their bowels full of wrath,
And ready mounted are they to spit forth
Their iron indignation.

SHAKESPEARE: *King John,* II, *c.* 1596

The last argument of kings. (Ultima ratio regum.)

Inscription engraved on French cannon by order of LOUIS XIV (1638–1715)

And rounder, rounder, rounder, roared the iron six-pounder,
Hurling death!

G. H. MCMASTER: *Carmen Bellicosum,* 1849

Cannon to right of them,
Cannon to left of them,
Cannon in front of them
Volley'd and thunder'd.

ALFRED TENNYSON: *The Charge of the Light Brigade,* 1854

[*See also* Artillery, Gun, War.

Cant

My dear friend, clear your mind of cant. You may *talk* as other people do, but don't *think* foolishly.

SAMUEL JOHNSON: *Boswell's Life,* May 15, 1783

The grand *primum mobile* of England is *cant;* cant political, cant poetical, cant religious, cant moral, but always cant, multiplied through all the varieties of life.

BYRON: *Letter to John Murray,* Feb. 7, 1821

Till cant cease, nothing else can begin.

THOMAS CARLYLE: *The French Revolution,* II, 1837

The English and the Americans cant beyond all other nations.

R. W. EMERSON: *English Traits,* XIII, 1856

The expression *cant* means untruthfulness, but joined to the feeling that one is truthful or telling the truth; the deceiving of others which is at the same time a self-deception.

MORITZ BUSCH: *Leaves from My Diary,* *c.* 1890

[*See also* Criticism, Doctrinaire, Happiness, Hypocrisy.

Capacity

Man's capacities have never been measured; nor are we to judge of what he can do by any precedents, so little has been tried.

H. D. THOREAU: *Walden,* 1854

[*See also* Ability, Expert, Talent.

Capital

Parsimony, and not industry, is the immediate cause of the increase of capital. Industry, indeed, provides the subject which parsimony accumulates. But whatever industry might acquire, if parsimony did not save and store up, the capital would never be the greater.

ADAM SMITH: *The Wealth of Nations,* II, 1776

Capital is that part of the wealth of a country which is employed in production, and consists of food, clothing, tools, raw materials, machinery, etc., necessary to give effect to labor.

DAVID RICARDO: *Principles of Political Economy,* V, 1817

In bourgeois society capital is independent and has individuality, while the living person is dependent and has no individuality.

KARL MARX and FRIEDRICH ENGELS: *The Communist Manifesto,* 1848

Without the accumulation of capital the arts could not progress, and it is chiefly through their power that the civilized races have extended, and are now everywhere extending their range, so as to take the place of the lower races.

CHARLES DARWIN: *The Descent of Man,* V, 1871

Abstinence from enjoyment is the only source of capital.

THOMAS BRASSEY: Speech at the Industrial Remuneration Conference, London, 1885

Capital has a right to a just share of the profits, but only to a just share.

WILLIAM CARDINAL O'CONNELL: *Pastoral Letter on the Laborer's Rights,* Nov. 23, 1912

[*See also* Books, Capital and Labor, Capitalism, Capitalist, Civilization, Communism, Exploitation, Family, Financier, Interest, Invention.

Capital and Labor

If a man successful in business expends a part of his income in things of no real use, while the poor employed by him pass through difficulties in getting the necessaries of life, this requires his serious attention.
JOHN WOOLMAN: *Remarks on Sundry Subjects,* 1773

The number of useful and productive laborers is everywhere in proportion to the quantity of capital stock which is employed in setting them to work, and to the particular way in which it is so employed.
ADAM SMITH: *The Wealth of Nations,* I, 1776

There is no way of keeping profits up but by keeping wages down.
DAVID RICARDO: *On Protection to Agriculture,* 1820

Labor in this country is independent and proud. It has not to ask the patronage of capital, but capital solicits the aid of labor.
DANIEL WEBSTER: Speech in the House of Representatives, April 2, 1824

Whatever things are destined to supply productive labor with the shelter, protection, tools and materials which the work requires, and to feed and otherwise maintain the laborer during the process, are capital.
J. S. MILL: *Principles of Political Economy,* I, 1848

Labor is prior to, and independent of, capital. Capital is only the fruit of labor, and could never have existed if labor had not first existed. Labor is the superior of capital, and deserves much the higher consideration.
ABRAHAM LINCOLN: Message to Congress, Dec. 3, 1861

Capital is dead labor that, vampire-like, lives only by sucking living labor, and lives the more, the more labor it sucks.
KARL MARX: *Das Kapital,* I, 1867

Capital is a result of labor, and is used by labor to assist it in further production. Labor is the active and initial force, and labor is therefore the employer of capital.
HENRY GEORGE: *Progress and Poverty,* III, 1879

Labor is the capital of our workingmen.
GROVER CLEVELAND: Message to Congress, Dec. 5, 1885

Each needs the other: capital cannot do without labor, nor labor without capital.
POPE LEO XIII: *Rerum novarum,* May 15, 1891

Labor, under capitalism, is doubly enslaved. It is directed toward ends which it has not chosen by means which are forced upon it.
JEAN JAURÈS: *Études socialistes,* I, 1902

We favor enactment and administration of laws giving labor and capital impartially their just rights. Capital and labor ought not to be enemies. Each is necessary to the other. Each has its rights, but the rights of labor are certainly no less "vested," no less "sacred," and no less "unalienable" than the rights of capital.
Democratic National Platform, 1904

When we oppose labor and capital, labor means the group that is selling its product, and capital all the other groups that are buying it.
O. W. HOLMES II: Speech in New York, Feb. 15, 1913

By treating the laborer first of all as a man, the employer will make him a better working man; by respecting his own moral dignity as a man, the laborer will compel the respect of his employer and of the community.
Pastoral Letter of the Roman Catholic Archbishops and Bishops of the United States, Feb. 22, 1920

[*See also* Employment, Labor.

Capital (=city)

Everything is best at capitals; the best masters, the best companions, and the best manners. Many other places are worth seeing, but capitals only are worth residing at.
LORD CHESTERFIELD: *Letter to his son,* Oct. 2, 1749

Capitalism

Capitalist production is not merely the production of commodities; it is essentially the production of surplus value.
KARL MARX: *Das Kapital,* I, 1867

The alarming development and aggressiveness of great capitalists and corporations, unless checked, will inevitably lead to the pauperization and hopeless degradation of the toiling masses. It is imperative, if we desire to enjoy the full blessings of life, that a check be placed upon unjust accumulation and the power for evil of aggregated wealth.
CONSTITUTION OF THE KNIGHTS OF LABOR, 1869

The basic law of capitalism is you or I, not both you and I.
KARL LIEBKNECHT: Speech before the Fourth Socialist Young People's Conference, Stuttgart, 1907

Except the tax levied for personal consumption, large ownership means investment, and investment means the direction of labor toward the production of the greatest returns — returns that so far as they are great show by that very fact that they are consumed by the many, not alone by the few.

O. W. HOLMES II: Speech in New York, Feb. 15, 1913

Industrial crisis, unemployment, waste, widespread poverty, these are the incurable diseases of capitalism.

JOSEPH STALIN: Speech before the conference of managers of the Soviet industry, Feb. 4, 1931

[*See also* Capital, Imperialism, Militarism.

Capitalist

In these days a great capitalist has deeper roots than a sovereign prince, unless he is very legitimate.

BENJAMIN DISRAELI: *Tancred,* XI, 1847

Capitalists are no more capable of self-sacrifice than a man is capable of lifting himself by his own bootstraps.

NIKOLAI LENIN: *Letters from Afar,* IV, 1917

It is just that any man who does a service to society and increases the general wealth should himself have a due share of the increased public riches, provided always that he respects the laws of God and the rights of his neighbor, and uses his property in accordance with the dictates of faith and right reason.

POPE PIUS XI: *Quadragesimo anno,* May 15, 1931

Communist come up, kill all capitalist. All capitalist lousy bunch, crooked bunch.

GUISEPPE ZANGARA: Last words before his execution for the assassination of Mayor Anton Cermak of Chicago, Raiford, Fla., March 20, 1933

[*See also* Communism, Peace.

Capitalization

It offends my eyes to see rome, france, caesar, henry the fourth, etc., begin with small letters; and I do not conceive that there can be any reason for doing it half so strong as the reason of long usage is to the contrary.

LORD CHESTERFIELD: *Letter to his son,* London, April 13, 1752

Capital Punishment

[*See* Punishment, Capital.

Captain

As many are soldiers that are not captains,
So many are captains that are no soldiers.

NATHANIEL FIELD: *A Woman Is a Weather-cock,* I, 1609

[*See also* Blasphemy.

Captivity

He that leadeth into captivity shall go into captivity. REVELATION XIII, 10, *c.* 95

Capuchin

If the emperor would merit immortal praise, he would utterly root out the order of the Capuchins, and, for an everlasting remembrance of their abominations, cause their books to remain in safe custody. 'Tis the worst and most poisonous sect. The Augustin and Bernardine friars are no way comparable with these confounded lice.

MARTIN LUTHER: *Table-Talk,* CCCCLXXXIV, 1569

[*See also* Faith.

Carcass

[*See* Grave.

Cardinal

The Bishop of Derry has renounced all religions to qualify himself for being a cardinal.

HORACE WALPOLE: *Letter to the Countess of Upper Ossory,* Dec. 30, 1783

What unheard-of misery have thousands suffered to purchase a cardinal's hat for an intriguing obscure adventurer who longed to be ranked with princes, or lord it over them by seizing the triple crown!

MARY WOLLSTONECRAFT: *A Vindication of the Rights of Woman,* I, 1792

Cards

The most patient man in loss, the most coldest that ever turned up ace.

SHAKESPEARE: *Cymbeline,* II, *c.* 1609

Cards are the Devil's books.

ENGLISH PROVERB, traced by Apperson to 1676

It is very wonderful to see persons of the best sense passing away a dozen hours together in shuffling and dividing a pack of cards, with no other conversation but what is made up of a few game phrases, and no other ideas but those of black or red spots ranged together in different figures.

JOSEPH ADDISON: *The Spectator,* June 16, 1711

Cards were at first for benefits designed,
Sent to amuse, not to enslave the mind.

DAVID GARRICK: *Epilogue to Edward Moore: The Gamester,* 1753

I am sorry I have not learned to play at cards. It is very useful in life: it generates kindness and consolidates society.

SAMUEL JOHNSON: *Boswell's Tour to the Hebrides,* Nov. 21, 1773

Pleased, the fresh packs on cloth of green they see,
And seizing, handle with preluding glee;
They draw, they sit, they shuffle, cut and deal,
Like friends assembled, but like foes to feel.

GEORGE CRABBE: *The Borough,* X, 1810

[*See also* Gambling, Luck, Racing, Unlucky.

Care

Care sits behind the horseman.
HORACE: *Carmina*, III, *c.* 20 B.C.

Small cares speak; great ones are dumb.
SENECA: *Phaedra*, *c.* 60

Care killed a cat.
ENGLISH PROVERB, traced by Apperson to the Shirburn Ballads, 1585

Past cure is . . . past care.
SHAKESPEARE: *Love's Labor's Lost*, V, *c.* 1595

Care keeps his watch in every old man's eye,
And where care lodges, sleep will never lie.
SHAKESPEARE: *Romeo and Juliet*, II, *c.* 1595

Care's an enemy to life.
SHAKESPEARE: *Twelfth Night*, I, *c.* 1601

When one is past, another care we have,
Thus woe succeeds a woe, as wave a wave.
ROBERT HERRICK: *Hesperides*, 1648

Care to our coffin adds a nail, no doubt,
And every grin so merry draws one out.
JOHN WOLCOT: *Expostulatory Odes*, *c.* 1780

Ye banks and braes o' bonnie Doon,
How can ye bloom sae fresh and fair;
How can ye chant, ye little birds,
And I sae weary fu' o' care!
ROBERT BURNS: *The Banks o' Doon*, *c.* 1792

It is a mistake to suppose that all care is wakeful. People sometimes sleep, as well as wake, by reason of their sorrow.
LEIGH HUNT: *The Indicator*, XXI, 1821

The night shall be filled with music
And the cares that infest the day
Shall fold their tents like the Arabs,
And as silently steal away.
H. W. LONGFELLOW: *The Day is Done*, 1845

[*See also* Children, Drudgery, Knowledge, Man and Woman, Sleep, Sorrow, Wine.

Carefulness

Be careful, and you will save many men from the sin of robbing you.
E. W. HOWE: *Country Town Sayings*, 1911

If you can't be good be careful.
AMERICAN PROVERB

Plenty of care never does any mischief. (Abundans cautela non nocet.)
LEGAL MAXIM

He that would climb the tree maun tak care o' his grip.
SCOTTISH PROVERB (*Maun*=must)

[*See also* Caution, Good.

Carelessness

The wife of a careless man is almost a widow.
HUNGARIAN PROVERB

[*See also* Fashion.

Carlyle, Thomas (1795–1881)

I lead a most dyspeptic, solitary, self-shrouded life: consuming, if possible in silence, my considerable daily allotment of pain; glad when any strength is left in me for working, which is the only use I can see in myself.
THOMAS CARLYLE: *Letter to R. W. Emerson*, Feb. 8, 1839

We have never had anything in literature so like earthquakes as the laughter of Carlyle.
R. W. EMERSON: *Carlyle's Past and Present*, 1843

The dynasty of British dogmatists, after lasting a hundred years and more, is on its last legs. Thomas Carlyle, third in the line of descent, finds an audience very different from those which listened to the silver speech of Samuel Taylor Coleridge and the sonorous phrases of Samuel Johnson . . . We smile at his clotted English.
O. W. HOLMES: *Scholastic and Bedside Teaching*, 1867 (Lecture at Harvard, Nov. 6)

Carlyle is a poet to whom nature has denied the faculty of verse.
ALFRED TENNYSON: *To W. E. Gladstone*, *c.* 1870

Rugged, mountainous, volcanic, he was himself more a French revolution than any of his volumes.
WALT WHITMAN: *Specimen Days*, Feb. 10, 1881

The "point of view" was imposed by Carlyle on the men he judged of in his writings with an austerity not only cruel but almost stupid. They are too often broken outright on the Procrustean bed; they are probably always disfigured.
R. L. STEVENSON: *Familiar Studies of Men and Books*, pref., 1882

Carlyle's eye was a terrible organ: he saw everything.
AUGUSTINE BIRRELL: *Obiter Dicta*, I, 1884

At bottom, Carlyle is simply an English atheist who makes it a point of honor not to be one.
F. W. NIETZSCHE: *The Twilight of the Idols*, 1889

[*See also* Emerson (R. W.).

Carnality

To be carnally minded is death.
ROMANS VIII, 6, *c.* 55

The carnal mind is enmity against God.
ROMANS VIII,

Carnation

[*See* Color.

Carnegie, Andrew (1835–1919)

There was no secret about his success: he was an idealist . . . Here was a man who represented American ideals.
CALVIN COOLIDGE: Speech at the Carnegie Institute, Pittsburgh, April 28, 1921

Carnival

'Tis known, at least it should be, that throughout
All countries of the Catholic persuasion,
Some weeks before Shrove Tuesday comes about,
The people take their fill of recreation,
And buy repentance, ere they grow devout,
However high their rank, or low their station,
With fiddling, feasting, dancing, drinking, masking,
And other things which may be had for asking.
BYRON: *Beppo*, 1818

Caroline of England (1768–1821)

Most gracious queen, we thee implore
To go away and sin no more,
But if that effort be too great,
To go away at any rate.
Anon.: Verse circulated in London on the trial of the queen for adultery, 1820

Carp

[*See* Hops.

Carpenter

Is not this the carpenter, the son of Mary, the brother of James and Joses, and of Juda, and Simon?
MARK VI, 3, *c.* 70

A carpenter's known by his chips.
JONATHAN SWIFT: *Polite Conversation*, II, 1738

Even Friar Giroflée performed some service: he was a very good carpenter, and even became a man of honor.
VOLTAIRE: *Candide*, XXX, 1759

Carpet

The soul of the apartment is in the carpet. From it are deduced not only the hues but the forms of all objects incumbent.
E. A. POE: *The Philosophy of Furniture*, 1840 (Burton's Gentleman's Magazine, May)

Carping

A rage for carping. (Cacœthes carpendi.)
LATIN PHRASE

Carthage

Moreover, I believe that Carthage must be destroyed. (Ceterum censeo Carthaginem esse delendam.)
CATO THE CENSOR: In the Roman Senate, *c.* 174 (Usually, shortened to "Delenda est Carthago." Plutarch says that Cato, after his return from Carthage in 174, added the sentence to every speech he made in the Senate)

Case

A rotten case abides no handling.
SHAKESPEARE: *II Henry IV*, IV, *c.* 1598

A celebrated case. (Cause célèbre.)
FRANÇOIS DE PETEVAL: Title of a book, 1734 (There used in the plural)

Hard cases make bad law.
ENGLISH PROVERB, not recorded before the XIX century

[*See also* Circumstance.

Cash

Cash is virtue.
BYRON: *Letter to Douglas Kinnaird*, Feb. 6, 1822

Cash never yet paid one man fully his deserts to another; nor could it, nor can it, now or henceforth to the end of the world.
THOMAS CARLYLE: *Past and Present*, III, 1843

Ah, take the cash, and let the credit go.
EDWARD FITZGERALD: Tr. of OMAR KHAYYÁM: *Rubáiyát* (*c.* 1100), 1857

In God we trust; all others must pay cash.
AMERICAN SAYING

Speak little, speak the truth; spend little, pay cash.
(Rede wenig, rede wahr,
Zehre wenig, zahle bar.)
GERMAN PROVERB

[*See also* Credit, Money.

Caste

[*See* Classes.

Castle

Castles in the air.
ENGLISH PHRASE, borrowed from ST. AUGUSTINE: *Sermon*, *c.* 400 (in aere aedificare)

Thou shalt make castles then in Spain,
And dream of joy, all but in vain.
GEOFFREY CHAUCER: *The Romaunt of the Rose*, *c.* 1370

A man's house is his castle, *et domus sua cuique tutissimum refugium;* for where shall a man be safe, if it be not in his house?
EDWARD COKE: *Institutes*, III, 1644

When we apply the maxim that every man's house is his castle we mean not to persuade the inhabiter of a poor hut that it is provided with drawbridges or portcullises, but only that it is under such sufficient protection as may provide for his security in a more pleasant, or perhaps, a better way — that it is fortified by the law.
LORD MANSFIELD: *Judgment in Lee* vs. *Gansell*, 1774

The splendor falls on castle walls
And snowy summits old in story.
ALFRED TENNYSON: *The Princess*, 1847

[*See also* House, Parley, Timidity.

Castlereagh, Viscount (1769–1822)

[*See* Epitaph, Statesman.

Castor-oil

[*See* Caution.

Casuist

There is a demand today for men who can make wrong appear right.

TERENCE: *Phormio*, VIII, *c.* 160 B.C.

He would make black white, and white black.

OVID: *Metamorphoses*, XI, *c.* 5

He could distinguish and divide
A hair 'twixt south and south-west side;
On either which he would dispute,
Confute, change hands, and still confute.

SAMUEL BUTLER: *Hudibras*, I, 1663

His tongue
Dropt manna, and could make the worse appear
The better reason.

JOHN MILTON: *Paradise Lost*, II, 1667

[*See also* Jesuit.

Casuistry

To prove by reason, in reason's despite,
That right is wrong, and wrong is right,
And white is black, and black is white.

ROBERT SOUTHEY: *All for Love*, IX, 1829

[*See also* Argument, Reason.

Cat

Owls, and swallows, and other birds fly upon their bodies, and upon their heads, and cats in like manner. Whereby you may know that they are no gods.

BARUCH VI, 21–22, *c.* 75

A cat has nine lives.

ENGLISH PROVERB, traced by Apperson to the XVI century

A cat may look on a king.

JOHN HEYWOOD: *Proverbs*, 1546 (Usually *at* is substituted for *on*)

When all candles be out all cats be grey.

IBID.

When the cat's away the mice will play.

ENGLISH PROVERB, traced by Apperson to 1578

When I play with my cat, who knows whether I do not make her more sport than she makes me?

MICHEL DE MONTAIGNE: *Essays*, II, 1580

Throw a cat over a house and it will land on its feet.

ENGLISH PROVERB, familiar since the XVII century

Send not a cat for lard.

GEORGE HERBERT: *Outlandish Proverbs*, 1640

Put an old cat to an old rat.

WILLIAM D'AVENANT: *Man's the Master*, I, 1669

There are some who, if a cat accidentally come into the room, though they neither see it nor are told of it, will presently be in a sweat and ready to die away.

INCREASE MATHER: *Remarkable Providences*, IV, 1684

The cat does play,
And after slay.

The New England Primer, *c.* 1688

While rain depends, the pensive cat gives o'er
Her frolics, and pursues her tail no more.

JONATHAN SWIFT: *A Description of a City Shower*, 1710

It is lost labor to play a jig to an old cat.

THOMAS FULLER: *Gnomologia*, 1732

Lauk! what a monstrous tail our cat has got!

HENRY CAREY: *The Dragon of Wantley*, II, 1737

Her conscious tail her joy declared.

THOMAS GRAY: *Ode on the Death of a Favorite Cat*, 1747

Ding, dong, bell,
Pussy's in the well;
Who put her in?
Little Tommy Green.
Who pulled her out?
Little Johnny Stout.

Anon.: *Nursery Rhyme*, *c.* 1750

There is not room to swing a cat.

TOBIAS SMOLLETT: *Humphrey Clinker*, II, 1771

What astonished him was that cats should have two holes cut in their coats exactly at the places where their eyes were.

G. C. LICHTENBERG: *Reflections*, 1799

The cat is the only non-gregarious domestic animal. It is retained by its extraordinary adhesion to the comforts of the house in which it is reared.

FRANCIS GALTON: *Inquiries Into Human Faculty*, 1883

Cats . . . have succeeded one another through the Tertiary epoch, therefore, for many thousands, or more probably, millions, of years, . . . [and], in their capacity of butchering machines, have undergone a steady though slow and gradual improvement.

T. H. HUXLEY: *Natural Rights and Political Rights*, 1890

I like little Pussy, her coat is so warm,
And if I don't hurt her she'll do me no harm;
So I'll not pull her tail, nor drive her away,
But Pussy and I very gently will play.

Author unidentified

A bad cat deserves a bad rat.

FRENCH PROVERB

The cat dreams of garbage.
HINDU PROVERB

Whatever is born of a cat will catch mice.
ITALIAN PROVERB

A cat dreams all night long of a sheep's tail.
PERSIAN PROVERB

[*See also* Aversion, Care, Cat and Dog, Dark, Experience, Kid, Kitten, Laughter, Merriment, Toilet.

Catalogue

[*See* Library.

Cat and Dog

By scratching and biting cats and dogs come together. JOHN HEYWOOD: *Proverbs*, 1546

Cat mighty dignified till de dog come by.
AMERICAN NEGRO PROVERB

Never was a cat or dog drowned that could see the shore. ITALIAN PROVERB

Red-haired cats, like red-haired dogs, are no good. SPANISH PROVERB

Cataract

And the wild cataract leaps in glory.
ALFRED TENNYSON: *The Princess*, 1847

Catarrh

[*See* Age (Old).

Catechism

[*See* Christianity.

Caterpillar

Tis an emblem of the Devil in its crawling walk, and bears his colors in its changing hue.
MARTIN LUTHER: *Table-Talk*, DLXXXV, 1569

An upholstered worm. Author unidentified

[*See also* Butterfly.

Cathedral

Mankind was never so happily inspired as when it made a cathedral.
R. L. STEVENSON: *An Inland Voyage*, 1878

One lingers about the cathedral a good deal, in Venice . . . Propped on its long row of low thick-legged columns, its back knobbed with domes, it seems like a vast warty bug taking a meditative walk.
S. L. CLEMENS (MARK TWAIN): *A Tramp Abroad*, XLIX, 1879

[*See also* Tree.

Catholicism, Roman

Here is everything which can lay hold of the eye, ear, and imagination — everything which can charm and bewitch the simple and ignorant. I wonder how Luther ever broke the spell.
JOHN ADAMS: *Letter to his wife*, Oct. 9, 1774

I am breeding one of my daughters a Catholic. . . . It is by far the most elegant worship, hardly excepting the Greek mythology. What with incense, pictures, statues, altars, shrines, relics, and the real presence, confession, absolution, — there is something sensible to grasp at. Besides, it leaves no possibility of doubt; for those who swallow their Deity, really and truly, in transubstantiation, can hardly find anything else otherwise than easy of digestion.
BYRON: *Letter to Thomas Moore*, March 8, 1822

The Catholic religion, even in the time of its utmost extravagance and atrocity, never wholly lost the spirit of the Great Teacher whose precepts form the noblest code, as His conduct furnished the purest example, of moral excellence. It is of religions the most poetical.
T. B. MACAULAY: *Dante*, 1824 (Knight's Quarterly Magazine, Jan.)

Look through the whole history of countries professing the Romish religion, and you will uniformly find the leaven of this besetting and accursed principle of action — that the end will sanction any means.
S. T. COLERIDGE: *Table-Talk*, Aug. 6, 1831

The Catholic religion is the only one that is true.
POPE LEO XIII: *Humanum genus*, April 20, 1884

Catholicism cannot be reconciled with naturalism or rationalism.
POPE LEO XIII: *Immortale Dei*, Nov. 1, 1885

Catholicism is eunuch-like, dirty, and Oriental. . . . Yes, Oriental; there is something even Chinese about it.
GEORGE MOORE: *Confessions of a Young Man*, VII, 1888

[*See also* Church (Roman Catholic), Popery, Protestantism.

Catholic, Roman

The ungodly papists prefer the authority of the church far above God's Word; a blasphemy abominable and not to be endured; wherewith, void of all shame and piety, they spit in God's face.
MARTIN LUTHER: *Table-Talk*, LVIII, 1569

I trust I am none of the wicked that eat fish a Friday.
JOHN MARSTON: *The Dutch Courtesan*, I, 1605

There was a Romish lady, brought up in popery,
Her mother always taught her the priest she must obey.

"Oh, pardon me, dear mother, I humbly pray thee now,
But unto these false idols I can no longer bow."
Anon.: *The Romish Lady, c.* 1650

In an age where every mouth is open for liberty of conscience it is equitable to show some regard to the conscience of a papist, who may be supposed, like other men, to think himself safest in his own religion.
SAMUEL JOHNSON: Address to the Electors of Great Britain, 1774

I am a Catholic, but not a papist.
DANIEL O'CONNELL (1775–1847)

It is lawful for Catholics to work in common with non-Catholics for the common welfare, provided the proper precaution is taken.
POPE PIUS X: *Letter to the German hierarchy,* Sept. 24, 1912

A good Catholic, precisely because of his Catholic principles, makes the better citizen, attached to his country, and loyally submissive to constituted civil authority in every legitimate form of government.
POPE PIUS XI: *Divini illius magistri,* Dec. 31, 1929

[*See also* Church (Roman Catholic), Convert, Irish, Knownothingism, Socialist.

Cato, Marcus Porcius (234–149 B.C.)

Heroic, stoic Cato, the sententious,
Who lent his lady to his friend Hortensius.
BRYON: *Don Juan,* VI, 1823

Cauliflower

Cauliflower is nothing but cabbage with a college education.
S. L. CLEMENS (MARK TWAIN): *Pudd'nhead Wilson,* V, 1894

Causality

All successful men have agreed in one thing, — they were causationists. They believed that things went not by luck, but by law; that there was not a weak or a cracked link in the chain that joins the first and last of things.
R. W. EMERSON: *The Conduct of Life,* II, 1860

Intellectual progress is by no one trait so adequately characterized as by development of the idea of causation.
HERBERT SPENCER: *The Data of Ethics,* IV, 1879

If there is anything in the world which I do firmly believe in it is the universal validity of the law of causation.
T. H. HUXLEY: *Science and Morals,* 1886

I firmly believe, in company with most physicists, that the quantum hypothesis will eventually find its exact expression in certain equations which will be a more exact formulation of the law of causality.
MAX PLANCK: *Where Is Science Going?,* V, 1932

[*See also* Cause and Effect, Determinism.

Cause

'Tis a bad cause that none dare speak in.
JOHN CLARKE: *Parœmiologia Anglo-Latina,* 1639

A man is a lion in his own cause.
DAVID FERGUSSON: *Scottish Proverbs,* 1641

Men are blind in their own cause. IBID.

The patriots of the cause I serve
Those services contemn;
Yet move me not, because I serve
The cause and not the men.
DANIEL DEFOE: *A Review of the Affairs of France and of All Europe,* VIII, 1712

One cause is good
Until the other's understood.
Anon.: *Poor Robin's Almanac,* 1731

They never fail who die
In a great cause.
BYRON: *Marino Faliero,* II, 1821

No man should be a judge in his own cause. (Nemo debet esse judex in propria causa.)
LEGAL MAXIM

A gude cause makes a strong arm.
SCOTTISH PROVERB

Cause and Effect

They have sown the wind, and they shall reap the whirlwind. HOSEA VII, 7, *c.* 740 B.C.

All human actions have one or more of these seven causes: chance, nature, compulsion, habit, reason, passion, desire.
ARISTOTLE: *Rhetoric,* I, *c.* 322 B.C.

Nothing can happen without a cause.
POLYBIUS: *Histories,* II, *c.* 125 B.C.

The mountain is in labor and brings forth a ridiculous mouse. (Parturiunt montes; nascetur ridiculus mus.)
HORACE: *De arte poetica, c.* 8. B.C.

The cause is hidden, but the effect is known. (Causa latet: vis est notissima.)
OVID: *Metamorphoses,* IV, *c.* 5

Whatsoever a man soweth, that shall he also reap. GALATIANS VI, 7, *c.* 50

The most important events are often determined by very trivial causes.
CICERO: *Orationes Philippicae,* V, *c.* 60 B.C.

How great a matter a little fire kindleth!
JAMES III, 5, *c.* 60

By their fruits ye shall know them.
MATTHEW VII, 20, *c.* 75

The Devil begat darkness; darkness begat ignorance; ignorance begat error and his brethren; error begat free-will and presumption; free-will begat works; works begat forgetfulness of God; forgetfulness begat transgression; transgression begat superstition; superstition begat satisfaction; satisfaction begat the mass-offering; the mass-offering begat the priest; the priest begat unbelief; unbelief begat hypocrisy; hypocrisy begat traffic in offerings for gain; traffic in offerings for gain begat Purgatory; Purgatory begat the annual solemn vigils; the annual vigils begat church-livings; church-livings begat avarice; avarice begat swelling superfluity; swelling superfluity begat fulness; fulness begat rage; rage begat licence; licence begat empire and domination; domination begat pomp; pomp begat ambition; ambition begat simony; simony begat the pope and his brethren, about the time of the Babylonish captivity.

MARTIN LUTHER: *Table-Talk*, D, 1569

There is one basic cause of all effects.

GIORDANO BRUNO: *De monade numero et figura*, II, 1591

There is occasions and causes why and wherefore in all things.

SHAKESPEARE: *Henry V*, V, *c.* 1599

If any strange accidents do happen either in the air or in the earth or in the waters we refer them to some natural cause or other, being unwilling (as it were) to acknowledge God to have a hand in them.

ROBERT GRAY: *An Alarum to England*, 1609

For want of a nail the shoe is lost; for want of a shoe the horse is lost; for want of a horse the rider is lost.

GEORGE HERBERT: *Outlandish Proverbs*, 1640 (Later versions add: "for want of a rider the battle is lost, for want of a battle the kingdom is lost")

A cause is the sum or aggregate of all such accidents, both in the agents and the patient, as concur to the producing of the effect propounded; all of which existing together, it cannot be understood but that the effect existeth with them; or that it can possibly exist if any one of them be absent.

THOMAS HOBBES: *Elements of Philosophy*, VI, 1656

All knowledge of causes is deductive, for we know none by simple intuition, but through the mediation of its effects.

JOSEPH GLANVILL: *The Vanity of Dogmatizing*, XX, 1661

Everything in nature is a cause from which there flows some effect.

BARUCH SPINOZA: *Ethica*, I, 1677

The knowledge of an effect depends on and involves the knowledge of a cause. IBID.

Nothing can happen without a sufficient reason.

G. W. LEIBNIZ: *The Monadology*, 1714

All our reasonings concerning causes and effects are derived from nothing but custom; and belief is more properly an act of the sensitive than of the cogitative part of our natures.

DAVID HUME: *A Treatise of Human Nature*, I, 1739

The universe shows us nothing save an immense and unbroken chain of cause and effect.

P. H. D. D'HOLBACH: *Le système de la nature*, I, 1770

To every existence another must be presupposed; to every condition another preceding condition.

J. G. FICHTE: *Die Bestimmung des Menschen*, I, 1800

It is a principle of law that a person intends to do that which is the natural effect of what he does.

LORD ELLENBOROUGH: *Judgment in Beckwith* vs. *Wood*, 1817

The thorns which I have reap'd are of the tree I planted.

BYRON: *Childe Harold*, IV, 1818

Cause and effect are two sides of one fact.

R. W. EMERSON: *Circles*, 1841

Cause and effect, means and ends, seed and fruit, cannot be severed; for the effect already blooms in the cause, the end preexists in the means, the fruit in the seed.

R. W. EMERSON: *Compensation*, 1841

That a cause leads to an effect is scarcely more certain than that, so far as morals are concerned, a repetition of effect tends to the generation of cause. Herein lies the principle of what we so vaguely term habit.

E. A. POE: *Fifty Suggestions*, *c.* 1848

Cause is simply everything without which the effect would not result, and with which it must result.

CHARLES BRADLAUGH: *A Plea for Atheism*, 1864

Christian Science explains all cause and effect as mental, not physical.

MARY BAKER G. EDDY: *Science and Health*, VI, 1908

Every effect becomes a cause.

BUDDHIST MAXIM

After this, therefore because of this. (Post hoc, ergo propter hoc.)

LATIN PHRASE (A familiar logical fallacy)

The cause being taken away, the effect is removed. (Sublata causa, tollitur effectus.)

LATIN PROVERB

[*See also* Accident, Causality, Chance, Determinism, Motion, War.

Cautery

[*See* Surgery.

Caution

The cautious seldom make mistakes.
CONFUCIUS: *Analects*, IV, *c.* 500 B.C.

It is always well to moor your ship with two anchors.
PUBLILIUS SYRUS: *Sententiae*, *c.* 50 B.C.

Look before you leap.
ENGLISH PROVERB, traced by Smith to *c.* 1350

A wise man does not trust all his eggs to one basket. CERVANTES: *Don Quixote*, I, 1605

Cautious without fear.
DANIEL DEFOE: *A Review of the Affairs of France and of All Europe*, VIII, 1712

He would not, with a peremptory tone,
Assert the nose upon his face his own.
WILLIAM COWPER: *Conversation*, 1782

Allah is Allah — but I have two anchors astern.
A Turkish admiral: To Lady Hester Stanhope, *c.* 1825

Think today and speak tomorrow.
H. G. BOHN: *Handbook of Proverbs*, 1855

It is generally understood that the sun does rise in the East, but I am in the habit of sleeping late and of my own knowledge I could not say positively where it rises.
Ascribed to MARTIN VAN BUREN (1782–1862)

Caution is the confidential agent of selfishness.
WOODROW WILSON: Speech at Chicago, Feb. 12, 1909

There are men who would even be afraid to commit themselves to the doctrine that castor oil is a laxative.
CAMILLE FLAMMARION (1842–1925)

Don't monkey with the buzz-saw.
AMERICAN PROVERB

Don't take any wooden money. IBID.

If your lips would keep from slips
Five things observe with care:
To whom you speak, of whom you speak,
And how, and when, and where.
Author unidentified

If there's no one at home don't leave clothes before the fire to dry. CHINESE PROVERB

Think much and often, speak little, and write less. ITALIAN PROVERB

If not chastely, then at least cautiously. (Nisi caste, saltem caute.) LATIN PROVERB

The most cautious woman gets the reputation of being the most chaste.
SPANISH PROVERB

Three things it is best to avoid: a strange dog, a flood, and a man who thinks he is wise.
WELSH PROVERB

[*See also* Adversity, Carefulness, Coward, Love, Prudence.

Cavalry

[*See* Army, Battle, General, Horse, Infantry, Soldier, War.

Caviare

The play, I remember, pleased not the million; 'twas caviare to the general.
SHAKESPEARE: *Hamlet*, II, *c.* 1601

There is an Italian sauce called *caviaro*, which begins to be in use with us, such vain affectors are we of novelties. It is prepared of the spawn of the sturgeon: the very name doth well express its nature, that it is good to beware of it.
TOBIAS VENNER: *Via recta*, 1620 (Latin *cave*=be careful)

Cedar

[*See* Tree.

Celibacy

The interdiction of marriage to priests was an act of impious tyranny, not only contrary to the word of God, but at war with every principle of justice.
JOHN CALVIN: *Institutes of the Christian Religion*, IV, 1536

Bishops, priests and deacons are not commanded by God's law either to vow the estate of a single life, or to abstain from marriage.
THE THIRTY-NINE ARTICLES, 1563

Christ with one sentence confutes all their arguments: God created them male and female.
MARTIN LUTHER: *Table-Talk*, CCCCXCI, 1569

Single blessedness.
SHAKESPEARE: *A Midsummer Night's Dream*, I, *c.* 1596

God hath prepared . . . a little coronet or special reward (extraordinary and beside the great crown of all faithful souls) for those who have not defiled themselves with women.
JEREMY TAYLOR: *The Rule and Exercises of Holy Living*, XI, 1650

A celibate, like the fly in the heart of an apple, dwells in a perpetual sweetness, but sits alone, and is confined and dies in singularity.
JEREMY TAYLOR: *Twenty-seven Sermons*, XVII, 1651

They that have grown old in a single state are generally found to be morose, fretful and captious, tenacious of their own practices and maxims.
SAMUEL JOHNSON: *The Rambler*, April 13, 1751

Marriage may often be a stormy lake, but celibacy is almost always a muddy horsepond.
THOMAS LOVE PEACOCK: *Melincourt*, VII, 1817

How deep a wound to morals and social purity has that accursed article of the celibacy of the clergy been! Even the best and most enlightened men in Romanist countries attach a notion of impurity to the marriage of a clergyman. And can such a feeling be without its effect on the estimation of the wedded life in general? Impossible! and the morals of both sexes in Spain, Italy, France, &c. prove it abundantly.
S. T. COLERIDGE: *Table-Talk*, April 18, 1833

The Church of Rome have an idea that the pope is St. Peter's successor, and that the clergy ought not to marry. But I would ask, if it was lawful for St. Peter to have a wife, why not lawful for another priest or preacher to have one?
LORENZO DOW: *Reflections on Matrimony*, 1833 (Cf. MATTHEW VIII, 14)

[*See also* Bachelor, Chastity, Continence, Marriage, Spinster, Vice, Virginity.

Cell

Every cell comes from a cell. (Omnis cellula e cellula.)
RUDOLF VIRCHOW: *Cellular-Pathologie*, I, 1858

The cell never acts; it *re*acts.
ERNST HAECKEL: *Generelle Morphologie*, 1866

What we call death is merely the bursting of a cell.
W. WINWOOD READE: *The Martyrdom of Man*, III, 1872

Every nucleus comes from a nucleus. (Omnis necleus e nucleo.)
WALTHER FLEMMING: *Zellsubstanz, Kern und Zelltheilung*, 1882 (Cf. VIRCHOW, *ante*, 1858)

[*See also* Body.

Celt

The Celts fear neither earthquakes nor the waves.
ARISTOTLE: *The Nicomachean Ethics*, III, *c.* 340 B.C. (Cited as a saying)

The Celts or Sidonides are an old family, of whose beginning there is no memory, and their end is likely to be still more remote in the future; for they have endurance and productiveness.
R. W. EMERSON: *English Traits*, IV, 1856

Cemetery

The fence around a cemetery is foolish, for those inside can't get out and those outside don't want to get in.
ARTHUR BRISBANE: *The Book of Today*, 1923

I have seen beautiful cemeteries. But it is a form of beauty I do not care for.
E. W. HOWE: *Sinner Sermons*, 1926

He who seeks equality should go to a cemetery.
GERMAN PROVERB

[*See also* Burial, Churchyard, Death, Epitaph, Funeral, Peace.

Censorship

Tell it not in Gath, publish it not in the streets of Askelon; lest the daughters of the Philistines rejoice, lest the daughters of the uncircumcised triumph.
II SAMUEL I, 21, *c.* 500 B.C.

The first thing will be to establish a censorship of fiction. Let the censors accept any tale that is good, and reject any that is bad.
PLATO: *The Republic*, *c.* 370 B.C.

Were nothing to pass the press but what were suited to the universal gusto, farewell typography!
JOSEPH GLANVILL: *The Vanity of Dogmatizing*, pref., 1661

If there had been a censorship of the press in Rome we should have had today neither Horace nor Juvenal, nor the philosophical writings of Cicero.
VOLTAIRE: *Letter to the Commissioner of Police of Paris*, June 20, 1733

I am mortified to be told that, in the United States of America, the sale of a book can become a subject of inquiry, and of criminal inquiry too, as an offence against religion; that a question like this can be carried before the civil magistrate. Is this then our freedom of religion?
THOMAS JEFFERSON: *Letter to M. Dufief*, 1814

Every burned book enlightens the world.
R. W. EMERSON: *Compensation*, 1841

The books of non-Catholics, *ex professo* treating of religion, are prohibited, unless they contain nothing opposed to the Catholic faith.
POPE LEO XIII: *General Decrees Concerning the Prohibition and Censorship of Books*, Jan. 25, 1897

[*See also* Books, Comstockery, Obscenity, Press (Free).

Censure

No man can justly censure or condemn another; because, indeed, no man truly knows another. This I perceive in myself; for I am in the dark to all the world, and my nearest friends behold me but in a cloud.
THOMAS BROWNE: *Religio Medici*, II, 1642

They have a right to censure that have a heart to help.
WILLIAM PENN: *Fruits of Solitude*, 1693

Censure is the tax a man pays to the public for being eminent.
JONATHAN SWIFT: *Thoughts on Various Subjects,* 1706

I find the pain of a little censure, even when it is unfounded, is more acute than the pleasure of much praise.
THOMAS JEFFERSON: *Letter to F. Hopkinson,* March 13, 1789

[*See also* Action, Applause, Critic, Criticism, Eminence.

Center

In the center of the center. (In centro centrilatentes.) MEDIEVAL LATIN PHRASE

Centipede

The centipede was happy, quite,
Until the frog for fun
Said, "Pray which foot comes after which,"
Which wrought his mind to such a pitch
He lay distracted in the ditch,
Considering how to run.
Author unidentified

Centralization

If ever this vast country is brought under a single government, it will be one of the most extensive corruption.
THOMAS JEFFERSON: *Letter to William T. Barry,* 1822

To bring about government by oligarchy, masquerading as democracy, it is fundamentally essential that practically all authority and control be centralized in our national government. The individual sovereignty of our states must first be destroyed.
F. D. ROOSEVELT: Radio address, March 2, 1930

[*See also* Paternalism, States' Rights.

Century

[*See* Eighteenth Century, etc.

Ceremony

When love begins to sicken and decay,
It useth an enforcéd ceremony.
SHAKESPEARE: *Julius Caesar,* IV, 1599

Ceremony was but devised at first
To set a gloss on faint deeds, hollow welcomes,
Recanting goodness, sorry ere 'tis shown.
SHAKESPEARE: *Timon of Athens,* I, *c.* 1607

Ceremony is an invention to take off the uneasy feeling which we derive from knowing ourselves to be less the object of love and esteem with a fellow-creature than some other person is. It endeavors to make up, by superior attentions in little points, for that invidious preference which it is forced to deny in the greater.
CHARLES LAMB: *A Bachelor's Complaint of the Behavior of Married People,* 1822 (London Magazine, Sept.)

[*See also* King.

Certainty

We love certainty. We like the pope to be infallible in faith, and the grave doctors to be infallible in morals, in order to have assurance.
BLAISE PASCAL: *Pensées,* XXIV, 1670

Next month I am certain to be on my legs for certain sure.
JOHN KEATS: *Letter to Taylor and Hessey,* June 10, 1817

The world is made up for the most part of morons and natural tyrants, sure of themselves, strong in their own opinions, never doubting anything.
CLARENCE DARROW: *Personal Liberty,* 1928

If you forsake a certainty and depend on an uncertainty, you will lose both the certainty and the uncertainty. SANSKRIT PROVERB

Ne'er quit certainty for hope.
SCOTTISH PROVERB

[*See also* Doubt, Taxes.

Cervantes, Miguel de (1547–1616)

Cervantes smiled Spain's chivalry away.
BYRON: *Don Juan,* XIII, 1823

Chain

Chains of steel or of silk – both are chains.
J. C. F. SCHILLER: *The Fiesco,* III, 1784

Chaldean

[*See* Magician.

Challenge

My hat is in the ring.
THEODORE ROOSEVELT: Announcement of his candidacy for the Presidency, Feb. 21, 1912

Put up or shut up. AMERICAN SAYING

To "Leave my house" and "What do you want with my wife?" there is no reply.
SPANISH PROVERB

Chambermaid

[*See* Love.

Chameleon

The chameleon . . . can feed on the air.
SHAKESPEARE: *Two Gentlemen of Verona,* II, *c.* 1595

Champagne

Here's to champagne, the drink divine
That makes us forget our troubles;
It's made of a dollar's worth of wine
And three dollars' worth of bubbles.
Author unidentified

[*See also* Brandy, Gentleman, Wine.

Chance

The race is not to the swift, nor the battle to the strong, neither yet bread to the wise, nor

yet riches to men of understanding, nor yet favor to men of skill; but time and chance happeneth to them all.
ECCLESIASTES IX, 11, *c.* 200 B.C.

Wisdom liketh not chance.
ENGLISH PROVERB, traced by Apperson to 1568

I have set my life upon a cast,
And I will stand the hazard of the die.
SHAKESPEARE: *Richard III,* V, *c.* 1592

As the unthought-on accident is guilty
To what we wildly do, so we profess
Ourselves to be the slaves of chance, and flies
Of every wind that blows.
SHAKESPEARE: *The Winter's Tale,* IV, *c.* 1611

A leap-frog chance.
BEN JONSON: *Bartholomew Fair,* I, 1614

That power
Which erring men call chance.
JOHN MILTON: *Comus,* 1637

Chance has something to say in everything, even how to write a good letter.
BALTASAR GRACIÁN: *The Art of Worldly Wisdom,* CXXXIX, 1647

Although men flatter themselves with their great actions, they are not so often the result of a great design as of chance.
LA ROCHEFOUCAULD: *Maxims,* 1665

A wise man turns chance into good fortune.
THOMAS FULLER: *Gnomologia,* 1732

All nature is but art unknown to thee;
All chance, direction which thou canst not see.
ALEXANDER POPE: *An Essay on Man,* I, 1732

Nothing was ever said with uncommon felicity but by the coöperation of chance; and therefore wit, as well as valor, must be content to share its honors with fortune.
SAMUEL JOHNSON: *The Idler,* May 26, 1759

Chance is a word devoid of sense; nothing can exist without a cause.
VOLTAIRE: *Philosophical Dictionary,* 1764

What is called chance is the instrument of Providence and the secret agent that counteracts what men call wisdom, and preserves order and regularity, and continuation in the whole.
HORACE WALPOLE: *Letter to the Countess of Upper Ossory,* Jan. 19, 1777

Chance is a nickname for Providence.
NICOLAS CHAMFORT: *Maximes et pensées,* *c.* 1785

There is no such thing as chance.
J. C. F. SCHILLER: *Wallenstein's Death,* II, 1799

Chance is blind and is the sole author of creation.
J. X. B. SAINTINE: *Picciola,* III, 1837

No more chance than a snowball in Hell.
AMERICAN SAYING

You have two chances —
One of getting the germ
And one of not.
And if you get the germ
You have two chances —
One of getting the disease
And one of not.
And if you get the disease
You have two chances —
One of dying
And one of not.
And if you die —
Well, you still have two chances!
Author unidentified

[*See also* Accident, Battle, Cause and Effect, Danger, Friend, Gambling, Hanging.

Change

Can the Ethiopian change his skin, or the leopard his spots?
JEREMIAH XIII, 23, *c.* 625 B.C.

One nation rises to supreme power in the world while another declines, and in a brief space of time the sovereign people change, transmitting, like Marathon racers, the torch of life to some other that is to succeed them.
LUCRETIUS: *De rerum natura,* II, 57 B.C.

Nothing maintains its bloom forever; age succeeds to age.
CICERO: *Orationes Philippicae,* XI, *c.* 60 B.C.

All things change; nothing perishes. (Omnia mutantur, nihil interit.)
OVID: *Metamorphoses,* XV, *c.* 5

All things change, and you yourself are constantly wasting away. So, also, is the universe.
MARCUS AURELIUS: *Meditations,* IX, *c.* 170

All things are changed, and we change with them. (Omnia mutantur nos et mutamur in illis.)
LOTHAIR I, *Holy Roman Emperor,* *c.* 840

Times change and men deteriorate. (Tempora mutantur et homines deteriorantur.)
The Gesta Romanorum, *c.* 1472

No joy so great but runneth to an end,
No hap so hard but may in fine amend.
ROBERT SOUTHWELL: *Times Go by Turns,* *c.* 1595

It's a long road that has no turning.
ENGLISH PROVERB, current since the XVII century

All things change except the love of change.
Anon.: *Madrigal,* 1601

This world is not for aye, nor 'tis not strange
That even our loves should with our fortunes change.
SHAKESPEARE: *Hamlet,* III, *c.* 1601

Full fathom five thy father lies;
Of his bones are coral made;
Those are pearls that were his eyes,
Nothing of him that doth fade,
But doth suffer a sea-change
Into something rich and strange.
SHAKESPEARE: *The Tempest,* I, 1611

Tomorrow to fresh woods, and pastures new.
JOHN MILTON: *Lycidas,* 1638

When it is not necessary to change, it is necessary not to change.
LUCIUS CARY (VISCOUNT FALKLAND): *A Discourse on the Infallibility of the Church of Rome,* 1660

Such is the state of life that none are happy but by the anticipation of change. The change itself is nothing: when we have made it the next wish is to change again.
SAMUEL JOHNSON: *Rasselas,* XLVII, 1759

Nothing in progression can rest on its original plan. We might as well think of rocking a grown man in the cradle of an infant.
EDMUND BURKE: *Letter to the sheriffs of Bristol,* 1777

There is a certain relief in change, even though it be from bad to worse; as I have found in traveling in a stage-coach, that it is often a comfort to shift one's position and be bruised in a new place.
WASHINGTON IRVING: *Tales of a Traveler,* 1824

Never swap horses crossing a stream.
AMERICAN PROVERB, traced to *c.* 1840

There are no birds in last year's nest.
H. W. LONGFELLOW: *It Is Not Always May,* 1841

Let the great world spin forever down the ringing grooves of change.
ALFRED TENNYSON: *Locksley Hall,* 1842

An individual is more apt to change, perhaps, than all the world around him.
DANIEL WEBSTER: Speech in the Senate, March 7, 1850

Let that which stood in front go behind,
Let that which was behind advance to the front,
Let bigots, fools, unclean persons, offer new propositions,
Let the old propositions be postponed.
WALT WHITMAN: *Reversals,* 1856

The dogmas of the quiet past are inadequate to the stormy present. . . . As our case is new, so we must think anew and act anew. We must disenthrall ourselves.
ABRAHAM LINCOLN: Message to Congress, Dec. 1, 1862

The old order changeth, yielding place to new.
ALFRED TENNYSON: *The Passing of Arthur,* 1869

It is an axiom of statesmanship, which the successful founders of tyranny have understood and acted upon, that great changes can best be brought about under old forms.
HENRY GEORGE: *Progress and Poverty,* VIII, 1879

Don't change barrels going over Niagara.
Slogan attributed (satirically) to the Republicans during the presidential campaign of 1932

The more it changes, the more it remains the same. (Plus ça change, plus c'est la même chose.) FRENCH PROVERB

Woman, wind, and luck soon change.
PORTUGUESE PROVERB

A Winter night, a woman's mind, and a laird's purpose aften change. SCOTTISH PROVERB

[*See also* Cause and Effect, Evolution, Expedience, Fashion, Fortune, French, Luck, Progress, Time.

Changeless

I am the Lord, I change not.
MALACHI III, 6, *c.* 300 B.C.

All things now are as they were in the day of those we have buried.
MARCUS AURELIUS: *Meditations,* IV, *c.* 170

Changeless march the stars above,
Changeless morn succeeds to even;
And the everlasting hills,
Changeless watch the changeless Heaven.
CHARLES KINGSLEY: *The Saint's Tragedy,* II, 1848

Chanticleer

[*See* Cock.

Chaos

The wrecks of matter, and the crash of worlds.
JOSEPH ADDISON: *Cato,* V, 1713

Lo, thy dread empire, Chaos, is restored;
Light dies before thy uncreating word:
Thy hand, great Anarch! lets the curtain fall;
And universal darkness buries all.
ALEXANDER POPE: *The Dunciad,* IV, 1742

Chaos could not more exist independent of a Creator than the present aptly disposed system of nature.
ETHAN ALLEN: *Reason the Only Oracle of Man,* I, 1784

Chaplain

[*See* Clergyman.

Chapman, George (1599?–1634?)

[*See* Homer.

Character

Character is that which reveals moral purpose, exposing the class of things a man chooses or avoids.
ARISTOTLE: *Rhetoric,* I, *c.* 322 B.C.

A good character carries with it the highest power of causing a thing to be believed.
IBID.

Every man's character is the arbiter of his fortune.
PUBLILIUS SYRUS: *Sententiae, c.* 50 B.C.

To adorn our characters by the charm of an amiable nature shows at once a lover of beauty and a lover of man.
EPICTETUS: *Encheiridion, c.* 100

The highest of characters is his who is as ready to pardon the moral errors of mankind as if he were every day guilty of them himself; and as cautious of committing a fault as if he never forgave one.
PLINY THE YOUNGER: *Letters,* VIII, *c.* 110

Unto ourselves our own life is necessary; unto others, our character.
ST. AUGUSTINE: *On the Good of Widowhood, c.* 413

Wolves do change their hair, but not their hearts. BEN JONSON: *Sejanus,* I, 1603

There's but the twinkling of a star
Between a man of peace and war;
A thief and justice, fool and knave,
A hugging off'cer and a slave;
A crafty lawyer and a pickpocket,
A great philosopher and a blockhead;
A formal preacher and a player,
A learn'd physician and man-slayer.
SAMUEL BUTLER: *Hudibras,* II, 1664

A man reveals his character even in the simplest thing he does. A fool does not enter a room, nor leave it, nor sit down, nor rise, nor is he silent, nor does he stand up, like a man of sense and understanding.
JEAN DE LA BRUYÈRE: *Caractères,* II, 1688

Let us not complain against men because of their rudeness, their ingratitude, their injustice, their arrogance, their love of self, their forgetfulness of others. They are so made. Such is their nature. To be annoyed with them is like denouncing a stone for falling, or a fire for burning.
JEAN DE LA BRUYÈRE: *Caractères,* XI

Most men follow nature no longer than while they are in their nightgowns, and all the busy part of the day are in characters which they neither become, nor act in with pleasure themselves, or their beholders.
RICHARD STEELE: *The Spectator,* Jan. 9, 1712

Mankind is made up of inconsistencies, and no man acts invariably up to his predominant character. The wisest man sometimes acts weakly, and the weakest sometimes wisely.
LORD CHESTERFIELD: *Letter to his son,* April 26, 1748

More knowledge may be gained of a man's real character by a short conversation with one of his servants than from a formal and studied narrative, begun with his pedigree and ended with his funeral.
SAMUEL JOHNSON: *The Rambler,* Oct. 13, 1750

Character must be kept bright, as well as clean.
LORD CHESTERFIELD: *Letter to his son,* Jan. 8, 1750

What a lofty spirit in a narrow breast!
J. W. GOETHE: *Torquato Tasso,* II, 1790

There is something in the character of every man which cannot be altered: it is the skeleton of his character. Trying to change it is like trying to train sheep to pull a cart.
G. C. LICHTENBERG: *Reflections,* 1799

A man never reveals his own character more vividly than when portraying the character of another.
JEAN PAUL RICHTER: *Titan,* CX, 1803

Character is higher than intellect. Thinking is the function. Living is the functionary.
R. W. EMERSON: *The American Scholar,* 1837

Character, even in the most distorted view taken of it by the most angry and prejudiced minds, generally retains something of its outline. No caricaturist ever represented Mr. Pitt as a Falstaff, or Mr. Fox as a skeleton; nor did any libeller ever impute parsimony to Sheridan, or profusion to Marlborough.
T. B. MACAULAY: *Sir William Temple,* 1838

All that a man does is physiognomical of him. You may see how a man would fight by the way in which he sings; his courage, or want of courage, is visible in the word he utters, in the opinion he has formed, no less than in the stroke he strikes. He is one; and preaches the same self abroad in all these ways.
THOMAS CARLYLE: *Heroes and Hero-Worship,* III, 1840 (Lecture in London, May 12)

That which we call character is a reserved force which acts directly by presence, and without means. It is conceived of as a certain undemonstrable force, a familiar or genius, by whose impulses the man is guided, but whose counsels he cannot impart.
R. W. EMERSON: *Character,* 1841

It is in trifles, and when he is off his guard, that a man best shows his character.
ARTHUR SCHOPENHAUER: *Parerga und Paralipomena,* I, 1851

One man is made of agate, another of oak; one of slate, another of clay. The education of the first is polishing; of the second, seasoning; of the third, rending; of the fourth moulding.
JOHN RUSKIN: *The Stones of Venice,* III, 1853

There are three Johns: 1, the real John; known only to his Maker; 2, John's ideal John, never the real one, and often very unlike him;

3, Thomas's ideal John, never the real John, nor John's John, but often very unlike either.
O. W. HOLMES: *The Autocrat of the Breakfast-Table*, III, 1858

A dome of brow denotes one thing; a pot-belly another; a squint, a pug-nose, mats of hair, the pigment of the epidermis, betray character.
R. W. EMERSON: *The Conduct of Life*, I, 1860

A fawn is not vulgar in being timid, nor a crocodile "gentle" because courageous.
JOHN RUSKIN: *Modern Painters*, IX, 1860

The things that really move liking in human beings are the gnarled nodosities of character, vagrant humors, freaks of generosity, some little unextinguishable spark of the aboriginal savage, some little sweet savor of the old Adam.
ALEXANDER SMITH: *Dreamthorp*, XII, 1863

Nobody is truly unassailable until his character is gone. Ascribed to BENJAMIN F. BUTLER (1818–93)

The sum of tendencies to act in a certain way.
T. H. HUXLEY: *Evolution and Ethics*, 1893 (Romanes Lecture)

If you will think about what you ought to do for other people, your character will take care of itself. Character is a by-product, and any man who devotes himself to its cultivation in his own case will become a selfish prig.
WOODROW WILSON: Address at Pittsburgh, Oct. 24, 1914

There is a kind of sweetness of character that stinks.
BENJAMIN DeCASSERES: *Fantasia Impromptu*, 1933

When wealth is lost, nothing is lost;
When health is lost, something is lost;
When character is lost, all is lost!
Author unidentified

Your character depends largely upon what the public doesn't know about you. IBID.

Never a Granville wanted loyalty, a Godolphin wit, or a Trelawny courage.
CORNISH PROVERB

[*See also* Author, Eccentricity, Feeling, Heredity, Talent, Voice.

Character, National

The French are wiser than they seem, and the Spaniards seem wiser than they are.
FRANCIS BACON: *Essays*, XXVI, 1612

The Irishman for his hand, the Welshman for a leg, the Englishman for a face, the Dutchman for a beard.
THOMAS DEKKER: *II The Honest Whore*, I, 1630 (Cited as "a saying")

It is true that the infinite wisdom of Heaven bestows a different genius on each people, but it is no less true that this law of Heaven changes according to time as well as to place.
PIERRE CORNEILLE: *Cinna*, II, 1639

The Italians are wise before the deed, the Germans in the deed, the French after the deed.
GEORGE HERBERT: *Outlandish Proverbs*, 1640

The Jews spend at Easter, the Moors at marriages, the Christians in suits. IBID.

Rage rules the Portuguese, and fraud the Scotch:
Revenge the Pole; and avarice the Dutch.
DANIEL DEFOE: *The True-Born Englishman*, I, 1701

The French have more real politeness, and the English the better method of expressing it.
DAVID HUME: *Letter to Michael Ramsay*, Sept. 12, 1734

God has so made the Germans and French that they both like good living.
VOLTAIRE: *Letter to Frederick the Great*, July, 1737

Where any accident, as a difference in language or religion, keeps two nations, inhabiting the same country, from mixing with one another, they will preserve during several centuries a distinct and even opposite set of manners. The integrity, gravity, and bravery of the Turks form an exact contrast to the deceit, levity and cowardice of the modern Greeks.
DAVID HUME: *Essays*, II, 1741

The English are proud; the French are vain.
J.-J. ROUSSEAU: *Émile*, VI, 1762

In settling an island, the first building erected by a Spaniard will be a church; by a Frenchman, a fort; by a Dutchman, a warehouse; and by an Englishman, an alehouse.
FRANCIS GROSE: *A Provincial Glossary*, 1797

As for France and England, with all their preeminence in science, the one is a den of robbers, and the other of pirates.
THOMAS JEFFERSON: *Letter to John Adams*, 1812

The English seem made of pure earth: the French have more air mixed with their clay, the Italians more fire, the Germans more water.
WILLIAM HAZLITT: *Traveling Abroad*, 1828 (New Monthly Magazine, June)

The Irish are hearty, the Scotch plausible, the French polite, the Germans good-natured, the Italians courtly, the Spaniards reserved and decorous — the English alone seem to exist in taking and giving offence.
WILLIAM HAZLITT: *Manners Make the Man*, 1829 (The Atlas, March 29)

We conceive distinctly enough the French, the Spanish, the German genius, and it is not the less real, that perhaps we should not meet in either of those nations a single individual who corresponded with the type.
R. W. EMERSON: *Nominalist and Realist,* 1841

An Englishman thinks it a deadly insult if you say he is no gentleman, or, still worse, a liar; a Frenchman if you call him a coward; a German if you say he is stupid.
ARTHUR SCHOPENHAUER: *Parerga und Paralipomena,* 1851

A Frenchman may possibly be clean: an Englishman is conscientiously clean.
R. W. EMERSON: *English Traits,* VI, 1856

Put an Englishman into the Garden of Eden, and he would find fault with the whole blarsted concern; put a Yankee in, and he would see where he could alter it to advantage; put an Irishman in, and he would want to boss the thing; put a Dutchman in, and he would proceed to plant it.
H. W. SHAW (JOSH BILLINGS): *Josh Billings, His Sayings,* 1865

A Frenchman drinks his native wine,
A German drinks his beer;
An Englishman his 'alf and 'alf,
Because it brings good cheer.
The Scotchman drinks his whiskey straight
Because it brings on dizziness;
An American has no choice at all —
He drinks the whole damn business.
Author unidentified

In America they say "How are you?" In England, "Who are you?" IBID.

Let a fly fall into a glass of beer, and the Englishman will throw away fly and beer, the German will take out the fly and drink the beer, and the Italian will throw away the beer and eat the fly. IBID.

The Englishman wants to be respected, but the Frenchman insists on being admired.
IBID.

Every Czech is a musician; every Italian, a doctor; every German, a trader; every Pole, a nobleman. POLISH PROVERB

[*See also* American, Armenian, Australian, Cheating, Corsican, Dutchman, Englishman, Fighting, Frenchman, Genoese, German, Greek, Hungarian, Irish, Irishman, Italian, Music, Pole, Portuguese, Scotsman, Slavery, Soldier, Spaniard.

Charity

When thou cuttest down thine harvest in thy field, and hast forgot a sheaf in the field, thou shalt not go again to fetch it: it shall be for the stranger, for the fatherless, and for the widow: that the Lord thy God may bless thee in all the work of thine hands.
DEUTERONOMY XXIV, 19, *c.* 650 B.C.

He that hath pity upon the poor lendeth unto the Lord; and that which he hath given will he pay him again.
PROVERBS XIX, 17, *c.* 350 B.C.

I was eyes to the blind, and feet was I to the lame. JOB XXIX, 15, *c.* 325 B.C.

The man who first proposed to support the poor increased the number of the miserable; it would have been simpler to let them die.
MENANDER: *Perinthis, c.* 300 B.C.

Blessed is he that considereth the poor.
PSALMS XLI, 1, *c.* 150 B.C.

Though I speak with the tongues of men and of angels, and have not charity, I am become as sounding brass, or a tinkling cymbal.
I CORINTHIANS XIII, 1, *c.* 55

Though I have all faith, so that I could remove mountains, and have not charity, I am nothing. I CORINTHIANS XIII, 2

Charity suffereth long and is kind; charity envieth not; charity vaunteth not itself, is not puffed up. I CORINTHIANS XIII, 4

Now abideth faith, hope, charity, these three; but the greatest of these is charity.
I CORINTHIANS XIII, 13

Put on charity, which is the bond of perfectness. COLOSSIANS III, 14, *c.* 60

Charity shall cover the multitude of sins.
I PETER IV, 8, *c.* 60

He that hath two coats, let him impart to him that hath none; and he that hath meat, let him do likewise. LUKE III, 11, *c.* 75

When thou doest alms, let not thy left hand know what thy right hand doeth.
MATTHEW VI, 3, *c.* 75

I was an hungred, and ye gave me meat; I was thirsty, and ye gave me drink: I was a stranger, and ye took me in.
MATTHEW XXV, 35

There was at Joppa a certain disciple named Tabitha, which by interpretation is called Dorcas: This woman was full of good works and almsdeeds which she did.
ACTS IX, 36, *c.* 75

The bread that you store up belongs to the hungry; the cloak that lies in your chest belongs to the naked; and the gold that you have hidden in the ground belongs to the poor. ST. BASIL (*c.* 330–379)

Charity begins at home.
ENGLISH PROVERB, borrowed from the Greek and traced by Apperson to *c.* 1380

He is truly great who hath a great charity.
THOMAS À KEMPIS: *Imitation of Christ,* I, *c.* 1420

Who can sever love from charity?
SHAKESPEARE: *Love's Labor's Lost*, IV, *c.* 1595

A tear for pity and a hand
Open as day for melting charity.
SHAKESPEARE: *II Henry IV*, IV, *c.* 1597

As cold as charity.
ENGLISH PHRASE, familiar since the XVII century

'Tis not enough to help the feeble up,
But to support him after.
SHAKESPEARE: *Timon of Athens*, I, *c.* 1607

True virtue has no limits, but goes on and on, and especially holy charity, which is the virtue of virtues, and which, having an infinite object, would become infinite if it could meet with a heart capable of infinity.
ST. FRANCIS DE SALES: *Introduction to the Devout Life*, I, 1609

Charity is a naked child, giving honey to a bee without wings.
FRANCIS QUARLES: *Enchiridion*, II, 1640

Give unto all, lest he, whom thou deni'st,
May chance to be no other man but Christ.
ROBERT HERRICK: *Noble Numbers*, 1648

There can be no greater argument to a man of his own power than to find himself able not only to accomplish his own desires, but also to assist other men in theirs; and this is that conception wherein consisteth charity.
THOMAS HOBBES: *On Human Nature*, IX, 1650

No man giveth, but with intention of good to himself; because gift is voluntary, and of all voluntary acts the object is to every man his own good.
THOMAS HOBBES: *Leviathan*, I, 1651

Poor for himself, rich for the poor, he wished to live, die and be buried among them.
INSCRIPTION ON THE TOMB OF J. P. CAMUS DE PONT-CARRÉ, BISHOP OF BELLEY, IN THE HOSPICE DES INCURABLES, Paris, 1652

It is good to be charitable — but to whom?
JEAN DE LA FONTAINE: *Fables*, VI, 1668

The charitable give out at the door, and God puts in at the window.
JOHN RAY: *English Proverbs*, 1670

He that bestows his goods upon the poor
Shall have as much again, and ten times more.
JOHN BUNYAN: *Pilgrim's Progress*, II, 1684

In necessary things, unity; in doubtful things, liberty; in all things, charity.
MOTTO OF RICHARD BAXTER (1615–91)

Charity . . . is kind, it is not easily provok'd, it thinks no evil, it believes all things, hopes all things.
COTTON MATHER: *The Wonders of the Invisible World*, I, 1693 (Cf. I CORINTHIANS XIII, 4, *c.* 55)

Lady Bountiful.
GEORGE FARQUHAR: Name of a character in *The Beaux' Stratagem*, 1707

Ambition, malice, rage and hate
Are strangers to my soul;
But peace and joy possess the parts,
And charity the whole.
DANIEL DEFOE: *A Review of the Affairs of France and of All Europe*, VIII, 1712

A man may bestow great sums on the poor and indigent without being charitable, and may be charitable when he is not able to bestow anything.
JOSEPH ADDISON: *The Guardian*, Sept. 21, 1713

Where has the Scripture made merit the rule or measure of charity?
WILLIAM LAW: *A Serious Call to a Devout and Holy Life*, VIII, 1728

You cannot heal all the sick, relieve all the poor; you cannot comfort all in distress, nor be a father to all the fatherless. IBID.

Charity and pride have different aims, yet both feed the poor.
THOMAS FULLER: *Gnomologia*, 1732

He that feeds upon charity has a cold dinner and no supper. IBID.

In faith and hope the world will disagree,
But all mankind's concern is charity.
ALEXANDER POPE: *An Essay on Man*, III, 1733

I hate nobody; I am in charity with the world.
JONATHAN SWIFT: *Polite Conversation*, 1738

Large was his bounty, and his soul sincere,
Heaven did a recompense as largely send;
He gave to misery (all he had) a tear,
He gain'd from Heaven ('twas all he wish'd) a friend.
THOMAS GRAY: *Elegy Written in a Country Churchyard*, 1750

He gives twice that gives soon; i.e., he will soon be called to give again.
BENJAMIN FRANKLIN: *Poor Richard's Almanac*, 1752

Charity is to will and do what is just and right in every transaction.
EMANUEL SWEDENBORG: *Heaven and Hell*, 1758

The most genuine and efficacious charity is that which greases the paws of the priests; such charity covers a multitude of sins.
VOLTAIRE: *Philosophical Dictionary*, 1764

Charity is a debt of honor.
IMMANUEL KANT: Lecture at Königsberg, 1775

You are much surer that you are doing good when you *pay* money to those who work, as the recompense of their labor, than when you *give* money merely in charity.

SAMUEL JOHNSON: *Boswell's Life*, April, 1776

I cannot describe to you the despairing sensation of trying to do something for a man who seems incapable or unwilling to do anything further for himself.

BYRON: *Letter to Thomas Moore*, April 2, 1823

It was his doctrine that the poor
Were always able, never willing;
And so the beggar at the door
Had first abuse and then a shilling.

W. M. PRAED: *Quince*, *c.* 1825

With one hand he put
A penny in the urn of poverty,
And with the other took a shilling out.

ROBERT POLLOK: *The Course of Time*, VIII, 1827

Charity, like nature, abhors a vacuum. Next to putting it into the bank, men like to squander their superfluous wealth on those to whom it is sure of doing the least possible good.

WILLIAM HAZLITT: *Butts of Different Sorts*, 1829 (The Atlas, Feb. 8)

In charity to all mankind, bearing no malice or ill-will to any human being, and even compassionating those who hold in bondage their fellow-men, not knowing what they do.

JOHN QUINCY ADAMS: *Letter to A. Bronson Alcott*, July 30, 1838

Do not tell me of my obligation to put all poor men in good situations. Are they *my* poor? I tell thee, thou foolish philanthropist, that I grudge the dollar, the dime, the cent I give to such men as do not belong to me and to whom I do not belong.

R. W. EMERSON: *Self-Reliance*, 1841

Alas! for the rarity
Of Christian charity
Under the sun.

THOMAS HOOD: *The Bridge of Sighs*, 1846

A strong argument for the religion of Christ is this — that offences against charity are about the only ones which men on their deathbeds can be made — not to understand — but to feel — as crimes.

E. A. POE: *Marginalia*, 1844–49

The worst of charity is that the lives you are asked to preserve are not worth preserving.

R. W. EMERSON: *The Conduct of Life*, VII, 1860

With malice toward none, with charity for all, with firmness in the right, as God gives us to see the right, let us strive on to finish the work we are in.

ABRAHAM LINCOLN: Inaugural address, March 4, 1865 (Cf. ADAMS, *ante*, 1838)

As for charity, it is a matter in which the immediate effect on the persons directly concerned, and the ultimate consequence to the general good, are apt to be at complete war with one another.

J. S. MILL: *The Subjection of Women*, IV, 1869

To look up and not down,
To look forward and not back,
To look out and not in — and
To lend a hand.

E. E. HALE: *Ten Times One is Ten*, IV, 1870

Here lies Estella, who transported a large fortune to Heaven in acts of charity, and has gone thither to enjoy it.

H. J. LORING: *Epitaphs Quaint, Curious and Elegant*, 1872

Charity has in it sometimes, perhaps often, a savor of superiority.

J. R. LOWELL: Speech in Westminster Abbey, Dec. 13, 1881

Whatever capital you divert to the support of a shiftless and good-for-nothing person is so much diverted from some other employment, and that means from somebody else.

W. G. SUMNER: *The Forgotten Man*, 1883

Organized charity, scrimped and iced,
In the name of a cautious, statistical Christ.

JOHN BOYLE O'REILLY: *In Bohemia*, 1886

I feel obliged to withhold my approval of the plan to indulge a benevolent and charitable sentiment through the appropriation of public funds for that purpose. I can find no warrant for such an appropriation in the Constitution.

GROVER CLEVELAND: Message to Congress vetoing "an act to enable the Commissioner of Agriculture to make a special distribution of seeds in the drought-stricken counties of Texas," Feb. 16, 1887

With one hand I take thousands of rubles from the poor, and with the other I hand back a few kopecks.

LYOF N. TOLSTOY: *What Shall We Do?*, 1891

The law of mutual charity perfects the law of justice.

POPE LEO XIII: *Graves de communi*, Jan. 18, 1901

Those who minister to poverty and disease are accomplices in the two worst of all the crimes.

GEORGE BERNARD SHAW: *Maxims for Revolutionists*, 1903

It is incumbent on the rich to help the poor. Those who give of their substance to Christ in the person of His poor will receive a most bountiful reward when He shall come to judge the world. Those who act to the contrary will pay the penalty.

POPE PIUS XI: *Casti connubii*, Dec. 31, 1930

Charity cannot take the place of justice unfairly withheld.
POPE PIUS XI: *Quadragesimo anno*, May 15, 1931

Charity sees the need; not the cause.
GERMAN PROVERB

Charity is the spice of riches.
HEBREW PROVERB

Give for the sake of God, even to the unbeliever.
MOROCCAN PROVERB

He who throws even a splinter to cover a widow's house will be protected by God.
RUSSIAN PROVERB

Charity begins at hame, but shouldna end there.
SCOTTISH PROVERB

[*See also* Alms, Altruism, Benefit, Benevolence, Church of England, Curiosity, Generosity, Gift, Giving, Home, Jew, Justice, Philanthropy, Pity, Poor, Priest, Sincerity, Society.

Charles II of England (1660–85)

Here lies our sovereign lord the king,
Whose word no man relies on;
He never says a foolish thing,
Nor ever does a wise one.
THE EARL OF ROCHESTER: Written on the bedroom door of Charles II, *c.* 1680

He took delight in having a number of little spaniels follow him and lie in his bedchamber, where he often suffered the bitches to puppy and give suck, which rendered it very offensive, and indeed made the whole court nasty and stinking.
JOHN EVELYN: *Diary*, Feb. 4, 1685

Charm

I bear a charmed life.
SHAKESPEARE: *Macbeth*, v, *c.* 1605

Thus slew they Hans the blue-eyed Dane,
Bull-throated, bare of arm,
But Anne of Austria looted first
The maid Ultruda's charm —
The little silver crucifix
That keeps a man from harm.
RUDYARD KIPLING: *The Ballad of Fisher's Boarding-House*, 1892

[*See also* Amulet, Passion.

Charmer

How happy I could be with either,
Were t'other dear charmer away!
JOHN GAY: *The Beggar's Opera*, I, 1728

Chasm

I accept your nomination in the confident trust that the masses of our countrymen, North and South, are eager to clasp hands across the bloody chasm which has so long divided them.
HORACE GREELEY: Speech of acceptance, May 20,1872

Chastening

As a man chasteneth his son, so the Lord thy God chasteneth thee.
DEUTERONOMY VIII, 5, *c.* 700 B.C.

Whom the Lord loveth he chasteneth.
HEBREWS XII, 6, *c.* 65

As many as I love, I rebuke and chasten.
REVELATION III, 19, *c.* 95

[*See also* Affliction.

Chastity

The master's wife cast her eyes upon Joseph; and she said, Lie with me. But he refused.
GENESIS XXXIX, 7–8, *c.* 700 B.C.

Once a woman has lost her chastity she will shrink from nothing.
TACITUS: *History*, IV, *c.* 100

We Christians regard a stain upon our chastity as more dreadful than any punishment, or even than death itself.
TERTULLIAN: *Apologeticus*, 197

For the preservation of chastity an empty and rumbling stomach and fevered lungs are indispensable.
ST. JEROME: *Letters*, XXII, *c.* 400

The chastity of widows and virgins is above the chastity of marriage.
ST. AUGUSTINE: *On the Good of Marriage*, *c.* 401

Women's virtue is founded upon a modest countenance, precise behavior, rectitude, and the want of temptation.
THE HITOPADESA, I, *c.* 500

I know not whether Caesar's exploits or Alexander's exceed in hardiness the resolution of a beautiful young woman, trained after our manner, in the open view and uncontrolled conversation of the world, solicited and battered by so many contrary examples, exposed to a thousand assaults and continual pursuits, and yet still holding herself good and unvanquished. There is no point of doing more thorny, nor more active, than this of not doing.
MICHEL DE MONTAIGNE: *Essays*, III, 1588

The fair, the chaste, and unexpressive she.
SHAKESPEARE: *As You Like It*, III, *c.* 1600

The very ice of chastity is in them.
IBID.

My chastity's the jewel of our house,
Bequeathed down from many ancestors.
SHAKESPEARE: *All's Well that Ends Well*, IV, *c.* 1602

There is no jewel in the world so valuable as a chaste and virtuous woman.
CERVANTES: *Don Quixote*, I, 1605

Chaste as the icicle
That's curdled by the frost from purest snow
And hangs on Dian's temple.
SHAKESPEARE: *Coriolanus*, v, *c.* 1607

Women are more willingly and more gloriously chaste when they are least restrained of their liberty.

JOHN WEBSTER: *The White Devil,* I, *c.* 1608

Chastity, the lily of virtues, makes men almost equal to angels. Nothing is beautiful but what is pure, and the purity of men is chastity.

ST. FRANCIS DE SALES: *Introduction to the Devout Life,* XII, 1609

Chaste women are often proud and forward, as presuming upon the merit of their chastity.

FRANCIS BACON: *Essays,* VIII, 1625

'Tis chastity, my brother, chastity:
She, that has that, is clad in complete steel;
And, like a quiver'd nymph with arrows keen,
May trace huge forests, and unharbor'd heaths,
Infamous hills, and sandy perilous wilds.

JOHN MILTON: *Comus,* 1637

So dear to Heaven is saintly chastity
That when a soul is found sincerely so
A thousand liveried angels lacky her,
Driving far off each thing of sin and guilt.

IBID.

Banish all objects of lust, shut up all youth into the severest discipline that can be exercised in any hermitage, ye cannot make them chaste, that came not thither so.

JOHN MILTON: *Areopagitica,* 1644

It is possible to meet with women who have never had an affair of gallantry; but it is rare to find any who have had only one.

LA ROCHEFOUCAULD: *Maxims,* 1665

If all the fornicators and adulterers in England were hanged by the neck till they be dead, John Bunyan, the object of their envy, would be still alive and well. I know not whether there be such a thing as a woman breathing under the copes of the whole heaven but by their apparel, their children or by common fame, except my wife.

JOHN BUNYAN: *Grace Abounding to the Chief of Sinners,* 1666

Temperance is the nurse of chastity.

WILLIAM WYCHERLEY: *Love in a Wood,* III, 1671

Your women of honor, as you call 'em, are only chary of their reputations, not their persons; and 'tis scandal that they would avoid, not men.

WILLIAM WYCHERLEY: *The Country Wife,* I, *c.* 1673

Lord, what fine notions of virtue do we women take up upon the credit of old foolish philosophers! Virtue's its own reward, virtue's this, virtue's that —. Virtue's an ass, and a gallant's worth forty on't.

JOHN VANBRUGH: *The Provok'd Wife,* I, 1697

A woman's resistance is no proof of her virtue; it is much more likely to be a proof of her experience. If we spoke sincerely, we should have to confess that our first impulse is to yield; we only resist on reflection.

NINON D'ENCLOS, *c.* 1700

Virgins, to keep chaste, must go
Abroad with such as are not so.

ALEXANDER POPE: *The Challenge,* 1717

Though she does not pique herself upon fidelity to any one man (which is but a narrow way of thinking), she boasts that she has always been true to her nation, and, notwithstanding foreign attacks, has always reserved her charms for the use of her own countrymen.

MARY WORTLEY MONTAGU: *Letter to the Countess of Pomfret,* Jan., 1739

A salamander is a kind of heroine in chastity that tread upon fire and live in the midst of flames, without being hurt.

JOSEPH ADDISON: *The Spectator,* Oct. 17, 1711

Be warm, but pure; be amorous, but be chaste.

BYRON: *English Bards and Scotch Reviewers,* 1809

Chastity is a monkish and evangelical superstition, a greater foe to natural temperance even than unintellectual sensuality; it strikes at the root of all domestic happiness, and consigns more than half of the human race to misery.

P. B. SHELLEY: *Queen Mab,* notes, 1813

If you still behave in dancing rooms and other societies as I have seen you, I do not want to live — if you have done so, I wish this coming night may be my last. I cannot live without you, and not only you but *chaste you; virtuous you.*

JOHN KEATS: *Letter to Fanny Brawne,* July 5, 1820

"Nay," quoth the maid, "the sultan's self shan't carry me
Unless his highness promises to marry me."

BYRON: *Don Juan,* V, 1821

There never was a drunken woman, or a woman who loved strong drink, who was chaste, if the opportunity of being the contrary presented itself to her.

WILLIAM COBBETT: *Advice to Young Men,* III, 1829

The most virtuous woman always has something within her that is not quite chaste.

BALZAC: *The Physiology of Marriage,* 1830

Is not chastity a virtue? Most undoubtedly, and a virtue of high deserving. And why? Not because it diminishes, but because it heightens enjoyment.

JEREMY BENTHAM: *Deontology,* 1834

There is no man who in his heart would not reverence a woman that chose to die rather than to be dishonored.
THOMAS DE QUINCEY: *On Suicide, c.* 1847

Q. Is continency preferable to marriage? *A.* A life of perfect chastity, embraced for God's sake, is a better and more blessed state.
JOHN MCCAFFREY: *A Catechism of Christian Doctrine for General Use,* 1866

There has never been a woman yet in the world who wouldn't have given the top of the milk-jug to some man, if she had met the right one.
Ascribed to LADY WILDE, mother of Oscar Wilde, *c.* 1870

The only really indecent people are the chaste.
J. K. HUYSMANS: *Certains,* 1889

Chastity is the cement of civilization and progress.
MARY BAKER G. EDDY: *Science and Health,* III, 1908

You may say . . . we need not expect young men to live up to the ideal of continence. If so, I cannot agree. It is a duty we cannot shirk to point to the true ideal, to chastity, to a single standard of morals for men and women.
JOSEPHUS DANIELS: Circular to all commanding officers of the Navy, Feb. 27, 1915

A reputation for chastity is necessary to a woman. Chastity itself is also sometimes useful. Author unidentified

Lord, make me pure and chaste — but not quite yet. IBID.

There are few chaste women who are not tired of their trade. FRENCH PROVERB

All women are chaste where there are no men.
SANSKRIT PROVERB

[*See also* Beauty, Calumny, Careful, Caution, Celibacy, English, Husband and Wife, Idleness, Lying, Marriage, May, Monasticism, Poverty, Purity, Virgin, Virginity, Virtue.

Chateaubriand, François de (1768–1848)

Chateaubriand is a miserable boaster without character, with a groveling soul and an itch for writing.
NAPOLEON I: To Barry E. O'Meara at St. Helena, Jan. 28, 1818

Chatterton, Thomas (1752–70)

He was an instance that a complete genius and a complete rogue can be formed before a man is of age.
HORACE WALPOLE: *Letter to William Mason,* July 24, 1778

In Chatterton there is nothing but the resolution to say again what has once been said.
SAMUEL JOHNSON: *Letter to Edmond Malone,* March 2, 1782

Chaucer, Geoffrey (c. 1340–1400)

Dan Chaucer, well of English undefiled,
On fame's eternal bede-roll worthy to be filed.
EDMUND SPENSER: *The Faerie Queene,* IV, *c.* 1589

I take unceasing delight in Chaucer. His manly cheerfulness is especially delicious to me in my old age. How exquisitely tender he is, and yet how perfectly free from the least touch of sickly melancholy or morbid drooping.
S. T. COLERIDGE: *Table-Talk,* March 15, 1834

Chaucer does not indulge in fine sentiment; he has no bravura passages; he is ever master of himself and of his subject. The light upon his page is the light of common day.
ALEXANDER SMITH: *Dreamthorp,* IV, 1863

[*See also* Sixty.

Cheapness

It is cheap enough to say, God help you.
THOMAS FULLER: *Gnomologia,* 1732

The cheap buyer takes bad meat. IBID.

What we obtain too cheap we esteem too lightly; it is dearness only that gives everything its value.
THOMAS PAINE: *The American Crisis,* I, 1776 (Pennsylvania Journal, Dec. 19)

Cheap and nasty.
ENGLISH PHRASE, applied to the products of Birmingham; not recorded before the XIX century

They buy goods cheap that bring naething hame. SCOTTISH PROVERB

[*See also* Antiquity, Buying and Selling.

Cheating

A false balance is an abomination to the Lord.
PROVERBS XI, 1, *c.* 350 B.C.

Cheat me in the price, but not in the goods.
THOMAS FULLER: *Gnomologia,* 1732

All tailors are cheats, and all men are tailors.
CHARLES LAMB: *Letter to B. W. Proctor,* Jan. 22, 1829

You can't cheat an honest man.
DAVID W. MAURER: *The Big Con,* I, 1940 (Quoted as a saying of confidence men)

It is more honorable to cheat than to steal.
GERMAN PROVERB

'Tis no sin to cheat a cheater. (Fallere fallentem non est fraus.)
MEDIEVAL LATIN PROVERB

It takes three Jews to cheat a Greek, three Greeks to cheat a Syrian, and three Syrians to cheat an Armenian.
LEVANTINE PROVERB

The German cheats the Pole; the Frenchman, the German; the Spaniard, the Frenchman; the Jew, the Spaniard; and the Devil only the Jew. POLISH PROVERB

A Russian can be cheated only by a gipsy, a gipsy by a Jew, a Jew by a Greek, and a Greek by the Devil. RUSSIAN PROVERB

One Jew is equal, in cheating, to two Greeks, and one Greek to two Armenians. IBID.

He that cheats me ance, shame fa' him; he that cheats me twice; shame fa' me.
SCOTTISH PROVERB

[*See also* Gambling, Jew, Lawyer, Man and Woman, Miser.

Check-book

Among the books with unhappy endings are check-books. Author unidentified

Checks and Balances

No man is a warmer advocate for proper restraints and wholesome checks in every department of government than I am; but I have never yet been able to discover the propriety of placing it absolutely out of the power of men to render essential services, because a possibility remains of their doing ill.
GEORGE WASHINGTON: *Letter to Bushrod Washington,* Nov. 10, 1787

The habits of thinking in a free country should inspire caution in those intrusted with its administration to confine themselves within their respective constitutional spheres, avoiding, in the exercise of the power of one department, to encroach upon another.
GEORGE WASHINGTON: Farewell Address, Sept. 17, 1796

The legislative, executive and judicial powers of government ought to be forever separate and distinct from each other; and no person exercising the functions of one of said departments shall assume or discharge the duties of any other.
DECLARATION OF RIGHTS OF MARYLAND, VIII, 1867

[*See also* Freedom, Government (American), Majority.

Cheek

How the red roses flush up in her cheeks,
And the pure snow, with goodly vermill stain.
EDMUND SPENSER: *Epithalamion,* 1595

See, how she leans her cheek upon her hand!
Oh, that I were a glove upon that hand,
That I might touch that cheek!
SHAKESPEARE: *Romeo and Juliet,* II, *c.* 1596

Thus is his cheek the map of days outworn.
SHAKESPEARE: *Sonnets,* LXVIII, 1609

He that still may see your cheeks,
Where all rareness still reposes,
Is a fool if e'er he seeks
Other lilies, other roses.
WILLIAM BROWNE: *Britannia's Pastorals,* II, 1616

The lilies
Contending with the roses in her cheeks,
Who most shall set them off.
PHILIP MASSINGER: *The Great Duke of Florence,* V, 1636

One ask'd me where the roses grew?
I bade him not go seek;
But forthwith bade my Julia shew
A bud in either cheek.
ROBERT HERRICK: *Hesperides,* 1648

To move the cheeks, puff them out, or slap them with the hands, are all exceedingly impolite, and entirely reprehensible.
ST. JOHN BAPTIST DE LA SALLE: *The Rules of Christian Manners and Civility,* I, 1695

His cheek hath laps like a fresh-singed swine.
ROBERT BROWNING: *Holy-Cross Day,* 1855

Girls with fat cheeks have hearts like flint.
PENNSYLVANIA GERMAN PROVERB

[*See also* Cosmetics, Dead, Drinking, Kiss, Laughter, Non-resistance, Nose, Tears.

Cheerfulness

Be of good cheer: this counsel is of Heaven.
HOMER: *Odyssey,* II, *c.* 800 B.C.

I exhort you to be of good cheer.
ACTS XXVII, 22, *c.* 75

The plainest sign of wisdom is a continual cheerfulness: her state is like that of things in the regions above the moon, always clear and serene.
MICHEL DE MONTAIGNE: *Essays,* I, 1580

A light heart lives long.
SHAKESPEARE: *Love's Labor's Lost,* V, *c.* 1595

A cheerful look makes a dish a feast.
GEORGE HERBERT: *Jacula Prudentum,* 1651

Cheerfulness keeps up a kind of daylight in the mind, and fills it with a steady and perpetual serenity.
JOSEPH ADDISON: *The Spectator,* May 17, 1712

Health and cheerfulness mutually beget each other.
JOSEPH ADDISON: *The Spectator,* May 24

Cheerful at morn he wakes from short repose,
Breathes the keen air, and carols as he goes.
OLIVER GOLDSMITH: *The Traveler,* 1764

There is nothing more beautiful than cheerfulness in an old face.
JEAN PAUL RICHTER: *Titan,* CXV, 1803

In my seventy-second year I am all cheerfulness, and neither anticipate the evil day till to do so is absolutely unavoidable.
WILLIAM GODWIN: *Letter to Mary Godwin Shelley,* 1827

I felt an earnest and humble desire, and shall do till I die, to increase the stock of harmless cheerfulness.
CHARLES DICKENS: Speech in Edinburgh, June 25, 1841

Cheer up! the worst is yet to come.
PHILANDER JOHNSON, *c.* 1900

[*See also* Happiness, Health, Hope, Humor (Good), Mirth, Philosopher, Wisdom.

Cheese

Cheese it is a peevish elf,
It digests all things but itself.
JOHN RAY: *English Proverbs,* 1670

A woman had such an antipathy against cheese that if she did but eat a piece of bread, cut with a knife which a little before had cut cheese, it would cause a deliquium.
INCREASE MATHER: *Remarkable Providences,* IV, 1684 (*Deliquium*=failure of the mind, fainting)

Cheese and salt meat should be sparingly eat.
BENJAMIN FRANKLIN: *Poor Richard's Almanac,* 1733

An apple-pie without some cheese
Is like a kiss without a squeeze.
OLD ENGLISH RHYME

[*See also* Bread and Cheese.

Chess

When a man's house is on fire it's time to break off chess.
THOMAS FULLER: *Gnomologia,* 1732

Life's too short for chess.
HENRY J. BYRON: *Our Boys,* I, 1874

A foolish expedient for making idle people believe they are doing something very clever, when they are only wasting their time.
GEORGE BERNARD SHAW: *The Irrational Knot,* XIV, 1880

Chesterfield, Earl of (1694–1773)

This man I thought had been a lord among wits, but I find he is only a wit among lords. [His letters to his son] teach the morals of a whore, and the manners of a dancing-master.
SAMUEL JOHNSON: *Boswell's Life,* 1754

The only Englishman who ever argued for the art of pleasing as the first duty of life.
VOLTAIRE: *Letter to Frederick the Great,* Aug. 16, 1774

I borrowed here a volume of Lord Chesterfield's letters, which I had heard very strongly commended. And what did I learn? — That he was a man of much wit, middling sense, and some learning; but as absolutely void of virtue as any Jew, Turk, or heathen that ever lived.
JOHN WESLEY: *Diary,* Oct. 11, 1775

Lord Chesterfield stands much lower in the estimation of posterity than he would have done if his letters had never been published.
T. B. MACAULAY: *Horace Walpole,* 1833

Chicago

Chicago sounds rough to the maker of verse;
One comfort we have — Cincinnati sounds worse.
O. W. HOLMES: *Welcome to the Chicago Commercial Club,* Jan. 14, 1880

Of all the places in the world, the one which from its literary societies sends me the most intelligent and thoughtful criticism upon my poetry is Chicago.
ROBERT BROWNING: *Letter to Chauncey M. Depew, c.* 1886

Hog butcher for the world,
Tool maker, stacker of wheat,
Player with railroads and the nation's freight handler;
Stormy, husky, brawling,
City of the big shoulders.
CARL SANDBURG: *Chicago,* 1916

[*See also* Paris.

Chick

[*See* Hen.

Chicken

If God grants me the usual length of life, I hope to make France so prosperous that every peasant will have a chicken in his pot on Sunday.
HENRY IV of France (1553–1610)

[*See also* Children, City, Hen, Preacher.

Chief

Hail to the chief who in triumph advances!
WALTER SCOTT: *The Lady of the Lake,* II, 1810

The recognized chief. (Facile princeps.)
LATIN PHRASE

Chief Justice

[*See* Judge.

Child

The wolf also shall dwell with the lamb, and the leopard shall lie down with the kid; and the calf and the young lion and the fatling together; and a little child shall lead them.
ISAIAH XI, 6, *c.* 700 B.C.

Train up a child in the way he should go; and when he is old he will not depart from it.
PROVERBS XXII, 6, *c.* 350 B.C.

Foolishness is bound in the heart of a child, but the rod of correction shall drive it from him. PROVERBS XXII, 15

When I was a child, I spake as a child, I understood as a child, I thought as a child; but when I became a man, I put away childish things. I CORINTHIANS XIII, 2, *c.* 55

The utmost reverence is due to a child.
JUVENAL: *Satires,* XIV, 128

A child tells in the street what its father and mother say at home.
THE TALMUD (*Succoth*), *c.* 200

Spare the rod and spoil the child.
ENGLISH PROVERB, borrowed from the Latin and traced by Smith to *c.* 1000 (Cf. PROVERBS XIII, 24: "He that spareth his rod hateth his son")

Many kiss the child for the nurse's sake.
ENGLISH PROVERB, traced by Smith to the XV century

A child, for his forgetful mind, expelleth kindness.
ALEXANDER BARCLAY: *The Ship of Fools,* 1509

What is a child save a lower animal in the form of a man?
LUIS DE GRANADA: *Guia de Peccadores,* *c.* 1555

How sharper than a serpent's tooth it is
To have a thankless child!
SHAKESPEARE: *King Lear,* I, 1606

A child is a man in a small letter, yet the best copy of Adam before he tasted of Eve or the apple.
JOHN EARLE (BISHOP OF SALISBURY): *Microcosmographie,* 1628

A naughty child is better sick than whole.
GEORGE HERBERT: *Outlandish Proverbs,* 1640

Better a snotty child than his nose wiped off.
IBID.

He that wipes the child's nose kisseth the mother's cheek. IBID.

To a child all weather is cold. IBID.

He that will not use the rod on his child his child shall be used as a rod on him.
THOMAS FULLER: *The Holy and the Profane State,* 1642

Put another man's child in your bosom and he'll creep out at your elbow.
JOHN RAY: *English Proverbs,* 1670

Ask the mother if the child be like the father.
THOMAS FULLER: *Gnomologia,* 1732

Behold the child, by nature's kindly law,
Pleased with a rattle, tickled with a straw.
ALEXANDER POPE: *An Essay on Man,* II, 1732

Teach your child to hold his tongue; he'll learn fast enough to speak.
BENJAMIN FRANKLIN: *Poor Richard's Almanac,* 1734

Don't set your wit against a child.
JONATHAN SWIFT: *Polite Conversation,* 1738

The lost child cries, but still he catches fireflies.
RYUSUI YOSHIDA: *The Lost Child, c.* 1750

Nothing is more absurd than an old child.
BENJAMIN WHICHCOTE: *Moral and Religious Aphorisms,* 1753

A child thinks 20 shillings and 20 years can scarce ever be spent.
BENJAMIN FRANKLIN: *Poor Richard's Almanac,* 1754

Lacking all sense of right and wrong, a child can do nothing which is morally evil, or which merits either punishment or reproof.
J.-J. ROUSSEAU: *Émile,* I, 1762

I should not have had much fondness for a child of my own. At least, I never wished to have a child.
SAMUEL JOHNSON: *Boswell's Life,* April 10, 1776

If there must be trouble let it be in my day, that my child may have peace.
THOMAS PAINE: *The American Crisis,* I, 1776 (Pennsylvania Journal, Dec. 19)

The child is father of the man.
WILLIAM WORDSWORTH: *My Heart Leaps Up,* 1807

A child is fed with milk and praise.
MARY LAMB: *The First Tooth,* 1809

Terrible child. (Enfant terrible.)
Author unidentified; the phrase gained currency through its use by Goethe, *c.* 1810

I thank the goodness and the grace
Which on my birth have smiled,
And made me, in these Christian days
A happy Christian child.
JANE TAYLOR: *A Child's Hymn of Praise,* *c.* 1810

Praise the child, and you make love to the mother.
WILLIAM COBBETT: *Advice to Young Men,* IV, 1829 (Quoted as "an old saying")

We have had a sick child, who, sleeping or not sleeping, next me, with a pasteboard partition between, killed my sleep. The little bastard is gone.
CHARLES LAMB: *Letter to Edward Moxon,* April 27, 1833

A curly, dimpled lunatic.
R. W. EMERSON: *Nature,* 1841

What power there is in the smile of a child, in its play, in its crying — in short, in its mere

existence. Are you able to resist its demand? Or do you hold out to it, as a mother, your breast, or, as a father, whatever it needs of your belongings?
MAX STIRNER: *The Ego and His Own,* 1845

A spoilt child never loves its mother.
HENRY TAYLOR: *Notes from Life,* 1847

Give a child his will, and a whelp his fill, and neither will thrive.
H. G. BOHN: *Handbook of Proverbs,* 1855

Backward, turn backward, O Time, in thy flight;
Make me a child again, just for tonight.
ELIZABETH CHASE (AKERS ALLEN): *Rock Me to Sleep,* 1860 (Saturday Evening Post, June 9)

Respect the child. Be not too much his parent. Trespass not on his solitude.
R. W. EMERSON: *Education,* 1865

Talk of Columbus and Newton! I tell you the child just born in yonder hovel is the beginning of a revolution as great as theirs. But you must have the believing and prophetic eye.
IBID.

Give a little love to a child, and you get a great deal back.
JOHN RUSKIN: *The Crown of Wild Olive,* II, 1866

I think that saving a little child
And bringing him to his own,
Is a derned sight better business
Than loafing around the Throne.
JOHN HAY: *Little Breeches,* 1871

The unresolved dissonances between the characters and sentiments of the parents survive in the child, and make up the history of its inner sufferings.
F. W. NIETZSCHE: *Human All-too-Human,* I, 1878

If you strike a child, take care that you strike it in anger, even at the risk of maiming it for life. A blow in cold blood neither can nor would be forgiven.
GEORGE BERNARD SHAW: *Maxims for Revolutionists,* 1903

Give us the child for eight years, and it will be a Bolshevist forever.
NIKOLAI LENIN: Speech to the Commissars of Education, Moscow, 1923

The fundamental theory of liberty upon which governments in this Union repose excludes any general power of the state to standardize its children by forcing them to accept instruction from public teachers only. The child is not the mere creature of the state.
Decision of the Supreme Court of the United States in the Oregon school case, 1925

You can usually account for a child before it comes, but once it's here — good Lord!
Author unidentified

There's only one pretty child in the world, and every mother has it.
CHESHIRE PROVERB

Beat your child once a day. If you don't know why, the child does.
CHINESE PROVERB

Give to a pig when it grunts and a child when it cries, and you will have a fine pig and a bad child.
DANISH PROVERB

A child remains a child until there is another child.
ESTONIAN PROVERB

The child that doesn't resemble its father shames its mother.
FRENCH PROVERB

A child that is loved has many names.
HUNGARIAN PROVERB

If you have a pet child, send him traveling.
JAPANESE PROVERB

Never give a child a sword. (Ne puero gladium.)
LATIN PROVERB

A child learns to talk quicker than to keep silent.
NORWEGIAN PROVERB

The house with no child in it is a house with nothing in it.
WELSH PROVERB

[*See also* Adult, Age (Old), Boy, Boy and Girl, Burnt, Childhood, Children, Damnation (Infant), Duty (Filial), Experience, Father and Child, Fireman, Girl, Grief, Imitation, Innocence, Life, Man and Woman, Mother and Child, Obedience, Paternalism, Precocity, Sun.

Childbirth

Unto the woman he said, I will greatly multiply thy sorrow and thy conception; in sorrow thou shalt bring forth children.
GENESIS III, 16, *c.* 700 B.C.

The Hebrew women are not as the Egyptian women, for they are lively, and are delivered ere the midwives come in unto them.
EXODUS I, 19, *c.* 700 B.C.

Three battles are not equal to the pangs of one childbirth.
EURIPIDES: *Medea,* 431 B.C.

A woman when she is in travail hath sorrow, because her hour is come: but as soon as she is delivered of the child she remembereth no more the anguish, for joy that a man is born into the world.
JOHN XVI, 21, *c.* 115

How often is a gold bed used by a woman having a child?
JUVENAL: *Satires,* VI, 116

And must I, Lord, bring forth a child
For Satan to devour?
CHARLES WESLEY: *For a Woman Near the Time of Her Travail,* 1767

But care and sorrow, and childbirth pain,
Left their traces on heart and brain.
J. G. WHITTIER: *Maud Muller,* 1854

Mr. Darrow — Do you believe that after Eve ate the apple, or gave it to Adam — which-

ever it was — God cursed Eve, and decreed that all womankind thenceforth and forever should suffer the pains of childbirth?
Mr. Bryan — I believe what it says.
Cross-Examination of W. J. Bryan by Clarence Darrow at the Scopes trial, Dayton, Tenn., July 21, 1925

What war is to man childbirth is to woman.
HINDU PROVERB

When there are seven nurses at a childbirth, the baby will be blind. RUSSIAN PROVERB

[*See also* Midwife.

Childhood

Childhood and youth are vanity.
ECCLESIASTES XI, 10, *c.* 200 B.C.

We were as twinn'd lambs that did frisk i' the sun,
And bleat the one at the other; what we chang'd
Was innocence for innocence; we knew not
The doctrine of ill-doing, nor dream'd
That any did.
SHAKESPEARE: *The Winter's Tale*, I, *c.* 1611

The age without pity.
JEAN DE LA FONTAINE: *Fables*, IX, 1671

The childhood shows the man
As morning shows the day.
JOHN MILTON: *Paradise Regained*, IV, 1671

Childhood is the sleep of reason.
J.-J. ROUSSEAU: *Émile*, II, 1762

I have had playmates, I have had companions,
In my days of childhood, in my joyful school-days;
All, all are gone, the old familiar faces.
CHARLES LAMB: *The Old Familiar Faces*, 1798

God-like childhood. (Die göttliche Kindheit.)
JEAN PAUL RICHTER: *Levana*, III, 1807

Heaven lies about us in our infancy.
WILLIAM WORDSWORTH: *Intimations of Immortality*, 1807

How dear to this heart are the scenes of my childhood,
When fond recollection presents them to view.
SAMUEL WOODWORTH: *The Old Oaken Bucket*, 1817

The heart of childhood is all mirth:
We frolic to and fro
As free and blithe, as if on earth
Were no such thing as woe.
JOHN KEBLE: *The Christian Year*, 1827

Childhood knows the human heart.
E. A. POE: *Tamerlane*, VII, 1827

Without, the frost, the blinding snow,
The storm-wind's moody madness —
Within, the firelight's ruddy glow
And childhood's nest of gladness.
C. L. DODGSON (LEWIS CARROLL): *Through the Looking-Glass*, 1871

What art can paint or gild any object in after-life with the glow which nature gives to the first baubles of childhood! St. Peter's cannot have the magical power over us that the red and gold covers of our first picture-book possessed.
R. W. EMERSON: *Domestic Life*, 1877

It is customary, but I think it is a mistake, to speak of happy childhood. Children are often overanxious and acutely sensitive. Man ought to be man and master of his fate; but children are at the mercy of those around them.
JOHN LUBBOCK (LORD AVEBURY): *The Pleasures of Life*, I, 1887

[*See also* Age, Ages, Boy, Child, Children, Error.

Child Labor

The young, young children, O my brothers,
They are weeping bitterly;
They are weeping in the playtime of the others
In the country of the free.
E. B. BROWNING: *The Cry of the Children*, 1843

Under modern industry all family ties among the proletarians are torn asunder, and children transformed into simple articles of commerce and instruments of labor.
KARL MARX and FRIEDRICH ENGELS: *The Communist Manifesto*, 1848

The golf links lie so near the mill
That almost every day
The laboring children can look out
And see the men at play.
SARAH N. CLEGHORN: In the Conning Tower, New York Tribune, Jan. 23, 1915

We favor the speedy enactment of an effective Federal child labor law.
Democratic National Platform, 1916

We favor the enactment and rigid enforcement of a Federal child labor law.
Republican National Platform, 1916

We urge coöperation with the states in the prohibition of child labor.
Democratic National Platform, 1920

The Republican party stands for a Federal child labor law and for its rigid enforcement. If the present law be found unconstitutional, we shall seek other means to enable Congress to prevent the evils of child labor.
Republican National Platform, 1920

[*See also* Labor.

Childless

The childless escape much misery.
EURIPIDES: *Medea*, 431 B.C.

There are three things which are unfilial, and to have no children is the greatest of them.
MENCIUS: *Discourses,* IV, *c.* 300 B.C.

It is better to die without children than to leave ungodly children.
ECCLESIASTICUS XVI, 4, *c.* 180 B.C.

Wretched is that orbity
And deprivation which yet never had
Or ever shall have issue.
THOMAS HEYWOOD: *Pleasant Dialogues and Dramas,* 1637

It is horrible to see oneself die without children.
NAPOLEON I: To Gaspard Gourgaud at St. Helena, Sept. 14, 1817

Soldier, robber, priest, atheist, courtesan, virgin, I care not what you are, if you have not brought children into the world to suffer your life has been as vain and as harmless as mine has been.
GEORGE MOORE: *Confessions of a Young Man,* XII, 1888

He that is childless has no light in his eyes.
PERSIAN PROVERB

[*See also* Child, Children.

Children

It is a great happiness to see our children rising round us, but from that good fortune spring the bitterest woes of man.
AESCHYLUS: *Agamemnon, c.* 490 B.C. (Quoted as " an old adage ")

What greater grief can there be for mortals than to see their children dead?
EURIPIDES: *The Suppliant Women, c.* 421 B.C.

Children cannot be happy, for they are not old enough to be capable of noble acts.
ARISTOTLE: *The Nicomachean Ethics,* I, *c.* 340 B.C.

Happy is the man that hath his quiver full of them. PSALMS CXXVII, 5, *c.* 150 B.C.

These are my jewels. (Haec ornamenta mea sunt.)
Ascribed to CORNELIA, the mother of the Gracchi, *c.* 135 B.C.

Suffer the little children to come unto me, and forbid them not; for of such is the kingdom of God.
MARK X, 14, *c.* 70 (Cf. MATTHEW XIX, 14, *c.* 75; LUKE XVIII, 16, *c.* 75)

It were better for him that a millstone were hanged about his neck, and he cast into the sea, than that he should offend one of these little ones. LUKE XVII, 2, *c.* 75

Little children, keep yourselves from idols. Amen. I JOHN V, 21, *c.* 115

Children are like leaves on a tree.
MARCUS AURELIUS: *Meditations,* X, *c.* 170

The children of the flesh can never be compared to the glory of holy virginity.
ST. AUGUSTINE: *On Holy Virginity, c.* 402

The children of most renowned and noble personages be for most part destructions to a commonwealth.
RICHARD TRAVERNER: Tr. of DESIDERIUS ERASMUS: *Adagia* (1508), 1539

Little pitchers have big ears.
ENGLISH PHRASE, traced by Apperson to 1546

Children and fools cannot lie.
JOHN HEYWOOD: *Proverbs,* 1546

And when with envy Time, transported,
Shall think to rob us of our joys,
You'll in your girls again be courted
And I'll go wooing in my boys.
Anon.: *Winifreda, c.* 1550

Take heed your children speak no words of villainy, nor show them much familiarity, and see that they use honest sports and games. Mark well what vice they are specially inclined to, and break it betimes.
HUGH RHODES: *Book of Nurture,* 1554

The great men and the doctors understand not the Word of God, but it is revealed to the humble and to children.
MARTIN LUTHER: *Table-Talk,* XIV, 1569

Children and chickens would ever be eating.
THOMAS TUSSER: *Five Hundred Points of Good Husbandry,* 1580

Children sweeten labors, but they make misfortunes more bitter. They increase the cares of life, but they mitigate the remembrance of death.
FRANCIS BACON: *Essays,* VII, 1597

He that hath wife and children hath given hostages to fortune, for they are impediments to great enterprises. IBID.

Some would have children: those that have them moan
Or wish them gone.
FRANCIS BACON: *Life* (poem), *c.* 1600

Children we think of affectionately, as divided pieces of our own bodies.
JOSEPH HALL: *Meditations and Vows,* IV, 1606

It is a great honor to you that are married that God, designing to multiply souls, which may bless and praise Him to all eternity, makes you coöperate with Him in so noble a work, by the production of the bodies into which He infuses immortal souls, like heavenly drops, as He creates them.
ST. FRANCIS DE SALES: *Introduction to the Devout Life,* XXXVIII, 1609

Children are poor men's riches.
ENGLISH PROVERB, traced by Apperson to 1611

It is
The fortune commonly of knavish children
To have the lovings't mothers.

THOMAS MIDDLETON: *Women Beware Women*, I, *c.* 1625

Children are certain cares and uncertain comforts.

ENGLISH PROVERB, traced by Apperson to 1639

When children stand quiet they have done some ill.

GEORGE HERBERT: *Outlandish Proverbs*, 1640

Some, admiring what motives to mirth infants meet with in their silent and solitary smiles, have resolved (how truly I know not) that then they converse with angels.

THOMAS FULLER: *A Pisgah-Sight of Palestine*, IV, 1650

He that hath children, all his morsels are not his own.

GEORGE HERBERT: *Jacula Prudentum*, 1651

Children are not endued with reason at all till they have attained the use of speech; but are called reasonable creatures for the possibility apparent of having the use of reason in time to come.

THOMAS HOBBES: *Leviathan*, V, 1651

No man can tell but he that loves his children how many delicious accents makes a man's heart dance in the pretty conversation of those dear pledges; their childishness, their stammering, their little angers, their innocence, their imperfections, their necessities, are so many little emanations of joy and comfort to him that delights in their persons and society.

JEREMY TAYLOR: *Twenty-seven Sermons*, XVII, 1651

Children are without pity.

JEAN DE LA FONTAINE: *Fables*, IX, *c.* 1670

Children and fools have merry lives.

JOHN RAY: *English Proverbs*, 1670

Children pick up words as pigeons peas
And utter them again as God shall please.

IBID.

Children, when they are little, they make parents fools; when great, mad. IBID.

Ah, there are no more children.

J. B. MOLIÈRE: *Le malade imaginaire*, II, 1673

Children suck the mother when they are young and the father when they are old.

ENGLISH PROVERB, traced by Apperson to 1678

If parents carry it lovingly towards their children, mixing their mercies with loving rebukes, and their loving rebukes with fatherly and motherly compassions, they are more likely to save their children than by being churlish and severe towards them.

JOHN BUNYAN: *The Life and Death of Mr. Badman*, 1680

Children have neither a past nor a future. Thus they enjoy the present — which seldom happens to us.

JEAN DE LA BRUYÈRE: *Caractères*, XI, 1688

I in the burying place may see
Graves shorter there than I;
From death's arrest no age is free,
Young children too may die.

New England Primer, *c.* 1688

Men are generally more careful of the breed of their horses and dogs than of their children.

WILLIAM PENN: *Fruits of Solitude*, 1693

Children should never be taken to church in a dress which would not be thought good enough for appearing before company.

ST. JOHN BAPTIST DE LA SALLE: *The Rules of Christian Manners and Civility*, II, 1695

I must whip my children for going into bad company instead of railing at bad company for ensnaring my children.

RICHARD STEELE: *The Tatler*, Oct. 4, 1709

Providence frequently punishes the self-love of men with children very much below their characters and qualifications, insomuch that they transmit their names to those who give daily proofs of the vanity of the labor and ambition of their progenitors.

RICHARD STEELE: *The Spectator*, July 9, 1712

Birds in their little nests agree;
And 'tis a shameful sight,
When children of one family
Fall out, and chide, and fight.

ISAAC WATTS: *Divine Songs for Children*, pref., 1715

But, children, you should never let
Such angry passions rise;
Your little hands were never made
To tear each other's eyes. IBID.

There oft are heard the tones of infant woe:
The short thick sob, loud scream, and shriller squall.

ALEXANDER POPE: *The Alley*, 1727 (Imitation of Edmund Spenser)

Happy is he that is happy in his children.

THOMAS FULLER: *Gnomologia*, 1732

Late children, early orphans.

BENJAMIN FRANKLIN: *Poor Richard's Almanac*, 1742

When children are doing nothing they are doing mischief.

HENRY FIELDING: *Tom Jones*, XV, 1749
(Cf. GEORGE HERBERT, *ante*, 1640)

There was an old woman who lived in a shoe, She had so many children she didn't know what to do. *Nursery Rhyme, c.* 1750

As soon as children are raised from the dead, which takes place immediately after they die, they are taken into Heaven and committed to the care of female angels who, in the life of the body, loved children tenderly, and also loved God.
EMANUEL SWEDENBORG: *Arcana Cœlestia,* 1756

What maintains one vice would bring up two children.
BENJAMIN FRANKLIN: *Poor Richard's Almanac,* 1758

The time has come to establish the principle that children belong to the Republic before they belong to their parents.
G. J. DANTON: Speech to the French Convention, 1791

Children should be seen and not heard.
ENGLISH PROVERB, not recorded before the XIX century, but familiar, with *maids* in place of *children,* since *c.* 1400

No considerations in this world would compensate to me a separation from yourself and your sister.
THOMAS JEFFERSON: *Letter to Mary Jefferson Eppes,* Jan., 1801

Children are horribly insecure; the life of a parent is the life of a gambler.
SYDNEY SMITH: *Letter to Francis Jeffrey, c.* 1803

That woman is contemptible who, having children, is ever bored.
JEAN PAUL RICHTER: *Levana,* IV, 1807

Children know,
Instinctive taught, the friend and foe.
WALTER SCOTT: *The Lady of the Lake,* II, 1810

Children are always ungrateful.
NAPOLEON I: To Gaspard Gourgaud at St. Helena, Dec. 22, 1816

Life is short, and provided a woman produces children, what more does a man want?
NAPOLEON I: To Gaspard Gourgaud at St. Helena, July 8, 1817

All children are by nature evil, and while they have none but the natural evil principle to guide them, pious and prudent parents must check their naughty passions in any way that they have in their power, and force them into decent and proper behavior and into what are called good habits.
MARTHA MARY BUTT: *The Fairchild Family,* 1818

I am determined my children shall be brought up in their father's religion, if they can find out what it is.
CHARLES LAMB: *Letter to John Chambers,* 1818

All children have wicked hearts when they are born: and that makes them so wicked when they grow up into life. Even little infants, that appear so innocent and pretty, are God's little enemies at heart.
SAMUEL SPRING: *Three Sermons to Little Children,* 1819

If you wish to study men you must not neglect to mix with the society of children.
JESSE TORREY: *The Moral Instructor,* 1819

When I consider how little of a rarity children are, — that every street and blind alley swarms with them, — that the poorest people commonly have them in most abundance, — how often they turn out ill, and defeat the fond hopes of their parents, taking to vicious courses, which end in poverty, disgrace, the gallows, &c. — I cannot for my life tell what cause for pride there can possibly be in having them.
CHARLES LAMB: *A Bachelor's Complaint of the Behavior of Married People,* 1822 (London Magazine, Sept.)

Of all people children are the most imaginative. They abandon themselves without reserve to every illusion. No man, whatever his sensibility may be, is ever affected by Hamlet or Lear as a little girl is affected by the story of poor Red Riding-hood.
J. B. MACAULAY: *Milton,* 1825 (Edinburgh Review, Aug.)

One must ask children and birds how cherries and strawberries taste.
J. W. GOETHE: *Conversations with Eckermann,* June 6, 1828

I care not for children till they care a little for me.
WALTER SCOTT: *Journal,* April 10, 1828

Children naturally want to be like their parents, and to do what they do.
WILLIAM COBBETT: *Advice to Young Men,* V, 1829

Children need models more than they need critics. JOSEPH JOUBERT: *Pensées,* 1842

Do ye hear the children weeping, O my brothers?
E. B. BROWNING: *The Cry of the Children,* 1843

Children are never too tender to be whipped: — like tough beefsteaks, the more you beat them the more tender they become.
E. A. POE: *Fifty Suggestions,* 1850 (Graham's Magazine, May–June)

Children have wide ears and long tongues.
H. G. BOHN: *Handbook of Proverbs,* 1855

He that has no children knows not what is love.
IBID.

How solemn they look there, stretch'd and still!
How quiet they breathe, the little children in their cradles!
WALT WHITMAN: *The Sleepers,* 1855

It is one of my rules in life not to believe a man who may happen to tell me that he feels no interest in children.
CHARLES DICKENS: Speech in London, Feb. 9, 1858

As soon as the children are good the mothers are scared, and think they are going to die.
R. W. EMERSON: *The Conduct of Life*, VII, 1860

Heaven protects children, sailors and drunken men.
THOMAS HUGHES: *Tom Brown at Oxford*, XII, 1861 (Quoted as a saying)

Between the dark and the daylight,
When the night is beginning to lower,
Comes a pause in the day's occupations
That is known as the children's hour.
H. W. LONGFELLOW: *The Children's Hour*, 1863

The hero does not always have heroic children, and is still less likely to have heroic grandchildren.
R. W. EMERSON: Lecture on Social Aims, Boston, Dec. 4, 1864

I devise to children the banks of the brooks and the golden sands beneath the waters thereof, and the odors of the willows that dip therein, and the white clouds that float high over the giant trees. And I leave to them the long days to be merry in, in a thousand ways, and the night and the moon, and the train of the Milky Way to wonder at.
CHARLES LOUNSBURY: Last will and testament, *c.* 1875

Children are a torment, and nothing else.
LYOF N. TOLSTOY: *The Kreutzer Sonata*, XIV, 1890

Children begin by loving their parents; after a time they judge them; rarely, if ever, do they forgive them.
OSCAR WILDE: *A Woman of No Importance*, II, 1893

When men otherwise capable of marriage enter upon it, it is wrong to stigmatize them as criminals because they will father only defective children.
POPE PIUS XI: *Casti connubii*, Dec. 31, 1930

All I need to make me happy
Two little young 'uns to call me pappy,
One named Biscuit, t'other named Gravy;
If I had another'n I'd call him Davy.
RAY WOOD: *Mother Goose in the Ozarks*, 1938

There are many loving parents in the world, but no loving children. CHINESE PROVERB

With one child you may walk, with two you may ride;
When you have three, at home you must bide.
CORNISH RHYME

Little children, little sorrows; big children, great sorrows. DANISH PROVERB

An only son — a dog; an only daughter — a bitch. ESTONIAN PROVERB

Neighbors' children are always the worst in the world. GERMAN PROVERB

Little children, headache; big children, heartache. ITALIAN PROVERB

Without children there is no real love.
IBID.

The reason why parents love the younger children best is because they have now so little hope that the elder will do well.
JAPANESE PROVERB

If a man leaves children behind him it is as if he did not die. MOROCCAN PROVERB

Children, chickens, priests and women never say "Enough." POLISH PROVERB

A house without children is only a cemetery.
SANSKRIT PROVERB

Better my bairns seek frae me than I beg frae them. SCOTTISH PROVERB

The best that can happen to a poor man is that ae bairn dee and the rest follow.
IBID. (ae=one)

Waly, waly! bairns are bonny;
One's enough, and twa's too mony.
SCOTTISH RHYME

The dearest child of all is the dead one.
SPANISH PROVERB

[*See also* Age (Old), Best, Boy, Boy and Girl, Brandy, Child, Damnation (Infant), Dancing, Faith, Family, Father, Fruitfulness, Girl, Graceful, Hell, Husband, Illegitimate, Infant, Kindness, Lying, Marriage, Merriment, Mother, Mother and Child, Parent, Pauperism, Precocity, Prophet, Truth, Twenty-five, Verse.

Chimney

There is not always good cheer where the chimney smokes.
THOMAS FULLER: *Gnomologia*, 1732

To talk of architecture is a joke,
Till you can build a chimney that won't smoke.
J. R. PLANCHÉ: *The Birds of Aristophanes*, 1846

Chimpanzee

The chimpanzee yearns for a tail.
WEST AFRICAN PROVERB

[*See also* Ape, Monkey.

Chin

His chin new reap'd,
Show'd like a stubble-land at harvest-home.
SHAKESPEARE: *I Henry IV*, I, *c.* 1598

A pointed chin bespeaks a cunning person.
GERMAN PROVERB

[*See also* Beard, Face.

China

What makes the value of dear china, but that 'tis so brittle? Were it not for that you might as well have stone mugs in your closet.
RICHARD STEELE: *The Funeral,* II, 1701

China-shop

[*See* Bull.

Chinese

The Chinese are cunning and ingenious; and have a great talent at bowing out ambassadors who come to visit them.
LEIGH HUNT: *The Indicator,* XVIII, 1821

If religion is held to mean more than mere ethics, I deny that the Chinese have a religion.
T. F. WADE: *The Hsin Ching Lu,* 1859

When I wish to remark —
And my language is plain —
That for ways that are dark
And for tricks that are vain,
The heathen Chinee is peculiar.
BRET HARTE: *Plain Language from Truthful James,* 1870

It is the immediate duty of Congress to fully investigate the effect of the immigration and importation of Mongolians upon the moral and material interests of the country.
Republican National Platform, 1876

To an American death is preferable to life on a par with the Chinaman. Treason is better than to labor beside a Chinese slave.
Manifesto of the Workingman's party of California, Oct. 16, 1876

American civilization demands that against the immigration or importation of Mongolians to these shores our gates be closed.
Democratic National Platform, 1884

Its absolute indifference to the profoundest spiritual truths in the nature of man is the most melancholy characteristic of the Chinese mind — its ready acceptance of a body without a soul, of a soul without a spirit, of a spirit without life, of a cosmos without a cause, a universe without a God.
A. H. SMITH: *Chinese Characteristics,* 1890

The testimony of Chinese persons is attended with great embarrassment arising from the loose notions entertained by witnesses of the obligation of an oath.
Decision of the Supreme Court of the United States in Li Sing vs. *U. S.,* 1900

We favor the continuance and strict enforcement of the Chinese exclusion law, and its application to the same classes of all Asiatic races.
Democratic National Platform, 1900

In all ages the Chinese find a peculiar and awful satisfaction in watching the agonies of the dying.
E. J. DINGLE: *Across China on Foot,* 1911

There are only two kinds of Chinese — those who give bribes and those who take them.
RUSSIAN PROVERB

Chinese Language

The ignorance of the Chinese may be attributed to their language. A literary Chinese must spend half his life in acquiring a thorough knowledge of it.
C. C. COLTON: *Lacon,* 1820

Chip

Am I not . . . a chip of the same block?
ROBERT SANDERSON (BISHOP OF LINCOLN): *Sermon,* 1627

How well dost thou now appear to be a chip of the old block?
JOHN MILTON: *Apology for Smectymnuus,* 1642

Chiropractic

The term chiropractic when used in this act shall be construed to mean . . . the study and application of a universal philosophy of biology, theology, theosophy, health, disease, death, the science of the cause of disease and art of permitting the restoration of the triune relationships between all attributes necessary to normal composite forms, to harmonious quantities and qualities, by placing in juxtaposition the abnormal concrete positions of definite mechanical portions with each other by hand, thus correcting all subluxations of the articulations of the spinal column, for the purpose of permitting the recreation of all normal cyclic currents through nerves that were formerly not permitted to be transmitted, through impingement, but have now assumed their normal size and capacity for conduction as they emanate through intervertebral foramina — the expressions of which were formerly excessive or partially lacking — named disease.
Act of the Legislature of New Jersey to regulate the practice of chiropractic, 1920

Chivalry

I shall maintain and defend the honest adoes and quarrels of all ladies of honor, widows, orphans and maids of good fame.
The Oath of a Knight (Sent by William Drummond of Hawthornden to Ben Jonson, July 1, 1619)

The age of chivalry is gone; that of sophisters, economists, and calculators has succeeded.
EDMUND BURKE: *Reflections on the Revolution in France,* III, 1790

[*See also* Cervantes (Miguel de)

Chocolate

The superiority of chocolate, both for health and nourishment, will soon give it the same preference over tea and coffee in America which it has in Spain.

THOMAS JEFFERSON: *Letter to John Adams,* 1785

Choice

There's small choice in rotten apples.

SHAKESPEARE: *The Taming of the Shrew,* I, 1594

No choice among stinking fish.

THOMAS FULLER: *Gnomologia,* 1732

I do not choose to run for President in 1928.

CALVIN COOLIDGE: Statement at Rapid City, S. D., Aug. 2, 1927

He who has a choice has trouble.

DUTCH PROVERB

Choir

Choristers bellow the tenor, as it were oxen; bark a counterpart, as it were a kennel of dogs; roar out a treble, as it were a sort of bulls; and grunt out a bass, as it were a number of hogs.

WILLIAM PRYNNE: *Histriomastix,* 1632

Chopin, F. F. (1810–49)

Hats off, gentlemen — a genius!

ROBERT SCHUMANN: Article in the Allegemeine Musikalische Zeitung, 1831

Chosen

Many are called, but few are chosen.

MATTHEW XXII, 14, *c.* 75

[*See also* Jew.

Christening

I proclaim you Thomas Luck, according to the laws of the United States and the state of California, so help me God.

BRET HARTE: *The Luck of Roaring Camp,* 1868 (Overland Monthly, Aug.)

[*See also* Baptism.

Christian

The disciples were called Christians first in Antioch.

ACTS XI, 26, *c.* 75

Almost thou persuadest me to be a Christian.

ACTS XXVI, 28

The Christians are unhappy men who are persuaded that they will survive death and live forever; in consequence, they despise death and are willing to sacrifice their lives to their faith.

LUCIAN: *On the Death of Peregrinus, c.* 166

The Christians do not commit adultery. They do not bear false witness. They do not covet their neighbor's goods. They honor father and mother. They love their neighbors. They judge justly. They avoid doing to others what they do not wish done to them. They do good to their enemies. They are kind.

ST. ARISTIDES: *Apology for the Christian Faith, c.* 160

"See," they say, "how these Christians love one another."

TERTULLIAN: *Apologeticus,* XIX, 197

The Christians to the lions! (Christianos ad leones.)

IBID. (Given as the cry of the Roman populace following any sort of public calamity)

A man becomes a Christian; he is not born one.

TERTULLIAN: *The Testimony of the Christian Soul, c.* 210

They are infidels who say, Verily God is Christ the son of Mary.

THE KORAN, V, *c.* 625

Kill all of them! God will recognize his own.

ABBOT ARNAULD OF CITEAUX: *At the siege of Beziers,* 1209

The barons, gentlemen, burgesses, and other true subjects of the realm, professing the Lord Jesus within the same.

Supplication to the Scotch Parliament, 1560

Men of simple understanding, little inquisitive and little instructed, make good Christians.

MICHEL DE MONTAIGNE: *Essays,* I, 1580

How like a fawning publican he looks!
I hate him for he is a Christian.

SHAKESPEARE: *The Merchant of Venice,* I, *c.* 1597

In converting Jews to Christians, you raise the price of pork.

SHAKESPEARE: *The Merchant of Venice,* III

Methinks sometimes I have no more wit than a Christian.

SHAKESPEARE: *Twelfth Night,* I, *c.* 1601

In every Christian
Hourly tempestuous persecutions grow.
Temptations martyr us alive. A man
Is to himself a Diocletian.

JOHN DONNE: *The Litany, c.* 1625

To make one a complete Christian he must have the works of a papist, the words of a Puritan, and the faith of a Protestant.

JAMES HOWELL: *Familiar Letters,* Aug. 25, 1635

A good Christian would rather be robbed than rob others — rather be murdered than murderer — martyred than tyrant.

Ascribed to ST. FRANCIS DE SALES (1567–1622) in J. P. CAMUS: *L'esprit de Saint François de Sales,* 1641

He that can apprehend and consider vice with all her baits and seeming pleasures, and yet abstain, and yet distinguish and prefer that which is truly better, he is the true warfaring Christian.

JOHN MILTON: *Areopagitica,* 1644

The egg's no chick by falling from the hen,
Nor man a Christian till he's born again.

JOHN BUNYAN: *A Book for Boys and Girls,* 1686

Lord, I ascribe it to thy grace
And not to chance as others do
That I was born of Christian race
And not a heathen or a Jew.
ISAAC WATTS: *Divine Songs for Children,* pref., 1715

To be like Christ is to be a Christian.
WILLIAM PENN: Last words, 1718

I have sent for you that you may see how a Christian can die.
JOSEPH ADDISON: On his deathbed, to his step-son, 1719

A very heathen in the carnal part,
Yet still a sad, good Christian at her heart.
ALEXANDER POPE: *Of the Characters of Women,* 1735

I think all Christians, whether papists or Protestants, agree in the essential articles, and that their differences are trivial, and rather political than religious.
SAMUEL JOHNSON: *Boswell's Life,* June 25, 1763

It is reasonably expected that there should be accord among those on earth who are citizens of Heaven.
BENJAMIN WHICHCOTE: *Moral and Religious Aphorisms,* 1753

All good Christians glory in the folly of the Cross. Nothing can be more contrary to religion and the clergy than reason and common sense.
VOLTAIRE: *Philosophical Dictionary,* 1764

Christians have been the most intolerant of all men. IBID.

Christians have burnt each other, quite persuaded
That all the Apostles would have done as they did. BYRON: *Don Juan,* I, 1819

Whatever makes men good Christians makes them good citizens.
DANIEL WEBSTER: Speech at Plymouth, N. H., Dec. 22, 1820

He who begins by loving Christianity better than truth will proceed by loving his own sect of church better than Christianity, and end in loving himself better than all.
S. T. COLERIDGE: *Aids to Reflection,* 1825

A Christian is God Almighty's gentleman.
J. C. HARE: *Guesses at Truth,* 1827

A Christian is commanded, under the strongest sanctions, to be just in all his dealings. Yet to how many of the twenty-four millions of professing Christians in these islands would any man in his senses lend a thousand pounds without security?
T. B. MACAULAY: *Civil Disabilities of the Jews,* 1831 (Edinburgh Review, Jan.)

Every Stoic was a Stoic; but in Christendom where is the Christian?
R. W. EMERSON: *Self-Reliance,* 1841

I never yet met with a Christian whose heart was thoroughly set upon the world to come, and, so far as human judgment could pronounce, perfect and right before God, who cared about art at all.
JOHN RUSKIN: *The Stones of Venice,* II, 1853

Onward, Christian soldiers,
Marching as to war,
With the cross of Jesus
Going on before.
S. BARING-GOULD: *Onward, Christian Soldiers,* 1866 (Church Times, Nov. 3)

It is a matter of surprise that men whose Christian honesty, purity, and self-devotedness are conceded on every hand, are often men with whom we do not like to associate.
J. G. HOLLAND: *Everyday Topics,* 1876

Out of terror the type has been willed, cultivated and attained: the domestic animal, the herd animal, the sick bruteman — the Christian.
F. W. NIETZSCHE: *The Antichrist,* III, 1888

The Christian, that *ultima ratio* of lying, is the Jew all over again — he is threefold the Jew.
F. W. NIETZSCHE: *The Antichrist,* XLIV

The Christian cannot promise to do or not do a given thing at a given time, for he cannot know what the law of love, which is the commanding principle of his life, will demand of him at that time.
LYOF N. TOLSTOY: *The Kingdom of God Is Within You,* 1893

The true Christian is the true citizen, lofty of purpose, resolute in endeavor, ready for a hero's deeds, but never looking down on his task because it is cast in the day of small things.
THEODORE ROOSEVELT: Speech in New York, Dec. 30, 1900

A federation of Christians is inconceivable in which each member retains his own opinions and private judgment in matters of faith.
POPE PIUS XI: *Mortalium animos,* Jan. 6, 1928

Pale faces, with drawn, retracted lips. It may be termed the Christian or pious *facies.*
HAVELOCK ELLIS: *The Mechanism of Detumescence,* IV, 1906

Venetian first, Christian afterward. (Pria Veneziani, poi Cristiani.) ITALIAN PROVERB

When Christians enter a town it is time for Moslems to go out and live on the riverbank.
MOROCCAN PROVERB

Nothing thicker than a Christian's head.
YIDDISH PROVERB

[*See also* Character (National), Chastity, Child, Christianity, Comfort, Conversation, Cuckold, Donne (John), Drinking, Faith, Golden Rule, Husband and Wife, Lawyer,

Marriage (Second), Philosopher, Piety, Pleasure, Politics, Pope, Promise, Self-Interest, Toleration, Warrior.

Christian, Early

The Christians in Rome were at first a class of men resembling the Quakers.
W. WINWOOD READE: *The Martyrdom of Man,* III, 1872

One would as little choose early Christians for companions as Polish Jews.
F. W. NIETZSCHE: *The Antichrist,* XLVI, 1888

Christianity

Christianity is the bastard progeny of Judaism. It is the basest of all national religions.
CELSUS: *A True Discourse, c.* 178

There was never law, or sect, or opinion did so magnify goodness as the Christian religion doth. FRANCIS BACON: *Essays,* 1597

The Christian religion teaches me two points — that there is a God whom men can know, and that their nature is so corrupt that they are unworthy of Him.
BLAISE PASCAL: *Pensées,* VIII, 1670

No nations are more warlike than those which profess Christianity.
PIERRE BAYLE: *Pensées sur la Comète,* 1682

Were it possible for anything in the Christian faith to be erroneous, I can find no ill consequences in adhering to it.
JOSEPH ADDISON: *The Spectator,* Oct. 3, 1711

I never saw, heard, nor read that the clergy were beloved in any nation where Christianity was the religion of the country.
JONATHAN SWIFT: *Thoughts on Religion,* 1728

Christianity is a scheme quite beyond our comprehension.
JOSEPH BUTLER: *The Analogy of Religion,* II, 1736

Christianity is part of the Common Law of England.
MATTHEW HALE: *History of the Pleas of the Crown,* 1736 (Also in WILLIAM BLACKSTONE: *Commentaries on the Laws of England,* IV, 1765)

Christianity is the highest perfection of humanity.
SAMUEL JOHNSON: *Letter to William Drummond,* Aug. 13, 1766

For seventeen hundred years the Christian sect has done nothing but harm.
VOLTAIRE: *Letter to Frederick the Great,* April 6, 1767

As to the Christian system of faith, it appears to me as a species of atheism — a sort of religious denial of God. It professes to believe in a man rather than in God. It is a compound made up chiefly of manism with but little deism, and is as near to atheism as twilight is to darkness.
THOMAS PAINE: *The Age of Reason,* I, 1794

The Christian religion is part of the law of the land. [England].
MR. CHIEF JUSTICE KENYON: *Decision in William's Case,* 1797 (Cf. HALE, *ante,* 1736)

The government of the United States of America is not, in any sense, founded on the Christian religion.
Treaty between the United States and Tripoli, XI, 1797 (This article has been accepted as authentic for years, and its authorship has been ascribed to Joel Barlow. But an Italian translation of the original Arabic text of the treaty, on file in the State Department, does not show the article)

I swear that never will I forgive Christianity . . . Oh, how I wish I were the Antichrist — that it were mine to crush the demon; to hurl him to his native Hell, never to rise again. I expect to gratify some of this insatiable feeling in poetry.
P. B. SHELLEY: *Letter to T. J. Hogg,* Jan. 3, 1811

The same means that have supported every other popular belief have supported Christianity. War, imprisonment, assassination, and falsehood; deeds of unexampled and incomparable atrocity have made it what it is.
P. B. SHELLEY: *Queen Mab,* notes, 1813

I would believe in Christianity if it dated from the beginning of the world.
NAPOLEON I: To Gaspard Gourgaud at St. Helena, 1815–1818

I'll be damned to Hell if I sit here to hear the Christian religion abused.
MR. JUSTICE BEST: Remark from the bench in *Rex* vs. *Carlile,* 1821

A wise man will always be a Christian, because the perfection of wisdom is to know where lies tranquillity of mind, and how to attain it, which Christianity teaches.
W. S. LANDOR: *Imaginary Conversations,* II, 1824

Christianity is not a theory, or a speculation; but a life; — not a philosophy of life, but a life and a living process.
S. T. COLERIDGE: *Aids to Reflection,* 1825

The real security of Christianity is to be found in its benevolent morality, in its exquisite adaptation to the human heart, in the facility with which its scheme accommodates itself to the capacity of every human intellect, in the consolation which it bears to the house

of mourning, in the light with which it brightens the great mystery of the grave.
T. B. MACAULAY: *Southey's Colloquies*, 1830

The flesh had become so insolent in the Roman world that Christian discipline was needed to chasten it. After the banquet of a Trimalchio the hunger-cure of Christianity was required.
HEINRICH HEINE: *Die romantische Schule*, 1836

Faith in an Invisible, not as real only, but as the only reality; time, through every meanest moment of it, resting on eternity; pagan empire of force displaced by a nobler supremacy, that of holiness.
THOMAS CARLYLE: *Heroes and Hero-Worship*, I, 1840 (Lecture in London, May 5)

We can never see Christianity from the catechism: — from the pastures, from a boat in the pond, from amidst the songs of wood-birds, we possibly may.
R. W. EMERSON: *Circles*, 1841

Bear witness, O Thou wrong and merciful One,
That earth's most hateful crimes have in Thy name been done.
J. G. WHITTIER: *The Gallows*, 1842

To pretend that Christianity was intended to stereotype existing forms of government and society, and protect them against change, is to reduce it to the level of Islamism and Brahminism. It is precisely because Christianity has not done this that it has been the religion of the progressive portion of mankind.
J. S. MILL: *The Subjection of Women*, II, 1869

Christianity is the complete negation of common sense and sound reason.
M. A. BAKUNIN: *Dieu et l'état*, 1871

Christianity is not in accordance with the cultivated mind; it can only be accepted by suppressing doubts, and by denouncing inquiry as sinful. It is therefore a superstition, and ought to be destroyed.
W. WINWOOD READE: *The Martyrdom of Man*, III, 1872

Protestantism has the method of Jesus with His secret too much left out of mind; Catholicism has His secret with His method too much left out of mind; neither has His unerring balance, His intuition, His sweet reasonableness. But both have hold of a great truth, and get from it a great power.
MATTHEW ARNOLD: *Literature and Dogma*, X, 1873

A man may carry the whole scheme of Christian truth in his mind from boyhood to old age without the slightest effect upon his character and aims. It has less influence than the multiplication table.
J. G. HOLLAND: *Everyday Topics*, 1876

Christianity is the enemy of liberty and of civilization. It has kept mankind in chains.
AUGUST BEBEL: Speech in the Reichstag, March 31, 1881

Christianity aims at mastering beasts of prey; its *modus operandi* is to make them ill — to make feeble is the Christian recipe for taming, for "civilizing."
F. W. NIETZSCHE: *The Antichrist*, XXII, 1888

Christianity has the rancor of the sick at its very core — the instinct against the healthy, against health. Everything that is well-constituted, proud, gallant and, above all, beautiful gives offence to its ears and eyes.
F. W. NIETZSCHE: *The Antichrist*, LI

I call Christianity the one great curse, the one great intrinsic depravity, the one great instinct of revenge, for which no means are venomous enough, or secret, subterranean and small enough — I call it the one immortal blemish upon the human race.
F. W. NIETZSCHE: *The Antichrist*, LXII

As an instrument of warfare against vice, or as a tool for making virtue, Christianity is a mere flint implement.
SAMUEL BUTLER: *Note-Books*, *c.* 1890

Civil society was renovated in every part by the teachings of Christianity. In the strength of that renewal the human race was lifted up to better things. Nay, it was brought back from death to life.
POPE LEO XIII: *Rerum novarum*, May 15, 1891

Christianity, with its doctrine of humility, of forgiveness, of love, is incompatible with the state, with its haughtiness, its violence, its punishments, its wars.
LYOF N. TOLSTOY: *The Kingdom of God Is Within You*, 1893

No religion ever proclaimed statements so obviously out of agreement with reason and contemporary human knowledge.
LYOF N. TOLSTOY: *What Is Religion?*, 1902

On all sides there are signs of the decay of the faith. People do not go to church, or, if they go, it is for the sake of the music, or for some non-religious motive. The evidence is overwhelming that the doctrines of Christianity have passed into the region of doubt.
LORD HUGH CECIL: Speech in the House of Commons, March 14, 1904

A shipwrecked sailor, landing on a lonely beach, observed a gallows. "Thank God," he exclaimed, "I am in a Christian country!"
Author unidentified

Christianity teaches a man to spend the best part of his life preparing for the worst.
IBID.

[*See also* Buddhism, Charity, Christian, Church (Christian), Deism, Faith, Jesus Christ,

Mercy, Miracle, Mohammedanism, Protestantism, Prudence, St. Paul, Sin, Skepticism, Sympathy.

Christian Science

Christian Science reveals incontrovertibly that Mind is All-in-all, that the only realities are the divine Mind and idea.
MARY BAKER G. EDDY: *Science and Health,* VI, 1908

[*See also* Cause and Effect.

Christ, Jesus

[*See* Jesus Christ.

Christmas

Come, all ye faithful, joyful and triumphant;
Come ye, come ye to Bethlehem;
Come and behold Him, born the king of angels;
Come and adore Him, come and adore Him,
Come and adore the Lord.
(Adeste fideles. Laeti triumphantes:
Venite, venite in Bethlehem.
Natum videte, Regem angelorum,
Venite, adoremus, venite, adoremus:
Venite, adoremus Dominus.)
Attributed to ST. BONAVENTURE (1221–1274), but probably much later.

At Christmas play, and make good cheer,
For Christmas comes but once a year.
THOMAS TUSSER: *Five Hundred Points of Good Husbandry,* 1580

This is the month, and this the happy morn,
Wherein the Son of Heaven's eternal King,
Of wedded maid and virgin mother born,
Our great redemption from above did bring.
JOHN MILTON: *On the Morning of Christ's Nativity,* 1629

A green Christmas makes a fat churchyard.
ENGLISH PROVERB, traced by Apperson to 1635

England was merry England, when
Old Christmas brought his sports again.
'Twas Christmas broach'd the mightiest ale;
'Twas Christmas told the merriest tale;
A Christmas gambol oft could cheer
The poor man's heart through half the year.
WALTER SCOTT: *Marmion,* VI, 1808

It came upon the midnight clear,
That glorious song of old,
From angels bending near the earth
To touch their harps of gold;
"Peace on the earth, good will to men
From Heaven's all-gracious King" –
The world in solemn stillness lay
To hear the angels sing.
E. H. SEARS: *Christmas Carol,* 1850 (The tune is by Richard S. Willis, 1851)

For Christ is born of Mary,
And gathered all above,
While mortals sleep, the angels keep
Their watch of wond'ring love.
O morning stars, together
Proclaim the holy birth!
And praises sing to God the King,
And peace to men on earth!
PHILLIPS BROOKS: *O Little Town of Bethlehem,* 1868 (The tune is by L. H. Redner)

God rest ye, little children; let nothing you affright,
For Jesus Christ, your Saviour, was born this happy night;
Along the hills of Galilee the white flocks sleeping lay,
When Christ, the Child of Nazareth, was born on Christmas day.
DIANA MULOCK CRAIK: *Christmas Carol,* 1881

Call a truce, then, to our labors – let us feast with friends and neighbors,
And be merry as the custom of our caste;
For if "faint and forced the laughter," and if sadness follow after,
We are richer by one mocking Christmas past.
RUDYARD KIPLING: *Christmas in India,* 1886

We would warn the young against giving countenance to such a Romanist practice as that of observing Christmas.
The Northern Presbytery of the Free Presbyterian Church of Scotland: *Opinion in the case of John Murray,* 1935

Green Christmas, white Easter. (Grüne Weihnacht, weisse Ostern.)
GERMAN PROVERB

Christmas is coming, the geese are getting fat,
Please to put a penny in the old man's hat;
If you haven't got a penny, a ha'penny will do,
If you haven't got a ha'penny, God bless you.
OLD ENGLISH CAROL

Christmas Eve

Silent night, holy night. (Stille Nacht, heilige Nacht.)
JOSEPH MOHR: *Die heilige Nacht,* first line, 1818 (The familiar tune is by Franz Gruber)

'Twas the night before Christmas, when all through the house
Not a creature was stirring, not even a mouse.
C. C. MOORE: *A Visit from St. Nicholas,* 1823

The time draws near the birth of Christ:
The moon is hid; the night is still;
The Christmas bells from hill to hill
Answer each other in the mist.
ALFRED TENNYSON: *In Memoriam,* XXVIII, 1850

Chronology

From the day when God made the Heaven and earth and the first man . . . unto the coming of Christ and his birth we found it to be . . . five thousand and five hundred years. *The Acts of Pilate,* XII, *c.* 325

Church

Church work goes on slowly.
ENGLISH PROVERB, traced by Apperson to the XVII century

The itch of disputing will prove the scab of churches.
HENRY WOTTON (1568–1639) (Wotton directed that this line be engraved on his tombstone in Latin: "Disputandi pruritus ecclesiarum scabies")

How glorious soever the church is, every one chooses out of it his own religion, by which he governs himself, and lets the rest alone.
JOHN SELDEN: *Table-Talk,* 1689

The kirk is aye greedy.
JAMES KELLY: *Complete Collection of Scottish Proverbs,* 1721

A Gothic church or a convent fill one with romantic dreams — but for the mysterious, the church in the abstract, it is a jargon that means nothing, or a great deal too much, and I reject it and its apostles.
HORACE WALPOLE: *Letter to William Cole,* July 12, 1778

I do not believe in the creed professed by the Jewish church, by the Roman church, by the Greek church, by the Turkish church, by the Protestant church, nor by any church that I know of. My own mind is my own church.
THOMAS PAINE: *The Age of Reason,* II, 1794

The church is an anvil that has worn out many hammers.
ENGLISH PROVERB, not recorded before the XIX century

A church is disaffected when it is persecuted, quiet when it is tolerated, and actively loyal when it is favored and cherished.
T. B. MACAULAY: *Hallam,* 1828 (Edinburgh Review, Sept.)

The poorer the church, the purer the church.
W. C. HAZLITT: *English Proverbs,* 1869

The church has always been willing to swap off treasures in Heaven for cash down.
R. G. INGERSOLL: Speech in Chicago, Sept. 20, 1880

The church does not die. (Ecclesia non moritur.)
LEGAL MAXIM

The church teaching. (Ecclesia docens.)
MEDIEVAL LATIN PHRASE

[*See also* Children, Excommunication, Magistrate.

Church and State

Render to Caesar the things that are Caesar's, and to God the things that are God's.
LUKE XII, 17, *c.* 70 (Also in MATTHEW XXII, 21, *c.* 75, and LUKE XX, 25, *c.* 75, with slight verbal changes)

I cannot give up my guidance to the magistrate, because he knows no more of the way to Heaven than I do, and is less concerned to direct me right than I am to go right.
THOMAS JEFFERSON: *Notes on Religion,* 1776

To compel a man to furnish contributions of money for the propagation of opinions which he disbelieves and abhors is sinful and tyrannical.
THOMAS JEFFERSON: *Virginia Statute of Religious Freedom,* 1779

Congress shall make no law respecting an establishment of religion, or prohibiting the free exercise thereof.
CONSTITUTION OF THE UNITED STATES, Amendment I, Dec. 15, 1791

The adulterous connection of church and state.
THOMAS PAINE: *The Age of Reason,* I, 1794

There are communities in which it would be as absurd to mix up theology with government as it would have been in the right wing of the allied army at Blenheim to commence a controversy with the left wing, in the middle of the battle, about Purgatory and the worship of images.
T. B. MACAULAY: *Gladstone on Church and State,* 1839 (Edinburgh Review, April)

A free church in a free state. (Libera chiesa in libero stato.)
CAMILLE CAVOUR: Speech in the Italian Parliament, March 27, 1861 (The same phrase, in French, was used by the Count de Montalembert at a Catholic congress at Malines, Aug. 20, 1863, and he is sometimes credited, erroneously, with originating it)

In any conflict between civil and ecclesiastical laws, the former should prevail.
Proposition condemned by POPE PIUS IX: *Syllabus of Errors,* XLII, Dec. 8, 1864

In spite of the intensity of Roman religious feeling, the religion of the state was always absolutely subject to the political authority.
W. A. HUNTER: *Exposition of Roman Law,* I, 1876

It is generally agreed that the Founder of the Church, Jesus Christ, wished the spiritual power to be distinct from the civil, and each to be free and unhampered in doing its own work, not forgetting, however, that it is expedient for both, and in the interest of everybody, that there be a harmonious relationship.
POPE LEO XIII: *Arcanum divinae sapientiae,* 1880

The church deems it unlawful to place all other religions on the same footing as the true religion.
POPE LEO XIII: *Immortale Dei,* Nov. 1, 1885

. . the fatal theory of the separation of church and state.

POPE LEO XIII: *Libertas praestantissimum,* June 20, 1888

The greatest achievement ever made in the cause of human progress is the total and final separation of the state from the church. If we had nothing else to boast of, we could claim with justice that first among the nations we of this country made it an article of organic law that the relations between man and his Maker were a private concern into which other men had no right to intrude.

D. D. FIELD: Speech in Chicago, 1893

In order to ensure to citizens freedom of conscience, the church in the U.S.S.R. is separated from the state, and the school from the church. Freedom of religious worship and freedom of anti-religious-worship propaganda is recognized for all citizens.

CONSTITUTION OF THE U.S.S.R., CXXIV, Jan. 31, 1924

[*See also* Godless.

Church, Christian

Upon this rock I will build my church, and the gates of Hell shall not prevail against it.

MATTHEW XVI, 18, *c.* 75

Where two or three are gathered together in my name, there am I in the midst of them.

MATTHEW XVIII, 20

He cannot have God for his father who refuses to have the church for his mother.

ST. AUGUSTINE: *De Symbolo,* XIII, *c.* 400

It is impossible for the Christian and true church to subsist without the shedding of blood, for her adversary, the Devil, is a liar and a murderer. The church grows and increases through blood; she is sprinkled with blood.

MARTIN LUTHER: *Table-Talk,* CCCLXXI, 1569

The church alone can digest ill-gotten gains.

J. W. GOETHE: *I Faust,* IX, 1808

The church is a sacred corporation for the promulgation and maintenance in Europe of certain Asian principles which, although local in their birth, are of divine origin and eternal application.

BENJAMIN DISRAELI: *Coningsby,* pref., 1844

The churches have killed their Christ.

ALFRED TENNYSON: *Maud,* 1855

I bring against the Christian church the most terrible of all the accusations that an accuser has ever had in his mouth. It is, to me, the greatest of all imaginable corruptions; it seeks to work the ultimate corruption, the worst possible corruption. The Christian church has left nothing untouched by its depravity; it has turned every value into worthlessness, every truth into a lie, and every integrity into baseness of soul.

F. W. NIETZSCHE: *The Antichrist,* LXII, 1888

The church founded by Jesus has *not* made its way; has *not* permeated the world — but *did* become extinct in the country of its birth — as Nazarenism and Ebionism.

T. H. HUXLEY: *Letter to Robert Taylor,* June 3, 1889

The Christian churches and Christianity have nothing in common save in name: they are utterly hostile opposites. The churches are arrogance, violence, usurpation, rigidity, death; Christianity is humility, penitence, submissiveness, progress, life.

LYOF N. TOLSTOY: *The Kingdom of God Is Within You,* 1893

Do not attack the church. Leave it alone. It is the only remaining bulwark against Christianity. Author unidentified

[*See also* Blood, Martyrdom.

Churches

I do not like to see the church and synagogue kissing and congeeing in awkward postures of affected civility.

CHARLES LAMB: *Essays on Elia,* 1823

Church-going

Christian people do run into the church as to a stage-play, where they may be delighted with piping and singing.

JOHN NORTHBROOKE: *Against Dicing,* 1577

[*See also* New York, Travel.

Church (house)

I was glad when they said unto me, Let us go into the house of the Lord.

PSALMS CXXII, 1, *c.* 150 B.C.

The nearer the church, the further from God.

ENGLISH PROVERB, traced by Smith to 1303

Where God builds a church the Devil has a chapel.

ENGLISH PROVERB, familiar before 1400

The steeple-house.

GEORGE FOX: *Journal,* 1694 (Used throughout to designate church)

Whenever God erects a house of prayer
The Devil always builds a chapel there;
And 'twill be found upon examination
The latter has the largest congregation.

DANIEL DEFOE: *The True-Born Englishman,* I, 1701

Who builds a church to God and not to fame
Will never mark the marble with his name.

ALEXANDER POPE: *Moral Essays,* III (Of the Use of Riches), 1732

If anything pass in a religious meeting seditiously and contrary to the public peace, let it be punished in the same manner and no otherwise than as if it had happened in a fair or market. These meetings ought not to be sanctuaries for faction and flagitiousness.
THOMAS JEFFERSON: *Notes on Religion,* 1776

Dear mother, dear mother, the church is cold,
But the ale-house is healthy and pleasant and warm.
WILLIAM BLAKE: *The Little Vagabond,* 1794

An instinctive taste teaches men to build their churches, in flat countries, with spire steeples, which, as they cannot be referred to any other object, point as with silent finger to the sky and star.
S. T. COLERIDGE: *The Friend,* I, 1818

Let all our churches be built plain and decent, and with free seats; but not more expensive than is absolutely unavoidable; otherwise the necessity of raising money will make rich men necessary to us.
The Doctrines and Discipline of the Methodist Episcopal Church, South, II, 1846

Your church is a baby-house made of blocks.
H. D. THOREAU: *An Essay on Civil Disobedience,* 1849

One should not go to church if one wants to breathe pure air.
F. W. NIETZSCHE: *Beyond Good and Evil,* 1886

Wherever there is one church there are two inns.
BULGARIAN PROVERB

There is little piety in big churches.
ITALIAN PROVERB

The Church is the mansion-house of the Omnipotent God. (Ecclesia est domus mansionalis Omnipotentis Dei.)
LEGAL MAXIM

[*See also* Architecture (Gothic), Hypocrisy, Thunder.

Church of England

This is the Catholick Faith: which except a man believe faithfully, he cannot be saved.
THE BOOK OF COMMON PRAYER (*Morning Prayer*), 1662

Charity and love is the known doctrine of the Church of England.
DANIEL DEFOE: *The Shortest Way With the Dissenters,* 1702

As for my religion, I die in the Holy Catholic and Apostolic Faith, professed by the whole church before the disunion of the East and the West; more particularly, I die in the communion of the Church of England, as it stands distinguished from all papal and Puritan innovations, and as it adheres to the doctrine of the Cross.
THOMAS KEN (BISHOP OF BATH AND WELLS): *Last will, c.* 1710

The Church of England hath a popish liturgy, a Calvinistic creed, and an Arminian clergy.
Ascribed to WILLIAM PITT (EARL OF CHATHAM) (1708–78)

Ours is a church reform'd, and now no more
Is aught for man to mend or to restore;
'Tis pure in doctrines, 'tis correct in creeds,
Has nought redundant, and it nothing needs;
No evil is therein — no wrinkle, spot,
Stain, blame, or blemish: — I affirm there's not.
GEORGE CRABBE: *Tales,* I (*The Dumb Orators*), 1812

Sir Richard Steele has observed, that there is this difference between the Church of Rome and the Church of England: the one professes to be infallible — the other to be never in the wrong.
C. C. COLTON: *Lacon,* 1820

A decorous simplicity is the characteristic of the Church of England.
MR. JUSTICE LUSHINGTON: *Judgment in Beal* vs. *Liddell,* 1855

The doctrine of the Old Testament is the religion of England. The first leaf of the New Testament it does not open. It believes in a Providence which does not treat with levity a pound sterling. They are neither transcendentalists nor Christians.
R. W. EMERSON: *English Traits,* XIII, 1856

The Church of England is not a mere depositary of doctrine. The Church of England is a part of England — it is a part of our strength and a part of our liberties, a part of our national character.
BENJAMIN DISRAELI: Speech in the House of Commons, Feb. 27, 1861

In the English church a man succeeds, not through his capacity for belief, but through his capacity for disbelief. Ours is the only church where the skeptic stands at the altar, and where St. Thomas is regarded as the ideal apostle.
OSCAR WILDE: *The Decay of Lying,* 1891

The state church seems more and more anxious to repudiate all complicity with the principles of the Protestant Reformation and to call itself Anglo-Catholic.
T. H. HUXLEY: *Controverted Questions,* 1892

[*See also* Episcopalian.

Church, Roman Catholic

I believe in the One, Holy, Catholic, and Apostolic Church.
THE NICAEAN CREED, 325

This is the Holy Church, the One Church, the True Church, the Catholic Church, which fights against all errors. She may be attacked, but cannot be overcome. The gates of Hell shall not prevail against her.
ST. AUGUSTINE: *De Symbolo, c.* 400

The church is a faithful and ever watchful guardian of the dogmas which have been committed to her charge. In this sacred deposit she changes nothing, she takes nothing from it, she adds nothing to it.

ST. VINCENT OF LÉRINS: *Commonitorium, c.* 450

The purple whore, . . . the beast of Babylon.

Anon.: *The Travels of Time,* 1624

It is less a religion than a priestly tyranny armed with the spoils of civil power which, on pretext of religion, it hath seized against the command of Christ Himself.

JOHN MILTON: *Treatise on Civil Power in Ecclesiastical Causes,* 1659

Abhor that arrant Whore of Rome,
And all her blasphemies;
And drink not of her cursed cup,
Obey not her decrees.

New England Primer, c. 1688

The church is the society of the faithful collected into one and the same body, governed by its legitimate pastors, of whom Jesus Christ is the invisible head — the pope, the successor of St. Peter, being His representative on earth.

ST. JOHN BAPTIST DE LA SALLE: *Les devoirs du chrétien,* x, 1703

I wish that you would crush this infamy. (Je voudrais que vous écrasassiez l'infâme.)

VOLTAIRE: *Letter to Jean le Rond D'Alembert,* June 23, 1760

A good man of a timorous disposition, in great doubt of his acceptance with God, and pretty credulous, may be glad to be of a church where there are so many helps to get to Heaven . . . I wonder that women are not all papists.

SAMUEL JOHNSON: *Boswell's Life,* June 10, 1784

The church is filled with men who are led into it merely by ambition, and who, though they might have been useful and respectable as laymen, are hypocritical and immoral as churchmen.

T. B. MACAULAY: *Letter from Rome,* Dec., 1838

She was great and respected before the Saxon had set foot on Britain, before the Frank had passed the Rhine, when Grecian eloquence still flourished in Antioch, when idols were still worshipped in the temple of Mecca. And she may still exist in undiminished vigor when some traveler from New Zealand shall, in the midst of a vast solitude, take his stand on a broken arch of London Bridge to sketch the ruins of St. Paul's.

T. B. MACAULAY: *Von Ranke,* 1840 (Edinburgh Review, Oct.)

The Catholic church holds it better for the sun and moon to drop from Heaven, for the earth to fail, and for all the many millions in it to die of starvation in extremest agony, as far as temporal affliction goes, than that one soul, I will not say, should be lost, but should commit one single venial sin, should tell one wilful untruth, or should steal one poor farthing without excuse.

J. H. NEWMAN: *Apologia pro vita sua,* II, 1864

Q. How long is the church on earth to last?
A. The Catholic church on earth will last to the end of the world.

JOHN MCCAFFREY: *A Catechism of Christian Doctrine for General Use,* 1866

The Latin church is the great fact which dominates the history of modern civilization.

H. C. LEA: *A History of Sacerdotal Celibacy,* III, 1867

The one great spiritual organization which is able to resist, and must, as a matter of life and death, resist, the progress of science and modern civilization.

T. H. HUXLEY: *Scientific Education,* 1869 (Speech in Liverpool)

The appeal from the living voice of the church to any tribunal whatsoever, human history included, is an act of private judgment and a treason, because that living voice is supreme; and to appeal from that supreme voice is also a heresy, because that voice, by divine assistance, is infallible.

HENRY CARDINAL MANNING: *Letter to the London Daily Telegraph,* Oct. 8, 1875

The church is not susceptible of being reformed in her doctrines. The church is the work of an Incarnate God. Like all God's works, it is perfect. It is, therefore, incapable of reform.

JAMES CARDINAL GIBBONS: *The Faith of Our Fathers,* VII, 1876

In matters of faith and morals God has made the church a sharer in the divine magistracy, and granted her, by a special privilege, immunity from error.

POPE LEO XIII: *Libertas praestantissimum,* June 20, 1888

When Socialism comes to power, the church will advocate Socialism with the same vigor it is now favoring feudalism and slavery. And it will find plenty of proof in the New Testament that the church has always been communistic.

AUGUST BEBEL: Speech at the congress of the Social-Democratic party, Jena, 1906

Both in the origin and in the exercise of her mission as educator of the young, the church is independent of any earthly power, not merely in regard to her lawful end and purpose, but also in regard to whatever means she may deem suitable and necessary to attain them.

POPE PIUS XI: *Divini illius magistri,* Dec. 31, 1929

The fundamental principles of Western civilization, individual liberty, human rights, the rights of private property, the integrity of human personality, derive from the doctrine now almost alone affirmed universally in the Western world by the Catholic church, that man at the core of his being is of a spiritual nature.
Resolution of National Catholic Alumni Federation, 1936

[*See also* Bloodshed, Catholic (Roman), Catholicism (Roman), Church of England, Dispute, Earth, Eucharist, Evolution, Faith, Historian, Infallibility (Papal), Infamy, Mass, Papacy, Pope, Sin, Transubstantiation.

Churchyard

The churchyard, like the sea and the gallows, receives all without asking questions.
ENGLISH PROVERB, not recorded before the XVIII century

I would rather sleep in the southern corner of a little country churchyard than in the tombs of the Capulets.
EDMUND BURKE: *Letter to Matthew Smith*, 1778

Nowhere probably is there more true feeling, and nowhere worse taste, than in a churchyard. BENJAMIN JOWETT (1817–93)

[*See also* Cemetery, Grave, Midnight.

Cicero (106–43 B.C.)

The letters of Cicero breathe the purest effusions of an exalted patriot.
THOMAS JEFFERSON: *Letter to John Adams*, 1819

A journalist in the worst sense of the word.
THEODOR MOMMSEN: *Römische Geschichte*, I, 1854

Cider

Cider smiles in your face, and then cuts your throat.
ENGLISH PROVERB, traced by Apperson to 1653

Cigar

Sublime tobacco! which from East to West,
Cheers the tar's labor or the Turkman's rest;
Divine in hookas, glorious in a pipe,
When tipp'd with amber, mellow, rich, and ripe;
Like other charmers wooing the caress,
More dazzling when daring in full dress;
Yet thy true lovers more adore by far
Thy naked beauties – Give me a cigar!
BYRON: *The Island*, II, 1823

Some sigh for this and that;
My wishes don't go far;
The world may wag at will,
So I have my cigar.
THOMAS HOOD: *The Cigar*, *c.* 1840

A good cigar is as great a comfort to a man as a good cry to a woman.
E. G. BULWER-LYTTON: *Darnley*, II, 1845

I do not believe that there was ever an Aunt Tabithy who could abide cigars.
DONALD G. MITCHELL (IK MARVEL): *Reveries of a Bachelor*, III, 1850

What smells so? Has somebody been burning a rag, or is there a dead mule in the backyard? No, the man is smoking a five-cent cigar.
EUGENE FIELD: *The Tribune Primer*, 1882

A woman is only a woman, but a good cigar is a smoke.
RUDYARD KIPLING: *The Betrothed*, 1886

What this country needs is a good five-cent cigar. THOMAS R. MARSHALL, *c.* 1920

[*See also* Cigarette, Pipe, Smoking, Tobacco.

Cigarette

A cigarette is the perfect type of a perfect pleasure. It is exquisite, and it leaves one unsatisfied.
OSCAR WILDE: *The Picture of Dorian Gray*, 1891

Cigarette-smoking is like drinking beer out of a thimble.
ELIZABETH AMY DILLWYN, who died at Swansea, Wales, *aet.* 90, 1935

[*See also* Tobacco.

Cigarmaker

When cigarmakers die they turn into jackasses.
AMERICAN CIGARMAKERS' PROVERB, *c.* 1880

Cincinnati

[*See* Chicago.

Circumcision

Ye shall circumcise the flesh of your foreskin; and it shall be a token of the covenant betwixt me and you.
GENESIS XVII, 11, *c.* 700 B.C.

If ye be circumcised, Christ shall profit you nothing. GALATIANS V, 2, *c.* 50

The Circumcision is an example of the power of poetry to raise the low and offensive.
R. W. EMERSON: *The Poet*, 1844

Circumlocution

Whatever was required to be done, the Circumlocution Office was before hand with all the public departments in the art of perceiving how not to do it.
CHARLES DICKENS: *Little Dorrit*, III, 1857

Circumstance

Men are dependent on circumstances, not circumstances on men.
HERODOTUS: *Histories*, VII, *c.* 430 B.C.

Men are the sport of circumstances.
BYRON: *Don Juan*, V, 1821

I am the very slave of circumstance.
BYRON: *Sardanapalus*, IV, 1821

Man is not the creature of circumstances. Circumstances are the creatures of men.
BENJAMIN DISRAELI: *Vivian Grey*, VI, 1827

Circumstances alter cases.
T. C. HALIBURTON: *The Old Judge*, 1837

Circumstances over which I have no control.
THE DUKE OF WELLINGTON: *Letter*, 1839

Witnesses may lie, but circumstances can't.
Author unidentified

[*See also* Evidence (Circumstantial), Pomp.

Circus

A good circus is an oasis of Hellenism in a world that reads too much to be wise, and thinks too much to be beautiful.
OSCAR WILDE: *London Models*, 1889 (English Illustrated Magazine, Jan.)

[*See also* Bread, Soldier.

Citizen

I am a citizen, not of Athens or Greece, but of the world.
Ascribed to SOCRATES (469–399 B.C.)

I am a Roman citizen. (Civis Romanus sum.)
CICERO: *Oration against Verres*, *c.* 60 B.C.

Paul said, I am a man which am a Jew of Tarsus, a city in Cilicia, a citizen of no mean city.
ACTS XXI, 39, *c.* 75

Civis, the most honorable name among the Romans; a citizen, a word of contempt among us.
JONATHAN SWIFT: *Thoughts on Various Subjects*, 1706

Every citizen is a king under a citizen king.
C. S. FAVART: *Les trois sultanes*, II, 1761

The free inhabitants of each of these states, paupers, vagabonds and fugitives from justice excepted, shall be entitled to all privileges and immunities of free citizens in the several states.
ARTICLES OF CONFEDERATION, IV, Nov. 15, 1777

The persons and property of our citizens are entitled to the protection of our government in all places where they may lawfully go.
THOMAS JEFFERSON: Official opinion as Secretary of State, 1793

Amongst the virtues of the good citizen are those of fortitude and patience.
WILLIAM COBBETT: *Advice to Young Men*, VI, 1829

The first requisite of a good citizen in this Republic of ours is that he shall be able and willing to pull his weight.
THEODORE ROOSEVELT: Speech in New York, Nov. 11, 1902

In this country of ours the man who has not raised himself to be a soldier, and the woman who has not raised her boy to be a soldier for the right — neither one of them is entitled to citizenship in the Republic.
THEODORE ROOSEVELT: Speech at Camp Upton, Nov. 18, 1917

Only such persons shall be citizens of the Reich who are of German or kindred stock and shall prove by their conduct that they are willing and fit loyally to serve the German people and the Reich.
German Law of Sept. 15, 1935

They are our citizens, aren't they? We can do what we like with them.
Reply of an official of the Russian Commissariat for Foreign Affairs to a protest against the oppression of German colonists in Siberia, 1929; quoted in W. H. CHAMBERLAIN: *Russia's Iron Age*, XIII, 1934

[*See also* Christian, Duty (Public), Soldier.

City

The first requisite to happiness is that a man be born in a famous city.
EURIPIDES: *Encomium on Alcibiades*, *c.* 415 B.C.

It is men who make a city, not walls or ships.
THUCYDIDES: *History*, VII, *c.* 410 B.C.

By the blessing of the upright the city is exalted, but it is overthrown by the mouth of the wicked.
PROVERBS XI, 11, *c.* 350 B.C.

Experience shows that a very populous city can seldom, if ever, be properly governed; all well-governed cities have a limited population.
ARISTOTLE: *Politics*, *c.* 322 B.C.

A city that is set on a hill cannot be hid.
MATTHEW V, 14, *c.* 75

You will confer the greatest benefits on your city, not by raising its roofs, but by exalting its souls. For it is better that great souls should live in small habitations than that abject slaves should burrow in great houses.
EPICTETUS: *Encheiridion*, *c.* 110

The people are the city.
SHAKESPEARE: *Coriolanus*, III, *c.* 1607

The chicken is the country's, but the city eats it.
GEORGE HERBERT: *Outlandish Proverbs*, 1640

Great cities seldom rest: if there be none
T'invade from far, they'll find worse foes at home.
ROBERT HERRICK: *Hesperides*, 1648

The air of cities is unfriendly to infants and children. Every animal is adapted to the use of fresh, natural and free air; the tolerance of artificial air (as that of cities) is the effect of habit, which young animals have not yet acquir'd.
JOHN ARBUTHNOT: *The Effect of Air on Human Bodies*, 1733

Cities are the abyss of the human species. At the end of a few generations in them races perish or degenerate, and it is necessary to renew them. This renewal always comes from the country.
J.-J. ROUSSEAU: *Émile*, I, 1762

In cities vice is hidden with most ease,
Or seen with least reproach; and virtue, taught
By frequent lapse, can hope no triumph there
Beyond th' achievement of successful flight.
WILLIAM COWPER: *The Task*, I, 1785

When we get piled upon one another in large cities, as in Europe, we shall become as corrupt as Europe.
THOMAS JEFFERSON: *Letter to James Madison*, Dec., 1787

I was rear'd
In the great city, pent mid cloisters dim,
And saw naught lovely but the sky and stars.
S. T. COLERIDGE: *Frost at Midnight*, 1798

We can be nowhere private except in the midst of London.
CHARLES LAMB: *Letter to Thomas Manning*, 1800

A rose-red city, half as old as time.
J. W. BURGON: Newdigate prize poem, 1825

If you would be known, and not know, vegetate in a village; if you would know, and not be known, live in a city.
C. C. COLTON: *Lacon*, 1820

I suspect the fifth act of life should be in great cities; it is there, in the long death of old age, that a man most forgets himself and his infirmities; receives the greatest consolation from the attention of friends, and the greatest diversion from external circumstances.
SYDNEY SMITH: *Letter to an unidentified woman*, 1835

Whatever events in progress shall go to disgust men with cities, and infuse into them the passion for country life, and country pleasures, will render a service to the whole face of this continent.
R. W. EMERSON: *The Young American*, 1844

Great cities must be obliterated from the earth.
OTTO VON BISMARCK: Speech in the Prussian Lower House, March 20, 1852

I loathe the squares and streets,
And the faces that one meets.
ALFRED TENNYSON: *Maud*, 1855

The great city is that which has the greatest man or woman;
If it be a few ragged huts, it is still the greatest city in the whole world.
WALT WHITMAN: *Song of the Broad-Ax*, 1856

Cities give us collision. London and New York take the nonsense out of man.
R. W. EMERSON: *The Conduct of Life*, IV, 1860

Comfort it is to say:
"Of no mean city am I!"
RUDYARD KIPLING: *To the City of Bombay*, 1894

A great city, a great solitude. (Magna civitas, magna solitudo.)
LATIN PROVERB

[*See also* Capital (=city), Classes, Farm, Garden, Mob, Parley, Physician, Town, Village.

City of God

Glorious things are spoken of thee, O city of God.
PSALMS LXXXVII, 3, *c.* 150 B.C.

The city of God. (De civitate Dei.)
ST. AUGUSTINE: Title of a book, 427

Civilian

[*See* Soldier.

Civility

Civility is a desire to receive it in turn, and to be accounted well bred.
LA ROCHEFOUCAULD: *Maxims*, 1665

Sleep not when others speak, sit not when others stand, speak not when you should hold your peace, walk not on when others stop.
GEORGE WASHINGTON: *Early copy-book*, before 1748

Be civil to all; sociable to many; familiar with few.
BENJAMIN FRANKLIN: *Poor Richard's Almanac*, 1756

He was so generally civil that nobody thanked him for it.
SAMUEL JOHNSON: *Boswell's Life*, 1777

Civility costs nothing.
ENGLISH PROVERB, not recorded before the XIX century

[*See also* Politeness.

Civilization

Civilized man is born, lives, and dies in slavery; at his birth he is confined in swaddling clothes; at death he is nailed in a coffin. So long as he retains the human form he is fettered by our institutions.
J.-J. ROUSSEAU: *Émile*, I, 1762

Civilized society . . . is a strange heterogeneous assemblage of vices and virtues, and of a variety of other principles, for ever at war, for ever jarring, for ever producing some dangerous, some distressing extreme.

ST. JOHN DE CRÈVECOEUR: *Letters from an American Farmer*, IX, 1782

The three great elements of modern civilization [are] gunpowder, printing and the Protestant religion.

THOMAS CARLYLE: *Lectures on German Literature*, 1837

We think our civilization near its meridian, but we are yet only at the cock-crowing and the morning star.

R. W. EMERSON: *Politics*, 1841

The civilized man has built a coach, but has lost the use of his feet. He is supported on crutches, but lacks so much support of muscle. He has a fine Geneva watch, but he fails of the skill to tell the hour by the sun.

R. W. EMERSON: *Self-Reliance*, 1841

Civilization is a progress from an indefinite, incoherent homogeneity toward a definite, coherent heterogeneity.

HERBERT SPENCER: *First Principles*, XVI, 1862

Civilization does not consist in the eschewing of garlic or the keeping clean of a man's finger-nails. It may lead to such delicacies, and probably will do so. But the man who thinks that civilization cannot exist without them imagines that the church cannot stand without the spire.

ANTHONY TROLLOPE: *North America*, I, 1862

The beginning of civilization is marked by an intense legality; that legality is the very condition of its existence, the bond which ties it together; but that legality — that tendency to impose a settled customary yoke upon all men and all actions — if it goes on, kills out the variability implanted by nature, and makes different men and different ages facsimilies of other men and other ages, as we see them so often.

WALTER BAGEHOT: *Physics and Politics*, 1869

A sufficient measure of civilization is the influence of good women.

R. W. EMERSON: *Civilization*, 1870

What does civilization itself rest upon — and what object has it, what its religions, arts, schools, &c., but rich, luxuriant, varied personalism?

WALT WHITMAN: *Democratic Vistas*, 1870

Increased means and increased leisure are the two civilizers of man.

BENJAMIN DISRAELI: Speech in Manchester, April 3, 1872

Civilization degrades the many to exalt the few.

A. BRONSON ALCOTT: *Table-Talk*, 1877

That civilization which conflicts with the doctrines of Holy Church is but a worthless imitation and a hollow name.

POPE LEO XIII: *Inscrutabili*, April 21, 1878

The greatness of modern, as compared with medieval or ancient civilization is that it possesses a larger stock of demonstrated truth.

J. R. SEELEY: *The Expansion of England*, 1883

I reckon I got to light out for the Territory, because Aunt Sally she's going to adopt me and civilize me and I can't stand it. I been there before.

S. L. CLEMENS (MARK TWAIN): *Huckleberry Finn*, XLIII, 1885

Civilization is carried on by superior men, and not by people in the mass; if nature sends no such men, civilization declines.

VICTOR DURUY: *Histoire des Romans*, VI, 1885

The purpose of all civilization is to convert man, a beast of prey, into a tame and civilized animal, a domestic animal.

F. W. NIETZSCHE: *The Genealogy of Morals*, I, 1887

Even the best of modern civilizations appears to me to exhibit a condition of mankind which neither embodies any worthy ideal nor even possesses the merit of stability.

T. H. HUXLEY: *Government*, 1890

The history of civilization details the steps by which men have succeeded in building up an artificial world within the cosmos.

T. H. HUXLEY: *Evolution and Ethics*, 1893 (Romanes Lecture)

All the civilizations we know have been created and directed by small intellectual aristocracies, never by people in the mass. The power of crowds is only to destroy.

GUSTAVE LEBON: *Psychologie des foules*, intro., 1895

I do not pin my dreams for the future to my country or even to my race. I think it probable that civilization somehow will last as long as I care to look ahead.

O. W. HOLMES II: Speech in New York, Feb. 15, 1913

All the blessings of civilization are either curses or superfluous.

AUGUST STRINDBERG: *Zones of the Spirit*, 1913

Civilization and profits go hand in hand.

CALVIN COOLIDGE: Speech in New York, Nov. 27, 1920

Mr. Darrow — Do you say that you do not believe that there were any civilizations on this earth that reach back beyond 5,000 years?

Mr. Bryan — I am not satisfied by any evidence that I have seen.

From the record of the Scopes trial, Dayton, Tenn., July 21, 1925

I believe from my heart that the cause which binds together my peoples and our gallant and faithful allies is the cause of Christian civilization.

KING GEORGE VI of England: Radio address, Dec. 25, 1939

[*See also* Americanism, Covetousness, Creed, Democracy, Poetry, Self-government, Socialism.

Claret

[*See* Wine (Claret).

Clarity

Clarity is the good faith of philosophers.

LUC DE VAUGENARGUES: *Réflexions,* 1746

Clarity is so clearly one of the attributes of truth that very often it passes for truth.

JOSEPH JOUBERT: *Pensées,* I, 1842

Everything that can be thought at all can be thought clearly. Everything that can be said can be said clearly.

LUDWIG WITTGENSTEIN: *Tractatus logico-philosophicus,* 1921

[*See also* Language, Profundity, Style.

Class-consciousness

[*See* Party.

Classes

The relation between superiors and inferiors is like that between the wind and the grass. The grass must bend when the wind blows over it.

CONFUCIUS: *Analects,* XII, *c.* 500 B.C.

To the lowly, the powerful and rich are as gods.

EURIPIDES: *Iphigenia in Tauris, c.* 413 B.C.

Any city, however small, is in fact divided into two, one the city of the poor, the other of the rich; these are at war with one another.

PLATO: *The Republic, c.* 370 B.C.

Some men labor with their minds and some with their muscles. Those who labor with their minds govern those who labor with their muscles.

MENCIUS: *Discourses,* III, *c.* 300 B.C.

Men of low degree are vanity, and men of high degree are a lie.

PSALMS LXII, 9, *c.* 150 B.C.

He that hath, to him shall be given; and he that hath not, from him shall be taken even that which he hath.

MARK IV, 25, *c.* 70 (Cf. MATTHEW XXV, 29, *c.* 75; LUKE VIII, 18; XIX, 26, *c.* 75)

If you are poor today you will always be poor. Only the rich now acquire riches.

MARTIAL: *Epigrams,* V, *c,* 95

One soweth, and another reapeth.

JOHN IV, 37, *c.* 115

Let them obey that know not how to rule.

SHAKESPEARE: *II Henry VI,* V, *c.* 1591

An two men ride of a horse, one must ride behind.

SHAKESPEARE: *Much Ado About Nothing,* III, *c.* 1599

A gentleman with his good gifts sits at the upper end of the table on a chair and a cushion, when a scholar with his good parts will be glad of a joint-stool in the lobby with the chambermaids.

Anon.: *Humor Out of Breath,* II, 1608

There are but two families in the world—Have-much and Have-little.

CERVANTES: *Don Quixote,* II, 1615

Half the world knows not how the other half lives.

GEORGE HERBERT: *Outlandish Proverbs,* 1640

Jupiter placed two tables in the world. The cunning, the vigilant and the strong eat at the first: the inferior have the leavings at the second.

JEAN DE LA FONTAINE: *Fables,* X, 1671

That some men are poorer than others ever was and ever will be; and that many are naturally querulous and envious is an evil as old as the world.

WILLIAM PETTY: *Political Arithmetic,* pref., *c.* 1677

The great Author distributed the ranks and offices in men in order to materially benefit and comfort, that one man should plow, another thresh, another grind, another labor at the forge, another knit or weave, another sail, another trade.

ISAAC DARROW: *Sermons,* 1679

I never could believe that Providence had sent a few men into the world, ready booted and spurred to ride, and millions ready saddled and bridled to be ridden.

RICHARD RUMBOLD: Speech on the scaffold, 1685

Heaven acts with wisdom in placing His creatures in differing ranks and classes in every part of the creation; nay, even in the celestial creature itself, we are told, there are different classes, even among the heavenly inhabitants themselves.

DANIEL DEFOE: *The Compleat English Gentleman, c.* 1730

The great and the little have need one of another.

THOMAS FULLER: *Gnomologia,* 1732

We are, by our occupations, education and habits of life, divided almost into different

species, which regard one another, for the most part, with scorn and malignity.
SAMUEL JOHNSON: *The Rambler*, Sept. 28, 1751

Nothing is more credible than that men's states should differ as much as their spirits and tempers do differ.
BENJAMIN WHICHOTE: *Moral and Religious Aphorisms*, 1753

One man is born with a silver spoon in his mouth, and another with a wooden ladle.
OLIVER GOLDSMITH: *The Citizen of the World*, 1762

For just experience tells, in every soil,
That those that think must govern those that toil.
OLIVER GOLDSMITH: *The Traveler*, 1764

The innocent class are always the victim of the few; they are in all countries and at all times the inferior agents, and must toil, and bleed, and are always sure of meeting with oppression and rebuke. It is for the sake of the great leaders on both sides that so much blood must be spilt; that of the people is counted as nothing.
ST. JOHN DE CRÈVECOEUR: *Letters from an American Farmer*, XII, 1782

All communities divide themselves into the few and the many. The first are the rich and well-born, the other the mass of the people.
ALEXANDER HAMILTON: Speech in the Federal Convention, June 18, 1787

Those who hold and those who are without property have ever formed distinct interests in society. Those who are creditors, and those who are debtors, fall under a like discrimination. A landed interest, a manufacturing interest, a mercantile interest, a moneyed interest, with many lesser interests, grow up of necessity in civilized nations, and divide them into different classes, actuated by different sentiments and views.
JAMES MADISON: *The Federalist*, X, 1787

Man differs from man in everything that can be supposed to lead to supremacy and subjection, as one star differs from another star in glory.
JONATHAN BOUCHER: *A View of the Causes and Consequences of the American Revolution*, XII, 1797

Men are not equal, and 'tis meet and right
That robes and titles our respect excite.
GEORGE CRABBE: *The Borough*, IV, 1810

Many faint with toil,
That few may know the cares and woe of sloth.
P. B. SHELLEY: *Queen Mab*, III, 1813

Such hath it been — shall be — beneath the sun
The many still must labor for the one.
BYRON: *The Corsair*, I, 1814

The rich and poor are fairly pitted. We shall see who can hang or burn fastest.
CHARLES LAMB: *Letter to George Dyer*, Dec. 20, 1830

Society is constantly advancing in knowledge. The tail is now where the head was some generations ago. But the head and the tail still keep their distance.
T. B. MACAULAY: *The War of the Succession in Spain*, 1833 (Edinburgh Review, Jan.)

The rich and the poor — the have-nots and the haves.
E. G. BULWER-LYTTON: *Athens*, I, 1836

Man has set man against man — washed against unwashed.
THOMAS CARLYLE: *The French Revolution*, II, 1837

It is as unjust to require that men of refinement and training should defer in their habits and associations to the notions of those who are their inferiors in these particulars, as it is to insist that political power should be the accompaniment of birth.
J. FENIMORE COOPER: *The American Democrat*, XIX, 1838

In every society some men are born to rule, and some to advise.
R. W. EMERSON: *The Young American*, 1844

A people is but the attempt of many
To rise to the completer life of one —
And those who live as models for the mass
Are singly of more value than they all.
ROBERT BROWNING: *Luria*, V, 1846

Why is one man richer than another? Because he is more industrious, more perservering, and more sagacious.
JOHN RUSKIN: *The Political Economy of Art*, II, 1857

In all social systems there must be a class to do the menial duties, to perform the drudgery of life. Its requisites are vigor, docility, fidelity. Such a class you must have, or you would not have that other class which leads progress, civilization and refinement. It constitutes the very mudsill of society and of political government.
J. H. HAMMOND: Speech in the Senate, March 4, 1858

Detestation of the high is the involuntary homage of the low.
CHARLES DICKENS: *A Tale of Two Cities*, I, 1859

A vulgar man may often be kind in a hard way, on principle, and because he thinks he ought to be; whereas, a highly-bred man, even when cruel, will be cruel in a softer way, understanding and feeling what he inflicts, and pitying his victim.
JOHN RUSKIN: *Modern Painters*, IX, 1860

Distribute the earth as you will, the principal question remains inexorable — Who is to dig it? Which of us, in brief word, is to do the hard and dirty work for the rest, and for what pay? Who is to do the pleasant and clean work, and for what pay? Who is to do no work, and for what pay?

JOHN RUSKIN: *Sesame and Lilies,* II, 1865

In theory it is desirable that the highest class of wealth and leisure should have an influence far out of proportion to its mere number: a perfect constitution would find for it a delicate expedient to make its fine thought tell upon the surrounding cruder thought.

WALTER BAGEHOT: *The English Constitution,* IX, 1867

The concessions of the privileged to the unprivileged are seldom brought about by any better motive than the power of the unprivileged to extort them.

J. S. MILL: *The Subjection of Women,* III, 1869

Hearts just as pure and fair
May beat in Belgrave Square
As in the lowly air
Of Seven Dials.

W. S. GILBERT: *Iolanthe,* I, 1882

For every man who consumes more than he creates there must of necessity be another man who has to consume less than he creates.

EDWARD CARPENTER: *England's Ideal,* 1887

It is the tendency of all social burdens to crush out the middle class, and to force society into an organization of only two classes, one at each social extreme.

W. G. SUMNER: *What Makes the Rich Richer and the Poor Poorer?,* 1887

The order of castes is merely the ratification of an order of nature, of a natural law of the first rank, over which no arbitrary fiat, no "modern idea," can exert any influence.

F. W. NIETZSCHE: *The Antichrist,* LVII, 1888

The great mistake is to take up with the notion that class is naturally hostile to class, and that the wealthy and the workingmen are intended by nature to live in conflict. So irrational and so false is this view that the direct contrary is the truth.

POPE LEO XIII: *Rerum novarum,* May 15, 1891

The world is divided into two classes, those who believe the incredible, and those who do the improbable.

OSCAR WILDE: *A Woman of No Importance,* II, 1893

The opposition between the men who have and the men who are is immemorial.

WILLIAM JAMES: *The Varieties of Religious Experience,* XI, 1902

Let Catholic writers take care when defending the cause of the proletariat and the poor not to use language calculated to inspire among the people aversion to the upper classes of society.

POPE PIUS X: *Apostolic Letter to the Bishops of Italy on Catholic Social Action,* Dec. 18, 1903

The relation of superior to inferior excludes good manners.

GEORGE BERNARD SHAW: *Maxims for Revolutionists,* 1903

The working class and the employing class have nothing in common. Between the two a struggle must go on until the workers of the world organize as a class, take possession of the earth and the machinery of production, and abolish the wage system.

Preamble to the constitution of the Industrial Workers of the World, adopted at Chicago, June, 1905

In the first-class compartment the conductor is polite and the passenger is gruff; in the second-class the conductor is polite and the passenger is polite; in the third-class the conductor is gruff and the passenger is polite.

GERMAN SAYING

[*See also* Authority, Boredom, Bourgeoisie, Capital and Labor, Class (Middle), Class Struggle, Communism, Englishman, Equality, Exploitation, Labor, Power, Proletariat, Prosperity, Rich and Poor, Society, State, Struggle for Existence, Virtue, Wealth.

Classic

A true classic is an author who has enriched the human mind, augmented its treasure, and made it advance a step.

C. A. SAINTE-BEUVE: *What Is a Classic?,* 1850

Class, Middle

There are three classes of citizens. The first are the rich, who are indolent and yet always crave more. The second are the poor, who have nothing, are full of envy, hate the rich, and are easily led by demagogues. Between the two extremes lie those who make the state secure and uphold the laws.

EURIPIDES: *The Suppliant Women, c.* 421 B.C.

The most perfect political community is one in which the middle class is in control, and outnumbers both of the other classes.

ARISTOTLE: *Politics,* IV, *c.* 322 B.C.

I am convinced that turbulence as well as every other evil temper of this evil age belong not to the lower but to the middle classes — those middle classes of whom in our folly we are so wont to boast.

LORD ROBERT CECIL (afterward MARQUIS OF SALISBURY): *Diary in Australia,* 1852

The state, it cannot too often be repeated, has nothing, and can give nothing, which it does

not take from somebody. Its victims must be those who have earned and saved, and they must be the broad, strong, middle classes, from whom alone any important contributions can be drawn.
W. G. SUMNER: *What Makes the Rich Richer and the Poor Poorer?*, 1887

A moderately honest man with a moderately faithful wife, moderate drinkers both, in a moderately healthy house: that is the true middle class unit.
GEORGE BERNARD SHAW: *Maxims for Revolutionists*, 1903

[*See also* Bourgeoisie, Classes.

Class Struggle

The history of all hitherto existing society is the history of class struggles.
KARL MARX and FRIEDRICH ENGELS: *The Communist Manifesto*, 1848

Some sort of violence is unavoidable. There is no possible choice between violence and non-violence. The only choice is between the two sides of the class struggle.
EARL BROWDER: *What Is Communism?*, 1936

[*See also* Classes, Communism, Rich and Poor.

Clay, Henry (1777–1852)

Clay is an eloquent man, with very popular manners and great political management. He is, like almost all the eminent men of this country, only half educated. His morals, public and private, are loose.
JOHN QUINCY ADAMS: *Diary*, March 9, 1821

Henry Clay, my beau-ideal of a statesman.
ABRAHAM LINCOLN: Speech in Ottawa, Ill., Aug. 21, 1858

Cleanliness

Wash ye, make you clean.
ISAIAH I, 16, *c.* 700 B.C.

What is man, that he should be clean?
JOB XV, 14, *c.* 325 B.C.

Respect for God demands that the face, the hands and the feet be washed once a day.
THE TALMUD (*Sabbath*), *c.* 200

Cleanness of body was ever deemed to proceed from a due reverence to God, to society, and to ourselves.
FRANCIS BACON: *The Advancement of Learning*, II, 1605

God requires corporal cleanliness in those that approach the altar.
ST. FRANCIS DE SALES: *Introduction to the Devout Life*, XXV, 1609

Let thy mind's sweetness have its operation
Upon thy body, clothes, and habitation.
GEORGE HERBERT: *The Temple*, 1633

'Tis much, among the filthy, to be clean.
ROBERT HERRICK: *Hesperides*, 1648

Wear not thy clothes foul, unsewed, dusty, nor old; look that they be brushed commonly once a day; take heed where thou sittest or kneelest, and whom thou approachest, for fear that there be dust or some uncleanness.
FRANCIS HAWKINS: *Youth's Behavior*, IV, 1663

Wash your hands always before you come to school.
WILLIAM MATHER: *The Young Man's Companion*, 1681

Cleanliness is indeed next to godliness.
JOHN WESLEY: *Sermon*, *c.* 1740

You might have eaten your dinner off the floor.
ENGLISH SAYING, not recorded before the XIX century

Cleanliness and order are not matters of instinct; they are matters of education, and like most great things — mathematics and classics — you must cultivate a taste for them.
BENJAMIN DISRAELI: Speech at Aylesbury, Sept. 21, 1865

"Cleanliness is next to godliness"; but washing should be only for the purpose of keeping the body clean, and this can be effected without scrubbing the whole surface daily. Water is not the natural habitat of humanity.
MARY BAKER G. EDDY: *Science and Health*, XII, 1908

[*See also* Character (National), Clothes, Dress, Gentleman.

Clearness

[*See* Clarity.

Clemency

Clemency is the best mark of a true monarch.
PIERRE CORNEILLE: *Cinna*, IV, 1639

[*See also* Grace (=clemency).

Clemens, S. L. (Mark Twain) (1835–1910)

I think he mainly misses fire: I think his life misses fire: he might have been something; he comes near to being something: but he never arrives.
WALT WHITMAN: *To Horace Traubel in Camden*, *c.* 1890

He never wrote a line that a father could not read to a daughter.
W. H. TAFT: Statement to the press on Clemens's death, 1910

Cleopatra (c. 69–30 B.C.)

[*See* Nose.

Clergy

Howl, ye ministers of the altar.
JOEL I, 13, *c.* 350 B.C.

We are ambassadors for Christ, as though God did beseech you by us.
II CORINTHIANS V, 20, *c.* 55

There are none harder nor hungrier than men of Holy Church.
WILLIAM LANGLAND: *Piers Plowman,* 1377

Who within the realm are more corrupt in life and manners than are they that are called the clergy, living in whoredom and adultery, deflowering virgins, corrupting matrons, and doing all abomination without fear of punishment?
Supplication to the Scotch Parliament, 1560

Many wear God's cloth that know not their Master.
JOSEPH HALL: *Meditations and Vows,* IV, 1606

Divines, if we observe them, have their postures, and their motions no less expertly, and with no less variety, than they that practise feats in the artillery-ground.
JOHN MILTON: *The Tenure of Kings and Magistrates,* 1649

That it may please thee to illuminate all bishops, priests, and deacons, with true knowledge and understanding of thy Word; and that both by their preaching and living they may set it forth, and show it accordingly; We beseech thee to hear us, good Lord.
THE BOOK OF COMMON PRAYER (*The Litany*), 1662

The clergy, if ever we would expect any edification from them, ought to be dieted and kept low, to be meek and humble.
JOHN EACHARD: *The Grounds and Occasions of the Contempt of the Clergy and Religion,* 1670

The clergy would have us believe them against our own reason, as the woman would have had her husband against his own eyes: What! will you believe your own eyes before your own sweet wife!
JOHN SELDEN: *Table-Talk,* 1689

There is no adjusting a quarrel with the clergy save by granting their demands. Their cause, they always pretend, is the cause of God, and they can therefore make no concession without sin.
PAUL DE RAPIN DE THOYRAS: *Histoire d'Angleterre,* I, 1724

It's kittle shooting at corbies and clergy.
ALLAN RAMSAY: *Scots Proverbs,* 1737
(*Kittle*=difficult, ticklish; *corbie*=crow)

To a philosophic eye the vices of the clergy are far less dangerous than their virtues.
EDWARD GIBBON: *The Decline and Fall of the Roman Empire,* I, 1776

Idle vermin who two or three times a day perform in the most slovenly manner a service which they think useless, but call their duty.
MARY WOLLSTONECRAFT: *A Vindication of the Rights of Woman,* XII, 1792

There are three classes of clergy: Nimrods, ramrods and fishing-rods.
ENGLISH PROVERB, not recorded before the XIX century

There is in the clergy of all the Christian denominations a time-serving, cringing, subservient morality, as wide from the spirit of the Gospel as it is from the intrepid assertion and vindication of truth.
JOHN QUINCY ADAMS: *Diary,* May 27, 1838

Is the glory of Heaven to be sung only by gentlemen in black coats? Must the truth be only expounded in gown and surplice, and out of those two vestments can nobody preach it?
W. M. THACKERAY: *The English Humorists,* III, 1853

Trade curses everything it handles; and though you trade in messages from Heaven, the whole curse of trade attaches to the business.
H. D. THOREAU: *Walden,* 1854

As the French say, there are three sexes,—men, women, and clergymen.
Ascribed to SYDNEY SMITH in *A Memoir of the Rev. Sydney Smith* by his daughter, Lady Holland, 1855

No minister or preacher of the gospel or of any religious creed or denomination shall be eligible as senator or delegate.
CONSTITUTION OF MARYLAND, III, 1867

The clergy are as like as peas.
R. W. EMERSON: *The Preacher,* 1867

The clergy are at present divisible into three sections: an immense body who are ignorant and speak out; a small proportion who know and are silent; and a minute minority who know and speak according to their knowledge.
T. H. HUXLEY: *Scientific Education,* 1869 (Speech in Liverpool)

This conference does not intend in future to elect brethren to deacon's or elder's orders unless they can read and write.
Resolution of the South Carolina Conference of the Methodist Episcopal Church, Jacksonville, Fla., 1870 (Methodist Advocate, Atlanta, Ga., Feb. 2)

It would be well if ecclesiastical persons would reflect that ordination, whatever deep-seated graces it may confer, has never been observed to be followed by any visible increase in the learning or the logic of its subject.
T. H. HUXLEY: *On the Hypothesis That Animals are Automata,* 1874

I cannot conceive anything better for the culture of a country than the presence in it of a body of men whose duty it is to believe in the supernatural, to perform daily miracles, and to keep alive that mythopoeic faculty which is so essential for the imagination.
OSCAR WILDE: *The Decay of Lying*, 1891

The chief meaning of the Christian teaching is the establishment of direct communion between God and man. Every man who takes upon himself the rôle of intercessor hinders those he wishes to guide from entering into direct communion with God, and himself loses completely the possibility of living in a Christian way.
LYOF N. TOLSTOY: *Letter to a Swiss pastor*, Aug. 26, 1901

Ministers of religion in their character as ministers of religion should not be used as comic characters or as villains.
A Code to Govern the Making of Motion and Talking Pictures by the Motion Picture Producers and Distributors of America, Inc., VIII, March 31, 1930

The British clergy are the wonder of the world. (Stupor mundi clerus Britannicus.)
MEDIEVAL LATIN PROVERB

[*See also* Abbot, Bishop, Christianity, Clergyman, Crime, Deacon, Laity, Preacher, Presbyterian, Priest.

Clergy, Benefit of

Touch not mine anointed, and do my prophets no harm.
I CHRONICLES XVI, 22, *c.* 300 B.C. (Benefit of clergy was based on this verse. Cf. PSALMS CV, 15, *c.* 150 B.C.)

The benefit of clergy. (Privilegium clericale.)
LEGAL PHRASE

Clergyman

No ecclesiastic should spend his time in hunting, gambling or feasting, or engage in commerce or usury, or be present at lewd dances.
JOHN CALVIN: *Institutes of the Christian Religion*, IV, 1536 (Credited to "the ancient bishops")

He has the canonical smirk and the filthy clammy palm of a chaplain.
WILLIAM WYCHERLEY: *The Country Wife*, IV, *c.* 1673

A little, round, fat, oily man of God.
JAMES THOMSON: *The Castle of Indolence*, II, 1748

It has been observed that physicians and lawyers are no friends to religion, and many conjectures have been formed to discover the reason. . . . The truth is, very few of them have thought about religion, but they have all seen a parson.
SAMUEL JOHNSON: *The Rambler*, April 17, 1750

A generic title under which is designated any Christian who consecrates himself to the service of God, and feels himself called upon to live without working at the expense of the rascals who work to live.
VOLTAIRE: *Philosophical Dictionary*, 1764

A man who is good enough to go to Heaven is good enough to be a clergyman.
SAMUEL JOHNSON: *Boswell's Life*, April 5, 1772

He that negotiates between God and man,
As God's ambassador, the grand concerns
Of judgment and of mercy, should beware
Of lightness in his speech.
WILLIAM COWPER: *The Task*, II, 1785

The sons of clergymen always turn out badly.
ENGLISH PROVERB, not recorded before the XIX century

Tempted by sins, let me their strength defy,
But have no second in a surplice by;
No bottle-holder, with officious aid,
To comfort conscience, weaken'd and afraid.
GEORGE CRABBE: *Tales*, II (*The Gentleman Farmer*), 1812

An average, ordinary, uninteresting minister; obese, dumpy, neither ill-natured nor good-natured; neither learned nor ignorant, striding over the stiles to church, with a second-rate wife — dusty and deliquescent — and four parochial children, full of catechism and bread and butter.
SYDNEY SMITH: *Letter to Archdeacon Singleton*, 1837

If you have offended a clergyman, kill him; else you will never have peace with him.
R. C. TRENCH (ARCHBISHOP OF DUBLIN): *Lessons in Proverbs*, 1853 (Quoted as a Bohemian proverb)

He was not ill-looking, according to the village standard, parted his hair smoothly, tied his white cravat carefully, was fluent, plausible, had a gift in prayer, was considered eloquent, was fond of listening to their spiritual experiences, and had a sickly wife.
O. W. HOLMES: *The Guardian Angel*, II, 1867

A Mr. Wilkinson, a clergyman.
ALFRED TENNYSON: Burlesque Wordsworthian line, *c.* 1870

A man who undertakes the management of our spiritual affairs as a method of bettering his temporal ones.
AMBROSE BIERCE: *The Devil's Dictionary*, 1906

As a career, the business of an orthodox preacher is about as successful as that of a celluloid dog chasing an asbestos cat through Hell.
ELBERT HUBBARD: *Roycroft Dictionary and Book of Epigrams*, 1923

[*See also* Altar, Celibacy, Clergy, Dean, Diet, Evolution, Parson, Preacher, Preaching, Priest, Pulpit, Smoking, Vicar, Vocation, Walking.

Clericalism

Clericalism, that is the enemy! (Le cléricalisme, voilà l'ennemi!)
ALPHONSE PEYRAT: Speech in the French Legislative Assembly, 1859 (Quoted by LÉON GAMBETTA: Speech at Grenoble, Sept. 26, 1872, and hence sometimes attributed to him)

Clerk

It is the justice's clerk that makes the justice.
THOMAS FULLER: *Gnomologia*, 1732

Cleveland, Grover (1837–1908)

I stand today to voice the sentiment of the young men of my state when I speak for Grover Cleveland. His name is upon their lips. His name is in their hearts. They love him, gentlemen, and respect him, and they love him and respect him not only for himself, for his character, for his integrity, for his iron will, but they love him most for the enemies he has made.
E. S. BRAGG of New York: Speech at the Democratic National Convention, Chicago, 1884

Harrison is a wise man,
  Cleveland is a fool;
Harrison rides a white horse
  Cleveland rides a mule.
Author unidentified: Campaign song in the Cleveland–Harrison campaign, 1892

Cleverness

Cleverness is not wisdom.
EURIPIDES: *The Bacchae*, *c.* 410 B.C.

Clever men are good, but they are not the best.
THOMAS CARLYLE: *Goethe*, 1828

Be good, sweet maid, and let who will be clever.
CHARLES KINGSLEY: *A Farewell*, 1858

Cleverness is serviceable for everything, sufficient for nothing.
H. F. AMIEL: *Journal*, Feb. 16, 1868

Client

He that pleads his own cause has a fool for his client.
ENGLISH PROVERB, not recorded before the XIX century

The best client is a scared millionaire.
Author unidentified

[*See also* Lawyer and Client.

Climate

Water shares the good or bad qualities of the land through which it flows, and man those of the climate in which he is born.
BALTASAR GRACIÁN: *The Art of Worldly Wisdom*, IX, 1647

A man who goes from one climate to another feels the change in spite of himself. He is like a plant that has transplanted itself: he either improves or degenerates.
J. O. DE LA METTRIE: *L'Homme machine*, 1748

In northern climates you will find people who have few vices, many virtues, and much sincerity and frankness. Go southward, and you will think that you have removed altogether from morality.
C. L. DE MONTESQUIEU: *The Spirit of the Laws*, XIV, 1748

No inconvenience is less superable by art or diligence than the inclemency of climates.
SAMUEL JOHNSON: *The Rambler*, Dec. 28, 1751

I wonder that any human being should remain in a cold country who could find room in a warm one.
THOMAS JEFFERSON: *Letter to Dr. Hugh Williamson*, 1801

Man is a creature fit for any climate, and necessity and determination soon reconcile him to anything.
FERDINAND WRANGELL: *Narrative of an Expedition to the Polar Sea in the Years 1820–23*, I, 1840

The hard soil and four months of snow make the inhabitant of the northern temperate zones wiser and abler than his fellow who enjoys the fixed smile of the tropics.
R. W. EMERSON: *Prudence*, 1841

What business have healthy people with climates?
SIDNEY LANIER: *Florida: Its Scenery, Climate and History*, 1875

[*See also* Adaptability, Buddhism, Coal, Government, Heaven and Hell, Language, Law, Liberty.

Closet

[*See* Skeleton.

Cloth

[*See* Measure.

Clothes

The woman shall not wear that which pertaineth unto a man, neither shall a man put on a woman's garment; for all that do so are abomination unto the Lord thy God.
DEUTERONOMY XXII, 5, *c.* 650 B.C.

Thou shalt not wear a garment of divers sort, as of woollen and linen together.
DEUTERONOMY XXII, 11

Clothed, and in his right mind.
MARK V, 15, *c.* 70 (Cf. LUKE VIII, 35, *c.* 75)

Blessed is he that watcheth, and keepeth his garments, lest he walk naked, and they see his shame. REVELATION XVI, 15, *c.* 95

Let thy attire be comely, but not costly.
JOHN LYLY: *Euphues*, 1579

Apes are apes, though clothed in scarlet.
BEN JONSON: *The Poetaster*, v, 1602

The soul of this man is his clothes.
SHAKESPEARE: *All's Well that Ends Well*, II, *c.* 1602

The greatest provocations of lust are from our apparel.
ROBERT BURTON: *The Anatomy of Melancholy*, III, 1621

Ever since we wear clothes we know not one another.
GEORGE HERBERT: *Outlandish Proverbs*, 1640

Clothes ought to be our remembrances of our lost innocency.
THOMAS FULLER: *The Holy State and The Profane State*, 1642

Whenas in silks my Julia goes,
Then, then, methinks, how sweetly flows
The liquefaction of her clothes!
ROBERT HERRICK: *Hesperides*, 1648

If thou art clean and warm it is sufficient, for more doth but rob the poor and please the wanton.
WILLIAM PENN: *Fruits of Solitude*, 1693

When clothing our body, we ought to remember that it bears the imprint of sin; we ought therefore to cover it with decency in accordance with the law of God.
ST. JOHN BAPTIST DE LA SALLE: *The Rules of Christian Manners and Civility*, II, 1695

How proud we are, how fond to show
Our clothes, and call them rich and new,
When the poor sheep and silkworms wore
That very clothing long before.
ISAAC WATTS: *Divine Songs for Children*, pref., 1715

Good clothes open all doors.
THOMAS FULLER: *Gnomologia*, 1732

So I be warm, let the people laugh. IBID.

Fortune in men has some small diff'rence made,
One flaunts in rags, one flutters in brocade;
The cobbler apron'd, and the parson gown'd,
The friar hooded, and the monarch crown'd.
ALEXANDER POPE: *An Essay on Man*, IV, 1734

She wears her clothes as if they were thrown on her with a pitchfork.
JONATHAN SWIFT: *Polite Conversation*, 1738

When you incline to have new clothes, look first well over the old ones, and see if you cannot shift with them another year, either by scouring, mending or even patching if necessary. Remember, a patch on your coat, and money in your pocket, is better and more creditable than a writ on your back, and no money to take it off.
BENJAMIN FRANKLIN: *Poor Richard's Almanac*, 1756

Fine clothes are good only as they supply the want of other means of procuring respect.
SAMUEL JOHNSON: *Boswell's Life*, 1776

Clothes gave us individuality, distinctions, social polity; clothes have made men of us.
THOMAS CARLYLE: *Sartor Resartus*, I, 1836

The fair Flora looked up with a pitiful air,
And answered quite promptly, "Why, Harry, *mon cher*,
I should like above all things to go with you there,
But really and truly — I've nothing to wear."
WILLIAM ALLEN BUTLER: *Nothing to Wear*, 1857

The clothes make the man. (Vestis virum facit.)
LATIN PROVERB

Becoming clothes are two-thirds of beauty.
WELSH PROVERB

[*See also* Apparel, Appearance, Bride, Cleanliness, Color, Dandy, Dress, Finery, Hygiene, Naked, Nothing, Tailor.

Cloud

There ariseth a little cloud out of the sea, like a man's hand.
I KINGS XVIII, 44, *c.* 500 B.C.

God gently driveth forward the clouds, and gathereth them together, and then layeth them on heaps.
THE KORAN, XXIV, *c.* 625

After clouds black, we shall have weather clear.
JOHN HEYWOOD: *Proverbs*, 1546

Every cloud has a silver lining.
ENGLISH PROVERB, familiar since the XVII century

Sometimes we see a cloud that's dragonish,
A vapor, sometime, like a bear or lion,
A tower'd citadel, a pendant rock,
A forked mountain, or blue promontory
With trees upon't, that nod unto the world
And mock our eyes with air.
SHAKESPEARE: *Antony and Cleopatra*, IV, *c.* 1606

Clouds are like Holy Writ, in which theologians cause the faithful or the crazy to see anything they please.
VOLTAIRE: *Philosophical Dictionary*, 1764

I consider the clouds above me but as a roof beautifully painted but unable to satisfy the mind.
CHARLES LAMB: *Letter to William Wordsworth*, Jan. 30, 1801

I wander'd lonely as a cloud.
WILLIAM WORDSWORTH: *Daffodils*, 1807

Far clouds of feathery gold,
Shaded with deepest purple, gleam
Like islands on a dark blue sea.
P. B. SHELLEY: *Queen Mab,* II, 1813

The white clouds go sailing by
Like colossal statues of the gods,
Of luminous marble.
HEINRICH HEINE: *Die Nordsee,* II, 1826

One cloud is enough to eclipse all the sun.
H. G. BOHN: *Handbook of Proverbs,* 1855

You could not see a cloud, because
No cloud was in the sky.
C. L. DODGSON (LEWIS CARROLL): *Through the Looking-Glass,* 1871

All clouds do not give rain.
DUTCH PROVERB

When clouds appear like rocks and towers,
The earth's refreshed by frequent showers.
ENGLISH WEATHER RHYME

Black clouds make a lot of noise but give little rain.
HINDU PROVERB

[*See also* Weather.

Clown

It is meat and drink to me to see a clown.
SHAKESPEARE: *As You Like It,* V, *c.* 1600

Club

An assembly of good fellows, meeting under certain conditions.
SAMUEL JOHNSON: *Dictionary,* 1755

On to the club, the scene of savage joys,
The school of coarse good-fellowship and noise.
WILLIAM COWPER: *Conversation,* 1782

The feeble coxcombry of club-houses.
JOHN RUSKIN: *The Stones of Venice,* I, 1851

No place in England where everyone can go is considered respectable. This is the genesis of the club — out of the Housewife by Respectability.
GEORGE MOORE: *Confessions of a Young Man,* IX, 1888

Coach

Go, call a coach, and let a coach be called;
And let the man who calleth be the caller;
And in the calling, let him nothing call,
But coach! coach! coach! Oh, for a coach, ye gods!
HENRY CAREY: *Chrononhotonthologos,* II, 1734

[*See also* Stage-Coach.

Coal

Coal is a portable climate. It carries the heat of the tropics to Labrador and the polar circle; and it is the means of transporting itself whithersoever it is wanted.
R. W. EMERSON: *The Conduct of Life,* III, 1860

Coal-miner

[*See* Collier.

Coast

The coast is clear.
ENGLISH PHRASE, traced by Smith to 1590

Coat

[*See* Dress, Thrift.

Coat-of-arms

[*See* Heraldry.

Cobbler

[*See* Drinker, Shoemaker.

Cock

The cock, that is the trumpet to the morn,
Doth with his lofty and shrill-sounding throat
Awake the god of day.
SHAKESPEARE: *Hamlet,* I, *c.* 1601

Hark, hark! I hear
The strain of strutting chanticleer
Cry, cock-a-diddle-dow.
SHAKESPEARE: *The Tempest,* I, 1611

[*See also* Hen, Husband and Wife, Influence, Morning.

Cock-fighting

Cock-fighting must be considered a barbarous diversion.
LORD ELLENBOROUGH: *Judgment in Squires* vs. *Whisken,* 1811

Cockney

He was born within the sound of Bow-bell.
THOMAS FULLER: *Worthies of England,* 1662

Let no native Londoner imagine that health, and rest, and innocent occupation, interchange of converse sweet, and recreative study, can make the country anything better than altogether odious and detestable.
CHARLES LAMB: *Letter to William Wordsworth,* Jan. 22, 1830

Cocktail

Cocktail is a stimulating liquor, composed of spirits of any kind, sugar, water and bitters.
Anon.: *In the New York Balance,* May 13, 1806

The cocktail is a pleasant drink;
It's mild and harmless — I don't think.
When you've had one you call for two,
And then you don't care what you do.
GEORGE ADE: The Sultan of Sulu, 1902

A little whiskey to make it strong,
A little water to make it weak,
A little lemon to make it sour,
A little sugar to make it sweet.
Anon.: Quoted by C. A. EATON in the House of Representatives, Jan. 9, 1935

Cocktails have all the disagreeability without the utility of a disinfectant.
SHANE LESLIE: *In the London Observer,* 1939

A cocktail is to a glass of wine as rape is to love.
Ascribed to PAUL CLAUDEL (1868–)

Co-education

The so-called method of co-education is false in theory and harmful to Christian training.
POPE PIUS XI: *Divini illius magistri,* Dec. 31, 1929

Coercion

Millions of innocent men, women and children, since the introduction of Christianity, have been burned, tortured, fined and imprisoned, yet we have not advanced one inch toward uniformity. What has been the effect of coercion? To make one-half of the world fools and the other half hypocrites.
THOMAS JEFFERSON: *Notes on Virginia,* 1782

Experience has taught us that men will not adopt and carry into execution measures the best calculated for their own good without the intervention of a coercive power.
GEORGE WASHINGTON: *Letter to John Jay,* Aug. 1, 1786

[*See also* Intolerance.

Coffee

Coffee, though a useful medicine, if drunk constantly will at length induce a decay of health, and hectic fever.
JESSE TORREY: *The Moral Instructor,* 1819

Why do they always put mud into coffee on board steamers? Why does the tea generally taste of boiled boots?
W. M. THACKERAY: *The Kickleburys on the Rhine,* 1850

Coffee has two virtues: it is wet and warm.
DUTCH PROVERB

Coffee should be black as Hell, strong as death, and sweet as love.
TURKISH PROVERB

[*See also* Racine (Jean), Tobacco.

Coffin

There's one thing in this world which a person don't ever try to jew you down on. That's a coffin.
S. L. CLEMENS (MARK TWAIN): *Life on the Mississippi,* XLIII, 1883

Get the coffin ready and the man won't die.
CHINESE PROVERB

Cogitation

His cogitative faculties immersed
In cogibundity of cogitation.
HENRY CAREY: *Chrononhotonthologos,* I, 1734

Coin

[*See* Cash, Currency.

Cold (=illness)

A May cold is a thirty-day cold.
ENGLISH PROVERB, not recorded before the XIX century

Stuff a cold and starve a fever. IBID.

[*See also* Death.

Cold (=temperature)

A woman's knee and a dog's snout are always cold. JAMES HOWELL: *Proverbs,* 1659

It snowed terribly all night, and is vengeance cold.
JONATHAN SWIFT: *The Journal to Stella,* Jan. 21, 1711

Cold is the source of more suffering to all animal nature than hunger, thirst, sickness, and all the other pains of life and of death itself put together.
THOMAS JEFFERSON: *Letter to William Dunbar,* Jan., 1801

St. Agnes Eve – Ah! bitter chill it was;
The owl, for all his feathers, was a-cold;
The hare limp'd trembling through the frozen grass,
And silent was the flock in woolly fold.
JOHN KEATS: *The Eve of St. Agnes,* 1820

As cold as the north side of a gravestone in Winter. AMERICAN SAYING, *c.* 1835

A hard, dull bitterness of cold.
J. G. WHITTIER: *Snow-Bound,* 1866

[*See also* Hunger, North.

Coleridge, S. T. (1772–1834)

My instincts are so far dog-like that I love being superior to myself better than my equals. S. T. COLERIDGE: *Notebooks,* 1805

How great a possibility; how small a realized result!
THOMAS CARLYLE: *Letter to R. W. Emerson,* Aug. 12, 1834

His general appearance would have led me to suppose him a dissenting minister. His hair was long and white and neglected; his complexion was florid, his features square, his eyes watery and hazy, his brow broad and massive, his build uncouth, his deportment grave and abstracted.
J. C. YOUNG: *A Memoir of Charles Mayne Young,* 1871

To tell the story of Coleridge without the opium is to tell the story of Hamlet without mentioning the ghost.
LESLIE STEPHEN: *Hours in a Library,* III, 1879

[*See also* Metaphysician.

Collar

We enjoin upon our priests as a matter of strict precept, that both at home and abroad, and whether they are residing in their own diocese or outside of it, they should wear the Roman collar.
Decrees of the Third Plenary Council of Baltimore, LXXVII, 1884

Collection

Jesus sat over against the treasury, and beheld how the people cast money into the treasury: and many that were rich cast in much.
MARK XII, 41, *c.* 70

Collective Bargaining

[*See* Labor Union.

Collector

Literature is in no way injured by the follies of collectors, since though they preserve the worthless, they necessarily protect the good.
ISAAC D'ISRAELI: *Curiosities of Literature,* 1834

A collector recently bought at public auction, in London, for one hundred and fifty-seven guineas, an autograph of Shakespeare: but for nothing a schoolboy can read "Hamlet."
R. W. EMERSON: *Experience,* 1841

[*See also* Auction, Bibliomania.

College

A set o' dull conceited hashes
Confuse their brains in college classes;
They gang in stirks, and come out asses.
ROBERT BURNS: *Epistle to J. Lapraik,* April 1, 1785 (*Stirk*=a bullock)

Our college friends are the dearest.
THOMAS JEFFERSON: *Letter to John Page,* 1804

It is, sirs, a small college, and yet there are those who love it.
DANIEL WEBSTER: Argument before the Supreme Court in the Dartmouth College case, 1819

Of all horned cattle, the most helpless in a printing-office is a college graduate.
HORACE GREELEY, *c.* 1860

The ideal college is Mark Hopkins on one end of a log and Mark Hopkins on the other.
Ascribed to JAMES A. GARFIELD: Speech in New York, Dec. 28, 1871 (It is very unlikely that the exact text of Garfield's remark has been preserved. Carrol A. Wilson, in The Colophon, Spring, 1938, argues that he probably said: "A log cabin in the woods, with a pine bench in it with Mark Hopkins at one end and me at the other, is a good enough college for me." Mark Hopkins (1802–87) was president of Williams College from 1836–1872)

[*See also* Education, School, University.

Collier

The Devil loves all colliers.
BRIAN MELBANCKE: *Philotinus,* 1583

Cologne

In Köhln, a town of monks and bones,
And pavements fank'd with murderous stones,
And rags, and hags, and hideous wenches;
I counted two and seventy stenches,
All well defined, and several stinks!
Ye nymphs that reign o'er sewers and sinks,
The river Rhine, it is well known,
Doth wash your city of Cologne;
But tell me, nymphs! what power divine
Shall henceforth wash the river Rhine?
S. T. COLERIDGE: *Cologne,* 1817

Colony

The best people in the mother-country will generally be the worst in the colonies; the worst at home will be the best abroad.
S. T. COLERIDGE: *Table-Talk,* Aug. 14, 1831

Colonies do not cease to be colonies because they are independent.
BENJAMIN DISRAELI: Speech in the House of Commons, Feb. 5, 1863

All colonies are oppressed peoples.
NIKOLAI LENIN: Instructions to the Soviet of Workers' and Soldiers' Deputies, May 19, 1917

Color

What value is given to cloth by adulteration with false colors? God likes not that which He Himself did not produce. Had He not the power to order that sheep should be born with purple or sky-blue fleeces? He had the power, but He did not wish; and what God did not wish certainly ought not to be produced artificially.
TERTULLIAN: *Women's Dress, c.* 220

The colors that show best by candlelight are white, carnation, and a kind of sea-water green.
FRANCIS BACON: *Essays,* XXXVII, 1625

Among the several kinds of beauty the eye takes most delight in colors. We nowhere meet with a more glorious or pleasing show in nature than what appears in the heavens at the rising and setting of the sun.
JOSEPH ADDISON: *The Spectator,* June 3, 1712

Colors speak all languages.
JOSEPH ADDISON: *The Spectator,* June 27, 1712

Colors are the smiles of nature. When they are extremely smiling, and break forth into other beauty besides, they are her laughs, as in the flowers.
LEIGH HUNT: *The Seer,* 1840

The purest and most thoughtful minds are those which love color the most.
JOHN RUSKIN: *The Stones of Venice,* II, 1851

Blue is true,
Yellow's jealous,
Green's forsaken,
Red's brazen,
White is love,
And black is death. Author unidentified

[*See also* Blue, Horse, Socialism.

Colt

The ragged colt may prove a good horse.
GEORGE CHAPMAN, BEN JONSON, and JOHN MARSTON: *Eastward Ho*, v, 1605

The kick of the dam hurts not the colt.
THOMAS FULLER: *Gnomologia*, 1732

[*See also* Horse.

Columbia University

The entrance of this college is thro' one of the streets where the most noted prostitutes live. This is certainly a temptation to the youth that have occasion to pass so often that way.
PATRICK M'ROBERTS: *Tour Through Part of the North Provinces of America*, I, 1775 (M'Roberts's reference was to King's College, now Columbia)

Columbus, Christopher (1451–1506)

How in God's name did Columbus get over
Is a pure wonder to me.
A. H. CLOUGH: *Columbus*, *c.* 1850

Every ship that comes to America got its chart from Columbus.
R. W. EMERSON: *Representative Men*, I, 1850

If Columbus had not sailed westward with the obstinacy of a maniac, he would not have encountered some pieces of wood, worked by the hand of man, twenty-four hours before he came to San Salvador, and that ridiculous circumstance would not have given courage to his crew, and he would have had to swallow his shame, return to Europe, and count himself lucky to get there.
HECTOR BERLIOZ: *Les grotesques de la musique*, 1859

Behind him lay the gray Azores,
Behind, the Gates of Hercules;
Before him not the ghost of shores;
Before him only shoreless seas.
The good mate said: "Now must we pray,
For lo! the very stars are gone.
Brave Admiral, speak; what shall I say?"
"Why, say 'Sail on! Sail on! and on!'"
CINCINNATUS HEINE (JOAQUIN MILLER): *Columbus*, 1871

When he started out he didn't know where he was going, when he got there he didn't know where he was, and when he got back he didn't know where he had been.
Author unidentified

[*See also* America.

Comb

Don't count the teeth of a comb; if you do they will all break out.
AMERICAN NEGRO PROVERB

Combination

When bad men combine, the good must associate.
EDMUND BURKE: *Thoughts on the Cause of the Present Discontents*, 1770

The paradox of all liberty is the necessity for the state to control liberty of association or combination in order to safeguard the liberty of the individual.
E. S. P. HAYNES: *The Case for Liberty*, VII, 1919

[*See also* Association.

Comedy

Comedy aims at representing men as worse, and tragedy as better, than in real life.
ARISTOTLE: *Poetics*, II, *c.* 322 B.C.

The debauching of virgins and the amours of strumpets are the subject of comedy.
LACTANTIUS: *Divinae institutiones*, VI, *c.* 310

The two great branches of ridicule in writing are comedy and burlesque. The first ridicules persons by drawing them in their proper characters, the other by drawing them quite unlike themselves.
JOSEPH ADDISON: *The Spectator*, Dec. 15, 1711

All comedies are ended by marriage.
BRYON: *Don Juan*, III, 1821

The human comedy. (La comédie humaine.)
BALZAC: Title of a series of novels, 1842

The essence of all jokes, of all comedy, seems to be an honest or well-intended halfness; a non-performance of what is pretended to be performed, at the same time that one is giving loud pledges of performance. The balking of the intellect, the frustrated expectation, the break of continuity in the intellect, is comedy and it announces itself in the pleasant spasms we call laughter.
R. W. EMERSON: *Letters and Social Aims*, 1875

Comedy is the fountain of sound sense.
GEORGE MEREDITH: *The Idea of Comedy*, 1877

The comic man is happy under any fate, and he says funny things at funerals, and when the bailiffs are in the house, or the hero is waiting to be hanged.
JEROME K. JEROME: *Stage-Land*, 1889

[*See also* Drama, Error, Humor, Laughter, Life, Man, Tragedy.

Comet

A comet is a star that runs, not being fixed like a planet, but a bastard among planets. It is

a haughty and proud star, engrossing the whole element, and carrying itself as if it were there alone.
MARTIN LUTHER: *Table-Talk*, CXXIV, 1569

Comfort

The superior man thinks always of virtue; the common man thinks of comfort.
CONFUCIUS: *Analects*, IV, *c.* 500 B.C.

Thy rod and thy staff they comfort me.
PSALMS XXIII, 4, *c.* 150 B.C.

Cold comfort.
ENGLISH PHRASE, in use since the XVII century

He that doth the ravens feed,
Yea, providently caters for the sparrow,
Be comfort to my age!
SHAKESPEARE: *As You Like It*, II, *c.* 1600

The man who has won his freedom tramples ruthlessly upon the kind of comfort which grocers, Christians, cows, women, Englishmen and other democrats worship in their dreams. The free man is a warrior.
F. W. NIETZSCHE: *The Twilight of the Idols*, 1889

The man who expects comfort in this life must be born deaf, dumb and blind.
TURKISH PROVERB

[*See also* Children, Love, Mind and Body, Virtue, Warrior.

Comforter

Miserable comforters are ye all.
JOB XVI, 2, *c.* 325 B.C. (From this derives the phrase " Job's comforter ")

The comforter's head never aches.
GEORGE HERBERT: *Outlandish Proverbs*, 1640

That it may please thee to strengthen such as do stand; and to comfort and help the weak-hearted; and to raise up those who fall; and finally to beat down Satan under our feet; We beseech thee to hear us, good Lord.
THE BOOK OF COMMON PRAYER (*The Litany*), 1662

Coming

Coming events cast their shadows before.
THOMAS CAMPBELL: *Lochiel's Warning*, 1803

Comity

Comity between nations. (Comitas inter gentes.)
LATIN PHRASE

Command

Who hath not served cannot command.
JOHN FLORIO: *First Fruites*, 1578

He commands enough that obeys a wise man.
GEORGE HERBERT: *Outlandish Proverbs*, 1640

There is great force hidden in a sweet command.
IBID.

No man is fit to command another that cannot command himself.
WILLIAM PENN: *No Cross, No Crown*, 1669

Command your man — and do it yourself.
JOHN RAY: *English Proverbs*, 1670

Every command is a slap in the face of liberty. Even when good is commanded it becomes evil in the light of sound morality, of human dignity, of true liberty.
M. A. BAKUNIN: *Dieu et l'état*, 1871

Little is done where many command.
DUTCH PROVERB

It is pleasant to command, though it be only a flock of sheep.
SPANISH PROVERB

[*See also* Ambition, Counsel, King, Learning, Obedience.

Commandment

(The Ten Commandments are in EXODUS XX, 2–17, *c.* 700 B.C. and in DEUTERONOMY V, 6–21, *c.* 650 B.C.)

Thou knowest the commandments, Do not commit adultery, Do not kill, Do not steal, Do not bear false witness, Defraud not, Honor thy father and mother.
MARK X, 19, *c.* 70 (Cf. LUKE XVIII, 20, *c.* 75)

Thou shalt love the Lord thy God with all thy heart, and with all thy soul, and with all thy mind, and with all thy strength: this is the first commandment.
MARK XII, 30 (Cf. MATTHEW XXII, 37–38, *c.* 75)

If ye love me, keep my commandments.
JOHN XIV, 15, *c.* 115

There never was at any time written a more excellent, complete, or compendious book of virtues than the Ten Commandments.
MARTIN LUTHER: *Table-Talk*, CCLXVIII, 1569

No mere man, since the Fall, is able in this life perfectly to keep the commandments.
THE BOOK OF COMMON PRAYER (*Shorter Catechism*), 1662

From the poetry of Lord Byron they drew a system of ethics compounded of misanthropy and voluptuousness, — a system in which the two great commandments were to hate your neighbor and to love your neighbor's wife.
T. B. MACAULAY: *Moore's Life of Byron*, 1831 (Edinburgh Review, June)

The Eleventh Commandment: Thou shalt not be found out.
GEORGE WHYTE-MELVILLE: *Holmby House*, XIV, 1860

I stand by the Ten Commandments. They are bully.
Ascribed to THEODORE ROOSEVELT (1858–1919) in ERNEST WEEKLEY: *Adjectives—and Other Words,* 1930

1. I be God your master. No get other God, only me.
2. (missing).
3. No talk God name for nothing.
4. Keep Sunday.
5. Hear for your father and your mother.
6. No kill.
7. No make bad.
8. No thief.
9. No lie.
10. No want other man his woman.

Anon.: Tr. of the Ten Commandments into Pidgin English

In vain we call old notions fudge
And bend our conscience to our dealing;
The Ten Commandments will not budge,
And stealing will continue stealing.
Author unidentified

The Eleventh Commandment: Mind your own business. IBID.

[*See also* Duty, Politics, Revelation.

Commerce

I am a bad Englishman, because I think the advantages of commerce are dearly bought for some by the lives of many more.
HORACE WALPOLE: *Letter to Horace Mann,* May 26, 1762

The selfish spirit of commerce knows no country, and feels no passion or principle but that of gain.
THOMAS JEFFERSON: *Letter to Larkin Smith,* 1809

Commerce is entitled to a complete and efficient protection in all its legal rights, but the moment it presumes to control a country, or to substitute its fluctuating expedients for the high principles of natural justice that ought to lie at the root of every political system, it should be frowned on, and rebuked.
J. FENIMORE COOPER: *The American Democrat,* XXXVI, 1838

In the pre-capitalist stages of society, commerce rules industry. The reverse is true of modern society.
KARL MARX: *Das Kapital,* III, 1895

[*See also* Business, Clergyman, England, Laissez-faire, Money, Prosperity, Trade (=commerce), Trade (Free).

Committee

A group of men who keep minutes and waste hours. Author unidentified

[*See also* Assembly, Board, Council.

Common

She is as common as a barber's chair.
THOMAS FULLER: *Gnomologia,* 1732

Common Law

[*See* Law (Common).

Common-sense

[*See* Sense (Common).

Commonwealth

[*See* Government.

Communion, Holy

[*See* Eucharist.

Communism

What is thine is mine, and all of mine is thine.
PLAUTUS: *Trinummus,* II, *c.* 190 B.C.

We who are united in heart and soul have no hesitation in sharing things. Among us all things are common except wives.
TERTULLIAN: *The Christian's Defence, c.* 215

What's mine is yours, and what is yours is mine.
SHAKESPEARE: *Measure for Measure,* V, 1604 (Cf. PLAUTUS, *ante, c.* 190 B.C.)

What's mine is my own; what's my brother's is his and mine.
THOMAS FULLER: *Gnomologia,* 1732

Were it possible to have a community of property, it would soon be found that no one would toil, but that men would be disposed to be satisfied with barely enough for the supply of their physical wants, since none would exert themselves to obtain advantages solely for the use of others.
J. FENIMORE COOPER: *The American Democrat,* XXVIII, 1838

The progress of society brings with it a necessity of sacrificing the ideal of what is excellent for the individual to the ideal of what is excellent for the whole.
THOMAS DE QUINCEY: *Superficial Knowledge, c.* 1847

All men have an equal right to the free development of their faculties; they have an equal right to the impartial protection of the state; but it is not true, it is against all the laws of reason and equity, it is against the eternal nature of things, that the indolent man and the laborious man, the spendthrift and the economist, the imprudent and the wise, should obtain and enjoy an equal amount of goods.
VICTOR COUSIN: *Justice et charité,* 1848

The theory of Communism may be summed up in one sentence: Abolish all private property.
KARL MARX and FRIEDRICH ENGELS: *The Communist Manifesto,* 1848

Whenever it ceases to be true that mankind, as a rule, prefer themselves to others, and those nearest to them to those more remote, from that moment Communism is not only practicable, but the only defensible form of society; and will, when that time arrives, be assuredly carried into effect.
J. S. MILL: *Representative Government*, III, 1861

Institutions grounded on Communism always have brilliant beginnings, for Communism involves a great exaltation; but they decline rapidly, for Communism is in conflict with human nature.
ERNEST RENAN: *Les apôtres*, 1866

The communism of combined wealth and capital, the outgrowth of overweening cupidity and selfishness which assiduously undermines the justice and integrity of free institutions, is not less dangerous than the communism of oppressed poverty and toil which, exasperated by injustice and discontent, attacks with wild disorder the citadel of misrule.
GROVER CLEVELAND: Message to Congress, Dec. 3, 1888

Communism will gradually come in, not by the collapse of the capitalistic bourgeoisie, but by the growth of the proletariat.
J. L. JAURÈS: *Études socialistes*, 1902

As soon as classes have been abolished, and the dictatorship of the proletariat has been done away with, the [Communist] party will have fulfilled its mission and can be allowed to disappear.
JOSEPH STALIN: Speech at Sverdloff University, April, 1924

Leninism is a combination of two things which Europeans have kept for some centuries in different compartments of the soul — religion and business.
J. M. KEYNES: *A Short View of Russia*, I, 1926

The riches and goods of Christians are not common, as touching the right, title and possession of the same, as some do falsely boast.
The Doctrines and Discipline of the Methodist Episcopal Church, I, 1932

Communism and religion are the two trades a fool may succeed at as well as the smartest practical man.
E. W. HOWE: *The Indignations of E. W. Howe*, 1933

The Japanese are only lice on the body of China, but Communism is a disease of the heart.
CHINESE SAYING, *c.* 1940

What's yours is mine, what's mine's my ain.
SCOTTISH PROVERB (Ain=own)

When two friends have a common purse, one sings and the other weeps.
SPANISH PROVERB

[*See also* Art, Communist, Individualism, Jesus Christ.

Communist

What is a Communist? One who hath yearnings
For equal division of unequal earnings.
Idler or bungler, or both, he is willing,
To fork out his copper and pocket your shilling.
EBENEZER ELLIOTT: *Epigram*, 1831

The Communist is a Socialist in a violent hurry.
G. W. GOUGH: *The Economic Consequences of Socialism*, I, 1926

One who has nothing, and is eager to share it with others.
Author unidentified

[*See also* Capitalist, Communism, Socialism, Socialist.

Community

The community is a fictitious body, composed of the individual persons who are considered as constituting, as it were, its members. The interest of the community, then, is what? The sum of the interests of the several members who compose it.
JEREMY BENTHAM: *The Principles of Morals and Legislation*, I, 1789

[*See also* Conformity, Majority, Society.

Companion

I am a brother to dragons, and a companion to owls.
JOB XXX, 29, *c.* 325 B.C.

There are people one loves — and people one would rather have as companions.
HENRIK IBSEN: *A Doll's House*, II, 1879

A mad dog neither drinks nor smokes, but it would be rash to conclude that he was therefore a safe and pleasant companion.
HENRY CABOT LODGE: Speech in the Senate, Jan. 6, 1915

With a good companion even Hell is as Heaven.
GERMAN PROVERB

The companion of my companion is not my companion. (Socii mei socius meus socius non est.)
LEGAL MAXIM

[*See also* Company, Misery, Solitude, Travel.

Company

Every man is like the company he keeps.
EURIPIDES: *The Phoenissaes*, *c.* 410 B.C.

The wise man will want to be ever with him who is better than himself.
PLATO: *Phaedo*, *c.* 360 B.C.

If a man could mount to Heaven and survey the mighty universe, his admiration of its beauties would be much diminished unless he had some one to share in his pleasure.
CICERO: *De amicitia*, *c.* 50 B.C.

The mind is depraved by the company of the low; it riseth to equality with equals; and to distinction with the distinguished.
The Hitopadesa, intro., *c.* 500

He that goeth to bed with dogs ariseth with fleas.
JOHN SANFORD: *Hours of Recreation*, 1572

It is better to be alone than in ill company.
GEORGE PETTIE: *Civil Conversations of Stefano Guazzo*, 1581

I had as lief have their room as their company.
ROBERT GREENE: *Farewell to Folly*, 1591

It easeth some, though none it ever cured,
To think their dolor others have endured.
SHAKESPEARE: *The Rape of Lucrece*, 1594

A man is known by the company he keeps.
ENGLISH PROVERB, current since the early XVII century (Cf. EURIPIDES, *ante*, *c.* 410 B.C.)

Frequent not the company of immodest persons, especially if they be also impudent, as is generally the case.
ST. FRANCIS DE SALES: *Introduction to the Devout Life*, XIII, 1609

Keep not ill company lest you increase the number.
GEORGE HERBERT: *Outlandish Proverbs*, 1640

Good company in a journey makes the way to seem the shorter.
IZAAK WALTON: *The Compleat Angler*, I, 1653

Tell me thy company, and I'll tell thee thy manners.
ROGER L'ESTRANGE: Tr. of FRANCISCO DE QUEVEDO: *Sueños* (1627), 1667

Company is an extreme provocative to fancy; and like a hot bed in gardening, is apt to make our imagination sprout too fast.
ANTHONY A. COOPER (EARL OF SHAFTESBURY): *Characteristics of Men, Manners, Opinions, Times*, I, *c.* 1713

The matron who conducts abroad
A willing nymph is thought a bawd;
And if a modest girl is seen
With one who cures a lover's spleen,
We guess her, not extremely nice,
And only wish to know her price.
JOHN GAY: *Fables*, I, 1727

Company in distress
Makes the sorrow less.
THOMAS FULLER: *Gnomologia*, 1732

Seven may be company, but nine are confusion.
IBID.

Who keep company with the wolf learn to howl.
IBID.

Associate yourself with men of good quality if you esteem your own reputation; for 'tis better to be alone than in bad company.
GEORGE WASHINGTON: *Early copy-book*, before 1748

Lay aside the best book whenever you can go into the best company; and depend upon it, you change for the better.
LORD CHESTERFIELD: *Letter to his son*, London, May 31, 1752

I live in the crowds of jollity, not so much to enjoy company as to shun myself.
SAMUEL JOHNSON: *Rasselas*, XVI, 1759

"Good company upon the road," says the proverb, "is the shortest cut."
OLIVER GOLDSMITH: *The Vicar of Wakefield*, XVIII, 1766

Two's a company, three's a crowd.
ENGLISH PROVERB, apparently not current until the XIX century

No company is far preferable to bad, because we are more apt to catch the vices of others than their virtues, as disease is far more contagious than health.
C. C. COLTON: *Lacon*, 1820

Introduce a base person among gentlemen; it is all to no purpose; he is not their fellow. Every society protects itself. The company is perfectly safe, and he is not one of them, though his body is in the room.
R. W. EMERSON: *Spiritual Laws*, 1841

Men of very great capacity will, as a rule, find the company of very stupid people preferable to that of the common run; for the same reason that the tyrant and the mob, the grandfather and the grandchildren, are natural allies.
ARTHUR SCHOPENHAUER: *Further Psychological Observations*, 1851

Intimate society between people radically dissimilar to one another is an idle dream. Unlikeness may attract, but it is likeness which retains.
J. S. MILL: *The Subjection of Women*, IV, 1869

A man is known by the company he avoids.
Author unidentified

The third person makes good company.
DUTCH PROVERB

The company makes the feast.
FRENCH PROVERB

Caught with; hanged with.
GERMAN PROVERB

'Tis for the sake of the company that dogs go to church.
IRISH PROVERB

He is known by his company. (Noscitur a sociis.)
LATIN PROVERB

Keep gude company, and ye'll be counted ane o' them.
SCOTTISH PROVERB

[*See also* Alone, Association, Companion, Conversation, Guest, Hanging, Ignorance, Marriage, Misery, Solitude.

Comparison

Comparisons turn friends into enemies.
PHILEMON: *Fragment, c.* 310 B.C.

Comparisons are odious.
JOHN FORTESCUE: *De laudibus legum Angliae, c.* 1462

Comparisons are odorous.
SHAKESPEARE: *Much Ado About Nothing,* III, *c.* 1599

Take thou heed that thou make no comparisons, and if any body happen to be praised for some brave act, or virtue, praise not another for the same virtue in his presence, for every comparison is odious.
FRANCIS HAWKINS: *Youth's Behavior,* VI, 1663

Nothing is good or bad but by comparison.
THOMAS FULLER: *Gnomologia,* 1732

To compare is not to prove.
FRENCH PROVERB

[*See also* Happiness.

Compassion

Be ye all of one mind, having compassion one of another.
I PETER, III, 8, *c.* 60

Bowels of compassion.
I JOHN III, 17, *c.* 115

We should only affect compassion, and carefully avoid having any.
LA ROCHEFOUCAULD: *Self-portrait,* 1658

Compassion is the fellow-feeling of the unsound.
GEORGE BERNARD SHAW: *Maxims for Revolutionists,* 1903

Compensation

For all our works a recompense is sure:
'Tis sweet to think on what was hard 't endure.
ROBERT HERRICK: *Hesperides,* 1648

Everything in the world is mingled with bitterness and charms; war has its sweets, Hymen its alarms.
JEAN DE LA FONTAINE: *Fables, c.* 1670

No pain, no palm; no thorns, no throne; no gall, no glory; no cross, no crown.
WILLIAM PENN: *No Cross, No Crown,* 1669

Since I must be old and have the gout, I have long turned those disadvantages to my own account, and plead them to the utmost when they will save me from doing anything I dislike.
HORACE WALPOLE: *Letter to Horace Mann,* Oct. 30, 1785

Competition

By competition the total amount of the supply is increased, and by increase of the supply a competition in the sale ensues, and this enables the consumer to buy at lower rates. Of all human powers operating on the affairs of mankind, none is greater than that of competition.
HENRY CLAY: Speech in the Senate, Feb. 2, 1832

Every child of the Saxon race is educated to wish to be first. It is our system; and a man comes to measure his greatness by the regrets, envies, and hatreds of his competitors.
R. W. EMERSON: *Representative Men,* I, 1850

Price-cutting and rebating, collecting information of the trade of competitiors, the operation of companies under other names to obviate prejudice or secure an advantage, or for whatever reason, are all legitimate methods of competition, whatever moral criticism they may justify. There is no rule of fairness or reasonableness which regulates competition.
JOHN G. JOHNSON and JOHN G. MILBURN: Brief for the Standard Oil Company, filed in the U. S. Circuit Court at St. Louis, 1909

Free competition, though within its limits it is productive of good results, cannot be the ruling principle of the economic world. It is necessary that economic affairs be brought once more into subjection to a true and effective guiding principle.
POPE PIUS XI: *Quadragesimo anno,* May 15, 1931

[*See also* Coöperation.

Complaisance

Give me a wench that will be easily had,
Not wooed with cost, and being sent for comes.
Anon.: *Nero,* I, 1624

A sweet and innocent compliance is the cement of love.
H. G. BOHN: *Handbook of Proverbs,* 1855

Complex, Inferiority

People hate those who make them feel their own inferiority.
LORD CHESTERFIELD: *Letter to his son,* April 30, 1750

Some men appear to feel that they belong to a pariah caste. They fear to offend, they bend and apologize, and walk through life with a timid step.
R. W. EMERSON: *The Conduct of Life,* V, 1860

Complexion

The dark in complexion are said to have a manly look, and the fair are called the children of the gods.
PLATO: *The Republic,* V, *c.* 350 B.C.

'Tis beauty truly blent, whose red and white
Nature's own sweet and cunning hand laid on.
SHAKESPEARE: *Twelfth Night*, I, *c.* 1601

I look like an old peeled wall.
WILLIAM CONGREVE: *The Way of the World*, III, 1700

The ladies of St. James's!
They're painted to the eyes;
Their white it stays for ever,
Their red it never dies;
But Phyllida, my Phyllida!
Her color comes and goes;
It trembles to a lily, —
It wavers to a rose.
AUSTIN DOBSON: *The Ladies of St. James*, 1885

Shun white Spaniards and black Englishmen.
DUTCH PROVERB

She looks like milk and blood.
GERMAN SAYING

[*See also* Cosmetics, Face, Night-life, Tears, Weeping.

Compliment

This was really a compliment to be pleased with — a nice little handsome pat of butter made up by a neat-handed Phillis of a dairy-maid instead of the grease fit only for cartwheels which one is dosed with by the pound.
WALTER SCOTT: *Diary*, Nov. 18, 1826 (On being complimented by Frances Burney d'Arblay)

Compliment is taken literally only by the savage. The accuracy of compliment is not that of algebra.
W. C. BROWNELL: *French Traits*, 1889

Women are never disarmed by compliments; men always are.
OSCAR WILDE: *An Ideal Husband*, III, 1895

Of a compliment only a third is meant.
WELSH PROVERB

[*See also* Friendship.

Composer

I always have a picture in my mind when I am composing, and I follow its outlines.
LUDWIG VAN BEETHOVEN: To Charles Neate, 1815

The composer is almost the only creative artist who must depend upon a horde of intermediate agents to present his work — some intelligent, some stupid; some friendly, some hostile; some energetic, some indolent; but all capable, from first to last, of either augmenting the brilliance of his work, or of disfiguring it, misrepresenting it, even destroying it altogether.
HECTOR BERLIOZ: *Traité d'instrumentation*, 1856

Builder and maker, thou, of houses not made with hands.
ROBERT BROWNING: *Abt Vogler*, 1864

Composure

The superior man is always composed; the ordinary man is uneasy and distressed.
CONFUCIUS: *Analects*, VII, *c.* 500 B.C.

Compromise

All government — indeed, every human benefit and enjoyment, every virtue and every prudent act — is founded on compromise and barter.
EDMUND BURKE: Speech on Conciliation with America, March 22, 1775

Compromise makes a good umbrella but a poor roof.
J. R. LOWELL: *Democracy*, 1884 (Address in Birmingham, England, Oct. 6)

Such an adjustment of conflicting interests as gives each adversary the satisfaction of thinking he has got what he ought not to have, and is deprived of nothing except what was justly his due.
AMBROSE BIERCE: *The Devil's Dictionary*, *c.* 1906

If you can't lick 'em, join 'em.
AMERICAN POLITICAL PROVERB

Better bend than break.
SCOTTISH PROVERB

[*See also* Lawsuit, Litigation.

Compulsion

I can do nothing else. (Ich kann nicht anders.)
MARTIN LUTHER: Speech to the Diet of Worms, April 18, 1521

[*See also* Cause and Effect.

Comstockery

Men, whose trade is rat-catching, love to catch rats; the bug-destroyer seizes on his bug with delight; and the suppressor is gratified by finding his vice.
SYDNEY SMITH: In the Edinburgh Review, 1810

I propose to add to a dictionary that is already too long the word *comstock;* its meaning will be apparent to everyone. If you associate dirt, filth and obscenity with an idea, a picture, a statue, or anything, why — you simply comstock it.
BERNARR MACFADDEN: In Physical Culture, May, 1917 (ANTHONY COMSTOCK, 1844–1915)

[*See also* Reformer.

Conceit

Seest thou a man wise in his own conceit? There is more hope of a fool than of him.
PROVERBS XXVI, 12, *c.* 350 B.C.

Be not wise in your own conceits.
ROMANS XII, 16, *c.* 55

Conceit in weakest bodies strongest works.
SHAKESPEARE: *Hamlet*, III, *c.* 1601

Conceit causes more conversation than wit.
LA ROCHEFOUCAULD: *Maxims*, 1665

Take away the self-conceited, and there will be elbow-room in the world.
BENJAMIN WHICHCOTE: *Moral and Religious Aphorisms*, 1753

I've never any pity for conceited people, because I think they carry their comfort about with them.
MARIAN EVANS (GEORGE ELIOT): *The Mill on the Floss*, V, 1860

Conceit is the finest armor a man can wear.
JEROME K. JEROME: *Idle Thoughts of an Idle Fellow*, 1889

[*See also* Diffidence, Error.

Concentration

Concentration is the secret of strength in politics, in war, in trade, in short in all management of human affairs.
R. W. EMERSON: *The Conduct of Life*, II, 1860

Concert

Nor cold, nor stern, my soul! yet I detest
These scented rooms, where, to a gaudy throng,
Heaves the proud harlot her distended breast
In intricacies of laborious song.
S. T. COLERIDGE: *Lines Composed in a Concert-Room*, 1799 (London Morning Post, Sept. 24)

Conclusion

Oh, most lame and impotent conclusion!
SHAKESPEARE: *Othello*, II, 1604

Concrete

Perhaps the efforts of the true poets, founders, religious, literatures, all ages, have been, and ever will be, our time and times to come, essentially the same — to bring people back from their persistent strayings and sickly abstractions, to the costless, average, divine, original concrete.
WALT WHITMAN: *Specimen Days*, May 6, 1882

Concubine

He took a knife, and laid hold on his concubine, and divided her, together with her bones, into twelve pieces.
JUDGES XIX, 29, *c.* 500 B.C.

[Solomon had] three hundred concubines.
I KINGS XI, 3, *c.* 500 B.C.

Concubinage even for the sake of offspring is unlawful.
ST. AUGUSTINE: *On the Good of Marriage*, *c.* 401

In heart and mind I did rejoice
That I had made so sweet a choice,
And therefore did my state resign
To be King Edward's concubine.
Anon.: JANE SHORE, *c.* 1600 (Jane Shore was the mistress of Edward IV. She died *c.* 1527)

Concubinage is almost universal. If it was morally wrong why was it permitted to the most pious men under the Old Testament? Why did our Saviour never say a word against it?
JAMES BOSWELL: *Letter to William Temple*, March 18, 1775

[*See also* Divorce, Wife.

Concupiscence

They were as fed horses in the morning; every one neighed after his neighbor's wife.
JEREMIAH V, 8, *c.* 625 B.C.

[*See also* Adam (Old).

Condescension

Mind not high things, but condescend to men of low estate. ROMANS XII, 16, *c.* 55

[He] bow'd his eminent top to their low ranks,
Making them proud of his humility.
SHAKESPEARE: *All's Well that Ends Well*, I, *c.* 1602

A lion-cub, of sordid mind,
Avoided all the lion kind;
Fond of applause, he sought the feasts
Of vulgar and ignoble beasts;
With asses all his time he spent,
Their club's perpetual president.
JOHN GAY: *Fables*, I, 1727

There is nothing more likely to betray a man into absurdity than condescension.
SAMUEL JOHNSON: *Boswell's Life*, 1780

On a certain condescension in foreigners.
J. R. LOWELL: Title of an essay, 1869

Condition

It is a condition which confronts us — not a theory.
GROVER CLEVELAND: Message to Congress, Dec. 6, 1887

Condolence

When we describe our sensations of another's sorrows, either in friendly or ceremonious condolence, the customs of the world seldom admit of rigid veracity.
SAMUEL JOHNSON: *The Idler*, March 31, 1759

Of all cruelties, those are the most intolerable that come under the name of condolence and consolation.
W. S. LANDOR: *Letter to Robert Southey* (after the death of his son), 1816

I pray that our Heavenly Father may assuage the anguish of your bereavement, and leave you only the cherished memory of the loved and lost, and the solemn pride that must be yours to have laid so costly a sacrifice upon the altar of freedom.

ABRAHAM LINCOLN: *Letter to Mrs. Bixby,* Nov. 21, 1864 (Lincoln was informed that Mrs. Bixby had lost five sons, all killed in battle. Actually, but two were killed. Of the rest, two were taken prisoner and one deserted. Of the two taken prisoner, one enlisted in the Confederate service, and was posted as a deserter)

In hasty condolences one usually finds a good deal of curiosity.

VICTOR HUGO: *Toilers of the Sea,* XIX, 1866

Conduct

A man is known by his conduct to his wife, to his family, and to those under him.

NAPOLEON I: To Barry E. O'Meara at St. Helena, March 25, 1817

We may give advice but we cannot give conduct.

BENJAMIN FRANKLIN: *Poor Richard's Almanac,* 1758

Conduct is three-fourths of our life and its largest concern.

MATTHEW ARNOLD: *Literature and Dogma,* I, 1873

Fully to understand human conduct as a whole, we must study it as a part of that larger whole constituted by the conduct of animate beings in general.

HERBERT SPENCER: *The Data of Ethics,* I, 1879

No conduct is hated by all.

MR. JUSTICE O. W. HOLMES: *Opinion in Peck* vs. *Tribune Company,* 1909

[*See also* Ethics, Inconsistency, Morality.

Conductor

A bad singer can spoil only his own part in a musical composition, but a bad conductor can ruin everything.

HECTOR BERLIOZ: *Traité d'instrumentation,* 1856

Confederate States

Maryland desires and consents to the recognition of the independence of the Confederate States.

Resolution of the Maryland Legislature, May 10, 1861

No hardier republicanism was generated in New England than in the slave states of the South, which produced so many great statesmen of America.

W. E. GLADSTONE: *Kin Beyond Sea,* 1878 (North American Review, Sept.–Oct.)

[*See also* Alone, Trade (Free).

Confederation

[*See* Treaty.

Confession

To confess a fault freely is the next thing to being innocent of it.

PUBLILIUS SYRUS: *Sententiae, c.* 50 B.C.

What madness to confess by day what was concealed by the darkness of night, and to relate openly what thou hast done secretly.

OVID: *Amores,* III, *c.* 10

What use to confess our faults at the moment the vessel is sinking?

CLAUDIUS CLAUDIANUS: *In Eutropium,* II, *c.* 400

Confess your sins to one another. (Confitemini alterutrum peccata vestra.)

THE VENERABLE BEDE: *Commentary on the Epistle of James, c.* 725

I confess to Almighty God, to the blessed Mary, ever Virgin, to blessed Michael the Archangel, to blessed John the Baptist, to the Holy Apostles Peter and Paul, and to all the saints, that I have sinned exceedingly in thought, word, and deed; through my fault, through my fault, through my most grievous fault.

THE ROMAN MASS: *The Confiteor* (It is first found in the present form in BERNOLD OF CONSTANCE: *Micrologus, c.* 1075)

A generous and free-minded confession doth disable a reproach and disarm an injury.

MICHEL DE MONTAIGNE: *Essays,* III, 1588

Confess and be hanged.

CHRISTOPHER MARLOWE: *The Jew of Malta,* IV, *c.* 1590 (Quoted as a proverb)

A fault confessed is more than half amended.

Anon.: *Arden of Feversham,* IV, 1592

Open confession, open penance.

ROBERT ARMIN: *A Nest of Ninnies,* 1608

It is an abuse to confess any kind of sin, whether mortal or venial, without a will to be delivered from it, since confession was instituted for no other end.

ST. FRANCIS DE SALES: *Introduction to the Devout Life,* XIX, 1609

Confession is the first step to repentance.

ENGLISH PROVERB, traced by Apperson to 1654

We have left undone those things which we ought to have done; and we have done those things which we ought not to have done.

THE BOOK OF COMMON PRAYER (*General Confession*), 1662

We confess our little faults only to persuade others that we have no great ones.

LA ROCHEFOUCAULD: *Maxims,* 1665

The Catholic religion does not oblige us to discover our sins indifferently to everybody: it allows us to remain concealed to all other men; but it excepts one alone, to whom it commands us to discover the bottom of our hearts, and to show ourselves as we are.
BLAISE PASCAL: *Pensées*, III, 1670

The devout spend so much time with their confessors because they like to talk about themselves — even to talk ill.
MARIE DE SÉVIGNE: *Letters*, *c.* 1690

Open confession is good for the soul.
JAMES KELLY: *Complete Collection of Scottish Proverbs*, 1721

It is forbidden for a confessor to ask a woman at confession where she lives, or when she will be alone, or to tell her to expect him at her home.
ALFONSO MARIA DI LIGUORI: *Theologia moralis*, V, 1753

There is something noble in publishing truth, though it condemns one's self.
SAMUEL JOHNSON: *Boswell's Tour to the Hebrides*, Sept. 15, 1773

The pope wanted me to confess, which I always evaded by saying, "Holy Father, I am too much occupied at present. When I get older."
NAPOLEON I: To Barry E. O'Meara at St. Helena, Nov. 9, 1816

I acknowledge the corn.
C. A. WICKLIFFE: Speech in the House of Representatives, 1828

There is no refuge from confession but suicide; and suicide is confession.
DANIEL WEBSTER: Argument at the trial of Capt. White for murder, April 6, 1830

It is the duty of nations as well as of men to confess their sins and transgressions in humble sorrow, yet with assured hope that genuine repentance will lead to mercy and pardon.
ABRAHAM LINCOLN: *Proclamation*, March 30, 1863

People think the confessional is unknown in Protestant churches. It is a great mistake. The principal change is, that there is no screen between the penitent and the father confessor.
O. W. HOLMES: *The Guardian Angel*, XIII, 1867

Confession may be good for the soul, but it doesn't get one much reputation for sense.
Author unidentified

A confession made in court is of greater effect than any proof. (Confessio facta in judicio omni probatione major est.)
LEGAL MAXIM

Under seal of the confessional. (Sub sigillo confessionis.) MEDIEVAL LATIN PHRASE

[*See also* Absolution, Fault, Penance, Sin, Suicide.

Confidant

We take a confidant to have an approver.
STANISLAUS LESZCZYNSKI (KING OF POLAND): *Oeuvres du philosophe bienfaisant*, 1763

Confidence

Confidence in an unfaithful man in time of trouble is like a broken tooth, and a foot out of joint. PROVERBS XXV, 19, *c.* 350 B.C.

Confidence is a plant of slow growth in an aged bosom.
WILLIAM PITT (EARL OF CHATHAM): Speech in the House of Commons, Jan. 14, 1766

Confidence is a thing not to be produced by compulsion. Men cannot be forced into trust.
DANIEL WEBSTER: Speech in the Senate, 1834

Men do not confide themselves to boys, or coxcombs, or pedants, but to their peers.
R. W. EMERSON: *Representative Men*, IV, 1850

Never confide in women or servants.
HEBREW PROVERB

[*See also* Despotism, Faithful.

Confined

I am cabin'd, cribb'd, confin'd.
SHAKESPEARE: *Macbeth*, III, *c.* 1605

Conflict

It is an irrepressible conflict between opposing and enduring forces.
WILLIAM H. SEWARD: Speech at Rochester, N. Y., Oct. 25, 1858

Conformity

When in Rome, do as the Romans do.
Author unknown (The saying is probably based upon some advice given to St. Augustine by St. Ambrose (*c.* 390): "When I am at Rome I fast on Saturdays; when I am at Milan I do not. Follow the custom of the church where you happen to be")

Conformity gives comeliness to things.
ROBERT HERRICK: *Hesperides*, 1648

Singularity in the right hath ruined many; happy those who are convinced of the general opinion.
BENJAMIN FRANKLIN: *Poor Richard's Almanac*, 1757

To think for himself! Oh, my God, teach him to think like other people!
MARY GODWIN SHELLEY: On being advised to send her son to a school where he would be taught to think for himself, *c.* 1825

The man who aims to speak as books enable, as synods use, as the fashion guides, and as interest commands, babbles. Let him hush.
R. W. EMERSON: Address at the Divinity College, Cambridge, Mass., July 15, 1838

The virtue in most request is conformity. Self-reliance is its aversion.
R. W. EMERSON: *Self-Reliance,* 1841

You must pay for conformity. All goes well as long as you run with conformists. But you, who are honest men in other particulars, know that there is alive somewhere a man whose honesty reaches to this point also, that he shall not kneel to false gods, and, on the day when you meet him, you sink into the class of counterfeits.
R. W. EMERSON: *English Traits,* XIII, 1856

Never say No when the world says Aye.
E. B. BROWNING: *Aurora Leigh,* I, 1857

Life cannot exist without a certain conformity to the surrounding universe — that conformity involves a certain amount of happiness in excess of pain. In short, as we live we are paid for living.
T. H. HUXLEY: *Letter to Charles Kingsley,* Sept. 23, 1860

The constitution of man is such that for a long time after he has discovered the incorrectness of the ideas prevailing around him he shrinks from openly emancipating himself from their domination; and, constrained by the force of circumstances, he publicly applauds what his private judgment condemns.
J. W. DRAPER: *History of the Intellectual Development of Europe,* 1863

The community in which each man acts like his neighbor is not yet a civilized community.
A. H. SAYCE: *Introduction to the Science of Language,* I, 1879

Either do as your neighbors do, or move away.
MOROCCAN PROVERB

To a question in Turkish the answer should be in Turkish.
PERSIAN PROVERB

[*See also* Fashion, Manners.

Confucian

[*See* Agnostic, Atheism.

Confucius (c. 551–478 B.C.)

Superior, and alone, Confucius stood,
Who taught that useful science, — to be good.
ALEXANDER POPE: *The Temple of Fame,* 1714

Confusion

If the whole conclave of Hell can so compolitise exadverse and diametrical contradictions as to compolitse such a multimonstrous maufrey of heteroclites and quicquidlibets quietly, I trust I may say with all humble reverence they can do more than the Senate of Heaven.
NATHANIEL WARD: *The Simple Cobbler of Aggawam,* 1646

With ruin upon ruin, rout on rout,
Confusion worse confounded.
JOHN MILTON: *Paradise Lost,* II, 1667

Congress

All legislative powers herein granted shall be vested in a Congress of the United States, which shall consist of a Senate and House of Representatives.
CONSTITUTION OF THE UNITED STATES, Art. I, 1789

Congress is the great commanding theatre of this nation, and the threshold to whatever department of office a man is qualified to enter.
THOMAS JEFFERSON: *Letter to William Wirt,* 1808

I have passed two hours in the Representatives' hall and Senate chamber today. I could learn nothing of the merits of any of the questions, but I had a preference, such as one feels in seeing two dogs fight, that one should beat.
AMOS LAWRENCE: *Diary,* Washington, May, 1836

Congress cannot properly even discuss a subject that Congress cannot legally control, unless it be to ascertain its own powers.
J. FENIMORE COOPER: *The American Democrat,* IV, 1838

Being elected to Congress, though I am very grateful to our friends for having done it, has not pleased me as much as I expected.
ABRAHAM LINCOLN: *Letter to J. F. Speed,* Oct. 22, 1846

I have been up to see Congress and they do not seem to be able to do anything except to eat peanuts and chew tobacco, while my army is starving.
R. E. LEE: *To his son Custis,* in Richmond, 1864 (The Confederate Congress)

Congress, you won't do. Go home, you mizzerable devils — go home!
C. F. BROWN (ARTEMUS WARD): *Artemus Ward: His Travels,* 1865

Though the President is commander-in-chief, Congress is his commander; and, God willing, he shall obey. He and his minions shall learn that this is not a government of kings and satraps, but a government of the people, and that Congress is the people.
THADDEUS STEVENS: Speech in the House of Representatives, Jan. 3, 1867

Some statesmen go to Congress and some go to jail. It is the same thing, after all.
EUGENE FIELD: *Tribune Primer,* 1882

We do not elect our wisest and best men to represent us in the Senate and the Congress.

In general, we elect men of the type that subscribes to only one principle — to get re-elected.
TERRY M. TOWNSEND: *The Doctor Looks at the Citizen*, 1940 (Address in New York, Jan. 30)

[*See also* Church and State, Slavery, Speech (Free).

Congress, Continental

The business of the Congress is tedious beyond expression. . . . Every man in it is a great man, an orator, a critic, a statesman; and therefore every man upon every question must show his oratory, his criticism, and his political abilities.
JOHN ADAMS: *Letter to his wife*, Oct. 9, 1774

Congressman

No person shall be a representative who shall not have attained to the age of 25 years, and have been seven years a citizen of the United States, and who shall not, when elected, be an inhabitant of that state in which he shall be chosen.
CONSTITUTION OF THE UNITED STATES, Art. I, 1789

You have no idea how destitute of talent are more than half of the members of Congress. Nine out of ten of your ordinary acquaintances are fully equal to them.
SERGEANT S. PRENTISS: *Letter to his sister*, Feb., 1833

Reader, suppose you were an idiot. And suppose you were a member of Congress. But I repeat myself.
S. L. CLEMENS (MARK TWAIN): Manuscript note, *c.* 1882 (Clemens used the idea in various speeches later)

A new Congressman must begin at the foot of the class and spell up.
CHAMP CLARK: Speech in Washington, March 16, 1916

Fleas can be taught nearly anything that a Congressman can.
S. L. CLEMENS (MARK TWAIN): *What Is Man?*, 1917

You can't use tact with a Congressman. A Congressman is a hog. You must take a stick and hit him on the snout.
HENRY ADAMS: *The Education of Henry Adams*, 1918 (Quoting an unnamed member of the Grant Cabinet, *c.* 1875)

After a man has been out of Congress awhile, people say, "You wouldn't think that man had been in Congress, would you?"
E. W. HOWE: *Sinner Sermons*, 1926

[*See also* Officeholder.

Congreve, William (1670–1729)

The characters of his dramas are profligates and strumpets, — the business of their brief existence, the undivided pursuit of lawless gallantry. No other spring of action, or possible motive of conduct, is recognized.
CHARLES LAMB: *Of the Artificial Comedy of the Last Century*, 1822 (London Magazine, April)

Conqueror

Conquered, we conquer. (Victi vincimus.)
PLAUTUS: *Casina*, I, *c.* 200 B.C.

A conqueror of conquerors. (Victor victorum.)
PLAUTUS: *Trinummus*, *c.* 190 B.C.

It is the law of war for conquerors to deal with the conquered at their pleasure.
JULIUS CAESAR: *The Gallic War*, I, *c.* 51 B.C.

I came, I saw, I conquered. (Veni, vidi, vici.)
JULIUS CAESAR: *Dispatch to the Roman Senate after the Battle of Zela*, 47 B.C.

I have conquered the universal conqueror. (Omnium victorem vici.)
INSCRIPTION ON A MEDAL COMMEMORATING DIANE OF POITIERS (1499–1566) (It shows her trampling underfoot the god of love)

The vanquished never yet spake well of the conqueror.
SAMUEL DANIEL: *A Defence of Rhyme*, 1602

I came, I saw, God conquered.
JOHN III SOBIESKI: Message to the pope after his defeat of the Turks at Vienna, Sept. 12, 1683 (Cf. JULIUS CAESAR, *ante*, 47 B.C.)

Most men cry, Long live the conqueror.
THOMAS FULLER: *Gnomologia*, 1732

The fame of a conqueror [is] a cruel fame.
LORD CHESTERFIELD: *Letter to his son*, Sept. 30, 1757

What millions died — that Caesar might be great!
THOMAS CAMPBELL: *The Pleasures of Hope*, II, 1799

The English conquered us, but they are far from being our equals.
NAPOLEON I: To Gaspard Gourgaud at St. Helena, 1815–1818

Rats and conquerors must expect no mercy in misfortune.
C. C. COLTON: *Lacon*, 1820

A conqueror, like a cannon-ball, must go on. If he rebounds, his career is over.
THE DUKE OF WELLINGTON: Quoted in SAMUEL ROGERS: *Recollections*, *c.* 1827

No men occupy so splendid a place in history as those who have founded monarchies on the ruins of republican institutions. The enterprise, be it good or bad, is one which requires a truly great man. It demands courage, activity, energy, wisdom, firmness, conspicuous virtues or vices so splendid and alluring as to resemble virtues.

T. B. MACAULAY: *Hallam,* 1828 (Edinburgh Review, Sept.)

The greatest conqueror is he who overcomes the enemy without a blow.

CHINESE PROVERB

[*See also* Death, Despair.

Conquest

To rejoice in conquest is to rejoice in murder.

LAO-TSZE: *The Tao Teh King, c.* 500 B.C.

A despised enemy has often maintained a sanguinary contest, and renowned states and kings have been conquered by a very slight effort.

HANNIBAL: Address to his army on the eve of Ticino, 218 B.C.

Moab is my washpot; over Edom will I cast out my shoe; over Philistia will I triumph.

PSALMS CVIII, 9, *c.* 150 B.C.

When we conquer enemies by kindness and justice we are more apt to win their submission than by victory in the field. In the one case, they yield only to necessity; in the other, by their own free choice.

POLYBIUS: *Histories,* V, *c.* 125 B.C.

Whoever conquers a free town and does not demolish it commits a great error, and may expect to be ruined himself; because whenever the citizens are disposed to revolt, they betake themselves of course to that blessed name of liberty, and the laws of their ancestors, which no length of time nor kind usage whatever will be able to eradicate.

NICCOLO MACHIAVELLI: *The Prince,* V, 1513

So many goodly cities ransacked and razed; so many nations destroyed and made desolate; so infinite millions of harmless people of all sexes, states and ages massacred, ravaged, and put to the sword; and the richest, the fairest, and the best part of the world topsiturvied, ruined and defaced for the traffic of pearls and pepper: Oh, base conquest!

MICHEL DE MONTAIGNE: *Essays,* III, 1588

To conquer without danger is to triumph without glory.

PIERRE CORNEILLE: *The Cid,* I, 1636

There is no such conquering weapon as the necessity of conquering.

GEORGE HERBERT: *Jacula Prudentum,* 1651

Conquest is the acquiring of the right of sovereignty by victory.

THOMAS HOBBES: *Leviathan,* conclusion, 1651

A conquest made by a democracy is always odious to the subject states. It becomes thereby monarchical by a fiction, but it is always more oppressive than a monarchy, as the experience of all times and ages shows.

C. L. DE MONTESQUIEU: *The Spirit of the Laws,* X, 1748

If there be one principle more deeply rooted than any other in the mind of every American, it is that we should have nothing to do with conquest.

THOMAS JEFFERSON: *Letter to William Short,* 1791

There is no state, the chief of which does not desire to secure to himself a constant state of peace by the conquest of the whole universe, if it were possible.

IMMANUEL KANT: *Perpetual Peace, Supplement I,* 1795

Even the final decision of a war is not to be regarded as absolute. The conquered nation often sees it as only a passing evil, to be repaired in after times by political combinations.

CARL VON CLAUSEWITZ: *Vom Kriege,* I, 1832

When nations attack one another, . . . and the one that gets the better seizes more or less of the other's territory and demands it as the price of peace, . . . we have a contract, a price paid for an article, to wit, peace.

T. H. HUXLEY: *On the Natural Inequality of Man,* 1890

Hail to the conquered. (Io victis.)

LATIN SAYING

[*See also* Conqueror, Imperialism, Sign, Victory, War.

Conquest, Norman

Twenty thousand thieves landed at Hastings. These founders of the House of Lords were greedy and ferocious dragoons, sons of greedy and ferocious pirates.

R. W. EMERSON: *English Traits,* IV, 1856

Consanguinity

None of you shall approach to any that is near of kin to him, to uncover their nakedness.

LEVITICUS XVIII, 6, *c.* 700 B.C. (A detailed list of the prohibited degrees follows, LEVITICUS XVIII, 7–18. It is also found in LEVITICUS XX, 11–21)

Conscience

When conscience discovers nothing wrong, what is there to be uneasy about, what is there to fear?

CONFUCIUS: *Analects,* XI, *c.* 500 B.C.

The wicked flee when no man pursueth.

PROVERBS XXVIII, 1, *c.* 350 B.C.

There is no witness so terrible, no accuser so potent, as the conscience that dwells in every man's breast.
POLYBIUS: *Histories,* XVIII, *c.* 125 B.C.

Conscience is a thousand witnesses.
RICHARD TAVERNER: *Proverbs,* 1539

The laws of conscience, though we ascribe them to nature, actually come from custom.
MICHEL DE MONTAIGNE: *Essays,* II, 1580

A clear conscience needeth no excuse, nor feareth any accusation.
JOHN LYLY: *Euphues,* 1579

A man cannot steal, but it accuseth him; he cannot swear, but it checks him; he cannot lie with his neighbor's wife, but it detects him: 'tis a blushing, shamefast spirit that mutinies in a man's bosom.
SHAKESPEARE: *Richard III,* I, *c.* 1592

The worm of conscience. IBID.

Conscience is but a word that cowards use,
Devised at first to keep the strong in awe.
SHAKESPEARE: *Richard III,* V

My conscience is my crown,
Contented thoughts my rest;
My heart is happy in itself;
My bliss is in my breast.
ROBERT SOUTHWELL: *Content and Rich,* *c.* 1595

A guilty conscience needs no accuser.
ENGLISH PROVERB, traced by Apperson to 1598

Conscience does make cowards of us all.
SHAKESPEARE: *Hamlet,* III, *c.* 1601

Your conscience is too nice,
And bites too hotly of the Puritan spice.
GEORGE CHAPMAN: *Bussy d'Ambois,* III, 1604

A guilty conscience feels continual fear.
MICHAEL DRAYTON: *The Owl,* 1604

I feel within me
A peace above all earthly dignities;
A still and quiet conscience.
SHAKESPEARE and JOHN FLETCHER: *Henry VIII,* III, 1613

A good conscience is a continual feast.
ROBERT BURTON: *The Anatomy of Melancholy,* II, 1621

There is another man within me that's angry with me.
THOMAS BROWNE: *Religio Medici,* II, 1642

Woe be to that man who shall tie himself so close to the letter of the law as to make shipwreck of conscience, that bird in his bosom.
JOSEPH HALL (BISHOP OF NORWICH): *Cases of Conscience,* II, *c.* 1645

Freedom of conscience is a natural right, both antecedent and superior to all human laws and institutions whatever: a right which laws never gave and which laws never take away.
JOHN GOODWIN: *Might and Right Well Met,* 1648

A man's conscience and his judgment is the same thing, and as the judgment, so also the conscience may be erroneous.
THOMAS HOBBES: *Leviathan,* II, 1651

Why should not conscience have vacation
As well as other courts o' th' nation?
SAMUEL BUTLER: *Hudibras,* II, 1664

O conscience, into what abyss of fears
And horrors hast thou driven me; out of which
I find no way, from deep to deeper plung'd!
JOHN MILTON: *Paradise Lost,* X, 1667

Conscience that can see without light, sits in the areopagy and dark tribunal of our hearts, surveying our thoughts and condemning their obliquities.
THOMAS BROWNE: *Christian Morals,* III, *c.* 1680

He that hath a scrupulous conscience is like a horse that is not well weigh'd: he starts at every bird that flies out of the hedge.
JOHN SELDEN: *Table-Talk,* 1689

Conscience, avaunt! Richard's himself again.
COLLEY CIBBER: Adaptation of SHAKESPEARE: *Richard III,* V, 1700

A quiet conscience sleeps in thunder.
THOMAS FULLER: *Gnomologia,* 1732

It is always term-time in the court of conscience. IBID.

Not to hear conscience is the way to silence it.
IBID.

A man that will enjoy a quiet conscience must lead a quiet life.
LORD CHESTERFIELD: *Letter to his son,* April 24, 1741

A good conscience is a continual Christmas.
BENJAMIN FRANKLIN: *Poor Richard's Almanac,* 1741 (Cf. BURTON, *ante,* 1621)

Labor to keep alive in your breast that little spark of celestial fire called conscience.
GEORGE WASHINGTON: *Early copy-book,* before 1748

Conscience without judgment is superstition.
BENJAMIN WHICHCOTE: *Moral and Religious Aphorisms,* 1753

In men it is necessary that the rational principle, or the intellectual discernment of right and wrong, should be aided by instinctive determinations. The dictates of mere reason, being slow and deliberate, would be otherwise much too weak.
RICHARD PRICE: *The Principal Questions in Morals,* II, 1758

Trust that man in nothing who has not a conscience in everything.
LAURENCE STERNE: *Tristram Shandy*, II, 1760

Whence do I get my rules of conduct? I find them in my heart. Whatever I feel to be good is good. Whatever I feel to be evil is evil. Conscience is the best of casuists.
J.-J. ROUSSEAU: *Émile*, X, 1762

Conscience admonishes as a friend before punishing us as a judge.
STANISLAUS LESZCYNSKI (KING OF POLAND): *Oeuvres du philosophe bienfaisant*, 1763

Conscience is a coward, and those faults it has not strength to prevent it seldom has justice enough to accuse.
OLIVER GOLDSMITH: *The Vicar of Wakefield*, XIII, 1766

In questions of law or of fact conscience is very often confounded with opinion. No man's conscience can tell him the rights of another man; they must be known by rational investigation or historical inquiry.
SAMUEL JOHNSON: Memorandum prepared for James Boswell, 1773

Conscience is an instinct to judge ourselves in the light of moral laws. It is not a mere faculty; it is an instinct.
IMMANUEL KANT: Lecture at Königsberg, 1775

It is inconsistent with the spirit of our laws and Constitution to force tender consciences.
THOMAS JEFFERSON: Proclamation concerning paroles, 1781

The worm of conscience keeps the same hours as the owl.
J. C. F. SCHILLER: *Kabala und Liebe*, V, 1784

The still small voice.
WILLIAM COWPER: *The Task*, V, 1785

In early days the conscience has in most
A quickness which in later life is lost.
WILLIAM COWPER: *Tirocinium*, 1785

Governments being, among other purposes, instituted to protect the consciences of men from oppression, it certainly is the duty of rulers, not only to abstain from it themselves, but, according to their stations, to prevent it in others.
GEORGE WASHINGTON: Address to the Quakers, 1785

The moral sense, or conscience, is as much a part of man as his leg or arm. It is given to all human beings in a stronger or weaker degree, as force of members is given them in a greater or less degree.
THOMAS JEFFERSON: *Letter to Peter Carr*, 1787

He that will judge of the first principles of morals must consult his conscience, or moral faculty, when he is calm and dispassionate, unbiased by interest, affection, or fashion.
THOMAS REID: *Essays on the Active Powers of Man*, III, 1788

We are bound, you, I, and every one, to make common cause, even with error itself, to maintain the common right of freedom of conscience.
THOMAS JEFFERSON: *Letter to Edward Dowse*, 1803

The wormwood of conscience embitters even sorrow.
JEAN PAUL RICHTER: *Titan*, XCIII, 1803

Conscience, that undying serpent, calls
Her venomous brood to their nocturnal task.
P. B. SHELLEY: *Queen Mab*, III, 1813

Conscience is but the pulse of reason.
S. T. COLERIDGE: *Zapolya*, I, 1817

A quiet conscience makes one so serene!
Christians have burnt each other, quite persuaded
That all the Apostles would have done as they did.
BYRON: *Don Juan*, I, 1819

Save me from curious conscience, that still lords
Its strength for darkness, burrowing like a mole.
JOHN KEATS: *To Sleep*, 1819

Conscience is a thing of fictitious existence, supposed to occupy a seat in the mind.
JEREMY BENTHAM: *Deontology*, I, 1834

Conscience is, in most men, an anticipation of the opinion of others.
HENRY TAYLOR: *The Statesman*, 1836

All men feel a necessity of being on some terms with their conscience, at their own expense, or at another's. If they cannot part with their faults, they will at least call them by their right names when they meet with such faults elsewhere.
J. A. FROUDE: *The Dissolution of the Monasteries*, 1857 (Fraser's Magazine)

The most miserable pettifogging in the world is that of a man in the court of his own conscience.
H. W. BEECHER: *Life Thoughts*, 1858

Conscience is an imitation within ourselves of the government without us.
ALEXANDER BAIN: *The Emotions and the Will*, 1859

Conscience is the chaos of chimeras, envies, and attempts, the furnace of dreams, the lurking-place of ideas we are ashamed of; it is the pandemonium of sophistry, the battlefield of the passions.
VICTOR HUGO: *Les Misérables*, LI, 1862

I desire so to conduct the affairs of this administration that if at the end, when I come to lay down the reins of power, I have lost every other friend on earth, I shall at least have one friend left, and that friend shall be down inside of me.

ABRAHAM LINCOLN: Reply to a committee proposing a plan of peace, 1864

Any animal whatever, endowed with well-marked social instincts, the parental and filial affections being here included, would inevitably acquire a moral sense or conscience, as soon as its intellectual powers had become as well, or nearly as well, developed as in man.

CHARLES DARWIN: *The Descent of Man*, IV, 1871

The sting of conscience, like the gnawing of a dog at a bone, is mere foolishness.

F. W. NIETZSCHE: *Human All-too-Human*, II, 1878

One may so train one's conscience that it kisses one when it bites.

F. W. NIETZSCHE: *Beyond Good and Evil*, 1886

A bad conscience is a kind of illness, in the sense that pregnancy is an illness.

F. W. NIETZSCHE: *The Genealogy of Morals*, II, 1887

Conscience and cowardice are really the same things. Conscience is the trade-name of the firm.

OSCAR WILDE: *The Picture of Dorian Gray*, 1891

Conscience makes egoists of us all. IBID.

A good conscience pays badly.

CHINESE PROVERB

Listen to conscience, and you will have nothing to eat. IBID.

There is no pillow so soft as a clear conscience.

FRENCH PROVERB

A clear conscience is like a wall of brass. (Murus aheneus conscientia sana.)

LATIN PROVERB

[*See also* Art, Courage, Digestion, Gallantry, Golden Rule, Guilt, Happiness, Health, Honor, Industry, Liberty, Millionaire, Morality, Politics, Skeptic, Villain.

Consciousness

There is no consciousness except when molecular disturbance is generated in the cerebrum and cerebellum faster than it can be drafted off to the lower centers.

JOHN FISKE: *The Destiny of Man*, V, 1884

It is the name of a nonentity, and has no right to a place among first principles. Those who still cling to it are clinging to a mere echo, the faint rumor left behind by the disappearing " soul " upon the air of philosophy.

WILLIAM JAMES: *Essays in Radical Empiricism*, I, 1912

Conscription

A military force cannot be raised in this manner but by the means of a military force.

DANIEL WEBSTER: Speech in the House of Representatives, Dec. 9, 1814

This republic has no place for a vast military service and conscription.

Democratic National Platform, 1900

They talk about conscription as being a democratic institution. Yes; so is a cemetery.

MEYER LONDON: Speech in House of Representatives, April 25, 1917

In order fully to protect the achievements of the workers' and peasants' revolution, the Russian Socialist Federated Republic declares it to be the duty of all the citizens of the Republic to protect their Socialist country and introduces conscription. The honorable right to defend the revolution by force of arms is bestowed only on the workers. Non-working elements have to carry out other military duties.

CONSTITUTION OF THE U.S.S.R., 1, 1924

[*See also* Army, Soldier.

Consecration

We cannot dedicate — we cannot consecrate — we cannot hallow — this ground. The brave men, living and dead, who struggled here have consecrated it far above our poor power to add or detract. The world will little note, nor long remember, what we say here, but it can never forget what they did here.

ABRAHAM LINCOLN: Gettysburg Address, Nov. 19, 1863

Consent

And whispering " I will ne'er consent " — consented. BYRON: *Don Juan*, I, 1819

Consent makes injury impossible. (Volenti non fit injuria.) LEGAL MAXIM

Long sufferance is equal to consent. (Longa patientia trahitur ad consensum.) IBID.

They do not consent who act under a mistake. (Non videntur qui errant consentire.)

IBID.

[*See also* Fraud, Silence.

Conservatism

Be not the first by whom the new are tried,
Nor yet the last to lay the old aside.

ALEXANDER POPE: *An Essay on Criticism*, II, 1711

There is always a certain meanness in the argument of conservatism, joined with a certain superiority in its fact.

R. W. EMERSON: *The Conservative*, 1841

All great peoples are conservative; slow to believe in novelties; patient of much error in actualities; deeply and forever certain of the greatness that is in law, in custom once solemnly established, and now long recognized as just and final.

THOMAS CARLYLE: *Past and Present*, III, 1843

A Conservative government is an organized hypocrisy.

BENJAMIN DISRAELI: Speech in the House of Commons, March 17, 1845

Conservatism defends those coercive arrangements which a still-lingering savageness makes requisite.

HERBERT SPENCER: *Social Statics*, III, 1851

The English power resides also in their dislike of change. They have difficulty in bringing their reason to act, and on all occasions use their memory first. As soon as they have rid themselves of some grievance, and settled the better practice, they make haste to fix it as a finality, and never wish to hear of alteration more.

R. W. EMERSON: *English Traits*, VI, 1856

What is conservatism? Is it not adherence to the old and tried, against the new and untried?

ABRAHAM LINCOLN: Speech in New York, Feb. 27, 1860

A bag with a hole in it.

H. W. SHAW (JOSH BILLINGS): *Josh Billings' Comical Lexicon*, 1877

Savages are the most conservative of human beings.

A. H. SAYCE: *Introduction to the Science of Language*, I, 1879

The Conservative party have always said that, on the whole, their policy meant that people had to fill up fewer forms than under the policies of other parties.

A. P. HERBERT: Speech in the House of Commons, Nov. 29, 1937

Conservative

A Conservative is only a Tory who is ashamed of himself.

Ascribed to J. HOOKHAM FRERE (1769–1846)

The man for whom the law exists — the man of forms, the Conservative, is a tame man.

H. D. THOREAU: *An Essay on Civil Disobedience*, 1849

All conservatives are such from personal defects. They have been effeminated by position or nature, born halt and blind, through luxury of their parents, and can only, like invalids, act on the defensive.

R. W. EMERSON: *The Conduct of Life*, I, 1860

The most conservative persons I ever met are college undergraduates.

WOODROW WILSON: Speech in New York, Nov. 19, 1905

A statesman who is enamored of existing evils, as distinguished from the Liberal, who wishes to replace them with others.

AMBROSE BIERCE: *The Devil's Dictionary*, 1906

A Conservative is a man with two perfectly good legs who, however, has never learned to walk.

F. D. ROOSEVELT: Radio speech, Oct. 26, 1939

Consistency

A foolish consistency is the hobgoblin of little minds, adored by little statesmen and philosophers and divines. With consistency a great soul has simply nothing to do.

R. W. EMERSON: *Self-Reliance*, 1841

Whoever in his public service is handcuffed and shackled by the vice of consistency will be a man not free to act as various questions come before him from time to time; he will be a statesman locked in a prison house the keys to which are in the keeping of days and events that are dead.

HENRY F. ASHURST: Speech in the Senate, Feb. 24, 1937

[*See also* Inconsistency.

Consolation

Grief is crowned with consolation.

SHAKESPEARE: *Antony and Cleopatra*, I, *c.* 1606

Before the affliction is digested consolation comes too soon, and after it is digested it comes too late.

LAURENCE STERNE: *Tristram Shandy*, III, 1761

Cry, baby, cry.
Take your little shirttail
And wipe your eye,
And go tell your mammy
To give you a piece of pie.

RAY WOOD: *Mother Goose in the Ozarks*, 1938

Do not try to console a man while the corpse is still in the house.

HEBREW PROVERB

[*See also* Condolence.

Consonant

[*See* Language.

Conspiracy

Whoso diggeth a pit shall fall therein.

PROVERBS XXVI, 27, *c.* 350 B.C.

Constancy

What is there in this vile earth that more commendeth a woman than constancy?

JOHN LYLY: *Euphues*, 1579

I am constant as the northern star,
Of whose true fix'd and resting quality
There is no fellow in the firmament.

SHAKESPEARE: *Julius Caesar*, III, 1599

Out upon it, I have loved
Three whole days together!
And am like to love three more,
If it prove fair weather.
JOHN SUCKLING: *Constancy,* 1638

Through perils both of wind and limb,
Through thick and thin she follow'd him.
SAMUEL BUTLER: *Hudibras,* I, 1663

Constancy is a perpetual inconstancy which causes our heart to attach itself to all the qualities of the person we love in succession, sometimes giving the preference to one, sometimes to another. This constancy is merely inconstancy fixed and limited to the same person.
LA ROCHEFOUCAULD: *Maxims,* 1665

There are two sorts of constancy in love — one arises from continually discovering in the loved person new subjects for love, the other arises from our making a merit of being constant. IBID.

The wife seldom rambles till the husband shows her the way.
JOHN VANBRUGH: *The Provok'd Wife,* V, 1697

Constancy is but a dull sleepy quality at best.
GEORGE FARQUHAR: *The Recruiting Officer,* I, 1706

When I am wearied with wand'ring all day,
To thee, my delight, in the evening I come:
No matter what beauties I saw in my way;
They were but my visits, but thou art my home.
MATTHEW PRIOR: *A Better Answer, to Chloe Jealous, c.* 1715

And I will luve thee still, my dear,
Till a' the seas gang dry:
Till a' the seas gang dry, my dear,
And the rocks melt wi' the sun;
I will luve thee still, my dear,
While the sands o' life shall run.
ROBERT BURNS: *A Red, Red Rose,* 1784

Constancy has nothing virtuous in itself, independently of the pleasure it confers.
P. B. SHELLEY: *Queen Mab,* notes, 1813

It is as absurd to say that a man can't love one woman all the time as it is to say that a violinist needs several violins to play the same piece of music.
BALZAC: *The Physiology of Marriage,* 1830

No lapse of moons can canker love,
Whatever fickle tongues may say.
ALFRED TENNYSON: *In Memoriam,* XXVI, 1850

[*See also* Courtship, Lover, Success.

Constantine the Great (274–337)

The Christian reptile.
P. B. SHELLEY: *Letter to T. L. Peacock,* Dec. 22, 1818

Constitution

Constitutions should consist only of general provisions; the reason is that they must necessarily be permanent, and that they cannot calculate for the possible change of things.
ALEXANDER HAMILTON: Speech in the Senate, June 28, 1788

A constitution is a thing antecedent to a government, and a government is only the creature of a constitution. The constitution of a country is not the act of its government, but of the people constituting a government.
THOMAS PAINE: *The Rights of Man,* I, 1791

The legislative authority of any country can only be restrained by its own municipal constitution. This is a principle that springs from the very nature of society; and the judicial authority can have no right to question the validity of a law unless such a jurisdiction is expressly given by the constitution.
JOHN MARSHALL: Argument as counsel in *Ware* vs. *Hilton,* 1796

The basis of our political systems is the right of the people to make and to alter their constitutions of government. But the constitution which at any time exists, until changed by an explicit and authentic act of the whole people, is sacredly obligatory upon all.
GEORGE WASHINGTON: Farewell Address, Sept. 17, 1776

In questions of power let no more be heard of confidence in man, but bind him down from mischief by the chains of the constitution.
THOMAS JEFFERSON: *Kentucky Resolutions,* Nov., 1798

A good constitution is infinitely better than the best despot.
T. B. MACAULAY: *Milton,* 1825 (Edinburgh Review, Aug.)

Sire, your character is itself a constitution.
ANNA LOUISE DE STÄEL: To Alexander I of Russia (1777–1825)

All trust in constitutions is grounded on the assurance they may afford, not that the depositories of power will not, but that they cannot, misemploy it.
J. S. MILL: *Representative Government,* VIII, 1861

The political constitution of a society is at once the expression and the consecration of its economic constitution.
P. A. KROPOTKIN: *Paroles d'un révolté,* 1884

It is very doubtful whether man is enough of a political animal to produce a good, sensible, serious and efficient constitution. All the evidence is against it.
GEORGE BERNARD SHAW: Address in New York, April 11, 1933

[*See also* Government (Free).

Constitutionality

I hope your committee will not permit doubts as to constitutionality, however reasonable, to block the suggested legislation.

F. D. ROOSEVELT: *Letter to the Ways and Means Committee of the House of Representatives* (on the Guffey-Snyder Coal Bill), July, 1935

Constitution, American

Should the states reject this excellent Constitution, the probability is that an opportunity will never again offer to make another in peace, — the next will be drawn in blood.

GEORGE WASHINGTON: Upon signing the Constitution, Sept. 17, 1787

There are very good articles in it, and very bad. I do not know which preponderate.

THOMAS JEFFERSON: *Letter to W. S. Smith,* Nov., 1787

The Constitution . . . is unquestionably the wisest ever yet presented to men.

THOMAS JEFFERSON: *Letter to David Humphreys,* March, 1789

If, in the opinion of the people, the distribution or modification of the constitutional powers be in any particular wrong, let it be corrected by an amendment in the way which the Constitution designates. But let there be no change by usurpation.

GEORGE WASHINGTON: Farewell Address, Sept. 17, 1796

The particular phraseology of the Constitution of the United States confirms and strengthens the principle, supposed to be essential to all written constitutions, that a law repugnant to the Constitution is void; and that courts, as well as other departments, are bound by that instrument.

JOHN MARSHALL: *Opinion as Chief Justice in Marburg* vs. *Madison,* 1802

By the tables of mortality, of the adults living at one moment of time, a majority will be dead in about nineteen years. At the end of that period, then, a new majority is come into place; or, in other words, a new generation. Each generation is as independent of the one preceding, as that was of all which had gone before. It has, then, like them, a right to choose for itself the form of government it believes most promotive of its own happiness; consequently, a solemn opportunity of doing this every nineteen or twenty years should be provided by the Constitution.

THOMAS JEFFERSON: *Letter to W. H. Torrance,* 1815

Some men look at constitutions with sanctimonious reverence, and deem them like the Ark of the Covenant, too sacred to be touched. They ascribe to the men of the preceding age a wisdom more than human, and suppose what they did to be beyond amendment. I knew that age well; I belonged to it, and labored with it. It deserved well of its country. It was very like the present, but without the experience of the present; and forty years of experience in government is worth a century of book-reading.

THOMAS JEFFERSON: *Letter to Samuel Kercheval,* July 12, 1816

I yield slowly and reluctantly to the conviction that our Constitution cannot last. Our opinions are incompatible with a united government, even among ourselves. The Union has been preserved thus far by miracles. I fear they cannot continue.

JOHN MARSHALL: *Letter to Joseph Story,* 1832

When the Constitution was first framed I predicted that it would last fifty years. I was mistaken. It will evidently last longer than that. But I was mistaken only in point of time. The crash will come, but not quite so quick as I thought.

Ascribed to AARON BURR in JAMES PARTON: *Life and Times of Aaron Burr,* 1858 (*c.* 1835)

We may be tossed upon an ocean where we can see no land — nor, perhaps, the sun or stars. But there is a chart and a compass for us to study, to consult, and to obey. That chart is the Constitution.

DANIEL WEBSTER: Speech at Springfield, Mass., Sept. 29, 1847

The Constitution of the United States was made not merely for the generation that then existed, but for posterity — unlimited, undefined, endless, perpetual posterity.

HENRY CLAY: Speech in the Senate, Feb. 6, 1850

There is a higher law than the Constitution.

W. H. SEWARD: Speech in the Senate, March 11, 1850

Your Constitution is all sail and no anchor.

T. B. MACAULAY: *Letter to H. S. Randall,* May 23, 1857

All that is valuable in the Constitution is one thousand years old.

WENDELL PHILLIPS: Speech at Boston, Feb. 17, 1861

The Constitution of the United States is a law for rulers and people, equally in war and in peace, and covers with the shield of its protection all classes of men, at all times and under all circumstances. No doctrine involving more pernicious consequences was ever invented by the wit of man than that any of its provisions can be suspended during any of the great exigencies of government.

MR. JUSTICE DAVID DAVIS: *Decision in* Ex parte *Milligan,* 1866

Outside of the Constitution we have no legal authority more than private citizens, and

within it we have only so much as that instrument gives us.
ANDREW JOHNSON: Message to the House of Representatives, March 2, 1867

The American Constitution is the most wonderful work ever struck off at a given time by the brain and purpose of man.
W. E. GLADSTONE: *Kin Beyond Sea,* 1878 (North American Review, Sept.–Oct.)

What's the Constitution among friends?
Ascribed to Congressman TIMOTHY CAMPBELL, of New York, *c.* 1885

A constitution is not intended to embody a particular economic theory. It is made for people of fundamentally differing views, and the accident of our finding certain opinions natural and familiar or novel and even shocking ought not to conclude our judgment upon the question whether statutes embodying them conflict with the Constitution of the United States.
MR. JUSTICE O. W. HOLMES: *Dissenting opinion in Lochner* vs. *New York,* 1904

We are under a Constitution, but the Constitution is what the judges say it is.
CHARLES E. HUGHES: Speech at Elmira, N. Y., May 3, 1907

Whenever the Constitution comes between men and the virtue of the white women of South Carolina, I say — to Hell with the Constitution!
COLE L. BLEASE: Public statement as Governor of South Carolina, 1911

The United States Constitution has proved itself the most marvelously elastic compilation of rules of government ever written.
F. D. ROOSEVELT: Radio speech, March 2, 1930

Our Constitution is so simple and practical that it is possible always to meet extraordinary needs by changes in emphasis and arrangement without loss of essential form.
F. D. ROOSEVELT: Inaugural address, March 4, 1933

When you came to examine the American Constitution, you found that it was not really a constitution, but a Charter of Anarchism. It was not an instrument of government: it was a guarantee to the whole American nation that it never should be governed at all. And that is exactly what the Americans wanted.
GEORGE BERNARD SHAW: Address in New York, April 11, 1933

Keep your eye on the Constitution. This is the guarantee, that is the safeguard, that is the night watchman of democratic representative government — freedom of speech, freedom of the press, the right of public assembly and the right to petition the government. Save all these things in the Constitution and let the Supreme Court stand behind it, and then you can get off all the hot air in Congress and in the Senate that you want to.
ALFRED E. SMITH: Speech at Harvard, June 22, 1933

If the Constitution is to be construed to mean what the majority at any given period in history wish the Constitution to mean, why a written Constitution and deliberate processes of amendment?
FRANK J. HOGAN: Presidential address before the American Bar Association, San Francisco, July 10, 1939

[*See also* Charity, Checks and Balances, Church and State, Fourteenth Amendment, Imperialism, Judiciary, Powers (Reserved), Rights (Bill of), Slavery, Treaty, Twentieth Amendment, Union (American), United States.

Constitution, English

The excellence of our constitution consists in the balance of three powers. Unfortunately it is the nature of a balance to fluctuate by a breath of air.
HORACE WALPOLE: *Letter to the Countess of Upper Ossory,* Dec. 9, 1790

England presents a singular phenomenon of an honest people whose constitution, from its nature, must render their government forever dishonest.
THOMAS JEFFERSON: *Letter to James Ronaldson,* 1810

We shall never make the constitution of England a strictly logical one, and I do not think that it is desirable that we should try.
BENJAMIN DISRAELI: Speech in the House of Commons, 1867

[*See also* Property.

Constructive

There is a prevalent idea that the constructive genius is in itself something grander than the critical, even though the former turns out to have merely made a symmetrical rubbish heap in the middle of the road of science, which the latter has to clear away before anybody can get forward.
T. H. HUXLEY: *Government,* 1890

[*See also* Criticism, Destruction.

Contemporary

[*See* Criticism.

Contempt

Contempt is the subtlest form of revenge.
BALTASAR GRACIÁN: *The Art of Worldly Wisdom,* CCV, 1647

When you cannot get a thing, then is the time to have contempt for it.
BALTASAR GRACIÁN: *The Art of Worldly Wisdom,* CCXX

I despise the pleasure of pleasing people that I despise.

MARY WORTLEY MONTAGU: *Letter to Wortley Montagu,* March 24, 1711

Many can bear adversity, but few contempt.

THOMAS FULLER: *Gnomologia,* 1732

There is nothing that people bear more impatiently, or forgive less, than contempt; and an injury is much sooner forgotten than an insult.

LORD CHESTERFIELD: *Letter to his son,* Oct. 9, 1746

Contempt is egotism in ill humor.

S. T. COLERIDGE: *Omniana,* CX, 1812

Contempt is the sharpest reproof.

H. G. BOHN: *Handbook of Proverbs,* 1855

Man is much more sensitive to the contempt of others than to self-contempt.

F. W. NIETZSCHE: *Human All-too-Human,* I, 1878

Contempt penetrates even the shell of the tortoise.

PERSIAN PROVERB

[*See also* Familiarity, Hatred, Laughter.

Contempt of Court

There are three different sorts of contempt. One kind is scandalizing the court itself. There may likewise be a contempt of this court in abusing parties who are concerned in causes here. There may be also a contempt of this court in prejudicing mankind against persons before the cause is heard.

LORD CHANCELLOR HARDWICKE: *Judgment in Roach* vs. *Garvan,* 1742

Judges and courts are alike open to criticism, and if reasonable argument or expostulation is offered against any judicial act as contrary to law or the public good, no court could or would treat it as contempt of court.

LORD RUSSELL OF KILLOWEN: *Judgment in Regina* vs. *Gray,* 1900

[*See also* Judge.

Contention

The beginning of strife is as when one letteth out water: therefore leave off contention, before it be meddled with.

PROVERBS XVII, 14, *c.* 350 B.C.

It is better to dwell in the wilderness than with a contentious and an angry woman.

PROVERBS XXI, 19

As coals are to burning coals, and wood to fire, so is a contentious man to kindle strife.

PROVERBS XXVI, 21

A continual dropping in a very rainy day and a contentious woman are alike.

PROVERBS XXVII, 15

In an hundred ells of contention there is not an inch of love.

GEORGE HERBERT: *Outlandish Proverbs,* 1640

Contentment

With only plain rice to eat, with only water to drink, and with only an arm for a pillow, I am still content.

CONFUCIUS: *Analects,* VII, *c.* 500 B.C.

The greatest wealth is to live content with little, for there is never want where the mind is satisfied.

LUCRETIUS: *De rerum natura,* V, 57 B.C.

I have learned, in whatsoever state I am, therewith to be content.

PHILIPPIANS IV, 11, *c.* 60

Be content with such things as ye have.

HEBREWS XIII, 5, *c.* 65

Fit thyself into the environment that thou findest on earth, and love the men with whom thy lot is cast.

MARCUS AURELIUS: *Meditations,* VI, *c.* 170

The contented mind is the only riches, the only quietness, the only happiness.

GEORGE PETTIE: *Petite Palace of Pettie His Pleasure,* 1576

Here below there is no satisfaction or content except for brutal or divine minds.

MICHEL DE MONTAIGNE: *Essays,* III, 1588

The noblest mind the best contentment has.

EDMUND SPENSER: *The Faerie Queene,* I, *c.* 1589

Sweet are the thoughts that savor of content,
The quiet mind is richer than a crown.

ROBERT GREENE: *Maesia's Song, c.* 1590

My crown is in my heart, not on my head;
Not deck'd with diamonds and Indian stones,
Nor to be seen: my crown is called content;
A crown it is that seldom kings enjoy.

SHAKESPEARE: *III Henry VI,* III, *c.* 1591

A contented mind is a continual feast.

ENGLISH PROVERB, traced by Apperson to 1592

I earn that I eat, get that I wear, owe no man hate, envy no man's happiness; glad of other men's good, content with my harm.

SHAKESPEARE: *As You Like It,* III, *c.* 1600

Poor and content is rich and rich enough.

SHAKESPEARE: *Othello,* III, 1604

I would do what I pleased, and doing what I pleased, I should have my will, and having my will, I should be contented; and when one is contented, there is no more to be desired; and when there is no more to be desired, there is an end of it.

CERVANTES: *Don Quixote,* I, 1605

'Tis better to be lowly born,
And range with humble livers in content,

Than to be perk'd up in a glistering grief,
And wear a golden sorrow.

SHAKESPEARE and JOHN FLETCHER: *Henry VIII*, II, 1613

Content is more than kingdom.

ENGLISH PROVERB, traced by Apperson to 1639

He that studies his content wants it.

GEORGE HERBERT: *Outlandish Proverbs*, 1640

Learn this of me, where e'r thy lot doth fall;
Short lot, or not, to be content with all.

ROBERT HERRICK: *Hesperides*, 1648

When we cannot find contentment in ourselves it is useless to seek it elsewhere.

LA ROCHEFOUCAULD: *Maxims*, 1665

He may well be contented who needs neither borrow nor flatter.

JOHN RAY: *English Proverbs*, 1670

The greatest wealth is contentment with a little.

IBID.

Happy the man, of mortals happiest he,
Whose quiet mind from vain desires is free;
Whom neither hopes deceive, nor fears torment,
But lives at peace, within himself content.

GEORGE GRANVILLE (LORD LANSDOWNE): *Epistle to Mrs. Higgins*, 1690

Happy the man whose wish and care
A few paternal acres bound,
Content to breathe his native air
In his own ground.
Whose herds with milk, whose fields with bread,
Whose flocks supply him with attire,
Whose trees in Summer yield him shade;
In Winter, fire.

ALEXANDER POPE: *Ode to Solitude*, *c.* 1700 (Pope says in a letter to Henry Cromwell, July 17, 1709, that it was written when he was " not twelve years old ")

The utmost we can hope for in this world is contentment; if we aim at anything higher, we shall meet with nothing but grief and disappointment.

JOSEPH ADDISON: *The Spectator*, Sept. 6, 1711

When the world trembles I'm unmoved,
When cloudy, I'm serene;
When darkness covers all without
I'm always bright within.

DANIEL DEFOE: *A Review of the Affairs of France and of All Europe*, VIII, 1712

Content is the philosopher's stone, which turns all it touches into gold.

THOMAS FULLER: *Gnomologia*, 1732

Contentment does not consist in heaping up more fuel, but in taking away some fire.

IBID.

Content makes poor men rich; discontent makes rich men poor.

BENJAMIN FRANKLIN: *Poor Richard's Almanac*, 1749

Who is rich? He that is content. Who is that? Nobody. IBID.

There was a jolly miller once,
Lived on the River Dee;
He worked and sang, from morn to night;
No lark so blithe as he.
And this the burden of his song,
Forever used to be, —
" I care for nobody, not I,
If no one cares for me."

ISAAC BICKERSTAFF: *Love in a Village*, I, 1762

Where wealth and freedom reign contentment fails.

OLIVER GOLDSMITH: *The Traveler*, 1764

My motto is " contented with little, yet wishing for more."

CHARLES LAMB: *Letter to William Wordsworth*, Oct. 13, 1800

Not loath to die, but yet to live content.

GEORGE CRABBE: *The Parish Register*, II, 1807

And Freedom, leaning on her spear,
Laughs louder than the laughing giant;
Some good bank-stock, some note of hand,
Or trifling railroad share, —
I only ask that fortune send
A little more than I shall spend.

O. W. HOLMES: *Contentment*, 1857 (In *The Autocrat of the Breakfast-Table*)

Contentment iz a kind ov moral laziness; if thare want ennything but kontentment in his world, man wouldn't be any more of a suck-cess than an angleworm iz.

H. W. SHAW (JOSH BILLINGS): *Josh Billings' Encyclopedia of Wit and Wisdom*, 1874

No man is content with his lot. (Nemo sua sorte contentus.) LATIN PROVERB

[*See also* Cosmetics, Happiness, Labor, Poor, Wages.

Continence

Continence is an angelic exercise.

ST. AUGUSTINE: *On the Good of Marriage*, *c.* 401

Continence is a greater good than marriage. But I am aware of some that murmur: if all men should abstain from intercourse, how will the human race exist? Would that all would abstain; much more speedily would the City of God be filled, and the end of the world hastened. IBID.

It is praiseworthy that even during the life of her husband, by his consent, a female vow continence unto Christ.

ST. AUGUSTINE: *On the Good of Widowhood*, *c.* 413

Me of my lawful pleasure she restrained
And prayed me oft forbearance; did it with
A pudency so rosy the sweet view on't
Might well have warmed old Saturn.

SHAKESPEARE: *Cymbeline*, II, *c.* 1609

Continence hath his joy; weigh both, and so,
If rottenness have more let Heaven go.

GEORGE HERBERT: *The Temple*, 1633

Rarely use venery but for health or offspring, never to dullness, weakness, or the injury of your own or another's peace or reputation.

BENJAMIN FRANKLIN: *Rules for his own conduct*, *c.* 1730

Continence, under some circumstances, is a duty, but is never a virtue, it being without any moral quality whatever.

R. G. WHITE: *Words and Their Uses*, V, 1870

[*See also* Celibacy, Chastity, Marriage, Piety.

Continental

In their ragged regimentals,
Stood the old Continentals,
Yielding not.

G. H. MCMASTER: *Carmen Bellicosum*, 1849

Contract

Covenants are ever made according to the present state of persons and of things; and have ever the more general laws of nature and of reason included in them, though not expressed.

JOHN MILTON: *The Tenure of Kings and Magistrates*, 1649

The definition of injustice is no other than the not performance of covenant.

THOMAS HOBBES: *Leviathan*, I, 1651

This is the epitome of all the contracts in the world betwixt man and man, betwixt prince and subject: they keep them as long as they like them, and no longer.

JOHN SELDEN: *Table-Talk*, 1689

Contracts between a nation and individuals are only binding on the conscience of the sovereign, and have no pretensions to a compulsive force.

ALEXANDER HAMILTON: *The Federalist*, LXXXI, 1788

No state shall . . . pass any . . . law impairing the obligation of contracts.

CONSTITUTION OF THE UNITED STATES, Art. I, 1789

In order that I may govern myself and be subject to no law save my own we must rebuild the edifice of society on the idea of contract.

P. J. PROUDHON: *Idée générale de la révolution*, 1851

Pretty much all law consists in forbidding men to do some things they want to do, and contract is no more exempt from law than other acts.

MR. JUSTICE O. W. HOLMES: *Dissenting opinion in Adkins* vs. *Children's Hospital*, 1922

The reservation of the reasonable exercise of the protective power of the state is read into all contracts.

MR. CHIEF JUSTICE CHARLES E. HUGHES: *Decision in Home Building & Loan Association* vs. *Blaisdell*, Jan. 8, 1934

An ambiguous contract ought to be construed against the seller. (Ambiguum pactum contra venditorem interpretandum est.)

LEGAL MAXIM

A contract arising out of a base consideration, or against morality, is null. (Contractus ex turpi causa vel contra bonos mores, nullus.)

IBID.

From a contract without consideration no right of action can arise. (Ex turpi causa non oritur actio.)

IBID.

[*See also* Justice, Marriage, Treaty.

Contradiction

Do I contradict myself?
Very well, then, I contradict myself;
(I am large — I contain multitudes.)

WALT WHITMAN: *Walt Whitman*, 1855

Contralto

A female singer who makes a low sort of music.

Author unidentified

Contrary

Mistress Mary, quite contrary.

Anon.: *Nursery Rhyme*, *c.* 1750

Contrast

I love to mark sad faces in fair weather,
And hear a merry laugh amid the thunder.

JOHN KEATS: *Fragment*, *c.* 1817

Evermore in the world is this marvelous balance of beauty and disgust, magnificence and rats.

R. W. EMERSON: *The Conduct of Life*, VII, 1860

Contrast increases the splendor of beauty, but it disturbs its influence; it adds to its attractiveness, but diminishes its power.

JOHN RUSKIN: *Modern Painters*, II, 1860

Controversy

There is scarce any truth, but its adversaries have made it an ugly vizard, by which it's exposed to the hate and disesteem of superficial examiners. For an opprobrious title, with vulgar believers, is as good as an argument.

JOSEPH GLANVILL: *Scepsis Scientifica*, 1665

One cause is good until the other's understood.

Anon.: *Poor Robin's Almanac*, 1731

Some great decorum, some fetish of a government, some ephemeral trade, or war, or man, is cried up by half mankind and cried down by the other half, as if all depended on this particular up or down. The odds are that the whole question is not worth the poorest thought which the scholar has lost in listening to the controversy. Let him not quit his belief that a popgun is a popgun, though the ancient and honorable of the earth affirm it to be the crack of doom.

R. W. EMERSON: *The American Scholar*, 1837

The dust of controversy, what is it but the falsehood flying off from all manner of conflicting true forces, and making such a loud dust-whirlwind, — that so the truths alone may remain, and embrace brother-like in some true resulting force?

THOMAS CARLYLE: *Past and Present*, I, 1843

[*See also* Dispute.

Convent

I like convents, but I wish they would not admit anyone under the age of fifty.

NAPOLEON I: To Gaspard Gourgaud at St. Helena, 1815–1818

[*See also* Nun.

Conversation

The more the bodily pleasures decrease, the greater grows the desire for the pleasure of conversation.

PLATO: *The Republic*, I, *c.* 350 B.C.

Conversation is the image of the mind. As the man is, so is his talk.

PUBLILIUS SYRUS: *Sententiæ*, *c.* 50 B.C.

Consider him with whom you converse in one of these three ways: either as your superior, or inferior, or equal. If superior, you ought to hear him and be convinced; if inferior, to convince him; if equal, to agree with him; and thus you will never be led into the love of strife.

EPICTETUS: *Encheiridion*, *c.* 110

It is good to vary, and mix speech of the present occasion with arguments, tales with reasons, asking of questions with telling of opinions, and jest with earnest.

FRANCIS BACON: *Essays*, II, 1597

Delectable and pleasant conversation, whose property is to move a kindly delight, and sometimes not without laughter.

BEN JONSON: *Cynthia's Revels*, V, 1601

Confidence contributes more than wit to conversation.

LA ROCHEFOUCAULD: *Maxims*, 1665

The reason why so few people are agreeable in conversation is that each is thinking more about what he intends to say than about what others are saying, and we never listen when we are eager to speak. IBID.

Nothing makes a man hate a woman more than her constant conversation.

WILLIAM WYCHERLEY: *The Country Wife*, II, *c.* 1673

If the minds of men were laid open, we should see but little difference between that of the wise man and that of the fool. The great difference is that the first knows how to pick and cull his thoughts for conversation, by suppressing some and communicating others; whereas the other lets them all indifferently fly out in words.

JOSEPH ADDISON: *The Spectator*, Nov. 17, 1711

The free conversation of a friend is what I would prefer to any entertainment.

DAVID HUME: *Letter to Michael Ramsay*, July 4, 1727

If thou hast a mind to get esteemed in company, have the art to edge about till thou canst get into a subject thou hast studied and art master of.

THOMAS FULLER: *Introductio ad Prudentiam*, I, 1731

When you speak to a man, look on his eyes; when he speaks to thee, look on his mouth.

BENJAMIN FRANKLIN: *Poor Richard's Almanac*, 1740

The pleasure which men are able to give in conversation holds no stated proportion to their knowledge or their virtue.

SAMUEL JOHNSON: *The Rambler*, Jan. 4, 1752

They would talk of nothing but high life and high-lived company, with other fashionable topics, such as pictures, taste, Shakespeare, and musical glasses.

OLIVER GOLDSMITH: *The Vicar of Wakefield*, IX, 1766

In conversation you never get a system. What is said upon a subject is to be gathered from a hundred people. The parts which a man gets thus are at such a distance from each other that he never attains to a full view.

SAMUEL JOHNSON: *Boswell's Life*, April 16, 1775

The happiest conversation is that of which nothing is distinctly remembered, but a general effect of pleasing impression.

SAMUEL JOHNSON: *Boswell's Life*, 1781

Words learned by rote a parrot may rehearse,
But talking is not always to converse.

WILLIAM COWPER: *Conversation*, 1782

Speak not but what may benefit others or yourself; avoid trifling conversation.

BENJAMIN FRANKLIN: *Autobiography*, 1798

Passion, prejudice, party, and even good-will tempt many who preserve a fair character with the world to deviate from truth in the laxity of conversation.

MR. JUSTICE LAWRENCE: *Judgment in the Berkeley Peerage Case,* 1811

It is a very bad sign (unless where it arises from singular modesty) when you cannot tell a man's profession from his conversation. Such persons either feel no interest in what concerns them most, or do not express what they feel.

WILLIAM HAZLITT: *The Round Table,* II, 1817

Man of great conversational powers almost universally practise a sort of lively sophistry and exaggeration which deceives, for the moment, both themselves and their auditors.

T. B. MACAULAY: *The Athenian Orators,* 1824

A single conversation across the table with a wise man is better than ten years' study of books.

H. W. LONGFELLOW: *Hyperion,* VII, 1830 (A Chinese proverb)

Two may talk and one may hear, but three cannot take part in a conversation of the most sincere and searching sort. In good company, there is never such discourse between two, across the table, as takes place when you leave them alone.

R. W. EMERSON: *Friendship,* 1841

Most people, in conversing, force us to curse our stars that our lot was not cast among the African nation mentioned by Eudoxus — the savages who, having no mouths, never opened them, as a matter of course.

E. A. POE: *Marginalia,* 1844–49

Conversation teaches more than meditation.

H. G. BOHN: *Handbook of Proverbs,* 1855

Conversation is an art in which a man has all mankind for his competitors.

R. W. EMERSON: *The Conduct of Life,* VII, 1860

"The time has come," the Walrus said,
"To talk of many things:
Of shoes — and ships — and sealing-wax —
Of cabbages — and kings —
And why the sea is boiling hot —
And whether pigs have wings."

C. L. DODGSON (LEWIS CARROLL): *Through the Looking-Glass,* 1871

Debate is masculine; conversation is feminine.

A. BRONSON ALCOTT: *Concord Days,* 1872

Conversation should touch everything but should concentrate itself on nothing.

OSCAR WILDE: *The Critic as Artist,* 1891

A man is seldom better than his conversation.

GERMAN PROVERB

[*See also* Author, Biography, Boor, Conceit, Debate, Garrulity, Gentleman, Heaven, Music, Pun, Wit.

Conversion

All men shall be Christians in this land hereafter, and shall believe in God the Father, the Son and the Holy Ghost; they shall not worship idols, or expose children to perish, or eat horseflesh. If any man shall do any of these things he shall be outlawed.

Resolution of the Althing (parliament) of Iceland, 1000

This day, my dear, I take a perilous leap.

HENRY IV of France: To his mistress, Gabrielle d'Estrées, on entering the Catholic Church, July, 1593 (Quoted by Voltaire, on his death-bed, May 30, 1778)

Jack he got Bob under
And he slugged him onct or twict;
And Bob confessed almighty quick
The divinity of Christ.

Anon.: *Jack the Evangelist, c.* 1850

You have not converted a man because you have silenced him.

JOHN MORLEY: *On Compromise,* 1874

[*See also* Jew.

Convert

Their busy teachers mingled with the Jews,
And raked for converts even the court and stews.

JOHN DRYDEN: *Absalom and Achitophel,* I, 1682

Charming women can true converts make:
We love the precepts for the teacher's sake.

GEORGE FARQUHAR: *The Constant Couple,* V, 1699

Converts and renegadoes of all kinds should take particular care to let the world see they act upon honorable motives, for whatever approbations they may receive from themselves, and applauses from those they converse with, they may be very well assured that they are the scorn of all good men, and the public marks of infamy and derision.

JOSEPH ADDISON: *The Spectator,* Sept. 5, 1711

A man who is converted from Protestantism to popery parts with nothing; he is only superadding to what he already had. But a convert from popery to Protestantism gives up as much of what he has held sacred as anything that he retains.

SAMUEL JOHNSON: *Boswell's Life,* Oct. 26, 1769

Those who were strangers to God, felt, as it were, a sword in their bones, constraining them to roar aloud.

JOHN WESLEY: *Journal,* June 4, 1772

It is a contradiction and an impossibility that any Catholic should turn Protestant through honest motives. We might as well talk of

committing a grievous and heinous sin through honest motives.
GIOVANNI PERRONE: *Popular Catechism,* xv, 1854

[*See also* Proselyte.

Conviction

When by reading or discourse we find ourselves thoroughly convinced of the truth of any article, and of the reasonableness of our belief in it, we should never after suffer ourselves to call it in question.
JOSEPH ADDISON: *The Spectator,* Aug. 23, 1712

The sorriest sophistical Bellarmine, preaching sightless faith and passive obedience, must first, by some kind of conviction, have abdicated his right to be convinced.
THOMAS CARLYLE: *Heroes and Hero-Worship,* IV, 1841

Convictions are more dangerous to truth than lies.
F. W. NIETZSCHE: *Human All-too-Human,* I, 1878

Men of fixed convictions do not count when it comes to determining what is fundamental in values and lack of values. Men of convictions are prisoners.
F. W. NIETZSCHE: *The Antichrist,* LIV, 1888

What was a lie in the father becomes a conviction in the son.
F. W. NIETZSCHE: *The Antichrist,* LV

Every conviction has its history, its primitive forms, its stage of tentativeness and error: it becomes a conviction only after having been, for a long time, not one, and then, for an even longer time, hardly one. IBID.

Convictions are the mainsprings of action, the driving powers of life. What a man lives are his convictions.
FRANCIS C. KELLEY (BISHOP OF OKLAHOMA CITY AND TULSA): Address at Oklahoma City, Okla., Nov. 28, 1933

[*See also* Persuasion.

Cook

It is no wonder that diseases are innumerable: count the cooks.
SENECA: *Epistulae morales ad Lucilium,* *c.* 63

You think I am cruel and gluttonous when I beat my cook for sending in a bad dinner. But if that is too trivial a cause, what other can there be for beating a cook?
MARTIAL: *Epigrams,* VIII, *c.* 95

It's a bad cook who can't lick his own fingers.
ENGLISH PROVERB, traced by Apperson to *c.* 1520

God sends meat but the Devil sends cooks.
ENGLISH PROVERB, traced by Apperson to 1542

Cookery is become an art, a noble science; cooks are gentlemen.
ROBERT BURTON: *The Anatomy of Melancholy,* I, 1621

Too many cooks spoil the broth.
ENGLISH PROVERB, traced by Apperson to 1662

His cook is his chief merit. The world visits his dinners, not him.
J. B. MOLIÈRE: *Le misanthrope,* II, 1666

We may live without poetry, music and art;
We may live without conscience, and live without heart;
We may live without friends; we may live without books;
But civilized man cannot live without cooks.
E. R. BULWER-LYTTON: *Lucile,* I, 1860

The French would be the best cooks in Europe if they had got any butcher's meat.
WALTER BAGEHOT: *Biographical Studies,* 1880 (Cited as " the old saying ")

Woman does not understand what food means, and yet she insists upon being a cook!
F. W. NIETZSCHE: *Beyond Good and Evil,* 1886

One cook's a cook, two cooks are half a cook, and three cooks are no cook at all.
Author unidentified

Too many cooks make the soup too salty.
DUTCH PROVERB

Cooks are made, roasters are born.
FRENCH PROVERB

The cook and butler are never enemies.
ITALIAN PROVERB

When a cook cooks a fly he keeps the best wing for himself. POLISH PROVERB

[*See also* Hunger, Peerage.

Cookery

Women cannot make a good book of cookery.
SAMUEL JOHNSON: *Boswell's Life,* April 15, 1778

Man is a cooking animal. The beasts have memory, judgment, and all the faculties and passions of our mind, in a certain degree; but no beast is a cook.
JAMES BOSWELL: *Boswell's Tour to the Hebrides,* 1785

The discovery of a new dish does more for human happiness than the discovery of a new star.
ANTHELME BRILLAT-SAVARIN: *Physiologie du goût,* 1825

[*See also* Hunger, Kitchen, Meat.

Cookery, English

The English diet, compared with the German, even with the French, is a sort of back-to-

nature diet, a return to cannibalism. This diet, I think, gives heavy feet to the mind — Englishwomen's feet.
F. W. NIETZSCHE: *Ecce Homo*, 1888

Cookery, German

German cooking, above all! — how much it has upon its conscience! Soup before the meal, meats cooked to death, fat and mealy vegetables! IBID.

Coöperation

Many hands make light work.
ENGLISH PROVERB, traced by Apperson to 1401

Three helping one another bear the burden of six. GEORGE HERBERT: *Jacula Prudentum*, 1651

When was ever honey made
With one bee in a hive?
THOMAS HOOD: *The Last Man*, 1826

It is evident that many great and useful objects can be attained in this world only by coöperation. It is equally evident that there cannot be efficient coöperation if men proceed on the principle that they must not coöperate for one object unless they agree about other objects.
T. B. MACAULAY: *Gladstone on Church and State*, 1839 (Edinburgh Review, April)

Social animals perform many little services for each other; horses nibble, and cows lick each other, on any spot which itches; monkeys search each other for external parasites.
CHARLES DARWIN: *The Descent of Man*, IV, 1871

Save possibly in education effects, coöperation can produce no general results that competition will not produce.
HENRY GEORGE: *Progress and Poverty*, VI, 1879

Two dogs will kill a lion. HEBREW PROVERB

Hand rubs hand and hand washes hand. (Manus manum fricat, et manus manum lavat.) LATIN PROVERB

Many hands make the burden light. (Multæ manus onus levius faciunt.) IBID.

[*See also* Help.

Copernicus, Nicolaus (1473–1543)

Copernicus . . . did not publish his book until he was on his deathbed. He knew how dangerous it is to be right when the rest of the world is wrong.
THOMAS B. REED: Speech at Waterville, Maine, July 30, 1885

Copy

The only good copies are those which exhibit the defects of bad originals.
LA ROCHEFOUCAULD: *Maxims*, 1665

Copyright

It is a kind of injustice that the long travels of an understanding brain, beside the loss of time and other expense, should be cast away upon men of no worth; or yield less benefit unto the author of a great work than to mere strangers; and perhaps his enemies.
WALTER RALEIGH: *Historie of the World*, V, 1614

Coquetry

Coquetry is of advantage only to the beautiful.
PROPERTIUS: *Elegies*, II, *c.* 20 B.C.

She that hath a rolling eye
And doth convey it well and wisely,
And thereto hath a wavering thought,
Trow you that this trull will not be bought?
EDWARD GOSYNHYLL (?): *A Dialogue Between the Common Secretary and Jealousy*, *c.* 1560

From waving fans, coy glances, glicks, cringes, and all such simpering humors, good Mercury defend us.
BEN JONSON: *Cynthia's Revels*, V, 1601
(*Glick*=a coquettish glance)

Henceforth forever I defy
The glances of a sinful eye,
Wavings of fans, treading of toes,
Wringing of fingers, biting the lip,
The wanton gait, th' alluring trip.
THOMAS MIDDLETON: *A Trick to Catch the Old One*, V, 1608

The superficies of lust.
JOHN WEBSTER: *The White Devil*, I, *c.* 1608

It is a kind of coquetry to make a show of never practising it.
LA ROCHEFOUCAULD: *Maxims*, 1665

Love's greatest miracle is the cure of coquetry. IBID.

No man has half that pleasure in possessing a mistress as a woman has in jilting a gallant.
JOHN VANBRUGH: *The Provok'd Wife*, I, 1697

By keeping men off, you keep them on.
JOHN GAY: *The Beggar's Opera*, I, 1728

Such is your cold coquette, who can't say "No,"
And won't say "Yes," and keeps you on and off-ing. BYRON: *Don Juan*, XII, 1823

Coquetry is the thorn that guards the rose — easily trimmed off when once plucked.
DONALD G. MITCHELL (IK MARVEL): *Reveries of a Bachelor*, 1850

[*See also* Coyness, Flirtation, Love.

Corn

A coming shower your shooting corns presage.
JONATHAN SWIFT: *A Description of a City Shower*, 1710

And when too short the modish shoes are worn,
You'll judge the seasons by your shooting corn.
JOHN GAY: *Trivia,* I, 1716

Cornet

Blow ye the cornet in Gibeah, and the trumpet in Ramah. HOSEA V, 8, *c.* 740 B.C.

[*See also* Kindness.

Cornishman

By Tre, Pol and Pen
You shall know the Cornish men.
ENGLISH SAYING, referring to the three syllables oftenest encountered in Cornish place and family-names

Corporation

Corporations are invisible, immortal and have no soul.
Ascribed to ROGER MANWOOD, chief baron of the English Exchequer, 1592

Corporations cannot commit treason, nor be outlawed, nor excommunicated, for they have no souls.
EDWARD COKE: *Reports,* V, 1605

Corporations . . . are many lesser commonwealths in the bowels of a greater, like worms in the entrails of a natural man.
THOMAS HOBBES: *Leviathan,* II, 1651

A corporation cannot blush.
Ascribed to HOWEL WALSH, an English lawyer, *c.* 1820

History proves that, owing to a change in social conditions, functions that were once performed by small bodies can be performed today only by large corporations. Nevertheless, just as it is wrong to take from the individual and commit to the community functions that private enterprise and industry can perform, so it is an injustice, a grave evil and a violation of right order for a large organization to arrogate to itself functions which could be performed efficiently by smaller ones.
PIUS XI: *Quadragesimo anno,* May 15, 1931

A corporation is just like any natural person, except that it has no pants to kick or soul to damn, and, by God, it ought to have both!
Ascribed to an unnamed Western judge in ERNST and LINDLEY: *Hold Your Tongue,* 1932

[*See also* Campaign Fund, Land.

Correspondence

One glimpse of the human face, and shake of the human hand, is better than whole reams of this cold, thin correspondence; yea, of more worth than all the letters that have sweated the fingers of sensibility, from Madame Sévigné and Balzac to Sterne and Shenstone.
CHARLES LAMB: *Letter to Thomas Manning,* Aug. 9, 1800

Correspondences are like smallclothes before the invention of suspenders: it is impossible to keep them up.
SYDNEY SMITH: *Letter to Mrs. Crowe,* Jan. 31, 1841

[*See also* Letter.

Corroboration

Merely corroborative detail, intended to give artistic verisimilitude to an otherwise bald and unconvincing narrative.
W. S. GILBERT: *The Mikado,* I, 1885

Corruption

God looked upon the earth, and, behold, it was corrupt; for all flesh had corrupted his way upon the earth.
GENESIS VI, 12, *c.* 700 B.C.

Evil communications corrupt good manners.
I CORINTHIANS XV, 33, *c.* 55

So when this corruptible shall have put on incorruption, and this mortal shall have put on immortality, then shall be brought to pass the saying that is written, Death is swallowed up in victory.
I CORINTHIANS XV, 54

If the chief party, whether it be the people, or the army, or the nobility, which you think most useful and of most consequence to you for the conservation of your dignity, be corrupt, you must follow their humor and indulge them, and in that case honesty and virtue are pernicious.
NICCOLO MACHIAVELLI: *The Prince,* XIX, 1513

When vice prevails, and impious men bear sway,
The post of honor is a private station.
JOSEPH ADDISON: *Cato,* IV, 1713

He that accuses all mankind of corruption ought to remember that he is sure to convict only one.
EDMUND BURKE: *Letter to the sheriffs of Bristol,* April 3, 1777

Corruption's not of modern date;
It hath been tried in ev'ry state.
JOHN GAY: *Fables,* II, 1738

The time to guard against corruption and tyranny is before they shall have gotten hold of us. It is better to keep the wolf out of the fold than to trust to drawing his teeth and talons after he shall have entered.
THOMAS JEFFERSON: *Notes on Virginia,* 1782

The best things, corrupted, become the worst. (Optima corrupta pessima.)
LATIN PROVERB

[*See also* Law, Obscenity, Politics.

Corset

God sent us women, and the Devil sent them corsets. FRENCH PROVERB

Corsican

Their prominent national character is never to forget a benefit or an injury. For the slightest insult in Corsica, a shot. Murders are consequently very common. At the same time, no people are more grateful for benefits conferred, and they will not scruple to sacrifice their lives for the person who bestowed them.

NAPOLEON I: To Barry E. O'Meara at St. Helena, May 24, 1817

Cortez, Hernando (1485–1547)

[*See* Discovery.

Cosmetics

Against Him those women sin who torment their skin with potions, stain their cheeks with rouge, and extend the line of their eyes with black coloring. Doubtless they are dissatisfied with God's plastic skill. In their own persons they convict and censure the Artificer of all things.

TERTULLIAN: *Women's Dress, c.* 220

Nature abhors to borrow from the mart,
Simples fit beauty, fie on drugs and art.

MICHAEL DRAYTON: *Endimion and Phoebe,* 1595

For whom does the blind man's wife paint herself?

ENGLISH SAYING, borrowed from the Spanish and traced to the XVII century

God has given you one face, and you make yourselves another.

SHAKESPEARE: *Hamlet,* III, *c.* 1601

The harlot's cheek, beautified with plastering art.

IBID.

From pargetting, painting, slicking, glazing, and renewing old rivelled faces, good Mercury, defend us.

BEN JONSON: *Cynthia's Revels,* v, 1601 (*Parget*=plaster; *rivelled*=wrinkled)

A painted face is the Devil's looking-glass. Painting is an enemy to blushing, which is virtue's color.

T. T.: *Of Painting the Face* (In *New Essays,* 1614)

She looks like an old coach newly painted.

WILLIAM WYCHERLEY: *The Plain Dealer,* II, *c.* 1674

Ancient Phillis has young graces,
'Tis a strange thing, but a true one:
Shall I tell you how?
She herself makes her own faces,
And each morning wears a new one;
Where's the wonder now?

WILLIAM CONGREVE: *The Double-Dealer,* III, 1694

A woman that paints puts up a bill that she is to be let.

THOMAS FULLER: *Gnomologia,* 1732

There are no ugly women; there are only women who do not know how to use cosmetics.

Ascribed to ANTOINE PIERRE BERRYER (1790–1868)

Contentment is the best powder for women's faces.

DUTCH PROVERB

Cold water, morning and evening, is the best of all cosmetics.

HEBREW PROVERB

A painted face fills the husband with suspicion and the gallant with hope.

SWEDISH PROVERB

[*See also* Blind, Complexion, Elizabeth of England, Face, Toilet.

Cosmology

How can I believe one who says that the sun is a red-hot mass of matter and the moon an earth?

TATIAN: *Oratio ad Graecos,* XXVII, *c.* 152

We should all laugh at a revealed cookery. But essentially the same ridicule, not more, and not less, applies to a revealed astronomy, or a revealed geology.

THOMAS DE QUINCEY: *The True Relations of the Bible to Merely Human Science, c.* 1845

If the human race at the present day, the world over, were to be asked to vote on the question as to whether the earth is round or flat, an overwhelming majority would be returned for a flat earth.

EDWIN LINTON: Article in School and Society, July 18, 1931

Cosmopolitan

I don't set up for being a cosmopolite, which to my mind signifies being polite to every country except your own.

THOMAS HOOD: *Up the Rhine,* 1839

I am a habitant of Vienna, St. Petersburg, Berlin, Constantinople;
I am of Adelaide, Sidney, Melbourne;
I am of London, Manchester, Bristol, Edinburgh, Limerick;
I am of Madrid, Cadiz, Barcelona, Oporto, Lyons, Brussels, Berne, Frankfort, Stuttgart, Turin, Florence.

WALT WHITMAN: *Salut au Monde,* 1856

To be really cosmopolitan a man must be at home even in his own country.

T. W. HIGGINSON: *Short Studies of American Authors,* 1879

Cossack

Take away his horse, and he is no longer a Cossack.

RUSSIAN PROVERB

Cost

Which of you, intending to build a tower, sitteth not down first and counteth the cost, whether he have sufficient to finish it?

LUKE XIV, 28, *c.* 75

What costs little is less esteemed.
THOMAS FULLER: *Gnomologia*, 1732

The cost of a thing is the amount of what I will call life which is required to be exchanged for it, immediately or in the long run.
H. D. THOREAU: *Walden*, 1854

Three things cost dear: the caresses of a dog, the love of a mistress, and the invasion of a host.
H. G. BOHN: *Handbook of Proverbs*, 1855

Cotes, Roger (1682–1716)

If Cotes had lived, we might have known something.
ISAAC NEWTON (1642–1727) (Cotes was the editor of the second edition of Newton's *Principia*, 1713, and a mathematician of great promise)

Cotton

Sir, you dare not make war on cotton. No power on earth dares make war upon it. Cotton is king. Until lately the Bank of England was king; but she tried to put her screws as usual, the Fall before last, upon the cotton crop, and was utterly vanquished. The last power has been conquered.
J. H. HAMMOND: Speech in the Senate, March, 1858

Gentlemen, there are Hottentots and there are Cottontots. A cottontot I take to be a person who, growing nothing but cotton, has to buy every earthly thing that he uses or consumes, consequently rarely if ever saves anything, and finds himself at the last of the year the property of his commission merchant — himself the property of the Northern man.
GEORGE W. BAGBY: Speech at Charleston, S. C., 1877

[*See also* Linen, Silk.

Cough

A dry cough is the trumpeter of death.
JOHN RAY: *English Proverbs*, 1670

In coughing, or sneezing, make not great noise, if it be possible, and send not forth any sigh, in such wise that others observe thee, without great occasion.
FRANCIS HAWKINS: *Youth's Behavior*, I, 1663

A convulsion of the lungs, vellicated by some sharp serosity.
SAMUEL JOHNSON: *Dictionary*, 1755

Love and a cough cannot be hid. (Amor tussisque non celantur.) LATIN PROVERB

Council

Call no council of war. It is proverbial that councils of war never fight.
H. W. HALLECK: *Telegram to G. G. Meade*, after Gettysburg, July 13, 1863

[*See also* Assembly, Board, Committee.

Counsel

In the multitude of counsellors there is safety.
PROVERBS XI, 14, *c.* 350 B.C. (Cf. PROVERBS XXIV, 6)

We took sweet counsel together.
PSALMS LV, 14, *c.* 150 B.C.

In cases of difficulty and when hopes are small, the boldest counsels are the safest.
LIVY: *History of Rome*, XXV, *c.* 10

Two heads are better than one.
ENGLISH PROVERB, borrowed from the Greek and current since the XVI century

'Tis not enough your counsel shall be true:
Blunt truths more mischief than nice falsehoods do.
ALEXANDER POPE: *An Essay on Criticism*, III, 1711

None goes to the gallows for giving ill counsel.
THOMAS FULLER: *Gnomologia*, 1732

The well-fed give better counsel than the hungry. FRENCH PROVERB

Give neither counsel nor salt till you are asked for it. ITALIAN PROVERB

Counsel is no command. SCOTCH PROVERB

[*See also* Advice, Folly, Friendship, Money.

Countenance

Let your countenance be pleasant, but in serious matters somewhat grave.
GEORGE WASHINGTON: *Early copy-book*, before 1748

The flexible muscles, growing daily more rigid, give character to the countenance; that is, they trace the operations of the mind with the iron pen of fate, and tell us not only what powers are within, but how they have been employed.
MARY WOLLSTONECRAFT: *A Vindication of the Rights of Woman*, IV, 1792

There is in every human countenance either a history or a prophecy, which must sadden, or at least soften, every reflecting observer.
S. T. COLERIDGE: *Omniana*, I, 1812

[*See also* Face, Merriment, Virtue.

Counterfeit

[*See* Imitation.

Country

The country of every man is that one where he lives best.
ARISTOPHANES: *Plutus*, 408 B.C.

Love of country is more potent than reason itself. OVID: *Epistulae ex Ponto*, I, c. 5

Nothing is sweeter than one's own country.
ST. JOHN CHRYSOSTOM: *Homily II*, *c.* 388

Had I a dozen sons, — each in my love alike, . . . I had rather have eleven die nobly for their country, than one voluptuously surfeit out of action.
SHAKESPEARE: *Coriolanus,* I, *c.* 1607

I do love
My country's good with a respect more tender,
More holy and profound, than mine own life.
SHAKESPEARE: *Coriolanus,* III

Our country is wherever we are well off.
JOHN MILTON: *Letter to Peter Heimbach,* Aug. 15, 1666 (Cf. ARISTOPHANES, *ante,* 408 B.C.)

What pity is it
That we can die but once to serve our country!
JOSEPH ADDISON: *Cato,* IV, 1713

We must love our country, even though it treats us with injustice.
VOLTAIRE: *Letter to J.-J. Rousseau,* Aug. 30, 1755

I am sure that I can save my country, and that nobody else can.
WILLIAM PITT: To the Duke of Devonshire, 1756

Who loves his country cannot hate mankind.
CHARLES CHURCHILL: *The Farewell,* 1764

The proper means of increasing the love we bear our native country is to reside some time in a foreign one.
WILLIAM SHENSTONE: *Of Men and Manners,* 1764

I only regret that I have but one life to lose for my country.
NATHAN HALE: Speech from the gallows, Sept. 22, 1776 (Cf. ADDISON, *ante,* 1713)

To make us love our country, our country ought to be lovely.
EDMUND BURKE: *Reflections on the Revolution in France,* III, 1790

My country is the world, and my religion is to do good.
THOMAS PAINE: *The Rights of Man,* V, 1791

O dream of joy! is this indeed
The lighthouse top I see?
Is this the hill? is this the kirk?
Is this mine own countree?
S. T. COLERIDGE: *The Ancient Mariner,* 1798

Breathes there the man with soul so dead,
Who never to himself hath said,
This is my own, my native land!
WALTER SCOTT: *The Lay of the Last Minstrel,* VI, 1805

Oh, my country! How I leave my country!
WILLIAM PITT: On his deathbed, shortly after the Battle of Austerlitz, 1806

The more I see of other countries, the more I love my own.
ANNA LOUISE DE STAËL: *Corinne,* III, 1807

My affections are first for my own country, and then, generally, for all mankind.
THOMAS JEFFERSON: *Letter to Thomas Law,* 1811

Our country: in her intercourse with foreign nations may she always be in the right; but our country, right or wrong!
STEPHEN DECATUR: Toast at a dinner at Norfolk, Va., April, 1816

He who loves not his country can love nothing.
BYRON: *The Two Foscari,* III, 1821

Let our object be, our country, our whole country, and nothing but our country.
DANIEL WEBSTER: Address on the laying of the cornerstone of the Bunker Hill Monument, June 17, 1825

I, for one, do not call the sod under my feet my country. But language, religion, laws, government, blood — identity of these makes men of one country.
S. T. COLERIDGE: *Table-Talk,* May 28, 1830

Our country is the world — our countrymen are mankind.
W. L. GARRISON: *Motto of the Liberator,* Jan. 1, 1831

My country, 'tis of thee,
Sweet land of liberty, —
Of thee I sing:
Land where our fathers died,
Land of the Pilgrim's pride,
From every mountain side
Let freedom ring.
SAMUEL F. SMITH: *America,* 1832

Next to the love of God, the love of country is the best preventive of crime.
GEORGE BORROW: *The Bible in Spain,* IV, 1843

Our country — whether bounded by the St. John's and the Sabine, or however otherwise bounded or described, and be the measurements more or less; — still our country, to be cherished in all our hearts, and to be defended by all our hands.
ROBERT C. WINTHROP: Toast at Faneuil Hall, July 4, 1845

I hope to find my country in the right: however, I will stand by her, right or wrong.
JOHN J. CRITTENDEN: Speech in the House of Representatives, May, 1846 (Cf. STEPHEN DECATUR, *ante,* 1816)

And say not thou " My country right or wrong,"
Nor shed thy blood for an unhallowed cause.
JOHN QUINCY ADAMS: *Congress, Slavery, and an Unjust War, c.* 1847

Let a person have nothing to do for his country, and he will not care for it.
J. S. MILL: *Representative Government,* III, 1861

O God — if there be a God — , save my country — if my country is worth saving.
Ascribed to " an old soldier," *c.* 1861

There is no such thing as a little country. The greatness of a people is no more determined by their number than the greatness of a man is determined by his height.
VICTOR HUGO: Speech, Nov. 17, 1862

You belong to your country as you belong to your own mother.
E. E. HALE: *The Man Without a Country,* 1863

It is no shame to a man that he should be as nice about his country as about his sweetheart.
J. R. LOWELL: *On a Certain Condescension in Foreigners,* 1869

Our country, right or wrong. When right, to be kept right; when wrong, to be put right.
CARL SCHURZ: Speech in the Senate, Jan. 17, 1872 (Cf. STEPHEN DECATUR, *ante,* 1816)

He serves his party best who serves the country best.
R. B. HAYES: Inaugural address, March 5, 1877

He loves his country best who strives to make it best.
R. G. INGERSOLL: Speech in New York, May 29, 1882

How can a man be said to have a country when he has no right to a square inch of soil?
HENRY GEORGE: *Social Problems,* II, 1884

"My country, right or wrong" is like saying, "My mother, drunk or sober."
G. K. CHESTERTON: *The Defendant,* 1901 (Cf. STEPHEN DECATUR, *ante,* 1816)

A wise man's country is that one where he is happiest. ITALIAN PROVERB

For country. (Pro patria.) LATIN PHRASE

The love of country. (Amor patriae.)
IBID.

Every man loves his own country best, even though it be Hell. PERSIAN PROVERB

[*See also* Civilization, Fatherland, Nationality, Party, Patriotism, Prophet, Proverb, Travel.

Countryside

God made the country, and man made the town.
WILLIAM COWPER: *The Task,* 1758

The country for a wounded heart.
ENGLISH PROVERB, not recorded before the XIX century

Fields, flowers, birds, and green lanes, I have no heart for. The bare road is cheerful, and almost good as a street.
CHARLES LAMB: *Letter to Thomas Manning,* May 10, 1834

I have no relish for the country; it is a kind of healthy grave.
SYDNEY SMITH: *Letter to Miss Harcourt,* 1838

The country, as discriminated from the woods, is of man's creation. The savage has no country.
A. BRONSON ALCOTT: *Tablets,* I, 1868

If you have not lived in the country, you do not know what hardship means.
CHINESE PROVERB

[*See also* Town.

Courage

My friends, quit ye like men, and be firm in the battle. HOMER: *Iliad,* VI, *c.* 800 B.C.

Be strong, and quit yourselves like men . . . and fight. I SAMUEL IV, 9, *c.* 500 B.C.

Courage is worth nothing if the gods withhold their aid.
EURIPIDES: *The Suppliant Women, c.* 421 B.C.

Courage may be taught, as a child is taught to speak. IBID.

Courage conquers all things. (Animus tamen omnia vincit.)
OVID: *Epistulae ex Ponto, c.* 5

Watch ye, stand fast in the faith, quit you like men, be strong.
I CORINTHIANS XVI, 13, *c.* 55

The strongest, most generous, and proudest of all virtues is true courage.
MICHEL DE MONTAIGNE: *Essays,* III, 1588

Courage mounteth with occasion.
SHAKESPEARE: *King John,* II, *c.* 1596

Screw your courage to the sticking-place.
SHAKESPEARE: *Macbeth,* I, *c.* 1605

Every man of courage is a man of his word.
PIERRE CORNEILLE: *Le menteur,* III, 1642

Perfect courage is to do unwitnessed what we should be capable of doing before all the world.
LA ROCHEFOUCAULD: *Maxims,* 1665

Courage is a virtue only so far as it is directed by prudence.
FRANÇOIS FÉNELON: *Aventures de Télémaque,* X, 1699

A man who has no good quality but courage is in a very ill way towards making an agreeable figure in the world, because that which he has superior to other people cannot be exerted without raising himself an enemy.
RICHARD STEELE: *The Spectator,* July 4, 1712

None are rash when they are not seen by anybody.
STANISLAUS LESZCZYNSKI (KING OF POLAND): *Œuvres du philosophe bienfaisant,* 1763

Courage is a quality so necessary for maintaining virtue that it is always respected, even when it is associated with vice.
SAMUEL JOHNSON: *Boswell's Life*, June 11, 1784

Often the test of courage is not to die but to live.
VITTORIO ALFIERI: *Oreste*, IV, *c.* 1785

Courage, considered in itself or without reference to its causes, is no virtue, and deserves no esteem. It is found in the best and the worst, and is to be judged according to the qualities from which it springs and with which it is conjoined.
W. E. CHANNING: *War*, 1835

Personal courage is really a very subordinate virtue – merely the distinguishing mark of a subaltern – a virtue, indeed, in which we are surpassed by the lower animals; or else you would not hear people say "as brave as a lion."
ARTHUR SCHOPENHAUER: *Position*, 1851

Courage ought to have eyes as well as arms.
H. G. BOHN: *Handbook of Proverbs*, 1855

I would define true courage to be a perfect sensibility of the measure of danger, and a mental willingness to endure it.
W. T. SHERMAN: *Memoirs*, II, 1875

The courage of the tiger is one, and of the horse another.
R. W. EMERSON: *Courage*, 1877

Courage without conscience is a wild beast.
R. G. INGERSOLL: Speech in New York, May 29, 1882

The red badge of courage.
STEPHEN CRANE: Title of a book, 1896

It is better to live one day as a lion than a hundred years as a sheep. (Meglio vivere un giorno da leone che cento anni da pecora.)
Motto on Italian 20-lire silver piece, *c.* 1930

Always do what you are afraid to do.
Author unidentified

Courage is often an effect of fear.
FRENCH PROVERB

Who has not courage needs legs.
ITALIAN PROVERB

By courage and faith. (Animo et fide.)
LATIN PHRASE

A man is a lion for his own cause.
SCOTTISH PROVERB

[*See also* Brandy, Bravery, Character, Coward, Cowardice, Daring, Kingly, Necessity, Patience, Soldier, Valor.

Court

The court ought to be in stead of counsel for the prisoner, to see that nothing be urged against him contrary to law and right.
EDWARD COKE: *Institutes*, III, 1644

Is not uncertainty and inconstancy in the highest degree disreputable to a court?
SAMUEL JOHNSON: Memorandum prepared for James Boswell, June 4, 1781

Courts of justice cautiously abstain from deciding more than what the immediate point submitted to their consideration requires.
MR. JUSTICE NICHOLL: *Judgment in the case of the goods of King George III, deceased*, 1822

It is one of the essential qualities of a court of justice that its proceedings should be public, and that all parties who may be desirous of hearing what is going on, if there be room in the place for that purpose – provided they do not interrupt the proceedings, and provided there is no specific reason why they should be removed – , have a right to be present for the purpose of hearing what is going on.
MR. JUSTICE BAGLEY: *Judgment in Daubney* vs. *Cooper*, 1829

When counsel addresses an argument on the ground of natural justice to a court of law, he addresses it to the wrong tribunal. It may be a good argument for inducing the legislature to alter the law; but in a court of law all that we can deal with is the law of the land as we find it.
MR. JUSTICE NORTH: *Judgment in* In re *Gregson*, 1887

A friend of the court. (Amicus curiae.)
LATIN PHRASE

[*See also* Judge, Judiciary, Law, Lawyer, Morality.

Court, Contempt of

[*See* Contempt of Court.

Courtesy

Much courtesy, much subtlety.
THOMAS NASHE: *The Unfortunate Traveler*, 1594 (Quoted as "an old adage")

I am the very pink of courtesy.
SHAKESPEARE: *Romeo and Juliet*, II, *c.* 1596

Dissembling courtesy! How fine this tyrant
Can tickle where she wounds!
SHAKESPEARE: *Cymbeline*, I, *c.* 1609

If a man be gracious and courteous to strangers it shows he is a citizen of the world.
FRANCIS BACON: *Essays*, XIII, 1612

The more courtesy, the more craft.
JOHN CLARKE: *Parœmiologia Anglo-Latina*, 1639

Courtesy on one side only lasts not long.
GEORGE HERBERT: *Outlandish Proverbs*, 1640

Courtesy is cumberous to them that know it not.
DAVID FERGUSSON: *Scottish Proverbs,* 1641

Truth, uttered with courtesy, is heaping coals of fire on the head; or, rather, throwing roses in the face.
Ascribed to ST. FRANCIS DE SALES (1567–1622) in J. P. CAMUS: *L'esprit de Saint François de Sales,* 1641

It is better to have too much courtesy than too little, provided you are not equally courteous to all, for that would be injustice.
BALTASAR GRACIÁN: *The Art of Worldly Wisdom,* CXVIII, 1647

Let thy ceremonies in courtesy be proper to the dignity and place of him with whom thou conversseth: for it is absurd to honor a clown with words courtly and of magnificence.
FRANCIS HAWKINS: *Youth's Behavior,* II, 1663

He may freely receive courtesies who knows how to requite them.
JOHN RAY: *English Proverbs,* 1670

Where there is o'er mickle courtesy there is little kindness.
JAMES KELLY: *Complete Collection of Scottish Proverbs,* 1721 (*Mickle*= much)

All doors are open to courtesy.
THOMAS FULLER: *Gnomologia,* 1732

Courtesy is not a falsehood or grimace; it need not be such.
THOMAS CARLYLE: *Heroes and Hero-Worship,* VI, 1840 (Lecture in London, May 22)

To speak kindly does not hurt the tongue.
FRENCH PROVERB

Cap in hand never did anyone harm.
ITALIAN PROVERB

An excess of courtesy is discourtesy.
JAPANESE PROVERB

The courteous man learns courtesy from the discourteous.
PERSIAN PROVERB

[*See also* Civility, Manner, Politeness, Retort.

Courtier

Who liveth in the court shall die in the straw.
JOHN LYLY: *Euphues,* 1579 (Quoted as "an old saying")

Oh, how wretched
Is that poor man that hangs on princes' favors!
There is, betwixt that smile we would aspire to,
That sweet aspect of princes, and their ruin,
More pangs and fears than wars and women have;
And when he falls, he falls like Lucifer,
Never to hope again.
SHAKESPEARE and JOHN FLETCHER: *Henry VIII,* III, 1613

He that eats the king's goose shall be choked with the feathers.
ENGLISH PROVERB, traced by Smith to 1629

The two maxims of any great man at court are, always to keep his countenance, and never to keep his word.
JONATHAN SWIFT: *Thoughts on Various Subjects,* 1706

To shake with laughter ere the jest they hear.
To pour at will the counterfeited tear;
And, as their patron hints the cold or heat,
To shake in dog-days, in December sweat.
SAMUEL JOHNSON: *London,* 1738

Notwithstanding appearances, there is not any description of men that despise monarchy so much as courtiers.
THOMAS PAINE: *The Rights of Man,* I, 1791

What are a courtier's duties? To place the king on the *chaise-percée* in the morning, and empty it over the head of the retiring minister of state in the afternoon.
Author unidentified

Courtship

Courting and wooing
Bring dallying and doing.
WILLIAM CAMDEN: *Remains Concerning Britain* (4th ed.), 1636

When words we want, love teacheth to indite,
And what we blush to speak she bids us write.
WILLIAM MATHER: *The Young Man's Companion,* 1681

Courtship to marriage is but as the music in the playhouse till the curtain's drawn.
WILLIAM CONGREVE: *The Old Bachelor,* V, 1693

Those marriages generally abound most with love and constancy that are preceded by a long courtship.
JOSEPH ADDISON: *The Spectator,* Dec. 29, 1711

He that goes a great way for a wife is either cheated or means to cheat.
THOMAS FULLER: *Gnomologia,* 1732

The place to carry on an affair with the daughter is behind her father's back. It is the lover's business to make her willing to see father and mother in Hell rather than lose him.
J. C. F. SCHILLER: *Kabale und Liebe,* I, 1784

When a man goes a-courting, and hopes for success, he must begin with doing, and not saying.
ROYALL TYLER: *The Contrast,* II, 1790

'Tis sweet to court, but, oh! how bitter,
To court a girl, and then not git her.
Anon.: *Favorite album verses, c.* 1845

A man pursuing a woman until she catches him. Author unidentified

[*See also* Lover, Marriage, Wooing.

Cousin

Call me cousin, but cozen me not.
THOMAS FULLER: *History of Cambridge University,* 1655

Nothing is so insufferable as a cousin's insult.
SANSKRIT PROVERB

[*See also* Relative.

Covenant

I will establish my covenant between me and thee, and thy seed after thee, in their generations, for an everlasting covenant, to be a God unto thee, and to thy seed after thee.
GENESIS XVII, 7, *c.* 700 B.C.

Open covenants of peace, openly arrived at, after which there shall be no private international understandings of any kind, but diplomacy shall proceed always frankly and in the public view.
WOODROW WILSON: Address to Congress, Jan. 8, 1918 (One of the Fourteen Points)

[*See also* Contract, Death.

Covent Garden

[*See* Lamb (Charles).

Covetousness

Thou shalt not covet thy neighbor's house, thou shalt not covet thy neighbor's wife, nor his manservant, nor his maidservant, nor his ox, nor his ass, nor anything that is thy neighbor's.
EXODUS XX, 17, *c.* 700 B.C. (Cf. DEUTERONOMY V, 21, *c.* 650 B.C.)

He that loveth silver shall not be satisfied with silver; nor he that loveth abundance with increase.
ECCLESIASTES V, 9, *c.* 200 B.C.

Take heed, and beware of covetousness: for a man's life consisteth not in the abundance of the things which he possesseth.
LUKE XII, 15, *c.* 75

The covetous man is full of fear; and he who lives in fear will ever be a bondman.
HORACE: *Epistles,* I, *c.* 20 B.C.

A covetous man doth no man good but when he dieth.
RICHARD TAVERNER: *Proverbs,* 1539

He was such a covetous monster that he would have flayed a louse to save the skin of it.
JOHN FLORIO: *Second Frutes,* 1591

I am Covetousness, begotten of an old churl in an old leathern bag; and might I have my wish, I would desire that this house and all the people in it were turn'd to gold, that I might lock you up in my good chest.
CHRISTOPHER MARLOWE: *Dr. Faustus,* II, 1604

If you have a longing desire to possess the goods which you have not, though you may say you would not possess them unjustly, you are, nevertheless, truly covetous.
ST. FRANCIS DE SALES: *Introduction to the Devout Life,* XIV, 1609

Though ye take from a covetous man all his treasure, he has yet one jewel left; ye cannot bereave him of his covetousness.
JOHN MILTON: *Areopagitica,* 1644

Covetous men live drudges to die wretches.
THOMAS FULLER: *Gnomologia,* 1732

Riches have made more covetous men than covetousness hath made rich men. IBID.

Covetousness has such a blinding power that all the arguments in the world will not convince a man that he is covetous.
THOMAS WILSON: *Maxims of Piety and of Christianity, c.* 1755

Covetousness bursts the sack and spills the grain.
WALTER SCOTT: *Kenilworth,* IV, 1821

Bare-faced covetousness was the moving spirit of civilization from its first dawn to the present day; wealth, and again wealth, and for the third time wealth; wealth, not of society, but of the puny individual, was its only and final aim.
FRIEDRICH ENGELS: *The Origin of the Family,* 1885

Covetousness has for its mother unlawful desire, for its daughter injustice, and for its friend violence. ARAB PROVERB

When all other vices grow old covetousness grows young. LATIN PROVERB

[*See also* Age (Old), Avarice, Miser, Property, Sin, Wealth.

Cow

A bellowing cow soon forgets her calf.
ENGLISH PROVERB, familiar in various forms since the XIV century

A cow is a very good animal in the field; but we turn her out of a garden.
SAMUEL JOHNSON: *Boswell's Life,* 1772

A red cow gives good milk.
ENGLISH PROVERB, not recorded before the XIX century

Thank you, pretty cow, that made
Pleasant milk to soak my bread,
Every day, and every night,
Warm, and fresh, and sweet, and white.
ANN and JANE TAYLOR: *Rhymes for the Nursery,* 1806

There was an old man who said, "How
Shall I flee from this horrible cow?
I will sit on this stile, and continue to smile,
Which may soften the heart of that cow."

EDMUND LEAR: *The Book of Nonsense*, 1846

I never saw a purple cow,
I never hope to see one;
But I can tell you anyhow
I'd rather see than be one.

GELETT BURGESS: *The Purple Cow*, 1895 (The Lark, San Francisco, May)

Has anyone ever seen a clean cow?

Author unidentified

My murderers shall come to grief,
Along with all who relish beef;
When I'm a man and you're a cow,
I'll eat you as you eat me now. IBID.

Milk the cow, but don't pull off her udder.

DUTCH PROVERB

The cow does not know the value of her tail till she has lost it. IBID.

[*See also* Coöperation, Definition, Devil, Easy, Heredity, Kiss, Luck, Milk, Talent, Warrior.

Coward

The coward calls himself cautious. (Timidus se vocat cautum.)

PUBLILIUS SYRUS: *Sententiæ, c.* 50 B.C.

It is the act of a coward to wish for death.

OVID: *Metamorphoses*, IV, *c.* 5

Ever will a coward show no mercy.

THOMAS MALORY: *Morte d'Arthur*, XVIII, 1485

Cowards fight when they can fly no further;
As doves do peck the falcon's piercing talons.

SHAKESPEARE: *III Henry VI*, I, *c.* 1591

You are the hare of whom the proverb goes,
Whose valor plucks dead lions by the beard.

SHAKESPEARE: *King John*, II, *c.* 1596

Cowards die many times before their deaths;
The valiant never taste of death but once.

SHAKESPEARE: *Julius Caesar*, II, 1599

Wouldst live a coward in thine own esteem,
Letting "I dare not" wait upon, "I would";
Like the poor cat i' the adage?

SHAKESPEARE: *Macbeth*, I, *c.* 1605

Few cowards know the extent of their fear.

LA ROCHEFOUCAULD: *Maxims*, 1665

Make a coward fight, and he will beat the Devil.

ENGLISH PROVERB, traced by Apperson to 1669

It is unwise to punish cowards with ignominy; for if they had regarded that, they would not have been cowards; death is their proper punishment, because they fear it most.

JONATHAN SWIFT: *Thoughts on Various Subjects*, 1706

I no more believe any man is born a coward than that he is born a knave. Truth makes a man of courage, and guilt makes that man of courage a coward.

DANIEL DEFOE: *A Review of the Affairs of France and of All Europe*, VIII, 1712

Cowards are cruel.

JOHN GAY: *Fables*, I, 1727

A coward's fear can make a coward valiant.

THOMAS FULLER: *Gnomologia*, 1732

Many would be cowards if they had courage enough. IBID.

He who fights and runs away
May live to fight another day;
But he who is in battle slain
Can never rise and fight again.

OLIVER GOLDSMITH: *The Art of Poetry on a New Plan*, 1761

The Summer soldier and the sunshine patriot.

THOMAS PAINE: *The Crisis*, I, 1776

Were one-half of mankind brave and one-half cowards, the brave would be always beating the cowards. Were all brave, they would lead a very uneasy life; all would be continually fighting; but being all cowards, we go on very well.

SAMUEL JOHNSON: *Boswell's Life*, 1778

A coward is much more exposed to quarrels than a man of spirit.

THOMAS JEFFERSON: *Letter to James Monroe*, 1785

The coward threatens only when he is safe.

J. W. GOETHE: *Torquato Tasso*, II, 1790

Like one that on a lonesome road
Doth walk in fear and dread,
And having once turned round, walks on,
And turns no more his head;
Because he knows a frightful fiend
Doth close behind him tread.

S. T. COLERIDGE: *The Ancient Mariner*, VI, 1798

That all men would be cowards if they dare,
Some men we know have courage to declare.

GEORGE CRABBE: *Tales*, I (*The Dumb Orators*), 1812

Cowards, 'tis said, in certain situations,
Derive a sort of courage from despair,
And then perform, from downright desperation,
Much more than many a bolder man would dare.

R. H. BARHAM: *The Ingoldsby Legends*, I, 1840

There is no such depth of poltroonery as that of the man who does not dare to run.

BENJAMIN R. TUCKER: *Instead of a Book*, 1893

One who in a perilous emergency thinks with his legs.

AMBROSE BIERCE: *The Devil's Dictionary*, 1906

No good luck ever comes to cowards.
GERMAN PROVERB

It is better to be a coward for a minute than dead the rest of your life. IRISH PROVERB

Of two cowards, the one who finds the other out first has the advantage.
ITALIAN PROVERB

Coward man keep sound bone.
JAMAICAN PROVERB

The coward is always in danger.
PORTUGUESE PROVERB

[*See also* Bravery, Bully, Conscience, Cowardice, Fear, Hero, Instinct, Nobility, Passion, Peace.

Cowardice

To know what is right and not do it is the worst cowardice.
CONFUCIUS: *Analects,* II, *c.* 500 B.C.

Cowardice is the mother of cruelty.
MICHEL DE MONTAIGNE: *Essays,* I, 1580

A cowardly act! What do I care about that? You may be sure that I should never fear to commit one if it were to my advantage.
NAPOLEON I: To Talleyrand, 1813

There is a cowardice which we do not despise because it has nothing base or treacherous in its elements; it betrays itself, not you: it is mere temperament; the absence of the romantic and the enterprising; it sees a lion in the way.
CHARLES LAMB: *The South-Sea House,* 1820 (London Magazine, Aug.)

Among ten men nine are sure to be women.
TURKISH PROVERB

[*See also* Alms, Coward, Pacifism, Valor.

Cowboy

Bubulcitate: to cry like a cow boy.
HENRY COCKERAM: *English Dictionary,* 1623

I want to be a cowboy and with the cowboys stand,
Big spurs upon my boot-heels and a lasso in my hand.
Anon.: *I Want to be a Cowboy, c.* 1875

Cowl

[*See* Dress, Monk.

Cowley, Abraham (1618–67)

Mr. Cowley has not left behind him a better man in England.
KING CHARLES II of England: On the death of Cowley, 1667

To him no author was unknown,
Yet what he wrote was all his own;
Horace's wit, and Virgil's state,
He did not steal, but emulate.
And when he would like them appear,
Their garb, but not their clothes, did wear.
JOHN DENHAM: *Elegy on Cowley,* 1667

Cowper, William (1731–1800)

I have no more right to the name of a poet than a maker of mouse-traps has to that of an engineer.
WILLIAM COWPER: To William Unwin, *c.* 1785

Coxcomb

[*See* Author, Dress, Knowledge.

Coyness

[*See* Coquetry.

Crabbe, William (1754–1832)

Crabbe knew men, but to read one of his poems seems to me all one with taking a dose of medicine.
R. W. EMERSON: *Journal,* July 21, 1837

Cradle

[*See* Children, Lullaby, Mother.

Crank

A crank is a little thing that makes revolutions.
Author unidentified

Crazy

I teach that all men are crazy. (Doceo insanire omnes.) HORACE: *Satires, c.* 25 B.C.

Everyone is crazy but me and thee, and sometimes I suspect thee a little.
Ascribed to an anonymous Quaker

[*See also* Lunatic.

Cream

Cream . . . is the very head and flower of milk: but it is somewhat of a gross nourishment, and by reason of the unctuosity of it, quickly cloyeth the stomach, relaxeth and weakeneth the retentive faculty thereof, and is easily converted into phlegm, and vaporous fumes.
TOBIAS VENNER: *Via recta,* 1620

[*See also* Milk.

Creation

In the beginning God created the Heaven and the earth. And the earth was without form, and void; and darkness was upon the face of the deep. And the Spirit of God moved upon the face of the waters. And God said, Let there be light; and there was light.
GENESIS I, 1–3, *c.* 700 B.C.

In the beginning was the Word, and the Word was with God, and the Word was God.
JOHN I, 1, *c.* 115

We believe that God hath made all things out of nothing: because, even although the world hath been made of some material, that very same material hath been made out of nothing.

ST. AUGUSTINE: *Of the Faith and of the Creed, c.* 393

Allah created man of congealed blood.

THE KORAN, XCVI, *c.* 625

Had I been present at the Creation, I would have given some useful hints for the better ordering of the universe.

Ascribed to ALPHONSO THE LEARNED, of Leon and Castile (1221–84)

The whole Creation is a mystery, and particularly that of man. At the blast of His mouth were the rest of the creatures made; and at His bare Word they started out of nothing: but in the frame of man (as the text describes it) He played the sensible operator, and seemed not so much to create as make him.

THOMAS BROWNE: *Religio Medici,* I, 1642

Heaven and earth, center and circumference were made in the same instant of time, and clouds full of water, and man was created by the Trinity on the 26th of October, 4004 B.C. at 9 o'clock in the morning.

JOHN LIGHTFOOT (vice-chancellor of Cambridge University), 1654

God said,
Let the earth bring forth soul living in her kind:
Cattle and creeping things, and beast of the earth,
Each in their kind. The earth obey'd, and straight
Op'ning her fertile womb, teem'd at a birth
Innumerous living creatures, perfect forms,
Limb'd and full grown.

JOHN MILTON: *Paradise Lost,* VII, 1667

It is easier to suppose that the universe has existed from all eternity than to conceive a Being beyond its limits capable of creating it. P. B. SHELLEY: *Queen Mab,* notes, 1813

The most serious parody I have ever heard was this: In the beginning was nonsense, and the nonsense was with God, and the nonsense was God.

F. W. NIETZSCHE: *Human All-too-Human,* II, 1878

[*See also* Evolution.

Credit

Credit is dead; bad pay killed it.

ENGLISH PROVERB, borrowed from the Italian and traced to the XVII century

He that hath lost his credit is dead to the world.

GEORGE HERBERT: *Outlandish Proverbs,* 1639

Who tells a lie to save his credit wipes his nose on his sleeve to save his napkin.

JAMES HOWELL: *Proverbs,* 1659

Credit lost is like a Venice-glass broken.

JOHN RAY: *English Proverbs,* 1670

Credit is undone in whispers. The tradesman's wound is received from one who is more private and more cruel than the ruffian with the lantern and dagger.

RICHARD STEELE: *The Spectator,* Nov. 9, 1711

In this institution of credit, which is as universal as honesty and promise in the human countenance, always some neighbor stands ready to be bread and land and tools and stock to the young adventurer.

R. W. EMERSON: *The Conservative,* 1841

Ah, take the cash, and let the credit go.

EDWARD FITZGERALD: Tr. of OMAR KHAYYÁM: *Rubáiyát* (*c.* 1100), 1857

I see before me the statue of a celebrated minister, who said that confidence was a plant of slow growth. But I believe, however gradual may be the growth of confidence, that of credit requires still more time to arrive at maturity.

BENJAMIN DISRAELI: Speech in the House of Commons, Nov. 9, 1867 (Cf. WILLIAM PITT under Confidence, *ante,* 1776)

Every dollar of fixed and stable value has, through the agency of confident credit, an astonishing capacity of multiplying itself in financial work. Every unstable and fluctuating dollar falls as a basis of credit and in its use begets gambling speculation and undermines the foundations of honest enterprise.

GROVER CLEVELAND: Message to Congress, Dec. 2, 1895

No man's credit is as good as his money.

E. W. HOWE: *Sinner Sermons,* 1926

Credit, like a looking-glass,
Broken once, is gone, alas!

Author unidentified

A pig bought on credit is forever grunting.

SPANISH PROVERB

[*See also* Cash.

Creditor

The creditor hath a better memory than the debtor. JAMES HOWELL: *Proverbs,* 1659

The creditors are a superstitious sect, great observers of set days and times.

BENJAMIN FRANKLIN: *Poor Richard's Almanac,* 1737

[*See also* Borrowing and Lending, Classes, Landlord.

Credit, Public

As a very important source of strength and security, cherish public credit. One method of preserving it is to use it as sparingly as possible.

GEORGE WASHINGTON: Farewell Address, Sept. 17, 1796

[*See also* Bankruptcy, Hamilton (Alexander).

Credo

To worship God and to leave every other man free to worship Him in his own way; to love one's neighbors, enlightening them if one can and pitying those who remain in error; to dismiss as immaterial all questions that would have given no trouble if no importance had been attached to them — this is my religion, and it is worth all your systems and symbols.

VOLTAIRE: *Letter to an unknown correspondent,* Jan. 5, 1759

My creed is: he is safe that does his best,
And death's a doom sufficient for the rest.

WILLIAM COWPER: *Hope,* 1782

I believe in one God, the creator of the universe. That He governs it by His providence. That He ought to be worshipped. That the most acceptable service we render to Him is doing good to His other children. That the soul of man is immortal and will be treated with justice in another life respecting its conduct in this.

BENJAMIN FRANKLIN: *Letter to Ezra Stiles,* 1789

I believe in one God, and no more; and I hope for happiness beyond this life. I believe in the equality of man; and I believe that religious duties consist in doing justice, loving mercy, and endeavoring to make our fellow creatures happy.

THOMAS PAINE: *The Age of Reason,* I, 1794

I still, and shall to eternity, embrace Christianity, and adore Him who is the express image of God.

WILLIAM BLAKE: *Letter to Captain Butts,* Nov. 22, 1802

Justice is the only worship;
Love is the only priest;
Ignorance is the only slavery;
Happiness is the only good;
The time to be happy is now,
The place to be happy is here,
The way to be happy is to make others so.

R. G. INGERSOLL: *Creed,* 1880

[*See also* American Creed, Creed.

Credulity

Your noblest natures are most credulous.

GEORGE CHAPMAN: *Bussy d'Ambois,* IV, 1604

If the world will be gulled, let it be gulled.

ROBERT BURTON: *The Anatomy of Melancholy,* III, 1621

He that knows nothing doubts nothing.

GEORGE HERBERT: *Outlandish Proverbs,* 1640

There are . . . heads that can credit the relations of mariners.

THOMAS BROWNE: *Religio Medici,* I, 1642

When you hear anything favorable keep a tight rein on your credulity; if unfavorable, give it the spur.

BALTASAR GRACIÁN: *The Art of Worldly Wisdom,* XXV, 1647

The world is naturally averse
To all the truth it sees or hears,
But swallows nonsense, and a lie
With greediness and gluttony.

SAMUEL BUTLER: *Hudibras,* III, 1664

The incredulous are the most credulous. They believe the miracles of Vespasian that they may not believe those of Moses.

BLAISE PASCAL: *Pensées,* II, 1670

What is it men cannot be made to believe!

THOMAS JEFFERSON: *Letter to Richard H. Lee,* 1786

Credulity is not a crime.

THOMAS PAINE: *The Age of Reason,* I, 1794

Wearied from doubt to doubt to flee,
We welcome fond credulity.

WALTER SCOTT: *Marmion,* III, 1808

Our credulity is not to be measured by the truth of the things we believe. When men believed the earth was flat, they were not credulous: they were using their common sense, and, if asked to prove that the earth was flat, would have said simply, "Look at it."

GEORGE BERNARD SHAW: *Androcles and the Lion,* pref., 1912

Better be too credulous than too skeptical.

CHINESE PROVERB

The world wants to be deceived. (Mundus vult decipi.)

LATIN PROVERB

[*See also* Belief, Disease, Philosophy.

Creed

The dust of creeds outworn.

P. B. SHELLEY: *Prometheus Unbound,* I, 1820

As men's prayers are a disease of the will, so are their creeds a disease of the intellect.

R. W. EMERSON: *Self-Reliance,* 1841

The better part of mankind have at all times practically regarded their creed as a sacred total to which nothing may be added, and from which nothing may be taken away.

J. A. FROUDE: *The Book of Job,* 1853 (Westminster Review)

When an age is found occupied in proving its creed, this is but a token that the age has ceased to have a proper belief in it.

MARK PATTISON: *Tendencies of Religious Thought in England,* 1860

But still my human hands are weak
To hold your iron creeds;

Against the words ye bid me speak
My heart within me pleads.
J. G. WHITTIER: *The Eternal Goodness,* 1867

The whole history of civilization is strewn with creeds and institutions which were invaluable at first, and deadly afterwards.
WALTER BAGEHOT: *Physics and Politics,* 1869

The Athanasian Creed is the most splendid ecclesiastical lyric ever poured forth by the genius of man.
BENJAMIN DISRAELI: *Endymion,* LIV, 1880

[*See also* American Creed, Calvinist, Credo.

Creed, American

[*See* American Creed.

Cremation

It is the best mode, as then the corpse does not produce any inconvenience; and as to the resurrection, that must be accomplished by a miracle, and it is easy to the Being who has it in His power to perform such a miracle to form again the ashes of the dead.
NAPOLEON I: To Barry E. O'Meara at St. Helena, Dec. 14, 1816

Cress

Eating cress makes one witty.
GREEK PROVERB

Cretan

[*See* Liar.

Crime

The land is full of bloody crimes, and the city is full of violence.
EZEKIEL VII, 23, *c.* 600 B.C.

The greatest crimes are caused by surfeit, not by want. Men do not become tyrants in order that they may not suffer cold.
ARISTOTLE: *Politics, c.* 322 B.C.

All go free when multitudes offend. (Quicquid multis peccatur, inultum est.)
LUCAN: *Pharsalia,* V, 65 B.C.

Crime is never founded on reason.
LIVY: *History of Rome,* XXVIII, *c.* 10

There is no crime without a precedent.
SENECA: *Hippolytus, c.* 60

What man was ever content with one crime?
JUVENAL: *Satires,* XIII, *c.* 125

No crime is rooted out once for all.
TERTULLIAN: *The Christian's Defence, c.* 215

A deed without a name.
SHAKESPEARE: *Macbeth,* IV, *c.* 1605

Crimes unwhipped of justice.
SHAKESPEARE: *King Lear,* III, 1606

The source of every crime is some defect of the understanding, or some error in reasoning, or some sudden force of the passions.
THOMAS HOBBES: *Leviathan,* II, 1651

Crimes become innocent and even glorious by their splendor, number and enormity.
LA ROCHEFOUCAULD: *Maxims,* 1665

If poverty is the mother of crime, then want of sense is its father.
JEAN DE LA BRUYÈRE: *Caractères,* XI, 1688

Successful crimes are praised very much like virtue itself. IBID.

The greater the man the greater the crime.
THOMAS FULLER: *Gnomologia,* 1732

The casuists of the Roman church, who gain, by confession, great opportunities of knowing human nature, have generally determined that what is a crime to do, it is a crime to think.
SAMUEL JOHNSON: *The Rambler,* April 14, 1750

There is not a crime but is placed among honest actions by the societies to which this crime is advantageous.
C. A. HELVÉTIUS: *De l'esprit,* II, 1758

In religion this term does not mean actions hurtful to society at large, but actions that are hurtful to the clergy. The greatest of all crimes is to be wanting in faith and in trust in that body, to question its opinions, to rob its churches, and to disdain its holy things.
VOLTAIRE: *Philosophical Dictionary,* 1764

A crime . . . is an act committed or omitted in violation of a public law either forbidding or commanding it.
WILLIAM BLACKSTONE: *Commentaries on the Laws of England,* IV, 1765

Providence sees to it that no man gets happiness out of crime.
VITTORIO ALFIERI: *Orestes,* I, *c.* 1785

The fruitful source of crimes consists in this circumstance: one man's possessing in abundance that of which another man is destitute.
WILLIAM GODWIN: *An Enquiry Concerning Political Justice,* 1793

The more religious a country is, the more crimes are committed in it.
NAPOLEON I: To Gaspard Gourgaud at St. Helena, Dec. 27, 1817

Commit a crime, and the earth is made of glass. Commit a crime, and it seems as if a coat of snow fell on the ground, such as reveals in the woods the track of every partridge and fox and squirrel and mole.
R. W. EMERSON: *Compensation,* 1841

Greed, love of pleasure, lust, idleness, anger, hatred, revenge: these are the chief causes of crime. These passions and desires are

shared by rich and poor alike, by the educated and uneducated. They are inherent in human nature; the germ is in every man.
A French judge, quoted by H. B. IRVING: *A Book of Remarkable Criminals,* 1918

Whoever profits by the crime is guilty of it.
FRENCH PROVERB

No one can live without crime. (Nemo sine crimine vivit.) LATIN PROVERB

In criminal acts the intent is to be regarded, not the result. (In maleficiis voluntas spectatur non exitus.) LEGAL MAXIM

[*See also* Blunder, Brotherhood, Diet, Drunkenness, End, History, Impeachment, Intention, Mistake, Moving-picture, Murder, Punishment, State, Treaty, Vulgarity.

Crime and Punishment

No man who commits a crime in secret can ever be sure that he will not be detected, even though he has escaped 10,000 times in the past.
EPICURUS: *Aphorisms, c.* 300 B.C.

The greatest incitement to crime is the hope of escaping punishment.
CICERO: *Pro Milone, c.* 50 B.C.

The punishment may be remitted; the crime will stand.
OVID: *Epistulae ex Ponto,* I, *c.* 5

I hear much of people's calling out to punish the guilty, but very few are concerned to clear the innocent.
DANIEL DEFOE: *An Appeal to Honor and Justice,* 1715

The lawgiver is undoubtedly allowed to estimate the malignity of an offence, not merely by the loss or pain which single acts may produce, but by the general alarm and anxiety arising from the fear of mischief, and insecurity of possession.
SAMUEL JOHNSON: *The Rambler,* April 20, 1751

It is not only vain, but wicked, in a legislator to frame laws in opposition to the laws of nature, and to arm them with the terrors of death. This is truly creating crimes in order to punish them.
THOMAS JEFFERSON: *Note on the Crimes Bill,* 1779

If hen-stealing prevail to a plainly unendurable extent, will you station police-officers at every hen-roost; and keep them watching and cruising incessantly to and fro over the parish, in the unwholesome dark, at enormous expense, with almost no effect? Or will you not try rather to discover where the fox's den is, and kill the fox?
THOMAS CARLYLE: *The Nigger Question,* 1849 (Fraser's Magazine, Dec.)

We have no time to make allowances; and the graduation of punishment by the scale of guilt is a mere impossibility. A thief is a thief in the law's eye though he has been trained from his cradle in the kennels of St. Giles's; and definite penalties must be attached to definite acts.
J. A. FROUDE: *Spinoza,* 1855 (Westminster Review)

A crowded police court docket is the surest of all signs that trade is brisk and money plenty.
S. L. CLEMENS (MARK TWAIN): *Roughing It,* LI, 1872

He grew up and married, and raised a large family, and brained them all with an ax one night, and got wealthy by all manner of cheating and rascality; and now he is the infernalest wickedest scoundrel in his native village, and is universally respected, and belongs to the Legislature.
S. L. CLEMENS (MARK TWAIN): *Story of the Bad Little Boy,* 1875

It is not the thief who is hanged, but one who was caught stealing. CZECH PROVERB

[*See also* Adultery, Crime, Criminal, Disgrace, Fear, Punishment.

Criminal

It is better that a criminal be not accused than that he be acquitted.
LIVY: *History of Rome,* XXXIV, *c.* 10

I shall do diligence, whenever I hear tell there is any traitors, murderers, rovers, and masterful thieves and outlaws, that suppress the poor, to bring them to the law at all my power.
The Oath of a Knight (Sent by William Drummond of Hawthornden to Ben Jonson, July 1, 1619)

If an Englishman, forgetting all laws, human, civil, and religious, offend against life and liberty, . . . he is no better than a Turk, a Saracen, a heathen.
JOHN MILTON: *The Tenure of Kings and Magistrates,* 1649

No Indian prince has to his palace
More followers than a thief to th' gallows.
SAMUEL BUTLER: *Hudibras,* II, 1664

Let me remember, when I find myself inclined to pity a criminal, that there is likewise a pity due to the country.
MATTHEW HALE: *History of the Pleas of the Crown,* 1736

The learned, the judicious, the pious Boerhaave relates that he never saw a criminal dragged to execution without asking himself, "Who knows whether this man is not less culpable than me?"
SAMUEL JOHNSON: *The Rambler,* April 20, 1751

When a felon's not engaged in his employment,
Or maturing his felonious little plans,

His capacity for innocent enjoyment
Is just as great as any honest man's.
W. S. GILBERT: *The Pirates of Penzance*, II, 1880

The criminal is the type of the strong man in unfavorable surroundings, the strong man made sick.
F. W. NIETZSCHE: *The Twilight of the Idols*, 1889

We enact many laws that manufacture criminals, and then a few that punish them.
BENJAMIN R. TUCKER: *Instead of a Book*, 1893

The criminal of today is the hero of our old legends. Author unidentified

All criminals turn preachers under the gallows.
ITALIAN PROVERB

The act is not criminal unless the mind is criminal. (Actus non facit reum, nisi mens sit rea.) LEGAL MAXIM

[*See also* Crime, Crime and Punishment, Justice, Punishment, Sterilization.

Cringing

Be cringing and commonplace, and anything is within your reach.
CARON DE BEAUMARCHAIS: *Le barbier de Séville*, III, 1775

Cripple

Little good can come from cripples; they generally take revenge on nature, and do as little honor to her as she has done to them.
BALTASAR GRACIÁN: *The Art of Worldly Wisdom*, CCLXXIII, 1647

Halt not before a cripple.
H. G. BOHN: *Handbook of Proverbs*, 1855

Cripples are aye better planners than workers.
SCOTTISH PROVERB

A cripple seldom disgraces himself.
WEST AFRICAN PROVERB

[*See also* Age (Old), Lunatic.

Crisis

These are the times that try men's souls.
THOMAS PAINE: *The American Crisis*, I, 1776 (Pennsylvania Journal, Dec. 19)

Critic

I am nothing if not critical.
SHAKESPEARE: *Othello*, II, 1604

Critics are like brushers of noblemen's clothes.
GEORGE HERBERT: *Jacula Prudentum*, 1651 (Often ascribed to Henry Wotton, 1568–1630)

They who write ill, and they who ne'er durst write,
Turn critics out of mere revenge and spite.
JOHN DRYDEN: *The Conquest of Granada*, prologue, 1670

I hear a great many of the fools are angry at me, and I am glad of it, for I write at them, not to them.
WILLIAM CONGREVE: *The Double Dealer*, dedication, 1695

Critics, as they are birds of prey, have ever a natural inclination to carrion.
ALEXANDER POPE: *Letter to William Wycherley*, Dec. 26, 1704

Every true critic is a hero born, descending in a direct line from a celestial stem by Momus and Hybris, who begat Zoilus, who begat Tigellius, who begat Etcetera the elder, who begat Bentley, and Rymer, and Wotton, and Perrault, and Dennis, who begat Etcetera the younger.
JONATHAN SWIFT: *A Tale of a Tub*, III, 1704

The generous critic fann'd the poet's fire,
And taught the world with reason to admire.
ALEXANDER POPE: *An Essay on Criticism*, I, 1711

The greatest critics among the ancients are those who have the most excelled in all other kinds of composition, and have shown the height of good writing even in the precepts which they have given for it.
JOSEPH ADDISON: *The Guardian*, July 23, 1713

When Jove was from his teeming head
Of wit's fair goddess brought to bed,
There follow'd at his lying-in
For afterbirth a sooterkin;
From hence the critic vermin sprung
With harpy claws and pois'nous tongue.
JONATHAN SWIFT: *To Dr. Delany*, 1729

A professed critic has a right to declare that his author wrote whatever he thinks he should have written.
THOMAS EDWARDS: *A Supplement to Mr. Warburton's Edition of Shakespeare*, 1748 (Written satirically)

The critic, rightly considered, is no more than the clerk whose office it is to transcribe the rules and laws laid down by those great judges whose vast strength of genius hath placed them in the light of legislators in the several sciences over which they presided.
HENRY FIELDING: *Tom Jones*, I, 1749

The genius, even when he endeavors only to entertain or instruct, yet suffers persecution from innumerable critics whose acrimony is excited merely by the pain of seeing others pleased, and of hearing applauses which another enjoys.
SAMUEL JOHNSON: *The Rambler*, Dec. 17, 1751

A fly, sir, may sting a stately horse, and make him wince; but one is but an insect, and the other is a horse still.
SAMUEL JOHNSON: *Boswell's Life*, 1754

A poet that fails in writing becomes often a morose critic. The weak and insipid white-wine makes at length excellent vinegar.
WILLIAM SHENSTONE: *On Writing and Books,* 1764

Every good poet includes a critic, but the reverse will not hold. IBID.

Blame where you must, be candid where you can,
And be each critic the good-natur'd man.
OLIVER GOLDSMITH: *The Good Natur'd Man,* epilogue, 1768

The man who is asked by an author what he thinks of his work is put to the torture, and is not obliged to speak the truth.
SAMUEL JOHNSON: *Boswell's Life,* April 25, 1778

Critics! — appalled I venture on the name,
Those cut-throat bandits in the paths of fame.
ROBERT BURNS: *Third Epistle to Mr. Graham of Fintry,* 1791

Critics in general are venomous serpents that delight in hissing.
W. B. DANIEL: *Rural Sports,* 1801

The whole effort of your mind is to destroy. Because others build slightly and eagerly, you employ yourself in kicking down their houses, and contract a sort of aversion for the more honorable, useful, and difficult task of building well yourself.
SYDNEY SMITH: *Letter to Francis Jeffrey,* 1804

Mercy on us, that God should give His favorite children, men, mouths to speak with, to discourse rationally, to promise smoothly, to flatter agreeably, to encourage warmly, to counsel wisely, to sing with, to drink with, and to kiss with, and that they should turn them into mouths of adders, bears, wolves, hyenas, and whistle like tempests, and emit breath through them like distillations of aspic poison, to asperse and vilify the innocent labors of their fellow-creatures who are desirous to please them!
CHARLES LAMB: *Letter to Thomas Manning,* Feb. 26, 1808

A man must serve his time to every trade
Save censure — critics all are ready made.
Take hackney'd jokes from Miller, got by rote,
With just enough of learning to misquote;
A mind well skill'd to find or forge a fault;
A turn for punning, call it Attic salt.
BYRON: *English Bards and Scotch Reviewers,* 1809

Fear not to lie — 'twill seem a lucky hit;
Shrink not from blasphemy — 'twill pass for wit;
Care not for feeling, pass your proper jest; —
And stand a critic, hated yet caress'd. IBID.

Reviewers are usually people who would have been poets, historians, biographers, if they could; they have tried their talents at one or the other, and have failed; therefore they turn critics.
S. T. COLERIDGE: *Lectures on Shakespeare and Milton,* 1812

All enmity, all envy, they disclaim,
Disinterested thieves of our good name:
Cool, sober murderers of their neighbors' fame.
S. T. COLERIDGE: *Modern Critics,* 1817

Reviewers, with some rare exceptions, are a most stupid and malignant race. As a bankrupt thief turns thief-taker in despair, so an unsuccessful author turns critic.
P. B. SHELLEY: *Adonais,* pref., 1821 (Shelley cancelled this passage before publication)

It may be laid down as an almost universal rule that good poets are bad critics. Their minds are under the tyranny of ten thousand associations imperceptible to others. The worst writer may easily happen to touch a spring which is connected in their minds with a long succession of beautiful images.
T. B. MACAULAY: *Dante,* 1824 (Knight's Quarterly Magazine, Jan.)

The title of ultracrepidarian critics has been given to those persons who find fault with small and insignificant details.
WILLIAM HAZLITT: *Table-Talk,* III, 1824

It is by giving faith to the creations of the imagination that a man becomes a poet. It is by treating those creations as deceptions, and by resolving them, as nearly as possible, into their elements, that he becomes a critic.
T. B. MACAULAY: *John Dryden,* 1828 (Edinburgh Review, Jan.)

For critics I care the five hundred thousandth part of the tythe of a half-farthing.
CHARLES LAMB: *Letter to Bernard Barton,* Aug. 30, 1830

Critic, spare thy vanity,
Nor show thy pompous parts,
To vex with odious subtlety
The cheerer of men's hearts.
R. W. EMERSON: *Saadi,* 1842

Nature fits all her children with something to do:
He who would write and can't write can surely review.
J. R. LOWELL: *A Fable for Critics,* 1848

Critics are sentinels in the grand army of letters, stationed at the corners of newspapers and reviews, to challenge every new author.
H. W. LONGFELLOW: *Kavanagh,* XIII, 1849

When we attend less to "authority" and more to principles, when we look less at merit and more at demerit, (instead of the converse, as some persons suggest,) we shall then be better critics than we are.
E. A. POE: *Marginalia,* 1844–49

"I'm an owl: you're another. Sir Critic, good day." And the barber kept on shaving.
JAMES T. FIELDS: *The Owl-Critic, c.* 1860

Poor devils! Where do they come from? At what age are they sent to the slaughter-house? What is done with their bones? Where do such animals pasture in the day-time? Do they have females, and young? How many of them handled the brush before being reduced to the broom?
HECTOR BERLIOZ: *Les grotesques de la musique,* 1859

Nature, when she invented, manufactured, and patented her authors, contrived to make critics out of the chips that were left.
O. W. HOLMES: *The Professor at the Breakfast-Table,* I, 1859

I refuse to admit that science has a place for men who make criticism their specialty, as in letters and in the arts. Criticism in science must be done by men of science themselves, and by the most eminent masters.
CLAUDE BERNARD: *Introduction à la médecine expérimentale,* 1865

The public is the only critic whose opinion is worth anything at all.
S. L. CLEMENS (MARK TWAIN): *A General Reply,* 1870 (Galaxy, Nov.)

A wise skepticism is the first attribute of a good critic.
J. R. LOWELL: *Among My Books,* 1870

The function of the aesthetic critic is to distinguish, to analyze, and separate from its adjuncts, the virtue by which a picture, a landscape, a fair personality in life or in a book, produces this special impression of beauty or pleasure, to indicate what the source of that impression is, and under what conditions it is experienced.
WALTER PATER: *Studies in the History of the Renaissance,* pref., 1873

There are men to whom the satisfaction of throwing down a triumphant fallacy is as great as that which attends the discovery of a new truth.
T. H. HUXLEY: *Joseph Priestly,* 1874 (Address at Birmingham)

The critic takes a book in one hand, and uses the other to paint himself with. When his work is done, we may fail to find the book in it, but we are sure to find him.
J. G. HOLLAND: *Everyday Topics,* 1876

Insects sting, not in malice, but because they want to live. It is the same with critics: they desire our blood, not our pain.
F. W. NIETZSCHE: *Human All-too-Human,* II, 1878

The dramatic critic is asleep. The play does not interest him. He will give it thunder in the paper.
EUGENE FIELD: *The Tribune Primer,* 1882

The first duty of an art critic is to hold his tongue at all times, and upon all subjects.
OSCAR WILDE: *The English Renaissance of Art,* 1882 (Lecture in New York, Jan. 9)

A critic is one who tells of the adventures of the soul among masterpieces.
JACQUES THIBAULT (ANATOLE FRANCE): *La vie littéraire,* pref., 1883

A man who writes about things he doesn't like.
Author unidentified

Critics are the stupid who discuss the wise.
IBID.

[*See also* Criticism, Damn, Masterpiece.

Criticism

It is easier to pull down than to build up.
ENGLISH PROVERB, popular, *c.* 1925, among American Rotarians, Kiwanians, etc.; traced by Apperson to JOHN BRIDGES: *A Defence of the Government Established in the Church of England,* 1587; it probably had a Latin origin: "Facilius est destruere quam construere"

The pleasure of criticism deprives us of that of being deeply moved by beautiful things.
JEAN DE LA BRUYÈRE: *Caractères,* II, 1688

Criticism is easy and art is difficult.
P. N. DESTOUCHES: *Le glorieux,* II, 1732

Criticism, though dignified from the earliest ages by the labors of men eminent for knowledge and sagacity, and, since the revival of polite literature, the favorite study of European scholars, has not yet attained the certainty and stability of science.
SAMUEL JOHNSON: *The Rambler,* Sept. 21, 1751

The critical taste does not depend upon a superior principle in men, but upon superior knowledge.
EDMUND BURKE: *The Sublime and Beautiful,* intro., 1756

As the arts advance towards their perfection, the science of criticism advances with equal pace.
EDMUND BURKE: *The Sublime and Beautiful,* I

Criticism is a study by which men grow important and formidable at very small expense.
SAMUEL JOHNSON: *The Idler,* June 9, 1759

Of all the cants that are canted in this world, though the cant of hypocrites may be the worst, the cant of criticism is the most tormenting.
LAURENCE STERNE: *Tristram Shandy,* III, 1761

The most agreeable of all amusements.
H. H. KAMES: *Elements of Criticism,* 1762

You may abuse a tragedy though you cannot write one. You may scold a carpenter who

has made you a bad table, though you cannot make a table. It is not your trade to make tables.
SAMUEL JOHNSON: *Boswell's Life,* June 25, 1763

If a man is often the subject of conversation he soon becomes the subject of criticism.
IMMANUEL KANT: Lecture at Königsberg, 1775

The worst thing you can do to an author is to be silent as to his works. An assault upon a town is a bad thing, but starving it is still worse; an assault may be unsuccessful, you may have more men killed than you kill, but if you starve the town you are sure of victory.
SAMUEL JOHNSON: *Boswell's Life,* 1791

Criticism strips the tree of both caterpillars and blossoms.
JEAN PAUL RICHTER: *Titan,* CV, 1803

I have always very much despised the artificial canons of criticism. When I have read a work in prose or poetry, or seen a painting, a statue, &c., I have only asked myself whether it gives me pleasure, whether it is animating, interesting, attaching? If it is, it is good for these reasons.
THOMAS JEFFERSON: *Letter to William Wirt,* 1816

The ultimate end of criticism is much more to establish the principles of writing than to furnish rules how to pass judgment on what has been written by others; if indeed it were possible that the two could be separated.
S. T. COLERIDGE: *Biographia Literaria,* XVIII, 1817

Three questions are essential to all just criticism: What is the author's object? How far has he accomplished it? How far is that objection worthy of approbation?
N. P. WILLIS: *Pencillings by the Way,* pref., 1835

In criticism I will be bold, and sternly, absolutely just with friend and foe. From this purpose nothing shall turn me. I shall aim at originality in the body of the work more than at any other especial quality.
E. A. POE: *Letter,* Jan. 17, 1841

You do not get a man's most effective criticism until you provoke him. Severe truth is expressed with some bitterness.
H. D. THOREAU: *Journal,* March 15, 1854

It is much easier to be critical than to be correct.
BENJAMIN DISRAELI: Speech in the House of Commons, Jan. 24, 1860

Most men endure criticism with commendable fortitude, just as most criminals when under the drop conduct themselves with calmness. They bleed, but they bleed inwardly.
ALEXANDER SMITH: *Dreamthorp,* VII, 1863

Criticism, carried to the height worthy of it, is a majestic office, perhaps an art, perhaps even a church.
WALT WHITMAN: *Criticism, c.* 1870

Criticism is above all a gift, an intuition, a matter of tact and flair; it cannot be taught or demonstrated, — it is an art.
H. F. AMIEL: *Journal,* May 19, 1878

Criticism itself is much criticized, — which logically establishes its title.
W. C. BROWNELL: *Criticism,* 1914

When criticism first propounded as its real concern the oft-repeated questions: "What has the poet tried to express, and how has he expressed it?" criticism prescribed for itself the only possible method.
J. E. SPINGARN: *Creative Criticism,* 1917

Criticism is based upon the decay of the art criticized. Author unidentified

[*See also* Author, Cant, Censure, Constructive, Critic, Dogma, Dryden (John), Judge, Standard.

Cromwell, Oliver (1599–1658)

In appearance extremely religious, he preaches eloquently to the soldiers, persuading them to live according to God's laws; and to render his persuasions more efficacious he avails himself of tears.
GIOVANNI SAGREDO: Report to the Venetian Senate, *c.* 1656

A perfect master of all the arts of simulation; and of dissimulation; who, turning up the whites of his eyes, and seeking the Lord with pious gestures, will weep and pray, and cant most devoutly, till an opportunity offers of dealing his dupe a knock-down blow under the short ribs.
Ascribed to GEORGE BATE, physician to Cromwell, *c.* 1660

That grand impostor, that loathsome hypocrite, that detestable traitor, that prodigy of nature, that opprobrium of mankind, that landscape of iniquity, that sink of sin, that compendium of baseness who now calls himself our Protector.
Address of the Anabaptists to Charles II, *c.* 1658

As he had all the wickedness against which damnation is denounced and for which hell-fire is prepared, so he had some virtues which have caused the memory of some men in all ages to be celebrated; and he will be looked upon by posterity as a brave bad man.
EDWARD HYDE (EARL OF CLARENDON): *The True Historical Narrative of the Rebellion and Civil Wars in England, c.* 1670

Cromwell was about to ravage all Christendom; the royal family was lost, and his own forever powerful, had it not been for a grain of sand that got into his ureter.
BLAISE PASCAL: *Pensées,* II, 1670

Cromwell, damned to everlasting fame.
ALEXANDER POPE: *An Essay on Man*, IV, 1734

Cromwell was the most terrible of all charlatans.
VOLTAIRE: *Philosophical Dictionary*, 1764

He stood bare, not cased in euphemistic coat-of-mail; he grappled like a giant, face to face, heart to heart, with the naked truth of things. I plead guilty to valuing such a man beyond all other sorts of men.
THOMAS CARLYLE: *Heroes and Hero-Worship*, VI, 1840 (Lecture in London, May 22)

He was simply a strong-minded, rough-built Englishman, with a character thoroughly English, and exceedingly good-natured.
THOMAS DE QUINCEY: *Falsification of English History*, *c.* 1847

He was a practical mystic, the most formidable and terrible of all combinations. A man who combines inspiration apparently derived — in my judgment, really derived — from close communion with the supernatural and the celestial, a man who has that inspiration and adds to it the energy of a mighty man of action, such a man as that lives in communion on a Sinai of his own, and when he pleases to come down to this world below seems armed with no less than the terrors and decrees of the Almighty Himself.
LORD ROSEBERY: Speech at the Cromwell Tercentenary, London, 1899

[*See also* Obscurity, Theocracy, Victory.

Cross

Whosoever will come after me, let him deny himself, and take up his cross, and follow me.
MARK VIII, 34, *c.* 70 (Cf. X, 21; MATTHEW XVI, 24, *c.* 75; LUKE IX, 23, *c.* 75)

He that taketh not his cross, and followeth after me, is not worthy of me.
MATTHEW X, 38, *c.* 75 (Cf. LUKE XIV, 27, *c.* 75)

No cross, no crown.
ENGLISH PROVERB, current since the XVI century (Title of a book by William Penn, 1669)

No man ought to lay a cross upon himself, or to adopt tribulation, as is done in popedom; but if a cross or tribulation come upon him, then let him suffer it patiently, and know that it is good and profitable for him.
MARTIN LUTHER: *Table-Talk*, DCXXXV, 1569

Crosses are ladders that lead to Heaven.
ENGLISH PROVERB, traced by Smith to 1616

Nothing in my hand I bring;
Simply to thy Cross I cling.
A. M. TOPLADY: *Hymn CCCXXXVII* (*Rock of Ages*), 1776

We do not attach any intrinsic virtue to the Cross; this would be sinful and idolatrous. Our veneration is referred to Him who died upon it.
JAMES CARDINAL GIBBONS: *The Faith of Our Fathers*, I, 1876

The way of the Cross is the way of light. (Via crucis via lucis.)
MEDIEVAL LATIN PROVERB

[*See also* Bishop, Crucifix, Gallows, Suffering.

Cross of Gold

You shall not press down upon the brow of labor this crown of thorns. You shall not crucify mankind upon a cross of gold.
W. J. BRYAN: Speech at the Democratic National Convention, Chicago, July 8, 1896

Cross, Sign of the

In all our actions, when we come in or go out, when we dress, when we wash, at our meals, before retiring to sleep, we make on our foreheads the sign of the cross. These practises are not committed by a formal law of Scripture, but tradition teaches them, custom confirms them, faith observes them.
TERTULLIAN: *De Corona*, III, *c.* 200

Crow

One crow never pulleth out another's eyes.
JAMES SANDFORD: *Hours of Recreation*, 1572

The crow doth sing as sweetly as the lark,
When neither is attended.
SHAKESPEARE: *A Merchant of Venice*, V, *c.* 1597

It's God that feeds the crows,
That neither tills, harrows, nor sows.
THOMAS FULLER: *Gnomologia*, 1732

Crow does not eat crow. LATIN PROVERB

[*See also* One.

Crowd

A crowd is not company, and faces are but a gallery of pictures.
FRANCIS BACON: *Essays*, XXVII, 1612

Whoever hath an ambition to be heard in a crowd must press, and squeeze, and thrust, and climb, with indefatigable pains, till he has exalted himself to a certain degree of altitude above them.
JONATHAN SWIFT: *A Tale of a Tub*, I, 1704

Observe any meetings of people, and you will always find their eagerness and impetuosity rise or fall in proportion to their numbers: when the numbers are very great, all sense and reason seem to subside, and one sudden frenzy to seize on all, even the coolest of them.
LORD CHESTERFIELD: *Letter to his son*, Sept. 13, 1748

Far from the madding crowd's ignoble strife.
THOMAS GRAY: *Elegy Written in a Country Churchyard,* 1750

Of all animals, men are the least fitted to live in herds. If they were crowded together as sheep are they would all perish in a short time. The breath of man is fatal to his fellows.
J.-J. ROUSSEAU: *Émile,* I, 1762

Large bodies are far more likely to err than individuals. The passions are inflamed by sympathy; the fear of punishment and the sense of shame are diminished by partition.
T. B. MACAULAY: *Hallam,* 1828 (Edinburgh Review, Sept.)

The individuals in a crowd, by their numbers, acquire a feeling of power which gives rein to instincts that, alone, they would have been forced to keep in check.
GUSTAVE LEBON: *Psychologies des foules,* I, 1895

Those who follow the crowd are quickly lost in it. Author unidentified

[*See also* Advice, Civilization, Company, Demagogue, Mob, Orator, Populace.

Crowing

[*See* Hen.

Crown

Uneasy lies the head that wears a crown.
SHAKESPEARE: *II Henry IV,* III, *c.* 1598

The most glorious crown is set with false diamonds.
PIERRE CORNEILLE: *Héraclius,* I, 1647

The royal crown cures not the headache.
BENJAMIN FRANKLIN: *Poor Richard's Almanac,* 1757

Every noble crown is, and on earth will forever be, a crown of thorns.
THOMAS CARLYLE: *Past and Present,* III, 1843

[*See also* Abdication, King.

Crown of Thorns

They clothed him with purple, and platted a crown of thorns, and put it about his head.
MARK XV, 17, *c.* 70 (Cf. MATTHEW XXVII, 29, *c.* 75; JOHN XIX, 2, *c.* 115)

[*See also* Cross of Gold, Crown.

Crucifix

And on his breast a bloody cross he bore,
The dear remembrance of his dying Lord.
EDMUND SPENSER: *The Faerie Queene,* I, *c.* 1589

On her white breast a sparkling cross she wore
Which Jews might kiss and infidels adore.
ALEXANDER POPE: *The Rape of the Lock,* II, 1714

The cross on the breast, and the Devil in the heart.
THOMAS FULLER: *Gnomologia,* 1732

Frantic priests waved the ill-omened cross
O'er the unhappy earth.
P. B. SHELLEY: *Queen Mab,* VII, 1813

Leave me to my crucifix,
Whose pallid burden, sick with pain, watches the world with weary eyes,
And weeps for every soul that dies, and weeps for every soul in vain.
OSCAR WILDE: *The Sphinx,* 1891

[*See also* Charm, Cross.

Crucifixion

Pilate said unto them, Why, what evil hath he done? And they cried out the more exceedingly, Crucify him.
MARK XV, 14, *c.* 70 (Cf. XV, 13; LUKE XXIII, 21, *c.* 75; JOHN XIX, 6, 15, *c.* 115)

And when they were come to the place which is called Calvary, there they crucified him.
LUKE XXIII, 33, *c.* 75

Cruelty

He who usurps the government of any state should execute and put in practice all the cruelties which he thinks material at once, that he may have no occasion to renew them often, but that by his discontinuance he may mollify the people, and by his benefits bring them over to his side.
NICCOLÒ MACHIAVELLI: *The Prince,* VIII, 1513

You are the cruell'st she alive.
SHAKESPEARE: *Twelfth Night,* I, *c.* 1601

I must be cruel, only to be kind.
SHAKESPEARE: *Hamlet,* III, *c.* 1601

Cruelty is more cruel if we defer the pain.
GEORGE HERBERT: *Jacula Prudentum,* 1651

Scarcely anything awakens attention like a tale of cruelty. The writer of news never fails to tell how the enemy murdered children and ravished virgins; and if the scene of action be somewhat distant, scalps half the inhabitants of a province.
SAMUEL JOHNSON: *The Idler,* Nov. 11, 1758

I would not enter on my list of friends
(Though graced with polish'd manners and fine sense,
Yet wanting sensibility) the man
Who needlessly sets foot upon a worm.
WILLIAM COWPER: *The Task,* VI, 1785

Those who are not adept in reading faces are always crueller and ruder than other people: that is why we find it easier to be cruel to animals than to men.
G. C. LICHTENBERG: *Reflections,* 1799

Man is little inferior to the tiger and hyena in cruelty and savagery.
ARTHUR SCHOPENHAUER: *Parerga und Paralipomena*, II, 1851

Cruelty is the first attribute of the Devil.
H. G. BOHN: *Handbook of Proverbs*, 1855

[*See also* Aristocracy, Avarice, Coward, Cowardice, Good and Evil, War and Peace.

Crutch

[*See* Foot.

Crying

[*See* Baby, Tears.

Cuba

I have ever looked on Cuba as the most interesting addition which could ever be made to our system of states. The control which, with Florida, this island would give us over the Gulf of Mexico, and the countries and isthmus bordering on it, as well as all those whose waters flow into it, would fill up the measure of our political well-being.
THOMAS JEFFERSON: *Letter to James Monroe*, 1823

Cuckold

To wear a horn and not know it will do me no more harm than to eat a fly and not see it.
JOHN LYLY: *Euphues*, 1579

The character of cuckoldry is perpetual; on whom it once fasteneth, it holdeth forever.
MICHEL DE MONTAIGNE: *Essays*, III, 1588

Pluck off the bull's horns and set them in my forehead: and let me be vilely painted; and in such great letters as they write, " Here is good horse to hire," let them signify under my sign, — " Here you may see Benedick the married man."
SHAKESPEARE: *Much Ado About Nothing*, I, *c.* 1599

He hath horrible sore eyes; and so hath every cuckold, for the roots of the horns spring in the eyeballs, and that's the reason the horn of a cuckold is as tender as his eye.
JOHN MARSTON: *The Malcontent*, I, 1604

The cuckold is the last that knows of it.
WILLIAM CAMDEN: *Remains Concerning Britain* (4th ed.), 1636

Company makes cuckolds.
JOHN CLARKE: *Parœmiologia Anglo-Latina*, 1639

I pray thee, O Lord, that I may not be married; but if I am to be married, that I may not be a cuckold; but if I am to be a cuckold, that I may not know it, but if I am to know, that I may not mind.
Anon.: *The Bachelor's Prayer*, *c.* 1650

Better to be a cuckold and no one know it, than to be none and yet to be thought so.
JAMES HOWELL: *Proverbs*, 1659

Cuckolds are kind to those who make them so.
MARY DE LA RIVIÈRE MANLEY: *The Lost Lover*, v, 1696

Cuckolds are Christians all the world over.
THOMAS FULLER: *Gnomologia*, 1732

He that thinks himself a cuckold carries live coals in his heart. IBID.

Call your husband cuckold in jest, and he'll never suspect you.
H. G. BOHN: *Handbook of Proverbs*, 1855

[*See also* Cuckoo.

Cuckoo

Cuccu, cuccu, well singes thu, cuccu:
Ne swike thu naver nu;
Sing cuccu, nu, sing cuccu,
Sing cuccu, sing cuccu, nu!
Anon.: *Cuckoo Song*, *c.* 1250

The cuckoo then on every tree,
Mocks married men; for thus sings he,
Cuckoo!
Cuckoo! Cuckoo! O word of fear,
Unpleasing to a married ear.
SHAKESPEARE: *Love's Labor's Lost*, v, *c.* 1595

Thrice welcome, darling of the Spring!
Even yet thou art to me
No bird, but an invisible thing,
A voice, a mystery.
WILLIAM WORDSWORTH: *To the Cuckoo*, 1807

The cuckoo comes in April,
Sings a song in May;
Then in June another tune,
And then she flies away. ENGLISH RHYME

Cucumber

A cucumber should be well sliced, and dressed with pepper and vinegar, and then thrown out, as good for nothing.
SAMUEL JOHNSON: *Boswell's Tour to the Hebrides*, Oct. 5, 1773 (Quoted as " a common saying of physicians in England ")

Culture

The great law of culture is, Let each become all that he was created capable of being; expand, if possible, to his full growth; resisting all impediments, casting off all foreign, especially all noxious adhesions, and show himself at length in his own shape and stature, be these what they may.
THOMAS CARLYLE: *J. P. F. Richter*, 1827

Culture inverts the vulgar views of nature, and brings the mind to call that apparent which it uses to call real, and that real, which it uses to call visionary.

R. W. EMERSON: *Nature,* VI, 1836

Culture, with us, ends in headache.

R. W. EMERSON: *Experience,* 1841

A cultivated mind is one to which the fountains of knowledge have been opened, and which has been taught, in any tolerable degree, to exercise its faculties.

J. S. MILL: *Utilitarianism,* II, 1863

Culture is properly described as the love of perfection; it is a study of perfection.

MATTHEW ARNOLD: *Culture and Anarchy,* I, 1869

Culture looks beyond machinery, culture hates hatred; culture has one great passion, — the passion for sweetness and light.

IBID. (The phrase "sweetness and light" is borrowed from JONATHAN SWIFT: *The Battle of the Books,* 1704. It is repeated by ARNOLD in *Literature and Dogma,* pref., 1873)

There are other forms of culture beside physical science; and I should be profoundly sorry to see the fact forgotten, or even to observe a tendency to starve, or cripple, literary, or aesthetic, culture for the sake of science.

T. H. HUXLEY: *Scientific Education,* 1869 (Speech in Liverpool)

Are not the processes of culture rapidly creating a class of supercilious infidels, who believe in nothing? Shall a man lose himself in countless masses of adjustments, and be so shaped with reference to this, that, and the other, that the simply good and healthy and brave parts of him are reduced and clipp'd away, like the bordering of a box in a garden?

WALT WHITMAN: *Democratic Vistas,* 1870

Culture is "to know the best that has been said and thought in the world."

MATTHEW ARNOLD: *Literature and Dogma,* pref., 1873

As culture comes in, faith goes out.

J. G. HOLLAND: *Everyday Topics,* 1876

We'll make culture hum.

Ascribed to the Chicago intelligentsia, *c.* 1890

Culture is what your butcher would have if he were a surgeon.

MARY PETTIBONE POOLE: *A Glass Eye at the Keyhole,* 1938

[*See also* Politeness, Soap.

Cunning

Cunning and treachery are the offspring of incapacity.

LA ROCHEFOUCAULD: *Maxims,* 1665

A cunning man is overmatched by a cunning man and a half.

BENJAMIN FRANKLIN: *Poor Richard's Almanac,* 1754

Nature has endowed some animals with cunning as a compensation for strength withheld; but it has provoked the malice of all others, as if avengers of public wrong.

R. W. EMERSON: *English Traits,* VIII, 1856

The most cunning are caught first.

FRENCH PROVERB

[*See also* Malice.

Cupid

This senior-junior, giant-dwarf, Dan Cupid:
Regent of love-rhymes, lord of folded arms,
The anointed sovereign of sighs and groans,
Liege of all loiterers and malcontents.

SHAKESPEARE: *Love's Labor's Lost,* III, *c.* 1595

Love's heralds should be thoughts,
Which ten times faster glide than the sun's beams,
Driving back shadows over low'ring hills:
Therefore do nimble-pinion'd doves draw love,
And therefore hath the wind-swift Cupid wings.

SHAKESPEARE: *Romeo and Juliet,* II, *c.* 1596

Some Cupid kills with arrows, some with traps.

SHAKESPEARE: *Much Ado About Nothing,* III, *c.* 1599

There is music even in the silent note which Cupid strikes, far sweeter than the sound of an instrument.

THOMAS BROWNE: *Religio Medici,* II, 1642

[*See also* Courtship, Love, Lover, Wooing.

Cure

It is part of the cure to wish to be cured. (Pars sanitatis velle sanari fuit.)

SENECA: *Phaedra, c.* 60

I dressed him; God cured him. (Je le pansay; Dieu le guarit.)

AMBROSE PARÉ: Concluding sentence of many of his surgical reports, 1552–73

Past cure is . . . past care.

SHAKESPEARE: *Love's Labor's Lost,* V, *c.* 1595

The cure is worse than the disease.

PHILIP MASSINGER: *The Bondman,* I, 1624

Who pays the physician does the cure.

GEORGE HERBERT: *Outlandish Proverbs,* 1640

Nature does not want to cure the man; she wants to put him in his coffin.

Ascribed to SIR WILLIAM GULL (1816–94) in T. H. HUXLEY: *The Struggle for Existence in Human Society,* 1888

The healing power of nature. (Vis medicatrix naturae.)

LATIN PHRASE

[*See also* Death, Disease, God, Like, Medicine, Physician, Prevention.

Curfew

The curfew tolls the knell of parting day,
The lowing herd winds slowly o'er the lea,
The plowman homeward plods his weary way,
And leaves the world to darkness and to me.
THOMAS GRAY: *Elegy Written in a Country Churchyard,* 1750

Curfew must not ring tonight.
ROSA H. THORPE: Title of a poem, 1882

[*See also* Bell.

Curiosity

Curiosity will always hurt women.
JOHN NORTHBROOKE: *Against Dicing,* 1577

Nothing is so curious and thirsty after knowledge of dark and obscure matters as the nature of man.
THOMAS WRIGHT: *The Passions of the Mind in General,* 1601

An itching humor or a kind of longing to see that which is not to be seen, to do that which ought not to be done, to know that secret which should not be known, to eat of the forbidden fruit.
ROBERT BURTON: *The Anatomy of Melancholy,* I, 1621

There are two sorts of curiosity: one is from interest, which makes us desire to know what may be useful to us; another is from pride, and arises from a desire of knowing what others are ignorant of.
LA ROCHEFOUCAULD: *Maxims,* 1665

Curiosity is only vanity. Most frequently we wish not to know, but to talk. We would not take a sea voyage for the sole pleasure of seeing without hope of ever telling.
BLAISE PASCAL: *Pensées,* II, 1670

Curiosity is delight.
WALTER CHARLETON: *The Natural History of the Passions,* 1674

Zaccheus, he
Did climb the tree,
His Lord to see.
NEW ENGLAND PRIMER, *c.* 1688

Curiosity is ill manners in another's house.
THOMAS FULLER: *Gnomologia,* 1732

Envy and idleness married together begot curiosity. IBID.

Curiosity is one of the permanent and certain characteristics of a vigorous intellect.
SAMUEL JOHNSON: *The Rambler,* March 12, 1751

The first and the simplest emotion which we discover in the human mind is curiosity.
EDMUND BURKE: *The Sublime and Beautiful,* I, 1756

I loathe that low vice — curiosity.
BYRON: *Don Juan,* I, 1819

Curiosity creeps into the homes of the unfortunate under the names of duty or pity.
F. W. NIETZSCHE: *Human All-too-Human,* I, 1878

Man's last agony and his last pulse of curiosity are one.
M. J. GUYAU: *L'irréligion de l'avenir,* III, 1887

Curiosity killed the cat.
AMERICAN PROVERB, not recorded in any English collection

The reason why most of us haven't committed suicide long ago. Author unidentified

[*See also* Inquisitive, Philosophy.

Currency

The crown has the sole right to issue money.
Decision of the English Privy Council, 1603

A positive law may render a shilling a legal tender for a guinea; because it may direct the courts of justice to discharge the debtor who has made that tender. But no positive law can oblige a person who sells goods, and who is at liberty to sell or not to sell, as he pleases, to accept of a shilling as equivalent to a guinea in the price of them.
ADAM SMITH: *The Wealth of Nations,* II, 1776

A great deal of small change is useful in a state, and tends to reduce the price of small articles.
THOMAS JEFFERSON: *Notes on a Money Unit,* 1784

Too great a quantity of cash in circulation is a much greater evil than too small a quantity.
NOAH WEBSTER: *Letter to the Maryland Journal,* Aug. 9, 1785

Depreciate paper as much as you will, and it will still serve all the purposes of barter. Tradesmen still keep shops, stock them with goods, and deliver their commodities for those coined rags. — Poor Reason, where art thou?
HORACE WALPOLE: *Letter to Hannah More,* Feb. 9, 1793

A cent is the representative of a certain quantity of corn or other commodity. Its value is in the necessities of the animal man. It is so much warmth, so much bread, so much water, so much land. The law may do what it will with the owner of property, its just power will still attach to the cent.
R. W. EMERSON: *Politics,* 1841

I believe gold and silver coin to be the money of the Constitution. No power was conferred on Congress to declare that either metal should not be money. Congress has therefore no power to demonetize silver any more than to demonetize gold.
JAMES G. BLAINE: Speech in the Senate, Feb. 7, 1878

No government can afford to be a clipper of coin.

R. G. INGERSOLL: Speech in New York, Oct. 23, 1880

We believe in honest money, the gold and silver coinage of the Constitution, and a circulating medium convertible into such money without loss.

Democratic National Platform, 1884

We have always recommended the best money known to the civilized world; and we urge that efforts should be made to unite all commercial nations in the establishment of an international standard, which shall fix for all the relative value of gold and silver coinage.

Republican National Platform, 1884

[*See also* Authority, Bimetallism, Cash, Coin, Dollar, Money.

Curse

Curse God, and die. JOB II, 9, *c.* 325 B.C.

Curse not the king, no not in thy thought; and curse not the rich in thy bedchamber: for a bird of the air shall carry the voice, and that which hath wings shall tell the matter.

ECCLESIASTES: X, 20, *c.* 200 B.C.

Curses come home to roost.

ENGLISH PROVERB, traced by Smith, in various forms, to the *Proverbs of Alfred, c.* 1275

I curse their head and all the hairs of their head. I curse their face, their eyes, their mouth, their nose, their tongue, their teeth, their shoulders, their back, and their heart, their arms, their legs, their hands, their feet, and every part of their body from the top of their head to the soles of their feet, before and behind, within and without . . . I curse them walking, and I curse them riding. I curse them eating, and I curse them drinking. I curse them within the house, and I curse them without the house. I curse their wives, their bairns and their servants . . . I curse their cattle, their wool, their sheep, their horses, their swine, their geese, and their hens. I curse their halls, their chambers, their stables, and their barns . . .

Curse on the English read by Scotch priests on the closing of the religious houses, *c.* 1530

Curses are a kind of prayers.

SAMUEL BUTLER: *Hudibras,* III, 1678

If any one's curse can effect damnation, it is not that of the pope, but that of the poor.

WILLIAM SHENSTONE: *Of Men and Manners,* 1764

Potz himmel tausend sakristey, Croaten schwere noth, Teufel, hexen, truden, kreuz-Battalion und kein End, Potz Element, Luft, Wasser, erd und feuer, Europa, asia, affrica und America, jesuiter, Augustiner, Benedictiner, Capuziner, minoriten, franziskaner, Dominicaner, Chartheuser, und heil: kreuzer herrn, Canonici Regulares und irregulares, und Bärnhäuter, Spitzbuben, hundsfütter, Cujonen und schwänz übereinander, Eseln, büffeln, ochsen, Narrn, Dulken und fuxen!

W. A. MOZART: *Letter to his cousin,* Nov. 13, 1777

An orphan's curse would drag to Hell
A spirit from on high;
But oh! more horrible than that
Is the curse in a dead man's eye.

S. T. COLERIDGE: *The Ancient Mariner,* IV, 1798

May his fate be that of the Sabbath men.

ARAB IMPRECATION (The Sabbath men are the Jews, who are doomed to Hell by the Koran)

To curse is to pray to the Devil.

GERMAN PROVERB

The lips that curse shall go hungry.

POLISH PROVERB

[*See also* Invective, Swearing.

Custom

Custom produces a kind of second nature.

CICERO: *De finibus,* V, *c.* 50 B.C.

Habit makes the custom.

OVID: *Metamorphoses,* XV, *c.* 5

Custom is second nature.

ENGLISH PROVERB, usually appearing as "Habit is second nature," traced by Apperson to *c.* 1390 (Cf. CICERO, *ante, c.* 50 B.C.)

Long sufferance begets custom; custom, consent and imitation.

MICHEL DE MONTAIGNE: *Essays,* III, 1588

Custom kills with feeble dint,
More by use than strength prevailing.

ROBERT SOUTHWELL: *Loss in Delay, c.* 1595

Labor by custom becometh easy.

JOHN DELONEY: *The Gentle Craft,* II, 1598

It is a custom
More honor'd in the breach than the observance.

SHAKESPEARE: *Hamlet,* I, *c.* 1601

Custom calls me to 't:
What custom wills, in all things should we do 't.

SHAKESPEARE: *Coriolanus,* II, *c.* 1607

Custom reconciles us to everything.

ROBERT BURTON: *The Anatomy of Melancholy,* XVIII, 1621

Custom without reason is only ancient error.

ENGLISH PROVERB, traced by Apperson to 1647

What gives us that fantastick fit,
That all our judgment and our wit
To vulgar custom we submit?

JOHN DENHAM: *Natura naturata,* 1668

Custom is the plague of wise men and the idol of fools.

THOMAS FULLER: *Gnomologia,* 1732

Customs, even the most foolish and the most cruel, have always their source in the real or apparent utility of the public.

C. A. HELVÉTIUS: *De l'esprit,* II, 1758

There's nothing like being used to a thing.

R. B. SHERIDAN: *The Rivals,* V, 1775

As the good writer forbears to depart from the common use of words, so the good citizen should avoid deviating too far from custom.

G. C. LICHTENBERG: *Reflections,* 1799

There is a deep meaning in all old customs.

J. C. F. SCHILLER: *Marie Stuart,* I, 1800

What custom hath endeared
We part with sadly, though we prize it not.

JOANNA BAILLIE: *Basil,* I, *c.* 1825

Marriage should war incessantly with a monster that is the ruin of everything. This is the monster of custom.

BALZAC: *The Physiology of Marriage,* 1830

Custom doth make dotards of us all.

THOMAS CARLYLE: *Sartor Resartus,* III, 1836

The favorite phrase of English law is, "a custom whereof the memory of man runneth not back to the contrary."

R. W. EMERSON: *English Traits,* VI, 1856

The despotism of custom is everywhere the standing hindrance to human advancement.

J. S. MILL: *On Liberty,* III, 1859

Customs may not be as wise as laws, but they are always more popular.

BENJAMIN DISRAELI: Speech in the House of Commons, March 11, 1870

The greatest barrier in this world is use and wont. To say that a thing has never yet been done among men is to erect a barrier stronger than reason, stronger than discussion.

THOMAS B. REED: Speech in the House of Representatives, April 12, 1878

There is a strong probability in favor of adherence to an existing custom, even if it be a bad one.

G. E. MOORE: *Principia Ethica,* V, 1903

Primitive man knew nothing of laws. He only knew customs.

MICHAEL J. DEE: *Conclusions,* III, 1917

Custom is the best interpreter of the law. (Consuetudo est optima legum interpres.)

THE CODE OF CANON LAW, II, May 19, 1918 (An ancient legal maxim)

Other times, other customs.

ITALIAN PROVERB

Custom is a tyrant. (Usus est tyrannus.)

LATIN PROVERB

Ancient custom has the force of law. (Vetustas pro lege semper habetur.)

LEGAL MAXIM

Custom may serve in place of law. (Consuetudo pro lege servatur.) IBID.

Custom rules the law. (Mos regit legem.)

IBID.

The custom of the place is to be observed. (Consuetudo loci est observanda.) IBID.

[*See also* Belief, Habit, Language, Law, Offense, Once, Peasant, Philosophy, Prejudice.

Customer

He is my friend that grindeth at my mill.

JOHN CLARKE: *Parœmiologia Anglo-Latina,* 1639

In all minor discussions between Statler employés and Statler guests, the employé is dead wrong.

E. M. STATLER: *Statler Hotel Service Code,* 1921

Cut

[*See* Unkindness.

Cyclopedia

In books a prodigy, they say,
A living cyclopedia.

COTTON MATHER: Epitaph on Anne Bradstreet, 1672

Cynic

The cynics, those canine philosophers, . . .

ST. AUGUSTINE: *The City of God,* XIV, 427

The cynic is one who never sees a good quality in a man, and never fails to see a bad one. He is the human owl, vigilant in darkness, and blind to light, mousing for vermin, and never seeing noble game.

H. W. BEECHER: *Proverbs from Plymouth Pulpit,* 1870

A cynic is a man who knows the price of everything, and the value of nothing.

OSCAR WILDE: *Lady Windermere's Fan,* II, 1892

A blackguard whose faulty vision sees things as they are, not as they ought to be.

AMBROSE BIERCE: *The Devil's Dictionary,* 1906

A cynic is one who is married to his first love.

Author unidentified

Cynicism

Cynicism is a small brass fieldpiece that eventually breaks and kills the cannoneer.

HENRY ALDRICH: *Artis logicae,* 1691

Cynicism is intellectual dandyism.
GEORGE MEREDITH: *The Egoist*, VII, 1879

Cynicism is the form in which base souls approach what they call honesty.
F. W. NIETZSCHE: *Beyond Good and Evil*, 1886

Cynicism such as one finds very frequently among the most highly educated young men and women of the West results from the combination of comfort with powerlessness.
BERTRAND RUSSELL: *The Conquest of Happiness*, X, 1930

[*See also* Animal.

Cypress

Know ye the land where the cypress and myrtle
Are emblems of deeds that are done in their clime?
BYRON: *The Bride of Abydos*, I, 1813

Czar

When the Czar gives an egg he takes a hen.
RUSSIAN PROVERB

When the Czar has a cold all Russia coughs.
IBID.

When the Czar has smallpox all Russia is pockmarked.
IBID.

Czech

Whoever is a Czech is a musician. (Co Czech to muzikant.)
CZECH PROVERB

[*See also* Character (National), German.

D

Dachshund

A dog and a half long and half a dog high.
Author unidentified

Daffodil

Daffodils,
That come before the swallow dares, and take
The winds of March with beauty.
SHAKESPEARE: *The Winter's Tale*, IV, *c.* 1611

Daisy

[*See* Spring.

Dalliance

Sweet dalliance keepeth wrinkles long away;
Repentance follows them that have refused.
HENRY CONSTABLE: *Sonnets to Diana*, *c.* 1592

The primrose path of dalliance.
SHAKESPEARE: *Hamlet*, I, *c.* 1601

Damage

The person who injures another must make good five kinds of damages: loss of bodily substance or function, pain, cost of healing, loss of income, and mental anguish.
THE TALMUD (*Baba Kamma*), *c.* 200

To what damage. (Ad quod damnum.)
LATIN PHRASE

Damn

Damn with faint praise, assent with civil leer,
And without sneering teach the rest to sneer.
ALEXANDER POPE: *An Epistle to Dr. Arbuthnot*, 1735

Damn braces. Bless relaxes.
WILLIAM BLAKE: *The Marriage of Heaven and Hell*, 1790

Though " Bother it " I may
Occasionally say,
I never never use a big, big D.
W. S. GILBERT: *H.M.S. Pinafore*, I, 1878

[*See also* Filipino, Independence, Invective.

Damnation

Wide is the gate and broad is the way that leadeth to destruction, and many there be which go in thereat.
MATTHEW VII, 13, *c.* 75

Depart from me, ye cursed, into everlasting fire, prepared for the Devil and his angels.
MATTHEW XV, 41

Ye serpents, ye generation of vipers, how can ye escape the damnation of hell?
MATTHEW XXIII, 33

God foreordained, for His own glory and the display of His attributes of mercy and justice, a part of the human race, without any merit of their own, to eternal salvation, and another part, in just punishment of their sin, to eternal damnation.
JOHN CALVIN: *Institutes of the Christian Religion*, 1536

I think the Devil will not have me damned, lest the oil that is in me should set Hell on fire.
SHAKESPEARE: *The Merry Wives of Windsor*, V, *c.* 1600

The primrose way to the everlasting bonfire.
SHAKESPEARE: *Macbeth*, II, *c.* 1605

Were't not for gold and women, there would be no damnation.
CYRIL TOURNEUR: *The Revenger's Tragedy*, I, 1607

The damned are in the abyss of Hell, as within a woeful city, where they suffer unspeakable torments in all their senses and members, because as they have employed all their senses and their members in sinning, so shall they suffer in each of them the punishment due to sin.
ST. FRANCIS DE SALES: *Introduction to the Devout Life*, XV, 1609

If poisonous minerals, and if that tree
Whose fruit threw death on else immortal us,

If lecherous goats, if serpents envious
Cannot be damned, alas! why should I be?
JOHN DONNE: *Holy Sonnets*, *c.* 1617

From all evil and mischief; from sin; from the crafts and assaults of the Devil; from Thy wrath, and from everlasting damnation, Good Lord, deliver us.
THE BOOK OF COMMON PRAYER (*The Litany*), 1662

A passage broad,
Smooth, easy, inoffensive, down to Hell.
JOHN MILTON: *Paradise Lost*, X, 1667

One of the confusions of the damned will be that they will be condemned by their own reason, which they now use to condemn Christianity.
BLAISE PASCAL: *Pensées*, 1670

When a damned soul shall have shed tears enough to fill all the rivers of the world, even if he should have shed but one a century, he will be no nearer deliverance after so many millions of years; he will only have begun to suffer.
DOMINIQUE BOUHOURS: *Pensées chrétiennes*, *c.* 1685

The bow of God's wrath is bent, and the arrow made ready on the string, and justice bends the arrow at your heart, and strains the bow, and there is nothing but the mere pleasure of God, and that of an angry God, without any promise or obligation at all, that keeps the arrow one moment from being made drunk with your blood.
JONATHAN EDWARDS: *Sinners in the Hands of an Angry God*, 1741 (Sermon, July 8)

All are damnable and damned;
Each one damning, damns the other;
They are damned by one another.
P. B. SHELLEY: *Peter Bell the Third*, III, 1819

O Mother, Mother, fare ye well;
Your wicked Polly's doomed to Hell.
The tears are lost you shed for me;
My soul is lost, I plainly see.
Anon.: *Wicked Polly*, *c.* 1820

I had rather be damned with Plato and Lord Bacon than go to Heaven with Paley and Malthus.
P. B. SHELLEY: *Prometheus Unbound*, pref., 1820

The idea of damnation is anything but disagreeable to some people; it gives them a kind of gloomy consequence in their own eyes. We must be something particular, they think, or God would hardly think it worth His while to torment us for ever.
GEORGE BORROW: *Wild Wales*, XLVII, 1862

Dearly beloved, unless you repent of your sins in a measure, and become converted in a degree, you will, I regret to say, be damned to a more or less extent.
Ascribed to a cautious clergyman of Detroit, *c.* 1928

[*See also* Anathema, Calvinism, Hell, Predestination.

Damnation, Infant

Therefore in bliss
You may not hope to dwell;
But unto you I shall allow
The easiest room in Hell.
MICHAEL WIGGLESWORTH: *The Day of Doom*, 1662

They are not too little to die; they are not too little to go to Hell.
JAMES JANEWAY: *A Token for Youth*, *c.* 1670

Hell is paved with infants' skulls.
Ascribed to RICHARD BAXTER (1615–91)

All children are by nature children of wrath, and are in danger of eternal damnation in Hell.
JONATHAN EDWARDS: *Sermon to Children*, 1740

Innocent babes writhed on thy stubborn spear,
And thou didst laugh to hear the mother's shriek
Of maniac gladness, as the sacred steel
Felt cold in her torn entrails!
P. B. SHELLEY: *Queen Mab*, VI, 1813

Though the [Roman Catholic] Church, in obedience to God's Word, declares that unbaptized infants are excluded from the Kingdom of Heaven, it should not hence be concluded that they are consigned to the place of the reprobate. . . . All that the church holds on this point is that unregenerate children are deprived of the beatific vision, or the possession of God, which constitutes the essential happiness of the blessed.
JAMES CARDINAL GIBBONS: *The Faith of Our Fathers*, XIX, 1876

Damozel

The blessed damozel leaned out
From the gold bar of Heaven.
D. G. ROSSETTI: *The Blessed Damozel*, 1850

Dancing

Through dancing many maidens have been unmaidened, whereby I may say it is the storehouse and nursery of bastardy.
JOHN NORTHBROOKE: *Against Dicing*, 1577

He capers nimbly in a lady's chamber
To the lascivious pleasing of a lute.
SHAKESPEARE: *Richard* III, 1, *c.* 1592

Let wantons, light of heart,
Tickle the senseless rushes with their heels.
SHAKESPEARE: *Romeo and Juliet*, I, *c.* 1596

You and I are past our dancing days. IBID.

A dance is a measured pace, as a verse is a measured speech.
FRANCIS BACON: *The Advancement of Learning*, II, 1605

You dance like a plumber's daughter.
THOMAS MIDDLETON: *A Chaste Maid in Cheapside*, I, *c.* 1607

I have the same opinion of dances that physicians have of mushrooms: the best of them are good for nothing.
ST. FRANCIS DE SALES: *Introduction to the Devout Life*, XXXIII, 1609

Let the concupiscence of jigs and dances reign as strong as it will amongst you.
BEN JONSON: *Bartholomew Fair*, I, 1614

Summer is in her face now, and she skippeth.
JOHN FLETCHER: *The Wild-Goose Chase*, II, 1621

Come and trip it as ye go,
On the light fantastic toe.
JOHN MILTON: *L'Allegro*, 1632

Come, knit hands, and beat the ground
In a light fantastic round.
JOHN MILTON: *Comus*, 1637

But oh, she dances such a way!
No sun upon an Easter-day,
Is half so fine a sight.
JOHN SUCKLING: *A Ballad upon a Wedding*, 1642

Tune her a jig and play it roundly, you shall see her bounce it away like a nimble frigate before a fresh gale.
GEORGE ETHEREGE: *She Would if She Could*, II, 1668

If you want to dance you must pay the piper.
ENGLISH PROVERB, traced by Apperson to 1681

Good dancers have mostly better heels than heads.
THOMAS FULLER: *Gnomologia*, 1732

In a fiddler's house all are dancers. IBID.

They love dancing well that dance barefoot upon thorns. IBID.

'Twas surely the Devil that taught women to dance and asses to bray. IBID.

Alike all ages: dames of ancient days
Have led their children through the mirthful maze;
And the gay grandsire, skill'd in gestic lore,
Has frisk'd beneath the burden of threescore.
OLIVER GOLDSMITH: *The Traveler*, 1764

On with the dance! Let joy be unconfined.
BYRON: *Childe Harold*, III, 1816

Dancing is a necessary accomplishment, although of short use; for the French rule is wise, that no lady dances after marriage. This is founded in solid physical reasons.
THOMAS JEFFERSON: *Letter to N. Burwell*, 1818

We have no adequate conception of the perfection of the ancient tragic dance. The pleasure which the Greeks received from it had for its basis difference; and the more unfit the vehicle, the more lively was the curiosity and intense the delight at seeing the difficulty overcome.
S. T. COLERIDGE: *Table-Talk*, June 5, 1824

The greater the fool the better the dancer.
THEODORE HOOK: *Sayings and Doings*, 1826

Dancing is at once rational and healthful: it gives animal spirits; it is the natural amusement of young people, and such it has been from the days of Moses.
WILLIAM COBBETT: *Advice to Young Men*, I, 1829

How inimitably graceful children are in general — before they learn to dance.
S. T. COLERIDGE: *Table-Talk*, Jan. 1, 1832

The Marquesan girls dance all over; not only do their feet dance, but their arms, hands, fingers, ay, their very eyes seem to dance in their heads.
HERMAN MELVILLE: *Typee*, XIX, 1846

All night have the roses heard
The flute, violin, bassoon;
All night has the casement jessamine stirr'd
To the dancers dancing in tune.
ALFRED TENNYSON: *Maud*, I, 1855

Will you, won't you, will you, won't you, will you join the dance?
Will you, won't you, will you, won't you, won't you join the dance?
C. L. DODGSON (LEWIS CARROLL): *Alice in Wonderland*, 1865

We lift up a solemn note of warning and entreaty . . . against dancing.
The Doctrines and Discipline of the Methodist Episcopal Church, III, 1932

Promiscuous dancing is a means of fostering the lust of the flesh, the lust of the eye, and the pride of life. These things are not of the Father, but are of the world.
The Northern Presbytery of the Free Presbyterian Church of Scotland: Opinion in the case of John Murray, 1935

He who cannot dance puts the blame on the floor. HINDU PROVERB

All dancing girls are nineteen years old.
JAPANESE PROVERB

[*See also* Actor, Clergyman, Eminence, Fiddler, French, Volcano.

Dandy

A dandy is a clothes-wearing man, a man whose trade, office, and existence consists in the wearing of clothes.
THOMAS CARLYLE: *Sartor Resartus*, III, 1836

Dane

The Danes are a nation without pride.
Ascribed to GEORGES CLEMENCEAU, 1915

[*See also* English, Englishman, Scandinavian.

Danger

Danger strikes the sooner when it is despised.
PUBLILIUS SYRUS: *Sententiæ*, *c.* 50 B.C.

The pitcher that goes too often to the well is broken at last.
ENGLISH PROVERB, traced by Smith to 1340

A man's wisdom is most conspicuous where he is able to distinguish among dangers and make choice of the least.
NICCOLÒ MACHIAVELLI: *The Prince*, XXI, 1513

To women's foreparts do not aspire,
From a mule's hind part retire,
And shun all parts of monk or friar.
JOHN FLORIO: *Second Frutes*, 1591

The blood more stirs
To rouse a lion than to start a hare.
SHAKESPEARE: *I Henry IV*, I, *c.* 1598

Out of this nettle, danger, we pluck this flower, safety.
SHAKESPEARE: *I Henry IV*, II

I spoke of most disastrous chances,
Of moving accidents by flood and field;
Of hair-breadth 'scapes i' the imminent deadly breach.
SHAKESPEARE: *Othello*, I, 1604

The more the danger, the more the honor.
JOHN FLETCHER: *Rule a Wife and Have a Wife*, IV, 1624 (Cited as a " Roman axiom ")

We triumph without glory when we conquer without danger.
PIERRE CORNEILLE: *The Cid*, II, 1636

The danger past, and God forgotten.
JOHN RAY: *English Proverbs*, 1670

There is nobody who is not dangerous for some one.
MARIE DE SÉVIGNÉ: *Letters*, *c.* 1690

The air is full of poniards.
Ascribed to JOSEPH FOUCHÉ (1763–1820), minister of police under Napoleon I

Keep yourself from the anger of a great man, from the tumult of a mob, from a man of ill fame, from a widow that has been thrice married, from a wind that comes in at a hole, and from a reconciled enemy.
H. G. BOHN: *Handbook of Proverbs*, 1855

Beware of a mule's hind foot, a dog's tooth, and a woman's tongue.
C. H. SPURGEON: *John Ploughman's Pictures*, 1880

He who risks needless danger dies the Devil's martyr.
DUTCH PROVERB

Without danger the game grows cold. (Sine periculo friget lusus.)
LATIN PROVERB

Hannibal is at the gates. (Hannibal ad portas.)
LATIN SAYING

[*See also* Conquest, Delay.

Daniel

[*See* Judge.

Dante Alighieri (1265–1321)

Dante is hard, and few can understand him.
BEN JONSON: *Volpone*, III, 1603

I still think of Dante as I thought when I first read him, that he is a superior poet to Milton; that he runs neck and neck with Homer; and that none but Shakespeare has gone decidedly beyond him.
T. B. MACAULAY: *Letter to T. F. Ellis*, July 1, 1834

Dante does not come before us as a large catholic mind; rather as a narrow, and even sectarian mind; it is partly the fruit of his age and position, but partly too of his own nature. His greatness has, in all senses, concentered itself into fiery emphasis and depth. He is world-great not because he is world-wide, but because he is world-deep.
THOMAS CARLYLE: *Heroes and Hero-Worship*, III, 1841 (Lecture in London, May 12)

I find him full of the *nobil volgare eloquenza* — that he knows *God damn*, and can be rowdy if he pleases, and he does please.
R. W. EMERSON: *Journal*, July 13, 1849

The hyena poetizing in tombs.
F. W. NIETZSCHE: *The Twilight of the Idols*, 1889

[*See also* Artist.

Danton, Georges Jacques (1759–94)

My name? It is Danton — a name tolerably well known in the Revolution. My dwelling? It will soon be annihilation. But my name will live in the Pantheon of history.
G. J. DANTON: To the French revolutionary tribunal, April 7, 1794

Dardanelles

The Dardanelles should be permanently opened as a free passage to the ships and commerce of all nations under international guarantees.
WOODROW WILSON: Address to Congress, Jan. 8, 1918 (One of the Fourteen Points)

Daring

By daring, great fears are concealed.
LUCAN: *Pharsalia*, IV, 65 B.C.

Nothing is too high for the daring of mortals: we storm Heaven itself in our folly.
HORACE: *Carmina*, I, *c.* 20 B.C.

And dar'st thou then
To beard the lion in his den,
The Douglas in his hall?
WALTER SCOTT: *Marmion*, VI, 1808

The will to do, the soul to dare.
WALTER SCOTT: *The Lady of the Lake*, I, 1810

[*See also* Boldness, Bravery, Courage, Valor.

Darkness

Darkness which may be felt.
EXODUS X, 21, *c.* 700 B.C.

The dark makes every woman beautiful.
OVID: *Ars amatoria*, I, *c.* 2 B.C.

Night makes no difference 'twixt the priest and clark;
Joan as my lady is as good i' th' dark.
ROBERT HERRICK: *Hesperides*, 1648 (Cf. OVID, *ante*, *c.* 2 B.C.)

It is always darkest just before the day dawneth.
THOMAS FULLER: *A Pisgah-Sight of Palestine*, II, 1650

He that gropes in the dark finds that he would not.
JOHN RAY: *English Proverbs*, 1670

No wonder if he breaks his shins that walks in the dark.
THOMAS FULLER: *Gnomologia*, 1732

'Tis very ill driving black hogs in the dark.
BENJAMIN FRANKLIN: *Poor Richard's Almanac*, 1748

[*See also* Blush, Dawn, Evening, Light, Morning, Night.

Darwin, Charles (1809–82)

The Abraham of science — a searcher as obedient to the command of truth as was the patriarch to the command of God.
JOHN TYNDALL: *Fragments of Science for Unscientific People*, II, 1871

[*See also* Darwinism, Evolution.

Darwinism

The question is this: Is man an ape or an angel? My lord, I am on the side of the angels. I repudiate with indignation and abhorrence the contrary view, which is, I believe, foreign to the conscience of humanity.
BENJAMIN DISRAELI: Speech to the Oxford Diocesan Society, Nov. 25, 1864

Darwinism is Malthus all over.
LOUIS AGASSIZ: Address before the Massachusetts State Board of Agriculture, 1872

The Darwinian theory, even when carried out to its extreme logical conclusion, not only does not oppose, but lends a decided support to, a belief in the spiritual nature of man. It shows us how man's body may have been developed from that of a lower animal form under the law of natural selection; but it also teaches us that we possess intellectual and moral faculties which could not have been so developed, but must have had another origin; and for this origin we can only find an adequate cause in the unseen universe of spirit.
A. R. WALLACE: *Darwinism*, 1889

[*See also* Evolution, Natural Selection, Struggle for Existence.

Daughter

The daughter of any priest, if she profane herself by playing the whore, she profaneth her father: she shall be burnt with fire.
LEVITICUS XXI, 9, *c.* 700 B.C.

Many daughters have done virtuously, but thou excellest them all.
PROVERBS XXXI, 29, *c.* 350 B.C.

A daughter is an embarrassing and ticklish possession.
MENANDER: *Perinthis*, *c.* 300 B.C.

The mother said to her daughter: "Daughter, bid thy daughter tell her daughter that her daughter's daughter hath a daughter."
GEORGE HAKEWILL: *Apologie of the Power & Providence of God*, III, 1627

Marry your son when you will; your daughter when you can.
GEORGE HERBERT: *Jacula Prudentum*, 1651

Two daughters and a back door are three arrant thieves.
JOHN RAY: *English Proverbs*, 1670

Daughters and dead fish do not keep well.
ENGLISH PROVERB, apparently no older than the XVIII century

The companion, the friend, and confidant of her mother, and the object of a pleasure something like the love between the angels to her father.
RICHARD STEELE: *The Tatler*, May 23, 1710

It is harder to marry a daughter well than to bring her up well.
THOMAS FULLER: *Gnomologia*, 1732

My son is my son till he have got him a wife,
But my daughter's my daughter all the days of her life.
IBID.

If a daughter you have, she's the plague of your life,

No peace shall you know, tho' you've buried your wife,
At twenty she mocks at the duty you taught her,
Oh, what a plague is an obstinate daughter.
R. B. SHERIDAN: *The Duenna,* I, 1775

I would by no means wish a daughter of mine to be a progeny of learning.
R. B. SHERIDAN: *The Rivals,* I, 1775

The younger your daughter, the more apt she is to love you.
E. W. HOWE: *Country Town Sayings,* 1911

Here lies a most dutiful daughter, honest and just,
Awaiting the resurrection, in hopes to be one of the first.
EPITAPH IN ST. GILES' CHURCHYARD, Northampton, England

Brilliant daughter, cranky wife.
DUTCH PROVERB

A house full of daughters is like a cellar full of sour beer. IBID.

They who are full of sin beget only daughters.
HINDU PROVERB

The daughter of a busy mother makes a bad housekeeper. IRISH PROVERB

The first child of a woman of good blood is always a girl. ITALIAN PROVERB

Daughters pay nae debts.
SCOTTISH PROVERB

The lucky man has a daughter as his first child.
SPANISH PROVERB

[*See also* Father and Daughter, Heredity, Learning, Mother and Daughter, Wife.

Daughter-in-law

If a daughter-in-law is ugly she can't conceal the fact from her mother-in-law.
CHINESE PROVERB

A bad daughter-in-law is worse than a thousand devils.
JAPANESE PROVERB

[*See also* Mother-in-law.

David (c. 1033–993 B.C.)

The thing that David had done displeased the Lord. II SAMUEL XI, 27, *c.* 500 B.C.

The Greek tragedies are not to be compared with the history of David.
MARTIN LUTHER: *Table-Talk,* DXLIII, 1569

[*See also* Age (Old).

Davis, Jefferson

[*See* Lincoln (Abraham).

Dawn

Night's candles are burnt out, and jocund day
Stands tiptoe on the misty mountain tops.
SHAKESPEARE: *Romeo and Juliet,* III, *c.* 1596

The gentle day
Dapples the drowsy East with spots of grey.
SHAKESPEARE: *Much Ado About Nothing,* V, *c.* 1599

The glow-worm shows the matin to be near,
And 'gins to pale his uneffectual fire.
SHAKESPEARE: *Hamlet,* I, *c.* 1601

It is always darkest just before the day dawneth.
THOMAS FULLER: *A Pisgah-Sight of Palestine,* II, 1650

The sun is not yet risen,
But the dawn lies red on the dew.
S. T. COLERIDGE: *Alice du Clos,* 1817

O'er night's brim day boils at last.
ROBERT BROWNING: *Pippa Passes,* intro., 1841

That single hour of the twenty-four, when crime ceases, debauchery is exhausted, and even desolation finds a shelter.
BENJAMIN DISRAELI: *Sybil,* XXI, 1845

And ghastly thro' the drizzling rain
On the bald streets breaks the blank day.
ALFRED TENNYSON: *In Memoriam,* VII, 1850

Come into the garden, Maud,
For the black bat, night, has flown.
ALFRED TENNYSON: *In Memoriam,* I

To behold the daybreak!
The little light fades the immense and diaphanous shadows;
The air tastes good to my palate.
WALT WHITMAN: *Walt Whitman,* 1855

The blood-red trouble of the dawn.
ELIZABETH CHASE (AKERS ALLEN): *Spring at the Capital,* 1864

And down the long and silent street
The dawn, with silver-sandalled feet,
Crept like a frightened girl.
OSCAR WILDE: *The Harlot's House,* 1885 (London Dramatic Review, April)

On the road to Mandalay
Where the flyin'-fishes play
An' the dawn comes up like thunder outer
China 'crost the Bay.
RUDYARD KIPLING: *Mandalay,* 1890

The time when men of reason go to bed.
AMBROSE BIERCE: *The Devil's Dictionary,* 1906

The dawn is the friend of the Muses.
LATIN PROVERB

[*See also* Day, Daybreak, Glow-worm, Morning, Sunrise.

Day

My days are swifter than a weaver's shuttle.
JOB VII, 6, *c.* 325 B.C.

O happy day. (O diem laetum.)
PLINY THE YOUNGER: *Letters,* VI, *c.* 110

The day is short and the work is long.
ENGLISH PROVERB, borrowed from the Greek and traced by Apperson to *c.* 1400

Be the day short or never so long,
At length it ringeth to evensong.
JOHN FOXE: *The Book of Martyrs,* VII, 1563

If you have lived one day you have seen everything; one day is the same as all others.
MICHEL DE MONTAIGNE: *Essays,* I, 1580

The gaudy, blabbing, and remorseful day.
SHAKESPEARE: *II Henry VI,* IV, *c.* 1591

Ah! when will this long weary day have end,
And lend me leave to come unto my love?
EDMUND SPENSER: *Epithalamion,* 1595

What hath this day deserv'd? What hath it done,
That it in golden letters should be set
Among the high tides in the calendar?
SHAKESPEARE: *King John,* III, *c.* 1596

The live-long day.
SHAKESPEARE: *Julius Cæsar,* I, 1599

The better the day, the better the deed.
THOMAS MIDDLETON: *The Phoenix,* I, 1607

Hide me from day's garish eye.
JOHN MILTON: *Il Penseroso,* 1632

Come day, go day, the day is long enough.
THOMAS DRAXE: *Bibliotheca scholastica instructissima,* 1633

Sweet day, so cool, so calm, so bright,
The bridal of the earth and sky,
The dew shall weep thy fall tonight;
For thou must die.
GEORGE HERBERT: *The Temple,* 1633

The better day, the worse deed.
MATTHEW HENRY: *Exposition of Genesis III,* 1704 (Cf. MIDDLETON, *ante,* 1607)

A day to come shows longer than a year that's gone.
THOMAS FULLER: *Gnomologia,* 1732

What a day may bring a day may take away.
IBID.

Is not every meanest day the confluence of two eternities?
THOMAS CARLYLE: *The French Revolution,* I, 1837

How troublesome is day!
It calls us from our sleep away;
It bids us from our pleasant dreams awake,
And sends us forth to keep or break
Our promises to pay.
How troublesome is day!
THOMAS LOVE PEACOCK: *Fly-by-Night,* 1837

The long days are no happier than the short ones.
P. J. BAILEY: *Festus,* 1839

It is possible that human folly should go the length of understanding by the Mosaical day, the mysterious day of that awful agency which molded the heavens and the heavenly host, no more than the ordinary nychthemeron or cycle of twenty-four hours?
THOMAS DE QUINCEY: *The True Relations of the Bible to Merely Human Science,* *c.* 1845

Each day is a little life; every waking and rising a little birth, every fresh morning a little youth, every going to rest and sleep a little death.
ARTHUR SCHOPENHAUER: *Our Relation to Ourselves,* 1851

O day! and is your mightiness
A sycophant to smug success?
Will the sweet sky and ocean broad
Be fine accomplices to fraud?
O sun! I curse thy cruel ray:
Back, back to chaos, harlot day!
R. W. EMERSON: *The Chartist's Complaint,* 1857

A little space of time ere time expire,
A little day, a little way of breath.
A. C. SWINBURNE: *Laus Veneris,* 1866

When one has much to put into them, a day has a hundred pockets.
F. W. NIETZSCHE: *Human All-too-Human,* I, 1878

Come day, go day, God send Sunday.
ENGLISH PROVERB (Cf. DRAXE, *ante,* 1633)

Wait till it is night before saying it has been a fine day.
FRENCH PROVERB

[*See also* Dawn, Deceit, Evening, Evil, Laughter, Night, Nightingale.

Day and Night

Night is sadder than day.
OVID: *Remedia amoris, c.* 10

But how so that the day be long,
The dark night cometh at last.
JOHN GOWER: *Confessio Amantis,* VI, *c.* 1390

Now welcome, night! thou night so long expected,
That long day's labor dost at last defray.
EDMUND SPENSER: *Epithalamion,* 1595

This night methinks is but the daylight sick.
SHAKESPEARE: *The Merchant of Venice,* V, *c.* 1597

The night is long that never finds the day.
SHAKESPEARE: *Macbeth,* V, *c.* 1605

The day has eyes; the night has ears.
DAVID FERGUSSON: *Scottish Proverbs*, 1641

It is never a bad day that hath a good night.
JOHN RAY: *English Proverbs*, 1670

The day always laughs at the night.
MODERN GREEK PROVERB

Daylight

We burn daylight.
THOMAS KYD: *The Spanish Tragedy*, III, 1592

It is a garish, broad, and peering day;
Loud, light, suspicious, full of eyes and ears,
And every little corner, nook, and hole
Is penetrated with the insolent light.
P. B. SHELLEY: *The Cenci*, II, 1819

Daylight will peer through a sma' hole.
SCOTTISH PROVERB

Days

We have seen better days.
SHAKESPEARE: *As You Like It*, II, *c.* 1600

Monday for wealth,
Tuesday for health,
Wednesday the best day of all:
Thursday for crosses,
Friday for losses,
Saturday no luck at all.
Old English rhyme

Monday is a saint's day,
Tuesday's just another such day,
Wednesday's the middle pin,
Thursday's too late to begin,
Friday we must fast and pray,
Saturday never was but half a day.
Another version

Monday is Sunday's brother,
Tuesday is such another,
Wednesday you must go to church and pray,
Thursday is half-holiday,
On Friday it is too late to begin to spin,
The Saturday is half-holiday agin. IBID.

[*See also* Birthday, Wedding-day.

Deacon

[Deacons] must be grave, not double-tongued, not given to much wine, not greedy of filthy lucre, holding the mystery of the faith in a pure conscience.
I TIMOTHY III, 8–9, *c.* 60

[*See also* Celibacy, Clergy, Clergyman.

Dead

I would rather be a slave to the poorest peasant than reign over the dead.
HOMER: *Odyssey*, XI, *c.* 800 B.C.

The angel of the Lord went forth, and smote in the camp of the Assyrians a hundred and fourscore and five thousand: and when they arose early in the morning, behold, they were all dead corpses.
ISAIAH XXXVII, 36, *c.* 700 B.C. (Cf. II KINGS XIX, 35, *c.* 500 B.C.)

Say nothing but good of the dead. (De mortuis nil nisi bonum.)
Ascribed to SOLON, *c.* 600 B.C., and to CHILON, *c.* 560 B.C. (It appears as a proverb in all European languages)

If we treat the dead as if they were wholly dead it shows want of affection; if we treat them as wholly alive it shows want of sense. Neither should be done.
CONFUCIUS: *The Book of Rites*, II, *c.* 500 B.C.

There are no toils for the dead.
SOPHOCLES: *Trachiniae*, *c.* 450 B.C.

The dead have no tears, and forget all sorrow.
EURIPIDES: *The Troades*, *c.* 415 B.C.

He shall return no more to his house, neither shall his place know him any more.
JOB VII, 10, *c.* 325 B.C.

Man lieth down, and riseth not: till the heavens be no more, they shall not awake, nor be raised out of their sleep.
JOB XIV, 12

The dead know not anything, neither have they any more reward; for the memory of them is forgotten.
ECCLESIASTES IX, 5, *c.* 200 B.C.

When the dead is at rest, let his remembrance rest.
ECCLESIASTICUS XXXVIII, 23, *c.* 180 B.C.

The dead praise not the Lord.
PSALMS CXV, 17, *c.* 150 B.C.

The life of the dead consists in being present in the minds of the living.
CICERO: *Orationes Philippicae*, IX, *c.* 60 B.C.

Nothing is easier than to blame the dead.
JULIUS CÆSAR: *The Gallic War*, VII, *c.* 51 B.C.

Time magnifies everything after death; a man's fame is increased as it passes from mouth to mouth after his funeral.
PROPERTIUS: *Elegies*, III, *c.* 20 B.C.

He that is dead is freed from sin.
ROMANS VI, 7, *c.* 55

Blessed are the dead which die in the Lord.
REVELATION, XIV, 13, *c.* 95

Art thou greater than our father Abraham, which is dead? and the prophets are dead.
JOHN VIII, 53, *c.* 115

Now he lives in Abraham's bosom. (Nunc ille vivit in sinu Abraham.)
ST. AUGUSTINE: *Confessions*, IX, *c.* 420

The dead do not know what is doing here, but afterward they hear of it from those who meet them in death.
ST. AUGUSTINE: *On the Care to be Had for the Dead*, *c.* 405

The dead have no friends.
ENGLISH PROVERB, traced by Apperson to 1303

As dead as a doornail.
ENGLISH PHRASE, traced by Smith to *c.* 1350

O lady, he is dead and gone;
  Lady, he's dead and gone;
And at his head a green grass turf,
  And at his heels a stone.
Anon.: *The Friar of Orders Gray, c.* 1550

A dead bee will make no honey.
JOHN FLORIO: *First Frutes,* 1578

Hares may pull dead lions by the beard.
THOMAS KYD: *The Spanish Tragedy,* I, *c.* 1586

Death, that hath suck'd the honey of thy breath,
Hath had no power yet upon thy beauty;
Thou art not conquer'd; beauty's ensign yet
Is crimson in thy lips, and in thy cheeks,
And death's pale flag is not advanced there.
SHAKESPEARE: *Romeo and Juliet,* V, *c.* 1596

But yesterday the word of Cæsar might
Have stood against the world; now lies he there,
And none so poor to do him reverence.
SHAKESPEARE: *Julius Cæsar, III,* 1599

Imperious Cæsar, dead and turn'd to clay,
Might stop a hole to keep the wind away:
Oh, that that earth, which kept the world in awe,
Should patch a wall to expel the Winter's flaw!
SHAKESPEARE: *Hamlet,* V, *c.* 1601

To what base uses we may return, Horatio! Why may not imagination trace the noble dust of Alexander, till we find it stopping a bung-hole? IBID.

If to behold
Those roses withered that set out her cheeks,
That pair of stars that gave her body light
Dark'ned and dim for ever, all those rivers
That fed her veins with warm and crimson streams
Frozen and dried up: if these be signs of death,
Then is she dead.
THOMAS DEKKER: *I The Honest Whore,* I, 1604

Duncan is in his grave;
After life's fitful fever he sleeps well;
Treason has done his worst: nor steel, nor poison,
Malice domestic, foreign levy, nothing
Can touch him further.
SHAKESPEARE: *Macbeth,* III, *c.* 1605

Mean and mighty, rotting
Together, have one dust.
SHAKESPEARE: *Cymbeline,* IV, *c.* 1609

The wind blows out, the bubble dies;
The Spring entombed in Autumn lies;
The dew dries up, the star is shot,
The flight is past, — and man forgot.
HENRY KING: *On the Life of Man, c.* 1625

Speak not of a dead man at the table.
GEORGE HERBERT: *Outlandish Proverbs,* 1640

The dead do not bite.
THOMAS FULLER: *Church History,* IX, 1655

Dead men tell no tales.
ENGLISH PROVERB, traced by Apperson to 1664

A dead mouse feels no cold.
JOHN RAY: *English Proverbs,* 1670

When our mortal frame shall be disjoin'd,
The lifeless lump uncoupled from the mind,
From sense of grief and pain we shall be free;
We shall not *feel,* because we shall not *be.*
JOHN DRYDEN: Tr. of LUCRETIUS: *De rerum natura* (57 B.C.), *c.* 1695

They are not *amissi,* but *præmissi;*
Not lost but gone before.
Ascribed to PHILIP HENRY (1631–1696), but probably much older

He sleeps, and life's poor play is over.
ALEXANDER POPE: *Eloisa to Abelard,* 1717

"Weep not," ye mourners, for the dead,
  But in this hope your spirits soar,
That ye can say of those ye mourn,
  They are not lost, but gone before.
ALEXANDER POPE: Epitaph for Elijah Fenton, East Hampstead, England, *c.* 1731 (Cf. HENRY, *ante,* 1696)

Dead folks are past fooling.
THOMAS FULLER: *Gnomologia,* 1732

Little birds may pick a dead lion. IBID.

Ha! Dead! Impossible! It cannot be!
I'd not believe it though himself should swear it.
HENRY CAREY: *Chrononhotonthologos,* II, 1734

Beneath those rugged elms, that yew-tree's shade,
  Where heaves the turf in many a mold'ring heap,
Each in his narrow cell for ever laid,
  The rude forefathers of the hamlet sleep.
THOMAS GRAY: *Elegy Written in a Country Churchyard,* 1750

Can storied urn or animated bust
  Back to its mansion call the fleeting breath?
Can honor's voice provoke the silent dust,
  Or flatt'ry soothe the dull cold ear of death?
IBID.

Nothing can be of less importance to any present interest than the fortune of those who have been long lost in the grave, and from whom nothing now can be hoped or feared.
SAMUEL JOHNSON: *The Rambler,* Oct. 1, 1751

Ah, lovely appearance of death!
No sight upon earth is so fair;
Not all the gay pageants that breathe
Can with a dead body compare.

GEORGE WHITEFIELD: *A Hymn to be Sung over His Own Corpse,* 1764

The dead ride fast. (Die Todten reiten schnell.) G. A. BÜRGER: *Leonore,* 1773

He is gone to Kingdom come.

FRANCIS GROSE: *A Classical Dictionary of the Vulgar Tongue,* 1785

Drive your cart and your plow over the bones of the dead.

WILLIAM BLAKE: *The Marriage of Heaven and Hell,* 1790

Flow gently, sweet Afton, among thy green braes;
Flow gently, I'll sing thee a song in thy praise;
My Mary's asleep by the murmuring stream,
Flow gently, sweet Afton, disturb not her dream.

ROBERT BURNS: *Flow Gently, Sweet Afton,* 1792

O pale, pale now, those rosy lips,
I aft hae kissed sae fondly,
And closed for aye the sparkling glance
That dwelt on me sae kindly;
And mouldering now in silent dust
That heart that loved me dearly,
And still within my bosom's core
Shall live my Highland Mary.

ROBERT BURNS: *Highland Mary,* 1792

What if a man is buried alive every now and then? For every one of them there are a hundred dead men walking the earth.

G. C. LICHTENBERG: *Reflections,* 1799

I do not amuse myself by thinking of dead people.

NAPOLEON I: To C. M. Talleyrand, at Berlin, on hearing of the death of a relative, 1806

Like the dew on the mountain,
Like the foam on the river,
Like the bubble on the fountain,
Thou art gone, and for ever.

WALTER SCOTT: *The Lady of the Lake,* III, 1810

The dead have no rights. They are nothing; and nothing cannot own something. Where there is no substance, there can be no accident.

THOMAS JEFFERSON: *Letter to Samuel Kerchival,* 1816

I doubt that we have any right to pity the dead for their own sakes.

BYRON: *Letter to John Murray,* Aug. 12, 1817

He lay like a warrior taking his rest,
With his martial cloak around him.

CHARLES WOLFE: *The Burial of Sir John Moore,* 1817

Those who live
Still fear the living, but a corse
Is merciless, and power doth give
To such pale tyrants half the spoil
He rends from those who groan and toil,
Because they blush not with remorse
Among their crawling worms.

P. B. SHELLEY: *Rosalind and Helen,* 1818

He has outsoared the shadow of our night;
Envy and calumny and hate and pain,
And that unrest which men miscall delight
Can touch him not and torture not again.

P. B. SHELLEY: *Adonais,* 1821

Bless me, how *little* you look. So shall we all look — kings, and kaisers — stripped for the last voyage.

CHARLES LAMB: *To the Shade of [R. W.] Elliston,* 1831 (The Englishman's Magazine, Aug.; Elliston was a popular comedian)

How very little the world misses anybody! How soon the chasm left by the best and wisest men closes!

T. B. MACAULAY: *Letter to Hannah M. Macaulay,* July 31, 1833

When once a man's dead
There's no more to be said.

R. H. BARHAM: *The Ingoldsby Legends,* I, 1840

If a man was great while living, he becomes tenfold greater when dead.

THOMAS CARLYLE: *Heroes and Hero-Worship,* I, 1840 (Lecture in London, May 5)

On fame's eternal camping-ground
Their silent tents are spread,
And glory guards, with solemn round,
The bivouac of the dead.

THEODORE O'HARA: *The Bivouac of the Dead,* 1847

Who ever really saw anything but horror in the smile of the dead?

E. A. POE: *Marginalia,* 1844–49

The dead advance as much as the living advance.

WALT WHITMAN: *Song of the Broad-Ax,* 1856

Strange, is it not, that of the myriads who
Before us pass'd the door of darkness through,
Not one returns to tell us of the road,
Which to discover we must travel too?

EDWARD FITZGERALD: Tr. of OMAR KHAYYÁM: *Rubáiyát* (*c.* 1100), 1857

In England the dead are dead to purpose. One cannot believe they ever were alive, or anything else than what they are now — names in school-books.

JOHN RUSKIN: *Modern Painters,* V, 1860

Wha lies here?
I, Johnny Dow.

Hoo! Johnny, is that you?
Ay, man, but a'm dead now.
Anon.: In NORFOLK's *Epitaphs,* 1861

I shall not see the shadows,
I shall not feel the rain;
I shall not hear the nightingale
Sing on, as if in pain:
And dreaming through the twilight
That doth not rise nor set,
Haply I may remember,
And haply may forget.
CHRISTINA ROSSETTI: *Song,* 1862

We should teach our children to think no more of their bodies when dead than they do of their hair when cut off, or of their old clothes when they have done with them.
GEORGE MACDONALD: *Annals of a Quiet Neighborhood,* 1866

The end is come of pleasant places,
The end of tender words and faces,
The end of all, the poppied sleep.
A. C. SWINBURNE: *Ilicit,* 1866

There ought to be little condonation of the foibles, and none at all of the moral obliquities of the dead.
JOHN MORLEY: *Voltaire,* III, 1872

Charlie died at daybreak, he died from a fall;
And he'll not see his mother when the work's all done this Fall.
Anon.: *When the Work's All Done This Fall, c.* 1875

Home is the sailor,
Home from the sea,
And the hunter home from the hill.
R. L. STEVENSON: *Requiem,* 1887

The dead are often just as living to us as the living are, only we cannot get them to believe it. They can come to us, but till we die we cannot go to them. To be dead is to be unable to understand that one is alive.
SAMUEL BUTLER: *Note-Books, c.* 1890

The dead they cannot rise, an' you'd better dry your eyes,
An' you'd best go look for a new love.
RUDYARD KIPLING: *Soldier, Soldier,* 1892

He's gone now, God spare us, and we'll not see him again.
J. M. SYNGE: *Riders to the Sea,* 1904

In the democracy of the dead, all men are equal. The poor man is as rich as the richest, and the rich man as poor as the pauper. The creditor loses his usury, and the debtor is acquitted of his obligation. There the proud man surrenders his dignity; the politician his honors; the worldling his pleasures; the invalid needs no physician; the laborer rests from toil. The wrongs of time are redressed; injustice is expiated, and the irony of fate is refuted.
Author unidentified

While we live, let's live in clover,
For when we're dead, we're dead all over.
IBID.

Time was I stood where thou dost now,
And view'd the dead, as thou dost me;
Ere long thou'lt be as low as I,
And others stand and look on thee.
Epitaph at Boughton, near Northampton, England

A beggar on his feet is worth more than an emperor in his grave.
FRENCH PROVERB

The dead have neither relatives nor friends.
IBID.

To the living we owe some consideration, but to the dead we owe only the truth.
IBID.

Dead dogs do not bite.
GERMAN PROVERB

The dead can do no harm.
GREEK PROVERB

Six feet of earth makes us all of one size.
ITALIAN PROVERB

Food for Acheron. (Pabulum Acherontis.)
LATIN PHRASE (*Acheron*=the place of the dead)

He has joined the majority. (Abiit ad majores.)
LATIN SAYING

Be happy while y'er leevin, for y'er a lang time dead.
SCOTTISH PROVERB

[*See also* Agnostic, Burial, Death, Dying, Epitaph, Forgotten, Grave, Heaven, Hell, Immortality, King, Sorrow.

Dead or Alive

We want Perdicaris alive or Raisuli dead.
JOHN HAY: Cablegram to the American consul in Morocco, June 22, 1904 (Perdicaris, a Greek naturalized as an American, had been kidnapped and held for ransom by Raisuli)

Deaf

Who is so deaf as he that will not hear?
JOHN HEYWOOD: *Proverbs,* 1546

Deaf men are quick-ey'd and distrustful.
THOMAS FULLER: *Gnomologia,* 1732

I found it impossible to say to others: "Speak louder! Shout! For I am deaf." How could I proclaim the deficiency of a sense which ought to have been more perfect in me than in other men — a sense which I once had in the highest perfection, and beyond all save a few of my profession?
LUDWIG VAN BEETHOVEN: *Letter to his brothers Carl and Johann,* Oct. 6, 1802

Deaf people always hear better than they say they do (or, than you think they do).
AMERICAN PROVERB

For foolish talk, deaf ears.
FRENCH PROVERB

[*See also* Age (Old), Belief, Hearing, Marriage.

Deal, Square

[*See* Square Deal.

Dean

The Devil and the dean begin with a letter;
When the Devil has the dean, the kirk will be better.

DAVID FERGUSSON: *Scottish Proverbs,* 1641

Death

Dust thou art, and unto dust shalt thou return.

GENESIS III, 19, *c.* 700 B.C.

We have made a covenant with death, and with hell are we at agreement.

ISAIAH XXVIII, 15, *c.* 700 B.C.

Keep thine eyes fixed upon the end of life.

Ascribed to SOLON, *c.* 600 B.C.

We end as a little heap of dust.

ANACREON: *Fragment, c.* 500 B.C.

Death is not the greatest of ills; it is worse to want to die, and not be able to.

SOPHOCLES: *Electra, c.* 450 B.C.

Death is a delightful hiding-place for weary men.

HERODOTUS: *Histories,* VII, *c.* 430 B.C.

No one knows but that death is the greatest of all good to man; yet men fear it, as if they well knew that it is the greatest of evils. Is not this the more reprehensible ignorance, to think that one knows what one does not know?

SOCRATES: In PLATO's *Apology of Socrates,* 399 B.C.

It is good to die before one has done anything deserving death.

ANAXANDRIDES: *Fragment, c.* 376 B.C.

No one has ever died who was ready to die.

ANTIPHANES: *Fragment, c.* 350 B.C.

A little sleep, a little slumber, a little folding of the hands to sleep.

PROVERBS VI, 10, *c.* 350 B.C. (Cf. XXIV, 33)

There the wicked cease from troubling; and there the weary be at rest.

JOB III, 17, *c.* 325 B.C.

I would not live alway. JOB VII, 16

Man dieth, and wasteth away; yea, man giveth up the ghost, and where is he?

JOB XIV, 10

The king of terrors. JOB XVIII, 14

He shall fly away as a dream, and shall not be found: yea, he shall be chased away as a vision of the night. JOB XX, 8

All flesh shall perish together, and man shall turn again into dust. JOB XXXIV, 15

Death, feared as the most awful of evils, is really nothing, for so long as we are, death has not come, and when it has come we are not.

EPICURUS: *Letter to Menoeceus, c.* 300 B.C.

Whom the gods love dies young.

MENANDER: *Moyostikhoi, c.* 300 B.C.

That which befalleth the sons of men befalleth beasts; even one thing befalleth them: as the one dieth, so dieth the other.

ECCLESIASTES III, 19, *c.* 200 B.C.

Man goes to his long home, and the mourners go about the streets. ECCLESIASTES XII, 5

He whom the gods favor dies young, while he is in his health, has his senses and his judgment sound.

PLAUTUS: *Bacchides,* IV, *c.* 200 B.C. (Cf. MENANDER, *ante, c.* 300 B.C.)

Judge none blessed before his death.

ECCLESIASTICUS XI, 28, *c.* 180 B.C.

Thales said there was no difference between life and death. "Why, then," said some one to him, "do not you die?" "Because," said he, "it makes no difference."

DIOGENES LAERTIUS: *Lives of the Philosophers, c.* 150. B.C.

What man is he that liveth, and shall not see death? PSALMS LXXXIX, 48, *c.* 150 B.C.

His breath goeth forth, he returneth to his earth; in that very day his thoughts perish.

PSALMS CXLVI, 4

No man can be ignorant that he must die, nor be sure that he may not this very day.

CICERO: *De senectute, c.* 78 B.C.

Why shed tears that thou must die? For if thy past life has been one of enjoyment, and if all thy pleasures have not passed through thy mind, as through a sieve, and vanished, leaving not a rack behind, why then dost thou not, like a thankful guest, rise cheerfully from life's feast, and with a quiet mind go take thy rest?

LUCRETIUS: *De rerum natura,* III, 57 B.C.

To die at the will of another is to die twice.

PUBLILIUS SYRUS: *Sententiæ, c.* 50 B.C.

I do not want to die, but I would not care if I were dead.

CICERO: *Tusculanae disputationes,* I, 45 B.C.

Wherever I look I see nothing but reminders of death. OVID: *Tristia,* I, *c.* 10 B.C.

Death is the last limit of all things. (Mors ultima linea rerum est.)

HORACE: *Epistles,* I, *c.* 5 B.C.

I see the rack and the scourge, and the instruments of torture adapted to every limb and every nerve; but I also see death. She stands

beyond my savage enemies, beyond my haughty countrymen. Against all the injuries of life, I have the refuge of death.
SENECA: *De brevitate vitae*, c. 49

The last enemy that shall be destroyed is death.
I CORINTHIANS XV, 26, c. 55

O death, where is thy sting? O grave, where is thy victory? I CORINTHIANS XV, 55

Death is a punishment to some, to some a gift, and to many a favor.
SENECA: *Hercules Oetaeus*, c. 60

O death! How thou followest the happy and fliest the wretched! IBID.

Prepare the couch; call for wine; crown thyself with roses; perfume thyself; the god bids thee remember death.
MARTIAL: *Epigrams*, II, 86

I looked, and behold a pale horse: and his name that sat on him was Death.
REVELATION VI, 8, c. 95

We pass away out of the world as grasshoppers.
II ESDRAS IV, 24, c. 100

What is death but a bugbear?
EPICTETUS: *Discourses*, II, c. 110

Death is a release from the impressions of the senses, and from desires that make us their puppets, and from the vagaries of the mind, and from the hard service of the flesh.
MARCUS AURELIUS: *Meditations*, VI, c. 170

Death ought to be our pleasure.
TERTULLIAN: *De spectaculis*, c. 200

There is nothing dreadful in that which delivers from all that which is to be dreaded.
TERTULLIAN: *The Testimony of the Christian Soul*, c. 210

It is a poor thing for anyone to fear that which is inevitable. IBID.

What is death at most? It is a journey for a season; a sleep longer than usual. If thou fearest death, thou shouldest also fear sleep.
ST. JOHN CHRYSOSTOM: *Homily* V, c. 388

Death levels all things. (Omnia mors æquat.)
CLAUDIUS CLAUDIANUS: *De raptu Proserpinæ*, II, c. 395

As death comes on we are like trees growing in the sandy bank of a widening river.
BHARTRIHARI: *The Vairagya Sataka*, c. 625

Better a thousand times to die with glory than live without honor.
Ascribed to LOUIS VI of France (1078–1137)

A good death does honor to a whole life.
FRANCESCO PETRARCH: *Canzoniere*, XVI, c. 1350

O death, rock me asleep! Bring me to quiet and rest;
Let pass my weary, guiltless life out of my careful breast;
Toll on the passing bell, ring out my doleful knell;
Let thy sound my death tell. Death doth draw me,
Death doth draw me. There is no remedy.
Ascribed to ANNE BOLEYN, c. 1536

How many sorts of deaths are in our bodies! Nothing is therein but death.
MARTIN LUTHER: *Table-Talk*, CXXIX, 1569

The deadest deaths are the best.
MICHEL DE MONTAIGNE: *Essays*, I, 1580

The premeditation of death is the premeditation of liberty; he who has learned to die has forgot what it is to be a slave. IBID.

Why, what is pomp, rule, reign, but earth and dust?
And, love we how we can, yet die we must.
SHAKESPEARE: *III Henry VI*, V, c. 1591

Cities fall, kingdoms perish, their pride and pomp lie buried in sand and grass. Then why should mortal man repine to die, whose life is as air, breath as wind, and body as glass?
TORQUATO TASSO: *Gerusalemme*, XV, 1592

Death, death; oh, amiable, lovely death!
Come, grin on me, and I will think thou smilest.
SHAKESPEARE: *King John*, III, c. 1596

Woe, destruction, ruin, and decay;
The worst is death, and death will have his day.
SHAKESPEARE: *Richard II*, III, c. 1596

Eyes, look your last!
Arms, take your last embrace! and lips, O you,
The doors of breath, seal with a righteous kiss
A dateless bargain to engrossing death.
SHAKESPEARE: *Romeo and Juliet*, V, c. 1596

That owest God a death.
SHAKESPEARE: *I Henry IV*, V, c. 1598

A man can die but once.
SHAKESPEARE: *II Henry IV*, III, c. 1598

O amiable, lovely death!
Thou odoriferous stench! sound rottenness!
Arise forth from the couch of lasting night,
Thou hate and terror to prosperity,
And I will kiss thy detestable bones;
And put my eyeballs in thy vaulty brows;
And ring these fingers with thy household worms;
And stop this gap of breath with fulsome dust,
And be a carrion monster like thyself.
SHAKESPEARE: *King John*, III, c. 1598

Cowards die many times before their deaths;
The valiant never taste of death but once.
Of all the wonders that I yet have heard,

It seems to me most strange that men should fear;
Seeing that death, a necessary end,
Will come when it will come.

SHAKESPEARE: *Julius Cæsar*, II, 1599

He that cuts off twenty years of life
Cuts off so many years of fearing death.

SHAKESPEARE: *Julius Cæsar*, III

That we shall die we know, 'tis but the time
And drawing days out, that men stand upon.

IBID.

There's a lean fellow beats all conquerors.

THOMAS DEKKER: *Old Fortunatus*, I, 1600

Strength stoops unto the grave,
Worms feed on Hector brave,
Swords may not fight with fate,
Earth still holds ope her gate.

THOMAS NASHE: *In Plague Time*, *c.* 1600

By a sleep to say we end
The heart-ache and the thousand natural shocks
That flesh is heir to, 'tis a consummation
Devoutly to be wished.

SHAKESPEARE: *Hamlet*, III, *c.* 1601

To die, to sleep;
To sleep: perchance to dream: ay, there's the rub;
For in that sleep of death what dreams may come
When we have shuffled off this mortal coil,
Must give us pause. IBID.

The rest is silence.

SHAKESPEARE: *Hamlet*, V

The jaws of death.

SHAKESPEARE: *Twelfth Night*, III, *c.* 1601

Ay, but to die, and go we know not where;
To lie in cold obstruction and to rot.

SHAKESPEARE: *Measure for Measure*, III, 1604

The sense of death is most in apprehension;
And the poor beetle that we tread upon,
In corporal sufferance feels a pang as great
As when a giant dies. IBID.

The weariest and most loathed worldly life
That age, ache, penury and imprisonment
Can lay on nature is a paradise
To what we fear of death. IBID.

Fear of death is worse than death itself.

Anon.: *King Leir*, 1605

Tomorrow, and tomorrow, and tomorrow,
Creeps in this petty pace from day to day,
To the last syllable of recorded time;
And all our yesterdays have lighted fools
The way to dusty death.

SHAKESPEARE: *Macbeth*, V, *c.* 1605

The stroke of death is as a lover's pinch,
Which hurts, and is desir'd.

SHAKESPEARE: *Antony and Cleopatra*, V, *c.* 1606

Oh, our lives' sweetness!
That we the pain of death would hourly die
Rather than die at once!

SHAKESPEARE: *King Lear*, V, 1606

I shall welcome death
As princes do some great ambassadors.

JOHN WEBSTER: *The White Devil*, V, *c.* 1608

This world's a city full of straying streets,
And death's the market-place where each one meets.

SHAKESPEARE and JOHN FLETCHER: *The Two Noble Kinsmen*, I, 1613

O eloquent, just, and mighty death! whom none could advise, thou hast persuaded; what none hath dared, thou hast done; and whom all the world hath flattered, thou only hast cast out of the world and despised: thou hast drawn together all the far stretched greatness, all the pride, cruelty and ambition of man, and covered it all over with these two narrow words, Hic jacet!

WALTER RALEIGH: *Historie of the World*, V, 1614

Death hath ten thousand several doors
For men to take their exit.

JOHN WEBSTER: *The Duchess of Malfi*, IV, *c.* 1614

Death devours lambs as well as sheep.

THOMAS SHELTON: Tr. of CERVANTES: *Don Quixote*, II, 1615

The iron sleep of death.

Anon.: *Nero*, III, 1624

Men fear death as children fear to go in the dark; and as that natural fear in children is increased with tales, so is the other.

FRANCIS BACON: *Essays*, II, 1625

Tremble to think how terrible the dream is
After this sleep of death.

PHILIP MASSINGER: *The Roman Actor*, III, 1629

Death hath a thousand doors to let out life.

PHILIP MASSINGER and JOHN FLETCHER: *A Very Woman*, V, 1634 (Cf. WEBSTER, *ante*, *c.* 1614)

All buildings are but monuments of death,
All clothes but winding sheets for our last knell,
All dainty fattings for the worms beneath,
All curious music but our passing bell;
Thus death is nobly waited on, for why?
All that we have is but death's livery.

Anon.: *Wit's Recreations*, 1640

Death keeps no calendar.

GEORGE HERBERT: *Outlandish Proverbs*, 1640

Deaths foreseen come not. IBID.

He that fears death lives not. IBID.

We all labor against our own cure, for death is the cure of all diseases.

THOMAS BROWNE: *Religio Medici*, IV, 1642

But here's the sunset of a tedious day.
These two asleep are; I'll but be undrest,
And so to bed. Pray wish us all good rest.

ROBERT HERRICK: Epitaph on Sir Edward Giles, *c.* 1650

Dear, beauteous death! the jewel of the just,
Shining nowhere, but in the dark;
What mysteries do lie beyond thy dust,
Could man outlook that mark!

HENRY VAUGHAN: *Silex scintellans,* I, 1650

Old men go to death; death comes to young men.

GEORGE HERBERT: *Jacula Prudentum,* 1651

Of all the evils of the world which are reproached with an evil character, death is the most innocent of its accusation.

JEREMY TAYLOR: *The Rule and Exercises of Holy Dying,* I, 1651

Rome can issue no dispensation from death.

J. B. MOLIÈRE: *l'Étourdi,* II, 1653 (An echo of a medieval proverb: "The pope can issue no bull against death")

Death quits all scores.

JAMES SHIRLEY: *Cupid and Death,* 1653

Welcome death, quoth the rat, when the trap fell down.

JAMES HOWELL: *Proverbs,* 1659

The glories of our blood and state
Are shadows, not substantial things;
There is no armor against fate;
Death lays its icy hand on kings;
Sceptre and crown
Must tumble down,
And in the dust be equal made
With the poor crooked scythe and spade.

JAMES SHIRLEY: *The Contention of Ajax and Ulysses,* 1659

From lightning and tempest; from plague, pestilence and famine; from battle and murder, and from sudden death, Good Lord, deliver us.

THE BOOK OF COMMON PRAYER (*The Litany*), 1662

In the midst of life we are in death.

THE BOOK OF COMMON PRAYER (*The Burial of the Dead*)

Everything has been written which could by possibility persuade us that death is not an evil, and the weakest men as well as heroes have given a thousand celebrated examples to support this opinion. Nevertheless, I doubt whether any man of good sense ever believed it.

LA ROCHEFOUCAULD: *Maxims,* 1665

Every door may be shut but death's door.

GIOVANNI TORRIANO: *Italian Proverbs,* 1666

I fled, and cry'd out, death!
Hell trembled at the hideous name, and sigh'd
From all her caves, and back resounded, death!

JOHN MILTON: *Paradise Lost,* II, 1667

The grisly terror. IBID.

Death in itself is nothing; but we fear
To be we know not what, we know not where.

JOHN DRYDEN: *Aurungzebe,* IV, 1676

Groans and convulsions, and discolor'd faces,
Friends weeping round us, blacks, and obsequies,
Make death a dreadful thing. The pomp of death
Is far more terrible than death itself.

NATHANIEL LEE: *Lucius Junius Brutus,* 1681

We shall never outwit nature: we shall all die as usual.

BERNARD DE FONTENELLE: *Dialogues des morts,* 1683

As a sweet odor, of a vast expense,
She vanished: we can scarcely say she died.

JOHN DRYDEN: *Ode to the Memory of Mrs. Anne Killegrew,* 1686

What is certain in death is somewhat softened by what is uncertain: it is the indefiniteness in the time which bears a certain relation to infinity, which is what is called eternity.

JEAN DE LA BRUYÈRE: *Caractères,* XI, 1688

Xerxes the great did die,
And so must you and I.

New England Primer, c. 1688

So softly death succeeded life in her,
She did but dream of Heaven, and she was there.

JOHN DRYDEN: *Eleonora,* 1692

A great leap in the dark.

JOHN VANBRUGH: *The Provok'd Wife,* V, 1697

To die is landing on some silent shore,
Where billows never break nor tempests roar;
Ere well we feel the friendly stroke 'tis o'er.

SAMUEL GARTH: *The Dispensary,* III, 1699

Death is the privilege of human nature;
And life without it were not worth our taking.
Thither the poor, the pris'ner, and the mourner
Fly for relief, and lay their burdens down.

NICHOLAS ROWE: *The Fair Penitent,* V, 1703

Strictly speaking, there is no absolute generation or absolute death. Generation is merely development or growth; death is envelopment and diminution.

G. W. LEIBNIZ: *The Monadology,* LXXIII, 1714

Death observes no ceremony.

JOHN WISE: *A Vindication of the Government of New England Churches,* II, 1717

The rest were vulgar deaths unknown to fame.

ALEXANDER POPE: Tr. of HOMER: *Iliad,* XI (*c.* 800 B.C.), 1718

Who dies in youth and vigor, dies the best.

ALEXANDER POPE: Tr. of HOMER: *Iliad,* XXII, 1720

About midnight my dear wife expired to our great astonishment, especially mine.
SAMUEL SEWALL: *Diary,* May 26, 1720

It is impossible that anything so natural, so necessary, and so universal as death should ever have been designed by Providence as an evil to mankind.
JONATHAN SWIFT: *Thoughts on Religion,* 1728

Death is the grand leveler.
THOMAS FULLER: *Gnomologia,* 1732

I know of nobody that has a mind to die this year. IBID.

Death is a law, not a punishment.
JEAN-BAPTISTE DUBOS: Last words, 1742

Death is the crown of life;
Were death denied, poor man would live in vain;
Were death denied, to live would not be life;
Were death denied, ev'n fools would wish to die.
EDWARD YOUNG: *Night Thoughts,* III, 1742

Death loves a shining mark, a signal blow.
EDWARD YOUNG: *Night Thoughts,* V

For who, to dumb forgetfulness a prey,
This pleasing anxious being e'er resign'd,
Left the warm precincts of the cheerful day,
Nor cast one longing ling'ring look behind?
THOMAS GRAY: *Elegy Written in a Country Churchyard,* 1750

Dogs, would you live forever? (Hunde, wollt ihr ewig leben?)
FREDERICK THE GREAT: To his wavering troops at Kolin, June 18, 1757

The truth is that every death is violent which is the effect of accident; every death which is not gradually brought on by the miseries of age, or when life is extinguished for any other reason than that it is burnt out. He that dies before sixty, of a cold or consumption, dies, in reality, but a violent death.
SAMUEL JOHNSON: *Letter to Bennet Langton,* Sept. 21, 1758

He who fears death dies every time he thinks of it.
STANISLAUS LESZCYNSKI (KING OF POLAND): *Œuvres du philosophe bienfaisant,* 1763

The state of man is not unlike that of a fish hooked by an angler. Death allows us a little line. We flounce, and sport, and vary our situation. But when we would extend our schemes, we discover our confinement, checked and limited by a superior hand, who drags us from our element whenever he pleases.
WILLIAM SHENSTONE: *Of Men and Manners,* 1764

That language, John Woolman is dead, meant no more than the death of my own will.
JOHN WOOLMAN: *Journal,* Aug. 26, 1772

Life! we've been long together
Through pleasant and through cloudy weather;
'Tis hard to part when friends are dear —
Perhaps 'twill cost a sigh, a tear;
Then steal away, give little warning,
Choose thine own time;
Say not good-night, — but in some brighter clime
Bid me good-morning.
ANNA LETITIA BARBAULD: *Ode to Life,* 1773

The better a man is, the more afraid he is of death.
SAMUEL JOHNSON: *Boswell's Life,* Sept. 16, 1777

Kate Macaulay was so unlucky as to die a few days ago.
HORACE WALPOLE: *Letter to Mary Berry,* June 28, 1791

If death did not exist today, it would be necessary to invent it.
J. B. MILHAUD: On voting in the French Convention for the execution of Louis XVI, Jan. 16, 1793

Death without phrases. (La mort sans phrase.)
Ascribed to E. J. SIEYÈS: On voting in the French Convention for the death of Louis XVI, Jan. 19, 1793

Death is an eternal sleep.
Motto on the gates of French cemeteries, placed there by order of Joseph Fouché, 1794

The first that died was Sister Jane;
In bed she moaning lay,
Till God released her of her pain;
And then she went away.
WILLIAM WORDSWORTH: *We Are Seven,* 1798

The certain end of all pain, and of all capacity to suffer pain, is death. Of all the things that man thinks of as evils, this is the least.
J. G. FICHTE: *Die Bestimmung des Menschen,* XVIII, 1800

We all look up to the blue sky for comfort, but nothing appears there, nothing comforts, nothing answers us, and so we die.
S. T. COLERIDGE: *Notebooks,* 1805

There is a fulness of time when men should go, and not occupy too long the ground to which others have a right to advance.
THOMAS JEFFERSON: *Letter to Dr. Benjamin Rush,* 1811

Count o'er the joys thine hours have seen,
Count o'er thy days from anguish free,
And know, whatever thou hast been,
'Tis something better not to be.
BYRON: *Euthanasia,* 1812

Death had he seen by sudden blow,
By wasting plague, by tortures slow,
By mine or breach, by steel or ball,
Knew all his shapes, and scorned them all.
WALTER SCOTT: *Rokeby,* I, 1813

How wonderful is death,
Death and his brother sleep!
One, pale as yonder waning moon
With lips of lurid blue!
The other, rosy as the morn
When throned on ocean's wave
It blushes o'er the world;
Yet both so passing wonderful!

P. B. SHELLEY: *Queen Mab*, I, 1813

Death is the only mercy that I crave,
Death soon and short, death and forgetfulness.

ROBERT SOUTHEY: *Roderick*, I, 1814

Man grows old, and dwindles, and decays,
And countless generations of mankind
Depart, and leave no vestige where they trod.

WILLIAM WORDSWORTH: *The Excursion*, IV, 1814

I enjoy good health: I am happy in what is around me, yet I assure you I am ripe for leaving all this year, this day, this hour.

THOMAS JEFFERSON: *Letter to John Adams*, 1816

Oh, God! it is a fearful thing
To see the human soul take wing.

BYRON: *The Prisoner of Chillon*, 1816

Oh, well, no matter what happens, there's always death.

NAPOLEON I: To Gaspard Gourgaud at St. Helena, June 11, 1817

I have been half in love with easeful death.

JOHN KEATS: *Ode to a Nightingale*, 1819

The lower creation learns death first in the moment of death; man proceeds onward with the knowledge that he is every hour approaching nearer to death, and this throws a feeling of uncertainty over life, even to the man who forgets in busy scenes that annihilation is awaiting him. It is for this reason chiefly that we have philosophies and religions.

ARTHUR SCHOPENHAUER: *The World as Will and Idea*, I, 1819

Death is the liberator of him whom freedom cannot release, the physician of him whom medicine cannot cure, and the comforter of him whom time cannot console.

C. C. COLTON: *Lacon*, 1820

First our pleasures die — and then
Our hopes, and then our fears — and when
These are dead, the debt is due,
Dust claims dust — and we die too.

P. B. SHELLEY: *Death*, 1820

It is a modest creed, and yet
Pleasant if one considers it,
To own that death itself must be,
Like all the rest, a mockery.

P. B. SHELLEY: *The Sensitive Plant*, 1820

The naked map of life is spread out before me, and in the emptiness and desolation I see death coming to meet me.

WILLIAM HAZLITT: *On the Fear of Death*, 1821

Of all impositions on the public the greatest seems to be death.

LEIGH HUNT: *The Indicator*, LI, 1821

I never had, and never could feel, any horror at death, simply as death.

S. T. COLERIDGE: *Table-Talk*, April 19, 1830

Leaves have their time to fall,
And flowers to wither at the North wind's breath,
And stars to set — but all,
Thou hast all seasons for thine own, O death.

FELICIA HEMANS: *The Hour of Death*, 1830

The crash of the whole solar and stellar systems could only kill you once.

THOMAS CARLYLE: *Letter to John Carlyle*, 1831

There are not ten people in the world whose deaths would spoil my dinner, but there are one or two whose deaths would break my heart.

T. B. MACAULAY: *Letter to Hannah M. Macaulay*, July 31, 1833

We sometimes congratulate ourselves at the moment of waking from a troubled dream: it may be so the moment after death.

NATHANIEL HAWTHORNE: *Journal*, Oct. 25, 1835

There is a reaper whose name is Death,
And with his sickle keen,
He reaps the bearded grain at a breath,
And the flowers that grow between.

H. W. LONGFELLOW: *The Reaper and the Flowers*, 1839

To every man upon this earth
Death cometh soon or late,
And how can man die better
Than facing fearful odds,
For the ashes of his fathers
And the temples of his gods?

T. B. MACAULAY: *Lays of Ancient Rome*, 1842

The play is the tragedy, "Man,"
And its hero the conqueror, Worm.

E. A. POE: *The Conqueror Worm*, 1843 (Graham's Magazine, March)

Oh! that we two lay sleeping
In our nest in the churchyard sod,
With our limbs at rest on the quiet earth's breast,
And our souls at home with God.

CHARLES KINGSLEY: *The Saint's Tragedy*, II, 1848

The fever called "living"
Is conquered at last.

E. A. POE: *For Annie*, 1849

Swing low, sweet chariot —
Comin' for to carry me home;
I looked over Jordan and what did I see?

A band of angels comin' after me —
Comin' for to carry me home.

American Negro spiritual, *c.* 1850

I strove with none; for none was worth my strife.
Nature I loved and, next to nature, art;
I warmed both hands before the fire of life;
It sinks, and I am ready to depart.

W. S. LANDOR: *On His Seventy-Fifth Birthday,* 1850

God's finger touch'd him, and he slept.

ALFRED TENNYSON: *In Memoriam,* LXXXV, 1850

The love of life is at bottom only the fear of death.

ARTHUR SCHOPENHAUER: *Our Relation to Ourselves,* 1851

There is no death to such as thou, dear Eva! neither darkness nor shadow of death; only such a bright fading as when the morning star fades in the golden dawn.

HARRIET BEECHER STOWE: *Uncle Tom's Cabin,* XXVII, 1852

Her cabin'd, ample spirit,
It flutter'd and fail'd for breath.
To-night it doth inherit
The vasty hall of death.

MATTHEW ARNOLD: *Requiescat,* 1853

He that died half a year ago is as dead as Adam.

H. G. BOHN: *Handbook of Proverbs,* 1855

The grand perhaps.

ROBERT BROWNING: *Bishop Blougram's Apology,* 1855

Has any one supposed it lucky to be born?
I hasten to inform him or her, it is just as lucky to die, and I know it.

WALT WHITMAN: *Walt Whitman,* 1855

One thing is certain and the rest is lies;
The flower that once has blown forever dies.

EDWARD FITZGERALD: Tr. of OMAR KHAYYÁM: *Rubáiyát* (*c.* 1100), 1857

Nothing can happen more beautiful than death.

WALT WHITMAN: *Starting from Paumanok,* 1860

The superb vistas of death.

WALT WHITMAN: *Song At Sunset,* 1860

Death squares all accounts.

CHARLES READE: *The Cloister and the Hearth,* XCII, 1861

There is no unmixed good in this world except dying.

H. W. BEECHER: *Eyes and Ears,* 1862

Close his eyes; his work is done.
What to him is friend or foeman,
Rise of moon, or set of sun,
Hand of man, or kiss of woman?

GEORGE H. BOKER: *Dirge for a Soldier,* 1862

If you wish to make a man look noble, your best course is to kill him. What superiority he may have inherited from his race, what superiority nature may have personally gifted him with, comes out in death.

ALEXANDER SMITH: *Dreamthorp,* III, 1863

A little while and I shall laugh; and then
I shall weep never and laugh not any more.

A. C. SWINBURNE: *Atalanta in Calydon,* 1865

Come, lovely and soothing death,
Undulate round the world, serenely arriving, arriving,
In the day, in the night, to all, to each,
Sooner or later, delicate death.

WALT WHITMAN: *When Lilacs Last in the Dooryard Bloom'd,* 1866

There is no god found stronger than death, and death is a sleep.

A. C. SWINBURNE: *Hymn to Proserpine,* 1866

From too much love of living,
From hope and fear set free,
We thank with brief thanksgiving
Whatever gods may be
That no life lives for ever;
That dead men rise up never;
That even the weariest river
Winds somewhere safe to sea.

A. C. SWINBURNE: *The Garden of Proserpine,* 1866

Turn the key and bolt the door,
Sweet is death forevermore.

R. W. EMERSON: *The Past,* 1867

While eating dinner, this dear little child
Was choked on a piece of beef,
Doctors came, tried their skill awhile,
But none could give relief.

JULIA A. MOORE (THE SWEET SINGER OF MICHIGAN): *The Sentimental Song Book,* 1876

There is no king more terrible than death.

AUSTIN DOBSON: *The Dance of Death,* 1877

The fear of the inevitable approach of death is a European malady.

FRANCIS GALTON: *Inquiries into Human Faculty,* 1883

I define death as an arrest of life, from which no revival of any length, whether of the whole or of any part, can take place.

AUGUST WEISMANN: *Ueber die Ewigkeit des Lebens,* 1883

Old men must die; or the world would grow moldy, would only breed the past again.

ALFRED TENNYSON: *Becket,* prologue, 1884

Is life a boon?
If so, it must befall
That death, whene'er he call,
Must call too soon.

W. S. GILBERT: *The Yeomen of the Guard,* I, 1888

Be not afraid, ye waiting hearts that weep,
For God still "giveth his beloved sleep,"
And if an endless sleep He wills, so best.

HENRIETTA HEATHORN HUXLEY: *Browning's Funeral,* 1889 (Inscribed on T. H. Huxley's gravestone, 1895)

Twilight and evening bell,
And after that the dark!
And may there be no sadness of farewell,
When I embark.

ALFRED TENNYSON: *Crossing the Bar,* 1889

Death and vulgarity are the only two facts in the Nineteenth Century that one cannot explain away.

OSCAR WILDE: *The Picture of Dorian Gray,* 1891

Whoever has lived long enough to find out what life is knows how deep a debt of gratitude we owe to Adam, the first great benefactor of our race. He brought death into the world.

S. L. CLEMENS (MARK TWAIN): *Pudd'nhead Wilson,* III, 1894

He who lives more lives than one
More deaths than one must die.

OSCAR WILDE: *The Ballad of Reading Gaol,* 1898

The passing on of William McKinley is an awful mystery. "Good-by," he said, "good-by to all. It is God's way."

JOHN WANAMAKER: On the death of McKinley, 1901

Our civilization is founded on the shambles, and every individual existence goes out in a lonely spasm of helpless agony.

WILLIAM JAMES: *The Varieties of Religious Experience,* VI, 1902

No man at all can be living forever, and we must be satisfied.

J. M. SYNGE: *Riders to the Sea,* 1904

Whether on the gallows high
Or where blood flows the reddest,
The noblest place for man to die —
Is where he dies the deadest.

AMBROSE BIERCE: *The Devil's Dictionary,* 1906

When a man dies, and his kin are glad of it, they say, "He is better off."

E. W. HOWE: *Country Town Sayings,* 1911

Why fear death? It is the most beautiful adventure in life.

CHARLES FROHMAN: Last words, May 7, 1915

And God said, Go down, Death, go down;
Go down to Savannah, Georgia,
Down to Yamacraw,
And find Sister Caroline.
She's borne the burden and the heat of the day,
She's labored long in my vineyard,
And she's tired —
She's weary —
Go down, Death, and bring her to me.

JAMES WELDON JOHNSON: *Go Down, Death,* 1927 (American Mercury, April)

The ole worl's rollin', rollin', rollin',
Well, I got on my travelin' shoes,
Some o' these mornin's bright an' fair,
Gonna hitch my wing an' try the air,
Death is in this land.

American Negro song, quoted by HOWARD W. ODUM: *Wings On My Feet,* III, 1929

Expect an early death — it will keep you busier.

MARTIN H. FISCHER (1879–)

We're here today and gone tomorrow.

AMERICAN PROVERB

Death rides a fast camel. ARAB PROVERB

The rose withers, the blossom blasteth,
The flower fades, the morning hasteth,
The sun sets, the shadow flies,
The gourd consumes; and man he dies.

Author unidentified

Death does not come with a trumpet.

DANISH PROVERB

Death keeps no almanac. DUTCH PROVERB

Shall wee all die?
Wee shall die all.
All die shall we?
Die all we shall.

Epitaph at Cunwallow, Cornwall, England

Death is a fisherman; the world we see
A fishpond is, and we the fishes be;
He sometimes angler-like doth with us play,
And slily takes us one by one away.

Epitaph at High Wycombe, England

Grim death took me without warning;
I was well at night, and dead in the morning.

Epitaph at Seven Oaks, Kent, England

A good life has a peaceful death.

FRENCH PROVERB

Death is the poor man's doctor.

GERMAN PROVERB

No herb grows that will cure death. IBID.

Death is sufficient punishment, even to an ant.

HINDU PROVERB

To die and to lose one's life are much the same thing. IRISH PROVERB

What is the world to a man when his wife is a widow? IBID.

After the game the king and the pawn go into the same box. ITALIAN PROVERB

What else is death but one brief sigh? IBID.

Remember you must die. (Memento mori.)

LATIN MOTTO

No one can escape death. (Mortem effugere nemo potest.) IBID.

The fear of death is worse than death. (Timor mortis morte pejor.) IBID.

The greatest king must at last be put to bed with a shovel. RUSSIAN PROVERB

When death lifts the curtain it's time to be startin'. SCOTTISH PROVERB

Oh! little did my mother think,
  That day she cradled me,
The lands that I should travel in,
  The deaths that I should dee.

SCOTTISH SONG

Death is deaf. SPANISH PROVERB

A man dies of the malady he fears most.
IBID.

Death is a black camel that kneels once at every man's door. TURKISH PROVERB

Death is always new.
WEST AFRICAN PROVERB

[*See also* Absence, Age (Old), Animal, Birth, Birth and Death, Blessed, Bravery, Cell, Christian, Coward, Day, Dead, Disease, Disgrace, Drinking, Dust, Dying, Epitaph, Escape, Fame, Fate, Fear, Good, Goodbye, Grave, Hell, Horse, Immortality, Jesuit, Judgment Day, Just, King, Life, Life and Death, Man, Morality, Mourning, Parting, Passion, Sin, Sleep, Soldier, Suicide, Virtue, Woman.

Deathbed

There is none so fortunate that there will not be one or two standing at his deathbed who will welcome the evil befalling him.
MARCUS AURELIUS: *Meditations*, x, *c.* 170

There is nothing in history which is so improving to the reader as those accounts which we meet with of the deaths of eminent persons, and of their behavior in that dreadful season.
JOSEPH ADDISON: *The Spectator*, Jan. 31, 1712

[*See also* Dying, Fame.

Debate

Debate is masculine; conversation is feminine.
A. BRONSON ALCOTT: *Concord Days*, 1872

Truth is lost with too much debating.
DUTCH PROVERB

[*See also* Argument, Discussion, Dispute.

Debauchery

Not joy but joylessness is the mother of debauchery.
F. W. NIETZSCHE: *Human All-too-Human*, II, 1878

Debs, Eugene (1855–1926)

While there is a lower class I am in it, while there is a criminal element I am of it, and while there is a soul in prison I am not free.
Speech during his trial at Canton, O., June 16, 1918

Debt

It is better to pay a creditor than to give to a friend.
ARISTOTLE: *The Nicomachean Ethics*, IX, *c.* 340 B.C.

Owe no man anything.
ROMANS XIII, 8, *c.* 55

Debt is the slavery of the free.
PUBLILIUS SYRUS: *Sententiæ*, *c.* 50 B.C.

The Lord forbid that I should be out of debt, as if, indeed, I could not be trusted.
RABELAIS: *Pantagruel*, III, 1533

Speak not of my debts unless you mean to pay them.
GEORGE HERBERT: *Outlandish Proverbs*, 1640

He pays the half, who does confess the debt.
ROBERT HERRICK: *Hesperides*, 1648

Debt is better than death.
JAMES HOWELL: *Proverbs*, 1659

Pride does not like to owe, and self-love does not like to pay.
LA ROCHEFOUCAULD: *Maxims*, 1665

Better go to bed supperless than rise in debt.
JOHN RAY: *English Proverbs*, 1670

Lying rides upon debt's back. IBID.

Out of debt, out of danger. IBID.

He has but a short Lent that must pay money at Easter.
THOMAS FULLER: *Gnomologia*, 1732

He that hath an hundred and one, and owes an hundred and two, the Lord have mercy on him. IBID.

Living upon trust is the way to pay double.
IBID.

Out of debt, out of danger. IBID.

Sins and debts are always more than we think them to be. IBID.

Small debts are like small shot; they are rattling on every side, and can scarcely be escaped without a wound: great debts are like cannon; of loud noise but little danger.
SAMUEL JOHNSON: *Letter to Joseph Simpson*, 1759

If you want the time to pass quickly, just give your note for 90 days.
R. B. THOMAS: *Farmers' Almanack*, 1797

Debt is a preceptor whose lessons are needed most by those who suffer from it most.
R. W. EMERSON: *Nature,* 1836

There are but two ways of paying debt — increase of industry in raising income, increase of thrift in laying out.
THOMAS CARLYLE: *Past and Present,* X, 1843

Debt is an evil conscience.
H. G. BOHN: *Handbook of Proverbs,* 1855

A man in debt is so far a slave.
R. W. EMERSON: *The Conduct of Life,* III, 1860

He is rich who owes nothing.
HUNGARIAN PROVERB

Better go without rice for a little than be in debt for long. JAPANESE PROVERB

Debts are like children: the smaller they are the more noise they make.
SPANISH PROVERB

[*See also* Anxiety, Bank, Borrower, Borrowing, Charity, Creditor, Debtor, Forgiveness.

Debt, Interallied

Well, they hired the money, didn't they?
CALVIN COOLIDGE: To Myron T. Herrick, American ambassador to France, at the White House, 1925, after Merrick had urged the lenient refunding of the French debt to the United States

We oppose cancellation of the debts owing to the United States by foreign nations.
Democratic National Platform, 1932

Debtor

The Russians have an excellent custom: they beat them on the shins that have money and will not pay their debts.
THOMAS DEKKER: *The Seven Deadly Sins of London,* I, 1606

Debtors are liars.
GEORGE HERBERT: *Outlandish Proverbs,* 1640

The debtor is always in the wrong.
ITALIAN PROVERB

A debtor is not presumed to give. (Debitor non presumitur donare.) LEGAL MAXIM

He who pays too late pays too little. (Qui tardius solvit, minus solvit.) IBID.

He who sleeps too long of a morning, let him borrow the pillow of a debtor.
SPANISH PROVERB

[*See also* Borrower, Borrowing, Classes, Creditor, Debt, Forgiveness.

Debt, Public

A national debt, if it is not excessive, will be to us a national blessing.
ALEXANDER HAMILTON: *Letter to Robert Morris,* April 30, 1781

I place economy among the first and most important of republican virtues, and public debt as the greatest of the dangers to be feared.
THOMAS JEFFERSON: *Letter to Governor Plumer,* 1816

The principle of spending money to be paid by posterity, under the name of funding, is but swindling futurity on a large scale.
THOMAS JEFFERSON: *Letter to John Taylor,* 1816

It is incumbent on every generation to pay its own debts as it goes — a principle which, if acted on, would save one-half the wars of the world.
THOMAS JEFFERSON: *Letter to Destutt Tracy,* 1820

If a national debt is considered a national blessing, then we can get on by borrowing. But as I believe it is a national curse, my vow shall be to pay the national debt.
ANDREW JACKSON: *Letter,* July 4, 1824

Public credit means the contracting of debts which a nation never can pay.
WILLIAM COBBETT: *Advice to Young Men,* II, 1829

We are opposed to the issuing of interest-bearing bonds of the United States in time of peace.
Democratic National Platform, 1896

I desire to go on record as predicting that we will never pay our public debt in full.
LEWIS H. HANEY: Speech at Detroit, Dec. 29, 1938

Decay

My flesh is clothed with worms and clods of dust; my skin is broken, and become loathsome. JOB VII, 6, *c.* 325 B.C.

It is a strange wood that has never a dead bough in it.
THOMAS FULLER: *Gnomologia,* 1732

[*See also* Decline, Degeneration, Mind and Body.

Deceit

O Lord, thou hast deceived me, and I was deceived. JEREMIAH XX, 7, *c.* 625 B.C.

Bread of deceit is sweet to a man, but afterwards his mouth shall be filled with gravel.
PROVERBS XX, 17, *c.* 350 B.C.

Whatever deceives seems to exercise a kind of magical enchantment.
PLATO: *The Republic,* III, *c.* 350 B.C.

Dost thou hate to be deceived? Do not deceive another.
ST. JOHN CHRYSOSTOM: *Homily* XIII, *c.* 388

Men are so simple and yield so readily to the wants of the moment that he who will trick will always find another who will suffer himself to be tricked.
NICCOLÒ MACHIAVELLI: *The Prince,* II, 1513

A quicksand of deceit.
SHAKESPEARE: *III Henry VI,* V, *c.* 1591

Oh, that deceit should steal such gentle shapes,
And with a virtuous vizard hide foul guile.
SHAKESPEARE: *Richard III,* II, *c.* 1592

O, that deceit should dwell
In such a gorgeous palace.
SHAKESPEARE: *Romeo and Juliet,* III, *c.* 1596

Sigh no more, ladies, sigh no more,
Men were deceivers ever.
SHAKESPEARE: *Much Ado About Nothing,* II, *c.* 1599

Deceit is the game of small minds, and is thus the proper pursuit of women.
PIERRE CORNEILLE: *Nicomède,* IV, 1651

From all inordinate and sinful affections; and from all the deceits of the world, the flesh, and the devil, Good Lord, deliver us.
THE BOOK OF COMMON PRAYER (*The Litany*), 1662

It is a double pleasure to deceive the deceiver.
JEAN DE LA FONTAINE: *Fables,* II, 1668

We never deceive for a good purpose. Knavery always adds malice to falsehood.
JEAN DE LA BRUYÈRE: *Caractères,* XI, 1688

It is vain to find fault with those arts of deceiving wherein men find pleasure to be deceived.
JOHN LOCKE: *Essay Concerning Human Understanding,* III, 1690

Deceit is the darling of the mind.
WILLIAM WARBURTON (BISHOP OF GLOUCESTER): *The Causes of Prodigies and Miracles,* I, 1727

Deceiving of a deceiver is no knavery.
THOMAS FULLER: *Gnomologia,* 1732

In three things a man may be easily deceived, viz.: in a man till known, a tree till down, and the day till done.
NATHANIEL BAILEY: *Etymological Dictionary,* 1736

An action cannot be supported for telling a bare naked lie: but that I define to be, saying a thing that is false, knowing or not knowing it to be so, and without any design to injure, cheat, or deceive another person. Every deceit comprehends a lie; but a deceit is more than a lie, on account of the view with which it is practised, its being coupled with some dealing, and the injury which it is calculated to occasion, and does occasion, to another person.
MR. JUSTICE BULLER: *Judgment in Pasley vs. Freeman,* 1789

Who is right — the man who believes that he is being deceived, or the man who believes that he is not?
G. C. LICHTENBERG: *Reflections,* 1799

Oh, what a tangled web we weave
When first we practise to deceive!
WALTER SCOTT: *Marmion,* VI, 1808

I defy any man to deceive me. He would have to be a real rogue to be as bad as I imagine him.
NAPOLEON I: To Gaspard Gourgaud at St. Helena, Dec. 12, 1816

You can fool some of the people all of the time, and all of the people some of the time, but you cannot fool all of the people all the time.
Ascribed to ABRAHAM LINCOLN, *c.* 1863, but not found in his published papers

The world wants to be deceived.
GERMAN PROVERB

If you deceive me once you are a scoundrel; if you deceive me often you are a smart man.
JUGO-SLAVIC PROVERB

He is not deceived who knows himself to be deceived. (Non decipitur qui scit se decipi.)
LEGAL MAXIM

[*See also* Credulity, Delirium, Fraud, Happiness, Haste, Heart, Inconstancy, Lying, Man and Woman, Marriage, Sincerity, Trust.

December

We shall hear
The rain and wind beat dark December.
SHAKESPEARE: *Cymbeline,* III, *c.* 1609

The sun, that brief December day,
Rose cheerless over hills of gray,
And, darkly circled, gave at noon
A sadder light than waning moon.
J. G. WHITTIER: *Snow-Bound,* 1866

If cold December gave you birth,
The month of snow and ice and mirth,
Place on your hand a turquoise blue,
Success will bless whate'er you do.
Author unidentified

[*See also* Age (Old), Months.

Decency

Let all things be done decently and in order.
I CORINTHIANS XIV, 40, *c.* 55

Decency is indecency's conspiracy of silence.
GEORGE BERNARD SHAW: *Maxims for Revolutionists,* 1903

[*See also* Immodesty, Vice.

Deception

[*See* Deceit.

Decision

Quick decisions are unsafe decisions.
SOPHOCLES: *Oedipus Tyrannus, c.* 450 B.C.

Let men decide firmly what they will not do, and they will be free to do vigorously what they ought to do.
MENCIUS: *Discourses,* IV, *c.* 300 B.C.

For what I will, I will, and there an end.
SHAKESPEARE: *Two Gentlemen of Verona,* I, *c.* 1595

Deck

The boy stood on the burning deck
Whence all but him had fled.
FELICIA HEMANS: *Casabianca,* 1826

Declaration of Independence

Yesterday the greatest question was decided which was ever debated in America; and a greater perhaps never was, nor will be, decided among men. A resolution was passed without one dissenting colony, that those United Colonies are, and of right ought to be, free and independent states.
JOHN ADAMS: *Letter to his wife,* July 3, 1776

The self-evident truths announced in the Declaration of Independence are not truths at all, if taken literally; and the practical conclusions contained in the same passage of that Declaration prove that they were never designed to be so received.
WILLIAM PINKNEY: Speech in the Senate, Feb. 15, 1820

This holy bond of our Union.
THOMAS JEFFERSON: *Letter to James Mease,* 1825

The glittering and sounding generalities of natural right which make up the Declaration of Independence.
RUFUS CHOATE: *Letter to the Whig committee of Maine,* 1856

[*See also* Jefferson (Thomas), Pledge.

Declaration of War

[*See* War (Declaration of).

Decline

The lives, not only of men, but of commonwealths and the whole world, run not upon a helix that still enlargeth; but on a circle where, arriving to their meridian, they decline in obscurity, and fall under the horizon again.
THOMAS BROWNE: *Religio Medici,* I, 1642

[*See also* Decay, Degeneration.

Decoration

In the court of the garden of the king's palace . . . were white, green and blue hangings, fastened with cords of fine linen and purple to silver rings and pillars of marble: the beds were of gold and silver, upon a pavement of red, and blue, and white, and black marble.
ESTHER I, 6, *c.* 125 B.C.

In full festoons the crimson curtains fell,
The sofas rose in bold elastic swell;
Mirrors in gilded frames display'd the tints
Of glowing carpets and of color'd prints;
The weary eye saw every object shine,
And all was costly, fanciful, and fine.
GEORGE CRABBE: *Tales,* II, (*The Gentleman Farmer*), 1812

The superfluities of house furniture are numerous and generally so conspicuous that it is only necessary to invite reflection on their impropriety. The gilding and ornamental work of looking-glasses and picture frames, books, chairs, &c. are expensive offerings to fancy and fashion.
JESSE TORREY: *The Moral Instructor,* 1819

The first spiritual want of a barbarous man is decoration, as indeed we still see among the barbarous classes in civilized countries.
THOMAS CARLYLE: *Sartor Resartus,* I, 1836

Wherever you can rest, there decorate; where rest is forbidden, so is beauty. You must not mix ornament with business, any more than you may mix play. Work first, and then rest.
JOHN RUSKIN: *The Seven Lamps of Architecture,* IV, 1849

[*See also* Ornament.

Decorum

Let them cant about decorum
Who have characters to lose.
ROBERT BURNS: *The Jolly Beggars,* 1785

[*See also* Vice.

Dedication

To the only honor and glory of God, my dear and blessed Saviour, (which hath done and suffered all these things for my soul,) his weak and unworthy servant humbly desires to consecrate himself and his poor labors; beseeching him to accept and bless them to the public good, and to the praise of his own glorious name.
JOSEPH HALL (BISHOP OF NORWICH): Sermon preached at Paul's Cross on Good Friday, April 14, 1609

In this, my book, tho' mean, you'll find
A good company for an honest mind.
WILLIAM MATHER: *The Young Man's Companion,* pref., 1681

A dedication is a wooden leg.
EDWARD YOUNG: *Love of Fame,* IV, 1728

There is the same difference between what a man says in a dedication and what he says

in a history as between a lawyer's pleading a case and reporting it.
SAMUEL JOHNSON: *Boswell's Tour to the Hebrides,* Oct. 5, 1773

Deed

Let deeds match words.
PLAUTUS: *Pseudolus,* I, *c.* 190 B.C.

How far that little candle throws his beams!
So shines a good deed in a naughty world.
SHAKESPEARE: *The Merchant of Venice,* V, *c.* 1597

A deed without a name.
SHAKESPEARE: *Macbeth,* IV, *c.* 1605

Deeds are males, words females are.
JOHN DAVIES: *The Scourge of Folly, c.* 1610

You must take the will for the deed.
JONATHAN SWIFT: *Polite Conversation,* 1738

Our deeds determine us, as much as we determine our deeds.
MARIAN EVANS (GEORGE ELIOT): *Adam Bede,* XXIX, 1859

Deeds are facts, and are forever and ever.
THOMAS B. REED: Speech in Portland, Maine, July 29, 1896

Deeds are masculine; words are feminine. (Fatti maschii; parole femine.)
MOTTO OF MARYLAND (in Italian), borrowed from the motto of the first Baron Baltimore, 1625 (Cf. DAVIES, *ante, c.* 1610)

[*See also* Abbot, Action, Doer.

Deep

Deep calleth unto deep.
PSALMS XLII, 7, *c.* 150 B.C.

Deeper than e'er plummet sounded.
SHAKESPEARE: *The Tempest,* III, 1611

[*See also* Still.

Defeat

Defeat in war is not the greatest of evils, but when that defeat is inflicted by an unworthy enemy then the evil is doubled.
AESCHINES: *Ctesiphontem,* 337 B.C.

If he that in the field is slain
Be in the bed of honor lain,
He that is beaten may be said
To lie in honor's truckle-bed.
SAMUEL BUTLER: *Hudibras,* I, 1663

I give the fight up; let there be an end,
A privacy, an obscure nook for me,
I want to be forgotten even by God.
ROBERT BROWNING: *Paracelsus,* V, 1835

It is defeat that turns bone to flint; it is defeat that turns gristle to muscle; it is defeat that makes men invincible.
H. W. BEECHER: *Royal Truths,* 1862

This has been a sad day for us, Colonel, a sad day; but we can't expect always to gain victories.
R. E. LEE: To Col. Fremantle of the British Army, at Gettysburg, July 3, 1863

[*See also* Honor.

Defect

It is the prerogative of great men to have great defects.
LA ROCHEFOUCAULD: *Maxims,* 1665

A man's personal defects will commonly have, with the rest of the world, precisely that importance which they have to himself. If he makes light of them, so will other men.
R. W. EMERSON: *English Traits,* VIII, 1856

Defendant

When the rights of the parties are obscure, the defendant is to be favored against the plaintiff. (Quum sunt partium jura obscura, reo potius favendum est quam auctori.)
LEGAL MAXIM

[*See also* Lawsuit.

Defender

[*See* Faith.

Defense

Even God himself did not pass sentence upon Adam before he was called upon to make his defense. "Adam," says God, "where art thou? Hast thou not eaten of the tree whereof I commanded thee that thou shouldst not eat?" And the same question was put to Eve also.
JOHN FORTESCUE: *De laudibus legum Angliæ, c.* 1462

[*See also* Trial by Jury.

Defense, National

Millions for defense, sir, but not one cent for tribute.
CHARLES C. PINCKNEY, Minister to France: To C. M. Talleyrand, on being told that a gift to the Directory might avert war with France, 1796

The nation that cannot resist aggression is constantly exposed to it. Its foreign policy is of necessity weak and its negotiations are conducted with disadvantage because it is not in condition to enforce the terms dictated by its sense of right and justice.
GROVER CLEVELAND: Message to Congress, Dec. 8, 1885

Defenseless

A man without a stick will be bitten even by a sheep.
HINDU PROVERB

Deference

He who would honor learning, and taste, and sentiment, and refinement of every sort, ought to respect its possessors, and, in all things but those which affect rights, defer to their superior advantages. This is the extent of the deference that is due from him who is not a gentleman, to him who is; but this much is due.

J. FENIMORE COOPER: *The American Democrat,* XIX, 1838

Defiance

I do defy him, and I spit at him;
Call him a slanderous coward and a villain.

SHAKESPEARE: *Richard II,* I, *c.* 1596

Come one, come all! this rock shall fly
From its firm base, as soon as I.

WALTER SCOTT: *The Lady of the Lake,* V, 1810

What are you going to do about it?

W. M. TWEED: On being confronted by proofs of his corruption, 1871

[*See also* Indomitable, Surrender.

Deficit

Let us have the courage to stop borrowing to meet continuing deficits. Stop the deficits.

F. D. ROOSEVELT: Radio Speech, July 30, 1932

[*See also* Bankruptcy, Borrowing.

Defilement

He that toucheth pitch shall be defiled therewith. ECCLESIASTICUS XIII, 1, *c.* 180 B.C.

Definition

Every definition is dangerous. (Omnis definitio periculosa est.)

DESIDERIUS ERASMUS: *Adagia,* 1508

The light of human minds is perspicuous words, but by exact definitions first snuffed, and purged from ambiguity.

THOMAS HOBBES: *Leviathan,* V, 1651

It is one of the maxims of the civil law that definitions are hazardous.

SAMUEL JOHNSON: *The Rambler,* May 28, 1751

I see a cow. I define her: *Animal quadrupes ruminans cornutum.* But a goat ruminates, and a cow may have no horns. *Cow* is plainer.

SAMUEL JOHNSON: *Boswell's Life,* April 7, 1778

A definition is no proof.

WILLIAM PINKNEY: Speech in the Senate, Feb. 15, 1820

A definition is that which so describes its object as to distinguish it from all others; it is no definition of any one thing if its terms are applicable to any one other.

E. A. POE: *The Rationale of Verse,* 1843 (The Pioneer, March)

Perhaps the reason why no satisfactory definitions can be given of goodness, beauty, truth, is that these ideas blend in our spiritual nature, so that, when we seek to distinguish them, we violate the unity of our higher self.

JOHN ADDINGTON SYMONDS: *On the Relation of Art to Science and Morality,* 1894

Defoe, Daniel (1660?–1731)

[*See* Ape.

Degeneration

Everything is good when it comes from the hands of the Almighty; everything degenerates in the hands of man.

J.-J. ROUSSEAU: *Émile,* I, 1762

[*See also* Decay, Decline, Inbreeding.

Deism

Slave to no sect, who takes no private road,
But looks through nature up to nature's God.

ALEXANDER POPE: *An Essay on Man,* IV, 1734

No honest man could be a Deist; for no man could be so after a fair examination of the proofs of Christianity.

SAMUEL JOHNSON: *Boswell's Life,* Feb., 1766

Deism teaches us, without the possibility of being deceived, all that is necessary or proper to be known. The creation is the Bible of the Deist. He there reads, in the handwriting of the Creator Himself, the certainty of His existence, and the immutability of His power, and all other Bibles and Testaments are to him forgeries.

THOMAS PAINE: *The Age of Reason,* III, 1794

Deity

The Supreme Power is not a Mind, but something higher than a mind; not a Force, but something higher than a force; not a Being, but something higher than a being.

W. WINWOOD READE: *The Martyrdom of Man,* III, 1872

[*See also* God.

Dejection

A man used to vicissitudes is not easily dejected.

SAMUEL JOHNSON: *Rasselas,* XII, 1759

Delaware

Delaware will probably remain what it ever has been, a mere county of England, conquered indeed, and held under by force, but always disposed to counter-revolution.

THOMAS JEFFERSON: *Letter to Bidwell,* 1806

A state that has three counties when the tide is out, and two when it is in.

J. J. INGALLS: Speech in the Senate, *c.* 1885

Delay

Delay is hateful, but it gives wisdom.

PUBLILIUS SYRUS: *Sententiæ, c.* 50 B.C.

Put it off: delay is an advantage.
OVID: *Fasti*, III, *c.* 5

Delays breed dangers.
JOHN LYLY: *Euphues*, 1579

Doubtful delay is worse than any fever.
HENRY CONSTABLE: *Sonnets to Diana*, *c.* 1592

Defer no time; delays have dangerous ends.
SHAKESPEARE: *I Henry VI*, III, 1592

Do not delay: the golden moments fly!
H. W. LONGFELLOW: *The Masque of Pandora*, VII, 1875

The law abhors delays. (Lex dilationes exhorret.) LEGAL MAXIM

It is a wise delay which makes the road safe.
SPANISH PROVERB

[*See also* Anarchy, Haste, Justice, Patience, War.

Delectable

They came to the Delectable Mountains.
JOHN BUNYAN: *Pilgrim's Progress*, I, 1684

Delegate

The delegate cannot delegate. (Delegatus non potest delegare.) LEGAL MAXIM

Deliberation

Think long when you may decide only once.
PUBLILIUS SYRUS: *Sententiæ*, *c.* 50 B.C.

The woman that deliberates is lost.
JOSEPH ADDISON: *Cato*, IV, 1713

[*See also* Opportunity.

Delicacy

An air of robustness and strength is very prejudicial to beauty. An appearance of delicacy, and even of fragility, is almost essential to it.
EDMUND BURKE: *The Sublime and Beautiful*, II, 1756

If a person has no delicacy, he has you in his power.
WILLIAM HAZLITT: *Literary Remains*, II, 1838

Delight

These violent delights have violent ends,
And in their triumphs, die; like fire and powder,
Which as they kiss, consume.
SHAKESPEARE: *Romeo and Juliet*, II, *c.* 1596

The race of delight is short, and pleasures have mutable faces.
THOMAS BROWNE: *Christian Morals*, *c.* 1680

[*See also* Desire, Phantom, Pleasure, Poetry.

Delirium

Delirium is our best deceiver.
BYRON: *The Spell is Broke*, 1810

Deluge

After us the deluge. (Après nous le déluge!)
MME. DE POMPADOUR: To Louis XV, after the battle of Rossbach, Nov. 5, 1757

Delusion

God shall send them strong delusion, that they should believe a lie.
II THESSALONIANS II, 11, *c.* 51

[*See also* Snare.

Demagogue

Every one that was in distress, and every one that was in debt, and every one that was discontented, gathered themselves unto him; and he became a captain over them.
I SAMUEL XXII, 2, *c.* 500 B.C. (David in the cave of Adullam)

A wise fellow who is also worthless always charms the rabble.
EURIPIDES: *Hippolytus*, 428 B.C.

The qualities necessary to a demagogue are these: to be foul-mouthed, base-born, a low, mean fellow.
ARISTOPHANES: *The Knights*, 424 B.C.

The demagogue, puffing up the people with words, sways them to his interest. When calamity follows he escapes from justice.
EURIPIDES: *The Suppliant Women*, *c.* 421 B.C.

A man of loose tongue, intemperate, trusting to tumult, leading the populace to mischief with empty words.
EURIPIDES: *Orestes*, 408 B.C.

The shortest way to ruin a country is to give power to demagogues.
DIONYSIUS OF HALICARNASSUS: *Antiquities of Rome*, VI, *c.* 20 B.C.

There have been many great men that have flattered the people, who ne'er loved them.
SHAKESPEARE: *Coriolanus*, II, *c.* 1607

As there are mountebanks for the natural body, so are there mountebanks for the politic body; men that undertake great cures, and, perhaps, have been lucky in two or three experiments, but want the grounds of science, and therefore cannot hold out.
FRANCIS BACON: *Essays*, XII, 1625

The chief demagogues and patrons of tumults.
JOHN GLAUDEN (BISHOP OF EXETER) (?): *Eikon Basilike*, 1648

The demagogue goes forth; the public eye is upon him; he frets his busy hour upon the stage; but soon either weariness, or bribe, or punishment, or disappointment bears him down, or drives him off, and he appears no more.

J. P. CURRAN: Speech to the jury at the trial of A. Hamilton Rowan, 1794

Who o'er the herd would wish to reign,
Fantastic, fickle, fierce, and vain?
Vain as the leaf upon the stream,
And fickle as a changeful dream;
Fantastic as a woman's mood,
And fierce as frenzy's fever'd blood —
Thou many-headed monster thing,
Oh, who would wish to be thy king?

WALTER SCOTT: *The Lady of the Lake*, v, 1810

The whole fabric of society presents a most threatening aspect. What is most ominous of an approaching change is the strength which the popular party have suddenly acquired, and the importance which the violence of demagogues has assumed.

P. B. SHELLEY: *Letter to Byron*, Nov. 20, 1816

A new race of men is springing up to govern the nation; they are the hunters after popularity, men ambitious, not of the honor so much as of the profits of office — the demagogues, whose principles hang laxly upon them, and who follow not so much what is right as what leads to a temporary vulgar applause.

JOSEPH STORY: *Commentaries on the Constitution of the United States*, 1833

If there be a vile thing in the world it is a plebeian advanced by patricians, not for the purpose of righting his own order, but for playing the pander to the worst interest of theirs.

E. G. BULWER-LYTTON: *Rienzi*, I, 1835

The demagogue is usually sly, a detractor of others, a professor of humility and disinterestedness, a great stickler for equality as respects all above him, a man who acts in corners, and avoids open and manly expositions of his course, calls blackguards gentlemen, and gentlemen folks, appeals to passions and prejudices rather than to reason, and is in all respects a man of intrigue and deception, of sly cunning and management.

J. FENIMORE COOPER: *The American Democrat*, XXI, 1838

The mean arts and unreasonable clamors of demagogues.

T. B. MACAULAY: *History of England*, I, 1848

The people are sovereign, but they are in the position of a sovereign eternally under age, who must therefore remain under tutelage, and cannot exercise his rights without grave danger. Like all minors, he is the sport of crafty scoundrels. These we call demagogues.

ARTHUR SCHOPENHAUER: *Parerga und Paralipomena*, II, 1851

In every age the vilest specimens of human nature are to be found among demagogues.

T. B. MACAULAY: *History of England*, IV, 1855

On one side is a statesman preaching patience, respect for vested rights, strict observance of public faith. On the other side is a demagogue ranting about the tyranny of capitalists and usurers, and asking why anybody should be permitted to drink champagne and to ride in a carriage while thousands of honest people are in want of necessaries. Which of the two candidates is likely to be preferred by a workingman who hears his children cry for bread?

T. B. MACAULAY: *Letter to H. S. Randall*, May 23, 1857

Critics should bear in mind that an orator does not speak chiefly to them or for their approval. He who writes, or speaks, or sings for thousands, must write, speak, or sing as those thousands would have him.

ANTHONY TROLLOPE: *North America*, I, 1862

The first-recorded judicial murder of a scientific thinker was compassed and effected, not by a despot, not by priests, but was brought about by eloquent demagogues.

T. H. HUXLEY: *Evidence as to Man's Place in Nature*, pref., 1863 (The reference is to Socrates)

Demagogues and agitators are very unpleasant, but they are incidents to a free and constitutional country, and you must put up with these inconveniences or do without many important advantages.

BENJAMIN DISRAELI: Speech in the House of Commons, April 12, 1867

The honest man, whether rich or poor, who earns his own living and tries to deal justly by his fellows, has as much to fear from the insincere and unworthy demagogue, promising much and performing nothing, or else performing nothing but evil, who would set on the mob to plunder the rich, as from the crafty corruptionist who, for his own ends, would permit the common people to be exploited by the very wealthy.

THEODORE ROOSEVELT: Message to Congress, Dec. 3, 1906

[*See also* Bryan (W. J.), Doctrinaire, Incompetence.

Demand

Demand is not a fixed quantity, that increases only as population increases. In each individual it rises with his power of getting the things demanded.

HENRY GEORGE: *Progress and Poverty*, IV, 1879

Democracy

A democracy is a state in which the poor, gaining the upper hand, kill some and banish

others, and then divide the offices among the remaining citizens equally, usually by lot.
PLATO: *The Republic,* VIII, *c.* 370 B.C.

Democracy is a charming form of government, full of variety and disorder, and dispensing a kind of equality to equals and unequals alike.
IBID.

Democracy arose from men thinking that if they are equal in any respect they are equal in all respects.
ARISTOTLE: *Politics,* V, *c.* 322 B.C.

A democracy is a government in the hands of men of low birth, no property, and vulgar employments. ARISTOTLE: *Politics,* VI

A democracy, when put to the strain, grows weak, and is supplanted by oligarchy.
ARISTOTLE: *Rhetoric,* I, *c.* 322 B.C.

When a state increases in wealth and luxury men indulge in ambitious projects and are eager for high dignities. Each feels ashamed that any of his fellow men should surpass him. The common people feel themselves oppressed by the grasping of some, and their vanity is flattered by others. Fired with evil passions, they are no longer willing to submit to control, but demand that everything be subject to their authority. The invariable result is that the government assumes the noble names of free and popular, but becomes in fact that most execrable thing, mob rule.
POLYBIUS: *Histories,* VI, *c.* 125 B.C.

Democracy is more cruel than wars or tyrants.
SENECA: *Epistulæ morales ad Lucilium,* CIV, *c.* 63

Another public weal was among the Athenians, where equality was of estate among the people. . . . This matter of governance was called in Greek *democratia.*
THOMAS ELYOT: *The Governour,* I, 1531

Democracy: when the multitude have government.
ABRAHAM FLEMING: *A Panoplie of Epistles,* 1576

Democracies do not nourish game and pleasures like unto monarchies.
EDWARD TOPSELL: *History of Fourfooted Beasts,* 1607

Democracies are commonly more quiet and less subject to sedition than where there are stirps of nobles.
FRANCIS BACON: *Essays,* XIV, 1625

The form of government established in Providence Plantations is democratical; that is to say, a government held by the free and voluntary consent of all, or the greater part, of the free inhabitants.
Records of Rhode Island, 1647

A democracy in effect is no more than an aristocracy of orators, interrupted sometimes with the temporary monarchy of one orator.
THOMAS HOBBES: *De corpore politico,* II, 1650

Public affairs ought to advance, and have a certain progress, neither too slow nor too quick. But the people have always too much action or too little. Sometimes, with 100,000 arms, they overturn everything; at other times, with 100,000 feet, they crawl like insects.
C. L. DE MONTESQUIEU: *The Spirit of the Laws,* II, 1748

Democracy has two excesses to be wary of: the spirit of inequality, which leads it to aristocracy, and the spirit of extreme equality, which leads it to despotism.
C. L. DE MONTESQUIEU: *The Spirit of the Laws,* VIII

If there were a nation of gods they would be governed democratically, but so perfect a government is not suitable to men.
J.-J. ROUSSEAU: *Du contrat social,* III, 1762

Democracy seems suitable only to a very little country.
VOLTAIRE: *Philosophical Dictionary,* 1764

The evils we experience flow from the excess of democracy. The people do not want virtue, but are the dupes of pretended patriots.
ELBRIDGE GERRY: Speech in the Constitutional Convention, 1787

It has been observed that a pure democracy, if it were practicable, would be the most perfect government. Experience has proved that no position is more false than this. The ancient democracies, in which the people themselves deliberated, never possessed one feature of good government. Their very character was tyranny; their figure deformity.
ALEXANDER HAMILTON: Speech in the Senate, June 21, 1788

In a democracy the people meet and exercise the government in person; in a republic, they assemble and administer it by their representatives and agents. A democracy, consequently, will be confined to a small spot. A republic may be extended over a large region.
JAMES MADISON: *The Federalist,* XIII, 1788

A perfect democracy is the most shameless thing in the world.
EDMUND BURKE: *Reflections on the Revolution in France,* 1790

Those who are subjected to wrong under multitudes are deprived of all external consolations. They seem deserted by mankind; overpowered by a conspiracy of their whole species.
IBID.

The tyranny of a multitude is a multiplied tyranny.
EDMUND BURKE: *Letter to Thomas Mercer,* Feb. 26, 1790

Under mere political liberty we are worse off than under despotism. . . . Formerly we had half a million despots; now we have a million oppressors.

J. P. MARAT: *Letter to Camille Desmoulins,* June 24, 1790

The most substantial democracy is that state in which the greatest number of men feel an interest in expressing opinion upon political questions, and in which the greatest number of judgments and wills concur in influencing public measures.

JAMES MACKINTOSH: *Vindiciae Gallicae,* 1791

Government of the people and for the people.

THOMAS COOPER: *Some Information Respecting America,* 1795

Democracy is necessarily despotism, as it establishes an executive power contrary to the general will; all being able to decide against one whose opinion may differ, the will of all is therefore not that of all: which is contradictory and opposite to liberty.

IMMANUEL KANT: *Perpetual Peace,* II, 1795

Democracy is Lovelace and the people is Clarissa.

JOHN ADAMS: *Letter to William Cunningham,* March, 1804

The government of the Union is emphatically and truly a government of the people. In form and in substance it emanates from them. Its powers are granted by them, and are to be exercised directly on them and for their benefit.

JOHN MARSHALL: *Decision in McCulloch* vs. *Maryland,* 1819

An aristocracy of blackguards.

BYRON: *Diary,* May, 1821

The people's government made for the people, made by the people, and answerable to the people.

DANIEL WEBSTER: Speech in the Senate, Jan. 26, 1830 (Cf. COOPER, *ante,* 1795)

Democracy is the healthful life-blood which circulates through the veins and arteries, which supports the system, but which ought never to appear externally, and as the mere blood itself.

S. T. COLERIDGE: *Table-Talk,* Sept. 19, 1830

The tendency of democracies is, in all things, to mediocrity.

J. FENIMORE COOPER: *The American Democrat,* XIV, 1838

Democracy is, by the nature of it, a self-cancelling business: and gives in the long run a net result of zero.

THOMAS CARLYLE: *Chartism,* VI, 1839

Democracy is morose, and runs to anarchy.

R. W. EMERSON: *Nominalist and Realist,* 1841

Fisher Ames . . . [said] . . . that a monarchy is a merchantman which sails well, but will sometimes strike on a rock and go to the bottom; whilst a republic is a raft which would never sink, but then your feet are always in the water.

R. W. EMERSON: *Politics,* 1841 (Fisher Ames, 1758–1808)

Democracy means despair of finding any heroes to govern you, and contented putting up with the want of them.

THOMAS CARLYLE: *Past and Present,* III, 1843

Democracy is nothing but a constitutional arbitrary power that has succeeded another constitutional arbitrary power.

P. J. PROUDHON: *Solution du problème social,* 1848

Democracies are prone to war, and war consumes them.

W. H. SEWARD: *Eulogy on John Quincy Adams,* 1848

Is it, or is it not a fact, that the air of a democracy agrees better with mere talent than with genius?

E. A. POE: *Marginalia,* 1844–49

If you establish a democracy, you must in due time reap the fruits of a democracy. You will in due season have great impatience of the public burdens, combined in due season with great increase of the public expenditure. You will in due season have wars entered into from passion and not from reason; and you will in due season submit to peace ignominiously sought and ignominiously obtained, which will diminish your authority and perhaps endanger your independence. You will in due season find your property is less valuable, and your freedom less complete.

BENJAMIN DISRAELI: Speech in the House of Commons, March 31, 1850

A government of all the people, by all the people, for all the people.

THEODORE PARKER: Speech at Boston, May 29, 1850 (Cf. COOPER, *ante,* 1795; WEBSTER, 1830)

I speak the pass-word primeval — I give the sign of democracy; My God! I will accept nothing which all cannot have their counterpart of on the same terms.

WALT WHITMAN: *Walt Whitman,* 1855

Institutions purely democratic must, sooner, or later, destroy liberty or civilization or both.

T. B. MACAULAY: *Letter to H. S. Randall,* May 23, 1857

I don't know where democracy will end, but it can't end in a quiet old age.

CLEMENS VON METTERNICH (1773–1859)

Ten million ignorances do not constitute one knowledge. IBID.

It has been evident for years that the country was doomed to run the full length of democracy.

R. E. LEE: *Letter to his wife,* Jan. 23, 1861

Democracy gives every man
The right to be his own oppressor.

J. R. LOWELL: *The Biglow Papers,* II, 1862

I will have never a noble,
No lineage counted great;
Fishers and choppers and plowmen
Shall constitute a state.

R. W. EMERSON: *Boston Hymn,* 1863 (Read in Music Hall Boston, Jan. 1)

Government of the people, by the people, for the people.

ABRAHAM LINCOLN: Gettysburg address, Nov. 19, 1863 (Cf. COOPER, *ante,* 1795; WEBSTER, 1830; PARKER, 1850)

Humble as I am, plebeian as I may be deemed, permit me in the presence of this brilliant assemblage to enunciate the truth that courts and cabinets, the President and his advisers, derive their power and their greatness from the people.

ANDREW JOHNSON: Speech in the Senate chamber on being sworn in as Vice-President, March 4, 1865 (Johnson was drunk at the time)

The world is weary of statesmen whom democracy has degraded into politicians.

BENJAMIN DISRAELI: *Lothair,* XVII, 1870

I say that democracy can never prove itself beyond cavil until it founds and luxuriantly grows its own forms of art, poems, schools, theology, displacing all that exists, or that has been produced anywhere in the past, under opposite influences.

WALT WHITMAN: *Democratic Vistas,* 1870

I do not deny the rights of democracy, but I have no illusions as to the uses that will be made of those rights so long as wisdom is rare and pride abundant.

H. F. AMIEL: *Journal,* June 12, 1871

Even in the purest democracies, such as the United States and Switzerland, a privileged minority stands against the vast enslaved majority.

M. A. BAKUNIN: *Dieu et l'état,* 1871

To put political power in the hands of men embittered and degraded by poverty is to tie firebrands to foxes and turn them loose amid the standing corn.

HENRY GEORGE: *Progress and Poverty,* X, 1879

She had got to the bottom of this business of democratic government and found out that it was nothing more than government of any other kind.

HENRY ADAMS: *Democracy,* 1880

Democracy most of all affiliates with the open air, is sunny and hardy and sane only with nature — just as much as art is. Something is required to temper both — to check them, restrain them from excess, morbidity.

WALT WHITMAN: *Specimen Days,* May 6, 1882

He who takes the oath today to preserve, protect and defend the Constitution of the United States only assumes the solemn obligation which every patriotic citizen — on the farm, in the workshop, in the busy marts of trade, and everywhere — should share with him. The Constitution which prescribes his oath, my countrymen, is yours; the government you have chosen him to administer for a time is yours; the suffrage which executes the will of free men is yours; the laws and the entire scheme of our civil rule, from the town meeting to the state capitols and the national capitol, is yours.

GROVER CLEVELAND: Inaugural address, March 4, 1885

Democracy has always been the death agony of the power of organization.

F. W. NIETZSCHE: *The Twilight of the Idols,* 1889

I should be very sorry to find myself on board a ship in which the voices of the cook and the loblolly boys counted for as much as those of the officers upon a question of steering, or reefing topsails; or where the " great heart " of the crew was called upon to settle the ship's course.

T. H. HUXLEY: *On the Natural Inequality of Man,* 1890

Democracy means simply the bludgeoning of the people by the people for the people.

OSCAR WILDE: *The Soul of Man Under Socialism,* 1891

In performing its functions, Christian democracy is most strictly bound to depend upon ecclesiastical authority, and to render full submission and obedience to the bishops and those who represent them.

POPE PIUS X: *Apostolic Letter to the Bishops of Italy on Catholic Social Action,* Dec. 18, 1903

Democracy substitutes election by the incompetent many for appointment by the corrupt few.

GEORGE BERNARD SHAW: *Maxims for Revolutionists,* 1903

I believe in democracy because it releases the energies of every human being.

WOODROW WILSON: Speech in New York, Sept. 4, 1912

A democracy is a state which recognizes the subjection of the minority to the majority, that is, an organization for the systematic use of violence by one class against the other, by one part of the population against another.

NIKOLAI LENIN: *The State and Revolution,* 1917

The world must be made safe for democracy.
WOODROW WILSON: Address to Congress, April 2, 1917

The democracy of the cemetery and the equality of the slaughter-house.
MEYER LONDON: Speech in the House of Representatives, April 25, 1917

Those who bewail the loss of personal liberty have not learned one of the essentials of a democracy. They should know that no one has the personal liberty in a republic to do what the majority has properly declared shall not be done.
WESLEY L. JONES of Washington: Speech in the Senate, Feb. 22, 1919

All lawful authority comes from God to the people.
CONSTITUTION OF THE IRISH FREE STATE, preamble, 1922

It would be folly to argue that the people cannot make political mistakes. They can and do make grave mistakes. They know it, they pay the penalty, but compared with the mistakes which have been made by every kind of autocracy they are unimportant.
CALVIN COOLIDGE: Speech in Evanston, Ill., Jan. 21, 1923

The evil of democracy is not the triumph of quantity, but the triumph of bad quality.
GUIDO DE RUGGIERO: *The History of European Liberalism,* II, 1927

Democracy is talking itself to death. The people do not know what they want; they do not know what is the best for them. There is too much foolishness, too much lost motion. I have stopped the talk and the nonsense. I am a man of action. Democracy is beautiful in theory; in practice it is a fallacy. You in America will see that some day.
BENITO MUSSOLINI: To Edwin L. James, of the New York Times, 1928

Envy is the basis of democracy.
BERTRAND RUSSELL: *The Conquest of Happiness,* VI, 1930

I have never spoken or listened at an election meeting without being ashamed of the whole sham democratic routine. The older I grow, the more I feel such exhibitions to be, as part of the serious business of the government of a nation, entirely intolerable and disgraceful to human nature and civic decency.
GEORGE BERNARD SHAW: Speech in New York, April 11, 1933

All the ills of democracy can be cured by more democracy.
ALFRED E. SMITH: Speech in Albany, June 27, 1933

Democracy, with its promise of international peace, has been no better guarantee against war than the old dynastic rule of kings.
JAN C. SMUTS: Address at St. Andrews University, Oct. 17, 1934

One of the weaknesses of a democracy, a system of which I am trying to make the best, is that until it is right up against it, it will never face the truth.
STANLEY BALDWIN: Speech in the House of Commons, Oct. 23, 1935

When everybody is somebody, then nobody is anybody. Author unidentified

[*See also* Art, Ballot, Conquest, Dead, Demagogue, Democrat, Despot, Election, English Language, Equality, Franchise, Government, Hell, Majority, Monarchy, Opinion (Public), Party, Press (Free), Proletariat, Puritanism, Republic, United States.

Democrat

The democratical man . . . is never quiet under any government.
Somers Tracts, I, 1686

We of the United States are constitutionally and conscientiously democrats.
THOMAS JEFFERSON: *Letter to Dupont de Nemours,* 1816

The proper antipode of a gentleman is to be sought for among the Anglo-American democrats.
S. T. COLERIDGE: *Biographia Literaria,* 1817

Democrats consider the people as the safest depository of power in the last resort; they cherish them, therefore, and wish to leave in them all the powers to the exercise of which they are competent.
THOMAS JEFFERSON: *Letter to William Short,* 1825

Soldiers are the only help against democrats.
WILHELM VON MERCKEL: *Die fünfte Zunft,* 1848

Thomas Jifferson was a squar' man,
A bawn dimokrat was he,
And him that 'ud be a squar' man
A bawn dimokrat must be.
JOHN MONTEITH: *Parson Brooks,* 1884

I am all kinds of a democrat, so far as I can discover — but the root of the whole business is this, that I believe in the patriotism and energy and initiative of the average man.
WOODROW WILSON: Speech at Philadelphia, June 29, 1916

How can one be a democrat and at the same time oppose the dictatorship of the proletariat?
NIKOLAI LENIN: In Pravda, May 12, 1917

[*See also* Comfort, Democracy, Liberal, Warrior, Whig.

Democratic Party

The Democratic party is like a mule. It has neither pride of ancestry nor hope of posterity.
IGNATIUS DONNELLY: Speech in the Minnesota Legislature, 1860

I never said all Democrats were saloonkeepers. What I said was that all saloonkeepers were Democrats. HORACE GREELEY, *c.* 1860

The Democratic party is like a man riding backward in a carriage. It never sees a thing until it has gone by.
BENJAMIN F. BUTLER, *c.* 1870

That party never had but two objects — grand and petit larcency.
R. G. INGERSOLL: Speech at Indianapolis, Sept. 21, 1876

We are Republicans, and don't propose to leave our party and identify ourselves with the party whose antecedents have been Rum, Romanism, and Rebellion.
S. D. BURCHARD: To James G. Blaine, speaking for a delegation, Oct. 29, 1884

A hopeless assortment of discordant differences, as incapable of positive action as it is capable of infinite clamor.
THOMAS B. REED: *Two Congresses Contrasted,* 1892 (North American Review, Aug.)

I am a Democrat, but not a revolutionist.
DAVID B. HILL: Statement at Chicago after the nomination of W. J. Bryan for the Presidency, July 11, 1896

I am a Democrat still — very still.
DAVID B. HILL: Statement after the second nomination of W. J. Bryan, 1900

The Democratic party stands for democracy; the Republican party has drawn to itself all that is aristocratic and plutocratic. The Democratic party is the champion of equal rights and opportunities to all; the Republican party is the party of privilege and private monopoly. The Democratic party listens to the voice of the whole people and gauges progress by the prosperity and advancement of the average man; the Republican party is subservient to the comparatively few who are the beneficiaries of governmental favoritism.
Democratic National Platform, 1908

In history the difference between Democracy and Republicanism is that one stood for debased currency, the other for honest money; the one for free silver, the other for honest currency; the one for free trade, the other for protection; the one for the contraction of American influence, the other for expansion. One has been forced to abandon every position it has taken on the great issues before the people; the other has held and vindicated all. In experience the difference between Democracy and Republicanism is that the one means adversity, while the other means prosperity. One means low wages; the other means high wages. One means doubt and debt; the other means confidence and thrift.
Republican National Platform, 1908

Can you let me know what positions you have at your disposal with which to reward deserving Democrats?
W. J. BRYAN: *Letter to Walker W. Vick, receiver-general of the Dominican Republic,* Aug. 20, 1913

[*See also* Democracy.

Demon

Never go out alone on Wednesday or Saturday nights, for demons are abroad then, and eighteen legions of them, commanded by Agrath the daughter of Machlath, seek whom they may devour.
THE TALMUD (*Pesachim*), *c.* 200 B.C.

I will begin by asking, why should we not worship demons? They are the creatures of God, and the worshipper of God is right to serve those who have His authority.
CELSUS: *A True Discourse, c.* 178

Demons are everywhere, and the cursing of them is universal.
TERTULLIAN: *The Testimony of the Christian Soul, c.* 210

Many demons are in woods, in waters, in wildernesses, and in dark pooly places, ready to hurt and prejudice people; some are also in the thick black clouds, which cause hail, lightning and thunder, and poison the air, the pastures and grounds.
MARTIN LUTHER: *Table-Talk,* DLXXIV, 1569

Gorgons and hydras and chimeras dire.
JOHN MILTON: *Paradise Lost,* I, 1667

It is not likely that every devil does know every language, or that every devil can do every mischief. 'Tis possible that the experience, or, if I may call it so, the education of all devils is not alike, and that there may be some differences in their abilities.
COTTON MATHER: *The Wonders of the Invisible World,* 1692

One devil often drubs another.
THOMAS FULLER: *Gnomologia,* 1732

It is not more strange that there should be evil spirits than evil men — evil unembodied spirits than evil embodied spirits.
SAMUEL JOHNSON: *Boswell's Tour to the Hebrides,* Aug. 16, 1773

Demonology is the shadow of theology.
R. W. EMERSON: *Demonology,* 1877

As a rule the devils have been better friends to man than the gods.
R. G. INGERSOLL: Speech in Boston, April 23, 1880

The belief in a demonic world is inculcated throughout the Gospels and the rest of the books of the New Testament; it pervades the whole patristic literature; it colors the theory and the practise of every Christian church down to modern times.

T. H. HUXLEY: *Controverted Questions,* 1892

Demons come from the northeast.

CHINESE PROVERB

[*See also* Angel, Devil, Fire, Night, Possession (Demoniacal), Spirit.

Demure

He maketh as though butter would not melt in his mouth.

JOHN PALSGRAVE: *L'Éclaircissement de la langue française,* 1530

Denial

[*See* Skepticism.

Dentist

He looks like a tooth-drawer, *i.e.,* very thin and meagre.

JOHN RAY: *English Proverbs,* 1670

A prestidigitator who, putting metal into your mouth, pulls coins out of your pocket.

AMBROSE BIERCE: *The Devil's Dictionary,* 1906

Depravity

The total depravity of inanimate things.

KATHERINE WALKER: Title of an essay, Atlantic Monthly, Sept., 1864

[*See also* Barère (Bertrand), Evil.

Derision

[*See* Laughter.

Dermatology

Dermatology is the best speciality. The patient never dies — and never gets well.

Author unidentified

Descartes, René (1596–1650)

The wonder of men.

JOSEPH GLANVILL: *The Vanity of Dogmatizing,* IV, 1661

The leading principle of Descartes's philosophy was, *Cogito, ergo sum* — "I think, therefore I exist"; and having laid this foundation-stone, he built an enormous building, the ruins of which lie scattered up and down among the sciences in disordered glory and venerable confusion.

SYDNEY SMITH: *Lecture on the Conduct of the Understanding,* I, 1806

Description

It beggar'd all description.

SHAKESPEARE: *Antony and Cleopatra,* II, *c.* 1606

Desertion

[*See* Divorce.

Déshabillé

Give me a face
That makes simplicity a grace:
Robes loosely flowing, hair as free;
Such sweet neglect more taketh me
Than all the adulteries of art;
They strike mine eyes, but not my heart.

BEN JONSON: *The Silent Woman,* I, 1609

[*See also* Dress.

Desire

Desire accomplished is sweet to the soul.

PROVERBS XIII, 19, *c.* 350 B.C.

Justice is noblest, and health is best,
But the heart's desire is the pleasantest.

Inscription at Delos, quoted by ARISTOTLE: *The Nicomachean Ethics,* I, *c.* 340 B.C.

We should aim rather at leveling down our desires than leveling up our means.

ARISTOTLE: *Politics,* II, *c.* 322 B.C.

If you want to make Pythocles happy do not augment his wealth but diminish his desires.

EPICURUS: *Aphorisms, c.* 300 B.C.

Nothing troubles you which you do not desire.

CICERO: *De senectute,* XIV, *c.* 78 B.C.

We desire most what we ought not to have.

PUBLILIUS SYRUS: *Sententiæ, c.* 50 B.C.

No one desires what is unknown.

OVID: *Ars amatoria,* III, *c.* 2 B.C.

Not going naked, nor matted hair, nor dirt, nor fasting, nor sleeping on the ground, nor rolling in the dust, nor sitting motionless can purify one who has not overcome desire.

The Dhammapada, X, *c.* 100

There is not a man in the world who doth not look at another's wife, if beautiful and young, with a degree of desire.

The Hitopadesa, II, *c.* 500

Desire dies in the same moment that beauty sickens, and beauty fadeth in the same instant that it flourisheth.

JOHN LYLY: *Endymion,* III, 1591

Is it not strange that desire should so many years outlive performance?

SHAKESPEARE: *II Henry IV,* II, *c.* 1598

Desire himself runs out of breath,
And getting, doth but gain his death;
Desire, nor reason hath, nor rest,
And blind, doth seldom choose the best;
Desire attained is not desire,
But as the cinders of the fire.

WALTER RALEIGH: *Affection and Desire, c.* 1602

He begins to die that quits his desires.

GEORGE HERBERT: *Outlandish Proverbs,* 1640

Desire and love are the same thing; save that by desire we always signify the absence of

the object; by love, most commonly the presence of the same.
THOMAS HOBBES: *Leviathan*, VI, 1651

Desires are nourished by delays.
JOHN RAY: *English Proverbs*, 1670

The uneasiness a man finds in himself upon the absence of anything whose present enjoyment carries the idea of delight with it is what we call desire.
JOHN LOCKE: *Essay Concerning Human Understanding*, II, 1690

The stoical scheme of supplying our wants by lopping off our desires is like cutting off our feet when we want shoes.
JONATHAN SWIFT: *Thoughts on Various Subjects*, 1706

The fewer desires, the more peace.
THOMAS WILSON: *Maxims of Piety and of Christianity*, c. 1755

Every desire is a viper in the bosom, who, while he was chill, was harmless; but when warmth gave him strength, exerted it in poison.
SAMUEL JOHNSON: *Letter to James Boswell*, Dec. 8, 1763

It is happy for human nature that there are desires which cannot be satisfied. Otherwise, the most sorry man would make himself master of the world.
STANISLAUS LESZCZYNSKI (KING OF POLAND): *Œuvres du philosophe bienfaisant*, 1763

The desire of a man for a woman is not directed at her because she is a human being, but because she is a woman. That she is a human being is of no concern to him.
IMMANUEL KANT: *Lecture at Königsberg*, 1775

Sooner murder an infant in his cradle than nurse unacted desires.
WILLIAM BLAKE: *The Marriage of Heaven and Hell*, 1790

The desire of the moth for the star,
Of the night for the morrow.
P. B. SHELLEY: *To* ——, 1824

From the desert I come to thee,
On a stallion shod with fire;
And the winds are left behind
In the speed of my desire.
BAYARD TAYLOR: *Bedouin Song*, 1854

Ah love! could you and I with Him conspire
To grasp this sorry scheme of things entire,
Would not we shatter it to bits — and then
Re-mold it nearer to the heart's desire!
EDWARD FITZGERALD: Tr. of OMAR KHAYYÁM: *Rubáiyát* (c. 1100), 1857

The sole evidence it is possible to produce that anything is desirable is that people actually desire it.
J. S. MILL: *Utilitarianism*, IV, 1863

The fundamental principle of human action — the law that is to political economy what the law of gravitation is to physics — is that men seek to gratify their desires with the least exertion.
HENRY GEORGE: *Progress and Poverty*, III, 1879

There are two tragedies in life. One is not to get your heart's desire. The other is to get it.
GEORGE BERNARD SHAW: *Man and Superman*, IV, 1903

A desire is the inward sign of a physical proclivity to act.
GEORGE SANTAYANA: *The Life of Reason*, I, 1905

[*See also* Belief, Cause and Effect, Death, Golden Rule, Good, Heart, Hell, King, Love, Man and Woman, Money, Temperance.

Desolation

The abomination of desolation.
MARK XIII, 14, c. 70 (Cf. MATTHEW XXIV, 15, c. 75. A quotation from DANIEL XI, 31 and XII, 11, c. 165 B.C.: "The abomination that maketh desolate")

Despair

Grim and comfortless despair.
SHAKESPEARE: *The Comedy of Errors*, V, 1593

Despair is one of Hell's catchpolls.
THOMAS DEKKER: *II The Honest Whore*, I, 1630

He who has resolved to conquer or die is seldom conquered; such noble despair perishes with difficulty.
PIERRE CORNEILLE: *Horace*, II, 1639

Despair doubles our strength.
JOHN RAY: *English Proverbs*, 1670

There was a castle called Doubting Castle, the owner whereof was Giant Despair.
JOHN BUNYAN: *Pilgrim's Progress*, I, 1678

I will indulge my sorrows, and give way
To all the pangs and fury of despair.
JOSEPH ADDISON: *Cato*, IV, 1713

Despair gives courage to a coward.
THOMAS FULLER: *Gnomologia*, 1732

Despair exaggerates not only our misery but also our weakness.
LUC DE VAUVENARGUES: *Réflexions*, 1746

Sir Ralph the rover tore his hair;
He cursed himself in his despair.
ROBERT SOUTHEY: *The Inchcape Rock*, 1801

It was at length the same to me,
Fetter'd or fetterless to be,
I learn'd to love despair.
BYRON: *The Prisoner of Chillon*, 1816

The nympholepsy of some fond despair.
BYRON: *Childe Harold*, IV, 1818

Chew my terbacker
And spit my juice;
Want to go to Heaven
But it ain't no use.

RAY WOOD: *Mother Goose in the Ozarks,* 1938

Despair of nothing. (Nil desperandum.)

LATIN PROVERB

[*See also* Doubt, Hell, Hope, Monk, Tears.

Desperation

A drowning man will catch at a straw.

ENGLISH PROVERB, familiar since the XVI century

I am one, my liege,
Whom the vile blows and buffets of the world
Have so incensed that I am reckless what
I do to spite the world.

SHAKESPEARE: *Macbeth,* III, *c.* 1605

The mass of men lead lives of quiet desperation. What is called resignation is confirmed desperation.

H. D. THOREAU: *Walden,* I, 1854

Despicable

It is only those who are despicable who fear being despised.

LA ROCHEFOUCAULD: *Maxims,* 1665

Despond

The name of the slough was Despond.

JOHN BUNYAN: *Pilgrim's Progress,* I, 1678

Despot

It is the old practice of despots to use a part of the people to keep the rest in order.

THOMAS JEFFERSON: *Letter to John Taylor,* 1798

There are three kinds of despots. There is the despot who tyrannizes over the body. There is the despot who tyrannizes over the soul. There is the despot who tyrannizes over the soul and body alike. The first is called the prince. The second is called the pope. The third is called the people.

OSCAR WILDE: *The Soul of Man Under Socialism,* 1891

[*See also* Dictator, Priest, Tyrant.

Despotism

To live by one man's will became the cause of all men's misery.

RICHARD HOOKER: *The Laws of Ecclesiastical Polity,* I, 1594

Fear is what is needed in a despotism. Virtue is not at all necessary, and honor would be dangerous.

C. L. DE MONTESQUIEU: *The Spirit of the Laws,* III, 1748

When the savages of Louisiana wish to gather fruit, they chop down the tree. This is precisely the course of a despotic government.

IBID.

It would be a dangerous delusion if our confidence in the men of our choice should silence our fears for the safety of our rights. Confidence is everywhere the parent of despotism. Free government is founded in jealousy, not in confidence.

THOMAS JEFFERSON: *Kentucky Resolutions,* Nov., 1798

He who studies history thoroughly will not fail to prefer a military despotism to a despotism of mere politicians.

H. W. HALLECK: *Elements of Military Art and Science,* intro., 1846

When the white man governs himself, that is self-government; but when he governs himself and also governs another man, that is more than self-government — that is despotism.

ABRAHAM LINCOLN: Speech at Peoria, Ill., Oct. 16, 1854

Arbitrary rule has its basis, not in the strength of the state or the chief, but in the moral weakness of the individual, who submits almost without resistance to the domineering power.

FRIEDRICH RATZEL: *History of Mankind,* I, 1868

Despotism has forever had a powerful hold upon the world. Autocratic government, not self-government, has been the prevailing state of mankind. . . . The record of past history is the record, not of the success of republics, but of their failure.

CALVIN COOLIDGE: Speech in Northampton, Mass., May 30, 1923

[*See also* Anarchy, Democracy, Dictator, Force, Government, Individualism, Liberty, Science, Tyranny, Tyrant.

Destiny

That shall be, shall be.

JOHN HEYWOOD: *Proverbs,* 1546

There is a divinity that shapes our ends,
Rough-hew them how we will.

SHAKESPEARE: *Hamlet,* V, *c.* 1601

'Tis vain to quarrel with our destiny.

THOMAS MIDDLETON: *A Trick to Catch the Old One,* IV, 1608

The event is never in the power of man.

ROBERT HERRICK: *Hesperides,* 1648

Often the prudent, far from making their destinies, succumb to them; it is destiny which makes them prudent.

VOLTAIRE: *Philosophical Dictionary,* 1764

I feel that I am the man of destiny.

J. C. F. SCHILLER: *Wallenstein's Death,* III, 1799

We ask action
And dream of arms and conflict; and string up
All self-devotion's muscles; and are set
To fold up papers.

A. H. CLOUGH: *Dipsychus,* 1850

For men must work, and women must weep,
And the sooner it's over, the sooner to sleep.
CHARLES KINGSLEY: *The Three Fishers,* 1856

If the red slayer think he slays,
Or if the slain think he is slain,
They know not well the subtle ways
I keep, and pass, and turn again.
R. W. EMERSON: *Brahma,* 1857 (Atlantic Monthly, Nov.)

Into this universe, and why not knowing,
Nor whence, like water willy-nilly flowing;
And out of it, as wind along the waste,
I know not whither, willy-nilly blowing.
EDWARD FITZGERALD: Tr. of OMAR KHAYYÁM: *Rubáiyát* (*c.* 1100), 1857

None can pierce the vast black veil uncertain
Because there is no light behind the curtain.
JAMES THOMSON: *The City of Dreadful Night,* 1874

Destiny is not a matter of chance, it is a matter of choice; it is not a thing to be waited for, it is a thing to be achieved.
W. J. BRYAN: Speech in Washington, Feb. 22, 1899

He that's born to be hanged needn't fear water.
IRISH PROVERB

No matter where an ox goes he must plow.
MONTENEGRAN PROVERB

[*See also* Battle, Determinism, Fate, Fortune, Opportunity.

Destruction

When a man takes the road to destruction, the gods help him along.
ÆSCHYLUS: *The Persians, c.* 490 B.C.

Wide is the gate, and broad is the way, that leadeth to destruction.
MATTHEW VII, 13, *c.* 75

[*See also* Criticism.

Desuetude

After an existence of nearly twenty years of almost innocuous desuetude these laws are brought forth.
GROVER CLEVELAND: Message to Congress, March 1, 1886

Detective

A detective policeman discovers a burglar from the marks made by his shoe, by a mental process identical with that by which Cuvier restored the extinct animals of Montmartre from fragments of their bones.
T. H. HUXLEY: *On the Educational Value of the Natural History Sciences,* 1854 (Lecture in London)

Determination

[*See* Resolution.

Determinism

Nothing happens without a cause. Everything has a cause and is necessary.
Ascribed to LEUCIPPES, *c.* 450 B.C.

Nothing has ever happened which has not been predestinated, and nothing will ever occur.
CICERO: *De divinatione,* I, *c.* 78 B.C.

There is nothing that the fates do not ordain; all things that happen, whatever they may be, are turned upon their spindles; the final event is always determined from the very first.
LUCIAN: *Zeus Cross-Examined, c.* 165

It lies not in our power to love or hate,
For will in us is overrul'd by fate.
CHRISTOPHER MARLOWE and GEORGE CHAPMAN: *Hero and Leander,* 1598

Our wills and fates do so contrary run
That our devices still are overthrown;
Our thoughts are ours, their ends none of our own.
SHAKESPEARE: *Hamlet,* III, *c.* 1601

There is no free will in the human mind: it is moved to this or that volition by some cause, and that cause has been determined by some other cause, and so on infinitely.
BARUCH SPINOZA: *Ethica,* 1677

For sure, whate'er we mortals hate or love,
Or hope or fear, depends on pow'rs above;
They move our appetites to good or ill,
And by foresight necessitate the will.
JOHN DRYDEN: *Palamon and Arcite, c.* 1698

We are little better than straws upon the water: we may flatter ourselves that we swim, when the current carries us along.
MARY WORTLEY MONTAGU: *Letter to James Steuart,* July 19, 1759

Necessity is not only all-powerful in the physical world; it also controls and regulates the moral world.
P. H. D. D'HOLBACH: *Le système de la nature,* I, 1770

My fate is determined; but I have not determined it.
ST. JOHN DE CRÈVECOEUR: *Letters from an American Farmer,* XII, 1782

All that I am and shall be I am and shall be of necessity, and it is impossible that I should be otherwise.
J. G. FICHTE: *Die Bestimmung des Menschen,* II, 1800

An intelligent being who, at a given instant, knew all the forces animating nature, and the relative positions of the beings within it would, if his intelligence were sufficiently capacious to understand these data, include in a single formula the movements of the largest bodies of the universe and those of its lightest atoms. Nothing would be uncertain for him; the future as well as the past would be present to his eyes.

P. S. LAPLACE: *Théorie analytique sur les probabilités,* 1812

With earth's first clay they did the last man's knead,
And then of the last harvest sowed the seed;
Yes, the first morning of creation wrote
What the last dawn of reckoning shall read.

EDWARD FITZGERALD: Tr. of OMAR KHAYYÁM: *Rubáiyát* (*c.* 1100), 1857

Spontaneity of thought and freedom of will, as characteristics of our species, are illusions of human pride, for even savages know that, from birth on, there is naught but unconscious reflexes and instincts.

RUDOLF VIRCHOW: *Cellular-Pathologie,* 1858

The world is mathematical, and has no casualty, in all its vast and flowing curve. Success has no more eccentricity than the gingham and muslin we weave in our mills.

R. W. EMERSON: *The Conduct of Life,* II, 1860

If we cannot follow the automatic machinery of nature into the mental and moral world, where it plays its part as much as in the bodily functions, without being accused of laying "all that we are evil in to a divine thrusting on," we had better return at once to our old demonology, and reinstate the Leader of the Lower House in his time-honored prerogatives.

O. W. HOLMES: *The Guardian Angel,* pref., 1867

It is just as impossible for the impartial and critical observer to detect a "wise providence" in the fate of individual human beings as a moral order in the history of peoples. Both are determined with iron necessity by a mechanical causality which connects every single phenomenon with one or more antecedent causes.

ERNST HAECKEL: *The Riddle of the Universe,* XIV, 1899

Determinism has faded out of theoretical physics.

ARTHUR EDDINGTON: *The Decline of Determinism,* 1932 (Address to the Mathematical Association)

[*See also* Accident, Causality, Cause and Effect, Destiny, Fate, Predestination, Will (Free).

Devil

How art thou fallen from Heaven, O Lucifer, son of the morning!

ISAIAH XIV, 12, *c.* 700 B.C.

Resist the devil, and he will flee from you.

JAMES IV, 7, *c.* 60

Be sober, be vigilant; because your adversary, the devil, as a roaring lion, walketh about, seeking whom he may devour.

I PETER V, 8, *c.* 60

Get thee behind me, Satan. (Vade retro, Satanas.)

MARK VIII, 33, *c.* 70 (Cf. MATTHEW XVI, 23, *c.* 75; LUKE IV, 8, *c.* 75. The Latin is from the Vulgate)

Get thee hence, Satan.

MATTHEW IV, 10, *c.* 75

He is a liar, and the father of it.

JOHN VIII, 44, *c.* 115

The Devil is God's ape. (Diabolus est Dei simia.)

ENGLISH PROVERB, borrowed from the Latin, and traced to Tertullian, *c.* 200

The Devil often transforms himself into an angel to tempt men, some for their instruction and some for their ruin.

ST. AUGUSTINE: *The City of God,* XV, 427

He that sups with the Devil must have a long spoon.

ENGLISH PROVERB, familiar since the XIV century

He must needs go that the Devil drives.

JOHN LYDGATE: *The Assembly of the Gods,* 1398

The Devil was sick;
The Devil a monk would be;
The Devil was well;
The Devil a monk was he.

ENGLISH RHYME, traced by Apperson, in a Latin form, to WALTER BOWER: *Scotichronicon,* II, *c.* 1450

The Devil is dead.

ENGLISH PROVERB, traced by Apperson to *c.* 1470

Give the Devil his due.

ENGLISH PROVERB, familiar since the XVI century

It is easier to raise the Devil than to lay him.

DESIDERIUS ERASMUS: *Adagia,* 1508

He is the most diligent preacher of all other; he is never out of his diocese.

HUGH LATIMER: *Sermons,* II, 1549

Every man before he dies shall see the Devil.

ENGLISH PROVERB, traced by Apperson to 1560

The Devil has two manner of shapes or forms, wherein he disguises himself; he either appears in the shape of a serpent, to affright and kill; or else in the form of a silly sheep, to lie and deceive; these are his two court colors.

MARTIN LUTHER: *Table-Talk,* DCCXVIII, 1569

Each man for himself, and the Devil for all.

JOHN FLORIO: *First Frutes,* 1578

Of three things the Devil makes his mess:
Of lawyers' tongues, of scriveners' fingers — you the third may guess.

JOHN FLORIO: *Second Frutes,* 1591

Devils are not so black as they be painted.
THOMAS LODGE: *A Margarite of America,* 1596

One sees more devils than vast Hell can hold.
SHAKESPEARE: *A Midsummer Night's Dream,* V, *c.* 1596

The Devil can cite Scripture for his purpose.
SHAKESPEARE: *The Merchant of Venice,* I, *c.* 1597

The Devil is kind to (or takes care of) his own.
JOHN DAY: *The Isle of Gulls,* II, 1606

The Prince of Darkness is a gentleman;
Modo he's called, and Mahu.
SHAKESPEARE: *King Lear,* III, 1606

What's got over the Devil's back must be spent under his belly.
THOMAS MIDDLETON: *Michaelmas Term,* IV, 1607

The Devil has a care of his footmen.
THOMAS MIDDLETON: *A Trick to Catch the Old One,* I, 1608 (Cf. DAY, *ante,* 1606)

The Devil take the hindmost.
BEAUMONT and FLETCHER: *Philaster,* V, 1611

The Devil can equivocate as well as a shopkeeper.
BEN JONSON: *Bartholomew Fair,* I, 1614

The Devil is an ass.
BEN JONSON: Title of a play, 1616

The author of confusion and lies.
ROBERT BURTON: *The Anatomy of Melancholy,* III, 1621

The scaly horror of his folded tail.
JOHN MILTON: *On the Morning of Christ's Nativity,* 1629

The Devil is good when he is pleased.
JOHN CLARKE: *Parœmiologia Anglo-Latina,* 1639

'Tis an ill company where the Devil bears the banner. IBID.

The Devil is a busy bishop in his own diocese.
DAVID FERGUSSON: *Scottish Proverbs,* 1641 (Cf. LATIMER, *ante,* 1549)

The heart of man is the place the Devil's in: I feel sometimes a Hell within myself.
THOMAS BROWNE: *Religio Medici,* I, 1642

Grant that he may have power and strength to have victory, and to triumph, against the Devil, the world, and the flesh.
THE BOOK OF COMMON PRAYER (*The Baptism of Infants*), 1662

Talk of the Devil, and he's presently at your elbow.
GIOVANNI TORRIANO: *Italian Proverbs,* 1666

When the Devil preaches the world's near an end.
ROGER L'ESTRANGE: Tr. of FRANCISCO DE QUEVEDO: *Sueños* (127), 1667

Him the almighty Power
Hurled headlong flaming from the ethereal sky,
With hideous ruin and combustion, down
To bottomless perdition, there to dwell
In adamantine chains and penal fire,
Who durst defy the Omnipotent to arms.
JOHN MILTON: *Paradise Lost,* I, 1667

The Devil hates holy water.
ENGLISH PROVERB, traced by Smith to 1676

How the Devil rebukes sin!
APHRA BEHN: *The Roundheads,* V, 1682

That there is a Devil is a thing doubted by none but such as are under the influences of the Devil. For any to deny the being of a Devil must be from an ignorance or profaneness worse than diabolical.
COTTON MATHER: *A Discourse on the Wonders of the Invisible World,* 1692 (Sermon, Aug. 4)

If I were a painter I would draw the Devil like an idiot, a driveller with a bib and bells: a man should have his head and horns, and woman the rest of him.
WILLIAM CONGREVE: *The Way of the World,* III, 1700

His laws are easy, and his gentle sway
Makes it exceeding pleasant to obey.
DANIEL DEFOE: *The True-Born Englishman,* I, 1701

The Devil bides his day.
JAMES KELLY: *Complete Collection of Scottish Proverbs,* 1721

The Devil's cow calves twice a year. IBID.

The Dee'l is no worse than he's called. IBID.

Man, woman, and Devil, are the three degrees of comparison.
THOMAS FULLER: *Gnomologia,* 1732

You would do little for God if the Devil were dead. IBID.

Why should the Devil have all the good tunes?
Ascribed to ROWLAND HILL, *c.* 1783

The Devil is subtle, yet weaves a coarse web.
R. C. TRENCH (ARCHBISHOP OF DUBLIN): *Lessons in Proverbs,* 1853

The Devil entangles youth with beauty, the miser with gold, the ambitious with power, the learned with false doctrine.
H. G. BOHN: *Handbook of Proverbs,* 1855

One of the principal objects of American reverence is the Devil. There are multitudes who are shocked to hear his name mentioned lightly, and who esteem such mention profanity.
J. G. HOLLAND: *Everyday Topics,* 1876

An apology for the Devil: It must be remembered that we have only heard one side of the case. God has written all the books.
SAMUEL BUTLER: *Note-Books, c.* 1890

The Devil and me, we don't agree;
I hate him; and he hates me.
Anon.: Salvation Army hymn, *c.* 1890

The hypothesis of a personal Devil has many advantages. It explains the whole of the facts; it avoids the postulation of two first causes; it vindicates the moral perfection of the Deity; and it allows the optimistic hope to be entertained that in the end good will triumph over evil.
CHARLES HARRIS: *A Text-Book of Apologetics,* 1905

Today is the festival of Michael the indomitable
Who expelled the Devil from Heaven,
And if the Devil had expelled Michael,
This would be the feast of the Devil.
Author unidentified

The Devil always leaves a stink behind him.
DANISH PROVERB

Never was hood so holy but the Devil could get his head in it. DUTCH PROVERB

The Devil has his martyrs among men. IBID.

When the Devil gets himself into the church, he seats himself on the altar. IBID.

The Devil paints himself black, but we see him rose-colored. FINNISH PROVERB

Where the Devil can't go he sends his grandmother. GERMAN PROVERB

It's no joke goin' to law with the Devil, and the court held in Hell. IRISH PROVERB

If you are afraid of the Devil, you will never be rich. ITALIAN PROVERB

When the priest's away the Devil will play.
RUSSIAN PROVERB

The Devil comes where money is; where it is not he comes twice. SWEDISH PROVERB

The Devil has three children: pride, falsehood and envy. WELSH PROVERB

[*See also* Adversary, Alone, Armenian, Asking, Atheism, Atheist, Basque, Books, Cause and Effect, Cheating, Church, Church (Christian), Church (house), Collier, Cruelty, Curse, Damnation, Damned, Dancing, Danger, Dean, Dice, Disease, Drunkard, Evil, Exorcism, Fact, Fanatic, Fear, Flatterer, Frenchman, God, Gold, Gravity, Haste, Heart, Hell, Hindmost, Hypocrisy, Idleness, Jew, Language, Lawyer, Luck, Lying, Magic, Man, Man and Woman, Marriage, Melancholy, Milton (John), Miracle, Mirror, Miser, Money, Mulatto, Music, Poetry, Poor, Prelate, Prudence, Song, Suicide, Thief, Tropics, Truth, Vicar, Voice, War, Wealth.

Devotion

Ruth said, Intreat me not to leave thee, or to return from following after thee: for whither thou goest, I will go: and where thou lodgest, I will lodge: thy people shall be my people, and thy God my God.
RUTH I, 16, *c.* 500 B.C.

A devout man, and one that feared God with all his house, which gave much alms to the people, and prayed to God always.
ACTS X, 2, *c.* 75

No humor is so easy to counterfeit as devotion.
MICHEL DE MONTAIGNE: *Essays,* III, 1588

Beads and prayer-books are the toys of age.
ALEXANDER POPE: *An Essay on Man,* II, 1732

Never yet, I believe, has there been such devotion shown by soldiers as mine have manifested for me. With the last drop of blood gushing out of their veins, they exclaimed, "God save the Emperor!"
NAPOLEON I: To Barry E. O'Meara at St. Helena, Nov. 12, 1816

A man cannot make a pair of shoes rightly unless he do it in a devout manner.
THOMAS CARLYLE: *Letter to Thomas Erskine,* Oct. 22, 1842

[*See also* Kingly, Man and Woman.

Dewdrop

I must go seek some dewdrops here,
And hang a pearl in every cowslip's ear.
SHAKESPEARE: *A Midsummer Night's Dream,* II, *c.* 1596

Stars of morning, dewdrops which the sun
Impearls on every leaf and every flower.
JOHN MILTON: *Paradise Lost,* V, 1667

Every dewdrop and raindrop had a whole heaven within it.
H. W. LONGFELLOW: *Hyperion,* III, 1839

Dewey, George (1837–1917)

Oh, dewy was the morning
Upon the first of May,
And Dewey was the admiral
Down in Manila Bay,
And dewy were the Regent's eyes,
Them orbs of royal blue,
And dew we feel discouraged?
I dew not think we dew.
EUGENE WARE: Lines without a title, first printed in the Topeka (Kansas) Capital, May 10, 1898

[*See also* Presidency.

Diagnosis

The first step toward cure is to know what the disease is. (Ad sanitatem gradus est novisse morbum.) LATIN PROVERB

Dialect

[*See* American language.

Diamond

None cuts a diamond but a diamond.

JOHN WEBSTER and JOHN MARSTON: *The Malcontent,* IV, 1604

Diamonds cut diamonds.

JOHN FORD: *The Lover's Melancholy,* I, 1628 (Usually used in the singular)

A rough diamond.

ENGLISH PHRASE, apparently first used by JOHN DRYDEN: *Fables Ancient and Modern,* pref., 1699 (There applied to Chaucer)

A diamond with a flaw is better than a common stone that is perfect.

CHINESE PROVERB

[*See also* April.

Diana

Great is Diana of the Ephesians.

ACTS XIX, 28, *c.* 75

Diaphragm

A muscular partition separating disorders of the chest from disorders of the bowels.

AMBROSE BIERCE: *The Devil's Dictionary,* 1906

Diary

In sea voyages, where there is nothing to be seen but sky and sea, men make diaries; but in land travel, wherein so much is to be observed, for the most part they omit it.

FRANCIS BACON: *Essays,* XVIII, 1625

The habit of recording is first of all likely to generate a desire to have something of some interest to record; it will exercise the memory and sharpen the understanding generally; and though the thoughts may not be very profound, nor the remarks very lively and ingenious, nor the narrative of exceeding interest, still the exercise is, I think, calculated to make the writer wiser and perhaps better.

CHARLES C. F. GREVILLE: *Diary,* Jan 2, 1838

Dice

Let the die be cast. (Jacta alea esto.)

JULIUS CÆSAR: On crossing the Rubicon on his return from Gaul, 49 B.C.

That sort of lottery is deceitful, abusive, illicitous and exceedingly scandalous. Never trust in it.

RABELAIS: *Pantagruel,* III, 1535

Dice-playing . . . is a door and window into all theft, murder, whoredom, swearing, blasphemy, banqueting, dancing, rioting, drunkenness, pride, covetousness, craft, deceit, lying, brawling, fighting, prodigality, nightwatchings, idleness, beggary, poverty, bankrupting, misery, prisonment, hanging, etc.

JOHN NORTHBROOKE: *Against Dicing,* 1577

The best throw at dice is to throw them away.

ENGLISH PROVERB, traced by Smith to *c.* 1590

The Devil is in the dice.

JOHN RAY: *English Proverbs,* 1670

Come on, bones, an' treat me nice,
Roll 'em, soldier, roll them dice.

American Negro song, quoted by HOWARD W. ODUM: *Wings On My Feet,* I, 1929

[*See also* Abbot, Chance, Expert, Friend, Gambling, Gaming, Life.

Dickens

I cannot tell what the dickens his name is.

SHAKESPEARE: *The Merry Wives of Windsor,* III, *c.* 1600

Dickens, Charles (1812–70)

Mr. Dickens writes too often and too fast. . . . If he persists much longer in this course, it requires no gift of prophecy to foretell his fate — he has risen like a rocket, and he will come down like a stick.

Anon.: Review of *The Pickwick Papers* in the Quarterly Magazine (London), 1838

Dickens, with preternatural apprehension of the language of manners, and the varieties of street life, with pathos and laughter, with patriotic and still enlarging generosity, writes London tracts. He is a painter of English details, like Hogarth; local and temporary in his tints and style, and local in his aims.

R. W. EMERSON: *English Traits,* XIV, 1856

I would much rather have written "Pickwick" than to be Chief Justice of England, or a peer in Parliament.

Ascribed to JOHN CAMPBELL, Chief Justice and Lord High Chancellor of England (1779–1861) in JOHN FORSTER: *The Life of Charles Dickens,* II, 1874

The good, the gentle, high-gifted, ever-friendly, noble Dickens — every inch of him an honest man.

THOMAS CARLYLE: *Letter to John Forster,* 1870

Dickens was the incarnation of cockneydom, a caricaturist who aped the moralist; he should have kept to short stories. If his novels are read at all in the future people will wonder what we saw in him.

GEORGE MEREDITH: *To Edward Clodd,* (Fortnightly Review, July, 1909), *c.* 1900

Dictator

Only those generals who gain successes can set up dictators.

ABRAHAM LINCOLN: *Letter to Joseph Hooker,* Jan. 26, 1863

In your dread of dictators you established a state of society in which every ward boss is

a dictator, every financier a dictator, every private employer a dictator, all with the livelihood of the workers at their mercy, and no public responsibility.
GEORGE BERNARD SHAW: Address in New York, April 11, 1933

We have nothing to fear in this country from a dictatorship. It cannot live here. We are not organized to carry it on. We have no desire for it.
ALFRED E. SMITH: Speech at Harvard, June 22, 1933

We know as a people, as a nation, that we are at the cross-roads in America. Soon we must determine whether or not we are going to preserve Anglo-Saxon institutions in this country or join the other nations of the earth under a dictator.
HATTON W. SUMNERS: Speech in the House of Representatives, July 13, 1937

Dictionary

To make dictionaries is dull work.
SAMUEL JOHNSON: *Dictionary*, pref., 1755

A dictionary is but an index to the literature of a given speech; or rather it bears to language the relation which a digest bears to a series of legal reports. Neither is an authority; and he is but a sorry lawyer who cites the one, an indifferent scholar who quotes the other as such.
G. P. MARSH: *Lectures on the English Language*, 1861

A malevolent literary device for cramping the growth of a language and making it hard and inelastic.
AMBROSE BIERCE: *The Devil's Dictionary*, 1906

Die

[*See* Dice.

Diet

Feed by measure, and defy the physician.
JOHN HEYWOOD: *Proverbs*, 1546

The kitchen is a good apothecaries' shop.
WILLIAM BULLEIN: *The Bulwark Against All Sickness*, 1562

Use three physicians still: first, Dr. Quiet, then Dr. Merry, and lastly, Dr. Diet.
JOHN HARINGTON: *The Englishman's Doctor*, 1608

[A parson's] fare is plain and common, but wholesome; what he hath is little, but very good. It consisteth most of mutton, beef and veal.
GEORGE HERBERT: *A Priest to the Temple*, I, 1632

A little with quiet is the only diet.
GEORGE HERBERT: *Outlandish Proverbs*, 1640

Whatsoever was the father of a disease, an ill diet was the mother.
GEORGE HERBERT: *Jacula Prudentum*, 1651

Nature delights in the most plain and simple diet. Every animal, but man, keeps to one dish.
JOSEPH ADDISON: *The Spectator*, Oct. 13, 1711

Kitchen physic is the best physic.
JONATHAN SWIFT: *Polite Conversation*, II, 1738

Sermons on diet ought to be preached in the churches at least once a week.
G. C. LICHTENBERG: *Reflections*, 1799

The allegory of Adam and Eve eating of the tree of evil, and entailing upon their posterity the wrath of God and the loss of everlasting life, admits of no other explanation than the disease and crime that have flowed from unnatural diet.
P. B. SHELLEY: *Queen Mab*, notes, 1813

If you wish to grow thinner, diminish your dinner,
And take to light claret instead of pale ale;
Look down with an utter contempt upon butter,
And never touch bread till it's toasted — or stale.
H. S. LEIGH: *Carols of Cockayne*, 1869

He that takes medicine and neglects to diet wastes the skill of his doctors.
CHINESE PROVERB

[*See also* Abstemiousness, Dinner, Doctor, Eating, Food, Spinach, Vegetarianism.

Difference

[*See* Opinion.

Difficulty

There is no excellence without difficulty.
OVID: *Ars amatoria*, II, *c.* 2 B.C.

It is hard to shave an egg.
THOMAS FULLER: *Gnomologia*, 1732

Difficulty, my brethren, is the nurse of greatness — a harsh nurse, who roughly rocks her foster-children into strength and athletic proportion.
W. C. BRYANT: Speech of welcome to Kossuth, Dec. 15, 1851

The best way out of a difficulty is through it.
Author unidentified

Three things are difficult: to know oneself, to conquer one's appetite, and to keep one's secret.
WELSH PROVERB

[*See also* Hard, Success.

Diffidence

A diffident man is much more intolerable than one who is conceited. The conceited allow

other people their deserts, but the diffident plainly despise those to whom they defer.
G. C. LICHTENBERG: *Reflections,* 1799

Digestion

A good eater must be a good man; for a good eater must have a good digestion, and a good digestion depends upon a good conscience.
BENJAMIN DISRAELI: *The Young Duke,* XII, 1831

Digestion is the great secret of life.
SYDNEY SMITH: *Letter to Arthur Kinglake,* Sept. 30, 1837

A man has often more trouble to digest meat than to get it.
H. G. BOHN: *A Handbook of Proverbs,* 1855

[*See also* Appetite, Cheese, Lean, Sleep.

Dignity

Ease with dignity. (Cum dignitate otium.)
CICERO: *Pro Sestio, c.* 50 B.C.

It is easier to increase in dignity than to acquire it in the first place.
PUBLILIUS SYRUS: *Sententiæ, c.* 50 B.C.

Let none presume
To wear an undeserved dignity.
SHAKESPEARE: *The Merchant of Venice,* II, *c.* 1597

It is more offensive to outshine in dignity than in personal attractions.
BALTASAR GRACIÁN: *The Art of Worldly Wisdom,* CVI, 1647

It is base and unworthy to live below the dignity of our nature.
BENJAMIN WHICHCOTE: *Moral and Religious Aphorisms,* 1753

By dignity I mean the absence of ludicrous and debasing associations.
S. T. COLERIDGE: *Biographia Literaria,* I, 1817

There is a healthful hardiness about real dignity that never dreads contact and communion with others, however humble.
WASHINGTON IRVING: *The Sketch-Book,* 1820

He never unbuttons himself.
Anon.: Said of Robert Peel (1788–1850)

We have exchanged the Washingtonian dignity for the Jeffersonian simplicity.
HENRY C. POTTER: Address in New York, April 30, 1889

[*See also* Beauty, Ease, Justice, Labor, Leisure, Money.

Dilatoriness

One of the four and twenty policies of a knave is to stay long at his errand.
JAMES HOWELL: *Proverbs,* 1659

Dilemma

Out of the frying-pan into the fire.
ENGLISH PHRASE, traced by Smith to 1546

In front a precipice, behind a wolf. (A fronte præcipitium, a tergo lupus.)
LATIN PROVERB

Dilettante

No man can be a true poet who writes for diversion only. These authors should be considered as versifiers and witty men rather than as poets.
ALEXANDER POPE: *Letter to Henry Cromwell,* Dec. 17, 1710

Diligence

Everything yields to diligence.
ANTIPHANES: *Fragment, c.* 350 B.C.

He becometh poor that dealeth with a slack hand, but the hand of the diligent maketh rich.
PROVERBS X, 4, *c.* 350 B.C.

The hand of the diligent shall bear rule.
PROVERBS XII, 24

The soul of the diligent shall be made fat.
PROVERBS XIII, 4

Seest thou a man diligent in his business? he shall stand before kings.
PROVERBS XXII, 29

Whatsoever thy hand findeth to do, do it with thy might.
ECCLESIASTES IX, 10, *c.* 200 B.C.

Make hay while the sun shines.
ENGLISH PROVERB, traced by Apperson to 1546

There hath grown no grass on my heel since I went hence.
NICHOLAS UDALL: *Ralph Roister Doister, c.* 1553

Diligence is the mother of good luck, and God gives all things to industry. Then plough deep while sluggards sleep, and you shall have corn to sell and to keep.
BENJAMIN FRANKLIN: *Poor Richard's Almanac,* 1757

Diligence is the greatest of teachers.
ARAB PROVERB

Without diligence, no prize. (Ohne Fleiss, kein Preis.)
GERMAN PROVERB

[*See also* Applause, Energy, Industry, Virtue.

Dimple

Love made those hollows.
SHAKESPEARE: *Venus and Adonis,* 1593

A dimple in the chin; a devil within.
IRISH PROVERB

[*See also* Lover.

Dinner

Better is a dinner of herbs where love is, than a stalled ox and hatred therewith.
PROVERBS XV, 17, *c.*. 350 B.C.

We should look for someone to eat and drink with before looking for something to eat and drink, for dining alone is leading the life of a lion or wolf.
EPICURUS: *Aphorisms, c.* 300 B.C.

At the dinner-table no one should be bashful.
PLAUTUS: *Trinummus*, II, *c.* 190 B.C.

In comparison with the stars, what is more trifling a matter than my dinner?
ST. AUGUSTINE: *Soliloquies*, I, *c.* 387

After dinner either rest or walk a mile. (Post coenam stabis vel passus mille meabis.)
Regimen Salernitanum, c. 1275

After dinner sit a while;
After supper walk a mile.
Author unidentified; it was already familiar in the XVI century

Dinners cannot be long where dainties want.
JOHN HEYWOOD: *Proverbs*, 1546

For whom he means to make an often guest
One dish will serve, and welcome make the rest.
JOSEPH HALL (BISHOP OF NORWICH): *Virgidemarium*, III, 1597

My wife had got ready a very fine dinner — *viz.*, a dish of marrow-bones; a leg of mutton; a loin of veal; a dish of fowl; three pullets and two dozen of larks all in a dish; a great tart, a neat's tongue, a dish of anchovies, a dish of prawns, and cheese.
SAMUEL PEPYS: *Diary*, Jan. 26, 1660

Strange to see how a good dinner and feasting reconciles everybody.
SAMUEL PEPYS: *Diary*, Nov. 9, 1665

A warmed-up dinner was never worth anything.
NICOLAS BOILEAU: *Le Lutrin*, I, 1674

Crowd not your table: let your numbers be
Not more than seven, and never less than three.
WILLIAM KING: *The Art of Cookery*, 1708

In my own memory dinner has crept by degrees from twelve to three, and where it will fix nobody knows.
RICHARD STEELE: *The Tatler*, Dec. 14, 1710

Nice eaters seldom meet with a good dinner.
THOMAS FULLER: *Gnomologia*, 1732

The family that dines the latest
Is in our street esteemed the greatest.
HENRY FIELDING: *Letter to Robert Walpole*, 1743

When a man is invited to dinner he is disappointed if he does not get something good.
SAMUEL JOHNSON: *Boswell's Life*, Sept. 22, 1777

A man seldom thinks with more earnestness of anything than he does of his dinner.
Ascribed to SAMUEL JOHNSON in *Mrs. Piozzi's Anecdotes*, 1786

Oh, the pleasure of eating my dinner alone!
CHARLES LAMB: *Letter to Mrs. Wordsworth*, Feb. 18, 1818

The hour of dinner includes everything of sensual and intellectual gratification which a great nation glories in producing.
SYDNEY SMITH: In the Edinburgh Review, 1819

That all-softening overpowering knell,
The tocsin of the soul, — the dinner bell.
BYRON: *Don Juan*, V, 1821

All human history attests
That happiness for man, — the hungry sinner! —
Since Eve ate apples, much depends on dinner.
BYRON: *Don Juan*, XIII, 1823

Even the great Napoleon could not eat his dinner twice.
ALPHONSE KARR: *Le chemin le plus court*, 1836

Serenely full, the epicure would say,
Fate cannot harm me, — I have dined today.
Ascribed to SYDNEY SMITH in *A Memoir of the Rev. Sydney Smith* by his daughter, LADY HOLLAND, 1855

Heavenly Father, bless us,
And keep us all alive,
There's ten of us to dinner
And not enough for five.
Anon.: *Hodge's Grace, c.* 1850

The rule for hospitality and Irish help, is, to have the same dinner every day throughout the year. At last, Mrs. O'Shaughnessy learns to cook it to a nicety, the host learns to carve it, and the guests are well served.
R. W. EMERSON: *The Conduct of Life*, II, 1860

Dinner was large, luminous, sumptuous.
THOMAS CARLYLE: *Reminiscences of Sundry*, 1867

Oil is best at the beginning, honey at the end, and wine in the middle.
DUTCH PROVERB

[*See also* Alone, Bell, Dish, Eating and Drinking, Exercise, Food, Hunger, Nap, Waiting, Washing.

Dinner-pail

[*See* Prosperity.

Diplomat

A diplomatic character is the narrowest sphere of society that man can act in. It forbids intercourse by a reciprocity of suspicion; and a diplomatist is a sort of unconnected atom, continually repelling and repelled.
THOMAS PAINE: *The Rights of Man*, I, 1791

Diplomatic agents are divided into three classes: (1) ambassadors, legates or nuncios; (2) envoys, ministers or other persons accredited to sovereigns; (3) chargés d'affaires accredited to ministers for foreign affairs.
THE CONGRESS OF VIENNA: Protocol of March 9, 1815, I

I always look upon diplomatists as the Hebrews of politics.
BENJAMIN DISRAELI: *Coningsby*, XXI, 1844

I have discovered the art of deceiving diplomats. I speak the truth, and they never believe me.
CAMILLO DI CAVOUR (1810–1861)

Nobody, not even the most rabid of democrats, can imagine without actual knowledge all the emptiness and quackery that passes for diplomacy.
OTTO VON BISMARCK (1815–1898)

A diplomat is a man who remembers a lady's birthday but forgets her age.
Author unidentified

When a diplomat says yes he means perhaps; when he says perhaps he means no; when he says no he is no diplomat.
Author unidentified

[*See also* Ambassador, Covenant.

Dirt

Every man must eat a peck of dirt before he dies.
ENGLISH PROVERB, familiar since the XVII century (Sometimes *ashes* appears in place of *dirt*)

Dirt parts company.
DAVID FERGUSSON: *Scottish Proverbs*, 1641

Fling dirt enough, and some will stick.
ENGLISH PROVERB, traced by Smith to 1678

Dirt defies the king.
JAMES KELLY: *Complete Collection of Scottish Proverbs*, 1721

He that deals in dirt has aye foul fingers.
ALLAN RAMSAY: *Scots Proverbs*, 1737

Man or boy that works or plays
In the fields or the highways
May, without offence or hurt,
From the soil contract a dirt.
MARY LAMB: *Cleanliness*, 1809

Dirt is dirtiest upon the fairest spots.
H. G. BOHN: *Handbook of Proverbs*, 1855

Matter in the wrong place.
Ascribed to LORD PALMERSTON (1784–1865)

Poverty comes from God, but not dirt.
HEBREW PROVERB

[*See also* Mole (animal).

Disagreement

Oh, shame to men! devil with devil damn'd
Firm concord holds, men only disagree
Of creatures rational.
JOHN MILTON: *Paradise Lost*, II, 1667

[*See also* Controversy, Debate, Discussion, Doctor.

Disappointment

Oft expectation fails and most oft there
Where most it promises, and oft it hits
Where hope is coldest and despair most fits.
SHAKESPEARE: *All's Well that Ends Well*, II, *c.* 1602

Blessed is he who expects nothing, for he shall never be disappointed.
ALEXANDER POPE: *Letter to John Gay*, Oct. 6, 1727

If the good people in their wisdom shall see fit to keep me in the background, I have been too familiar with disappointment to be much chagrined.
ABRAHAM LINCOLN: Announcement of his candidacy for the Illinois Legislature, 1832

[*See also* Ambition.

Disaster

Unmerciful disaster
Followed fast and followed faster.
E. A. POE: *The Raven*, 1845 (New York Evening Mirror, Jan. 29)

[*See also* Calamity.

Disciple

The disciple is not above his master.
MATTHEW X, 24, *c.* 75 (Cf. LUKE VI, 40, *c.* 75)

If any man come to me, and hate not his father, and mother, and wife, and children, and brethren, and sisters, yea, and his own life also, he cannot be my disciple.
LUKE XIV, 26, *c.* 75

I had better never see a book than to be warped by its attraction clean out of my own orbit, and made a satellite instead of a system.
R. W. EMERSON: *The American Scholar*, 1837

No true disciple of mine will ever be a Ruskinian; he will follow, not me, but the instincts of his own soul, and the guidance of its Creator.
JOHN RUSKIN: *St. Mark's Rest*, 1877

Thou seekest disciples? Then thou seekest ciphers.
F. W. NIETZSCHE: *The Twilight of the Idols*, 1889

To speak of Tolstoyism, to seek guidance, to inquire about my solution of questions, is a great and a gross error.
LYOF N. TOLSTOY: *Diary*, *c.* 1900

[*See also* Apostle, Biography, Follower, Martyrdom.

Discipline

Submit your neck to the yoke, and let your soul receive discipline.
ECCLESIASTICUS LI, 34, *c.* 180 B.C.

The man that designs his son to honor and to triumphs, to consular dignities, and presidencies of councils, loves to see him pale with study, or panting with labor, hardened with sufferings, or eminent by dangers.
JEREMY TAYLOR: *The Rule and Exercises of Holy Dying,* I, 1651

Love well, whip well.
BENJAMIN FRANKLIN: *Poor Richard's Almanac,* 1733

Man must be disciplined, for he is by nature raw and wild.
IMMANUEL KANT: Lecture at Königsberg, 1775

Law, order, duty an' restraint, obedience, discipline.
RUDYARD KIPLING: *M'Andrew's Hymn,* 1893

The bird that can sing and won't sing must be made to sing. GERMAN PROVERB

[*See also* Aristocracy, Army, Order.

Discontent

We are never satisfied with our own.
TERENCE: *Phormio,* I, *c.* 160 B.C.

Now is the Winter of our discontent.
SHAKESPEARE: *Richard III,* I, *c.* 1592

I see your brows are full of discontent.
SHAKESPEARE: *Richard II,* IV, *c.* 1596

If we murmur here, we may at the next melancholy be troubled that God did not make us to be angels or stars.
JEREMY TAYLOR: *The Rule and Exercises of Holy Living,* 1650

Let thy discontents be thy secrets; — if the world knows them 't will despise thee and increase them.
BENJAMIN FRANKLIN: *Poor Richard's Almanac,* 1741

Where the people have no power, they enter into no contests, and are not anxious to know how they shall use it. The spirit of discontent becomes torpid for want of employment, and sighs itself to rest.
FISHER AMES: *Oration on Washington,* 1799

Discontent is the want of self-reliance; it is infirmity of will.
R. W. EMERSON: *Self-Reliance,* 1841

Does he paint? he fain would write a poem, —
Does he write? he fain would paint a picture.
ROBERT BROWNING: *One Word More,* 1855

Discontent is the first step in the progress of a man or a nation.
OSCAR WILDE: *A Woman of No Importance,* II, 1893

[*See also* Contentment, Debate, Demagogue.

Discord

Medicine, to produce health, must know disease; music, to produce harmony, must know discord. PLUTARCH: *Lives, c.* 100

Discord oft in music makes the sweeter lay.
EDMUND SPENSER: *The Faerie Queene,* III, *c.* 1589

I never heard
So musical a discord, such sweet thunder.
SHAKESPEARE: *A Midsummer Night's Dream,* IV, *c.* 1596

Straining harsh discords and unpleasing sharps.
SHAKESPEARE: *Romeo and Juliet,* III, *c.* 1596

Discords make the sweetest airs.
SAMUEL BUTLER: *Hudibras,* III, 1678

[*See also* Abomination.

Discouragement

Nothing resembles pride so much as discouragement.
H. F. AMIEL: *Journal,* Dec. 30, 1850

Discourtesy

Discourtesy is not a single vice of the mind, but a product of several — foolish vanity, ignorance of obligation, indolence, stupidity, destruction, contempt of others, jealousy.
JEAN DE LA BRUYÈRE: *Caractères,* XI, 1688

[*See also* Courtesy.

Discovery

What so truly suits with honor and honesty as the discovering things unknown? erecting towns, peopling countries, informing the ignorant, reforming things unjust, teaching virtue; and gain to our native mother-country a kingdom to attend her: find employment for those that are idle, because they know not what to do?
JOHN SMITH: *A Description of New England,* 1616

No great discovery was ever made without a bold guess.
Ascribed to ISAAC NEWTON (1642–1727)

I do not much wish well to discoveries, for I am always afraid they will end in conquest and robbery.
SAMUEL JOHNSON: *Letter to W. S. Johnson of Connecticut,* March 4, 1773

It is in the nature of human affairs that great alterations take place suddenly, and great discoveries are made unexpectedly, as it were accidentally.

WILLIAM GODWIN: *An Enquiry Concerning Political Justice,* 1793

Or like stout Cortez when with eagle eyes
He stared at the Pacific — and all his men
Look'd at each other with a wild surmise —
Silent, upon a peak in Darien.

JOHN KEATS: *On First Looking into Chapman's Homer,* 1816

A great discovery is a fact whose appearance in science gives rise to shining ideas, whose light dispels many obscurities and shows us new paths.

CLAUDE BERNARD: *Introduction à la médecine expérimentale,* 1865

[*See also* Columbus (Christopher).

Discretion

Discretion is valor. A daring pilot is dangerous to a ship.

EURIPIDES: *The Suppliant Women, c.* 421 B.C.

Consult nothing so much upon every occasion as discretion. It is more discreet to be silent than to speak.

EPICTETUS: *Encheiridion, c.* 110

Discretion is the better part of valor.

ENGLISH PROVERB, traced by Apperson to the XV century (Cf. EURIPIDES, *ante, c.* 421 B.C.)

A wise man sees as much as he ought, not as much as he can.

MICHEL DE MONTAIGNE: *Essays,* II, 1580

Let your own discretion be your tutor: suit the action to the word, the word to the action.

SHAKESPEARE: *Hamlet,* III, *c.* 1601

Let's teach ourselves that honorable stop
Not to outsport discretion.

SHAKESPEARE: *Othello,* II, 1604

He hath a wisdom that doth guide his valor
To act in safety.

SHAKESPEARE: *Macbeth,* III, *c.* 1605

Though a man has all other perfections, and wants discretion, he will be of no great consequence in the world; but if he has this single talent in perfection, and but a common share of others, he may do what he pleases in his particular station of life.

JOSEPH ADDISON: *The Spectator,* Nov. 17, 1711

There is a time to wink as well as to see.

THOMAS FULLER: *Gnomologia,* 1732

He who fights and runs away
May live to fight another day.

OLIVER GOLDSMITH: *The Art of Poetry on a New Plan,* 1761

Discretion means, when it is said that something is to be done within the discretion of the authorities, that that something is to be done according to the rules of reason and justice, not according to private opinion; according to law and not humor. It is to be, not arbitrary, vague, and fanciful, but legal and regular. And it must be exercised within the limit to which an honest man, competent to the discharge of his office, ought to confine himself.

LORD HALSBURY: *Judgment in Sharp* vs. *Wakefield,* 1891

A man in Georgia pulled a gun
An' took a shot at me.
Jes' as he took the second shot
I passed through Tennessee.

American Negro song, quoted by HOWARD W. ODUM: *Wings on My Feet,* XVII, 1929

I'd rather hear them say " There he goes " than " Here he lies."

AMERICAN PROVERB

The age of discretion is reached when one has learned to be indiscreet discreetly.

Author unidentified

A dram of discretion is worth more than a pound of knowledge.

ITALIAN PROVERB

[*See also* Caution, Fool, Judge, Philosophy, Prudence, Valor.

Discussion

Friendly free discussion calling forth
From the fair jewel, truth, its latent ray.

JAMES THOMSON: *Liberty,* II, 1736

Men are never so likely to settle a question rightly as when they discuss it freely.

T. B. MACAULAY: *Southey's Colloquies,* 1830

In one case out of a hundred a point is excessively discussed because it is obscure; in the ninety-nine remaining it is obscure because excessively discussed.

E. A. POE: *The Rationale of Verse,* 1843 (The Pioneer, March)

A method of confirming others in their errors.

AMBROSE BIERCE: *The Devil's Dictionary,* 1906

[*See also* Argument, Controversy, Debate, Dispute, Obscurity, Speech (Free).

Disease

There are more pernicious diseases of the soul than of the body.

CICERO: *Tusculanae disputationes,* III, 45 B.C.

Desperate diseases require desperate remedies.

ENGLISH PROVERB, traced by Apperson to 1539

Our bodies are always exposed to the attacks of Satan. The maladies I suffer are not natural, but Devil's spells.

MARTIN LUTHER: *Table-Talk,* DLXXXIII, 1569

Before the curing of a strong disease,
Even in the instant of repair and health,
The fit is strongest.

SHAKESPEARE: *King John,* III, *c.* 1596

Ruptures, catarrhs, loads o' gravel i' the back, lethargies, cold palsies, raw eyes, dirt-rotten livers, wheezing lungs, bladders full of posthume, sciaticas, incurable bone-aches.

SHAKESPEARE: *Troilus and Cressida,* V, *c.* 1601

Diseases crucify the soul of man, attenuate our bodies, dry them, wither them, shrivel them up like old apples, make them as so many anatomies.

ROBERT BURTON: *The Anatomy of Melancholy,* I, 1621

Man hath as many diseases as a horse.

JAMES HOWELL: *The Parley of Beasts,* 1660

Convulsions, epilepsies, fierce catarrhs,
Intestine stone and ulcer, colic pangs,
Demoniac phrenzy, moping melancholy,
And moon-struck madness, pining atrophy,
Marasmus, and wide-wasting pestilence,
Dropsies, and asthmas, and joint-racking rheums.

JOHN MILTON: *Paradise Lost,* XI, 1667

Diseases are the interests of pleasures.

JOHN RAY: *English Proverbs,* 1670

Nature, in the production of disease, is uniform and consistent, so much so, that for the same disease in different persons the symptoms are for the most part the same; and the selfsame phenomena that you would observe in the sickness of a Socrates you would observe in the sickness of a simpleton.

THOMAS SYDENHAM (1624–89)

Disease generally begins that equality which death completes.

SAMUEL JOHNSON: *The Rambler,* Sept. 1, 1750

Disease is very old and nothing about it has changed. It is we who change as we learn to recognize what was formerly imperceptible.

J. M. CHARCOT: *De l'expectation en médecine,* 1857

A conflict of citizens in a cell state, brought about by external forces.

RUDOLF VIRCHOW: *Cellular-Pathologie,* 1858

The whipping post and branding iron of luxury.

H. W. SHAW (JOSH BILLINGS): *Josh Billings' Comical Lexicon,* 1877

The symptoms of disease are marked by purpose, and the purpose is beneficent. The processes of disease aim not at the destruction of life, but at the saving of it.

FREDERICK TREVES: Address to the Edinburgh Philosophical Institution, Oct. 31, 1905

Disease is an experience of so-called mortal mind. It is fear made manifest on the body.

MARY BAKER G. EDDY: *Science and Health,* XIV, 1908

Diseases are not species, such as dogs and cats, but abnormal, though not altogether irregular, behavior of animals and plants.

THOMAS C. ALLBUTT (1836–1925)

The causes of all diseases are to be found in the blood. HEBREW PROVERB

A long disease doesn't lie. It always kills at last.

IRISH PROVERB

Every disease is a doctor. IBID.

[*See also* Age (Old), Cure, Death, Diet, Doctor, Gluttony, Health, Medicine, Mouth, Patient, Physician, Sickness, Sleep, Vegetarianism.

Disfranchisement

Persons who cannot elect or be elected are: (*a*) People employing hired labor for the purpose of making profit; (*b*) persons living on unearned incomes such as interest on capital, income from enterprises, receipts from property, etc.; (*c*) private traders and middlemen; (*d*) monks and clergy of all persuasions and denominations for whom this occupation is a profession.

CONSTITUTION OF THE U.S.S.R., Jan. 31, 1924

Disgrace

Disgrace is immortal, and lives long after one thinks it is dead.

PLAUTUS: *Persa,* III, *c.* 200 B.C.

We should prefer death to disgrace.

CICERO: *De officiis,* I, 78 B.C.

When men disgraces share,
The lesser is the care.

BEN JONSON: *Cynthia's Revels,* V, 1601

Disgraces are like cherries: one draws another.

GEORGE HERBERT: *Jacula Prudentum,* 1651

Disgrace does not consist in the punishment, but in the crime.

VITTORIO ALFIERI: *Antigone,* I, 1785

Come, death, and snatch me from disgrace.

E. G. BULWER-LYTTON: *Richelieu,* IV, 1838

[*See also* Family, Honor.

Disguise

The voice is Jacob's voice, but the hands are the hands of Esau.

GENESIS XXVII, 22, *c.* 700 B.C.

Disgust

Disgust is a sort of synthesis which attaches to the total form of objects, and which must diminish and disappear as scientific analysis

separates into facts what, as a whole, is so repugnant.
C. R. RICHET: *Les causes du dégoût*, 1884

Dish

A dish fit for the gods.
SHAKESPEARE: *Julius Cæsar*, II, 1599

[*See also* Eating.

Dishonesty

What is come by dishonestly vanishes in profligacy.
CICERO: *Orationes Philippicæ*, II, *c.* 60 B.C.

The hidden things of dishonesty.
II CORINTHIANS IV, 2, *c.* 55

The man who is dishonest as a statesman would be a dishonest man in any station.
THOMAS JEFFERSON: *Letter to George Logan*, Nov., 1816

Dishonor

A man dishonored is worse than dead.
CERVANTES: *Don Quixote*, I, 1605

There is no death, however slow and painful, that I would not prefer to dishonor.
NAPOLEON I: To Barry E. O'Meara at St. Helena, Oct. 7, 1817

His honor rooted in dishonor stood,
And faith unfaithful kept him falsely true.
ALFRED TENNYSON: *Elaine*, 1859

[*See also* Honor.

Disillusion

I was taught to think, and I was willing to believe, that genius was not a bawd, that virtue was not a mask, that liberty was not a name, that love had its seat in the human heart. Now I would care little if these words were struck out of the dictionary, or if I had never heard them. They are become to my ears a mockery and a dream.
WILLIAM HAZLITT: *On the Pleasure of Hating*, 1821

Disobedience

Disobedience in the eyes of any one who has read history is man's original virtue. It is through disobedience that progress has been made, through disobedience and through rebellion.
OSCAR WILDE: *The Soul of Man Under Socialism*, 1891

Disobedience, the rarest and most courageous of the virtues, is seldom distinguished from neglect, the laziest and commonest of the vices.
GEORGE BERNARD SHAW: *Maxims for Revolutionists*, 1903

[*See also* Obedience.

Dispatch

Dispatch is the soul of business; and nothing contributes more to dispatch than method. Lay down a method for everything, and stick to it inviolably, as far as unexpected incidents may allow.
LORD CHESTERFIELD: *Letter to his son*, Feb. 5, 1750

Dispersion

[*See* Jew.

Dispute

He is proud, knowing nothing, but doting about questions and strifes of words, whereof cometh envy, strife, railings, evil surmisings, perverse disputings of men of corrupt minds.
I TIMOTHY VI, 4–5, *c.* 60

A good cause needs not to be patroned by passion, but can sustain itself upon a temperate dispute.
THOMAS BROWNE: *Religio Medici*, V, 1642

I never saw an instance of one of two disputants convincing the other by argument. I have seen many, on their getting warm, becoming rude, and shooting one another.
THOMAS JEFFERSON: *Letter to Thomas Jefferson Randolph*, 1808

[*See also* Argument, Controversy, Debate, Division, Opinion.

Disraeli, Benjamin (1804–81)

He is a liar in action and words. His life is a living lie. He is a disgrace to his species. . . . England is degraded in tolerating or having upon the face of her society a miscreant of his abominable, foul and atrocious nature. If there be harsher terms in the British language I should use them.
DANIEL O'CONNELL: Speech at Dublin, 1835

Dissension

Civil dissension is a viperous worm
That gnaws the bowels of the commonwealth.
SHAKESPEARE: *I Henry VI*, III, 1592

Dissimulation

I hate as I hate the gates of Hell that man whose words conceal his thoughts.
HOMER: *Iliad*, IX, *c.* 800 B.C.

To know how to dissemble is the knowledge of kings.
ARMAND CARDINAL RICHELIEU: *Mirame*, *c.* 1625

Men of the world, knowing that there are few things so unpopular as penetration, take care to wear the appearance of being imposed upon.
HENRY TAYLOR: *The Statesman*, 1836

He who knows not how to dissemble knows not how to live. (Qui nescit dissimulare nescit vivere.)
Author unknown (Sometimes *regnare* (rule) is substituted for *vivere*)

[*See also* Man.

Distance

Far from our eyes th' enchanting objects set,
Advantage by the friendly distance get.
Anon.: *A Poet Against Fruition*, 1685

If a man makes me keep my distance, the comfort is, he keeps his at the same time.
JONATHAN SWIFT: *Thoughts on Various Subjects*, 1706

'Tis distance lends enchantment to the view.
THOMAS CAMPBELL: *The Pleasures of Hope*, I, 1799

Over there, where you are not — there is happiness. G. P. SCHMIDT VON LÜBECK: *Des Fremdlings Abendlied*, 1808

The pathos of distance.
F. W. NIETZSCHE: *Beyond Good and Evil*, 1886 (Also in *The Antichrist*, 1888, and *The Twilight of the Idols*, 1889). JAMES HUNEKER: Title of a book, 1913

Hills look green that are far away.
IRISH PROVERB

Distinction

Among all excellent and illustrious men those are most praiseworthy who have been the authors of religion and divine worship; next come the founders of states; then come successful generals who have enlarged their own kingdom or the dominion of their country. To these are to be added literary men of all kinds, according to their several degrees; and lastly, as being the greatest number, come the artificers and mechanics.
NICCOLÒ MACHIAVELLI: *Discorsi*, I, 1531

There lurks in every human heart a desire of distinction, which inclines every man first to hope, and then to believe, that Nature has given him something peculiar to himself.
SAMUEL JOHNSON: *Letter to James Boswell*, Dec. 8, 1763

[*See also* Eminence, Fame, Man and Woman, Reputation.

Diversity

So many men, so many minds. (Quot homines, tot sententiæ.)
TERENCE: *Phormio*, *c.* 160 B.C.

So many heads, so many kinds of advice.
FRENCH PROVERB

So many heads, so many brains.
ITALIAN PROVERB

[*See also* Variety.

Divine Right

God and my right. (Dieu et mon droit.)
Motto on the royal arms of England, first used by Richard I at the Battle of Gisors, 1198

Not all the water in the rough rude sea
Can wash the balm from an anointed king;
The breath of worldly men cannot depose
The deputy elected by the Lord.
SHAKESPEARE: *Richard II*, III, *c.* 1596

How can any Christian man derive his kingship from Christ, but with worse usurpation than the pope his headship over the church, since Christ not only hath not left the least shadow of a command for any such vicegerence from Him in the state, as the pope pretends for his in the church, but hath expressly declared that such regal dominion is from the Gentiles, not from Him, and hath strictly charged us not to imitate them therein?
JOHN MILTON: *The Ready and Easy Way to Establish a Free Commonwealth*, 1660

Unto my flock I daily preach'd,
Kings are by God appointed,
And damn'd are those who dare resist,
Or touch the Lord's anointed.
Anon.: *The Vicar of Bray*, 1734

Can I choose my own king? I can choose my own King Popinjay, and play what farce or tragedy I may with him; but he who is to be my ruler, whose will is to be higher than my will, was chosen for me in Heaven.
THOMAS CARLYLE: *Sartor Resartus*, III, 1836

The Prussian kings hold their crown, not by the gift of the people, but by the grace of God.
OTTO VON BISMARCK: Speech in the Prussian Reichstag, 1847

The rights and interests of the laboring man will be protected and cared for, not by labor agitators, but by the Christian men to whom God in His infinite wisdom has given the control of the property interests of the country.
GEORGE F. BAER (president of the Philadelphia and Reading Railway): *Letter to the Rev. W. F. Clark* of Wilkes-Barré, Pa., July 17, 1902

The national polity of our nation was elucidated in the command given to the Imperial Grandson by the Sun Goddess Amaterasu-O-Mikami, that the land shall be reigned over and governed by an unbroken line of emperors for ages eternal. Sovereignty lies absolutely with the emperor.
DECREE OF THE JAPANESE CABINET, Aug. 3, 1935

[*See also* Government, King, Monarchy, Sovereignty.

Divinity

What is there of the divine in a load of bricks? What . . . in a barber's shop? . . . Much. All.
R. W. EMERSON: *Journal*, July 18, 1834

[*See also* Dogma, Theology.

Division

Divide and rule. (Divide et impera.)
Ascribed to PHILIP OF MACEDON (382–336 B.C.)

If a house be divided against itself, that house cannot stand.
MARK III, 25, *c.* 70

A house divided against itself cannot stand. I believe this government cannot endure permanently half-slave and half-free.
ABRAHAM LINCOLN: Speech accepting the Republican nomination as Senator from Illinois, June 17, 1858

Two captains sink the ship.
TURKISH PROVERB

[*See also* Arithmetic, Cook, Doctor, Goat.

Divorce

If a man set his face to put away a concubine who has borne him children or a wife who has given him children, they shall return to that woman her dowry and shall give to her part of field, garden and goods, and she shall bring up her children.
THE CODE OF HAMMURABI, *c.* 2030 B.C.

When a man hath taken a wife, and married her, and it come to pass that she find no favor in his eyes, because he hath found some uncleanness in her: then let him write her a bill of divorcement, and give it in her hand, and send her out of his house.
DEUTERONOMY XXIV, 1, *c.* 650 B.C.

Divorce is not honorable to women.
EURIPIDES: *Medea*, 431 B.C.

If she go not as thou wouldst have her, cut her off from thy flesh, and give her a bill of divorce, and let her go.
ECCLESIASTICUS XXV, 26, *c.* 180 B.C.

Whosoever shall put away his wife, and marry another, committeth adultery.
MARK X, 11, *c.* 70 (Cf. LUKE XVI, 18, *c.* 75)

It hath been said, Whosoever shall put away his wife, let him give her a writing of divorcement: But I say unto you, That whosoever shall put away his wife, saving for the cause of fornication, causeth her to commit adultery: and whosoever shall marry her that is divorced committeth adultery.
MATTHEW V, 31–32, *c.* 75

Whosoever shall put away his wife, except it be for fornication, and shall marry another, committeth adultery.
MATTHEW XIX, 9, *c.* 75 (Cf. MARK X, 11, *ante.* The insertion of an exception will be noted)

A man is guilty of adultery if he marries a divorced woman; and so is he who divorces his wife, save on the ground of misconduct, in order to marry again.
LACTANTIUS: *Divinae Institutiones*, VI, *c.* 310

It is wrong to leave a wife who is sterile in order to take another by whom children may be had. Anyone doing this is guilty of adultery.
ST. AUGUSTINE: *Conjugal Adultery*, I, *c.* 400

If a man leaves his wife and she marries another, she commits adultery.
ST. AUGUSTINE: *On the Good of Marriage*, *c.* 401

If anyone shall say that on account of heresy, or the hardships of cohabitation, or the deliberate abuse of one party by the other the marriage tie may be broken, let him be anathema.
DECREES OF THE COUNCIL OF TRENT, XXIV, 1564

There are two causes of divorce: first adultery; but first, Christians ought to labor and to use diligent persuasions to reconcile the married pair; sharply, withal, reproving the guilty person. The second cause is much like: when one runs away from the other, and after returning runs away again. Such have commonly mates in other places, and richly deserve to be punished.
MARTIN LUTHER: *Table-Talk*, DCCXLVII, 1569

He counsels a divorce; a loss of her
That, like a jewel, has hung twenty years
About his neck, yet never lost her lustre.
SHAKESPEARE and JOHN FLETCHER: *Henry VIII*, II, 1613

Defender of marriage. (Defensor vinculi.)
Officer appointed by Pope Benedict XIV to oppose suits for annulment, 1741

Divorce is entirely to the disadvantage of women. If a man has had several wives, he shows no sign of it, whereas a woman several times married fades completely.
NAPOLEON I: To Gaspard Gourgaud at St. Helena, Jan. 9, 1817

Draw up the papers, lawyer, and make 'em good and stout,
For things are running crossways, and Betsey and I are out.
WILL CARLETON: *Betsey and I Are Out*, 1873

Divorce is born of perverted morals, and leads, as experience shows, to vicious habits in public and private life.
POPE LEO XIII: *Arcanum divinæ sapientiæ*, Feb. 10, 1880

Husbands and wives should never separate if there is no Christian demand for it. It is better to await the logic of events than for a wife precipitately to leave her husband, or for a husband to leave his wife.
MARY BAKER G. EDDY: *Science and Health*, III, 1908

It is the function of the state to determine the grounds upon which a valid divorce may be granted. We recognize as lawful a divorce granted by the state.
The Doctrines and Discipline of the Methodist Episcopal Church, II, 1932

Divorce is the sacrament of adultery.
FRENCH PROVERB

From bed and board. (A mensa et toro.)
LEGAL PHRASE

From the bonds of matrimony. (A vinculo matrimonii.) IBID.

[*See also* Adultery, Marriage.

Dixie

I wish I was in Dixie! Hooray! Hooray!
In Dixie's land we'll take our stand,
And lib and die in Dixie.
Away! Away!
Away down south in Dixie!
DANIEL D. EMMETT: *Dixie's Land,* 1859

Doctor

Diaulus, once a doctor, is now an undertaker; what he does as an undertaker he used to do also as a doctor.
MARTIAL: *Epigrams,* IX, *c.* 95

Frightened patients when they want a cure,
Bid any price, and any pain endure;
But when the doctor's remedies appear
The cure's too easy, and the price too dear.
DANIEL DEFOE: *The True-Born Englishman,* II, 1701

You tell your doctor that y' are ill,
And what does he but write a bill?
MATTHEW PRIOR: *Alma,* III, *c.* 1716

If the doctor cures the sun sees it; if he kills the earth hides it.
JAMES KELLY: *Complete Collection of Scottish Proverbs,* 1721

" Is there no hope? " the sick man said,
The silent doctor shook his head,
And took his leave with signs of sorrow,
Despairing of his fee tomorrow.
JOHN GAY: *Fables,* I, 1727

That patient is not like to recover who makes the doctor his heir.
THOMAS FULLER: *Gnomologia,* 1732

Who shall decide when doctors disagree?
ALEXANDER POPE: *Moral Essays,* III (Of the Use of Riches), 1732

God heals and the doctor takes the fee.
BENJAMIN FRANKLIN: *Poor Richard's Almanac,* 1736

The best doctor is the one you run for and can't find.
DENIS DIDEROT: *Pensées philosophiques,* 1746

The term *doctor* . . . distinguishes him to whom it is granted as a man who has attained such knowledge of his profession as qualifies him to instruct others.
SAMUEL JOHNSON: *Boswell's Life,* May 6, 1775

Doctors like fees no doubt, — ought to like them; yet if they are brave and well-educated, the entire object of their lives is not fees. They, on the whole, desire to cure the sick; and, — if they are good doctors, and the choice were fairly put to them, — would rather cure their patient and lose their fee than kill him and get it.
JOHN RUSKIN: *The Crown of Wild Olive,* I, 1866

Doctors are oxydable products, and the schools must keep furnishing new ones as the old ones turn into oxyds; some of first-rate quality that burn with a great light; some of a lower grade of brilliancy; some honestly, unmistakably, by the grace of God, of moderate gifts, or in simpler phrase, dull.
O. W. HOLMES: *Scholastic and Bedside Teaching,* 1867 (Lecture at Harvard, Nov. 6)

When a doctor looks me square in the face and kant see no money in me, then i am happy.
H. W. SHAW (JOSH BILLINGS): *Josh Billings' Encyclopedia of Wit and Wisdom,* 1874

What sort of a doctor is he? Well, I don't know much about his ability, but he's got a very good bedside manner.
GEORGE DU MAURIER: Lines under a drawing in Punch, March 15, 1884

A single doctor like a sculler plies,
And all his art and all his physic tries;
But two physicians, like a pair of oars,
Conduct you soonest to the Stygian shores.
Author unidentified

Patients worry over the beginning of an illness; doctors worry over its end.
CHINESE PROVERB

A doctor should have a falcon's eye, a girl's hand, and a lion's heart.
DUTCH PROVERB

After death the doctor. FRENCH PROVERB

The presence of the doctor is the first part of the cure. IBID.

A young doctor means a new graveyard.
GERMAN PROVERB

Good doctors do not like big bottles. IBID.

No doctor at all is better than three. IBID.

A doctor and a clown know more than a doctor alone. ITALIAN PROVERB

A doctor's mistake is the will of God. IBID.

If the patient dies, the doctor killed him; if he gets well, the saints cured him. IBID.

While the doctor is considering the patient dies.
IBID.

Death defies the doctor. LATIN PROVERB

There is more danger from the doctor than from the disease. IBID.

Before a doctor can cure one patient he must kill ten. POLISH PROVERB

If your friend is a doctor, send him to the house of your enemy.
PORTUGUESE PROVERB

The more doctors, the more sickness. IBID.

A doctor gets less work from six men than from one woman. SPANISH PROVERB

Heaven defend me from a busy doctor.
WELSH PROVERB

[*See also* Ape, Apple, Cure, Diet, Friend, Grammarian, Health, Medicine, Physician, Sunshine, Surgeon, Undertaker, Vaccination, Vocation.

Doctor of Divinity

[*See* Ass.

Doctor of Laws

Then stood there up one in the council, a Pharisee, named Gamaliel, a doctor of the law. ACTS V, 34, *c.* 75

A leather medal his reward should be,
A leather medal and an LL.D.
Anon.: *Harvardiana,* III, 1837

[*See also* Lawyer.

Doctrinaire

The American doctrinaire is the converse of the American demagogue, and, in his way, is scarcely less injurious to the public. The first deals in poetry, the last in cant.
J. FENIMORE COOPER: *The American Democrat,* XXI, 1838

Doctrine

Henceforth be no more children, tossed to and fro, and carried about with every wind of doctrine. EPHESIANS IV, 14, *c.* 60

Doctrines do not necessarily die from being killed.
T. H. HUXLEY: *Natural Rights and Political Rights,* 1890

If you want a war, nourish a doctrine. Doctrines are the most fearful tyrants to which men ever are subject, because doctrines get inside of a man's own reason and betray him against himself. Civilized men have done their fiercest fighting for doctrines.
W. G. SUMNER: *War,* 1903

[*See also* Lama.

Doer

[*See* Doing.

Dog

Thou shalt not bring the hire of a whore, or the price of a dog, into the house of the Lord thy God for any vow: for even both these are abomination unto the Lord thy God.
DEUTERONOMY XXIV, 18, *c.* 650 B.C.

Are dogs divided into hes and shes, or do they both share equally in hunting and in keeping watch and in the other duties of dogs?
PLATO: *The Republic,* VIII, *c.* 370 B.C.

Dogs are like their mistresses.
IBID. (Cited as a proverb)

A dog returneth to his vomit.
PROVERBS XXVI, 11, *c.* 350 B.C.

A living dog is better than a dead lion.
ECCLESIASTES IX, 4, *c.* 200 B.C.

They went their way, and the dog went after them. TOBIT XI, 4, *c.* 180 B.C.

Beware of dogs. PHILIPPIANS III, 2, *c.* 60

Give not that which is holy unto the dogs.
MATTHEW VII, 6, *c.* 75

The dogs eat of the crumbs which fall from their master's table. MATTHEW XV, 27

The dogs came and licked his sores.
LUKE XVI, 21, *c.* 75

Fierce in the woods, gentle in the house.
MARTIAL: *Epigrams,* II, 86

There are five signs of a mad dog: its mouth hangs open, its saliva drips, its ears fall, its tail is between its legs, and it slinks along the wall. THE TALMUD (*Yomah*), *c.* 200

The dog is devoid of shame.
ST. JOHN CHRYSOSTOM: *Homily* XII, c. 388

Love me, love my dog. (Qui me amat, amat et canem meum.)
ST. BERNARD: *Sermon, c.* 1155

A still dog bites sore.
ENGLISH PROVERB, traced by Apperson to the *Proverbs of Alfred, c.* 1270

A barking dog seldom bites.
ENGLISH PROVERB, traced by Apperson to *c.* 1350

Like a dog in the manger.
ENGLISH PHRASE, in use since the XVI century

Every dog has his day.
ENGLISH PROVERB, borrowed from the Greek, and familiar since the XVI century

Dogs bark by custom.
ENGLISH PROVERB, familiar since the XVI century

What delight can there be, and not rather displeasure in hearing the barking and howling of dogs? Or what greater pleasure is there to be felt when a dog followeth a hare than when a dog followeth a dog?
THOMAS MORE: *Utopia,* 1516

Keep running after a dog, and he will never bite you.
RABELAIS: *Gargantua,* I, 1535

An old dog biteth sore.
JOHN HEYWOOD: *Proverbs,* 1546

A stick is quickly found to beat a dog with.
ENGLISH PROVERB, traced by Apperson to 1563

Dogs bark boldly at their own master's door.
EDMUND TILNEY: *Duties in Marriage,* 1568

Who sleepeth with dogs shall rise with fleas.
JOHN FLORIO: *First Frutes,* 1578

I had rather be a dog, and bay the moon,
Than such a Roman.
SHAKESPEARE: *Julius Cæsar,* IV, 1599

It is hard to teach an old dog new tricks.
WILLIAM CAMDEN: *Remains Concerning Britain,* 1605

Mastiff, greyhound, mongrel grim,
Hound or spaniel, brach or lym,
Or bobtail tyke or trundle-tail.
SHAKESPEARE: *King Lear,* III, 1606 (*Brach* =a hound bitch; *lym*=a bloodhound; *tyke*=a cur; *trundle-tail*=a cur)

The little dogs and all,
Tray, Blanche, and Sweetheart, see, they bark at me.
IBID.

Dogs fawn on a man no longer than he feeds them.
RANDLE COTGRAVE: *French-English Dictionary,* 1611

A good dog deserves a good bone.
BEN JONSON: *A Tale of a Tub,* II, 1633

A dog's nose is ever cold.
JOHN CLARKE: *Parœmiologia Anglo-Latina,* 1639

In every country dogs bite.
GEORGE HERBERT: *Outlandish Proverbs,* 1640

Look not for musk in a dog's kennel. IBID.

Who hath no more bread than need must not keep a dog. IBID.

If the old dog barks he gives counsel.
GEORGE HERBERT: *Jacula Prudentum,* 1651

The dog will not bite for being struck with a bone. JAMES HOWELL: *Proverbs,* 1659

Hunger and ease is a dog's life.
GIOVANNI TORRIANO: *Italian Proverbs,* 1666

A dog's nose and a maid's knees are always cold.
JOHN RAY: *English Proverbs,* 1670 (Cf. CLARKE, *ante,* 1639)

He that would hang his dog gives out first that he is mad. IBID.

The dog that licks ashes trust not with meal.
IBID.

Let sleeping dogs lie.
ENGLISH PROVERB, traced by Smith to 1681

The dog teaches thee fidelity.
JOHN HORNECK: *The Crucifixion of Jesus,* 1686

Histories are more full of examples of the fidelity of dogs than of friends.
ALEXANDER POPE: *Letter to H. Cromwell,* Oct. 9, 1709

Let dogs delight to bark and bite,
For God hath made them so.
ISAAC WATTS: *Divine Songs for Children,* 1715

He that strikes my dog would strike me if he durst.
JAMES KELLY: *Complete Collection of Scottish Proverbs,* 1721

Silence, ye wolves! while Ralph to Cynthia howls,
And makes night hideous.
ALEXANDER POPE: *The Dunciad,* III, 1728

Lo, when two dogs are fighting in the streets,
With a third dog one of the two dogs meets;
With angry teeth he bites him to the bone,
And this dog smarts for what that dog has done.
HENRY FIELDING: *Tom Thumb,* I, 1730

I am his Highness' dog at Kew;
Pray tell me, sir, whose dog are you?
ALEXANDER POPE: *On the Collar of a Dog,* *c.* 1730

Of all the dogs array'd in fur,
Hereunder lies the truest cur.
He knew no tricks, he never flatter'd:
Nor those he fawn'd upon bespatter'd.
JONATHAN SWIFT: *Epitaph on His Dog,* *c.* 1730

Dogs bark as they are bred, and fawn as they are fed.
THOMAS FULLER: *Gnomologia,* 1732

Dogs never go into mourning when a horse dies. IBID.

If you want a pretence to whip a dog, it is enough to say he ate up the frying-pan.
IBID.

It's a hard Winter when dogs eat dogs. IBID.

Silly dogs are more angry with the stone than with the hand that flung it. IBID.

He asks no angel's wing, no seraph's fire,
But thinks, admitted to that equal sky,
His faithful dog shall bear him company.
ALEXANDER POPE: *An Essay on Man,* I, 1732

With countenance blithe,
And with a courtly grin, the fawning hound
Salutes thee cowering, his wide opening nose
Upward he curls, and his large sloe-black eyes
Melt in soft blandishments and humble joy.
WILLIAM SOMERVILLE: *The Chase,* I, 1735

Bow, wow, wow;
Whose dog art thou?
Little Tom Tinker's dog;
Bow, wow, wow.

Anon.: *Nursery Rhyme, c.* 1750

Give a dog an ill name and hang him.

GEORGE COLMAN THE ELDER: *Polly Honeycombe,* 1760

Dogs have not the power of comparing. A dog will take a small piece of meat as readily as a large, when both are before him.

SAMUEL JOHNSON: *Boswell's Life,* Oct. 19, 1769

A dog is made fat in two meals.

ENGLISH PROVERB, not recorded before the XIX century

Every dog is entitled to one bite. IBID.

Thy lap-dog, Rufa, is a dainty beast,
It don't surprise me in the least
To see thee lick so dainty clean a beast.
But that so dainty clean a beast licks thee,
Yes — that surprises me.

S. T. COLERIDGE: In the *Annual Anthology,* II, 1800

A dog starv'd at his master's gate
Predicts the ruin of the state.

WILLIAM BLAKE: *Auguries of Innocence, c.* 1802

Near this spot
Are deposited the remains of one
Who possessed beauty without vanity,
Strength without insolence,
Courage without ferocity,
And all the virtues of man without his vices.
This praise, which would be unmeaning flattery
If inscribed over human ashes,
Is but a just tribute to the memory of
Boatswain, a dog.

BYRON: Epitaph for a dog buried at Newstead Abbey, 1808

When thieves come, I bark: when gallants, I am still —
So perform both my master's and mistress's will.

S. T. COLERIDGE: *For a House-Dog's Collar,* 1809

'Tis sweet to hear the watch-dog's honest bark
Bay deep-mouth'd welcome as we draw near home;
'Tis sweet to know there is an eye will mark
Our coming, and look brighter when we come.

BYRON: *Don Juan,* I, 1819

One of the animals which a generous and sociable man would soonest become is a dog. A dog can have a friend; he has affections and character, he can enjoy equally the field and the fireside; he dreams, he caresses, he propitiates; he offends, and is pardoned; he stands by you in adversity; he is a good fellow.

LEIGH HUNT: *The Indicator,* LXIV, 1821

Has he bit any of the children yet? If he has, have them shot, and keep him for curiosity, to see if it was the hydrophobia.

CHARLES LAMB: *Letter to P. G. Patmore,* Sept., 1827

The dog alone, of all brute animals, has an affection upwards to man.

S. T. COLERIDGE: *Table-Talk,* May 2, 1830

The dog may have a spirit, as well as his brutal master;
A spirit to live in happiness: for why should he be robbed of his existence?
Hath he not a conscience of evil, a glimmer of moral sense,
Love and hatred, courage and fear, and visible shame and pride?

MARTIN F. TUPPER: *Proverbial Philosophy,* I, 1837

To carry children or dogs with one on a visit of ceremony is altogether vulgar. Even in half-ceremonious visits it is necessary to leave one's dog in the ante-room.

Anon.: *Etiquette for Ladies,* 1838

Like a dog, he hunts in dreams.

ALFRED TENNYSON: *Locksley Hall,* 1842

Old dog Tray's ever faithful,
Grief cannot drive him away;
He's gentle, he's kind; I'll never, never find
A better friend than old dog Tray.

S. C. FOSTER: *Old Dog Tray,* 1853

Dogs begin in jest and end in earnest.

H. G. BOHN: *Handbook of Proverbs,* 1855

Every dog is a lion at home. IBID.

If you wish the dog to follow you, feed him. IBID.

It is an ill-bred dog that will beat a bitch. IBID.

Many dogs soon eat up a horse. IBID.

One barking dog sets all the street a barking. IBID.

I don't like dogs. I always expect them to go mad.

Ascribed to SYDNEY SMITH in *A Memoir of the Rev. Sydney Smith* by his daughter, LADY HOLLAND, 1855

The one absolutely unselfish friend that man can have in this selfish world, the one that never deserts him, the one that never proves ungrateful or treacherous, is his dog. . . . He will kiss the hand that has no food to offer; he will lick the wounds and sores that come in encounter with the roughness of the world. . . . When all other friends desert, he remains.

GEORGE G. VEST: Speech at Warrensburg, Mo., Sept. 23, 1870

I agree with Agassiz that dogs possess something very like a conscience.

CHARLES DARWIN: *The Descent of Man,* IV, 1871

Newfoundland dogs are good to save children from drowning, but you must have a pond of water handy and a child, or else there will be no profit in boarding a Newfoundland.
H. W. SHAW (JOSH BILLINGS): Lecture at San Francisco, 1885

The great pleasure of a dog is that you may make a fool of yourself with him and not only will he not scold you, but he will make a fool of himself too.
SAMUEL BUTLER: *Note-Books, c.* 1890

Our German forefathers had a very kind religion. They believed that, after death, they would meet again all the good dogs that had been their companions in life. I wish I could believe that too.
OTTO VON BISMARCK (1815–1898)

Every time I come to town
The boys keep kicking my dog around;
Even if he is a hound
They've got to stop kicking my dog around.
Anon.: Campaign-song of Champ Clark of Missouri in his campaign for the Presidency, 1912

A dog knows his master, but not his master's master. ABYSSINIAN PROVERB

Call a dog a dog; he won't bite you for it.
AMERICAN NEGRO SAYING

I'd ruther drink swampy water
An' sleep in a holler log
Than have a feller feed me
That wouldn't feed mah dog.
AMERICAN NEGRO SONG

The dog is the only animal who has seen his god. Author unidentified

The more I see of men, the more I like dogs.
IBID.

To a dog the whole world is a smell. IBID.

A hunting dog always dies a violent death.
CHINESE PROVERB

Dogs do not dislike poor families. IBID.

The dog that is idle barks at his fleas, but the dog that is hunting does not feel them.
IBID.

A hungry dog and a thirsty horse pay no heed to blows. DANISH PROVERB

Pet your dog and he'll spoil your clothes.
DUTCH PROVERB

Major
Born a dog
Died a gentleman.
Epitaph on a dog's grave in Maryland

Who does not feed the dog feeds the thief.
ESTONIAN PROVERB

It is home to a dog after he has been there three nights. FINNISH PROVERB

A dog in the kitchen asks for no company.
FRENCH PROVERB

A dog may look at a bishop. IBID.

A good dog never gets a good bone. IBID.

Don't snap your fingers at the dog before you get out of the village. IBID.

Only a dog and a Frenchman go walking after they have eaten. IBID.

The best thing about a man is his dog. IBID.

A dog does not remain tied to a sausage long.
GERMAN PROVERB

Once a dog is bitten all other dogs bite him.
IBID.

If the dog barks, go in; if the bitch barks, go out. HEBREW PROVERB

Never disturb a dog eating or a man sleeping.
ITALIAN PROVERB

There is no dog so bad but he will wag his tail.
IBID.

Before dog go without supper him eat cockroach. JAMAICAN PROVERB

A lean dog shames its master.
JAPANESE PROVERB

If a man be great even his dog will wear a proud look. IBID.

If you must be a dog it's best to be the dog of a samurai. IBID.

The dog's power of scent. (Odora canum vis.)
LATIN PHRASE

Beware the dog. (Cave canem.) IBID.

Beware of the silent dog and still water.
LATIN PROVERB

The leaner the dog the fatter the flea.
POLISH PROVERB

A house without either a dog or a cat is the house of a scoundrel.
PORTUGUESE PROVERB

Barking dogs make poor hunters. IBID.

A dog is wiser than a woman; it does not bark at its master. RUSSIAN PROVERB

A' are no' thieves that dogs bark at.
SCOTTISH PROVERB

They're keen o' company that taks the dog on their back. IBID.

Meat never hangs so high but a dog will try his legs. SPANISH PROVERB

A lonely dog will make a companion of his tail. WELSH PROVERB

Growling dogs have foul hides. IBID.

A dog is not insulted when called a dog.
WEST AFRICAN PROVERB

[*See also* Authority, Beating, Cabbage, Cat, Cat and Dog, Caution, Children, Cold, Companion, Coöperation, Cost, Danger, Dead, Eminence, Fiddler, Fight, Fighting, Flea, Fool, Friend, Gentleman, Good, Grain, Hand, Head, Home, Horse, Host, Hunger, Hunting, Industry, Infidel, Lawyer, Longevity, Love, Lover, Luck, Malice, Man, Moon, Name, News, Pride, Quarrel, Quarrelsome, Silence, Sleeping, Trade (=commerce), Trust, Welcome.

Doggedness

It's dogged as does it.
ANTHONY TROLLOPE: *The Last Chronicles of Barset*, I, 1867

Dogma

It is gross ignorance that produces the dogmatic spirit. The man who knows next to nothing is always eager to teach what he has just learned; the man who knows a lot scarcely believes that what he is saying can be unknown to others, and in consequence he speaks with diffidence.
JEAN DE LA BRUYÈRE: *Caractères*, V, 1688

For modes of faith let graceless zealots fight;
His can't be wrong whose life is in the right.
ALEXANDER POPE: *An Essay on Man*, III, 1733

From the age of fifteen, dogma has been the fundamental principle of my religion. I know of no other religion; I cannot enter into the idea of any other sort of religion; religion, as a mere sentiment, is to me a dream and a mockery.
J. H. NEWMAN: *Apologia pro vita sua*, II, 1864

Dogmatic theology is an attempt at both literary and scientific criticism of the highest order; and the age which developed dogma had neither the resources nor the faculty for such a criticism.
MATTHEW ARNOLD: *Literature and Dogma*, IX, 1873

[*See also* Laughter, Theology.

Doing

The doer must suffer for the deed.
ÆSCHYLUS: *Choephori*, *c.* 490 B.C. (Quoted as a proverb)

Whatever thy hand findeth to do, do it with thy might.
ECCLESIASTES IX, 10, *c.* 200 B.C.

They can because they think they can. (Possunt, quia posse videntur.)
VIRGIL: *Æneid*, V, 19 B.C.

Be ye doers of the word, and not hearers only, deceiving your own selves.
JAMES I, 22, *c.* 60

Easier said than done.
ENGLISH PROVERB, first recorded in 1546

Saying and doing are two things.
JOHN HEYWOOD: *Proverbs*, 1546

If to do were as easy as to know what were good to do, chapels had been churches, and poor men's cottages princes' palaces.
SHAKESPEARE: *The Merchant of Venice*, I, *c.* 1597

Let each man do his best.
SHAKESPEARE: *I Henry IV*, I, *c.* 1598

Oh, what men dare do! what men may do! what men daily do, not knowing what they do!
SHAKESPEARE: *Much Ado About Nothing*, IV, *c.* 1599

Things won are done; joy's soul lies in the doing.
SHAKESPEARE: *Troilus and Cressida*, I, *c.* 1601

Let's meet and either do or die.
JOHN FLETCHER: *The Island Princess*, II, 1621

A man must do as he can when he cannot as he would.
THOMAS DRAXE: *Bibliotheca scholastica instructissima*, 1633

What we do, let's do suddenly.
THOMAS HEYWOOD: *The Wise-Woman of Hogsden*, I, 1638

Say well and do well end with one letter;
Say well is good, but do well is better.
JOHN CLARKE: *Parœmiologia Anglo-Latina*, 1639

In doing we learn.
GEORGE HERBERT: *Outlandish Proverbs*, 1640 (More often: "We learn by doing")

The shortest answer is doing.
GEORGE HERBERT: *Jacula Prudentum*, 1651

All may do what has by man been done.
EDWARD YOUNG: *Night Thoughts*, VI, 1744

What can be done will be done. (Was gemacht werden kann, wird gemacht.)
GERMAN PROVERB, traced by Büchmann to 1811 and probably much older

Let us then be up and doing.
H. W. LONGFELLOW: *A Psalm of Life*, 1839

Theirs not to make reply,
Theirs not to reason why,
Theirs but to do or die.
ALFRED TENNYSON: *The Charge of the Light Brigade*, 1854

It is not book-learning young men need, nor instruction about this and that, but a stiffening of the vertebrae which will cause them to be loyal to a trust, to act promptly, concentrate their energies, do a thing — carry a message to Garcia.

ELBERT HUBBARD: *A Message to Garcia,* 1900

What you can't do in one day you must do in two. EAST ANGLIAN PROVERB

One can only do by doing. (On ne peut faire qu'en faisant.) FRENCH PROVERB

From saying to doing is a long step.

ITALIAN PROVERB

More trouble is caused by doing nothing than by doing too much. IBID.

Do it, and then make an excuse. (Fac et excusa.) LATIN PROVERB

Let the doer beware. (Caveat actor.) IBID.

Better do it than wish it done.

SCOTTISH PROVERB

[*See also* Achievement, Action, Done, Intention.

Dollar

The almighty dollar.

WASHINGTON IRVING: *The Creole Village,* 1836 (The New Yorker, Nov. 12)

A dollar goes on increasing in value with all the genius, and all the virtue of the world. A dollar in a university is worth more than a dollar in a jail.

R. W. EMERSON: *The Conduct of Life,* III, 1860

Each dollar is a soldier that does your bidding.

Ascribed to VINCENT ASTOR by HARVEY O'CONNOR: *The Astors,* IV, 1941

[*See also* Credit, Currency, Done, Money.

Domestication

[*See* Civilization.

Domesticity

[*See* Home.

Dominican

[*See* Friar.

Done

That char is charred, as the goodwife said when she had hanged her husband (or, as the boy said when he killed his father).

ENGLISH SAYING, current in various forms since the XV century (*Char*=job)

That is sooner said than done.

JOHN HEYWOOD: *Proverbs,* 1546

What's done can't be undone.

SHAKESPEARE: *Macbeth,* V, *c.* 1605

Well done, soon done.

DAVID FERGUSSON: *Scottish Proverbs,* 1641

And now the matchless deed's achiev'd,
Determined, dared, and done.

CHRISTOPHER SMART: *A Song to David,* 1763

All is over but the charges of fraud.

AMERICAN SAYING

All is over but the shouting. IBID.

[*See also* Doing.

Donkey

There's another thing that no man never see, and that's a dead donkey.

CHARLES DICKENS: *The Pickwick Papers,* LI, 1837

[*See also* Ass, Irishman, Monk.

Donne, John (1572–1631)

He was an orthodox Christian only because he could have been an infidel more easily; and therefore willed to be a Christian.

S. T. COLERIDGE: *Donne,* 1818

Doomsday

Everyone's death day is his Doomsday.

JOHN LYLY: *Euphues,* 1579

A thousand pounds and a bottle of hay
Is all one thing at Doomsday.

JOHN RAY: *English Proverbs,* 1670 (*Bottle*=bundle)

No man has learned anything rightly, until he knows that every day is Doomsday.

R. W. EMERSON: *Society and Solitude,* 1870

[*See also* Judgment Day.

Door

Here is the door, and there is the way.

Anon.: *Mankind, c.* 1483

There lies your way: you see the door.

BEN JONSON: *The Staple of News,* III, 1625

Doorkeeper

At the door of the monastery shall be placed a man of age and wisdom who shall know how to receive a reply and how to return one, and whose ripeness of years will not permit him to trifle. When any one knocks he shall answer "Thanks be to God!" and give a blessing.

THE RULE OF ST. BENEDICT, *c.* 529

Double-faced

May the man be damned and never grow fat
Who wears two faces under one hat.

ENGLISH RHYME

Doubt

He that doubteth is damned.

ROMANS XIV, 23, *c.* 55

O thou of little faith, wherefore didst thou doubt? MATTHEW XIV, 31, *c.* 75

[Thomas] said unto them, Except I shall see in his hands the print of the nails, and put my finger into the print of the nails, and thrust my hand into his side, I will not believe.

JOHN XX, 25, *c.* 115 (The origin of "doubting Thomas")

When men are in doubt they always believe what is most agreeable.

FLAVIUS ARRIANUS: *The Anabasis of Alexander the Great, c.* 150

Modest doubt is call'd
The beacon of the wise.

SHAKESPEARE: *Troilus and Cressida,* II, *c.* 1601

Our doubts are traitors,
And make us lose the good we oft might win,
By fearing to attempt.

SHAKESPEARE: *Measure for Measure,* I, 1604

I am cabin'd, cribb'd, confin'd, bound in
To saucy doubts and fears.

SHAKESPEARE: *Macbeth,* III, *c.* 1605

He that knows nothing doubts nothing.

GEORGE HERBERT: *Outlandish Proverbs,* 1640

Uncertain ways unsafest are,
And doubt a greater mischief than despair.

JOHN DENHAM: *Cooper's Hill,* 1642

If you would be a real seeker after truth, it is necessary that at least once in your life you doubt, as far as possible, all things.

RENÉ DESCARTES: *Principles of Philosophy,* I, 1644

Doubts are more cruel than the worst of truths.

J. B. MOLIÈRE: *Le misanthrope,* II, 1666

Seeking to know is only too often learning to doubt.

ANTOINETTE DESHOULIÈRES: *Réflexion sur le jeu, c.* 1675

You'll not believe him bald till you see his brains.

THOMAS FULLER: *Gnomologia,* 1732

I learn more from your doubts than from all that the divine Aristotle, the wise Plato, and the incomparable Descartes have affirmed so lightly.

FREDERICK THE GREAT: *Letter to Voltaire,* Sept. 21, 1737

To believe with certainty we must begin with doubting.

STANISLAUS LESZCZYNSKI (KING OF POLAND): *Œuvres du philosophe bienfaisant,* 1763

Melt and dispel, ye spectre-doubts, that roll
Cimmerian darkness o'er the parting soul!

THOMAS CAMPBELL: *The Pleasures of Hope,* II, 1799

Doubt everything at least once — even the proposition that two and two are four.

G. C. LICHTENBERG: *Reflections,* 1799

He who shall teach the child to doubt
The rotting grave shall ne'er get out.
He who respects the infant's faith
Triumphs over Hell and death.

WILLIAM BLAKE: *Auguries of Innocence, c.* 1802

The testimony of those who doubt the least is not unusually that very testimony that ought most to be doubted.

C. C. COLTON: *Lacon,* 1820

I've stood upon Achilles' tomb,
And heard Troy doubted: time will doubt of Rome.

BYRON: *Don Juan,* IV, 1821

He who dallies is a dastard; he who doubts is damned.

Ascribed to GEORGE MCDUFFIE of South Carolina (1790–1851), in the House of Representatives, *c.* 1830 (Cf. ROMANS, *ante, c.* 55)

Happy are those who have no doubt of themselves.

GUSTAVE FLAUBERT: *Letter to Louise Colet,* 1845

There lives more faith in honest doubt,
Believe me, than in half the creeds.

ALFRED TENNYSON: *In Memoriam,* XCVI, 1850

I am the doubter and the doubt,
And I the hymn the Brahmin sings.

R. W. EMERSON: *Brahma,* 1857 (Atlantic Monthly, Nov.)

"I doubt it," said the carpenter,
"And shed a bitter tear."

C. L. DODGSON (LEWIS CARROLL): *Through the Looking-Glass,* 1871

What a state of society is this in which freethinker is a term of abuse, and in which doubt is regarded as a sin!

W. WINWOOD READE: *The Martyrdom of Man,* III, 1872

Of that there is no manner of doubt —
No probable, possible shadow of doubt —
No possible doubt whatever.

W. S. GILBERT: *The Gondoliers,* I, 1889

I respect faith, but doubt is what gets you an education.

WILSON MIZNER (1876–1933)

Some say she do, and some say she don't.

AMERICAN NEGRO SAYING

If the sun and the moon should doubt
They'd immediately go out.

Author unidentified

He who knows the most believes the least.

ITALIAN PROVERB

When in danger or in doubt
Run in circles, yell and shout.

NAVAL ACADEMY COUPLET

Doubt is the key to knowledge.
PERSIAN PROVERB

Among the safe courses, the safest of all is to doubt. SPANISH PROVERB

[*See also* Belief, Believer, Credulity, Faith, Gold, Jealousy, Skeptic, Skepticism.

Douglas, Stephen A. (1813–61)

At the House, Douglas of Illinois . . . had taken the floor. . . . His face was convulsed, his gesticulation frantic, and he lashed himself into such a heat that if his body had been made of combustible matter it would have been burnt out. In the midst of his roaring, to save himself from choking, he stripped and cast away his cravat, unbuttoned his waistcoat, and had the air and aspect of a half-naked pugilist.
JOHN QUINCY ADAMS: *Diary*, Feb. 14, 1844

Dove

Oh that I had wings like a dove! for then would I fly away, and be at rest.
PSALMS LV, 6, *c.* 150 B.C.

In constancy and nuptial love
I learn my duty from the dove.
JOHN GAY: *Fables*, intro., 1727

[*See also* Alliteration, Eagle, Voice.

Down

He that is down can fall no lower.
SAMUEL BUTLER: *Hudibras*, I, 1663

He that's down, down with him.
JOHN RAY: *English Proverbs*, 1670

The tree is no sooner down but every one runs for his hatchet.
THOMAS FULLER: *Gnomologia*, 1732

Lord, I been down so long,
Down don't worry me.
American Negro song, quoted by HOWARD W. ODUM: *Wings On My Feet*, V, 1929

Kick him again; he's down.
AMERICAN PROVERB

[*See also* Fall.

Downfall

From morn
To noon he fell, from noon to dewy eve,
A Summer's day; and with the setting sun
Dropt from the zenith like a falling star.
JOHN MILTON: *Paradise Lost*, I, 1667

Downhill

It is easy to bowl downhill.
JOHN CLARKE: *Parœmiologia Anglo-Latina*, 1639

Going downhill no one is old.
JAPANESE PROVERB

Dowry

Why, give him gold enough and marry him to a puppet, or an aglet-baby; or an old trot with ne'er a tooth in her head, though she have as many diseases as two and fifty horses! why, nothing comes amiss, so money comes withal.
SHAKESPEARE: *The Taming of the Shrew*, I, 1594

Gi'e me a lass with a lump of land,
And we for life shall hang togither;
Tho' daft or wise I'll never demand,
Or black or fair it maks na whether.
ALLAN RAMSAY: *Give Me a Lass*, 1728

A fair wife without a fortune is a fine house without furniture.
THOMAS FULLER: *Gnomologia*, 1732

Bring something, lass, along with thee,
If thou intend to live with me. IBID.

The dowry goes with the wind, and the ugliness stays with the wife. IRISH PROVERB

The virtue of the parents is the best dowry.
LATIN PROVERB

Better a tocher in her than wi' her.
SCOTTISH PROVERB (*Tocher*=dowry)

A great dowry is a bed full of brambles.
SPANISH PROVERB

[*See also* Bride.

Doxology

Praise God from whom all blessings flow;
Praise Him, all creatures here below;
Praise him above, ye heavenly host;
Praise Father, Son and Holy Ghost.
THOMAS KEN: *Evening Hymn*, *c.* 1690

Praise John from whom oil blessings flow;
Praise him, oil creatures here below;
Praise him above, ye heavenly host;
Praise Archbold too, but John the most.
Anon.: Sung by students of the University of Chicago on its reopening as a result of benefactions by John D. Rockefeller and John D. Archbold, 1892

Draft

He who sits with his back to a draft sits with his face to a coffin. SPANISH PROVERB

Dragon

The dragon stood before the woman which was ready to be delivered, for to devour her child as soon as it was born.
REVELATION XII, 4, *c.* 95

Drama

The drama's laws the drama's patrons give.
For we that live to please must please to live.
SAMUEL JOHNSON: Prologue written for the opening of Drury Lane Theatre, 1747

Through all the drama — whether damn'd or not —
Love gilds the scene, and women guide the plot.

R. B. SHERIDAN: *The Rivals,* epilogue, 1775

All the greatest masterpieces of the dramatic art have been composed in direct violation of the unities, and could never have been composed if the unities had not been violated.

T. B. MACAULAY: *Moore's Life of Lord Byron,* 1831 (Edinburgh Review, June)

There can be no great drama without a noble national life, and the commercial spirit of England has killed that.

OSCAR WILDE: *The English Renaissance of Art,* 1882 (Lecture in New York, Jan.)

It is an extremely difficult thing to put on the stage anything which runs contrary to the opinions of a large body of people.

GEORGE BERNARD SHAW: Evidence before the Joint Select Committee on the Stage Plays, July 30, 1909

What makes the difference between the drama and all other kinds of art is that you crowd a mass of people together, not as you would crowd them in the streets, but as you would crowd them in a prison, in such a manner that it is humiliating for anybody present to make any protest.

G. K. CHESTERTON: Evidence before the Joint Select Committee on the Stage Plays, Sept. 24, 1909

The drama, like the symphony, does not teach or prove anything.

J. M. SYNGE (1871–1909)

[*See also* Acting, Actor, Dramatist, Evidence, Fiction, Play (=drama), Theatre.

Dramatist

Hope never tells a more flattering tale than in the ear of a dramatic author.

LE SAGE: *Gil Blas,* XI, 1735

The business of the dramatist is to keep out of sight, and to let nothing appear but his characters. As soon as he attracts notice to his personal feelings, the illusion is broken. The effect is as unpleasant as that which is produced on the stage by the voice of a prompter or the entrance of a scene-shifter.

T. B. MACAULAY: *Milton,* 1825 (Edinburgh Review, Aug.)

Of all imitators, dramatists are the most perverse, the most unconscionable, or the most unconscious, and have been so time out of mind.

E. A. POE: *Marginalia,* 1844–49

The dramatic author is enclosed in a rigid frame. . . . The solitary reader tolerates everything, goes where he is led, even when he is disgusted; but the spectators taken *en masse* are seized with prudishness, with frights, with sensibilities of which the author must take notice under pain of a certain failure.

ÉMILE ZOLA: *Mes haines,* 1866

The dramatic author has to paint his beaches with real sand: real live men and women move about the stage; we hear real voices; what is feigned merely puts a sense upon what is; we do actually see a woman go behind a screen as Lady Teazle, and, after a certain interval, we do actually see her very shamefully produced again.

R. L. STEVENSON: *Familiar Studies of Men and Books,* I, 1882

The success may justify the dramatist, but it may not be so easy to justify the success.

Author unidentified

Drawing

A faculty of drawing, like that of playing upon a musical instrument, cannot be acquired but by an infinite number of acts.

JOSHUA REYNOLDS: *Discourses,* II, 1769 (Lecture at the Royal Academy, London, Dec. 11)

Without drawing, I feel myself but half invested with language.

S. T. COLERIDGE: *Notebooks,* 1803

The art of drawing is of more real importance to the human race than that of writing, because people can hardly draw anything without being of some use both to themselves and others, and can hardly write anything without wasting their own time and that of others.

JOHN RUSKIN: *Modern Painters,* IV, 1856

Writing is a form of drawing, therefore if you give the same attention and trouble to drawing as you do to writing, depend on it, there is nobody who cannot be made to draw.

T. H. HUXLEY: Address at Liverpool, 1882

[*See also* Painter.

Dread

[*See* Fear.

Dream

Dreams are made up mainly of matters that have been in the dreamer's thoughts during the day.

HERODOTUS: *Histories,* VII, *c.* 430 B.C.

Your old men shall dream dreams, your young men shall see visions.

JOEL II, 28, *c.* 350 B.C.

In sleep every dog dreams of food, and I, a fisherman, dream of fish.

THEOCRITUS: *Idylls,* XXI, *c.* 270 B.C.

Dreams lift up fools.

ECCLESIASTICUS XXXIV, 1, *c.* 180 B.C.

After midnight dreams are true.

HORACE: *Satires,* I, *c.* 25 B.C.

Dreams go by contraries.
ENGLISH PROVERB, traced by Smith to *c.* 1400

We see sleeping what we wish for waking.
GEORGE PETTIE: *Petite Palace of Pettie His Pleasure,* 1576

Dreams are the true interpreters of our inclinations; but there is art required to sort and understand them.
MICHEL DE MONTAIGNE: *Essays,* III, 1588

Oh! I have pass'd a miserable night,
So full of ugly sights, of ghastly dreams,
That, as I am a Christian faithful man,
I would not spend another such a night,
Though 'twere to buy a world of happy days.
SHAKESPEARE: *Richard III,* I, *c.* 1592

I have had a dream, past the wit of man to say what dream it was.
SHAKESPEARE: *A Midsummer Night's Dream,* IV, *c.* 1596

Dreams are the children of an idle brain,
Begot of nothing but vain fantasy,
Which is as thin of substance as the air
And more inconstant than the wind.
SHAKESPEARE: *Romeo and Juliet,* I, *c.* 1596

A dream itself is but a shadow.
SHAKESPEARE: *Hamlet,* II, *c.* 1601

We are such stuff
As dreams are made on, and our little life
Is rounded with a sleep.
SHAKESPEARE: *The Tempest,* IV, 1611

After a dream of weddings comes a corpse.
JOHN CLARKE: *Parœmiologia Anglo-Latina,* 1639

Here we are all, by day; by night we're hurled
By dreams, each one, into a sev'ral world.
ROBERT HERRICK: *Hesperides,* 1648

Old men commonly dream oftener, and have their dreams more painful, than young.
THOMAS HOBBES: *Human Nature,* III, 1651

That man was prettily and fantastically troubled, who, having used to put his trust in dreams, one night dreamed that all dreams were vain; for he considered, if so, then this was vain, and the dreams might be true for all this. But if they might be true, then this dream might be so upon equal reason. And then dreams were vain, because this dream, which told him so, was true; and so round again.
JEREMY TAYLOR: *The Deceitfulness of the Heart,* 1653

At break of day dreams, they say, are true.
JOHN DRYDEN: *The Spanish Friar,* III, 1681

Dreams and prophecies make a man go on with boldness and courage upon a danger or a mistress; if he obtains, he attributes much to them; if he miscarries, he thinks no more of them, or is no more thought of himself.
JOHN SELDEN: *Table-Talk,* 1689

All dreams, as in old Galen I have read,
Are from repletion and complexion bred,
From rising fumes of indigested food,
And noxious humors that infect the blood.
JOHN DRYDEN: *Fables Ancient and Modern,* 1699

A change came o'er the spirit of my dream.
BYRON: *The Dream,* 1816

She had dreams all yesternight
Of her own betrothed knight —
Dreams that made her moan and leap
As on her bed she lay in sleep.
S. T. COLERIDGE: *Christabel,* I, 1816

I arise from dreams of thee
In the first sweet sleep of night,
When the winds are breathing low,
And the stars are shining bright.
P. B. SHELLEY: *The Indian Serenade,* 1822

We sometimes from dreams pick up some hint worth improving by . . . reflection.
THOMAS JEFFERSON: *Letter to James Monroe,* 1823

If there were dreams to sell
What would you buy?
T. L. BEDDOES: *Dream-Pedlary, c.* 1830

I dreamt that I dwelt in marble halls,
With vassals and serfs at my side.
ALFRED BUNN: *The Bohemian Girl,* I, 1843

Is the goal so far away?
Far, how far no tongue can say,
Let us dream our dream to-day.
ALFRED TENNYSON: *Ode Sung at the Opening of the International Exhibition, London,* 1862

Dear Lord, please send us blessed dreams,
And let them all come true.
ELIZABETH CHASE (AKERS ALLEN): *Blessed Dreams,* 1866

Dreams are excursions to the limbo of things, a semi-deliverance from the human prison.
H. F. AMIEL: *Journal,* Nov. 8, 1872

Dreams retain the infirmities of our character. The good genius may be there or not; our evil genius is sure to stay.
R. W. EMERSON: *Demonology,* 1877

Men never cling to their dreams with such tenacity as at the moment when they are losing faith in them, and know it, but do not dare yet to confess it to themselves.
W. G. SUMNER: *The Banquet of Life,* 1887

In a dream one gets what one covets awake.
GERMAN PROVERB

Dreams are a sixtieth part of prophecy.
HEBREW PROVERB

[*See also* Dreamer, Fox, Funeral, Hope, Midsummer, Supper, Vision.

Dreamer

Oh! that we two sat dreaming
On the sward of some sheep-trimmed down
Watching the white mist steaming
Over river and mead and town.

CHARLES KINGSLEY: *The Saint's Tragedy*, II, 1848

The fisher droppeth his net in the stream,
And a hundred streams are the same as one;
And the maiden dreameth her love-lit dream;
And what is it all, when all is done?
The net of the fisher the burden breaks,
And always from dreaming the dreamer wakes.

ALICE CARY: *The Lover's Diary*, 1867

Let me dream as of old by the river,
And be loved by the dream alway;
For a dreamer lives forever,
And a toiler dies in a day.

JOHN BOYLE O'REILLY: *The Cry of the Dreamer*, 1873

We are the music makers,
We are the dreamers of dreams,
Wandering by lone sea-breakers,
And sitting by desolate streams —
World-losers and world-forsakers,
On whom the pale moon gleams.

ARTHUR O'SHAUGHNESSY: *Ode*, 1874

A dreamer is one who can only find his way by moonlight, and his punishment is that he sees the dawn before the rest of the world.

OSCAR WILDE: *The Critic as Artist*, 1891

Dress

The woman shall not wear that which pertaineth unto a man, neither shall a man put on a woman's garment: for all that do so are abomination unto the Lord thy God.

DEUTERONOMY XXII, 5, *c.* 650 B.C.

The desire to please by outward charms, which we know naturally invite lust, does not spring from a sound conscience. Why should you rouse an evil passion?

TERTULLIAN: *Women's Dress, c.* 220

There goes but a pair of shears betwixt an emperor and the son of a bagpiper: only the dyeing, dressing, pressing, glossing, makes the difference.

JOHN MARSTON: *The Malcontent*, IV, 1604

She steals and robs each part o' th' world
With borrowed beauties to inflame thine eye;
The sea to fetch her pearl is dived into,
The diamond rocks are cut to make her shine,
To plume her pride the birds do naked sing.

Anon.: *Nero*, I, 1624

Fine dressing is a foul house swept before the door.

GEORGE HERBERT: *Outlandish Proverbs*, 1640

A sweet disorder in the dress
Kindles in clothes a wantonness.

ROBERT HERRICK: *Hesperides*, 1648

A studious gallantry in clothes cannot make a wise man love his wife the better. Such gayeties are fit for tragedies, but not for the uses of life.

JEREMY TAYLOR: *The Mysteriousness of Marriage*, 1651

Ever be modest in thy apparel, rather seeking to accommodate nature than curious by art to procure admiration: clothes may give thee ornament, but the judicious will never seek thy perfection on thy outside, and I'm sure if decency be the only aim thou wilt be sure to shoulder off the censure of a phantastic.

FRANCIS HAWKINS: *Youth's Behavior*, IV, 1663

Singularity in dress is ridiculous; in fact, it is generally looked upon as a proof that the mind is somewhat deranged. The fashion of the country wherein one lives is the rule which should be followed in the choice and form of dress.

ST. JOHN BAPTIST DE LA SALLE: *The Rules of Christian Manners and Civility*, II, 1695

I have always a sacred veneration for anyone I observe to be a little out of repair in his person, as supposing him either a poet or a philosopher.

JONATHAN SWIFT: *A Letter of Advice to a Young Poet*, Dec. 1, 1720

Without black velvet breeches, what is man?

JAMES BRAMSTON: *Men of Taste, c.* 1730

It is not the cowl that makes the friar.

THOMAS FULLER: *Gnomologia*, 1732

It is not the fine coat that makes the fine gentleman.

IBID.

Eat to please thyself, but dress to please others.

BENJAMIN FRANKLIN: *Poor Richard's Almanac*, 1738

Take great care always to be dressed like the reasonable people of your own age, in the place where you are; whose dress is never spoken of one way or another, as either too negligent or too much studied.

LORD CHESTERFIELD: *Letter to his son*, Oct. 9, 1746

In dress one should always keep below one's means.

C. L. DE MONTESQUIEU: *Pensées, c.* 1750

All such dresses are forbidden which incite irregular desires.

THOMAS WILSON: *Maxims of Piety and of Christianity, c.* 1755

I cannot see why a person should be esteemed haughty on account of his taste for fine clothes, any more than one who discovers a fondness for birds, flowers, moths or butterflies.

WILLIAM SHENSTONE: *On Dress*, 1764

Taste in dress is certainly one of the lowest subjects to which this word is applied; yet

there is a right even here, however narrow its foundation, respecting the fashion of any particular nation.
JOSHUA REYNOLDS: *Discourses*, VII, 1774 (Lecture at the Royal Academy, London, Dec. 10, 1776)

Some ladies think they may, under the privileges of the *déshabillé*, be loose and negligent of their dress in the morning. But be you, from the moment you rise till you go to bed, as cleanly and properly dressed as at the hours of dinner or tea.
THOMAS JEFFERSON: *Letter to Martha Jefferson*, 1783

Dress drains our cellar dry,
And keeps our larder lean; puts out our fires
And introduces hunger, frost, and woe,
Where peace and hospitality might reign.
WILLIAM COWPER: *The Task*, II, 1785

Immense sums are continually wasted by almost all classes of both sexes, in superfluities of dress. Two thirds of the expense of hats might be saved if they were manufactured with a view to utility and durability, instead of fashion and fancy.
JESSE TORREY: *The Moral Instructor*, 1819

It is not every man that can afford to wear a shabby coat; worldly wisdom dictates to her disciples the propriety of dressing somewhat beyond their means, but of living within them; for every one sees how we dress, but none see how we live, except we choose to let them. C. C. COLTON: *Lacon*, 1820

Poets, artists, and men of genius in general are seldom coxcombs, but often slovens; for they find something out of themselves better worth studying than their own persons.
WILLIAM HAZLITT: *The Plain Speaker*, I, 1826

Let your dress be as cheap as may be without shabbiness; think more about the color of your shirt than about the gloss or texture of your coat; be always as clean as your occupation will, without inconvenience, permit.
WILLIAM COBBETT: *Advice to Young Men*, I, 1829

In all my journeys through the country, the only well-dressed men that I saw were the Western miners. Their wide-brimmed hats, which shaded their faces from the sun and protected them from the rain, and the cloak, which is by far the most beautiful piece of drapery ever invented, may well be dwelt on with admiration. Their high boots, too, were sensible and practical. They wore only what was comfortable, and therefore beautiful.
OSCAR WILDE: *House Decoration*, 1882 (Lecture in New York, May 11)

Has a woman who knew that she was well-dressed ever caught a cold?
F. W. NIETZSCHE: *The Twilight of the Idols*, 1889

Woman's first duty in life is to her dressmaker. What the second duty is no one has yet discovered.
OSCAR WILDE: *An Ideal Husband*, III, 1895

Little girl, you look so small;
Don't you wear no clothes at all?
Don't you wear no chemise shirt?
Don't you wear no petty-skirt?
Don't you wear no underclothes
But your corset and your hose?
W. A. SUNDAY: *Sermon*, c. 1912

Eat what you will, but dress as others do.
ARAB PROVERB

A really rich man is careless of his dress.
CHINESE PROVERB

Three-tenths of a woman's good looks are due to nature, seven-tenths to dress. IBID.

Dress slowly when you are in a hurry.
FRENCH PROVERB

Always be well dressed, even when begging.
HINDU PROVERB

An ape's an ape, a varlet's a varlet,
Though they be clad in silk and scarlet.
OLD ENGLISH RHYME

A stick dressed up doesn't look like a stick.
SPANISH PROVERB

[*See also* Adornment, Affectation, Apparel, Appearance, Children, Clothes, Deference, Déshabillé, Finery, Maiden, Ornament, Sloven, Thirty.

Drink

The priest and the prophet have erred through strong drink, they are swallowed up of wine, they are out of the way through strong drink; they err in vision, they stumble in judgment. ISAIAH XXVIII, 7, c. 700 B.C.

Give strong drink unto him that is ready to perish, and wine unto those that be of heavy hearts. PROVERBS XXXI, 6, c. 350 B.C.

I care right nought, I take no thought
For clothes to keep me warm;
Have I good drink, I surely think
Nothing can do me harm.
Anon.: *A Song of Ale*, c. 1500

O God, that men should put an enemy in their mouths to steal away their brains!
SHAKESPEARE: *Othello*, II, 1604

The wild anarchy of drink.
BEN JONSON: *Underwoods*, 1640

Better belly burst than good drink lost.
JOHN RAY: *English Proverbs*, 1670 (Or *good meat*)

Bacchus hath drowned more men than Neptune.
THOMAS FULLER: *Gnomologia*, 1732

In cold countries the aqueous part of the blood is exhaled only slightly by perspiration; it remains in great abundance. One can therefore use alcoholic liquors without danger of the blood coagulating.

C. L. DE MONTESQUIEU: *The Spirit of the Laws,* XIV, 1748

Drink does not drown care, but waters it, and makes it grow faster.

BENJAMIN FRANKLIN: *Poor Richard's Almanac,* 1749

Fermented spirits please our common people because they banish care and all consideration of future or present evils.

EDMUND BURKE: *The Sublime and Beautiful,* intro., 1756

A bumper of good liquor
Will end a contest quicker
Than justice, judge or vicar.

R. B. SHERIDAN: *The Duenna,* II, 1775

Inspiring bold John Barleycorn!
What dangers thou canst make us scorn!

ROBERT BURNS: *Tam o' Shanter,* 1790

Tell me I hate the bowl —
Hate is a feeble word:
I loathe, abhor — my very soul
With strong disgust is stirred
When'er I see, or hear, or tell
Of the dark beverage of Hell!

Anon.: *The Drunkard's Daughter, c.* 1850

Drink washes off the daub, and discovers the man.

H. G. BOHN: *Handbook of Proverbs,* 1855

Punches and juleps, cobblers and smashes,
To make the tongue waggle with wit's merry flashes.

HARRY HILL: Legend over the door of his "club house" in Houston street, New York, *c.* 1867

When drink's in, wit's out.

SCOTTISH PROVERB

[*See also* Ale, Beer, Brandy, Champagne, Cider, Drinker, Drinking, Drunk, Katzenjammer, Whiskey, Wine.

Drinker

Cobblers and tinkers are the best ale drinkers.

JOHN RAY: *English Proverbs,* 1670

He has a hole under his nose that all his money runs into.

THOMAS FULLER: *Gnomologia,* 1732

I'm the very infant that refused its milk before its eyes were open, and called out for a bottle of old rye. W-h-o-o-p! I'm that little cupid!

MORGAN NEVILLE: *The Last of the Boatmen,* 1829

"Cold water is the best of drinks,"
Let temperance poets sing.
But who am I that I should have
The best of everything?
Let poets revel at the pump
And peers debauch on tea;
But whiskey, beer, or even wine
Is good enough for me.

Author unidentified

I drink; therefore I am. (Bibo, ergo sum.)

IBID.

Master of the drinkers. (Arbiter bibendi.)

LATIN PHRASE

He who goes to bed, and goes to bed sober,
Falls as the leaves do, and dies in October;
But he who goes to bed, and goes to bed mellow,
Lives as he ought to do, and dies an honest fellow.

OLD ENGLISH RHYME

He speaks in his drink what he thinks in his drouth.

SCOTTISH PROVERB

Under a tattered cloak you will generally find a good drinker.

SPANISH PROVERB

[*See also* Drunk, Drunkard, Lips.

Drinking

Do not drink wine nor strong drink, thou, nor thy sons with thee, when ye go into the tabernacle of the congregation, lest ye die.

LEVITICUS X, 9, *c.* 700 B.C.

Come ye, say they, I will fetch wine, and we will fill ourselves with strong drink; and tomorrow shall be as this day, and much more abundant.

ISAIAH LVI, 12, *c.* 700 B.C.

They shall drink, and make a noise as through wine.

ZECHARIAH IX, 15, *c.* 520 B.C.

The man who is master of himself drinks gravely and wisely.

CONFUCIUS: *The Book of Poetry, c.* 500 B.C.

Let him drink, and forget his poverty, and remember his misery no more.

PROVERBS XXXI, 7, *c.* 350 B.C.

Drink and be merry, for our time on earth is short, and death lasts forever.

AMPHIS: *Fragment, c.* 330 B.C.

It is meet before we partake of food to bless the Maker of all things, and to sing when we drink.

CLEMENT OF ALEXANDRIA: *Paedagogus, c.* 190

Whoever gulps down wine as a horse gulps down water is called a Scythian.

ATHENAEUS: *Deipnosophistae, c.* 230 (*Scythians*=a barbarous people inhabiting the plains to the northeast of Greece)

So was their jolly whistle well y-wet.

GEOFFREY CHAUCER: *The Canterbury Tales* (The Reeve's Tale), *c.* 1386

I do not drink more than a sponge.
RABELAIS: *Gargantua*, I, 1535

I wet, I humect, I moisten my gullet, I drink, and all for fear of dying. Drink always, and you shall never die. IBID.

Long quaffing maketh a short life.
JOHN LYLY: *Euphues*, 1579

Drink down all unkindness.
SHAKESPEARE: *The Merry Wives of Windsor*, I, *c.* 1600

Toss the pot, toss the pot; let us be merry,
And drink till our cheeks be as red as a cherry.
Anon.: *Toss the Pot*, *c.* 1600

I have very poor and unhappy brains for drinking; I could wish courtesy would invent some other custom of entertainment.
SHAKESPEARE: *Othello*, II, 1604

We did sleep day out of countenance, and make the night light with drinking.
SHAKESPEARE: *Antony and Cleopatra*, II, 1606

I told you, sir, they were red-hot with drinking;
So full of valor that they smote the air
For breathing in their faces; beat the ground
For kissing of their feet.
SHAKESPEARE: *The Tempest*, IV, 1611

I drink when I have occasion for it, and sometimes when I have not.
CERVANTES: *Don Quixote*, II, 1615

Come landlord, fill a flowing bowl until it does run over,
Tonight we will all merry be — tomorrow we'll get sober.
JOHN FLETCHER and BEN JONSON: *The Bloody Brother*, II, *c.* 1616

Drink today, and drown all sorrow;
You shall perhaps not do it tomorrow;
Best, while you have it, use your breath;
There is no drinking after death. IBID.

Drink to me only with thine eyes,
And I will pledge with mine;
Or leave a kiss but in the cup,
And I'll not look for wine.
BEN JONSON: *To Celia*, 1616

Drinking will make a man quaff,
Quaffing will make a man sing,
Singing will make a man laugh,
And laughing long life doth bring.
Anon.: *Old Sir Simon the King*, *c.* 1620

Drink not the third glass.
GEORGE HERBERT: *The Temple*, 1633

Let's warm our brains with half a dozen healths,
And then hang cold discourse, for we'll speak fireworks.
JOHN FLETCHER: *The Elder Brother*, I, 1637

That I call immoderation that is beside or beyond that order of good things for which God hath given us the use of drink.
JEREMY TAYLOR: *The Rule and Exercises of Holy Living*, 1650

Nothing in Nature's sober found,
But an eternal health goes round.
Fill up the bowl then, fill it high,
Find all the glasses there, for why
Should every creature drink but I,
Why, man of morals, tell me why?
ABRAHAM COWLEY: *Anacreontiques*, 1656

Drink not with meat in thy mouth; call not for drink then, speak not then; fill not thy glass to drink, and drink not while thy next companion drinketh, or he who sitteth at the upper end of the table.
FRANCIS HAWKINS: *Youth's Behavior*, VII, 1663

A night of good drinking
Is worth a year's thinking.
CHARLES COTTON: *Chanson à Boire*, *c.* 1665

You must drink as much after an egg as after an ox. JOHN RAY: *English Proverbs*, 1670

He that dares drink, and for that drink dares die,
And, knowing this, dares yet drink on, am I.
GEORGE VILLIERS (DUKE OF BUCKINGHAM): *The Rehearsal*, IV, 1671

Drinking with women is as unnatural as scolding with 'em.
WILLIAM WYCHERLEY: *The Country Wife*, II, *c.* 1673

Make me a bowl, a mighty bowl,
Large as my capacious soul,
Vast as my thirst is; let it have
Depth enough to be my grave.
JOHN OLDHAM: *Satire Against Virtue*, 1681

He that drinks well, does sleep well; he that sleeps well, doth think well;
He that drinks well, doth do well; he that does well, must drink well.
Anon.: *The Loyal Garland*, 1686

Bacchus' blessings are a treasure,
Drinking is the soldier's pleasure.
JOHN DRYDEN: *Alexander's Feast*, I, 1697

To drink is a Christian diversion,
Unknown to the Turk or the Persian.
WILLIAM CONGREVE: *The Way of the World*, IV, 1700

An Englishman will fairly drink as much
As will maintain two families of Dutch.
DANIEL DEFOE: *The True-Born Englishman*, II, 1701

I believe more people break their brains by drinking than study: for tho' the latter may be troublesome enough, yet a book is not so hard as a bottle.
BERNARD DE MANDEVILLE: *A Dissertation Upon Drunkenness*, 1708

Money we want, and cannot borrow;
Yet drink we must, to slacken sorrow.
THOMAS FULLER: *Gnomologia*, 1732

When an old man will not drink, you may safely promise him a visit in the next world.
IBID.

He that drinks fast, pays slow.
BENJAMIN FRANKLIN: *Poor Richard's Almanac*, 1733

The feast of reason and the flow of soul.
ALEXANDER POPE: *The First Satire of the Second Book of Horace*, 1733

Then toss off your glasses, and scorn the dull asses
Who, missing the kernel, still gnaw the shell;
What's love, rule or riches? Wise Solomon teaches
They're vanity, vanity, vanity still.
Cho. Friends and a bottle still bear the bell.
BENJAMIN FRANKLIN: *Drinking Song*, *c.* 1740 (In a letter to the Abbé de La Roche, giving the text and probably written in 1779, he says that he wrote the song "forty years ago")

I always naturally hated drinking; and yet I have often drunk, with disgust at the time, attended by great sickness the next day, only because I then considered drinking as a necessary qualification for a fine gentleman, and a man of pleasure.
LORD CHESTERFIELD: *Letter to his son*, March 27, 1747

When Methodist preachers come down
A-preaching that drinking is sinful,
I'll wager the rascals a crown
They always preach best with a skinful.
OLIVER GOLDSMITH: *She Stoops to Conquer*, II, 1773

Count all the trees that crown Jamaica's hills,
Count all the stars that through the heavens you see,
Count every drop that the wide ocean fills;
Then count the pleasures Bacchus yields to me.
PHILIP FRENEAU: *The Jamaica Funeral*, 1776

A man who has been drinking wine at all freely should never go into a new company. With those who have partaken of wine with him he may be pretty well in unison, but he will probably be offensive, or appear ridiculous, to other people.
SAMUEL JOHNSON: *Boswell's Life*, March 16, 1776

Then trust me there's nothing like drinking,
So pleasant on this side the grave:
It keeps the unhappy from thinking,
And makes e'en the valiant more brave.
CHARLES DIBDIN: *Nothing Like Grog*, *c.* 1780

When neebors angry at a plea,
And just as wud as wud can be,
How easy can the barley-bree
Cement the quarrel!
It's aye the cheapest lawyer's fee
To taste the barrel.
ROBERT BURNS: *Scotch Drink*, 1785 (*Wud*=angry)

Therefore drink! (Ergo bibamus!)
J. W. GOETHE: *Ergo bibamus*, refrain, 1810

He bids the ruddy cup go round
Till sense and sorrow both are drowned.
WALTER SCOTT: *Rokeby*, III, 1813

There are two reasons for drinking: one is, when you are thirsty, to cure it; the other, when you are not thirsty, to prevent it.
THOMAS LOVE PEACOCK: *Melincourt*, XVI, 1817

What's drinking?
A mere pause from thinking.
BYRON: *The Deformed Transformed*, III, 1824

Never mix your liquor.
CHARLES DIBDIN: *Ben the Boatswain*, 1830

It's a damn long time between drinks.
EDWARD B. DUDLEY, *Governor of North Carolina:* To Pierce Mason Butler, Governor of South Carolina, 1838. (They are said to have met in the home of Mrs. Nancy Anne Jones, midway between Raleigh and Durham, N. C.)

We've drunk down the sun, boys! let's drink down the moon!
R. H. BARHAM: *The Ingoldsby Legends*, I, 1840

Let us make our glasses kiss;
Let us quench the sorrow-cinders.
R. W. EMERSON: *From the Persian of Hafiz*, 1851

Drink! for you know not whence you came, nor why:
Drink! for you know not why you go, nor where.
EDWARD FITZGERALD: Tr. of OMAR KHAYYÁM: *Rubáiyát* (*c.* 1100), 1857

It's all right to drink like a fish — if you drink what a fish drinks.
MARY PETTIBONE POOLE: *A Glass Eye at the Keyhole*, 1938

There was an old hen
And she had a wooden leg,
And every damned morning
She laid another egg;
She was the best damned chicken
On the whole damned farm —
And another little drink
Wouldn't do us no harm.
AMERICAN FOLKSONG

Drink, drink — brothers, drink! Let sorrow stay at home. (Trink, Trink — Brüderlein trink. Lass' doch die Sorgen zu Haus.)
Anon.: *Brüderlein Trink* (A German students' song of unknown date)

Drink? Die! Drink not? Die anyhow! Therefore, drink! (Saufst? Stirbst! Saufst net? Stirbst 'a! Also, sauf!)

BAVARIAN PROVERB

When the arm bends the mouth opens.

DANISH PROVERB

After all mourning one drinks.

FRENCH PROVERB

Who drinks will drink again. (Qui a bu, boira.)

IBID.

A thousand drink themselves to death before one dies of thirst.
(Es trinken tausend sich den Tod
Ehe einer stirbt vor Durstes Noth.)

GERMAN PROVERB

Drinking a little too much is drinking a great deal too much. IBID.

The Old Germans always drank one more. (Die alten Deutschen tranken immer noch eins.)

GERMAN STUDENTS' SLOGAN

It is a bad man who remembers what went on at a drinking bout. GREEK PROVERB

If the husband drinks, half the house is afire; if the wife drinks, the whole house.

RUSSIAN PROVERB

They that drink langest live langest.

SCOTTISH PROVERB

[*See also* Appetite, Barroom, Bartender, Chastity, Dinner, Drink, Drunk, Drunkard, Drunkenness, Eating and Drinking, Forty, Hygiene, Inn, Katzenjammer, Love, Soldier, Temperance, Thirst, Toast, Wine.

Driving

Like the driving of Jehu, the son of Nimshi: for he driveth furiously.

II KINGS IX, 20, *c.* 500 B.C.

Drought

The hay is withered away, the grass faileth, there is no green thing.

ISAIAH XV, 6, *c.* 700 B.C.

Drowned

Full fathom five thy father lies;
Of his bones are coral made.

SHAKESPEARE: *The Tempest*, I, 1611

Drowning

A drowning man will catch at a straw.

ENGLISH PROVERB, familiar since the XVII century (Sometimes *twig* appears in place of *straw*)

He goes a great voyage that goes to the bottom of the sea.

H. G. BOHN: *Handbook of Proverbs*, 1855

The drowning man will always scream, though there be none to hear him.

ITALIAN PROVERB

[*See also* Hanging, Swimming.

Drudgery

How many a rustic Milton has passed by,
Stifling the speechless longings of his heart,
In unremitting drudgery and care!

P. B. SHELLEY: *Queen Mab*, V, 1813

Drugs

Drugs, cataplasms and whiskey are stupid substitutes for the dignity and potency of divine Mind, and its efficacy to heal.

MARY BAKER G. EDDY: *Science and Health*, VI, 1908

There is only one reason why men become addicted to drugs; they are weak men. Only strong men are cured, and they cure themselves.

MARTIN H. FISCHER (1879–)

[*See also* Medicine, Physician.

Drum

The double double double beat
Of the thundering drum
Cries, Hark! the foes come.

JOHN DRYDEN: *A Song for St. Cecilia's Day*, 1687

The noisy drum hath nothing in it but mere air. THOMAS FULLER: *Gnomologia*, 1732

And grummer, grummer, grummer, rolled the roll of the drummer
Through the morn!

G. H. MCMASTER: *Carmen bellicosum*, 1849

I hear the great drums pounding,
And the small drums steady whirring;
And every blow of the great convulsive drums,
Strikes me through and through.

WALT WHITMAN: *Dirge for Two Veterans*, 1865

Drummer

A drummer is a soldier with a drum.

MR. JUSTICE DENISON: *Judgment in Lloyd vs. Wooddall*, 1748

Drunk

A drunken man staggereth in his vomit.

ISAIAH XIX, 14, *c.* 700 B.C.

They are drunken, but not with wine; they stagger, but not with strong drink.

ISAIAH XXIX, 9

All my bones shake: I am like a drunken man, and like a man whom wine hath overcome.

JEREMIAH XXIII, 9, *c.* 625 B.C.

An old man is twice a child, and so is a drunken man. PLATO: *Laws*, I, *c.* 360 B.C.

He maketh them to stagger like a drunken man.

JOB XII, 25, *c.* 325 B.C.

The drunken man is a living corpse.

ST. JOHN CHRYSOSTOM: *Homilies*, I, *c.* 388

He that killeth a man when he is drunk shall be hanged when he is sober.

JOHN HEYWOOD: *Proverbs*, 1546

That which the sober man keeps in his breast the drunken man lets out at the lips. Astute people, when they want to ascertain a man's true character, make him drunk.
MARTIN LUTHER: *Table-Talk*, DCXCIX, 1569

Drunken men never take harm.
GEORGE CHAPMAN, BEN JONSON and JOHN MARSTON: *Eastward Ho*, III, 1605 (Quoted as a popular saying)

Bacchus had given them such an overthrow
Their bodies lay like slaughtered carcasses.
NATHANIEL FIELD: *A Woman Is a Weathercock*, IV, 1609

He that is drunken may his mother kill,
Big with his sister; he hath lost the reins,
Is outlawed by himself.
GEORGE HERBERT: *The Temple*, 1633

One whom the brewer's horse hath bit.
THOMAS HEYWOOD: *Philocothonista*, 1635

The variety of behavior in men that have drunk too much is the same with that of madmen: some of them being raging, others loving, others laughing, all extravagantly, but according to their several domineering passions.
THOMAS HOBBES: *Leviathan*, VIII, 1651

Then hasten to be drunk, — the business of the day.
JOHN DRYDEN: *Cymon and Iphigenia*, 1699

Today it is our pleasure to be drunk.
HENRY FIELDING: *Tom Thumb*, I, 1730

Who can help sickness, quoth the drunken wife, when she fell into the gutter.
THOMAS FULLER: *Gnomologia*, 1732

Drunk for a penny, dead drunk for tuppence, clean straw for nothing.
Sign on gin-shops in London, *c.* 1750

I write this reeling,
Having got drunk exceedingly today,
So that I seem to stand upon the ceiling.
BYRON: *Don Juan*, I, 1819

Man, being reasonable, must get drunk;
The best of life is but intoxication.
BYRON: *Don Juan*, II

Not drunk is he who from the floor
Can rise alone and still drink more;
But drunk is he who prostrate lies,
Without the power to drink or rise.
THOMAS LOVE PEACOCK: *The Misfortunes of Elphin*, 1829

Drunk, I speak of purity;
Beggar, I of lordship speak.
R. W. EMERSON: *From the Persian of Hafiz*, 1851

It's bad enough to see a man drunk — but a woman!
AMERICAN PROVERB, apparently first recorded by GELETT BURGESS: *Are You a Bromide?* 1907

There comes a night
When we all get tight.
AMERICAN PROVERB

No man is drunk so long as he can lie on the floor without holding on.
Author unidentified

What a man says drunk he has thought sober.
FLEMISH PROVERB

A drunken woman is an open door.
GERMAN PROVERB

When everybody says you are drunk go to bed.
ITALIAN PROVERB

Carefree and drunk. (Securus et ebrius.)
LATIN PHRASE

A drunken man thinks the sea is only knee-deep.
RUSSIAN PROVERB

[*See also* Ale, Chastity, Children, Drink, Drinking, Drunkard, Lamb (Charles), Manly, Merriment.

Drunkard

Woe unto them that rise up early in the morning, that they may follow strong drink; that continue until night, till wine inflame them.
ISAIAH V, 11, *c.* 700 B.C.

Woe to . . . the drunkards of Ephraim, whose glorious beauty is a fading flower.
ISAIAH XXVIII, 1

The drunkard and the glutton shall come to poverty, and drowsiness shall clothe a man with rags.
PROVERBS XXIII, 20, *c.* 350 B.C.

Awake, ye drunkards, and weep; and howl, all ye drinkers of wine.
JOEL I, 5, *c.* 350 B.C.

He is a drunkard who takes more than three glasses, though he be not drunk.
EPICTETUS: *Encheiridion*, *c.* 110

There are more old drunkards than old physicians.
RABELAIS: *Gargantua*, I, 1535

I never heard praise ascribed to a drunkard, but the well-bearing of his liquor, which is a better commendation for a brewer's horse.
WILLIAM CECIL (LORD BURLEIGH): *Advice to His Son*, *c.* 1555

Nor have we one or two kinds of drunkards only, but eight kinds. The first is ape drunk, and he leaps, and sings, and hollows, and danceth for the heavens: the second is lion drunk, and he flings the pots about the house, calls his hostess whore, breaks the glass windows with his dagger, and is apt to quarrel with any man that speaks to him: the third is swine drunk, heavy, lumpish, and sleepy, and cries for a little more drink, and a few more clothes: the fourth is sheep drunk, wise in his own conceit, when he cannot bring forth a right word: the fifth is maudlin drunk, when a fellow will weep for kindness

in the midst of his ale, and kiss you, saying; By God, Captain I love thee, go thy ways, thou dost not think so often of me as I do of thee; I would (if it pleased God) could I not love thee so well as I do, and then he puts his finger in his eye, and cries: the sixth is martin drunk, when a man is drunk and drinks himself sober ere he stir: the seventh is goat drunk, when in his drunkenness he hath no mind but on lechery: the eighth is fox drunk, when he is crafty drunk, as many of the Dutch men be, will never bargain but when they are drunk.
THOMAS NASHE: *Pierce Pennilesse*, 1592

Sweet fellowship in shame!
One drunkard loves another of the name.
SHAKESPEARE: *Love's Labor's Lost*, IV, *c.* 1595

The Devil has no power over a drunkard.
HENRY GLAPTHORNE: *Lady Mother*, III, 1635

With the merry Greeks . . . he that drank immoderately and above his strength had the denomination of Philocothonista.
THOMAS HEYWOOD: *Philocothonista*, 1635

He that will be a drunkard must have money, either of his own or of some other man's; either of his father's, mother's, master's, or at the highway, or some way.
JOHN BUNYAN: *The Life and Death of Mr. Badman*, 1680

Let the drunkard alone, and by and by he'll fall of himself.
THOMAS FULLER: *Gnomologia*, 1732

Often drunk and seldom sober
Falls like the leaves in October. IBID.

Some frolic drunkard, reeling from a feast,
Provokes a broil, and stabs you for a jest.
SAMUEL JOHNSON: *London*, 1738

If we take habitual drunkards as a class, their heads and their hearts will bear an advantageous comparison with those of any other class.
ABRAHAM LINCOLN: Speech in Springfield, Ill., Feb. 22, 1842

Drunkards have a fool's tongue and a knave's heart.
H. G. BOHN: *Handbook of Proverbs*, 1855

Where have you disposed of their carcasses?
Those drunkards and gluttons of so many generations;
Where have you drawn off all the foul liquid and meat?
WALT WHITMAN: *This Compost*, 1856

A drunkard in the gutter is just where he ought to be.
W. G. SUMNER: *The Forgotten Man*, 1883

A drunkard who has taken the pledge should never be locked up in a wine-cellar.
FRENCH PROVERB

[*See also* Drink, Drinker, Drinking, Drunkenness, Father, Gambler, Incredible, Nose. Portuguese, Prohibition, Trust.

Drunkenness

There is death in the pot.
II KINGS IV, 40, *c.* 500 B.C.

Drunkenness is simply voluntary insanity.
SENECA: *Epistulae morales ad Lucilium*, *c.* 63

Drunkenness is the ruin of reason. It is premature old age. It is temporary death.
ST. BASIL: *Homilies*, XIV, *c.* 375

The immoderate drinking of wine produces not fewer diseases of body and soul than much drinking of water, but far more and severer.
ST. JOHN CHRYSOSTOM: *Homilies*, I, *c.* 388

Drunkenness is very sepulchre
Of man's wit and his discretion.
GEOFFREY CHAUCER: *The Canterbury Tales* (The Pardoner's Tale), *c.* 1386

Drunkenness both aggravates the crime and makes it more clearly a crime.
EDWIN COKE: *Institutes*, I, 1628

Drunkenness is a vice which is painful and sickly in the very acting of it.
JEREMY TAYLOR: *Twenty-seven Sermons*, 1651

By drunkenness men do oftentimes shorten their days; go out of the ale-house drunk, and break their necks before they come home. Instances, not a few, might be given of this, but this is so manifest a man need say nothing.
JOHN BUNYAN: *The Life and Death of Mr. Badman*, 1680

Drunkenness spoils health, dismounts the mind, and unmans men. It reveals secrets, is quarrelsome, lascivious, impudent, dangerous and mad.
WILLIAM PENN: *Fruits of Solitude*, 1693

You must allow that drunkenness, which is equally destructive to body and mind, is a fine pleasure.
LORD CHESTERFIELD: *Letter to his son*, Oct. 9, 1746

I have a partiality for drunkenness, though I never practised it: it is a reality; but what is sobriety, only the absence of drunkenness?
HORACE WALPOLE: *Letter to Mary and Agnes Berry*, July 9, 1789

Drunkenness is the vice of a good constitution, or of a bad memory; of a constitution so treacherously good that it never bends until it breaks; or of a memory that recollects the pleasures of getting drunk, but forgets the pains of getting sober.
C. C. COLTON: *Lacon*, 1820

Such men as will get drunk and then abuse their wives do not deserve the name of men, for they have not the principle of men, but may be called the Devil's swill-tub walking upright, and such deserve a dose of eel tea, *i.e.*, spirituous liquor in which a living eel has been slimed.

LORENZO DOW: *Reflections on Matrimony*, 1833

Drunkenness makes some men fools, some beasts, and some devils.

H. G. BOHN: *Handbook of Proverbs*, 1855

Drunken days have all their tomorrows.

SAMUEL SMILES: *Thrift*, 1875 (Cited as "the old proverb")

Shame lost and shame found.

H. W. SHAW (JOSH BILLINGS): *Josh Billings' Comical Lexicon*, 1877

Drunkenness is a joy reserved for the gods: so men do partake of it impiously, and so they are very properly punished for their audacity.

JAMES BRANCH CABELL: *Jurgen*, XVIII, 1919

Drunkenness is temporary suicide: the happiness that it brings is merely negative, a momentary cessation of unhappiness.

BERTRAND RUSSELL: *The Conquest of Happiness*, I, 1930

The best cure for drunkenness is, sober, to look at a drunken man. CHINESE PROVERB

Drunkenness kills more than the sword.

LATIN PROVERB

[*See also* Ale, Children, Drink, Drinker, Drunk, Flesh, Germany, Katzenjammer, Prohibition.

Dryden, John (1631–1700)

Ev'n copious Dryden wanted, or forgot,
The last and greatest art — the art to blot.

ALEXANDER POPE: *The First Epistle of the Second Book of Horace*, 1737

Dryden may be properly considered as the father of English criticism, as the writer who first taught us to determine upon principles the merit of composition.

SAMUEL JOHNSON: *Lives of the Poets* (Dryden), 1778

The distinguishing characteristic of Dryden's genius seems to have been the power of reasoning and of expressing the result in appropriate language. This may seem slender praise; yet these were the talents that led Bacon into the recesses of philosophy and conducted Newton to the cabinet of nature.

WALTER SCOTT: *Life of Dryden*, 1808

His mind was of a slovenly character, — fond of splendor, but indifferent to neatness. Hence most of his writings exhibit the sluttish magnificence of a Russian noble, all vermin and diamonds, dirty linen and inestimable sables.

T. B. MACAULAY: *John Dryden*, 1828 (Edinburgh Review, Jan.)

We only know Dryden by quotations, and these are found only in books that have long since had their day.

An unnamed American: To FRANCES TROLLOPE (quoted in her *Domestic Manners of the Americans*, IX, 1832), *c.* 1830

Dryden's genius was of that sort which catches fire by its own motion; his chariot wheels get hot by driving fast.

S. T. COLERIDGE: *Table-Talk*, Nov. 1, 1833

Duchess

A duchess is never more than 30 to a bourgeois.

Ascribed to an unidentified French duchess

[*See also* Love.

Duck

Serve a duck whole, but eat only the breast and neck; the rest send back to the cook.

MARTIAL: *Epigrams*, XII, *c.* 100

Dudevant, Armantine (George Sand) (1804–76)

Lactae ubertas, or the milch-cow with the grand manner.

F. W. NIETZSCHE: *The Twilight of the Idols*, 1889

Duelling

A nobleman may accept a challenge to a duel in order to avoid the imputation of cowardice.

Doctrine condemned by Pope Alexander VII, Sept. 24, 1665

When you meet your antagonist, do everything in a mild and agreeable manner. Let your courage be as keen, but at the same time as polished, as your sword.

R. B. SHERIDAN: *The Rivals*, III, 1775

Whosoever committeth murder by way of duel shall suffer death by hanging; and if he were the challenger, his body, after death, shall be gibbetted. He who removeth it from the gibbet shall be guilty of a misdemeanor, and the officer shall see that it be replaced.

THOMAS JEFFERSON: *Crimes Bill*, 1779

It is too bad that death often results from duelling, for duels otherwise help keep up politeness in society.

NAPOLEON I: To Gaspard Gourgaud at St. Helena, 1815–1818

Due Process

No state . . . shall . . . deprive any person of life, liberty or property without due process of law.

CONSTITUTION OF THE UNITED STATES, Amendment XIV, July 28, 1868

[*See also* Mob.

Dulcimer

A damsel with a dulcimer
In a vision once I saw:

It was an Abyssinian maid,
And on her dulcimer she play'd.
S. T. COLERIDGE: *Kubla Khan,* 1816

Dullness

The midwife laid her hand on his thick skull,
With this prophetic blessing, "Be thou dull."
JOHN DRYDEN: *Absalom and Achitophel,* II, 1682

Authors have established it as a kind of rule that a man ought to be dull sometimes.
JOSEPH ADDISON: *The Spectator,* July 23, 1711

Born a goddess, dullness never dies.
ALEXANDER POPE: *The Dunciad,* I, 1728

Slow dastard dullness is his native vice.
WILLIAM WARBURTON (BISHOP OF GLOUCESTER): *A Fragment from Claudian's First Book Against Rufinus, Imitated, c.* 1740

Learn'd, without sense, and venerably dull.
CHARLES CHURCHILL: *The Rosciad,* 1761

He is not only dull himself, but the cause of dullness in others.
SAMUEL FOOTE: Of an unnamed law-lord, reported in BOSWELL'S *Life of Johnson,* 1783

Peter was dull — he was at first
Dull — oh, so dull — so very dull!
Whether he talkt, wrote, or rehearst —
Still with this dullness was he curst —
Dull — beyond all conception — dull.
P. B. SHELLEY: *Peter Bell the Third,* VII, 1819

A dull ax never loves grindstones.
H. W. BEECHER: *Royal Truths,* 1862

Dullness is the coming of age of seriousness.
OSCAR WILDE: *Phrases and Philosophies for the Use of the Young,* 1891

[*See also* Boredom, Fool.

Duluth

Duluth! the word fell upon my ear with a peculiar and indescribable charm, like the gentle murmur of a low fountain stealing forth in the midst of roses; or the soft, sweet accents of an angel's whisper in the bright, joyous dream of sleeping innocence.
J. PROCTOR KNOTT: Speech in the House of Representatives, Jan. 21, 1871

Dumpy

I hate a dumpy woman.
BYRON: *Don Juan,* I, 1819

Dunce

A wit with dunces and a dunce with wits.
ALEXANDER POPE: *The Dunciad,* IV, 1742

[*See also* Fool.

Dupe

Men would not live long in society if they were not the dupes of each other.
LA ROCHEFOUCAULD: *Maxims,* 1665

The dupeability of men.
THOMAS CARLYLE: *Heroes and Hero-Worship,* VI, 1840 (Lecture in London, May 22)

[*See also* Gambling, Love.

Durability

Nothing is more durable than a hog's snout.
AMERICAN PROVERB

Duress

He that complies against his will,
Is of his own opinion still.
SAMUEL BUTLER: *Hudibras,* III, 1678

Dust

Dust shalt thou eat all the days of thy life.
GENESIS III, 14, *c.* 700 B.C.

Dust thou art, and unto dust shalt thou return.
GENESIS III, 19

All are of the dust, and all turn to dust again.
ECCLESIASTES III, 20, *c.* 200 B.C.

They die, and return to their dust.
PSALMS CIV, 29, *c.* 150 B.C.

Golden lads and girls all must,
As chimney-sweepers, come to dust.
SHAKESPEARE: *Cymbeline,* IV, *c.* 1609

The glories of our blood and state
Are shadows, not substantial things;
There is no armor against fate,
Death lays his icy hand on kings.
Scepter and crown
Must tumble down,
And, in the dust, be equal made
With the poor crooked scythe and spade.
JAMES SHIRLEY: *The Contention of Ajax and Ulysses,* 1659

Earth to earth, ashes to ashes, dust to dust.
THE BOOK OF COMMON PRAYER (*The Burial of the Dead*), 1662

A heap of dust remains of thee:
'Tis all thou art, and all the proud shall be.
ALEXANDER POPE: *Elegy to the Memory of an Unfortunate Lady,* 1717

The dust in smaller particles arose,
Than those which fluid bodies do compose.
Contraries in extremes do often meet;
It was so dry that you might call it wet.
JOHN ARBUTHNOT: *On a Dusty Day, c.* 1725

First our pleasures die — and then
Our hopes, and then our fears — and when
These are dead, the debt is due,
Dust claims dust — and we die too.
P. B. SHELLEY: *Death,* 1820

Mud with the juice squeezed out.
Author unidentified

[*See also* Death, March, Mortality, Odessa, Victory.

Dutch

Many do so magnify the Hollanders as if they were more, and all other nations less, than men, as to matters of trade and policy; making them angels, and others fools, brutes and sots in those particulars.
WILLIAM PETTY: *Political Arithmetic*, I, *c.* 1677

The Dutch are a stupid people.
NAPOLEON I: *Diary of Pulteney Malcolm at St. Helena*, Sept. 21, 1816

In matters of commerce, the fault of the Dutch
Is offering too little and asking too much.
GEORGE CANNING: Despatch to the English ambassador in Holland, Jan. 31, 1826

The Dutch seem very happy and comfortable, certainly; but it is the happiness of animals. In vain do you look for the sweet breath of hope and advancement among them.
S. T. COLERIDGE: *Table-Talk*, May 4, 1830

There are three kinds of Dutch: the Dutch, the damned Dutch, and the hog Dutch.
AMERICAN SAYING, *c.* 1855

The Dutch companee is the best companee
That ever came over from old Germanee;
There's the Amsterdam Dutch and the Rotterdam Dutch,
The Potsdam Dutch and the other dam Dutch.
American popular song, *c.* 1875

[*See also* Anchor, Character (National), English, Holland, Irish, Pilgrim, Tobacco.

Dutch Language

[*See* Language.

Duty

Fear God, and keep his commandments: for this is the whole duty of man.
ECCLESIASTES XII, 13, *c.* 200 B.C.

It is better to begin doing our duty late than never.
DIONYSIUS OF HALICARNASSUS: *Antiquities of Rome*, IX, *c.* 20 B.C.

We have done that which was our duty to do.
LUKE XVII, 10, *c.* 75

At daybreak, when loath to rise, have this thought in thy mind: I am rising for a man's work.
MARCUS AURELIUS: *Meditations*, V, *c.* 170

Who would dig and delve from morn till evening? Who would travail and toil with the sweat of his brows? Yea, who would, for his king's pleasure, adventure and hazard his life, if wit had not so won men that they thought nothing more needful in this world nor anything whereunto they were more bounden than here to live in their duty and to train their whole life, according to their calling?
THOMAS WILSON: *The Arte of Rhetorique*, 1553

The right, practical divinity is this: Believe in Christ, and do thy duty in that state of life to which God has called thee.
MARTIN LUTHER: *Table-Talk*, VII, 1569

I do perceive here a divided duty.
SHAKESPEARE: *Othello*, I, 1604

Do your duty, and leave the rest to the gods.
PIERRE CORNEILLE: *Horace*, II, 1639

To do my duty in that state of life unto which it shall please God to call me.
THE BOOK OF COMMON PRAYER (*The Catechism*), 1662

When I'm not thank'd at all, I'm thank'd enough,
I've done my duty, and I've done no more.
HENRY FIELDING: *Tom Thumb*, I, 1730

Honor and shame from no condition rise;
Act well your part: there all the honor lies.
ALEXANDER POPE: *An Essay on Man*, IV, 1734

An act of duty is law in practise.
BENJAMIN WHICHCOTE: *Moral and Religious Aphorisms*, 1753

Reason shows us our duty; he who can make us love our duty is more powerful than reason itself.
STANISLAUS LESZCYNSKI (KING OF POLAND): *Œuvres du philosophe bienfaisant*, 1763

No man is obliged to do as much as he can do. A man is to have part of his life to himself.
SAMUEL JOHNSON: *Boswell's Life*, 1766

He trespasses against his duty who sleeps upon his watch as well as he that goes over to the enemy.
EDMUND BURKE: *Thoughts on the Cause of the Present Discontents*, 1770

Only aim to do your duty, and mankind will give you credit where you fail.
THOMAS JEFFERSON: *The Rights of British America*, 1774

Duty is the obligation to act in reverence for law.
IMMANUEL KANT: *Grundlegung zur Metaphysik der Sitten*, I, 1785

We ought to use the best means we can to be well informed of our duty.
THOMAS REED: *Essays on the Active Powers of Man*, V, 1788

My great wish is to go on in a strict but silent performance of my duty; to avoid attracting notice, and to keep my name out of newspapers.
THOMAS JEFFERSON: *Letter to F. Hopkinson*, 1789

Duty is that mode of action on the part of the individual which constitutes the best possible application of his capacity to the general benefit.

WILLIAM GODWIN: *An Enquiry Concerning Political Justice,* 1793

It is my duty to represent in my own person, in so far as I am able, the most complete and perfect humanity.

J. G. FICHTE: *Die Bestimmung des Menschen,* XVIII, 1800

England expects every officer and man to do his duty this day.

HORATIO NELSON: Signal to the English fleet before the Battle of Trafalgar, Oct. 21, 1805

Stern daughter of the voice of God.

WILLIAM WORDSWORTH: *Ode to Duty,* 1807

The primal duties shine aloft, like stars;
The charities that soothe, and heal, and bless,
Are scattered at the feet of man, like flowers,
The generous inclination, the just rule,
Kind wishes, and good actions and pure thoughts;
No mystery is here!

WILLIAM WORDSWORTH: *The Excursion,* IX, 1814

The trivial round, the common task,
Would furnish all we ought to ask —
Room to deny ourselves; a road
To bring us, daily, nearer God.

JOHN KEBLE: *The Christian Year,* 1827

There is no evil that we cannot either face or fly from, but the consciousness of duty disregarded. A sense of duty pursues us ever. It is omnipresent, like the Deity.

DANIEL WEBSTER: Argument at the trial of John F. Knapp, 1830

I have my own stern claims and perfect circle. It denies the name of duty to many offices that are called duties.

R. W. EMERSON: *Self-Reliance,* 1841

There's life alone in duty done,
And rest alone in striving.

J. G. WHITTIER: *The Drovers,* 1847

Never to tire, never to grow cold; to be patient, sympathetic, tender; to look for the budding flower and the opening heart; to hope always; like God, to love always, — this is duty.

H. F. AMIEL: *Journal,* May 27, 1849

I slept and dreamed that life was beauty;
I woke and found that life was duty.

Anon.: *Duty, c.* 1850

The best security for people's doing their duty is that they should not know anything else to do.

WALTER BAGEHOT: *Letter to the London Inquirer,* 1851

Theirs not to make reply,
Theirs not to reason why,
Theirs but to do and die.

ALFRED TENNYSON: *The Charge of the Light Brigade,* 1854

To live without duties is obscene.

R. W. EMERSON: *English Traits,* XI, 1856

Our duty is to submit ourselves with all humility to the established limits of our intelligence; and not perversely to rebel against them. Let those who can, believe that there is eternal war set between our intellectual faculties and our moral obligations. I, for one, admit no such radical vice in the constitution of things.

HERBERT SPENCER: *First Principles,* I, 1862

So nigh is grandeur to our dust,
So near is God to man,
When duty whispers low, *Thou must,*
The youth replies, *I can.*

R. W. EMERSON: *Voluntaries,* III, 1863 (Atlantic Monthly, Oct.)

He seen his duty, a dead-sure thing —
And went for it thar and then;
And Christ ain't a-going to be too hard
On a man that died for men.

JOHN HAY: *Jim Bludso,* 1871

For duty, duty must be done;
The rule applies to everyone,
And painful though that duty be,
To shirk the task were fiddle-de-dee.

W. S. GILBERT: *Ruddigore,* I, 1887

A nation goes to pieces when it confounds its duty with the general concept of duty.

F. W. NIETZSCHE: *The Antichrist,* XI, 1888

Duty is what one expects from others.

OSCAR WILDE: *A Woman of No Importance,* II, 1893

A legal duty so-called is nothing but a prediction that if a man does or omits certain things he will be made to suffer in this or that way by judgment of the court.

O. W. HOLMES II: Speech at the Boston University School of Law, 1897

Duty can only be defined as that action which will cause more good to exist in the universe than any possible alternative.

G. E. MOORE: *Principia Ethica,* v, 1903

Duty is lighter than a feather, but heavier than a mountain.

EMPEROR MEIJI TENNO of Japan (1852–1912)

Duties are not performed for duty's sake, but because their neglect would make the man uncomfortable. A man performs but one duty — the duty of contenting his spirit, the duty of making himself agreeable to himself.

S. L. CLEMENS (MARK TWAIN): *What Is Man?* II, 1917

England expects every American to do his duty.

AMERICAN SAYING, 1917

A sense of duty is useful in work, but offensive in personal relations.
BERTRAND RUSSELL: *The Conquest of Happiness*, x, 1930

He seen his duty and he done it.
AMERICAN SAYING

The path of duty lies in what is near, but men seek it in what is remote.
CHINESE PROVERB

[*See also* Curiosity, Husband and Wife, Justice, Labor, Law, Obligation, Order.

Duty, Filial

Honor thy father and thy mother: that thy days may be long upon the land which the Lord thy God giveth thee.
EXODUS XX, 12, *c.* 700 B.C. (Cf. DEUTERONOMY V, 16, *c.* 650 B.C.)

There are three thousand offenses punished by the five punishments, but the greatest of them all is to be unfilial.
CONFUCIUS: *The Book of Filial Piety*, XI, *c.* 500 B.C.

Unhappy the child who forgets his duty to his parents, for his own children, in their turn, will repay him in the same coin.
EURIPIDES: *The Suppliant Women*, *c.* 421 B.C.

A lively and lasting sense of filial duty is more effectually impressed on the mind of a son or daughter by reading "King Lear," than by all the dry volumes of ethics and divinity that ever were written.
THOMAS JEFFERSON: *Letter to Robert Skipwith*, 1771

The absurd duty, too often inculcated, of obeying a parent only on account of his being a parent, shackles the mind, and prepares it for a slavish submission to any power but reason.
MARY WOLLSTONECRAFT: *A Vindication of the Rights of Woman*, IX, 1792

[*See also* Father, Mother.

Duty, Parental

To have voluntarily become to any being the occasion of its existence produces an obligation to make that existence happy.
SAMUEL JOHNSON: *The Rambler*, Aug. 17, 1751

Duty, Public

Render therefore to all their dues: tribute to whom tribute is due; custom to whom custom; fear to whom fear; honor to whom honor.
ROMANS XIII, 7, *c.* 55

Render therefore unto Cæsar the things which are Cæsar's; and unto God the things that are God's.
MATTHEW XXII, 21, *c.* 75 (Cf LUKE XX, 25, *c.* 75)

Renounce your domestic comforts for a few months, and reflect that to be a good husband and good father at this moment you must be also a good citizen.
THOMAS JEFFERSON: *Letter to Elbridge Gerry*, 1797

Every man is under the natural duty of contributing to the necessities of society; and this is all the laws should enforce on him.
THOMAS JEFFERSON: *Letter to F. W. Gilmer*, 1816

No personal consideration should stand in the way of performing a public duty.
U. S. GRANT: On the Whiskey Ring, July 29, 1875

Dvořák, Antonin (1841–1904)

He smells of the pure, open air — a milkman's composer.
JAMES HUNEKER: *Old Fogy*, XVI, 1913

Dying

He gathered up his feet into the bed, and yielded up the ghost, and was gathered unto his people.
GENESIS XLIX, 33, *c.* 700 B.C.

Let me die the death of the righteous, and let my last end be like his.
NUMBERS XXIII, 10, *c.* 700 B.C.

The hour of departure has arrived, and we go our ways — I to die, and you to live. Which is the better, God only knows.
SOCRATES: In PLATO'S *Apology of Socrates*, 399 B.C.

Yea, though I walk through the valley of the shadow of death, I will fear no evil: for thou art with me; thy rod and thy staff they comfort me.
PSALMS XXIII, 4, *c.* 350 B.C.

On my eyelids is the shadow of death.
JOB XVI, 16, *c.* 325 B.C.

Of all the boons that man asks of the gods, he prays most fervently for an easy death.
POSIDIPPUS: *Fragment*, *c.* 275 B.C.

I am unwilling to die, but I care not if I were dead.
CICERO: *Tusculanae disputationes*, I, 45 B.C.

Happy the man who has trampled underfoot his fears and can laugh at the approach of all-subduing death.
VIRGIL: *Georgics*, II, 30 B.C.

May I be granted the boon of dying in my native land.
OVID: *Tristia*, I, *c.* 10

I end a life of consummate misery by a death the most revolting.
GERMANICUS: On his deathbed in Antioch, 19

To die well is to die willingly.
SENECA: *Epistulae morales ad Lucilium*, LXI, *c.* 63

It doesn't hurt, Paetus. (Paete, non dolet.)
ARRIA, wife of the Stoic Thrasea Paetus: Last words to her husband, 65

Hail Cæsar; we who are about to die salute you. (Ave Cæsar, morituri te salutant.)
Salutation of Roman gladiators on entering the arena, *c.* 100

The act of dying is also one of the acts of life.
MARCUS AURELIUS: *Meditations,* VI, *c.* 170

Receive death with gladness, as one of the things that nature wills.
MARCUS AURELIUS: *Meditations,* IX

There is no man so fortunate that there shall not be by him when he is dying some who are pleased with what is going to happen.
MARCUS AURELIUS: *Meditations,* X

O wretched little soul of mine, imprisoned in an unworthy body, go forth, be free!
CORNIFICIA, daughter to Marcus Aurelius: On being put to death by the Emperor Caracalla, 215

What, I pray you, is dying? Just what it is to put off a garment. For the body is about the soul as a garment; and after laying this aside for a short time by means of death, we shall resume it again with the more splendor.
ST. JOHN CHRYSOSTOM: *Homilies, V, c.* 388

I have lived in doubt, I die in anxiety, I know not whither I go. (Vixi dubius, anxius morior, nescio quo vada.)
Author unidentified, *c.* 1400

Father Abbot, I am come to lay my weary bones among you.
THOMAS WOLSEY: On halting at Leicester Abbey on his way to London to answer a charge of treason, Nov. 26, 1529 (He died Nov. 30)

O death! rock me on sleep,
  Bring me on quiet rest;
Let pass my very guiltless ghost
  Out of my careful breast:
Toll on the passing bell,
Ring out the doleful knell.
Let the sound my death tell,
    For I must die,
    There is no remedy,
    For now I die.
ANNE BOLEYN: *Death, c.* 1536

Lord! Lord! make an end! make an end! (Domine! Domine! fac finem! fac finem!)
DESIDERIUS ERASMUS: Last words, 1536

I am going to seek a great perhaps. Draw the curtain: the farce is played out.
Ascribed to FRANÇOIS RABELAIS: On his deathbed, April 9, 1553 (?)

I have not lived eighty years without learning how to stand dying for a quarter of an hour.
THE CONSTABLE DE MONTMORENCI: On receiving a mortal wound, 1567

If I were a writer of books I would compile a register, with a commentary, of the different deaths that men die, for he who would teach them how to die would also teach them how to live.
MICHEL DE MONTAIGNE: *Essays,* II, 1580

If you know not how to die, take no care for it. Nature herself will fully and sufficiently teach you in the proper time, she will exactly discharge that work for you; trouble not yourself with it.
MICHEL DE MONTAIGNE: *Essays,* III, 1588

Close up his eyes and draw the curtain close;
And let us all to meditation.
SHAKESPEARE: *II Henry VI,* III, *c.* 1591

Make me die a good old man:
That is the butt-end of a mother's blessing.
SHAKESPEARE: *Richard III,* II, *c.* 1592

'Tis a vile thing to die, my gracious lord,
When men are unprepared and look not for it.
SHAKESPEARE: *Richard III,* III

It is as natural to die as to be born.
FRANCIS BACON: *Essays,* II, 1597

Many times death passeth with less pain than the torture of a limb; for the most vital parts are not the quickest of sense.
IBID.

A man can die but once.
SHAKESPEARE: *II Henry IV,* III, *c.* 1598

How oft when men are at the point of death
They have been merry, which their keepers call
A lightning before death.
SHAKESPEARE: *Romeo and Juliet,* V, *c.* 1598

My life is run his compass.
SHAKESPEARE: *Julius Cæsar,* V, 1599

If I must die
I will encounter darkness as a bride,
And hug it in mine arms.
SHAKESPEARE: *Measure for Measure,* III, 1604

Here is my journey's end, here is my butt,
And very sea-mark of my utmost sail.
SHAKESPEARE: *Othello,* V, 1604

Nothing in his life
Became him like the leaving it; he died
As one that had been studied in his death
To throw away the dearest thing he ow'd,
As 't were a careless trifle.
SHAKESPEARE: *Macbeth,* I, *c.* 1605

I saw him now going the way of all flesh.
JOHN WEBSTER and THOMAS DEKKER: *Westward Hoe,* 1605

I thank my God heartily that he hath brought me into the light to die, and not suffered me to die in the dark.
WALTER RALEIGH: Speech on the scaffold, Oct. 29, 1618

And make her tug with death
Until her soul sweat.
JAMES SHIRLEY: *The Cardinal,* v, 1641

Take away but the pomps of death, the disguises, and solemn bugbears, and the actings by candlelight, and proper and phantastic ceremonies, the minstrels and the noisemakers, the women and the weepers, the swoonings and the shriekings, the nurses and the physicians, the dark room and the ministers, the kindred and the watches, and then to die is easy, ready, and quitted from its troublesome circumstances.
JEREMY TAYLOR: *The Rule and Exercises of Holy Dying,* III, 1651

The long habit of living indisposeth us for dying.
THOMAS BROWNE: *Urn Burial,* II, 1658

My desire is to make what haste I may to be gone.
OLIVER CROMWELL: Last words, 1658

Death is but a little word, but 'tis a great work to die.
HARRY VANE: On the scaffold, 1662

Dying is ceasing to be afraid.
WILLIAM WYCHERLEY: *The Plain Dealer,* I, *c.* 1674

I see myself now at the end of my journey; my toilsome days are ended. I am going now to see that head that was crowned with thorns, and that face that was spit upon for me.
JOHN BUNYAN: *Pilgrim's Progress,* II, 1678

Now I am about to take my last voyage, a great leap in the dark.
THOMAS HOBBES: On his deathbed, Dec. 4, 1679

Suppose that one man should die quietly, another should die suddenly, and a third should die under great consternation of spirit, no man can judge of their eternal condition by the manner of any of these kinds of deaths.
JOHN BUNYAN: *The Life and Death of Mr. Badman,* 1680

Don't let poor Nelly starve.
CHARLES II of England: Last words, referring to Nell Gwynn, 1685

So was she soon exhaled, and vanished hence;
As a sweet odor, of a vast expense.
She vanished, we can scarcely say she died.
JOHN DRYDEN: *Ode to the Memory of Mrs. Anne Killegrew,* 1686

When I can read my title clear
To mansions in the skies,
I'll bid farewell to every fear
And wipe my weeping eyes.
ISAAC WATTS: *Hymns and Spiritual Songs,* II, 1707

There is nothing in history which is so improving to the reader as those accounts which we meet with of the death of eminent persons, and their behavior in that dreadful season.
JOSEPH ADDISON: *The Spectator,* Jan. 31, 1712

I imagined it was more difficult to die. (J'avais cru plus difficile de mourir.)
LOUIS XIV of France: Last words, to Madame de Maintenon, 1715

See my lips tremble and my eyeballs roll,
Suck my last breath, and catch my flying soul.
ALEXANDER POPE: *Eloisa to Abelard,* 1717

Resolved, To think much, on all occasions, of my own dying, and of the common circumstances which attend death.
JONATHAN EDWARDS: *Resolutions,* 1722

While there is life there's hope (he cried,)
Then why such haste? — so groan'd and died.
JOHN GAY: *The Sick Man and The Angel,* 1727

Is this dying? Is this all? Is this what I feared when I prayed against a hard death? Oh, I can bear this! I can bear it!
COTTON MATHER: On his deathbed, 1728

He hath lived ill that knows not how to die well.
THOMAS FULLER: *Gnomologia,* 1732

He is miserable that dieth not before he desires to die. IBID.

I know of nobody that has a mind to die this year. IBID.

Don't look like a calf that has just had its throat cut.
GEORGE II of England: To his wife, Caroline of Brandenburg-Anspach, at her deathbed, Nov. 15, 1737

I am dying, sir, of a hundred good symptoms.
ALEXANDER POPE: On his deathbed, 1744

The conscience of the dying man calumniates his life.
LUC DE VARVENARGUES: *Réflexions,* 1746

In life's last scene what prodigies surprise,
Fears of the brave, and follies of the wise!
From Marlborough's eyes the streams of dotage flow,
And Swift expires a driveller and a show.
SAMUEL JOHNSON: *The Vanity of Human Wishes,* 1749

For who, to dumb forgetfulness a prey,
This pleasing anxious being e'er resign'd.
Left the warm precincts of the cheerful day,
Nor cast one longing ling'ring look behind?
THOMAS GRAY: *Elegy Written in a Country Churchyard,* 1750

He left a world he was weary of with the cool indifference you quit a dirty inn, to continue your journey to a place where you hope for better accommodation.
MARY WORTLEY MONTAGU: *Letter to James Steuart,* July 19, 1759

It matters not how a man dies, but how he lives. The act of dying is of no importance, it lasts so short a time.

SAMUEL JOHNSON: *Boswell's Life,* Oct. 26, 1769

No rational man can die without uneasy apprehensions.

SAMUEL JOHNSON: *Boswell's Life,* April 15, 1778

I go to see the sun for the last time.

J.-J. ROUSSEAU: Last words, July 21, 1778

It will be but a momentary pang.

JOHN ANDRÉ: Last words on the scaffold, 1780

Perhaps nature wants us, at the end of our days, to be disgusted with life, so that we may leave this world with less regret.

FREDERICK THE GREAT: *Letter to Jean le Rond D'Alembert,* Sept. 30, 1783

If I had the strength to hold a pen I would write down how easy and pleasant it is to die.

WILLIAM HUNTER: Last words, 1783

I do not like the apparatus [of death] at all, and hope I shall know no more of my going out of the world than I did of my coming into it. Life is a farce, and should not end with a mourning scene.

HORACE WALPOLE: *Letter to the Countess of Upper Ossory,* Jan. 19, 1784

I am extremely afraid of dying.

SAMUEL JOHNSON: *Letter to James Boswell,* Feb. 11, 1784

The mountain is passed; now we shall get on better. (La montagne est passée; nous irons mieux.)

FREDERICK THE GREAT: Last words, 1786

A dying man can do nothing easy.

BENJAMIN FRANKLIN: On his deathbed, April 17, 1790

Their souls did from their bodies fly —
They fled to bliss or woe
And every soul, it pass'd me by
Like the whizz of my cross-bow.

S. T. COLERIDGE: *The Ancient Mariner,* III, 1798

I think I'll make a long sleep of it. (Ich denke einen langen Schlaf zu thun.)

J. C. F. SCHILLER: *Wallenstein's Death,* v, 1799

Doctor, I die hard, but I am not afraid to go.

GEORGE WASHINGTON: Last words, Dec. 14, 1799

Let there be no inscription upon my tomb. Let no man write my epitaph. No man can write my epitaph. I am here ready to die. I am not allowed to vindicate my character; and when I am prevented from vindicating myself, let no man dare calumniate me. Let my character and motives repose in obscurity and peace, till other times and other men can do them justice.

ROBERT EMMET: Speech at his trial, 1803

I have lived an honest and useful life to mankind; my time has been spent in doing good; and I die in perfect composure and resignation to the will of my Creator.

THOMAS PAINE: *Last will,* 1809

Soldiers, straight at my heart! (Soldats, droit au cœur!)

MICHEL NEY: Last words at his execution, Dec. 7, 1815

He is an ignoble man who doesn't know how to die. I knew it as a boy of fifteen.

LUDWIG VAN BEETHOVEN: To Fanny Giannastasio del Rio, 1816

I am perfectly resigned. I am surrounded by my family, I have served my country, I have reliance upon God, and am not afraid of the Devil.

HENRY GRATTAN: Last words, 1820

There is a great difference between going off in warm blood like Romeo, and making one's exit like a frog in a frost.

JOHN KEATS: *Letter to Fanny Brawne,* March, 1820

So live that when thy summons comes to join
The innumerable caravan that moves
To the pale realm of shade, where each shall take
His chamber in the silent halls of death,
Thou go not like the quarry-slave at night,
Scourged to his dungeon, but, sustained and soothed
Like one who wraps the drapery of his couch
About him, and lies down to pleasant dreams.

W. C. BRYANT: *Thanatopsis,* 1821 (The poem first appeared in the North American Review in 1811, but the lines here quoted were not added until 1821)

Then out spake brave Horatius,
The captain of the gate:
"To every man upon this earth
Death cometh soon or late;
And how can man die better
Than facing fearful odds
For the ashes of his fathers
And the temples of his gods?"

T. B. MACAULAY: *Horatius,* 1842

We thought her dying when she slept,
And sleeping when she died.

THOMAS HOOD: *The Deathbed,* 1846

This is the last of earth! I am content.

JOHN QUINCY ADAMS: On his deathbed, Feb. 23, 1848

I strove with none; for none was worth my strife,
Nature I loved, and next to nature, art;
I warmed both hands before the fire of life,
It sinks, and I am ready to depart.

W. S. LANDOR: *On His Seventy-Fifth Birthday,* 1853

As the last bell struck, a peculiar sweet smile shone over his face, and he lifted up his head a little, and quickly said, "Adsum!" and fell back. It was the word we used at school when names were called.
W. M. THACKERAY: *The Newcomes*, II, 1855

The dull nights go over, and the dull days also,
The soreness of lying so much in bed goes over,
The physician, after long putting off, gives the silent and terrible look for an answer,
The children come hurried and weeping, and the brothers and sisters are sent for.
WALT WHITMAN: *To Think of Time*, 1855

I am ready at any time. Do not keep me waiting.
JOHN BROWN: Last words on the scaffold, 1859

Let us go over the river, and sit in the shade of the trees.
T. J. (STONEWALL) JACKSON: Last words, 1863

The dying are nearly as reticent as the dead.
ALEXANDER SMITH: *Dreamthorp*, III, 1863

The finest sight beneath the sky
Is to see how bravely a man can die.
ROBERT BUCHANAN: *London Poems*, 1866

It was the eleventh of December,
On a cold and windy day,
Just at the close of evening,
When the sunlight fades away;
Little Henry he was dying,
In his little crib he lay,
With soft winds round him sighing
From the morn till close of day.
JULIA A. MOORE (THE SWEET SINGER OF MICHIGAN): *The Sentimental Song Book*, 1876

It is not true that the dying man is generally more honest than the living. On the contrary, by the solemn attitude of the bystanders and the flowing or repressed streams of tears, everyone present is inveigled into a comedy of vanity, now conscious, now unconscious.
F. W. NIETZSCHE: *Human All-too-Human*, II, 1878

Glory hallelujah! I am going to the Lord! I come! Ready! Go!
CHARLES J. GUITEAU: Last words on the scaffold, June 30, 1882

Now comes the mystery.
HENRY WARD BEECHER: Last words, 1887

I haven't time now to be tired.
WILHELM I of Germany: On his deathbed, March 8, 1888

Don't cheer, boys; the poor devils are dying.
Ascribed to J. W. PHILIP, captain of the battleship Texas, at the Battle of Santiago, July 4, 1898

So much to do; so little done.
CECIL RHODES: On his deathbed, 1902

I have careful records of about 500 deathbeds, studied particularly with reference to the modes of death and the sensations of the dying. . . . Ninety suffered bodily pain or distress of one sort or another, eleven showed mental apprehension, two positive terror, one expressed spiritual exaltation, one bitter remorse. The great majority gave no sign one way or the other; like birth, their death was a sleep and a forgetting.
WILLIAM OSLER: *Science and Immortality*, II, 1904

We need more courage to die alone. Everybody wants to die with the regiment.
MARTIN H. FISCHER (1879–)

What's the matter with you guys? Do you want to live forever?
Commonly ascribed to an American sergeant in the World War, addressing soldiers reluctant to make a charge, but in former years it was credited to FREDERICK THE GREAT (Wollt ihr immer leben?), and is probably ancient

Wisdom is on the lips of those about to die.
FRENCH PROVERB

The best way to get praise is to die.
ITALIAN PROVERB

The more you think of dying the better you will live.
IBID.

In the act of dying. (In articulo mortis.)
LATIN PHRASE

The dying salute those who are about to die. (Morituri morituros salutant.)
LATIN PROVERB

No one is presumed to trifle at the point of death. (Nemo praesumitur ludere in extremis.)
LEGAL MAXIM

[*See also* Alone, Bishop, Brandy, Chinese, Christian, Coffin, Death, Doubt, Grave, Emperor, King.

Dyspeptic

Drinking and sweating is the life of a dyspeptic.
SENECA: *Epistulae morales ad Lucilium*, IV, *c.* 63

E

Eagle

Her young ones also suck up blood; and where the slain are, there is she.
JOB XXXIX, 30, *c.* 325 B.C.

Wheresoever the carcass is, there will the eagles be gathered together.
MATTHEW XXIV, 28, *c.* 75 (Cf. LUKE XVII, 37, *c.* 75)

The eagle suffers little birds to sing,
And is not careful what they mean thereby.
SHAKESPEARE: *Titus Andronicus*, IV, 1594

I wish the bald eagle had not been chosen as the representative of our country: he is a bird of bad moral character, . . . he is generally poor, and often very lousy.
BENJAMIN FRANKLIN: *Letter to Sarah Bache*, Jan. 26, 1784

When thou seest an eagle, thou seest a portion of genius; lift up thy head.
WILLIAM BLAKE: *The Marriage of Heaven and Hell*, 1790

Eagles don't breed doves. DUTCH PROVERB

An eagle's old age is as good as a sparrow's youth. GREEK PROVERB

Eagles catch no flies. (Aquila non captat muscas.) LATIN PROVERB

[*See also* Alone, Enigma, Mystery.

Ear

I have got a wolf by the ear.
TERENCE: *Phormio*, III, *c.* 160 B.C.

Nature has given man one tongue, but two ears, that we may hear twice as much as we speak.
DIOGENES LAERTIUS: *Lives of the Philosophers* (Zeno), *c.* 150 B.C.

He that hath ears to hear, let him hear.
MARK IV, 9, *c.* 70 (Cf. MARK IV, 23)

It went in at one ear and out at the other.
ENGLISH SAYING, borrowed from the Latin, and current since the XIV century

To put a flea in his ear.
ENGLISH PHRASE, familiar since the XV century

Friends, Romans, countrymen, lend me your ears.
SHAKESPEARE: *Julius Cæsar*, III, 1599

Give every man thy ear, but few thy voice.
SHAKESPEARE: *Hamlet*, I, *c.* 1601

The ears are two music-rooms.
THOMAS DEKKER: *The Gull's Hornbook*, III, 1609

More is meant than meets the ear.
JOHN MILTON: *Il Penseroso*, 1632

I was all ear. JOHN MILTON: *Comus*, 1637

One pair of ears draws dry a hundred tongues.
GEORGE HERBERT: *Outlandish Proverbs*, 1640

The ears should be kept perfectly clean; but it must never be done in company. It should never be done with a pin, and still less with the fingers, but always with an ear-picker.
ST. JOHN BAPTIST DE LA SALLE: *The Rules of Christian Manners and Civility*, I, 1695

The wise pretend to make it clear,
'Tis no great loss to lose an ear.
Why are we then so fond of two,
When, by experience, one would do?
JONATHAN SWIFT: *To Dr. Delany*, 1729

[*See also* Error, Eye and Ear, Hearing.

Earl

The nation looked upon him as a deserter, and he shrunk into insignificancy and an earldom.
LORD CHESTERFIELD: *Character of Pulteney*, 1763

An earl by right, by courtesy a man.
ALFRED AUSTIN: *The Season*, 1861

Early

The early bird catches the worm.
ENGLISH PROVERB, traced by Apperson to 1605

Early sow, early mow.
JOHN CLARKE: *Parœmiologia Anglo-Latina*, 1639

Early Rising

[*See* Rising (Early).

Earnestness

[*See* Virtue.

Earth

The four corners of the earth.
ISAIAH XI, 12, *c.* 700 B.C.

The earth is a round body in the center of the heavens, and has no need of air or any other thing for its support, but is kept in place by the equability of the surrounding heavens and its own equipoise.
PLATO: *Phaedo*, *c.* 360 B.C.

Speak to the earth, and it shall teach thee.
JOB XII, 8, *c.* 325 B.C.

All things come from earth, and to earth they all return.
MENANDER: *Moyostikhoi*, *c.* 300 B.C.

One generation passeth away, and another generation cometh: but the earth abideth forever. ECCLESIASTES I, 4, *c.* 200 B.C.

The earth is the Lord's, and the fulness thereof.
PSALMS XXIV, 1, *c.* 150 B.C.

What is the earth but a lump of clay surrounded by water?
BHARTRIHARI: *The Vairagya Sataka*, *c.* 625

One should not consider the earth, any more than any other planet, as the center of the universe.
GIORDANO BRUNO: *Del infinito, universo e mondi*, V, 1584

This goodly frame, the earth, seems to me a sterile promontory.
SHAKESPEARE: *Hamlet*, II, *c.* 1601

This earth is the grave and Golgotha wherein all things that live must rot; 't is but the draught wherein the heavenly bodies discharge their corruption; the very muck-hill on which the sublunary orbs cast their excrements.
JOHN MARSTON: *The Malcontent*, IV, 1604

With a sincere regard for the learned of the church, I demonstrate by means of philosophy that the earth is round, and is inhabited on all sides; that it is insignificantly small, and is borne through the stars.
JOHANN KEPLER: *Astronomia nova*, 1609

It is a bawdy planet.
SHAKESPEARE: *The Winter's Tale*, I, *c.* 1611

All our pomp the earth covers.
GEORGE HERBERT: *Outlandish Proverbs*, 1640

Nevertheless, it moves! (E pur si muove!)
Attributed, probably apocryphally, to Galileo (1564–1642), as he rose from his knees after formally recanting the Copernican cosmology

This little point of earth.
JOHN WILKINS (BISHOP OF CHESTER): *Discourse that the Earth May Be a Planet*, 1640

Six feet of earth make all men equal.
JAMES HOWELL: *Proverbs*, 1659

This earth, a spot, a grain, an atom.
JOHN MILTON: *Paradise Lost*, VIII, 1667

This congregated ball.
ALEXANDER POPE: *The First Epistle of the First Book of Horace*, 1735

To her full breasts, me Mother Earth receives;
Cheaply I'll riot on the wealth she gives.
WILLIAM WARBURTON (BISHOP OF GLOUCESTER): *A Fragment From Claudian's First Book Against Rufinus, Imitated*, *c.* 1740

On this little shell how very few are the spots where man can live and flourish! Even under those mild climates which seem to breathe peace and happiness, the poison of slavery, the fury of despotism, and the rage of superstition are all combined against man.
ST. JOHN DE CRÈVECOEUR: *Letters from an American Farmer*, IX, 1782

The earth is given as a common stock for man to labor and live on.
THOMAS JEFFERSON: *Letter to James Madison*, 1785

The hills
Rock-ribbed and ancient as the sun, — the vales
Stretching in pensive quietness between;
The venerable woods — rivers that move
In majesty, and the complaining brooks
That make the meadows green; and, poured round all,
Old Ocean's gray and melancholy waste, —
Are but the solemn decorations all
Of the great tomb of man.
W. C. BRYANT: *Thanatopsis*, 1811 (North American Review)

There's not one atom of yon earth
But once was living man;
Nor the minutest drop of rain,
That hangeth in its thinnest cloud,
But flowed in human veins.
P. B. SHELLEY: *Queen Mab*, II, 1813

He saw with his own eyes the moon was round,
Was also certain that the earth was square.
Because he had journey'd fifty miles, and found
No sign that it was circular anywhere.
BYRON: *Don Juan*, V, 1821

This earth
Spins like a fretful midge.
D. G. ROSSETTI: *The Blessed Damosel*, 1850

Now I am terrified at the earth! It is calm and patient,
It grows such sweet things out of such corruptions,
It turns harmless and stainless on its axis, with such endless successions of diseas'd corpses.
WALT WHITMAN: *This Compost*, 1856

We find out of any group of men selected at random some who are crippled, insane, idiotic and otherwise born incurably imperfect in body or mind, and it is possible that this world may rank among other worlds as one of these.
FRANCIS GALTON: *Inquiries Into Human Faculty*, 1883

The lunatic asylum of the solar system.
S. PARKES CADMAN: Speech in New York, Nov. 17, 1935

The earth has room for all. WELSH PROVERB

[*See also* Cosmology, Heart, Man, Sun.

Earthquake

The earth opened her mouth, and swallowed them up, and their houses, and all the men that appertained unto Korah, and all their goods. NUMBERS XVI, 32, *c.* 700 B.C.

Nation shall rise against nation, and kingdom against kingdom: and there shall be famines, and pestilences, and earthquakes, in divers places. MATTHEW XXIV, 7, *c.* 75

When mountains fall headlong over hollow places they shut in the air within their caverns, and this air, in order to escape, breaks through the earth, and so produces earthquakes.
LEONARDO DA VINCI: *Notebooks*, *c.* 1500

Plenty of winds gotten in the bowels, holes and corners of the earth, bursting out of the earth, and the earth closing again, causeth the shaking, or earthquake, and is a token of ensuing war.
JOHN TULLY: *Almanack*, 1693

Sometimes the ground has gap'd so wide
Houses have sunk beneath,
Shatter'd to bits, or keeping whole,
The people starv'd to death.

Anon.: *Earthquakes Improved,* 1755

[*See also* English.

Ease

It is the mark of a superior man that he will take no harmful ease.

CONFUCIUS: *The Book of History,* V, *c.* 500 B.C.

What is sweeter than lettered ease (otio litterato).

CICERO: *Tusculanae disputationes,* V, 45 B.C.

Ignoble ease. (Ignobilis oti.)

VIRGIL: *Georgics,* IV, 30 B.C.

Itch and ease can no man please.

JOHN HEYWOOD: *Proverbs,* 1546

Let each man keep his heart at ease:
No man dies of that disease.

BEAUMONT and FLETCHER: *The Knight of the Burning Pestle,* II, 1609

Honor and ease are seldom bedfellows.

JOHN CLARKE: *Parœmiologia Anglo-Latina,* 1639

He that is at ease seeks dainties.

GEORGE HERBERT: *Outlandish Proverbs,* 1640

God laughs at a man who says to his soul, Take thy ease.

ABRAHAM COWLEY: *Of Myself,* 1665

When men are easy in themselves, they let others remain so.

ANTHONY A. COOPER (EARL OF SHAFTESBURY): *Characteristics of Men, Manners, Opinions, Times,* III, *c.* 1713

They wrong man greatly who say he is to be seduced by ease. Difficulty, abnegation, martyrdom, death are the allurements that act on the heart of man.

THOMAS CARLYLE: *Heroes and Hero-Worship,* II, 1840 (Lecture in London, May 8)

Never do anything standing that you can do sitting, or anything sitting that you can do lying down.

CHINESE PROVERB

Ease with dignity. (Otium cum dignitate.)

LATIN PHRASE

[*See also* Honor, Inn.

East

The East only awaits a man.

NAPOLEON I: To Gaspard Gourgaud at St. Helena, April 23, 1816

The trade of the East has always been the richest jewel in the diadem of commerce. All nations, in all ages, have sought it; and those which obtained it, or even a share of it, attained the highest degree of opulence, refinement, and power.

T. H. BENTON: Speech in the Senate, 1847

The East bow'd low before the blast,
In patient, deep disdain.
She let the legions thunder past,
And plunged in thought again.

MATTHEW ARNOLD: *Obermann Once More,* 1855

Always the East — old, how incalculably old!

WALT WHITMAN: *Specimen Days,* July 22, 1878

Experience has shown us that the trade of the East is the key to national wealth and influence.

CHESTER A. ARTHUR: Message to the Senate, April 4, 1882

The urge toward the East. (Der Drang nach Osten.)

The phrase is not listed in Büchman, and its author remains unidentified; it was first heard in Germany during the discussion of plans for the Bagdad Railway, *c.* 1888

If you've 'eard the East a-callin', you won't never 'eed naught else.

RUDYARD KIPLING: *Mandalay,* 1890

Ship me somewheres east of Suez, where the best is like the worst,
Where they aren't no Ten Commandments an' a man can raise a thirst.

IBID.

From the East, light. (Ex Oriente lux.)

LATIN PHRASE

[*See also* Dawn.

East and West

Too far East is West.

R. C. TRENCH (ARCHBISHOP OF DUBLIN): *Lessons in Proverbs,* 1853

Oh, East is East, and West is West, and never the twain shall meet,
Till earth and sky stand presently at God's great Judgment Seat.

RUDYARD KIPLING: *The Ballad of East and West,* 1889

Easter

A solemn feast celebrated by Christians in remembrance of the resurrection of a God who was publicly hanged. To the end of celebrating this great day with all due honor, the Christians eat their God, doubtless to ascertain if, like the phoenix, He will spring into life from that which has devoured Him.

VOLTAIRE: *Philosophical Dictionary,* 1764

At Easter let your clothes be new
Or else be sure you will it rue.

OLD ENGLISH RHYME

[*See also* Christmas, Debauchery.

Easy

Anyone can steer the ship when the sea is calm.
PUBLILIUS SYRUS: *Sententiæ*, *c.* 50 B.C.

Easy come, easy go.
ENGLISH PROVERB, not recorded in its present form before the XIX century, but familiar as " Lightly come, lightly go " since the XIV

It is as easy as lying.
SHAKESPEARE: *Hamlet*, III, *c.* 1601

Going downhill a cow can pull as much as an ox. FRENCH PROVERB

[*See also* Doing.

Eating

Leave off first for manners' sake; and be not unsatiable, lest thou offend.
ECCLESIASTICUS XXXI, 17, *c.* 180 B.C.

Eating should be done in silence, lest the windpipe open before the gullet, and life be in danger. THE TALMUD (*Ta'anit*), *c.* 200

Eat to live, and do not live to eat.
ENGLISH PROVERB, traced by Smith to *c.* 1410

Feed by measure and defy the physician.
JOHN HEYWOOD: *Proverbs*, 1546

A man should not so much respect what he eateth as with whom he eateth.
MICHEL DE MONTAIGNE: *Essays*, III, 1588

Persons of honor never think of eating but at sitting down at table, and after dinner wash their hands and their mouths, that they may neither retain the taste nor the scent of what they have been eating.
ST. FRANCIS DE SALES: *Introduction to the Devout Life*, XXXIX, 1609

Jack Sprat could eat no fat,
His wife could eat no lean,
And so between the two of them
They licked the platter clean.
ENGLISH NURSERY RHYME, first recorded in 1639

A full gorged belly never produced a sprightly mind.
JEREMY TAYLOR: *Twenty-seven Sermons*, XVI, 1651

Often and little eating makes a man fat.
JOHN RAY: *English Proverbs*, 1670

If it were not for the belly the back might wear gold.
THOMAS FULLER: *Gnomologia*, 1732

To eat well is no whoredom; and to starve is no gentility. IBID.

Fingers were made before forks, and hands before knives.
JONATHAN SWIFT: *Polite Conversation*, 1738

Lord, Madame, I have fed like a farmer, I shall grow as fat as a porpoise. IBID.

Some people have a foolish way of not minding, or pretending not to mind, what they eat. For my part, I mind my belly very studiously and very carefully, for I look upon it that he who does not mind his belly will hardly mind anything else.
SAMUEL JOHNSON: *Boswell's Life*, Aug. 5, 1763

Tell me what you eat, and I will tell you what you are. (Dis-moi ce que tu manges, je te dirai ce que tu es.)
ANTHELME BRILLAT-SAVARIN: *Physiologie du goût*, 1825

Quick at meals, quick at work, is a saying as old as the hills.
WILLIAM COBBETT: *Advice to Young Men*, III, 1829

We do not eat for the good of living, but because the meat is savory and the appetite is keen. R. W. EMERSON: *Nature*, 1836

Man is what he eats. (Der Mensch ist, was er isst.)
L. A. FEUERBACH: Review of MOLESCHOTT'S *Lehre der Nahrungsmittel für das Volk*, 1850

He that eats till he is sick must fast till he is well.
H. G. BOHN: *Handbook of Proverbs*, 1855

There is no love sincerer than the love of food.
GEORGE BERNARD SHAW: *Man and Superman*, I, 1903

I eat, therefore I am. (Edo, ergo sum.)
Anon.: *Parody of Descartes' " Cogito, ergo sum "*

The destiny of nations depends on what they eat. FRENCH PROVERB

Stop eating when you are enjoying it most.
GERMAN PROVERB

Spread the table and the quarrel will end.
HEBREW PROVERB

Eating while seated makes one large of size; eating while standing makes one strong.
HINDU PROVERB

[*See also* Abstemiousness, Abstinence, Alone, Appetite, Belly, Breakfast, Children, Diet, Digestion, Dinner, Dish, Dress, Drinking, Eating and Drinking, Edible, Emesis, Exercise, Fat, Feasting, Forty, Gluttony, Gourmet, Hygiene, Lady, Love, Manners, Merriment, Modesty, Pheasant, Short, Sleep, Stomach, Supper.

Eating and Drinking

Let us eat and drink; for tomorrow we shall die.
ISAIAH XXII, 13, *c.* 700 B.C. (Cf. I CORINTHIANS XV, 32, *c.* 55)

There is nothing better for a man, than that he should eat and drink, and that he should make his soul enjoy good in his labor.
ECCLESIASTES II, 24, *c.* 200 B.C.

Every man should eat and drink and enjoy the fruit of all his labor; it is the gift of God.
ECCLESIASTES III, 13

A man hath no better thing under the sun than to eat, and to drink, and to be merry.
ECCLESIASTES VIII, 15

Take no thought for your life, what ye shall eat, or what ye shall drink.
MATTHEW VI, 25, *c.* 75

The Son of man came eating and drinking, and they say, Behold a man gluttonous, and a winebibber, a friend of publicans and sinners.
MATTHEW XI, 19

In eating, a third of the stomach should be filled with food, a third with drink, and the rest left empty.
THE TALMUD (*Gittin*), *c.* 200

Up to the age of forty, eating is beneficial; after forty, drinking.
THE TALMUD (*Sabbath*), *c.* 200

He that eateth well drinketh well, he that drinketh well sleepeth well, he that sleepeth well sinneth not, and he that sinneth not goeth straight through Purgatory to Paradise.
WILLIAM LITHGOW: *Rare Adventures*, 1609

Eat at pleasure, drink by measure.
RANDLE COTGRAVE: *French-English Dictionary*, 1611

What they want in meat, let them take out in drink.
THOMAS HEYWOOD: *The Fair Maid of the West*, II, 1617 (Cited as an "old proverb")

The choleric drinks, the melancholic eats, the phlegmatic sleeps.
GEORGE HERBERT: *Outlandish Proverbs*, 1640

Eat well is drink well's brother.
JAMES KELLY: *Complete Collection of Scottish Proverbs*, 1721

He was an ingenious man that first found out eating and drinking.
JONATHAN SWIFT: *Polite Conversation*, 1738

He who eats and drinks, but does not bless the Lord, is a thief.
HEBREW PROVERB

[*See also* Appetite, Eating, Drinking, Merriment, Temperance.

Eavesdropper

Listeners ne'er hear good of themselves.
JOHN RAY: *English Proverbs*, 1670

Listen at the hole, and you'll hear news of yourself.
THOMAS FULLER: *Gnomologia*, 1732

He who peeps through a hole may see what will vex him.
H. G. BOHN: *Handbook of Proverbs*, 1855

Eccentricity

Eccentricity has always abounded when and where strength of character has abounded; and the amount of eccentricity in a society has been proportional to the amount of genius, mental vigor, and moral courage it contained.
J. S. MILL: *On Liberty*, III, 1859

A man may say what he likes on a public platform — he may publish whatever opinion he chooses — but he dare not wear a peculiar fashion of hat on the street. Eccentricity is an outlaw.
ALEXANDER SMITH: *Dreamthorp*, XII, 1863

Echo

To an echo you owe the pleasure of hearing yourself talk.
WILLIAM CONGREVE: *The Way of the World*, II, 1700

A million horrible bellowing echoes broke
From the red-ribb'd hollow behind the wood,
And thunder'd up into Heaven.
ALFRED TENNYSON: *Maud*, XXIII, 1855

The echo always has the last word.
GERMAN PROVERB

[*See also* Bugle.

Eclipse

These late eclipses in the sun and moon portend no good to us. Love cools, friendship falls off, brothers divide: in cities, mutinies; in countries, discord; in palaces, treason; and the bond cracked between son and father.
SHAKESPEARE: *King Lear*, I, 1606

Economics

What we might call, by way of eminence, the dismal science.
THOMAS CARLYLE: *The Nigger Question*, 1849 (Fraser's Magazine, Dec.)

Annual income twenty pounds, annual expenditure nineteen nineteen six, result happiness. Annual income twenty pounds, annual expenditure twenty pound ought and six, result misery.
CHARLES DICKENS: *David Copperfield*, XXII, 1849

No nation ever made its bread either by its great arts, or its great wisdoms. By its minor arts or manufactures, by its practical knowledges, yes: but its noble scholarship, its noble philosophy, and its noble art are always

to be bought as a treasure, not sold for a livelihood.
JOHN RUSKIN: *The Crown of Wild Olive,* IV, 1866

Economy

Learn on how little man may live.
LUCAN: *Pharsalia,* IV, 65 B.C.

Let us all be happy and live within our means, even if we have to borrer the money to do it with.
C. F. BROWNE (ARTEMUS WARD): *Natural History,* 1866

The love of economy is the root of all virtue.
GEORGE BERNARD SHAW: *Maxims for Revolutionists,* 1903

I would rather have my people laugh at my economies than weep for my extravagance.
KING OSCAR II OF SWEDEN (1829–1907)

After order and liberty, economy is one of the highest essentials of a free government. . . . Economy is always a guarantee of peace.
CALVIN COOLIDGE: Speech in Northampton, Mass., May 30, 1923

Any government, like any family, can for a year spend a little more than it earns. But you and I know that a continuance of that habit means the poorhouse.
F. D. ROOSEVELT: Radio Speech, July 30, 1932

[*See also* Frugality, Thrift.

Edible

Good to eat, and wholesome to digest, as a worm to a toad, a toad to a snake, a snake to a pig, a pig to a man, and a man to a worm.
AMBROSE BIERCE: *The Devil's Dictionary,* 1906

Edinburgh

That most picturesque (at a distance) and nastiest (when near) of all capital cities.
THOMAS GRAY: *Letter to Dr. Wharton,* Sept., 1765

Pompous the boast, and yet a truth it speaks:
A Modern Athens — fit for modern Greeks.
JAMES HANNAY: *On Edinburgh, c.* 1860

Editor

Who would not be an editor? To write
The magic *we* of such enormous might;
To be so great beyond the common span
It takes the plural to express the man.
J. G. SAXE: *The Press,* 1855

A person employed on a newspaper, whose business it is to separate the wheat from the chaff, and to see that the chaff is printed.
ELBERT HUBBARD: *Roycroft Dictionary and Book of Epigrams,* 1923

[*See also* Journalism, Journalist, Newspaper, Press.

Education

Do not train boys to learning by force and harshness, but lead them by what amuses them, so that they may better discover the bent of their minds.
PLATO: *The Republic,* VII, *c.* 370 B.C.

There are two kinds of arguments, the true and the false. The young should be instructed in both — but the false first.
PLATO: *The Republic,* I, *c.* 350 B.C.

Children should be led into the right paths, not by severity, but by persuasion.
MENANDER: *Adelphoi, c.* 300 B.C.

On one occasion Aristotle was asked how much educated men were superior to those uneducated: "As much," said he, "as the living are to the dead."
DIOGENES LAERTIUS: *Lives of the Philosophers* (Aristotle), *c.* 150 B.C.

I call a complete and generous education that which fits a man to perform justly, skilfully, and magnanimously all the offices, both private and public, of peace and war.
JOHN MILTON: *Tractate on Education,* 1644

There is nothing so monstrous to which education cannot form our ductile minority; it can lick us into shapes beyond the monstrosities of Africa.
JOSEPH GLANVILL: *The Vanity of Dogmatizing,* XIV, 1661

A well-trained mind is made up, so to speak, of all the minds of past ages: only a single mind has been educated during all that time.
BERNARD DE FONTENELLE: *Digression sur les anciens et les modernes,* 1688

It is the great end of education to raise ourselves above the vulgar.
RICHARD STEELE: *The Tatler,* Sept. 7, 1709

Education is a companion which no misfortune can depress, no crime can destroy, no enemy can alienate, no despotism can enslave. At home a friend, abroad an introduction, in solitude a solace, and in society an ornament. It chastens vice, it guides virtue, it gives, at once, grace and government to genius. Without it, what is man? A splendid slave, a reasoning savage.
JOSEPH ADDISON: *The Spectator,* Nov. 6, 1711

No education can be of true advantage to young women but that which trains them up in humble industry, in great plainness of living, in exact modesty of dress.
WILLIAM LAW: *A Serious Call to a Devout and Holy Life,* XIX, 1728

'Tis education forms the common mind;
Just as the twig is bent the tree's inclined.
ALEXANDER POPE: *Moral Essays,* I (Of the Knowledge and Characters of Men), 1733

It is reported of the Persians, by an ancient writer, that the sum of their education consisted in teaching youth to ride, to shoot with the bow, and to speak truth.

SAMUEL JOHNSON: *The Rambler*, Feb. 15, 1751

The great secret of education is to direct vanity to proper objects.

ADAM SMITH: *The Theory of Moral Sentiments*, VI, 1759

The inward development of our faculties and organs is the education of nature; the use which we are taught to make of this development is the education of men; and that we gain from our own experience of the objects around us is the education of things.

J.-J. ROUSSEAU: *Émile*, I, 1762

I hate by-roads in education. Education is as well known, and has long been as well known, as ever it can be.

SAMUEL JOHNSON: *Boswell's Life*, 1775

Wisdom and knowledge, as well as virtue, diffused generally among the body of the people, being necessary for the preservation of their rights and liberties, and as these depend on spreading the opportunities and advantages of education in the various parts of the country and among the different orders of the people, it shall be the duty of the legislatures and magistrates, in all future periods of this commonwealth, to cherish the interest of literature and the sciences, and of all seminaries of them.

CONSTITUTION OF MASSACHUSETTS, 1780

The tax which will be paid for the purpose of education is not more than the thousandth part of what will be paid to kings, priests and nobles who will rise up among us if we leave the people in ignorance.

THOMAS JEFFERSON: *Letter to George Wythe*, 1786

I have never thought a boy should undertake abstruse or difficult sciences, such as mathematics in general, till fifteen years of age at soonest. Before that time, they are best employed in learning the languages, which is merely a matter of memory.

THOMAS JEFFERSON: *Letter to Ralph Izard*, 1788

There is but one method of preventing crimes, and of rendering a republican form of government durable, and that is, by disseminating the seeds of virtue and knowledge through every part of the state by means of proper places and modes of education, and this can be done effectually only by the interference and aid of the Legislature.

BENJAMIN RUSH: *The Influence of Physical Causes Upon the Moral Faculty*, 1788

A competent number of schools ought to be maintained in each town for the convenient instruction of youth.

CONSTITUTION OF VERMONT, 1791

Education, however indispensable in a cultivated age, produces nothing on the side of genius. When education ends, genius often begins.

ISAAC D'ISRAELI: *Essay on the Literary Character*, VI, 1795

Every man who rises above the common level has received two educations: the first from his teachers; the second, more personal and important, from himself.

EDWARD GIBBON: *Memoirs*, 1795

The General Assembly shall make such provisions by taxation or otherwise as, with the income arising from the school trust fund, will secure a thorough and efficient system of common schools throughout the state; but no religious or other sect or sects shall ever have any exclusive right or control of any part of the school funds of this state.

CONSTITUTION OF OHIO, 1802

Repetition is the mother of education.

JEAN PAUL RICHTER: *Levana*, I, 1807

The great use of education is to give us confidence, and to make us think ourselves on a level with other men. An uneducated man thinks there is a magic in it, and stands in awe of those who have had the benefit of it. It does little for us. No man, as Selden says, is the wiser for his learning.

Ascribed to J. HORNE TOOKE (1736–1812) in G. H. POWELL: *Reminiscences and Table-Talk of Samuel Rogers*, 1903

The General Assembly shall provide by law for a general and uniform system of common schools.

CONSTITUTION OF INDIANA, 1816

Anyone who has passed through the regular gradations of a classical education, and is not made a fool by it, may consider himself as having had a very narrow escape.

WILLIAM HAZLITT: *The Ignorance of the Learned*, 1821

Education makes a people easy to lead, but difficult to drive; easy to govern, but impossible to enslave.

HENRY BROUGHAM (LORD BROUGHAM AND VAUX): *The Present State of the Law*, 1828

The things taught in schools and colleges are not an education, but the means of education.

R. W. EMERSON: *Journal*, July 15, 1831

It is an axiom in political science that unless a people are educated and enlightened it is idle to expect the continuance of civil liberty or the capacity for self-government.

TEXAS DECLARATION OF INDEPENDENCE, March, 2, 1836

We are students of words: we are shut up in schools, and colleges, and recitation-rooms, for ten or fifteen years, and come out at last with a bag of wind, a memory of words, and do not know a thing.

R. W. EMERSON: *The New England Reformers,* 1844

A general diffusion of knowledge being essential to the preservation of the rights and liberties of the people, it shall be the duty of the Legislature of this state to make suitable provision for the support and maintenance of public schools.

CONSTITUTION OF TEXAS, 1845

A whale ship was my Yale College and my Harvard.

HERMAN MELVILLE: *Moby Dick,* XXIV, 1851

No child under the age of fifteen should receive instruction in subjects which may possibly be the vehicle of serious error, such as philosophy or religion, for wrong notions imbibed early can seldom be rooted out, and of all the intellectual faculties, judgment is the last to arrive at maturity. The child should give its attention either to subjects where no error is possible at all, such as mathematics, or to those in which there is no particular danger in making a mistake, such as languages, natural science, history, and so on.

ARTHUR SCHOPENHAUER: *On Education,* 1851 (Cf. JEFFERSON, *ante,* 1786)

All things now are to be learned at once, not first one thing, then another, not one well but many badly. Learning is to be without exertion, without attention, without toil; without grounding, without advance, without finishing.

J. H. NEWMAN: *On the Scope and Nature of University Education,* v, 1852

Education is the leading human souls to what is best, and making what is best out of them; and these two objects are always attainable together, and by the same means; the training which makes men happiest in themselves also makes them most serviceable to others.

JOHN RUSKIN: *Stones of Venice,* III, 1853

No mother's mark is more permanent than the mental nævi and moles, and excrescences, and mutilations, that students carry with them out of the lecture room.

O. W. HOLMES: *The Contagiousness of Puerperal Fever,* revised ed., 1855

A child's education should begin at least one hundred years before he was born.

O. W. HOLMES: *The Autocrat of the Breakfast-Table,* I, 1858

The idea of a girl's education is whatever qualifies her for going to Europe.

Ascribed to "an eminent teacher of girls" by R. W. EMERSON: *The Conduct of Life,* IV, 1860

You send your child to the schoolmaster, but 'tis the schoolboys who educate him. You send him to the Latin class, but much of his tuition comes, on his way to school, from the shop-windows.

R. W. EMERSON: *The Conduct of Life,* IV, 1860

If there were to be any difference between a girl's education and a boy's, I should say that of the two the girl should be earlier led, as her intellect ripens faster, into deep and serious subjects: and that her range of literature should be, not more, but less frivolous.

JOHN RUSKIN: *Sesame and Lilies,* II, 1865

Man can be set free from the yoke of his own nature only by education. It alone can make it possible for him to subordinate the impulses of his body to the guidance of his developing mind.

M. A. BAKUNIN: *Dieu et l'état,* 1871

Wherever is found what is called a paternal government, there is found state education. It has been discovered that the best way to insure implicit obedience is to commence tyranny in the nursery.

BENJAMIN DISRAELI: Speech in the House of Commons, June 15, 1874

In large states public education will always be mediocre, for the same reason that in large kitchens the cooking is usually bad.

F. W. NIETZSCHE: *Human All-too-Human,* I, 1878

Next in importance to freedom and justice is popular education, without which neither freedom nor justice can be permanently maintained.

JAMES A. GARFIELD: *Letter of Acceptance,* July 12, 1880

The important thing is not so much that every child should be taught, as that every child should be given the wish to learn.

JOHN LUBBOCK (LORD AVEBURY): *The Pleasures of Life,* X, 1887

Education is fatal to any one with a spark of artistic feeling. Education should be confined to clerks, and even them it drives to drink. Will the world learn that we never learn anything that we did not know before?

GEORGE MOORE: *Confessions of a Young Man,* VII, 1888

What is the task of all higher education? To make man into a machine. What are the means employed? He is taught how to suffer being bored.

F. W. NIETZSCHE: *The Twilight of the Idols,* 1889

Education is an admirable thing, but it is well to remember from time to time that nothing that is worth knowing can be taught.

OSCAR WILDE: *The Critic as Artist,* 1891

We are opposed to state interference with parental rights and rights of conscience in the education of children as an infringement of the fundamental Democratic doctrine that the largest individual liberty consistent with the rights of others insures the highest type of American citizenship and the best government.

Democratic National Platform, 1892

In educating the young it is not sufficient that religious instruction be given to them at fixed times; it is necessary also that every other subject that is taught to them be permeated with Christian piety. If this is wanting, little good can be expected from any kind of learning.

POPE LEO XIII: *Militantis ecclesiæ,* 1897

The great difficulty in education is to get experience out of ideas.

GEORGE SANTAYANA: *The Life of Reason,* I, 1905

We need education in the obvious more than investigation of the obscure.

O. W. HOLMES II: Speech in New York, Feb. 15, 1913

The constitution of Soviet Russia must ensure state aid to all students, in the forms of food, clothing, and school supplies.

NIKOLAI LENIN: *Materials Relating to the Revision of the Party Programme,* 1917

The state has a right to insist that its citizens shall be educated.

Pastoral Letter of the American Roman Catholic hierarchy, Feb., 1920

The parents have a right to say that no teacher paid by their money shall rob their children of faith in God and send them back to their homes skeptical, or infidels, or agnostics, or atheists.

W. J. BRYAN: Testimony at the Scopes trial, Dayton, Tenn., July 16, 1925

Every method of education founded, wholly or in part, on the denial or forgetfulness of original sin and of grace, and relying on the sole powers of human nature, is unsound.

POPE PIUS XI: *Divini illius magistri,* Dec. 31, 1929

The effects of infantile instruction are, like those of syphilis, never completely cured.

ROBERT BRIFFAULT: *Sin and Sex,* VIII, 1931

Education is the process of driving a set of prejudices down your throat.

MARTIN H. FISCHER (1879–)

Classical education in the English public schools consists of casting sham pearls before real swine. Author unidentified

To reverence superiority and accept a fact though it slay him are the final tests of an educated man. IBID.

[*See also* Animal, Character, Cleanliness, Coeducation, College, Family, Flogging, Freedom (Academic), Gentleman, Manual training, Militia, Nature, Nature *vs.* Nurture, Pedagogue, School, Society, Teacher.

Edwards, Jonathan (1703–58)

I have a constitution in many respects peculiarly unhappy, attended with flaccid solids, vapid, sizy, and scarce fluids, and a low tide of spirits; often occasioning a kind of childish weakness and contemptibleness of speech, presence, and demeanor, with a disagreeable dullness and stiffness.

JONATHAN EDWARDS: Letter to the trustees of New Jersey College, 1757

He believed in the worst God, preached the worst sermons, and had the worst religion of any human being who ever lived on this continent.

M. M. RICHTER: *Jonathan Edwards,* 1920

Eel

[*See* Habit, Mud.

Effect

[*See* Cause and Effect.

Efficiency

Did nothing in particular,
And did it very well.

W. S. GILBERT: *Iolanthe,* II, 1882

There was ease in Casey's manner as he stepped into his place;
There was pride in Casey's bearing, and a smile on Casey's face.
And when, responding to the cheers, he lightly doffed his hat,
No stranger in the crowd could doubt 'twas Casey at the bat.

ERNEST L. THAYER: *Casey at the Bat,* 1888 (San Francisco Examiner, June 3)

The best carpenters make the fewest chips.

GERMAN PROVERB

Egg

Is there any taste in the white of an egg?

JOB VI, 6, *c.* 325 B.C.

A priests' rule that is true:
Those eggs are best are long and white and new.

JOHN HARINGTON: *The Englishman's Doctor,* 1608

The egg's . . . a chicken *in potentia.*

BEN JONSON: *The Alchemist,* II, 1612

Every living thing comes from an egg. (Omne vivum ex ovo.)

WILLIAM HARVEY (1578–1657)

The vulgar boil, the learned roast an egg.

ALEXANDER POPE: *The Second Epistle of the Second Book of Horace,* 1738

I never see an egg brought on my table but I feel penetrated with the wonderful change it would have undergone but for my gluttony; it might have been a gentle, useful hen,

leading her chickens with a care and vigilance which speaks shame to many women.
ST. JOHN DE CRÈVECOEUR: *Letters from an American Farmer*, II, 1782

A hen is only an egg's way of making another egg.
SAMUEL BUTLER: *Life and Habit*, 1877

You can't unscramble scrambled eggs.
AMERICAN PROVERB

Better to have an egg today than a hen tomorrow. ITALIAN PROVERB

[*See also* Ale, Apple, Best, Caution, Christian, Hen, Heredity, Innocence.

Egoism

It is easy for me to curry favor with myself.
PHAEDRUS: *Fabulae Aesopiae*, V, *c.* 40

I would that all men were even as I myself.
ST. PAUL: In *I Corinthians VII*, 7, *c.* 55

I to myself am dearer than a friend.
SHAKESPEARE: *Two Gentlemen of Verona*, II, *c.* 1595

All the courses of my life do show
I am not in the roll of common men.
SHAKESPEARE: *I Henry IV*, III, *c.* 1598

If she think not well of me,
What care I how fair she be?
GEORGE WITHER: *The Author's Resolution*, 1617

Such is the nature of man that howsoever they may acknowledge many others to be more witty, or more eloquent, or more learned, yet they will hardly believe there may be many so wise as themselves.
THOMAS HOBBES: *Leviathan*, I, 1651

I am clever; and make no scruple of declaring it; why should I?
LA ROCHEFOUCAULD: *Self-Portrait*, 1658

We love our friends because they are our image; and we love our God because we are His.
JOSEPH GLANVILL: *The Vanity of Dogmatizing*, XIII, 1661

We would rather speak ill of ourselves than not talk of ourselves at all.
LA ROCHEFOUCAULD: *Maxims*, 1665

We cannot possibly feel for others; it is solely for ourselves that we feel. It is not father or mother, wife or child, that we love, but the agreeable emotions that they set up in us — emotions of pride and self-love.
G. C. LICHTENBERG: *Reflections*, 1799

Every man regards his own life as the New Year's Eve of time.
JEAN PAUL RICHTER: *Levana*, II, 1807

No man would, I think, exchange his existence with any other man, however fortunate. We had as lief not be, as not be ourselves.
WILLIAM HAZLITT: *On the Fear of Death*, 1821

I, too, am a king.
LUDWIG VAN BEETHOVEN (1770–1827)

Let a man know his worth, and keep things under his feet. Let him not peep or steal, or skulk up and down with the air of a charity-boy, a bastard, or an interloper, in the world which exists for him.
R. W. EMERSON: *Self-Reliance*, 1841

I love and honor Epaminondas, but I do not wish to be Epaminondas.
R. W. EMERSON: *Spiritual Laws*, 1841

Nothing is more to me than myself.
MAX STIRNER: *The Ego and His Own*, 1845

Whether what I think and do is Christian, what do I care? Whether it is human, humane, liberal, or inhuman, inhumane, illiberal, what do I care about that? IBID.

I find no sweeter fat than sticks to my own bones.
WALT WHITMAN: *Song of Myself*, 1855

If the egotist is weak, his egotism is worthless. If the egotist is strong, acute, full of distinctive character, his egotism is precious, and remains a possession of the race.
ALEXANDER SMITH: *Dreamthorp*, 1863

Egoism is the very essence of a noble soul.
F. W. NIETZSCHE: *Beyond Good and Evil*, 1886

Other people are quite dreadful. The only possible society is one's self.
OSCAR WILDE: *An Ideal Husband*, III, 1895

From his cradle to his grave a man never does a single thing which has any first and foremost object save one — to secure peace of mind, spiritual comfort, for himself.
S. L. CLEMENS (MARK TWAIN): *What Is Man?* 1906

I am my world.
LUDWIG WITTGENSTEIN: *Tractatus Logico-Philosophicus*, 1921

Every bird loves to hear himself sing.
GERMAN PROVERB

Every man thinks his own geese swans. IBID.

I, by myself, on me. (Ich, über mich, von mir.)
GERMAN SAYING

Every man can tout best on his own horn.
SCOTTISH PROVERB (*Tout*=blow)

[*See also* Apology, Contempt, Laissez faire, Self-love.

Egypt

Bury me not, I pray thee, in Egypt.
GENESIS XLVII, 29, *c.* 700 B.C.

Egypt is like a very fair heifer.
JEREMIAH XLVI, 20, *c.* 625 B.C.

Egypt is all the country covered by the inundations of the Nile, and all men who drink Nile water are Egyptians.
HERODOTUS: *Histories*, II, *c.* 430 B.C.

There sits drear Egypt, mid beleaguering sands,
Half woman and half beast,
The burnt-out torch within her mouldering hands
That once lit all the East.
J. R. LOWELL: *To the Past*, 1845

The riches of Egypt all go to foreigners.
ARAB PROVERB

[*See also* Fleshpots, Pyramid, Travel.

Egyptian

Ye shall spoil the Egyptians.
EXODUS III, 22, *c.* 700 B.C.

The Egyptians will I give over into the hand of a cruel lord; and a fierce king shall rule over them. ISAIAH XIX, 4, *c.* 700 B.C.

The Egyptians were universally atheists and anarchists.
RALPH CUDWORTH: *The True Intellectual System of the Universe*, 1678

Eighteenth Century

The putrid Eighteenth Century: such an ocean of sordid nothingness, shams and scandalous hypocrisies as never weltered in the world before.
THOMAS CARLYLE: *Letter to R. W. Emerson*, April 8, 1854

Eight-hour Day

Eight hours for work,
Eight hours for sleep,
Eight hours for what you will.
Slogan of the American labor movement, *c.* 1885

Eight hours for work, eight for play, eight for sleep — and eight shillings a day.
Slogan of the English labor movement, *c.* 1885

We favor the eight-hour day on all government work.
Democratic National Platform, 1908

The eight-hour day now undoubtedly has the sanction of the judgment of society in its favor and should be adopted as a basis for wages even where the actual work to be done cannot be completed within eight hours.
WOODROW WILSON: Statement to the press, Aug. 19, 1916

We declare our faith in the principle of the eight-hour day.
Republican National Platform, 1924

[*See also* Labor.

Eighty

The days of our years are threescore years and ten; and if by reason of strength they be fourscore years, yet is their strength labor and sorrow; for it is soon cut off, and we fly away. PSALMS XC, 10, *c.* 150 B.C.

My eightieth year warns me to pack my bags before I leave this life.
VARRO: *Rerum rusticarum*, 26 B.C.

Cato learned Greek at eighty; Sophocles
Wrote his grand Œdipus, and Simonides
Bore off the prize for verse from his compeers,
When each had numbered more than fourscore years.
H. W. LONGFELLOW: *Morituri Salutamus*, 1875

[*See also* Age (Old), Ages, Dying.

Ejaculation

Ejaculations are short prayers darted up to God on emergent occasions.
THOMAS FULLER: *Good Thoughts in Bad Times*, 1645

Elbow-grease

Elbow-grease is the best polish.
ENGLISH PROVERB, apparently not recorded before the XIX century

Election

Those who can fairly carry an election can also suppress a rebellion.
ABRAHAM LINCOLN: Message to Congress, June 4, 1861

An honest election, under democracy, is an act of innocence which does not take place more than once in the history of a given nation.
JOSÉ MARÍE GIL ROBLES: Speech in Madrid, 1933

[*See also* Ballot, English.

Electioneering

You see, in elections for members to sit in Parliament, how far saluting rows of old women, drinking with clowns, and being upon a level with the lowest part of mankind in that wherein they themselves are lowest, their diversions, will carry a candidate.
RICHARD STEELE: *The Spectator*, April 4, 1712

We will spend and spend, and tax and tax, and elect and elect.
Ascribed to HARRY L. HOPKINS: To Max Gordon at the Empire race-track, Yonkers, N. Y., Aug., 1938

Electricity

I'll put a girdle round the earth
In forty minutes.
SHAKESPEARE: *A Midsummer Night's Dream*, II, *c.* 1596

We call that fire of the black thunder-cloud electricity, and lecture learnedly about it, and grind the like of it out of glass and silk: but *what* is it? What made it? Whence comes it? Whither goes it?

THOMAS CARLYLE: *Heroes and Hero-Worship,* I, 1841 (Lecture in London, May 5)

Elegance

Elegant, pure and aerial minds.

JOHN KEATS: *To Some Ladies,* 1817

Arbiter of elegance. (Arbiter elegantiarum.)

LATIN PHRASE

Elegy

Take one of your neighbors who has lately departed this life; it is no great matter at what age the party died, but it will be best if he went away suddenly, being kill'd, drown'd, or froze to death.

BENJAMIN FRANKLIN: *Receipt to Make a New-England Funeral Elegy,* 1722

Element

There is one element, of which all things are made up.

GIORDANO BRUNO: *De monade numero et figura,* II, 1591

Elephant

Behold now behemoth, which I made with thee: he eateth grass as an ox. Lo now, his strength is in his loins, and his force is in the navel of his belly. He moveth his tail like a cedar: the sinews of his stones are wrapped together. His bones are as strong as pieces of brass; his bones are like bars of iron.

JOB XL, 15–18, *c.* 325 B.C.

The elephant hath joints, but none for courtesy; his legs are legs for necessity, not for flexure.

SHAKESPEARE: *Troilus and Cressida,* II, *c.* 1601

The elephant, although a gross beast, is yet the most decent and most sensible of any other upon earth. Although he never changes his female, and hath so tender a love for her whom he hath chosen, yet he never couples with her but at the end of every three years, and then only for the space of five days.

ST. FRANCIS DE SALES: *Introduction to the Devout Life,* XXXIX, 1609

They that govern elephants never appear before them in white.

JEREMY TAYLOR: *The Mysteriousness of Marriage,* 1651

It was six men of Indostan,
To learning much inclined,
Who went to see the elephant,
Though all of them were blind.

J. G. SAXE: *The Blind Men and the Elephant,* 1849

I do not mean to call an elephant a vulgar animal; but if you think about him carefully, you will find that his non-vulgarity consists in such gentleness as is possible to elephantine nature; not in his insensitive hide, nor in his clumsy foot; but in the way he will lift his foot if a child lies in his way; and in his sensitive trunk, and still more sensitive mind, and capability of pique on points of honor.

JOHN RUSKIN: *Modern Painters,* IX, 1860

Elephants a-pilin teak
In the sludgy, squdgy creek.

RUDYARD KIPLING: *Mandalay,* 1890

I asked my mother for fifteen cents
To see the elephant jump the fence;
He jumped so high he touched the sky,
And never came back 'till the Fourth of July.

AMERICAN FOLK-RHYME; date undetermined

An elephant never forgets an injury.

AMERICAN PROVERB

When an elephant is in trouble even a frog will kick him.

HINDU PROVERB

[*See also* Ugliness.

Elf

And the elves also,
Whose little eyes glow
Like sparks of fire, befriend thee.

ROBERT HERRICK: *Night-Piece to Julia,* 1648

Elia

[*See* Lamb (Charles).

Elijah

[*See* Leather.

Eliot, George (Marian Evans) (1819–80)

George Eliot had the heart of Sappho; but the face, with the long proboscis, the protruding teeth of the Apocalyptic horse, betrayed animality.

GEORGE MEREDITH: To Edward Clodd (Fortnightly Review, July, 1909), *c.* 1900

Elizabeth of England (1558–1603)

She hath abused her body, against God's laws, to the disgrace of princely majesty and the whole nation's reproach, by unspeakable and incredible variety of lust, which modesty suffereth not to be remembered.

WILLIAM CARDINAL ALLEN: *Admonition to the Nobility and People of England and Ireland,* 1588

Elizabeth, our dread sovereign and gracious queen, is not only a liberal patron unto poets, but an excellent poet herself; whose learned, delicate and noble muse surmounteth, be it in ode, elegy, epigram; or in any other kind of poem, heroic or lyric.

FRANCIS MERES: *Pallidas Tamia,* 1598

Queen Elizabeth never saw herself after she became old in a true glass; they painted her, and sometimes would vermilion her nose.
WILLIAM DRUMMOND of Hawthornden: *Informations and Manners of Ben Jonson,* 1618

Elocutionist

There are few men elocutionists, because when a man is a nuisance, he is told the truth.
E. W. HOWE: *Country Town Sayings,* 1911

Eloquence

It is not what the speaker says but who he is that gives weight to eloquence.
EURIPIDES: *Hecuba, c.* 426 B.C.

He is an eloquent man who can treat subjects of an humble nature with delicacy, lofty things impressively, and moderate things temperately.
CICERO: *De oratore, c.* 80 B.C.

The mistress of all the arts. (Omnium artium domina.)
TACITUS: *De oratoribus,* XXXVI, *c.* 76

Such force hath the tongue, and such is the power of eloquence and reason, that most men are forced even to yield in that which most standeth against their will.
THOMAS WILSON: *The Arte of Rhetorique,* 1553

That eloquence prejudices the subject it would advance which wholly attracts us to itself.
MICHEL DE MONTAIGNE: *Essays,* I, 1580

Aged ears play truant at his tales,
And younger hearings are quite ravished;
So sweet and voluble is his discourse.
SHAKESPEARE: *Love's Labor's Lost,* II, *c.* 1595

Oh, that my tongue were in the thunder's mouth!
Then with a passion would I shake the world.
SHAKESPEARE: *King John III, c.* 1596

Talking and eloquence are not the same: to speak, and to speak well are two things. A fool may talk, but a wise man speaks.
BEN JONSON: *Discoveries, c.* 1635

Eloquent speakers are inclined to ambition; for eloquence seemeth wisdom, both to themselves and others.
THOMAS HOBBES: *Leviathan,* XI, 1651

Eloquence is the painting of thought.
BLAISE PASCAL: *Pensées,* XXIV, 1670

Eloquence, smooth and cutting, is like a razor whetted with oil.
JONATHAN SWIFT: *Thoughts on Various Subjects,* 1706

Eloquence
That might have soothed a tiger's rage,
Or thawed the cold heart of a conqueror.
P. B. SHELLEY: *Queen Mab,* I, 1813

In a country and government like ours, eloquence is a powerful instrument, well worthy of the special pursuit of our youth.
THOMAS JEFFERSON: *Letter to G. W. Summers,* 1822

True eloquence does not consist in speech. Words and phrases may be marshalled in every way, but they cannot compass it. It must consist in the man, in the subject, and in the occasion. It comes, if it comes at all, like the outbreaking of a fountain from the earth, or the bursting forth of volcanic fires, with spontaneous, original, native force.
DANIEL WEBSTER: Speech in Boston, Aug. 2, 1826

We love eloquence for its own sake, and not for any truth which it may utter, or any heroism it may inspire.
H. D. THOREAU: *Cape Cod,* 1865

Can there be a more horrible object in existence than an eloquent man not speaking the truth?
THOMAS CARLYLE: Speech at Edinburgh, 1866

Every man is eloquent once in his life.
R. W. EMERSON: *Eloquence,* 1877

The finest eloquence is that which gets things done; the worst is that which delays them.
DAVID LLOYD GEORGE: At the Paris Peace Conference, Jan., 1919

Eloquence is logic on fire.
Author unidentified

Who can speak well can also lie well.
JAPANESE PROVERB

[*See also* Man and Woman, Preacher.

Elopement

To elope is cowardly; it is running away from danger; and danger has become so rare in modern life.
OSCAR WILDE: *A Woman of No Importance,* II, 1893

Emancipation

On the first day of January, in the year of our Lord 1863, all persons held as slaves within any state, or designated part of a state, the people whereof shall then be in rebellion against the United States, shall be then, thenceforward, and forever free.
ABRAHAM LINCOLN: Proclamation, Sept. 22, 1862

I do order and declare that all persons held as slaves within said designated states and parts of states are and henceforward shall be free; and that the executive government of the United States, including the military and naval authorities thereof, will recognize and maintain the freedom of said persons.
ABRAHAM LINCOLN: Emancipation Proclamation, Jan. 1, 1863

No more auction block for me;
Many thousand gone.
No more peck o' corn for me;
No more driver's lash for me;
No more pint o' salt for me:
Etc.

American Negro spiritual, *c.* 1863

[*See also* Freedom, Negro, Slave, Slavery, Union.

Embalming

Joseph commanded his servants the physicians to embalm his father.

GENESIS L, 2, *c.* 700 B.C.

Embryo

The karygranulomes, not the idiogranulomes or microsomenstratum in the protoplasm of the spermatogonia, unite into the idiosphacrosome, acrosoma of Lenhossék, a protean phase, as the idiosphacrosome differentiates into an idiocrytosome and an idiocalyptosome, both surrounded by the idiosphacrotheca, the archoplasmic vesicle; but the idioectosome disappears in the metamorphosis of the spermatid into a sphere, the idiophtharosome.

WILLIAM OSLER: Address before the Classical Association at Oxford, May 16, 1919 (It need not be added that this was concocted as burlesque)

Emerald

[*See* May.

Emerson, R. W. (1803–82)

A young man named Ralph Waldo Emerson, a classmate of my lamented son George, after failing in the everyday avocations of a Unitarian preacher and schoolmaster, starts a new doctrine of Transcendentalism, declares all the old revelations superannuated and worn out, and announces the approach of new revelations and prophecies.

JOHN QUINCY ADAMS: *Diary,* Aug. 2, 1840

Emerson's writing has a cold, cheerless glitter, like the new furniture in a warehouse, which will come of use by and by.

ALEXANDER SMITH: *Dreamthorp,* IX, 1863

A gap-toothed and hoary-headed ape, carried at first into notice on the shoulder of Carlyle, and who now in his dotage spits and chatters from a dirtier perch of his own finding and fouling: coryphaeus or choragus of his Bulgarian tribe of autocoprophagous baboons, who make the filth they feed on.

A. C. SWINBURNE: *Letter,* Jan. 30, 1874

A just man, poised on himself, all-loving, all-inclosing, and sane and clear as the sun.

WALT WHITMAN: *Specimen Days,* May 6, 1882

Emerson is one who lives instinctively on ambrosia — and leaves everything indigestible on his plate.

F. W. NIETZSCHE: *The Twilight of the Idols,* 1889

Emesis

If thou hast been forced to eat much, arise, go out, and vomit; and it shall refresh thee, and thou shalt not bring sickness upon the body.

ECCLESIASTICUS XXXI, 25, *c.* 180 B.C.

Eminence

They that stand high have many blasts to shake them.

SHAKESPEARE: *Richard III,* I, *c.* 1592

Not to know me argues yourselves unknown.

JOHN MILTON: *Paradise Lost,* IV, 1667

A man does not rise to eminence in the world who is merely a good singer and dancer.

J.-J. ROUSSEAU: *Confessions,* V, 1766

That you have enemies you must not doubt, when you reflect that you have made yourself eminent.

THOMAS JEFFERSON: *Letter to James Steptoe,* 1782

He who surpasses or subdues mankind
Must look down on the hate of those below.

BYRON: *Childe Harold,* III, 1816

Who knows not noble Valdez
Hath never heard of Spain.

RUDYARD KIPLING: *The Song of Diego Valdez,* 1902

Let a dog bite a poor scholar and no one cares, but if a scorpion sting a mandarin sympathisers come in crowds.

CHINESE PROVERB

Nearest the king, nearest the gallows.

DANISH PROVERB

Eminence shortens life. HEBREW PROVERB

It's the biggest cherry-tree that attracts the wind. JAPANESE PROVERB

[*See also* Censure, Distinction, Envy, Fame, High, Merit, Tall.

Emotion

There are moments in life when the heart is so full of emotion
That if by chance it be shaken, or into its depths like a pebble
Drops some careless word, it overflows, and its secret,
Spilt on the ground like water, can never be gathered together.

H. W. LONGFELLOW: *The Courtship of Miles Standish,* VI, 1858

The advantage of the emotions is that they lead us astray.

OSCAR WILDE: *The Picture of Dorian Gray,* 1891

The secret of remaining young is never to have an emotion that is unbecoming. IBID.

[*See also* Art, Curiosity, Music, Poetry, Tragedy.

Emperor

Because I pillage with one little ship I am called a pirate; because you do it with a great navy you are called an emperor.
A captured pirate to Alexander of Macedon, *c.* 330 B.C.

An emperor ought to die standing.
VESPASIAN, EMPEROR OF ROME: On his deathbed, 79

[*See also* Abdication, Dead, Hunting, Husband and Wife, King.

Empire

The Empire is peace. (L'empire c'est la paix.)
NAPOLEON III (then President of France): Speech before the Chamber of Commerce at Bordeaux, Oct. 9, 1852

The day of small nations has passed away; the day of empires has come.
JOSEPH CHAMBERLAIN: Speech at Birmingham, May 13, 1904

[*See also* Aristocracy, Imperialism, Peace, West.

Employment

A man who qualifies himself well for his calling never fails of employment in it.
THOMAS JEFFERSON: *Letter to Peter Carr,* 1792

Employment gives health, sobriety, and morals. Constant employment and well-paid labor produce, in a country like ours, general prosperity, content, and cheerfulness.
DANIEL WEBSTER: Speech in the Senate, July 25, 1846

The man who gives me employment, which I must have or suffer, that man is my master, let me call him what I will.
HENRY GEORGE: *Social Problems,* v, 1884

[*See also* Capital and Labor, Vocation.

Empty

Empty barrels make the most noise.
ENGLISH PROVERB, traced by Apperson to JOHN LYLY: *Euphues,* 1579

An empty bag cannot stand upright.
H. G. BOHN: *Handbook of Proverbs,* 1855

Empty wagons make the most noise.
DANISH PROVERB

Emulation

When a certain worthy died one man copied his way of wearing his hat, another his way of carrying his sword, a third the cut of his beard and a fourth his walk, but not one tried to be the honest man he was.
G. C. LICHTENBERG: *Reflections,* 1799

The little snake studies the ways of the big serpent.
JAPANESE PROVERB

End

Remember the end.
Attributed to CHILO of Sparta, *c.* 600 B.C.

Remember the end, and thou shalt never do amiss.
ECCLESIASTICUS III, 36, *c.* 180 B.C.

No man ever undertakes an art or a science merely to acquire knowledge of it. In all human affairs there is always an end in view — of pleasure, or honor, or advantage.
POLYBIUS: *Histories,* III, *c.* 125 B.C.

Crime is honest in a good cause. (Honesta turpitudo est pro causa bona.)
PUBLILIUS SYRUS: *Sententiæ,* *c.* 50 B.C.

The end is not yet.
MATTHEW XXIV, 6, *c.* 75 (Sometimes *thereof* is inserted after *end,* possibly by assimilation from PROVERBS XX, 21: "The end thereof shall not be blessed")

Indifferent acts are judged by their ends; sins are judged by themselves.
ST. AUGUSTINE: *To Consentius, Against Lying,* *c.* 400

The end proveth everything.
JOHN GOWER: *Confessio Amantis,* VI, *c.* 1390

If the end be well, all will be well. (Si finis bonus est, totum bonum erit.)
GESTA ROMANORUM, *c.* 1472

All is well that ends well.
JOHN HEYWOOD: *Proverbs,* 1546

All things tend toward one final end.
GIORDANO BRUNO: *De monade numero et figura,* II, 1591

The end crowns all;
And that old common arbitrator, Time,
Will one day end it.
SHAKESPEARE: *Troilus and Cressida,* IV, *c.* 1601

All's well that ends well.
SHAKESPEARE: Title of a play, *c.* 1602 (Cf. GESTA ROMANORUM, *ante,* *c.* 1472; HEYWOOD, 1546)

The be-all and the end-all.
SHAKESPEARE: *Macbeth,* I, *c.* 1605

If the end is licit the means are licit. (Cum finis est licitus etiam media sunt licita.)
HERMANN BUSENBAUM: *Medulla theologiae moralis,* 1645 (This seems to be the source of "The end justifies the means")

A morning sun and a wine-bred child and a Latin-bred woman seldom end well.
GEORGE HERBERT: *Jacula Prudentum,* 1651

We should look to the end in all things.
JEAN DE LA FONTAINE: *Fables,* III, 1668

The end must justify the means.
MATTHEW PRIOR: *Hans Carvel*, c. 1710

Everything hath an end, and a pudding hath two.
THOMAS FULLER: *Gnomologia*, 1732

Let the intermediate ends be warrantable, and the ultimate end worthy.
BENJAMIN WHICHCOTE: *Moral and Religious Aphorisms*, 1753

The end directs and sanctifies the means.
LORD CHIEF JUSTICE WILMOT: *Judgment in Collins* vs. *Blantern*, 1767

He who wills the end wills the means.
ENGLISH PROVERB, not recorded before the XIX century

It is the beginning of the end. (C'est le commencement de la fin.)
C. M. TALLEYRAND: Said during the Hundred Days, March 20–June 28, 1815

What signifies the ladder, provided one rise and attain the end?
C. A. SAINTE-BEUVE: *Letter to the Abbé Eustache Barbe*, July 26, 1829

To accomplish anything excellent, the will must work for catholic and universal ends.
R. W. EMERSON: *Civilization*, 1870

May God make our end better than our beginning. ARAB SAYING

The end praises the work. (La fin loue l'œuvre.) FRENCH PROVERB

End good, all good. (Ende gut, alles gut.)
GERMAN PROVERB

To the end. (Ad finem.) LATIN PHRASE

Look to the end. (Respice finem.)
LATIN PROVERB

[*See also* Beginning, Catholicism (Roman), Church (Roman Catholic), Fool, Progress.

Endogamy

Every daughter, that possesseth an inheritance in any tribe of the children of Israel, shall be wife unto one of the family of the tribe of her father, that the children of Israel may enjoy every man the inheritance of his fathers. NUMBERS XXXVI, 8, c. 700 B.C.

Endurance

What can't be cured must be endured.
ENGLISH PROVERB (Apperson traces early forms to WILLIAM LANGLAND: *Piers Plowman*, c. 1375)

The first thing a child should learn is how to endure. It is what he will have most need to know. J.-J. ROUSSEAU: *Émile*, II, 1762

Fate gave to man the courage of endurance.
LUDWIG VAN BEETHOVEN: *Diary*, 1814

He conquers who endures.
ITALIAN PROVERB

Enemy

A man's enemies are the men of his own house.
MICAH VII, 6, c. 700 B.C.

I have pursued mine enemies, and destroyed them; and turned not again until I had consumed them.
II SAMUEL XXII, 38, c. 500 B.C.

The worst enemy is the one that fears the gods.
ÆSCHYLUS: *The Seven Against Thebes*, c. 490 B.C.

The Spartans do not ask how many the enemy number, but where they are.
Ascribed to AGIS II, KING OF SPARTA, c. 415 B.C.

Wise men learn much from their enemies.
ARISTOPHANES: *The Birds*, 414 B.C.

An enemy has his due also, namely, evil.
PLATO: *The Republic*, I, c. 350 B.C.

If thine enemy be hungry, give him bread to eat; and if he be thirsty, give him water to drink: for thou shalt heap coals of fire upon his head, and the Lord shall reward thee.
PROVERBS XXV, 21–22, c. 350 B.C. (Cf. ROMANS XII, 20, c. 55)

Rejoice not over thy greatest enemy being dead.
ECCLESIASTICUS VII, 7, c. 180 B.C.

Mine enemies are lively, and they are strong: and they that hate me wrongfully are multiplied. PSALMS XXXVIII, 19, c. 150 B.C.

A man has no enemy worse than himself.
CICERO: *Ad Atticum*, X, c. 50 B.C.

Love your enemies, bless them that curse you, do good to them that hate you, and pray for them which despitefully use you, and persecute you.
MATTHEW V, 44, c. 75 (Cf. LUKE VI, 27–28, c. 75)

It's hard to trust an enemy. (Cale creditur hosti.) OVID: *Fasti*, II, c. 5 B.C.

A dead enemy always smells good. (Optime olere occisum hostem.)
ALUS VITELLIUS: On visiting the battlefield of Bedriacum, 69 (Also ascribed to CHARLES IX of France, on the night of St. Bartholomew, 1571)

A father who contracteth debts is an enemy, and a mother false to her bed; a beautiful wife is an enemy; an ignorant son is an enemy. *The Hitopadesa*, intro., c. 500

Avoid that which an enemy tells you to do; for if you follow his advice, you will smite your knees with the hand of sorrow. If he shows you a road straight as an arrow, turn from it and go the other way.
SADI: *The Gulistan*, 1258

A man that is well advised dreadeth his least enemy.
GEOFFREY CHAUCER: *The Canterbury Tales* (Melibœus's Tale), *c.* 1386

In cases of defence 'tis best to weigh
The enemy more mighty than he seems.
SHAKESPEARE: *Henry V*, II, *c.* 1599

Heat not a furnace for your foe so hot
That it do singe yourself.
SHAKESPEARE and JOHN FLETCHER: *Henry VIII*, I, 1613

You have many enemies, that know not
Why they are so, but, like to village-curs,
Bark when their fellows do.
SHAKESPEARE and JOHN FLETCHER: *Henry VIII*, II

To a flying enemy a silver bridge.
THOMAS SHELTON: Tr. of CERVANTES: *Don Quixote*, II (1615), 1620

He is no man's enemy but his own.
JOHN CLARKE: *Parœmiologia Anglo-Latina*, 1639

Take heed of wind that comes in at a hole, and a reconciled enemy.
GEORGE HERBERT: *Outlandish Proverbs*, 1640

How pleasant it is to pity the fate of an enemy when we have nothing more to fear from him.
PIERRE CORNEILLE: *La mort de Pompée*, V, 1643

One enemy is too much.
GEORGE HERBERT: *Jacula Prudentum*, 1651

If any two men desire the same thing, which nevertheless they cannot both enjoy, they become enemies.
THOMAS HOBBES: *Leviathan*, I, 1651

Believe no tales from an enemy's tongue.
JAMES HOWELL: *Proverbs*, 1659

Take heed of enemies reconciled, and of meat twice boiled.
JOHN RAY: *English Proverbs*, 1670 (Smith traces the thought to Chaucer, *c.* 1386)

Our enemies will tell the rest with pleasure.
WILLIAM FLEETWOOD (BISHOP OF ST. ASAPH): *Free Sermons*, pref., 1712 (The House of Commons ordered this preface to be burned, but Steele reprinted it in the Spectator for May 21, 1712)

The gifts of an enemy are justly to be dreaded.
VOLTAIRE: *La Henriade*, II, 1723

If we are bound to forgive an enemy, we are not bound to trust him.
THOMAS FULLER: *Gnomologia*, 1732

If you have no enemies it is a sign fortune has forgot you.
IBID.

Though thy enemy seems a mouse, yet watch him like a lion.
IBID.

There is no little enemy.
BENJAMIN FRANKLIN: *Poor Richard's Almanac*, 1733

I may not be an enemy; I would not have one. To be an enemy is a sin; to have one is a temptation.
BENJAMIN WHICHCOTE: *Moral and Religious Aphorisms*, 1753

There is not a more prudent maxim than to live with one's enemies as if they may one day become one's friends.
LORD CHESTERFIELD: *Letter to his son*, Dec. 31, 1757

We wish no evil to those we despise, but only to those who have a right to despise us.
STANISLAUS LESZCYNSKI (KING OF POLAND): *Œuvres du philosophe bienfaisant*, 1763

My prayer to God is a very short one "Oh Lord, make my enemies ridiculous!" God has granted it.
VOLTAIRE: *Letter to M. Damilaville*, May, 1767

You are a member of Parliament, and one of that majority which has doomed my country to destruction. — You have begun to burn our towns, and murder our people. — Look upon your hands! They are stained with the blood of your relations! — You and I were long friends: — You are now my enemy, — and I am yours.
BENJAMIN FRANKLIN: *Letter to William Strahan*, July 5, 1775 (Written but not sent)

He who loves his enemies betrays his friends;
This surely is not what Jesus intends.
WILLIAM BLAKE: *The Everlasting Gospel*, *c.* 1810

Earth could not hold us both, nor can one heaven
Contain my deadliest enemy and me.
ROBERT SOUTHEY: *Roderick*, XXI, 1814

To affirm that a vicious man is only his own enemy, is about as wise as to affirm that a virtuous man is only his own friend.
C. C. COLTON: *Lacon*, 1820

Our greatest enemies are those who rob us of our good opinion of ourselves.
WILLIAM HAZLITT: *Traveling Abroad*, 1828 (New Monthly, May–June)

Our friends, the enemy. (Nos amis, les ennemis.)
P. J. BÉRANGER: *L'Opinion de ces demoiselles*, *c.* 1830

Learning from one's enemies is the best way to love them, for it puts one into a grateful mood toward them.
F. W. NIETZSCHE: *Human All-too-Human*, II, 1878

A man cannot be too careful in the choice of his enemies.
OSCAR WILDE: *The Picture of Dorian Gray,* 1891

If you attend to your work, and let your enemy alone, some one else will come along some day, and do him up for you.
E. W. HOWE: *Country Town Sayings,* 1911

Do not despise a small wound, a poor relative, or an humble enemy. DANISH PROVERB

There is no little enemy. FRENCH PROVERB

The best enemies are those who make threats.
GERMAN PROVERB

Many enemies, much honor. IBID.

A wise enemy is better than a foolish friend.
MODERN GREEK PROVERB

The gate of a town may be shut, but not the mouth of an enemy. PERSIAN PROVERB

He that does you an ill turn will ne'er forgie you. SCOTTISH PROVERB

[*See also* Author, Conquest, Danger, Enmity, Envy, Foe, Forgiveness, Friend and Enemy, Gift, God, Grave, Hatred, House, Hypocrisy, Kiss, Laughter, Prayer, Reconciliation, Revenge, Soldier, Spoils, Victory.

Energy

Energy is the only life, and is from the body; and reason is the bound or outward circumference of energy. Energy is eternal delight.
WILLIAM BLAKE: *The Marriage of Heaven and Hell,* 1790

Energy may be turned to bad uses; but more good may always be made of an energetic nature than of an indolent and impassive one.
J. S. MILL: *On Liberty,* III, 1859

[*See also* Diligence.

Engineer

Engineers are more clever than artillerymen.
NAPOLEON I: To Gaspard Gourgaud at St. Helena, Nov. 7, 1817

[*See also* Infantry.

England

Merry England.
ENGLISH PHRASE, traced by Smith to *c.* 1300

England is the paradise of women, the purgatory of men, and the hell of horses.
JOHN FLORIO: *Second Frutes,* 1591 (Cf. FULLER, *post,* 1642)

This England never did, nor never shall,
Lie at the proud foot of a conqueror.
SHAKESPEARE: *King John,* V, *c.* 1596

This royal throne of kings, this scepter'd isle,
This earth of majesty, this seat of Mars,
This other Eden, demi-paradise,
This fortress built by nature for herself
Against infection and the hand of war;
This happy breed of men, this little world,
This precious stone set in the silver sea,
Which serves it in the office of a wall,
Or as a moat defensive to a house,
Against the envy of less happy lands;
This blessed plot, this earth, this realm, this England.
SHAKESPEARE: *Richard II,* II, *c.* 1596

He who would England win
In Ireland must begin.
ENGLISH RHYME, traced by Apperson to the XVI century

O England, full of sin, but most of sloth,
Spit out thy phlegm, and fill thy breast with glory.
GEORGE HERBERT: *The Temple,* 1633

Let not England forget her precedence of teaching nations how to live.
JOHN MILTON: *Doctrine and Discipline of Divorce,* 1633

England is a prison for men, a paradise for women, a purgatory for servants, a hell for horses.
THOMAS FULLER: *The Holy State and the Profane State,* 1642 (Cf. FLORIO, *ante,* 1591)

England, ah! perfidious England! (L'Angleterre, ah! la perfide Angleterre!)
J. B. BOSSUET: Sermon at Metz, 1652 (During the Napoleonic era the phrase became converted into "La perfide Albion")

The first impediment of England's greatness is that the territories thereunto belonging are too far asunder, and divided by the sea into many several islands and countries.
WILLIAM PETTY: *Political Arithmetic,* V, *c.* 1677

O debauchery, debauchery, what hast thou done in England! Thou hast corrupted our young men, and hast made our old men beasts; thou hast deflowered our virgins, and hast made matrons bawds.
JOHN BUNYAN: *The Life and Death of Mr. Badman,* 1680

England is a little garden full of sour weeds.
Ascribed to LOUIS XIV of France, *c.* 1706

'Tis to thy sovereign grace I owe
That I was born on British ground,
Where streams of heavenly mercy flow
And words of sweet salvation sound.
ISAAC WATTS: *Divine Songs for Children,* pref., 1715

Hail, happy land, whose fertile grounds
The liquid fence of Neptune bounds.
JOHN GAY: *Fables,* II, 1738

All things human have their ends, and some day England will lose its liberty, and perish.

It will perish when its legislative power becomes more corrupt than its executive power.

C. L. DE MONTESQUIEU: *The Spirit of the Laws*, XI, 1748

The land of scholars, and the nurse of arms.

OLIVER GOLDSMITH: *The Traveler*, 1764

The sun of her glory is fast descending to the horizon.

THOMAS JEFFERSON: *Notes on Virginia*, 1782

England, with all thy faults I love thee still.

WILLIAM COWPER: *The Task*, II, 1785

Slaves cannot breathe in England; if their lungs
Receive our air, that moment they are free.

IBID.

England is a nation which nothing but views of interest can govern.

THOMAS JEFFERSON: *Letter to James Madison*, 1785

England is a moon shone upon by France. France has all things within herself; and she possesses the power of recovering from the severest blows. England is an artificial country: take away her commerce, and what has she?

Ascribed to EDMUND BURKE (1729–97) in ALEXANDER DYCE: *Recollections of the Table-Talk of Samuel Rogers*, 1856

Oh, it's a snug little island!
A right little, tight little island!
Search the globe round, none can be found
So happy as this little island.

CHARLES DIBDIN: *The Snug Little Island*, 1797

In England there are sixty different religions, and only one sauce.

FRANCESCO CARACCIOLI (1752–99)

Great Britain is fighting our battles and the battles of mankind, and France is combatting for the power to enslave and plunder us and all the world.

FISHER AMES: *Letter to Theodore Dwight*, Oct. 31, 1803

It is now three centuries since an English pig has fallen in a fair battle upon English ground, or a farmhouse been rifled, or a clergyman's wife been subjected to any other proposals of love than the connubial endearments of her sleek and orthodox mate.

SYDNEY SMITH: *Peter Plymley's Letters*, 1808

You cannot imagine, you say, that England will ever be ruined and conquered; and for no other reason that I can find, but because it seems so very odd it should be ruined and conquered. Alas! so reasoned, in their time, the Austrian, Russian and Prussian Plymleys. But the English are brave; so were all these nations.

IBID.

A pirate spreading misery and ruin over the face of the ocean.

THOMAS JEFFERSON: *Letter to Walter Jones*, 1810

I consider the government of England as totally without morality, insolent beyond bearing, inflated with vanity and ambition, aiming at the exclusive dominion of the sea, lost in corruption, of deep-rooted hatred towards us, hostile to liberty wherever it endeavors to show its head, and the eternal disturber of the peace of the world.

THOMAS JEFFERSON: *Letter to Thomas Leiper*, June, 1815

The extremes of opulence and of want are more remarkable, and more constantly obvious, in this country than in any other that I ever saw.

JOHN QUINCY ADAMS: *Diary*, Nov. 8, 1816

In my opinion the only thing which can save England will be abstaining from meddling in Continental affairs, and by withdrawing her army from the Continent . . . You are superior in maritime force to all the world united; and while you confine yourself to that arm, you will always be powerful and be dreaded.

NAPOLEON I: To Barry E. O'Meara at St. Helena, May 27, 1817

I am sure my bones would not rest in an English grave, or my clay mix with the earth of that country. I believe the thought would drive me mad on my deathbed, could I suppose that any of my friends would be base enough to convey my carcass back to your soil.

BYRON: *Letter to John Murray*, June 7, 1819

I have no great cause to love that spot of earth
Which holds what *might have been* the noblest nation;
But though I owe it little but my birth,
I feel a mixed regret and veneration
For its decaying fame and former worth.

BYRON: *Don Juan*, X, 1823

It was never good times in England since the poor began to speculate upon their condition.

CHARLES LAMB: *Letter to George Dyer*, Dec. 20, 1830

England stands at the head of modern civilization, as a whole, although many countries surpass her in particular parts. The higher tastes of England are not as refined and cultivated, perhaps, as those of Italy and France, but the base of society is infinitely more advanced.

J. FENIMORE COOPER: *The American Democrat*, XXXIV, 1838

England is preëminently the country of pauperism.

KARL MARX: *On the King of Prussia and Social Reform*, 1845

That mountain of shams.

MARGARET FULLER OSSOLI: *Letter to R. W. Emerson,* Nov. 16, 1846

Oh, to be in England
Now that April's there.

ROBERT BROWNING: *Home Thoughts from Abroad,* 1847

If there be one test of national genius universally accepted, it is success; and if there be one successful country in the universe for the last millennium, that country is England.

R. W. EMERSON: *English Traits,* III, 1856

Oh, England is a pleasant place for them that's rich and high,
But England is a cruel place for such poor folks as I.

CHARLES KINGSLEY: *The Last Buccaneer,* 1857

In bad years there is plenty of grumbling here, and sometimes a little rioting. But it matters little, for here the sufferers are not the rulers. The supreme power is in the hands of a class, numerous indeed, but select — of an educated class, of a class which is, and knows itself to be, deeply interested in the security of property and the maintenance of order.

T. B. MACAULAY: *Letter to H. S. Randall,* May 23, 1857

The greatness of England is now all collective; individually small, we only appear capable of anything great by our habit of combining.

J. S. MILL: *On Liberty,* III, 1859

England is the mother of parliaments.

JOHN BRIGHT: Speech at Birmingham, Jan. 18, 1865

In England it [is] enough for a man to try and produce any serious beautiful work to lose all his rights as a citizen.

OSCAR WILDE: *The English Renaissance of Art,* 1882 (Lecture in New York, Jan. 9)

England and the United States are natural allies, and should be the best of friends.

U. S. GRANT: *Personal Memoirs,* conclusion, 1885

The disease from which the nation is suffering is dishonesty. What we have all been trying to do is to live at the expense of other people's labor, without giving an equivalent of our own labor in return. Some succeed, others only try; but it comes to much the same thing.

EDWARD CARPENTER: *England's Ideal,* 1887

What should they know of England who only England know?

RUDYARD KIPLING: *The English Flag,* 1891

God punish England! (Gott strafe England!)

ALFRED FUNKE: *Schwert und Myrte,* 1914 (This work was a novel published serially in the Sonntagszeitung für das deutsche Haus. The phrase became popular in Germany at once)

To fight England is like fighting fate.

LORD DUNSANY: *A Word in Season,* 1940 (London Times, May 13)

A scientist says: Roast beef made England what she is today. Moral: Eat more vegetables. Author unidentified

England is every dog's spiritual home. IBID.

On a fine day the climate of England is like looking up a chimney; on a foul day, like looking down one. IBID.

The heart of England.

ENGLISH PHRASE, usually applied to Warwickshire

England is a good land with a bad people.

FRENCH PROVERB

The three wonders of England are the churches, the women and the wool (ecclesia, foemina, lana).

MEDIEVAL LATIN SAYING

[*See also* Alliance, Austrian, Ballad, Britain, British, Canada, Cant, Character (National), Dead, Duty, English, Englishman, Exile, France, Freedom, French, Gluttony, Government (English), Great Britain, Home, Ireland, Isolation, Leadership, Liberty, Oats, Oxford University, Navy (British), Parliament, Party, Pension, Poor, Protestantism, Punishment, Puritanism, Slave, Sportsmanship, Tobacco-chewing, Travel, United States, Wales.

English

Who dare compare the English, the most degraded of all the races under Heaven, with the Welsh?

GIRALDUS CAMBRENSIS (1147–1222)

The English are the apes of the French.

ENGLISH PROVERB, traced by Apperson to the early XVII century

The English take their pleasures sadly.

First found, in the form of "They amuse themselves sadly" (Ils s'amusent tristement) in MAXIMILIEN DE BÉTHUNE (DUC DE SULLY): *Mémoires,* 1630

A nation not slow and dull, but of a quick, ingenious, and piercing spirit; acute to invent, subtile and sinewy to discourse, not beneath the reach of any point the highest that human capacity can soar to.

JOHN MILTON: *Areopagitica,* 1644

These are the heroes who despise the Dutch,
And rail at new-come foreigners so much;
Forgetting that themselves are all deriv'd
From the most scoundrel race that ever liv'd.

DANIEL DOFOE: *The True-Born Englishman,* I, 1701

The Pict has made them sour; the Dane, morose;
False from the Scot, and from the Norman worse;
What honesty they have, the Normans gave them;
And that, now they grow old, begins to leave them.

DANIEL DEFOE: *The True-Born Englishman*, II

No panegyric needs their praise record,
An Englishman ne'er wants his own good word.

IBID.

Raw meat makes animals fierce, and it has the same effect on man. The English, who eat their meat red and bloody, show the savagery that goes with such food.

J. O. DE LA METTRIE: *L'Homme machine*, 1748

The English are never so weak as at home, nor so easy to conquer.

C. L. MONTESQUIEU: *The Spirit of the Laws*, IX, 1748 (Quoted as "the *mot* of the Sieur de Coucy to Charles V" of France (1337–80); Enguerrand VII de Coucy was married to Isabel, the elder daughter of Edward III of England, and remained neutral in the war between England and France)

The English are a busy people. They haven't the time to become polished.

C. L. MONTESQUIEU: *Pensées, c.* 1750

The people of England are never so happy as when you tell them they are ruined.

ARTHUR MURPHY: *The Upholsterer*, II, 1758

I think it owing to the good sense of the English that they have not painted better.

WILLIAM HOGARTH: *Letter to Horace Walpole*, 1761

The English think they are free, but they are only so during the election of members of Parliament. Afterward they are slaves, they are nothing. During the brief moment of their liberty, the use which they make of it merits well that they should lose it.

J.-J. ROUSSEAU: *Du contrat social*, III, 1761

The English are close friends, but distant acquaintance.

RICHARD CUMBERLAND: *The West Indian*, II, 1771

Froth at the top, dregs at bottom, but the middle excellent.

Ascribed to VOLTAIRE (1694–1778)

This selfish race, from all the world disjoin'd,
Perpetual discord spread throughout mankind,
Aim to extend their empire o'er the ball,
Subject, destroy, absorb, and conquer all.

PHILIP FRENEAU: *The British Prison Ship*, III, 1781

Bug: a nickname given by the Irish to Englishmen, bugs having (as it is said) been introduced into Ireland by the English.

FRANCIS GROSE: *A Classical Dictionary of the Vulgar Tongue*, 1785 (*Bug*=Eng. for bedbug)

A nation of shopkeepers. (Une nation boutiquière.)

NAPOLEON I, *c.* 1795; cf. 1817 *post.* (Edward Latham, in Famous Sayings and Their Authors, calls attention to the following in ADAM SMITH: *The Wealth of Nations*, II, 1776: "To found a great empire for the sole purpose of raising up a people of customers may at first sight appear a project fit only for a nation of shopkeepers. It is, however, a project altogether unfit for a nation of shopkeepers; but extremely fit for a nation whose government is influenced by shopkeepers. Such statesmen, and such statesmen only, are capable of fancying that they will find some advantage in employing the blood and treasure of their fellow-citizens to found and maintain such an empire")

The English never know when they are beaten.

ENGLISH PROVERB, not recorded before the XIX century

I thank the goodness and the grace,
  Which on my birth have smiled,
And made me, in these Christian days,
  A happy English child!

ANN and JANE TAYLOR: *Rhymes for the Nursery*, 1806

God-damn! I love the English! (Goddam! moi j'aime les Anglais.)

P. J. BÉRANGER: *Les boxeurs*, 1814

You were greatly offended with me for having called you a nation of shopkeepers. Had I meant by this that you were a nation of cowards, you would have had reason to be displeased, even though it were ridiculous and contrary to historical facts; but no such thing was ever intended. I meant that you were a nation of merchants.

NAPOLEON I: To Barry E. O'Meara at St. Helena, May 31, 1817

The English have no exalted sentiments. They can all be bought.

NAPOLEON I: To Gaspard Gourgaud at St. Helena, Sept. 26, 1817

The English are the most disagreeable of all the nations of Europe, — more surly and morose, with less disposition to please, to exert themselves for the good of society, to make small sacrifices, and to put themselves out of their way.

SYDNEY SMITH: In the Edinburgh Review, 1818

The good people of England do all that in them lies to make their king a puppet; and then, with their usual consistency, detest him if he

is not what they would make him, and despise him if he is.
C. C. COLTON: *Lacon,* 1820

Though I love my country, I do not love my countrymen.
BYRON: *Letter to Count d'Orsay,* April 22, 1823

The English are the only people to whom the term blackguard is peculiarly applicable — by which I understand a reference of everything to violence, and a contempt for the feelings and opinions of others.
WILLIAM HAZLITT: *English Characteristics,* 1829 (The Atlas, July 5)

Everybody knows that it is only necessary to raise a bugbear before the English imagination in order to govern it at will. Whatever they hate or fear, they implicitly believe in, merely from the scope it gives to their passions.
WILLIAM HAZLITT: *The Life of Napoleon Bonaparte,* III, 1830

The English travel about all the time, looking at battlefields, waterfalls, ruined masonry, and dull classical relics.
J. W. GOETHE: *II Faust,* II, 1832

The English are a dumb people. They can do great acts, but not describe them. Like the old Romans and some few others, their epic poem is written on the earth's surface: England her mark!
THOMAS CARLYLE: *Past and Present,* III, 1843

The people of English stock, in all countries, are a solid people, wearing good hats and shoes, and owners of land whose title-deeds are properly recorded.
R. W. EMERSON: *The Superlative,* 1847

Twenty-seven millions, mostly fools.
THOMAS CARLYLE: *Latter-Day Pamphlets,* VI, 1850

They doubt a man's sound judgment if he does not eat with appetite, and shake their heads if he is particularly chaste.
R. W. EMERSON: *English Traits,* VIII, 1856

When they live with other races they do not take their language, but bestow their own. They subsidize other nations, and are not subsidized. They proselyte, and are not proselyted. They assimilate other races to themselves, and are not assimilated. IBID.

The English nation is never so great as in adversity.
BENJAMIN DISRAELI: Speech in the House of Commons, Aug. 11, 1857

If an earthquake were to engulf England tomorrow, the English would manage to meet and dine somewhere among the rubbish, just to celebrate the event.
Ascribed to DOUGLAS W. JERROLD (1803–57)

The British working class grows more and more bourgeois, so that this most bourgeois of nations is apparently aiming at having eventually a bourgeois aristocracy and a bourgeois proletariat as well as a bourgeoisie.
FRIEDRICH ENGELS: *Letter to Karl Marx,* 1858

The English have more good sense than any other nation — and they are fools.
CLEMENS VON METTERNICH (1773–1859)

The English are eminently a nation of vagabonds. The sun paints English faces with all the colors of his climes. The Englishman is ubiquitous.
ALEXANDER SMITH: *Dreamthorp,* XII, 1863

England is the country in which social discipline has most succeeded, not so much in conquering, as in suppressing whatever is most liable to conflict with it. The English, more than any other people, not only act but feel according to rule.
J. S. MILL: *The Subjection of Women,* III, 1869

The English always manage to muddle through.
Author unidentified; first heard *c.* 1885

They are not a philosophical race, the English.
F. W. NIETZSCHE: *Beyond Good and Evil,* 1886

The English have mind enough; but they have not taste enough.
W. D. HOWELL: *Criticism and Fiction,* 1892

We, the English nation, have an ethic, a morality, and if we had not we should never have been a nation at all.
G. K. CHESTERTON: Evidence before the Joint Select Committee on the Stage Plays, Sept. 24, 1909

The real English resemble Romans. They do not want London to be world-famous for her lectures, her halls of science, her preachers, her public statues, or her national galleries. These things we prefer bad. We pride ourselves on our train service, our shops, our policemen, our Rugby football matches and our race meetings.
VISCOUNT HARBERTON: *How to Lengthen Our Ears,* 1917

We are always serene in times of difficulty. We have staying power; we are not rattled.
STANLEY BALDWIN: Radio Speech, Sept. 25, 1933

[*See also* American, Anglomania, Austrian, Aviation, British, Cant, Character (National), Conservatism, Englishman, Home, India, Irish, Meat, Mob, Morality, November, Pilgrim, Soldier, Sunday, Water.

English Language

The king's English.
THOMAS WILSON: *The Arte of Rhetorique,* 1553

I am of this opinion, that our tongue should be written clean and pure, unmixt and unmangled with borrowing of other tongues, wherein if we take not heed betimes, ever borrowing and never paying, she shall be fain to keep her house as bankrupt.

JOHN CHEKE: *Letter to Thomas Hoby,* 1557

The most English words are of one syllable, so that the more monosyllables you use, the truer Englishman you shall seem, and the less you shall smell of the inkhorn.

GEORGE GASCOIGNE: *Steel Glass,* 1576

Whosoever shall become of the English state, the English tongue cannot prove fairer than it is at this day.

RICHARD MUNCASTER: *The First Part of the Elementarie,* 1582

Our English tongue of all languages most swarmeth with the single money of monosyllables, which are the only scandal of it. Books written in them and no other seem like shopkeepers' boxes, that contain nothing else save halfpence, three-farthings and twopences.

THOMAS NASHE: *Christ's Tears Over Jerusalem,* 1593

I know that some will say it is a mingle tongue. And why not so much the better, taking the best of both and the other? Another will say that it lacks grammar. Nay, truly, it has that praise that it does not want grammar; for grammar it might have, but needs it not; being so easy of itself, and so void of those cumbersome differences of cases, moods, genders and tenses, which I think was a piece of the tower of Babylon's curse that a man should be put to school to learn his mother tongue.

PHILIP SIDNEY: *Apologie for Poetrie,* 1598

And who (in time) knows whither we may vent
The treasure of our tongue? To what strange shores
The gain of our best glory shall be sent,
T' enrich unknowing nations with our stores?
What worlds in th' yet unformed occident
May come refin'd with th' accents that are ours?

SAMUEL DANIEL: *Musophilus,* 1599

Great, verily, was the glory of our tongue before the Norman conquest in this: that the old English could express most aptly all the conceptions of the mind in their own speech without borrowing from any.

WILLIAM CAMDEN: *Remains Concerning Britain,* 1605

When substantialness combineth with delightfulness, fullness with fineness, seemliness with portliness, and courrantness with staidness, how can the language which consisteth of all these sound other than most full of sweetness?

RICHARD CAREW: *Epistle on the Excellency of the English Tongue,* 1605

Our language hath no law but use, and still
Runs blind, unbridled at the vulgars' will.

JOSHUA SYLVESTER: Tr. of BARTAS: *Divine Week,* 1606

Albeit our tongue hath not received dialects, or accentual notes as the Greek, nor any certain or established rule either of grammar or true writing, is notwithstanding very copious, and few there be that have the most proper graces thereof.

EDMUND BOLTON: *Hypercritica,* 1610

English is the language of men ever famous and foremost in the achievements of liberty.

JOHN MILTON: *Areopagitica,* 1644

I have endeavor'd to write English as near as I could distinguish it from the tongue of pedants and that of affected travelers. Only I am sorry that (speaking so noble a language as we do) we have not a more certain measure for it, as they have in France, where they have an Academy erected for that purpose.

JOHN DRYDEN: *The Rival Ladies,* dedication, 1664

English is the language with which we are swaddled and rocked asleep.

JOHN EACHARD: *The Grounds and Occasions of the Contempt of the Clergy and Religion,* 1670

I have labored to refine our language to grammatical purity, and to clear it from colloquial barbarisms, licentious idioms, and irregular combinations.

SAMUEL JOHNSON: *The Rambler,* March 14, 1752

English, . . . in spite of its energy, plenty, and the crowd of excellent writers this nation has produced, does yet retain too much of its barbarous original to adapt itself to musical composition.

THOMAS GRAY: *Letter to Count Algarotti,* Sept. 9, 1763

Good English is plain, easy and smooth in the mouth of an unaffected English gentleman.

SAMUEL JOHNSON: *Boswell's Life,* March, 1772

English is destined to be in the next and succeeding centuries more generally the language of the world than Latin was in the last or French is in the present age.

JOHN ADAMS: *Letter to the President of Congress,* Sept. 5, 1780

I wish you would write in English, because it is a better language than Latin, and because the disuse of English as a living and literary language would be the greatest evil that could befall mankind.

ROBERT SOUTHEY: *Letter to W. S. Landor,* May 2, 1808

It may be doubted whether a composite language like the English is not a happier instrument of expression than a homogeneous one like the German. We possess a wonderful richness and variety of modified meanings in our Saxon and Latin quasi-synonyms, which the Germans have not.

S. T. COLERIDGE: *Table-Talk,* Aug. 19, 1832

English is the most difficult, arbitrary and careful of all languages.

MATTHEW FONTAINE MAURY: *Scraps from the Lucky Bag,* 1840

When I see painful professors of Greek, poring in their sumptuous Oxfords over dead Greek for a thousand years or more, and leaving live English all the while to develop itself under charge of Pickwicks and Sam Wellers, as if *it* were nothing and the other were all things: this, and the like of it everywhere, fills me with reflections.

THOMAS CARLYLE: *Letter to R. W. Emerson,* July 7, 1846

When we consider the richness, good sense and strict economy of English, none of the other living languages can be put beside it.

JAKOB GRIMM: *Ueber den Ursprung der Sprache,* 1851

Wondrous the English language, language of live men,
Language of ensemble, powerful language of resistance,
Language of a proud and melancholy stock, and of all who aspire,
Language of growth, faith, self-esteem, rudeness, justice, friendliness, prudence, decision, exactitude, courage.

WALT WHITMAN: *As I Sat Alone,* 1856

English as she is spoke.

P. CAROLINO: Title of a " guide of the conversation in Portuguese and English," 1882

View'd freely, the English language is the accretion and growth of every dialect, race and range of time, and is both the free and compacted composition of all.

WALT WHITMAN: *Slang in America,* 1885

There is one expression that continually comes to my mind whenever I think of the English language and compare it with others: it seems to me positively and expressly masculine. It is the language of a grown-up man and has very little childish or feminine about it.

OTTO JESPERSEN: *The Growth and Structure of the English Language,* I, 1905

The English have no respect for their language, and will not teach their children to speak it. It is impossible for an Englishman to open his mouth without making some other Englishman hate or despise him.

GEORGE BERNARD SHAW: *Pygmalion,* pref., 1912

Every immigrant who comes here should be required within five years to learn English or leave the country.

THEODORE ROOSEVELT: Article in the Kansas City Star, April 27, 1918

English has shown itself a useful instrument for a country setting out to learn the habits of democracy. It is most convenient for the politician to be able to employ a language with only one word (instead of three or even four) for *you.*

R. C. GOFFIN: *Some Notes on Indian English,* 1934

Nothing makes one so angry as when one is tired and comes home and must speak English. (Nix mach's man so bös als wenn man müd ist und häm kemmt und mus' English schwetza.)

PENNSYLVANIA GERMAN SAYING

[*See also* American Language, French Language, German Language, Grammar, Language, Slang.

Englishman

An Englishman hath three qualities: he can suffer no partner in his love, no stranger to be his equal, nor to be dared by any.

JOHN LYLY: *Euphues,* 1579

An Englishman Italianate is a devil incarnate.

ENGLISH PROVERB, traced by Apperson to OVERTON: *Jacob's Troublesome Journey,* 1586

The Englishman, of many other nations, is least atheistical, and bears a natural disposition of much reverence and awe towards the Deity.

JOHN MILTON: *The Reason of Church Government,* I, 1641

But Lord! to see the absurd nature of Englishmen, that cannot forbear laughing and jeering at everything that looks strange.

SAMUEL PEPYS: *Diary,* Nov. 28, 1662

When I see an Englishman subtle and full of lawsuits, I say " There is a Norman, who came in with William the Conqueror." When I see any man good-natured and polite, " That is one who came with the Plantagenets "; a brutal character, " That is a Dane."

VOLTAIRE: *Lettres philosophiques sur les Anglais,* 1733

That silly, sanguine notion which is firmly entertained here, that one Englishman can beat three Frenchmen, encourages, and has sometimes enabled, one Englishman in reality to beat two.

LORD CHESTERFIELD: *Letter to his son,* Feb. 7, 1749

There is no one instance of an Englishman's having ever been suspected of a gallantry with a French woman of condition, though

every French woman of condition is more than suspected of having a gallantry.
LORD CHESTERFIELD: *Letter to his son,* June 5, 1750

Not only England, but every Englishman is an island.
FRIEDRICH VON HARDENBERG (NOVALIS): *Fragments,* 1799

Asses, swine, have litter spread,
And with fitting food are fed;
All things have a home but one:
Thou, O Englishman, hast none!
P. B. SHELLEY: *The Masque of Anarchy,* 1819

All Englishmen are, as such, without reflection, properly so called; distractions and party spirit will not permit them to perfect themselves in quiet. But they are great as practical men.
J. W. GOETHE: *Conversations with Eckermann,* Feb. 24, 1825

Ill manners make the Englishman.
WILLIAM HAZLITT: *Manners Make the Man,* 1829 (The Atlas, March 29)

How hard it is to make an Englishman acknowledge that he is happy.
W. M. THACKERAY: *Pendennis,* I, 1849

An Englishman shows no mercy to those below him in the social scale, as he looks for none from those above him; any forbearance from his superiors surprises him, and they suffer in his good opinion.
R. W. EMERSON: *English Traits,* XI, 1856

A low Englishman is the lowest of the low.
GEORGE BORROW: *Wild Wales,* LXV, 1862

One has often wondered whether upon the whole earth there is anything so unintelligent, so unapt to perceive how the world is really going, as an ordinary young Englishman of the upper class.
MATTHEW ARNOLD: *Culture and Anarchy,* I, 1869

Nothing equals my thankfulness when I meet an Englishman who is not like every other.
J. R. LOWELL: *On a Certain Condescension in Foreigners,* 1869

He is an Englishman!
For he himself has said it,
And it's greatly to his credit,
That he's an Englishman!
For he might have been a Rooshian
A French or Turk or Prooshian,
Or perhaps Itali-an.
But in spite of all temptations
To belong to other nations,
He remains an Englishman.
W. S. GILBERT: *H.M.S. Pinafore,* I, 1878

There is nothing so bad or so good that you will not find Englishmen doing it; but you will never find an Englishman in the wrong. He does everything on principle. He fights you on patriotic principles; he robs you on business principles; he enslaves you on imperial principles.
GEORGE BERNARD SHAW: *The Man of Destiny,* 1898

Englishmen never will be slaves; they are free to do whatever the government and public opinion allow them to do.
GEORGE BERNARD SHAW: *Man and Superman,* II, 1903

Mad dogs and Englishmen go out in the noonday sun. Author unidentified

When the sun comes out in England, the Englishman says: "What a beautiful day! Let's go out and kill something." IBID.

Don't trust any Englishman who speaks French with a correct accent. FRENCH PROVERB

The Englishman is a drunkard. (Inglés borracho.) SPANISH SAYING

[*See also* Ale, Anglo-Saxon, British, Briton, Character (National), Comfort, Complexion, Criminal, Cromwell (Oliver), Drinking, English, Fortune, French Language, Frenchman, Ireland, Italianized, Morality, Peerage, Portuguese, Press (Free), Soldier, Steam, Taxes, Warrior, Weather.

Englishwoman

The English lady cannot dress herself.
BEN JONSON. *Volpone,* III, 1605

Nor shall my verse the brighter sex defame,
For English beauty will preserve her name.
Beyond dispute, agreeable and fair,
And modester than other nations are,
For when the vice prevails the great temptation
Is want of money more than inclination.
DANIEL DEFOE: *The True-Born Englishman,* II, 1701

England produces under favorable conditions of ease and culture the finest women in the world. And, as the men are affectionate and true-hearted, the women inspire and refine them.
R. W. EMERSON: *English Traits,* VI, 1856

Enigma

There be three things which are too wonderful for me, yea, four which I know not: The way of an eagle in the air; the way of a serpent upon a rock; the way of a ship in the midst of the sea; and the way of a man with a maid.
PROVERBS XXX, 18–19, *c.* 350 B.C.

Enjoyment

Who can enjoy alone?
JOHN MILTON: *Paradise Lost,* VIII, 1667

True enjoyment cannot be described.
J.-J. ROUSSEAU: *Confessions,* VIII, 1766

The first half of life consists of the capacity to enjoy without the chance; the last half consists of the chance without the capacity.
S. L. CLEMENS (MARK TWAIN): *Letter to Edward L. Dimmitt,* July 19, 1901

[*See also* Delight, Morality, Pleasure.

Enmity

Enmity concealed is the most dangerous; avowed, it loses the chance for revenge.
SENECA: *Medea, c.* 60

All that most maddens and torments; all that stirs up the lees of things; all truth with malice in it; all that cracks the sinews and cakes the brain; all the subtle demonisms of life and thought; all evil, to crazy Ahab, were visibly personified, and made practically assailable in Moby Dick.
HERMAN MELVILLE: *Moby Dick,* XL, 1851

[*See also* Animosity, Enemy, Envy.

Ennui

[*See* Boredom.

Enough

Enough is abundance to the wise.
EURIPIDES: *The Phoenissae, c.* 410 B.C.

Nothing is enough for the man to whom enough is too little.
EPICURUS: *Aphorisms, c.* 300 B.C.

Enough is as good as a feast.
ENGLISH PROVERB, borrowed from the Greek and traced to the XV century (A Latin form, " Satis quod sufficit," is older)

Enough is enough.
JOHN HEYWOOD: *Proverbs,* 1546

He that knoweth when he hath enough is no fool.
IBID.

'Tis not so deep as a well, nor so wide as a church door; but 'tis enough, 'twill serve.
SHAKESPEARE: *Romeo and Juliet,* III, *c.* 1596

The poor have little, — beggars none;
The rich too much — enough not one.
BENJAMIN FRANKLIN: *Poor Richard's Almanac,* 1740

Enough! or too much!
WILLIAM BLAKE: *The Marriage of Heaven and Hell,* 1790

Enough is better than too much.
FRENCH PROVERB

Enough, more than enough. (Satis, superque.)
LATIN PHRASE

Whatever suffices is enough. (Satis quod sufficit.)
LATIN PROVERB

Enough of this. (Jam satis.)
LATIN SAYING

[*See also* Fortune, Money, Once.

Entente

Cordial understanding. (Entente cordiale.)
Commonly applied to the understanding between France and Great Britain, *c.* 1904–1940 (The phrase was first used by KING LOUIS PHILIPPE of France in a speech from the throne, 1843)

Enterprise

[*See* Laissez-faire.

Entertainment

That which might pass for raillery and entertertainment in heathenism is detestable in Christianity.
JEREMY COLLIER: *A Short View of the Immorality and Profaneness of the English Stage,* intro., 1698

[*See also* Amusement.

Enthusiasm

There is a melancholy which accompanies all enthusiasm.
ANTHONY A. COOPER (EARL OF SHAFTESBURY): *Characteristics of Men, Manners, Opinions, Times,* I, *c.* 1713

Enthusiasm is that temper of the mind in which the imagination has got the better of the judgment.
WILLIAM WARBURTON (BISHOP OF GLOUCESTER): *The Divine Legation of Moses,* I, 1737

The sense of this word among the Greeks affords the noblest definition of it: enthusiasm signifies God in us.
ANNA LOUISE DE STAËL: *De l'Allemagne,* IV, 1810

Rash enthusiasm in good society
Were nothing but a moral inebriety.
BYRON: *Don Juan,* XIII, 1823

Nothing great was ever achieved without enthusiasm. The way of life is wonderful; it is by abandonment.
R. W. EMERSON: *Circles,* 1841

[*See also* Patriotism.

Enthusiast

A gloomy, hair-brained enthusiast, after his death, may have a place in the calendar, but will scarcely ever be admitted, when alive, into intimacy and society except by those who are as delirious and dismal as himself.
DAVID HUME: *Enquiry Concerning the Principles of Morals,* IX, 1751

No wild enthusiast ever yet could rest,
Till half mankind were like himself possess'd.
WILLIAM COWPER: *The Progress of Error,* 1782

Opposition always inflames the enthusiast, never converts him.
J. C. F. SCHILLER: *Kabale und Liebe,* III, 1784

Enticement

My son, if sinners entice thee, consent thou not. PROVERBS I, 10, *c.* 350 B.C.

[*See also* Temptation.

Environment

The alligator, matchless as he is, when he quitteth the water is without power. Were the lion to forsake the forests, he would be upon a level with the jackal.
The Hitopadesa, III, *c.* 500

A good herb, transplanted into a soil very different from her nature, doth much sooner conform itself to the soil than it reformeth the same to itself.
MICHEL DE MONTAIGNE: *Essays*, III, 1588

Men are like plants; the goodness and flavor of the fruit proceeds from the peculiar soil and exposition in which they grow. We are nothing but what we derive from the air we breathe, the climate we inhabit, the government we obey, the system of religion we profess, and the nature of our employment.
ST. JOHN DE CRÈVECOEUR: *Letters from an American Farmer*, III, 1782

He who passes his life surrounded by solemn, lofty oaks must be a different man from him who lives among airy birches.
J. W. GOETHE: *Conversations with Eckermann*, April 2, 1829

People are not the better for the sun and moon, the horizon and the trees; as it is not observed that the keepers of Roman galleries, or the valets of painters, have any elevation of thought, or that librarians are wiser men than others.
E. W. EMERSON: *Spiritual Laws*, 1841

Wherever the material condition of the laboring classes has been improved, improvement in their personal qualities has followed, and wherever their material condition has been depressed, deterioration in these qualities has been the result.
HENRY GEORGE: *Progress and Poverty*, VI, 1879

Place an infant in the heart of China, and but for the angle of the eye or the shade of the hair, the Caucasian would grow up as those around him, using the same speech, thinking the same thoughts, exhibiting the same tastes. Change Lady Vere de Vere in her cradle with an infant of the slums, and will the blood of a hundred earls give you a refined and cultured woman?
HENRY GEORGE: *Progress and Poverty*, IX

[*See also* Education, Luther (Martin), Nature *vs.* Nurture, Socialism, Voltaire.

Envy

Do not envy the wealth of your neighbor.
HOMER: *Odyssey*, XVIII, *c.* 800 B.C.

The potter envies the potter; the carpenter, the carpenter; the poor man is jealous of the poor man; the bard, of the bard.
HESIOD: *Works and Days*, *c.* 700 B.C.

Few men have the strength of character to rejoice in a friend's success without a touch of envy.
ÆSCHYLUS: *Agamemnon*, *c.* 490 B.C.

Those who are not envied are never wholly happy. IBID.

It is a nobler fate to be envied than to be pitied.
PINDAR: *Pythian Odes*, I, *c.* 475 B.C.

Envy crawls before the rich.
SOPHOCLES: *Ajax*, *c.* 450 B.C.

It is much better to be envied than pitied.
HERODOTUS: *Histories*, III, *c.* 430 B.C.

Men can endure the praise of others so long as they believe that the actions praised are within their own power; they envy whatever they consider to be beyond it.
THUCYDIDES: *History*, II, *c.* 410 B.C.

A sound heart is the life of the flesh, but envy the rottenness of the bones.
PROVERBS XIV, 30, *c.* 350 B.C.

Wrath is cruel, and anger is outrageous; but who is able to stand before envy?
PROVERBS XXVII, 4

All the tyrants of Sicily never invented a worse torment than envy.
HORACE: *Epistles*, I, *c.* 5 B.C.

Envy is to be overcome only by death.
HORACE: *Epistles*, II

Envy, the meanest of vices, creeps on the ground like a serpent.
OVID: *Epistulae ex Ponto*, III, *c.* 5

Envy, like flame, soars upward.
LIVY: *History of Rome*, VIII, *c.* 10

The vulgar bark at men of mark, as dogs bark at strangers.
SENECA: *De vita beata*, XIX, *c.* 58

Where envying and strife is, there is confusion, and every evil work. JAMES III, 16, *c.* 60

Envy is the adversary of the fortunate.
EPICTETUS: *Encheiridion*, *c.* 110

Since we cannot attain to greatness, let us revenge ourselves by railing at it.
MICHEL DE MONTAIGNE: *Essays*, III, 1588

Envy with a pale and meager face (whose body was so lean that one might tell all her bones, and whose garment was so tatter'd that it was easy to number every thread) stood shooting at stars, whose darts fell down again on her own face. JOHN LYLY: *Endymion*, V, 1591

Let high attempts dread envy, and ill tongues.
JOSEPH HALL (BISHOP OF NORWICH): *Virgidemarium*, prologue, 1597

No metal can,
No, not the hangman's ax, bear half the keenness
Of thy sharp envy.
SHAKESPEARE: *The Merchant of Venice,* IV, *c.* 1597

I am Envy, begotten of a chimneysweeper and an oysterwife. I cannot read, and therefore wish all books were burnt. I am lean with seeing others eat.
CHRISTOPHER MARLOWE: *Dr. Faustus,* VI, 1604

If on the sudden he begins to rise:
No man that lives can count his enemies.
THOMAS MIDDLETON: *A Trick to Catch the Old One,* I, 1608

Envy will ever be hatched where multitudes are drawn together.
HENRY PERCY (EARL OF NORTHUMBERLAND): *Advice to His Son,* 1609

He is weary of his earldom if there be a duke in the land.
THOMAS ADAMS: *Diseases of the Soul,* 1616

Every other sin hath some pleasure annexed to it, or will admit of an excuse: envy alone wants both.
ROBERT BURTON: *The Anatomy of Melancholy,* I, 1621

Deformed persons and eunuchs, and old men and bastards, are envious, for he that cannot possibly mend his own case, will do what he can to impair another's.
FRANCIS BACON: *Essays,* IX, 1625

A man shall never be enriched by envy.
THOMAS DRAXE: *Bibliotheca scholastica instructissima,* 1633

Envy not greatness, for thou mak'st thereby
Thyself the worse, and so the distance greater.
GEORGE HERBERT: *The Temple,* 1633

The envious man shall never want woe.
WILLIAM CAMDEN: *Remains Concerning Britain* (4th ed.), 1636

From envy, hatred, and malice, and all uncharitableness, Good Lord deliver us.
THE BOOK OF COMMON PRAYER (*The Litany*), 1662

The envious will die, but envy never.
J. B. MOLIÈRE: *Le Tartuffe,* V, 1664

Envy is more irreconcilable than hatred.
LA ROCHEFOUCAULD: *Maxims,* 1665

Our envy always outlives the happiness of those we envy. IBID.

The truest mark of being born with great qualities is being born without envy. IBID.

We often make a parade of passions, even of the most criminal; but envy is a timid and shameful passion which we never dare to avow. IBID.

Honor is always attended on by envy.
WILLIAM WINSTANLEY: *England's Worthies,* 1684

Envy and hatred are always united. They gather strength from each other by being engaged upon the same object.
JEAN DE LA BRUYÈRE: *Caractères,* XI, 1688

Envy is a criminal sorrow for the welfare of our neighbor.
ST. JOHN BAPTIST DE LA SALLE: *Les devoirs du chrétien,* XIV, 1703

Envy will merit as its shade pursue,
But like a shadow proves the substance true.
ALEXANDER POPE: *An Essay on Criticism,* II, 1711

The reason why men of true good sense envy less than others, is, because they admire themselves with less hesitation than fools and silly people.
BERNARD DE MANDEVILLE: *The Fable of the Bees,* XIV, 1714

Envy is a kind of praise.
JOHN GAY: *Fables,* I, 1727

Envy's a sharper spur than pay. IBID.

Envy is not an original temper, but the natural, necessary and unavoidable effect of emulation, or a desire of glory.
WILLIAM LAW: *A Serious Call to a Devout and Holy Life,* XVIII, 1728

To all my foes, dear fortune, send
Thy gifts! but never to my friend:
I tamely can endure the first;
But this with envy makes me burst.
JONATHAN SWIFT: *On the Death of Dr. Swift,* 1731

Envy shooteth at others and woundeth herself.
THOMAS FULLER: *Gnomologia,* 1732

Nothing sharpens sight like envy. IBID.

Envy, to which th' ignoble mind's a slave,
Is emulation in the learn'd or brave.
ALEXANDER POPE: *An Essay on Man,* II, 1732

Whenever I encounter envy I always try to provoke it: before an envious man I always praise those who make him turn pale.
C. L. DE MONTESQUIEU: *Pensées, c.* 1750

Most of the misery which the defamation of blameless actions or the obstruction of honest endeavors brings upon the world is inflicted by men that propose no advantage to themselves but the satisfaction of poisoning the banquet which they cannot taste, and blasting the harvest which they have no right to reap.
SAMUEL JOHNSON: *The Rambler,* Dec. 17, 1751

There is but one man who can believe himself free from envy, and it is he who has never examined his own heart.
C. A. HELVÉTIUS: *De l'esprit,* 1758

There are just two creatures I would envy — a horse in his wild state traversing the forests of Asia, or an oyster on some of the desert shores of Europe.
ROBERT BURNS: *Letter to Miss Chalmers,* Dec. 19, 1787

The hate which we all bear with the most Christian patience is the hate of those who envy us. C. C. COLTON: *Lacon,* 1820

Envy writhes; it don't laugh.
BYRON: *Letter to John Murray,* Feb. 7, 1821

Even in envy may be discerned something of an instinct of justice, something of a wish to see fair play, and things on a level.
LEIGH HUNT: *The Indicator,* LI, 1821

Envy, among other ingredients, has a mixture of the love of justice in it. We are more angry at undeserved than at deserved good fortune.
WILLIAM HAZLITT: *Characteristics,* VI, 1823

An envious man is a squint-ey'd fool.
H. G. BOHN: *Handbook of Proverbs,* 1855

'Twere better my enemy envy me than I him.
IBID.

Probably the greatest harm done by vast wealth is the harm that we of moderate means do ourselves when we let the vices of envy and hatred enter deep into our own nature.
THEODORE ROOSEVELT: Speech in Providence, R. I., Aug. 23, 1902

The dog with the bone is always in danger.
AMERICAN PROVERB

If envy were a fever, all mankind would be ill.
DANISH PROVERB

Envy is stronger than avarice.
FRENCH PROVERB

Envy is the sorrow of fools.
GERMAN PROVERB

All kinds of enmity are curable save that which flows out of envy. HEBREW PROVERB

Envy and anger shorten life. IBID.

When all men praised the peacock for his tail, the birds cried out "Look at his legs! and what a voice!" JAPANESE PROVERB

The blood of the black cuttlefish. (Migrae succus loliginus.) LATIN PHRASE

Without envy. (Sine invidia.) IBID.

Envy is the enemy of honor.
LATIN PROVERB

[*See also* Ambition, Classes, Curiosity, Democracy, Devil, Eminence, Fame, Greed, Hatred, Jealousy, Johnson (Samuel), King, Merit, Poet, Praise, Pride, Sin, Wealth.

Epic

[*See* Poetry.

Epictetus (c. 50–?)

[*See* Gentleman.

Epicure

[*See* Dinner.

Epicurean

I am an Epicurean. I consider the genuine (not the imputed) doctrines of Epicurus as containing everything rational in moral philosophy which Greek and Rome have left us.
THOMAS JEFFERSON: *Letter to William Short,* 1819

Epigram

It is with epigrams as with other inventions: the best are those which annoy us because we did not think of them ourselves.
G. C. LICHTENBERG: *Reflections,* 1799

What is an epigram? A dwarfish whole,
Its body brevity, and wit its soul.
S. T. COLERIDGE: In the London Morning Post, Sept. 23, 1802

In Pope's day men wore rapiers, and their weapons they carried with them into literature, and frequently unsheathed them too. They knew how to stab to the heart with an epigram.
ALEXANDER SMITH: *Dreamthorp,* II, 1863

Short, it is easily retained in the memory; pithy, it contains in the compass of a few lines the sum of an argument; and the result of experience it often expresses the wisdom of ages.
H. P. DODD: *The Epigrammatists,* intro., 1870

The qualities rare in a bee that we meet
In an epigram never should fail;
The body should always be little and sweet,
And a sting should be left in its tail.
(Omne epigramma sit instar apis: sit aculeus illi;
Sint sua mella; sit et corporis exigui.)
Author and translator unidentified

A platitude with vine-leaves in its hair.
Author unidentified

[*See also* Wit.

Epilogue

A good play needs no epilogue.
SHAKESPEARE: *As You Like It,* epilogue, *c.* 1600

Episcopalian

The great majority of our members are woefully ignorant so far as any real knowledge of the Christian religion or the church is concerned. Judged by any standard to determine their Christian intelligence, they are in the moron class.

HENRY W. HOBSON (BISHOP OF SOUTHERN OHIO): Address at the annual convention of the Protestant Episcopal diocese of Chicago, Feb., 1935

[*See also* Church of England.

Epitaph

Go tell the Spartans, thou that passeth by,
That here, obedient to the laws, we lie.

SIMONIDES: Epitaph for the Spartans who fell at Thermopylæ, 480 B.C.

Here, lapped in hallowed slumber, Saon lies,
Asleep, not dead; a good man never dies.

CALLIMACHUS, *c.* 250 B.C.

May the earth lie light upon thee. (Sit tibi terra levis.)

Epitaph common on Roman tombs, often abbreviated to S.T.T.L.

So may he rest: his faults lie gently on him!

SHAKESPEARE and JOHN FLETCHER: *Henry VIII,* IV, 1613

Underneath this stone doth lie
As much beauty as could die:
Which in life did harbor give
To more virtue than doth live.

BEN JONSON: *On Elizabeth L. H.,* 1616

Good friend for Jesus sake, forebaere,
To digg the dust encloased heare
Blest be ye man yt spares thes stones,
And curst be he yt moves my bones.

SHAKESPEARE: Epitaph chosen (though probably not written) by himself for his tomb at Stratford-on-Avon, 1616

She was — but room forbids to tell thee what —
Sum all perfection up, and she was — that.

FRANCIS QUARLES: Epitaph on Lady Luchyn, *c.* 1630

A sumptuous pyramid of golden verse
Over the ruins of an ignoble hearse.

JOHN DAY: *The Parliament of Bees,* v, 1641

Underneath this sable hearse
Lies the subject of all verse,
Sydney's sister, Pembroke's mother;
Death, ere thou hast slain another
Learn'd and fair, and good as she,
Time shall throw a dart at thee.

BEN JONSON: *On the Countess of Pembroke,* 1641

All hope of never dying here lies dead.

RICHARD CRASHAW: *On the Death of Mr. Herrys,* 1646

Here a pretty baby lies
Sung asleep with lullabies:
Pray be silent, and not stir
Th' easy earth that covers her.

ROBERT HERRICK: *Hesperides,* 1648

Here a solemn fast we keep,
While all beauty lies asleep,
Husht be all things; no noise here,
But the toning of a tear;
Or a sigh of such as bring
Cowslips for her covering.

IBID.

For a man to say all the excellent things that can be said upon one, and call that his epitaph, is as if a painter should make the handsomest piece he can possibly make, and say 'twas my picture.

JOHN SELDEN: *Table-Talk,* 1689

Interr'd beneath this marble stone,
Lie Saunt'ring Jack, and Idle Joan.
While rolling threescore years and one
Did round this globe their courses run;
If human things went ill or well;
If changing empires rose or fell;
The morning past, the evening came,
And found this couple still the same.

MATTHEW PRIOR: *An Epitaph,* 1718

The body of Benjamin Franklin, printer, (like the cover of an old book, its contents torn out and stript of its lettering and gilding), lies here, food for worms; but the work shall not be lost, for it will (as he believed) appear once more in a new and more elegant edition, revised and corrected by the Author.

BENJAMIN FRANKLIN: Epitaph on himself, written in 1728

Tom Smith is dead, and here he lies,
Nobody laughs and nobody cries;
Where his soul's gone, or how it fares,
Nobody knows, and nobody cares.

Anon.: Epitaph on Tom Smith, of Newbury (England), 1742

Here lies Fred,
Who was alive and is dead;
Had it been his father
I had much rather;
Had it been his brother,
Still better than the other;
Had it been his sister,
No one would have missed her;
Had it been the whole generation,
All the better for the nation;
But since 'tis only Fred,
That was alive and is dead,
Why, there's no more to be said.

Anon.: Epitaph on Frederick, Prince of Wales, 1751

David Hume
Born 1711 Died 1776
Leaving it to posterity to add the rest.

Epitaph of David Hume, written by himself, 1775

In lapidary inscriptions a man is not upon oath.

SAMUEL JOHNSON: *Boswell's Life,* 1775

In sex a woman, in abilities a man. (Sexu femina, ingenio vir.)

Epitaph of Maria Theresa of Austria, at Vienna, 1780

My name, my country — what are they to thee?
What, whether base or proud, my pedigree?
Perhaps I far surpassed all other men;

Perhaps I fell below them all; what then?
Suffice it, stranger, that thou seest a tomb;
Thou know'st its use; it hides no matter whom.
WILLIAM COWPER: Tr. from the Greek, *c.* 1782

Here Holy Willie's sair-worn clay
Taks up its last abode;
His saul has ta'en some other way —
I fear the left-hand road.
ROBERT BURNS: *Holy Willie's Prayer,* 1785

Pain could not sour, whom blessings had not spoil'd;
Nor death affright, whom not a vice had soil'd.
HORACE WALPOLE: Epigraph for Lady Dysart, 1789

Let my epitaph be, "Here lies Joseph, who failed in everything he undertook."
JOSEPH II, HOLY ROMAN EMPEROR: Last words, 1790

No lengthen'd scroll, no praise-encumber'd stone;
My epitaph shall be my name alone.
BYRON: *A Fragment,* 1803

Come knock your heads against this stone,
For sorrow that poor John Thompson's gone.
WILLIAM BLAKE: *An Epitaph, c.* 1808

An excellent adage commands that we should
Relate of the dead that alone which is good;
But of the great lord who here lies in lead
We know nothing good but that he is dead.
S. T. COLERIDGE: In the Friend, Nov. 9, 1809

My friends, believe that I sleep. (Mes amis, croyez que je dors.)
Epitaph of the Chevalier Stanislas de Boufflers, written by himself, *c.* 1815

Names neatly carved for glory —
The patient stone bears all.
LUDWIG UHLAND: *Minster Tradition, c.* 1820

Posterity will ne'er survey
A nobler grave than this:
Here lies the bones of Castlereagh:
Stop, traveler, ——.
BYRON: *Epitaph,* 1821

Here lies Sir Jenkin Grout, who loved his friend, and persuaded his enemy; what his mouth ate, his hand paid for: what his servants robbed, he restored: if a woman gave him pleasure, he supported her in pain: he never forgot his children: and whoso touched his finger, drew after it his whole body.
Epitaph quoted by R. W. EMERSON: *Manners,* 1841

When fades at length our lingering day,
Who cares what pompous tombstones say?
Read on the hearts that love us still,
Hic jacet Joe. *Hic jacet* Bill.
O. W. HOLMES: *Bill and Joe,* 1851

Unawed by opinion
Unseduced by flattery
Undismayed by disaster
He confronted life with antique courage
And death with Christian hope
Epitaph of James Petigru, Charleston, S. C., 1863

Here lies a man whose crown was won
By blowing in an empty gun.
Author unidentified, *c.* 1880

And when I lie in the green kirkyard,
With the mold upon my breast,
Say not that she did well, or ill,
Only, She did her best.
DINAH MULOCK CRAIK: Epitaph for herself, *c.* 1887

This be the verse you grave for me:
Here he lies where he longed to be;
Home is the sailor, home from the sea,
And the hunter home from the hill.
R. L. STEVENSON: *Requiem,* 1887 (Written in 1880)

Warm Summer sun, shine kindly here;
Warm southern wind, blow softly here;
Green sod above, lie light, lie light —
Good night, dear heart, good night, good night.
S. L. CLEMENS (MARK TWAIN): Epitaph for his young daughter, adopted from one by Robert Richardson, *c.* 1885

He slept beneath the moon,
He basked beneath the sun;
He lived a life of going-to-do,
And died with nothing done.
JAMES ALBERRY: Epitaph for himself, 1889

An inscription on a tomb, showing that virtues acquired by death have a retroactive effect.
AMBROSE BIERCE: *The Devil's Dictionary,* 1906

Here lies the body of
Lady O'Looney,
Great-niece of Burke, commonly
called the Sublime
She was
Bland, passionate, and deeply religious;
Also she painted in water colors,
And sent several pictures to the Exhibition.
She was first cousin to Lady Jones,
And of such is the Kingdom of Heaven.
Epitaph at Pewsey, Bedfordshire, England

This turf has drank
A widow's tear;
Three of her husbands
Slumber here.
Epitaph in a churchyard in Staffordshire, England

Against his will
Here lies George Hill,
Who from a cliff
Fell down quite stiff.

When it happen'd is not known,
Therefore not mention'd on this stone.
Epitaph in St. Peter's Churchyard, Isle of Thanet, England

It is so soon that I am done for,
I wonder what I was begun for.
Epitaph on a child's grave at Cheltenham, England

Here lies the body of Bob Dent;
He kicked up his heels and to Hell he went.
Epitaph on a tombstone in Grand Gulf Cemetery, near Port Gibson, Miss.

Here lies. (Hic jacet.) LATIN PHRASE

[*See also* Agnostic, Angel, Architect, Dead, Fame, Keats (John), Monument, Tomb.

Equality

The only stable state is the one in which all men are equal before the law.
ARISTOTLE: *Politics*, v, *c.* 322 B.C.

So far as the natural law is concerned, all men are equal.
DOMITIUS ULPIANUS: *Liber singularis regularum*, *c.* 220

All men, among themselves, are by nature equal. The inequality we now discern hath its spring from the civil law.
THOMAS HOBBES: *Philosophical Rudiments Concerning Government and Society*, I, 1651

It follows as a common law of nature that every man esteem and treat another as one who is naturally his equal, and who is a man as well as he.
JOHN WISE: *A Vindication of the Government of New England Churches*, II, 1717

It is not true that equality is a law of nature. Nature knows no equality. Its sovereign law is subordination and dependence.
LUC DE VARVENARGUES: *Réflexions*, 1746

All men have equal rights to liberty, to their property, and to the protection of the laws.
VOLTAIRE: *Essai sur les mœurs*, 1754

The nature of things continually tends to the destruction of equality.
J.-J. ROUSSEAU: *Du contrat social*, I, 1761

Your levellers wish to level down as far as themselves, but they cannot bear levelling up to themselves.
SAMUEL JOHNSON: *Boswell's Life*, 1763

It is better that some should be unhappy than that none should be happy, which would be the case in a general state of equality.
SAMUEL JOHNSON: *Boswell's Life*, April 7, 1776

We hold these truths to be self-evident: that all men are created equal; that they are endowed by their Creator with inalienable rights; that among these are life, liberty, and the pursuit of happiness.
THOMAS JEFFERSON: *The Declaration of Independence*, 1776

The foundation on which all [our constitutions] are built is the natural equality of man, the denial of every preëminence but that annexed to legal office, and particularly the denial of a preëminence by birth.
THOMAS JEFFERSON: *Letter to George Washington*, 1784

Men are born and always continue free and equal in respect of their rights. Civil distinctions, therefore, can only be founded on public utility.
Declaration of the Rights of Man by the French National Assembly, I, 1789

Equality in a state is the relation of the citizens to one another, according to which one cannot compel another juridically without he subjects himself also to the law, by which in his turn he may also be compelled in the same manner.
IMMANUEL KANT: *Perpetual Peace*, II, 1795

A musical instrument composed of chords, keys or pipes, all perfectly equal in size and power, might as well be expected to produce harmony as a society composed of members all perfectly equal to be productive of peace and order.
JONATHAN BOUCHER: *A View of the Causes and Consequences of the American Revolution*, XII, 1797

Men are entitled to equal rights — but to equal rights to unequal things.
CHARLES JAMES FOX (1749–1806)

The best way to make every one poor is to insist on equality of wealth.
NAPOLEON I: To Gaspard Gourgaud at St. Helena, Jan. 29, 1817

Equality, in a social sense, may be divided into that of condition and that of rights. Equality of condition is incompatible with civilization, and is found only to exist in those communities that are but slightly removed from the savage state. In practice, it can only mean a common misery.
J. FENIMORE COOPER: *The American Democrat*, VI, 1838

All men have an equal right to the free development of their faculties; they have an equal right to the impartial protection of the state; but it is not true, it is against all the laws of reason and equity, it is against the eternal nature of things, that the indolent man and the laborious man, the spendthrift and the economist, the imprudent and the wise, should obtain and enjoy an equal amount of goods.
VICTOR COUSIN: *Justice et charité*, 1848

Six of one and half a dozen of the other.
CHARLES DICKENS: *Bleak House,* XXIV, 1853

I think the authors of the Declaration of Independence intended to include *all* men, but they did not intend to declare all men equal *in all respects.*
ABRAHAM LINCOLN: Speech at Springfield, Ill., June 26, 1857

Certainly the Negro is not our equal in color — perhaps not in many other respects; still, in the right to put into his mouth the bread that his own hands have earned he is the equal of every other man, white or black.
ABRAHAM LINCOLN: Speech at Springfield, Ill., July 17, 1858

Of equality — As if it harm'd me, giving others the same chances and rights as myself — As if it were not indispensable to my own rights that others possess the same.
WALT WHITMAN: *Thought,* 1860

Four score and seven years ago our fathers brought forth on this continent a new nation, conceived in liberty, and dedicated to the proposition that all men are created equal.
ABRAHAM LINCOLN: *Gettysburg Address,* Nov. 19, 1863

Popular privileges are consistent with a state of society in which there is great inequality of position. Democratic rights, on the contrary, demand that there should be equality of condition as the fundamental basis of the society they regulate.
BENJAMIN DISRAELI: Speech in the House of Commons, March 18, 1867

Men of culture are the true apostles of equality.
MATTHEW ARNOLD: *Culture and Anarchy,* 1869

The puniest infant that comes wailing into the world in the squalidest room of the most miserable tenement-house becomes at that moment seized of an equal right with the millionaires. And it is robbed if the right is denied.
HENRY GEORGE: *Progress and Poverty,* VII, 1879

The duke, the jockey-boy, and the artist are exactly alike; they are dressed by the same tailor, they dine at the same clubs, they swear the same oaths, they speak equally bad English, they love the same women.
GEORGE MOORE: *Confessions of a Young Man,* IX, 1888

The defect of equality is that we only desire it with our superiors.
HENRY BECQUE: *Querelles litteraires,* 1890

The doctrine that all men are, in any sense, or have been, at any time, free and equal, is an utterly baseless fiction.
T. H. HUXLEY: *On the Natural Inequality of Man,* 1890

The equality existing among the various social members consists only in this: that all men have their origin in God the Creator, have been redeemed by Jesus Christ, and are to be judged and rewarded or punished by God exactly according to their merits or demerits.
POPE PIUS X: *Apostolic Letter to the Bishops of Italy on Catholic Social Action,* Dec. 18, 1903

The doctrine of equality seldom embraces those who are worse off than its exponents.
R. A. PIDDINGTON: *The Next British Empire,* 1938

I am just as good as you are, and a damned sight better. AMERICAN SAYING

The five fingers are not all equal.
ARMENIAN PROVERB

The only real equality is in the cemetery.
GERMAN PROVERB

All men are born equal. (Omnes pari sorte nascimur.) LATIN PROVERB

All men are equal before the law of nature. (Quod ad jus naturale attinet, omnes homines æquales sunt.) LEGAL MAXIM

An equal has no power over an equal. (Par in parem imperium non habet.) IBID.

[*See also* Classes, Credo, Democracy, Disease, Friend, Judge, Justice, Liberty, Marriage, Nation, Negro, Sleep, Society, Superiority.

Equator

No one minds what Jeffrey says — it is not more than a week ago that I heard him speak disrespectfully of the equator.
Ascribed to SYDNEY SMITH in *A Memoir of the Rev. Sydney Smith* by his daughter, Lady Holland, 1855

Afternoon. Crossed the equator. In the distance it looked like a blue ribbon stretched across the ocean. Several passengers kodak'd it.
S. L. CLEMENS (MARK TWAIN): *Following the Equator,* IV, 1897

Equity

Equity, though it is a kind of justice, is not legal justice, but a rectification of legal justice.
ARISTOTLE: *The Nicomachean Ethics,* V, *c.* 340 B.C.

There's no equity stirring.
SHAKESPEARE: *I Henry IV,* II, *c.* 1598

Equity is a rougish thing; for law we have a measure. Equity is according to the conscience of him that is chancellor; and as that is larger or narrower, so is equity.
JOHN SELDEN: *Table-Talk,* 1689

Equity is abatement of legal right upon reasonable considerations.
BENJAMIN WHICHCOTE: *Moral and Religious Aphorisms,* 1753

Law, without equity, though hard and disagreeable, is much more desirable for the public good than equity without law.
WILLIAM BLACKSTONE: *Commentaries on the Laws of England,* I, 1765

A man must come into a court of equity with clean hands.
MR. JUSTICE EYRE: *Judgment in Dering* vs. *Winchelsea,* 1787

Nothing can be politically right that is morally wrong; and no necessity can sanctify a law that is contrary to equity.
BENJAMIN RUSH: *The Influence of Physical Causes Upon the Moral Faculty,* 1788

Law and equity are two things which God hath joined, but which man hath put asunder.
C. C. COLTON: *Lacon,* 1820

A party who seeks equity must do equity.
LORD CHANCELLOR COTTENHAM: *Judgment in Sturgis* vs. *Champneys,* 1839

Simply a matter of the length of the judge's ears.
ELBERT HUBBARD: *Roycroft Dictionary and Book of Epigrams,* 1923

Equity does not demand that its suitors shall have led blameless lives.
MR. JUSTICE BRANDEIS: *Decision in Loughran* vs. *Loughran* et al., April 30, 1934

The rules of equity. (Jus aequum.)
LATIN PHRASE

Equity considers that to have been done which ought to have been done. (Aequitas factum habet quod fieri oportuit.) LEGAL MAXIM

Equity follows the law. (Aequitas sequitur legem.) IBID.

[*See also* Just, Land, Law, Law (Common), Law (Natural).

Equivocation

Equivocation is half way to lying, as lying is the whole way to Hell.
WILLIAM PENN: *Fruits of Solitude,* 1693

[*See also* Lying.

Erasmus, Desiderius (1466–1536)

Erasmus is the enemy to true religion, the open adversary of Christ, the complete and faithful picture and image of Epicurus and of Lucian.
MARTIN LUTHER: *Table-Talk,* DCLXXX, 1569

Erasmus laid the egg which Luther hatched.
Author unidentified, *c.* 1600

Error

All mortals err.
SOPHOCLES: *Antigone, c.* 450 B.C.

Who can understand his errors?
PSALMS XIX, 12, *c.* 350 B.C.

Remember that I am a frail mortal, and therefore I have erred.
TERENCE: *Adelphi,* IV, *c.* 160 B.C.

To err is human. (Humanum est errare.)
SENECA: *Naturales quaestiones,* IV, *c.* 63

The last error shall be worse than the first.
MATTHEW XXVII, 64, *c.* 75

The comedy of errors.
SHAKESPEARE: Title of a play, 1593

O hateful error, melancholy's child,
Why dost thou show to the apt thoughts of men
The things that are not?
SHAKESPEARE: *Julius Cæsar,* V, 1599

Who says he does not err, errs in conceit.
JOHN NORDEN: *Surveyors' Dialogue,* 1607

Next to truth, a confirmed error does well.
BEN JONSON: *Bartholomew Fair,* intro., 1614

Who errs and mends, to God himself commends.
THOMAS SHELTON: Tr. of CERVANTES: *Don Quixote,* II (1615), 1620

The chief cause of human errors is to be found in the prejudices picked up in childhood.
RENÉ DESCARTES: *Principles of Philosophy,* I, 1644

Who is so stupid as both to mistake in geometry, and also to persist in it, when another detects his error to him?
THOMAS HOBBES: *Leviathan,* V, 1651

He that assures himself he never errs will always err.
JOSEPH GLANVILLE: *The Vanity of Dogmatizing,* XXIII, 1661 (Cf. NORDEN, *ante,* 1607)

You have a wrong sow by the ear.
SAMUEL BUTLER: *Hudibras,* II, 1664

Man is a being filled with error. This error is natural, and, without grace, ineffaceable. Nothing shows him the truth; everything deceives him.
BLAISE PASCAL: *Pensées,* IV, 1670

Errors, like straws, upon the surface flow;
He who would search for pearls must dive below.
JOHN DRYDEN: *All for Love,* prologue, 1678

To err is human, to forgive divine.
ALEXANDER POPE: *An Essay on Criticism,* II, 1711 (Cf. SENECA, *ante, c.* 63)

The best may err.
JOSEPH ADDISON: *Cato,* V, 1713

Error is always in haste.
THOMAS FULLER: *Gnomologia,* 1732

Honest error is to be pitied, not ridiculed.
LORD CHESTERFIELD: *Letter to his son,* Feb. 16, 1748

Rivers rush to the ocean no faster than man rushes into error.
VOLTAIRE: *Philosophical Dictionary,* 1764

Man is made for error; it enters his mind naturally, and he discovers a few truths only with the greatest effort.
FREDERICK THE GREAT: *Letter to Voltaire,* June 29, 1771

Error of opinion may be tolerated where reason is left free to combat it.
THOMAS JEFFERSON: Inaugural Address, March 4, 1801

One error almost compels another.
S. T. COLERIDGE: *Notebooks,* 1805

It is almost as difficult to make a man unlearn his errors as his knowledge. Mal-information is more hopeless than non-information; for error is always more busy than ignorance.
C. C. COLTON: *Lacon,* 1820

There is no error so crooked, but it hath in it some lines of truth.
MARTIN F. TUPPER: *Proverbial Philosophy,* I, 1837

Error, wounded, writhes with pain,
And dies among his worshippers.
W. C. BRYANT: *The Battlefield,* 1839

Sometimes we may learn more from a man's errors than from his virtues.
H. W. LONGFELLOW: *Hyperion,* IV, 1839

Error is got out of the minds that cherish it as the taenia is removed from the body, one joint, or a few joints at a time, for the most part; rarely the whole evil at once.
O. W. HOLMES: *The Contagiousness of Puerperal Fever,* revised ed., 1855 (*Taenia*=a variety of tapeworm)

When a learned man errs he makes a learned error. ARAB PROVERB

An old error is always more popular than a new truth. GERMAN PROVERB

A common error becomes the law. (Communis error facit jus.) LEGAL MAXIM

[*See also* Cause and Effect, Experience, Human, Ignorance, Judgment, Logic, Mend, Opinion, Truth and Error.

Erudition

[*See* Learning.

Escape

I am escaped with the skin of my teeth.
JOB XIX, 20, *c.* 325 B.C. (Usually *by* is substituted for *with*)

Men, not having been able to cure death, misery, and ignorance, have imagined to make themselves happy by not thinking of these things.
BLAISE PASCAL: *Pensées,* II, 1670

[*See also* Danger, Gone.

Essayist

Some turn over all books, and are equally searching in all papers; they write out of what they presently find or meet, without choice. Such are all essayists, even their master Montaigne.
BEN JONSON: *Discoveries, c.* 1615

Estate, Fourth

[*See* Journalism.

Esteem

Our merit gains us the esteem of the virtuous — our star that of the public.
LA ROCHEFOUCAULD: *Maxims,* 1665

Esteem has more engaging charms than friendship, or even love. It captivates hearts better, and never makes ingrates.
STANISLAUS LESZCYNSKI (KING OF POLAND): *Œuvres du philosophe bienfaisant,* 1763

We are usually mistaken in esteeming men too much; rarely in esteeming them too little.
IBID.

[*See also* Love.

Eternal Recurrence

While the earth remaineth, seed-time and harvest, and cold and heat, and summer and winter, and day and night shall not cease.
GENESIS VIII, 22, *c.* 700 B.C.

The thing that hath been, it is that which shall be; and that which is done is that which shall be done: and there is no new thing under the sun.
ECCLESIASTES I, 9, *c.* 200 B.C.

How many ages hence
Shall this our lofty scene be acted over
In states unborn and accents yet unknown?
SHAKESPEARE: *Julius Cæsar,* III, 1599

At dinner-time I was strangely haunted by what I would call the sense of preëxistence — videlicet, a confused idea that nothing that passed was said for the first time, that the same topics had been discussed, and the same persons had stated the same opinions on the same subjects.
WALTER SCOTT: *Journal,* Feb. 17, 1828

To be, in any form — what is that?
(Round and round we go, all of us, and ever come back thither.)
WALT WHITMAN: *Walt Whitman,* 1855

All things return eternally, and ourselves with them: We have already existed times without number, and all things with us.
F. W. NIETZSCHE: *Thus Spake Zarathustra,* LVII, 1885

It is only three generations from shirtsleeves to shirtsleeves. AMERICAN PROVERB

Worka like hell
To earna de mon

To buy de spaget
To getta de streng'
To worka like hell
To earna de mon, &c. Author unidentified

[*See also* Predestination.

Eternity

The sum of all sums is eternity. (Summarum summa est aeternum.)
LUCRETIUS: *De rerum natura,* III, 57 B.C.

The created world is but a small parenthesis in eternity.
THOMAS BROWNE: *Christian Morals,* III, *c.* 1680

Eternity! thou pleasing dreadful thought!
Through what variety of untried being,
Through what new scenes and changes must
we pass!
JOSEPH ADDISON: *Cato,* V, 1713

We can have but a little sense of what an eternal duration is; it swallows up all thought and imagination: if we set ourselves to think upon it, we are presently lost.
JONATHAN EDWARDS: *Sinners in Zion Tenderly Warned,* 1740

If the human mind, by any future improvement of its sensibility, should become conscious of an infinite number of ideas in a minute, that minute would be eternity.
P. B. SHELLEY: *Queen Mab,* notes, 1813

Then star nor sun shall waken
Nor any change of light:
Nor sound of waters shaken,
Nor any sound or sight:
Nor wintry leaves nor vernal,
Nor days nor things diurnal;
Only the sleep eternal
In an eternal night.
A. C. SWINBURNE: *The Garden of Proserpine,* 1866

The monotone of everlastingness.
D. S. MACCOLL: *Carthage,* 1882

The Sunday of time.
ELBERT HUBBARD: *Roycroft Dictionary and Book of Epigrams,* 1923

What is not now was not before; what was not before is not now. BUDDHIST MAXIM

[*See also* Present.

Ether

The ether of space is nothing but the nominative of the verb to undulate.
Author unidentified

Ethics

Ethics is the art of living well and happily.
HENRY MORE: *Enchiridion ethicum,* I, 1667

Our whole dignity consists in thought. Let us endeavor, then, to think well: this is the principle of ethics.
BLAISE PASCAL: *Pensées,* II, 1670

In law a man is guilty when he violates the rights of another. In ethics he is guilty if he only thinks of doing so.
IMMANUEL KANT: Lecture at Königsberg, 1775

I have but one system of ethics for men and for nations, — to be grateful, to be faithful to all engagements and under all circumstances, to be open and generous, promoting in the long run even the interests of both.
THOMAS JEFFERSON: *Letter to the Duchesse D'Auville,* 1790

The aim of ethics is to render scientific — *i.e.,* true, and as far as possible systematic — the apparent cognitions that most men have of the rightness or reasonableness of conduct, whether the conduct be considered as right in itself, or as the means to some end conceived as ultimately reasonable.
HENRY SIDGWICK: *The Methods of Ethics,* I, 1874

Ethical systems are roughly distinguishable according as they take for their cardinal ideas (1) the character of the agent; (2) the nature of the motive; (3) the quality of his deeds; and (4) the results.
HERBERT SPENCER: *The Data of Ethics,* III, 1879

[*See also* Comfort, Morality, Right and Wrong.

Ethics, Professional

We must hold a man amenable to reason for the choice of his daily craft or profession. It is not an excuse any longer for his deeds, that they are the custom of his trade. What business has he with an evil trade?
R. W. EMERSON: *Spiritual Laws,* 1841

Ethiopian

[*See* Change, Miscegenation, Skin.

Eucharist

As they were eating, Jesus took bread, and blessed it, and brake it, and gave it to the disciples, and said, Take, eat; this is my body. MATTHEW XXVI, 26, *c.* 75

The bread that I will give is my flesh.
JOHN VI, 51, *c.* 115

Whoso eateth my flesh, and drinketh my blood, hath eternal life; and I will raise him up at the last day. JOHN VI, 54

He that eateth my flesh, and drinketh my blood, dwelleth in me and I in him. JOHN VI, 56

As the bread, when it is consecrated, is no longer mere bread but the eucharist and thus two things, earthly and heavenly, so our bodies, when we receive the eucharist, are no longer corruptible, but have the hope of eternal life.
IRENÆUS: *Adversus hæreses,* IV, *c.* 180

He was the Word that spake it:
He took the bread and brake it;
And what that Word did make it
I do believe and take it.

JOHN DONNE: *On the Sacrament, c.* 1610

Beware of him on the days when he takes communion.

JACQUES DU LORENS: *Satires,* I, *c.* 1625

At the times of the Holy Communion he takes order with the church wardens, that the elements be of the best, not cheap or coarse, much less ill-tasted or unwholesome.

GEORGE HERBERT: *A Priest to the Temple,* I, 1632 (On the duties of a parson)

Bring the holy crust of bread,
Lay it underneath the head;
'Tis a certain charm to keep
Hags away, while children sleep.

ROBERT HERRICK: *Hesperides,* 1648

The body and blood of Christ . . . are verily and indeed taken and received by the faithful in the Lord's Supper.

THE BOOK OF COMMON PRAYER (*The Catechism*), 1662

How I hate this folly of not believing in the eucharist, etc! If the gospel be true, if Jesus Christ be God, what difficulty is there?

BLAISE PASCAL: *Pensées,* 1670

Such sav'ry deities must needs be good
As serv'd at once for worship and for food.

JOHN DRYDEN: *Absalom and Achitophel,* I, 1682

This day so cold that the sacramental bread is frozen pretty hard, and rattles sadly as broken into the plates.

SAMUEL SEWALL: *Diary,* Jan. 24, 1685

Neither antiquity nor any other sect of the present day has imagined a more atrocious and blasphemous absurdity than that of eating God. It is a most revolting dogma, insulting to the Supreme Being, the height of madness and folly.

FREDERICK THE GREAT: *Letter to Voltaire,* March 19, 1776

[*See also* Catholicism (Roman), Transubstantiation.

Euclid

[*See* Geometry, Intelligence.

Eugenics

The best of either sex should be united with the best as often, and the inferior with the inferior as seldom, as possible.

PLATO: *The Republic, c.* 370 B.C.

Study your race, or the soil of your family will dwindle into cits or esquires, or run up into wits or madmen.

RICHARD STEELE: *The Tatler,* Oct. 1, 1709

If we forbade the discontented, the sullen, the atrabilious to propagate their kind we might transform the world into a garden of happiness.

F. W. NIETZSCHE: *Human All-too-Human,* II, 1878

[*See also* Sterilization.

Eunuch

He that is wounded in the stones, or hath his privy member cut off, shall not enter into the congregation of the Lord.

DEUTERONOMY XXIII, 1, *c.* 650 B.C.

There are some eunuchs, which were so born from their mother's womb: and there are some eunuchs, which were made eunuchs of men: and there be eunuchs, which have made themselves eunuchs for the kingdom of heaven's sake. MATTHEW XIX, 12, *c.* 75

The kingdom of Heaven is thrown open to all eunuchs.

TERTULLIAN: *De monogamia, c.* 212

[*See also* Beard, Envy, Gout.

Euripides (480–406 B.C.)

A poet whom Socrates called his friend, whom Aristotle lauded, whom Menander admired, and for whom Sophocles and the city of Athens put on mourning on hearing of his death, must certainly have been something.

J. W. GOETHE: *Conversations with Eckermann,* March 28, 1827

Europe

I take Europe to be worn out. When Voltaire dies we may say "Good-night."

HORACE WALPOLE: *Letter to Horace Mann,* Nov. 24, 1774

Europe has a set of primary interests, which to us have none, or a very remote relation. Hence, she must be engaged in frequent controversies the causes of which are essentially foreign to our concerns.

GEORGE WASHINGTON: Farewell Address, Sept. 19, 1796

Roll up the map of Europe; it will not be wanted these ten years.

WILLIAM PITT: On his deathbed, 1806

Better fifty years of Europe than a cycle of Cathay.

ALFRED TENNYSON: *Locksley Hall,* 1842

The state system of Europe is a system akin to the system of cages in an impoverished provincial zoo.

LEON TROTSKY: *What Next?,* 1932

Either Europe will be reorganized on a revolutionary basis or it will not survive.

NAHUM GOLDMANN: Address to the World Jewish Congress, Washington, Feb., 1940

[*See also* Asia, City, Foreign Relations, Freedom, History, King, Monarchy, Napoleon I, Travel, War.

Europe, Northern

The workshop of the human race. (Humani generis officinam.)

C. L. DE MONTESQUIEU: *The Spirit of the Laws*, XVII, 1748 (Quoted from "the Goth Jornandez")

Euxine

[*See* Black Sea.

Eve (c. 4000 B.C.?)

Eve exceeded all women in sorrow and misery. Never came into the world a more miserable woman; she saw that for her sake we were all to die.

MARTIN LUTHER: *Table-Talk*, DLVIII, 1569

Mr. Darrow — Do you believe that the first woman was Eve?
Mr. Bryan — Yes.
Mr. Darrow — Do you believe she was literally made out of Adam's rib?
Mr. Bryan — I do.

At the Scopes trial, Dayton, Tenn., July 21, 1925

[*See also* Adam and Eve, Childbirth, Ugliness.

Even

"Now we are even," quoth Stephen, when he gave his wife six blows for one.

JONATHAN SWIFT: *Journal to Stella*, Jan. 20, 1711

Evening

The evening crowns the day.

GEORGE CHAPMAN: *All Fools*, II, 1605

Light thickens; and the crow
Makes wing to the rooky wood:
Good things of day begin to droop and drowse;
Whiles night's black agents to their preys do rouse.

SHAKESPEARE: *Macbeth*, III, *c.* 1605

Now came still evening on, and twilight gray
Had in her sober livery all things clad;
Silence accompany'd; for beast and bird,
They to their grassy couch, these to their nests,
Were slunk, all but the wakeful nightingale.

JOHN MILTON: *Paradise Lost*, IV, 1667

The curfew tolls the knell of parting day,
The lowing herd winds slowly o'er the lea,
The ploughman homeward plods his weary way,
And leaves the world to darkness and to me.

THOMAS GRAY: *Elegy Written in a Country Churchyard*, 1750

The holy time is quiet as a nun
Breathless with adoration.

WILLIAM WORDSWORTH: *It Is a Beauteous Evening*, 1807

Parting day
Dies like the dolphin, whom each pang imbues
With a new color as it gasps away,
The last still loveliest, till — 'tis gone, and all is gray.

BYRON: *Childe Harold*, IV, 1818

The day is done, and the darkness
Falls from the wings of night,
As a feather is wafted downward
From an eagle in its flight.

H. W. LONGFELLOW: *The Day Is Done*, 1845

Every evening we are poorer by a day.

ARTHUR SCHOPENHAUER: *Parerga und Paralipomena*, 1851

To me at least was never evening yet
But seemed far beautifuller than its day.

ROBERT BROWNING: *The Ring and the Book*, I, 1868

[*See also* Landscape, Night, Sunset, Twilight.

Evensong

Though the day be never so long,
At last the bells ring for evensong.

STEPHEN HAWES: *The Pastime of Pleasure*, 1555

Event

The gravest events dawn with no more noise than the morning star makes in rising.

H. W. BEECHER: *Royal Truths*, 1862

[*See also* Narrative, Thinker.

Everlasting

[*See* Eternity, Hell.

Everywhere

He that is everywhere is nowhere. (Nusquam est, qui ubique est.)

SENECA: *Epistulæ morales ad Lucilium*, II, *c.* 63

Here and everywhere. (Hic et ubique.)

LATIN PHRASE

So everywhere. (Sic passim.) IBID.

Evidence

They who shall accuse their wives of adultery, and shall have no witnesses thereof besides themselves, the testimony which shall be required by one of them shall be that he swear four times by God that he speaketh the truth, and the fifth time that he imprecate the curse of God on him if he be a liar. And it shall avert the punishment from the wife if she swear four times by God that he is a liar, and if the fifth time she imprecate the wrath of God on her if he speaketh the truth.

THE KORAN, XXIV, *c.* 625

[On the stage] the evidence of one prejudiced witness, of shady antecedents, is quite sufficient to convict the most stainless and irreproachable old gentleman of crimes for the commital of which he could have had no possible motive.

JEROME K. JEROME: *Stage-Land*, 1889

It is for ordinary minds, and not for psychoanalysts, that our rules of evidence are framed. They have their source very often

in considerations of administrative convenience, of practical expediency, and not in rules of logic.
MR. JUSTICE B. N. CARDOZO: *Opinion in Shepard* vs. *the United States,* Nov. 6, 1933

[*See also* Eye-witness, Miracle, Proof.

Evidence, Circumstantial

Some circumstantial evidence is very strong, as when you find a trout in the milk.
H. D. THOREAU: *Journal,* Nov. 11, 1854

Circumstantial evidence only raises a probability.
MR. JUSTICE POLLOCK: *Judgment in Regina* vs. *Rowton,* 1865

[*See also* Circumstance.

Evil

The imagination of man's heart is evil from his youth.
GENESIS VIII, 21, *c.* 700 B.C.

I make peace, and create evil: I the Lord do all these things.
ISAIAH XLV, 7, *c.* 700 B.C.

The gods can either take away evil from the world and will not, or, being willing to do so cannot; or they neither can nor will, or lastly, they are both able and willing. If they have the will to remove evil and cannot, then they are not omnipotent. If they can, but will not, then they are not benevolent. If they are neither able nor willing, then they are neither omnipotent nor benevolent. Lastly, if they are both able and willing to annihilate evil, how does it exist?
EPICURUS: *Aphorisms, c.* 300 B.C.

One evil flows from another. (Aliud ex alio malum.)
TERENCE: *Eunuchus,* V, *c.* 160 B.C.

An evil life is a kind of death.
OVID: *Epistulæ ex Ponto,* III, *c.* 5

The evil best known is the most tolerable.
LIVY: *History of Rome,* XXIII, *c.* 10

Abstain from all appearances of evil.
I THESSALONIANS V, 22, *c.* 51

Evil communications corrupt good manners.
I CORINTHIANS, XV, 33, *c.* 55

Be not overcome of evil, but overcome evil with good.
ROMANS XII, 21, *c.* 55

Sufficient unto the day is the evil thereof.
MATTHEW VI, 34, *c.* 75

Although it be with truth thou speakest evil, this also is a crime.
ST. JOHN CHRYSOSTOM: *Homilies,* III, *c.* 388

God judged it better to bring good out of evil than to suffer no evil to exist.
ST. AUGUSTINE: *Enchiridion,* XXVII, 421

Shame to him who evil thinks. (Honi soit qui mal y pense.)
Motto of the Order of the Garter, established by Edward III of England, April 23, 1349

Of two evils we should always choose the less.
THOMAS À KEMPIS: *Imitation of Christ,* III, *c.* 1420

Whoever takes it upon himself to establish a commonwealth and prescribe laws must presuppose all men naturally bad, and that they will yield to their innate evil passions as often as they can do so with safety.
NICCOLÒ MACHIAVELLI: *Discorsi,* I, 1531

There are three all-powerful evils: lust, anger and greed.
TULSĪ DĀS: *Rāmāyan,* 1574

Evils have their life, their limits; their diseases and their health.
MICHEL DE MONTAIGNE: *Essays,* III, 1588

A beast is but like itself, but an evil man is half a beast and half a devil.
JOSEPH HALL (BISHOP OF NORWICH): *Meditations and Vows,* II, 1606

All evils become equal when they are extreme.
PIERRE CORNEILLE: *Horace,* III, 1639

There are men of whom we can never believe evil without having seen it. Yet there are few in whom we should be surprised to see it.
LA ROCHEFOUCAULD: *Maxims,* 1665

So farewell hope, and with hope, farewell fear,
Farewell remorse; all good to me is lost.
Evil, be thou my good.
JOHN MILTON: *Paradise Lost,* IV, 1667

That which is evil is soon learn't.
JOHN RAY: *English Proverbs,* 1670

If plagues or earthquakes break not Heav'n's design,
Why then a Borgia or a Catiline?
ALEXANDER POPE: *An Essay on Man,* I, 1732

No evil without its advantages.
WILLIAM HONE: *Every-Day Book,* 1827

As to pure evil or malignity for its own sake, apart from some procurement or notion of good, nothing which we see in all nature induces us to suppose it possible.
LEIGH HUNT: *The Seer,* LII, 1840

There is no pure lie, no pure malignity in nature. The entertainment of the proposition of depravity is the last profligacy and profanation. There is no skepticism, no atheism, but that.
R. W. EMERSON: *The New England Reformers,* 1844

"Resist not evil" means "Do not resist the evil man," which is to say, "Never offer violence to another," which is to say, "Never commit an act that is contrary to love."
LYOF N. TOLSTOY: *On Life,* 1887

What is evil? — Whatever springs from weakness.
F. W. NIETZSCHE: *The Antichrist*, II, 1888

Every evil comes to us on wings and goes away limping. FRENCH PROVERB

The three evils are the sea, fire, and woman.
GREEK PROVERB

The beginning of the evil. (Origo mali.)
LATIN PHRASE

To what evil will it lead? (Cui malo?) IBID.

For every evil under the sun,
There is a remedy or there is none;
If there be one, try and find it;
If there be none, never mind it.
OLD ENGLISH RHYME

What is evil lives forever. SPANISH PROVERB

[*See also* Appearance, Child, Example, Fear, Good and Evil, Learning, Money, Nonresistance, Progress.

Evildoing

Evil deeds never prosper.
HOMER: *Odyssey*, VIII, *c.* 800 B.C.

It is not noble to return evil for evil; at no time ought we do an injury to our neighbors.
PLATO: *Crito*, X, *c.* 350 B.C.

Fret not thyself because of evildoers, neither be thou envious against the workers of iniquity, for they shall soon be cut down like the grass, and wither as the green herb.
PSALMS XXXVII, 1–2, *c.* 150 B.C.

The way to evildoing always runs through evildoing. SENECA: *Agamemnon*, *c.* 60

No man is clever enough to know all the evil he does.
LA ROCHEFOUCAULD: *Maxims*, 1665

Men never do evil so completely and cheerfully as when they do it from religious conviction. BLAISE PASCAL: *Pensées*, 1670

The curse of an evil deed is that it must always engender more evil.
J. C. F. SCHILLER: *The Piccolomini*, V, 1799

Multitudes think they like to do evil; yet no man ever really enjoyed doing evil since God made the world.
JOHN RUSKIN: *Stones of Venice*, I, 1851

Better suffer a great evil than do a little one.
H. G. BOHN: *Handbook of Proverbs*, 1855

A little excuse is enough for doing evil.
GREEK PROVERB

One may not do evil that good may come of it. (Non faciat malum, ut inde veniat bonum.)
LEGAL MAXIM

[*See also* Hatred.

Evil Eye

[*See* Eye (Evil).

Evolution

Men first appeared as fishes. When they were able to help themselves they took to the land.
Ascribed to ANAXIMANDER (610–546 B.C.)

And from the dead, corporeal mass,
Thro' each progressive order pass
To instinct, reason, God.
MARK AKENSIDE: *Hymn to Science*, 1739

Lord Monboddo, the Scotch judge, has lately written a strange book about the origin of language, in which he traces monkeys up to men, and says that in some countries the human species have tails like other beasts.
SAMUEL JOHNSON: *Letter to Hester Thrale*, Aug. 25, 1773

Each of us is aware, if he looks back upon his own history, that he was a theologian in his childhood, a metaphysician in his youth, and a natural philosopher in his manhood.
AUGUSTE COMTE: *Cours de philosophie positive*, I, 1830

Man, made of the dust of the world, does not forget his origin; and all that is yet inanimate will one day speak and reason. Unpublished nature will have its whole secret told.
R. W. EMERSON: *Uses of Great Men*, 1850

The changes which God causes in His lower creatures are almost always from worse to better, while the changes which God allows man to make in himself are very often quite the other way.
JOHN RUSKIN: *Lectures on Architecture and Painting*, IV, 1853

We declare it to be clearly opposed to the Holy Scriptures and the Faith to say that the human body was produced by successive and spontaneous transformations of less perfect forms into more perfect forms.
Decree of the Provincial Council of Cologne, 1860

Man's derived supremacy over the earth; man's power of articulate speech; man's gift of reason; man's free will and responsibility; man's faith and man's redemption; the incarnation of the Eternal Son, the indwelling of the Eternal Spirit — all are equally and utterly irreconcilable with the degrading notion of the brute origin of him who was created in the image of God, and redeemed by the Eternal Son.
SAMUEL WILBERFORCE (BISHOP OF OXFORD): *Sermon at Oxford*, 1860

Evolution is a change from an incoherent homogeneity to a coherent heterogeneity, accompanying the dissipation of motion and integration of matter.
HERBERT SPENCER: *First Principles*, III, 1862

[It is a] shabby-genteel sentiment . . . which makes men prefer to believe that they are degenerated angels rather than elevated apes.

W. WINWOOD READE: *The Martyrdom of Man*, III, 1872

Evolution is not a force but a process, not a cause but a law.

JOHN MORLEY: *On Compromise*, 1874

Every individual alive today, the highest as well as the lowest, is derived in an unbroken line from the first and lowest forms.

AUGUST WEISMANN: *Dauer des Lebens*, 1881

The conditions that direct the order of . . . the living world . . . are marked by their persistence in improving the birthright of successive generations. They determine, at much cost of individual comfort, that each plant and animal shall, on the general average, be endowed at its birth with more suitable natural faculties than those of its representative in the preceding generation.

FRANCIS GALTON: *Inquiries Into Human Faculty*, 1883

Out of the dusk a shadow,
Then a spark;
Out of the cloud a silence,
Then a lark;
Out of the heart a rapture,
Then a pain;
Out of the dead, cold ashes
Life again.

JOHN B. TABB: *Evolution*, 1884

We are very little changed
From the semi-apes who ranged
India's prehistoric clay.

RUDYARD KIPLING: *A General Summary*, 1886

It is an error to imagine that evolution signifies a constant tendency to increased perfection. That process undoubtedly involves a constant remodeling of the organism in adaptation to new conditions; but it depends on the nature of those conditions whether the direction of the modifications effected shall be upward or downward.

T. H. HUXLEY: *The Struggle for Existence in Human Society*, 1888

In due time the evolution theory will have to abate its vehemence, cannot be allow'd to dominate everything else, and will have to take its place as a segment of the circle, the cluster — as but one of many theories, many thoughts, of profoundest value — and readjusting and differentiating much, yet leaving the divine secrets just as inexplicable and unreachable as before — maybe more so.

WALT WHITMAN: *Notes Left Over, c.* 1888

Species do not evolve toward perfection, but quite the contrary. The weak, in fact, always prevail over the strong, not only because they are in the majority, but also because they are the more crafty.

F. W. NIETZSCHE: *The Twilight of the Idols*, 1889

As a docile son of the Church, resolved to live and die in the Faith, and obedient in this case to authority, I hereby declare that I disavow, retract and denounce all that I have said, written and published in favor of this [the Darwinian] theory.

M. D. LEROY: In Le Monde (Paris), Feb. 26, 1895 (Father Leroy, a Dominican, had published in 1891 a book called *L'Évolution restreinte aux espèces organiques*, in which he argued that it was sufficient to believe that God had specially created the human soul — that the evolution of the body might be believed in. In 1895 he was called to Rome, and soon afterward published his recantation)

The probable fact is that we are descended not only from monkeys but from monks.

ELBERT HUBBARD: *Roycroft Dictionary and Book of Epigrams*, 1923

It shall be unlawful for any teacher in any of the universities, normals, and all other public schools in the state, which are supported in whole or in part by the public school funds of the state, to teach the theory that denies the story of the divine creation of man as taught in the Bible, and to teach instead that man has descended from a lower order of animals.

Act of the Legislature of Tennessee, March 21, 1925

What shall we say of the intelligence, not to say religion, of those who are so particular to distinguish between fishes and reptiles and birds, but put a man with an immortal soul in the same circle with the wolf, the hyena, and the skunk? What must be the impression made upon children by such a degradation of man?

W. J. BRYAN: Statement issued in Dayton, Tenn., July 28, 1925

If a minister believes and teaches evolution, he is a stinking skunk, a hypocrite, and a liar.

W. A. (BILLY) SUNDAY: Statement to the press, 1925

[*See also* Darwin (Charles), Darwinism, Man, Natural Selection, Plant, Progress, Struggle for Existence.

Exactness

Delusive exactness is a source of fallacy throughout the law.

MR. JUSTICE O. W. HOLMES: *Dissenting opinion in Traux vs. Corrigan*, 1921

Exactness is the sublimity of fools.

Author unidentified

Exaggeration

Exaggeration is a department of lying.

BALTASAR GRACIÁN: *The Art of Worldly Wisdom*, XLI, 1647

There is no one who does not exaggerate.
R. W. EMERSON: *Nominalist and Realist,* 1841

[*See also* Jealousy, Journalism.

Examination

Examinations are formidable even to the best prepared, for the greatest fool may ask more than the wisest man can answer.
C. C. COLTON: *Lacon,* 1820

Example

Example is better than precept.
ENGLISH PROVERB, traced by Apperson to 1400

Example is often a mirror that deceives.
PIERRE CORNEILLE: *Cinna,* II, 1639

Example is a dangerous lure: where the wasp got through the gnat is stuck.
JEAN DE LA FONTAINE: *Fables,* II, *c.* 1670

The example of Alexander's chastity has not made so many continent as that of his drunkenness has made intemperate.
BLAISE PASCAL: *Pensées,* VIII, 1670

Example draws where precept fails,
And sermons are less read than tales.
MATTHEW PRIOR: *Poems on Several Occasions,* 1708

A good example is the best sermon.
THOMAS FULLER: *Gnomologia,* 1732

Setting too good an example is a kind of slander seldom forgiven; 't is *scandalum magnatum.*
BENJAMIN FRANKLIN: *Poor Richard's Almanac,* 1753

Example is the school of mankind, and they will learn at no other.
EDMUND BURKE: *Letters on a Regicide Peace,* I, 1797

Example is an eloquent orator.
CZECH PROVERB

[*See also* Abbot, Age (Old), History, Imitation, Influence.

Excellence

Excellent things are rare.
PLATO: *The Republic,* IV, *c.* 370 B.C. (Cited as a proverb)

By different methods different men excel,
But where is he who can do all things well?
CHARLES CHURCHILL: *Epistle to William Hogarth,* 1763

Nothing is fine but the ideal; or rather, excellence exists only by abstraction.
WILLIAM HAZLITT: *The Prose Album,* 1829 (Monthly Magazine, July)

If a man has good corn, or wood, or boards, or pigs to sell, or can make better chairs or knives, crucibles, or church organs, than anybody else, you will find a broad, hard-beaten road to his house, though it be in the woods.
R. W. EMERSON: *Journal,* Feb., 1855

[*See also* Mousetrap.

Excelsior

The shades of night were falling fast,
As through an Alpine village passed
A youth, who bore, 'mid snow and ice
A banner with the strange device,
Excelsior!
H. W. LONGFELLOW: *Excelsior,* 1841

Exception

No rule is so general which admits not some exception.
ROBERT BURTON: *The Anatomy of Melancholy,* I, 1621

The exception proves the rule.
JOHN WILSON: *The Cheats,* 1664

Excess

Nothing in excess.
Ascribed to THALES (*c.* 624–546 B.C.), to SOLON (*c.* 638–558 B.C.), to CLEOBULUS (*c.* 628–558 B.C.) and to SOCRATES (469–399 B.C.)

To gild refined gold, to paint the lily,
To throw a perfume on the violet,
To smooth the ice, or add another hue
Unto the rainbow, or with taper-light
To seek the beauteous eye of Heaven to garnish,
Is wasteful, and ridiculous excess.
SHAKESPEARE: *King John,* IV, *c.* 1596

Thou tiest but wings to a swift grayhound's heel
And add'st to a running chariot a fifth wheel.
THOMAS DEKKER: *Match Me in London,* I, 1631

He does nothing who endeavors to do more than is allowed to humanity.
SAMUEL JOHNSON: *Rasselas,* 1759

The road of excess leads to the palace of wisdom.
WILLIAM BLAKE: *The Marriage of Heaven and Hell,* 1790

It never rains but it pours.
ENGLISH PROVERB, apparently not recorded before the XVIII century

Even nectar is poison if taken to excess.
HINDU PROVERB

Nothing to excess. (Ne quid nimis.)
LATIN PHRASE, borrowed from the Greek

The law condemns excess. (Excessus in jure reprobatur.)
LEGAL MAXIM

Moderation is a fatal thing; nothing succeeds like excess.
OSCAR WILDE: *A Woman of No Importance,* II, 1893

[*See also* Intemperance, Moderation, Pride, Too Much.

Exchange

A fair exchange is no robbery.
ENGLISH PROVERB, traced by Apperson to 1546

Excitement

[*See* Pleasure.

Exclusiveness

This gallows is for us and our children.
Notice on a gallows in England; origin undetermined, *c.* 1700

Excommunication

Do to the book, quench the candle, ring the bell. Form of excommunication, *c.* 1200 (*Do to*=close)

Excommunications are merely external punishments, and they do not deprive one of the common prayers of the Church.
MARTIN LUTHER: Ninety-five theses, posted on the church door at Wittenberg, XXIII, Oct. 31, 1517

Although the sword of excommunication is the chief weapon of ecclesiastical discipline, and very useful for keeping the people to their duties, it is to be used only with sobriety and circumspection, for experience teaches that if it be used rashly and for small reason it will be more despised than feared, and will work more evil than good.
DECREES OF THE COUNCIL OF TRENT, XXV, Dec. 4, 1563

They first read him out of their church, and next minute
Turned round and declared he had never been in it.
J. R. LOWELL: *A Fable for Critics*, 1848

[*See also* Actor.

Excuse

Better a bad excuse than none.
NICHOLAS UDALL: *Ralph Roister Doister*, V, *c.* 1553

Who excuses, accuses. (Qui s'excuse, s'accuse.)
FRENCH PROVERB

Execution

Sir, executions are intended to draw spectators. If they do not draw spectators they don't answer their purpose.
SAMUEL JOHNSON: *Boswell's Life*, 1783

An execution is sheer horror to all concerned — sheriffs, halbertmen, chaplain, spectators, Jack Ketch, and culprit; but out of all this, and towering behind the vulgar and hideous accessories of the scaffold, gleams the majesty of implacable law.
ALEXANDER SMITH: *Dreamthorp*, V, 1863

[*See also* Boleyn (Anne), Gallows, Hanging.

Executioner

All power, all discipline, are based upon the executioner. He is at once the horror of human society and the tie that holds it together. Take this incomprehensible agent out of the world and at that instant order will yield to chaos, thrones will fall, and society will disappear.
JOSEPH DE MAISTRE: *Soirées de Saint-Petersbourg*, 1821

Behold the Lord High Executioner!
A personage of noble rank and title —
A dignified and potent officer,
Whose functions are particularly vital.
W. S. GILBERT: *The Mikado*, I, 1885

Executive

[*See* Legislature, War and Peace.

Exegesis

We must be on guard against giving interpretations of Scripture that are far-fetched or opposed to science, and so exposing the word of God to the ridicule of unbelievers.
ST. AUGUSTINE: *De Genesi ad litteram*, *c.* 410

Study and pains were now no more their care;
Texts were explained by fasting and by prayer.
JOHN DRYDEN: *Religio laici*, 1682

Exercise

Let exercise come before meals, not after.
HIPPOCRATES: *Aphorisms*, *c.* 400 B.C.

Bodily exercise profiteth little.
I TIMOTHY IV, 8, *c.* 60

Exercise ferments the humors, casts them into their proper channels, throws off redundancies, and helps nature in those secret distributions, without which the body cannot subsist in its vigor, nor the soul act with cheerfulness.
JOSEPH ADDISON: *The Spectator*, July 12, 1711

After dinner sit a while;
After supper walk a mile.
THOMAS FULLER: *Gnomologia*, 1732

Use now and then a little exercise a quarter of an hour before meals, as to swing a weight, or swing your arms about with a small weight in each hand; to leap, or the like, for that stirs the muscles of the breast.
BENJAMIN FRANKLIN: *Poor Richard's Almanac*, 1742

Health is the vital principle of bliss,
And exercise, of health.
JAMES THOMSON: *The Castle of Indolence*, II, 1748

Not less than two hours a day should be devoted to exercise.
THOMAS JEFFERSON: *Letter to T. M. Randolph, Jr.*, 1786

Those who do not find time for exercise will have to find time for illness.
THE EARL OF DERBY: Address in Liverpool, 1873

There are temptations which strong exercise best enables us to resist.
JOHN LUBBOCK (LORD AVEBURY): *The Pleasures of Life,* VI, 1887

Faddists are continually proclaiming the value of exercise: four people out of five are more in need of rest than exercise.
LOGAN CLENDENING: *Modern Methods of Treatment,* I, 1924

Whenever I feel like exercise I lie down until the feeling passes.
Ascribed to ROBERT M. HUTCHINS by J. P. MCEVOY: *Young Man Looking Backwards,* 1938 (American Mercury, Dec.)

[*See also* Athlete, Horse, Labor, Medicine, Riding, Walking.

Exile

He shall return no more to his house, neither shall his place know him any more.
JOB VII, 10, *c.* 325 B.C.

Exile is death. (Exilium mors est.)
OVID (43 B.C.–18 A.D.): On his exile to the delta of the Danube, 8 A.D.

I have loved justice and hated iniquity; therefore I die in exile.
POPE GREGORY VII: On his deathbed, May, 1085

By foreign hands thy dying eyes were clos'd,
By foreign hands thy decent limbs compos'd,
By foreign hands thy humble grave adorn'd,
By strangers honor'd, and by strangers mourn'd!
ALEXANDER POPE: *To the Memory of an Unfortunate Lady,* 1717

And more true joy Marcellus exiled feels
Than Cæsar with a senate at his heels.
ALEXANDER POPE: *An Essay on Man,* IV, 1734

A man had better have ten thousand pounds at the end of ten years passed in England than twenty thousand pounds at the end of ten years passed in India.
SAMUEL JOHNSON: *Boswell's Life,* Oct. 10, 1779

Exile is life. (Exilium vita est.)
VICTOR HUGO (1802–1885): Inscribed over his door on his exile to the Island of Jersey, 1851

Exiles are on the whole men of considerable force of character; a quiet man would endure and succumb; he would not have energy to transplant himself, or to become so conspicuous as to be an object of general attack.
FRANCIS GALTON: *Inquiries Into Human Faculty,* 1883

[*See also* Europe, Justice, Mind.

Existence

There is nothing in the essence of man which makes his existence necessary; it may equally well happen that this or that man does or does not exist.
BARUCH SPINOZA: *Ethica,* 1677

Mere existence is so much better than nothing that one would rather exist even in pain than not exist.
SAMUEL JOHNSON: *Boswell's Life,* April 15, 1778

I existed. (J'ai vécu.)
E. J. SIEYÈS: On being asked what he did during the Reign of Terror, *c.* 1795

Exorcism

In my name shall they cast out devils.
MARK XVI, 17, *c.* 70

He cast out the spirits with his word.
MATTHEW VIII, 16, *c.* 75

Paul, being grieved, turned and said to the spirit, I command thee in the name of Jesus Christ to come out of her. And he came out the same hour. ACTS XVI, 18, *c.* 75

I exorcise thee, Satan (O cross, purify me) in the name of the living God, that thou mayest never leave again thy abode. Pronounced in the house of her whom I have anointed.
Inscription in an amulet found in Syria, probably dating from *c.* 200; the earliest known form of Christian exorcism

I charge thee, Satan, hous'd within this man,
To yield possession to my holy prayers,
And to thy state of darkness hie thee straight;
I conjure thee by all the saints in Heaven!
SHAKESPEARE: *The Comedy of Errors,* IV, 1593

As it is unlawful to entreat witches to heal bewitched persons, because they cannot do this but by Satan, so is it very sinful, by scratching, or burnings, or detention of urine, etc., to endeavor to constrain them to unbewitch any, for this is to put them upon seeking to the Devil.
INCREASE MATHER: *Remarkable Providences,* VIII, 1684

[*See also* Miracle, Possession (Demoniacal).

Expansion

[*See* Imperialism.

Expectation

Oft expectation fails and most oft there
Where most it promises, and oft it hits
Where hope is coldest and despair most fits.
SHAKESPEARE: *All's Well that Ends Well,* II, *c.* 1602

'Tis expectation makes a blessing dear;
Heaven were not Heaven, if we knew what it were.
JOHN SUCKLING: *Against Fruition, c.* 1640

Blessed is he who expects nothing, for he shall never be disappointed.
ALEXANDER POPE: *Letter to John Gay,* Oct. 6, 1727

We must expect everything and fear everything from time and men.
LUC DE VAUVENARGUES: *Réflexions,* 1746

All expectation hath something of torment.
BENJAMIN WHICHCOTE: *Moral and Religious Aphorisms,* 1753

Something will turn up.
BENJAMIN DISRAELI: *Popanilla,* VII, 1827
(Quoted as the "national motto" of England)

[*See also* Anticipation, Disappointment, Uncertainty.

Expected

It is always nice to be expected and not to arrive.
OSCAR WILDE: *An Ideal Husband,* IV, 1895

Expedience

All things are lawful unto me, but all things are not expedient.
I CORINTHIANS VI, 12, *c.* 55 (Cf. X, 23)

[*See also* Age (Old), Justice, Swapping.

Experience

The reward of suffering is experience.
AESCHYLUS: *Agamemnon, c.* 490 B.C.

You shall know by experience. (Experiundo scies.) TERENCE: *Heautontimoroumenos, c.* 160 B.C.

Every day learns from that which preceded it.
PUBLILIUS SYRUS: *Sententiæ, c.* 50 B.C.

Experience is the teacher of fools.
LIVY: *History of Rome,* XXII, *c.* 10

Experience teaches. (Experientia docet.)
TACITUS: *History,* V, *c.* 100

The stone that is thrown into the air is none the worse for falling down, and none the better for going up.
MARCUS AURELIUS: *Meditations,* IX, *c.* 170

A burnt child dreads the fire.
ENGLISH PROVERB, in common use since the XIV century

It is costly wisdom that is bought by experience. . . . Learning teacheth more in one year than experience in twenty.
ROGER ASCHAM: *The Scolemaster, c.* 1560

Experience is the mother of all things.
JOHN FLORIO: *First Frutes,* 1578

A scalded dog fears even cold water.
RANDLE COTGRAVE: *French-English Dictionary,* 1611

Experience is nothing but memory.
THOMAS HOBBES: *Elements of Philosophy,* I, 1656

We arrive complete novices at the different ages of life, and we often want experience in spite of our years.
LA ROCHEFOUCAULD: *Maxims,* 1665

Experience: in that all our knowledge is founded; and from that it ultimately derives itself.
JOHN LOCKE: *Essay Concerning Human Understanding,* II, 1690

Experience is the mistress of knaves as well as of fools.
ROGER L'ESTRANGE: Tr. of AESOP: *Fables,* 1692

Experience teaches fools, and he is a great one that will not learn by it.
THOMAS FULLER: *Gnomologia,* 1732

Experience joined with common sense
To mortals is a providence.
MATTHEW GREEN: *The Spleen,* 1737

Experience keeps a dear school, yet fools will learn in no other.
BENJAMIN FRANKLIN: *Poor Richard's Almanac,* 1743

I have but one lamp by which my feet are guided, and that is the lamp of experience.
PATRICK HENRY: Speech in the Virginia Convention, March 23, 1775

Man really knows nothing save what he has learned by his own experience.
C. M. WIELAND: *Oberon,* II, 1780

A sadder and a wiser man,
He rose the morrow morn.
S. T. COLERIDGE: *The Ancient Mariner,* 1798

Forty years of experience in government is worth a century of book-reading.
THOMAS JEFFERSON: *Letter to Samuel Kerchival,* 1816

To most men, experience is like the stern lights of a ship, which illumine only the track it has passed.
S. T. COLERIDGE: *To Thomas Allsop, c.* 1820

Nobody will use other people's experience, nor have any of his own till it is too late to use it.
NATHANIEL HAWTHORNE: *American Note-Books,* Oct. 25, 1836

Experience teacheth many things, and all men are his scholars:
Yet is he a strange tutor, unteaching that which he hath taught.
MARTIN F. TUPPER: *Proverbial Philosophy,* I, 1838

Necessity has no law, and experience is often one form of necessity.
J. H. NEWMAN: *On the Scope and Nature of University Education,* I, 1852

Experience without learning is better than learning without experience.
H. G. BOHN: *Handbook of Proverbs,* 1855

Experience inkreases our wizdum but don't reduse our phollys.
H. W. SHAW (JOSH BILLINGS): *Josh Billings' Encyclopedia of Wit and Wisdom,* 1874

A burnt child loves the fire.
OSCAR WILDE: *The Picture of Dorian Gray,* 1891

Experience is of no ethical value; it is simply the name we give our mistakes. It demonstrates that the future will be the same as the past. IBID.

Men are wise in proportion, not to their experience, but to their capacity for experience.
GEORGE BERNARD SHAW: *Maxims for Revolutionists,* 1903

Experience cannot deliver to us necessary truths; truths completely demonstrated by reason. Its conclusions are particular, not universal.
JOHN DEWEY: *The Quest for Certainty,* II, 1929

A new net will not catch an old bird.
DANISH PROVERB

Blacksmith's children are not afraid of sparks.
IBID.

A scalded cat dreads even cold water.
FRENCH PROVERB

Experience is good medicine, but it is never taken until the sickness is over.
GERMAN PROVERB

He who has burnt his mouth blows his soup.
IBID.

He who lives near the woods is not frightened by owls. IBID.

He who has been bitten by a snake is afraid of an eel.
IBID. (A Hindu proverb makes it " of a rope " and a Russian proverb " of worms ")

Experience is the fruit of the tree of errors.
PORTUGUESE PROVERB

Experience is the fool's best teacher; the wise do not need it. WELSH PROVERB

[*See also* Art, Insight, Knowledge, Law, Learning, Marriage (Second).

Experiment

Prove all things; hold fast that which is good.
I THESSALONIANS V, 21, *c.* 51 (*Try* is often substituted for *prove* in quotation)

All true and fruitful natural philosophy hath a double scale or ladder, ascendent and descendent, ascending from experiments to the invention of causes, and descending from causes to the invention of new experiments.
FRANCIS BACON: *The Advancement of Learning,* II, 1605

All experiments are not worth the making. 'Tis much better to be ignorant of a disease than to catch it. Who would wound himself for information about pain, or smell a stench for the sake of the discovery?
JEREMY COLLIER: *A Short View of the Immorality and Profaneness of the English Stage,* intro., 1698

Why think? Why not try the experiment?
JOHN HUNTER: *Letter to Edward Jenner,* Aug. 2, 1775

The observer listens to nature; the experimenter questions and forces her to reveal herself. G. L. C. F. CUVIER (1769–1832)

No facts are to me sacred; none are profane; I simply experiment, an endless seeker, with no past at my back.
R. W. EMERSON: *Circles,* 1841

Man is naturally metaphysical and arrogant, and is thus capable of believing that the ideal creations of his mind, which express his feelings, are identical with reality. From this it follows that the experimental method is not really natural to him.
CLAUDE BERNARD: *Introduction à la médecine expérimentale,* 1865

The true worth of an experimenter consists in his pursuing not only what he seeks in his experiment, but also what he did not seek.
IBID.

As soon as you injure an animal or remove it from the physiological conditions of its life, the experiments performed upon it are practically worthless. The great discoveries in physiology are the result of work with sound organs in sound animals.
MARTIN H. FISCHER (1879–)

I am always glad to try anything once.
AMERICAN SAYING, not recorded before the XIX century

There is nothing I more deprecate than the use of the Fourteenth Amendment beyond the absolute compulsion of its words to prevent the making of social experiments that an important part of the community desires, in the insulated chambers afforded by the several states, even though the experiments may seem futile or even noxious to me and to those whose judgment I most respect.
MR. JUSTICE O. W. HOLMES II: Dissenting opinion in *Truax* vs. *Corrigan,* 1914

It is common sense to take a method and try it. If it fails, admit it frankly and try another. But above all, try something.
F. D. ROOSEVELT: Speech at Oglethorpe University, May 22, 1932

[*See also* Prohibition, Research, Science.

Expert

The best partner for dice-playing is not a just man, but a good dice-player.
PLATO: *The Republic,* I, *c.* 370 B.C.

Let every man practise the art that he knows best.
CICERO: *Tusculanae disputationes*, I, 45 B.C.

Always believe the expert. (Experto credite.)
VIRGIL: *Æneid*, XI, 19 B.C.

The shoemaker makes a good shoe because he makes nothing else.
R. W. EMERSON: *Letters and Social Aims*, 1875

An ordinary man, away from home, giving advice. Author unidentified

Every skilled person is to be believed with reference to his own art. (Cuilibet in arte sua perito est credendum.) LEGAL MAXIM

[*See also* Profession, Trade, Vocation.

Explanation

I am an enemy of long explanations: they deceive either the one party or the other, and usually both.
J. W. GOETHE: *Goetz von Berlichingen*, I, 1771

I fear explanations explanatory of things explained.
Ascribed to ABRAHAM LINCOLN by CARL SANDBURG: *Abraham Lincoln: The War Years*, II, 1939 (*c.* 1863)

[*See also* Apology.

Exploitation

The history of all past society has consisted in the development of class antagonisms, antagonisms that assumed different forms at different epochs. But whatever form they may have taken, one fact is common to all past ages, *viz.*, the exploitation of one part of society by the other.
KARL MARX and FRIEDRICH ENGELS: *The Communist Manifesto*, 1848

It violates right order whenever capital so employs the working or wage-earning classes as to divert business and economic activity entirely to its own arbitrary will and advantage, without any regard to the human dignity of the workers, the social character of economic life, social justice, and the common good.
POPE PIUS XI: *Quadragesimo anno*, May 15, 1931

[*See also* Capital and Labor, Law.

Exploration

[*See* Discovery.

Expression

When we are understood, it is proof that we speak well; and all your learned gabble is mere nonsense.
J. B. MOLIÈRE: *Les femmes savantes*, II, 1672

Whatever we conceive well we express clearly, and words flow with ease.
NICOLAS BOILEAU: *L'Art poétique*, I, 1674

Fit expression is so rare that mankind have a superstitious value for it, and it would seem the whole human race agree to value a man precisely in proportion to his power of expression; and to the most expressive man that has existed, namely, Shakespeare, they have awarded the highest place.
R. W. EMERSON: *The Superlative*, 1847

[*See also* Style.

Extermination

War of extermination. (Bellum ad exterminationem.) LATIN PHRASE

Extinction

I am the last of my race. My race ends with me.
J. C. F. SCHILLER: *Wilhelm Tell*, II, 1804

Extortion

Whether we force a man's property from him by pinching his stomach or pinching his fingers makes some difference anatomically; morally, none whatsoever.
JOHN RUSKIN: *The Two Paths*, 1859

Extravagance

He who gives his milk to his cat must drink water. GERMAN PROVERB

He who buys what he needs not, sells what he needs. JAPANESE PROVERB

[*See also* Economy.

Extremes

Avoid extremes.
Ascribed to CLEOBULUS OF LINDUS, *c.* 575 B.C.

Our senses can grasp nothing that is extreme. Too much noise deafens us; too much light blinds us; too far or too near prevents us seeing; too long or too short is beyond understanding; too much truth stuns us.
BLAISE PASCAL: *Pensées*, I, 1670

Extremes meet.
HORACE WALPOLE: *Letter to the Countess of Upper Ossory*, June 12, 1780

[*See also* Man and Woman.

Extremity

Man's extremity is God's opportunity.
THOMAS ADAMS: *Sermon*, 1629

[*See also* Law.

Eye

The eye that mocketh at his father, and despiseth to obey his mother, the ravens of the valley shall pick it out, and the young eagles shall eat it. PROVERBS XXX, 17, *c.* 350 B.C.

The eye is not satisfied with seeing.
ECCLESIASTES I, 8, *c.* 200 B.C.

His eyes are as the eyes of doves by the rivers of waters, washed with milk, and fitly set.
SOLOMON'S SONG, V, 12, *c.* 200 B.C.

In the twinkling of an eye.
I CORINTHIANS XV, 52, *c.* 55

If thy right eye offend thee, pluck it out, and cast it from thee. MATTHEW V, 29, *c.* 75

The light of the body is the eye.
MATTHEW VI, 22

Their eyes seemed like rings from which the gems had been dropped.
DANTE: *Purgatorio,* XXIII, *c.* 1320

The eye hath ever been thought the pearl of the face. JOHN LYLY: *Euphues,* 1579

Her eyes are sapphires set in snow.
THOMAS LODGE: *Rosalynde,* 1590

A lover's eyes will gaze an eagle blind.
SHAKESPEARE: *Love's Labor's Lost,* IV, *c.* 1595

Where is any author in the world
Teaches such beauty as a woman's eye?
IBID.

In the glasses of thine eyes I see thy grieved heart.
SHAKESPEARE: *Richard II,* I, *c.* 1596

Alack, there lies more peril in thine eye
Than twenty of their swords.
SHAKESPEARE: *Romeo and Juliet,* II, *c.* 1596

Her eyes in Heaven
Would through the airy region stream so bright,
That birds would sing and think it were not night. IBID.

I have a good eye, uncle; I can see a church by daylight.
SHAKESPEARE: *Much Ado About Nothing,* II, *c.* 1599

There is murder in mine eye.
SHAKESPEARE: *As You Like It,* III, *c.* 1600

Bugle eyeballs.
IBID. (*Bugle*=a tubular bead, usually black, used to trim women's clothes)

Never touch your eye but with your elbow.
ENGLISH PROVERB, familiar since the XVII century

An eye like Mars, to threaten and command.
SHAKESPEARE: *Hamlet,* III, *c.* 1601

The error of our eye directs our mind.
SHAKESPEARE: *Troilus and Cressida,* V, *c.* 1601

Eyes can speak and eyes can understand.
GEORGE CHAPMAN: *The Gentleman Usher,* II, 1606

What the eye ne'er sees the heart ne'er rues.
SAMUEL ROWLANDS: *A Pair of Spy-Knaves,* *c.* 1613

A rolling eye, a roving heart.
THOMAS ADAMS: *Sermon,* 1629

She that has good eyes
Has good thighs.
JOHN SUCKLING: *The Goblins,* 1638

The eyes have one language everywhere.
GEORGE HERBERT: *Jacula Prudentum,* 1651

The eye is a shrew.
JOHN RAY: *English Proverbs,* 1670

'Tis ill jesting with your eye and religion.
SAMUEL PALMER: *Moral Essays on Proverbs,* 1710

Who has but one eye is always wiping it.
THOMAS FULLER: *Gnomologia,* 1732

Why has not man a microscopic eye?
For this plain reason: man is not a fly.
ALEXANDER POPE: *An Essay on Man,* I, 1732

The sight of you is good for sore eyes.
JONATHAN SWIFT: *Polite Conversation,* 1738

The harvest of a quiet eye.
WILLIAM WORDSWORTH: *A Poet's Epitaph,* 1800

That eye was in itself a soul.
BYRON: *The Bride of Abydos,* I, 1813

I dislike an eye that twinkles like a star. Those only are beautiful which, like the planets, have a steady, lambent light, — are luminous, but not sparkling.
H. W. LONGFELLOW: *Hyperion,* III, 1839

Nor brighter was his eye, nor moister
Than a too-long opened oyster.
ROBERT BROWNING: *The Pied Piper,* IV, 1842

A small hurt in the eye is a great one.
H. G. BOHN: *Handbook of Proverbs,* 1855

An eye can threaten like a loaded and leveled gun, or can insult like hissing or kicking; or, in its altered mood, by beams of kindness, it can make the heart dance with joy.
R. W. EMERSON: *The Conduct of Life,* V, 1860

Her large, sweet, asking eyes.
J. G. WHITTIER: *Snow-Bound,* 1866

Every shut eye ain't asleep.
AMERICAN NEGRO PROVERB

When the right eye throbs, it's mother or sister coming; when the left eye throbs, it's brother or husband coming. ITALIAN PROVERB

Where love is, there the eye wanders. (Ubi amor, ibi oculus.) LATIN PROVERB

What the eye does not admire,
The heart does not desire.

OLD ENGLISH RHYME

Great men's eyes are dim.

TURKISH PROVERB

[*See also* Age (Old), Cat, Crime and Punishment, Drinking, Eye and Ear, Foot, Heart, Love, Lover.

Eye and Ear

That which is conveyed through the ear affects us less than what the eye receives.

HORACE: *De arte poetica, c.* 8 B.C.

What a mercy it would be if we were able to open and close our ears as easily as we open and close our eyes!

G. C. LICHTENBERG: *Reflections,* 1799

Never buy a horse with your ears, but with your eyes. CZECH PROVERB

The eyes believe themselves; the ears believe other people. GERMAN PROVERB

Eyebrow

Black brows they say
Become some women best, so that there be not
Too much hair there, but in a semicircle
Or a half-moon made with a pen.

SHAKESPEARE: *The Winter's Tale,* II, *c.* 1611

My wife and I quarreled about her pulling her brows. She threatened she would not go to Williamsburg if she might not pull them; I refused, however, and got the better of her and maintained my authority.

WILLIAM BYRD: *Diary,* Feb. 5, 1711

Eye, Evil

Eat thou not the bread of him that hath an evil eye, neither desire thou his dainty meats.

PROVERBS XXIII, 6, *c.* 350 B.C.

For one that dies of natural causes ninety-nine die of the evil eye.

THE TALMUD (*Baba Metzia*), *c.* 200

Eye-witness

One eye-witness is worth more than ten who tell what they have heard.

PLAUTUS: *Truculentus,* II, *c.* 190 B.C.

F

Fable

Fables were the first pieces of wit that made their appearance in the world.

JOSEPH ADDISON: *The Spectator,* Sept. 29, 1711

A fable is a bridge which leads to truth.

ARAB PROVERB

[*See also* History, Novel.

Face

The face is the image of the soul. (Imago animi vultus est.)

CICERO: *De oratore,* III, *c.* 80 B.C.

A pleasant face is a silent recommendation.

PUBLILIUS SYRUS: *Sententiæ, c.* 50 B.C.

A silent face often expresses more than words.

OVID: *Ars amatoria,* I, *c.* 2 B.C.

Your face counts your years.

JUVENAL: *Satires,* VI, 116

God hath done his part: she hath a good face.

JOHN HEYWOOD: *The Spider and the Flie,* 1556

Her angel's face,
As the great eye of Heaven shined bright,
And made a sunshine in the shady place.

EDMUND SPENSER: *The Faerie Queene,* I, *c.* 1589

You have such a February face,
So full of front, of storm, of cloudiness.

SHAKESPEARE: *Much Ado About Nothing,* V, *c.* 1599

God has given you one face, and you make yourselves another.

SHAKESPEARE: *Hamlet,* III, *c.* 1601

Was this the face that launched a thousand ships,
And burnt the topless towers of Ilium?

CHRISTOPHER MARLOWE: *Dr. Faustus,* XIV, 1604

His face is the worst thing about him.

SHAKESPEARE: *Measure for Measure,* II, 1604

He had a face like a benediction.

CERVANTES: *Don Quixote,* I, 1605

I have seen better faces in my time
Than stands on any shoulder that I see.

SHAKESPEARE: *King Lear,* II, 1606

There is a garden in her face
Where roses and white lilies blow.

THOMAS CAMPION: *Cherry-Ripe,* 1610

Oh, that I were a veil upon that face
To hide it from the world; methinks I could
Envy the very sun for gazing on you.

SHAKERLEY MARMION: *The Antiquary,* 1641

It is the common wonder of all men, how among so many million of faces there should be none alike.

THOMAS BROWNE: *Religio Medici,* II, 1642

The face is often only a smooth impostor.

PIERRE CORNEILLE: *Le Menteur,* II, 1642

Her face is like the milky way i' the sky —
A meeting of gentle lights without name.

JOHN SUCKLING: *Brennoralt,* III, 1646

The ruins of a house may be repaired: why not those of a face?

JEAN DE LA FONTAINE: *Fables,* VII, 1671

If to her share some female errors fall
Look on her face, and you'll forget 'em all.

ALEXANDER POPE: *The Rape of the Lock,* II, 1712

If it was the fashion to go naked, the face would be hardly observed.

MARY WORTLEY MONTAGU: *Letter to an unidentified correspondent,* April 1, 1717

People unused to the world have babbling countenances; and are unskillful enough to show what they have sense enough not to tell.

LORD CHESTERFIELD: *Letter to his son,* April 30, 1752

Oh! why was I born with a different face?
Why was I not born like the rest of my race?

WILLIAM BLAKE: *To Thomas Butts, c.* 1802

The face of every one
That passes by me is a mystery.

WILLIAM WORDSWORTH: *The Prelude,* 1805

His face was of the doubtful kind,
That wins the eye, but not the mind.

WALTER SCOTT: *Rokeby,* V, 1813

The sea of upturned faces.

WALTER SCOTT: *Rob Roy,* XX, 1817

If, for silver or for gold,
You could melt ten thousand pimples
Into half a dozen dimples,
Then your face we might behold,
Looking, doubtless, much more smugly;
Yet even then 'twould be d——d ugly.

BYRON: *Epigram from the French,* 1819

The women pardoned all except her face.

BYRON: *Don Juan,* V, 1821

[Some] faces are books in which not a line is written, save perhaps a date.

H. W. LONGFELLOW: *Hyperion,* I, 1839

A face like a ferret
Betoken'd her spirit.

R. H. BARHAM: *The Ingoldsby Legends,* I, 1840

Trust not a man's word if you please, or you may come to very erroneous conclusions; but at all times place implicit confidence in a man's countenance, in which there is no deceit, and of necessity there can be none.

GEORGE BORROW: *Lavengro,* XXII, 1851

This face is a dog's snout, sniffing for garbage;
Snake's nest in that mouth — I hear the sibilant threat.

WALT WHITMAN: *Faces,* 1855

The Methodists have acquired a face; the Quakers, a face; the nuns, a face.

R. W. EMERSON: *English Traits,* IV, 1856

There never was a face
So suited, in its way,
A clergyman to grace
As Mr. Parks', M.A.

W. S. GILBERT: *The Phantom Head, c.* 1865

A man of fifty is responsible for his face.

EDWIN M. STANTON, *c.* 1865

She was a lady of incisive features bound in stale parchment.

GEORGE MEREDITH: *Diana of the Crossways,* XIV, 1885

As a beauty I am not a star,
There are others more handsome by far,
But my face, I don't mind it,
For I am behind it;
It's the people in front get the jar.

Commonly ascribed to WOODROW WILSON (1856–1924), who was fond of quoting it; but probably erroneously. It has also been ascribed to ANTHONY EUWER (?–?)

The Christian face. (Facies Christiana.)

HAVELOCK ELLIS: *Autobiography,* IV, 1939 (Term applied to "the face which tells of natural instinct repressed by a perpetual stern control imprinting on the mouth the fixed lines of high tension")

The face is the index of the mind. (Vultus est index animi.)

LATIN PROVERB

"What is your fortune, my pretty maid?"
"My face is my fortune, sir," she said.

Nursery rhyme

[*See also* Cheek, Complexion, Cosmetics, Countenance, Heart, Laughter, Pale, Perspiration, Physiognomy.

Fact

Believe the facts. (Credite rebus.)

OVID: *Fasti,* II, *c.* 5

The credibility, or the certain truth of a matter of fact does not immediately prove anything concerning the wisdom or goodness of it.

JOSEPH BUTLER: *The Analogy of Religion,* 1736

Facts are stubborn things.

TOBIAS SMOLLETT: Tr. of A. R. LE SAGE: *Gil Blas,* X, 1750

No matter of fact can be mathematically demonstrated, though it may be proved in such a manner as to leave no doubt on the mind.

RICHARD WHATELY: *Logic,* IV, 1826

Facts are not truths; they are not conclusions; they are not even premisses, but in the nature and parts of premisses. The truth depends on, and is only arrived at, by a legitimate deduction from all the facts which are truly material.

S. T. COLERIDGE: *Table-Talk,* Dec. 27, 1831

I grow daily to honor facts more and more, and theory less and less. A fact, it seems to me, is a great thing — a sentence printed, if not by God, then at least by the Devil.
THOMAS CARLYLE: *Letter to R. W. Emerson*, April 29, 1836

A little fact is worth a whole limbo of dreams.
R. W. EMERSON: *The Superlative*, 1847

Sit down before fact as a little child, be prepared to give up every preconceived notion, follow humbly wherever and to whatever abyss nature leads, or you shall learn nothing.
T. H. HUXLEY: *Letter to Charles Kingsley*, Sept. 23, 1860

In this life we want nothing but facts, sir; nothing but facts.
CHARLES DICKENS: *Hard Times*, I, 1854

Why does the statement of a new fact always leave us cold? Because our minds have to take in something which deranges our old ideas. We are all like that in this miserable world.
J. M. CHARCOT: *De l'expectation en médecine*, 1857

Facts are contrary 'z mules.
J. R. LOWELL: *The Biglow Papers*, II, 1862

Let us not underrate the value of a fact; it will one day flower into a truth.
H. D. THOREAU: *Excursions*, 1863

A fact in itself is nothing. It is valuable only for the idea attached to it, or for the proof which it furnishes.
CLAUDE BERNARD: *Introduction à la médecine expérimentale*, 1865

Facts are facts and flinch not.
ROBERT BROWNING: *The Ring and the Book*, II, 1868

A world of fact lies outside and beyond the world of words.
T. H. HUXLEY: *Lay Sermons*, 1870

There are no eternal facts, as there are no absolute truths.
F. W. NIETZSCHE: *Human All-too-Human*, I, 1878

Her taste exact
For faultless fact
Amounts to a disease.
W. S. GILBERT: *The Mikado*, II, 1885

Those who refuse to go beyond fact rarely get as far as fact.
T. H. HUXLEY: *The Progress of Science*, 1887

Just statin' eevidential facts beyon' all argument.
RUDYARD KIPLING: *M'Andrew's Hymn*, 1893

I know of no greater folly than trying to live a spiritual life in a world undoubtedly material. The really spiritual nations are notoriously worthless; before we do the best we can, we must first look facts in the face, and act upon them.
E. W. HOWE: *The Blessing of Business*, 1918

Science proceeds from facts to the uniformities in facts. These are themselves facts.
L. H. HENDERSON: *Science, Logic and Human Intercourse*, 1933

The fact speaks for itself. (Res ipsa loquitur.)
LEGAL MAXIM

[*See also* Falsehood, Judge, Jury, Probability, Science, Truth.

Faction

A spirit of faction, which is apt to mingle its poison in the deliberations of all bodies of men, will often hurry the persons of whom they are composed into improprieties and excesses for which they would blush in a private capacity.
ALEXANDER HAMILTON: *The Federalist*, 1788

As we wax hot in faction,
In battle we wax cold;
Wherefore men fight not as they fought
In the brave days of old.
T. B. MACAULAY: *Lays of Ancient Rome*, 1842

[*See also* Party.

Factory

Dead matter leaves the factory ennobled and transformed, whereas men are corrupted and degraded.
POPE PIUS XI: *Quadragesimo anno*, May 15, 1931

Faerie Queene, The

[*See* Allegory.

Failure

In great attempts it is glorious even to fail.
LONGINUS: *On the Sublime*, III, *c.* 250 (Cited as a proverb)

He that is used to go forward, and findeth a stop, faileth out of his own favor, and is not the thing he was.
FRANCIS BACON: *Essays*, 1597

He is good that failed never.
DAVID FERGUSSON: *Scottish Proverbs*, 1641

There is not a fiercer hell than the failure in a great object.
JOHN KEATS: *Endymion*, pref., 1818

Half the failures in life arise from pulling in one's horse as he is leaping.
J. C. and A. W. HARE: *Guesses at Truth*, I, 1827

In the lexicon of youth, which fate reserves
For a bright manhood, there is no such word
As — fail.
E. G. BULWER-LYTTON: *Richelieu*, II, 1838

Failure in a great enterprise is at least a noble fault. GREEK PROVERB

The world laughs at those who fail.
WELSH PROVERB

[*See also* Ambition, Napoleon I.

Faint-heart

Faint heart never won fair lady.
ENGLISH PROVERB, traced by Apperson to JOHN GOWER: *Confessio Amantis, c.* 1390

Fair

Behold, thou art fair, my love; behold, thou art fair.
SOLOMON'S SONG I, 15, *c.* 200 B.C. (Also in IV, 1)

Fair as the moon. SOLOMON'S SONG VI, 10

She that is fair hath half her portion.
THOMAS DRAXE: *Bibliotheca scholastica instructissima,* 1633

[*See also* Beauty, Bravery.

Fair Play

Thou shouldst not decide until thou hast heard what both have to say.
ARISTOPHANES: *The Wasps,* 422 B.C. (Credited to "a wise man")

Hear the other side. (Audi alteram partem.)
ST. AUGUSTINE: *De duabus animabus, c.* 390

All is fair in love and war.
ENGLISH PROVERB, apparently unrecorded in its present form before the XIX century; in BEAUMONT and FLETCHER: *The Lovers' Progress,* V, 1623, it appears as "All stratagems in love, and that the sharpest war, are lawful"

What is sauce for the goose is sauce for the gander.
ENGLISH PROVERB, traced by Smith to 1670

Turn about is fair play.
ENGLISH PROVERB, not recorded before the XIX century

Fair play's a jewel.
WALTER SCOTT: *Redgauntlet,* XXI, 1824

One should always play fairly when one has the winning cards.
OSCAR WILDE: *An Ideal Husband,* IV, 1895

The love of fair play is a spectator's virtue, not a principal's.
GEORGE BERNARD SHAW: *Maxims for Revolutionists,* 1903

Hands aff is fair play. SCOTTISH PROVERB

[*See also* Exchange.

Fairy

They are fairies; he that speaks to them shall die. SHAKESPEARE: *The Merry Wives of Windsor,* V, *c.* 1600

Fairyland

Charm'd magic casements, opening on the foam
Of perilous seas, in faery lands forlorn.
JOHN KEATS: *To a Nightingale,* 1819

Fairy-tale

Child of the pure unclouded brow
And dreaming eyes of wonder,
Though time be fleet, and I and thou
Are half a life asunder,
Thy loving smile will surely hail
The love-gift of a fairy-tale.
C. L. DODGSON (LEWIS CARROLL): *Through the Looking-Glass,* 1871

Faith

Nowhere is there faith on earth. (Nusquam tuta fides.) VIRGIL: *Æneid,* IV, *c.* 19 B.C.

We walk by faith, not by sight.
II CORINTHIANS V, 7, *c.* 55

By grace are ye saved through faith; and that not of yourselves: it is the gift of God.
EPHESIANS: II, 8, *c.* 60

For as the body without the spirit is dead, so faith without works is dead also.
JAMES II, 26, *c.* 60

Faith is the substance of things hoped for, the evidence of things not seen.
HEBREWS XI, 1, *c.* 65

Daughter, thy faith hath made thee whole; go in peace, and be whole of thy plague.
MARK V, 34, *c.* 70 (Cf. LUKE VIII, 48, *c.* 75)

Lord, I believe; help thou mine unbelief.
MARK IX, 24

If ye have faith as a grain of mustard seed, ye shall say unto this mountain, Remove hence to yonder place; and it shall remove: and nothing shall be impossible unto you.
MATTHEW XVII, 20, *c.* 75

Blessed are they that have not seen, and yet have believed. JOHN XX, 29, *c.* 115

The man without faith is a walking corpse.
POPE XYSTUS I: *The Ring, c.* 150

What is faith save to believe what you do not see? (Quid est enim fides, nisi credere quod non vides?)
ST. AUGUSTINE: *Homilies on St. John,* XL, *c.* 416

Faith has to do with things that are not seen, and hope with things that are not in hand.
THOMAS AQUINAS: *Summa theologiae,* LVII, *c.* 1265

Faith is required of thee, and a sincere life, not loftiness of intellect, nor deepness in the mysteries of God.
THOMAS À KEMPIS: *Imitation of Christ,* IV, *c.* 1420

Believe that you have it, and you have it. (Credo quod habes, et habes.)
DESIDERIUS ERASMUS: *Letter to Thomas More, c.* 1500

Faith is a knowledge of the benevolence of God toward us, and a certain persuasion of His veracity.
JOHN CALVIN: *Institutes of the Christian Religion,* III, 1536

We should always be disposed to believe that that which appears to us to be white is really black, if the hierarchy of the Church so decides.
IGNATIUS LOYOLA: *Exercitia spiritualia,* 1541

A capuchin says: wear a grey coat and a hood, a rope round thy body, and sandals on thy feet. A cordelier says: put on a black hood. An ordinary papist says: do this or that work, hear mass, pray, fast, give alms, &c. But a true Christian says: I am justified and saved only by faith in Christ, without any works or merits of my own. Compare these together, and judge which is the true righteousness.
MARTIN LUTHER: *Table-Talk,* CCCVI, 1569

How many things that were articles of faith yesterday are fables today.
MICHEL DE MONTAIGNE: *Essays,* I, 1580

Nothing is so firmly believed as what we least know.
IBID.

He wears his faith but as the fashion of his hat; it ever changes with the next block.
SHAKESPEARE: *Much Ado About Nothing,* I, *c.* 1599

The best philosopher, by all the demonstration in the world, can conceive nothing of the mysteries of godliness, because he utterly wants the eye of faith.
JOSEPH HALL (BISHOP OF NORWICH): *Meditations and Vows,* I, 1606

To believe only possibilities is not faith, but mere philosophy.
THOMAS BROWNE: *Religio Medici,* I, 1642

Faith is a thing that's four-square; let it fall
This way or that, it not declines at all.
ROBERT HERRICK: *Hesperides,* 1648

Faith is a gift of God which man can neither give nor take away by promise of rewards or menaces of torture.
THOMAS HOBBES: *Leviathan,* XLII, 1651

The eagles will be where the carcass is, and that shall have the faith of most which is best able to pay them for 't.
JOSEPH GLANVILL: *The Vanity of Dogmatizing,* XIV, 1661

An outward and visible sign of an inward and spiritual grace.
THE BOOK OF COMMON PRAYER (*Catechism*), 1662

Faith affirms what the senses do not affirm, but not the contrary of what they perceive. It is above, and not contrary to.
BLAISE PASCAL: *Pensées,* XIV, 1670

Faith is not built on disquisitions vain;
The things we must believe are few and plain.
JOHN DRYDEN: *Religio laici,* 1682

'Twas an unhappy division that has been made between faith and works. Tho' in my intellect I may divide them, just as in the candle I know there is both light and heat; but yet put out the candle, and they are both gone; one remains not without the other: So 'tis betwixt faith and works. Nay, in a right conception, *fides est opus;* if I believe a thing because I am commanded, that is opus.
JOHN SELDEN: *Table-Talk,* 1689

A person may be qualified to do greater good to mankind, and become more beneficial to the world, by morality without faith than by faith without morality.
JOSEPH ADDISON: *The Spectator,* Aug. 16, 1712

Faith is kept alive in us, and gathers strength, more from practise than from speculations.
JOSEPH ADDISON: *The Spectator,* Aug. 23, 1712

For modes of faith let graceless zealots fight,
He can't be wrong whose life is in the right.
ALEXANDER POPE: *An Essay on Man,* I, 1732

Faith builds a bridge across the gulf of death,
To break the shock blind nature cannot shun.
EDWARD YOUNG: *Night Thoughts,* IV, 1745

It is neither necessary, nor indeed possible, to understand any matter of faith farther than it is revealed.
BENJAMIN WHICHCOTE: *Moral and Religious Aphorisms,* 1753

In the affairs of this world, men are saved, not by faith, but by the want of it.
BENJAMIN FRANKLIN: *Poor Richard's Almanac,* 1758

The way to see by faith is to shut the eye of reason.
IBID.

Faith separate from love is not faith, but mere science, which in itself is void of spiritual life.
EMANUEL SWEDENBORG: *Heaven and Hell,* 1758

Faith is a necessary fraud at best.
CHARLES CHURCHILL: *Gotham,* II, 1763

No man has power to let another prescribe his faith. Faith is not faith without believing.
THOMAS JEFFERSON: *Notes on Religion,* 1776

If anyone doubts my veracity I can only say that I pity his want of faith.
R. E. RASPE: *Baron Münchhausen's Narrative of His Marvellous Travels and Campaigns in Russia,* VI, 1785

His Majesty is not disposed to rest the security of his state upon the stupidity of his subjects.
BARON VON ZEDLITZ (Prussian Minister of Religion under Frederick the Great): Reply to a memorial from the Breslau Consistory arguing that "those who believe most are the best subjects," 1785

What is it the New Testament teaches us? To believe that the Almighty committed debauchery with a woman engaged to be married; and the belief of this debauchery is called faith.
THOMAS PAINE: *The Age of Reason*, III, 1794

The faith that looks through death.
WILLIAM WORDSWORTH: *Intimations of Immortality*, 1807

I hear the message well enough; what I lack is faith.
J. W. GOETHE: *I Faust*, I, 1808

One in whom persuasion and belief
Had ripened into faith, and faith become
A passionate intuition.
WILLIAM WORDSWORTH: *The Excursion*, 1814

Faith, fanatic faith, once wedded fast
To some dear falsehood, hugs it to the last.
THOMAS MOORE: *Lalla Rookh*, 1817

Whatever may be thought of the genuineness or authority of any part of the book of Daniel, it makes no difference in my belief in Christianity; for Christianity is within a man, even as he is a being gifted with reason; it is associated with your mother's chair, and with the first-remembered-tones of her blessed voice.
S. T. COLERIDGE: *Table-Talk*, Jan. 6, 1823

Lavater believed in Cagliostro and his wonders. When the impostor was unmasked, Lavater maintained, "This is another Cagliostro; the Cagliostro who did the wonders was a holy person."
J. W. GOETHE: *Conversations with Eckermann*, Feb. 17, 1829

My faith looks up to Thee,
Thou Lamb of Calvary,
Saviour divine!
RAY PALMER: *The Lamb of God*, 1832

Faith and love are apt to be spasmodic in the best minds. Men live on the brink of mysteries and harmonies into which they never enter, and with their hand on the door-latch they die outside.
R. W. EMERSON: *Letter to Thomas Carlyle*, March 12, 1835

Faith is loyalty to some inspired teacher, some spiritual hero.
THOMAS CARLYLE: *Heroes and Hero-Worship*, I, 1840 (Lecture in London, May 5)

Faith is like love: it cannot be forced.
ARTHUR SCHOPENHAUER: *Parerga und Paralipomena*, II, 1851

The saddest thing that can befall a soul
Is when it loses faith in God and woman.
ALEXANDER SMITH: *A Life Drama*, 1853

Faith sees by the ears.
H. G. BOHN: *Handbook of Proverbs*, 1855

Faith is the antiseptic of the soul.
WALT WHITMAN: *Leaves of Grass*, pref., 1855

Let us have faith that right makes might; and in that faith let us dare to do our duty as we understand it.
ABRAHAM LINCOLN: Speech in New York, Feb. 21, 1859

We cannot live on probabilities. The faith in which we can live bravely and die in peace must be a certainty, so far as it professes to be a faith at all, or it is nothing.
J. A. FROUDE: *A Plea for the Free Discussion of Theological Difficulties*, 1863 (Fraser's Magazine)

Q. Why must we believe what the Catholic Church teaches? A. We must believe all the Catholic Church teaches because God has revealed it, who can neither deceive nor be deceived.
JOHN MCCAFFREY: *A Catechism of Christian Doctrine for General Use*, 1866

Without faith a man can do nothing. But faith can stifle all science.
H. F. AMIEL: *Journal*, Feb. 7, 1872

The beast faith lives on its own dung.
A. C. SWINBURNE: *Dirae*, VIII, 1875

In our windy world
What's up is faith, what's down is heresy.
ALFRED TENNYSON: *Harold*, I, 1876

Whoever has theological blood in his veins is shifty and dishonorable in all things. The pathetic thing that grows out of this condition is called faith.
F. W. NIETZSCHE: *The Antichrist*, IX, 1888

To yearn for a strong faith is not the proof of a strong faith, but the reverse. If a man really have strong faith he can indulge in the luxury of skepticism.
F. W. NIETZSCHE: *The Twilight of the Idols*, 1889

I can believe anything, provided it is incredible.
OSCAR WILDE: *The Picture of Dorian Gray*, 1891

O faith that meets ten thousand cheats,
Yet drops no jot of faith.
RUDYARD KIPLING: *To the True Romance*, 1893

Belief without evidence in what is told by one who speaks without knowledge, of things without parallel.
AMBROSE BIERCE: *The Devil's Dictionary*, 1906

About 999 in 1000 believe everything; the other one believes nothing – except that it is a good thing for human society that the 999 believe everything.
MICHAEL J. DEE: *Conclusions*, v, 1917

Whoever disturbs the pupil's faith in any way does him grave wrong, inasmuch as he abuses the trust which children place in their teachers, and takes unfair advantage of their inexperience and of their natural craving for unrestrained liberty, at once illusory and false.
POPE PIUS XI: *Divini illius magistri*, Dec. 31, 1929

Faith is believing what you know ain't so.
Author unidentified

By faith and love. (Fide et amore.)
LATIN PHRASE

In good faith. (In bona fide.) IBID.

Faith has no fear. (Fides non timet.)
LATIN PROVERB

Faith is the sister of justice. (Justitiae soror fides.) IBID.

Defender of the faith. (Fidei defensor.)
MEDIEVAL LATIN PHRASE

Faith before intellect. (Fides ante intellectum.)
MEDIEVAL LATIN PROVERB

Faith alone is sufficient. (Sola fides sufficit.)
IBID.

[*See also* Belief, Believer, Bible, Charity, Christianity, Credulity, Culture, Doubt, Evolution, Good, Hope, Humanity, Infallibility (Papal), Infamy, Kindness, Morality, Pasteur (Louis), Persuasion, Skeptic, Skepticism, Superstition, Truth.

Faithful

I have fought a good fight, I have finished my course, I have kept the faith.
II TIMOTHY IV, 7, *c.* 65

Be thou faithful unto death.
REVELATION II, 10, *c.* 95

The seas they shall run dry,
And rocks melt into sands;
Then I'll love you still, my dear,
When all those things are done.
Anon.: *The Young Man's Farewell to His Love*, *c.* 1600

To thine own self be true,
And it must follow, as the night the day,
Thou canst not then be false to any man.
SHAKESPEARE: *Hamlet*, I, *c.* 1601

The fidelity of most men is merely an invention of self-love to win confidence; a method to place us above others and to render us depositaries of the most important matters.
LA ROCHEFOUCAULD: *Maxims*, 1665

Among the faithless faithful only be.
JOHN MILTON: *Paradise Lost*, v, 1667

Those who are faithless know the pleasures of love; it is the faithful who know love's tragedies.
OSCAR WILDE: *The Picture of Dorian Gray*, 1891

Young men want to be faithful and are not; old men want to be faithless and cannot. IBID.

I have been faithful to thee, Cynara, in my fashion.
ERNEST DOWSON: *No Sum Qualis*, 1896

Always faithful. (Semper fidelis.)
LATIN PHRASE

Faithful unto death. (Fidelis ad urnum.)
IBID.

[*See also* Belief.

Faith-healing

The prayer of faith shall save the sick.
JAMES V, 15, *c.* 60

Faithless

Yet do not my folly reprove:
She was fair – and my passion begun;
She smil'd – and I could not but love;
She is faithless – and I am undone.
WILLIAM SHENSTONE: *Disappointment*, *c.* 1750

The faith of Carthaginians. (Fides Punica.)
LATIN PHRASE (The Romans alleged that the Carthaginians were faithless)

[*See also* Faithful.

Fall

How art thou fallen from heaven, O Lucifer, son of the morning!
ISAIAH XIV, 12, *c.* 700 B.C.

How are the mighty fallen!
II SAMUEL I, 19, *c.* 500 B.C. (Cf. verses 25 and 27)

A just man falleth seven times, and riseth up again. PROVERBS XXIV, 16, *c.* 350 B.C.

In the place where the tree falleth, there it shall be. ECCLESIASTES XI, 3, *c.* 200 B.C.

But oh, how pale his lady looked,
Frae aff the castle wa',
When down before the Scottish spear
She saw proud Percy fa'.
Anon.: *The Battle of Otterburn*, *c.* 1400

Who climbeth highest, most dreadful is his fall.
JOHN LYDGATE: *Miscellaneous Poems*, *c.* 1440

Better sit still than rise and fall.
JOHN HEYWOOD: *Proverbs*, 1546

He that never climbed never fell. IBID.

But as the tree is great and tall,
The great and mightier is his fall.
Anon.: *The Life of Man*, *c.* 1550

Ay me, how many perils do enfold
The righteous man, to make him daily fall.
EDMUND SPENSER: *The Faerie Queene*, I, *c.* 1589

The ripest fruit first falls.
SHAKESPEARE: *Richard II*, II, *c.* 1596

But yesterday, the word of Cæsar might
Have stood against the world: now lies he there,
And none so poor to do him reverence.
SHAKESPEARE: *Julius Cæsar*, III, 1599

Oh, what a fall was there, my countrymen!
IBID.

He that lies upon the ground can fall no lower.
ENGLISH PROVERB, borrowed from the Latin and familiar since the XVII century

Men that fall low must die,
As well as men cast headlong from the sky.
GEORGE CHAPMAN: *Bussy d'Ambois*, I, 1604

From that full meridian of my glory
I haste now to my setting; I shall fall
Like a bright exhalation in the evening,
And no man see me more.
SHAKESPEARE and JOHN FLETCHER: *Henry VIII*, II, 1613

He falls like Lucifer,
Never to rise again.
SHAKESPEARE and JOHN FLETCHER: *Henry VIII*, III (Cf. ISAIAH XIV, *c.* 700 B.C.)

He that is fallen cannot help him that is down.
GEORGE HERBERT: *Outlandish Proverbs*, 1640

While leanest beasts in pastures feed,
The fattest ox the first must bleed.
ROBERT HERRICK: *Hesperides*, 1648

From morn
To noon he fell, from noon to dewy eve,
A Summer's day; and with the setting sun
Dropp'd from the zenith, like a falling star.
JOHN MILTON: *Paradise Lost*, I, 1667

Flutt'ring his pinions vain, plumb down he drops.
JOHN MILTON: *Paradise Lost*, II

Fallen, fallen, fallen, fallen,
Fallen from his high estate,
And welt'ring in his blood;
Deserted at his utmost need,
By those his former bounty fed;
On the bare earth expos'd he lies,
With not a friend to close his eyes.
JOHN DRYDEN: *Alexander's Feast*, 1697

Humpty-Dumpty sat on a wall,
Humpty-Dumpty had a great fall.
Nursery Rhyme, *c.* 1750

One never falls but on the side toward which one leans.
F. P. G. GUIZOT: Speech in the French Chamber of Deputies, May 5, 1837

Look high, and fall low.
H. G. BOHN: *Handbook of Proverbs*, 1855

Oaks may fall, when reeds brave the storm.
IBID.

The bigger they are the further they fall.
JACK JOHNSON (heavy-weight champion of the world): Before his fight with Jess Willard at Havana, April 5, 1915

The harder you fall the higher you bounce.
AMERICAN PROVERB

A fall does not hurt those who fly low.
CHINESE PROVERB

The best riders have the hardest falls. IBID.

When the ox falls everyone whets his knife.
HEBREW PROVERB

[*See also* Down, High, Man and Woman, Pride, Stuck-up, Tree.

Fallibility

[*See* Judgment.

Falsehood

Oh, what a goodly outside falsehood hath!
SHAKESPEARE: The Merchant of Venice, I, *c.* 1597

Falsehood and fraud shoot up on every soil,
The product of all climes.
JOSEPH ADDISON: *Cato*, IV, 1713

The united voice of millions cannot lend the smallest foundation to falsehood.
OLIVER GOLDSMITH: *The Vicar of Wakefield*, VIII, 1766

Falsehood is fire in stubble; — it turns all the light stuff around it into its own substance for a moment, one crackling blazing moment, — and then dies; and all its converts are scattered in the wind, without place or evidence of their existence, as viewless as the wind which scatters them.
S. T. COLERIDGE: *Omniana*, 1812

We ought neither to say that a person sees, if he sees falsely, nor speaks, if he speaks falsely. For seeing falsely is worse than blindness, and speaking falsely, than silence.
JOHN RUSKIN: *Modern Painters*, V, 1860

The beginning of all is to have done with falsity — to eschew falsity as death eternal.
THOMAS CARLYLE: *Journal*, June 23, 1870

False facts are highly injurious to the progress of science, for they often endure long; but false views, if supported by some evidence, do little harm, for everyone takes a salutary pleasure in proving their falseness; and when this is done, one path toward error is closed and the road to truth is often at the same time opened.
CHARLES DARWIN: *The Descent of Man*, XXI, 1871

Falsehood has beauty if it works for good.
ITALIAN PROVERB

False in one thing, false in everything. (Falsus in uno, falsus in omnibus.)
LEGAL MAXIM

[*See also* Bulletin, Devil, Faith, Lying, Man, Truth and Falsehood.

Fame

The wise man thinks of fame just enough to avoid being despised.
EPICURUS: *Aphorisms, c.* 300 B.C.

Let us now praise famous men.
ECCLESIASTICUS XLIV, 1, *c.* 180 B.C.

I have raised a monument more lasting than brazen statues, and higher than the royal pyramids, a monument which shall not be destroyed by the wasting rain, the fury of the north wind, or the flight of ages.
HORACE: *Carmina,* III, *c.* 20 B.C.

Fame due to the achievements of the mind never perishes.
PROPERTIUS: *Elegies,* III, *c.* 20 B.C.

He who disdains fame enjoys it in its purity.
LIVY: *History of Rome,* XXII, *c.* 10

The love of fame puts spurs to the mind.
OVID: *Tristia,* V, *c.* 10

How sweet it is to have people point and say, "There he is." PERSIUS: *Satires,* I, *c.* 60

I do not like the man who squanders life for fame. MARTIAL: *Epigrams,* I, 86

If fame is to come only after death, I am in no hurry for it. MARTIAL: *Epigrams,* V, 95

Those who desire fame are fond of praise and flattery, though it comes from their inferiors.
PLINY THE YOUNGER: *Letters,* IV, *c.* 110

The desire for fame is the last weakness wise men put off. TACITUS: *Annals,* IV, *c.* 110

It is misery to live on the fame of others.
JUVENAL: *Satires,* VIII, 118

Life is warfare and a pilgrim's brief sojourn, and fame after death is only forgetfulness.
MARCUS AURELIUS: *Meditations,* II, *c.* 170

Consider how many do not even know your name, and how many will soon forget it, and how those who now praise you will presently blame you. Fame after death is of no value, and neither is reputation now, nor anything else. MARCUS AURELIUS: *Meditations,* IX

The desire for fame tempts even noble minds.
ST. AUGUSTINE: *The City of God,* V, 427

The man who spends his life without winning fame leaves such mark of himself on earth as smoke in air or foam on water.
DANTE: *Inferno,* XXIV, *c.* 1320

Honor, glory, praise, renown, and fame — each is but an echo, a shade, a dream, a flower that is blasted with every wind and spoiled with every shower.
TORQUATO TASSO: *Gerusalemme,* XIV, 1592

Let fame, that all hunt after in their lives,
Live register'd upon our brazen tombs.
And then grace us in the disgrace of death.
SHAKESPEARE: *Love's Labor's Lost,* I, *c.* 1595

Contempt of fame begets contempt of virtue.
BEN JONSON: *Sejanus,* I, 1603

There's hope a great man's memory may outlive his life half a year.
SHAKESPEARE: *Hamlet,* III, *c.* 1601

Fame is but wind.
THOMAS CORYATE: *Crudities,* 1611

Fame is a liar, and was never other.
GEORGE WITHER and WILLIAM BROWNE: *The Shepherd's Pipe,* VII, 1614

Fame is like a river, that beareth up things light and swoln, and drowns things weighty and solid. FRANCIS BACON: *Essays,* L, 1625

For my name and memory, I leave it to men's charitable speeches, to foreign nations, and to the next ages.
FRANCIS BACON: *Last will,* 1626

That last infirmity of noble minds.
JOHN MILTON: *Lycidas,* 1638 (Cf. TACITUS, *ante, c.* 110)

He hath not lived that lives not after death.
GEORGE HERBERT: *Outlandish Proverbs,* 1640

Who knows whether the best of men be known, or whether there be not more remarkable persons forgot, than any that stand remembered in the known account of time?
THOMAS BROWNE: *Urn Burial,* V, 1658

The fame of men ought always to be estimated by the means used to acquire it.
LA ROCHEFOUCAULD: *Maxims,* 1665

Fame is a revenue payable only to our ghosts.
GEORGE MACKENZIE: *A Moral Essay Preferring Solitude to Public Employment,* 1665

Not to know me argues yourselves unknown.
JOHN MILTON: *Paradise Lost,* IV, 1667

We are so presumptuous that we wish to be known by all the world, and even by people who will live after we are gone; and we are so vain that the good opinion of five or six persons near us delights and contents us.
BLAISE PASCAL: *Pensées,* II, 1670

Fame has the drawback that it compels its votaries to order their lives according to the opinions of their fellowmen, shunning what

others usually shun, and seeking what they usually seek.
BARUCH SPINOZA: *De intellectus emendatione*, 1670

Fame, if not double fac'd, is double mouth'd,
And with contrary blast proclaims most deeds;
On both his wings, one black, the other white.
JOHN MILTON: *Samson Agonistes*, 1671

The aspiring youth that fired the Ephesian dome
Outlives in fame the pious fool that rais'd it.
COLLEY CIBBER: Adaptation of SHAKESPEARE: *Richard III*, III, 1700

Fame and rest are utter opposites.
RICHARD STEELE: *The Funeral*, V, 1701

Fame can never make us lie down contentedly on a deathbed.
ALEXANDER POPE: *Letter to William Trumbull*, March 12, 1713

Fame, impatient of extremes, decays
Not more by envy than excess of praise.
ALEXANDER POPE: *The Temple of Fame*, 1714

Nor fame I slight, nor for her favors call;
She comes unlooked for, if she comes at all.
IBID.

What a heavy burden is a name that becomes famous too soon.
VOLTAIRE: *La Henriade*, III, 1723

All fame is dangerous: good bringeth envy; bad, shame.
THOMAS FULLER: *Gnomologia*, 1732

Fame is a magnifying-glass. IBID.

Fame is but the breath of the people, and that often unwholesome. IBID.

From fame to infamy is a beaten road.
IBID.

What's fame? A fancied life in others' breath;
A thing beyond us, ev'n before our death; . . .
All that we feel of it begins and ends
In the small circle of our foes or friends.
ALEXANDER POPE: *An Essay on Man*, IV, 1734

And what is fame? The meanest have their day;
The greatest can but blaze and pass away.
ALEXANDER POPE: *The First Epistle of the First Book of Horace*, 1735

The best-concerted schemes men lay for fame,
Die fast away: only themselves die faster.
ROBERT BLAIR: *The Grave*, 1743

If we look back into past times, we find innumerable names of authors once in high reputation, read perhaps by the beautiful, quoted by the witty, and commented on by the grave; but of whom we now know only that they once existed.
SAMUEL JOHNSON: *The Rambler*, May 29, 1750

When fate writ my name it made a blot.
HENRY FIELDING: *Amelia*, II, 1752

What is fame? an empty bubble.
JAMES GRAINGER: *Solitude*, 1755

All hunt for fame; but most mistake the way.
CHARLES CHURCHILL: *The Rosciad*, 1761

Fame is the advantage of being known by people of whom you yourself know nothing, and for whom you care as little.
STANISLAUS LESZCYNSKI (KING OF POLAND): *Œuvres du philosophe bienfaisant*, 1763

Of praise a mere glutton, he swallow'd what came,
And the puff of a dunce he mistook for fame.
OLIVER GOLDSMITH: *Retaliation*, 1774

What rage for fame attends both great and small!
Better be d——n'd than mentioned not at all.
JOHN WOLCOT (PETER PINDAR): *To the Royal Academicians*, 1783

The novelty of a poet in my obscure situation, without any of those advantages which are reckoned necessary for that character, at least at this time of day, has raised a partial tide of public notice which has borne me to a height where I am absolutely, feelingly certain, my abilities are inadequate to support me; and too surely do I see that time when the same tide will leave me and recede perhaps as far below the mark of truth.
ROBERT BURNS: *Letter to Mrs. Dunlop*, Jan. 15, 1787

A good part of the fame of most celebrated men is due to the short-sightedness of their admirers. The realization by such men that they are seen through by a few who have less reputation but more genius must spoil all the fame they enjoy.
G. C. LICHTENBERG: *Reflections*, 1799

I awoke one morning and found myself famous.
BYRON: After the publication of *Childe Harold*, 1812

The temple of fame stands upon the grave: the flame that burns upon its altars is kindled from the ashes of dead men.
WILLIAM HAZLITT: *The English Poets*, VIII, 1816

What is the end of fame? 'tis but to fill
A certain portion of uncertain paper:
Some liken it to climbing up a hill,
Whose summit, like all hills, is lost in vapor:
For this men write, speak, preach, and heroes kill,
And bards burn what they call their midnight taper,
To have, when the original is dust,
A name, a wretched picture, and worse bust.
BYRON: *Don Juan*, I, 1819

Artists who have won fame are embarrassed by it; thus their first works are often their best.
LUDWIG VAN BEETHOVEN: *Conversation Book*, 1820

There are names written in her immortal scroll at which fame blushes.
WILLIAM HAZLITT: *Characteristics,* XXII, 1823

One of the few, the immortal names,
That were not born to die.
FITZ-GREENE HALLECK: *Marco Bozzaris,* 1825

Fame is no sure test of merit, but only a probability of such: it is an accident, not a property of a man.
THOMAS CARLYLE: *Goethe,* 1828 (Foreign Review, July)

Lives of great men all remind us
We can make our lives sublime,
And departing, leave behind us
Footprints on the sands of time.
H. W. LONGFELLOW: *A Psalm of Life,* 1839

Happy is the man who hath never known what it is to taste of fame — to have it is a purgatory, to want it is a hell.
E. G. BULWER-LYTTON: *The Last of the Barons,* I, 1843

Ah, pensive scholar, what is fame?
A fitful tongue of leaping flame;
A giddy whirlwind's fickle gust,
That lifts a pinch of mortal dust;
A few swift years, and who can show
What dust was Bill and which was Joe?
O. W. HOLMES: *Bill and Joe,* 1851

Fame, like a river, is narrowest at its source and broadest afar off.
H. G. BOHN: *Handbook of Proverbs,* 1855

Fame usually comes to those who are thinking about something else.
O. W. HOLMES: *The Autocrat of the Breakfast-Table,* XII, 1858

Fame, the being known, though in itself one of the most dangerous things to man, is nevertheless the true and appointed air, element, and setting of genius and its works.
GERARD MANLEY HOPKINS: *Letter to Robert Bridges,* Oct., 1886

A little heap of dust,
A little streak of rust,
A stone without a name —
Lo! hero, sword and fame!
AMBROSE BIERCE: *Fame,* 1898

Fame is the beauty-parlor of the dead.
BENJAMIN DECASSERES: *Fantasia Impromptu,* 1933

The final test of fame is to have a crazy person imagine he is you. Author unidentified

The only real life is the life of fame.
SANSKRIT PROVERB

Fame is a calamity. TURKISH PROVERB

[*See also* Ale, Ambition, Distinction, Eminence, Envy, Famous, Happiness, Lafayette (Marquis de), Mousetrap, Napoleon I, Profit, Quotation.

Familiarity

Familiarity breeds contempt.
PUBLILIUS SYRUS: *Sententiæ, c.* 50 B.C.

Be thou familiar, but by no means vulgar.
SHAKESPEARE: *Hamlet,* I, *c.* 1601

Sweets grown common lose their dear delight.
SHAKESPEARE: *Sonnets,* CII, 1609

He chooseth rather to be counted a spy than not a politician, and maintains his reputation by naming great men familiarly.
SIR THOMAS OVERBURY: *Characters,* 1614

Indiscriminate familiarity either offends your superiors, or else dubs you their dependent, and led-captain. It gives your inferiors just, but troublesome and improper claims of equality.
LORD CHESTERFIELD: *Letter to his son,* Aug. 30, 1749

The man who enters his wife's dressing-room is either a philosopher or a fool.
BALZAC: *The Physiology of Marriage,* 1830

The familiarity of superiors causes bitterness, for it may not be returned.
F. W. NIETZSCHE: *Beyond Good and Evil,* 1886

[*See also* Husband and Wife, Manners.

Family

The son dishonoreth the father, the daughter riseth up against her mother, the daughter in law against her mother in law; a man's enemies are the men of his own house.
MICAH VII, 6, *c.* 700 B.C.

There is little less trouble in governing a private family than a whole kingdom. Wherever the mind is perplexed it is in an entire disorder, and domestic employments are no less troublesome for being less important.
MICHEL DE MONTAIGNE: *Essays,* I, 1580

It is a reverend thing to see an ancient castle or building not in decay: or to see a fair timber tree sound and perfect. How much more to behold an ancient and noble family which hath stood against the waves and weathers of time.
FRANCIS BACON: *Essays,* XIV, 1625

Generations pass while some trees stand, and old families last not three oaks.
THOMAS BROWNE: *Urn Burial,* V, 1658

There's no family but there's a whore or a knave of it.
JAMES HOWELL: *Proverbs,* 1659

The building up of a family is a manufacture very little above the building of a house of cards. Time and accidents are sure to furnish a blast to blow it down.
GEORGE SAVILE (MARQUESS OF HALIFAX): *Political, Moral and Miscellaneous Reflections, c.* 1690

He that has no fools, knaves, nor beggars in his family was begot by a flash of lightning.
THOMAS FULLER: *Gnomologia,* 1732

The happiest moments of my life have been the few which I have passed at home in the bosom of my family.
THOMAS JEFFERSON: *Letter to Francis Willis,* 1790

The family consists of those who live under the same roof with the paterfamilias; those who form (if I may use the expression) his fireside.
LORD KENYON: *Judgment in Rex* vs. *Inhabitants of Darlington,* 1792

A fine family is a fine thing
(Provided they don't come in after dinner);
'Tis beautiful to see a matron bring
Her children up (if nursing them don't thin her).
BYRON: *Don Juan,* III, 1821

On what foundation is the present family, the bourgeois family, based? On capital, on private gain. . . . The bourgeois family will vanish as a matter of course with the vanishing of capital.
KARL MARX and FRIEDRICH ENGELS: *The Communist Manifesto,* 1848

I go (always other things being equal) for the man that inherits family traditions and the cumulative humanities of at least four or five generations.
O. W. HOLMES: *The Autocrat of the Breakfast-Table,* I, 1858

All happy families are alike, but every unhappy one is unhappy in its own way.
LYOF N. TOLSTOY: *Anna Karenina,* I, 1876

The family is a society limited in numbers, but nevertheless a true society, anterior to every state or nation, with rights and duties of its own, wholly independent of the commonwealth.
POPE LEO XIII: *Rerum novarum,* May 15, 1891

The family is more sacred than the state, and men are begotten not for the earth and for time, but for Heaven and eternity.
POPE PIUS XI: *Casti connubii,* Dec. 31, 1930

Nobody's family can hang out the sign, "Nothing the matter here." CHINESE PROVERB

The larger your family, the more disgrace is in store for you. HINDU PROVERB

None but a mule denies his family.
MOROCCAN PROVERB

Large family; quick help. SERBIAN PROVERB

[*See also* Accident, Ancestry, Children, Father, Like, Marriage, Mother, Property, State, Wife and Child.

Famine

Half-starved spiders prey'd on half-starved flies.
CHARLES CHURCHILL: *The Prophecy of Famine,* 1763

There was no corn — in the wide market-place
All loathliest things, even human flesh, was sold;
They weighed it in small scales — and many a face
Was fixt in eager horror then; his gold
The miser brought; the tender maid, grown bold
Through hunger, bared her scornèd charms in vain.
P. B. SHELLEY: *The Revolt of Islam,* X, 1818

[*See also* Farmer, Fasting.

Fanatic

Fanatics are picturesque, and mankind prefers observing poses to listening to reasons.
F. W. NIETZSCHE: *The Antichrist,* LV, 1888

A fanatic is the Devil's plaything.
ARMENIAN PROVERB

[*See also* Enthusiast.

Fanaticism

There is only one step from fanaticism to barbarism.
DENIS DIDEROT: *Essai sur le mérite et la vertu,* 1746

Which is the more dangerous, fanaticism or atheism? Fanaticism is certainly a thousand times more deadly; for atheism inspires no bloody passion, whereas fanaticism does: atheism is not opposed to crime, but fanaticism causes crimes to be committed.
VOLTAIRE: *Philosophical Dictionary,* 1764

We know the crimes that fanaticism in religion has caused; let us be careful not to introduce fanaticism in philosophy.
FREDERICK THE GREAT: *Letter to Voltaire, c.* 1775

Fanaticism is always the child of persecution.
NAPOLEON I: To Barry E. O'Meara at St. Helena, Jan. 27, 1817

The victim of the fanatical persecutor will find that the stronger the motives he can urge for mercy are, the weaker will be his chance of obtaining it, for the merit of his destruction will be supposed to rise in value in proportion as it is effected at the expense of every feeling, both of justice and of humanity.
C. C. COLTON: *Lacon,* 1820

Fanaticism is an evil, but it is not the greatest of evils. It is good that a people should be roused by any means from a state of utter torpor; — that their minds should be diverted from objects merely sensual to meditations, however erroneous, on the mysteries of the moral and intellectual world; and from interests which are immediately selfish to those which relate to the past, the future, and the remote.

T. B. MACAULAY: *Dante*, 1824 (Knight's Quarterly Magazine, Jan.)

[*See also* Monomania.

Fancy

Tell me where is fancy bred,
Or in the heart or in the head?
How begot, how nourished?
Reply, reply.
It is engender'd in the eyes,
With grazing fed; and fancy dies
In the cradle where it lies.

SHAKESPEARE: *The Merchant of Venice*, III, *c.* 1597

So full of shapes is fancy,
That it alone is high fantastical.

SHAKESPEARE: *Twelfth Night*, I, *c.* 1601

All power of fancy over reason is a degree of insanity.

SAMUEL JOHNSON: *Rasselas*, XLIV, 1759

Only fancy has perpetual May.

J. C. F. SCHILLER: *Lied an die Freude*, 1786

Fancy is a wilful, imagination a spontaneous act; fancy, a play as with dolls and puppets which we choose to call men and women; imagination, a perception and affirming of a real relation between a thought and some material fact. Fancy amuses; imagination expands and exalts us.

R. W. EMERSON: *Poetry and Imagination*, 1876

[*See also* Husband and Wife, Insanity.

Fancy-free

In maiden meditation, fancy-free.

SHAKESPEARE: *A Midsummer Night's Dream*, II, *c.* 1596

Faneuil Hall

When liberty is in danger Faneuil Hall has the right, it is her duty, to strike the key-note for these United States.

WENDELL PHILLIPS: Speech on the murder of Elijah P. Lovejoy, Faneuil Hall, Boston, Dec. 8, 1837 (Lovejoy was killed by a mob at Alton, Ill., Nov. 7)

Far

So far, so good.

ENGLISH PHRASE, apparently not recorded before the XVIII century

O'er the hills and far away.

THOMAS D'URFEY: *Pills to Purge Melancholy*, 1719

Farce

[*See* Drama.

Farewell

Sir, fare you well:
Hereafter, in a better world than this,
I shall desire more love and knowledge of you.

SHAKESPEARE: *As You Like It*, I, *c.* 1600

Fare thee well;
The elements be kind to thee, and make
Thy spirits all of comfort!

SHAKESPEARE: *Antony and Cleopatra*, III, *c.* 1606

Once more farewell!
If e'er we meet hereafter, we shall meet
In happier climes, and on a safer shore.

JOSEPH ADDISON: *Cato*, IV, 1713

And fare thee weel, my only luve!
And fare thee weel a while!
And I will come again, my luve,
Tho' it were ten thousand mile.

ROBERT BURNS: *A Red, Red Rose*, 1794

Fare thee well! and if for ever,
Still for ever, fare thee well.

BYRON: *Fare Thee Well*, 1816

All farewells should be sudden, when forever.

BYRON: *Sardanapalus*, V, 1821

Farewell and adieu to you, Spanish ladies!
Farewell and adieu to you, ladies of Spain!

HERMAN MELVILLE: *Moby Dick*, XXXIX, 1851

[*See also* Good-bye, Good-night, Parting.

Farm

It makes but little difference whether you are committed to a farm or a county jail.

H. D. THOREAU: *Walden*, 1854

I know few things more pleasing to the eye, or more capable of affording scope and gratification to a taste for the beautiful, than a well-situated, well-cultivated farm.

EDWARD EVERETT: Speech at Buffalo, Oct. 9, 1857

Through the ample open door of the peaceful country barn,
A sun-lit pasture field, with cattle and horses feeding;
And haze, and vista, and the far horizon, fading away.

WALT WHITMAN: *A Farm Picture*, 1865

Burn down your cities and leave our farms, and your cities will spring up again as if by magic; but destroy our farms, and the grass will grow in the streets of every city in the country.

W. J. BRYAN: Speech at the Democratic National Convention, Chicago, July 8, 1896

[*See also* Agriculture, Farmer, Farming, Pirate.

Farmer

When there are too many farmers the excess will be of the better kind; when there are too many mechanics and laborers, of the worst.

ARISTOTLE: *Politics*, IV, *c.* 322 B.C.

A farmer is always going to be rich next year.
PHILEMON: *Fragment, c.* 300 B.C.

It is from the tillers of the soil that spring the best citizens, the staunchest soldiers. Farmers are, of all men, the least given to vice.
CATO: *De re rustica, c.* 200 B.C.

How can he get wisdom who holdeth the plow?
ECCLESIASTICUS XXXVIII, 25, *c.* 180 B.C.

The husbandman that laboreth must be first partaker of the fruits.
II TIMOTHY II, 6, *c.* 65

The farmer's eye is the best fertilizer.
PLINY THE ELDER: *Natural History,* XVIII, *c.* 79

A plain country fellow is one that manures his ground well, but lets himself lie fallow and untilled. He has reason enough to do his business, and not enough to be idle or melancholy.
JOHN EARLE (BISHOP OF SALISBURY): *Microcosmographie,* 1628

Farmers fatten most when famine reigns.
SAMUEL GARTH: *The Dispensary,* II, 1699

Whoever could make two ears of corn, or two blades of grass, to grow upon a spot of ground where only one grew before, would deserve better of mankind, and do more essential service to his country, than the whole race of politicians put together.
JONATHAN SWIFT: *Gulliver's Travels,* II, 1726

He that by the plow would thrive
Himself must either hold or drive.
BENJAMIN FRANKLIN: *Poor Richard's Almanac,* 1747

Farmers are often worthless fellows. They have all the sensual vices of the nobility, with cheating into the bargain.
SAMUEL JOHNSON: *Boswell's Life,* May 14, 1778

Those who labor in the earth are the chosen people of God, if He ever had a chosen people, whose breasts He has made His peculiar deposit for substantial and genuine virtue.
THOMAS JEFFERSON: *Notes on Virginia,* 1782

Our farmers round, well pleased with constant gain,
Like other farmers, flourish and complain.
GEORGE CRABBE: *The Parish Register,* I, 1807

All country people hate each other. They have so little comfort that they envy their neighbors the smallest pleasure or advantage. . . . If you do anyone a favor, the whole neighborhood is up in arms; the clamor is like that of a rookery.
WILLIAM HAZLITT: *The Round Table,* II, 1817

Here once the embattled farmers stood
And fired the shot heard round the world.
R. W. EMERSON: Hymn sung at the completion of the Concord monument, April 19, 1836

When tillage begins, other arts follow. The farmers, therefore, are the founders of civilization.
DANIEL WEBSTER: Speech at Boston, Jan. 13, 1840

Farmers are respectable and interesting to me in proportion as they are poor — poor farmers.
H. D. THOREAU: *Walden,* 1854

The Golden Age of the small farmer is over. He can barely get along. He is in debt to the cattle-dealer, the land speculator, the usurer. Mortgages ruin whole communities, even more than taxes.
P. A. KROPOTKIN: *Paroles d'un révolté,* 1884

Even if a farmer intends to loaf, he gets up in time to get an early start.
E. W. HOWE: *Country Town Sayings,* 1911

Nobody can discuss agriculture so learnedly as a farmer who hasn't paid the interest on his mortgage for eight years.
H. L. DAVIS: *Honey in the Horn,* XIX, 1935

Hope sustains the farmer. (Spes alit agricolas.)
LATIN PROVERB

[*See also* Agriculture, Farm, Farming, Industry, Peasant.

Farming

Farming is a senseless pursuit, a mere laboring in a circle. You sow that you may reap, and then you reap that you may sow. Nothing ever comes of it.
JOANNES STOBAEUS: *Florilegium, c.* 500

Q. What is the best business a man can do? A. Tilling the ground, or farming.
NOAH WEBSTER: *The Rudiments of English Grammar,* 1790

No occupation is so delightful to me as the culture of the earth.
THOMAS JEFFERSON: *Letter to C. W. Peale,* 1811

The first receipt to farm well is to be rich.
SYDNEY SMITH: *Letter to John Wishaw,* April 13, 1818

You think farm buildings and broad acres a solid property: but its value is flowing like water. It requires as much watching as if you were decanting wine from a cask.
R. W. EMERSON: *The Conduct of Life,* III, 1860

Some people tell us that there ain't no Hell,
But they never farmed, so how can they tell?
Anon.: *Down on the Farm,* 1940 (Congressional Record, Sept. 26)

[*See also* Agriculture, Countryside, Farm, Farmer, Peasant.

Farther

I may go farther, and fare worse.
JAMES SHIRLEY: *Love in a Maze*, II, 1632

Fascism

Fascism is nothing but capitalist reaction; from the point of view of the proletariat the differences between types of reaction are meaningless.
LEON TROTSKY: *What Next?*, VII, 1932

Fascism, before being a party, is a religion.
BENITO MUSSOLINI: Radio broadcast from Rome, Aug. 20, 1937

[*See also* Art, Individualism, Violence, Work.

Fashion

The fashion of this world passeth away.
I CORINTHIANS VII, 31, *c.* 55

A wise man ought to withdraw and retire his soul from the crowd, and there keep it at liberty, and in power to judge freely of things; but, as to his outward garb and appearance, absolutely follow and conform himself to the fashion of the time. It is the rule of rules, and the general law of laws, that every one observe those of the place wherein he lives.
MICHEL DE MONTAIGNE: *Essays*, I, 1580

The fashion wears out more apparel than the man.
SHAKESPEARE: *Much Ado About Nothing*, III, *c.* 1599

The glass of fashion and the mold of form,
The observ'd of all observers.
SHAKESPEARE: *Hamlet*, III, *c.* 1601

Let's do it after the high Roman fashion.
SHAKESPEARE: *Antony and Cleopatra*, IV, *c.* 1606

He is only fantastical that is not in fashion.
ROBERT BURTON: *The Anatomy of Melancholy*, 1621

Nothing is thought rare
Which is not new, and follow'd; yet we know
That what was worn some twenty years ago
Comes into grace again.
BEAUMONT (?) and FLETCHER: *The Noble Gentleman*, prologue, 1626

As good out of the world as out of the fashion.
JOHN CLARKE: *Parœmiologia Anglo-Latina*, 1639

What is in fashion is handsome and pleasant, though never so uncouth to an unconcern'd beholder.
JOSEPH GLANVILL: *The Vanity of Dogmatizing*, XIV, 1661

Every age has its own fashion, in pleasure, in wit, in manners.
NICOLAS BOILEAU: *L'Art poétique*, III, 1674

Be not the first by whom the new are tried,
Nor yet the last to lay the old aside.
ALEXANDER POPE: *An Essay on Criticism*, II, 1711

Fools may invent fashions that wise men will wear.
THOMAS FULLER: *Gnomologia*, 1732

The more careless the more modish.
JONATHAN SWIFT: *Polite Conversation*, 1738

Have the courage to prefer propriety to fashion — one is but the abuse of the other.
STANISLAUS LESZCZYNSKI (KING OF POLAND): *Œuvres du philosophe bienfaisant*, 1763

Fashion [is] an idiot painter that seems industrious to place staring fools and unprincipled knaves in the foreground of its picture, while men of sense and honesty are too often thrown in the dimmest shades.
ROBERT BURNS: *Letter to William Smellie*, Jan. 22, 1792

Fashion is the veriest goddess of semblance and of shade; to be happy is of far less consequence to her worshippers than to appear so; even pleasure itself they sacrifice to parade, and enjoyment to ostentation.
C. C. COLTON: *Lacon*, 1820

Fashion is gentility running away from vulgarity, and afraid of being overtaken.
WILLIAM HAZLITT: *Conversations of James Northcote, R.A.*, 1830

No woman can look as well out of the fashion as in it.
S. L. CLEMENS (MARK TWAIN): *Letter from New York to the Alta Californian* (San Francisco), April 16, 1867

Fashion is that by which the fantastic becomes for a moment universal.
OSCAR WILDE: *The Picture of Dorian Gray*, 1891

Fashion is what one wears oneself. What is unfashionable is what other people wear.
OSCAR WILDE: *An Ideal Husband*, III, 1895

Follow fashion make monkey cut him tail.
JAMAICAN PROVERB

What has been the fashion once will come into fashion again.
JAPANESE PROVERB

[*See also* Clothes, Dress, Language.

Fasting

When ye fast, be not, as the hypocrites, of a sad countenance.
MATTHEW VI, 16, *c.* 75

Let not your fasts be with hypocrites, for they fast on Mondays and Thursdays, but do you fast on Wednesdays and Fridays.
The Didache, or Teaching of the Twelve Apostles, *c.* 125

Fasting is better than prayer.
ST. CLEMENT: *Second Epistle to the Corinthians*, c. 150

Fasting is a medicine.
ST. JOHN CHRYSOSTOM: *Homilies*, III, c. 388

When war, pestilence or famine begins to rage, or any other calamity threatens a country and people, it is the duty of pastors to exhort the church to fasting, that they may deprecate the wrath of the Lord.
JOHN CALVIN: *Institutes of the Christian Religion*, IV, 1536

The popish fasting is murder, whereby many people have been destroyed, observing the fasts strictly, and, chiefly, by eating one sort of food, so that nature's strength is thereby weakened.
MARTIN LUTHER: *Table-Talk*, DVII, 1569

He that feeds barely fasts sufficiently.
RANDLE COTGRAVE: *French-English Dictionary*, 1611

Q. If a man cannot sleep without taking supper, is he bound to fast? A. By no means.
ANTONIO ESCOBAR: *Summula casuum conscientiæ*, I, 1627

Though a man eat fish till his guts crack, yet if he eat no flesh he fasts.
JOHN TAYLOR: *Jack-a-Lent*, 1630

What an idiot is man to believe that abstaining from flesh, and eating fish, which is so much more delicate and delicious, constitutes fasting.
NAPOLEON I: To Barry E. O'Meara at St. Helena, April 3, 1817

He who fasteth and doeth no good, saveth his bread, but loseth his soul.
H. G. BOHN: *Handbook of Proverbs*, 1855

It is good fasting when the table is covered with fish.
DANISH PROVERB

Fasting today makes the food good tomorrow.
GERMAN PROVERB

A fast is better than a bad meal.
IRISH PROVERB

Who fasts but does no other good saves his bread but goes to Hell.
ITALIAN PROVERB

One good deed is better than three days of fasting.
JAPANESE PROVERB

[*See also* Abstemiousness, Abstinence, Asceticism, Breakfast, Eating, Exegesis, Friar, Labor, Meal.

Fat

Eglon was a very fat man.
JUDGES III, 17, c. 500 B.C.

Fat men are more likely to die suddenly than the slender.
HIPPOCRATES: *Aphorisms*, c. 400 B.C.

He that putteth his trust in the Lord shall be made fat.
PROVERBS XXVIII, 25, c. 350 B.C.

The fat is in the fire.
ENGLISH SAYING, familiar since the XIV century (Smith notes that at first it indicated failure, but now means that there will be an explosion)

Fat paunches have lean pates, and dainty bits
Make rich the ribs, but bankrupt quite the wits.
SHAKESPEARE: *Love's Labor's Lost*, I, c. 1595

A gross fat man — as fat as butter.
SHAKESPEARE: *I Henry IV*, II, c. 1598

Let me have men about me that are fat,
Sleek-headed men, and such as sleep o' nights.
SHAKESPEARE: *Julius Cæsar*, I, 1599

Oh, that this too too solid flesh would melt,
Thaw and resolve itself into a dew!
SHAKESPEARE: *Hamlet*, I, c. 1601

They are more sickly that have gross and full bodies.
TOBIAS VENNER: *Via recta*, 1620

I am resolved to grow fat, and look young till forty.
JOHN DRYDEN: *Secret Love*, III, 1668

Fat sorrow is better than lean sorrow.
JOHN RAY: *English Proverbs*, 1670

Often and little eating makes a man fat.
IBID.

The fatter the sow, the more she desires the mire.
JOHN BUNYAN: *Pilgrim's Progress*, II, 1678

Fat flesh freezes soon.
JAMES KELLY: *Complete Collection of Scottish Proverbs*, 1721

Fat housekeepers make lean executors.
IBID.

I shall grow as fat as a porpoise.
JONATHAN SWIFT: *Polite Conversation*, II, 1738

I cannot but bless the memory of Julius Cæsar, for the great esteem he expressed for fat men, and his aversion to lean ones.
DAVID HUME: *Letter to Mrs. Dysart*, March 19, 1751

Who drives fat oxen should himself be fat.
SAMUEL JOHNSON: *Boswell's Life*, 1784

Who ever hears of fat men heading a riot, or herding together in turbulent mobs?
WASHINGTON IRVING: *Knickerbocker's History of New York*, III, 1809

Nobody loves a fat man.
AMERICAN PROVERB

A fat man is no good in war; he can neither fight nor run away.
IBID.

Fat hens lay few eggs. GERMAN PROVERB

Fat heads, lean brains. ITALIAN PROVERB

A fat man has a thin soul. WELSH PROVERB

[*See also* Cheek, Eating, Fire, Forty, Gentleman, Health, Hen, Laughter, Mind and Body, Perspiration.

Fatalism

[*See* Fate.

Fatality

I never nurs'd a dear gazelle,
  To glad me with its soft black eye,
But when it came to know me well,
  And love me, it was sure to die.

THOMAS MOORE: *The Fire Worshippers,* 1817

Fate

All things come alike to all: there is one event to the righteous, and to the wicked; to the good and to the clean, and to the unclean; to him that sacrificeth, and to him that sacrificeth not: as is the good, so is the sinner; and he that sweareth, as he that feareth an oath.

ECCLESIASTES IX, 2, *c.* 200 B.C.

The fates are calling. (Fata vocant.)

VIRGIL: *Georgics,* IV, 30 B.C.

Fate with impartial hand turns out the doom of high and low; her capacious urn is constantly shaking out the names of all mankind.

HORACE: *Carmina,* III, *c.* 20 B.C.

Fate will find a way. (Fata viam invenient.)

VIRGIL: *Æneid,* X, 19 B.C.

Little folks become their little fate.

HORACE: *Epistles,* I, *c.* 5 B.C.

Fate leads the willing, and drags along those who hang back.

SENECA: *Epistulæ morales ad Lucilium,* CVII, *c.* 63

He who remembers what man is can be discontented at nothing that happens.

EPICTETUS: *Encheiridion, c.* 110

If by fate anyone means the will or power of God, let him keep his meaning but mend his language: for fate commonly means a necessary process which will have its way apart from the will of God and of men.

ST. AUGUSTINE: *The City of God,* V, 427

The possession which the Creator has written on our forehead, be it small or great, we shall surely attain, even in the desert; and more than this we can never get, though we be on Mount Meru, whose sides are packed with gold.

BHARTRIHARI: *The Vairagya Sataka, c.* 625

Our wills and fates do so contrary run
That our devices still are overthrown;
Our thoughts are ours, their ends none of our own.

SHAKESPEARE: *Hamlet,* III, *c.* 1601

Fate, show thy force; ourselves we do not owe;
What is decreed must be, and be this so.

SHAKESPEARE: *Twelfth Night,* I, *c.* 1601

Who can control his fate?

SHAKESPEARE: *Othello,* V, 1604

The glories of our blood and state
  Are shadows, not substantial things,
There is no armor against fate;
  Death lays his icy hand on kings.

JAMES SHIRLEY: *Death the Leveler,* 1659

Here's a sigh to those who love me,
  And a smile to those who hate;
And whatever sky's above me,
  Here's a heart for every fate.

BYRON: *Letter to John Murray,* June 4, 1817

Every clod of loam beneath us
Is a skull of Alexander;
Oceans are the blood of princes;
Desert sands the dust of beauties.

R. W. EMERSON: *From the Persian of Hafiz,* 1851

We are all, like swimmers in the sea,
Poised on the top of a huge wave of fate,
Which hangs uncertain to which side to fall;
And whether it will heave us up to land,
Or whether it will roll us out to sea.

MATTHEW ARNOLD: *Sohrab and Rustum,* 1853

The moving finger writes; and having writ,
Moves on; nor all your piety nor wit
  Shall lure it back to cancel half a line,
Nor all your tears wash out a word of it.

EDWARD FITZGERALD: Tr. of OMAR KHAYYÁM: *Rubáiyát* (*c.* 1100), 1857

Up from earth's centre through the seventh gate
I rose, and on the throne of Saturn sate,
  And many a knot unravell'd by the road.
But not the master-knot of human fate.

IBID.

Fate is a name for facts not yet passed under the fire of thought; for causes which are unpenetrated.

R. W. EMERSON: *Fate,* 1860

What is written is written. (El maktub maktub.) ARAB PROVERB

Fate does not work in trivialities.

WELSH PROVERB

[*See also* Destiny, Determinism, Dust, Fortune, God, Predestination.

Father

If a man strike his father his hand shall be cut off.

THE CODE OF HAMMURABI, *c.* 2250 B.C.

He that begetteth a fool doeth it to his sorrow: and the father of a fool hath no joy.

PROVERBS XVII, 21, *c.* 350 B.C.

Hearken unto thy father that begat thee.

PROVERBS XXIII, 22

Call no man your father upon the earth: for one is your Father, which is in heaven.
MATTHEW XXIII, 9, *c.* 75

Father of his country. (Pater patriæ.)
Title given to Cicero by Cato and Catullus, after his consulship, 63–4 B.C.; also applied to Washington

No love to a father's.
GEORGE HERBERT: *Outlandish Proverbs,* 1640

One father is more than a hundred schoolmasters.
IBID.

It is impossible to please all the world and also one's father.
JEAN DE LA FONTAINE: *Fables,* II, *c.* 1670

A father, when punishing, is always a father; a slight punishment suffices for his anger.
JEAN RACINE: *Phèdre,* III, 1677

He was scarce of news that told his father was hanged.
JAMES KELLY: *Complete Collection of Scottish Proverbs,* 1721

Please sell no more drink to my father,
It makes him so strange and so wild;
Heed the prayers of my heart-broken mother
And pity the poor drunkard's child.
MRS. FRANK B. PRATT: *The Drunkard's Child, c.* 1850

Father, dear father, come home with me now;
The clock in the steeple strikes one;
You promised, dear father, that you would come home
As soon as your day's work was done;
Our fire has gone out, our house is all dark,
And mother's been watching since tea,
With poor brother Benny so sick in her arms
And no one to help her but me.
HENRY CLAY WORK: *Father, Dear Father, Come Home With Me Now, c.* 1860

Father is drinking again.
Anon.: Title of a popular song, *c.* 1880

The blow almost killed father.
JEAN HAVEZ: Title of a popular song, *c.* 1895

Fathers should be neither seen nor heard. That is the only proper basis for family life.
OSCAR WILDE: *An Ideal Husband,* III, 1895

With the growth of modern civilization the rôle of the father is being increasingly taken over by the state, and there is reason to think that a father may cease before long to be biologically advantageous, at any rate in the wage-earning class.
BERTRAND RUSSELL: *Marriage and Morals,* I, 1929

A father is a banker provided by nature.
FRENCH PROVERB

He is the father whom the marriage points to. (Est pater ille quem nuptia demonstrant.)
LEGAL MAXIM

[*See also* Blessing, Child, Duty (Filial), Eye, Family, Father and Child, Father and Daughter, Father and Mother, Father and Son, Heredity, Judge, Man and Woman, Misfortune, Mother, Mother and Child, Sorrow.

Father and Child

My mother says that he is my father, but myself I do not know, for no man can know who was his father.
HOMER: *Odyssey,* I, *c.* 800 B.C.

Child's pig; father's bacon.
ENGLISH PROVERB, traced by Smith to *c.* 1350

Wise is the child that knows its father.
ENGLISH PROVERB, borrowed from the Greek, and current since the XVI century

Happy is that child whose father goes to the Devil.
ENGLISH PROVERB, traced by Smith to 1552

It is a wise father that knows his own child.
SHAKESPEARE: *The Merchant of Venice,* II, *c.* 1597

The first service a child doth his father is to make him foolish.
GEORGE HERBERT: *Outlandish Proverbs,* 1640

There are fathers so unnatural that the whole of their lives seems to be devoted to giving their children reason for being consoled when they die.
JEAN DE LA BRUYÈRE: *Caractères,* XI, 1688

What a father says to his children is not heard by the world, but it will be heard by posterity.
JEAN PAUL RICHTER: *Levana,* pref., 1807

Up to twenty-one, I hold a father to have power over his children as to marriage; after that age, authority and influence only.
S. T. COLERIDGE: *Table-Talk,* June 10, 1824

It's a dull child that knows less than its father.
Author unidentified

It is better that the child should weep than the father.
GERMAN PROVERB

One father takes better care of ten children than ten children take care of one father.
IBID.

[*See also* Father, Heaven and Hell, Paternity.

Father and Daughter

Nothing is dearer to an old father than a daughter. Sons have spirits of higher pitch, but they are not given to fondness.
EURIPIDES: *The Suppliant Woman, c.* 421 B.C.

It is no new observation, I believe, that a lover in most cases has no rival so much to be feared as the father.
CHARLES LAMB: *The Wedding,* 1833

[*See also* Daughter.

Father and Mother

Honor thy father and thy mother: that thy days may be long upon the land which the Lord thy God giveth thee.
EXODUS XX, 12, *c.* 700 B.C. (Cf. DEUTERONOMY V, 16, *c.* 650 B.C.; MARK VII, 10, *c.* 70; MATTHEW XIX, 19, *c.* 75; LUKE VI, 2, *c.* 75)

The eye that mocketh at his father, and despiseth to obey his mother, the ravens of the valley shall pick it out, and the young eagles shall eat it.
PROVERBS XXX, 17, *c.* 350 B.C.

Honor thy father and mother both in word and deed, that a blessing may come upon thee from them.
ECCLESIASTICUS I, 2, *c.* 180 B.C.

He that curseth father or mother, let him die the death. MATTHEW XV, 4, *c.* 75

[*See also* Duty (Filial).

Father and Son

If a man set his face to disinherit his son and say to the judges, " I will disinherit my son," the judges shall inquire into his past, and if the son have not committed a crime sufficiently grave to cut him off from the sonship, the father may not cut off his son from sonship.
THE CODE OF HAMMURABI, *c.* 2250 B.C.

Saul and Jonathan were lovely and pleasant in their lives, and in their death they were not divided. II SAMUEL I, 23, *c.* 500 B.C.

Thy love to me was wonderful, passing the love of women. II SAMUEL I, 26

What greater ornament to a son than a father's glory, or to a father than a son's honorable conduct?
SOPHOCLES: *Antigone, c.* 450 B.C.

A wise son maketh a glad father.
PROVERBS X, 1, *c.* 350 B.C.

A foolish son is a grief to his father, and bitterness to her that bare him.
PROVERBS XVII, 25

A foolish son is the calamity of his father.
PROVERBS XIX, 13

Like father, like son. (Qualis pater talis filius.)
LATIN PROVERB, familiar in English since the XIV century

Such a father, such a son.
WILLIAM CAMDEN: *Remains Concerning Britain,* 1605

Diogenes struck the father when the son swore.
ROBERT BURTON: *The Anatomy of Melancholy,* III, 1621

One father is enough to govern one hundred sons, but not a hundred sons one father.
GEORGE HERBERT: *Outlandish Proverbs,* 1640

There must always be a struggle between a father and son, while one aims at power and the other at independence.
SAMUEL JOHNSON: *Boswell's Life,* July 14, 1763

As happy as the boy who killed his father.
AMERICAN SAYING

He is his father's son. (Patris est filius.)
LATIN PHRASE

[*See also* Duty (Filial), Son.

Fatherland

How dear to all good hearts is their fatherland.
VOLTAIRE: *Tancrède,* III, 1760

A fatherland is an association on the same soil of the living and the dead, with those yet to be born.
JOSEPH DE MAISTRE: *Étude sur la souveraineté,* 1794

With God for King and Fatherland. (Mit Gott für König und Vaterland.)
Motto of the German Landwehr (army reserve), adopted by a general order of March 17, 1813

[*See also* Country, Patriotism.

Fatherless

That it may please thee to defend, and provide for, the fatherless children, and widows, and all who are desolate and oppressed; We beseech thee to hear us, good Lord.
THE BOOK OF COMMON PRAYER (*The Litany*), 1662

The fatherless child is half an orphan; the motherless child is all one.
FINNISH PROVERB

[*See also* Charity, Orphan, Vineyard.

Fatigue

Fatigue is the best pillow. HINDU PROVERB

Fault

When anyone told Isze-loo that he had a fault, he rejoiced.
MENCIUS: *Discourses,* II, *c.* 300 B.C.

He who overlooks one fault invites another.
PUBLILIUS SYRUS: *Sententiæ, c.* 50 B.C.

When we try to avoid one fault we are led to the opposite, unless we be very careful.
HORACE: *De arte poetica, c.* 8 B.C.

I have not hated the man, but his faults.
MARTIAL: *Epigrams,* II, 86

His only fault is that he has no fault.
PLINY THE YOUNGER: *Letters,* IX, *c.* 110

There are six faults which a man ought to avoid: the desire of riches, drowsiness, sloth, idleness, tediousness, fear, and anger.
The Hitopadesa, I, *c.* 500

A fault excused is twice committed.
ENGLISH PROVERB, traced by Apperson to *c.* 1590

A fault confessed is more than half amended.
Anon.: *Arden of Feversham,* IV, 1592

I will chide no breather in the world but myself, against whom I know most faults.
SHAKESPEARE: *As You Like It,* III, *c.* 1600

A fault to Heaven,
A fault against the dead, a fault to nature,
To reason most absurd.
SHAKESPEARE: *Hamlet,* I, *c.* 1601

Condemn the fault, and not the actor of it.
SHAKESPEARE: *Measure for Measure,* II, 1604

They say, best men are molded out of faults,
And, for the most, become much more the better
For being a little bad.
SHAKESPEARE: *Measure for Measure,* V

Every man has his fault.
SHAKESPEARE: *Timon of Athens,* III, *c.* 1607

Bad men excuse their faults; good men will leave them.
BEN JONSON: *Catiline,* III, 1611

Great men's faults are never small.
JOHN CLARKE: *Parœmiologia Anglo-Latina,* 1639

Faults are thick where love is thin.
JAMES HOWELL: *Proverbs,* 1659

If we had no faults, we should not take so much pleasure in noting those of others.
LA ROCHEFOUCAULD: *Maxims,* 1665

In the intercourse of life, we please more by our faults than by our good qualities. IBID.

It belongs only to great men to have great faults. IBID.

We confess to small faults to persuade others that we are free of great ones. IBID.

We often take credit for faults opposite to those we have; when we are weak we boast of being obstinate. IBID.

If a friend tell thee a fault, imagine always that he telleth thee not the whole.
THOMAS FULLER: *Introductio ad Prudentiam,* I, 1731

Everyone lays his faults upon the time.
THOMAS FULLER: *Gnomologia,* 1732

The first faults are theirs that commit them;
The second faults are theirs that permit them.
IBID.

There are some faults so nearly allied to excellence that we can scarce weed out the vice without eradicating the virtue.
OLIVER GOLDSMITH: *The Good Natur'd Man,* I, 1768

The pleasure I get out of observing one of my faults is often greater than the chagrin caused by the fault itself.
G. C. LICHTENBERG: *Reflections,* 1799

A fault confessed
Is a new virtue added to a man.
J. S. KNOWLES: *The Love-Chase,* I, 1837

The greatest of faults is to be conscious of none.
THOMAS CARLYLE: *Heroes and Hero-Worship,* II, 1840 (Lecture in London, May 8)

Every man in his lifetime needs to thank his faults.
R. W. EMERSON: *Compensation,* 1841

We forget a fault when we have confessed it, but the person to whom we confess doesn't forget it.
F. W. NIETZSCHE: *Human All-too-Human,* I, 1878

Justifying a fault doubles it.
FRENCH PROVERB

Conscious of no fault. (Non conscire sibi.)
LATIN PHRASE

No one is prevented by his own faults from pointing out those of another.
LATIN PROVERB

He who loves not the loved one's faults does not truly love. SPANISH PROVERB

[*See also* Friendship.

Faultless

Whoever thinks a faultless piece to see,
Thinks what ne'er was, nor is, nor e'er shall be.
ALEXANDER POPE: *An Essay on Criticism,* II, 1711

Faultless to a fault.
ROBERT BROWNING: *The Ring and the Book,* IX, 1868

He's lifeless that's faultless.
SCOTTISH PROVERB

[*See also* Fault, Perfection.

Favor

Accept a favor, and you sell your liberty.
PUBLILIUS SYRUS: *Sententiæ, c.* 50 B.C.

The feelings of men looking for favors are very different from those of the same men after obtaining them.
DIONYSIUS OF HALICARNASSUS: *Antiquities of Rome*, V, *c.* 20 B.C.

The first favor that is refused wipes out all that have been granted.
PLINY THE YOUNGER: *Letters*, III, *c.* 110

A favor which is tardily bestowed is no favor at all. AUSONIUS: *Epigrams*, *c.* 360

Oh, how wretched
Is that poor man that hangs on princes' favors!
There is betwixt that smile we would aspire to,
That sweet aspect of princes, and their ruin,
More pangs and fears than wars or women have. SHAKESPEARE and JOHN FLETCHER: *Henry VIII*, III, 1613

Almost everyone takes pleasure in repaying small favors, and many people are grateful also for moderate ones, but hardly anyone fails to show ingratitude for great ones.
LA ROCHEFOUCAULD: *Maxims*, 1665

Men are shamed by favors.
IMMANUEL KANT: Lecture at Königsberg, 1775

Those who have had, and who may yet have, occasion to ask great favors, should never ask small ones.
THOMAS JEFFERSON: *Letter to General Lafayette*, 1786

Men are never attached to you by favors.
NAPOLEON I: To Gaspard Gourgaud at St. Helena, 1815–1818

A denial of a favor is not an invasion of a right.
J. FENIMORE COOPER: *The American Democrat*, XI, 1838

Ask a favor in the day-time.
WEST AFRICAN PROVERB

[*See also* Gratitude, Kiss, Prince.

Fawning

[*See* Flattery.

Fear

He that fleeth from the fear shall fall into the pit; and he that getteth up out of the pit shall be taken in the snare.
JEREMIAH XLVIII, 44, *c.* 625 B.C.

The fear of the Lord is the beginning of knowledge.
PROVERBS I, 7, *c.* 350 B.C. (Cf. PSALMS CXI, 10, *c.* 150 B.C., where *knowledge* is changed to *wisdom*. Cf. also JOB XXVIII, 28, *c.* 325 B.C.; PROVERBS X, 27; XIV, 26; XV, 33; XIX, 23)

Fear is pain arising from the anticipation of evil.
ARISTOTLE: *Rhetoric*, BOOK II, *c.* 322 B.C.

No one can love the man he fears. IBID.

He who does not blush and has no fear has the first principles of every kind of baseness.
Ascribed to DIPHILUS, *c.* 300 B.C.

Fear is a bad guardian for a thing that ought to last. CICERO: *De officiis*, II, 78 B.C.

In times of peril fear has no pity.
JULIUS CÆSAR: *The Gallic War*, VII, 51 B.C.

Who can love either him whom he fears, or him by whom he thinks he is feared?
CICERO: *De amicitia*, *c.* 50 B.C.

He who is feared by many must fear many.
PUBLILIUS SYRUS: *Sententiæ*, *c.* 50 B.C.

Fear always represents objects in their worst light. LIVY: *History of Rome*, XXVII, *c.* 10

He who has vain fears deserves those that are real. SENECA: *Oedipus*, *c.* 60

Fear is a feeling that is stronger than love.
PLINY THE YOUNGER: *Letters*, I, *c.* 110

Sudden terrors alarm even the bravest.
TACITUS: *Annals*, XV, *c.* 110

Fear is the foundation of safety.
TERTULLIAN: *Women's Dress*, *c.* 220

If fear were not a good thing, fathers would not have set schoolmasters over their children, nor lawgivers magistrates for cities.
ST. JOHN CHRYSOSTOM: *Homilies*, XV, *c.* 388

Men do with less remorse offend against those who desire to be beloved than against those who are ambitious of being feared, and the reason is because love is fastened only by a ligament of obligation, which the ill-nature of mankind breaks upon every occasion that is presented to his profit; but fear depends upon an apprehension of punishment, which is never to be dispelled.
NICCOLÒ MACHIAVELLI: *The Prince*, XVII, 1513

Fear oftentimes restraineth words, but makes not thoughts to cease.
THOMAS VAUX: *Content*, *c.* 1550

He that feareth every bush must never go a-birding.
JOHN LYLY: *Euphues and His England*, 1580

Who feareth to suffer, suffereth already, because he feareth.
MICHEL DE MONTAIGNE: *Essays*, III, 1588

The souls of men are full of dread.
SHAKESPEARE: *Richard III*, II, *c.* 1592

They spake not a word;
But, like dumb statues, or breathing stones,
Gazed each on other, and look'd deadly pale.
SHAKESPEARE: *Richard III*, III

In the night, imagining some fear,
How easy is a bush supposed a bear.
SHAKESPEARE: *A Midsummer Night's Dream,* V, *c.* 1596

I have a faint cold fear thrills through my veins,
That almost freezes up the heat of life.
SHAKESPEARE: *Romeo and Juliet,* IV, *c.* 1596

To fear the worst oft cures the worst.
SHAKESPEARE: *Troilus and Cressida,* III, *c.* 1601

Our fears do make us traitors.
SHAKESPEARE: *Macbeth,* IV, *c.* 1605

Fear has many eyes.
CERVANTES: *Don Quixote,* II, 1615

Those who love to be feared, fear to be loved; they themselves are of all people the most abject; some fear them, but they fear every one.
Ascribed to ST. FRANCIS DE SALES (1567–1622) in J. P. CAMUS: *L'esprit de Saint François de Sales,* 1641

Fear is the love that's due to gods and princes.
Anon.: *Nero,* II, 1624

He that knows no guilt can know no fear.
PHILIP MASSINGER: *The Great Duke of Florence,* IV, 1636

There is no medicine for fear.
DAVID FERGUSSON: *Scottish Proverbs,* 1641

How often the fear of one evil leads us into a worse!
NICOLAS BOILEAU: *L'Art poétique,* I, 1674

There is no fear without some hope, and no hope without some fear.
BARUCH SPINOZA: *Ethica,* III, 1677

Do you think I was born in a wood to be afraid of an owl?
JONATHAN SWIFT: *Polite Conversation,* 1738

Fear follows crime, and is its punishment.
VOLTAIRE: *Sémiramis,* I, 1748

Everything is dangerous to him that is afraid of it.
BENJAMIN WHICHCOTE: *Moral and Religious Aphorisms,* 1753

The man who fears nothing is as powerful as he who is feared by everybody.
J. C. F. SCHILLER: *The Robbers,* I, 1781

Nothing is so rash as fear; and the counsels of pusillanimity very rarely put off, whilst they are always sure to aggravate, the evils from which they should fly.
EDMUND BURKE: *Letters on a Regicide Peace,* I, 1797

Like one, that on a lonesome road
Doth walk in fear and dread,
And having once turned round, walks on,
And turns no more his head;
Because he knows a frightful fiend
Doth close behind him tread.
S. T. COLERIDGE: *The Ancient Mariner,* VI, 1798

As a man grows older it is harder and harder to frighten him.
JEAN PAUL RICHTER: *Levana,* III, 1807

The first duty of man is that of subduing fear. We must get rid of fear; we cannot act at all till then. A man's acts are slavish, not true but specious; his very thoughts are false, he thinks too as a slave and coward, till he have got fear under his feet.
THOMAS CARLYLE: *Heroes and Hero-Worship,* I, 1840 (Lecture in London, May 5)

We are afraid of truth, afraid of fortune, afraid of death, and afraid of each other.
R. W. EMERSON: *Self-Reliance,* 1841

He has not learned the lesson of life who does not every day surmount a fear.
R. W. EMERSON: *Courage,* 1877

The only thing we have to fear is fear itself.
F. D. ROOSEVELT: Inaugural address, March 4, 1933

In a love without fear there is something wanting. ARAB PROVERB

Fear gives intelligence even to fools.
FRENCH PROVERB

Fear is the greatest of all inventors. IBID.

A coward's fear makes a brave man braver.
SCOTTISH PROVERB

Fear always goeth armed.
SPANISH PROVERB

Three fears weaken the heart: fear of the truth, fear of poverty, and fear of the Devil.
WELSH PROVERB

[*See also* Animal, Belief, Caution, Courage, Coward, Daring, Death, Despotism, Doubt, Faith, Fault, Hatred, Hell, Hero, Hope, Humanity, Joy, Law, Love, Moderation, Money, Morality, Motive, Nobility, Perplexity, Poor, Populace, Religion, Society, Strength, Superiority, Travel, Trembling, Weakness.

Fearfully

I am fearfully and wonderfully made.
PSALMS CXXXIX, 14, *c.* 150 B.C.

Feast

Small cheer and great welcome makes a merry feast.
SHAKESPEARE: *The Comedy of Errors,* III, 1593

As much valor is to be found in feasting as in fighting, and some of our city captains and carpet knights will make this good, and prove it.
ROBERT BURTON: *The Anatomy of Melancholy,* I, 1621

The feast of reason, and the flow of soul.
ALEXANDER POPE: *The First Satire of the Second Book of Horace*, 1733

Dutch feast: where the entertainer gets drunk before his guests.
FRANCIS GROSE: *A Classical Dictionary of the Vulgar Tongue*, 1785

[*See also* Clergyman, Eating, Haste.

February

All the months in the year,
Curse a fair Februeer.
THOMAS FULLER: *Gnomologia*, 1732

February brings the rain,
Thaws the frozen lake again.
SARA COLERIDGE: *Pretty Lessons in Verse*, 1834

The February born will find
Sincerity and peace of mind;
Freedom from passion and from care
If they the pearl will wear.
Author unidentified (Sometimes *amethyst* is substituted for *pearl*)

If February give much snow
A fine Summer it doth foreshow.
ENGLISH RHYME

Rain in February is as good as manure.
FRENCH PROVERB

February, the shortest month in the year, is also the worst. ITALIAN PROVERB

[*See also* Months.

Fecundity

[*See* Fruitfulness.

Fee

[*See* Lawsuit, Lawyer, Physician.

Feeble-minded

[*See* Sterilization.

Feeling

Those who would make us feel must feel themselves.
CHARLES CHURCHILL: *The Rosciad*, 1761

Some feelings are to mortals given,
With less of earth in them than Heaven.
WALTER SCOTT: *The Lady of the Lake*, II, 1810

Feeling is any portion of consciousness which occupies a place sufficiently large to give it a perceivable individuality.
HERBERT SPENCER: *The Principles of Psychology*, II, 1855

The ennobling difference between one man and another, — between one animal and another, — is precisely in this, that one feels more than another.
JOHN RUSKIN: *Sesame and Lilies*, I, 1865

Only one absolute certainty is possible to man, namely, that at any given moment the feeling which he has exists.
T. H. HUXLEY: *Letter to J. G. T. Sinclair*, July 21, 1890

It is the hardest thing in the world to put feeling, and deep feeling, into words. From the standpoint of expression, it is easier to write a "Das Kapital" in four volumes than a simple lyric of as many stanzas.
JACK LONDON: To Anna Strunsky Walling, Dec. 27, 1899

Individuality is founded in feeling; and the recesses of feeling, the darker, blinder strata of character, are the only places in the world in which we catch real fact in the making.
WILLIAM JAMES: *The Varieties of Religious Experience*, XX, 1902

[*See also* Art, Music.

Feeling, Good

The Era of Good Feeling.
The period from 1817 to 1824, when party enmities were abated in the United States; the term was first used in the Boston Centinel, July 12, 1817

Feet

[*See* Foot.

Fellow-feeling

A fellow-feeling makes one wondrous kind.
DAVID GARRICK: Prologue written for his last performance, June 10, 1776

Fellowship

They gave to me and Barnabas the right hands of fellowship. GALATIANS II, 9, *c.* 50

What men call . . . good fellowship is commonly but the virtue of pigs in a litter, which lie close together to keep each other warm.
H. D. THOREAU: *Journal*, Oct. 23, 1852

Fellowship is Heaven, and lack of fellowship is Hell; fellowship is life, and lack of fellowship is death; and the deeds that ye do upon the earth, it is for fellowship's sake that ye do them.
WILLIAM MORRIS: *The Dream of John Ball*, 1888

Female

The female contains all qualities, and tempers them — she is in her place, and moves with perfect balance;
She is all things duly veil'd — she is both passive and active.
WALT WHITMAN: *I Sing the Body Electric*, 1855

The female of the species is more deadly than the male.
RUDYARD KIPLING: *The Female of the Species*, 1911 (Ladies' Home Journal, Nov.)

[*See also* Woman.

Feminine

The eternal feminine. (Das Ewig-Weibliche.)
J. W. GOETHE: *II Faust*, II, 1832

[*See also* Moon, Woman.

Ferry

No toll for the use of a ferry shall be paid by a hermit, a student who is a Brahmin, or a woman more than two months pregnant.
THE CODE OF MANU, VIII, *c.* 100

I have always had a passion for ferries; to me they afford inimitable, streaming, never-failing, living poems.
WALT WHITMAN: *Specimen Days*, 1882

[*See also* Haste.

Fetter

No man loveth his fetters, be they made of gold.
JOHN HEYWOOD: *Proverbs*, 1546

So free we seem, so fettered fast we are!
ROBERT BROWNING: *Andrea del Sarto*, 1855

Feudalism

[*See* Church (Roman Catholic).

Fever

By a superabundance of bile fever is produced.
ST. JOHN CHRYSOSTOM: *Homilies*, X, *c.* 388

So, when a raging fever burns,
We shift from side to side by turns;
And 't is a poor relief we gain
To change the place, but keep the pain.
ISAAC WATTS: *Hymns and Spiritual Songs*, 1707

Fevers are errors of various types. The quickened pulse, coated tongue, febrile heat, dry skin, pain in the head and limbs, are pictures drawn on the body by a mortal mind.
MARY BAKER G. EDDY: *Science and Health*, XII, 1908

[*See also* Bleeding.

Few

[*See* Many.

Fickleness

[*See* Fortune, French.

Fiction

If this were played upon a stage now, I could condemn it as an improbable fiction.
SHAKESPEARE: *Twelfth Night*, III, *c.* 1601

I am reading an idle tale, not expecting wit or truth in it, and very glad it is not metaphysics to puzzle my judgment, or history to mislead my opinion.
MARY WORTLEY MONTAGU: *Letter to the Countess of Bute*, Sept. 30, 1757

Fiction lags after truth.
EDMUND BURKE: Speech on Conciliation with America, March 22, 1775

Fiction, unlike history, has the softenings of fancy and sentiment; and we read on in the hope of something like poetical justice to be done at last, which is more than we can reckon upon in reality.
WILLIAM HAZLITT: *The Influence of Books on the Progress of Manners*, 1828 (New Monthly Magazine, May)

Every writer of fiction, although he may not adopt the dramatic form, writes in effect for the stage.
CHARLES DICKENS: Speech in Edinburgh, March 26, 1858

The good end happily, the bad unhappily. That is what fiction means.
OSCAR WILDE: *The Importance of Being Earnest*, III, 1895

[*See also* Tragedy, Truth.

Fiddler

There were three roaring fiddlers
Came lately out of France,
That light and nimbly can
Teach maidens how to dance.
Anon.: *Choice of Inventions*, II, *c.* 1575

Fiddlers, dogs and flies come to feasts uncalled.
DAVID FERGUSSON: *Scottish Proverbs*, 1641

Fiddlers' fare: meat, drink, and money.
JOHN TAYLOR: *Wandering to See the Wonders of the West*, 1649

In the house of a fiddler all fiddle.
GEORGE HERBERT: *Outlandish Proverbs*, 1640

The least boy always carries the greatest fiddle.
JOHN RAY: *English Proverbs*, 1670

He was a fiddler, and consequently a rogue.
JONATHAN SWIFT: *Journal to Stella*, July 25, 1711

There is nothing, I think, in which the power of art is shown so much as in playing the fiddle. In all other things we can do something at first. Any man will forge a bar of iron, if you give him a hammer; not so well as a smith, but tolerably. A man will saw a piece of wood, and make a box, though a clumsy one; but give him a fiddle and a fiddle-stick, and he can do nothing.
SAMUEL JOHNSON: *Boswell's Life*, April 15, 1773

Old King Cole was a merry old soul,
And a merry old soul was he;
He called for his pipe and he called for his bowl,
And he called for his fiddlers three.
Author unidentified

In the fiddler's house all are dancers.
FRENCH PROVERB

[*See also* Author, Dancer, King Cole, Musician, Violin.

Fidelity

Fidelity that is bought with money may be overcome by money.
SENECA: *Agamemnon, c.* 60

[*See also* Faithful.

Fielding, Henry (1707–54)

Richardson used to say that had he not known who Fielding was he should have believed he was an ostler.
SAMUEL JOHNSON: *Boswell's Life,* April 6, 1772

He was a blockhead. IBID.

What a master of composition Fielding was! Upon my word, I think the "Oedipus Tyrannus," the "Alchemist," and "Tom Jones" the three most perfect plots ever planned. And how charming, how wholesome, Fielding always is! To take him up after Richardson is like emerging from a sick room heated by stoves into an open lawn, on a breezy day in May.
S. T. COLERIDGE: *Table-Talk,* July 5, 1834

Fiend

[*See* Hell.

Fierceness

The fiercer animals are, the less intelligence they have.
J. O. DE LA METTRIE: *L'Homme machine,* 1748

Make your faces fierce. (Faccia feroce.)
Command in the Neapolitan Army, 1848

Fife

The vile squeaking of his wry-necked fife.
SHAKESPEARE: *The Merchant of Venice,* II, *c.* 1597

Fifty

He who at fifty is a fool
Is far too stubborn grown for school.
CHARLES COTTON: *Visions,* 1670

At fifty one can no longer love.
NAPOLEON I: To Gaspard Gourgaud at St. Helena, April 7, 1817

At fifty years, 'tis said, afflicted citizens lose their sick headaches.
R. W. EMERSON: *Society and Solitude,* 1870

After a man is fifty you can fool him by saying he is smart, but you can't fool him by saying he is pretty.
E. W. HOWE: *Country Town Sayings,* 1911

[*See also* Ages, Husband, Superannuation.

Fifty-five

If truth in spite of manners must be told,
Why really fifty-five is something old.
THOMAS PARNELL: *To an Old Beauty,* 1722

Fighter

A man that will fight may find a cudgel in every hedge.
JOHN CLARKE: *Parœmiologia Anglo-Latina,* 1639

So 'ere's to you, Fuzzy-Wuzzy, at your 'ome in the Soudan;
You're a pore benighted 'eathen but a first-class fightin' man.
RUDYARD KIPLING: *Fuzzy-Wuzzy,* 1890

Fighting

Even the bravest cannot fight beyond his strength. HOMER: *Iliad,* XIII, *c.* 800 B.C.

Fight on, my men, Sir Andrew says,
A little I'm hurt, but yet not slain;
I'll but lie down and bleed awhile,
And then I'll rise and fight again.
Anon.: *Sir Andrew Barton, c.* 1550

It is fighting at great disadvantage to fight those who have nothing to lose.
FRANCESCO GUICCIARDINI: *Storia d'Italia,* 1564

Fight dog, fight bear.
ENGLISH PROVERB, traced by Apperson to 1583

'Tis no festival unless there be some fighting.
THOMAS HALL: *Funebria Florae,* 1660

He that is valiant and dare fight,
Though drubbed, can lose no honor by 't.
SAMUEL BUTLER: *Hudibras,* I, 1663

It is impossible to express unto another how a smart sea-fight elevates the spirits of a man, and makes him despise all dangers. In and after all sea-fights I have been very thirsty.
THOMAS BROWNE II: *Letter to his father,* July 16, 1666

Most sorts of diversion in men, children, and other animals, are in imitation of fighting.
JONATHAN SWIFT: *Thoughts on Various Subjects,* 1706

There is a time to pray and a time to fight. This is the time to fight.
JOHN P. G. MUHLENBERG: Sermon at Woodstock, Va., 1775

One fights well when one's heart is light.
NAPOLEON I: To Gaspard Gourgaud at St. Helena, Feb. 17, 1816

An Irishman fights before he reasons, a Scotchman reasons before he fights, an Englishman is not particular as to the order of precedence, but will do either to accommodate his customers. C. C. COLTON: *Lacon,* 1820

It is the ignorant and childish part of mankind that is the fighting part. Idle and vacant minds want excitement, as all boys kill cats.
R. W. EMERSON: *War,* 1849

There was a blow. Somebody fell. We got up. Turning upon our antagonist, we then suc-

ceeded in winding his arms around our waist, and by a quick manoeuvre threw him on top of us, bringing our back at the same time in contact with the bed of the printing-press. Then, inserting our nose between his teeth, and our hands in his hair, we had him.
Ascribed to an unnamed Iowa editor, *c.* 1855

Go in anywhere, Colonel! You'll find lovely fighting along the whole line.
PHILIP KEARNY: At the battle of Seven Pines, May 31, 1862

You should never wear your best trousers when you go out to fight for liberty and truth.
HENRIK IBSEN: *An Enemy of the People,* V, 1882

For the Lord abideth back of me to guide my fighting arm.
RUDYARD KIPLING: *Mulholland's Contract,* 1894

Do not get into a fight if you can possibly avoid it. If you get in, see it through. Don't hit if it is honorably possible to avoid hitting, but never hit soft. Don't hit at all if you can help it; don't hit a man if you can possibly avoid it; but if you do hit him, put him to sleep.
THEODORE ROOSEVELT: Speech in Washington, Jan. 24, 1918

It isn't the size of the dog in the fight that counts; it's the size of the fight in the dog.
Author unidentified

Thrice is he armed that hath his quarrel just;
And four times he who gets his fist in fust.
IBID.

When a man fights it means that a fool has lost his argument. CHINESE PROVERB

It's an ill fight where he that wins has the warst o't. SCOTTISH PROVERB

[*See also* Antagonist, Battle, Discretion, Fight, German, Irishman, Pistol, Pride, Soldier, War.

Fig-leaf

The eyes of them both were opened, and they knew that they were naked; and they sewed fig leaves together, and made themselves aprons. GENESIS III, 7, *c.* 700 B.C.

[*See also* Breeches.

Fig-tree

Judah and Israel dwelt safely, every man under his vine and under his fig tree, from Dan even to Beer-sheba.
I KINGS IV, 25, *c.* 500 B.C.

Figures

Figures never lie.
ENGLISH PROVERB, apparently not recorded before the XIX century

You may prove anything by figures.
THOMAS CARLYLE: *Chartism,* II, 1839

Figures are not party men.
BENJAMIN DISRAELI: Speech in the House of Commons, July 28, 1846

Figures don't lie, but liars figure.
Author unidentified

[*See also* Statistics.

Filipino

Damn, damn, damn the Filipinos!
Cross-eyed kakiak ladrones!
Underneath the starry flag
Civilize 'em with a Krag,
And return us to our own belovèd homes.
Anon.: Chorus of song sung by American troops in the Philippines, 1899

There was once a Filipino *hombre*
Who ate rice, *pescado y legumbre.*
His trousers were wide
And his shirt hung outside,
And that was his regular *costumbre.*
Anon.: *The Filipino Hombre, c.* 1900

We favor an immediate declaration of the nation's purpose to give the Filipinos, first, a stable form of government; second, independence, and third, protection from outside interference, such as has been given for nearly a century to the republics of Central and South America.
Democratic National Platform, 1900

[*See also* Philippines.

Finance

Financial sense is knowing that certain men will promise to do certain things, and fail.
E. W. HOWE: *Sinner Sermons,* 1926

Finance, Public

No money shall be drawn from the treasury but in consequence of appropriations made by law; and a regular statement and account of the receipts and expenditures of all public money shall be published from time to time.
CONSTITUTION OF THE UNITED STATES, Art. I, 1789

The accounts of the United States ought to be, and may be made, as simple as those of a common farmer, and capable of being understood by common farmers.
THOMAS JEFFERSON: *Letter to James Madison,* 1796

Financier

A financier is a pawnbroker with imagination.
A. W. PINERO: *The Second Mrs. Tanqueray,* II, 1893

Financiers live in a world of illusion. They count on something which they call the capital of the country, which has no existence. Every five dollars they count as a hundred dollars; and that means that every financier, every banker, every stockbroker, is 95% a lunatic. And it is in the hands of these lunatics that you leave the fate of your country!
GEORGE BERNARD SHAW: Address in New York, April 11, 1933

Finding

Findings are keepings.

ENGLISH PROVERB, apparently not recorded before the XIX century

Finding things is not forbidden anywhere.

WEST AFRICAN PROVERB

Finery

Can a maid forget her ornaments, or a bride her attire? JEREMIAH II, 32, *c.* 625 B.C.

A woman's appearance depends upon two things: the clothes she wears and the time she gives to her toilet. . . . Against the first we bring the charge of ostentation, against the second of harlotry.

TERTULLIAN: *Women's Dress, c.* 220

With silken coats, and caps, and golden rings,
With ruffs, and cuffs, and farthingales, and things;
With scarfs, and fans, and double change of bravery,
With amber-bracelets, beads, and all this knavery.

SHAKESPEARE: *The Taming of the Shrew,* IV, 1594

Fine feathers make fine birds.

ENGLISH PROVERB, traced by Apperson to JOHN DAVIES: *The Scourge of Folly, c.* 1610

There is a desire in women to go neat and fine, and it is a comely thing to be adorned with that that in God's sight is of great price.

JOHN BUNYAN: *Pilgrim's Progress,* II, 1678

If lust and wanton eyes are the death of the soul, can any women think themselves innocent who, with naked breasts, patched faces, and every ornament of dress, invite the eye to offend?

WILLIAM LAW: *A Serious Call to a Devout and Holy Life,* XIX, 1728

A modest woman, dressed out in all her finery, is the most tremendous object of the whole creation.

OLIVER GOLDSMITH: *She Stoops to Conquer,* II, 1773

I found that my ribbons and gew-gaws were dragging me down to Hell, and so I took them off and gave them to my sister.

S. L. CLEMENS (MARK TWAIN): *Letter from New York to the Alta Californian* (San Francisco), May 18, 1867 (Ascribed to "a pious girl")

[*See also* Dress, Jewelry, Ornament.

Finger

The bones of her fingers ran out at length when you prest 'em, they are so gently delicate.

BEN JONSON: *Cynthia's Revels,* V, 1601

Fingers were made before forks, and hands before knives.

JONATHAN SWIFT: *Polite Conversation,* II, 1738

I am shocked sometimes at the shape of my own fingers, not for their resemblance to the ape tribe (which is something), but for the exquisite adaptation of them to the purposes of picking, fingering, etc. No one that is so framed, I maintain it, but should tremble.

CHARLES LAMB: *Letter to Bernard Barton,* Dec. 1, 1824

A boy born with fingers like a girl will make an easy living. CHINESE PROVERB

A pointing finger never says "Look here"; it says "Look there." JAMAICAN PROVERB

[*See also* Eating.

Finger-nail

Cut them on Monday, cut them for health;
Cut them on Tuesday, cut them for wealth;
Cut them on Wednesday, cut them for news;
Cut them on Thursday, a pair of new shoes;
Cut them on Friday, cut them for sorrow;
Cut them on Saturday, see your true love tomorrow;
Cut them on Sunday your safety seek,
The Devil will have you the rest of the week.

OLD ENGLISH RHYME

Finland

Finland is the country of the Devil.

RUSSIAN PROVERB

Fire

Behold, how great a matter a little fire kindleth.

JAMES III, 5, *c.* 60

Fire and pride cannot be hid.

ENGLISH PROVERB, traced by Apperson to *c.* 1375

As the spirits of darkness be stronger in the dark, so good spirits are augmented not only by the divine light of the sun, but also by our common wood-fire; and as the celestial fire drives away dark spirits, so also this our fire of wood doth the same.

CORNELIUS AGRIPPA VON NITTESHEIM: *De occulta philosophia,* I, 1510

A little fire is quickly trodden out;
Which, being suffer'd, rivers cannot quench.

SHAKESPEARE: *III Henry VI,* IV, *c.* 1591

Fire that's closest kept burns most of all.

SHAKESPEARE: *Two Gentlemen of Verona,* I, *c.* 1595

One fire burns out another's burning.

SHAKESPEARE: *Romeo and Juliet,* I, *c.* 1596

The fat's in the fire.

JOHN MARSTON: *What You Will,* 1607

A fair fire makes a room gay.

JOHN RAY: *English Proverbs,* 1670

If you light your fire at both ends the middle will shift for itself.

ENGLISH PROVERB, quoted in *The Spectator,* Jan. 3, 1712, as "the old kitchen proverb"

Heap logs and let the blaze laugh out.
ROBERT BROWNING: *Paracelsus,* III, 1835

I hear the alarm at dead of night,
I hear bells — shouts! — I pass the crowd — I run!
The sight of the flames maddens me with pleasure.
WALT WHITMAN: *Poem of Joys,* 1860

What matter how the night behaved?
What matter how the North-wind raved?
Blow high, blow low, not all its snow
Could quench our hearth-fire's ruddy glow.
J. G. WHITTIER: *Snow-Bound,* 1866

If the fire roars there will be a quarrel in the family. AMERICAN PROVERB

A crooked log makes a better fire than a straight one. FRENCH PROVERB

[*See also* Cause and Effect, Evil, Experience, Fire and Water, Frying-pan, Iron, Smoke, Water.

Fire and Water

Fire is love and water sorrow.
ENGLISH PROVERB, traced by Apperson to 1590

Fire and water are good servants but bad masters.
ENGLISH PROVERB, traced by Apperson and Smith to 1692 (The *water* half goes back to 1562)

When fire and water are at war it is the fire that always loses. SPANISH PROVERB

[*See also* Ship.

Firearms

[*See* Cannon, Gun.

Fireman

What ye cannot quench, pull down;
Spoil a house to save a town.
ROBERT HERRICK: *Hesperides,* 1648

She's the only gal I love,
With a face like a horse and buggy:
Leaning up against the lake,
O fireman, save my child!
Anon.: *Fireman, Save My Child, c.* 1875

Fireside

[*See* Home.

Firmament

This most excellent canopy, the air, look you, this brave o'erhanging firmament, this majestical roof fretted with golden fire, why it appears no other thing to me than a foul and pestilent congregation of vapors.
SHAKESPEARE: *Hamlet,* II, *c.* 1601

[*See also* Sky.

Firmness

The superior man is firm in the right way, and not merely firm.
CONFUCIUS: *Analects,* XV, *c.* 500 B.C.

Be like a rocky headland on which the waves break incessantly, but it stands fast and the waters sink to rest.
MARCUS AURELIUS: *Meditations,* IV, *c.* 170

Stand firm as a tower, which never shakes its top, no matter what winds are blowing.
DANTE: *Purgatorio,* V, *c.* 1320

I will neither yield to the song of the siren nor the voice of the hyena, the tears of the crocodile nor the howling of the wolf.
GEORGE CHAPMAN, BEN JONSON and JOHN MARSTON: *Eastward Ho,* V, 1605

[*See also* King, Resolution.

First

Many that are first shall be last; and the last shall be first.
MARK X, 31, *c.* 70 A.D. (Cf. MATTHEW XIX, 30; XX, 16, *c.* 75; LUKE XIII, 30, *c.* 75)

First come, first served.
HENRY PORTER: *Two Angry Women of Abingdon,* IV, 1599

The first blow is as much as two.
GEORGE HERBERT: *Jacula Prudentum,* 1651

The first men in the world were a gardener, a plowman and a grazier.
THOMAS FULLER: *Gnomologia,* 1732

First amongst his equals. (Primus inter pares.)
LATIN PHRASE

First amongst them all. (Primus inter omnes.)
IBID.

The first is most right. RUSSIAN PROVERB

[*See also* Last, Meal.

First-born

All the firstborn are mine; for on the day that I smote all the firstborn in the land of Egypt I hallowed unto me all the firstborn in Israel, both man and beast: mine shall they be: I am the Lord. NUMBERS III, 13, *c.* 700 B.C.

First born, first fed.
THOMAS DRAXE: *Bibliotheca scholastica instructissima,* 1633

Fish

Like a fish out of water.
ENGLISH PHRASE, borrowed from the Greek, and familiar since the XIV century

There are as good fish in the sea as ever came out of it.
ENGLISH PROVERB, familiar in various forms since the XIV century

The great fish [eat] the small.
ALEXANDER BARCLAY: *The Ship of Fools,* 1509

All is fish that comes to the net.
ENGLISH PROVERB, traced by Apperson to *c.* 1520 (Sometimes " all is not ")

She is neither fish, nor flesh, nor good red herring. JOHN HEYWOOD: *Proverbs,* 1546

The sea hath fish for every man.
WILLIAM CAMDEN: *Remains Concerning Britain,* 1605

The best fish swim near the bottom.
JOHN CLARKE: *Parœmiologia Anglo-Latina,* 1639

I have other fish to fry.
ENGLISH PHRASE, traced by Apperson and Smith to 1660

Fish must swim thrice — once in the water, a second time in the sauce, and a third time in wine in the stomach.
JOHN RAY: *English Proverbs,* 1670

Ye monsters of the bubbling deep
Your Maker's praises spout;
Up from the sands ye codlings peep
And wag your tails about.
COTTON MATHER: *Hymn, c.* 1700

It is a silly fish that is caught twice with the same bait.
THOMAS FULLER: *Gnomologia,* 1732

That fish will soon be caught that nibbles at every bait. IBID.

Who hears the fishes when they cry?
H. D. THOREAU: *A Week on the Concord and Merrimack Rivers,* 1849

No human being, however great or powerful, was ever so free as a fish.
JOHN RUSKIN: *The Two Paths,* v, 1859

The biggest fish he ever caught were those that got away.
EUGENE FIELD: *Our Biggest Fish,* 1889

As lacking in privacy as a goldfish.
AMERICAN PHRASE, *c.* 1900

In still waters are the largest fish.
DANISH PROVERB

Little fish are sweet. DUTCH PROVERB

It is the sauce that makes the fish edible.
FRENCH PROVERB

The bigger the river the bigger the fish.
PORTUGUESE PROVERB

Nothing is so clean as a fish.
WELSH PROVERB

[*See also* Best, Evolution, Fasting, Fisherman, Fishing, Guest, Head, Herring, Old, Property, Struggle for Existence, Trout, Visiting.

Fisherman

The fishers also shall mourn, and all they that cast angle into the brooks shall lament, and they that spread nets upon the waters shall languish. ISAIAH XIX, 8, *c.* 700 B.C.

And he saith unto them, Follow me, and I will make you fishers of men.
MATTHEW IV, 19, *c.* 75

I am, sir, a brother of the angle.
IZAAK WALTON: *The Compleat Angler,* I, 1653

All that are lovers of virtue, and dare trust in His providence, and be quiet, and go a-angling.
IZAAK WALTON: *The Compleat Angler,* XXI

A fisherman's walk: three steps and overboard.
ENGLISH PHRASE, not recorded before the XIX century

Wha'll buy my caller herrin'?
The're no brought here without brave darin'.
Buy my caller herrin',
Ye little ken their worth.
Wha'll buy my caller herrin'?
Oh, you may ca' them vulgar farin',
Wives and mithers maist despairin'
Ca' them lives o' men.
Ascribed to CAROLINA, LADY NAIRNE (1766–1845)

Fishing

Canst thou draw out leviathan with an hook?
JOB XLI, 1, *c.* 325 B.C.

He was astonished, and all that were with him, at the draught of the fishes which they had taken. LUKE V, 9, *c.* 75

Simon Peter saith unto them, I go a fishing. They say unto him, We also go with thee. They went forth, and entered into a ship immediately, and that night they caught nothing. JOHN XXI, 3, *c.* 115

To fish in troubled waters.
ENGLISH PHRASE, familiar since the XVI century (Sometimes *muddied* is substituted for *troubled*)

All fish are not caught with flies.
JOHN LYLY: *Euphues,* 1579

A man may fish with the worm that hath eat of a king, and eat of the fish that hath fed of that worm.
SHAKESPEARE: *Hamlet,* IV, *c.* 1601

Give me mine angle, we'll to the river; there,
My music playing far off, I will betray
Tawny-finn'd fishes; my bended hook shall pierce
Their slimy jaws.
SHAKESPEARE: *Antony and Cleopatra,* II, *c.* 1606

If you swear you will catch no fish.
ENGLISH PROVERB, traced by Apperson to *c.* 1607

Angling may be said to be so like the mathematics that it can never be fully learnt.
IZAAK WALTON: *The Compleat Angler,* pref., 1653

Angling is somewhat like poetry, — men are to be born so.
IZAAK WALTON: *The Compleat Angler,* I

You will find angling to be like the virtue of humility, which has a calmness of spirit and a world of other blessings attending upon it.
IBID.

Of all the world's enjoyments
That ever valued were,
There's none of our employments
With fishing can compare.
THOMAS D'URFEY: *Pills to Purge Melancholy,* 1719

Still he fishes that catches one.
THOMAS FULLER: *Gnomologia,* 1732

Simple Simon went a-fishing
For to catch a whale,
But all the water he had got
Was in his mother's pail.
Nursery Rhyme, c. 1750

A stick and a string with a fly at one end and a fool at the other.
Author unidentified; familiar since the early XIX century

He minded not his friends' advice
But followed his own wishes;
And one most cruel trick of his
Was that of catching fishes.
JANE TAYLOR: *The Little Fisherman,* 1804

Old Peter Grimes made fishing his employ;
His wife he cabined with him and his boy,
And seemed that life laborious to enjoy.
GEORGE CRABBE: *Peter Grimes, c.* 1805

Anglers boast of the innocence of their pastime; yet it puts fellow-creatures to the torture. They pique themselves on their meditative faculties; and yet their only excuse is a want of thought.
LEIGH HUNT: *The Indicator,* XI, 1821

In other localities certain places in the streams are much better than others, but at Niagara one place is just as good as another, for the reason that the fish do not bite anywhere.
S. L. CLEMENS (MARK TWAIN): *Niagara,* 1875

Fish or cut bait. AMERICAN SAYING

When the wind is in the East,
Then the fishes bite the least;
When the wind is in the West,
Then the fishes bite the best;
When the wind is in the North,
Then the fishes do come forth;
When the wind is in the South,
It blows the bait in the fish's mouth.
OLD ENGLISH RHYME

[*See also* Fish, Fisherman, Frog, Trout.

Fist

I feel an army in my fist.
J. C. F. SCHILLER: *The Robbers,* II, 1781

[*See also* Bellicosity.

Fit

He's as fit as a fiddle.
ENGLISH SAYING, traced by Apperson to 1616

Flag

Have not I myself known five hundred living soldiers sabred into crows' meat for a piece of glazed cotton which they called their flag; which, had you sold it in any market-cross, would not have brought above three groschen?
THOMAS CARLYLE: *Sartor Resartus,* III, 1836

Trade follows the flag.
ENGLISH PROVERB, not recorded before the last quarter of the XIX century

[*See also* Jew.

Flag, American

And the star-spangled banner, oh, long may it wave,
O'er the land of the free and the home of the brave.
F. S. KEY: *The Star-Spangled Banner,* 1814 (Baltimore American, Sept. 16)

When Freedom from her mountain height
Unfurled her standard to the air,
She tore the azure robe of night
And set the stars of glory there.
J. R. DRAKE: *The American Flag,* 1819 (New York Evening Post, May 29)

Old Glory.
The first use of the name is ascribed to WILLIAM DRIVER, a ship captain, 1831

Ay, tear her tattered ensign down!
Long has it waved on high,
And many an eye has danced to see
That banner in the sky.
O. W. HOLMES: *Old Ironsides,* 1836

If anyone attempts to haul down the American flag, shoot him on the spot.
JOHN A. DIX: Order to the commandant at New Orleans, Jan. 29, 1861

A star for every state, and a state for every star.
R. C. WINTHROP: Speech in Boston, 1862

We'll rally round the flag, boys, we'll rally once again,
Shouting the battle-cry of freedom.
G. F. ROOT: *The Battle-Cry of Freedom,* 1863

"Shoot, if you must, this old gray head,
But spare your country's flag," she said.
J. G. WHITTIER: *Barbara Frietchie,* 1863 (Atlantic Monthly, Oct.)

Thick-sprinkled bunting! Flag of stars!
Long yet your road, fateful flag! – long yet your road, and lined with bloody death.

WALT WHITMAN: *Drum-Taps*, 1865

White is for purity, red for valor, blue for justice.

CHARLES SUMNER: *Are We a Nation?*, 1867

[*See also* Americanism, Merchant Marine.

Flag, Confederate

Furl that banner, for 'tis weary;
Round its staff 'tis drooping dreary;
Furl it, fold it, it is best;
For there's not a man to wave it,
And there's not a sword to save it,
And there's not one left to lave it
In the blood which heroes gave it;
And its foes now scorn and brave it;
Furl it, hide it, let it rest!

A. J. RYAN: *The Conquered Banner*, 1866

Flag, English

Where is the flag of England?
Go sail where rich galleons come
With shoddy and "loaded" cottons,
And beer and Bibles and rum;
Go, too, where brute force has triumphed,
And hypocrisy makes its lair;
And your question will find its answer,
For the flag of England is there.

HENRY LABOUCHÈRE: *Where Is the Flag of England?*, 1885

Flattery

A flattering mouth worketh ruin.

PROVERBS XXVI, 28, *c.* 350 B.C.

A man that flattereth his neighbor spreadeth a net for his feet. PROVERBS XXIX, 5

All flatterers are mercenary, and all low-minded men are flatterers.

ARISTOTLE: *Nicomachean Ethics*, IV, *c.* 340 B.C.

A flatterer is a friend who is your inferior, or pretends to be so.

ARISTOTLE: *Nicomachean Ethics*, VIII

Their throat is an open sepulchre; they flatter with their tongue.

PSALMS V, 9, *c.* 150 B.C.

Let flattery, the handmaid of vice, be kept out of friendship.

CICERO: *De amicitia*, *c.* 50 B.C.

Crows pick out the eyes of the dead, when they are no longer of any use. But flatterers destroy the souls of the living by blinding their eyes. EPICTETUS: *Encheiridion*, *c.* 110

But when I tell him he hates flatterers,
He says he does, being then most flattered.

SHAKESPEARE: *Julius Cæsar*, II, 1599

Why should the poor be flatter'd?
No, let the candied tongue lick absurd pomp,
And crook the pregnant hinges of the knee,
Where thrift may follow fawning.

SHAKESPEARE: *Hamlet*, III, *c.* 1601

He that loves to be flattered is worthy of the flatterer.

SHAKESPEARE: *Timon of Athens*, I, *c.* 1607

Flatterers look like friends, as wolves like dogs.

GEORGE CHAPMAN: *The Conspiracy of Byron*, III, 1608

The flatterer is blear-eyed to ill, and cannot see vices, and his tongue walks ever in one track of unjust praises, and can no more tell how to discommend than to speak true.

JOSEPH HALL (BISHOP OF NORWICH): *Characterisms of Vices*, 1608

Flattery is more dangerous than hatred.

BALTASAR GRACIÁN: *The Art of Worldly Wisdom*, LXXXIV, 1647

Take heed thou beest not a flatterer, for such an one showeth to have little opinion of the judgment of him whom he flattereth, holding him for a simple fellow.

FRANCIS HAWKINS: *Youth's Behavior*, I, 1663

If we did not flatter ourselves, the flattery of others would not hurt us.

LA ROCHEFOUCAULD: *Maxims*, 1665

When we think we hate flattery we only hate the manner of the flatterer. IBID.

When flatterers meet, the Devil goes to dinner.

JOHN RAY: *English Proverbs*, 1678

Love of flattery, in most men, proceeds from the mean opinion they have of themselves; in women, from the contrary.

JONATHAN SWIFT: *Thoughts on Various Subjects*, 1706

Among all the diseases of the mind, there is not one more epidemical, or more pernicious, than the love of flattery. First we flatter ourselves, and then the flattery of others is sure of success.

RICHARD STEELE: *The Spectator*, Dec. 3, 1711

There is no man of what capacity or penetration soever that is wholly proof against the witchcraft of flattery, if artfully performed and suited to his abilities.

BERNARD DE MANDEVILLE: *An Inquiry Into the Origin of Moral Virtue*, 1723

I love flattery so well, I would fain have some circumstances of probability added to it, that I might swallow it with comfort.

MARY WORTLEY MONTAGU: *Letter to the Countess of Mar*, 1725

He that rewards flattery begs it.

THOMAS FULLER: *Gnomologia*, 1732

Women have, in general, but one object, which is their beauty; upon which, scarce any

flattery is too gross for them to swallow. Nature has hardly formed a woman ugly enough to be insensible to flattery upon her person.
LORD CHESTERFIELD: *Letter to his son,* Oct. 16, 1747

Just praise is only a debt, but flattery is a present.
SAMUEL JOHNSON: *The Rambler,* Sept. 10, 1751

Every woman is infallibly to be gained by every sort of flattery, and every man by one sort or other.
LORD CHESTERFIELD: *Letter to his son,* March 16, 1752

Flattery is no more than what raises in a man's mind an idea of a preference which he has not.
EDMUND BURKE: *The Sublime and Beautiful,* I, 1756

When he whom everybody else flatters, flatters me, I then am truly happy.
SAMUEL JOHNSON: *Boswell's Life,* April 21, 1773

Let those flatter who fear: it is not an American art.
THOMAS JEFFERSON: *The Rights of British America,* 1774

Flattery corrupts both the receiver and the giver.
EDMUND BURKE: *Reflections on the Revolution in France,* 1790

He who says he hates all kinds of flattery, and says so in earnest, simply says that he has not yet become acquainted with all kinds of it. G. C. LICHTENBERG: *Reflections,* 1799

A little flattery will support a man through great fatigue.
JAMES MONROE: On being asked if he were not worn out by the attentions shown him as President, 1817 (ABIGAIL ADAMS: *Letter to F. A. Vanderkemp,* Jan. 24, 1818)

The flattery of the fool is always pungent and delicious.
W. M. PRAED: *On True Friendship, c.* 1830

Domestic flattery is the most dangerous of all flatteries.
HENRY TAYLOR: *The Statesman,* 1836

It is possible to be below flattery as well as above it. One who trusts nobody will not trust sycophants. One who does not value real glory will not value its counterfeit.
T. B. MACAULAY: *History of England,* II, 1848

What really flatters a man is that you think him worth flattering.
GEORGE BERNARD SHAW: *John Bull's Other Island,* IV, 1904

When a woman thinks she can't be flattered, tell her it's true; that flatters her.
Author unidentified

Flatterers, like cats, lick and then scratch.
GERMAN PROVERB

If you want to lick the old woman's pot, scratch her back. JAMAICAN PROVERB

[*See also* Epitaph, Fame, Friendship, Imitation, Poet, Praise, Prince, Slander, Song, Swift (Jonathan), Tyrant.

Flaubert, Gustave (1821–80)

Cheer up, old fellow! After all, you are Flaubert!
I. S. TURGENEV: To Flaubert, *c.* 1875

Flaubert bores me. What nonsense has been talked about him! Impersonal! Nonsense, he is the most personal writer I know. That odious pessimism! How sick I am of it! It never ceases, it is lugged in *à tout propos,* and the little lyrical phrase with which he winds up every paragraph, how boring it is.
GEORGE MOORE: *Confessions of a Young Man,* XI, 1888

Flea

He has a flea in his ear.
ENGLISH SAYING, familiar since the XV century (*i.e.,* he has something to think about)

That's a valiant flea that dare eat his breakfast on the lip of a lion.
SHAKESPEARE: *Henry V,* III, *c.* 1599

We shall have rain: the fleas bite.
JOHN CLARKE: *Parœmiologia Anglo-Latina,* 1639

Kill not a flea or other unclean vermin in the presence of others.
FRANCIS HAWKINS: *Youth's Behavior,* I, 1663

So, naturalists observe, a flea
Hath smaller fleas that on him prey;
And these have smaller still to bite 'em,
And so proceed *ad infinitum.*
JONATHAN SWIFT: *On Poetry,* 1712

Well washed and combed domestic pets grow dull; they miss the stimulus of fleas.
FRANCIS GALTON: *Inquiries Into Human Faculty,* 1883

A little flea sat on a rock,
Making a lonesome sound;
He did not know what to do with himself,
There being no dog around.
Ascribed to ROBINSON NEWBOLD, *c.* 1900

Kill a flea in March and you kill a hundred in Summer. AMERICAN PROVERB

When eager bites the thirsty flea
Clouds and rain you sure shall see.
OLD ENGLISH RHYME

[*See also* Dog, Fly, Haste, Horse, Precedence.

Flesh

The end of all flesh.
GENESIS VI, 13, *c.* 700 B.C.

All flesh is grass.
ISAIAH XL, 6, *c.* 700 B.C. (Cf. I PETER I, 24, *c.* 60)

The works of the flesh are manifest, which are these, Adultery, fornication, uncleanness, lasciviousness, idolatry, witchcraft, hatred, variance, emulations, wrath, strife, seditions, heresies, envyings, murders, drunkenness, revellings, and such like.
GALATIANS V, 19–21, *c.* 50

I see another law in my members, warring against the law of my mind, and bringing me into captivity to the law of sin which is in my members. ROMANS VII, 23, *c.* 55

All flesh is not the same flesh: but there is one kind of flesh of men, another flesh of beasts, another of fishes, and another of birds.
I CORINTHIANS XV, 39, *c.* 55

The spirit indeed is willing, but the flesh is weak. MATTHEW XXVI, 41, *c.* 75

Nothing good is engendered of the flesh.
POPE XYSTUS I: *The Ring*, *c.* 150

No one ever hated his own flesh.
ST. AUGUSTINE: *Of Continence*, *c.* 425

O flesh, flesh, how art thou fishified!
SHAKESPEARE: *Romeo and Juliet*, II, *c.* 1596

This bond is forfeit;
And lawfully by it this the Jew may claim
A pound of flesh.
SHAKESPEARE: *The Merchant of Venice*, IV, *c.* 1597

I have more flesh than another man; and therefore more frailty.
SHAKESPEARE: *I Henry IV*, III, *c.* 1598

The way of all flesh.
JOHN WEBSTER and THOMAS DEKKER: *Westward Ho*, II, 1605

"All flesh," says Paul, "is not the same flesh. There is one flesh of men; another of beasts; another of fishes; and another of birds." And what then? — nothing. A cook could have said as much.
THOMAS PAINE: *The Age of Reason*, II, 1794 (Cf. I CORINTHIANS, *ante*, *c.* 55)

I always see the Garden, and God there,
A-making man's wife — and, my lesson learned,
The value and significance of flesh,
I can't unlearn ten minutes afterwards.
ROBERT BROWNING: *Fra Lippo Lippi*, 1855

I believe in the flesh and the appetites;
Seeing, hearing, feeling, are miracles, and each part and tag of me is a miracle.
WALT WHITMAN: *Walt Whitman*, 1855

The horse bit the parson!
How came it to pass?
The horse heard the parson say,
"All flesh is grass."
H. J. LOARING: *Epitaphs Quaint, Curious and Elegant*, 1872

[*See also* Death, Fat, Fish, Meat.

Flesh and Blood

Am I but what I seem, mere flesh and blood,
A branching channel, with a mazy flood? . . .
I call it mine, not me.
JOHN ARBUTHNOT: *Know Thyself*, 1734

[*See also* Body, Bread.

Fleshpots

The fleshpots of Egypt.
ENGLISH PHRASE, borrowed from EXODUS XVI, 3, *c.* 700 B.C.

Flight

One pair of heels is worth two pair of hands.
THOMAS FULLER: *Gnomologia*, 1732

He who flees judgment confesses his guilt. (Fatetur facinus qui judicium fugit.)
LEGAL MAXIM

[*See also* Discretion.

Flirtation

Flirtation is at the bottom of woman's nature, although all do not practise it, some being restrained by fear, others by sense.
LA ROCHEFOUCAULD: *Maxims*, 1665

It is more difficult for woman to resign flirtations than love. IBID.

One kind of flirtation is to boast we never flirt.
IBID.

Attention without intention.
Author unidentified

Flogging

A man who has not been flogged has not been educated.
MENANDER: *Moyostikhoi*, *c.* 300 B.C.

There is now less flogging in our great schools than formerly — but then less is learned there; so that what the boys get at one end they lose at the other.
SAMUEL JOHNSON: *Boswell's Life*, 1775

O ye! who teach the ingenious youth of nations,
Holland, France, England, Germany or Spain,
I pray ye flog them upon all occasions,
It mends their morals, never mind the pain.
BYRON: *Don Juan*, II, 1819

It used to take me all vacation to grow a new hide in place of the one they flogged off me during school term.
S. L. CLEMENS (MARK TWAIN): *Letter from New York to the Alta Californian* (San Francisco), May 28, 1867

[*See also* Child, Children.

Flood

In the six hundredth year of Noah's life, in the second month, the seventeenth day of the month, the same day were all the fountains of the great deep broken up, and the windows of heaven were open. And the rain was upon the earth forty days and forty nights. GENESIS VII, 11–12, *c.* 700 B.C.

One good flood is better than a hundred baskets of manure. HINDU PROVERB

[*See also* Caution.

Florida

In Summer the crackers live off yams; in Winter they live off Yanks. FLORIDA SAYING

Flower

As welcome as the flowers in May.
JAMES HOWELL: *Familiar Letters,* April 28, 1645

Nobody is fond of fading flowers.
THOMAS FULLER: *Gnomologia,* 1732

The Infinite has written its name on the heavens in shining stars, and on the earth in tender flowers.
JEAN PAUL RICHTER: *Hesperus,* XXV, 1795

To me the meanest flower that blows can give
Thoughts that do often lie too deep for tears.
WILLIAM WORDSWORTH: *Intimations of Immortality,* 1807

Where are the flowers, the fair young flowers,
That lately sprang and stood
In brighter light and softer airs, a beauteous sisterhood?
W. C. BRYANT: *The Death of the Flowers,* 1825

The flower of sweetest smell is shy and lowly.
WILLIAM WORDSWORTH: *Not Love, Not War,* 1827

There is material enough in a single flower for the ornament of a score of cathedrals.
JOHN RUSKIN: *Stones of Venice,* I, 1851

I sometimes think that never blows so red
The rose as where some buried Cæsar bled;
That every hyacinth the garden wears
Dropt in her lap from some once lovely head.
EDWARD FITZGERALD: Tr. of OMAR KHAYYÁM: *Rubáiyát* (*c.* 1100), 1857

Flowers are the sweetest things that God ever made, and forgot to put a soul into.
H. W. BEECHER: *Life Thoughts,* 1858

The flowers that bloom in the Spring, tra la,
Have nothing to do with the case.
W. S. GILBERT: *The Mikado,* II, 1885

I feel really frightened when I sit down to paint a flower. HOLMAN HUNT (1827–1910)

Say it with flowers.
Advertising slogan of the Society of American Florists, ascribed to P. F. O'KEEFE and adopted 1917

[*See also* Color, May, Spring, Weed.

Flute

The flute is not an instrument with a good moral effect. It is too exciting.
ARISTOTLE: *Politics,* VIII, *c.* 322 B.C.

The music of the flute is enervating to the mind.
OVID: *Remedia amoris, c.* 10

Alcibiades refused to learn the flute, as a sordid thing, and not becoming a free citizen; saying that to play on the lute or the harp does not in any way disfigure a man's body or face, but one is hardly to be known by the most intimate friends when playing on the flute. PLUTARCH: *Lives, c.* 100

The soft complaining flute
In dying notes discovers
The woes of hopeless lovers.
JOHN DRYDEN: *A Song for St. Cecilia's Day,* 1687

An ill wind that blows nobody good.
Author unidentified

A tutor who tooted a flute
Tried to teach two young tutors to toot;
Said the two to the tutor:
Is it harder to toot, or
To tutor two tutors to toot? IBID.

What is worse than a flute? Two flutes. IBID.

[*See also* Dancing.

Fly

Hungry flies bite sore.
JOHN HEYWOOD: *Proverbs,* 1546

The flies go to lean horses.
JAMES SANDFORD: *Hours of Recreation,* 1572

Even a fly hath a spleen.
ENGLISH PROVERB, borrowed from the Latin, and traced by Smith to 1584 (*Spleen*=anger)

The fly sate upon the axletree of the chariot wheel, and said, What a dust do I raise.
FRANCIS BACON: *Essays,* XXI, 1612 (Credited to Æsop)

Cover yourself with honey, and you shall see the flies will eat you.
THOMAS SHELTON: Tr. of CERVANTES: *Don Quixote,* II (1615), 1620

To a boiling pot flies come not.
GEORGE HERBERT: *Outlandish Proverbs,* 1640

Some men are more vexed with a fly than with a wound.
JEREMY TAYLOR: *The Mysteriousness of Marriage,* 1651

He capers like a fly in a tar-box.
JOHN RAY: *English Proverbs,* 1670

King James said to the fly, Have I three kingdoms and thou must needs fly into my eye?
JOHN SELDEN: *Table-Talk,* 1689

It is easier to catch flies with honey than with vinegar.
ENGLISH PROVERB, not recorded before the XVIII century

Let that fly stick in the wall: when the dirt's dry it will rub out.
TOBIAS SMOLLETT: *The Reprisal,* II, 1757 (An English proverb; often *flea* is substituted for *fly*)

A fly is as untamable as a hyena.
R. W. EMERSON: *The Conduct of Life,* VII, 1860

Shoo fly, don't bodder me!
T. B. BISHOP: Title of a popular song, *c.* 1868

Put cream and sugar on a fly, and it tastes very much like a black raspberry.
E. W. HOWE: *Country Town Sayings,* 1911

A fly on your nose;
You slap, and it goes;
If it comes back again
It will bring a good rain.
OLD ENGLISH RHYME

Kill a fly in May,
You've kept thousands away.
Kill a fly in June,
They'll be scarce soon.
Kill a fly in July,
You've killed just one fly. IBID.

[*See also* Amber, Blind, Cajolery, Eagle, Fiddler, Flea, Honey, Horse, Hurry, Ointment, Toilet, Trout.

Foe

The stern joy which warriors feel
In foeman worthy of their steel.
WALTER SCOTT: *The Lady of the Lake,* V, 1810

And where are the foes who so vauntingly swore
That the havoc of war and the battle's confusion
A home and a country should leave us no more?
Their blood has washed out their foul footsteps' pollution.
F. S. KEY: *The Star-Spangled Banner,* 1814 (Baltimore American, Sept. 16)

[*See also* Enemy.

Fog

A Summer fog for fair, a Winter fog for rain.
ENGLISH PROVERB

A fan cannot dispel a fog. JAPANESE PROVERB

Foible

We consecrate a great deal of nonsense, because it was allowed by great men. There is none without his foible. I verily believe if an angel should come to chant the chorus of moral law, he would eat too much gingerbread, or take liberties with private letters, or do some precious atrocity.
R. W. EMERSON: *Nominalist and Realist,* 1841

Folk-song

A folk-song is a song that nobody ever wrote.
Author unidentified

The only thing to do with a folk-melody, once you have played it, is to play it louder.
IBID.

Follower

I beseech you, be ye followers of me.
I CORINTHIANS IV, 16, *c.* 55 (Cf. XI, 1)

A man who tries to surpass another may perhaps succeed in equalling if not actually surpassing him, but one who merely follows can never quite come up with him: a follower, necessarily, is always behind.
QUINTILIAN: *De institutione oratoria,* X, *c.* 90

I light my candle from their torches.
ROBERT BURTON: *The Anatomy of Melancholy,* III, 1621

With pack-horse constancy we keep the road
Crooked or straight, through quags or thorny dells,
True to the jingling of our leader's bells.
WILLIAM COWPER: *Tirocinium,* 1785

Thou seekest followers? Then seek ciphers.
F. W. NIETZSCHE: *The Twilight of the Idols,* 1889

[*See also* Disciple.

Folly

The foolishness of fools is folly.
PROVERBS XIV, 24, *c.* 350 B.C.

Their folly shall be manifest to all men.
II TIMOTHY III, 9, *c.* 65

The shortest follies are the best.
PIERRE CHARRON: *De la sagesse,* I, 1601

The common curse of mankind, — folly and ignorance.
SHAKESPEARE: *Troilus and Cressida,* II, *c.* 1601

Does he not return wisest who comes home whipt by his own follies?
THOMAS MIDDLETON: *A Trick to Catch the Old One,* II, 1608

Folly is wise in her own eyes.
Anon.: *A Book of Merry Riddles,* 1629

Folly grows without watering.
GEORGE HERBERT: *Outlandish Proverbs,* 1640

If folly were grief, every house would weep.
IBID.

The chief disease that reigns this year is folly.
IBID.

Folly pursues us in every period of life. If any one appears wise, it is only because his follies are proportioned to his age and fortune.
LA ROCHEFOUCAULD: *Maxims*, 1665

He who lives without folly is not so wise as he thinks.
IBID.

There are follies as catching as infections.
IBID.

Alas! we see that at all times the little have suffered for the follies of the great.
JEAN DE LA FONTAINE: *Fables*, II, *c.* 1670

Happy is he who knows his follies in his youth.
JOHN RAY: *English Proverbs*, 1670

Men of all ages have the same inclinations, and over them reason has no control. Thus wherever men are found there are follies, and they are always the same follies.
BERNARD DE FONTENELLE: *Dialogues des morts*, 1683

The follies of the fathers are no warning to the children.
IBID.

I know of nothing in the world that is not a monument to the folly of mankind.
BERNARD DE FONTENELLE: *Entretiens sur la pluralité des mondes*, II, 1686

Till follies become ruinous, the world is better with them than it would be without them.
GEORGE SAVILE (MARQUESS OF HALIFAX): *Political, Moral and Miscellaneous Reflections*, *c.* 1690

With endless pain this man pursues
What, if he gain'd, he could not use:
And t'other fondly hopes to see
What never was, nor e'er shall be.
MATTHEW PRIOR: *Alma*, *c.* 1716

I enjoy vast delight in the folly of mankind; and, God be praised, that is an inexhaustible source of entertainment.
MARY WORTLEY MONTAGU: *Letter to the Countess of Mar*, 1725

Shoot folly as it flies.
ALEXANDER POPE: *An Essay on Man*, I, 1732

If I can please myself with my own follies, have not I plentiful provision for life?
COLLEY CIBBER: *Apology for His Life*, I, 1740

The first degree of folly is to conceit one's self wise; the second to profess it; the third to despise counsel.
BENJAMIN FRANKLIN: *Poor Richard's Almanac*, 1754

The seeds of folly shoot forth rank and bold,
And ev'ry seed brings forth a hundred fold.
CHARLES CHURCHILL: *The Farewell*, 1764

The word folly is perhaps the prettiest word in the language.
WILLIAM SHENSTONE: *Of Men and Manners*, 1764

When lovely woman stoops to folly,
And finds too late that men betray,
What charm can soothe her melancholy?
What art can wash her guilt away?
OLIVER GOLDSMITH: *The Vicar of Wakefield*, XXIV, 1766

The hours of folly are measur'd by the clock; but of wisdom, no clock can measure.
WILLIAM BLAKE: *The Marriage of Heaven and Hell*, 1790

The follies of the fool are known to the world, but are hidden from himself; the follies of the wise are known to himself, but hidden from the world.
C. C. COLTON: *Lacon*, 1820

He who hath not a dram of folly in his mixture hath pounds of much worse matter.
CHARLES LAMB: *All Fools' Day*, 1820

Every man's follies are the caricature resemblances of his wisdom.
JOHN STERLING: *Essays and Tales*, 1840

Each age has its own follies, as its majority is made up of foolish young people.
R. W. EMERSON: *Carlyle's Past and Present*, 1843

Folly hath eagle's wings but the eyes of an owl.
DUTCH PROVERB

He who shows himself a sheep the wolf will eat.
ITALIAN PROVERB

[*See also* Beauty, Dog, Fool, History, Ignorance, Jollity, Mirth, Nonsense, Wisdom, Wise.

Food

Why is not a rat as good as a rabbit? Why should men eat shrimps and neglect cockroaches?
H. W. BEECHER: *Eyes and Ears*, 1862

I might glorify my bill of fare until I was tired; but after all, the Scotchman would shake his head and say, "Where's your haggis?" and the Fijian would sigh and say, "Where's your missionary?"
S. L. CLEMENS (MARK TWAIN): *A Tramp Abroad*, XLIX, 1879

There is no love sincerer than the love of food.
GEORGE BERNARD SHAW: *Man and Superman*, I, 1903

It is not the horse that draws the cart, but the oats.
RUSSIAN PROVERB

[*See also* Eating, Metabolism, Nothing, Poison, Population, Value.

Fool

I have played the fool.
I SAMUEL XXVI, 21, *c.* 500 B.C.

There is always a majority of fools.
Ascribed to HERACLITUS (*c.* 540–475 B.C.)

The fool speaks only folly.
EURIPIDES: *The Bacchae, c.* 410 B.C.

The wise shall inherit glory: but shame shall be the promotion of fools.
PROVERBS III, 35, *c.* 350 B.C.

Every fool will be meddling.
PROVERBS XX, 3

A whip for the horse, a bridle for the ass, and a rod for the fool's back. PROVERBS XXVI, 3

Answer not a fool according to his folly, lest thou also be like unto him.
PROVERBS XXVI, 4

Answer a fool according to his folly, lest he be wise in his own conceit. PROVERBS XXVI, 5

As a dog returneth to his vomit, so a fool returneth to his folly. PROVERBS XXVI, 11

Though thou shouldest bray a fool in a mortar among wheat with a pestle, yet will not his foolishness depart from him.
PROVERBS XXVII, 22

The wise man's eyes are in his head; but the fool walketh in darkness.
ECCLESIASTES II, 14, *c.* 200 B.C.

He that teacheth a fool is like one who glueth a potsherd together.
ECCLESIASTICUS XXII, 7, *c.* 180 B.C.

The fool hath said in his heart, There is no God.
PSALMS XIV, 1, *c.* 150 B.C. (Cf. LIII, 1)

Who is not a fool? (Qui non stultus?)
HORACE: *Satires,* II, *c.* 25 B.C.

A fool is overbearing when he is flattered, but he yields when he is looked in the face.
DIONYSIUS OF HALICARNASSUS: *Antiquities of Rome,* V, *c.* 20 B.C.

We are fools for Christ's sake.
I CORINTHIANS IV, 10, *c.* 55

Whosoever shall say, Thou fool, shall be in danger of hell fire. MATTHEW V, 22, *c.* 75

There is no fellowship with a fool.
The Dhammapada, IV, *c.* 100

Though a fool spend all his life with wise men, he will know the truth no more than a spoon knows the taste of soup.
The Dhammapada, V

Of the child unborn, the dead, and the fool, the two first, and not the last, are the least to be lamented; for the two first cause but a transient sorrow, whilst the last is an eternal plague. *The Hitopadesa,* intro., *c.* 500

It is better to roam the mountains with the wild beasts than to live in a palace with a fool.
BHARTRIHARI: *The Niti Sataka, c.* 625

A fool's bolt is soon shot.
ENGLISH PROVERB, traced by Smith to *c.* 1225

Fool's paradise.
ENGLISH PHRASE, in use since the XV century

A man may know a fool by his much clattering.
RICHARD WYDEVILLE (EARL RIVERS): Tr. of CHRISTINE DE PISE: *Moral Proverbs,* 1477

A fool beholdeth only the beginning of his works, but a wise man taketh heed to the end.
Anon.: *Dialogues of Creatures, c.* 1535

God sendeth fortune to fools.
JOHN HEYWOOD: *Proverbs,* 1546

There is no fool to the old fool. IBID.

There is nothing more fulsome than a she-fool.
WILLIAM CECIL (LORD BURLEIGH): *Advice to His Son, c.* 1555

Fools are fortunate.
ENGLISH PROVERB, traced by Apperson to *c.* 1568

Fools make feasts, and wise men enjoy them.
JAMES SANDFORD: *Hours of Recreation,* 1572

A fool will laugh even when he is drowning.
ENGLISH PROVERB, traced by Apperson to 1577

A fool and his money are soon parted.
ENGLISH PROVERB, traced by Apperson and Smith to 1580

Fools and little dogs are ladies' playfellows.
BRIAN MELBANCKE: *Philotinus,* 1583

He who hath only been a very fool shall at no time prove very wise.
MICHEL DE MONTAIGNE: *Essays,* III, 1588

Fools please women best.
JOHN LYLY: *Song of Accius and Silena, c.* 1594

What fools these mortals be!
SHAKESPEARE: *A Midsummer Night's Dream,* III, *c.* 1596

We play the fool with the time, and the spirits of the wise sit in the clouds and mock us.
SHAKESPEARE: *II Henry IV,* II, *c.* 1598

The dullness of the fool is the whetstone of the wits.
SHAKESPEARE: *As You Like It,* I, *c.* 1600

A fool, a fool! I met a fool i' the forest,
A motley fool, a miserable world!
As I do live by food, I met a fool;
Who laid him down and bask'd him in the sun.
SHAKESPEARE: *As You Like It,* II

The fool doth think he is wise, but the wise man knows himself to be a fool.
SHAKESPEARE: *As You Like It*, v

Those that are fools, let them use their talents.
SHAKESPEARE: *Twelfth Night*, I, *c.* 1601

This fellow is wise enough to play the fool;
And to do that well craves a kind of wit.
SHAKESPEARE: *Twelfth Night*, III

Fools set stools for wise folk to stumble at.
WILLIAM CAMDEN: *Remains Concerning Britain*, 1605

To be a fool born is a disease incurable.
BEN JONSON: *Volpone*, II, 1605

Fools are wise until they speak.
RANDLE COTGRAVE: *French-English Dictionary*, 1611

There is in human nature, generally more of the fool than of the wise.
FRANCIS BACON: *Essays*, XII, 1612

Fools and madmen tell commonly truth.
ROBERT BURTON: *The Anatomy of Melancholy*, II, 1621

Fools are a family over all the world.
JAMES SHIRLEY: *The Lady of Pleasure*, IV, 1637

Fools tie knots, and wise men loose them.
JOHN CLARKE: *Parœmiologia Anglo-Latina*, 1639

If all fools wore white caps we should seem a flock of geese.
GEORGE HERBERT: *Outlandish Proverbs*, 1640

None is a fool always; everyone sometimes.
IBID.

He is not the fool that the fool is, but he that with the fool deals.
DAVID FERGUSSON: *Scottish Proverbs*, 1641

Let Providence provide for fools; 'tis not partiality, but equity, in God, who deals with us but as our natural parents. Those that are able of body and mind He leaves to their deserts; to those of weaker merits He imparts a larger portion; and pieces out the defect of one by the excess of the other.
THOMAS BROWNE: *Religio Medici*, I, 1642

To make a trade of laughing at a fool is the highway to become one.
THOMAS FULLER: *The Holy State and the Profane State*, 1642

He who does not know a fool when he sees one is himself a fool.
BALTASAR GRACIÁN: *The Art of Worldly Wisdom*, CXCVII, 1647

Fools will still be fools.
ROBERT HEATH: *Satires*, 1650

Every man hath a fool in one sleeve.
GEORGE HERBERT: *Jacula Prudentum*, 1651

He hath great need of a fool that plays the fool himself.
IBID.

One fool makes a hundred.
IBID.

It is sometimes necessary to play the fool to avoid being deceived by smart fellows.
LA ROCHEFOUCAULD: *Maxims*, 1665

Only a few things are needed to make a wise man happy, but nothing can satisfy a fool: that is why nearly all men are miserable.
IBID.

Some fools have wit, but none have discretion.
IBID.

There are no fools so tiresome as those who have some wit.
IBID.

A fool may ask more than seven wise men can answer.
GIOVANNI TORRIANO: *Italian Proverbs*, 1666

Men are so necessarily fools, that it would be being a fool in a higher strain of folly not to be a fool.
BLAISE PASCAL: *Pensées*, XXIV, 1670

A fool may ask more questions in an hour than a wise man can answer in seven years.
JOHN RAY: *English Proverbs*, 1670 (Cf. TORRIANO, *ante*, 1666)

A learned fool is more foolish than an ignorant one.
J. B. MOLIÈRE: *Les femmes savantes*, III, 1672

A fool always finds a greater fool to admire him.
NICOLAS BOILEAU: *L'art poétique*, I, 1674

Do you think we human beings are the only fools in the universe?
BERNARD DE FONTENELLE: *Entretiens sur la pluralité des mondes*, II, 1686

A fool does not enter a room, nor leave it, nor sit down, nor rise up, nor is he silent, nor does he stand on his legs, like a man of sense.
JEAN DE LA BRUYÈRE: *Caractères*, II, 1688

A fool is an automaton. He is a machine worked by a spring. Irresistible natural forces make him move and turn, always at the same pace and never stopping. He is never inconsistent with himself. Whoever has seen him once has seen him at all times. He is fixed and immovable by nature.
JEAN DE LA BRUYÈRE: *Caractères*, XI

I hear a great many of the fools are angry at me, and I am glad of it, for I write at them, not to them.
WILLIAM CONGREVE: *The Double Dealer*, dedication, 1694

None are fools always, though every one sometimes.
THOMAS D'URFEY: *The Comical History of Don Quixote*, I, 1694

I am a fool, I know it; and yet, God help me,
I'm poor enough to be a wit.
WILLIAM CONGREVE: *Love for Love*, I, 1695

A fool hath no dialogue within himself; the first thought carrieth him without the reply of a second.
GEORGE SAVILE (MARQUESS OF HALIFAX): *Political, Moral and Miscellaneous Reflections*, c. 1690

Fools rush in where angels fear to tread.
ALEXANDER POPE: *An Essay on Criticism*, III, 1711

You beat your pate, and fancy wit will come;
Knock as you please, there's nobody at home.
ALEXANDER POPE: *Epigram*, c. 1720

Few follow wisdom or her rules;
Fools in derision follow fools.
JOHN GAY: *Fables*, I, 1727

My boys, let us be grave: here comes a fool.
Ascribed to SAMUEL CLARKE (1675–1729) by Boswell in the dedication to his *Life of Johnson*, 1791; Dr. Clarke is said to have made the remark on observing Beau Nash approaching

Hated by fools, and fools to hate,
Be that my motto, and my fate.
JONATHAN SWIFT: *To Dr. Delany*, 1729

A fool can dance without a fiddle.
THOMAS FULLER: *Gnomologia*, 1732

A fool is happier in thinking well of himself than a wise man in others thinking well of him. IBID.

A fool's tongue is long enough to cut his own throat. IBID.

A nod for a wise man and a rod for a fool. IBID.

The fool saith, Who would have thought it? IBID.

Wise men learn by other men's harms; fools by their own. IBID.

The fool is happy that he knows no more.
ALEXANDER POPE: *An Essay on Man*, II, 1732

No creature smarts so little as a fool.
ALEXANDER POPE: *An Epistle to Dr. Arbuthnot*, 1735

Who knows a fool must know his brother;
For one will recommend another.
BENJAMIN FRANKLIN: *Poor Richard's Almanac*, 1740

To be intimate with a foolish friend is like going to bed to a razor.
BENJAMIN FRANKLIN: *Poor Richard's Almanac*, 1754

It is ill-manners to silence a fool, and cruelty to let him go on.
BENJAMIN FRANKLIN: *Poor Richard's Almanac*, 1757

Fool beckons fool, and dunce awakens dunce.
CHARLES CHURCHILL: *The Apology*, 1761

A fool's paradise is better than a wiseacre's purgatory.
GEORGE COLEMAN THE ELDER: *The Deuce Is in Him*, I, 1763

The greatest, the most dangerous and the least endurable of fools are the reasoning ones. Without being any the less foolish, they conceal from the unreflecting the disorder in their heads by the dexterity of their tongues, and are accepted as wise because they rave more coherently than their brethren in the asylum.
C. M. WIELAND: *Die Abderiten*, II, 1774

A fool must now and then be right by chance.
WILLIAM COWPER: *Conversation*, 1782

I am a fool by profession.
ROBERT BURNS: *The Jolly Beggars*, 1785

Fools rushed on fools, as waves succeed to waves.
Author unidentified (Quoted by ROBERT BURNS: *Letter to Mrs. McLehose*, Jan. 20, 1788)

A fool sees not the same tree that a wise man sees.
WILLIAM BLAKE: *The Marriage of Heaven and Hell*, 1790

If the fool would persist in his folly he would become wise. IBID.

Fools and modest people are alike innocuous. Only half-fools and half-wise are really dangerous.
J. W. GOETHE: *Elective Affinities*, II, 1808

Fools are my theme, let satire be my song.
BYRON: *English Bards and Scotch Reviewers*, 1809

Ever since Adam fools have been in the majority.
CASIMIR DELAVIGNE: *L'Étude fait-elle le bonheur?*, 1820

I am always afraid of a fool. One cannot be sure that he is not a knave as well.
WILLIAM HAZLITT: *Characteristics*, LXXXV, 1823

No combination of statesmen is a match for a general combination of fools.
T. B. MACAULAY: *Letter to Macvey Napier*, Nov. 24, 1843

I have great faith in fools: — self-confidence my friends will call it.
E. A. POE: *Marginalia*, 1844–49

Every man a little beyond himself is a fool.
H. G. BOHN: *Handbook of Proverbs*, 1855

Fools are wise men in the affairs of women.
IBID.

A fool wants to kill space and kill time.
JOHN RUSKIN: *Modern Painters,* IV, 1856

Hain't we got all the fools in town on our side? And ain't that a big enough majority in any town?
S. L. CLEMENS (MARK TWAIN): *Huckleberry Finn,* XXVI, 1884

I may be crazy, but I ain't no fool.
BERT WILLIAMS: Title of a song, *c.* 1900

The first man you meet is a fool. If you do not think so ask him, and he will prove it.
AMBROSE BIERCE: *Collected Works,* VIII, 1911

The best way to silence any friend of yours whom you know to be a fool is to induce him to hire a hall.
WOODROW WILSON: Speech, Jan. 27, 1916

Every man is a damn fool for at least five minutes every day. Wisdom consists in not exceeding the limit.
ELBERT HUBBARD: *Roycroft Dictionary and Book of Epigrams,* 1923

Don't be mean to the fool; put a penny in his cup, as you do for the blind beggar.
E. W. HOWE: *Sinner Sermons,* 1926

Don't give yo' aigs to a fool to carry.
AMERICAN NEGRO SAYING

The fool in a hurry drinks his tea with chopsticks.
CHINESE PROVERB

There is no need to hang a bell to a fool.
DANISH PROVERB

Praise a fool, and you may make him useful.
IBID.

A fool's head never grows white.
FRENCH PROVERB

Only God understands the fool.
IBID.

Everybody must wear out at least one pair of fool's shoes.
GERMAN PROVERB

It is better to be silent like a fool than to talk like one.
IBID.

It is better to deal with a whole fool than with a half fool.
IBID.

Women and luck always favor fools.
IBID.

Better to be the enemy of a wise man than the friend of a fool.
HINDU PROVERB

" God help the fool," said the idiot.
IRISH PROVERB

A fool delights to give advice.
ITALIAN PROVERB

When wise men play the fool they do it thoroughly.
IBID.

One half of the human race spends its time in laughing at the other half, and all are fools.
JAPANESE PROVERB

All fools are slaves. (Stuli omnes servi.)
LATIN PROVERB

Even a fool sometimes speaks well. (Interdum stultus bene loquitur.)
IBID.

The limbo of fools. (Limbus fatuorum.)
MEDIEVAL LATIN PHRASE (The *Limbus fatuorum* was the post-mortem abiding place of those too lacking in merit for Heaven and too lacking in blame for Hell. It was thus somewhat like the *Limbus infantum,* where unbaptized infants were incarcerated)

Do not try to teach a fool; as well try to cure the dead.
RUSSIAN PROVERB

When a fool shoots, God guides the bullet.
IBID.

If you want to win a fool over to your side, tell him a story.
SANSKRIT PROVERB

Fools are aye fond o' flittin', and wise men o' sittin'.
SCOTTISH PROVERB

Forbid a fool a thing, an' that he'll do.
IBID.

Every man is a fool in some man's opinion.
SPANISH PROVERB

If every fool wore a crown, we'd all be kings.
WELSH PROVERB

[*See also* Acting, Advice, Ages, Character, Children, Dancer, Dog, Dream, Enemy, Envy, Exactness, Examination, Experience, Familiarity, Fashion, Father, Fifty, Fighting, Figures, Flattery, Folly, Foolishness, Fortune, Forty, Friar, Gravity, Hair (White), Heart, Hero, Home, House, Hurry, Husband and Wife, Idleness, Ignorance, Jester, Judgment, Knave, Latin Language, Laughter, Lawyer, Learning, Liar, Limbo, Lord, Luck, Lying, Man, Manners, Market, Marriage, Martyrdom, Meddling, Melancholy, Memory, Merriment, Mirror, Mirth, Mischief, Name, Nod, Opinion (Public), Parliament, Philosopher, Poet, Prayer, Promise, Prophet, Proverb, Public, Self-satisfaction, Self-taught, Silence, Sleep, Tongue, Travel, Truth, Truth-telling, Wealth, Weather, Wine Woman and Song, Wisdom, Wise, Young and Old.

Foolishness

God hath chosen the foolish things of the world to confound the wise; and God hath chosen the weak things of the world to confound the things which are mighty.
I CORINTHIANS I, 27, *c.* 55

It's a foolish sheep that makes the wolf his confessor.
JOHN RAY: *English Proverbs,* 1670

Nothing is more dangerous than a foolish friend.
FRENCH PROVERB

If foolishness were a disease, there would be groaning in every house.
SPANISH PROVERB

[*See also* Folly, Fool, Insolence.

Foot

To a foot in a shoe the whole world seems to be paved with leather.
The Hitopadesa, I, *c.* 500

There's language in her eye, her cheek, her lip,
Nay, her foot speaks.
SHAKESPEARE: *Troilus and Cressida*, IV, *c.* 1601

Dry feet, warm head,
Bring safe to bed.
GEORGE HERBERT: *Outlandish Proverbs*, 1640

Her feet beneath her petticoat,
Like little mice, stole in and out,
As if they feared the light.
JOHN SUCKLING: *A Ballad Upon a Wedding*, 1642

Her pretty feet
Like snails did creep
A little out, and then,
As if they played at bo-peep
Did soon draw in again.
ROBERT HERRICK: *Hesperides*, 1648

One foot is better than two crutches.
GEORGE HERBERT: *Jacula Prudentum*, 1651

Where e'er you tread your foot shall set
The primrose and the violet.
SAMUEL BUTLER: *Hudibras*, I, 1663

Keep your mouth wet, feet dry.
BENJAMIN FRANKLIN: *Poor Richard's Almanac*, 1733

A pretty foot is one of the greatest gifts of nature.
J. W. GOETHE: *Elective Affinities*, I, 1808

How's your poor feet?
ENGLISH CATCH-PHRASE, *c.* 1900

Don't sweep a person's feet: it will make him lazy; so will hitting them with a straw.
AMERICAN NEGRO PROVERB

[*See also* Happiness, Head, Shoe, Warm, Washing.

Football

He played at the balloon, and made it bound in the air, both with fist and foot.
RABELAIS: *Gargantua*, I, 1535

As concerning football, I protest unto you that it may rather be called a friendly kind of fight than a play or recreation — a bloody and murthering practise than a fellowly sport or pastime.
PHILIP STUBBES: *The Anatomie of Abuses*, 1583

Foraging

A twice-born man who, on his travels, falls in need of food shall not be punished if he take not more than two stalks of sugar-cane or two roots of vegetable from a field.
THE CODE OF MANU, VIII, *c.* 100

Forbearance

I was weary with forbearance.
JEREMIAH XX, 9, *c.* 625 B.C.

Forbearance is a part of justice.
MARCUS AURELIUS: *Meditations*, IV, *c.* 170

Bear and forbear.
THOMAS TUSSER: *Five Hundred Points of Good Husbandry*, 1580

Forbear to judge, for we are sinners all.
SHAKESPEARE: *II Henry VI*, III, *c.* 1591

There is a limit at which forbearance ceases to be a virtue.
EDMUND BURKE: *Observations on a Late State of the Nation*, 1769

Next to knowing when to seize an opportunity, the most important thing in life is to know when to forego an advantage.
BENJAMIN DISRAELI: *The Infernal Marriage*, 1834

[*See also* Happiness.

Forbidden

Forbidden things have a secret charm.
TACITUS: *Annals*, XIII, *c.* 110

Forbidden fruit is sweet.
H. G. BOHN: *Handbook of Proverbs*, 1855

Women have a much better time than men in this world; there are far more things forbidden to them.
OSCAR WILDE: *A Woman of No Importance*, II, 1893

Force

Force, unaccompanied by prudence, sinks under its own weight. The gods give effect to force regulated by wisdom; they pursue with wrath bold, unhallowed schemes.
HORACE: *Carmina*, III, *c.* 20 B.C.

Whatever, against our will and without our empowering the same, is by greater force done upon our body, is no lewdness.
ST. AUGUSTINE: *On Lying*, *c.* 395

Where wisdom is called for, force is of little use.
HERODOTUS: *Histories*, III, *c.* 430 B.C.

There are two ways of contending, by law and by force: the first is proper to men; the second to beasts; but because many times the first is insufficient, recourse must be had to the second.
NICCOLÒ MACHIAVELLI: *The Prince*, XI, 1513

Who overcomes
By force, hath overcome but half his foe.
JOHN MILTON: *Paradise Lost*, I, 1667

Force rules the world, and not opinion; but opinion is that which makes use of force.
BLAISE PASCAL: *Pensées,* XXIV, 1670

Force cannot give right.
THOMAS JEFFERSON: *The Rights of British America,* 1774

Neither philosophy, nor religion nor morality, nor wisdom, nor interest will ever govern nations or parties against their vanity, their pride, their resentment or revenge, or their avarice or ambition. Nothing but force and power and strength can restrain them.
JOHN ADAMS: *Letter to Thomas Jefferson,* Oct. 9, 1787

Our judgment will always suspect those weapons that can be used with equal prospect of success on both sides. Therefore we should regard all force with aversion.
WILLIAM GODWIN: *An Enquiry Concerning Political Justice,* 1793

Force [is] the vital principle and immediate parent of despotism.
THOMAS JEFFERSON: First Inaugural Address, 1801

Right resolves itself into its natural nothingness when it is swallowed up by force.
MAX STIRNER: *The Ego and His Own,* 1845

I feel that the true way of dealing with the matter is by a force which is overwhelming and prevents any attempt at resistance.
RICHARD OLNEY: Instructions to Edwin Walker, special U. S. district attorney at Chicago, during the Pullman strike, June 30, 1894

Germany has once more said that force, and force alone, shall decide whether justice and peace shall reign in the affairs of men, whether right as America conceives it, or dominion as she conceives it, shall determine the destinies of mankind. There is, therefore, but one response possible from us: force, force to the uttermost, force without stint or limit, the righteous and triumphant force which shall make right of the law of the world and cast every selfish dominion down in the dust.
WOODROW WILSON: Speech in Baltimore, April 6, 1918

At the turning points of history, it is force, and force alone, which makes the crucial decision.
BENITO MUSSOLINI: Speech in Naples, Oct. 26, 1922

Where force is necessary, there it must be applied boldly, decisively and completely. But one must know the limitations of force; one must know when to blend force with a maneuver, the blow with an agreement.
LEON TROTSKY: *What Next?,* XIV, 1932

[*See also* Gentleness, Knowledge, Majority, Might, Money, Navel, Opinion, Patience, Right and Might, Right and Wrong, State, War.

Forefather

Beneath those rugged elms, that yew-tree's shade,
Where heaves the turf in many a mold'ring heap,
Each in his narrow cell for ever laid,
The rude forefathers of the hamlet sleep.
THOMAS GRAY: *Elegy Written in a Country Churchyard,* 1750

[*See also* Ancestry, Dead.

Forefront

Set ye Uriah in the forefront of the hottest battle, and retire ye from him, that he may be smitten, and die.
II SAMUEL XI, 15, *c.* 500 B.C.

Forehead

Foreheads villainous low.
SHAKESPEARE: *The Tempest,* IV, 1611

The dome of thought.
BYRON: *Childe Harold,* II, 1812

A fair forehead outshines its diamond diadem.
JOHN RUSKIN: *Modern Painters,* V, 1860

[*See also* Brow.

Foreign Relations

It is the sincere wish of United America to have nothing to do with the political intrigues, or the squabbles of European nations.
GEORGE WASHINGTON: *Letter to the Earl of Buchan,* April 22, 1793

My ardent desire is, and my aim has been, to comply strictly with all our engagements, foreign and domestic; but to keep the United States free from political connections with every other country, to see them independent of all and under the influence of none.
GEORGE WASHINGTON: *Letter to Patrick Henry,* Oct. 9, 1795

It is a fact too notorious to be denied that the greatest embarrassments under which the administration of this government labors proceed from the counteraction of people among ourselves, who are more disposed to promote the views of another nation than to establish national character of their own.
GEORGE WASHINGTON: *Letter to C. C. Pinckney,* July 8, 1796

Against the insidious wiles of foreign influence, I conjure you to believe me, fellow-citizens, the jealousy of a free people ought to be constantly awake, since history and experience prove that foreign influence is one of the most baneful foes of republican government.
GEORGE WASHINGTON: Farewell Address, Sept. 17, 1796

Why quit our own to stand upon foreign ground? Why, by interweaving our destiny with that of any part of Europe, entangle our peace and prosperity in the toils of European ambition, rivalship, interest, humor, or caprice?
IBID.

Nations that want protectors will have masters.
FISHER AMES: *Oration in Boston,* 1800 (Feb. 8)

The less we have to do with the amities or enmities of Europe, the better.
THOMAS JEFFERSON: *Letter to Thomas Leiper,* 1815

I have ever deemed it fundamental for the United States never to take active part in the quarrels of Europe. Their political interests are entirely distinct from ours. Their mutual jealousies, their balance of power, their complicated alliances, their forms and principles of government, are all foreign to us. They are nations of eternal war.
THOMAS JEFFERSON: *Letter to James Monroe,* 1823

Hope nothing from foreign governments. They will never be really willing to aid you until you have shown that you are strong enough to conquer without them.
GIUSEPPE MAZZINI: *On the Duties of Man,* 1840

We declare for a constructive foreign policy based on these principles: (*a*) Outlawry of war and an abhorrence of militarism, conquest, and imperialism. (*b*) Freedom from entangling political alliances with foreign nations. (*c*) Protection of American lives and rights. (*d*) Noninterference with the elections or other internal political affairs of any foreign nation.
Democratic National Platform, 1928

[*See also* Alliance, Imperialism, Neutrality, Union (American).

Foresight

In respect to foresight and firmness, the people are more prudent, more stable, and have better judgment than princes.
NICCOLÒ MACHIAVELLI: *Discorsi,* I, 1531

To know
That which before us lies in daily life,
Is the prime wisdom.
JOHN MILTON: *Paradise Lost,* VIII, 1667

The first years of man must make provision for the last. SAMUEL JOHNSON: *Rasselas,* 1759

A miser of sixty refuses himself necessaries that he may not want them when he is a hundred. Almost all of us make ourselves unhappy by too much foresight.
STANISLAUS LESZCZYNSKI (KING OF POLAND): *Œuvres du philosophe bienfaisant,* 1763

Human foresight often leaves its proudest possessor only a choice of evils.
C. C. COLTON: *Lacon,* 1820

He who can see three days ahead will be rich for three thousand years.
JAPANESE PROVERB

The wise man looks ahead. (Sapiens qui prospicit.) LATIN PROVERB

[*See also* Forethought, Hindsight, Prudence.

Forest

The green-haired forest.
R. W. EMERSON: *The World-Soul,* 1847

This is the forest primeval. The murmuring pines and the hemlocks,
Bearded with moss, and in garments green, indistinct in the twilight,
Stand like Druids of eld, with voices sad and prophetic,
Stand like harpers hoar, with beards that rest on their bosoms.
H. W. LONGFELLOW: *Evangeline,* 1847

A forest of all manner of trees is poor, if not disagreeable in effect: a mass of one species of tree is sublime.
JOHN RUSKIN: *Modern Painters,* III, 1856

[*See also* Latin, Tree, Woods.

Forethought

Take time by the forelock.
Ascribed to THALES, *c.* 575 B.C.

Ke Wan Tze thought thrice before acting. Twice would have been enough.
CONFUCIUS: *Analects,* V, *c.* 500 B.C.

Look before you leap.
ENGLISH PROVERB, traced by Smith to *c.* 1350

Yet is one good forewit worth two afterwits.
JOHN HEYWOOD: *Proverbs,* 1546

Excessive forethought and too great solicitude for the future are often productive of misfortune; for the affairs of the world are subject to so many accidents that seldom do things turn out as even the wisest predicted; and whoever refuses to take advantage of present good from fear of future danger, provided the danger be not certain and near, often discovers to his annoyance and disgrace that he has lost opportunities full of profit and glory, from dread of dangers which have turned out to be wholly imaginary.
FRANCESCO GUICCIARDINI: *Storia d'Italia,* 1564

As a man without forethought scarcely deserves the name of man, so forethought without reflection is but a metaphorical phrase for the instinct of a beast.
S. T. COLERIDGE: *Aids to Reflection,* 1825

Dig a well before you are thirsty.
CHINESE PROVERB

[*See also* Foresight.

Forever

For ever, and a day.
SHAKESPEARE: *As You Like It,* IV, *c.* 1600

May it last forever. (Esto perpetua.)
MOTTO OF IDAHO, adopted March 5, 1886

Forewarned

Forewarned, forearmed. (Praemonitus, praemunitus.)
LATIN PROVERB

Forgetfulness

It is often wise to forget what you know.
PUBLILIUS SYRUS: *Sententiæ*, c. 50 B.C.

Men are men; the best sometimes forget.
SHAKESPEARE: *Othello*, II, 1604

We never forget things so well as when we are tired of talking of them.
LA ROCHEFOUCAULD: *Maxims*, 1665

Of all affliction taught a lover yet,
'Tis sure the hardest science to forget.
ALEXANDER POPE: *Eloisa to Abelard*, 1717

Blessed are those who forget, for they thus surmount even their mistakes.
F. W. NIETZSCHE: *Beyond Good and Evil*, 1886

Lord God of Hosts, be with us yet,
Lest we forget — lest we forget!
RUDYARD KIPLING: *Recessional*, 1897 (London Times, July 17)

[*See also* Injury, Promise.

Forgiveness

There is nothing so advantageous to a man as a forgiving disposition.
TERENCE: *Adelphi*, V, c. 160 B.C.

Forgive others many things, yourself nothing.
PUBLILIUS SYRUS: *Sententiæ*, c. 50 B.C.

Be ye kind one to another, tender-hearted, forgiving one another, even as God for Christ's sake hath forgiven you.
EPHESIANS IV, 32, c. 60

Forgive us our debts as we forgive our debtors.
MATTHEW VI, 12, c. 75

If ye forgive not men their trespasses, neither will your Father forgive your trespasses.
MATTHEW VI, 15

Father, forgive them; for they know not what they do. LUKE XXIII, 34, c. 75

Neither do I condemn thee: go and sin no more. JOHN VIII, 11, c. 115

He who forgiveth, and is reconciled unto his enemy, shall receive his reward from God.
THE KORAN, XLII, c. 625

Forgive and forget.
ENGLISH PHRASE, in common use since the XIV century

In taking revenge a man is but even with his enemy, but in passing it over he is superior, for it is a prince's part to pardon.
FRANCIS BACON: *Essays*, IV, 1597

He who forgives easily invites offense.
PIERRE CORNEILLE: *Cinna*, IV, 1639

Forgive us our trespasses as we forgive those who trespass against us.
THE BOOK OF COMMON PRAYER (*The Lord's Prayer*), 1662

That it may please thee to forgive our enemies, persecutors, and slanderers, and to turn their hearts; We beseech thee to hear us, good Lord.
THE BOOK OF COMMON PRAYER (*The Litany*), 1662

We forgive so long as we love.
LA ROCHEFOUCAULD: *Maxims*, 1665

She hugg'd the offender, and forgave the offence.
JOHN DRYDEN: *Cymon and Iphigenia*, 1699

The truest joys they seldom prove,
Who free from quarrels live;
'Tis the most tender part of love,
Each other to forgive.
JOHN SHEFFIELD (DUKE OF BUCKINGHAM): *Song*, 1701

To err is human, to forgive divine.
ALEXANDER POPE: *An Essay on Criticism*, II, 1711

To forgive no enemy; but to be cautious and often dilatory in revenge.
HENRY FIELDING: *Jonathan Wild*, IV, 1743 (Maxim of Wild for the attainment of greatness)

A wise man will make haste to forgive, because he knows the true value of time, and will not suffer it to pass away in unnecessary pain.
SAMUEL JOHNSON: *The Rambler*, Dec. 24, 1751

Forgive what you can't excuse.
MARY WORTLEY MONTAGU: *Letter to James Steuart*, Oct. 13, 1759

Before we extol a man for his forgiving temper, we should inquire whether he is above revenge, or below it.
T. B. MACAULAY: *Hallam*, 1828 (Edinburgh Review, Sept.)

O Thou, who man of baser earth didst make,
And ev'n with Paradise devise the snake;
For all the sin wherewith the face of man
Is blacken'd — man's forgiveness give, — and take!
EDMUND FITZGERALD: Tr. of OMAR KHAYYÁM: *Rubáiyát* (c. 1100), 1857

Life has taught me to forgive much, but to seek forgiveness still more.
OTTO VON BISMARCK: In the autograph album of Count Enzenberg, c. 1875

In a village in the country,
There her parents now do live,
Drinking port wine that she sends 'em —
But they never can forgive.
Anon.: *She Was Poor but She Was Honest* (Sung by British soldiers, 1914–18)

A woman may consent to forget and forgive, but she never will drop the habit of referring to the matter now and then.
Author unidentified

Forgiving the unrepentant is like drawing pictures on water. JAPANESE PROVERB

Forgive others often, but yourself never. (Ignoscito sæpe alteri, nunquam tibi.)
LATIN PROVERB

[*See also* Character, Injury, Judgment, Pardon.

Forgotten

I am forgotten as a dead man out of mind: I am like a broken vessel.
PSALMS XXXI, 12, *c.* 150 B.C.

Unminded, unmoaned.
JOHN HEYWOOD: *Proverbs,* 1546

Die two months ago, and not forgotten yet?
SHAKESPEARE: *Hamlet,* III, *c.* 1601

The world forgetting, by the world forgot,
ALEXANDER POPE: *Eloisa to Abelard,* 1717

I want to be forgotten even by God.
ROBERT BROWNING: *Paracelsus,* V, 1835

Forgotten Man

Who is the Forgotten Man? He is the clean, quiet, virtuous, domestic citizen, who pays his debts and his taxes and is never heard of out of his little circle.
W. G. SUMNER: *The Forgotten Man,* 1883

[*See also* Philanthropy.

Fork

[*See* Eating, Finger.

Form

It is meritorious to insist on forms; religion and all else naturally clothes itself in forms. Everywhere the formed world is the only habitable one.
THOMAS CARLYLE: *Heroes and Hero-Worship,* VI, 1840 (Lecture in London, May 22)

True greatness is the most ready to recognize and most willing to obey those simple outward laws which have been sanctioned by the experience of mankind, and we suspect the originality which cannot move except on novel paths.
J. A. FROUDE: *Arnold's Poems,* 1854 (Westminster Review)

Formality

His life was formal. His actions seemed ruled with a ruler.
CHARLES LAMB: *The South-Sea House,* 1820 (London Magazine, Aug.)

Of all formal things in the world, a clipped hedge is the most formal; and of all the informal things in the world, a forest-tree is the most informal.
H. W. BEECHER: *Royal Truths,* 1862

[*See also* Form.

Fornication

This is the will of God, even your sanctification, that ye should abstain from fornication.
I THESSALONIANS IV, 3, *c.* 51

It is reported commonly that there is fornication among you. I CORINTHIANS V, 1, *c.* 55

Flee fornication. I CORINTHIANS VI, 18

Fornication is a lapse from one marriage into many.
CLEMENT OF ALEXANDRIA: *Stromateis,* *c.* 193

The fornicator is not worthy of compassion, but deserves to be derided, and made a mockery of, since he is more irrational than a woman, and a harlot besides.
ST. JOHN CHRYSOSTOM: *Homilies,* XIV, *c.* 388

Thou has committed
Fornication: but that was in another country,
And besides, the wench is dead.
CHRISTOPHER MARLOWE: *The Jew of Malta,* I, *c.* 1590

All men will naturally commit fornication, as all men will naturally steal.
SAMUEL JOHNSON: *Boswell's Life,* April 5, 1776

[*See also* Adultery, Flesh, Harlot, Marriage, Murder, Sin, Theatre.

Forsaken

My God, my God, why hast thou forsaken me?
PSALMS XXII, 1, *c.* 150 B.C.

And at the ninth hour Jesus cried with a loud voice, saying, Eloi, Eloi, lama sabachthani? which is, being interpreted, My God, My God, why hast thou forsaken me?
MARK XV, 34, *c.* 70 (Cf. MATTHEW XXVII, 46, *c.* 75. A quotation from PSALMS XXII, 1, *ante*)

Fort

Hold the fort; I am coming.
W. T. SHERMAN: Signal to General John M. Corse, at the Battle of Allatoona, Ga., Oct. 5, 1864 (What Sherman really wigwagged from Kenesaw Mountain was: "Sherman says hold fast. We are coming." The message was given its present form by P. P. Bliss, who wrote a popular hymn, using it as the title, in 1870. This hymn is often ascribed, erroneously, to MOODY and SANKEY, who used it during their evangelical tour of the British Isles, 1873)

Fortitude

Bear all inward and outward sufferings in silence, complaining only to God.
E. L. GRUBER: *Rules for the Examination of Our Daily Lives,* 1715

By suffering willingly what we cannot avoid, we secure ourselves from vain and immoderate disquiet; we preserve for better purposes that strength which would be unprofitably wasted in wild efforts of desperation, and maintain that circumspection which may enable us to seize every support, and improve every alleviation.
SAMUEL JOHNSON: *The Rambler,* Aug. 24, 1751

By fortitude and prudence. (Fortitudine et prudentia.) LATIN PHRASE

[*See also* Adversity, Kingly, Soldier, Virtue.

Fortunate

Even God can scarcely beat the fortunate.
PUBLILIUS SYRUS: *Sententiæ, c.* 50 B.C.

Those men are indeed fortunate who, in the depths of Winter, can afford to have plenty of milk and ghee on their tables, wear thick garments, anoint their bodies with saffron, tire themselves with pleasant exercises, sleep in the arms of beautiful women, and repose at their ease within their dwellings, chewing a leaf of betel mixed with spices.
BHARTRIHARI: *The Sringa Sataka, c.* 625

Fortune

When fortune brings up one blessing it pours out three evils.
DEMETRIUS: *Fragment, c.* 415 B.C.

Fortune can take from us nothing but what she gave us.
PUBLILIUS SYRUS: *Sententiæ, c.* 50 B.C.

Fortune is as brittle as glass. IBID.

Fortune, when she caresses a man too much, makes him a fool. IBID.

Man's life is ruled by fortune, not by wisdom.
CICERO: *Tusculanae disputationes,* LIX, 45 B.C.

Every man is the architect of his own fortune.
SALLUST: *De republica ordinanda, c.* 40 B.C.

Fortune, swooping with the dash of an eagle, snatches the imperial diadem from this man, and delights to place it on the head of some other. HORACE: *Carmina,* I, *c.* 20 B.C.

The most miserable fortune is the safest, for there is no fear of anything worse.
OVID: *Epistulæ ex Ponto,* II, *c.* 5

Not many men have both good fortune and good sense.
LIVY: *History of Rome,* XXX, *c.* 10

Nothing is more perilous to men than a sudden change of fortune.
QUINTILIAN: *De institutione oratoria,* CCLX, *c.* 90

Fortune gives many too much, but none enough. MARTIAL: *Epigrams,* XII, *c.* 100

Fortune is an evil chain to the body, and vice to the soul.
EPICTETUS: *Encheiridion, c.* 110

When we review what goes on in the world, is it not evident that in all human transactions the caprices of fortune turn wisdom into a jest? TACITUS: *Annals,* III, *c.* 110

Fortune may have the arbitrament of one-half of our actions, but she leaves the other half, or little less, to be governed by ourselves.
NICCOLÒ MACHIAVELLI: *The Prince,* XXV, 1513

Men may second fortune, but they cannot thwart her — they may weave her web, but they cannot break it.
NICCOLÒ MACHIAVELLI: *Discorsi,* II, 1531

It is an ill wind that blows nobody good.
ENGLISH PROVERB, traced by Smith to 1546

God sendeth fortune to fools.
JOHN HEYWOOD: *Proverbs,* 1546

Fortune knocks at least once at every man's door.
ENGLISH PROVERB, traced by Apperson to 1567

He danceth well enough to whom fortune pipeth.
JAMES SANDFORD: *Hours of Recreation,* 1572

Events, especially in war, do for the most part depend upon fortune, who will not be governed by, nor submit unto, human reason or prudences.
MICHEL DE MONTAIGNE: *Essays,* I, 1580

When fortune smiles, I smile to think
How quickly she will frown.
ROBERT SOUTHWELL: *Content and Rich, c.* 1595

When fortune means to men most good
She looks upon them with a threatening eye.
SHAKESPEARE: *King John,* III, 1596

O fortune, fortune! all men call thee fickle.
SHAKESPEARE: *Romeo and Juliet,* III, *c.* 1596

Oh, I am fortune's fool. IBID.

Fortune is painted blind, with a muffler afore her eyes.
SHAKESPEARE: *Henry V,* III, *c.* 1599

There is a tide in the affairs of men
Which, taken at the flood, leads on to fortune.
SHAKESPEARE: *Julius Cæsar,* IV, 1599

Fortune, the great commandress of the world,
Hath divers ways to advance her followers.
To some she gives honor without deserving,
To other some, deserving without honor.
GEORGE CHAPMAN: *All Fools,* V, 1605

Fortune, that arrant whore,
Ne'er turns the key to the poor.
SHAKESPEARE: *King Lear*, II, 1606

A good man's fortune may grow out at heels.
IBID.

Fortune's a right whore:
If she give aught, she deals it in small parcels,
That she may take away all at one swoop.
JOHN WEBSTER: *The White Devil*, I, *c.* 1608

He is but a stone tossed up into the air by fortune's sling, to receive the greater fall.
THOMAS ADAMS: *Diseases of the Soul*, 1616

There is no fence for ill fortune.
WILLIAM CAMDEN: *Remains Concerning Britain*, 1636

It is a law of the gods, never broken, to sell somewhat dearly the great benefits they confer upon us.
PIERRE CORNEILLE: *Cinna*, II, 1639

Fortune pays sometimes for the intensity of her favors by the shortness of their duration.
BALTASAR GRACIÁN: *The Art of Worldly Wisdom*, XXXVIII, 1647

Fortune to one is mother, to another is stepmother.
GEORGE HERBERT: *Jacula Prudentum*, 1651

Great fortune brings with it great misfortune.
IBID.

Fortune always seems blind to those she never favors. LA ROCHEFOUCAULD: *Maxims*, 1665

We need greater virtue to sustain good than evil fortune. IBID.

He who hath no ill fortune is cloyed with good.
JOHN RAY: *English Proverbs*, 1670

Fortune is always on the side of the largest battalions.
MARIE DE SÉVIGNÉ: *Letter to her daughter, Countess de Grignan*, *c.* 1690

I can enjoy her while she's kind;
But when she dances in the wind,
And shakes the wings, and will not stay,
I puff the prostitute away.
JOHN DRYDEN: *Imitations of Horace*, I, 1693

O fortune, fortune, thou art a bitch!
JOHN VANBRUGH: *The Relapse*, I, 1696

Fortune and love don't always favor the most deserving.
ENGLISH PROVERB, not recorded before the XVIII century

The quality of fortune, though a man has less reason to value himself upon it than on that of the body or mind, is, however, the kind of quality which makes the most shining figure in the eye of the world.
JOSEPH ADDISON: *The Spectator*, Nov. 10, 1711

Flee never so fast, you cannot flee your fortune.
JAMES KELLY: *Complete Collection of Scottish Proverbs*, 1721

Fortune rarely brings good or evil singly.
THOMAS FULLER: *Gnomologia*, 1732

He is a good man whom fortune makes better.
IBID.

When fortune knocks, be sure to open the door.
NATHANIEL BAILEY: *Etymological Dictionary*, 1736

A change of fortune hurts a wise man no more than a change of the moon.
BENJAMIN FRANKLIN: *Poor Richard's Almanac*, 1756

Fortune often delights to dignify what nature has neglected.
SAMUEL JOHNSON: *Thoughts Respecting Falkland's Islands*, 1771

Good fortune is far worse than bad.
THOMAS CARLYLE: *Letter to R. W. Emerson*, Feb. 3, 1835

An Englishman who has lost his fortune is said to have died of a broken heart.
R. W. EMERSON: *English Traits*, X, 1856

A son of fortune. (Fortunae filius.)
LATIN PHRASE

A fraudulently acquired fortune never reaches the third heir. LATIN PROVERB

Flee as fast as you will, your fortune will be at your tail. SCOTTISH PROVERB

[*See also* Bold, Brave, Bravery, Change, Character, Destiny, Determinism, Enemy, Face, Fate, Friend, God, Hero, Industry, Luck, Manners, Merit, Misfortune, Opportunity, Predestination, Riches, Self-help, Self-made.

Fortune-teller

And here is one, the Sibyl of the Row,
Who knows all secrets, or affects to know.
Seeking their fate, to her the simple run,
To her the guilty, theirs awhile to shun;
Mistress of worthless arts, depraved in will,
Her care unblest and unrepaid her skill,
Slave to the tribe, to whose command she stoops,
And poorer than the poorest maid she dupes.
GEORGE CRABBE: *The Parish Register*, I, 1807

Forty

If a man reach forty and has not made himself heard of, he is not worth regarding with respect.
CONFUCIUS: *Analects*, IX, *c.* 500 B.C.

At forty I attained to an unperturbed mind.
MENCIUS: *Discourses*, II, *c.* 300 B.C.

I am resolved to grow fat and look young till forty.
JOHN DRYDEN: *The Maiden Queen* (or *Secret Love*), III, 1668

Every man at forty is a fool or physician.
JOHN RAY: *English Proverbs,* 1670

At the age of forty she is very far from being cold and insensible: her fire may be covered with ashes, but it is not extinguished.
MARY WORTLEY MONTAGU: *Letter to Lady* ——, Jan. 13, 1716

A fool at forty is a fool indeed.
EDWARD YOUNG: *Love of Fame,* II, 1728

At thirty man suspects himself a fool;
Knows it at forty, and reforms his plan.
EDWARD YOUNG: *Night Thoughts,* I, 1742

Fat, fair and forty were all the toasts of the young men.
JOHN O'KEEFE: *Irish Minnie,* II, 1795

Forty times over let Michaelmas pass,
Grizzling hair the brain doth clear, —
Then you know a boy is an ass,
Then you know the worth of a lass,
Once you have come to forty year.
W. M. THACKERAY: *The Age of Wisdom,* 1840

On passing his fortieth year, any man of the slightest power of mind — any man, that is, who has more than the sorry share of intellect with which nature has endowed five-sixths of mankind — will hardly fail to show some trace of misanthropy.
ARTHUR SCHOPENHAUER: *The Ages of Life,* 1851

Men over forty are no judges of a book written in a new spirit.
R. W. EMERSON: *The Man of Letters,* 1863

Every man over forty is a scoundrel.
GEORGE BERNARD SHAW: *Maxims for Revolutionists,* 1903

The comparative uselessness of men over forty years of age.
WILLIAM OSLER: Speech in Baltimore, Feb. 22, 1905 (This led to the misapprehension that Dr. Osler proposed to retire, or even chloroform, all men at 40, and to the appearance of the verb *to oslerize*)

The dangerous age. (Den farlige alder.)
Title of a book in Danish by KARIN MICHAELIS, 1910 (The dangerous age is 40)

[*See also* Age (Middle), Ages, Eating and Drinking, Fat, Thirty.

Forty-five

[*See* Spinster.

Forty-nine

[*See* Body and Mind.

Forty-three

She may very well pass for forty-three,
In the dusk with a light behind her.
W. S. GILBERT: *Trial by Jury,* 1875

Today is my forty-third birthday. I have thus long passed the peak of life where the waters divide.
ESAIAS TEGNÉR: *Letter to F. M. Franzén,* Nov. 13, 1825

Foul

It's a bad bird that fouls its own nest.
ENGLISH PROVERB, traced by Apperson to *c.* 1250

Foul water will quench fire as well as fair.
JOHN HEYWOOD: *Proverbs,* 1546

Fourteen Points

[*See* Covenant, Dardanelles, League of Nations, Poland, Sea.

Fourth of July

[*See* July Fourth.

Fowl

[*See* Hen.

Fox

The foxes, the little foxes, that spoil the vine.
SOLOMON'S SONG II, 14, *c.* 200 B.C.

The tail is enough to bewray the fox.
WILLIAM LAMBARDE: *Peramulation of Kent,* 1576 (*Bewray*=reveal)

A crafty fox never preyeth near his den.
JOHN CLARKE: *Parœmiologia Anglo-Latina,* 1639

Reynard is still Reynard, though he put on a cowl. THOMAS FULLER: *Gnomologia,* 1732

Many foxes grow gray, but few grow good.
BENJAMIN FRANKLIN: *Poor Richard's Almanac,* 1749

A sleeping fox counts hens in his dreams.
RUSSIAN PROVERB

The quick brown fox jumps over the lazy dog.
Sentence used by typewriter repairmen to test machines (It contains every letter in the alphabet)

If a fox crosses on the ice you can take a cannon over. SERBIAN PROVERB

[*See also* Hypocrisy, Lion, Trial.

Fox-hunter

[He pursues] with earnestness and hazard something not worth the catching.
ALEXANDER POPE: *Letter to William Wycherley,* Oct. 26, 1705

Fox-hunters who have all day long tried in vain to break their necks join at night in a second attempt on their lives by drinking.
BERNARD DE MANDEVILLE: *The Fable of the Bees,* I, 1714

D'ye ken John Peel with his coat so gay?
D'ye ken John Peel at the break of day?

D'ye ken John Peel when he's far, far away,
With his hounds and his horn in the morning?
J. W. GRAVES: *D'Ye Ken John Peel, c.* 1750

The world may be divided into people that read, people that write, people that think, and fox-hunters.
WILLIAM SHENSTONE: *On Writing and Books,* 1764

Though the fox he follows may be tamed,
A mere fox-follower never is reclaimed.
WILLIAM COWPER: *Conversation,* 1782

The English country gentleman galloping after a fox — the unspeakable in full pursuit of the uneatable.
OSCAR WILDE: *A Woman of No Importance,* I, 1893

[*See also* Hunting.

Fox-hunting

Samson went and caught three hundred foxes, and took firebrands, and turned tail to tail, and put a firebrand in the midst between two tails. JUDGES XV, 4, *c.* 500 B.C.

Hounds and horses devour their masters.
JOHN CLARKE: *Parœmiologia Anglo-Latina,* 1639

Fox-hunting in my opinion deserves a place with the graver, more serious professions, among the great illusions of men.
LORD DUNSANY: *My Ireland,* XXVI, 1938

[*See also* Hunting, Racing.

Fragility

If you drop 'em they bust.
AMERICAN SAYING

Frailty

Frailty, thy name is woman!
SHAKESPEARE: *Hamlet,* I, *c.* 1601

Frailty is the incurable nature of mankind.
GEORGE SAVILE (MARQUESS OF HALIFAX): *Political, Moral and Miscellaneous Reflections, c.* 1690

The first time a woman is frail, she should be somewhat nice, methinks, for then or never is her time to make her fortune.
JOHN GAY: *The Beggar's Opera,* I, 1728

To step aside is human.
ROBERT BURNS: *An Address to the Unco Guid,* 1785

[*See also* Flesh, Judge, Love.

France

If I were God and had two sons, the eldest would have to be God after me, but I'd made the second King of France.
Ascribed to MAXIMILIAN I, HOLY ROMAN EMPEROR (1459–1519)

The day of the ruin of France is the eve of the ruin of England.
THOMAS OVERBURY: *Characters,* 1614

Ye talk of France — a slight unseason'd country.
JOHN FLETCHER: *The Wild-Goose Chase,* I, 1621

France is a meadow that cuts thrice a year.
GEORGE HERBERT: *Jacula Prudentum,* 1651

I am a citizen of the world; but if I were to adopt any country, it would be that in which I live at present [France], and from which I am determined never to depart, unless a war drive me to Switzerland or Italy.
DAVID HUME: *Letter to Gilbert Elliot,* Sept. 22, 1764

They order this matter better in France.
LAURENCE STERNE: *A Sentimental Journey,* I, 1768

France is worse than Scotland in everything but climate.
SAMUEL JOHNSON: *Boswell's Life,* 1775

The government of France is an absolute monarchy tempered by songs.
An anonymous French wit to Nicolas Chamfort, *c.* 1780

France, freed from that monster, Bonaparte, must again become the most agreeable country on earth. It would be the second choice of all whose ties of family and fortune give a preference to some other one, and the first choice of all not under those ties.
THOMAS JEFFERSON: *Letter to William Short,* 1814

A curse is on thee, France! from far and wide
It hath gone up to Heaven; all lands have cried
For vengeance upon thy detested head;
All nations curse thee, France! for wheresoe'er
In peace or war thy banner hath been spread,
All forms of human woe have follow'd there.
ROBERT SOUTHEY: *Ode Against Napoleon,* Jan., 1814

Trifles are great things in France — reason nothing.
NAPOLEON I: *Diary of Pulteney Malcolm at St. Helena,* Jan. 11, 1817

Who can help loving the land that has taught us
Six hundred and eighty-five ways to dress eggs?
THOMAS MOORE: *The Fudge Family,* 1818

France always has plenty men of talent, but it is always deficient in men of action and high character.
NAPOLEON I: To Gaspard Gourgaud at St. Helena, 1815–1818

France was long a despotism tempered by epigrams.
THOMAS CARLYLE: *The French Revolution,* I, 1837

The further off from England, the nearer is to France.
C. L. DODGSON (LEWIS CARROLL): *Alice's Adventures in Wonderland,* X, 1865

Whoever seems a little more distinguished than another has been to France.
GEORGE MOORE: *Confessions of a Young Man*, XI, 1888

France is a nation of ciphers — a mere crowd. It has wealth and elegance, but no individual men. They only act in the mass. They are nothing more than thirty million of obedient Kaffirs.
OTTO VON BISMARCK, *c.* 1865

I have traveled a good deal through France, but I don't ever recall having seen a pretty country girl.
IBID.

Like God in France. (Wie Gott in Frankreich.)
GERMAN SAYING

[*See also* Ballad, Belgium, Character (National), England, French, Frenchman, Italy, Kiss, Luxury, Opinion (Public), Patriotism, Scotland, Taste, War (Civil).

Franchise

I say no body of men are fit to make Presidents, judges and generals, unless they themselves supply the best specimens of the same; and that supplying one or two such specimens illuminates the whole body for a thousand years.
WALT WHITMAN: *Notes Left Over*, *c.* 1888

[*See also* Ballot, Vote.

Franciscan

[*See* Friar.

Franklin, Benjamin (1706–90)

He snatched the thunderbolt from Heaven, the sceptre from tyrants. (Eripuit caelo fulmen, mox sceptra tyrannis.)
A. R. J. TURGOT: Inscription for a bust of Franklin by J. A. Houdon, Paris, 1778

If to be venerated for benevolence, if to be admired for talents, if to be esteemed for patriotism, if to be beloved for philanthropy, can gratify the human mind, you must have the pleasing consolation to know that you have not lived in vain. And I flatter myself that it will not be ranked among the least grateful occurrences of your life to be assured that, so long as I retain my memory, you will be thought on with respect, veneration, and affection by your sincere friend.
GEORGE WASHINGTON: *Letter to Benjamin Franklin*, Sept. 23, 1789

The greatest man and ornament of the age and country in which he lived.
THOMAS JEFFERSON: *Letter to Samuel Smith*, 1798

A philosophical Quaker full of mean and thrifty maxims.
JOHN KEATS: *Letter to George and Georgiana Keats*, Oct. 14–31, 1818

[*See also* Epitaph, Greatness.

Fraternity

[*See* Liberty.

Fratricide

Oh, my offence is rank, it smells to Heaven;
It hath the primal eldest curse upon 't, —
A brother's murder.
SHAKESPEARE: *Hamlet*, III, *c.* 1601

Fraud

A pious fraud. (Pia fraus.)
OVID: *Metamorphoses*, IX, *c.* 5

Fraud and deceit abound in these days more than in former times.
EDWARD COKE: *Reports* (*Twyne's Case*), 1602

No court has ever attempted to define fraud.
MR. JUSTICE LINDLEY: *Judgment in Allcard* vs. *Skinner*, 1887

Fraud is infinite in variety; sometimes it is audacious and unblushing; sometimes it pays a sort of homage to virtue, and then it is modest and retiring; it would be honesty itself if it could only afford it.
LORD MACNAGHTEN: *Judgment in Reddaway* vs. *Banham*, 1896

A fraud is not perfect unless it be practised on clever persons.
ARAB PROVERB

Fraud vitiates everything. (Fraus vitiat omnia.)
LEGAL MAXIM

It is fraud to conceal fraud. (Fraus est celare fraudem.)
IBID.

No one can defraud those who know and consent. (Fraudare eos qui sciunt et consentiunt nemo videtur.)
IBID.

No right of action can arise out of a fraud. (Ex dolo malo non oritur actio.)
IBID.

[*See also* Falsehood, Frost, Haste, Law, War.

Freak

A freak of nature. (Lusus naturae.)
LATIN PHRASE

Frederick the Great of Prussia (1712–86)

As to his being an author, I have not looked at his poetry; but his prose is poor stuff. He writes just as you may suppose Voltaire's foot-boy to do, who has been his amanuensis.
SAMUEL JOHNSON: *Boswell's Life*, July 18, 1763

We hardly know any instance of the strength and weakness of human nature so striking and so grotesque as the character of this haughty, vigilant, resolute, sagacious blue-stocking, half Mithridates and half Trissotin, bearing up against a world in arms, with an ounce of poison in one pocket and a quire of bad verses in the other.
T. B. MACAULAY: *Frederick the Great*, 1842 (Edinburgh Review, April)

Freedom

No one is free save Jove.
ÆSCHYLUS: *Prometheus Bound, c.* 490 B.C.

No man is wholly free. He is a slave to wealth, or to fortune, or the laws, or the people restrain him from acting according to his will alone. EURIPIDES: *Hecuba, c.* 426 B.C.

Who, then, is free? The wise who can command his passions, who fears not want, nor death, nor chains, firmly resisting his appetites and despising the honors of the world, who relies wholly on himself, whose angular points of character have all been rounded off and polished. HORACE: *Satires,* II, *c.* 25 B.C.

Paul said, But I was free born.
ACTS XXII, 28, *c.* 75

Freedom all solace to man gives;
He lives at ease, that freely lives.
JOHN BARBOUR: *The Bruce, c.* 1375

I remember a proverb said of old: Who loseth his freedom, in faith he loseth all.
JOHN LYDGATE: *London Lickpenny, c.* 1430

Pray you use your freedom,
And, so far as you please, allow me mine,
To hear you only; not to be compelled
To take your moral potions.
PHILIP MASSINGER: *The Duke of Milan,* IV, 1623

If I have freedom in my love,
And in my soul am free,
Angels alone, that soar above,
Enjoy such liberty.
RICHARD LOVELACE: *To Althea from Prison,* 1642

No man who knows aught can be so stupid to deny that all men naturally were born free, being the image and resemblance of God Himself, and were, by privilege above all the creatures, born to command, and not to obey.
JOHN MILTON: *The Tenure of Kings and Magistrates,* 1649

None can love freedom heartily but good men; the rest love not freedom, but license.
IBID.

A free man is he that, in those things which by his strength and wit he is able to do, is not hindered to do what he has a will to.
THOMAS HOBBES: *Leviathan,* XXI, 1651

I am as free as nature first made man,
Ere the base laws of servitude began,
When wild in woods the noble savage ran.
JOHN DRYDEN: *The Conquest of Granada,* I, 1670

It is not good to be too free. It is not good to have everything one wants.
BLAISE PASCAL: *Pensées,* XXV, 1670

Only that thing is free which exists by the necessities of its own nature, and is determined in its actions by itself alone.
BARUCH DE SPINOZA: *Ethica,* I, 1677

Men are not naturally free.
ROBERT FILMER: *Patriarcha,* 1680

Free I was born, have lived, and will die.
Motto on a medal struck by Queen Christina of Sweden (1626–89)

Freedom of men under government is to have a standing rule to live by, common to every one of that society, and made by the legislative power vested in it; a liberty to follow my own will in all things, when the rule prescribes not, and not to be subject to the inconstant, uncertain, unknown, arbitrary will of another man.
JOHN LOCKE: *Treatises on Government,* II, 1690

The freedom princes owe their people is the freedom of law.
J. B. MASSILLON: *To Louis XV,* 1719

Who rule o'er freemen should themselves be free.
HENRY BROOKE: *The Earl of Essex,* I, 1749

It is a general prejudice, and has been propagated for these sixteen hundred years, that arts and sciences cannot flourish under an absolute government; and that genius must necessarily be cramped where freedom is restrained. This sounds plausible, but is false in fact.
LORD CHESTERFIELD: *Letter to his son,* Feb. 7, 1749

We are only so free that others may be free as well as we.
BENJAMIN WHICHCOTE: *Moral and Religious Aphorisms,* 1753

The power, opportunity, or advantage that anyone has to do as he pleases.
JONATHAN EDWARDS: *Freedom of the Will,* I, 1754

Man is born free — and everywhere he is in irons.
J.-J. ROUSSEAU: *Du contrat social,* I, 1761

He is truly free who wishes only for that which he is able to accomplish, and does whatever pleases him.
J.-J. ROUSSEAU: *Émile,* I, 1762

God Almighty . . . has given to all men a natural right to be free, and they have it ordinarily in their power to make themselves so, if they please.
JAMES OTIS: *The Rights of the British Colonies Asserted and Proved,* 1764

Who are a free people? Not those over whom government is reasonably exercised, but those who live under a government so constitutionally checked and controlled that proper provision is made against its being otherwise exercised.
JOHN DICKINSON: *Farmer's Letters,* VII, 1767

Depend upon it that the lovers of freedom will be free.
EDMUND BURKE: Speech to the electors of Bristol, Nov. 3, 1774

Under God we are determined that wheresoever, whensoever, or howsoever we shall be called to make our exit, we will die free men.
JOSIAH QUINCY: *Observations on the Boston Port Bill,* 1774

Freedom is that faculty which enlarges the usefulness of all other faculties.
IMMANUEL KANT: Lecture at Königsberg, 1775

Freedom hath been hunted round the globe. Asia and Africa have long expelled her. Europe regards her like a stranger, and England hath given her warning to depart. Oh, receive the fugitive, and prepare in time an asylum for mankind!
THOMAS PAINE: *Common Sense,* 1776

Freedom has a thousand charms to show,
That slaves, howe'er contented, never know.
WILLIAM COWPER: *Table-Talk,* 1782

Since the general civilization of mankind, I believe there are more instances of the abridgment of the freedom of the people by gradual and silent encroachments of those in power than by violent and sudden usurpations.
JAMES MADISON: Speech in the Virginia Convention, June 16, 1788

Free countries are those in which the rights of man are respected, and the laws, in consequence, are just.
M. M. I. ROBESPIERRE: Speech in the French Constituent Assembly, May 30, 1791

I, Sebastien-Roch-Nicolas Chamfort, herewith declare that I prefer to die a free man rather than be led a slave to prison.
NICOLAS CHAMFORT: Declaration to the police, signed with his blood, on attempting suicide with dagger and pistol, 1794 (The attempt succeeded, and he died April 13)

This is a free country.
ENGLISH SAYING, not recorded before the XIX century

Freedom is conceivable only of intelligence.
J. G. FICHTE: *Die Bestimmung des Menschen,* IV, 1800

Freedom exists only in the land of dreams, and the beautiful blooms only in song.
J. C. F. SCHILLER: *Der Antritt des neuen Jahrhunderts,* 1800

Freedom is as little lost in a day as won in a day. JEAN PAUL RICHTER: *Titan,* CV, 1803

Man free, man working for himself, with choice
Of time, and place, and object.
WILLIAM WORDSWORTH: *The Prelude,* VIII, 1805

Thus freedom now so seldom wakes,
The only throb she gives,
Is when some heart indignant breaks,
To show that still she lives.
THOMAS MOORE: *The Harp that Once through Tara's Halls,* 1808

Who would be free, themselves must strike the blow. BYRON: *Childe Harold,* II, 1812

Freedom's battle, once begun,
Bequeath'd by bleeding sire to son,
Though baffled oft is ever won.
BYRON: *The Giaour,* 1813

Yes, freedom! yet thy banner, torn, but flying,
Streams like the thunder-storm against the wind. BYRON: *Childe Harold,* IV, 1818

If a man has freedom enough to live healthy, and work at his craft, he has enough; and so much all can easily obtain.
J. W. GOETHE: *Conversations with Eckermann,* Jan. 18, 1827

Sir, there have existed, in every age and every country, two distinct orders of men — the lovers of freedom and the devoted advocates of power.
ROBERT Y. HAYNE: Speech in the Senate, Jan. 21, 1830

Freedom cannot be granted. It must be taken.
MAX STIRNER: *The Ego and His Own,* 1845

Freedom may lead to many transgressions, but it lends even to vices a less ignoble form.
K. W. VON HUMBOLDT: *Die Grenzen der Wirksamkeit des Staates,* 1851

The cause of freedom is identified with the destinies of humanity, and in whatever part of the world it gains ground, by and by it will be a common gain to all those who desire it.
LOUIS KOSSUTH: Speech in New York, 1851

Every man has freedom to do all that he wills, provided he infringes not the equal freedom of any other man.
HERBERT SPENCER: *Social Statics,* II, 1851

No one can be perfectly free till all are free.
IBID.

My faith in the proposition that each man should do precisely as he pleases with all which is exclusively his own lies at the foundation of the sense of justice there is in me. I extend the principle to communities of men as well as to individuals. I so extend it because it is politically wise, as well as naturally just: politically wise in saving us from broils about matters which do not concern us.
ABRAHAM LINCOLN: Speech at Peoria, Ill., Oct. 16, 1854

I would rather sit on a pumpkin, and have it all to myself, than to be crowded on a velvet cushion. I would rather ride on earth in an ox-cart with a free circulation than go to

Heaven in the fancy car of an excursion train and breathe a malaria all the way.

H. D. THOREAU: *Walden*, 1854

Free soil, free men, free speech, Frémont!

Slogan of the Republican party in the national campaign of 1856

I am for those that have never been master'd!
For men and women whose tempers have never been master'd,
For those whom laws, theories, conventions, can never master.

WALT WHITMAN: *As I Sat Alone*, 1856

Those who deny freedom to others deserve it not for themselves, and, under a just God, cannot long retain it.

ABRAHAM LINCOLN: *Letter to H. L. Pierce*, April 6, 1859

The only freedom which deserves the name is that of pursuing our own good in our own way, so long as we do not attempt to deprive others of theirs, or impede their efforts to obtain it.

J. S. MILL: *On Liberty*, I, 1859

In the beauty of the lilies Christ was born across the sea,
With a glory in His bosom that transfigures you and me;
And He died to make men holy, let us die to make men free,
While God is marching on.

JULIA WARD HOWE: *Battle Hymn of the Republic*, 1861

I intend no modification of my oft-expressed wish that all men everywhere could be free.

ABRAHAM LINCOLN: *Letter to Horace Greeley*, Aug. 22, 1862

In giving freedom to the slave we assure freedom to the free, — honorable alike in what we give and what we preserve.

ABRAHAM LINCOLN: Message to Congress, Dec. 1, 1862

Freedom all winged expands,
Nor perches in a narrow place;
Her broad van seeks unplanted lands;
She loves a poor and virtuous race.

R. W. EMERSON: *Voluntaries*, 1863 (Atlantic Monthly, Oct.)

Yes, we'll rally round the flag, boys, we'll rally once again,
Shouting the battle-cry of freedom.

G. F. ROOT: *The Battle-Cry of Freedom*, 1863

Glad to strike one free blow,
Whether for weal or woe;
Glad to breathe one free breath,
Though on the lips of death.

GEORGE H. BOKER: *The Black Regiment*, 1864

What that energy which is the life of genius, above everything demands and insists upon, is freedom; entire independence of all authority, prescription and routine — the fullest room to expand as it will.

MATTHEW ARNOLD: *The Literary Influence of Academies*, 1865

The freedom of a government does not depend upon the quality of its laws, but upon the power that has the right to create them.

THADDEUS STEVENS: Speech in the House of Representatives, Jan. 3, 1867

What citizen of a free country would listen to any offers of good and skillful administration in return for the abdication of freedom?

J. S. MILL: *The Subjection of Women*, IV, 1869

I am free only in so far as I recognize the humanity and respect the liberty of all the men surrounding me.

M. A. BAKUNIN: *Dieu et l'état*, 1871

If I want to be free from any other man's dictation, I must understand that I can have no other man under my control.

W. G. SUMNER: *The Forgotten Man*, 1883

The highest type of free man must be sought where the greatest resistance has to be overcome — five paces away from tyranny, on the very threshold of thraldom.

F. W. NIETZSCHE: *The Twilight of the Idols*, 1889

All we have of freedom — all we use or know —
This our fathers bought for us, long and long ago.

RUDYARD KIPLING: *The Old Issue*, 1899 (London Times, Sept. 29)

Freedom exists only where the people take care of the government.

WOODROW WILSON: Speech in New York, Sept. 4, 1912

No amount of political freedom will satisfy the hungry masses.

NIKOLAI LENIN: Draft of Bolshevik Theses, March 17, 1917

Every generation must wage a new war for freedom against new forces which seek through new devices to enslave mankind.

Platform of the Progressive party, 1924

I express many absurd opinions. But I am not the first man to do it; American freedom consists largely in talking nonsense.

E. W. HOWE: *Preaching from the Audience*, 1926

Oh, Lord, I want to be free, want to be free;
Rainbow round my shoulder, wings on my feet.

American Negro song, quoted by HOWARD W. ODUM: *Wings on My Feet*, IX, 1929

Real freedom means good wages, short hours, security in employment, good homes, opportunity for leisure and recreation with family and friends.

OSWALD MOSELY: *Fascism*, 1936

Better to be a free bird than a captive king.
DANISH PROVERB

[*See also* Democracy, Fish, French, Government, Health, Ignorance, Kosciusko (Tadeusz), Liberty, Mind, Prohibition, Slave, Society.

Freedom, Academic

A university studies politics, but it will not advocate fascism or communism. A university studies military tactics, but it will not promote war. A university studies peace, but it will not organize crusades of pacifism. It will study every question that affects human welfare, but it will not carry a banner in a crusade for anything except freedom of learning.
L. D. COFFMAN, president of the University of Minnesota: In the Journal of the American Association of University Women, Jan., 1936

Academic freedom is simply a way of saying that we get the best results in education and research if we leave their management to people who know something about them.
ROBERT M. HUTCHINS: *The Higher Learning in America,* I, 1936

Freedom, Religious

No person now or at any time hereafter living in this province who shall confess and acknowledge one Almighty God to be the Creator, Upholder and Ruler of the World, and who professes him or herself obliged in conscience to live peaceably and quietly under the civil government, shall in any case be molested or prejudiced for his or her conscientious persuasion or practise.
Law of Pennsylvania, Dec. 10, 1682

That state that will give liberty of conscience in matters of religion must give liberty of conscience and conversation in their moral laws, or else the fiddle will be out of tune, and some of the strings crack.
NATHANIEL WARD: *The Simple Cobbler of Aggawam,* 1646

All religions must be tolerated, and the sole concern of the authorities should be to see that one does not molest another, for here every man must be saved in his own way.
FREDERICK THE GREAT: *Cabinet Order,* June 22, 1740

No person shall be compelled to frequent or maintain any religious institution.
THOMAS JEFFERSON: *Proposed Constitution for Virginia,* June, 1776

All men shall be free to profess, and by argument to maintain, their opinion in matters of religion; and . . . the same shall in no wise diminish, enlarge, or affect their civil capacities.
THOMAS JEFFERSON: *Virginia Statute of Religious Freedom,* 1779

Every man, conducting himself as a good citizen, and being accountable to God alone for his religious opinions, ought to be protected in worshipping the Deity according to the dictates of his own conscience.
GEORGE WASHINGTON: *Letter to the United Baptist Chamber of Virginia,* May, 1789

Congress shall make no law respecting an establishment of religion, or prohibiting the free exercise thereof.
CONSTITUTION OF THE UNITED STATES, Amendment I, Dec. 15, 1791

I am for freedom of religion and against all maneuvers to bring about a legal ascendancy of one sect over another.
THOMAS JEFFERSON: *Letter to Elbridge Gerry,* 1799

Ay, call it holy ground,
The soil where first they trod;
They have left unstained what there they found, —
Freedom to worship God.
FELICIA HEMANS: *The Landing of the Pilgrim Fathers,* 1826

Nobody ever heard an Evangelical admit a High Churchman's right to be a High Churchman or a Catholic's right to be a Catholic.
J. A. FROUDE: *A Plea for the Free Discussion of Theological Difficulties,* 1863 (Fraser's Magazine)

Everyone is free to adopt and profess that religion which, guided by the light of reason, he holds to be true.
Proposition condemned by Pope Pius IX, Dec. 8, 1864

The United States, knowing no distinction of her own citizens on account of religion or nativity, naturally believes in a civilization the world over which will secure the same universal views.
U. S. GRANT: *Letter appointing Benjamin F. Peixotto consul at Bucharest,* Dec. 8, 1870

It is not within the power of the President, nor of Congress, nor of any judicial tribunal of the United States, to take or even hear testimony or in any mode to inquire into or decide upon the religious belief of any official.
THOMAS F. BAYARD (Secretary of State): *Note to Baron Ignatz von Schaeffer, Austro-Hungarian Minister to the United States,* May, 1885

[*See also* Censorship, Toleration.

Freemason

A set of imbeciles who meet to make good cheer and perform ridiculous fooleries.
NAPOLEON I: To Barry E. O'Meara at St. Helena, Nov. 2, 1816

Masons never tell. Author unidentified

No Mason is ever hanged. IBID.

Free Speech

[*See* Speech (Free).

Freethinker

[*See* Agnostic, Atheist, Doubt.

Freethinking

By freethinking I mean the use of the understanding in endeavoring to find out the meaning of any proposition whatsoever, in considering the nature of the evidence for or against, and in judging of it according to the seeming force or weakness of the evidence.
ANTHONY COLLINS: *A Discourse of Freethinking,* 1713

French

Have the French for friends, but not for neighbors.
NICEPHORUS I (BYZANTINE EMPEROR), *c.* 805

The French are naturally more fierce and hot than dexterous and strong, and if resisted handsomely in their first charge they slacken and cool, and grow as timorous as women. They are likewise impatient of distress or incommodity, and grow so careless by degrees that it is no hard matter, finding them in disorder, to master and overcome them.
NICCOLÒ MACHIAVELLI: *The State of France, c.* 1520

It hath been an opinion that the French are wiser than they seem.
FRANCIS BACON: *Essays,* XXVI, 1625

The character of the French demands seriousness in their sovereign.
JEAN DE LA BRUYÈRE: *Caractères,* X, 1688

Ungovern'd passion settled first in France,
Where mankind lives in haste, and thrives by chance,
A dancing nation, fickle and untrue:
Have oft undone themselves, and others too.
DANIEL DEFOE: *The True-Born Englishman,* I, 1701

The French are the only people, except the Greeks, who have been at once philosophers, poets, orators, historians, painters, architects, sculptors, and musicians.
DAVID HUME: *Of Civil Liberty,* 1740

What a number of sins does the cheerful, easy good-breeding of the French frequently cover! Many of them want common sense, many more common learning; but in general, they make up so much by their manner, for those defects, that frequently they pass undiscovered.
LORD CHESTERFIELD: *Letter to his son,* March 6, 1747

The toast of each Briton in war's dread alarms,
O'er bottle or bowl, is " Success to our arms."
Attack'd, put to flight, and forc'd from each trench,
" Success to our legs " is the toast of the French.
Anon.: *The Defeats of the French Army,* 1759

I hate the French because they are all slaves and wear wooden shoes.
OLIVER GOLDSMITH: *The History of a Disabled Soldier,* 1760

The French are an indelicate people; they will spit upon any place.
SAMUEL JOHNSON: *Boswell's Life,* 1775

The French are a gross, ill-bred, untaught people; a lady there will spit on the floor and rub it with her foot.
SAMUEL JOHNSON: *Boswell's Life,* May 14, 1778

A nation of right merry fellows, possessing the true secret of being happy, which is nothing more than thinking of nothing, talking about anything, and laughing at everything.
WASHINGTON IRVING: *Salmagundi,* Feb. 13, 1807

The French are not capable of freedom.
S. T. COLERIDGE: *Omniana,* CXXI, 1812

It is in the French character to insult kings.
NAPOLEON I: To Gaspard Gourgaud at St. Helena, Feb. 8, 1816

The French are not a religious nation.
NAPOLEON I: *Diary of Pulteney Malcolm at St. Helena,* July 25, 1816

The French are a fickle nation.
NAPOLEON I: *Diary of Pulteney Malcolm at St. Helena,* Jan. 11, 1817

The French have vanity, levity, independence, and caprice, with an unconquerable passion for glory. They will as soon do without bread as without glory.
NAPOLEON I: To Barry E. O'Meara at St. Helena, Feb. 17, 1817

The French, though an amiable and intelligent people, are not an imaginative one. The greatest height they go is in a balloon.
LEIGH HUNT: *The Indicator,* XVIII, 1821

The French have understanding and *esprit,* but neither a solid basis nor piety. What serves the moment, what helps his party, seems right to the Frenchman.
J. W. GOETHE: *Conversations with Eckermann,* Nov. 24, 1824

French honesty arises not perhaps from the love of justice, but from a repugnance to violence or force. They are a complaisant people, and would not rob you without first asking your consent, and making you an accomplice in your own wrong.
WILLIAM HAZLITT: *Traveling Abroad,* 1828 (New Monthly Magazine, May–June)

Fickle in everything else, the French have been faithful in one thing only, — their love of change.

ARCHIBALD ALISON: *History of Europe During the French Revolution,* 1833

I hate the hollowness of French principles; I hate the republicanism of French politics; I hate the hostility of the French people to revealed religion; I hate the artificiality of French cooking; I hate the acidity of French wines; I hate the flimsiness of the French language.

Ascribed to S. T. COLERIDGE (1772–1834) in J. C. YOUNG: *A Memoir of Charles Mayne Young,* 1871

The French are a pleasure-loving people, fond of dancing and light wines.

Author unidentified; said to have appeared in an American school geography, *c.* 1840

French ignorance is often more amusing than the wisdom of other people.

H. C. LODGE: *French Opinions of the United States,* 1884

The French are irreconcilable, savage foes; and, if you strip them of the cook, the tailor, and the hairdresser, you will find nothing left in them but copper-skinned Indians.

OTTO VON BISMARCK, *c.* 1880

The French are a people on the down grade.

WILLIAM II OF GERMANY: To A. Fendrich, 1912

When the Ethiopian turns white the French will love the English. ENGLISH PROVERB

The friendship of the French is like their wine: it is pleasant but it does not last long.

GERMAN PROVERB

They do everything; they know nothing. (Tutto fanno; niente sanno.) ITALIAN SAYING

[*See also* Aviation, Character (National), Cook, English, Mayonnaise, Patriotism, Pilgrim, Politeness, Soldier.

French Language

Unless a man knows French, he is held of little account [in England].

ROBERT OF GLOUCESTER: *Chronicle,* 1298

And French she spake full fair and fetishly,
After the school of Stratford-atte-bowe.

GEOFFREY CHAUCER: *The Canterbury Tales,* prologue, *c.* 1386

Jack would be a gentleman if he could speak French. JOHN HEYWOOD: *Proverbs,* 1546

Gentlemen's children are taught to speak French from the time they are rocked in their cradles.

RANULF HIGDEN: *Polychronicon, c.* 1350 (By 1387, according to John de Trevisa, who translated the Polychronicon into English, this fashion for French had died out, and English was taught)

The principal function of the academy shall be to labor with all care and diligence to give certain rules to our language, and to render it pure, eloquent, and capable of treating the arts and sciences.

Statutes of the Académie Française, XXIV, 1635

Very polished languages, and such as are praised for their superior clearness and perspicuity, are generally deficient in strength. The French language has that perfection and that defect.

EDMUND BURKE: *The Sublime and Beautiful,* IV, 1756

The French, though now spoken in all the courts of Europe, cannot lay claim either to the conciseness, purity or strength of expression to be found in the English; its softness may suit the disposition of those who are born slaves, but it is neither suitable to the free and manly sentiment of English kings or English subjects.

DANIEL FENNING: *A Royal English Dictionary,* dedication, 1761

If only this damned French language were not so badly fitted for music!

W. A. MOZART: *Letter to his father,* July 9, 1778

You will learn to speak it better from women and children in three months than from men in a year.

THOMAS JEFFERSON: *Letter to T. M. Randolph,* 1787

The most meagre and inharmonious of all languages.

HORACE WALPOLE: *Letter to Hannah More,* Oct. 14, 1787

French . . . is, perhaps, the most perspicuous and pointed language in the world.

S. T. COLERIDGE: *Miscellaneous,* 1811

An Englishman understates, avoids the superlative, checks himself in compliments, alleging that in the French language one cannot speak without lying.

R. W. EMERSON: *English Traits,* IX, 1856

Whene'er I hear French spoken as I approve
I find myself quietly falling in love.

E. R. BULWER-LYTTON (OWEN MEREDITH): *Lucile,* I, 1860

[*See also* English Language, Language.

Frenchman

The passion of nearly every Frenchman is to pass for a wit.

C. L. DE MONTESQUIEU: *Persian Letters,* LXVI, 1721

We . . . are now so degenerated that three Frenchmen can evidently beat one Englishman.

HORACE WALPOLE: *Letter to George Montagu,* July 13, 1745

A Frenchman who, with a fund of virtue, learning and good sense, has the manners and good breeding of his country, is the perfection of human nature.
LORD CHESTERFIELD: *Letter to his son,* March 6, 1747

One Englishman is able to beat five Frenchmen at any time.
OLIVER GOLDSMITH: *The Citizen of the World,* CXX, 1762

The Frenchman, easy, debonair, and brisk,
Give him his lass, his fiddle, and his frisk,
Is always happy, reign whoever may,
And laughs the sense of mis'ry far away.
WILLIAM COWPER: *Table-Talk,* 1782

A true German can't endure a Frenchman, but he likes French wine.
J. W. GOETHE: *I Faust,* I, 1808

Frenchmen are like grains of gunpowder — each by itself smutty and contemptible, but mass them together and they are terrible indeed.
S. T. COLERIDGE: *Table-Talk,* July 30, 1831

Everything French suits exactly every Frenchman.
W. C. BROWNELL: *French Traits,* 1889

Set him to write poetry, he is limited, artificial and impotent; set him to write prose, he is free, natural and effective.
MATTHEW ARNOLD: *The Literary Influence of Academies,* 1865

Give a Frenchman twenty-five lashes, and if you only make a fine speech to him about the freedom and dignity of man he will persuade himself that he is not lashed at all.
OTTO VON BISMARCK, *c.* 1875

The French they are a peculiar race,
Parley-vous!
Anon.: *Mademoiselle from Armenteers,* 1915

Forty million Frenchmen can't be wrong.
Author unidentified (The saying was popular among the American soldiers during the World War, 1917–18. Sometimes *thirty* or *fifty* appears in place of *forty*)

When a Frenchman sleeps the Devil rocks him.
FRENCH PROVERB

A Frenchman runs away even from a she-goat.
RUSSIAN PROVERB

A Frenchman's legs are thin, his soul is little, he is fickle as the wind.
IBID.

No one so frightened as a frightened Frenchman.
IBID.

The Frenchman is a scoundrel. (Francés gabacho.)
SPANISH PROVERB

[*See also* Attack, Character (National), Cheating, Englishman, German, Pole.

Frenchwoman

It is not a fashion for the maids in France to kiss before they are married.
SHAKESPEARE: *Henry V,* V, *c.* 1599

[*See also* Englishman.

Frenzy

[*See* Poet.

Friar

The fasting of the friars is more easy to them than our eating to us. For one day of fasting there are three of feasting. Every friar for his supper has two quarts of beer, a quart of wine, and spice-cakes, or bread prepared with spice and salt, the better to relish their drink.
MARTIN LUTHER: *Table-Talk,* CCCCLXXXIII, 1569

A friar, a liar.
ENGLISH PROVERB, traced to the XVII century

Do as the friar saith, not as he doth.
JOHN CLARKE: *Parœmiologia Anglo-Latina,* 1639

The friar preached against stealing, and had a goose in his sleeve.
GEORGE HERBERT: *Jacula Prudentum,* 1651

Embryos and idiots, eremites and friars,
White, black, and gray, with all their trumpery.
JOHN MILTON: *Paradise Lost,* III, 1667

The numerous vermin of mendicant friars, Franciscans, Dominicans, Augustins, who swarmed in this century [the Thirteenth] with habits and institutions variously ridiculous, disgraced religion, learning, and common sense. They seized on Scholastic philosophy as a science peculiarly suited to their minds; and, excepting only Friar Bacon, they all preferred words to things.
EDWARD GIBBON: *Outlines of the History of the World, c.* 1760

What baron or squire
Or knight of the shire
Lives half so well as a holy friar?
JOHN O'KEEFE: *I Am a Friar of Orders Gray,* 1785

I hated friars, and was for the annihilation of them and of their receptacles of crime, the monasteries, where every vice was practised with impunity. A set of miscreants, who in general are a dishonor to the human race.
NAPOLEON I: To Barry E. O'Meara at St. Helena, April 4, 1817

[*See also* Danger, Dress, Monk.

Friday

He that sings on Friday will weep on Sunday.
GEORGE HERBERT: *Outlandish Proverbs,* 1640

Now Friday came. Your old wives say,
Of all the week's the unluckiest day.

RICHARD FLECKNOE: *Diarium*, 1656

Alas! you know the cause too well;
The salt is spilt, to me it fell.
Then to contribute to my loss,
My knife and fork were laid across;
On Friday, too! the day I dread;
Would I were safe at home, in bed!

JOHN GAY: *Fables*, I, 1727

Fine on Friday, fine on Sunday;
Wet on Friday, wet on Sunday.

OLD ENGLISH RHYME

Friday's a day as'll have his trick,
The fairest or foulest day o' the wik. IBID.

[*See also* Days, Nail, Sneezing, Thursday, Wedding-day.

Friend

My friend should honor him who honors me.

HOMER: *Iliad*, IX, *c.* 800 B.C.

And one shall say unto him, What are these wounds in thine hands? Then he shall answer, Those with which I was wounded in the house of my friends.

ZECHARIAH XIII, 6, *c.* 520 B.C.

Have no friends not equal to yourself.

CONFUCIUS: *Analects*, IX, *c.* 500 B.C.

He who throws away a friend is as bad as he who throws away his life.

SOPHOCLES: *Oedipus Tyrannus*, *c.* 450 B.C.

When ill befalls a friend's kind eye beams comfort. EURIPIDES: *Ion*, *c.* 420 B.C.

When fortune smiles, what need of friends?

EURIPIDES: *Orestes*, 408 B.C.

There is a friend that sticketh closer than a brother. PROVERBS XVIII, 24, *c.* 350 B.C.

One has remained a boy in mind, while the other has become a man of high ability. How can they continue friends?

ARISTOTLE: *The Nicomachean Ethics*, IX, *c.* 340 B.C.

A faithful friend is a strong defense: and he that hath found such an one hath found a treasure.

ECCLESIASTICUS VI, 14, *c.* 180 B.C.

Forsake not an old friend, for the new is not comparable unto him.

ECCLESIASTICUS, IX, 10

Mine own familiar friend, in whom I trusted, which did eat of my bread, hath lifted up his heel against me.

PSALMS XLI, 9, *c.* 150 B.C.

A friend is, as it were, a second self. (Amicus est tanquam alter idem.)

CICERO: *De amicitia*, XXI, *c.* 50 B.C.

Never injure a friend, even in jest. IBID.

The vulgar estimate friends by the advantage to be derived from them.

OVID: *Epistulæ ex Ponto*, II, *c.* 5

In prosperity it is very easy to find a friend; in adversity, nothing is so difficult.

EPICTETUS: *Encheiridion*, *c.* 110

Instead of herds of oxen, endeavor to assemble flocks of friends about your house. IBID.

Greater love hath no man than this, that a man lay down his life for his friends.

JOHN XV, 13, *c.* 115

A friend in need is a friend indeed.

ENGLISH PROVERB, traced by Apperson to the XIII century

Reprove a friend in secret, but praise him before others.

LEONARDO DA VINCI: *Notebooks*, *c.* 1500

A friend is long a-getting, and soon lost.

JOHN LYLY: *Euphues*, 1579

Time draweth wrinkles in a fair face, but addeth fresh colors to a fast friend, which neither heat, nor cold, nor misery, nor place, nor destiny, can alter or diminish.

JOHN LYLY: *Endymion*, III, 1591

To wail friends lost
Is not by much so wholesome — profitable,
As to rejoice at friends but newly found.

SHAKESPEARE: *Love's Labor's Lost*, V, *c.* 1595

Two lovely berries molded on one stem:
So, with two seeming bodies, but one heart.

SHAKESPEARE: *A Midsummer Night's Dream*, III, *c.* 1596

I would be friends with you and have your love.

SHAKESPEARE: *The Merchant of Venice*, I, *c.* 1597

A friend should bear his friend's infirmities.

SHAKESPEARE: *Julius Cæsar*, IV, 1599

We have slept together,
Rose at an instant, learn'd, play'd, eat together;
And wheresoe'er we went, like Juno's swans,
Still we went coupled and inseparable.

SHAKESPEARE: *As You Like It*, I, *c.* 1600

Let them be good that love me, though but few.

BEN JONSON: *Cynthia's Revels*, III, 1601

Those friends thou hast, and their adoption tried,
Grapple them to thy soul with hoops of steel,
But do not dull thy palm with entertainment
Of each new hatched, unfledged comrade.

SHAKESPEARE: *Hamlet*, I, *c.* 1601

Where shall man have a worse friend than he brings from home?

WILLIAM CAMDEN: *Remains Concerning Britain*, 1605

Friends are thieves of time. (Amici fures temporis.)
LATIN PROVERB, quoted in FRANCIS BACON: *The Advancement of Learning*, II, 1605

I am not of that feather to shake off
My friend when he must need me.
SHAKESPEARE: *Timon of Athens*, I, *c.* 1607

I am wealthy in my friends.
SHAKESPEARE: *Timon of Athens*, II

Those you make friends,
And give your hearts to, when they once perceive
The least rub in your fortunes, fall away
Like water from ye.
SHAKESPEARE and JOHN FLETCHER: *Henry VIII*, II, 1613

To find friends when we have no need of them, and to want them when we have, are both alike easy and common. In prosperity, who will not profess to love a man? In adversity, how few will show that they do indeed?
OWEN FELLTHAM: *Resolves*, I, *c.* 1620

All men's friend, no man's friend.
JOHN WODROEPHE: *Spared Hours*, 1623

A man cannot speak to his son but as a father, to his wife but as a husband, to his enemy but upon terms; whereas a friend may speak as the case requires, and not as it sorteth with the person.
FRANCIS BACON: *Essays*, XXVII, 1625

You may take sarza to open the liver; steel to open the spleen; flowers of sulphur for the lungs; castoreum for the brain; but no receipt openeth the heart but a true friend, to whom you may impart griefs, joys, fears, hopes, suspicions, counsels, and whatsoever lieth upon the heart to oppress it, in a kind of civil shrift or confession. IBID.

He is my friend that grindeth at my mill.
THOMAS DRAXE: *Bibliotheca scholastica instructissima*, 1633

Thy friend put in thy bosom; wear his eyes
Still in thy heart, that he may see what's there.
GEORGE HERBERT: *The Temple*, 1633

I hold he loves me best that calls me Tom.
THOMAS HEYWOOD: *Hierarchie of the Blessed Angells*, 1635

All are not friends that speak us fair.
JAMES CLARKE: *Parœmiologia Anglo-Latina*, 1639

It is good to have some friends both in Heaven and Hell.
GEORGE HERBERT: *Outlandish Proverbs*, 1640

Life without a friend is death without a witness.
IBID.

Many friends in general; one in special.
IBID.

I have loved my friends as I do virtue, my soul, my God.
THOMAS BROWNE: *Religio Medici*, II, 1642

Friends are a second existence.
BALTASAR GRACIÁN: *The Art of Worldly Wisdom*, CXI, 1647

A man is judged by his friends, for the wise and foolish have never agreed.
BALTASAR GRACIÁN: *The Art of Worldly Wisdom*, CLVI

Wilt thou my true friend be?
Then love not mine, but me.
ROBERT HERRICK: *Hesperides*, 1648

When a friend asks there is no tomorrow.
GEORGE HERBERT: *Jacula Prudentum*, 1651

Although I love my friend because he is worthy, yet he is not worthy if he can do me no good.
JEREMY TAYLOR: *Twenty-seven Sermons*, I, 1651

Trust not a reconciled friend, for good turns cannot blot out old grudges.
GEORGE CHAPMAN: *Alphonsus*, I, 1654

I am complaisant towards friends, and put up patiently with their ill humors, but I never take much pains to please them when they visit me, and I am never much disquieted by their absence.
LA ROCHEFOUCAULD: *Self-portrait*, 1658

Choose thy friends like thy books, few but choice. JAMES HOWELL: *Proverbs*, 1659

Make not thy friend too cheap to thee, nor thyself too dear to him. IBID.

In the adversity of our best friends we often find something which does not displease us.
LA ROCHEFOUCAULD: *Maxims*, 1665

He who is the friend of all humanity is not my friend. J. P. MOLIÈRE: *Alceste*, I, 1666

It is good to have friends, but bad to need them.
Anon.: *New Help to Discourse*, 1669

If we all told what we know of one another there would not be four friends in the world.
BLAISE PASCAL: *Pensées*, VI, 1670

Happy is he whose friends were born before him. JOHN RAY: *English Proverbs*, 1670

New friends, like new mistresses, are got by disparaging old ones.
WILLIAM WYCHERLEY: *The Plain Dealer*, I, *c.* 1674

Old friends are best. King James used to call for his old shoes; they were easiest for his feet. JOHN SELDEN: *Table-Talk*, 1689

A true friend unbosoms freely, advises justly, assists readily, adventures boldly, takes all patiently, defends courageously, and continues a friend unchangeably.
WILLIAM PENN: *Fruits of Solitude*, 1693

When we are old, our friends find it difficult to please us, and are less concerned whether we be pleased or not.
JONATHAN SWIFT: *Thoughts on Various Subjects*, 1706

Histories are more full of examples of the fidelity of dogs than of friends.
ALEXANDER POPE: *Letter to Henry Cromwell*, Oct. 19, 1709

I am weary of friends, and friendships are all monsters.
JONATHAN SWIFT: *Journal to Stella*, Oct. 23, 1710

Real friends are our greatest joy and our greatest sorrow. It were almost to be wished that all true and faithful friends should expire on the same day.
FRANÇOIS FÉNELON: On the death of the Duc de Chevreuse, Aug. 13, 1714

Seem only to regard your friends.
But use them for your private ends.
JOHN GAY: *Fables*, I, 1727

Why do we grieve that friends should die?
No loss more easy to supply.
JONATHAN SWIFT: *On the Death of Dr. Swift*, 1731

Even reckonings keep long friends.
THOMAS FULLER: *Gnomologia*, 1732

He is my friend that succoreth me, not he that pitieth me. IBID.

If you have one true friend you have more than your share. IBID.

May it please God not to make our friends so happy as to forget us! IBID.

No man can be happy without a friend, nor be sure of his friend till he is unhappy. IBID.

There is no better looking-glass than an old friend. IBID.

My guide, philosopher, and friend.
ALEXANDER POPE: *An Essay on Man*, IV, 1734 (Also in the First Epistle of the First Book of Horace, 1735)

There are three faithful friends — an old wife, an old dog, and ready money.
BENJAMIN FRANKLIN: *Poor Richard's Almanac*, 1738

Fly, my friends, with treacherous speed,
Melt as snow before the sun;
Leave me at my greatest need,
Leave me to my God alone.
CHARLES WESLEY: *On the Loss of His Friends*, 1749

A brother may not be a friend, but a friend will always be a brother.
BENJAMIN FRANKLIN: *Poor Richard's Almanac*, 1752

Be slow in choosing a friend, slower in changing. BENJAMIN FRANKLIN: *Poor Richard's Almanac*, 1757

The loss of a beloved deserving friend is the hardest trial of philosophy.
MARY WORTLEY MONTAGU: *Letter to James Steuart*, Nov. 27, 1759

There is no word in the Latin language that signifies a female friend. *Amica* means a mistress: and perhaps there is no friendship betwixt the sexes wholly disunited from a degree of love.
WILLIAM SHENSTONE: *On Writing and Books*, 1764

He cast off his friends, as a huntsman his pack;
For he knew, when he pleas'd, he could whistle them back.
OLIVER GOLDSMITH: *Retaliation*, 1774

If a man does not make new acquaintance as he advances through life he will soon find himself alone. A man should keep his friendship in constant repair.
SAMUEL JOHNSON: To Joshua Reynolds, 1775

He that has friends has no friend.
SAMUEL JOHNSON: *Boswell's Life*, 1778 (Ascribed to " an old Greek." Cf. April 24, 1779)

If it is abuse, why one is always sure to hear of it from one damned good-natured friend or another.
R. B. SHERIDAN: *The Critic*, I, 1779

One friend must in time lose the other.
SAMUEL JOHNSON: *Letter to Mrs. William Strahan*, April 23, 1781

Officious, innocent, sincere,
Of every friendless name the friend.
SAMUEL JOHNSON: *On the Death of Robert Levet*, 1783

A friend may be often found and lost, but an old friend never can be found, and nature has provided that he cannot easily be lost.
SAMUEL JOHNSON: To Hester Thrale, Nov. 13, 1783

Now, sir, if ye hae friends enow,
Though real friends I b'lieve are few,
Yet, if your catalogue be fou,
I'se no insist,
But gif ye want ae friend that's true,
I'm on your list.
ROBERT BURNS: *Epistle to J. Lapraik*, April 1, 1785

I want someone to laugh with me, someone to be grave with me, someone to please me and help my discrimination with his or her own remark, and at times, no doubt, to admire my acuteness and penetration.
ROBERT BURNS: *Commonplace-Book*, April 9, 1787

I find as I grow older that I love those most whom I loved first.
THOMAS JEFFERSON: *Letter to Mrs. John Bolling,* 1787

I never considered a difference of opinion in politics, in religion, in philosophy, as cause for withdrawing from a friend.
THOMAS JEFFERSON: *Letter to William Hamilton,* 1800

Our very best friends have a tincture of jealousy even in their friendship; and when they hear us praised by others, will ascribe it to sinister and interested motives if they can.
C. C. COLTON: *Lacon,* 1820

When we have lost a favorite horse or a dog, we usually endeavor to console ourselves by the recollection of some bad qualities they happened to possess; and we are very apt to tranquilize our minds by similar reminiscences on the death of those friends who have left us nothing. IBID.

Let no man grumble when his friends fall off,
As they will do like leaves at the first breeze:
When your affairs come round, one way or t'other,
Go to the coffee-house, and take another.
BYRON: *Don Juan,* XIV, 1823

Of all plagues, good Heaven, thy wrath can send,
Save, save, oh! save me from the candid friend.
GEORGE CANNING: *The New Morality,* 1823

I like a friend the better for having faults that one can talk about.
WILLIAM HAZLITT: *The Plain Speaker,* I, 1826

Green be the turf above thee,
Friend of my better days!
None knew thee but to love thee,
Nor named thee but to praise.
FITZ-GREENE HALLECK: *On the Death of Joseph Rodman Drake,* 1827

We never know the true value of friends. While they live we are too sensitive of their faults: when we have lost them we only see their virtues.
J. C. and A. W. HARE: *Guesses at Truth,* 1827

The best way to keep your friends is to never borrow from them and never lend them anything.
PAUL DE KOCK: *Homme aux trois culottes,* 1830

We want but two or three friends, but these we cannot do without, and they serve us in every thought we think.
R. W. EMERSON: *Letter to Thomas Carlyle,* Sept. 17, 1836

A man's growth is seen in the successive choirs of his friends.
R. W. EMERSON: *Circles,* 1841

A friend is a person with whom I may be sincere. Before him I may think aloud.
R. W. EMERSON: *Friendship,* 1841

The most I can do for my friend is simply to be his friend.
H. D. THOREAU: *Journal,* Feb. 7, 1841

Never have a friend that's poorer than yourself.
DOUGLAS JERROLD: *Bubbles of the Day,* II, 1842

Nothing makes the earth seem so spacious as to have friends at a distance: they make the latitudes and longitudes.
H. D. THOREAU: *Letter to Mrs. E. Castleton,* May 22, 1843

Friends are the thermometers by which we may judge the temperature of our fortunes.
Ascribed to the COUNTESS OF BLESSINGTON (1789–1849)

My best friend would be the man who would blow my brains out with a pistol.
E. A. POE: On his deathbed, as recorded by Dr. J. J. Moran, Oct. 7, 1849

Can't I be your friend, but I must be your fool too?
H. G. BOHN: *Handbook of Proverbs,* 1855

Few there are that will endure a true friend.
IBID.

Friends are the nearest relations. IBID.

Friends got without desert will be lost without cause. IBID.

He that ceaseth to be a friend never was a good one. IBID.

When two friends have a common purse, one sings and the other weeps. IBID.

Between me and my friend what unfathomable distance! All mankind, like motes and insects, are between us.
H. D. THOREAU: *Journal,* Feb. 24, 1857

There is no man so friendless but what he can find a friend sincere enough to tell him disagreeable truths.
E. G. BULWER-LYTTON: *What Will He Do With It?,* II, 1858

I desire so to conduct the affairs of this administration that if at the end, when I come to lay down the reins of power, I have lost every other friend on earth, I shall at least have one friend left, and that friend shall be down inside of me.
ABRAHAM LINCOLN: Reply to Missouri Committee of Seventy, 1864

Granting that we had both the will and the sense to choose our friends well, how few of us have the power. Nearly all our associations are determined by chance, or necessity; and restricted within a narrow circle.
JOHN RUSKIN: *Sesame and Lilies,* I, 1865

Fellowship in joy, not sympathy in sorrow, is what makes friends.
F. W. NIETZSCHE: *Human All-too-Human,* I, 1878

As I picked up books, so I picked up my friends. I read friends and books with the same passion, with the same avidity; and as I discarded my books when I had assimilated as much of them as my system required, so I discarded my friends when they ceased to be of use to me.
GEORGE MOORE: *Confessions of a Young Man,* II, 1888

Friends are generally of the same sex, for when men and women agree, it is only in their conclusions; their reasons are always different.
GEORGE SANTAYANA: *The Life of Reason,* II, 1905

While your friend holds you affectionately by both your hands you are safe, for you can watch both his.
AMBROSE BIERCE: *The Devil's Dictionary,* 1906

Every friend is a possible temptation.
Maxim for newspaper men, ascribed to W. R. NELSON (1841–1915), publisher of the Kansas City Star

Probably no man ever had a friend he did not dislike a little; we are all so constituted by nature no one can possibly entirely approve of us.
E. W. HOWE: *The Indignations of E. W. Howe,* 1933

A friend is one who dislikes the same people that you dislike. Author unidentified

Friends help; others pity. IBID.

When we lose a friend we die a little. IBID.

You can hardly make a friend in a year, but you can easily lose one in an hour.
CHINESE PROVERB

Everyman's friend is everyman's fool.
DUTCH PROVERB

The friends of my friends are my friends.
FLEMISH PROVERB

It is worse to mistrust a friend than to be deceived by him. FRENCH PROVERB

They only are true friends who think as one.
IBID.

There are three kinds of friends: those who love you, those who hate you, and those who care nothing about you.
GERMAN PROVERB

They are not all friends who laugh with you.
IBID.

These can never be true friends: hope, dice, a prostitute, a robber, a cheat, a goldsmith, a monkey, a doctor, and a distiller.
HINDU PROVERB

What a friend gets is not lost.
IRISH PROVERB

The character of a man depends on whether he has good or bad friends.
JAPANESE PROVERB

A friend is another self. (Alter ipse amicus.)
LATIN PROVERB

Friends are thieves of time. (Amici fures temporis.) IBID.

One God, no more,
But friends good store. OLD ENGLISH RHYME

When we go up the hill of fortune may we never meet a friend coming down.
OLD ENGLISH TOAST

It is better to be in chains with friends than in a garden with strangers.
PERSIAN PROVERB

Beware of a friend you have offended.
PORTUGUESE PROVERB

An untried friend is like an uncracked nut.
RUSSIAN PROVERB

If you seek friends who can be trusted, go to the cemetery. IBID.

Be a friend to yourself, and others will.
SCOTTISH PROVERB

Before ye choose a friend, eat a peck o' salt wi' him. IBID.

Change your friend e'er you hae need.
IBID.

Love your friend and look to yourself. IBID.

[*See also* Acquaintance, Adversity, Alone, Best, Conversation, Customer, Dead, Dog, Enemy, Flatterer, Flattery, Foolishness, Frenchman, Friend and Enemy, Friendship, Golden Rule, Guide, Happiness, Heaven and Hell, House, Husband and Wife, Jest, Louse, Lover, Mirror, Money, Old, Old and New, Physician, Politics, Privacy, Prosperity, Relative.

Friend and Enemy

It is better to mediate between enemies than between friends, for one of the friends is sure to become an enemy and one of the enemies a friend.
Ascribed to BIAS, *c.* 550 B.C.

An enemy should be hated only so far as one may be hated who may one day be a friend.
SOPHOCLES: *Ajax, c.* 450 B.C.

Treat your friend as if he will one day be your enemy, and your enemy as if he will one day be your friend.
LABERIUS: *Fragment, c.* 45 B.C.

He that is not with me is against me.
LUKE XI, 23, *c.* 75

God save me from my friends; I can take care of my enemies.
ENGLISH PROVERB, traced by Apperson to 1477

The friend that faints is a foe.
JOHN DAVIES: *The Scourge of Folly,* 1611

A wise man gets more out of his enemies than a fool gets out of his friends.
BALTASAR GRACIÁN: *The Art of Worldly Wisdom,* LXXXIV, 1647

Nothing is so dangerous as an ignorant friend; a wise enemy is much better.
JEAN DE LA FONTAINE: *Fables,* VIII, 1671

One enemy can do more hurt than ten friends can do good.
JONATHAN SWIFT: *Journal to Stella,* June 30, 1711

Never trust much to a new friend or an old enemy.
JAMES KELLY: *Complete Collection of Scottish Proverbs,* 1721

No friend to a bosom friend; no enemy to a bosom enemy.
IBID.

Nature teaches us to love our friends, but religion our enemies.
THOMAS FULLER: *Gnomologia,* 1732

Our friends abandon us only too easily, and our enemies are implacable.
VOLTAIRE: *Letter to Charles Palissot,* Sept. 24, 1760

An injured friend is the bitterest of foes.
THOMAS JEFFERSON: *French Treaties Opinion,* 1793

Thy friendship oft has made my heart to ache:
Do be my enemy — for friendship's sake.
WILLIAM BLAKE: *To H., c.* 1808

If you want enemies, excel others; if you want friends, let others excel you.
C. C. COLTON: *Lacon,* 1820

Speak well of your friend; of your enemy say nothing.
H. G. BOHN: *Handbook of Proverbs,* 1855

Trust not the praise of a friend or the contempt of an enemy.
IBID.

Whatever the number of a man's friends, there will be times in his life when he has one too few; but if he has only one enemy, he is lucky indeed if he has not one too many.
E. G. BULWER-LYTTON: *What Will He Do With It?,* IX, 1858

I choose my friends for their good looks, my acquaintances for their characters, and my enemies for their brains.
OSCAR WILDE: *The Picture of Dorian Gray,* 1891

The enemy of my enemy is my friend.
FRENCH PROVERB

A needle's eye is wide enough for two friends; the whole world is too narrow for two enemies.
PERSIAN PROVERB

Beware of the friend who was once your foe.
PORTUGUESE PROVERB

Better be friends at a distance than enemies at hame.
SCOTTISH PROVERB

[*See also* Enemy, Friend, Historian, House, Misfortune, Money, Obsequiousness, Physician, Preparedness.

Friendless

My familiar friends have forgotten me.
JOB XIX, 14, *c.* 325 B.C.

There is no desert like being friendless.
BALTASAR GRACIÁN: *The Art of Worldly Wisdom,* CLVIII, 1647

A friendless man is like a left hand without a right.
HEBREW PROVERB

Friendly

For thus the royal mandate ran
When first the human race began:
The social, friendly, honest man,
Whate'er he be,
'Tis he fulfils great nature's plan,
And none but he.
ROBERT BURNS: *Epistle to J. Lapriak,* April 1, 1785

Friendship

There are three friendships which are advantageous, and three which are injurious. Friendship with the upright; friendship with the sincere; and friendship with the man of much observation; these are advantages. Friendship with the man of specious airs; friendship with the insinuatingly soft; and friendship with the glib-tongued; these are injurious.
CONFUCIUS: *Analects,* XVI, *c.* 500 B.C.

The perfect friendship is that between good men, alike in their virtue.
ARISTOTLE: *The Nicomachean Ethics,* VIII, *c.* 340 B.C.

When men are friends there is no need of justice between them, but though they be just they still need friendship.
IBID.

Life is nothing without friendship. (Sine amicitia vitam esse nullam.)
Ascribed by Cicero to QUINTUS ENNIUS (239–169 B.C.)

Friendship can exist only where men harmonize in their views of things human and divine.
CICERO: *De amicitia,* XI, *c.* 50 B.C.

Friendship always benefits; love sometimes injures.
SENECA: *Epistulæ morales ad Lucilium, c.* 63

We ought to flee the friendship of the wicked, and the enmity of the good.
EPICTETUS: *Encheiridion, c.* 110

The virtue is no less to conserve friendship gotten, than the wisdom was great to get and win the same.
WILLIAM PAINTER: *The Palace of Pleasure,* II, 1567

O friendship! of all things the most rare, and therefore most rare because most excellent, whose comfort in misery is always sweet, and whose counsels in prosperity are ever fortunate.
JOHN LYLY: *Endymion,* III, 1591

When adversities flow, then love ebbs; but friendship standeth stiffly in storms. IBID.

There is flattery in friendship.
SHAKESPEARE: *Henry V,* III, *c.* 1599

Friendship is constant in all other things,
Save in the office and affairs of love.
SHAKESPEARE: *Much Ado About Nothing,* II, *c.* 1599

Most friendship is feigning.
SHAKESPEARE: *As You Like It,* II, *c.* 1600

If I do vow a friendship, I'll perform it
To the last article.
SHAKESPEARE: *Othello,* III, 1604

Friendship's full of dregs.
SHAKESPEARE: *Timon of Athens,* I, *c.* 1607

Without reciprocal mildness and temperance there can be no continuance of friendship. Every man will have something to do for his friend, and something to bear with in him.
OWEN FELLTHAM: *Resolves,* II, *c.* 1620

Friendship is but a word.
PHILIP MASSINGER: *A New Way to Pay Old Debts,* II, 1633

Friendship is the allay of our sorrows, the ease of our passions, the discharge of our oppressions, the sanctuary to our calamities, the counsellor of our doubts, the clarity of our minds, the emission of our thoughts, the exercise and improvement of what we meditate.
JEREMY TAYLOR: *Of the Nature and Offices of Friendship,* 1660

In friendship, as in love, we are often more happy from the things we are ignorant of than from those we are acquainted with.
LA ROCHEFOUCAULD: *Maxims,* 1665

What causes the majority of women to be so little touched by friendship is that it is insipid when they have once tasted of love.
IBID.

What men have given the name of friendship to is nothing but an alliance, a reciprocal accommodation of interests, an exchange of good offices; in fact, it is nothing but a system of traffic, in which self-love always proposes to itself some advantage. IBID.

Sudden friendship, sure repentance.
JOHN RAY: *English Proverbs,* 1670

Ceremony and great professing renders friendship as much suspect as it does religion.
WILLIAM WYCHERLEY: *The Plain Dealer,* I, *c.* 1674

Friendship, of itself a holy tie,
Is made more sacred by adversity.
JOHN DRYDEN: *The Hind and the Panther,* III, 1687

In friendship we see only those faults which may injure our friend; in love we see only those which injure ourselves.
JEAN DE LA BRUYÈRE: *Caractères,* V, 1688

There can be no friendship where there is no freedom. Friendship loves a free air, and will not be fenced up in straight and narrow enclosures.
WILLIAM PENN: *Fruits of Solitude,* I, 1693

Great souls by instinct to each other turn,
Demand alliance, and in friendship burn.
JOSEPH ADDISON: *The Campaign,* 1705

Friendship is a strong and habitual inclination in two persons to promote the good and happiness of one another.
EUSTACE BUDGELL: *The Spectator,* May 22, 1712

The friendships of the world are oft
Confederacies in vice, or leagues of pleasure.
JOSEPH ADDISON: *Cato,* III, 1713

Friendship's a noble name, 'tis love refined.
SUSANNAH CENTLIVRE: *The Stolen Heiress,* II, 1715

Friendship, gift of Heaven, delight of great souls; friendship, which kings, so distinguished for ingratitude, are unhappy enough not to know.
VOLTAIRE: *La Henriade,* VIII, 1723

Friendship, like love, is but a name,
Unless to one you stint the flame.
The child, whom many fathers share.
Hath seldom known a father's care.
JOHN GAY: *Fables,* I, 1727

The strongest friendship yields to pride,
Unless the odds be on our side.
JONATHAN SWIFT: *On the Death of Dr. Swift,* 1731

A broken friendship may be solder'd, but will never be sound.
THOMAS FULLER: *Gnomologia,* 1732

Friendship is not to be bought at a fair.
IBID.

Friendship's the wine of life.
EDWARD YOUNG: *Night Thoughts,* II, 1742

Friendship, peculiar boon of Heav'n,
The noble mind's delight and pride,

To men and angels only giv'n,
 To all the lower world denied.

SAMUEL JOHNSON: *Friendship: an Ode*, 1743

There is nothing that is meritorious but virtue and friendship; and, indeed, friendship itself is only a part of virtue.

ALEXANDER POPE: On his deathbed, 1744

Friendship is a slow grower, and never thrives unless ingrafted upon a stock of known and reciprocal merit.

LORD CHESTERFIELD: *Letter to his son*, Oct. 9, 1747

Friendship between mortals can be contracted on no other terms than that one must some time mourn for the other's death.

SAMUEL JOHNSON: *The Rambler*, May 15, 1750

If a man does not make new acquaintance as he advances through life, he will soon find himself left alone. A man, sir, should keep his friendship in constant repair.

SAMUEL JOHNSON: *Boswell's Life*, 1755

Friendship is the marriage of the soul; and this marriage is subject to divorce.

VOLTAIRE: *Philosophical Dictionary*, 1764

And what is friendship but a name,
 A charm that lulls to sleep;
A shade that follows wealth or fame,
 And leaves the wretch to weep?

OLIVER GOLDSMITH: *The Hermit*, 1764

Friendship is a disinterested commerce between equals.

OLIVER GOLDSMITH: *The Good-Natur'd Man*, I, 1768

Friendship is the hobby-horse of all the moral rhetoricians; it is nectar and ambrosia to them.

IMMANUEL KANT: Lecture at Königsberg, 1775

Friendship is the bond of reason.

R. B. SHERIDAN: *The Duenna*, I, 1775

True friendship is a plant of slow growth, and must undergo and withstand the shocks of adversity before it is entitled to the appelation.

GEORGE WASHINGTON: *Letter to Bushrod Washington*, Jan. 15, 1783

Most friendships are formed by caprice or by chance — mere confederacies in vice or leagues in folly.

SAMUEL JOHNSON: *Boswell's Life*, May 19, 1784

The happiest moments my heart knows are those in which it is pouring forth its affections to a few esteemed characters.

THOMAS JEFFERSON: *Letter to Mrs. Trist*, 1786

Should auld acquaintance be forgot,
 And never brought to mind?
Should auld acquaintance be forgot,
 And days o' lang syne?

ROBERT BURNS: *Auld Lang Syne*, 1788

The bird a nest, the spider a web, man friendship.

WILLIAM BLAKE: *The Marriage of Heaven and Hell*, 1790

A sudden thought strikes me, — let us swear an eternal friendship.

J. HOOKHAM FRERE: *The Rovers*, 1798

I find friendship to be like wine, raw when new, ripened with age, the true old man's milk and restorative cordial.

THOMAS JEFFERSON: *Letter to Benjamin Rush*, 1811

Old friendships are like meats served up repeatedly, cold, comfortless, and distasteful. The stomach turns against them.

WILLIAM HAZLITT: *On the Pleasure of Hating*, 1821

The discussing the characters and foibles of common friends is a great sweetener and cement of friendship.

WILLIAM HAZLITT: *Table-Talk*, II, 1824

No friendship is so cordial or so delicious as that of girl for girl; no hatred so intense and immovable as that of woman for woman.

W. S. LANDOR: *Imaginary Conversations*, I, 1824

A woman's friendship borders more closely on love than man's. Men affect each other in the reflection of noble or friendly acts; whilst women ask fewer proofs and more signs and expressions of attachment.

S. T. COLERIDGE: *Table-Talk*, 1827

Friendship closes its eyes rather than see the moon eclipst; while malice denies that it is ever at the full.

J. C. and A. W. HARE: *Guesses at Truth*, 1827

Friendship often ends in love; but love, in friendship — never.

C. C. COLTON: *Lacon*, 1820

The condition which high friendship demands is ability to do without it.

R. W. EMERSON: *Friendship*, 1841

With most people there will be no harm in occasionally mixing a grain of disdain with your treatment of them; that will make them value your friendship all the more.

ARTHUR SCHOPENHAUER: *Our Relation to Others*, 1851

Friendship's blind service, in the hour of need,
Wipes the pale face — and lets the victim bleed.

O. W. HOLMES: *A Sentiment*, 1855

Friendships multiply joys, and divide griefs.

H. G. BOHN: *Handbook of Proverbs*, 1855

Friendship that flames goes out in a flash.
IBID.

There is a magic in the memory of a schoolboy friendship; it softens the heart, and even affects the nervous system of those who have no heart.
BENJAMIN DISRAELI: *Endymion,* LII, 1880

An acquaintance that begins with a compliment is sure to develop into a real friendship.
OSCAR WILDE: *An Ideal Husband,* II, 1895

Friendship is like two clocks keeping time.
Author unidentified

Friendship is love without his wings. IBID.

Where obligations begin, friendship ends.
IBID.

Friendship is honey — but don't eat it all.
MOROCCAN PROVERB

[*See also* Absence, Adversity, Anarchy, Breeding, Esteem, French, Friend, Laughter, Love, Man and Woman, Visiting.

Frog

I marvel why frogs and snails are with some people, and in some countries, in great account, and judged wholesome food, whereas indeed they have in them nothing else but a cold, gross, slimy and excremental juice.
TOBIAS VENNER: *Via recta,* 1620

Put your hook through your frog's mouth, and out at his gills, and then with a fine needle and silk sew the upper part of his leg with only one stitch to the arming wire of your hook, or tie the frog's leg above the upper joint to the armed wire; and in so doing use him as though you loved him.
IZAAK WALTON: *The Compleat Angler,* I, 1653

The frog by nature is both damp and cold,
Her mouth is large, her belly much will hold.
JOHN BUNYAN: *A Book for Boys and Girls,* 1686

The frog sings, and yet she has neither hair nor wool to cover her.
THOMAS FULLER: *Gnomologia,* 1732

I have been in France, and have eaten frogs.
The nicest little rabbity things you ever tasted.
CHARLES LAMB: *Letter to John Clare,* Aug. 31, 1822

I don't see no p'ints about that frog that's any better'n any other frog.
S. L. CLEMENS (MARK TWAIN): *The Celebrated Jumping Frog of Calaveras County,* 1865 (Saturday Press, New York, Nov. 18)

A frog in a well knows nothing of the high seas.
JAPANESE PROVERB

When the frog flies into a passion, the pond knows nothing of it.
MODERN GREEK PROVERB

[*See also* Elephant, If.

Frontier

There, remote from the power of example and check of shame, many families exhibit the most hideous parts of our society. They are a kind of forlorn hope, preceding by ten or twelve years the most respectable army of veterans which come after them.
ST. JOHN DE CRÈVECOEUR: *Letters from an American Farmer,* III, 1782

[*See also* Pioneer.

Frost

Frost and fraud have always foul ends.
WILLIAM CAMDEN: *Remains Concerning Britain,* 1605

The first and last frosts are the worst.
GEORGE HERBERT: *Outlandish Proverbs,* 1640

The secret ministry of frost.
S. T. COLERIDGE: *Frost at Midnight,* 1798

[*See also* Hail, Moon, Weed.

Frowardness

They that are of a froward heart are abomination to the Lord.
PROVERBS XI, 20, *c.* 350 B.C.

Frown

Say that she frown; I'll say she looks as clear
As morning roses newly wash'd with dew.
SHAKESPEARE: *The Taming of the Shrew,* II, 1594

Frugality

Frugality is misery in disguise.
PUBLILIUS SYRUS: *Sententiæ, c.* 50 B.C.

Frugality includes all the other virtues.
CICERO: *Tusculanae disputationes,* III, 45 B.C.

Frugality is a handsome income.
DESIDERIUS ERASMUS: *Colloquia,* 1524

The frugal crone, whom praying priests attend,
Still strives to save the hallow'd taper's end,
Collects her breath, as ebbing life retires.
ALEXANDER POPE: *Moral Essays,* I (Of the Knowledge and Characters of Men), 1733

Frugality is necessary even to complete the pleasure of expense.
SAMUEL JOHNSON: *The Rambler,* Sept. 18, 1750

Without frugality none can be rich, and with it very few would be poor. IBID.

Make no expense but to do good to others or yourself; i.e., waste nothing.
BENJAMIN FRANKLIN: *Autobiography,* 1798

[*See also* Economy, Industry, Liberality, Manners, Thrift, Travel.

Fruit

By their fruits ye shall know them.
MATTHEW VII, 20, *c.* 75

The tree is known by his fruit.
MATTHEW XII, 33

The ripest fruit first falls.
SHAKESPEARE: *Richard II*, II, *c.* 1596

He that would have the fruit must climb the tree. THOMAS FULLER: *Gnomologia*, 1732

Fruit is gold in the morning, silver in the afternoon, and lead at night.
ENGLISH PROVERB, not recorded before the XIX century

Fruit out of season,
Sorrow out of reason. OLD ENGLISH RHYME

[*See also* Fall, Low, Tree.

Fruitfulness

Be ye fruitful, and multiply; bring forth abundantly in the earth, and multiply therein.
GENESIS IX, 7, *c.* 700 B.C. (Cf. I, 22; I, 28; XXXV, 11)

Thy wife shall be as a fruitful vine by the sides of thine house: thy children like olive plants round about thy table.
PSALMS CXXVIII, *c.* 150 B.C.

The world must be peopled.
SHAKESPEARE: *Much Ado About Nothing*, II, *c.* 1599

[*See also* Jew, Philoprogenitiveness.

Frying-pan

He leaped from the frying-pan into the fire.
ENGLISH PROVERB, borrowed from the Greek, and traced by Apperson to 1528

Fugue

The preachers are desired not to encourage the singing of fugue tunes in our congregations.
The Doctrines and Discipline of the Methodist Episcopal Church, South, I, 1846

[*See also* Training.

Fuller, Margaret (1810–50)

Yesternight there came a bevy of Americans from Emerson, one Margaret Fuller, the chief figure of them, a strange lilting lean old maid, not nearly such a bore as I expected.
THOMAS CARLYLE: *Journal*, Oct. 8, 1846

Fun

The fun . . . grew fast and furious.
ROBERT BURNS: *Tam O'Shanter*, 1790

[*See also* Merriment, Mirth, Revelry.

Funeral

It is of no consequence to the dead what his funeral is; costly obsequies are the affectation of the living.
EURIPIDES: *The Troades*, *c.* 415 B.C.

Man goeth to his long home, and the mourners go about the streets.
ECCLESIASTES XII, 5, *c.* 200 B.C.

According to his virtue let us use him,
With all respect and rites of burial.
SHAKESPEARE: *Julius Cæsar*, V, 1599

When I am dead
Save charge; let me be buried in a nook;
No guns, no pompous whining; these are fooleries.
JOHN FORD: *The Lover's Melancholy*, II, 1628

The pomp of funerals feeds rather the vanity of the living than does honor to the dead.
LA ROCHEFOUCAULD: *Maxims*, 1665

When we attend a funeral, we are apt to comfort ourselves with the happy difference that is betwixt us and our dead friend.
THOMAS WILSON: *Maxims of Piety and of Christianity*, *c.* 1755

The marquise will not have good weather for her journey.
LOUIS XV of France: As the funeral of Mme. de Pompadour passed his window, in a pelting rain, April 18, 1764

Dream of a funeral and you hear of a marriage.
ENGLISH PROVERB, not recorded before the XIX century

One funeral makes another. IBID.

Of all
The fools who flock'd to swell or see the show
Who car'd about the corpse? The funeral
Made the attraction, and the black the woe.
BYRON: *The Vision of Judgment*, 1823

I have been to a funeral, where I made a pun, to the consternation of the rest of the mourners. I can't describe to you the howl which the widow set up at proper intervals.
CHARLES LAMB: *Letter to P. G. Patmore*, July 19, 1827

Funeral eloquence
Rattles the coffin-lid.
R. W. EMERSON: *Ode Inscribed to W. H. Channing*, 1846

Here lies one who for med'cines would not give
A little gold, and so his life he lost;
I fancy now he'd wish again to live,
Could he but guess how much his funeral cost.
H. J. LOARING: *Epitaphs Quaint, Curious, and Elegant*, 1872

No, but I approve of it.
GEORGE F. HOAR: On being asked if he was going to attend Benjamin F. Butler's funeral, 1893

Burn me and scatter the ashes where they will, and let there be no abracadabra of ritual, is my wish about myself.

GEORGE MEREDITH: *To Edward Clodd*, *c.* 1900 (Fortnightly Review, July, 1909)

I direct that I be given a modest funeral, either at sunrise or at sunset, with no pomp, no singing, no music.

GIUSEPPE VERDI: Last will, May 14, 1900

Look down po' lonesome road,
Hacks all dead in line;
Some give a nickel, some give a dime
To bury this po' body o' mine.

American Negro Song, quoted by HOWARD W. ODUM: *Rainbow Round My Shoulder*, XVI, 1928

Funeral sermon, lying sermon. (Leichenpredigt, Lügenpredigt.) GERMAN PROVERB

[*See also* Burial.

Fur

Friend, once 'twas fame that led thee forth
To brave the tropic heat, the frozen North,
Late it was gold, then beauty was the spur;
But now our gallants venture but for fur.

Anon: Restoration quatrain, *c.* 1670

The fur that warms a monarch warmed a bear.

ALEXANDER POPE: *An Essay on Man*, III, 1733

[*See also* Mitten.

Fury

Beware the fury of a patient man.

JOHN DRYDEN: *Absalom and Achitophel*, I, 1682

Every stroke our fury strikes is sure to hit ourselves at last.

WILLIAM PENN: *Fruits of Solitude*, 1693

[*See also* Anger, Patience, Peace, Woman.

Futility

We ought not to stretch either our legs or our hopes for a point they cannot reach.

EPICTETUS: *Encheiridion*, *c.* 110

Sue a beggar and get a louse.

JOHN CLARKE: *Parœmiologia Anglo-Latina*, 1639

I have spent my life laboriously doing nothing. (Vitam perdidi laboriose agendo.)

HUGO GROTIUS: On his deathbed, 1645

Most men eddy about
Here and there, eat and drink,
Chatter and love and hate,
Gather and squander, are raised
Aloft, are hurled in the dust,
Striving blindly, achieving
Nothing; and then they die, —
Perish and no one asks
Who or what they have been.

MATTHEW ARNOLD: *Rugby Chapel*, 1867

It ain't no use sayin': " Please give me a glass of milk! " to de cow.

AMERICAN NEGRO SAYING

It's no use making shoes for geese.

DANISH PROVERB

It's no use. ('S gibt gar kein Use.)

PENNSYLVANIA GERMAN SAYING

Two baldhead men are fighting over a comb.

RUSSIAN SAYING

It's needless pouring water on a drowned mouse. SCOTTISH PROVERB

[*See also* Milk.

Future

We know what we are, but know not what we may be.

SHAKESPEARE: *Hamlet*, IV, *c.* 1601

The never-ending flight
Of future days.

JOHN MILTON: *Paradise Lost*, II, 1667

I know of no way of judging the future but by the past.

PATRICK HENRY: Speech in the Virginia Convention, 1775

I like the dreams of the future better than the history of the past.

THOMAS JEFFERSON: *Letter to John Adams*, 1816

There's a good time coming.

WALTER SCOTT: *Rob Roy*, XXXII, 1817

The future is a great land; a man cannot go around it in a day; he cannot measure it with a bound; he cannot bind its harvests into a single sheaf. It is wider than the vision, and has no end.

DONALD G. MITCHELL (IK MARVEL): *Reveries of a Bachelor*, IV, 1850

The future is no more uncertain than the present.

WALT WHITMAN: *Song of the Broad-Ax*, 1856

The future comes like an unwelcome guest.

EDMUND GOSSE: *May-Day*, 1873

No one can forbid us the future.

INSCRIPTION ON THE BASE OF THE MONUMENT TO LÉON GAMBETTA (1838–82) IN PARIS, *c.* 1883

Hats off to the past; coats off to the future.

AMERICAN PROVERB

The future has no cure for the past.

Author unidentified

[*See also* Action, Experience, Forethought, Happiness, Husband and Wife, Past and Present.

G

Gaiety

Gaiety makes us gods.
FREDERICK THE GREAT: *Letter to Voltaire,* Sept. 21, 1737

[*See also* Innocence, Merriment, Virtue.

Gain

[*See* Profit.

Gait

By her gait the goddess was known. (Incessu patuit Dea.) VERGIL: *Æneid,* I, 19 B.C.

A proper gait is one in which there is an appearance of authority, weight, dignity, and tranquility.
ST. AMBROSE: *Clergymen's Duties,* I, *c.* 390

Galilean

[*See* Jesus Christ.

Galileo

[*See* Kepler (Johann).

Gallantry

I hold him but a fool that will endanger
His body for a girl that loves him not.
SHAKESPEARE: *Two Gentlemen of Verona,* V, *c.* 1595

Gallantry consists in saying empty things in an agreeable manner.
LA ROCHEFOUCAULD: *Maxims,* 1665

Conscience has no more to do with gallantry than it has with politics.
R. B. SHERIDAN: *The Duenna,* II, 1775

I could not exactly play the Stoic with a woman who had scrambled eight hundred miles to unphilosophize me.
BYRON: *Letter to Augusta Leigh,* Sept. 8, 1816

[*See also* Bible, Chastity.

Gallop

I sprang to the stirrup, and Joris, and he;
I galloped, Dirck galloped, we galloped all three.
ROBERT BROWNING: *How They Brought the Good News from Ghent to Aix,* 1845

Gallows

A horse that was foaled of an acorn.
ENGLISH PHRASE, familiar since the XVII century

No Indian prince has to his palace
More followers than a thief to the gallows.
SAMUEL BUTLER: *Hudibras,* II, 1664

He has the gallows in his face.
OLIVER GOLDSMITH: *The Good Natur'd Man,* V, 1768

On the gallows everyone is a preacher.
DUTCH PROVERB

The cross and the gallows are alike made of wood. POLISH PROVERB

[*See also* Brave, Christianity, Churchyard, Criminal, Eminence, Exclusiveness, Execution, Hanging, Liberty, Lying, Orator, Scaffold, Theft, Thief.

Galumphing

He went galumphing back.
C. L. DODGSON (LEWIS CARROLL): *Through the Looking-Glass,* 1871

Gambler

I'll tell thee what it says; it calls me villain, a treacherous husband, a cruel father, a false brother; one lost to nature and her charities; or to say all in one short word, it calls me — gamester.
EDWARD MOORE: *The Gamester,* II, 1753

No gambler was ever yet a happy man.
WILLIAM COBBETT: *Advice to Young Men,* I, 1829

A hundred drunkards are better than one gambler. MOROCCAN PROVERB

[*See also* Slang.

Gambling

Let the king prohibit gambling and betting in his kingdom, for these are vices that destroy the kingdoms of princes.
THE CODE OF MANU, IX, *c.* 100

Heads I win; tails you lose.
ENGLISH SAYING, traced to the XVII century

He that puts confidence in . . . dice, cards, balls, bowls, or any game lawful or unlawful doth adventure to be laughed at for a fool, or die a beggar unpitied.
JOHN TAYLOR: *A Kicksey Winsey,* 1619

Play not for gain, but sport. Who plays for more
Than he can lose with pleasure stakes his heart.
GEORGE HERBERT: *The Temple,* 1633

Such and such a man spends his life playing every day for a small stake. Give him every morning the money that he may gain during the day, on condition that he does not play — you will make him unhappy. It will perhaps be said that what he seeks is the amusement of play, not gain. Let him play then for nothing; he will lose his interest and be wearied.
BLAISE PASCAL: *Pensées,* V, 1670

We begin as dupes and end as scoundrels.
ANTOINETTE DESHOULIÈRES: *Réflexion sur le jeu, c.* 1675

A man gets no thanks for what he loseth at play.
THOMAS FULLER: *Gnomologia,* 1732

Shake off the shackles of this tyrant vice;
Hear other calls than those of cards and dice:
Be learn'd in nobler arts than arts of play;
And other debts than those of honor pay.
DAVID GARRICK: *Prologue to* EDWARD MOORE: *The Gamester,* 1753

The familiarities of the gaming-table contribute very much to the decay of politeness. . . . The pouts and quarrels that naturally arise from disputes must put an end to all complaisance, or even good will towards one another.
MARY WORTLEY MONTAGU: *Letter to the Countess of Bute,* June 24, 1759

Gaming is a principle inherent in human nature. It belongs to us all.
EDMUND BURKE: Speech in the House of Commons, Feb. 11, 1780

The child of avarice, the brother of iniquity, and the father of mischief.
GEORGE WASHINGTON: *Letter,* Jan. 15, 1783

Gaming corrupts our dispositions, and teaches us a habit of hostility against all mankind.
THOMAS JEFFERSON: *Letter to Martha Jefferson,* 1787

The winner's shout, the loser's curse,
Dance before dead England's hearse.
WILLIAM BLAKE: *Auguries of Innocence,* c. 1802

Man is a gaming animal.
CHARLES LAMB: *Mrs. Battle's Opinions on Whist,* 1820

When for a time all other books are abandoned for the betting book, when I herd with the vilest and stupidest and most degraded of beings, and am occupied with the mysteries and craft of the stable to the exclusion of all other interests, pursuits and occupations, I am tormented with a sensation of self-reproach, of shame and of remorse, which is exactly akin to what the drunkard feels in his sober intervals.
CHARLES C. F. GREVILLE: *Diary,* Jan. 2, 1838

The roulette table pays nobody except him who keeps it. Nevertheless a passion for gaming is common, though a passion for keeping roulette tables is unknown.
GEORGE BERNARD SHAW: *Maxims for Revolutionists,* 1903

The only man who makes money following the races is the one who does so with a broom and shovel.
ELBERT HUBBARD: *Roycroft Dictionary and Book of Epigrams,* 1923

All trading contains in it some elements of chance — faulty judgment of persons holding positions of trust, of circumstances which may arise, and of actual values. Elements of chance do not, therefore, necessarily indicate gambling.
JAMES CANNON, JR.: *Unspotted from the World,* Aug. 3, 1929

To continue to gamble is to weaken the best qualities in the individual, no matter what the form of gambling may be, whether on the race track, in the popular sport of the day, at the card tables, or on the stock market.
Resolution of the General Conference of the Methodist Episcopal Church South, Dallas, Texas, May, 1930

It signifies nothing to play well if you lose.
Author unidentified

Money goes to the gambling-house as criminals go to execution.
CHINESE PROVERB

Gambling is the child of avarice and the father of despair.
FRENCH PROVERB

[*See also* Betting, Business, Cards, Chance, Clergyman, Dice, Gambler, Loser, Speculation, Stock-market, Wager.

Game (=food)

Game is cheaper in the market than in the fields and woods.
THOMAS FULLER: *Gnomologia,* 1732

Game (=play)

The game is not worth the candle.
ENGLISH SAYING, traced by Smith to 1603

Those games in which the gain serves as a recompense for the dexterity and industry of the body or of the mind, such as tennis ball, pall-mall, running at the ring, chess, and backgammon, are recreations in themselves good and lawful.
ST. FRANCIS DE SALES: *Introduction to the Devout Life,* XXXI, 1609

Who leaves the game loses it.
FRENCH PROVERB

Gander

The wild gander leads his flock through the cool night;
Ya-honk! he says, and sounds it down to me like an invitation.
WALT WHITMAN: *Walt Whitman,* 1855

[*See also* Sauce.

Gang

Hail! Hail! The gang's all here!
What the hell do we care? What the hell do we care?
Hail! Hail! The gang's all here!
What the hell do we care now?
American popular song, *c.* 1885

Garden

The Lord God planted a garden eastward in Eden; and there he put the man whom he had formed.
GENESIS II, 8, *c.* 700 B.C.

I know a bank where the wild thyme blows,
Where ox-lips, and the nodding violet grows;
Quite over-canopied with luscious woodbine,
With sweet musk-roses, and with eglantine.

SHAKESPEARE: *A Midsummer Night's Dream,* II, *c.* 1596

God Almighty first planned a garden; and indeed it is the purest of human pleasures.

FRANCIS BACON: *Essays,* XLVI, 1625

A garden must be looked into, and dressed as the body.

GEORGE HERBERT: *Outlandish Proverbs,* 1640

God the first garden made, and the first city Cain.

ABRAHAM COWLEY: *The Garden,* V, 1664

I never had any other desire so strong and so like to covetousness, as that one which I have had always, that I might be master at last of a small house and large garden. IBID.

This rule in gardening never forget:
To sow dry and to set wet.

JOHN RAY: *English Proverbs,* 1670

No garden without its weeds.

THOMAS FULLER: *Gnomologia,* 1732

"'Tis well said," replied Candide, "but we must cultivate our gardens."

VOLTAIRE: *Candide,* XXX, 1759

The works of a person that builds begin immediately to decay; while those of him who plants begin directly to improve. In this, planting promises a more lasting pleasure than building.

WILLIAM SHENSTONE: *Unconnected Thoughts on Gardening,* 1764

No one is ever at ease in a garden unless it looks like open country.

J. W. GOETHE: *Elective Affinities,* II, 1808

A farm, however large, is not more difficult to direct than a garden, and does not call for more attention or skill.

THOMAS JEFFERSON: *Letter to J. B. Stuart,* 1817

A garden was the primitive prison, till man, with Promethean felicity and boldness, luckily sinned himself out of it.

CHARLES LAMB: *Letter to William Wordsworth,* Jan. 22, 1830

I have never, for any eight months together, during my whole life, been without a garden.

WILLIAM COBBETT: *A Year's Residence in America,* 1837

Come into the garden, Maud,
 For the black bat, night, has flown,
Come into the garden, Maud,
 I am here at the gate alone;
And the woodbine spices are wafted abroad,
 And the musk of the rose is blown.

ALFRED TENNYSON: *Maud,* I, 1855

A garden is like those pernicious machineries which catch a man's coat-skirt or his hand, and draw in his arm, his leg, and his whole body to irresistible destruction.

R. W. EMERSON: *The Conduct of Life,* VIII, 1860

In a garden the first of our race was deceived;
In a garden the promise of grace he received;
In a garden was Jesus betray'd to His doom;
In a garden His body was laid in the tomb.

GEORGE BORROW: Tr. of ROBERT WILLIAMS: *Pethau a wnaed mewn Gardd* (*Wild Wales,* XLVI), 1862

It is curious, pathetic almost, how deeply seated in the human heart is the liking for gardens and gardening.

ALEXANDER SMITH: *Dreamthorp,* XI, 1863

A little garden square and wall'd;
And in it throve an ancient evergreen,
A yew-tree, and all round it ran a walk
Of shingle, and a walk divided it.

ALFRED TENNYSON: *Enoch Arden,* 1864

A garden is a lovesome thing, God wot.

T. E. BROWNE: *My Garden,* 1887

More things grow in the garden than the gardener sows. SPANISH PROVERB

[*See also* Labor, Market, Weed.

Gardener

There is no ancient gentlemen but gardeners.

SHAKESPEARE: *Hamlet,* V, *c.* 1601

Eat your fill, and pouch none, is gardener's law.

JAMES KELLY: *Complete Collection of Scottish Proverbs,* 1721

What a man needs in gardening is a cast-iron back, with a hinge in it.

C. D. WARNER: *My Summer in a Garden,* III, 1870

[*See also* First.

Garlic

We remember the fish, which we did eat in Egypt freely; the cucumbers, the melons, and the leeks, and the onions, and the garlic.

NUMBERS XI, 5, *c.* 700 B.C.

Garlic makes a man wink, drink, and stink.

ENGLISH PROVERB, traced by Apperson to 1594

Our apothecary's shop is our garden full of potherbs, and our doctor is a clove of garlic.

Anon.: *A Deep Snow,* 1615

[*See also* Hatred.

Garner, John N. (1868–)

A labor-baiting, poker-playing, whiskey-drinking, evil old man.

JOHN L. LEWIS: Statement to the press, Washington, July 27, 1939

Garnet

[*See* January.

Garrick, David (1717–79)

Here lies David Garrick, describe him who can?
An abridgment of all that was pleasant in man; . . .
On the stage he was natural, simple, affecting;
'Twas only that when he was off he was acting.
OLIVER GOLDSMITH: *Retaliation,* 1774

Dr. Johnson sends most respectful condolence to Mrs. Garrick, and wishes that any endeavor of his could enable her to support a loss which the world cannot repair.
SAMUEL JOHNSON: *Letter to Mrs. Garrick,* Feb. 2, 1779 (Garrick died Jan. 20)

In declamation he never charmed me; nor could he be a gentleman. . . . Applause had turned his head, and yet he was never content even with that prodigality. His jealousy and envy were unbounded.
HORACE WALPOLE: *Letter to the Countess of Upper Ossory,* Feb. 1, 1779

[*See also* Actor.

Garrulity

His conversation was marked by its happy abundance.
MARY GODWIN SHELLEY: Preface to the first Collected Edition of Shelley, 1839

He had a most amazing fertility in words, but unfortunately that gift was unaccompanied by any correlated gift of selection or compression of his matter.
MR. JUSTICE G. P. LANGTON: *Judgment in Hall* vs. *Hall,* 1939

Garter, Order of

[*See* Evil, Honors.

Gary, Elbert H. (1846–1927)

Judge Gary never saw a blast furnace until after his death.
BENJAMIN STOLBERG: *The Story of the CIO,* III, 1938

Gas-light

Gas is totally inadmissible within doors. Its harsh and unsteady light offends. No one having both brains and eyes will use it.
E. A. POE: *The Philosophy of Furniture,* 1840 (Burton's Gentleman's Magazine, May)

Gaul

All Gaul is divided into three parts.
JULIUS CÆSAR: *The Gallic War,* I, 51 B.C.

Gauls

Almost all the Gauls are fond of change, and easily excited to war, but at the same time they are attached to liberty and hate slavery.
JULIUS CÆSAR: *The Gallic War,* III

In their first efforts they are more than men, yet in their last they are less than women.
LIVY: *History of Rome,* X, *c.* 10

Gautier, Théophile (1811–72)

His ideas were born duchesses. No one could torment a fancy more delicately than he; he scented a new one afar like a truffle, and from the morgue of the dictionary he dragged forgotten beauties.
EDGAR SALTUS: *Tales Before Supper,* intro., 1887

Gay, John

[*See* Epitaph.

Gazelle

[*See* Fatality.

Genealogist

One who traces back your family as far as your money will go. Author unidentified

Genealogy

And Aram begat Aminadab; and Aminadab begat Naasson; and Naasson begat Salmon; and Salmon begat Booz of Rachab; and Booz begat Obed of Ruth; and Obed begat Jesse.
MATTHEW I, 4–5, *c.* 75 (Cf. LUKE III, 23 ff., *c.* 75)

The Fitzpatricks are so ancient that the best Irish antiquaries affirm that they reckoned many generations before the first man was created.
HORACE WALPOLE: *Letter to the Countess of Upper Ossory,* Aug. 27, 1783

We seem to have lived in the persons of our forefathers; it is the labor and reward of vanity to extend the term of this ideal longevity.
EDWARD GIBBON: *Memoirs,* 1795

An account of one's descent from an ancestor who did not particularly care to trace his own.
AMBROSE BIERCE: *The Devil's Dictionary,* 1906

[*See also* Ancestry, Heraldry.

General

A general, said Socrates, must be skilful in preparing the materials of war and in supplying his soldiers; he must be a man of mechanical ingenuity, careful, persevering, sagacious, kind and yet severe, open yet crafty, careful of his own but ready to steal from others, profuse yet rapacious, cautious yet enterprising.
XENOPHON: *Memorabilia,* III, *c.* 390 B.C.

A good general not only sees the way to victory; he also knows when victory is impossible. POLYBIUS: *Histories* I, *c.* 125 B.C.

Comrades, you have lost a good captain to make a bad general.
Ascribed to SATURNINUS (?–100 B.C.)

Adversity reveals the genius of a general; good fortune conceals it.
HORACE: *Satires,* II, *c.* 25 B.C.

To a good general luck is not important.
LIVY: *History of Rome*, XXII, *c.* 10

The proper arts of a general are judgment and prudence. TACITUS: *Annals*, III, *c.* 110

'Tis fit a general
Should not endanger his own person oft;
So that he make a noise when he's a' horseback.
JOHN WEBSTER: *The White Devil*, II, *c.* 1608

There is only one great general in a century.
BALTASAR GRACIÁN: *The Art of Worldly Wisdom*, CCIII, 1647

Our gen'rals now, retired to their estates,
Hang their old trophies o'er the garden gates.
ALEXANDER POPE: *The First Epistle of the First Book of Horace*, 1735

We should try to make war without leaving anything to hazard. In this lies the talent of a general.
MAURICE DE SAXE: *Mes rêveries*, 1757

Soldiers only make risings and riots; they are generals and colonels who make rebellions.
HORACE WALPOLE: *Letter to Mrs. Carter*, July 25, 1789

I think with the Romans of old, that the general of today should be a common soldier tomorrow, if necessary.
THOMAS JEFFERSON: *Letter to James Madison*, 1797

The Creator has not thought proper to mark those in the forehead who are of stuff to make good generals. We are first, therefore, to seek them blindfold, and let them learn the trade at the expense of great losses.
THOMAS JEFFERSON: *Letter to General Bailey*, Feb., 1813

The mind of a general ought to resemble and be as clear as the field-glass of a telescope.
NAPOLEON I: To Barry E. O'Meara at St. Helena, Sept. 20, 1817

A general who sees with the eyes of others will never be able to command an army as it should be.
NAPOLEON I: To Barry E. O'Meara at St. Helena, Dec. 9, 1817

Generals should mess with the common soldiers. The Spartan system was a good one.
NAPOLEON I: To Gaspard Gourgaud at St. Helena, 1815–1818

I do not deserve more than half credit for the battles I have won. Soldiers generally win battles; generals get credit for them. IBID.

The best generals are those who have served in the artillery. IBID.

Military talent is greatly overrated by the world, because the means by which it shows itself are connected with brute force and the most terrible results; and men's faculties are dazzled and beaten down by a thunder and lightning so formidable to their very existence. If playing a game of chess involved the blowing up of gunpowder and the hazard of laying waste a city, men would have the same grand idea of a game of chess.
LEIGH HUNT: *The Companion*, XIII, 1828

Hail, ye indomitable heroes, hail!
Despite of all your generals ye prevail.
W. S. LANDOR: *The Crimean Heroes*, 1856

I am the very pattern of a modern major-general.
I've information vegetable, animal and mineral;
I know the kings of England, and I quote the fights historical,
From Marathon to Waterloo, in order categorical.
W. S. GILBERT: *The Pirates of Penzance*, I, 1880

The prize of the general is not a bigger tent, but command.
O. W. HOLMES II: Speech in New York, Feb. 15, 1913

Generals always die in bed.
Saying of the English soldiers in France, 1914–18

One bad general is better than two good ones.
FRENCH PROVERB

[*See also* Army, Battle, Cavalry, Command, Dictator, Distinction, Infantry, Sixty, Soldier, War.

Generality

It is the nature of the mind of man, to the extreme prejudice of knowledge, to delight in the spacious liberty of generalities.
FRANCIS BACON: *The Advancement of Learning*, II, 1605

The glittering generalities of the speaker have left an impression more delightful than permanent.
F. J. DICKMAN: In the Providence Journal, Dec. 14, 1849 (Notice of a lecture by Rufus Choate; apparently the first occurrence of the phrase)

Fraud lurks in generalities. (Fraus latet in generalibus.) LEGAL MAXIM

Generalization

Men are more apt to be mistaken in their generalizations than in their particular observations.
NICCOLÒ MACHIAVELLI: *Discorsi*, I, 1531

A few generalizations always circulate in the world, whose authors we do not rightly know, which astonish, and appear to be avenues to vast kingdoms of thought.
R. W. EMERSON: *English Traits*, VII, 1856

General propositions do not decide concrete cases.
MR. JUSTICE O. W. HOLMES: Dissenting opinion in *Lochner* vs. *New York*, 1904

[*See also* Theory.

Generation

They are a perverse and crooked generation.
DEUTERONOMY XXXII, 5, *c.* 700 B.C.

The man who sees two or three generations is like one who sits in the conjuror's booth at a fair, and sees the tricks two or three times. They are meant to be seen only once.
ARTHUR SCHOPENHAUER: *Parerga und Paralipomena*, III, 1851

[*See also* Earth.

Generosity

Generosity goes with good birth.
PIERRE CORNEILLE: *Héraclius*, V, 1647

What is called generosity is usually only the vanity of giving; we enjoy the vanity more than the thing given.
LA ROCHEFOUCAULD: *Maxims*, 1665

The world is beholden to generous mistakes for the greatest part of the good that is done in it.
GEORGE SAVILE (MARQUIS OF HALIFAX): *Political, Moral and Miscellaneous Reflections*, *c.* 1690

Though the generous man care the least for wealth, yet he will be the most galled with the want of it.
THOMAS FULLER: *Gnomologia*, 1732

Humanity is the virtue of a woman, generosity of a man. The fair sex, who have commonly much more tenderness than ours, have seldom so much generosity.
ADAM SMITH: *The Theory of Moral Sentiments*, IV, 1759

A man is sometimes more generous when he has but a little money than when he has plenty, perhaps thro' fear of being thought to have but little.
BENJAMIN FRANKLIN: *Autobiography*, 1798

It is recorded of many great men, who did not end their days in a workhouse, that they were non-retentive of money. Schiller, when he had nothing else to give away, gave the clothes from his back, and Goldsmith the blankets from his bed. Tender hands found it necessary to pick Beethoven's pockets at home before he walked out.
E. G. BULWER-LYTTON: *The Caxtons*, XIII, 1849

The quickest generosity is the best.
ARAB PROVERB

It is easy to be generous with other people's property.
LATIN PROVERB

[*See also* Alms, Charity, Giving, Just, Man and Woman, Stockbroker.

Genesis

Take away from Genesis the belief that Moses was the author, on which only the strange belief that it is the word of God has stood, and there remains nothing of Genesis but an anonymous book of stories, fables, and traditionary or invented absurdities, or of downright lies.
THOMAS PAINE: *The Age of Reason*, II, 1794

Genius

There is no great genius without a touch of dementia.
SENECA: *De tranquillitate animi*, XV, *c.* 62

Genius may sometimes need the spur, but more often he needs a curb.
LONGINUS: *On the Sublime*, II, *c.* 250

Great geniuses have their empire, their renown, their greatness, their victory, and their lustre, and have no need of material grandeurs, with which they have no relation. They are not seen with the eyes, but with the mind; that is enough.
BLAISE PASCAL: *Pensées*, XIX, 1670

The great despise men of genius who have nothing but genius; men of genius despise the great who have nothing but greatness; the upright pity all who have either greatness or genius without virtue.
JEAN DE LA BRUYÈRE: *Caractères*, IX, 1688

Time, place, and action may with pains be wrought;
But genius must be born, and never can be taught.
JOHN DRYDEN: *To Mr. Congreve*, 1694

When a true genius appears in the world, you may know him by this sign, that the dunces are all in confederacy against him.
JONATHAN SWIFT: *Thoughts on Various Subjects*, 1706

One science only will one genius fit,
So vast is art, so narrow human wit.
ALEXANDER POPE: *An Essay on Criticism*, I, 1711

Every great genius seems to ride upon mankind like Pyrrhus on his elephant.
JONATHAN SWIFT: *A Letter of Advice to a Young Poet*, Dec. 1, 1720

A fine genius, in his own country, is like gold in the mine.
BENJAMIN FRANKLIN: *Poor Richard's Almanac*, 1733

I have always thought geniuses much inferior to the plain sense of a cookmaid, who can make a good pudding and keep the kitchen in order.
MARY WORTLEY MONTAGU: *Letter to the Countess of Pomfret*, March, 1739

The animal kingdom costs nature no more effort than the vegetable, and the most splendid genius no more than a blade of wheat.
J. O. DE LA METTRIE: *L'Homme machine,* 1748

I dare say there are very few captains of foot who are not much better company than ever Descartes or Sir Isaac Newton were. I honor and respect such superior geniuses; but I desire to converse with people of this world.
LORD CHESTERFIELD: *Letter to his son,* Sept. 19, 1752

Genius is patience. (Le génie, c'est la patience.)
GEORGE DE BUFFON: *Discours sur le style,* 1753

The man of understanding reasons only according to what he has learned; but the man of genius according to himself.
STANISLAUS LESZCZYNSKI (KING OF POLAND): *Œuvres du philosophe bienfaisant,* 1763

A genius never can be quite still.
SAMUEL JOHNSON: To Hester Thrale, July 17, 1775

The true genius is a mind of large general powers, accidentally determined to some particular direction.
SAMUEL JOHNSON: *Lives of the Poets* (Cowley), 1778

Genius is nothing more than knowing the use of tools, but there must be tools for it to use. A man who has spent all his life in this room will give a very poor account of what is contained in the next.
SAMUEL JOHNSON: To Frances Burney, Nov. 25, 1784

The lamp of genius burns away quicker than the lamp of life.
J. C. F. SCHILLER: *The Fiesco,* II, 1784

When the man of genius returns to the cares, the duties, the vexations, and the amusements of life, his companions behold him as one of themselves — the creature of habits and infirmities.
ISAAC D'ISRAELI: *Essay on the Literary Character,* XVI, 1795

At least once a year everyone is a genius.
G. C. LICHTENBERG: *Reflections,* 1799

Sometimes men come by the name of genius in the same way that certain insects come by the name of centipede — not because they have a hundred feet, but because most people can't count above fourteen. IBID.

Genius is reason made sublime.
M. J. DE CHÉNIER: *Épître à Voltaire,* 1806

Men of genius are ethereal chemicals operating on the mass of neutral intellect.
JOHN KEATS: *Letter to Benjamin Bailey,* Nov. 22, 1817

There was a time when, in Germany, a genius was always thought of as short, weak, or hunch-backed; but commend me to a genius who has a well-proportioned body.
J. W. GOETHE: *Conversations with Eckermann,* March 11, 1828

The world has a standing pique against genius.
WILLIAM HAZLITT: *The Ruling Passion,* 1829 (The Atlas, Jan. 18)

You will find this a good gauge or criterion of genius — whether it progresses and evolves, or only spins upon itself.
S. T. COLERIDGE: *Table-Talk,* Aug. 6, 1832

Men of genius are rarely much annoyed by the company of vulgar people, because they have a power of looking at such persons as objects of amusement of another race altogether.
S. T. COLERIDGE: *Table-Talk,* Aug. 20, 1833

The most precious gift that Heaven can give to the earth; a man of genius as we call it; the soul of a man actually sent down from the skies with a God's-message to us, — this we waste away as an idle artificial firework, sent to amuse us a little, and sink it into ashes, wreck and ineffectuality.
THOMAS CARLYLE: *Heroes and Hero-Worship,* II, 1840 (Lecture in London, May 8)

In every work of genius we recognize our own rejected thoughts: they come back to us with a certain alienated majesty.
R. W. EMERSON: *Self-Reliance,* 1841

Genius is the power to labor better and more availably.
R. W. EMERSON: *The Transcendentalist,* 1842

Genius is the clearer presence of God Most High in a man. Dim, potential in all men; in this man it has become clear, actual.
THOMAS CARLYLE: *Past and Present,* IV, 1843

Discrowned and timid, thoughtless, worn,
The child of genius sits forlorn:
Between two sleeps a short day's stealth,
'Mid many ails a brittle health,
A cripple of God, half true, half formed.
R. W. EMERSON: *The Poet,* 1844

Genius melts many ages into one, and thus effects something permanent, yet still with a similarity of office to that of the more ephemeral writer. A work of genius is but the newspaper of a century, or perchance of a hundred centuries.
NATHANIEL HAWTHORNE: *Mosses from an Old Manse,* 1846

What the world calls genius is the state of mental disease arising from the undue predominance of some one of the faculties. The works of such genius are never sound in

themselves, and, in especial, always betray the general mental insanity.
E. A. POE: *Fifty Suggestions,* 1845 (Graham's Magazine, May)

Men of genius are far more abundant than is supposed. In fact, to appreciate thoroughly the work of what we call genius, is to possess all the genius by which the work was produced.
E. A. POE: *Marginalia,* 1844–49

Genius is not a single power, but a combination of great powers. It reasons, but it is not reasoning; it judges, but it is not judgment; it imagines, but it is not imagination; it feels deeply and fiercely, but it is not passion. It is neither, because it is all.
E. P. WHIPPLE: *Literature and Life,* 1849

Great geniuses have the shortest biographies. Their cousins can tell you nothing about them. They lived in their writings, and so their house and street life was trivial and commonplace.
R. W. EMERSON: *Representative Men,* II, 1850

The great men never know how or why they do things. They have no rules; cannot comprehend the nature of rules; — do not, usually, even know, in what they do, what is best or what is worst: to them it is all the same; something they cannot help saying or doing, — one piece of it as good as another, and none of it (it seems to *them*) worth much.
JOHN RUSKIN: *Modern Painters,* IV, 1856

Genius can only breathe freely in an atmosphere of freedom. Persons of genius are, *ex vi termini,* more individual than other people — less capable, consequently, of fitting themselves, without hurtful compression, into any of the small number of molds which society provides in order to save its members the trouble of forming their own character.
J. S. MILL: *On Liberty,* III, 1859

The transcendent capacity of taking trouble.
THOMAS CARLYLE: *Frederick the Great,* IV, 1860

Your man of genius pays dearly for his distinction. His head runs up into a spire, and instead of a healthy man, merry and wise, he is some mad dominie.
R. W. EMERSON: *The Conduct of Life,* IV, 1860

Genius is mainly an affair of energy.
MATTHEW ARNOLD: *The Literary Influence of Academies,* 1865

Genius has somewhat of the infantine;
But of the childish not a touch or taint.
ROBERT BROWNING: *Prince Hohenstiel-Schwangau,* 1871

Genius, as an explosive power, beats gunpowder hollow.
T. H. HUXLEY: *Administrative Nihilism,* 1871

Genius is nothing more than our common faculties refined to a greater intensity. There are no astonishing ways of doing astonishing things. All astonishing things are done by ordinary materials.
B. R. HAYDON: *Table-Talk,* 1876

High original genius is always ridiculed on its first appearance; most of all by those who have won themselves the highest reputation in working on the established lines. Genius only commands recognition when it has created the taste which is to appreciate it.
J. A. FROUDE: *Thomas Carlyle,* II, 1882

I have nothing to declare but my genius.
OSCAR WILDE: To a customs officer on landing in New York, Jan., 1882

It is the privilege of genius that to it life never grows commonplace as to the rest of us.
J. R. LOWELL: Address at Taunton, Eng., Sept. 4, 1883

Geniuses are explosive material, in which an immense amount of power is accumulated. They result from the fact that for long ages energy has been collected, hoarded up, preserved for their use — and no explosion has taken place.
F. W. NIETZSCHE: *The Twilight of the Idols,* 1889

The public is wonderfully tolerant. It forgives everything except genius.
OSCAR WILDE: *The Critic as Artist,* 1891

Geniuses are commonly believed to excel other men in their power of sustained attention . . . But it is their genius making them attentive, not their attention making geniuses of them.
WILLIAM JAMES: *Psychology, Briefer Course,* XIII, 1892

Genius is one per cent inspiration and ninety-nine per cent perspiration.
THOMAS A. EDISON, *c.* 1895

These are the prerogatives of genius: to know without having learned; to draw just conclusions from unknown premises; to discern the soul of things.
AMBROSE BIERCE: *Collected Works,* VIII, 1911

Genius is no snob. It does not run after titles or seek by preference the high circles of society.
WOODROW WILSON: Speech at Hodgenville, Ky., Sept. 4, 1916

Genius is of three types. In one class, the abilities are nearly complete at birth and burn out between 30 and 35 (Schubert, maybe Shakespeare). In a second class, complete development is not achieved until after 35 (Darwin, Clive, Gladstone). In the third class, perfection appears early and continues to old age.

(Goethe wrote at four and was writing at 84).

WILLIAM FEATHER: In The William Feather Magazine, March, 1940 (Credited to "an English correspondent")

Genius is the infinite capacity for taking pains.

Author unidentified (Ascribed to Charles Dickens, and various others, but without ground. Cf. CARLYLE, *ante*, 1860)

Genius only genius can explain.

WELSH PROVERB

[*See also* Books, Business, Cain, Critic, Democracy, Education, German, Greatness, Industry, Patience, Philosophy, Poe (E. A.), Poet, Prayer, Solitude, Talent and Genius, Taste, University, Vacillation.

Genoa

There are in Genoa mountains without wood, sea without fish, women without shame, and men without conscience.

JAMES HOWELL: *Instructions for Foreign Travel,* VIII, 1642 (Cited as a proverb)

[*See also* California.

Genoese

It takes nine Jews to equal one Genoese.

ITALIAN PROVERB

Genteel

The genteel thing is the genteel thing any time, if as be that a gentleman bes in a concatenation accordingly.

OLIVER GOLDSMITH: *She Stoops to Conquer,* I, 1773

Too proud to beg, too honest to steal,
I know what it is to be wanting a meal;
My tatters and rags I try to conceal:
I'm one of the shabby genteel.

ENGLISH POPULAR SONG, *c.* 1865

Gentility

A man can buy nothing in the market with gentility.

WILLIAM CECIL (LORD BURLEIGH): *Advice to His Son, c.* 1555

Gentility is nothing but ancient riches.

GEORGE HERBERT: *Jacula Prudentum,* 1651

Gentility without ability is worse than plain beggary.

JOHN RAY: *English Proverbs,* 1670

[*See also* Birth (High), Fashion, Gentleman.

Gentleman

When Adam delved and Eve span,
Who was then the gentleman?

Author unidentified; traced to the XIV century

He is gentle that doth gentle deeds.

GEOFFREY CHAUCER: *The Canterbury Tales* (The Wife of Bath's Tale), *c.* 1386

Well born, well dressed, and moderately learned. (Bene nati, bene vestiti, et mediocriter docti.)

Statute of All Souls College, Oxford, *c.* 1440, stating the qualifications of a fellow, and often quoted as a definition of gentleman

Gentlemen and rich men are venison in Heaven.

JOHN NORTHBROOKE: *Against Dicing,* 1577

He cannot be a gentleman which loveth not a dog. IBID.

Who can live idly and without manual labor, and will bear the port, charge and countenance of a gentleman, he alone should be called master and be taken for a gentleman.

THOMAS SMITH: *De republica Anglorum,* 1583

He be a dunghill gentleman, or a gentleman of the first head, as they used to term them.

PHILIP STUBBES: *The Anatomy of Abuses,* 1583

Since every Jack became a gentleman,
There's many a gentle person made a Jack.

SHAKESPEARE: *Richard III,* I, *c.* 1592

He is complete in feature, and in mind,
With all good grace to grace a gentleman.

SHAKESPEARE: *Two Gentlemen of Verona,* II, c. 1595

All the wealth I had
Ran in my veins; I was a gentleman.

SHAKESPEARE: *The Merchant of Venice,* III, *c.* 1597

A gentleman born, Master Parson; who writes himself *armigero;* in any bill, warrant, quittance, or obligation, *armigero.*

SHAKESPEARE: *The Merry Wives of Windsor,* I, *c.* 1600.

(From the Latin *armiger,* signifying the squire of a knight, and hence one entitled to bear heraldic arms)

My master hath been an honorable gentleman; tricks he hath had in him which gentlemen have.

SHAKESPEARE: *All's Well that Ends Well,* V, *c.* 1602

The best of men
That e'er wore earth about him was a sufferer;
A soft, meek, patient, humble, tranquil spirit,
The first true gentleman that ever breathed.

THOMAS DEKKER: *I The Honest Whore,* I, 1604

I can make a lord, but only God Almighty can make a gentleman.

JAMES I OF ENGLAND, *c.* 1604

The prince of darkness is a gentleman.

SHAKESPEARE: *King Lear,* III, 1606

We are gentlemen,
That neither in our hearts nor outward eyes
Envy the great, nor do the low despise.

SHAKESPEARE: *Pericles,* II, *c.* 1608

A gentleman loves clean napery.
JAMES SHIRLEY: *Hyde Park*, I, 1637

Is he not a complete gentleman? His family came in with the Conqueror.
GEORGE CHAPMAN and JAMES SHIRLEY: *The Ball*, I, 1639

A gentleman without money is a pudding without suet. JAMES HOWELL: *Proverbs*, 1659

A gentleman may love like a lunatic, but not like a beast.
LA ROCHEFOUCAULD: *Maxims*, 1665

The qualifications of a fine gentleman are to eat *à la mode*, drink champagne, dance jigs, and play at tennis.
THOMAS SHADWELL: *The Sullen Lovers*, II, 1668

A gentleman without living is like a pudding without suet.
JOHN RAY: *English Proverbs*, 1670

What's a gentleman but his pleasure? IBID.

His tribe were God Almighty's gentlemen.
JOHN DRYDEN: *Absalom and Achitophel*, I, 1682

When y'ave said a gentleman, you have said all.
JOHN CROWNE: *Sir Courtly Nice*, I, 1685

Gentlemen have ever been more temperate in their religion than the common people, as having more reason, the others running in a hurry. In the beginning of Christianity the Fathers writ *Contra gentes* and *Contra gentiles;* they were all one.
JOHN SELDEN: *Table-Talk*, 1689

Ours are a sort of modest, inoffensive people, who neither have sense nor pretend to any, but enjoy a jovial sort of dullness; they are commonly known in the world by the name of honest, civil gentlemen.
ALEXANDER POPE: *Letter to William Wycherley*, Oct. 26, 1705

You see, among men who are honored with the common appellation of gentleman, many contradictions to that character.
RICHARD STEELE: *The Tatler*, Sept. 10, 1709

Men of courage, men of sense and men of letters are frequent, but a true fine gentleman is what one seldom sees.
RICHARD STEELE: *The Guardian*, April 20, 1713

Genteel in personage,
Conduct, and equipage;
Noble by heritage,
Generous and free.
HENRY CAREY: *The Contrivances*, I, 1715

The first thing a bare gentleman calls for in the morning is a needle and a thread.
JAMES KELLY: *Complete Collection of Scottish Proverbs*, 1721

A thief passes for a gentleman when stealing has made him rich.
THOMAS FULLER: *Gnomologia*, 1732

Education begins a gentleman; conversation completes him. IBID.

Manners and money make a gentleman.
IBID.

The true pleasures of a gentleman are those of the table, but within the bound of moderation; good company, that is to say, people of merit; moderate play, which amuses, without any interested views; and sprightly gallant conversations with women of fashion and sense.
LORD CHESTERFIELD: *Letter to his son*, Oct. 9, 1746

A gentleman is one who understands and shows every mark of deference to the claims of self-love in others, and exacts it in return from them.
WILLIAM HAZLITT: *Table-Talk*, 1824

The social duties of a gentleman are of a high order. The class to which he belongs is the natural repository of the manners, tastes, tone, and, to a certain extent, of the principles of a country.
J. FENIMORE COOPER: *The American Democrat*, XIX, 1838

A gentleman makes no noise; a lady is serene.
R. W. EMERSON: *Manners*, 1844

Who misses or who wins the prize.
Go, lose or conquer as you can;
But if you fail, or if you rise,
Be each, pray God, a gentleman.
W. M. THACKERAY: *The End of the Play*, 1848

It is a vulgar error to suppose that a gentleman must be ready to fight. The utmost that can be demanded of him is that he be incapable of a lie.
R. W. EMERSON: *Journal*, Dec. 14, 1850

It takes three generations to make a gentleman.
Ascribed to ROBERT PEEL (1788–1850) by WALTER BAGEHOT: *Biographical Studies*, 1880

And thus he bore without abuse
The grand old name of gentleman,
Defamed by every charlatan,
And soil'd with all ignoble use.
ALFRED TENNYSON: *In Memoriam*, CXI, 1850

It is almost a definition of a gentleman to say he is one who never inflicts pain.
J. H. NEWMAN: *On the Scope and Nature of University Education*, VI, 1852

Once a gentleman, always a gentleman.
CHARLES DICKENS: *Little Dorrit*, II, 1857

A gentleman's first characteristic is that fineness of structure in the body which renders it

capable of the most delicate sensation; and of structure in the mind which renders it capable of the most delicate sympathies—one may say, simply, fineness of nature.
JOHN RUSKIN: *Modern Painters*, VI, 1860

The gentleman does not needlessly and unnecessarily remind an offender of a wrong he may have committed against him. He can not only forgive, he can forget; and he strives for that nobleness of self and mildness of character which impart sufficient strength to let the past be but the past. A true man of honor feels humbled himself when he cannot help humbling others.
ROBERT E. LEE: Memorandum found in his military valise after his death; probably written *c.* 1862

A man may learn from his Bible to be a more thorough gentleman than if he had been brought up in all the drawing-rooms in London.
CHARLES KINGSLEY: *The Water Babies*, III, 1863

None of you has ever seen a gentleman.
CHARLES ELIOT NORTON: Lecture to his class at Harvard University, *c.* 1880

Nature's gentlemen are the worst type of gentlemen I know.
OSCAR WILDE: *Lady Windermere's Fan*, II, 1892

If a man is a gentleman, he knows quite enough, and if he is not a gentleman, whatever he knows is bad for him.
OSCAR WILDE: *A Woman of No Importance*, III, 1893

One's duty as a gentleman should never interfere with one's pleasures in the slightest degree.
OSCAR WILDE: *The Importance of Being Earnest*, IV, 1895

No gentleman ever weighs over two hundred pounds.
THOMAS B. REED: To David B. Henderson, in the House lobby, *c.* 1895

The fatal reservation of the gentleman is that he sacrifices everything to his honor except his gentility.
GEORGE BERNARD SHAW: *Maxims for Revolutionists*, 1903

A man may wear a red necktie, a green vest and tan shoes, and still be a gentleman.
E. M. STATLER: *Statler Hotel Service Code*, 1921

One never thinks of Habukkuk, John the Baptist, Epictetus, Martin Luther or Calvin as gentlemen; they were prophets, saints, heroes, if you like, but not gentlemen.
H. D. SEDGWICK: *In Praise of Gentlemen*, XI, 1935

A gentleman is a man who can disagree without being disagreeable.
Author unidentified

A gentleman is a man who never strikes a woman without provocation. IBID.

The true gentleman is God's servant, the world's master, and his own man. IBID.

Gentlemen and dogs leave doors open behind them. GERMAN PROVERB

Gentlemen are born, noblemen are made.
ITALIAN PROVERB

Gude breeding and siller mak our sons gentlemen. SCOTTISH PROVERB (*Siller*=silver)

[*See also* Adam and Eve, Blonde, Brother (Younger), Candor, Classes, Company, Democrat, Drinking, Dress, French Language, Gentility, George IV of England, Jesus Christ, Knowledge, Liberality, Navy (British), Patrick (St.), Priest, Riding, Shirtsleeves, Sport, Sportsmanship, Swiss, Tobacco-chewing.

Gentleness

We were gentle among you, even as a nurse cherisheth her children.
I THESSALONIANS II, 7, *c.* 51

The servant of the Lord must . . . be gentle unto all men. II TIMOTHY II, 24, *c.* 65

Let gentleness my strong enforcement be.
SHAKESPEARE: *As You Like It*, II, *c.* 1600

What would you have? your gentleness shall force
More than your force move us to gentleness.
IBID.

This milky gentleness.
SHAKESPEARE: *King Lear*, I, 1606

They are as gentle
As zephyrs blowing below the violet.
SHAKESPEARE: *Cymbeline*, IV, *c.* 1609

A gentle heart is tied with an easy thread.
GEORGE HERBERT: *Outlandish Proverbs*, 1640

It is only persons of firmness that can have real gentleness; those who appear gentle are in general only of a weak character, which easily changes into asperity.
LA ROCHEFOUCAULD: *Maxims*, 1665

Gentle to others, to himself severe.
SAMUEL ROGERS: *The Voyage of Columbus*, VI, 1810

The great mind knows the power of gentleness,
Only tries force because persuasion fails.
ROBERT BROWNING: *Prince Hohenstiel-Schwangau*, 1871

[*See also* Gentleman, Husband and Wife, Meekness.

Gentry

[*See* Head.

Geology

[*See* Cosmology.

Geometry

Let no one enter here who is ignorant of geometry.

PLATO: Inscription over the door of the Academy at Athens, *c.* 380 B.C.

Geometry was born in Egypt, where the inundations of the Nile, by obliterating the bounds of the fields, made the people invent exact measures to distinguish every man's land from his neighbor's.

BERNARD DE FONTENELLE: *Entretiens sur la pluralité des mondes,* I, 1686

Geometry is that part of universal mechanics which accurately proposes and demonstrates the art of measuring.

ISAAC NEWTON: *The Mathematical Principles of Natural Philosophy,* II, 1687

Happy the youth in Euclid's axioms tried,
Though little versed in any art beside.

BYRON: *A College Examination,* 1806

[*See also* Mathematics.

George III of England (1738–1820)

A man of piety and candor in religion, a friend of liberty and property in government, and a patron of merit. . . . These are the sentiments worthy of a king — a patriot king

JOHN ADAMS: *Diary,* Feb., 1761

The heart of Britain still beats kindly for George III, not because he was wise and just, but because he was pure in life, honest in intent, and because according to his lights he worshipped Heaven.

W. M. THACKERAY: *The Four Georges,* 1860

[*See also* Georges (Four).

George IV of England (1762–1830)

A noble, nasty race he ran,
Superbly filthy and fastidious;
He was the world's first gentleman,
And made the appellation hideous.

W. M. PRAED: Proposed epitaph on George IV, 1825

[*See also* Georges (Four).

George, Henry (1839–97)

Did you ever read Henry George's book, "Progress and Poverty"? It is more damneder nonsense than poor Rousseau's blether.

T. H. HUXLEY: *Letter to James Knowles,* Dec. 14, 1889

It has been said that it marks an epoch in history when God lets loose a thinker in the world. And such a thinker was Henry George.

W. J. BRYAN: Speech at *Progress and Poverty* anniversary dinner, New York, Jan. 24, 1905

Henry George was one of the great prophets of the world. I won't mention them all — Moses, Jesus, Goethe, Henry George.

CLARENCE DARROW: Address before the Chicago Single Tax Club, Sept. 19, 1913

Henry George set me on the economic trail, the trail of political science.

GEORGE BERNARD SHAW: Address in New York, April 11, 1933

Georges, Four

I sing the Georges Four,
For Providence could stand no more.
Some say that far the worst
Of all the Four was George the First.
But yet by some 'tis reckoned
That worser still was George the Second.
And what mortal ever heard
Any good of George the Third?
When George the Fourth from earth descended,
Thank God the line of Georges ended.

W. S. LANDOR: On hearing Thackeray's lectures on the Four Georges, *c.* 1856

Georgia

Until we can repopulate Georgia, it is useless for us to occupy it; but the utter destruction of its roads, houses and people will cripple their military resources. I can make this march, and make Georgia howl.

W. T. SHERMAN: Telegram to U. S. Grant from Atlanta, Sept. 9, 1864

Marching through Georgia.

HENRY CLAY WORK: Title of a song, 1865

Geranium

Everything is handsome about the geranium, not excepting its name.

LEIGH HUNT: *The Seer,* VII, 1840

German

Germans are honest men.

SHAKESPEARE: *The Merry Wives of Windsor,* IV, *c.* 1600

The German's wit is in his fingers.

GEORGE HERBERT: *Outlandish Proverbs,* 1640

Ah, a German and a genius! A prodigy! Admit him!

JONATHAN SWIFT: On meeting Händel, *c.* 1745

The Germans are very seldom troubled with any extraordinary ebullitions or effervescences of wit, and it is not prudent to try it upon them.

LORD CHESTERFIELD: *Letter to his son,* July 21, 1752

A German loves fighting for its own sake.
HORACE WALPOLE: *Letter to H. S. Conway*, Oct. 4, 1762

The German's special forte is original work in fields wherein others have prepared the way. He possesses in a superlative degree the art of being original by imitation.
G. C. LICHTENBERG: *Reflections*, 1799

High deeds, O Germans, are to come from you.
WILLIAM WORDSWORTH: *A Prophecy*, 1807

A true German can't endure a Frenchman, but he likes French wine.
J. W. GOETHE: *I Faust*, I, 1808

German scholars dive deeper and come up muddier than any others.
RICHARD PORSON (1759–1808)

Germans, you can fall, but you cannot sink.
THEODOR KÖRNER: *Leier und Schwert*, 1814

Christianity has somewhat softened the brutal Germanic lust of battle, but could not destroy it.
HEINRICH HEINE: *History of Religion and Philosophy in Germany*, 1834

An appeal to fear never finds an echo in German hearts.
OTTO VON BISMARCK: Speech in the Zollverein Parliament, May 18, 1868

Members of the German race . . . look upon beer drinking as an essential element in man's social and moral nature, and think everybody a Puritan or fanatic who holds different views.
J. E. STEBBINS: *Fifty Years History of the Temperance Cause*, XIX, 1874

The Irish, the Irish,
They don't amount to much,
But they's a damned sight better than
The dirty, dirty Dutch.
AMERICAN FOLK-RHYME, *c.* 1875 (*Dutch*= German)

Everything that is ponderous, viscous and pompously clumsy, all long-winded and wearying kinds of style, are developed in great variety among Germans.
F. W. NIETZSCHE: *Beyond Good and Evil*, XXVIII, 1886

The profound and icy mistrust which the German arouses whenever he gets any power into his hands is the aftermath of that vast horrible fear with which, for long centuries, Europe dreaded the wrath of the Teutonic blond beast.
F. W. NIETZSCHE: *The Genealogy of Morals*, I, 1887

It is my ambition to be looked upon as a despiser of Germans *par excellence*. . . . The Germans are *canaille.*
F. W. NIETZSCHE: *Ecce Homo*, 1888

We Germans fear God, but nothing else in the world. (Wir Deutsche fürchten Gott, aber sonst nichts in der Welt.)
OTTO VON BISMARCK: Speech in the Reichstag, Feb. 6, 1888

The German is a hero born, and believes that he can hack and hew his way through life.
HEINRICH VON TREITSCHKE: *Politik*, II, 1897

The German people are the chosen of God.
WILLIAM II: Speech to soldiers, Aug. 4, 1914

The Germans naturally hate the republican form of government.
BENITO MUSSOLINI: Speech in Udine, Sept. 20, 1922

We Germans will never produce another Goethe, but we may produce another Cæsar.
OSWALD SPENGLER: *Bemühungen*, 1925

Where the German sets his foot the earth bleeds for a hundred years.
Where the German draws and drinks water the springs rot for a hundred years.
Where the German draws a breath the pest rages for a hundred years.
He betrays the strong and robs the weak and rules them.
If there were a direct road to Heaven he would not hesitate to dethrone God.
And we shall yet see that the German steals the sun from Heaven.
Ascribed to LUCIAN RYDLA, a Polish poet, by Prelate Klos in a speech at Posen, July 2, 1929

When a snake warms himself on ice a German will begin to wish well to a Czech.
CZECH PROVERB

Wherever there are three Germans there are always four opinions. GERMAN PROVERB

Wherever Germans are, it is unhealthy for Italians. ITALIAN PROVERB

The German may be a good fellow, but it is better to hang him. RUSSIAN PROVERB

[*See also* Aviation, Character (National), Cheating, Citizen, Dutch, Frenchman, Immigrant, Invention, Land, Scandinavian, Singer, Thief, Wagner (Richard).

German Language

Life is too short to learn German.
Ascribed to RICHARD PORSON (1759–1808)

When one is polite in German one lies.
J. W. GOETHE: *II Faust*, II, 1832

German is inferior to English in modifications of expression of the affections, but superior to it in modifications of expression of all objects of the senses.
S. T. COLERIDGE: *Table-Talk*, May 18, 1833

German gives me a cold in the head.
E. R. BULWER-LYTTON (OWEN MEREDITH): *Lucile*, I, 1860

Some German words are so long that they have a perspective. Observe these examples: Freudschaftsbezeigungen, Dilletantenaufdringlichkeiten, Stadtverordnetenversammlungen.
S. L. CLEMENS (MARK TWAIN): *A Tramp Abroad*, Appendix D, 1879

[*See also* English Language, Language.

Germany

Germany is like a brave and gallant horse, highly fed, but without a good rider; as the horse runs here and there, astray, unless he have a rider to rule him, so Germany is also a powerful, rich, and brave country, but needs a good head and government.
MARTIN LUTHER: *Table-Talk*, DCCCLXXXV, 1569

I'll have them wall all Germany with brass.
CHRISTOPHER MARLOWE: *Dr. Faustus*, I, 1604

Drunkenness, the darling favorite of Hell,
Chose Germany to rule; and rules so well,
No subjects more obsequiously obey,
None please so well, or are so pleas'd as they.
DANIEL DEFOE: *The True-Born Englishman*, I, 1701

Germany, Germany above all — above all in the world. (Deutschland, Deutschland über alles — über alles in der Welt.)
A. H. HOFFMANN VON FALLERSLEBEN: *Das Lied der Deutschen*, Aug. 26, 1841 (The tune is that of the Austrian national hymn, *Gott erhalte Franz den Kaiser*, set by Josef Haydn, 1797)

Germany is Hamlet.
FERDINAND FREILIGRATH: *Ein Glaubensbekenntnis*, 1844

Let us put Germany in the saddle!
OTTO VON BISMARCK: Speech in the Parliament of the Confederation, 1867

Made in Germany.
The use of this label on goods imported from Germany was first ordained by the British Merchandise Marks Act of Aug. 23, 1887; it did not appear in the United States until some time later

Germany's future lies on the water.
WILHELM II: Speech at Stettin, Sept. 23, 1898

We are now about to accept gauge of battle with this natural foe to liberty.
WOODROW WILSON: Message to Congress, April 2, 1917

Germany has reduced savagery to a science, and this great war for the victorious peace of justice must go on until the German cancer is cut clean out of the world body.
THEODORE ROOSEVELT: Speech at Johnstown, Pa., Sept. 30, 1917

If the German people, in their historic development, had possessed tribal unity like other nations, the German Reich today would be the master of the entire world.
ADOLF HITLER: *Mein Kampf*, I, 1925

The development of European history is inconceivable without Germany.
BENITO MUSSOLINI: Speech at Milan, Oct. 6, 1934

[*See also* Battle, Jew, Land, Poland.

Gesture

There was language in their very gesture.
SHAKESPEARE: *The Winter's Tale*, V, *c.* 1611

Let the gestures of thy body be agreeable to the matter of thy discourse, for it hath been ever held a solecism in oratory to point to the earth when thou talkest of Heaven.
FRANCIS HAWKINS: *Youth's Behavior*, I, 1663

Gettysburg, Battle of (July 1–3, 1863)

Never mind, General, all this has been *my* fault; it is *I* that have lost this fight, and you must help me out of it in the best way you can.
R. E. LEE: To Gen. C. M. Wilcox, July 3, 1863

Ghost

When Jesus therefore had received the vinegar, he said, It is finished: and he bowed his head, and gave up the ghost.
JOHN XIX, 30, *c.* 115

Ghosts do fear no laws,
Nor do they care for popular applause.
Anon.: *Thomas Nash His Ghost*, *c.* 1600

The graves stood tenantless, and the sheeted dead
Did squeak and gibber in the Roman streets.
SHAKESPEARE: *Hamlet*, I, *c.* 1601

Avaunt! and quit my sight! let the earth hide thee!
Thy bones are marrowless, thy blood is cold;
Thou hast no speculation in those eyes
Which thou dost glare with!
SHAKESPEARE: *Macbeth*, III, *c.* 1605

It is wonderful that five thousand years have now elapsed since the creation of the world, and still it is undecided whether or not there has ever been an instance of the spirit of any person appearing after death. All argument is against it, but all belief is for it.
SAMUEL JOHNSON: *Boswell's Life*, March 31, 1778

How many children, and how many men, are afraid of ghosts, who are not afraid of God!
T. B. MACAULAY: *Dante*, 1824 (Knight's Quarterly Magazine, Jan.)

The outward and visible sign of an inward fear.
AMBROSE BIERCE: *The Devil's Dictionary*, 1906

I believes in a ghost, I believes in a ha'nt,
Good God-a-mighty, I ain't no saint,
Ain't got no arms, ain't got no haid,
Don't stop to count them tracks I made.
American Negro song, quoted by HOWARD W. ODUM: *Wings on My Feet*, XVI, 1929

[*See also* Midnight, Spirits.

Ghost, Holy

[*See* Holy Ghost.

Giant

There were giants in the earth in those days.
GENESIS VI, 4, *c.* 700 B.C.

[Ammon] was accounted a land of giants: giants dwelt therein in old time; and the Ammonites call them Zamzummin.
DEUTERONOMY II, 20, *c.* 650 B.C.

Oh, it is excellent
To have a giant's strength; but it is tyrannous
To use it like a giant.
SHAKESPEARE: *Measure for Measure*, II, 1604

It is impossible to suppose a giant the object of love.
EDMUND BURKE: *The Sublime and Beautiful*, IV, 1756

[*See also* Abraham, Strength.

Gibbon, Edward (1737–94)

It is difficult to comprehend his meaning and the chain of his ideas, as fast as we naturally read. . . . The mind of the reader is constantly dazzled by a glare or ornament, or charmed from the subject by the music of the language.
NOAH WEBSTER: *Dissertations on the English Language*, 1789

Heard of the death of Mr. Gibbon, the calumniator of the despised Nazarene, the derider of Christianity. Awful dispensation! He too was my acquaintance. Lord, I bless thee, considering how much infidel acquaintance I have had, that my soul never came into their secret! How many souls have his writings polluted! Lord preserve others from their contagion!
HANNAH MORE: *Diary*, Jan. 19, 1794

It was on the night of June 27, 1787, between the hours of eleven and twelve, that I wrote the last lines of the last page, in a Summerhouse in my garden. . . . I will not dissemble the first emotions of joy on the recovery of my freedom, and perhaps, the establishment of my fame. But my pride was soon humbled, and a sober melancholy was spread over my mind, by the idea that I had taken an everlasting leave of an old and agreeable companion, and that whatsoever might be the future fate of my History, the life of the historian must be short and precarious.
EDWARD GIBBON: *Memoirs*, 1795 (Written *c.* 1792; the reference, of course, is to *The Decline and Fall of the Roman Empire*)

[*See also* Books, Style.

Gibraltar

I know not why you set so great a value upon Gibraltar, as it is a bad harbor, and costs an enormous sum of money. From it you cannot prevent a fleet from passing into the Mediterranean.
NAPOLEON I: To Barry E. O'Meara at St. Helena, Feb. 10, 1817

Gift

It is not good to refuse a gift.
HOMER: *Odyssey*, XVIII, *c.* 800 B.C.

Thou shalt take no gift; for the gift bindeth the wise, and perverteth the words of the righteous.
EXODUS XXIII, 8, *c.* 700 B.C.

The gifts of enemies are not gifts, but mischiefs.
SOPHOCLES: *Ajax*, *c.* 450 B.C. (Cited as a proverb)

The gift of a bad man can bring no good.
EURIPIDES: *Medea*, 431 B.C.

A gift is as a precious stone in the eyes of him that hath it.
PROVERBS XVII, 8, *c.* 350 B.C.

A man's gift maketh room for him, and bringeth him before great men.
PROVERBS XVIII, 16

Every man is a friend to him that giveth gifts.
PROVERBS XIX, 6

A gift in secret pacifieth anger.
PROVERBS XXI, 14

A gift destroyeth the heart.
ECCLESIASTES VII, 7, *c.* 200 B.C.

Gifts prevail over both gods and men; even Jupiter is soothed by them.
OVID: *Ars amatoria*, III, *c.* 2 B.C.

The gift derives its value from the rank of the giver.
OVID: *Epistulæ ex Ponto*, IV, *c.* 5

Every good gift and every perfect gift is from above, and cometh down from the Father of lights.
JAMES I, 17, *c.* 60

They presented unto him gifts: gold, and frankincense, and myrrh.
MATTHEW II, 11, *c.* 75

Gifts are like fish-hooks.
MARTIAL: *Epigrams*, V, *c.* 95

Whoever makes great gifts wishes great gifts to be made to him in return.
IBID.

Never look a gift horse in the mouth. (Equi donati dentes non inspiciuntur.)
ST. JEROME: *On the Epistle to the Ephesians, c.* 420 (Quoted as "a vulgar proverb." The English form has been in common use since the XV century)

Nothing is freer than a gift.
ENGLISH PROVERB, traced by Smith to *c.* 1470

Throw no gift again at the giver's head;
Better is half a loaf than no bread.
JOHN HEYWOOD: *Proverbs,* 1546

Fain would I have a pretty thing
To give unto my lady;
I mean no hurt, I mean no harm,
But as pretty a thing as may be.
CLEMENT ROBINSON (?): *A Handful of Pleasant Delights,* 1584

Win her with gifts, if she respect not words;
Dumb jewels often in their silent kind
More than quick words do move a woman's mind.
SHAKESPEARE: *Two Gentlemen of Verona,* III, *c.* 1595

Rich gifts wax poor when givers prove unkind.
SHAKESPEARE: *Hamlet,* III, *c.* 1601

A gift much expected is paid, not given.
GEORGE HERBERT: *Outlandish Proverbs,* 1640

A wicked man's gift hath a touch of his master.
IBID.

Gifts enter everywhere without a wimble.
IBID. (*Wimble*=gimlet)

He that gives thee a capon, give him the leg and wing.
IBID.

She that takes gifts herself she sells.
DAVID FERGUSSON: *Scottish Proverbs,* 1641

Saints themselves will sometimes be,
Of gifts that cost them nothing, free.
SAMUEL BUTLER: *Hudibras,* I, 1663

Nothing costs so much as what is given us.
THOMAS FULLER: *Gnomologia,* 1732

People seldom read a book which is given to them.
SAMUEL JOHNSON: *Boswell's Life,* April 27, 1773

If a man with his eyes open, and without any means used to deceive him, gives me a thing, I am not to let him have it again when he grows wiser.
SAMUEL JOHNSON: *Boswell's Tour to the Hebrides,* Oct. 15, 1773

Whatever a man has is in the end only a gift.
C. M. WIELAND: *Oberon,* II, 1780

To receive a present handsomely and in a right spirit, even when you have none to give in return, is to give one in return.
LEIGH HUNT: *The Seer,* XLIX, 1840

We do not quite forgive a giver. The hand that feeds us is in some danger of being bitten.
R. W. EMERSON: *Gifts,* 1841

The gift without the giver is bare.
J. R. LOWELL: *The Vision of Sir Launfal,* II, 1848

The greatest grace of a gift, perhaps, is that it anticipates and admits of no return.
H. W. LONGFELLOW: *Letter to Mrs. J. T. Fields,* Feb. 28, 1871

Gifts should be handed, not thrown.
DANISH PROVERB

Gifts break rocks.
PORTUGUESE PROVERB

Whatever is bought is cheaper than a gift.
SPANISH PROVERB

Never look a gift horse in the eye.
WELSH PROVERB

[*See also* Enemy, Giving, Greek, Thanks.

Gin

No gin, no king!
Cry of the mob in London on the passage of the act laying an excise tax of 20 shillings a gallon on gin, 1736

[*See also* Byron (Lord), Lamb (Charles), Teetotaler.

Gipsy

Gipsies . . . tell men of losses, and the next time they look for their purses they find their words true.
WYE SALTONSTALL: *Picturae Loquentes,* XXI, 1631

Men and women who are in life as the wild river and the night-owl, as the blasted tree and the wind over ancient graves.
C. G. LELAND: *The Gipsies,* V, 1882

The white moth to the closing vine,
The bee to the open clover,
And the gipsy blood to the gipsy blood
Ever the wide world over.
RUDYARD KIPLING: *The Gipsy Trail,* 1892 (The Century, Dec.)

A gipsy tells the truth once in his life, and immediately repents.
RUSSIAN PROVERB

[*See also* Bargaining, Cheating, Like.

Girl

An unlesson'd girl, unschool'd, unpractis'd;
Happy in this, she is not yet so old
But she may learn.
SHAKESPEARE: *The Merchant of Venice,* III, *c.* 1597

One of those little prating girls,
Of whom fond parents tell such tedious stories.
JOHN DRYDEN: *The Rival Ladies,* I, 1664

Girls we love for what they are; young men for what they promise to be.
J. W. GOETHE: *Dichtung und Wahrheit*, III, 1831

You cannot hammer a girl into anything. She grows as a flower does, — she will wither without sun; she will decay in her sheath as a narcissus will if you do not give her air enough; she may fall and defile her head in dust if you leave her without help at some moments of her life; but you cannot fetter her; she must take her own fair form and way if she take any.
JOHN RUSKIN: *Sesame and Lilies*, 1865

There was a little girl,
Who had a little curl
Right in the middle of her forehead;
And when she was good
She was very, very good,
But when she was bad she was horrid.
H. W. LONGFELLOW: (no title), 1871

The whisper of a pretty girl can be heard further than the roar of a lion.
ARAB PROVERB

Girls and glass are always in danger.
ITALIAN PROVERB

[*See also* Boy, Boy and Girl, Child, Children, Education, Friendship, Giving, Hazlitt (William), Maiden, Virgin.

Giving

God loveth a cheerful giver.
II CORINTHIANS IX, 7, *c.* 55

Give, and it shall be given unto you; good measure, pressed down, and shaken together, and running over. LUKE VI, 38, *c.* 75

It is more blessed to give than to receive.
ACTS XX, 35, *c.* 75

If in carnal wealth, how much more in spiritual does God love a cheerful giver?
ST. AUGUSTINE: *Of the Catechizing of the Unlearned*, *c.* 400

Better an apple given than eaten.
THE PROVERBS OF HENDYNG, *c.* 1300

He giveth twice that giveth quickly.
RICHARD TAVERNER: *Proverbs*, 1539

He that is long a giving knows not how to give.
GEORGE HERBERT: *Outlandish Proverbs*, 1640

Who gives to all, denies all. IBID.

No man giveth but with intention of good to himself, because giving is voluntary, and of all voluntary acts the object is to every man his own good.
THOMAS HOBBES: *Leviathan*, I, 1651

When you give,
Give not by halves.
PHILIP MASSINGER: *The Bashful Lover*, II, 1655

The hand that gives, gathers.
JAMES HOWELL: *Proverbs*, 1659

He who gives away his goods before he is dead
Take a beetle and knock him on the head.
JOHN RAY: *English Proverbs*, 1670
(*Beetle*=a paving rammer)

Giving is the business of the rich.
J. W. GOETHE: *Hermann und Dorothea*, I, 1797

Give and spend
And God will send.
H. G. BOHN: *Handbook of Proverbs*, 1855

He gives nothing who does not give himself.
FRENCH PROVERB

A man cannot give what he hasn't got. (Nil dat quod non habet.) LATIN PROVERB

Let him who exhorts others to give, give himself. (Qui suadet, sua det.) IBID.

All that we can hold in our dead hands is what we have given away. SANSKRIT PROVERB

Gie is a gude fellow, but he soon wearies.
SCOTTISH PROVERB (*Gie*=give)

[*See also* Alms, Benefit, Charity, French, Generosity, Gift, Lending, Liberality.

Gladness

The hope of the righteous shall be gladness.
PROVERBS X, 28, *c.* 350 B.C.

Thou hast put off my sackcloth, and girded me with gladness. PSALMS XXX, 11, *c.* 150 B.C.

Let the nations be glad and sing for joy.
PSALMS LXVII, 4

Gladness of heart is the life of man.
ECCLESIASTICUS XXX, 22, *c.* 180 B.C.

A man of gladness seldom falls into madness.
JOHN RAY: *English Proverbs*, 1670

[*See also* May.

Gladstone, W. E. (1809–98)

He has one gift most dangerous to a speculator, a vast command of a kind of language, grave and majestic, but of vague and uncertain import.
T. B. MACAULAY: *Gladstone on Church and State*, 1839 (Edinburgh Review, April)

If Gladstone fell in the Thames, that would be a misfortune. But if someone fished him out again, that would be a calamity.
Ascribed to BENJAMIN DISRAELI, *c.* 1867
(Similar sayings have been levelled at many other statesmen since)

A sophistical rhetorician, inebriated with the exuberance of his own verbosity.
BENJAMIN DISRAELI: Speech in London, July 27, 1878

If you were to put that man on a moor with nothing on but his shirt, he could become whatever he pleased.
T. H. HUXLEY: To John Morley, *c.* 1880

The grand old man.
W. VERNON HARCOURT: Speech at Derby, April 25, 1882

I don't object to the G.O.M. having the ace of trumps up his sleeve, but I do object to his saying the Almighty put it there.
HENRY LABOUCHÈRE, *c.* 1885

He could convince others of many things, and himself of anything. Author unidentified

Glass

We see through a glass, darkly.
I CORINTHIANS XIII, 12 *c.* 55

[*See also* House.

Glitter

[*See* Appearance.

Gloaming

In the gloaming, O, my darling!
When the lights are dim and low,
And the quiet shadows falling
Softly come and softly go.
META ORRED: *In the Gloaming, c.* 1875

Gloom

[*See* Austerity.

Glory

It is the brave man's part to live with glory, or with glory die.
SOPHOCLES: *Ajax, c.* 450 B.C.

The heavens declare the glory of God.
PSALMS XIX, 1, *c.* 150 B.C.

Whether therefore ye eat, or drink, or whatever ye do, do all to the glory of God.
I CORINTHIANS X, 31, *c.* 55

There is one glory of the sun, and another glory of the moon, and another glory of the stars: for one star differeth from another star in glory.
I CORINTHIANS XV, 41

There is a sufficient glory in the very consciousness of a noble deed.
CICERO: *Orationes Philippicæ,* II, *c.* 60 B.C.

How hard it is to maintain inherited glory.
PUBLILIUS SYRUS: *Sententiæ, c.* 50 B.C.

He has true glory who despises it.
LIVY: *History of Rome,* X, *c.* 10

The love of glory gives strength to the mind, and the desire of praise inspires men with eloquence.
OVID: *Tristia,* V, *c.* 10

Glory is a torch to kindle the noble mind.
SILIUS ITALICUS: *Punica,* VI, *c.* 75

Glory comes too late when it comes only to our ashes.
MARTIAL: *Epigrams,* I, 86

Glory is wont to exalt, not to humble.
TERTULLIAN: *Women's Dress, c.* 220

Man is often vainglorious about his contempt of glory.
ST. AUGUSTINE: *Confessions,* X, *c.* 420

To the greater glory of God. (Ad maiorem Dei gloriam.)
POPE GREGORY THE GREAT: *Dialogues,* I, *c.* 593 (Motto of the Jesuits, 1539)

How quickly passes away the glory of this world. (O quam cito transit gloria mundi.)
THOMAS À KEMPIS: *Imitation of Christ,* I, *c.* 1420

Who is there that does not voluntarily exchange health, repose, and life itself for reputation and glory, the most useless, frivolous, and false coin that passes current amongst us?
MICHEL DE MONTAIGNE: *Essays,* I, 1580

Glory is like a circle in the water.
Which never ceaseth to enlarge itself
Till, by broad spreading it disperse to nought.
SHAKESPEARE: *I Henry VI,* I, *c.* 1592

When the moon shone, we did not see the candle;
So doth the greater glory dim the less.
SHAKESPEARE: *The Merchant of Venice,* V, *c.* 1597

Like madness is the glory of this life.
SHAKESPEARE: *Timon of Athens,* I, *c.* 1607

Glories, like glow-worms, afar off shine bright,
But look'd too near have neither heat nor light.
JOHN WEBSTER: *The White Devil,* IV, *c.* 1608

Some glory in their birth, some in their skill,
Some in their wealth, some in their bodies' force,
Some in their garments, though new-fangled ill;
Some in their hawks and hounds, some in their horse.
SHAKESPEARE: *Sonnets,* XCI, 1609

I make no haste to have my numbers read.
Seldom comes glory till a man be dead.
ROBERT HERRICK: *Hesperides,* 1648

The garlands wither on your brow;
Then boast no more your mighty deeds!
Upon death's purple altar now
See where the victor-victim bleeds.
JAMES SHIRLEY: *The Contention of Ajax and Ulysses,* 1659

There is no road of flowers leading to glory.
JEAN DE LA FONTAINE: *Fables,* X, 1671

The greatest baseness of man is his seeking for glory: but even this is the greatest indication of his excellence; for, whatever possession he may have on earth, whatever health

and essential comfort he may have, he is not satisfied without the esteem of men.
BLAISE PASCAL: *Pensées*, II, 1670

Hasty glory goes out in a snuff.
THOMAS FULLER: *Gnomologia*, 1732

Who pants for glory finds but short repose;
A breath revives him, or a breath o'erthrows.
ALEXANDER POPE: *The First Epistle of the Second Book of Horace*, 1737

The paths of glory lead but to the grave.
THOMAS GRAY: *Elegy Written in a Country Churchyard*, 1750

When we examine what glory is, we discover that it is nearly nothing. To be judged by the ignorant and esteemed by imbeciles, to hear one's name spoken by a rabble who approve, reject, love or hate without reason – that is nothing to be proud of.
FREDERICK THE GREAT: *Letter to Voltaire*, Jan. 3, 1773

One crowded hour of glorious life
Is worth an age without a name.
Anon.: *The Bee*, Oct. 12, 1791

Before this time tomorrow I shall have gained a peerage or Westminster Abbey.
HORATIO NELSON: Before the Battle of the Nile, Aug. 1, 1798

Not in utter nakedness,
But trailing clouds of glory do we come.
WILLIAM WORDSWORTH: *Intimations of Immortality*, 1807

Where is it now, the glory and the dream?
IBID.

It is through glory that free nations are brought to slavery.
FRANÇOIS CHATEAUBRIAND: Speech in the French Chamber, March 2, 1818

The glory that was Greece
And the grandeur that was Rome.
E. A. POE: *To Helen*, 1836 (Southern Literary Messenger, March)

The glory dies not, and the grief is past.
S. E. BRYDGES: *On the Death of Sir Walter Scott*, 1832

The deed is everything, not the glory.
J. W. GOETHE: *II Faust*, IV, 1832

Glory, glory, hallelujah.
C. S. HALL: *John Brown's Body*, refrain, 1860

Mine eyes have seen the coming of the glory of the Lord.
JULIA WARD HOWE: *Battle Hymn of the Republic*, 1861

The thirst for glory is an epidemic which robs a people of their judgment, seduces their vanity, cheats them of their interests, and corrupts their consciences.
W. G. SUMNER: *The Conquest of the United States by Spain*, 1899

Holy Father, so passes away the glory of this world. (Pater sancte, sic transit gloria mundi.)
Author and date unknown (Büchmann says that "when a new pope goes to be crowned at St. Peter's the master of ceremonies thrice lights a bundle of oakum on a reed staff," and each time calls out this admonition)

When glory comes, loss of memory follows.
FRENCH PROVERB

Born to glory. (Natus ad gloriam.)
LATIN PHRASE

Glory is the shadow of virtue. (Gloria virtutis umbra.)
LATIN PROVERB

To God be all the glory. (Soli Deo gloria.)
MEDIEVAL LATIN PHRASE, often appearing at the ends of books

[*See also* Ambition, Battlefield, Conquest, Death, Fame, God, Hair, Literature, Man and Woman, Popularity, Pride, War.

Glove

Ask'd her to acquit me of rudeness if I drew off her glove. Enquiring the reason, I told her 'twas great odds between handling a dead goat and a living lady.
SAMUEL SEWALL: *Diary*, Oct. 12, 1720

An iron hand in a velvet glove.
Author unidentified; sometimes ascribed to NAPOLEON I

[See also Cheek, Kiss.

Glow-worm

The glow-worm shows the matin to be near,
And 'gins to pale his uneffectual fire.
SHAKESPEARE: *Hamlet*, I, *c.* 1601

Gluttony

Be not among . . . riotous eaters of flesh.
PROVERBS XXIII, 20, *c.* 350 B.C.

Gluttony hinders chastity.
POPE XYSTUS I: *The Ring*, *c.* 150

Gluttony slays more than the sword.
ENGLISH PROVERB, traced by Apperson to *c.* 1535

Two hungry meals make the third a glutton.
JOHN HEYWOOD: *Proverbs*, 1546

None is happy but a glutton.
JOHN LYLY: *A Serving Men's Song*, *c.* 1584

He hath eaten me out of house and home.
SHAKESPEARE: *II Henry IV*, II, *c.* 1598

I am Gluttony. My parents are all dead, and the devil a penny they have left me, but a bare pension, and that is thirty meals a day – a small trifle to suffice nature. I come of a royal parentage! My grandfather was a gam-

mon of bacon, my grandmother a hogshead of claret wine.
CHRISTOPHER MARLOWE: *Dr. Faustus*, II, 1604

Great eaters and great sleepers are incapable of anything else that is great.
HENRY IV OF FRANCE (1553–1610)

He was a man of an unbounded stomach.
SHAKESPEARE and JOHN FLETCHER: *Henry VIII*, IV, 1613

Swinish gluttony
Ne'er looks to Heav'n amidst his gorgeous feast,
But with besotted base ingratitude
Crams, and blasphemes his feeder.
JOHN MILTON: *Comus*, 1637

Who hastens a glutton, chokes him.
GEORGE HERBERT: *Outlandish Proverbs*, 1640

Gluttony is the sin of England.
THOMAS FULLER: *Sermons*, 1640

Formidable is the state of an intemperate man whose employment is the same with the work of the sheep or the calf, always to eat.
JEREMY TAYLOR: *Twenty-seven Sermons*, XV, 1651

Gluttony is no sin if it doesn't injure health.
Doctrine condemned by Pope Alexander VII, Sept. 24, 1665

It is easier to fill a glutton's belly than his eye.
THOMAS FULLER: *Gnomologia*, 1732

More die by food than famine. IBID.

What slaughter'd hecatombs, what floods of wine
Fill the capacious squire and deep divine.
ALEXANDER POPE: *Moral Essays*, III (Of the Use of Riches), 1732

A glutton digs his grave with his teeth.
FRENCH PROVERB

Many dishes, many diseases. (Multa fercula, multos morbos.) LATIN PROVERB

[*See also* Belly, Drunkard, Eating, Gourmet, Sin.

Gnat

[To] strain at a gnat and swallow a camel.
MATTHEW XXIII, 24, *c.* 75

He formed this gnat who built the sky.
JAMES MONTGOMERY: *The Gnat*, *c.* 1830

Goat

These are the beasts which we shall eat: the ox, the sheep, and the goat.
DEUTERONOMY XIV, 4, *c.* 650 B.C.

Mine anger was kindled against the shepherds, and I punished the goats.
ZECHARIAH X, 3, *c.* 520 B.C.

A shepherd divideth his sheep from his goats.
MATTHEW XXV, 32, *c.* 75

They stinken as a goat.
GEOFFREY CHAUCER: *The Canterbury Tales* (The Canon's Yeoman's Tale), *c.* 1386

No goat ever died of hunger.
FRENCH PROVERB

If you have no trouble, buy a goat.
PERSIAN PROVERB

No botanist ever had half the knowledge of a goat. WELSH PROVERB

A goat should not concern itself with the quarrels of sheep. WEST AFRICAN PROVERB

[*See also* Beard, Boy, Candle-light, God, Kid, Lean, Lust, Merriment.

God

God will provide.
GENESIS XXII, 8, *c.* 700 B.C.

God said unto Moses, I am that I am.
EXODUS III, 14, *c.* 700 B.C.

The Lord is greater than all gods.
EXODUS XVIII, 11

I am the Lord thy God, which have brought thee out of the land of Egypt, out of the house of bondage. Thou shalt have no other gods before me.
EXODUS XX, 2–3 (Cf. DEUTERONOMY V, 6–7, *c.* 650 B.C.)

The Lord the Lord God, merciful and gracious, longsuffering, and abundant in goodness and truth. EXODUS XXXIV, 6

I am God, and there is none else.
ISAIAH XLV, 22, *c.* 700 B.C. (Cf. XLV, 18; XLVI, 9)

The Lord your God is God of gods, and Lord of lords, a great God, a mighty, and a terrible. DEUTERONOMY X, 17, *c.* 650 B.C.

God, if He be good, is not the author of all things, but of a few things only, and not of most things that occur to man.
PLATO: *The Republic*, *c.* 370 B.C.

He was a wise man who invented God.
PLATO: *Sisyphus*, *c.* 360 B.C. (Probably spurious)

A man's heart deviseth his way: but the Lord directeth his steps.
PROVERBS XVI, 9, *c.* 350 B.C.

The heavens declare the glory of God; and the firmament showeth his handiwork.
PSALMS XIX, 1, *c.* 150 B.C.

God is our refuge and strength, a very present help in trouble. PSALMS XLVI, 1

God standeth in the congregation of the mighty; he judgeth among the gods.
PSALMS LXXXII, 1

The lord is a great God, and a great King above all gods. PSALMS XCV, 3

Worship him, all ye gods. PSALMS XCVII, 7

There is nothing which God cannot accomplish. CICERO: *De divinatione*, II, *c.* 78 B.C.

Nature herself has imprinted on the minds of all the idea of a God.
CICERO: *De natura deorum*, I, 45 B.C.

There is a God within us, and we glow when He stirs us. OVID: *Fasti*, VI, *c.* 5

If God be my friend I cannot be wretched.
OVID: *Tristia*, I, *c.* 10

All things work together for good to them that love God. ROMANS VIII, 28, *c.* 55

If God be for us, who can be against us?
ROMANS VIII, 31

O the depth of the riches both of the wisdom and knowledge of God! how unsearchable are his judgments, and his ways past finding out! ROMANS XI, 33

The foolishness of God is wiser than men, and the weakness of God is stronger than men.
I CORINTHIANS I, 25, *c.* 55

There is none other God but one.
I CORINTHIANS VIII, 1

Fear God. I PETER II, 17, *c.* 60

Call it nature, fate, fortune: all are but names of the one and same God.
SENECA: *De beneficiis*, IV, *c.* 63

God never repents His first decision.
SENECA: *De beneficiis*, VI

Whom the Lord loveth he chasteneth.
HEBREWS XII, 6, *c.* 65

Our God is a consuming fire.
HEBREWS XII, 29

There is one God; and there is none other but he. MARK XII, 32, *c.* 70

With God nothing shall be impossible.
LUKE I, 37, *c.* 75

God is no respecter of persons.
ACTS X, 34, *c.* 75 (Cf. ROMAN II, 11, *c.* 55)

Ye men of Athens, I perceive that in all things ye are too superstitious. For as I passed by, and beheld your devotions, I found an altar with this inscription, TO THE UNKNOWN GOD. Whom therefore ye ignorantly worship, him declare I unto you.
ACTS XVII, 22–23

I am Alpha and Omega, the beginning and the end, the first and the last.
REVELATION XXII, 13, *c.* 95

God is the ruler of all. (Regnator omnium Deus.) TACITUS: *Germany*, 99

No man hath seen God at any time.
JOHN I, 18, *c.* 115

God is a spirit: and they that worship him must worship him in spirit and in truth.
JOHN IV, 24

We have one Father, even God.
JOHN VIII, 41

God is love; and he that dwelleth in love dwelleth in God, and God in him.
I JOHN IV, 16, *c.* 115

God is not the name of God, but an opinion about Him.
POPE XYSTUS I: *The Ring*, *c.* 150

When you speak of God, you are being judged by God. IBID.

It makes no difference whether you call Zeus the Most High, or Zeus, or Adonaios, or Sabaoth, or Amon like the Egyptians, or Papaios like the Scythians.
CELSUS: *A True Discourse*, *c.* 178

There is an enmity between what is of God and what is of man.
TERTULLIAN: *The Christian's Defence*, *c.* 215

God must not be thought of as a physical being, or as having any kind of body. He is pure mind. He moves and acts without needing any corporeal space, or size, or form, or color, or any other property of matter.
ORIGEN: *De principiis*, I, *c.* 254

God is best known in not knowing Him.
ST. AUGUSTINE: *De ordine*, *c.* 387

We can know what God is not, but we cannot know what He is.
ST. AUGUSTINE: *De trinitate*, *c.* 410

We praise thee, O God; we acknowledge thee to be the Lord. (Te Deum laudamus; te Dominum confitemur.)
Anon.: *Te Deum* (This ancient hymn has been ascribed to ST. AMBROSE, *c.* 400, but without ground A more probable author is ST. CAESARIUS, *c.* 500)

There is no God but God.
THE KORAN, III, *c.* 625

Man thinks, God directs. (Homo cogitat, Deus indicat.) ALCUIN: *Epistles*, *c.* 800

Time does not contain Him, nor space hold Him. No intelligence can grasp Him, nor imagination figure Him. Nothing is like Him. But still He hears and sees all things.
ABDALLAH IBN TUMART: *Tauhid, or Confession of Faith*, *c.* 1140

God is over all things, under all things; outside all; within but not enclosed; without but not excluded; above but not raised up; below but not depressed; wholly above, pre-

siding; wholly beneath, sustaining; wholly without, embracing; wholly within, filling.
HILDEBERT OF LAVARDIN (ARCHBISHOP OF TOURS): *Epistles, c.* 1125

Man proposes, but God disposes.
ENGLISH PROVERB, borrowed from the Latin and based on PROVERBS XVI, 9 (Cf. *ante, c.* 350 B.C. The Latin form, "Homo proponit, sed Deus disponit," is in THOMAS À KEMPIS: *Imitation of Christ,* I, *c.* 1420)

To God, most good, most great. (Deo optimo maximo.)
Legend on every bottle of Bénédictine liqueur, abbreviated as D.O.M., *c.* 1510

A mighty fortress is our God. (Ein' feste Burg ist unser Gott.)
MARTIN LUTHER: *Ein' feste Burg,* 1529

God is no botcher.
JOHN HEYWOOD: *Proverbs,* 1546

When God contemplates some great work, He begins it by the hand of some poor, weak, human creature, to whom He afterwards gives aid, so that the enemies who seek to obstruct it are overcome.
MARTIN LUTHER: *Table-Talk,* LXIX, 1569

God comes with leaden feet, but strikes with iron hands.
ENGLISH PROVERB, traced by Smith to 1579

God shall be my hope,
My stay, my guide and lantern to my feet.
SHAKESPEARE: *II Henry VI,* II, *c.* 1591

Our soundest knowledge is to know that we know Him not as indeed He is, neither can know Him; and our safest eloquence concerning Him is our silence, when we confess without confession that His glory is inexplicable, His greatness above our capacity and reach.
RICHARD HOOKER: *The Laws of Ecclesiastical Polity,* I, 1594

God's a good man.
SHAKESPEARE: *Much Ado About Nothing,* III, *c.* 1599

The servant of God hath a good master.
RANDLE COTGRAVE: *French-English Dictionary,* 1611

Had I but served my God with half the zeal
I served my king, he would not in mine age
Have left me naked to mine enemies.
SHAKESPEARE and JOHN FLETCHER: *Henry VIII,* III, 1613

God makes; man shapes.
ROBERT BURTON: *The Anatomy of Melancholy,* III, 1621

God is a sure paymaster.
JOHN CLARKE: *Parœmiologia Anglo-Latina,* 1639

Man doth what he can, and God what He will.
IBID.

God comes to see without a bell.
GEORGE HERBERT: *Outlandish Proverbs,* 1640

God oft hath a great share in a little house.
IBID.

God strikes with His finger, and not with all His arm.
IBID.

Have God and have all.
DAVID FERGUSSON: *Scottish Proverbs,* 1641

He is poor that God hates.
IBID.

You would do little for God, an the Devil were dead.
IBID.

God is like a skilful geometrician.
THOMAS BROWNE: *Religio Medici,* I, 1642

I fear God, yet am not afraid of Him.
IBID.

Our idea of God implies necessary and eternal existence; the manifest conclusion then is that God does exist.
RENÉ DESCARTES: *Principles of Philosophy,* I, 1644

God has His whips here to a two-fold end —
The bad to punish, and the good t' amend.
ROBERT HERRICK: *Noble Numbers,* 1647

God is all fore-part, for we never see
Any part backward in the Deity.
IBID.

That there's a God we all do know,
But what God is we cannot show.
IBID.

God gives His wrath by weight, and without weight His mercy.
GEORGE HERBERT: *Jacula Prudentum,* 1651

By denying the existence, or providence of God, men may shake off their ease, but not their yoke.
THOMAS HOBBES: *Leviathan,* XXXI, 1651

The God of Christians is not a God who is simply the author of mathematical truths: that is believed only by Epicureans and heathen.
BLAISE PASCAL: *Pensées,* 1670

Just are the ways of God,
And justifiable to men.
JOHN MILTON: *Samson Agonistes,* 1671

If we think of God, it follows that He exists.
NICOLAS MALEBRANCHE: *Conversations métaphysiques et chrétiennes,* 1677

God is a being absolutely infinite; a substance consisting of infinite attributes, each of which expresses His eternal and infinite essence.
BARUCH SPINOZA: *Ethica,* I, 1677

God is a thing that thinks.
IBID.

I have loved to hear my Lord spoken of; and wherever I have seen the print of His shoe in the earth, there I have coveted to set my foot too.

JOHN BUNYAN: *Pilgrim's Progress*, II, 1678

God is infallible in His own nature: He cannot be subject to error or sin, for He is His own light, and His own law; reason is consubstantial with Him, He understands it perfectly, and loves it invincibly.

NICOLAS MALEBRANCHE: *Traité de morale*, I, 1684

I feel that there is a God, and I do not feel that there is none. For me that is enough.

JEAN DE LA BRUYÈRE: *Caractères*, XVI, 1688

We have a more certain knowledge of the existence of a God than of anything our senses have not immediately discovered to us. Nay, I presume I may say that we more certainly know that there is a God than that there is anything else without us.

JOHN LOCKE: *Essay Concerning Human Understanding*, IV, 1690

I fear my God, and I fear none other.

JEAN RACINE: *Athalie*, III, 1690

The Being of God is so comfortable, so convenient, so necessary to the felicity of mankind, that (as Tully admirably says) *Dii immortales ad usum hominum fabricati paene videantur* – if God were not a necessary Being of Himself, He might almost seem to be made on purpose for the use and benefit of men.

JOHN TILLOTSON (ARCHBISHOP OF CANTERBURY): *Sermons*, XCIII, 1694

The existence of God is far more evidently perceived than the existence of men, because the effects of nature are infinitely more numerous and considerable than those ascribed to human agents.

GEORGE BERKELEY: *The Principles of Human Knowledge*, 1710

God is to His creatures, not only what an inventor is to his machine, but also what a prince is to his subjects and a father is to his children.

G. W. LEIBNIZ: *The Monadology*, LXXXIV, 1714

Our God, our help in ages past,
Our hope for years to come,
Our shelter from the stormy blast,
And our eternal home.

ISAAC WATTS: *The Psalms of David*, 1719

If the triangles made a god, they would give him three sides.

C. L. DE MONTESQUIEU: *Persian Letters*, III, 1721

I believe there is one supreme, most perfect Being, Author and Father of the gods themselves. For I believe that man is not the most perfect being but one, rather that as there are many degrees of beings his inferiors, so there are many degrees of beings superior to him.

BENJAMIN FRANKLIN: *Articles of Belief and Acts of Religion*, Nov. 20, 1728

Let him say what he will, men have spoken well of God before now.

THOMAS FULLER: *Gnomologia*, 1732

Laugh where we must, be candid where we can,
But vindicate the ways of God to man.

ALEXANDER POPE: *An Essay on Man*, I, 1732

To Him no high, no low, no great, no small;
He fills, He bounds, connects and equals all!

IBID.

Who sees with equal eye, as God of all,
A hero perish or a sparrow fall,
Atoms or systems into ruin hurled
And now a bubble burst, and now a world.

IBID.

Nor God alone in the still calm we find;
He mounts the storm, and walks upon the wind.

ALEXANDER POPE: *An Essay on Man*, II

Slave to no sect, who takes no private road,
But looks through nature up to nature's God.

ALEXANDER POPE: *An Essay on Man*, IV

My reason tells me that God exists, but it also tells me that I can never know what he is.

VOLTAIRE: *Letter to Frederick the Great*, Oct. 1737

Father of all! in every age,
In every clime adored,
By saint, by savage, and by sage,
Jehovah, Jove, or Lord!

ALEXANDER POPE: *The Universal Prayer*, 1738

The God that holds you over the pit of Hell, much as one holds a spider, or some loathsome insect, over the fire, abhors you, and is dreadfully provoked; His wrath towards you burns like fire; He looks upon you as worthy of nothing else but to be cast into the fire; He is of purer eyes than to bear to have you in His sight; you are ten thousand times more abominable in His eyes than the most hateful venomous serpent is in ours.

JONATHAN EDWARDS: *Sinners in the Hands of an Angry God*, 1741 (Sermons, July 8)

The Deity . . . is not the natural object of any passion or affection.

DAVID HUME: *Letter to William Mure*, June 30, 1743

God Himself is not an absolute but a limited monarch, limited by the rule which infinite wisdom prescribes to infinite power.

HENRY BOLINGBROKE (VISCOUNT BOLINGBROKE): *The Idea of a Patriot King*, 1749

From Thee, great God, we spring, to Thee we tend, —
Path, motive, guide, original, and end.
SAMUEL JOHNSON: *Motto for The Rambler*, VII, 1749

To believe there is a God is to believe the existence of all possible good and perfection in the universe, and it is to be resolved upon this: that things either are, or finally shall be, as they should be.
BENJAMIN WHICHCOTE: *Moral and Religious Aphorisms*, 1753

The most perfect idea of God that we can form in this life is that of an independent, unique, infinite, eternal, omnipotent, immutable, intelligent and free First Cause, whose power extends over all things.
E. B. DE CONDILLAC: *Traité des animaux*, VI, 1755

Whenever an important event, a revolution, or a calamity turns to the profit of the church, such is always signalized as the Finger of God.
VOLTAIRE: *Philosophical Dictionary*, 1764

If God didn't exist, man would have to invent Him. (Si Dieu n'existait pas, il faudrait l'inventer.)
VOLTAIRE: *Épître à l'auteur du nouveau livre des trois imposteurs*, 1769 (Cf. VOLTAIRE, *post*, Nov. 10, 1770)

It is said that God is always on the side of the heaviest battalions.
VOLTAIRE: *Letter to M. le Riche*, Feb. 6, 1770 (Borrowed from Marie de Sévigné, but Mme. de Sévigné said *fortune*, not *God*. Cf. Sévigné, under Fortune, *c*. 1690)

" If God did not exist it would be necessary to invent Him." — I am rarely satisfied with my lines, but I confess that I have a father's tenderness for that one.
VOLTAIRE: To M. Saurin, Nov. 10, 1770 (Cf. VOLTAIRE, *ante*, 1769)

God's perfections are marvellous but not lovable.
IMMANUEL KANT: Lecture at Königsberg, 1775

God moves in a mysterious way
His wonders to perform.
WILLIAM COWPER: *Light Shining Out of Darkness*, 1779

Every conjecture we can form with regard to the works of God has as little probability as the conjectures of a child with regard to the works of a man.
THOMAS REID: *Essays on the Intellectual Powers*, I, 1785

The pride of the peacock is the glory of God.
The lust of the goat is the bounty of God.
The wrath of the lion is the wisdom of God.
The nakedness of woman is the work of God.
WILLIAM BLAKE: *The Marriage of Heaven and Hell*, 1790

The only idea man can affix to the name of God is that of a first cause, the cause of all things. Incomprehensible and difficult as it is for a man to conceive what a first cause is, he arrives at the belief of it from the tenfold greater difficulty of disbelieving it.
THOMAS PAINE: *The Age of Reason*, I, 1794

What renders the principle of equality inapplicable to our relations with God, is, that of all beings, it is He alone who cannot be represented as subject to duty.
IMMANUEL KANT: *Perpetual Peace*, II, 1795

Sire, I had no need for that hypothesis.
P. S. LAPLACE: On being asked by Napoleon I what room there was for God in the cosmology of his *Mécanique céleste*, I, 1799

After all, is our idea of God anything more than personified incomprehensibility?
G. C. LICHTENBERG: *Reflections*, 1799

There lives a God to punish and avenge.
J. C. F. SCHILLER: *Wilhelm Tell*, IV, 1804

A vengeful, pitiless, and almighty fiend,
Whose mercy is a nickname for the rage
Of tameless tigers hungering for blood.
P. B. SHELLEY: *Queen Mab*, IV, 1813

The being called God bears every mark of a veil woven by philosophical conceit, to hide the ignorance of philosophers even from themselves. They borrow the thread of its texture from the anthropomorphism of the vulgar.
P. B. SHELLEY: *Queen Mab*, notes

Then conquer we must when our cause it is just,
And this be our motto, " In God is our trust! "
F. S. KEY: *The Star-Spangled Banner*, 1814 (Baltimore American, Sept. 16)

I believe in God and in His wisdom and benevolence.
JOHN ADAMS: *Letter to Thomas Jefferson*, Dec. 8, 1818

If I had believed in a God of rewards and punishments, I might have lost courage in battle.
NAPOLEON I: To Gaspard Gourgaud at St. Helena, 1815–1818

God is the perfect poet,
Who in His person acts His own creations.
ROBERT BROWNING: *Paracelsus*, II, 1835

Time and space are not God, but creations of God; with God, as it is a universal Here, so is it an everlasting Now.
THOMAS CARLYLE: *Sartor Resartus*, III, 1836

Nearer, my God, to Thee,
Nearer to Thee;

E'en though it be a cross
That raiseth me.

SARAH F. ADAMS: *Nearer, My God, To Thee,* 1841 (The familiar tune was written by Lowell Mason, 1856)

God's in His Heaven —
All's right with the world.

ROBERT BROWNING: *Pippa Passes,* I, 1841

There is no longer any God for us. God's laws are become a greatest-happiness principle, a parliamentary expediency: the Heavens overarch us only as an astronomical time-keeper; a butt for Herschel-telescopes to shoot science at, to shoot sentimentalities at.

THOMAS CARLYLE: *Past and Present,* III, 1843

After reading all that has been written, and after thinking all that can be thought, on the topics of God and the soul, the man who has a right to say that he thinks at all will find himself face to face with the conclusion that, on these topics, the most profound thought is that which can be the least easily distinguished from the most superficial sentiment.

E. A. POE: *Marginalia,* 1844–49

And almost every one, when age,
Disease, or sorrows strike him,
Inclines to think there is a God,
Or something very like Him.

ARTHUR H. CLOUGH: *Dipsychus,* 1850

The word God is a theology in itself, indivisibly one, inexhaustibly various, from the vastness and simplicity of its meaning. Admit a God, and you introduce among the subjects of your knowledge a fact encompassing, closing in upon, absorbing, every other fact conceivable.

J. H. NEWMAN: *On the Scope and Nature of University Education,* 1852

A voice in the wind I do not know;
A meaning on the face of the high hills
Whose utterance I cannot comprehend.
A something is behind them: that is God.

GEORGE MACDONALD: *Within and Without,* I, 1855

God will forgive me; it is His trade.

HEINRICH HEINE: On his deathbed, 1856

Whoever fears God, fears to sit at ease.

E. B. BROWNING: *Aurora Leigh,* VIII, 1857

In great contests each party claims to act in accordance with the will of God. Both may be, and one must be wrong. God cannot be for and against the same thing at the same time.

ABRAHAM LINCOLN: *Memorandum,* Sept. 30, 1862

I know not where his islands lift
Their fronded palms in air;
I only know I cannot drift
Beyond His love and care.

J. G. WHITTIER: *The Eternal Goodness,* 1867

Is it more unphilosophical to believe in a personal God, omnipotent and omniscient, than in natural forces unconscious and irresistible? Is it unphilosophical to combine power with intelligence?

BENJAMIN DISRAELI: *Lothair,* IX, 1870

Priests, kings, statesmen, soldiers, bankers, and public functionaries of all sorts; policemen, jailers and hangmen; capitalists, usurers, business men and property-owners; lawyers, economists and politicians — all of them, down to the meanest grocer, repeat in chorus the words of Voltaire, that if there were no God it would be necessary to invent Him.

M. A. BAKUNIN: *Dieu et l'état,* 1871

The assumed instinctive belief in God has been used by many persons as an argument for His existence. But this is a rash argument, as we should thus be compelled to believe in the existence of many cruel and malignant spirits, only a little more powerful than man; for the belief in them is far more general than in a beneficent Deity.

CHARLES DARWIN: *The Descent of Man,* XXI, 1871

As men in the days of ignorance endeavored to discover perpetual motion and the philosopher's stone, so now they endeavor to define God.

W. WINWOOD READE: *The Martyrdom of Man,* III, 1872

The word God is used in most cases as by no means a term of science or exact knowledge, but a term of poetry and eloquence, a term thrown out, so to speak, at a not fully grasped object of the speaker's consciousness, — a literary term, in short; and mankind mean different things by it as their consciousness differs.

MATTHEW ARNOLD: *Literature and Dogma,* I, 1873

God Himself does not speak prose, but communicates with us by hints, omens, inference and dark resemblances in objects lying all around us.

R. W. EMERSON: *Poetry and Imagination,* 1876

An honest God is the noblest work of man.

R. G. INGERSOLL: *The Gods, and Other Lectures,* 1876

God is not only true, but Truth itself.

POPE LEO XIII: *Aeterni patris,* Aug. 4, 1879

Whatever may be God's future, we cannot forget His past.

W. H. MALLOCK: *Is Life Worth Living?,* 1879

Every man recognizes within himself a free and rational spirit, independent of his body. This spirit is what we call God.

LYOF N. TOLSTOY: *The Gospel in Brief,* 1880

It is the fool that saith in his heart there is no God. But what shall we call the man who tells us that with this sort of a world God bids us be content?

HENRY GEORGE: *Social Problems,* 1884

We are most unfair to God: we do not allow Him to sin.

F. W. NIETZSCHE: *Beyond Good and Evil,* 1886

What is it: is man only a blunder of God, or God only a blunder of man?

F. W. NIETZSCHE: *The Twilight of the Idols,* 1889

What would be the value of a god who knew nothing of anger, revenge, envy, scorn, cunning, violence? who had perhaps never experienced the rapturous ardeurs of victory and of destruction?

F. W. NIETZSCHE: *The Antichrist,* XVI, 1888

The Christian concept of a god — the god as the patron of the sick, the god as a spinner of cobwebs, the god as a spirit — is one of the most corrupt concepts that has ever been set up in the world: it probably touches low-water mark in the ebbing evolution of the god-type.

F. W. NIETZSCHE: *The Antichrist,* XVIII

We deny that God is God.

F. W. NIETZSCHE: *The Antichrist,* XLVII

If we ever encountered a god who always cured us of a cold in the head at just the right time, or got us into our carriage at the very instant heavy rain began to fall, he would seem so absurd a god that he'd have to be abolished even if he existed.

F. W. NIETZSCHE: *The Antichrist,* LII

It must be remembered that we have heard only one side of the case. God has written all the books.

SAMUEL BUTLER: *Note-Books, c.* 1890

Lord God of hosts, be with us yet,
Lest we forget, lest we forget.

RUDYARD KIPLING: *Recessional,* 1897 (London Times, July 17)

To search for God and to find the Devil — that is what happened to me.

AUGUST STRINDBERG: *Inferno,* 1897

We thus arrive at the paradoxical conception of God as a gaseous vertebrate.

ERNST HAECKEL: *The Riddle of the Universe,* XV, 1899

Our monistic God, the all-embracing essence of the world, the nature-god of Spinoza and Goethe, is identical with eternal, all-inspiring energy, and one, in eternal and infinite substance, with space-filling matter.

ERNST HAECKEL: *Der Kampf um den Entwickelungsgedanken,* III, 1905

God is Love.

MARY BAKER G. EDDY: *Science and Health,* I, 1908 (Cf. I JOHN IV, 16, *ante, c.* 115)

The John Doe of philosophy and religion.

ELBERT HUBBARD: *Roycroft Dictionary and Book of Epigrams,* 1923

Belief in God is the unshaken foundation of all social order and of all responsible action on earth.

POPE PIUS XI: *Caritate Christi compulsi,* May 3, 1932

The mystery of God may be unfathomable, His power and majesty beyond reckoning, His ways not as our ways; but if He is a God, He is not absolute and infinite.

PAUL ELMER MORE: *Pages from an Oxford Diary,* 1937

God gets only the women that men do not want. Author unidentified

Let us thank God that there is no God. IBID.

God is a busy worker, but He loves help.

BASQUE PROVERB

God is slow in paying, but He always pays.

DUTCH PROVERB

Better deal with God directly than with His saints. FRENCH PROVERB

God does well what He does. IBID.

God is not as severe as He is said to be.

IRISH PROVERB

God never shuts one door but He opens another. IBID.

He who leaves God out of his reckoning does not know how to count.

ITALIAN PROVERB

God is believed in because no one can see Him.

JAPANESE PROVERB

God assisting us. (Deo juvante.)

LATIN PHRASE

God favoring us. (Deo favente.) IBID.

God willing. (Deo volente.) IBID.

My hope is in God. (Spes mea in Deo.)

IBID.

God notices pure hands, not full ones. (Puras Deus non plenas aspicit manus.)

LATIN PROVERB

God can shave without soap.

POLISH PROVERB

God soon or late dries all things that are wet.

RUSSIAN PROVERB

We talk, but God does what He pleases.

SPANISH PROVERB

Whom God loves, his bitch brings forth pigs.

IBID.

There are three things that only God knows: the beginning of things, the cause of things, and the end of things. WELSH PROVERB

[*See also* Act of God, Age (Old), Agnostic, Atheist, Blind, Bread, Calvinism, Cause and Effect, Church, Credo, Danger, Deity, Devil, Faith, German, Gods, Good and Evil, Greek Language, Guest, Immortality, Jew, Judgment, Just, Kindness, King, Lamb, Law, Law (Natural), Learning, Light, Love, Luxury, Mammon, Man, Mercy, Microbe, Moment, Monotheism, Mother, Nature, Nest, Ocean, Optimism, Pantheism, Pardon, Poor, Power, Prayer, Providence, Prudence, Revelation, Revenge, Sin, Skeptic, Theologian, Trinity, Trust, Truth, War.

Goddess

Solomon went after Ashtoreth, the goddess of the Zidonians. I KINGS XI, 5, *c.* 500 B.C.

Great is Diana of the Ephesians.
ACTS XIX, 28, *c.* 75

Goddess excellently bright.
BEN JONSON: *Hymn to Diana,* 1601

[*See also* Gait.

Godliness

Great is the mystery of godliness.
I TIMOTHY III, 16, *c.* 60

Godliness is profitable unto all things, having promise of the life that now is, and of that which is to come. I TIMOTHY IV, 8

Godliness with contentment is great gain.
I TIMOTHY VI, 6

Ye may be godly, but ye'll ne'er be cleanly.
SCOTTISH PROVERB

[*See also* Cleanliness, Hypocrisy.

Godmother

Horse godmother: a large masculine woman, a gentleman-like kind of a lady.
FRANCIS GROSE: *A Classical Dictionary of the Vulgar Tongue,* 1785

Gods

The issue lies in the laps of the gods.
HOMER: *Iliad,* XVII, *c.* 800 B.C.

The eternal gods do not lightly change their minds. HOMER: *Odyssey,* III, *c.* 800 B.C.

Every nation made gods of their own.
II KINGS XVII, 29, *c.* 500 B.C.

Do not take liberties with the gods, or weary them.
CONFUCIUS: *The Book of Rites,* XV, *c.* 500 B.C.

When calamity befalls a state the gods are forgotten and no one bothers to honor them.
EURIPIDES: *The Troades, c.* 415 B.C.

Manifestly there are gods, but what the multitude believes of them is not true, for what the multitude believes changes from time to time.
EPICURUS: *Letter to Menoeceus, c.* 300 B.C.

It was a man who first made men believe in gods. CRITIAS: *Fragment, c.* 425 B.C.

We serve the gods—whatever the gods may be. EURIPIDES: *The Orestes,* 408 B.C.

The gods are not sorcerers who change themselves from time to time, nor are they misled by the machinations of others, either in word or deed.
PLATO: *The Republic,* II, *c.* 370 B.C.

Even the gods love their jokes.
PLATO: *Cratylus, c.* 360 B.C.

The gods play games with men as balls.
PLAUTUS: *Captivi, c.* 200 B.C.

When the gods like a man they throw some profit in his way.
PLATO: *Persa,* IV, *c.* 200 B.C.

The gods have always been, and never were born.
CICERO: *De natura deorum,* I, 45 B.C.

It is expedient that gods should exist: since it is expedient, let us believe they do.
OVID: *Ars amatoria,* I, *c.* 2 B.C.

The gods have no time to attend to small matters. OVID: *Tristia,* II, *c.* 10

The gods are come down to us in the likeness of men. ACTS XIV, 11, *c.* 75

It was fear in the world that created the gods.
STATIUS: *Thebaid,* III, *c.* 90

Nay, but there *are* gods, and they *do* concern themselves with human affairs.
MARCUS AURELIUS: *Meditations,* II, *c.* 170

Perhaps the world is governed by various gods, and divided into provinces. If so, then each nation is run as it ought to be run.
CELSUS: *A True Discourse, c.* 178

A god does not change his ways.
TERTULLIAN: *The Christian's Defence, c.* 215

Man cannot make a worm, yet he will make gods by the dozen.
MICHEL DE MONTAIGNE: *Essays,* II, 1580

Come, let us march against the powers of Heaven,
And set black streamers in the firmament
To signify the slaughter of the gods.
CHRISTOPHER MARLOWE: *I Tamburlaine,* I, *c.* 1588

A god is not so glorious as a king.
I think the pleasure they enjoy in Heaven
Cannot compare with kingly joys in earth.
CHRISTOPHER MARLOWE: *I Tamburlaine,* II

Though Heaven bears
A face far from us, gods have most long ears;
Jove has a hundred marble marble hands.
JOHN MARSTON: *Sophonisba,* I, 1606

As flies to wanton boys, are we to the gods;
They kill us for their sport.
SHAKESPEARE: *King Lear*, IV, 1606

The gods are just, and of our pleasant vices
Make instruments to plague us.
SHAKESPEARE: *King Lear*, V

The gods are easy and condemn
All such as are not soft like them.
ROBERT HERRICK: *Hesperides*, 1648

Gods meet gods, and justle in the dark.
JOHN DRYDEN and NATHANIEL LEE: *Œdipus*, IV, 1679

A god alone can comprehend a god.
EDWARD YOUNG: *Night Thoughts*, IX, 1745

The pagan theology is universally received as matter for writing and conversation, though believed now by nobody; and we talk of Jupiter, Mars, Apollo, etc., as gods, though we know, that if they ever existed at all, it was only as mere mortal men.
LORD CHESTERFIELD: *Letter to his son*, April 26, 1748

Ignorance of natural causes created the gods, and priestly impostures made them terrible.
P. H. D. D'HOLBACH: *Le système de la nature*, II, 1770

As nations improve, so do their gods.
G. C. LICHTENBERG: *Reflections*, 1799

In the history of the world there will not again be any man, never so great, whom his fellow-men will take for a god.
THOMAS CARLYLE: *Heroes and Hero-Worship*, II, 1840 (Lecture in London, May 8)

I have a right to overthrow Zeus, Jehovah and company if I can. If I cannot, then they remain in the right as against me.
MAX STIRNER: *The Ego and His Own*, 1845

A Greek never entered a wood without expecting to meet a god in it.
JOHN RUSKIN: *Modern Painters*, IV, 1856

The god of the cannibals will be a cannibal, of the crusaders a crusader, and of the merchants a merchant.
R. W. EMERSON: *The Conduct of Life*, VI, 1860

Wonderful verse of the gods,
Of one import, of varied tone;
They chant the bliss of their abodes
To man imprisoned in his own.
R. W. EMERSON: *My Garden*, 1866

For the gods we know not of, who give us our daily breath,
We know they are cruel as love or life, and lovely as death.
A. C. SWINBURNE: *Hymn to Proserpine*, 1866

When half-gods go,
The gods arrive.
R. W. EMERSON: *Give All to Love*, 1867

The Ethiop gods have Ethiop lips,
Bronze cheeks, and woolly hair;
The Grecian gods are like the Greeks,
As keen-eyed, cold and fair.
WALTER BAGEHOT: *Literary Studies*, II, 1879

The deities of one age are the by-words of the next.
R. G. INGERSOLL: Speech in Boston, April 23, 1880

If there were gods, how could I endure it to be no god? Therefore, there are no gods!
F. W. NIETZSCHE: *Thus Spake Zarathustra*, 1885

All gods hitherto have been sanctified, rebaptized devils.
F. W. NIETZSCHE: *Beyond Good and Evil*, 1886

Gods are fond of the ridiculous. They can't help laughing, even at the most holy matters.
IBID.

The Greeks knew no more piquant seasoning for the happiness of their gods than the joys of cruelty. What final meaning have the Trojan war and like tragic horrors? It is impossible to be in any doubt about it: they were intended to be festival games for the gods, and, in so far as a poet is more godlike than other men, as festival games also for the poets.
F. W. NIETZSCHE: *The Genealogy of Morals*, II, 1887

A man is grateful for his own existence: to that end he needs a god.
F. W. NIETZSCHE: *The Antichrist*, XVI, 1888

Two thousand years have come and gone—and not a single new god!
F. W. NIETZSCHE: *The Antichrist*, XIX

The pig is taught by sermons and epistles
To think the god of swine has snout and bristles.
AMBROSE BIERCE: *The Devil's Dictionary*, 1906

Never burn bad incense before good gods.
CHINESE PROVERB

There are some gods who abandon men; they are the gods who know men.
JAPANESE PROVERB

The nature of the gods. (Natura Deorum.)
LATIN PHRASE

When one god presses hard, another brings relief.
LATIN PROVERB

Worship the gods as if they were present.
Motto inscribed over the doors of Chinese temples

[*See also* Angel, Aspiration, Bold, Cat, Deity, Destruction, Enemy, Evil, Fear, God, Gold, Happiness, Help, Man, Necessity, Prosperity, Ugliness, Vice.

Goethe, J. W. (1749–1832)

From early youth I have had admiration, love and reverence for the one and immortal Goethe.
LUDWIG VAN BEETHOVEN: *Letter to Goethe,* Feb. 8, 1823

The gods pass out: Goethe is dead.
HEINRICH HEINE: On the death of Goethe, 1832

When he is told such a thing must be so, there is immense authority and custom in favor of its being so, it has been held to be so for a thousand years, he answers, with Olympian politeness, "But *is* it so? is it so to *me?*"
MATTHEW ARNOLD: *Heinrich Heine,* 1865

No mere German, but a European event.
F. W. NIETZSCHE: *The Twilight of the Idols,* 1889

Goethe, politically, was a skunk.
AUGUSTINE BIRRELL: Written in the margin of his copy of GEORG BRANDES: *Main Currents in Nineteenth Century Literature,* 1918

When he suffered from a spiritual ailment of any kind he got rid of it by inoculating others with it.
IRVING BABBITT: *Rousseau and Romanticism,* 1919

[*See also* German, Idiot, Kant (Immanuel), Nietzsche (F. W.).

Going

Rise, let us be going.
MATTHEW XXVI, 46, *c.* 75

Stand not upon the order of your going,
But go at once.
SHAKESPEARE: *Macbeth,* III, *c.* 1605

[*See also* Gone.

Gold

Gold is tried with a touchstone, and men by gold. Ascribed to CHILON, *c.* 560 B.C.

Gold hath been the ruin of many.
ECCLESIASTICUS XXI, 6, *c.* 180 B.C.

Gold can make its way through the midst of guards, and break through the strongest barriers more easily than the lightning's bolt.
HORACE: *Carmina,* III, *c.* 20 B.C.

Men now worship gold to the neglect of the gods. By gold good faith is banished and justice is sold.
PROPERTIUS: *Elegies,* III, *c.* 20 B.C.

Silver and gold have I none; but such as I have give I thee. ACTS III, 6, *c.* 75

Not Philip, but Philip's gold, took the cities of Greece.
PLUTARCH: *Lives* (*Paulus Æmilius*), *c.* 100

It is not all gold that shineth.
Anon.: *The Proverbs of Hending, c.* 1300
(Borrowed from a Latin proverb: "Non omne quod nitet aurum est")

It is not all gold that glareth.
GEOFFREY CHAUCER: *The House of Fame,* I, *c.* 1384

A man may buy gold too dear.
JOHN HEYWOOD: *Proverbs,* 1546

All is not gold which glisteneth.
GEORGE PETTIE: *Petite Palace of Pettie His Pleasure,* 1576

Bell, book and candle shall not drive me back,
When gold and silver becks me to come on.
SHAKESPEARE: *King John,* III, *c.* 1596

All is not gold that glisters.
WILLIAM CAMDEN: *Remains Concerning Britain,* 1605

This yellow slave
Will knit and break religions; bless the accurs'd,
Make the hoar leprosy ador'd; place thieves,
And give them title, knee, and approbation
With senators on the bench.
SHAKESPEARE: *Timon of Athens,* IV, *c.* 1607

The purest gold is most ductile.
OWEN FELLTHAM: *Resolves, c.* 1620

An ass laden with gold will go lightly uphill.
THOMAS SHELTON: Tr. of CERVANTES: *Don Quixote,* II (1615), 1620

If gold knew what gold is
Gold would get gold, I wis.
GEORGE HERBERT: *Outlandish Proverbs,* 1640

No lock will hold against the power of gold.
IBID.

That is gold which is worth gold. IBID.

Gold gives to even the ugliest a certain pleasing charm.
J. B. MOLIÈRE: *Sganarelle,* I, 1660

Gold goes in at any gate except Heaven's.
JOHN RAY: *English Proverbs,* 1670

Gold is a wonderful clearer of the understanding; it dissipates every doubt and scruple in an instant, accommodates itself to the meanest capacities, silences the loud and clamorous, and brings over the most obstinate and inflexible.
JOSEPH ADDISON: *The Spectator,* Dec. 4, 1711

Gold defiles with frequent touch;
There's nothing fouls the hand so much.
JONATHAN SWIFT: *The Fable of Midas,* 1712

He is worth gold that can win it.
JAMES KELLY: *Complete Collection of Scottish Proverbs,* 1721

An ass laden with gold overtakes everything.
THOMAS FULLER: *Gnomologia,* 1732

Man was made the standing jest of Heav'n,
And gold but sent to keep the fools in play,
For some to heap, and some to throw away.
ALEXANDER POPE: *Moral Essays,* III (Of the Use of Riches), 1732

O cursed lust of gold! when, for thy sake,
The fool throws up his interest in both worlds;
First starved in this, then damned in that to come.
ROBERT BLAIR: *The Grave,* 1743

The lust of gold, unfeeling and remorseless!
The last corruption of degenerate man.
SAMUEL JOHNSON: *Irene,* I, 1749

All is not gold that glitters.
DAVID GARRICK: Prologue to OLIVER GOLDSMITH: *She Stoops to Conquer,* 1773 (Apparently the first appearance of the saying in the form now most familiar. Cf. CHAUCER, *c.* 1384; PETTIE, 1576; CAMDEN, *c.* 1605. With *glisters* the proverb is in SHAKESPEARE: *The Merchant of Venice,* II, *c.* 1597)

Gold is a living god.
P. B. SHELLEY: *Queen Mab,* V, 1813

Man seeks for gold in mines, that he may weave
A lasting chain for his own slavery.
P. B. SHELLEY: *The Revolt of Islam,* VIII, 1818

Gold and iron are good
To buy iron and gold.
R. W. EMERSON: *Politics,* 1841

A grain of gold will gild a great surface, but not so much as a grain of wisdom.
H. D. THOREAU: *Life Without Principle,* 1863 (Atlantic Monthly, Oct.)

Like liberty, gold never stays where it is undervalued.
J. S. MORRILL: Speech in the Senate, Jan. 28, 1878

Where gold is, there the Devil is.
GERMAN PROVERB

When gold speaks every tongue is silent.
ITALIAN PROVERB

[*See also* Appearance, Damnation, Devil, Labor, Money, Riches, Wealth.

Golden Age

The Golden Age never was the present age.
THOMAS FULLER: *Gnomologia,* 1732

In the reign of Saturn. (Saturno rege.)
LATIN PHRASE

Golden Rule

What you do not want others to do to you, do not do to others.
CONFUCIUS: *The Doctrine of the Mean,* XIII, *c.* 500 B.C.

Do not do to others what would anger you if done to you by others.
Ascribed to ISOCRATES, *c.* 375 B.C.

What thou thyself hatest, do to no man.
TOBIT IV, 14, *c.* 180 B.C.

The question was once put to Aristotle how we ought to behave to our friends; and his answer was, "As we should wish them to behave to us."
DIOGENES LAERTIUS: *Lives of the Philosophers, c.* 150 B.C.

This is the sum of all true righteousness: deal with others as thou wouldst thyself be dealt by. Do nothing to thy neighbor which thou wouldst not have him do to thee hereafter.
THE MAHABHARATA, *c.* 150 B.C.

Whatsoever thou wouldst that men should not do to thee, do not do that to them. This is the whole Law. The rest is only explanation.
HILLEL HA-BABLI: *The Sabbath,* XXXI, *c.* 30 B.C.

All things whatsoever ye would that men should do to you, do ye even so to them: for this is the law and the prophets.
MATTHEW VII, 12, *c.* 75

As ye would that men should do to you, do ye also to them likewise.
LUKE VI, 31, *c.* 75

What thou avoidest suffering thyself seek not to impose on others.
EPICTETUS: *Encheiridion, c.* 100

Whatsoever ye do not wish should be done unto you, do not do to others.
ACTS XV, 29 (This passage does not appear in the accepted canon of the New Testament, but it is to be found in a MS. supposed to date from *c.* 125, and is quoted in one of the Dooms of King Alfred of England, *c.* 875)

All things whatsoever that thou wouldst not wish to be done to thee, do thou also not to another.
The Didache, or Teaching of the Twelve Apostles, c. 135

Whatever the Christians do not wish to be done to them they do not do to another.
ST. ARISTIDES: *Apology for the Christian Faith,* XV, *c.* 160

As ye will that men do to you, and do ye to them in like manner.
JOHN WYCLIF: Tr. of LUKE VI, 31, 1389

Do as ye wald be done to.
DAVID FERGUSSON: *Scottish Proverbs,* 1641

Whatsoever you require that others should do to you, that do ye to them.
THOMAS HOBBES: *Leviathan,* I, 1651

My duty towards my neighbor is to love him as myself, and to do all men as I would they should do unto me.
THE BOOK OF COMMON PRAYER (*Catechism*), 1662

The evil which you do not wish done to you, you ought to refrain from doing to another, so far as may be done without injury to some third person.
HENRY MORE: *Encheiridion ethicum*, IV, 1667

Desire nothing for yourself which you do not desire for others.
BARUCH SPINOZA: *Ethica*, IV, 1677

If the prisoner should ask the judge whether he would be content to be hanged, were he in his case, he would answer no. Then, says the prisoner, do as you would be done to.
JOHN SELDEN: *Table-Talk*, 1689

Should that most unshaken rule of morality, and foundation of all social virtue, "that one should do as he would be done unto," be proposed to one who never heard of it before, but yet is of capacity to understand its meaning, might he not without any absurdity ask a reason why?
JOHN LOCKE: *Essay Concerning Human Understanding*, I, 1690

Be you to others kind and true,
As you'd have others be to you;
And neither do nor say to men
Whate'er you would not take again.
ISAAC WATTS: *Divine Songs for Children*, pref., 1715

If a man any ways doubt whether what he is going to do to another man be agreeable to the law of nature, then let him suppose himself to be in that other man's room.
JOHN WISE: *A Vindication of the Government of New England Churches*, II, 1717

Do as you would be done by, is the surest method of pleasing.
LORD CHESTERFIELD: *Letter to his son*, Oct. 16, 1747

To do as you would be done by, is the plain, sure, and undisputed rule of morality and justice.
LORD CHESTERFIELD: *Letter to his son*, Sept. 27, 1748

No man doth think others will be better to him that he is to them.
BENJAMIN WHICHCOTE: *Moral and Religious Aphorisms*, 1753

I must always act in such a way that I can at the same time will that the maxim by which I act should become a universal law.
IMMANUEL KANT: *Grundlegung zur Metaphysik der Sitten*, I, 1785

We ought to act that part towards another which we would judge to be right in him to act toward us, if we were in his circumstances and he in ours.
THOMAS REID: *Essays on the Active Powers*, V, 1788

The duty of man . . . is plain and simple, and consists of but two points: his duty to God, which every man must feel, and with respect to his neighbor, to do as he would be done by.
THOMAS PAINE: *The Rights of Man*, I, 1791

He has observ'd the golden rule,
Till he's become the golden fool.
WILLIAM BLAKE: *Epigram*, c. 1808

Do other men, for they would do you.
CHARLES DICKENS: *Martin Chuzzlewit*, XI, 1844

To do as one would be done by, and to love one's neighbor as one's self, constitute the ideal perfection of utilitarian morality.
J. S. MILL: *Utilitarianism*, II, 1863

Our conscience teaches us it is right, our reason teaches us it is useful, that men should live according to the Golden Rule.
W. WINWOOD READE: *The Martyrdom of Man*, III, 1872

Reason shows me that if my happiness is desirable and a good, the equal happiness of any other person must be equally desirable.
HENRY SIDGWICK: *The Methods of Ethics*, III, 1874

Do unto others as you would have others do unto you in like case.
P. A. KROPOTKIN: *La morale anarchiste*, 1891

Do not do unto others as you would that they should do unto you. Their tastes may not be the same.
GEORGE BERNARD SHAW: *Maxims for Revolutionists*, 1903

Do others or they will do you.
AMERICAN PROVERB (Cf. DICKENS, *ante*, 1844)

Do unto others as they would do unto you if they had the chance.
Author unidentified

Do as you would be done by.
ENGLISH PROVERB, obviously based on MATTHEW VII, 12, *c.* 75 (It appears in various other forms, e.g., Do unto others as you would have others do unto you)

When we and ours have it in our power to do for you and yours what you and yours have done for us and ours, then we and ours will do for you and yours what you and yours have done for us and ours.
OLD ENGLISH TOAST

[*See also* Politics.

Goldfish

[*See* Privacy.

Goldsmith, Oliver (1730–74)

It is amazing how little Goldsmith knows. He seldom comes where he is not more ignorant than any one else.
SAMUEL JOHNSON: *Boswell's Life,* April 30, 1773

Here lies Nolly Goldsmith, for shortness called Noll,
Who wrote like an angel, and talk'd like poor Poll.
DAVID GARRICK: Impromptu epitaph on Goldsmith, 1774

Let not his faults be remembered; he was a very great man.
SAMUEL JOHNSON: *Letter to Bennet Langton,* July 5, 1774

Poet, naturalist, and historian,
Who left scarcely any style of writing untouched,
And touched none that he did not adorn.
(Poetae, physici, historici,
Qui nullum fere scribendi genus
Non tetigit,
Nullum quod tetigit non ornavit.)
SAMUEL JOHNSON: Epitaph on Goldsmith, 1774

Goldsmith was a man who, whatever he wrote, did it better than any other man could do.
SAMUEL JOHNSON: *Boswell's Life,* 1778

No man was more foolish when he had not a pen in his hand, or more wise when he had.
SAMUEL JOHNSON: *Boswell's Life,* 1780

Goldsmith did everything happily.
S. T. COLERIDGE: *Table-Talk,* Jan. 4, 1823

An inspired idiot.
WILLIAM HAZLITT: *The Ruling Passion,* 1829 (The Atlas, Jan. 18)

Goldsmith could not be termed a thinker; but everything he touched he brightened, as, after a month of dry weather, the shower brightens the dusty shrubbery of a suburban villa.
ALEXANDER SMITH: *Dreamthorp,* II, 1863

Gold Standard

We renew our allegiance to the principle of the gold standard and declare our confidence in the wisdom of the legislation of the Fifty-sixth Congress, by which the parity of all our money and the stability of our currency upon a gold basis has been secured.
Republican National Platform, 1900

We believe it to be the duty of the Republican party to uphold the gold standard and the integrity and value of our national currency.
Republican National Platform, 1904

The Republican party established and will continue to uphold the gold standard and will oppose any measure which will undermine the government's credit or impair the integrity of our national currency. Relief by currency inflation is unsound in principle and dishonest in results.
Republican National Platform, 1932

[*See also* Bimetallism, Money, Silver (Free).

Golf

It is unjust to claim the privileges of age, and retain the playthings of childhood.
SAMUEL JOHNSON: *The Rambler,* Sept. 8, 1750

[*See also* Child Labor.

Gone

He has gone, he has made off, he has escaped, he has broken away. (Abiit, excessit, evasit, erupit.)
CICERO: *Oration in Catilinam, c.* 50 B.C.

Gone is gone. (Hin ist hin.)
GERMAN PROVERB, traced by Büchmann to MARTIN LUTHER, 1524

Like the dew on the mountain,
Like the foam on the river,
Like the bubble on the fountain,
Thou art gone, and forever!
WALTER SCOTT: *The Lady of the Lake,* III, 1810

Off agin, on agin,
Gone agin, Finnigin.
S. W. GILLILAN: *Finnigin to Flannigan,* 1908

[*See also* Here.

Good

The good man is his own friend.
SOPHOCLES: *Oedipus Coloneus, c.* 450 B.C.

Every art and every inquiry, as well as every practical pursuit, seems to aim at some good, whereby it has been well said that the good is that at which all things aim.
ARISTOTLE: *The Nicomachean Ethics,* I, *c.* 340 B.C.

Good has two meanings: it means both that which is good absolutely and that which is good for somebody.
ARISTOTLE: *The Nicomachean Ethics,* VII

In goodness there are all kinds of wisdom.
EURIPIDES: *Alcestis,* 438 B.C.

The proof of a well-trained mind is that it rejoices in which is good and grieves at the opposite.
CICERO: *De amicitia,* XIII, *c.* 50 B.C.

To whose good? (Cui bono?)
CICERO: *Pro Sistio, c.* 50 B.C.

The good hate sin from an innate love of virtue.
HORACE: *Epistles,* I, *c.* 5 B.C.

Prove all things; hold fast that which is good.
I THESSALONIANS V, 21, *c.* 51

All things work together for good to them that love God. ROMANS VIII, 28, *c.* 55

It is not goodness to be better than the worst.
SENECA: *Epistulæ ad Lucilium*, c. 63

Do good to them that hate you.
MATTHEW V, 44, c. 75

There was a man named Joseph, a counseller; and he was a good man, and a just.
LUKE XXIII, 50, c. 75

He was a good man, and full of the Holy Ghost and of faith.
ACTS II, 24, c. 75

A good man doubles the length of his existence. To have lived so as to look back with pleasure on life is to have lived twice.
MARTIAL: *Epigrams*, X, c. 95

If you would be good, first believe that you are bad.
EPICTETUS: *Encheiridion*, c. 110

Let us put an end, once for all, to this discussion of what a good man should be — and be one.
MARCUS AURELIUS: *Meditations*, X, c. 170

That which is good, provided it be full and true, loves not darkness; it rejoices in being seen and exults over pointing fingers.
TERTULLIAN: *Women's Dress*, c. 220

Good wine needs no bush.
ENGLISH PROVERB, familiar since the XV century

It was too good to be true.
JOHN LYLY: *Mother Bombie*, 1594

Naught so vile that on the earth doth live
But to the earth some special good doth give.
SHAKESPEARE: *Romeo and Juliet*, II, c. 1596

Can one desire too much of a good thing?
SHAKESPEARE: *As You Like It*, IV, c. 1600

That which is not good is not delicious.
JOHN MILTON: *Comus*, 1637

Goodness and greatness go not always together.
JOHN CLARKE: *Parœmiologia Anglo-Latina*, 1639

Good find good.
GEORGE HERBERT: *Outlandish Proverbs*, 1640

Whatsoever is the object of any man's appetite or desire, that is it which he for his part calleth good.
THOMAS HOBBES: *Leviathan*, I, 1651

No man so good, but another may be as good as he.
THOMAS FULLER: *Worthies of England*, 1662 (Quoted as "a country proverb")

No man deserves to be praised for his goodness unless he has strength of character to be wicked. All other goodness is generally nothing but indolence or impotence of will.
LA ROCHEFOUCAULD: *Maxims*, 1665

Abashed the Devil stood,
And felt how awful goodness is, and saw
Virtue in her shape how lovely.
JOHN MILTON: *Paradise Lost*, IV, 1667

Good, the more
Communicated, more abundant grows.
JOHN MILTON: *Paradise Lost*, V

A good is that which is pleasant, agreeable and well-suited to any perceptive life or grade of such life, and which involves the preservation of the recipient.
HENRY MORE: *Encheiridion ethicum*, IV, 1667

That is my good that does me good.
JOHN RAY: *English Proverbs*, 1670

The osseous and solid part of goodness, which gives stability and rectitude to all the rest.
THOMAS BROWNE: *Christian Morals*, III, c. 1680

All their luxury was doing good.
SAMUEL GARTH: *Cleremont*, 1715

Bode good and get it.
JAMES KELLY: *Complete Collection of Scottish Proverbs*, 1721 (*Bode*= expect)

Good for the liver may be bad for the spleen.
THOMAS FULLER: *Gnomologia*, 1732

Good men must die, but death cannot kill them quite.
IBID.

He cannot be good that knows not why he is good.
IBID.

There is no such thing as good small beer, good brown bread, or a good old woman.
JONATHAN SWIFT: *Polite Conversation*, 1738

Some things must be good in themselves, else there could be no measure whereby to lay out good and evil.
BENJAMIN WHICHCOTE: *Moral and Religious Aphorisms*, 1753

While I can crawl upon this planet I think myself obliged to do what good I can, in my narrow domestic spheres, to my fellow creatures, and to wish them all the good I cannot do.
LORD CHESTERFIELD: *Letter to the Bishop of Waterford*, Jan. 22, 1760

Doing good,
Disinterested good, is not our trade.
WILLIAM COWPER: *The Task*, I, 1785

A glass is good, and a lass is good,
And a pipe to smoke in cold weather;
The world is good, and the people are good,
And we're all good fellows together.
JOHN O'KEEFE: *Sprigs of Laurel*, II, 1785

The ground that a good man treads is hallowed.
J. W. GOETHE: *Torquato Tasso*, I, 1790

The good die young.

ENGLISH PROVERB, not recorded before the XIX century and perhaps derived from WORDSWORTH, *post*, 1814

The good is the enemy of the best.

ENGLISH PROVERB, not recorded before the XIX century

To be good only is to be
A god or else a Pharisee.

WILLIAM BLAKE: *The Everlasting Gospel*, *c.* 1810

The good die first.

WILLIAM WORDSWORTH: *The Excursion*, I, 1814

I know nothing more moral, more sublime, more worthy of your preservation than David's description of the good man in the Fifteenth Psalm.

THOMAS JEFFERSON: *Letter to Isaac Englebrecht*, 1824

The smallest actual good is better than the most magnificent promises of impossibilities. The wise man of the Stoics would, no doubt, be a grander object than a steam-engine. But there are steam-engines. And the wise man of the Stoics is yet to be born.

T. B. MACAULAY: *Lord Bacon*, 1837

Howe'er it be, it seems to me,
'Tis only noble to be good,
Kind hearts are more than coronets,
And simple faith than Norman blood.

ALFRED TENNYSON: *Lady Clara Vere de Vere*, 1842

Be good, sweet maid, and let who will be clever.

CHARLES KINGSLEY: *A Farewell*, 1858

Good in all,
In the satisfaction and aplomb of animals,
In the annual return of the reasons,
In the hilarity of youth,
In the strength and flush of manhood.

WALT WHITMAN: *Song At Sunset*, 1860

I live for those who love me,
For those who know me true;
For the Heaven that smiles above me,
And awaits my spirit too;
For the cause that lacks assistance,
For the wrong that needs resistance,
For the future in the distance,
And the good that I can do.

G. LINNAEUS BANKS: *What I Live For*, *c.* 1870

Reason teaches us that what is good is good for something, and that what is good for nothing is not good at all.

F. H. BRADLEY: *Ethical Studies*, II, 1876

What is good? — Whatever augments the feeling of power, the will to power, power itself, in man.

F. W. NIETZSCHE: *The Antichrist*, II, 1888

Be good, and you will be lonesome.

S. L. CLEMENS (MARK TWAIN): *Following the Equator*, inscription on frontispiece, 1897

If I am asked, "What is good?" my answer is that good is good, and that is the end of the matter. Or if I am asked, "How is good to be defined?" my answer is that it cannot be defined, and that is all I have to say about it.

G. E. MOORE: *Principia Ethica*, I, 1903

If you can't be good, be sanitary.

Saying of the American soldiers in France, 1917–20

Be good. And if you can't be good, be careful.

AMERICAN PROVERB

I expect to pass through this world but once; any good thing, therefore, that I can do, or any kindness that I can show to my fellow-creatures, let me do it now; let me not defer or neglect it, for I shall not pass this way again.

Author unidentified (It has been ascribed to many authors, but its source remains undetermined)

The good cry easily. GREEK PROVERB

Be good yourself and the world will be good.

HINDU PROVERB

Good is when I steal other people's wives and cattle; bad is when they steal mine.

HOTTENTOT PROVERB

For the Lord Jesus Christ's sake,
Do all the good you can,
To all the people you can,
In all the ways you can,
As long as ever you can.

Inscription on a tombstone at Shrewsbury, England

He is so good that he is good for nothing.

ITALIAN PROVERB

A common good. (Commune bonum.)

LATIN PHRASE

The greatest good. (Summum bonum.)

IBID.

The gude dog doesna aye get the best bane.

SCOTTISH PROVERB

The gude man's no aye the best man. IBID.

Twa gudes seldom meet — what's gude for the plant is ill for the peat. IBID.

Every man is good, but not for everything.

SPANISH PROVERB

[*See also* Beautiful, Careful, Fox, Good and Bad, Good and Evil, Pleasure, Three, Truth, Virtue.

Good and Bad

The bad will be bad for evermore, and the good will be good.

EURIPIDES: *Hecuba*, *c.* 426 B.C.

It is not every bad man that will ever be good, but there will be no good man who was not at some time bad.
ST. AUGUSTINE: *The City of God,* XV, 427

Goodness is simple; badness is manifold.
ARISTOTLE: *The Nicomachean Ethics,* II, *c.* 340 B.C.

None are known to be good until they have opportunity to be bad.
BENJAMIN WHICHCOTE: *Moral and Religious Aphorisms,* 1753

When bad men combine, the good must associate; else they will fall, one by one, an unpitied sacrifice in a contemptible struggle.
EDMUND BURKE: *Thoughts on the Cause of the Present Discontents,* 1770

He that is good will infallibly become better, and he that is bad will as certainly become worse; for vice, virtue, and time are three things that never stand still.
C. C. COLTON: *Lacon,* 1820

Good and bad are but names very readily transferable to that or this.
R. W. EMERSON: *Self-Reliance,* 1841

Thy mind the mosque and cool kiosk,
Spare fast and orisons;
Mine me allows the drinking-house,
And sweet chase of the nuns.
R. W. EMERSON: *Ghazelle,* 1851

There is no odor so bad as that which arises from goodness tainted. It is human, it is divine, carrion.
H. D. THOREAU: *Walden,* 1854

Nothing is good or bad, but by comparison.
H. G. BOHN: *Handbook of Proverbs,* 1855

Nothing so bad as not to be good for something.
IBID.

Nothing out of its place is good and nothing in its place is bad.
WALT WHITMAN: *Leaves of Grass,* pref., 1855

Most of the things we do are not to be judged as either good or bad in respect of either ends or means.
HERBERT SPENCER: *The Data of Ethics,* I, 1879

Those doings of men which, morally considered, are indifferent we class as good or bad according to their success or failure. A good jump is a jump which, remoter ends ignored, well achieves the immediate purpose of a jump.
HERBERT SPENCER: *The Data of Ethics,* III

If you are a good man you want a bad one to convert; if you are a bad man you want a bad one to go out on the spree with.
GEORGE MOORE: *Confessions of a Young Man,* XII, 1888

A man is as good as he has to be, and a woman as bad as she dares.
ELBERT HUBBARD: *Roycroft's Dictionary and Book of Epigrams,* 1923

There is so much good in the worst of us,
And so much bad in the best of us,
That it ill behooves any of us
To find fault with the rest of us.
Author unidentified

The usual choice is not between the good and the bad but between the bad and the worse.
FRENCH PROVERB

He hurts the good who spares the bad.
LATIN PROVERB

[*See also* Affliction, Bad, Conscience, Good, Good and Evil, Housewife, Judge, Law, Mercy, Opinion, Organization, Pardon, Punishment, Sleep, Thinking, Tragedy.

Good and Evil

The Lord God commanded the man, saying, Of every tree of the garden thou mayest freely eat: but of the tree of the knowledge of good and evil, thou shalt not eat of it: for in the day that thou eatest thereof thou shalt surely die.
GENESIS II, 16–17, *c.* 700 B.C.

Your eyes shall be opened, and ye shall be as gods, knowing good and evil.
GENESIS III, 5

Woe unto them that call evil good, and good evil.
ISAIAH V, 20, *c.* 700 B.C.

Out of the mouth of the Most High proceedeth not evil and good?
LAMENTATIONS III, 38, *c.* 585 B.C.

Good and evil do not befall men without reason. Heaven sends them happiness or misery according to their conduct.
CONFUCIUS: *The Book of History,* IV, *c.* 500 B.C.

It will never be possible to get rid of evil altogether, for there must always be something opposite to good.
PLATO: *Theaeteus, c.* 360 B.C.

Be not overcome of evil, but overcome evil with good.
ROMANS XII, 21, *c.* 55

Men are less sensible of good than of evil.
LIVY: *History of Rome,* XXX, *c.* 10

The power of choosing good and evil is within the reach of all.
ORIGEN: *De principiis,* II, *c.* 254

He that is good is free, though he be a slave; he that is evil is a slave, though he be a king.
ST. AUGUSTINE: *The City of God,* IV, 427

In human affairs there is no evil that has not some good mixed with it.
FRANCESCO GUICCIARDINI: *Storia d'Italia,* 1564

Whoever imitates evil always goes beyond the example; whoever imitates good always falls short. IBID.

Suffer the ill, and look for the good.
JAMES SANDFORD: *Hours of Recreation*, 1572

The evil that men do lives after them;
The good is oft interred with their bones.
SHAKESPEARE: *Julius Cæsar*, III, 1599

There is some soul of goodness in things evil,
Would men observingly distil it out.
SHAKESPEARE: *Henry V*, IV, *c.* 1599

Bear with evil and expect good.
GEORGE HERBERT: *Outlandish Proverbs*, 1640

Better good afar off than evil at hand. IBID.

He that hopes not for good fears not evil. IBID.

Good and evil we know in the field of this world grow up together almost inseparably; and the knowledge of good is so involved and interwoven with the knowledge of evil, and in so many cunning resemblances hardly to be discerned, that those confused seeds which were imposed upon Psyche as an incessant labor to cull out, and sort asunder, were not more intermixed.
JOHN MILTON: *Areopagitica*, 1644

Evil no nature hath; the loss of good
Is that which gives to sin a livelihood.
ROBERT HERRICK: *Noble Numbers*, 1647

These words of good, evil, and contemptible are ever used with relation to the person that useth them: there being nothing simply and absolutely so; nor any common rule of good and evil, to be taken from the nature of the objects themselves.
THOMAS HOBBES: *Leviathan*, I, 1651

There are heroes in evil as well as in good.
LA ROCHEFOUCAULD: *Maxims*, 1665

We often do good in order that we may do evil with impunity. IBID.

All good to me is lost;
Evil, be thou my good.
JOHN MILTON: *Paradise Lost*, IV, 1667

A good is that which is pleasant, agreeable and well-suited to any perceptive life or grade of such life, and which involves the preservation of the recipient. On the other hand, what is unpleasant, disagreeable, and unsuited to any perceptive life or grade of such life, is an evil.
HENRY MORE: *Encheiridion ethicum*, IV, 1667

What shall we say is good? Celibacy? I say no; for the world would come to an end. Marriage? No, continence is better. Not to kill? No; for disorders would be horrible, and the wicked would kill the good. To kill? No; for that destroys nature. We have neither the true nor the good but in part, and mixed with the false and the evil.
BLAISE PASCAL: *Pensées*, VIII, 1670

No man better knows what good is than he who hath endured evil.
JOHN RAY: *English Proverbs*, 1670

Things are called good or evil only in reference to pleasure or pain. That we call good which is apt to cause or increase pleasure, or diminish pain, in us; or else to procure or preserve us the possession of any other good, or absence of any evil.
JOHN LOCKE: *Essay Concerning the Human Understanding*, II, 1690

Two urns by Jove's high throne have ever stood,
The source of evil, one, and one of good.
ALEXANDER POPE: Tr. of HOMER: *Iliad*, XXIV (*c.* 800 B.C.), 1720

Nothing is morally good or evil, just or unjust, by mere will without nature, because everything is what it is by nature, and not by will.
RALPH CUDWORTH: *Concerning Eternal and Immutable Morality*, II, 1731

Good and evil are chiefly in the imagination.
THOMAS FULLER: *Gnomologia*, 1732

There is not the thickness of a sixpence between good and evil. IBID.

The chance to do evil is found a hundred times a day, and that of doing good once a year.
VOLTAIRE: *Zadig*, 1748

Man, as man, is averse to what is evil and wicked, for evil is unnatural and good is connatural to man.
BENJAMIN WHICHCOTE: *Moral and Religious Aphorisms*, 1753

"There is," said Candide, "a great amount of evil in the world." "What does it matter," said the dervish, "whether it is good or evil? When His Highness sends a ship to Egypt does he worry about the comfort or discomfort of the rats aboard?"
VOLTAIRE: *Candide*, XXX, 1759

The little merit man can plead
In doing well dependeth still
Upon his power of doing ill.
CHARLES CHURCHILL: *The Ghost*, IV, 1763

As it is said of the greatest liar that he tells more truth than falsehood, so it may be said of the worst man that he does more good than evil.
SAMUEL JOHNSON: *Boswell's Life*, April 3, 1778

We ought to prefer a greater good, though more distant, to a less; and a less evil to a greater.
THOMAS REID: *Essays on the Active Powers*, V, 1788

Pleasure is in itself a good; nay, even setting aside immunity from pain, the only good. Pain is in itself an evil, and indeed, without exception the only evil; or else the words good and evil have no meaning.
JEREMY BENTHAM: *The Principles of Morals and Legislation,* X, 1789

The depravity of hating what is good for its own sake, and choosing evil because it is evil, for the mere love of it, I cannot ascribe to any human creature.
J. G. FICHTE: *Die Bestimmung des Menschen,* XVIII, 1800

Good and bad men are each less so than they seem.
S. T. COLERIDGE: *Table-Talk,* April 19, 1830

What we all love is good touched up with evil —
Religion's self must have a spice of devil.
A. H. CLOUGH: *Dipsychus,* 1850

Oh, yet we trust that somehow good
Will be the final goal of ill,
To pangs of nature, sins of will
Defects of doubt and taints of blood.
ALFRED TENNYSON: *In Memoriam,* LIV, 1850

He who does no good does evil enough.
R. C. TRENCH (ARCHBISHOP OF DUBLIN): *Lessons in Proverbs,* 1853

The first lesson of history is the good of evil.
R. W. EMERSON: *The Conduct of Life,* I, 1860

Evil saith to good: My brother.
A. C. SWINBURNE: *Hymn to Proserpine,* 1866

The Author of the world invented not only the good but also the evil in the world; He invented cruelty; He invented sin. If He invented sin how can He be otherwise than sinful? And if He invented cruelty how can He be otherwise than cruel?
W. WINWOOD READE: *The Martyrdom of Man,* III, 1872

There is only one way to put an end to evil, and that is to do good for evil.
LYOF N. TOLSTOY: *What I Believe,* 1884

One good deed is enough to wipe out a hundred evil ones. CHINESE PROVERB

[*See also* Evil, Good, Good and Bad, Hero, Life, Love, Napoleon I, Necessity, Punishment, Tree, Virtue and Vice.

Goodbye

To say, Farewell, be hanged! — that's twice goodbye.
JOHN DUNTON: *Athenian Sport,* 1707

Goodbye to flattery's fawning face;
To grandeur with his wise grimace;
To upstart wealth's averted eye;
To supple office, low and high;
To crowded halls, to court and street;
To frozen hearts and hasting feet;
To those who go, and those who come;
Goodbye, proud world! I'm going home.
R. W. EMERSON: *Goodbye,* 1839

Every time a nigger says goodbye he ain't gone.
AMERICAN NEGRO PROVERB

Until we meet again. (Auf Wiedersehen.)
GERMAN PHRASE (The French "Au revoir" is identical in meaning)

[*See also* Farewell, Parting.

Good, Common

The common good of all is the supreme law.
RICHARD CUMBERLAND: *De legibus naturæ,* I, 1672

The affection of a creature toward the good of the species or common nature is as proper and natural to him as it is to any organ, part or member of an animal body, or mere vegetable, to work in its known course, and regular way of growth.
ANTHONY A. COOPER (EARL OF SHAFTESBURY): *An Inquiry Concerning Virtue or Merit,* II, 1699

For the public good. (Pro bono publico.)
LATIN PHRASE

[*See also* Law.

Good-nature

Nothing is rarer than true good nature; they who are reputed to have it are generally only pliant or weak.
LA ROCHEFOUCAULD: *Maxims,* 1665

Good-nature is stronger than tomahawks.
R. W. EMERSON: *Clubs,* 1877

Good-night

Good-night, ladies.
SHAKESPEARE: *Hamlet,* IV, *c.* 1601

Many good-nights is loth away.
JAMES KELLY: *Complete Collection of Scottish Proverbs,* 1721

Good-will

It is very difficult to gain good-will; but once you have it, it is easy to keep it.
BALTASAR GRACIÁN: *The Art of Worldly Wisdom,* CXII, 1647

Gude-will should be taken in part payment.
SCOTTISH PROVERB

Goose

The goose gabbles amid the melodious swans.
VIRGIL: *Eclogues,* IX, 37 B.C.

The goose that laid the golden egg.
ENGLISH PHRASE, derived from ÆSOP: *Fables, c.* 600 B.C., and in common use since the XV century

Goose liver for the lickerous Roman.
JOSEPH HALL (BISHOP OF NORWICH): *Virgidemarium*, III, 1597

Thou cream-faced loon,
Where got'st thou that goose look?
SHAKESPEARE: *Macbeth*, V, *c.* 1605

While man exclaims, "See all things for my use!"
"See man for mine!" replies a pampered goose.
ALEXANDER POPE: *An Essay on Man*, III, 1733

I should not think of keeping a goose in a cage, that I might hang him up in the parlor for the sake of his melody, but a goose upon a common, or in a farmyard, is no bad performer.
WILLIAM COWPER: *Letter to John Newton*, Sept. 18, 1784

The wild goose is more cosmopolite than we; he breaks his fast in Canada, takes a luncheon in the Susquehanna, and plumes himself for the night in a Louisiana bayou.
H. D. THOREAU: *Journal*, March 21, 1840

Feather by feather the goose is plucked.
ITALIAN PROVERB

[*See also* Anthropomorphism, Lean, Market, Sauce.

Gospel

The gospel of Jesus Christ, the Son of God.
MARK I, 1, *c.* 70

Go ye unto all the world, and preach the gospel to every creature. MARK XVI, 15

His word was gospel.
NICHOLAS DE GUILDFORD: *The Owl and the Nightingale*, *c.* 1250

The gospel belongs to the poor and sorrowful, and not to princes and courtiers who live in continual joy and delight, in security, void of all tribulation.
MARTIN LUTHER: *Table-Talk*, CCCCVI, 1569

It is a strange and sickly world into which the gospels lead us — a world apparently out of a Russian novel.
F. W. NIETZSCHE: *The Antichrist*, XXXI, 1888

[*See also* Bible, Heresy.

Gossip

Tell it not in Gath, publish it not in the streets of Askelon. II SAMUEL I, 20, *c.* 500 B.C.

Hast thou heard a word against thy neighbor? Let it die within thee, trusting that it will not burst thee.
ECCLESIASTICUS XIX, 10, *c.* 180 B.C.

The wise man indulges himself not in gossip with women, not even his own wife.
THE TALMUD (*Pirke Aboth*), *c.* 200

To tell tales out of school: that is her great lust.
JOHN HEYWOOD: *Proverbs*, 1546

They haif said. Quhat say they? Lat thame say.
Inscription over the entrance of Marischal College, University of Aberdeen, Scotland, *c.* 1593

'Tis merry when gossips meet.
SAMUEL ROWLANDS: Title of a play, 1602

Foul whisperings are abroad.
SHAKESPEARE: *Macbeth*, V, *c.* 1605

Gossips are frogs: they drink and talk.
GEORGE HERBERT: *Outlandish Proverbs*, 1640

If all men knew what others say of them, there would not be four friends in the world.
BLAISE PASCAL: *Pensées*, VIII, 1670

I have told all the chambermaids, waiting-women, tire-women and old women of my acquaintance, and whispered it as a secret to 'em, so that you need not doubt 'twill spread.
WILLIAM WYCHERLEY: *The Country Wife*, I, *c.* 1673

And all who told it added something new,
And all who heard it made enlargements too;
In ev'ry ear it spread, on ev'ry tongue it grew.
ALEXANDER POPE: *The Temple of Fame*, 1714

Gossiping and lying go together.
THOMAS FULLER: *Gnomologia*, 1732

"They say so" is half a lie. IBID.

There is only one thing in the world worse than being talked about, and that is not being talked about.
OSCAR WILDE: *The Picture of Dorian Gray*, 1891

It is perfectly monstrous the way people go about nowadays saying things against one, behind one's back, that are absolutely and entirely true.
OSCAR WILDE: *A Woman of No Importance*, II, 1893

If what we see is doubtful, how can we believe what is spoken behind the back?
CHINESE PROVERB

Little people like to talk about what the great are doing. GERMAN PROVERB

Whoever gossips to you will gossip of you.
SPANISH PROVERB

[*See also* Scandal, Talebearer.

Gotham

Three wise men of Gotham
Went to sea in a bowl,
And if the bowl had been stronger
My song would be longer.
OLD ENGLISH RHYME (These legendary fools have been familiar in English folk-lore since the XIV century)

Gothic

[*See* Architecture (Gothic).

Gourmet

The heads of parrots, tongues of nightingales,
The brains of peacocks, and of ostriches,
Shall be our food; and, could we get the phoenix,
Though nature lost her kind, she were our dish.

BEN JONSON: *Volpone*, III, 1605

My footboy shall eat pheasants, calver'd salmons,
Knots, godwits, lampreys. I myself will have
The beards of barbels serv'd instead of salads,
Oil'd mushrooms, and the swelling unctuous paps
Of a fat pregnant sow, newly cut off.

BEN JONSON: *The Alchemist*, II, 1612

His dinner is his other work, for he sweats at it as much as at labor; he is a terrible fastener on a piece of beef, and you may have hope to stave the guard off sooner.

JOHN EARLE (BISHOP OF SALISBURY): *Microcosmographie*, 1628

Nice eaters seldom meet with a good dinner.

THOMAS FULLER: *Gnomologia*, 1732

They were at once dainty and voracious, understood the right and the wrong of every dish, and alike emptied the one and the other.

FRANCES BURNEY: *Evelina*, I, 1778

I have been a great observer and I can truly say that I have never known a man "fond of good eating and drinking," as it is called; that I have never known such a man (and hundreds I have known) who was not worthy of respect.

WILLIAM COBBETT: *Advice to Young Men*, I, 1829

Gourmets dig their graves with their teeth.

FRENCH PROVERB

[*See also* Eating, Gluttony.

Gout

There is no pain like the gout.

NICHOLAS BRETON: *Crossing of Proverbs*, 1616

Gout is the distemper of a gentleman; whereas the rheumatism is the distemper of a hackney-coachman or chairman, who is obliged to be out in all weathers and at all hours.

LORD CHESTERFIELD: *Letter to his son*, Nov. 28, 1765

This disease seldom attacks eunuchs, and when it does, they seem to be those who happen to be of a robust habit, to lead an indolent life, and to live very full.

WILLIAM CULLEN: *First Lines of the Practice of Physic*, I, 1774

Pangs arthritic that infest the toe
Of libertine excess.

WILLIAM COWPER: *The Task*, 1783

What a very singular disease gout is! It seems as if the stomach fell down into the feet. The smallest deviation from right diet is immediately punished by limping and lameness, and the innocent ankle and blameless instep are tortured for the vices of the nobler organs.

SYDNEY SMITH: *Letter to the Countess of Carlisle*, 1840

With respect to the gout,
The physician is but a lout.

H. G. BOHN: *Handbook of Proverbs*, 1855

[*See also* Age (Old), Ages, Wine.

Government

In a country well governed poverty is something to be ashamed of. In a country badly governed wealth is something to be ashamed of.

CONFUCIUS: *Analects*, VIII, *c.* 500 B.C.

To govern means to rectify.

CONFUCIUS: *Analects*, XII

If anyone at all is to have the privilege of lying, the rulers of the state should be such persons.

PLATO: *The Republic*, V, *c.* 370 B.C.

Until philosophers take to government, or those who now govern become philosophers, so that government and philosophy unite, there will be no end to the miseries of states.

IBID.

When good government prevails men of little worth submit to men of great worth. When bad government prevails men of little power submit to men of great power.

MENCIUS: *Discourses*, IV, *c.* 300 B.C.

Monarchy degenerates into tyranny, aristocracy into oligarchy, and democracy into savage violence and anarchy.

POLYBIUS: *Histories*, V, *c.* 125 B.C.

That form of government is the best which includes monarchy, aristocracy, and democracy.

POLYBIUS: *Histories*, VI

A good government produces citizens distinguished for courage, love of justice, and every other good quality; a bad government makes them cowardly, rapacious, and the slaves of every foul desire.

DIONYSIUS OF HALICARNASSUS: *Antiquities of Rome*, II, *c.* 20 B.C.

In a change of government, the poor seldom change anything except the name of their master.

PHAEDRUS: *Fabulae Aesopiae*, I, *c.* 40

Let no wise man estrange himself from the government of the state; for it is both wicked to withdraw from being useful to the needy, and cowardly to give way to the worthless.

EPICTETUS: *Encheiridion*, *c.* 110

Whatsoever moveth is stronger than that which is moved, and whatsoever governeth is stronger than that which is governed.

ST. ARISTIDES: *Apology for the Christian Faith*, *c.* 160

All well-governed states and wise princes have taken care not to reduce the nobility to despair, nor the people to discontent.
NICCOLÒ MACHIAVELLI: *The Prince*, XIX, 1513

He who wishes to be a tryant, and does not slay Brutus, and he who wishes to establish a free state, and does not slay the sons of Brutus, maintains his work for only a short time.
NICCOLÒ MACHIAVELLI: *Discorsi*, III, 1531

The world is ruled by a certain few, even as a little boy of twelve years old rules, governs, and keeps a hundred great and strong oxen upon a pasture.
MARTIN LUTHER: *Table-Talk*, CLVII, 1569

Government is a sign of the divine grace, of the mercy of God, who has no pleasure in murdering, killing, and strangling. If God left all things to go which way they would, as among the Turks and other nations, without good government, we should quickly dispatch one another out of this world.
MARTIN LUTHER: *Table-Talk*, DCCLV

All public regimen, of what kind soever, seemeth evidently to have risen from the deliberate advice, consultation and composition between men.
RICHARD HOOKER: *The Laws of Ecclesiastical Polity*, I, 1594

I will govern according to the common weal, but not according to the common will.
JAMES I OF ENGLAND: *Reply to the House of Commons*, 1621

He that would govern others, first should be
The master of himself.
PHILIP MASSINGER: *The Bondman*, I, 1624

All kinds of government are not suited to all climates.
PIERRE CORNEILLE: *Cinna*, II, 1639

Democracy, I do not conceive that ever God did ordain as a fit government either for church or commonwealth. If the people be governors, who shall be governed? As for monarchy, and aristocracy, they are both of them clearly approved, and directed in Scripture, yet so as referreth the sovereignty to Himself, and setteth theocracy in both, as the best form of government in the commonwealth, as well as in the church.
JOHN COTTON: *The Bloody Tenant Washed and Made White in the Blood of the Lamb*, 1647

There are very few so foolish that they had not rather govern themselves than be governed by others.
THOMAS HOBBES: *Leviathan*, I, 1651

You do not know, my son, with how little wisdom the world is governed. (An nescis, mi fili, quantilla prudentia mundus regatur.)
Commonly ascribed to BISHOP AXEL OXENSTJERNA, Chancellor of Sweden (1583–1654), but Büchman says in *Geflügelte Worte* that it probably orignated with Pope Julius III, who said to a Portuguese monk: "If you knew with how little expenditure of sense the world is governed, you would wonder"

God has left nations unto the liberty of setting up such governments as best please themselves.
ALGERNON SIDNEY: Speech on the scaffold, Dec. 7, 1683

It is safest and most reasonable to accept the government under which we live as the best of all, and to submit to it quietly.
JEAN DE LA BRUYÈRE: *Caractères*, X, 1688

The great and chief end of men, . . . putting themselves under government, is the preservation of their property.
JOHN LOCKE: *Treatises on Government*, 1690

If men be good, government cannot be bad.
WILLIAM PENN: *Fruits of Solitude*, 1693

No system of government was ever so ill devised that, under proper men, it wouldn't work well enough. IBID.

We may observe in the republic of dogs that the whole state is ever in the profoundest peace after a full meal; and that civil broils arise among them when it happens for one great bone to be seized on by some leading dog; who either divides it among the few, and then it falls to an oligarchy; or keeps it to himself, and then it runs up to a tyranny.
JONATHAN SWIFT: *The Battle of the Books*, 1704

That particular form of government is necessary which best suits the temper and inclination of a people. Nothing can be God's ordinance but what He has particularly declared to be such; there is no particular form of civil government described in God's Word, neither does nature prompt it.
JOHN WISE: *A Vindication of the Government of New England Churches*, II, 1717

Salus populi, or the happiness of the people, is the end of its being, or main business to be attended and done. IBID.

For forms of government let fools contest:
Whate'er is best administr'd is best.
ALEXANDER POPE: *An Essay on Man*, III, 1733

Nothing appears more surprising to those who consider human affairs with a philosophical eye than the easiness with which the many are governed by the few.
DAVID HUME: *Essays Moral and Political*, I, 1741

When a government lasts a long while it deteriorates by insensible degrees.
C. L. DE MONTESQUIEU: *The Spirit of the Laws*, V, 1748

Republics end through luxury; monarchies through poverty.

C. L. DE MONTESQUIEU: *The Spirit of the Laws*, VII

The deterioration of every government begins with the decay of the principles on which it was founded.

C. L. DE MONTESQUIEU: *The Spirit of the Laws*, VIII

In rivers and bad governments the lightest things swim at top.

BENJAMIN FRANKLIN: *Poor Richard's Almanac*, 1754

What institution of government could tend so much to promote the happiness of mankind as the general prevalence of wisdom and virtue? All government is but an imperfect remedy for the deficiency of these.

ADAM SMITH: *The Theory of Moral Sentiments*, IV, 1759

Government originated in the attempt to find a form of association that defends and protects the person and property of each with the common force of all.

J.-J. ROUSSEAU: *Du contrat social*, I, 1761

In all sorts of government man is made to believe himself free, and to be in chains.

STANISLAUS LESZCZYNSKI (KING OF POLAND): *Œuvres du philosophe bienfaisant*, 1763

In every government, though terrors reign,
Though tyrant kings or tyrant laws restrain,
How small, of all that human hearts endure,
That part which laws or kings can cause or cure!

OLIVER GOLDSMITH: *The Traveler*, 1764

Tyranny, bad as it is, is better than anarchy; and the worst of governments is more tolerable than no government at all.

LORD CHIEF JUSTICE CAMDEN: *Judgment in the Case of the Seizure of Papers*, 1765

'Tis a political maxim that all government tends to despotism, and like the human frame brings at its birth the latent seed which finally shall destroy the constitution. This is a melancholy truth — but such is the lot of humanity.

JOSIAH QUINCY, JR.: *Letter to the Boston Gazette*, 1767

Government will not, perhaps, soon arrive at such purity and excellence but that some connivance at least will be indulged to the triumphant and successful cheat.

SAMUEL JOHNSON: *Thoughts Respecting Falkland's Islands*, 1771

I would not give half a guinea to live under one form of government rather than another.

SAMUEL JOHNSON: *Boswell's Life*, March 31, 1772

All government, indeed every human benefit and enjoyment, every virtue, and every prudent act, is founded on compromise and barter.

EDMUND BURKE: Speech on Conciliation with America, March 22, 1775

Those who bear equally the burdens of government should equally participate of its benefits.

THOMAS JEFFERSON: *Address to Lord Dunmore*, 1775

All government is ultimately and essentially absolute.

SAMUEL JOHNSON: *Taxation No Tyranny*, 1775

Governments [derive] their just powers from the consent of the governed.

THOMAS JEFFERSON: *The Declaration of Independence*, 1776

Society in every state is a blessing, but government, even in its best stage, is but a necessary evil; in its worst state an intolerable one.

THOMAS PAINE: *Common Sense*, 1776

All governments depend upon the good will of the people.

JOHN ADAMS: *Letter to E. C. E. Genêt*, May 15, 1780

The operations of government have little influence upon the private happiness of private men.

SAMUEL JOHNSON: *Letter to Robert Chambers*, April 19, 1783

When a people shall have become incapable of governing themselves, and fit for a master, it is of little consequence from what quarter he comes.

GEORGE WASHINGTON: *Letter to Lafayette*, April 28, 1788

In framing a government which is to be administered by men over men the great difficulty lies in this: You must first enable the government to control the governed, and in the next place, oblige it to control itself.

ALEXANDER HAMILTON: *The Federalist*, Feb. 8, 1788

Why has government been instituted at all? Because the passions of men will not conform to the dictates of reason and justice without constraint.

IBID.

The natural progress of things is for liberty to yield and government to gain ground.

THOMAS JEFFERSON: *Letter to E. Carrington*, 1788

Government is a contrivance of human wisdom to provide for human wants. Men have a right that these wants should be provided for by this wisdom.

EDMUND BURKE: *Reflections on the Revolution in France*, 1790

Every age and generation must be as free to act for itself, *in all cases*, as the ages and generations which preceded it. The vanity and pre-

sumption of governing beyond the grave is the most ridiculous and insolvent of all tyrannies.
THOMAS PAINE: *The Rights of Man*, I, 1791

Society performs for itself almost everything which is ascribed to government. IBID.

It is for the good of nations, and not for the emolument or aggrandizement of particular individuals, that government ought to be established, and that mankind are at the expense of supporting it. The defects of every government and constitution both as to principle and form, must, on a parity of reasoning, be as open to discussion as the defects of a law, and it is a duty which every man owes to society to point them out.
THOMAS PAINE: *The Rights of Man*, II

Government can have no more than two legitimate purposes — the suppression of injustice against individuals within the community, and the common defense against external invasion.
WILLIAM GODWIN: *An Enquiry Concerning Political Justice*, 1793

Government is, abstractedly taken, an evil, a usurpation upon the private judgment and individual conscience of mankind. IBID.

Society is produced by our wants, and government by our wickedness. IBID.

I have no ambition to govern men. It is a painful and thankless office.
THOMAS JEFFERSON: *Letter to John Adams*, 1796

As soon as there were some to be governed there were also some to govern.
JONATHAN BOUCHER: *A View of the Causes and Consequences of the American Revolution*, XII, 1797

Men still have to be governed by deception.
G. C. LICHTENBERG: *Reflections*, 1799

Away with the cant of "Measures, not men!" — the idle supposition that it is the harness and not the horses that draw the chariot along. If the comparison must be made, if the distinction must be taken, men are everything, measures comparatively nothing.
GEORGE CANNING: Speech in the House of Commons, 1801

Government has hardened into a tyrannical monopoly, and the human race in general becomes as absolutely property as beasts in the plow.
JOHN DICKINSON: *Letter to Thomas McKean*, Nov. 22, 1802

That government is the strongest of which every man feels himself a part.
THOMAS JEFFERSON: *Letter to H. D. Tiffin*, 1807

The ordinary affairs of a nation offer little difficulty to a person of any experience.
THOMAS JEFFERSON: *Letter to James Sullivan*, 1808

Every nation has the government that it deserves.
JOSEPH DE MAISTRE: *Letter*, Aug. 27, 1811

While all other sciences have advanced, that of government is at a standstill — little better understood, little better practised now than three or four thousand years ago.
JOHN ADAMS: *Letter to Thomas Jefferson*, July 9, 1813

No government can be maintained without the principle of fear as well as of duty. Good men will obey the last, but bad ones the former only. If our government ever fails it will be from this weakness.
THOMAS JEFFERSON: *Letter to J. W. Eppes*, 1814

A single good government is a blessing to the whole earth.
THOMAS JEFFERSON: *Letter to George Flower*, 1817

Governments connive at many things which they ought to correct, and correct many things at which they ought to connive.
C. C. COLTON: *Lacon*, 1820

That is the best government which desires to make the people happy, and knows how to make them happy.
T. B. MACAULAY: *Milford's History of Greece*, 1824

Government must be framed for man as he is, and not for man as he should be if he were free from vice.
JAMES KENT: *Commentaries on American Law*, I, 1826

Government is emphatically a machine: to the discontented a "taxing machine," to the contented a "machine for securing property."
THOMAS CARLYLE: *Signs of the Times*, 1829

Government is a trust, and the officers of the government are trustees; and both the trust and the trustees are created for the benefit of the people.
HENRY CLAY: Speech at Lexington, Ky., May 16, 1829

The maxim that governments ought to train the people in the way in which they should go sounds well. But is there any reason for believing that a government is more likely to lead the people in the right way than the people to fall into the right way of themselves?
T. B. MACAULAY: *Southey's Colloquies*, 1830

Government exists for the purpose of keeping the peace, for the purpose of compelling us to settle our disputes by arbitration instead of settling them by blows, for the purpose of compelling us to supply our wants by industry instead of supplying them by rapine.

T. B. MACAULAY: *Civil Disabilities of the Jews,* 1831 (Edinburgh Review, Jan.)

The three great ends which a statesman ought to propose to himself in the government of a nation are: (1) security to possessors; (2) facility to acquirers; and (3) hope to all.

S. T. COLERIDGE: *Table-Talk,* June 25, 1831

The necessity for external government to man is in an inverse ratio to the vigor of his self-government. Where the last is most complete, the first is least wanted. Hence, the more virtue the more liberty.

S. T. COLERIDGE: *Table-Talk,* June 15, 1833

Whatever government is not a government of laws is a despotism, let it be called what it may.

DANIEL WEBSTER: Speech at Bangor, Me., Aug. 25, 1835

The form of government which prevails is the expression of what cultivation exists in the population which permits it. The law is only a memorandum.

R. W. EMERSON: *Politics,* 1841

The less government we have the better.

IBID.

The only legitimate right to govern is an express grant of power from the governed.

W. H. HARRISON: Inaugural Address, March 4, 1841

It may be laid as an universal rule that a government which attempts more than it ought will perform less.

T. B. MACAULAY: *Comic Dramatists of the Restoration,* 1841

What is the end of government? To suppress all noise and disturbance, whether of Puritan preaching, Cameronian psalm-singing, thieves'-riot, murder, arson, or what noise soever, and — be careful that supplies do not fail!

THOMAS CARLYLE: *Past and Present,* III, 1843

Government, as the most conspicuous object in society, is called upon to give signal of what shall be done; and, in many ways, to preside over, further, and command the doing of it. But the government cannot do, by all its signaling and commanding, what the society is radically indisposed to do.

THOMAS CARLYLE: *Past and Present,* IV

Government has been a fossil; it should be a plant.

R. W. EMERSON: *The Young American,* 1844

The object of the state is always the same: to limit the individual, to tame him, to subordinate him, to subjugate him.

MAX STIRNER: *The Ego and His Own,* 1845

The executive of the modern state is but a committee for managing the common affairs of the bourgeoisie.

KARL MARX and FRIEDRICH ENGELS: *The Communist Manifesto,* 1848

To be governed is to be watched, inspected, spied upon, directed, law-ridden, regulated, penned up, indoctrinated, preached at, checked, appraised, seized, censured, commanded, by beings who have neither title, nor knowledge, nor virtue. To be governed is to have every operation, every transaction, every movement noted, registered, counted, rated, stamped, measured, numbered, assessed, licensed, refused, authorized, indorsed, admonished, prevented, reformed, redressed, corrected.

P. J. PROUDHON: *Confessions d'un révolutionaire,* 1849

Whoever lays his hand on me to govern me is a usurper and tyrant, and I declare him my enemy.

IBID.

The authority of government . . . can have no pure right over my person and property but what I concede to it.

H. D. THOREAU: *An Essay on Civil Disobedience,* 1849

The state should avoid all solicitude for the positive welfare of its citizens, and not proceed a step further than is necessary for their mutual security and their protection against foreign enemies. It should impose restrictions on freedom for no other purpose.

K. W. VON HUMBOLDT: *Die Grenzen der Wirksamkeit des Staates,* 1851

The best government is that in which the law speaks instead of the lawyer.

M. L. BYRN: *The Repository of Wit and Humor,* 1852

That government, and that alone, is just which enforces and defends all of man's natural rights and protects him against wrongs of his fellow men.

GALUSHA A. GROW: Speech in the House of Representatives, 1852

No man is good enough to govern another man without that other's consent.

ABRAHAM LINCOLN: Speech at Peoria, Ill., Oct. 16, 1854

I do not subscribe to the doctrine that the people are the slaves and property of their government. I believe that government is for the use of the people, and not the people for the use of government.

GERRIT SMITH: Speech in the House of Representatives, June 27, 1854

Governments exist to protect the rights of minorities. The loved and the rich need no protection, — they have many friends and few enemies.

WENDELL PHILLIPS: Speech at Boston, Dec. 21, 1860

Government consists of acts done by human beings; and if the agents, or those who choose the agents, or those to whom the agents are responsible, or the lookers-on whose opinion ought to influence and check all these, are mere masses of ignorance, stupidity, and baleful prejudice, every operation of government will go wrong.

J. S. MILL: *Representative Government,* II, 1861

Protection is the price of obedience everywhere, in all countries. It is the only thing that makes government respectable. Deny it and you cannot have free subjects or citizens; you may have slaves.

ROBERT TOOMBS: Speech in the Senate, Jan. 7, 1861

Perpetuity is implied, if not expressed, in the fundamental law of all national governments. It is safe to assert that no government proper ever had a provision in its organic law for its own termination.

ABRAHAM LINCOLN: Inaugural address, March 4, 1861

Must a government, of necessity, be too strong for the liberties of its own people, or too weak to maintain its own existence?

ABRAHAM LINCOLN: Message to Congress, July 4, 1861 (This also appears in a speech delivered at Washington, Nov. 10, 1864)

God reigns, and the government at Washington still lives.

JAMES A. GARFIELD: Speech in New York on the assassination of Lincoln, April 15, 1865

The divine right of kings may have been a plea for feeble tyrants, but the divine right of government is the keystone of human progress, and without it government sinks into police and a nation into a mob.

BENJAMIN DISRAELI: *Lothair,* pref., 1870

I say the mission of government, henceforth, in civilized lands, is not repression alone, and not authority alone, not even of law, nor by that favorite standard of the eminent writer, the rule of the best men, the born heroes and captains of the race (as if such ever, or one time out of a hundred, get into the big places, elective or dynastic) — but higher than the highest arbitrary rule, to train communities through all their grades, beginning with individuals and ending there again, to rule themselves.

WALT WHITMAN: *Democratic Vistas,* 1870

All government is evil.

B. R. HAYDON: *Table-Talk,* 1876

The government of the world is carried on by sovereigns and statesmen, and not by anonymous paragraph writers or the hairbrained chatter of irresponsible frivolity.

BENJAMIN DISRAELI: Speech in London, Nov. 9, 1878

The best system [of government] is to have one party govern and the other party watch.

THOMAS B. REED: Speech in the House of Representatives, 1880

There are times when a government must be liberal and times when it must be dictatorial: here everything changes, and there is no eternity.

OTTO VON BISMARCK: Speech in the Reichstag, Feb. 24, 1881

I do not think that it is possible to find a perfect moral foundation for the authority of any government, be it the government of an emperor or a republic. They are all of the nature of an usurpation, though I think, when confined within certain exact limits, of a justifiable usurpation.

AUBERON HERBERT: *The Right and Wrong Way of Compulsion by the State,* 1885

The right to rule is not necessarily bound up with any special mode of government. It may take this form or that, provided only that it be of a nature to insure the general welfare.

POPE LEO XIII: *Immortale Dei,* Nov. 1, 1885

Good government, and especially the government of which every American citizen boasts, has for its objects the protection of every person within its care in the greatest liberty consistent with the good order of society, and his perfect security in the enjoyment of his earnings with the least possible diminution for public needs.

GROVER CLEVELAND: Message to Congress, Dec. 6, 1886

The government is not an almoner of gifts among the people, but an instrumentality by which the people's affairs should be conducted upon business principles, regulated by the public needs.

GROVER CLEVELAND: Message to the House of Representatives, Feb. 26, 1887

A Genghis Khan with telegraphs.

Ascribed to ALEXANDER HERZEN (1812–70) in LYOF N. TOLSTOY: *The Kingdom of God Is Within You,* 1893

Government is an association of men who do violence to the rest of us.

LYOF N. TOLSTOY: *The Kingdom of God Is Within You,* 1893

Government is the assumption of authority over a given area and all within it, exercised generally for the double purpose of more complete oppression of its subjects and extension of its boundaries.

BENJAMIN R. TUCKER: *Instead of a Book,* 1893

The government is us; we are the government, you and I.
THEODORE ROOSEVELT: Speech at Asheville, N. C., Sept. 9, 1902

The firm basis of government is justice, not pity.
WOODROW WILSON: Inaugural Address, March 4, 1913

Accountancy – that is government.
LOUIS D. BRANDEIS: Statement before the House Committee on Interstate and Foreign Commerce, Jan. 30, 1914

In relation to society and government it may be repeated that new ideas are rare; in regard to the latter, perhaps not more than two really large and new ideas have been developed in as many millenniums.
H. C. LODGE: Address in Schenectady, N. Y., June 9, 1915

Government is merely an attempt to express the conscience of everybody, the average conscience of the nation, in the rules that everybody is commanded to obey. That is all it is. If the government is going faster than the public conscience, it will presently have to pull up; if it is not going as fast as the public conscience, it will presently have to be whipped up.
WOODROW WILSON: Speech in Washington, Jan. 29, 1915

No man ever saw a government. I live in the midst of the government of the United States, but I never saw the government of the United States. Its personnel extends through all the nations, and across the seas, and into every corner of the world.
WOODROW WILSON: Speech in Pittsburgh, Jan. 29, 1916

Government is not an exact science.
MR. JUSTICE LOUIS D. BRANDEIS: *Opinion in Truax* vs. *Corrigan,* 1921

The cost of government will continue to increase, I care not what party is in power.
REED SMOOT: Speech in the Senate, 1925

The government is mainly an expensive organization to regulate evildoers, and tax those who behave: government does little for fairly respectable people except annoy them.
E. W. HOWE: *Notes for My Biographer,* 1926

Experience teaches us to be most on our guard to protect liberty when the government's purposes are beneficent.
MR. JUSTICE LOUIS D. BRANDEIS: *Opinion in Olmstead* vs. *U. S.,* 1928

[We advocate] the removal of government from all fields of private enterprise except where necessary to develop public works and natural resources in the common interest.
Democratic National Platform, 1932

For three long years I have been going up and down this country preaching that government . . . costs too much. I shall not stop that preaching.
F. D. ROOSEVELT: Speech of Acceptance, July 2, 1932

If a people be well fed and well housed it cares nothing about the form of government under which it lives or the honesty or rottenness of that government.
BENJAMIN DECASSERES: *Fantasia Impromptu,* 1933

Today the nations of the world may be divided into two classes – the nations in which the government fears the people, and the nations in which the people fear the government.
AMOS R. E. PINCHOT: *Open letter,* April 16, 1935

Fire, water and government know nothing of mercy.
ALBANIAN PROVERB

What I must not do, the government must not do.
Author unidentified

A government within a government. (Imperium in imperio.)
LATIN PHRASE

Only fools are glad when governments change.
RUMANIAN PROVERB

[*See also* Absolutism, Accountancy, Anarchist, Authority, Bureaucracy, Centralization, City, Classes, Compromise, Conservative, Constitution, Democracy, Despotism, Experience, Family, Freedom, Government (Free), History, Injustice, Justice, King, Laissez-faire, Law, Law (Natural), Lean, Liberty, Marriage, Minority, Monarchy, Morality, Multitude, Nationality, Newspaper, Office, Oligarchy, Opinion, Opinion (Public), Opposition, Oppression, Order, Papacy, Party, Paternalism, People, Police, Politics, Press (Free), Propaganda, Republic, Society, Sovereignty, Spain, State, Tryanny.

Government, American

I have no fear but that the result of our experiment will be that men may be trusted to govern themselves without a master. Could the contrary of this be proved I should conclude either that there is no God, or that He is a malevolent Being.
THOMAS JEFFERSON: *Letter to David Hartley,* 1787

With all the imperfections of our present government, it is without comparison the best existing, or that ever did exist.
THOMAS JEFFERSON: *Letter to E. Carrington,* 1787

The national government possesses those powers which it can be shown the people have conferred on it, and no more. All the rest belongs to the state governments, or to the people themselves.
DANIEL WEBSTER: Speech in the Senate, Jan. 26, 1830

How does it become a man to behave towards the American government today? I answer, that he cannot without disgrace be associated with it.
H. D. THOREAU: *An Essay on Civil Disobedience,* 1849

What was once a constitutional federal republic is now converted, in reality, into one as absolute as that of the autocrat of Russia, and as despotic in its tendency as any absolute government that ever existed.
JOHN C. CALHOUN: Speech in the Senate, March 4, 1850

Government, English

The mob are statesmen, and their statesmen sots.
DANIEL DEFOE: *The True-Born Englishman,* II, 1701

I consider [the English] government as the most flagitious which has existed since the days of Philip of Macedon, whom they make their model. It is not only founded in corruption itself, but insinuates the same poison into the bowels of every other, corrupts its councils, nourishes factions, stirs up revolutions, and places its own happiness in fomenting commotions and civil wars among others, thus rendering itself truly the *hostis humani generis.*
THOMAS JEFFERSON: *Letter to John Adams,* 1816

Our whole political machinery presupposes a people so fundamentally at one that they can safely afford to bicker.
A. J. BALFOUR, *c.* 1905 (Quoted in the Political Quarterly, London, Dec. 1939)

Government, Federal

[*See* States' Rights.

Government, Free

Free government is the true nurse of genius.
LONGINUS: *On the Sublime,* XLIV, *c.* 250

The worst government is popular government.
PIERRE CORNEILLE: *Cinna,* II, 1639

A free commonwealth without single person or house of lords is by far the best government.
JOHN MILTON: *The Ready and Easy Way to Establish a Free Commonwealth,* 1660

Let the people think they govern and they will be governed.
WILLIAM PENN: *Fruits of Solitude,* 1693

If any ask me what a free government is, I answer, that, for any practical purpose, it is what the people think so.
EDMUND BURKE: *Letter to the Sheriffs of Bristol,* 1777

The basis of our political systems is the right of the people to make and to alter their constitutions of government.
GEORGE WASHINGTON: Farewell Address, Sept. 17, 1796

Free government is founded in jealousy, and not in confidence; it is jealousy, and not confidence, which prescribes limited constitutions, to bind down those whom we are obliged to trust with power.
THOMAS JEFFERSON: *Kentucky Resolutions,* Nov., 1798

The will of the people is the only legitimate foundation of any government, and to protect its free expression should be our first object.
THOMAS JEFFERSON: *Letter to Benjamin Waring,* March, 1801

All free governments are the creatures of volition — a breath can make them and a breath can destroy them.
A. H. STEPHENS: Speech in the House of Representatives, Aug. 6, 1850

Government over all, by all, and for the sake of all.
THEODORE PARKER: Speech before the Anti-Slavery Society, Boston, May 13, 1854

All government of right originates from the people, is founded on compact only, and instituted solely for the good of the whole; and they have at all times the inalienable right to alter, reform or abolish their form of government in such manner as they may deem expedient.
DECLARATION OF RIGHTS OF MARYLAND, I, 1867

No government can be free that does not allow all its citizens to participate in the formation and execution of her laws. There are degrees of tyranny; but every other government is a despotism.
THADDEUS STEVENS: Speech in the House of Representatives, June 3, 1867

All free governments are managed by the combined wisdom and folly of the people.
JAMES A. GARFIELD: *Letter,* April 21, 1880

[*See also* Democracy, Government (Representative), People.

Government Ownership

It may be said generally that businesses which are in their nature monopolies are properly part of the functions of the state, and should be assumed by the state. There is the same reason why government should carry telegraphic messages as that it should carry letters; that railroads should belong to the public as that common roads should.
HENRY GEORGE: *Progress and Poverty,* VIII, 1879

I do not believe in government ownership or anything which can with propriety be left in private hands, and in particular I should most strenuously object to government ownership of railroads.
THEODORE ROOSEVELT: Speech in Raleigh, N. C., Oct. 19, 1905

The right of the government to regulate, supervise and control public utilities in the public interest we believe should be strengthened, but we are firmly opposed to the nationalization or government ownership of public utilities. Republican National Platform, 1924

The Socialists contend rightly that certain forms of property should be reserved to the state, since possession of them carries with it a kind of power too great to be left to private individuals without grave danger to the community in general. Just demands of this sort contain nothing that is opposed to Christian truth. POPE PIUS XI: *Quadragesimo anno,* May 15, 1931

[*See also* Monopoly.

Government, Popular

[*See* Government (Free), People.

Government, Representative

To be fully comformable to the principle of right, the form of government must be representative. This is the only one that permits republicanism, without which the government is arbitrary and despotic, whatever the constitution may be.
IMMANUEL KANT: *Perpetual Peace,* II, 1795

Representative institutions are of little value, and may be a mere instrument of tyranny or intrigue, when the generality of electors are not sufficiently interested in their own government to give their vote, or, if they vote at all, do not bestow their suffrages on public grounds, but sell them for money, or vote at the beck of some one who has control over them, or whom for private reasons they desire to propitiate.
J. S. MILL: *Representative Government,* I, 1861

[*See also* Democracy, Government (Free), Republic.

Governor

Under our present system, the chief duty of the governor of Alabama is running an employment agency.
FRANK DIXON: Inaugural Address as Governor of Alabama, Jan. 17, 1938

Grace (=clemency)

He giveth grace unto the lowly.
PROVERBS III, 34, *c.* 350 B.C.

Ye are fallen from grace.
GALATIANS V, 4, *c.* 50

Shall we continue in sin, that grace may abound? God forbid.
ROMANS VI, 1–2, *c.* 55

Abundant grace.
II CORINTHIANS IV, 15, *c.* 55

By grace are ye saved through faith; and that not of yourselves: it is the gift of God.
EPHESIANS II, 8, *c.* 60

Unto every one of us is given grace according to the measure of the gift of Christ.
EPHESIANS IV, 7

God resisteth the proud, but giveth grace unto the humble. JAMES IV, 6, *c.* 60

The law detects, grace alone conquers, sin.
ST. AUGUSTINE: *Of Continence, c.* 425

Princes should leave things of injustice and envy to the ministry and execution of others, but acts of favor and grace are to be performed by themselves.
NICCOLÒ MACHIAVELLI: *The Prince,* XIX, 1513

There, but for the grace of God, goes ———.
Author unknown, but commonly credited to JOHN BRADFORD (1510–55). (He is said to have applied the words to himself on seeing a criminal pass by on the way to the gallows. He himself was burned at Smithfield, July 1, 1555. The saying is also attributed to RICHARD BAXTER (1615–91), JOHN BUNYAN (1628–88) and JOHN ESLEY (1703–91))

Hail to thee, lady! and the grace of Heaven,
Before, behind thee and on every hand,
Enwheel thee round!
SHAKESPEARE: *Othello,* II, 1604

Divine grace was never slow.
GEORGE HERBERT: *Outlandish Proverbs,* 1640

Nor can a man with grace his soul inspire,
More than the candles set themselves on fire.
JOHN BUNYAN: *A Book For Boys and Girls,* 1686

God is in debt to none; and if He gives to some that He is not in debt to, because it is His pleasure, that does not bring Him into debt to others.
JONATHAN EDWARDS: *The Justice of God in the Damnation of Sinners,* 1734

Plenteous grace with Thee is found,
Grace to cover all my sin;
Let the healing streams abound;
Make and keep me pure within.
CHARLES WESLEY: *Refuge,* 1740

I need Thy presence every passing hour:
What but Thy grace can foil the tempter's power?
Who like Thyself my guide and stay can be?
Through cloud and sunshine, oh abide with me!
H. F. LYTE: *Abide with Me,* 1847 (The tune is by W. H. Monk, 1861)

By the grace of God. (Dei gratia.)
LATIN PHRASE

God does not refuse grace to one who does what he can. (Facienti quod in se est Deus non denegat gratiam.)
MEDIEVAL LATIN PROVERB

[*See also* Affliction, Antinomianism, Benediction, Grace and Works, Salvation, Will (Free).

Grace (=thanksgiving)

What God gives, and what we take,
'Tis a gift for Christ His sake:
Be the meal of beans and pease,
God be thank'd for those, and these:
Have we flesh, or have we fish,
All are fragments from His dish.

ROBERT HERRICK: *Noble Numbers,* 1647

Thee let us taste, nor toil below
For perishable meat;
The manna of Thy love bestow,
Give us Thy flesh to eat.

CHARLES WESLEY: *Grace Before Meat,* 1739

Some hae meat and canna eat,
And some would eat that want it;
But we hae meat and we can eat,
Sae let the Lord be thankit.

ROBERT BURNS: *Grace Before Meat,* c. 1795

She leaped upon a pile, and lifted high
Her mad looks to the lightning, and cried: "Eat!"

P. B. SHELLEY: *The Revolt of Islam,* VI, 1818

The custom of saying grace at meals had, probably, its origin in the early times of the world, and the hunter-state of man, when dinners were precarious things, and a full meal was something more than a common blessing; when a bellyful was a windfall, and looked like a special providence.

CHARLES LAMB: *Grace Before Meat,* 1821 (London Magazine, Nov.)

For what we are about to receive the Lord make us truly thankful, for Christ's sake. Amen. OLD ENGLISH GRACE

[*See also* Thanksgiving.

Grace and Works

If by grace, then it is no more of works: otherwise grace is no more grace. But if it be of works, then it is no more grace: otherwise work is no more work.

ROMANS XI, 6, *c.* 55

Graceful

Grace is the ornament of ornament. Without it, beauty is lifeless.

BALTASAR GRACIÁN: *The Art of Worldly Wisdom,* CXXVII, 1647

Grace was in all her steps, Heaven in her eye,
In every gesture dignity and love.

JOHN MILTON: *Paradise Lost,* VIII, 1667

What's a fine person, or a beauteous face,
Unless deportment gives them decent grace?

CHARLES CHURCHILL: *The Rosciad,* 1761

Every natural action is graceful.

R. W. EMERSON: *Nature,* 1836

He said, "She has a lovely face;
God in his mercy lend her grace."

ALFRED TENNYSON: *The Lady of Shalott,* 1852

Grace of God

[*See* Grace (=clemency).

Grammar

Cæsar is not above the grammarians. (Caesar non supra grammaticos.)

Ascribed by SUETONIUS: *Lives of Eminent Grammarians,* to the Emperor Tiberius (42 B.C.–37 A.D.)

I am the King of Rome, and above grammar. (Ego sum rex Romanus, et supra grammaticam.)

THE EMPEROR SIGISMUND: At the Council of Constance, 1414

Boyhood is distracted for years with precepts of grammar that are infinitely prolix, perplexed and obscure.

JOHANN COMENIUS: *Orbis sensualium pictus,* 1658

Grammar lords it over kings, and with a high hand makes them obey its laws.

J. B. MOLIÈRE: *Les femmes savantes,* II, 1672

The first thing you should attend to is, to speak whatever language you do speak in its greatest purity, and according to the rules of grammar; for we must never offend against grammar.

LORD CHESTERFIELD: *Letter to his son,* Oct. 17, 1739

It is not the business of grammar, as some critics seem preposterously to imagine, to give law to the fashions which regulate our speech. On the contrary, from its conformity to these, and from that alone, it derives all its authority and value.

GEORGE CAMPBELL: *The Philosophy of Rhetoric,* 1776

Our modern grammars have done much more hurt than good. The authors have labored to prove what is obviously absurd, viz., that our language is not made right; and in pursuance of this idea, have tried to make it over again, and persuade the English to speak by Latin rules, or by arbitrary rules of their own.

NOAH WEBSTER: *Dissertations on the English Language,* pref., 1789

Where strictness of grammar does not weaken expression, it should be attended to. . . . But where, by small grammatical negligences, the energy of an idea is condensed, or a word stands for a sentence, I hold grammatical rigor in contempt.

THOMAS JEFFERSON: *Letter to James Madison,* 1801

In the immense field of knowledge innumerable are the paths, and grammar is the gate of entrance to them all.
WILLIAM COBBETT: *Grammar of the English Language*, pref., 1823

The established practise of the best speakers and writers of any language is the standard of grammatical accuracy in the use of that language.
SAMUEL KIRKHAM: *English Grammar in Familiar Lectures*, I, 1829

I am free to confess I don't know grammar. . . . I detest grammar. . . . Oh, the delicious blunders one sees when they are irretrievable!
E. G. BULWER-LYTTON: Quoted in N. P. WILLIS: *Pencilling by the Way*, LXIX, 1835

Grammar is the analysis of language.
E. A. POE: *The Rationale of Verse*, 1843 (The Pioneer, March)

A man's grammar, like Cæsar's wife, must not only be pure, but above suspicion of impurity. E. A. POE: *Marginalia*, 1844–49

The principles and rules of grammar are the means by which the forms of language are made to correspond with the universal forms of thought.
J. S. MILL: Inaugural Address as Lord Rector of St. Andrew's University, 1867

Grammar is a science or nothing. It has the outward forms of a science and its difficulties spring out of its scientific character.
ALEXANDER BAIN: *A First English Grammar*, pref., 1872

Grammar, like other sciences, deals only with what can be brought under general laws and stated in the form of general rules, and ignores isolated phenomena.
HENRY SWEET: *A New English Grammar*, intro., 1891

That sure is a great school. It's practical. They don't teach no goddam grammar there.
A Kansas farmer: To Nelson Antrim Crawford, *c.* 1915

Bad grammar does not vitiate a deed. (Mala grammatica non vitiat chartam.)
LEGAL MAXIM

The art of speaking and writing correctly. (Ars bene dicendi et bene scribendi.)
MEDIEVAL DEFINITION

[*See also* Language.

Grammarian

Saving only the doctors, there are none more stupid than the grammarians.
HERACLITUS: *Fragment*, *c.* 500 B.C.

Grammarians dispute, and the question is still undecided.
HORACE: *De arte poetica*, *c.* 8 B.C.

To break Priscian's head: to write or speak false grammar. Priscian was a famous grammarian who flourished at Constantinople in the year 525, and who was so devoted to his favorite study that to speak false Latin in his company was as disagreeable to him as to break his head.
FRANCIS GROSE: *A Classical Dictionary of the Vulgar Tongue*, 1785

Thou eunuch of language: thou butcher, imbruing thy hands in the bowels of orthography: thou arch-heretic in pronunciation: thou pitch-pipe of affected emphasis: thou carpenter, mortising the awkward joints of jarring sentences: thou squeaking dissonance of cadence; thou pimp of gender: thou scape-gallows from the land of syntax: thou scavenger of mood and tense: thou murderous accoucheur of infant learning: thou *ignis fatuus*, misleading the steps of benighted ignorance: thou pickle-herring in the puppet-show of nonsense.
ROBERT BURNS: Memorandum on an unidentified critic, *c.* 1791

He settled *hoti's* business — let it be! —
Properly based *oun* —
Gave us the doctrine of the enclitic *de*,
Dead from the waist down.
ROBERT BROWNING: *A Grammarian's Funeral*, 1855 (*Hoti*=a statement introduced by *because; oun*=archaic spelling of *un-*)

Devotees of grammatical studies have not been distinguished for any very remarkable felicities of expression.
A. BRONSON ALCOTT: *Tablets*, I, 1868

[*See also* Grammar.

Grandeur

There is grandeur in the growling of the gale.
W. S. GILBERT: *The Mikado*, II, 1885

[*See also* King.

Grandfather

[*See* Dancing, Heredity.

Grandmother

A grandam's name is little less in love
Than is the doting title of a mother.
SHAKESPEARE: *Richard III*, IV, *c.* 1592

Go teach your grandam to suck eggs.
JONATHAN SWIFT: *Polite Conversation*, I, 1738

[*See also* Devil.

Grant, U. S. (1822–85)

I wish some of you would tell me the brand of whiskey that Grant drinks. I would like to send a barrel of it to my other generals.
Ascribed to ABRAHAM LINCOLN, 1863 (This is supposed to have been his reply on receiving a complaint about Grant's

drinking. The story was invented by a reporter, and appeared in the New York Herald, Nov. 26)

Since Vicksburg they have not a word to say against Grant's habits. He has the disagreeable habit of not retreating before irresistible veterans.
MARY BOYKIN CHESNUT: *Diary*, Richmond, Va., Jan. 1, 1864

He is a scientific Goth, resembling Alaric, destroying the country as he goes and delivering the people over to starvation. Nor does he bury his dead, but leaves them to rot on the battlefield.
JOHN TYLER: *Letter to Sterling Price*, June 7, 1864

When Grant once gets possession of a place, he holds on to it as if he had inherited it.
ABRAHAM LINCOLN: To Benjamin F. Butler, June 22, 1864

I am more of a farmer than a soldier. I take little or no interest in military affairs.
U. S. GRANT: To Otto von Bismarck at a military review at Potsdam, 1879

How those old Greeks would have seized upon him! The gods, the destinies, seem to have concentrated upon him.
WALT WHITMAN: *Specimen Days*, Sept. 28, 1879

You ask me what state he comes from. My answer shall be, he hails from Appomattox and its famous apple tree.
ROSCOE CONKLING: Speech nominating Grant for a third term, 1880

[*See also* Brotherhood, Determination.

Grape

The fathers have eaten a sour grape, and the children's teeth are set on edge.
JEREMIAH XXXI, 29, *c.* 625 B.C. (Cf. EZEKIEL XVIII, 2, *c.* 600 B.C.; cited as a proverb)

The grapes are sour.
ENGLISH SAYING, borrowed from ÆSOP: *Fables* (The Fox and the Grapes), *c.* 600 B.C.

The vines with the tender grape give a good smell.
SOLOMON'S SONG II, 13, *c.* 200 B.C.

There is a devil in every berry of the grape.
ENGLISH PROVERB, said to be of Turkish origin, and traced by Smith to 1634

Better be jocund with the fruitful grape
Than sadden after none, or bitter, fruit.
EDWARD FITZGERALD: Tr. of OMAR KHAYYÁM: *Rubáiyát* (*c.* 1100), 1857

The grape that can with logic absolute
The two-and-seventy jarring sects confute:
The sovereign alchemist that in a trice
Life's leaden metal into gold transmute.
IBID.

[*See also* Fox, Vine, Vineyard, Wine.

Grapefruit

A grapefruit is a lemon that had a chance and took advantage of it.
Author unidentified

Grass

God said, Let the earth bring forth grass.
GENESIS I, 11, *c.* 700 B.C.

They shall soon be cut down like the grass.
PSALMS XXXVII, 2, *c.* 150 B.C.

Grass is the hair of the earth.
THOMAS DEKKER: *The Gull's Hornbook*, III, 1609

How lush and lusty the grass looks! how green!
SHAKESPEARE: *The Tempest*, II, 1611

If the grass grow in Janiveer
It grows the worse for't all the year.
JOHN RAY: *English Proverbs*, 1670

A blade of grass is always a blade of grass, whether in one country or another.
SAMUEL JOHNSON: *Mrs. Piozzi's Anecdotes*, 1786

The murmur that springs
From the growing of grass.
E. A. POE: *Al Aaraaf*, II, 1829

A child said, What is the grass? fetching it to me with full hands;
How could I answer the child? I do not know what it is, any more than he.
WALT WHITMAN: *Walt Whitman*, 1855

Grass is the forgiveness of nature — her constant benediction. . . . Forests decay, harvests perish, flowers vanish, but grass is immortal.
JOHN J. INGALLS: Speech in the Senate, 1874

Grass is hard and lumpy and damp, and full of dreadful black insects.
OSCAR WILDE: *The Decay of Lying*, 1891

Nearer the rock, the sweeter the grass.
SCOTTISH PROVERB

[*See also* Drought, Farm, Farmer, High, Nature, Turk.

Grasshopper

Even these . . . ye may eat: . . . the grasshopper after his kind.
LEVITICUS XI, 22, *c.* 700 B.C.

[*See also* Death.

Gratitude

Gratitude is not only the greatest of virtues, but the parent of all the others.
CICERO: *Pro Plancio*, 54 B.C.

Gratitude, in most men, is only a strong and secret hope of greater favors.
LA ROCHEFOUCAULD: *Maxims*, 1665

Gratitude is like the good faith of traders: it maintains commerce, and we often pay, not because it is just to discharge our debts, but that we may more readily find people to trust us. IBID.

A grateful mind
By owing owes not, but still pays, at once
Indebted and discharg'd.
JOHN MILTON: *Paradise Lost*, IV, 1667

He that gives to a grateful man puts out at usury.
THOMAS FULLER: *Gnomologia*, 1732

You may believe anything that is good of a grateful man. IBID.

The gratitude of place-expectants is a lively sense of future favors.
Ascribed to ROBERT WALPOLE (1676–1745)

There are minds so impatient of inferiority that their gratitude is a species of revenge, and they return benefits, not because recompense is a pleasure, but because obligation is a pain.
SAMUEL JOHNSON: *The Rambler*, Jan. 15, 1751

Every acknowledgement of gratitude is a circumstance of humiliation; and some are found to submit to frequent mortifications of this kind, proclaiming what obligations they owe, merely because they think it in some measure cancels the debt.
OLIVER GOLDSMITH: *The Citizen of the World*, LXVI, 1762

Gratitude is a burden upon our imperfect nature.
LORD CHESTERFIELD: *Letter to his son*, Nov. 7, 1765

Sweet is the breath of vernal shower,
The bee's collected treasures sweet,
Sweet music's melting fall, but sweeter yet
The still small voice of gratitude.
THOMAS GRAY: *Ode for Music*, 1769

Gratitude is a fruit of great cultivation; you do not find it among gross people.
SAMUEL JOHNSON: *Boswell's Journal of a Tour to the Hebrides*, Sept. 20, 1773

William Kingston, the man born without arms, came to see me of his own accord. Some time since he received a clear sense of the favor of God.
JOHN WESLEY: *Journal*, Aug. 31, 1790

The bridegroom may forget the bride,
  Was made his wedded wife yestreen;
The monarch may forget the crown
  That on his head an hour has been;
The mother may forget the child
  That smiles sae sweetly on her knee;
But I'll remember thee, Glencairn,
  And a' that thou hast done for me.
ROBERT BURNS: *Lament for James, Earl of Glencairn*, 1791

Praise the bridge that carried you over.
GEORGE COLMAN THE YOUNGER: *The Heir-at-Law*, 1797

Alas! the gratitude of men
Hath often left me mourning.
WILLIAM WORDSWORTH: *Simon Lee*, 1798

No metaphysician ever felt the deficiency of language so much as the grateful.
C. C. COLTON: *Lacon*, 1820

Next to ingratitude, the most painful thing to bear is gratitude.
H. W. BEECHER: *Proverbs from Plymouth Pulpit*, 1870

One can put some trust in the gratitude of a sovereign, and also in that of his family; under certain conditions, one can even rely upon it; but one can never expect anything from the gratitude of a nation.
OTTO VON BISMARCK (1815–98)

Lambs have the grace to suck kneeling.
CHINESE PROVERB

Gratitude is the heart's memory.
FRENCH PROVERB

These three are never grateful: a lover, a son-in-law, and a nephew. HINDU PROVERB

Give a grateful man more than he asks.
PORTUGUESE PROVERB

Gratitude preserves auld friendships and begets new. SCOTTISH PROVERB

Grave

Whosoever toucheth . . . a grave shall be unclean seven days.
NUMBERS XIX, 16, *c.* 700 B.C.

He made his grave with the wicked, and with the rich. ISAIAH LIII, 9, *c.* 700 B.C.

He that goeth down to the grave shall come up no more. JOB VII, 9, *c.* 325 B.C.

The grave is mine house: I have made my bed in the darkness. JOB XVII, 13

To lack a grave matters little.
VIRGIL: *Æneid*, II, 19 B.C.

O death, where is thy sting? O grave, where is thy victory? I CORINTHIANS XV, 55, *c.* 55

Lay me a green sod under my head,
  And another at my feet;
And lay my bent bow by my side,
  Which was my music sweet;
And make my grave of gravel and green,
  Which is most right and meet.
Anon.: *Robin Hood's Death*, *c.* 1500

I'll give my jewels for a set of beads;
My gorgeous palace for a hermitage, . . .
And my large kingdom for a little grave,
A little little grave, an obscure grave.
SHAKESPEARE: *Richard II*, III, *c.* 1596

Let's talk of graves, of worms, and epitaphs.
IBID.

That small model of the barren earth
Which serves as paste and cover to our bones.
IBID.

Still as the grave.
SHAKESPEARE: *Othello*, V, 1604

So be my grave my peace.
SHAKESPEARE: *King Lear*, I, 1606

Mean and mighty, rotting
Together, have one dust.
SHAKESPEARE: *Cymbeline*, IV, *c.* 1609

Dust and an endless darkness.
JOHN FLETCHER: *Thierry and Theodoret*, IV, 1620

Our lives are but our marches to the grave.
JOHN FLETCHER: *The Humorous Lieutenant*, III, *c.* 1620

The grave's a fine and private place,
But none, I think, do there embrace.
ANDREW MARVELL: *To His Coy Mistress*, *c.* 1648

A piece of a churchyard fits everybody.
GEORGE HERBERT: *Jacula Prudentum*, 1651

Go to the dull churchyard and see
Those hillocks of mortality.
Where proudest man is only found
By a small swelling in the ground.
THOMAS FLATMAN: *A Doomsday Thought*, 1659

Teach me to live that I may dread
The grave as little as my bed.
THOMAS KEN: *Evening Hymn*, *c.* 1690

Hark! from the tombs a doleful sound.
ISAAC WATTS: First line of a hymn, 1707

The grave unites; where e'en the great find rest,
And blended lie th' oppressor and th' oppressed.
ALEXANDER POPE: *Windsor Forest*, 1713

Yet shall thy grave with rising flow'rs be dressed,
And the green turf lie lightly on thy breast;
There shall the morn her earliest tears bestow,
There the first roses of the year shall blow.
ALEXANDER POPE: *Elegy to the Memory of an Unfortunate Lady*, 1717

Graves are of all sizes.
THOMAS FULLER: *Gnomologia*, 1732

In the grave, dust and bones jostle not for the wall.
IBID.

The grave is the general meeting-place.
IBID.

The solitary, silent, solemn scene,
Where Cæsars, heroes, peasants, hermits lie,
Blended in dust together; where the slave
Rests from his labors; where th' insulting proud
Resigns his powers; the miser drops his hoard.
Where human folly sleeps.
JOHN DYER: *The Ruins of Rome*, 1740

The bodies of those that made such a noise and tumult when alive, when dead, lie as quietly among the graves of their neighbors as any others.
JONATHAN EDWARDS: *Procrastination*, *c.* 1740

The knell, the shroud, the mattock and the grave,
The deep, damp vault, the darkness, and the worm.
EDWARD YOUNG: *Night Thoughts*, IV, 1742

The boast of heraldry, the pomp of power,
And all that beauty, all that wealth e'er gave,
Await alike th' inevitable hour,
The paths of glory lead but to the grave.
THOMAS GRAY: *Elegy Written in a Country Churchyard*, 1750

Each in his narrow cell forever laid,
The rude forefathers of the hamlet sleep.
IBID.

Bring me an ax and spade,
Bring me a winding sheet;
When I my grave have made,
Let winds and tempests beat.
WILLIAM BLAKE: *Song*, 1783

The man we celebrate must find a tomb,
And we that worship him, ignoble graves.
WILLIAM COWPER: *The Task*, III, 1785

It is enough to make —— turn over in his grave.
ENGLISH SAYING, not recorded before the XIX century

Who can look down upon the grave even of an enemy, and not feel a compunctious throb, that he should ever have warred with the poor handful of earth that lies mouldering before him.
WASHINGTON IRVING: *The Sketch-Book*, 1820

Art is long, and Time is fleeting,
And our hearts, though stout and brave,
Still, like muffled drums, are beating
Funeral marches to the grave.
H. W. LONGFELLOW: *A Psalm of Life*, 1839

The good, the brave, the beautiful,
How dreamless is their sleep,
Where rolls the dirge-like music
Of the ever-tossing deep.
Or where the hurrying night-winds
Pale Winter's robes have spread
Above their narrow palaces,
In the cities of the dead.
PARK BENJAMIN: *The Departed*, *c.* 1844

We bargain for the graves we lie in.
JAMES R. LOWELL: *The Vision of Sir Launfal*, 1848

Of all the pulpits from which the human voice is ever sent forth there is none from which it reaches so far as from the grave.
JOHN RUSKIN: *The Seven Lamps of Architecture*, VI, 1849

The grave itself is but a covered bridge,
Leading from light to light, through a brief darkness.

H. W. LONGFELLOW: *The Golden Legend*, v, 1851

Dust into dust, and under dust, to lie,
Sans wine, sans song, sans singer, and — sans end.

EDWARD FITZGERALD: Tr. of OMAR KHAYYÁM: *Rubáiyát* (*c.* 1100), 1857

The man who has a grave or two in his heart does not need to haunt churchyards.

ALEXANDER SMITH: *Dreamthorp*, III, 1863

Under the wide and starry sky,
Dig the grave and let me lie.

R. L. STEVENSON: *Requiem*, 1887

They are moving grandpa's grave to build a sewer.

Anon.: Title of a popular song, *c.* 1895

Bartley will have a fine coffin out of the white boards, and a deep grave surely. What more can we want than that? No man at all can be living forever, and we must be satisfied.

J. M. SYNGE: *Riders to the Sea*, 1904

What a jolly life a corpse must lead
In the grave so calm and cool,
Scorning the trifles that mortals most heed
And pitying the sage and fool.

Author unidentified

In the grave the prince is no more comfortable than the peasant. GERMAN PROVERB

[*See also* Age (Old), Burial, Cemetery, Churchyard, Dead, Death, Dying, Epitaph, Funeral, Gluttony, Life and Death, Midnight, Monument, Mortality, Moses, Sleep, Tomb.

Gravedigger

The houses that he makes last till Doomsday.

SHAKESPEARE: *Hamlet*, v, *c.* 1601

[*See also* Pleasure.

Grave-robber

If anyone shall dig up and plunder a buried corpse he shall be outlawed until he comes to an agreement with the relatives of the dead man, and they ask that he be allowed to come among men again.

The Salic Law, *c.* 490

Graveyard

[*See* Cemetery, Churchyard, Equality, Grave.

Gravity

What doth gravity out of his bed at midnight?

SHAKESPEARE: *I Henry IV*, II, *c.* 1598

'Tis not for gravity to play at cherry-pit with Satan.

SHAKESPEARE: *Twelfth Night*, III, *c.* 1601

Gravity is a mysterious carriage of the body invented to conceal the want of mind.

LA ROCHEFOUCAULD: *Maxims*, 1665

Grave as an owl in a barn.

GEORGE FARQUHAR: *The Inconstant*, III, 1702

Gravity is of the very essence of imposture.

ANTHONY A. COOPER (EARL OF SHAFTESBURY): *Characteristics of Men, Manners, Opinions, Times*, *c.* 1713

The gravest fish is an oyster; the gravest bird's an owl; the gravest beast's an ass; and the gravest man's a fool.

ALLAN RAMSAY: *Scots Proverbs*, 1737

To maintain a constant gravity in his countenance and behavior, and to affect wisdom on all occasions.

HENRY FIELDING: *Jonathan Wild*, IV, 1743 (Maxim of Wild for the attainment of greatness)

The very essence of gravity was design, and, consequently, deceit; it was a taught trick to gain credit of the world for more sense and knowledge than a man was worth.

LAURENCE STERNE: *Tristram Shandy*, I, 1760 (Following this, Sterne quotes La Rochefoucauld, *ante*, 1665)

[*See also* Human, Spaniard, Virtue.

Gravity (force of)

Gravity is nothing else than a natural force implanted by the Creator of the world into its parts, so that, coming together in the shape of a sphere, they might form a unified whole.

NICOLAUS COPERNICUS: *De revolutionibus orbium coelestium*, 1543

Gravity and lightness are only attraction and flight. Nothing is naturally heavy or light.

GIORDANO BRUNO: *Del infinito, universo, e mondi*, v, 1584

Gravity is a natural corporeal attraction between bodies toward a connection, so that the earth attracts a stone much more than a stone attracts the earth.

JOHANN KEPLER: *Astronomia nova*, 1609

Gravy

With such a gravy one could eat one's own father.

Ascribed to an unnamed French epicure

Gray

[*See* Hair (Gray).

Gray, Thomas (1716–71)

I would prefer being the author of that poem to the glory of beating the French tomorrow.

JAMES WOLFE: Before the Battle of Quebec, Sept. 13, 1759 (Said of Gray's *Elegy Written in a Country Churchyard*, 1750)

I do not think Gray a first-rate poet. He has not a bold imagination, nor much command of words. His "Elegy in a Churchyard" has a happy selection of images, but I don't like what are called his great things.

SAMUEL JOHNSON: *Boswell's Life,* June 25, 1763

I shall be but a shrimp of an author.

THOMAS GRAY: To Horace Walpole, Feb. 25, 1768, seventeen years after the publication of *An Elegy Written in a Country Churchyard*

Great Britain

Men who content themselves with the semblance of truth, and a display of words, talk much of our obligations to Great Britain for protection. Had she a single eye to our advantage? A nation of shopkeepers are very seldom so disinterested.

SAMUEL ADAMS: Speech on American independence, Philadelphia, Aug. 1, 1776

Great Britain's governing principles are conquest, colonization, commerce, monopoly.

THOMAS JEFFERSON: *Letter to William Carmichael,* 1790

Like a bubble, Great Britain expanded rapidly and then burst. It has since been expanding again. Can we avoid the obvious inference?

J. R. SEELEY: *The Expansion of England,* 1883

[*See also* Britain, British, England.

Greatness

Great men are not always wise.

JOB XXXII, 9, *c.* 325 B.C.

The man of true greatness never loses his child's heart.

MENCIUS: *Discourses,* IV, *c.* 300 B.C.

Mordecai the Jew was next unto King Ahasuerus, and great among the Jews.

ESTHER X, 3, *c.* 125 B.C.

It is the duty of a great man, in a revolutionary age, to punish the guilty, to be kind to the lowest orders, and in all states of fortune to do what is straightforward and honorable.

CICERO: *De officiis,* I, 78 B.C.

Great is he who uses earthenware as if it were silver; no less great is he who uses silver as if it were earthenware.

SENECA: *Epistulæ morales ad Lucilium,* V, *c.* 63

Idleness, women, disorder, a foolish partiality for one's own native place, discontent and timidity are six obstructions to greatness.

The Hitopadesa, II, *c.* 500

Many small make a great.

GEOFFREY CHAUCER: *The Canterbury Tales* (The Parson's Tale), *c.* 1386 (Quoted as a proverb)

Greatness knows itself.

SHAKESPEARE: *I Henry IV,* IV, *c.* 1598

Upon what meat doth this our Cæsar feed,
That he is grown so great?

SHAKESPEARE: *Julius Cæsar,* I, 1599

He doth bestride the narrow world
Like a colossus, and we petty men
Walk under his huge legs.

IBID.

Rightly to be great
Is not to stir without great argument,
But greatly to find quarrel in a straw
When honor's at the stake.

SHAKESPEARE: *Hamlet,* IV, *c.* 1601

Some are born great, some achieve greatness, and some have greatness thrust upon them.

SHAKESPEARE: *Twelfth Night,* II, *c.* 1601

Farewell! a long farewell, to all my greatness!
This is the state of man: today he puts forth
The tender leaves of hope; tomorrow blossoms,
And bears his blushing honors thick upon him:
The third day comes a frost, a killing frost,
And, when he thinks, good easy man, full surely
His greatness is a-ripening, nips his root,
And then he falls, as I do.

SHAKESPEARE and JOHN FLETCHER: *Henry VIII,* III, 1613

Seem not greater than thou art.

ROBERT BURTON: *The Anatomy of Melancholy,* II, 1621

There would be no great ones if there were no little ones.

GEORGE HERBERT: *Outlandish Proverbs,* 1640

Nothing can cover his high fame but Heaven;
No pyramids set off his memories
But the eternal substance of his greatness;
To which I leave him.

JOHN FLETCHER: *The False One,* II, 1647

Great and small have the same accidents, and the same vexations, and the same passions; but one is at the circumference of the wheel, and the other near the center, and thus less agitated by the same movements.

BLAISE PASCAL: *Pensées,* VIII, 1670

The nearer we come to great men the more clearly we see that they are only men. They rarely seem great to their valets.

JEAN DE LA BRUYÈRE: *Caractères,* 1688

How mean must the most exalted potentate upon earth appear to that eye which takes in innumerable orders of blessed spirits, differing in glory and perfection.

GEORGE BERKELEY: *The Guardian,* June 1, 1713

None think the great unhappy, but the great.

EDWARD YOUNG: *Love of Fame,* I, 1728

It is a grand mistake to think of being great without goodness; and I pronounce it as certain that there was never yet a truly great man that was not at the same time truly virtuous.

BENJAMIN FRANKLIN: *The Busy-Body,* Feb. 18, 1729

A great man will not trample upon a worm, nor sneak to an emperor.
THOMAS FULLER: *Gnomologia*, 1732

Great hopes make great men. IBID.

Who noble ends by noble means obtains,
Or, failing, smiles in exile or in chains,
Like good Aurelius let him reign, or bleed
Like Socrates — that man is great indeed.
ALEXANDER POPE: *An Essay on Man*, IV, 1734

Greatness consists in power, pride, insolence, and doing mischief to mankind. . . . A great man and a great rogue are synonymous.
HENRY FIELDING: *Jonathan Wild*, IV, 1743

The merit of great men is not understood but by those who are formed to be such themselves: genius speaks only to genius.
STANISLAUS LESZCYNSKI (KING OF POLAND): *Œuvres du philosophe bienfaisant*, 1763

Great, valiant, pious, good, and clean,
Sublime, contemplative, serene,
Strong, constant, pleasant, wise.
CHRISTOPHER SMART: *A Song to David*, 1763

As a madman is apt to think himself grown suddenly great, so he that grows suddenly great is apt to borrow a little from the madman.
SAMUEL JOHNSON: Memorandum prepared for James Boswell, June 4, 1781

The greatest man is he who forms the taste of a nation; the next greatest is he who corrupts it.
Ascribed to JOSHUA REYNOLDS (1723–92)

No man who wanted to be a great man ever was a great man.
JOHN HUNTER (1728–93)

The defects of great men are the consolation of dunces.
ISAAC D'ISRAELI: *Essay on the Literary Character*, 1795

He that is truly wise and great
Lives both too early and too late.
ENGLISH PROVERB, not recorded before the XIX century

Homer and Virgil and Milton, and Locke and Bacon and Newton, are as great as the hills and the streams; and endure till Heaven and earth shall pass away, and the whole fabric of nature is shaken into dissolution and eternal ashes.
SYDNEY SMITH: *Lectures on Moral Philosophy*, 1804

Subtract from a great man all that he owes to opportunity, and all that he owes to chance; all that he has gained by the wisdom of his friends, and by the folly of his enemies; and our Brobdignag will often become a Lilliputian. C. C. COLTON: *Lacon*, 1820

He who comes up to his own idea of greatness must always have had a very low standard of it in his mind.
WILLIAM HAZLITT: *Table-Talk*, 1824

The spirit of the age is the very thing that a great man changes.
BENJAMIN DISRAELI: *The Infernal Marriage*, IX, 1834

The world knows nothing of its greatest men.
HENRY TAYLOR: *Philip Van Artevelde*, I, 1834

Not he is great who can alter matter, but he who can alter my state of mind.
R. W. EMERSON: *The American Scholar*, 1837

The greatest man is he who chooses the right with invincible resolution, who resists the sorest temptations from within and without, who bears the heaviest burdens cheerfully, who is calmest in storms and most fearless under menace and frowns, whose reliance on truth, on virtue, on God, is most unfaltering; and is this a greatness which is apt to make a show, or which is most likely to abound in conspicuous station?
W. E. CHANNING: *Self-Culture*, 1838

I console myself in the poverty of my thoughts, in the paucity of great men, in the malignity and dullness of the nations, by seeing what the prolific soul could beget on actual nature; — seeing that Plato was, and Shakespeare, and Milton, — three irrefragable facts.
R. W. EMERSON: *Literary Ethics*, 1838

We all love great men; love, venerate and bow down submissive before great men: nay, can we honestly bow down to anything else?
THOMAS CARLYLE: *Heroes and Hero-Worship*, I, 1840 (Lecture in London, May 5)

He fought a thousand glorious wars,
And more than half the world was his,
And somewhere, now, in yonder stars,
Can tell, mayhap, what greatness is.
W. M. THACKERAY: *The Chronicle of the Drum*, 1840

The great man is not convulsible or tormentable; events pass over him without much impression. R. W. EMERSON: *Circles*, 1841

Who can tell if Washington be a great man, or no? Who can tell if Franklin be? Yes, or any but the twelve, or six, or three great gods of fame?
R. W. EMERSON: *Nominalist and Realist*, 1841

Every great man is a unique.
R. W. EMERSON: *Self-Reliance*, 1841

Great men serve us as insurrections do in bad governments.
R. W. EMERSON: *Character*, 1844

The great are great only because we are on our knees. Let us rise!
MAX STIRNER: *The Ego and His Own,* 1845

Every great man is always being helped by everybody, for his gift is to get good out of all things and all persons.
JOHN RUSKIN: *Modern Painters,* II, 1846

That individuals have soared above the plane of their race is scarcely to be questioned; but, in looking back through history for traces of their existence we should pass over all biographies of "the good and the great," while we search carefully the slight records of wretches who died in prison, in Bedlam, or upon the gallows.
E. A. POE: *Marginalia,* 1844–49

He is great who . . . never reminds us of others.
R. W. EMERSON: *Representative Men,* I, 1850

Great men are more distinguished by range and extent than by originality.
R. W. EMERSON: *Representative Men,* V

Great minds are like eagles, and build their nest in some lofty solitude.
ARTHUR SCHOPENHAUER: *Our Relation to Others,* 1851

All things that great men do are well done.
H. G. BOHN: *Handbook of Proverbs,* 1855

Great minds are easy in prosperity, and quiet in adversity. IBID.

A great man,
Leaves clean work behind him, and requires
No sweeper up of the chips.
E. B. BROWNING: *Aurora Leigh,* V, 1857

All great men come out of the middle classes.
R. W. EMERSON: *Considerations By The Way,* 1860

The great man is the man who does a thing for the first time.
ALEXANDER SMITH: *Dreamthorp,* VIII, 1863

Great men are the real men: in them nature has succeeded.
H. F. AMIEL: *Journal,* Aug. 13, 1865

The hero is not fed on sweets,
Daily his own heart he eats;
Chambers of the great are jails,
And head-winds right for royal sails.
R. W. EMERSON: *Heroism,* 1867

Greatness is a spiritual condition worthy to excite love, interest, and admiration; and the outward proof of possessing greatness is that we excite love, interest, and admiration.
MATTHEW ARNOLD: *Culture and Anarchy,* I, 1869

Great men are rarely isolated mountain peaks; they are the summits of ranges.
T. W. HIGGINSON: *Atlantic Essays,* 1871

A great man is made up of qualities that meet or make great occasions.
J. R. LOWELL: *My Study Windows,* 1871

A great man is only an actor playing out his own ideal.
F. W. NIETZSCHE: *Beyond Good and Evil,* 1886

Great men, like great ages, are explosive material.
F. W. NIETZSCHE: *The Twilight of the Idols,* 1889

After all, Attila was a greater man than John Bright. He has left a greater name in history.
OTTO VON BISMARCK (1815–98)

If a great man could make us understand him we should hang him.
GEORGE BERNARD SHAW: *Maxims for Revolutionists,* 1903

If you would be accounted great by your contemporaries, be not too much greater than they.
AMBROSE BIERCE: *Collected Works,* VIII, 1911

Buildings are measured by their shadows, and great men by their calumniators.
CHINESE PROVERB

It is dangerous to eat cherries with the great; they throw the stones at your head.
DANISH PROVERB

It is permissible for great men to joke with saints. GERMAN PROVERB

[*See also* Fault, Good, Inspiration.

Greece

Greece appears to me to be the fountain of knowledge; Rome of elegance.
SAMUEL JOHNSON: *Boswell's Life,* April 29, 1778

Fair Greece! sad relic of departed worth!
Immortal, though no more! though fallen, great!
BYRON: *Childe Harold,* II, 1812

The isles of Greece, the isles of Greece!
Where burning Sappho loved and sung,
Eternal Summer gilds them yet,
But all except their sun is set.
BYRON: *Don Juan,* III, 1821

We are all Greeks. Our laws, our literature, our religion, our arts have their roots in Greece.
P. B. SHELLEY: *Hellas,* pref., 1821

The glory that was Greece.
E. A. POE: To Helen, 1836 (Southern Literary Messenger, March)

Greed

They are greedy dogs which can never have enough.
ISAIAH LVI, 11, *c.* 700 B.C.

Greedy folks have long arms.
JAMES KELLY: *Complete Collection of Scottish Proverbs,* 1721

Need makes greed. IBID.

The greedy man and the gileynour are soon agreed. IBID. (*Gileynour*=swindler)

[*See also* Church, Crime, Evil, Laissez-faire.

Greek

Never trust a Greek.
EURIPIDES: *Iphigenia in Aulis, c.* 410 B.C.

I fear the Greeks, even when they bring gifts. (Timeo Danaos et dona ferentes.)
VIRGIL: *Æneid,* II, 19 B.C.

There is no difference between the Jew and the Greek. ROMANS X, 12, *c.* 55

Among the Greeks every man is an actor. Do you smile? Then his sides burst with laughter. Does he spy a tear in a friend's eye? Then he melts in tears, though in reality he feels no grief. If at mid-Winter you ask for a little fire, he calls for his greatcoat. If you say I am hot, he breaks into a sweat.
JUVENAL: *Satires,* III, *c.* 110

When Greeks joined Greeks, then was the tug of war!
NATHANIEL LEE: *The Rival Queens,* IV, 1677 (Usually, "When Greek meets Greek, then comes the tug of war")

Demosthenes . . . spoke to an assembly of brutes; to a barbarous people.
SAMUEL JOHNSON: *Boswell's Life,* 1773

From what we know of the Greeks, it does not appear that they knew or studied any language but their own, and this was one cause of their becoming so learned; it afforded them more time to apply themselves to better studies.
THOMAS PAINE: *The Age of Reason,* I, 1794

I like the Greeks, who are plausible rascals — with all the Turkish vices, without their courage.
BYRON: *Letter to Henry Drury,* May 3, 1810

I hate all Greeks.
HEINRICH HEINE: *Die Nordsee,* II, 1826

The polished Greeks, the world's masters in the delights of language, and in range of thought, . . . were little more than splendid savages.
CHARLES SUMNER: Speech at Boston, July 4, 1845

The Grecian individual is superior to the modern; but the Grecian whole is inferior.
THOMAS DE QUINCEY: *Superficial Knowledge, c.* 1847

Perhaps the Greek mind may be best imagined by taking, as its groundwork, that of a good, conscientious, but illiterate, Scotch Presbyterian Border farmer of a century or two back.
JOHN RUSKIN: *Modern Painters,* IV, 1856

There is abundant evidence that the Greeks were of old, as their descendants and successors still are, one of the most excitable of the races of mankind.
J. S. MILL: *The Subjection of Women,* III, 1869

If an ancient Greek were to come to life now he would be found far oftener at the circus than at the theatre.
OSCAR WILDE: *London Models,* 1889 (English Illustrated Magazine, Jan.)

After shaking hands with a Greek count your fingers. ALBANIAN PROVERB

Beware of Greeks bearing gifts.
LATIN PROVERB, apparently derived from VIRGIL, *ante,* 19 B.C.

Greeks tell the truth, but only once a year.
RUSSIAN PROVERB

[*See also* Armenian, Character (National), Cheating, French, Gods.

Greek Language

It is Greek; it can't be read. (Graecum est; non potest legi.) MEDIEVAL LATIN SAYING

It was Greek to me.
SHAKESPEARE: *Julius Cæsar,* I, 1599

The language of the Holy Ghost.
ROBERT SOUTH: *Sermons,* 1679

I knew this was heathen Greek to them.
JOHN WESLEY: *Journal,* July 1, 1769

I will say nothing of Greek; I should irritate myself too much.
HEINRICH HEINE: *Reisebilder,* II, 1826

It is hardly possible to conceive a language more perfect than the Greek.
S. T. COLERIDGE: *Table-Talk,* July 7, 1832

It is strange that God learned Greek when He desired to turn author — and stranger that He did not learn it better.
F. W. NIETZSCHE: *Beyond Good and Evil,* 1886

[*See also* Education, Language, Linguist, Unintelligible.

Greek Literature

The tragedies of the Greeks seem to me to be the work of schoolboys when put beside the sublime scenes of Corneille and the perfect tragedies of Racine.
VOLTAIRE: *Letter to Horace Walpole,* July 15, 1768

[*See also* Latin Literature.

Greeley, Horace (1811–72)

A self-made man who worships his creator.
HENRY CLAPP, *c.* 1858

Mr. Greeley would be the greatest journalist in America if he did not aim to be one of the leading politicians of America.
JOHN RUSSELL YOUNG, *c.* 1861

Green

Green wood makes a hot fire.
ENGLISH PROVERB, traced by Apperson to 1477

All thing is gay that is green.
JOHN HEYWOOD: *Proverbs,* 1546

No white nor red was ever seen
So amorous as this lovely green.
ANDREW MARVELL: *Thoughts in a Garden, c.* 1650

[*See also* Blue, Color, Wedding.

Greenwood

[*See* Tree.

Greeting

This is General Lee, I presume?
The spokesman of a women's committee of welcome: To General R. E. Lee when he entered Maryland at Williamsport, June 25, 1863

Dr. Livingston, I presume?
H. M. STANLEY: To Livingston at Ujiji, Lake Tanganyika, Nov. 10, 1871

Gregariousness

[*See* Author.

Grief

Time will soften thy grief; he that is dead is nothing.
EURIPIDES: *Alcestis,* 438 B.C.

Grief is a tree that has tears for its fruit.
PHILEMON: *Fragment, c.* 300 B.C.

All his days are sorrows, and his travail grief.
ECCLESIASTES II, 23, *c.* 200 B.C.

My life is spent with grief, and my years with sighing.
PSALMS XXXI, 10, *c.* 150 B.C.

Grief conquers the unconquered man.
OVID: *Metamorphoses,* XIII, *c.* 5

That is a light grief which can take counsel.
SENECA: *Medea,* I, *c.* 60

Grief and death were born of sin, and devour sin.
ST. JOHN CHRYSOSTOM: *Homilies* V, *c.* 388

Time and thinking tame the strongest grief.
ENGLISH PROVERB, borrowed from the Latin, and familiar in various forms since the XIV century

There is no greater grief than, in misery, to recall happier times.
DANTE: *Inferno,* V, *c.* 1320

The revealing of griefs is, as it were, a renewing of sorrow.
JOHN LYLY: *Endymion,* III, 1591

Grief softens the mind
And makes it fearful and degenerate.
SHAKESPEARE: *II Henry VI,* IV, *c.* 1591

Mighty griefs are dumb.
SAMUEL DANIEL: *The Complaynt of Rosamond,* 1592

Grief best is pleased with grief's society.
SHAKESPEARE: *The Rape of Lucrece,* 1594

True grief is fond and testy as a child. IBID.

Grief fills the room up of my absent child,
Lies in his bed, walks up and down with me,
Puts on his pretty looks, repeats his words,
Remembers me of all his gracious parts,
Stuffs out his vacant garments with his form:
Then have I reason to be fond of grief.
SHAKESPEARE: *King John,* III, *c.* 1596

Each substance of a grief hath twenty shadows.
SHAKESPEARE: *Richard II,* II, *c.* 1596

My grief lies all within;
And these external manners of laments
Are merely shadows to the unseen grief
That swells with silence in the tortur'd soul.
SHAKESPEARE: *Richard II,* IV

One pain is lessen'd by another's anguish;
One desperate grief cures with another's languish.
SHAKESPEARE: *Romeo and Juliet,* I, *c.* 1596

Some grief shows much of love;
But much of grief shows still some want of wit.
SHAKESPEARE: *Romeo and Juliet,* III

Every one can master a grief but he that has it.
SHAKESPEARE: *Much Ado About Nothing,* III, *c.* 1599

The grief is fine, full, perfect, that I taste.
SHAKESPEARE: *Troilus and Cressida,* IV, *c.* 1601

My particular grief
Is of so flood-gate and o'erbearing nature
That it engluts and swallows other sorrows.
SHAKESPEARE: *Othello,* I, 1604

Give sorrow words; the grief that does not speak
Whispers the o'er-fraught heart and bids it break.
SHAKESPEARE: *Macbeth,* IV, *c.* 1605

Some griefs are medicinable.
SHAKESPEARE: *Cymbeline,* III, *c.* 1609

Alas, I am nothing but a multitude
Of walking griefs.
BEAUMONT and FLETCHER: *The Maid's Tragedy,* III, 1611

What's gone and what's past help
Should be past grief.
SHAKESPEARE: *The Winter's Tale,* III, 1611

I ran from grief; grief ran and overtook me.
FRANCIS QUARLES: *Emblems,* II, 1635

Never grieve for that you cannot help.
JOHN CLARKE: *Parœmiologia Anglo-Latina,* 1639

All griefs with bread are less.
GEORGE HERBERT: *Outlandish Proverbs,* 1640

Do you wish to be fed with milk and pap instead of solid food? Have you not teeth to masticate bread, even the bitter bread of grief?
Ascribed to ST. FRANCIS DE SALES (1567–1622) in J. P. CAMUS: *L'esprit de Saint François de Sales,* 1641

Nothing speaks our grief so well
As to speak nothing.
RICHARD CRASHAW: *On the Death of Mr. Herrys,* 1646

Consider sorrows, how they are aright;
Grief, if't be great, 'tis short; if long, 'tis light.
ROBERT HERRICK: *Hesperides,* 1648

The grief of the head is the grief of griefs.
JAMES HOWELL: *Proverbs,* 1659

No day passeth without some grief.
JOHN RAY: *English Proverbs,* 1670

Grief is so far from retrieving a loss that it makes it greater; but the way to lessen it is by a comparison with others' losses.
WILLIAM WYCHERLEY: *Love in a Wood,* v, 1673

People will pretend to grieve more than they really do, and that takes off from their true grief.
JONATHAN SWIFT: *Letter to Mrs. Dingley,* Jan. 14, 1712

Grief has a natural eloquence belonging to it, and breaks out in more moving sentiments than can be supplied by the finest imagination.
JOSEPH ADDISON: *The Spectator,* June 5, 1712

New grief awakens the old.
THOMAS FULLER: *Gnomologia,* 1732

The silent manliness of grief.
OLIVER GOLDSMITH: *The Deserted Village,* 1770

There is a solemn luxury in grief.
WILLIAM MASON: *The English Garden,* 1772

All grief for what cannot in the course of nature be helped soon wears away.
SAMUEL JOHNSON: *Boswell's Life,* Sept. 14, 1777

Grief is itself a medicine.
WILLIAM COWPER: *Charity,* 1782

A grief without a pang, void, dark and drear,
A stifled, drowsy, unimpassioned grief,
Which finds no natural outlet, no relief,
In word, or sigh, or tear.
S. T. COLERIDGE: *Dejection,* 1802

No more will I count over, link by link,
My chain of grief.
JOHN KEATS: *Endymion,* I, 1818

The ocean has her ebbings — so has grief.
THOMAS CAMPBELL: *Theodric,* 1824

Grief is the agony of an instant: the indulgence of grief the blunder of a life.
BENJAMIN DISRAELI: *Vivian Grey,* VI, 1827

There is no grief like the grief which does not speak.
H. W. LONGFELLOW: *Hyperion,* II, 1839

There is a calm, a holy feeling,
Vulgar minds can never know,
O'er the bosom softly stealing, —
Chasten'd grief, delicious woe.
R. H. BARHAM: *The Ingoldsby Legends,* I, 1840

No man ever stated his griefs as lightly as he might. Allow for exaggeration in the most patient and sorely ridden hack that ever was driven.
R. W. EMERSON: *Spiritual Laws,* 1841

The only cure for grief is action.
G. H. LEWES: *The Spanish Drama,* II, 1846

We hear the rain fall, but not the snow. Bitter grief is loud, calm grief is silent.
BERTHOLD AUERBACH: *Auf der Höhe,* 1865

Before the beginning of years
There came to the making of man
Time with a gift of tears,
Grief with a glass that ran.
A. C. SWINBURNE: *Atalanta in Calydon,* 1865

Those who have known grief seldom seem sad.
BENJAMIN DISRAELI: *Endymion,* IV, 1880

The more you grieve the greater your loss.
PERSIAN PROVERB

Compare your griefs with other men's and they will seem less.
SPANISH PROVERB

Concealed grief has no remedy.
TURKISH PROVERB

[*See also* Age (Old), Children, Happiness, Hope, Joy, Proverb, Sigh, Sorrow, Tears, Woe.

Grindstone

To hold one's nose to the grindstone.
ENGLISH PHRASE, traced by the New English Dictionary to 1532

Grotesque

I believe that there is no test of greatness in periods, nations, or men, more sure than the development, among them or in them, of a noble grotesque, and no test of comparative smallness or limitation, of one kind or another, more sure than the absence of grotesque invention, or incapability of understanding it.
JOHN RUSKIN: *Stones of Venice,* III, 1853

Growed

I 'spect I grow'd. Don't think nobody ever made me. HARRIET BEECHER STOWE: Topsy, in *Uncle Tom's Cabin*, XX, 1852

Grudge

The high-minded man does not bear grudges, for it is not the mark of a great soul to remember injuries, but to forget them.
ARISTOTLE: *The Nicomachean Ethics*, IV, *c.* 340 B.C.

Grudge not one against another.
JAMES V, 9, *c.* 60

If I can catch him once upon the hip,
I will feed fat the ancient grudge I bear him.
SHAKESPEARE: *The Merchant of Venice*, I, *c.* 1597

A strong grudge does not remain secret long.
WELSH PROVERB

[*See also* Friend.

Grumbling

Be not a grumbler, for this leads to blasphemy.
The Didache, or Teaching of the Twelve Apostles, *c.* 135

Grundy, Mrs.

What will Mrs. Grundy say?
THOMAS MORTON: *Speed the Plough*, I, 1800

Guard, Old

[*See* Surrender.

Guess

Once I guessed right,
And I got credit by't;
Thrice I guessed wrong,
And I kept my credit on.
Author unidentified (Quoted by JONATHAN SWIFT, 1710)

[*See also* Discovery, Prophet.

Guest

Withdraw thy foot from thy neighbor's house, lest he be weary of thee, and hate thee.
PROVERBS XXV, 17, *c.* 350 B.C.

No one can be so welcome a guest that he will not annoy his host after three days.
PLAUTUS: *Miles Gloriosus*, III, 205 B.C.

Whether he who is come to thy house be of the highest or of the lowest rank, he is to be treated with respect; for of all men thy guest is the superior. *The Hitopadesa*, I, *c.* 500

Every guest who comes to the monastery shall be received as if he were Christ Himself.
THE RULE OF ST. BENEDICT, *c.* 529

An unbidden guest knoweth not where to sit.
JOHN HEYWOOD: *Proverbs*, 1546

Fish and guests in three days are stale.
JOHN LYLY: *Euphues*, 1579 (Usually encountered in the form "Fish and company stink in three days." Cf. PLAUTUS, *ante*, 205 B.C.)

Unbidden guests
Are often welcomest when they are gone.
SHAKESPEARE: *II Henry VI*, II, *c.* 1591

Here's our chief guest,
If he had been forgotten,
It had been as a gap in our great feast.
SHAKESPEARE: *Macbeth*, III, *c.* 1605

See, your guests approach:
Address yourself to entertain them sprightly,
And let's be red with mirth.
SHAKESPEARE: *The Winter's Tale*, IV, *c.* 1611

The greater the kindness of my host, the greater my anxiety not to impose on it.
VOLTAIRE: *Letter to Baron de Bretuil*, Dec., 1723

Welcome the coming, speed the parting guest.
ALEXANDER POPE: Tr. of HOMER: *Odyssey* (*c.* 800 B.C.), XV, 1726

A constant guest is never welcome.
THOMAS FULLER: *Gnomologia*, 1732

It is an ill guest that never drinks to his hostess.
IBID.

After three days men grow weary of a wench, a guest, and rainy weather.
BENJAMIN FRANKLIN: *Poor Richard's Almanac*, 1733

The merry but unlooked for guest
Full often proves to be the best.
WILLIAM COMBE: *Dr. Syntax in Search of the Picturesque*, XXIX, 1809

To the house of a friend if you're pleased to retire,
You must all things admit, you must all things admire;
You must pay with observance the price of your treat,
You must eat what is praised, and must praise what you eat.
GEORGE CRABBE: *The Borough*, XI, 1810

Every guest hates the others, and the host hates them all. ALBANIAN PROVERB

When the ass was invited to a wedding he said: They must need some more wood and water.
BOSNIAN PROVERB

Better slight a guest than starve him.
CHINESE PROVERB

The host is happy when the guest has gone.
IBID.

A guest in the house: God in the house.
CZECH PROVERB

The guest of the hostess gets better fare than the guest of the host. FINNISH PROVERB

The eye should be blind in the house of another. IRISH PROVERB

Only a dog barks guests away from his own door. MOROCCAN PROVERB

The guest is subject to the rule of the host.
IBID.

The master of the house is the servant of the guest.
PERSIAN PROVERB

Hail, guest, we ask not what thou art;
If friend, we greet thee, hand and heart;
If stranger, such no longer be;
If foe, our love shall conquer thee.
WELSH RHYME

[*See also* Visiting.

Guide

My guide, philosopher, and friend.
ALEXANDER POPE: *An Essay on Man*, IV, 1734 (Also in *The First Epistle of the First Book of Horace*, 1735)

O Lord direct us. (Domine dirige nos.)
MOTTO OF THE CITY OF LONDON

Guillotine

He that invented the maiden first hanselled it.
JAMES KELLY: *Complete Collection of Scottish Proverbs*, 1721 (*Maiden*=an early form of guillotine; *hansel*=to use for the first time)

My machine will take off a head in a twinkling, and the victim will feel nothing but a sense of refreshing coolness. We cannot make too much haste, gentlemen, to allow the nation to enjoy this advantage.
J. I. GUILLOTIN: To the French National Assembly, 1789

In 1794 the guillotine appeared to be the only institution left in France.
ALPHONSE DE LAMARTINE: *Historie des Girondins*, 1847

A machine which makes a Frenchman shrug his shoulders with good reason.
AMBROSE BIERCE: *The Devil's Dictionary*, 1906

Guilt

Guilt is present in the hesitation, even though the deed be not committed.
CICERO: *De officiis*, III, 78 B.C.

Alas! how difficult it is not to betray guilt by our countenance!
OVID: *Metamorphoses*, II, *c.* 5

Men's minds are very ingenious in palliating guilt in themselves.
LIVY: *History of Rome*, XXVIII, *c.* 10

Whosoever shall keep the whole law, and yet offend in one point, he is guilty of all.
JAMES II, 10, *c.* 60

He is not guilty who did not will guilt.
SENECA: *Hercules Oetaeus*, *c.* 60

Nobody becomes guilty by fate.
SENECA: *Oedipus*, *c.* 60

It is proper for the guilty to tremble.
SENECA: *Epistulæ morales ad Lucilium*, *c.* 63

By the verdict of his own breast no guilty man is ever acquitted.
JUVENAL: *Satires*, XIII, *c.* 125

A guilty conscience needs no accuser.
ENGLISH PROVERB, traced by Apperson to the XVI century

Suspicion always haunts the guilty mind;
The thief doth fear each bush an officer.
SHAKESPEARE: *III Henry VI*, V, *c.* 1591

Use every man after his desert, and who should
'Scape whipping!
SHAKESPEARE: *Hamlet*, II, *c.* 1601

Guilt is the source of sorrow, 'tis the fiend,
Th' avenging fiend, that follows us behind
With whips and stings.
NICHOLAS ROWE: *The Fair Penitent*, III, 1703

The guilty is he who merely meditates a crime.
VITTORIO ALFIERI: *Antigone*, II, 1785

Guilt was never a rational thing; it distorts all the faculties of the human mind, it perverts them, it leaves a man no longer in the free use of his reason, it puts him into confusion.
EDMUND BURKE: Speech in the House of Commons, Feb. 17, 1788

God hath yoked to guilt
Her pale tormentor, misery.
W. C. BRYANT: *Inscription for the Entrance to a Wood*, 1817

Guilt was my grim chamberlain,
That lighted me to bed,
And drew my midnight curtains round
With fingers bloody red.
THOMAS HOOD: *Eugene Aram*, 1829

Not guilty — but don't do it again.
AMERICAN SAYING

[*See also* Crime, Fear, Innocence, Judge, Justice, Punishment.

Guitar

A guitar has moonlight in it.
JAMES M. CAIN: *Serenade*, IX, 1937

Guiteau, Charles J. (?–1882)

One, two, three, four, five, six, seven;
All good children go to Heaven;
All the rest go below
To keep company with Guiteau.
AMERICAN CHILDREN'S RHYME, 1882 (Guiteau shot James A. Garfield July 2, 1881, and was hanged June 30, 1882)

Gullet

[*See* Eating.

Gun

The men behind the guns.
J. J. ROONEY: Title of a poem, 1898

One gun on land is worth ten at sea.
FRENCH MILITARY MAXIM

[*See also* Arms, Artillery, Cannon, Club, Shooting.

Gustavus Adolphus II of Sweden (1594–1632)

Consider the great Gustavus Adolphus! In eighteen months he won one battle, lost a second, and was killed in the third. His fame was won at a cheap rate.

NAPOLEON I: To Gaspard Gourgaud at St. Helena, 1815–1818

H

Habeas Corpus

The privilege of the writ of habeas corpus shall not be suspended, unless when in cases of rebellion or invasion the public safety may require it.

CONSTITUTION OF THE UNITED STATES, Art. I, 1789

The most stringent curb that ever legislation imposed on tyranny.

T. B. MACAULAY: *History of England,* I, 1848

Habit

The nature of men is always the same; it is their habits that separate them.

CONFUCIUS: *Analects,* I, *c.* 500 B.C.

Habit is a sort of second nature.

CICERO: *De finibus,* V, *c.* 50 B.C.

Nothing is more powerful than habit.

OVID: *Ars amatoria,* II, *c.* 2 B.C.

Habit makes the custom.

OVID: *Metamorphoses,* II, *c.* 5

Nothing is in reality either pleasant or unpleasant by nature; but all things become so through habit.

EPICTETUS: *Encheiridion, c.* 110

Habit is second nature.

ENGLISH PROVERB, borrowed from the Latin of CICERO, *ante, c.* 50 B.C., and traced to JOHN GOWER: *Confessio Amantis, c.* 1390

Habit is overcome by habit.

THOMAS À KEMPIS: *Imitation of Christ,* I, *c.* 1420

How use doth breed a habit in a man!

SHAKESPEARE: *Two Gentlemen of Verona,* V, *c.* 1595

Refrain tonight,
And that shall lend a kind of easiness
To the next abstinence: the next more easy;
For use almost can change the stamp of nature.

SHAKESPEARE: *Hamlet,* III, *c.* 1601

Habits are the daughters of action, but then they nurse their mother, and produce daughters after her image, but far more beautiful and prosperous.

JEREMY TAYLOR: *Twenty-five Sermons,* 1653

We are never so ridiculous from the habits we have as from the habits that we affect to have.

LA ROCHEFOUCAULD: *Maxims,* 1665

Ill habits gather by unseen degrees, —
As brooks make rivers, rivers run to seas.

JOHN DRYDEN: Tr. of OVID: *Metamorphoses* (*c.* 5), *c.* 1695

'Tis nothing when you are used to it, as the eels said when they were being skinned alive.

ENGLISH SAYING, not recorded before the XIX century

Habit with him was all the test of truth;
"It must be right: I've done it from my youth."

GEORGE CRABBE: *The Borough,* III, 1810

The capacity for forming habits is the kindest device that God uses for the preservation of His creatures.

ERNST VON FEUCHTERSLEBEN: *Zur Diätetik der Seele,* I, 1838

Whether people are happy or miserable, poor or prosperous, still we sweep the stairs of a Saturday.

JOHN RUSKIN: *Modern Painters,* V, 1860

For the ordinary business of life an ounce of habit is worth a pound of intellect.

THOMAS B. REED: Speech at Bowdoin College, Maine, July 25, 1902

Habit is a shirt made of iron.

CZECH PROVERB

Habit is all-powerful, even in love.

FRENCH PROVERB

Man is an animal of habit. (Der Mensch ist ein Gewohnheitstier.)

GERMAN PROVERB

If the peasant should become a king, he would not remove his basket from his hand.

HEBREW PROVERB

He who changes his habits will soon be dead.

PORTUGUESE PROVERB

Habits are at first cobwebs, then cables.

SPANISH PROVERB

[*See also* Cause and Effect, Custom, Motive.

Hail

There fell upon men a great hail out of heaven, every stone about the weight of a talent: the men blasphemed God because of the plague of the hail.

REVELATION XVI, 21, *c.* 95

Hail brings frost i' th' tail.

JOHN RAY: *English Proverbs,* 1670

Hail Mary

The angel being come in, said unto her: Hail, full of grace, the Lord is with thee: Blessed art thou among women.

LUKE I, 28, *c.* 75 (The Douay Version)

Hair

A large head of hair makes the handsome more graceful and the ugly more terrible.
Ascribed to LYCURGUS, *c.* 850 B.C.

The hair of my flesh stood up.
JOB IV, 15, *c.* 325 B.C.

Doth not even nature itself teach you that if a man have long hair it is a shame unto him?
I CORINTHIANS XI, 14, *c.* 55

If a woman have long hair it is a glory to her, for her hair is given her for a covering.
I CORINTHIANS XI, 15

The very hairs of your head are all numbered.
MATTHEW X, 30, *c.* 75

Of what service to your salvation is all the anxious care you spend in arraying your hair? TERTULLIAN: *Women's Dress, c.* 220

A hair of the dog that bit him.
ENGLISH PHRASE, traced by Smith to 1546

The hair is the finest ornament women have. Of old, virgins used to wear it loose, except when they were in mourning. I like women to let their hair fall down their back; 'tis a most agreeable sight.
MARTIN LUTHER: *Table-Talk,* DCCLI, 1569

More hair than wit.
SHAKESPEARE: *The Comedy of Errors,* II, 1593

Her sunny locks
Hang on her temples like a golden fleece.
SHAKESPEARE: *The Merchant of Venice,* I, *c.* 1597

And each particular hair to stand on end,
Like quills upon the fretful porpentine.
SHAKESPEARE: *Hamlet,* I, *c.* 1601
(*Porpentine*=porcupine)

Do but look on her hair; it is bright
As love's star when it riseth.
BEN JONSON: *The Devil Is an Ass,* 1616

Nature herself abhors to see a woman shorn or polled; a woman with cut hair is a filthy spectacle, and much like a monster.
WILLIAM PRYNNE: *Histriomastix,* 1632

When I lie tangled in her hair
And fettered with her eye.
RICHARD LOVELACE: *To Althea from Prison,* 1642

One hair of a woman can draw more than a hundred pair of oxen.
JAMES HOWELL: *Familiar Letters,* II, 1647

Fair tresses man's imperial race insnare,
And beauty draws us with a single hair.
ALEXANDER POPE: *The Rape of the Lock,* II, 1712

Kissing her hair I sat against her feet,
Wove and unwove it, wound and found it sweet;
Made fast therewith her hands, drew down her eyes,
Deep as deep flowers and dreamy like dim skies;
With her own tresses bound and found her fair,
Kissing her hair.
A. C. SWINBURNE: *Rondel,* 1866

Her hair had smells of all the sunburned South.
A. C. SWINBURNE: *Laus Veneris,* 1866

Don't comb your hair at night; it will make you forgetful. AMERICAN NEGRO PROVERB

Long hair, little sense. FRENCH PROVERB

The beauty of the heavens is the stars; the beauty of women is their hair.
ITALIAN PROVERB

[*See also* Brow, Maiden, Shadow.

Hair, Black

His locks are bushy, and black as a raven.
SOLOMON'S SONG, V, 11, *c.* 200 B.C.

[*See also* Beard.

Haircomb

A scabbed head doth never love the comb.
JOHN WODROEPHE: *Spared Hours,* 1623

Hair, Dark

There is a prevalence of dark hair among men of atrabilious and sour temperament.
FRANCIS GALTON: *Inquiries Into Human Faculty,* 1883

Hair, Gray

Then shall ye bring down my gray hairs with sorrow to the grave.
GENESIS XLII, 38, *c.* 700 B.C. (Cf. XLIV, 31)

The hoary head is a crown of glory.
PROVERBS XVI, 31, *c.* 350 B.C.

The beauty of old men is the gray head.
PROVERBS XX, 29

Now also when I am old and gray-headed, O God, forsake me not.
PSALMS LXXI, 18, *c.* 150 B.C.

Gray hairs are death's blossoms.
ENGLISH PROVERB, traced by Apperson to 1588

Hold off! Unhand me, gray-beard loon!
S. T. COLERIDGE: *The Ancient Mariner,* 1798

Thy silver locks, once auburn bright,
Are still more lively in my sight
Than golden beams of orient light.
WILLIAM COWPER: To Mary, 1793

"Who touches a hair of yon gray head
Dies like a dog! March on!" he said.
J. G. WHITTIER: *Barbara Frietchie,* 1863

There is a sinking of the soul,
A sudden shock of age and care;
As one who in a mirror sees
The first gray streaking of his hair.
R. H. NEWELL (ORPHEUS C. KERR): *The Man of Feeling,* 1864

Gray hair is a sign of age, not of wisdom.
GREEK PROVERB

If you pull out a gray hair seven will come to its funeral.
PENNSYLVANIA GERMAN PROVERB

[*See also* Bald, Fox, Lunatic, Marriage.

Hair, Red

A red-headed man will make a good stallion.
JOHN RAY: *English Proverbs,* 1670

There was never a saint with red hair.
RUSSIAN PROVERB

[*See also* Beard, Cat.

Hair, White

These hairs now blossom whiter than the swan.
ARISTOPHANES: *The Wasps,* 422 B.C.

His head and his hairs were white like wool, as white as snow. REVELATION I, 14, *c.* 95

How ill white hairs become a fool and jester!
SHAKESPEARE: *II Henry IV,* V, *c.* 1597

A fool's hair never turns white.
FRENCH PROVERB

[*See also* Age (Old), Bald, Beard.

Hairy

Jacob said to Rebekah his mother, Behold, Esau my brother is a hairy man, and I am a smooth man. GENESIS XXVII, 11, *c.* 700 B.C.

A hairy body and arms indicate a manly soul.
JUVENAL: *Satires,* II, *c.* 110

A hairy man's a geary man, but a hairy wife's a witch.
SCOTTISH PROVERB (*Geary*=wealthy)

[*See also* Leather.

Halcyon

I remembered the halcyon days.
GEORGE JOYCE: *Exposition of Daniel,* 1545

Half

They are fools who know not that the half is better than the whole.
HESIOD: *Works and Days, c.* 700 B.C.

Better is half a loaf than no bread.
JOHN HEYWOOD: *Proverbs,* 1546

My dear, my better half.
PHILIP SIDNEY: *Arcadia,* III, 1590 (Meaning, of course, wife)

Half a tale is enough to a wise man.
DAVID FERGUSSON: *Scottish Proverbs,* 1641

Never do things by halves.
ENGLISH PROVERB, not recorded before the XVIII century

Half the truth is often a great lie.
BENJAMIN FRANKLIN: *Poor Richard's Almanac,* 1758

[*See also* Gods.

Halo

[*See* Moon.

Hamilton, Alexander (1757–1804)

I consider Napoleon, Fox, and Hamilton the three greatest men of our epoch, and I do not hesitate to award first place to Hamilton.
Ascribed to C. M. TALLEYRAND, 1794

Hamilton was honest as a man, but, as a politician, believed in the necessity of either force or corruption to govern men.
THOMAS JEFFERSON: *Letter to Benjamin Rush,* Jan., 1811

The bastard brat of a Scotch peddler.
Ascribed to JOHN ADAMS (1735–1826)

He smote the rock of the national resources, and abundant streams of revenue gushed forth. He touched the dead corpse of public credit, and it sprung upon its feet.
DANIEL WEBSTER: Speech in the Senate, March 10, 1831

Hamlet

I saw "Hamlet, Prince of Denmark" played, but now the old plays begin to disgust this refined age.
JOHN EVELYN: *Diary,* Nov. 26, 1661

[*See also* Acting.

Hammer

Hammer of the monks (malleus monachorum); hammer of witches (malleus maleficarum).
MEDIEVAL LATIN PHRASES

Hammer and Anvil

Between the hammer and the anvil. (Inter malleum et incudem.)
LATIN PHRASE, taken into English in the XVI century

When you are anvil hold you still;
When you are hammer strike your fill.
JOHN FLORIO: *Second Frutes,* 1591

For a hard anvil, a hammer of feathers.
JOHN WODREOPHE: *Spared Hours,* 1623

In this world a man must be either anvil or hammer.
H. W. LONGFELLOW: *Hyperion,* IV, 1839

The anvil is not afraid of the hammer.
C. H. SPURGEON: *John Ploughman's Talks,* XXI, 1869

The anvil lasts longer than the hammer.
ITALIAN PROVERB

Hand

Let not thy left hand know what thy right hand doeth. MATTHEW VI, 3, *c.* 75

Fine Italian hand.
ENGLISH PHRASE, probably dating from the XVI century, when Italian diplomacy had a high reputation for subtlety; also used to designate the Italian fashion in handwriting

There's no better sign of a brave mind than a hard hand.
SHAKESPEARE: *II Henry VI,* IV, *c.* 1591

Without the bed her other fair hand was
On the green coverlet, whose perfect white
Showed like an April daisy on the grass,
With pearly sweat, resembling dew of night.
SHAKESPEARE: *The Rape of Lucrece,* 1594

Hands off.
ENGLISH PHRASE, familiar since the XVII century

The hand of little employment hath the daintier sense. SHAKESPEARE: *Hamlet,* V, *c.* 1601

Two parts of us successively command;
The tongue in peace; but when in war the hand.
ROBERT HERRICK: *Hesperides,* 1648

An iron hand in a velvet glove.
ENGLISH PHRASE, not recorded before the XIX century; commonly ascribed to NAPOLEON I, but apparently without ground

There is a hand that has no heart in it, there is a claw or paw, a flipper or fin, a bit of wet cloth to take hold of, a piece of unbaked dough on the cook's trencher, a cold clammy thing we recoil from or greedy clutch with the heat of sin, which we drop as a burning coal.
C. A. BARTOL: *The Rising Faith,* 1875

Don't wash the inside of a baby's hand; you will wash his luck away.
AMERICAN NEGRO PROVERB

Is the hand quicker than the eye?
Call of swindlers challenging rustics to three-card monte, or shell games, in the American backwoods, *c.* 1850

Cold hand, warm heart. GERMAN PROVERB

[*See also* Finger, Handshake, Head, Kiss, Possession, Washing.

Händel, G. F. (1685–1759)

Händel knows how to produce an effect better than any of us. When he chooses to strike, he strikes like a thunderbolt.
W. A. MOZART: To J. F. Rochlitz, *c.* 1790

Händel is the greatest composer who ever lived. I uncover my head and kneel at his grave.
LUDWIG VAN BEETHOVEN: To J. A. Stumpff, 1823

From him I can still learn. Bring me the books!
LUDWIG VAN BEETHOVEN: On his deathbed, to Gerhard von Breuning, 1827

[*See also* German, Music, Tweedledum and Tweedledee.

Handkerchief

Men, who never cry, carry handkerchiefs big enough for a whale to weep into.
Author unidentified

Handsaw

A handsaw is a good thing, but not to shave with. THOMAS FULLER: *Gnomologia,* 1732

[*See also* Hawk.

Handshake

To offer one's hand to a superior would be impolite; but if they choose to give that proof of good-will, it should be received with respect and gratitude, inclining the head.
ST. JOHN BAPTIST DE LA SALLE: *The Rules of Christian Manners and Civility,* I, 1695

[*See also* Hand.

Handsome

It is a misery to be too handsome a man.
PLAUTUS: *Miles Gloriosus,* I, 205 B.C.

He is handsome that handsome doth.
JOHN RAY: *English Proverbs,* 1670 (The usual form is "Handsome is as handsome does")

She that is born handsome is born married.
IBID.

A handsome woman should be English to the neck, French to the waist, and Dutch below.
Author unidentified

No handsome man is ever really poor.
SPANISH PROVERB

[*See* Ages, Beauty.

Handwriting

A quick and legible hand is no mean accomplishment.
QUINTILIAN: *De institutione oratoria,* I, *c.* 90

Who'er writ it writes a hand like a foot.
JONATHAN SWIFT: *Polite Conversation,* 1738

There is something to me repugnant at any time in written hand. The test never seems determinate. Print settles it.
CHARLES LAMB: *Oxford in the Vacation,* note, 1820 (London Magazine, Oct.)

The handwriting on the wall.
ENGLISH PHRASE, derived from DANIEL V, 5, *c.* 165 B.C.

Hanging

He that is hanged is accursed of God.
DEUTERONOMY XXI, 23, *c.* 650 B.C. (Cf. GALATIANS III, 13, *c.* 50)

Go and hang yourself. (Exige, ac suspende te.)
PLAUTUS: *Bacchides, c.* 200 B.C.

So they hanged Haman on the gallows that he had prepared for Mordecai.
ESTHER VII, 10, *c.* 125 B.C.

He that is born to be hanged will never be drowned.
ENGLISH PROVERB, traced by Smith to the XVI century

Hanging and wiving go by destiny.
Anon.: *The Schoolhouse for Women,* 1541

Suits hang half a year in Westminster Hall;
At Tyburn half an hour's hanging endeth all.
JOHN HEYWOOD: *Proverbs,* 1546

There is no man so good, who, were he to submit all his thoughts and actions to the laws, would not deserve hanging ten times in his life.
MICHEL DE MONTAIGNE: *Essays,* II, 1580

A man is never undone till he be hanged.
SHAKESPEARE: *Two Gentlemen of Verona,* II, *c.* 1595

As well be hanged for a sheep as a lamb.
ENGLISH PROVERB, current since the XVII century

Last nicht I dressed Queen Mary,
An' pit on her braw silken goon,
An' a' the thanks I'v gat this nicht
Is tae be hanged in Edinboro town.
Anon.: *Mary Hamilton, c.* 1600

He hath no drowning mark upon him; his complexion is perfect gallows.
SHAKESPEARE: *The Tempest,* I, 1611

Three merry boys, and three merry boys,
And three merry boys are we,
As ever did sing in a hempen string
Under the gallow-tree.
BEN JONSON and JOHN FLETCHER: *The Bloody Brother,* III, *c.* 1616

I had rather hang in a woman's company than in a man's; because if we should go to Hell together, I should scarce be letten in, for all the devils are afraid to have any women come amongst them.
THOMAS DEKKER: *II The Honest Whore,* V, 1630

Hanging is the worst use man can be put to.
HENRY WOTTON: *Reliquae Wottonianae,* 1651

He that is hanged on a crab tree will never love verjuice.
JAMES HOWELL: *Proverbs,* 1659 (*Verjuice*=crab-apple cider)

I went out to Charing Cross to see Major General Harrison hanged, drawn, and quartered; which was done there, he looking as cheerful as any man could do in that condition.
SAMUEL PEPYS: *Diary,* Oct. 13, 1660

No Indian prince has to his palace
More followers than a thief to the gallows.
SAMUEL BUTLER: *Hudibras,* II, 1664

An old thief desires a new halter.
JOHN RAY: *English Proverbs,* 1670

Nay, nay, quoth Stringer, when his neck was in the halter.
IBID.

We hang men for trifles, and banish them for things not worth naming.
DANIEL DEFOE: *The Shortest Way with the Dissenters,* 1702

Clever Tom Clinch, while the rabble was bawling,
Rode stately through Holborn to die in his calling,
He stopt at the George for a bottle of sack,
And promis'd to pay for it when he came back.
JONATHAN SWIFT: *On Tom Clinch Going to be Hanged,* 1727

I hang your husband, child, 'tis true,
But with him hang your care.
Twang dang dillo dee.
JOHN GAY: *The Beggar's Opera,* II, 1728

All are not hanged that are condemned.
THOMAS FULLER: *Gnomologia,* 1732

He's up too soon
That's hanged e'er noon.
IBID.

Take courage! younger than thou have been hanged.
IBID.

We must all hang together, or assuredly we shall all hang separately.
BENJAMIN FRANKLIN: To John Hancock, on signing the Declaration of Independence, July 4, 1776

No man 'er felt the halter draw
With good opinion of the law.
JOHN TRUMBULL: *McFingal,* III, 1782

Sae rantingly, sae wantonly,
Sae dauntingly gaed he;
He played a spring, and danced it round,
Below the gallows-tree.
ROBERT BURNS: *Macpherson's Farewell,* 1788 (*Spring*=a lively tune)

A necktie party.
AMERICAN PHRASE, not recorded before the XIX century

They set him high upon a cart —
The hangman rode below —
They drew his hands behind his back,
And bared his noble brow.
W. E. AYTOUN: *The Execution of Montrose,* 1848

And folks are beginning to think it looks odd,
To choke a poor scamp for the glory of God.
J. R. LOWELL: *A Fable for Critics,* 1848

Hang me, oh hang me, and I'll be dead and gone,

Hang me, oh hang me, and I'll be dead and gone,
I wouldn't mind the hanging, it's bein' gone so long,
It's layin' in my grave so long.
Anon.: *The Gambler, c.* 1870

The sheriff took Frankie to the gallows,
Hung her until she died;
They hung her for killing Johnnie,
And the undertaker waited outside;
She killed her man, 'cause he done her wrong.
Anon.: *Frankie and Johnnie, c.* 1875

Jerked to Jesus.
W. F. STOREY: Headline on a report of four hangings, Chicago Times, Nov. 27, 1875

Hanging is a sharp argument.
R. L. STEVENSON: *Familiar Studies of Men and Books,* VI, 1882

They're hangin' Danny Deever in the mornin'!
RUDYARD KIPLING: *Danny Deever,* 1896

It is sweet to dance to violins
When love and life are fair:
To dance to flutes, to dance to lutes
Is delicate and rare:
But it is not sweet with nimble feet
To dance upon the air.
OSCAR WILDE: *The Ballad of Reading Goal,* 1898

The sentence of the court upon you is that you be taken from this place to a lawful prison and thence to the place of execution, and that you be there hanged by the neck until you are dead; and that your body be afterward buried within the precincts of the prison in which you shall have been confined before your execution. And may the Lord have mercy on your soul.
Formula used by English judges in sentencing a prisoner to death, adopted 1903

This will surely be a lesson to me.
Speech of a Tennessee Negro on the gallows, recorded by Irvin S. Cobb, *c.* 1915

They put that coon upon the gallows
And told him he would die;
He crossed his legs and winked his eye
And sailed up in the sky.
American Negro song, quoted by HOWARD W. ODUM: *Rainbow Round My Shoulder,* XIV, 1928

It's not the drop that's going to worry me; it's the sudden stop.
KENNETH NEU: To the hangman, before being hanged at New Orleans, Jan. 2, 1935

He stood upon nothing and kicked at the United States. Author unidentified

Company's good if you are going to be hanged.
CORNISH PROVERB

Big thieves hang the little ones.
CZECH PROVERB

Caught with, hanged with. (Mitgefangen, mitgehangen.) GERMAN PROVERB

"Bad company brings me to this," said the felon as he went to the gallows between the hangman and a priest. GERMAN SAYING

There is a remedy for everything except a broken neck. ITALIAN PROVERB

Let him be hanged by the neck. (Suspendatur per collum.)
Medieval form of death sentence

No one is ever hanged with money in his pocket. RUSSIAN PROVERB

Hanging gaes by hap.
SCOTTISH PROVERB (*Hap*=chance)

[*See also* Baker, Bankrupt, Base, Beaumarchais, Company, Crime and Punishment, Destiny, Drunk, Execution, Freemason, Gallows, Golden Rule, Jury, Lincoln (Abraham), Marriage, Mother, Name, News, November, Punishment (Capital), Rope, Scaffold, Suicide, Thief, Traitor, Unity.

Hangman

A hangman is a good trade; he doth his work by daylight.
JOHN RAY: *English Proverbs,* 1670

A man may be capable, as Jack Ketch's wife said of his servant, of a plain piece of work, a bare hanging; but to make a malefactor die sweetly was only belonging to her husband.
JOHN DRYDEN: *Discourse Concerning the Original and Progress of Satire,* 1693

[*See also* Pleasure.

Hannibal

[*See* Danger.

Happiness

Wherefore are all they happy that deal very treacherously?
JEREMIAH XII, 1, *c.* 625 B.C.

Who save the gods can be happy all life long?
ÆSCHYLUS: *Agamemnon, c.* 490 B.C.

No one is happy all his life long.
EURIPIDES: *The Suppliant Women, c.* 421 B.C.

He that keepeth the law, happy is he.
PROVERBS, XXIX, 18, *c.* 350 B.C.

Happiness is at once the best, the noblest and the pleasantest of things.
ARISTOTLE: *The Nicomachean Ethics,* I, *c.* 340 B.C.

Happy is the man whom God correcteth: therefore despise not thou the chastening of the Almighty. JOB V, 17, *c.* 325 B.C.

Happiness may be defined as good fortune joined to virtue, or as independence, or as a life that is both agreeable and secure, or as plenty of property and slaves, with the capacity to get more.

ARISTOTLE: *Rhetoric,* I, *c.* 322 B.C.

No man is happy unless he believes he is.

PUBLILIUS SYRUS: *Sententiæ, c.* 50 B.C.

If thou art sound in stomach, side, and feet, the riches of a king will add nothing to thy happiness. HORACE: *Epistles,* I, *c.* 5 B.C.

Mankind differ in their notions of happiness; but in my opinion he truly possesses it who lives in the anticipation of honest fame, and the glorious figure he shall make in the eyes of posterity.

PLINY THE YOUNGER: *Letters,* IX, *c.* 110

Here we are called happy when we have peace, such little peace as can be had in a good life; but that happiness, in comparison with our final happiness, is altogether misery.

ST. AUGUSTINE: *The City of God,* XIX, 427

I have now reigned about fifty years in victory or peace, beloved by my subjects, dreaded by my enemies, and respected by my allies. Riches and honors, power and pleasure, have waited on my call, nor does any earthly blessing appear to have been wanting to my felicity. In this situation I have diligently numbered the days of pure and genuine happiness which have fallen to my lot: they amount to fourteen.

Ascribed to ABD-ER-RAHMAN III of Spain, *c.* 960

I were but little happy if I could say how much.

SHAKESPEARE: *Much Ado About Nothing,* II, *c.* 1599

Oh, how bitter a thing it is to look into happiness through another man's eyes!

SHAKESPEARE: *As You Like It,* V, *c.* 1600

Happiness makes us base.

JOHN MARSTON: *Sophonisba,* II, 1606

We never enjoy perfect happiness; our most fortunate successes are mingled with sadness; some anxieties always perplex the reality of our satisfaction.

PIERRE CORNEILLE: *The Cid,* III, 1636

He that talks much of his happiness summons grief.

GEORGE HERBERT: *Outlandish Proverbs,* 1640

How happy is he born and taught
That serveth not another's will;
Whose armor is his honest thought,
And simple truth his utmost skill.

HENRY WOTTON: *The Character of a Happy Life,* 1651

It is a kind of happiness to know to what extent we may be unhappy.

LA ROCHEFOUCAULD: *Maxims,* 1665

The happiness or unhappiness of men depends no less upon their dispositions than on their fortunes. IBID.

We are more interested in making others believe we are happy than in trying to be happy ourselves. IBID.

We are never so happy, nor so unhappy, as we think we are. IBID.

Happiness is that pleasure which flows from the sense of virtue and from the consciousness of right deeds.

HENRY MORE: *Encheiridion ethicum,* II, 1667

The past and present are only our means; the future is always our end. Thus we never really live, but only hope to live. Always looking forward to being happy, it is inevitable that we should never be so.

BLAISE PASCAL: *Pensées,* III, 1670

All men have happiness as their object: there is no exception. However different the means they employ, they all aim at the same end.

BLAISE PASCAL: *Pensées,* VIII

Unbroken happiness is a bore: it should have ups and downs.

J. B. MOLIÈRE: *Les fourberies de Scapin,* III, 1671

There is no other way by which the individual can attain to his own happiness than that which leads to the common happiness of all.

RICHARD CUMBERLAND: *De legibus naturae,* I, 1672

Happy the man who, unknown to the world, lives content with himself in some retired nook, whom the love of this nothing called fame has never intoxicated with its vain smoke; who makes all his pleasure dependent on his liberty of action, and gives an account of his leisure to no one but himself.

NICOLAS BOILEAU: *Épîtres,* VI, 1670

No man is happy but by comparison.

THOMAS SHADWELL: *The Virtuoso,* II, 1676

To enjoy true happiness we must travel into a very far country, and even out of ourselves.

THOMAS BROWNE: *Christian Morals,* *c.* 1680

Friends, books, a cheerful heart, and conscience clear
Are the most choice companions we have here.

WILLIAM MATHER: *The Young Man's Companion,* pref., 1681

To be happy one must have a good stomach and a bad heart.

BERNARD DE FONTENELLE: *Dialogues des morts,* 1683

Happiness, in its full extent, is the utmost pleasure we are capable of, and misery the utmost pain; and the lowest degree of what can be called happiness is so much ease from pain, and so much present pleasure, as without which any one cannot be content.

JOHN LOCKE: *Essay Concerning Human Understanding*, II, 1690

The natural affections duly established in a rational creature being the only means which can procure him a constant series or succession of the mental enjoyments, they are the only means which can procure him a certain and solid happiness.

ANTHONY A. COOPER (EARL OF SHAFTESBURY): *An Inquiry Concerning Virtue or Merit*, II, 1699

If we take an examination of what is generally understood by happiness, as it has respect either to the understanding or the senses, we shall find all its properties and adjuncts will herd under this short definition, that it is a perpetual possession of being well deceived.

JONATHAN SWIFT: *A Tale of a Tub*, IX, 1704

True happiness is of a retired nature, and an enemy to pomp and noise.

JOSEPH ADDISON: *The Spectator*, March 17, 1711

Resigned to Heaven, we may with joy
To any state submit,
And in the world of miseries
Have happiness complete.

DANIEL DEFOE: *A Review of the Affairs of France and of All Europe*, VIII, 1712

That action is best which procures the greatest happiness for the greatest numbers.

FRANCIS HUTCHESON: *An Inquiry into the Original of our Ideas of Beauty and Virtue*, II, 1725 (Cf. BECCARIA, *post*, 1765)

He is happy that knoweth not himself to be otherwise.

THOMAS FULLER: *Gnomologia*, 1732

O happiness! our being's end and aim!
Good, pleasure, ease, content! whate'er thy name:
That something still which prompts th' eternal sigh,
For which we bear to live, or dare to die.

ALEXANDER POPE: *An Essay on Man*, IV, 1734

Reason's whole pleasure, all the joys of sense,
Life in three words, — health, peace, and competence.

IBID.

How sad a sight is human happiness,
To those whose thought can pierce beyond an hour!

EDWARD YOUNG: *Night Thoughts*, I, 1742

Happy are the people whose annals are tiresome.

C. L. DE MONTESQUIEU: *Pensées*, *c.* 1750

Happiness means, for queens, fertility — but for maidens, sterility.

IBID.

Every period of life is obliged to borrow its happiness from the time to come. In youth we have nothing past to entertain us, and in age we derive little from retrospect but hopeless sorrow.

SAMUEL JOHNSON: *The Rambler*, Feb. 25, CCIII, 1752

Every being must desire happiness for himself.

RICHARD PRICE: *The Principal Questions in Morals*, I, 1758

One would suffer a great deal to be happy.

MARY WORTLEY MONTAGU: *Letter to James Steuart*, July 19, 1759

However great a happiness is, there is still one greater, which is that of being worthy of the happiness enjoyed.

STANISLAUS LESZCYNSKI (KING OF POLAND): *Œuvres du philosophe bienfaisant*, 1763

The greatest happiness of the greatest number. (La massima felicità divisa nel maggior numero.)

C. B. BECCARIA: *Trattato dei delitti e delle pene*, intro., 1765 (Cf. HUTCHESON, *ante*, 1725)

That all who are happy are equally happy is not true. A peasant and a philosopher may be equally satisfied, but not equally happy. Happiness consists in the multiplicity of agreeable consciousness. A peasant has not capacity for having equal happiness with a philosopher.

SAMUEL JOHNSON: *Boswell's Life*, Feb., 1766

I firmly believe, notwithstanding all our complaints, that almost every person upon earth tastes upon the totality more happiness than misery.

HORACE WALPOLE: *Letter to the Countess of Upper Ossory*, Jan. 19, 1777

Our greatest happiness . . . does not depend on the condition of life in which chance has placed us, but is always the result of a good conscience, good health, occupation, and freedom in all just pursuits.

THOMAS JEFFERSON: *Notes on Virginia*, 1782

If happiness hae not her seat
  And centre in the breast,
We may be wise, or rich, or great,
  But never can be blest.

ROBERT BURNS: *Epistle to Davie*, 1785

Domestic happiness, thou only bliss
Of Paradise that hast survived the Fall.

WILLIAM COWPER: *The Task*, III, 1785

He is happiest of whom the world says least, good or bad.

THOMAS JEFFERSON: *Letter to John Adams*, 1786

If the happiness of the mass of mankind can be secured at the expense of a little tempest

now and then, or even of a little blood, it will be a precious purchase.
THOMAS JEFFERSON: *Letter to Ezra Stiles,* 1786

It is neither wealth nor splendor, but tranquillity and occupation, which give happiness.
THOMAS JEFFERSON: *Letter to Mrs. A. S. Marks,* 1788

True happiness must arise from well-regulated affections, and an affection includes a duty.
MARY WOLLSTONECRAFT: *A Vindication of the Rights of Woman,* IX, 1792

Human felicity is produced not so much by great pieces of good fortune that seldom happen, as by little advantages that occur every day.
BENJAMIN FRANKLIN: *Autobiography,* 1798

A long happiness loses by its mere length.
G. C. LICHTENBERG: *Reflections,* 1799

For the happy the hour never strikes. (Dem Glücklichen schlägt keine Stunde.)
GERMAN PROVERB, borrowed from J. C. F. SCHILLER: *The Piccolomini,* III, 1799

In the child happiness dances; in the man, at most, it only smiles or weeps.
JEAN PAUL RICHTER: *III Levana,* IV, 1807

The greatest happiness of all those whose interest is in question [is] the right and proper, and only right and proper and universally desirable, end of human action.
JEREMY BENTHAM: Note on his *Principles of Morals and Legislation* (1789), 1812 (Cf. HUTCHESON, *ante,* 1725; BECCARIA, 1765)

All men have the same share of happiness.
NAPOLEON I: To Gaspard Gourgaud at St. Helena, Feb. 7, 1817

Happiness was born a twin.
BYRON: *Don Juan,* II, 1819

Happiness is much more equally divided than some of us imagine.
C. C. COLTON: *Lacon,* 1820

He that thinks himself the happiest man, really is so.
IBID.

Mark Antony sought for happiness in love; Brutus in glory; Cæsar in dominion: the first found disgrace, the second disgust, the last ingratitude, and each destruction.
IBID.

There comes
For ever something between us and what
We deem our happiness.
BYRON: *Sardanapalus,* I, 1821

So long as there are differences between one moment of pleasure and another a man can go on being happy with the same woman.
BALZAC: *The Physiology of Marriage,* 1830

There is ev'n a happiness
That makes the heart afraid.
THOMAS HOOD: *To Melancholy, c.* 1830

Man is the artificer of his own happiness.
H. D. THOREAU: *Journal,* Jan. 21, 1838

Mankind are always happy for having been happy; so that, if you make them happy now, you make them happy twenty years hence by the memory of it.
SYDNEY SMITH: *Benevolent Affections,* 1839

To fill the hour – that is happiness.
R. W. EMERSON: *Experience,* 1841

Happy, my brother? First of all, what difference is it whether thou art happy or not! Today becomes yesterday so fast, all tomorrows become yesterdays; and then there is no question whatever of happiness.
THOMAS CARLYLE: *Past and Present,* III, 1843

The only happiness a brave man ever troubled himself with asking much about was happiness enough to get his work done.
IBID.

The first requisite for the happiness of the people is the abolition of religion.
KARL MARX: *A Criticism of the Hegelian Philosophy of Right,* 1844

The only way to be happy is to shut yourself up in art, and count everything else as nothing.
GUSTAVE FLAUBERT: *Letter to Louise Colet,* 1845

Happiness is white and pink.
THÉOPHILE GAUTIER: *Caprices et zigzags,* 1845

Man's real life is happy, chiefly because he is ever expecting that it soon will be so.
E. A. POE: *Marginalia,* 1844–49

Man is never happy, but spends his whole life in striving after something which he thinks will make him so; he seldom attains his goal, and when he does, it is only to be disappointed; he is mostly shipwrecked in the end, and comes into harbor with masts and rigging gone.
ARTHUR SCHOPENHAUER: *The Vanity of Existence,* 1851

Happiness in this world, when it comes, comes incidentally. Make it the object of pursuit, and it leads us a wild-goose chase, and is never attained. Follow some other object, and very possibly we may find that we have caught happiness without dreaming of it.
NATHANIEL HAWTHORNE: *American Note-Books,* Nov., 1852

The sun and stars that float in the open air;
The apple-shaped earth, and we upon it –
surely the drift of them is something grand!
I do not know what it is, except that it is grand,
and that it is happiness.
WALT WHITMAN: *Carol of Occupations,* 1855

Happy the people whose annals are blank.
THOMAS CARLYLE: *Frederick the Great,* I, 1858 (Cf. MONTESQUIEU, *ante, c.* 1750)

The happiest women, like the happiest nations, have no history.
MARIAN EVANS (GEORGE ELIOT): *The Mill on the Floss,* VI, 1860

Unquestionably, it is possible to do without happiness; it is done involuntarily by nineteen-twentieths of mankind.
J. S. MILL: *Utilitarianism,* II, 1863

When a man is happy, every effort to express his happiness mars its completeness. I am not happy at all unless I am happier than I know.
ALEXANDER SMITH: *Dreamthorp,* VII, 1863

Make us happy and you make us good.
ROBERT BROWNING: *The Ring and the Book,* IV, 1869

Most ov the happiness in this world konsists in possessing what others kant git.
H. W. SHAW (JOSH BILLINGS): *Josh Billings' Encyclopedia of Wit and Wisdom,* 1874

What right have we to happiness?
HENRIK IBSEN: *Ghosts,* I, 1881

Happiness is a woman.
F. W. NIETZSCHE: *Thus spake Zarathustra,* XLVII, 1885

What is happiness? — The feeling that power increases — that resistance is overcome.
F. W. NIETZSCHE: *The Antichrist,* II, 1888

There is nothing of permanent value (putting aside a few human affections), nothing that satisfies quiet reflection, except the sense of having worked according to one's capacity and light to make things clear and get rid of cant and shams of all sorts.
T. H. HUXLEY: To W. Platt Ball, Oct. 27, 1890

Pleasure is the only thing to live for. Nothing ages like happiness.
OSCAR WILDE: *An Ideal Husband,* II, 1895

When I count up the rare minutes of real happiness in my life, I do not believe they make more than twenty-four hours in all.
OTTO VON BISMARCK (1815–98)

Melchisedec was a really happy man. He was without father, without mother and without descent. He was an incarnate bachelor. He was a born orphan.
SAMUEL BUTLER: *Note-Books, c.* 1890

Happiness, like every other emotional state, has blindness and insensibility to opposing facts given it as its instinctive weapon for self-protection against disturbance.
WILLIAM JAMES: *The Varieties of Religious Experience,* IV, 1902

The secret of happiness is this: let your interests be as wide as possible, and let your reactions to the things and persons that interest you be as far as possible friendly rather than hostile.
BERTRAND RUSSELL: *The Conquest of Happiness,* X, 1930

Much happiness is overlooked because it doesn't cost anything. Author unidentified

Success is getting what you want; happiness is wanting what you get. IBID.

Once in every man's life happiness passes him by. GERMAN PROVERB

Looking for happiness is like clutching the shadow or chasing the wind.
JAPANESE PROVERB

God does not love the man who is always happy. JUGO-SLAVIC PROVERB

Always happy. (Semper felix.)
LATIN PHRASE

Better be happy than wise.
SCOTTISH PROVERB

If you want to have a good day, take a shave; a good month, slay a pig; a good year, marry; but if you want all your days to be good, become a priest. SPANISH PROVERB

There are three sureties of happiness: good habits, amiability, and forbearance.
WELSH PROVERB

[*See also* Action, Ambition, Bagpipe, Bliss, Bride, Children, Comfort, Credo, Death, Distance, Drunkenness, Equality, Escape, Ethics, Eugenics, Family, Friend, Golden Rule, History, Home, Hope, Husband and Wife, Indolence, Inn, Justice, Knowledge, Laughter, Law, Life, Marriage, Memory, Mind, Misery, Mortality, Opportunity, Poor, Power, Pride, Property, Providence, Science, Trifle, Utilitarianism, Virtue, Wealth, Wisdom.

Hapsburg

The Hapsburgs have become powerful by plundering older families — the Hungarians, for instance. At bottom they are only a family of police spies who made their fortune by confiscations.
OTTO VON BISMARCK (1815–98)

Hard

Is anything too hard for the Lord?
GENESIS XVIII, 14, *c.* 700 B.C.

As hard as to find a needle in a haystack.
ENGLISH PHRASE, familiar in various forms since the XVI century

It is hard to teach an old dog new tricks.
ENGLISH PROVERB, familiar since the XVI century

It is hard to pull a stocking off a bare leg.
ENGLISH PROVERB, familiar since the XVII century

It's very hard to shave an egg.
JOHN CLARKE: *Parœmiologia Anglo-Latina,* 1639

It is hard to make a good web of a bottle of hay.
JOHN RAY: *English Proverbs,* 1670 (*Bottle*=bundle)

It is hard to sit in Rome and strive against the pope.
JAMES KELLY: *Complete Collection of Scottish Proverbs,* 1721

It is hard to get blood out of a turnip.
ENGLISH PROVERB, not recorded before the XIX century

It is hard to please everyone. (Durum est omnibus placere.) LATIN PROVERB

Things hard to come by are much esteemed. (Quae rarissima carissima.) IBID.

Harding, Warren G. (1865–1923)

A fitting representative of the common aspirations of his fellow citizens.
CALVIN COOLIDGE: Speech of Acceptance, July 27, 1920

Hare

Hare, a black meat, is melancholy and hard of digestion.
ROBERT BURTON: *The Anatomy of Melancholy,* I, 1621

[*See also* Madness.

Harlot

The hire of a harlot. MICAH I, 7, *c.* 700 B.C.

Thou hast played the harlot with many lovers.
JEREMIAH III, 1, *c.* 625 B.C.

The lips of a strange woman drop as a honeycomb, and her mouth is smoother than oil.
PROVERBS V, 3, *c.* 350 B.C.

He that keepeth company with harlots spendeth his substance. PROVERBS XXIX, 3

Verily I say unto you that the publicans and the harlots go into the kingdom of God before you. MATTHEW XXI, 31, *c.* 75

The harlot knows not how to love but only to ensnare; her kiss hath poison, and her mouth a pernicious drug.
ST. JOHN CHRYSOSTOM: *Homilies,* XIV, *c.* 388

For a harlot to turn honest is one of Hercules' labors. It was more easy for him in one night to make fifty queans than to make one of them honest again in fifty years.
THOMAS DEKKER: *I The Honest Whore,* III, 1604

Sweetmeats which rot the eater; in man's nostril,
Poison'd perfumes; they are coz'ning alchemy;
Shipwrecks in calmest weather.
JOHN WEBSTER: *The White Devil,* III, 1608

Phryne had talents for mankind;
Open she was, and unconfin'd,
Like some free port of trade.
ALEXANDER POPE: *Phryne,* 1727 (Imitation of the Earl of Dorset)

Samson with his strong body had a weak head, or he would not have laid it in a harlot's lap.
BENJAMIN FRANKLIN: *Poor Richard's Almanac,* 1756

In silk and scarlet walks many a harlot.
W. C. HAZLITT: *English Proverbs,* 1869

A harlot repents as often as water turns to sour milk. ARAB PROVERB

When the harlot reforms it is only to become a procuress. IBID.

Young harlot, old devotee. (Junge Bettschwester, alte Betschwester.) GERMAN PROVERB

Young harlot, old procuress. IBID.

"Virtue in the middle," said the Devil as he sat down between two old harlots.
GERMAN SAYING (Sometimes *priests* is substituted for *harlots*)

If you spit in a harlot's face, she says it's raining. YIDDISH PROVERB

[*See also* Cosmetics, Fornication, Jealousy, May, Modesty, Prostitute, Virginity, Whore.

Harm

The number of people who can do us good is very small; but almost anyone can do us harm.
BALTASAR GRACIÁN: *The Art of Worldly Wisdom,* CCLVII, 1647

Harmonica

I am very much pleased with your project on the harmonica, and the prospect of your succeeding in the application of keys to it. It will be the greatest present which has been made to the musical world this century, not excepting the pianoforte.
THOMAS JEFFERSON: *Letter to Francis Hopkinson,* 1786

Harmony

From harmony, from heavenly harmony,
This universal frame began:
From harmony to harmony
Through all the compass of the notes it ran,
The diapason closing full in man.
JOHN DRYDEN: *A Song for St. Cecilia's Day,* 1687

The soul obeys its own laws, and the body also follows its own laws. The two agree in virtue of the preëstablished harmony between all substances, for they are all representations of one and the same universe.
G. W. LEIBNIZ: *The Monadology,* LXXVIII, 1714

If there be two perfect equal circles, or globes, together, there is something more of beauty

than if they were of unequal, disproportionate magnitudes. And if two parallel lines be drawn the beauty is greater than if they were obliquely inclined without proportion, because there is equality of distance.
JONATHAN EDWARDS: *Notes on the Mind*, c. 1718

That sort of beauty which is called natural, as of vines, plants, trees, etc., consists of a very complicated harmony; and all the natural motions, and tendencies, and figures of bodies in the universe are done according to proportion, and therein is their beauty. IBID.

Harp

We hanged our harps upon the willows.
PSALMS CXXXVII, 2, *c.* 150 B.C.

The harp that once thro' Tara's halls
  The soul of music shed,
Now hangs as mute on Tara's walls
  As if that soul were fled.
THOMAS MOORE: *The Harp that Once*, 1808

[*See also* Ascetic, Flute, Heart.

Harper

His brother's name was Jubal: he was the father of all such as handle the harp and organ.
GENESIS IV, 21, *c.* 700 B.C.

I heard the voice of harpers harping with their harps. REVELATION XIV, 2, *c.* 95

As blind as a harper.
JOHN LYLY: *Sapho and Phao*, IV, 1584

I ha' harpit ye up to the Throne o' God,
  I ha' harpit your midmost soul in three;
I ha' harpit ye down to the hinges o' Hell,
  And — ye — would — make — a knight o' me!
RUDYARD KIPLING: *The Last Rhyme of True Thomas*, 1893

Harrowing

I could a tale unfold whose lightest word
Would harrow up thy soul.
SHAKESPEARE: *Hamlet*, I, *c.* 1601

Harvard University

They have a college at Cambridge, about four miles from Boston, where divinity, mathematics, philosophy and the oriental languages are taught.
PATRICK M'ROBERTS: *Tour Through Part of the North Provinces of America*, III, 1775

If this boy passes the examinations he will be admitted; and if the white students choose to withdraw, all the income of the college will be devoted to his education.
EDWARD EVERETT: Answer, as president of Harvard, to a protest against the admission of a Negro student, Beverly Williams, 1848

This celebrated institootion of learnin' is pleasantly situated in the barroom of Parker's, in School street, and has poopils from all over the country.
C. F. BROWNE (ARTEMUS WARD): *Artemus Ward: His Book*, 1862

You can always tell a Harvard man, but you can't tell him much.
Ascribed to JAMES BARNES (1866–1936)

[*See also* Education.

Harvest

The harvest truly is plenteous, but the laborers are few. MATTHEW IX, 37, *c.* 75

Dry August and warm,
Doth harvest no harm.
THOMAS TUSSER: *Five Hundred Points of Good Husbandry*, 1580

[*See also* March, Misfortune.

Has-been

It is better to be a has-been than a never-was.
AMERICAN PROVERB (The New English Dictionary traces *has-been* to 1606)

Haste

Make speed, haste, stay not.
I SAMUEL XX, 38, *c.* 500 B.C.

He that is hasty of spirit exalteth folly.
PROVERBS XIV, 29, *c.* 350 B.C.

He that hasteth with his feet sinneth.
PROVERBS XIX, 2

Make haste, O God, to deliver me; make haste to help me, O Lord.
PSALMS LXX, 1, *c.* 150 B.C.

What is done hastily cannot be done prudently.
PUBLILIUS SYRUS: *Sententiæ*, *c.* 50 B.C.

Nothing is seen clearly and certainly by a man in a hurry; haste is improvident and blind.
LIVY: *History of Rome*, XXII, *c.* 10

Every delay, however trifling, seems too long to a man in haste.
SENECA: *Agamemnon*, *c.* 60

The more haste the less speed.
ENGLISH PROVERB, traced by Smith to *c.* 1350

There is no workman, whosoe'er he be,
That may both work well and hastily.
GEOFFREY CHAUCER: *The Canterbury Tales* (The Merchant's Tale), c. 1386

Haste makes waste.
ENGLISH PROVERB, familiar since the XV century

Hasty man lacketh never woe.
RICHARD HILLES: *Commonplace book*, *c.* 1535

Hasty love is soon hot and soon cold.
Anon.: *Wit and Science*, *c.* 1570 (Quoted as a proverb)

Hasty climbers soon do fall.
EDWARD DYER: *My Mind to Me a Kingdom Is,* 1588

Too swift arrives as tardy as too slow.
SHAKESPEARE: *Romeo and Juliet,* II, *c.* 1596

Wisely, and slow; they stumble that run fast.
IBID.

Good and quickly seldom meet.
GEORGE HERBERT: *Outlandish Proverbs,* 1640

Who hath no haste in his business, mountains to him seem valleys. IBID.

It's no use making haste; the thing to do is to set out in time.
JEAN DE LA FONTAINE: *Fables,* VI, 1668

Haste makes waste, and waste makes want, and want makes strife between the good man and his wife.
JOHN RAY: *English Proverbs,* 1670

Hasty climbers have sudden falls. IBID.

Marry in haste and repent at leisure. IBID.

Nothing must be done hastily but killing of fleas. IBID.

Haste trips up his own heels.
THOMAS FULLER: *Gnomologia,* 1732

Fraud and deceit are always in haste.
H. G. BOHN: *Handbook of Proverbs,* 1855

Three things only are well done in haste: flying from the plague, escaping quarrels, and catching fleas. IBID.

Nothing is more vulgar than haste.
R. W. EMERSON: *The Conduct of Life,* V, 1860

The hasty and the slow meet at the ferry.
ARAB PROVERB

You run too fast you run two time.
JAMAICAN PROVERB

Make haste slowly. (Festina lente.)
LATIN PROVERB, borrowed from the Greek

Hasty justice is the stepmother of misfortune. (Festinatio justitiæ est noverca infortunii.)
LEGAL MAXIM

All haste is from the Devil. (Omni festinatio est a diabolo.) MEDIEVAL LATIN PROVERB

Haste is of the Devil; God works slowly.
PERSIAN PROVERB

Haste and anger hide gude counsel.
SCOTTISH PROVERB

Three things must not be carried on in haste: war, feasting and argument.
WELSH PROVERB

[*See also* Error, Gluttony, Hurry, Judgment, Marriage, Midwife, Slow.

Hastings, Warren (1732–1818)

I impeach him in the name and by virtue of those eternal laws of justice which he has violated. I impeach him in the name of human nature itself, which he has cruelly outraged, injured and oppressed, in both sexes, in every age, rank, situation and condition of life.
EDMUND BURKE: *The Trial of Hastings,* Feb. 19, 1788

Hat

A man indeed ought not to cover his head, forasmuch as he is the image and glory of God: but the woman is the glory of the man.
I CORINTHIANS XI, 7, *c.* 55

If he be not in love with some woman, there is no believing old signs: a' brushes his hat o' mornings; what should that bode?
SHAKESPEARE: *Much Ado About Nothing,* III, *c.* 1599

A hat is not made for one shower.
GEORGE HERBERT: *Outlandish Proverbs,* 1640

We are not fond of a new hat. There is a certain insolence about it.
LEIGH HUNT: *The Indicator,* XXVIII, 1821

The hat is the *ultimatum moriens* of respectability.
O. W. HOLMES: *The Autocrat of the Breakfast Table,* VIII, 1858

Where did you get that hat?
J. J. SULLIVAN: Title of a popular song, 1888 (Applied derisively to Benjamin Harrison, who was said to be seeking to impress the voters in his grandfather's hat)

[*See also* Challenge, Politeness.

Hatchet

[*See* Washington (George).

Hathaway, Ann (1556–1623)

She hath a way so to control,
To rapture the imprisoned soul,
And sweetest Heaven on earth display,
That to be Heaven Ann hath a way;
She hath a way,
Ann Hathaway,—
To be Heaven's self Ann hath a way.
CHARLES DIBDIN: *A Love Ditty,* 1795

Hatred

Thou shalt not hate thy brother in thy heart.
LEVITICUS XIX, 17, *c.* 700 B.C.

Better is a dinner of herbs where love is than a stalled ox and hatred therewith.
PROVERBS XV, 17, *c.* 350 B.C.

The bloodthirsty hate the upright.
PROVERBS XLIV, 10

A time to love, and a time to hate.
ECCLESIASTES III, 8, *c.* 200 B.C.

They hate me with cruel hatred.
PSALMS XXV, 19, *c.* 150 B.C.

I hate them with perfect hatred.
PSALMS CXXXIX, 22

Open and avowed hatred far more becomes a man of straightforward character than concealing his sentiments with a smooth brow.
CICERO: *De amicitia, c.* 50 B.C.

Take care that no one hate you justly.
PUBLILIUS SYRUS: *Sententiæ, c.* 50 B.C.

Hatred is inveterate anger.
CICERO: *Tusculanae disputationes,* IV, 45 B.C.

Let them hate me, if they only fear me. (Oderint dum metuant.)
Ascribed to CALIGULA (12–41)

Do good to them that hate you.
MATTHEW V, 44, *c.* 75 (Cf. LUKE VI, 27, *c.* 75)

It is human to hate those whom we have injured.
TACITUS: *Life of Agricola, c.* 98

He that hateth his brother is in darkness, and walketh in the darkness, and knoweth not whither he goeth, because that darkness hath blinded his eyes.
I JOHN II, 11, *c.* 115

Whosoever hateth his brother is a murderer.
I JOHN III, 15

Love as in time to come thou shouldst hate, and hate as thou shouldst in time to come love.
RICHARD TAVERNER: *Proverbs,* 1539

These two sins, hatred and pride, deck and trim themselves out, as the Devil clothed himself in the Godhead. Hatred will be godlike; pride will be truth. These two are right deadly sins: hatred is killing; pride is lying.
MARTIN LUTHER: *Table-Talk,* CCLIII, 1569

Hatreds are the cinders of affection.
WALTER RALEIGH: *Letter to Robert Cecil,* May 10, 1593

I do hate him as I hate the Devil.
BEN JONSON: *Every Man Out of His Humor,* I, 1600

I do hate him as I do hell-pains.
SHAKESPEARE: *Othello,* I, 1604

In time we hate that which we often fear.
SHAKESPEARE: *Antony and Cleopatra,* I, *c.* 1606

There's no hate lost between us.
THOMAS MIDDLETON: *The Witch,* IV, *c.* 1625

He who is hated by all can't hope to live long.
PIERRE CORNEILLE: *Cinna,* I, 1639

The evil that we do does not attract to us so much persecution and hatred as our good qualities.
LA ROCHEFOUCAULD: *Maxims,* 1665

When our hatred is too keen it places us beneath those we hate.
IBID.

All men naturally hate each other.
BLAISE PASCAL: *Pensées,* XXIV, 1670

He could eat my heart with garlic.
JOHN RAY: *English Proverbs,* 1670

In so far as men are tormented by anger, envy, or any passion implying hatred, they are drawn asunder and made contrary one to another, and therefore are so much the more to be feared, as they are more powerful, crafty and cunning than the other animals. And because men are in the highest degree liable to these passions, therefore men are naturally enemies.
BARUCH SPINOZA: *Tractatus theologico-politicus,* II, 1677

Hatred is blind as well as love.
THOMAS FULLER: *Gnomologia,* 1732

The greatest hate springs from the greatest love.
IBID.

What so great misery as to be hated, and to know that we deserve to be hated?
ADAM SMITH: *The Theory of Moral Sentiments,* III, 1759

Men hate more steadily than they love.
SAMUEL JOHNSON: *Boswell's Life,* Sept. 15, 1777

I like a good hater.
SAMUEL JOHNSON: *Mrs. Piozzi's Anecdotes,* 1786

Like the greatest virtue and the worst dogs, the fiercest hatred is silent.
JEAN PAUL RICHTER: *Hesperus,* XII, 1795

We not only love ourselves in others, but hate ourselves in others too.
G. C. LICHTENBERG: *Reflections,* 1799

It is as natural to hate as to love, to despise as to admire, to express our hatred or contempt as our love or admiration.
WILLIAM HAZLITT: *On Poetry in General,* 1821

Hatred is by far the longest pleasure;
Men love in haste, but they detest at leisure.
BYRON: *Don Juan,* XII, 1823

National hatred is something peculiar. You will always find it strongest and most violent where there is the lowest degree of culture.
J. W. GOETHE: *Conversations with Eckermann,* March 14, 1830

The doctrine of hatred must be preached as the counteraction of the doctrine of love, when that pules and whines.
R. W. EMERSON: *Self-Reliance,* 1841

We've practised loving long enough,
Let's come at last to hate.
(Wir haben lang genug geliebt,
Und wollen endlich hassen.)
GEORG HERWEGH: *Lied vom Hasse,* 1841

Hatred and contempt are mutually exclusive. In not a few cases hatred of a person has its roots in nothing save unwilling esteem for his virtues.
ARTHUR SCHOPENHAUER: *Parerga und Paralipomena,* 1851

Folks never understand the folks they hate.
J. R. LOWELL: *The Biglow Papers,* II, 1862

Men hate those to whom they have to lie.
VICTOR HUGO: *Toilers of the Sea,* I, 1866

Women learn how to hate as they forget how to charm.
F. W. NIETZSCHE: *Beyond Good and Evil,* 1886

It does not matter much what a man hates provided he hates something.
SAMUEL BUTLER: *Note-Books, c.* 1890

We have but one, one only hate,
We love as one, we hate as one,
We have one foe and one alone.
(Wir haben nur einen einzigen Hass,
Wir lieben vereint, wir hassen vereint,
Wir haben nur einen einzigen Feind.)
ERNST LISSAUER: *Hassgesang gegen England,* 1914

We must hate — hatred is the basis of Communism. Children must be taught to hate their parents if they are not Communists.
NIKOLAI LENIN: Speech to the Commissars of Education, Moscow, 1923

The most sublime force in life is hatred. To love is to surrender; to hate is to carry on.
Author unidentified

Hatred watches while friendship sleeps.
FRENCH PROVERB

If you hate a man, don't kill him, but let him live. HINDU PROVERB

Short is the road that leads from fear to hate.
ITALIAN PROVERB

Without hatred. (Sine odio.)
LATIN PHRASE

[*See also* Charity, Crime, Culture, Envy, Fault, Flattery, Flesh, Injury, Laughter, Love, Lover, Patriotism, Reason, Victory, Wealth.

Hatter

[*See* Madness.

Hatteras, Cape

The graveyard of the Atlantic.
Author unidentified

If the Bermuda let you pass
You must beware of Hatteras.
SAILORS' RHYME

Haughtiness

The daughters of Zion are haughty, and walk with stretched forth necks and wanton eyes, walking and mincing as they go, and making a tinkling with their feet.
ISAIAH III, 16, *c.* 700 B.C.

Pride goeth before destruction, and a haughty spirit before a fall.
PROVERBS XVI, 18, *c.* 350 B.C.

The avenging gods follow close upon the haughty. SENECA: *Hercules Furens, c.* 50

She holds up her head like a hen drinking.
JAMES KELLY: *Complete Collection of Scottish Proverbs,* 1721

[*See also* Humility.

Have and Have-not

[*See* Classes, Possession.

Having

Using and enjoying is the true having.
BENJAMIN WHICHCOTE: *Moral and Religious Aphorisms,* 1753

Hawk

I am but mad north-north-west; when the wind is southerly, I know a hawk from a hand-saw.
SHAKESPEARE: *Hamlet,* II, *c.* 1601

Hawthorn

And every shepherd tells his tale
Under the hawthorn in the dale.
JOHN MILTON: *L'Allegro,* 1632

The hawthorn-bush, with seats beneath the shade
For talking age and whispering lovers made.
OLIVER GOLDSMITH: *The Deserted Village,* 1770

Hawthorne, Nathaniel (1804–64)

I read no newspapers, and hardly remember who is President; and feel as if I had no more concern with what other people trouble themselves about than if I dwelt in another planet.
NATHANIEL HAWTHORNE: *Journal,* Brook Farm, April 28, 1841

Although a Yankee, he partakes of none of the characteristics of a Yankee. His thinking and his style have an antique air. His roots strike down through the visible mold of the present, and draw sustenance from the generations under ground.
ALEXANDER SMITH: *Dreamthorp,* IX, 1863

[*See also* Ape, Poe (E. A.).

Hay

The hay appeareth, and the tender grass sheweth itself. PROVERBS XXVII, 25, *c.* 350 B.C.

Make hay while the sun shines.
ENGLISH PROVERB, traced by Smith to 1509

Maud Muller on a Summer's day
Raking the meadow sweet with hay.
J. G. WHITTIER: *Maud Muller*, 1854

[*See also* Opportunity.

Haydn, Josef (1732–1809)

Haydn's . . . symphonies lead us through boundless green woods, among a merry gay crowd of happy people. Young men and maidens pass by dancing: laughing children, peeping from behind trees and rosebushes, playfully throw flowers at one another. A life full of love, of felicity, eternally young, as before the fall: no suffering, no sorrow, only a sweet melancholy longing for the beloved form that floats in the glow of the sunset.
E. T. A. HOFFMAN: *Kreisleriana*, 1821

So far as genius can exist in a man who is merely virtuous, Haydn had it. He went as far as the limits that morality sets to intellect.
F. W. NIETZSCHE: *Human All-too-Human*, II, 1878

[*See also* Music.

Hay-fever

I am suffering from my old complaint, the hay-fever. My fear is, perishing by deliquescence; I melt away in nasal and lachrymal profluvia. My remedies are warm pediluvium, cathartics, topical application of a watery solution of opium to eyes, ears, and the interior of the nostrils. The membrane is so irritable that light, dust, contradiction, an absurd remark, the sight of a Dissenter — anything, sets me sneezing.
SYDNEY SMITH: *Letter to Dr. Holland*, June 1835

Hazlitt, William (1778–1830)

William Hazlitt . . . owned he could not bear young girls; they drove him mad. So I took him home to my old nurse, where he recovered perfect tranquility.
CHARLES LAMB: *Letter to William Wordsworth*, June 26, 1806

[*See also* Ape.

Head

Oh, what a rare head if only it had brains!
PHAEDRUS: *Fabulae Aesopiae*, *c*. 50

Two heads are better than one.
ENGLISH PROVERB, borrowed from the Greek, and familiar since the XVI century (Before the XVIII century *wits* commonly appeared in place of *heads*. Sometimes followed by other phrases, e.g., " even if one is a sheep's " and " quoth the old woman when she took her dog to market ")

Better be the head of a lizard than the tail of a lion.
GEORGE HERBERT: *Outlandish Proverbs*, 1640 (*Dog* usually appears in place of *lizard*)

He that hath a head of wax must not walk in the sun.
IBID.

It is no time to stoop when the head is off.
DAVID FERGUSSON: *Scottish Proverbs*, 1641

Mickle head, little wit. IBID. (*Mickle*=big)

Better be the head of the yeomanry than the tail of the gentry.
JOHN RAY: *English Proverbs*, 1670

Off with his head! so much for Buckingham!
COLLEY CIBBER: Adaptation of SHAKESPEARE: *Richard III*, IV, 1700

It is a sound head that has not a soft piece in it.
JAMES KELLY: *Complete Collection of Scottish Proverbs*, 1721

One good head is better than a hundred strong hands.
THOMAS FULLER: *Gnomologia*, 1732

Where Macgregor sits, there is the head of the table.
Ascribed to ROBERT MACGREGOR, a Scotch outlaw (1671–1734), commonly known as Rob Roy

Thou hast a head, and so has a pin.
JONATHAN SWIFT: *Polite Conversation*, I, 1738

An old head upon young shoulders.
ENGLISH PHRASE, not recorded before the XIX century

The dome of thought, the palace of the soul.
BYRON: *Childe Harold*, II, 1812

The fish begins to stink at the head.
ARMENIAN PROVERB

Unless your head is solid bone, do not put it out of a car window. Author unidentified

Head cool and feet warm, keep the doctor poor.
GERMAN PROVERB

Fat heads, lean brains. ITALIAN PROVERB

Her head looks as if it had worn out two bodies.
NEW ENGLAND SAYING

Where the head gaes the tail will follow.
SCOTTISH PROVERB

There is no sore as big as the head cut off.
WEST AFRICAN PROVERB

[*See also* Cabbage, Foot, Head and Heart, Lamb (Charles), Learning, Money, Sixty, Tongue, Warm, Washing.

Headache

When the head aches all the body is out of tune.
THOMAS SHELTON: Tr. of CERVANTES: *Don Quixote*, I (1605), 1620

When the officer reached me [with Lee's request for a meeting, at Appomattox, April 9,

1865] I was still suffering with the sick headache; but the instant I saw the contents of the note I was cured.
U. S. GRANT: *Personal Memoirs*, LXVII, 1885

If the head aches all the limbs grow weak.
LATIN PROVERB

[*See also* Children, Crown.

Head and Heart

Bad mind, bad heart.
TERENCE: *Andria*, I, *c.* 160 B.C.

The head is always the dupe of the heart.
LA ROCHEFOUCAULD: *Maxims*, 1665

The heart has its reasons which reason cannot know. BLAISE PASCAL: *Pensées*, IV, 1670

Hearts may agree though heads differ.
THOMAS FULLER: *Gnomologia*, 1732

Nine times in ten the heart governs the understanding.
LORD CHESTERFIELD: *Letter to his son*, May 15, 1749

A good heart is better than all the heads in the world.
E. G. BULWER-LYTTON: *The Disowned*, 1828

The brave, impetuous heart yields everywhere
To the subtle, contriving head.
MATTHEW ARNOLD: *Empedocles on Etna*, 1852

[*See also* Head, Heart, Humor, Lover, Madness, Man and Woman, Money, Virtue and Vice.

Healing

[*See* Medicine.

Health

There is a limit to the best of health: disease is always a near neighbor.
ÆSCHYLUS: *Agamemnon*, *c.* 490 B.C.

Too much attention to health is a hindrance to learning, to invention and to studies of any kind, for we are always feeling suspicious shootings and swimmings in our heads, and we are prone to blame our studies for them.
PLATO: *The Republic*, III, *c.* 370 B.C.

To lose one's health renders science null, art inglorious, strength unavailing, wealth useless, and eloquence powerless.
HEROPHILUS: *Fragment*, *c.* 300 B.C.

A man in good health is always full of advice to the sick.
MENANDER: *Andria*, *c.* 300 B.C.

Health and good estate of body are above all gold. ECCLESIASTICUS XXX, 15, *c* 180 B.C.

Life is not merely being alive, but being well.
MARTIAL: *Epigrams*, VI, *c.* 95

A sound mind in a sound body. (Mens sana in corpore sano.) JUVENAL: *Satires*, X, *c.* 125

Without health life is not life; it is not living life. Without health life is only a state of languor and an image of death.
RABELAIS: *Pantagruel*, IV, 1533

A man's own observation, what he finds good of, and what he finds hurt of, is the best physic to preserve health.
FRANCIS BACON: *Essays*, VII, 1597

Health is better than wealth.
ENGLISH PROVERB, familiar since the XVII century

O health, health! The blessing of the rich! the riches of the poor! who can buy thee at too dear a rate?
BEN JONSON: *Volpone*, II, 1605

Gold that buys health can never be ill spent.
JOHN WEBSTER and THOMAS DEKKER: *Westward Ho*, V, 1605

Health and an able body are two jewels.
JOHN FLETCHER: *The Wild-Goose Chase*, II, 1621

Health is no other (as the learned hold)
But a just measure both of heat and cold.
ROBERT HERRICK: *Hesperides*, 1648

Look to your health, and if you have it, praise God, and value it next to a good conscience.
IZAAK WALTON: *The Compleat Angler*, I, 1653

It is a boresome disease to try to keep health by following a too strict regimen.
LA ROCHEFOUCAULD: *Maxims*, 1665

I am as sound as a bell — fat, plump and juicy.
CHARLES SEDLEY: *Bellamira*, III, 1687

I need no salts for my stomach, no hartshorn for my head, nor wash for my complexion; I can gallop all the morning after the hunting-horn, and all the evening after a fiddle.
GEORGE FARQUHAR: *The Recruiting Officer*, I, 1706

I have good health, good thoughts, and good humor, thanks be to God Almighty.
WILLIAM BYRD: *Diary*, Nov. 2, 1709 (A frequent entry in his diary)

Health and cheerfulness mutually beget each other.
JOSEPH ADDISON: *The Spectator*, May 24, 1712

Health without wealth is half a sickness.
THOMAS FULLER: *Gnomologia*, 1732

He who was never sick dies the first fit.
IBID.

Health is the vital principle of bliss.
JAMES THOMSON: *The Castle of Indolence*, II, 1748

Among the innumerable follies by which we lay up in our youth repentance and remorse for the succeeding part of our lives, there is scarce any against which warnings are of less efficacy than the neglect of health.
SAMUEL JOHNSON: *The Rambler*, Sept. 1, 1750

Health is beauty, and the most perfect health is the most perfect beauty.
WILLIAM SHENSTONE: *Of Men and Manners*, 1764

Health is the absence of disease, and consequently of all those kinds of pain which are among the symptoms of disease. A man may be said to be in a state of health when he is not conscious of any uneasy sensations, the primary seat of which can be perceived to be anywhere in his body.
JEREMY BENTHAM: *The Principles of Morals and Legislation*, VI, 1789

Health is worth more than learning.
THOMAS JEFFERSON: *Letter to John Garland Jefferson*, 1790

I am in a moment of prettywellness.
HORACE WALPOLE: *Letter to the Countess of Upper Ossory*, Jan. 14, 1792

The feeling of health is acquired only by sickness.
G. C. LICHTENBERG: *Reflections*, 1799

The poorest man would not part with health for money, but the richest would gladly part with all their money for health.
C. C. COLTON: *Lacon*, 1820

The ground-work of all happiness is health.
LEIGH HUNT: *The Indicator*, XXX, 1821

What have I gained by health? Intolerable dullness. What by early hours and moderate meals? A total blank.
CHARLES LAMB: *Letter to William Wordsworth*, Jan. 22, 1830

Give me health and a day, and I will make the pomp of emperors ridiculous.
R. W. EMERSON: *Nature*, 1836

Men of great abilities are generally of a large and vigorous animal nature.
HENRY TAYLOR: *The Statesman*, 1836

Beneath her torn hat glowed the wealth
Of simple beauty and rustic health.
J. G. WHITTIER: *Maud Muller*, 1854

He who hath good health is young.
H. G. BOHN: *Handbook of Proverbs*, 1855

Measure your health by your sympathy with morning and Spring.
H. D. THOREAU: *Journal*, Feb. 25, 1859

The first wealth is health. Sickness is poor-spirited, and cannot serve anyone.
R. W. EMERSON: *The Conduct of Life*, II, 1860

In health there is freedom. Health is the first of all liberties.
H. F. AMIEL: *Journal*, April 3, 1866

A call loan.
H. W. SHAW (JOSH BILLINGS): *Josh Billings' Comical Lexicon*, 1877

Health — silliest word in our language, and one knows so well the popular idea of health. The English country gentleman galloping after a fox — the unspeakable in full pursuit of the uneatable.
OSCAR WILDE: *A Woman of No Importance*, I, 1893

The sound body is the product of the sound mind.
GEORGE BERNARD SHAW: *Maxims for Revolutionists*, 1903 (Cf. JUVENAL, *ante*, *c.* 125)

Health is not a condition of matter, but of Mind.
MARY BAKER G. EDDY: *Science and Health*, VI, 1908

He who has health has hope, and he who has hope has everything. ARAB PROVERB

We are usually the best men when we are in the worst health. Author unidentified

Better pay the butcher than the doctor.
GERMAN PROVERB

One moment of good health is as good as a thousand blessings. HINDU PROVERB

O blessed health! (O beata sanitas!)
LATIN PROVERB

To a healthy man everything seems healthy.
RUSSIAN PROVERB

If you would live in health be old early.
SPANISH PROVERB

[*See also* Appetite, Atheism, Character, Cheerfulness, Desire, Exercise, Freedom, Happiness, Illness, Interruption, Labor, Money, Philosophy, Physician, Poverty, Prince, Rising (Early), Sleep, Thirst, Wealth.

Hearing

We have two ears and only one tongue in order that we may hear more and speak less.
DIOGENES LAERTIUS: *Lives of the Philosophers* (*Zeno*), *c.* 150 B.C.

Hear, and see, and be still.
Anon.: *The Proverbs of Wisdom*, *c.* 1450

None so deaf as those who will not hear.
ENGLISH PROVERB, traced by Smith to 1546

Hear much; speak little.
ROBERT BURTON: *The Anatomy of Melancholy*, II, 1621

When all men speak, no man hears.
JAMES KELLY: *Complete Collection of Scottish Proverbs*, 1721

I will sit down now, but the time will come when you will hear me.
BENJAMIN DISRAELI: Maiden speech in the House of Commons, Dec. 7, 1837

Hear the other party. (Audi alteram partem.)
LATIN PROVERB

[*See also* Belief, Ear, Faculty, Flesh, Seeing.

Hearsay

Hearsay is half a lie. GERMAN PROVERB

[*See also* Eye-witness.

Hearse

Don't drive a hearse, or you will be the next to die. AMERICAN NEGRO PROVERB

Father Time's delivery van.
Author unidentified

Heart

I am pained at my very heart; my heart maketh a noise in me. JEREMIAH IV, 19, *c.* 625 B.C.

The heart is deceitful above all things, and desperately wicked. JEREMIAH XVII, 9

A sound heart is the life of the flesh.
PROVERBS XIV, 30, *c.* 350 B.C.

A wise man's heart is at his right hand; but a fool's heart at his left.
ECCLESIASTES X, 2, *c.* 200 B.C.

God . . . knoweth the secrets of the heart.
PSALMS XLIV, 21, *c.* 150 B.C.

The heart is deep. PSALMS LXIV, 6

My heart was in my mouth.
PETRONIUS ARBITER: *Satyricon, c.* 50

Where your treasure is, there will your heart be also.
MATTHEW VI, 21, *c.* 75 (Cf. LUKE XII, 34, *c.* 75)

Out of the abundance of the heart the mouth speaketh. MATTHEW XII, 34

Out of the heart proceed evil thoughts, murders, adulteries, fornications, thefts, false witness, blasphemies. MATTHEW XV, 19

The heart is the most noble of all the members of our body.
ST. JOHN CHRYSOSTOM: *Homilies,* XI, *c.* 388

My heart was in my boots.
ENGLISH SAYING, familiar since the XV century (Until the XVIII century *hose* commonly appeared in place of *boots*)

Not to eat our hearts — that is, we should not vex ourselves with thoughts.
JOHN LYLY: *Euphues,* 1579

My heart is turn'd to stone.
SHAKESPEARE: *II Henry VI,* V, *c.* 1591

My heart is true as steel.
SHAKESPEARE: *A Midsummer Night's Dream,* II, *c.* 1596

A honey tongue, a heart of gall.
WALTER RALEIGH: *The Nymph's Reply, c.* 1599

He hath a heart as sound as a bell and his tongue is the clapper, for what his heart thinks his tongue speaks.
SHAKESPEARE: *Much Ado About Nothing,* III, *c.* 1599

Hearts of oak.
ENGLISH PHRASE, in common use since the XVII century

I will wear my heart upon my sleeve
For daws to peck at.
SHAKESPEARE: *Othello,* I, 1604

Faint heart never won fair lady.
WILLIAM CAMDEN: *Remains Concerning Britain,* 1605

The heart dreams not of what the eye sees not.
THOMAS SHELTON: Tr. of CERVANTES: *Don Quixote,* II (1615), 1620

The heart of man is the place the Devil dwells in.
THOMAS BROWNE: *Religio Medici,* I, 1642

Who hath sailed about the world of his own heart, sounded each creek, surveyed each corner, but that there still remains therein much terra incognita to himself?
THOMAS FULLER: *The Holy State and the Profane State,* 1642

A fair face and a foul heart.
JAMES HOWELL: *Proverbs,* 1659

How hollow and full of ordure is the heart of man! BLAISE PASCAL: *Pensées,* V, 1670

The guts uphold the heart, and not the heart the guts.
THOMAS FULLER: *Gnomologia,* 1732

When the heart is afire, some sparks will fly out of the mouth. IBID.

With all my heart, and a piece of my liver.
JONATHAN SWIFT: *Polite Conversation,* 1738

That hideous sight, a naked human heart.
EDWARD YOUNG: *Night Thoughts,* III, 1742

The heart is like a viper, hissing, and spitting poison at God.
JONATHAN EDWARDS: *The Freedom of the Will,* 1754

No sky is heavy if the heart be light.
CHARLES CHURCHILL: *The Prophecy of Famine,* 1763

Some hearts are hidden, some have not a heart.
GEORGE CRABBE: *The Borough,* X, 1810

His heart was one of those which most enamor us,
Wax to receive, and marble to retain.
BYRON: *Beppo*, 1818

There is an awful warmth about my heart like a load of immortality.
JOHN KEATS: *Letter to J. H. Reynolds*, Sept. 22, 1818

Worse than a bloody hand is a hard heart.
P. B. SHELLEY: *The Cenci*, V, 1819

Their hearts are in the right place.
BENJAMIN DISRAELI: *The Infernal Marriage*, I, 1834

A heart for any fate.
H. W. LONGFELLOW: *A Psalm of Life*, 1839

Would you have your songs endure?
Build on the human heart!
ROBERT BROWNING: *Sordello*, II, 1840

Kind hearts are more than coronets.
ALFRED TENNYSON: *Lady Clara Vere de Vere*, 1842

Warm, live, improvident, indecent hearts.
E. B. BROWNING: *Aurora Leigh*, III, 1857

Whatever comes from the heart carries the heat and color of its birthplace.
O. W. HOLMES: *The Professor at the Breakfast-Table*, VI, 1859

My heart is like a singing bird
Whose nest is in a water'd shoot;
My heart is like an apple-tree
Whose boughs are bent with thick-set fruit;
My heart is like a rainbow shell
That paddles in a halycon sea;
My heart is gladder than all these,
Because my love is come to me.
CHRISTINA G. ROSSETTI: *A Birthday*, *c.* 1860

Look into the heart of any man, and you will always find at least one black spot.
HENRIK IBSEN: *Pillars of Society*, III, 1879

Heart speaks to heart. (Cor ad cor loquitur.)
Motto adopted by J. H. NEWMAN for his coat-of-arms as cardinal, 1879 (It was suggested by his long friendship for Ambrose St. John, *d.* 1875)

Still stands thine ancient sacrifice —
An humble and a contrite heart.
RUDYARD KIPLING: *Recessional*, 1897 (London Times, July 17)

In each human heart there are a tiger, a pig, an ass, and a nightingale. Diversity of character is due to their unequal activity.
AMBROSE BIERCE: *The Devil's Dictionary*, 1906

The heart never lies.
DUTCH PROVERB

The heart of a maiden is a dark forest.
RUSSIAN PROVERB

When the heart's fu' the tongue canna speak.
SCOTTISH PROVERB

The heart, like the eye, is never satisfied.
WEST AFRICAN PROVERB

[*See also* Absence, Adamant, Devil, Head and Heart, Innocence, Joy, Passion, Standing, Stomach, Theologian, Thinking, Tongue.

Heartache

The whole head is sick and the whole heart faint.
ISAIAH I, 5, *c.* 700 B.C.

Heaviness in the heart of man maketh it stoop.
PROVERBS XII, 25, *c.* 350 B.C.

The heart knoweth its own bitterness.
PROVERBS XIV, 10

Let not your heart be troubled.
JOHN XIV, 1, *c.* 115

Every heart hath its own ache.
THOMAS FULLER: *Gnomologia*, 1732

My heart is sair — I dare na tell —
My heart is sair for somebody.
ROBERT BURNS: *Somebody*, 1790

Hearts live by being wounded.
OSCAR WILDE: *A Woman of No Importance*, III, 1893

[*See also* Children, Heartbreak, Hope.

Heartbreak

The Lord is nigh unto them that are of a broken heart.
PSALMS XXXIV, 18, *c.* 150 B.C.

Thou hast cleft my heart in twain.
SHAKESPEARE: *Hamlet*, III, *c.* 1601

My old heart cracked.
SHAKESPEARE: *King Lear*, II, 1606

Had we never loved sae kindly,
Had we never loved sae blindly!
Never met — or never parted,
We had ne'er been broken-hearted.
ROBERT BURNS: *Song*, 1791

Broken hearts die slow.
THOMAS CAMPBELL: *Theodric*, 1824

Never morning wore
To evening but some heart did break.
ALFRED TENNYSON: *In Memoriam*, VI, 1850

[*See also* Heartache.

Hearthstone

I'm going to my own hearthstone,
Bosomed in yon green hills alone, —
A secret nook in a pleasant land,
Whose groves the frolic fairies planned.
R. W. EMERSON: *Good-by*, 1839

Look well to the hearthstone; therein all hope for America lies.
CALVIN COOLIDGE: Speech of Acceptance, July 27, 1920

[*See also* Fire, Fireplace, Home.

Heat

My skin is black upon me, and my bones are burned with heat. JOB XXX, 30, *c.* 325 B.C.

They must hunger in frost that will not work in heat. JOHN HEYWOOD: *Proverbs,* 1546

It was so dreadful here that I found there was nothing left for it but to take off my flesh and sit in my bones.
Ascribed to SYDNEY SMITH in *A Memoir of the Rev. Sydney Smith* by his daughter, LADY HOLLAND, 1855

American lads and lasses are all pale. Men at thirty and women at twenty-five have had all semblance of youth baked out of them. Infants even are not rosy, and the only shades known on the cheeks of children are those composed of brown, yellow, and white. All this comes of those damnable hot-air pipes with which every tenement in America is infested.
ANTHONY TROLLOPE: *North America,* I, 1862

[*See also* Burden.

Heathen

I will execute vengeance in anger and fury upon the heathen, such as they have not heard. MICAH V, 15, *c.* 700 B.C.

A reproach unto the heathen.
EZEKIEL XXII, 4, *c.* 600 B.C.

Deliver us from the heathen.
I CHRONICLES XVI, 35, *c.* 300 B.C.

Why do the heathen rage, and the people imagine a vain thing?
PSALMS II, 1, *c.* 150 B.C. (Cf. ACTS IV, 25, *c.* 75)

The heathens, when they died, went to bed without a candle.
THOMAS FULLER: *Gnomologia,* 1732

The heathen in his blindness
Bows down to wood and stone.
REGINALD HERBER: *Missionary Hymn,* 1827 (Quoted in KIPLING: *The 'Eathen,* 1892)

I am not merely an opponent of Christianity; I am a heathen — and proud of it.
ERICH LUDENDORFF: Press interview, April, 1935

In heathen parts. (In partibus infidelium.)
LATIN PHRASE, attached to the titles of Roman Catholic dioceses in non-Christian countries

[*See also* Agnostic, Atheist, Zeal.

Heaven

There the wicked cease from troubling, and there the weary be at rest.
JOB III, 17, *c.* 325 B.C.

I knew a man . . . caught up to the third heaven. II CORINTHIANS XII, 2, *c.* 55

Lay up for yourselves treasures in heaven, where neither moth nor rust doth corrupt and where thieves do not break through nor steal.
MATTHEW VI, 20, *c.* 75

The street of the city was pure gold.
REVELATION XXI, 21, *c.* 95

In my Father's house are many mansions.
JOHN XIV, 2, *c.* 115

On the palm-trees in Heaven each cluster yields ten thousand dates, and on the fig-trees each shoot yields ten thousand figs, and if three men were to partake of one fig all of them would be satisfied. On each ear of the wheat there are ten thousand grains, and each grain yields six measures of flour.
Apocalypse of James the Brother of Jesus, c. 350 (The words are ascribed to JESUS)

We have created over you seven Heavens.
THE KORAN, II, *c.* 625

The way to Heaven out of all places is of like length and distance.
THOMAS MORE: *Utopia,* 1516

Heaven is our heritage,
Earth but a player's stage.
THOMAS NASHE: *In Plague Time, c.* 1600

Heaven's face doth glow.
SHAKESPEARE: *Hamlet,* III, *c.* 1601

There trees for evermore bear fruit
And evermore do spring;
There evermore the angels sit,
And evermore do sing.
F. B. P.: *Jerusalem, My Happy Home, c.* 1624

No coming to Heaven with dry eyes.
THOMAS ADAMS: *Sermon,* 1629

We cannot go to Heaven on beds of down.
RICHARD BRATHWAITE: *The English Gentlemen,* 1631

Angels, thy old friends, there shall greet thee,
Glad at their own home now to meet thee.
RICHARD CRASHAW: *Hymn to the Adorable St. Teresa, c.* 1640

Heaven were not Heaven if we knew what it were.
JOHN SUCKLING: *Against Fruition, c.* 1640

All we know
Of what the blessèd do above,
Is that they sing, and that they love.
EDMUND WALLER: *While I Listen to Thy Voice,* 1645

God hath this world for many made, 'tis true:
But He hath made the world to come for few.
ROBERT HERRICK: *Noble Numbers,* 1647

The glory of the next world will never wear out.
JOHN BUNYAN: *Pilgrim's Progress,* I, 1678

There is a land of pure delight
Where saints immortal reign·

Infinite day excludes the night,
And pleasures banish pain.

ISAAC WATTS: *Hymns and Spiritual Songs,* II, 1707

When I can read my title clear
To mansions in the skies,
I'll bid farewell to every fear,
And wipe my weeping eyes.

IBID.

Thither, where sinners may have rest, I go,
Where flames refin'd in breasts seraphic glow.

ALEXANDER POPE: *Eloisa and Abelard,* 1717

And rest at last where souls unbodied dwell,
In ever-flowing meads of asphodel.

ALEXANDER POPE: Tr. of HOMER: *Odyssey,* XXIV (*c.* 800 B.C.), 1720

Heaven is a cheap purchase, whatever it cost.

THOMAS FULLER: *Gnomologia,* 1732

Heaven will make amends for all. IBID.

He will never get to Heaven who desires to go thither alone. IBID.

No man was ever scared into Heaven. IBID.

There is no going to Heaven in a sedan. IBID.

The way to Heaven is ascending; we must be content to travel up hill, though it be hard and tiresome, and contrary to the natural bias of our flesh.

JONATHAN EDWARDS: *The Christian Pilgrim, c.* 1745

Entrance into Heaven is not at the hour of death, but at the moment of conversion.

BENJAMIN WHICHCOTE: *Moral and Religious Aphorisms,* 1753

No man must go to Heaven who has not sent his heart thither before.

THOMAS WILSON: *Maxims of Piety and of Christianity, c.* 1755

One of the wonders of Heaven is that no one there is ever permitted to stand behind another and look at the back of his head.

EMANUEL SWEDENBORG: *Heaven and Hell,* 1758

The happiness of an unembodied spirit will consist in a consciousness of the favor of God, in the contemplation of truth, and in the possession of felicitating ideas.

SAMUEL JOHNSON: *Boswell's Life,* March, 1772

Lord, I believe thou hast prepar'd
(Unworthy tho' I be)
For me a blood-brought free reward,
A golden harp for me.

WILLIAM COWPER: *Olney Hymns,* 1779

What can be more ridiculous than to suppose that Omnipotent Goodness and Wisdom created, and will select the most virtuous of its creatures to sing His praises to all eternity? — it is an idea that I should think could never have entered but into the head of a king, who might delight to have his courtiers sing birthday odes for ever.

HORACE WALPOLE: *Letter to William Mason,* Nov. 8, 1783

A Persian's Heaven is easily made;
'Tis but black eyes and lemonade.

THOMAS MOORE: *Intercepted Letters,* VI, 1813

That prophet ill sustains his holy call,
Who finds not Heavens to suit the tastes of all.

THOMAS MOORE: *Lalla Rookh,* 1817

In Heaven roast geese fly round with gravy-boats in their bills; tarts grow wild like sunflowers; everywhere there are brooks of bouillon and champagne, everywhere trees on which napkins flutter, and you eat and wipe your lips and eat again without injury to your stomach; you sing psalms, or flirt with the dear, delicate little angels.

HEINRICH HEINE: *Reisebilder,* II, 1826

Heav'n but the vision of fulfill'd
Desire.

EDWARD FITZGERALD: Tr. of OMAR KHAYYÁM: *Rubáiyát* (*c.* 1100), 1857

Sydney Smith said that his idea of Heaven was eating *foie gras* to the sound of trumpets.

SAMUEL ROGERS: *Table-Talk,* 1856

Heaven might be defined as the place which men avoid.

H. D. THOREAU: *Excursions,* 1863

In our English popular religion the common conception of a future state of bliss is that of . . . a kind of perfected middle-class home, with labor ended, the table spread, goodness all around, the lost ones restored, hymnody incessant.

MATTHEW ARNOLD: *Literature and Dogma,* XII, 1873

Heaven is the presence of God.

CHRISTINA ROSSETTI: *Seek and Find,* 1879

Hello, Central! Give me Heaven.

CHARLES K. HARRIS: Title of song, 1901

When she was dying, and her children about her, the priest said to her: "Mrs. Gallagher, it's in Heaven you'll be at 12 o'clock tomorrow."

AUGUSTA GREGORY: *Poets and Dreamers,* 1903

You will eat bye and bye
In that glorious land above the sky;
Work and pray, live on hay,
You'll get pie in the sky when you die.

JOE HILL: *The Preacher and the Slave, c.* 1906

The Coney Island of the Christian imagination.

ELBERT HUBBARD: *Roycroft Dictionary and Book of Epigrams,* 1923

I'm gwine to Heaven on eagle's wing;
All don't see me, goin' to hear me sing.
American Negro song

Men do not go to Heaven laughing.
DUTCH PROVERB

We all hope he is where we all know he ain't.
Funeral sermon ascribed to a Negro clergyman

If God were not willing to forgive sin Heaven would be empty. GERMAN PROVERB

[*See also* African, Expectation, Friend, Gold, Hereafter, Idiot, Immortality, Kentucky, Paradise, Party, Resurrection.

Heaven and Hell

I desire to go to Hell, not to Heaven. In Hell I shall enjoy the company of popes, kings and princes, but in Heaven are only beggars, monks, hermits and apostles.
NICCOLÒ MACHIAVELLI: On his deathbed, 1530

It is good to have some friends in both Heaven and Hell.
GEORGE HERBERT: *Outlandish Proverbs*, 1640

They that be in Hell ween there is none other Heaven. JOHN HEYWOOD: *Proverbs*, 1546

The way to Hell's a seeming Heav'n.
FRANCIS QUARLES: *Emblems*, II, 1635

Better to reign in Hell than serve in Heaven.
JOHN MILTON: *Paradise Lost*, I, 1667

Better go to Heaven in rags than to Hell in embroidery.
THOMAS FULLER: *Gnomologia*, 1732

Hell was built on spite, and Heav'n on pride.
ALEXANDER POPE: *An Essay on Man*, III, 1733

The doctrine of a future state of rewards and punishments is not to be found in, nor did it make part of, the Mosaic dispensation.
WILLIAM WARBURTON (BISHOP OF GLOUCESTER): *The Divine Legation of Moses*, I, 1737

Can the believing husband in Heaven be happy with his unbelieving wife in Hell? Can the believing father in Heaven be happy with his unbelieving children in Hell? Can the loving wife in Heaven be happy with her unbelieving husband in Hell? I tell you yea! Such will be their sense of justice that it will increase rather than diminish their bliss.
JONATHAN EDWARDS: *Discourses on Various Important Subjects*, 1738

Plucked from the roaring lion's teeth,
Caught up from the eternal fire,
Snatched from the gates of Hell I breathe,
And lo! to Heaven I still aspire.
CHARLES WESLEY: *At the Approach of Temptation*, 1740

A man may go to Heaven with half the pains which it costs him to purchase Hell.
HENRY FIELDING: *Jonathan Wild*, IV, 1743

I hope to merit Heaven by making earth a Hell. BYRON: *Childe Harold*, I, 1812

I sent my soul through the invisible,
Some letter of that after-life to spell:
And by and by my soul return'd to me,
And answer'd "I myself am Heav'n and Hell."
EDWARD FITZGERALD: Tr. of OMAR KHAYYÁM: *Rubáiyát* (*c.* 1100), 1857

To beings constituted as we are the monotony of singing psalms would be as great an affliction as the pains of Hell, and might be even pleasantly interrupted by them.
BENJAMIN JOWETT: Intro. to PLATO: *Phaedo*, 1871

Hell is Heaven enjoying itself.
Author unidentified

Heaven for climate; Hell for society. (Himmel für Klima; Hölle für Gesellschaft.)
GERMAN SAYING

If there were no Hell, no one would worry about Heaven. WELSH PROVERB

[*See also* Heaven, Hell, Hereafter, Immortality, Lawyer, Paradise, Power, Soul.

Heavens

The heavens declare the glory of God; and the firmament showeth his handiwork.
PSALMS XIX, 1, *c.* 150 B.C.

Hebrew

A Hebrew or a Hebrewess.
JEREMIAH XXXIV, 9, *c.* 625 B.C.

I am a Hebrew, and I fear the Lord.
JONAH I, 9, *c.* 400 B.C.

[*See also* Childbirth, Jew, Moses, Paul (St.).

Hebrew Language

Their children . . . could not speak in the Jews' language, but according to the language of each people.
NEHEMIAH XIII, 24, *c.* 300 B.C.

The words of the Hebrew tongue have a peculiar energy. It is impossible to convey so much so briefly in any other language.
MARTIN LUTHER: *Table-Talk*, XXXIV, 1569

It's all Hebrew to me: I can't understand a word. J. B. MOLIÈRE: *L'Étourdi*, III, 1653

[*See also* Aspiration, Greek Language.

Hecuba

[*See* Indifference.

Heed

Take heed of an ox before, an ass behind, and a monk on all sides.
JOHN RAY: *English Proverbs*, 1670

Heine, Heinrich (1797–1856)

Blackguard Heine is worth very little.
THOMAS CARLYLE: *Letter to R. W. Emerson,* Nov. 5, 1836

Heinrich Heine has fulfilled my highest conception of a lyric poet. I have sought in vain through all the centuries for an equally sweet and passionate music. He possesses that divine malice without which I cannot imagine perfection. And how he handles German!
F. W. NIETZSCHE: *Ecce Homo,* 1888

Heir

The tears of an heir are masked laughter.
PUBLILIUS SYRUS: *Sententiæ, c.* 50 B.C.

The next heir is always suspected and disliked.
TACITUS: *History,* I, *c.* 100

Who wait for dead men go long barefoot.
JOHN HEYWOOD: *Proverbs,* 1546

He pulls with a long rope that waits for another's death.
GEORGE HERBERT: *Outlandish Proverbs,* 1640

Our teeth have time to grow while we wait for a dead man's shoes.
J. B. MOLIÈRE: *Le médecin malgré lui,* II, 1666

"Yet doth he live," exclaims the impatient heir,
And sighs for sables that he may not wear.
BYRON: *Lara,* I, 1814

I, the heir of all the ages, in the foremost files of time.
ALFRED TENNYSON: *Locksley Hall,* 1842

Ill-gotten goods never descend to the third heir.
LATIN PROVERB

God alone, and not man, can make an heir. (Deus solus haeredem facere potest, non homo.)
LEGAL MAXIM

He who is in the womb is held as already born, whenever his benefit is in question. (Qui in utero est pro jam nato habetur, quoties de ejus commodo quaeritur.)
IBID.

[*See also* Doctor, Onion, Physician.

Hell

Hell hath enlarged herself, and opened her mouth without measure.
ISAIAH V, 14, *c.* 700 B.C.

Hell from beneath is moved for thee to meet thee at thy coming.
ISAIAH XIV, 9

The way of sinners is made plain with stones, but at the end thereof is the pit of hell.
ECCLESIASTICUS XXI, 10, *c.* 180 B.C.

The wicked shall be turned into hell, and all the nations that forget God.
PSALMS IX, 17, *c.* 150 B.C.

The descent to Avernus is easy.
VIRGIL: *Ænied,* VI, 19 B.C.

Where their worm dieth not, and the fire is not quenched.
MARK IX, 44, *c.* 75

In the regions below there are no corn-fields, no clustering vines, but fierce Cerberus and the filthy ferryman of the Stygian waters.
TIBULLUS: *Elegies,* I, *c.* 20 B.C.

The fire of Gehenna is sixty times as hot as the fire of this earth.
THE TALMUD (*Berachoth*), *c.* 200

Hell is paved with the skulls of priests.
ST. JOHN CHRYSOSTOM: *De sacerdotio, c.* 390

He fashioned Hell for the inquisitive. (Curiosis fabricavit infernos.)
ST. AUGUSTINE: *Confessions,* XI, *c.* 420

They who believe not shall have garments of fire fitted unto them; boiling water shall be poured on their heads; their bowels shall be dissolved thereby, and also their skins; and they shall be beaten with maces of iron.
THE KORAN, XXII, *c.* 625

The best man in Hell hath such comfort as if the whole world were on fire, even to the firmament on high, and he were in the midst of that fire in his shirt or stark naked. But another man may have it tenfold worse, or thirtyfold, or sixtyfold, or an hundredfold, or a thousandfold, or sixty thousandfold worse, for the more his sins the deeper his place in Hell and the hotter his fire.
BERTHOLD OF REGENSBURG: *Sermon, c.* 1260

That the saints may enjoy their beatitude and the grace of God more abundantly, they are permitted to see the punishment of the damned in Hell.
THOMAS AQUINAS: *Summa theologiæ,* III, *c.* 1265

Abandon every hope, ye who enter here. (Lasciate ogni speranza voi ch'entrate.)
DANTE: *Inferno,* III, *c.* 1320 (Inscription over the gate of Hell)

Here sighs, plaints, and voices of the deepest woe resounded through the starless sky. Strange languages, horrid cries, accents of grief and wrath, voices deep and hoarse, with hands clenched in despair, made a commotion which whirled forever through that air of everlasting gloom, even as sand when whirlwinds sweep the ground.
IBID.

The hound of Hell, in Greek, is called Cerberus; in Hebrew, Scorphur: he has three throats — sin, the law, and death.
MARTIN LUTHER: *Table-Talk,* DCXXVI, 1569

Hell is full of good desires.
EDWARD HELLOWES: Tr. of ANTONIO DE GUEVARA: *Familiar Letters,* 1574

A Hell as hopeless and as full of fears
As are the blasted banks of Erebus,
Where shaking ghosts with ever-howling groans
Hover about the ugly ferryman.

CHRISTOPHER MARLOWE: *I Tamburlaine*, v, *c.* 1588

Hell's broken loose.

ROBERT GREENE: *Friar Bacon and Friar Bungay*, IV, 1594 (Cf. MILTON, *post*, 1667)

Black is the badge of Hell,
The hue of dungeons and the suit of night.

SHAKESPEARE: *Love's Labor's Lost*, IV, *c.* 1595

Represent to yourself a city involved in darkness, burning with brimstone and stinking pitch, and full of inhabitants who cannot make their escape.

ST. FRANCIS DE SALES: *Introduction to the Devout Life*, XV, 1609

That's the greatest torture souls feel in Hell,
That they must live, and cannot die.

JOHN WEBSTER: *The Duchess of Malfi*, IV, *c.* 1614

I see a brimstone sea of boiling fire,
And fiends, with knotted whips of flaming wire,
Torturing poor souls, that gnash their teeth in vain,
And gnaw their flame-tormented tongues for pain.

FRANCIS QUARLES: *Emblems*, 1635

God is a consuming fire against thee, and there is but one paper wall of thy body between thy soul and eternal flames.

THOMAS SHEPARD: *The Sincere Convert*, 1641

I thank God, and with joy I mention it, I was never afraid of Hell, nor never grew pale at the description of that place.

THOMAS BROWNE: *Religio Medici*, I, 1642

Hell is no other but a soundless pit,
Where no one beam of comfort peeps in it.

ROBERT HERRICK: *Noble Numbers*, 1647

Oh, loth am I to burn and fry in Hell!

JOHN BUNYAN: *Sighs from Hell*, 1648

When thou art scorching in thy flames, when thou art howling in thy torments, then God shall laugh, and His saints shall sing and rejoice, that His power and wrath are thus made known to thee.

CHRISTOPHER LOVE: *Hell's Torments*, *c.* 1650

Hell is full of good meanings and wishings.

GEORGE HERBERT: *Jacula Prudentum*, 1651

Hell could not be Hell without the despair of accursed souls; for any hope were a refreshment, and a drop of water, which would help to allay those flames, which as they burn intolerably, so they must burn forever.

JEREMY TAYLOR: *Twenty-seven Sermons*, 1651

Hell is full of good intentions and meanings.

RICHARD WHITLOCK: *Zoötomia*, 1654

A crime it is, therefore in bliss
You may not hope to dwell,
But unto you I shall allow
The easiest room in Hell.

MICHAEL WIGGLESWORTH: *The Day of Doom*, 1662 (God, to the children damned for Adam's fall)

Here meets them now the worm that gnaws
And plucks their bowels out;
The pit, too, on them shuts her jaws —
This dreadful is, no doubt.

JOHN BUNYAN: *One Thing Is Needful*, 1665

A dungeon horrible on all sides round,
As one great furnace, flamed; yet from those flames
No light, but rather darkness visible
Serv'd only to discover sights of woe,
Regions of sorrow, doleful shades, where peace
And rest can never dwell, hope never comes
That comes to all; but torture without end.

JOHN MILTON: *Paradise Lost*, I, 1667

All Hell broke loose.

JOHN MILTON: *Paradise Lost*, IV (Cf. GREENE, *ante*, 1594)

'Tis pity such a pretty maid
As I should go to Hell.

ABRAHAM CHEAR: *A Looking-Glass for Children*, *c.* 1670

Hell is a terrible place, that's worse a thousand times than whipping.

JAMES JANEWAY: *A Token for Youth*, *c.* 1670

The fear of Hell, or aiming to be blest,
Savors too much of private interest.
This moved not Moses, nor the zealous Paul,
Who for their friends abandoned soul and all.

EDMUND WALLER: *Of Divine Love*, 1685

Hell will never be full till you be in it.

JAMES KELLY: *Complete Collection of Scottish Proverbs*, 1721

Pillars of flame in spiral volume rise,
Like fiery snakes, and lick the infernal skies;
Sulphur, the eternal fuel unconsumed,
Vomits redounding smoke, thick, unillumed.

JOSEPH TRAPP: *The Four Last Things*, *c.* 1725

There is nothing that keeps wicked men at any one moment out of Hell, but the mere pleasure of God.

JONATHAN EDWARDS: *Sinners in the Hands of an Angry God*, 1741 (Sermon, July 8)

We find it easy to tread on and crush a worm that we see crawling on the earth; so it is as easy for us to cut or singe a slender thread that anything hangs by: thus easy it is for God, when He pleases, to cast His enemies down to Hell. IBID.

Let him go abroad to a distant country; let him go to some place where he is not known. Don't let him go to the Devil, where he is known.
SAMUEL JOHNSON: *Boswell's Journal of a Tour to the Hebrides,* Aug. 18, 1773

Hell is paved with good intentions.
SAMUEL JOHNSON: *Boswell's Life,* April 14, 1775 (Quoted as a proverb. Cf. HELLOWES, *ante,* 1574; HERBERT, 1651; WHITLOCK, 1654)

The most licentious man, were Hell open before him, would not take the most beautiful strumpet to his arms.
SAMUEL JOHNSON: *Boswell's Life,* June 3, 1781

The fear o' Hell's a hangman's whip,
To haud the wretch in order.
ROBERT BURNS: *Epistle to a Young Friend,* 1786

A vast, unbottomed, boundless pit,
Filled fou o' lowin' brunstane,
Wha's ragin' flame, and scorchin' heat,
Wad melt the hardest whunstane!
ROBERT BURNS: *The Holy Fair,* 1786 (*Whunstone*=a stone used in the game of curling)

Ah, Tam! ah, Tam! Thou'll get thy fairin';
In Hell they'll roast thee like a herrin'.
ROBERT BURNS: *Tam O'Shanter,* 1790

Spaces of fire, and all the yawn of Hell.
JOHN KEATS: *Hyperion,* I, 1819

Hell is a city much like London.
P. B. SHELLEY: *Peter Bell the Third,* III, 1819

A lake of fire and brimstone whose flames are unquenchable, and whose smoke ascendeth up forever and ever.
THE BOOK OF MORMON (*Jacob VI,* 10), 1830

Hell is more bearable than nothingness.
P. J. BAILEY: *Festus,* 1839

We, the undersigned presbyters and deacons in holy orders in the Church of England and Ireland, feel it to be our bounden duty to the Church and to the souls of men to declare our firm belief that the Church, in common with the whole Catholic Church . . . teaches, in the words of our Blessed Lord, that the "punishment" of the "cursed," equally with the "life" of the "righteous," is "everlasting."
Manifesto drawn up by E. B. PUSEY in answer to *Essays and Reviews,* by FREDERICK TEMPLE, ROWLAND WILLIAMS, H. B. WILSON, BENJAMIN JOWETT and others (1860), and signed by 11,000 clergymen, 1864

The heat of Hell is waxen seven times hot.
A. C. SWINBURNE: *Laus Veneris,* 1866

The German word for Hell—*Hölle*—sounds more like *helly* than anything else; therefore, how necessarily chipper, frivolous and unimpressive it is.
S. L. CLEMENS (MARK TWAIN): *A Tramp Abroad,* Appendix D, 1879

Children have so little fear of Hell that if they could see it they would admire it.
VICTOR HUGO: *Ninety-Three,* 1879

Hell is the work of prigs, pedants and professional truth-tellers.
SAMUEL BUTLER: *Note-Books, c.* 1890

The Hell which a thoroughly bad man dreads can only be a Hell of physical suffering; and, if he abstains from crime through fear of fire, he is not a good man, but a bad man in chains.
LESLIE STEPHEN: *Agnostic Annual,* 1895

It doesn't matter what they preach
Of high or low degree;
The old Hell of the Bible
Is Hell enough for me.
F. L. STANTON: *Enough for Him, c.* 1898

O Death, where is thy sting-a-ling-a-ling,
O Grave, thy victoree?
The bells of Hell go ting-a-ling-a-ling
For you but not for me.
Anon.: British soldiers' song, popular in 1914–18

The religion of Hell is patriotism, and the government is an enlightened democracy.
JAMES BRANCH CABELL: *Jurgen,* XXXVIII, 1919

If there is no Hell, a good many preachers are obtaining money under false pretenses.
WILLIAM A. SUNDAY (1863–1936)

Oh, Hell is deep an' Hell is wide
An' Hell ain't got no bottom or side.
American Negro song

Cheer up; there ain't no Hell!
AMERICAN PROVERB

There are no fans in Hell. ARAB PROVERB

Hell is paved with monks' cowls, priests' robes, and spike-helmets. GERMAN PROVERB

The Acherusian bog. (Acherusia palus.)
LATIN PHRASE (*Acheron*=the place of the dead)

Hell is paved with good intentions and roofed with lost opportunities.
PORTUGUESE PROVERB

One can get used to everything, even to Hell.
RUSSIAN PROVERB

Hell is full of the ungrateful.
SPANISH PROVERB

[*See also* Children, Damnation, Damned, Devil, Fan, Friend, Heaven and Hell, Hereafter, Hopeless, Immortality, Inquisitive,

Judgment Day, Liar, Music, Priest, Protestantism, Prussia, Sinner, Texas.

Help

For a man to help another is to be a god.
PLINY THE ELDER: *Natural History*, II, 77

He who is the cause of another's advancement is thereby the cause of his own ruin: for that advancement is founded either upon the conduct or the power of the donor, and both of these become suspect in the eyes of him who has been advanced.
NICCOLÒ MACHIAVELLI: *The Prince*, III, 1513

No one is so rich that he does not need another's help; no one so poor as not to be useful in some way to his fellow man; and the disposition to ask assistance from others with confidence, and to grant it with kindness, is part of our very nature.
POPE LEO XIII: *Graves de communi*, Jan. 18, 1901

One rooster can't help another to scratch the same piece of ground. AFRICAN PROVERB

Three helping one another will do as much as six men singly. SPANISH PROVERB

Hen

A black hen lays a white egg.
JOHN RAY: *English Proverbs*, 1670 (Cited as " a French proverb ")

A crooning cow, a crowing hen, and a whistling maid boded never luck to a house.
JAMES KELLY: *Complete Collection of Scottish Proverbs*, 1721

If you would have a hen lay you must bear with her cackling.
THOMAS FULLER: *Gnomologia*, 1732

It is no good hen that cackles in your house and lays in another's. IBID.

Higgledy, piggledy, my black hen,
She lays eggs for gentlemen.
Anon.: *Nursery Rhyme*, *c.* 1750

It is a bad hen that lays her eggs away from the farm. DANISH PROVERB

Hens like to lay where they see an egg.
DUTCH PROVERB

Fat hens are aye ill layers. SCOTTISH PROVERB

The hen never forgets him who has stolen her chicks. WEST AFRICAN PROVERB

[*See also* Busy, Christian, Fat, Heredity, Husband and Wife, Luck, Sitting, Whistling.

Hen-pecked

They are sorry houses where the hens crow, and the cock holds his peace.
JOHN FLORIO: *First Frutes*, 1578

Henry VIII of England (1491–1547)

Bluff Harry the Eight to six spouses was wedded:
One died, one survived, two divorced, two beheaded. Anon.: *Nursery Rhyme*, *c.* 1750

Heraldry

The heralds tell us that certain scutcheons and bearings denote certain conditions, and that to put colors on colors, or metals on metals, is false blazonry. If all this were reversed, if every coat-of-arms in Europe were new-fashioned, if it were decreed that *or* should never be placed but on *argent*, or *argent* but on *or*, that illegitimacy should be denoted by a lozenge, and widowhood by a bend, the new science would be just as good as the old science, because both the new and old would be good for nothing.
T. B. MACAULAY: *Moore's Life of Lord Byron*, 1831 (Edinburgh Review)

The science of fools with long memories.
J. R. PLANCHÉ: *The Pursuivant of Arms*, 1852

Hercules

Hercules was not begot in one night.
GREEK PROVERB, quoted by JOHN MILTON: *A Declaration, or Letters Patent of the Lection of the Present King of Poland*, 1674

Herd

[*See* Crowd, Majority, Mob, Rabble.

Here

Here and there.
ENGLISH PHRASE, traced by the New English Dictionary to *c.* 1300

Neither here nor there.
ENGLISH PHRASE, traced by the New English Dictionary to *c.* 1583

Here, there and everywhere.
CHRISTOPHER MARLOWE: *Dr. Faustus*, IV, 1604

Better say " Here it is " nor " Here it was."
DAVID FERGUSSON: *Scottish Proverbs*, 1641

We're here because we're here because we're here because we're here.
Anon.: Refrain of an American folk-song, popular among college students, Elks, Kiwanians and other convivial groups; also sung by the British Army, 1914–18

Hereafter

Hereafter comes not yet.
JOHN HEYWOOD: *Proverbs*, 1546

When I lay sucking at my mother's breasts, I had no notion how I should afterwards eat, drink, or live. Even so we on earth have no idea what the life to come will be.
MARTIN LUTHER: *Table-Talk*, DCCXCIX, 1569

Who would fardels bear,
To grunt and sweat under a weary life,
But that the dread of something after death,
The undiscover'd country from whose bourn
No traveler returns, puzzles the will,
And makes us rather bear those ills we have
Than fly to others that we know not of?

SHAKESPEARE: *Hamlet*, III, *c.* 1601

'Twill be all one a thousand years hence.

JONATHAN SWIFT: *Polite Conversation*, 1738

[*See also* Heaven, Heaven and Hell, Hell, Immortality.

Heredity

The fathers have eaten sour grapes, and the children's teeth are set on edge.

EZEKIEL XVII, 2, *c.* 600 B.C.

Neither roses nor hyacinths spring from the squill, nor is a high-spirited child born of a bondwoman.

THEOGNIS: *Elegies*, *c.* 550 B.C.

Noble fathers have noble children.

EURIPIDES: *Fragment*, *c.* 425 B.C.

Fierce eagles do not produce timorous doves.

HORACE: *Carmina*, IV, *c.* 13 B.C.

A good tree cannot bring forth evil fruit, neither can a corrupt tree bring forth good fruit.

MATTHEW VII, 18, *c.* 75

It will not out of the flesh that is bred in the bone.

JOHN HEYWOOD: *Proverbs*, 1546

Where the cow and bull are both milk-white,
They never do beget a coal-black calf.

SHAKESPEARE: *Titus Adronicus*, V, 1594

Was never fox but wily cubs begets,
The bear his fierceness to his brood besets,
Nor fearful hare falls out of lion's seed,
Nor eagle wont the tender dove to breed.

JOSEPH HALL (BISHOP OF NORWICH): *Virgidemarium*, IV, 1598

As for the most part, we see children of noble personages to bear the lineaments and resemblance of their parents, so in like manner, for the most part, they possess their virtues and noble dispositions, which even in their tenderest years will bud forth, and discover itself.

HENRY PEACHAM: *The Compleat Gentleman*, 1622

He's a chip o' th' old block.

WILLIAM ROWLEY: *A Match at Midnight*, I, 1633

Like hen, like chicken.

PHILIP MASSINGER: *The City Madam*, I, 1658

We are our reanimated ancestors, and antedate their resurrection.

JOSEPH GLANVILL: *The Vanity of Dogmatizing*, XV, 1661

What a figure is the young heir likely to make who is a dunce both by father and mother's side?

JOSEPH ADDISON: *The Guardian*, Sept. 8, 1713

We come into the world with the mark of our descent, and with our characters about us.

A. R. LE SAGE: *Gil Blas*, X, 1735

There are some hereditary strokes of character by which a family may be as clearly distinguished as by the blackest features of the human face.

Letters of Junius, May 30, 1769

Helvétius maintains that men are born with approximately the same talents. This is contradicted by experience. The character of men is fixed indelibly at birth.

FREDERICK THE GREAT: *Letter to Jean le Rond D'Alembert*, Aug. 13, 1777

He was not merely a chip of the old block, but the old block itself.

EDMUND BURKE: Speech in the House of Commons, Feb. 26, 1781

A good cow may have a bad calf.

NOAH WEBSTER: *A Grammatical Institute of the English Language*, 1783

A wild goose never laid a tame egg.

H. G. BOHN: *Handbook of Proverbs*, 1855

The greatness or smallness of a man is, in the most conclusive sense, determined for him at his birth, as strictly as it is determined for a fruit whether it is to be a currant or an apricot.

JOHN RUSKIN: *Modern Painters*, IV, 1856

I go always (other things being equal) for the man who inherits family traditions and the cumulative humanities of at least four or five generations.

O. W. HOLMES: *The Autocrat of the Breakfast Table*, I, 1858

How shall a man escape from his ancestors, or draw off from his veins the black drop which he drew from his father's or his mother's life?

R. W. EMERSON: *The Conduct of Life*, I, 1860

There is something frightful in the way in which not only characteristic qualities, but particular manifestations of them, are repeated from generation to generation.

O. W. HOLMES: *The Guardian Angel*, pref., 1867

Blood is a destiny. One's genius descends in the stream from long lines of ancestry.

A. BRONSON ALCOTT: *Tablets*, II, 1868

Though it be false and mischievous to speak of hereditary vice, it is most true and wise to observe the mysterious fact of hereditary temptation.

WALTER BAGEHOT: *Literary Studies*, I, 1879

It runs in the blood like wooden legs.
CHESHIRE SAYING

What is born of a hen will scratch.
ITALIAN PROVERB

Bad hen, bad egg. (Mala gallina, malum ovum.) LATIN PROVERB

If you know his father and grandfather you may trust his son. MOROCCAN PROVERB

Clever father, clever daughter; clever mother, clever son. RUSSIAN PROVERB

An ill cow may hae a gude calf.
SCOTTISH PROVERB

[*See also* Ancestry, Aristocracy, Birth (High), Child, Children, Heritage, Like, Nobility, Rank, Sterilization.

Heresy

Though we, or an angel from heaven, preach any other gospel unto you than that which we have preached unto you, let him be accursed. GALATIANS I, 8, *c.* 50

A man that is a heretic, after the first and second admonition, reject. TITUS III, 10, *c.* 60

Damnable heresies. II PETER II, 1, *c.* 60

Ignorance is the mark of the heathen, knowledge of the true church, and conceit of the heretics.
CLEMENT OF ALEXANDRIA: *Stromateis,* I, *c.* 193

It often happens that when it becomes necessary to defend certain points of Catholic doctrine against the insidious attacks of heresy, they are more carefully studied, they become more clearly understood, they are more earnestly inculcated; and so the very questions raised by heretics give occasion to a more thorough knowledge of the subject in question.
ST. AUGUSTINE: *The City of God,* XVI, 427

The toleration of heretics is more injurious than the devastation of the provinces by the barbarians.
POPE GELASIUS (reigned 492–96)

If I had a brother, I would rather he had slain a hundred men than that he were in a single heresy. I would rather that my sister had had a hundred men, and that my brother had slain all his children with his own hand.
BERTHOLD OF REGENSBURG: Sermon, *c.* 1260

If forgers and other malefactors are put to death by the secular power, there is much more reason for excommunicating and even putting to death one convicted of heresy.
THOMAS AQUINAS: *Summa theologicæ,* II, *c.* 1265

Faith is not to be held with heretics.
CHRISTOPHER MARLOWE: *The Jew of Malta,* II, *c.* 1590

From heresy, frenzy and jealousy, good Lord, deliver me.
JOHN HARINGTON: Tr. of LUDOVICO ARIOSTO: *Orlando Furioso* (1532), 1591

Blessed shall be he that doth revolt from his allegiance to a heretic.
SHAKESPEARE: *King John,* III, *c.* 1596

In religion,
What damned error, but some sober brow
Will bless it and approve it with a text.
SHAKESPEARE: *The Merchant of Venice,* III, *c.* 1597

Heresies perish not with their authors, but, like the river Arethusa, though they lose their currents in one place, they rise up again in another.
THOMAS BROWNE: *Religio Medici,* I, 1642

A man may be a heretic in the truth; and if he believes things only because his pastor says so, or the assembly so determines, without knowing other reason, though his belief be true, yet the very truth he holds becomes his heresy. JOHN MILTON: *Areopagitica,* 1644

For the same man to be a heretic and a good subject is incompossible.
GEORGE HERBERT: *Jacula Prudentum,* 1651

Heresy may be easier kept out than shook off.
IBID.

From all false doctrine, heresy, and schism, Good Lord, deliver us.
THE BOOK OF COMMON PRAYER (*The Litany*), 1662

Among theologians heretics are those who are not backed with a sufficient array of battalions to render them orthodox.
VOLTAIRE: *Philosophical Dictionary,* 1764

Every society has a right to preserve public peace and order, and therefore has a good right to prohibit the propagation of opinions which have a dangerous tendency. . . . No member of a society has a right to teach any doctrine contrary to what the society holds to be true.
SAMUEL JOHNSON: *Boswell's Life,* May 7, 1773

If the propagation of religious truth be a principal end of government, as government; if it be the duty of a government to employ for that end its constitutional power; if the constitutional power of governments extends, as it most unquestionably does, to the making of laws for the burning of heretics; if burning be, as it most assuredly is, in many cases, a most effectual mode of suppressing opinions; why should we not burn?
T. B. MACAULAY: *Gladstone on Church and State,* 1839 (Edinburgh Review, April)

The law knows no heresy.
Decision of the Supreme Court of the United States in *Watson* vs. *Jones,* Dec., 1871

If special honor is claimed for any, then heresy should have it as the truest servitor of human kind.

CHARLES BRADLAUGH: Speech in London, Sept. 25, 1881

Books of apostates, heretics, schismatics, and all other writers defending heresy or schism or in any way attacking the foundations of religion, are altogether prohibited.

POPE LEO XIII: *General Decrees Concerning the Prohibition and Censorship of Books*, Jan. 25, 1897

With the Bible one becomes a heretic.

ITALIAN PROVERB

[*See also* Agnostic, Atheist, Church (Roman Catholic), Faith, Flesh, Huss (John), Jerome (St.), Jew, Lying, Magic, Sin.

Heritage

The lines are fallen unto me in pleasant places; yea, I have a goodly heritage.

PSALMS XVI, 6, *c.* 150 B.C.

What we have inherited from our fathers and mothers is not all that walks in us. There are all sorts of dead ideas and lifeless old beliefs.

HENRIK IBSEN: *Ghosts*, I, 1881

[*See also* Birth (High), Family, Heir, Inheritance, Wisdom.

Hermit

Far in a wild, unknown to public view,
From youth to age a reverend hermit grew;
The moss his bed, the cave his humble cell,
His food the fruits, his drink the crystal well:
Remote from man, with God he pass'd the days,
Prayer all his business, all his pleasure praise.

THOMAS PARNELL: *The Hermit*, *c.* 1715

How blest the solitary's lot,
Who, all-forgetting, all-forgot,
  Within his humble cell,
The cavern wild with tangling roots,
Sits o'er his newly-gathered fruits,
  Beside his crystal well.

ROBERT BURNS: *Despondency*, 1786

For years upon a mountain's brow,
A hermit lived, the Lord knows how;
A robe of sackcloth he did bear,
And got his food, the Lord knows where.
Hardships and penance were his lot;
He often pray'd, the Lord knows what.
At length this holy man did die;
He left this world, the Lord knows why.
He's buried in this gloomy den,
And he shall rise, the Lord knows when.

H. J. LOARING: *Epitaphs Quaint, Curious and Elegant*, 1872

[*See also* Ferry, Heaven and Hell, Nun.

Hero

Barren countries produce the most heroes.

Ascribed to MENANDER (342–291 B.C.)

Who is the noblest hero? The man who conquers his senses.

BHARTRIHARI: *The Niti Sataka*, *c.* 625

  They have sat
The live-long day, with patient expectation,
To see great Pompey pass the streets of Rome.

SHAKESPEARE: *Julius Cæsar*, I, 1599

There are heroes of evil as well as of good.

LA ROCHEFOUCAULD: *Maxims*, 1665

Shakespeare ought not to have made Othello black; for the hero of a tragedy ought always to be white.

THOMAS RYMER: *A Short View of Tragedy*, 1692

No man is a hero to his valet.

Ascribed by Smith to MME. CORNUEL, *c.* 1694 (The idea is to be found in the Greeks)

Whoe'er excels in what we prize,
Appears a hero in our eyes.

JONATHAN SWIFT: *Cadenus and Vanessa*, 1713

Heroes are much the same, the point's agreed,
From Macedonia's madman to the Swede;
The whole strange purpose of their lives, to find
Or make an enemy of all mankind.

ALEXANDER POPE: *An Essay on Man*, IV, 1734

See the conquering hero comes!
Sound the trumpet, beat the drums!

THOMAS MORELL: *Judas Maccabaeus*, 1747 (Set to music by G. F. HÄNDEL)

A light supper, a good night's sleep, and a fine morning have sometimes made a hero of the same man who, by an indigestion, a restless night, and rainy morning would have proved a coward.

LORD CHESTERFIELD: *Letter to his son*, April 26, 1748

Two persons threw themselves into a gulf: this was an action common to Sappho and Curtius. But the first did it to put an end to the torments of love and the other to save Rome: Sappho was therefore a fool and Curtius a hero.

C. A. HELVÉTIUS: *De l'esprit*, II, 1758

Your hero always should be tall.

CHARLES CHURCHILL: *The Rosciad*, 1761

The boy stood on the burning deck
  Whence all but he had fled;
The flame that lit the battle's wreck,
  Shone round him o'er the dead.

FELICIA HEMANS: *Casabianca*, 1826

Hero-worship exists, has existed, and will forever exist, universally among mankind.

THOMAS CARLYLE: *Sartor Resartus*, III, 1836

Worship of a hero is transcendent admiration of a great man.

THOMAS CARLYLE: *Heroes and Hero-worship,* 1840 (Lecture in London, May 5)

It will never make any difference to a hero what the laws are. His greatness will shine and accomplish itself unto the end, whether they second him or not.

R. W. EMERSON: *The Conservative,* 1841

Thou and I, my friend, can, in the most flunky world, make, each of us, one non-flunky, one hero, if we like; that will be two heroes to begin with.

THOMAS CARLYLE: *Past and Present,* I, 1843

The legacy of heroes, — the memory of a great name, and the inheritance of a great example.

BENJAMIN DISRAELI: Speech in the House of Commons, Feb. 1, 1849

Every hero becomes a bore at last. Perhaps Voltaire was not bad-hearted, yet he said of the good Jesus, even, "I pray you, let me never hear that man's name again."

R. W. EMERSON: *Representative Men,* I, 1850

A hero cannot be a hero unless in an heroic world.

NATHANIEL HAWTHORNE: *American Note-Books,* May 7, 1850

'Tis fortune chiefly that makes heroes.

H. G. BOHN: *Handbook of Proverbs,* 1855

Each man is a hero and an oracle to somebody.

R. W. EMERSON: *Letters and Social Aims,* 1875

A great style of hero draws equally all classes, all the extremes of society, till we say the very dogs believe in him.

R. W. EMERSON: *Greatness,* 1876

Here is a hero who did nothing but shake the tree when the fruit was ripe. Do you think that was a small thing to do? Well, just look at the tree he shook.

F. W. NIETZSCHE: *Human All-too-Human,* II, 1878

Everyone is the chief personage, the hero, of his own baptism, his own wedding, and his own funeral.

O. W. HOLMES: *Some of My Early Teachers,* 1882 (Farewell lecture at the Harvard Medical School, Nov. 28)

No man is a hero to his own wife; no woman is a wife to her own hero.

Author unidentified

A hero is one who knows how to hang on one minute longer. NORWEGIAN PROVERB

[*See also* Agamemnon, Beer, Children, Greatness, Hero-worship.

Heroism

Times of heroism are generally times of terror.

R. W. EMERSON: *Heroism,* 1841

Heroism is the brilliant triumph of the soul over the flesh: that is to say, over fear: fear of poverty, of suffering, of calumny, of sickness, of isolation, and of death.

H. F. AMIEL: *Journal,* Oct. 1, 1849

The greatest obstacle to being heroic is the doubt whether one may not be going to prove one's self a fool; the truest heroism is to resist the doubt, and the profoundest wisdom to know when it ought to be resisted, and when to be obeyed.

NATHANIEL HAWTHORNE: *The Blithedale Romance,* II, 1852

When the will defies fear, when duty throws the gauntlet down to fate, when honor scorns to compromise with death — this is heroism.

R. G. INGERSOLL: Speech in New York, May 29, 1882

[*See also* Bravery, Courage, Hero.

Herring

Of all the fish in the sea herring is the king.

JAMES HOWELL: *Proverbs,* 1659

To draw a herring across the trail.

AMERICAN PHRASE, not recorded before the XIX century (In England *track* is usually substituted for *trail*)

A land with lots of herring can get along with few doctors. DUTCH PROVERB

[*See also* Fish, Miser.

Hesitation

How long halt ye between two opinions? If the Lord be God, follow him: but if Baal, then follow him. I KINGS XVIII, 21, *c.* 500 B.C.

Ares hates those who hesitate.

EURIPIDES: *Heraclidae, c.* 425 B.C. (*Ares*=Mars)

No man, having put his hand to the plow, and looking back, is fit for the kingdom of God.

LUKE IX, 62, *c.* 75

And while I at length debate and beat the bush
There shall step in other men and catch the birds. JOHN HEYWOOD: *Proverbs,* 1546

I am at war 'twixt will and will not.

SHAKESPEARE: *Measure for Measure,* II, 1604

Far better never to have heard the name
Of zeal and just ambition, than to live
Baffled and plagued by a mind that every hour
Turns recreant to her task: takes heart again,
Then feels immediately some hollow thought
Hang like an interdict upon her hopes.

WILLIAM WORDSWORTH: *The Prelude,* I, 1805

The man who hesitates is lost; so is the woman who doesn't. Author unidentified

[*See also* Deliberation, Indecision.

Heterodoxy

[*See* Orthodoxy, Trade (=commerce).

Hexameter

These lame hexameters the strong-wing'd music of Homer!
No — but a most burlesque barbarous experiment.
When was a harsher sound ever heard, ye Muses, in England?
When did a frog coarser croak upon our Helicon?

ALFRED TENNYSON: *On Translations of Homer,* 1863

Hiccup

Sneezing will stop a hiccup.
HIPPOCRATES: *Aphorisms, c.* 400 B.C.

[*See also* Laughter.

High

They that stand high have many blasts to shake them;
And if they fall, they dash themselves to pieces.
SHAKESPEARE: *Richard III,* I, *c.* 1592

The higher the plum-tree, the sweeter the plum.
JOHN CLARKE: *Parœmiologia Anglo-Latina,* 1639

The higher the hill, the lower the grass.
JAMES KELLY: *Complete Collection of Scottish Proverbs,* 1721

The highest branch is not the safest roost.
H. G. BOHN: *Handbook of Proverbs,* 1855

[*See also* Fall.

Highland

[*See* Nostalgia.

Highlander

Highlandmen hate tools and taxes.
ROBERT BURNS: *To William S[impson],* May, 1785

It's ill taking the breeks aff a Hielandman.
WALTER SCOTT: *Rob Roy,* XXVII, 1817 (*Breeks*=breeches)

My heart's in the Highlands, my heart is not here;
My heart's in the Highlands a-chasing the deer;
A-chasing the wild deer, and following the roe —
My heart's in the Highlands wherever I go.
ROBERT BURNS: *My Heart's in the Highlands,* 1790

Highlands

Speak weel o' the Hielands, but dwell in the Laigh.
SCOTTISH PROVERB (*Laigh*=Lowlands)

Highway

The king's highway.
ENGLISH PHRASE (The New English Dictionary's first example is dated 1604)

No man can make a stable-yard of the king's highway.
LORD ELLENBOROUGH: *Judgment in Rex* vs. *Cross,* 1812 (Probably the earliest parking decision)

He that builds a house by the highway finds it either too high or too low.
ITALIAN PROVERB

Hill

A city that is set on a hill cannot be hid.
MATTHEW V, 14, *c.* 75

The everlasting hills do not change like the faces of men. TACITUS: *Annals,* XIV, *c.* 110

Wonder at hills; keep on the plain.
JOHN FLORIO: *Second Frutes,* 1591

Hills peep o'er hills, and Alps on Alps arise.
ALEXANDER POPE: *An Essay on Criticism,* II, 1711

The king of France and twenty thousand men
Went up the hill, and then came down again.
Author unidentified (*Home* sometimes appears in place of *down*)

Jack and Jill went up the hill
To fetch a pail of water;
Jack fell down and broke his crown,
And Jill came tumbling after.
NURSERY RHYME, probably of Norse origin

Green hills are blue from a distance.
IRISH PROVERB

[*See also* High, Mountain.

Himself

Conscience avaunt, Richard's himself again.
COLLEY CIBBER: Adaptation of SHAKESPEARE: *Richard III,* V, 1700

Hind

A hind let loose.
GENESIS XLIX, 21, *c.* 700 B.C.

Hindmost

The Devil take the hindmost.
BEAUMONT and FLETCHER: *Philaster,* V, 1611

Hindsight

Their hindsight was better than their foresight.
Ascribed to H. W. BEECHER by W. S. WALSH: *The International Encyclopedia of Prose and Poetical Quotations,* 1908

When you're thirsty it's too late to think about digging a well. JAPANESE PROVERB

Hip

He smote them hip and thigh.
JUDGES XV, 8, *c.* 500 B.C.

I have thee on the hip.
SHAKESPEARE: *The Merchant of Venice,* IV, *c.* 1597

[*See also* Kiss, Lip.

Hippocrates (c. 460–357 B.C.)

Hippocrates was the first to be both physician and philosopher — the first to recognize what nature does.
GALEN: *On the Natural Faculties,* I, *c.* 175

Hippopotamus

I have seen the hippopotamus, both asleep and awake; and I can assure you that, awake or asleep, he is the ugliest of the works of God.
T. B. MACAULAY: *Letter to Macvey Napier,* March 9, 1850

He thought he saw a banker's clerk
 Descending from the bus;
He looked again, and found it was
 A hippopotamus.
" If this should stay to dine," he said,
 " There won't be much for us."
C. L. DODGSON (LEWIS CARROLL): *Sylvie and Bruno,* 1889

Hire

[*See* Labor.

Hiss

A hundred hisses outweigh a thousand claps. The former come more directly from the heart.
CHARLES LAMB: *Letter to William Wordsworth,* Dec. 11, 1806

Historian

It is natural for a good man to love his country and his friends, and to hate the enemies of both. But when he writes history he must abandon such feelings, and be prepared to praise enemies who deserve it and to censure the dearest and most intimate friends.
POLYBIUS: *Histories,* I, *c.* 125 B.C.

The first law is that the historian shall never dare to set down what is false; the second, that he shall never dare to conceal the truth; the third, that there shall be no suspicion in his work of either favoritism or prejudice.
CICERO: *De oratore,* II, *c.* 80 B.C.

It is a noble employment to rescue from oblivion those who deserve to be remembered, and by extending the reputation of others, to advance at the same time our own.
PLINY THE YOUNGER: *Letters,* V, *c.* 110

The historian should be fearless and incorruptible; a man of independence, loving frankness and truth; one who, as the poet says, calls a fig a fig and a spade a spade. He should yield to neither hatred nor affection, but should be unsparing and unpitying. He should be neither shy nor deprecating, but an impartial judge, giving each side all it deserves but no more. He should know in his writings no country and no city; he should bow to no authority and acknowledge no king. He should never consider what this or that man will think, but should state the facts as they really occurred.
LUCIAN: *How History Should be Written,* *c.* 170

So long as Poggio lauds his country and reviles its enemies, he escapes being either a bad citizen or a good historian.
JACOPO SANNAZARO: *Epigram on Poggio Bracciolini,* author of a history of Florence, *c.* 1500

The historian makes himself a poet . . . in painting, for the effects, the motions, the whisperings of the people, which though in disputation, one might say were true — yet who will mark them well shall find them taste of a poetical vein, and in that kind are gallantly to be marked — for though perchance, they were not so, yet it is enough they might be so.
PHILIP SIDNEY: *Letter to Robert Sidney,* Oct. 18, 1580

If an historian were to relate truthfully all the crimes, weaknesses and disorders of mankind, his readers would take his work for satire rather than for history.
PIERRE BAYLE: *Dictionary,* 1697

It is the most agreeable talent of an historian to be able to draw up his armies and fight his battles in proper expressions, to set before our eyes the divisions, cabals, and jealousies of great men.
JOSEPH ADDISON: *The Spectator,* July 2, 1712

The man who ventures to write contemporary history must expect to be attacked both for everything he has said and everything he has not said.
VOLTAIRE: *Letter to Bertin de Rocheret,* April 14, 1732

Historians relate, not so much what is done, as what they would have believed.
BENJAMIN FRANKLIN: *Poor Richard's Almanac,* 1739

The first quality of an historian is to be true and impartial; the next to be interesting.
DAVID HUME: *Letter to William Mure,* Oct., 1754

Great abilities are not requisite for an historian, for in historical composition all the greatest powers of the human mind are quiescent. He has facts ready to his hand, so there is no exercise of invention. Imagination is not required to any high degree — only about as much as is used in the lower kinds of poetry.
SAMUEL JOHNSON: *Boswell's Life,* July 6, 1763

An historian is a prophet in retrospect.
A. W. VON SCHLEGEL: *In the Athenäum* (Berlin), 1798

The historian's first duties are sacrilege and the mocking of false gods. They are his indispensable instruments for establishing the truth.

JULES MICHELET: *Histoire de France*, I, 1833

A historian stands in a fiduciary position towards his readers, and if he withholds from them important facts likely to influence their judgment, he is guilty of fraud, and, when justice is done in this world, will be condemned to refund all moneys he has made by his false professions, with compound interest. This sort of fraud is unknown to the law, but to nobody else.

AUGUSTINE BIRRELL: *Obiter Dicta*, I, 1884

The historian reports to us, not events themselves, but the impressions they have made on him.

HEINRICH VON SYBEL: Memorial address on Leopold von Ranke, 1886

The historian looks backward. In the end he also believes backward.

F. W. NIETZSCHE: *The Twilight of the Idols*, 1889

[*See also* History, Philosopher, Thucydides.

History

And Bela died, and Jobab the son of Zeräh of Bozrah reigned in his stead.
And Jobab died, and Husham of the land of Temani reigned in his stead.
And Husham died, and Hadad the son of Bedad, who smote Midian in the field of Moab, reigned in his stead.
And Hadad died, and Samlah of Masrekah reigned in his stead.
And Samlah died, and Saul of Rehoboth by the river reigned in his stead.
And Saul died, and Baalhanan the son of Achbor reigned in his stead.
And Baalhanan the son of Achbor died, and Hadar reigned in his stead.

GENESIS XXXVI, 33–39, *c.* 700 B.C.

History repeats itself.

ENGLISH PROVERB, found also in other languages, and apparently derived from THUCYDIDES: *History*, I, *c.* 410 B.C.

History offers the best training for those who are to take part in public affairs.

POLYBIUS: *Histories*, I, *c.* 125 B.C.

The aim of history is to assemble real facts and real speeches, to the end that lovers of knowledge may be instructed and persuaded.

POLYBIUS: *Histories*, II

History is now an organic whole. The affairs of Italy and Africa are intermingled with those of Asia and Greece, and all move to one end.

POLYBIUS: *Histories*, III

History is the witness of the times, the torch of truth, the life of memory, the teacher of life, the messenger of antiquity.

CICERO: *De oratore*, II, *c.* 80 B.C.

Not to know what happened before one was born is always to be a child. IBID.

History is philosophy teaching by examples.

DIONYSIUS OF HALICARNASSUS: *Antiquities of Rome*, *c.* 20 B.C.

Oratory and poetry are of little value unless they reach the highest perfection; but history, in whatever way it may be executed, is a source of pleasure.

PLINY THE YOUNGER: *Letters*, V, *c.* 110

The only good histories are those written by those who had command in the events they describe.

MICHEL DE MONTAIGNE: *Essays*, II, 1580

It is the true office of history to represent the events themselves, together with the counsels, and to leave the observations and conclusions thereupon to the liberty and faculty of every man's judgment.

FRANCIS BACON: *The Advancement of Learning*, II, 1605

We are much beholden to Machiavel[li] and others, that write what men do, and not what they ought to do. IBID.

We may gather out of history a policy no less wise than eternal, by the comparison and application of other men's forepassed miseries with our own like errors and ill deservings.

WALTER RALEIGH: *Historie of the World*, pref., 1614

What he wanteth in sense he supplies in history.

THOMAS ADAMS: *Diseases of the Soul*, 1616

History deals with the irregular effects of the passions and caprices of men.

BERNARD DE FONTENELLE: *Histoire du renouvellement de l'Académie des Sciences*, pref., 1708

Anything but history, for history must be false.

ROBERT WALPOLE: On his deathbed, on being asked what should be read to him, 1715

History, the longer it runs, contracts the more filth, and retains in it the additional ordure of every soil through which it passes.

WILLIAM WARBURTON (BISHOP OF GLOUCESTER): *The Causes of Prodigies and Miracles*, I, 1727

History can be well written only in a free country.

VOLTAIRE: *Letter to Frederick the Great*, May 27, 1737

History is only a confused heap of facts.

LORD CHESTERFIELD: *Letter to his son*, Feb. 5, 1750

The history of the great events of this world is hardly more than the history of crimes.

VOLTAIRE: *Essai sur les mœurs*, 1754

History is only a picture of crimes and misfortunes.
VOLTAIRE: *L'Ingénu*, x, 1757

My dear Smollett . . . disgraces his talent by writing those stupid romances commonly called history.
MARY WORTLEY MONTAGU: *Letter to the Countess of Bute*, Oct. 3, 1758 (SMOLLETT'S *History of England* appeared in 1756)

On whatever side we regard the history of Europe, we shall perceive it to be a tissue of crimes, follies, and misfortunes.
OLIVER GOLDSMITH: *The Citizen of the World*, XLII, 1762

Happy is the nation that has no history.
C. B. BECCARIA: *Trattato dei delitti e delle pene*, intro., 1764

How much charlatanry has been put into history, either by astonishing the reader with prodigies, by titillating human malignity with satire, or by flattering the families of tyrants with infamous praise!
VOLTAIRE: *Philosophical Dictionary*, 1764

We are very uncorrupt and tolerably enlightened judges of the transactions of past ages; where no passions deceive and where the whole train of circumstances, from the trifling cause to the tragical event, is set in an orderly series before us. Few are the partisans of departed tyranny; and to be a Whig on the business of an hundred years ago is very consistent with every advantage of present servility.
EDMUND BURKE: *Thoughts on the Cause of the Present Discontents*, 1770

There is but a shallow stream of thought in history.
SAMUEL JOHNSON: *Boswell's Life*, April 19, 1772

All history, so far as it is not supported by contemporary evidence, is romance.
SAMUEL JOHNSON: *Boswell's Tour to the Hebrides*, Nov. 20, 1773

That certain kings reigned and certain battles were fought we can depend upon as true, but all the coloring, all the philosophy of history is conjecture.
SAMUEL JOHNSON: *Boswell's Life*, April 11, 1775

History . . . is little more than the register of the crimes, follies and misfortunes of mankind.
EDWARD GIBBON: *The Decline and Fall of the Roman Empire*, I, 1776 (Cf. VOLTAIRE, *ante*, 1754 and 1757)

This is my history; like all other histories, a narrative of misery.
SAMUEL JOHNSON: *Letter to Bennet Langton*, Aug. 25, 1784

Some write a narrative of wars and feats,
Of heroes little known, and call the rant
A history. Describe the man, of whom
His own coevals took but little note,
And paint his person, character and views,
As they had known him from his mother's womb.
WILLIAM COWPER: *The Task*, III, 1785

History makes one shudder and laugh by turns.
HORACE WALPOLE: *Letter to Lord Strafford*, 1786

The histories of mankind that we possess are histories only of the higher classes.
T. R. MALTHUS: *The Principle of Population*, II, 1798

The important events in the world are not deliberately brought about; they simply occur.
G. C. LICHTENBERG: *Reflections*, 1799

History, in general, only informs us what bad government is.
THOMAS JEFFERSON: *Letter to John Narvell*, 1807

I am determined to apply myself to a study that is hateful and disgusting to my very soul, but which is, above all studies, necessary for him who would be listened to as a mender of antiquated abuses. I mean that record of crimes and miseries — history.
P. B. SHELLEY: *Letter to Thomas Hookham*, Dec. 17, 1812

History's pen its praise or blame supplies,
And lies like truth, and still most truly lies.
BYRON: *Lara*, I, 1814

A morsel of genuine history is a thing so rare as to be always valuable.
THOMAS JEFFERSON: *Letter to John Adams*, 1817

There is the moral of all human tales;
'Tis but the same rehearsal of the past,
First freedom, and then glory — when that fails,
Wealth, vice, corruption, — barbarism at last.
BYRON: *Childe Harold*, IV, 1818

History fades into fable; fact becomes clouded with doubt and controversy; the inscription molders from the tablet: the statue falls from the pedestal. Columns, arches, pyramids, what are they but heaps of sand; and their epitaphs, but characters written in the dust?
WASHINGTON IRVING: *The Sketch-Book*, 1820

The public history of all countries, and all ages, is but a sort of mask, richly colored. The interior working of the machinery must be foul.
JOHN QUINCY ADAMS: *Diary*, Nov. 9, 1822

Man is fed with fables through life, and leaves it in the belief he knows something of what has been passing, when in truth he has known nothing but what has passed under his own eye.
THOMAS JEFFERSON: *Letter to Thomas Cooper*, 1823

The historic muse, from age to age,
Through many a waste heart-sickening page
Hath traced the works of man.

JOHN KEBLE: *The Christian Year,* 1827

I should like much to tell the truth; but if I did, I should be torn to pieces, here or abroad.

THE DUKE OF WELLINGTON: Quoted in SAMUEL ROGERS: *Recollections,* c. 1827

History, at least in its state of ideal perfection, is a compound of poetry and philosophy. It impresses general truths on the mind by a vivid representation of particular characters and incidents.

T. B. MACAULAY: *Hallam,* 1828 (Edinburgh Review, Sept.)

To come to the true history of a country you must read its laws; you must read books treating of its usages and customs in former times; and you must particularly inform yourself as to prices of labor and of food.

WILLIAM COBBETT: *Advice to Young Men,* II, 1829

Peoples and government have never learned anything from history, or acted on principles deducible from it.

G. W. F. HEGEL: *The Philosophy of History,* 1832

It is part of my creed that the only poetry is history, could we tell it right.

THOMAS CARLYLE: *Letter to R. W. Emerson,* Aug. 12, 1834

Universal history, the history of what man has accomplished in this world, is at bottom the history of the great men who have worked here.

THOMAS CARLYLE: *Heroes and Hero-Worship,* I, 1840 (Lecture in London, May 5)

Histories are a kind of distilled newspapers.

THOMAS CARLYLE: *Heroes and Hero-Worship,* III (Lecture in London, May 12)

The two parties which divide the state, the party of conservatism and that of innovation, are very old, and have disputed the possession of the world ever since it was made. This quarrel is the subject of civil history.

R. W. EMERSON: *The Conservative,* 1841

I am ashamed to see what a shallow village tale our so-called history is.

R. W. EMERSON: *History,* 1841

There is less intention in history than we ascribe to it. We impute deep-laid, far-sighted plans to Cæsar and Napoleon; but the best of their power was in nature, not in them.

R. W. EMERSON: *Spiritual Laws,* 1841

The last phase of a world historical figure is generally comical. History takes this course in order that mankind may break away from its past in good spirits.

KARL MARX: *A Criticism of the Hegelian Philosophy of Right,* 1844

History, showing us the life of nations, has nothing to record save wars and revolutions: the peaceful years appear only as brief pauses or interludes, scattered here and there.

ARTHUR SCHOPENHAUER: *Parerga und Paralipomena,* II, 1851

The study of history is said to enlarge and enlighten the mind. Why? Because, as I conceive, it gives it a power of judging of passing events, and of all events, and a conscious superiority over them, which before it did not possess.

J. H. NEWMAN: *On the Scope and Nature of University Education,* v, 1852

The only history worth reading is that written at the time of which it treats, the history of what was done and seen, heard out of the mouths of the men who did and saw.

JOHN RUSKIN: *Stones of Venice,* III, 1853

He that would know what shall be, must consider what hath been.

H. G. BOHN: *Handbook of Proverbs,* 1855

History is all party pamphlets.

R. W. EMERSON: *Journal,* Feb. 18, 1855

Not that which men do worthily, but that which they do successfully, is what history makes haste to record.

H. W. BEECHER: *Life Thoughts,* 1858

History has the great virtue of soothing.

VICTOR DURUY: *Instruction ministérielle,* Sept. 4, 1863

There is no law of history any more than of a kaleidoscope.

JOHN RUSKIN: *Letter to J. A. Froude,* Jan., 1864

History is a voice forever sounding across the centuries the laws of right and wrong.

J. A. FROUDE: *The Science of History,* 1864 (Lecture in London, Feb. 5)

Happy the people whose annals are blank in history-books.

THOMAS CARLYLE: *Frederick the Great,* XVI, 1865 (Cf. BECCARIA, *ante,* 1764)

The march of Providence is so slow and our desires so impatient; the work of progress is so immense and our means of aiding it so feeble; the life of humanity is so long, that of the individual so brief, that we often see only the ebb of the advancing ways, and are thus discouraged. It is history that teaches us to hope.

ROBERT E. LEE: *Letter to Charles Marshall,* c. 1866

The time is not come for impartial history. If the truth were told just now it would not be credited.

ROBERT E. LEE: To David Macrae (quoted in MACRAE: *The Americans at Home,* I), c. 1868

The whole history of civilization is strewn with creeds and institutions which were invaluable at first, and deadly afterward.
WALTER BAGEHOT: *Physics and Politics*, 1869

History is a record of the gradual negation of man's original bestiality by the evolution of his humanity.
M. A. BAKUNIN: *Dieu et l'état*, 1871

I don't believe the truth will ever be known, and I have a great contempt for history.
GEORGE G. MEADE: On being asked to write his memoirs of the Civil War, 1871 (Cf. WELLINGTON, *ante*, *c.* 1827; LEE, 1868)

The masses of worthless gossip furnished us by historians.
HERBERT SPENCER: *The Data of Ethics*, IV, 1879

When a history book contains no lies it is always tedious.
JACQUES THIBAULT (ANATOLE FRANCE): *Le crime de Sylvestre Bonnard*, 1881

All history is only one long story to this effect: men have struggled for power over their fellow-men in order that they might win the joys of earth at the expense of others, and might shift the burdens of life from their own shoulders upon those of others.
W. G. SUMNER: *The Forgotten Man*, 1883

History is a pageant and not a philosopher.
AUGUSTINE BIRRELL: *Obiter Dicta*, II, 1887

Anybody can make history. Only a great man can write it.
OSCAR WILDE: *The Critic as Artist*, 1891

History is merely gossip.
OSCAR WILDE: *Lady Windermere's Fan*, II, 1892

The memorable events of history are the visible effects of invisible changes in human thought.
GUSTAVE LEBON: *Psychologie des foules*, intro., 1895

History is simply a piece of paper covered with print; the main thing is still to make history, not to write it.
OTTO VON BISMARCK (1815–98)

A boy who hears a lesson in history ended by the beauty of peace, and how Napoleon brought ruin upon the world and that he should be forever cursed, will not long have much confidence in his teacher. He wants to hear more about the fighting and less about the peace negotiations.
WILLIAM LEE HOWARD: *Peace, Dolls and Pugnacity*, 1903

An account mostly false, of events unimportant, which are brought about by rulers mostly knaves, and soldiers mostly fools.
AMBROSE BIERCE: *The Devil's Dictionary*, 1906

Every student during his academic period ought to get up one bit of history thoroughly from the ultimate sources, in order to convince himself what history is not.
W. G. SUMNER: *Folkways*, 1907

History is bunk.
Ascribed to HENRY FORD, *c.* 1915 (On the stand during the trial of his suit against the Chicago *Tribune*, July 15, 1919, Mr. Ford denied the use of the word *bunk*, but was somewhat vague about what he did say. The following is from the record: *Q.* You said in 1915 and 1916, didn't you, that you did not take any stock in history; it was tradition? *A.* Yes. *Q.* You think so more now than then? *A.* I do, yes. *Q.* Did you mean to support your argument by a reference to history, the thing that you said was bunk? *A.* I say Mr. Delavigne added that. I don't remember ever reading it. *Q.* Those are not your sentiments? *A.* Well, I don't know about that. *Q.* You don't believe in history? *A.* I don't say I don't believe in it)

History is a fairy tale whose end is death.
Author unidentified (Quoted in J. A. CRAMB: *The Origins and Destiny of Imperial Britain*, I, 1915)

People think too historically. They are always living half in a cemetery.
ARISTIDE BRIAND (1862–1932)

It is not the neutrals or the lukewarms who make history.
ADOLF HITLER: Speech in Berlin, April 23, 1933

The history of the world is the judge of the world.
HERMANN ULLMANN: Article in Geist der Zeit (Berlin), 1938

History is a tired old man with a long beard.
Author unidentified

History is something that never happened, written by a man who wasn't there. IBID.

Of all history the most instructive to a man is his own. IBID.

The history of the world is only the opinion of the world. GERMAN PROVERB

Human history is similar to the heroic tales pigs relate of swine. WELSH PROVERB

[*See also* Historian, Pedagogue, Poetry, Progress, Sin.

History, Materialistic Conception of

The method of production of the material things of life generally determines the social, political, and spiritual currents of life. It is not the consciousness of men which determines their mode of existence; rather, it is

their social existence which determines the nature of their consciousness.
KARL MARX: *A Contribution to the Critique of Political Economy*, pref., 1859

The materialist conception of history starts from the proposition that the production of the means to support human life and, next to production, the exchange of things produced, is the basis of all social structure. . . . From this point of view the final causes of all social changes and political revolutions are to be sought . . . in changes in the modes of production and exchange.
FRIEDRICH ENGELS: *Socialism, Utopian and Scientific*, 1891

The economic interpretation of history does not necessarily mean that all events are determined solely by economic forces. It simply means that economic facts are the ever recurring decisive forces, the chief points in the process of history.
EDWARD BERNSTEIN: *Evolutionary Socialism*, I, 1899

[*See also* Idea.

Hit

A hit, a very palpable hit.
SHAKESPEARE: *Hamlet*, V, *c.* 1601

The vulgar will keep no account of your hits, but of your misses.
THOMAS FULLER: *Gnomologia*, 1732

Hobbes, Thomas (1588–1679)

Here lies Tom Hobbes, the bugbear of the nation,
Whose death has frightened atheism out of fashion.
Anon.: *Broadside*, 1679

Hobbes is perhaps the first of whom we can say that he is a good English writer.
HENRY HALLAM: *Introduction to the Literature of Europe in the Fifteenth, Sixteenth and Seventeenth Centuries*, IV, 1838

Hobby

Everyone to his hobby. (Chacun à sa marotte.)
FRENCH PROVERB

Hobo

A hobo is a man who builds palaces and lives in shacks;
He builds Pullmans and rides the rods;
He builds automobiles and pushes a wheelbarrow;
He serves T-bone steaks and gets the soup bone.
Anon.: *What Is a Hobo?*, *c.* 1920

Hog

The hog is never good but when he is in the dish.
LEONARD MASCALL: *The Book of Cattle*, 1587

A hog in armor is still but a hog.
THOMAS FULLER: *Gnomologia*, 1732

The hog that plows not, nor obeys thy call,
Lives on the labor of this lord of all.
ALEXANDER POPE: *An Essay on Man*, III, 1733

[*See also* Durable, Living, Pig, Pollution, Ship.

Hogarth, William (1697–1764)

If genius warm thee, reader, stay,
If merit touch thee, shed a tear;
Be vice and dullness far away!
Great Hogarth's honor'd dust is here.
SAMUEL JOHNSON: Epitaph for Hogarth, suggested in a letter to David Garrick, Dec. 12, 1771

Holiday

If all the year were playing holidays,
To sport would be as tedious as to work.
SHAKESPEARE: *I Henry IV*, I, *c.* 1598

I am in a holiday humor.
SHAKESPEARE: *As You Like It*, IV, *c.* 1600

Certain days set apart by the church to be spent in holy idleness, which is favorable to piety. . . . The safest way of passing such days is to sit and yawn your head off.
VOLTAIRE: *Philosophical Dictionary*, 1764

Butcher'd to make a Roman holiday.
BYRON: *Childe Harold*, IV, 1818

The day is never so holy that the pot refuses to boil.
DANISH PROVERB

[*See also* Laziness, Monday.

Holiness

Holy, holy, holy, is the Lord of hosts: the whole earth is full of his glory.
ISAIAH VI, 3, *c.* 700 B.C.

The captain of the Lord's host said unto Joshua, Loose thy shoe from off thy foot; for the place whereon thou standest is holy. And Joshua did so.
JOSHUA V, 15, *c.* 500 B.C.

There are two sorts of holiness, substantial and accidental. St. Francis was once substantially holy by his faith in Jesus Christ, but afterwards he became infatuated with the accidental holiness of the hood, an accessory wholly foreign to holiness.
MARTIN LUTHER: *Table-Talk*, DVIII, 1569

A holy habit cleanseth not a foul soul.
GEORGE HERBERT: *Outlandish Proverbs*, 1640

There is no true holiness without humility.
THOMAS FULLER: *Gnomologia*, 1732

He that sees the beauty of holiness, or true moral good, sees the greatest and most important thing in the world. . . . Unless this is seen nothing is seen that is worth seeing: for there is no other true excellence or beauty.
JONATHAN EDWARDS: *Treatise of Religious Affections*, 1746

Everything that lives is holy.
WILLIAM BLAKE: *The Marriage of Heaven and Hell,* 1790

Divine am I inside and out, and I make holy whatever I touch or am touch'd from;
The scent of these arm-pits, aroma finer than prayer.
WALT WHITMAN: *Walt Whitman,* 1855

Holy of holies. (Sanctum sanctorum.)
LATIN PHRASE

Holland

The very cockpit of Christendom, the school of arms, and rendezvous of all adventurous spirits.
JAMES HOWELL: *Instructions for Foreign Travel,* 1642

A country that draws fifty foot of water,
In which men live as in the hold of nature;
And when the sea does in upon them break,
And drowns a province, does not spring a leak.
SAMUEL BUTLER: *The Character of Holland,* 1665

A country naturally cold, moist and unpleasant.
WILLIAM PETTY: *Political Arithmetic,* I, 1677

Where the broad ocean leans against the land.
OLIVER GOLDSMITH: *The Traveler,* 1764

Holland and the Netherlands ought to be seen once, because no other country is like them. Everything is artificial. It is interesting to see a country and a nature made, as it were, by man, and to compare it with God's nature.
S. T. COLERIDGE: *Table-Talk,* May 4, 1830

God made the ocean, but the Dutch made Holland.
DUTCH PROVERB

[*See also* Netherlands.

Hollander

[*See* Dutch.

Hollywood

They know only one word of more than one syllable here, and that is *fillum.*
Ascribed to LOUIS SHERWIN, on leaving Hollywood, *c.* 1920

A place where the inmates are in charge of the asylum.
Ascribed to LAURENCE STALLINGS, *c.* 1930

What I like about Hollywood is that one can get along by knowing two words of English – *swell* and *lousy.*
Ascribed to VICKI BAUM, *c.* 1933

[*See also* California.

Holy

[*See* Holiness.

Holy Ghost

He that shall blaspheme against the Holy Ghost hath never forgiveness, but is in danger of eternal damnation.
MARK III, 29, *c.* 70

She was found with child of the Holy Ghost.
MATTHEW I, 18, *c.* 75 (Cf. v, 20)

He that shall speak against the Holy Ghost, it shall not be forgiven him, neither in this world nor in the world to come.
MATTHEW XII, 32

Elizabeth was filled with the Holy Ghost.
LUKE I, 41, *c.* 75 (This phenomenon is described in various other places in the New Testament: cf. LUKE I, 67; IV, 1; ACTS II, 4; IV, 8; VI, 5; VII, 55; XIII, 9)

He said unto them, Have ye received the Holy Ghost since ye believed? And they said unto him, We have not so much as heard whether there be any Holy Ghost.
ACTS XIX, 2, *c.* 75

The Holy Ghost is not of an inferior nature to the Father and the Son, but, so to say, cosubstantial and coeternal.
ST. AUGUSTINE: *Of the Faith and of the Creed, c.* 393

Come, Holy Ghost, our souls inspire,
And lighten with celestial fire.
Thou the anointing Spirit art,
Who dost thy seven-fold gifts impart.
Thy blessed unction from above
Is comfort, life, and fire of love.
RABANUS MAURUS (ARCHBISHOP OF MAINZ): *Veni Creator Spiritus, c.* 825

When the flames and hellish cries
Fright mine ears, and fright mine eyes,
And all terrors me surprise;
  Sweet Spirit, comfort me!
ROBERT HERRICK: *Noble Numbers,* 1647

The Holy Ghost, proceeding from the Father and the Son, is of one substance, majesty, and glory with the Father and the Son, very and very eternal God.
The Doctrine and Discipline of the Methodist Episcopal Church, IV, 1932

[*See also* Bible, Blasphemy, Body, Sin, Trinity.

Home

Be not long away from home.
HOMER: *Odyssey,* III, *c.* 800 B.C.

They shall sit every man under his vine and under his fig-tree.
MICAH, IV, 4, *c.* 700 B.C.

As a bird that wandereth from her nest, so is a man that wandereth from his place.
PROVERBS XXVII, 8, *c.* 350 B.C.

Here is our home, here our country. (Hic domus, haec patria est.)
VIRGIL: *Æneid,* VII, 19 B.C.

If any man hunger, let him eat at home.
I CORINTHIANS XI, 34, *c.* 55

A man's foes shall be they of his own household.
MATTHEW X, 36, *c.* 75

What is the perfect way to happiness? To stay at home.
BHARTRIHARI: *The Niti Sataka, c.* 625

Home is home, be it never so homely.
ENGLISH PROVERB, traced by Apperson to *c.* 1300

Men are merriest when they are from home.
SHAKESPEARE: *Henry V,* I, *c.* 1599

When I was at home, I was in a better place.
SHAKESPEARE: *As You Like It,* II, *c.* 1600

Every bird likes its own nest best.
RANDLE COTGRAVE: *French-English Dictionary,* 1611

Every groom is a king at home.
JOHN DAVIES: *The Scourge of Folly,* 1611

Charity and beating begin at home.
JOHN FLETCHER: *Wit Without Money,* V, *c.* 1614

A saint abroad, at home a fiend.
PHINEAS FLETCHER: *The Purple Island,* VII, 1633

A fool knows more in his own house than a wise man in another's.
GEORGE HERBERT: *Outlandish Proverbs,* 1640

Dry bread at home is better than roast meat abroad.
IBID.

Every dog is a lion at home.
GIOVANNI TORIANO: *Italian Proverbs,* 1666

Happy the man, whose wish and care
A few paternal acres bound,
Content to breathe his native air,
In his own ground.
ALEXANDER POPE: *Ode on Solitude, c.* 1700

To be happy at home is the ultimate result of all ambition, the end to which every enterprise and labor tends, and of which every desire prompts the prosecution.
SAMUEL JOHNSON: *The Rambler,* Nov. 10, 1750

If solid happiness we prize,
Within our breast this jewel lies,
And they are fools who roam.
The world has nothing to bestow;
From our own selves our joys must flow,
And that dear hut, our home.
NATHANIEL COTTON: *The Fireside,* 1751

The poorest man may in his cottage bid defiance to all the force of the Crown. It may be frail, its roof may shake; the wind may blow through it; the storms may enter, — the rain may enter, — but the King of England cannot enter; all his forces dare not cross the threshold of the ruined tenement.
WILLIAM PITT (EARL OF CHATHAM): Speech in the House of Commons, 1760

Abstracted from home, I know no happiness in this world.
THOMAS JEFFERSON: *Letter to Lieut. de Unger,* 1780

He seemed to consider his own home merely as an hotel, where at any hour of the night he might disturb the family to claim admittance, where letters and messages might be left for him; where he dined when no other dinner was offered him, and where, when he made an appointment, he was to be met with.
FRANCES BURNEY: *Cecilia,* I, 1782

Oh dream of joy, is this indeed
The lighthouse top I see?
Is this the hill? is this the kirk?
Is this mine own countree?
S. T. COLERIDGE: *The Ancient Mariner,* VI, 1798

The sober comfort, all the peace which springs
From the large aggregate of little things;
On these small cares of daughter, wife or friend,
The almost sacred joys of home depend.
HANNAH MORE: *Sensibility, c.* 1800

The happiness of the domestic fireside is the first boon of Heaven; and it is well it is so, since it is that which is the lot of the mass of mankind.
THOMAS JEFFERSON: *Letter to John Armstrong,* Feb., 1813

The approach of home to husbands and to sires,
After long traveling by land or water,
Most naturally some small doubt inspires —
A female family's a serious matter.
BYRON: *Don Juan,* III, 1821

'Mid pleasures and palaces though we may roam,
Be it ever so humble, there's no place like home.
J. H. PAYNE: *Home, Sweet Home,* 1823 (The song occurs in his opera, *Clari, or, The Maid of Milan,* with music by Henry R. Bishop, London, May 8)

The largest part of mankind are nowhere greater strangers than at home.
S. T. COLERIDGE: *Aids to Reflection,* 1825

The stately homes of England,
How beautiful they stand!
Amidst their tall ancestral trees,
O'er all the pleasant land.
FELICIA HEMANS: *The Homes of England,* 1826

Sweet is the smile of home; the mutual look,
When hearts are of each other sure.
JOHN KEBLE: *The Christian Year,* 1827

In happy homes he saw the light
Of household fires gleam warm and bright.
H. W. LONGFELLOW: *Excelsior,* 1841

Weep no more, my lady;
  Oh, weep no more today!
We will sing one song for the old Kentucky home,
  For the old Kentucky home, far away.
S. C. FOSTER: *My Old Kentucky Home,* 1853

East or west, home is best.
H. G. BOHN: *Handbook of Proverbs,* 1855

Domesticity is the taproot which enables the English to branch wide and high. The motive and end of their trade and empire is to guard the independence and privacy of their homes.
R. W. EMERSON: *English Traits,* VI, 1856

As the homes, so the state.
A. BRONSON ALCOTT: *Tablets,* I, 1868

The best security for civilization is the dwelling, and upon proper and becoming dwellings depends more than anything else the improvement of mankind. Such dwellings are the nursery of all domestic virtues, and without a becoming home the exercise of those virtues is impossible.
BENJAMIN DISRAELI: Speech in London, July 18, 1874

Home as we now conceive it was the creation of the Puritan. Wife and child rose from being mere dependents on the will of husband or father, as husband or father saw in them saints like himself, souls hallowed by the touch of a divine Spirit, and called with a divine calling like his own.
J. R. GREEN: *A Short History of the English People,* VIII, 1874

O fortunate, O happy day,
When a new household finds its place
Among the myriad homes of earth,
Like a new star just sprung to birth.
H. W. LONGFELLOW: *The Hanging of the Crane,* 1874

Perhaps you have a mother, likewise a sister too,
Perhaps you have a sweetheart to weep and mourn for you.
If this be your condition I advise you to never roam,
I advise you by experience you had better stay at home.
Anon.: *The Texas Ranger, c.* 1875

The final culmination of this vast and varied republic will be the production and perennial establishment of millions of comfortable city homesteads and moderate-sized farms, healthy and independent, single separate ownership, fee simple, life in them complete but cheap, within reach of all.
WALT WHITMAN: *Notes Left Over, c.* 1888

Through all the seas of all Thy world, slambangin' home again.
RUDYARD KIPLING: *M'Andrew's Hymn,* 1893

Home is the girl's prison and the woman's workhouse.
GEORGE BERNARD SHAW: *Maxims for Revolutionists,* 1903

Home life is no more natural to us than a cage is natural to a cockatoo.
GEORGE BERNARD SHAW: *Getting Married,* pref., 1908

The sun shines warmer at home.
ALBANIAN PROVERB

Home ain't nothing like this.
AMERICAN CATCH-PHRASE, c. 1900

Any old place I hang my hat is home, sweet home to me. AMERICAN SAYING

Even when you are looking for trouble, there's no place like home. Author unidentified

Home is where the great are small, and the small are great. IBID.

Home is where the heart is. IBID.

Home is where you slip in the bathtub and break your neck. IBID.

No place is home until two people have latchkeys. IBID.

The smoke of a man's own house is better than the fire of his neighbors. SPANISH PROVERB

There is no home that is not twice as beautiful as the most beautiful city.
WEST AFRICAN PROVERB

[*See also* Charity, Homesickness, House, Husband, Land, Merriment, Patriot, Piety, Prophet, Sixty, Travel, Wages.

Homeless

The foxes have holes, and the birds of the air have nests; but the Son of Man hath not where to lay his head.
MATTHEW VIII, 20, *c.* 75

He dwells nowhere that dwells everywhere.
MARTIAL: *Epigrams,* VII, *c.* 95

Homeopathy

Homeopathy is insignificant as an art of healing, but of great value as criticism on the hygeia or medical practice of the time.
R. W. EMERSON: *Nominalist and Realist,* 1841

The vulgar quackeries drop off, atrophied, one after another. Homeopathy has long been encysted, and is carried on the body medical as quietly as an old wen.
O. W. HOLMES: *Scholastic and Bedside Teaching,* 1867 (Lecture at Harvard, Nov. 6)

Homer (c. 800 B.C.)

Homer has taught all other poets the art of telling lies skillfully.
ARISTOTLE: *Poetics,* XXIV, *c.* 322 B.C.

Homer nods. (Dormitat Homerus.)
HORACE: *De arte poetica, c.* 8 B.C.

In the Odyssey we may liken Homer to the setting sun: his glory remains, but the heat of his beams has abated.
LONGINUS: *On the Sublime,* IX, *c.* 250

The lord of the sublimest song soaring over the others like an eagle.
DANTE: *Inferno,* IV, *c.* 1320

In his books he contained, and most perfectly expressed, not only the documents martial and discipline of arms, but also incomparable wisdoms, and instructions for politic governance of people.
THOMAS ELYOT: *The Governour,* 1531

Even Homer sometimes nods.
ENGLISH PROVERB, derived from HORACE, *ante, c.* 8 B.C., and familiar since the XVII century

Seven cities warr'd for Homer, being dead,
Who, living, had no roof to shroud his head.
THOMAS HEYWOOD: *Hierarchie of the Blessed Angels,* 1635 (The cities, according to Greek legend, were Athens, Smyrna, Rhodes, Colophon, Salamis, Argos and Chios)

I can no more believe old Homer blind,
Than those who say the sun hath never shined;
The age wherein he lived was dark, but he
Could not want sight who taught the world to see.
JOHN DENHAM: *The Progress of Learning, c.* 1650

Read Homer once, and you can read no more,
For all books else appear so mean, so poor,
Verse will seem prose; but still persist to read,
And Homer will be all the books you need.
JOHN SHEFFIELD (DUKE OF BUCKINGHAM): *An Essay on Poetry, c.* 1680

Be Homer's works your study and delight;
Read them by day, and meditate by night.
ALEXANDER POPE: *An Essay on Criticism,* I, 1711

The divine Homer, who recorded the bloody battles the most in fashion, appears to me either to have been extremely mistaken or extremely mercenary.
MARY WORTLEY MONTAGU: *Letter to James Steuart,* July 19, 1759

Homer, in point of purity, is a most blameless writer; and though he was not an enlightened man, has interspersed many great and valuable truths throughout both his poems.
WILLIAM COWPER: *Letter to John Newton,* Dec. 3, 1785

My veneration for his genius is equal to that of his most idolatrous readers; but my reflections on the history of human errors have forced upon me the opinion that his existence has really proved one of the signal misfortunes of mankind.
JOEL BARLOW: *The Columbiad,* pref., 1807

Oft of one wide expanse had I been told
That deep-brow'd Homer ruled as his demesne,
Yet did I never breathe its pure serene
Till I heard Chapman speak out loud and bold:
Then felt I like some watcher of the skies
When a new planet swims into his ken;
Or like stout Cortez when with eagle eyes
He stared at the Pacific, and all his men
Look'd at each other with a wild surmise
Silent, upon a peak in Darien.
JOHN KEATS: *On First Looking Into Chapman's Homer,* 1819

There is no moral, little or big, foul or fair, to the Iliad.
THOMAS DE QUINCEY: *Milton* vs. *Southey and Landor, c.* 1847

A man who has not read Homer is like a man who has not seen the ocean. There is a great object of which he has no idea.
WALTER BAGEHOT: *Literary Studies,* I, 1879

[*See also* Artist, Dante Alighieri, Greatness, Hexameter, Nodding, Novel.

Homesickness

Homesickness is a wasting pang.
S. T. COLERIDGE: *Homesick,* 1798

Hame, hame, hame, O hame fain wad I be —
O hame, hame, hame, to my ain countree!
ALLAN CUNNINGHAM: *Hame,* 1810

All up and down de whole creation,
Sadly I roam,
Still longing for de old plantation,
And for de old folks at home.
S. C. FOSTER: *Old Folks at Home,* 1851

Lawd, I wonder, huh,
Lawd, I wonder, huh,
Will I ever git back home?
American Negro song, quoted by HOWARD W. ODUM: *Wings On My Feet,* I, 1929

[*See also* Home, Nostalgia.

Honesty

No man is really honest; none of us is above the influence of gain.
ARISTOPHANES: *Plutus,* 408 B.C.

Let us walk honestly, as in the day.
ROMANS XIII, 13, *c.* 55

Honesty is often in the wrong.
LUCAN: *Pharsalia,* VIII, 65

In an honest man there is always something of a child. MARTIAL: *Epigrams,* XII, *c.* 100

You are as honest a man as any is in the cards — if the kings were out.
BRIAN MELBANCKE: *Philotimus,* 1583

His words are bonds, his oaths are oracles.
SHAKESPEARE: *Two Gentlemen of Verona,* II, *c.* 1595

Honesty is the best policy.
ENGLISH PROVERB, traced by Apperson to 1599

I thank God I am as honest as any man living that is an old man and no honester than I.
SHAKESPEARE: *Much Ado About Nothing,* III, *c.* 1599

To be honest, as this world goes, is to be one man picked out of ten thousand.
SHAKESPEARE: *Hamlet,* II, *c.* 1601

I am myself indifferent honest.
SHAKESPEARE: *Hamlet,* III

No legacy is so rich as honesty.
SHAKESPEARE: *All's Well that Ends Well,* III, *c.* 1602

I have but little more to say, sir, of his honesty; he has everything that an honest man should not have; what an honest man should have, he has nothing.
SHAKESPEARE: *All's Well that Ends Well,* IV

Honesty is but an art to seem so.
JOHN MARSTON: *The Malcontent,* V, 1604

Honesty's a fool.
SHAKESPEARE: *Othello,* III, 1604

Take note, take note, O world,
To be direct and honest is not safe. IBID.

Were there no Heaven nor Hell
I should be honest.
JOHN WEBSTER: *The Duchess of Malfi,* I, *c.* 1614

Honesty is ill to thrive by.
JOHN CLARKE: *Parœmiologia Anglo-Latina,* 1639

Here lies a truly honest man.
RICHARD CRASHAW: *Epitaph Upon Mr. Ashton,* 1648

A man never surfeits of too much honesty.
JOHN RAY: *English Proverbs,* 1670

He is wise that is honest. IBID.

Of all crafts, to be an honest man is the master craft. IBID.

The honester man, the worse luck. IBID.

Honest men
Are the soft, easy cushions on which knaves
Repose and fatten.
THOMAS OTWAY: *Venice Preserved,* I, 1682

To be honest is nothing; the reputation of it is all.
WILLIAM CONGREVE: *The Old Bachelor,* V, 1693

He is only honest who is not discovered.
SUSANNA CENTLIVRE: *The Artifice,* V, 1710

Heav'n, that made me honest, made me more
Than ever king did, when he made a lord.
NICHOLAS ROWE: *Jane Shore,* II, 1714

Honesty may be dear bought, but can never be an ill pennyworth.
JAMES KELLY: *Complete Collection of Scottish Proverbs,* 1721

Honest men fear neither the light nor the dark.
THOMAS FULLER: *Gnomologia,* 1732

Honesty is a fine jewel, but much out of fashion. IBID.

An honest man's the noblest work of God.
ALEXANDER POPE: *An Essay on Man,* IV, 1734 (Quoted by ROBERT BURNS: *The Cotter's Saturday Night,* 1785)

Our great error is that we suppose mankind more honest than they are.
ALEXANDER HAMILTON: Speech in the Constitutional Convention, June 22, 1787

The honest man, though e'er so poor
Is king o' men for a' that.
ROBERT BURNS: *For a' That and a' That,* 1795

Men are disposed to live honestly, if the means of doing so are open to them.
THOMAS JEFFERSON: *Letter to M. de Marbois,* 1817

An honest man may be "the noblest work of God," but he is not the noblest product of humanity.
EDWARD DICEY: *Six Months in the Federal States,* 1863

"Honesty is the best policy," but he who acts on that principle is not an honest man.
RICHARD WHATELY (ARCHBISHOP OF DUBLIN): *Easy Lessons on Morals,* 1845

I do not remember that in my whole life I ever wilfully misrepresented anything to anybody at any time. I have never knowingly had connection with a fraudulent scheme.
J. PIERPONT MORGAN I: Press interview, 1910

The natural man has a difficult time getting along in this world. Half the people think he is a scoundrel because he is not a hypocrite.
E. W. HOWE: *Sinner Sermons,* 1926

Honesty is praised, but it starves.
LATIN PROVERB

Honesty is true honor. (Probitas verus honor.)
IBID.

Honesty never repents. IBID.

A thread will tie an honest man better than a rope will do a rogue. SCOTTISH PROVERB

[*See also* Cynicism, French, Honor, Lawyer, Poor.

Honey

A land flowing with milk and honey.
EXODUS III, 8, *c.* 700 B.C.

What is sweeter than honey?
JUDGES XIV, 18, *c.* 500 B.C.

My son, eat thou honey, because it is good.
PROVERBS XXIV, 13, *c.* 350 B.C.

Dear is bought the honey that is licked of the thorn. THE PROVERBS OF HENDYNG, *c.* 1300

A fly followeth the honey.
THOMAS HOCCLEVE: *De regimine principum, c.* 1425

A dead bee maketh no honey.
JAMES SANDFORD: *Hours of Recreation,* 1572

Every bee's honey is sweet.
GEORGE HERBERT: *Outlandish Proverbs,* 1640

The best oil is in the top, the best wine in the middle, and the best honey in the bottom.
THOMAS FULLER: *Worthies of England,* 1662

Honey is sweet, but the bee stings.
JOHN RAY: *English Proverbs,* 1670

He who shareth honey with the bear hath the least part of it.
THOMAS FULLER: *Gnomologia,* 1732

Make yourself all honey, and the flies will eat you. ITALIAN PROVERB

[*See also* Ascetic, Bee, Cajolery, Dead, Fly, John the Baptist, Milk, Money.

Honeymoon

Honeymoon: applied to those married persons that love well at first, and decline in affection afterward; it is honey now, but it will change as the moon.
THOMAS BLOUNT: *Glossographia,* 1656

When a couple are newly married the first month is honeymoon, or smick smack.
JOHN RAY: *English Proverbs,* 1670

The first month after marriage, when there is nothing but tenderness and pleasure.
SAMUEL JOHNSON: *Dictionary,* 1755

Don't tell me of the honeymoon; it is harvest-moon with me.
HORACE WALPOLE: *Letter to George Montagu,* May 19, 1756 (Quotation from a nobleman about to marry a rich wife)

Of all the lunar things that change
The one that shows most fickle and strange
And takes the most eccentric range
Is the moon, so called, of honey.
THOMAS HOOD: *Miss Kilmansegg,* 1840

A honeymoon is a good deal like a man laying off to take an expensive vacation, and coming back to a different job.
E. W. HOWE: *Sinner Sermons,* 1926

The honeymoon is the period during which the bride trusts the bridegroom's word of honor.
Author unidentified

Honor

Honor and dishonor are the matters with which the high-minded man is especially concerned.
ARISTOTLE: *The Nicomachean Ethics,* IV, *c.* 340 B.C.

It is the nature of the many to be amenable to fear but not to the sense of honor. IBID.

Leave not a stain in thine honor.
ECCLESIASTICUS XXXIII, 22, *c.* 180 B.C.

He who has lost honor can lose nothing more.
PUBLILIUS SYRUS: *Sententiæ, c.* 50 B.C.

Who that in youth no virtue useth,
In age all honor him refuseth.
Anon.: *Proverbs of Wisdom, c.* 1450

There is nothing left to me but honor, and my life, which is saved.
FRANCIS I of France: To his mother, after the Battle of Pavia, Feb. 24, 1525; the quotation usually appears as "All is lost save honor" (Tout est perdu fors l'honneur)

That name, that idle name of wind, that empty sound called honor.
SAMUEL DANIEL: *A Pastoral,* 1592

Mine honor is my life; both grow in one;
Take honor from me and my life is done.
SHAKESPEARE: *Richard II,* I, *c.* 1596

Can honor set a leg? no: or an arm? no: or take away the grief of a wound? no. Honor hath no skill in surgery, then? no. What is honor? a word. What is that word honor? air. Who hath it? he that died o' Wednesday. Doth he feel it? no. Doth he hear it? no. It is insensible, then? Yes, to the dead. But will it not live with the living? no. Therefore, I'll none of it. Honor is a mere scutcheon; and so ends my catechism.
SHAKESPEARE: *I Henry IV,* V, *c.* 1598

If it be a sin to covet honor,
I am the most offending soul alive.
SHAKESPEARE: *Henry V,* IV, *c.* 1599

Set honor in one eye and death i' the other
And I will look on both indifferently;
For let the gods so speed me as I love
The name of honor more than I fear death.
SHAKESPEARE: *Julius Cæsar,* I, *c.* 1599

Rightly to be great,
Is . . . greatly to find quarrel in a straw,
When honor's at the stake.

SHAKESPEARE: *Hamlet,* IV, *c.* 1601

Honor travels in a strait so narrow
Where one but goes abreast.

SHAKESPEARE: *Troilus and Cressida,* III, *c.* 1601

See that you come
Not to woo honor, but to wed it.

SHAKESPEARE: *All's Well that Ends Well,* II, *c.* 1602

A scar nobly got, or a noble scar, is a good livery of honor.

SHAKESPEARE: *All's Well that Ends Well,* IV

If I lose mine honor,
I lose myself.

SHAKESPEARE: *Antony and Cleopatra,* III, *c.* 1606

Honor is a baby's rattle.

THOMAS RANDOLPH: *The Muses' Looking Glass,* III, 1638

Honor and ease are seldom bedfellows.

JOHN CLARKE: *Parœmiologia Anglo-Latina,* 1639

The proud and gloomy sense of honor.

PIERRE CORNEILLE: *Horace,* II, 1639

An ill deed cannot bring honor.

GEORGE HERBERT: *Outlandish Proverbs,* 1640

Honor and profit lie not in one sack. IBID.

Honor without profit is a ring on the finger.

IBID.

I could not love thee, dear, so much,
Loved I not honor more.

RICHARD LOVELACE: *To Lucasta, on Going to the Wars,* 1642

If honor cannot restrain a man, virtue will not.

BALTASAR GRACIÁN: *The Art of Worldly Wisdom,* CXVI, 1647

Honor's the moral conscience of the great.

WILLIAM D'AVENANT: *Gondibert,* 1651

Honor is like a widow, won
With brisk attempt and putting on.

SAMUEL BUTLER: *Hudibras,* II, 1664

Honor is like a rocky island without a landing-place; once we leave it we can't get back.

NICOLAS BOILEAU: *Satires du Sieur D,* X, 1666

Godlike erect, with native honor clad.

JOHN MILTON: *Paradise Lost,* IV, 1667

Without money honor is nothing but a malady.

JEAN RACINE: *Les plaideurs,* I, 1668

Honor will buy no beef.

THOMAS SHADWELL: *The Sullen Lovers,* V, 1668 (Cited as a proverb)

Whoever would not die to preserve his honor would be infamous.

BLAISE PASCAL: *Pensées,* III, 1670

Honor is a public enemy, and conscience a domestic; and he that would secure his pleasure, must pay a tribute to one, and go halves with t'other.

WILLIAM CONGREVE: *Love for Love,* III, 1695

Honor is but an empty bubble.

JOHN DRYDEN: *Alexander's Feast,* 1697

When honor's lost, 'tis a relief to die;
Death's but a sure retreat from infamy.

SAMUEL GARTH: *The Dispensary,* V, 1699

Honor's a fine imaginary notion,
That draws in raw and unexperienced men
To real mischiefs.

JOSEPH ADDISON: *Cato,* II, 1713

When vice prevails and impious men bear sway,
The post of honor is a private station.

JOSEPH ADDISON: *Cato,* IV

The religious man fears, the man of honor scorns, to do an ill action.

JOSEPH ADDISON: *The Guardian,* Sept. 15, 1713

In points of honor to be try'd,
All passions must be laid aside:
Ask no advice, but think alone;
Suppose the question not your own:
How shall I act? is not the case;
But how would Brutus in my place?
In such a cause would Cato bleed?
And how would Socrates proceed?

JONATHAN SWIFT: To Stella, 1727

That I may have a constant regard to honor and probity, that I may possess a perfect innocence and a good conscience, and at length become truly virtuous and magnanimous, — help me, good God; help me, O Father!

BENJAMIN FRANKLIN: *Articles of Belief and Acts of Religion,* Nov. 20, 1728

Honor and shame from no condition rise;
Act well your part, there all the honor lies.

ALEXANDER POPE: *An Essay on Man,* IV, 1734

True, conscious honor is to feel no sin;
He's armed without that's innocent within.

ALEXANDER POPE: *The First Epistle of the First Book of Horace,* 1735

No man can justly aspire to honor but at the hazard of disgrace.

SAMUEL JOHNSON: *The Rambler,* Feb. 5, 1751

The difference there is betwixt honor and honesty seems to be chiefly in the motive. The

mere honest man does that from duty which the man of honor does for the sake of character.
WILLIAM SHENSTONE: *Of Men and Manners,* 1764

Tho fear o' Hell's a hangman's whip,
To hand the wretch in order;
But where ye feel your honor's grip,
Let that aye be your border.
ROBERT BURNS: *Epistle to a Young Friend,* 1786

It is gone, that sensibility of principle, that chastity of honor, which felt a stain like a wound.
EDMUND BURKE: *Reflections on the Revolution in France,* 1790

Nothing is lost except our honor.
BYRON: *Letter to Thomas Moore,* May 14, 1821

To those whose god is honor, disgrace alone is sin.
J. C. and A. W. HARE: *Guesses at Truth,* 1827

Honor is venerable to us because it is no ephemeris. It is always ancient virtue.
R. W. EMERSON: *Self-Reliance,* 1841

The jingling of the guinea helps the hurt that honor feels.
ALFRED TENNYSON: *Locksley Hall,* 1842

Honor is, on its objective side, other people's opinion of what we are worth; on its subjective side it is the respect we pay to this opinion.
ARTHUR SCHOPENHAUER: *Position,* 1851

The louder he talked of his honor the faster we counted our spoons.
R. W. EMERSON: *The Conduct of Life,* VI, 1860

No man sacrifices his honor, even for one he loves.
HENRIK IBSEN: *A Doll's House,* III, 1879

As to honor — you know — it's a very fine medieval inheritance, which women never get hold of. JOSEPH CONRAD: *Chance,* II, 1914

All is lost — including honor.
Author unidentified

The honor that is lost in a moment cannot be restored in a hundred years.
ITALIAN PROVERB

Honor trusts honor. RUSSIAN PROVERB

[*See also* Age (Old), Backside, Charity, Danger, Death, Defeat, Despotism, Envy, Fame, Honorable, Industry, Love, Money, Peace, Poor, Profit, Prophet, Thief.

Honorable

Whatever is most honorable is also safest.
LIVY: *History of Rome,* XXXIV, *c.* 10

For Brutus is an honorable man;
So are they all, all honorable men.
SHAKESPEARE: *Julius Cæsar,* III, 1599

Honorable is whatsoever possession, action, or quality is an argument and sign of power.
THOMAS HOBBES: *Leviathan,* X, 1651

Not every thing which the law allows is honorable. (Non omne quod licet honestum est.)
LEGAL MAXIM

Be honorable yourself if you wish to associate with honorable people. WELSH PROVERB

[*See also* Ancient, Honor, Just, Marriage, Opinion.

Honors

As snow in summer, and as rain in harvest, so honor is not seemly for a fool.
PROVERBS XXVI, 1, *c.* 350 B.C.

A man naturally expects honor for anything in which he excels.
ARISTOTLE: *Rhetoric,* Book II, *c.* 322 B.C.

An honor prudently declined often comes back with increased lustre.
LIVY: *History of Rome,* II, *c.* 10

I receive not honor from men.
JOHN V, 41, *c.* 115

If I honor myself, my honor is nothing.
JOHN VIII, 54

The honors of this world, what are they but puff, and emptiness, and peril of falling?
ST. AUGUSTINE: *Of the Catechizing of the Unlearned, c.* 400

Honors change manners.
ENGLISH PROVERB, borrowed from the Greek, and traced by Apperson to *c.* 1430

One honor won is a surety for more.
LA ROCHEFOUCAULD: *Maxims,* 1665

I have seen enough of political honors to know that they are but splendid torments.
THOMAS JEFFERSON: *Letter to Martha Jefferson Randolph,* 1797

I like the Garter; there is no damned merit in it.
Ascribed to WILLIAM LAMB, VISCOUNT MELBOURNE (1779–1848) (Order of the Garter)

I read in the *Perseveranz* that I am to be given the title of Marquis. I appeal to you, as an artist, to do all you can to prevent it.
GIUSEPPE VERDI: *Letter to Ferdinando Martini,* Italian Minister of Public Instruction, Feb. 11, 1893

Honors run into money. FRENCH PROVERB

Honor follows him who flees it. (Honor sequitur fugientem.) LATIN PROVERB

[*See also* Beloved, Title.

Hope

Prisoners of hope.

ZECHARIAH IX, 12, *c.* 520 B.C.

Hope deferred maketh the heart sick.

PROVERBS XIII, 12, *c.* 350 B.C.

Hope for the living, but none for the dead.

THEOCRITUS: *Idylls,* IV, *c.* 270 B.C.

I do not buy hope with money.

TERENCE: *Adelphi,* II, *c.* 160 B.C.

While there's life there's hope.

ENGLISH PROVERB, borrowed from CICERO: *Ad Atticum,* IX, *c.* 50 B.C.

Hope ever tells us tomorrow will be better.

TIBULLUS: *Elegies,* II, *c.* 20 B.C.

Who against hope believed in hope.

ROMANS IV, 18, *c.* 55

Hope that is seen is not hope; for what a man seeth, why doth he yet hope for?

ROMANS VIII, 24

A ship ought not to be held by one anchor, nor life by a single hope.

EPICTETUS: *Encheiridion, c.* 110

What can be hoped for which is not believed?

ST. AUGUSTINE: *On Faith, Hope, and Charity, c.* 421

If it were not for hope the heart would break.

ENGLISH PROVERB, traced by Smith to *c.* 1200

As wisdom without courage is futile, even so faith without hope is nothing worth; for hope endures and overcomes misfortune and evil.

MARTIN LUTHER: *Table-Talk,* CCXCVII, 1569

Everything that is done in the world is done by hope. No husbandman would sow one grain of corn if he hoped not it would grow up and become seed; no bachelor would marry a wife if he hoped not to have children; no merchant or tradesman would set himself to work if he did not hope to reap benefit thereby.

MARTIN LUTHER: *Table-Talk,* CCXCVIII, 1569

Hope for the best, but prepare for the worst.

ENGLISH PROVERB, traced by Apperson to 1587

Hope is the fawning traitor of the mind, while, under color of friendship, it robs it of its chief force of resolution.

PHILIP SIDNEY: *Arcadia,* III, 1590

Hope, like the hyena, coming to be old,
Alters his shape, is turned into despair.

HENRY CONSTABLE: *Sonnets to Diana, c.* 1592

True hope is swift, and flies with swallow's wings;
Kings it makes gods, and meaner creatures kings.

SHAKESPEARE: *Richard III,* V, *c.* 1592

Hope is a lover's staff; walk hence with that
And manage it against despairing thoughts.

SHAKESPEARE: *Two Gentlemen of Verona,* III, *c.* 1595

Hope is a good breakfast but a bad supper.

ENGLISH PROVERB, familiar since the early XVII century

The miserable have no other medicine
But only hope.

SHAKESPEARE: *Measure for Measure,* III, 1604

Hope never leaves a wretched man that seeks her.

BEAUMONT and FLETCHER: *The Captain,* II, *c.* 1612

He who lives on hope will die fasting.

ENGLISH PROVERB, traced by Apperson to 1623

It is a certain sign of a wise government and proceeding when it can hold men's hearts by hopes when it cannot by satisfaction.

FRANCIS BACON: *Essays,* XV, 1625

My nature is
That I incline to hope rather than fear,
And gladly banish squint suspicion.

JOHN MILTON: *Comus,* 1637

He that lives in hope dances without music.

GEORGE HERBERT: *Outlandish Proverbs,* 1640

Hope! of all ills that men endure,
The only cheap and universal cure.

ABRAHAM COWLEY: *The Mistress,* 1647

Hope is a great falsifier.

BALTASAR GRACIÁN: *The Art of Worldly Wisdom,* XIX, 1647

Hope is the poor man's bread.

GEORGE HERBERT: *Jacula Prudentum,* 1651

Appetite, with an opinion of attaining, is called hope; the same, without such opinion, despair.

THOMAS HOBBES: *Leviathan,* I, 1651

Hope and fear are inseparable.

LA ROCHEFOUCAULD: *Maxims,* 1665

When I consider life, 'tis all a cheat,
Yet, fooled with hope, men favor the deceit;
Trust on, and think tomorrow will repay.
Tomorrow's falser than the former day;
Lies worst, and while it says we shall be blest
With some new joys, cuts off what we possessed.

JOHN DRYDEN: *Aurengzebe,* IV, 1676

Hope is a very thin diet.

THOMAS SHADWELL: *Bury Fair,* III, 1689

The faint glimmering of a doubtful hope.

JOSEPH ADDISON: *Cato,* III, 1713

Hope is but the dream of those that wake.
MATTHEW PRIOR: *Solomon on the Vanity of the World*, III, 1718

Great hopes make great men.
THOMAS FULLER: *Gnomologia*, 1732

He that wants hope is the poorest man alive.
IBID.

Hope is as cheap as despair. IBID.

Hope is worth any money. IBID.

Hope springs eternal in the human breast;
Man never is, but always to be, blest.
ALEXANDER POPE: *An Essay on Man*, I, 1732

Know then, whatever cheerful and serene
Supports the mind, supports the body too;
Hence, the most vital movement mortals feel
Is hope, the balm and lifeblood of the soul.
JOHN ARMSTRONG: *The Art of Preserving Health*, IV, 1744

And hope enchanted smiled, and waved her golden hair.
WILLIAM COLLINS: *Ode on the Passions*, 1747

The natural flights of the human mind are not from pleasure to pleasure, but from hope to hope. SAMUEL JOHNSON: *The Rambler*, March 24, 1749

It is necessary to hope, though hope should always be deluded; for hope itself is happiness, and its frustrations, however frequent, are yet less dreadful than its extinction.
SAMUEL JOHNSON: *The Idler*, May 26, 1759

Hope! thou nurse of young desire.
ISAAC BICKERSTAFF: *Love in a Village*, I, 1762

Hope is a flatterer: but the most upright of all parasites; for she frequents the poor man's hut as well as the palace of his superior.
WILLIAM SHENSTONE: *On Writing and Books*, 1764

A Christian virtue which consists in our despising all poor things here below in the expectation of enjoying in an unknown country unknown joys which our priests promise us for the worth of our money.
VOLTAIRE: *Philosophical Dictionary*, 1764

If hoping does you any good, hope on.
C. M. WIELAND: *Oberon*, IV, 1780

To hope is to enjoy.
JACQUES DELILLE: *Les jardins*, I, 1782

Hope springs exulting on triumphant wing.
ROBERT BURNS: *The Cotter's Saturday Night*, 1785

Auspicious hope! in thy sweet garden grow
Wreaths for each toil, a charm for every woe.
THOMAS CAMPBELL: *The Pleasures of Hope*, I, 1799

The rose is fairest when 'tis budding new,
And hope is brightest when it dawns from fears.
WALTER SCOTT: *The Lady of the Lake*, IV, 1810

Sweet hope, ethereal balm upon me shed,
And wave thy silver pinions o'er my head.
JOHN KEATS: *To Hope*, 1815

A hope beyond the shadow of a dream.
JOHN KEATS: *Endymion*, I, 1818

Hopes, what are they? — Beads of morning
  Strung on slender blades of grass;
Or a spider's web adorning
  In a straight and treacherous pass.
WILLIAM WORDSWORTH: *Inscriptions Supposed to be Found In and Near a Hermit's Cell*, 1818

Worse than despair,
Worse than the bitterness of death, is hope.
P. B. SHELLEY: *The Cenci*, V, 1819

Cold hopes swarm like worms within our living clay. P. B. SHELLEY: *Adonais*, 1821

  Through the sunset of hope,
  Like the shapes of a dream,
What paradise islands of glory gleam!
P. B. SHELLEY: *Hellas*, 1822

Something will turn up.
BENJAMIN DISRAELI: *Popanilla*, VII, 1827
(Cited as the national motto of England)

The hope, and not the fact, of advancement is the spur to industry.
HENRY TAYLOR: *The Statesman*, 1836

We should deal with ourselves as a wise physician is said to have dealt with his patients: those who were incurable lost their lives, but they never lost hope.
ERNEST VON FEUCHTERSLEBEN: *Zur Diätetik der Seele*, XII, 1838

The old hope is hardest to be lost.
E. B. BROWNING: *The Cry of the Children*, 1843

The heart bowed down by weight of woe
To weakest hope will cling.
ALFRED BUNN: *The Bohemian Girl*, II, 1843

The mighty hopes that make us men.
ALFRED TENNYSON: *In Memoriam*, LXXXV, 1850

Hope is grief's best music.
H. G. BOHN: *Handbook of Proverbs*, 1855

The worldly hope men set their hearts upon
Turns ashes — or it prospers; and anon,
  Like snow upon the desert's dusty face
Lighting a little hour or two — is gone.
EDWARD FITZGERALD: Tr. of OMAR KHAYYÁM: *Rubáiyát* (*c.* 1100), 1857

Hope is the parent of faith.
C. A. BARTOL: *Radical Problems*, 1872

Hope is the worst of evils, for it prolongs the torment of man.
F. W. NIETZSCHE: *Human All-too-Human*, I, 1878

There is yet hope.
JAMES MUNYON (patent medicine manufacturer): Advertising slogan, *c.* 1895

There is fear in every hope, and hope in every fear.
ARAB PROVERB

Hope is a waking dream.
Ascribed to ARISTOTLE, PLATO and other Greeks, but not to be found in their extant works

No disease like hope.
HINDU PROVERB

The last thing ever lost is hope.
ITALIAN PROVERB

More pleasure in hope than in fulfilment.
JAPANESE PROVERB

In this sign is my hope. (In hoc signo mea spes.)
LATIN PHRASE

While I breathe, I hope. (Dum spiro, spero.)
MEDIEVAL LATIN PROVERB

In the land of hope there is never any Winter.
RUSSIAN PROVERB

A good hope is better than a poor possession.
SPANISH PROVERB

[*See also* Admiration, Age (Old), Ages, Animal, Certainty, Charity, Expectation, Faith, Fear, Health, Humanity, Love, Marriage (Second), Patience, Success, Vow, Waiting.

Hopeless

My days are swifter than a weaver's shuttle, and are spent without hope.
JOB VII, 6, *c.* 325 B.C.

Is there no hope? the sick man said;
The silent doctor shook his head.
JOHN GAY: *The Sick Man and the Angel*, 1727

The setting of a great hope is like the setting of the sun. The brightness of our life is gone.
H. W. LONGFELLOW: *Hyperion*, I, 1839

Where the heart is past hope, the face is past shame.
H. G. BOHN: *Handbook of Proverbs*, 1855

Something was dead in each of us,
And what was dead was hope.
OSCAR WILDE: *The Ballad of Reading Gaol*, 1898

[*See also* Hell.

Hops

Hops and turkeys, carp and beer,
Came into England all in one year.
OLD ENGLISH RHYME, traced by Apperson, in various forms, to the end of the XVI century; the year is supposed to have been 1520

Horace (65–8 B.C.)

Horace still charms with graceful negligence,
And without method talks us into sense.
ALEXANDER POPE: *An Essay on Criticism*, III, 1711

Horn

The horn, the horn, the lusty horn.
SHAKESPEARE: *As You Like It*, IV, *c.* 1600

Little Boy Blue, come blow your horn,
The sheep's in the meadow, the cow's in the corn.
Anon.: *Nursery Rhyme*, *c.* 1750

All are not hunters that blow the horn.
MEDIEVAL LATIN PROVERB

[*See also* Bugle, Hunting.

Hornet

I will send hornets before thee, which shall drive out the Hivite, the Canaanite, and the Hittite, from before thee.
EXODUS XXIII, 28, *c.* 700 B.C.

Horror

I could a tale unfold whose lightest word
Would harrow up thy soul, freeze thy young blood,
Make thy two eyes, like stars, start from their spheres,
Thy knotted and combined locks to part
And each particular hair to stand on end,
Like quills upon the fretful porpentine.
SHAKESPEARE: *Hamlet*, I, *c.* 1601 (*Porpentine*=porcupine)

On horror's head horrors accumulate.
SHAKESPEARE: *Othello*, III, 1604

Horse

Solomon had 40,000 stalls of horses for his chariots, and 12,000 horsemen.
I KINGS IV, 26, 500 B.C. (II CHRONICLES IX, 25, *c.* 300 B.C. says 4000 stalls)

Hast thou given the horse strength? Hast thou clothed his neck with thunder?
JOB XXXIX, 19, *c.* 325 B.C.

He saith among the trumpets, Ha, ha! and he smelleth the battle afar off, the thunder of the captains, and the shouting.
JOB XXXIX, 25

Behold a pale horse, and his name that sat on him was Death.
REVELATION VI, 8, *c.* 95

The horse is the strength of the army. The horse is a moving bulwark.
The Hitopadesa, III, *c.* 500

You may lead a horse to water but you can't make him drink.
ENGLISH PROVERB, traced by Smith to *c.* 1175

A horse! a horse! my kingdom for a horse!
Ascribed to RICHARD III of England, at Bosworth Field, Aug. 23, 1485 (It appears in SHAKESPEARE: *Richard III*, V, *c.* 1592)

It be a good horse that never stumbleth.
JOHN HEYWOOD: *Proverbs*, 1546

Of a ragged colt there cometh a good horse.
IBID.

The flies go to lean horses.
JAMES SANDFORD: *Hours of Recreation*, 1572

A flea-bitten horse never tires.
ENGLISH PROVERB, traced by Apperson to 1577

Round-hoofed, short-jointed, fetlocks shag and long,
Broad breast, full eye, small head, and nostril wide,
High crest, short ears, straight legs, and passing strong,
Thin mane, thick tail, broad buttock, tender hide.
SHAKESPEARE: *Venus and Adonis*, 1593

He doth nothing but talk of his horse; and he makes it a great appropriation to his own good parts, that he can shoe him himself. I am much afraid, my lady, his mother play'd false with a smith.
SHAKESPEARE: *The Merchant of Venice*, I, *c.* 1597

His mane thin-haired, his neck high-crested,
Small ear, short head, and burly-breasted.
R. S.: *Phillis and Flora*, 1598

I will not change my horse with any that treads but on four pasterns. Ça, ha! he bounds from the earth, as if his entrails were hairs, le cheval volant, the Pegasus, chez les narines de feu! When I bestride him, I soar, I am a hawk; he trots the air; the earth sings when he touches it.
SHAKESPEARE: *Henry V*, III, *c.* 1599

Why brook'st thou, ignorant horse, subjection?
JOHN DONNE: *Holy Sonnets*, XII, *c.* 1617

They say princes learn no art truly, but the art of horsemanship. The reason is, the brave beast is no flatterer. He will throw a prince as soon as his groom.
BEN JONSON: *Discoveries*, *c.* 1635

Good horses make short miles.
GEORGE HERBERT: *Outlandish Proverbs*, 1640

The fault of the horse is put upon the saddle.
IBID.

There is no good horse of a bad color.
IZAAK WALTON: *The Compleat Angler*, V, 1653

A galled horse will not endure the comb.
JOHN RAY: *English Proverbs*, 1670

It's an ill horse can neither whinny nor wag his tail.
IBID.

Let a horse drink when he will, not what he will.
IBID.

He's a gentle horse that never cast his rider.
JAMES KELLY: *Complete Collection of Scottish Proverbs*, 1721

Up hill spare me,
Down hill forbear me;
Plain way, spare me not,
Nor let me drink when I am hot.
THOMAS FULLER: *Gnomologia*, 1732

Would you treat your horse with a peck of oysters?
IBID.

The bounding steed you pompously bestride
Shares with his lord the pleasure and the pride.
ALEXANDER POPE: *An Essay on Man*, III, 1733

A horse gives but a kind of half exercise.
THOMAS JEFFERSON: *Letter to T. M. Randolph, Jr.*, 1786

The horse appears to be content with as few ideas as a domestic animal can well have.
LEIGH HUNT: *The Indicator*, LXIV, 1821

'Orses and dorgs is . . . wittles and drink to me.
CHARLES DICKENS: *David Copperfield*, XIX, 1849

A young trooper should have an old horse.
H. G. BOHN: *Handbook of Proverbs*, 1855

'Tis the abilities of a horse that occasion his slavery.
IBID.

The ways of a man with a maid be strange, yet simple and tame
To the ways of a man with a horse, when selling or racing the same.
RUDYARD KIPLING: *Certain Maxims of Hafiz*, 1886

Care, and not fine stables, makes a good horse.
DANISH PROVERB

Better a blind horse than an empty halter.
DUTCH PROVERB

The blind nag goes straight ahead.
GERMAN PROVERB

The leaner the horse, the less kicking he does.
ITALIAN PROVERB

One white foot — buy him;
Two white feet — try him;
Three white feet — look well about him;
Four white feet — go without him.
OLD ENGLISH RHYME

One white foot, keep him not a day;
Two white feet, send him soon away;
Three white feet, sell him to a friend;
Four white feet, keep him to the end.
Another version

[*See also* Adventure, Arms, Ass, Blind, Cause and Effect, Change, Children, Colt, Coöperation, Disease, Dog, England, Expedience, Fly, Food, Jealousy, Late, Longevity Man, Mare, Mule, Poet, Riding, Swapping, Trust, Weariness.

Horsehair

Steep horsehair certain weeks
In water: there will be produced a snake.

ROBERT BROWNING: *The Ring and the Book,* IX, 1868

Horseleech

[*See* Begging.

Horse-race

Chance and skill enter into card-playing; chance and knowledge into horse-racing.

JAMES CANNON, JR.: *Unspotted from the World,* Aug. 3, 1929

[*See also* Opinion, Racing.

Hospital

In the Year of Christ
MDCCLV
George the Second Happily Reigning
(For He Sought the Happiness of His People)
Philadelphia Flourishing
(For Its Inhabitants Were Publick Spirited)
This Building
By the Bounty of the Government
And of Many Private Persons
Was Piously Founded
For the Relief of the Sick and Miserable;
May the God of Mercies
Bless the Undertaking.

BENJAMIN FRANKLIN: Inscription for the cornerstone of the Pennsylvania Hospital, Philadelphia, 1755

I think it frets the saints in Heaven to see
How many desolate creatures on the earth
Have learnt the simple dues of fellowship
And social comfort in a hospital.

E. B. BROWNING: *Aurora Leigh,* III, 1857

The indigent sick of this city and its environs, without regard to sex, age or color, who may require surgical or medical treatment, and who can be received into the hospital without peril to the other inmates, and the poor of this city and state, of all races, who are stricken down by any casualty, shall be received into the hospital, without charge, for such period of time and under such regulations as you may prescribe.

JOHNS HOPKINS: *Letter of instruction to the first trustees of the Johns Hopkins Hospital,* Baltimore, March, 1873

[*See also* Brothel.

Hospitality

Axylos, the son of Teuthranos, was a man of substance and dear to his fellow men, for his house was by the side of the road, and he welcomed all who passed by.

HOMER: *The Iliad,* VI, *c.* 800 B.C.

Receive a stranger in, and he shall overthrow thee with a whirlwind, and shall turn thee out of thy own.

ECCLESIASTICUS XI, 36, *c.* 180 B.C.

The Lord give mercy unto the house of Onesiphorus; for he oft refreshed me, and was not ashamed of my chain.

II TIMOTHY I, 16, *c.* 60

Use hospitality to one another without grudging.

I PETER IV, 9, *c.* 60

Be not forgetful to entertain strangers, for thereby some have entertained angels unawares.

HEBREWS XIII, 2, *c.* 65

I was hungered, and ye gave me meat: I was thirsty, and ye gave me drink: I was a stranger, and ye took me in.

MATTHEW XXV, 35, *c.* 75

Hospitality is to be shown even towards an enemy. The tree doth not withdraw its shade, even from the wood-cutter.

The Hitopadesa, I, *c.* 500

Never dine with a patient who is in your debt, but get your dinner at an inn: otherwise he will deduct his hospitality from your bill.

HENRI DE MONDEVILLE: *Treatise on Surgery,* 1316

Be bright and jovial among your guests.

SHAKESPEARE: *Macbeth,* III, *c.* 1605

I charge thee, invite them all; let in the tide
Of knaves once more; my cook and I'll provide.

SHAKESPEARE: *Timon of Athens,* III, *c.* 1607

Don't set up for what is called hospitality. If your house be like an inn, nobody cares for you. A man who stays a week with another makes him a slave for a week.

SAMUEL JOHNSON: *Boswell's Life,* May 15, 1783

Hospitality consists in a little fire, a little food, and an immense quiet.

R. W. EMERSON: *Journal,* 1856

When there is room in the heart there is room in the house.

DANISH PROVERB

In hospitality the chief thing is the good will.

GREEK PROVERB

Hospitality to strangers is greater than reverence for the name of God.

HEBREW PROVERB

He that bids me to meat wishes me to live.

SCOTTISH PROVERB

[*See also* Angel, Guest, Host, Hostess, Inhospitable, Paris, Stranger, Visiting, Welcome.

Host

A host is like a general: it takes a mishap to reveal his genius.

HORACE: *Satires,* II, *c.* 25 B.C.

In good company, you need not ask who is the master of the feast. The man who sits in the lowest place, and who is always industrious in helping every one, is certainly the man.

DAVID HUME: *Essays, Moral and Political,* I, 1741

If you are a host to your guest, be a host to his dog also. RUSSIAN PROVERB

[*See also* Guest, Hospitality.

Hostess

A woeful hostess brooks not merry guests.
SHAKESPEARE: *The Rape of Lucrece,* 1594

[*See also* Guest, Visiting.

Hotel

It used to be a good hotel, but that proves nothing — I used to be a good boy.
S. L. CLEMENS (MARK TWAIN): *Letter from New York to the Alta Californian (San Francisco)*, April 19,1867

This ain't the Waldorf; if it was you wouldn't be here.
Sign displayed in American country hotels, *c.* 1900

[*See also* Customer.

Hour

The hours fly round the circle.
MARCUS MANILIUS: *Astronomica,* III, *c.* 40 B.C.

Every part has his hour: we wake at six and look about us, that's eye-hour; at seven we should pray, that's knee-hour; at eight walk, that's leg-hour; at nine gather flowers and pluck a rose, that's nose-hour; at ten we drink, that's mouth-hour; at eleven lay about us for victuals, that's hand-hour; at twelve go to dinner, that's belly-hour.
THOMAS MIDDLETON and WILLIAM ROWLEY: *The Changeling,* I, *c.* 1623

Soft silken hours.
RICHARD CRASHAW: *Wishes to His Supposed Mistress,* 1646

An hour of pain is as long as a day of pleasure.
THOMAS FULLER: *Gnomologia,* 1732

It happens in an hour that comes not in an age. IBID.

Wingless, crawling hours.
P. B. SHELLEY: *Prometheus Unbound,* I, 1820

An hour may destroy what an age was building.
H. G. BOHN: *Handbook of Proverbs,* 1855

[*See also* Minute, Moment.

Hour-glass

An hour-glass is a reminder not only of time's quick flight, but also of the dust to which we must at last return.
G. C. LICHTENBERG: *Reflections,* 1799

House

The rain descended, and the floods came, and the winds blew, and beat upon that house; and it fell not: for it was founded upon a rock. MATTHEW VII, 25, *c.* 75

A foolish man . . . built his house upon the sand. MATTHEW VII, 26

Better an empty house than a bad tenant.
ENGLISH PROVERB, first recorded in the XVII century

He that lives in a glass house must not throw stones.
ENGLISH PROVERB, familiar since the XVII century (At earlier periods " has a glass head " was more common)

The house of every one is to him as his castle and fortress, as well for his defense against injury and violence as for his repose.
EDWARD COKE: *Semayne's Case,* 1605

Houses are built to live in, and not to look on.
FRANCIS BACON: *Essays,* XLV, 1625

I in my own house am an emperor,
And will defend what's mine.
PHILIP MASSINGER: *The Roman Actor,* I, 1629

My house, my house, though thou art small,
Thou art to me the Escurial.
GEORGE HERBERT: *Outlandish Proverbs,* 1640

The house shows the owner.
GEORGE HERBERT: *Jacula Prudentum,* 1651

Fools build houses, and wise men buy them.
JOHN RAY: *English Proverbs,* 1670

Better one's house be too little one day than too big all the year after.
THOMAS FULLER: *Gnomologia,* 1732

He that buys a house ready wrought,
Has many a pin and nail for nought. IBID.

Were you to tell men who live without houses how we pile brick upon brick, and rafter upon rafter, and that after a house is raised to a certain height a man tumbles off a scaffold and breaks his neck, he would laugh heartily at our folly in building; but it does not follow that men are better without houses.
SAMUEL JOHNSON: *Boswell's Life,* May 7, 1773

A comfortable house is a great source of happiness. It ranks immediately after health and a good conscience.
SYDNEY SMITH: To Lord Murray, Sept. 29, 1843

That is an honest house which has the owner's honor built into its apartments, and whose appointments are his proper ornaments.
A. BRONSON ALCOTT: *Tablets,* I, 1868

The first year let your house to your enemy; the second, to your friend; the third, live in it yourself.
W. C. HAZLITT: *English Proverbs,* 1869

A house kept to the end of prudence is laborious without joy; a house kept to the end of dis-

play is impossible to all but a few women, and their success is dearly bought.
R. W. EMERSON: *Domestic Life*, 1877

I prefer houses to the open air. In a house we all feel of the proper proportions. Everything is subordinated to us, fashioned for our use and our pleasure.
OSCAR WILDE: *The Decay of Lying*, 1891

The best way to realize the pleasure of feeling rich is to live in a smaller house than your means would entitle you to have.
EDWARD CLARKE: *The Story of My Life*, 1918

The most difficult mountain to cross is the threshold of a house. DANISH PROVERB

Half a house is half a hell.
GERMAN PROVERB

We shall have a house without a fault in the next world. ITALIAN PROVERB

A man's house is his best refuge. (Domus sua cuique est tutissimum refugium.)
LEGAL MAXIM

The public laws favor the privacy of the house. (Jura publica favent privata domus.)
IBID.

Three things damn a house: a leaky roof, an evil woman, and smoke. (Sunt tria damna domus: imber, mala femina, fumus.)
MEDIEVAL LATIN PROVERB

The owner has one house, the renter a thousand. PERSIAN PROVERB

Don't buy the house; buy the neighbor.
RUSSIAN PROVERB

A wee house has a wide throat.
SCOTTISH PROVERB

[*See also* Achievement, Bugle, Builder, Building, Castle, Child, Children, Highway, Home, Household, Housekeeping, Housewife, Order, Priest, Property.

Household

A man's foes shall be they of his own household. MATTHEW X, 36, *c.* 75

The household is a school of power.
R. W. EMERSON: *Education*, 1865

[*See also* Home.

Housekeeping

Everything is of use to a housekeeper.
GEORGE HERBERT: *Outlandish Proverbs*, 1640

Marriage is honorable, but housekeeping's a shrew. JOHN RAY: *English Proverbs*, 1670

[*See also* Housewife.

House of Commons

The House of Commons is called the Lower House in twenty acts of Parliament; but what are twenty acts of Parliament amongst friends? JOHN SELDEN: *Table-Talk*, 1689

House of Lords

That hospital of incurables, the House of Lords.
LORD CHESTERFIELD: *Letter to his son*, Aug. 1, 1766

House of Representatives

The House of Representatives shall be composed of members chosen every second year by the people of the several states, and the electors in each state shall have the qualifications requisite for electors of the most numerous branch of the state Legislature.
CONSTITUTION OF THE UNITED STATES, Art. I, 1789

Housewife

She looketh well to the ways of her household, and eateth not the bread of idleness.
PROVERBS XXXI, 27, *c.* 350 B.C.

Bare walls make giddy housewives.
JOHN CLARKE: *Parœmiologia Anglo-Latina*, 1639

There is but an hour in a day between a good housewife and a bad.
JOHN RAY: *English Proverbs*, 1670

On household cares intent, with many a sigh
She turns the pancake, and she molds the pie;
Melts into sauces rich the savory ham;
From the crush'd berry strains the lucid jam.
GEORGE CANNING and J. HOOKHAM FRERE: *The Anti-Jacobin*, April 2, 1798

Here lies a poor woman, who always was tired;
She lived in a house where help was not hired.
Her last words on earth were: "Dear friends, I am going
Where washing ain't done, nor sweeping, nor sewing;
But everything there is exact to my wishes;
For where they don't eat there's no washing of dishes."
Anon.: *The Housewife's Epitaph*, *c.* 1825

A good housewife is of necessity a humbug.
W. M. THACKERAY: *Vanity Fair*, I, 1848

The uglier the woman, the better the housewife. GERMAN PROVERB

[*See also* Housekeeping.

Howells, W. D. (1837–1920)

Henry James went to France and read Turgenev. W. D. Howells stayed at home and read Henry James.
GEORGE MOORE: *Confessions of a Young Man*, X, 1888

Howling

Howl ye, for the day of the Lord is at hand.
ISAIAH XIII, 6, *c.* 700 B.C.

The howling wilderness.
DEUTERONOMY XXXII, 10, *c.* 650 B.C.

Hugging

Imparadis'd in one another's arms.
JOHN MILTON: *Paradise Lost,* IV, 1667

The river rolls, the crickets sing,
The lightning-bug he flash his wing,
Then like a rope my arms I fling
Round Rose of Alabama.
Anon.: *Rose of Alabama,* 1856

Let him rebuke who ne'er has known the pure Platonic grapple,
Or hugged two girls at once behind a chapel.
EZRA POUND: *L'Homme moyen sensuel,* 1910

Hugo, Victor (1802–1885)

A glittering humbug.
THOMAS CARLYLE: To Henry B. Stanton, 1840

He had not the time to acquire taste.
ERNEST RENAN: *Essais de morale et de critique,* 1859

Hugo was a cross between an Italian improvisatore and a metaphysical German student.
GEORGE MOORE: *Confessions of a Young Man,* IV, 1888

The lighthouse on the sea of nonsense.
F. W. NIETZSCHE: *The Twilight of the Idols,* 1889

Alas, Victor Hugo!
PAUL VERLAINE: On being asked, on his deathbed, to name the greatest French poet of the XIX century, 1896

Human

I am a man; and nothing human is foreign to me. (Homo sum; humani nihil a me alienum puto.) TERENCE: *Heautontimoroumenos, c.* 160 B.C.

Horrible, hairy, human.
RUDYARD KIPLING: *The Truce of the Bear,* 1898

To err is human. (Humanum est errare.)
LATIN PROVERB

[*See also* Humanity, Man.

Humanitarianism

When any man is more stupidly vain and outrageously egotistic than his fellows, he will hide his hideousness in humanitarianism.
GEORGE MOORE: *Confessions of a Young Man,* XII, 1888

[*See also* Philanthropy.

Humanity

Humanity is very uniform.
SAMUEL JOHNSON: *Taxation No Tyranny,* 1775

The still, sad music of humanity.
WILLIAM WORDSWORTH: *Tintern Abbey,* 1798

I cannot think of the present state of humanity as that in which it is destined to remain; I am absolutely unable to conceive of this as its complete and final vocation. Then, indeed, were all a dream and a delusion; and it would not be worth the trouble to have lived, and played out this ever-repeated game, which tends to nothing and signifies nothing. Only in so far as I can regard this state as the means toward a better, as the transition-point to a higher and more perfect state, has it any value in my eyes.
J. G. FICHTE: *Die Bestimmung des Menschen,* 1800

Love, hope, fear, faith — these make humanity;
These are its sign and note and character.
ROBERT BROWNING: *Paracelsus,* 1835

Humanity is a pigsty where liars, hypocrites and the obscene in spirit congregate.
GEORGE MOORE: *Confessions of a Young Man,* IX, 1888

Humanity must remain as it is.
POPE LEO XIII: *Quadragesimo anno,* May 15, 1931

[*See also* Man.

Human Nature

[*See* Nature (Human).

Hume, David (1711–76)

I always lived on good terms with Mr. Hume, though I have frankly told him I was not clear that it was right in me to keep company with him. But (said I) how much better are you than your books!
JAMES BOSWELL: *Tour to the Hebrides,* Aug. 15, 1773

A certain coldness of temperament, not unmixed with aristocratical pride, or at least with a great aversion from everything like vulgar credulity, rendered his skepticism so extreme that it became a sort of superstition in turn, and blinded him to the claims of every species of enthusiasm, civil as well as religious.
LEIGH HUNT: *The Indicator,* V, 1821

He is an extraordinary ordinary man.
Ascribed to SIR JAMES MACINTOSH (1765–1832) by THOMAS ALLSOP: *Letters, Conversations and Recollections of S. T. Coleridge,* 1836

[*See also* Blackstone (William), Epitaph, Skeptic.

Humility

Before honor is humility.
PROVERBS XV, 33, *c.* 350 B.C.

Better is it to be of an humble spirit with the lowly than to divide the spoil with the proud.
PROVERBS XVI, 19

By humility, and the fear of the Lord, are riches, and honor, and life.
PROVERBS XXII, 4

The higher we are placed, the more we should be humble. CICERO: *De officiis*, I, 78 B.C.

God resisteth the proud, but giveth grace unto the humble. JAMES IV, 6, *c.* 60

He that shall humble himself shall be exalted.
MATTHEW XXIII, 12, *c.* 75 (Cf. LUKE XIV, 11, *c.* 75)

There is something in humility which strangely exalts the heart.
ST. AUGUSTINE: *The City of God*, XIV, 427

Humble thyself in all things.
THOMAS À KEMPIS: *Imitation of Christ*, III, *c.* 1420

The humility of hypocrites is, of all pride, the greatest and most haughty.
MARTIN LUTHER: *Table-Talk*, CCCCXVI, 1569

He loves humility in all men but himself, as if he did wish well to all souls but his own.
THOMAS ADAMS: *Diseases of the Soul*, 1616

Professions of humility are the very cream, the very essence of pride; the really humble man wishes to be, and not to appear so. Humility is timorous, and starts at her shadow; and so delicate that if she hears her name pronounced it endangers her existence.
Ascribed to ST. FRANCIS DE SALES (1567–1622) in J. P. CAMUS: *L'esprit de Saint François de Sales*, 1641

Humble we must be, if to Heaven we go:
High is the roof there; but the gate is low:
When e're thou speak'st, look with a lowly eye:
Grace is increased by humility.
ROBERT HERRICK: *Noble Numbers*, 1647

Plenty of people want to be pious, but no one yearns to be humble.
LA ROCHEFOUCAULD: *Maxims*, 1665

Humility is often only a feigned submission, of which we make use to render others submissive. It is an artifice of pride which abases in order to exalt itself. IBID.

The more noble, the more humble.
JOHN RAY: *English Proverbs*, 1670

He that is down needs fear no fall;
He that is low, no pride;
He that is humble ever shall
Have God to be his guide.
JOHN BUNYAN: *Pilgrim's Progress*, II, 1678

Humility is a virtue all preach, none practise, and yet everybody is content to hear. The master thinks it good doctrine for his servant, the laity for the clergy, and the clergy for the laity. JOHN SELDEN: *Table-Talk*, 1689

It is hard to be high and humble.
THOMAS FULLER: *Gnomologia*, 1732

It is not a sign of humility to declaim against pride. IBID.

To be humble to superiors is duty, to equals courtesy, to inferiors nobleness.
BENJAMIN FRANKLIN: *Poor Richard's Almanac*, 1735

A fault which humbles a man is of more use to him than a good action which puffs him up.
THOMAS WILSON: *Maxims of Piety and of Christianity*, *c.* 1755

The Devil did grin, for his darling sin
Is pride that apes humility.
S. T. COLERIDGE: *The Devil's Thoughts*, 1799

I have not the slightest feeling of humility towards the public, or to anything in existence but the Eternal Being, the principle of beauty, and the memory of great men.
JOHN KEATS: *Letter to J. H. Reynolds*, April 9, 1818

Humility, that low, sweet root,
From which all heavenly virtues shoot.
THOMAS MOORE: *Loves of the Angels*, 1823

'Umble we are, 'umble we have been, 'umble we shall ever be.
CHARLES DICKENS: *David Copperfield*, I, 1849

Never be haughty to the humble; never be humble to the haughty.
JEFFERSON DAVIS: Speech in Richmond, July 22, 1861

Extremes meet, and there is no better example than the haughtiness of humility.
R. W. EMERSON: *Letters and Social Aims*, 1875

You've no idea what a poor opinion I have of myself – and how little I deserve it.
W. S. GILBERT: *Ruddigore*, I, 1887

The trodden worm curls up. Thus it reduces its chance of being stepped on again. In the language of morality – humility.
F. W. NIETZSCHE: *The Twilight of the Idols*, 1889

Life is a long lesson in humility.
JAMES M. BARRIE: *The Little Minister*, III, 1891

The tumult and the shouting dies,
The captains and the kings depart;
Still stands thine ancient sacrifice,
A humble and a contrite heart.
RUDYARD KIPLING: *Recessional*, 1897 (London Times, July 17)

The fruits of humility are love and peace.
HEBREW PROVERB

[*See also* Holiness, Learning, Life, Pride, Virtue.

Humor

'Twas the saying of an ancient sage that humor was the only test of gravity, and gravity of humor. For a subject which would not bear raillery was suspicious: and a jest which would not bear a serious examination was certainly false wit.

ANTHONY A. COOPER (EARL OF SHAFTESBURY): *Essay on the Freedom of Wit and Humor*, v, 1709

True humor springs not more from the head than from the heart; it is not contempt, its essence is love; it issues not in laughter, but in still smiles, which lie far deeper. It is a sort of inverse sublimity, exalting, as it were, into our affections what is below us, while sublimity draws down into our affections what is above us.

THOMAS CARLYLE: *J. P. F. Richter*, 1827 (Edinburgh Review, June)

Humor is consistent with pathos, whilst wit is not.

S. T. COLERIDGE: *Allsop's Letters, Conversations, and Recollections of S. T. Coleridge*, 1836

It is not humor to be malignant. (Non est jocus esse malignum.) LATIN PROVERB

[*See also* Jest, Joke, Laughter, Mirth, Wit.

Humor, Good

[*See* Cheerfulness.

Humpty Dumpty

[*See* Fall.

Hungarian

The Hungarian is far too lazy ever to be bored.

GERMAN PROVERB

Wherever there is a Hungarian there is a quarrel. POLISH PROVERB

Hungary

Outside Hungary there is no life; if there is any it is not the same. HUNGARIAN PROVERB

[*See also* Indifference, Poland.

Hunger

A hungry stomach will not allow its owner to forget it, whatever his cares and sorrows.

HOMER: *Odyssey*, VII, *c.* 800 B.C.

Death in all its shapes is hateful to unhappy man, but the worst is death from hunger.

HOMER: *Odyssey*, XII

They that be slain with the sword are better than they that be slain with hunger.

LAMENTATIONS IV, 9, *c.* 585 B.C.

Men do not despise a thief if he steal to satisfy his soul when he is hungry.

PROVERBS VI, 30, *c.* 350 B.C.

If thine enemy be hungry, give him bread to eat. PROVERBS XXV, 21

Hunger is the best sauce.

CICERO: *De finibus*, II, *c.* 50 B.C. (Credited to SOCRATES)

Of all diseases, hunger is the worst.

The Dhammapada, XV, *c.* 100

Hunger will break stone walls.

ENGLISH PROVERB, traced by Smith to *c.* 1350

I am so sore forhungered that my belly weeneth my throat is cut.

JOHN PALSGRAVE: *Alcolastus*, 1540

A hungry dog eats dirty puddings.

ENGLISH PROVERB, borrowed from the Latin and traced by Apperson to 1546

Hunger forceth the wolf out of his den.

WILLIAM PAINTER: *The Palace of Pleasure*, 1567

Yon Cassius has a lean and hungry look.

SHAKESPEARE: *Julius Cæsar*, I, 1599

A murrain on all proverbs. They say hunger breaks through stone walls; but I am as gaunt as lean-ribbed famine, yet I can burst through no stone walls.

JOHN MARSTON: *Antonio's Revenge*, V, 1602

They said they were an-hungry; sigh'd forth proverbs,
That hunger broke stone walls, that dogs must eat,
That meat was made for mouths, that the gods sent not
Corn for the rich men only: with these shreds
They vented their complainings.

SHAKESPEARE: *Coriolanus*, I, *c.* 1607

Hunger is good kitchen meat.

DAVID FERGUSSON: *Scottish Proverbs*, 1641

Cold and hunger never yet
Co'd a noble verse beget.

ROBERT HERRICK: *Hesperides*, 1648

A hungry man is an angry man.

JAMES HOWELL: *Proverbs*, 1659

Hunger knows no friend.

DANIEL DEFOE: *Robinson Crusoe*, II, 1719

Hunger is insolent.

ALEXANDER POPE: Tr. of HOMER: *Odyssey*, VII (*c.* 800 B.C.), 1726

Hunger is not dainty.

THOMAS FULLER: *Gnomologia*, 1732

Hungry men think the cook lazy. IBID.

My stomach serves me instead of a clock.

JONATHAN SWIFT: *Polite Conversation*, 1738

Hunger finds no fault with the cookery.

H. G. BOHN: *Handbook of Proverbs*, 1855

Hunger iz a slut hound on a fresh track.

H. W. SHAW (JOSH BILLINGS): *Josh Billings' Encyclopedia of Wit and Wisdom*, 1874

Hunger does not breed reform; it breeds madness, and all the ugly distempers that make an ordered life impossible.
WOODROW WILSON: Address to Congress, Nov. 11, 1918

Better cross an angry man than a hungry man.
DANISH PROVERB

Hunger is the first course of a good dinner.
FRENCH PROVERB

To a hungry man there is no bad bread.
IBID.

Hunger has no taste. HINDU PROVERB

A blind man can see his mouth.
IRISH PROVERB

Hunger makes beans taste like almonds.
ITALIAN PROVERB

Even Fuji is without beauty to a hungry man.
JAPANESE PROVERB

Death by hunger is worse than death by fire.
JUGO-SLOVAK PROVERB

Hunger is the best cook. (Fames est optimus coquus.) LATIN PROVERB

[*See also* Appetite, Charity, Fly, Home, Measles, Poverty.

Hunter

[*See* Horn, Hunting.

Hunting

He was a mighty hunter before the Lord: wherefore it is said, Even as Nimrod the mighty hunter before the Lord.
GENESIS X, 9, *c.* 700 B.C.

There is no one exercise that enableth the body more for the wars than hunting, by teaching you to endure heat, cold, hunger, thirst, to rise early, watch late, lie and fare badly.
HENRY PEACHAM: *The Compleat Gentleman*, 1622

Good and much company, and a good dinner; most of their discourse was about hunting, in a dialect I understood very little.
SAMUEL PEPYS: *Diary*, Nov. 22, 1663

Soon as Aurora drives away the night,
And edges eastern clouds with rosy light,
The healthy huntsman, with the cheerful horn,
Summons the dogs, and greets the dappled morn.
JOHN GAY: *Rural Sports*, II, 1713

Proud Nimrod first the bloody chase began,
A mighty hunter, and his prey was man.
ALEXANDER POPE: *Windsor Forest*, 1713

The dusky night rides down the sky,
And ushers in the morn;
The hounds all join in glorious cry,
The huntsman winds his horn;
And a-hunting we will go.
HENRY FIELDING: *Don Quixote in England*, II, 1733

The sport of kings.
WILLIAM SOMERVILLE: *The Chase*, 1735

In the woods and on the moors I seek my joy. I am a hunter. (Im Wald und auf der Heide, da such ich meine Freude: ich bin ein Jägersmann.)
Anon.: *Im Wald und auf der Heide*, *c.* 1750

Bye, Baby Bunting,
Daddy's gone a-hunting
To get a little rabbit skin
To wrap the Baby Bunting in.
Anon.: *Nursery Rhyme, c.* 1750

It is very strange and very melancholy that the paucity of human pleasures should persuade us ever to call hunting one of them.
SAMUEL JOHNSON: *Mrs. Piozzi's Anecdotes*, 1786

The horn of the hunter is heard on the hill.
JULIA CRAWFORD: *Kathleen Mavourneen*, *c.* 1840

The hare, the partridge, and the fox must be preserved first, in order that they may be killed afterwards.
JOHN LUBBOCK (LORD AVEBURY): *The Pleasures of Life*, IX, 1887

The emperor who is a huntsman soon loses his throne. CHINESE PROVERB

[*See also* Clergyman, Fox-hunter, Fox-hunting, Sport, War.

Hunt, Leigh (1784–1859)

One of those happy souls
Which are the salt of the earth, and without whom
This world would smell like what it is — a tomb.
P. B. SHELLEY: *Letter to Maria Gisborne*, July 1, 1820

Hurricane

Then up and spake an old sailor,
Had sailed to the Spanish Main,
"I pray thee, put into yonder port,
For I fear a hurricane."
H. W. LONGFELLOW: *The Wreck of the Hesperus*, 1841

Why is a hurricane an act of God when by our weather-signals we are able to anticipate hurricanes?
FRANCIS WHARTON: *On the Law of Negligence*, 1878

Hurry

Hurry is the weakness of fools.
BALTASAR GRACIÁN: *The Art of Worldly Wisdom*, LIII, 1647

Whoever is in a hurry shows that the thing he is about is too big for him.
LORD CHESTERFIELD: *Letter to his son*, Aug. 20, 1749

A man of sense may be in haste, but can never be in a hurry, because he knows that what-

ever he does in a hurry he must necessarily do very ill.
LORD CHESTERFIELD: *Letter to his son,* Aug. 28, 1751

Move slowly; never negotiate in a hurry.
Ascribed to AARON BURR in JAMES PARTON: *Life and Times of Aaron Burr,* 1858 (*c.* 1835)

Let us leave hurry to slaves. The compliments and ceremonies of our breeding should recall, however remotely, the grandeur of our destiny. R. W. EMERSON: *Manners,* 1844

Hurry is slow. (Festinatio tarda est.)
LATIN PROVERB

Hurry is good only for catching flies.
RUSSIAN PROVERB

[*See also* Haste, Late, Lawyer, Slow.

Husband

Would it not grieve a woman to be overmaster'd with a piece of valiant dust? to make an account of her life to a clod of wayward marl?
SHAKESPEARE: *Much Ado About Nothing,* II, *c.* 1599

Men are April when they woo, December when they wed.
SHAKESPEARE: *As You Like It,* IV, *c.* 1600

No worse a husband than the best of men.
SHAKESPEARE: *Antony and Cleopatra,* II, *c.* 1606

If the husband be not at home there is nobody.
GEORGE HERBERT: *Outlandish Proverbs,* 1640

There's no form of prayer in the Liturgy against bad husbands.
GEORGE FARQUHAR: *The Beaux's Stratagem,* II, 1707

'Tis the established custom [in Vienna] for every lady to have two husbands, one that bears the name, and another that performs the duties.
MARY WORTLEY MONTAGU: *Letter to Lady Rich,* Sept. 20, 1716

God give me a rich husband, though he be an ass. THOMAS FULLER: *Gnomologia,* 1732

Husband, don't believe what you see, but what I tell you. IBID.

Sorrow for a husband is like a pain in the elbow, sharp and short. IBID.

I have known many single men I should have liked in my life (if it had suited them) for a husband; but very few husbands have I ever wished was mine.
MARY LAMB: *Letter to Sarah Stoddart,* June 2, 1806

A real husband always is suspicious.
BYRON: *Don Juan,* I, 1819

The truant husband should return and say
"My dear, I was the first who came away."
IBID.

Wedded she was some years, and to a man
Of fifty, and such husbands are in plenty;
And yet, I think, instead of such a one
'T were better to have two of five-and-twenty. IBID.

A good husband is never the first to go to sleep at night or the last to awake in the morning.
BALZAC: *The Physiology of Marriage,* 1830

It is necessary to be almost a genius to make a good husband. IBID.

The majority of husbands remind me of an orang-utang trying to play the violin.
IBID.

Thou are mated with a clown,
And the grossness of his nature will have weight to drag thee down.
He will hold thee, when his passion shall have spent its novel force,
Something better than his dog, a little dearer than his horse.
ALFRED TENNYSON: *Locksley Hall,* 1842

I should like to see any kind of a man, distinguishable from a gorilla, that some good and even pretty woman could not shake a husband out of.
O. W. HOLMES: *The Professor at the Breakfast-Table,* VII, 1859

If there were no husbands, who would look after our mistresses?
GEORGE MOORE: *Confessions of a Young Man,* X, 1888

A husband is a sort of promissory note — a woman is tired of meeting him.
OSCAR WILDE: *A Woman of No Importance,* II, 1893

One who, having dined, is charged with the care of the plate.
AMBROSE BIERCE: *The Devil's Dictionary,* 1906

Do married men make the best husbands?
Ascribed to JAMES HUNEKER (1860–1921)

Every husband is my enemy. IBID.

All husbands are alike, but they have different faces so you can tell them apart.
Author unidentified

A husband is simply a lover with a two-days' growth of beard, his collar off, and a bad cold in the head. IBID.

Some men are husbands merely because some women disliked to be called old maids.
IBID.

A woman needs three husbands: one to support her, one to love her, and one to beat her.
BULGARIAN PROVERB

A good poet makes a bad husband.
FRENCH PROVERB

A jovial friend makes a bad husband. IBID.

Mother, I must have a husband or I shall set fire to the house. GERMAN PROVERB

A rakish bachelor makes a jealous husband.
ITALIAN PROVERB

It is nothing; they are only killing my husband.
PORTUGUESE PROVERB

Happy's the maid that's married to a mitherless son. SCOTTISH PROVERB

[*See also* Artist, Bachelor, Beauty, Husband and Wife, Jealousy, Lover, Man and Woman, Marriage, War, Wife.

Husband and Wife

The woman which hath an husband is bound by the law to her husband so long as he liveth; but if the husband be dead, she is loosed from the law of her husband.
ROMANS VII, 2, *c.* 55

Let the husband render unto the wife due benevolence. I CORINTHIANS VII, 3, *c.* 55

Wives, submit yourselves unto your own husbands, as unto the Lord. For the husband is the head of the wife, even as Christ is the head of the church.
EPHESIANS V, 22–23, *c.* 60

As the church is subject unto Christ, so let the wives be to their own husbands in every-thing. EPHESIANS V, 24

Husbands, love your wives, even as Christ also loved the church, and gave himself for it.
EPHESIANS V, 25

Wives, submit yourselves unto your own husbands, as it is fit in the Lord.
COLOSSIANS III, 18, *c.* 60

Husbands, love your wives, and be not bitter against them. COLOSSIANS III, 19

Ye wives, be in subjection to your own husbands. I PETER III, 1, *c.* 60

A wife must worship her husband as if he were a god, though he may be without virtue or other good qualities, and seek pleasure with other women.
THE CODE OF MANU, V, *c.* 100

When a husband goes abroad on a pious pilgrimage his wife must wait for him eight years; when he goes abroad to acquire learning she must wait six years; when he goes abroad for pleasure, three years.
THE CODE OF MANU, IX

Every husband exacts chastity from his wife; but beauty a believing Christian does not require.
TERTULLIAN: *Women's Dress, c.* 220

It's a sad house where the hen crows louder than the cock.
ENGLISH PROVERB, traced to the XVI century

A good wife maketh a good husband.
JOHN HEYWOOD: *Proverbs,* 1546

The naturalest and first conjunction of two towards the making a society of continuance is of the husband and wife, each having care of the family: the man to get, to travel abroad, to defend; the wife to save, to stay at home, and distribute that which is gotten for the nurture of the children and family.
THOMAS SMITH: *De republica Anglorum,* I, 1583

Thou art an elm, my husband, I, a vine.
SHAKESPEARE: *The Comedy of Errors,* II, 1593

I will attend my husband, be his nurse,
Diet his sickness, for it is my office.
SHAKESPEARE: *The Comedy of Errors,* V

Thy husband is thy lord, thy life, thy keeper,
Thy head, thy sovereign: one that cares for thee,
And for thy maintenance commits his body
To painful labor, both by sea and land;
To watch the night in storms, the day in cold,
While thou liest warm at home, secure and safe;
And craves no other tribute at thy hands,
But love, fair looks, and true obedience;
Too little payment for so great a debt.
SHAKESPEARE: *The Taming of the Shrew,* V, 1594

Such duty as the subject owes the prince,
Even such a woman oweth to her husband.
IBID.

A light wife doth make a heavy husband.
SHAKESPEARE: *The Merchant of Venice,* V, *c.* 1597

Men are April when they woo, December when they wed: maids are May when they are maids, but the sky changes when they are wives.
SHAKESPEARE: *As You Like It,* IV, *c.* 1600

Let the woman take
An elder than herself: so wears she to him,
So sways she level in her husband's heart:
For, boy, however we do praise ourselves,
Our fancies are more giddy and unfirm,
More longing, wavering, sooner lost and worn
Than women's are.
SHAKESPEARE: *Twelfth Night,* II, *c.* 1601

The calmest husbands make the stormiest wives.
THOMAS DEKKER: *I The Honest Whore,* V, 1604

Let husbands know
Their wives have sense like them: they see, and smell,
And have their palates both for sweet and sour,
As husbands have.
SHAKESPEARE: *Othello,* IV, 1604

O wives! love tenderly and cordially the husbands whom God has given you, but with a respectful love, and full of reverence; for therefore did God create them of a sex more vigorous and predominant.
ST. FRANCIS DE SALES: *Introduction to the Devout Life,* XXXVIII, 1609

Man and wife make one fool.
BEN JONSON: *Bartholomew Fair,* I, 1614

In the husband, wisdom; in the wife, gentleness.
GEORGE HERBERT: *Outlandish Proverbs,* 1640

It is a silly flock where the ewe bears the bell.
DAVID FERGUSSON: *Scottish Proverbs,* 1641

Every married woman shall be free from bodily correction or stripes by her husband, unless it be in his own defence upon her assault.
LAW OF MASSACHUSETTS, 1641

She commandeth her husband, in any equal matter, by constant obeying him.
THOMAS FULLER: *The Holy and Profane State,* 1642

A true wife accounts her subjection her honor and freedom, and would not think her condition safe and free but in her subjection to her husband's authority.
JOHN WINTHROP: *Journal,* 1645

A husband's power over his wife is paternal and friendly, not magisterial and despotic.
JEREMY TAYLOR: *The Mysteriousness of Marriage,* 1651

Let husband and wife infinitely avoid a curious distinction of mine and thine, for this hath caused all the laws, and all the suits, and all the wars in the world. IBID.

What a delight to have a husband at night beside you; were it for nothing save the pleasure of having one to salute you and say, God protect you, when you sneeze.
J. B. MOLIÈRE: *Sganarelle,* I, 1660

The obedience which the soldier, instructed in his duty, shows to his general, the valet to his master, a child to his father, the lowest friar to his superior, does not approach the docility, the obedience, the humility and the profound respect which a wife should show to her husband, chief, lord and master.
J. B. MOLIÈRE: *L'École des femmes,* III, 1662

The wife, where danger or dishonor lurks,
Safest and seemliest by her husband stays,
Who guards her, or with her the worst endures.
JOHN MILTON: *Paradise Lost,* IX, 1667

When the wife drinks to the husband all is well.
JOHN RAY: *English Proverbs,* 1670

God's universal law
Gave to the man despotic power
Over his female in due awe.
JOHN MILTON: *Samson Agonistes,* 1671

'Tis as much a husband's prudence to provide innocent diversion for a wife as to hinder her unlawful pleasures.
WILLIAM WYCHERLEY: *The Country Wife,* I, *c.* 1673

If ever two were one, they surely we.
If ever man were lov'd by wife, then thee;
If ever wife was happy in a man,
Compare with me, ye women, if you can.
ANNE BRADSTREET: *To My Dear and Loving Husband,* 1678

Th' one is but the other's bail,
Like Roman jailers, when they slept
Chained to the prisoners they kept.
SAMUEL BUTLER: *Hudibras,* III, 1678

Husband! thou dull unpitied miscreant,
Wedded to noise, to misery, and want;
Sold an eternal vassal for thy life,
Oblig'd to cherish and to heat a wife:
Repeat thy loath'd embraces every night
Prompted to act by duty not delight.
Anon.: *Against Marriage, c.* 1690

They think of each other in absence with a confidence unknown to the highest friendship; their satisfactions are doubled, their sorrows lessened, by participation.
RICHARD STEELE: *The Tatler,* Aug. 2, 1709

In the married state, the world must own,
Divided happiness was never known,
To make it mutual, nature points the way:
Let husbands govern: gentle wives obey.
JOHN VANBRUGH and COLLEY CIBBER: *The Provok'd Husband,* V, 1728

As the goodman saith, so say we:
But as the goodwife saith, so it must be.
THOMAS FULLER: *Gnomologia,* 1732

The reason why the law will not suffer a wife to be a witness against her husband is to preserve the peace of families.
LORD HARDWICKE: *Judgment in Barker* vs. *Dixie,* 1735

One good husband is worth two good wives; for the scarcer things are the more they're valued.
BENJAMIN FRANKLIN: *Poor Richard's Almanac,* 1742

If ever a man and his wife, or a man and his mistress, who pass nights as well as days together, absolutely lay aside all good-breeding, their intimacy will soon degenerate into a coarse familiarity, infallibly productive of contempt or disgust.
LORD CHESTERFIELD: *Letter to his son,* Nov. 3, 1749

A man will sometimes rage at his wife when in reality his mistress has offended him, and a lady complain of the cruelty of her husband when she has no other enemy than bad cards.
SAMUEL JOHNSON: *The Rambler,* May 19, 1750

To make a good husband is but one branch of a man's duty, but it is the chief duty of a woman to make a good wife.
H. H. KAMES: *Loose Hints Upon Education,* 1781

A husband and wife ought to continue so long united as they love each other: any law which should bind them to cohabitation for one moment after the decay of their affection would be a most intolerable tyranny, and the most unworthy of toleration.
P. B. SHELLEY: *Queen Mab,* notes, 1813

A wife is the slave of her husband.
NAPOLEON I: To Gaspard Gourgaud at St. Helena, 1815–1818

Emperors are only husbands in wives' eyes.
BYRON: *Don Juan,* V, 1821

That moral centaur, man and wife.
IBID. (The stanza containing this line was omitted from the first edition, apparently by accident)

Husband and wife come to look alike at last.
O. W. HOLMES: *The Professor at the Breakfast-Table,* VII, 1859

In less than law, her master;
In more than name, her friend.
R. H. NEWELL (ORPHEUS C. KERR): *The Perfect Husband,* 1864

A man who is married to a woman his inferior in intelligence finds her a perpetual dead weight, or, worse than a dead weight, a drag, upon every aspiration of his to be better than public opinion requires him to be.
J. S. MILL: *The Subjection of Women,* IV, 1869

By the laws of England, by the laws of Christianity, and by the constitution of society, when there is a difference of opinion between husband and wife, it is the duty of the wife to submit to the husband.
VICE-CHANCELLOR MALINS: *Judgment in Agar-Ellis* vs. *Lascelles,* 1878

Women always intrigue in secret against the higher souls of their husbands; they are always willing to cheat them out of their future for the sake of a painless and comfortable present.
F. W. NIETZSCHE: *Human All-too-Human,* I, 1878

The husband is the chief of the family and the head of the wife.
POPE LEO XIII: *Arcanum divinae sapientiae,* Feb. 10, 1880

The husband represents Christ, and the wife represents the church. IBID.

Husband twice as old as wife,
Argues ill for married life.
W. S. GILBERT: *The Princess Ida,* I, 1884

It is most dangerous nowadays for a husband to pay any attention to his wife in public. It always makes people think that he beats her when they are alone.
OSCAR WILDE: *Lady Windermere's Fan,* II, 1892

One can always recognize women who trust their husbands. They look so thoroughly unhappy. IBID.

When a man lends a helping hand to some noble woman, struggling alone with adversity, his wife should not say, "It is never well to interfere with your neighbor's business."
MARY BAKER G. EDDY: *Science and Health,* III, 1908

A man should be taller, older, heavier, uglier, and hoarser than his wife.
E. W. HOWE: *Country Town Sayings,* 1911

There is only one thing for a man to do who is married to a woman who enjoys spending money, and that is to enjoy earning it.
IBID.

The subjection of the wife to the husband may vary in its degree and manner according to the conditions of person, place and time. If the husband neglect his duty, it falls to the wife to take his place as directing head of the family.
POPE PIUS XI: *Casti connubii,* 1930

A woman worries about the future until she gets a husband; a man begins to worry about it when he gets a wife.
Author unidentified

When the husband earns well the wife spins well. DUTCH PROVERB

A good husband should be deaf and a good wife blind. FRENCH PROVERB

A woman is to her husband what her husband has made her. IBID.

The better the workman, the worse the husband. GERMAN PROVERB

If the husband is without learning, the wife is without pride. HINDU PROVERB

When a wife sins the husband is never innocent. ITALIAN PROVERB

A good wife shows the workmanship of a good husband. SPANISH PROVERB

[*See also* Bride, Bridegroom, Divorce, Drinking, Familiarity, Haste, Heaven and Hell, Hero, Husband, Marriage, Modesty, Mother-in-law, Obedience, Partnership, Union, Wife.

Husbandman

Noah began to be a husbandman, and he planted a vineyard.
GENESIS IX, 20, *c.* 700 B.C.

The industrious husbandman plants trees of which he himself will never see a berry.
CICERO: *Tusculanae disputationes,* I, 45 B.C.

The husbandman that laboreth must be the first partaker of the fruits.
II TIMOTHY II, 6, *c.* 65

[*See also* Farmer, Farming, Profession, Vineyard.

Huss, John (c. 1370–1415)

If John Huss was a heretic, then there is not a single Christian under the sun.
MARTIN LUTHER: *The Letters of John Huss,* pref., 1537

Huxley, T. H. (1825–95)

Kicked into the world a boy without guide or training, or with worse than none, I confess to my shame that few men have drunk deeper of all kinds of sin than I.
T. H. HUXLEY: *Letter to Charles Kingsley,* Sept. 23, 1860

Huysmans, J. K. (1848–1907)

Huysmans goes to my soul like a gold ornament of Byzantine workmanship; there is in his style the yearning charm of arches, a sense of ritual, the passion of the mural, of the window.
GEORGE MOORE: *Confessions of a Young Man,* XI, 1888

Hyena

There, fiercer from the keeper's lashes,
His teeth the fell hyena gnashes.
MARY LAMB: *The Beasts in the Tower,* 1809

[*See also* Laughter.

Hygiene

Clothe warm, eat little, drink well, so shalt thou live.
JOHN FLORIO: *First Frutes,* 1578

To avoid illness eat less: to have a long life worry less. CHINESE PROVERB

[*See also* Health, Washing.

Hymn

Let the word of Christ dwell in you richly in all wisdom; teaching and admonishing one another in psalms and hymns and spiritual songs. COLOSSIANS III, 16, *c.* 60

And when they had sung an hymn, they went out into the Mount of Olives.
MATTHEW XXVI, 30, *c.* 75

Hymns devout and holy psalms
Singing everlastingly.
JOHN MILTON: *At a Solemn Music,* 1645

A soft blending
Of dulcet instruments came charmingly;
And then a hymn.
JOHN KEATS: *Endymion,* III, 1818

A great race is not only that race which creates its god in its own image, but that race which also knows how to create its own hymn for its god.
GABRIELLE D'ANNUNZIO: *Constitution of the Free State of Fiume,* Aug. 27, 1920

[*See also* Anthem.

Hyperbole

Hyperboles are the peculiar property of young men; they betray a vehement nature.
ARISTOTLE: *Rhetoric,* III, *c.* 322 B.C.

Hyphen

The one being abhorrent to the powers above the earth and under them is the hyphenated American — the German-American, the Irish-American, or the native-American. Be American, pure and simple.
THEODORE ROOSEVELT: Speech in Buffalo, N. Y., Sept. 10, 1895 (Apparently the first appearance of *hyphenated American*)

Some Americans need hyphens in their names, because only part of them has come over; but when the whole man has come over, heart and thought and all, the hyphen drops of its own weight out of his name.
WOODROW WILSON: Address in Washington, May 16, 1914

A hyphenated American is not an American at all. . . . Our allegiance must be purely to the United States. We must unsparingly condemn any man who holds any other allegiance.
THEODORE ROOSEVELT: Speech in New York, Oct. 12, 1915

I am exactly as much opposed to English-Americans as to German-Americans. I oppose all kinds of hyphenated Americanism.
THEODORE ROOSEVELT: Speech in Detroit, May 19, 1916

Hypochondria

It is . . . the manner of hypochondriacs to change often their physician; and indeed they often do it consistently, for a physician who does not admit the reality of the disease cannot be supposed to take much pains to cure it, or to avert the danger of which he entertains no apprehension.
WILLIAM CULLEN: *First Lines of the Practice of Physic,* II, 1774

My hypochondria, in the last analysis, is simply a knack for extracting, for personal application, the greatest amount of venom from any and every incident of life, no matter what it may be.
G. C. LICHTENBERG: *Reflections,* 1799

Hypochondria is a species of torment which not only makes us unreasonably cross with the things of the present; not only fills us with groundless anxiety on the score of future misfortunes entirely of our own manufacture; but also leads to unmerited self-reproach for what we have done in the past.
ARTHUR SCHOPENHAUER: *Further Psychological Observations,* 1851

Hypocrisy

The joy of a hypocrite is but for a moment.
JOB XX, 5, *c.* 325 B.C.

Hypocrisy, by acquiring a foundation of credit in smaller matters, prepares for itself the opportunity of deceiving in greater.
LIVY: *History of Rome,* XXVIII, *c.* 110

When thou prayest, thou shalt not be as the hypocrites are: for they love to pray standing in the synagogues and in the corners of the streets, that they may be seen of men.
MATTHEW VI, 5, *c.* 75

Thou hypocrite, first cast out the beam out of thine own eye; and then shalt thou see clearly to cast out the mote out of thy brother's eye.
MATTHEW VII, 5

Woe unto you, scribes and Pharisees, hypocrites.
MATTHEW XXIII, 13 (Jesus's bill of particulars against the scribes and Pharisees follows, 13–39. Cf. LUKE XII, 44, *c.* 75)

It is of great consequence to disguise your inclination, and to play the hypocrite well; and men are so simple in their temper and so submissive to their present necessities, that he that is neat and cleanly in his collusions shall never want people to practise them upon.
NICCOLÒ MACHIAVELLI: *The Prince,* XI, 1513

I can smile, and murder whiles I smile,
And cry "Content" to that which grieves my heart;
And wet my cheeks with artificial tears,
And frame my face to all occasions.
SHAKESPEARE: *III Henry VI,* III, *c.* 1591

One may smile, and smile, and be a villain.
SHAKESPEARE: *Hamlet,* I, *c.* 1601

God has given you one face, and you make yourselves another.
SHAKESPEARE: *Hamlet,* III

The hypocrite doth vizard all his villainy with the mask or veil of virtue.
JOHN TAYLOR: *Parts of This Summer's Travels, c.* 1635

A hypocrite is in himself both the archer and the mark, in all actions shooting at his own praise or profit.
THOMAS FULLER: *The Holy State and the Profane State,* V, 1642

Compound for sins they are inclin'd to,
By damning those they have no mind to.
SAMUEL BUTLER: *Hudibras,* I, 1663

Hypocrisy is the homage which vice renders to virtue.
LA ROCHEFOUCAULD: *Maxims,* 1665

Neither man nor angel can discern
Hypocrisy, the only evil that walks
Invisible, except to God alone.
JOHN MILTON: *Paradise Lost,* III, 1667

Hypocrisy itself does great honor, or rather justice, to religion, and tacitly acknowledges it to be an ornament to human nature.
JOSEPH ADDISON: *The Spectator,* Dec. 8, 1711

Hypocrisy at the fashionable end of the town is very different from hypocrisy in the city. The modish hypocrite endeavors to appear more vicious than he really is; the other kind of hypocrite more virtuous.
JOSEPH ADDISON: *The Spectator,* May 28, 1712

No rogue like to the godly rogue.
THOMAS FULLER: *Gnomologia,* 1732

His son he cheats; he leaves his bail i' th' lurch:
Where is the rascal gone — he's gone to church.
Anon.: *Epigrams in Distich,* 1740

Joe hates a hypocrite: which shows
Self-love is not a fault of Joe's.
Anon.: *On a Hypocrite, c.* 1780

Oh, for a forty-parson power to chant
Thy praise, hypocrisy! Oh, for a hymn
Loud as the virtues thou dost loudly vaunt,
Not practise!
BYRON: *Don Juan,* X, 1823

The only vice that cannot be forgiven is hypocrisy. The repentance of a hypocrite is itself hypocrisy.
WILLIAM HAZLITT: *Characteristics,* 1823

He was a man
Who stole the livery of the court of Heaven
To serve the Devil in.
ROBERT POLLOK: *The Course of Time,* VIII, 1827

Beads about the neck and the Devil in the heart.
H. G. BOHN: *Handbook of Proverbs,* 1855

If we must be enemies, let us be men, and fight it out as we propose to do, and not deal in hypocritical appeals to God and humanity.
W. T. SHERMAN: *Letter to J. H. Hood,* Atlanta, Sept. 10, 1864

It is a very noble hypocrisy not to talk of one's self.
F. W. NIETZSCHE: *Human All-too-Human,* I, 1878

I hope you have not been leading a double life, pretending to be wicked, and being really good all the time. That would be hypocrisy.
OSCAR WILDE: *The Importance of Being Earnest,* II, 1895

If you give him time man often succeeds in living up to his hypocrisies.
Author unidentified; quoted by J. A. SPENDER: *These Times,* 1934

A mouth that prays, a hand that kills.
ARAB PROVERB

Better be a sinner than a hypocrite.
DANISH PROVERB

When the fox preaches look to your geese.
GERMAN PROVERB

A hypocrite has the face of an archbishop and the heart of a miller.
MODERN GREEK PROVERB

[*See also* Affectation, Calumny, Cant, Cause and Effect, Criticism, Dissimulation, Pleasure, Prayer, Sinner, Wilson (Woodrow).

Hypothesis

It is the first duty of a hypothesis to be intelligible.
T. H. HUXLEY: *Evidence as to Man's Place in Nature*, II, 1863

A hypothesis is an inference based on knowledge which is insufficient to prove its high probability.
FREDERICK BARRY: *The Scientific Habit of Thought*, II, 1927

Hysteria

For hysterical maidens I prescribe marriage, for they are cured by pregnancy.
HIPPOCRATES: *Aphorisms, c.* 400 B.C.

I

Ibsen, Henrik (1828–1906)

[*See* Nationality.

Ice

And ice, mast-high, came floating by,
As green as emerald.
S. T. COLERIDGE: *The Ancient Mariner*, 1798

[*See also* Fox, Rich and Poor.

Iceland

There are no snakes to be met with throughout the whole island.
Said by SAMUEL JOHNSON: *Boswell's Life*, 1778, to be the whole sixty-second chapter of *The Natural History of Iceland*, by one Horrebow

Iceman

How'd you like to be the iceman?
AMERICAN CATCH-PHRASE, *c.* 1900

Ice-water

Full many a man, both young and old,
Is brought to his sarcophagus
By pouring water, icy cold,
Adown his warm esophagus.
Author unidentified

Idea

As there are misanthropists or haters of men, so also are there misologists or haters of ideas.
PLATO: *Phaedo, c.* 360 B.C.

It is not in the power of the most exalted wit or enlarged understanding, by any quickness or variety of thought, to invent or frame one new simple idea.
JOHN LOCKE: *Essay Concerning Human Understanding*, II, 1690

There seems to be a constant decay of all our ideas; even of those which are struck deepest, and in minds the most retentive, so that if they be not sometimes renewed by repeated exercises of the senses, or reflection on those kinds of objects which at first occasioned them, the print wears out, and at last there remains nothing to be seen. IBID.

To ask at what time a man has first any ideas is to ask when he begins to perceive; having ideas and perception being the same thing.
IBID.

That fellow seems to me to possess but one idea, and that a wrong one.
SAMUEL JOHNSON: *Boswell's Life*, 1770

Nothing affects me but an abstract idea.
WILLIAM HAZLITT: Quoted in B. R. HAYDON: *Journal*, Oct. 13, 1828

The wise only possess ideas; the greater part of mankind are possessed by them.
S. T. COLERIDGE: *Defoe*, 1830

Men's ideas are the direct emanations of their material state. This is true in politics, law, morality, religion, metaphysics, etc.
KARL MARX: *The German Ideology*, 1846

One of the greatest pains to human nature is the pain of a new idea.
WALTER BAGEHOT: *Physics and Politics*, 1869

No army can withstand the strength of an idea whose time has come.
VICTOR HUGO (1802–85)

Every new idea has something of the pain and peril of childbirth about it; ideas are just as mortal and just as immortal as organized beings are.
SAMUEL BUTLER: *Note-Books, c.* 1890

An idea, to be suggestive, must come to the individual with the force of a revelation.
WILLIAM JAMES: *The Varieties of Religious Experience*, 1902

An idea that is not dangerous is unworthy of being called an idea at all.
ELBERT HUBBARD: *Roycroft Dictionary and Book of Epigrams*, 1923

Every idea is an incitement. It offers itself for belief and if believed it is acted on unless some other belief outweighs it or some failure of energy stifles the movement at its birth.
MR. JUSTICE O. W. HOLMES: *Dissenting opinion in Gitlow* vs. *People of New York*, 1924

There is no adequate defense, except stupidity, against the impact of a new idea.
P. W. BRIDGMAN: *The Intelligent Individual and Society*, III, 1938

[*See also* Age (Old), Brain, Press (Free), Sincerity.

Ideal

All human things do require to have an ideal in them; to have some soul in them, were it only to keep the body unputrefied. And wonderful it is to see how the ideal or soul, place it in what ugliest body you may, will irradiate said body with its own nobleness; will gradually, incessantly, mold, modify, new-form or reform said ugliest body, and make it at last beautiful, and to a certain degree divine.
THOMAS CARLYLE: *Past and Present,* III, 1843

The greatness of human actions is proportioned to the inspiration that engenders them. Happy is he who bears within himself a God, an ideal of beauty, and who obeys it: ideal of art, ideal of science, ideal of country, ideal of the evangelical virtues. These are the living wells of great thoughts and great actions. All of them reflect light from the Infinite.
LOUIS PASTEUR: Address to the Académie Française, 1885

I looked for great men, but all I found were the apes of their ideals.
F. W. NIETZSCHE: *The Twilight of the Idols,* 1889

An ideal cannot wait for its realization to prove its validity.
GEORGE SANTAYANA: *The Life of Reason,* I, 1905

There is no force so democratic as the force of an ideal.
CALVIN COOLIDGE: Speech in New York, Nov. 27, 1920

[*See also* Excellence.

Idealism

[*See* Carnegie (Andrew).

Idealist

The idealist is incorrigible: if he be thrown out of his Heaven he makes an ideal of his Hell.
F. W. NIETZSCHE: *Human All-too-Human,* II, 1878

Sometimes people call me an idealist. Well, that is the way I know I am an American. America is the only idealistic nation in the world.
WOODROW WILSON: Speech at Sioux Falls, N. D., Sept. 8, 1919

Pare an idealist to the quick and you'll find a Nero.
BENJAMIN DeCASSERES: *Fantasia Impromptu,* 1933

Ideology

[*See* Doctrine.

Idiom

Correct idiom is the foundation of good style.
ARISTOTLE: *Rhetoric,* III, *c.* 322 B.C.

Idiot

The souls of idiots, not being responsible for their sins, will go to Heaven; the souls of such men as Goethe and Rousseau are in danger of Hell-fire; therefore it is better to be born an idiot than to be born a Goethe or a Rousseau.
W. WINWOOD READE: *The Martyrdom of Man,* III, 1872

[*See also* Fool, Moron, Physician, Untameable.

Idleness

Idleness is disgrace.
HESIOD: *Works and Plays, c.* 700 B.C.

Abundance of idleness was in her.
EZEKIEL XVI, 49, *c.* 600 B.C.

Through idleness of the hands the house droppeth through.
ECCLESIASTES X, 18, *c.* 200 B.C.

They do nothing laboriously. (Operose nihil agunt.)
SENECA: *De brevitate vitae,* 49

Why stand ye here all the day idle?
MATTHEW XX, 6, *c.* 75

The mother of vices.
JOHN LYDGATE: *The Fall of Princes,* II, *c.* 1440

Idleness is the mistress of wanton appetites, and fortress of lust's gate.
JOHN NORTHBROOKE: *Against Dicing,* 1577

There is a beastly and slothful idleness which idle persons get to themselves, not for labors, but for pleasures and delights; there is also an honest and necessary idleness whereby good men are made more apt and ready to do their labors and vocations whereunto they are called.
IBID.

The nurse of sin.
EDMUND SPENSER: *The Fairie Queene,* I, *c.* 1589

Love is idleness.
SHAKESPEARE: *The Taming of the Shrew,* I, 1594

I rather would entreat thy company,
To see the wonders of the world abroad
Than living, dully sluggardized at home,
Wear out thy youth with shapeless idleness.
SHAKESPEARE: *Two Gentlemen of Verona,* I, *c.* 1595

Man (doubtless) was not created to be an idle fellow; he was not set in this universal orchard to stand still as a tree.
THOMAS DEKKER: *The Seven Deadly Sins of London,* IV, 1606

Ten thousand harms, more than the ills I know
My idleness doth hatch.
SHAKESPEARE: *Antony and Cleopatra,* I, *c.* 1606

Idleness is an appendix to nobility.
ROBERT BURTON: *The Anatomy of Melancholy,* I, 1621

Without business, debauchery.
GEORGE HERBERT: *Outlandish Proverbs,* 1640

Of all our faults, the one that we excuse most easily is idleness.
LA ROCHEFOUCAULD: *Maxims,* 1665

Idleness is the key of beggary.
JOHN RAY: *English Proverbs,* 1670

Idleness is the root of all evil.
GEORGE FARQUHAR: *The Beaux's Stratagem,* I, 1707

The insupportable labor of doing nothing.
RICHARD STEELE: *The Spectator,* May 2, 1711

An idle man is a kind of monster in the creation. All nature is busy about him; every animal he sees reproaches him.
JOSEPH ADDISON: *The Guardian,* Sept. 10, 1713

Satan finds some mischief still
For idle hands to do.
ISAAC WATTS: *Divine Songs for Children,* pref., 1715

If the Devil find a man idle he'll set him to work.
JAMES KELLY: *Complete Collection of Scottish Proverbs,* 1721

He that is busy is tempted by but one devil; he that is idle, by a legion.
THOMAS FULLER: *Gnomologia,* 1732

Idle brains are the Devil's workhouses. IBID.

Idle people take the most pains. IBID.

Idle men are dead all their life long. IBID.

When we do ill the Devil tempteth us; when we do nothing, we tempt him. IBID.

And heard thy everlasting yawn confess
The pains and penalties of idleness.
ALEXANDER POPE: *The Dunciad,* IV, 1742

Their only labor was to kill time,
And labor dire it is, and weary woe.
JAMES THOMSON: *The Castle of Indolence,* I, 1748

Idleness is the refuge of weak minds, and the holiday of fools.
LORD CHESTERFIELD: *Letter to his son,* July 20, 1749

Every man is, or hopes to be, an idler.
SAMUEL JOHNSON: *The Idler,* April 15, 1758

Idleness and pride tax with a heavier hand than kings and parliaments.
BENJAMIN FRANKLIN: *Letter,* July 11, 1765

Absence of occupation is not rest,
A mind quite vacant is a mind distress'd.
WILLIAM COWPER: *Retirement,* 1782

An idler is a watch that wants both hands —
As useless if it goes as if it stands. IBID.

Expect poison from standing water.
WILLIAM BLAKE: *The Marriage of Heaven and Hell,* 1790

Idle people have the least leisure.
ENGLISH PROVERB, not recorded before the XIX century

There is one piece of advice, in a life of study, which I think no one will object to; and that is, every now and then to be completely idle, — to do nothing at all.
SYDNEY SMITH: *Lectures on Moral Philosophy,* 1804

He who saddens
At thought of idleness cannot be idle,
And he's awake who thinks himself asleep.
JOHN KEATS: *Letter to J. H. Reynolds,* Feb. 19, 1818

One monster there is in the world: the idle man.
THOMAS CARLYLE: *Past and Present,* III, 1843

The occupation most becoming to a civilized man is to do nothing.
THÉOPHILE GAUTIER: *Caprices et zigzags,* 1845

It has been said that idleness is the parent of mischief, which is very true; but mischief itself is merely an attempt to escape from the dreary vacuum of idleness.
GEORGE BORROW: *Lavengro,* XIV, 1851

Doing nothing is doing ill.
H. G. BOHN: *Handbook of Proverbs,* 1855

I am not an actor, I am a spectator only. My sole occupation is sight-seeing. In a certain imperial idleness, I amuse myself with the world.
ALEXANDER SMITH: *Dreamthorp,* XI, 1863

An idle man has so much to do
That he never has time to be sad.
JOHN HAY: *The Enchanted Shirt,* 1871

If I rest, I rust. (Rast' ich, so rost' ich.)
Motto adopted by WILLIAM II of Germany as a schoolboy, *c.* 1872

Man must be doing something, or fancy that he is doing something, for in him throbs the creative impulse; the mere basker in the sunshine is not a natural, but an abnormal man.
HENRY GEORGE: *Progress and Poverty,* IX, 1879

It is impossible to enjoy idling thoroughly unless one has plenty of work to do.
JEROME K. JEROME: *Idle Thoughts of an Idle Fellow,* 1889

To do nothing at all is the most difficult thing in the world, the most difficult and the most intellectual.

OSCAR WILDE: *The Critic as Artist,* 1891

When you kill a chicken, save me the feet;
When you think I'm workin' I'm walkin' the street.

American Negro song

An idle person has the Devil for a playfellow.

ARAB PROVERB

When I am doing nothing I differ in nothing from my lazy groom.

Ascribed to various Greek sages and rulers

Idleness is the Devil's pillow.

DANISH PROVERB

The sweetness of idleness. (Dolce far niente.)

ITALIAN PHRASE

Doing nothing is doing ill.

JAPANESE PROVERB

Idleness is the cause of all the vices. (Otia omnia vitia parit.) LATIN PROVERB

Idleness is the ruin of chastity. IBID.

There is no god of the idle. IBID.

Better be idle than ill doing.

SCOTTISH PROVERB

Better sit idle than work for nought. IBID.

Idle young, needy auld. IBID.

An idler's breath withers all that blooms.

WELSH PROVERB

[*See also* Busy, Crime, Curiosity, Fault, Indolence, Industry, Laziness, Leisure, Loafing, Love, Sloth, Sluggard.

Idolatry

Ephraim is joined to idols: let him alone.

HOSEA IV, 17, *c.* 740 B.C. (Usually: "Ephraim is wedded to his idols")

Thou shalt not make unto thee any graven image, or any likeness of anything that is in heaven above, or that is in the earth beneath, or that is in the water under the earth.

EXODUS XX, 4, *c.* 700 B.C. (Cf. DEUTERONOMY V, 8, *c.* 650 B.C.)

Ye shall make you no idols nor graven image, neither rear you up a standing image, neither shall ye set up any image of stone in your land, to bow down unto it: for I am the Lord your God.

LEVITICUS XXVI, 1, *c.* 700 B.C.

We easily fall into idolatry, for we are inclined thereunto by nature, and coming to us by inheritance, it seems pleasant.

MARTIN LUTHER: *Table-Talk,* CLXXV, 1569

Four species of idols beset the human mind: idols of the tribe, idols of the den, idols of the market, and idols of the theatre.

FRANCIS BACON: *Novum Organon,* II, 1620

All men are idolaters, some of fame, others of self-interest, most of pleasure.

BALTASAR GRACIÁN: *The Art of Worldly Wisdom,* XXVI, 1647

All worship whatsoever must proceed by symbols, by idols: — we may say, all idolatry is comparative, and the worst idolatry is only more idolatrous.

THOMAS CARLYLE: *Heroes and Hero-Worship,* IV, 1840 (Lecture in London, May 15)

I see her first a-smokin' of a whackin' white cheroot,
An' a-wastin' Christian kisses on an 'eathen idol's foot.

RUDYARD KIPLING: *Mandalay,* 1890

He who slays a king and he who dies for him are alike idolaters.

GEORGE BERNARD SHAW: *Maxims for Revolutionists,* 1903

[*See also* Children, Flesh, Image.

If

I knew when seven justices could not make up a quarrel, but when the parties were met themselves, one of them thought but of an *if,* as, "If you said so then I said so"; and they shook hands and swore brothers. Your *if* is the only peacemaker; much virtue in *if.*

SHAKESPEARE: *As You Like It,* V, *c.* 1600

If the sky fall, we shall catch larks.

JOHN RAY: *English Proverbs,* 1670

If and *an* spoils many a good charter.

JAMES KELLY: *Complete Collection of Scottish Proverbs,* 1721 (*An*=archaic form of *if*)

If my aunt had been a man she'd have been my uncle.

ENGLISH PROVERB, not recorded before the XIX century

If all the world were apple-pie,
And all the sea were ink,
And all the trees were bread and cheese,
What would we have to drink?

JOSEPH RITSON: *Gammer Gurton's Garland,* 1810

If a frog had wings he wouldn't bump his backside every time he jumps.

AMERICAN PROVERB

With enough *ifs* we could put Paris into a bottle. FRENCH PROVERB

If my aunt had wheels, she would be an omnibus. GERMAN PROVERB

Ignorance

They are all ignorant, they are all dumb dogs.
ISAIAH XLVI, 10, *c.* 700 B.C.

To the ignorant even the words of the wise seem foolishness.
EURIPIDES: *The Bacchae, c.* 410 B.C.

If any man be ignorant, let him be ignorant.
I CORINTHIANS XIV, 38, *c.* 55

You do ill if you praise, but worse if you censure, what you do not rightly understand.
LEONARDO DA VINCI: *Notebooks, c.* 1500

Better unborn than untaught.
JOHN HEYWOOD: *Proverbs,* 1546

Ignorance is the mother of devotion.
HENRY COLE (DEAN OF ST. PAUL'S): *Disputation at Westminster,* 1559

He knows not a B from a battledore.
JOHN FOXE: *The Book of Martyrs,* II, 1563

There is an abecedarian ignorance that precedes knowledge, and a doctoral ignorance that comes after it; an ignorance which knowledge creates and begets, as she dispatches and destroys the first.
MICHEL DE MONTAIGNE: *Essays,* I, 1580

Many abuses are engendered into the world; or, to speak more boldly, all the abuses of the world are engendered upon this, that we are taught to fear to make profession of our ignorance, and are bound to accept and allow all that we cannot refute.
MICHEL DE MONTAIGNE: *Essays,* III, 1588

Ignorance is the curse of God.
SHAKESPEARE: *II Henry VI, c.* 1591

O thou monster, ignorance, how deformed dost thou look!
SHAKESPEARE: *Love's Labor's Lost,* IV, *c.* 1595

Ignorance is a voluntary misfortune.
NICHOLAS LING: *Politeuphuia,* 1597

There is no darkness but ignorance.
SHAKESPEARE: *Twelfth Night,* IV, *c.* 1601

Ignorance is the mother of admiration.
GEORGE CHAPMAN: *Widow's Tears,* II, 1612

There are infirmities not only of body, but of soul and fortunes, which do require the merciful hand of our abilities. I cannot contemn a man for ignorance, but behold him with as much pity as I do Lazarus.
THOMAS BROWNE: *Religio Medici,* II, 1642

Ignorance never gets beyond wonder.
BALTASAR GRACIÁN: *The Art of Worldly Wisdom,* XXVIII, 1647

It is often the greatest wisdom to be ignorant.
IBID.

The ignorant hath an eagle's wings and an owl's eyes.
GEORGE HERBERT: *Jacula Prudentum,* 1651

Ignorance of the law excuses no man: not that all men know the law, but because 'tis an excuse everyone will plead, and no man can tell how to refute him.
JOHN SELDEN: *Table-Talk,* 1689

A man may live long, and die at last in ignorance of many truths which his mind was capable of knowing, and that with certainty.
JOHN LOCKE: *Essay Concerning Human Understanding,* I, 1690

From ignorance our comfort flows,
The only wretched are the wise.
MATTHEW PRIOR: *To the Hon. Charles Montague,* 1692

The fool is happy that he knows no more.
ALEXANDER POPE: *An Essay on Man,* II, 1732

Where ignorance is bliss
'Tis folly to be wise.
THOMAS GRAY: *Ode on a Distant Prospect of Eton College,* 1747

Oh, more than Gothic ignorance!
HENRY FIELDING: *Tom Jones,* VII, 1749

He that neither knows himself nor thinks he can learn of others is not fit for company.
BENJAMIN WHICHCOTE: *Moral and Religious Aphorisms,* 1753

Ignorance, madam, pure ignorance.
SAMUEL JOHNSON: To a woman who asked him to account for an error in his Dictionary, 1755

Ignorance is mere privation by which nothing can be produced: it is a vacuity in which the soul sits motionless and torpid for want of attraction; and, without knowing why, we always rejoice when we learn, and grieve when we forget.
SAMUEL JOHNSON: *Rasselas,* XI, 1759

Mankind have a great aversion to intellectual labor; even supposing knowledge to be easily attainable, more people would be content to be ignorant than would take even a little trouble to acquire it.
SAMUEL JOHNSON: *Boswell's Life,* May 24, 1763

Ignorance is preferable to error; and he is less remote from the truth who believes nothing than he who believes what is wrong.
THOMAS JEFFERSON: *Notes on Virginia,* 1782

Ignorance is of a peculiar nature; once dispelled, it is impossible to reëstablish it. It is not originally a thing of itself, but is only the absence of knowledge; and though man may be kept ignorant, he cannot be made ignorant.
THOMAS PAINE: *The Rights of Man,* I, 1791

If a nation expects to be ignorant and free, in a state of civilization, it expects what never was and never will be.
THOMAS JEFFERSON: *Letter to Charles Yancey,* 1816

Ignorance lies at the bottom of all human knowledge, and the deeper we penetrate the nearer we arrive unto it.
C. C. COLTON: *Lacon,* 1820

A plowman is not an ignorant man because he does not know how to read; if he knows how to plow he is not to be called an ignorant man.
WILLIAM COBBETT: *Advice to Young Men,* III, 1829

Ignorance and impudence always go together; for in proportion as we are unacquainted with other things, must we feel a want of respect for them.
WILLIAM HAZLITT: *Manners Make the Man,* 1829 (The Atlas, March)

To be conscious that you are ignorant is a great step to knowledge.
BENJAMIN DISRAELI: *Sybil,* I, 1845

Blind and naked ignorance
Delivers brawling judgments, unashamed,
On all things all day long.
ALFRED TENNYSON: *Merlin and Vivien,* 1859

Better a reverent ignorance
Than knowledge atheistic.
ALEXANDER SMITH: *Dreamthorp,* XI, 1863

A man's ignorance sometimes is not only useful, but beautiful, — while his knowledge, so called, is oftentimes worse than useless, besides being ugly.
H. D. THOREAU: *Excursions,* 1863

Ignorance never settles a question.
BENJAMIN DISRAELI: Speech in the House of Commons, May 14, 1866

I am thankful that the good God created us all ignorant. I am glad that when we change His plans in this regard we have to do it at our own risk.
S. L. CLEMENS (MARK TWAIN): *Letter from New York to the Alta Californian* (*San Francisco*), May 28, 1867

Our lives are universally shortened by our ignorance.
HERBERT SPENCER: *Principles of Biology,* VI, 1867

The ignorant classes are the dangerous classes. Ignorance is the womb of monsters.
H. W. BEECHER: *Proverbs from Plymouth Pulpit,* 1870

A man's ignorance is as much his private property, and as precious in his own eyes, as his family Bible.
O. W. HOLMES: *The Young Practitioner,* 1871 (Lecture in New York, March 2)

There are many things of which a wise man might wish to be ignorant.
R. W. EMERSON: *Demonology,* 1877

A body without knowledge is like a house without a foundation. HEBREW PROVERB

Ignorance of the law excuses no one. (Ignorantia legis excusat neminem.)
LEGAL MAXIM (Or, perhaps more commonly, "Ignorance of the law is no excuse" — Ignorantia juris non excusat. Cf. SELDEN, *ante,* 1689)

[*See also* Art, Bold, Credo, Credulity, Double, Education, Folly, Knowledge, Law, Lawyer, Opinion.

Iliad

There are few books which are fit to be remembered in our wisest hours, but the Iliad is brightest in the serenest days, and embodies still all the sunlight that fell on Asia Minor.
H. D. THOREAU: *A Week on the Concord and Merrimack Rivers,* 1849

Illegitimate

There are no illegitimate children — only illegitimate parents.
JUDGE LÉON R. YANKWICH, of the United States District Court for the Southern District of California: *Decision in Zipkin* vs. *Mozon,* June, 1928

[*See also* Mulatto.

Ill-gotten

Ill gotten, ill spent.
ENGLISH PROVERB, borrowed from the Latin, and in common use since the XVI century

One ill-gotten penny corrupts a whole fortune.
GERMAN PROVERB

Illinois

[*See* American Language.

Illiteracy

For the protection of the quality of our American citizenship and of the wages of our workingmen against the fatal competition of low-priced labor we demand that the immigration laws be thoroughly enforced, and so extended as to exclude from entrance to the United States those who can neither read nor write.
Republican National Platform, 1896

Illiterate

The life of an illiterate man is death. (Vita hominis sine literis mors est.)
LATIN PROVERB

[*See also* King.

Illness

A long illness between life and death makes death a comfort both to those who die and to those who remain.
JEAN DE LA BRUYÈRE: *Caractères,* XI, 1688

An ill man is worst when he appeareth good.
THOMAS FULLER: *Gnomologia,* 1732

Be not sick too late, nor well too soon.
BENJAMIN FRANKLIN: *Poor Richard's Almanac,* 1734

Physical ills are the taxes laid upon this wretched life; some are taxed higher, and some lower, but all pay something.
LORD CHESTERFIELD: *Letter to his son,* Nov. 22, 1757

What poor things does a fever-fit or an overflowing of the bile make of the masters of creation.
WALTER SCOTT: *Journal,* Jan. 10, 1826

My bedfellows are cough and cramp; we sleep three in a bed.
CHARLES LAMB: *Letter to Edward Moxon,* April 27, 1833

Illness tells us what we are.
ITALIAN PROVERB

We are usually the best men when we are in the worst health. SPANISH PROVERB

[*See also* Disease, Hygiene, Invalid, Sickness.

Ill-Starred

The stars in their courses fought against Sisera.
JUDGES V, 19, *c.* 500 B.C.

Image

The Holy Synod commands that images of Christ, of the Mother of God and of the other saints be kept in churches, and that due honor and reverence be paid to them, not because it is believed that there is any divinity in them, or that anything may be asked from them, but because the honor which is done to them is done to the prototypes they represent.
DECREES OF THE COUNCIL OF TRENT, XXV, 1564

The pagans looked upon an idol as a god endowed with intelligence, and the other attributes of the Deity. Catholic Christians know that a holy image has no intelligence or power to hear and help them.
JAMES CARDINAL GIBBONS: *The Faith of Our Fathers,* XV, 1876

[*See also* Idolatry.

Imagination

The imagination of man's heart is evil from his youth. GENESIS VIII, 21, *c.* 700 B.C.

Imagination is a sort of faint perception.
ARISTOTLE: *Rhetoric,* I, *c.* 322 B.C.

Nature has implanted in our souls an inextinguishable love of everything great and exalted, of everything which appears beyond our comprehension. Whence it comes to pass, that even the whole world is not sufficient for the depth and rapidity of the human imagination, which often sallies forth beyond the limits of all that surrounds us.
LONGINUS: *On the Sublime, c.* 250

Such tricks hath strong imagination,
That if it would but apprehend some joy,
It comprehends some bringer of that joy;
Or in the night, imagining some fear,
How easy is a bush supposed a bear!
SHAKESPEARE: *A Midsummer Night's Dream,* V, *c.* 1596

The lunatic, the lover and the poet
Are of imagination all compact. IBID.

This is a gift that I have, a foolish extravagant spirit, full of forms, figures, shapes, objects, ideas, apprehensions, motions, revolutions; these are begot in the ventricle of memory, nourished in the womb of *pia mater,* and delivered upon the mellowing of occasion.
SHAKESPEARE: *Love's Labor's Lost,* IV, *c.* 1595

In my mind's eye, Horatio.
SHAKESPEARE: *Hamlet,* I, *c.* 1601

My imaginations are as foul
As Vulcan's stithy.
SHAKESPEARE: *Hamlet,* III

Give me an ounce of civet, good apothecary, to sweeten my imagination.
SHAKESPEARE: *King Lear,* IV, 1606

After the object is removed, or the eye shut, we still retain an image of the thing seen, though more obscure than when we see it. And this is it, the Latins call imagination, from the image made in seeing. . . . Imagination, therefore, is nothing but decaying sense; and is found in men, and many other living creatures, as well sleeping, as waking.
THOMAS HOBBES: *Leviathan,* II, 1651

Wit in the poet is no other than the faculty of imagination, which, like a nimble spaniel, beats over and ranges through the field of memory till it springs the quarry it hunted after.
JOHN DRYDEN: *Annus Mirabilis,* 1667

Imagination is the deceptive part in man, the mistress of error and falsehood, and so much the more deceitful as she is not always so; for she would be an infallible rule of truth if she were an infallible one of falsehood. But being most frequently false, she gives no mark of her quality, marking with the same character the true and the false.
BLAISE PASCAL: *Pensées,* IV, 1670

A man of a polite imagination is let into a great many pleasures that the vulgar are not capable of receiving. He can converse with a picture, and find an agreeable companion in a statue. He meets with a secret refreshment in a description, and often feels a greater satisfaction in the prospect of fields and meadows than another does in the possession.
JOSEPH ADDISON: *The Spectator,* June 21, 1712

Were it not for imagination a man would be as happy in the arms of a chambermaid as of a duchess.
SAMUEL JOHNSON: *Boswell's Life,* May 9, 1778

There is nothing more fearful than imagination without taste.
J. W. GOETHE: *Maxims,* III, 1790

I am certain of nothing but the holiness of the heart's affections, and the truth of imagination. What the imagination seizes as beauty must be truth — whether it existed before or not. . . . The imagination may be compared to Adam's dream — he awoke and found it truth.
JOHN KEATS: *Letter to Benjamin Bailey,* Nov. 22, 1817

The great instrument of moral good is the imagination.
P. B. SHELLEY: *The Defense of Poetry,* 1821

Imagination is the eye of the soul.
JOSEPH JOUBERT: *Pensées,* 1842

The virtue of the imagination is its reaching, by intuition and intensity of gaze (not by reasoning, but by its authoritative opening and revealing power), a more essential truth than is seen at the surface of things.
JOHN RUSKIN: *Modern Painters,* I, 1843

Imagination is the result of heredity. It is simply concentrated race-experience.
OSCAR WILDE: *The Critic as Artist,* 1891

[*See also* Enthusiasm, Evil, Fancy, Irish, Love, Memory, Poet, Poetry, Travel, Verse (Blank).

Imbecile

[*See* Moron.

Imitation

O imitators, servile herd! (O imitatores, servum pecus!) HORACE: *Epistles,* I, *c.* 20 B.C.

Go, and do thou likewise. LUKE X, 37, *c.* 75

A great part of art consists in imitation. For the whole conduct of life is based on this: that what we admire in others we want to do ourselves.
QUINTILIAN: *De institutione oratoria,* X, *c.* 90

Agesilaus, being invited once to hear a man who admirably imitated the nightingale, declined, saying he had heard the nightingale itself.
PLUTARCH: *Lives (Agesilaus), c.* 100

We all learn easily to imitate what is base and depraved. JUVENAL: *Satires,* XIV, 128

Before we use either to write or speak eloquently, we must dedicate our minds wholly to follow the most wise and learned men, and seek to fashion as well their speech and gesturing as their wit or inditing. The which when we earnestly mind to do we cannot but in time appear somewhat like them.
THOMAS WILSON: *The Arte of Rhetorique,* 1553

He who imitates an evil example generally goes beyond it; he who imitates a good example generally falls short of it.
FRANCESCO GUICCIARDINI: *Historia d'Italia,* 1564

In imitating great authors I have always excelled myself.
JOSEPH ADDISON: *The Guardian,* Sept. 4, 1713

It is impossible to imitate Voltaire without being Voltaire.
FREDERICK THE GREAT: *Letter to Voltaire,* Aug. 8, 1736

There is much difference between imitating a good man, and counterfeiting him.
BENJAMIN FRANKLIN: *Poor Richard's Almanac,* 1738

We are more than half what we are by imitation. The great point is to choose good models and to study them with care.
LORD CHESTERFIELD: *Letter to his son,* Jan. 18, 1750

Almost all absurdity of conduct arises from the imitation of those whom we cannot resemble.
SAMUEL JOHNSON: *The Rambler,* July 2, 1751

No man ever yet became great by imitation.
SAMUEL JOHNSON: *The Rambler,* Sept. 7, 1751

To copy faults is want of sense.
CHARLES CHURCHILL: *The Rosciad,* I, 1761

He who confines himself to the imitation of an individual, as he never proposes to surpass, so he is not likely to equal, the object of his imitation. He professes only to follow; and he that follows must necessarily be behind.
JOSHUA REYNOLDS: *Discourses,* VI, 1774 (Lecture at the Royal Academy, London, Dec. 10)

To do exactly the opposite is also a form of imitation.
G. C. LICHTENBERG: *Reflections,* 1799

Man is an imitative creature.
J. C. F. SCHILLER: *Wallenstein's Death,* III, 1799

Imitation is the sincerest of flattery.
C. C. COLTON: *Lacon,* 1820

What the child imitates he is trying to understand.
F. W. A. FROEBEL: *Menschenerziehung,* 1826

If you see a great master you will always find that he has used what was good in his predecessors, and that it was this which made him great.

J. W. GOETHE: *Conversations with Eckermann,* Jan. 4, 1827

All great poets have been gross imitators. It is, however, a mere *non distributio medii* to infer that all great imitators are poets.

E. A. POE: *Marginalia,* 1844–49

Fish is good, but fishy is always bad. Nothing is more offensive than the coloring that a weak writer always receives from the last strong man he has read.

J. G. HOLLAND: *Everyday Topics,* 1876

In matters of art it is dangerous to learn to do as others do.

RENÉ LENORMAND: *Étude sur l'harmonie moderne,* 1913

An imitator is a man who succeeds in being an imitation.

ELBERT HUBBARD: *Roycroft Dictionary and Book of Epigrams,* 1923

Hens lay where they see an egg.

DUTCH PROVERB

[*See also* Admiration, Ape, Artist, German, Plagiarism, Poetry.

Immaculate Conception

We define that the Blessed Virgin Mary in the first moment of her conception, by the singular grace and privilege of Almighty God, in virtue of the merits of Jesus Christ, the Saviour of the human race, was preserved free from every stain of Original Sin.

POPE PIUS IX: *Ineffabilis Deus,* Dec. 8, 1854

Immigrant

If anyone wish to migrate to another village, and if one or more who live in that village do not wish to receive him, if there be only one who objects he shall not move there.

THE SALIC LAW, *c.* 490

'Tis not likely that any man of a plentiful estate should voluntarily abandon a happy certainty to roam after imaginary advantages in a new world.

ROBERT BEVERLEY: *History and Present State of Virginia,* 1705

The duteous son, the sire decayed,
The modest matron, and the blushing maid,
Forc'd from their homes, a melancholy train,
To traverse climes beyond the Western main.

OLIVER GOLDSMITH: *The Traveler,* 1764

Out of twelve families of immigrants of each country, generally seven Scotch will succeed, nine German, and four Irish.

ST. JOHN DE CRÈVECOEUR: *Letters from an American Farmer,* III, 1782

My opinion with respect to immigration is that, except of useful mechanics and some particular descriptions of men or professions, there is no need of encouragement, while the policy or advantage of its taking place in a body (I mean the settling of them in a body) may be much questioned; for, by so doing, they retain the language, habits and principles (good or bad) which they bring with them.

GEORGE WASHINGTON: Address to Congress, Nov. 19, 1794

The German and Irish millions, like the Negro, have a great deal of guano in their destiny. They are ferried over the Atlantic, and carted over America, to ditch and to drudge, to make corn cheap, and then to lie down prematurely to make a spot of green grass on the prairie.

R. W. EMERSON: *The Conduct of Life,* I, 1860

Foreign immigration, which in the past has added so much to the wealth, development of resources, and increase of power to the nation — the asylum of the oppressed of all nations — should be fostered and encouraged by a liberal and just policy.

Republican National Platform, 1864

The admitted right of a government to prevent the influx of elements hostile to its internal peace and security may not be questioned, even where there is no treaty stipulation on the subject.

GROVER CLEVELAND: Message to Congress, Dec. 8, 1885

We heartily approve all legitimate efforts to prevent the United States from being used as the dumping ground for the known criminals and professional paupers of Europe.

Democratic National Platform, 1892

It would be a sight hitherto unknown on earth if men forsook their home without being either pushed or pulled.

THOMAS B. REED: Speech in the House of Representatives, Nov. 1, 1894

An unenlightened person who thinks one country better than another.

AMBROSE BIERCE: *The Devil's Dictionary,* 1906

[*See also* Pioneer.

Immodesty

Immodest words admit of no defence,
For want of decency is want of sense.

WENTWORTH DILLON (EARL OF ROSCOMMON): *Essay on Translated Verse,* 1684

Immortality

There is yet something remaining for the dead, and some far better thing for the good than for the evil.

PLATO: *Phaedo, c.* 360 B.C.

Let us not lament too much the passing of our friends. They are not dead, but simply gone before us along the road which all must travel.

ANTIPHANES: *Fragment, c.* 350 B.C.

If a man die, shall he live again?
JOB XIV, 14, *c.* 325 B.C.

The spirit shall return unto God who gave it.
ECCLESIASTES XII, 7, *c.* 200 B.C.

God created man to be immortal, and made him to be an image of his own eternity.
WISDOM OF SOLOMON II, 23, *c.* 100 B.C.

If I err in my belief that the souls of men are immortal, I err gladly, and I do not wish to lose so delightful an error.
CICERO: *De senectute,* XXIII, *c.* 78 B.C.

Without the hope of immortality no one would ever face death for his country.
CICERO: *Tusculanae disputationes,* I, 45 B.C.

Whatever it is that feels, and knows and wills, and has the power of growth, is celestial and divine, and for that reason must be immortal.
IBID.

This corruptible must put on incorruption, and this mortal must put on immortality.
I CORINTHIANS IX, 25, *c.* 55

They are not lost but sent before. (Non amittuntur sed præmittuntur.)
SENECA: *Epistulæ morales ad Lucilium,* *c.* 63

This day, which thou fearest as thy last, is the birthday of eternity. IBID.

Our Saviour Jesus Christ . . . hath abolished death, and hath brought life and immortality to light through the gospel.
II TIMOTHY I, 10, *c.* 65

We maintain that after life has passed away thou still remainest in existence, and lookest forward to a day of judgment, and according to thy deserts are assigned to misery or bliss.
TERTULLIAN: *The Testimony of the Christian Soul,* *c.* 210

After the royal throne comes death; after the dunghill comes the Kingdom of Heaven.
ST. JOHN CHRYSOSTOM: *Homilies,* V, *c.* 388

After the resurrection of the body shall have taken place, being set free from the condition of time, we shall enjoy eternal life, with love ineffable and steadfastness without corruption.
ST. AUGUSTINE: *Of the Faith and of the Creed,* *c.* 393

Death came through Eve; life has come through Mary.
ST. JEROME: *The Virgin's Professions,* *c.* 420

If I had been with God Almighty before He created the world, I could not have advised Him how out of nothing to make this globe, the firmament, and that glorious sun, which in its swift course gives light to the whole earth; how, in such manner, to create man and woman, all which He did for us, without our counsel. Therefore ought we justly to give Him the honor, and leave to His divine power and goodness the new creation of the life to come, and not presume to speculate thereon.
MARTIN LUTHER: *Table-Talk,* CXXI, 1569

Her immortal part with angels lives.
SHAKESPEARE: *Romeo and Juliet,* V, *c.* 1596

Farewell, brave relics of a complete man!
Look up and see thy spirit made a star.
GEORGE CHAPMAN: *Bussy d'Ambois,* V, 1604

Death, be not proud, though some have called thee
Mighty and dreadful, for thou art not so,
For those whom thou think'st thou doest overthrow
Die not, poor Death, nor yet canst thou kill me . . .
One short sleep past, we wake eternally,
And Death shall be no more; Death, thou shalt die.
JOHN DONNE: *Holy Sonnets,* VIII, *c.* 1617

To immortality. (A l'immortalité.)
MOTTO OF THE FRENCH ACADEMY, adopted 1635

I shall rise from the dead, from the dark station, from the prostration, from the prosternation of death, and never miss the sun, which shall then be put out, for I shall see the Son of God, the Sun of glory, and shine myself, as that sun shines.
JOHN DONNE: *Sermons,* 1650

He felt through all his fleshly dress
Bright shoots of everlastingness.
HENRY VAUGHN: *Silex scintillans,* I, 1650

They eat, they drink, and in communion sweet
Quaff immortality and joy.
JOHN MILTON: *Paradise Lost,* V, 1667

When I can read my title clear
To mansions in the skies,
I'll bid farewell to every fear,
And wipe my weeping eyes.
ISAAC WATTS: *Hymns and Spiritual Songs,* II, 1707

It must not be supposed that they who assert the natural immortality of the soul are of opinion that it is absolutely incapable of annihilation, even by the infinite power of the Creator who first gave it being, but only that it is not liable to be broken or dissolved by the ordinary laws of nature or motion.
GEORGE BERKELEY: *The Principles of Human Knowledge,* 1710

The stars shall fade away, the sun himself
Grow dim with age, and nature sink in years,
But thou shalt flourish in immortal youth,

Unhurt amidst the wars of elements,
The wrecks of matter, and the crush of worlds.
JOSEPH ADDISON: *Cato,* v, 1713

I can easily overlook any present momentary sorrow when I reflect that it is in my power to be happy a thousand years hence. If it were not for this thought I had rather be an oyster than a man.
GEORGE BERKELEY: *The Guardian,* June 23, 1713

That we are to live hereafter is just as reconcilable with the scheme of atheism, and as well accounted for by it, as that we are now alive is; and therefore nothing can be more absurd than to argue from that scheme that there can be no future state.
JOSEPH BUTLER: *The Analogy of Religion,* I, 1736

Still seems it strange, that thou shouldst live forever?
Is it less strange, that thou shouldst live at all?
This is a miracle; and that no more.
EDWARD YOUNG: *Night Thoughts,* VII, 1745

As shipwrecked mariners desire
With eager grasp to reach the shore,
As hirelings long to obtain their hire,
And veterans wish their warfare o'er,
I languish from this earth to flee,
And gasp for immortality.
CHARLES WESLEY: *Desiring Death,* 1749

Surely there is something pleasing in the belief that our separation from those whom we love is merely corporeal; and it may be a great incitement to virtuous friendship if it can be made probable that the union that has received the divine approbation shall continue to eternity.
SAMUEL JOHNSON: *Letter to James Elphinston,* Sept. 25, 1750

Shall I be left abandon'd in the dust,
When fate, relenting, lets the flower revive?
Shall nature's voice, to man alone unjust,
Bid him, though doom'd to perish, hope to live?
JAMES BEATTIE: *The Minstrel,* I, 1771

Life! We've been long together . . .
Say not good-night, but in some brighter clime
Bid me good-morning.
ANNA LETITIA BARBAULD: *Ode to Life,* 1773

The belief of immortality is impressed upon all men, and all men act under an impression of it, however they may talk, and though, perhaps, they may be scarcely sensible of it.
SAMUEL JOHNSON: *Boswell's Life,* April 14, 1775

I trouble not myself about the manner of future existence. I content myself with believing, even to positive conviction, that the power that gave me existence is able to continue it, in any form and manner he pleases, either with or without this body; and it appears more probable to me that I shall continue to exist hereafter than that I should have had existence, as I now have, before that existence began.
THOMAS PAINE: *The Age of Reason,* I, 1794

Mortal man thinks of himself as immortal because his race is immortal: he confuses the drop in the stream with the stream itself.
JEAN PAUL RICHTER: *Hesperus,* XXXV, 1795

The super-sensual world is no future world; it is now present; it can at no point of finite existence be more present than at another; not more present after an existence of myriads of lives than at this moment.
J. G. FICHTE: *Die Bestimmung des Menschen,* III, 1800

Though inland far we be
Our souls have sight of that immortal sea
Which brought us hither.
WILLIAM WORDSWORTH: *Intimations of Immortality,* 1807

Death is a gate of dreariness and gloom,
That leads to azure isles and beaming skies
And happy regions of eternal hope.
P. B. SHELLEY: *Queen Mab,* IX, 1813

We see by the glad light
And breathe the sweet air of futurity;
And so we live, or else we have no life.
WILLIAM WORDSWORTH: *The Excursion,* IX, 1814

I cannot conceive that [God] could make such a species as the human merely to live and die on this earth. If I did not believe in a future state, I should believe in no God.
JOHN ADAMS: *Letter to Thomas Jefferson,* Dec. 8, 1818

The term is not very distant at which we are to deposit in the same cerement our sorrows and suffering bodies, and to ascend in essence to an ecstatic meeting with the friends we have loved and lost, and whom we shall still love and never lose again.
THOMAS JEFFERSON: *Letter to John Adams,* 1818

A hope beyond the shadow of a dream.
JOHN KEATS: *Endymion,* I, 1818

I long to believe in immortality.
JOHN KEATS: *Letter to Fanny Brawne,* 1818

When we are dead, we are dead.
NAPOLEON I: To Gaspard Gourgaud at St. Helena, Jan. 10, 1818

Those that he loved so long and sees no more,
Loved and still loves — not dead, but gone before,
He gathers round him.
SAMUEL ROGERS: *Human Life,* 1819

To desire immortality is to desire the perpetuation of a great mistake.
ARTHUR SCHOPENHAUER: *The World as Will and Idea,* II, 1819

Let him who believes in immortality enjoy his happiness in silence, without giving himself airs about it.
J. W. GOETHE: *Conversations with Eckermann*, Feb. 25, 1824

One of the few, the immortal names
That were not born to die.
FITZ-GREENE HALLECK: *Marco Bozzaris*, 1825

If I stoop
Into a dark tremendous sea of cloud,
It is but for a time. I shall emerge one day.
ROBERT BROWNING: *Paracelsus*, conclusion, 1835

And with the morn those angel faces smile
Which I have loved long since, and lost awhile.
J. H. NEWMAN: *Light in the Darkness*, 1836

I've got a home out yonder;
Few days, few days;
I've got a home out yonder;
I am going home.
Anon.: *The Negro Singer's Own Book*, 1841

To him who believes in an eternal heavenly life, the present life loses its value — or rather, it has already lost its value; belief in the heavenly life is belief in the worthlessness and nothingness of this life.
L. A. FEUERBACH: *Das Wesen des Christentums*, 1841

The thought of life that ne'er shall cease
Has something in it like despair.
H. W. LONGFELLOW: *The Golden Legend*, I, 1851

The grand perhaps.
ROBERT BROWNING: *Bishop Blougram's Apology*, 1855

There is no death! What seems so is transition;
This life of mortal breath
Is but a suburb of the life elysian,
Whose portal we call death.
H. W. LONGFELLOW: *Resignation*, 1855

I swear I think now that everything without exception has an eternal soul —
The trees have, rooted in the ground; the weeds of the sea have; the animals.
WALT WHITMAN: *To Think of Time*, 1855

Ah, Christ, that it were possible
For one short hour to see
The souls we loved, that they might tell us
What and where they be!
ALFRED TENNYSON: *Maud*, II, 1855

I neither deny nor affirm the immortality of man. I see no reason for believing in it, but, on the other hand, I have no means of disproving it.
T. H. HUXLEY: *Letter to Charles Kingsley*, Sept. 23, 1860

Sleep that no pain shall wake,
Night that no morn shall break.
CHRISTINA ROSSETTI: *Dream-Land*, 1862

There is no death! the stars go down
To rise upon some fairer shore.
J. L. MCCREERY: *There Is No Death*, 1863 (Arthur's Home Magazine, July)

Pale, beyond porch and portal,
Crowned with calm leaves, she stands
Who gathers all things mortal
With cold immortal hands.
A. C. SWINBURNE: *The Garden of Proserpine*, 1866

Alas for him who never sees
The stars shine through his cypress-trees!
Who, hopeless, lays his dead away,
Nor looks to see the breaking day
Across the mournful marbles play!
J. G. WHITTIER: *Snow-Bound*, 1866

Oh, may I join the choir invisible
Of those immortal dead who live again.
MARIAN EVANS (GEORGE ELIOT): *The Choir Invisible*, 1867

The insatiableness of our desires asserts our personal imperishableness.
A. BRONSON ALCOTT: *Tablets*, II, 1868

I am a better believer, and all serious souls are better believers, in immortality than we can give grounds for.
R. W. EMERSON: *Immortality*, 1876

Our hope of immortality does not come from any religions, but nearly all religions come from that hope.
R. G. INGERSOLL: Interview in the Chicago Times, Nov. 14, 1879

The only evidence, so far as I know, about another life is, first, that we have no evidence; and, secondly, that we are rather sorry that we have not, and wish we had. IBID.

The high multicellular organisms with well-differentiated organs have in them the germs of death, but the low unicellular organisms are potentially immortal.
AUGUST WEISMANN: *Dauer des Lebens*, 1881

I believe in the immortality of the soul, not in the sense in which I accept the demonstrable truths of science, but as a supreme act of faith in the reasonableness of God's work.
JOHN FISKE: *The Destiny of Man*, XVI, 1884

Never did Christ utter a single word attesting to a personal resurrection and a life beyond the grave.
LYOF N. TOLSTOY: *What I Believe*, 1884

I am the tadpole of an archangel.
VICTOR HUGO (1802–85)

For tho' from out our bourne of time and place
The flood may bear me far,
I hope to see my Pilot face to face
When I have crost the bar.
ALFRED TENNYSON: *Crossing the Bar*, 1889

If a man has sent his teeth and his hair and perhaps two or three limbs to the grave before him, the presumption should be that, as he knows nothing further of these when they have once left him, so will he know nothing of the rest of him when it too is dead. The whole may surely be argued from the parts.
SAMUEL BUTLER: *Note-Books, c.* 1890

The desire for immortality seems never to have had a very strong hold upon mankind, and the belief is less widely held than is usually stated.
WILLIAM OSLER: *Science and Immortality,* II, 1904

[*See also* Annihilation, Aspiration, Corruptible, Credo, Death, Dying, Epitaph, Eternity, Heaven, Heaven and Hell, Hell, Hereafter.

Impartiality

I will not make flesh of one and fish of the other.
JOHN CLARKE: *Parœmiologia Anglo-Latina,* 1639

[*See also* Judge, Neutrality.

Impatience

The cat always catches the impatient mouse.
MOROCCAN PROVERB

Impatience is incurable. WELSH PROVERB

Impeachment

I own the soft impeachment.
R. B. SHERIDAN: *The Rivals,* V, 1775

Judgment in cases of impeachment shall not extend further than to removal from office, and disqualification to hold and enjoy any office of honor, trust or profit under the United States; but the party convicted shall nevertheless be liable and subject to indictment, trial, judgment and punishment according to law.
CONSTITUTION OF THE UNITED STATES, Art. I, 1789

The President, Vice-President and all civil officers of the United States shall be removed from office on impeachment for, and conviction of, treason, bribery, or other high crimes and misdemeanors.
CONSTITUTION OF THE UNITED STATES, Art. II

Experience has already shown that the impeachment the Constitution has provided is not even a scarecrow.
THOMAS JEFFERSON: *Letter to Spencer Roane,* 1819

[*See also* Hastings (Warren).

Imperfection

There was never a good town but had a mire at one end of it.
JAMES KELLY: *Complete Collection of Scottish Proverbs,* 1721

All things are literally better, lovelier, and more beloved for the imperfections which have been divinely appointed, that the law of human life may be effort, and the law of human judgment mercy.
JOHN RUSKIN: *Stones of Venice,* II, 1853

Even the best firewood has some ants on it.
WEST AFRICAN PROVERB

Imperialism

It is very obvious, and no more than natural, for princes to desire to extend their dominions, and when they attempt nothing but what they are able to achieve they are applauded, at least not upbraided thereby; but when they are unable to compass it, and yet will be doing, then they are condemned, and indeed not unworthily.
NICCOLÒ MACHIAVELLI: *The Prince,* III, 1513

If barbarians appear to be intellectually immature, so that they lack not only the liberal arts but even the mechanical ones as well, and seem unfit for the government of a republic, and even for the carrying on of a decent family life, a foreign prince may assume their administration for their own benefit and set up his own governors in their cities and provinces.
FRANCESCO VICTORIA: *De Indis,* II, 1585

Whatsoever God, by the ministration of nature, hath created on earth, was, at the beginning, common among men; may it not then be lawful now to attempt the possession of such lands as are void of Christian inhabitants, for Christ's sake?
WILLIAM STRACHEY: *The Historie of Travaile into Virginia Britannia, c.* 1620

The desire to gain a more extensive territory, to conquer or to hold in awe our neighboring states, to surpass them in arts or arms, is a desire founded on prejudice and error. Power is not happiness. Security and peace are more to be desired than a name at which nations tremble.
WILLIAM GODWIN: *An Enquiry Concerning Political Justice,* 1793

This Constitution never was, and never can be, strained to lap over all the wilderness of the West, without essentially affecting both the rights and convenience of its real proprietors. It was never constructed to form a covering for the inhabitants of the Missouri and Red river country. And whenever it is attempted to be stretched over them, it will rend asunder.
JOSIAH QUINCY: Speech in the House of Representatives, Jan. 14, 1811

The great nations, like lions roused from their lairs, are roaring and springing upon the prey, and the little nations, like packs of hungry wolves, are standing by, licking their jaws, and waiting for their share of the spoils.
H. W. BEECHER: *Life Thoughts,* 1858

The whites land. The cannon! One must submit to baptism, clothes, work.
ARTHUR RIMBAUD: *Une saison en enfer,* 1873

Maintaining, as I do, the tenets of a line of precedents from Washington's day, which proscribe entangling alliances with foreign states, I do not favor a policy of acquisition of new and distant territory or the incorporation of remote interests with our own.
GROVER CLEVELAND: Message to Congress, Dec. 8, 1885

Wherever there's wealth to covet,
Or land that can be possessed;
Wherever are savage races,
To cozen, coerce and scare,
Ye shall find the vaunted ensign,
For the English flag is there.
HENRY LABOUCHERE: *Where Is the Flag of England?,* 1885

The mission of the United States is one of benevolent assimilation.
WILLIAM MCKINLEY: *Letter to H. G. Otis,* Dec. 21, 1898

Take up the white man's burden —
Send forth the best ye breed —
Go bind your sons to exile
To serve your captives' need.
RUDYARD KIPLING: *The White Man's Burden,* 1899

We assert that no nation can long endure half republic and half empire, and we warn the American people that imperialism abroad will lead quickly and inevitably to despotism at home.
Democratic National Platform, 1900

The evacuation of Boston was not simply that one flag went down and another flag went up over the Province House and the Old State House; that soldiers in homespun followed down to the wharves other soldiers in red coats. On the 17th day of March, 1776, republicanism under George Washington drove imperialism under Sir William Howe out of Boston, never to come back.
GEORGE F. HOAR: Speech in the Senate, March 18, 1901

The conquest of the earth, which mostly means the taking it away from those who have a different complexion or slightly flatter noses than ourselves, is not a pretty thing when you look into it.
JOSEPH CONRAD: *Heart of Darkness,* 1902

Learn to think imperially.
JOSEPH CHAMBERLAIN: Speech at the Guildhall, London, Jan. 19, 1904

Imperialism, in a sense, is the transition stage from capitalism to Socialism. . . . It is capitalism dying, not dead.
NIKOLAI LENIN: *Materials Relating to the Revision of the Party Programme,* 1917

Imperialism is absolutely necessary to a people which desires spiritual as well as economic expansion.
BENITO MUSSOLINI: Speech in Milan, March 23, 1919

The rich man gains a market; the poor man loses a leg. RUSSIAN PROVERB

Yankee imperialism. (Imperialismo yanqui.)
SPANISH PHRASE (Latin America)

[*See also* Conquest, Foreign Relations, War (Mexican).

Imponderable

In politics the influence of imponderables is often greater than that of either military power or money.
OTTO VON BISMARCK: Speech in the Reichstag, Feb. 1, 1868

Importance

He's the whole team, and the little dog under the wagon. NEW ENGLAND SAYING

Imports

As wine and oil are imported to us from abroad, so must ripe understanding, and many civil virtues, be imported into our minds from foreign writings; — we shall else miscarry still, and come short in the attempts of any great enterprise.
JOHN MILTON: *History of Britain,* III, 1669

Impossiblity

Nothing is impossible to a willing heart.
JOHN HEYWOOD: *Proverbs,* 1546

God does not ask the impossible.
Decrees of the Council of Trent, VI, 1564

The task he undertakes
Is numbering sands and drinking oceans dry.
SHAKESPEARE: *Richard II,* II, *c.* 1596

You can't get blood out of a turnip [or a stone].
ENGLISH PROVERB, borrowed from the Latin and traced by Apperson to 1599

Who'll wrest water from a flinty stone?
JOHN WEEVER: *Epigrams in the Oldest Cut,* 1599

You can't make a silk purse out of a sow's ear.
ENGLISH PROVERB, first recorded in 1611

You cannot make a windmill go with a pair of bellows.
GEORGE HERBERT: *Outlandish Proverbs,* 1639

Few things are impossible in themselves: application to make them succeed fails us more often than the means.
LA ROCHEFOUCAULD: *Maxims,* 1665

Impossibilities are all equal, and admit no degrees.
ROBERT HOWARD: *The Duke of Lerma,* pref., 1668

Man is so made that when anything fires his soul impossibilities vanish.
JEAN DE LA FONTAINE: *Fables*, VIII, 1671

You cannot make a hunting horn of a fox's tail.
THOMAS FULLER: *Gnomologia*, 1732

You cannot make velvet of a sow's ear. IBID.

You can't sell the cow and have her milk too.
IBID.

Few things are impossible to diligence and skill.
SAMUEL JOHNSON: *Rasselas*, XII, 1759

Impossible is a word that I never utter.
J. F. COLIN D'HARLEVILLE: *Malice pour malice*, I, 1793

Nothing is impossible, as the old woman said when they told her the calf had swallowed the grindstone.
ENGLISH SAYING, not recorded before the XIX century

You write, "It is impossible": that is not French.
NAPOLEON I: *Letter to Count Lemarois*, July 9, 1813

It is not a lucky word, this *impossible;* no good comes of those that have it often in their mouth.
THOMAS CARLYLE: *The French Revolution*, III, 1837

I can answer in two words — im possible.
Ascribed to an American movie magnate, 1930

You can't shoe a running horse.
DUTCH PROVERB

One cannot be and have been.
FRENCH PROVERB

You can't both ring the bells and march in the procession. IBID.

A mouse's nest in a cat's ear.
FRENCH SAYING

No one can blow and swallow at the same time.
GERMAN PROVERB

A thousand men can't undress a naked man.
GREEK PROVERB

By asking for the impossible we obtain the best possible. ITALIAN PROVERB

No one is bound to do the impossible. (Ad impossibile nemo tenetur.)
LEGAL MAXIM; other forms are: "No one is bound by the impossible" (Nemo tenetur ad impossibile), "The law requires no one to do the impossible" (Lex neminem cogit ad impossibile), "There can be no obligation to perform the impossible" (Impossibilium nulla obligatio), and "The law excuses impossibility" (Impotentia excusat legem)

You can't make corn-cakes without breaking eggs. SPANISH PROVERB

[*See also* Belief, Unnatural.

Imprisonment

Every man being presumed innocent till he has been convicted, whenever his detention becomes indispensable, all rigor to him, more than is necessary to secure his person, ought to be provided against by the law.
Declaration of the Rights of Man by The French National Assembly, IX, 1789

He must pay with his body who cannot pay in money. (Luat in corpore, qui non habet in ære.) LEGAL MAXIM

[*See also* Law, Prison.

Improbable

[*See* Belief.

Impromptu

His impromptus smell of the lamp.
PYTHEAS: Said of Demosthenes' orations, *c.* 330 B.C.

I'll make you an impromptu at my leisure.
J. B. MOLIÈRE: *Les précieuses ridicules*, XII, 1659

Improvidence

If any provide not for his own, and especially for those of his own house, he hath denied the faith and is worse than an infidel.
I TIMOTHY V, 8, *c.* 60

Give not that which is holy unto the dogs, neither cast ye your pearls before swine.
MATTHEW VII, 6, *c.* 75

Lightly come, lightly go.
ENGLISH PROVERB, current since the XV century (Sometimes *easy* appears in place of *lightly*)

Spare at the spigot, and let out at the bunghole. JOHN RAY: *English Proverbs*, 1670

If it should rain porridge, he'd want a dish.
THOMAS FULLER: *Gnomologia*, 1732

Buy what thou hast no need of, and ere long thou shalt sell thy necessaries.
BENJAMIN FRANKLIN: *Poor Richard's Almanac*, 1757

They killed the goose that laid the golden egg.
ENGLISH SAYING, borrowed from the Greek

[*See also* Spendthrift, Thrift.

Impudence

Impudence is the worst of all human diseases.
EURIPIDES: *Medea*, 431 B.C.

The contempt of good reputation is called impudence.
THOMAS HOBBES: *Leviathan*, VI, 1651

I don't say it is impossible for an impudent man not to rise in the world; but a moderate merit, with a large share of impudence, is more probable to be advanced than the greatest qualifications without it.
MARY WORTLEY MONTAGU: *Letter to Wortley Montagu,* Sept. 24, 1714

[*See also* Ignorance, Modesty.

Impulse

Impulse manages everything badly.
STATIUS: *Theibaid,* x, *c.* 90

Impunity

The hope of impunity is the greatest inducement to do wrong.
CICERO: *Pro Milano, c.* 50 B.C.

Impunity encourages worse offences. (Impunitas semper ad deteriora invitat.)
LEGAL MAXIM

Inbreeding

By the universal economy of nature it is known, and by the instance of the Jews it is proved, that the human species has a tendency to degenerate, in any small number of persons, when separated from the general stock of society, and intermarrying constantly with each other.
THOMAS PAINE: *The Rights of Man,* I, 1791

Incarnation

The Father is in me, and I in him.
JOHN X, 38, *c.* 115 (Cf. XIV, 11)

The Word of God, Jesus Christ, on account of his great love for mankind, became what we are in order to make us what he is himself.
IRENAEUS: *Adversus hæreses,* v, *c.* 180

The one thoroughly laid down and safe way to avoid all going wide of truth is the doctrine of the Incarnation — that one and the same person is God and man; as God, the end of our going; as man, the way we are to go.
ST. AUGUSTINE: *The City of God,* XI, 427

The mystery of the humanity of Christ, that He sunk Himself into our flesh, is beyond all human understanding.
MARTIN LUTHER: *Table-Talk,* CLXXXIII, 1569

God clothed Himself in vile man's flesh that so He might be weak enough to suffer woe.
JOHN DONNE: *Holy Sonnets,* XI, *c.* 1617

By the mystery of thy holy Incarnation; by thy holy Nativity and Circumcision; by thy Baptism, Fasting, and Temptation, Good Lord, deliver us.
THE BOOK OF COMMON PRAYER (*The Litany*), 1662

Age crept on: one God would not suffice
For senile puerility; thou framedst
A tale to suit thy dotage, and to glut
Thy misery-thirsting soul, that the mad fiend
Thy wickedness had pictured might afford
A plea for sating the unnatural thirst
For murder, rapine, violence, and crime.
P. B. SHELLEY: *Queen Mab,* VI, 1813

Incense

I like incense; it makes the churches smell so sweet.
NAPOLEON I: *Diary of Pulteney Malcolm at St. Helena,* Jan. 31, 1817

Inch

Give an inch, and you'll take an ell.
HENRY PORTER: *Two Angry Women of Abingdon,* IV, 1599 (Usually, "Give him an inch, and he'll take an ell." *Ell*=a measure now archaic; about 45 inches)

Income

If I am the greatest benefactor of the human race, is that a reason for giving me what I do not need, especially when my superfluity might be of the greatest use to thousands?
WILLIAM GODWIN: *An Enquiry Concerning Political Justice,* 1793

The ideal income is a thousand dollars a day — and expenses.
Ascribed to PIERRE LORILLARD, *c.* 1885

[*See also* Money.

Incompetence

He that hath not the craft let him shut up shop.
GEORGE HERBERT: *Outlandish Proverbs,* 1640

One's own incompetence is a difficult fact to accept. So the citizen is prone to believe the demagogue who tells him the fault is not in himself. He wants to believe he can work less and earn more, save less and have more, go in debt and not have to pay it.
TERRY M. TOWNSEND: *The Doctor Looks at the Citizen,* 1940 (Address in New York, Jan. 30)

Incomprehensible

Nothing so easily persuades people of little sense as that which they cannot understand.
JEAN CARDINAL RETZ: *Conjuration de Fiesque,* 1632

[*See also* Greek Language, Hebrew Language.

Incongruity

[*See* Laughter.

Inconsistency

Nothing that is not a real crime makes a man appear so contemptible and little in the eyes of the world as inconsistency, especially when it regards religion or party.
JOSEPH ADDISON: *The Spectator,* Sept. 5, 1711

Man is so inconsistent a creature that it is impossible to reason from his belief to his conduct, or from one part of his belief to another.
T. B. MACAULAY: *Hallam,* 1828 (Edinburgh Review, Sept.)

Inconsistencies of opinion, arising from changes of circumstances, are often justifiable.
DANIEL WEBSTER: Speech in the Senate, July 25, 1846

[*See also* Character, Consistency.

Inconstancy

Afore you're off wi' the auld love
It's best to be on wi' the new.
Anon.: *It's Gude to be Merry and Wise*, *c.* 1550

My merry, merry, merry roundelay
Concludes with Cupid's curse,
They that do change old love for new,
Pray gods they change for worse.
GEORGE PEEL: *The Arraignment of Paris*, I, *c.* 1581

As one nail by strength drives out another,
So the remembrance of my former love
Is by a newer object quite forgotten.
SHAKESPEARE: *Two Gentlemen of Verona*, II, *c.* 1595

Sigh no more, ladies, sigh no more,
Men were deceivers ever,
One foot in sea and one on shore;
To one thing constant never.
SHAKESPEARE: *Much Ado About Nothing*, II, *c.* 1599

I do confess thou'rt sweet, yet find
Thee such an unthrift of thy sweets,
Thy favors are but like the wind,
Which kisses everything it meets.
ROBERT AYTON: *An Inconstant Mistress*, *c.* 1600

Oh, female faith!
Go sow the ingrateful sand, and love a woman!
JOHN MARSTON: *The Malcontent*, IV, 1604

Inconstancy no sin will prove
If we consider that we love
But the same beauty in another face,
Like the same body in another place.
LORD HERBERT OF CHERBURY: *Inconstancy*, *c.* 1610

I loved a lass, a fair one,
As fair as e'er was seen;
She was indeed a rare one,
Another Sheba queen:
But, fool as then I was,
I thought she loved me too:
But now, alas! she's left me,
Falero, lero, loo!
GEORGE WITHER: *I Loved a Lass*, *c.* 1615

It is not, Celia, in our power
To say how long our love will last;
It may be we within this hour
May lose those joys we now do taste:
The blesséd, that immortal be,
From change in love are only free.
GEORGE ETHEREDGE: To a Lady, *c.* 1670

I hate inconstancy – I loathe, detest,
Abhor, condemn, abjure the mortal made
Of such quicksilver clay that in his breast
No permanent foundation can be laid.
BYRON: *Don Juan*, II, 1819

Other towns; other girls. (Andere Städtchen, andere Mädchen.)
ALBERT SCHLIPPENBACH: *Liederbuch für deutsche Künstler*, 1833

Inconvenience

Better once a mischief than ever an inconvenience.
JOHN CLARKE: *Parœmiologia Anglo-Latina*, 1639

There's no inconvenience but has its convenience.
SAMUEL RICHARDSON: *Clarissa*, II, 1748

Incredible

There are three things that are not to be credited: a woman when she weeps, a merchant when he swears, nor a drunkard when he prays.
BARNABE RICH: *My Lady's Looking-Glass*, 1616

[*See also* Belief, Faith.

Incredulity

As incredulous as those who think none bald till they see his brains.
JOHN LYLY: *Euphues and His England*, 1580

Lukewarm incredulity acts as an emetic on secrets.
BALTASAR GRACIÁN: *The Art of Worldly Wisdom*, CCXIII, 1647

[*See also* Credulity, Doubt, Philosophy.

Incurable

Past cure, past care.
MICHEL DRAYTON: *England's Heroic Epistles*, 1598

[*See also* Hope.

Indecency

Want of decency is want of sense.
WENTWORTH DILLON (EARL OF ROSCOMMON): *Essay on Translated Verse*, 1684

The most virtuous woman is often indecent without knowing it.
BALZAC: *The Physiology of Marriage*, 1830

Indecency and fun are old cronies.
S. S. COX: *Why We Laugh*, IV, 1876

[*See also* Decency, Immodesty, Innuendo, Laughter.

Indecision

How long halt ye between two opinions?
I KINGS XVIII, 21, *c.* 500 B.C.

There is grief in indecision.
CICERO: *De officiis*, III, 78 B.C.

While we ponder when to begin it becomes too late to do.
QUINTILIAN: *De institutione oratoria,* XII, c. 90

Some craven scruple
Of thinking too precisely on the event.
SHAKESPEARE: *Hamlet,* IV, c. 1601

Of all the small annoyances that weight our mental buoyances,
No chaff or cold derision is so sad as indecision is.
W. S. GILBERT: *The Bab Ballads,* 1869

[*See also* Deliberation, Hesitation.

Indecorum

Has this fellow no feeling of his business, that he sings at grave-making?
SHAKESPEARE: *Hamlet,* V, c. 1601

Indelicacy

Public practice of any art, and staring in men's faces, is very indelicate in a female.
SAMUEL JOHNSON: *Boswell's Life,* April 11, 1775

Independence

Let every vat stand upon its own bottom.
WILLIAM BULLEIN: *Dialogue Against the Fever Pestilence,* 1564

Call me what instrument you will, though you can fret me, yet you cannot play upon me.
SHAKESPEARE: *Hamlet,* III, c. 1601

This man is free from servile bands,
Of hope to rise, or fear to fall:
Lord of himself, though not of lands,
And, having nothing, yet hath all.
HENRY WOTTON: *The Character of a Happy Life,* 1651

Often I've been by power oppressed,
And with deep sorrow tried;
By the same power I've been caressed,
And I have both defied.
DANIEL DEFOE: *A Review of the Affairs of France and of All Europe,* VIII, 1712

As long as I live I'll spit in my parlor.
THOMAS FULLER: *Gnomologia,* 1732

Studious of ease, and fond of humble things,
Below the smiles, below the frowns of kings:
Thanks to my stars, I prize the sweets of life,
No sleepless nights I count, no days of strife.
I rest, I wake, I drink, I sometimes love,
I read, I write, I settle, or I rove;
Content to live, content to die unknown,
Lord of myself, accountable to none.
BENJAMIN FRANKLIN: *Poor Richard's Almanac,* 1742

We, therefore, the representatives of the United States of America, in General Congress assembled, appealing to the Supreme Judge of the world for the rectitude of our intentions, do, in the name and by the authority of the good people of these colonies, solemnly publish and declare that these United Colonies are, and of right ought to be, free and independent states.
THOMAS JEFFERSON: *Declaration of Independence,* 1776

Nothing short of independence, it appears to me, can possibly do. A peace on other terms would, if I may be allowed the expression, be a peace of war.
GEORGE WASHINGTON: *Letter to John Banister,* April 21, 1778

Every tub must stand upon its bottom.
CHARLES MACKLIN: *The Man of the World,* I, 1781 (Cf. BULLEIN, *ante,* 1564)

Men feel their weakness, and to numbers run,
Themselves to strengthen, or themselves to shun;
But though to this our weakness may be prone,
Let's learn to live, for we must die, alone.
GEORGE CRABBE: *The Borough,* X, 1810

I am of a sect by myself, as far as I know.
THOMAS JEFFERSON: *Letter to Ezra Stiles,* 1819

Independence forever!
JOHN ADAMS: On his deathbed, July 4, 1826

It is my living sentiment, and by the blessing of God it shall be my dying sentiment, — independence now and independence forever.
DANIEL WEBSTER: *Eulogy on Adams and Jefferson,* Aug. 2, 1826

His brow is wet with honest sweat,
He earns whate'er he can,
And looks the whole world in the face,
For he owes not any man.
H. W. LONGFELLOW: *The Village Blacksmith,* 1841

I was not born to be forced. I will breathe after my own fashion. . . . If a plant cannot live according to its nature, it dies; and so a man.
H. D. THOREAU: *An Essay on Civil Disobedience,* 1849

All we ask is to be let alone.
JEFFERSON DAVIS: Message to the Confederate Congress, April 29, 1861

Follow your own path, no matter what people say.
KARL MARX: *Das Kapital,* pref., 1867

To be independent is the business of a few only; it is the privilege of the strong.
F. W. NIETZSCHE: *Beyond Good and Evil,* 1886

Independence is good, but isolation is too high a price to pay for it.
BENJAMIN R. TUCKER: *Instead of a Book,* 1893

No man of letters is further apart from circles and cliques than I am. For twenty years I have worked and struggled in absolute independence, and so it will be to the end.

GEORGE GISSING: *Letter to H. H. Sturmer,* Dec. 20, 1897

Neither the clamor of the mob nor the voice of power will ever turn me by the breadth of a hair from the course I mark out for myself, guided by such knowledge as I can obtain, and controlled and directed by a solemn conviction of right and duty.

ROBERT M. LaFOLLETTE, SR.: Speech in the Senate, Oct. 6, 1917

There is something better, if possible, that a man can give than his life. That is his living spirit to a service that is not easy, to resist counsels that are hard to resist, to stand against purposes that are difficult to stand against.

WOODROW WILSON: Speech at Suresnes Cemetery, France, May 30, 1919

Eat when I can git it, sleep all the time,
Don't give a dam if sun never shines.
Ain't nobody's business but my own.

American Negro song, quoted by HOWARD W. ODUM: *Wings On My Feet,* XVI, 1929

I don't give a damn for any damned man that don't give a damn for me.

AMERICAN SAYING

So lead your life that you can look any man in the eye and tell him to go to Hell. IBID.

[*See also* Declaration of Independence, Individualism, Self-help, Self-reliance.

Independence Day

The second day of July, 1776, will be the most memorable epocha in the history of America. I am apt to believe that it will be celebrated by succeeding generations as the great anniversary festival. It ought to be commemorated, as the day of deliverance, by solemn acts of devotion to God Almighty. It ought to be solemnized with pomp and parade, with shows, games, sports, guns, bells, bonfires, and illuminations, from one end of this continent to the other, from this time forward forevermore.

JOHN ADAMS: *Letter to Mrs. Adams,* July 3, 1776

[*See also* Declaration of Independence, July Fourth.

Independence, Declaration of

[*See* Declaration of Independence.

Index

'Tis a pitiful piece of knowledge that can be learnt from an index, and a poor ambition to be rich in the inventory of another's treasure.

JOSEPH GLANVILL: *The Vanity of Dogmatizing,* XV, 1661

An index is a necessary implement, and no impediment, of a book except in the same sense wherein the carriages of an army are termed impediments. Without this, a large author is but a labyrinth, without a clue to direct the reader therein.

THOMAS FULLER: *Worthies of England,* 1662

The most accomplished way of using books at present is twofold: either, first, to serve them as men do lords, — learn their titles exactly and then brag of their acquaintance; or, secondly, which is, indeed, the choicer, the profounder and politer method, to get a thorough insight into the index, by which the whole book is governed and turned, like fishes by the tail.

JONATHAN SWIFT: *A Tale of a Tub,* 1704

[The] modern device of consulting indexes . . . is to read books Hebraically, and begin where others usually end.

JONATHAN SWIFT: *A Letter of Advice to a Young Poet,* Dec. 1, 1720

Index-learning turns no student pale,
Yet holds the eel of science by the tail.

ALEXANDER POPE: *The Dunciad,* I, 1728

There are the men who pretend to understand a book by scouting through the index: as if a traveler should go about to describe a palace when he had seen nothing but the privy.

JONATHAN SWIFT: *On the Mechanical Operation of the Spirit, c.* 1740

So essential did I consider an index to be to every book that I proposed to bring a bill into Parliament to deprive an author who published a book without an index of the privilege of copyright, and moreover, to subject him for his offense to a pecuniary penalty.

JOHN CAMPBELL (BARON CAMPBELL): *Lives of the Chief Justices of England,* III, 1846

One may recollect generally that certain thoughts or facts are to be found in a certain book; but without a good index such a recollection may hardly be more available than that of the cabin-boy who knew where the ship's tea-kettle was because he saw it fall overboard. In truth a very large part of every man's reading falls overboard, and unless he has good indexes he will never find it again.

HORACE BINNEY: *Letter to S. A. Allibone,* Feb. 20, 1866

India

I have been reading three volumes on India. What rascals those English are!

NAPOLEON I: To Gaspard Gourgaud at St. Helena, 1815–1818

The temper of chums, the love of your wife, and a new piano's tune —
Which of the three will you trust at the end of an Indian June?

RUDYARD KIPLING: *Certain Maxims of Hafiz,* 1886

The playground of the sons of English capitalists.

EDWARD CARPENTER: *England's Ideal,* 1887

[*See also* Exile.

Indian

By our Apostolic authority we define and proclaim that the Indians, or any other peoples who may be hereafter discovered by Catholics, although they be not Christian, must in no way be deprived of their liberty or their possessions.

POPE PAUL III: *Letter to the Archbishop of Toledo,* 1537

They approach like foxes, fight like lions, and fly away like birds.

A Jesuit description of the Iroquois, *c.* 1600

Lo, the poor Indian! whose untutored mind
Sees God in clouds, or hears him in the wind.

ALEXANDER POPE: *An Essay on Man,* I, 1732

He is neither more defective in ardor, nor impotent with his female, than the white reduced to the same diet and exercise.

THOMAS JEFFERSON: *Notes on Virginia,* 1782

I believe the Indian to be in body and mind equal to the white man.

THOMAS JEFFERSON: *Letter to F. J. Chastellux,* 1785

Ask a Northern Indian what is beauty, and he will answer: a broad, flat face; small eyes, high cheek-bones, three or four broad black lines across each cheek; a low forehead, a large, broad chin; a clumsy hook nose, a tawny hide, and breasts hanging down to the belt.

SAMUEL HEARNE: *A Journey from Prince of Wales Fort in Hudson's Bay to the Northern Ocean,* 1795

Impassive — fearing but the name of fear —
A stoic of the woods — a man without a tear.

THOMAS CAMPBELL: *Gertrude of Wyoming,* I, 1809

The Cooper Indians are dead — died with their creator. The kind that are left are of altogether a different breed, and cannot be successfully fought with poetry, and sentiment, and soft soap, and magnanimity.

S. L. CLEMENS (MARK TWAIN): *Letter from New York to the Alta Californian* (San Francisco), May 28, 1867

The only good Indians I ever saw were dead.

W. T. SHERMAN: Reply to an Indian at Fort Cobb, I. T., who said "Me good Indian," Jan., 1869

The Pilgrim Fathers landed on the shores of America and fell upon their knees. Then they fell upon the aborigines.

Author unidentified

[*See also* Slavery.

Indiana

I come from Indiana, the home of more first-rate second-class men than any state in the Union.

Ascribed to THOMAS R. MARSHALL (1854–1925)

Indictment

I do not know the method of drawing up an indictment against a whole people.

EDMUND BURKE: Speech on Conciliation with America, March 22, 1775

I can't arraign before a court, civil or military, a whole brigade.

GENERAL O. M. MITCHEL: To a committee of citizens complaining of outrages by his men of the Army of the Ohio in Alabama, May, 1862

Indifference

What's Hecuba to him, or he to Hecuba,
That he should weep for her?

SHAKESPEARE: *Hamlet,* II, *c.* 1601

I care not three skips of a louse.

BEN JONSON: *A Tale of a Tub,* 1633

At length the morn and cold indifference came.

NICHOLAS ROWE: *The Fair Penitent,* I, 1703

I care for nobody, no, not I,
If no one cares for me.

ISAAC BICKERSTAFFE: *Love in a Village,* I, 1762

There's no love lost between us.

OLIVER GOLDSMITH: *She Stoops to Conquer,* IV, 1773

Shall I weep if a Poland fall? shall I shriek if a Hungary fail?
Or an infant civilization be ruled with rod or with knout?
I have not made the world, and He that made it will guide.

ALFRED TENNYSON: *Maud,* 1855

Indignation

His lips are full of indignation.

ISAIAH XXX, 27, *c.* 700 B.C.

The capacity of indignation makes an essential part of the outfit of every honest man.

J. R. LOWELL: *On a Certain Condescension in Foreigners,* 1869

No one lies so boldly as the man who is indignant.

F. W. NIETZSCHE: *Beyond Good and Evil,* 1886

Indignation is the privilege of the Chandala.

F. W. NIETZSCHE: *The Antichrist,* LVII, 1888 (*Chandala*=the lowest caste of Hindus)

[*See also* Laughter, Lying, Poetry.

Indiscretion

As a jewel of gold in a swine's snout, so is a fair woman which is without discretion.

PROVERBS XI, 22, *c.* 350 B.C.

It is indiscreet for a rat to gnaw at a tiger's tail.
CHINESE PROVERB

[*See also* Discretion, Innocence.

Individualism

When two do the same thing it is never quite the same thing.
PUBLILIUS SYRUS: *Sententiæ, c.* 50 B.C.

I never submitted the whole system of my opinions to the creed of any party of men whatever, in religion, in philosophy, in politics, or in anything else, where I was capable of thinking for myself. Such an addiction is the last degradation of a free and moral agent. If I could not go to Heaven but with a party, I would not go there at all.
THOMAS JEFFERSON: *Letter to Francis Hopkinson,* 1789

Individuality is to be preserved and respected everywhere, as the root of everything good.
JEAN PAUL RICHTER: *Titan,* CXII, 1803

Common natures do not suffice me. Good people, as they are called, won't serve. I want individuals.
CHARLES LAMB: *Letter to William Wordsworth,* March 20, 1822

Individuality is the aim of political liberty. By leaving to the citizen as much freedom of action and of being as comports with order and the rights of others, the institutions render him truly a freeman. He is left to pursue his means of happiness in his own manner.
J. FENIMORE COOPER: *The American Democrat,* XLII, 1838

We fancy men are individuals; so are pumpkins; but every pumpkin in the field goes through every point of pumpkin history.
R. W. EMERSON: *Nominalist and Realist,* 1841

Nature never rhymes her children, nor makes two men alike.
R. W. EMERSON: *Character,* 1844

There will never be a really free and enlightened state until the state comes to recognize the individual as a higher and independent power, from which all its own power and authority are derived, and treats him accordingly.
H. D. THOREAU: *An Essay on Civil Disobedience,* 1849

Humanity is alone real; the individual is an abstraction.
AUGUSTE COMTE: *Catéchisme positiviste,* 1852

An individual is as superb as a nation when he has the qualities which make a superb nation.
WALT WHITMAN: *Leaves of Grass,* pref., 1855

Whatever crushes individuality is despotism, by whatever name it may be called.
J. S. MILL: *On Liberty,* III, 1859

A people, it appears, may be progressive for a certain length of time, and then stop. When does it stop? When it ceases to possess individuality.
IBID.

Must not the virtue of modern individualism, continually enlarging, usurping all, seriously affect, perhaps keep down entirely, in America, the like of the ancient virtue of patriotism, the fervid and absorbing love of general country?
WALT WHITMAN: *Democratic Vistas,* 1870

That cause is strong which has not a multitude, but one strong man behind it.
J. R. LOWELL: Speech at Chelsea, Mass., Dec. 22, 1885

When the war closed . . . we were challenged with a peacetime choice between the American system of rugged individualism and a European philosophy of . . . paternalism and State Socialism.
HERBERT HOOVER: Speech in New York, Oct. 22, 1928

Any power must be the enemy of mankind which enslaves the individual by terror and force, whether it arises under a Fascist or Communist flag. All that is valuable in human society depends upon the opportunity for development accorded to the individual.
ALBERT EINSTEIN: Public statement in England, Sept. 15, 1933

[*See also* Business, Communism, Community, Independence, Liberty, Public, State.

Indolence

Of all our faults, that which we most readily admit is indolence. We persuade ourselves that it cherishes all the peaceful virtues; and that, without entirely destroying the others, it merely suspends their functions.
LA ROCHEFOUCAULD: *Maxims,* 1665

Indolence is the sleep of the mind.
LUC DE VAUVENARGUES: *Réflexions,* 1746

The greater part of human misery is caused by indolence.
G. C. LICHTENBERG: *Reflections,* 1799

For poesy! — no, — she has not a joy, —
At least for me, — so sweet as drowsy noons,
And evenings steep'd in honied indolence.
JOHN KEATS: *Ode on Indolence,* 1819

The love of indolence is universal, or next to it.
S. T. COLERIDGE: *Table-Talk,* June 8, 1833

[*See also* Idleness, Sloth, Sluggard.

Indomitable

Here I stand! I can do nothing else. God help me! Amen! (Hier stehe ich! Ich kann nicht anders. Gott helfe mir! Amen.)
MARTIN LUTHER: Speech to the Diet at Worms, April 18, 1521

Sink or swim, live or die, survive or perish, I give my heart and my hand to this vote.
Ascribed to JOHN ADAMS in a speech by Daniel Webster, Aug. 2, 1826, a month after Adams's death; it seems to have been based on some remarks of Adams to Jonathan Sewall in 1774

To love, and bear; to hope till hope creates
From its own wreck the thing it contemplates;
Neither to change, nor falter, nor repent.
P. B. SHELLEY: *Prometheus Unbound*, IV, 1820

Never say die.
CHARLES DICKENS: *The Pickwick Papers*, II, 1837

I have begun several times many things, and have often succeeded at last. I will sit down now, but the time will come when you shall hear me.
BENJAMIN DISRAELI: Maiden speech in the House of Commons, Dec. 7, 1837

I am short a cheek-bone and an ear, but am able to whip all Hell yet.
JOHN M. CORSE: *Dispatch to L. M. Dayton*, aide-de-camp to W. T. Sherman, from the battlefield at Alatoona, Ga., Oct. 6, 1864

[*See also* Defiance, Resolution.

Induction

The inductive method has been practised ever since the beginning of the world by every human being. It is constantly practised by the most ignorant clown, by the most thoughtless schoolboy, by the very child at the breast. The very infant, we imagine, is led by induction to expect milk from his mother or nurse, and none from his father.
T. B. MACAULAY: *Lord Bacon*, 1837

Industry

Whatsoever thy hand findeth to do, do it with thy might. ECCLESIASTES IX, 10, *c.* 200 B.C.

Nothing so difficult but it may be won by industry.
TERENCE: *Heautontimoroumenos*, IV, *c.* 160 B.C.

Industry is fortune's right hand, and frugality her left.
JOHN RAY: *English Proverbs*, 1670

Much industry and little conscience make a man rich. IBID.

He that would eat the fruit must climb the tree.
JAMES KELLY: *Complete Collection of Scottish Proverbs*, 1721

Lose no time; be always employ'd in something useful; cut off all unnecessary actions.
BENJAMIN FRANKLIN: *Rules for his own conduct*, *c.* 1730

In every rank, or great or small,
'Tis industry supports us all.
JOHN GAY: *Fables*, II, 1738

Know the true value of time; snatch, seize, and enjoy every moment of it. No idleness, no laziness, or procrastination: never put off till tomorrow what you can do today.
LORD CHESTERFIELD: *Letter to his son*, Dec. 26, 1749

Industry need not wish.
BENJAMIN FRANKLIN: *Poor Richard's Almanac*, 1758

If you have great talents industry will improve them; if you have but moderate abilities industry will supply their deficiency.
JOSHUA REYNOLDS: *Discourses*, II, 1769 (Lecture at the Royal Academy, London, Dec. 11)

My motto is *Nulla dies sine linea.* If I ever let the muse go to sleep it is only that she may wake refreshed.
LUDWIG VAN BEETHOVEN: *Letter to Otto Wegeler*, Oct. 7, 1826

Each morning sees some task begun,
Each evening sees it close;
Something attempted, something done,
Has earned a night's repose.
H. W. LONGFELLOW: *The Village Blacksmith*, 1841

Sick, irritated, and the prey to a thousand discomforts, I go on with my labor like a true workingman, who, with sleeves rolled up, in the sweat of his brow, beats away at his anvil, not caring whether it rains or blows, hails or thunders.
GUSTAVE FLAUBERT: *Letter to Louise Colet*, 1845

In the ordinary business of life industry can do anything which genius can do, and very many things which it cannot.
H. W. BEECHER: *Proverbs from Plymouth Pulpit*, 1870

Industry is the root of all ugliness.
OSCAR WILDE: *Phrases and Philosophies for the Use of the Young*, 1891

The foot of the farmer is the best manure for his land. GERMAN PROVERB

The dog that trots about finds a bone.
GIPSY PROVERB

By industry and honor. (Labore et honore.)
LATIN PHRASE

To industry nothing is impossible. (Industriæ nil impossibile.) LATIN PROVERB

[*See also* Capital, Commerce, Diligence, Energy, Labor, Nobility, Property, Work.

Inequality

It is the nature of things to be unequal. One is worth twice, or five times, or ten, or a hundred, or a thousand, or ten thousand times as much as another. To think of them as equal is to upset the whole scheme of things. Who would make shoes if big ones were of the same price as small ones?

MENCIUS: *Discourses, c.* 300 B.C.

Though all men were made of one metal, yet they were not cast all in the same mold.

THOMAS FULLER: *Gnomologia,* 1732

There is an inequality of right and authority which emanates from God Himself.

POPE LEO XIII: *Quod apostolici muneris,* Dec. 28, 1878

[*See also* Classes, Equality.

Inevitable

What will be, will be. (Che sarà, sarà.)

ITALIAN PROVERB

[*See also* Death.

Inexactitude

Some risk of terminological inexactitude.

WINSTON CHURCHILL: Speech in the House of Commons, Feb. 22, 1906

Infallibility

When we received the word of God which ye heard of us, ye received it not as the word of men, but, as it is in truth, the word of God.

I THESSALONIANS II, 13, *c.* 51

This is the scripture whereof there is no doubt.

THE KORAN, II, *c.* 625

[*See also* Certainty, Church of England.

Infallibility, Papal

The Roman Church has never erred, nor will it err to all eternity, the Scriptures being witness thereof.

POPE GREGORY VII, *c.* 1080

They who believe in the infallibility of the pope and openly say so are blasphemers.

JOHN HUSS: *De ecclesia,* 1412

A supereminent prodigious power sent upon earth to encounter and master a great evil.

J. H. NEWMAN: *Apologia pro vita sua,* II, 1864

The Roman pontiff, when he speaks *ex cathedra* — that is, when, in the exercise of his office as pastor and teacher of all Christians, he defines, by virtue of his supreme apostolic authority, a doctrine of faith or morals for the whole Church — is, by reason of the divine assistance promised to him in blessed Peter, possessed of that infallibility with which the Divine Redeemer wished His Church to be endowed in defining doctrines of faith and morals; consequently, such definitions are irreformable of their own nature, and not by reason of the Church's consent.

Decree of the Vatican Council, July 18, 1870

What is the real doctrine of infallibility? It simply means that the pope, as successor of St. Peter, Prince of the Apostles, by virtue of the promises of Jesus Christ, is preserved from error of judgment when he promulgates to the Church a decision on faith or morals.

JAMES CARDINAL GIBBONS: *The Faith of Our Fathers,* XI, 1876

All true followers of Christ believe in the infallibility of the Roman pontiff in the sense defined by the Vatican Council with the same faith as they believe the Incarnation of our Lord.

POPE PIUS XI: *Mortalium animos,* Jan. 6, 1928

[*See also* Certainty.

Infamy

Down with the infamy! (Écrasez l'infâme!)

VOLTAIRE: *Letter to Jean le Rond d'Alembert,* Jan. 27, 1762 (The phrase is frequently encountered in his letters of the period, and also occurs in those of Frederick the Great. On Nov. 28, 1762, Voltaire wrote to d'Alembert that by *infâme* he meant superstition, "not the Christian religion, which I love and respect." But he sometimes used it in such a way that it unquestionably referred to Catholicism)

[*See also* Fame, Honor.

Infancy

Heaven lies about us in our infancy.

WILLIAM WORDSWORTH: *Intimations of Immortality,* V, 1807

Infant

[*See* Baby, Child, Damnation (Infant), Limbo.

Infantry

Infantry is the nerve of an army.

FRANCIS BACON: *Essays,* XXIX, 1625

Infantry is the arm which in the end wins battles. The rifle and the bayonet are the infantryman's chief weapons. The battle can be won in the last resort only by means of these weapons.

British Field Service Regulations, 1924

The infantry, the infantry, with dirt behind the ears,
The infantry, the infantry, can drink their weight in beers;
The cavalry, the artillery and the God-damned engineers
Can never beat the infantry in a hundred thousand years.

Anon.: American soldiers' song

[*See also* Army, Battle, Cavalry, General, War.

Inferiority

[*See* Breeding, Classes, Complex (Inferiority), Familiarity, Indignation, Politeness, Superiority.

Inferiority Complex

[*See* Complex (Inferiority).

Infidel

He hath denied the faith, and is worse than an infidel. I TIMOTHY V, 8, *c.* 60

It is the reward of infidels that on them shall fall the curse of God, and of the angels, and of all mankind, and they shall remain under the same forever, save those who repent and amend, for God is gracious and merciful.
THE KORAN, III, *c.* 625

Whatever excellent endowments appear in infidels are divine gifts.
JOHN CALVIN: *Institutes of the Christian Religion,* II, 1536

There may be salvation for a virtuous infidel.
JOSEPH ADDISON: *The Spectator,* Aug. 16, 1712

As hard as it is to recover a papist, it is still harder to recover an infidel.
JOHN WESLEY: *Journal,* June 25, 1737

He is an infidel as a dog is an infidel; that is to say, he has never thought upon the subject.
SAMUEL JOHNSON: *Boswell's Life,* Oct. 19, 1769

The wonder is, always and always, how there can be a mean man or an infidel.
WALT WHITMAN: *Walt Whitman,* 1855

In the land of the infidel. (In partibus infidelium.)
LATIN PHRASE affixed to the titles of Roman Catholic bishops assigned to titular dioceses in non-Christian countries

[*See also* Antichrist, Atheism, Atheist, Culture, Education, Gibbon (Edward), Improvidence, Jew, Magician, Progress, Skeptic.

Infidelity

A sin so fearful that for the committing it both land and people must be destroyed, as it went with Jerusalem, with Rome, Greece, and other kingdoms.
MARTIN LUTHER: *Table-Talk,* CCXLVII, 1569

The great pillars and supporters of infidelity are either a vanity of appearing wiser than the rest of mankind, or an ostentation of courage in despising the terrors of another world.
JOSEPH ADDISON: *The Spectator,* Oct. 3, 1711

Infidelity has emanated chiefly from the learned.
EMANUEL SWEDENBORG: *Heaven and Hell,* 1758

Wise men wonder at the present growth of infidelity. They should have consider'd, when they taught people to doubt the authority of newspapers and the truth of predictions in almanacs, that the next step might be a disbelief in the well vouch'd acts of ghosts, witches, and doubts even of the truths of the Creed.
BENJAMIN FRANKLIN: *Letter to a London newspaper,* May 20, 1765

The spirit of infidelity has the heart of a wolf, the fangs of a tiger, and the talons of a vulture. Blood is its proper nourishment: and it scents its prey with the nerves of a hound, and cowers over the field of death on the sooty pinions of a fiend.
TIMOTHY DWIGHT: *A Discourse in Two Parts,* 1812

[*See also* Agnosticism, Atheism, Skepticism, Unfaithfulness.

Infinity

Whatsoever we imagine is finite. Therefore, there is no idea, or conception of any thing we call infinite. No man can have in his mind an image of infinite magnitude; nor conceive infinite swiftness, infinite time, infinite force, or infinite power. When we say anything is infinite, we signify only that we are not able to conceive the ends and bounds of the thing named; having no conception of the thing, but of our own inability.
THOMAS HOBBES: *Leviathan,* III, 1651

That which is infinite is as much above what is great as it is above what is small. Thus God, being infinitely great, He is as much above kings as He is above beggars; He is as much above the highest angel as He is above the meanest worm.
JONATHAN EDWARDS: *Great Guilt No Obstacle to the Pardon of the Returning Sinner, c.* 1733

To infinity. (Ad infinitum.) LATIN PHRASE

[*See also* God.

Inflation

Inflation is repudiation.
CALVIN COOLIDGE: Speech before the Hamilton Club, Chicago, Jan. 11, 1922

[*See also* Gold Standard.

Influence

A cock has great influence on his own dunghill.
PUBLILIUS SYRUS: *Sententiæ, c.* 50 B.C.

A little leaven leaveneth the whole lump.
GALATIANS V, 9, *c.* 50 (Cf. I CORINTHIANS V, 6, *c.* 55)

The rotten apple spoils his companions.
BENJAMIN FRANKLIN: *Poor Richard's Almanac,* 1736

A constant influence, a peculiar grace.
WILLIAM WORDSWORTH: *Character of the Happy Warrior,* 1807

Thou art the framer of my nobler being,
Nor does there live one virtue in my soul,
One honorable hope, but calls thee father.
S. T. COLERIDGE: *Zapolya,* I, 1817

Lives of great men all remind us
We can make our lives sublime,
And, departing, leave behind us
Footprints on the sands of time.
H. W. LONGFELLOW: *A Psalm of Life,* 1839

I breathed a song into the air,
It fell to earth, I know not where . . .
And the song, from beginning to end,
I found again in the heart of a friend.
H. W. LONGFELLOW: *The Arrow and the Song,* 1841

Every life is a profession of faith, and exercises a silent but inevitable influence.
H. F. AMIEL: *Journal,* May 2, 1852

There is no such thing as good influence. All influence is immoral — immoral from the scientific point of view.
OSCAR WILDE: *The Picture of Dorian Gray,* 1891

[*See also* Example.

Influenza

There reigns an epidemical distemper, called by the genteel name of *l'influenza.* It is a little fever, of which scarcely anybody dies; and it generally goes off with a little looseness.
LORD CHESTERFIELD: *Letter to his son,* July 9, 1767

Information

Information appears to stew out of me naturally, like the precious ottar of roses out of the otter.
S. L. CLEMENS (MARK TWAIN): *Roughing It,* pref., 1872

[*See also* Knowledge, Newspaper.

Ingratitude

One ungrateful man does an injury to all who need help.
PUBLILIUS SYRUS: *Sententiæ, c.* 50 B.C.

You too, Brutus my son! (Et tu, Brute fili.)
JULIUS CÆSAR: On being stabbed by Brutus, March 15, 44 B.C. (Quoted by SHAKESPEARE: *Julius Cæsar,* III, 1599)

The earth produces nothing worse than an ingrate. AUSONIUS: *Epigrams, c.* 360

There might I see ingratitude with an hundred eyes gazing for benefits, and with a thousand teeth gnawing on the bowels wherein she was bred.
JOHN LYLY: *Endymion,* V, 1591

What, would'st thou have a serpent sting thee twice?
SHAKESPEARE: *The Merchant of Venice,* IV, *c.* 1597

This was the most unkindest cut of all;
For when the noble Cæsar saw him stab,
Ingratitude, more strong than traitor's arms,
Quite vanquish'd him; then burst his mighty heart.
SHAKESPEARE: *Julius Cæsar,* III, 1599

Blow, blow, thou Winter wind,
Thou art not so unkind
As man's ingratitude.
SHAKESPEARE: *As You Like It,* II, *c.* 1600

Time hath, my lord, a wallet at his back,
Wherein he puts alms for oblivion,
A great-sized monster of ingratitudes;
Those scraps are good deeds past; which are devour'd
As fast as they are made, forgot as soon
As done.
SHAKESPEARE: *Troilus and Cressida,* III, *c.* 1601

I hate ingratitude more in a man,
Than lying, vainness, babbling, drunkenness,
Or any taint of vice.
SHAKESPEARE: *Twelfth Night,* III, *c.* 1601

Ingratitude! thou marble-hearted fiend.
SHAKESPEARE: *King Lear,* I, 1606

Base ingratitude.
JOHN MILTON: *Comus,* 1637

You can call a man no worse than unthankful.
JOHN CLARKE: *Parœmiologia Anglo-Latina,* 1639

An ingrate is something less to blame for his ingratitude than the one who did him the favor. LA ROCHEFOUCAULD: *Maxims,* 1665

Too great haste to repay an obligation is a kind of ingratitude. IBID.

We seldom find people ungrateful as long as we are in a condition to render them further services. IBID.

As to the ungrateful, there is not one who does not at last die miserable.
JEAN DE LA FONTAINE: *Fables,* VI, 1668

He that's ungrateful has no guilt but one,
And other crimes may pass for virtues in him.
EDWARD YOUNG: *Busiris,* I, 1719

A hog never looks up to him that threshes down the acorns.
THOMAS FULLER: *Gnomologia,* 1732

Ingratitude is treason to mankind.
JAMES THOMSON: *Coriolanus,* 1748

We set ourselves to bite the hand that feeds us.
EDMUND BURKE: *Thoughts on the Cause of the Present Discontents,* 1770

A man is very apt to complain of the ingratitude of those who have risen far above him.
SAMUEL JOHNSON: *Boswell's Life,* 1776

It is the nature of corrupt and unregenerate man to dislike his benefactors, who, by conferring benefits upon him, mortify in the most generous manner his miserable vanity.
GEORGE BORROW: *The Bible in Spain,* VII, 1843

I have heard much about the ingratitude and selfishness of the world. It may have been my

good fortune, but I have never experienced either of these unfeeling conditions.
JAMES NASMYTH: *Autobiography*, 1883

Do no good — and you will suffer no ingratitude. ARAB PROVERB

Ingratitude is the daughter of pride.
FRENCH PROVERB

Ingratitude is the reward of the world.
GERMAN PROVERB

Do a man a good turn, and he'll never forgie you. SCOTTISH PROVERB

He who has drunk his fill turns his back on the well. SPANISH PROVERB

[*See also* Favor, Gratitude, Office-seeker.

Inheritance

If a man die, and have no son, then ye shall cause his inheritance to pass unto his daughter. And if he have no daughter, then ye shall give his inheritance unto his brethren. And if he have no brethren, then ye shall give his inheritance unto his father's brethren. And if his father have no brethren, then ye shall give his inheritance unto his kinsman that is next to him of his family, and he shall possess it. NUMBERS XXVII, 8–11, *c.* 700 B.C.

A good man leaveth an inheritance to his children's children: and the wealth of the sinner is laid up for the just.
PROVERBS XIII, 22, *c.* 350 B.C.

A son can bear with equanimity the loss of his father, but the loss of his inheritance may drive him to despair.
NICCOLÒ MACHIAVELLI: *The Prince*, XVII, 1513

Man's natural right of possessing and transmitting property by inheritance must remain intact and cannot be taken away by the state.
POPE PIUS XI: *Quadragesimo anno*, May 15, 1931

[*See also* Heir, Heritage, Law (Salic), Wealth, Wisdom.

Inhumanity

Man's inhumanity to man
Makes countless thousands mourn.
ROBERT BURNS: *Man Was Made to Mourn*, 1785

Iniquity

They that plow iniquity . . . reap the same.
JOB IV, 8, *c.* 325 B.C.

I was shapen in iniquity, and in sin did my mother conceive me.
PSALMS LI, 5, *c.* 150 B.C.

Iniquity is the greatest evil (summum malum).
BENJAMIN WHICHCOTE: *Moral and Religious Aphorisms*, 1753

[*See also* Evildoer.

Injunction

We object to government by injunction as a new and highly dangerous form of oppression by which Federal judges, in contempt of the laws of the states and rights of citizens, become at once legislators, judges, and executioners.
Democratic National Platform, 1896

Injury

The injury we do and the one we suffer are not weighed in the same scales.
ÆSOP: *Fables* (*The Partial Judge*), *c.* 600 B.C.

The best remedy for an injury is to forget it.
PUBLILIUS SYRUS: *Sententiæ*, *c.* 50 B.C.

It is better to suffer an injury than to do one.
CICERO: *Tusculanæ disputationes*, V, 45 B.C.

He who injured you was either stronger or weaker. If he was weaker, spare him; if he was stronger, spare yourself.
SENECA: *De Ira*, III, *c.* 43

It is human nature to hate those you have injured. TACITUS: *Life of Agricola*, *c.* 98

If an injury has to be done to a man it should be so severe that his vengeance need not be feared.
NICCOLÒ MACHIAVELLI: *The Prince*, III, 1513

He threatens many that hath injured one.
BEN JONSON: *Sejanus*, II, 1603

An injury engraves itself on metal; a benefit is written on the waves.
JEAN BERTAUT: *Recueil de quelques vers amoureux*, 1606

Injuries are writ in brass, and not to be forgotten.
PHILIP MASSINGER: *The Duke of Milan*, V, 1623

To have done more hurt to a man than he can, or is willing to expiate, inclineth the doer to hate the sufferer. For he must expect revenge, or forgiveness; both of which are hateful.
THOMAS HOBBES: *Leviathan*, XI, 1651

Forgiveness to the injured does belong,
But they ne'er pardon who have done the wrong.
JOHN DRYDEN: *I The Conquest of Granada*, II, 1670

To make critical notes upon injuries, and be too acute in their apprehension, is to add unto our own tortures, to feather the arrows of our enemies, and to resolve to sleep no more.
THOMAS BROWNE: *Christian Morals*, III, *c.* 1680

Injury is to be measured by malice.
THOMAS FULLER: *Gnomologia*, 1732

Christianity commands us to pass by injuries; policy, to let them pass by us.
BENJAMIN FRANKLIN: *Poor Richard's Almanac,* 1741

It costs no more to resent injuries than to bear them.
THOMAS WILSON: *Maxims of Piety and of Christianity, c.* 1755

A readiness to resent injuries is a virtue only in those who are slow to injure.
R. B. SHERIDAN: *A Trip to Scarborough,* v, 1777

An individual, thinking himself injured, makes more noise than a state.
THOMAS JEFFERSON: *Letter to the Georgia delegates in Congress,* 1785

If you injure your neighbor, better not do it by halves.
GEORGE BERNARD SHAW: *Maxims for Revolutionists,* 1903

Write injuries in sand, but benefits in marble.
FRENCH PROVERB

No one should benefit by an injury done by himself. (Commodum ex injuria sua nemo habere debet.)
LEGAL MAXIM

[*See also* Contempt, Forgiveness, Grudge, Hatred, Insult, Irony, Meekness, Patience.

Injustice

A kingdom founded on injustice never lasts.
SENECA: *Medea, c.* 60

Whoever does injustice does injustice to himself, for to that extent he makes himself bad.
MARCUS AURELIUS: *Meditations,* IX, *c.* 170

The definition of injustice is no other than the not performance of covenant.
THOMAS HOBBES: *Leviathan,* XV, 1651

Injustice swift, erect and unconfin'd,
Sweeps the wide earth, and tramples o'er mankind.
ALEXANDER POPE: Tr. of HOMER: *Iliad,* IX (*c.* 800 B.C.), 1717

However small the object of an injustice may be, the injustice itself may be very great.
IMMANUEL KANT: *Perpetual Peace,* Appendix II, 1795

If the injustice is part of the necessary friction of the machine of government, let it go, let it go: perchance it will wear smooth.
H. D. THOREAU: *An Essay on Civil Disobedience,* 1849

There is a passion in the human heart stronger than the desire to be free from injustice and wrong, and that is the desire to inflict injustice and wrong upon others, and men resent more keenly an attempt to prevent them from oppressing other people than they do the oppression from which they themselves suffer.
LORD PALMERSTON: *Letter to Lord Clarendon,* Dec. 2, 1859

There is but one blasphemy, and that is injustice.
R. G. INGERSOLL: Speech in Chicago, Sept. 20, 1880

Every immortal deed was an act of fearful injustice; the world of grandeur, of triumph, of courage, of lofty aspiration, was built up on injustice.
GEORGE MOORE: *Confessions of a Young Man,* VIII, 1888

The strictest administration of the law works the greatest injustice. (Summum jus, summa injuria.)
LEGAL MAXIM

[*See also* Government, Justice, Lawyer, Society.

Inn

When you go to an inn let it not be with the feeling that you must have whatever you ask for.
CONFUCIUS: *The Book of Rites,* I, *c.* 500 B.C.

There was no room for them in the inn.
LUKE II, 7, *c.* 75

If die I must, let me die drinking in an inn.
WALTER MAP (OR MAPES): *De nugis curialium, c.* 1200

To let the world wag, and take mine ease in mine inn.
JOHN HEYWOOD: *Proverbs,* 1546

Shall I not take mine ease in mine inn?
SHAKESPEARE: *I Henry IV,* III, *c.* 1598

Now spurs the lated traveler apace
To gain the timely inn.
SHAKESPEARE: *Macbeth,* III, *c.* 1605

Choose not a house near an inn.
GEORGE HERBERT: *Outlandish Proverbs,* 1640

He goes not out of his way that goes to a good inn.
IBID.

Archbishop Leighton used often to say that if he were to choose a place to die in, it should be an inn; it looking like a pilgrim's going home, to whom this world was all as an inn, and who was weary with the noise and confusion in it.
GILBERT BURNET: *The History of My Own Times,* 1724

Whoe'er has traveled life's dull round,
Where'er his stages may have been,
May sigh to think he still has found
The warmest welcome at an inn.
WILLIAM SHENSTONE: Written on the window of an inn at Henley, 1758

There is nothing which has been contrived by man by which so much happiness is produced as by a good tavern or inn.
SAMUEL JOHNSON: *Boswell's Life,* March 21, 1776

How oft doth man, by care oppressed,
Find in an inn a place of rest.
WILLIAM COMBE: *Dr. Syntax in Search of the Picturesque,* IX, 1809

Stay, traveler! (Siste, viator!)
INSCRIPTION ON ROMAN INNS

[*See also* Church (=house), Journey, Tavern.

Innocence

The innocent are God's elect.
ST. CLEMENT: *First Epistle to the Corinthians, c.* 125

Until a child is one year old it is incapable of sin. THE TALMUD (*Yomah*), *c.* 200

Innocence beareth her defense with her.
JOHN FLORIO: *First Frutes,* 1578

What judgment shall I dread, doing no wrong?
SHAKESPEARE: *The Merchant of Venice,* IV, *c.* 1597

The day is not more clear than the bottom of my heart. JEAN RACINE: *Phèdre,* IV, 1677

Without unspotted, innocent within,
She feared no danger, for she knew no sin.
JOHN DRYDEN: *The Hind and the Panther,* I, 1687

When an innocent man is condemned it is the affair of every man.
JEAN DE LA BRUYÈRE: *Caractères,* XIV, 1688

Innocence is no protection.
THOMAS FULLER: *Gnomologia,* 1732

You are as innocent as a devil of two years old.
JONATHAN SWIFT: *Polite Conversation,* I, 1738

She was innocent as the child unborn.
JONATHAN SWIFT: *Directions to Servants,* 1745

To dread no eye, and to suspect no tongue, is the greatest prerogative of innocence.
SAMUEL JOHNSON: *The Rambler,* Nov. 10, 1750

Innocence is ashamed of nothing.
J.-J. ROUSSEAU: *Émile,* IV, 1762

It is better that ten guilty persons escape than that one innocent suffer,
WILLIAM BLACKSTONE: *Commentaries on the Laws of England,* IV, 1765

Innocence is plain, direct, and simple; guilt is a crooked, intricate, inconstant, and various thing.
EDMUND BURKE: Speech on the impeachment of Warren Hastings, Feb. 15, 1788

The innocent are gay.
WILLIAM COWPER: *The Task,* I, 1785

Oh, mirth and innocence! Oh, milk and water!
BYRON: *Beppo,* 1818

Innocence is as an armed heel
To trample accusation.
P. B. SHELLEY: *The Cenci,* IV, 1819

As innocent as a new-laid egg.
W. S. GILBERT: *Engaged,* I, 1877

Nothing looks so like innocence as an indiscretion.
OSCAR WILDE: *Lady Windermere's Fan,* II, 1892

The first age of man is when he thinks of all the wicked things he is going to do. This is called the age of innocence.
Author unidentified

Innocence is the chief of virtues; modesty comes second. GREEK PROVERB

[*See also* Blush, Guilt, Imprisonment, Jew, Virtue.

Innovation

As the births of living creatures at first are ill-shapen, so are all innovations, which are the births of time.
FRANCIS BACON: *Essays,* XXIV, 1625

Toward the preservation of your government and the permanency of your present happy state it is requisite, not only that you steadily discountenance irregular opposition to its acknowledged authority, but also that you resist with care the spirit of innovation upon its principles, however specious the pretext.
GEORGE WASHINGTON: Farewell Address, Sept. 17, 1796

Great innovations should not be forced on slender majorities.
THOMAS JEFFERSON: *Letter to General Kosciusko,* 1808

Innuendo

The older dramatists found their fun in obscenity; the moderns employ innuendo, which marks a great advance in decorum.
ARISTOTLE: *The Nicomachean Ethics,* IV, *c.* 340 B.C.

Inquisitiveness

An inquisitive person is always ill-natured.
PLAUTUS: *Stichus,* 200 B.C.

Shun the inquisitive man, for thou wilt find him leaky; open ears do not keep what has been intrusted to them.
HORACE: *Epistles,* I, *c.* 5 B.C.

Hell was made for the inquisitive.
ST. AUGUSTINE: *Confessions,* XI, *c.* 420

[*See also* Curiosity, Hell.

Insanity

Now see that noble and most sovereign reason,
Like sweet bells jangled, out of tune and harsh.
SHAKESPEARE: *Hamlet,* III, *c.* 1601

There is a pleasure sure
In being mad which none but madmen know.
JOHN DRYDEN: *The Spanish Friar,* III, 1681

There is not a sight in nature so mortifying as that of a distracted person, when his imagination is troubled, and his whole soul disordered and confused. Babylon in ruins is not so melancholy a spectacle.
JOSEPH ADDISON: *The Spectator,* July 3, 1712

In individuals, insanity is rare, but in groups, parties, nations and epochs it is the rule.
F. W. NIETZSCHE: *Beyond Good and Evil,* 1886

A madman has no free will. (Furiosi nulla voluntas est.) LEGAL MAXIM

Not of sound mind. (Non compos mentis.)
LEGAL PHRASE

[*See also* Lunatic, Murderer.

Insect

It is possible, in insects, to demonstrate the existence of memory, of the association of sensory images, of perception, attention, habit-forming, simple inference from analogy, the use of experience, and other distinct though feeble evidences of deliberation and adaptation.
AUGUSTE FOREL: *Die physischen Fähigkeiten der Ameisen,* 1901

Something in the insect seems to be alien to the habits, morals and psychology of this world, as if it had come from some other planet, more monstrous, more energetic, more insensate, more atrocious, more infernal than our own.
MAURICE MAETERLINCK: *J. H. Fabre et son œuvre,* 1911

[*See also* Beetle, Bug.

Insight

A moment's insight is sometimes worth a life's experience.
O. W. HOLMES: *The Professor at the Breakfast Table,* x, 1859

[*See also* Ages.

Insincerity

Insincerity in a man's own heart must make all his enjoyments, all that concerns him, unreal; so that his whole life must seem like a merely dramatic representation.
NATHANIEL HAWTHORNE: *American Note-Books,* Dec. 6, 1837

Insincerity is merely a method by which we can multiply our personalities.
OSCAR WILDE: *The Picture of Dorian Gray,* 1891

Insolence

The more foolish, the more insolent. (Quo quisque stulitor, eo magis insolescit.)
LATIN PROVERB

The insolent are always in trouble.
TURKISH PROVERB

[*See also* Greatness, Office, Prosperity, Wealth.

Insomnia

When I lie down, I say, When shall I arise, and the night be gone? and I am full of tossings to and fro unto the dawning of the day.
JOB VII, 4, *c.* 325 B.C.

O sleep, O gentle sleep,
Nature's soft nurse, how have I frighted thee,
That thou no more wilt weigh my eyelids down
And steep my senses in forgetfulness?
SHAKESPEARE: *II Henry IV,* III, *c.* 1598

He that thinks in his bed has a day without a night. SCOTTISH PROVERB

[*See also* Sleep.

Inspiration

No man was ever great without a touch of divine afflatus (adflatu divino).
CICERO: *De natura deorum,* II, 45 B.C.

A god has his abode within our breast; when he rouses us, the glow of inspiration warms us; this holy rapture springs from the seeds of the divine mind sown in man.
OVID: *Fasti,* VI, *c.* 5

Gie me a spark o' nature's fire —
That's a' the learning I desire.
ROBERT BURNS: *Epistle to J. Lapraik,* April 1, 1785

There is something in our minds like sunshine and the weather, which is not under our control. When I write, the best things come to me from I know not where.
G. C. LICHTENBERG: *Reflections,* 1799

Beneath whose looks did my reviving soul
Riper in truth and virtuous daring grow?
Whose eyes have I gazed fondly on,
And loved mankind the more?
P. B. SHELLEY: *Queen Mab,* I, 1813

At Canterbury I hope the remembrance of Chaucer will set me forward like a billiard ball.
JOHN KEATS: *Letter to Taylor and Hessey,* May 16, 1817

I become a transparent eyeball; I am nothing; I see all; the currents of the Universal Being circulate through me; I am part or particle of God. R. W. EMERSON: *Nature,* 1836

[*See also* Genius, Poet.

Instigator

The instigator is more guilty than the doer. (Plus peccat auctor quam actor.)
LEGAL MAXIM

Instinct

Instinct is a great matter; I was a coward on instinct.
SHAKESPEARE: *I Henry IV,* II, *c.* 1598

Let him make use of instinct who cannot make use of reason.
JOHN RAY: *English Proverbs,* 1670

How instinct varies in the grov'ling swine,
Compar'd, half-reasoning elephant, with thine!
'Twixt that and reason what a nice barrier!
Forever sep'rate, yet forever near.

ALEXANDER POPE: *An Essay on Man*, I, 1732

Instinct preceded wisdom.

GEORGE LILLO: *Fatal Curiosity*, I, 1736

As the intelligence improves, the instincts decay.

J. O. DE LA METTRIE: *L'homme machine*, 1748

Instinct is intelligence incapable of self-consciousness.

JOHN STERLING: *Thoughts and Images*, *c.* 1840

All our progress is an unfolding, like the vegetable bud. You have first an instinct, then an opinion, then a knowledge, as the plant has root, bud, and fruit. Trust the instinct to the end, though you can render no reason.

R. W. EMERSON: *Intellect*, 1841

Instinct is untaught ability.

ALEXANDER BAIN: *The Senses and the Intellect*, 1855

My natural instinct teaches me.

W. S. GILBERT: *The Princess Ida*, II, 1884

I call an animal, a species, an individual corrupt, when it loses its instincts, when it chooses, when it prefers, what is injurious to it.

F. W. NIETZSCHE: *The Antichrist*, VI, 1888

Many instincts ripen at a certain age and then fade away.

WILLIAM JAMES: *Psychology, Briefer Course*, XXV, 1892

The general principle upon which the newer morality differs from the traditional morality of Puritanism is this: We believe that instinct should be trained rather than thwarted.

BERTRAND RUSSELL: *Marriage and Morals*, XXI, 1929

[*See also* Animal, Bird, Brain, Conscience, Living, Man, Reason.

Institution

An institution is the lengthened shadow of one man; as, the Reformation, of Luther; Quakerism, of Fox; Methodism, of Wesley, Abolition, of Clarkson.

R. W. EMERSON: *Self-Reliance*, 1841

I love mankind, but I hate the institutions of the dead unkind.

H. D. THOREAU: *A Week on the Concord and Merrimack Rivers*, 1849

As a snow-drift is formed where there is a lull in the wind, so, one would say, where there is a lull of truth an institution springs up. But the truth blows right on over it, nevertheless, and at length blows it down.

H. D. THOREAU: *Cape Cod*, 1865

Individuals may form communities, but it is institutions alone that can create a nation.

BENJAMIN DISRAELI: Speech at Manchester, 1866

[*See also* Creed, Nation, Opinion, Progress, State.

Insult

If you utter insults you will also hear them.

PLAUTUS: *Pseudolus*, IV, *c.* 190 B.C.

Thou hast added insult to injury.

PHAEDRUS: *Fabulae Aesopiae*, V, *c.* 40

An insult is either sustained or destroyed, not by the disposition of those who insult, but by the disposition of those who bear it.

ST. JOHN CHRYSOSTOM: *Homilies*, II, *c.* 388

He who permits himself to be insulted deserves the insult.

PIERRE CORNEILLE: *Héraclius*, I, 1647

The art of returning insult for insult belongs to street-porters.

FREDERICK THE GREAT: *Letter to Voltaire*, Dec. 25, 1738

Fate never wounds more deep the gen'rous heart
Than when a blockhead's insult points the dart.

SAMUEL JOHNSON: *London*, 1738

An injury is much sooner forgotten than an insult.

LORD CHESTERFIELD: *Letter to his son*, Oct. 9, 1746

No holiness requires us to submit to insult.

J. W. GOETHE: *Torquato Tasso*, III, 1790

One insult pocketed soon produces another.

THOMAS JEFFERSON: *Letter to George Washington*, 1790

Injuries accompanied with insults are never forgiven; all men on these occasions are good haters, and lay out their revenge at compound interest; they never threaten until they can strike, and smile when they cannot.

C. C. COLTON: *Lacon*, 1820

If he is insulted, he can be insulted; all his affair is not to insult.

R. W. EMERSON: *The Conduct of Life*, VI, 1860

Do not insult the mother alligator until after you have crossed the river.

HAITIAN PROVERB

[*See also* Affront, Contempt, Cousin, Irony.

Insurance

Contributors for Insuring Houses, Chambers or Rooms from Loss by Fire by Amicable Contribution Within the Cities of London and Westminster and the Liberties Thereof and the Place Thereunto Adjoining.

Corporate name of the first insurance company, organized in London, Nov. 12, 1696

Insurrection

When the government violates the people's rights, insurrection is, for the people and for each portion of the people, the most sacred of rights and the most indispensable of duties.

THE MARQUIS DE LAFAYETTE: Speech to the French Constituent Assembly, Feb. 20, 1790

Insurrection of thought always precedes insurrection of arms.

WENDELL PHILLIPS: Speech at Brooklyn, Nov. 1, 1859

[*See also* Rebellion, Revolution.

Integrity

The just man walketh in his integrity.

PROVERBS XX, 7, *c.* 350 B.C.

Integrity is praised, and starves.

JUVENAL: *Satires,* I, *c.* 110

Integrity of life is fame's best friend,
Which nobly, beyond death, shall crown the end.

JOHN WEBSTER: *The Duchess of Malfi,* V, *c.* 1614

Integrity without knowledge is weak and useless, and knowledge without integrity is dangerous and dreadful.

SAMUEL JOHNSON: *Rasselas,* XLI, 1759

A little integrity is better than any career.

R. W. EMERSON: *The Conduct of Life,* V, 1860

Intellect

[*See* Character, Intelligence, Mind, Skepticism.

Intelligence

He that is among the reasonable, of all the most reasonable; and among the witty, of all the most witty; and among the eloquent, of all the most eloquent: him, think I, among all men, not only to be taken for a singular man, but rather to be counted for half a god.

THOMAS WILSON: *The Arte of Rhetorique,* 1553

The more mind we have, the more original men do we discover there are. Common people find no difference between men.

BLAISE PASCAL: *Pensées,* IX, 1670

The amount of intelligence necessary to please us is a most accurate measure of the amount of intelligence we have ourselves.

C. A. HELVÉTIUS: *De l'esprit,* 1758

Honest, unaffected distrust of the powers of man is the surest sign of intelligence.

G. C. LICHTENBERG: *Reflections,* 1799

Nothing is finer for the purpose of great productions than a very gradual ripening of the intellectual powers.

JOHN KEATS: *Letter to his brothers,* Jan. 23, 1818

The intelligent have a right over the ignorant; namely, the right of instructing them.

R. W. EMERSON: *Representative Men,* II, 1850

Great intellectual gifts mean an activity preeminently nervous in its character, and consequently a very high degree of susceptibility to pain in every form.

ARTHUR SCHOPENHAUER: *Personality,* 1851

We think of Euclid as of fine ice; we admire Newton as we admire the Peak of Teneriffe. Even the intensest labors, the most remote triumphs of the abstract intellect, seem to carry us into a region different from our own — to be in a *terra incognita* of pure reasoning, to cast a chill on human glory.

WALTER BAGEHOT: *Literary Studies,* II, 1879

In order to acquire intellect one must need it. One loses it when it is no longer necessary.

F. W. NIETZSCHE: *The Twilight of the Idols,* 1889

The best human intelligence is still decidedly barbarous; it fights in heavy armor and keeps a fool at court.

GEORGE SANTAYANA: *The Life of Reason,* I, 1905

The moral obligation to be intelligent.

JOHN ERSKINE: Title of a book, 1915

[*See also* Books, Brain, Character, Freedom, Habit, Instinct, Man and Woman, Mind, Modesty, Suicide, Thinking, Unsociability.

Intemperance

Choler and grips are with an intemperate man.

ECCLESIASTICUS XXXI, 23, *c.* 180 B.C.

There is no so just and lawful pleasure wherein intemperance and excess is not to be condemned.

MICHEL DE MONTAIGNE: *Essays,* I, 1580

Every inordinate cup is unblessed and the ingredient is a devil.

SHAKESPEARE: *Othello,* II, 1604

Of all calamities this is the greatest.

THOMAS JEFFERSON: *Letter to Mary Jefferson Eppes,* 1798

[*See also* Drunkenness, Gluttony.

Intention

The intention makes the crime.

ARISTOTLE: *Rhetoric,* I, *c.* 322 B.C.

To mean well is nothing without to do well.

PLAUTUS: *Trinummus,* II, *c.* 190 B.C.

In honorable dealing we must consider what we intended, not what we said.
CICERO: *De officiis,* I, 78 B.C.

A benefit consists not in that which is done or given, but in the intention of the giver or doer. SENECA: *De beneficiis,* I, *c.* 63

Stain not fair acts with foul intentions.
THOMAS BROWNE: *Christian Morals,* I, *c.* 1680

There's nothing we read of in torture's inventions
Like a well-meaning dunce with the best of intentions.
J. R. LOWELL: *A Fable for Critics,* 1848

All men mean well.
GEORGE BERNARD SHAW: *Maxims for Revolutionists,* 1903

Every act must be judged by the doer's intention. (Omne actum ab agentis intentione judicandum.) LEGAL MAXIM

Outward acts show the inward intent. (Acta exteriora indicant interiora secreta.) IBID.

The intention is punished, although the consequence do not follow. (Affectus punitur licet non sequatur effectus.) IBID.

[*See also* Hell.

Intercourse

Every animal is sad after intercourse. (Omne animale post coitu triste.)
LATIN PROVERB

Interdependence

Interdependence absolute, foreseen, ordained, decreed.
RUDYARD KIPLING: *M'Andrew's Hymn,* 1893

Interest

No law can reduce the common rate of interest below the lowest ordinary market rate at the time when that law is made.
ADAM SMITH: *The Wealth of Nations,* II, 1776

Every half-year's interest costs half a year of life.
HORACE WALPOLE: *Letter to the Countess of Upper Ossory,* Nov. 10, 1793

Interest springs from the power of increase which the reproductive forces of nature give to capital. It is not an arbitrary, but a natural thing; it is not the result of a particular social organization, but of laws of the universe which underlie society. It is, therefore, just.
HENRY GEORGE: *Progress and Poverty,* III, 1879

[*See also* Investment, Usury.

Internationalism

To deem of ev'ry country as the same
Is rank rebellion 'gainst the lawful claim
Of nature, and such dull indifference
May be philosophy, but can't be sense.
CHARLES CHURCHILL: *The Farewell,* 1764

I believe that our Great Maker is preparing the world, in His own good time, to become one nation, speaking one language.
GROVER CLEVELAND: Inaugural address, March 4, 1893

The man who loves other countries as much as his own stands on a level with the man who loves other women as much as he loves his own wife.
THEODORE ROOSEVELT: Speech in New York, Sept. 6, 1918

Internationalism is a luxury which only the upper classes can afford; the common people are hopelessly bound to their native shores.
BENITO MUSSOLINI: Speech in the Italian Chamber, June 21, 1921

Interpreter

Egad, I think the interpreter is the hardest to be understood of the two.
R. B. SHERIDAN: *The Critic,* I, 1779

[*See also* Translation, Translator.

Interruption

For sleep, health and wealth to be truly enjoyed, they must be interrupted.
JEAN PAUL RICHTER: *Flower, Fruit, and Thorn Pieces,* VIII, 1796

[*See also* Life.

Intimacy

They're as thick as three in a bed.
SCOTTISH SAYING

Intolerance

For he was of that stubborn crew
Of errant saints whom all men grant
To be the true Church Militant;
Such as do build their faith upon
The holy text of pike and gun;
Decide all controversies by
Infallible artillery;
And prove their doctrine orthodox
By apostolic blows and knocks.
SAMUEL BUTLER: *Hudibras,* I, 1663

Undoubtedly a certain amount of truth, and hence a certain utility, lies at the bottom of religious intolerance. Our philosophers talk of it as if it could be reasoned away, but that it assuredly cannot be.
G. C. LICHTENBERG: *Reflections,* 1799

I have seen gross intolerance shown in support of toleration.
S. T. COLERIDGE: *Biographia Literaria,* 1817

So long as there are earnest believers in the world, they will always wish to punish opin-

ions, even if their judgment tells them it is unwise, and their conscience that it is wrong.
WALTER BAGEHOT: *Literary Studies*, II, 1879

[*See also* Bigotry, Coercion, Toleration.

Intrusion

I hope I don't intrude.
JOHN POOLE: *Paul Pry*, 1825 (The sentence is a tag in the play)

Come not to council unbidden.
SCOTTISH PROVERB

Intuition

Intuition and demonstration are the degrees of our knowledge; whatever comes short of one of these, with what assurance soever embraced, is but faith, or opinion, but not knowledge, at least in all general truths.
JOHN LOCKE: *Essay Concerning Human Understanding*, IV, 1690

[*See also* Faith.

Invalid

A sick man wishes to be where he is not.
SAMUEL JOHNSON: *Letter to William Windham*, Oct. 2, 1784

He lies pitying himself, hoping and moaning to himself; he yearneth over himself; his bowels are even melted within him, to think what he suffers; he is not ashamed to weep over himself.
CHARLES LAMB: *The Convalescent*, 1825 (London Magazine, July)

The modern sympathy with invalids is morbid. Illness of any kind is hardly a thing to be encouraged in others.
OSCAR WILDE: *The Importance of Being Earnest*, II, 1895

[*See also* Illness, Patient, Sickness.

Invasion

All the armies of Europe, Asia and Africa combined, with all the treasure of the earth (our own excepted) in their military chest, with a Bonaparte for a commander, could not by force take a drink from the Ohio or make a track on the Blue Ridge in a trial of a thousand years.
ABRAHAM LINCOLN: Speech at Springfield, Ill., Jan. 27, 1837

Invective

Thou flea! thou nit, thou Winter-cricket thou!
SHAKESPEARE: *The Taming of the Shrew*, IV, 1594

She speaks poniards, and every word stabs: if her breath were as terrible as her terminations, there were no living near her; she would infect to the north star.
SHAKESPEARE: *Much Ado About Nothing*, II, *c.* 1599

Thou art an ape of an ape.
JOHN FORD: *The Lover's Melancholy*, I, 1628

A round pox confound you!
This is court rhetoric at the back stairs.
JAMES SHIRLEY: *The Cardinal*, V, 1641

Sir, your wife, under pretense of keeping a bawdy-house, is a receiver of stolen goods.
SAMUEL JOHNSON: To a Thames waterman, reported by Bennet Langton to James Boswell, 1780

Oh, you arch-ass — you double-barreled ass!
LUDWIG VAN BEETHOVEN: Written in the margin of a copy of *Cäcelia*, beside an article by Gottfried Weber attacking MOZART'S *Requiem*, 1825

God damn your god damned old hellfired god damned soul to hell god damn you and goddam your god damned family's god damned hellfired god damned soul to hell and good damnation god damn them and god damn your god damn friends to hell.
Letter to Abraham Lincoln, dated Fillmore, La., Nov. 25, 1860, and signed PETE MUGGINS

Invention

They have sought out many inventions.
ECCLESIASTES VII, 29, *c.* 200 B.C.

The inventions dictated by necessity are older than those suggested by pleasure.
CICERO: *De oratore*, *c.* 80 B.C.

Nothing is invented and perfected at the same time.
JOHN RAY: *English Proverbs*, 1670

The greatest inventions were produced in the times of ignorance, as the use of the compass, gunpowder, and printing; and by the dullest nations, as the Germans.
JONATHAN SWIFT: *Thoughts on Various Subjects*, 1706

Want is the mistress of invention.
SUSANNAH CENTLIVRE: *The Busybody*, I, 1709

All our inventions have endowed material forces with intellectual life, and degraded human life into a material force.
KARL MARX: Speech in London, April 14, 1856

Invention breeds invention.
R. W. EMERSON: *Society and Solitude*, 1870

If the works of the great poets teach anything, it is to hold mere invention somewhat cheap. It is not the finding of a thing, but the making something out of it after it is found, that is of consequence.
J. R. LOWELL: *My Study Windows*, 1871

The first book tyrannizes over the second. Read Tasso, and you think of Virgil; read Virgil, and you think of Homer; and Milton forces you to reflect how narrow are the limits of human invention. " Paradise Lost " had never existed but for these precursors.
R. W. EMERSON: *Quotation and Originality*, 1876

Invention consists in avoiding the constructing of useless combinations and in constructing the useful combinations which are in infinite minority. To invent is to discern, to choose.
HENRI POINCARÉ (1854–1912)

[*See also* America, Machine, Necessity, Progress.

Inventor

He had been eight years upon a project for extracting sunbeams out of cucumbers, which were to be put in phials hermetically sealed, and let out to warm the air in raw, inclement Summers.
JONATHAN SWIFT: *Gulliver's Travels*, III, 1726

Investment

In investing money the amount of interest you want should depend on whether you want to eat well or sleep well.
J. KENFIELD MORLEY: *Some Things I Believe*, 1937

Let every man divide his money into three parts, and invest a third in land, a third in business, and a third let him keep by him in reserve. HEBREW PROVERB

[*See also* Capitalism.

Invitation

" Come, will ye dine with me this holy day? "
I yielded — though he hoped I would say nay.
JOSEPH HALL (BISHOP OF NORWICH): *Virgidemarium*, III, 1597

[*See also* Thanks.

Ireland

The diseases of Ireland are many, and the sickness is grown to that contagion that it is almost past cure.
BARNABE RICH: *The Anothomy of Ireland*, 1615

He that will England win
Must with Ireland first begin.
FYNES MORYSON: *Itinerary*, 1617

Her own sons native, worse than strangers born,
They have their mother's entrails rent and torn.
JOHN TAYLOR: *Mad Fashions*, 1642

The Emerald Isle.
Anon.: *Erin*, *c.* 1795 (The phrase reappeared in JAMES and HORACE SMITH: *Rejected Addresses*, 1812, and soon gained common currency)

England's danger is Ireland's opportunity.
ENGLISH PROVERB, not recorded before the XIX century

I am quite sure that no dangers are to be feared by England from the disannexing and independence of Ireland at all comparable with the evils which have been, and will yet be, caused to England by the union.
S. T. COLERIDGE: *Table-Talk*, Dec. 17, 1831

Ireland is in a state of social decomposition.
BENJAMIN DISRAELI: Speech in the House of Commons, July 2, 1849

Far hence amid an isle of wondrous beauty,
Crouching over a grave an ancient sorrowful mother,
Once a queen, now lean and tatter'd seated on the ground,
Her old white hair drooping dishevel'd round her shoulders.
WALT WHITMAN: *Old Ireland*, 1861

Ulster for a soldier,
Connaught for a thief,
Munster for learning,
And Leinster for beef.
GEORGE BORROW: *Wild Wales*, *c.* 1862 (Cited as " the old song ")

We declare our sympathy with the efforts of those noble patriots who, led by Gladstone and Parnell, have conducted their grand and peaceful contest for home rule in Ireland.
Democratic National Platform, 1888

We earnestly hope that we may soon congratulate our fellow citizens of Irish birth upon the peaceful recovery of home rule for Ireland.
Republican National Platform, 1888

Ireland is a fatal disease — fatal to Englishmen and doubly fatal to Irishmen.
GEORGE MOORE: *Confessions of a Young Man*, XI, 1888

Ireland is a country in which the probable never happens and the impossible always does.
Ascribed to J. P. MAHAFFY (1839–1919)

Resolved, That the Senate of the United States express its sympathy with the aspirations of the Irish people for a government of their own choice.
Resolution of the Senate, May 29, 1919

[*See also* Christianity, England, Scotland.

Irish

This savage manner of incivility amongst the Irish is bred in the bone; they have it by nature, and so I think of their inhuman cruelty, that are so apt to run into rebellion, and so ready to attempt any other kind of mischief.
BARNABE RICH: *The Anothomy of Ireland*, 1615

A servile race in folly nursed,
Who truckle most when treated worst.
JONATHAN SWIFT: *On the Death of Dr. Swift*, 1731

The Irish mix better with the English than the Scotch do; their language is nearer to English.
SAMUEL JOHNSON: *Boswell's Life*, May 1, 1773

The Irish are a fair people; they never speak well of one another.
SAMUEL JOHNSON: *Boswell's Life*, Feb., 1775

The Irish from different parts of that kingdom are very different. One would think on so small an island an Irishman must be an Irishman: yet it is not so: they are different in their aptitude to, and in their love of labor.
ST. JOHN DE CRÈVECOEUR: *Letters from an American Farmer*, III, 1782

Irish assurance: a bold, forward behavior. It is said that a dipping in the river Shannon totally annihilates bashfulness.
FRANCIS GROSE: *A Classical Dictionary of the Vulgar Tongue*, 1785

The Irish have the best hearts in the three kingdoms.
HORACE WALPOLE: *Letter to Hannah More*, June 15, 1787

Had you English not persecuted the Catholics in Ireland, in all probability the greatest number of them would before now have become Protestants.
NAPOLEON I: To Barry E. O'Meara at St. Helena, Sept. 8, 1817

The Irish are irascible, prone to debt, and to fight, and very impatient of the restraints of law.
SYDNEY SMITH: In the Edinburgh Review, 1820

How often have the Irish started to try to achieve something, but every time they have been crushed, politically and industrially. By consistent oppression they have been artificially converted into an utterly demoralized nation, and now fulfill the notorious function of supplying England, America, Australia, etc., with prostitutes, casual laborers, pimps, thieves, swindlers, beggars and other rabble.
FRIEDRICH ENGELS: *Letter to Karl Marx*, 1856

The dirty, dirty Dutch,
They don't amount to much,
But they're a damned sight better than the Irish.
AMERICAN FOLK RHYME, *c.* 1875 (*Dutch*=German)

The Irish are an imaginative race, and it is said that imagination is too often accompanied by somewhat irregular logic.
BENJAMIN DISRAELI: Speech at the Guildhall, London, Nov. 9, 1879

The ambition of the Irish is to say a thing as everybody says it, only louder.
GERARD MANLEY HOPKINS: *Letter to Robert Bridges*, March, 1888

What a pack of liars! That is at the bottom of the whole Irish question. The Irish cannot tell the truth.
T. H. HUXLEY: To Frank Harris, *c.* 1892

A fighting race who never won a battle, a race of politicians who cannot govern themselves, a race of writers without a great one of native strain, an island race who have yet to man a fleet for war, for commerce or for the fishing banks and to learn how to build ships, a pious race excelling in blasphemy, who feel most wronged by those they have first injured, who sing of love and practise fratricide, preach freedom and enact suppression, a race of democrats who sweat the poor, have a harp for an emblem and no musicians, rebelled on foreign gold and cringed without it, whose earlier history is myth and murder, whose later, murder, whose tongue is silver and whose heart is black, a race skilled in idleness, talented in hate, inventive only in slander, whose land is a breeding-ground of modern reaction and the cradle of Western crime.
TOM PENHALIGON: *The Impossible Irish*, dedication, 1935

Hit him again: he's Irish. MANX PROVERB

More Irish than the Irish. (Hibernicis ipsis Hibernior.) MEDIEVAL LATIN PHRASE

[*See also* Ballad, Character (National), German, Immigrant, Irishman, Pilgrim, Scandinavian, Wheelbarrow.

Irishman

Will any but an Irishman hang a wooden kettle over the fire?
THOMAS FULLER: *Gnomologia*, 1732

An Irishman's obligation is all on one side.
ENGLISH SAYING, not recorded before the XIX century

Every Irishman has a potato in his head.
J. C. and A. W. HARE: *Guesses at Truth*, 1827

Give an Irishman lager for a month, and he's a dead man. An Irishman is lined with copper, and the beer corrodes it. But whiskey polishes the copper and is the saving of him.
S. L. CLEMENS (MARK TWAIN): *Life on the Mississippi*, XXIII, 1883

My one claim to originality among Irishmen is that I have never made a speech.
GEORGE MOORE: *Confessions of a Young Man*, IV, 1888

Put an Irishman on the spit and you can always get another Irishman to turn him.
GEORGE BERNARD SHAW: *John Bull's Other Island*, pref., 1907 (Cited as a proverb)

An Irishman, before answering a question, always asks another.
P. W. JOYCE: *English As We Speak It In Ireland*, 1910

Take away an Irishman's religion, and you make a devil of him. Author unidentified

An Irishman is never at peace except when he's fighting. IRISH PROVERB

Every time a donkey brays an Irishman dies.
IBID.

[*See also* Character (National), Ireland, Lawyer, Soldier.

Iron

The iron did swim. II KINGS VI, 6, *c.* 500 B.C.

The iron entered into his soul. (Ferrum pertransiit animam ejus.)
PSALMS CV, 18, *c.* 150 B.C. (A faulty translation in the Vulgate. In the Authorized Version it is, correctly, "he was laid in iron," i.e., manacled)

Strike while the iron is hot.
THE GREEK ANTHOLOGY, *c.* 80 B.C.

He shall rule them with a rod of iron.
REVELATION II, 27, *c.* 95 (Cf. XII, 5; XIX, 15)

He had too many irons in the fire.
ENGLISH PHRASE, traced by Smith to 1549

Ay me! what perils do environ
The man that meddles with cold iron!
SAMUEL BUTLER: *Hudibras,* I, 1663

[*See also* Gold, Hot, Opportunity.

Irony

Nothing is so insulting as to add irony to injury.
NAPOLEON I: To Barry E. O'Meara at St. Helena, Dec. 6, 1816

An ironic man, with his sly stillness, and ambuscading ways, may be viewed as a pest to society.
THOMAS CARLYLE: *Sartor Resartus,* II, 1836

Irony is an insult conveyed in the form of a compliment.
E. P. WHIPPLE: *Literature and Life,* 1849

Life's little ironies.
THOMAS HARDY: Title of a book, 1894

[*See also* Absolute.

Irrelevance

One of the principal features of my entertainment is that it contains so many things that don't have anything to do with it.
C. F. BROWNE (ARTEMUS WARD): *Lecture on the Mormons,* 1863

Irremediable

What's gone and what's past help
Should be past grief.
SHAKESPEARE: *The Winter's Tale,* III, *c.* 1611

What's past help is beyond prevention.
PHILIP MASSINGER: *The Unnatural Combat,* II, 1639

It's no use crying over spilt milk.
ENGLISH PROVERB, traced by Smith to 1659

Irresolution

How happy could I be with either
Were t'other dear charmer away!
JOHN GAY: *The Beggar's Opera,* II, 1728

Irving, Henry (1838–1905)

[*See* Leg.

Irving, Washington (1783–1859)

I do not go to bed two nights out of the seven without taking Washington Irving under my arm.
CHARLES DICKENS: Speech in New York, Feb. 18, 1842

Island

[*See* Relatives-in-law.

Isolation

Isolation is the sum-total of wretchedness to man. To be cut off, to be left solitary: to have world alien, not your world; all a hostile camp for you; not a home at all, of hearts and faces who are yours, whose you are! It is the frightfulest enchantment; too truly a work of the Evil One.
THOMAS CARLYLE: *Past and Present,* IV, 1843

In these troublous days the great Mother Empire stands splendidly isolated in Europe.
G. E. FOSTER: Speech in the Canadian House of Commons, Jan. 16, 1896

[*See also* Independence, Solitude.

Israel

[*See* Jew.

Italian

God placed popedom in Italy not without cause, for the Italians can make out many things to be real and true which in truth are not so: they have crafty and subtle brains.
MARTIN LUTHER: *Table-Talk,* CCCCLIX, 1569

The Italians are all thieves. (Gli Italiani tutti ladroni.)
Ascribed to NAPOLEON I, *c.* 1800 (To it a woman is reputed to have replied with the pun, "Non tutti, ma buona parte" — Not all, but a good part)

A race corrupted by a bad government and a bad religion, long renowned for skill in the arts of voluptuousness, and tolerant of all the caprices of sensuality.
T. B. MACAULAY: *Moore's Life of Lord Byron,* 1831 (Edinburgh Review, June)

The Italians have voices like peacocks.
E. R. BULWER-LYTTON (OWEN MEREDITH): *Lucile,* I, 1860

The Italians are fond of red clothes, peacock plumes, and embroidery; and I remember one rainy morning in the city of Palermo, the street was in a blaze with scarlet umbrellas.
R. W. EMERSON: *The Conduct of Life*, IV, 1860

The Italians have not sense or patience enough to taste a ripe peach. . . . They are sunk beneath all sympathy and have become detestable — down to the very children.
JOHN RUSKIN: *Letter to Jean Ingelow*, July 19, 1869

[*See also* Austrian, Character (National), German, Hand, Italy.

Italianized

An Englishman Italiante is a devil incarnate.
ENGLISH PROVERB, traced by Apperson to OVERTON: *Jacob's Troublesome Journey*, 1586

Italian Language

It is a general opinion among those who know little or nothing of the subject that this admirable language is adapted only to the effeminate cant of sonneteers, musicians and connoisseurs.
T. B. MACAULAY: *Dante*, 1824 (Knight's Quarterly Magazine, Jan.)

Italian is the sweetest and softest language.
S. T. COLERIDGE: *Miscellaneous*, 1811

That soft bastard Latin,
Which melts like kisses from a female mouth.
BYRON: *Beppo*, 1818

The Tuscan's siren tongue —
That music in itself, whose sounds are song,
The poetry of speech.
BYRON: *Childe Harold*, IV, 1818

[*See also* Language.

Italics

Never italicize.
R. W. EMERSON: *The Superlative*, 1847

Italy

Beyond the Alps lies Italy.
ENGLISH SAYING, apparently borrowed from LIVY: *History of Rome*, XXI, *c.* 10

Ah, servile Italy, thou inn of grief, ship without pilot in a mighty storm, no longer queen of provinces, but a brothel.
DANTE: *Purgatorio*, VI, *c.* 1320

Suffer not thy sons to pass the Alps, for they shall learn nothing there but pride, blasphemy, and atheism.
WILLIAM CECIL (LORD BURLEIGH): *Advice to His Son*, *c.* 1555

Italy is a paradise for horses, a hell for women.
ROBERT BURTON: *The Anatomy of Melancholy*, III, 1621 (Quoted as a proverb)

Wheresoe'er I turn my ravished eyes
Gay gilded scenes and shining prospects rise.
Poetic fields encompass me around,
And still I seem to tread on classic ground.
JOSEPH ADDISON: *Letter from Italy*, 1701

A man who has not been to Italy is always conscious of his inferiority.
SAMUEL JOHNSON: *Boswell's Life*, April 11, 1776

Know'st thou the land where the lemon-trees bloom,
And the golden orange glows in the thicket's dark gloom?
(Kennst du das Land wo die Citronen blühn,
Im dunkeln Laub die Gold-Orangen glühn?)
J. W. GOETHE: *Wilhelm Meisters Lehrjahre*, III, 1795

Know ye the land where the cypress and myrtle
All emblems of deeds that are done in their clime;
Where the rage of the vulture, the love of the turtle,
Now melt into sorrow, now madden to crime?
BYRON: *The Bride of Abydos*, I, 1813

Italy is only a geographical expression.
CLEMENS VON METTERNICH: Memorandum for the chancelleries of Europe, Aug. 2, 1814

Italia! Oh Italia! thou who has
The fatal gift of beauty.
BYRON: *Childe Harold*, IV, 1818

We go to see Italy, not the Italians.
C. C. COLTON: *Lacon*, 1820

The seed of blood and misery has been sown in Italy, and a more vigorous race is arising to go forth to the harvest.
P. B. SHELLEY: *Hellas*, pref., 1821

We came to Italy. I felt
A yearning for its sunny sky;
My very spirit seem'd to melt
As swept its first warm breezes by.
From lip and cheek a chilling mist,
From life and soul a frozen rime,
By every breath seem'd softly kiss'd —
God's blessing on its radiant clime.
N. P. WILLIS: *Melanie*, II, 1835

You may have the universe if I may have Italy.
GIUSEPPI VERDI: *Attila*, I, 1846

Italy, my Italy!
Queen Mary's saying serves for me —
(When fortune's malice
Lost her Calais) —
Open my heart and you will see
Graved inside of it, " Italy."
ROBERT BROWNING: *De Gustibus*, 1855

Midnight, and love, and youth, and Italy!
E. R. BULWER-LYTTON: *The Wanderer*, prologue, 1857

The Creator made Italy from designs by Michael Angelo.
S. L. CLEMENS (MARK TWAIN): *Innocents Abroad,* III, 1869

It is to the Roman popes that Italy owes her glory and majesty.
POPE LEO XIII: *Inscrutabili,* April 21, 1878

Italy to be born in, France to live in, and Spain to die in. SPANISH PROVERB

[*See also* Ballad, Christianity, Genoa, Papacy, Patriotism, Poland, Rome, Travel.

Itch

[*See* Love, Palm.

Ivy

The creeping, dirty, courtly ivy.
ALEXANDER POPE: *The Dunciad,* I, 1728

Creeping ivy clings to wood or stone,
And hides the ruin that it feeds upon.
WILLIAM COWPER: *The Progress of Error,* 1782

J

Jack and Jill

Jack and Jill.
Generic name for any youth and girl, traced by Smith to *c.* 1450; in the form of Ienken and Iulyan it is still older

Every Jack has his Jill.
ENGLISH PROVERB, familiar since the XVI century

Jack shall pipe and Jill shall dance.
GEORGE WITHER: *Christmas,* 1622

Jack and Jill went up the hill
To fetch a pail of water;
Jack fell down and broke his crown,
And Jill came tumbling after.
Anon.: *Nursery Rhyme, c.* 1750

Every Jack will find a Jill, gang the world as it may.
WALTER SCOTT: *St. Ronan's Well,* II, 1824

Jack-of-all-trades

Some broken citizen . . . hath well played Jack-of-all-trades.
GEOFFREY MYNSHUL: *Essays and Characters of a Prison and Prisoners,* 1618

Jack of all trades is of no trade.
THOMAS FULLER: *Gnomologia,* 1732 (More usually, " Jack of all trades; master of none ")

A man of many trades begs his bread on Sunday. SCOTCH PROVERB

Jack Robinson

I'd do it as soon as say Jack Robinson.
FRANCES BURNEY: *Evelina,* 1778

Jackson, Andrew (1767–1845)

I feel much alarmed at the prospect of seeing General Jackson President. He is one of the most unfit men I know of for such a place.
THOMAS JEFFERSON: To Daniel Webster, 1824

He is one of our tribe of great men who turn disease to commodity, like John Randolph, who for forty years was always dying. Jackson, ever since he became a mark of public attention, has been doing the same thing. He is so ravenous of notoriety that he craves the sympathy for sickness as a portion of his glory.
JOHN QUINCY ADAMS: *Diary,* June 27, 1833

Where is there a chief magistrate of whom so much evil has been predicted, and from whom so much good has come?
THOMAS H. BENTON: Speech in the Senate, Jan. 12, 1837

He was the most American of Americans — an embodied Declaration of Independence — the Fourth of July incarnate.
JAMES PARTON: *Life of Andrew Jackson,* I, 1859

Andrew Jackson spelled *God* with a small *g,* and Europe *Urope;* but he was a great general, an incorruptible judge, and a capable President. He always believed the earth was flat instead of round, and insisted that the proper pronunciation of *development* was *devil-ope-ment,* but he had great ruling qualities nevertheless.
W. P. BROWNLOW: Speech in the House of Representatives, Jan 11, 1898

Jackson, T. J. (Stonewall) (1824–63)

Look at Jackson — there he stands like a stone wall.
BRIG.-GEN. B. E. BEE: To Capt. Porter King at the Battle of Bull Run, July 21, 1861 (Bee was killed the same day)

Says he, " That's Banks, he's fond of shell,
Lord save his soul! we'll give him —; " well,
That's Stonewall Jackson's way.
J. W. PALMER: *Stonewall Jackson's Way,* 1862 (Written Sept. 17, during the Battle of Antietam)

My opinion of the merits of General Jackson has been greatly enhanced during this expedition. He is true, honest and brave; has a single eye to the good of the service, and spares no exertion to accomplish his object.
R. E. LEE: Report to Jefferson Davis after the first invasion of Maryland, Oct., 1862

If General Lee had Grant's resources he would soon end the war; but Old Jack can do it without resources.
GEORGE E. PICKETT: *Letter to his fiancée,* Oct. 11, 1862

You are better off than I am, for while you have lost your *left,* I have lost my *right* arm.
R. E. LEE: *Letter to Jackson,* May 4, 1863 (Jackson was wounded at Chancellorsville, May 2, his left arm was amputated May 3, and he died May 10)

One year after the war the household goods of the dead hero were allowed to be sold in the town of Lexington under the hammer of the auctioneer.
E. A. POLLARD: *The Virginia Tourist,* I, 1870

Jade

Let the galled jade wince; our withers are unwrung. SHAKESPEARE: *Hamlet,* III, *c.* 1601

Jail

I think a jail a school of virtue is,
A house of study, and of contemplation:
A place of discipline and reformation.
JOHN TAYLOR: *The Virtue of a Jail,* 1630

Taken from the county jail
By a set of curious chances;
Liberated then on bail,
On my own recognizances.
W. S. GILBERT: *The Mikado,* I, 1885

[*See also* Congress, Ship.

Jailer

Old thieves make good jailers.
GERMAN PROVERB

James, G. P. R. (1799–1860)

What wonderful fertility of imagination! What prodigious depth of thought! In this he is far beyond the best novelists, his contemporaries. W. S. LANDOR: *Letter to Robert Browning,* July, 1863)

James, Henry (1843–1916)

His whole book is one long flutter near to the one magical and unique word, but the word is not spoken; and for want of the word his characters are never resolved out of the haze of nebulæ. GEORGE MOORE: *Confessions of a Young Man,* X, 1888

Henry James writes fiction as if it were a painful duty.
OSCAR WILDE: *The Decay of Lying,* 1891

He has created a genre of his own. He has the distinction that makes the scientist a savant; he has contributed something to the sum, the common stock.
W. C. BROWNELL: *American Prose Masters,* 1909

[*See also* Howells, W. D.

January

January brings the snow,
Makes our feet and fingers glow.
SARA COLERIDGE: *Pretty Lessons in Verse,* 1834

Pale January lay
In its cradle day by day,
Dead or living, hard to say.
ALFRED AUSTIN: *Primroses,* 1882

By her who in this month is born,
No gems save garnets should be worn;
They will insure her constancy,
True friendship and fidelity.
Author unidentified

A warm January; a cold May.
WELSH PROVERB

[*See also* Grass, Months.

Japanese

Even the Japanese are becoming Christian and respectable; in another quarter of a century silk hats and pianos will be found in every house in Jeddo.
GEORGE MOORE: *Confessions of a Young Man,* IX, 1888

The probability is that, were a Japanese gentleman a devout adherent of any particular form of religion, he would rather conceal it than make a display of it.
KENCHO SUYEMATSU: *The Religions of Japan,* 1905

[*See also* Metaphysics.

Jaundice

All looks yellow to the jaundiced eye.
ALEXANDER POPE: *An Essay on Criticism,* II, 1711

[*See also* Jealousy.

Jawbone

Samson said, With the jawbone of an ass, heaps upon heaps, with the jawbone of an ass have I slain a thousand men.
JUDGES XV, 16, *c.* 500 B.C.

Jay

What, is the jay more precious than the lark,
Because his feathers are more beautiful?
SHAKESPEARE: *The Taming of the Shrew,* IV, 1594

Remember this, and bear in mind:
A jaybird's tail sticks up behind.
Album verse, c. 1845

Jealousy

The race of men is of a jealous temperament.
HOMER: *Odyssey,* VII, *c.* 800 B.C.

Jealousy is cruel as the grave; the coals thereof are coals of fire.
SOLOMON'S SONG VIII, 6, *c.* 200 B.C.

Though jealousy be produced by love, as ashes are by fire, yet jealousy extinguishes love as ashes smother the flame.
MARGARET OF NAVARRE: *Heptameron,* 1559

He that a white horse and a fair wife keepeth,
For fear, for care, for jealousy scarce sleepeth.
JOHN FLORIO: *Second Frutes,* 1591

Melampus, when will love be void of fears?
When jealousy hath neither eyes nor ears.
GEORGE PEELE: *Song of Coridon and Melampus, c.* 1591

The venom clamors of a jealous woman
Poisons more deadly than a mad dog's tooth.
SHAKESPEARE: *The Comedy of Errors,* V, 1593

I had rather be a toad,
And live upon the vapor of a dungeon,
Than keep a corner in the thing I love
For others' uses.
SHAKESPEARE: *Othello,* III, 1604

The green-eyed monster. IBID.

Trifles light as air
Are to the jealous confirmations strong
As proofs of holy writ. IBID.

Wedlock's yellow sickness.
THOMAS MIDDLETON: *The Phoenix,* II, 1607

Jealousy is always born with love, but does not always die with it.
LA ROCHEFOUCAULD: *Maxims,* 1665

Jealousy is in some ways just and reasonable, for its object is only to preserve a good that belongs to us, or that we think belongs to us.
IBID.

Jealousy is the greatest of all evils, and the least pitied by those who cause it. IBID.

Jealousy lives upon doubt, and comes to an end or becomes a fury as soon as it passes from doubt to certainty. IBID.

No persons escape causing jealousy who are worthy of exciting it. IBID.

There is more self-love than love in jealousy.
IBID.

Hunger, revenge, to sleep are petty foes,
But only death the jealous eyes can close.
WILLIAM WYCHERLEY: *Love in a Wood,* I, 1673

The jaundice of the soul.
JOHN DRYDEN: *The Hind and the Panther,* III, 1687

Jealousy's a thing unknown among people of quality.
JOHN VANBRUGH: *The Confederacy,* 1705

Jealousy shuts one door and opens two.
SAMUEL PALMER: *Moral Essays on Proverbs,* 1710

The great unhappiness of this passion is that it naturally tends to alienate the affection which it is so solicitous to engross: and that for these two reasons: because it lays too great a constraint on the words and actions of the suspect person; and, at the same time, shows you have no honorable opinion of her; both of which are strong motives to aversion.
JOSEPH ADDISON: *The Spectator,* Sept. 14, 1711

It is jealousy's peculiar nature,
To swell small things to great, nay, out of nought,
To conjure much; and then to lose its reason
Amid the hideous phantoms it has form'd.
EDWARD YOUNG: *The Revenge,* III, 1721

No man is greatly jealous who is not in some measure guilty.
BENJAMIN WHICHCOTE: *Moral and Religious Aphorisms,* 1753

A jealous love lights his torch from the firebrands of the furies.
EDMUND BURKE: Speech in the House of Commons, Feb. 11, 1780

Jealousy is the great exaggerator.
J. C. F. SCHILLER: *The Fiesco,* I, 1784

Doubts and jealousies often beget the facts they fear. THOMAS JEFFERSON: *Letter to Albert Gallatin,* 1806

Love may exist without jealousy, although this is rare; but jealousy may exist without love, and this is common: for jealousy can feed on that which is bitter, no less than on that which is sweet, and is sustained by pride, as often as by affection.
C. C. COLTON: *Lacon,* 1820

Jealousy is said to be the offspring of love. Yet, unless the parent makes haste to strangle the child, the child will not rest till it has poisoned the parent.
J. C. and A.W. HARE: *Guesses at Truth,* 1827

A lewd bachelor makes a jealous husband.
H. G. BOHN: *Handbook of Proverbs,* 1855

The woman's natural jealousy is not at a man's loving another, but at his forsaking her.
JAMES HINTON: *Life in Nature,* 1862

The jealousy of the harlot is shown by adultery; that of the virtuous woman by tears.
ARAB PROVERB

Jealousy does more harm than witchcraft.
GERMAN PROVERB

A woman's jealousy sets the whole house on fire. (Incendit omnem feminæ zelus domum.) LATIN PROVERB

Jealousy and love are sisters.
RUSSIAN PROVERB

Jealousy knows no loyalty. SPANISH PROVERB

[*See also* Artist, Bachelor, Despotism, Friend.

Jeffersonian

We have exchanged the Washingtonian dignity for the Jeffersonian simplicity, which was in truth only another name for the Jeffersonian vulgarity.

H. C. POTTER (BISHOP OF NEW YORK): Speech in New York, April 30, 1889

Jefferson, Thomas (1743–1826)

A man of profound ambition and violent passions.

ALEXANDER HAMILTON: *Letter to Edward Carrington*, 1792

He is in his person tall, meager, emaciated; his muscles relaxed, and his joints so loosely connected as not only to disqualify him, apparently, for any vigorous exertion of body, but to destroy everything like elegance and harmony in his air and movement.

WILLIAM WIRT: *The Letters of the British Spy*, 1803

The name of Jefferson will be hailed with gratitude, his memory honored and cherished as the second founder of the liberties of the people.

HENRY CLAY: Speech in the House of Representatives, Jan. 8, 1813

Here was buried Thomas Jefferson, author of the Declaration of American Independence, of the statute of Virginia for religious freedom, and father of the University of Virginia.

Epitaph of Jefferson at Charlottesville, Va., written by himself, *c.* 1825

If not an absolute atheist, he had no belief in a future existence. All his ideas of obligation or retribution were bounded by the present life. His duties to his neighbor were under no stronger guarantee than the laws of the land and the opinions of the world. The tendency of this condition upon a mind of great compass and powerful resources is to produce insincerity and duplicity, which were his besetting sins through life.

JOHN QUINCY ADAMS: *Diary*, Jan. 11, 1831

The moral character of Jefferson was repulsive. Continually puling about liberty, equality, and the degrading curse of slavery, he brought his own children to the hammer, and made money of his debaucheries.

THOMAS HAMILTON: *Men and Manners in America*, IX, 1833

I incline to the opinion that he was not altogether conscious of his own insincerity, and deceived himself as well as others. His success through a long life, and especially from his entrance upon the office of Secretary of State under Washington until he reached the Presidential chair, seems, to my imperfect vision, a slur upon the moral government of the world.

JOHN QUINCY ADAMS: *Diary*, July 29, 1836

I cannot reckon Jefferson among the benefactors of mankind.

T. B. MACAULAY: *Letter to H. S. Randal of New York*, May 25, 1857

The principles of Jefferson are the definitions and axioms of free society.

ABRAHAM LINCOLN: *Letter to H. L. Pierce*, April 6, 1859

The immortality of Jefferson does not lie in any one of his achievements, but in his attitude toward mankind.

WOODROW WILSON: Speech at Washington, April 13, 1916

[*See also* Ambition, Dignity.

Jehovah

[*See* God, Gods.

Jeopardy

Nor shall any person be subject for the same offense to be twice put in jeopardy of life or limb.

CONSTITUTION OF THE UNITED STATES, Amendment V, Dec. 15, 1791

Jerome, St. (c. 340–420)

Jerome should not be numbered among the teachers of the Church, for he was a heretic; yet I believe that he is saved through faith in Christ.

MARTIN LUTHER: *Table-Talk*, DXXXIX, 1569

Jerusalem

If I forget thee, O Jerusalem, let my right hand forget her cunning.

PSALMS CXXXVII, 5, *c.* 150 B.C.

O Jerusalem, Jerusalem, thou that killest the prophets, and stonest them which are sent unto thee, how often would I have gathered thy children together, even as a hen gathereth her chickens under her wings, and ye would not! MATTHEW XXIII, 37, *c.* 75

Ten measures of beauty came into the world; Jerusalem received nine measures, and the rest of the world one. HEBREW PROVERB

Jest

Let us never adopt the maxim, Rather lose our friend than our jest.

QUINTILIAN: *De institutione oratoria*, VI, *c.* 90

Many a true word is spoken in jest.

ENGLISH PROVERB, current since Chaucer's time, *c.* 1385

A jest's prosperity lies in the ear
Of him that hears it, never in the tongue
Of him that makes it.

SHAKESPEARE: *Love's Labor's Lost*, V, *c.* 1595

Some things are privileged from jest — namely, religion, matters of state, great persons, all men's present business of importance, and any case that deserves pity.

FRANCIS BACON: *Essays*, II, 1597

Jests and scoffs do lessen majesty and greatness, and should be far from great personages and men of wisdom.
HENRY PEACHAM: *The Compleat Gentleman,* 1622

All things are big with jest.
GEORGE HERBERT: *The Temple,* 1633

Jest not with the eye, or with religion.
GEORGE HERBERT: *Outlandish Proverbs,* 1640

Long jesting was never good. IBID.

Harmless mirth is the best cordial against the consumption of the spirits: wherefore jesting is not unlawful if it trespasseth not in quantity, quality or season.
THOMAS FULLER: *The Holy State and the Profane State,* 1642

Leave jesting while it pleaseth, lest it turn to earnest.
GEORGE HERBERT: *Jacula Prudentum,* 1651

Neither mock nor scoff in any thing of importance, nor be reproachful, nor also break a jest, biting like a dog; but if thou deliverest thy conceit which is ready, and not too much premeditated, and without offence to any body, thou mayst do well.
FRANCIS HAWKINS: *Youth's Behavior,* III, 1663

The cream of the jest.
JOHN EACHARD: *The Grounds and Occasions of the Contempt of the Clergy and Religion,* 1670 (JAMES BRANCH CABELL: Title of a novel, 1917)

The truest jests sound worst in guilty ears.
JOHN RAY: *English Proverbs,* 1670

The wise make jests and fools repeat them.
IBID.

Jesting is often only indigence of intellect.
JEAN DE LA BRUYÈRE: *Caractères,* 1688

Men aim rightest when they shoot in jest.
JOHN DRYDEN: *Discourse Concerning the Original and Progress of Satire,* 1693

I laugh at nobody's jest but my own or a lady's.
WILLIAM CONGREVE: *The Double Dealer,* I, 1694

I love my jest, an the ship were sinking.
WILLIAM CONGREVE: *Love for Love,* III, 1695

He that laughs at his own jest mars all the mirth of it.
JAMES KELLY: *Complete Collection of Scottish Proverbs,* 1721

Too late the forward youth shall find
That jokes are sometimes paid in kind;
Or if they canker in the breast,
He makes a foe who makes a jest.
JOHN GAY: *Fables,* I, 1727

Leave a jest when it pleases you best.
THOMAS FULLER: *Gnomologia,* 1732

Of all the griefs that harass the distress'd,
Sure the most bitter is a scornful jest.
SAMUEL JOHNSON: *London,* 1738

If you give a jest you must take a jest.
JONATHAN SWIFT: *Polite Conversation,* 1738

A jest breaks no bones.
SAMUEL JOHNSON: *Boswell's Life,* 1781

Good jests bite like lambs, not like dogs.
H. G. BOHN: *Handbook of Proverbs,* 1855

Never jest with God, death, or the Devil.
ARAB PROVERB

Many a friend has been lost by a jest, but none has ever been got by one. CZECH PROVERB

[*See also* Humor, Joke, Laughter, Wit.

Jester

Alas, poor Yorick! I knew him, Horatio: a fellow of infinite jest, of most excellent fancy.
SHAKESPEARE: *Hamlet,* V, *c.* 1601

Jesters do oft prove prophets.
SHAKESPEARE: *King Lear,* V, 1606

A jester is an evil character.
BLAISE PASCAL: *Pensées,* VI, 1670

Where you see a jester a fool is not far off.
THOMAS FULLER: *Gnomologia,* 1732

Jesuit

They will talk so divinely, with fancies to feed you,
And rattle out rhetoric your minds to amaze,
With learning and logic they'll seem for to lead you
Even straight into Heaven, so grave is their grace.
WILLIAM ELDERTON: *A Triumph for True Subjects,* 1581

Rome's caterpillars.
Anon.: *The Travels of Time,* 1624

Jesuits, seminary priests, and all others that have taken orders by any authority derived from the see of Rome [shall], before the fourteenth day of June next ensuing, make their repair to some of His Majesty's ports within the realm, and from thence transport themselves out of the same with the first opportunity of wind and weather into some foreign parts beyond the sea, and never after return into this realm.
JAMES I: *Proclamation,* May 6, 1624

They are a society of men, or rather let us call them angels, predicted by Isaiah in these words, "Go, ye swift and ready angels." They have the spirit of eagles; they are a flock of phœnixes; they have changed the face of Christendom.

Anon.: *L'image du premier siècle de la Société de Jésus*, 1640 (The reference is to ISAIAH XVIII, 2; in the Authorized Version: "Go, ye swift messengers." In the Vulgate it is "angeli veloces")

The voluminous Jesuits, those Laplanders of Peripateticism, do but subtly trifle; and their philosophic undertakings are much like his who spent his time in darting cummin seeds through the eye of a needle.

JOSEPH GLANVILL: *The Vanity of Dogmatizing*, XVI, 1661

It began to be rumored up and down among the people that I was a witch, a Jesuit, a highwayman, and the like.

JOHN BUNYAN: *Grace Abounding to the Chief of Sinners*, 1666

No religion that I know of in all the world ever had such lewd and scandalous casuists. Their main business seems to be, not to keep men from sin, but to teach them how near they might lawfully come, without sinning.

JOHN TILLOTSON (ARCHBISHOP OF CANTERBURY): *Sermons*, 1694

Have you made an acquaintance with some eminent Jesuits? I know no people in the world more instructive.

LORD CHESTERFIELD: *Letter to his son*, March 8, 1750

The Jesuits pass for smart politicians, and have succeeded in getting themselves turned out of three countries, just for a beginning. They little deserve their reputation.

VOLTAIRE: *Letter to Mme. du Deffand*, May 18, 1767

The Society of Jesus is the most dangerous of orders, and has done more mischief than all the others.

NAPOLEON I: To Barry E. O'Meara at St. Helena, Nov. 2, 1816

I do not like the reappearance of the Jesuits. If ever there was a body of men who merited damnation on earth and in Hell it is this society of Loyola's. Nevertheless, we are compelled by our system of religious toleration to offer them an asylum.

JOHN ADAMS: *Letter to Thomas Jefferson*, 1816

The Jesuits constantly inculcated a thorough contempt of worldly things in their doctrines, but eagerly grasped at them in their lives.

C. C. COLTON: *Lacon*, 1820

The Society of Jesus is a sword whose handle is in Rome and the point everywhere.

ANDRÉ DUPIN: Speech in the French Chamber of Deputies, 1825

Sow a Jesuit, and you reap a rebel.

JÉRÔME BONAPARTE: Speech in the French Chamber of Deputies, 1877

Not even the clearest and most precise logic makes a man a match for a Jesuit.

ERNST HAECKEL: *Der Kampf um den Entwickelungsgedanken*, 1905

Deaths among Jesuits occur in groups of threes.

JESUIT SAYING

[*See also* Missionary.

Jesus Christ

We preach Christ crucified, unto the Jews a stumblingblock, and unto the Greeks foolishness. I CORINTHIANS I, 23, *c.* 55

As in Adam all die, even so in Christ shall all be made alive. I CORINTHIANS XV, 21

Christ is all, and in all.

COLOSSIANS III, 11, *c.* 60

Jesus . . . was made a little lower than the angels. HEBREWS II, 9, *c.* 65

Jesus Christ the same yesterday, and today, and forever. HEBREWS XIII, 8

Thou hast conquered, Galilean! (Vicisti, Galilæe!)

Ascribed, apocryphally, to JULIAN THE APOSTATE, on his deathbed, 363

Christ is the best husband.

ST. AUGUSTINE: *On Holy Virginity*, *c.* 402

Christ will remain a priest and king, though He was never consecrated by any papist bishop or greased by any of those shavelings; but He was ordained and consecrated by God Himself, and by Him anointed.

MARTIN LUTHER: *Table-Talk*, CXC, 1569

When Jesus Christ utters a word, He opens His mouth so wide that it embraces all Heaven and earth, even though that word be but in a whisper.

MARTIN LUTHER: *Table-Talk*, CCXXX

The best of men
That e'er wore earth about Him was a sufferer,
A soft, meek, patient, humble tranquil spirit,
The first true gentleman that ever breath'd.

THOMAS DEKKER: *I The Honest Whore*, V, 1604

Commander-in-chief of the Celestial Army, King of Zion, Eternal Emperor, Pontifex Maximus of the Christian Church, Archbishop of All Souls, Elector of Truth, Archduke of Glory, Duke of Life, Prince of Peace, Defender of the Gates of Hell, Conqueror of Death, Hereditary Lord of All Nations, Lord of Justice, and Head of the Sacred Council of the Heavenly Father.

H. D.: *Sacred Geography*, 1704 (The book is dedicated to Jesus Christ and two contemporary princes, and these titles appear in the dedication. The identity of the author is unknown)

Jesus shall reign where e'er the sun
Does his successive journeys run;

His kingdom stretch from shore to shore
Till moons shall wax and wane no more.
ISAAC WATTS: *The Psalms of David,* 1719

Jesus, lover of my soul,
Let me to Thy bosom fly,
While the nearer waters roll,
While the tempest still is high.
CHARLES WESLEY: *In Temptation,* 1740

Christ is God clothed with human nature.
BENJAMIN WHICHCOTE: *Moral and Religious Aphorisms,* 1753

As to Jesus of Nazareth, I think His system of morals and His religion, as He left them to us, the best the world ever saw or is like to see; but I apprehend it has received various corrupting changes, and I have, with most of the present dissenters in England, some doubts as to His divinity.
BENJAMIN FRANKLIN: *Letter to President Stiles of Yale,* 1789

His parentage was obscure; His condition poor; His education null; His natural endowments great; His life correct and innocent; He was meek, benevolent, patient, firm, disinterested, and of the sublimest eloquence.
THOMAS JEFFERSON: *An Estimate of the Merit of the Doctrines of Jesus Compared with Those of Others,* 1803

He did not die with Christian ease,
Asking pardon of His enemies.
WILLIAM BLAKE: *The Everlasting Gospel,* *c.* 1810

A parish demagogue.
P. B. SHELLEY: *Queen Mab,* VII, 1813

Stand up, stand up for Jesus.
GEORGE DUFFIELD: Title of hymn, 1818

I do not think Jesus Christ ever existed.
NAPOLEON I: To Gaspard Gourgaud at St. Helena, 1815–1818

Jesus astonishes and overpowers sensual people. They cannot unite Him to history or reconcile Him with themselves.
R. W. EMERSON: *History,* 1841

The Lord from Heaven,
Born of a village girl, carpenter's son,
Wonderful, Prince of Peace, the mighty God.
ALFRED TENNYSON: *Aylmer's Field,* 1864

Thou hast conquered, O pale Galilean!
The world has grown grey from Thy breath.
A. C. SWINBURNE: *Hymn to Proserpine,* 1866 (Cf. JULIAN, *ante,* 363)

In politics He was a leveller or communist; in morals He was a monk; He believed that only the poor and despised would inherit the kingdom of God.
W. WINWOOD READE: *The Martyrdom of Man,* III, 1872

Into the woods my Master went,
Clean forspent, forspent,
Into the woods my Master came,
Forspent with love and shame.
But the olives they were not blind to Him,
The little gray leaves were kind to Him;
The thorn-tree had a mind to Him,
When into the woods He came.
SIDNEY LANIER: *A Ballad of Trees and the Master,* 1877

Jesus died too soon. He would have repudiated His doctrine if He had lived to my age.
F. W. NIETZSCHE: *Thus Spake Zarathustra,* XXI, 1885

He is what we should call an artist and a Bohemian in His manner of life.
GEORGE BERNARD SHAW: *Androcles and the Lion,* pref., 1912

Christ is my hope. (Spes mea Christus.)
LATIN PHRASE

Jesus the Saviour of men. (Jesus hominum Salvator.)
LATIN PHRASE (Usually only the initials, I. H. S., are used)

[*See also* Anathema, Bible, Charity, Christianity, Church (Roman Catholic), Gentleman, Hero, Jew, Liar, Meekness, Paul (St.), Sect, Tears, Transubstantiation, War.

Jew

I will make of thee a great nation, and I will bless thee, and make thy name great.
GENESIS XII, 2, *c.* 700 B.C. (Cf. XLVI, 3; EXODUS XXXII, 10, *c.* 700 B.C.)

The children of Israel were fruitful, and increased abundantly, and multiplied, and waxed exceedingly mighty; and the land was filled with them. EXODUS I, 7, *c.* 700 B.C.

Ye shall be a peculiar treasure unto me above all people. EXODUS XIX, 5

Ye shall be unto me a kingdom of priests, and a holy nation. EXODUS XIX, 6

I have seen this people, and behold, it is a stiffnecked people.
EXODUS XXXII, 9 (Cf. XXXIII, 3, 5, 9; DEUTERONOMY IX, 6, 13, *c.* 650 B.C.)

Thou art an holy people unto the Lord thy God, and the Lord hath chosen thee to be a peculiar people unto himself, above all the nations that are upon the earth.
DEUTERONOMY XIV, 2, *c.* 650 B.C.

Thou shalt become an astonishment, a proverb, and a by-word among all nations whither the Lord shall lead thee.
DEUTERONOMY XXVIII, 37

The Lord shall scatter thee among all people, from the one end of the earth even to the other, and there thou shalt serve other gods, which neither thou nor thy fathers have known, even gods of wood and stone.
DEUTERONOMY XXVIII, 64

I will . . . deliver them to be removed to all the kingdoms of the earth, to be a curse, and an astonishment, and a hissing, and a reproach, among all the nations whither I have driven them.
JEREMIAH XXIX, 18, *c.* 625 B.C.

Israel shall be a proverb and a by-word among all people.
I KINGS IX, 7, *c.* 500 B.C. (Cf. DEUTERONOMY XXVIII, *ante, c.* 650 B.C.

Rezin king of Syria . . . drave the Jews from Elath. II KINGS XVI, 6, *c.* 500 B.C.

Certain Chaldeans came near, and accused the Jews. DANIEL III, 8, *c.* 165 B.C.

Haman sought to destroy all the Jews that were throughout the whole kingdom of Ahasuerus.
ESTHER III, 6, *c.* 125 B.C.

The fear of the Jews fell upon them.
ESTHER VIII, 17

They have penetrated to every country, and it would be hard to find anywhere in the world a place that has not had to endure this race, and in which it did not strive for mastery.
STRABO: *Geography*, XII, *c.* 20 B.C.

The Jews . . . both killed the Lord Jesus, and their own prophets, and have persecuted us; and they please not God, and are contrary to all men. I THESSALONIANS II, 14–15, *c.* 51

What advantage then hath the Jew? or what is there of circumcision?
ROMANS III, 1, *c.* 55

Are they Hebrews? so am I. Are they Israelites? so am I. Are they the seed of Abraham? so am I. II CORINTHIANS XI, 22, *c.* 55

Salvation is of the Jews. JOHN IV, 22, *c.* 115

A people that adopts an unsocial way of life, refuses to sit at table with others, or to take part in the common prayers and offerings, is as remote from the rest of us as the Susans and Bactrians, or even as the distant Indians.
Ascribed to APOLLONIUS of Tyana, c. 50

When the number of the disciples were multiplied, there arose a murmuring of the Grecians against the Hebrews.
ACTS VI, 1, *c.* 75

Claudius . . . commanded all Jews to depart from Rome. ACTS XVIII, 2

A people given to superstition and opposed to religion. TACITUS: *Annals*, V, *c.* 110

The Jews are a race apart. They have made laws according to their own fashion, and keep them.
CELSUS: *A True Discourse*, *c.* 178

In the Jews' olive tree we have been grafted.
TERTULLIAN: *The Testimony of the Christian Soul*, *c.* 210

Pilate said unto the Jews, Your nation is always seditious, and rebels against your benefactors. THE ACTS OF PILATE, IX, *c.* 325

The nefarious sect. (Secta nefaria.)
Designation of the Jews in edicts of the Roman Emperors after 326

The Jews themselves, and all that is theirs, belong to the king.
Law of EDWARD THE CONFESSOR of England, *c.* 1180

The Jews, like Cain, are doomed to wander the earth as fugitives and vagabonds, and their faces are covered with shame.
POPE INNOCENT III: *Letter to the Count de Nevers*, *c.* 1200

What a shame it is they should be more miserable under Christian princes than their ancestors were under Pharaoh.
POPE INNOCENT IV: *Letter in defense of the Jews*, 1247

If all the seas were ink, and all the reeds pens, and all the people scribes, it would not be enough to record all the misfortunes of the Jews in a single year.
Gloss to the *Migilat Taanit*, *c.* 1400

We decree and order that from now on, and for all time, Christians shall not eat or drink with Jews, nor admit them to feasts, nor cohabit with them, nor bathe with them. Christians shall not allow Jews to hold civil honors over Christians, or to exercise public offices in the state.
POPE EUGENIUS IV: *Decree*, 1442

Innocent or not, let the Jew be fried.
PEDRO ARBUÉS (Spanish inquisitor): To his officers, *c.* 1480

Jews and papists are ungodly wretches; they are two stockings made of one piece of cloth.
MARTIN LUTHER: *Table-Talk*, CCLXXV, 1569

If a Jew, not converted at heart, were to ask baptism at my hands, I would take him on to the bridge, tie a stone round his neck, and hurl him into the river; for these wretches are wont to make a jest of our religion.
MARTIN LUTHER: *Table-Talk*, CCCLVI

We order that each and every Jew of both sexes in our temporal dominions, and in all the cities, lands, places and baronies subject to them, shall depart completely out of the confines thereof within the space of three months after these letters shall have been made public. POPE PIUS IV: *Decree*, 1569

To undo a Jew is charity, and not sin.
CHRISTOPHER MARLOWE: *The Jew of Malta*, IV, *c.* 1590

Sufferance is the badge of all our tribe.
SHAKESPEARE: *The Merchant of Venice*, I, *c.* 1597

I am a Jew: Hath not a Jew eyes? hath not a Jew hands, organs, dimensions, senses, affections, passions? fed with the same food, hurt with the same weapons, subject to the same diseases, healed by the same means, warmed and cooled by the same Winter and Summer, as a Christian is?

SHAKESPEARE: *The Merchant of Venice,* III

In converting Jews to Christians, you raise the price of pork. IBID.

I took by the throat the circumcised dog
And smote him.

SHAKESPEARE: *Othello,* V, 1604

Our English proverb: to look like a Jew, whereby is meant sometimes a weather-beaten, wasp-like fellow, sometimes a frenetic and lunatic person, sometimes one discontented.

THOMAS CORYAT: *Crudities,* 1611

The Jew is obstinate in all fortunes; the persecution of fifteen hundred years hath but confirmed them in their error. They have already endured whatsoever may be inflicted; and have suffered, in a bad cause, even to the condemnation of their enemies.

THOMAS BROWNE: *Religio Medici,* I, 1642

Have mercy upon all Jews, Turks, infidels and heretics.

THE BOOK OF COMMON PRAYER (*Good Friday*), 1662

I will use you as bad as a Jew.

THOMAS FULLER: *Worthies of England,* 1662 (Quoted as a common saying)

The carnal Jews hold a middle place between the Christians and the pagans. The pagans do not know God, and love only the earth. The Jews know the true God, and love only the earth. The Christians know the true God, and do not love the earth.

BLAISE PASCAL: *Pensées,* XV, 1670

The Jews, a headstrong, moody, murm'ring race
As ever tried th' extent and stretch of grace;
God's pampered people, whom, debauched with ease,
No king could govern nor no God could please.

JOHN DRYDEN: *Absalom and Achitophel,* I, 1682

Talk what you will of the Jews, that they are cursed: they thrive wherever they come; they are able to oblige the prince of their country by lending him money; none of them beg; they keep together; and as for their being hated, why Christians hate one another as much.

JOHN SELDEN: *Table-Talk,* 1689

Wherever there is money there are Jews.

C. L. DE MONTESQUIEU: *Persian Letters,* LX, 1721

A people long since abandoned of God.

WILLIAM WARBURTON (BISHOP OF GLOUCESTER): *The Divine Legation of Moses,* II, dedication, 1737

This is the Jew that Shakespeare drew.

ALEXANDER POPE: On seeing Charles Macklin as Shylock, Feb. 14, 1741

If it were permitted to reason consistently in religious matters, it is clear that we all ought to become Jews, because Jesus Christ our Saviour was born a Jew, lived a Jew, died a Jew, and He said expressly that He was fulfilling the Jewish religion.

VOLTAIRE: *Philosophical Dictionary,* 1764

He left his old religion for an estate, and has not had time to get a new one, but stands like a dead wall between church and synagogue, or like the blank leaves between the Old and New Testament.

R. B. SHERIDAN: *The Duenna,* I, 1775

Their system was deism; that is, belief of only one God. But their ideas of Him and of His attributes were degrading and injurious.

THOMAS JEFFERSON: *An Estimate of the Merit of the Doctrines of Jesus Compared with Those of Others,* 1803

The idea of a Jew (which our pious ancestors held in horror) has nothing in it now revolting. We have found the claws of the beast, and pared its nails, and now we take it to our arms, fondle it, write plays to flatter it: it is visited by princes, affects a taste, patronizes the arts, and is the only liberal and gentleman-like thing in Christendom.

CHARLES LAMB: *Specimens of the English Dramatic Poets,* 1808

A people still, whose common ties are gone;
Who, mixed with every race, are lost in none.

GEORGE CRABBE: *The Borough,* IV, 1810

Beat my Jew, and I'll beat your Jew. (Haust du meinen Juden, so haue ich deinen Juden.)

GERMAN PROVERB, apparently derived from J. P. HEBEL: *Die zwei Postillione,* 1811

I wish your name may be admitted to all the privileges of citizens in every country of the world. This country has done much. I wish it may do more; and annul every narrow idea in religion, government and commerce.

JOHN ADAMS: *Letter to Mordecai M. Noah,* July 31, 1818

The Jews were a cowardly and cruel people.

NAPOLEON I: To Gaspard Gourgaud at St. Helena, 1815–1818

I have, in the abstract, no disrespect for Jews. They are a piece of stubborn antiquity, compared with which Stonehenge is in its nonage. They date beyond the pyramids. But I should not care to be in habits of familiar intercourse with any of that nation.

CHARLES LAMB: *Imperfect Sympathies,* 1821 (London Magazine, Aug.)

A hopeless faith, a homeless race.

JOHN KEBLE: *The Christian Year,* 1827

The religion of the Jews is, indeed, a light; but it is as the light of the glow-worm, which gives no heat, and illumines nothing but itself.

S. T. COLERIDGE: *Table-Talk*, April 13, 1830

The point of view of the Semite is subjective and egoistic. His poetry is lyrical, and hence subjective. In his religion he is self-seeking and exclusive.

CHRISTIAN LASSEN: *Indische Alterthumskunde*, I, 1847

1. No Jew, without exception, is permitted to settle, to carry on commerce, trade, or any handicraft in the canton.
2. Any citizen who admits a Jew into his house, be it for commercial purposes, as clerk or servant, or in any other capacity, or for what other purpose soever, is liable to a fine of 300 francs.

Law of the Canton of Basel, Switzerland, Nov. 17, 1851

They are an ancient people, a famous people, an enduring people, and a people who in the end have generally attained their objects. I hope Parliament may endure for ever, and sometimes I think it will; but I cannot help remembering that the Jews have outlived Assyrian kings, Egyptian Pharaohs, Roman Cæsars, and Arabian Caliphs.

BENJAMIN DISRAELI: Speech in the House of Commons, May 25, 1854

If the duration of afflictions and the patience with which they are borne ennoble, the Jews may vie with the aristocracy of any land. If a literature which owns a few classical tragedies is deemed rich, what place should be assigned to a tragedy which extends over fifteen centuries and in which the poets and actors were also the heroes?

LEOPOLD ZUNZ: *Die synagogale Poesie des Mittelalters*, 1855

The ruler of the rulers of the earth.

R. W. EMERSON: *The Conduct of Life*, I, 1860

If it hadn't been for just such damned cusses as you, our Lord Jesus Christ would be alive and well to this day.

GENERAL EBENEZER DUMONT, U.S.A.: To a Jewish sutler at Muldraugh's Hill, Ky., 1861

Jews are not fit for Heaven, but on earth they are most useful.

MARIAN EVANS (GEORGE ELIOT): *The Spanish Gypsy*, I, 1868

The Jew everywhere feels himself a cosmopolitan.

FRIEDRICH VON HELLWALD: *Zur Characteristik des jüdischen Volkes*, 1872

Every country has the sort of Jew it deserves.

K. E. FRANZOS: *Tote Seelen*, 1875 (Vienna Neue Freie Presse, March 31)

The Jew is about to strangle the native idealism of Old Germany; the Jew threatens to corrupt German character, German fidelity, German purity, German probity.

Resolution of the Assembly of Anti-Semites, Berlin, July 15, 1877

The Jews are our misfortune.

HEINRICH VON TREITSCHKE: *Ein Wort über unser Judenthum*, 1880

It is to the Jewish nation that humanity owes the deepest debt of gratitude, and it is on that nation that humanity has inflicted the deepest wrongs.

F. W. FARRAR: Speech at the Mansion House, London, Feb. 1, 1882

A race in which ability seems as natural and hereditary as the curve of their noses.

J. R. LOWELL: *Democracy*, 1884 (Address in Birmingham, England, Oct. 6)

Anti-Semitism is the final consequence of Judaism.

F. W. NIETZSCHE: *The Antichrist*, XXIV, 1888

Nobody can ever make the Americans think ill of the Jews as a class or as a race.

JOHN HAY: Speech in Washington, June 15, 1903

Wars are the Jew's harvests.

WERNER SOMBART: *Die Juden und das Wirtschaftsleben*, 1911

Jews are a distinct nationality of which every Jew, whatever his country, his station or his shade of belief, is necessarily a member.

LOUIS D. BRANDEIS: Address to the Eastern Council of the Central Conference of Reform Rabbis, June 28, 1915

His Majesty's government view with favor the establishment in Palestine of a national home for the Jewish people, and will use their best endeavor to facilitate the achievement of this object, it being clearly understood that nothing shall be done which may prejudice the civil and religious rights of existing non-Jewish communities in Palestine or the rights and political status enjoyed by the Jews in any other country.

A. J. BALFOUR: *Letter to Lord Rothschild*, Nov. 2, 1917

The Jewish bourgeoisie are our enemies, not as Jews but as bourgeoisie. The Jewish worker is our brother.

NIKOLAI LENIN: Speech before the Council of People's Commissars, Aug. 9, 1918

Unless Bolshevism is nipped in the bud immediately, it is bound to spread in one form or another over Europe and the whole world, for it is organized and worked by Jews who have no nationality, and whose object is to destroy for their own ends the existing order of things.

THE NETHERLANDS MINISTER at Petrograd: *Letter to A. J. Balfour*, Sept. 18, 1918

None but members of the nation may be citizens of the state. None but those of German blood, whatever their creed, may be members of the nation. No Jew, therefore, may be a member of the nation.
National Programme of the Nazis, ratified Feb. 25, 1920

The Jew may hang on to a dollar when dealing with the enemy, but he does not dole out pittances to his wife, alternately humor and cuff his children, nor request, by his manner, that elderly people who are not up to date shall get off the earth.
ELBERT HUBBARD: *Roycroft Dictionary and Book of Epigrams,* 1923

Slaughter the Jews! (Juda verrecke!)
Slogan of the Austrian Nazis, *c.* 1933

1. Marriages between Jews and citizens of German or kindred stock shall be prohibited. Marriages concluded despite the law shall be considered void even when they were concluded abroad.
2. Non-marital sexual intercourse between Jews and citizens of German or kindred stock shall be prohibited.
3. Jews shall not employ in their households female citizens of German or kindred stock under 45 years of age.
4. Jews shall not hoist the Reich and national flag, nor display the Reich colors. They are, however, permitted to display the Jewish colors.
GERMAN LAW of Sept. 15, 1935

It is not possible for Christians to take part in anti-Semitism. We are Semites spiritually.
POPE PIUS XI: To a group of Belgian pilgrims, Sept., 1938

The world is divided into two groups of nations — those which want to expel the Jews and those which do not want to receive them.
Ascribed to CHAIM WEIZMANN, *c.* 1938

Anti-Semitism means hating the Jews more than is necessary.
Author unidentified

Half of Christendom worships a Jew, and the other half a Jewess.
IBID.

How odd
Of God
To choose
The Jews.
HOWLAND SPENCER, 1915

Jews are like everybody else, only more so.
IBID.

When you baptize a Jew hold him under water for five minutes.
BULGARIAN PROVERB

It doesn't matter; the Jew is burned.
GERMAN PROVERB

Only a Jew can cheat a Jew.
IBID.

Whoever loves Jews hates Germans.
IBID.

Affliction is the ornament of the Jews.
HEBREW PROVERB

The law of the land is the law of the Jew.
IBID.

These three are the marks of a Jew — a tender heart, self-respect, and charity.
IBID.

When a Jew smiles at a Moslem it is a sign that he is preparing to cheat him.
MOROCCAN PROVERB

The peasant earns the money, the noble spends it, and the Jew gets it in the end.
POLISH PROVERB

Only the Devil can cheat a Jew.
IBID.

Cheat a Jew and he will kiss you; kiss a Jew and he will cheat you.
RUSSIAN PROVERB

Give a Jew the rope free, and he will let you hang him.
IBID.

It lifts forty sins from the soul to kill a Jew.
UKRAINIAN PROVERB

A nation that persecutes Jews cannot last long.
YIDDISH PROVERB

No more vicious anti-Semite than a Jewish anti-Semite.
IBID.

A Galician Jew is worse than a Christian.
YIDDISH PROVERB, common among German Jews

German Jews are half Christians.
YIDDISH PROVERB, common among Russian Jews

[*See also* Armenian, Bible, Character (National), Cheating, Chesterfield (Earl of), Christian, Christian (Early), Curse, Diplomat, Genoese, Hebrew, Hebrew Language, Inbreeding, Judaism, Physician, Poland, Puritan, Toleration, Trust, Uproar, War, Worst, Yankee, Zionism.

Jewelry

The Utopians wonder how many men should be taken with the glaring doubtful lustre of a jewel or stone that can look up to a star, or to the sun itself.
THOMAS MORE: *Utopia,* 1516

Infinite riches in a little room.
CHRISTOPHER MARLOWE: *The Jew of Malta,* I, *c.* 1590

Orators of love.
SAMUEL DANIEL: *The Complaynt of Rosamond,* 1592

Dumb jewels often, in their silent kind,
More than quick words, do move a woman's mind.
SHAKESPEARE: *Two Gentlemen of Verona,* III, *c.* 1595

Like a rich jewel in an Ethiop's ear.
SHAKESPEARE: *Romeo and Juliet,* I, *c.* 1596

[*See also* Finery, Gift.

Jingo

We don't want to fight,
But, by Jingo, if we do,
We've got the ships, we've got the men,
We've got the money too.
Anon.: *English Music Hall Song, c.* 1877

Job, Book of (c. 325 B.C.)

The book of Job is pure Arab poetry of the highest and most antique cast.
S. T. COLERIDGE: *Table-Talk,* May 9, 1830

A noble book; all men's book! It is our first, oldest statement of the never-ending problem, — men's destiny, and God's ways with him here in this earth. And all in such free flowing outlines; grand in its sincerity, in its simplicity; in its epic melody, and repose of reconcilement.
THOMAS CARLYLE: *Heroes and Hero-Worship,* II, 1840 (Lecture in London, May 8)

John

John — How that name smacks! What an honest, full, English, and yet withal holy and apostolic sound it bears.
CHARLES LAMB: *Letter to J. B. Dibdin,* Sept. 18, 1827

John Bull

The world is a bundle of hay,
Mankind are the asses who pull;
Each tugs it a different way,
And the greatest of all is John Bull.
BYRON: *Epigram,* 1821

Johnson, Samuel (1709–84)

That great Cham of literature.
TOBIAS SMOLLETT: *Letter to John Wilkes,* March 16, 1759

Pomposo, insolent and loud,
Vain idol of a scribbling crowd, . . .
Whose cursory flattery is the tool
Of every fawning, flattering fool;
Who wit with jealous eye surveys,
And sickens at another's praise; . . .
Who to increase his native strength
Draws words six syllables in length,
With which, assisted with a frown,
By way of club, he knocks us down.
CHARLES CHURCHILL: *The Ghost,* 1763

A superstitious dog.
Ascribed to VOLTAIRE by James Boswell, 1763

Dr. Johnson's sayings would not appear so extraordinary were it not for his bow-wow way.
THE EARL OF PEMBROKE: To James Boswell, *c.* 1770

If you were to make little fishes talk they would talk like whales.
OLIVER GOLDSMITH: To Johnson, *c.* 1773

I can now look back upon threescore and four years, in which little has been done, and little has been enjoyed; a life diversified by misery, spent part in the sluggishness of penury, and part under the violence of pain, in gloomy discontent or importunate distress.
SAMUEL JOHNSON: *Letter to Hester Thrale,* Sept. 21, 1773

Johnson deals so much in tribal tautology, or the fault of repeating the same sense in three different phrases, that I believe it would be possible, taking the ground-work for all three, to make one of his Ramblers into three different papers, that should all have exactly the same purport and meaning, but in different phrases.
HORACE WALPOLE: *Letter to the Countess of Upper Ossory,* Feb. 1, 1779

Here Johnson lies — a sage by all allowed
Whom to have bred, may well make England proud;
Who many a noble gift from Heaven possessed
And faith at last, alone worth all the rest.
Oh, made immortal by a double prize
By fame on earth — by glory in the skies.
WILLIAM COWPER: *Epitaph on Johnson, c.* 1785

Envy (the mother of many vices) was the bosom serpent of this literary despot.
WILLIAM HAYLEY: *Letter to Anna Seward,* 1785

I own I like not Johnson's turgid style,
That gives an inch the importance of a mile,
Casts of manure a wagon-load around
To raise a simple daisy from the ground;
Uplifts the club of Hercules, for what?
To crush a butterfly or brain a gnat!
JOHN WOLCOT: *On Dr. Samuel Johnson,* 1785

Here lies poor Johnson. Reader! have a care,
Tread light, lest you rouse a sleeping bear.
Religious, moral, gen'rous and humane,
He was, but self-conceited, rude, and vain:
Ill-bred, and overbearing in dispute,
A scholar and a Christian, yet a brute.
SOAME JENYNS: *Epitaph on Johnson,* 1786

Johnson made coxcombs of all his friends, and they in return made him a coxcomb.
WILLIAM COWPER: *Letter to Samuel Rose,* June 5, 1789

His style is a mixture of Latin and English; an intolerable composition of Latinity, affected smoothness, scholastic accuracy, and roundness of periods.
NOAH WEBSTER: *Dissertations on the English Language,* 1789

Rabelais and all other wits are nothing compared with him. You may be diverted by them; but Johnson gives you a forcible hug, and shakes laughter out of you, whether you will or no.
Ascribed to DAVID GARRICK by James Boswell, 1791

Johnson made the most brutal speeches to living persons; for though he was good-natured

at bottom, he was very ill-natured at top. He loved to dispute to show his superiority. If his opponents were weak, he told them they were fools; if they vanquished him, he was scurrilous.
HORACE WALPOLE: *Letter to Mary Berry,* May 26, 1791

All his books are written in a learned language, in a language which nobody hears from his mother or his nurse, in a language in which nobody ever quarrels, or drives bargains, or makes love, in a language in which nobody ever thinks.
T. B. MACAULAY: *Samuel Johnson,* 1831 (Edinburgh Review, Sept.)

The characteristic peculiarity of his intellect was the union of great powers with low prejudices. If we judged of him by the best parts of his mind, we should place him almost as high as he was placed by the idolatry of Boswell; if by the worst parts of his mind, we should place him even below Boswell himself.
IBID.

I have always considered him to be, by nature, one of our great English souls. A strong and noble man; so much left undeveloped in him to the last: in a kindlier element what might he not have been, — poet, priest, sovereign, ruler!
THOMAS CARLYLE: *Heroes and Hero-Worship,* v, 1840 (Lecture in London, May 19)

[*See also* Boswell (James), Style.

John the Baptist

John was clothed with camel's hair, and with a girdle of a kid about his loins; and he did eat locusts and wild honey.
MARK I, 6, *c.* 70

He was a burning and a shining light.
JOHN V, 35, *c.* 115

[*See also* Gentleman.

Joke

In joking one must be moderate.
CICERO: *De oratore,* II, *c.* 80 B.C.

Joking aside. (Omissis jocis.)
PLINY THE YOUNGER: *Letters,* VI, *c.* 110

A joke never gains over an enemy, but often loses a friend.
THOMAS FULLER: *Gnomologia,* 1732

Joke went out and brought home his fellow, and they two began a quarrel.
BENJAMIN FRANKLIN: *Poor Richard's Almanac,* 1741

Vivacity and wit make a man shine in company, but trite jokes and loud laughter reduce him to a buffoon.
LORD CHESTERFIELD: *Letter to his son,* Feb. 5, 1750

A joke's a very serious thing.
CHARLES CHURCHILL: *The Ghost,* 1763

A joke loses everything when the joker laughs himself.
J. C. F. SCHILLER: *The Fiesco,* I, 1784

Nothing better reveals a man's character than the joke he takes in bad part.
G. C. LICHTENBERG: *Reflections,* 1799

One doesn't joke with a man about to be murdered.
NAPOLEON I: To Gaspard Gourgaud at St. Helena, Sept. 26, 1817

Someone is generally sure to be the sufferer by a joke. What is sport to one is death to another.
WILLIAM HAZLITT: *Lectures on the English Comic Writers,* I, 1819

Extry charg fur this larst remark. It's a goak.
C. F. BROWNE (ARTEMUS WARD): *Artemus Ward: His Book,* 1865

The essence of all jokes, of all comedy, seems to be an honest or well-intended halfness; a non-performance of what is pretended to be performed, at the same time that one is giving loud pledges of performance.
R. W. EMERSON: *The Comic,* 1876

The stupidest book in the world is a book of jokes.
J. G. HOLLAND: *Everyday Topics,* 1876

Jokes should have sheep's teeth, not dog's.
CZECH PROVERB

[*See also* Humor, Gods, Jest, Mirth, Wit.

Joker

A joker is near akin to a buffoon; and neither of them is the least related to wit.
LORD CHESTERFIELD: *Letter to his son,* Aug. 30, 1749

Jonah

[*See* Miracle.

Jonson, Ben (1572–1637)

He is a great lover and praiser of himself; a contemner and scorner of others; given rather to lose a friend than a jest; jealous of every word and action of those about him, especially after drink, which is one of the elements in which he liveth.
WILLIAM DRUMMOND of Hawthornden: *Note on Ben Jonson,* Jan. 19, 1619

O rare Ben Jonson!
JOHN YOUNG: *Epitaph in Westminster Abbey,* 1637

And now fierce Jonson's gone, we well may say
The stage hath seen her glory and decay.
OWEN FELLTHAM: *Jonsonus Virbius,* 1638

If I would compare him with Shakespeare I must acknowledge him the more correct poet,

but Shakespeare the greater wit. Shakespeare was the Homer, or father of our dramatic poets; Jonson was the Virgil, the pattern of elaborate writing. I admire him, but I love Shakespeare.
JOHN DRYDEN: *Of Dramatic Poesy*, 1668

Ben Jonson is a great borrower from the works of others, and a plagiarist even from nature; so little freedom is there in his imitations of her, and he appears to receive her bounty like an alms.
WILLIAM HAZLITT: *Lectures on the English Comic Writers*, II, 1819

Ben Jonson was the greatest man after Shakespeare in that age of dramatic genius.
S. T. COLERIDGE: *Table-Talk*, Feb. 17, 1833

[*See also* Nickname, Shakespeare (William).

Joseph II, Holy Roman Emperor (1741–90)

[*See* Epitaph.

Journalese

Translated from journalese into plain English.
Anon.: In the Pall Mall Gazette, April 2, 1882 (This is the earliest use of the term recorded in the New English Dictionary. Its first example of *newspaperese* is dated in 1889, and its first example of *newspaper English* 1888. The analogue *Zeitungsdeutsch* was used by ARTHUR SCHOPENHAUER in *Materialien zu einer Abhandlung über den argen Unfug, der in jetziger Zeit mit der deutschen Sprache getrieben wird*, 1864)

Journalism

A fourth estate, of able editors, springs up.
THOMAS CARLYLE: *The French Revolution*, II, 1837

Great is journalism. Is not every able editor a ruler of the world, being the persuader of it?
IBID.

It is often made a matter of boasting, that the United States contain so many public journals. It were wiser to make it a cause of mourning, since the quality, in this instance, diminishes in an inverse ratio to the quantity.
J. FENIMORE COOPER: *The American Democrat*, XXVII, 1838

Exaggeration of every kind is as essential to journalism as it is to the dramatic art, for the object of journalism is to make events go as far as possible.
ARTHUR SCHOPENHAUER: *On Some Forms of Literature*, 1851

To the wholesome training of severe newspaper work, when I was a very young man, I constantly refer my first successes.
CHARLES DICKENS: Speech in London, April 18, 1868

In a world of daily — nay, almost hourly — journalism every clever man, every man who thinks himself clever, or whom anybody else thinks clever, is called upon to deliver his judgment point-blank and at the word of command on every conceivable subject of human thought.
J. R. LOWELL: *Democracy*, 1884 (Address in Birmingham, England, Oct. 6)

Modern journalism justifies its own existence by the great Darwinian principle of the survival of the vulgarest.
OSCAR WILDE: *The Critic as Artist*, 1891

The difference between literature and journalism is that journalism is unreadable, and literature is not read. IBID.

Yellow journalism.
Phrase apparently coined by ERVIN WARDMAN, editor of the New York Press, in the Spring of 1896; R. F. Outcault's Yellow Kid had appeared in the comic section of the New York World a year before

Journalism consists in buying white paper at two cents a pound and selling it at ten cents a pound. CHARLES A. DANA (1819–97)

In our country I am inclined to think that almost, if not quite, the most important profession is that of the newspaper man, including the man of the magazines, especially the cheap magazines, and the weeklies.
THEODORE ROOSEVELT: Speech in Milwaukee, Sept. 7, 1910

[*See also* Editor, Friend, Literature, Newspaper, Press.

Journalist

Upon my tongues continual slanders ride,
The which in every language I pronounce,
Stuffing the ears of men with false reports.
SHAKESPEARE: *II Henry IV*, induction, *c.* 1598

Ask how to live? Write, write, write anything;
The world's a fine believing world, write news!
JOHN FLETCHER: *Wit Without Money*, II, *c.* 1614

I am a printer, and a printer of news; and I do hearken after them, wherever they be at any rates; I'll give anything for a good copy now, be it true or false, so it be news.
BEN JONSON: *News from the New World*, 1621

A newswriter is a man without virtue, who writes lies at home for his own profit. To these compositions is required neither genius nor knowledge, neither industry nor sprightliness; but contempt of shame and indifference to truth are absolutely necessary.
SAMUEL JOHNSON: *The Idler*, Nov. 11, 1758

A chiel's amang you taking notes,
And, faith, he'll prent it.
ROBERT BURNS: *On Captain Grose's Peregrinations Through Scotland*, 1789 (*Chiel*=fellow)

A would-be satirist, a hired buffoon,
A monthly scribbler of some low lampoon,
Condemn'd to drudge, the meanest of the mean,
And furbish falsehoods for a magazine.
BYRON: *English Bards and Scotch Reviews,* 1809

They are a sort of assassins who sit with loaded blunderbusses at the corner of streets and fire them off for hire or for sport at any passenger they select.
JOHN QUINCY ADAMS: *Diary,* Sept. 7, 1820

It is one of the essential duties of a newspaper correspondent to conceal as much as possible from the public the sources of his information.
MOWBRAY MORRIS (manager of the London Times): *Letter to P. O'Brien* (correspondent at Athens), July 25, 1850

A journalist is a man who has missed his calling.
Ascribed to OTTO VON BISMARCK (In this form he never said it. But on Nov. 10, 1862, in a statement printed in a newspaper on the island of Rügen, he spoke of the opposition press as being "in large part in the hands of Jews and malcontents who have missed their calling")

In centuries before ours the public nailed the ears of journalists to the pump. In this century journalists have nailed their own ears to the keyhole.
OSCAR WILDE: *The Soul of Man Under Socialism,* 1891

There is no such thing as an independent press. You know it, and I know it. I am paid $150 a week for keeping honest opinions out of the paper. We are intellectual prostitutes, and our time and our talents are the property of other men.
A New York editor, quoted in E. W. Howe's Monthly, June, 1917

Writing good editorials is chiefly telling the people what *they* think, not what *you* think.
ARTHUR BRISBANE (1864–1936)

Man's a vapor,
Full of woes;
Starts a paper,
Up he goes.
Author unidentified

Journey

A prosperous journey.
ROMANS I, 10, *c.* 55

Jesus commanded them that they should take nothing for their journey, save a staff only; no scrip, no bread, no money in their purse.
MARK VI, 8, *c.* 70 (Cf. LUKE IX, 3, *c.* 75)

Journeys end in lovers' meeting.
SHAKESPEARE: *Twelfth Night,* II, *c.* 1601

It is a great journey to the world's end.
JOHN RAY: *English Proverbs,* 1670

A man knows his companion in a long journey and a little inn.
THOMAS FULLER: *Gnomologia,* 1732

[*See also* Travel.

Jowett, Benjamin (1817–93)

I come first. My name is Jowett.
There's no knowledge but I know it.
I am Master of this College.
What I don't know isn't knowledge.
Anon.: *The Masque of Balliol,* 1881

Joy

The man from whom the joys of life have departed is living no more, but should be counted with the dead.
SOPHOCLES: *Antigone, c.* 450 B.C.

The joyfulness of a man prolongeth his days.
ECCLESIASTICUS XXX, 22, *c.* 180 B.C.

Joy cometh in the morning.
PSALMS XXX, 5, *c.* 150 B.C.

All seek joy, but it is not found on earth.
ST. JOHN CHRYSOSTOM: *Homilies,* XVIII, *c.* 388

The heart, with excessive joy, is inwardly dilated, and suffereth a manifest resolution of the vital spirits, which may go on so far that it may thereby be deprived of its nourishment, and by consequence of life itself, by this pericharie or extremity of gladness.
RABELAIS: *Gargantua,* I, 1535

Unmingled joys here to no man befall;
Who least, hath some; who most, hath never all.
ROBERT SOUTHWELL: *Times Go By Turns, c.* 1595

I wish you all the joy that you can wish.
SHAKESPEARE: *The Merchant of Venice,* III, *c.* 1597

Silence is the perfectest herald of joy:
I were but little happy if I could say how much.
SHAKESPEARE: *Much Ado About Nothing,* II, *c.* 1599

Joy delights in joy.
SHAKESPEARE: *Sonnets,* VIII, 1609

Great joys, like griefs, are silent.
SHAKERLEY MARMION: *Holland's Leaguer,* V, 1632

Who bathes in worldly joys, swims in a world of fears.
PHINEAS FLETCHER: *The Purple Island,* VIII, 1633

Awake, my heart, and sing!
PAUL GERHARDT: *Morgenlied,* 1648

It is a fine seasoning for joy to think of those we love.
J. B. MOLIÈRE: *La misanthrope,* V, 1666

A joy that's shared is a joy made double.
JOHN RAY: *English Proverbs,* 1670

Joy is the life of man's life.
BENJAMIN WHICHCOTE: *Moral and Religious Aphorisms,* 1753

Joy makes us giddy.
G. E. LESSING: *Minna von Barnhelm,* II, 1767

O God, may I live to have one day of unsullied joy!
LUDWIG VAN BEETHOVEN: *The Testament of Heiligenstadt,* Oct. 6, 1802

When the power of imparting joy
Is equal to the will, the human soul
Requires no other Heaven.
P. B. SHELLEY: *Queen Mab,* II, 1813

I have drunken deep of joy,
And I will taste no other wine tonight.
P. B. SHELLEY: *The Cenci,* I, 1819

Joys too exquisite to last,
And yet more exquisite when past.
JAMES MONTGOMERY: *The Little Cloud,* c. 1830

For compassion a human heart suffices; but for full and adequate sympathy with joy an angel's only.
S. T. COLERIDGE: *Table-Talk,* Aug. 30, 1833

All life is activity, and joy is the normal accompaniment of that activity.
ERNST VON FEUCHTERSLEBEN: *Zur Diätetik der Seele,* VIII, 1838

Joys are bubble-like: what makes them bursts them too. P. J. BAILEY: *Festus,* 1839

Joy was duty and love was law.
J. G. WHITTIER: *Maud Muller,* 1854

No joy without alloy.
H. G. BOHN: *Handbook of Proverbs,* 1855

All great joys are serious.
ALEXANDER SMITH: *Dreamthorp,* III, 1863

He chortled in his joy.
C. L. DODGSON (LEWIS CARROLL): *Through the Looking Glass,* 1871

Joy, like the ague, has one good day between two bad ones. DANISH PROVERB

[*See also* Change, Charity, Debauchery, Friend, Leap, Morning, Prostitute, Tears.

Joy and Sorrow

I will turn their mourning into joy, and will comfort them, and make them rejoice from their sorrow.
JEREMIAH XXXI, 13, *c.* 625 B.C.

They that sow in tears shall reap in joy.
PSALMS CXXVI, 5, *c.* 150 B.C.

The latter end of joy is woe.
GEOFFREY CHAUCER: *The Canterbury Tales (The Nun's Priest's Tale),* c. 1386

My plenteous joys
Wanton in fullness, seek to hide themselves
In drops of sorrow.
SHAKESPEARE: *Macbeth,* I, *c.* 1605

We pick our sorrows out of the joys of other men, and from their sorrows we derive our joys.
OWEN FELLTHAM: *Resolves,* I, *c.* 1620

God send you joy, for sorrow will come fast enough.
JOHN CLARKE: *Parœmiologia Anglo-Latina,* 1639

Every inch of joy has an ell of annoy.
JOHN RAY: *English Proverbs,* 1670

Our present joys are sweeter for past pain.
GEORGE GRANVILLE (LORD LANSDOWNE): *The British Enchanters,* V, 1706

It seems but reasonable that we should be capable of receiving joy from what is no real good to us, since we can retrieve grief from what is no real evil.
JOSEPH ADDISON: *The Spectator,* Dec. 15, 1711

Joys impregnate. Sorrows bring forth.
WILLIAM BLAKE: *The Marriage of Heaven and Hell,* 1790

Sorrow is brief but joy is endless.
J. C. F. SCHILLER: *Die Jungfrau von Orleans,* V, 1801

Sorrows remembered sweeten present joy.
ROBERT POLLOK: *The Course of Time,* I, 1827

One can endure sorrow alone, but it takes two to be glad.
ELBERT HUBBARD: *Roycroft Dictionary and Book of Epigrams,* 1923

Judaism

The punishment of children for the crimes of their parents . . . can be only well explained and vindicated on the principle of no future state in the religion of Moses.
WILLIAM WARBURTON (BISHOP OF GLOUCESTER): *The Divine Legation of Moses,* dedication of Vol. II, 1737

[*See also* Christianity, Jew.

Judas

[*See* Bible, Biography, Bishop.

Judge

If a judge pronounce a judgment and afterward reverse it, he shall pay twelvefold the damages which were awarded, and they shall expel him from his seat of judgment, and he shall not return.
THE CODE OF HAMMURABI, *c.* 2250 B.C.

If one man sin against another, the judge shall judge him. I SAMUEL II, 25, *c.* 500 B.C.

Give thy servant an understanding heart to judge thy people, that I may discern between good and bad. I KINGS III, 9, *c.* 500 B.C.

A judge should not be a youth, but old.
PLATO: *The Republic,* III, *c.* 370 B.C.

The function of the judge is to restore equality. If we represent the matter at dispute by a line divided into two unequal parts, it is his business to take from the longer part the amount whereby it exceeds half of the whole line, and to add it to the shorter part.
ARISTOTLE: *The Nicomachean Ethics,* V, *c.* 340 B.C.

Be instructed, ye judges of the earth. Serve the Lord with fear.
PSALMS II, 10–11, *c.* 150 B.C.

He shall judge the poor of the people, he shall save the children of the needy, and shall break in pieces the oppressor.
PSALMS LXII, 4

No one should be judge in his own case.
PUBLILIUS SYRUS: *Sententiæ, c.* 50 B.C.

The judge is condemned when the guilty is acquitted. IBID.

The law is relaxed when the judge shows pity.
IBID.

A good and faithful judge prefers what is right to what is expedient.
HORACE: *Carmina,* IV, *c.* 13 B.C.

The good judge condemns the crime but does not revile the criminal.
SENECA: *De Ira,* I, *c.* 43

A judge is unjust who hears but one side of a case, even though he decide it justly.
SENECA: *Medea, c.* 60

No one is ever innocent when his opponent is the judge. LUCAN: *Pharsalia,* VII, 65

Judges are best in the beginning; they deteriorate as time passes.
TACITUS: *Annals,* XV, *c.* 110

There must always be a goodly number of judges, for few will always do the will of the few.
NICCOLÒ MACHIAVELLI: *Discorsi,* I, 1531

Of the same paper whereon a judge writ but even now the condemnation against an adulterer he will tear a portion, thereon to write some love lines to his fellow judge's wife.
MICHEL DE MONTAIGNE: *Essays,* III, 1588

A Daniel come to judgment! yea, a Daniel!
O wise young judge, how I do honor thee!
SHAKESPEARE: *The Merchant of Venice,* IV, *c.* 1597

And then the justice
In fair round belly with good capon lined.
SHAKESPEARE: *As You Like It,* II, *c.* 1600

A judge were better a briber than a respecter of persons, for a corrupt judge offendeth not so highly as a facile.
FRANCIS BACON: *The Advancement of Learning,* I, 1605

Thieves for their robbery have authority
When judges steal themselves.
SHAKESPEARE: *Measure for Measure,* II, 1604

Look with thine eyes: see how yond justice rails upon yond simple thief. Hark, in thine ear: change places; and, handy-dandy, which is the justice, which is the thief?
SHAKESPEARE: *King Lear,* IV, 1606

Who wear out a good wholesome forenoon in hearing a cause between an orange-wife and a fosset-seller; and then rejourn the controversy of threepence to a second day of audience.
SHAKESPEARE: *Coriolanus,* II, *c.* 1607

He who has the judge for his father goes into court with an easy mind.
CERVANTES: *Don Quixote,* II, 1615

When a judge departs from the letter of the law he becomes a lawbreaker.
FRANCIS BACON: *De augmentis scientiarum,* 1623

Judges ought to remember that their office is *jus dicere,* and not *jus dare* — to interpret law, and not to make law, or give law.
FRANCIS BACON: *Essays,* LVI, 1625

Judges do not answer questions of fact, juries do not answer questions of law.
EDWARD COKE: *Institutes,* I, 1628

He hath put off the person of a judge that puts on the person of a friend.
THOMAS ADAMS: *Sermon,* 1629 (Credited to CICERO)

'Tis a maxim in our politics,
A judge destroys a mighty practiser:
When they grow rich and lazy they are ripe
For honor.
JAMES SHIRLEY: *Honoria and Mammon, c.* 1635

When a judge puts on his robes he puts off his relations to any, and, like Melchisedech, becomes without pedigree.
THOMAS FULLER: *The Holy State and the Profane State,* 1642 (Cf. HEBREWS VII, 1–3)

If thou be a severe, sour-complexioned man, then I disallow thee to be a competent judge.
IZAAK WALTON: *The Compleat Angler,* pref., 1653

I shall no more mind you than a hungry judge does a cause after the clock has struck one.
WILLIAM WYCHERLEY: *The Plain Dealer,* I, *c.* 1674

The duty of a judge is to render justice; his art is to delay it.
JEAN DE LA BRUYÈRE: *Caractères*, XIV, 1688

No action will lie against a judge of record for any matter done by him in the exercise of his judicial functions.
MR. JUSTICE POWEL: *Judgment in Gwinne* vs. *Poole*, 1692

The good judge, tickled with the proceeding, simpers upon a great beard, and fidgets off and on his cushion as if he had swallowed cantharides, or sat upon a cow-itch.
WILLIAM CONGREVE: *The Way of the World*, V, 1700

Judges' commissions shall be made *quando se bene gesserit* (during good behavior).
Act of Parliament (12 and 13 William III), 1702

The judge is nothing but the law speaking.
BENJAMIN WHICHCOTE: *Moral and Religious Aphorisms*, 1753

A man may judge impartially even in his own cause.
LORD MANSFIELD: *Judgment in Rex* vs. *Cowle*, 1759

Next to permanency in office, nothing can contribute more to the independence of the judges than a fixed provision for their support.
ALEXANDER HAMILTON: *The Federalist*, 1788

The judges, both of the Supreme and inferior courts, shall hold their offices during good behavior, and shall at stated times receive for their services a compensation which shall not be diminished during their continuance in office.
CONSTITUTION OF THE UNITED STATES, Art. III, 1789

To vindicate the policy of the law is no necessary part of the office of a judge.
MR. JUSTICE SCOTT: *Judgment in Evans* vs. *Evans*, 1790

As anger does not become a judge, so neither doth pity; for one is the mark of a foolish woman, as the other is of a passionate man.
MR. JUSTICE SCROGGS: *Judgment in Rex* vs. *Johnson*, 1794

Knowing that religion does not furnish grosser bigots than law, I expect little from old judges.
THOMAS JEFFERSON: *Letter to Thomas Cooper*, 1810

I cannot properly give advice to anybody. It is very often supposed judges can give advice, and I therefore take this public opportunity of saying that a judge cannot do it.
MR. JUSTICE BAYLEY: Obiter dictum during the trial of Dewhurst, 1820

What a wretched thing a Lord Chief Justice is, always was, and will be!
CHARLES LAMB: *Letter to Bernard Barton*, Jan. 23, 1824

He delights to balance a straw, to see a feather turn the scale or make it even again; and divides a scruple to the smallest fraction. He hugs indecision to his breast, and takes home a modest doubt or a nice point to solace himself with it in protracted, luxurious dalliance. Delay seems, in his mind, to be of the very essence of justice.
WILLIAM HAZLITT: *The Spirit of the Times*, 1825 (Said of Lord Eldon, Lord High Chancellor of England, *d.* 1838)

The world has produced fewer instances of truly great judges than it has of great men in almost every other department of civilized life.
HORACE BINNEY: *The Life and Character of Chief Justice Marshall*, 1835

Fill the seats of justice
With good men, not so absolute in goodness
As to forget what human frailty is.
T. N. TALFOURD: *Ion*, V, 1835

The Chief Justice was rich, quiet, and infamous.
T. B. MACAULAY: *Warren Hastings*, 1841 (Edinburgh Review, Oct.)

The judge is always supposed to be on the prisoner's side.
The Doctrines and Discipline of the Methodist Episcopal Church South, I, 1846

It is the province of the judge to expound the law only – the written from the statute, the unwritten or common law from the decisions of our predecessors and of our existing courts – from the text-writers of acknowledged authority, and upon the principles to be clearly deduced from them by sound reason and just inference – not to speculate upon what is the best, in his opinion, for the advantage of the community.
LORD JUSTICE COLERIDGE: *Judgment in Brownlow* vs. *Egerton*, 1854

Maud Muller looked and sighed: "Ah me!
That I the judge's bride might be!
He would dress me up in silks so fine,
And praise and toast me at his wine."
J. G. WHITTIER: *Maud Muller*, 1854

The judge weighs the arguments, and puts a brave face on the matter, and since there must be a decision, decides as he can, and hopes he has done justice.
R. W. EMERSON: *The Conduct of Life*, VII, 1860

We must remember that we have to make judges out of men, and that by being made judges their prejudices are not diminished and their intelligence is not increased.
R. G. INGERSOLL: Speech in Washington, Oct. 22, 1883

Judges, like Cæsar's wife, should be above suspicion.
MR. JUSTICE BOWEN: *Judgment in Leeson vs. the General Council of Medical Education,* 1889

Judges are apt to be naïve, simple-minded men.
O. W. HOLMES II: Speech in New York, Feb. 15, 1913

Our judges have been, on the whole, both able and upright public servants. . . . But their whole training and the aloofness of their position on the bench prevent their having, as a rule, any real knowledge of, or understanding sympathy with, the lives and needs of the ordinary hard-working toiler.
THEODORE ROOSEVELT: Speech in Santiago, Chile, Nov. 22, 1913

There are no more reactionary people in the world than judges.
NIKOLAI LENIN: *Political Parties and the Proletariat,* 1917

During his whole official career a judge never talks to a fellow-creature and no one ever talks to him. Counsel address him, he rules for or against his old friend at the bar, or sums up, or gives judgment against him, but he never talks to him. . . . The rules forbid even a witness to speak. He has to be examined or cross-examined. But if he attempts to speak the truth he is at once stopped, and threatened with penalties, and told that what he is about to say is not evidence.
EDWARD PARRY (JUDGE OF THE COUNTY COURT OF KENT): *My Own Way,* 1932

Courts and judges are not, and should not be, above criticism, and as long as they are not impeded in the conduct of judicial business by publications having the effect of obstructing enforcement of their orders and judgments, or of impairing the justice and impartiality of verdicts, there is no right to enforce a contempt proceeding.
CHIEF JUSTICE JAMES P. HUGHES OF THE INDIANA SUPREME COURT: *Decision in the State* vs. *Don Nixon,* Jan. 9, 1935

Law is what a judge dispenses. The judge, however, is no character of the everyday scene. He is no representative of the average man's commonsense. A certain remoteness from the experiences of everyday life and a certain rigidity of viewpoint are essential to his rôle as judge.
GERHART HUSSERL: *Everyday Life and the Law,* 1940 (Journal of Social Philosophy, July)

The best law leaves the least discretion to the judge. LATIN PROVERB

It is for a judge to declare, not to make the law. (Judicis est jus dicere non dare.)
LEGAL MAXIM (Cf. BACON, *ante,* 1625)

It is the business of a good judge to enlarge his authority. (Boni judicis est ampliare suam auctoritatem.) IBID.

It is the duty of a good judge to prevent litigation. (Boni judicis est causas litium dirimere.) IBID.

A judge and a stomach do their asking in silence. RUSSIAN PROVERB

Tell God the truth, but give the judge money. IBID.

The thing to fear is not the law but the judge. IBID.

[*See also* Cause, Golden Rule, Injunction, Judgment, Judiciary, Jury, Law, Lawsuit, Magistrate, Officeholder, Sobriety, Supreme Court.

Judgment

We should be gentle with those who err, not in will, but in judgment.
SOPHOCLES: *Trachiniae, c.* 450 B.C.

Thou art weighed in the balances, and art found wanting. DANIEL V, 27, *c.* 165 B.C.

Men judge the affairs of other men better than their own.
TERENCE: *Heautontimoroumenos, c.* 160 B.C.

The judgments of the Lord are true and righteous altogether. More to be desired are they than gold, yea, than much fine gold: sweeter also than honey and the honeycomb.
PSALMS XIX, 9–10, *c.* 150 B.C.

In giving judgment haste is criminal.
PUBLILIUS SYRUS: *Sententiæ, c.* 50 B.C.

All men judge the acts of others by what they would have done themselves.
DIONYSIUS OF HALICARNASSUS: *Antiquities of Rome,* V, *c.* 20 B.C.

The judgment of man is fallible.
OVID: *Fasti,* V, *c.* 5

If you judge, investigate. (Si judicas, cognosce.) SENECA: *Medea, c.* 60

Judge not, that ye be not judged.
MATTHEW VII, 1, *c.* 75

Judge not, and ye shall not be judged: condemn not, and ye shall not be condemned: forgive, and ye shall be forgiven.
LUKE VI, 37, *c.* 75

Then said Paul, I stand at Cæsar's judgment seat, where I ought to be judged.
ACT XXV, 10, *c.* 75

Judge not according to the appearance, but judge righteous judgment.
JOHN VII, 24, *c.* 115

O mortal men, be wary how ye judge.
DANTE: *Paradiso,* XX, *c.* 1320

All general judgments are loose and imperfect.
MICHEL DE MONTAIGNE: *Essays,* III, 1588

A man had need of tough ears to hear himself freely judged. IBID.

Forbear to judge, for we are sinners all.
SHAKESPEARE: *II Henry VI,* III, *c.* 1591

O judgment, thou art fled to brutish beasts,
And men have lost their reason.
SHAKESPEARE: *Julius Cæsar,* III, 1599

Give every man thy ear, but few thy voice;
Take each man's censure, but reserve thy judgment.
SHAKESPEARE: *Hamlet,* I, *c.* 1601

Men's judgments are
A parcel of their fortunes; and things outward
Do draw the inward quality after them,
To suffer all alike.
SHAKESPEARE: *Antony and Cleopatra,* III, *c.* 1606

Men's judgments sway of that side fortune leans.
GEORGE CHAPMAN: *Widow's Tears,* 1612

Every one complains of his memory, and no one complains of his judgment.
LA ROCHEFOUCAULD: *Maxims,* 1665

Sometimes a fool has talent, but never judgment.
IBID.

When we are too young our judgment is weak; when we are too old, ditto.
BLAISE PASCAL: *Pensées,* III, 1670

He that judges without informing himself to the utmost that he is capable, cannot acquit himself of judging amiss.
JOHN LOCKE: *Essay Concerning Human Understanding,* II, 1690

Knowledge is the treasure, but judgment the treasurer of a wise man. He that has more knowledge than judgment is made for another man's use more than his own.
WILLIAM PENN: *Fruits of Solitude,* 1693

'Tis with our judgments as our watches: none
Go just alike, yet each believes his own.
ALEXANDER POPE: *An Essay on Criticism,* I, 1711

Liberty of judgment? No iron chain, or outward force of any kind, could ever compel the soul of a man to believe or to disbelieve: it is his own indefeasible light, that judgment of his; he will reign, and believe there, by the grace of God alone.
THOMAS CARLYLE: *Heroes and Hero-Worship,* IV, 1840 (Lecture in London, May 15)

He hath a good judgment that relieth not wholly on his own.
H. G. BOHN: *Handbook of Proverbs,* 1855

The perceptions of worth and worthlessness are not conclusions of reasoning, but immediate sensations like those of seeing and hearing.
J. A. FROUDE: *Spinoza,* 1855 (Westminster Review)

He has sounded forth the trumpet that shall never call retreat
He is sifting out the hearts of men before His Judgment Seat.
JULIA WARD HOWE: *Battle Hymn of the Republic,* 1861

I dimly guess from blessings known
Of greater out of sight,
And, with the chastened Psalmist, own
His judgments too are right.
J. G. WHITTIER: *The Eternal Goodness,* 1867

No nation is fit to sit in judgment upon any other nation.
WOODROW WILSON: Speech in New York, April 20, 1915

One cool judgment is worth a thousand hasty counsels. The thing to do is to supply light and not heat.
WOODROW WILSON: Speech in Pittsburgh, Jan. 29, 1916

Let the faithful be on their guard against the overrated independence of private judgment and the false autonomy of human reason.
POPE PIUS XI: *Casti connubii,* Dec. 31, 1930

The judgment of God. (Judicium Dei.)
LATIN PHRASE

Judgment should follow the laws, not the precedents. (Judicandum est legibus non exemplis.)
LEGAL MAXIM

[*See also* Affection, Conscience, Enthusiasm, General, Judge, Memory, Mercy, Mote and Beam, Opinion, Opinion (Public), Orator, Peer, People, Policy.

Judgment Day

Therefore be ye also ready: for in such an hour as ye think not the Son of man cometh.
MATTHEW XXIV, 44, *c.* 75

In those days shall men seek death, and shall not find it, and shall desire to die, and death shall flee from them.
REVELATION IX, 6, *c.* 95

Day of wrath. (Dies irae.)
THOMAS OF CELANO: Latin hymn, *c.* 1250

The cuckoo is good for something, in that its appearance gives tidings that Summer is at hand; so the pope serves to show us that the Day of Judgment approaches.
MARTIN LUTHER: *Table-Talk,* CCCCLXI, 1569

I believe that the angels are all up in arms, are putting on their harness, and girding their swords about them. For the Last Judgment draws nigh, and the angels prepare themselves for the combat, and to strike down Turk and pope into the bottomless pit.
MARTIN LUTHER: *Table-Talk,* DLXXIII

The aged earth aghast
With terror of that blast
Shall from the surface to the center shake,
When, at the world's last session,
The dreadful Judge in middle air shall spread
His throne.
JOHN MILTON: *On the Morning of Christ's Nativity,* 1629

God hides from man the reck'ning Day, that he
May fear it ever for uncertainty:
That being ignorant of that one, he may
Expect the coming of it ev'ry day.
ROBERT HERRICK: *Noble Numbers,* 1647

Some hide themselves in caves and delve
In places under ground:
Some rashly leap into the deep,
To escape by being drown'd:
Some to the rocks (O senseless blocks!)
And wooded mountains run,
That there they might this fearful sight,
And dreaded Presence shun.
MICHAEL WIGGLESWORTH: *The Day of Doom,* 1662

A thousand pounds and a bottle of hay
Is all one thing at Doomsday.
JOHN RAY: *English Proverbs,* 1670

When rattling bones together fly
From the four corners of the sky.
JOHN DRYDEN: *Ode to the Memory of Mrs. Anne Killegrew,* 1686

Hark the shrill outcries of the guilty wretches!
Lively bright horror and amazing anguish
Stare thro' their eyelids, while the living worm lies
Gnawing within them.
ISAAC WATTS: *The Day of Judgment,* 1707

Are you ready? Are you ready?
Ready for the Judgment Day?
When the saints and the sinners
Shall be parted right and left —
Are you ready for the Judgment Day?
Anon.: Methodist hymn, *c.* 1800

Yonder comes my Lord,
Bible in His hand,
A crown upon His head;
He's come to judge the world,
The living and the dead;
Looks like Judgment Day.
Anon.: Negro spiritual, *c.* 1840

Till the sun grows cold,
And the stars are old,
And the leaves of the Judgment Book unfold.
BAYARD TAYLOR: *Bedouin Song,* 1855

Under the sod and the dew,
Waiting the Judgment Day;
Under the one the Blue;
Under the other, the Gray.
FRANCIS M. FINCH: *The Blue and the Gray,* 1867

He weren't no saint, but at Jedgment
I'd run my chance with Jim
'Longside of some pious gentlemen
That wouldn't shook hands with him.
JOHN HAY: *Jim Bludso,* 1871

And when the Last Great Bugle Call adown the Hurnai throbs,
And the last grim joke is entered in the big black Book of Jobs,
And Quetta graveyards give again their victims to the air,
I shouldn't like to be the man who sent Jack Barrett there.
RUDYARD KIPLING: *The Story of Uriah,* 1886

God will not look you over for medals, degrees or diplomas, but for scars.
ELBERT HUBBARD: *Roycroft Dictionary and Book of Epigrams,* 1923

One o' these days 'bout twelve o'clock,
This ole worl' gonna reel an' rock;
I'm gonna leave, I'm gonna ride,
Six white horses side by side.
American Negro song, quoted by HOWARD W. ODUM: *Wings On My Feet,* II, 1929

[*See also* Immortality.

Judiciary

There is no liberty if the power of judging be not separated from the legislative and executive powers.
C. L. DE MONTESQUIEU: *The Spirit of the Laws,* IV, 1748

The judicial power of the United States shall be vested in one Supreme Court, and in such inferior courts as the Congress may from time to time ordain and establish.
CONSTITUTION OF THE UNITED STATES, Art. III, 1789

This member of the government was at first considered as the most harmless and helpless of all its organs. But it has proved that the power of declaring what the law is, *ad libitum,* by sapping and mining, slyly, and without alarm, the foundations of the Constitution, can do what open force would not dare to attempt.
THOMAS JEFFERSON: *Letter to Edward Livingston,* 1825

[*See also* Judge, Law.

Jug

I know of nothing uglier than the ordinary jug or pitcher. A museum could be filled with the different kinds of water vessels which are used in hot countries. Yet we continue to submit to the depressing jug with the handle all on one side.
OSCAR WILDE: *House Decoration,* 1882 (Lecture in New York, May 11)

Julep

[*See* Drink.

July

If the first of July be rainy weather,
It will rain, more or less, for four weeks together.
JOHN RAY: *English Proverbs,* 1670

Hot July brings cooling showers,
Apricots and gillyflowers.
SARA COLERIDGE: *Pretty Lessons in Verse,* 1834

The glowing ruby should adorn
Those who in warm July are born,
Then will they be exempt and free
From love's doubt and anxiety.
Author unidentified

[*See also* Bathing, Fly, Months.

July Fourth

That which distinguishes this day from all others is that then both orators and artillerymen shoot blank cartridges.
JOHN BURROUGHS: *Journal,* July 4, 1859

A safe and sane Fourth.
Ascribed by Stevenson to TOM MASSON: *Editorial in Life,* 1896

[*See also* Adams (John), Independence Day.

Jump

Yeesus, what a yump!
Exclamation of a legendary Swedish-American who made a wild leap to board a steamship that was leaving its pier, landed on his head, and on recovering consciousness and looking back found that he was half a mile from shore

June

The leafy month of June.
S. T. COLERIDGE: *The Ancient Mariner,* V, 1798

June brings tulips, lilies, roses,
Fills the children's hands with posies.
SARA COLERIDGE: *Pretty Lessons in Verse,* 1834

It is the month of June,
The month of leaves and roses,
When pleasant sights salute the eyes,
And pleasant scents the noses.
N. P. WILLIS: *The Month of June,* 1844

What is so rare as a day in June?
Then, if ever, come perfect days.
J. R. LOWELL: *The Vision of Sir Launfal,* I, 1848

On a morn in June
When the dew glistens on the pearled ears,
A shiver runs through the deep corn for joy.
MATTHEW ARNOLD: *Sohrab and Rustum,* 1853

Who comes with Summer to this earth
And owes to June her day of birth,
With ring of agate on her hand,
Can health, wealth, and long life command.
Author unidentified

[*See also* Bathing, Brook, Fly, Months.

Jungle

Here are cool mosses deep,
And thro' the moss the ivies creep,
And in the stream the long-leaved flowers weep,
And from the craggy ledge the poppy hangs in sleep.
ALFRED TENNYSON: *The Lotos-Eaters,* 1833

Jupiter

[*See* Gods.

Jurisprudence

The gladsome light of jurisprudence.
EDWARD COKE: *Institutes,* I, 1628

Jurisprudence, in effect, is a special branch of the science of transcendental nonsense.
FELIX S. COHEN: *Transcendental Nonsense and the Functional Approach,* 1935

[*See also* Law.

Jury

He who gives judgment in a case where the law has been violated is that day giving judgment on his own liberties.
AESCHINES: *Ctesiphontem,* 337 B.C.

Are you good men and true?
SHAKESPEARE: *Much Ado About Nothing,* III, *c.* 1598

The jury, passing on the prisoner's life,
May in the sworn twelve have a thief or two
Guiltier than him they try.
SHAKESPEARE: *Measure for Measure,* II, 1604

Then went the jury out, whose names were Mr. Blind-man, Mr. No-good, Mr. Malice, Mr. Love-lust, Mr. Live-loose, Mr. Heady, Mr. High-mind, Mr. Enmity, Mr. Liar, Mr. Cruelty, Mr. Hate-light, and Mr. Implacable, who every one gave in his private verdict against him among themselves, and afterwards unanimously concluded to bring him in guilty before the judge.
JOHN BUNYAN: *Pilgrim's Progress,* I, 1678

The man who laugh'd but once, to see an ass
Mumbling to make the cross-grain'd thistles pass;
Might laugh again, to see a jury chaw
The prickles of an unpalatable law.
JOHN DRYDEN: *The Medal,* 1682

The hungry judges soon the sentence sign,
And wretches hang that jurymen may dine.
ALEXANDER POPE: *The Rape of the Lock,* III, 1712

It is better to toss up cross and pile in a cause than to refer it to a judge whose mind is warped by any motive whatever, in that particular case. But the common sense of twelve honest men gives a still better chance of just decision than the hazard of cross and pile.
THOMAS JEFFERSON: *Notes on Virginia,* 1782

The trial of all crimes, except in cases of impeachment, shall be by jury.
CONSTITUTION OF THE UNITED STATES, Art. III, 1789

In my mind, he was guilty of no error, he was chargeable with no exaggeration, he was betrayed by his fancy into no metaphor, who once said that all we see about us, kings, lords, and commons, the whole machinery of the state, all the apparatus of the system, and its varied workings, end in simply bringing twelve good men into a box.
LORD BROUGHAM: *The Present State of the Law,* 1828

A jury too frequently has at least one member more ready to hang the panel than to hang the traitor.
ABRAHAM LINCOLN: *Letter to Erastus Corning and others,* June 12, 1863

The jury system puts a ban upon intelligence and honesty, and a premium upon ignorance, stupidity and perjury.
S. L. CLEMENS (MARK TWAIN): *Roughing It,* XLVIII, 1872

We, the jury, find our client not guilty.
Verdict of a jury in the Municipal Court at Fort Smith, Ark., in a drunkenness case, Dec. 2, 1933

For racial discrimination to result in the exclusion from jury service of otherwise qualified groups not only violates our Constitution and the laws enacted under it but is at war with our basic concepts of a democratic society and a representative government.
MR. JUSTICE HUGO L. BLACK: *Opinion in Smith* vs. *State of Texas,* Nov. 25, 1940

Jurors are the judges of fact. (Juratores sunt judices facti.) LEGAL MAXIM

[*See also* Judge, Lawsuit, Lawyer, Peer, Trial.

Just

Noah was a just man and perfect in his generations, and Noah walked with God.
GENESIS VI, 9, *c.* 700 B.C.

Heaven gives long life to the just and the intelligent.
CONFUCIUS: *The Book of History,* V, *c.* 500 B.C.

He that ruleth over men must be just.
II SAMUEL XXIII, 3, *c.* 500 B.C.

The path of the just is as the shining light, that shineth more and more unto the perfect day.
PROVERBS IV, 18, *c.* 350 B.C.

The memory of the just is blessed.
PROVERBS X, 7

The tongue of the just is as choice silver.
PROVERBS X, 20

There shall be no evil happen to the just.
PROVERBS XII, 21

The just man walketh in his integrity; his children are blessed after him.
PROVERBS XX, 7

By the just we mean that which is lawful and that which is fair and equitable.
ARISTOTLE: *The Nicomachean Ethics,* V, *c.* 340 B.C.

The just man, first to his purpose, is not to be shaken from his resolve by the fury of a mob laying upon him its impious behests, nor by the frown of a threatening tyrant, nor by the dangers of the ocean, nor by the loud peals of thunder as they rend the sky; even if the universe were to fall in pieces around him, the ruins would strike him undismayed.
HORACE: *Carmina,* III, *c.* 20 B.C.

The spirits of just men made perfect.
HEBREWS XII, 23, *c.* 65

What is against truth cannot be just.
ST. AUGUSTINE: *To Consentius, Against Lying, c.* 400

Thrice is he arm'd that hath his quarrel just.
SHAKESPEARE: *II Henry VI,* III, *c.* 1591

Be just and fear not.
SHAKESPEARE and JOHN FLETCHER: *Henry VIII,* III, 1613

The bad man's death is horror; but the just
Keeps something of his glory in the dust.
WILLIAM HABINGTON: *Elegies,* VIII, 1635

Only the actions of the just
Smell sweet and blossom in the dust.
JAMES SHIRLEY: *The Contention of Ajax and Ulysses,* 1659

Just are the ways of God,
And justifiable to men.
JOHN MILTON: *Samson Agonistes,* 1671

The sweet remembrance of the just
Shall flourish when he sleeps in dust.
NAHUM TATE and NICHOLAS BRADY: *Metrical version of Psalms CXII,* 1696 (Cf. PSALMS CXII, 6: "The righteous shall be in everlasting remembrance")

He who is only just is stern.
VOLTAIRE: *Letter to Frederick the Great,* 1740

We cannot be just if we are not kind-hearted.
LUC DE VAUVENARGUES: *Réflexions,* 1746

Be just before you are generous.
R. B. SHERIDAN: *The School for Scandal,* IV, 1777

The memory of the just survives in Heaven.
WILLIAM WORDSWORTH: *The Excursion,* VII, 1814

Thrice is he armed that hath his quarrel just;
And four times he who gets his fist in fust.
H. W. SHAW (JOSH BILLINGS): *Josh Billings: His Sayings,* 1865 (Cf. SHAKESPEARE, *ante,* 1591)

What is just and honorable. (Quid verum atque decens.) LATIN PHRASE

[*See also* Friendship, Justice, Law.

Justice

None calleth for justice, nor any pleadeth for truth: they trust in vanity, and speak lies; they conceive mischief, and bring forth iniquity. ISAIAH XLIX, 4, *c.* 700 B.C.

Every virtue is included in the idea of justice, and every just man is good.
THEOGNIS: *Elegies, c.* 550 B.C.

There is a point beyond which even justice becomes unjust.
SOPHOCLES: *Electra, c.* 450 B.C.

In a really just cause the weak conquer the strong.
SOPHOCLES: *Œdipus Coloneus, c.* 450 B.C.

Justice is a contract of expediency, entered upon to prevent men harming or being harmed. EPICURUS: *Aphorisms, c.* 300 B.C.

Justice is the crowning glory of the virtues.
CICERO: *De officiis,* I, 78 B.C.

The fundamentals of justice are that no one shall suffer wrong, and that the public good be served. IBID.

The aim of justice is to give everyone his due.
CICERO: *De legibus,* I, *c.* 50 B.C.

Though justice moves slowly, it seldom fails to overtake the wicked.
HORACE: *Carmina,* III, *c.* 20 B.C.

Learn to do justice. (Discite justitiam.)
VERGIL: *Æneid,* VI, 19 B.C.

Justice is the earnest and constant will to render to every man his due. The precepts of the law are these: to live honorably, to injure no other man, to render to every man his due.
The Institutes of Justinian, intro., 533

I have loved justice and hated iniquity; therefore I die an exile.
POPE GREGORY VII: *Last words,* 1085

We will deny justice to none, nor delay it.
MAGNA CARTA, 1215

Justice is a certain rectitude of mind whereby a man does what he ought to do in the circumstances confronting him.
THOMAS AQUINAS: *Summa theologiae,* LXI, *c.* 1265

Let justice be done, though the world perish. (Fiat justitia, et pereat mundus.)
MOTTO of FERDINAND I, HOLY ROMAN EMPEROR (1503–64)

The extremity of justice is extreme injustice.
RICHARD GRAFTON: *Chronicle at Large,* 1568

Use every man after his desert, and who should 'Scape whipping?
SHAKESPEARE: *Hamlet,* II, *c.* 1601

Even-handed justice.
SHAKESPEARE: *Macbeth,* I, *c.* 1605

Plate sins with gold,
And the strong lance of justice hurtless breaks;
Arm it in rags, a pigmy's straw does pierce it.
SHAKESPEARE: *King Lear,* IV, 1606

It is because of justice that man is a god to man and not a wolf.
FRANCIS BACON: *De augmentis scientiarum,* 1623

Justice in her very essence is all strength and activity; and hath a sword put into her hand, to use against all violence and oppression on the earth.
JOHN MILTON: *Eikonoklastes,* XXVIII, 1649

Justice [consists] in taking from no man what is his.
THOMAS HOBBES: *Leviathan,* II, 1651

Justice may wink a while, but see at last.
THOMAS MIDDLETON: *The Mayor of Quinborough,* V, 1651

Love of justice in the generality of men is only the fear of suffering from injustice.
LA ROCHEFOUCAULD: *Maxims,* 1665

Justice is what is established.
BLAISE PASCAL: *Pensées,* VII, 1670

Justice, though she's painted blind,
Is to the weaker side inclined.
SAMUEL BUTLER: *Hudibras,* III, 1678

Justice is lame as well as blind.
THOMAS OTWAY: *Venice Preserved,* I, 1682

Justice, and keeping of contracts, is that which most men seem to agree in.
JOHN LOCKE: *Essay Concerning Human Understanding,* I, 1690

Angry justice shows her awful face,
Where little villains must submit to fate,
That great ones may enjoy the world in state.
SAMUEL GARTH: *The Dispensary,* 1699

Justice is the end of government.
DANIEL DEFOE: *The True-Born Englishman,* II, 1701

Justice is always violent to the party offending, for every man is innocent in his own eyes.
DANIEL DEFOE: *The Shortest Way With Dissenters,* 1702

Justice, with change of interest, learns to bow,
And what was merit once is murder now.
DANIEL DEFOE: *A Hymn to the Pillory,* 1703

We are to look upon all the vast apparatus of our government as having ultimately no other object or purpose but the distribution of justice. Kings and parliaments, fleets and armies, officers of the court and revenue, ambassadors, ministers and privy councillors, are all subordinate in the end to this part of administration. Even the clergy, as their duty leads them to inculcate morality, may justly be thought, so far as regards this world, to have no other useful object of their institution.

DAVID HUME: *Essays, Moral and Political,* I, 1741

To withdraw ourselves from the law of the strong, we have found ourselves obliged to submit to justice. Justice or might, we must choose between these two masters: so little are we made to be free.

LUC DE VAUVENARGUES: *Réflexions,* 1746

There are men whom a happy disposition, a strong desire of glory and esteem, inspire with the same love for justice and virtue which men in general have for riches and honors. . . . But the number of these men is so small that I only mention them in honor of humanity.

C. A. HELVÉTIUS: *De l'esprit,* II, 1758

God aims at satisfying justice in the eternal damnation of sinners.

JONATHAN EDWARDS: *God's Chief End in Creation,* 1765

Justice is the end of government. It is the end of civil society. It ever has been and ever will be pursued until it be obtained, or until liberty be lost in the pursuit.

ALEXANDER HAMILTON: *The Federalist,* 1788

Justice is the great standing policy of civil society; and any eminent departure from it, under any circumstances, lies under the suspicion of being no policy at all.

EDMUND BURKE: *Reflections on the Revolution in France,* I, 1790

Justice is the sum of all moral duty.

WILLIAM GODWIN: *An Enquiry Concerning Political Justice,* 1793

The sword of the law should never fall but on those whose guilt is so apparent as to be pronounced by their friends as well as foes.

THOMAS JEFFERSON: *Letter to Sarah Mease,* March, 1801

I believe that justice is instinct and innate, that the moral sense is as much a part of our constitution as that of feeling, seeing, or hearing.

THOMAS JEFFERSON: *Letter to John Adams,* 1816

In civilized nations, the most arbitrary governments have generally suffered justice to have a free course in private suits.

T. B. MACAULAY: *Hallam,* 1828 (Edinburgh Review, Sept.)

There is no happiness, there is no liberty, there is no enjoyment of life, unless a man can say, when he rises in the morning, I shall be subject to the decision of no unwise judge today.

DANIEL WEBSTER: Speech in New York, March 10, 1831

One man's justice is another's injustice.

R. W. EMERSON: *Circles,* 1841

Justice is truth in action.

JOSEPH JOUBERT: *Pensées,* 1842

Foolish men imagine that because judgment for an evil thing is delayed, there is no justice, but an accidental one, here below. Judgment for an evil thing is many times delayed some day or two, some century or two, but it is sure as life, it is sure as death.

THOMAS CARLYLE: *Past and Present,* I, 1843

Justice is the great interest of man on earth. It is the ligament which holds civilized beings and civilized nations together.

DANIEL WEBSTER: Speech at the funeral of Mr. Justice Story, Sept. 12, 1845

I departed from legality only to return to justice.

NAPOLEON III: Explanation of the *coup d'état* of Dec. 2, 1851

Truth is justice's handmaid, freedom is its child, peace is its companion, safety walks in its steps, victory follows in its train.

Ascribed to SYDNEY SMITH in *A Memoir of the Rev. Sydney Smith* by his daughter, LADY HOLLAND, 1855

Justice is spontaneous respect, mutually guaranteed, for human dignity, in whatever person it may be compromised and under whatever circumstances, and to whatever risk its defense may expose us.

P. J. PROUDHON: *De la justice dans la révolution,* I, 1858

Justice is a faculty that may be developed. This development is what constitutes the education of the human race. IBID.

Liberty, equality — they are bad principles. The only true principle for mankind is justice. H. F. AMIEL: *Journal,* Dec. 4, 1863

Whoever fights, whoever falls,
Justice conquers evermore.

R. W. EMERSON: *Voluntaries,* IV, 1863 (Atlantic Monthly, Oct.)

Judging from the main portions of the history of the world, so far, justice is always in jeopardy.

WALT WHITMAN: *Democratic Vistas,* 1870

That which is above justice must be based on justice, and include justice, and be reached through justice.

HENRY GEORGE: *Social Problems,* IX, 1884

If mankind does not relinquish at once, and forever, its vain, mad, and fatal dream of justice, the world will lapse into barbarism.

GEORGE MOORE: *Confessions of a Young Man,* VIII, 1888

No system of judicature can be suggested in which occasionally failure to insure complete justice may not arise.
MR. JUSTICE HAWKINS: *Judgment in Rex* vs. *Miles,* 1890

To heal the breach between the rich and the poor, it is necessary to distinguish between justice and charity. There can be no claim for redress except where justice is violated.
POPE PIUS X: *Apostolic Letter to the Bishops of Italy on Catholic Social Action,* Dec. 18, 1903

Justice has nothing to do with expediency. It has nothing to do with any temporary standard whatever. It is rooted and grounded in the fundamental instincts of humanity.
WOODROW WILSON: Speech in Washington, Feb. 26, 1916

Justice, though due to the accused, is due to the accuser also. The concept of fairness must not be strained till it is narrowed to a filament. We are to keep the balance true.
MR. JUSTICE B. N. CARDOZO: *Decision in Snyder* vs. *Commonwealth of Massachusetts,* Jan. 8, 1934

There is no such thing as justice – in or out of court.
CLARENCE DARROW: To a newspaper interviewer, April 18, 1936

One hour of justice is worth a hundred of prayer.
ARAB PROVERB

Every man loves justice at another man's expense.
Author unidentified

Justice has a nose of wax.
GERMAN PROVERB

Justice is founded in the rights bestowed by nature upon man. Liberty is maintained in the security of justice.
INSCRIPTION ON THE DEPARTMENT OF JUSTICE BUILDING, Washington

Justice is the queen of virtues. (Justitia virtutum regina.)
LATIN PROVERB

Justice knows neither father nor mother, but concerns itself only with truth. (Justitia non novit patrem nec matrem; solum veritatem spectat.)
LEGAL MAXIM

Let justice be done, though the heavens fall. (Fiat justitia, ruat coelum.)
IBID.

Justice to all. (Justitia omnibus.)
MOTTO OF THE DISTRICT OF COLUMBIA

[*See also* Charity, Credo, Desire, Envy, Equity, Faith, Forbearance, Gold, Golden Rule, Haste, Judge, Kingly, Law, Law (Natural), Lawyer, Liberty, Majority, Mercy, People, Right and Might, Society, Virtue.

Justice and Mercy

He injures the good who spares the bad.
PUBLILIUS SYRUS: *Sententiæ, c.* 50 B.C.

Sparing justice feeds iniquity.
SHAKESPEARE: *The Rape of Lucrece,* 1594

He that's merciful unto the bad is cruel to the good.
THOMAS RANDOLPH: *The Muses' Looking-Glass,* 1636

I shall temper . . . justice with mercy.
JOHN MILTON: *Paradise Lost,* X, 1667

Justice must tame whom mercy cannot win.
GEORGE SAVILE (MARQUESS OF HALIFAX): *On the Death of Charles II,* 1685

Justice, Social

[*See* Exploitation.

K

Kansas

The roosters lay eggs in Kansas.
The roosters lay eggs as big as beer kegs.
And the hair grows on their legs in Kansas.
Anon.: Popular song, *c.* 1880

Kansas is the navel of the nation. Diagonals drawn from Duluth to Galveston, from Washington to San Francisco, from Tallahassee to Olympia, from Sacramento to Augusta, intersect it in its center.
J. J. INGALLS: Speech in the Senate, *c.* 1885

What is the matter with Kansas?
W. A. WHITE: Editorial in the Emporia Gazette, Aug. 15, 1896

Kant, Immanuel (1724–1804)

Kant never read a book in his life. . . . No, none at all; no book whatsoever.
THOMAS DE QUINCEY: *Kant in His Miscellaneous Essays, c.* 1830

Kant became an idiot. And such a man was a contemporary of Goethe!
F. W. NIETZSCHE: *The Antichrist,* XI, 1888

Katharsis

[*See* Tragedy.

Katydid

The katydid works her chromatic reed
On the walnut-tree over the well.
WALT WHITMAN: *Song of Myself,* 1855

Katzenjammer

A hair of the same dog next morning
Is best to quench our fev'rish burning.
EDWARD WARD: *British Wonders,* 1717

Let us have wine and women, mirth and laughter,
Sermons and soda-water the day after.
BYRON: *Don Juan,* II, 1819

[*See also* Drinking, Drunk, Drunkenness.

Keats, John (1795–1821)

It is a better and a wiser thing to be a starved apothecary than a starved poet; so back to the shop, Mr. John, back to "plasters, pills, and ointment boxes," etc. But, for Heaven's sake, young Sangrado, be a little more sparing of extenuatives and soporifics in your practice than you have been in your poetry.
J. G. LOCKHART: *Review of Endymion in Blackwood's,* Aug., 1818

That dirty little blackguard.
BYRON: On Keats, 1820

If I should die I have left no immortal work behind me — nothing to make my friends proud of my memory, — but I have loved the principle of beauty in all things, and if I had had time I would have made myself remembered.
JOHN KEATS: *Letter to Fanny Brawne,* Feb., 1820 (Keats died Feb. 23, 1821)

Where is Keats now? I am anxiously expecting him in Italy, when I shall take care to bestow every attention on him. . . . I am aware, in part, that I am nourishing a rival who will far surpass me, and this is an additional motive, and will be an added pleasure.
P. B. SHELLEY: *Letter to Leigh Hunt,* Nov., 1820

This grave contains all that was mortal of a young English poet, who, on his deathbed, in the bitterness of his heart at the malicious power of his enemies, desired these words to be graven on his tombstone, "Here lies one whose name was writ in water."
EPITAPH OF KEATS ON HIS TOMBSTONE AT ROME, *c.* 1821

One of the noblest specimens of the workmanship of God.
P. B. SHELLEY: *Adonais,* pref., 1821

The kind of man that Keats was gets ever more horrible to me.
THOMAS CARLYLE: *Diary,* 1848

[*See also* Name.

Keeper

Am I my brother's keeper?
GENESIS IV, 9, *c.* 700 B.C.

Kentuckian

Great, tall, raw-boned Kentuckians, attired in hunting-shirts, and trailing their loose joints over a vast extent of territory, with the easy lounge peculiar to the race.
HARRIET BEECHER STOWE: *Uncle Tom's Cabin,* XI, 1852

Kentucky

It is a Kentucky of a place.
Description of Heaven by a Kentucky preacher, *c.* 1840

My old Kentucky home.
S. C. FOSTER: Title of a song, 1853

[*See also* Home, Lincoln (Abraham).

Kepler, Johann (1571–1630)

Galileo was a great genius, and so was Newton; but it would take two or three Galileos and Newtons to make one Kepler.
S. T. COLERIDGE: *Table-Talk,* Oct. 8, 1830

Kettle

[*See* Recrimination.

Kibitzer

He that sits to work in the market-place shall have many teachers.
THOMAS FULLER: *Gnomologia,* 1732

[*See also* Spectator.

Kick

It is hard for thee to kick against the pricks.
ACTS IX, 5, *c.* 75 (Cf. XXVI, 14)

It is contrary to decency and to Christian mildness to kick any one, no matter who it may be.
ST. JOHN BAPTIST DE LA SALLE: *The Rules of Christian Manners and Civility,* I, 1695

A kick that scarce would move a horse,
May kill a sound divine.
WILLIAM COWPER: *Yearly Distress, c.* 1790

Kid

He shall sacrifice one kid of the goats for a sin offering.
LEVITICUS XXIII, 19, *c.* 700 B.C. (Cf. NUMBERS VII, 16, 22 and 28, *c.* 700 B.C.)

A piece of a kid is worth two of a cat.
JOHN HEYWOOD: *Proverbs,* 1546

Where the dam leaps over the kid follows.
THOMAS FULLER: *Gnomologia,* 1732

[*See also* Merriment, Milk.

Kidnaping

He that stealeth a man, and selleth him, or if he be found in his hand, he shall surely be put to death.
EXODUS XXI, 16, *c.* 700 B.C.

Kidney

A man of my kidney.
SHAKESPEARE: *The Merry Wives of Windsor,* III, *c.* 1600

Killing

[*See* Murder.

Kindness

Kindness begets kindness.
SOPHOCLES: *Ajax, c.* 450 B.C.

In her tongue is the law of kindness.
PROVERBS XXXI, 26, *c.* 350 B.C.

Wherever there is a human being there is a chance for a kindness.
SENECA: *Thyestes, c.* 60

Who is a stranger to those who have the habit of speaking kindly?
The Hitopadesa, II, *c.* 500

A little more than kin, and less than kind.
SHAKESPEARE: *Hamlet,* I, *c.* 1601

A woman killed with kindness.
THOMAS HEYWOOD: Title of a play, 1603 ("To kill a wife with kindness" is in SHAKESPEARE: *The Taming of the Shrew,* IV, 1594)

Kindness in women, not their beauteous looks,
Shall win my love.
SHAKESPEARE: *The Taming of the Shrew,* IV, 1594

The milk of human kindness.
SHAKESPEARE: *Macbeth,* I, *c.* 1605

The unkindest beast [is] more kinder than mankind.
SHAKESPEARE: *Timon of Athens,* IV, *c.* 1607

Kind hearts are soonest wronged.
NICHOLAS BRETON: *Crossing of Proverbs,* 1616

Kindness is lost that's bestowed on children and old folks.
JOHN CLARKE: *Parœmiologia Anglo-Latina,* 1639

The more kindness we heap upon one who hates us, the more we arm him to betray us.
PIERRE CORNEILLE: *Cinna,* I, 1639

A kindness of which one is reminded always seems a reproach.
JEAN RACINE: *Iphigénie,* IV, 1674

Kind as kings upon their coronation day.
JOHN DRYDEN: *The Hind and the Panther,* I, 1687

Who does a kindness is not therefore kind;
Perhaps prosperity becalm'd his breast;
Perhaps the wind just shifted from the East.
ALEXANDER POPE: *Moral Essays,* II (Of the Knowledge and Characters of Men), 1733

Obscurely wise and coarsely kind.
SAMUEL JOHNSON: *On the Death of Robert Levet,* 1783

We'll take a cup o' kindness yet
For auld lang syne.
ROBERT BURNS: *Auld Lang Syne,* 1788 (Based on an old Scotch song, and first found in a letter to Mrs. Dunlop, Dec. 17)

That best portion of a good man's life, —
His little, nameless, unremembered acts
Of kindness.
WILLIAM WORDSWORTH: *Tintern Abbey,* 1798

A part of kindness consists in loving people more than they deserve.
JOSEPH JOUBERT: *Pensées,* 1842

Kind hearts are more than coronets,
And simple faith than Norman blood.
ALFRED TENNYSON: *Lady Clara Vere de Vere,* 1842

Little deeds of kindness, little words of love,
Help to make earth happy like the Heaven above.
JULIA A. F. CARNEY: *Little Things,* 1845

Kindness is very indigestible. It disagrees with very proud stomachs.
W. M. THACKERAY: *The Adventures of Philip,* II, 1862

One can always be kind to people one cares nothing about.
OSCAR WILDE: *The Picture of Dorian Gray,* 1891

I expect to pass through this world but once. Any good therefore that I can do, or any kindness that I can show to any fellow creature, let me do it now. Let me not defer or neglect it, for I shall not pass this way again.
Author unidentified

Kindness is a language the deaf can hear and the dumb can understand.
IBID.

Father and mother are kind, but God is kinder.
DANISH PROVERB

Kindness grows old fast.
FRENCH PROVERB

Kindness is the beginning and the end of the law.
HEBREW PROVERB

He who does kindly deeds becomes rich.
HINDU PROVERB

One kind word can warm three Winter months.
JAPANESE PROVERB

The gardens of kindness never fade.
MODERN GREEK PROVERB

God is merciful to those who are kind.
MOROCCAN PROVERB

A kind word is better than a big pie.
RUSSIAN PROVERB

Kindness is like cress-seed; it grows fast.
SCOTTISH PROVERB

Kindness will creep where it canna gang.
IBID. (*Gang*=go)

Always repay kindness with even more kindness.
WELSH PROVERB

[*See also* Just, Violence, Virtue.

King

Kings are happy in many things, but mainly in this: that they can do and say whatever they please.
SOPHOCLES: *Antigone, c.* 450 B.C.

God save the king.
I SAMUEL X, 24, *c.* 500 B.C. (In the Vulgate it appears as "Vivat rex" — May the king live)

The wrath of a king is as messengers of death.
PROVERBS XVI, 14, *c.* 350 B.C.

Is it fit to say to the king, Thou art wicked?
JOB XXXIV, 18, *c.* 325 B.C.

Better is a poor and a wise child than an old and foolish king, who will no more be admonished.
ECCLESIASTES IV, 13, *c.* 200 B.C.

The first art that a king must learn is to endure envy. SENECA: *Hercules Furens, c.* 50

Fear God. Honor the king.
I PETER II, 17, *c.* 60

A king is one who fears nothing and desires nothing. SENECA: *Thyestes, c.* 60

It is the lot of a king to do well and be ill spoken of.
MARCUS AURELIUS: *Meditations,* VII, *c.* 170

I am not an actor; I am not a singer; I am not a mountebank; I am not a courtesan. What, then, have I to do in the palaces of kings?
BHARTRIHARI: *The Vairagya Sataka, c.* 625

An illiterate king is a crowned donkey.
Ascribed to FOULQUES II, COUNT OF ANJOU (*c.* 890–958)

The king is dead, long live the king! (Le roi est mort, vive le roi!)
Form of proclamation on the death of a French king, first used on the death of Charles VII, 1461

A king is appointed to protect his subjects in their lives, properties and laws. For this purpose he has a delegation of power from the people, and he has no just claim to any other power.
JOHN FORTESQUE: *De laudibus legum Angliae, c.* 1462

Good king, avaricious king. (Bon roi, roi avare.)
Ascribed to LOUIS XII of France (1462–1515)

The strange lustre that surrounds a king conceals and shrouds him from us.
MICHEL DE MONTAIGNE: *Essays,* III, 1588

It is preposterous and most unlawful to condemn a king if not found guilty by a jury of kings.
Anon.: *A Brief Discourse in Praise of King Richard the Third, c.* 1590

Let us sit upon the ground
And tell sad stories of the death of kings:
How some have been depos'd, some slain in war,
Some haunted by the ghosts they have depos'd.
Some poison'd by their wives, some sleeping kill'd,
All murder'd.
SHAKESPEARE: *Richard II,* III, *c.* 1596

The dread and fear of kings.
SHAKESPEARE: *The Merchant of Venice,* IV, *c.* 1597

It is atheism and blasphemy to dispute what God can do; good Christians content themselves with His will revealed in His Word; so it is presumption and contempt to dispute what a king can do, or say that a king cannot do this or that.
JAMES I of England: *Basilikon Doron,* 1599

What infinite heart's ease
Must kings neglect that private men enjoy!
And what have kings that privates have not too,
Save ceremony, save general ceremony?
SHAKESPEARE: *Henry V,* IV, *c.* 1599

A king of shreds and patches.
SHAKESPEARE: *Hamlet,* III, *c.* 1601

There's such divinity doth hedge a king,
That treason can but peep to what it would.
SHAKESPEARE: *Hamlet,* IV

The king's a beggar, now the play is done.
SHAKESPEARE: *All's Well that Ends Well,* epilogue, *c.* 1602

A king's a king, do fortune what she can.
MICHAEL DRAYTON: *The Barons' Wars,* V, 1603

The king-becoming graces,
As justice, verity, temperance, stableness,
Bounty, perseverance, mercy, lowliness,
Devotion, patience, courage, fortitude,
I have no relish of them.
SHAKESPEARE: *Macbeth,* IV, *c.* 1605

The king reigns, but does not govern. (Rex regnat, sed non gubernat.)
JAN ZAMOJSKI: Speech in the Polish parliament, June, 1605 (The reference is to Sigismund III of Poland and Sweden, who had tried, against the opposition of Zamojski, to introduce legislation by majority vote in the Polish parliament)

Ay, every inch a king.
SHAKESPEARE: *King Lear,* IV, 1606

All kings that are not tyrants, or perjured, will be glad to bound themselves within the limits of their laws. And they that persuade them the contrary are vipers and pests both against them and the commonwealth.
JAMES I of England: Speech to Parliament, 1609

Alas, what are we kings?
Why do you gods place us above the rest,
To be serv'd, flatter'd, and ador'd, till we
Believe we hold within our hands your thunder?
And when we come to try the power we have,
There's not a leaf shakes at our threat'nings.
BEAUMONT and FLETCHER: *Philaster,* IV, 1611

Thou traitor, that dar'st confine thy king to things
Possible and honest! IBID.

Had I but served my God with half the zeal
I served my king, he would not in mine age
Have left me naked to mine enemies.
SHAKESPEARE and JOHN FLETCHER: *Henry VIII*, III, 1613

It is a miserable state of mind to have few things to desire and many things to fear, and yet that commonly is the case of kings.
FRANCIS BACON: *Essays*, XIX, 1625

Kings and bears oft worry their keepers.
DAVID FERGUSSON: *Scottish Proverbs*, 1641

There is a quadrobulary saying which passes current in the Western world, that the [Holy Roman] emperor is king of kings; the Spaniard, king of men; the French, king of asses; the king of England, king of devils.
NATHANIEL WARD: *The Simple Cobbler of Aggawam*, 1646

If wars go well, each for a part lays claim:
If ill, then kings, not soldiers, bear the blame.
ROBERT HERRICK: *Hesperides*, 1648

It is not, neither ought to be, the glory of a Protestant state, never to have put their king to death; it is the glory of a Protestant king never to have deserved death.
JOHN MILTON: *The Tenure of Kings and Magistrates*, 1649

The king's cheese goes half away in parings.
JAMES HOWELL: *Proverbs*, 1659

It is impossible for the king to have things done as cheap as other men.
SAMUEL PEPYS: *Diary*, July 21, 1662

Who finds himself unhappy is not being a king, except a king dethroned.
BLAISE PASCAL: *Pensées*, II, 1670

He that eats the king's goose shall be choked with the feathers.
JOHN RAY: *English Proverbs*, 1670

In a monarchy the king must by necessity be above the laws.
ROBERT FILMER: *Patriarcha*, 1680

The people have a right supreme
To make their kings; for kings are made for them.
JOHN DRYDEN: *Absalom and Achitophel*, I, 1682

A king is a thing men have made for their own sakes, for quietness' sake.
JOHN SELDEN: *Table-Talk*, 1689

The king can do no wrong. IBID.

Titles are shadows; crowns are empty things;
The good of subjects is the end of kings.
DANIEL DEFOE: *The True-Born Englishman*, II, 1701

Kings are commonly said to have long hands;
I wish they had as long ears.
JONATHAN SWIFT: *Thoughts on Various Subjects*, 1706

What is a king? — a man condemn'd to bear
The public burthen of the nation's care;
From the first blooming of his ill-taught youth,
Nourish'd in flattery, and estrang'd from truth.
MATTHEW PRIOR: *Solomon on the Vanity of the World*, 1718

Nothing resembles a man more than a king.
Ascribed to CHARLES XII of Sweden (1682–1718)

Sail, quoth the king; hold, quoth the wind.
JAMES KELLY: *Complete Collection of Scottish Proverbs*, 1721

God save our gracious king,
Long live our noble king,
God save the king.
HENRY CAREY: *God Save the King*, 1740 (Cf. I SAMUEL, *ante*, *c.* 500 B.C.)

All the kings of the earth, before God, are as grasshoppers; they are nothing, and less than nothing: both their love and their hatred is to be despised.
JONATHAN EDWARDS: *Sinners in the Hands of an Angry God*, 1741 (Sermon, July 8)

May you, may Cam and Isis preach it long:
"The right divine of kings to govern wrong."
ALEXANDER POPE: *The Dunciad*, IV, 1742

The first king was a fortunate soldier.
VOLTAIRE: *Mérope*, I, 1743

Let us strangle the last king with the guts of the last priest.
DENIS DIDEROT: *Dithyrambe sur la fête de rois*, *c.* 1750

The king was in his counting-house,
Counting out his money;
The queen was in the parlor,
Eating bread and honey.
Anon.: *Nursery rhyme*, *c.* 1750

The more happy I am, the more I pity kings.
VOLTAIRE: *Letter to Lord Keith*, Oct. 4, 1759

That the king can do no wrong is a necessary and fundamental principle of the English constitution.
WILLIAM BLACKSTONE: *Commentaries on the Laws of England*, III, 1765 (Cf. SELDEN, *ante*, 1689)

The king never dies.
WILLIAM BLACKSTONE: *Commentaries on the Laws of England*, IV

Good kings are slaves and their subjects are free.
Ascribed to MARIE of France (1703–68)

He is a good king that preserves his people.
HORACE WALPOLE: *Letter to William Mason*, July 4, 1778

A king ought never fall from his throne save when the throne itself falls.

VITTORIO ALFIERI: *Polinice*, I, 1780

Kings are naturally lovers of low company.

EDMUND BURKE: Speech in the House of Commons, Feb. 11, 1780

There is no king who, with sufficient force, is not always ready to make himself absolute.

THOMAS JEFFERSON: *Letter to George Wythe*, 1786

No race of kings has ever presented above one man of common sense in twenty generations.

THOMAS JEFFERSON: *Letter to Benjamin Hawkins*, 1787

If any of our countrymen wish for a king, give them Æsop's fable of the frogs who asked a king; if this does not cure them, send them to Europe. They will come back good republicans.

THOMAS JEFFERSON: *Letter to David Ramsay*, 1787

There is not a crowned head in Europe whose talents or merits would entitle him to be elected a vestryman by the people of any parish in America.

THOMAS JEFFERSON: *Letter to George Washington*, 1788

Kings will be tyrants from policy when subjects are rebels from principle.

EDMUND BURKE: *Reflections on the Revolution in France*, 1790

Kings are in the moral order what monsters are in the natural.

HENRI GREGOIRE: Speech to the French National Convention, Sept. 21, 1792

The king can do no wrong; he cannot constitutionally be supposed capable of injustice.

MR. JUSTICE JOHN NICHOLL: *Judgment in the case of the goods of King George III, deceased, 1822* (Cf. SELDEN, *ante*, 1689)

Kings are like stars — they rise and set, they have
The worship of the world, but no repose.

P. B. SHELLEY: *Hellas*, 1822

That which is called firmness in a king is called obstinacy in a donkey.

Ascribed to THOMAS ERSKINE (1750–1823)

A king should die standing.

LOUIS XVIII of France: On his deathbed, 1824

The king is the least independent man in his dominions.

J. C. and A. W. HARE: *Guesses at Truth*, 1827

Every attorney's clerk and every forward schoolboy on an upper form knows that, by a fundamental maxim of our policy, the king can do no wrong; that every court is bound to suppose his conduct and his sentiments to be, on every occasion such as they ought to be; and that no evidence can be received for the purpose of setting aside this loyal and salutary presumption.

H. B. MACAULAY: *Hallam*, 1828 (Edinburgh Review, Sept.)

King is Kön-ning, Kan-ning, man that knows or cans.

THOMAS CARLYLE: *Heroes and Hero-Worship*, I, 1840 (Lecture in London, May 5)

Strip your Louis Quatorze of his king-gear, and there is left nothing but a poor forked radish with a head fantastically carved.

THOMAS CARLYLE: *Heroes and Hero-Worship*, V, 1840 (Lecture in London, May 19)

When a Parisian of the Seventeenth Century was told that there was no king in Venice he could not get over his astonishment and thought he would die of laughing.

P. J. PROUDHON: *Qu'est-ce que la propriété?*, 1840

Kings are for nations in their swaddling clothes.

VICTOR HUGO: Speech in the French Constituent Assembly, 1848

It is the misfortune of kings that they will not hear the truth.

JOHANN JACOBY: To King Friedrich Wilhelm IV of Prussia, Nov. 2, 1848

A king promises, but observes only when he pleases.

H. G. BOHN: *Handbook of Proverbs*, 1855

God said, I am tired of kings,
I suffer them no more;
Up to my ear the morning brings
The outrage of the poor.

R. W. EMERSON: *Boston Hymn*, 1863 (Read in Music Hall, Boston, Jan. 1)

Under kings women govern, but under queens, men.

J. S. MILL: *The Subjection of Women*, III, 1869 (Quoted as "a bad joke")

Kings is mostly rapscallions.

S. L. CLEMENS (MARK TWAIN): *Huckleberry Finn*, XXIII, 1884

Everyone is born a king, and most people die in exile.

OSCAR WILDE: *A Woman of No Importance*, III, 1893

An honest king's the noblest work of God.

EDMUND BLUNDEN: *Elegy on King George V of England*, 1936

A good king is better than an old law.

DANISH PROVERB

A king gets blamed before he does any wrong, and is praised before he does any good.

FINNISH PROVERB

The king (or the queen) wills it. (Le roi (or la reine) le veult.)
Form of royal assent, in England, to bills passed by Parliament

Today a king, tomorrow nothing.
FRENCH PROVERB

Kings have long arms. GREEK PROVERB

The king cannot deceive or be deceived. (Rex non potest fallere nec falli.)
LATIN PROVERB

The king can do nothing save what he may do by law. (Nihil potest rex nisi quod de jure potest.) LEGAL MAXIM

The king can do no wrong. (Rex non potest peccare.)
LEGAL MAXIM (Cf. SELDEN, *ante*, 1689, and BLACKSTONE, 1765)

The king never dies. (Rex nunquam moritur.)
LEGAL MAXIM (Cf. BLACKSTONE, *ante*, 1765)

It is kingly to do good and to be spoken of evilly. (Bene facere et male audire regium est.)
Motto on the Town Hall of Zittau, Saxony

If the king says at noonday, "It is night," the wise man says, "Behold the stars!"
PERSIAN PROVERB

What the king commands is obeyed, but not executed. SPANISH PROVERB

[*See also* Abdication, Advice, Ague, American, Ancestry, Assassination, Attack, Bishop, Blind, Cannon, Cat, Citizen, Dirt, Dust, Eminence, Freedom, Gods, Good and Evil, Grammar, Heaven and Hell, Kingly, Law, Legislature, Lese-Majesty, Like, Lying, Monarchy, Music, Must, Peace, Philosopher, Punctuality, Queen, Right (Divine), Soldier, Sovereign, Subject, Theft, Throne, Tyrant, War.

King Cole

Old King Cole was a merry old soul,
And a merry old soul was he;
He called for his pipe
And he called for his bowl
And he called for his fiddlers three.
Anon.: *Nursery rhyme, c.* 1750

Kingdom

My kingdom is not of this world.
JOHN XIX, 36, *c.* 115

[*See also* Injustice.

Kipling, Rudyard (1865–1936)

When the Rudyards cease from Kipling
And the Haggards ride no more.
J. K. STEPHEN: *Lapsus Calami*, 1891

Kirk

[*See* Church.

Kiss

So she caught him, and kissed him.
PROVERBS VII, 13, *c.* 350 B.C.

The kisses of an enemy are deceitful.
PROVERBS XXVII, 6

Greet all the brethren with a holy kiss.
I THESSALONIANS V, 26, *c.* 51

Judas, one of the twelve, . . . drew near Jesus to kiss him. But Jesus said unto him, Judas, betrayest thou the Son of man with a kiss?
LUKE XXII, 47–48, *c.* 75

He who kisses you, Philaenis, sins against nature.
MARTIAL: *Epigrams*, II, 86 (Philaenis was bald and one-eyed)

Teach not thy lips such scorn; for they were made
For kissing, lady, not for such contempt.
SHAKESPEARE: *Richard III*, I, *c.* 1592

Their lips were four red roses on a stalk,
Which in their Summer beauty kiss'd each other.
SHAKESPEARE: *Richard III*, IV

Ten kisses short as one, one long as twenty.
SHAKESPEARE: *Venus and Adonis*, I, 1593

He took the bride about the neck
And kiss'd her lips with such a clamorous smack
That at the parting, all the church did echo.
SHAKESPEARE: *The Taming of the Shrew*, III, 1594

Upon thy cheek lay I this zealous kiss,
As seal to this indenture of my love.
SHAKESPEARE: *King John*, II, *c.* 1596

It is not a fashion for the maids in France to kiss before they are married.
SHAKESPEARE: *Henry V*, V, *c.* 1599

Were kisses all the joys in bed,
One woman would another wed.
SHAKESPEARE (?): *The Passionate Pilgrim*, 1599

His kissing is as full of sanctity as the touch of holy bread.
SHAKESPEARE: *As You Like It*, III, *c.* 1600

Sweet Helen, make me immortal with a kiss.
CHRISTOPHER MARLOWE: *Dr. Faustus*, XIV, 1604

[He] kiss me hard,
As if he pluck'd up kisses by the roots,
That grew upon my lips.
SHAKESPEARE: *Othello*, III, 1604

Kissing goes by favor.
ENGLISH PROVERB, traced by Apperson to 1605

We have kiss'd away
Kingdoms and provinces.
SHAKESPEARE: *Antony and Cleopatra*, III, *c.* 1606

The slowest kiss makes too much haste.
THOMAS MIDDLETON: *A Chaste Maid in Cheapside*, IV, *c.* 1607

A kiss,
Long as my exile, sweet as my revenge.
SHAKESPEARE: *Coriolanus*, V, *c.* 1607

Graze on my lips, and when those mounts are dry,
Stray lower, where the pleasant fountains lie.
GERVASE MARKHAM and LEWIS MACHIN: *The Dumb Knight*, 1608

Kiss till the cows come home.
BEAUMONT and FLETCHER: *The Scornful Lady*, II, 1610

Brothers and sisters lawfully may kiss.
BEAUMONT and FLETCHER: *A King and No King*, IV, 1611

Kissing with inside lip.
SHAKESPEARE: *The Winter's Tale*, I, *c.* 1611

Wanton kisses are the keys of sin.
NICHOLAS BRETON: *Crossing of Proverbs*, 1616

Drink to me only with thine eyes
And I will pledge with mine.
Or leave a kiss but in the cup,
And I'll not look for wine.
BEN JONSON: *To Celia*, 1616

These poor half-kisses kill me quite.
MICHAEL DRAYTON: *To His Coy Love*, 1631

After kissing comes more kindness.
JOHN CLARKE: *Parœmiologia Anglo-Latina*, 1639

Free of her lips, free of her hips.
JOHN RAY: *English Proverbs*, 1640

Anthea bade me tie her shoe;
I did, and kissed the instep too;
And would have kissed unto her knee,
Had not her blush rebuked me.
ROBERT HERRICK: *Hesperides*, 1648

Give me a kiss, and to that kiss a score;
Then to that twenty, add a hundred more;
A thousand to that hundred; so kiss on,
To make that thousand up a million;
Treble that million, and when that is done,
Let's kiss afresh, as when we first begun.
IBID.

What is a kiss? Why this, as some approve:
The sure sweet cement, glue, and lime of love.
IBID.

He is a fool that kisseth the maid when he may kiss the mistress.
JAMES HOWELL: *Proverbs*, 1659

Who would refuse to kiss a lapdog, if it were preliminary to the lips of his lady?
WILLIAM CONGREVE: *The Old Bachelor*, I, 1693

You must not kiss and tell.
WILLIAM CONGREVE: *Love for Love*, II, 1695

A chuck under the chin is worth two kisses.
JONATHAN SWIFT: *Polite Conversation*, I, 1738

I had rather give a knave a kiss, for once, than be troubled with him.
IBID.

Lord! I wonder what fool it was that first invented kissing.
JONATHAN SWIFT: *Polite Conversation*, II

Those who can number their kisses
Will always with few be content.
C. H. WILLIAMS: *On Lady Ilchester's Asking Lord Ilchester How Many Kisses He Would Have*, 1740

Do thou snatch treasures from my lips,
And I'll take kingdoms back from thine.
R. B. SHERIDAN: *The Duenna*, III, 1775

I am just two and two, I am warm, I am cold,
And the parent of numbers that cannot be told;
I am lawful, unlawful – a duty, a fault;
I am often sold dear, good for nothing when bought,
An extraordinary boon, and a matter of course,
And yielded with pleasure – when taken by force.
WILLIAM COWPER: *Riddle in a letter to John Newton*, July 30, 1780

I'll kiss thee yet, yet,
And I'll kiss thee o'er again,
And I'll kiss thee yet, yet,
My bonnie Peggy Alison!
ROBERT BURNS: *Bonnie Peggy Alison*, 1788

Gin a body meet a body
Comin' through the rye,
Gin a body kiss a body,
Need a body cry?
ROBERT BURNS: *Comin' Through the Rye*, *c.* 1792

Come, lay thy head upon my breast,
And I will kiss thee into rest.
BYRON: *The Bride of Abydos*, I, 1813

A long, long kiss, – a kiss of youth and love.
BYRON: *Don Juan*, II, 1819

She took me to her elfin grot,
And there she wept, and sigh'd full sore,
And there I shut her wild, wild eyes
With kisses four.
JOHN KEATS: *La Belle Dame Sans Merci*, 1819

The sunlight clasps the earth
And the moonbeams kiss the sea:
What are all these kissings worth
If thou kiss not me?
P. B. SHELLEY: *Love's Philosophy*, 1819

Soul meets soul on lovers' lips.
P. B. SHELLEY: *Prometheus Unbound*, II, 1820

What lies lurk in kisses!
HEINRICH HEINE: *In den Küssen, welche Lüge*, 1827

The maiden who ventures to kiss a sleeping man wins of him a pair of gloves.
WALTER SCOTT: *The Fair Maid of Perth*, V, 1828

Jenny kissed me when we met,
 Jumping from the chair she sat in;
Time, you thief, who love to get
 Sweets into your list, put that in.
Say I'm weary, say I'm sad,
 Say that health and wealth have missed me;
Say I'm growing old, but add
 Jenny kissed me.
LEIGH HUNT: *Jenny Kissed Me*, 1838

Our spirits rushed together at the touching of the lips.
ALFRED TENNYSON: *Locksley Hall*, 1842

The kiss is nestling on my lip —
 The last, my love, you gave me;
And dying thus, the doctors say,
 Another kiss might save me.
Anon.: Favorite album verses, *c*. 1845

Dear as remember'd kisses after death,
And sweet as those by hopeless fancy feign'd.
ALFRED TENNYSON: *The Princess*, IV, 1847

First time he kiss'd me, he but only kiss'd
The fingers of this hand wherewith I write;
And ever since it grew more clean and white.
E. B. BROWNING: *Sonnets from the Portuguese*, 1847

Do not make me kiss, and you will not make me sin.
H. G. BOHN: *Handbook of Proverbs*, 1855

The sound of a kiss is not so loud as that of cannon, but its echo lasts a great deal longer.
O. W. HOLMES: *The Professor at the Breakfast Table*, XI, 1859

The waste wedlock of a sterile kiss.
A. C. SWINBURNE: *Hermaphroditus*, 1863

 Her neck,
Kissed over close, wears yet a purple speck,
 Wherein the pained blood falters and goes out;
Soft, and stung softly — fairer for a fleck.
A. C. SWINBURNE: *Laus Veneris*, 1866

Rose kissed me today,
 Will she kiss me tomorrow?
Let it be as it may,
Rose kissed me today.
AUSTIN DOBSON: *A Kiss*, 1873

A tender, sensitive young female tells how she felt when first he kissed her — like a tub of roses swimming in honey, cologne, nutmeg, and blackberries.
S. S. COX: *Why We Laugh*, IV, 1876

The woman that cries hush bids kiss:
 I learnt
So much of her that taught me kissing.
A. C. SWINBURNE: *Marino Faliero*, I, 1885

Plucky lot she cared for idols when I kissed her where she stud!
RUDYARD KIPLING: *Mandalay*, 1890

A kiss is now attestedly a quite innocuous performance, with nothing very fearful about it one way or the other. It even has its pleasant side.
JAMES BRANCH CABELL: *Jurgen*, XIV, 1919

I kiss the [your] hand, gracious lady. (Küss die Hand, gnädige Frau.)
AUSTRIAN SALUTATION

Some women blush when they are kissed; some call for the police; some swear; some bite. But the worst are those who laugh.
Author unidentified

When the girl you kiss gives as good as you give, you are not getting firsts. IBID.

The kiss of Judas.
ENGLISH PHRASE, based on LUKE XXII, 47–48, *ante*, *c*. 75

No one can object to an honorable kiss.
GERMAN PROVERB

A kiss is worth nothing until it's divided between two. GYPSY PROVERB

When a knave kisses you count your teeth.
HEBREW PROVERB

A kiss and a drink o' water mak but a wersh breakfast.
SCOTTISH PROVERB (*Wersh*=tasteless)

Kiss and be kind; the fiddler is blind. IBID.

[*See also* Aunt, Bachelor, Bride, Drinking, Frenchwoman, Hair, Learning, Lisp.

Kitchen

The taste of the kitchen is better than the smell.
THOMAS FULLER: *Gnomologia*, 1732

He who would not lose his appetite should not go into the kitchen. GERMAN PROVERB

[*See also* Cookery.

Kitten

Do you see that kitten chasing so prettily her own tail? If you could look with her eyes, you might see her surrounded with hundreds of figures performing complex dramas, with tragic and comic issues, long conversations, many characters, many ups and downs of fate. R. W. EMERSON: *Experience*, 1841

[*See also* Cat, Diet, Merriment.

Knave

More knave than fool.
CHRISTOPHER MARLOWE: *The Jew of Malta*, I, *c*. 1590

A whoreson, beetle-headed, flap-ear'd knave!
SHAKESPEARE: *The Taming of the Shrew*, IV, 1594

We are arrant knaves all.
SHAKESPEARE: *Hamlet*, III, c. 1601

A poor, decayed, ingenious, foolish, rascally knave.
SHAKESPEARE: *All's Well that Ends Well*, IV, c. 1602

A slippery and subtle knave; a finder of occasions, that has an eye can stamp and counterfeit advantages, though true advantage never present itself: a devilish knave!
SHAKESPEARE: *Othello*, II, 1604

A knave; a rascal; an eater of broken meats; a base, proud, shallow, beggarly, three-suited, hundred-pound, filthy, worsted-stocking knave. SHAKESPEARE: *King Lear*, II, 1606

When knaves fall out, true men come by their own. JOHN RAY: *English Proverbs*, 1670

Every knave has a fool in his sleeve.
SAMUEL PALMER: *Moral Essays on Proverbs*, 1710

Let a knave propose to deceive men, and he will never lack dupes.
FREDERICK THE GREAT: *Letter to Voltaire*, June 29, 1771

The first of the nine orders of knaves is he that tells his errand before he goes it.
H. G. BOHN: *Handbook of Proverbs*, 1855

He is no small knave who knows a great one.
DANISH PROVERB

There's naething sae like an honest man as an arrant knave. SCOTTISH PROVERB

[*See also* Coward, Family, Laughter, Learning, Man.

Knee

Up to the knee is free. (Bis an d'Kni ist fri.)
LOW GERMAN PROVERB

[*See also* Cold, Dog.

Kneeling

[Jesus] kneeled down, and prayed.
LUKE XXII, 41, *c.* 75 (Cf. ACTS VII, 60; IX, 46; XX, 36, *c.* 75)

Knight

He was a very parfit gentle knight.
GEOFFREY CHAUCER: *The Canterbury Tales*, prologue, *c.* 1386

Knight without fear and without reproach. (Chevalier sans peur et sans reproche.)
Applied to the Chevalier Pierre du Terrail Bayard (1476–1524)

What knight-errant ever paid custom, poll-tax, subsidy, quit-rent, porterage or ferry-boat? What tailor ever brought him a bill for making his clothes? What governor, that lodged him in his castle, ever made him pay a reckoning? What king did not seat him at his table? What damsel was not in love with him and did not yield herself up to his whole pleasure and will?
CERVANTES: *Don Quixote*, I, 1605

You shall hardly see a fool upon the stage, but he's a knight.
WILLIAM WYCHERLEY: *The Country Wife*, III, *c.* 1673

So faithful in love, and so dauntless in war,
There never was knight like the youth Lochinvar. WALTER SCOTT: *Marmion*, V, 1808

[*See also* Blaine (James G.), Chivalry.

Knock

Knock, and it shall be opened unto you.
MATTHEW VII, 7, *c.* 75 (Cf. LUKE XI, 9, *c.* 75)

Every knock is a boost.
Ascribed to ELBERT HUBBARD, *c.* 1900

Knowledge

The tree of knowledge.
GENESIS II, 9, *c.* 700 B.C. (Cf. II, 17)

When you know a thing, to hold that you know it, and when you do not know it, to admit that you do not — this is true knowledge.
CONFUCIUS: *Analects*, I, *c.* 500 B.C.

As for me, all I know is that I know nothing.
Ascribed to SOCRATES in PLATO: *Phaedrus*, *c.* 360 B.C.

Knowledge is the food of the soul.
PLATO: *Protagoras*, *c.* 360 B.C.

The fear of the Lord is the beginning of knowledge. PROVERBS I, 7, *c.* 350 B.C.

Through knowledge shall the just be delivered.
PROVERBS XI, 9

The lips of knowledge are a precious jewel.
PROVERBS XX, 15

A wise man is strong; yea, a man of knowledge increaseth strength. PROVERBS XXIV, 5

"Know thyself" is a good saying, but not in all situations. In many it is better to say "Know others."
MENANDER: *Thrasyleon*, *c.* 300 B.C.

He that increaseth knowledge increaseth sorrow. ECCLESIASTES I, 18, *c.* 200 B.C.

Many shall run to and fro, and knowledge shall be increased. DANIEL XII, 4, *c.* 165 B.C.

Knowledge is not knowledge until someone else knows that one knows.
LUCILIUS: *Fragment*, *c.* 125 B.C.

No one can know everything. (Nec scire fas est omnia.) HORACE: *Carmina*, IV, *c.* 13 B.C.

Knowledge puffeth up.
I CORINTHIANS VIII, 1, *c.* 55

It is better to have useless knowledge than to know nothing.
SENECA: *Epistulæ morales ad Lucilium, c.* 63

Nature has given to us the seeds of knowledge, but not knowledge itself.
IBID.

All wish to know, but none want to pay the price.
JUVENAL: *Satires,* VII, 118

It is not lawful or proper for you to know everything.
LUCIAN: *Zeus Cross-Examined, c.* 165

When my knowledge was small I swelled with pride like an elephant blinded by passion, and it seemed to me that there was nothing I did not know. But when I learned more I became aware of my foolishness, and my excitement subsided.
BHARTRIHARI: *The Vairagya Sataka, c.* 625

Nothing is more excellent than knowledge.
JOHN OF DAMASCUS: *Dialectica,* I, *c.* 730

What harm is there in getting knowledge and learning, were it from a sot, a pot, a fool, a Winter mitten, or an old slipper?
RABELAIS: *Pantagruel,* III, 1533

Before Noah's flood the world was highly learned, by reason men lived a long time, and so attained great experience and wisdom; now, ere we begin rightly to come to the true knowledge of a thing, we lie down and die. God will not have it that we should attain a higher knowledge of things.
MARTIN LUTHER: *Table-Talk,* CLX, 1569

It is not the business of knowledge to enlighten a soul that is dark of itself; nor to make a blind man to see. Her business is not to find a man eyes, but to guide, govern, and direct his steps, provided he has found feet and straight legs to go upon.
MICHEL DE MONTAIGNE: *Essays,* I, 1580

He will be ignorant of nothing, though it be a shame to know it.
THOMAS ADAMS: *Diseases of the Soul,* 1616

Knowledge and human power are synonymous, since the ignorance of the cause frustrates the effect.
FRANCIS BACON: *Novum Organum,* I, 1620

Knowledge is power.
ENGLISH PROVERB, apparently based on FRANCIS BACON, *ante,* 1620

We must not think to make a staple commodity of all the knowledge in the land, to mark and license it like our broadcloth and our woolpacks.
JOHN MILTON: *Areopagitica,* 1644

All knowledge is remembrance.
THOMAS HOBBES: *Human Nature,* VI, 1651

He knew what's what.
SAMUEL BUTLER: *Hudibras,* I, 1663

It is much better to know something about everything than to know everything about one thing.
BLAISE PASCAL: *Pensées,* I, 1670

Let the fools say what they please: knowledge is worth something.
JEAN DE LA FONTAINE: *Fables,* VIII, 1671

Knowledge in a coxcomb becomes impertinence.
J. B. MOLIÈRE: *Les femmes savantes,* III, 1672

There is knowledge and knowledge: knowledge that resteth in the bare speculation of things, and knowledge that is accompanied with the grace of faith and love, which puts a man upon doing even the will of God from the heart.
JOHN BUNYAN: *Pilgrim's Progress,* I, 1678

Knowledge that puffs up the possessor's mind
Is ever more of a pernicious kind.
WILLIAM MATHER: *The Young Man's Companion,* pref., 1681

No man's knowledge, here, can go beyond his experience.
JOHN LOCKE: *Essay Concerning Human Understanding,* II, 1690

Knowledge seems to me to be nothing but the perception of the connexion and agreement, or disagreement and repugnancy, of any of our ideas. In this alone it consists. Where this perception is, there is knowledge; and where it is not, there, though we may fancy, guess, or believe, yet we always come short of knowledge.
JOHN LOCKE: *Essay Concerning Human Understanding,* IV

The struggling for knowledge hath a pleasure in it like that of wrestling with a fine woman.
GEORGE SAVILE (MARQUESS OF HALIFAX): *Political, Moral and Miscellaneous Reflections, c.* 1690

All knowledge resolves itself into probability.
DAVID HUME: *A Treatise of Human Nature,* I, 1739

Knowledge is a comfortable and necessary retreat and shelter for us in advanced age; and if we do not plant it while young it will give us no shade when we grow old.
LORD CHESTERFIELD: *Letter to his son,* Dec. 11, 1747

Manners must adorn knowledge, and smooth its way through the world. Like a great rough diamond, it may do very well in a closet by way of curiosity, and also for its intrinsic value; but it will never be worn, nor shine, if it is not polished.
LORD CHESTERFIELD: *Letter to his son,* July 1, 1748

Of all kinds of knowledge that we can ever obtain, the knowledge of God and the knowledge of ourselves are the most important.
JONATHAN EDWARDS: *Freedom of Will*, pref., 1754

To be proud of knowledge is to be blind with light.
BENJAMIN FRANKLIN: *Poor Richard's Almanac*, 1756

Knowledge is more than equivalent to force.
SAMUEL JOHNSON: *Rasselas*, XIII, 1759

The desire of knowledge, like the thirst of riches, increases ever with the acquisition of it.
LAURENCE STERNE: *Tristram Shandy*, II, 1760

Knowledge is, in most of those who cultivate it, a species of money, which is valued greatly, but only adds to our well-being in proportion as it is communicated, and is only good in commerce. Take from the wise the pleasure of being listened to, and knowledge would be nothing to them.
J.-J. ROUSSEAU: *La nouvelle Héloïse*, XII, 1761

A desire of knowledge is the natural feeling of mankind; and every human being whose mind is not debauched will be willing to give all that he has to get knowledge.
SAMUEL JOHNSON: *Boswell's Life*, July 30, 1763

Knowledge always desires increase: it is like fire, which must first be kindled by some external agent, but which will afterwards propagate itself.
SAMUEL JOHNSON: *Letter to William Drummond*, Aug. 13, 1766

All knowledge is of itself of some value. There is nothing so minute or inconsiderable that I would not rather know it than not.
SAMUEL JOHNSON: *Boswell's Life*, April 14, 1775

Knowledge is of two kinds; we know a subject ourselves, or we know where we can find information upon it.
SAMUEL JOHNSON: *Boswell's Life*, April 15, 1775

Who knows much hath many cares.
G. E. LESSING: *Nathan der Weise*, IV, 1779

Someone once said of Tobias Mayer, the mathematician, that even he himself did not know that he knew so much.
G. C. LICHTENBERG: *Reflections*, 1799 (JOHANN TOBIAS MAYER, 1723–62)

I know what I can know, and I am not troubled about what I cannot know.
J. G. FICHTE: *Die Bestimmung des Menschen*, XVIII, 1800

And so we all of us in some degree
Are led to knowledge, wheresoever led,
And howsoever.
WILLIAM WORDSWORTH: *The Prelude*, VIII, 1805

All that we know is, nothing can be known.
BYRON: *Childe Harold*, II, 1812 (Ascribed to " Athena's wisest son ")

An extensive knowledge is needful to thinking people — it takes away the heat and fever; and helps, by widening speculation, to ease the burden of the mystery.
JOHN KEATS: *Letter to J. H. Reynolds*, May 3, 1818

Knowledge enormous makes a god of me.
JOHN KEATS: *Hyperion*, III, 1819

All that men really understand is confined to a very small compass; to their daily affairs and experience, to what they have an opportunity to know, and motives to study or practise. The rest is affectation and imposture.
WILLIAM HAZLITT: *The Ignorance of the Learned*, 1821

The worth and value of knowledge is in proportion to the worth and value of its object.
S. T. COLERIDGE: *Aids to Reflection*, 1825

Knowledge is the great sun of the firmament. Life and power are scattered with all its beams.
DANIEL WEBSTER: Address on laying the cornerstone of Bunker Hill Monument, June 17, 1825

Each of our leading conceptions, — each branch of our knowledge, — passes successively through three different theoretical conditions: the theological, or fictitious; the metaphysical, or abstract; the scientific, or positive.
AUGUSTE COMTE: *Cours de philosophie positive*, I, 1830

He half knows everything.
T. B. MACAULAY: *Letter to Macvey Napier*, Dec. 17, 1830 (Alluding to Lord Brougham)

Knowledge is the knowing that we cannot know.
R. W. EMERSON: *Representative Men*, IV, 1850 (Cf. BYRON, *ante*, 1812)

Who loves not knowledge? Who shall rail
Against her beauty? May she mix
With men and prosper! Who shall fix
Her pillars? Let her work prevail.
ALFRED TENNYSON: *In Memoriam*, CXIV, 1850

I am chargeable with no paradox when I speak of a knowledge which is its own end, when I call it literal knowledge, or a gentleman's knowledge, when I educate for it, and make it the scope of a university.
J. H. NEWMAN: *On the Scope and Nature of University Education*, IV, 1852

You must be above your knowledge, not under it, or it will oppress you; and the more you have of it the greater will be the load.
J. H. NEWMAN: *On the Scope and Nature of University Education,* v

The real animating power of knowledge is only in the moment of its being first received, when it fills us with wonder and joy; a joy for which, observe, the previous ignorance is just as necessary as the present knowledge.
JOHN RUSKIN: *Stones of Venice,* III, 1853

In science, as in life, learning and knowledge are distinct, and the study of things, and not of books, is the source of the latter.
T. H. HUXLEY: *A Lobster, or The Study of Zoölogy,* 1861

What is most of our boasted so-called knowledge but a conceit that we know something, which robs us of the advantage of our actual ignorance?
H. D. THOREAU: *Excursions,* 1863

What is all our knowledge worth? We do not even know what the weather will be tomorrow.
BERTHOLD AUERBACH: *Auf der Höhe,* 1865

Mediocre men often have the most acquired knowledge.
CLAUDE BERNARD: *Introduction à la médecine expérimentale,* 1865

When a man's knowledge is not in order, the more of it he has the greater will be his confusion.
HERBERT SPENCER: *The Study of Sociology,* I, 1873

It is better to know nothing than to know what ain't so.
H. W. SHAW (JOSH BILLINGS): *Josh Billings' Encyclopedia of Wit and Wisdom,* 1874

Our knowledge is the amassed thought and experience of innumerable minds.
R. W. EMERSON: *Letters and Social Aims,* 1875

Banish me from Eden when you will, but first let me eat of the fruit of the tree of knowledge.
R. G. INGERSOLL: *The Gods, and Other Lectures,* 1876

He who knows not and knows not he knows not, he is a fool — shun him;
He who knows not and knows he knows not, he is simple — teach him;
He who knows and knows not he knows, he is asleep — wake him;
He who knows and knows he knows, he is wise — follow him!
RICHARD BURTON: Tr. from the Arabic, *c.* 1880

Better know nothing than half-know many things.
F. W. NIETZSCHE: *Thus Spake Zarathustra,* IV, 1885

Knowledge is recognition of something absent; it is a salutation, not an embrace.
GEORGE SANTAYANA: *The Life of Reason,* I, 1905

Strange how much you've got to know
Before you know how little you know.
Author unidentified

What you don't know, somebody else is getting paid for knowing. IBID.

He who knows should rule, and he who does not know should obey. ITALIAN PROVERB

The pope and a peasant know more between them than the pope alone. IBID.

Who knows most, knows least. IBID.

The happiest life is to know nothing. (Nihil scire est vita jucundissima.)
LATIN PROVERB

Many know many things, no one everything. (Multi multa, nemo omnia novit.)
LEGAL MAXIM

[*See also* Authority, Curiosity, Discretion, Doubt, Experience, Ignorance, Information, Integrity, Intuition, Judgment, Knowledge and Ignorance, Knowledge *vs.* Wisdom, Learning, Life, Nature, Newspaper, Opinion, Philosophy, Reticence, Self-knowledge, Tree, Wisdom.

Knowledge and Ignorance

The only good is knowledge, and the only evil ignorance.
DIOGENES LAERTIUS: *Lives of the Philosophers (Socrates), c.* 150 B.C.

A seeming ignorance is often a most necessary part of worldly knowledge.
LORD CHESTERFIELD: *Letter to his son,* Jan. 15, 1753

The only thing we can never know is to know how to ignore what we can never know.
J.-J. ROUSSEAU: *Émile,* IV, 1762

Knowledge is not happiness, and science
But an exchange of ignorance for that
Which is another kind of ignorance.
BYRON: *Manfred,* II, 1817

To be conscious that you are ignorant is a great step to knowledge.
BENJAMIN DISRAELI: *Sybil,* I, 1845

[*See also* Ignorance, Knowledge.

Knowledge vs. Wisdom

The greatest clerks be not the wisest men.
GEOFFREY CHAUCER: *The Canterbury Tales (The Reeve's Tale), c.* 1386

There is no great concurrence between learning and wisdom.
FRANCIS BACON: *The Advancement of Learning,* I, 1605

Knowledge without wisdom is double folly.
BALTASAR GRACIÁN: *The Art of Worldly Wisdom,* XVI, 1647

We live and learn, but not the wiser grow.
JOHN POMFRET: *Collected Poems,* 1702

Deign on the passing world to turn thine eyes,
And pause a while from letters, to be wise.
SAMUEL JOHNSON: *The Vanity of Human Wishes,* 1749

Knowledge dwells
In heads replete with thoughts of other men;
Wisdom in minds attentive to their own.
WILLIAM COWPER: *The Task,* VI, 1785

Knowledge is proud that he has learned so much;
Wisdom is humble that he knows no more.
IBID.

Knowledge comes, but wisdom lingers.
ALFRED TENNYSON: *Locksley Hall,* 1842

It is the province of knowledge to speak, and it is the privilege of wisdom to listen.
O. W. HOLMES: *The Poet at the Breakfast-Table,* X, 1872

Knowledge is a process of piling up facts; wisdom lies in their simplification.
MARTIN H. FISCHER (1879–)

[*See also* Knowledge, Wisdom, Wise.

Know-Nothingism

Our progress in degeneracy appears to me to be pretty rapid. As a nation, we began by declaring that "all men are created equal." . . . When the Know-Nothings get control, it will read, "all men are created equal except Negroes and foreigners and Catholics."
ABRAHAM LINCOLN: *Letter to J. F. Speed,* Aug. 24, 1855

Knox, John (1505–72)

One is tempted almost to say that there was more of Jesus in St. Theresa's little finger than in John Knox's whole body.
MATTHEW ARNOLD: *Literature and Dogma,* X, 1873

Koran

The Alcoran of the Turks (I speak without prejudice) is an ill-composed piece containing in it vain and ridiculous errors in philosophy, impossibilities, fictions, and vanities beyond laughter, maintained by evident and open sophisms, the policy of ignorance, deposition of universities, and banishment of learning.
THOMAS BROWNE: *Religio Medici,* I, 1642

They must have a mean opinion of the Christian religion, or be but ill-grounded therein, who can apprehend any danger from so manifest a forgery.
GEORGE SALE: Tr. of the KORAN (To the Reader), 1734

A wearisome confused jumble, crude, incondite; endless iterations, long-windedness, entanglement; most crude, incondite; — insupportable stupidity, in short! Nothing but a sense of duty could carry any European through the Koran.
THOMAS CARLYLE: *Heroes and Hero-Worship,* II, 1840 (Lecture in London, May 8)

[*See also* Library.

Kosciusko, Tadeusz (1746–1817)

Freedom shrieked as Kosciusko fell.
THOMAS CAMPBELL: *The Pleasures of Hope,* 1799 (Referring to Kosciusko's defeat, wounding and capture at the battle of Maciejowice, Oct. 10, 1794)

The original liberty Pole.
Author unidentified

Kosher

Whatsoever parteth the hoof, and is clovenfooted, and cheweth the cud, among the beasts, that shall ye eat.
LEVITICUS XI, 3, *c.* 700 B.C. (Cf. DEUTERONOMY XIV, 6, *c.* 650 B.C.)

These shall ye eat of all that are in the waters: whatsoever hath fins and scales in the waters, in the seas, and in the rivers, them shall ye eat.
LEVITICUS XI, 9 (Cf. DEUTERONOMY XIV, 9, *c.* 650 B.C.)

[*See also* Unclean.

L

Labor

In the sweat of thy face shalt thou eat bread, till thou return unto the ground; for out of it wast thou taken.
GENESIS III, 19, *c.* 700 B.C.

Six days shalt thou labor, and do all thy work.
EXODUS XX, 9, *c.* 700 B.C. (Cf. DEUTERONOMY V, 12, *c.* 650 B.C.)

Labor is no disgrace.
HESIOD: *Works and Days, c.* 700 B.C.

In all labor there is profit.
PROVERBS XIV, 23, *c.* 350 B.C.

He that laboreth, laboreth for himself.
PROVERBS XVI, 26

Man is born to labor and the bird to fly.
JOB V, 7, *c.* 325 B.C. (The Douay Version)

What hath man of all his labor, and of the vexation of his heart, wherein he hath labored under the sun?
ECCLESIASTES II, 22, *c.* 200 B.C. (Cf. I, 3)

To rejoice in his labor: this is the gift of God.
ECCLESIASTES V, 19

He that would eat the nut must crack the shell.
PLAUTUS: *Curculio, c.* 200 B.C.

Man goeth forth unto his work, and to his labor until the evening.
PSALMS CIV, 23, *c.* 150 B.C.

Thou shalt eat the labor of thine hands.
PSALMS CXXVIII, 2

What is there illustrious that is not attended by labor?
CICERO: *Tusculanæ disputationes,* III, 45 B.C.

Labor is a pleasure in itself.
MARCUS MANILIUS: *Astronomica,* IV, *c.* 40 B.C.

Labor conquers all things. (Labor omnia vincit.)
VIRGIL: *Georgics,* I, 30 B.C.

Life gives nothing to man without labor.
HORACE: *Satires,* I, *c.* 25 B.C.

Labor of love.
I THESSALONIANS I, 3, *c.* 51

Every man shall receive his own reward according to his own labor.
I CORINTHIANS III, 8, *c.* 55

Come unto me, all ye that labor and are heavy laden, and I will give you rest.
MATTHEW XII, 28, *c.* 75

Labor is a powerful medicine.
ST. JOHN CHRYSOSTOM: *Homilies,* II, *c.* 388

Labor is our portion lest we should make this world our rest and not hope for the hereafter.
ST. JOHN CHRYSOSTOM: *Homilies,* VI

To labor is to pray. (Laborare est orare.)
MOTTO OF THE BENEDICTINES, *c.* 529

He who labors as he prays lifts his heart to God with his hands.
ST. BERNARD: *Ad sororem, c.* 1130

God sells us all things at the price of labor.
LEONARDO DA VINCI: *Notebook, c.* 1500

Who will not suffer labor in this world, let him not be born.
JOHN FLORIO: *First Frutes,* 1578

Honest labor bears a lovely face.
THOMAS DEKKER and HENRY CHETTLE: *Patient Grissil,* I, 1603

The labor we delight in physics pain.
SHAKESPEARE: *Macbeth,* II, *c.* 1605

Labor, as well as fasting, serves to mortify and subdue the flesh. Provided the labor you undertake contributes to the glory of God and your own welfare, I would prefer that you should suffer the pain of labor rather than that of fasting.
ST. FRANCIS DE SALES: *Introduction to the Devout Life,* XXIII, 1609

A little labor, much health.
GEORGE HERBERT: *Outlandish Proverbs,* 1640

He that labors and thrives spins gold.
IBID.

Let us go forth and resolutely dare with sweat of brow to toil our little day.
JOHN MILTON: *Tractate on Education,* 1644

To labor is the lot of man below;
And when Jove gave us life, he gave us woe.
ALEXANDER POPE: Tr. of HOMER: *Iliad,* X (*c.* 800 B.C.), 1717

Everything in the world is purchased by labor, and our passions are the only causes of labor.
DAVID HUME: *A Treatise of Human Nature,* I, 1739

The fruits of labor are the sweetest of all pleasures.
LUC DE VAUVENARGUES: *Réflexions,* 1746

Nature recompenses men for their sufferings; it renders them laborious, because to the greatest toils it attaches the greatest rewards. But if arbitrary power take away the rewards of nature, man resumes his disgust for labor, and inactivity appears to be the only good.
C. L. DE MONTESQUIEU: *The Spirit of the Laws,* XIII, 1748

Labor's face is wrinkled with the wind, and swarthy with the sun.
SAMUEL JOHNSON: *The Rambler,* July 10, 1750

Labor is a surmounting of difficulties, an exertion of the contracting power of the muscles; and as such resembles pain, which consists in tension or contraction, in everything but degree.
EDMUND BURKE: *The Sublime and Beautiful,* IV, 1756

No man loves labor for itself.
SAMUEL JOHNSON: *Boswell's Life,* Oct. 26, 1769

From labor health, from health contentment springs.
JAMES BEATTIE: *The Minstrel,* I, 1771

The value of any commodity to the person who possesses it, and who means not to use or consume it himself, but to exchange it for other commodities, is equal to the quantity of labor which it enables him to purchase or command. Labor, therefore, is the real measure of the exchangeable value of all commodities.
ADAM SMITH: *The Wealth of Nations,* I, 1776

Labor is exercise continued to fatigue; exercise is labor used only while it produces pleasure.
SAMUEL JOHNSON: *Letter to Hester Piozzi,* 1788

Take not from the mouth of labor the bread it has earned.
THOMAS JEFFERSON: Inaugural Address, March 4, 1801

There is no real wealth but the labor of man. Were the mountains of gold and the valleys of silver, the world would not be one grain of corn the richer; no one comfort would be added to the human race.
P. B. SHELLEY: *Queen Mab,* notes, 1813

Such hath it been — shall be — beneath the sun:
The many still must labor for the one.
BYRON: *The Corsair,* I, 1814

Let us then be up and doing,
With a heart for any fate;
Still achieving, still pursuing,
Learn to labor and to wait.
H. W. LONGFELLOW: *A Psalm of Life,* 1839

Each morning sees some task begun,
Each evening sees it close;
Something attempted, something done,
Has earned a night's repose.
H. W. LONGFELLOW: *The Village Blacksmith,* 1841

Labor is the curse of the world, and nobody can meddle with it without becoming proportionately brutified.
NATHANIEL HAWTHORNE: *American Note-Books,* Aug. 12, 1841

Labor is not joyous but grievous.
THOMAS CARLYLE: *The Nigger Question,* 1849 (Fraser's Magazine, Dec.)

When I go into my garden with a spade, and dig a bed, I feel such an exhilaration and health that I discover that I have been defrauding myself all this time in letting others do for me what I should have done with my own hands.
R. W. EMERSON: *Man the Reformer,* 1849

As labor is the common burden of our race, so the effort of some to shift their share of the burden on to the shoulders of others is the great durable curse of the race.
ABRAHAM LINCOLN: Fragment written about July 1, 1854

There is rough work to be done, and rough men must do it; there is gentle work to be done, and gentlemen must do it; and it is physically impossible that one class should do, or divide, the work of the other. And it is of no use to try to conceal this sorrowful fact by fine words, and to talk to the workman about the honorableness of manual labor, and the dignity of humanity.
JOHN RUSKIN: *The Crown of Wild Olive,* I, 1866

The Democratic party is the friend of labor and the laboring man, and pledges itself to protect him alike against the cormorant and the commune.
Democratic National Platform, 1880

A truly American sentiment recognizes the dignity of labor and the fact that honor lies in honest toil.
GROVER CLEVELAND: *Letter of acceptance,* Aug. 18, 1884

We denounce the importation of contract labor, whether from Europe or Asia, as an offense against the spirit of American institutions.
Republican National Platform, 1884

We favor the establishment of a national bureau of labor; the enforcement of the eight-hour law.
IBID.

There is no boon in nature. All the blessings we enjoy are the fruits of labor, toil, self-denial, and study.
W. G. SUMNER: *The Boon of Nature,* 1887

Even if man had never fallen from the state of innocence he would not have been wholly idle; but the labor which would have been his free choice in that case, and his delight, became compulsory by his sin, and a painful expiation of it.
LEO XIII: *Rerum novarum,* May 15, 1891

It is only by the labor of workingmen that states grow rich.
IBID.

We favor the enactment by the states of laws for abolishing the notorious sweating system; for abolishing contract convict labor, and for prohibiting the employment in factories of children under 15 years of age.
Democratic National Platform, 1892

We recommend that Congress create a Department of Labor, in charge of a secretary with a seat in the Cabinet.
Democratic National Platform, 1900

We cannot afford to let any group of citizens, any individual citizens, live or labor under conditions which are injurious to the common welfare. Industry must submit to such public regulation as will make it a means of life and health, not of death or inefficiency.
THEODORE ROOSEVELT: Speech in Chicago, Aug. 6, 1912

The labor of a human being is not a commodity or article of commerce.
The Clayton Antitrust Act, VI, Oct. 15, 1914

Sweating, slums, the sense of semi-slavery in labor, must go. We must cultivate a sense of manhood by treating men as men.
DAVID LLOYD GEORGE: Speech in the House of Commons, Dec. 6, 1919

Labor, even the most humble and the most obscure, if it is well done, tends to beautify and embellish the world.
GABRIELLE D'ANNUNZIO: *Constitution of the Free State of Fiume,* Aug. 27, 1920

Laws regulating hours of labor and conditions under which labor is performed are just assertions of the national interest in the welfare of the people.
Democratic National Platform, 1920

The Russian Socialist Federated Soviet Republic declares labor the duty of all citizens of the republic.
CONSTITUTION OF THE U.S.S.R., I, Jan. 31, 1924

We favor collective bargaining and laws regulating hours of labor and conditions under which labor is performed.
Democratic National Platform, 1924

The only kind of labor which gives the workingman a title to all its fruits is that which he does as his own master.
POPE PIUS XI: *Quadragesimo anno,* 1931

No form of labor is a disgrace. Labor is, on the contrary, the highest degree of nobility for anyone who faithfully coöperates through it and with it in constructing the life of the community and in preserving the nation.
ADOLF HITLER: Speech in Berlin, May 1, 1934

Whether you work by the piece or the day,
Decreasing the hours increases the pay.
Author unidentified

The labor's forgotten when the sweat dries.
JAPANESE PROVERB

[*See also* Aristocracy, Capital, Capital and Labor, Child Labor, Civilization, Cross of Gold, Custom, Eight-hour Day, Employment, Idleness, Industry, Invention, Labor Union, Land, Pauperism, Property, Rest, Sixty, Slave, Slavery, Sweat, Temperance, Wages, Wealth, Work, Worker.

Laboratory

Put off your imagination, as you put off your overcoat, when you enter the laboratory. But put it on again, as you put on your overcoat, when you leave.
CLAUDE BERNARD: *Introduction à la médecine expérimentale,* 1865

Without laboratories men of science are soldiers without arms.
LOUIS PASTEUR (1822–95)

Laborer

[*See* Worker.

Labor Union

The bad workmen, who form the majority of the operatives in many branches of industry, are decidedly of opinion that bad workmen ought to receive the same wages as good.
J. S. MILL: *On Liberty,* IV, 1859

The methods by which a trade union can alone act are necessarily destructive; its organization is necessarily tyrannical.
HENRY GEORGE: *Progress and Poverty,* VI, 1879

We favor the repeal of all laws restricting the free action of labor, and the enactment of laws by which labor organizations may be incorporated.
Democratic National Platform, 1884

Trade unions are the only means by which workmen can protect themselves from the tyranny of those who employ them. But the moment that trade unions become tyrants in their turn they are engines for evil: they have no right to prevent people from working on any terms that they choose.
MR. JUSTICE LINDLEY: *Judgment in Lyons vs. Wilkins,* 1896

It is essential that there should be organizations of labor. This is an era of organization. Capital organizes and therefore labor must organize.
THEODORE ROOSEVELT: Speech in Milwaukee, Oct. 14, 1912

[The right] to make non-membership in a union a condition of employment . . . is a part of the constitutional right of personal liberty and private property, not to be taken away even by legislation.
MR. JUSTICE MAHLON PITNEY: *Opinion in Hitchman Coal and Coke Co.* vs. *Mitchell,* 1917

Facts show that politically independent trade unions do not exist anywhere. There have never been any. Experience and theory say that there never will be any.
LEON TROTSKY: *Communism and Syndicalism,* 1929

Lady

I shall be a lady forever.
ISAIAH XLVII, 7, *c.* 700 B.C.

Methought I saw a lady passing fair, but very mischievous, who in the one hand carried a knife with which she offered to cut my throat, and in the other a looking-glass wherein, seeing how ill anger became ladies, she refrained from intended violence.
JOHN LYLY: *Endymion,* V, 1591

Some men must love my lady and some Joan.
SHAKESPEARE: *Love's Labor's Lost,* III, *c.* 1595

There is nothing of so tender a nature as the reputation and conduct of ladies.
JONATHAN SWIFT: *The Tatler,* Sept. 13, 1709

There is scarce a lady of quality in Great Britain that ever saw the sun rise.
RICHARD STEELE: *The Tatler,* Dec. 14, 1710

Far-fetched and dear-bought is fit for ladies.
JONATHAN SWIFT: *Polite Conversation,* 1738

Is that manners, to show your learning before ladies?
IBID.

Ladies set no value on the moral character of men who pay their addresses to them: the greatest profligate will be as well received as the man of the greatest virtue, and this by a very good woman, by a woman who says her prayers three times a day.
SAMUEL JOHNSON: *Boswell's Life,* June 10, 1784

As eating a great deal is deemed indelicate in a lady (for her character should be rather divine than sensual), it will be ill manners to help her to a large slice of meat at once, or fill her plate too full.

JOHN TURSLER: *The Honors of the Table,* 1788

Women all want to be ladies, which is simply to have nothing to do, but listlessly to go they scarcely care where, for they cannot tell what.

MARY WOLLSTONECRAFT: *A Vindication of the Rights of Woman,* IX, 1792

I met a lady in the meads.
Full beautiful — a faery's child,
Her hair was long, her foot was light,
And her eyes were wild.

JOHN KEATS: *La Belle Dame Sans Merci,* 1819

A fine lady; by which term I wish to express the result of that perfect education in taste and manner, down to every gesture, which Heaven forbid I, professing to be a poet, should undervalue. It is beautiful, and therefore I welcome it in the name of the author of beauty.

CHARLES KINGSLEY: *Alton Locke,* XIII, 1850

That monster of European civilization and Teutonico-Christian stupidity.

ARTHUR SCHOPENHAUER: *Parerga und Paralipomena,* 1851

When a lady says no she means perhaps; when she says perhaps she means yes; when she says yes she is no lady.

Author unidentified

If you are a lady, and I am a lady, who is to look after the sow? SPANISH PROVERB

[*See also* Gentleman, Timidity.

Lafayette, Marquis de (1757–1834)

He has a canine appetite for popularity and fame.

THOMAS JEFFERSON: *Letter to James Madison,* Jan. 30, 1787

Lafayette, we are here!

CHARLES E. STANTON: Speech at the tomb of Lafayette in Paris, July 4, 1917

Laissez-faire

Liberty of action and liberty of movement. (Laissez faire et laissez passer.)

Ascribed to J. C. M. V. DE GOURNAY (1712–59)

It is not the policy of the government in America to give aid to works of any kind. They let things take their natural course without help or impediment, which is generally the best policy.

THOMAS JEFFERSON: *Letter to Thomas Digges,* 1788

Agriculture, manufactures, commerce, and navigation, the four pillars of our prosperity, are the most thriving when left most free to individual enterprise.

THOMAS JEFFERSON: Message to Congress, 1801

Laissez-faire, supply-and-demand, — one begins to be weary of all that. Leave all to egoism, to ravenous greed of money, of pleasure, of applause; — it is the gospel of despair.

THOMAS CARLYLE: *Past and Present,* III, 1843

Lama

Every lama has his own doctrine.

TIBETAN PROVERB

[*See also* Buddhism.

Lamb

One lamb thou shalt offer in the morning; and the other lamb thou shalt offer at even.

EXODUS XXIX, 39, *c.* 700 B.C. (Cf. NUMBERS XXVIII, 4, *c.* 700 B.C.)

Like lambs to the slaughter.

JEREMIAH LI, 40, *c.* 625 B.C

Little lamb, who made thee?
Dost thou know who made thee?
Gave thee life and bid thee feed
By the stream and o'er the mead;
Gave thee clothing of delight,
Softest clothing, woolly, bright;
Gave thee such a tender voice,
Making all the vales rejoice?
Little lamb, who made thee?
Dost thou know who made thee?

WILLIAM BLAKE: *The Lamb,* 1789

Mary had a little lamb,
Its fleece was white as snow,
And everywhere that Mary went
The lamb was sure to go.

SARAH J. HALE: *Mary's Lamb,* 1830 (Juvenile Miscellany, Sept.)

God tempers the wind to the shorn lamb.

ENGLISH PROVERB, commonly ascribed to LAURENCE STERNE: *A Sentimental Journey,* II, 1768, where it is quoted, but traced by Apperson to a French original of 1594, and in English to 1640

[*See also* May, Peace.

Lamb, Charles (1775–1834)

Slow of speech, and reserved of manners, no one seeks or cares for my society and I am left alone.

CHARLES LAMB: *Letter to S. T. Coleridge,* June 10, 1796

Charles was drunk last night, and drunk the night before.

MARY LAMB: *Letter to Sarah Stoddart,* Nov. 30, 1810

Poor Elia (Call him Ellia)!

CHARLES LAMB: *Letter to J. Taylor,* July 30, 1821

A clever fellow, certainly; but full of villainous and abortive puns, which he miscarries of every minute.
THOMAS HOOD: *Diary*, April 4, 1823

Mr. Lamb has a distaste to new faces, to new books, to new buildings, to new customs.
WILLIAM HAZLITT: *The Spirit of the Age*, 1825

Charles Lamb had a head worthy of Aristotle, with as fine a heart as ever beat in human bosom, and limbs very fragile to sustain it.
LEIGH HUNT: *Autobiography*, 1850

Charles Lamb's essays are scented with the primroses of Covent Garden.
ALEXANDER SMITH: *Dreamthorp*, II, 1863

Insuperable proclivity to gin in poor old Lamb. His talk contemptibly small, indicating wondrous ignorance and shallowness, even when it was serious and good-mannered, which it seldom was, usually ill-mannered (to a degree), screwed into frosty artificialities, ghastly make-believe of wit, in fact more like " diluted insanity " (as I defined it) than anything of real jocosity, humor, or geniality.
THOMAS CARLYLE: *Letter to Jane Welsh Carlyle*, 1866

He conquered poverty and hereditary madness, and won an imperishable name in English literature, all in silence and with a smile.
W. C. HAZLITT: *Mary and Charles Lamb*, conclusion, 1874

[*See also* Ape.

Lame

The halt and the blind. LUKE XIV, 21, *c.* 75

In a retreat the lame are foremost.
GEORGE HERBERT: *Outlandish Proverbs*, 1640

A lame traveler should get out betimes.
THOMAS FULLER: *Gnomologia*, 1732

The lame foot overtakes the swift one in the end. GREEK PROVERB

If you live with the lame you will learn to limp. LATIN PROVERB

[*See also* Charity, Priest.

Lamentation

A doleful lamentation.
MICAH II, 4, *c.* 700 B.C.

Lancashire

[*See* Example.

Land

The land shall not be sold for ever: for the land is mine; for ye are strangers and sojourners with me. LEVITICUS XXV, 23, *c.* 700 B.C.

The land is more dangerous than the ocean.
OVID: *Tristia*, I, *c.* 10

I would give a thousand furlongs of sea for an acre of barren ground.
SHAKESPEARE: *The Tempest*, I, 1611

Being on sea, sail; being on land, settle.
GEORGE HERBERT: *Outlandish Proverbs*, 1640

Who buys land buys war.
GIOVANNI TORRIANO: *Italian Proverbs*, 1666

He that hath some land must have some labor.
JOHN RAY: *English Proverbs*, 1670

The balance of power in a society accompanies the balance of property in land.
JOHN ADAMS: *Letter to James Sullivan*, May 26, 1776

The small landholders are the most precious part of a state.
THOMAS JEFFERSON: *Letter to James Madison*, 1785

Man was born on shore, and it is natural for him to like it.
NAPOLEON I: To Barry E. O'Meara at St. Helena, May 7, 1817

Land belongs to these two: To the Almighty God; and to all His children of men that have ever worked well on it, or that shall ever work well on it.
THOMAS CARLYLE: *Past and Present*, III, 1843

The land of every country belongs to the people of that country. The individuals called landowners have no right in morality and justice to anything but the rent, or compensation for its salable value.
J. S. MILL: *Principles of Political Economy*, I, 1848

Equity . . . does not permit property in land.
HERBERT SPENCER: *Social Statics*, II, 1851

If a man own land, the land owns him.
R. W. EMERSON: *Wealth*, 1860

We are opposed to all further grants of lands to railroads or other corporations. The public domain should be held sacred to actual settlers. Democratic National Platform, 1872

We are opposed to further grants of the public lands to corporations and monopolies, and demand that the national domain be set apart for free homes for the people.
Republican National Platform, 1872

The possession of land involves and carries with it the duty of cultivating that land.
CHARLES BRADLAUGH: *The Land, the People, and the Coming Struggle*, 1876

The most valuable lands on the globe, the lands which yield the highest rent, are not lands of surpassing natural fertility, but lands to which a surpassing utility has been given by the increase of population.
HENRY GEORGE: *Progress and Poverty*, IV, 1879

The equal right of all men to the use of land is as clear as their equal right to breathe the air — it is a right proclaimed by the fact of their existence. For we cannot suppose that some men have a right to be in this world, and others no right.

HENRY GEORGE: *Progress and Poverty*, VII

What is necessary for the use of land is not its private ownership, but the security of improvements. It is not necessary to say to a man, "this land is yours," in order to induce him to cultivate or improve it. It is only necessary to say to him, "whatever your labor or capital produces on this land shall be yours."

HENRY GEORGE: *Progress and Poverty*, VIII

Only German people may be the owners of German land.

National Programme of the Nazis, March 6, 1930

A lord without land is like a cask without wine.

DANISH PROVERB

He is not a full man who does not own a piece of land. HEBREW PROVERB

That which is built upon the land goes with the land. (Aedificatum solo, solo cedit.)

LEGAL MAXIM

[*See also* Ale, Aristocracy, Master, Missionary, Nobility.

Landlord

There is a disadvantage belonging to land, compared with money. A man is not so much afraid of being a hard creditor as of being a hard landlord.

SAMUEL JOHNSON: *Boswell's Life*, March 21, 1783

Who is the landlord? The landlord is a gentleman who does not earn his wealth. He does not even take the trouble to receive his wealth. He has a host of people around him to do the actual spending for him. He never sees it until he comes to enjoy it. His sole function, his chief pride, is stately consumption of wealth produced by others.

DAVID LLOYD GEORGE: Speech at Limehouse, July 30, 1909

The only trustworthy landlord is a dead one.

RUSSIAN PROVERB

Landmark

Remove not the ancient landmark, which thy fathers have set.

PROVERBS XXII, 28, *c.* 350 B.C. (Cf. XXIII, 10)

Landowner

[*See* Land, Landlord, Law.

Landscape

There is in woods and waters a certain enticement and flattery, together with a failure to yield a present satisfaction. This disappointment is felt in every landscape.

R. W. EMERSON: *Nature*, 1836

We can double the true beauty of an actual landscape by half closing our eyes as we look at it. The naked senses sometimes see too little — but then always they see too much.

E. A. POE: *Marginalia*, 1844–49

An evening light is generally the best for all landscapes.

ANTHONY TROLLOPE: *North America*, I, 1862

Lane

[*See* Long.

Language

The whole earth was of one language, and of one speech. GENESIS XI, 1, *c.* 700 B.C.

Language, like money, when it receives the public stamp, ought to have currency.

QUINTILIAN: *De institutione oratoria*, I, *c.* 90

The chief virtue that language can have is clearness, and nothing detracts from it so much as the use of unfamiliar words.

GALEN: *On the Natural Faculties*, I, *c.* 175

Man is the one name belonging to every nation on earth; there is one soul and many tongues, one spirit and many sounds; every country has its own speech, but the subjects of speech are common to all.

TERTULLIAN: *The Testimony of the Christian Soul*, *c.* 210

Man has great power of speech, but the greater part thereof is empty and deceitful. The animals have little, but that little is useful and true; and better is a small and certain thing than a great falsehood.

LEONARDO DA VINCI: *Notebook*, *c.* 1500

A man is worth as many men as he knows languages.

Ascribed to CHARLES V, *Holy Roman Emperor* (1500–58)

There are eight famous and chief languages: Hebrew, Greek, Latin, Syriac, Arabic, Italian, Spanish, and French.

FRANCIS MERES: *Pallidas Tamia*, 1598

The Italian is pleasant, but without sinews, as a still reflecting water; the French delicate, but even nice as a woman, scarce daring to open her lips for fear of marring her countenance; the Spanish majestical but fulsome, running too much on the *o*, and terrible like the Devil in a play; the Dutch manlike, but withal very harsh, as one ready at every word to pick a quarrel.

RICHARD CAREW: *Epistle on the Excellency of the English Tongue*, 1605

When the language in common use in any country becomes irregular and depraved, it is followed by their ruin and their degradation.
JOHN MILTON: *Letter to Bendetto Buonmattai*, Sept. 10, 1638

Custom is the most certain mistress of language, as the public stamp makes the current money.
BEN JONSON: *Grammar*, 1640

Speak not in an unknown language, or in what thou knowest not well, be it not in case of necessity to be better understood, but use thine own natural tongue, as men of quality of the town speak it, nor like the mean sort.
FRANCIS HAWKINS: *Youth's Behavior*, VI, 1663

Every living language, like the perspiring bodies of living creatures, is in perpetual motion and lateration; some words go off, and become obsolete; others are taken in, and by degrees grow into common use; or the same word is inverted to a new sense and notion, which in tract of time makes as observable a change in the air and features of a language as age makes in the lines and mien of a face.
RICHARD BENTLEY: *Dissertation Upon the Epistles of Phalaris*, 1697

[Women] should be taught languages, as particularly French and Italian; and I would venture the injury of giving a woman more tongues than one.
DANIEL DEFOE: *An Essay Upon Projects*, 1697

Custom is, and will be, sovereign over all the forms of writing and speaking.
ISAAC WATTS: *The Art of Reading and Writing English*, 1721

The air has an influence in forming the languages of mankind. The serrated, close way of speaking of Northern nations may be owing to their reluctance to open their mouth wide in cold air, which must make their language abound in consonants; whereas from a contrary cause, the inhabitants of warmer climates, opening their mouths, must form a softer language, abounding in vowels.
JOHN ARBUTHNOT: *The Effect of Air on Human Bodies*, 1733

Knowing any language imperfectly is very little better than not knowing it at all.
LORD CHESTERFIELD: *Letter to his son*, Dec. 29, 1747

It is with language as with manners: they are both established by the usage of people of fashion; it must be imitated, it must be complied with.
LORD CHESTERFIELD: *Letter to his son*, April 5, 1754

Language is the only instrument of science, and words are but the signs of ideas.
SAMUEL JOHNSON: *Dictionary*, pref., 1755

Language is purely a species of fashion, in which by the general, but tacit, consent of the people of a particular state or country, certain sounds come to be appropriated to certain things as their signs.
GEORGE CAMPBELL: *The Philosophy of Rhetoric*, III, 1776

I am always sorry when any language is lost, because languages are the pedigrees of nations.
SAMUEL JOHNSON: *Boswell's Life*, 1776

No grammatical rules have sufficient authority to control the firm and established usage of language. Established custom, in speaking and writing, is the standard to which we must at last resort for determining every controverted point in language and style.
HUGH BLAIR: *Lectures on Rhetoric and Belles Lettres*, 1783

I am of opinion that there never was an instance of a man's writing or speaking his native tongue with elegance, who passed from fifteen to twenty years of age out of the country where it was spoken.
THOMAS JEFFERSON: *Letter to J. Bannister*, 1785

In general, I am of opinion, that till the age of about sixteen, we are best employed on languages: Latin, Greek, French, and Spanish. . . . I think Greek the least useful.
THOMAS JEFFERSON: *Letter to J. W. Eppes*, 1787

As there is now nothing new to be learned from the dead languages, all the useful books being already translated, the languages are becoming useless, and the time expended in teaching and learning them is wasted. So far as the study of languages may contribute to the progress and communication of knowledge, it is only in the living languages that new knowledge is to be found.
THOMAS PAINE: *The Age of Reason*, I, 1794

As the Greek was subtle in thought and sensuously refined in feeling — as the Roman was serious and practical rather than speculative — as the Frenchman is popular and sociable — as the Briton is profound and the German philosophic — so are also the languages of these nations.
D. JENISCH: *Vergleichung von vierzehn Sprachen*, 1796

Language originated before philosophy, and that is what is the matter with philosophy.
G. C. LICHTENBERG: *Reflections*, 1799

If I had a son, I should endeavor to make him familiar with French and German authors. Greek and Latin are only luxuries.
Ascribed to RICHARD PORSON (1759–1808)

The care of the national language is at all times a sacred trust and a most important privilege of the higher orders of society. Every man of education should make it the object of his unceasing concern to preserve his language pure and entire, to speak it, so far as is in his power, in all its beauty and perfection.

FRIEDRICH VON SCHLEGEL: *Geschichte der alten und neuen Literatur,* 1815

Language is the armory of the human mind; and at once contains the trophies of its past, and the weapons of its future conquests.

S. T. COLERIDGE: *Biographia Literaria,* XVI, 1817

I believe that the process of thought might be carried on independent and apart from spoken or written language. I do not in the least doubt that if language had been denied or withheld from man, thought would have been a process more simple, more easy, and more perfect than at present.

S. T. COLERIDGE: To Thomas Allsop, *c.* 1820

The tedious time we moderns employ in acquiring the language of the ancient Greeks and Romans, which cost them nothing, is the principal reason why we cannot arrive at that grandeur of soul and perfection of knowledge that was in them.

C. C. COLTON: *Lacon,* 1820

Language is a perpetual Orphic song,
Which rules with Dædal harmony a throng
Of thought and forms, which else senseless and
shapeless were.

P. B. SHELLEY: *Prometheus Unbound,* IV, 1820

The vocabulary of an enlightened society is philosophical, that of a half-civilized people is poetical.

T. B. MACAULAY: *Milton,* 1825 (Edinburgh Review, Aug.)

Language, as well as the faculty of speech, was the immediate gift of God.

NOAH WEBSTER: *American Dictionary,* pref., 1828

My way of learning a language is always to begin with the Bible, which I can read without a dictionary. After a few days passed in this way I am master of all the common particles, the common rules of syntax, and a pretty large vocabulary. Then I fall on some good classical work.

T. B. MACAULAY: *Letter to Macvey Napier,* Nov. 26, 1836

Colleges and books only copy the language which the field and the workyard made.

R. W. EMERSON: *The American Scholar,* 1837

We infer the spirit of the nation in great measure from the language, which is a sort of monument to which each forcible individual in a course of many hundred years has contributed a stone.

R. W. EMERSON: *Nominalist and Realist,* 1841

No noble work of the imagination, as far as we recollect, was ever composed by any man, except in a dialect which he had learned without remembering how or when, and which he had spoken with perfect ease before he had ever analysed its structure. Romans of great abilities wrote Greek verses; but how many of those verses have deserved to live?

T. B. MACAULAY: *Frederick the Great,* 1842 (Edinburgh Review, April)

Language is the archives of history, and, if we must say it, a sort of tomb of the muses. For, though the origin of most of our words is forgotten, each word was at first a stroke of genius.

R. W. EMERSON: *The Poet,* 1844

The phraseology of every nation has a taint of drollery about it to the ears of every nation speaking a different tongue.

E. A. POE: *Marginalia,* 1844–49

Language — human language — after all, is but little better than the croak and cackle of fowls, and other utterances of brute nature — sometimes not so adequate.

NATHANIEL HAWTHORNE: *American Note-Book,* July 14, 1850

Language! the blood of the soul, sir, into which our thoughts run, and out of which they grow.

O. W. HOLMES: *The Professor at the Breakfast Table,* II, 1859

The half-art, half-instinct of language.

CHARLES DARWIN: *The Descent of Man,* IV, 1871

Language signifies certain instrumentalities whereby men consciously and with intention represent their thought, to the end, chiefly, of making it known to other men.

W. D. WHITNEY: *The Life and Growth of Language,* I, 1875

Language is no artificial product, contained in books and dictionaries and governed by the strict rules of impersonal grammarians. It is the living expression of the mind and spirit of a people, ever changing and shifting, whose sole standard of correctness is custom and the common usage of the community.

A. H. SAYCE: *Introduction to the Science of Language,* II, 1879

Language is but a poor bull's-eye lantern wherewith to show off the vast cathedral of the world; and yet a particular thing once said in words is so definite and memorable that it makes us forget the absence of the many which remain unexpressed.

R. L. STEVENSON: *Familiar Studies of Men and Books,* III, 1882

Language is not an abstract construction of the learned, or of dictionary-makers, but is something arising out of the work, needs, ties, joys, affections, tastes, of long generations of humanity, and has its bases broad and low, close to the ground.

WALT WHITMAN: *Slang in America,* 1885

Language is everywhere diseased, and the burden of this disease rests heavily upon human progress.
F. W. NIETZSCHE: *The Case of Wagner*, 1888

Language is the expression of ideas by means of speech-sounds combined into words.
HENRY SWEET: *A New English Grammar*, intro., 1891

No man fully capable of his own language ever masters another.
GEORGE BERNARD SHAW: *Maxims for Revolutionists*, 1903

Language, like all art, becomes pale with years; words and figures of speech lose their contagious and suggestive power.
GEORGE SANTAYANA: *The Life of Reason*, I, 1905

Language is a purely human and non-instinctive method of communicating ideas, emotions and desires by means of a system of voluntarily produced symbols.
EDWARD SAPIR: *Language*, I, 1921

In his whole life man achieves nothing so great and so wonderful as what he achieved when he learnt to talk.
Ascribed to " a Danish philosopher " in OTTO JESPERSEN: *Language*, V, 1922

Mr. Darrow — And you say that all those languages of all the sons of men have come on the earth not over 4,150 years ago?
Mr. Bryan — I have seen no evidence that would lead me to put it any farther back than that.
From the record of the Scopes trial, Dayton, Tenn., July 21, 1925

Any man who does not make himself proficient in at least two languages other than his own is a fool. Such men have the quaint habit of discovering things fifty years after all the world knows about them — because they read only their own language.
MARTIN H. FISCHER (1879–)

So long as the language lives the nation lives too. CZECH PROVERB

Language changes every eighteen or twenty miles. HINDU PROVERB

Arabic is a language, Persian a sweetmeat, and Turkish an art. PERSIAN PROVERB

Arabic is for flattery, Turkish for reproof, and Persian for convincing. IBID.

Spanish is the language for lovers, Italian for singers, French for diplomats, German for horses, and English for geese.
SPANISH PROVERB

[*See also* Accent, Grammar, Internationalism, Metaphor, Mother-tongue, Nation, Neologism, Slang, Speech, Style, Travel.

Lap

[*See* Mother.

Lark

The busy lark, the messenger of day.
GEOFFREY CHAUCER: *The Canterbury Pilgrims* (*The Knight's Tale*), *c.* 1386

When the sky falleth we shall have larks.
JOHN HEYWOOD: *Proverbs*, 1546

It was the lark, the herald of the morn.
SHAKESPEARE: *Romeo and Juliet*, III, *c.* 1596

Hark! hark! the lark at Heaven's gate sings.
SHAKESPEARE: *Cymbeline*, II, *c.* 1609

And now the herald lark
Left his ground-nest, high tow'ring to descry
The morn's approach, and greet her with his song.
JOHN MILTON: *Paradise Regained*, II, 1671

Up springs the lark,
Shrill-voiced, and loud, the messenger of morn.
JAMES THOMPSON: *The Seasons*, II, 1727

O singing lark,
That singest like an angel in the clouds.
S. T. COLERIDGE: *Fears in Solitude*, 1798

The music soars within the little lark,
And the lark soars.
E. B. BROWNING: *Aurora Leigh*, III, 1857

[*See also* Jay, Rising (Early), Skylark.

Last

Many that are first shall be last; and the last first.
MARK X, 31, *c.* 70 (Cf. MATTHEW XIX, 30; XX, 16, *c.* 75; LUKE XIII, 30, *c.* 75)

Last, but not least.
ENGLISH PHRASE, first recorded in the XVI century

It is the last straw that breaks the camel's back.
ENGLISH PROVERB, borrowed from the Latin and familiar in English, often with *horse* in place of *camel*, since the XVII century

The last act crowns the play.
FRANCIS QUARLES: *Emblems*, I, 1635

He that pays last never pays twice.
JOHN RAY: *English Proverbs*, 1670

To the last [at the feast] the bones. (Au dernier les os.) FRENCH PROVERB

[*See also* First, Laughter.

Late

Better late than never. (Potius sero quam nunquam.) LIVY: *History of Rome*, IV, *c.* 10

It's too late to shut the stable-door when the horse is stolen.
ENGLISH PROVERB, borrowed from the French, and traced to the XIV century

It's never too late to mend.
ENGLISH PROVERB, familiar since the XVI century

Who cometh late lodgeth ill.
JOHN FLORIO: *First Frutes,* 1578

It is no time to stoop when the head is off.
DAVID FERGUSSON: *Scottish Proverbs,* 1641

He that riseth late must trot all day, and shall scarce overtake his business at night.
BENJAMIN FRANKLIN: *Poor Richard's Almanac,* 1757

I have been five minutes too late all my lifetime.
HANNAH COWLEY: *The Belle's Stratagem,* I, 1780

You come late — but you come.
J. C. F. SCHILLER: *The Piccolomini,* I, 1799

Good that comes too late is good as nothing.
H. G. BOHN: *Handbook of Proverbs,* 1855

Late, late, so late! and dark the night and chill!
Late, late, so late! but we can enter still.
Too late, too late! ye cannot enter now.
ALFRED TENNYSON: *Guinevere,* 1859

A little too late is much too late.
GERMAN PROVERB

It is better to hurry always than to be late once.
HUNGARIAN PROVERB

"You spoke too late," as the fool said when he swallowed a bad egg and heard the chicken chirp going down his throat.
IRISH SAYING

Who doesn't come at the right time must take what is left. (Wer net kummt zu rechter Zeit muss hemma was iwwerich bleibt.)
PENNSYLVANIA GERMAN PROVERB

A late messenger brings bad news.
WELSH PROVERB

[*See also* Hindsight, Learning, Mend, Might-have-been.

Latin

The Latin has no feeling for the beauty of a forest. When he takes his repose in it he lies upon his belly, while we [the Germans] rest upon our backs.
HEINRICH VON TREITSCHKE: *Politik,* I, 1897

The Latin race is now used up. I admit that in its time it has done great things, but its mission is now at an end; it is now fated to dwindle, and possibly even to disappear altogether — as a whole at least.
OTTO VON BISMARCK (1815–98)

Latin Language

Away with him, away with him! he speaks Latin.
SHAKESPEARE: *II Henry VI,* IV, *c.* 1591

To smatter Latin with an English mouth is as ill a hearing as law French.
JOHN MILTON: *Tractate on Education,* 1644

What's Latin but the language of the beast?
Anon.: *Lay-Lecture,* 1647

With a florin, Latin, and a good nag one may find out the way in any country.
GIOVANNI TORRIANO: *Italian Proverbs,* 1666

The Romans would never have found time to conquer the world if they had been obliged first to learn Latin.
HEINRICH HEINE: *Reisebilder,* II, 1826

A fool, unless he knows Latin, is never a great fool.
SPANISH PROVERB

[*See also* Education, English Language, Language, Linguist, Patient.

Latin Literature

When Greek authors began to be read in the original, interest in Latin literature as literature vanished.
RUDOLF VIRCHOW: Address on assuming the rectorship of the University of Berlin, Oct. 15, 1892

Laughter

The pleasantest laughter is at the expense of our enemies.
SOPHOCLES: *Ajax, c.* 450 B.C.

I said of laughter, It is mad: and of mirth, What doeth it?
ECCLESIASTES II, 2, *c.* 200 B.C.

As the crackling of thorns under a pot, so is the laughter of a fool.
ECCLESIASTES VII, 6

A fool lifteth up his voice with laughter, but a wise man doth scarce smile a little.
ECCLESIASTES XXI, 20

Laughter has its springs in some kind of meanness or deformity.
CICERO: *De oratore,* II, *c.* 80 B.C.

Nothing is sillier than silly laughter.
CATULLUS: *Carmina,* XXXIX, *c.* 60 B.C.

He burst his sides with laughter.
PETRONIUS: *Satyricon, c.* 50

The capacity for laughter has never been granted to man before the fortieth day from his birth, and then it is looked upon as a miracle of precocity.
PLINY THE ELDER: *Natural History,* VII, *c.* 77

If you are wise, laugh. (Ride si sapis.)
MARTIAL: *Epigrams,* I, 86

Sayings designed to raise a laugh are generally untrue and never complimentary. Laughter is never far removed from derision.
QUINTILIAN: *De institutione oratoria,* VI, *c.* 90

It is easy to condemn with a laugh.
JUVENAL: *Satires,* X, *c.* 125

Laughter does not seem to be a sin, but it leads to sin.
ST. JOHN CHRYSOSTOM: *Homilies,* XV, *c.* 388

They laugh that win.
JOHN HEYWOOD: *Proverbs,* 1546

He laughed in his sleeve.
THOMAS HARMON: *A Caveat or Warning for Common Vagabonds,* 1567

I am stabb'd with laughter.
SHAKESPEARE: *Love's Labor's Lost,* V, *c.* 1595

Laugh and grow fat.
ENGLISH PROVERB, traced by Apperson to 1596 (*Laugh and Be Fat* is the title of a tract by JOHN TAYLOR, 1615)

You shall see him laugh till his face be like a wet cloak ill laid up.
SHAKESPEARE: *II Henry IV,* V, *c.* 1598

Laughter almost ever cometh of things most disproportioned to ourselves, and nature; laughter hath a scornful tickling.
PHILIP SIDNEY: *Apologie for Poetrie,* 1598

My lungs begin to crow like chanticleer.
SHAKESPEARE: *As You Like It,* II, *c.* 1600

I will laugh like a hyena.
SHAKESPEARE: *As You Like It,* IV

Laughter should dimple the cheek, and not furrow the brow with ruggedness.
OWEN FELTHAM: *Resolves, c.* 1620

Laugh not too much: the witty man laughs least.
GEORGE HERBERT: *The Temple,* 1633

Wrinkle not thy face with too much laughter. Profuseness of laughter is the city of fools.
FRANCIS QUARLES: *Enchyridion,* 1640

He who laughs at everything is as big a fool as he who weeps at everything.
BALTASAR GRACIÁN: *The Art of Worldly Wisdom,* CCIX, 1647

Laughter is nothing else but sudden glory arising from some sudden conception of some eminency in ourselves, by comparison with the infirmity of others, or with our own formerly.
THOMAS HOBBES: *On Human Nature,* IX, 1650 (The same idea is developed in *Leviathan,* I, 1651)

That laughter consisteth in wit, or, as they call it, in jest, experience confuteth, for men laugh at mischances and indecencies wherein there lieth no wit nor jest at all. IBID.

Laugh not aloud and to the disfiguring of thy countenance, or without subject, only by custom.
FRANCIS HAWKINS: *Youth's Behavior,* 1663

Two similar faces, neither of which alone causes laughter, cause laughter when they are together, by their resemblance.
BLAISE PASCAL: *Pensées,* IX, 1670

A maid that laughs is half taken.
JOHN RAY: *English Proverbs,* 1670

He laughs ill that laughs himself to death.
IBID.

Laughter is the hiccup of a fool. IBID.

A man hates what he laughs at.
BARUCH SPINOZA: *Ethica,* IV, 1677

We must laugh before we are happy for fear of dying without laughing at all.
JEAN DE LA BRUYÈRE: *Caractères,* IV, 1688

There is nothing more unbecoming to a man of quality than to laugh. When I laugh, I always laugh alone.
WILLIAM CONGREVE: *The Double Dealer,* I, 1694

He laughs best who laughs last.
ENGLISH PROVERB, not recorded before the XVIII century; it was apparently derived from the French, but it is to be found in nearly all European languages

When a man of wit makes us laugh it is by betraying some oddness or infirmity in his own character, or in the representation which he makes of others, and when we laugh at a brute or even at an inanimate thing it is at some action or incident that bears a remote analogy to any blunder or absurdity in reasonable creatures.
JOSEPH ADDISON: *The Spectator,* April 24, 1711

Laughter, while it lasts, slackens and unbraces the mind, weakens the faculties, and causes a kind of remissness and dissolution in all the powers of the soul.
JOSEPH ADDISON: *The Spectator,* Dec. 15 1712

Man is distinguished from all other creatures by the faculty of laughter.
JOSEPH ADDISON: *The Spectator,* Sept. 26, 1712

He who laughs, and is himself ridiculous, bears a double share of ridicule.
ANTHONY A. COOPER (EARL OF SHAFTESBURY): *Characteristics of Men, Manners, Opinions, Times,* I, *c.* 1713

Every land has its own laugh.
JAMES KELLY: *Complete Collection of Scottish Proverbs,* 1721

He is not laughed at that laughs at himself first.
THOMAS FULLER: *Gnomologia*, 1732

He who laugheth too much hath the nature of a fool; he that laugheth not at all hath the nature of an old cat.
IBID.

In laughter there is always a kind of joyousness that is incompatible with contempt or indignation.
VOLTAIRE: *L'Enfant prodigue*, pref., 1736

I am neither of a melancholy nor a cynical disposition, and am as willing and as apt to be pleased as anybody; but I am sure that, since I have had the full use of my reason, nobody has ever heard me laugh.
LORD CHESTERFIELD: *Letter to his son*, March 9, 1748

Loud laughter is the mirth of the mob, who are only pleased with silly things; for true wit or good sense never excited a laugh since the creation of the world. A man of parts and fashion is therefore only seen to smile, but never heard to laugh.
LORD CHESTERFIELD: *Letter to his son*, Oct. 19, 1748

Laughter is a nascent cry, stopped of a sudden.
DAVID HARTLEY: *Observations on Man*, I, 1749

That frolic which shakes one man with laughter will convulse another with indignation.
SAMUEL JOHNSON: *The Rambler*, Sept. 28, 1751

We seldom ever laugh without crime.
THOMAS WILSON: *Maxims of Piety and of Christianity*, c. 1755

No natural defect can be a cause of laughter, because it is a misfortune to which we ourselves are liable. We only laugh at those instances of moral absurdity to which we are conscious we ourselves are not liable.
OLIVER GOLDSMITH: *Polite Learning in Europe*, XI, 1759

'Tis not deemed so great a crime by half
To violate a vestal as to laugh.
CHARLES CHURCHILL: *The Rosciad*, 1761

The loud laugh that spoke the vacant mind.
OLIVER GOLDSMITH: *The Deserted Village*, 1770

The day most wholly lost is the one on which one does not laugh.
NICOLAS CHAMFORT: *Maximes et pensées*, c. 1785

Laughter is an affection arising from the sudden transformation of a strained expectation into nothing.
IMMANUEL KANT: *Kritik der Urtheilskraft*, 1790

No one is sadder than the man who laughs too much.
JEAN PAUL RICHTER: *Hesperus*, XIX, 1795

No man ever distinguished himself who could not bear to be laughed at.
MARIA EDGEWORTH: *Tales of Fashionable Life* (*Ennui*), 1812

I am convinced that there can be no entire regeneration of mankind until laughter is put down.
P. B. SHELLEY: To T. J. Hogg, *c.* 1813

Laughter may be defined to be a sort of convulsive and involuntary movement, occasioned by mere surprise or contrast (in the absence of any more serious emotion) before it has time to reconcile its belief to contradictory appearances.
WILLIAM HAZLITT: *Lectures on the English Comic Writers*, I, 1819

The cause of laughter is simply the sudden perception of the incongruity between a concept and the real object.
ARTHUR SCHOPENHAUER: *The World as Will and Idea*, I, 1819

Laughter is little more than an expression of self-satisfied shrewdness.
G. W. F. HEGEL: *The Philosophy of Art*, *c.* 1820

Few men are much worth loving in whom there is not something well worth laughing at.
J. C. and A. W. HARE: *Guesses at Truth*, 1827

To resolve laughter into an expression of contempt is contrary to fact, and laughable enough. Laughter is a convulsion of the nerves; and it seems as if nature cut short the rapid thrill of pleasure on the nerves by a sudden convulsion of them, to prevent the sensation becoming painful.
S. T. COLERIDGE: *Table-Talk*, Aug. 25, 1833

Laughter [is] the cipher-key wherewith we decipher the whole man.
THOMAS CARLYLE: *Sartor Resartus*, I, 1836

The man who cannot laugh is not only fit for treasons, stratagems, and spoils, but his whole life is already a treason and a stratagem.
IBID.

Laughter means sympathy; good laughter is not the crackling of thorns under the pot.
THOMAS CARLYLE: *Heroes and Hero-Worship*, III, 1840 (Lecture in London, May 12)

How wonderfully, since Shakespeare's time, have we lost the power of laughing at bad jests! The very finish of our wit belies our gaiety.
JOHN RUSKIN: *Modern Painters*, IV, 1856

The silv'ry fabric of a laugh.
R. H. NEWELL (ORPHEUS C. KERR): *The Palace Beautiful*, 1864

Laffing iz the sensation ov pheeling good all over, and showing it principally in one spot.
H. W. SHAW (JOSH BILLINGS): *Josh Billings' Comical Lexicon*, 1877

Laughing has always been considered by theologians as a crime.
R. G. INGERSOLL: Speech in Chicago, Nov. 26, 1882

The mere possibility of employing laughter as a weapon shows that it involves the idea of power.
HARALD HÖFFDING: *Psykologiske Undersögelser*, 1889

He who laughs best today will also laugh last.
F. W. NIETZSCHE: *The Twilight of the Idols*, 1889

Laughter is not a bad beginning for a friendship, and it is the best ending for one.
OSCAR WILDE: *The Picture of Dorian Gray*, 1891

Man alone suffers so excruciatingly in the world that he was compelled to invent laughter.
F. W. NIETZSCHE: *The Will to Power*, I, 1896

The attitudes, gestures and movements of a human body are laughable in exact proportion as they make it remind us of a machine.
HENRI BERGSON: *Le rire*, 1900

Laughter is the bark of delight of a gregarious animal at the proximity of his kind. . . . Laughter is the female of tragedy. . . . Laughter is the mind sneezing.
WYNDHAM LEWIS: *Inferior Religions*, 1920

He was born with the gift of laughter and a sense that the world was mad.
RAFAEL SABATINI: *Scaramouche*, I, 1921 (This sentence is inscribed over the entrance to the Sterling Hall of Graduate Studies at Yale University, though without credit to Sabatini)

Progress is nothing but the victory of laughter over dogma.
BENJAMIN DECASSERES: *Fantasia Impromptu*, 1933

He who laughs, lasts.
MARY PETTIBONE POOLE: *A Glass Eye at the Keyhole*, 1938

Ef yo' take a cat to chu'ch, de folks gwine to laugh. AMERICAN NEGRO SAYING

We must laugh before we are happy, lest we should die without having laughed.
FRENCH PROVERB

Too much laughter deadens the mind.
HEBREW PROVERB

A man with a loud laugh makes truth itself seem folly. IRISH PROVERB

Laughter makes good blood.
ITALIAN PROVERB

He that laughs alane will mak sport in company. SCOTTISH PROVERB

One who is always laughing is a fool; and one who never laughs a knave.
SPANISH PROVERB

The laughter of a fool is like that of a horse.
WELSH PROVERB

[*See also* Anarchy, Anger, Comedy, Drinking, Fool, Jest, Man, Medicine, Merry, Mirth, Sorrow.

Laughter and Tears

Even in laughter the heart is sorrowful; and the end of that mirth is heaviness.
PROVERBS XIV, 13, *c.* 350 B.C.

Woe unto you that laugh now! for ye shall mourn and weep. LUKE VI, 25, *c.* 75

Learn weeping, and thou shalt gain laughing.
GEORGE HERBERT: *Outlandish Proverbs*, 1640

He who laughs on Friday will weep on Sunday.
JEAN RACINE: *Les plaideurs*, I, 1668

He can laugh and cry, and both in a wind.
JOHN RAY: *English Proverbs*, 1670

I am forced to try to make myself laugh that I may not cry: for one or other I must do; and is it not philosophy carried to the highest pitch for a man to conquer such tumults of soul as I am sometimes agitated by, and in the very height of the storm to quaver out a horselaugh?
SAMUEL RICHARDSON: *Clarissa*, LXXXIV, 1748

I laugh at everything, for fear of being obliged to weep.
CARON DE BEAUMARCHAIS: *Le barbier de Séville*, I, 1775

Laughter and tears are meant to turn the wheels of the same sensibility; one is a wind-power and the other water-power, that is all.
O. W. HOLMES: *The Autocrat of the Breakfast-Table*, IV, 1858

Laugh, and the world laughs with you;
Weep, and you weep alone.
For the sad old earth must borrow its mirth,
But has troubles enough of its own.
ELLA WHEELER WILCOX: *Solitude*, 1883

An onion can make people cry, but there is yet to be invented a vegetable that can make them laugh. Author unidentified

[*See also* Widow, Woman.

Lavender

Let's go to that house, for the linen looks white, and smells of lavender, and I long to lie in a pair of sheets that smell so.
IZAAK WALTON: *The Compleat Angler*, IV, 1653

Law

Ye shall have one manner of law, as well for the stranger, as for one of your own country.
LEVITICUS XXIV, 22, *c.* 700 B.C.

Laws, like cobwebs, entangle the weak, but are broken by the strong.
Ascribed to SOLON, *c.* 575 B.C.

The more mandates and laws are enacted, the more there will be thieves and robbers.
LAO-TSZE: *The Tao Teh King, c.* 500 B.C.

The safety of the people is the highest law.
The Twelve Tables, XII, 450 B.C.

Laws can never be enforced unless fear supports them. SOPHOCLES: *Ajax, c.* 450 B.C.

The commands of the law are conventional and have no root in nature.
ANTIPHON: *Orations, c.* 435 B.C.

The makers of laws are the majority who are weak; they make laws and distribute praises and censures with a view to themselves and to their own interests; and they terrify the stronger sort of men, and those who are able to get the better of them, in order that they may not get the better of them.
PLATO: *Gorgias, c.* 360 B.C.

The law is light.
PROVERBS VI, 23, *c.* 350 B.C.

It makes no difference whether a good man has defrauded a bad man or a bad man defrauded a good man, or whether a good or a bad man has committed adultery: the law can look only to the amount of damage done.
ARISTOTLE: *The Nicomachean Ethics,* V, *c.* 340 B.C.

The actions ordained by law are just actions only accidentally. IBID.

The law is reason free from passion.
ARISTOTLE: *Politics,* III, *c.* 322 B.C.

Ancient laws remain in force long after the people have the power to change them.
ARISTOTLE: *Politics,* IV

Good law means good order.
ARISTOTLE: *Politics,* VII

It is best that laws should be so constructed as to leave as little as possible to the decision of those who judge.
ARISTOTLE: *Rhetoric,* I, *c.* 322 B.C.

Law is a pledge that the citizens of a state will do justice to one another.
Ascribed to LYCOPHRON by ARISTOTLE: *Politics,* III, *c.* 322 B.C.

The law follows custom.
PLAUTUS: *Trinummus,* IV, *c.* 190 B.C.

According to the law of the Medes and Persians, which altereth not.
DANIEL VI, 8, *c.* 165 B.C. (Also in verse 12)

Law is nothing else but right reason, calling us imperiously to our duty, and prohibiting every violation of it.
CICERO: *Orationes Philippicae,* XI, *c.* 60 B.C.

The laws put the safety of all above the safety of one. CICERO: *De finibus,* II, *c.* 50 B.C.

The foundation of law is not opinion but nature. CICERO: *De legibus, c.* 50 B.C.

Time is the best interpreter of every doubtful law.
DIONYSIUS OF HALICARNASSUS: *Antiquities of Rome,* II, *c.* 20 B.C.

The purpose of law is to prevent the strong always having their way.
OVID: *Fasti,* III, *c.* 5

Law is deaf, inexorable, calculated rather for the safety and advantage of the poor than of the rich, and admits of no relaxation or indulgence if its bounds are transgressed.
LIVY: *History of Rome,* II, *c.* 10

No law perfectly suits the convenience of every member of the community; the only consideration is, whether upon the whole it be profitable to the greater part.
LIVY: *History of Rome,* XXXIV

What a slight foundation for virtue it is to be good only from fear of the law!
SENECA: *De Ira,* II, *c.* 43

The law is good, if a man use it lawfully.
I TIMOTHY I, 8, *c.* 60

The law is not made for a righteous man, but for the lawless and disobedient, for the ungodly and for sinners, for unholy and profane, for murderers of fathers and murderers of mothers, for manslayers.
I TIMOTHY I, 9

Laws do not persuade because they threaten.
SENECA: *Epistulæ morales ad Lucilium, c.* 63

The law is open. ACTS XIX, 38, *c.* 75

The more corrupt the state, the more numerous the laws. TACITUS: *History,* III, *c.* 100

As physicians are the preservers of the sick, so are the laws of the injured.
EPICTETUS: *Encheiridion, c.* 110

Good men need no laws, and bad men are not made better by them.
Ascribed to DEMONAX OF CYPRUS, *c.* 150

The precepts of the law are these: to live honorably, to injure no other man, to render to every man his due.
THE INSTITUTES OF JUSTINIAN, 533

No freeman shall be taken, or imprisoned, or disseized, or outlawed, or exiled, or in any way harmed, nor will we go upon or send upon him, save by the lawful judgment of his peers or by the law of the land.
MAGNA CARTA, XXXIX, 1215

Law is a regulation in accord with reason, issued by a lawful superior for the common good.
THOMAS AQUINAS: *Summa theologicæ,* I, *c.* 1265

The law is lordly.
WILLIAM LANGLAND: *Piers Plowman,* 1377

Lawmakers ought not to be law-breakers.
ENGLISH PROVERB, traced by Apperson to CHAUCER: *The Canterbury Pilgrims* (*The Man of Law's Tale*), *c.* 1386

There is nothing more difficult to undertake, more uncertain to succeed, and more dangerous to manage, than to prescribe new laws. Because he who innovates in that manner has for his enemies all those who made any advantage by the old laws; and those who expect to benefit by the new will be but cool and lukewarm in his defence.
NICCOLÒ MACHIAVELLI: *The Prince,* VI, 1513

All laws are promulgated for this end: that every man may know his duty; and therefore the plainest and most obvious sense of the words is that which must be put on them.
THOMAS MORE: *Utopia,* 1516

The law of God, which we call the moral law, must alone be the scope, and rule, and end, of all laws.
JOHN CALVIN: *Institutes of the Christian Religion,* IV, 1536

Little money, little law.
Anon.: *The Parliament of Byrdes, c.* 1550

The law groweth of sin, and doth punish it.
JOHN FLORIO: *First Frutes,* 1578

It is the rule of rules and the general law of laws that every man shall obey that of the place where he is.
MICHEL DE MONTAIGNE: *Essays,* I, 1580

For law, king, people. (Pro lege, rege, grege.)
MOTTO OF WILLIAM OF ORANGE (1533–1584)

It would be better to have no laws at all than it is to have so many as we have.
MICHEL DE MONTAIGNE: *Essays,* III, 1588

Laws are now maintained in credit, not because they are essentially just, but because they are laws. It is the mystical foundation of their authority; they have none other. They are often made by fools; more often by men who in hatred of equality have want of equity; but ever by men who are vain and irresolute. There is nothing so grossly and largely offending, nor so ordinarily wrongful, as the laws.
IBID.

No man is so exquisitely honest or upright but he brings his actions and thoughts within compass and danger of the laws, and that ten times in his life might not lawfully be hanged.
IBID.

There is one law governing all things.
GIORDANO BRUNO: *De monade numero et figura,* II, 1591

For the most part laws are but like spiders' webs, taking the small gnats, or perhaps sometimes the fat flesh flies, but hornets that have sharp stings and greater strength break through.
JOHN HARINGTON: Tr. of LUDOVICO ARIOSTO: *Orlando Furioso,* XXXII (1532), 1591

I have perhaps some shallow spirit of judgment,
But in these nice sharp quillets of the law,
Good faith, I am no wiser than a daw.
SHAKESPEARE: *I Henry VI,* II, *c.* 1591

Law, logic and Switzers may be hired to fight for anybody.
ENGLISH PROVERB, traced by Apperson to 1593

Of law there can be no less acknowledged than that her seat is the bosom of God, her voice the harmony of the world.
RICHARD HOOKER: *Of the Laws of Ecclesiastical Polity,* I, 1594

Laws they are not which public approbation hath not made so.
IBID.

In law, what plea so tainted and corrupt
But being season'd with a gracious voice
Obscures the show of evil?
SHAKESPEARE: *The Merchant of Venice,* III, *c.* 1597

Old father antic, the law.
SHAKESPEARE: *I Henry IV,* I, *c.* 1598

In the corrupted currents of this world,
Offence's gilded hand may shove by justice;
And oft 'tis seen the wicked prize itself
Buys out the law.
SHAKESPEARE: *Hamlet,* III, *c.* 1601

Who to himself is law, no law doth need,
Offends no law, and is a king indeed.
GEORGE CHAPMAN: *Bussy D'Ambois,* II, 1604

We must not make a scarecrow of the law,
Setting it up to fear the birds of prey,
And let it keep one shape, till custom make it
Their perch and not their terror.
SHAKESPEARE: *Measure for Measure,* II, 1604

Some say men on the back of law
May ride and rule it like a patient ass,
And with a golden bridle in the mouth
Direct it into anything they please.
NATHANIEL FIELD: *A Woman Is a Weathercock,* II, 1609

New lords, new laws.
JOHN HARINGTON: *Nugæ Antiquæ, c.* 1610

The law is blind, and speaks in general terms.
THOMAS MAY: *The Heir, c.* 1620

He that goes to law holds a wolf by the ear.
ROBERT BURTON: *The Anatomy of Melancholy,* 1621 (Quoted as a proverb)

That which is a law today is none tomorrow.
IBID.

Law is a pickpurse.
JAMES HOWELL: *Familiar Letters*, I, 1645 (March 20, 1621)

That law may be set down as good which is certain in meaning, just in precept, convenient in execution, agreeable to the form of government, and productive of virtue in those that live under it.
FRANCIS BACON: *De augmentis scientiarum*, VIII, 1623

The law obliges us to do what is proper, not simply what is just.
HUGO GROTIUS: *De jure belli ac pacis*, I, 1625

No freeman whatsoever ought to be imprisoned but according to the law of the land.
JOHN SELDEN: *Argument in Darnel's Case*, 1627

Extremity of law is extremity of wrong.
JOHN CLARKE: *Parœmiologia Anglo-Latina*, 1639

Here the great art lies, to discern in which the law is to bid restraint and punishment, and in what things persuasion only is to work.
JOHN MILTON: *Areopagitica*, 1644

The law is not the same at morning and at night.
GEORGE HERBERT: *Jacula Prudentum*, 1651

With customs we live well, but laws undo us.
IBID.

Where there is no common power there is no law. THOMAS HOBBES: *Leviathan*, I, 1651

A good law is that which is needful for the good of the people, and withal perspicuous.
THOMAS HOBBES: *Leviathan*, II

All the sentences of precedent judges that have ever been cannot altogether make a law contrary to natural equity. IBID.

Unnecessary laws are not good laws, but traps for money. IBID.

The law, being made, is but words and paper without the hands and swords of men.
JAMES HARRINGTON: *The Commonwealth of Oceana*, 1656

Law can discover sin, but not remove.
JOHN MILTON: *Paradise Lost*, XII, 1667

In a thousand pounds of law there's not an ounce of love.
JOHN RAY: *English Proverbs*, 1670

The common good of all is the supreme law.
RICHARD CUMBERLAND: *De legibus naturæ*, I, 1672

Too many matters have been regulated by laws, which nature, long custom and general consent ought only to have governed.
WILLIAM PETTY: *Political Arithmetic*, pref., *c.* 1677

Let not the law of thy country be the non-ultra of thy honesty; nor think that always good enough which the law will make good.
THOMAS BROWNE: *Christian Morals*, I, *c.* 1680

Law is nothing else but the will of him that hath the power of the supreme father.
ROBERT FILMER: *Patriarcha*, 1680

No written laws can be so plain, so pure,
But wit may gloss and malice may obscure.
JOHN DRYDEN: *The Hind and the Panther*, II, 1687

The pretended power of suspending of laws or the execution of laws by regal authority without consent of Parliament is illegal.
THE ENGLISH BILL OF RIGHTS, I, Dec., 1689

What are twenty acts of Parliament amongst friends? JOHN SELDEN: *Table-Talk*, 1689

If anything be imprinted on the mind of all men as a law, all men must have a certain and unavoidable knowledge that certain and unavoidable punishment will attend a breach of it.
JOHN LOCKE: *Essay Concerning Human Understanding*, I, 1690

Law is but a heathen word for power.
DANIEL DEFOE: *The History of the Kentish Petition*, 1701

The voice of nations and the course of things
Allow that laws superior are to kings.
DANIEL DEFOE: *The True-Born Englishman*, II, 1701

Law, in a free country, is, or ought to be, the determination of the majority of those who have property in land.
JONATHAN SWIFT: *Thoughts on Various Subjects*, 1706

Law is a bottomless pit.
JOHN ARBUTHNOT: Title of a pamphlet, 1712

A penny-weight of love is worth a pound of law.
JAMES KELLY: *Complete Collection of Scottish Proverbs*, 1721 (Cf. RAY, *ante*, 1670)

New laws are too apt to be voluminous, and so perplexed and mutable, from whence proceeds neglect, contempt and ignorance.
WILLIAM WARBURTON (BISHOP OF GLOUCESTER): *The Causes of Prodigies and Miracles*, I, 1727

Be you never so high, the law is above you.
THOMAS FULLER: *Gnomologia*, 1732

Ill kings make many good laws. IBID.

Law cannot persuade where it cannot punish. IBID.

Much law, but little justice. IBID.

The more laws, the more offenders. IBID.

Force first made conquest, and that conquest law.
ALEXANDER POPE: *An Essay on Man*, III, 1733

By length of time and continuance laws are so multiplied and grown to that excessive variety that there is a necessity of a reduction of them, or otherwise it is not manageable.
MATTHEW HALE: *History of the Pleas of the Crown*, 1736

Law [is] licensed breaking of the peace.
MATTHEW GREEN: *The Spleen*, 1737

Laws can have no further effect than to restrain men from an open violation of right, while what is done amiss in private, though equally tending to the public prejudice, escapes their animadversion.
WILLIAM WARBURTON (BISHOP OF GLOUCESTER): *The Divine Legation of Moses*, I, 1737

The laws of a country ought to bear reference to its physical character, to the climate, whether warm, cold, or temperate; to the quality of the soil, to its situation, to its size, to the kind of life led by the people, whether farmers, hunters, or laborers.
C. L. DE MONTESQUIEU: *The Spirit of the Laws*, I, 1748

Laws undertake to punish only overt acts.
C. L. DE MONTESQUIEU: *The Spirit of the Laws*, XII

Right is the rule of law, and law is declaratory of right.
BENJAMIN WHICHCOTE: *Moral and Religious Aphorisms*, 1753

Laws too gentle are seldom obeyed; too severe, seldom executed.
BENJAMIN FRANKLIN: *Poor Richard's Almanac*, 1756

The law is a sort of hocus-pocus science, that smiles in yer face while it picks yer pocket.
CHARLES MACKLIN: *Love à la Mode*, II, 1759 (Cf. HOWELL, *ante*, 1621)

Laws are always useful to persons of property, and hurtful to those who have none.
J.-J. ROUSSEAU: *Du contrat social*, I, 1761

Good laws lead to the making of better ones; bad ones bring in worse.
J.-J. ROUSSEAU: *Du contrat social*, III

Just to the windward of the law.
CHARLES CHURCHILL: *The Ghost*, III, 1763

Laws should be made by legislators, not by judges.
C. B. BECCARIA: *Trattato dei delitti e delle pene*, 1764

The law doth punish man or woman
That steals the goose from off the common,
But lets the greater felon loose
That steals the common from the goose.
Author unidentified, *c.* 1764

Laws grind the poor, and rich men rule the law.
OLIVER GOLDSMITH: *The Traveler*, 1764

How small, of all that human hearts endure,
That part which kings or laws can cause or cure!
SAMUEL JOHNSON: Inserted in OLIVER GOLDSMITH: *The Traveler*, 1764

Laws are generally nets of such a texture as the little creep through, the great break through, and the middle-sized alone are entangled in.
WILLIAM SHENSTONE: *Of Men and Manners*, 1764

Let all the laws be clear, uniform and precise: to interpret laws is almost always to corrupt them.
VOLTAIRE: *Philosophical Dictionary*, 1764

Let the law never be contradictory to custom: for if the custom be good, the law is worthless. IBID.

A rule of civil conduct, prescribed by the supreme power in a state, commanding what is right and prohibiting what is wrong.
WILLIAM BLACKSTONE: *Commentaries on the Laws of England*, I, 1765

Where law ends, tyranny begins.
WILLIAM PITT (EARL OF CHATHAM): Speech in the House of Lords, in defense of John Wilkes, Jan. 9, 1770

When any people are ruled by laws in framing which they have no part, that are to bind them to all intents and purposes, without, in the same manner, binding the legislators themselves, they are, in the strictest sense, slaves; and the government, with respect to them, is despotic.
ALEXANDER HAMILTON: *The Farmer Refuted*, 1775

Laws are formed by the manner and exigencies of particular times, and it is but accidental that they last longer than their causes.
SAMUEL JOHNSON: *Letter to James Boswell*, Feb. 3, 1775

Whenever the offence inspires less horror than the punishment, the rigor of penal law is obliged to give way to the common feelings of mankind.
EDWARD GIBBON: *The Decline and Fall of the Roman Empire*, I, 1776

Laws are not made for particular cases, but for men in general.
SAMUEL JOHNSON: *Boswell's Life*, 1776

People, crushed by law, have no hopes but from power. If laws are their enemies, they will be enemies to laws; and those who have much to hope and nothing to lose, will always be dangerous, more or less.
EDMUND BURKE: *Letter to Charles James Fox*, Oct. 8, 1777

The law is to us precisely what I am in my barnyard, a bridle and check to prevent the strong and greedy from oppressing the timid and weak.
ST. JOHN DE CRÈVECOEUR: *Letters from an American Farmer*, II, 1782

No man e'er felt the halter draw
With good opinion of the law.
JOHN TRUMBULL: *M'Fingal*, III, 1782

The law does not consist in particular instances, though it is explained by particular instances and rules, but the law consists of principles which govern specific and individual cases as they happen to arise.
LORD MANSFIELD: *Judgment in Rex* vs. *Bembridge*, 1783

Miserable is the condition of individuals, dangerous is the condition of the state, if there is no certain law, or, which is the same thing, no certain administration of law, to protect individuals or to guard the state.
LORD MANSFIELD: *Judgment in Rex* vs. *Shipley*, 1784

The first maxim of a free state is that the laws be made by one set of men, and administered by another; in other words, that the legislative and judicial characters be kept separate.
WILLIAM PALEY: *The Principles of Moral and Political Philosophy*, VI, 1785

The law is the last result of human wisdom acting upon human experience for the benefit of the public.
SAMUEL JOHNSON: *Mrs. Piozzi's Anecdotes*, 1786

Ignorance of the law is no excuse in any country. If it were, the laws would lose their effect, because it can be always pretended.
THOMAS JEFFERSON: *Letter to M. Limozin*, 1787

The sober second thought of the people shall be law.
FISHER AMES: Speech in Congress, 1788

Law and arbitrary power are in eternal enmity.
EDMUND BURKE: Speech on the impeachment of Warren Hastings, Feb. 15, 1788

It will be of little avail to the people that the laws are made by men of their own choice if the laws be so voluminous that they cannot be read, or so incoherent that they cannot be understood; if they be repealed or revised before they are promulgated, or undergo such incessant changes that no man, who knows what the law is today can guess what it will be tomorrow.
ALEXANDER HAMILTON: *The Federalist*, 1788

The general object which all laws have, or ought to have, in common, is to augment the total happiness of the community; and therefore, in the first place, to exclude, so far as may be, everything that tends to subtract from that happiness: in other words, to exclude mischief.
JEREMY BENTHAM: *The Principles of Morals and Legislation*, XIII, 1789

The law ought to prohibit only actions hurtful to society. What is not prohibited by the law should not be hindered, nor should any one be compelled to that which the law does not require.
Declaration of the Rights of Man by the French National Assembly, V, 1789

The law is an expression of the will of the community. All citizens have a right to concur, either personally or by their representatives, in its formation. It should be the same to all, whether it protects or punishes.
Declaration of the Rights of Man by the French National Assembly, VI

No man should be accused, arrested, or held in confinement except in cases determined by the law, and according to the forms which it has prescribed. All who promote, solicit, execute, or cause to be executed, arbitrary orders, ought to be punished; and every citizen called upon or apprehended by virtue of the law ought immediately to obey, and not render himself culpable by resistance.
Declaration of the Rights of Man by the French National Assembly, VII

The execution of the laws is more important than the making them.
THOMAS JEFFERSON: *Letter to the Abbé Arnond*, 1789

One law for the lion and ox is oppression.
WILLIAM BLAKE: *The Marriage of Heaven and Hell*, 1790

A law not repealed continues in force, not because it cannot be repealed, but because it is not repealed, and the non-repealing passes for consent.
THOMAS PAINE: *The Rights of Man*, I, 1791

Laws, not blood!
M. J. DE CHÉNIER: *Caius Gracchus*, 1792

As new cases occur the law is perpetually found deficient. It is therefore perpetually necessary to make new laws.
WILLIAM GODWIN: *An Enquiry Concerning Political Justice*, 1793

Laws always lose in energy what the government gains in extent.
IMMANUEL KANT: *Perpetual Peace*, Supplement I, 1795

It is always justifiable, in examining the principle of a law, to inquire what other laws can be passed with equal reason, and to impute to it all the mischiefs for which it may be used as a precedent.

JOHN NICHOLAS: Speech in the House of Representatives, Feb. 25, 1799

The glorious uncertainty of the law.

ENGLISH PHRASE, not recorded before the XIX century

When I hear any man talk of an unalterable law, the only effect it produces upon me is to convince me that he is an unalterable fool.

SYDNEY SMITH: *Peter Plymley's Letters,* I, 1807

Every law which originated in ignorance and malice, and gratifies the passions from which it sprang, we call the wisdom of our ancestors.

SYDNEY SMITH: *Peter Plymley's Letters,* V

Laws are inherited like diseases.

J. W. GOETHE: *I Faust,* I, 1808

No man has a natural right to commit aggression on the equal rights of another, and this is all from which the laws ought to restrain him; every man is under the natural duty of contributing to the necessities of society, and this is all the laws should enforce on him; and no man having a natural right to be the judge between himself and another, it is his natural duty to submit to the umpirage of an impartial third.

THOMAS JEFFERSON: *Letter to F. W. Gilmor,* 1816

Laws were made to be broken.

JOHN WILSON: *Noctes Ambrosianæ,* XXIV, 1822

Laws are made for men of ordinary understanding, and should therefore be construed by the ordinary rules of common sense. Their meaning is not to be sought for in metaphysical subtleties, which may make anything mean everything or nothing, at pleasure.

THOMAS JEFFERSON: *Letter to William Johnson,* 1823

What are laws but expressions of the opinion of some class which has power over the rest of the community? By what was the world ever governed but by the opinion of some person or persons? By what else can it ever be governed?

T. B. MACAULAY: *Southey's Colloquies,* 1830

Laws exist in vain for those who have not the courage and the means to defend them.

T. B. MACAULAY: *Burleigh and His Times,* 1832 (Edinburgh Review, April)

Law is whatever is boldly asserted and plausibly maintained.

Ascribed to AARON BURR in JAMES PARTON: *Life and Times of Aaron Burr,* 1858 (*c.* 1835)

The law is a ass, a idiot.

CHARLES DICKENS: *Oliver Twist,* LI, 1838

Good men must not obey the laws too well.

R. W. EMERSON: *Politics,* 1841

The law is only a memorandum. IBID.

I am beginning to think with Horsley — that " the people have nothing to do with the laws but to obey them."

E. A. POE: *Fifty Suggestions,* 1845 (Graham's Magazine, May–June)

It is not desirable to cultivate a respect for the law so much as for the right.

H. D. THOREAU: *An Essay on Civil Disobedience,* 1849

The law is for the protection of the weak more than the strong.

MR. JUSTICE ERLE: *Judgment in Regina* vs. *Woolley,* 1850

I will have no laws. I will acknowledge none. I protest against every law which an authority calling itself necessary imposes upon my free will.

P. J. PROUDHON: *Idée générale de la révolution,* 1851

The clash between what the law forbids and what society not only tolerates but seeks after, is one of the essential features of a state of society which is on the verge of ruin.

LOUIS DE LOMÉNIE: *Beaumarchais and His Times,* 1855

We bury men when they are dead, but we try to embalm the dead body of laws, keeping the corpse in sight long after the vitality has gone. It usually takes a hundred years to make a law; and then, after it has done its work, it usually takes a hundred years to get rid of it.

H. W. BEECHER: *Life Thoughts,* 1858

The law does not generate justice. The law is nothing but a declaration and application of what is already just.

P. J. PROUDHON: *De la justice dans la révolution,* I, 1858

The laws and just restraints are to a noble nation, not chains, but chain mail — strength and defence, though something also of an encumbrance.

JOHN RUSKIN: *The Two Paths,* V, 1859

No laws, however stringent, can make the idle industrious, the thriftless provident, or the drunken sober.

SAMUEL SMILES: *Self-Help,* I, 1859

The lawless science of our law,
That codeless myriad of precedent,
That wilderness of single instances.

ALFRED TENNYSON: *Aylmer's Field,* 1864

No state shall make or enforce any law which shall abridge the privileges or immunities of citizens of the United States; nor shall any state deprive any person of life, liberty or property without due process of law, nor deny to any person within its jurisdiction the equal protection of the laws.

CONSTITUTION OF THE UNITED STATES, Amendment XIV, July 28, 1868

The beginning of civilization is marked by an intense legality; that legality is the very condition of its existence, the bond which ties it together; but that legality — that tendency to impose a settled customary yoke upon all men and all actions, if it goes on, kills the variability implanted by nature, and makes different men and different ages facsimiles of other men and other ages.

WALTER BAGEHOT: *Physics and Politics,* 1869

Laws and institutions require to be adapted, not to good men, but to bad.

J. S. MILL: *The Subjection of Women,* II, 1869

Laws never would be improved if there were not numerous persons whose moral sentiments are better than the existing laws.

IBID.

I know no method to secure the repeal of bad or obnoxious laws so effective as their stringent execution.

U. S. GRANT: Inaugural address, March 4, 1869

Numbers make the laws, but the good has nothing to do with figures.

H. F. AMIEL: *Journal,* June 12, 1871

All law has for its object to confirm and exalt into a system the exploitation of the workers by a ruling class.

M. A. BAKUNIN: *Dieu et l'état,* 1871

Laws are like medicines: they usually cure the disease only by setting up another that is lesser or more transient.

OTTO VON BISMARCK: Speech in the Prussian Upper House, March 6, 1872

The law is the true embodiment
Of everything that's excellent.

W. S. GILBERT: *Trial By Jury,* 1875

Men would be great criminals did they need as many laws as they make.

C. J. DARLING: *Scintillæ Juris,* 1877

Law is an alliance of those who have farsight and insight against the shortsighted.

RUDOLF VON JHERING: *Der Zweck im Recht,* VIII, 1877

In a criminal proceeding the question is not alone whether substantial justice has been done, but whether justice has been done according to law.

MR. JUSTICE COCKBURN: *Judgment in Martin* vs. *Mackonochie,* 1878

It is far more important the law should be administered with absolute integrity than that in this case or in that the law should be a good law or a bad one.

LORD COLERIDGE: *Judgment in Regina* vs. *Ramsey,* 1883

The law is an adroit mixture of customs that are beneficial to society, and would be followed even if no law existed, and others that are of advantage to a ruling minority but harmful to the masses of men, and can be enforced on them only by terror.

P. A. KROPOTKIN: *Paroles d'un révolté,* 1884

The law has no claim to human respect. It has no more civilizing mission; its only purpose is to protect exploitation. IBID.

The law condemns and punishes only actions that fall within certain definite and narrow limits; it thereby justifies, in a way, all similar actions that lie outside those limits.

LYOF N. TOLSTOY: *What I Believe,* 1884

Laws come before men live together in society, and have their origin in the natural and consequently in the eternal law.

POPE LEO XIII: *Libertas praestantissimum,* June 20, 1888

The authority of the law is grounded on the thesis: God gave it, and the fathers lived it.

F. W. NIETZSCHE: *The Antichrist,* LVII, 1888

Laws only bind when they are in accordance with right reason, and hence with the eternal law of God.

POPE LEO XIII: *Rerum novarum,* May 15, 1891

We know how laws are made — we who have been behind the scenes. They are the products of selfishness, deception and party prejudice. True justice is not in them, and cannot be in them.

LYOF N. TOLSTOY: *The Kingdom of God Is Within You,* 1893

The attempt to guard adult man by law is a bad education for the battle of life.

W. E. H. LECKY: *Democracy and Liberty,* 1896

The reign of law.

JAMES LANE ALLEN: Title of a novel, 1900

It is difficult to make our material condition better by the best laws, but it is easy enough to ruin it by bad laws.

THEODORE ROOSEVELT: Speech in Providence, R. I., Aug. 23, 1902

While there still is doubt, while opposite convictions still keep a battlefront against each other, the time for law has not come.
O. W. HOLMES II: Speech in New York, Feb. 15, 1913

Law is the expression and the perfection of common sense.
Ascribed to JOSEPH H. CHOATE (1832–1917) in G. J. CLARK: *Great Sayings by Great Lawyers,* 1922

The passing of an unjust law is the suicide of authority.
Pastoral Letter of the American Roman Catholic Hierarchy, Feb., 1920

A year ago, if I had $100 in gold in my pocket, I was a law-abiding citizen; if I perchance had a pint of whiskey I was a criminal. To-day, if I have the whiskey, I am a law-abiding citizen; but if I have the gold I am a criminal violating the law.
L. J. DICKINSON: Speech at Cleveland, O., Jan. 5, 1934

Legal concepts are supernatural entities which do not have a verifiable existence except to the eyes of faith.
FELIX S. COHEN: *Transcendental Nonsense and the Functional Approach,* 1935

The law of blood (jus sanguinis); canon law (jus canonicum); the civil law (jus civile, *or* lex civile); the law for the government of the church (jus ecclesiasticum); the law of commerce (jus commercii); the common law (jus commune *or* lex communis); the law of contract (lex contractus); the divine law (jus divinum); the law divine and human (lex divina ac humana); the general law (lex generalis); the law of the Germans (lex Germanica); the law of God (lex Domini); the law of human society (jus humanae societatis); international law (jus inter gentes); the law of the land (lex terrae); the law of the majority (lex majoris partis); the law of mankind (jus hominum); the law merchant (lex mercatoria); the law of Moses (lex Moysi); municipal law (jus privatum); the law of nations (jus gentium); natural law (jus naturæ); the law of Parliament (lex parliamenti); the law of the place where a man has his domicile (lex domicilii); the law of the place where an action is brought (lex actus, lex fori, lex ordinandi, lex reisitae, *or* lex situs); private law (lex privata); public law (jus publicum, *or* lex publica); the law of religion (jus ponticium); the law of retaliation (lex talionis); sumptuary law (lex sumptuaria); the law of things (jus rerum); the unwritten law (lex non scripta); the law of war (jus belli); the written law (lex scripta).
LATIN PHRASES

The law protects everybody who can afford to hire a good lawyer. Author unidentified

The more by law, the less by right.
DANISH PROVERB

The law has a wax nose. FRENCH PROVERB

New laws are followed by new tricks.
GERMAN PROVERB

The more laws the less justice. IBID.

Thus is the law written. (Ita lex scripta est.)
LATIN PHRASE

Laws are made by the conqueror, and accepted by the conquered. LATIN PROVERB

Law is king. (Lex rex.) IBID.

Let the people obey the magistrates, and the magistrates the laws. IBID.

The more law, the less justice. (Summum jus, summa injuria.) IBID.

No punishment without law. (Nulla poena sine lege.) LEGAL MAXIM

The later decisions are the stronger in law. (Judicia posteriora sunt in lege fortiora.)
IBID.

The law forces no one to do vain or useless things. (Lex neminem cogit ad vana seu inutilia peragenda.) IBID.

The law looks forward, not backward. (Lex prospicit non respicit.) IBID.

The law regards the course of nature. (Lex spectat naturae ordinem.) IBID.

The laws are adapted to those cases which most frequently arise. (Ad ea quae frequentius accidunt jura adaptantur.) IBID.

The laws grow by litigation. (Litigando jura crescunt.) IBID.

The laws keep the vigilant, not those who sleep. (Vigilantibus, non dormientibus, subveniunt jura.) IBID.

The law will always furnish a remedy. (Lex semper dubit remedium.) IBID.

The niceties of the law are not the law. (Apices juris non sunt jura.) IBID.

Wherever there is society there is law. (Ubi societas ibi lex.) IBID.

Wretched is the slavery where the law is changeable or uncertain. (Misera est servitus ubi jus est vagum aut incertum.) IBID.

Like king, like law; like law, like people.
PORTUGUESE PROVERB

[*See also* Aggression, Arms, Ballad, Constitution, Court, Crime, Crime and Punishment, Criminal, Custom, Disciple, Equity, Error, Evil, Execution, Freedom, Golden Rule, Habeas Corpus, Hanging, Hell, Ignorance, Injustice, Judge, Judiciary, Jurisprudence,

Jury, King, Law (Natural), Lawyer, Liberty, Litigation, Magistrate, Man and Woman, Manners, Maxim, Monk, Moving-picture, Nicety, Opinion, Possession, Precedent, Prince, Property, Punishment, Sin, Song, State, Supreme Court, Trifle, Tyranny, Vigilance, War.

Law-abiding

He that keepeth the law, happy is he.
PROVERBS XXIX, 18, *c.* 350 B.C.

Render therefore unto Cæsar the things which are Cæsar's. MATTHEW XXII, 21, *c.* 75

Fear God, and offend not the prince nor his laws,
And keep thyself out of the magistrate's claws.
THOMAS TUSSER: *Five Hundred Points of Good Husbandry,* 1580

Follow law, and forms of law, as far as convenient.
ABRAHAM LINCOLN: Instructions to U. S. Grant, Oct. 21, 1862

The observance of the law is the greatest solvent of public ills.
CALVIN COOLIDGE: Speech of acceptance, July 27, 1920

It is the duty of a citizen not only to observe the law but to let it be known that he is opposed to its violation.
CALVIN COOLIDGE: Message to Congress, Dec. 6, 1923

Lawbreaker

[*See* Criminal.

Law, Canon

The canon law is a body of Roman ecclesiastical law relative to such matters as that church either has, or pretends to have, the proper jurisdiction.
WILLIAM BLACKSTONE: *Commentaries on the Laws of England,* I, 1765

Law, Common

Reason is the life of the law; nay, the Common Law itself is nothing but reason.
EDWARD COKE: *Institutes,* I, 1628

The Common Law is the custom of the kingdom, and we are bound to know it, and must be all governed by it.
MR. CHIEF JUSTICE NORTH: *Judgment in Whitebread's Case,* 1679

I consider all the encroachments made on the Constitution heretofore as nothing, as mere retail stuff, compared with the wholesale doctrine that there is a Common Law in force in the United States, of which, and of all the cases within its provisions, their courts have cognizance.
THOMAS JEFFERSON: *Letter to Charles Pinckney,* Oct., 1799

The Common Law is not a brooding omnipresence in the sky but the articulate voice of some sovereign or quasi-sovereign that can be identified.
MR. JUSTICE O. W. HOLMES: *Dissenting opinion in Southern Pacific Company* vs. *Jensen,* 1916

A fortuitous concourse of atoms.
Author unidentified

At Common Law you are done for at once; in equity you are not so easily disposed of. The former is a bullet which is instantaneously and charmingly effective; the latter, the angler's hook, which plays with the victim before it kills him. Common Law is prussic acid; equity is laudanum. IBID.

[*See also* Christianity, Law.

Law, Divine

[*See* Law (Natural).

Law Enforcement

No man is above the law and no man is below it, nor do we ask any man's permission when we require him to obey it.
THEODORE ROOSEVELT: Message to Congress, Jan., 1904

Violations of law weaken and threaten government itself. No honest government can condone such actions on the part of its citizens. The Republican party pledges the full strength of the government for the maintenance of these principles by the enforcement of the Constitution and of all laws.
Republican National Platform, 1924

If the law is upheld only by government officials, then all law is at an end.
HERBERT HOOVER: Message to Congress, 1929

[*See also* Law.

Law, English

There is no pretense to say or insinuate to the contrary but that the laws and customs of England are not only good but the very best.
JOHN FORTESCUE: *De laudibus legum Angliae, c.* 1462

The law of England is the greatest grievance of the nation, very expensive and dilatory.
GILBERT BURNET (BISHOP OF SALISBURY): *The History of My Own Times,* 1724

Every man who comes into England is entitled to the protection of the English law, whatever oppression he may heretofore have suffered, and whatever may be the color of his skin.
LORD MANSFIELD: *Judgment in the case of James Somersett, a Negro,* June 22, 1772

There is no presumption in this country [England] that every person knows the law: it would be contrary to common sense and reason if it were so.

MR. JUSTICE MAULE: *Judgment in Martindale* vs. *Faulkner,* 1846

[*See also* Law.

Law, French

[*See* Latin Language.

Law, Martial

The will of the commander-in-chief for the time being.

Ascribed to the DUKE OF WELLINGTON (1769–1852)

Law, Natural

The consent of all nations is the law of nature.

CICERO: *Tusculanæ disputationes,* I, 45 B.C.

All things are subject to fixed laws. (Certis legibus omnia parent.)

MARCUS MANILIUS: *Astronomica,* I, *c.* 40 B.C.

The law which nature has taught to all living creatures, so that it is common to man and beast.

DOMITIUS ULPIANUS: *Institutiones,* I, *c.* 220

Nature in man's heart her laws doth pen.

JOHN DAVIES: *Nosci Teipsum,* 1599

The law of nature is so unalterable that it cannot be changed by God Himself.

HUGO GROTIUS: *De jure belli ac pacis,* I, 1625

The course of nature God seldom alters or perverts; but, like an excellent artist, hath so contrived His work that, with the self-same instrument, without a new creation, He may effect His obscurest designs.

THOMAS BROWNE: *Religio Medici,* I, 1642

The laws of nature, as justice, equity, modesty, mercy, and, in sum, doing to others as we would be done to, of themselves, without the terror of some power to cause them to be observed, are contrary to our natural passions, that carry us to partiality, pride, revenge, and the like.

THOMAS HOBBES: *Leviathan,* XVII, 1651

The law of nature is the only law of laws truly and properly to all mankind fundamental; the beginning and the end of all government.

JOHN MILTON: *The Ready and Easy Way to Establish a Free Commonwealth,* 1660

There is an omnipresent eternal Mind, which knows and comprehends all things, and exhibits them to our view in such a manner, and according to such rules, as He Himself hath ordained, and are by us termed the laws of nature.

GEORGE BERKELEY: *Dialogues Between Hylas and Philonous,* III, 1713

The Universal Cause
Acts to one end, but acts by various laws.

ALEXANDER POPE: *An Essay on Man,* III, 1733

Laws, in their most general signification, are the necessary relations arising from the nature of things. In this sense all beings have their laws; the Deity His laws, the material word its laws, the intelligences superior to man their laws, beasts their laws, man his laws.

C. L. DE MONTESQUIEU: *The Spirit of the Laws,* I, 1748

Everything in nature acts in conformity with law.

IMMANUEL KANT: *Grundlegung zur Metaphysik der Sitten,* II, 1785

Search out the wisdom of nature, there is depth in all her doings;
She seemeth prodigal of power, yet her rules are the maxims of frugality.

M. F. TUPPER: *Proverbial Philosophy,* I, 1838

Nature is an endless combination and repetition of a very few laws. She hums the old well known air through innumerable variations.

R. W. EMERSON: *History,* 1841

The common sense of most shall hold a fretful realm in awe,
And the kindly earth shall slumber, lapt in universal law.

ALFRED TENNYSON: *Locksley Hall,* 1842

Those rights to which every man is entitled equally, and which depend on the law of nature, unfettered by the restrictions of mankind or a state of civilized society.

PATRICK COLQUHOUN: *A Summary of the Roman Civil Law,* I, 1849

Nature's rules have no exceptions.

HERBERT SPENCER: *Social Statics,* 1851

The law of the past cannot be eluded,
The law of the present and future cannot be eluded,
The law of the living cannot be eluded — it is eternal.

WALT WHITMAN: *To Think of Time,* 1855

The sharp-hoof'd moose of the north, the cat on the house-sill, the chickadee, the prairie-dog,
The litter of the grunting sow as they tug at her teats,
The brood of the turkey-hen, and she with her half-spread wings;
I see in them and myself the same old law.

WALT WHITMAN: *Walt Whitman,* 1855

We do not believe the less in astronomy and vegetation because we are writhing and roaring in our beds with rheumatism.

R. W. EMERSON: *The Sovereignty of Ethics,* 1878

The law of nature is the same thing as the eternal law, implanted in rational creatures,

and inclining them to their right action and end; and can be nothing else but the eternal reason of God, the Creator and Ruler of all the world.
POPE LEO XIII: *Libertas praestantissimum,* June 20, 1888

The laws of nature and of the Gospel . . . must remain absolutely free from political parties, and have nothing to do with the various changes of administration which may occur in a nation.
POPE LEO XIII: *Graves de communi,* Jan. 18, 1901

[*See also* Equality, Nature, Opinion (Public), Property, Vow.

Law, Salic

Of Salic land no portion of an inheritance shall ever come to a woman, but the whole inheritance of the land shall come to the male heirs.
THE SALIC LAW, *c.* 490

Lawsuit

Suits at court are like Winter nights, long and wearisome.
THOMAS DELONEY: *Jack of Newbury,* VI, 1597

Agree, for the law is costly.
WILLIAM CAMDEN: *Remains Concerning Britain,* 1605

To go to law is for two persons to kindle a fire, at their own cost, to warm others and singe themselves to cinders.
OWEN FELLTHAM: *Resolves, c.* 1620

Sue a beggar and get a louse.
JOHN CLARKE: *Parœmiologia Anglo-Latina,* 1639

He that hath right, fears; he that hath wrong, hopes.
GEORGE HERBERT: *Outlandish Proverbs,* 1640

Lawsuits consume time and money and rest and friends. IBID.

One suit breeds twenty. IBID.

He that loves law will get his fill of it.
JAMES KELLY: *Complete Collection of Scottish Proverbs,* 1721

A lean award is better than a fat judgment.
BENJAMIN FRANKLIN: *Poor Richard's Almanac,* 1753

Fees to judges, puisne judges, clerks, protonotaries, philizers, chirographers, underclerks, proclamators, counsel, witnesses, jurymen, marshals, tipstaffs, criers, porters; for enrollings, exemplifications, bails, vouchers, returns, caveats, examinations, filings of words, entries, declarations, replications, recordats, nolle prosequis, certioraris, mittimus, demurrers, special verdicts, informations, scire facias, supersedeas, habeas corpus, coach hire, treating of witnesses, etc.
JOHN ARBUTHNOT: *Law is a Bottomless Pit,* XI, 1712

To set an attorney to work to worry and torment another man is a very base act; to alarm his family as well as himself, while you are sitting quietly at home.
WILLIAM COBBETT: *Advice to Young Men,* II, 1829

A machine which you go into as a pig and come out of as a sausage.
AMBROSE BIERCE: *The Devil's Dictionary,* 1906

Nearly every lawsuit is an insult to the intelligence of both plaintiff and defendant.
E. W. HOWE: *Sinner Sermons,* 1926

Going to law is losing a cow for the sake of a cat. CHINESE PROVERB

Win your lawsuit and lose your money. IBID.

One goes to court with one lawsuit and comes home with two. DANISH PROVERB

If you've a good case, try to compromise; if a bad one, take it into court. FRENCH PROVERB

Go to law for a sheep – and lose your cow. GERMAN PROVERB

A lawsuit is a fruit-tree planted in a lawyer's garden. ITALIAN PROVERB

A personal action dies with the person. (Actio personalis moritur cum persona.) LEGAL MAXIM

It is for the public good that there be an end of litigation. (Expedit reipublicae ut sit finis litium.) IBID.

A happy death is better than a lawsuit. SPANISH PROVERB

[*See also* Litigant.

Law, Sumptuary

It is the highest impertinence and presumption in kings and ministers to pretend to watch over the economy of private people, and to restrain their expense, either by sumptuary laws or by prohibiting the importation of foreign luxuries. They are themselves always, and without any exception, the greatest spendthrifts in the society.
ADAM SMITH: *The Wealth of Nations,* II, 1776

Lawyer

The lawyer is always in a hurry.
PLATO: *Theætetus, c.* 360 B.C.

Zenas the lawyer. TITUS III, 13, *c.* 60

The lawyers rejected the counsel of God.
LUKE VII, 30, *c.* 75

Woe unto ye also, ye lawyers! for ye lade men with burdens grievous to be born, and ye yourselves touch not the burdens with one of your fingers.
LUKE XI, 46

Woe unto you, lawyers! for ye have taken away the key of knowledge: ye entered not in yourselves, and them that were entering in ye hindered.
LUKE XI, 52

Then stood there up one in the council, a Pharisee, named Gamaliel, a doctor of the law.
ACTS V, 34, *c.* 75

The Devil makes his Christmas pie of lawyers' tongues.
ENGLISH PROVERB, traced to the XVI century

Lawyers use the law as shoemakers use leather; rubbing it, pressing it, and stretching it with their teeth, all to the end of making it fit their purposes.
Ascribed to LOUIS XII of France (1462–1515)

[The Utopians] have no lawyers among them, for they consider them as a sort of people whose profession it is to disguise matters.
THOMAS MORE: *Utopia,* 1516

God has not given laws to make out of right wrong, and out of wrong right, as the un-Christianlike lawyers do, who study law only for the sake of gain and profit.
MARTIN LUTHER: *Table-Talk,* DCCCXXX, 1569

From the physician and attorney keep not the truth hidden.
JOHN FLORIO: *First Frutes,* 1578

Lawyers and physicians are an ill provision for any country.
MICHEL DE MONTAIGNE: *Essays,* III, 1588

Of three things the Devil makes his mess:
Of lawyers' tongues, of scriveners' fingers —
You the third may guess.
JOHN FLORIO: *Second Frutes,* 1591

The first thing we do, let's kill all the lawyers.
SHAKESPEARE: *II Henry VI,* IV, *c.* 1591

Adversaries . . . in law
Strive mightily, but eat and drink as friends.
SHAKESPEARE: *The Taming of the Shrew,* I, 1594

May not that be the skull of a lawyer? Where be his quiddities now, his quillets, his cases, his tenures, and his tricks?
SHAKESPEARE: *Hamlet,* V, *c.* 1601

You wear out a good wholesome forenoon in hearing a cause between an orange-wife and a fosset-seller, and then return to the controversy of three pence to a second day of audience.
SHAKESPEARE: *Coriolanus,* II, *c.* 1607

See the galleons, the galleasses, the great armadas of the law; then there be hoys and petty vessels, oars and scullers.
THOMAS MIDDLETON: *A Trick to Catch the Old One,* I, 1608

A man may as well open an oyster without a knife as a lawyer's mouth without a fee.
BARTEN HOLYDAY: *Technogamia,* 1618

Few lawyers die well; few physicians live well.
WILLIAM CAMDEN: *Remains Concerning Britain* (4th ed.), 1636

Go not for . . . every quarrel to the lawyer, nor for every thirst to the pot.
GEORGE HERBERT: *Outlandish Proverbs,* 1640

Lawyers are accounted knaves over all the country.
Anon.: *The Countryman's Care,* 1641

Lawyers, like bread, [are best] when they are young and new.
THOMAS FULLER: *The Holy State and the Profane State,* 1642

Your pettifoggers damn their souls,
To share with knaves in cheating fools.
SAMUEL BUTLER: *Hudibras,* I, 1663

No good attorney will ever go to law.
GIOVANNI TORRIANO: *Italian Proverbs,* 1666

A good lawyer, an evil neighbor.
JOHN RAY: *English Proverbs,* 1670

Fair and softly, as lawyers go to Heaven.
IBID.

A man without money needs no more fear a crowd of lawyers than a crowd of pickpockets.
WILLIAM WYCHERLEY: *The Plain Dealer,* III, *c.* 1674

Of lawyers and physicians I shall say nothing, because this country is very peaceable and healthy. Long may it so continue, and never have occasion for the tongue of the one nor the pen of the other, both equally destructive of men's estates and lives.
GABRIEL THOMAS: *An Historical and Geographical Account of the Province and Country of Pennsylvania and of West New Jersey,* 1698

What's the first excellence in a lawyer? Tautology. What the second? Tautology. What the third? Tautology.
RICHARD STEELE: *The Funeral,* I, 1701

These are the mountebanks of state, . . .
The mastiffs of a government,
To worry and run down the innocent.
DANIEL DEFOE: *A Hymn to the Pillory,* 1703

Sometimes a man who deserves to be looked down upon because he is a fool is despised only because he is a lawyer.

C. L. DE MONTESQUIEU: *Persian Letters*, XLIV, 1721

Laws are best explained, interpreted and applied by those whose interest and abilities lie in perverting, confounding and eluding them.

JONATHAN SWIFT: *Gulliver's Travels*, II, 1726

God works wonders now and then;
Behold! a lawyer, an honest man.

BENJAMIN FRANKLIN: *Poor Richard's Almanac*, 1733

The fell attorney prowls for prey.

SAMUEL JOHNSON: *London*, 1738

There have been lawyers that were orators, philosophers, historians. There have been Bacons and Clarendons. There will be none such any more till, in some better age, true ambition or the love of fame prevails over avarice, and men find leisure and encouragement to prepare themselves for the exercise of this profession by climbing up to the vantage ground — so my Lord Bacon calls it — of science, instead of grovelling all their lives below in a mean but gainful application to all the little arts of chicane.

HENRY ST. JOHN (VISCOUNT BOLINGBROKE): *The Study of History*, 1752

The laws I love; the lawyers I suspect.

CHARLES CHURCHILL: *The Farewell*, 1764

I question not but there are many attorneys born with open and honest hearts: but I know not one that has had the least practice who is not selfish, trickish, and disingenuous.

WILLIAM SHENSTONE: *Of Men and Manners*, 1764

It is unjust, sir, to censure lawyers for multiplying words when they argue; it is often necessary for them to multiply words.

SAMUEL JOHNSON: *Boswell's Life*, 1781

These men are more properly law-givers than interpreters of the law; and have united the skill and dexterity of the scribe with the power and ambition of the prince: who can tell where this may lead in a future day?

ST. JOHN DE CRÈVECOEUR: *Letters from an American Farmer*, IX, 1782

I would be loth to speak ill of any person who I do not know deserves it, but I am afraid he is an attorney.

SAMUEL JOHNSON: *Mrs. Piozzi's Anecdotes*, 1786

Yes, Jamie, he was a bad man, but he might have been worse; he was an Irishman, but he might have been a Scotchman; he was a priest, but he might have been a lawyer.

SAMUEL PARR: Said of James O'Coighy, hanged for treason on June 7, 1798

He saw a lawyer killing a viper
On a dunghill hard by his own stable,
And the Devil smiled, for it put him in mind
Of Cain and his brother Abel.

S. T. COLERIDGE: *The Devil's Thoughts*, 1799

A lawyer's opinion is worth nothing unless paid for.

ENGLISH PROVERB, not recorded before the XIX century

A lawyer art thou? Draw not nigh!
Go, carry to some fitter place
The keenness of that practised eye,
The hardness of that sallow face.

WILLIAM WORDSWORTH: *A Poet's Epitaph*, 1800

Young lawyers attend the courts, not because they have business there but because they have no business anywhere else.

WASHINGTON IRVING: *Salmagundi*, June 27, 1807

By law's dark by-ways he had stored his mind
With wicked knowledge how to cheat mankind.

GEORGE CRABBE: *The Borough*, VI, 1810

Who calls a lawyer rogue, may find, too late,
On one of these depends his whole estate.

GEORGE CRABBE: *Tales*, II (*The Gentleman Farmer*), 1812

A lawyer without history or literature is a mechanic, a mere working mason; if he possesses some knowledge of these, he may venture to call himself an architect.

WALTER SCOTT: *Guy Mannering*, XXXVII, 1815

I think we may class the lawyer in the natural history of monsters.

JOHN KEATS: *Letter to George and Georgiana Keats*, March 13, 1819

If you cannot avoid a quarrel with a blackguard let your lawyer manage it rather than yourself. No man sweeps his own chimney but employs a chimney-sweeper who has no objection to dirty work, because it is his trade.

C. C. COLTON: *Lacon*, 1820

Lawyers are the only civil delinquents whose judges must of necessity be chosen from themselves.

IBID.

A barrister of extended practise, if he has any talents at all, is the best companion in the world.

WALTER SCOTT: *Journal*, April 30, 1828

He is no lawyer who cannot take two sides.

CHARLES LAMB: *Letter to Samuel Rogers*, Dec., 1833

The profession of the law is the only aristocracy that can exist in a democracy without doing violence to its nature.

ALEXIS DE TOCQUEVILLE: *Democracy in America*, I, 1835

Every person who enters into a learned profession undertakes to bring to the exercise of it a reasonable degree of care and skill. He does not undertake, if he is an attorney, that at all events you shall gain your case; nor does he undertake to use the highest possible degree of skill: there may be persons who have higher education and greater advantages than he has. But he undertakes to bring a fair, reasonable, and competent degree of skill.

LORD CHIEF JUSTICE TINDAL: *Judgment in Lanphier and wife* vs. *Phipos,* 1838

If there were no bad people there would be no good lawyers.

CHARLES DICKENS: *The Old Curiosity Shop,* LVI, 1841

An eminent lawyer cannot be a dishonest man. Tell me a man is dishonest, and I will answer he is no lawyer. He cannot be, because he is careless and reckless of justice; the law is not in his heart, is not the standard and rule of his conduct.

DANIEL WEBSTER: Speech at Charleston, S. C., May 10, 1847

Most good lawyers live well, work hard, and die poor. IBID.

Weary lawyers with endless tongues.

J. G. WHITTIER: *Maud Muller,* 1854

Fools and obstinate men make lawyers rich.

H. G. BOHN: *Handbook of Proverbs,* 1855

The law . . . is a profession which abounds with honorable men, and in which I believe there are fewer scamps than in any other.

GEORGE BORROW: *Wild Wales,* LV, 1862

It is a strange trade, that of advocacy. Your intellect, your highest heavenly gift, hung up in the shop window like a loaded pistol for sale, will either blow out a pestilent scoundrel's brains, or the scoundrel's salutary sheriff's officer's (in a sense), as you please to choose for your guinea.

THOMAS CARLYLE: *Lord Jeffrey,* 1867

He was a knowing man enough, a keen country lawyer, but honest.

O. W. HOLMES: *The Guardian Angel,* XXXI, 1867

Thus wrangled, brangled, jangled they a month.

ROBERT BROWNING: *The Ring and the Book,* I, 1868

Here lies John Shaw,
Attorney-at-law;
And when he died,
The Devil cried,
"Give us your paw,
John Shaw
Attorney-at-law!"

H. J. LOARING: *Epitaphs Quaint, Curious and Elegant,* 1872

The longer I practise law, and the more success I have, the more it seems to me to depend upon luck and the fancy of people.

Ascribed to JOSEPH H. CHOATE, *c.* 1878

The weapon of the advocate is the sword of the soldier, not the dagger of the assassin.

Ascribed to ALEXANDER COCKBURN (1805–80)

The mere advocate, however brilliant, will lose the most cases, though he may win the most verdicts.

B. F. BUTLER: *Autobiography and Personal Reminiscences,* 1892

Whether you're an honest man or whether you're a thief
Depends on whose solicitor has given me a brief.

W. S. GILBERT: *Utopia Limited,* I, 1893

The only man in whom ignorance of the law is not punished.

ELBERT HUBBARD: *Roycroft Dictionary and Book of Epigrams,* 1923

I will not counsel or maintain any suit or proceeding which shall appear to me to be unjust, nor any defense except such as I believe to be honestly debatable under the law of the land.

Model oath for candidates for admission to the bar, prepared by the American Bar Association, *c.* 1925

A lawyer must first get on, then get honor, and then get honest. Author unidentified

A town that can't support one lawyer can always support two. IBID.

By birth and interest lawyers belong to the people; by habit and taste to the aristocracy. Thus they proclaim themselves a logical connecting link between the two. IBID.

The animals are not so stupid as is thought: they have no lawyers. IBID.

"Virtue in the middle," said the Devil, as he sat down between two lawyers.

DANISH PROVERB

The better lawyer, the worst Christian.

DUTCH PROVERB

God save us from a lawyer's etcetera.

FRENCH PROVERB

No lawyer will ever go to Heaven so long as there is room for more in Hell. IBID.

A lawyer and a wagon-wheel must be well greased. GERMAN PROVERB

Lawyers and soldiers are the Devil's playmates. IBID.

Love all men — but not lawyers.

IRISH PROVERB

A bad agreement is better than a good lawyer.

ITALIAN PROVERB

An unprincipled orator [i.e. lawyer] subverts the laws. (Orator improbus leges subvertit.)
LATIN PROVERB

When God wanted to chastise mankind He invented lawyers. RUSSIAN PROVERB

It's an ill cause that the lawyer thinks shame o'.
SCOTTISH PROVERB

Fools and stubborn men make wealthy lawyers.
SPANISH PROVERB

[*See also* Accessory, Accomplice, Character, Clergyman, Devil, Government, Law, Lawsuit, Lawyer and Client, Profession, Soldier, Vocation.

Lawyer and Client

Orphans around his bed the lawyer sees,
And takes the plaintiff's and defendant's fees.
His fellow pick-purse, watching for a job,
Fancies his fingers in the cully's fob.
JONATHAN SWIFT: *On Dreams,* 1724

Lawyers are always more ready to get a man into troubles than out of them.
OLIVER GOLDSMITH: *The Good Natur'd Man,* III, 1768

A lawyer has no business with the justice or injustice of the cause which he undertakes unless his client asks his opinion, and then he is bound to give it honestly. The justice or injustice of the cause is to be decided by the judge.
SAMUEL JOHNSON: *Boswell's Tour to the Hebrides,* Aug. 15, 1773

If the advocate refuses to defend from what he may think of the charge or of the defense, he assumes the character of the judge; nay, he assumes it before the hour of judgment; and, in proportion to his rank and reputation, puts the heavy influence of, perhaps, a mistaken opinion into the scale against the accused.
THOMAS ERSKINE (LORD ERSKINE): On the trial of THOMAS PAINE for publishing *The Rights of Man,* 1792

A counsel is not to speak of that which he knows; he is not called upon to consider whether the facts with which he is dealing are true or false. What he has to do is to argue as best he can, without degrading himself, in order to maintain the proposition which will carry with it either the protection or the remedy which he desires for his client. If, amidst the difficulties of his position, he were to be called upon during the heat of his argument to consider whether what he says is true or false, whether what he says is relevant or irrelevant, he would have his mind so embarrassed that he could not do the duty which he is called upon to perform.
MR. JUSTICE BEST: *Judgment in Munster* vs. *Lamb,* 1833

Lawyers' gowns are lined with the wilfulness of their clients.
H. G. BOHN: *Handbook of Proverbs,* 1855

The good lawyer is not the man who has an eye to every side and angle of contingency, and qualifies all his qualifications, but who throws himself on your part so heartily that he can get you out of a scrape.
R. W. EMERSON: *The Conduct of Life,* II, 1860

A lawyer starts life giving $500 worth of law for $5, and ends giving $5 worth for $500.
Ascribed to BENJAMIN H. BREWSTER, Attorney-General of the United States (1816–88)

Lawyers have been known to wrest from reluctant juries triumphant verdicts of acquittal for their clients, even when those clients, as often happens, were clearly and unmistakably innocent.
OSCAR WILDE: *The Decay of Lying,* 1889

A lawyer collected $641 for a client. The agreement was that the lawyer was to have 10% as a commission. How much did the client receive?
ELBERT HUBBARD: *Roycroft Dictionary and Book of Epigrams,* 1923

When two dogs fight for a bone and the third runs off with it, there's a lawyer among the dogs. GERMAN PROVERB

A peasant between two lawyers is like a fish between two cats. SPANISH PROVERB

[*See also* Lawyer, Litigation.

Lawyer, Philadephia

Three Philadelphia lawyers are a match for the Devil.
NEW ENGLAND PROVERB (Thornton's first example of its appearance in print in this form is dated 1924, but he traces the notion of the Philadelphia lawyer's extraordinary shrewdness back to 1803, and it is probably older)

Layman

Antiquity teaches us that laymen are in a high degree hostile to the clergy.
POPE BONIFACE VIII: *Clericis laicos,* 1296

Laziness

If long, she is lazy; if little, she is loud.
JOHN FLORIO: *Second Frutes,* 1591

Lazybones.
ENGLISH TERM, traced by the New English Dictionary to 1592

The lazy man the most doth love.
ROBERT HERRICK: *Hesperides,* 1648

Lazy people take the most pains.
ENGLISH PROVERB, common since the XVIII century

A lazy ox is little better for the goad.
THOMAS FULLER: *Gnomologia,* 1732

A lazy sheep thinks its wool heavy. IBID.

Laziness travels so slowly that poverty soon overtakes him.
BENJAMIN FRANKLIN: *Poor Richard's Almanac,* 1756

Laziness is premature death.
STANISLAUS LESZCYNSKI (KING OF POLAND): *Œuvres du philosophe bienfaisant,* 1763

Laziness is often mistaken for patience.
FRENCH PROVERB

Lazy people are always eager to be doing something. IBID.

It is always holiday to the lazy. (Ignavis semper feriæ sunt.) LATIN PROVERB

A lazy man is never lucky. PERSIAN PROVERB

Lazy youth makes lousy age.
SCOTTISH PROVERB

Only the crazy give aid to the lazy.
WELSH PROVERB

[*See also* Blame, Hungarian, Idleness, Industry, Leisure, Poverty, Property, Sloth.

Leadership

The leaders of this people cause them to err; and they that are led of them are destroyed.
ISAIAH IX, 16, *c.* 700 B.C.

If the trumpet give an uncertain sound, who shall prepare himself to the battle?
I CORINTHIANS XIV, 8, *c.* 55

If the blind lead the blind, both shall fall into the ditch.
MATTHEW XV, 14, *c.* 75 (Cf. LUKE VI, 39, *c.* 75)

He that leadeth into captivity shall go into captivity. REVELATION XIII, 10, *c.* 95

Reason and judgment are the qualities of a leader. TACITUS: *History,* III, *c.* 100

In all legislative assemblies the greater the number composing them may be, the fewer will be the men who will in fact direct their proceedings.
ALEXANDER HAMILTON: *The Federalist,* 1788

Whoever is foremost leads the herd.
J. C. F. SCHILLER: *Wallenstein's Death,* III, 1799

When we think we lead we most are led.
BYRON: *The Two Foscari,* II, 1821

A man Cæsar is born, and for ages after we have a Roman Empire. Christ is born, and millions of minds so grow and cleave to His genius, that He is confounded with virtue and the possible of man. An institution is the lengthened shadow of one man.
R. W. EMERSON: *Self-Reliance,* 1841

If human progress had been merely a matter of leadership we should be in Utopia today.
THOMAS B. REED: Speech at Colby University, June 30, 1885

An army of stags led by a lion would be better than an army of lions led by a stag.
LATIN PROVERB

[*See also* Boss, First.

Leaf

[*See* Ugliness.

League of Nations

A general association of nations must be formed under specific covenants for the purpose of affording mutual guarantees of political independence and territorial integrity to great and small states alike.
WOODROW WILSON: Address to Congress, Jan. 8, 1918 (One of the Fourteen Points)

The Democratic party favors the League of Nations as the surest, if not the only practicable means of maintaining the peace of the world and terminating the insufferable burden of great military and naval establishments. It was for this that America broke away from traditional isolation and spent her blood and treasure to crush a colossal scheme of conquest.
Democratic National Platform, 1920

The League exists as a foreign agency. We hope it will be helpful. But the United States sees no reason to limit its own freedom and independence of action by joining it.
CALVIN COOLIDGE: Message to Congress, Dec. 6, 1923

The Democratic party renews its declaration of confidence in the ideal of world peace, the League of Nations and the World Court of Justice as together constituting the supreme effort of the statesmanship and religious conviction of our time to organize the world for peace.
Democratic National Platform, 1924

The Republican party maintains the traditional American policy of noninterference in the political affairs of other nations. This government has definitely refused membership in the League of Nations and to assume any obligations under the covenant of the League. On this we stand.
Republican National Platform, 1928

[*See also* Peace (International).

Leak

A sma' leak will sink a great ship.
SCOTTISH PROVERB

Lean

My leanness, my leanness, woe unto me!
ISAIAH XXIV, 16, *c.* 700 B.C.

Yond Cassius has a lean and hungry look.
SHAKESPEARE: *Julius Cæsar,* I, 1599

Men of a lean habit of body are commonly a long time healthy, having good appetites and strong stomachs for digestion.
TOBIAS VENNER: *Via recta,* 1620

As the lean people are the most active, unquiet, and ambitious, they everywhere govern the world, and may certainly oppress their antagonists whenever they please.
DAVID HUME: *Letter to Mrs. Dysart,* March 19, 1751

A goose, a woman, and a goat are bad things lean. PORTUGUESE PROVERB

[*See also* Age (Old), Fat, Horse, Hunger, Thin, Thinking.

Leap

Rejoice thee in that day, and leap for joy.
LUKE VI, 23, *c.* 75

Look before you leap.
ENGLISH PROVERB, traced by Smith to *c.* 1350

By a leap. (Per saltum.) LATIN PHRASE

[*See also* Jump.

Learning

He who remembers from day to day what he has yet to learn, and from month to month what he has learned already, may be said to have a love of learning.
CONFUCIUS: *Analects,* XIX, *c.* 500 B.C.

What is most needed for learning is an humble mind.
CONFUCIUS: *The Book of History,* IV, *c.* 500 B.C.

Learning is ever young, even in old age.
ÆSCHYLUS: *Agamemnon, c.* 490 B.C.

A wise man will hear, and will increase in learning. PROVERBS I, 5, *c.* 350 B.C.

There is no royal road to learning.
A corruption of Euclid's saying to Ptolemy I: "There is no royal road to geometry," *c.* 300 B.C.

A man of learning has riches within him.
PHAEDRUS: *Fabulæ Æsopiæ,* IV, *c.* 40

The mind is slow to unlearn what it has been long in learning. SENECA: *Troades, c.* 60

Men learn while they teach. (Homines, dum docent, discunt.)
SENECA: *Epistulæ morales ad Lucilium, c.* 63

Ever learning, and never able to come to the knowledge of the truth.
II TIMOTHY III, 7, *c.* 65

Much learning doth make thee mad.
ACTS XXVI, 24, *c.* 75

If the heavens were all parchment, and the trees of the forest all pens, and every human being were a scribe, it would still be impossible to record all that I have learned from my teachers.
Ascribed to JOCHANAN BEN ZAKKAI, *c.* 75

A man without learning grows old like an ox; his flesh grows, but not his wisdom.
The Dhammapada, XI, *c.* 100

Learning is a name superior to beauty; learning is better than hidden treasure. Learning is a companion on a journey to a strange country; learning is strength inexhaustible. A man in this world without learning is as a beast of the field.
The Hitopadesa, intro., *c.* 500

Commonly those that be unfittest for learning be chiefly set to learning.
ROGER ASHAM: *Toxiphilus,* 1545

Learning teacheth more in one year than experience in twenty.
ROGER ASHAM: *The Scolemaster, c.* 1560

I am still learning. (Ancora imparo.)
Favorite saying of MICHELANGELO (1474–1563)

To what purpose do we so arm and steel ourselves with these laboring efforts of learning? Let us survey the surface of the earth, and consider so many simple people as we see toiling, sweltering, and drooping about their business, which never heard of Aristotle nor of Plato. From those doth nature daily draw and afford us effects of constancy and patterns of patience, more pure and forcible than are those we so curiously study for in schools.
MICHEL DE MONTAIGNE: *Essays,* III, 1588

Oh, this learning, what a thing it is!
SHAKESPEARE: *The Taming of the Shrew,* I, 1594

The burden of lean and wasteful learning.
SHAKESPEARE: *As You Like It,* III, *c.* 1600

No knave to the learned knave.
FYNES MORYSON: *Itinerary,* III, 1617

Live and learn.
ENGLISH PROVERB, traced by Apperson to *c.* 1620

Learning hath his infancy, when it is but beginning, and almost childish; then his youth, when it is luxuriant and juvenile; then his strength of years, when it is solid and reduced; and, lastly, his old age, when it waxeth dry and exhaust.
FRANCIS BACON: *Essays,* LVIII, 1625

When a great learned man, who is long in making, dieth, much learning dieth with him.
EDWARD COKE: *Institutes,* I, 1628

Learning is the eye of the mind.
THOMAS DRAXE: *Bibliotheca scholastica instructissima,* 1633

Much learning, much sorrow.
JOHN CLARKE: *Parœmiologia Anglo-Latina,* 1639

That which is naught is soon learned. IBID.

A handful of good life is better than a bushel of learning.
GEORGE HERBERT: *Outlandish Proverbs,* 1640

Learn young, learn fair.
DAVID FERGUSSON: *Scottish Proverbs,* 1641

The end of learning is to repair the ruins of our first parents by regaining to know God aright, and out of that knowledge to love Him, to imitate Him, to be like Him, as we may the nearest by possessing our souls of true virtue, which being united to the heavenly grace of faith, makes up the highest perfection.
JOHN MILTON: *Tractate on Education,* 1644

The love of learning and the love of money rarely meet.
GEORGE HERBERT: *Jacula Prudentum,* 1651

A man is never too old to learn.
THOMAS MIDDLETON: *The Mayor of Quinborough,* V, 1651

Learning, that cobweb of the brain,
Profane, erroneous, and vain.
SAMUEL BUTLER: *Hudibras,* I, 1663

Learning makes the wise wiser and the fool more foolish.
JOHN RAY: *English Proverbs,* 1670

That which is evil is soon learned. IBID.

Most men's learning is nothing but history dully taken up. JOHN SELDEN: *Table-Talk,* 1689

No man is the wiser for his learning: it may administer matter to work in, or objects to work upon; but wit and wisdom are born with a man. IBID.

I am of those who must be taught, and am seeking for teachers.
PETER THE GREAT of Russia: Motto adopted 1697

Words are but wind; and learning is nothing but words; ergo, learning is nothing but wind.
JONATHAN SWIFT: *A Tale of a Tub,* VIII, 1704

A little learning is a dangerous thing;
Drink deep, or taste not the Pierian spring:
There shallow draughts intoxicate the brain,
And drinking largely sobers us again.
ALEXANDER POPE: *An Essay on Criticism,* II, 1711

Never too late to learn.
JAMES KELLY: *Complete Collection of Scottish Proverbs,* 1721

Learning by study must be won;
'Twas ne'er entail'd from son to son.
JOHN GAY: *Fables,* I, 1727

Learning makes a good man better, and an ill man worse.
THOMAS FULLER: *Gnomologia,* 1732 (Cf. RAY, *ante,* 1670)

Ask of the learn'd the way: the learn'd are blind.
ALEXANDER POPE: *An Essay on Man,* IV, 1734

Of learned fools I have seen ten times ten; of unlearned wise men, I have seen a hundred.
BENJAMIN FRANKLIN: *Poor Richard's Almanac,* 1735

Most learned men are like courtiers. Sometimes they are just as greedy, intriguing, treacherous, and cruel; and the only difference between the pests of the court and the pests of the school is that the latter are the more ridiculous.
VOLTAIRE: *Letter to Frederick the Great,* Aug. 26, 1736

Much learning shows how little mortals know.
EDWARD YOUNG: *Night Thoughts,* VI, 1744

Wear your learning, like your watch, in a private pocket; and do not pull it out and strike it, merely to show that you have one. If you are asked what o'clock it is, tell it; but do not proclaim it hourly and unasked, like the watchman.
LORD CHESTERFIELD: *Letter to his son,* Feb. 22, 1748

Tim was so learned that he could name a horse in nine languages. So ignorant that he bought a cow to ride on.
BENJAMIN FRANKLIN: *Poor Richard's Almanac,* 1750

Learning is acquired by reading books; but the much more necessary learning, the knowledge of the world, is only to be acquired by reading men, and studying all the various editions of them.
LORD CHESTERFIELD: *Letter to his son,* March 16, 1752

And still they gazed, and still the wonder grew
That one small head should carry all he knew.
OLIVER GOLDSMITH: *The Deserted Village,* 1770

When we are young we learn much because we are universally ignorant; we observe everything because everything is new.
SAMUEL JOHNSON: *Letter to Hester Thrale,* Aug. 5, 1775

I would by no means wish a daughter of mine to be a progeny of learning.
R. B. SHERIDAN: *The Rivals,* I, 1775

Gie me ae spark o' nature's fire:
That's a' the learning I desire.
ROBERT BURNS: *Epistle to J. Lapraik*, April 1, 1785

A man of learning is never bored.
JEAN PAUL RICHTER: *Hesperus*, VIII, 1795

In the republic of learning everyone wants to command.
G. C. LICHTENBERG: *Reflections*, 1799

With just enough of learning to misquote.
BYRON: *English Bards and Scotch Reviewers*, 1809

Learning is the knowledge of that which none but the learned know. He is the most learned man who knows the most of what is farthest removed from common life and actual observation, that is of the least practical utility, and least liable to be brought to the test of experience, and that, having been handed down through the greatest number of intermediate stages, is the most full of uncertainty, difficulties, and contradictions.
WILLIAM HAZLITT: *The Ignorance of the Learned*, 1821

Learn to unlearn.
BENJAMIN DISRAELI: *Contarini Fleming*, I, 1832

Bees are sometimes drowned (or suffocated) in the honey which they collect. So some writers are lost in their collected learning.
NATHANIEL HAWTHORNE: *American Note-Books*, 1842

Soon learnt, soon forgotten.
H. G. BOHN: *Handbook of Proverbs*, 1855

We do not learn by inference and deduction and the application of mathematics to philosophy, but by direct intercourse and sympathy. H. D. THOREAU: *Excursions*, 1863

All learning which is the outgrowth of sound reason, and in conformity with the truth of things, serves to confirm what we believe on the authority of God.
POPE LEO XIII: *Libertas praestantissimum*, June 20, 1888

A learned man is an idler who kills time by study.
GEORGE BERNARD SHAW: *Maxims for Revolutionists*, 1903

A little general learning has come to be a useful thing in a world where from its infrequency it has ceased to be dangerous.
W. C. BROWNELL: *Standards*, 1916

Be eager for learning, even if it comes from the snout of a hog. ARAB PROVERB

To be fond of learning is to be at the gate of knowledge. CHINESE PROVERB

The learned are seldom lucky.
GERMAN PROVERB

He who is learned but does not fear God is like a woman without manners.
HEBREW PROVERB

One hour of learning and good works in this world is better than all the joys of the hereafter. IBID.

Learning without wisdom is a load of books on an ass's back. JAPANESE PROVERB

Learning breeds difficulty. (Difficultatem facit doctrina.) LATIN PROVERB

When house and land are gone and spent,
Then learning is most excellent.
OLD ENGLISH RHYME

What we first learn we best ken.
SCOTTISH PROVERB

Learn young, learn fair;
Learn auld, learn mair. SCOTTISH RHYME

[*See also* Books, Devil, Experience, Fool, Health, Inspiration, Knowledge, Knowledge *vs.* Wisdom, Lady, Pedant, Philosophy, Printing, Teaching, Wisdom.

Least

Inasmuch as ye have done it unto one of the least of these my brethren, ye have done it unto me.
MATTHEW XXV, 40, *c.* 75 (Cf. XXV, 45)

He that is least among you all, the same shall be great. LUKE IX, 48, *c.* 75

The least foolish is wise.
GEORGE HERBERT: *Outlandish Proverbs*, 1640

[*See also* Evil, Last.

Leather

[Elijah] was a hairy man, and girt with a girdle of leather. II KINGS I, 8, *c.* 500 B.C.

There's nothing like leather.
ENGLISH PROVERB, traced by Smith to 1692

Leaven

A little leaven leaveneth the whole lump.
GALATIANS V, 9, *c.* 50

Lecture

The lecturer stands on a large raised platform, on which sit around him the bald and hoary-headed and superlatively wise. Ladies come in large numbers, especially those who aspire to soar above the frivolities of the world.
ANTHONY TROLLOPE: *North American*, I, 1862

Lee, Robert E. (1807–70)

He is almost unapproachable, and yet no man is more simple, or less ostentatious, hating all pretension. It would be impossible for an officer to be more reverenced, admired and respected. He eats the rations of the soldier and quarters alone in his tent.
JOHN TYLER: *Letter to Sterling Price*, June 7, 1864

Whatever General Lee's feelings were I do not know. As he was a man of much dignity, with an impassable face, it was impossible to say whether he felt inwardly glad that the end had finally come, or felt sad over the result and was too manly to show it.

U. S. GRANT: *Personal Memoirs,* LXVII, 1885 (He is describing his meeting with Lee at Appomattox, April 9, 1865)

I am now considered such a monster that I hesitate to darken with my shadow the doors of those I love best, lest I should bring upon them misfortune.

ROBERT E. LEE: *Letter to Martha Custis Williams,* April 7, 1866

Lefthanded

Ehud, the son of Gera, a Benjamite, a man lefthanded. JUDGES III, 15, *c.* 500 B.C.

There were seven hundred chosen men lefthanded; every one could sling stones at a hair breadth, and not miss. JUDGES XX, 16

Leg

His legs are as pillars of marble, set upon sockets of fine gold.

SOLOMON'S SONG V, 15, *c.* 200 B.C.

Her legs were such Diana shows,
When tuckt up she a-hunting goes;
With buskins shortened to descry
The happy dawning of her thigh.

ROBERT HERRICK: *Hesperides,* 1648

As to my health, thanks be to God, as long as I sit still I am without pain, but if I do but walk a little I have pains in my legs, but that is, I think, caused by former colds, and because they have carried my body so long.

ANTONY VAN LEEUWENHOEK: *Letter to J. Chamberlayne,* May 17, 1707

[Henry] Irving's legs are limpid and utter. Both are delicately intellectual, but his left leg is a poem.

Ascribed to OSCAR WILDE, *c.* 1879

Bad legs and ill wives should stay at hame.

SCOTTISH PROVERB

[*See also* Belly.

Legend

History has its truth; and so has legend hers.

VICTOR HUGO: *Ninety-Three,* II, 1879

Legislation

The people are not qualified to legislate. With us, therefore, they only choose the legislators.

THOMAS JEFFERSON: *Letter to L'Abbé Arnond,* 1789

The best public measures are seldom adopted from previous wisdom, but forc'd by the occasion.

BENJAMIN FRANKLIN: *Autobiography,* 1798

No good measure was ever proposed which, if duly pursued, failed to prevail in the end.

THOMAS JEFFERSON: *Letter to Edward Coles,* 1814

Foolish legislature is a rope of sand which perishes in the twisting.

R. W. EMERSON: *Politics,* 1841

No man with a genius for legislation has appeared in America. They are rare in the history of the world.

H. D. THOREAU: *Cape Cod,* 1865

One of the greatest delusions in the world is the hope that the evils in this world are to be cured by legislation.

THOMAS B. REED: Speech in the House of Representatives, 1886

Blundering experiments in legislation cannot be simply abandoned if they do not work well; even if they are set aside, they leave their effects behind; and they create vested interests which make it difficult to set them aside.

W. G. SUMNER: *Federal Legislation on Railroads,* 1887

[*See also* Law, Legislature, Party.

Legislature

Kings govern by means of popular assemblies only when they cannot do without them.

CHARLES JAMES FOX: Speech in the House of Commons, Oct. 31, 1776

The more multitudinous a representative assembly may be rendered, the more it will partake of the infirmities incident to collective meetings of the people. Ignorance will be the dupe of cunning, and passion the slave of sophistry and declamation. The people can never err more than in supposing that by multiplying their representatives beyond a certain limit, they strengthen the barrier against the government of a few.

ALEXANDER HAMILTON: *The Federalist,* 1788

If the upper house agrees with the lower, it is superfluous; if it disagrees, it ought to be abolished.

E. J. SIEYÈS: *Qu'est-ce que le tiers état?,* 1789

The executive in our government is not the sole, it is scarcely the principal object of my jealousy. The tyranny of the legislatures is the most formidable dread at present and will be for many years. That of the executive will come in its turn, but it will be at a remote period.

THOMAS JEFFERSON: *Letter to James Madison,* 1789

[*See also* Assembly, Congress, Judiciary, Leadership, Opinion (Public), Parliament.

Leibniz, G. W. (1646–1716)

There are such people as Leibnizes on this earth; and their office seems not that of

planets — to revolve within the limits of one system; but that of comets — to connect different systems together.
THOMAS DE QUINCEY: *Superficial Knowledge, c.* 1847

Leisure

The wisdom of a learned man cometh by opportunity of leisure; and he that hath little business shall become wise.
ECCLESIASTICUS XXXVIII, 24, *c.* 180 B.C.

He was never less at leisure than when he was at leisure. CICERO: *De officiis,* III, 78 B.C.

Leisure with dignity. (Cum dignitate otium.)
CICERO: *Pro Sestio, c.* 50 B.C.

Who has more leisure than a worm?
SENECA: *Epistulæ morales ad Lucilium, c.* 63

They had no leisure so much as to eat.
MARK VI, 31, *c.* 70

Leisure is the mother of philosophy.
THOMAS HOBBES: *Leviathan,* IV, 1651

Idle folks have the least leisure.
JOHN RAY: *English Proverbs,* 1670

Leisure is pain; take off our chariot wheels;
How heavily we drag the load of life!
EDWARD YOUNG: *Night Thoughts,* II, 1742

A life of leisure and a life of laziness are two things.
BENJAMIN FRANKLIN: *Poor Richard's Almanac,* 1746

Leave us leisure to be good.
THOMAS GRAY: *Hymn to Adversity,* 1753

All intellectual improvement arises from leisure; all leisure arises from one working for another.
SAMUEL JOHNSON: *Boswell's Life,* April 13, 1773

What the banker sighs for, the meanest clown may have, — leisure and a quiet mind.
H. D. THOREAU: *Journal,* Jan. 18, 1841

It would be glorious to see mankind at leisure for once. It is nothing but work, work, work. I cannot easily buy a blankbook to write thoughts in; they are commonly ruled for dollars and cents.
H. D. THOREAU: *Life Without Principle,* 1863 (Atlantic Monthly, Oct.)

Increased means and increased leisure are the two civilizers of man.
BENJAMIN DISRAELI: Speech at Manchester, April 3, 1872

The advantage of leisure is mainly that we may have the power of choosing our own work, not certainly that it confers any privilege of idleness.
JOHN LUBBOCK (LORD AVEBURY): *The Pleasures of Life,* VI, 1887

A workman ought to have leisure in proportion to the wear and tear of his strength.
POPE LEO XIII: *Rerum novarum,* May 15, 1891

To be able to fill leisure intelligently is the last product of civilization.
BERTRAND RUSSELL: *The Conquest of Happiness,* 1930

[*See also* Busy, Civilization, Idleness.

Lemon

I'll be with you in the squeezing of a lemon.
OLIVER GOLDSMITH: *She Stoops to Conquer,* I, 1773

It was actually twelve miles from a lemon.
Ascribed to SYDNEY SMITH in *A Memoir of the Rev. Sydney Smith* by his daughter, Lady Holland, 1855

[*See also* Cocktail, Grapefruit.

Lemonade

This lemonade is as insipid as your soul — try it.
J. C. F. SCHILLER: *Kabale und Liebe,* V, 1784

[*See also* Heaven.

Lending

A good man showeth favor, and lendeth.
PSALMS CXII, 5, *c.* 150 B.C.

If thou wilt lend this money, lend it not
As to thy friends; for when did friendship take
A breed of barren metal of his friend?
But lend it rather to thine enemy;
Who, if he break, thou mayst with better face
Exact the penalty.
SHAKESPEARE: *The Merchant of Venice,* I, *c.* 1597

He that lends, gives.
GEORGE HERBERT: *Outlandish Proverbs,* 1640

Lend and lose; so play fools.
JOHN RAY: *English Proverbs,* 1670

The leeful man is the beggar's brother.
JAMES KELLY: *Complete Collection of Scottish Proverbs,* 1721 (*Leeful*= ready to lend)

Better give a shilling than lend and lose half a crown.
THOMAS FULLER: *Gnomologia,* 1732

Lend money to an enemy, and thou'lt gain him; to a friend, and thou'lt lose him.
BENJAMIN FRANKLIN: *Poor Richard's Almanac,* 1740

If you lend you either lose the money or gain an enemy. ALBANIAN PROVERB

Lending to a spendthrift is pelting a dog with meat balls. CHINESE PROVERB

Lending to God or the soil pays good interest.
DANISH PROVERB

Money lent to a friend must be recovered from an enemy. GERMAN PROVERB

It is better to give one lire than to lend twenty. ITALIAN PROVERB

Lend money to a city, but never to a man. JAPANESE PROVERB

Never lend a horse, a razor, or your wife. POLISH PROVERB

If you have had enough of your friend, lend him some money. RUSSIAN PROVERB

These three should never be lent: a weapon, a wife, and a dog. IBID.

[*See also* Acquaintance, Borrowing and Lending, Friend.

Leninism

Leninism has added no new principles to Marxism, nor abolished any of its old principles. Leninism is only Marxism brought up to date. It is the active Marxism of the era of imperialism and proletarian revolutions.

JOSEPH STALIN: Interview with the first American Labor Delegation in Russia, Sept. 9, 1927

Lent

The cutthroat butchers, wanting throats to cut,
At Lent's approach their bloody shambles shut;
For forty days their tyranny doth cease,
And men and beasts take truce and live at peace.

JOHN TAYLOR: *Jack-a-Lent*, 1630

After a carnival Lent ever follows.

PHILIP MASSINGER: *The City Madam*, IV, 1658

He has but a short Lent that must pay money at Easter.

THOMAS FULLER: *Gnomologia*, 1732

Marry in Lent, and you'll live to repent.

ENGLISH PROVERB, not recorded before the XIX century

A full stomach praises Lent.

DANISH PROVERB

[*See also* Debauchery.

Lentil

I hate with a bitter hatred the names of lentils and haricots — those pretentious cheats of the appetite, those tabulated humbugs, those certificated aridities calling themselves human food!

GEORGE GISSING: *The Private Papers of Henry Ryecroft*, 1903

Leopard

[*See* Change.

Leper

The leper in whom the plague is, his clothes shall be rent, and his head bare, and he shall put a covering upon his upper lip, and shall cry, Unclean, unclean.

LEVITICUS XIII, 45, *c.* 700 B.C.

Jesus put forth his hand, and touched him, saying, . . . Be thou clean. And immediately his leprosy was cleansed.

MATTHEW VIII, 3, *c.* 75

Le Sage, A. R. (1668–1747)

One may say of his novels that they suggest having been written in a café, by a domino player, after the theatre.

JOSEPH JOUBERT: *Pensées*, 1842

Lese-Majesty

A king who desires his own welfare will forgive the following when they inveigh against him: disappointed litigants, children, aged men, and the sick.

THE CODE OF MANU, VIII, *c.* 100

The slander of majesty shall not be punished, for if it proceed from levity it is to be despised; if from madness, to be pitied; if from malice, forgiven.

CODEX THEODOSIANUS, 438

Lesson

I shall the effect of this good lesson keep,
As watchman to my heart.

SHAKESPEARE: *Hamlet*, I, *c.* 1601

One man's fault is another man's lesson.

H. G. BOHN: *Handbook of Proverbs*, 1855

[*See also* Example, Hanging.

Letter

His letters . . . are weighty and powerful; but his bodily presence is weak, and his speech contemptible.

II CORINTHIANS X, 10, *c.* 55

You say there is nothing to write about. Then write to me that there is nothing to write about.

PLINY THE YOUNGER: *Letters*, I, *c.* 110

The letter is too long by half a mile.

SHAKESPEARE: *Love's Labor's Lost*, V, *c.* 1595

A letter is a deliberate and written conversation.

BALTASAR GRACIÁN: *The Art of Worldly Wisdom*, CXLVIII, 1647

I have made this letter longer than usual because I lack the time to make it shorter.

BLAISE PASCAL: *Provincial Letters*, XVI, 1657

A short letter to a distant friend is, in my opinion, an insult like that of a slight bow or cursory salutation; — a proof of unwillingness to do much, even where there is a necessity of doing something.

SAMUEL JOHNSON: *Letter to Joseph Baretti*, June 10, 1761

In a man's letters his soul lies naked.

SAMUEL JOHNSON: *Letter to Hester Thrale*, Oct. 27, 1777

Beasts may convey, and tuneful birds may sing,
Their mutual feelings, in the opening Spring;
But man alone has skill and power to send
The heart's warm dictates to the distant friend.
GEORGE CRABBE: *The Library,* 1781

I find by experience that it is much more rational, as well as easy, to answer a letter of real business by the return of the post.
EDWARD GIBBON: *Letter to Lord Sheffield,* Sept. 9, 1789

Essays that act the part of letters are mighty insipid things, and when one has nothing occasional to say, it is better to say nothing.
HORACE WALPOLE: *Letter to Mary Berry,* Sept. 18, 1789

Oh, the glory, the freedom, the passion of a letter! It is worth all the lip-talk in the world.
DONALD G. MITCHELL (IK MARVEL): *Reveries of a Bachelor,* II, 1850

I have received no more than one or two letters in my life that were worth the postage.
H. D. THOREAU: *Walden,* 1854

He thought he saw an elephant
That practised on a fife;
He looked again and found it was
A letter from his wife.
"At length I realize," he said,
"The bitterness of life."
C. L. DODGSON (LEWIS CARROLL): *The Hunting of the Snark,* 1876

Any man who does not write books, has plenty of time to think, and lives in unsatisfying society is likely to be a good letter-writer.
F. W. NIETZSCHE: *Human All-too-Human,* I, 1878

A letter is an unannounced visit, and the postman is thus the agent of impolite surprises. Every week we ought to have an hour for receiving letters — and then go and take a bath. F. W. NIETZSCHE: *Human All-too-Human,* II

The only kind of letters a woman likes to receive from a man are those which should not have been written. Author unidentified

Letters written after dinner are read in Hell.
TURKISH PROVERB

[*See also* Anger, Chance, Postoffice, Postscript.

Letters

The republic of letters. (La république des lettres.)
J. B. MOLIÈRE: *Le mariage forcé,* VI, 1664

[*See also* Literature.

Lettuce

It is of all herbs, the best and wholesomest for hot seasons, for young men, and them that abound with choler, and also for the sanguine, and such as have hot stomachs.
TOBIAS VENNER: *Via recta,* 1620

Lettuce is like conversation: it must be fresh and crisp, and so sparkling that you scarcely notice the bitter in it.
C. D. WARNER: *My Summer in a Garden,* IX, 1870

Leviathan

Canst thou draw out leviathan with an hook?
JOB XLI, 1, *c.* 325 B.C.

[*See also* Mayor.

Lewdness

Lewd did I live, & evil I did dwel.
Ascribed to P. T. BARNUM (1810–91): it reads the same both ways

[*See also* Uproar.

Lewes, George Henry (1817–78)

He was the son of a clown. He had the legs of his father in his brain.
GEORGE MEREDITH: To Edward Clodd (Fortnightly Review, July, 1909), *c.* 1900

Lexicographer

Every other author may aspire to praise; the lexicographer can only hope to escape reproach, and even this negative recompense has been yet granted to very few.
SAMUEL JOHNSON: *Dictionary,* pref., 1755

Liar

Zeus gives no aid to liars.
HOMER: *Iliad,* IV, *c.* 800 B.C.

A sword is upon the liars; and they shall dote.
JEREMIAH L, 36, *c.* 625 B.C.

A poor man is better than a liar.
PROVERBS XIX, 22, *c.* 350 B.C.

I hate a liar. (Mendacem odi.)
PLAUTUS: *Mostellaria,* I, *c.* 200 B.C.

I said in my haste, All men are liars.
PSALMS CXVI, 11, *c.* 150 B.C.

We give no credit to a liar, even when he speaks the truth.
CICERO: *De divinatione,* II, *c.* 78 B.C.

Let God be true, but every man a liar.
ROMANS III, 4, *c.* 55

The Cretans are always liars.
TITUS I, 12, *c.* 60

A liar must have a good memory.
QUINTILIAN: *De institutione oratoria,* IV, *c.* 90

All liars shall have their part in the lake which burneth with fire and brimstone.
REVELATION XXI, 8, *c.* 95

Without are dogs, and sorcerers, and whoremongers, and murderers, and idolaters, and whosoever loveth and maketh a lie.
REVELATION XXII, 15

When he speaketh a lie, he speaketh of his own: for he is a liar, and the father of it.
JOHN VIII, 44, *c.* 115

Who is a liar but he that denieth that Jesus is the Christ? I JOHN II, 22, *c.* 115

He shall not prosper who deviseth lies.
THE KORAN, XX, *c.* 625

She will lie as fast as a dog will lick a dish.
JOHN HEYWOOD: *Proverbs*, 1546

An egg is not so full of meat as she is full of lies.
JOHN STILL (BISHOP OF BATH AND WELLS) (?): *Gammer Gurton's Needle*, v, 1566

A liar is far worse, and does greater mischief, than a murderer on the highways; for a liar and false teacher deceives people, seduces souls, and destroys them.
MARTIN LUTHER: *Table-Talk*, DCXC, 1569

I love to hear him lie.
SHAKESPEARE: *Love's Labor's Lost*, I, *c.* 1595

Thou liest in thy throat.
SHAKESPEARE: *Twelfth Night*, III, *c.* 1601

He will lie, sir, with such volubility that you would think truth were a fool.
SHAKESPEARE: *All's Well that Ends Well*, IV, *c.* 1602

Show me a liar, and I will show thee a thief.
THOMAS ADAMS: *Sermon*, 1629

He never lies but when the holly is green.
DAVID FERGUSSON: *Scottish Proverbs*, 1641
(The holly is always green)

A liar is always lavish of oaths.
PIERRE CORNEILLE: *Le menteur*, III, 1642

Ferdinand Mendez Pinto was but a type of thee, thou liar of the first magnitude!
WILLIAM CONGREVE: *Love for Love*, II, 1695

The Lord delights in them that speak
The words of truth; but every liar
Must have his portion in the lake
That burns with brimstone and with fire.
ISAAC WATTS: *Divine Songs for Children*, pref., 1715

The greatest fools are the greatest liars.
LORD CHESTERFIELD: *Letter to his son*, Feb. 17, 1754

Whoever tells a lie is not pure of heart, and such a person cannot cook a clear soup.
LUDWIG VAN BEETHOVEN: *Letter to Mme. Streicher*, 1820

The most mischievous liars are those who keep sliding on the verge of truth.
J. C. and A. W. HARE: *Guesses at Truth*, 1827

Woe unto the liar, for he shall be thrust down to Hell.
THE BOOK OF MORMON (*II Nephi IX*, 34), 1830

If you have reason to suspect that a person is telling you a lie, look as though you believed every word he said. This will give him courage to go on; he will become more vehement in his assertions, and in the end betray himself.
ARTHUR SCHOPENHAUER: *Our Relation to Others*, 1851

He never speaks — and always lies.
THE EARL OF COWLEY (British ambassador to France): On Napoleon III, *c.* 1865

Even a liar tells a hundred truths to one lie; he has to, to make the lie good for anything.
H. W. BEECHER: *Proverbs from Plymouth Pulpit*, 1870

No one is such a liar as the man who is indignant.
F. W. NIETZSCHE: *Beyond Good and Evil*, 1886

The Swabians are the best liars in Germany: they lie innocently.
F. W. NIETZSCHE: *The Antichrist*, X, 1888

The aim of the liar is simply to charm, to delight, to give pleasure. He is the very basis of civilized society.
OSCAR WILDE: *The Decay of Lying*, 1891

Snake, he ain't got no friend; neither de long-tongue liar. AMERICAN NEGRO SAYING

To a liar, a liar and a half. (A menteur, menteur et demi.) FRENCH PROVERB

The liar is caught as quickly as a cripple.
ITALIAN PROVERB

Let the liar forget, and then ask him.
MOROCCAN PROVERB

[*See also* Blaine (James G.), Boasting, Devil, Friar, Good and Evil, Irish, Lie, Lying, Poet.

Libel

The greater the truth, the greater the libel.
Ascribed to LORD ELLENBOROUGH, Lord Chief Justice of England (1750–1818); also to LORD MANSFIELD (1704–93)

It is not the truth or falsehood that makes a libel, but the temper with which it is published.
MR. JUSTICE BEST: *Judgment in Rex* vs. *Burdett*, 1820

Why are libels against individuals prosecuted? Because they have a tendency to provoke the party to whom they are sent to a breach of the peace. IBID.

I despair of any definition of libel which shall exclude no publications which ought to be suppressed, and include none which ought to be omitted.
JOHN CAMPBELL (BARON CAMPBELL): *Argument for the defense in Regina* vs. *The Times newspaper*, 1838

A man may utter with impunity that which he cannot publish with impunity. The distinction arises from the greater circulation, and the greater power to injure, of a published libel than of a spoken slander. The editor of a journal, therefore, does not possess the same immunities as an editor that he possesses as a private citizen.
J. FENIMORE COOPER: *The American Democrat,* XXVI, 1838

Everything printed or written which reflects on the character of another, and is published without lawful justification or excuse, is a libel, whatever the intention may have been.
MR. JUSTICE PARKE: *Judgment in O'Brien vs. Clement,* 1846

What's the good of a libel suit? They might prove it on you.
Ascribed to TIMOTHY D. SULLIVAN, *c.* 1900

[*See also* Slander.

Liberal

I consider it a great homage to public opinion to find every scoundrel nowadays professing himself a liberal.
BENJAMIN DISRAELI: *The Infernal Marriage,* 1834

A liberal is one who believes in more laws and more jobholders, therefore in higher taxes and less liberty.
Anon.: Editorial in the Baltimore Evening Sun, Nov. 24, 1932

A liberal is a man who is willing to spend somebody else's money.
CARTER GLASS: Associated Press interview, Sept. 24, 1938

We are against people who push other people around, just for the fun of it.
RALPH INGERSOLL: Definition of a liberal in a press interview, April 13, 1940

A liberal is a Christian Scientist with a boil.
Author unidentified

[*See also* Conservative, Democrat, Radical, Whig.

Liberalism

The natural tendency of every young man who is conscious of powers and capabilities above his station is to adopt what are called popular or liberal opinions. He peculiarly feels the disadvantage of his own class, and is tempted to look with jealousy on all those who, with less natural talent, enjoy superior privileges.
GEORGE CRABBE, JR.: *Life of the Rev. George Crabbe,* VII, 1834

A gentlemen . . . is liberal in his attainments, opinions, practices and concessions. He asks for himself no more than he is willing to concede to others.
J. FENIMORE COOPER: *The American Democrat,* XIX, 1838

The tone and tendency of liberalism . . . is to attack the institutions of the country under the name of reform and to make war on the manners and customs of the people under the pretext of progress.
BENJAMIN DISRAELI: Speech in London, June 24, 1872

Liberalism is too often merely a way of speaking.
OSCAR I. JANOWSKY: *People at Bay,* III, 1938

[*See also* Socialism.

Liberality

The liberal soul shall be made fat: and he that watereth shall be watered also himself.
PROVERBS XI, 25, *c.* 350 B.C.

Of all the varieties of virtue, liberality is the most beloved.
ARISTOTLE: *The Nicomachean Ethics,* IV, *c.* 340 B.C.

The giving away of other men's goods is called liberality.
JOHN NORTHBROOKE: *Against Dicing,* 1577

What is called liberality is most often only the vanity of giving, which we like better than the thing we give.
LA ROCHEFOUCAULD: *Maxims,* 1665

Liberality consists less in giving much than in giving at the right moment.
JEAN DE LA BRUYÈRE: *Caractères,* IV, 1688

All liberality should have for its basis and support frugality.
RICHARD STEELE: *The Spectator,* April 7, 1712

[*See also* Generosity, Giving.

Liberator

The shepherd drives the wolf from the sheep's throat, for which the sheep thanks the shepherd as his liberator, while the wolf denounces him for the same act as the destroyer of liberty.
ABRAHAM LINCOLN: Speech in Baltimore, April 18, 1864

Libertine

The synagogue of the Libertines.
ACTS VI, 9, *c.* 75

[*See also* Nun, Press.

Liberty

Proclaim liberty throughout all the land unto all the inhabitants thereof.
LEVITICUS XXV, 10, *c.* 700 B.C. (The inscription on the Liberty Bell at Philadelphia, recast in its present form in June, 1753)

Thus saith the Lord: Ye have not hearkened unto me, in proclaiming liberty, every one to his brother, and every man to his neighbor: behold, I proclaim a liberty for you, saith the Lord, to the sword, to the pestilence, and to the famine.

JEREMIAH XXXIV, 17, *c.* 625 B.C.

O sweet name of liberty. (O nomen dulce libertatis.)

CICERO: *Oration Against Verres, c.* 60 B.C.

A love of liberty is planted by nature in the breasts of all men.

DIONYSIUS OF HALICARNASSUS: *Antiquities of Rome,* IV, *c.* 20 B.C.

No favor produces less permanent gratitude than the gift of liberty, especially among people who are ready to make a bad use of it.

LIVY: *History of Rome,* XXXIX, *c.* 10

Brethren, ye have been called unto liberty; only use not liberty for an occasion to the flesh, but by love serve one another.

GALATIANS V, 13, *c.* 50

Where the spirit of the Lord is, there is liberty.

II CORINTHIANS III, 17, *c.* 55

Thou inquirest what liberty is? To be slave to nothing, to no necessity, to no accident, to keep fortune at arm's length.

SENECA: *Epistulæ morales ad Lucilium, c.* 63

Only in states in which the power of the people is supreme has liberty any abode.

CICERO: *De republica,* I, *c.* 50 B.C.

Liberties and masters are not easily combined.

TACITUS: *History,* IV, *c.* 100

Nature gives liberty even to dumb animals.

IBID.

I tell you true, liberty is the best of all things; never live beneath the noose of a servile halter.

WILLIAM WALLACE: Address to the Scots, *c.* 1300

Every subject's duty is the king's; but every subject's soul is his own.

SHAKESPEARE: *Henry V,* IV, *c.* 1599

I must have liberty
Withal, as large a charter as the wind,
To blow on whom I please.

SHAKESPEARE: *As You Like It,* II, *c.* 1600

Liberty plucks justice by the nose.

SHAKESPEARE: *Measure for Measure,* I, 1604

Much liberty brings men to the gallows.

RANDLE COTGRAVE: *French-English Dictionary,* 1611

Liberty is the power that we have over ourselves.

HUGO GROTIUS: *De jure belli ac pacis,* I, 1625

I do here declare that those things which have been done whereby men had some cause to suspect the liberty of the subjects to be entrenched upon shall not hereafter be drawn into example for your prejudice; and in time to come, in the word of a king, you shall not have the like cause to complain.

CHARLES I of England: Speech to Parliament, 1628

Civil or federal liberty is the proper end and object of authority, and cannot exist without it; and it is a liberty to that which is good, just and honest.

JOHN WINTHROP: *Journal,* 1635

Liberty, which appears so dear, is often only an imaginary good.

PIERRE CORNEILLE: *Cinna,* II, 1639

A bean in liberty is better than a comfit in prison.

GEORGE HERBERT: *Outlandish Proverbs,* 1640

Give me the liberty to know, to utter, and to argue freely according to conscience, above all liberties.

JOHN MILTON: *Areopagitica,* 1644

When complaints are freely heard, deeply considered, and speedily reformed, then is the utmost bound of civil liberty obtained that wise men look for.

IBID.

Civil liberties and proprieties admeasured, to every man to his true *suum,* are the *prima pura principia, propria quarto modo,* the *sine quibus* of human states, without which men are but women.

NATHANIEL WARD: *The Simple Cobbler of Aggawam,* 1646

By liberty is understood the absence of external impediments; which impediments may take away part of a man's power to do what he would, but cannot hinder him from using the power left him, according as his judgment and reason shall dictate to him.

THOMAS HOBBES: *Leviathan,* I, 1651

Above all things — liberty!

MOTTO OF JOHN SELDEN (1584–1654)

Lean liberty is better than fat slavery.

JOHN RAY: *English Proverbs,* 1670

Liberty is a great pleasure.

WILLIAM WYCHERLEY: *The Country Wife,* IV, *c.* 1673

More liberty begets desire of more,
The hunger still increases with the store.

JOHN DRYDEN: *The Hind and the Panther,* I, 1687

Liberty is not idleness, but the free use of time. It is the chance of work and exercise.

JEAN DE LA BRUYÈRE: *Caractères,* XII, 1688

A man on the rack is not at liberty to lay by the idea of pain, and divert himself with other contemplations.

JOHN LOCKE: *Essay Concerning Human Understanding,* II, 1690

Freedom of men under government is to have a standing rule to live by, common to every one of that society, and made by the legislative power vested in it; a liberty to follow my own will in all things, when the rule prescribes not, and not to be subject to the inconstant, uncertain, unknown, arbitrary will of another man.

JOHN LOCKE: *Treatises on Government*, X, 1690

Liberty should reach every individual of a people, as they all share one common nature: if it only spreads among particular branches, there had better be none at all, since such a liberty only aggravates the misfortune of those who are deprived of it, by setting before them a disagreeable subject of comparison.

JOSEPH ADDISON: *The Spectator*, Jan. 29, 1712

A day, an hour of virtuous liberty,
Is worth a whole eternity in bondage.

JOSEPH ADDISON: *Cato*, II, 1713

Liberty or death. IBID.

Give me again my hollow tree,
A crust of bread, and liberty.

ALEXANDER POPE: *The Sixth Satire of the Second Book of Horace*, 1714

Liberty of conscience is nowadays not only understood to be the liberty of believing what men please, but also of endeavoring to propagate that belief as much as they can.

JONATHAN SWIFT: *Sermon on the Testimony of Conscience*, c. 1715

His safety must his liberty restrain.

ALEXANDER POPE: *An Essay on Man*, III, 1733

Liberty is the right to do what the laws allow. If a citizen had a right to do what they forbid it would no longer be liberty, for everyone else would have the same right.

C. L. DE MONTESQUIEU: *The Spirit of the Laws*, XI, 1748

In constitutional states liberty is but a compensation for the heaviness of taxation. In despotic states the equivalent for liberty is the lightness of taxation.

C. L. DE MONTESQUIEU: *The Spirit of the Laws*, XIII

In those few places where men enjoy what they call liberty, it is continually in a tottering situation, and makes greater and greater strides to that fault of despotism which at last swallows up every species of government.

EDMUND BURKE: *A Vindication of Natural Society*, 1756

They that can give up essential liberty to obtain a little temporary safety deserve neither liberty nor safety.

BENJAMIN FRANKLIN: Motto of the Historical Review of Pennsylvania, 1759

Liberty is obedience to the law which one has laid down for oneself.

J.-J. ROUSSEAU: *Du contrat social*, I, 1761

Free people, remember this maxim: we may acquire liberty, but it is never recovered if it is once lost.

J.-J. ROUSSEAU: *Du contrat social*, II

Liberty is not a fruit that grows in all climates, and so it is not within the reach of all people.

J.-J. ROUSSEAU: *Du contrat social*, III

Liberty is a more invigorating cordial than tokay.

WILLIAM SHENSTONE: *Of Men and Manners*, 1764

They make a rout about universal liberty without considering that all that is to be valued, or indeed can be enjoyed by individuals, is private liberty. Political liberty is good only so far as it produces private liberty.

SAMUEL JOHNSON: *Boswell's Life*, May, 1768

The God who gave us life gave us liberty at the same time.

THOMAS JEFFERSON: *The Rights of British America*, 1774

Abstract liberty, like other mere abstractions, is not to be found.

EDMUND BURKE: Speech on Conciliation with America, March 22, 1775

Natural liberty is a gift of the beneficent Creator to the whole human race, and . . . civil liberty is founded in that, and cannot be wrested from any people without the most manifest violation of justice.

ALEXANDER HAMILTON: *The Farmer Refuted*, 1775

Is life so dear or peace so sweet as to be purchased at the price of chains and slavery? Forbid it, Almighty God! I know not what course others may take, but as for me, give me liberty, or give me death.

PATRICK HENRY: Speech in the Virginia Convention, March 23, 1775 (Cf. ADDISON, *ante*, 1713)

Among a people generally corrupt liberty cannot long exist.

EDMUND BURKE: *Letter to the sheriffs of Bristol*, April 3, 1777

Liberty must be limited in order to be possessed. IBID.

We are all agreed as to our own liberty; we would have as much of it as we can get; but we are not agreed as to the liberty of others: for in proportion as we take it, others must lose.

SAMUEL JOHNSON: *Boswell's Life*, April 8, 1779

A zeal [for liberty] sometimes disguises from the world, and not rarely from the mind

which it possesses, an envious desire of plundering wealth or degrading greatness.
SAMUEL JOHNSON: *Lives of the Poets* (*Mark Akenside*), 1780

Where liberty dwells, there is my country.
BENJAMIN FRANKLIN: *Letter to B. Vaughan,* March 14, 1783

The people never give up their liberties but under some delusion.
EDMUND BURKE: Speech at a meeting in Buckinghamshire, 1784

'Tis liberty alone that gives the flower
Of fleeting life its lustre and perfume;
And we are weeds without it.
WILLIAM COWPER: *The Task,* v, 1785

The tree of liberty must be refreshed from time to time with the blood of patriots and tyrants. It is its natural manure.
THOMAS JEFFERSON: *Letter to W. S. Smith,* Nov. 13, 1787

The natural progress of things is for liberty to yield and government to gain ground.
THOMAS JEFFERSON: *Letter to E. Carrington,* 1788

Political liberty consists in the power of doing whatever does not injure another. The exercise of the natural rights of every man has no other limits than those which are necessary to secure to every other man the free exercise of the same rights; and these limits are determinable only by law.
Declaration of the Rights of Man by the French National Assembly, IV, 1789

The great half truth, liberty.
WILLIAM BLAKE: *The Marriage of Heaven and Hell,* 1790

But what is liberty without wisdom, and without virtue? It is the greatest of all possible evils; for it is folly, vice, and madness, without tuition or restraint.
EDMUND BURKE: *Reflections on the Revolution in France,* I, 1790

We are not to expect to be translated from despotism to liberty in a featherbed.
THOMAS JEFFERSON: *Letter to Lafayette,* 1790

Of what use is political liberty to those who have no bread? It is of value only to ambitious theorists and politicians.
J. P. MARAT: *Letter to Camille Desmoulins,* June 24, 1790

The condition upon which God hath given liberty to a man is eternal vigilance.
J. P. CURRAN: Speech in Dublin, July 10, 1790

The tree of liberty grows only when watered by the blood of tyrants.
BERTRAND BARÈRE: Speech in the French National Convention, 1792 (Cf. JEFFERSON, *ante,* 1787)

It requires some experience of liberty to know how to use it.
H. H. BRACKENRIDGE: *Modern Chivalry,* 1792

O Liberty! what crimes are committed in thy name!
Ascribed to MME. ROLAND: On passing a statue of Liberty on her way to the guillotine, Nov. 8, 1793

Liberty, equality, fraternity. (Liberté, égalité, fraternité.)
MOTTO OF THE FRENCH REPUBLIC, usually ascribed to ANTOINE-FRANÇOIS MOMORO (1756–94); it was abandoned in 1940

The ball of liberty is now so well in motion that it will roll round the globe.
THOMAS JEFFERSON: *Letter to Tench Coxe,* 1795

True liberty is a liberty to do everything that is right, and the being restrained from doing anything that is wrong.
JONATHAN BOUCHER: *A View of the Causes and Consequences of the American Revolution,* XII, 1797

Liberty in England is a sort of idol; people are bred up in the belief and love of it, but see little of its doings. They walk about freely, but it is between high walls.
GEORGE WASHINGTON: To John Bernard (Quoted in BERNARD: *Retrospections of America, 1811,* v, *c.* 1798)

How did mankind ever come by the idea of liberty? What a grand thought it was!
G. C. LICHTENBERG: *Reflections,* 1799

Our liberty depends on our education, our laws, and habits to which even prejudices yield; on the dispersion of our people on farms and on the almost equal diffusion of property.
FISHER AMES: Oration in Boston, 1800 (Feb. 8)

I have from my first outset in public life been deeply affected by the charms of liberty, and from that early period to my old age been without fee or reward an advocate for her slandered righteous cause.
JOHN DICKINSON: *Letter to Thomas McKean,* March 4, 1801

"Make way for liberty!" he cried —
"Make way for liberty!" — and died.
JAMES MONTGOMERY: *Arnold Winkelried,* 1806

Eternal spirit of the chainless mind!
Brightest in dungeons, Liberty! thou art.
BYRON: *The Prisoner of Chillon,* 1816

The lightning of the nations.
P. B. SHELLEY: *Ode to Liberty,* 1819

Nations will more readily part with the essentials than with the forms of liberty; and Napoleon might have died an emperor in reality if he had been contented to have lived a consul in name.

C. C. COLTON: *Lacon,* 1820

The disease of liberty is catching.

THOMAS JEFFERSON: *Letter to Lafayette,* 1820

To die for liberty is a pleasure, not a pain.

MARCO BOZZARIS: Last words, 1823

Liberty here means to do each as he pleases; to care for nothing and nobody, and cheat everybody.

WILLIAM FAUX: *Memorable Days in America,* 1823

If liberty produces ill-manners and want of taste, she is a very excellent parent with two very disagreeable daughters.

WILLIAM HAZLITT: *Covent Garden Theatre,* 1829 (The Atlas, Oct. 4)

Liberty *and* Union, now and for ever, one and inseparable!

DANIEL WEBSTER: Speech in the Senate, Jan. 26, 1830

God grants liberty only to those who love it, and are always ready to guard and defend it.

DANIEL WEBSTER: Speech in the Senate, June 3, 1834

All this of liberty and equality, electoral suffrages, independence and so forth, we will take to be a temporary phenomenon, by no means a final one. Though likely to last a long time, with sad enough embroilments for us all, we must welcome it as the penalty of sins that are past, the pledge of inestimable benefits that are coming.

THOMAS CARLYLE: *Heroes and Hero-Worship,* IV, 1840 (Lecture in London, May 15)

Let your cry be for free souls rather than for free men. Moral liberty is the one really important liberty.

JOSEPH JOUBERT: *Pensées,* 1842

The men of future generations will yet win many a liberty of which we do not even feel the want.

MAX STIRNER: *The Ego and His Own,* 1845

Liberty is worth whatever country is worth. It is by liberty that a man has a country; it is by liberty he has rights.

HENRY GILES: *The Worth of Liberty,* 1847

Our liberties we prize and our rights we will maintain.

MOTTO OF IOWA, adopted Feb. 25, 1847

While I trust that liberty and free institutions, as we have experienced them, may ultimately spread over the globe, I am by no means sure that all people are fit for them; nor am I desirous of imposing or forcing our peculiar forms upon any other nation that does not wish to embrace them.

DANIEL WEBSTER: Speech at Springfield, Mass., Sept. 29, 1847

No more parties, no more authority, absolute liberty of man and citizen — that is my political and social confession of faith.

P. J. PROUDHON: *Confessions d'un révolutionaire,* 1849

That treacherous phantom which men call liberty.

JOHN RUSKIN: *The Seven Lamps of Architecture,* VIII, 1849

The only obligation which I have a right to assume is to do at any time what I think right.

H. D. THOREAU: *An Essay on Civil Disobedience,* 1849

I fear you will laugh when I tell you what I conceive to be about the most essential mental quality for a free people, whose liberty is to be progressive, permanent, and on a large scale: it is much stupidity.

WALTER BAGEHOT: *Letter to the London Inquirer,* 1851

By civil liberty is meant, not only the absence of individual restraint, but liberty within the social system and political organism — a combination of principles and laws which acknowledge, protect, and favor the dignity of man.

FRANCIS LIEBER: *Civil Liberty and Self-Government,* 1852

Liberty is the sovereignty of the individual.

JOSIAH WARREN: *Equitable Commerce,* 1852

Liberty has never built a durable political edifice; it simply crowns what the times have erected.

NAPOLEON III: Speech to the French Parliament, Feb. 14, 1853

Liberty — precious boon of Heaven — is meek and reasonable. She admits that she belongs to all — to the high and the low; the rich and the poor; the black and the white — and that she belongs to them all equally.

GERRIT SMITH: Speech in the House of Representatives, June 27, 1854

I am for the people of the whole nation doing just as they please in all matters which concern the whole nation; for that of each part doing just as they choose in all matters which concern no other part; and for each individual doing just as he chooses in all matters which concern nobody else.

ABRAHAM LINCOLN: Speech, Oct. 1, 1858

The liberty of the individual must be thus far limited: he must not make himself a nuisance to other people.

J. S. MILL: *On Liberty,* III, 1859

Whether in chains or in laurels, liberty knows nothing but victories.

WENDELL PHILLIPS: Speech at Harper's Ferry, Nov. 1, 1859

Nothing is more disgusting than the crowing about liberty by slaves, as most men are, and the flippant mistaking for freedom of some paper preamble like a Declaration of Independence, or the statute right to vote, by those who have never dared to think or to act.

R. W. EMERSON: *The Conduct of Life,* I, 1860

The things required for prosperous labor, prosperous manufactures, and prosperous commerce are three. First, liberty; second, liberty; third, liberty.

H. W. BEECHER: Address at Liverpool, Oct. 16, 1863

Four score and seven years ago our fathers brought forth on this continent a new nation, conceived in liberty and dedicated to the proposition that all men are created equal.

ABRAHAM LINCOLN: *Gettysburg Address,* Nov. 19, 1863

The world has never had a good definition of the word liberty.

ABRAHAM LINCOLN: Speech in Baltimore, April 18, 1864

One evening, when I was yet in my nurse's arms, I wanted to touch the tea-urn, which was boiling merrily. . . . My nurse would have taken me away from the urn, but my mother said " Let him touch it." So I touched it — and that was my first lesson in the meaning of liberty.

JOHN RUSKIN: *The Story of Arachne,* 1870 (Lecture in London, Dec. 13)

Liberty means that a man is recognized as free and treated as free by those who surround him.

M. A. BAKUNIN: *Dieu et l'état,* 1871

A natural right to liberty, irrespective of the ability to defend it, exists in nations as much as and no more than it exists in individuals.

J. A. FROUDE: *The English in Ireland in the Eighteenth Century,* I, 1872

The more liberty you give away the more you will have.

R. G. INGERSOLL: Speech in Boston, Sept. 20, 1880

Civil liberty is the status of the man who is guaranteed by law and civil institutions the exclusive employment of all his own powers for his own welfare.

W. G. SUMNER: *The Forgotten Man,* 1883

If men use their liberty in such a way as to surrender their liberty, are they thereafter any the less slaves? If people by a plebiscite elect a man despot over them, do they remain free because the despotism was of their own making?

HERBERT SPENCER: *The New Toryism,* 1884

Give me your tired, your poor,
Your huddled masses, yearning to breathe free,
The wretched refuse of your teeming shore:
Send these, the homeless, tempest tossed, to me:
I lift my lamp beside the golden door.

INSCRIPTION ON STATUE OF LIBERTY, New York harbor, unveiled Oct. 28, 1886

Liberty belongs only to those who have the gift of reason.

POPE LEO XIII: *Libertas praestantissimum,* June 20, 1888

The German historians are convinced that Rome was synonymous with despotism, and that the Germanic peoples brought the spirit of liberty into the world. What is the difference between this conviction and a lie?

F. W. NIETZSCHE: *The Antichrist,* LV, 1888

Equal liberty, in the property sphere, is such a balance between the liberty to take and the liberty to keep that the two liberties may coexist without conflict or invasion.

BENJAMIN R. TUCKER: *Instead of a Book,* 1893

Liberty means responsibility. That is why most men dread it.

GEORGE BERNARD SHAW: *Maxims for Revolutionists,* 1903

The liberty of the citizen to do as he likes so long as he does not interfere with the liberty of others to do the same, which has been a shibboleth for some well-known writers, is interfered with by school laws, by the Post Office, by every state or municipal institution which takes his money for purposes thought desirable, whether he likes it or not.

MR. JUSTICE O. W. HOLMES: *Dissenting opinion in Lochner* vs. *New York,* 1904

Liberty is not a means to a higher political end. It is itself the highest political end.

J. E. E. DALBERG (LORD ACTON): *Lectures on Modern History,* 1906

The very forces that liberty has set free work against the dangerous consequences of liberty.

ELLEN KEY: *Love and Ethics,* 1911

The history of liberty is a history of resistance. The history of liberty is a history of limitations of governmental power, not the increase of it.

WOODROW WILSON: Speech in New York, Sept. 9, 1912

I have always in my own thought summed up individual liberty, and business liberty, and every other kind of liberty, in the phrase that is common in the sporting world, "A free field and no favor."

WOODROW WILSON: Speech in Washington, Jan. 29, 1915

Sworn to no party,
Of no sect am I;
I won't keep quiet
And I will not lie.

ADMIRAL LORD FISHER, R.N. (1841–1920)

Things have come to a hell of a pass
When a man can't wallop his own jackass.

Author unidentified; often quoted by HENRY WATTERSON (1840–1921)

Mankind is tired of liberty.

BENITO MUSSOLINI: In the Gerarchia, April, 1923

We have no liberty except liberty to behave ourselves. And it is a right no one questions, or we wouldn't have that.

E. W. HOWE: *Sinner Sermons,* 1926

The greatest dangers to liberty lurk in insidious encroachment by men of zeal, well-meaning but without understanding.

MR. JUSTICE LOUIS D. BRANDEIS: *Opinion in Olmstead* vs. *United States,* 1928

Modern liberty begins in revolt.

H. M. KALLEN: Lecture at the New School for Social Research, New York, 1928

You have set up in New York harbor a monstrous idol which you call Liberty. The only thing that remains to complete that monument is to put on its pedestal the inscription written by Dante on the gate of Hell: "All hope abandon, ye who enter here."

GEORGE BERNARD SHAW: Address in New York, April 11, 1933

Of what we call liberty in its full human meaning — freedom of thought, speech, action, self-expression — there is today less in Europe than there has been during the last 2000 years.

JAN C. SMUTS: Address at St. Andrews University, Oct. 17, 1934

Liberty is the only thing you cannot have unless you are willing to give it to others.

WILLIAM ALLEN WHITE: In the Emporia (Kansas) Gazette, Oct. 24, 1940

Liberty is like health: from the moment you think about it you no longer enjoy it.

Author unidentified

No liberty is worth a damn which doesn't allow a man to do wrong now and then. IBID.

Liberty is ancient; it is despotism that is new.

FRENCH PROVERB

True liberty reigns only among the brutes.

IBID.

Dear is country, but liberty is dearer still. (Patria cara, carior libertas.)

LATIN PROVERB

Liberty is the best of all things. (Libertas optima rerum.) MEDIEVAL LATIN PROVERB

[*See also* Art, Charity, Chastity, Combination, Command, Death, Democracy, Education, Equality, Faith, Faneuil Hall, Fighting, Freedom, Happiness, Individualism, Judgment, Judiciary, Jury, Justice, Laissez-faire, Liberator, License, Literature, Marriage, People, Press (Free), Priest, Prison, Property, Slavery, Speech (Free), Taxation, Taxes, Travel, Union (American), Voltaire, Wealth.

Liberty-Hall

This is Liberty-Hall. You may do just as you please here.

OLIVER GOLDSMITH: *She Stoops to Conquer,* II, 1773

Liberty, Religious

[*See* Freedom (Religious).

Librarian

His work is to be a factor and trader for helps to learning, and a treasurer to keep them, and a dispenser to apply them to use or see them well used, or at least not abused.

JOHN DURY: *Letter to William Dugard,* 1649 (Dury was deputy keeper of the king's medals and library)

Unlearned men of books assume the care,
As eunuchs are the guardians of the fair.

EDWARD YOUNG: *Love of Fame,* II, 1728

[*See also* Environment.

Library

Burn the libraries, for all their value is in the Koran.

THE CALIPH OMAR: On the fall of Alexandria, 641

The aggregation of large libraries tends to divert men's thoughts from the one great book, the Bible, which ought, day and night, to be in every one's hand. My object, my hope, in translating the Scriptures, was to check the so prevalent production of new works.

MARTIN LUTHER: *Table-Talk,* DCCCCXI, 1569

Come, and take choice of all my library,
And so beguile thy sorrow.

SHAKESPEARE: *Titus Andronicus,* IV, 1594

Were I not a king, I would be an university man; and, if it were so that I must be made a prisoner, I would have no other prison than this library, and be chained together with all these goodly authors.

JAMES I of England: On visiting the Bodleian Library, Oxford, 1604

Libraries are as the shrines where all the relics of the ancient saints, full of true virtue, and that without delusion or imposture, are preserved and reposed.

FRANCIS BACON: *The Advancement of Learning,* II, 1605

My library
Was dukedom large enough.
SHAKESPEARE: *The Tempest*, I,1611

I no sooner come into the library, but I bolt the door to me, excluding lust, avarice, and all such vices, whose nurse is idleness, the mother of ignorance, and melancholy herself, and in the very lap of eternity, amongst so many divine souls, I take my seat, with so lofty a spirit and sweet content that I pity all our great ones and rich men that know not this happiness.
ROBERT BURTON: *The Anatomy of Melancholy*, II, 1621

To desire to have many books, and never to use them, is like a child that will have a candle burning by him all the while he is asleep.
HENRY PEACHAM: *The Compleat Gentleman*, 1622

That place that does contain
My books, the best companions, is to me
A glorious court, where hourly I converse
With the old sages and philosophers;
And sometimes, for variety, I confer
With kings and emperors, and weight their counsels.
JOHN FLETCHER and PHILIP MASSINGER: *The Elder Brother*, I, 1635

It is a vanity to persuade the world one hath much learning, by getting a great library.
THOMAS FULLER: *The Holy State and the Profane State*, 1642

A few good books is better than a library.
WILLIAM RAMESEY: *The Gentleman's Companion*, 1672

No place affords a more striking conviction of the vanity of human hopes than a public library. SAMUEL JOHNSON: *The Rambler*, March 23, 1751

A circulating library in a town is as an evergreen tree of diabolical knowledge.
R. B. SHERIDAN: *The Rivals*, I, 1775

Calvin grows gentle in this silent coast,
Nor finds a single heretic to roast;
Here, their fierce rage subdued, and lost their pride,
The pope and Luther slumber side by side.
GEORGE CRABBE: *The Library*, 1781 (Original version, not published)

Let every man, if possible, gather some good books under his roof, and obtain access for himself and family to some social library. Almost any luxury should be sacrificed to this.
W. E. CHANNING: Address in Boston, 1838

The true university of these days is a collection of books.
THOMAS CARLYLE: *Heroes and Hero-Worship*, V, 1840 (Lecture in London, May 19)

A library is not worth anything without a catalogue — it is a Polyphemus without any eye in his head.
THOMAS CARLYLE: Testimony before the Commissioners Appointed to Inquire Into the Constitution and Government of the British Museum, Feb., 1849

A library is but the soul's burial-ground. It is the land of shadows.
H. W. BEECHER: *Star Papers*, 1855

A great library contains the diary of the human race.
GEORGE DAWSON: Address at the opening of the Birmingham, Eng., library, Oct. 26, 1866

Every library should try to be complete on something, if it were only the history of pinheads.
O. W. HOLMES: *The Poet at the Breakfast-Table*, VIII, 1872

The richest minds need not large libraries.
A. BRONSON ALCOTT: *Table-Talk*, I, 1877

A man's library is a sort of harem, and I observe that tender readers have a great pudency in showing their books to a stranger.
R. W. EMERSON: *Books*, 1877

A hospital for the mind.
INSCRIPTION ON THE LIBRARY AT ALEXANDRIA, EGYPT

Food for the soul. (Nutrimentum spiritus.)
INSCRIPTION ON THE STATE LIBRARY AT BERLIN

Medicine for the soul.
INSCRIPTION ON THE LIBRARY AT THEBES

[*See also* Books.

License

What is called liberty in some is called license in others.
QUINTILIAN: *De institutione oratoria*, III, *c.* 90

As it becomes none but great poets to make use of the poetic license, so it is intolerable that any but men of great and illustrious souls should be privileged above the authority of custom.
MICHEL DE MONTAIGNE: *Essays*, I, 1580

License they mean when they cry liberty.
JOHN MILTON: *Sonnet*, *c.* 1645

Liberty will ever be more free and secure, in proportion as license is kept in restraint.
POPE LEO XIII: *Libertas praestantissimum*, June 20, 1888

[*See also* Freedom, Liberty.

Licentiousness

There is no air a man draws so greedily, or sucks so gluttonously, and that more spreads

itself, or penetrates more deeply, than licentiousness.
MICHEL DE MONTAIGNE: *Essays*, III, 1588

[*See also* Hell.

Lie

[*See* Liar, Lying.

Life

Life runs as fast as a chariot's wheel.
ANACREON: *Fragment*, *c.* 500 B.C.

Life is a theatre in which the worst people often have the best seats.
Ascribed to ARISTONYMUS by JOANNES STOBAEUS: *Florilegium*, *c.* 500 B.C.

Life is not truly life, but only misery.
EURIPIDES: *Alcestis*, 438 B.C.

The trials of living and the pangs of disease make even the short span of life too long.
HERODOTUS: *Histories*, VII, *c.* 430 B.C.

Life is a struggle.
EURIPIDES: *The Suppliant Women*, *c.* 421 B.C.

Life is like a game at dice.
ALEXIS: *Fragment*, *c.* 325 B.C.

All that a man hath will be given for his life.
JOB II, 4, *c.* 325 B.C.

The life of man on earth is a warfare.
JOB VII, 1

My days are swifter than a weaver's shuttle, and are spent without hope. JOB VII, 6

My life is wind. JOB VII, 7

I would not live alway; let me alone; for my days are vanity. JOB VII, 16

We are but of yesterday, and know nothing, because our days upon earth are a shadow.
JOB VIII, 9

No man is sure of life. JOB XXIV, 22

Our days on the earth are as a shadow, and there is none abiding.
I CHRONICLES XXIX, 15, *c.* 300 B.C.

What man is he that desireth life, and loveth many days? PSALMS XXIV, 12, *c.* 150 B.C.

We spend our years as a tale that is told.
PSALMS XC, 9

The days of our years are three-score years and ten; and if by reason of strength they be four-score years, yet is their strength labor and sorrow; for it is soon cut off and we fly away. PSALMS XC, 10

O misery of men! O blinded fools! in what dark mazes, in what dangers we walk this little journey of our life!
LUCRETIUS: *De rerum natura*, II, 57 B.C.

Life is long to the miserable, but short to the happy.
PUBLILIUS SYRUS: *Sententiæ*, *c.* 50 B.C.

Nature has given us life at interest like money, with no day fixed for repayment.
CICERO: *Tusculanæ disputationes*, I, 45 B.C.

We are always beginning to live, but we are never living.
MARCUS MANILIUS: *Astronomica*, IV, *c.* 40 B.C.

Life is like a school of gladiators, where men live and fight with one another.
SENECA: *De Ira*, II, *c.* 43

Life, if well used, is long enough.
SENECA: *De brevitate vitae*, II, 49

What is your life? It is even a vapor, that appeareth for a little time, and then vanisheth away. JAMES IV, 14, *c.* 60

Life is neither a good nor an evil, but simply the scene of good and evil.
SENECA: *Epistulæ morales ad Lucilium*, *c.* 63

Life is war.
IBID. (Cf. JOB VII, 1, *ante*, *c.* 325 B.C.)

Nature has given man nothing better than the shortness of his life.
PLINY THE ELDER: *Natural History*, VII, 77

The blessings of life are not equal to its ills, though the number of the two may be equal; nor can any pleasure compensate for the least pain. IBID.

To a longer and worse life, a shorter and better is by all means to be preferred.
EPICTETUS: *Encheiridion*, *c.* 110

Blessed is he that hath a short life.
ST. CLEMENT: *First Epistle to the Corinthians*, *c.* 125

Life is warfare, and the sojourn of a stranger in a strange land.
MARCUS AURELIUS: *Meditations*, II, *c.* 170

The longest life and the shortest amount to the same. For the present is of equal duration for all, and what we lose is not ours. IBID.

To contemplate human life for forty years is the same as contemplating it for ten thousand. In ten thousand, what more will you see?
MARCUS AURELIUS: *Meditations*, VII

Life is that force which holds matter together.
PORPHYRY: *On Abstinence from Animal Food*, *c.* 270

The utmost span of a man's life is a hundred years. Half of it is spent in night, and of the rest half is lost by childhood and old age. Work, grief, longing and illness make up what remains.
BHARTRIHARI: *The Vairagya Sataka*, *c.* 625

Life is sweet.
ENGLISH PROVERB, traced by Apperson to *c.* 1350

This life is fickle, frail and vain.
Anon.: *The Life of Man, c.* 1550

In our sad condition, our only consolation is the expectation of another life. Here below all is incomprehensible.
MARTIN LUTHER: *Table-Talk,* CXXXII, 1569

Life is a tender thing, and easy to be distempered.
MICHEL DE MONTAIGNE: *Essays,* III, 1588

The sands are number'd that make up my life.
SHAKESPEARE: *III Henry VI,* I, *c.* 1591

Life is as tedious as a twice-told tale,
Vexing the dull ear of a drowsy man.
SHAKESPEARE: *King John,* III, *c.* 1596

Let life be short; else shame will be too long.
SHAKESPEARE: *Henry V,* IV, *c.* 1599

The world's a bubble, and the life of man
Less than a span;
In his conception wretched, from the womb
So to the tomb;
Curst from the cradle, and brought up to years
With cares and fears.
Who then to frail mortality shall trust,
But limns the water, or but writes in dust.
FRANCIS BACON: *Life, c.* 1600

And so, from hour to hour, we ripe and ripe,
And then, from hour to hour, we rot and rot;
And thereby hangs a tale.
SHAKESPEARE: *As You Like It,* II, *c.* 1600

Life is a shuttle.
SHAKESPEARE: *The Merry Wives of Windsor,* V, *c.* 1600

I do not set my life at a pin's fee.
SHAKESPEARE: *Hamlet,* I, *c.* 1601

A man's life's no more than to say " One."
SHAKESPEARE: *Hamlet,* V

The web of our life is of a mingled yarn, good and ill together.
SHAKESPEARE: *All's Well that Ends Well,* IV, *c.* 1602

Reason thus with life:
If I do lose thee, I do lose a thing
That none but fools would keep.
SHAKESPEARE: *Measure for Measure,* III, 1604

Life is a poet's fable
And all her days are lies.
Anon.: *Song, c.* 1605

Out, out, brief candle!
Life's but a walking shadow, a poor player
That struts and frets his hour upon the stage,
And then is heard no more; it is a tale
Told by an idiot, full of sound and fury,
Signifying nothing.
SHAKESPEARE: *Macbeth,* V, *c.* 1605

When we are born, we cry, that we are come
To this great stage of fools.
SHAKESPEARE: *King Lear,* IV, 1606

Like as the waves make toward the pebbled shore,
So do our minutes hasten to their end.
SHAKESPEARE: *Sonnets,* LX, 1609

The longer life, the greater grief.
RANDLE COTGRAVE: *French-English Dictionary,* 1611

Our life is nothing but a Winter's day;
Some only break their fasts, and so, away:
Others stay dinner, and depart full fed;
The deepest age but sups, and goes to bed.
FRANCIS QUARLES: *Emblems,* 1635

Life is a dream. (La vida es sueño.)
PEDRO CALDERON: Title of a play, 1636

Life is half spent before we know what it is.
GEORGE HERBERT: *Outlandish Proverbs,* 1640

I have spent my life laboriously doing nothing.
HUGO GROTIUS: Last words, 1645

We have more days to live than pleasures.
BALTASAR GRACIÁN: *The Art of Worldly Wisdom,* CLXXIV, 1647

We are in the world like men playing at tables; the chance is not in our power, but to play it is; and when it is fallen, we must manage it as we can.
JEREMY TAYLOR: *The Rule and Exercises of Holy Living,* 1650

These are the thoughts of mortals, this is the end and sum of all their designs: a dark night and an ill guide, a boisterous sea and a broken cable, a hard rock and a rough wind.
JEREMY TAYLOR: *The Rule and Exercises of Holy Dying,* 1651

Life's but a petty stake, scarce worth the prize.
EDWARD BENLOWES: *Theophila,* 1652

Life is a pure flame, and we live by an invisible sun within us.
THOMAS BROWNE: *Urn Burial,* V, 1658

A short life and a merry.
JOHN TATHAM: *The Rump,* I, 1660

Let nature and let art do what they please,
When all is done, life's an incurable disease.
ABRAHAM COWLEY: *Ode to Dr. Scarborough,* 1663

Between us and Hell or Heaven there is nothing but life, which of all things is the frailest.
BLAISE PASCAL: *Pensées,* I, 1670

Sit the comedy out, and that done,
When the play's at an end, let the curtain fall down.
THOMAS FLATMAN: *The Whim,* 1674

When I consider life, 'tis all a cheat;
Yet, fooled with hope, men favor the deceit.
JOHN DRYDEN: *Aurengzebe*, IV, 1676

Why are we so fond of a life that begins with a cry and ends with a groan?
MARY, COUNTESS OF WARWICK: On her deathbed, 1678

Human life is at the greatest and the best but like a forward child, that must be played with, and humored a little, to keep it quiet, till it falls asleep, and then the care is over.
WILLIAM TEMPLE: *Of Poetry*, 1680

Life is a sleep.
JEAN DE LA BRUYÈRE: *Caractères*, XI, 1688

Most men employ the first part of life to make the rest miserable. IBID.

When life is miserable it is painful to endure it; when it is happy it is horrible to lose it.
IBID.

As runs the glass
Man's life doth pass.
The New England Primer, c. 1688

Life is a tragedy wherein we sit as spectators for awhile, and then act out our part in it.
JONATHAN SWIFT: *Thoughts on Various Subjects*, 1706

Amid two seas, on one small point of land,
Wearied, uncertain, and amazed we stand.
MATTHEW PRIOR: *Solomon on the Vanity of the World*, III, 1718

Who breathes must suffer, and who thinks must mourn;
And he alone is blessed who ne'er was born.
IBID.

No man hath a lease of his life.
JAMES KELLY: *Complete Collection of Scottish Proverbs*, 1721

A little rule, a little sway,
A sunbeam in a Winter's day,
Is all the proud and mighty have
Between the cradle and the grave.
JOHN DYER: *Grongar Hill*, 1726

Our whole life is but a greater and longer childhood.
THOMAS FULLER: *Gnomologia*, 1732

We are born crying, live complaining, and die disappointed. IBID.

Life is a jest, and all things show it;
I thought so once, and now I know it.
JOHN GAY: Couplet by himself, following Alexander Pope's epitaph on him in Westminster Abbey; probably written in 1732

A mighty maze, but not without a plan.
ALEXANDER POPE: *An Essay on Man*, I, 1733

Life can little more supply
Than just to look about us and to die. IBID.

We are all like vessels tossed on the bosom of the deep; our passions are the winds that sweep us impetuously onward; each pleasure is a rock; the whole of life is a wide ocean.
PIETRO METASTASIO: *Olimpiade*, II, 1735

What shall we call this undetermin'd state,
This narrow isthmus 'twixt two boundless oceans,
That whence we came, and that to which we tend?
GEORGE LILLO: *Arden of Feversham*, III, c. 1735

My life is a combat.
VOLTAIRE: *Mahomet*, II, 1742

Life is most enjoyed
When courted least; most worth, when disesteemed.
EDWARD YOUNG: *Night Thoughts*, III, 1742

Still seems it strange, that thou shouldst live for ever?
Is it less strange, that thou shouldst live at all?
This is a miracle, and *that* no more.
EDWARD YOUNG: *Night Thoughts*, VII, 1744

Reflect that life, like every other blessing,
Derives its value from its use alone.
SAMUEL JOHNSON: *Irene*, III, 1749

The main of life is composed of small incidents and petty occurrences; of wishes for objects not remote, and grief for disappointments of no fatal consequence; of insect vexations which sting us and fly away, impertinences which buzz a while about us, and are heard no more; of meteorous pleasures which dance before us and are dissipated; of compliments which glide off the soul like other music, and are forgotten by him that gave and him that received them.
SAMUEL JOHNSON: *The Rambler*, Nov. 10, 1750

Life may as properly be called an art as any other, and the great incidents in it are no more to be considered as mere accidents than the severest members of a fine statue or a noble poem.
HENRY FIELDING: *Amelia*, I, 1752

A good man's life is all of a piece.
BENJAMIN WHICHCOTE: *Moral and Religious Aphorisms*, 1753

Life is a game of chance.
VOLTAIRE: *Letter to M. Tronchin*, Nov. 24, 1755

Human life is everywhere a state in which much is to be endured, and little to be enjoyed.
SAMUEL JOHNSON: *Rasselas*, XI, 1759

Life is tedious.
SAMUEL JOHNSON: *Boswell's Life*, June 10, 1761

Let us make the best of that bad bargain of being born in this vile planet, where we may find, however (God be thanked), much to laugh at, though little to approve.

MARY WORTLEY MONTAGU: *Letter to James Steuart,* Jan. 13, 1761

What is the life of man? Is it not to shift from side to side — from sorrow to sorrow — to button up one cause of vexation and unbutton another?

LAURENCE STERNE: *Tristram Shandy,* V, 1761

After all, monseigneur, I must live!
I don't see the necessity for it.

The protest was made by a priest accused of publishing libels; the answer was by the Count d'Argenson (1696–1764), one of the ministers of Louis XV

Philosophers there are who try to make themselves believe that this life is happy; but they believe it only while they are saying it, and never yet produced conviction in a single mind.

SAMUEL JOHNSON: *Letter to Hester Thrale,* Sept. 30, 1773

Man lives in the world but once. (Man lebt nur einmal in der Welt.)

J. W. GOETHE: *Clavigo,* I, 1774

Life is the faculty of spontaneous activity, the awareness that we have powers.

IMMANUEL KANT: Lecture in Königsberg, 1775

Brother, I have watched men: their insect cares and giant projects — their godlike plans and their mouselike employments — their eager race after happiness; this one trusting to the swiftness of his horse — another to the nose of his ass — a third to his own legs; this checkered lottery of life, on which so many stake their innocence and Heaven to snatch a prize, and — blanks are all they draw; for they find to their disappointment that there was no prize in the wheel.

J. C. F. SCHILLER: *The Robbers,* III, 1781

A painful passage o'er a restless flood,
A vain pursuit of fugitive false good,
A sense of fancied bliss and heartfelt care,
Closing at last in darkness and despair.

WILLIAM COWPER: *Hope,* 1782

Men deal with life as children with their play,
Who first misuse, then cast their toys away.

IBID.

What is life, I ask myself, is it a gracious gift? No, it is too bitter; a gift means something valuable conferred, but life appears to be a mere accident, and of the worst kind: we are born to be victims of diseases and passions, of mischances and death.

ST. JOHN DE CRÈVECOEUR: *Letters from an American Farmer,* XII, 1782

Life, as Cowley seems to say, ought to resemble a well-ordered poem; of which one rule generally received is, that the exordium should be simple, and should promise little.

SAMUEL JOHNSON: *Boswell's Life,* Sept. 7, 1782

Life is not measured by the time we live.

GEORGE CRABBE: *The Village,* II, 1783

Thus we build on the ice, thus we write on the waves of the sea; the roaring waves pass away, the ice melts, and away goes our palace, like our thoughts.

J. C. VON HERDER: *Ideen zur Philosophie der Geschichte der Menschheit,* II, 1784

Life is all a variorum.

ROBERT BURNS: *The Jolly Beggars,* 1785

The art of life is the art of avoiding pain.

THOMAS JEFFERSON: *Letter to Mrs. Cosway,* 1786

A useless life is an early death.

J. W. GOETHE: *Iphigenia auf Tauris,* I, 1787

Life is still beautiful. (Das Leben ist doch schön.)

J. C. F. SCHILLER: *Don Carlos,* IV, 1787

Life is but a day at most.

ROBERT BURNS: *Lines Written in Friars' Carse Hermitage,* 1788

Were it offered to my choice, I should have no objection to a repetition of the same life from its beginning, only asking the advantages authors have in a second edition to correct some faults of the first.

BENJAMIN FRANKLIN: *Autobiography,* 1798

The dreary intercourse of daily life.

WILLIAM WORDSWORTH: *Tintern Abbey,* 1798

Every man has a rainy corner in his life.

JEAN PAUL RICHTER: *Titan,* 1803

Life is not the supreme good.

J. C. F. SCHILLER: *Die Braut von Messina,* 1803

Life is but a day:
A fragile dewdrop on its perilous way
From a tree's summit.

JOHN KEATS: *Sleep and Poetry,* 1817

We wither from our youth, we gasp away —
Sick — sick; unfound the boon, unslaked the thirst,
Though to the last, in verge of our decay,
Some phantom lures, such as we sought at first —
But all too late, — so are we doubly curst.

BYRON: *Childe Harold,* IV, 1818

What a bore life is! What a cross!

NAPOLEON I: To Gaspard Gourgaud at St. Helena, Jan. 16, 1818

The painted veil which those who live
Call life.

P. B. SHELLEY: *Sonnet,* 1818

A man's life of any worth is a continual allegory, and very few eyes can see the mystery of his life — a life like the Scriptures, figurative — which such people can no more make out than they can the Hebrew Bible.
JOHN KEATS: *Letter to George Keats,* Feb. 18, 1819

The weariness, the fever, and the fret,
Here where men sit and hear each other groan.
JOHN KEATS: *To a Nightingale,* 1819

Life to the great majority is only a constant struggle for mere existence, with the certainty of losing it at last.
ARTHUR SCHOPENHAUER: *The World as Will and Idea,* IV, 1819

Short as life is, some find it long enough to outlive their characters, their constitutions and their estates. C. C. COLTON: *Lacon,* 1820

A day of gold from out an age of iron
Is all that life allows the luckiest sinner.
BYRON: *Don Juan,* III, 1821

Life, like a dome of many-colored glass,
Stains the white radiance of eternity.
P. B. SHELLEY: *Adonais,* LII, 1821

Between two worlds, life hovers like a star
'Twixt night and morn, upon the horizon's verge,
How little do we know that which we are!
How less what we may be!
BYRON: *Don Juan,* XV, 1824

Life is the one universal soul, which by virtue of the enlivening Breath, and the informing Word, all organized bodies have in common, each after its kind.
S. T. COLERIDGE: *Aids to Reflection,* 1825

Human life may be regarded as a succession of frontispieces. The way to be satisfied is never to look back.
WILLIAM HAZLITT: *The Prose Album,* 1829 (The Monthly Magazine, July)

Life is the two-fold internal movement of composition and decomposition, at once general and continuous.
H. M. DUCROTAY DE BLAINVILLE: *Cours de physiologie générale,* I, 1833

Life is that power in the individual which can force external forces to obey an internal law.
ERNST VON FEUCHTERSLEBEN: *Zur Diätetik der Seele,* I, 1838

Do you desire to master the art of prolonging life? Rather apply yourself to the art of enduring it.
ERNST VON FEUCHTERSLEBEN: *Zur Diätetik der Seele,* XII

A bridge of groans across a stream of tears.
P. J. BAILEY: *Festus,* 1839

Tell me not in mournful numbers,
Life is but an empty dream.
H. W. LONGFELLOW: *A Psalm of Life,* 1839

Life is real! Life is earnest!
And the grave is not its goal. IBID.

A little gleam of time between two eternities; no second chance to us forever more!
THOMAS CARLYLE: *Heroes and Hero-Worship,* V, 1840 (Lecture in London, May 19)

Life is a series of surprises.
R. W. EMERSON: *Circles,* 1841

Life is a festival only to the wise. Seen from the nook and chimney-side of prudence, it wears a ragged and dangerous front.
R. W. EMERSON: *Heroism,* 1841

My life is not an apology, but a life. It is for itself and not for a spectacle. I much prefer that it should be of a lower strain, so it be genuine and equal, than that it should be glittering and unsteady.
R. W. EMERSON: *Self-Reliance,* 1841

My life hath been the poem I would have writ,
But I could not both live, and live to utter it.
H. D. THOREAU: *Journal,* Aug. 28, 1841

Every thing admonishes us how needlessly long life is.
R. W. EMERSON: *The Transcendentalist,* 1842

Life was never a May-game for men: in all times the lot of the dumb millions born to toil was defaced with manifold sufferings, injustices, heavy burdens, avoidable and unavoidable; not play at all, but hard work that made the sinews sore, and the heart sore.
THOMAS CARLYLE: *Past and Present,* III, 1843

Such is life.
CHARLES DICKENS: *Martin Chuzzlewit,* XXIX, 1844

Youth is a blunder; manhood a struggle; old age a regret.
BENJAMIN DISRAELI: *Coningsby,* III, 1844

Life is simply a process of combustion.
M. J. SCHLEIDEN: *Die Pflanze und ihr Leben,* 1848

Life makes strange bedfellows.
E. G. BULWER-LYTTON: *The Caxtons,* IV, 1849

Man's real life is happy, chiefly because he is ever expecting that it soon will be so.
E. A. POE: *Marginalia,* 1844–49

My life is like a stroll upon the beach.
H. D. THOREAU: *A Week on the Concord and Merrimack Rivers,* 1849

Life is eating us up. We shall be fables presently. Keep cool: it will be all one a hundred years hence.
R. W. EMERSON: *Representative Men,* IV, 1850

Life is March weather, savage and serene in one hour. IBID.

Life's well enough, but we shall be glad to get out of it, and they will all be glad to have us. IBID.

Life, a fury slinging flame.
ALFRED TENNYSON: *In Memoriam*, L, 1850

Knowledge, love, power, — there is the complete life.
H. F. AMIEL: *Journal*, April 7, 1851

Life is made up of marble and mud.
NATHANIEL HAWTHORNE: *The House of the Seven Gables*, II, 1851

Life is an unprofitable disturbance in the calm of nonexistence.
ARTHUR SCHOPENHAUER: *Parerga und Paralipomena*, 1851

I do not snivel that snivel the world over,
That months are vacuums, and the ground but wallow and filth;
That life is a suck and a sell, and nothing remains at the end but threadbare crape, and tears.
WALT WHITMAN: *Walt Whitman*, 1855

Life is an apprenticeship to constant renunciations, to the steady failure of our claims, our hopes, our powers, our liberty.
H. F. AMIEL: *Journal*, Oct. 22, 1856

I came like water, and like wind I go.
EDWARD FITZGERALD: Tr. of OMAR KHAYYÁM: *Rubáiyát* (*c.* 1100), 1857

The wine of life keeps oozing drop by drop,
The leaves of life keep falling one by one.
IBID.

Life isn't all beer and skittles.
THOMAS HUGHES: *Tom Brown's School-days*, I, 1857 (*Skittles*=a game resembling ten-pins)

Life, as we call it, is nothing but the edge of the boundless ocean of existence where it comes on soundings.
O. W. HOLMES: *The Professor at the Breakfast-Table*, v, 1859

Life is an ecstasy.
R. W. EMERSON: *The Conduct of Life*, I, 1860

Does the road wind up-hill all the way?
Yes, to the very end.
Will the day's journey take the whole long day?
From morn to night, my friend.
CHRISTINA ROSSETTI: *Up-Hill*, 1862

Life is a watch or a vision
Between a sleep and a sleep.
A. C. SWINBURNE: *Atalanta in Calydon*, 1865

Every form of human life is romantic.
T. W. HIGGINSON: *A Plea for Culture*, 1867

[Life is] the definite combination of heterogeneous changes, both simultaneous and successive, in correspondence with external coexistences and sequences.
HERBERT SPENCER: *The Principles of Biology*, I, 1867

Life is a wave which in no two consecutive moments of its existence is composed of the same particles.
JOHN TYNDALL: *Fragments of Science for Unscientific People*, II, 1871

Life is a fatal complaint, and an eminently contagious one.
O. W. HOLMES: *The Poet at the Breakfast-Table*, XII, 1872

Life's more amusing than we thought.
ANDREW LANG: *Ballade of Middle Age*, 1872

Life is one long tragedy; creation is one great crime.
W. WINWOOD READE: *The Martyrdom of Man*, III, 1872

To procure life, to obtain a mate, and to rear offspring: such is the real business of life.
IBID.

Human existence is girt round with mystery: the narrow region of our experience is a small island in the midst of a boundless sea. To add to the mystery, the domain of our earthly existence is not only an island of infinite space, but also in infinite time. The past and the future are alike shrouded from us: we neither know the origin of anything which is, nor its final destination.
J. S. MILL: *Three Essays on Religion*, III, 1874

Life iz like a mountain: after climbing up one side and sliding down the other, put up the sled.
H. W. SHAW (JOSH BILLINGS): *Josh Billings' Encyclopedia of Wit and Wisdom*, 1874

One moment of a man's life is a fact so stupendous as to take the lustre out of all fiction.
R. W. EMERSON: *Demonology*, 1877

We live embosomed in sounds we do not hear, scents we do not smell, spectacles we see not.
IBID.

Life is an abyss.
VICTOR HUGO: *The History of a Crime*, 1877

Lo! as the wind is, so is mortal life —
A moan, a sigh, a sob, a storm, a strife.
EDWIN ARNOLD: *The Light of Asia*, 1879

Life is a school of probability.
WALTER BAGEHOT: *Literary Studies*, II, 1879

Life's a chameleon,
Whose color is fit argument for fools.
ALFRED AUSTIN: *Savonarola*, I, 1881

Life is made up of interruptions.
W. S. GILBERT: *Patience*, I, 1881

Life is a shadowy, strange, and winding road.
R. G. INGERSOLL: Speech in Chicago, Nov. 26, 1882

To most of us the real life is the life we do not lead.
OSCAR WILDE: *The English Renaissance of Art*, 1882 (Lecture in New York, Jan. 9)

Life in general may be looked upon as a republic where the individuals are for the most part unconscious that while they are working for themselves they are also working for the public good.
FRANCIS GALTON: *Inquiry Into Human Faculty*, 1883

The great business of life is to be, to do, and to do without, and to depart.
JOHN MORLEY: Address in Edinburgh, Nov., 1887

Life is an instinct for growth, for survival, for the accumulation of forces, for power.
F. W. NIETZSCHE: *The Antichrist*, VI, 1888

Life's a pleasant institution;
Let us take it as it comes.
W. S. GILBERT: *The Gondoliers*, I, 1889

Thanks in old age — thanks ere I go,
For health, the midday sun, the impalpable air — for life, mere life,
For precious ever-lingering memories (of you my mother dear — you, father — you, brothers, sisters, friends),
For all my days — not those of peace alone — the days of war the same.
WALT WHITMAN: *Thanks in Old Age*, 1889

Life imitates art far more than art imitates life.
OSCAR WILDE: *The Decay of Lying*, 1889

Life is one long process of getting tired.
SAMUEL BUTLER: *Note-Books*, *c.* 1890

Life is the art of drawing sufficient conclusions from insufficient premisses. IBID.

Life is a long lesson in humility.
JAMES M. BARRIE: *The Little Minister*, III, 1891

To suffer and to endure is the lot of humankind. Let them strive as they may, they will never summon up enough strength and cunning to throw off the ills and troubles which beset them.
POPE LEO XIII: *Rerum novarum*, May 15, 1891

I spend my life thus: I eat, talk and listen; I eat, write and read — that is, talk and listen again; I eat and play; I eat, talk and listen again; I eat and go to bed; and so on, day after day.
LYOF N. TOLSTOY: *What Shall We Do?*, 1891

Life is terribly deficient in form. Its catastrophes happen in a wrong way and to the wrong people. There is a grotesque horror about its comedies, and its tragedies seem to culminate in farce.
OSCAR WILDE: *The Critic as Artist*, 1891

One should absorb the color of life, but one should never remember its details.
OSCAR WILDE: *The Picture of Dorian Gray*, 1891

Life is far too important a thing ever to talk seriously about.
OSCAR WILDE: *Lady Windermere's Fan*, II, 1892

Life consists in penetrating the unknown, and fashioning our actions in accord with the new knowledge thus acquired.
LYOF N. TOLSTOY: *The Kingdom of God Is Within You*, 1893

Life is simply a mauvais quart d'heure made up of exquisite moments.
OSCAR WILDE: *A Woman of No Importance*, II, 1893

When a man says he has exhausted life one always knows life has exhausted him. IBID.

Men know life too early, women know life too late.
OSCAR WILDE: *A Woman of No Importance*, III

A wisp of fog betwixt us and the sun;
A call to battle, and the battle done
Ere the last echo dies within our ears;
A rose choked in the grass; an hour of fears;
The gusts that past a darkening shore do beat;
The burst of music down an unlistening street.
LIZETTE WOODWORTH REESE: *Tears*, 1899

Life . . . is a combat without grandeur, without happiness, fought in solitude and silence.
ROMAIN ROLLAND: *Beethoven*, 1903

That life is worth living is the most necessary of assumptions, and, were it not assumed, the most impossible of conclusions.
GEORGE SANTAYANA: *The Life of Reason*, I, 1905

Do not try to live forever. You will not succeed.
GEORGE BERNARD SHAW: *The Doctor's Dilemma*, pref., 1906

Life does not proceed by the association and addition of elements, but by dissociation and division.
HENRI BERGSON: *L'évolution créatrice*, I, 1907

The vital glow. (L'élan vital.) IBID.

Tell me not in mournful wish-wash
Life's a sort of sugared dish-wash.
EZRA POUND: *L'Homme moyen sensuel*, 1910 (Cf. LONGFELLOW, *ante*, 1839)

"You scoundrel, you have wronged me," hissed the philosopher. "May you live forever!"
AMBROSE BIERCE: *Collected Works*, VIII, 1911

Life is a romantic business. It is painting a picture, not doing a sum – but you have to make the romance. And it will come to the question how much fire you have in your belly.
O. W. HOLMES II: *Letter to Oswald Ryan*, June 5, 1911

The ice of life is slippery.
GEORGE BERNARD SHAW: *Fanny's First Play*, pref., 1911

We are encamped like bewildered travelers in a garish, unrestful hotel.
JOSEPH CONRAD: *Victory*, 1915

You think I am fighting for wages. For pay. For a glass more of beer. For better cigars. For costlier clothes. To get rid of rags. Well, so I am. But only incidentally. I am really fighting for life.
HORACE TRAUBEL: *Chants Communal*, 1915

Life is simply one damned thing after another.
Ascribed to FRANK WARD O'MALLEY (1876–1932); also to ELBERT HUBBARD (1859–1915)

All life is an experiment. Every year if not every day we have to wager our salvation upon some prophecy based upon imperfect knowledge.
MR. JUSTICE O. W. HOLMES: *Dissenting opinion in Abrams* vs. *United States*, 1919

Life is a disease; and the only difference between one man and another is the stage of the disease at which he lives.
GEORGE BERNARD SHAW: *Back to Methuselah*, I, 1921

Soliloquy of a new-born child: Out of Nothing into a Something; out of a No into a Yes; out of Where was I? into What am I?; out of a possibility into a maybe; out of a sleep into a sweat; out of Nullity into Bolony.
BENJAMIN DECASSERES: *Fantasia Impromptu*, 1933

Life is like that.
AMERICAN SAYING, current *c.* 1935

Life is like a fire; it begins in smoke, and ends in ashes.
ARAB PROVERB

All life comes from life. (Omne vivum e vivo.)
Author unidentified

Life consists in wanting something. When a man is satisfied he is as good as dead.
IBID.

Life is a jig saw puzzle with most of the pieces missing.
IBID.

Life is a one-way street.
IBID.

There may be a Heaven;
There must be a Hell;
Meanwhile, we have our life here –
Well?
IBID.

Spell *live* backward, and you have *evil.*
IBID.; it seems to be derived from a German saying to the same purport, based on *Leben* (life) and *Nebel* (cloud)

Man's life is like a candle in the wind.
CHINESE PROVERB

Life is an onion, and one peels it crying.
FRENCH PROVERB

The life of man consists of yesterday, today and tomorrow.
IBID.

Life means struggle. (Das Leben heisst Streben.)
GERMAN PROVERB

The life of man is like a long journey with a heavy load on the back.
JAPANESE PROVERB

Man's journey through life is like that of a bee through blossoms.
JUGO-SLAVIC PROVERB

To every man his own life is a mystery. (Sua cuique vita obscura est.)
LATIN PROVERB

Life is like drunkenness: the pleasure passes away, but the headache remains.
PERSIAN PROVERB

[*See also* Ages, Art, Day, Duty, Emotion, Evil, Existence, Fame, Health, Hope, Humanity, Humility, Immortality, Life and Death, Living, Longevity, Man, Misery, Misfit, Morality, Pain, Strenuous, Suicide, Tedious, Woman, World.

Life and Death

The race of men is like the race of leaves. As one generation flourishes another decays.
HOMER: *Iliad*, VI, *c.* 800 B.C.

It is best for man not to be born, nor to see the rays of the bright sun; next best is to die quickly, and lie neath the earth.
THEOGNIS: *Elegies*, *c.* 550 B.C.

Thou canst not judge the life of man until death hath ended it.
SOPHOCLES: *Trachiniæ*, *c.* 450 B.C. (Cited as an old saying)

The man who prays for death is mad. There is nothing so good in death as the misery of life.
EURIPIDES: *Iphigenia in Tauris*, *c.* 413 B.C.

Man that is born of woman is of few days, and full of trouble. He cometh forth like a flower, and is cut down; he fleeth also as a shadow, and continueth not.
JOB XIV, 1–2, *c.* 325 B.C.

Life is nothing but a journey to death.
SENECA: *Ad Polybium de consolatione*, *c.* 44

It is a misery to be born, a pain to live, and anguish to die. (Nasci miserum, vivere pœna, angustia mori.)
Ascribed to ST. BERNARD (1090–1153)

Of evil life cometh evil ending.
Anon.: *King Alisaunder, c.* 1300

So long as we may, let us enjoy this breath,
For naught doth kill a man so soon as death.
Author unidentified; familiar since the XVI century

He who should teach men to die would at the same time teach them to live.
MICHEL DE MONTAIGNE: *Essays,* I, 1580

My prime of youth is but a frost of cares,
My feast of joy is but a dish of pain,
My crop of corn is but a field of tares,
And all my good is but vain hope of gain;
The day is past, and yet I saw no sun,
And now I live, and now my life is done.
CHIDIOCK TICHBORNE: *Elegy, c.* 1586

Let us live, laugh, and be merry amongst our friends, but die and yield up the ghost amongst strangers, and such as we know not.
MICHEL DE MONTAIGNE: *Essays,* III, 1588

Life is a frost of cold felicity,
And death the thaw of all our vanity.
THOMAS BASTARD: *Chrestoleros,* IV, 1598

He that cuts off twenty years of life
Cuts off so many years of fearing death.
SHAKESPEARE: *Julius Cæsar,* III, 1599

The child was born, and cried;
Became a man, after fell sick, and died.
Anon.: *The London Prodigal,* I, 1605

To-morrow, and to-morrow, and to-morrow,
Creeps in this petty pace from day to day
To the last syllable of recorded time,
And all our yesterdays have lighted fools
The way to dusty death.
SHAKESPEARE: *Macbeth,* V, 1605

Golden lads and girls all must,
As chimney-sweepers, come to dust.
SHAKESPEARE: *Cymbeline,* IV, *c.* 1609

We are such stuff
As dreams are made on; and our little life
Is rounded with a sleep.
SHAKESPEARE: *The Tempest,* IV, 1611

Our lives are but our marches to the grave.
JOHN FLETCHER: *The Humorous Lieutenant,* III, *c.* 1620

He that begins to live begins to die.
FRANCIS QUARLES: *Hieroglyphics of the Life of Man,* 1638

Such a life, such a death.
JOHN CLARKE: *Parœmiologia Anglo-Latina,* 1639

Life without a friend; death without a witness.
GEORGE HERBERT: *Outlandish Proverbs,* 1640

Learn to live well, that thou mayst die so too;
To live and die is all we have to do.
JOHN DENHAM: *Of Prudence,* 1650

I was born without knowing why, I have lived without knowing why, and I am dying without either knowing why or how.
PIERRE GASSENDI: Last words, 1655

Let one imagine a number of men in chains, and all condemned to death, some of whom, being beheaded every day in the sight of the others, those who remain see their own condition in that of their fellows, and, regarding each other with grief, and without hope, await their turn: this is a picture of the condition of men.
BLAISE PASCAL: *Pensées,* II, 1670

For man there are only three events — to be born, to live and to die. He doesn't know it when he is born; he suffers at death, and he forgets how to live.
JEAN DE LA BRUYÈRE: *Caractères,* XI, 1688

Our days begin with trouble here,
Our life is but a span,
And cruel death is always near,
So frail a thing is man.
The New England Primer, c. 1688

Teach me to live that I may dread
The grave as little as my bed.
THOMAS KEN: *Evening Hymn, c.* 1690

It is as natural to die as to be born.
THOMAS FULLER: *Gnomologia,* 1732

Life can little more supply
Than just to look about us and to die.
ALEXANDER POPE: *An Essay on Man,* I, 1732

As soon as man, expert from time, has found
The key of life, it opes the gates of death.
EDWARD YOUNG: *Night Thoughts,* IV, 1742

Life! we've been long together,
Through pleasant and through cloudy weather;
'Tis hard to part when friends are dear,
Perhaps 'twill cost a sigh, a tear;
Then steal away, give little warning;
Choose thine own time;
Say not "Good-night"; but in some brighter clime
Bid me "Good-morning."
ANNA LETITIA BARBAULD: *Ode to Life,* 1773

Man has two and a half minutes on earth — one to laugh, one to sigh, and half a minute to love: in the midst of this last he dies.
JEAN PAUL RICHTER: *Hesperus,* IV, 1792

How calm and sweet the victories of life,
How terrorless the triumph of the grave.
P. B. SHELLEY: *Queen Mab,* VI, 1813

We live and die,
But which is best you know no more than I.
BYRON: *Don Juan,* VII, 1823

Death is a cool night; life is a sultry day.
HEINRICH HEINE: *Der Tod ist die kühle Nacht*, 1827

'Tis not the whole of life to live,
Nor all of death to die.
JAMES MONTGOMERY: *The Issues of Life and Death*, *c.* 1830

Life is as the current spark on the miner's wheel of flints;
Whiles it spinneth there is light; stop it, all is darkness.
M. F. TUPPER: *Proverbial Philosophy*, I, 1838

Out of sleeping a waking,
Out of waking a sleep.
R. W. EMERSON: *The Sphinx*, 1841 (Dial, Jan.)

Born in throes, 'tis fit that man should live in pains and die in pangs.
HERMAN MELVILLE: *Moby Dick*, IV, 1851

'Tis but a tent where takes his one-day's rest
A sultan to the realm of death addrest;
The sultan rises, and the dark ferrásh
Strikes, and prepares it for another guest.
EDWARD FITZGERALD: Tr. of OMAR KHAYYÁM: *Rubáiyát* (*c.* 1100), 1857

Ah, for the weariness that comes of living
There is no cure but death.
ELIZABETH CHASE (AKERS ALLEN): *The City of the Living*, 1866

A little season of love and laughter,
Of light and life, and pleasure and pain,
And a horror of outer darkness after,
And the dust returneth to dust again.
A. L. GORDON: *The Swimmer*, 1867

Life is the tillage, and death is the harvest according.
WALT WHITMAN: *As I Watch'd the Plowman Plowing*, 1871

The thought of death certainly influences the conduct of life less than might have been expected.
JOHN LUBBOCK (LORD AVEBURY): *The Pleasures of Life*, II, 1887

The two old, simple problems ever intertwined,
Close home, elusive, present, baffled, grappled,
By each successive age insoluble, passed on
To ours today — and we pass on the same.
WALT WHITMAN: *Life and Death*, 1889

Live your own life, for you will die your own death.
LATIN PROVERB

[*See also* Death, Life, Living, Longevity, Morality, Religion.

Light

God said, Let there be light: and there was light.
GENESIS I, 3, *c.* 700 B.C.

The light of the world.
MATTHEW V, 14, *c.* 75 (Cf. JOHN VIII, 12, *c.* 115)

The light shineth in darkness.
JOHN I, 5, *c.* 115

Everyone that doeth evil hateth the light.
JOHN III, 20

He was a burning and a shining light.
JOHN V, 35

Walk while ye have the light, lest darkness come upon you.
JOHN XII, 35

Light, even though it passes through pollution, is not polluted.
ST. AUGUSTINE: *Homilies on St. John*, I, *c.* 416

You stand in your own light.
JOHN HEYWOOD: *Proverbs*, 1546

A dim religious light.
JOHN MILTON: *Il Penseroso*, 1632

Where the light is brightest the shadows are deepest.
J. W. GOETHE: *Goetz von Berlichingen*, II, 1771

The light that never was on sea or land.
WILLIAM WORDSWORTH: *Elegiac Stanzas Suggested by a Picture of Peele Castle in a Storm*, 1807

Even the minutest molecule of light,
That in an April sunbeam's fleeting glow
Fulfils its destined, though invisible work,
The universal Spirit guides.
P. B. SHELLEY: *Queen Mab*, VI, 1813

Open the shutters in the bedroom, and let in more light. (Macht doch den Fensterladen im Schlafgemach auf, damit mehr Licht herein komme.)
J. W. GOETHE: On his deathbed, 1832 (The words are commonly reduced to "Light! more light!" (Licht! mehr Licht!)

Lead, kindly Light, amid the encircling gloom,
Lead Thou me on!
The night is dark, and I am far from home —
Lead Thou me on!
Keep Thou my feet; I do not ask to see
The distant scene, — one step enough for me.
J. H. NEWMAN: *Light in the Darkness*, 1833 (The tune is by J. B. Dykes, 1865)

Light is the first of painters. There is no object so foul that intense light will not make it beautiful.
R. W. EMERSON: *Nature*, 1836

The light that failed.
RUDYARD KIPLING: Title of a novel, 1891

[*See also* Culture.

Light-hearted

A light heart lives long.
SHAKESPEARE: *Love's Labor's Lost*, V, *c.* 1595

Lighthouse

The lighthouse lifts its massive masonry,
A pillar of fire by night, of cloud by day.
H. W. LONGFELLOW: *The Lighthouse*, 1850

The coastwise lights of England watch the ships of England go.
RUDYARD KIPLING: *The Coastwise Lights,* 1893

A tall building on the seashore in which the government maintains a lamp and the friend of a politician.
AMBROSE BIERCE: *The Devil's Dictionary,* 1906

At the foot of a lighthouse one finds darkness.
SPANISH PROVERB

Lightning

The lightnings lightened the world: the earth trembled and shook.
PSALMS LXXVII, 18, *c.* 150 B.C.

The lightning, which doth cease to be
Ere one can say " It lightens."
SHAKESPEARE: *Romeo and Juliet,* II, *c.* 1596

Lightning seems to be this: An almost infinitely fine, combustible matter, that floats in the air, that takes fire by a sudden and mighty fermentation, that is some way promoted by the cool and moisture, and perhaps attraction, of the clouds. By this sudden agitation, this fine, floating matter is driven forth with a mighty force.
JONATHAN EDWARDS: *Notes on Natural Science, c.* 1718

Lightning never strikes twice in the same place.
AMERICAN PROVERB

Lightning strikes the loftiest tree first.
HINDU PROVERB

Beware of an oak:
It draws the stroke;
Avoid an ash:
It counts the flash;
Creep under the thorn:
It can save you from harm.
OLD ENGLISH RHYME

Forked lightning at night:
The next day clear and bright. IBID.

[*See also* Oak.

Lightning-Bug

The lightning-bug is a wondrous sight,
But you'd think it has no mind;
It pumps around in the darkest night,
With its headlight on behind.
Author unidentified

Like

One rogue leads another on: the gods link like with like.
HOMER: *Odyssey,* XVI, *c.* 800 B.C.

Like people, like priest.
HOSEA IV, 9, *c.* 740 B.C.

Cicala loves cicala, ant loves ant, and hawk loves hawk.
THEOCRITUS: *Idylls,* IX, *c.* 270 B.C.

As like as two drops of milk.
PLAUTUS: *Miles Glorioso,* 205 B.C.

All flesh consorteth according to kind, and a man will cleave to his like.
ECCLESIASTICUS XIII, 6, *c.* 180 B.C.

It is an old proverb that like and like draw together.
CICERO: *De senectute,* III, *c.* 78 B.C.

Like master, like man.
PETRONIUS ARBITER: *Satyricon, c.* 50

Like to like.
ENGLISH PROVERB, borrowed from the Latin, and traced by Apperson and Smith to *c.* 1375

Birds of a feather flock together.
ENGLISH PROVERB, borrowed from HOMER: *Odyssey,* XVII, and current since the XVI century

Like mother, like daughter.
ENGLISH PROVERB, traced by Apperson to 1509 (Cf. EZEKIEL XVI, 44, under Mother and Daughter)

The like delighteth in the like.
RICHARD TAVERNER: Tr. of DESIDERIUS ERASMUS: *Adagia* (1508), 1539

Such saint, such shrine.
JOHN BALE: *Acts of English Votaries,* 1546

Like lord, like chaplain.
JOHN BALE: *King Johan,* 1548

Like mistress, like maid.
ENGLISH PROVERB, traced by Apperson to 1557

Like cow, like calf.
WILLIAM BULLEIN: *Dialogue Against the Fever Pestilence,* 1564

Like will to like, quoth the Devil to the collier.
ULPIAN FULWELL: *Like Will to Like,* 1568

As like as one pease is to another.
JOHN LYLY: *Euphues and His England,* 1580

Such mistress, such Nan;
Such masters, such man.
THOMAS TUSSER: *Five Hundred Points of Good Husbandry,* 1580

Such saints, such service.
THOMAS HOWELL: *Howell His Devises,* 1581

Such beef, such broth.
FRANCIS MERES: *Palladis Tamia,* 1598

Every like is not the same.
SHAKESPEARE: *Julius Cæsar,* II, 1599

I shall not look upon his like again.
SHAKESPEARE: *Hamlet,* I, *c.* 1601

As the princes are, so are the people.
ROBERT BURTON: *The Anatomy of Melancholy,* 1621

Like blood, like goods, and like age
Make the happiest marriage.
JOHN CLARKE: *Parœmiologia Anglo-Latina,* 1639

Likeness causeth liking. IBID.

Like saint, like offering. IBID.

Like will to like, each creature loves his kind.
ROBERT HERRICK: *Hesperides,* 1648

Like hen, like chicken.
PHILIP MASSINGER: *The City Madam,* I, 1658

Like author, like book.
JOHN RAY: *English Proverbs,* 1670

Like to like, and Nan to Nicholas. IBID.

Like priest, like people.
THOMAS FULLER: *Gnomologia,* 1732 (Cf. HOSEA, *ante, c.* 740 B.C.)

She's as like her husband as if she were spit out of his mouth.
JONATHAN SWIFT: *Polite Conversation,* III, 1738 (The idea has been traced by Smith to *c.* 1400)

Like cures like. (Similia similibus curantur.)
LATIN PROVERB, adopted as the motto of homeopathy by SAMUEL HAHNEMANN: *Organon der Rationellen Heilkunde,* 1810

Like breeds like.
ALFRED TENNYSON: *Walking to the Mail,* 1842 (Cited as a common saying)

One crow will not pick out another crow's eyes.
H. G. BOHN: *Handbook of Proverbs,* 1855

Like pot, like lid. ARMENIAN PROVERB

Pretty children sing pretty songs.
DANISH PROVERB

Gipsy with gipsy, gentile with gentile. (Rom romesa, gajo gajesa.) GIPSY PROVERB

Like crow, like egg. GREEK PROVERB

Like father, like son. (Qualis pater, talis filius.)
LATIN PROVERB

Like king, like people. (Qualis rex, talis grex.)
IBID.

No likeness is the same. (Nullum simile est idem.)
IBID. (Cf. SHAKESPEARE, *ante,* 1599)

Like likes like. (Simili gaudet simili.)
MEDIEVAL LATIN PROVERB

[*See also* Pity, Pride, Same, Society.

Lilac

When lilacs last in the dooryard bloom'd.
WALT WHITMAN: Title and first line of a poem, 1865–6

Lily

Consider the lilies of the field, how they grow; they toil not, neither do they spin. And yet I say unto you, That even Solomon in all his glory was not arrayed like one of these.
MATTHEW VI, 28–29, *c.* 75 (Cf. LUKE XII, 27, *c.* 75)

Lilies that fester smell far worse than weeds.
SHAKESPEARE: *Sonnets,* XCIV, 1609

Lilies are whitest in a blackamoor's hand.
THOMAS FULLER: *Gnomologia,* 1732

Limbo

The limbo of fools. (Limbus fatuorum.)
MEDIEVAL LATIN PHRASE (The *post-mortem* abiding place of fools and half-wits, neither Heaven nor Hell)

The limbo of infants. (Limbus infantum.)
MEDIEVAL LATIN PHRASE (The *post-mortem* abiding place of unbaptized infants. Also called the *Limbus patrum* or *Limbus puerorum.* It is not to be confused with Purgatory)

[*See also* Fool.

Limping

[*See* Lame.

Lincoln, Abraham (1809–65)

Lincoln is one of those peculiar men who perform with admirable skill everything which they undertake.
STEPHEN A. DOUGLAS: Speech at Ottawa, Ill., Aug. 21, 1858

The tycoon.
Nickname applied to Abraham Lincoln by his secretaries, J. G. NICOLAY and JOHN HAY, 1861

He is . . . an enemy of the human race, and deserves the execration of all mankind.
ROBERT TOOMBS: Speech in the Senate, Jan. 7, 1861

The august baboon.
Anon.: In New Orleans Delta, April 29, 1861

[Lincoln] ought to hang somebody, and get a name for will or decisiveness of character. Let him hang some child or woman if he has not the courage to hang a man.
W. H. HERNDON: *Letter to Lyman Trumbull,* Nov. 21, 1861

Jeffdavise rides a white horse,
Lincoln rides a mule;
Jeffdavise is a gentleman,
And Lincoln is a fule.
Anon.: Lines said to have been sent to a Confederate prisoner at Fort Morton, Indianapolis, by his girl at home, *c.* 1863

Fox populi.
Anon.: In Vanity Fair (London), 1863

The most striking thing is the absence of personal loyalty to the President. It does not exist. He has no admirers, no enthusiastic supporters, none to bet on his head. If a Republican convention were to be held tomorrow, he would not get the vote of a state.
R. H. DANA: *Letter from Washington to Charles Francis Adams,* March, 1863

Lincoln was born in Kentucky, and laid the foundation of his honesty in Kentucky. He is honest, with that allowance.
WENDELL PHILLIPS: Speech in New York, May, 1863

I will make a prophecy that may now sound peculiar. In fifty years, perhaps much sooner, Lincoln's name will be inscribed close to Washington's on this Republic's roll of honor.
CARL SCHURZ: *Letter to Theodor Petrasch,* Oct. 12, 1864

Blackguard and buffoon as he is, he has pursued his end with an energy as untiring as an Indian, and a singleness of purpose that might almost be called patriotic.
Anon.: In the Charleston Mercury, Jan. 10, 1865

Now he belongs to the ages.
EDWIN M. STANTON: On being told of Lincoln's death, April 15, 1865

You lay a wreath on murdered Lincoln's bier,
You, who, with mocking pencil, wont to trace
Broad for self-complacent British sneer,
His length of shambling limb, his furrowed face.
TOM TAYLOR: *Abraham Lincoln Foully Assassinated,* 1865 (Punch, May 6)

It is the great boon of such characters as Mr. Lincoln's, that they reunite what God has joined together and man has put asunder. In him was vindicated the greatness of real goodness and the goodness of real greatness.
PHILLIPS BROOKS: Sermon in Philadelphia, 1865

I am sure if this man had ruled in a period of less facility of printing, he would have become mythological in a very few years, like Æsop or Pilpay, or one of the Seven Wise Masters, by his fables and proverbs.
R. W. EMERSON: *Abraham Lincoln,* 1865

O comrade lustrous with silver face in the night.
WALT WHITMAN: *When Lilacs Last in the Dooryard Bloom'd,* 1865–6

His heart was as great as the world, but there was no room in it to hold the memory of a wrong.
R. W. EMERSON: *Letters and Social Aims,* 1875

Lincoln was a very normal man with very normal gifts, but all upon a great scale, all knit together in loose and natural form, like the great frame in which he moved and dwelt.
WOODROW WILSON: Speech at Chicago, Feb. 12, 1909

Linen

Choose not a woman, nor linen clothes, by the candle[light].
JAMES SANDFORD: *Hours of Recreation,* 1572

All animal substances are less cleanly than vegetables. I have often thought that, if I kept a seraglio, the ladies should all wear linen gowns — or cotton; I mean stuffs made of vegetable substances. I would have no silk; you cannot tell when it is clean: it will be very nasty before it is perceived to be so. Linen detects its own dirtiness.
SAMUEL JOHNSON: *Boswell's Tour of the Hebrides,* 1785

Dirty linen should be washed at home, not in public.
NAPOLEON I: To the French Legislative Assembly, 1815

[*See also* Lavender, Silk.

Liner

The liner she's a lady, and 'er route is cut an' dried;
The man-o'-war's 'er 'usband, an' 'e always keeps beside.
RUDYARD KIPLING: *The Liner She's a Lady,* 1894

Linguist

Every man heard them speak in his own language.
ACTS II, 6, *c.* 75 (The Apostles on the day of Pentecost)

Besides 'tis known he could speak Greek
As naturally as pigs squeak;
That Latin was no more difficile
Than to a blackbird 'tis to whistle.
SAMUEL BUTLER: *Hudibras,* I, 1663

Men who can speak a number of different tongues are notorious for having little to say in any of them.
H. R. HUSE: *The Illiteracy of the Literate,* 1933

[*See also* Language.

Lion

The lion does not always feast. Strong though he be, he sometimes fears hunger.
THEOGNIS: *Elegies, c.* 550 B.C.

A lion . . . is strongest among beasts, and turneth not away for any.
PROVERBS XXX, 30, *c.* 350 B.C.

The young lions roar after their prey, and seek their meat from God.
PSALMS CIV, 21, *c.* 150 B.C.

Do not pluck the beard of a dead lion.
MARTIAL: *Epigrams,* III, *c.* 95

It is not good to wake a sleeping lion.
PHILIP SIDNEY: *Arcadia,* IV, 1590

Small curs are not regarded when they grin;
But great men tremble when the lion roars.
SHAKESPEARE: *II Henry VI,* III, *c.* 1591

Think you a little din can daunt mine ears?
Have I not in my time heard lions roar?
SHAKESPEARE: *The Taming of the Shrew,* V, 1594

A lion among ladies is a most dreadful thing.
SHAKESPEARE: *A Midsummer Night's Dream,* III, *c.* 1596

There is not a more fearful wild-fowl than your lion living.
SHAKESPEARE: *A Midsummer Night's Dream,* V

Well roared, lion. IBID.

Who nourisheth a lion must obey him.
BEN JONSON: *Sejanus,* III, 1603

The lion is not so fierce as he is painted.
THOMAS FULLER: *Historie of the Holy Warre,* V, 1639

The tawny lion, pawing to get free
His hinder parts.
JOHN MILTON: *Paradise Lost,* VII, 1667

The lion's share.
ENGLISH PHRASE, not recorded before the XVIII century

The lion is (beyond dispute)
Allow'd the most majestic brute;
His valor and his gen'rous mind
Prove him superior of his kind.
JOHN GAY: *Fables,* II, 1738

The fox provides for himself, but God provides for the lion.
WILLIAM BLAKE: *The Marriage of Heaven and Hell,* 1790

Woe to the hapless neighborhood
When he is pressed by want of food.
Of man, or child, or bull, or horse
He makes his prey: such is his force.
MARY LAMB: *The Beasts in the Tower,* 1809

[*See also* Bold, Coöperation, Daring, Dead, Dog, Flea, God, Head, Home, Leadership.

Lips

Thy lips are like a thread of scarlet.
SOLOMON'S SONG IV, 3, *c.* 200 B.C.

Free of her lips, free of her hips.
ENGLISH PROVERB, traced by Apperson to 1576

Teach not thy lips such scorn; for they were made
For kissing, lady, not for such contempt.
SHAKESPEARE: *Richard III,* I, *c.* 1592

He that had the grace to print a kiss on these lips should taste wine and rose-leaves.
BEN JONSON: *Cynthia's Revels,* V, 1601

Some ask'd me where the rubies grew?
And nothing I did say:
But with my finger pointed to
The lips of Julia.
ROBERT HERRICK: *Hesperides,* 1648

Our spirits rushed together at the touching of the lips.
ALFRED TENNYSON: *Locksley Hall,* 1842

The prim, pursed-up mouth's protruding lips.
ROBERT BROWNING: *The Ring and the Book,* XI, 1872

The lips that touch liquor must never touch mine.
Anon.: (No title), *c.* 1880 (First appeared in *Standard Recitations,* 1884)

[*See also* Foot, Kiss, Mouth.

Liquor

[*See* Belly, Drink, Drinking, Lips.

Lisp

A lisping lass is good to kiss.
JOHN RAY: *English Proverbs,* 1670

[*See also* Macaulay (T. B.).

List

He's got 'em on the list — he's got 'em on the list;
And they'll none of 'em be missed.
W. S. GILBERT: *The Mikado,* I, 1885

Listener

No siren did ever so charm the ear of the listener as the listening ear has charmed the soul of the siren.
HENRY TAYLOR: *The Statesman,* 1836

It takes a great man to make a good listener.
ARTHUR HELPS: *Brevia,* 1871

A good listener is not only popular everywhere, but after a while he knows something.
WILSON MIZNER (1876–1933)

From listening comes wisdom, and from speaking repentance. ITALIAN PROVERB

Liszt, Franz (1811–86)

A venerable man with a purple nose — a Cyrano de Cognac nose.
JAMES HUNEKER: *Old Fogy,* IX, 1913

[*See also* Tschaikovsky (P. I.).

Literature

Whatsover things were written aforetime were written for our learning.
ROMANS XV, 4, *c.* 55

Thieves cannot destroy it, and it is improved by time; it is the only monument that is proof against death.

MARTIAL: *Epigrams*, x, *c.* 95

The only reward to be expected from the cultivation of literature is contempt if one fails and hatred if one succeeds.

VOLTAIRE: *Letter to Mlle. Quinault*, Aug. 16, 1738

Literature is a kind of intellectual light which, like the light of the sun, may sometimes enable us to see what we do not like.

SAMUEL JOHNSON: *A Project for the Employment of Authors*, 1756

It is after public passion has subsided that our most celebrated writers have produced their *chef d'œuvres;* as it is after the eruption of a volcano that the land in its vicinity is the most fertile.

STANISLAUS LESZCYNSKI (KING OF POLAND): *Œuvres du philosophe bienfaisant*, 1763

Literature is an avenue to glory ever open for those ingenious men who are deprived of honors or of wealth.

ISAAC D'ISRAELI: *Essay on the Literary Character*, xxiv, 1795

Literature has been the charm of my life, and, could I have carved out my own fortunes, to literature would my whole life have been devoted.

JOHN QUINCY ADAMS: *Diary*, Dec. 25, 1820

Literature becomes free institutions. It is the graceful ornament of civil liberty, and a happy restraint on the asperities which political controversies sometimes occasion.

DANIEL WEBSTER: Speech at Plymouth, Mass., Dec. 22, 1820

National literature is now rather an unmeaning term; the epoch of world literature is at hand, and every one must strive to hasten its approach.

J. W. GOETHE: *Conversations with Eckermann*, Jan. 31, 1827

All literature is yet to be written. Poetry has scarce chanted its first song. The perpetual admonition of nature to us is, "The world is new, untried. Do not believe the past. I give you the universe a virgin today."

R. W. EMERSON: *Literary Ethics*, 1838

When literature is the sole business of life it becomes a drudgery; when we are able to resort to it only at certain hours it is a charming relaxation.

SAMUEL ROGERS: *Table-Talk*, 1856

In literature, in these days, the masonry is good but the architecture is poor.

JOSEPH JOUBERT: *Pensées*, 1842

Literature is a noble calling, but only when the call obeyed by the aspirant issues from a world to be enlightened and blessed, not from a void stomach clamoring to be gratified and filled.

HORACE GREELEY: *Letter to Robert Dale Owen*, March 5, 1860

The power of French literature is in its prose writers; the power of English literature is in its poets.

MATTHEW ARNOLD: *The Literary Influence of Academies*, 1865

When I first took literature as my profession . . . I made a compact with myself that in my person literature should stand by itself, of itself, and for itself.

CHARLES DICKENS: Speech in Liverpool, April 10, 1869

Literature, strictly consider'd, has never recognized the people, and, whatever may be said, does not today. Speaking generally, the tendencies of literature, as hitherto pursued, have been to make mostly critical and querulous men.

WALT WHITMAN: *Democratic Vistas*, 1870

Our high respect for a well-read man is praise enough of literature.

R. W. EMERSON: *Letters and Social Aims*, 1875

Writing is not literature unless it gives to the reader a pleasure which arises not only from the things said, but from the way in which they are said; and that pleasure is only given when the words are carefully or curiously or beautifully put together into sentences.

STOPFORD BROOKE: *Primer of English Literature*, 1876

Delicacy — a sad, sad false delicacy — robs literature of the best two things among its belongings: family-circle narrative and obscene stories.

S. L. CLEMENS (MARK TWAIN): *Letter to W. D. Howells*, Sept. 19, 1877

The benignities of literature defy fortune and outlive calamity. They are beyond the reach of thief or moth or rust. As they cannot be inherited, so they cannot be alienated.

J. R. LOWELL: Address in Chelsea, Mass., Dec. 22, 1885

In literature, as in every other product of human skill, . . . wherever the producer so modifies his work as, over and above its primary use or intention, to make it pleasing (to himself, of course, in the first instance) there "fine" as opposed to merely serviceable art exists.

WALTER PATER: *Style*, 1888

The difference between literature and journalism is that journalism is unreadable, and literature is not read.

OSCAR WILDE: *The Critic as Artist*, 1891

Literature always anticipates life. It does not copy it, but molds it to its purpose.

OSCAR WILDE: *The Decay of Lying*, 1891

The man who writes about himself and his own time is the only man who writes about all people and about all time.
GEORGE BERNARD SHAW: *The Sanity of Art,* 1895

Literature is printed nonsense.
AUGUST STRINDBERG: *Zones of the Spirit,* 1913

Great literature is the creation, for the most part, of disreputable characters, many of whom looked rather seedy, some of whom were drunken blackguards, a few of whom were swindlers or perpetual borrowers, rowdies, gamblers or slaves to a drug.
ALEXANDER HARVEY: *William Dean Howells,* 1917

Literature is news that stays news.
EZRA POUND: *How to Read,* 1931

Literature exists for the sake of the people — to refresh the weary, to console the sad, to hearten the dull and downcast, to increase man's interest in the world, his joy of living, and his sympathy in all sorts and conditions of man.
JUDGE M. T. MANTON: *Dissenting opinion in United States* vs. *One Book Entitled " Ulysses,"* 1934

'Ere is literature with a capital Hell!
Ascribed to an unnamed cockney

[*See also* Books, Journalism, Letters, Novel, Politics.

Literature, American

The curious have observed that the progress of humane literature (like the sun) is from the East to the West; thus has it traveled thro' Asia and Europe, and now is arrived at the eastern shore of America.
NATHANIEL AMES: *Almanac,* 1758

Our authors and scholars are generally men of business, and make their literary pursuits subservient to their interests.
BENJAMIN RUSH: *Letter to an English friend,* April 16, 1790

In the four quarters of the globe, who reads an American book? Or goes to an American play?
SYDNEY SMITH: In the Edinburgh Review, Jan.–May, 1820

As the blood of all nations is mingling with our own, so will their thoughts and feelings finally mingle in our literature. We shall draw from the Germans, tenderness; from the Spaniards, passion; from the French, vivacity; to mingle more and more with our English solid sense.
H. W. LONGFELLOW: *Kavanagh,* 1849

Literature, English

I may say of our literature that it has one characteristic which distinguishes it from almost all the other literatures of modern Europe, and that is its exuberant reproductiveness.
BENJAMIN DISRAELI: Speech in London, May 6, 1868

Literature, German

Apart from Goethe's writings, and especially his conversations with Eckermann (the best German book in existence), what German prose remains that is worth reading over and over? Lichtenberg's aphorisms, the first book of Jung-Stilling's autobiography, Adalbert Stifter's " Der Nachsommer " and Gottfried Keller's " Die Leute von Seldwyla " — and there, for the present, the list must end.
F. W. NIETZSCHE: *Human All-too-Human,* II, 1878

Lithuanian

The Lithuanian is as stupid as a pig and as cunning as a serpent. POLISH PROVERB

Litigant

Those who come into a court of justice to seek redress must come with clean hands.
LORD KENYON: *Judgment in Petrie* vs. *Hannay,* 1789

A person about to give up his skin for the hope of retaining his bones.
AMBROSE BIERCE: *The Devil's Dictionary,* 1906

Litigation

[*See* Law, Lawsuit, Lawyer, Litigant.

Little

The ox, though vast in bulk, is kept on the road by a little whip.
SOPHOCLES: *Ajax, c.* 450 B.C.

He that contemneth small things shall fall by little and little.
ECCLESIASTICUS XIX, 1, *c.* 180 B.C.

He is always a slave who cannot live on little.
HORACE: *Satires,* II, *c.* 25 B.C.

Many a little makes a mickle.
ENGLISH PROVERB, traced to the XIII century (*Mickle*=a large quantity)

Little pot, soon hot.
JOHN HEYWOOD: *Proverbs,* 1546

A little saint best fits a little shrine.
ROBERT HERRICK: *Hesperides,* 1648

Little wealth, little care.
GEORGE HERBERT: *Jacula Prudentum,* 1651

Little and often fills the purse.
GIOVANNI TORRIANO: *Italian Proverbs,* 1666

A little thing comforts us because a little thing afflicts us.
BLAISE PASCAL: *Pensées,* VI, 1670

A little house well filled, a little land well tilled, and a little wife well willed.
JOHN RAY: *English Proverbs,* 1670

Little bodies have great souls. IBID.

Little strokes fell great oaks. IBID.

Little dogs have long tails.
JAMES KELLY: *Complete Collection of Scottish Proverbs,* 1721

Little gear, less care. IBID.

He's a little fellow, but every bit of that little is bad.
THOMAS FULLER: *Gnomologia,* 1732

Little boats must keep the shore. IBID.

No viper so little but hath its venom. IBID.

There could be no great ones if there were no little ones. IBID.

There is nothing too little for so little a creature as man.
SAMUEL JOHNSON: *Boswell's Life,* July, 1763

Little things are great to little man.
OLIVER GOLDSMITH: *The Traveler,* 1764

Every little helps.
JOHN O'KEEFFE: *Wild Oats,* v, 1791

Little drops of water, little grains of sand,
Make the mighty ocean and the pleasant land.
JULIA A. F. CARNEY: *Little Things,* 1845

Little things affect little minds.
BENJAMIN DISRAELI: *Sybil,* III, 1845

Little things attract light minds.
H. G. BOHN: *Handbook of Proverbs,* 1855

Of a little take a little and leave a little.
IBID.

Little potatoes are hard to peel.
AMERICAN PROVERB

God gives little folks little gifts.
DANISH PROVERB

Little pots soon run over. DUTCH PROVERB

From little, one comes to great.
FRENCH PROVERB

Little pedlar, little pack. IBID.

Little and often make much in the end.
GERMAN PROVERB

Little people have big hearts. IBID.

A little nest is warmer than a big nest.
IRISH PROVERB

Little toads are also poisonous.
PENNSYLVANIA GERMAN PROVERB

While the tall maid is stooping the little one has swept the house. SPANISH PROVERB

[*See also* Dog, Fate, Fish, Laziness, Living, Much, Small, Tall.

Liver

The liver is the lazaret of bile.
BYRON: *Don Juan,* II, 1819

A large red organ thoughtfully provided by nature to be bilious with.
AMBROSE BIERCE: *The Devil's Dictionary,* 1906

A man's liver is his carburetor.
Author unidentified

It is the liver that makes one love.
MEDIEVAL LATIN PROVERB

[*See also* Calvinist, Heart, Love.

Living

The land of the living.
JOB XXVIII, 13, *c.* 325 B.C.

To him that is joined to all the living there is hope; for a living dog is better than a dead lion. ECCLESIASTES IX, 4, *c.* 200 B.C.

Live according to nature. (Secundum naturam vivere.)
MOTTO OF THE STOICS, *c.* 200 B.C.

It matters not how long you live, but how well.
PUBLILIUS SYRUS: *Sententiæ, c.* 50 B.C.

Live to thyself, and fly from fortune.
OVID: *Tristia,* III, *c.* 10

Live with men as if God saw you; converse with God as if men heard you.
SENECA: *Epistulæ morales ad Lucilium, c.* 63

To live is not a blessing, but to live well.
IBID.

To be able to look back upon one's past life with satisfaction is to live twice.
MARTIAL: *Epigrams,* X, *c.* 95

Short is the little which remains to thee of life. Live as on a mountain.
MARCUS AURELIUS: *Meditations,* X, *c.* 170

Let us live then, and be glad
While young life's before us
After youthful pastime had,
After old age hard and sad,
Earth will slumber o'er us.
(Gaudeamus igitur,
Juvenes dum sumus
Post jucundam juventutem,
Post molestam senectutem,
Nos habebit humus.)
Medieval students' song, traced to 1267, but revised in the XVIII century

They lived long that have lived well.
THOMAS WILSON: *The Arte of Rhetorique,* 1553

There be three kinds of lives. One is occupied in action and doing; the second in knowledge

and study; the third in oblectation and fruition of pleasures and wanton pastimes.
JOHN NORTHBROOKE: *Against Dicing*, 1577
(*Oblectation*=enjoyment)

If you would live well for a week, kill a hog; if you would live well for a month, marry; if you would live well all your life, turn priest.
ENGLISH PROVERB, current in various forms since the XVII century

It is silliness to live when to live is torment.
SHAKESPEARE: *Othello*, I, 1604

He that lives well is learned enough.
GEORGE HERBERT: *Outlandish Proverbs*, 1640

Where life is more terrible than death, it is then the truest valor to dare to live.
THOMAS BROWNE: *Religio Medici*, XLIV, 1642

Learn to live well, that thou may'st die so too;
To live and die is all we have to do.
JOHN DENHAM: *Of Prudence*, 1650

One half the world knows not how the other half lives.
GEORGE HERBERT: *Jacula Prudentum*, 1651

Live while ye may.
JOHN MILTON: *Paradise Lost*, IV, 1667

It is not how long but how well we live.
JOHN RAY: *English Proverbs*, 1670

They seldom live well who think they shall live long.
THOMAS FULLER: *Gnomologia*, 1732

To die's a lesson we shall know
Too soon without a master;
Then let us only study now
How we may live the faster.
LORD CHESTERFIELD: *Verses Upon Death*, 1733

My object is to have you fit to live; which, if you are not, I do not desire that you should live at all.
LORD CHESTERFIELD: *Letter to his son*, Dec. 18, 1747

So live, that sinking in thy last long sleep,
Calm thou mayst smile, while all around thee weep.
WILLIAM JONES: *From the Persian, c.* 1775

I sought the simple life that nature yields.
GEORGE CRABBE: *The Village*, I, 1783

To be able to breathe freely is not enough to make one live.
J. W. GOETHE: *Iphigenie auf Tauris*, I, 1787

Live and let live. (Leben und leben lassen.)
J. C. F. SCHILLER: *Wallenstein's Camp*, VI, 1799

Plain living and high thinking are no more.
WILLIAM WORDSWORTH: *Sonnets Dedicated to Liberty*, XIII, 1802

I live, which is the main point.
HEINRICH HEINE: *Reisebilder*, II, 1826

A man may live upon little, but he can't live upon nothing.
H. G. BOHN: *Handbook of Proverbs*, 1855

'Twas a jolly old pedagogue, long ago,
Tall and slender, and sallow and dry;
His form was bent, and his gait was slow,
His long thin hair was white as snow,
But a wonderful twinkle shone in his eye;
And he sang every night as he went to bed,
"Let us be happy down here below;
The living should live, though the dead be dead,"
Said the jolly old pedagogue long ago.
GEORGE ARNOLD: *The Jolly Old Pedagogue*, 1867

A living thing is distinguished from a dead thing by the multiplicity of the changes at any moment taking place in it.
HERBERT SPENCER: *Principles of Biology*, I, 1867

The world, as a world, barely makes a living.
Ascribed to HORACE GREELEY (1811–72)

In certain cases it is indecent to go on living. To continue to vegetate in a state of cowardly dependence upon doctors, once the meaning of life, the right to life, has been lost, ought to be regarded with the greatest contempt by mankind.
F. W. NIETZSCHE: *The Twilight of the Idols*, 1889

To live is like to love — all reason is against it, and all healthy instinct for it.
SAMUEL BUTLER: *Note-Books, c.* 1890

The men who start out with the notion that the world owes them a living generally find that the world pays its debt in the penitentiary or the poorhouse.
W. G. SUMNER: *Earth Hunger*, 1896

To live is to function. That is all there is in living.
O. W. HOLMES II: Speech on his 91st birthday, Washington, March 8, 1932

Fear less, hope more; eat less, chew more; whine less, breathe more; talk less, say more; hate less, love more; and all good things are yours. Author unidentified

While we live, let us live. (Dum vivimus, vivamus.)
MEDIEVAL LATIN PROVERB

[*See also* Character, Dying, Ethics, Life, Life and Death, Longevity, Thinking.

LL.D.

[*See* Doctor of Laws.

Loaf

[*See* Bread.

Loafing

I loaf and invite my soul;
I lean and loaf at my ease, observing a spear of Summer grass.

WALT WHITMAN: *Walt Whitman,* 1855

[*See also* Idleness.

Lobbying

Lobbying is declared to be a crime.

CONSTITUTION OF THE STATE OF GEORGIA, 1877

Locke, John (1632–1704)

Against Locke's philosophy I think it an unanswerable objection that, although he carried his throat about with him in this world for seventy-two years, no man ever condescended to cut it.

THOMAS DE QUINCEY: *On Murder Considered as One of the Fine Arts,* 1827

[*See also* Greatness.

Locomotive

Fierce-throated beauty!
Roll through my chant with all thy lawless music, thy swinging lamps at night,
Thy mad-whistled laughter, echoing, rumbling like an earthquake, rousing all.

WALT WHITMAN: *To a Locomotive in Winter,* 1876

Where is there a woman whose form is more splendid than that of a locomotive?

J. K. HUYSMANS: *A rebours,* III, 1884

Locust

Even these of them ye may eat: the locust after his kind, and the bald locust after his kind.

LEVITICUS XI, 22, *c.* 700 B.C.

[*See also* Honey, John the Baptist.

Lodging-house

Oh, that I had in the wilderness a lodging place of wayfaring men.

JEREMIAH IX, 2, *c.* 625 B.C.

Logic

The application of whips, racks, gibbets, galleys, dungeons, fire and faggot in a dispute may be looked upon as popish refinements upon the old heathen logic.

JOSEPH ADDISON: *The Spectator,* Dec. 4, 1711

Logic is nothing more than a knowledge of words.

CHARLES LAMB: *Letter to Thomas Manning,* 1801

Logic is a large drawer, containing some useful instruments, and many more that are superfluous. C. C. COLTON: *Lacon,* 1820

The philosophy of reasoning, to be complete, ought to comprise the theory of bad as well as of good reasoning.

J. S. MILL: *A System of Logic,* 1843

There is something in the vanity of logic which addles a man's brains.

E. A. POE: *Marginalia,* 1844–49

Logic is logic. That's all I say.

O. W. HOLMES: *The One-Hoss Shay,* 1858

Logic is neither a science nor an art, but a dodge.

Ascribed to BENJAMIN JOWETT (1817–93), *c.* 1870

Logical consequences are the scarecrows of fools and the beacons of wise men.

T. H. HUXLEY: *On the Hypothesis that Animals Are Automata,* 1874

Logic is founded upon suppositions which do not correspond to anything in the actual world — for example, the supposition of the equality of things, and that of the identity of the same thing at different times.

F. W. NIETZSCHE: *Human All-too-Human,* I, 1878

Error has its logic as well as truth.

GEORGE PLECHANOFF: *Anarchism and Socialism,* 1910

Logic, like whiskey, loses its beneficial effect when taken in too large quantities.

LORD DUNSANY: *My Ireland,* XIX, 1938

[*See also* Eloquence, Law.

Logician

He was in logic a great critic,
Profoundly skill'd in analytic;
He could distinguish and divide
A hair 'twixt south and south-west side.

SAMUEL BUTLER: *Hudibras,* I, 1663

When all is said and done, the rapt saint is found the only logician.

R. W. EMERSON: *The Method of Nature,* 1849 (Address at Waterville College, Maine, Aug. 11)

Your true logician gets, in time, to be logicalized, and then, so far as regards himself, the universe is one word. A thing, for him, no longer exists. He deposits upon a sheet of paper a certain assemblage of syllables, and fancies that their meaning is riveted by the act of deposition.

E. A. POE: *Marginalia,* 1844–49

Logrolling

We have had quite enough of puffing and flattering each other in the Review. It is a vile taste for men united in one literary undertaking to exchange their favors.

T. B. MACAULAY: *Letter to Macvey Napier,* Aug. 19, 1830

Loins

Let your loins be girded about, and your lights burning. LUKE XII, 35, *c.* 75

[*See also* Strength.

London

Gem of all joy, jasper of jocundity;
Most mighty carbuncle of virtue and valor.
WILLIAM DUNBAR: *In Honor of the City of London, c.* 1502

Is there not reigning in London as much pride, as much covetousness, as much cruelty, as much oppression, as much superstition, as was in Nebo? Yes, I think, and much more, too. Therefore I say, Repent, O London, repent, repent!
HUGH LATIMER: *Sermon on the Ploughers,* 1549 (*Nebo*=city destroyed by King Mesha of Moab)

London's the dining-room of Christendom.
THOMAS MIDDLETON: *Civitatis Amor,* 1616

London, thou great emporium of our isle,
Oh, thou too bounteous, thou too fruitful Nile,
How shall I praise or curse to thy desert,
Or separate thy sound, from thy corrupted part?
JOHN DRYDEN: *The Medal,* 1682

Dear, damn'd, distracting town, farewell:
Thy fools no more I'll tease;
This year in peace, ye critics, dwell;
Ye harlots, sleep at ease.
ALEXANDER POPE: *A Farewell to London,* 1715

The worst place in the world for a good woman to grow better in.
JOHN VANBRUGH: *A Journey to London,* I, *c.* 1725

Here malice, rapine, accident, conspire,
And now a rabble rages, now a fire;
Their ambush here relentless ruffians lay,
And here the fell attorney prowls for prey;
Here falling houses thunder on your head,
And here a female atheist talks you dead.
SAMUEL JOHNSON: *London,* 1738

By seeing London I have seen as much of life as the world can show.
SAMUEL JOHNSON: *Boswell's Tour to the Hebrides,* Oct. 12, 1773

When a man is tired of London he is tired of life.
SAMUEL JOHNSON: *Boswell's Life,* Sept. 20, 1777

O thou, resort and mart of all the earth,
Chequer'd with all complexions of mankind,
And spotted with all crimes; in which I see
Much that I love, and more that I admire,
And all that I abhor; thou freckl'd fair,
That pleasest and yet shock'st me.
WILLIAM COWPER: *The Task,* III, 1785

The city of London, though handsomer than Paris, is not so handsome as Philadelphia.
THOMAS JEFFERSON: *Letter to John Page,* 1786

Oh, London is a fine town,
A very famous city,
Where all the streets are paved with gold,
And all the maidens pretty.
GEORGE COLMAN THE YOUNGER: *The Heir-at-Law,* I, 1797

Oh, her lamps of a night! her rich goldsmiths, print-shops, toy-shops, mercers, hardwaremen, pastry-cooks, St. Paul's Churchyard, the Strand, Exeter Change, Charing Cross, with the man upon a black horse! These are thy gods, O London!
CHARLES LAMB: *Letter to Thomas Manning,* Nov. 28, 1800

A mighty mass of brick, and smoke, and shipping,
Dirty and dusty, but as wide as eye
Could reach, with here and there a sail just skipping
In sight, then lost amidst the forestry
Of masts; a wilderness of steeples peeping
On tiptoe through their sea-coal canopy;
A huge, dun cupola, like a foolscap crown
On a fool's head — and there is London Town.
BYRON: *Don Juan,* X, 1823

That monstrous tuberosity of civilized life, the capital of England.
THOMAS CARLYLE: *Sartor Resartus,* III, 1836

London is a modern Babylon.
BENJAMIN DISRAELI: *Tancred,* V, 1847

There is fiercer crowded misery
In garret-toil and London loneliness
Than in cruel islands 'mid the far-off sea.
JOHN FORSTER: *Life and Adventures of Oliver Goldsmith,* dedication, 1848

Out of La Trappe, which does not suit a Protestant man, there is perhaps no place where one can be so perfectly alone.
THOMAS CARLYLE: *Letter to R. W. Emerson,* Sept. 9, 1853

London is the epitome of our times, and the Rome of today.
R. W. EMERSON: *English Traits,* IX, 1856

That great foul city of London there, — rattling, growling, smoking, stinking, — a ghastly heap of fermenting brickwork, pouring out poison at every pore, — you fancy it is a city of work? Not a street of it! It is a great city of play; very nasty play, and very hard play, but still play.
JOHN RUSKIN: *The Crown of Wild Olive,* I, 1866

London — a nation, not a city.
BENJAMIN DISRAELI: *Lothair,* XXVII, 1870

A city of cities, an aggregation of humanity, that probably has never been equaled in any period of the history of the world, ancient or modern.
BENJAMIN DISRAELI: Speech in the House of Commons, May 1, 1873

There never was such a great city with such small houses.
BENJAMIN DISRAELI: *Endymion,* III, 1880

The night was dark and stormy,
But blithe of heart were they,
For shining in the distance
The lights o' London lay.

G. R. SIMS: *The Lights O' London,* 1881

In London we may suffer, but no one has any excuse for being dull.

JOHN LUBBOCK (LORD AVEBURY): *The Pleasures of Life,* VI, 1887

The imagination cannot conceive a viler criminal than he who should build another London like the present one, nor a greater benefactor than he who should destroy it.

GEORGE BERNARD SHAW: *Maxims for Revolutionists,* 1903

London is the clearing-house of the world.

JOSEPH CHAMBERLAIN: Speech at the Guildhall, London, Jan. 19, 1904

[*See also* City, Cockney, English, Hell, Park.

London Bridge

[*See* Church (Roman Catholic).

Londoner

[*See* Cockney.

London Times

Is not the Times newspaper an open forum, open as never forum was before, where all mortals vent their opinion, state their grievance?

THOMAS CARLYLE: *Latter-Day Pamphlets,* VI, 1850

It has been said that one copy of the Times contains more useful information than the whole of the historical works of Thucydides.

RICHARD COBDEN: Speech in Manchester, Dec. 27, 1850

If I desired to leave to remote posterity some memorial of existing British civilization, I would prefer, not our docks, not our railways, not our public buildings, not even the palace in which we now hold our sittings; I would prefer a file of the Times newspaper.

E. G. BULWER-LYTTON: Speech in the House of Commons, March 26, 1855

If only it dared to cleave to the right, to show the right to be the only expedient, and feed its batteries from the central heart of humanity, it might not have so many men of rank among its contributors, but genius would be its cordial and invincible ally; it might now and then bear the brunt of formidable combinations, but no journal is ruined by wise courage.

R. W. EMERSON: *English Traits,* XV, 1856

Loneliness

I wandered lonely as a cloud.

WILLIAM WORDSWORTH: First line of a poem written at Grasmere in 1804; published 1807

"I am a lone lorn creetur," were Mrs. Gummidge's words.

CHARLES DICKENS: *David Copperfield,* I, 1849

Why should I feel lonely? Is not our planet in the Milky Way?

H. D. THOREAU: *Walden,* 1854

The surest sign of age is loneliness.

A. BRONSON ALCOTT: *Tablets,* I, 1868

[*See also* Alone, Misery.

Lonesome

[*See* Alone, Good, Loneliness.

Long

The long and the short of it.

ENGLISH PHRASE, traced by Smith to *c.* 1330

Long ailments wear out pain, and long hopes joy.

STANISLAUS LESZCZYNSKI (KING OF POLAND): *Œuvres du philosophe bienfaisant,* 1763

It's a long lane that has no turning.

SAMUEL FOOTE: *A Trip to Calais,* II, 1778

[*See also* Tall.

Longevity

All the days of Methuselah were nine hundred sixty and nine years; and he died.

GENESIS V, 27, *c.* 700 B.C.

The whole age of Jacob was a hundred forty and seven years.

GENESIS XLVII, 28

Among many evils and naughty affections which follow the nature of man, corrupted by sin, none bringeth greater inconvenience than the inordinate hope of long life. This is the cause why we defer the reformation of our lives, and remember not that we have an account to make at the last day.

JOHN NORTHBROOKE: *Against Dicing,* 1577

I love long life better than figs.

SHAKESPEARE: *Antony and Cleopatra,* I, *c.* 1606

The longer thread of life we spin,
The more occasion still to sin.

ROBERT HERRICK: *Noble Numbers,* 1647

A cool mouth and warm feet live long.

GEORGE HERBERT: *Jacula Prudentum,* 1651

"Enlarge my life with multitude of days!"
In health, in sickness, thus the suppliant prays:
Hides from himself its state, and shuns to know,
That life protracted is protracted woe.

SAMUEL JOHNSON: *The Vanity of Human Wishes,* 1749

He that lives longest lives but a little while.

SAMUEL JOHNSON: *The Rambler,* Nov. 2, 1750

Dr. Rush, or somebody else, says that nobody lives long without having one parent, at least, an old stager.
BYRON: *Letter to Thomas Moore,* Oct. 1, 1821

He lives long that lives till all are weary of him.
H. G. BOHN: *Handbook of Proverbs,* 1855

Long life hath long misery. IBID.

A horse lives forty years, a blackbird eighteen, a mouse six, and many insects only a few weeks or even days.
AUGUST WEISMANN: *Dauer des Lebens,* 1881

Uncommon extension of the fear of death.
AMBROSE BIERCE: *The Devil's Dictionary,* 1906

He who is not dead at twenty-three, drowned at twenty-four, or killed at twenty-five will live long. DUTCH PROVERB

A fence lasts three years; a dog, three fences; a horse, three dogs; a man three horses.
GERMAN PROVERB

He who would live long must sometimes change his way of living.
ITALIAN PROVERB

[*See also* Abraham, Cheerfulness, Life, Life and Death, Living, Merriment, Methuselah, Mirth, Moses.

Longfellow, H. W. (1807–82)

Longfellow for rich color, graceful forms and incidents – all that makes life beautiful and love refined.
WALT WHITMAN: *Specimen Days,* April 16, 1881

A white man, but no poet.
Author unidentified

Longing

I have
Immortal longings in me.
SHAKESPEARE: *Antony and Cleopatra,* v, *c.* 1606

And the stately ships go on
To their haven under the hill;
But oh, for the touch of a vanish'd hand,
And the sound of a voice that is still!
ALFRED TENNYSON: *Break, Break, Break,* 1842

A feeling of sadness and longing,
That is not akin to pain,
And resembles sorrow only
As the mist resembles the rain.
H. W. LONGFELLOW: *The Day Is Done,* 1845

Come to me in my dreams, and then
By day I shall be well again,
For then the night will more than pay
The hopeless longing of the day.
MATTHEW ARNOLD: *Longing,* 1852

A nameless longing filled her breast.
J. G. WHITTIER: *Maud Muller,* 1854

Look

From looking, men get to loving.
CLEMENT OF ALEXANDRIA: *Paedagogus,* III, *c.* 190

Ah, 'tis the silent rhetoric of a look
That works the league betwixt the states of hearts.
SAMUEL DANIEL: *The Queen's Arcadia,* v, 1615

One look is worth more than a hundred reports.
JAPANESE PROVERB

[*See also* Leap.

Looker-on

The looker-on sees most of the game.
ENGLISH PROVERB, borrowed from the Latin of Seneca, and quoted as familiar by FRANCIS BACON: *Essays,* 1597

My business in this state made me a looker-on here in Vienna.
SHAKESPEARE: *Measure for Measure,* v, 1604

[*See also* Advice, Kibitzer.

Loony

Who's loony now?
JOHN ARMSTRONG CHALONER: To his brother, Robert Chanler, when it became known that the latter had been divorced by his wife, Lina Cavalieri, and that he had mortgaged his property for $200,000 to meet the costs of the action, Dec., 1911; Chaloner had been declared insane in New York but sane in Virginia

[*See also* Crazy, Insane.

Loose

[*See* Hind.

Loquacity

Loquacious people seldom have much sense.
BALTASAR GRACIÁN: *The Art of Worldly Wisdom,* CV, 1647

Loquacity and lying are cousins.
GERMAN PROVERB

[*See also* Taciturnity.

Lord

There will never be any good time in England until we have done with lords.
OLIVER CROMWELL, 1650

A nod from a lord is breakfast for a fool.
THOMAS FULLER: *Gnomologia,* 1732

Ye see yon birkie, ca'd a lord,
Wha struts, and stares, and a' that;
Though hundreds worship at his word,
He's but a coof for a' that.
ROBERT BURNS: *For a' That and a' That,* 1795 (*Birkie*=a smart youth; *coof*=fool)

The lord is the peasant that was,
The peasant the lord that shall be;
The lord is hay, the peasant grass,
One dry, and one the living tree.

R. W. EMERSON: *Woodnotes*, II, 1841

Most lords are feeble and forlorn.

WALTER BAGEHOT: *The English Constitution*, 1867

[*See also* Nod, Peerage.

Lord Chancellor

[*See* Sitting.

Lord's Prayer

(The text is in MATTHEW VI, 9–13, *c.* 75; a shortened form is in LUKE XI, 2–4.)

The Lord's prayer is the prayer above all prayers. It is a prayer which the most high Master taught us, wherein are comprehended all spiritual and temporal blessings, and the strongest comforts in all trials, temptations, and troubles, even in the hour of death.

MARTIN LUTHER: *Table-Talk*, CCLXVII, 1569

Lord's Supper

[*See* Eucharist.

Loser

The loser is always suspicious.

PUBLILIUS SYRUS: *Sententiæ*, *c.* 50 B.C.

Give losers leave to talk.

ENGLISH PROVERB, traced by Smith to 1546

Give losers leave to speak and winners to laugh.

THOMAS FULLER: *Gnomologia*, 1732

It signifies nothing to play well if you lose.

H. G. BOHN: *Handbook of Proverbs*, 1855

The loser is always in the wrong.

SPANISH PROVERB

Loss

Nothing hurts worse than the loss of money.

LIVY: *History of Rome*, XXX, *c.* 10

I hold it true, whate'er befall,
I feel it when I sorrow most;
'Tis better to have loved and lost,
Than never to have loved at all.

ALFRED TENNYSON: *In Memoriam*, XXVII, 1850

Cut your losses and let your profits run.

AMERICAN PROVERB

[*See also* Profit and Loss.

Lost

What is lost is lost. (Quod periit, periit.)

PLAUTUS: *Cistellaria*, IV, *c.* 250 B.C.

"We are lost!" the captain shouted
As he staggered down the stair.

JAMES T. FIELDS: *The Ballad of the Tempest*, 1849

Loud

[*See* Laughter.

Louis XIV of France (1638–1715)

Louis XIV was the only king of France worthy of the name.

NAPOLEON I: To Gaspard Gourgaud at St. Helena, 1815–1818

[*See also* Name.

Louis XV of France (1710–74)

Louis XV was a man of talent, but he had no heart.

NAPOLEON I: To Gaspard Gourgaud at St. Helena, 1815–1818

Louse

All the dust of the land became lice throughout all the land of Egypt. . . . There were lice upon man, and upon beast.

EXODUS VIII, 17–18, *c.* 700 B.C.

It is a familiar beast to man, and signifies — love.

SHAKESPEARE: *The Merry Wives of Windsor*, I, *c.* 1600

No friend like to a bosom friend, as the man said when he pulled out a louse.

THOMAS FULLER: *Gnomologia*, 1732

Nits will be lice.

Ascribed to OLIVER CROMWELL in ISAAC D'ISRAELI: *Curiosities of Literature*, 1823

Starved lice bite the hardest.

DUTCH PROVERB

A louse in the cabbage is better than no meat at all.

PENNSYLVANIA GERMAN PROVERB

Every man has his louse.

POLISH PROVERB

One finger cannot catch a louse.

WEST AFRICAN PROVERB

[*See also* Futility, Lawsuit, Precedence, Priest.

Love

[*See under the rubrics following; also, see* Absence, Affection, Age (Old), Ages, Anger, Aversion, Bold, Boy, Ceremony, Change, Children, Compliance, Constancy, Credo, Cupid, Desire, Drama, Esteem, Fair Play, Faith, Faithful, Fault, Fear, Fifty, Fire, Flirtation, Fortune, Friend, Friendship, Gentleman, Giant, God, Habit, Haste, Hatred, Honor, Humanity, Humility, Husband and Wife, Inconstancy, Jealousy, Kindness, Kiss, Life, Liver, Look, Loss, Louse, Man and Woman, Marriage, Moderation, Modesty, Money, Music, Night, Novel, Pity, Pleasure, Poet, Poetry, Poverty, Prosperity, Prudence, Reason, Soldier, Soup, Spring, Tears, Trust, Unlucky, War, Youth and Age.

Love and Hatred

Better is a dinner of herbs where love is, than a stalled ox and hatred therewith.

PROVERBS XV, 17, *c.* 350 B.C.

Love as in time to come thou shouldst hate, and hate as thou shouldst in time to come love.
RICHARD TAVERNER: Tr. of DESIDERIUS ERASMUS: *Adagia* (1508), 1539

If we judge of love by the majority of its results, it rather resembles hatred than friendship. LA ROCHEFOUCAULD: *Maxims*, 1665

The more we love a woman the nearer we are to hating her. IBID.

We are nearer loving those who hate us than those who love us more than we like.
IBID.

Love and hatred are natural exaggerators.
HEBREW PROVERB

There was never great love that was not followed by great hatred. IRISH PROVERB

He who loves you will make you weep, but he who hates you may make you laugh.
SPANISH PROVERB

Love and Marriage

Love is often a fruit of marriage.
J. B. MOLIÈRE: *Sganarelle*, I, 1660

Who marrieth for love without money hath good nights and sorry days.
JOHN RAY: *English Proverbs*, 1670

We poor, common folk must take wives whom we love and who love us.
W. A. MOZART: *Letter to his father*, Feb. 7, 1778

One should always be in love. That is the reason one should never marry.
OSCAR WILDE: *A Woman of No Importance*, III, 1893

Let those about to enter into wedlock pray diligently for divine help, so that they may make their choice in accordance with Christian prudence, not led by the blind and unrestrained impulse of lust, nor by any desire for riches, nor by any other base influence, but by a true and noble love and sincere affection for the future partner.
POPE PIUS XI: *Casti connubii*, Dec. 31, 1930

He who is in love with an ugly maiden is in love with money too. FRENCH PROVERB

Who marries for love has to live with sorrow.
SPANISH PROVERB

[*See also* Marriage.

Love, Divine

God is love. I JOHN IV, 8, *c.* 115

If we love one another, God dwelleth in us, and his love is perfected in us.
I JOHN IV, 12

The angel wrote, and vanished. The next night
It came again, with a great awakening light,
And showed the names of whom the love of God had blessed, —
And, lo! Ben Adhem's name led all the rest.
LEIGH HUNT: *Abou Ben Adhem*, 1834

I know not where His islands lift
Their fronded palms in air;
I only know I cannot drift
Beyond His love and care.
J. G. WHITTIER: *The Eternal Goodness*, 1867

Love: In General

Love is not properly nor naturally in season, save in the age next unto infancy.
MICHEL DE MONTAIGNE: *Essays*, III, 1588

Down on your knees,
And thank Heaven, fasting, for a good man's love.
SHAKESPEARE: *As You Like It*, III, *c.* 1600

Men have died from time to time and worms have eaten them, but not for love.
SHAKESPEARE: *As You Like It*, IV

O coz, coz, coz, my pretty little coz, that thou didst know how many fathom deep I am in love! But it cannot be sounded; my affection hath an unknown bottom, like the bay of Portugal. IBID.

Nature is fine in love: and where 'tis fine,
It sends some precious instance of itself
After the thing it loves.
SHAKESPEARE: *Hamlet*, IV, *c.* 1601

Love sought is good, but given unsought is better.
SHAKESPEARE: *Twelfth Night*, III, *c.* 1601

There's beggary in the love that can be reckon'd.
SHAKESPEARE: *Antony and Cleopatra*, I, *c.* 1606

Love and lordship like no fellowship.
JOHN CLARKE: *Parœmiologia Anglo-Latina*, 1639 (Borrowed from the Latin)

Love is a circle that doth restless move
In the same sweet eternity of love.
ROBERT HERRICK: *Hesperides*, 1648

Love is a thing most nice; and must be fed
To such a height; but never surfeited. IBID.

Love is a boy, by poets styled;
Then spare the rod, and spoil the child.
SAMUEL BUTLER: *Hudibras*, II, 1664

It is difficult to love those we do not esteem, but it is no less so to love those whom we esteem much more than ourselves.
LA ROCHEFOUCAULD: *Maxims*, 1665

It is with true love as with ghosts. Everyone talks of it, but few have ever seen it. IBID.

There is no passion wherein self-love reigns so powerfully as in love, and one is always more ready to sacrifice the peace of the loved one than one's own. IBID.

Can a mouse fall in love with a cat?
THOMAS FULLER: *Gnomologia,* 1732

Love is wont rather to ascend than descend.
IBID.

I love him for himself alone.
R. B. SHERIDAN: *The Duenna,* I, 1775

With all thy faults I love thee still.
WILLIAM COWPER: *The Task,* 1785

Children of the future age,
Reading this indignant page,
Know that in a former time,
Love, sweet love, was thought a crime.
WILLIAM BLAKE: *A Little Girl Lost, c.* 1792

If I love you, what business is it of yours?
J. W. GOETHE: *Wilhelm Meister's Lehrjahre,* IV, 1795

I have lived and loved. (Ich habe gelebt und geliebet.)
J. C. F. SCHILLER: *The Piccolomini,* III, 1799

You, you, lie in my heart; you, you lie in my mind. (Du, du liegst mir im Herzen; du, du liegst mir im Sinn.)
Anon.: *Du, Du liegst mir im Herzen, c.* 1800

I have never loved anyone for love's sake, except, perhaps, Josephine — a little.
NAPOLEON I: To Gaspard Gourgaud at St. Helena, April 7, 1817

God be thanked, the meanest of his creatures
Boasts two soul-sides, one to face the world with,
One to show a woman when he loves her.
ROBERT BROWNING: *One Word More,* 1855

Whoever lives true life will love true love.
E. B. BROWNING: *Aurora Leigh,* I, 1857

If love were what the rose is,
And I were like the leaf,
Our lives would grow together
In sad or singing weather,
Blown fields or flowerful closes,
Green pleasure or gray grief.
A. C. SWINBURNE: *A Match,* 1866

Love affairs have always greatly interested me, but I do not greatly care for them in books or moving pictures. In a love affair I wish to be the hero, with no audience present.
E. W. HOWE: *Sinner Sermons,* 1926

With love. (Con amore.) ITALIAN PHRASE

A man is not where he lives, but where he loves. (Homo not est ubi animat, sed amat.)
LATIN PROVERB

Ah, Celeste, my pretty jewel, I love you as a pig loves the mud! Louisiana Creole song

Where there is love there is no sin.
MONTENEGRIN PROVERB

The greatest love is a mother's; then comes a dog's; then comes a sweetheart's.
POLISH PROVERB

An old man in love is like a flower in Winter.
PORTUGUESE PROVERB

A pennyweight o' love is worth a pound o' law.
SCOTTISH PROVERB

He who finds not love finds nothing.
SPANISH PROVERB

It is easy for them who have never been loved to sneer at love. WELSH PROVERB

Love: In Man and Woman

Love loves truth, which women hate.
ROBERT DEVEREUX (EARL OF ESSEX): *Change, c.* 1600

In their first passion women are in love with their lovers; in all others they are in love with love.
LA ROCHEFOUCAULD: *Maxims,* 1665

In matters of love a woman's oath is no more to be minded than a man's.
JOHN VANBRUGH: *The Relapse,* III, 1696

It is commonly a weak man who marries for love. SAMUEL JOHNSON: *Boswell's Life,* March 28, 1776

Love is the whole history of a woman's life; it is only an episode in man's.
ANNA LOUISE DE STAËL: *De l'influence des passions,* 1796 (Cf. BYRON, *post,* 1819)

Love diminishes the delicacy of women and increases that of men.
JEAN PAUL RICHTER: *Titan,* XXXIV, 1803

A maid in love grows bold without knowing it.
JEAN PAUL RICHTER: *Titan,* LXXI

Man's love is of man's life a thing apart,
'Tis woman's whole existence.
BYRON: *Don Juan,* I, 1819 (Cf. DE STAËL, *ante,* 1796)

Woman likes to believe that love can achieve anything. It is her peculiar superstition.
F. W. NIETZSCHE: *Beyond Good and Evil,* 1886

A woman who loves sacrifices her honor; a God who loved became a Jew.
F. W. NIETZSCHE: *The Twilight of the Idols,* 1889

Men always want to be a woman's first love — women like to be a man's last romance.
OSCAR WILDE: *A Woman of No Importance,* II, 1893

Women love men for their defects; if men have enough of them women will forgive them everything, even their gigantic intellects.
IBID.

When a man has once loved a woman he will do anything for her except continue to love her.

OSCAR WILDE: *An Ideal Husband*, I, 1895

The fickleness of the woman I love is only equaled by the infernal constancy of the women who love me.

GEORGE BERNARD SHAW: *The Philanderer*, II, 1898

Women in love are less ashamed than men. They have less to be ashamed of.

AMBROSE BIERCE: *The Devil's Dictionary*, 1906

Love: Its Beginnings

Love is a product of habit.

LUCRETIUS: *De rerum natura*, IV, 57 B.C.

Whoever loved that loved not at first sight?

CHRISTOPHER MARLOWE and GEORGE CHAPMAN: *Hero and Leander*, I, 1598

No sooner met but they looked, no sooner looked but they loved, no sooner loved but they sighed, no sooner sighed but they asked one another the reason, no sooner knew the reason but they sought the remedy.

SHAKESPEARE: *As You Like It*, V, *c.* 1600

She loved me for the dangers I had passed
And I loved her that she did pity them.

SHAKESPEARE: *Othello*, I, 1604

Love not at the first look.

JOHN CLARKE: *Parœmiologia Anglo-Latina*, 1639

There are people who would never have been in love if they had never heard of love.

LA ROCHEFOUCAULD: *Maxims*, 1665

Love is wont to be the loadstone of love.

GIOVANNI TORRIANO: *Italian Proverbs*, 1666

Why did she love him? Curious fool! — be still —
Is human love the growth of human will?

BYRON: *Lara*, II, 1814

Love at first sight is only realizing an imagination that has always haunted us; or meeting with a face, or figure, or cast of expression in perfection that we have seen and admired in a less degree or in less favorable circumstances a hundred times before.

WILLIAM HAZLITT: *The Prose Album*, 1829 (The Monthly Magazine, July)

There is nothing holier, in this life of ours, than the first consciousness of love — the first fluttering of its silken wings.

H. W. LONGFELLOW: *Hyperion*, III, 1839

It is difficult to know at what moment love begins; it is less difficult to know that it has begun.

H. W. LONGFELLOW: *Kavanagh*, XXI, 1849

Eating huckleberries all day long
And learning how to love.

Author unidentified; it seems to be from an American popular song, *c.* 1875

Love cannot be commanded. (Amor cogi non potest.)

LATIN PROVERB

Loving comes by looking. (Ex visu amor.)

IBID.

The beginning of love is bad and the end is worse.

PORTUGUESE PROVERB

Love and eggs are best when they are fresh.

RUSSIAN PROVERB

Love: Its Causes

We love no one but for adventitious qualities.

BLAISE PASCAL: *Pensées*, VI, 1670

Congruity is the mother of love.

H. G. BOHN: *Handbook of Proverbs*, 1855

We love our lost loves for the love we gave them.
And not for anything they gave our love.

E. R. BULWER-LYTTON: *The Wanderer*, prologue, 1857

Love: Its Course

Hot love is soon cold.

RICHARD WHITFORD: *Work for Householders*, 1537

Though the beginning of love bring delight, the end bringeth destruction.

JOHN LYLY: *Euphues*, 1579

The course of true love never did run smooth.

SHAKESPEARE: *A Midsummer Night's Dream*, I, *c.* 1595

Time goes on crutches till love have all his rites.

SHAKESPEARE: *Much Ado About Nothing*, II, *c.* 1599

There lives within the very flame of love
A kind of wick or snuff that will abate it.

SHAKESPEARE: *Hamlet*, IV, *c.* 1601

Love cometh in at the window and goeth out at the door.

WILLIAM CAMDEN: *Remains Concerning Britain*, 1605

There are very few people who, when their love is over, are not ashamed of having been in love.

LA ROCHEFOUCAULD: *Maxims*, 1665

Love is never without jealousy.

JAMES KELLY: *Complete Collection of Scottish Proverbs*, 1721

Love, like man himself, dies of overeating much oftener than of hunger.

JEAN PAUL RICHTER: *Quintus Fixlein*, VIII, 1796

The soul of man becomes weary, and never loves the same object long and fully. There are always some points upon which two hearts do not agree, and in the end those points suffice to render life insupportable.

F. A. R. DE CHATEAUBRIAND: *René*, 1802

No more we meet in yonder bowers;
Absence has made me prone to roving;

But older, firmer hearts than ours,
Have found monotony in loving.
BYRON: To Lesbia, 1806

Love will expire — the gay, the happy dream
Will turn to scorn, indiff'rence, or esteem:
Some favor'd pairs, in this exchange, are blest,
Nor sigh for raptures in a state of rest.
GEORGE CRABBE: *Tales*, IV (Procrastination), 1812

Soon or late love is his own avenger.
BYRON: *Don Juan*, IV, 1821

A man has choice of beginning love, but not to end it.
H. G. BOHN: *Handbook of Proverbs*, 1855

Day by day he gazed upon her,
Day by day he sighed with passion,
Day by day his heart within him
Grew more hot with love and longing.
H. W. LONGFELLOW: *Hiawatha*, II, 1855

" Soldier, soldier come from the wars,
I'll up an' tend to my true love! "
" 'E's lying on the dead with a bullet through 'is 'ead,
An' you'd best go look for a new love."
RUDYARD KIPLING: *Soldier, Soldier*, 1892

Yet each man kills the thing he loves,
By each let this be heard,
Some do it with a bitter look,
Some with a flattering word,
The coward does it with a kiss,
The brave man with a sword.
OSCAR WILDE: *The Ballad of Reading Gaol*, 1898

Cold broth hot again, that loved I never;
Old love renewed again, that loved I ever.
OLD ENGLISH RHYME

Love is like war: you begin when you like and leave off when you can. SPANISH PROVERB

Perfect love sometimes does not come till the first grandchild. WELSH PROVERB

Love: Its Duration

Whither thou goest, I will go; and where thou lodgest, I will lodge; thy people shall be my people, and thy God my God.
RUTH I, 16, *c.* 500 B.C.

Many waters cannot quench love, neither can the floods drown it.
SOLOMON'S SONG VIII, 7, *c.* 200 B.C.

Without good eating and drinking love grows cold. TERENCE: *Eunuchus*, IV, *c.* 160 B.C.

To love is in our power, but not to stop loving.
PUBLILIUS SYRUS: *Sententiæ*, *c.* 50 B.C.

Love lasteth as long as the money endureth.
WILLIAM CAXTON: *The Game and Play of Chess*, 1476 (Cited as " a common proverb ")

Love me little, love me long.
JOHN HEYWOOD: *Proverbs*, 1546 (CHARLES READE: title of a novel, 1859)

'Tis good to be off wi' the old love
Before you are on wi' the new.
RICHARD EDWARDS: *Damon and Pithias*, 1571 (Borrowed by WALTER SCOTT: *The Bride of Lammermoor*, XXIX, 1819, and others, usually with *good* changed to *best*)

It is against the nature of love not to be violent, and against the condition of violence to be constant.
MICHEL DE MONTAIGNE: *Essays*, III, 1588

Friendship is constant in all other things,
Save in the office and affairs of love.
SHAKESPEARE: *Much Ado About Nothing*, II, *c.* 1599

Let me not to the marriage of true minds
Admit impediments: love is not love
Which alters when it alteration finds.
SHAKESPEARE: *Sonnets*, CXVI, 1609

If love lives on hope, it dies with it; it is a fire which goes out for want of fuel.
PIERRE CORNEILLE: *The Cid*, I, 1636

When poverty comes in at doors, love leaps out at windows.
JOHN CLARKE: *Parœmiologia Anglo-Latina*, 1639

A wall between preserves love.
SAMUEL PALMER: *Moral Essays on Proverbs*, 1710

The chains of love are never so binding as when the links are made of gold.
ROYALL TYLER: *The Contrast*, II, 1790

As fair art thou, my bonny lass,
So deep in luve am I;
And I will luve thee still, my dear,
Till a' the seas gang dry.
Till a' the seas gang dry, my dear,
And the rocks melt wi' the sun,
I will luve thee still, my dear,
While the sands o' life shall run.
ROBERT BURNS: *A Red, Red Rose*, 1794

The magic of first love is our ignorance that it can ever end.
BENJAMIN DISRAELI: *Henrietta Temple*, IV, 1837

Bind the sea to slumber stilly,
Bind its odor to the lily,
Bind the aspen ne'er to quiver,
Then bind love to last for ever.
THOMAS CAMPBELL: *How Delicious Is the Winning*, 1842

I love thee with a love I seemed to lose
With my lost saints, — I love thee with the breath,
Smiles, tears, of all my life! — and, if God choose,
I shall but love thee better after death.
E. B. BROWNING: *Sonnets from the Portuguese*, 1847

And love, grown faint and fretful,
With lips but half regretful,
Sighs, and with eyes forgetful
Weeps that no loves endure.

A. C. SWINBURNE: *The Garden of Proserpine,* 1863

If you love me as I love you
What knife can cut our love in two?

RUDYARD KIPLING: *An Old Song,* 1886 (An old rhyme)

The only difference between a caprice and a life-long passion is that the caprice lasts a little longer.

OSCAR WILDE: *The Picture of Dorian Gray,* 1891

Love is a delightful day's journey. At the farther end kiss your companion and say farewell.

AMBROSE BIERCE: *Collected Works,* VIII, 1911

Time
is
Too slow for those who wait,
Too swift for those who fear,
Too long for those who grieve,
Too short for those who rejoice,
But for those who love, time is
Eternity.
Hours fly,
Flowers die,
New days,
New ways,
Pass by.
Love stays.

Anon.: Inscription on a sundial at the University of Virginia, Charlottesville

Man loves but once. (Der Mensch liebt nur einmal.) GERMAN PROVERB

Old love rusts not. IBID.

Love: Its Effects

Can there be a love which does not make demands on its object?

CONFUCIUS: *Analects,* XIV, *c.* 500 B.C.

At the touch of love every one becomes a poet.

PLATO: *Symposium, c.* 360 B.C.

Love blinds all men alike, both the reasonable and the foolish.

MENANDER: *Andria, c.* 300 B.C.

Even a god, falling in love, could not be wise.

PUBLILIUS SYRUS: *Sententiæ, c.* 50 B.C.

Let the man who does not wish to be idle fall in love. OVID: *Amoris,* I, *c.* 10

There is no fear in love; but perfect love casteth out fear. I JOHN IV, 18, *c.* 115

He that loveth is void of all reason.

ALEXANDER BARCLAY: *The Ship of Fools,* 1509

There hath none pleased mine eye but Cynthia, none delighted mine ears but Cynthia, none possessed my heart but Cynthia. I have forsaken all other fortunes to follow Cynthia, and here I stand ready to die, if it please Cynthia. JOHN LYLY: *Endymion,* V, 1588

I do love; and it hath taught me to rhyme, and to be melancholy.

SHAKESPEARE: *Love's Labor's Lost,* IV, *c.* 1595

Except I be by Sylvia in the night,
There is no music in the nightingale.

SHAKESPEARE: *Two Gentlemen of Verona,* III, *c.* 1595

Love always makes those eloquent that have it.

CHRISTOPHER MARLOWE: *Hero and Leander,* II, 1598

If thou remember'st not the slightest folly
That ever love did make thee run into,
Thou hast not loved.

SHAKESPEARE: *As You Like It,* II, *c.* 1600

O powerful love! that in some respects, makes a beast a man, in some other, a man a beast.

SHAKESPEARE: *The Merry Wives of Windsor,* V, *c.* 1600

This is the very ecstasy of love,
Whose violent property foredoes itself,
And leads the will to desperate undertakings.

SHAKESPEARE: *Hamlet,* II, *c.* 1601

In my youth I suffered much extremity for love.

IBID.

Doubt love, 'tis good, but 'tis not good to fear it;
Love hurts them most that least of all come near it. Anon.: *Humor Out of Breath,* II, 1608

If it be love
To sit cross-arm'd and think away the day,
Mingled with starts, crying your name as loud
And hastily as men i' the streets do fire;
Then, madam, I dare swear he loves you.

BEAUMONT and FLETCHER: *Philaster,* II, 1611

We sat and sigh'd,
And look'd upon each other, and conceiv'd
Not what we ail'd; yet something we did ail;
And yet were well; and yet we were not well:
And what was our disease we could not tell.

SAMUEL DANIEL: *Hymen's Triumph,* 1615

Love all love of other sights controls,
And makes one little room an everywhere.

JOHN DONNE: *Good-Morrow, c.* 1615

Love is the tyrant of the heart; it darkens
Reason, confounds discretion; deaf to counsel,
It runs a headlong course to desperate madness.

JOHN FORD: *The Lover's Melancholy,* III, 1628

He that hath love in his breast hath spurs in his sides.

GEORGE HERBERT: *Outlandish Proverbs,* 1640

Love and business teach eloquence. IBID.

Love makes a good eye squint. IBID.

Love makes all hard hearts gentle. IBID.

Love makes one fit for any work. IBID.

As love becomes more confident, respect recedes.
BALTASAR GRACIÁN: *The Art of Worldly Wisdom,* CCXC, 1647

I bring ye love: *Quest.* What will love do?
Ans. Love will be-fool ye:
I bring ye love: *Quest.* What will love do?
Ans. Heat ye to cool ye.
ROBERT HERRICK: *Hesperides,* 1648

No man, at one time, can be wise, and love.
IBID.

We are easily duped by those we love.
J. B. MOLIÈRE: *Le Tartuffe,* IV, 1664

All the passions make us commit faults, but love makes us commit the most ridiculous ones. LA ROCHEFOUCAULD: *Maxims,* 1665

In love we often doubt what we most believe.
IBID.

Love's greatest miracle is the cure of coquetry.
IBID.

Ah, love, love! When thou seizeth us we may well say, Goodbye, prudence!
JEAN DE LA FONTAINE: *Fables,* IV, 1668

Love wrecked Troy.
JEAN DE LA FONTAINE: *Fables,* VII, 1671

Love either finds equality or makes it;
Like death, he knows no difference in degrees,
But planes and levels all.
JOHN DRYDEN: *Marriage à la Mode,* III, 1672

She ne'er loved who durst not venture all.
JOHN DRYDEN: *Aurengzebe,* V, 1676

At the beginning and at the end of love the two lovers are embarrassed to find themselves alone.
JEAN DE LA BRUYÈRE: *Caractères,* IV, 1688

When a man is really in love he looks insufferably silly.
JOHN VANBRUGH: *The Provok'd Wife,* III, 1697

Love taught him shame, and shame with love at strife
Soon taught the sweet civilities of life.
JOHN DRYDEN: *Fables, Ancient and Modern,* 1699

To love her is a liberal education.
RICHARD STEELE: *The Tatler,* Aug. 2, 1709
(Said of Lady Elizabeth Hastings, under the name of Aspasia)

The most ordinary plebeian or mechanic in love bleeds and pines away with a certain elegance and tenderness of sentiments which this passion naturally inspires.
JOSEPH ADDISON: *The Spectator,* May 13, 1712

Love is not to be reason'd down, or lost
In high ambition, and a thirst of greatness;
'Tis second life, it grows into the soul,
Warms every vein, and beats in every pulse.
JOSEPH ADDISON: *Cato,* I, 1713

All men are thieves in love.
JOHN GAY: *The Beggar's Opera,* I, 1728

Love and pride stock Bedlam.
THOMAS FULLER: *Gnomologia,* 1732

The first sigh of love is the last of wisdom.
ANTOINE BRET: *L'école amoureuse,* VII, 1760

Love sets the heart aching so delicately there's no taking a wink of sleep for the pleasure of the pain.
GEORGE COLEMAN THE YOUNGER: *The Mountaineers,* I, 1793

Whatever you love, you live.
J. G. FICHTE: *Religionslehre,* 1806

O, love, love, love!
Love is like a dizziness;
It winna let a poor body
Gang about his business!
JAMES HOGG: *Love Is Like a Dizziness,* 1807

Love is a symbol of eternity. It wipes out all sense of time, destroying all memory of a beginning and all fear of an end.
ANNA LOUISE DE STAËL: *Corinne,* VIII, 1807

Who loves, raves.
BYRON: *Childe Harold,* IV, 1818

Common as light is love,
And its familiar voice wearies not ever.
Like the wide heaven, the all-sustaining air,
It makes the reptile equal to the god.
P. B. SHELLEY: *Prometheus Unbound,* II, 1820

It is awful work, this love, and prevents all a man's projects of good or glory.
BYRON: *Letter to Thomas Moore,* Sept. 19, 1821

Whoso loves believes the impossible.
E. B. BROWNING: *Aurora Leigh,* V, 1857

When a man is in love with one woman in a family, it is astonishing how fond he becomes of every person connected with it. He ingratiates himself with the maids; he is bland with the butler; he interests himself about the footman; he runs on errands for the daughters; he gives advice and lends money to the young son at college; he pats little dogs which he would kick otherwise; he smiles at old stories which would make him break out in yawns, were they uttered by any one but papa.
W. M. THACKERAY: *The Virginians,* XX, 1858

Love is the state in which man sees things most decidedly as they are not.
F. W. NIETZSCHE: *The Antichrist,* XXIII, 1888

In love humanity has found the form of selection most conducive to the ennoblement of the species.
ELLEN KEY: *Love and Ethics,* 1911

The heart that loves is always young.
GREEK PROVERB

Love is a thing that sharpens all our wits.
ITALIAN PROVERB

Who loves, fears. (Chi ama, teme.) IBID.

A man in love mistakes a harelip for a dimple.
JAPANESE PROVERB

He who loves is a slave; he who is loved is master. POLISH PROVERB

They that love maist speak least.
SCOTTISH PROVERB (*Maist*=most)

No one acts more foolishly than a wise man in love. WELSH PROVERB

Love: Its Joys

Jacob served seven years for Rachel; and they seemed unto him but a few days, for the love he had to her.
GENESIS XXIX, 20, *c.* 700 B.C.

Ah! what is love? It is a pretty thing,
As sweet unto a shepherd as a king,
And sweeter too;
For kings have cares that wait upon a crown,
And cares can make the sweetest love to frown.
ROBERT GREENE: *The Shepherd's Wife's Song, c.* 1590

Love in my bosom like a bee
Doth suck his sweet.
THOMAS LODGE: *Rosalynde,* 1590

Love comforteth like sunshine after rain.
SHAKESPEARE: *Venus and Adonis,* 1593

And when love speaks, the voice of all the gods
Makes heaven drowsy with the harmony.
SHAKESPEARE: *Love's Labor's Lost,* IV, *c.* 1595

Come live with me and be my love,
And we will all the pleasures prove,
That valleys, groves, or hills, or fields,
Or woods and steepy mountains yields.
CHRISTOPHER MARLOWE: *The Passionate Shepherd to His Love,* 1599

Come, my Celia, let us prove,
While we can, the sports of love.
Time will not be ours for ever,
He, at length, our good will sever.
BEN JONSON: *Volpone,* III, 1605

Sweet is the love purchased with difficulty.
NATHANIEL FIELD: *A Woman Is a Weathercock,* II, 1609

Though love and all his pleasures are but toys,
They shorten tedious nights.
THOMAS CAMPION: *Book of Airs,* I, 1610

The pleasure of love is in loving; we are happier in the passion we feel than in that we inspire.
LA ROCHEFOUCAULD: *Maxims,* 1665

One hour of downright love is worth an hour of dully living on.
APHRA BEHN: *II The Rover,* V, 1681

Love is love's reward.
JOHN DRYDEN: *Palamon and Arcite, c.* 1698 (Cited as a maxim)

If there's delight in love, 'tis when I see
That heart, which others bleed for, bleed for me.
WILLIAM CONGREVE: *The Way of the World,* III, 1700

If Heaven a draught of heavenly pleasure spare,
One cordial in this melancholy vale,
'Tis when a youthful, loving, modest pair
In other's arms breathe out the tender tale.
ROBERT BURNS: *The Cotter's Saturday Night,* 1785

That delicious passion, in spite of acid disappointment, gin-house prudence and bookworm philosophy, I hold to be the first of human joys, our dearest blessing here below.
ROBERT BURNS: Autobiographical memorandum prepared for Dr. John Moore, Aug., 1787

It would be hard indeed if the gratification of so delightful a passion as virtuous love did not sometimes more than counterbalance all its attendant evils.
T. R. MALTHUS: *The Principle of Population,* IV, 1798

There's nothing half so sweet in life
As love's young dream.
THOMAS MOORE: *Love's Young Dream, c.* 1815

It is best to love wisely, no doubt; but to love foolishly is better than not to be able to love at all.
W. M. THACKERAY: *Pendennis,* VI, 1849

It is more useful to be loved than to be venerated.
ARTHUR SCHOPENHAUER: *Our Relation to Others,* 1851

Take away love, and our earth is a tomb.
ROBERT BROWNING: *Fra Lippo Lippi,* 1855

A book of verses underneath the bough,
A jug of wine, a loaf of bread — and thou
Beside me singing in the wilderness —
Oh, wilderness were Paradise enow!
EDWARD FITZGERALD: Tr. of OMAR KHAYYÁM: *Rubáiyát* (*c.* 1100), 1857

Love alone can lend young people rapture, however transiently, in a world wherein the

result of every human endeavor is transient, and the end of all is death.
JAMES BRANCH CABELL: *Jurgen*, VIII, 1919

Love is the most fun you can have without laughing. Author unidentified

Love is half the feast. WELSH PROVERB

Love: Its Mutuality

Let him not think himself loved by any who loves none.
EPICTETUS: *Encheiridion*, c. 100

These things I command you, that ye love one another. JOHN XV, 17, c. 115

To be loved, love. (Ut ameris, ama.)
AUSONIUS: *Epigrams*, c. 360

There is no greater invitation to love than loving first, and that soul is sterner than it ought which, even if it were unwilling to bestow love, is also unwilling to repay it.
ST. AUGUSTINE: *Of the Catechizing of the Unlearned*, c. 400

Love begets love.
ROBERT HERRICK: *Hesperides*, 1648 (Borrowed from the Latin)

Love is love's reward.
JOHN DRYDEN: *Palamon and Arcite*, II, c. 1698

No person who is in love can ever be entirely persuaded that the passion is not reciprocal; as no one who does not feel it ever believes that it is sincere in others.
WILLIAM HAZLITT: *The Prose Album*, 1829 (The Monthly Magazine, July)

Oh! how delighted 'tis to see
A youth and maid in love agree.
Anon.: *Favorite album verses*, c. 1845

It was many and many a year ago,
In a kingdom by the sea,
That a maiden there lived whom you may know
By the name of Annabel Lee;
And this maiden she lived with no other thought
Than to love and be loved by me.
E. A. POE: *Annabel Lee*, 1849 (New York Tribune, Oct. 9)

Rosemary's green, diddle diddle, lavender's blue;
If you'll love me, diddle diddle, I will love you.
OLD ENGLISH RHYME

Love: Its Nature

Love is perfidious.
PLAUTUS: *Cistellaria*, I, c. 205 B.C.

Now I know what love is. (Nunc scio quid sit amor.) VIRGIL: *Eclogues*, IX, 37 B.C.

Love is the same in all.
VIRGIL: *Georgics*, III, 30 B.C.

In love there are two evils: war and peace.
HORACE: *Satires*, II, c. 25 B.C.

Love is fostered by confidence and constancy; he who is able to give much is able also to love much.
PROPERTIUS: *Elegies*, II, c. 20 B.C.

Love is a kind of warfare.
OVID: *Ars amatoria*, I, c. 2 B.C.

Love is a credulous thing. (Credula res amor est.) OVID: *Metamorphoses*, VII, c. 10

Love can be afraid of nothing.
SENECA: *Medea*, c. 60

Love can deny nothing to love.
ANDREAS CAPELLANUS: *De amore*, c. 1200

Love is free.
GEOFFREY CHAUCER: *The Canterbury Tales* (*The Knight's Tale*), c. 1386

Love is blind.
GEOFFREY CHAUCER: *The Canterbury Tales* (*The Merchant's Tale*)

Love is swift, sincere, pious, pleasant, gentle, strong, patient, faithful, prudent, long-suffering, manly, and never seeking her own; for wheresoever a man seeketh his own, there he falleth from love.
THOMAS À KEMPIS: *Imitation of Christ*, III, c. 1420

They do not love that do not show their love.
JOHN HEYWOOD: *Proverbs*, 1546

Love knoweth no laws.
JOHN LYLY: *Euphues*, 1579

As love is without law, so it is without respect, either of friends or foe.
BARNABE RICH: *Rich His Farewell*, 1581

Love is nothing save an insatiate thirst to enjoy a greedily desired object.
MICHEL DE MONTAIGNE: *Essays*, III, 1588

A bitter sweet, a folly worst of all
That forceth wisdom to be folly's thrall.
ROBERT GREENE: *Menaphon's Song*, c. 1589

Love is but an eye-worm, which only tickleth the head with hopes and wishes.
JOHN LYLY: *Endymion*, III, c. 1591

Love is a fiend, a fire, a heaven, a hell,
Where pleasure, pain, and sad repentance dwell.
RICHARD BARNFIELD: *The Affectionate Shepherd*, 1594

How wayward is this foolish love,
That, like a testy babe, will scratch the nurse
And presently, all humbled, kiss the rod.
SHAKESPEARE: *Two Gentlemen of Verona*, I, c. 1595

Oh, how this Spring of love resembleth
Th' uncertain glory of an April day,
Which now shows all the beauty of the sun,
And by and by a cloud takes all away.
IBID.

Didst thou but know the inly touch of love;
Thou wouldst as soon go kindle fire with snow,
As seek to quench the fire of love with words.
SHAKESPEARE: *Two Gentlemen of Verona,* II

Love looks not with the eyes, but with the mind;
And therefore is winged Cupid painted blind.
SHAKESPEARE: *A Midsummer Night's Dream, c.* 1596

Love is a smoke rais'd with the fume of sighs;
Being purg'd, a fire sparkling in lovers' eyes;
Being vex'd, a sea nourish'd with lovers' tears:
What is it else? A madness most discreet,
A choking gall, and a preserving sweet.
SHAKESPEARE: *Romeo and Juliet,* I, *c.* 1596

Love is sweetest seasoned with suspect.
GEORGE CLIFFORD (EARL OF CUMBERLAND): To Cynthia, 1597

Love is blind, and lovers cannot see
The pretty follies that themselves commit.
SHAKESPEARE: *The Merchant of Venice,* II, *c.* 1597

Love is merely a madness; and, I tell you, deserves as well a dark house and whip as madmen do; and the reason why they are not so punished and cured is that the lunacy is so ordinary that the whippers are in love too.
SHAKESPEARE: *As You Like It,* III, *c.* 1600

Love is ever sick, and yet is never dying;
Love is ever true, and yet is ever lying;
Love does doat in liking, and is mad in loathing;
Love indeed is anything, yet indeed is nothing.
THOMAS MIDDLETON: *Blurt, Master Constable,* II, 1601

Love is a razor, cleansing being well us'd,
But fetcheth blood still being the least abus'd.
GEORGE CHAPMAN: *Bussy d'Ambois,* III, 1604

Oh, what a Heaven is love! Oh, what a Hell!
THOMAS DEKKER: *I The Honest Whore,* I, 1604

Tell me, dearest, what is love?
'T is a lightning from above;
'T is an arrow, 't is a fire,
'T is a boy they call desire.
BEAUMONT and FLETCHER: *The Knight of the Burning Pestle,* III, 1609

Love is a sickness full of woes,
All remedies refusing;
A plant that with most cutting grows,
Most barren with best using.
SAMUEL DANIEL: *Hymen's Triumph,* 1615

Love is a spiritual coupling of two souls,
So much more excellent, as it least relates
Unto the body.
BEN JONSON: *The New Inn,* III, 1629

Love is like linen — often changed, the sweeter.
PHINEAS FLETCHER: *Sicelides,* III, 1631

Love hath swifter wings than time.
EDMUND WALLER: *To Phyllis,* 1645

Love and honor make poor companions.
BALTASAR GRACIÁN: *The Art of Worldly Wisdom,* CCXC, 1647

Love's the noblest frailty of the mind.
JOHN DRYDEN: *The Indian Emperor,* II, 1665

A fire celestial, chaste, refin'd,
Conceiv'd and kindled in the mind;
Which, having found an equal flame,
Unites, and both become the same.
JONATHAN SWIFT: *Cadenus and Vanessa,* 1713

Whene'er she speaks, my ravish'd ear
No other voice but hers can hear,
No other wit but hers approve:
Tell me, my heart, if this be love?
GEORGE, BARON LYTTELTON: *Song,* 1732

Love is a talkative passion.
THOMAS WILSON: *Sacra Privata, c.* 1755

The object of the mixed passion which we call love is the beauty of the sex. Men are carried to the sex in general, as it is the sex, and by the common law of nature; but they are attached to particulars by personal beauty.
EDMUND BURKE: *The Sublime and Beautiful,* I, 1756

That love in its essence is heat is evident from the fact that the mind, and thence the body, becomes warm from love, and according to its degree and quality; and this man experiences alike in Winter as in Summer.
EMANUEL SWEDENBORG: *Heaven and Hell,* 1758

Love withers under constraint: its very essence is liberty: it is compatible neither with obedience, jealousy, nor fear: it is there most pure, perfect, and unlimited where its votaries live in confidence, equality and unreserve.
P. B. SHELLEY: *Queen Mab,* notes, 1813

That profound and complicated sentiment which we call love is the universal thirst for a communion not merely of the senses, but of our whole nature, intellectual, imaginative and sensitive. . . . The sexual impulse, which is only one, and often a small part of those claims, serves, from its obvious and external nature, as a kind of type of expression of the rest, a common basis, an acknowledged and visible link.
P. B. SHELLEY: *Fragment,* 1818

Love is very timid when 'tis new.
BYRON: *Don Juan,* I, 1819

Love's a capricious power: I've known it hold
Out through a fever caused by its own heat,
But be much puzzled by a cough and cold,
And find a quinsy very hard to treat.
BYRON: *Don Juan,* II

Love is a spaniel that prefers even punishment from one hand to caresses from another.
C. C. COLTON: *Lacon*, 1820

I look upon love as a sort of hostile transaction, very necessary to keep the world going, but by no means a sinecure to the parties concerned.
BYRON: *Letter to Lady ——*, Nov. 10, 1822

A person once said to me that he could make nothing of love, except that it was friendship accidentally combined with desire. Whence I concluded that he had never been in love. For what shall we say of the feeling which a man of sensibility has towards his wife with her baby at her breast? How pure from sensual desire! yet how different from friendship!
S. T. COLERIDGE: *Table-Talk*, Sept. 27, 1830

Sympathy constitutes friendship; but in love there is a sort of antipathy, or opposing passion. Each strives to be the other, and both together make up one whole. IBID.

Every one who has been in love knows that the passion is strongest, and the appetite weakest, in the absence of the beloved object, and that the reverse is the case in her presence.
S. T. COLERIDGE: *Table-Talk*, May 14, 1833

Love is the business of the idle, but the idleness of the busy.
E. G. BULWER-LYTTON: *Rienzi*, IV, 1835

Love is not altogether a delirium, yet has it many points in common therewith.
THOMAS CARLYLE: *Sartor Resartus*, II, 1836

Love is the May-day of the heart.
BENJAMIN DISRAELI: *Henriette Temple*, IV, 1837

Love: — what a volume in a word, an ocean in a tear,
A seventh heaven in a glance, a whirlwind in a sigh,
The lightning in a touch, a millenium in a moment.
M. F. TUPPER: *Proverbial Philosophy*, I, 1838

Ask not of me, love, what is love?
Ask what is good of God above —
Ask of the great sun what is light —
Ask what is darkness of the night —
Ask sin of what may be forgiven —
Ask what is happiness of Heaven —
Ask what is folly of the crowd —
Ask what is fashion of the shroud —
Ask what is sweetness of thy kiss —
Ask of thyself what beauty is.
P. J. BAILEY: *Festus*, 1839

Love is fabled to be blind; but kindness is necessary to perception; love is not a hood, but an eye-water.
R. W. EMERSON: *Prudence*, 1841

Love is a flame — ruminated I; and (glancing round the room) how a flame brightens up a man's habitation!
DONALD G. MITCHELL (IK MARVEL): *Reveries of a Bachelor*, I, 1850

O lyric love, half angel and half bird,
And all a wonder and a wild desire!
ROBERT BROWNING: *The Ring and the Book*, I, 1868

The affirmative of affirmatives is love.
R. W. EMERSON: *Success*, 1877

Love is like measles: you can get it only once, and the later in life it occurs the tougher it goes.
H. W. SHAW (JOSH BILLINGS): Lecture in San Francisco, 1885

True love always involves renunciation of one's personal comfort.
LYOF N. TOLSTOY: *On Life*, 1887

I have noticed that there are times when every second woman likes you. Is love, then, a magnetism which we sometimes possess and exercise unconsciously, and sometimes do not possess?
GEORGE MOORE: *Confessions of a Young Man*, XI, 1888

Love is only half an illusion; the lover, but not his love, is deceived.
GEORGE SANTAYANA: *The Life of Reason*, II, 1905

We cannot permit love to run riot; we must build fences around it, as we do around pigs.
E. W. HOWE: *Preaching from the Audience*, 1926

Love is a conflict between reflexes and reflections.
MAGNUS HIRSCHFELD: *Sex in Human Relationship*, 1935

A season pass on the shuttle between Heaven and Hell. Author unidentified

Love is an egotism of two. IBID.

Love is like a well: a good thing to drink out of, but a bad thing to fall into. IBID.

Love is one damned fool after another. IBID.

Love is such a funny thing;
It's very like a lizard;
It twines itself around your heart
And penetrates your gizzard. IBID.

Love is a contact of epidermises.
FRENCH PROVERB

Try to reason about love, and you will lose your reason. IBID.

Calf love,
Half love;
Old love,
Cold love. OLD ENGLISH RHYME

Love: Its Pains

How miserable is the man who loves.
PLAUTUS: *Asinaria*, c. 200 B.C.

It is good to love in a moderate degree, but it is not good to love to distraction.
PLAUTUS: *Curculio*, I, c. 200 B.C.

Stay me with flagons, comfort me with apples: for I am sick of love.
SOLOMON'S SONG II, 5, c. 200 B.C.

In love, pain and pleasure are always at war.
PUBLILIUS SYRUS: *Sententiæ*, c. 50 B.C.

Love enjoys the falling tear.
PROPERTIUS: *Elegies*, I, c. 25 B.C.

There are as many sorrows in love as seashells on the shore.
OVID: *Ars amatoria*, II, c. 2 B.C.

In love there is more aloes than honey.
JUVENAL: *Satires*, VI, 116

Love is the crocodiles in the river of desire.
BHARTRIHARI: *The Vairagya Sataka*, c. 625

Love is a thing aye full of busy dread.
GEOFFREY CHAUCER: *Troylus and Cryseyde*, c. 1374

Though the beginning of love bring delight, the end bringeth destruction.
JOHN LYLY: *Euphues*, 1579

Love is a sour delight, a sugared grief,
A living death, an ever-dying life,
A breach of reason's law.
THOMAS WATSON: *Ecatompathia*, 1582

True be it said, whatever man it said,
That love with gall and honey doth abound.
EDMUND SPENSER: *The Faerie Queene*, IV, c. 1589

To live in Hell, and Heaven to behold;
To welcome life, and die a living death;
To sweat with heat, and yet be freezing cold;
To grasp at stars, and lie the earth beneath;
To tread a maze that never shall have end;
To burn in sighs, and starve in daily tears.
HENRY CONSTABLE: *Sonnets to Diana*, 1592

Love is a familiar. Love is a devil. There is no evil angel but love.
SHAKESPEARE: *Love's Labor's Lost*, I, c. 1595

I have done penance for contemning love;
Whose high imperious thoughts have punish'd me
With bitter fasts, with penitential groans,
With nightly tears, and daily heart-sore sighs.
SHAKESPEARE: *Two Gentlemen of Verona*, II, c. 1595

O brawling love! O hating love!
SHAKESPEARE: *Romeo and Juliet*, I, c. 1596

Love is the mind's strong physic, and the pill
That leaves the heart sick and o'erturns the will.
THOMAS MIDDLETON: *Blurt, Master-Constable*, III, 1601

One that loved not wisely, but too well.
SHAKESPEARE: *Othello*, V, 1604

Never was a story of more woe
Than this of Juliet and her Romeo.
IBID. Last lines. Quoted by ROBERT BARTON: *The Anatomy of Melancholy*, 1621

Love doth much mischief — sometimes like a siren, sometimes like a fury.
FRANCIS BACON: *Essays*, X, 1625

The sweets of love are mix'd with tears.
ROBERT HERRICK: *Hesperides*, 1648

Faults are thick where love is thin.
JAMES HOWELL: *Proverbs*, 1659

In the old age of love, as in that of life, we still live for its evils, but no longer for its pleasures. LA ROCHEFOUCAULD: *Maxims*, 1665

Pains of love be sweeter far
Than all other pleasures are.
JOHN DRYDEN: *Tyrannic Love*, IV, 1669

Love and pease-pottage will make their way, because one breaks the belly, the other the heart. JOHN RAY: *English Proverbs*, 1670

Soft scenes of solitude no more can please:
Love enters there, and I'm my own disease.
ALEXANDER POPE: *Sappho to Phaon*, 1713

The rose is sweetest washed with morning dew,
And love is loveliest when embalmed in tears.
WALTER SCOTT: *The Lady of the Lake*, IV, 1810

Love in a hut, with water and a crust,
Is — love, forgive us! — cinders, ashes, dust.
JOHN KEATS: *Lamia*, II, 1820

And most of all would I flee from the cruel madness of love —
The honey of poison-flowers and all the measureless ill.
ALFRED TENNYSON: *Maud*, I, 1855

The mind has a thousand eyes
And the heart but one;
Yet the light of a whole life dies
When love is done.
F. W. BOURDILLON: *The Night Has a Thousand Eyes*, 1873

Those who are faithful know only the trivial side of love; it is the faithless who know love's tragedies.
OSCAR WILDE: *The Picture of Dorian Gray*, 1891

I plucked a lemon in the garden of love.
American popular song and saying, c. 1895

He who falls in love has come to the end of happiness. JAPANESE PROVERB

He that loves Glass without a G,
Take away L and that is he.

OLD ENGLISH RHYME

Love: Its Power

O love, resistless in thy might, thou triumphest even over gold!

SOPHOCLES: *Antigone*, *c.* 450 B.C.

Love is strong as death.

SOLOMON'S SONG VIII, 6, *c.* 200 B.C.

Love conquers all. (Omnia vincit amor.)

VIRGIL: *Eclogues*, X, 37 B.C.

Every creature on earth, man and beast, fish, cattle, and birds — all rush into the fire of love. Love is the lord of all.

VIRGIL: *Georgics*, III, 30 B.C.

Love will find a way.

ENGLISH PROVERB, current since the XVI century

Were beauty under twenty locks kept fast,
Yet love breaks through and picks them all at last.

SHAKESPEARE: *Venus and Adonis*, 1593

Stony limits cannot keep love out:
And what love can do, that dares love attempt.

SHAKESPEARE: *Romeo and Juliet*, II, *c.* 1595

Love finds a way.

ENGLISH PROVERB, familiar since the XVII century

To enlarge or illustrate the power and effect of love is to set a candle in the sun.

ROBERT BURTON: *The Anatomy of Melancholy*, II, 1621

No cord nor cable can so forcibly draw, or hold so fast, as love can do with a twined thread.

ROBERT BURTON: *The Anatomy of Melancholy*, III

Love, thou art absolute sole lord
Of life and death.

RICHARD CRASHAW: *Hymn to the Adorable St. Teresa*, *c.* 1640

Love rules his kingdom without a sword.

GEORGE HERBERT: *Outlandish Proverbs*, 1640

Where there is no place
For the glow-worm to lie;
Where there is no space
For receipt of a fly;
Where the midge dares not venture
Lest herself fast she lay;
If love come, he will enter
And soon find out his way.

Anon.: *The Great Adventurer*, *c.* 1650

Love can do much, but money can do more.

GIOVANNI TORRIANO: *Italian Proverbs*, 1666

Love makes the world go round.

ENGLISH PROVERB, apparently borrowed from the French; not found before the XIX century

Love demands all, and has a right to all.

LUDWIG VAN BEETHOVEN: *Letter to the Countess Giulietta Guicciardi*, July 6, 1800

Love laughs at locksmiths.

GEORGE COLMAN THE YOUNGER: Title of a play, 1803

Love rules the court, the camp, the grove,
And men below, and saints above.

WALTER SCOTT: *The Lay of the Last Minstrel*, III, 1805

The power of love consists mainly in the privilege of coining, circulating, and making current those falsehoods between man and woman that would not pass for one moment, either between woman and woman, or man and man.

C. C. COLTON: *Lacon*, 1820

He that shuts love out, in turn shall be
Shut out from love, and on her threshold lie
Howling in outer darkness.

ALFRED TENNYSON: *The Palace of Art*, 1830

It is hardly an argument against a man's general strength of character that he should be mastered by love. A fine constitution doesn't insure one against smallpox.

MARIAN EVANS (GEORGE ELIOT): *Adam Bede*, I, 1859

I have found it impossible to carry the heavy burden of responsibility and to discharge my duties as king as I would wish to do without the help and support of the woman I love.

EDWARD VIII: Radio broadcast, Dec. 11, 1936

Love teaches even asses to dance.

FRENCH PROVERB

Who travels for love finds a thousand miles not longer than one.

JAPANESE PROVERB

Love cures the wound it makes. (Amoris vulnus idem sanat.)

LATIN PROVERB

Love made the world. (Amor mundum fecit.)

IBID.

Love: Its Symptoms

Four things cannot be kept close: love, the cough, fire, and sorrow.

JAMES SANDFORD: *Hours of Recreation*, 1572 (Borrowed, as to the cough, from a Latin proverb, *post*)

They love indeed who quake to say they love.

PHILIP SIDNEY: *Astrophel and Stella*, 1591

If he be not in love with some woman, there is no believing old signs: a' brushes his hat o' mornings; what should that bode?

SHAKESPEARE: *Much Ado About Nothing*, III, *c.* 1599

A murderous guilt shows not itself more soon
Than love that would seem hid; love's night is noon.

SHAKESPEARE: *Twelfth Night*, III, *c.* 1601

Love and murder will out.
WILLIAM CONGREVE: *The Double Dealer*, IV, 1694

Love and light cannot be hid.
JAMES KELLY: *Complete Collection of Scottish Proverbs*, 1721

Everyone talks of what he loves.
THOMAS FULLER: *Gnomologia*, 1732

Love and a red nose cannot be hid.
THOMAS HOLCROFT: *Duplicity*, II, 1781

There are three things that can never be hidden — love, a mountain, and one riding on a camel. ARAB PROVERB

Love and smoke are two things which can't be concealed. FRENCH PROVERB

He who is not impatient is not in love.
ITALIAN PROVERB

Love and a cough cannot be hid. (Amor tussique non celantur.) LATIN PROVERB

Love: Its Technic

Love hates delays and does not submit to them. SENECA: *Hercules Furens*, *c.* 50

Those that love most speak least.
GEORGE PETTIE: *Petite Palace of Pettie His Pleasure*, 1576

The sweetest honey
Is loathsome in its own deliciousness,
And in the taste confounds the appetite:
Therefore, love moderately.
SHAKESPEARE: *Romeo and Juliet*, II, *c.* 1595

Speak low, if you speak love.
SHAKESPEARE: *Much Ado About Nothing*, II, *c.* 1598

I do love her just as a man holds a wolf by the ears: but, for fear of turning upon me and pulling out my throat, I would let her go to the Devil.
JOHN WEBSTER: *The White Devil*, V, *c.* 1608

Love and war are the same thing, and stratagems and policy are as allowable in the one as in the other.
CERVANTES: *Don Quixote*, II, 1615

A man of sense may love like a madman, but never like a fool.
LA ROCHEFOUCAULD: *Maxims*, 1665

Follow love and it will flee,
Flee love and it will follow thee.
JOHN RAY: *English Proverbs*, 1670

They love too much that die for love. IBID.

Whom we love best, to them we can say least.
IBID.

O brute! The drudgery of loving!
WILLIAM CONGREVE: *The Old Bachelor*, I, 1693

Words are the weak support of cold indifference; love has no language to be heard.
WILLIAM CONGREVE: *The Double Dealer*, IV, 1694

It requires far more genius to make love than to command armies.
Ascribed to NINON DE L'ENCLOS (1616–1706)

Fanned fire and forced love never did well yet.
JAMES KELLY: *Complete Collection of Scottish Proverbs*, 1721

In love's wars he who flieth is conqueror.
THOMAS FULLER: *Gnomologia*, 1732

If you would be loved, love and be lovable.
BENJAMIN FRANKLIN: *Poor Richard's Almanac*, 1755

Nothing makes love sweeter and tenderer than a little scolding and freezing, just as the grape-clusters acquire by a frost, before vintage, thinner skins and better must.
JEAN PAUL RICHTER: *Hesperus*, XXXV, 1795

All is fair in love and war.
ENGLISH PROVERB, apparently unrecorded in its present form before the XIX century; in BEAUMONT and FLETCHER: *The Lovers' Progress*, V, 1623, it appears as "All stratagems in love, and that the sharpest war, are lawful"

To speak of love is to make love.
BALZAC: *The Physiology of Marriage*, 1830

To love I must have something I can put my arms around.
H. W. BEECHER: *Royal Truths*, 1862

Such ever was love's way; to rise, it stoops.
ROBERT BROWNING: *A Death in the Desert*, 1864

What is done for love is always beyond good and evil.
F. W. NIETZSCHE: *Beyond Good and Evil*, 1886

Love 'em and leave 'em.
AMERICAN SAYING, *c.* 1910

If there is any one thing that a man should do in private, it is his loving.
E. W. HOWE: *Country Town Sayings*, 1911

Love is a game in which both players always cheat. IBID.

Of all forms of caution, caution in love is perhaps the most fatal to true happiness.
BERTRAND RUSSELL: *The Conquest of Happiness*, XII, 1930

Follow love, and it will flee;
Flee, and it will follow thee.
OLD ENGLISH RHYME

Seek love, and it will shun you;
Haste away, and 'twill outrun you. IBID.

Blue eyes say, "Love me or I die"; black eyes say, "Love me or I kill thee."
SPANISH PROVERB

If love be timid it is not true. IBID.

Love tells us many things that are not so.
UKRAINIAN PROVERB

Love: Its Universality

Love lurks as soon about a sheepcote as a palace. THOMAS LODGE: *Rosalynde,* 1590

Let those love now, who never loved before;
And those who always loved, now love the more.
THOMAS PARNELL: Tr. of *Pervigilium Veneris* (*c.* 200), *c.* 1700

The strong, the brave, the virtuous, and the wise,
Sink in the soft captivity together.
JOSEPH ADDISON: *Cato,* III, 1713

He that does not love a woman sucked a sow.
THOMAS FULLER: *Gnomologia,* 1732

We are all born for love; it is the principle of existence and its only end.
BENJAMIN DISRAELI: *Sybil,* V, 1845

Love well who will, love wise who can,
But love, be loved.
CINCINNATUS HEINE (JOAQUIN MILLER): *With Walker in Nicaragua,* III, 1871

Love is as warm amang cottars as courtiers.
SCOTTISH PROVERB

Loveliness

Loveliness
Needs not the foreign aid of ornament,
But is when unadorn'd, adorn'd the most.
JAMES THOMPSON: *The Seasons* (*Autumn*), 1728

I fill this cup to one made up
Of loveliness alone.
E. C. PINKNEY: *A Health,* 1825

[*See also* Beauty.

Lover

He is not a lover who does not love forever.
EURIPIDES: *The Troades, c.* 415 B.C.

Find me a reasonable lover and I'll give you his weight in gold.
PLAUTUS: *Curculio,* I, *c.* 200 B.C.

A great lover of women. (Magnus amator mulierum.)
PLAUTUS: *Menaechmi, c.* 200 B.C.

Lover, lunatic. (Amans, amens.)
PLAUTUS: *Mercator, c.* 200 B.C.

The quarrels of lovers are the renewal of love.
TERENCE: *Andria,* III, *c.* 160 B.C.

Jupiter laughs at the perjuries of lovers.
OVID: *Ars amatoria,* I, *c.* 2 B.C.

Lovers remember everything.
OVID: *Heroides, c.* 10

Every lover is a kind of soldier.
OVID: *Remedia amoris, c.* 10

He that loveth is void of all reason.
ALEXANDER BARCLAY: *The Ship of Fools,* I, 1509

Lovers live by love, as larks live by leeks.
JOHN HEYWOOD: *Proverbs,* 1546

Foul words and frowns must not repel a lover.
SHAKESPEARE: *Venus and Adonis,* 1593

A lover's eyes will gaze an eagle blind.
SHAKESPEARE: *Love's Labor's Lost,* IV, *c.* 1595

How silver-sweet sound lovers' tongues by night,
Like soft music to attending ears.
SHAKESPEARE: *Romeo and Juliet,* II, *c.* 1596

And then the lover,
Sighing like a furnace, with a woeful ballad
Made to his mistress' eyebrow.
SHAKESPEARE: *As You Like It,* II, *c.* 1600

It is as easy to count atomies as to resolve the propositions of a lover.
SHAKESPEARE: *As You Like It,* III

The sight of lovers feedeth those in love.
IBID.

Lovers swear more performance than they are able, and yet reserve an ability that they never perform; vowing more than the perfection of ten, and discharging less than the tenth part of one.
SHAKESPEARE: *Troilus and Cressida,* III, *c.* 1601

If ever thou shalt love,
In the sweet pangs of it remember me;
For such as I am all true lovers are;
Unstaid and skittish in all motions else,
Save in the constant image of the creature
That is belov'd.
SHAKESPEARE: *Twelfth Night,* II, *c.* 1601

Lovers' oaths are like mariners' prayers, uttered in extremity; but when the tempest is o'er and the vessel leaves tumbling, they fall from protesting to drinking.
JOHN WEBSTER: *The White Devil,* V, *c.* 1608

There was never proud man thought so absurdly well of himself as the lover doth of the person loved; and therefore it was well said that it is impossible to love and to be wise.
FRANCIS BACON: *Essays,* X, 1625

Why so pale and wan, fond lover,
Prithee, why so pale?
Will, when looking well can't move her,
Looking ill prevail?
Prithee, why so pale?
JOHN SUCKLING: *Song,* 1637

A poor beauty finds more lovers than husbands.
GEORGE HERBERT: *Outlandish Proverbs,* 1640

Lovers never tire of each other — they always speak of themselves.
LA ROCHEFOUCAULD: *Maxims,* 1665

Lovers, when they lose their breath,
Bleed away in easy death.
JOHN DRYDEN: *Tyrannic Love,* 1669

A lover even tries to stand well with the house dog.
J. B. MOLIÈRE: *Les femmes savantes,* I, 1672

There is no hiding from lovers' eyes.
JOHN CROWNE: *The Destruction of Jerusalem,* IV, 1677

Lovers, like sick people, may say what they please.
JEREMY COLLIER: *A Short View of the Immorality and Profaneness of the English Stage,* intro., 1698

One may like the love and despise the lover.
GEORGE FARQUHAR: *The Recruiting Officer,* III, 1706

I never knew a lover that would not willingly secure his interest as well as his mistress, or had not the prudence (among all his distractions) to consider that a woman was but a woman, and money was a thing of more real merit than the whole sex put together.
MARY PIERREPONT: *Letter to E. Wortley Montagu,* Aug., 1710

Beauty soon grows familiar to the lover,
Fades in his eye, and palls upon the sense.
JOSEPH ADDISON: *Cato,* I, 1713

Of all affliction taught a lover yet,
'Tis sure the hardest science to forget.
ALEXANDER POPE: *Eloisa to Abelard,* 1717

Lovers complain of their hearts, but the distemper is in their heads.
THOMAS FULLER: *Gnomologia,* 1732

The lover in the husband may be lost.
GEORGE, BARON LYTTELTON: *Advice to a Lady,* c. 1760

Bring me yew to deck my grave:
Such end true lovers have.
WILLIAM BLAKE: *Song,* 1783

He was a lover of the good old school
Who still becomes more constant as they cool.
BYRON: *Beppo,* 1818

Lovers may be, and, indeed, generally are enemies, but they never can be friends.
BYRON: *Letter to Lady* ——, Nov. 10, 1822

I've seen your stormy seas and stormy women,
And pity lovers rather more than seamen.
BYRON: *Don Juan,* VI, 1823

It is easier to be a lover than a husband, for the same reason that it is more difficult to show a ready wit all day long than to say a good thing occasionally.
BALZAC: *The Physiology of Marriage,* 1830

A lover always thinks of his mistress first and himself second; with a husband it runs the other way. IBID.

A lover tells a woman all that a husband hides from her. IBID.

A woman's little affections always fool her lover, and he goes into ecstasies over things which only make her husband shrug his shoulders. IBID.

The lover is the husband's instrument of revenge. IBID.

The accepted and betrothed lover has lost the wildest charm of his maiden in her acceptance of him. She was Heaven whilst he pursued her as a star; she cannot be Heaven if she stoops to such a one as he.
R. W. EMERSON: *Nature,* 1836

Have I a lover
Who is noble and free? —
I would he were nobler
Than to love me.
R. W. EMERSON: *The Sphinx,* 1841 (Dial, Jan.)

All mankind love a lover.
R. W. EMERSON: *Spiritual Laws,* 1841 (Usually, "All the world loves a lover")

Two souls with but a single thought,
Two hearts that beat as one.
(Zwei Seelen und ein Gedanke,
Zwei Herzen und ein Schlag.)
E. F. J. VON MÜNCH-BELLINGHAUSEN (FRIEDRICH HALM): *Der Sohn der Wildnis,* II, 1843 (Tr. as *Ingomar* by MARIA A. LOVELL)

A lover without indiscretion is no lover at all.
THOMAS HARDY: *The Hand of Ethelberta,* XX, 1876

Prithee, pretty maiden — prithee tell me true,
(Hey, but I'm doleful, willow willow waly!)
Have you e'er a lover a dangling after you?
Hey willow waly O!
W. S. GILBERT: *Patience,* I, 1881

All the world loves a lover; but not while the love-making is going on.
ELBERT HUBBARD: *Roycroft Dictionary and Book of Epigrams,* 1923

Round her waist she wore a yaller ribbon;
She wore it in September, and in the month of May;
And when I ast her where the hell she got it —
"I got it from a lover who is fur, fur away."
American folksong

A good hater; a good lover. FRENCH PROVERB

In the eyes of a lover pockmarks are dimples.
JAPANESE PROVERB

Lovers are madmen. (Amantes sunt amentes.)
LATIN PROVERB

Friends are like those of one father; lovers, like those of one mother.
MALAY PROVERB

[*See also* Absence, Alone, Beauty, Courtship, Cupid, Flute, Gratitude, Harlot, Husband, Imagination, Journey, Love, Lunatic, Mourning, Poet, Spring.

Love, Unrequited

The less my hope the warmer my love.
TERENCE: *Eunuchus,* IV, *c.* 160 B.C.

As good love comes as goes.
ROBERT HENRYSON: *Moral Fables,* III, *c.* 1470

She never told her love,
But let concealment, like a worm i' the bud,
Feed on her damask cheek; she pin'd in thought,
And with a green and yellow melancholy
She sat like patience on a monument,
Smiling at grief.
SHAKESPEARE: *Twelfth Night,* II, *c.* 1601

A mighty pain to love it is,
And 'tis a pain that pain to miss;
But of all pains the greatest pain
It is to love, but love in vain.
ABRAHAM COWLEY: *Anacreontiques,* 1656

When we can't get what we love we must love what we have.
ROGER DE BUSSY-RABUTIN: *Letter to Marie de Sévigné,* 1667

Say what you will, 'tis better to be left
Than never to have loved.
WILLIAM CONGREVE: *The Way of the World,* II, 1700

Ah! woe's me, that I should love and conceal;
Long have I wish'd, but never dare reveal,
Even though severely love's pains I feel;
Xerxes that great, was't free from Cupid's dart,
And all the greatest heroes felt the smart.
GEORGE WASHINGTON: Untitled poem written some time before 1748

Of the uses of adversity which are sweet, none are sweeter than those which grow out of disappointed love.
HENRY TAYLOR: *Notes from Life,* 1847

'Tis better to have loved and lost,
Than never to have loved at all.
ALFRED TENNYSON: *In Memoriam,* XXXVII, 1850 (Cf. CONGREVE, *ante,* 1700)

When a woman says she loves a man,
The man must hear her, though he love her not.
E. B. BROWNING: *Aurora Leigh,* IX, 1856

The more cause the girl finds to regret that she did not marry you, the more comfortable you will feel over it. It isn't poetical, but it is mighty sound doctrine.
S. L. CLEMENS (MARK TWAIN): *Answers to Correspondents,* 1875

Love feeds on hope, they say, or love will die —
Ah, miserie!
Yet my love lives, although no hope have I!
Ah, miserie!
W. S. GILBERT: *Patience,* I, 1881

Nobody loves me. I am going into the garden and eat worms.
Author unidentified; a favorite motto at the time of the button craze, *c.* 1905

Love unrequited is like a question without an answer.
ITALIAN PROVERB

To love a woman who scorns you is to lick honey from a thorn.
WELSH PROVERB

Low

The boughs that bear most hang lowest.
THOMAS FULLER: *Gnomologia,* 1732

Low Countries

[*See* Belgium, Holland, Netherlands.

Lowell

[*See* Boston.

Lowland

Praise the high country, but plant your crop in the lowlands.
UKRAINIAN PROVERB

[*See also* Highlands.

Lowly

He giveth grace unto the lowly.
PROVERBS III, 34, *c.* 350 B.C.

Though the Lord be high, yet hath he respect unto the lowly.
PSALMS CXXXVIII, 6, *c.* 150 B.C.

It is dangerous for a man of lowly birth to grumble in public.
PHAEDRUS: *Fabulæ Æsopiæ, c.* 40

Low niggers and poor white trash set uneasy in fine chairs.
AMERICAN NEGRO PROVERB

Loyalty

Master, go on, and I will follow thee,
To the last gasp, with truth and loyalty.
SHAKESPEARE: *As You Like It,* II, *c.* 1600

Whose bread I eat, his song I sing. (Wes Brot ich ess, des Lied ich sing.)
MIDDLE HIGH GERMAN SAYING

Luck

A lucky man is rarer than a white crow.
JUVENAL: *Satires,* VII, 118

The Devil's children have the Devil's luck.
ENGLISH PROVERB, familiar since the XVII century

As good luck would have it.
SHAKESPEARE: *The Merry Wives of Windsor*, III, *c.* 1600

The more knave, the better luck.
WILLIAM CAMDEN: *Remains Concerning Britain* (4th ed.), 1636

Luck long lasting was ever suspicious.
BALTASAR GRACIÁN: *The Art of Worldly Wisdom*, XXXVIII, 1647

Is he lucky? (Est-il heureux?)
CARDINAL MARAZIN (1602–61): Asked of all men who sought service under him

Luck and temper rule the world.
LA ROCHEFOUCAULD: *Maxims*, 1665

Ill luck is worse than found money.
JOHN RAY: *English Proverbs*, 1670

A crooning cow, a crowing hen and a whistling woman boded never luck to a house.
JAMES KELLY: *Complete Collection of Scottish Proverbs*, 1721

He came safe from the East Indies, and was drowned in the Thames.
THOMAS FULLER: *Gnomologia*, 1732

Better luck next time.
ENGLISH SAYING, not recorded before the XIX century

There's luck in odd numbers.
SAMUEL LOVER: *Rory O'More*, 1836

Good luck reaches farther than long arms.
H. G. BOHN: *Handbook of Proverbs*, 1855

Lucky men need no counsel. IBID.

The only sure thing about luck is that it will change.
BRET HARTE: *The Outcasts of Poker Flat*, 1869

Throw a lucky man into the sea, and he will come up with a fish in his mouth.
ARAB PROVERB

Good luck is a lazy man's estimate of a worker's success. Author unidentified

If a horse gets no wild grass it never becomes fat; if a man is not lucky he never becomes rich. CHINESE PROVERB

Luck has but a slender anchorage.
DANISH PROVERB

Luck stops at the door and inquires whether prudence is within. IBID.

A lucky man always ends as a fool.
GERMAN PROVERB

Luck sometimes visits a fool, but never sits down with him. IBID.

Too much luck is bad luck. IBID.

Behind bad luck comes good luck.
GIPSY PROVERB

Luck is one-half of success. HINDU PROVERB

Good luck beats early rising. IRISH PROVERB

It's better to be lucky than wise. IBID.

He who gets the little luck gets the big luck.
IBID.

He who is lucky in love should never play cards. ITALIAN PROVERB

He who is lucky passes for a wise man, too.
IBID.

Even the street-dog has his lucky days.
JAPANESE PROVERB

To wait for luck is the same as waiting for death. IBID.

One ounce of good luck is better than a ton of brains. JUGO-SLAVIC PROVERB

Luck is always borrowed, not owned.
NORWEGIAN PROVERB

See a pin and pick it up:
All the day you'll have good luck.
OLD ENGLISH RHYME

If you were born lucky even your rooster will lay eggs. RUSSIAN PROVERB

Better be the lucky man than the lucky man's son. SCOTTISH PROVERB

Give your son luck, and throw him into the sea. SPANISH PROVERB

Luck never gives; it only lends.
SWEDISH PROVERB

Good luck comes to the saucy and bold.
WELSH PROVERB

[*See also* Age (Old), Bold, Change, Coward, Cowardice, Daughter, Deserving, Diligence, Knave, Laziness, Learning, Numbers (Odd), Physician, Pin, Spider.

Ludicrous

The ludicrous is merely a subdivision of the ugly. It consists in some defect which is neither painful nor destructive.
ARISTOTLE: *Poetics*, V, *c.* 322 B.C.

[*See also* Laughter.

Lukewarmness

[*See* Moderation.

Lullaby

Rock-a-bye baby, on the tree top,
When the wind blows the cradle will rock;
When the bough breaks the cradle will fall;
Down will come baby, cradle and all.
ENGLISH NURSERY RHYME, *c.* 1650

Hush, my dear, lie still and slumber,
Holy angels guard thy bed!

Heavenly blessings without number
Gently falling on thy head.
ISAAC WATTS: *Divine Songs for Children,* 1715

Sweet and low, sweet and low,
Wind of the western sea,
Low, low, breathe and blow,
Wind of the western sea!
Over the rolling waters go,
Come from the dying moon, and blow,
Blow him again to me;
While my little one, while my pretty one sleeps.
ALFRED TENNYSON: *The Princess,* II, 1847

[*See also* Mother.

Lump

If you don't like it you can lump it.
AMERICAN SAYING, not recorded before the XIX century (*Lump*=endure)

Lunacy

There is only one kind of common sense, but forty varieties of lunacy.
WEST AFRICAN PROVERB

[*See also* Genius, Insanity.

Lunatic

Every lunatic thinks all other men are crazy.
PUBLILIUS SYRUS: *Sententiæ, c.* 50 B.C.

It is jolly at times to play the lunatic.
SENECA: *De tranquillitate animi, c.* 62

The lunatic, the lover, and the poet,
Are of imagination all compact.
SHAKESPEARE: *A Midsummer Night's Dream,* V, *c.* 1596

Whence comes it that a cripple does not irritate us, and a crippled mind does irritate us? Because a cripple recognizes that we go straight, and a crippled spirit says that it is we who limp; were it not for this we should have pity for him and not anger.
BLAISE PASCAL: *Pensées,* VI, 1670

Babylon in ruins is not so melancholy a spectacle.
JOSEPH ADDISON: *The Spectator,* July 3, 1712

The various admirable movements in which I have been engaged have always developed among their members a large lunatic fringe.
THEODORE ROOSEVELT: *Letter to H. C. Lodge,* Feb. 27, 1913

Lunatics never grow gray. GERMAN PROVERB

[*See also* Crazy, Imagination, Insanity, Madness, Philosopher.

Lust

Dearly beloved, I beseech you, as strangers and pilgrims, abstain from fleshly lusts, which war against the soul. I PETER II, 11, *c.* 60

Lust is an appetite of the mind by which temporal goods are preferred to eternal goods.
ST. AUGUSTINE: *On Lying, c.* 395

Sinful lust is not nature, but a disease of nature.
ST. AUGUSTINE: *Of Continence, c.* 425

Love comforteth, like sunshine after rain,
But lust's effect is tempest after sun.
SHAKESPEARE: *Venus and Adonis,* 1593

It subverts kingdoms, overthrows cities, towns, families; mars, corrupts and makes a massacre of men. Thunder and lightning, wars, fires, plagues, have not done that mischief to mankind as this burning lust, this brutish passion.
ROBERT BURTON: *The Anatomy of Melancholy,* III, 1621

As concerning lust or incontinency, it is a short pleasure, bought with long pain, a honeyed poison, a gulf of shame, a pickpurse, a breeder of diseases, a gall to the conscience, a corrosive to the heart, turning man's wit into foolish madness, the body's bane, and the soul's perdition.
JOHN TAYLOR: *The Unnatural Father,* 1621

Beware of lust; it doth pollute and foul
Whom God in baptism washed in His own blood.
GEORGE HERBERT: *The Temple,* 1633

When lust,
By unchaste looks, loose gestures, and foul talk,
But most by lewd and lavish arts of sin,
Lets in defilement to the inward parts,
The soul grows clotted by contagion,
Imbodies and imbrutes, till she quite lose
The divine property of her first being.
JOHN MILTON: *Comus,* 1637

The sages figured lust in the form of a satyr; of shape, part human, part bestial; to signify that the followers of it prostitute the reason of a man to pursue the appetites of a beast.
RICHARD STEELE: *The Tatler,* Aug. 2, 1709

Everything that lives is holy. . . . The lust of the goat is the glory of God.
WILLIAM BLAKE: *The Marriage of Heaven and Hell,* 1790

When the heart's full of lust the mouth's full of leasings.
JAMES KELLY: *Complete Collection of Scottish Proverbs,* 1721 (*Leasing*=lie)

[*See also* Appetite, Clothes, Crime, Evil, Idleness, Man, Sin, Vice.

Lute

The lascivious pleasing of a lute.
SHAKESPEARE: *Richard III,* I, *c.* 1592

It is the little rift within the lute
That by and by will make the music mute.
ALFRED TENNYSON: *Merlin and Vivien,* 1859

[*See also* Dancer.

Luther, Martin (1483–1546)

Luther was the foulest of monsters.
POPE GREGORY XV: *Bull canonizing Ignatius Loyola*, 1622

At the time when Luther died all the possessed people in the Netherlands were quiet: the devils in them said the reason was because Luther had been a great friend of theirs, and they owed him that respect as to go as far as Germany to attend his funeral.
INCREASE MATHER: *Cases of Conscience Concerning Evil Spirits Personating Men*, 1693

The only fit commentator on Paul was Luther — not by any means such a gentleman as the Apostle, but almost as great a genius.
S. T. COLERIDGE: *Table-Talk*, June 15, 1833

A rude plebeian face; with his huge crag-like brows and bones, the emblem of rugged energy; at first, almost a repulsive face. Yet in the eyes especially there is a wild silent sorrow; an unnamable melancholy, the element of all gentle and fine affections; giving to the rest the true stamp of nobleness. Laughter was in this Luther; but tears also were there.
THOMAS CARLYLE: *Heroes and Hero-Worship*, IV, 1840 (Lecture in London, May 15)

[*See also* Erasmus (Desiderius), Gentleman, Institution, Reformation.

Luxury

Solomon's provision for one day was thirty measures of fine flour, and threescore measures of meal, ten fat oxen, and twenty oxen out of the pastures, and an hundred sheep, besides harts and roebucks, and fallow deer, and fatted fowl.
I KINGS IV, 22–23, *c.* 500 B.C.

Faint-hearted men are the fruit of luxurious countries. The same soil never produces both delicacies and heroes.
HERODOTUS: *Histories*, IX, *c.* 430 B.C.

Luxury and avarice — these pests have been the ruin of every state.
CATO THE CENSOR: In support of the Oppian Law, 215 B.C.

If you wish to destroy avarice, you must destroy luxury, which is its mother.
CICERO: *De oratore*, II, *c.* 80 B.C.

Luxury is a criminal affection for pleasures opposed to Christian chastity.
ST. JOHN BAPTIST DE LA SALLE: *Les devoirs du chrétien*, XIV, 1703

Silks and satins, scarlet and velvets, put out the kitchen fire.
BENJAMIN FRANKLIN: *Poor Richard's Almanac*, 1758

People have declaimed against luxury for 2000 years, in verse and in prose, and people have always delighted in it.
VOLTAIRE: *Philosophical Dictionary*, 1764

O luxury! thou curs'd by Heaven's decree,
How do thy potions, with insidious joy,
Diffuse their pleasures only to destroy.
OLIVER GOLDSMITH: *The Deserted Village*, 1770

No nation was ever hurt by luxury; for . . . it can reach but to a very few.
SAMUEL JOHNSON: *Boswell's Life*, April 13, 1773

Every degree of luxury hath some connection with evil.
JOHN WOOLMAN: *Journal*, III, 1774

The friends of humanity cannot but wish that in all countries the laboring classes should have a taste for comforts and enjoyments, and that they should be stimulated by all legal means in their exertions to procure them. There cannot be a better security against a superabundant population.
DAVID RICARDO: *Principles of Political Economy*, V, 1817

The most universal, mischievous, expensive and inexcusable customs of the present age of luxury and extravagance are those of adopting sugar, tea and coffee, ardent spirits and tobacco as articles of daily consumption.
JESSE TORREY: *The Moral Instructor*, 1819

For them the Ceylon diver held his breath
And went all naked to the hungry shark,
For them his ears gushed blood; for them in death,
The seal on the cold ice with piteous bark
Lay full of darts: for them alone did seethe
A thousand men in troubles wide and dark.
JOHN KEATS: *Isabella*, 1820

I dreamt that I dwelt in marble halls,
With vassals and serfs at my side.
ALFRED BUNN: *The Bohemian Girl*, II, 1843 (Drury Lane, Nov. 27)

Most of the luxuries, and many of the so-called comforts of life, are not only not indispensable, but positive hindrances to the elevation of mankind.
H. D. THOREAU: *Walden*, 1854

Give us the luxuries of life, and we will dispense with its necessaries.
O. W. HOLMES: *The Autocrat of the Breakfast-Table*, VI, 1858

Them as ha' never had a cushion don't miss it.
MARIAN EVANS (GEORGE ELIOT): *Adam Bede*, XL, 1859

He lives like God in France. (Er lebt wie Gott in Frankreich.) GERMAN SAYING

Curly locks! Curly locks!
Wilt thou be mine?

Thou shalt not wash dishes
  Nor yet feed the swine.
But sit on a cushion
  And sew a fine seam
And feed upon strawberries
  Sugar and cream. OLD ENGLISH RHYME

[*See also* Art, Avarice, Grief, Law (Sumptuary), Monasticism, Republic.

Lying

A lie is useful only as a medicine to men. The use of such medicines should be confined to physicians.
PLATO: *The Republic, c.* 370 B.C.

Lying lips are abomination to the Lord.
PROVERBS XII, 22, *c.* 350 B.C.

A lying tongue hateth those that are afflicted by it. PROVERBS XXVI, 28

The best lie, I hear, is a hot one.
PLAUTUS: *Mostellaria, c.* 200 B.C.

One lie treads on another's heels.
TERENCE: *Andria, c.* 160 B.C.

I hate and abhor lying.
PSALMS CXIX, 163, *c.* 150 B.C.

If the truth of God hath more abounded through my lie unto his glory, why yet am I also judged as a sinner?
ROMANS III, 7, *c.* 55

Wherefore putting away lying, speak every man truth with his neighbor: for we are members one of another. EPHESIANS IV, 25, *c.* 60

Peter said, Ananias, why hath Satan filled thine heart to lie to the Holy Ghost? . . . And Ananias hearing these words fell down, and gave up the ghost. ACTS III, 3–5, *c.* 75

There is no lie so reckless that it lacks all support.
PLINY THE ELDER: *Natural History,* VIII, 77

Lying is wrong even to save chastity.
ST. AUGUSTINE: *On Lying, c.* 395

He who says that some lies are just, must be judged to say no other than that some sins are just, and therefore some things are just which are unjust: than which what can be more absurd?
ST. AUGUSTINE: *To Consentius, Against Lying, c.* 400

Lying is forbidden, even for the detection of heretics. IBID.

It is even a sin to lie against the Devil.
ENGLISH PROVERB, traced to the XVI century

Children and fools cannot lie.
JOHN HEYWOOD: *Proverbs,* 1546

In time and place a harmless lie is a great deal better than a hurtful truth.
ROGER ASCHAM: *Letter to C. Howe, c.* 1550

The Devil has two occupations, to which he applies himself incessantly, and which are the foundation stones of his kingdom – lying and murder.
MARTIN LUTHER: *Table-Talk,* DCXIII, 1569

He who is not sure of his memory should avoid lying.
MICHEL DE MONTAIGNE: *Essays,* I, 1580

Tell a lie, and a blister will come upon your tongue.
ENGLISH PROVERB, traced by Smith to 1584

When was truth so beautiful that it could be preferred to a magnanimous lie?
TORQUATO TASSO: *Gerusalemme,* II, 1592

Who speaks not truly, lies.
SHAKESPEARE: *King John,* IV, *c.* 1596

It is not the lie that passeth through the mind, but the lie that sinketh in, and settleth in it, that doth the hurt.
FRANCIS BACON: *Essays,* I, 1597

For my part, if a lie may do thee grace,
I'll gild it with the happiest terms I have.
SHAKESPEARE: *I Henry IV,* II, *c.* 1598

If I tell thee a lie, spit in my face; call me horse.
IBID.

These lies are like the father that begets them; gross as a mountain, open, palpable. IBID.

Lord, Lord, how this world is given to lying!
SHAKESPEARE: *I Henry IV,* V

How subject we old men are to this vice of lying!
SHAKESPEARE: *II Henry IV,* III, *c.* 1598

No law against lying.
ENGLISH PROVERB, familiar since the XVII century

The lie with circumstance; the lie direct.
SHAKESPEARE: *As You Like It,* V, *c.* 1600

'Tis as easy as lying.
SHAKESPEARE: *Hamlet,* III, *c.* 1601

You told a lie, an odious, damned lie:
Upon my soul, a lie, a wicked lie.
SHAKESPEARE: *Othello,* V, 1604

Lying is father to falsehood, and grandsire to perjury; fraud (with two faces) is his daughter, a very monster; treason (with hairs like snakes) is his kinsman.
THOMAS DEKKER: *The Seven Deadly Sins of London,* II, 1606

To lapse in fulness
Is sorer than to lie for need, and falsehood
Is worse in kings than beggars.
SHAKESPEARE: *Cymbeline,* III, *c.* 1609

Lying . . . becomes none but tradesmen.
SHAKESPEARE: *The Winter's Tale,* IV, *c.* 1611

Nothing can need a lie.
GEORGE HERBERT: *The Temple*, 1633

One lie will destroy a whole reputation for integrity.
BALTASAR GRACIÁN: *The Art of Worldly Wisdom*, CLXXXI, 1647

Half the world knows not how the other half lies.
GEORGE HERBERT: *Jacula Prudentum*, 1651

Breaking of an oath, and lying
Is but a kind of self-denying.
SAMUEL BUTLER: *Hudibras*, II, 1664

Although persons may have no interest in what they are saying, we must not thence conclude absolutely that they are not lying; for there are people who lie simply for the sake of lying. BLAISE PASCAL: *Pensées*, VIII, 1670

As universal a practice as lying is, and as easy a one as it seems, I do not remember to have heard three good lies in all my conversation, even from those who were most celebrated in that faculty.
JONATHAN SWIFT: *Thoughts on Various Subjects*, 1706

Never was it given to mortal man
To lie so boldly as we women can.
ALEXANDER POPE: *The Wife of Bath*, 1714

Lie you for me, and I'll swear for you.
JAMES KELLY: *Complete Collection of Scottish Proverbs*, 1721

Stint not to truth the flow of wit:
Be prompt to lie whene'er 'tis fit.
JOHN GAY: *Fables*, I, 1727

Men were born to lie, and women to believe them.
JOHN GAY: *The Beggar's Opera*, II, 1728

Ask me no questions, and I'll tell you no fibs.
OLIVER GOLDSMITH: *She Stoops to Conquer*, III, 1773

A man had rather have a hundred lies told of him than one truth which he does not wish should be told.
SAMUEL JOHNSON: *Boswell's Life*, April 15, 1773

Weaklings have to lie.
JEAN PAUL RICHTER: *Hesperus*, IV, 1795

The man who fears no truths has nothing to fear from lies.
THOMAS JEFFERSON: *Letter to George Logan*, 1816

It is a great misery for a man to lie, even unconsciously, even to himself.
THOMAS CARLYLE: *Letter to his wife*, Nov. 2, 1835

Man everywhere is the born enemy of lies.
THOMAS CARLYLE: *Heroes and Hero-Worship*, I, 1840 (Lecture in London, May 5)

There is no lie that many men will not believe; there is no man who does not believe many lies; and there is no man who believes only lies.
JOHN STERLING: *Essays and Tales*, 1840

Every violation of truth is not only a sort of suicide in the liar, but is a stab at the health of human society.
R. W. EMERSON: *Prudence*, 1841

It is astonishing what force, purity and wisdom it requires for a human being to keep clear of falsehoods.
MARGARET FULLER OSSOLI: *Letter to W. H. Channing*, July, 1842

A man who has never been within the tropics does not know what a thunderstorm means; a man who has never looked on Niagara has but a faint idea of a cataract; and he who has not read Barère's Memoirs may be said not to know what it is to lie.
T. B. MACAULAY: *The Mémoires de Bertrand Barère*, 1843

The credit got by a lie lasts only till the truth comes out.
H. G. BOHN: *Handbook of Proverbs*, 1855

Sin has many tools, but a lie is the handle which fits them all.
O. W. HOLMES: *The Autocrat of the Breakfast-Table*, VI, 1858

Can there be a more horrible object in existence than an eloquent man not speaking the truth?
THOMAS CARLYLE: Address as Lord Rector of Edinburgh University, 1866

The essence of lying is in deception, not in words; a lie may be told by silence, by equivocation, by the accent on a syllable, by a glance of the eyes attaching a peculiar significance to a sentence; and all these kinds of lies are worse and baser by many degrees than a lie plainly worded.
JOHN RUSKIN: *Modern Painters*, IX, 1872

The cruelest lies are often told in silence.
R. L. STEVENSON: *Virginibus Puerisque*, 1881

I never seed anybody but lied, one time or another.
S. L. CLEMENS (MARK TWAIN): *Huckleberry Finn*, I, 1885

It is merely corroborative detail, intended to give verisimilitude to an otherwise bald and unconvincing narrative.
W. S. GILBERT: *The Mikado*, II, 1885

If there be trouble to herward, and a lie of the blackest can clear,
Lie, while thy lips can move, or a man is alive to hear.
RUDYARD KIPLING: *Certain Maxims of Hafiz*, 1886

There is an innocence about lying that is a sign of good faith in a cause.
F. W. NIETZSCHE: *Beyond Good and Evil*, 1886

The most common sort of lie is that by which a man deceives himself: the deception of others is a relatively rare offence.
F. W. NIETZSCHE: *The Antichrist*, LV, 1888

What is a fine lie? Simply that which is its own evidence. If a man is sufficiently unimaginative to produce evidence in support of a lie, he might just as well speak the truth at once.
OSCAR WILDE: *The Decay of Lying*, 1889

Any fool can tell the truth, but it requires a man of some sense to know how to lie well.
SAMUEL BUTLER: *Note-Books*, *c.* 1890

Terminological inexactitude.
WINSTON CHURCHILL: Speech in the House of Commons, Feb. 22, 1906

I lie; therefore I persist. The art of survival is the art of lying to yourself heroically, continuously, creatively. The senses lie to the mind; the mind lies to the senses. The truth-seeker is a liar; he is hunting for happiness, not truth.
BENJAMIN DeCASSERES: *Fantasia Impromptu*, 1933

An abomination unto the Lord, but a very present help in time of trouble.
Author unidentified (Cf. PROVERBS XII, *ante*, *c.* 350 B.C.; the second half is from PSALMS XLVI, 1)

Better a lie that soothes than a truth that hurts.
CZECH PROVERB

If lies were Latin, there would be many scholars.
DANISH PROVERB

Lying is the first step to the gallows.
GERMAN PROVERB

A woman may tell ninety-nine lies, but the hundredth will betray her.
HAUSSA PROVERB

A lie looks the better of having a witness.
IRISH PROVERB

One lie draws ten after it.
ITALIAN PROVERB

The cleverest of lies lasts only a week.
JAPANESE PROVERB

Tell a lie and you will hear the truth.
SPANISH PROVERB

Lying and boasting are the same.
WELSH PROVERB

One lie can kill a thousand truths.
WEST AFRICAN PROVERB

[*See also* Abomination, Age (Old), Ambassador, American, Art, Boasting, Debt, Easy, Eloquence, Equivocation, Exaggeration, Falsehood, Gossip, Government, Indignation, Liar, Metternich (Clemens von), Monk, Morality, Oath, Orator, Poet, Politician, Praise, Promise, Sin, Slander, Soup, Statistics, Travel, Traveler, Truth, Truth and Falsehood, Truth-telling, Washington (George), Whisper.

Lynching

We urge the Congress to enact at the earliest possible date a Federal anti-lynching law, so that the full influence of the Federal government may be wielded to exterminate this hideous crime.
Republican National Platform, 1924

Lynching has always been the means for protection, not of white women, but of profits.
WALTER WHITE: *Rope and Faggot*, V, 1929

My grand-daughter's gone to the lynching;
My son and his wife are there, too.
I would fain have been out there to watch it,
But God brought me down with the flu.
So — bring back, bring back,
Bring back a finger to me!
GEORGE S. SCHUYLER: *The Old-Fashioned Way*, 1934

Lyric

I co'd rehearse
A lyric verse.
ROBERT HERRICK: *Hesperides*, 1648

M

Macaulay, T. B. (1800–59)

An ugly, cross-made, splay-footed, shapeless little dumpling of a fellow, with a featureless face too — except indeed a good expansive forehead — sleek, puritanical, sandy hair — large glimmering eyes — and a mouth from ear to ear. He has a lisp and a burr.
Anon.: In Blackwood's, 1831

I wish I were only as sure about anything as Tom Macaulay is about everything.
WILLIAM LAMB (VISCOUNT MELBOURNE), *c.* 1845

Macaulay is like a book in breeches.
Ascribed to SYDNEY SMITH in *A Memoir of the Rev. Sydney Smith* by his daughter, Lady Holland, 1855

His "Lays of Ancient Rome" are clever, but the word lays is inapplicable to the poetry of antiquity. His history is partial, his criticism superficial, his style fantastic.
W. S. LANDOR: *Letter to Robert Browning*, 1860

A Scottish sycophant and fine talker.
KARL MARX: *Das Kapital*, I, 1867

Macaulay is like the military king who never suffered himself to be seen, even by the attendants in his bed-chamber, until he had

had time to put on his uniform and jack-boots.
JOHN MORLEY: *Critical Miscellanies*, I, 1871

A sentence of Macaulay's may have no more sense in it than a blot pinched between doubled paper.
JOHN RUSKIN: *Praeterita*, I, 1885

MacDonald, J. Ramsay (1866–1939)

There are no professions he ever made, no pledges he ever gave to the country, and no humiliation to which he would not submit if they would only allow him still to be called the Prime Minister.
VISCOUNT SNOWDEN: Speech in the House of Lords, July 3, 1934

Macedonian

[*See* Plainspeaking.

Machiavelli, Niccolò (1468–1527)

Out of his surname they have coined an epithet for a knave, and out of his Christian name a synonym for the Devil.
T. B. MACAULAY: *Machiavelli*, 1827

[*See also* History.

Machine

The increase of net incomes, estimated in commodities, which is always the consequence of improved machinery, will lead to new savings and accumulations. These savings are annual, and must soon create a fund much greater than the gross revenue originally lost by the discovery of the machine, when the demand for labor will be as great as before.
DAVID RICARDO: *Principles of Political Economy*, XXXI, 1817

Subdivision of labor improves the art, but debilitates the artist, and converts the man into a mere breathing part of that machinery by which he works.
C. C. COLTON: *Lacon*, 1820

Man is a tool-using animal.
THOMAS CARLYLE: *Sartor Resartus*, I, 1836

Men have become the tools of their tools.
H. D. THOREAU: *Walden*, 1854

The great mechanical impulses of the age, of which most of us are so proud, are a mere passing fever, half-speculative, half-childish.
JOHN RUSKIN: *Modern Painters*, IV, 1856

Faith in machinery is our besetting danger; often in machinery most absurdly disproportioned to the end which this machinery, if it is to do any good at all, is to serve; but always in machinery, as if it had a value in and for itself.
MATTHEW ARNOLD: *Culture and Anarchy*, I, 1869

A tool is but the extension of a man's hand, and a machine is but a complex tool. He that invents a machine augments the power of a man and the well-being of mankind.
H. W. BEECHER: *Proverbs from Plymouth Pulpit*, 1870

The evil that machinery is doing is not merely in the consequences of its work but in the fact that it makes men themselves machines also.
OSCAR WILDE: Press interview in Omaha, 1882 (Weekly Herald, March 22)

The world is dying of machinery; that is the great disease, that is the plague that will sweep away and destroy civilization; man will have to rise against it sooner or later.
GEORGE MOORE: *Confessions of a Young Man*, VII, 1888

One machine can do the work of fifty ordinary men. No machine can do the work of one extraordinary man.
ELBERT HUBBARD: *Roycroft Dictionary and Book of Epigrams*, 1923

[*See also* Agriculture, Body, Culture, Man, Tool.

Madman

[*See* Lover, Lunatic.

Madness

Whom Jupiter would destroy he first makes mad.
SOPHOCLES: *Antigone*, *c.* 450 B.C. (Quoted as a proverb; familiar in English as "Whom the gods would destroy they first make mad")

As mad as a March hare.
ENGLISH PHRASE, in common use since the XIV century

Men are mad so unavoidably that not to be mad would constitute one a madman of another order of madness.
BLAISE PASCAL: *Pensées*, VI, 1670

I am but mad north-north-west; when the wind is southerly I know a hawk from a handsaw.
SHAKESPEARE: *Hamlet*, II, *c.* 1601

That he is mad, 'tis true; 'tis true 'tis pity;
And pity 'tis 'tis true. IBID.

Though this be madness, yet there is method in't. IBID.

This is very midsummer madness.
SHAKESPEARE: *Twelfth Night*, III, *c.* 1601

That way madness lies.
SHAKESPEARE: *King Lear*, III, 1606

It is better to be mad with the rest of the world than to be wise alone.
BALTASAR GRACIÁN: *The Art of Worldly Wisdom*, CXXXIII, 1647

Moon-struck madness.
JOHN MILTON: *Paradise Lost*, XI, 1667

There is a pleasure sure
In being mad which none but madmen know.
JOHN DRYDEN: *The Spanish Friar,* II, 1681

Great wits are sure to madness near alli'd
And thin partitions do their bounds divide.
JOHN DRYDEN: *Absalom and Achitophel,* I, 1682

As mad as a hatter.
ENGLISH PHRASE, not recorded before the XIX century (The New English Dictionary traces "as a weaver," now obsolete, to 1609)

His madness was not of the head, but heart.
BYRON: *Lara,* I, 1814

[*See also* Anger, Fool, Greatness, Insanity, Lunatic, Moon, Poet.

Magic

If we condemn natural magic, or the wisdom of nature, because the Devil (who knoweth more than any man) doth also teach witches and poisoners the harmful parts of herbs, drugs, minerals and excrements, then we may by the same rule condemn the physician and the art of healing.
WALTER RALEIGH: *Historie of the World,* I, 1614

We ought to be very cautious in the prosecution of magic and heresy. The attempt to put down these two crimes may be extremely perilous to liberty, and may be the origin of a number of petty acts of tyranny if the legislator be not on his guard; for as such an accusation does not bear directly on the overt acts of a citizen, but refers to the idea we entertain of his character, it becomes dangerous in proportion to the ignorance of the people; and therefore a citizen is ever in danger, because the most correct conduct in the world, the purest morals, the strictest performance of every duty, are no guarantee against the suspicion of such crimes.
C. L. DE MONTESQUIEU: *The Spirit of the Laws,* XII, 1748

Magician

Then came the magicians, the astrologers, the Chaldeans, and the soothsayers.
DANIEL IV, 7, *c.* 165 B.C.

The magician is an infidel, but his magic is truth.
HINDU PROVERB

Magistrate

The magistrate is a speaking law, and the law is a silent magistrate.
CICERO: *De legibus,* III, *c.* 50 B.C.

The civil magistrate has no authority in ecclesiastical matters. He is only a member of the church, the government of which ought to be committed to the clergy.
EDWIN SANDYS (BISHOP OF LONDON): *Letter to Henry Bullinger of Zürich,* setting forth the principles of the Puritans, 1573

The magistrate beareth not his sword for naught, for he is God's minister, and a father of the country, appointed of God to punish offenders.
JOHN NORTHBROOKE: *Against Dicing,* 1577

Art thou a magistrate? Then be severe.
GEORGE HERBERT: *The Temple,* 1633

I entreat you to consider that when you choose magistrates you take them from among yourselves, men subject to like passions as you are.
JOHN WINTHROP: *Journal,* 1645

Magistrates, having no right to interfere with matters of conscience, have only to look to outward conduct.
BLAISE PASCAL: *Provincial Letters,* 1657

It is good to obey a magistrate in matters ethically indifferent, even when there is no fear of punishment.
HENRY MORE: *Enchiridion Ethicum,* IV, 1667

[*See also* Judge, Law, Prince.

Magna Charta

Magna Charta is the law, and let the king look out.
INSCRIPTION ON A MONUMENT IN TEWKESBURY ABBEY, *c.* 1250

Magna Charta is such a fellow that he will have no sovereign.
EDWARD COKE: Speech in the House of Commons, May 17, 1628

[*See also* Bill of Rights.

Magnanimity

Magnanimity becomes a man of fortune.
PUBLILIUS SYRUS: *Sententiæ,* *c.* 50 B.C.

He who commands the vanquisht, speaks the power,
And glorifies the worthy conqueror.
ROBERT HERRICK: *Hesperides,* 1648

Magnanimity despises everything to gain everything.
LA ROCHEFOUCAULD: *Maxims,* 1665

Magnanimity in politics is not seldom the truest wisdom; and a great empire and little minds go ill together.
EDMUND BURKE: Speech on Conciliation with America, March 22, 1775

Magnanimity is often more a matter of culture than of disposition. A man is magnanimous rather for the sake of showing off than out of goodness of heart. Those who really have it in their nature rarely see anything noteworthy about being magnanimous.
G. C. LICHTENBERG: *Reflections,* 1799

[*See also* Virtue.

Magnificat, The

My soul doth magnify the Lord.
LUKE I, 46, *c.* 75 (The text runs to v. 55)

Magnificence

The magnificent man is an artist in expenditure; he can discern what is seemly, and spend great sums in good taste.
ARISTOTLE: *The Nicomachean Ethics*, IV, *c.* 340 B.C.

Everything unknown is taken for magnificent.
TACITUS: *Life of Agricola*, *c.* 98

Mahomet

[*See* Mohammed.

Maiden

The maid, like Paradise, undressed, untilled,
Bears crops of native virtue in her breast.
JOHN DAVIES: *A Contention Betwixt a Wife, a Widow, and a Maid*, 1602

Wives are fair apples served in golden dishes,
Widows good wine, which time makes better much,
But maids are grapes desired by many wishes,
But that they grow so high as none can touch.
IBID.

A maid and a virgin is not all one.
JOHN CLARKE: *Parœmiologia Anglo-Latina*, 1639

It is enough she is willing to be married when the fifth act requires it.
JOHN DRYDEN: *Essay of Dramatic Poesy*, 1668

A maid oft seen and a gown oft worn
Are disesteemed and held in scorn.
JOHN RAY: *English Proverbs*, 1670

Maidens must be mild and meek,
Swift to hear and soft to speak.
JAMES KELLY: *Complete Collection of Scottish Proverbs*, 1721

Maidens should be meek until they be married, and then burn kirks.
IBID.

A tender, timid maid, who knew not how
To pass a pig-sty, or to face a cow.
GEORGE CRABBE: *Tales of the Hall*, 1819

Standing, with reluctant feet,
Where the brook and river meet.
H. W. LONGFELLOW: *Maidenhood*, 1841

When maidens sue, men live like gods.
H. G. BOHN: *Handbook of Proverbs*, 1855

Three little maids from school are we,
Pert as a schoolgirl well can be,
Filled to the brim with girlish glee,
Three little maids from school.
W. S. GILBERT: *The Mikado*, I, 1885

I've a neater, sweeter maiden in a cleaner, greener land.
RUDYARD KIPLING: *Mandalay*, 1890

Tell me, pretty maiden, are there any more at home like you?
OWEN HALL: *Florodora*, II, 1900 (The music was by Leslie Stuart)

One hair of a maiden's head pulls harder than ten yoke of oxen.
DANISH PROVERB

It is what a maiden doesn't know that adorns her.
RUSSIAN PROVERB

A dink maiden aft maks a dirty wife.
SCOTTISH PROVERB (*Dink*=neat)

All meat's to be eaten, all maids to be wed.
SPANISH PROVERB

[*See also* Body, Cold, Dog, Enigma, Fancy-free, Frenchwoman, Girl, Happiness, Heart, Kiss, Laughter, No, Spinster, Tears, Virgin.

Maid, Old

[*See* Spinster.

Maine

As Maine goes, so goes the country.
AMERICAN POLITICAL MAXIM, first recorded *c.* 1888

Here's to the state of Maine, the land of the bluest skies, the greenest earth, the richest air, the strongest, and what is better, the sturdiest men, the fairest, and what is best of all, the truest women under the sun.
THOMAS B. REED: Speech at Portland, Maine, Aug. 7, 1900

As Maine goes, so goes Vermont.
JAMES A. FARLEY: Statement to the press, Nov. 4, 1936 (Maine and Vermont were the only states carried by Alfred M. Landon, Republican candidate for the Presidency)

[*See also* Blaine (James G.).

Majority

In a republic this rule ought always to be observed, that the greatest number should not have the predominant power.
CICERO: *De republica*, II, *c.* 50 B.C.

What is done publicly by the majority is to be attributed to the whole.
DOMITIUS ULPIANUS: *Liber singularis regularum*, *c.* 210

When any number of men have, by the consent of every individual, made a community, they have thereby made that community one body, with a power to act as one body, which is only by the will and determination of the majority. For that which acts any community, being only the consent of the individuals of it, and it being one body must move one way, it is necessary the body should move that way the greater force carries it, which is the consent of the majority.
JOHN LOCKE: *Treatises on Government*, II, 1690

It is my principle that the will of the majority should always prevail.
THOMAS JEFFERSON: *Letter to James Madison*, Dec. 20, 1787

I readily suppose my opinion wrong, when opposed by the majority.
THOMAS JEFFERSON: *Letter to James Madison,* 1788

The voice of the majority is no proof of justice.
J. C. F. SCHILLER: *Mary Stuart,* II, 1800

Life to the great majority is only a constant struggle for mere existence, with the certainty of losing it at last.
ARTHUR SCHOPENHAUER: *The World as Will and Idea,* IV, 1819

The majority, compose them how you will, are a herd, and not a very nice one.
WILLIAM HAZLITT: *Butts of Different Sorts,* 1829 (The Atlas, Feb. 8)

The great majority of men seem to be minors.
R. W. EMERSON: *The Poet,* 1844

A majority is always the best repartee.
BENJAMIN DISRAELI: *Tancred,* II, 1847

A government in which the majority rule in all cases cannot be based on justice, even as far as men understand it.
H. D. THOREAU: *An Essay on Civil Disobedience,* 1849

Decision by majorities is as much an expedient as lighting by gas.
W. E. GLADSTONE: Speech in the House of Commons, Jan. 21, 1858

One, on God's side, is a majority.
WENDELL PHILLIPS: Speech at Harper's Ferry, Nov. 1, 1859

A majority held in restraint by constitutional checks and limitations, and always changing easily with deliberate changes of popular opinions and sentiments, is the only true sovereign of a free people.
ABRAHAM LINCOLN: Inaugural address, March 4, 1861

The fact disclosed by a survey of the past that majorities have been wrong, must not blind us to the complementary fact that majorities have usually not been entirely wrong.
HERBERT SPENCER: *First Principles,* I, 1862

Neither current events nor history show that the majority rules, or ever did rule.
JEFFERSON DAVIS: To J. F. Jaquess and J. R. Gilmore, July 17, 1864

One, with God, is always a majority, but many a martyr has been burned at the stake while the votes were being counted.
THOMAS B. REED: Speech in the House of Representatives, 1885 (Cf. PHILLIPS, *ante,* 1859)

Rule is evil, and it is none the better for being majority rule.
BENJAMIN R. TUCKER: *Instead of a Book,* 1893

The voice of the majority saves bloodshed, but it is no less the arbitrament of force than is the decree of the most absolute of despots backed by the most powerful armies.
IBID.

I not only believe majority rule is just, I believe it is best. All men know more than a few; all experience is better than new and untried theory.
E. W. HOWE: *Success Easier Than Failure,* 1917

One with the law is a majority.
CALVIN COOLIDGE: Speech of acceptance, July 27, 1920

Seven never wait for one. RUSSIAN PROVERB

[*See also* Ballot, Blood and Iron, Innovation, Law, Majority and Minority, Mob, Public.

Majority and Minority

In all companies there are more fools than wise men, and the greater part always get the better of the wiser.
RABELAIS: *Pantagruel,* II, 1533

On a candid examination of history, we shall find that turbulence, violence, and abuse of power, by the majority trampling on the rights of the minority, have produced factions and commotions which, in republics, have, more frequently than any other cause, produced despotism.
JAMES MADISON: Speech in the Virginia Convention, June 16, 1788

Though the will of the majority is in all cases to prevail, that will, to be rightful, must be reasonable; the minority possess their equal rights, which equal laws must protect, and to violate would be oppression.
THOMAS JEFFERSON: Inaugural address, March 4, 1801

The minority of a country is never known to agree, except in its efforts to reduce and oppress the majority.
J. FENIMORE COOPER: *The American Democrat,* VIII, 1838

Shall we judge a country by the majority, or by the minority? By the minority, surely.
R. W. EMERSON: *The Conduct of Life,* VII, 1860

The history of most countries has been that of majorities — mounted majorities, clad in iron, armed with death, treading down the tenfold more numerous minorities.
O. W. HOLMES: Address to the Massachusetts Medical Society, Boston, May 30, 1860

If by the mere force of numbers a majority should deprive a minority of any clearly written constitutional right, it might in a moral point of view, justify revolution — certainly would if such a right were a vital one.
ABRAHAM LINCOLN: Inaugural address, March 4, 1861

The numerical majority is ready, is eager to delegate its power of choosing its ruler to a certain select minority. It abdicates in favor of its elite, and consents to obey whoever that elite may confide in.
WALTER BAGEHOT: *The English Constitution,* IX, 1867

The oppression of a majority is detestable and odious: the oppression of a minority is only by one degree less detestable and odious.
W. E. GLADSTONE: Speech in the House of Commons, Feb. 8, 1870

A minority may be right; a majority is always wrong.
HENRIK IBSEN: *An Enemy of the People,* IV, 1882

The majority submits to principles consciously, because they meet the demands of reason, and the minority unconsciously, because they have become public opinion.
LYOF N. TOLSTOY: *The Kingdom of God Is Within You,* 1893

When great changes occur in history, when great principles are involved, as a rule the majority are wrong. The minority are right.
EUGENE V. DEBS: Speech before the jury in the Federal court, Cleveland, Sept. 12, 1918

The moment a mere numerical superiority by either states or voters in this country proceeds to ignore the needs and desires of the minority, and for their own selfish purpose or advancement, hamper or oppress that minority, or debar them in any way from equal privileges and equal rights – that moment will mark the failure of our constitutional system.
F. D. ROOSEVELT: Radio address, March 2, 1930

The thing we have to fear in this country, to my way of thinking, is the influence of the organized minorities, because somehow or other the great majority does not seem to organize. They seem to feel that they are going to be effective because of their known strength, but they give no expression of it.
ALFRED E. SMITH: Speech at Harvard, June 22, 1933

Minorities are the stars of the firmament; majorities, the darkness in which they float.
MARTIN H. FISCHER (1879–)

[*See also* Democracy, Minority.

Malaria

[*See* Ague.

Male and Female

Male and female created he them.
GENESIS I, 27, *c.* 700 B.C.

The male is by nature superior to the female.
ARISTOTLE: *Politics, c.* 322 B.C.

As deep drinketh the goose as the gander.
JOHN HEYWOOD: *Proverbs,* 1546

[Male birds] are almost always the wooers; and they alone are armed with special weapons for fighting with their rivals. They are generally stronger and larger than the females, and are endowed with the requisite qualities of courage and pugnacity.
CHARLES DARWIN: *The Descent of Man,* XXI, 1871

All females save woman seek the male only in the Spring.
FRENCH PROVERB

[*See also* Celibacy, Dog, Envy, Female, Man and Woman, Propriety, Sex.

Malefactor

Malefactors of great wealth.
THEODORE ROOSEVELT: Speech at Provincetown, Mass., Aug. 20, 1907

Malevolence

The malevolent have secret teeth.
PUBLILIUS SYRUS: *Sententiæ, c.* 50 B.C.

[*See also* Woman.

Malice

Malice is cunning.
CICERO: *De natura deorum,* III, 45 B.C.

Malice is blind.
LIVY: *History of Rome,* XXXVIII, *c.* 10

Wit larded with malice, and malice forced with wit.
SHAKESPEARE: *Troilus and Cressida,* V, *c.* 1601

Speak of me as I am; nothing extenuate,
Nor set down aught in malice.
SHAKESPEARE: *Othello,* V, 1604

Malice is mindful.
JOHN CLARKE: *Parœmiologia Anglo-Latina,* 1639

Malice hath a strong memory.
THOMAS FULLER: *A Pisgah-Sight of Palestine,* III, 1650

Malice drinketh up the greater part of its own poison.
THOMAS FULLER: *Gnomologia,* 1732

Malice will always find bad motives for good actions.
THOMAS JEFFERSON: *Letter to James Madison,* 1810

Malice seldom wants a mark to shoot at.
H. G. BOHN: *Handbook of Proverbs,* 1855

A blind mule kicking by guess.
H. W. SHAW (JOSH BILLINGS): *Josh Billings' Comical Lexicon,* 1877

[*See also* Charity, Friendship, Injury, Murder.

Malignity

That pure malignity can exist is the extreme proposition of unbelief. It is not to be entertained by a rational agent; it is atheism; it is the last profanation.
R. W. EMERSON: *Representative Men*, III, 1850

[*See also* Evil, Humor.

Malpractise

Malpractise is a great misdemeanor and offense at Common Law, whether it be for curiosity and experiment, or by neglect; because it breaks the trust which the party has placed in his physician, and tends to the patient's destruction.
WILLIAM BLACKSTONE: *Commentaries on the Laws of England*, IV, 1765

Malta

Malta would be a pleasant place if every priest on it were a tree. MALTESE PROVERB

[*See also* Sicilian.

Malthusianism

I solemnly declare that I do not believe that all the heresies and sects and factions which the ignorance and the weakness and the wickedness of man have ever given birth to, were altogether so disgraceful to man as a Christian, a philosopher, a statesman, or citizen, as this abominable tenet.
S. T. COLERIDGE: *Table-Talk*, Aug. 12, 1832

It furnishes a philosophy by which Dives as he feasts can shut out the image of Lazarus who faints with hunger at his door; by which wealth may complacently button up its pocket when poverty asks an alms, and the rich Christian bend on Sundays in a nicely upholstered pew to implore the good gifts of the All Father without any feeling of responsibility for the squalid misery that is festering but a square away.
HENRY GEORGE: *Progress and Poverty*, II, 1879

Malthus, T. R. (1766–1834)

Philosopher Malthus came here last week. I got an agreeable party for him of unmarried people. There was only one lady who had had a child; but he is a good-natured man, and, if there are no appearances of approaching fertility, is civil to every lady.
SYDNEY SMITH: *Letter to Lady Holland*, 1831

[*See also* Darwinism.

Mammon

Ye cannot serve God and mammon.
MATTHEW VI, 24, *c.* 75 (Cf. LUKE XVI, 13, *c.* 75)

The mammon of unrighteousness.
LUKE XVI, 9, *c.* 75

Mammon has two properties; it makes us secure, first, when it goes well with us, and then we live without fear of God at all; secondly, when it goes ill with us, then we tempt God, fly from him, and seek after another God.
MARTIN LUTHER: *Table-Talk*, CLXI, 1569

Man

Of all the creatures that creep and breathe on earth there is none more wretched than man. HOMER: *Iliad*, XVII, *c.* 800 B.C.

The earth produces nothing feebler than man.
HOMER: *Odyssey*, XVIII, *c.* 800 B.C.

God created man in his own image, in the image of God created he him; male and female created he them. GENESIS I, 27, *c.* 700 B.C.

The Lord God formed man of the dust of the ground, and breathed into his nostrils the breath of life; and man became a living soul.
GENESIS II, 7

Thus saith the Lord: Cursed be the man that trusteth in man.
JEREMIAH XVII, 5, *c.* 625 B.C.

Most men are bad.
Ascribed to BIAS OF PRIENE, one of the Seven Sages of Greece, *c.* 550 B.C.

Man is a shadow and a dream.
PINDAR: *Pythian Odes*, VIII, *c.* 475 B.C.

There are many wonderful things in nature, but the most wonderful of all is man.
SOPHOCLES: *Antigone*, *c.* 450 B.C.

Man is the measure of all things.
Ascribed to PROTAGORUS, *c.* 450 B.C.

Men fade like the leaves. They are emblems of imbecility, images of clay, a race lightsome and without substance, creatures of a day, without wings.
ARISTOPHANES: *The Birds*, 414 B.C.

Man is a tame, a domesticated animal.
PLATO: *Laws*, VI, *c.* 360 B.C.

Man is a biped without feathers.
PLATO: *Politicus*, *c.* 360 B.C.

Man is born unto trouble, as the sparks fly upward. JOB V, 7, *c.* 325 B.C.

Man that is born of a woman is of few days, and full of trouble. JOB XIV, 1

Man . . . is a worm. JOB XXV, 6

Man is by nature a political animal.
ARISTOTLE: *Politics*, I, *c.* 322 B.C.

At his best man is the noblest of all animals; separated from law and justice, he is the worst. IBID.

Does man differ from the other animals? Only in posture. The rest are bent, but he is a wild beast who walks upright.
PHILEMON: *Fragment*, *c.* 310 B.C.

Man was not intended by nature to live in communities and be civilized.
EPICURUS: *Aphorisms, c.* 300 B.C.

God hath made man upright; but they have sought out many inventions.
ECCLESIASTES VII, 29, *c.* 200 B.C.

Man is a wolf to man. (Homo homini lupus.)
PLAUTUS: *Asinaria,* II, *c.* 200 B.C.

I am a man, and nothing human is foreign to me. TERENCE: *Heautontimoroumenos, c.* 160 B.C.

Thou hast made him a little lower than the angels.
PSALMS VIII, 5, *c.* 150 B.C. (Quoted in HEBREWS II, 7, *c.* 65)

As for man his days are as grass; as a flower of the field so he flourisheth.
PSALMS CIII, 15

I am fearfully and wonderfully made.
PSALMS CXXXIX, 14

Man is like to vanity: his days are as a shadow that passeth away. PSALMS CXLIV, 4

Men are a hard, laborious species.
VIRGIL: *Georgics,* I, 30 B.C.

We are dust and shadow.
HORACE: *Carmina,* IV, *c.* 13 B.C.

Man is of the earth, earthy.
I CORINTHIANS XV, 47, *c.* 55

Man is a social animal.
SENECA: *De beneficiis,* VII, *c.* 63

Man is a reasoning animal. (Rationale animal est homo.)
SENECA: *Epistulæ morales ad Lucilium,* XLI, *c.* 63

Man is the only animal that knows nothing, and can learn nothing without being taught. He can neither speak nor walk nor eat, nor do anything at the prompting of nature, but only weep.
PLINY THE ELDER: *Natural History,* VII, 77

Lions do not fight with one another; serpents do not attack serpents, nor do the wild monsters of the deep rage against their like. But most of the calamities of man are caused by his fellow-man. IBID.

Some are good, some are middling, but the greater part are bad.
MARTIAL: *Epigrams,* I, 86

Man is more precious in the sight of God than the angels.
POPE XYSTUS I: *The Ring, c.* 120

I say to myself in the morning: before the day is out I shall encounter the busybody, the ingrate, the bully, the traitor, the man of envy, the bad neighbor.
MARCUS AURELIUS: *Meditations,* I, *c.* 170

Nature never intended man to be a low, grovelling creature. From the moment of his birth she implants in him an inextinguishable love for the noble and the good.
LONGINUS: *On the Sublime,* XXV, *c.* 250

Man is a gentle animal.
ST. JOHN CHRYSOSTOM: *Homilies,* XI, *c.* 388

Cursed is every one who placeth his hope in man.
ST. AUGUSTINE: *On the Christian Conflict, c.* 397

We are black by nature.
ST. JEROME: *The Virgin's Profession, c.* 420

An earthly animal, but worthy of Heaven.
ST. AUGUSTINE: *The City of God,* XXII, 427

The heavens and earth and sea and all that is in them are the works of the Lord, but man is His work in a special sense, for to make him the Lord used His hands. For the other things it sufficed for the Lord to speak and they were made, but for man He took clay and fashioned it with His own hands.
RUPERT, ABBOT OF DEUTZ: *Commentary on the Prophets, c.* 1130

Man is nothing else than . . . a sack of dung, the food of worms.
ST. BERNARD: *Meditationes piissimæ, c.* 1140

Man and the animals are merely a passage and channel for food, a tomb for other animals, a haven for the dead, giving life by the death of others, a coffer full of corruption.
LEONARDO DA VINCI: *Notebooks, c.* 1500

Speaking generally, men are ungrateful, fickle, hypocritical, fearful of danger, and covetous of gain.
NICCOLÒ MACHIAVELLI: *The Prince,* XVII, 1513

Man is the only animal who injures his mate.
LODOVICO ARIOSTO: *Orlando Furioso,* V, 1532

Man is but a bubble, or bladder of the water.
RICHARD TAVERNER: Tr. of DESIDERIUS ERASMUS: *Adagia* (1508), 1539

Man is a microcosm, or a little world, because he is an extract from all the stars and planets of the whole firmament, from the earth and the elements; and so he is their quintessence.
THEOPHRASTUS BOMBAST VON HOHENHEIM (PARACELSUS): *Archidoxies,* I, *c.* 1525

We have altogether a confounded, corrupt, and poisoned nature, both in body and soul; throughout the whole of man is nothing that is good.
MARTIN LUTHER: *Table-Talk,* CCLXII, 1569

Man is a being wonderfully vain, changeable and vacillating.
MICHEL DE MONTAIGNE: *Essays,* I, 1580

Man sees himself lodged here in the mud and filth of the world, nailed and fastened to the most lifeless and stagnant part of the universe, in the lowest story of the house, at the furthest distance from the vault of Heaven, with the vilest animals; and yet, in his imagination, he places himself above the circle of the moon, and brings Heaven under his feet. MICHEL DE MONTAIGNE: *Essays,* II

Man is sin.
ROBERT GREENE: *The Penitent Palmer's Ode, c.* 1590

Lords of the wide world, and wild watery seas,
Imbued with intellectual sense and souls,
Of more preeminence than fish and fowls.
SHAKESPEARE: *The Comedy of Errors,* II, 1593

A blast of wind, a momentary breath,
A watery bubble symbolized with air,
A sun-blown rose, but for a season fair,
A ghostly glance, a skeleton of death.
BARNABE BARNES: *Divine Century of Spiritual Sonnets,* 1595

Men are but gilded loam or painted clay.
SHAKESPEARE: *Richard II,* I, *c.* 1596

There's no trust,
No faith, no honesty in men; all perjured,
All forsworn, all naught, all dissemblers.
SHAKESPEARE: *Romeo and Juliet,* III, *c.* 1596

God made him, and therefore let him pass for a man.
SHAKESPEARE: *The Merchant of Venice,* I, *c.* 1597

A man! A man! My kingdom for a man!
JOHN MARSTON: *The Scourge of Villainie,* 1598

I know my life's a pain and but a span,
I know my sense is mocked with everything;
And to conclude, I know myself a man,
Which is a proud, and yet a wretched thing.
JOHN DAVIES: *Nosce Teipsum,* 1599

His life was gentle, and the elements
So mix'd in him that Nature might stand up,
And say to all the world, This was a man!
SHAKESPEARE: *Julius Cæsar,* V, 1599

Unless above himself he can
Erect himself, how poor a thing is man!
SAMUEL DANIEL: *To the Countess of Cumberland, c.* 1600

The true science and study of man is man.
PIERRE CHARRON: *De la sagesse,* I, 1601
(Cf. POPE, *post,* 1733)

He was a man, take him for all in all,
I shall not look upon his like again.
SHAKESPEARE: *Hamlet,* I, *c.* 1601

What a piece of work is man! how noble in reason! how infinite in faculty! in form and moving how express and admirable! in action how like an angel! in apprehension how like a god! the beauty of the world! the paragon of animals! And, yet, to me, what is this quintessence of dust? Man delights not me: no, nor woman either.
SHAKESPEARE: *Hamlet,* II

What is a man,
If his chief good and market of his time
Be but to sleep and feed?
SHAKESPEARE: *Hamlet,* IV

Every man is odd.
SHAKESPEARE: *Troilus and Cressida,* IV, *c.* 1601

Man is the slime of this dung-pit.
JOHN MARSTON: *The Malcontent,* IV, 1604

Every man is as Heaven made him, and sometimes a great deal worse.
CERVANTES: *Don Quixote,* I, 1605

Mankind hath within itself his goats, chameleons, salamanders, camels, wolves, dogs, swine, moles and whatever sorts of beasts: there are but a few men amongst men.
JOSEPH HALL: *Meditations and Vows,* II, 1606

As flies to wanton boys, are we to the gods;
They kill us for their sport.
SHAKESPEARE: *King Lear,* IV, 1606

I wonder men dare trust themselves with men.
SHAKESPEARE: *Timon of Athens,* I, *c.* 1607

We are such stuff
As dreams are made on.
SHAKESPEARE: *The Tempest,* IV, 1611

What's he, born to be sick, so always dying,
That's guided by inevitable fate;
That comes in weeping, and that goes out crying;
Whose calendar of woes is still in date;
Whose life's a bubble, and in length a span;
A concert still in discords? 'Tis a man.
WILLIAM BROWNE: *Britannia's Pastorals,* I, 1613

This is the state of man: today he puts forth
The tender leaves of hope; tomorrow blossoms,
And bears his blushing honors thick upon him:
The third day comes a frost, a killing frost,
And, when he thinks, good easy man, full surely
His greatness is a-ripening, nips his root,
And then he falls, as I do.
SHAKESPEARE and JOHN FLETCHER: *Henry VIII,* III, 1613

A man alone is either a saint or a devil.
ROBERT BURTON: *The Anatomy of Melancholy,* I, 1621 (Quoted in Latin)

Man is one world, and hath another to attend him. GEORGE HERBERT: *The Temple,* 1633

A man has his hour and a dog his day.
BEN JONSON: *A Tale of a Tub,* 1633

Man's state implies a necessary curse;
When not himself, he's mad; when most himself, he's worse.
FRANCIS QUARLES: *Emblems*, II, 1635

Men are not angels.
JOHN CLARKE: *Parœmiologia Anglo-Latina*, 1639

A man is known to be mortal by two things, sleep and lust.
GEORGE HERBERT: *Outlandish Proverbs*, 1640

Nature tells me I am the image of God, as well as Scripture. He that understands not thus much hath not his introduction or first lesson, and is yet to begin the alphabet of man.
THOMAS BROWNE: *Religio Medici*, II, 1642

Man is a watch, wound up at first, but never
Wound up again: once down, he's down for ever.
ROBERT HERRICK: *Hesperides*, 1648

A map of misery.
JOHN TAYLOR: *The Certain Travails of an Uncertain Journey*, 1653

Man is a noble animal, splendid in ashes and pompous in the grave.
THOMAS BROWNE: *Urn Burial*, v, 1658

Of all the creatures that fly in the air, walk on the ground or swim in the sea, from Paris to Peru and from Japan to Rome, the most foolish, in my opinion, is man.
NICOLAS BOILEAU: *Satires du Sieur D*, VIII, 1666

There wanted yet the master work, the end
Of all yet done: a creature who, not prone
And brute as other creatures, but endued
With scantity of reason, might erect
His stature, and upright with front serene
Govern the rest.
JOHN MILTON: *Paradise Lost*, VII, 1667

Man is but a reed, the most feeble thing in nature, but he is a thinking reed. The entire universe need not arm itself to crush him. A vapor, a drop of water suffices to kill him. But if the universe were to crush him man would still be more noble than that which killed him, because he knows that he dies, and the advantage which the universe has over him: the universe knows nothing of this.
BLAISE PASCAL: *Pensées*, I, 1670

Man is naturally credulous and incredulous, timid and rash. IBID.

Man is neither an angel nor a brute, and the very attempt to raise him to the level of the former sinks him to that of the latter. IBID.

What is man in nature? A nothing when compared to infinity; a whole when compared to nothing; a middle point between nothing and whole. IBID.

Man, to himself, is the most prodigious object in nature. BLAISE PASCAL: *Pensées*, III

What a chimera is man! what a nonesuch, what a monster, what a chaos, what a contradiction, what a prodigy! Judge of all things, and imbecile maggot; depository of truth, and sewer of uncertainty and error, the glory and rubbish of the universe!
BLAISE PASCAL: *Pensées*, VIII

Man is ice to the truth and fire to falsehood.
JEAN DE LA FONTAINE: *Fables*, IX, 1671

A spirit free, to choose for my own share,
What sort of flesh and blood I pleas'd to wear,
I'd be a dog, a monkey or a bear,
Or anything, but that vain animal,
Who is so proud of being rational.
JOHN WILMOT (EARL OF ROCHESTER): *A Satire Against Mankind*, 1675

Men are but children of a larger growth.
JOHN DRYDEN: *All for Love*, IV, 1678

Man, false man, smiling, destructive man!
NATHANIEL LEE: *Theodosius*, III, 1680

Trust not a man; we are by nature false,
Dissembling, subtle, cruel and unconstant.
THOMAS OTWAY: *The Orphan*, II, 1680

We are rational creatures; our virtue and perfection is to love reason, or rather to love order.
NICOLAS MALEBRANCHE: *Traité de morale*, I, 1684

From God he's a backslider;
Of ways, he loves the wider;
With wickedness a sider;
More venom than a spider;
In sin he's a confider;
A make-bate and divider;
Blind reason is his guider;
The Devil is his rider.
JOHN BUNYAN: *A Book for Boys and Girls*, 1686 (*Make-bate*=a breeder of strife)

Man's like a candle in a candlestick,
Made up of tallow, and a little wick. IBID.

Man is a mere character in a comedy.
JEAN DE LA BRUYÈRE: *Caractères*, VIII, 1688

That filthy, awkward, two-legged creature, man.
WILLIAM CONGREVE: *The Old Bachelor*, II, 1693

How dull, and how insensible a beast
Is man.
JOHN DRYDEN: *Discourse Concerning the Origin and Progress of Satire*, I, 1693

Man is the merriest species of the creation; all above and below him are serious.
JOSEPH ADDISON: *The Spectator*, Dec. 15, 1711

A sinful, an ignorant, a miserable being.
JOSEPH ADDISON: *The Guardian*, Sept. 5, 1713

What dust we dote on when 'tis man we love.
ALEXANDER POPE: *Eloisa to Abelard*, 1717

Man is the favorite animal on earth.
JOHN WISE: *A Vindication of the Government of New England Churches,* II, 1717

It is a good world, but they are ill that are on it.
JAMES KELLY: *Complete Collection of Scottish Proverbs,* 1721

What, then, is man? The smallest part of nothing.
EDWARD YOUNG: *The Revenge,* IV, 1721

The most pernicious race of little odious vermin that nature ever suffered to crawl upon the surface of the earth.
JONATHAN SWIFT: *Gulliver's Travels,* VI, 1726

Man is practised in disguise;
He cheats the most discerning eyes.
JOHN GAY: *Fables,* intro., 1727

Man is placed in a world full of a variety of things; his ignorance makes him use many of them as absurdly as the man that put dust in his eyes to relieve his thirst, or put on chains to remove pain.
WILLIAM LAW: *A Serious Call to a Devout and Holy Life,* XI, 1728

For what are men who grasp at praise sublime,
But bubbles on the rapid stream of time,
That rise, and fall, that swell, and are no more,
Born, and forgot, ten thousand in an hour?
EDWARD YOUNG: *Love of Fame,* II, 1728

Vain humankind! fantastic race!
Thy various follies who can trace?
Self-love, ambition, envy, pride,
Their empire in our hearts divide.
JONATHAN SWIFT: *On the Death of Dr. Swift,* 1731

The best metal is iron; the best vegetable, wheat; but the worst animal is man.
THOMAS FULLER: *Gnomologia,* 1732

Each beast, each insect, happy in its own,
Is Heav'n unkind to man, and man alone?
Shall he alone whom rational we call
Be pleased with nothing if not blest with all?
ALEXANDER POPE: *An Essay on Man,* I, 1733

Great lord of all things, yet a prey to all;
Sole judge of truth, in endless error hurled;
The glory, jest and riddle of the world!
ALEXANDER POPE: *An Essay on Man,* II

The proper study of mankind is man.
IBID. (Cf. CHARRON, *ante,* 1601)

Men may be read, as well as books, too much.
ALEXANDER POPE: *Moral Essays,* I (Of the Knowledge and Characters of Men), 1733

Thou still retain'st some sparks of heavenly fire,
Too faint to mount, yet restless to aspire;
Angel enough to seek thy bliss again,
And brute enough to make thy search in vain.
JOHN ARBUTHNOT: *Know Thyself,* 1734

A little, wretched, despicable creature; a worm, a mere nothing, and less than nothing; a vile insect that has risen up in contempt against the majesty of Heaven and earth.
JONATHAN EDWARDS: *The Justice of God in the Damnation of Sinners,* 1734

We are an inferior part of the creation of God. There are natural appearances of our being in a state of degradation.
JOSEPH BUTLER: *The Analogy of Religion,* I, 1736

When nature made us men she made us blessed.
WILLIAM WARBURTON (BISHOP OF GLOUCESTER): *A Fragment From Claudian's First Book Against Rufinus, Imitated,* c. 1740

How poor, how rich, how abject, how august,
How complicate, how wonderful, is man!
EDWARD YOUNG: *Night Thoughts,* I, 1742

Oh, what a miracle to man is man. IBID.

Ah! how unjust to nature, and himself,
Is thoughtless, thankless, inconsistent man.
EDWARD YOUNG: *Night Thoughts,* II

Man wants but little, nor that little long.
EDWARD YOUNG: *Night Thoughts,* IV

To none man seems ignoble, but to man.
IBID.

Say, why was man so eminently raised
Amid the vast creation? why ordained
Through life and death to dart his piercing eye,
With thoughts beyond the limit of his frame?
MARK AKENSIDE: *The Pleasures of Imagination,* I, 1744

Man's a poor deluded bubble,
Wand'ring in a midst of lies.
ROBERT DODSLEY: *Song,* 1745

What is the difference between man and ape, based on natural history? Most definitely I see no difference. I wish some one could show me even one distinction.
CAROLUS LINNAEUS: *Letter to J. G. Gmelin,* Feb. 14, 1747

Men, who are knaves individually, are in the mass very honorable.
C. L. DE MONTESQUIEU: *The Spirit of the Laws,* XXV, 1748

Mankind are very odd creatures: one half censure what they practise, the other half practise what they censure; the rest always say and do as they ought.
BENJAMIN FRANKLIN: *Poor Richard's Almanac,* 1752

Man is a wonder to himself; he can neither govern nor know himself.
BENJAMIN WHICHCOTE: *Moral and Religious Aphorisms,* 1753

There is nothing proper and peculiar to man but the use of reason and exercise of virtue.
IBID.

To each his suff'rings: all are men,
Condemn'd alike to groan,
The tender for another's pain;
Th' unfeeling for his own.

THOMAS GRAY: *Ode on a Distant Prospect of Eton College*, 1755

Every man has a wild beast within him.

FREDERICK THE GREAT: *Letter to Voltaire*, 1759

Man wants but little here below,
Nor wants that little long.

OLIVER GOLDSMITH: *The Hermit*, 1764 (Cf. YOUNG, *ante*, 1742)

A man has generally the good or ill qualities which he attributes to mankind.

WILLIAM SHENSTONE: *Of Men and Manners*, 1764

Dividing the world into an hundred parts, I am apt to believe the calculation might be thus adjusted:

Pedants	15
Persons of common sense	40
Wits	15
Fools	15
Persons of a wild uncultivated taste	10
Persons of original taste, improved by art	5

IBID.

At every moment of his life man is only a passive instrument in the hands of necessity.

P. H. D. D'HOLBACH: *Le système de la nature*, I, 1770

Alas! we are ridiculous animals.

HORACE WALPOLE: *Letter to Horace Mann*, May 14, 1777

What shadows we are, and what shadows we pursue.

EDMUND BURKE: Speech at Bristol, Sept. 10, 1780

Man originates in muck, wades a while in muck, makes muck, and in the end returns to muck.

J. C. F. SCHILLER: *The Robbers*, IV, 1781

One must confess it: man is more sensible than reasonable.

FREDERICK THE GREAT: *Letter to Jean le Rond D'Alembert*, Sept. 8, 1782

The bulk of mankind are schoolboys through life.

THOMAS JEFFERSON: *Notes on a Money Unit*, 1784

We are poor silly animals: we live for an instant upon a particle of a boundless universe, and are much like a butterfly that should argue about the nature of the seasons and what creates their vicissitudes, and does not exist itself to see one annual revolution of them.

HORACE WALPOLE: *Letter to the Earl of Strafford*, Aug. 6, 1784

Man was made to mourn.

ROBERT BURNS: Title and refrain of a song, 1785

You don't know the damned [human] race. (Du kennst die verdammte Rasse nicht.)

Ascribed to FREDERICK THE GREAT (1712–86)

The mass of men are neither wise nor good.

JOHN JAY: *Letter to George Washington*, June 27, 1786

Take mankind in general: they are vicious, their passions may be operated upon.

ALEXANDER HAMILTON: Speech in the Federal Convention, June 22, 1787

Are we a piece of machinery that, like the Æolian harp, passive, takes the impression of the passing accident? Or do these workings argue something within us above the trodden clod?

ROBERT BURNS: *Letter to Mrs. Dunlop*, Jan. 1, 1789

He that is born to be a man neither should nor can be anything nobler, greater or better than a man.

C. M. WIELAND: *Peregrinus Proteus*, 1791

The more I see of men, the more I admire dogs.

Ascribed to MADAME ROLAND (1754–93)

Man is an intellect served by organs.

L. G. A. DE BONALD: *Théorie du pouvoir politique et religieux*, 1796

Man is a digestive tube.

PIERRE CABANIS: *Rapports du physique et du moral de l'homme*, I, 1796

Man must make the angels laugh.

CHARLES LAMB: *Letter to S. T. Coleridge*, Oct. 24, 1796

What is man? Half beast, half angel.

JOACHIM LORENZ EVERS: *Vierhundert Lieder*, 1797

I think I may fairly make two postulata — first, that food is necessary to the existence of man; secondly, that the passion between the sexes is necessary, and will remain nearly in its present state.

T. R. MALTHUS: *The Principle of Population*, I, 1798

In every man there is a little of all men.

G. C. LICHTENBERG: *Reflections*, 1799

Man is half mind and half matter in the same way as a polyp is half plant and half animal. The strangest creatures are always found on the borderlines of species.

IBID.

Man is simply a bulb with thousands of roots. It is his nerves alone that feel; the rest of him merely holds them together, and makes it more convenient to carry them about. All we see is the pot in which the man is planted.

IBID.

Man is the cruelest enemy of man.

J. G. FICHTE: *Die Bestimmung des Menschen*, XII, 1800

Man is like a ball tossed betwixt the wind and the billows.

J. C. F. SCHILLER: *Wilhelm Tell*, IV, 1804

O man! thou feeble tenant of an hour,
Debased by slavery, or corrupt by power,
Who knows thee well must quit thee with disgust,
Degraded mass of animated dust!
Thy love is lust, thy friendship all a cheat,
Thy smiles hypocrisy, thy words deceit!
By nature vile, ennobled but by name,
Each kindred brute might bid thee blush for shame.

BYRON: *On the Monument of a Newfoundland Dog*, 1808

Each turns round in his own small circle, like a kitten playing with its tail.

J. W. GOETHE: *I Faust*, I, 1808

When Prometheus made man, he had used up all the water in making other animals; so he mingled his clay with tears.

Ascribed to RICHARD PORSON (1759–1808) in SAMUEL ROGERS: *Recollections*, 1859

[Man] fabricates
The sword which stabs his peace; he cherisheth
The snakes that gnaw his heart; he raiseth up
The tyrant whose delight is in his woe,
Whose sport is in his agony.

P. B. SHELLEY: *Queen Mab*, III, 1813

Thou knowest how great is man
Thou knowest his imbecility. IBID.

A creature squalid, vengeful, and impure;
Remorseless, and submissive to no law
But superstitious fear and abject sloth.

WILLIAM WORDSWORTH: *The Excursion*, IX, 1814

Let us take men as they are, not as they ought to be.

FRANZ SCHUBERT: *Diary*, June 16, 1816

Man is merely a more perfect animal than the rest. He reasons better.

NAPOLEON I: To Barry E. O'Meara at St. Helena, Nov. 9, 1816

Half dust, half deity.

BYRON: *Manfred*, I, 1817

Man!
Thou pendulum betwixt a smile and a tear.

BYRON: *Childe Harold*, IV, 1818

I believe that man was produced by the action of the heat of the sun upon the mud.

NAPOLEON I: To Gaspard Gourgaud at St. Helena, 1815–1818

Man is the only animal that laughs and weeps; for he is the only animal that is struck with the difference between what things are, and what they ought to be.

WILLIAM HAZLITT: *Lectures on the English Comic Writers*, I, 1819

Vain man! Mind your own business! Do no wrong! Do all the good you can! Eat your canvas-back ducks! drink your Burgundy! Sleep your siesta, when necessary, and trust in God.

JOHN ADAMS: *Letter to Thomas Jefferson*, March 14, 1820

Men are the same.

C. C. COLTON: *Lacon*, 1820

Man is an embodied paradox, a bundle of contradictions. IBID.

To despise our species is the price we must too often pay for our knowledge of it. IBID.

What a Bedlamite is man!

THOMAS JEFFERSON: *Letter to John Adams*, 1821

Man is an intellectual animal, and therefore an everlasting contradiction to himself. His senses center in himself, his ideas reach to the end of the universe; so that he is torn in pieces between the two, without a possibility of its ever being otherwise.

WILLIAM HAZLITT: *Characteristics*, LXIII, 1823

Man is a fallen god who remembers the heavens.

ALPHONSE DE LAMARTINE: *Nouvelles méditations poétiques*, 1823

Is not man the only automaton on earth? The things usually called so are in fact heteromatous.

A. W. and J. C. HARE: *Guesses at Truth*, 1827

Where every prospect pleases
And only man is vile.

REGINALD HEBER: *From Greenland's Icy Mountains*, 1827

The whole history of the species is made up of little except crimes and errors.

T. B. MACAULAY: *Hallam*, 1828 (Edinburgh Review, Sept.)

If a man is not rising upwards to be an angel, depend upon it, he is sinking downwards to be a devil. He cannot stop at the beast. The most savage of men are not beasts; they are worse, a great deal worse.

S. T. COLERIDGE: *Table-Talk*, Aug. 30, 1833

Man is not man as yet.

ROBERT BROWNING: *Paracelsus*, V, 1835

Man is a tool-using animal.

THOMAS CARLYLE: *Sartor Resartus*, I, 1836

An omniverous biped that wears breeches. IBID.

A feeble unit in the middle of a threatening Infinitude.

THOMAS CARLYLE: *Sartor Resartus*, II

Alas, poor devil! spectres are appointed to haunt him; one age, he is hagridden, bewitched; the next, priestridden, befooled; in all ages, bedeviled. And now the Genius of Mechanism smothers him worse than any

nightmare did; till the soul is nigh choked out of him, and only a kind of digestive, mechanic life remains.
THOMAS CARLYLE: *Sartor Resartus,* III

Man is a god in ruins.
R. W. EMERSON: *Nature,* 1836

A man must have aunts and cousins; must buy carrots and turnips, must have barn and woodshed, must go to market and to the blacksmith's shop, must saunter and sleep and be inferior and silly.
R. W. EMERSON: *Journal,* June 8, 1838

We may pause in sorrow and silence over the depths of darkness that are in man, if we rejoice in the heights of purer vision he has attained to.
THOMAS CARLYLE: *Heroes and Hero-Worship,* I, 1840 (Lecture in London, May 5)

Men are not philosophers, but are rather very foolish children, who, by reason of their partiality, see everything in the most absurd manner, and are the victims at all times of the nearest object.
R. W. EMERSON: *The Conservative,* 1841

A man is a golden impossibility.
R. W. EMERSON: *Experience,* 1841

Not in nature but in man is all the beauty and worth he sees. The world is very empty, and is indebted to this gilding, exalting soul for all its pride.
R. W. EMERSON: *Spiritual Laws,* 1841

Man is cheap.
R. W. EMERSON: *The Transcendentalist,* 1842

Mankind are earthen jugs with spirits in them.
NATHANIEL HAWTHORNE: *American Note-Books,* 1842

A two-legged animal without feathers.
THOMAS CARLYLE: *Past and Present,* I, 1843 (Cf. PLATO, *ante, c.* 360 B.C.)

Spiders can spin, beavers can build and show contrivance; the ant lays up accumulation of capital, and has, for aught I know, a Bank of Antland. If there is no soul in man higher than all that, did it reach to sailing on the cloud-rack and spinning sea-sand; then I say, man is but an animal, a more cunning kind of brute: he has no soul, but only a succedaneum for salt.
THOMAS CARLYLE: *Past and Present,* III

Nature never rhymes her children, nor makes two men alike.
R. W. EMERSON: *Character,* 1844

Every man is a history of the world for himself.
MAX STIRNER: *The Ego and His Own,* 1845

Man is "called" to nothing in this world. He has no destiny, no function, no vocation, any more than a plant or a dumb brute. IBID.

I like man, but not men.
R. W. EMERSON: *Journal,* March, 1846

After all, man is the great poet, and not Homer nor Shakespeare; and our language itself, and the common arts of life, are his work.
H. D. THOREAU: *A Week on the Concord and Merrimack Rivers,* 1849

Man can paint, or make, or think nothing but man.
R. W. EMERSON: *Representative Men,* I, 1850

Men resemble their contemporaries even more than their progenitors. IBID.

Seat thyself sultanically among the moons of Saturn, and take high abstracted man alone, and he seems a wonder, a grandeur, and a woe. But from the same point take mankind in mass, and for the most part they seem a mob of unnecessary duplicates, both contemporary and hereditary.
HERMAN MELVILLE: *Moby Dick,* CVI, 1851

Man is a burlesque of what he should be.
ARTHUR SCHOPENHAUER: *Parerga und Paralipomena,* II, 1851

Man is at bottom a wild and terrible animal. We know him only as what we call civilization has tamed and trained him; hence we are alarmed by the occasional breaking out of his true nature. But whenever the locks and chains of law and order are cast off, and anarchy comes in, he shows himself for what he really is. IBID.

Be neither saint nor sophist led, but be a man.
MATTHEW ARNOLD: *Empedocles on Etna,* 1852

However we brave it out, we men are a little breed. ALFRED TENNYSON: *Maud,* I, 1855

What creature else
Conceives the circle, and then walks the square?
Loves things proved bad, and leaves a thing proved good?
E. B. BROWNING: *Aurora Leigh,* VII, 1857

Nothing but a cloud of elements organic,
C, O, H, N, Ferrum, Chlor., Flu., Sil., Potassa,
Calc., Sod., Phosph., Mag., Sulphur, Mang.,
Alumin, Cuprum,
Such as man is made of.
O. W. HOLMES: *The Professor at the Breakfast-Table,* 1859

Man is in the most literal sense of the word a *zoön politikon,* not only a social animal, but an animal which can develop into an individual only in society.
KARL MARX: *A Contribution to the Criticism of Political Economy,* 1859

Who touches this, touches a man.
WALT WHITMAN: *So Long,* 1860

That great Alps and Andes of the living world.
T. H. HUXLEY: *Evidence as to Man's Place in Nature,* II, 1863

It is better to be a human being dissatisfied than a pig satisfied.
J. S. MILL: *Utilitarianism*, I, 1863

Nature they say, doth dote,
And cannot make a man
Save on some worn-out plan,
Repeating us by rote.
J. R. LOWELL: *Commemoration Ode*, July 21, 1865

As an organism increases in perfection the conditions of its life become more complex. Man is the most complex of the products of nature.
WALTER PATER: *Coleridge*, 1865

Before the beginning of years,
There came to the making of man
Time, with a gift of tears;
Grief, with a glass that ran;
Pleasure, with pain for leaven;
Summer, with flowers that fell;
Remembrance fallen from Heaven,
And madness risen from Hell;
Strength without hands to smite;
Love that endures for a breath;
Night, the shadow of light,
And life, the shadow of death.
A. C. SWINBURNE: *Atalanta in Calydon*, 1865

O man, strange composite of Heaven and earth!
Majesty dwarf'd to baseness! fragrant flower
Running to poisonous seed! and seeming worth
Cloaking corruption! weakness mastering power!
J. H. NEWMAN: *The Dream of Gerontius*, 1866

Lord, what are we, and what are our children, but a generation of vipers?
O. W. HOLMES: *The Medical Profession in Massachusetts*, 1869 (Lecture in Boston, Jan. 29. Quoted from MATTHEW III, 7; XII, 34, *c.* 75; LUKE III, 7, *c.* 75)

Like our huge earth itself, which, to ordinary scansion, is full of vulgar contradictions and offence, man, viewed in the lump, displeases, and is a constant puzzle and affront to the merely educated classes.
WALT WHITMAN: *Democratic Vistas*, 1870

Man, with all his noble qualities, with sympathy which feels for the most debased, with benevolence which extends not only to other men but to the humblest living creature, with his god-like intellect which has penetrated into the movements and constitution of the solar system — with all these exalted powers — man still bears in his bodily frame the indelible stamp of his lowly origin.
CHARLES DARWIN: *The Descent of Man*, XXI, 1871

Man is developed from an ovule about 1–125th of an inch in diameter, which differs in no respect from the ovules of other animals.
IBID.

Man by nature bears within himself
Nobility that makes him half a god.
CINCINNATUS HEINE (JOAQUIN MILLER): *Ida*, II, 1871

There is a great deal of human nature in man.
CHARLES KINGSLEY: *At Last*, 1871

God give us men! A time like this demands
Strong minds, great hearts, true faith, and ready hands.
Men whom the lust of office does not kill;
Men whom the spoils of office cannot buy;
Men who possess opinions and a will;
Men who have honor; men who will not lie.
J. G. HOLLAND: *Wanted*, 1872

There is only one man upon the earth; what we call men are not individuals but components.
W. WINWOOD READE: *The Martyrdom of Man*, III, 1872

We have the aspirations of creators and the propensities of quadrupeds. IBID.

The history of man is a series of conspiracies to win from nature some advantage without paying for it.
R. W. EMERSON: *Demonology*, 1877

Live dirt.
H. W. SHAW (JOSH BILLINGS): *Josh Billings' Comical Lexicon*, 1877

Man is not an ox, who, when he has eaten his fill, lies down to chew the cud; he is the daughter of the horse leech, who constantly asks for more.
HENRY GEORGE: *Progress and Poverty*, IV, 1879

The history of the world shows that when a mean thing was done, man did it; when a good thing was done, man did it.
R. G. INGERSOLL: Speech in Pittsburgh, Oct. 14, 1879

The most essential feature of man is his improvableness.
JOHN FISKE: *The Destiny of Man*, X, 1884

Man is nature's sole mistake.
W. S. GILBERT: *The Princess Ida*, I, 1884

Man is more of an ape than many of the apes.
F. W. NIETZSCHE: *Thus Spake Zarathustra*, prologue, 1885

Man is a rope stretching from the animal to the superman — a rope over an abyss.
IBID.

The earth has a skin, and that skin has diseases. One of those diseases is called man.
F. W. NIETZSCHE: *Thus Spake Zarathustra*, XL

We are very slight changed
From the semi-apes who ranged
India's prehistoric clay.
RUDYARD KIPLING: *Departmental Ditties*, 1886

Man is a complex, mendacious, artful, and inscrutable animal.
F. W. NIETZSCHE: *Beyond Good and Evil,* 1886

The breeding of an animal that can promise — is not this precisely the task that nature has set herself in man?
F. W. NIETZSCHE: *The Genealogy of Morals,* II, 1887

Man, relatively speaking, is the most botched of all the animals and the sickliest, and he has wandered the most dangerously from his instincts.
F. W. NIETZSCHE: *The Antichrist,* XIV, 1888

What we know of man today is limited precisely by the extent to which we have regarded him as a machine. IBID.

There are times when one would like to hang the whole human race, and finish the farce.
S. L. CLEMENS (MARK TWAIN): *A Connecticut Yankee at King Arthur's Court,* 1889

Is man only a blunder of God? Or God only a blunder of man?
F. W. NIETZSCHE: *The Twilight of the Idols,* 1889

We are like billiard balls in a game played by unskilful players, continually being nearly sent into a pocket, but hardly ever getting right into one, except by a fluke.
SAMUEL BUTLER: *Note-Books, c.* 1890

Though I've belted you and flayed you,
By the livin' Gawd that made you,
You're a better man than I am, Gunga Din.
RUDYARD KIPLING: *Gunga Din,* 1890

Man is a rational animal who always loses his temper when he is called upon to act in accordance with the dictates of reason.
OSCAR WILDE: *The Critic as Artist,* 1891

Men become old, but they never become good.
OSCAR WILDE: *Lady Windermere's Fan,* I, 1892

Man, so far as natural science by itself is able to teach us, is no longer the final cause of the universe, the Heaven-descended heir of all the ages. His very existence is an accident, his story a brief and transitory episode in the life of one of the meanest of the planets.
A. J. BALFOUR: *The Foundations of Belief,* I, 1895

Men, my dear, are very queer animals — a mixture of horse-nervousness, ass-stubbornness and camel-malice.
T. H. HUXLEY: *Letter to Mrs. W. K. Clifford,* Feb. 10, 1895

Man has no single mental faculty which is his exclusive prerogative. His whole psychic life differs from that of the nearest related mammals only in degree, and not in kind; quantitatively, not qualitatively.
ERNST HAECKEL: *The Riddle of the Universe,* VI, 1899

Man is not matter: he is not made up of brain, blood, bones and other material elements. The Scriptures inform us that man is made in the image and likeness of God. Matter is not that likeness.
MARY BAKER G. EDDY: *Science and Health,* XIV, 1908

Nothing is more romantic than nature, except nature plus man. But the exception is prodigious.
W. C. BROWNELL: *American Prose Masters,* 1909

A poor degenerate from the ape,
  Whose hands are four, whose tail's a limb,
I contemplate my flaccid shape.
  And know I may not rival him.
ALDOUS HUXLEY: *First Philosopher's Song,* 1920

There is no more reason to believe that man descended from some inferior animal than there is to believe that a stately mansion has descended from a small cottage.
W. J. BRYAN: Statement issued in Dayton, Tenn., July 28, 1925

We are not really native to this world, except in respect to our bodies.
GEORGE SANTAYANA: *The Genteel Tradition at Bay,* II, 1931

My studies in speculative philosophy, metaphysics and science are all summed up in the image of a mouse called man running in and out of every hole in the cosmos hunting for the Absolute Cheese.
BENJAMIN DeCASSERES: *Fantasia Impromptu,* 1933

Man as we know him in the whole of recorded human history is, and ever has been, of an unchanging and unchangeable nature; all the discoveries of science and the inventions of the mechanical age, all the changes in forms and concepts of government, of economic and of social life have not in the least affected or changed the essential nature of man as man.
Resolution of National Catholic Alumni Federation, 1936

The world is a pot, and man is a spoon in it.
ARMENIAN PROVERB

A man weighing 150 pounds approximately contains 3500 cubic feet of gas, oxygen, hydrogen and nitrogen in his constitution, which at 70 cents per 1000 cubic feet would be worth $2.45 for illuminating purposes. He also contains the necessary fats to make a 15-pound candle, and thus, with his 3500 cubic feet of gases, he possesses great illuminating possibilities. His system contains 22 pounds and 10 ounces of carbon, or enough to make 780 dozen, or 9360 lead pencils.

There are about 50 grains of iron in his blood and the rest of the body would supply enough to make one spike large enough to hold his weight. A healthy man contains 54 ounces of phosphorus. This deadly poison would make 800,000 matches or enough poison to kill 500 persons. Author unidentified

Man is the only animal that eats when he is not hungry, drinks when he is not thirsty, and makes love at all seasons. IBID.

There is so much good in the worst of us,
And so much bad in the best of us,
That it ill behooves any of us
To find fault with the rest of us. IBID.

There was a young man who said " Damn!
It is borne upon me that I am
An engine which moves
In predestinate grooves;
I'm not even a bus; I'm a tram! " IBID.

The tallest man must stretch sometimes, and the shortest must stoop. DANISH PROVERB

Men are carried by horses, fed by cattle, clothed by sheep, defended by dogs, imitated by monkeys, and eaten by worms.
HUNGARIAN PROVERB

Man is more fragile than an egg and harder than rock. JUGO-SLAVIC PROVERB

The nature of man. (Natura hominum.)
LATIN PHRASE

Man is tougher than iron, harder than stone, and more delicate than the rose.
TURKISH PROVERB

A man is what he is, not what he was.
YIDDISH PROVERB

[*See also* Authority, Birth, Civilization, Crowd, Curiosity, Darwinism, Death, Dying, Earth, Evil, Evolution, Fate, Good and Evil, Habit, Human, Humanity, Laughter, Life, Living, Man and Woman, Mankind, Man (Old), Mind, Nature (Human), Parasite, Society, Suffering, Thinking, World.

Man and Woman

The man said, The woman whom thou gavest to be with me, she gave me of the tree, and I did eat. GENESIS III, 12, *c.* 700 B.C.

The woman is destined to follow the man. In her youth she follows her father and her elder brother. Married, she follows her husband. Widowed, she follows her son.
CONFUCIUS: *The Book of Rites,* IX, *c.* 500 B.C.

All the pursuits of men are the pursuits of women also, but in all of them a woman is inferior to a man.
PLATO: *The Republic, c.* 370 B.C.

By means of a whorish woman a man is brought to a piece of bread,
PROVERBS VI, 26, *c.* 350 B.C.

Ye must know that women have dominion over you: do ye not labor and toil, and give and bring all to the women?
I ESDRAS IV, 22, *c.* 100 B.C.

The man is not of the woman; but the woman of the man. Neither was the man created for the woman; but the woman for the man.
I CORINTHIANS II, 8–9, *c.* 55

The woman is the glory of the man.
I CORINTHIANS XI, 7

So long as a man desires women his mind is in bondage, as a calf is in bondage to its mother.
The Dhammapada, XX, *c.* 100

Woman is the confusion of man.
VINCENT OF BEAUVAIS: *Speculum historiale,* X, *c.* 1250

The nobility both of England and Scotland [are] inferior to brute beasts, for they do that to women which no male among the common sort of beasts can be proved to do to their females; that is, they reverence them, and quake at their presence; they obey their commandments, and that against God.
JOHN KNOX: *The First Blast of the Trumpet Against the Monstrous Regiment of Women,* 1558

The intelligence of woman is inferior to that of man, and every woman who tries to deny it proves it.
COUNTESS DIANE OF POITIERS (1499–1566)

Men have broad and large chests, and small narrow hips, and more understanding than women, who have but small and narrow chests, and broad hips, to the end they should remain at home, sit still, keep house, and bear and bring up children.
MARTIN LUTHER: *Table-Talk,* DCCXXV, 1569

Were women never so fair, men would be false. Were women never so false, men would be fond.
JOHN LYLY: *Alexander and Campaspe,* III, 1584

A man of straw is worth more than a woman of gold.
JOHN FLORIO: *Second Frutes,* 1591

Men have marble, women waxen, minds.
SHAKESPEARE: *The Rape of Lucrece,* 1594

However we do praise ourselves,
Our fancies are more giddy and unfirm,
More longing, wavering, sooner lost and worn
Than women's are.
SHAKESPEARE: *Twelfth Night,* II, *c.* 1601

[Men] are all but stomachs, and we all but food;
They eat us hungerly, and when they are full
They belch us.
SHAKESPEARE: *Othello,* III, 1604

Were there no women, men might live like gods.
THOMAS DEKKER: *II The Honest Whore*, III, 1630

Men are more eloquent than women made,
But women are more powerful to persuade.
THOMAS RANDOLPH: *Amyntas*, 1638

Man is the whole world and the breath of God; woman the rib and crooked piece of man.
THOMAS BROWNE: *Religio Medici*, II, 1642

Women were created for the comfort of men.
JAMES HOWELL: *Familiar Letters*, III, 1650

Words are women, deeds are men.
GEORGE HERBERT: *Jacula Prudentum*, 1651

For contemplation he and valor formed,
For softness she, and sweet attractive grace.
JOHN MILTON: *Paradise Lost*, IV, 1667

If we do not cheat women they'll cheat us.
WILLIAM WYCHERLEY: *The Country Wife*, IV, *c.* 1673

A man no more believes a woman when she says she has an aversion for him than when she says she'll cry out.
WILLIAM WYCHERLEY: *The Plain Dealer*, II, *c.* 1674

A woman is a solitary, helpless creature without a man.
THOMAS SHADWELL: *A True Widow*, II, 1679

O woman! lovely woman! Nature made thee
To temper man: we had been brutes without you.
THOMAS OTWAY: *Venice Preserved*, I, 1682

It is because of men that women dislike one another.
JEAN DE LA BRUYÈRE: *Caractères*, III, 1688

Women always run to extremes. They are either better or worse than men. IBID.

What hogs men turn when they grow weary of women!
JOHN VANBRUGH: *The Provok'd Wife*, III, 1697

There are more well-pleased old women than old men.
RICHARD STEELE: *The Tatler*, Dec. 21, 1710

It is the male that gives charms to womankind, that produces an air in their faces, a grace in their motions, a softness in their voices, and a delicacy in their complexions.
JOSEPH ADDISON: *The Spectator*, July 17, 1712

If the heart of a man is depress'd with cares,
The mist is dispell'd when a woman appears.
JOHN GAY: *The Beggar's Opera*, II, 1728

A man is always afraid of a woman who loves him too well.
JOHN GAY: *The Beggar's Opera*, III

Man is fire and woman tow: the Devil comes and sets them ablaze.
THOMAS FULLER: *Gnomologia*, 1732

Man, woman and Devil are the three degrees of comparison. IBID.

There's not so bad a Jill,
But there's as bad a Will. IBID.

In men we various ruling passions find;
In women two almost divide the kind;
Those only fix'd, they first or last obey,
The love of pleasure and the love of sway.
ALEXANDER POPE: *Moral Essays*, II (Of the Characters of Women), 1735

It is the man and woman united that makes the complete human being. Separate, she wants his force of body and strength of reason; he, her softness, sensibility and acute discernment. Together, they are most likely to succeed in the world.
BENJAMIN FRANKLIN: *Letter to a young man*, June 25, 1745

No man is so much abstracted from common life as not to feel a particular pleasure from the regard of the female world.
SAMUEL JOHNSON: *The Rambler*, April 21, 1750

Man is born to be intellectual, thus to think from the understanding; woman is born to be voluntary, thus to think from the will.
EMANUEL SWEDENBORG: *Heaven and Hell*, 1758

Our sex's weakness you expose and blame,
Of every prating fop the common theme;
Yet from this weakness you suppose is due
Sublimer virtue than your Cato knew.
From whence is this unjust distinction shown?
Are we not formed with passions like your own?
Nature with equal fire our souls endued:
Our minds as lofty, and as warm our blood.
MARY WORTLEY MONTAGU: *Letter to James Steuart*, July 19, 1759

Humanity is the virtue of a woman, generosity of a man. The fair sex, who have commonly much more tenderness than ours, have seldom so much generosity.
ADAM SMITH: *The Theory of Moral Sentiments*, IV, 1759

But for her sex, a woman is a man; she has the same organs, the same needs, the same faculties. The machine is the same in its construction; its parts, its working, and its appearance are similar. Regard it as you will, the difference is only in degree.
J.-J. ROUSSEAU: *Émile*, V, 1762

Men speak of what they know; women of what pleases them. J.-J. ROUSSEAU: *Émile*, XI

Men of sense in all ages abhor those customs which treat us only as the vassals of your sex.
ABIGAIL ADAMS: *Letter to John Adams*, March 31, 1776

I am very tender-hearted on love-cases, especially to women, whose happiness does really depend, for some time at least, on the accomplishment of their wishes: they cannot conceive that another swain might be just as charming. I am not so indulgent to men, who do know that one romance is as good as another.
HORACE WALPOLE: *Letter to Horace Mann*, July 30, 1783

There's nought but care on every hand,
In every hour that passes, O;
What signifies the life o' man,
An 'twere na for the lasses, O?
ROBERT BURNS: *Green Grow the Rashes*, 1784

Women have a perpetual envy of our vices; they are less vicious than we, not from choice, but because we restrict them.
SAMUEL JOHNSON: *Boswell's Life*, June 10, 1784

Women trade with the weaknesses and follies of men, not with their reason.
NICOLAS CHAMFORT: *Maximes et pensées*, *c.* 1785

The two sexes mutually corrupt and improve each other.
MARY WOLLSTONECRAFT: *A Vindication of the Rights of Woman*, VIII, 1792

What is it men in women do require?
The lineaments of gratified desire.
What is it women do in men require?
The lineaments of gratified desire.
WILLIAM BLAKE: *A Question Answered*, *c.* 1793

Love is the history of a woman's life; it is only an episode in man's.
ANNA LOUISE DE STAËL: *De l'influence des passions*, 1796 (Cf. BYRON, *post*, 1819)

Without the smile from partial beauty won,
Oh! what were man! — a world without a sun.
THOMAS CAMPBELL: *The Pleasures of Hope*, II, 1799

A man may brave opinion; a woman must submit to it.
ANNA LOUISE DE STAËL: *Delphine*, motto, 1802

The old age of women is sadder and more lonely than that of men.
JEAN PAUL RICHTER: *Titan*, XXXIV, 1803 (Cf. STEELE, *ante*, 1710)

A woman's feeling for a man inferior to herself is pity rather than love.
ANNA LOUISE DE STAËL: *Corinne*, VI, 1807

It is necessary to the natural and social order that men should protect and women be protected. IBID.

The flower, I doubt not, receives a fair guerdon from the bee — its leaves blush deeper in the next Spring —, and who shall say between man and woman which is the most delighted?
JOHN KEATS: *Letter to J. H. Reynolds*, Feb. 19, 1818

Man's love is of man's life a thing apart,
'Tis woman's whole existence.
BYRON: *Don Juan*, I, 1819 (Cf. DE STAËL, *ante*, 1796)

Women do not transgress the bounds of decorum so often as men, but when they do they go greater lengths. For with reason somewhat weaker, they have to contend with passions somewhat stronger; besides, a female by one transgression forfeits her place in society forever; if once she falls, it is the fall of Lucifer.
C. C. COLTON: *Lacon*, 1820

A man and a woman make far better friendships than can exist between two of the same sex; but with this condition, that they never have made, or are to make, love with each other.
BYRON: *Letter to Lady ——*, Nov. 10, 1822

The man's desire is for the woman; but the woman's desire is rarely other than for the desire of the man.
S. T. COLERIDGE: *Table-Talk*, July 23, 1827

Let any woman, neither old nor ugly, and passing for modest, throw herself (as the phrase is) at any man's head she meets with, and she may set him down as her own from that time forward, unless he be either very wise or very stupid.
WILLIAM HAZLITT: *Coquettes*, 1829 (The Atlas, March 22)

Physically, a man is a man for a much longer time than a woman is a woman.
BALZAC: *The Physiology of Marriage*, 1830

A woman's head is usually over ears in her heart. Man seems to have been designed for the superior being of the two; but as things are, I think women are generally better creatures than men. They have, taken universally, weaker appetites and weaker intellects, but they have much stronger affections. A man with a bad heart has been sometimes saved by a strong head; but a corrupt woman is lost for ever.
S. T. COLERIDGE: *Table-Talk*, May 5, 1830

Women have a less accurate measure of time than men. There is a clock in Adam: none in Eve.
R. W. EMERSON: *Journal*, Feb. 8, 1836

Woman is the lesser man, and all thy passions, match'd with mine,
Are as moonlight unto sunlight, and as water unto wine.
ALFRED TENNYSON: *Locksley Hall*, 1842

No man is a match for a woman till he's married.
R. S. SURTEES: *Handley Cross*, LVII, 1843

Man's game for woman; fly where he will,
Over clover, grass or stubble,
She'll wing you, feather you, or kill,
Just as she takes the trouble.
Anon.: *Favorite album verses, c.* 1845

Man's fate and woman's are contending powers;
Each tries to dupe the other in the game.
E. G. BULWER-LYTTON: *The New Timon,* 1846

Man is the hunter; woman is his game; . . .
We hunt them for the beauty of their skins.
ALFRED TENNYSON: *The Princess,* V, 1847

In the long years liker must they grow;
The man be more of woman, she of man.
ALFRED TENNYSON: *The Princess,* VII

In their hearts all women believe that it is the business of men to earn money and their own to spend it — if possible, while their husbands live, but if not, then afterward.
ARTHUR SCHOPENHAUER: *Parerga und Paralipomena,* 1851

That women is by nature meant to obey may be seen by the fact that every woman who is placed in the unnatural position of complete independence immediately attaches herself to some man, by whom she allows herself to be guided and ruled. If she is young, it will be a lover; if she is old, a priest.
IBID.

As unto the bow the cord is,
So unto the man is woman;
Though she bends him she obeys him,
Though she draws him, yet she follows,
Useless each without the other.
H. W. LONGFELLOW: *Hiawatha,* X, 1855

For men must work, and women must weep,
And the sooner it's over, the sooner to sleep.
CHARLES KINGSLEY: *The Three Fishers,* 1856

A man is a great thing upon the earth and through eternity, but every jot of the greatness of man is unfolded out of woman;
First the man is shaped in the woman; he can then be shaped in himself.
WALT WHITMAN: *Unfolded Out of the Folds,* 1856

We sew, sew, prick our fingers, dull our sight,
Producing what? . . . A cushion, where you lean
And sleep, and dream of something we are not,
But would be for your sake.
E. B. BROWNING: *Aurora Leigh,* I, 1857

Men, the very best of men, can only suffer, while women can endure.
DINAH MULOCK CRAIK: *John Halifax, Gentleman,* 1857

Man has his will, — but woman has her way.
O. W. HOLMES: *The Autocrat of the Breakfast-Table,* I, 1858

Men, at most, differ as Heaven and earth,
But women, worst and best, as Heaven and Hell.
ALFRED TENNYSON: *Merlin and Vivien,* 1859

Most men and most women are merely one couple more.
R. W. EMERSON: *The Conduct of Life,* I, 1860

Men are deceived about women because they forget that they and women do not speak the same language.
H. F. AMIEL: *Journal,* Dec. 26, 1868

It is only a man here and there who has any tolerable knowledge of the character even of the women of his own family.
J. S. MILL: *The Subjection of Women,* I, 1869

Woman seems to differ from man in mental disposition, chiefly in her greater tenderness and less selfishness.
CHARLES DARWIN: *The Descent of Man,* XIX, 1871

A woman never forgets her sex. She would rather talk with a man than an angel, any day.
O. W. HOLMES: *The Poet at the Breakfast-Table,* IV, 1872

There are two kinds of moral law, two kinds of conscience, in man and woman, and they are altogether different. The two sexes do not understand each other. But in practical life, the woman is judged by man's law, as if she were a man, not a woman.
HENRIK IBSEN: *Notes for A Doll's House, made in Rome,* Oct. 19, 1878

After a quarrel between a man and a woman the man suffers chiefly from the thought that he has wounded the woman; the woman suffers from the thought that she has not wounded the man enough.
F. W. NIETZSCHE: *Human All-too-Human,* I, 1878

Men who do not make advances to women are apt to become victims to women who make advances to them.
WALTER BAGEHOT: *Biographical Studies,* 1880

Woman's dearest delight is to wound man's self-conceit, though man's dearest delight is to gratify hers.
GEORGE BERNARD SHAW: *An Unsocial Socialist,* V, 1883

Man is for woman a means: the end is always the child.
F. W. NIETZSCHE: *Thus Spake Zarathustra,* XVIII, 1885

In revenge as in love woman is always more barbarous than man.
F. W. NIETZSCHE: *Beyond Good and Evil,* 1886

The substance of our lives is woman. All other things are irrelevancies, hypocrisies, subterfuges. We sit talking of sports and politics, and all the while our hearts are filled with memories of women and the capture of women.

GEORGE MOORE: *Confessions of a Young Man*, IX, 1888

A male figure rises to the head, and is a symbol of the intelligence; a woman's figure sinks to the inferior parts of the body, and is expressive of generation.

GEORGE MOORE: *Confessions of a Young Man*, XIII

Woman is unspeakably more wicked than man, also cleverer. Goodness in woman is really nothing but a form of degeneracy.

F. W. NIETZSCHE: *Ecce Homo*, 1888

The Book of Life begins with a man and a woman in a garden. It ends with Revelation.

OSCAR WILDE: *A Woman of No Importance*, I, 1893

Hogamus higamus,
Men are polygamous,
Higamus hogamus,
Women monogamous.

Anon.: Doggerel in circulation in the American colleges, *c.* 1895

If every woman in the world was weeping her heart out, men would be found dining, feeding, feasting.

A. W. PINERO: *The Benefit of the Doubt*, I, 1895

All women become like their mothers. That is their tragedy. No man does. That is his.

OSCAR WILDE: *The Importance of Being Earnest*, I, 1895

The only way for a woman to provide for herself decently is for her to be good to some man that can afford to be good to her.

GEORGE BERNARD SHAW: *Mrs. Warren's Profession*, II, 1898

The whole world is strewn with snares, traps, gins and pitfalls for the capture of men by women.

GEORGE BERNARD SHAW: *Man and Superman*, epistle dedicatory, 1903

The maternal instinct leads a woman to prefer a tenth share in a first rate man to the exclusive possession of a third rate one.

GEORGE BERNARD SHAW: *Maxims for Revolutionists*, 1903

I may define man as a male human being and woman as a female human being. What the early Christians did was to strike the " male " out of the definition of man, and " human being " out of the definition of woman.

JAMES DONALDSON: *Woman*, 1907

What a woman most admires in a man is distinction among men. What a man most admires in a woman is devotion to himself.

AMBROSE BIERCE: *Collected Works*, VIII, 1911

There never lived a woman who did not wish she were a man. There never lived a man who wished he were a woman.

E. W. HOWE: *Country Town Sayings*, 1911

With women, men are the enemy; they abuse them as a nation abuses a people with whom it is at war, with old stories told in other wars.

IBID.

If a woman doesn't chase a man a little, she doesn't love him.

E. W. HOWE: *Sinner Sermons*, 1926

If the man is the head of the family, the woman is the heart, and as he occupies the chief place in ruling, so she may and ought to claim for herself the chief place in love.

POPE PIUS XI: *Casti connubii*, Dec. 31, 1930

If a man has sworn to injure you, you may sleep at night; if a woman, keep awake.

ARAB PROVERB

A man is as old as he feels; a woman is as old as she looks.

Author unidentified (The first half is borrowed from SENECA, *c.* 50)

A man's age commands veneration; a woman's demands tact.

IBID.

Friendship is impossible between a man and a woman, for, unless he becomes more than a friend she becomes less.

IBID.

The difference between a man and a woman is that a man looks forward, and a woman remembers.

IBID.

There is one thing common to both man and woman. Both exist exclusively for the happiness of the man.

IBID.

Women's faults are many,
Men have only two;
Everything they say,
And everything they do.

IBID.

Man is the head, but woman turns it.

CHESHIRE PROVERB

A woman can carry more out of a house in her apron than a man can bring in in a hay-cart.

DUTCH PROVERB

If you would understand man, study woman.

FRENCH PROVERB

Men make laws, women make manners.

IBID.

A woman without a man is like a garden without a fence.

GERMAN PROVERB

When men meet they listen; when women meet they look.

IBID.

A man comes into the world with a loaf of bread in his hand; a woman comes into the world with both hands empty.

HEBREW PROVERB

An old man in the house is a snare in the house; an old woman in the house is a treasure in the house. IBID.

In man mortal sins are venial; in woman venial sins are mortal. ITALIAN PROVERB

Love enters a man through his eyes; a woman, through her ears. POLISH PROVERB

Outdoors for man and dog; indoors for woman and cat. RUSSIAN PROVERB

He who has one woman has all women; he who has all women has no woman.
SPANISH PROVERB

[*See also* Age (Old), Awkwardness, Cannibalism, Chastity, Cigar, Clothes, Compliment, Conversation, Coquetry, Devil, Divorce, Drink, Enigma, Flattery, Forbidden, Friend, Generosity, Good and Bad, Hair, Hat, Letter, Life, Love, Lying, Male and Female, Man (Old), Misfortune, Modesty, Monogamy, Opposites, Pain, Praise, Sleep, Telling, Unchastity, Virtue.

Manchuria

Manchuria produces two products: soya beans and bandits. CHINESE PROVERB

Mandarin

[*See* Eminence.

Manila, Battle of (May 1, 1898)

[*See* Dewey (George).

Mankind

How beauteous mankind is! O brave new world
That has such people in it.
SHAKESPEARE: *The Tempest*, v, 1611

If we lived upon the moon and were not men, but rational creatures, could we imagine such fantastical beings as mankind? Could we have any idea of so strange a compound of foolish passions and wise reflections?
BERNARD DE FONTENELLE: *Entretiens sur la pluralité des mondes*, II, 1686

He who deals with mankind on the square,
Is his own bubble, and undoes himself.
GEORGE LILLO: *Fatal Curiosity*, I, 1736

I hate mankind with all the fury of an old maid. Indeed, most women of my age do.
MARY WORTLEY MONTAGU: *Letter to James Steuart*, Nov. 27, 1759

[*See also* Humanity, Man, Man and Woman, Passion.

Manliness

I will have only those glorious manly pleasures of being very drunk and very slovenly.
WILLIAM WYCHERLEY: *The Country Wife*, I, *c.* 1673

Not fortune's worshipper, nor fashion's fool,
Not lucre's madman, nor ambition's tool,
Not proud nor servile, be one poet's praise
That, if he pleased, he pleased by manly ways.
ALEXANDER POPE: *An Epistle to Dr. Arbuthnot*, 1735

[*See also* Deeds.

Manner

It is not ill-bred to adopt a high manner with the great and powerful, but it is vulgar to lord it over humble people.
ARISTOTLE: *The Nicomachean Ethics*, IV, *c.* 340 B.C.

Suit your manner to the man.
TERENCE: *Adelphi*, III, *c.* 160 B.C.

A man's natural manner best becomes him.
CICERO: *De officiis*, I, 78 B.C.

I am native here,
And to the manner born.
SHAKESPEARE: *Hamlet*, I, *c.* 1601

A bad manner spoils everything, even reason and justice.
BALTASAR GRACIÁN: *The Art of Worldly Wisdom*, XIV, 1647

In everything the manner is fully as important as the matter.
LORD CHESTERFIELD: *Letter to his son*, Nov. 19, 1750

My lords, we are vertebrate animals, we are mammalia! My learned friend's manner would be intolerable in Almighty God to a black beetle.
Ascribed to various English lawyers, protesting against the hectoring of opponents at the bar

Manner, Bedside

[*See* Doctor.

Manners

It is good manners which make the excellence of a neighborhood. No wise man will settle where they are lacking.
CONFUCIUS: *Analects*, IV, *c.* 500 B.C.

Evil communications corrupt good manners.
MENANDER: *Moyostikhoi*, *c.* 300 B.C. (Cf. I CORINTHIANS XV, *post*, *c.* 55)

Manners go on deteriorating.
PLAUTUS: *Mercator*, *c.* 200 B.C.

Oh, the times! oh, the manners! (O tempora! O mores!)
CICERO: *Oration in Catalinam*, *c.* 50 B.C. (*Mores* may also mean morals)

Evil communications corrupt good manners.
I CORINTHIANS XV, 33, *c.* 55 (Cf. MENANDER, *ante*, *c.* 300 B.C.)

What once were vices are now manners.
SENECA: *Epistulæ morales ad Lucilium*, *c.* 63

Do you expect a mother to teach her children manners which differ from her own?
JUVENAL: *Satires*, VI, 116

Manners make the man.

ENGLISH PROVERB, traced by Smith to *c.* 1350 (" Manners maketh man " was the motto of WILLIAM OF WYKEHAM, Bishop of Winchester and Chancellor of England, 1324–1404)

Foul words corrupt good manners.

JOHN PALSGRAVE: *L'éclaircissement de la langue française,* 1530

As laws are necessary that good manners may be preserved, so good manners are necessary that laws may be maintained.

NICCOLÒ MACHIAVELLI: *Discorsi,* I, 1531

A man by nothing is so well bewrayed
As by his manners.

EDMUND SPENSER: *The Faerie Queene,* VI, *c.* 1589 (*Bewray*=reveal)

Gentle blood will gentle manners breed.

IBID.

Among a man's equals a man shall be sure of familiarity, and therefore it is good a little to keep state; among a man's inferiors a man shall be sure of reverence, and therefore it is good a little to be familiar.

FRANCIS BACON: *Essays,* III, 1597

Those that are good manners at the court are as ridiculous in the country as the behavior of the country is mockable at the court.

SHAKESPEARE: *As You Like It,* III, *c.* 1600

Fit for the mountains and the barb'rous caves,
Where manners ne'er were preach'd.

SHAKESPEARE: *Twelfth Night,* IV, *c.* 1601

Men's evil manners live in brass: their virtues
We write in water.

SHAKESPEARE and JOHN FLETCHER: *Henry VIII,* IV, 1613

You must practise
The manners of the time if you intend
To have favor from it.

PHILIP MASSINGER: *The Unnatural Combat,* I, 1639

Manners know distance.

ROBERT HERRICK: *Hesperides,* 1648

To sleep when others speak, to sit when others stand, to walk on when others stay, to speak when one should hold his peace, or hear others, are all things of ill manners.

FRANCIS HAWKINS: *Youth's Behavior,* I, 1663

Being set at the table, scratch not thy self, and take thou heed as much as thou canst to spit, cough, and to blow at thy nose; but if it be needful, do it dexterously without much noise, turning thy face sideling.

FRANCIS HAWKINS: *Youth's Behavior,* VII

Manners make often fortunes.

JOHN RAY: *English Proverbs,* 1670

It is impolite to hold the fork, the knife, or the spoon raised in the hand, to make motions with any of those things, to carry a piece of bread to the mouth with the knife, to make use at the same time of the spoon and fork, to wipe them with the tongue, or to thrust them into the mouth. Nothing is more impolite than to lick the fingers.

ST. JOHN BAPTIST DE LA SALLE: *The Rules of Christian Manners and Civility,* II, 1695

Our manners, like our faces, though ever so beautiful, must differ in their beauty.

ANTHONY A. COOPER (EARL OF SHAFTESBURY): *Characteristics of Men, Manners, Opinions, Times,* III, *c.* 1713

Good manners is the art of making those people easy with whom we converse. Whoever makes the fewest persons uneasy is the best bred in the company.

JONATHAN SWIFT: *A Treatise on Good Manners and Good Breeding, c.* 1720

" After you " is good manners.

JAMES KELLY: *Complete Collection of Scottish Proverbs,* 1721

Manners and money make a gentleman.

THOMAS FULLER: *Gnomologia,* 1732

Never seem wiser or more learned than the people you are with.

LORD CHESTERFIELD: *Letter to his son,* Feb. 22, 1748

Manners must adorn knowledge and smooth its way through the world.

LORD CHESTERFIELD: *Letter to his son,* July 1, 1748

At play and at fire it's good manners to give place to the last comer, and affect not to speak louder than ordinary.

GEORGE WASHINGTON: *Early copy-book,* before 1748

Good manners are, to particular societies, what good morals are to society in general: their cement and their security.

LORD CHESTERFIELD: *Letter to his son,* Nov. 3, 1749

Manners speak the idiom of their soil.

THOMAS GRAY: *The Alliance of Education and Government, c.* 1750

There is one rule relative to behavior that ought to regulate every other; and it is simply to cherish such an habitual respect for mankind as may prevent us from disgusting a fellow-creature for the sake of a present indulgence.

MARY WOLLSTONECRAFT: *A Vindication of the Rights of Woman,* VIII, 1792

Manners are of more importance than laws. Upon them, in a great measure, the laws depend. The law touches us but here and there, and now and then. Manners are what vex or soothe, corrupt or purify, exalt or debase, barbarize or refine us, by a constant, steady,

uniform, insensible operation, like that of the air we breathe in.
EDMUND BURKE: *Letters on a Regicide Peace*, I, 1797

The manners of every nation are standard of orthodoxy within itself. But these standards being arbitrary, reasonable people in all allow free toleration for the manners, as for the religion, of others.
THOMAS JEFFERSON: *Letter to Jean Baptiste Say*, 1815

He was the mildest manner'd man
That ever scuttled ship or cut a throat.
BYRON: *Don Juan*, III, 1821

The manners of all nations are equally bad.
JOHN WILSON: *Noctes Ambrosianæ*, XXXIX, 1822

In the days of old
Men made the manners; manners now make men.
BYRON: *Don Juan*, XV, 1824

There are men whose manners have the same essential splendor as the simple and awful sculpture on the friezes of the Parthenon.
R. W. EMERSON: *History*, 1841

One man lies in his work, and gets a bad reputation; another in his manners, and enjoys a good one.
H. D. THOREAU: *Journal*, June 25, 1852

A contrivance of wise men to keep fools at a distance.
R. W. EMERSON: *The Conduct of Life*, V, 1860 (Quoted from an unnamed source)

Manners are the happy ways of doing things.
IBID.

Good manners are made up of petty sacrifices.
R. W. EMERSON: *Letters and Social Aims*, 1875

The stately manners of the old school.
H. W. LONGFELLOW: *Michael Angelo*, I, 1883

Manners before morals.
OSCAR WILDE: *Lady Windermere's Fan*, IV, 1892

Never pick your nose or your ear save with your elbow.
CHINESE PROVERB

Other times, other manners. (Autres temps, autres mœurs.)
FRENCH PROVERB

Good manners are better than good birth.
MOROCCAN PROVERB

One learns manners from those who have none.
PERSIAN PROVERB

[*See also* Brain, Civility, Classes, Company, Corruption, Courtesy, Fashion, Honors, Knowledge, Lady, Man and Woman, Politeness, Times, Well-bred.

Man, Old

Thou shalt rise up before the hoary head, and honor the face of the old man.
LEVITICUS XIX, 32, *c.* 700 B.C.

The race of old men is naturally hasty, choleric and impatient of control.
EURIPIDES: *Andromache*, *c.* 427 B.C.

An old man is but a voice and a shadow.
EURIPIDES: *Fragment*, *c.* 425 B.C.

Old men have more regard for expediency than for honor.
ARISTOTLE: *Rhetoric*, II, *c.* 322 B.C.

No man is ever so old but he thinks he can live another year.
CICERO: *De senectute*, VII, *c.* 78 B.C.

You must begin to be an old man early if you wish to be an old man long.
CICERO: *De senectute*, XX

Aged men [should] be sober, grave, temperate, sound in faith, in charity, in patience.
TITUS II, 2, *c.* 60

When a man sees his skin wrinkled and his hair white, and has looked upon the sons of his sons, he may abandon wife and family, go to the forest, and abandon himself to religious exercises.
THE CODE OF MANU, VI, *c.* 100

Old men all look alike.
JUVENAL: *Satires*, X, *c.* 125

An old man and a cripple, what can I do but praise God?
Ascribed to ARRIAN (*c.* 96–*c.* 180)

Auld men will die, and bairns will soon forget.
Anon.: *Black-Letter Ballads*, *c.* 1570

Care keeps his watch in every old man's eye.
SHAKESPEARE: *Romeo and Juliet*, II, *c.* 1596

Have you not a moist eye, a dry hand, a yellow cheek, a white beard, a decreasing leg, an increasing belly? Is not your voice broken, your wind short, your chin double, your wit single, and every part about you blasted with antiquity?
SHAKESPEARE: *II Henry IV*, I, *c.* 1598

Lord, Lord, how subject we old men are to the vice of lying!
SHAKESPEARE: *II Henry IV*, III

The sixth age shifts
Into the lean and slipper'd pantaloon,
With spectacles on nose and pouch on side,
His youthful hose, well saved, a world too wide
For his shrunk shank; and his big manly voice,
Turning again toward childish treble, pipes
And whistles in his sound.
SHAKESPEARE: *As You Like It*, II, *c.* 1600

Last scene of all,
That ends this strange eventful history,
Is second childishness and mere oblivion,

Sans teeth, sans eyes, sans taste, sans everything. IBID.

An old man is twice a child.
SHAKESPEARE: *Hamlet*, II, *c.* 1601

The satirical rogue says here that old men have gray beards; that their faces are wrinkled; their eyes purging thick amber and plum-tree gum; and that they have a plentiful lack of wit, together with most weak hams.
IBID.

Pray do not mock me:
I am a very foolish, fond old man,
Fourscore and upward.
SHAKESPEARE: *King Lear*, IV, 1606

Men of age object too much, consult too long, adventure too little, repent too soon, and seldom drive business home to the full period, but content themselves with a mediocrity of success.
FRANCIS BACON: *Essays*, XLII, 1625

Young I was, but now am old,
But I am not yet grown cold;
I can play, and I can twine
'Bout a virgin like a vine:
In her lap too I can lie
Melting, and in fancy die:
And return to life, if she
Claps my cheek, or kisseth me;
Thus, and thus it now appears
That our love outlasts our years.
ROBERT HERRICK: *Hesperides*, 1648

Before a man comes to be wise he is half dead with gouts and consumption, with catarrhs and aches, with sore eyes and a worn-out body.
JEREMY TAYLOR: *The Rule and Exercises of Holy Dying*, I, 1651

An old man is a bed full of bones.
JOHN RAY: *English Proverbs*, 1670

Old men are only walking hospitals.
WENTWORTH DILLON (EARL OF ROSCOMMON): Tr. of HORACE: *De arte poetica* (*c.* 8 B.C.), 1680

Most men in years, as they are generally discouragers of youth, are like old trees that, being past bearing themselves, will suffer no young plants to flourish beneath them.
ALEXANDER POPE: *Letter to William Wycherley*, March 25, 1705

Old men and comets have been reverenced for the same reason: their long beards, and pretenses to foretell events.
JONATHAN SWIFT: *Thoughts on Various Subjects*, 1706

When men grow virtuous in their old age they are merely making a sacrifice to God of the Devil's leavings. IBID.

Old men are soon angry.
THOMAS FULLER: *Gnomologia*, 1732

Every old man complains of the growing depravity of the world, of the petulance and insolence of the rising generation.
SAMUEL JOHNSON: *The Rambler*, Sept. 8, 1750

Man can have only a certain number of teeth, hair and ideas; there comes a time when he necessarily loses his teeth, hair and ideas.
VOLTAIRE: *Philosophical Dictionary*, 1764

A man grows better humored as he grows older.
SAMUEL JOHNSON: *Boswell's Tour to the Hebrides*, Sept. 15, 1773

There is a wicked inclination in most people to suppose an old man decayed in his intellects. If a young or middle-aged man, when leaving a company, does not recollect where he laid his hat, it is nothing; but if the same inattention is discovered in an old man people will shrug up their shoulders and say: "His memory is going."
SAMUEL JOHNSON: *Boswell's Life*, 1783

I hold it a prudery becoming old men (the reverse of that of old women) not to trouble myself about or censure the frolics of the young.
HORACE WALPOLE: *Letter to the Countess of Upper Ossory*, Sept. 6, 1787

John Anderson my jo, John,
When we were first acquent,
Your locks were like the raven,
Your bonnie brow was brent;
But now your brow is beld, John,
Your locks are like the snaw;
But blessings on your frosty pow,
John Anderson my jo.
ROBERT BURNS: *John Anderson*, 1790
(*Brent*=unwrinkled; *beld*=bald; *pow*=head)

He's always compleenin' frae mornin' to e'enin',
He hoasts and he hirples the weary day lang;
He's doyl't and he's dozin', his bluid it is frozen,
O dreary's the night wi' a crazy auld man!
ROBERT BURNS: *What Can a Young Lassie?*, 1792 (*Hoast*=to cough; *hirple*=to limp)

Good wishes are all an old man has to offer to his country or his friends.
THOMAS JEFFERSON: *Letter to Thomas Law*, 1811

Old men are testy, and will have their way.
P. B. SHELLEY: *The Cenci*, I, 1819

An old man, like a spider, can never make love without beating his own deathwatch.
C. C. COLTON: *Lacon*, 1820

An old man never wants a tale to tell.
H. G. BOHN: *Handbook of Proverbs*, 1855

A man in old age is like a sword in a shop window. H. W. BEECHER: *Life Thoughts*, 1858

A person is always startled when he hears himself seriously called an old man for the first time.

O. W. HOLMES: *The Autocrat of the Breakfast-Table*, x, 1858

We do not count a man's years until he has nothing else to count.

R. W. EMERSON: *Society and Solitude*, 1870

Don't you stay at home of evenings?
Don't you love a cushioned seat
In a corner, by the fireside, with your slippers on your feet?
Don't you wear warm fleecy flannels?
Don't you muffle up your throat?
Don't you like to have one help you when you're putting on your coat?

O. W. HOLMES: *The Archbishop and Gil Blas*, 1879 (Read at the annual meeting of the Harvard class of 1829, Jan. 6)

Love for an old man is sunlight on the snow: it dazzles more than it warms.

Author unidentified

An old man loved is Winter with flowers.

GERMAN PROVERB

It is useless to physic the dead or to advise an old man. GREEK PROVERB

[*See also* Age (Old), Man and Woman, Superannuation, Woman (Old), Youth and Age.

Man, Primitive

Some lived by spoil, some like brute beasts grazed upon the ground, some went naked, some roamed like woodwoses, none did anything by reason, but most did what they could by manhood.

THOMAS WILSON: *The Arte of Rhetorique*, 1553 (*Woodwose*=a satyr or faun)

Mansion

In my Father's house are many mansions.

JOHN XIV, 2, *c.* 115

Man, Young

The eyes of young men are curious and penetrating, their imaginations are of a roving nature, and their passion under no discipline or restraint.

JOSEPH ADDISON: *The Guardian*, July 6, 1713

[*See also* Youth and Age.

Manual Training

The first thing obvious to children is what is sensible; and that we make no part of their rudiments. We press their memory too soon, and puzzle, strain and load them with words and rules, to know grammar and rhetoric, and a strange tongue or two, that it is ten to one may never be useful to them, leaving their natural genius to mechanical and physical or natural knowledge uncultivated and neglected, which would be of exceeding use and pleasure to them through the whole course of their lives.

WILLIAM PENN: *Fruits of Solitude*, 1693

Manufactures

My idea is that we should encourage home manufactures to the extent of our own consumption of everything of which we raise the raw material.

THOMAS JEFFERSON: *Letter to David Humphreys*, 1809

[*See also* Laissez-faire.

Many

Many men, many minds. (Quot homines, tot sententiæ.)

TERENCE: *Phormio*, II, *c.* 160 B.C.

Many be called, but few are chosen.

MATTHEW XX, 16, *c.* 75

Many strokes overthrow the tallest oak.

JOHN LYLY: *Euphues*, 1579

Many a little makes a mickle.

WILLIAM CAMDEN: *Remains Concerning Britain*, 1605

Many heads are better than one.

JAMES KELLY: *Complete Collection of Scottish Proverbs*, 1721

He who commences many things finishes but few.

H. G. BOHN: *Handbook of Proverbs*, 1855

It takes many drops to make a lake.

ARMENIAN PROVERB

Marathon, Battle of (490 B.C.)

That man is little to be envied whose patriotism would not gain force upon the plain of Marathon.

SAMUEL JOHNSON: *A Journey to the Western Islands of Scotland*, 1775

Marble

Marble is eminently a solid and massive substance. Unless you want mass and solidity, don't work in marble. If you wish for lightness, take wood; if for freedom, take stucco; if for ductility, take glass.

JOHN RUSKIN: *The Two Paths*, v, 1859

The discovery of marble quarries gave the Greeks the opportunity for that intensified vitality of action, that more sensuous and simple humanism, to which the Egyptian sculptor working laboriously in the hard porphyry and rose-colored granite of the desert could not attain.

OSCAR WILDE: *The English Renaissance of Art*, 1882 (Lecture in New York, Jan. 9)

[*See also* Rome.

March

One bushel of March dust is worth a king's ransom.

JOHN HEYWOOD: *A Play of the Weather*, 1533

Beware the ides of March.
SHAKESPEARE: *Julius Cæsar*, I, 1599

March comes in like a lion and goes out like a lamb.
ENGLISH PROVERB, apparently first quoted in print in JOHN FLETCHER: *A Wife for a Month*, 1624

March brings breezes loud and shrill,
Stirs the dancing daffodil.
SARA COLERIDGE: *Pretty Lessons in Verse*, 1834

The bleak wind of March
Made her tremble and shiver.
THOMAS HOOD: *The Bridge of Sighs*, 1846

Who in this world of ours their eyes
In March first open shall be wise;
In days of peril firm and brave,
And wear a bloodstone to their grave.
Author unidentified

[*See also* February, Flea, Months, Thunder.

Marching

Mountains are worse obstacles in marching than rivers.
NAPOLEON I: To Gaspard Gourgaud at St. Helena, 1815–1818

Marching along, fifty-score strong,
Great-hearted gentlemen, singing this song.
ROBERT BROWNING: *Cavalier Tunes*, I, 1842

Mare

The gray mare is the better horse.
JOHN HEYWOOD: *Proverbs*, 1546 (Gray Flemish mares were much esteemed in England in the XVI century)

Mare's nest.
ENGLISH PHRASE, traced by Smith to 1582

The old gray mare, she ain't what she used to be.
American popular song, *c.* 1880

Margin

In getting my books, I have been always solicitous of an ample margin; this not so much through any love of the thing itself, however agreeable, as for the facility it affords me of penciling suggested thoughts, agreements, and differences of opinion, or brief critical comments in general.
E. A. POE: *Marginalia*, 1844–49

Marine

Tell that to the marines — the sailors won't believe it.
WALTER SCOTT: *Redgauntlet*, XIII, 1824 (Quoted as a saying)

'E isn't one o' the reg'lar line, nor 'e isn't one of the crew;
'E's a kind of a giddy harumfrodite — soldier an' sailor too.
RUDYARD KIPLING: *Soldier an' Sailor Too*, 1892

Mark

God save the mark.
SHAKESPEARE: *I Henry IV*, I, *c.* 1598

Mark Antony (83–30 B.C.)

As Helen was to the Trojans, so has that man been to this republic — the cause of war, the cause of mischief, the cause of ruin.
CICERO: *Second Oration Against Mark Antony*, 44 B.C.

Market

Good ware makes quick markets.
NICHOLAS BRETON: *Crossing of Proverbs*, 1616

The market is the best garden.
GEORGE HERBERT: *Outlandish Proverbs*, 1640

A man must sell his ware after the rates of the market.
JOHN RAY: *English Proverbs*, 1670

Game is cheaper in the market than in the fields and woods.
THOMAS FULLER: *Gnomologia*, 1732

Three women and a goose make a market.
ITALIAN PROVERB

If fools never went to market bad goods would never be sold.
SPANISH PROVERB

Two women make a market; three make a fair.
UKRAINIAN PROVERB

The market-house is the women's courthouse.
WEST INDIAN PROVERB

[*See also* Game.

Marlowe, Christopher (1564–93)

Marlowe was happy in his buskin Muse —
Alas, unhappy in his life and end;
Pity it is that wit so ill should dwell,
Wit lent from Heaven, but vices sent from Hell.
Anon.: *The Return from Parnassus*, 1606

Marlowe's mighty line.
BEN JONSON: *To the Memory of My Beloved, the Author Mr. William Shakespeare* (in the First Folio Shakespeare), 1623

[*See also* Atheist.

Marriage

It is not good that the man should be alone; I will make him a help meet for him.
GENESIS II, 18, *c.* 700 B.C.

Let them marry to whom they think best; only to the family of the tribe of their father shall they marry.
NUMBERS XXXVI, 6, *c.* 700 B.C.

Marry in the Springtime of thy life, neither much above or below the age of thirty. Thy wife should be a virgin in her nineteenth year.
HESIOD: *Works and Days*, *c.* 700 B.C.

Marriage lies at the bottom of all government.
CONFUCIUS: *The Book of Rites*, XXIV, *c.* 500 B.C.

It is best by far to marry in one's own class.
ÆSCHYLUS: *Prometheus Bound, c.* 490 B.C.

A man, though he be gray-haired, can always get a wife. But a woman's time is short.
ARISTOPHANES: *Lysistrata,* 411 B.C.

The age of eighteen is the best time for women to marry, and the age of thirty-seven, or a little less, for men.
ARISTOTLE: *Politics,* VII, *c.* 322 B.C.

He who would marry is on the road to repentance. PHILEMON: *Fragment, c.* 310 B.C.

Marriage, to tell the truth, is an evil, but it is a necessary evil.
MENANDER: *Fragment, c.* 300 B.C.

The first bond of society is marriage; the next, children; then the family.
CICERO: *De officiis,* I, 78 B.C.

It is mind, not body, that makes marriage last.
PUBLILIUS SYRUS: *Sententiæ, c.* 50 B.C.

If thou wouldst marry wisely, marry thy equal.
OVID: *Heroides,* IX, *c.* 10

To avoid fornication, let every man have his own wife, and let every woman have her own husband. I CORINTHIANS VII, 2, *c.* 55

It is better to marry than to burn.
I CORINTHIANS VII, 9

If thou marry, thou hast not sinned; and if a virgin marry, she hath not sinned. Nevertheless such shall have trouble in the flesh: but I spare you. I CORINTHIANS VII, 28

He that is married careth for the things that are of the world, how he may please his wife.
I CORINTHIANS VII, 33

She that is married careth for the things of the world, how she may please her husband.
I CORINTHIANS VII, 34

For this cause shall a man leave his father and mother, and shall be joined unto his wife, and they two shall be one flesh.
EPHESIANS V, 31, *c.* 60

I will therefore that the younger women marry, bear children, guide the house, give none occasion to the adversary to speak reproachfully. I TIMOTHY V, 14, *c.* 60

Marriage is honorable in all.
HEBREWS XIII, 4, *c.* 65

What therefore God hath joined together, let not man put asunder.
MARK X, 9, *c.* 70 (Cf. MATTHEW XIX, 6 *c.* 75)

When they shall rise from the dead, they neither marry, nor are given in marriage; but are as the angels which are in heaven.
MARK XII, 25, *c.* 70 (Cf. XXII, 30, *c.* 75; LUKE XX, 35; usually misquoted: "In Heaven there is neither marriage nor giving in marriage")

If you are really devoted to one woman, then bow your head and yield your neck to the yoke. JUVENAL: *Satires,* VI, 116

Let the wedlock of the faithful be a rivalry in continence.
POPE XYSTUS I: *The Ring, c.* 150

It is better to marry only because it is worse to burn. It is still better neither to marry nor to burn. TERTULLIAN: *Ad uxorem, c.* 205

The Apostle Paul is a witness that marriage is for the sake of generation. "I wish," he says, "young women to marry." And, as if some one asked him why, he adds immediately: "to bear children, to be the mothers of families."
ST. AUGUSTINE: *On the Good of Marriage, c.* 401 (Cf. I TIMOTHY V, 14, *ante, c.* 60)

Marriage is not a good, but it is a good in comparison with fornication. IBID.

I praise wedlock, I praise marriage; but it is because they produce me virgins.
ST. JEROME: *The Virgin's Profession, c.* 420

Renounce marriage, and imitate the angels.
JOHN OF DAMASCUS: *Dialectica, c.* 730

Better be an old man's darling than a young man's slave.
ENGLISH PROVERB, current since the XVI century

To hang or wed: both hath an hour;
And whether it be, I am well sure
Hanging is better of the twain:
Sooner done, and shorter pain.
Anon.: *The Schoolhouse for Women,* 1541

He that weddeth ere he be wise shall die ere he thrive. JOHN HEYWOOD: *Proverbs,* 1546

More things belong [to marriage] than four bare legs in a bed. IBID.

Whoever saith that marriage is to be put above virginity or celibacy, and that it is not more blessed to remain chaste than to marry, let him be anathema.
Decree of the Council of Trent, XXIV, 1564

Marry in haste, repent at leisure.
ENGLISH PROVERB, traced by Apperson to 1566

No man is so virtuous as to marry a wife only to have children.
MARTIN LUTHER: *Table-Talk,* CCLVII, 1569

The state of matrimony is the chief in the world after religion; but people shun it because of its inconveniences, like one who, running out of the rain, falls into the river.
MARTIN LUTHER: *Table-Talk,* DCCXXI

On what pretence can man have interdicted marriage, which is a law of nature? 'Tis as though we were forbidden to eat, to drink, to sleep. 'Tis the most certain sign of God's

enmity to popedom, that He has allowed it to assail the conjugal union of the sexes.
MARTIN LUTHER: *Table-Talk,* DCCXXVIII

I have seen marriages where, at first, husband and wife seemed as though they would eat one another up: in six months they have separated in mutual disgust. 'Tis the Devil inspires this evanescent ardor, in order to divert the parties from prayer.
MARTIN LUTHER: *Table-Talk,* DCCXXXII

Amongst all the bonds of benevolence and goodwill there is none more honorable, ancient or honest than marriage.
GEORGE PETTIE: *Petite Palace of Pettie His Pleasure,* 1576

In marriage the husband should have two eyes, and the wife but one.
JOHN LYLY: *Euphues and His England,* 1580

Marriages are made in Heaven. IBID.

A good marriage (if there be any) refuseth the company and conditions of love; it endeavoreth to present those of amity. It is a sweet society of life, full of constancy, of trust, and an infinite number of profitable and solid offices, and mutual obligations.
MICHEL DE MONTAIGNE: *Essays,* III, 1588

She's not well married that lives married long,
But she's best married that dies married young.
SHAKESPEARE: *Romeo and Juliet,* IV, *c.* 1596

Hanging and wiving go by destiny.
SHAKESPEARE: *The Merchant of Venice,* II, *c.* 1597 (Quoted as " the ancient saying ")

Men are April when they woo, December when they wed; maids are May when they are maids, but the sky changes when they are wives.
SHAKESPEARE: *As You Like It,* IV, *c.* 1600

I will marry her, sir, at your request; but if there be no great love in the beginning, yet Heaven may decrease it upon better acquaintance. I hope, upon familiarity will grow more contempt; I will marry her, that I am freely dissolved, and dissolutely.
SHAKESPEARE: *The Merry Wives of Windsor,* I, *c.* 1600

If thou wilt needs marry, marry a fool.
SHAKESPEARE: *Hamlet,* III, *c.* 1601

A young man married is a man that's marred.
SHAKESPEARE: *All's Well that Ends Well,* II, *c.* 1602

The nun is kept in cloister, not the wife:
Wedlock alone doth make the virgin free.
JOHN DAVIES: *A Contention betwixt a Wife, a Widow, and a Maid,* 1602

Wedlock indeed hath oft comparèd been
To public feasts, where meet a public rout;
Where they that are without would fain go in,
And they that are within would fain go out.
IBID.

Marriage is but a ceremonial toy.
CHRISTOPHER MARLOWE: *Dr. Faustus,* II, 1602

Oh, curse of marriage,
That we can call these delicate creatures ours,
And not their appetites! I had rather be a toad,
And live upon the vapor of a dungeon,
Than keep a corner in the thing I love
For others' uses.
SHAKESPEARE: *Othello,* III, 1604

Age and wedlock lames man and beast.
WILLIAM CAMDEN: *Remains Concerning Britain,* 1605

Reverend and honorable matrimony,
Mother of lawful sweets, unshamed mornings,
Dangerless pleasures!
THOMAS MIDDLETON: *The Phoenix,* II, 1607

That ever man should marry! For one Hypermnestra that saved her lord and husband, forty-nine of her sisters cut their husbands' throats all in one night.
JOHN WEBSTER: *The White Devil,* V, *c.* 1608

Let me not to the marriage of true minds
Admit impediments.
SHAKESPEARE: *Sonnets,* CXVI, 1609

Nothing is more natural than to marry.
MR. CHIEF JUSTICE HOBART: *Judgment in Sheffield* vs. *Ratcliffe,* 1617

One was never married, and that's his hell; another is, and that's his plague.
ROBERT BURTON: *The Anatomy of Melancholy,* I, 1621

Hast thou any mind to marriage?
We'll provide thee some soft-natured wench,
that's dumb too.
JOHN FLETCHER: *The Wild-Goose Chase,* I, 1621

To all married men be this a caution:
Neither to dote too much, nor doubt a wife.
PHILIP MASSINGER: *The Picture,* V, 1630

Married once,
A man is staked or poun'd, and cannot graze
Beyond his own hedge.
PHILIP MASSINGER and NATHANIEL FIELD: *The Fatal Dowry,* IV, 1632

How like a lottery these weddings are.
BEN JONSON: *A Tale of a Tub,* I, 1633

The sum of all that makes a just man happy
Consists in the well-choosing of his wife:
And there, well to discharge it, does require
Equality of years, of birth, of fortune.
PHILIP MASSINGER: *A New Way to Pay Old Debts,* IV, 1633

First thrive and then wive.
JOHN CLARKE: *Parœmiologia Anglo-Latina,* 1639

Like blood, like goods, and like age,
Makes the happiest marriage. IBID.

Advise none to marry or go to war.
GEORGE HERBERT: *Outlandish Proverbs*, 1640

He that marries for wealth sells his liberty.
IBID.

Marriage is a school and exercise of virtue.
JEREMY TAYLOR: *The Mysteriousness of Marriage*, 1651

Marriage hath in it less of beauty, but more of safety than the single life; it hath more care, but less danger; it is more merry, and more sad; is fuller of sorrows, and fuller of joys: it lies under more burdens, but is supported by all the strengths of love and charity, and those burdens are delightful.
JEREMY TAYLOR: *Twenty-seven Sermons*, XVII, 1651

Honest men marry, but not wise ones.
ENGLISH PROVERB, traced by Apperson to 1659

The holy state of matrimony was ordained by Almighty God in Paradise, before the Fall of Man, signifying to us that mystical union between Christ and His Church; and so it is the first relation; and when two persons are joined in that holy state, they twain become one flesh, and so it is the nearest relation.
MR. JUSTICE HYDE: *Judgment in Manby* vs. *Scott*, 1659

To have and to hold from this day forward, for better, for worse, for richer, for poorer, in sickness and in health, to love and to cherish, till death us do part.
THE BOOK OF COMMON PRAYER (*The Solemnization of Holy Marriage*), 1662 (This is the man's vow; in the woman's " and to obey " follows " to cherish ")

There may be good, but there are no pleasant marriages.
LA ROCHEFOUCAULD: *Maxims*, 1665

Hail, wedded love! mysterious law, true source
Of human offspring, sole propriety,
In Paradise of all things common else.
JOHN MILTON: *Paradise Lost*, IV, 1667

For what thou art is mine:
Our state cannot be sever'd; we are one,
One flesh; to lose thee were to lose myself.
JOHN MILTON: *Paradise Lost*, IX

Marriage is good for nothing but to make friends fall out.
THOMAS SHADWELL: *The Sullen Lovers*, II, 1668

One year of joy, another of comfort, and all the rest of content.
JOHN RAY: *English Proverbs*, 1670 (Described as " a marriage wish ")

When a couple are newly married, the first month is honeymoon or smick smack; the second is hither and thither; the third is thwick thwack; the fourth, the Devil take them that brought thee and I together.
IBID.

I am to be married within these three days; married past redemption.
JOHN DRYDEN: *Marriage à la Mode*, I, 1672

'Tis my maxim, he's a fool that marries; but he's a greater that does not marry a fool.
WILLIAM WYCHERLY: *The Country Wife*, I, *c.* 1673

Of all actions of a man's life, his marriage does least concern other people; yet of all actions of our life, 'tis most meddled with by other people. JOHN SELDEN: *Table-Talk*, 1689

Marriage is a desperate thing. The frogs in Æsop were extreme wise; they had a great mind to some water, but they would not leap into the well, because they could not get out again. IBID.

The happiness of married life depends upon making small sacrifices with readiness and cheerfulness. IBID.

By day 'tis nothing but an endless noise;
By night the echo of forgotten joys:
Ye gods! that man by his own slavish law,
Should on himself such inconvenience draw.
Anon.: *Against Marriage*, *c.* 1690

Every man plays the fool once in his life, but to marry is playing the fool all one's life long.
WILLIAM CONGREVE: *The Old Bachelor*, III, 1693

Never marry but for love, but see that thou lov'st what is lovely.
WILLIAM PENN: *Fruits of Solitude*, 1693

There is a poor sordid slavery in marriage that turns the flowing tide of honor, and sinks it to the lowest ebb of infamy. 'Tis a corrupted soil; ill-nature, avarice, sloth, cowardice and dirt are all its product.
JOHN VANBRUGH: *The Provok'd Wife*, I, 1697

If I were married to a hogshead of claret, matrimony would make me hate it.
JOHN VANBRUGH: *The Provok'd Wife*, II,

Tho' marriage be a lottery in which there are a wondrous many blanks, yet there is one inestimable lot in which the only heaven on earth is written.
JOHN VANBRUGH: *The Provok'd Wife*, V

Marry first, and love will come afterwards.
Anon.: *Poor Robin's Almanac*, 1699 (Quoted as a proverb)

Wedlock is hell if at least one side does not love.
RICHARD STEELE: *The Funeral*, I, 1701

I don't think matrimony consistent with the liberty of the subject.

GEORGE FARQUHAR: *The Twin Rivals*, V, 1702

The reason why so few marriages are happy is because young ladies spend their time in making nets, not in making cages.

JONATHAN SWIFT: *Thoughts on Various Subjects*, 1706

Venus, a beautiful, good-natured lady, was the goddess of love; Juno, a terrible shrew, the goddess of marriage: and they were always mortal enemies. IBID.

Grave authors say and witty poets sing
That honest wedlock is a glorious thing.

ALEXANDER POPE: *January and May*, 1709

The common design of parents is to get their girls off as well as they can, and they make no conscience of putting into our hands a bargain for our whole life which will make our hearts ache every day of it.

RICHARD STEELE: *The Tatler*, Nov. 9, 1710

Those marriages generally abound most with love and constancy that are preceded by a long courtship.

JOSEPH ADDISON: *The Spectator*, Dec. 29, 1711

Marriage enlarges the scene of our happiness and miseries. A marriage of love is pleasant; a marriage of interest easy; and a marriage where both meet, happy. A happy marriage has in it all the pleasures of friendship, all the enjoyments of sense and reason; and indeed all the sweets of life. IBID.

Very few people that have settled entirely in the country, but have grown at length weary of one another. The lady's conversation generally falls into a thousand impertinent effects of idleness; and the gentleman falls in love with his dogs and his horses, and out of love with everything else.

MARY WORTLEY MONTAGU: *Letter to Edward Wortley Montagu*, shortly before their marriage on Aug. 12, 1712

They dream in courtship, but in wedlock wake.

ALEXANDER POPE: *The Wife of Bath*, 1714

Do you think your mother and I should have lived comfortably so long together if ever we had been married?

JOHN GAY: *The Beggar's Opera*, I, 1728

Be not hasty to marry; it's better to have one plow going than two cradles; and more profit to have a barn filled than a bed.

THOMAS FULLER: *Introductio ad Prudentiam*, II, 1731

Keep thy eyes wide open before marriage; and half shut afterward. IBID.

He that is needy when he is married,
Shall not be rich when he is buried.

THOMAS FULLER: *Gnomologia*, 1732

It is hard to wive and thrive both in a year. IBID.

She that marries ill never wants something to say for it. IBID.

Where there's marriage without love, there will be love without marriage.

BENJAMIN FRANKLIN: *Poor Richard's Almanac*, 1734

I believe it will be found that those who marry late are best pleased with their children, and those who marry early with their partners.

SAMUEL JOHNSON: *Rasselas*, 1759

I do not . . . pretend to have discovered that life has any thing more to be desired than a prudent and virtuous marriage.

SAMUEL JOHNSON: *Boswell's Life*, Dec. 21, 1762

Men and women, in marrying, make a vow to love one another. Would it not be better for their happiness if they made a vow to please one another?

STANISLAUS LESZCZYNSKI (KING OF POLAND): *Œuvres du philosophe bienfaisant*, 1763

"Lo! here's the bride, and there's the tree,
Take which of these best liketh thee."
"The bargain's bad on either part —
But, hangman, come — drive on the cart."

Anon.: *The Festoon*, 1767

It is so far from being natural for a man and woman to live in a state of marriage that we find all the motives which they have for remaining in that connection, and the restraints which civilized society imposes to prevent separation, are hardly sufficient to keep them together.

SAMUEL JOHNSON: *Boswell's Life*, March 31, 1772

'Tis safest in matrimony to begin with a little aversion.

R. B. SHERIDAN: *The Rivals*, II, 1775

I believe marriages would in general be as happy, and often more so, if they were all made by the Lord Chancellor, upon a due consideration of the characters and circumstances, without the parties having any choice in the matter.

SAMUEL JOHNSON: *Boswell's Life*, March 22, 1776

Marriage is the best state for man in general; and every man is a worse man in proportion as he is unfit for the married state. IBID.

Zounds! madam, you had no taste when you married me!

R. B. SHERIDAN: *The School for Scandal*, II, 1777

Nine unhappy marriages in ten spring from faults on the husband's side. Women acquire liberty by marrying, find themselves happier than they were, and love the author.

HORACE WALPOLE: *Letter to George Hardinge*, July 9, 1777

It is clear that marriage, even in the state of nature and certainly long before it was raised to the dignity of a sacrament, was divinely instituted in such a way that it should be a perpetual and indissoluble bond, which cannot therefore be dissolved by any civil law.

POPE PIUS VI: *Rescript to the Bishop of Agria*, 1789

Love without marriage is like a bird of passage alight upon the mast of a ship at sea. For my part, I prefer a fine green tree with its own roots, and room in its branches for a nest.

JEAN PAUL RICHTER: *Titan*, CXXV, 1803

Taught by care, the patient man and wife
Agree to share the bitter-sweet of life.

GEORGE CRABBE: *The Parish Register*, II, 1807

What man of sense can marriage-rites approve?
What man of spirit can be bound to love?
Forced to be kind! compell'd to be sincere!
Do chains and fetters make companions dear?

GEORGE CRABBE: *Tales*, II (*The Gentleman Farmer*), 1812

A system could not well have been devised more studiously hostile to human happiness than marriage.

P. B. SHELLEY: *Queen Mab*, notes, 1813

The best thing a woman can do is to marry. It appears to me that even quarrels with one's husband are preferable to the ennui of a solitary existence.

ELIZABETH PATTERSON BONAPARTE: *Letter to Lady Charles Morgan*, Aug. 11, 1817 (Elizabeth Patterson married Jerome Bonaparte Dec. 24, 1803; he deserted her in 1805)

The roaring of the wind is my wife and the stars through the window pane are my children. The mighty abstract idea I have of beauty in all things stifles the more divided and minute domestic happiness.

JOHN KEATS: *Letter to George and Georgiana Keats*, Oct. 21, 1818

Wishing each other, not divorced, but dead;
They live respectably as man and wife.

BYRON: *Don Juan*, I, 1819

Marriage is a feast where the grace is sometimes better than the dinner.

C. C. COLTON: *Lacon*, 1820

When a man marries, dies, or turns Hindu,
His best friends hear no more of him.

P. B. SHELLEY: *Letter to Maria Gisborne*, July 1, 1820

All tragedies are finish'd by a death,
All comedies are ended by a marriage.

BYRON: *Don Juan*, III, 1821

I knew a very interesting Italian lady last Winter, but now she is married.

P. B. SHELLEY: *Letter to T. J. Hogg*, Oct. 22, 1821

Marriage by its best title is a monopoly, and not of the least invidious sort.

CHARLES LAMB: *A Bachelor's Complaint of the Behavior of Married People*, 1822 (London Magazine, Sept.)

Marriage was instituted by God himself for the purpose of preventing promiscuous intercourse of the sexes, for promoting domestic felicity, and for securing the maintenance and security of children.

NOAH WEBSTER: *An American Dictionary of the English Language*, 1828

No man should marry until he has studied anatomy and dissected at least one woman.

BALZAC: *The Physiology of Marriage*, 1830

Some people believe in a decree, viz., that God has determined in all cases that particular men and women should be married to each other, and that it is impossible they should marry any other person. But I say, hush! for if that be the case, then God appoints all matches; but I believe the Devil appoints a great many.

LORENZO DOW: *Reflections on Matrimony*, 1833

The marriage vow is an absurdity imposed by society.

ARMANTINE DUDEVANT (GEORGE SAND): *Jacques*, 1834

The most happy marriage I can picture or imagine to myself would be the union of a deaf man to a blind woman.

S. T. COLERIDGE: *Allsop's Letters, Conversations, and Recollections of S. T. Coleridge*, 1836

There is no condition (evil as it may be in the eye of reason) which does not include, or seem to include, when it has become familiar, some good, some redeeming or reconciling qualities. I agree, however, that marriage is not one of these. IBID.

Whatever woman may cast her lot with mine, should any ever do so, it is my intention to do all in my power to make her happy and contented; and there is nothing I can imagine that would make me more unhappy than to fail in the effort.

ABRAHAM LINCOLN: *Letter to Mary S. Owens*, May 7, 1837

I have come to the conclusion never again to think of marrying, and for this reason: I can never be satisfied with anyone who would be blockhead enough to have me.

ABRAHAM LINCOLN: *Letter to Mrs. O. H. Browning*, April 1, 1838

Nothing new here except my marrying, which to me is a matter of profound wonder.

ABRAHAM LINCOLN: *Letter to Samuel Marshall*, Nov. 11, 1842

Two we are, and one we'll be,
If you consent to marry me.
Anon.: *Favorite album verses, c.* 1845

Needles and pins, needles and pins,
When a man marries his trouble begins.
J. O. HALLIWELL-PHILLIPPS: *Nursery Rhymes and Nursery Tales of England,* 1845

Advice to persons about to marry — Don't.
HENRY MAYHEW: *Mr. Punch's Almanac,* 1845

Neither sex alone
Is half itself, and in true marriage lies
Nor equal, nor unequal: each fulfills
Defect in each, and always thought in thought,
Purpose in purpose, will in will, they grow,
The single pure and perfect animal.
ALFRED TENNYSON: *The Princess,* VII, 1847

Marriage is the life-long miracle,
The self-begetting wonder, daily fresh.
CHARLES KINGSLEY: *The Saint's Tragedy,* II, 1848

Our bourgeois, not content with having the wives and daughters of the proletarians at their disposal, not to speak of common prostitutes, take the greatest pleasure in seducing one another's wives. Bourgeois marriage is in reality a system of wives in common.
KARL MARX and FRIEDRICH ENGELS: *The Communist Manifesto,* 1848

As to marriage, I think the intercourse of heart and mind may be fully enjoyed without entering into this partnership of daily life.
MARGARET FULLER OSSOLI: *Letter to her sister,* 1848

A woman with fair opportunities, and without an absolute hump, may marry whom she likes.
W. M. THACKERAY: *Vanity Fair,* I, 1848

Remember, it's as easy to marry a rich woman as a poor woman.
W. M. THACKERAY: *Pendennis,* XXVIII, 1849

Age and wedlock tame man and beast.
H. G. BOHN: *Handbook of Proverbs,* 1855

Where one is wise, two are happy. IBID.

Never marry unless you can do so into a family that will enable your children to feel proud of both sides of the house.
ROBERT E. LEE: To John B. Hood, at Camp Cooper, Tex., 1856

It doesn't much signify whom one marries, for one is sure to find next morning that it was someone else.
SAMUEL ROGER: *Table-Talk,* 1856

Marriage must be a relation either of sympathy or of conquest.
MARIAN EVANS (GEORGE ELIOT): *Romola,* XLVIII, 1863

Marriage is neither Heaven nor Hell. It is simply Purgatory.
Ascribed to ABRAHAM LINCOLN, 1864 (Cf. LINCOLN, *ante,* 1837, 1838, 1842)

Marriage by its very nature is subject to the regulation of the civil power.
Proposition condemned by POPE PIUS IX: *Syllabus of Errors,* LXXIV, Dec. 8, 1864

Marriage is something you have to give your whole mind to.
HENRIK IBSEN: *The League of Youth,* IV, 1869

What marriage may be in the case of two persons of cultivated faculties, identical in opinions and purposes, between whom there exists that best kind of equality, similarity of powers and capacities with reciprocal superiority in them, so that each can enjoy the luxury of looking up to the other, and can have alternatively the pleasure of leading and of being led in the path of development — I will not attempt to describe.
J. S. MILL: *The Subjection of Women,* IV, 1869

Every woman should marry — and no man.
BENJAMIN DISRAELI: *Lothair,* XXX, 1870

Man scans with scrupulous care the character and pedigree of his horses, cattle, and dogs before he matches them; but when he comes to his own marriage he rarely, or never, takes any such care.
CHARLES DARWIN: *The Descent of Man,* XXI, 1871

Marriage iz a fair transaction on the face ov it. But thare iz quite too often put up jobs in it.
H. W. SHAW (JOSH BILLINGS): *Josh Billings' Encyclopedia of Wit and Wisdom,* 1874

Marriage is the most inviolable and irrevocable of all contracts that were ever formed. Every human compact may be lawfully dissolved but this.
JAMES CARDINAL GIBBONS: *The Faith of Our Fathers,* XXXI, 1876

In marriage, talk occupies most of the time.
F. W. NIETZSCHE: *Human All-too-Human,* I, 1878

Marriage was not instituted by man, but by God.
POPE LEO XIII: *Arcanum divinæ sapientiæ,* Feb. 10, 1880

When Christianity is rejected, marriage inevitably sinks into the slavery of man's vile passions. IBID.

In marriage a man becomes slack and selfish, and undergoes a fatty degeneration of his moral being.
R. L. STEVENSON: *Virginibus Puerisque,* I, 1881

Pleasant the snaffle of courtship, improving the manners and carriage.

But the colt who is wise will abstain from the terrible thorn-bit of marriage.
RUDYARD KIPLING: *Certain Maxims of Hafiz,* 1886

A married philosopher is a comic character.
F. W. NIETZSCHE: *The Genealogy of Morals,* III, 1887

Marriage — what an abomination! Love — yes, but not marriage. Love cannot exist in marriage, because love is an ideal; that is to say, something not quite understood — transparencies, color, light, a sense of the unreal. But a wife — you know all about her — who her father was, who her mother was, what she thinks of you and her opinion of the neighbors over the way.
GEORGE MOORE: *Confessions of a Young Man,* VII, 1888

It's an experiment
Frequently tried.
W. S. GILBERT: *The Gondoliers,* II, 1889

No human law can abolish the natural and inherent right of marriage, or limit in any way its chief and principal purpose, ordained by God from the beginning, which is to increase and multiply.
POPE LEO XIII: *Rerum novarum,* May 15, 1891

A more or less durable connection between male and female lasting beyond the mere act of propagation till after the birth of the offspring.
EDWARD WESTERMARCK: *The History of Human Marriage,* I, 1891

A man can be happy with any woman as long as he does not love her.
OSCAR WILDE: *The Picture of Dorian Gray,* 1891

The one charm of marriage is that it makes a life of deception necessary for both parties.
IBID.

Now, if you must marry, take care she is old —
A troop-sergeant's widow's the nicest I'm told —
For beauty won't help if your vittles is cold.
RUDYARD KIPLING: *The Young British Soldier,* 1892

The world has grown suspicious of anything that looks like a happy married life.
OSCAR WILDE: *Lady Windermere's Fan,* II, 1892

Twenty years of romance make a woman look like a ruin, but twenty years of marriage make her something like a public building.
OSCAR WILDE: *A Woman of No Importance,* I, 1893

The happiness of a married man depends on the people he has not married.
OSCAR WILDE: *A Woman of No Importance,* II

Women have become so highly educated that nothing should surprise them except happy marriages.
IBID.

Men marry because they are tired, women because they are curious; both are disappointed.
OSCAR WILDE: *A Woman of No Importance,* III

In married life three is company and two is none.
OSCAR WILDE: *The Importance of Being Earnest,* I, 1895

It is a woman's business to get married as soon as possible, and a man's to keep unmarried as long as he can.
GEORGE BERNARD SHAW: *Man and Superman,* II, 1903

Marriage is possible because it combines the maximum of temptation with the maximum of opportunity.
GEORGE BERNARD SHAW: *Maxims for Revolutionists,* 1903

The state or condition of a community consisting of a master, a mistress and two slaves, making in all, two.
AMBROSE BIERCE: *The Devil's Dictionary,* 1906

They stood before the altar and supplied
The fire themselves in which their fat was fried.
IBID.

An exclusive relation of one or more men to one or more women, based on custom, recognized and supported by public opinion, and where law exists, by law.
LORD AVEBURY: *Marriage, Totems and Religion,* 1911

A bad marriage is like an electrical thrilling machine: it makes you dance, but you can't let go.
AMBROSE BIERCE: *Collected Works,* VIII, 1911

The greatest sacrifice in marriage is the sacrifice of the adventurous attitude toward life: the being settled.
GEORGE BERNARD SHAW: *Androcles and the Lion,* pref., 1912

The primary end of marriage is the procreation and education of children.
THE CODE OF CANON LAW, MXIII, May 19, 1918

A marriage is likely to be what is called happy if neither party ever expected to get much happiness out of it.
BERTRAND RUSSELL: *Marriage and Morals,* X, 1929

The more civilized people become the less capable they seem of lifelong happiness with one partner.
IBID.

The sanctity of the institution of marriage and the home shall be upheld. Pictures shall not infer that low forms of sex relationship are the accepted or common thing.
A CODE TO GOVERN THE MAKING OF MOTION AND TALKING PICTURES BY THE MOTION PICTURE PRODUCERS AND DISTRIBUTORS OF AMERICA, INC., II, March 31, 1930

By holy matrimony the souls of the contracting parties are joined and knit together more directly and intimately than their bodies, not by any passing whim of either sense or spirit but by a deliberate act of the will, and from this union of souls by God's decree a sacred and inviolable bond arises.
POPE PIUS XI: *Casti connubii,* Dec. 31, 1930

To be entirely happy in marriage, the same thing must be important to both.
MARIE OF RUMANIA: *The Story of My Life,* 1934

Marriage is not made for everybody, nor attractive to everybody, nor good for everybody who embarks on it.
EDWARD WESTERMARCK: *The Future of Marriage in Western Civilization,* 1936

It is better for a woman to marry a man who loves her than a man she loves.
ARAB PROVERB

Bigamy is having one wife too many. Monogamy is the same. Author unidentified

It begins with a prince kissing an angel. It ends with a baldheaded man looking across the table at a fat woman. IBID.

Love is the star men look up to as they walk along, and marriage is the coal-hole they fall into. IBID.

Marriage is a condition that most women aspire to and most men submit to. IBID.

Marriage is a public confession of a private intention. IBID.

Marriage is a romance in which the hero dies in the first chapter. IBID.

Marriage is not a word but a sentence. IBID.

Marriage makes two one — but which one?
IBID.

The gods gave man fire, and man invented fire engines. They gave him love, and he invented marriage. IBID.

A man should marry a woman half his age, plus seven years. CHINESE SAYING

Take no notice of what you hear said on the pillow. IBID.

In marrying and taking pills it is best not to think about it too much. DUTCH PROVERB

To marry once is a duty; twice, foolishness; thrice, lunacy. IBID.

Love is the flower; marriage is the fruit.
FINNISH PROVERB

Love makes passion, but money makes marriage. FRENCH PROVERB

Marriage means to eat and drink and sleep together. IBID.

Marriage puts every one in his place. IBID.

He who marries changes. GERMAN PROVERB

If you want a good year, marry; if you want two, refrain. IBID.

Maidenhood is sun, chastity moon, and marriage night. IBID.

Marriage is a school in which the pupil learns too late. IBID.

Marriage is fever in reverse: it starts with heat and ends with cold. IBID.

Marriage is Heaven and Hell. IBID.

Marriage is the hospital of love. IBID.

The bachelor is a peacock, the engaged man a lion, and the married man a jackass.
IBID.

Wedlock, woe. (Ehestand, Wehestand.)
IBID.

When God wants to punish a man He makes him think of marriage. IBID.

Marriage is the only evil that man pray for.
GREEK PROVERB

If you marry at all, marry last year.
IRISH PROVERB

It is lucky to marry when the moon is full and when the tide is high. IBID.

Take a vine of good soil, and the daughter of a good mother ITALIAN PROVERB

The tie of marriage. (Vinculum matrimonii.)
LATIN PHRASE

Consent, not cohabitation, constitutes marriage. (Consensus, non concubitus, facit matrimonium.) LEGAL MAXIM

The presumption is always in favor of the validity of a marriage. (Semper præsumitur pro matrimonio.) IBID.

Always marry a short woman; her clothes will cost you less. MOROCCAN PROVERB

My little old man and I fell out.
I'll tell you what 'twas all about;
I had money and he had none,
And that's the way the row begun.
Nursery rhyme

O mother, I shall be married
To Mr. Punchinello,
To Mr. Punch,
To Mr. Joe,

To Mr. Nell,
To Mr. Lo,
Mr. Punch, Mr. Joe,
Mr. Nell, Mr. Lo,
To Mr. Punchinello. IBID.

Before going to war say a prayer; before going to sea say two; before getting married say three. POLISH PROVERB

There were two brothers who were smart and a third who got married. IBID.

Marriage is the tomb of love. RUSSIAN PROVERB

No matter how fiery love may be, it is cooled by marriage. IBID.

A dish o' married love grows soon cauld. SCOTTISH PROVERB

A man may woo where he will, but he will wed where his hap is. IBID.

He that married a beggar gets a louse for a tocher. IBID. (*Tocher*=dowry)

Ne'er marry a penniless maiden that's proud o' her pedigree. IBID.

Bachelor, a peacock; betrothed, a lion; married, a donkey. SPANISH PROVERB

For a woman marriage consists of spinning, bearing children, and crying. IBID.

He who marries at a distance either deceives or is deceived. IBID.

He who marries badly becomes a widower late. IBID.

Marriage is reaching into a bag of snakes in the hope of catching an eel. IBID.

If you are married on Monday or Wednesday, you will have a miserable wedded life. YIDDISH PROVERB

[*See also* Advice, Bride, Bridegroom, Celibacy, Chastity, Comedy, Courtship, Custom, Cynic, Dancing, Daughter, Divorce, Endogamy, Funeral, Hanging, Haste, Housekeeping, Husband, Husband and Wife, Hysteria, Jealousy, Lent, Living, Love, Man and Woman, Marriage (Early), Marriage (Late), Marriage (Second), May, Monogamy, Mother-in-law, Nihilism, No, Poverty, Priest, Teetotaler, Virgin, Virginity, Wedding, Wedding-day, Widow, Wife, Wooing.

Marriage Bell

[*See* Merriment.

Marriage, Early

A child's birds and a boy's wife are well used.
JOHN RAY: *English Proverbs,* 1670

Honest men marry soon; wise men not at all. IBID.

Early marriage, long love. GERMAN PROVERB

Marry very young, or become a monk very young. MODERN GREEK PROVERB

[*See also* Marriage.

Marriage, Late

He that marries late marries ill.
ENGLISH PROVERB, quoted as " common " by Thomas Nashe, 1589

Now he in Charon's barge a bride doth seek.
JOSEPH HALL (BISHOP OF NORWICH): *Virgidemarium,* IV, 1598

It is good to marry late, or never.
JOHN CLARKE: *Parœmiologia Anglo-Latina,* 1639

They that marry ancient people, merely in expectation to bury them, hang themselves, in hope that one will come and cut the halter.
THOMAS FULLER: *The Holy State and the Profane State,* III, 1642

Grave authors say, and witty poets sing,
That honest wedlock is a glorious thing,
But depth of judgment most in him appears
Who wisely weds in his maturer years.
ALEXANDER POPE: *January and May,* 1709

Ye guardian powers of love and fame,
This chaste, harmonious pair behold;
And thus reward the generous flame
Of all who barter vows for gold.
O bloom of youth! O tender charms!
Well-buried in a dotard's arms.
MARK AKENSIDE: *To a Gentleman Whose Mistress Had Married an Old Man,* 1745

Old men, when they marry young women, are said to make much of death.
SAMUEL RICHARDSON: *Clarissa,* IV, 1748

A childless old man . . . may prefer a boy born in his own house, though he knows it not his own, to disrespectful or worthless nephews or nieces.
MARY WORTLEY MONTAGU: *Letter to the Countess of Bute,* May 22, 1759

When an ancient gentleman marries, it is his best excuse that he wants a nurse.
HORACE WALPOLE: *Letter to Mary Berry,* Sept. 30, 1789

So two sere trees, dry, stunted, and unsound,
Each other catch, when dropping to the ground;
Entwine their wither'd arms 'gainst wind and weather,
And shake their leafless heads and drop together.
GEORGE CRABBE: *The Parish Register,* II, 1807

A young woman married to an old man must behave like an old woman.
H. G. BOHN: *Handbook of Proverbs,* 1855

When men marry late they love their Autumn child with a twofold affection, — father's and grandfather's both in one.
O. W. HOLMES: *The Guardian Angel*, IV, 1867

At the marriage of an old man, death laughs.
GERMAN PROVERB

A young wife is an old man's post-horse to the grave. IBID.

A young wife is an old man's ticket to Hell.
IBID.

A late marriage is always somewhat shameful.
IBID.

[*See also* Marriage.

Marriage, Mixed

Everywhere and with the greatest strictness the Church forbids marriage between baptized persons, one of whom is a Catholic and the other a member of a schismatical or heretical sect. If there is any danger of the falling away of the Catholic party and the perversion of the children such a marriage is forbidden by the divine law also.
THE CODE OF CANON LAW, MLX, May 19, 1918

Marriage, Second

A woman who marries a second time forgets her dead husband and his children.
HOMER: *Odyssey*, XV, *c.* 800 B.C.

The wife is bound by the law as long as her husband liveth; but if her husband be dead, she is at liberty to be married to whom she will; only in the Lord.
I CORINTHIANS VII, 39, *c.* 55

The younger widows, . . . when they have begun to wax wanton against Christ, they will marry. I TIMOTHY V, 11, *c.* 60

First marriages are of better desert than second.
ST. AUGUSTINE: *On the Good of Widowhood*, *c.* 413

The instances that second marriage move
Are base respects of thrift, but none of love.
SHAKESPEARE: *Hamlet*, III, *c.* 1601

He loves his bonds who, when the first are broke,
Submits his neck unto a second yoke.
ROBERT HERRICK: *Hesperides*, 1648

He that marries a widow and three children marries four thieves.
JOHN RAY: *English Proverbs*, 1670

Importunate suspicions are the usual fruits of a second marriage.
JEAN RACINE: *Phèdre*, II, 1677

No pious Christian ought to marry twice.
ALEXANDER POPE: *The Wife of Bath*, 1714

Women who have been happy in a first marriage are most apt to venture upon a second.
JOSEPH ADDISON: *The Drummer*, II, 1715

The triumph of hope over experience.
SAMUEL JOHNSON: *Boswell's Life*, 1770 (Collectanea of the Rev. Dr. Maxwell)

Second marriages, unless the first one has been dissolved by death, are crimes.
POPE LEO XIII: *Arcanum divinæ sapientiæ*, Feb. 10, 1880

There's no cure for laziness, but I've known a second wife to hurry it some.
H. W. SHAW (JOSH BILLINGS): Lecture at San Francisco, 1885

When a man makes a mistake in his first marriage the victim is his second wife.
Author unidentified

He who has not married a second time is never really poor. CHINESE PROVERB

Marriage, Trial

Give us a set term and a set marriage, that we may find out if we are fit for the great marriage.
F. W. NIETZSCHE: *Thus Spake Zarathustra*, LVI, 1885

Mars

[*See* Gods.

Marshal

[*See* Soldier.

Marshall, John (1755–1835)

His twistifications in the case of Marbury, in that of Burr, and the Yazoo case show how dexterously he can reconcile law to his personal biases.
THOMAS JEFFERSON: *Letter to James Madison*, 1810

A crafty chief judge, who sophisticates the law to his mind by the turn of his own reasoning.
THOMAS JEFFERSON: *Letter to Thomas Ritchie*, 1820

Martyrdom

The blood of the martyrs is the seed of the Church.
Adapted from TERTULLIAN: *Apologeticus*, 197: "Semen est sanguis Christianorum" — The blood of Christians is seed

The ashes of martyrs drive away demons.
ST. JOHN CHRYSOSTOM: *Homilies*, VIII, *c.* 388

As for me, I have no inclination to risk my life for the truth. . . . Popes and emperors must settle the creeds. If they settle them well, so much the better; if ill, I shall keep on the safe side.
DESIDERIUS ERASMUS: *Letter to Archbishop Warham of Canterbury*, *c.* 1500

It is not the suffering but the cause which makes a martyr.
ENGLISH PROVERB, traced by Smith to 1644

There's no religion so irrational but can boast its martyrs.

JOSEPH GLANVILL: *The Vanity of Dogmatizing*, XIV, 1661

Th' Egyptians worshipp'd dogs, and for
Their faith made fierce and zealous war.
Others ador'd a rat, and some
For that church suffer'd martyrdom.

SAMUEL BUTLER: *Hudibras*, I, 1663

There are three kinds of martyrdom, the first both in will and deed, which is the highest; the second in will but not in deed; the third in deed but not in will. The church commemorates these martyrs in the same order: St. Stephen first, who suffered death both in will and deed; St. John the Evangelist next, who suffered in will but not in deed; the Holy Innocents last, who suffered in deed but not in will.

CHARLES WHEATLY: *The Church of England Man's Companion*, V, 1710

The only method by which religious truth can be established is by martyrdom.

SAMUEL JOHNSON: *Boswell's Life*, May 7, 1773

I am very fond of truth, but not at all of martyrdom.

VOLTAIRE: *Letter to Jean le Rond D'Alembert*, Feb., 1776

He that dies a martyr proves that he was not a knave, but by no means that he was not a fool.

C. C. COLTON: *Lacon*, 1820

The martyrs to vice far exceed the martyrs to virtue, both in endurance and in number.

IBID.

They never fail who die
In a great cause: the block may soak their gore;
Their heads may sodden in the sun; their limbs
Be strung to city gates and castle walls —
But still their spirit walks abroad.

BYRON: *Marino Faliero*, II, 1821

Those corpses of young men,
Those martyrs that hang from the gibbets — those hearts pierc'd by the gray lead,
Cold and motionless as they seem, live elsewhere with unslaughter'd vitality.

WALT WHITMAN: *Europe*, 1850

A pale martyr in his shirt of fire.

ALEXANDER SMITH: *A Life Drama*, II, 1853

The torments of martyrdoms are probably most keenly felt by the bystanders. The torments are illusory. The first suffering is the last suffering, the later hurts being lost on insensibility.

R. W. EMERSON: *Courage*, 1877

The disciples of a martyr suffer much more than the martyr.

F. W. NIETZSCHE: *Human All-too-Human*, I, 1878

Tortured for the republic. (Strangulatus pro republica.)

JAMES A. GARFIELD: Said to have been written, in Latin, on his deathbed, 1882

Blood is the worst of all testimonies to the truth.

F. W. NIETZSCHE: *Thus Spake Zarathustra*, II, 1885

It is so little true that martyrs offer any support to the truth of a cause that I am inclined to deny that any martyr has ever had anything to do with the truth at all.

F. W. NIETZSCHE: *The Antichrist*, LIII, 1888

A thing is not necessarily true because a man dies for it.

OSCAR WILDE: *The Portrait of Mr. W. H.*, 1889

[*See also* Admiration, Blood, Danger.

Marvel

A man likes marvelous things; so he invents them, and is astonished.

E. W. HOWE: *Sinner Sermons*, 1926

Marx, Karl (1818–83)

I thank you for the honor which you have done me by sending me your great work on "Capital."

CHARLES DARWIN: *Letter to Karl Marx*, Oct. 1, 1873

Mankind is now shorter by a head. It has lost the greatest head of our time.

FRIEDRICH ENGELS: *Letter to Sorge*, March 15, 1883, the day after Marx's death

Karl Marx was a mighty prophet.

GEORGE BERNARD SHAW: Address in New York, April 11, 1933

Marxism

The most important element in the foundation of Marxism is the materialistic interpretation of history. With it Marxism stands or falls.

EDWARD BERNSTEIN: *Evolutionary Socialism*, I, 1899

[*See also* Leninism.

Mary

[*See* Virgin Mary.

Maryland

Rivers, Heaven and earth never agreed better to frame a place for man's habitation, were it fully manured and inhabited by industrious people.

JOHN SMITH: *General Historie of Virginia*, VI, 1624

Here the Roman Catholic and the Protestant Episcopal, whom the world would persuade have proclaimed open wars against each other, contrariwise concur in an unanimous parallel of friendship.

GEORGE ALSOP: *The Character of the Province of Maryland*, 1666

Maryland, my Maryland.

JAMES RYDER RANDALL: Title of a song, 1861 (The familiar tune is that of the German song, "O Tannenbaum")

Mask

Beauty masked, like the sun in eclipse, gathers together more gazers than if it shined out.
WILLIAM WYCHERLEY: *The Country Wife,* II, *c.* 1673

Mason

[*See* Freemason.

Mass

No priest, no mass.
ENGLISH PROVERB, first recorded in the XVI century

The mass is the greatest blaspheming of God, and the highest idolatry upon earth, an abomination the like to which has never been in Christendom since the time of the Apostles.
MARTIN LUTHER: *Table-Talk,* CLXXI, 1569

No law can be made to oblige curates to say mass every day; for such a law would expose them to the danger of saying it sometimes in mortal sin.
ETIENNE BAUMY: *The Summary of Sins,* 1633

The performance of high mass . . . must impress every mind, where a spark of fancy glows, with that awful melancholy, that sublime tenderness, so near akin to devotion.
MARY WOLLSTONECRAFT: *A Vindication of the Rights of Woman,* XII, 1792

Many a rascal has attended regularly at mass, and many a good man has never gone at all.
P. B. SHELLEY: *Address to the Irish People,* 1812

The mass was nearly over. I staid to the end, wondering that so many reasonable beings could come together to see a man bow, drink, bow again, wipe a cup, wrap up a napkin, spread his arms, and gesticulate with his hands; and to hear a low muttering which they could not understand, interrupted by the occasional jingling of a bell.
T. B. MACAULAY: *Diary,* Lyons, Oct. 28, 1838

The lasses of Havana ride to mass in coaches yellow,
But ere they go they ask if the priest's a handsome fellow.
GEORGE BORROW: Tr. of a Spanish song, *El Punto de la Vana* (*Wild Wales,* L), 1862

A copper coin in the plate, a copper mass.
GERMAN PROVERB

A mass is just as good said as sung.
ITALIAN PROVERB

[*See also* White.

Massachusetts

Sir, I confess it: the first public love of my heart is the Commonwealth of Massachusetts.
JOSIAH QUINCY: Speech in the House of Representatives, Jan. 14, 1811

I shall enter on no encomium upon Massachusetts; she needs none. There she is. Behold her, and judge for yourselves. There is her history; the world knows it by heart.
DANIEL WEBSTER: Speech in the Senate, Jan. 26, 1831

Have faith in Massachusetts!
CALVIN COOLIDGE: Speech in the State Senate, Jan. 7, 1914

Massacre

Go ye after him through the city, and smite: let not your eye spare, neither have ye pity; slay utterly old and young, both maids, and little children.
EZEKIEL IX, 5–6, *c.* 600 B.C.

Masses

[*See* Mob, Multitude, People, Populace, Public, Rabble, Slavery.

Master

The eyes and footsteps of the master are the things that most benefit the land.
COLUMELLA: *De re rustica,* IV, *c.* 70

No man can serve two masters.
MATTHEW VI, 24, *c.* 75

The choice and master spirits of this age.
SHAKESPEARE: *Julius Cæsar,* III, 1599

No man is his craft's master the first day.
JOHN CLARKE: *Parœmiologia Anglo-Latina,* 1639

Where every man is master the work goes to wrack.
IBID.

To be ruled by weaker people, to have a fool for one's master, is the fate of miserable and unblessed people.
JEREMY TAYLOR: *The Mysteriousness of Marriage,* 1651

Masters should be sometimes blind and sometimes deaf.
THOMAS FULLER: *Gnomologia,* 1732

The eye of the master will do more work than both his hands.
BENJAMIN FRANKLIN: *Poor Richard's Almanac,* 1758

He that is master of himself will soon be master of others.
H. G. BOHN: *Handbook of Proverbs,* 1855

The measure of a master is his success in bringing all men round to his opinion twenty years later.
R. W. EMERSON: *The Conduct of Life,* IV, 1860

I am glad the old masters are all dead, and I only wish they had died sooner.
S. L. CLEMENS (MARK TWAIN): *Letter from New York to the Alta Californian* (San Francisco), May 28, 1867

The master's eye is the best currycomb.
IRISH PROVERB

No one is born a master. ITALIAN PROVERB

He who serves two masters has to lie to one of them. PORTUGUESE PROVERB

[*See also* Husband and Wife, Like, Master and Servant.

Master and Servant

If a man smite his servant, or his maid, with a rod, and he die under his hand; he shall be surely punished. Notwithstanding, if he continue a day or two, he shall not be punished: for he is his money.
EXODUS XXI, 20–21, *c.* 700 B.C.

If you must be a slave, choose a master of long-established opulence, for they who have reaped a rich harvest unexpectedly are harsh to their slaves.
ÆSCHYLUS: *Agamemnon, c.* 490 B.C.

The master who dreads his servants is lower than a servant.
PUBLILIUS SYRUS: *Sententiæ, c.* 50 B.C.

Servants, be obedient to them that are your masters according to the flesh, with fear and trembling, in singleness of your heart, as unto Christ. EPHESIANS VI, 5, *c.* 60

Exhort servants to be obedient unto their own masters, and to please them well in all things; not answering again; not purloining, but shewing all good fidelity; that they may adorn the doctrine of God our Saviour in all things. TITUS II, 9–10, *c.* 60

Servants, be subject to your masters with all fear; not only to the good and gentle, but also to the froward. I PETER II, 18, *c.* 60

One eye of the master sees more than ten of the servant.
GEORGE HERBERT: *Outlandish Proverbs,* 1640

A servant is known by his master's absence.
THOMAS FULLER: *Gnomologia,* 1732

It is the law of nature between master and servant that the servant shall spoil or plunder the master.
JOHN QUINCY ADAMS: *Diary,* Dec. 17, 1810

The servant is the most implacable enemy of his master.
NAPOLEON I: To Gaspard Gourgaud at St. Helena, Jan. 29, 1817

More have been ruined by their servants than by their masters.
C. C. COLTON: *Lacon,* 1820

Whoever employs, with the right to command, is a master; and, whoever serves, with an obligation to obey, a servant.
J. FENIMORE COOPER: *The American Democrat,* XIX, 1838

The man who gives me employment, which I must have or suffer, that man is my master, let me call him what I will.
HENRY GEORGE: *Social Problems,* v, 1884

Judge the master by his servant.
GERMAN PROVERB

No one knows less about his servants than their master. ITALIAN PROVERB

Woe to the master whom the servant teaches.
JUGO-SLAVIC PROVERB

An ill servant ne'er made a gude maister.
SCOTTISH PROVERB

A servant, at the end of one year, has all the habits of his master. SPANISH PROVERB

[*See also* Servant.

Masterpiece

Whoever has accomplished an immortal work will be as little hurt by its reception from the public or the opinions of critics as a sane man in a madhouse is affected by the upbraidings of the insane.
ARTHUR SCHOPENHAUER: *Notebooks, c.* 1840

Masterpieces have never been produced by men given to obscenity or lustful thoughts — men who have no Master.
M. T. MANTON, J.: *Dissenting opinion in United States* vs. *One Book Entitled "Ulysses,"* 1934

Mastery

The voice of them that shout for mastery.
EXODUS XXXII, 18, *c.* 700 B.C.

Materialism

I am very certain that I am not double; I consider myself as one single being; I know that I am a material, animated and organized animal which thinks. Hence I conclude that animated matter may think.
FREDERICK THE GREAT: *Letter to Voltaire,* Dec. 4, 1775

To talk of immaterial existences is to talk of nothings. To say that the human soul, angels, God, are immaterial, is to say they are nothings, or that there is no God, no angels, no soul. I cannot reason otherwise.
THOMAS JEFFERSON: *Letter to John Adams,* 1820

Man's ideas, views, and conceptions, in one word, man's consciousness, changes with every change in the conditions of his material existence, in his social relations and in his social life.
KARL MARX and FRIEDRICH ENGLES: *The Communist Manifesto,* 1848

[*See also* Atheism, Atheist, Determinism, Fact, History (Materialistic Conception of), Matter, Mysticism, Predestination.

Materialist

The materialist is a Calvinist without a God.
EDWARD BERNSTEIN: *Evolutionary Socialism*, I, 1899

[*See also* Pacifism.

Materia Medica

[*See* Medicine.

Mathematician

I have hardly ever known a mathematician who was able to reason.
PLATO: *The Republic*, VII, *c.* 370 B.C.

In mathematics he was greater
Than Tycho Brahe or Erra Pater;
For he by geometric scale
Could take the size of pots of ale;
Resolve by sines and tangents, straight
If bread or butter wanted weight;
And wisely tell what hour o' th' day
The clock does strike, by algebra.
SAMUEL BUTLER: *Hudibras*, I, 1663

The mathematician proceeds upon propositions which he has once demonstrated, and though the demonstration may have slipped out of his memory he builds upon the truth, because he knows it was demonstrated.
JOSEPH ADDISON: *The Spectator*, Aug. 23, 1712

A great science is mathematics, but mathematicians are often only blockheads.
G. C. LICHTENBERG: *Reflections*, 1799

An addict to mathematics always neglects the gods. LATIN PROVERB

Mathematics

And for mathematical sciences, he that doubts their certainty hath need of a dose of hellebore.
JOSEPH GLANVILL: *The Vanity of Dogmatizing*, XX, 1661

Mathematics contains much that will neither hurt one if one does not know it nor help one if one does know it.
J. B. MENCKEN: *De charlataneria eruditorum*, II, 1715

The study of mathematics, like the Nile, begins in minuteness, but ends in magnificence.
C. C. COLTON: *Lacon*, 1820

Mathematics has not a foot to stand upon which is not purely metaphysical. It begins in metaphysics; and their several orbits are continually intersecting.
THOMAS DE QUINCEY: *Kant in His Miscellaneous Essays*, *c.* 1830

The validity of mathematical propositions is independent of the actual world — the world of existing subject-matters —, is logically prior to it, and would remain unaffected were it to vanish from being.
CASSIUS J. KEYSER: *The Pastures of Wonder*, II, 1929

[*See also* Education.

Matrimony

[*See* Marriage.

Matter

All matter depends on motion.
RENÉ DESCARTES: *Principles of Philosophy*, II, 1644

The earth and the heavens are composed of the same matter. IBID.

I have no reason for believing the existence of matter. I have no immediate intuition thereof: neither can I immediately, from my sensations, ideas, notions, actions, or passions, infer an unthinking, unperceiving, inactive substance — either by probable deduction or necessary consequence.
GEORGE BERKELEY: *Dialogues Between Hylas and Philonous*, III, 1713

Every portion of matter may be looked upon as a garden full of plants, and a pond full of fishes.
G. W. LEIBNIZ: *The Monadology*, LXVII, 1714

We stood talking for some time together of Bishop Berkeley's ingenious sophistry to prove the non-existence of matter, and that everything in the universe is merely ideal. . . . I shall never forget the alacrity with which Johnson answered, striking his foot with mighty force against a large stone, till he rebounded from it, — " I refute it thus."
JAMES BOSWELL: *Life of Johnson*, Aug. 6, 1763

If anyone asks where matter came from we can only answer that it has always existed.
P. H. D. D'HOLBACH: *Le système de la nature*, II, 1770

Everything is more or less organized matter. To think so is against religion, but I think so just the same.
NAPOLEON I: To Gaspard Gourgaud at St. Helena, 1815–1818

When Bishop Berkeley said " there was no matter "
And proved it — 'twas no matter what he said.
BYRON: *Don Juan*, XI, 1823

Matter exists only as attraction and repulsion — attraction and repulsion *are* matter.
E. A. POE: *Eureka*, 1848

Earth to a chamber of mourning turns —
I hear the o'er weening, mocking voice:
Matter is conqueror — matter, triumphant only, continues onward.
WALT WHITMAN: *Yet, Yet, Ye Downcast Hours*, 1860

[*See also* Mind and Matter.

Maturity

Maturity hath her defects, as well as greenness, and worse.
MICHEL DE MONTAIGNE: *Essays*, III 1588

Maxim

It is unbecoming for young men to utter maxims. ARISTOTLE: *Rhetoric*, II, *c.* 322 B.C.

What can the use be of sawing about a set of maxims to which there are a complete set of antagonist maxims?
SYDNEY SMITH: *Lecture on the Conduct of the Understanding*, I, 1806

A man of maxims only is like a Cyclops with one eye, and that eye placed in the back of his head.
S. T. COLERIDGE: *Table-Talk*, June 24, 1827

Maxims are the condensed good sense of nations.
JAMES MACKINTOSH: *Progress of Ethical Philosophy*, 1830

A good maxim is never out of season.
H. G. BOHN: *Handbook of Proverbs*, 1855

Maxims are to the intellect what laws are to actions; they do not enlighten, but they guide and direct, and, although themselves blind, are protective.
JOSEPH JOUBERT: *Pensées*, 1864

The mind of man, when its daily maxims are put before it, revolts from anything so stupid, so mean, so poor.
WALTER BAGEHOT: *Literary Studies*, 1879

I detest any attempt to bring the law into maxims. Maxims are invariably wrong, that is, they are so general and large that they always include something which is not intended to be included.
LORD ESHER: *Judgment in Yarmouth* vs. *France*, 1887

[*See also* Proverb.

May

The vulgar say that it is unlucky to marry in May. OVID: *Fasti*, V, *c.* 5

Hard is his heart that loveth naught in May.
GEOFFREY CHAUCER: *The Romaunt of the Rose*, *c.* 1370

And May was come, the month of gladness.
JOHN LYDGATE: *Troy-Book*, *c.* 1415

All nature's imps triumph whiles joyful May dost last;
When May is gone, of all the year the pleasant time is past.
RICHARD EDWARDS: *May*, *c.* 1576

The merry month of May.
NICHOLAS BRETON: *Phillida and Carydon*, 1591

Rough winds do shake the darling buds of May.
SHAKESPEARE: *Sonnets*, XVIII, 1609

He that is in town in May loseth his Spring.
GEORGE HERBERT: *Outlandish Proverbs*, 1640

A hot May makes a fat churchyard.
ENGLISH PROVERB, first recorded in 1659

The Marchioness of S—— . . . said . . . that though she would promise to be chaste in every month besides, she could not engage for herself in May.
EUSTACE BLUDGELL: *The Spectator*, April 29, 1712

In the wonderfully beautiful month of May.
(Im wunderschönen Monat Mai.)
HEINRICH HEINE: *Lyrische Intermezzo*, I, 1823

May brings flocks of pretty lambs,
Skipping by their fleecy dams.
SARA COLERIDGE: *Pretty Lessons in Verse*, 1834

The word May is a perfumed word. It is an illuminated initial. It means youth, love, song, and all that is beautiful in life.
H. W. LONGFELLOW: *Journal*, May 1, 1861

In all the branches full-fledged May did sing,
Caught the light-flitting winds in flowery mesh,
And poured its spreading smile o'er everything.
ALFRED AUSTIN: *The Human Tragedy*, IV, 1862

Who first beholds the light of day
In Spring's sweet flowery month of May
And wears an emerald all her life,
Shall be a loved and happy wife.
Author unidentified

If you are sick in May, you'll be well the rest of the year. FRENCH PROVERB

Harlots and scoundrels marry in May.
GERMAN PROVERB

May is the month to marry bad wives.
LATIN PROVERB

A dry May and a leaking June
Make the farmer whistle a merry tune.
OLD ENGLISH RHYME

Flowers before May bring bad luck.
WELSH PROVERB

[*See also* April, Bathing, Cold (Illness), Flower, Fly, January, Maying, Months.

Maybe

And I don't mean maybe.
AMERICAN SAYING, *c.* 1920

Maybe's a big book. SCOTTISH PROVERB

What may be may na be. IBID.

Mayhem

Anyone who bites off a free man's nose must pay an indemnity of a pound of silver, and give his farm buildings as security.
THE HITTITE CODE, *c.* 1350 B.C.

Maying

Oh! that we two were Maying
Down the stream of the soft Spring breeze;

Like children with violets playing,
In the shade of the whispering trees.
CHARLES KINGSLEY: *The Saint's Tragedy,* II, 1848

Mayonnaise

One of the sauces which serve the French in place of a state religion.
AMBROSE BIERCE: *The Devil's Dictionary,* 1906

Mayor

It's a mad life to be a lord mayor; it's a stirring life, a fine life, a velvet life, a careful life.
THOMAS DEKKER: *The Shoemaker's Holiday,* V, 1599

Commentators on Job have been puzzled to find out a meaning for Leviathan. 'Tis a whale, say some; a crocodile, say others. In my simple conjecture, Leviathan is neither more nor less than the Lord Mayor of London for the time being.
CHARLES LAMB: *Letter to Robert Southey,* May 20, 1799

May Queen

You must wake and call me early, call me early, mother dear;
Tomorrow 'ill be the happiest time of all the blythe Newyear;
Of all the glad Newyear, mother, the maddest, merriest day —
For I'm to be Queen o' the May, mother, I'm to be Queen o' the May.
ALFRED TENNYSON: *The May Queen,* 1833

McKinley, William (1843–1901)

McKinley has no more backbone than a chocolate eclair.
THEODORE ROOSEVELT: On McKinley's reluctance to enter upon war with Spain, 1898

[*See also* Assassination.

Meadow

The meadows of Gibeah.
JUDGES XX, 33, *c.* 500 B.C.

Meadows trim with daisies pied.
JOHN MILTON: *L'Allegro,* 1632

Meal

Better are meals many than one too merry.
JOHN HEYWOOD: *Proverbs,* 1546

Two hungry meals make the third a glutton.
IBID.

The wholesomest meal is at another man's cost.
JAMES HOWELL: *Proverbs,* 1659

Long meals, short prayers.
CZECH PROVERB

The best part of every meal is its first part.
IRISH PROVERB

He fasts enough that has a bad meal.
ITALIAN PROVERB

[*See also* Dinner, Eating, Exercise, Food, Merriment, Supper.

Mean

The mean is best.
Ascribed to CLEOBULUS OF LINDOS, *c.* 575 B.C.

There is a mean in all things; there are, in short, certain fixed limits, on either side of which what is right cannot exist.
HORACE: *Satires,* I, *c.* 25 B.C.

Whoever cultivates the golden mean (aurea mediocritas) avoids both the poverty of a hovel and the envy of a palace.
HORACE: *Carmina,* II, *c.* 20 B.C.

The golden mean.
ENGLISH PHRASE, borrowed from HORACE, *ante,* and traced by Apperson to the Ancrene Riwle (Rule of Anchoresses), *c.* 1225

[*See also* Middle.

Meaning

One may know your meaning by your gaping.
JOHN RAY: *English Proverbs,* 1670

The meaning of meaning.
C. K. OGDEN and I. A. RICHARDS: Title of a book, 1923

The meaning of a word in general use is determined, not by pundits, still less by official action of any kind, but by the people. It is the duty of the professional linguist to find out, by investigation, what the usage of the people is, in this particular matter, and to record his findings.
KEMP MALONE: *On Defining Mahogany,* 1940

Meanness

Meanness is incurable; it cannot be cured by old age, or by anything else.
ARISTOTLE: *The Nicomachean Ethics,* IV, *c.* 340 B.C.

He is mean enough to steal acorns from a blind hog.
AMERICAN SAYING, *c.* 1835

Means

He who wills the end wills the means.
ENGLISH PROVERB, not recorded before the XIX century

Him, only him, the shield of Jove defends
Whose means are fair and spotless as his ends.
WILLIAM WORDSWORTH: *Dion,* VI, 1820

Most of the great results of history are brought about by discreditable means.
R. W. EMERSON: *The Conduct of Life,* VII, 1860

[*See also* Catholicism (Roman), Church (Roman Catholic), End.

Measles

Hunger is best for the measles, and plenty of food for the smallpox.
CHINESE PROVERB

Measure

A perfect and just measure shalt thou have: that thy days may be lengthened in the land which the Lord thy God giveth thee.
DEUTERONOMY XXV, 15, *c.* 650 B.C.

In everything there lieth measure.
GEOFFREY CHAUCER: *Troylus and Cryseyde, c.* 1375

Measure for measure.
SHAKESPEARE: Title of a play, 1604

When many strike on an anvil they must strike by measure.
JOHN RAY: *English Proverbs,* 1670

It is no sin to sell dear, but a sin to give ill measure.
JAMES KELLY: *Complete Collection of Scottish Proverbs,* 1721

Don't measure yourself; it will make you die.
AMERICAN NEGRO PROVERB

In buying cloth measure it ten times; it can be cut but once. RUSSIAN PROVERB

[*See also* Man, Weights and Measures.

Meat

Thou mayest eat flesh, whatsoever thy soul lusteth after.
DEUTERONOMY XII, 20, *c.* 650 B.C.

Strong meat belongeth to them that are of full age. HEBREWS V, 14, *c.* 65

The nearer the bone, the sweeter the meat.
ENGLISH PROVERB, traced by Smith to 1559 (Cf. KELLY, *post,* 1721)

It is meat and drink to me.
SHAKESPEARE: *As You Like It,* V, *c.* 1600

All flesh is not venison.
GEORGE HERBERT: *Outlandish Proverbs,* 1640

The flesh is aye fairest that is farthest from the bone.
JAMES KELLY: *Complete Collection of Scottish Proverbs,* 1721 (Cf. ENGLISH PROVERB, *ante,* 1559)

Much meat, much malady.
THOMAS FULLER: *Gnomologia,* 1732

It is a fact that great eaters of meat are in general more cruel and ferocious than other men; this observation holds good in all places and at all times; the barbarism of the English is well known.
J.-J. ROUSSEAU: *Émile,* I, 1762

But we hae meat, and we can eat,
Sae let the Lord be thankit.
ROBERT BURNS: *Grace Before Meat, c.* 1795

It is only by softening and disguising dead flesh by culinary preparation that it is rendered susceptible of mastication or digestion; and that the sight of its bloody juices and raw horror does not excite intolerable loathing and disgust.
P. B. SHELLEY: *Queen Mab,* notes, 1813

If you buy meat cheap, you will smell what you have saved when it boils. ARAB PROVERB

White meat, white wine; red meat, red wine.
FRENCH PROVERB

They who eat much meat talk too much.
HEBREW PROVERB

Old meat makes good soup.
ITALIAN PROVERB

Who eats the meat can pick the bone.
SPANISH PROVERB

[*See also* Bone, Cook, English, Flesh, Goat, Poison.

Meddling

Every fool will be meddling.
PROVERBS XX, 3, *c.* 350 B.C.

Never put your hand between the bark and the tree.
ENGLISH PROVERB, current in various forms since the XVI century

Meddlers are the Devil's body-lice; they fetch blood from those that feed them.
THOMAS FULLER: *Gnomologia,* 1732

Meddlesome Matty.
ANN and JANE TAYLOR: *Original Poems for Infant Minds,* I, 1804

[*See also* Busy, Fool, Midwifery.

Medes and Persians

[*See* Law.

Medicine

Natural forces within us are the true healers of disease.
HIPPOCRATES: *Aphorisms, c.* 400 B.C.

Wherever the art of medicine is loved, there also is love of humanity. IBID.

Medicine may be regarded generally as the knowledge of the loves and desires of the body, and how to satisfy them or not.
PLATO: *Symposium, c.* 360 B.C.

The most High hath created medicines out of the earth, and a wise man will not abhor them.
ECCLESIASTICUS XXXVIII, 4, *c.* 180 B.C.

Because all the sick do not recover, therefore medicine is no art.
CICERO: *De natura deorum,* II, 45 B.C.

Time is the best medicine.
OVID: *Remedia amoris, c.* 10

Medicine is a conjectural art. It has almost no rules.

AULUS CORNELIUS CELSUS: *De medicina*, *c.* 10

Medicine is not only a science; it is also an art. It does not consist of compounding pills and plasters; it deals with the very processes of life, which must be understood before they may be guided.

THEOPHRASTUS BOMBAST VON HOHENHEIM (PARACELSUS): *Die grosse Wunderartzney*, 1530

Strong disease requires a strong medicine.

RICHARD TAVERNER: *Proverbs*, 1539

'Tis wonderful how God has put such excellent physic in mere muck; we know by experience that swine's dung stints the blood; horse's serves for the pleurisy; man's heals wounds and black blotches; asses' is used for the bloody flux, and cow's with preserved roses serves for epilepsy, or for convulsions of children.

MARTIN LUTHER: *Table-Talk*, XCII, 1569

Patience is the best medicine.

JOHN FLORIO: *First Frutes*, 1578

Throw physic to the dogs; I'll none of it.

SHAKESPEARE: *Macbeth*, V, *c.* 1605

I find the medicine worse than the malady.

BEAUMONT and FLETCHER: *Love's Cure*, III, *c.* 1610

If you fly physic in health altogether, it will be too strange for your body when you shall need it; if you make it too familiar, it will work no extraordinary effect when sickness cometh.

FRANCIS BACON: *Essays*, XXX, 1625

The physician looks with another eye on the medicinal herb than the grazing ox which swoops it in with the common grass.

JOSEPH GLANVILL: *The Vanity of Dogmatizing*, XXIV, 1661

In physic things of melancholic hue and quality are used against melancholy, sour against sour, salt to remove salt humors.

JOHN MILTON: *Samson Agonistes*, pref., 1671

Nearly all men die of their medicines, not of their diseases.

J. B. MOLIÈRE: *Le malade imaginaire*, III, 1673

Apollo was held the god of physic, and sender of diseases. Both were originally the same trade, and still continue.

JONATHAN SWIFT: *Thoughts on Various Subjects*, 1706

Physic, for the most part, is nothing else but the substitute of exercise or temperance.

JOSEPH ADDISON: *The Spectator*, Oct. 13, 1711

There is a common argument that is both false and fatal. "So-and-so," one hears, "has been cured by such-and-such a treatment, and I have his disease; *ergo*, I must try his remedy." How many people die by reasoning thus! What they overlook is that the diseases which afflict us are as different as the features of our faces.

VOLTAIRE: *Letter to Baron de Bretuil*, Dec., 1723

Learn from the beasts the physic of the field.

ALEXANDER POPE: *An Essay on Man*, III, 1733

Much are we beholden to physicians, who only prescribe the bark of the quinquina, when they might oblige their patients to swallow the whole tree.

Ascribed to DAVID DALRYMPLE (LORD HAILES), *c.* 1785

Medicines are fit only for old people.

NAPOLEON I: To Barry E. O'Meara at St. Helena, Aug. 19, 1816

Take a dose of medicine once, and in all probability you will be obliged to take an additional hundred afterward.

NAPOLEON I: To Barry E. O'Meara at St. Helena, Sept. 26, 1817

Throw out opium, which the Creator himself seems to prescribe, for we often see the scarlet poppy growing in the cornfields, as if it were foreseen that wherever there is hunger to be fed there must also be pain to be soothed; throw out a few specifics which our art did not discover, and is hardly needed to apply; throw out wine, which is a food, and the vapors which produce the miracle of anesthesia, and I firmly believe that if the whole *materia medica, as now used,* could be sunk to the bottom of the sea, it would be all the better for mankind – and all the worse for the fishes.

O. W. HOLMES: Address to the Massachusetts Medical Society, Boston, May 30, 1860

A stone flung down the Bowery to kill a dog in Broadway.

AMBROSE BIERCE: *The Devil's Dictionary*, 1906

Medicine is the only profession that labors incessantly to destroy the reason for its own existence.

JAMES BRYCE: Speech in New York, March 23, 1914

Medicine is the one place where all the show is stripped off the human drama. You, as doctors, will be in a position to see the human race stark naked – not only physically, but mentally and morally as well.

MARTIN H. FISCHER (1879–)

Some day when you have time, look into the business of prayer, amulets, baths, and poultices, and discover for yourself how much valuable therapy the medical profession has cast out of the window. IBID.

Medicine can cure only curable diseases.
CHINESE PROVERB

A good laugh and a long sleep are the best cures in the doctor's book. IRISH PROVERB

Good medicine always has a bitter taste.
JAPANESE PROVERB

If you want to be cured of I don't know what, take this herb of I don't know what name, apply it I don't know where, and you will be cured I don't know when.
Medieval jocosity, source unknown

Who lives by medicine lives miserably. (Qui medice vivit misere vivit.)
MEDIEVAL LATIN PROVERB

[*See also* Cure, Dermatologist, Disease, Doctor, Drugs, Labor, Merriment, Monk, Nihilism, Osteopathy, Physic, Physician, Remedy, Surgeon, Time.

Mediocrity

O mediocrity, thou priceless jewel.
JOHN FLETCHER and PHILIP MASSINGER: *The Queen of Corinth*, III, *c.* 1616

Mediocrity obtains more with application than superiority without it.
BALTASAR GRACIÁN: *The Art of Worldly Wisdom*, XVIII, 1647

There are certain things in which mediocrity is insupportable — poetry, music, painting, public speaking.
JEAN DE LA BRUYÈRE: *Caractères*, I, 1688

A very good or very bad poet is remarkable; but a middling one, who can bear!
THOMAS FULLER: *Gnomologia*, 1732

The world is a republic of the mediocrities, and always was.
THOMAS CARLYLE: *Letter to R. W. Emerson*, May 13, 1853

The general average of mankind are not only moderate in intellect, but also moderate in inclinations: they have no tastes or wishes strong enough to incline them to do anything unusual, and they consequently do not understand those who have, and class all such with the wild and intemperate whom they are accustomed to look down upon.
J. S. MILL: *On Liberty*, III, 1859

To the mediocre mediocrity is a form of happiness; they have a natural instinct for mastering one thing, for specialization.
F. W. NIETZSCHE: *The Antichrist*, LVII, 1888

[*See also* Mean, Moderation, State, United States.

Meekness

The man Moses was very meek, above all the men which were upon the face of the earth.
NUMBERS XII, 3, *c.* 700 B.C.

The meek shall inherit the earth.
PSALMS XXXVII, 11, *c.* 150 B.C.

The meekness and gentleness of Christ.
II CORINTHIANS X, 1, *c.* 55

Blessed are the meek, for they shall inherit the earth.
MATTHEW V, 5, *c*, 75 (Cf. PSALMS XXXVII, 11, *ante*, *c.* 150 B.C.)

Unto him that smiteth thee on the one cheek offer also the other; and him that taketh away thy cloak forbid not to take thy coat also. LUKE VI, 29, *c.* 75

Meekness takes injuries like pills, not chewing, but swallowing them down.
THOMAS BROWNE: *Christian Morals*, III, *c.* 1680

Let bishops, deans and prebendaries swell
With pride and fatness till their hearts rebel:
I'm meek and modest.
GEORGE CRABBE: *The Borough*, IV, 1810

Do not trust the meek with your money.
SPANISH PROVERB

If some one hits you with a stone, hit him back with a piece of cotton. TURKISH PROVERB

[*See also* Candor, Maiden, Moses, Temperance, Virtue.

Meeting

Journeys end in lovers meeting.
SHAKESPEARE: *Twelfth Night*, II, *c.* 1601

When shall we three meet again
In thunder, lightning, or in rain?
SHAKESPEARE: *Macbeth*, I, *c.* 1605

The joys of meeting pay the pangs of absence.
NICHOLAS ROWE: *Tamerlane*, II, 1702

The sight of you is good for sore eyes.
JONATHAN SWIFT: *Polite Conversation*, 1738

Ships that pass in the night, and speak each other in passing,
Only a signal shown and a distant voice in the darkness.
H. W. LONGFELLOW: *Tales of a Wayside Inn*, 1863

[*See also* Crowd.

Melancholy

All heaviness of mind and melancholy come of the Devil; especially these thoughts: that God is not gracious unto him, that God will have no mercy upon him, etc. Whosoever thou art, possessed with such heavy thoughts, know for certain, that they are a work of the

Devil. God sent His Son into the world, not to affright, but to comfort.
MARTIN LUTHER: *Table-Talk*, DCXXXIV, 1569

Melancholy is the nurse of frenzy.
SHAKESPEARE: *The Taming of the Shrew*, induction, 1594

I am as melancholy as a gib cat.
SHAKESPEARE: *I Henry IV*, I, *c.* 1598 (*Gib*=castrated)

I can suck melancholy out of a song.
SHAKESPEARE: *As You Like It*, II, *c.* 1600

I have neither the scholar's melancholy, which is emulation; nor the musician's, which is fantastical; nor the courtier's, which is proud; nor the soldier's, which is ambitious; nor the lawyer's, which is politic; nor the lady's, which is nice; nor the lover's, which is all these; but it is a melancholy of mine own, compounded of many simples, extracted from many objects, and, indeed, the sundry contemplation of my travels, in which my often rumination wraps me in a most humorous sadness.
SHAKESPEARE: *As You Like It*, IV

Aristotle said melancholy men of all others are the most witty.
ROBERT BURTON: *The Anatomy of Melancholy*, I, 1621

If there is a hell upon earth it is to be found in a melancholy man's heart. IBID.

Hence, loathéd melancholy,
Of Cerberus and blackest midnight born,
In Stygian cave forlorn,
'Mongst horrid shapes, and shrieks, and sights unholy!
JOHN MILTON: *L'Allegro*, 1632

There's naught in this life sweet,
If man were wise to se 't,
But only melancholy;
O sweetest melancholy!
JOHN FLETCHER and THOMAS MIDDLETON: *The Nice Valor*, III, 1647

He is a fool that is not melancholy once a day.
ENGLISH PROVERB, traced by Smith to 1678

Make not a bosom friend of a melancholy sad soul: he goes always heavy loaded, and thou must bear half.
THOMAS FULLER: *Introductio at Prudentiam*, I, 1731

There is a kindly mood of melancholy
That wings the soul.
JOHN DYER: *The Ruines of Rome*, 1740

Melancholy marked him for her own.
THOMAS GRAY: *Elegy Written in a Country Churchyard*, 1750

Melancholy, silent maid,
With leaden eye that loves the ground.
THOMAS GRAY: *Hymn to Adversity*, 1753

That affection does not deserve the epithet of chaste which does not receive a sublime gloom of tender melancholy.
MARY WOLLSTONECRAFT: *A Vindication of the Rights of Woman*, VII, 1792

There's such a charm in melancholy
I would not if I could be gay.
SAMUEL ROGERS: *To* ——, *c.* 1810

Melancholy is the pleasure of being sad.
VICTOR HUGO: *The Toilers of the Sea*, III, 1866

[*See also* Beauty, Eating and Drinking, Enthusiasm, Hare, Love, Night, Song.

Melanchthon, Philipp (1497–1560)

Melanchthon is a better logician than myself; he argues better. My superiority lies rather in the rhetorical way.
MARTIN LUTHER: *Table-Talk*, XLV, 1569

Mellon, Andrew W. (1855–1937)

The finances of this nation have been managed with a genius and a success unmatched since the days of Hamilton.
CALVIN COOLIDGE: Speech of acceptance, Aug. 14, 1924

Melodrama

[*See* Tragedy.

Melody

Melody is the very essence of music. When I think of a good melodist I think of a fine race-horse. A contrapuntist is only a post-horse.
W. A. MOZART: To Michael Kelly, 1786

Heard melodies are sweet, but those unheard
Are sweeter.
JOHN KEATS: *On a Grecian Urn*, *c.* 1819

[*See also* Music.

Memory

Memory is the mother of all wisdom.
ÆSCHYLUS: *Prometheus Bound*, *c.* 490 B.C.

If I do not remember thee, let my tongue cleave to the roof of my mouth.
PSALMS CXXXVII, 6, *c.* 150 B.C.

Memory is the treasury and guardian of all things. CICERO: *De oratore*, I, *c.* 80 B.C.

The things that were hardest to bear are sweetest to remember.
SENECA: *Hercules Furens*, *c.* 50

There is no greater sorrow than to recall happiness in times of misery.
DANTE: *Inferno*, V, *c.* 1320

Of fortune's sharp adversity
The worst kind of infortune is this:
A man to have been in prosperity,
And it remember, when it passed is.
GEOFFREY CHAUCER: *Troylus and Cryseyde*, *c.* 1374

A good memory is generally joined to a weak judgment.
MICHEL DE MONTAIGNE: *Essays*, I, 1580

Women are often weak in memory.
ROBERT GREENE: *Friar Bacon and Friar Bungay*, I, 1594

There's hope a great man's memory may outlive his life half a year.
SHAKESPEARE: *Hamlet*, III, *c.* 1601

A lasting, high and happy memory.
BEN JONSON: *Sejanus*, I, 1603

Imagination and memory are but one thing, which for divers considerations hath divers names.
THOMAS HOBBES: *Leviathan*, II, 1651

Memory is . . . like a sepulchre furnished with a load of broken and discarnate bones.
JOSEPH GLANVILL: *The Vanity of Dogmatizing*, XV, 1661

Everyone complains of his lack of memory but no one of his lack of judgment.
LA ROCHEFOUCAULD: *Maxims*, 1665

He that admires the proficiency of another always attributes it to the happiness of his memory, and he that laments his own defects concludes with a wish that his memory were better.
SAMUEL JOHNSON: *The Idler*, Sept. 15, 1759

Time whereof the memory of man runneth not to the contrary.
WILLIAM BLACKSTONE: *Commentaries on the Laws of England*, I, 1765

I would not wish you to possess that kind of memory which retains with accuracy and certainty all names and dates. I never knew it to accompany much invention or fancy. It is almost the exclusive blessing of dullness.
AARON BURR: *Letter to his wife*, Dec., 1791

Of all the faculties of the human mind that of memory is the first which suffers decay from age.
THOMAS JEFFERSON: *Letter to B. H. Latrobe*, 1812

Oft in the stilly night
E'er slumber's chain has bound me,
Fond memory brings the light
Of other days around me.
THOMAS MOORE: *Oft in the Stilly Night*, *c.* 1815

Nothing is more common than a fool with a strong memory.
C. C. COLTON: *Lacon*, 1820

Of all the faculties of the mind memory is the first that flourishes, and the first that dies.
IBID.

The memory strengthens as you lay burdens upon it, and becomes trustworthy as you trust it.
THOMAS DE QUINCEY: *Confessions of an English Opium-Eater*, I, 1822

How cruelly sweet are the echoes that start
When memory plays an old tune on the heart.
ELIZA COOK: *Lays of a Wild Harp*, 1835

Mankind are always happier for having been happy; so that if you make them happy now, you make them happy twenty years hence by the memory of it.
SYDNEY SMITH: *The Benevolent Affections*, 1839

There was an old man of Khartoum
Who kept two tame sheep in his room,
" For," he said, " they remind me
Of one left behind me,
But I cannot remember of whom."
Author unidentified

Tho' lost to sight, to mem'ry dear.
Author unidentified; it appears in a song by George Linley, 1840, but it was not original with him

A sorrow's crown of sorrows is remembering happier things.
ALFRED TENNYSON: *Locksley Hall*, 1842

The library of the mind.
FRANCIS FAUVEL-GOURAND: *Phreno-Mnemotechnic Dictionary*, 1844

Around me shall hover,
In sadness or glee,
'Til life's dream be over,
Sweet memories of thee.
Anon.: *Favorite album verses*, *c.* 1845

You can't order remembrance out of a man's mind.
W. M. THACKERAY: *The Virginians*, X, 1858

Memories vague of half-forgotten things,
Not true nor false, but sweet to think upon.
WILLIAM MORRIS: *The Earthly Paradise*, 1868

Many a man fails as an original thinker simply because his memory is too good.
F. W. NIETZSCHE: *Human All-too-Human*, II, 1878

The one who thinks over his experiences most, and weaves them into systematic relations with each other will be the one with the best memory.
WILLIAM JAMES: *Psychology, Briefer Course*, XVIII, 1892

Memory in a woman is the beginning of dowdiness.
OSCAR WILDE: *A Woman of No Importance*, III, 1893

Memory is the diary that chronicles things that never have happened and couldn't possibly have happened.
OSCAR WILDE: *The Importance of Being Earnest*, I, 1895

Memory is the power to gather roses in Winter.
Author unidentified

People with good memories seldom remember anything worth remembering. IBID.

The palest ink is better than the best memory.
CHINESE PROVERB

[*See also* Age (Old), Alms, Creditor, Experience, Fame, Judgment, Knowledge, Malice, Monument, Poet, Preacher, Remembrance, Smell.

Mend

It's never too late to mend.
ENGLISH PROVERB, borrowed from the Greek, and current since the XVI century

Who errs and mends
To God himself commends.
THOMAS SHELTON: Tr. of CERVANTES: *Don Quixote*, II (1615), 1620

If everyone would mend one, all would be amended.
JOHN RAY: *English Proverbs*, 1670

Mendacity

[*See* Lying, Miracle.

Mendicant

[*See* Begging.

Menial

A pampered menial forced me from the door,
To seek a shelter in an humbler shed.
THOMAS MOSS: *The Beggar's Petition*, 1768 (It is said that Oliver Goldsmith, to whom Moss had shown the poem, substituted "pampered menial" for "liveried servant," which was in the original)

Mercenary

In times of peace they plunder, and in times of war they desert.
NICCOLÒ MACHIAVELLI: *The Prince*, XII, 1513

Standing armies are sometimes (I would by no means say generally, much less universally) composed of persons who have rendered themselves unfit to live in civil society; who have no other motives of conduct than those which a desire of the present gratification of their passions suggests; who have no property in any country; men who have given up their own liberties, and envy those who enjoy liberty; who are equally indifferent to the glory of a George or a Louis; who, for the addition of one penny a day to their wages, would desert from the Christian cross and fight under the crescent of the Turkish sultan.
JOHN HANCOCK: Speech on the Boston Massacre, Boston, 1774

[*See also* Swiss.

Merchant

Tyre, the crowning city, whose merchants are princes, whose traffickers are the honorable of the earth. ISAIAH XXIII, 8, *c.* 700 B.C.

Merchants love nobody.
THOMAS JEFFERSON: *Letter to John Langdon*, 1785

Merchants are the least virtuous citizens and possess the least of the *amor patriæ*.
THOMAS JEFFERSON: *Letter to M. de Meunier*, 1786

The craft of the merchant is bringing a thing from where it abounds to where it is costly.
R. W. EMERSON: *The Conduct of Life*, III, 1860

If you would be a merchant fine,
Beware o' auld horses, herring, and wine.
SCOTTISH PROVERB

[*See also* Business, Gods, Profession, Trade (=commerce), Trade (Free).

Mercy

The merciful man doeth good to his own soul.
PROVERBS XI, 17, *c.* 350 B.C.

He that hath mercy on the poor, happy is he.
PROVERBS XIV, 21

Have mercy upon me, O Lord; for I am weak: O Lord, heal me; for my bones are vexed.
PSALMS VI, 2, *c.* 150 B.C.

Surely goodness and mercy shall follow me all the days of my life: and I will dwell in the house of the Lord forever.
PSALMS XXIII, 6

A good man is ever merciful.
PSALMS XXXVII, 26

God be merciful unto us, and bless us; and cause his face to shine upon us; Selah.
PSALMS LXVII, 1

The mercy of the Lord is from everlasting to everlasting upon them that fear Him.
PSALMS CIII, 17

Mercy will soon pardon the meanest.
WISDOM OF SOLOMON VI, 6, *c.* 100 B.C.

Nothing is more praiseworthy, nothing more suited to a great and illustrious man than a merciful disposition.
CICERO: *De officiis*, I, 78 B.C.

It is a bad cause that asks for mercy.
PUBLILIUS SYRUS: *Sententiæ*, *c.* 50 B.C.

Mercy rejoiceth against judgment.
JAMES II, 13, *c.* 60

Blessed are the merciful: for they shall obtain mercy. MATTHEW V, 7, *c.* 75

God be merciful to me a sinner.
LUKE XVIII, 13, *c.* 75

It is noble to give the vanquished their lives.
STATIUS: *Thebaid*, VI, *c.* 90

Dost thou wish to receive mercy? Show mercy to thy neighbor.
ST. JOHN CHRYSOSTOM: *Homilies*, XIII, *c.* 388

Mercy imitates God, and disappoints Satan.
ST. JOHN CHRYSOSTOM: *Homilies,* XXI

Mercy passeth right.
GEOFFREY CHAUCER: *Troylus and Cryseyde, c.* 1374

Who will not mercy unto others show,
How can he mercy ever hope to have?
EDMUND SPENSER: *The Faerie Queene,* V, *c.* 1589

Wilt thou draw near the nature of the gods?
Draw near them in being merciful;
Sweet mercy is nobility's true badge.
SHAKESPEARE: *Titus Andronicus,* I, 1594

Mercy but murders, pardoning those that kill.
SHAKESPEARE: *Romeo and Juliet,* III, *c.* 1596

The quality of mercy is not strain'd,
It droppeth as the gentle rain from Heaven
Upon the place beneath: it is twice blest;
It blesseth him that gives and him that takes;
'Tis mightiest in the mightiest; it becomes
The thronéd monarch better than his crown . . .
Mercy is above this sceptred sway;
It is enthronéd in the hearts of kings,
It is an attribute to God himself.
SHAKESPEARE: *The Merchant of Venice,* IV, *c.* 1597

Whereto serves mercy
But to confront the visage of offense?
SHAKESPEARE: *Hamlet,* III, *c.* 1601

Not the king's crown, nor the deputed sword,
The marshal's truncheon, nor the judge's robe,
Become them with one half so good a grace,
As mercy does.
SHAKESPEARE: *Measure for Measure,* II, 1604

Nothing emboldens sins so much as mercy.
SHAKESPEARE: *Timon of Athens,* III, *c.* 1607

The greatest attribute of Heaven is mercy;
And 'tis the crown of justice, and the glory,
Where it may kill with right, to save with pity.
JOHN FLETCHER and PHILIP MASSINGER: *The Lover's Progress,* III, 1623

Mercies that are ordinary we swallow, and take small notice of them.
Anon.: *A True and Certain Relation of a Strange Birth,* 1635

Our offences being mortal, and deserving not only death but damnation, if the goodness of God be content to traverse and pass them over with a loss, misfortune, or disease, what frenzy were it to term this a punishment, rather than an extremity of mercy, and to groan under the rod of His judgments rather than admire the sceptre of His mercies!
THOMAS BROWNE: *Religio Medici,* I, 1642

The dimensions of this mercy are above my thoughts. It is, for aught I know, a crowning mercy.
OLIVER CROMWELL: Dispatch after the Battle of Worcester, Sept. 4, 1651

Less pleasure take brave minds in battles won,
Than in restoring such as are undone;
Tigers have courage, and the rugged bear,
But man alone can, whom he conquers, spare.
EDMUND WALLER: *To My Lord Protector,* 1654

That it may please thee to have mercy upon all men; we beseech thee to hear us, good Lord.
THE BOOK OF COMMON PRAYER (*The Litany*), 1662

I shall temper justice with mercy.
JOHN MILTON: *Paradise Lost,* X, 1667

As you are stout be merciful.
JAMES KELLY: *Complete Collection of Scottish Proverbs,* 1721

Cowards are cruel, but the brave
Love mercy and delight to save.
JOHN GAY: *Fables,* I, 1727

To kill is a power common to the vilest of the earth; but mercy belongs to gods and kings alone.
PIETRO METASTASIO: *La Clemenza di Tito,* III, *c.* 1735

A God all mercy is a God unjust.
EDWARD YOUNG: *Night Thoughts,* IV, 1742

There is a mercy which is weakness, and even treason against the common good.
MARIAN EVANS (GEORGE ELIOT): *Romola,* III, 1863

What would be the use of laws against murder if the condemned criminal could obtain his liberty by apologizing to the queen? Yet such is the Christian system, which, though in one sense beautiful on account of its mercy, is also immoral on account of its indulgence.
W. WINWOOD READE: *The Martyrdom of Man,* III, 1872

In case of doubt it is best to lean to the side of mercy. (In dubiis benigniora sunt semper præferenda.)
LEGAL MAXIM

[*See also* Coward, God, Justice and Mercy, King, Law (Natural), Sinner, Sympathy.

Meredith, George (1828–1909)

In George Meredith there is nothing but crack-jaw sentences, empty and unpleasant in the mouth as sterile nuts. I do not know any book more tedious than "Tragic Comedians," more pretentious, more blatant; it struts and screams, stupid in all its gaud and absurdity as a cockatoo.
GEORGE MOORE: *Confessions of a Young Man,* X, 1888

Meredith is only a prose Browning.
Ascribed to OSCAR WILDE, *c.* 1890 (Someone replied "So was Browning")

His style is chaos illuminated by flashes of lightning. As a writer he has mastered everything, except language; as a novelist he can

do everything, except tell a story; as an artist he is everything, except articulate.
OSCAR WILDE: *The Decay of Lying,* 1891

Mr. Meredith's world . . . is not a real world. It is a fantastic one treated realistically.
W. C. BROWNELL: *Victorian Prose Masters,* 1901

Merit

The sufficiency of merit is to know that my merit is not sufficient.
FRANCIS QUARLES: *Emblems,* 1635

The more merit, the less affectation.
BALTASAR GRACIÁN: *The Art of Worldly Wisdom,* CXXIII, 1647

Nature makes merit, but fortune sets it to work.
LA ROCHEFOUCAULD: *Maxims,* 1665

The merit of men has its season, as fruits have.
IBID.

There are people whose merits disgust us.
IBID.

There is merit with eminence, but there is no eminence without some merit. IBID.

The test of extraordinary merit is to see those who envy it the most yet obliged to praise it.
IBID.

The world far oftener favors false merit than it accords justice to true merit. IBID.

Where he falls short, 'tis Nature's fault alone
Where he succeeds, the merit's all his own.
CHARLES CHURCHILL: *The Rosciad,* 1761

Merit, God knows, is very little rewarded.
CHARLES LAMB: *Letter to William Wordsworth,* Oct. 13, 1804

Towers are measured by their shadows, and men of merit by those who are envious of them. CHINESE PROVERB

[*See also* Esteem, Fortune, Honors, Modesty, Virtue, Worth.

Mermaid

Once I sat upon a promontory,
And heard a mermaid on a dolphin's back
Uttering such dulcet and harmonious breath,
That the rude sea grew civil at her song;
And certain stars shot madly from their spheres,
To hear the sea-maid's music.
SHAKESPEARE: *A Midsummer Night's Dream,* II, *c.* 1596

Merriment

Be content, I pray thee, and tarry all night, and let thine heart be merry.
JUDGES XIX, 6, *c.* 500 B.C.

Nabal's heart was merry within him, for he was very drunken.
I SAMUEL XXV, 36, *c.* 500 B.C.

A merry heart maketh a cheerful countenance.
PROVERBS XV, 13, *c.* 350 B.C.

He that is of a merry heart hath a continual feast. PROVERBS XV, 15

A merry heart doeth good like a medicine.
PROVERBS XVII, 22

A man hath no better thing under the sun, than to eat, and to drink, and to be merry.
ECCLESIASTES VIII, 15, *c.* 200 B.C.

Is any merry? Let him sing psalms.
JAMES V, 13, *c.* 60

Take thine ease, eat, drink, and be merry.
LUKE XII, 19, *c.* 75

Let us eat, and be merry. LUKE XV, 23

If you are wise, be merry.
MARTIAL: *Epigrams,* II, 86

It is merry in hall
When beards wag all.
OLD ENGLISH RHYME, traced by Smith to *c.* 1300

As merry as a cricket.
ENGLISH PHRASE, familiar since the XVI century

As long liveth the merry man, they say,
As doth the sorry man, and longer by a day.
NICHOLAS UDALL: *Ralph Roister Doister,* I, *c.* 1553

It is good to be merry at meat (or meals).
ENGLISH PROVERB, familiar since the XVII century

Small cheer and great welcome makes a merry feast.
SHAKESPEARE: *The Comedy of Errors,* III, 1593

A merrier man,
Within the limit of becoming mirth,
I never spent an hour's talk withal.
SHAKESPEARE: *Love's Labor's Lost,* II, *c.* 1595

Why should a man whose blood is warm within
Sit like his grandsire cut in alabaster?
SHAKESPEARE: *The Merchant of Venice,* I, *c.* 1597

Put on
Your boldest suit of mirth, for we have friends
That purpose merriment.
SHAKESPEARE: *The Merchant of Venice,* II

A merry heart lives long-a.
SHAKESPEARE: *II Henry IV,* V, *c.* 1598

Men are merriest when they are from home.
SHAKESPEARE: *Henry V,* I, 1599

As merry as the day is long.
SHAKESPEARE: *Much Ado About Nothing,* II, *c.* 1599

A short life and a merry one.
ENGLISH PHRASE, familiar since the XVII century

I had rather have a fool to make me merry than experience to make me sad.
SHAKESPEARE: *As You Like It*, IV, *c.* 1600

Children and fools have merry lives.
JOHN RAY: *English Proverbs*, 1670

Resolve to be merry though the ship were sinking.
SUSANNA CENTLIVRE: *The Artifice*, v, 1710

Be always merry as ever you can,
For none delights in a sorrowful man.
THOMAS FULLER: *Gnomologia*, 1732

A merry fellow was never yet a respectable man.
LORD CHESTERFIELD: *Letter to his son*, Aug. 20, 1749

Nothing is more hopeless than a scheme of merriment.
SAMUEL JOHNSON: *The Idler*, May 26, 1759

All went merry as a marriage bell.
BYRON: *Childe Harold*, III, 1816

Merry is only a mask of sad.
R. W. EMERSON: *Waldeinsamkeit*, 1858 (Atlantic Monthly, Oct.)

When we are merriest is the time to go home.
CZECH PROVERB

The three merriest things in the world are a cat's kitten, a goat's kid, and a young widow.
IRISH PROVERB

Merry have we met, and merry have we been;
Merry let us part, and merry meet again;
With our merry sing-song, happy, gay, and free,
With a merry ding-dong, happy let us be!
OLD ENGLISH RHYME

[*See also* Doctor, Drinking, England, Gaiety, Meal, Mirth, More, Revelry, Singer, Three.

Mesmerism

Mesmerism is high life below stairs; Momus playing Jove in the kitchens of Olympus.
R. W. EMERSON: *Demonology*, 1877

Metabolism

Food eaten is sundered in three. The thickest stock thereof becometh excrement, the middling flesh, and thinnest mind. Water drunk is sundered in three. The thickest stock thereof becometh the body's water, the middling blood, and the thinnest breath. Heat eaten is sundered in three. The thickest stock thereof becometh bone, the middling marrow, the thinnest speech.
THE PRASNA UPANISHAD, *c.* 500 B.C.

Metaphor

The greatest thing in style is to have a command of metaphor. This power cannot be acquired; it is a mark of genius, for to make good metaphors implies an eye for resemblances.
ARISTOTLE: *Poetics*, XXII, *c.* 322 B.C.

Metaphor is of the highest value in both prose and poetry, but one must give especial attention to the use of metaphor in prose, for the resources of prose are less abundant than those of poetry.
ARISTOTLE: *Rhetoric*, III, *c.* 322 B.C.

A noble metaphor, when it is placed to an advantage, casts a kind of glory round it, and darks a lustre through a whole sentence.
JOSEPH ADDISON: *The Spectator*, July 3, 1712

She sees a mob of metaphors advance,
Pleas'd with the madness of the mazy dance.
ALEXANDER POPE: *The Dunciad*, I, 1728

Examine language; what, if you except some few primitive elements (of natural sounds), what is it all but metaphors, recognized as such, or no longer recognized; still fluid and florid, or now solid-grown and colorless?
THOMAS CARLYLE: *Sartor Resartus*, I, 1836

Metaphysician

He turn'd, without perceiving his condition,
Like Coleridge, into a metaphysician.
BYRON: *Don Juan*, I, 1819

He has spent all his life in letting down empty buckets into empty wells, and he is frittering away his age in trying to draw them up again.
Ascribed to SYDNEY SMITH in *A Memoir of the Rev. Sydney Smith* by his daughter, Lady Holland, 1855

Metaphysicians, like all other men who cannot give convincing reasons for their statements, are usually not very polite in controversy. One's success against them may be measured approximately by the increasing want of politeness in their replies.
HERMANN VON HELMHOLTZ: *Das Denken in der Medizin*, 1877 (Address in Berlin, Aug. 2)

A metaphysician is a man who goes into a dark cellar at midnight without a light looking for a black cat that is not there.
Ascribed to BARON BOWEN of Colwood (1835–94)

[*See also* Evolution, Philosopher.

Metaphysics

Much wrangling in things needless to be known.
Anon.: *Nero*, I, 1624

He knew what's what, and that's as high
As metaphysic wit can fly.
SAMUEL BUTLER: *Hudibras*, I, 1663

Others apart sat on a hill retir'd,
In thoughts more elevate, and reasoned high
Of Providence, foreknowledge, will and fate,

Fixed fate, free will, foreknowledge absolute;
And found no end, in wand'ring mazes lost.
JOHN MILTON: *Paradise Lost*, II, 1667

The metaphysical proofs of God are so remote from the reasoning of men, and so complicated, that they make but little impression; and even were this to serve some persons, it would be only during the instant of their seeing the demonstration, and an hour afterwards they would fear they had been deceived. BLAISE PASCAL: *Pensées*, XI, 1670

Let us next consider the subject of metaphysics. Alas, what an immensity of nonsense awaits us!
J. B. MENCKEN: *De charlanteria eruditorum*, II, 1715

Metaphysics consists of two parts, first, that which all men of sense already know, and second, that which they can never know.
VOLTAIRE: *Letter to Frederick the Great*, April 17, 1737

Metaphysics is a science which treats of being in general and its properties; of forms abstracted from matter; of immaterial things, as God, angels, &c.
ZACHARY GREY: Note in his edition of SAMUEL BUTLER: *Hudibras*, 1744

It is by metaphysical arguments only we are able to prove that the rational soul is not corporeal, that lead and sand cannot think; that thoughts are not square or round, or do not weigh a pound. . . . Indeed, we have no strict demonstration of anything, except mathematical truths, but by metaphysics.
JONATHAN EDWARDS: *Freedom of the Will*, I, 1754

In metaphysics the ancients have said everything. We coincide with them, or we repeat them. All modern books of this kind are only repetitious.
VOLTAIRE: *Philosophical Dictionary*, 1764

When the man speaking and the man spoken to do not understand each other, that is metaphysics. IBID.

Metaphysics, rightly shown,
But teach how little can be known.
JOHN TRUMBULL: *The Progress of Dullness*, 1773

If Shakespeare had been condemned to write a system of metaphysics explanatory of his magic influence over all the passions of the mind, it would have been a dull and unsatisfactory work; a heavy task, both to the reader and to the writer.
C. C. COLTON: *Lacon*, 1820

Metaphysics pleases me because it is never ending.
PROSPER MÉRIMÉE: *Lettres à une inconnue*, 1854

I hate metaphysics worse than physics.
W. S. LANDOR: *Letter to Robert Browning*, 1860

In rude and primitive ages man believed that when he dreamed he entered a second actual world. Herein lies the origin of all metaphysics. Without dreams there would have appeared no reason for a dualistic world.
F. W. NIETZSCHE: *Human All-too-Human*, I, 1878

Metaphysics is the finding of bad reasons for what we believe upon instinct.
F. H. BRADLEY: *Appearance and Reality*, 1893

There are no more metaphysics among the educated Japanese. Why should there be among us? MICHAEL J. DEE: *Conclusions*, V, 1917

[*See also* Knowledge, Mathematics, Philosophy.

Metempsychosis

A man may fish with the worm that hath eat of a king, and eat of the fish that hath fed of that worm.
SHAKESPEARE: *Hamlet*, IV, *c.* 1601

Or ever the knightly years were gone
With the old world to the grave,
I was a king in Babylon
And you were a Christian slave.
W. F. HENLEY: *Echoes*, 1888

Method

Though this be madness, yet there is method in 't. SHAKESPEARE: *Hamlet*, II, *c.* 1601

Lay down a method for everything, and stick to it inviolably, as far as unexpected incidents may allow.
LORD CHESTERFIELD: *Letter to his son*, Feb. 5, 1750

Methodism

Spiritual influenza.
GEORGE CRABBE: *The Borough*, IV, intro., 1810

It is no fault in others that the Methodist Church sends more soldiers to the field, more nurses to the hospital, and more prayers to Heaven than any. God bless the Methodist Church.
ABRAHAM LINCOLN: Speech to a Methodist delegation, Washington, May 14, 1864

Whenever a reporter is assigned to cover a Methodist conference he comes home an atheist. AMERICAN NEWSPAPER PROVERB

[*See also* Institution.

Methodist

They violently strain their eyeballs inward, half closing the lids; then, as they sit, they are in a perpetual motion of fee-faw, making long hums at proper periods, and continuing the sound at equal height; choosing their time in those intermissions while the preacher is at ebb.
JONATHAN SWIFT: *On the Mechanical Operation of the Spirit*, *c.* 1740

If the choice rested with us, we should say, — Give us back our wolves again — restore our Danish invaders — curse us with any evil but the evil of a canting, deluded, and Methodistical populace.

SYDNEY SMITH: In the Edinburgh Review, 1809

A lean, strait-locked, whey-faced Methodist.

CHARLES LAMB: *Letter to Bernard Barton,* Dec., 1827

As a general rule the Episcopal minister went to the family mansion, and the Methodist missionary preached to the Negroes and dined with the overseer at his house.

MARY BOYKIN CHESTNUT: *Diary,* Feb. 26, 1865 (Ascribed to a "Miss Daniel")

[*See also* Boarding-school, Drinking, Face.

Metternich, Clemens von (1773–1859)

One or two lies are sometimes necessary, but Metternich is all lies.

NAPOLEON I: To Barry E. O'Meara at St. Helena, April 6, 1817

[*See also* Statesman.

Mexico

I stood looking at it and thought that never in the world would there be discovered other lands such as these.

BERNAL DÍAZ: On the valley of Mexico, 1519

The want of a stable, responsible government in Mexico, capable of repressing and punishing marauders and bandit bands, who have not only taken the lives and seized and destroyed the property of American citizens in that country, but have insolently invaded our soil, made war upon and murdered our people thereon, has rendered it necessary temporarily to occupy, by our armed forces, a portion of the territory of that friendly state.

Democratic National Platform, 1916

We should not recognize any Mexican government, unless it be a responsible government willing and able to give sufficient guarantees that the lives and property of American citizens are respected and protected; that wrongs will be promptly corrected and just compensation will be made for injury sustained.

Republican National Platform, 1920

Michaelangelo (1475–1564)

I do not want Michelangelo for breakfast — for luncheon — for dinner — for tea — for supper — for between meals.

S. L. CLEMENS (MARK TWAIN): *Innocents Abroad,* III, 1869

Microbe

I tell thee that those viewless beings,
Whose mansion is the smallest particle
Of the impassive atmosphere,
Think, feel and live like man.

P. B. SHELLEY: *Queen Mab,* II, 1813

Adam
Had 'em.

STRICKLAND GILLILAN: *The Antiquity of Microbes,* 1904 (Baltimore American)

In the Nineteenth Century men lost their fear of God and acquired a fear of microbes.

Author unidentified

Middle

The middle course is the safest. (Medio tutissimus ibis.)

OVID: *Metamorphoses,* c. 5

[*See also* Mean.

Middle Ages

[*See* Ages (Middle).

Middle Class

[*See* Class (Middle).

Midnight

It came to pass at midnight, that the man was afraid.

RUTH III, 8, *c.* 500 B.C.

The noon of night.

DANTE: *Purgatorio,* XV, *c.* 1320

The dreadful dead of dark midnight.

SHAKESPEARE: *The Rape of Lucrece,* 1593

The iron tongue of midnight hath told twelve;
Lovers, to bed, 'tis almost fairy time.

SHAKESPEARE: *A Midsummer Night's Dream,* V, *c.* 1596

The dead vast and middle of the night.

SHAKESPEARE: *Hamlet,* I, *c.* 1601

'Tis now the very witching time of night,
When churchyards yawn and Hell itself breathes out
Contagion to this world.

SHAKESPEARE: *Hamlet,* III

Midnight brought on the dusky hour
Friendliest to sleep and silence.

JOHN MILTON: *Paradise Lost,* V, 1667

This is the dumb and dreary hour,
When injur'd ghosts complain;
When yawning graves give up their dead
To haunt the faithless swain.

DAVID MALLET: *William and Margaret,* 1723

Once upon a midnight dreary, while I pondered weak and weary,
Over many a quaint and curious volume of forgotten lore.

E. A. POE: *The Raven,* 1845 (New York Evening Mirror, Jan. 24)

I stood on the bridge at midnight,
As the clocks were striking the hour,
And the moon rose o'er the city,
Behind the dark church-tower.

H. W. LONGFELLOW: *The Bridge,* 1846

The gaunt lonesomeness of this midnight hour, in the ugly universal snoring hum of the overfilled, deep-sunk posterity of Adam. . . .
THOMAS CARLYLE: *Letter to R. W. Emerson*, May 13, 1853

[*See also* Night, Sleep.

Midst

Into the midst of things. (In medias res.)
LATIN PHRASE

Midsummer

A midsummer night's dream.
SHAKESPEARE: Title of a play, c. 1596

[*See also* Madness.

Midwife

The midwives feared God.
EXODUS I, 17, *c.* 700 B.C.

God dealt well with the midwives; and the people multiplied, and waxed very mighty.
EXODUS I, 20

Hasty people will never make good midwives.
JOHN RAY: *English Proverbs*, 1670

When there are two midwives the baby's head is mashed.
PERSIAN PROVERB

[*See also* Childbirth.

Midwifery

Meddlesome midwifery is bad.
MEDICAL MAXIM, not recorded before the XIX century

Might

The gods love to humble the mighty.
HERODOTUS: *Histories*, VII, *c.* 430 B.C.

Whatsoever thy hand findeth to do, do it with thy might.
ECCLESIASTES IX, 10, *c.* 200 B.C.

Then the Lord awakened as one out of sleep, and like a mighty man that shouteth by reason of wine. And he smote his enemies in the hinder parts.
PSALMS LXXVIII, 65–66, *c.* 150 B.C.

The reasoning of the mightiest is always the best.
JEAN DE LA FONTAINE: *Fables*, I, 1668

Might makes a weird sound of its own stillness.
P. B. SHELLEY: *Alastor*, 1816

[*See also* Diligence, Fall, Force, Justice, Right and Might, Strength.

Might and Right

[*See* Right and Might.

Might-have-been

The world which credits what is done,
Is cold to all that might have been.
ALFRED TENNYSON: *In Memoriam*, LXXV, 1850

Of all the sad words of tongue or pen,
The saddest are these: It might have been.
J. G. WHITTIER: *Maud Muller*, 1854

My name is Might-have-been;
I am also called No-more, Too-late, Farewell.
D. G. ROSSETTI: *Sonnets*, 1881

Militarism

My life's amusements have been just the same
Before and after standing armies came.
ALEXANDER POPE: *The Second Satire of the Second Book of Horace*, 1733

The spirit of this country is totally adverse to a large military force.
THOMAS JEFFERSON: *Letter to Chandler Price*, 1807

We oppose militarism. It means conquest abroad and intimidation and oppression at home. It means the strong arm which has ever been fatal to free institutions. It is what millions of our citizens have fled from in Europe.
Democratic National Platform, 1900

[*See also* Army, Buddhism, Cannon, Monarchy, War.

Militia

Raw in the fields the rude militia swarms,
Mouths without hands; maintain'd at vast expense,
In peace a charge, in war a weak defence.
JOHN DRYDEN: *Cymon and Iphigenia*, 1699

The Congress shall have power . . . to provide for organizing, arming and disciplining the militia, and for governing such part of them as may be employed in the service of the United States, reserving to the states respectively the appointment of the officers, and the authority of training the militia according to the discipline prescribed by Congress.
CONSTITUTION OF THE UNITED STATES, Art. I, 1789

A well-regulated militia being necessary to the security of a free state, the right of the people to keep and bear arms shall not be infringed.
CONSTITUTION OF THE UNITED STATES, Amendment II, Dec. 15, 1791

For a people who are free, and who mean to remain so, a well organized and armed militia is their best security.
THOMAS JEFFERSON: Message to Congress, Nov., 1808

We must train and classify the whole of our male citizens, and make military instruction a regular part of collegiate education. We can never be safe till this is done.
THOMAS JEFFERSON: *Letter to James Monroe*, 1813

[*See also* Army.

Milk

A land flowing with milk and honey.
EXODUS III, 8, *c.* 700 B.C. (Cf. III, 17; XIII, 5; XXXIII, 3; JEREMIAH XI, 5; XXXII, 22, *c.* 625 B.C.; EZEKIEL XX, 6; XX, 15, *c.* 600 B.C.)

Thou shalt not seethe a kid in his mother's milk.
EXODUS XXIII, 19 (Cf. DEUTERONOMY XIV, 21, *c.* 650 B.C.)

Everyone that useth milk is unskilful in the word of righteousness: for he is a babe.
HEBREWS V, 13, *c.* 65

A red cow gives good milk.
ENGLISH PROVERB, familiar since the XVII century

It's no use crying over spilt milk. IBID.

Milk . . . causeth the body to wax gross, and for amending of a dry constitution, and for them that are extenuated by long sickness, or are in a consumption, it is by reason of the excellent moistening, cooling and nourishing faculty of it, of singular efficacy.
TOBIAS VENNER: *Via recta,* 1620

What the French call Christian milk — milk which has been baptized.
S. L. CLEMENS (MARK TWAIN): *A Tramp Abroad,* XLIX, 1879

That delightful substance which comes out of the wonderful chemistry which God has given the cow for the delight of the world and the sustenance of children.
CHAUNCEY M. DEPEW: Speech in the Senate, April 2, 1902

Milk before wine
I would 'twere mine;
Milk taken after,
Is poison's daughter. OLD ENGLISH RHYME

[*See also* Beer, Bread and Butter, Child, Cow, Cream, Kid, Snake.

Milkmaid

A fair and happy milkmaid is a country wench that is so far from making herself beautiful by art that one look of hers is able to put all face-physic out of countenance.
THOMAS OVERBURY: *Characters,* 1614

"Where are you going my pretty maid?"
"I'm going a-milking, sir," she said.
Anon.: *Nursery rhyme, c.* 1750

Mill

[*See* Water.

Miller

There was a jolly miller once,
Lived on the River Dee;
He worked and sang, from morn to night;
No lark so blithe as he.
And this the burden of his song,
Forever used to be. —
"I care for nobody, not I,
If no one care for me."
ISAAC BICKERSTAFFE: *Love in a Village,* I, 1762

The only honest miller is the one with hair on his teeth. GERMAN PROVERB

[*See also* Thief.

Millionaire

Superior want of conscience . . . is often the determining quality which makes a millionaire out of one who otherwise might have been a poor man.
HENRY GEORGE: *Progress and Poverty,* VI, 1879

The reason why I defend the millions of the millionaire is not that I love the millionaire, but that I love my own wife and children, and that I know no way in which to get the defense of society for my hundreds, except to give my help, as a member of society, to protect his millions.
W. G. SUMNER: *The Family and Property,* 1888

[*See also* Equality, Patient, Rich.

Milton, John (1608–74)

Three poets in three distant ages born,
Greece, Italy, and England did adorn.
The first in loftiness of thought surpass'd;
The next, in majesty; in both, the last.
The force of nature could no further go;
To make a third, she join'd the former two.
JOHN DRYDEN: *Under Mr. Milton's Picture,* 1688

His fame is gone out like a candle in a snuff, and his memory will always stink, which might have lived in honorable repute, had he not been a notorious traitor, and most impiously and villainously belied that blessed martyr, King Charles I.
WILLIAM WINSTANLEY: *Lives of the Most Famous English Poets,* 1687

Milton's strong pinion now not Heaven can bound,
Now serpent-like, in prose he sweeps the ground,
In quibbles, angel and archangel join,
And God the Father turns a school-divine.
ALEXANDER POPE: *The First Epistle of the Second Book of Horace,* 1737

An acrimonious and surly republican.
SAMUEL JOHNSON: *Lives of the Poets (Milton),* III, 1778

Was there ever anything so delightful as the music of the Paradise Lost? It is like that of a fine organ; has the fullest and the deepest tones of majesty with all the softness and elegance of the Dorian flute: variety without end, and never equaled, unless perhaps by Virgil.
WILLIAM COWPER: *Letter to William Unwin,* Oct. 31, 1779

Milton was a genius that could cut a colossus from a rock, but could not carve heads upon cherry-stones.
SAMUEL JOHNSON: *Boswell's Life,* June 13, 1784 (On Milton as a sonnet writer)

The reason Milton wrote in fetters when he wrote of angels and God, and at liberty when of devils and Hell, is because he was a true poet and of the Devil's party without knowing it.
WILLIAM BLAKE: *The Marriage of Heaven and Hell,* 1790

That mighty orb of song,
The divine Milton.
WILLIAM WORDSWORTH: *The Excursion,* I, 1814

Milton's the prince of poets, so we say:
A little heavy, but no less divine;
An independent being in his day;
Learned, pious, temperate in love and wine.
BYRON: *Don Juan,* III, 1821

Milton was a great poet, but a bad divine, and a miserable politician.
JOHN WILSON: *Noctes Ambrosianæ,* I, 1822

It is to be regretted that the prose writings of Milton should in our time, be so little read. As compositions, they deserve the attention of every man who wishes to become acquainted with the full power of the English language. They abound with passages compared with which the finest declamations of Burke sink into insignificance. They are a perfect field of cloth of gold. The style is stiff with gorgeous embroidery.
T. B. MACAULAY: *Milton,* 1825 (Edinburgh Review, Aug.)

Milton was the stair or high tableland to let down the English genius from the summits of Shakespeare.
R. W. EMERSON: *English Traits,* V, 1856

Reading Milton is like dining off gold plate in a company of kings; very splendid, very ceremonious, and not a little appalling.
ALEXANDER SMITH: *Dreamthorp,* IX, 1863

O mighty-mouth'd inventor of harmonies,
O skill'd to sing of time or eternity,
God-gifted organ-voice of England,
Milton, a name to resound for ages.
ALFRED TENNYSON: *Milton,* 1863

[*See also* Burke (Edmund), Dante Alighieri, Greatness, Invention, Newton (Isaac), Obscurity.

Mind

Rule your mind or it will rule you.
HORACE: *Carmina,* I, *c.* 20, B.C.

Only the mind cannot be sent into exile.
OVID: *Epistulæ ex Ponto,* IV, *c.* 5

O ye gods! what thick encircling darkness blinds the minds of men!
OVID: *Metamorphoses,* VI, *c.* 5

A good mind is lord of a kingdom.
SENECA: *Thyestes,* II, *c.* 60

In his right mind.
MARK V, 15, *c.* 70 (Cf. LUKE VIII, 35, *c.* 75)

In reading profane authors we should be reminded by the admirable light of truth which appears in them that the human mind, however much fallen and perverted from its original integrity, is still adorned and invested with gifts from its Creator.
JOHN CALVIN: *Institutes of the Christian Religion,* II, 1536

It is good to rub and polish your mind against the minds of others.
MICHEL DE MONTAIGNE: *Essays,* I, 1580

My mind to me a kingdom is,
Such perfect joy therein I find
As far exceeds all earthly bliss
That God or nature hath assigned.
EDWARD DYER: *My Mind to Me a Kingdom Is,* 1588

The worth of the mind consisteth not in going high, but in marching orderly.
MICHEL DE MONTAIGNE: *Essays,* III, 1588

There is one Mind. It is absolutely omnipresent, giving mentality to all things.
GIORDANO BRUNO: *De monade numero et figura,* II, 1591

'Tis but a base, ignoble mind
That mounts no higher than a bird can soar.
SHAKESPEARE: *II Henry VI,* II, *c.* 1591

Man's mind a mirror is of heavenly sights,
A brief wherein all marvels summed lie.
ROBERT SOUTHWELL: *Content and Rich,* *c.* 1595

In my mind's eye.
SHAKESPEARE: *Hamlet,* I, *c.* 1601

The flash and outbreak of a fiery mind.
SHAKESPEARE: *Hamlet,* II

Thy mind is a very opal.
SHAKESPEARE: *Twelfth Night,* II, *c.* 1601

The mind is free, whate'er afflict the man.
MICHAEL DRAYTON: *The Barons' War,* V, 1603

Canst thou not minister to a mind diseas'd;
Pluck from the memory a rooted sorrow;
Raze out the written troubles of the brain;
And, with some sweet oblivious antidote,
Cleanse the stuff'd bosom of that perilous matter
Which weighs upon the heart?
SHAKESPEARE: *Macbeth,* V, *c.* 1605

There is one principal and, as it were, radical distinction between different minds, in respect of philosophy and the sciences; which is this: that some minds are stronger and apter to mark the differences of things, others to mark their resemblances.
FRANCIS BACON: *Novum Organum,* I, 1620

The mind is its own place, and in itself
Can make a heaven of Hell, a hell of Heaven.

JOHN MILTON: *Paradise Lost,* I, 1667

All bodies, the firmament, the stars, the earth and its kingdoms, are not equal to the lowest mind; for mind knows all these and itself; and these bodies nothing.

BLAISE PASCAL: *Pensées,* 1670

As for my feeble mind, that I will leave behind me, for that I have no need of that in the place whither I go; nor is it worth bestowing upon the poorest pilgrim; wherefore, when I am gone, I desire that you would bury it in a dunghill.

JOHN BUNYAN: *Pilgrim's Progress,* II, 1678

Love, hope, and joy, fair pleasure's smiling train,
Hate, fear, and grief, the family of pain,
These mix'd with art, and to due bounds confin'd
Make and maintain the balance of the mind.

ALEXANDER POPE: *An Essay on Man,* II, 1732

No prelate's lawn, with hair-shirt lined,
Is half so incoherent as my mind.

ALEXANDER POPE: *The First Epistle of the First Book of Horace,* 1735

What we call a mind is nothing but a heap or collection of different perceptions, united together by certain relations, and supposed, though falsely, to be endowed with a perfect simplicity and identity.

DAVID HUME: *A Treatise of Human Nature,* I, 1739

The mind is but a barren soil — a soil which is soon exhausted, and will produce no crop, or only one, unless it be continually fertilized and enriched with foreign matter.

JOSHUA REYNOLDS: *Discourses,* VI, 1774 (Lecture at the Royal Academy, London, Dec. 10)

The march of the human mind is slow.

EDMUND BURKE: Speech on Conciliation with America, March 22, 1775

The true and strong and sound mind is the mind that can embrace equally great things and small.

SAMUEL JOHNSON: *Boswell's Life,* 1778

The knowledge of external nature, and the sciences which that knowledge requires or includes, are not the great or the frequent business of the human mind.

SAMUEL JOHNSON: *Lives of the Poets (Milton),* 1778

A mind forever
Voyaging through strange seas of thought alone.

WILLIAM WORDSWORTH: *The Prelude,* III, 1805

The caverns of the mind are obscure, and shadowy, or pervaded with a lustre, beautifully bright indeed, but shining not beyond their portals.

P. B. SHELLEY: *Speculations on Metaphysics,* 1815

Happiness, or misery, is in the mind. It is the mind that lives.

WILLIAM COBBETT: *Grammar of the English Language,* 1823

Mind is the great lever of all things; human thought is the process by which human ends are ultimately answered.

DANIEL WEBSTER: Address on laying the cornerstone of the Bunker Hill Monument, June 17, 1825

My mind is unChristian, for it keeps no day of rest.

ESAIAS TEGNÉR: *Letter to F. M. Franzén,* Jan., 1826

The mind is like a sheet of white paper in this: that the impressions it receives the oftenest, and retains the longest, are black ones.

J. C. and A. W. HARE: *Guesses at Truth,* 1827

Measure your mind's height by the shade it casts.

ROBERT BROWNING: *Paracelsus,* II, 1835

It is mind which does the work of the world, so that the more there is of mind, the more work will be accomplished.

W. E. CHANNING: *Self-Culture,* 1838

There is an unseemly exposure of the mind, as well as of the body.

WILLIAM HAZLITT: *Sketches and Essays,* 1839

How can we speak of the action of the mind under any divisions, as of its knowledge, of its ethics, of its works, and so forth, since it melts will into perception, knowledge into act? Each becomes the other. Itself alone is.

R. W. EMERSON: *Intellect,* 1841

It is good to learn to look without wonder or disgust on the weaknesses which are to be found in the strongest minds.

T. B. MACAULAY: *Warren Hastings,* 1841 (Edinburgh Review, Oct.)

A chief event of life is the day in which we have encountered a mind that startled us.

R. W. EMERSON: *Character,* 1844

On earth there is nothing great but man; in man there is nothing great but mind.

WILLIAM HAMILTON: *Lectures on Metaphysics, c.* 1850

A great mind is a good sailor, as a great heart is.

R. W. EMERSON: *English Traits,* II, 1856

Man is a soul informed by divine ideas, and bodying forth their image. His mind is the unit and measure of things visible and invisible.

A. BRONSON ALCOTT: *Tablets,* II, 1868

The mind can weave itself warmly in the cocoon of its own thoughts, and dwell a hermit anywhere.

J. R. LOWELL: On a Certain Condescension in Foreigners, 1869

There is no fundamental difference between man and the higher animals in their mental faculties.

CHARLES DARWIN: *The Descent of Man,* X, 1871

The mind of man may be compared to a musical instrument with a certain range of tones, beyond which in both directions we have an infinitude of silence.

JOHN TYNDALL: *Fragments of Science for Unscientific People,* II, 1871

If we look into ourselves we discover propensities which declare that our intellects have arisen from a lower form; could our minds be made visible we should find them tailed.

W. WINWOOD READE: *The Martyrdom of Man,* III, 1872

All progress of mind consists for the most part in differentiation, in the resolution of an obscure and complex subject into its component aspects.

WALTER PATER: *Style,* 1888

A mysterious form of matter secreted by the brain. Its chief activity consists in the endeavor to ascertain its own nature, the futility of the attempt being due to the fact that it has nothing but itself to know itself with.

AMBROSE BIERCE: *The Devil's Dictionary,* 1906

Mind, issued from the monkey's womb,
Is still umbilical to earth.

ALDOUS HUXLEY: *First Philosopher's Song,* 1920

Little minds are interested in the extraordinary; great minds in the commonplace.

ELBERT HUBBARD: *Roycroft Dictionary and Book of Epigrams,* 1923

Great minds are interested in ideas, average minds in events, small minds in people.

Author unidentified

What the mind is at the age of five it will be at the age of twenty-five. HINDU PROVERB

A man's mind is the man himself. (Mens cujusque is est quisque.) LATIN PROVERB

A man's mind is a mirk mirror.

SCOTTISH PROVERB. (*Mirk*=dark)

[*See also* Algebra, Brain, Christian Science, Education, Eternity, Face, God, Head and Heart, Health, Indolence, Learning, Library, Man, Mind and Body, Mind and Matter, Moderation, Poetry, Progress, Thinking, Thought, Time.

Mind and Body

The body is at its best between the ages of thirty and thirty-five; the mind is at its best about the age of forty-nine.

ARISTOTLE: *Rhetoric, c.* 322 B.C.

The earthy tabernacle weigheth down the mind that museth upon many things.

WISDOM OF SOLOMON IX, 15, *c.* 100 B.C.

In the same way that the strength of the mind surpasses that of the body, the sufferings of the mind are more severe than the pains of the body.

CICERO: *Orationes Philippicæ,* XI, *c.* 60 B.C.

The mind grows and decays with the body.

LUCRETIUS: *De rerum natura,* III, 57 B.C.

Pain of mind is worse than pain of body.

PUBLILIUS SYRUS: *Sententiæ, c.* 50 B.C.

The mind, when it is sick, is more sick than the sick body. OVID: *Tristia,* IV, *c.* 10

I delight in the law of God after the inward man; but I see another law in my members, warring against the law of my mind, and bringing me into captivity to the law of sin.

ROMANS VII, 22, *c.* 55

A sound mind in a sound body. (Mens sana in corpore sano.)

JUVENAL: *Satires,* X, *c.* 125

'Tis the mind that makes the body rich.

SHAKESPEARE: *The Taming of the Shrew,* IV, 1594

Fat bodies, lean brains.

BEAUMONT and FLETCHER: *Love's Cure,* II, *c.* 1610

Strength and weakness of mind are badly named — they are, in fact, nothing more than the good or bad arrangement of the organs of the body.

LA ROCHEFOUCAULD: *Maxims,* 1665

All our perceptions are dependent on our organs and the disposition of our nerves and animal spirits.

DAVID HUME: *A Treatise of Human Nature,* I, 1739

A feeble body weakens the mind.

J.-J. ROUSSEAU: *Émile,* I, 1762

Every . . . state of the mind [is] connected with a certain state of the body, which must be inquired into in order to its being treated as a disease by the art of physic.

WILLIAM CULLEN: *First Lines of the Practice of Physic,* II, 1774

When it comes to the body, there are as many imaginary invalids as invalids in fact. When it comes to the mind, there are as many who are only supposed to have sound ones as there are persons who have them in fact.

G. C. LICHTENBERG: *Reflections,* 1799

Body and mind, like man and wife, do not always agree to die together.
C. C. COLTON: *Lacon,* 1820

The mind may undoubtedly affect the body; but the body also affects the mind. There is a reaction between them; and by lessening it on either side, you diminish the pain on both.
LEIGH HUNT: *The Indicator,* VII, 1821

Minds, like bodies, will often fall into a pimpled, ill-conditioned state from mere excess of comfort.
CHARLES DICKENS: *Barnaby Rudge,* VII, 1840

Our mental conditions are simply the symbols in consciousness of the changes which take place automatically in the organism.
T. H. HUXLEY: *On the Hypothesis that Animals Are Automata,* 1874

Mortal mind and body are one. Neither exists without the other, and both must be destroyed by immortal Mind.
MARY BAKER G. EDDY: *Science and Health,* VI, 1908

The body may be cured, but not the mind.
CHINESE PROVERB

[*See also* Body, Body and Soul, Marriage, Pleasure, Sickly.

Mind and Matter

No barriers, no masses of matter however enormous, can withstand the powers of the mind; the remotest corners yield to them; all things succumb; the very Heaven itself is laid open.
MARCUS MANILIUS: *Astronomica,* I, *c.* 40 B.C.

Mind moves matter. (Mens agitat molem.)
VIRGIL: *Æneid,* VI, 19 B.C.

All the choir of Heaven and furniture of earth . . . have not any substance without a mind.
GEORGE BERKELEY: *The Principles of Human Knowledge,* 1710

The ultimate forms of existence which we distinguish in our little speck of the universe are, possibly, only two out of infinite varieties of existence, not only analogous to matter and analogous to mind, but of kinds which we are not competent so much as to conceive.
T. H. HUXLEY: *Evidence as to Man's Place in Nature,* II, 1863

What is mind? No matter. What is matter? Never mind.
Ascribed to THOMAS H. KEY (1799–1875)

[*See also* Matter.

Mine and Thine

If it were not for *mine* and *thine* the world would be Heaven.
GERMAN PROVERB

Mine and thine. (Meum et tuum.)
LATIN PHRASE

[*See also* Communism, Husband and Wife, Property.

Minority

Every new opinion, at its starting, is precisely in a minority of one.
THOMAS CARLYLE: *Heroes and Hero-Worship,* II, 1840 (Lecture in London, May 8)

Great truths always dwell a long time with small minorities, and the real voice of God is often that which rises above the masses, not that which follows them.
FRANCIS LIEBER: *Civil Liberty and Self-Government,* 1852

Governments exist to protect the rights of minorities. The loved and the rich need no protection, — they have many friends and few enemies.
WENDELL PHILLIPS: Speech at Boston, Dec. 21, 1860

Minorities must suffer.
AUGUSTINE BIRRELL: Speech in the House of Commons, 1906

If a man is in a minority of one we lock him up.
O. W. HOLMES II: Speech in New York, Feb. 15, 1913

[*See also* Majority, Majority and Minority, Opinion, Truth.

Minstrel

A wandering minstrel I —
A thing of shreds and patches.
W. S. GILBERT: *The Mikado,* I, 1885

Minute

Take care of the minutes, for the hours will take care of themselves.
LORD CHESTERFIELD: *Letter to his son,* Oct. 9, 1746

[*See also* Moment.

Miracle

In my name shall they cast out devils; they shall speak with new tongues; they shall take up serpents; and if they drink any deadly thing, it shall not hurt them; they shall lay hands on the sick, and they shall recover.
MARK XVI, 17–18, *c.* 70

What is easy to understand we despise; we need prodigies and miracles.
SYNESIUS: *Egyptian Tales, c.* 400

Why, they ask, do not those miracles, which you preach of as past events, happen nowadays? I might reply that they were necessary before the world believed, to bring the world to believe; but whoever is still looking for prodigies to make him believe is himself a great prodigy for refusing to believe where the world believes.

ST. AUGUSTINE: *The City of God,* XXII, 427

Miracles appear to be so, according to our ignorance of nature, and not according to the essence of nature.

MICHEL DE MONTAIGNE: *Essays,* I, 1580

They say miracles are past.

SHAKESPEARE: *All's Well that Ends Well,* II, *c.* 1602

There was never miracle wrought by God to convert an atheist, because the light of nature might have led him to confess a God: but miracles have been wrought to convert idolaters and the superstitious, because no light of nature extendeth to declare the will and true worship of God.

FRANCIS BACON: *The Advancement of Learning,* II, 1605

That miracles have been, I do believe; that they may yet be wrought by the living, I do not deny; but I have no confidence in those which are fathered on the dead.

THOMAS BROWNE: *Religio Medici,* I, 1642

Miracles are the swaddling-clothes of infant churches.

THOMAS FULLER: *Church History,* II, 1655

A miracle is an effect which exceeds the natural force of the means employed for it.

BLAISE PASCAL: *Pensées,* XXII, 1670

Had it not been for the miracles, there would have been no sin in not believing in Jesus Christ.

IBID.

So the miracle be wrought, what matter if the Devil did it?

THOMAS FULLER: *Gnomologia,* 1732

The Old Testament affords us the same historical evidence of the miracles of Moses and of the prophets as of the common civil history of Moses and the kings of Israel, or as of the affairs of the Jewish nation.

JOSEPH BUTLER: *The Analogy of Religion,* II, 1736

What is a miracle? — 'Tis a reproach,
'Tis an implicit satire on mankind.

EDWARD YOUNG: *Night Thoughts,* IX, 1745

There is not to be found, in all history, any miracle attested by a sufficient number of men, of such unquestioned goodness, education, and learning as to secure us against all delusion in themselves; of such undoubted integrity as to place them beyond all suspicion of any design to deceive others; of such credit and reputation in the eyes of mankind as to have a great deal to lose in case of their being detected in any falsehood; and at the same time attesting facts, performed in such a public manner, and in so celebrated a part of the world, as to render the detection unavoidable.

DAVID HUME: *An Enquiry Concerning the Human Understanding,* III, 1748

The story of the whale swallowing Jonah, though a whale is large enough to do it, borders greatly on the marvelous; but it would have approached nearer to the idea of miracle if Jonah had swallowed the whale.

THOMAS PAINE: *The Age of Reason,* I, 1794

The happy do not believe in miracles.

J. W. GOETHE: *Hermann und Dorothea,* II, 1797

Many a man who is now willing to be shot down for the sake of his belief in a miracle would have doubted, if he had been present, the miracle itself.

G. C. LICHTENBERG: *Reflections,* 1799

Miracles are not the proofs, but the necessary results, of revelation.

S. T. COLERIDGE: *Omniana,* 1812

Our reason can never admit the testimony of men who not only declare that they were eye-witnesses of miracles, but that the Deity was irrational; for He commanded that He should be believed, He proposed the highest rewards for faith, eternal punishment for disbelief.

P. B. SHELLEY: *Queen Mab,* notes, 1813

The question before the human race is whether the God of nature shall govern the world by His own laws, or whether priests and kings shall rule it by fictitious miracles.

THOMAS JEFFERSON: *Letter to John Adams,* 1815

The word miracle, as pronounced by Christian churches, gives a false impression; it is a monster. It is not one with the blowing clover and the falling rain.

R. W. EMERSON: Address at the Divinity College, Cambridge, Mass., July 15, 1838

The age of miracles past? The age of miracles is forever here!

THOMAS CARLYLE: *Heroes and Hero-Worship,* IV, 1840 (Lecture in London, May 15)

Every cubic inch of space is a miracle.

WALT WHITMAN: *Miracles,* 1856

No miracle has ever taken place under conditions which science can accept. Experience shows, without exception, that miracles occur only in times and in countries in which miracles are believed in, and in the presence of persons who are disposed to believe them.

ERNEST RENAN: *Vie de Jésus,* intro., 1863

However skilfully the modern ingenuity of semi-belief may have tampered with supernatural interpositions, it is clear to every

honest and unsophisticated mind that, if miracles be incredible, Christianity is false.
F. W. FARRAR: *The Witness of History to Christ,* 1870

It is almost impossible to exaggerate the proneness of the human mind to take miracles as evidence, and to seek for miracles as evidence.
MATTHEW ARNOLD: *Literature and Dogma,* v, 1873

Miracles are the children of mendacity.
R. G. INGERSOLL: Speech in New York, April 25, 1881

An act or event out of the order of nature and unaccountable, as beating a hand of four kings and an ace with four aces and a king.
AMBROSE BIERCE: *The Devil's Dictionary,* 1906

There is as much evidence that the miracles occurred as that the battle of Waterloo occurred, or that a large body of Russian troops passed through England in 1914 to take part in the war on the Western front.
GEORGE BERNARD SHAW: *Androcles and the Lion,* pref., 1912

Miracle seems vastly more reasonable, to all but one mind out of 100,000, than any rationalistic material explanation whatsoever.
MICHAEL J. DEE: *Conclusions,* IV, 1917

One miracle is just as easy to believe as another.
W. J. BRYAN: From the court records of the Scopes trial, Dayton, Tenn., July 21, 1925

Miracles happen only to those who believe in them.
FRENCH PROVERB

No one believes in the saint unless he works miracles.
ITALIAN PROVERB

[*See also* Flesh, Prayer.

Mirror

There was never yet fair woman but she made mouths in a glass.
SHAKESPEARE: *King Lear,* III, 1606

The more women look in their glass, the less they look to their house.
GEORGE HERBERT: *Outlandish Proverbs,* 1640

The Devil's behind the glass.
H. G. BOHN: *Handbook of Proverbs,* 1855

The best mirror is a friend's eye.
GAELIC PROVERB

A mirror eats donkeys and spits out fools.
GERMAN PROVERB

Mirth

The heart of fools is in the house of mirth.
ECCLESIASTES VII, 4, *c.* 200 B.C.

How difficult it is to imitate mirth; how difficult to mimic cheerfulness with a sad heart.
TIBULLUS: *Elegies,* III, *c.* 20 B.C.

Mirth prolongeth life, and causeth health.
NICHOLAS UDALL: *Ralph Roister Doister,* *c.* 1553

Mirth cannot move a soul in agony.
SHAKESPEARE: *Love's Labor's Lost,* v, *c.* 1595

From the crown of his head to the sole of his foot, he is all mirth.
SHAKESPEARE: *Much Ado About Nothing,* III, *c.* 1599

Let's be red with mirth.
SHAKESPEARE: *The Winter's Tale,* IV, *c.* 1611

I love such mirth as does not make friends ashamed to look upon one another next morning.
IZAAK WALTON: *The Compleat Angler,* v, 1653

Mirth to a prudent man should always be accidental. It should naturally arise out of the occasion, and the occasion seldom be laid for it.
RICHARD STEELE: *The Spectator,* Oct. 15, 1711

In the time of mirth take heed.
THOMAS FULLER: *Gnomologia,* 1732

Mustard is good sauce, but mirth is better.
IBID.

Where lives the man that has not tried
How mirth can into folly glide,
And folly into sin?
WALTER SCOTT: *The Bridal of Triermain,* I, 1813

The end of mirth is the beginning of sorrow.
CZECH PROVERB

[*See also* Guest, Humor, Jest, Laughter, Merriment, Wit.

Miscegenation

Moses . . . married an Ethiopian woman.
NUMBERS XII, 1, *c.* 700 B.C.

Turtles and doves of diff'rent hues unite,
And glossy jet is paired with shining white.
ALEXANDER POPE: *Sappho to Phaon,* 1712

[*See also* Mulatto.

Mischief

A heart that deviseth wicked imaginings, feet that be swift in running to mischief.
PROVERBS VI, 18, *c.* 350 B.C. (Listed among things " the Lord doth hate ")

It is sport to a fool to do mischief.
PROVERBS X, 23

His mischief shall return upon his own head, and his violent dealing shall come down upon his own pate.
PSALMS VII, 16, *c.* 150 B.C.

Thy tongue deviseth mischiefs, like a sharp razor, working deceitfully. PSALMS LII, 2

He who wishes to do mischief is never without a reason.
PUBLILIUS SYRUS: *Sententiæ, c.* 50 B.C.

Mischief, thou art afoot,
Take thou what course thou wilt.
SHAKESPEARE: *Julius Cæsar,* III, 1599

He that mischief hatcheth mischief catcheth.
WILLIAM CAMDEN: *Remains Concerning Britain,* 1636

He had a head to contrive, a tongue to persuade, and a hand to execute any mischief.
EDWARD HYDE (EARL OF CLARENDON): *The True Historical Narrative of the Rebellion and Civil Wars in England,* III, *c.* 1670

Mischief comes by the pound, and goes away by the ounce.
THOMAS FULLER: *Gnomologia,* 1732

Never to do more mischief to another than was necessary to the effecting his purpose; for that mischief was too precious a thing to be thrown away.
HENRY FIELDING: *Jonathan Wild,* IV, 1743 (Maxim of Wild for the attainment of greatness)

In every deed of mischief he had a heart to resolve, a head to contrive, and a hand to execute.
EDWARD GIBBON: *The Decline and Fall of the Roman Empire,* II, 1781 (Cf. HYDE, *ante, c.* 1670)

The mair mischief the better sport.
SCOTTISH PROVERB

[*See also* Ability, Abomination, Priest.

Miser

Misers are neither relations, nor friends, nor citizens, nor Christians, nor perhaps even human beings.
JEAN DE LA BRUYÈRE: *Caractères,* VI, 1688

The Devil lies brooding in the miser's chest.
THOMAS FULLER: *Gnomologia,* 1732

Misers are very good people; they amass wealth for those who wish their death.
STANISLAUS LESZCYNSKI (KING OF POLAND): *Œuvres du philosophe bienfaisant,* 1763

No man was born a miser, because no man was born to possession. Every man is born *cupidus* — desirous of getting; but not *avarus* — desirous of keeping.
SAMUEL JOHNSON: *Boswell's Life,* April 25, 1778

Nature laughs at a miser.
HENRY GEORGE: *Progress and Poverty,* IX, 1879

Every miser has a spendthrift son.
FRENCH PROVERB

In a city full of misers the cheats have plenty to eat. HINDU PROVERB

The miser's wedding — a potato and a herring.
IRISH SAYING

[*See also* Avarice, Covetousness, Devil, Foresight.

Misery

The misery of man is great upon him.
ECCLESIASTES VIII, 6, *c.* 200 B.C.

It is hard for the happy to understand misery.
QUINTILIAN: *De institutione oratoria,* IX, *c.* 90

I am miserable from no cause save that of my ignorance, and if knowledge also shall cause me misery, then misery is eternal.
ST. AUGUSTINE: *Soliloquies,* II, *c.* 387

It is good to have companions in misery.
JOHN GOWER: *Confessio Amantis,* II, *c.* 1390

Sharp misery had worn him to the bone.
SHAKESPEARE: *Romeo and Juliet,* V, *c.* 1596

Misery acquaints a man with strange bedfellows.
SHAKESPEARE: *The Tempest,* II, 1611 (Usually quoted "makes" instead of "acquaints a man with")

Man is so full of misery that, if it were not repugnant to the Christian religion, we might assume that evil spirits had passed into human form and were now atoning for their sins.
LUCILIO VANINI: *De admirandis naturæ reginæ deaeque mortalium arcanis,* L, 1616

It is misery enough to have once been happy.
JOHN CLARKE: *Parœmiologia Anglo-Latina,* 1639

God doth not promise here to man, that He
Will free him quickly from his misery;
But in His own time, and when He thinks fit,
Then He will give a happy end to it.
ROBERT HERRICK: *Noble Numbers,* 1647

The greatness of man lies in the fact that he knows himself miserable. A tree does not know itself miserable. It is to be miserable to know ourselves miserable; but it is to be great to know that we are miserable.
BLAISE PASCAL: *Pensées,* II, 1670

Misery loves company.
JOHN RAY: *English Proverbs,* 1670 (Cf. GOWER, *ante, c.* 1390)

Let us embrace, and from this very moment
Vow an eternal misery together.
THOMAS OTWAY: *The Orphan,* IV, 1680

He's miserable indeed that must lock up his miseries.
THOMAS FULLER: *Gnomologia,* 1732

Life and misery began together. IBID.

Many of our miseries are merely comparative; we are often made unhappy, not by the presence of any real evil, but by the absence of some fictitious good.
SAMUEL JOHNSON: *The Adventurer,* Nov. 27, 1753

I fly from pleasure, because pleasure has ceased to please; I am lonely because I am miserable.
SAMUEL JOHNSON: *Rasselas,* III, 1759

Misery seeks not man, but man misery.
FRANCES BURNEY: *Cecilia,* VIII, 1782

It is strange that misery, when viewed in others, should become to us a sort of real good.
ST. JOHN DE CRÈVECOEUR: *Letters from an American Farmer,* II, 1782

Misery travels free throughout the world.
J. C. F. SCHILLER: *Wallenstein's Death,* IV, 1799

If misery loves company, misery has company enough.
H. D. THOREAU: *Journal,* Sept. 1, 1851

He bears misery best that hides it most.
H. G. BOHN: *Handbook of Proverbs,* 1855

If, during thirty years, the annoyances connected with shirt-buttons found missing when you are hurriedly dressing for dinner were gathered into a mass and endured at once, it would be misery equal to a public execution.
ALEXANDER SMITH: *Dreamthorp,* VII, 1863

There are a good many real miseries in life that we cannot help smiling at, but they are the smiles that make wrinkles and not dimples.
O. W. HOLMES: *The Poet at the Breakfast-Table,* III, 1872

The miserable are very talkative.
HINDU PROVERB

There is no pleasure like misery — when it does not last long. IBID.

No misery can long be kept secret.
WELSH PROVERB

[*See also* Civilization, Despotism, Escape, Friendship, Guilt, Happiness, Hatred, History, Indolence, Longevity, Mind, Misfortune, Mockery, Pain, Presidency, Rich, Trifle.

Misfit

The job called for an accountant, but a dancer got it.
CARON DE BEAUMARCHAIS: *Le barbier de Séville,* IV, 1775

If you choose to represent the various parts in life by holes upon a table, of different shapes, — some circular, some triangular, some square, some oblong, — and the persons acting these parts by bits of wood of similar shapes, we shall generally find that the triangular person has got into the square hole, the oblong into the triangular, and a square person has squeezed himself into the round hole.
SYDNEY SMITH: *Lectures on Moral Philosophy,* 1804

Misfortune

It costs a man only a little exertion to bring misfortune on himself.
MENANDER: *Thessala, c.* 300 B.C.

We can profit only by our own misfortunes and those of others. The former, though they may be the more beneficial, are also the more painful; let us turn, then, to the latter.
POLYBIUS: *Histories,* I, *c.* 125 B.C.

The wise man sees in the misfortunes of others what he should avoid.
PUBLILIUS SYRUS: *Sententiæ, c.* 50 B.C.

Not ignorant of misfortune, I learn from my own woes to succor others who are wretched.
VIRGIL: *Æneid,* I, *c.* 19 B.C.

Misfortunes test friends, and detect enemies.
EPICTETUS: *Encheiridion, c.* 110

There is no misfortune, but to bear it nobly is good fortune.
MARCUS AURELIUS: *Meditations,* IV, *c.* 170

Misfortunes never come singly.
ENGLISH PROVERB, traced by Apperson to *c.* 1300

We feel a kind of bitter-sweet pricking of malicious delight in contemplating the misfortunes of others.
MICHEL DE MONTAIGNE: *Essays,* III, 1588

By speaking of our misfortunes we relieve them.
PIERRE CORNEILLE: *Polyeucte,* I, 1642

Philosophy triumphs easily over misfortunes past and to come, but present misfortunes triumph over philosophy.
LA ROCHEFOUCAULD: *Maxims,* 1665

We have all of us sufficient fortitude to bear the misfortunes of others. IBID.

Misfortunes tell us what fortune is.
THOMAS FULLER: *Gnomologia,* 1732

When misfortune is asleep, let no one wake her.
IBID.

We have a degree of delight, and that no small one, in the real misfortunes and pains of others.
EDMUND BURKE: *The Sublime and Beautiful,* I, 1758

Misfortunes, like the owl, avoid the light.
CHARLES CHURCHILL: *The Night,* 1762

If a great man struggling with misfortunes is a noble object, a little man that despises them is no contemptible one.
WILLIAM COWPER: *Letter to Clotworthy Rowley,* Sept. 2, 1762

Depend upon it that if a man talks of his misfortunes there is something in them that is not disagreeable to him; for where there is nothing but pure misery there never is any recourse to the mention of it.
SAMUEL JOHNSON: *Boswell's Life,* 1780

Every man has a rainy corner in his life, from which bad weather besets him.
JEAN PAUL RICHTER: *Titan,* 1803

Man bears misfortune without complaint—and so it pains him the more.
FRANZ SCHUBERT: *Diary,* June 16, 1816

Most of our misfortunes are more supportable than the comments of our friends upon them. C. C. COLTON: *Lacon,* 1820

In general, the greatest reverses of fortune are the most easily borne from a sort of dignity belonging to them.
WILLIAM HAZLITT: *The Life of Napoleon Bonaparte,* IV, 1830

Misfortune comes to all men and most women.
CHINESE PROVERB

There are three great misfortunes: in youth to lose one's father, in middle age to lose one's wife, and in old age to have no sons. IBID.

Misfortunes always come in by a door that has been left open for them. CZECH PROVERB

One misfortune always carries another on its back. DUTCH PROVERB

The great storm always comes at harvest time.
FRENCH PROVERB

Blessed is that misfortune which comes alone.
ITALIAN PROVERB

When a man is falling, every saint pushes him.
IBID.

Wherever men are, there misfortune is.
UKRAINIAN PROVERB

Misfortunes come by forties.
WELSH PROVERB

Misfortunes come in with a gallop, and go out with a crawl. IBID.

[*See also* Affliction, Blessing, Calamity, Fortune, History, Jew, Wisdom.

Misogynist

One woman is fair, yet I am well; another is wise, yet I am well: another virtuous, yet I am well; but till all graces be in one woman, one woman shall not come in my grace.
SHAKESPEARE: *Much Ado About Nothing,* II, *c.* 1599

Let such a one know that he is making fools merry and wise men sick; and that, in the eye of considering persons, he hath less compunction than the common hangman, and less shame than a prostitute.
RICHARD STEELE: *The Guardian,* June 3, 1713

Like all rogues, he was a great calumniator of the fair sex.
WALTER SCOTT: *The Heart of Midlothian,* XVIII, 1818

Misquotation

I am met with a whole ging of words and phrases not mine, for he hath maimed them, and, like a sly depraver, mangled them in this his wicked limbo.
JOHN MILTON: *An Apology for Smectymnuus,* 1642 (*Ging*=gang)

Miss

Hit or miss.
SHAKESPEARE: *Troilus and Cressida,* I, *c.* 1601

An inch in a miss is as good as an ell.
WILLIAM CAMDEN: *Remains Concerning Britain,* 1605

The vulgar will keep no account of your hits, but of your misses.
THOMAS FULLER: *Gnomologia,* 1732

A miss is as good as a mile.
WALTER SCOTT: *Journal,* Dec. 3, 1825

Missionary

They are the messengers of the churches, and the glory of Christ.
II CORINTHIANS VIII, 23 *c.* 55

I robbed other churches, taking wages of them, to do you service. II CORINTHIANS XI, 8

Though Jesuits, etc. travel to distant east and west to propagate their religion and traffic, I never heard of one that made a journey into Asia or Africa to preach the doctrines of liberty, though those regions are so deplorably oppressed.
HORACE WALPOLE: *Letter to Hannah More,* Sept. 22, 1788

If I were a cassowary
On the plains of Timbuctoo,
I would eat a missionary,
Bible and hymn-book too.
Ascribed to SAMUEL WILBERFORCE (1805–73)

At first we had the land and the white man had the Bible. Now we have the Bible and the white man has the land. BANTU SAYING

Mississippi River

The Father of Waters.
Origin unknown (The name of the river is derived from the Algonquian *misi,* meaning great, and *sipi,* meaning river. LE PAGE DU PRATZ, in his *Histoire de la Lou-*

isiane, 1758, translated the words, erroneously, as *le vieux père des rivières,* and this error may have given rise to the English phrase)

The Big Drink.

Author unidentified; traced by Thornton to 1846

The Father of Waters again goes unvexed to the sea.

ABRAHAM LINCOLN: *Letter to J. C. Conkling,* Aug. 26, 1863 (The reference is to the fall of Vicksburg, July 4)

Missouri

I'm from Missouri; you must show me.

Ascribed to WILLARD D. VANDIVER; it was first heard generally in the Presidential campaign of 1912, when Champ Clark of Missouri was a Democratic candidate

Mistake

Do not be ashamed of mistakes — and so make them crimes.

CONFUCIUS: *The Book of History,* IV, *c.* 500 B.C.

The shortest mistakes are always the best.

J. B. MOLIÈRE: *L'étourdi,* IV, 1653

It is worse than a crime; it is a blunder. (C'est pire qu'un crime; c'est une faute.)

JOSEPH FOUCHÉ: On the execution of the Duc d'Enghien, March 21, 1804

He who makes no mistakes never makes anything.

ENGLISH PROVERB, not recorded before the XIX century

The only things one never regrets are one's mistakes.

OSCAR WILDE: *The Picture of Dorian Gray,* 1891

I entreat you by the mercies of Christ to imagine that you may be mistaken.

W. R. BOWIE: Sermon at Grace Church, New York, 1934

He is always right who suspects that he makes mistakes. SPANISH PROVERB

[*See also* Caution, Experience, Forgetfulness.

Mistress

He thought the use of a maid nothing in comparison to the wantonness of a wife, and would never have any other mistress.

WILLIAM DRUMMOND of Hawthornden: *Informations and Manners of Ben Jonson,* 1618

He that makes his mistress a goldfinch may make her a wagtail.

ENGLISH PROVERB, traced by Smith to 1647

What I fancy, I approve,
No dislike there is in love:
Be my mistress short or tall,
And distorted therewithal:
Be her forehead, and her eyes
Full of incongruities:
Has she thin hair, hath she none,
She's to me a paragon.

ROBERT HERRICK: *Hesperides,* 1648

A mistress should be like a little country retreat near the town — not to dwell in constantly, but only for a night and away.

WILLIAM WYCHERLEY: *The Country Wife,* I, *c.* 1673

Next to the pleasure of making a new mistress is that of being rid of an old one. IBID.

Every man believes that mistresses are unfaithful, and patrons capricious; but he excepts his own mistress, and his own patron.

SAMUEL JOHNSON: *Boswell's Life,* Dec. 21, 1762

[*See also* Cost, Husband, Kiss, Like.

Mistrust

Mistrust carries one much further than trust.

GERMAN PROVERB

Misunderstanding

Is it so bad, then, to be misunderstood? Pythagoras was misunderstood, and Socrates, and Jesus, and Luther, and Copernicus, and Galileo, and Newton, and every pure and wise spirit that ever took flesh. To be great is to be misunderstood.

R. W. EMERSON: *Self-Reliance,* 1841

Misuse

[*See* Abuse.

Mite

[*See* Widow.

Mob

The mob is easily led and may be moved by the smallest force, so that its agitations have a wonderful resemblance to those of the sea.

POLYBIUS: *Histories,* XI, *c.* 125 B.C.

The mob is the mother of tyrants.

DIONYSIUS OF HALICARNASSUS: *Antiquities of Rome,* VII, *c.* 20 B.C.

A many-headed beast.

HORACE: *Epistles,* I, *c.* 5 B.C.

Nothing is so difficult to form a judgment of as the mind of the mob.

LIVY: *History of Rome,* XXXI, *c.* 10

There is nothing so little to be hoped for from that many-headed monster, the mob, when stirred up, as humanity and good nature; it is much more capable of reverence and fear.

MICHEL DE MONTAIGNE: *Essays,* I, 1580

O great and wise, be ill at ease when your deeds please the mob.

BALTASAR GRACIÁN: *The Art of Worldly Wisdom,* XXVIII, 1647

The mob has many heads, but no brains.
THOMAS FULLER: *Gnomologia,* 1732

The number of the malefactors authorizes not the crime.
IBID.

A mob's a monster.
BENJAMIN FRANKLIN: *Poor Richard's Almanac,* 1747

Every numerous assembly is mob, let the individuals who compose it be what they will.
LORD CHESTERFIELD: *Letter to his son,* March 18, 1751

The mob does not deserve to be enlightened.
FREDERICK THE GREAT: *Letter to Voltaire,* Aug. 7, 1766

I am not fond of mobs, Madam.
HORACE WALPOLE: *Letter to the Countess of Upper Ossory,* Feb. 17, 1779

The mob, which everywhere is the majority, will always let itself be led by scoundrels.
FREDERICK THE GREAT: *Letter to Jean le Rond D'Alembert,* Sept. 8, 1782

The mobs of great cities add just so much to the support of pure government as sores do to the strength of the human body.
THOMAS JEFFERSON: *Notes on Virginia,* 1782

Mobs will never do to govern states or command armies.
JOHN ADAMS: *Letter to Benjamin Hichborn,* Jan. 27, 1787

An English mob, which, to a foreigner, might convey the belief of an impending massacre, is often contented by the demolition of a few windows.
SYDNEY SMITH: In the Edinburgh Review, 1803

It is an easy and a vulgar thing to please the mob, and no very arduous task to astonish them; but essentially to benefit and to improve them is a work fraught with difficulty, and teeming with danger.
C. C. COLTON: *Lacon,* 1820

A few men may make a mob as well as many.
WENDELL PHILLIPS: Speech on the murder of E. P. Lovejoy, Boston, Dec. 8, 1837 (Lovejoy was killed Nov. 7)

A mob is a society of bodies voluntarily bereaving themselves of reason, and traversing its work. The mob is man voluntarily descending to the nature of the beast.
R. W. EMERSON: *Compensation,* 1841

A mob cannot be a permanency; everybody's interest requires that it should not exist.
R. W. EMERSON: *Politics,* 1841

The nose of a mob is its imagination. By this, at any time, it can be quietly led.
E. A. POE: *Marginalia,* 1844–49

Against the wild-fire of the mob there is no defence.
H. G. BOHN: *Handbook of Proverbs,* 1855

You can talk a mob into anything.
JOHN RUSKIN: *Sesame and Lilies,* I, 1865

Fill a theatre with a thousand Renans and a thousand Herbert Spencers, and the combination of these two thousand brains of genius will produce only the soul of a concierge.
OCTAVE UZANNE: *Les zigzags d'un curieux,* 1889

All assemblages of men are different from the men themselves. Neither intelligence nor culture can prevent a mob from acting as a mob. The wise man and the knave lose their identity and merge themselves into a new being.
THOMAS B. REED: Speech at Bowdoin College, Maine, July 25, 1902

Mob law does not become due process of law by securing the assent of a terrorized jury.
MR. JUSTICE O. W. HOLMES: *Dissenting opinion in Frank* vs. *Mangum,* 1914

The world is made up of a great mob, and nothing will influence it so much as the lash.
E. W. HOWE: *Success Easier Than Failure,* 1917

[*See also* Crowd, Demagogue, Masses, Morality, Multitude, Nation, Orator, People, People (Common), Populace, Proletariat, Rabble.

Mockery

Whoso mocketh the poor reproacheth his Maker: and he that is glad at calamities shall not be unpunished.
PROVERBS XVII, 5, *c.* 350 B.C.

Mock not a cobbler for his black thumbs.
THOMAS FULLER: *The Holy State and the Profane State,* III, 1642

Mock not, quoth Mumford, when his wife called him a cuckold.
ENGLISH PROVERB, traced by Smith to 1659

Mockery is only too often mere poverty of wit.
JEAN DE LA BRUYÈRE: *Caractères,* V, 1688

Mocking is catching.
JAMES KELLY: *Complete Collection of Scottish Proverbs,* 1721

[*See also* Delusion.

Mocking-Bird

Then from a neighboring thicket the mocking-bird, wildest of singers,
Swinging aloft on a willow spray that hung o'er the water,
Shook from his little throat such floods of delirious music,

That the whole air and the woods and the waves seemed silent to listen.
H. W. LONGFELLOW: *Evangeline*, II, 1847

[*See also* Nightingale.

Moderation

Moderation lasts. (Moderata durant.)
SENECA: *Troades*, *c.* 60

A great soul prefers moderation to excess.
SENECA: *Epistulæ morales ad Lucilium*, *c.* 63

I love temperate and moderate natures. An immoderate zeal, even for that which is good, though it does not offend, does astonish me, and puts me to study what name to give it.
MICHEL DE MONTAIGNE: *Essays*, I, 1580

Some have too much, yet still they crave;
I little have, yet seek no more;
They are but poor, though much they have,
And I am rich with little store.
EDWARD DYER: *My Mind to Me a Kingdom Is*, 1588

Be moderate.
SHAKESPEARE: *Troilus and Cressida*, IV, *c.* 1601

Moderation is the silken string running through the pearl-chain of all virtues.
THOMAS FULLER: *The Holy State and the Profane State*, III, 1642

Fear and dull disposition, lukewarmness and sloth, are not seldom wont to cloak themselves under the affected name of moderation.
JOHN MILTON: *An Apology for Smectymnuus*, 1642

Let moderation on thy passions wait
Who loves too much, too much the lov'd will hate.
ROBERT HERRICK: *Hesperides*, 1648

Men have made a virtue of moderation to limit the ambition of the great, and to console people of mediocrity for their want of fortune and of merit.
LA ROCHEFOUCAULD: *Maxims*, 1665

Moderation is the languor and sloth of the soul; ambition is its activity and heat.
IBID.

Who wishes to travel far spares his mount.
JEAN RACINE: *Les plaideurs*, I, 1668

It is very possible to practise moderation in some things, in drink and the like — to restrain the appetites — but can a man restrain the affections of his mind, and tell them, so far you shall go, and no farther?
GEORGE BORROW: *Lavengro*, LXVI, 1851

Moderation is the reason of politics.
LÉON GAMBETTA: Speech, Feb. 26, 1875

Sheer the sheep, but don't flay them.
DUTCH PROVERB

Moderation is best. (Optimus modus.)
LATIN PROVERB

[*See also* Abstinence, Enough, Excess, Mean, Temperance, Too Much.

Modesty

Modesty is of no use to a beggar.
HOMER: *Odyssey*, XVII, *c.* 800 B.C.

The superior man is distressed by the limitations of his ability; he is not distressed by the fact that men do not recognize the ability that he has.
CONFUCIUS: *Analects*, XV, *c.* 500 B.C.

Modesty is hardly to be described as a virtue. It is a feeling rather than a disposition. It is a kind of fear of falling into disrepute.
ARISTOTLE: *The Nicomachean Ethics*, IV, *c.* 340 B.C.

It is sometimes wise to forget who we are.
PUBLILIUS SYRUS: *Sententiæ*, *c.* 50 B.C.

Once gone, modesty never returns.
IBID.

Modesty in human beings is praised because it is not a matter of nature, but of will.
LACTANTIUS: *Divinæ institutiones*, VI, *c.* 310

Modesty is ruin to a harlot.
The Hitopadesa, III, *c.* 500

Once a wise man was asked, What is intelligence? He answered, modesty. Then he was asked, What is modesty? And he answered, intelligence.
SOLOMON BEN JUDAH IBN GABIROL: *The Improvement of Character*, III, *c.* 1050

Her modest eyes, abashéd to behold
So many gazers as on her do stare,
Upon the lowly ground affixéd are.
EDMUND SPENSER: *Epithalamion*, 1595

The bounds of modesty.
SHAKESPEARE: *Romeo and Juliet*, IV, *c.* 1596

Modesty may more betray our sense
Than woman's lightness.
SHAKESPEARE: *Measure for Measure*, II, 1604

I have done no braver thing
Than all the worthies did;
And yet a braver yet doth spring,
Which is, to keep that hid.
JOHN DONNE: *The Undertaking*, *c.* 1610

She that hath a wise husband must entice him to an eternal dearness by the veil of modesty.
JEREMY TAYLOR: *The Mysteriousness of Marriage*, 1651

Modesty is to merit what the shade is to the figures in a painting; it gives it strength and makes it stand out.
JEAN DE LA BRUYÈRE: *Caractères*, II, 1688

A just and reasonable modesty . . . sets off every talent which a man can be possessed

of. . . . Like the shades of paintings, it raises and rounds every figure, and makes the colors more beautiful, though not so glowing as they would be without it.
JOSEPH ADDISON: *The Spectator,* Nov. 24, 1711

I take it to be the highest instance of a noble mind to bear great qualities without discovering in a man's behavior any consciousness that he is superior to the rest of the world.
RICHARD STEELE: *The Spectator,* March 31, 1712

Modesty gives the maid greater beauty than even the bloom of youth, it bestows on the wife the dignity of a matron, and reinstates the widow in her virginity.
JOSEPH ADDISON: *The Guardian,* July 6, 1713

No modest man ever did or ever will make a fortune.
MARY WORTLEY MONTAGU: *Letter to Wortley Montagu,* Sept. 24, 1714

What should a Christian woman be but a plain, unaffected, modest, humble creature, averse to everything in her dress and carriage that can draw the eyes of beholders, or gratify the passions of lewd and amorous persons?
WILLIAM LAW: *A Serious Call to a Devout and Holy Life,* XIX, 1728

Women commend a modest man, but like him not. THOMAS FULLER: *Gnomologia,* 1732

Modesty is the only sure bait when you angle for praise.
LORD CHESTERFIELD: *Letter to his son,* May 8, 1750

What is modesty, if it deserts from truth? Of what use is the disguise by which nothing is concealed?
SAMUEL JOHNSON: *Letter to Samuel Richardson,* Sept. 26, 1753

Modesty ought to be the virtue of those who are deficient in other virtues.
STANISLAUS LESZCZYNSKI (KING OF POLAND): *Œuvres du philosophe bienfaisant,* 1763

Modesty makes large amends for the pain it gives the persons who labor under it, by the prejudice it affords every worthy person in their favor.
WILLIAM SHENSTONE: *Of Men and Manners,* 1764

Modesty seldom resides in a breast that is not enriched with nobler virtues.
OLIVER GOLDSMITH: *She Stoops to Conquer,* I, 1773

An impudent fellow may counterfeit modesty, but I'll be hanged if a modest man can ever counterfeit impudence.
OLIVER GOLDSMITH: *She Stoops to Conquer,* II

I have conversed with medical men on anatomical subjects, and compared the proportions of the human body with artists, yet such modesty did I meet with that I was never reminded by a word or look of my sex.
MARY WOLLSTONECRAFT: *A Vindication of the Rights of Woman,* VII, 1792

When anyone remains modest, not after praise but after blame, then his modesty is real.
JEAN PAUL RICHTER: *Hesperus,* 1795

Goodness blows no trumpet, nor desires to have it blown. We should be modest for a modest man — as he is for himself.
CHARLES LAMB: *Letter to Mrs. Basil Montagu,* 1828

A modest man is the natural butt of impertinence.
WILLIAM HAZLITT: *Butts of Different Sorts,* 1829 (The Atlas, Feb. 8)

Modesty, itself a ramification and evidence of chastity, what is it but an invention by which pleasure is augmented? Modesty dictates concealment; concealment stimulates curiosity; curiosity augments desire, and with previous desire subsequent gratification increases.
JEREMY BENTHAM: *Deontology,* 1834

With people of only moderate ability modesty is mere honesty; but with those who possess great talent it is hyprocrisy.
ARTHUR SCHOPENHAUER: *Further Psychological Observations,* 1851

Modesty is what ails me. That's what's kept me under.
C. F. BROWNE (ARTEMUS WARD): *Artemus Ward: His Travels,* 1865

Modesty is an ornament, but you go further without it. GERMAN PROVERB

Never be modest in eating or in business.
HINDU PROVERB

Without offence to modesty. (Salvo pudore.)
LATIN PHRASE

Modesty is of no use to a man in want. (Verecundia inutilis viro egenti.)
LATIN PROVERB

The enemies of modesty are love and sickness.
SPANISH PROVERB

[*See also* Bashfulness, Innocence, Law (Natural), Poet.

Mohammed (c. 570–632)

As Mohammed gave his Arabs the best religion he could, as well as the best laws, preferable, at least, to those of the ancient pagan lawgivers, I confess I cannot see why he deserves not equal respect, though not with Moses or Jesus Christ, whose laws came really from Heaven, yet with Minos or Numa.
GEORGE SALE: Tr. of THE KORAN (*To the Reader*), 1734

Withal I like Mahomet for his total freedom from cant. He is a rough self-helping son of the wilderness; does not pretend to be what he is not. There is no ostentatious pride in him; but neither does he go much upon humility: he is there as he can be, in cloak and shoes of his own clouting.

THOMAS CARLYLE: *Heroes and Hero-Worship*, II, 1840 (Lecture in London, May 8)

[*See also* Mountain.

Mohammedan

The worshipping of images and the doctrine of transubstantiation are great stumbling-blocks to the Mohammedans, and the church which teacheth them is very unfit to bring those people over.

GEORGE SALE: Tr. of THE KORAN (*To the Reader*), 1734

One Mohammedan is no Mohammedan; two are half a one; three are one.

CHINESE PROVERB

[*See also* Christian, Jew, Teetotaler.

Mohammedanism

The kingdom of Mohammed is a kingdom of revenge, of wrath, and desolation.

MARTIN LUTHER: *Table-Talk*, CCXXI, 1569

Mohammedanism is less ridiculous than Christianity.

NAPOLEON I: To Gaspard Gourgaud at St. Helena, Aug. 28, 1817

A bastard kind of Christianity, but a living kind; with a heart-life in it; not dead, chopping barren logic merely.

THOMAS CARLYLE: *Heroes and Hero-Worship*, II, 1840 (Lecture in London, May 8)

Molasses

[*See* Policy.

Mole (=animal)

The mole's a creature very smooth and sleek,
She digs i' th' dirt, but 'twill not on her stick.

JOHN BUNYAN: *A Book for Boys and Girls*, 1686

Mole (=growth)

A mole on the neck:
You shall have money by the peck.

OLD ENGLISH RHYME

If you've got a mole above your chin
You'll never be beholden to any of your kin.

IBID.

Mole-hill

[*See* Mountain.

Molière, J. B. (1622–73)

I have known and loved Molière from my youth, and have learned from him during my whole life. I never fail to read some of his plays every year, that I may keep up a constant intercourse with what is excellent.

J. W. GOETHE: *Conversations with Eckermann*, March 28, 1827

Mollycoddle

[*See* Sport.

Moment

There are moments in life worth purchasing with worlds.

HENRY FIELDING: *Amelia*, III, 1752

Moments big as years.

JOHN KEATS: *Hyperion*, 1819

God works in moments. FRENCH PROVERB

[*See also* Hour, Minute.

Mona Lisa

Hers is the head upon which "all the ends of the world have come," and the eyelids are a little weary. . . . She is older than the rocks among which she sits; like the vampire, she has been dead many times, and learned the secrets of the grave; and has been a diver in deep seas, and keeps her fallen day about her.

WALTER PATER: *Notes on Leonardo da Vinci*, 1869 (Fortnightly Review, Nov.)

Monarch

I am monarch of all I survey,
My right there is none to dispute;
From the center all round to the sea
I am lord of the fowl and the brute.

WILLIAM COWPER: *Verses Supposed to Have Been Written by Alexander Selkirk*, 1782

Who lord it o'er their fellowmen
With most prevailing tinsel: who unpen
Their baaing vanities, to browse away
The comfortable green and juicy hay
From human pastures.

JOHN KEATS: *Endymion*, III, 1818

[*See also* Beggar, King, Republic, Right (Divine), Song.

Monarchy

Certainly that people must needs be mad or strangely infatuated that build the chief hope of their common happiness or safety on a single person; who, if he happen to be good, can do no more than another man; if to be bad, hath in his hands to do more evil without check than millions of other men.

JOHN MILTON: *The Ready and Easy Way to Establish a Free Commonwealth*, 1660

In monarchies things go by whimsy.

JOHN VANBRUGH: *The Provok'd Wife*, III, 1697

Though liberty be preferable to slavery in almost every case; yet I should rather wish to see an absolute monarch than a republic in this island.

DAVID HUME: *Essays, Moral and Political,* I, 1741

The mode of government by one may be ill adapted to a small society, but is best for a great nation.

SAMUEL JOHNSON: *Boswell's Life,* April 26, 1776

I was much an enemy to monarchy before I came to Europe. I am ten thousand times more so since I have seen what they are. There is scarcely an evil known in these countries which may not be traced to their king as its source, nor a good which is not derived from the small fibers of republicanism existing among them.

THOMAS JEFFERSON: *Letter to George Washington,* 1788

All the monarchical governments are military. War is their trade; plunder and revenue their objects. While such governments continue, peace has not the absolute security of a day.

THOMAS PAINE: *The Rights of Man,* II, 1791

Kingly power, wisely limited, is the surest safeguard of the rights and liberties of a great nation.

Address of Oxford University to GEORGE III, June, 1792

It is to arraign the dispositions of Providence Himself to suppose that He has created beings incapable of governing themselves, and to be trampled on by kings.

HENRY CLAY: Speech in the House of Representatives, March 24, 1818

A monarchical government, it is said, is natural to man, because it is an instinct of nature: the very bees have it.

LEIGH HUNT: *The Indicator,* I XIV, 1821

A monarchy is the most expensive of all forms of government, the regal state requiring a costly parade, and he who depends on his own power to rule must strengthen that power by bribing the active and enterprising whom he cannot intimidate.

J. FENIMORE COOPER: *The American Democrat,* XII, 1838

The monarchical form of government is natural to men, as it is to bees, ants, migratory birds, wandering elephants, wolves on the prowl, and other animals, all of which appoint one to lead their undertakings.

ARTHUR SCHOPENHAUER: *Parerga und Paralipomena,* II, 1851

No form of existing government, no form of government that ever did exist, gives or has given so large a measure of individual freedom to all who live under it as a constitutional monarchy in which the crown is divested of direct political power.

ANTHONY TROLLOPE: *North America,* I, 1862

An absolute monarchy is one in which the monarch does as he pleases so long as he pleases the assassins.

AMBROSE BIERCE: *The Devil's Dictionary,* 1906

It is as good to have a constitutional monarchy as to have a Hitler or a Mussolini — or much better; better than to have a President of the French Republic; better than having a Roosevelt, who is a political boss and is intended to be a political boss, who has more power than his ministers because they are personally appointed by him; and better than Stalin.

STAFFORD CRIPPS, leader of the Left Wing Socialists of England: Public statement, 1935

[*See also* Absolutism, Despotism, Divine Right, Government, King, Prussia.

Monasticism

He who wants to lead a life of luxury that even a king would envy, let him enter a monastery.

JOHN HUSS: *De ecclesia,* 1412

It is hard to find one monastery in ten that is not rather a brothel than a sanctuary of chastity.

JOHN CALVIN: *Institutes of the Christian Religion,* IV, 1536

I do not wonder that, where the monastic life is permitted, every order finds votaries, and every monastery inhabitants. Men will submit to any rule by which they may be exempted from the tyranny of caprice and of chance.

SAMUEL JOHNSON: *Letter to Joseph Baretti,* June 10, 1761

Monasticism represented something more positive than a protest against the world. We believe it to have been the realization of the infinite loveliness and beauty of personal purity.

J. A. FROUDE: *The Lives of the Saints,* 1852 (Eclectic Review)

The nearer the monastery, the poorer the peasant.

GERMAN PROVERB

[*See also* Friar, Monk.

Monday

Monday [is] the holiday of preachers.

THOMAS FULLER: *Worthies of England,* I, 1662

As Monday goes, so goes all the week.

GERMAN PROVERB

[*See also* Days, Nail, Sneezing, Wedding-Day.

Money

Money is life to us wretched mortals.

HESIOD: *Works and Days,* c. 700 B.C.

Money lays waste cities; it sets men to roaming from home; it seduces and corrupts honest

men and turns virtue to baseness; it teaches villainy and impiety.
SOPHOCLES: *Antigone, c.* 450 B.C.

Money is a guarantee that we may have what we want in the future. Though we need nothing at the moment it insures the possibility of satisfying a new desire when it arises.
ARISTOTLE: *The Nicomachean Ethics,* V, *c.* 340 B.C.

Money is a defense.
ECCLESIASTES VII, 12, *c.* 200 B.C.

Money answereth all things.
ECCLESIASTES X, 19

Nothing is a greater proof of a narrow and grovelling disposition than to be fond of money, while nothing is more noble and exalted than to despise it, if thou hast it not; and if thou hast it, to employ it in beneficence and liberality.
CICERO: *De officiis,* I, 78 B.C.

Money is the sinews of war.
CICERO: *Orationes Philippicæ,* V, *c.* 60 B.C.

The populace may hiss me, but when I go home and think of my money I applaud myself.
HORACE: *Epistles,* I, *c.* 25 B.C.

Nothing stings more deeply than the loss of money. LIVY: *History of Rome,* XXX, *c.* 10

Filthy lucre.
I TIMOTHY III, 3, *c.* 60 (Cf. TITUS I, 7, *c.* 60)

The love of money is the root of all evil.
I TIMOTHY VI, 10 (Sometimes shortened to "money is the root of all evil")

Thy money perish with thee, because thou hast thought that the gift of God may be purchased with money. ACTS VIII, 20, *c.* 75

Money is mourned with deeper sorrow than friends or kindred.
JUVENAL: *Satires,* XIII, 128

Nothing that is God's is obtainable by money.
TERTULLIAN: *The Christian's Defence, c.* 215

Love of money is the disease which makes men most grovelling and pitiful.
LONGINUS: *On the Sublime,* XLIV, *c.* 250

Let us keep a firm grip upon our money, for without it the whole assembly of virtues are but as blades of grass.
BHARTRIHARI: *The Niti Sataka, c.* 625

Money makes the man.
GREEK PROVERB, traced to the V century B.C.; familiar in English since the XVI century

Money talks.
ENGLISH PROVERB, recent in its present form, but the idea goes back to the XVI century

Unto money be all things obedient.
RICHARD TAVERNER: *Proverbs,* 1539

Money makes the mare go.
ENGLISH PROVERB, traced by Smith to 1572

My money doth make me full merry to be,
And without my money none careth for me.
THOMAS DELONEY: *Jack of Newbury,* I, 1597

She is the sovereign queen of all delights;
For her the lawyer pleads, the soldier fights.
RICHARD BARNFIELD: *The Encomium of Lady Pecunia,* 1598

If money go before, all ways do lie open.
SHAKESPEARE: *The Merry Wives of Windsor,* II, *c.* 1600

Money is a good soldier, sir, and will on.
IBID.

Oh, what a world of vile ill-favor'd faults
Looks handsome in three hundred pounds a year!
SHAKESPEARE: *The Merry Wives of Windsor,* III

Money is a fruit that is always ripe.
ENGLISH PROVERB, traced by Smith to 1616

Money is like muck, not good unless spread.
FRANCIS BACON: *Essays,* XV, 1625

Money never cometh out of season.
THOMAS DRAXE: *Bibliotheca scholastica instructissima,* 1633

When we want money we want all. IBID.

Why is the form of money round? Because it is to run from every man.
Anon.: *A Helpe to Discourse,* 1640

To have money is a fear; not to have it, a grief.
GEORGE HERBERT: *Jacula Prudentum,* 1651

He that hath money in his purse cannot want a head for his shoulders.
JAMES HOWELL: *Proverbs,* 1659

What is worth in anything
But so much money as 'twill bring?
SAMUEL BUTLER: *Hudibras,* II, 1664

Money gives an appearance of beauty even to ugliness; but everything becomes frightful with poverty.
NICOLAS BOILEAU: *Satires du Sieur D.,* VIII, 1666

Money begets money.
GIOVANNI TORRIANO: *Italian Proverbs,* 1666

It is pretty to see what money will do.
SAMUEL PEPYS: *Diary,* March 21, 1667

Money brings honor, friends, conquest, and realms.
JOHN MILTON: *Paradise Regained,* II, 1671

Money makes up in a measure all other wants in men.
WILLIAM WYCHERLEY: *The Country Wife,* II, *c.* 1673

Money, th' only power
That all mankind falls down before.
SAMUEL BUTLER: *Hudibras,* III, 1678

Money makes a man laugh.
JOHN SELDEN: *Table-Talk,* 1689

He that serves God for money will serve the Devil for better wages.
ROGER L'ESTRANGE: Tr. of ÆSOP: *Fables,* 1692

How sweetly one guinea rhymes to another, and how they dance to the music of their own clink!
WILLIAM CONGREVE: *The Old Bachelor,* III, 1693

No man will take counsel, but every man will take money: therefore money is better than counsel.
JONATHAN SWIFT: *Thoughts on Various Subjects,* 1706

A man who is furnished with arguments from the mint will convince his antagonist much sooner than one who draws them from reason and philosophy.
JOSEPH ADDISON: *The Spectator,* Dec. 4, 1711

Money, the life-blood of the nation,
Corrupts and stagnates in the veins,
Unless a proper circulation
Its motion and its heat maintains.
JONATHAN SWIFT: *The Run Upon the Bankers,* 1720

God send some money, for they are little thought of that want it, quoth the Earl of Eglinton at his prayer.
JAMES KELLY: *Complete Collection of Scottish Proverbs,* 1721

Like Heav'n, it hears the orphans' cries,
And wipes the tears from widows' eyes.
JOHN GAY: *Fables,* I, 1727

Money was made for the free-hearted and generous.
JOHN GAY: *The Beggar's Opera,* II, 1728

A man without money is a bow without an arrow.
THOMAS FULLER: *Gnomologia,* 1732

A man without money is no man at all. IBID.

He that gets money before he gets wit
Will be but a short while master of it. IBID.

I wot well how the world wags;
He is most loved that hath most bags. IBID.

Money in purse will always be in fashion.
IBID.

Money is a merry fellow. IBID.

Money is the best bait to fish for man with.
IBID.

Money is the sinew of love as well as of war.
IBID.

Money makes not so many true friends as real enemies. IBID.

Money will say more in one moment than the most eloquent lover can in years.
HENRY FIELDING: *The Miser,* III, 1733

Nothing but money is sweeter than honey.
BENJAMIN FRANKLIN: *Poor Richard's Almanac,* 1735

Money is of a prolific generating nature. Money can beget money, and its offspring can beget more.
BENJAMIN FRANKLIN: *Letter to My Friend A. B.,* 1748

He that is of opinion money will do everything may well be suspected of doing everything for money.
BENJAMIN FRANKLIN: *Poor Richard's Almanac,* 1753

They may be false who languish and complain,
But they who sigh for money never feign.
MARY WORTLEY MONTAGU: *Letter to James Steuart,* Nov. 27, 1759

There are some sensible folks who having great estates have wisdom enough too to spend them properly; there are others who are not less wise, perhaps, as knowing how to shift without 'em. Between these two degrees are they who spend their money dirtily, or get it so.
WILLIAM COWPER: *Letter to Clotworthy Rowley,* Sept. 2, 1762

The contempt of money is no more a virtue than to wash one's hand is one; but one does not willingly shake hands with a man that never washes his.
HORACE WALPOLE: *Letter to William Mason,* April 18, 1777

I suppose there is not a man in the world who, when he becomes a knave for a thousand thalers, would not rather have remained honest for half the money.
G. C. LICHTENBERG: *Reflections,* 1799

O money, money, how blindly thou hast been worshipped, and how stupidly abused! Thou art health, and liberty, and strength; and he that has thee may rattle his pockets at the foul fiend.
CHARLES LAMB: *Letter to S. T. Coleridge,* June 7, 1809

Money, and not morality, is the principle of commercial nations.
THOMAS JEFFERSON: *Letter to John Langdon,* 1810

They say that knowledge is power. I used to think so, but I now know that they meant money. . . . Every guinea is a philosopher's stone. . . . Cash is virtue.

BYRON: *Letter to Douglas Kinnaird*, Feb. 6, 1822

Ready money is Aladdin's lamp.

BYRON: *Don Juan*, XII, 1823

The power which money gives is that of brute force; it is the power of the bludgeon and the bayonet.

WILLIAM COBBETT: *Advice to Young Men*, I, 1829

I am not fond of money, or anxious about it. But, though every day makes me less and less eager for wealth, every day shows me more and more strongly how necessary a competence is to a man who desires to be either great or useful.

T. B. MACAULAY: *Letter to Hannah M. Macaulay*, Aug. 17, 1833

Whoso has sixpence is sovereign (to the length of sixpence) over all men; commands cooks to feed him, philosophers to teach him, kings to mount guard over him, — to the length of sixpence.

THOMAS CARLYLE: *Sartor Resartus*, I, 1836

One is weary of hearing about the omnipotence of money. I will say rather that, for a genuine man, it is no evil to be poor.

THOMAS CARLYLE: *Heroes and Hero-Worship*, V, 1840 (Lecture in London, May 19)

As for money, enough is enough; no man can enjoy more.

ROBERT SOUTHEY: *The Doctor*, XX, 1840

Money, which represents the prose of life, and which is hardly spoken of in parlors without an apology, is, in its effects and laws, as beautiful as roses.

R. W. EMERSON: *Nominalist and Realist*, 1841

The jingling of the guinea helps the hurt that honor feels.

ALFRED TENNYSON: *Locksley Hall*, 1842

After all, money, as they say, is miraculous.

THOMAS CARLYLE: *Past and Present*, III, 1843

We often buy money very much too dear.

W. M. THACKERAY: *Barry Lyndon*, XIII, 1844

Money is a good servant but a bad master.

H. G. BOHN: *Handbook of Proverbs*, 1855

I haven't any time to make money, and I don't want any anyhow. Money is more trouble than it's worth. HORACE GREELEY, *c.* 1860

The force of the guinea you have in your pocket depends wholly on the default of a guinea in your neighbor's pocket. If he did not want it, it would be of no use to you.

JOHN RUSKIN: *Unto This Last*, II, 1862

Whenever money is the principal object of life with either man or nation, it is both got ill, and spent ill; and does harm both in the getting and spending.

JOHN RUSKIN: *The Crown of Wild Olive*, I, 1866

Money entails duties. How shall we get the money and forget the duties? Voilà the great problem!

EDWARD CARPENTER: *England's Ideal*, 1887

Money is always on the brain so long as there is a brain in reasonable order.

SAMUEL BUTLER: *Note-Books, c.* 1890

Money is a new form of slavery, and distinguishable from the old simply by the fact that it is impersonal — that there is no human relation between master and slave.

LYOF N. TOLSTOY: *What Shall We Do?*, 1891

He who has money has in his pocket those who have none.

LYOF N. TOLSTOY: *Money*, 1895

When I think of all the sorrow and the barrenness that has been wrought in my life by want of a few more pounds per annum than I was able to earn, I stand aghast at money's significance.

GEORGE GISSING: *The Private Papers of Henry Ryecroft*, 1903

Money is indeed the most important thing in the world; and all sound and successful personal and national morality should have this fact for its basis.

GEORGE BERNARD SHAW: *The Irrational Knot*, 1905

When a man says money can do anything, that settles it: he hasn't any.

E. W. HOWE: *Sinner Sermons*, 1926

Six long months have passed
Since I have slept in bed.
I ain't eat a square meal o' vittles in three long weeks;
Money thinks I'm dead.

American Negro song

Money is sweet balm. ARAB PROVERB

God made bees, and bees made honey,
God made man, and man made money.

Author unidentified

Money is honey, my little sonny,
And a rich man's joke is always funny.

IBID.

Money never goes to jail. IBID.

Even the blind can see money.

CHINESE PROVERB

He that is without money might as well be buried in rice with his mouth sewed up.

IBID.

Money gives a man thirty years more of dignity.
IBID.

If you have no money, be polite.
DANISH PROVERB

Money is more eloquent than a dozen members of Parliament. IBID.

One bag of money is stronger than two bags of truth. IBID.

A man without money is like a wolf without teeth. FRENCH PROVERB

Peace makes money and money makes war.
IBID.

Mention money and the whole world is silent.
GERMAN PROVERB

Money is the man. (Geld ist der Mann.)
IBID.

No money, no fear. IBID.

No man ever had enough money.
GIPSY PROVERB

Money makes everything legitimate, even bastards. HEBREW PROVERB

A heavy purse makes a light heart.
IRISH PROVERB

Money swore an oath that nobody who didn't love it should ever have it. IBID.

Health without money is half sickness.
ITALIAN PROVERB

Money begets money. IBID.

Public money is like holy water; everyone helps himself. IBID.

The money you refuse will never do you any good. IBID.

When money is not a servant it is a master.
IBID.

Money has no ears, but it hears.
JAPANESE PROVERB

Money has no legs, but it runs. IBID.

Money is another kind of blood. (Pecunia alter sanguis.) LATIN PROVERB

Money smells good no matter what its source.
IBID.

Ready money, ready medicine. IBID.

Too much money is the worst of tribulations.
MOROCCAN PROVERB

Who hath money hath fear; who hath none hath sorrow. PERSIAN PROVERB

When I had money everyone called me brother.
POLISH PROVERB

When money speaks the truth is silent.
RUSSIAN PROVERB

Money is flat and meant to be piled up.
SCOTTISH PROVERB

Money makes a man free ilka where.
IBID. (*Ilka*=every)

Money makes and money mars. IBID.

Muck and money gae thegither. IBID.

No mountain is so high that an ass loaded with gold cannot climb it. SPANISH PROVERB

Say what you will against money, it is always a good Catholic. IBID.

Money is like an eel in the hand.
WELSH PROVERB

Money is the best messenger.
YIDDISH PROVERB

[*See also* American, Aristocracy, Authorship, Cash, Credit, Currency, Devil, Dollar, Fool, Gentleman, Gold, Gold Standard, Hanging, Honor, Husband and Wife, Imprisonment, Inflation, Jew, Law, Loss, Lover, Mammon, Man and Woman, Monkey, Peasant, Power, Purse, Riches, Silver (Free), Trust, War, Wealth.

Money-changer

Jesus went into the temple, . . . overthrew the tables of the money changers, and the seats of them that sold doves.
MARK XI, 15, *c.* 70 (Cf. MATTHEW XXI, 12, *c.* 75; JOHN II, 15, *c.* 115)

Money-getting

Get money by fair means if you can; if not, get money.
HORACE: *Epistles,* I, *c.* 20 B.C.

Get money first; virtue comes afterward.
IBID.

Money falls into the hands of some men as a *denarius* falls down a sewer.
SENECA: *Epistulæ morales ad Lucilium,* *c.* 63

No matter how the money comes, money you must have. JUVENAL: *Satires,* XIV, 128

If thou wouldst keep money, save money;
If thou wouldst reap money, sow money.
THOMAS FULLER: *Gnomologia,* 1732

Get place and wealth, if possible with grace;
If not, by any means get wealth and place.
ALEXANDER POPE: *The First Epistle of the First Book of Horace,* 1735

There are few ways in which a man can be more innocently employed than in getting money.
SAMUEL JOHNSON: *Boswell's Life,* March 27, 1775

It is a common observation that any fool can get money; but they are not wise that think so. C. C. COLTON: *Lacon,* 1820

The art of getting rich consists not in industry, much less in saving, but in a better order, in timeliness, in being at the right spot.
R. W. EMERSON: *The Conduct of Life,* III, 1860

What is eating one's bread in the sweat of one's brow but making money? I will believe no man who tells me that he would not sooner earn two loaves than one — and if two, then two hundred. I will believe no man who tells me that he would sooner earn one dollar a day than two — and if two, then two hundred.
ANTHONY TROLLOPE: *North America,* I, 1862

The first of all English games is making money.
JOHN RUSKIN: *The Crown of Wild Olive,* I, 1866

The money-getter who pleads his love of work has a lame defense, for love of work at money-getting is a lower taste than love of money.
AMBROSE BIERCE: *Collected Works,* VIII, 1911

The money-getter is never tired.
CHINESE PROVERB

Getting money is like digging with a needle; spending it is like water soaking into sand.
JAPANESE PROVERB

[*See also* Miser.

Mongolian

The yellow peril.
ENGLISH PHRASE, traced by the New English Dictionary to 1900

Mongrel

The combination of swarthiness with stature above the average and a long skull confer upon me the serene impartiality of a mongrel.
T. H. HUXLEY: *On the Aryan Question,* 1890 (Nineteenth Century, Nov.)

Monk

There are two classes a monk should avoid: women and bishops.
JOHANNES CASSIANUS: *De institutis coenobiorum,* 420

The monks shall sleep clothed, and girt with belts or with ropes: and they shall not have their knives at their sides while they sleep, lest perchance in a dream they wound other sleepers.
THE RULE OF ST. BENEDICT, *c.* 529

Monks shall not study law or medicine.
Decree of the Council of Ratisbon, 877

A monk out of his monastery is like a fish out of water.
GRATIAN: *Decretum Gratiani, c.* 1125

If thou wouldst be a monk thou must be content, for Christ's sake, to be esteemed a fool in this world.
THOMAS À KEMPIS: *Imitation of Christ,* I, *c.* 1420 (A reference to I CORINTHIANS IV, 10)

A right monk, if there ever was any, since the monking world monked a monkery.
RABELAIS: *Gargantua,* I, 1535

What frugality is there in their food? They are exactly like so many swine fattening in a sty.
JOHN CALVIN: *Institutes of the Christian Religion,* IV, 1536

They must rise early, yes, not sleep at all, who overreach monks in matter of profit.
THOMAS FULLER: *Worthies of England,* 1662

I like a church; I like a cowl;
I love a prophet of the soul;
And on my heart monastic aisles
Fall like sweet strains, or pensive smiles;
Yet not for all his faith can see
Would I that cowlèd churchman be.
R. W. EMERSON: *The Problem,* 1840 (The Dial, July)

It takes more than a hood and sad eyes to make a monk.
ALBANIAN PROVERB

Everyone to his trade: dogs bark, wolves howl, and monks lie.
GERMAN PROVERB

Offend one monk, and the monks of all Christendom will know it.
IBID.

A runaway monk never praises his convent.
ITALIAN PROVERB

He that can do no better must be a monk.
MEDIEVAL ENGLISH PROVERB

Despair makes the monk. (Desperatio facit monachum.)
MEDIEVAL LATIN PROVERB

The cowl does not make the monk. (Cucullus non facit monachum.)
IBID.

Beware of a bull when you are in front of him, of a donkey when you are behind, and of a monk wherever you are.
RUSSIAN PROVERB

[*See also* Abbot, Danger, Devil, Evolution, Heaven and Hell, Monasticism, Physician, Rome.

Monkey

What pretty things men will make for money, quoth the old woman, when she saw a monkey.
THOMAS FULLER: *Gnomologia,* 1732

Monkeys, warm with envious spite,
Their most obliging friends will bite.
BENJAMIN FRANKLIN: *Poor Richard's Almanac,* 1741

I dislike monkeys. They always remind me of poor relations.
HENRY LUTTRELL: *Advice to Julia,* 1820

The monkey is an organized sarcasm upon the human race.
H. W. BEECHER: *Eyes and Ears,* 1862

A monkey with his tail cut off is still a monkey.
WEST AFRICAN PROVERB

No monkey ever laughs at another. IBID.

[*See also* Ape, Coöperation, Evolution, Fashion, Friend, Man.

Monogamy

I am persuaded that if God had not ordained marriage, but had left men to associate with the first women they met, they themselves would very speedily have become tired of this disorderly course, and have prayed for marriage, since 'tis the very prohibition to do wrong which most excites to wrong.
MARTIN LUTHER: *Table-Talk,* DCCXXXVI, 1569

Whether the law of marriage be instituted or not, the dictate of nature and virtue seems to be an early attachment to one woman.
T. R. MALTHUS: *The Principle of Population,* II, 1798

The institution of monogamy, and the laws of marriage which it entails, bestow upon the woman an unnatural position of privilege, by considering her throughout as the full equivalent of the man, which is by no means the case.
ARTHUR SCHOPENHAUER: *On Women,* 1851

Even in civilized mankind faint traces of a monogamic instinct can sometimes be perceived.
BERTRAND RUSSELL: *Marriage and Morals,* X, 1929

[*See also* Man and Woman, Marriage.

Monopoly

It is better to abolish monopolies in all cases than not to do it in any.
THOMAS JEFFERSON: *Letter to James Madison,* 1788

All forms of personal excellence, superiority, skill and distinguished attainment constitute natural monopolies and find their reward under applications of the monopoly principle.
W. G. SUMNER: *A Group of Natural Monopolies,* 1888

It is not competition, but monopoly, that deprives labor of its product. Wages, inheritance, gifts and gambling aside, every process by which men acquire wealth rests upon a monopoly, a prohibition, a denial of liberty.
BENJAMIN R. TUCKER: *Why I Am an Anarchist,* 1892

Where a trust becomes a monopoly the state has an immediate right to interfere.
THEODORE ROOSEVELT: Message to the New York Legislature, Jan. 3, 1900

We pledge the Democratic party to an unceasing warfare in nation, state, and city against private monopoly in every form.
Democratic National Platform, 1900

A private monopoly is indefensible and intolerable.
Democratic National Platform, 1904

A private monopoly is indefensible and intolerable.
Democratic National Platform, 1908

A private monopoly is indefensible and intolerable.
Democratic National Platform, 1912

Monopoly has generally evolved into state monopoly.
NIKOLAI LENIN: Speech before the All-Russian Conference of the Russian Social-Democratic Labor party, May 7, 1917

This country would not be a land of opportunity, America would not be America, if the people were shackled with government monopolies.
CALVIN COOLIDGE: Speech of acceptance, Aug. 14, 1924

[*See also* Government Ownership, Land, Nature, Newspaper, Trusts.

Monosyllable

Monosyllabic lines, unless very artfully managed, are stiff or languishing, but may be beautiful to express melancholy, slowness or labor.
ALEXANDER POPE: *Letter to William Walsh,* Oct. 22, 1706

[*See also* English Language.

Monotheism

One Lord, one faith, one baptism, one God and Father of all, who is above all, and through all, and in you all. EPHESIANS IV, 5, *c.* 60

There is but one God, to whom the name of God alone belongs, from whom all things come, and who is Lord of the whole universe.
TERTULLIAN: *The Testimony of the Christian Soul, c.* 210

I believe in one God, and no more.
THOMAS PAINE: *The Age of Reason,* I, 1794

Monotheistic religions alone furnish the spectacle of religious wars, religious persecutions, heretical tribunals, that breaking of idols and destruction of images of the gods, that razing of Indian temples and Egyptian colossi, which had looked on the sun 3000 years;

just because a jealous god had said, "Thou shalt make no graven image."
ARTHUR SCHOPENHAUER: *Religion: A Dialogue,* 1851

According to the teaching of monotheism, God is an individual, self-dependent, all-perfect, unchangeable Being; intelligent, living, personal, and present; almighty, all-seeing, all-remembering, between whom and His creatures there is an infinite gulf; who has no origin, who is all-sufficient for Himself; who created and upholds the universe; who will judge every one of us, sooner or later, according to that law of right and wrong which He has written on our hearts.
J. H. NEWMAN: *On the Scope and Nature of University Education,* I, 1852

[*See also* God.

Monotony

Every day with me is literally another yesterday, for it is exactly the same.
ALEXANDER POPE: *Letter to Henry Cromwell,* March 18, 1708

[*See also* Boredom, Nothing.

Monroe Doctrine

We consider the interests of Cuba, Mexico and ours as the same, and that the object of both must be to exclude all European influence from this hemisphere.
THOMAS JEFFERSON: *Letter to W. C. C. Claiborne,* Oct., 1808

We should consider any attempt [by the European Powers] to extend their system to any portion of this hemisphere as dangerous to our peace and safety. With the existing colonies or dependencies of any European Power we have not interfered, and shall not interfere. But with the governments who have declared their independence, and maintained it, . . . we could not view any interposition for the purpose of oppressing them, or controlling, in any other manner, their destiny, by any European Power, in any other light than as the manifestation of an unfriendly disposition towards the United States.
JAMES MONROE: Message to Congress, Dec. 2, 1823

Monroe, James (1758–1831)

He is a man whose soul might be turned wrong side outwards, without discovering a blemish to the world.
THOMAS JEFFERSON: *Letter to W. T. Franklin,* 1786

Gouging still flourishes. His Excellency, Mr. Monroe, while a young man, constantly kept his hair closely shorn, in order that his head might be less exposed to this brutal practise.
WILLIAM FAUX: *Memorable Days in America,* 1823

Mr. Monroe is a very remarkable instance of a man whose life has been a continued series of the most extraordinary good fortune, who has never met with any known disaster, has gone through a splendid career of public service, has received more pecuniary reward from the public than any other man since the existence of the nation, and is now dying, at the age of seventy-two, in wretchedness and beggary.
JOHN QUINCY ADAMS: *Diary,* April 27, 1831

President Monroe died on the fourth of July — a respectable man, I believe.
R. W. EMERSON: *Journal,* July 6, 1831

Monster

A monster frightful, formless, immense. (Monstrum horrendum, informe, ingens.)
VIRGIL: *Æneid,* III, 19 B.C.

Neither in the case of monsters which are born and live, how quickly soever they die, will it be denied that they will rise again, or is it to be believed that they will rise again so, and not rather with their nature corrected and freed from fault.
ST. AUGUSTINE: *On Faith, Hope, and Charity, c.* 421

Montagu, Mary Wortley (1689–1762)

Lady Mary Wortley is arrived; I have seen her. Her dress, like her languages, is a *galimatias* of several countries; the groundwork, rags; and the embroidery, nastiness. She wears no cap, no handkerchief, no gown, no petticoat, no shoes. An old black-laced hood represents the first; the fur of a horseman's coat, which replaces the third, serves for the second; a dimity petticoat is deputy, and officiates for the fourth; and slippers act the part of the last.
HORACE WALPOLE: *Letter to George Montagu,* Dec. 30, 1761

Montaigne, Michel de (1533–92)

There have been men with deeper insight; but, one would say, never a man with such abundance of thoughts: he is never dull, never insincere, and has the genius to make the reader care for all that he cares for.
R. W. EMERSON: *Representative Men,* IV, 1850

[*See also* Ape.

Mont Blanc

Remote, serene, and inaccessible.
P. B. SHELLEY: *Mont Blanc,* 1816

Mont Blanc is the monarch of mountains;
They crown'd him long ago
On a throne of rocks, in a robe of clouds,
With a diadem of snow.
BYRON: *Manfred,* I, 1817

Montesquieu, C. L. de (1689–1755)

Montesquieu sometimes mistakes an epigram for a definition, and an antithesis for a novel idea, but for all that he remains a profound and Heaven-sent genius, who knows how to think himself and make his readers think.

VOLTAIRE: *Letter to an unknown correspondent,* Jan. 5, 1759

Months

Thirty days hath November,
April, June and September,
February has twenty-eight alone,
And all the rest have thirty-one.

OLD ENGLISH RHYME, appearing in various forms; author unidentified, but it has been traced to the XVI century

Thirty days hath September,
April, June, and November;
All the rest have thirty-one
Excepting February alone:
Which hath but twenty-eight, in fine,
Till leap year gives it twenty-nine.

Another version

Thirty days hath September,
April, June, and November,
February has twenty-eight alone,
All the rest have thirty-one;
Excepting leap-year, — that the time
When February's days are twenty-nine.

IBID.

[*See also* Oyster.

Monument

I would rather have men ask, after I am dead, why I have no monument than why I have one.

Ascribed to MARCUS PORCIUS CATO THE ELDER (234–149 B.C.)

Monuments are made for victories over strangers: domestic troubles should be covered with the veil of sadness.

JULIUS CÆSAR: After the battle of Pharsalia, wherein he destroyed Pompey's army, 48 B.C.

It is superfluous to raise a monument; if our lives deserve it our memories will endure.

PLINY THE YOUNGER: *Letters,* IX, *c.* 110

If a man do not erect his own tomb ere he dies he shall live no longer in monument than the bell rings and the widow weeps.

SHAKESPEARE: *Much Ado About Nothing,* V, *c.* 1599

Tombs are the clothes of the dead. A grave is but a plain suit, and a rich monument is one embroidered.

THOMAS FULLER: *The Holy State and the Profane State,* III, 1642

If you would see his monument, look around. (Si monumentum requiris, circumspice.)

Epitaph of Christopher Wren in St. Paul's Cathedral, London, *c.* 1725 (Wren was the architect of the cathedral)

The most lasting monuments are the paper monuments.

THOMAS FULLER: *Gnomologia,* 1732

Let not a monument give you or me hopes,
Since not a pinch of dust remains of Cheops.

BYRON: *Don Juan,* I, 1819

Those only deserve a monument who do not need one.

WILLIAM HAZLITT: *Characteristics,* 1823

A reminder of one who has been forgotten.

Author unidentified

[*See also* Fame, Tomb.

Moon

He appointed the moon for seasons.

PSALMS CIV, 19, *c.* 150 B.C.

He made his friends believe that the moon is made of green cheese.

DESIDERIUS ERASMUS: *Adagia,* 1508

Late, late yestreen I saw the new moon,
Wi' the auld moon in her arm.

Anon.: *Sir Patrick Spence, c.* 1550

With how sad steps, O moon, thou climb'st the skies!
How silently, and with how wan a face!

PHILIP SIDNEY: *Astrophel and Stella,* XXXI, 1591

Oh, swear not by the moon, the inconstant moon,
That monthly changes in her circled orb.

SHAKESPEARE: *Romeo and Juliet,* II, *c.* 1596

I'd rather be a dog and bay the moon
Than such a Roman.

SHAKESPEARE: *Julius Cæsar,* IV, 1599

Queen and huntress, chaste and fair,
Now the sun is laid to sleep,
Seated in thy silver chair,
State in wonted manner keep:
  Hesperus entreats thy light,
  Goddess, excellently bright.

BEN JONSON: *Cynthia's Revels,* V, 1601

It is the very error of the moon:
She comes more nearer earth than she was wont
And makes men mad.

SHAKESPEARE: *Othello,* V, 1604

Doth the moon care for the barking of a dog?

ROBERT BURTON: *The Anatomy of Melancholy,* II, 1621

You meaner beauties of the night,
  That poorly satisfy our eyes
More by your number than your light;
  You common people of the skies, —
What are you when the moon shall rise?

HENRY WOTTON: *You Meaner Beauties of the Night,* 1651

Though I believe the moon is inhabited, I live on civil terms with those who do not.

BERNARD DE FONTENELLE: *Entretiens sur la pluralité des mondes,* II, 1686

Soon as the evening shades prevail,
The moon takes up the wondrous tale;
And nightly, to the listening earth,
Repeats the story of her birth.

JOSEPH ADDISON: *The Spectator,* Aug. 23, 1712

Cynthia, named fair regent of the night.

JOHN GAY: *Trivia,* III, 1716

Once in a blue moon.

ENGLISH PHRASE, not recorded before the XIX century

Or the coy moon, when in the waviness
Of whitest clouds she does her beauty dress,
And staidly paces higher up, and higher,
Like a sweet nun in holiday attire.

JOHN KEATS: *Epistle to My Brother George,* 1816

Thou wast the river — thou wast glory won;
Thou wast my clarion's blast — thou wast my steed —
My goblet full of wine — my topmost deed: —
Thou wast the charm of women, lovely moon!

JOHN KEATS: *Endymion,* III, 1818

What is there in thee, moon, that thou shouldst move
My heart so potently? IBID.

The moon does not so clearly demand a feminine as the sun does a masculine sex: it might be considered negatively or neuter — yet if the reception of its light from the sun were known, that would have been a good reason for making her feminine, as being the recipient body.

S. T. COLERIDGE: *Table-Talk,* May 7, 1830

The man who has seen the rising moon break out of the clouds at midnight has been present like an archangel at the creation of light and of the world.

R. W. EMERSON: *History,* 1841

Yon rising moon that looks for us again —
How oft hereafter will she wax and wane;
How oft hereafter rising look for us
Through this same garden — and for one in vain!

EDWARD FITZGERALD: Tr. of OMAR KHAYYÁM: *Rubáiyát* (*c.* 1100), 1857

Lo, the moon ascending,
Up from the east the silvery round moon,
Beautiful over the house-tops, ghastly, phantom moon,
Immense and silent moon.

WALT WHITMAN: *Dirge for Two Veterans,* 1865–6

A halo round the moon is a sign of wind.

CHINESE PROVERB

Clear moon,
Frost soon. OLD ENGLISH RHYME

Pale moon doth rain,
Red moon doth blow,
White moon doth neither
Rain nor snow. IBID.

The moon shines, but it does not warm.

UKRAINIAN PROVERB

[*See also* Cosmology, Moonlight, Night, Philosopher, Star.

Moonlight

How sweet the moonlight sleeps upon this bank!
Here will we sit and let the sounds of music
Creep in our ears.

SHAKESPEARE: *The Merchant of Venice,* V, *c.* 1596

When the moon shone, we did not see the candle;
So doth the greater glory dim the less. IBID.

Now glowed the firmament
With living sapphires; Hesperus, that led
The starry host, rode brightest, till the moon,
Rising in clouded majesty, at length
Apparent queen, unveiled her peerless light,
And o'er the dark her silver mantle threw.

JOHN MILTON: *Paradise Lost,* IV, 1667

I have beheld two lovers in a night,
Hatched o'er with moonshine.

ROBERT HERRICK: *Farewell Unto Poetrie,* *c.* 1670

Girls and boys, come out to play,
The moon is shining as light as day.

Anon.: *Nursery rhyme, c.* 1750

There is not a day
The longest, not the twenty-first of June,
Sees half the business in a wicked way
On which three single hours of moonshine smile.

BYRON: *Don Juan,* I, 1819

A moon that, just
In crescent, dimly rain'd about the leaf
Twilights of airy silver.

ALFRED TENNYSON: *Ardley Court,* 1842

It glimmers on the forest tips
And through the dewy foliage drips
In little rivulets of light.

H. W. LONGFELLOW: *The Golden Legend,* VI, 1851

Moonlight is sculpture.

NATHANIEL HAWTHORNE: *American Note-Books,* 1863

On moonlight nights the Recording Angel uses shorthand. Author unidentified

Moor

The moor has done his work, the Moor may go.

J. C. F. SCHILLER: *The Fiesco,* III, 1784

[*See also* Character (National), Portuguese.

Moral

To point a moral, or adorn a tale.

SAMUEL JOHNSON: *The Vanity of Human Wishes,* 1749

"Tut, tut, child!" said the Duchess, "every thing's got a moral, if you only can find it."
C. L. DODGSON (LEWIS CARROLL): *Alice's Adventures in Wonderland*, IX, 1865

Moralist

Come, you are too severe a moraler.
SHAKESPEARE: *Othello*, II, 1604

Moralists, from whatever different principles they set out, commonly meet in their conclusions.
WILLIAM PALEY: *The Principles of Moral and Political Philosophy*, II, 1785

It would be strange to demand of a moralist that he teach no other virtue than those he himself possesses.
ARTHUR SCHOPENHAUER: *The World as Will and Idea*, IV, 1819

The moralist can advance such propositions only as will be found to be generally true, for none are so universally.
C. C. COLTON: *Lacon*, 1820

I never came across anyone in whom the moral sense was dominant who was not heartless, cruel, vindictive, log-stupid and entirely lacking in the smallest sense of humanity.
OSCAR WILDE: *Letter to Leonard Smithers*, 1897

Morality

I conceive that when a man deliberates whether he shall do a thing or not do it, he does nothing else but consider whether it be better for himself to do it or not to do it.
THOMAS HOBBES: *Questions Concerning Liberty*, 1656

There cannot any one moral rule be proposed whereof a man may not justly demand a reason; which would be perfectly ridiculous and absurd if they were innate, or so much as self-evident.
JOHN LOCKE: *Essay Concerning Human Understanding*, I, 1690

All the civilized nations of the world agree in the great points of morality.
JOSEPH ADDISON: *The Spectator*, Aug. 16, 1712

The greatest part of morality is of a fixed eternal nature, and will endure when faith shall fail.
IBID.

The first rudiments of morality, broached by skillful politicians, to render men useful to each other as well as tractable, were chiefly contrived that the ambitious might reap the more benefit from and govern vast numbers of them with the greatest ease and security.
BERNARD DE MANDEVILLE: *An Inquiry Into the Origin of Moral Virtue*, 1723

The notion of morals implies some sentiment common to all mankind, which recommends the same object to general approbation, and makes every man, or most men, agree in the same opinion or decision concerning it.
DAVID HUME: *An Enquiry Concerning the Principles of Morals*, IX, 1751

In morality we are sure as in mathematics.
BENJAMIN WHICHCOTE: *Moral and Religious Aphorisms*, 1753

Morality is eternal and immutable.
RICHARD PRICE: *The Principal Questions in Morals*, I, 1758

One should not destroy an insect, one should not quarrel with a dog, without a reason sufficient to vindicate one through all the courts of morality.
WILLIAM SHENSTONE: *Of Men and Manners*, 1764

Whatever is contrary *bonos mores et decorum* the principles of our law prohibit, and the king's court, as the general censor and guardian of the public manners, is bound to restrain and punish.
LORD MANSFIELD: *Judgment in Jones* vs. *Randall*, 1774

It is God's will, not merely that we should *be* happy, but that we should *make* ourselves happy. This is the true morality.
IMMANUEL KANT: Lecture at Königsberg, 1775

To enjoy and give enjoyment, without injury to yourself or others: this is true morality.
NICOLAS CHAMFORT: *Maxims et pensées*, *c.* 1785

Whenever you are to do a thing, though it can never be known but to yourself, ask yourself how you would act were all the world looking at you, and act accordingly.
THOMAS JEFFERSON: *Letter to Peter Carr*, 1785

In every case I must so act that I can at the same time will that the maxim behind my act should become a universal law.
IMMANUEL KANT: *Grundlegung zur Metaphysik der Sitten*, I, 1785

Morality, thou deadly bane,
Thy tens o' thousands thou hast slain!
Vain in his hope whose stay and trust is
In moral mercy, truth, and justice!
ROBERT BURNS: To Gavin Hamilton, 1786

The testimony of our moral faculty, like that of the external senses, is the testimony of nature, and we have the same reason to rely upon it.
THOMAS REED: *Essays on the Active Powers of Man*, III, 1788

Policy says, "Be wise as serpents"; morality adds thereto the restrict: "and harmless (without falsehood) as doves."
IMMANUEL KANT: *Perpetual Peace*, Appendix I, 1795

If only a tenth part of the morality that is in books existed in the heart!
G. C. LICHTENBERG: *Reflections,* 1799

I never did, or countenanced, in public life, a single act inconsistent with the strictest good faith; having never believed there was one code of morality for a public, and another for a private man.
THOMAS JEFFERSON: *Letter to Don Valentine de Feronda,* 1809

A man may have no religion, and yet be moral.
NAPOLEON I: To Gaspard Gourgaud at St. Helena, 1815–1818

Morality for the upper classes; the scaffold for the mob. IBID.

There are two principles of established acceptance in morals; first, that self-interest is the mainspring of all our actions, and secondly, that utility is the test of their value.
C. C. COLTON: *Lacon,* 1820

The great secret of morals is love.
P. B. SHELLEY: *The Defence of Poetry,* 1821

In general, morality may be compared to the consonant; prudence to the vowel. The former cannot be uttered (reduced to practice) but by means of the latter.
S. T. COLERIDGE: *Aids to Reflection,* 1825

We know no spectacle so ridiculous as the British public in one of its periodical fits of morality.
T. B. MACAULAY: *Moore's Life of Lord Byron,* 1831 (Edinburgh Review, June)

Morality without religion is only a kind of dead reckoning, — an endeavor to find our place on a cloudy sea by measuring the distance we have run, but without any observation of the heavenly bodies.
H. W. LONGFELLOW: *Kavanagh,* XIII, 1849

The analogy of morals is rather with art than with geometry.
J. A. FROUDE: *Reynard the Fox,* 1852 (Fraser's Magazine)

Aim above morality. Be not simply good; be good for something.
H. D. THOREAU: *Walden,* 1854

The time always comes at which moral principles originally adopted have been carried to all their legitimate conclusions, and then the system founded on them becomes rigid, unexpansive and liable to fall behind moral progress.
HENRY MAINE: *Ancient Law,* I, 1861

The moral feelings are not innate, but acquired.
J. S. MILL: *Utilitarianism,* III, 1863

He is immoral who is acting to any private end. He is moral whose aim or motive may become a universal rule.
R. W. EMERSON: *Character,* 1844 (Cf. KANT, *ante,* 1785)

Morality is character and conduct such as is required by the circle or community in which the man's life happens to be placed. It shows how much good men require of us.
H. W. BEECHER: *Life Thoughts,* 1858

I believe that the experiences of utility, organized and consolidated through all the past generations of the human race, have been producing corresponding modifications, which, by continued transmission and accumulation, have become in us certain faculties of moral intuition — certain emotions responding to right and wrong conduct which have no apparent basis in the individual experience of utility.
HERBERT SPENCER: *Letter to J. S. Mill,* 1868

Neither the individuals nor the ages most distinguished for intellectual achievements have been most distinguished for moral excellence.
W. E. H. LECKY: *History of European Morals,* I, 1869

The morals of men are more governed by their pursuits than by their opinions. A type of virtue is first formed by circumstances, and men afterwards make it the model upon which their theories are framed. IBID.

If men were reared under precisely the same conditions as hive-bees, there can hardly be a doubt that our unmarried females would, like the worker-bees, think it a sacred duty to kill their brothers, and mothers would strive to kill their fertile daughters; and no one would think of interfering.
CHARLES DARWIN: *The Descent of Man,* IV, 1871

Man . . . derives his moral sense from the social feelings which are instinctive or innate in the lower animals. IBID.

A moral being is one who is capable of reflecting on his past actions and their motives — of approving of some and disapproving of others.
CHARLES DARWIN: *The Descent of Man,* XXI

Morality represents for everybody a thoroughly definite and ascertained idea: — the idea of human conduct regulated in a certain manner. MATTHEW ARNOLD: *Literature and Dogma,* I, 1873

Every one of us, whatever our speculative opinions, knows better than he practises, and recognizes a better law than he obeys.
J. A. FROUDE: *On Progress,* 1882

The foundation of morality is to have done, once and for all, with lying.

T. H. HUXLEY: *Science and Morals*, 1886

Fear is the mother of morality.

F. W. NIETZSCHE: *Beyond Good and Evil*, 1886

It is not surprising that lambs should bear a grudge against birds of prey, but that is no reason for blaming birds of prey for pouncing on lambs.

F. W. NIETZSCHE: *The Genealogy of Morals*, I, 1887

What is Jewish, what is Christian morality? Chance robbed of its innocence; unhappiness polluted with the idea of " sin "; well-being represented as a danger, as a " temptation "; a physiological disorder produced by the canker worm of conscience.

F. W. NIETZSCHE: *The Antichrist*, XXV, 1888

Morality is the best of all devices for leading mankind by the nose.

F. W. NIETZSCHE: *The Antichrist*, XLIV

There are no such things as moral facts.

F. W. NIETZSCHE: *The Twilight of the Idols*, 1889

Morality turns on whether the pleasure precedes or follows the pain. Thus it is immoral to get drunk because the headache comes after the drinking, but if the headache came first, and the drunkenness afterwards, it would be moral to get drunk.

SAMUEL BUTLER: *Note-Books, c.* 1890

Morality is simply the attitude we adopt toward people whom we personally dislike.

OSCAR WILDE: *An Ideal Husband*, III, 1895

All moral laws are merely statements that certain kinds of actions will have good effects.

G. E. MOORE: *Principia Ethica*, V, 1903

An Englishman thinks he is moral when he is only uncomfortable.

GEORGE BERNARD SHAW: *Man and Superman*, III, 1903

Religious morality is a morality of sacrifice, which is dear to the weak and degenerate, but to all other people is a species of slavery.

BENITO MUSSOLINI: Speech in Lausanne, July, 1904

For the preservation of the moral order neither the laws and sanctions of the temporal power are sufficient nor the beauty of virtue and the expounding of its necessity. A religious authority must enter in to enlighten the mind, to direct the will, and to strengthen human frailty by the aid of divine grace.

POPE PIUS XI: *Casti connubii*, Dec. 31, 1930

Absolutism in morals is a guarantee of objectional morals in the same way as absolutism in government is a guarantee of objectionable government.

ROBERT BRIFFAULT: *Sin and Sex*, II, 1931

[*See also* British, Buddhism, Chastity, Darwinism, Ethics, Faith, Golden Rule, Good and Bad, Good and Evil, Infallibility (Papal), Infamy, Instinct, Justice, Manners, Money, Moralist, Nihilism, Pleasure, Revelation, Scotsman, Spaniard, Taste.

Morality, National

The established rules of morality and justice are applicable to nations as well as to individuals; . . . the former as well as the latter are bound to keep their promises; to fulfill their engagements to respect the rights of property which others have acquired under contracts with them.

ALEXANDER HAMILTON: *Vindication of the Funding System*, 1791

Let us with caution indulge the supposition that morality can be maintained without religion. Whatever may be conceded to the influence of refined education on minds of peculiar structure, reason and experience both forbid us to expect that national morality can prevail in exclusion of religious principle.

GEORGE WASHINGTON: Farewell Address, Sept. 17, 1796

The nation, being in effect a licensed predatory concern, is not bound by the decencies of that code of law and morals that governs private conduct.

THORSTEIN VEBLEN: *Absentee Ownership*, I, 1923

[*See also* Nation.

Moravian

The Moravians . . . certainly exceed all mankind in absurdity of principles and madness of practise, yet these people walk erect, and are numbered among rational beings.

MARY WORTLEY MONTAGU: *Letter to James Steuart*, Oct. 13, 1759

More

The more the merrier.

JOHN PALSGRAVE: *L'éclaircissement de la langue française*, 1530

A man can do no more than he can.

JOHN RAY: *English Proverbs*, 1670

The more the merrier; the fewer, the better cheer.

THOMAS FULLER: *Gnomologia*, 1732

Please, sir, I want some more.

CHARLES DICKENS: *Oliver Twist*, II, 1838

[*See also* Much.

Moreau, Jean Victor (1763–1813)

Moreau is like a drum, which nobody hears of except it be beaten.

Author unidentified (Moreau became famous because of his retreats to the Rhine, 1796, and in Italy, 1799)

Mormonism

The political power of the Mormon Church in the territories as exercised in the past is a menace to free institutions, a danger no longer to be suffered. Therefore we pledge the Republican party to appropriate legislation asserting the sovereignty of the nation in all territories where the same is questioned, and in furtherance of that end to place upon the statute books legislation stringent enough to divorce the political from the ecclesiastical power, and thus stamp out the attendant wickedness of polygamy.

Republican National Platform, 1888

Morning

Weeping may endure for a night, but joy cometh in the morning.

PSALMS XXX, 5, *c.* 150 B.C.

The wings of the morning.

PSALMS CXXXIX, 9

The morning is a friend to the muses.

DESIDERIUS ERASMUS: *Colloquia,* 1524

Cloudy mornings turn to clear afternoons.

JOHN HEYWOOD: *Proverbs,* 1546

See how the morning opes her golden gates,
And takes her farewell of the glorious sun.
How well resembles it the prime of youth,
Trimm'd like a younker prancing to his love.

SHAKESPEARE: *III Henry VI,* II, *c.* 1591

The grey-eyed morn smiles on the frowning night.

SHAKESPEARE: *Romeo and Juliet,* II, *c.* 1596

All the speed is in the morning.

GABRIEL HARVEY: *Commonplace-Book,* *c.* 1600

But look, the morn, in russet mantle clad,
Walks o'er the dew of yon high eastward hill.

SHAKESPEARE: *Hamlet,* I, *c.* 1601

The cock, that is the trumpet to the morn,
Doth with his lofty and shrill-sounding throat
Awake the god of day.

IBID.

Full many a glorious morning have I seen
Flatter the mountain tops with sovereign eye,
Kissing with golden face the meadows green,
Gilding pale streams with heavenly alchemy.

SHAKESPEARE: *Sonnets,* XXXIII, 1609

Pack, clouds, away, and welcome day,
  With night we banish sorrow;
Sweet air, blow soft, mount, lark, aloft
  To give my love good-morrow!

THOMAS HEYWOOD: *The Rape of Lucrece,* 1608

Mornings are mysteries.

HENRY VAUGHAN: *Silex scintillans,* I, 1650

Sweet is the breath of morn, her rising sweet,
With charm of earliest birds; pleasant the sun
When first on this delightful land he spreads
His orient beams on herb, tree, fruit, and flower.

JOHN MILTON: *Paradise Lost,* IV, 1667

Morn,
Wak'd by the circling hours, with rosy hand
Unbarr'd the gates of light.

JOHN MILTON: *Paradise Lost,* VI

At length the morn and cold indifference came.

NICHOLAS ROWE: *The Fair Penitent,* I, 1703

The hour in which the cat-organ of an irritable viscerage is substituted for the brain as the mind's instrument.

S. T. COLERIDGE: To Thomas Allsop, *c.* 1820

'Tis always morning somewhere in the world.

R. H. HORNE: *Orion,* III, 1843

Lose an hour in the morning, and you will be all day hunting for it.

RICHARD WHATELY: *Easy Lessons on Morals,* 1845

Morn in the white wake of the morning star
Came furrowing all the orient into gold.

ALFRED TENNYSON: *The Princess,* III, 1847

All memorable events transpire in morning time and in a morning atmosphere.

H. D. THOREAU: *Walden,* 1854

An hour in the morning is worth two in the evening.

H. G. BOHN: *Handbook of Proverbs,* 1855

For a breeze of morning moves,
  And the plant of love is on high,
Beginning to faint in the light that she loves
  On a bed of daffodil sky.

ALFRED TENNYSON: *Maud,* I, 1855

And like a soul belated,
In Hell and Heaven unmated,
By cloud and mist abated
  Comes out of darkness morn.

A. C. SWINBURNE: *The Garden of Proserpine,* 1866

The first hour of the morning is the rudder of the day.

H. W. BEECHER: *Proverbs from Plymouth Pulpit,* 1870

I hear the trumpets of the morning blowing.

H. W. LONGFELLOW: *The Two Rivers,* 1873

The morning hours have gold in their mouths. (Die Morgenstunde hat Gold im Munde.)

GERMAN PROVERB

The morning is wiser than the evening.

RUSSIAN PROVERB

[*See also* Day, Dawn, Indifference, Joy, Lark, Pastime, Sun, Sunrise, Weather.

Moron

Coriantor was the son of Moron. And Moron was the son of Ethem.
THE BOOK OF MORMON (*Ether I*, 7–8), 1830

A thing that grieves not and that never hopes,
Stolid and stunned, a brother to the ox.
EDWIN MARKHAM: *The Man With the Hoe,* 1899

Resolved, That the feeble-minded be divided into three classes, viz.:
Idiots. — Those so deeply defective that their mental development never exceeds that of a normal child of about two years.
Imbeciles. — Those whose mental development is above that of an idiot but does not exceed that of a normal child of about seven years.
Morons. — Those whose mental development is above that of an imbecile but does not exceed that of a normal child of about twelve years.
Resolutions of the American Association for the Study of the Feeble-Minded, Lincoln, Ill., May, 1910

See the happy moron;
He doesn't give a damn:
I wish I were a moron —
My God, perhaps I am!
Anon.: In the Eugenics Review, July, 1929

[*See also* Certainty.

Mortality

Your fathers, where are they? and the prophets, do they live forever?
ZECHARIAH I, 5, *c.* 520 B.C.

All flesh shall perish together, and man shall turn again unto dust.
JOB XXXIV, 15, *c.* 325 B.C.

The wind passeth over it, and it is gone; and the place thereof shall know it no more.
PSALMS CIII, 16, *c.* 150 B.C.

When hope and hap, when health and wealth, are highest, then woe and wrack, disease and death, are nighest.
GEORGE PETTIE: *Petite Palace of Pettie His Pleasure,* 1576

All that in this world is great or gay
Doth as a vapor vanish and decay.
EDMUND SPENSER: *The Ruines of Time,* 1591

It smells of mortality.
SHAKESPEARE: *King Lear,* IV, 1606

To smell of a turf of fresh earth is wholesome for the body; no less are thoughts of mortality cordial to the soul.
THOMAS FULLER: *The Holy State and the Profane State,* 1642

All hope of never dying here lies dead.
RICHARD CRASHAW: *On the Death of Mr. Herrys,* 1646

Fifteen is full as mortal as threescore.
EDWARD YOUNG: *Love of Fame,* VI, 1728

All men think all men mortal but themselves.
EDWARD YOUNG: *Night Thoughts,* I, 1742

They that creep and they that fly
Shall end where they began.
THOMAS GRAY: *Ode to Spring,* 1748

If any purpose of nature be clear, we may affirm that the whole scope and intention of man's creation, so far as we can judge by natural reason, is limited to the present life.
DAVID HUME: *On the Immortality of the Soul,* 1777

Hills sink to plains, and man returns to dust,
That dust supports a reptile or a flower;
Each changeful atom by some other nurs'd
Takes some new form, to perish in an hour.
PHILIP FRENEAU: *The House of Night,* 1779

At this point I become mortal.
J. C. F. SCHILLER: *Don Carlos,* I, 1787

Oh, why should the spirit of mortal be proud?
Like a fast-flitting meteor, a fast-flying cloud,
A flash of the lightning, a break of the wave,
He passes from life to his rest in the grave.
WILLIAM KNOX: *Mortality,* 1824

[*See also* Death, Earth, Flesh, Grave, Life.

Mortgage

Once a mortgage, always a mortgage, and nothing but a mortgage.
LEGAL MAXIM

Moses (c. 1400 B.C.)

The man Moses was very meek, above all the men which were upon the face of the earth.
NUMBERS XII, 3, *c.* 700 B.C.

He buried him in a valley in the land of Moab, over against Beth-peor; but no man knoweth of his sepulchre unto this day.
DEUTERONOMY XXXIV, 6, *c.* 650 B.C.

Moses was a hundred and twenty years old when he died: his eye was not dim, nor his natural force abated.
DEUTERONOMY XXXIV, 7

An Egyptian priest named Moses, who possessed a portion of Lower Egypt, being dissatisfied with the established institutions there, left it and came to Judea with a large body of people who worshipped the Most High.
STRABO: *Geography,* XVI, *c.* 20 B.C.

Moses with his law is most terrible; there never was any equal to him in perplexing, affrighting, tyrannizing, threatening, preaching, and thundering.
MARTIN LUTHER: *Table-Talk,* CCLXXVI, 1569

Go down, Moses,
'Way down in Egypt lan';

Tell ole Pharaoh
To let my people go.
Negro spiritual, *c.* 1840

A pillar of light on the threshold of history.
ASHER GINZBERG (AHAD HA'AM): *Al Parashat Derakim,* 1895

The greatest Hebrew who never lived.
ABRAM LEON SACHER: *A History of the Jew,* II, 1930 (Dr. Sacher reports this saying, but does not subscribe to it)

[*See also* Hell.

Moslem

[*See* Mohammedan.

Mosquito

They are too delicate and unfitte to begine new plantations and collonies that cannot enduer the biting of a muskeeto.
Anon.: *Answers to Objections Made Against the Plymouth Colony,* XII, Jan. 24, 1623

Good-night; sleep tight;
Don't let the mosquitoes bite.
AMERICAN NURSERY RHYME

Mote

There are infinitely more assignable real parts on the surface of a particle of light than there are particles of dust, water and stone on the surface of the terrestrial globe.
JONATHAN EDWARDS: *Freedom of the Will,* I, 1754

I tell thee that those viewless beings,
Whose mansion is the smallest particle
Of the impassive atmosphere,
Think, feel and live like man.
P. B. SHELLEY: *Queen Mab,* III, 1813

Mote and Beam

Why beholdest thou the mote that is in thy brother's eye, but considerest not the beam that is in thine own eye?
MATTHEW VII, 3, *c.* 75 (Cf. LUKE VI, 41, *c.* 75)

Mother

A mother in Israel.
JUDGES V, 7, *c.* 500 B.C. (Cf. II SAMUEL XX, 19, *c.* 500 B.C.)

Despise not thy mother when she is old.
PROVERBS XXIII, 22, *c.* 350 B.C.

Begin, little boy, to recognize your mother with a smile. VIRGIL: *Eclogues,* II, 37 B.C.

And all my mother came into mine eyes
And gave me up to tears.
SHAKESPEARE: *Henry V,* IV, *c.* 1598

The mother is a matchless beast.
JAMES KELLY: *Complete Collection of Scottish Proverbs,* 1721

Not a week passes (perhaps I might with equal veracity say a day) in which I do not think of her. Such was the impression her tenderness made upon me, though the opportunity she had for showing it was so short.
WILLIAM COWPER: *Letter to Joseph Hill,* Nov., 1784 (On his mother: she died in 1737, when he was six years old)

For God, who lives above the skies,
Would look with vengeance in His eyes,
If I should ever dare despise
My mother.
ANN and JANE TAYLOR: *Original Poems for Infant Minds,* I, 1804

A mother is a mother still,
The holiest thing alive.
S. T. COLERIDGE: *The Three Graves,* 1818

Happy he
With such a mother. Faith in womankind
Beats with his blood, and trust in all things high
Comes easy to him.
ALFRED TENNYSON: *The Princess,* VII, 1847

The shrill-edged shriek of a mother.
ALFRED TENNYSON: *Maud,* I, 1855

Over my slumbers your loving watch keep;
Rock me to sleep, mother; rock me to sleep.
ELIZABETH CHASE (AKERS ALLEN): *Rock Me to Sleep,* 1860 (Saturday Evening Post, June 9)

Mother, thou sole and only, thou not these,
Keep me in mind a little when I die.
A. C. SWINBURNE: *Atalanta in Calydon,* 1865

The hand that rocks the cradle
Is the hand that rules the world.
W. R. WALLACE: *What Rules the World,* 1865

If I were hanged on the highest hill,
Mother o' mine, O mother o' mine!
I know whose love would follow me still,
Mother o' mine, O mother o' mine!
RUDYARD KIPLING: *Mother o' Mine,* 1894 (Today, London, June 2)

Mother knows best.
EDNA FERBER: Title of a story, 1927 (The saying has been familiar in the United States for many years)

One may desert one's father, though he be a high official, but not one's mother, though she be a beggar. CHINESE PROVERB

It is safer in a mother's lap than in a lord's bed.
ESTONIAN PROVERB

He is bare of news who speaks ill of his mother.
IRISH PROVERB

No bones are ever broken by a mother's beating. RUSSIAN PROVERB

An ounce of mother is worth a ton of priest.
SPANISH PROVERB

God could not be everywhere, so He made mothers. YIDDISH PROVERB

[*See also* Birth, Child, Children, Daughter, Duty (Filial), Eye, Faith, Father, Heredity, Love, Man and Woman, Manners, Mother and Child, Mother and Daughter, Mother and Son, Sorrow, War, Wife, Wooing.

Mother and Child

Can a woman forget her sucking child, that she should not have compassion on the son of her womb? yea, they may forget.
ISAIAH XLIX, 15, *c.* 700 B.C.

Her children arise up and call her blessed.
PROVERBS XXXI, 28, *c.* 350 B.C.

Mothers are fonder of their children than fathers, for they remember the pain of bringing them forth, and are surer that they are their own.
ARISTOTLE: *The Nicomachean Ethics,* IX, *c.* 340 B.C.

What tigress is there that does not purr over her young ones, and fawn upon them in tenderness?
ST. AUGUSTINE: *The City of God,* XV, 427

He that wipes the child's nose kisseth the mother's cheek.
GEORGE HERBERT: *Outlandish Proverbs,* 1640

Mothers soften their children with kisses and imperfect noises, with the pap and breast-milk of soft endearments; they rescue them from tutors, and snatch them from discipline, they desire to keep them fat and warm, and their feet dry, and their bellies full, and then the children govern, and cry, and prove fools and troublesome.
JEREMY TAYLOR: *The Rule and Exercises of Holy Dying,* III, 1651

A child may have too much of his mother's blessing.
JOHN RAY: *English Proverbs,* 1670

My opinion is that the future good or bad conduct of a child entirely depends upon the mother.
NAPOLEON I: To Barry E. O'Meara at St. Helena, June 10, 1817

Praise the child, and you make love to the mother.
WILLIAM COBBETT: *Advice to Young Men,* IV, 1829 (Cited as "an old saying." Cf. HERBERT, *ante,* 1640)

Like mother, like child.
FREDERICK MARRYAT: *Jacob Faithful,* XXIII, 1834 (Quoted as a proverb)

A spoilt child never loves its mother.
HENRY TAYLOR: *Notes from Life,* 1847

Mother is the name for God in the lips and hearts of little children.
W. M. THACKERAY: *Vanity Fair,* II, 1848

The mother's heart is the child's schoolroom.
H. W. BEECHER: *Life Thoughts,* 1858

The female of one of the emus (*Dromæus irroratus*), as soon as she catches sight of her progeny, becomes violently agitated, and, notwithstanding the resistance of the father, appears to use her utmost endeavors to destroy them.
CHARLES DARWIN: *The Descent of Man,* II, 1871

Some mothers need happy children; others need unhappy ones — otherwise they cannot prove their maternal virtues.
F. W. NIETZSCHE: *Human All-too-Human,* I, 1878

In the eyes of its mother every beetle is a gazelle. MOROCCAN PROVERB

[*See also* Heredity, Manners, Mother, Music, Suckling.

Mother and Daughter

The daughter riseth up against her mother.
MICAH VII, 6, *c.* 700 B.C. (Cf. MATTHEW X, 35, *c.* 75; LUKE XII, 53, *c.* 75)

As is the mother, so is her daughter.
EZEKIEL XVI, 44, *c.* 600 B.C. (Quoted as a proverb)

I warned my son against taking home the foal of a bad mother.
EURIPIDES: *Andromache, c.* 427 B.C.

O loveliest daughter of a lovely mother. (O matre pulchra filia pulchrior.)
HORACE: *Carmina,* IV, *c.* 13 B.C.

Thou art thy mother's glass, and she in thee
Calls back the lovely April of her prime.
SHAKESPEARE: *Sonnets,* III, 1609

A light-heel'd mother makes a heavy-heel'd daughter.
JOHN RAY: *English Proverbs,* 1670

He that would the daughter win
Must with the mother first begin. IBID.

Ewe follows ewe; as the acts of the mother, so are the acts of the daughter.
HEBREW PROVERB

[*See also* Like, Mother.

Mother and Son

A father is proud of those sons who have merit, and puts the rest lower. But a mother, though she is proud too of the former, cherishes the latter.
CONFUCIUS: *The Book of Rites,* XXIX, *c.* 500 B.C.

Where yet was ever found a mother
Who'd give her booby for another?
JOHN RAY: *Fables,* I, 1727

Mothers' darlings make but milksop heroes.
THOMAS FULLER: *Gnomologia,* 1732

Men are what their mothers make them.
R. W. EMERSON: *The Conduct of Life*, I, 1860

[*See also* Father and Son, Mother, Mother and Child, Son.

Motherhood

[Motherhood] is the keystone of the arch of matrimonial happiness.
THOMAS JEFFERSON: *Letter to Martha Jefferson Randolph*, 1791

Womanliness means only motherhood;
All love begins and ends there.
ROBERT BROWNING: *The Inn Album*, VII, 1875

Mother-in-law

Happy is she who marries the son of a dead mother.
JAMES KELLY: *Complete Collection of Scottish Proverbs*, 1721

The mother-in-law remembers not that she was a daughter-in-law.
THOMAS FULLER: *Gnomologia*, 1732

She was to me all that a mother could be, and I yield to none in admiration for her character, love of her virtues, and veneration for her memory.
R. E. LEE: *Letter*, 1853 (Speaking of his mother-in-law, Mary Custis, lately dead)

I know a mother-in-law who sleeps in her spectacles, the better to see her son-in-law suffer in her dreams.
ERNEST COQUELIN (1848–1909)

However much you dislike your mother-in-law you must not set fire to her.
ERNEST WILD (Recorder of London): To a culprit before him, *c.* 1925

The husband's mother is the wife's devil.
GERMAN PROVERB

The only good mother-in-law wears a green dress [i.e., is dead and buried]. IBID.

Be civil to a mother-in-law and she will come to your house three times a day.
JAPANESE PROVERB

Never rely on the glory of the morning or the smile of your mother-in-law. IBID.

A mother-in-law and a daughter-in-law in one house are like two cats in a bag.
YIDDISH PROVERB

[*See also* Arkansas, Daughter-in-law.

Motherless

Baby Jesus, who dost lie
Far above that stormy sky,
In Thy mother's pure caress,
Stoop and save the motherless.
CHARLES KINGSLEY: *The Saint's Tragedy*, I, 1848

[*See also* Husband, Orphan.

Motherwit

No delusion is greater than the notion that method and industry can make up for lack of motherwit, either in science or in practical life.
T. H. HUXLEY: *The Progress of Science*, 1887

An ounce of motherwit is worth a pound of clergy. SCOTTISH PROVERB

Motion

Whatever moves is moved by another. (Quod movetur ab alio movetur.)
THOMAS AQUINAS: *Summa theologicæ*, I, *c.* 1265

[*See also* Matter.

Motionless

Day after day, day after day,
We stuck, nor breath nor motion;
As idle as a painted ship
Upon a painted ocean.
S. T. COLERIDGE: *The Ancient Mariner*, 1798

Motion-picture

[*See* Moving-picture.

Motive

Pleasure and nobility between them supply the motives of all actions whatsoever.
ARISTOTLE: *The Nicomachean Ethics*, III, *c.* 340 B.C.

In vain the sage, with retrospective eye,
Would from th' apparent what conclude the why,
Infer the motive from the deed, and show
That what we chanced was what we meant to do.
ALEXANDER POPE: *Moral Essays*, I (Of the Knowledge and Characters of Men), 1733

There is no such thing as any sort of motive that is in itself a bad one.
JEREMY BENTHAM: *The Principles of Morals and Legislation*, X, 1789

An action is essentially good if the motive of the agent be good, regardless of the consequences.
IMMANUEL KANT: *Grundlegung zur Metaphysik der Sitten*, II, 1785

Often we think we believe a thing, and yet do not believe it. Nothing is more impenetrable than the motivation of our actions.
G. C. LICHTENBERG: *Reflections*, 1799

We must judge a man's motives from his overt acts. LORD KENYON: *Judgment in Rex vs. Waddington*, 1800

If no action is to be deemed virtuous for which malice can imagine a sinister motive, then there never was a virtuous action; no, not even in the life of our Saviour Himself. But He has taught us to judge the tree by its

fruit, and to leave motives to Him who can alone see into them.
THOMAS JEFFERSON: *Letter to Martin Van Buren,* 1824

Motives are symptoms of weakness, and supplements for the deficient energy of the living principle, the law within us. Let them then be reserved for those momentous acts and duties in which the strongest and best balanced natures must feel themselves deficient, and where humility, no less than prudence, prescribes deliberation.
S. T. COLERIDGE: *Aids to Reflection,* 1825

One will not go far wrong if one attributes extreme actions to vanity, average ones to habit, and petty ones to fear.
F. W. NIETZSCHE: *Human All-too-Human,* I, 1878

Whenever a man does a thoroughly stupid thing it is always from the noblest motive.
OSCAR WILDE: *The Picture of Dorian Gray,* 1891

[*See also* Action, End, Morality.

Mountain

The mountains skipped like rams, and the little hills like lambs.
PSALMS CXIV, 4, *c.* 150 B.C.

The mountain was in labor and brought forth a [ridiculous] mouse. (Parturiunt montes, nascetur ridiculus mus.)
HORACE: *De arte poetica, c.* 8 B.C.

If the mountain won't come to Mohammed, Mohammed must go to the mountain.
ENGLISH PROVERB, familiar since the XVII century

A mountain and a river are good neighbors.
GEORGE HERBERT: *Jacula Prudentum,* 1651

The Delectable Mountains.
JOHN BUNYAN: *Pilgrim's Progress,* I, 1678

Hills peep o'er hills, and Alps on Alps arise.
ALEXANDER POPE: *An Essay on Criticism,* II, 1711

Mountains interposed
Make enemies of nations, who had else
Like kindred drops been mingled into one.
WILLIAM COWPER: *The Task,* II, 1785

Separate from the pleasure of your company, I don't much care if I never see a mountain in my life.
CHARLES LAMB: *Letter to William Wordsworth,* Jan. 30, 1801

This wall of eagle-baffling mountain,
Black, wintry, dead, unmeasured; without herb,
Insect, or beast, or shape or sound of life.
P. B. SHELLEY: *Prometheus Unbound,* I, 1820

Mountains are to the rest of the body of the earth what violent muscular action is to the body of man. The muscles and tendons of its anatomy are, in the mountain, brought out with force and convulsive energy, full of expression, passion, and strength; the plains and the lower hills are the repose and the effortless motion of the frame.
JOHN RUSKIN: *Modern Painters,* II, 1846

The Rocky-Candy Mountains.
Anon.: *The Paul Bunyan Legend, c.* 1875

There are many paths to the top of the mountain, but the view is always the same.
CHINESE PROVERB

Mountains live longer than kings.
DUTCH PROVERB

To make a mountain of a mole-hill.
ENGLISH PHRASE, borrowed from the Greek of Lucian

[*See also* Cause and Effect, Marching, Mont Blanc, Volcano.

Mountaineer

The loud torrent and the whirlwind's roar
But bind him to his native mountains more.
OLIVER GOLDSMITH: *The Traveler,* 1764

Mountaineers always love their country.
NAPOLEON I: *Diary of Pulteney Malcolm at St. Helena,* March 25, 1817

Mountaineers are always free. (Montani semper liberi.)
MOTTO OF WEST VIRGINIA, adopted Sept. 26, 1863

Mourning

I will wail and howl, I will go stripped and naked: I will make a wailing like the dragons, and mourning as the owls.
MICAH I, 8, *c.* 700 B.C.

They shall make themselves utterly bald for thee, and gird them with sackcloth, and they shall weep for thee with bitterness of heart and bitter wailing.
EZEKIEL XXVII, 31, *c.* 600 B.C.

It is better to go to the house of mourning than to go to the house of feasting: for that is the end of all men; and the living will lay it to his heart. ECCLESIASTES VII, 2, *c.* 200 B.C.

Blessed are they that mourn: for they shall be comforted. MATTHEW V, 4, *c.* 75

None mourn more ostentatiously than those who most rejoice.
TACITUS: *Annals,* II, *c.* 110

The house of mourning teaches charity and wisdom.
ST. JOHN CHRYSOSTOM: *Homilies,* XV, *c.* 388

Mourning
Helps not the mourned, yet hurts them that mourn.
THOMAS DEKKER: *The Shoemaker's Holiday,* IV, 1599

We must be patient; but I cannot choose but weep, to think they should lay him i' the cold ground.

SHAKESPEARE: *Hamlet*, IV, *c.* 1601

The generality of women mourn the death of their lovers not so much from the love they bore them as to appear more worthy of being loved.

LA ROCHEFOUCAULD: *Maxims*, 1665

There are some persons whom, when we lose, we regret more than we mourn; and others whom we mourn and scarcely regret.

IBID.

If a man will observe as he walks the streets, I believe he will find the merriest countenances in mourning coaches.

JONATHAN SWIFT: *Thoughts on Various Subjects*, 1706

Man was made to mourn.

ROBERT BURNS: Title of a poem, 1785

What, madam, have you not forgiven God Almighty yet?

Ascribed to JOHN WESLEY (1703–91) on meeting a widow in deep mourning two years after her husband's death

We seldom indulge long in depression and mourning except when we think secretly that there is something very refined in it.

WILLIAM GODWIN: *Letter to Mary Godwin Shelley*, Oct. 27, 1818

I count it crime
To mourn for any overmuch.

ALFRED TENNYSON: *In Memoriam*, LXXXV, 1850

We do not die with those we mourn.

ELIZABETH CHASE (AKERS ALLEN): *Endurance*, 1861

For a little child a little mourning.

FRENCH PROVERB

[*See also* Death, Drinking, Funeral, Grave, Laughter, Widow.

Mouse

A mouse never trusts his life to one hole only.

PLAUTUS: *Truculentus*, IV, *c.* 190 B.C.

When a building is about to fall, all the mice desert it.

PLINY THE ELDER: *Natural History*, VIII, 77

It had need to be a wily mouse that should breed in a cat's ear.

JOHN HEYWOOD: *Proverbs*, 1546

Mice and rats and such small deer.

SHAKESPEARE: *King Lear*, III, 1606

No house without mouse.

JOHN RAY: *English Proverbs*, 1670

Hickory, dickory, dock,
The mouse ran up the clock.

Anon.: *Nursery rhyme*, *c.* 1750

Three blind mice, see how they run.

IBID.

Wee, sleekit, cow'rin', tim'rous beastie,
Oh, what a panic's in thy breastie!
Thou need na start awa' sae hasty,
Wi' bickering brattle!
I wad be laith to rin and chase thee,
Wi' murd'ring prattle!

ROBERT BURNS: *To a Mouse*, 1785

A cube of cheese no larger than a die
May bait the trap to catch a nibbling mie.

AMBROSE BIERCE: *The Devil's Dictionary*, 1906

[*See also* Cause and Effect, Longevity, Love, Mountain, Mouse-trap.

Mouse-trap

If a man can write a better book, preach a better sermon, or make a better mouse-trap than his neighbor, though he builds his house in the woods, the world will make a beaten path to his door.

SARAH S. B. YULE: *Borrowings*, 1889 (The quotation is ascribed to EMERSON by Mrs. Yule, and it resembles a passage in his *Journals*, 1855, but the reference to the mouse-trap does not appear in the latter. Cf. EMERSON, 1856, under Excellence)

Mouth

The mouth is a snare of death.

The Didache, or Teaching of the Twelve Apostles, *c.* 135

Look to the mouth; diseases enter there.

GEORGE HERBERT: *The Temple*, 1633

A close mouth catches no fleas.

WILLIAM CAMDEN: *Remains Concerning Britain* (4th ed.), 1636

A wise head makes a close mouth.

JOHN RAY: *English Proverbs*, 1670

In man, the gateway to the soul; in woman, the outlet of the heart.

AMBROSE BIERCE: *The Devil's Dictionary*, 1906

A shut mouth is as good as a priest's blessing.

IRISH SAYING

You never open your mouth but you put your foot in it.

IBID.

Teeth placed before the tongue give good advice.

ITALIAN PROVERB

A shut mouth keeps out of strife.

PORTUGUESE PROVERB

[*See also* Heart, Silence, Taciturnity.

Moving

I never saw an oft-removed tree,
Nor yet an oft-removed family,
That throve so well as those that settled be.

BENJAMIN FRANKLIN: *Poor Richard's Almanac*, 1758

Three removes are as bad as a fire. IBID.

Moving-picture

Assemblies rage in this part of the world. I now and then peep upon these things with the same coldness I would do on a moving picture.

MARY WORTLEY MONTAGU: *Letter to the Countess of Mar,* March, 1727

No picture shall be produced which will lower the moral standards of those who see it. Hence the sympathy of the audience should never be thrown to the side of crime, wrong-doing, evil or sin. Correct standards of life shall be presented on the screen, subject only to necessary dramatic contrasts. Law, natural or human, should not be ridiculed, nor shall sympathy be created for its violation.

A CODE TO GOVERN THE MAKING OF MOTION AND TALKING PICTURES BY THE MOTION PICTURE PRODUCERS OF AMERICA, INC., March 31, 1930

[*See also* Marriage, Murder, Nakedness, Obscenity, Passion.

Mozart, W. A. (1756–91)

I tell you before God and on my word as an honest man that your son is the greatest composer I have ever heard of.

JOSEPH HAYDN: To Leopold Mozart, in Vienna, Feb. 12, 1785

O Mozart, immortal Mozart, what countless images of a brighter and better world thou hast stamped upon our souls!

FRANZ SCHUBERT: *Diary,* June 13, 1816

[*See also* Music.

Much

The much runs ever to the more.

MICHAEL DRAYTON: *I Polyolbion,* 1612

Much of a muchness.

JOHN VANBRUGH and COLLEY CIBBER: *The Provok'd Husband,* I, 1728

Much in little. (Multum in parvo.)

LATIN PHRASE

[*See also* Ado, Too Much.

Muckraker

The men with the muckrakes are often indispensable to the well-being of society; but only if they know when to stop raking the muck, and to look upward to the celestial crown above them, to the crown of worthy endeavor. There are beautiful things above and round about them; and if they gradually grow to feel that the whole world is nothing but muck, their power of usefulness is gone.

THEODORE ROOSEVELT: Address in Washington, April 14, 1906

Mud

Mud chokes no eels.

THOMAS FULLER: *Gnomologia,* 1732

Mudsill

[*See* Proletariat.

Mugwump

A mugwump is a person educated beyond his intellect.

HORACE PORTER: To an interviewer during the Cleveland-Blaine campaign, 1884

A mugwump is one of those boys who always has his mug on one side of the political fence and his wump on the other.

ALBERT J. ENGEL: Speech in the House of Representatives, April 23, 1935

Mulatto

God made the white man and the black man, but the Devil made the mulatto.

ENGLISH PROVERB, not recorded before the XIX century

Many colored women think it more disgraceful to be black than to be illegitimate. . . . A mulatto girl deemed it beneath her to associate with her half sister, a black, and the daughter of her mother's husband, her own father being a white man.

ROBERT DALE OWEN and others: Report of the American Freedmen's Inquiry Commission to the Secretary of War, June, 1863

A child of two races, ashamed of both.

AMBROSE BIERCE: *The Devil's Dictionary,* 1906

Mule

Be ye not as the horse or the mule, which have no understanding.

PSALMS XXXII, 9, *c.* 150 B.C.

Forty [or ten] acres and a mule.

Author unidentified: Promise cherished by American Negroes after emancipation; possibly based upon a field order of W. T. Sherman at Savannah, Jan. 16, 1865; cf. that date under Negro

Is this not a mule? Tickle his heel and see.

EUGENE FIELD: *The Tribune Primer,* 1882

I've known mules to be good for six months so as to get a chance to kick.

H. W. SHAW (JOSH BILLINGS): Lecture at San Francisco, 1885

A mule is an animal that has neither pride of ancestry nor hope of posterity.

Author unidentified

The mule always keeps a kick in reserve for its master. FRENCH PROVERB

He who looks for a mule without a fault must go on foot. SPANISH PROVERB

[*See also* Adventure, Danger, Family.

Multiplication

[*See* Arithmetic.

Multitude

The . . . multitude . . . fell a lusting.
NUMBERS XI, 4, *c.* 700 B.C.

A great multitude, which no man could number, of all nations, and kindreds, and peoples, and tongues. REVELATION VII, 9, *c.* 95

The blunt monster with uncounted heads,
The still-discordant wavering multitude.
SHAKESPEARE: *II Henry IV*, induction, *c.* 1598

The many-headed multitude.
SHAKESPEARE: *Coriolanus*, II, *c.* 1607

If there be any among those common objects of hatred I do contemn and laugh at, it is that great enemy of reason, virtue, and religion, the multitude; that numerous piece of monstrosity, which, taken asunder, seem men, and the reasonable creatures of God, but, confused together, make but one great beast, and a monstrosity more prodigious than Hydra.
THOMAS BROWNE: *Religio Medici*, II, 1642

Preposterous is that government, (and rude)
When kings obey the wider multitude.
ROBERT HERRICK: *Hesperides*, 1648

The multitude is always in the wrong.
WENTWORTH DILLON (EARL OF ROSCOMMON): *Essay on Translated Verse*, 1684

The multitude grows neither old nor wise; it always remains in its infancy.
J. W. GOETHE: *Egmont*, IV, 1788

The fickle multitude, which veers with every wind! Woe to him who leans on such a reed!
J. C. F. SCHILLER: *Maria Stuart*, IV, 1800

Beneath thy broad, impartial eye
How fade the lines of caste and birth;
How equal in their suffering lie
The groaning multitudes of earth.
J. G. WHITTIER: *Democracy*, 1841

[*See also* Masses, Mob, Opinion (Public), People, Populace, Proletariat, Rabble, Tyranny.

Mum

Mum's the word.
ENGLISH PHRASE, in use since the early XVIII century

Murder

Thou shalt not kill.
EXODUS XX, 13, *c.* 700 B.C. (Cf. DEUTERONOMY V, 17, *c.* 650 B.C.)

Jesus said, Thou shalt do no murder.
MATTHEW XIX, 18, *c.* 75

Murder will out.
GEOFFREY CHAUCER: *The Canterbury Tales* (*The Nun's Priest's Tale*), *c.* 1386

Murder most foul.
SHAKESPEARE: *Hamlet*, I, *c.* 1601

Murder, though it have no tongue, will speak
With most miraculous organ.
SHAKESPEARE: *Hamlet*, II

Blood hath been shed ere now i' the olden time,
Ere human statute purged the gentle weal;
Aye, and since too, murders have been performed
Too terrible for the ear.
SHAKESPEARE: *Macbeth*, III, *c.* 1605

Other sins only speak; murder shrieks out.
JOHN WEBSTER: *The Duchess of Malfi*, IV, *c.* 1614

Murder is when a person of sound memory and discretion unlawfully killeth any reasonable creature in being, and under the king's peace, with malice aforethought, either express or implied.
EDWARD COKE: *Institutes*, III, 1628

When there has been a murder committed an apparition of the slain party, accusing of any man, altho' such apparitions have oftener spoke true than false, is not enough to convict the man as guilty of that murder; but yet it is a sufficient reason for magistrates to make a particular inquiry whether such a man have afforded any ground for such an accusation.
COTTON MATHER: *The Wonders of the Invisible World*, I, 1693

No sane mind in a sane body resolves upon a real crime. It is a man of violent passions, bloodshot eyes, and swollen veins that alone can grasp the knife of murder.
P. B. SHELLEY: *Queen Mab*, notes, 1813

They cut his throat from ear to ear,
His head they battered in,
His name was Mr. William Weare,
He dwelt in Lyon's inn.
Anon.: *Recollections of John Thurtell, Executed at Hartford for the Murder of Mr. W. Weare*, 1824

They loved murder and would drink the blood of beasts.
THE BOOK OF MORMON (*Jarom*, 6), 1830

Every unpunished murder takes away something from the security of every man's life.
DANIEL WEBSTER: Argument in the trial of Joseph White, Salem, Mass., 1830

Anatomists tell us that never again
Shall life revisit the foully slain,
When once they've been cut through the jugular vein.
R. H. BARHAM: *The Ingoldsby Legends*, I, 1840

Murder, in the murderer, is no such ruinous thought as poets and romancers will have it; it does not unsettle him, or fright him from his ordinary notice of trifles.
R. W. EMERSON: *Experience*, 1841

Simply to kill a man is not murder.
THOMAS DE QUINCEY: *On Suicide, c.* 1847

I am a murdered man, altho' not yet dead.
W. S. LANDOR: *Letter to Robert Browning,* Dec., 1859

Murder, like talent, seems occasionally to run in families.
G. H. LEWES: *The Physiology of Common Life,* XII, 1859

Murder, gentlemen, is when a man is murderously killed.
Ascribed to "a Western judge" in WILLIAM MATHEWS: *Words; Their Use and Abuse,* I, 1876

If the punishment of murder were abolished, the number of murders would not increase by so many as one. On the contrary, it would decrease to the number now committed by habitual criminals who have been corrupted in prison.
P. A. KROPOTKIN: *Paroles d'un révolté,* 1884

I wonder why murder is considered less immoral than fornication in literature.
GEORGE MOORE: *Confessions of a Young Man,* XI, 1888

Lizzie Borden took an ax
And gave her mother forty whacks;
When she saw what she had done
She gave her father forty-one.
Anon.: Jingle in circulation after the trial of Lizzie Borden at Fall River, Mass., 1893

When we say that murder in general is to be avoided, we only mean that it is so, so long as the majority of mankind will certainly not agree to it, but will persist in living.
G. E. MOORE: *Principia Ethica,* V, 1903

The technique of murder must be presented in a way that will not inspire imitation.
A CODE TO GOVERN THE MAKING OF MOTION AND TALKING PICTURES BY THE MOTION PICTURE PRODUCERS AND DISTRIBUTORS OF AMERICA, INC., I, March 31, 1930

No one ever commits murder with a golden dagger.
HINDU PROVERB

[*See also* Assassination, Cain, Drunk, Flesh, King, Lying, Mercy, Natural Selection, Sin.

Murderer

When any man commits a murder, and the son of the murdered man says "Let him die," he shall die, but if the son says "Let him pay an indemnity" he shall pay an indemnity.
TELIPINUS (KING OF THE HITTITES): *Proclamation, c.* 1650 B.C.

He that smiteth a man, so that he die, shall be surely put to death.
EXODUS XXI, 12 *c.* 700 B.C.

If he smite him with an instrument of iron, so that he die, he is a murderer: the murderer shall surely be put to death.
NUMBERS XXXV, 16, *c.* 700 B.C.

Ye shall take no satisfaction for the life of a murderer, which is guilty of death: but he shall be surely put to death.
NUMBERS XXXV, 31

My soul is wearied because of murderers.
JEREMIAH IV, 31, *c.* 625 B.C.

Murderers . . . shall have their part in the lake which burneth with fire and brimstone: which is the second death.
REVELATION XXI, 8, *c.* 95

Whosoever hateth his brother is a murderer.
I JOHN III, 15, *c.* 115

Whosoever slays a man on shipboard shall be bound to the dead man and thrown into the sea. Whosoever slays a man on land shall be bound to the dead man and buried in the earth.
RICHARD COEUR DE LION: *Laws for the crusaders of the Third Crusade,* 1189

Will all great Neptune's ocean wash this blood
Clean from my hand? No, this my hand will rather
The multitudinous seas incarnadine.
SHAKESPEARE: *Macbeth,* II, *c.* 1605

Blood, though it sleep a time, yet never dies.
The gods on murderers fix revengeful eyes.
GEORGE CHAPMAN: *Widow's Tears,* V, 1612

Carcasses bleed at the sight of the murderer.
ROBERT BURTON: *The Anatomy of Melancholy,* 1621

If once a man indulges himself in murder, very soon he comes to think little of robbing; and from robbing he next comes to drinking and Sabbath-breaking, and from that to incivility and procrastination.
THOMAS DE QUINCEY: *On Murder Considered as One of the Fine Arts,* 1827

Everybody is a potential murderer. I've never killed any one, but I frequently get satisfaction reading the obituary notices.
CLARENCE DARROW: Newspaper interview in Chicago, April 18, 1937

A murderer is one who is presumed to be innocent until he is proved insane.
Author unidentified

[*See also* Criminal, Hatred, Law, Revenge.

Museum

A museum is seldom a cheerful place — oftenest induces the feeling that nothing could ever have been young.
WALTER PATER: *Sir Thomas Browne,* 1886

An artist may visit a museum, but only a pedant can live there.
GEORGE SANTAYANA: *The Life of Reason,* IV, 1905

Mushroom

[*See* Ascetic, Dancing.

Music

Music produces a kind of pleasure which human nature cannot do without.

CONFUCIUS: *The Book of Rites,* XVII, *c.* 500 B.C.

Indulged in to excess, music emasculates instead of invigorating the mind, causing a relaxation of the intellectual faculties, and debasing the warrior into an effeminate slave, destitute of all nerve and energy of soul.

PLATO: *The Republic,* VI, *c.* 370 B.C.

David spake to the chief of the Levites to appoint their brethren to be the singers with instruments of music, psalteries and harps and cymbals, sounding, by lifting up the voice with joy.

I CHRONICLES XV, 16, *c.* 300 B.C.

If the king loves music, there is little wrong in the land.

MENCIUS: *Discourses, c.* 300 B.C.

All the daughters of music shall be brought low. ECCLESIASTES XII, 4, *c.* 200 B.C.

Ye hear the sound of the cornet, flute, harp, sackbut, psaltery, and all kinds of music.

DANIEL III, 5, *c.* 165 B.C.

Where griping griefs the heart would wound
And doleful dumps the mind oppress,
There music with her silver sound
With speed is wont to send redress.

RICHARD EDWARDS: *A Song to the Lute, c.* 1550

I always loved music; whoso has skill in this art is of a good temperament, fitted for all things. We must teach music in schools; a schoolmaster ought to have skill in music, or I would not regard him; neither should we ordain young men as preachers unless they have been well exercised in music.

MARTIN LUTHER: *Table-Talk,* DCCCXXXVIII, 1569

There are certain pleasures which only fill the outward senses, and there are others also which pertain only to the mind or reason; but music is a delectation so put in the midst that both by the sweetness of the sounds it moveth the senses, and by the artificiousness of the number and proportions it delighteth reason itself.

JOHN NORTHBROOKE: *Against Dicing,* 1577

A lamentable tune is the sweetest music to a woeful mind.

PHILIP SIDNEY: *Arcadia,* II, 1590

Preposterous ass, that never read so far
To know the cause why music was ordain'd!
Was it not to refresh the mind of man,
After his studies or his usual pain?

SHAKESPEARE: *The Taming of the Shrew,* III, 1594

I have a reasonable good ear in music:
Let's have the tongs and the bones.

SHAKESPEARE: *A Midsummer Night's Dream,* IV, *c.* 1596

Music do I hear?
Ha! Ha! keep time: how sour sweet music is,
When time is broke and no proportion kept!

SHAKESPEARE: *Richard II,* V, *c.* 1596

How sweet the moonlight sleeps upon this bank!
Here will we sit and let the sounds of music
Creep in our ears: soft stillness, and the night
Becomes the touches of sweet harmony.

SHAKESPEARE: *The Merchant of Venice,* V, *c.* 1597

I am never merry when I hear sweet music.

IBID.

The man that hath no music in himself,
Nor is not moved with concord of sweet sounds,
Is fit for treasons, stratagems and spoils.

IBID.

Naught so stockish, hard and full of rage,
But music for the time doth change his nature.

IBID.

The loadstone draweth iron unto it, but the stone of Ethiopia called Theamedes driveth it away: so there is a kind of music that doth assuage and appease the affections, and a kind that doth kindle and provoke the passions.

FRANCIS MERES: *Pallidas Tamia,* 1598

If music be the food of love, play on;
Give me excess of it, that, surfeiting,
The appetite may sicken, and so die.

SHAKESPEARE: *Twelfth Night,* I, *c.* 1601

There's no music when a woman is in the concert.

THOMAS DEKKER: *I The Honest Whore,* II, 1604

When that our Saviour Christ was born
In Bethlehem, that fair city,
To save mankind that was forlorn
The angels sang continually;
Thus saints and angels in Heaven above
And godly men do music love.

Anon.: *A Song in Praise of Music, c.* 1605

Give me some music; music, moody food
Of us that trade in love.

SHAKESPEARE: *Antony and Cleopatra,* II, *c.* 1606

The world's a body, every liberal art
A needful member, music the soul and heart.

Anon.: *Humor Out of Breath,* I, 1608

I am advised to give her music o' mornings; they say it will penetrate.

SHAKESPEARE: *Cymbeline,* II, *c.* 1609

[Music] is a principal means of glorifying our merciful Creator, it heightens our devotion, it gives delight and ease to our traveler, it expelleth sadness and heaviness of spirit, preserveth people in concord and amity, allayeth fierceness and anger, and lastly, is the best physic for many melancholy diseases.

HENRY PEACHAM: *The Compleat Gentleman,* 1622

Generally, music feedeth the disposition of spirit which it findeth.

FRANCIS BACON: *Sylva Sylvarum,* II, 1627

Such music (as 'tis said)
Before was never made
But when of old the sons of morning sung.

JOHN MILTON: *On the Morning of Christ's Nativity,* 1629

Lap me in soft Lydian airs.

JOHN MILTON: *L'Allegro,* 1632

Such sweet compulsion doth in music lie.

JOHN MILTON: *Arcades, c.* 1633

The music of the spheres.

THOMAS BROWNE: *Religio Medici,* II, 1642

Who shall silence all the airs and madrigals that whisper softness in chambers?

JOHN MILTON: *Areopagitica,* 1644

The mellow touch of music most doth wound
The soul when it doth rather sigh, then sound.

ROBERT HERRICK: *Hesperides,* 1648

Music helps not the toothache.

GEORGE HERBERT: *Jacula Prudentum,* 1651

Music is nothing else but wild sounds civilized into time and tune.

THOMAS FULLER: *Worthies of England,* X, 1662

Music and women I cannot but give way to, whatever my business is.

SAMUEL PEPYS: *Diary,* March 9, 1666

The greatest strokes make not the best music.

JOHN RAY: *English Proverbs,* 1670

Music, like balm, eases grief's smarting wound.

SAMUEL PORDAGE: *The Siege of Babylon,* IV, 1678

The sweetness and delightfulness of music has a natural power to lenify melancholy passions.

INCREASE MATHER: *Remarkable Providences,* VIII, 1684 (*Lenify*=to mitigate)

What passion cannot music raise and quell?

JOHN DRYDEN: *A Song for St. Cecilia's Day,* 1687

Music hath charms to soothe a savage breast,
To soften rocks, or bend a knotted oak.

WILLIAM CONGREVE: *The Mourning Bride,* I, 1697

Music is almost as dangerous as gunpowder; and it may be requires looking after no less than the press, or the mint. 'Tis possible a public regulation might not be amiss.

JEREMY COLLIER: *A Short View of the Immorality and Profaneness of the English State,* intro., 1698

Warriors she fires with animated sounds,
Pours balm into the bleeding lover's wounds.

ALEXANDER POPE: *Ode for Musick on St. Cecilia's Day,* 1708

Nothing is capable of being well set to music that is not nonsense.

JOSEPH ADDISON: *The Spectator,* March 21, 1711

Music resembles poetry: in each
Are nameless graces which no methods teach,
And where a master-hand alone can reach.

ALEXANDER POPE: *An Essay on Criticism,* I, 1711

Music has charms alone for peaceful minds.

ALEXANDER POPE: *Sappho to Phaon,* 1712

Music is a kind of counting performed by the mind without knowing that it is counting.

G. W. LEIBNIZ: *The Monadology,* 1714

Music's force can tame the furious beast;
Can make the wolf or foaming boar restrain
His rage; the lion drop his crested mane
Attentive to the song.

MATTHEW PRIOR: *Solomon on the Vanity of the World,* II, 1718

Give the piper a penny to play, and twopence to leave off.

THOMAS FULLER: *Gnomologia,* 1732

Light quirks of music, broken and uneven,
Make the soul dance upon a jig to Heav'n.

ALEXANDER POPE: *Moral Essays,* IV (Of the Use of Riches), 1732

There's sure no passion in the human soul
But finds its food in music.

GEORGE LILLO: *Fatal Curiosity,* I, 1736

To music's pipe the passions dance.

MATTHEW GREEN: *The Spleen,* 1737

Music exalts each joy, allays each grief,
Expels diseases, softens every pain,
Subdues the rage of passion and the plague.

JOHN ARMSTRONG: *The Art of Preserving Health,* IV, 1744

The best, most beautiful, and most perfect way that we have of expressing a sweet concord of mind to each other is by music. When I would form, in my mind, ideas of a society in the highest degree happy, I think of them as expressing their love, their joy, and the inward concord, and harmony, and spiritual beauty of their souls, by sweetly singing to each other.

JONATHAN EDWARDS: *Miscellaneous Observations on Important Theological Subjects,* 1747

O music! sphere-descended maid,
Friend of pleasure, wisdom's aid.

WILLIAM COLLINS: *Ode on the Passions,* 1747

A certain music, never known before,
Here lulled the pensive, melancholy mind.

JAMES THOMSON: *The Castle of Indolence,* I, 1748

Listed into the cause of sin,
Why should a good be evil?
Music, alas! too long has been
Pressed to obey the Devil.
Drunken, or lewd, or light, the lay
Flower to the soul's undoing;
Widened, and strewed with flowers the way
Down to eternal ruin.

CHARLES WESLEY: *The True Use of Music,* 1749

Rings on her fingers and bells on her toes,
And so she makes music wherever she goes.

Anon.: *Nursery rhyme, c.* 1750

The Most High has a decided taste for vocal music, provided it be lugubrious and gloomy enough.

VOLTAIRE: *Philosophical Dictionary,* 1764

Is there a heart that music cannot melt?
Ah me! how is that rugged heart forlorn!

JAMES BEATTIE: *The Minstrel,* I, 1771

Music, to a nice ear, is a hazardous amusement, as long attention to it is very fatiguing.

WILLIAM CULLEN: *First Lines of the Practice of Physic,* II, 1774

Much of the effect of music, I am satisfied, is owing to the association of ideas. Scotch reels, though brisk, make me melancholy, whereas the airs in "The Beggar's Opera," many of which are very soft, never fail to render me gay, because they are associated with the warm sensations and high spirits of London.

SAMUEL JOHNSON: *Boswell's Life,* 1777

The still sweet fall of music far away.

THOMAS CAMPBELL: *The Pleasures of Hope,* II, 1799

Music is the moonlight in the gloomy night of life.

JEAN PAUL RICHTER: *Titan,* CXXV, 1803

The music in my heart I bore,
Long after it was heard no more.

WILLIAM WORDSWORTH: *The Solitary Reaper,* 1807

Music is a higher revelation than philosophy.

LUDWIG VAN BEETHOVEN: *Letter to Bettina von Arnim,* 1810

Only the flint of a man's mind can strike fire in music.

LUDWIG VAN BEETHOVEN: *Letter to Bettina von Arnim,* Aug., 1812

When music arose with its voluptuous swell,
Soft eyes look'd love to eyes which spake again,
And all went merry as a marriage bell.

BYRON: *Childe Harold,* III, 1816

Silver key of the fountain of tears,
Where the spirit drinks till the brain is wild;
Softest grave of a thousand fears,
Where their mother, Care, like a drowsy child,
Is laid asleep in flowers.

P. B. SHELLEY: *To Music,* 1817

Let me have music dying, and I seek
No more delight.

JOHN KEATS: *Endymion,* IV, 1818

Music stands quite alone. It is cut off from all the other arts. . . . It does not express a particular and definite joy, sorrow, anguish, horror, delight, or mood of peace, but joy, sorrow, anguish, horror, delight, peace of mind *themselves,* in the abstract, in their essential nature, without accessories, and therefore without their customary motives. Yet it enables us to grasp and share them fully in this quintessence.

ARTHUR SCHOPENHAUER: *The World as Will and Idea,* II, 1819

A carpenter's hammer, in a warm Summer noon, will fret me into more than midsummer madness. But those unconnected, unset sounds are nothing to the measured malice of music.

CHARLES LAMB: *A Chapter on Ears,* 1821 (London Magazine, March)

The only universal tongue.

SAMUEL ROGERS: *Italy,* 1822

Music, indeed! Give me a mother singing to her clean and fat and rosy baby.

WILLIAM COBBETT: *Advice to Young Men,* III, 1829

Some cry up Haydn, some Mozart,
Just as the whim bites. For my part,
I do not care a farthing candle
For either of them, or for Handel.

CHARLES LAMB: *Letter to Mrs. William Hazlitt,* May 24, 1830

An ear for music is a very different thing from a taste for music. I have no ear whatever; I could not sing an air to save my life; but I have the intensest delight in music, and can detect good from bad.

S. T. COLERIDGE: *Table-Talk,* Oct. 5, 1830

The best sort of music is what it should be,— sacred; the next best, the military, has fallen to the lot of the Devil.

S. T. COLERIDGE: *Table-Talk,* July 6, 1833

Music that gentlier on the spirit lies
Than tir'd eyelids upon tir'd eyes.

ALFRED TENNYSON: *The Lotos-Eaters,* 1833

The Americans are almost ignorant of the art of music, one of the most elevating, innocent and refining of human tastes, whose influence on the habits and morals of a people is of the most beneficial tendency.

J. FENIMORE COOPER: *The American Democrat*, XXXVI, 1838

Who is there that, in logical words, can express the effect music has on us? A kind of inarticulate unfathomable speech, which leads us to the edge of the Infinite and lets us for moments gaze into that.

THOMAS CARLYLE: *Heroes and Hero-Worship*, III, 1840 (Lecture in London, May 12)

Music hath caught a higher pace than any virtue that I know. It is the arch-reformer.

H. D. THOREAU: *Journal*, Jan. 8, 1842

Scientific music has no claim to intrinsic excellence — it is fit for scientific ears only. In its excess it is the triumph of the physique over the morale of music. The sentiment is overwhelmed by the sense.

E. A. POE: *The Rationale of Verse*, 1843 (The Pioneer, March)

If I were to begin life again, I would devote it to music. It is the only cheap and unpunished rapture upon earth.

SYDNEY SMITH: *Letter to the Countess of Carlisle*, Aug., 1844

It is in music, perhaps, that the soul most nearly attains the great end for which, when inspired by the poetic sentiment, it struggles — the creation of supernal beauty.

E. A. POE: *The Poetic Principle*, 1845

For music any words are good enough.

J. R. PLANCHÉ: *The Birds of Aristophanes*, I, 1846 (Cf. ADDISON, *ante*, 1711)

Indefinitiveness is an element of true music — I mean of true musical expression. Give to it any undue decision — imbue it with any very determinate tone — and you deprive it, at once, of its ethereal, its ideal, its intrinsic and essential character. You dispel its luxury of dream. You dissolve the atmosphere of the mystic upon which it floats. You exhaust it of its breath of faëry.

E. A. POE: *Marginalia*, 1844–49

When I hear music, I fear no danger. I am invulnerable. I see no foe. I am related to the earliest times, and to the latest.

H. D. THOREAU: *Journal*, Jan. 13, 1857

I struck one chord of music
Like the sound of a great Amen.

ADELAIDE A. PROCTOR: *The Lost Chord*, 1861

I love Wagner; but the music I prefer is that of a cat hung up by its tail outside a window, and trying to stick to the panes of glass with its claws.

CHARLES BAUDELAIRE (1821–67)

Music sweeps by me as a messenger
Carrying a message that is not for me.

MARIAN EVANS (GEORGE ELIOT): *The Spanish Gypsy*, III, 1868

Who hears music, feels his solitude
Peopled at once.

ROBERT BROWNING: *Balaustion's Adventure*, 1871

Music arouses in us various emotions, but not the more terrible ones of horror, fear, rage, etc. It awakens rather the gentler feelings of tenderness and love, which readily passes into devotion. . . . It likewise stirs up in us the sense of triumph and the glorious ardor for war.

CHARLES DARWIN: *The Descent of Man*, XIX, 1871

There is no music in nature, neither melody or harmony. Music is the creation of man.

H. R. HAWEIS: *Music and Morals*, I, 1871

Music is love in search of a word.

SIDNEY LANIER: *The Symphony*, 1875

Music is the art in which form and matter are always one, the art whose subject cannot be separated from the method of its expression, the art which most completely realizes the artistic ideal, and is the condition to which all the other arts are constantly aspiring.

OSCAR WILDE: *The English Renaissance of Art*, 1882 (Lecture in New York, Jan. 9)

Music [is] the ideal of all art whatever, because in music it is impossible to distinguish the form from the substance or matter, the subject from the expression.

WALTER PATER: *Style*, 1888

If musical sounds affect us more powerfully than the sounds of nature, the reason is that nature confines itself to expressing feelings, whereas music suggests them to us.

HENRI BERGSON: *Time and Free Will*, I, 1889

Without music life would be a mistake.

F. W. NIETZSCHE: *The Twilight of the Idols*, 1889

If one hears bad music it is one's duty to drown it by one's conversation.

OSCAR WILDE: *The Picture of Dorian Gray*, 1891

If one plays good music people don't listen, and if one plays bad music people don't talk.

OSCAR WILDE: *The Importance of Being Earnest*, III, 1895

Music is another planet.

ALPHONSE DAUDET (1840–97)

Hell is full of musical amateurs. Music is the brandy of the damned.

GEORGE BERNARD SHAW: *Man and Superman*, III, 1903

Cathedrals in sound.
ALFRED BRUNEAU: Said of the music of Cesar Franck at the unveiling of a statue to the composer in Paris, Oct. 22, 1904

What most people relish is hardly music; it is rather a drowsy reverie relieved by nervous thrills.
GEORGE SANTAYANA: *The Life of Reason,* IV, 1905

When people hear good music, it makes them homesick for something they never had, and never will have.
E. W. HOWE: *Country Town Sayings,* 1911

Music is, first of all, motion; after that emotion. I like movement, rhythmical variety, polyphonic life.
JAMES HUNEKER: *Old Fogy,* X, 1913

Modern music is as dangerous as cocaine.
PIETRO MASCAGNI: Interview in Berlin, Dec., 1927

Music rots when it gets too far from the dance.
EZRA POUND: *How to Read,* 1931

It is easier to understand a nation by listening to its music than by learning its language.
Author unidentified

Music is an incitement to love. (Incitamentum amoris musica.) LATIN PROVERB

Where there is music there can be no harm.
SPANISH PROVERB

As the music is, so are the people of the country. TURKISH PROVERB

[*See also* Art, Bell, Concert, Discord, Drum, Harp, Mediocrity, Melody, Opera, Painting, Patient, Piper, Poet, Poetry, Song, Wagner (Richard).

Musician

He must be a poor sort of a man, for otherwise he would not be so good a piper.
Ascribed to ANTISTHENES (*c.* 450–380 B.C.)

We shall never become musicians unless we understand the ideals of temperance, fortitude, liberality and magnificence.
PLATO: *The Republic,* III, *c.* 370 B.C.

You make as good music as a wheelbarrow.
THOMAS FULLER: *Gnomologia,* 1732

If you love music, hear it; go to operas, concerts, and pay fiddlers to play to you; but I insist upon your neither piping nor fiddling yourself. It puts a gentleman in a very frivolous, contemptible light.
LORD CHESTERFIELD: *Letter to his son,* April 19, 1749

Feed the musician, and he's out of tune.
GEORGE CRABBE: *The Newspaper,* 1785

A musician, the most skillful, can only divert himself and a few others.
WILLIAM COWPER: *Letter to Lady Hesketh,* Jan. 16, 1786

Musicians take all the liberties they can.
LUDWIG VAN BEETHOVEN: *Letter to Bettina von Arnim,* Aug., 1812

Musical people are so absurdly unreasonable. They always want one to be perfectly dumb at the very moment when one is longing to be absolutely deaf.
OSCAR WILDE: *An Ideal Husband,* II, 1895

These three take crooked ways: carts, boats, and musicians. HINDU PROVERB

Music-lover

Of the ladies that sparkle at a musical performance, a very small number has any quick sensibility of harmonious sounds. But every one that goes has the pleasure of being supposed to be pleased with a refined amusement, and of hoping to be numbered among the votaresses of harmony.
SAMUEL JOHNSON: *The Idler,* Aug. 12, 1758

Musk

[*See* Smell.

Mussolini, Benito (1883–)

Mussolini is like a man on a bicycle; he must keep going on the path of persecution or he must fall.
JULES SAUERWEIN: Lecture at the University of Chicago, June 26, 1933

Must

Must is for kings.
THOMAS DEKKER and HENRY CHETTLE: *Patient Grissil,* IV, 1603

Must is a hard nut. (Muss ist eine harte Nuss.)
GERMAN PROVERB

Mustard

[*See* Beef.

Mute

Why so dull and mute, young sinner?
Prythee, why so mute?
Will, when speaking well can't win her,
Saying nothing do't?
Prythee, why so mute?
JOHN SUCKLING: *Encouragements to a Lover,* 1638

Nature is a mute, and man, her articulate, speaking brother, lo! he is also a mute.
R. W. EMERSON: *The Method of Nature,* 1841

Mutton

Let us return to our muttons. (Revenons à nos moutons.)
Anon.: *Maistre Pierre Patelin, c.* 1450 (The original text says " à ces moutons," but as the saying became proverbial the change to " à nos " was made. The mean-

ing is "Let us return to the subject at issue." In the original, one Guillaume, a cloth dealer, prosecutes a shepherd for stealing some of his sheep. In court he discovers that his lawyer, Patelin, is wearing clothes made of cloth also stolen from him. Whenever he refers to this cloth the judge says "Revenons à ces moutons." The French word *mouton* means both sheep and mutton. Hence the familiar English mistranslation)

Flesh of a mutton is food for a glutton.
RANDLE COTGRAVE: *French-English Dictionary,* 1611

Of all birds, give me mutton.
THOMAS FULLER: *Gnomologia,* 1732

The leg of mutton of Wales beats the leg of mutton of any other country.
GEORGE BORROW: *Wild Wales,* IX, 1862

Muzzle

Thou shalt not muzzle the ox when he treadeth out the corn.
DEUTERONOMY XXV, 4, *c.* 650 B.C.

Mystery

There be three things which are too wonderful for me, yea, four which I know not: the way of an eagle in the air; the way of a serpent upon a rock; the way of a ship in the midst of the sea; and the way of a man with a maid. PROVERBS XXX, 18–19, *c.* 350 B.C.

Methinks there be not impossibilities enough in religion for an active faith; the deepest mysteries ours contains have not only been illustrated, but maintained, by syllogism and the rule of reason. I love to lose myself in a mystery; to pursue my reason to an *O altitudo!*
THOMAS BROWNE: *Religio Medici,* I, 1642

Mix a little mystery with everything, and the very mystery arouses veneration.
BALTASAR GRACIÁN: *The Art of Worldly Wisdom,* III, 1647

Mystery is the wisdom of blockheads.
HORACE WALPOLE: *Letter to Horace Mann,* Jan. 2, 1761

Mystery is the antagonist of truth. It is a fog of human invention that obscures truth, and represents it in distortion. Truth never envelops itself in mystery; and the mystery in which it is at any time enveloped is the work of its antagonist, and never of itself.
THOMAS PAINE: *The Age of Reason,* I, 1794

There was the door to which I found no key,
There was the veil through which I might not see.
EDWARD FITZGERALD: Tr. of OMAR KHAYYÁM: *Rubáiyát* (*c.* 1100), 1857

[*See also* Enigma, Siren.

Mysticism

The more mysterious, the more imperfect: that which is mystically spoken is but half spoken.
BENJAMIN WHICHCOTE: *Moral and Religious Aphorisms,* 1753

From mystics proceed religious revelations; from mystics, philosophy; mysticism is the common source of both.
K. R. E. VON HARTMANN: *The Philosophy of the Unconscious,* I, 1869

And everyone will say
As you walk your mystic way,
If this young man expresses himself in terms too deep for me,
Why, what a very singularly deep young man this deep young man must be.
W. S. GILBERT: *Patience,* I, 1881

Mysticism has been thoroughly investigated millions of years by millions of men, and without result, except to prove the unrelenting truth of materialism.
E. W. HOWE: *Sinner Sermons,* 1926

N

Nail

Gnaw not thy nails in the presence of others, nor bite them with thy teeth.
FRANCIS HAWKINS: *Youth's Behavior,* I, 1663

Hippocrates has left direction how we should cut our nails — even with the ends of the fingers, neither shorter nor longer.
H. D. THOREAU: *Walden,* I, 1854

Cut them on Monday, you cut them for health;
Cut them on Tuesday, you cut them for wealth;
Cut them on Wednesday, you cut them for news;
Cut them on Thursday, a new pair of shoes;
Cut them on Friday, you cut them for sorrow;
Cut them on Saturday, see your true love tomorrow.
But he that on Sunday cuts his horn,
Better that he had never been born.
OLD ENGLISH RHYME

[*See also* Cause and Effect, Fingernail, Name.

Nakedness

They were both naked, the man and his wife, and were not ashamed.
GENESIS II, 25, *c.* 700 B.C.

Naked came I out of my mother's womb, and naked shall I return thither.
JOB I, 21, *c.* 325 B.C.

When a' was naked, he was, for all the world, like a forked radish with a head fantastically carved.
SHAKESPEARE: *II Henry IV,* III, *c.* 1598

No beauty she doth miss
When all her robes are on:
But beauty's self she is
When all her robes are gone.
Anon.: *Madrigal*, 1602

Our first parents, so long as they went naked, were suffered to dwell in Paradise, but after they got coats on their backs they were turned out of doors.
THOMAS DEKKER: *The Gull's Hornbook*, II, 1609

Nakedness is uncomely, as well in mind as body. FRANCIS BACON: *Essays*, VI, 1625

Beauty when most unclothed is clothed best.
PHINEAS FLETCHER: *Sicelides*, II, 1631

An hundred thieves cannot strip one naked man, especially if his skin's off.
BENJAMIN FRANKLIN: *Poor Richard's Almanac*, 1755

The angels in the innermost Heaven are naked, because they are in innocence, and innocence corresponds to nakedness.
EMANUEL SWEDENBORG: *Heaven and Hell*, 1758

Her gentle limbs did she undress,
And lay down in her loveliness.
S. T. COLERIDGE: *Christabel*, I, 1816

Lives the man that can figure a naked Duke of Windlestraw addressing a naked House of Lords?
THOMAS CARLYLE: *Sartor Resartus*, I, 1836

Who goes there? hankering, gross, mystical, nude.
WALT WHITMAN: *Walt Whitman*, 1855

Is not nakedness indecent? No, not inherently. It is your thought, your sophistication, your fear, your respectability, that is indecent. There come moods when these clothes of ours are not only too irksome to wear, but are themselves indecent.
WALT WHITMAN: *Specimen Days*, Aug. 27, 1877

Complete nudity is never permitted. This includes nudity in fact or in silhouette, or any lecherous or licentious notice thereof by other characters in the picture.
A CODE TO GOVERN THE MAKING OF MOTION AND TALKING PICTURES BY THE MOTION PICTURE PRODUCERS AND DISTRIBUTORS OF AMERICA, INC., March 31, 1930

Anything will fit a naked man.
IRISH SAYING

In a state of nature. (In puris naturalibus.)
LATIN PHRASE

[*See also* Fig-leaf.

Name

Adam gave names to all cattle, and to the fowl of the air, and to every beast of the field.
GENESIS II, 20, *c.* 700 B.C.

As his name is, so is he.
I SAMUEL XXV, 25, *c.* 500 B.C.

A good name is rather to be chosen than great riches. PROVERBS XXII, 1, *c.* 350 B.C.

A good name is better than precious ointment.
ECCLESIASTES VII, 1, *c.* 200 B.C.

So long as the wild boar delights in the mountain tops, the fish in the rivers, and the bees feed on thyme, so long will the glory of thy name remain. VIRGIL: *Eclogues*, V, 37 B.C.

An illustrious and ancient name.
LUCAN: *Pharsalia*, IX, 65

The shadow of a mighty name. IBID.

Well is him that hath a good name.
Anon.: *Proverbs of Wisdom*, *c.* 1450

He that hath an ill name is half hanged.
JOHN HEYWOOD: *Proverbs*, 1546

I cannot say the crow is white,
But needs must call a spade a spade.
HUMPHREY GIFFORD: *Song*, *c.* 1580

What's in a name? that which we call a rose
By any other name would smell as sweet.
SHAKESPEARE: *Romeo and Juliet*, II, *c.* 1596

Generally things are ancienter than the names whereby they are called.
RICHARD HOOKER: *The Laws of Ecclesiastical Polity*, V, 1597

What should be in that "Cæsar"?
Why should that name be sounded more than yours?
Write them together: yours is as fair a name;
Sound them: it doth become the mouth as well.
SHAKESPEARE: *Julius Cæsar*, I, 1599

I name no names.
ENGLISH PHRASE, familiar since the XVII century

"What is thy name, faire maid?" quoth he.
"Penelophon, O king," quoth she.
Anon.: *King Cophetua and the Beggar-Maid*, *c.* 1600

Who steals my purse steals trash; 'tis something, nothing;
'Twas mine, 'tis his, and has been slave to thousands;
But he that filches from me my good name
Robs me of that which not enriches him,
And makes me poor indeed.
SHAKESPEARE: *Othello*, III, 1604

In *ford*, in *ham*, in *ley* and *ton*
The most of English surnames run.
RICHARD VERSTEGEN: *Restitution of Decayed Intelligence in Antiquities Concerning the English Nation*, 1605

For my name and memory, I leave it to men's charitable speeches, to foreign nations, and the next ages.
FRANCIS BACON: *Last will*, 1626

Names and natures do often agree.
JOHN CLARKE: *Parœmiologia Anglo-Latina,* 1639

An ill wound is cured, not an ill name.
GEORGE HERBERT: *Outlandish Proverbs,* 1640

Round the whole world his dread name shall sound,
And reach to worlds that must not yet be found.
ABRAHAM COWLEY: *The Davideis,* II, 1656

I must call everything by its name. I call a cat a cat, and Rolet a scoundrel.
NICOLAS BOILEAU: *Satires du Sieur D,* I, 1666

A good name keeps its lustre in the dark.
JOHN RAY: *English Proverbs,* 1670

He is a fool and ever shall, that writes his name upon a wall. IBID.

The evil wound is cured, but not the evil name. IBID.

Take away my good name and take away my life. IBID.

Louis XIV of France spent his life in turning a good name into a great.
JONATHAN SWIFT: *Thoughts on Various Subjects,* 1706

O name forever sad, forever dear.
ALEXANDER POPE: *Eloisa to Abelard,* 1717

It is a heavy burden to bear a name that is too famous.
VOLTAIRE: *La Henriade,* III, 1723

Fools' names, like fools' faces,
Are often seen in public places.
THOMAS FULLER: *Gnomologia,* 1732

He's born in a good hour who gets a good name. IBID.

He left a name at which the world grew pale,
To point a moral, or adorn a tale.
SAMUEL JOHNSON: *The Vanity of Human Wishes,* 1749

When fate writ my name it made a blot.
HENRY FIELDING: *Amelia,* II, 1752

How many Cæsars and Pompeys, by mere inspiration of the names, have been rendered worthy of them! And how many are there who might have done exceeding well in the world, had not their characters and spirits been totally depressed and Nicodemus'd into nothing.
LAURENCE STERNE: *Tristram Shandy,* I, 1760

The fascination of a name.
WILLIAM COWPER: *The Task,* VI, 1785

The magic of a name.
THOMAS CAMPBELL: *The Pleasures of Hope,* II, 1799

Sticks and stones will break my bones, but names will never hurt me.
ENGLISH PROVERB, not recorded before the XIX century

I agree with you entirely in condemning the mania of giving names to objects of any kind after persons still living. Death alone can seal the title of any man to this honor, by putting it out of his power to forfeit it.
THOMAS JEFFERSON: *Letter to Benjamin Rush,* 1800

I am the last of my race. My name ends with me.
J. C. F. SCHILLER: *Wilhelm Tell,* I, 1804

He left a corsair's name to other times,
Linked with one virtue and a thousand crimes.
BYRON: *The Corsair,* III, 1814

The glory and the nothing of a name.
BYRON: *Churchill's Grave,* 1816

Here lies one whose name was writ in water.
JOHN KEATS: Written for his own gravestone, *c.* 1820

One of the few, the immortal names,
That were not born to die.
FITZ-GREENE HALLECK: *Marco Bozzaris,* 1825

His name admonished him of what he owed to his country.
J. C. and A. W. HARE: *Guesses at Truth,* 1827

The nothing of a name.
E. A. POE: *Tamerlane,* VIII, 1827

All poetry is but a giving of names.
THOMAS CARLYLE: *Journal,* May 18, 1832

Never take an iambus as a Christian name. A trochee, or tribach, will do very well. Edith and Rotha are my favorite names for women.
S. T. COLERIDGE: *Table-Talk,* July 8, 1832

And lo, Ben Adhem's name led all the rest.
LEIGH HUNT: *Abou Ben Adhem,* 1834

Men are the constant dupes of names, while their happiness and well-being mainly depend on things.
J. FENIMORE COOPER: *The American Democrat,* XLVI, 1838

Few men have grown unto greatness whose names are allied to ridicule.
M. F. TUPPER: *Proverbial Philosophy,* I, 1838

A town may have been named Dartmouth because it is situated at the mouth of the Dart. But it is no part of the signification of the word Dartmouth to be situated at the mouth of the Dart. If sand should choke up the mouth of the river, or an earthquake change its course, and remove it to a distance from the town, the name of the town would not necessarily be changed.
J. S. MILL: *A System of Logic,* I, 1843

Good men must die, but death cannot kill their names.
H. G. BOHN: *Handbook of Proverbs*, 1855

I would rather make my name than inherit it.
W. M. THACKERAY: *The Virginians*, I, 1858

Names are much more persistent than the functions upon which they were originally bestowed.
WOODROW WILSON: *Congressional Government*, intro., 1885

Where a man calls himself by a name which is not his name he is telling a falsehood.
LORD ESHER: *Judgment in Reddaway* vs. *Banham*, 1895

She was poor but she was honest
And her parents was the same
Till she came up to the city
And she lost her honest name.
Anon.: *She Was Poor but She Was Honest* (Sung by British soldiers, 1914–18)

A name never harms a man if the man does not harm the name. ESTONIAN PROVERB

A good name is better than a golden girdle.
FRENCH PROVERB

In your own country, your name; abroad, your clothes. HEBREW PROVERB

When a tiger dies he leaves his skin; when a man dies, his name. JAPANESE PROVERB

An error as to a name is nothing when there is a certainty as to the person. (Nihil facit error nominis cum de corpore constat.)
LEGAL MAXIM

Names are the marks of things. (Nomina sunt notae rerum.) IBID.

A bad wound may heal, but a bad name will kill. SCOTTISH PROVERB

A gude name is sooner tint than won.
IBID. (*Tint*=lost)

Naething is got without pains but an ill name and lang nails. IBID.

[*See also* Blame, Child, Cornishman, Nickname, Reputation.

Nantucket

Nantucket! Take out your map and look at it — a mere hillock, and elbow of sand; all beach, without a background. Some gamesome wights will tell you that they have to plant weeds there, they don't grow naturally; that pieces of wood in Nantucket are carried about like bits of the true cross in Rome; that one blade of grass makes an oasis, three blades in a day's walk a prairie.
HERMAN MELVILLE: *Moby Dick*, XIV, 1851

Nap

I never take a nap after dinner but when I have had a bad night, and then the nap takes me.
SAMUEL JOHNSON: *Boswell's Life*, 1775

Napkin

Put your napkin upon your lap, covering your knees. It is out of date, and now looked upon as a vulgar habit, to put your napkin up over your breast.
C. B. HARTLEY: *The Gentlemen's Book of Etiquette*, III, 1873

The napkin in the collar. (La serviette au cou.)
Motto of Les Amis d'Escoffier, New York, 1936

Naples

Naples sitteth by the sea, keystone of an arch of azure.
M. F. TUPPER: *Proverbial Philosophy*, 1838

See Naples and die. (Vedi Napoli e poi muori.)
ITALIAN PROVERB

Napoleon I (1769–1821)

He is of middle size, rather slim, of a tawny complexion, and there is nothing particular in his appearance, except his black eyes, which are extremely brilliant, and habitually fixed on the ground.
Anon.: Editorial in the London Times, Aug. 4, 1797

Napoleon was, I will not say made, but permitted, for a cat-o'nine-tails to inflict ten thousand lashes upon the back of Europe as divine vengeance for the atheism, infidelity, fornications, adulteries, incests, sodomies, as well as briberies, robberies, murders, thefts, intrigues, and fradulent speculations of her inhabitants.
ABIGAIL ADAMS: *Letter to Mrs. Mercy Warren*, March 9, 1807

In my youth we used to march and countermarch all the Summer without gaining or losing a square league, and then we went into Winter quarters. And now comes an ignorant, hot-headed young man who flies about from Boulogne to Ulm, and from Ulm to the middle of Moravia, and fights battles in December. The whole system of his tactics is monstrously incorrect.
Ascribed to "an old German officer (*c.* 1810) by T. B. MACAULAY: *Moore's Life of Byron*, 1831 (Edinburgh Review, June)

I know not how it has been with former conquerors during their lives, but I believe there never was a human being who united against himself such a mass of execration and abhorrence as this man has done. There is indeed, on the other hand, an admiration of him equally enthusiastic, as for every great conqueror there always must be; but I have never yet seen the person by whom he was regarded with affection.
JOHN QUINCY ADAMS: *Diary*, Nov. 4, 1812

The bile-suffused cheek of Bonaparte, his wrinkled brow, and yellow eye, the ceaseless inquietude of his nervous system, speak no

less plainly the character of his unresting ambition than his murders and his victories.
P. B. SHELLEY: *Queen Mab*, notes, 1813

Evil was his good.
ROBERT SOUTHEY: *Ode Against Napoleon*, Jan., 1814

Bonaparte was a lion in the field only. In civil life, a cold-blooded, calculating, unprincipled usurper, without a virtue; no statesman, knowing nothing of commerce, political economy, or civil government, and supplying ignorance by bold presumption.
THOMAS JEFFERSON: *Letter to John Adams*, July, 1814

Waterloo is cast in my teeth. . . . I ought to have died in Moscow.
NAPOLEON I: To Gaspard Gourgaud at St. Helena, April 23, 1816

What is most extraordinary, and I believe unparalleled in history, is that I rose from being a private person to the astonishing height of power I possessed without having committed a single crime to obtain it. If I were on my deathbed, I could make the same declaration.
NAPOLEON I: To Barry E. O'Meara at St. Helena, Dec. 5, 1816

Had I succeeded, I should have died with the reputation of the greatest man that ever existed. As it is, although I have failed, I shall be considered as an extraordinary man. I have fought fifty pitched battles, almost all of which I have gained. I have framed and carried into effect a code of laws that will bear my name to the most distant posterity.
NAPOLEON I: To Barry E. O'Meara at St. Helena, March 3, 1817

What a fine iron binding Bonaparte has round his face, as if it had been cased in steel!
WILLIAM HAZLITT: *Table-Talk*, 1821

I wish my ashes to be deposited on the banks of the Seine, in the midst of the French people I have loved so well.
NAPOLEON I: Codicil to his will, April 16, 1821

Yes! where is he, the champion and the child
Of all that's great or little, wise or wild?
Whose game was empires, and whose stakes were thrones,
Whose table earth — whose dice were human bones?
BYRON: *The Age of Bronze*, 1823

Bonaparte I never saw; though during the Battle of Waterloo we were once, I understood, within a quarter of a mile of each other. I regret it much; for he was a most extraordinary man. To me he seems to have been at his acme at the Peace of Tilsit, and gradually to have declined afterwards.
THE DUKE OF WELLINGTON: Quoted in SAMUEL ROGERS: *Recollections*, *c.* 1827

Always enlightened, always clear and decided, he was endowed at every hour with sufficient energy to carry into effect whatever he considered advantageous and necessary. His life was the stride of a demi-god, from battle to battle, and from victory to victory.
J. W. GOETHE: *Conversations with Eckermann*, March 11, 1828

The French emperor is among conquerors what Voltaire is among writers, a miraculous child. His splendid genius was frequently clouded by fits of humor as absurdly perverse as those of the pet of the nursery, who quarrels with his food, and dashes his playthings to pieces.
T. B. MACAULAY: *Hallam*, 1828 (Edinburgh Review, Sept.)

Napoleon will live when Paris is in ruins; his deeds will survive the dome of the Invalides: no man can show the tomb of Alexander.
ARCHIBALD ALISON: *History of Europe During the French Revolution*, 1833

I call Napoleon the agent or attorney of the middle class of modern society; of the throng who fill the markets, shops, counting-houses, manufactories, ships, of the modern world, aiming to be rich.
R. W. EMERSON: *Napoleon*, 1850

God was bored by him.
VICTOR HUGO: *Les châtiments*, 1853

Napoleon was, of all the men in the world, the one who most profoundly despised the race. He had a marvelous insight into the weaker sides of human nature.
CLEMENS VON METTERNICH (1773–1859)

The outward mask of civilization Bonaparte wore, and he could use political and social ideas for the purposes of his ambition as dexterously as cannon; but in character he was a Corsican and as savage as any bandit of his isle. If utter selfishness, if the reckless sacrifice of humanity to your own interest and passions be vileness, history has no viler name.
GOLDWIN SMITH: *Three English Statesmen*, 1867

Napoleon seems to have ended by regarding mankind as a troublesome pack of hounds only worth keeping for the sport of hunting with them.
GEORGE BERNARD SHAW: *The Revolutionist's Handbook*, III, 1903

[*See also* Abdication, History.

Narrative

Narrative teases me. I have little concern in the progress of events.
CHARLES LAMB: *Mackery End in Hertfordshire*, 1821 (London Magazine, July)

Narrow

Narrow is the way which leadeth unto life, and few there be that find it.
MATTHEW VII, 14, *c.* 75

Wide will wear but narrow will tear.
JOHN RAY: *English Proverbs,* 1670

Nation

A nation scattered and peeled, . . . a nation meted out and trodden down.
ISAIAH XVIII, 2, *c.* 700 B.C.

The nations are as a drop of a bucket, and are counted as the small dust of the balance.
ISAIAH XL, 15

Blessed is the nation whose God is the Lord.
PSALMS XXXIII, 12, *c.* 150 B.C.

Nations are changed by time; they flourish and decay; by turns command and obey.
OVID: *Metamorphoses,* XV, *c.* 5

A crooked and perverse nation.
PHILIPPIANS II, 15, *c.* 60

Methinks I see in my mind a noble and puissant nation rousing herself like a strong man after sleep, and shaking her invincible locks; methinks I see her as an eagle mewing her mighty youth, and kindling her undazzled eyes at the full midday beam.
JOHN MILTON: *Areopagitica,* 1644

A small country and few people may be equivalent in wealth and strength to a far greater people and territory.
WILLIAM PETTY: *Political Arithmetic,* I, *c.* 1677

Satiate with power, of fame and wealth possess'd,
A nation grows too glorious to be blest;
Conspicuous made, she stands the mark of all,
And foes join foes to triumph in her fall.
GEORGE CRABBE: *The Library,* 1781

Nations are equal in respect to each other, and entitled to claim equal consideration for their rights, whatever may be their relative dimensions or strength, or however greatly they may differ in government, religion, or manners.
JAMES KENT: *Commentaries on American Law,* I, 1826

A true nation loves its vernacular tongue. A completed nation will not import its religion.
R. W. EMERSON: *Character,* 1844

All the great things have been done by little nations.
BENJAMIN DISRAELI: *Tancred,* 1847

Nations have lost their old omnipotence; the patriotic tie does not hold. Nations are getting obsolete, we go and live where we will. Steam has enabled men to choose what law they will live under. Money makes place for them.
R. W. EMERSON: *English Traits,* II, 1856

A nation never falls but by suicide.
R. W. EMERSON: *Journal,* 1861

A nation may be said to consist of its territory, its people and its laws. The territory is the only part which is of certain durability.
ABRAHAM LINCOLN: Message to Congress, Dec. 1, 1862

Nations, like individuals, are subjected to punishments and chastisements in this world.
ABRAHAM LINCOLN: Proclamation, March 30, 1863

No nation can last which has made a mob of itself, however generous at heart.
JOHN RUSKIN: *Sesame and Lilies,* 1865

Individualities may form communities, but it is institutions alone that can create a nation.
BENJAMIN DISRAELI: Speech at Manchester, 1866

A group of men who speak one language and read the same newspapers.
F. W. NIETZSCHE: Notes for *Beyond Good and Evil, c.* 1885

A nation is a detour of nature to arrive at six or seven great men — and then get round them.
F. W. NIETZSCHE: *Beyond Good and Evil,* 1886

There is such a thing as a nation being so right that it does not need to convince others by force that it is right.
WOODROW WILSON: Speech at Philadelphia, May 10, 1915

There is no nation on earth so dangerous as a nation fully armed, and bankrupt at home.
H. C. LODGE: Speech before the National Security League, Washington, Jan. 22, 1916

[*See also* Adversity, Change, Empire, Family, Insanity, Institution, Judgment, Language, Morality (National), Nationality, Prosperity, Sovereignty, Union (American).

Nationalism

National differences, and antagonisms between peoples, are daily more and more vanishing, owing to the development of the bourgeoisie, to freedom of commerce, to the world-market, to uniformity in the mode of production, and in the conditions of life corresponding thereto.
KARL MARX and FRIEDRICH ENGELS: *The Communist Manifesto,* 1848

Nationalism is an infantile disease. It is the measles of mankind.
ALBERT EINSTEIN: To George Sylvester Viereck, 1921

Born in iniquity and conceived in sin, the spirit of nationalism has never ceased to bend human institutions to the service of dissension and distress.
THORSTEIN VEBLEN: *Absentee Ownership,* I, 1923

Nationality

There is a great difference between nationality and race. Nationality is the miracle of political independence. Race is the principle of physical analogy.

BENJAMIN DISRAELI: Speech in the House of Commons, Aug. 9, 1848

A portion of mankind may be said to constitute a nationality if they are united among themselves by common sympathies which do not exist between them and any others — which makes them coöperate with each other more willingly than with other people, desire to be under the same government, and desire that it should be government by themselves or a portion of themselves exclusively.

J. S. MILL: *Representative Government*, XVI, 1861

I began by feeling that I was a Norwegian, then changed into a Scandinavian, and have now arrived at being a generalized Germanic.

HENRIK IBSEN: *Letter to Georg Brandes*, Oct. 30, 1888

The difference between a nation and a nationality is clear. Likeness between members is the essence of a nationality, but the members of a nation may be very different.

LOUIS D. BRANDEIS: Address to the Eastern Council of the Central Conference of Reform Rabbis, June 28, 1915

Why do people speak of great men in terms of nationality? Great Germans, great Englishmen? Goethe always protested against being called a German poet. Great men are simply men.

ALBERT EINSTEIN: Article in the New York Times, 1926

You can take a man out of a country, but you can't take a country out of a man.

Author unidentified

[*See also* Character (National), Jew.

Naturalization

We advocate . . . the independent naturalization of married women. An American woman, resident in the United States, should not lose her citizenship by marriage to an alien.

Republican National Platform, 1920

Only those who will be loyal to our institutions, who are here in conformity with our laws, and who are in sympathy with our national traditions, ideals, and principles should be naturalized.

Republican National Platform, 1928

Naturalness

Nothing so much prevents our being natural as the desire of appearing so.

LA ROCHEFOUCAULD: *Maxims*, 1665

Being natural is simply a pose.

OSCAR WILDE: *The Picture of Dorian Gray*, 1891

Nothing that is natural is disgraceful. (Naturalia non sunt turpia.)

LATIN PROVERB

Natural Selection

I have called this principle, by which each slight variation, if useful, is preserved, by the term natural selection. . . . But the expression often used by Mr. Herbert Spencer, of the survival of the fittest, is more accurate.

CHARLES DARWIN: *The Origin of Species*, III, 1859

From the war of nature, from famine and death, the most exalted object which we are capable of conceiving, namely, the production of the higher animals, directly follows. There is grandeur in this view of life.

CHARLES DARWIN: *The Origin of Species*, XV

This hypothesis may or may not be sustainable hereafter: it may give way to something else, and higher science may reverse what science has here built up with so much skill and patience, but its sufficiency must be tried by the tests of science *alone* if we are to maintain our position as the heirs of Bacon, and the acquitters of Galileo.

T. H. HUXLEY: *Letter to the London Times*, Dec. 26, 1859

Natural selection . . . implies that the individuals which are best fitted for the complex and changing conditions to which, in the course of ages, they are exposed, generally survive and procreate their kind.

CHARLES DARWIN: *The Variation of Animals and Plants Under Domestication*, XX, 1868

Of all the animals that are born a few only can survive; and it is owing to this law that development takes place. The law of murder is the law of growth.

W. WINWOOD READE: *The Martyrdom of Man*, 1872

Nature has made up her mind that what cannot defend itself shall not be defended.

R. W. EMERSON: *Courage*, 1877

Compare the strong bull of Bashan with a salt-water smelt. Who doubts the superiority of the bull? Yet, if you drop them both into the Atlantic ocean, I will take my chances with the smelt.

THOMAS B. REED: Speech in the House of Representatives, Feb. 1, 1894

[*See also* Darwin (Charles), Darwinism, Environment, Evolution, Progress, Struggle for Existence.

Nature

Nature is immovable.

EURIPIDES: *Electra*, *c.* 415

It is in the nature of a stone to move downward, and it cannot be trained to move up-

ward, even though one throw it into the air ten thousand times.
ARISTOTLE: *The Nicomachean Ethics,* II, *c.* 340 B.C.

Whatever befalls in the course of nature should be considered good.
CICERO: *De senectute,* XIX, *c.* 78 B.C.

Nature without education has oftener raised man to glory and virtue than education without natural abilities.
CICERO: *Pro archia poeta,* 62 B.C.

Nature resolves everything into its component elements, but annihilates nothing.
LUCRETIUS: *De rerum natura,* I, 57 B.C.

Those things are better which are perfected by nature than those which are finished by art.
CICERO: *De natura deorum,* II, 45 B.C.

Drive out nature with a pitchfork, and she will always come back.
HORACE: *Satires,* I, *c.* 25 B.C.

God made the beauties of nature like a child playing in the sand.
Ascribed to APOLLONIUS OF TYANA (*c.* 10 B.C.–80 A.D.)

It is difficult to change nature. (Naturam mutare difficile est.)
SENECA: *De Ira,* II, *c.* 43

It is hard to make out whether [nature] is a kind parent or a harsh stepmother to man.
PLINY THE ELDER: *Natural History,* VII, *c.* 79

Never does nature say one thing and wisdom another. JUVENAL: *Satires,* XIV, 128

All nature is good.
ST. AUGUSTINE: *Of Continence, c.* 425

Nature is the art of God Eternal.
DANTE: *De monarchia, c.* 1320

Nature never breaks her own laws.
LEONARDO DA VINCI: *Notebooks, c.* 1500

Nature is the right law.
JOHN FLORIO: *First Frutes,* 1578

Let us permit nature to have her way: she understands her business better than we do.
MICHEL DE MONTAIGNE: *Essays,* III, 1588

The prodigality of nature.
SHAKESPEARE: *Richard III,* I, *c.* 1592

Such is the nature of the beast.
ENGLISH SAYING, traced to the XVII century

To hold, as 't were, the mirror up to nature.
SHAKESPEARE: *Hamlet,* III, *c.* 1601

Nature her custom holds,
Let shame say what it will.
SHAKESPEARE: *Hamlet,* IV

One touch of nature makes the whole world kin.
SHAKESPEARE: *Troilus and Cressida,* III, *c.* 1601

Nothing in nature is unserviceable,
No, not even inutility itself.
JOHN MARSTON: *Sophonisba,* II, 1606

Thou, nature, art my goddess; to thy law
My services are bound.
SHAKESPEARE: *King Lear,* I, 1606

Nature's above art.
SHAKESPEARE: *King Lear,* IV

In nature's infinite book of secrecy
A little I can read.
SHAKESPEARE: *Antony and Cleopatra,* I, *c.* 1606

Nature uses as little as possible of anything.
JOHANN KEPLER: *Astronomia nova,* 1609

How hard it is to hide the sparks of nature!
SHAKESPEARE: *Cymbeline,* III, *c.* 1609

Nature is often hidden, sometimes overcome, seldom extinguished.
FRANCIS BACON: *Essays,* XXXVIII, 1612

Nature is not governed except by obeying her.
FRANCIS BACON: *De augmentis scientiarum,* III, 1623

Nature is no botcher.
JOHN CLARKE: *Parœmiologia Anglo-Latina,* 1639

There are no grotesques in nature; not anything framed to fill up empty cantons, and unnecessary spaces.
THOMAS BROWNE: *Religio Medici,* XV, 1642

Nature is not at variance with art, nor art with nature, they being both servants of His providence: art is the perfection of nature; were the world now as it was the sixth day, there were yet a chaos; nature hath made one world, and art another. In brief, all things are artificial; for nature is the art of God.
THOMAS BROWNE: *Religio Medici,* XVI

Nature seldom gives us the very best; for that we must have recourse to art.
BALTASAR GRACIÁN: *The Art of Worldly Wisdom,* XII, 1647

Accuse not nature, she hath done her part;
Do thou but thine!
JOHN MILTON: *Paradise Lost,* VIII, 1667

Nature has some perfections, to show that she is the image of God; and some defects, to show that she is only His image.
BLAISE PASCAL: *Pensées,* XXIV, 1670

Nature has no goal in view, and final causes are only human imaginings.
BARUCH DE SPINOZA: *Ethica,* I, 1677

The beauty, symmetry, regularity and order seen in the universe are the effects of a blind, unintelligent nature.

PIERRE BAYLE: *Pensées diverses,* 1680

I always think of nature as a great spectacle, somewhat resembling the opera.

BERNARD DE FONTENELLE: *Entretiens sur la pluralité des mondes,* I, 1686

Nature is a good housewife. She always makes use of what is cheapest, let the difference be never so slight, and yet her frugality goes with an extraordinary magnificence, shining through all her works. That is to say, she is magnificence in design but frugal in execution — and what could be more praiseworthy than a great design achieved at small expense? IBID.

Nature never makes excellent things for mean, or no uses.

JOHN LOCKE: *Essay Concerning Human Understanding,* II, 1690

Nature, like liberty, is but restrained
By the same laws which first herself ordained.

ALEXANDER POPE: *An Essay on Criticism,* I, 1711

In nature there can never be two beings which are exactly alike.

G. W. LEIBNIZ: *The Monadology,* IX, 1714

Chase nature away, and it returns at a gallop.

P. N. DESTOUCHES: *Le glorieux,* IV, 1732

He that follows nature is never out of his way.

THOMAS FULLER: *Gnomologia,* 1732

Wolves may lose their teeth, but not their nature. IBID.

All are but parts of one stupendous whole,
Whose body nature is, and God the soul.

ALEXANDER POPE: *An Essay on Man,* I, 1732

Nature will always maintain her rights, and prevail in the end over any abstract reasoning whatsoever.

DAVID HUME: *Essays Moral and Political,* I, 1741

The volume of nature is the book of knowledge.

OLIVER GOLDSMITH: *The Citizen of the World,* IV, 1762

It can't be nature, for it is not sense.

CHARLES CHURCHILL: *The Farewell,* 1764

Men argue, nature acts.

VOLTAIRE: *Philosophical Dictionary,* 1764

There is not a sprig of grass that shoots uninteresting to me.

THOMAS JEFFERSON: *Letter to Martha Jefferson Randolph,* 1790

Never, no never, did nature say one thing and wisdom say another.

EDMUND BURKE: *Letters on a Regicide Peace,* III, 1797

Nature never did betray
The heart that loved her.

WILLIAM WORDSWORTH: *Tintern Abbey,* 1798

The nearer we get to any natural object the more incomprehensible it becomes. A grain of sand is undoubtedly not what I take it to be.

G. C. LICHTENBERG: *Reflections,* 1799

Nature is one connected whole. At any given moment every part must be precisely what it is, because all other parts are what they are, and not a grain of sand could be moved from its place without changing something throughout all parts of the immeasurable whole.

J. G. FICHTE: *Die Bestimmung des Menschen,* I, 1800

I must confess that I am not romance-hit about nature. The earth, the sea, and sky (when all is said) is but as a house to dwell in.

CHARLES LAMB: *Letter to Thomas Manning,* Nov. 28, 1800

Nature is perfect, wherever we look, but man always deforms it.

J. C. F. SCHILLER: *Die Braut von Messina,* 1803

To nature's great command
All human laws are frail and weak.

GEORGE CRABBE: *The Hall of Justice,* I, 1807

Nature has an etiquette all her own.

LUDWIG VAN BEETHOVEN: *Letter to Breitkopf and Haertel,* Sept. 17, 1812

Art, glory, freedom fail, but nature still is fair.

BYRON: *Childe Harold,* II, 1812

I love not man the less, but nature more.

BYRON: *Childe Harold,* IV, 1818

Nature had a robe of glory on.

P. B. SHELLEY: *The Revolt of Islam,* III, 1818

To him who in the love of nature holds
Communion with her visible forms, she speaks
A various language; for his gayer hours
She has a voice of gladness, and a smile
And eloquence of beauty, and she glides
Into his darker musings, with a mild
And healing sympathy that steals away
Their sharpness ere he is aware.

W. C. BRYANT: *Thanatopsis,* 1821

Nature is not lavish of her beauties; they are widely scattered, and occasionally displayed, to be selected with care, and gathered with difficulty.

BYRON: *Letter to John Murray,* Feb. 7, 1821

I love snow, and all the forms
Of the radiant frost;
I love waves, and winds, and storms,
Every thing almost

Which is nature's, and may be
Untainted by man's misery.

P. B. SHELLEY: *Song*, 1822

Nature goes her own way, and all that to us seems an exception is really according to order.

J. W. GOETHE: *Conversations with Eckerman*, Dec. 9, 1824

Nature is the term in which we comprehend all things that are representable in the forms of time and space, and subjected to the relations of cause and effect: and the cause of the existence of which, therefore, is to be sought for perpetually in something antecedent.

S. T. COLERIDGE: *Aids to Reflection*, 1825

There is no pause or chasm in the activities of nature. IBID.

Nature, which is the time-vesture of God and reveals Him to the wise, hides Him from the foolish.

THOMAS CARLYLE: *Sartor Resartus*, III, 1836

There are no fixtures in nature. The universe is fluid and volatile.

R. W. EMERSON: *Circles*, 1841

Nature hates monopolies and exceptions.

R. W. EMERSON: *Compensation*, 1841

Nature is an endless combination and repetition of a very few laws. She hums the old well-known air through innumerable variations. R. W. EMERSON: *History*, 1841

For nature ever faithful is
To such as trust her faithfulness.
When the forest shall mislead me,
When the night and morning lie,
When sea and land refuse to feed me,
'T will be time enough to die.

R. W. EMERSON: *Woodnotes*, I, 1841

Nature encourages no looseness, pardons no errors.

R. W. EMERSON: *The Superlative*, 1847

Nature admits no lie.

THOMAS CARLYLE: *Latter-Day Pamphlets*, V, 1850

Nature red in tooth and claw.

ALFRED TENNYSON: *In Memoriam*, LVI, 1850

Down with pulpit, down with priest,
And give us nature's teaching.

J. G. WHITTIER: *A Sabbath Scene*, 1850

Nature never half does her work. She goes over it, and over it, to make assurance sure, and makes good her ground with wearying repetition.

J. A. FROUDE: *The Lives of the Saints*, 1852 (Eclectic Review)

What nature does generally, is sure to be more or less beautiful; what she does rarely, will either be *very* beautiful, or absolutely ugly.

JOHN RUSKIN: *Lectures on Architecture and Painting*, 1853

I believe a leaf of grass is no less than the journey-work of the stars,
And the pismire is equally perfect, and a grain of sand, and the egg of the wren,
And the tree-toad is a chef-d'oeuvre for the highest,
And the running blackberry would adorn the parlors of Heaven,
And the narrowest hinge in my hand puts to scorn all machinery.

WALT WHITMAN: *Walt Whitman*, 1855

Our old mother nature has pleasant and cheery tones enough for us when she comes in her dress of blue and gold over the eastern hilltops; but when she follows us upstairs to our beds in her suit of black velvet and diamonds, every creak of her sandals and every whisper of her lips is full of mystery and fear. O. W. HOLMES: *The Professor at the Breakfast-Table*, VII, 1859

Nature is no spendthrift, but takes the shortest way to her ends.

R. W. EMERSON: *Fate*, 1860

Nature is the tyrannous circumstance, the thick skull, the sheathed snake, the ponderous rock-like jaw.

R. W. EMERSON: *The Conduct of Life*, I, 1860

Nature tells every secret once.

R. W. EMERSON: *The Conduct of Life*, V

Nature is profoundly imperturbable. We may adjust the beating of our hearts to her pendulum if we will and can, but we may be very sure that she will not change the pendulum's rate of going because our hearts are palpitating.

O. W. HOLMES: Address to the Massachusetts Medical Society, Boston, May 30, 1860

Nature never quite goes along with us. She is sombre at weddings, sunny at funerals, and she frowns on ninety-nine out of a hundred picnics.

ALEXANDER SMITH: *Dreamthorp*, V, 1863

I wonder nature don't retire
From public life disgusted.

W. S. GILBERT: *Margate*, *c.* 1865

The investigation of nature is an infinite pleasure-ground, where all may graze, and where the more bite, the longer the grass grows, the sweeter is its flavor, and the more it nourishes.

T. H. HUXLEY: *Administrative Nihilism*, 1871

As the nature of any given thing is the aggregate of its powers and properties, so nature in the abstract is the aggregate of the powers and properties of all things. Nature means the sum of all phenomena, together with the causes which produce them; including not only all that happens, but all that is capable of happening.

J. S. MILL: *Three Essays on Religion*, IV, 1874

One touch of nature may make the whole world kin, but two touches of nature will destroy any work of art.

OSCAR WILDE: *The Decay of Lying*, 1889 (Cf. SHAKESPEARE: *Troilus and Cressida*, *ante*, *c.* 1600)

The more we study art, the less we care for nature. What art really reveals to us is nature's lack of design, her curious crudities, her extraordinary monotony, her absolutely unfinished condition. IBID.

Nature is very rarely right; to such an extent even, that it might also be said that nature is usually wrong.

J. MCN. WHISTLER: *The Gentle Art of Making Enemies*, 1890

Nature has no one distinguishable ultimate tendency with which it is possible to feel a sympathy.

WILLIAM JAMES: *The Varieties of Religious Experience*, XX, 1902

Nature aborts all her works to make room for more. She never finishes anything nor permits anything to become perfect.

MICHAEL J. DEE: *Conclusions*, I, 1917

Ain't nature grand [or wonderful]!

AMERICAN PHRASE

Nature is a hanging judge.

Author unidentified

Nature and love will out. GERMAN PROVERB

Nature does nothing in vain. (Natura nihil agit frustra.) LATIN PROVERB

Nature does not proceed by leaps. (Natura non facit saltus.) IBID.

[*See also* Annihilation, Art, Artist, Cause and Effect, Culture, Cure, Death, Equality, God, Law (Natural), Living, Nature *vs.* Nurture, Necessity, Pantheism, Physician, Poetry, Struggle for Existence, Vacuum.

Nature-faker

The nature-faker is an object of derision to every scientist worthy of the name, to every real lover of the wilderness, to every faunal naturalist, to every true hunter or nature-lover.

THEODORE ROOSEVELT: In Everybody's Magazine, Sept., 1907 (Apparently the first appearance of the term)

Nature, Good

[*See* Good-nature.

Nature, Human

Every bias, instinct, propension within is a natural part of our nature, but not the whole: add to these the superior faculty whose office it is to adjust, manage and preside over them, and take in this its natural superiority, and you complete the idea of human nature.

JOSEPH BUTLER: *Sermons Upon Human Nature*, III, 1726

Human nature is the same all over the world, but its operations are so varied by education and habit that one must see it in all its dresses in order to be entirely acquainted with it.

LORD CHESTERFIELD: *Letter to his son*, Oct. 2, 1747

All men are born with a sufficiently violent liking for domination, wealth and pleasure, and with much taste for idleness; consequently, all men want the money and the wives or daughters of others, to be their master, to subject them to all their caprices, and to do nothing, or at least to do only very agreeable things.

VOLTAIRE: *Philosophical Dictionary*, 1764

Long ages of dreary monotony are the first facts in the history of human communities, but those ages were not lost to mankind, for it was then that was formed the comparatively gentle and guidable thing which we now call human nature.

WALTER BAGEHOT: *Physics and Politics*, 1869

There is a great deal of human nature in man.

CHARLES KINGSLEY: *At Last*, 1871

[*See also* Jesus Christ, Originality.

Nature vs. Nurture

Education altereth nature.

JOHN LYLY: *Euphues*, 1579

A born devil, on whose nature nurture can never stock.

SHAKESPEARE: *The Tempest*, IV, 1611

Nurture is above nature.

JOHN CLARKE: *Parœmiologia Anglo-Latina*, 1639

Nature passes nurture.

DAVID FERGUSSON: *Scottish Proverbs*, 1641

Man is so educable an animal that it is difficult to distinguish between that part of his character which has been acquired through education and circumstance, and that which was in the original grain of his constitution.

FRANCIS GALTON: *Inquiry Into Human Faculty*, 1883

Nature is stronger than rearing.

IRISH PROVERB

[*See also* Environment, Heredity, Nature.

Naught

[*See* Nothing.

Naughty

A naughty person . . . walketh with a froward mouth.

PROVERBS VI, 12, *c.* 350 B.C.

Wholesome meats to a vitiated stomach differ little or nothing from unwholesome; and best books to a naughty mind are not unapplicable to occasions of evil.

JOHN MILTON: *Areopagitica*, 1644

I gave her cakes, I gave her wine,
I gave her sugar-candy,
But oh, the naughty little girl,
She asked me for some brandy.

MARY GODWIN SHELLEY: *Letter to Maria Gisborne*, March 7, 1882 (Cited as "a nursery rhyme")

Navel

His force is in the navel of his belly.

JOB XL, 16, *c.* 325 B.C.

[*See also* Adam and Eve, Body.

Navigation

[*See* Laissez-faire, Sea.

Navigator

[*See* Ability.

Navy

King Solomon made a navy of ships in Ezion-geber, which is beside Eloth, on the shore of the Red sea.

I KINGS IX, 26, *c.* 500 B.C.

The most sincere neutrality is not a sufficient guard against the depredations of nations at war. To secure a respect to a neutral flag requires a naval force organized and ready to vindicate it from insult or aggression.

GEORGE WASHINGTON: Address to Congress, Dec. 7, 1796

It is no part of our policy to create and maintain a navy able to cope with that of the other great powers of the world.

CHESTER A. ARTHUR: Message to Congress, Dec. 4, 1883

We must have a navy so strong and so well proportioned and equipped, so thoroughly ready and prepared, that no enemy can gain command of the sea and effect a landing in force on either our western or our eastern coast.

Republican National Platform, 1916

[*See also* Army and Navy, Marine.

Navy, British

The dominion of the sea, as it is an ancient and undoubted right of the crown of England, so is it the best security of the land. The wooden walls are the best walls of this kingdom.

THOMAS COVENTRY: Speech in the House of Commons, June 17, 1635

It is upon the navy under the good Providence of God that the safety, honor and welfare of this realm do chiefly depend.

CHARLES II of England: *Articles of War*, preamble, *c.* 1672

The royal navy of England has ever been its greatest defence and ornament; it is its ancient and natural strength; the floating bulwark of the island.

WILLIAM BLACKSTONE: *Commentaries on the Laws of England*, I, 1765

There were gentlemen and there were seamen in the navy of Charles II. But the seamen were not gentlemen; and the gentlemen were not seamen.

T. B. MACAULAY: *History of England*, I, 1848

Stick close to your desks and never go to sea,
And you all may be rulers of the queen's navee.

W. S. GILBERT: *H.M.S. Pinafore*, I, 1878

Nazareth

Can there any good thing come out of Nazareth?

JOHN I, 46, *c.* 115

Neapolitan

The Neapolitan will embrace you with one arm, and rip your guts with the other.

THOMAS DEKKER: *The Gull's Hornbook*, II, 1609

Near

My shirt is near me, but my skin is nearer.

ENGLISH PROVERB, traced by Apperson to 1539

Nearest, dearest.

GERMAN PROVERB

Necessary

There is no such thing as a necessary man.

FRENCH PROVERB

Necessity

Necessity is stronger far than any art.

ÆSCHYLUS: *Prometheus Bound*, *c.* 490 B.C.

Even the gods can't resist necessity.

Ascribed to SIMONIDES (556–468 B.C.)

Nothing is stronger than necessity.

EURIPIDES: *Helena*, 412 B.C. (Credited to "the sage")

Necessity knows no law.

PUBLILIUS SYRUS: *Sententiæ*, *c.* 50 B.C.

Necessity makes laws, but does not obey them.

IBID.

Necessity makes even the timid brave.

SALLUST: *Catilina*, *c.* 40 B.C.

Necessity is stronger than human nature.

DIONYSIUS OF HALICARNASSUS: *Antiquities of Rome*, V, *c.* 20 B.C.

Necessity is the last and strongest weapon.

LIVY: *History of Rome*, IV, *c.* 10

You make a virtue of necessity.
ST. JEROME: *Apologeticum adversus Rufinum,* III, 401

I shall cut my coat after my cloth.
JOHN HEYWOOD: *Proverbs,* 1546

The school of necessity is kept by a violent mistress.
MICHEL DE MONTAIGNE: *Essays,* I, 1580

Teach thy necessity to reason thus:
There is no virtue like necessity.
SHAKESPEARE: *Richard II,* I, *c.* 1596

Grim necessity.
SHAKESPEARE: *Richard II,* V

Necessity's sharp pinch.
SHAKESPEARE: *King Lear,* II, 1606

The tyrant's plea.
JOHN MILTON: *Paradise Lost,* IV, 1667

Necessity is the mother of invention.
JONATHAN SWIFT: *Gulliver's Travels,* IV, 1726

Necessity never made a good bargain.
BENJAMIN FRANKLIN: *Poor Richard's Almanac,* 1735

A man who is in extreme necessity may steal enough of another's goods to relieve his necessity.
ALPHONSUS MARIA DI LIGOURI: *Theologia moralis,* IV, 1753

Whatever necessity lays upon thee, endure; whatever she commands, do.
J. W. GOETHE: *Iphigenie auf Tauris,* IV, 1787

Necessity has a stern face.
J. C. F. SCHILLER: *Wallenstein's Death,* I, 1799

Necessity, thou mother of the world!
P. B. SHELLEY: *Queen Mab,* VI, 1813

Pain and pleasure, good and evil join,
To do the will of strong necessity. IBID.

Necessity is the constant scourge of the lower orders; ennui that of the higher classes.
ARTHUR SCHOPENHAUER: *The World as Will and Idea,* I, 1819

Necessity is the mother of courage, as of invention.
WALTER SCOTT: *Quentin Durward,* XXIII, 1823

Manhood begins when we have, in a way, made truce with necessity; begins, at all events, when we have surrendered to necessity, as the most part only do; but begins joyfully and hopefully only when we have reconciled ourselves to necessity, and thus, in reality, triumphed over it, and felt that in necessity we are free.
THOMAS CARLYLE: *Burns,* 1828 (Edinburgh Review, Dec.)

Nature must obey necessity.
H. G. BOHN: *Handbook of Proverbs,* 1855

Necessity knows neither law nor Constitution, and never did in this country.
JOHN F. FOLLETT of Ohio: Speech in the House of Representatives, Feb. 11, 1884

If any man should wish to construct a pond of human blood for the purpose of enabling sick wealthy people under the advice of medical men to bathe in it, I think he would be able to arrange it without hindrance so long as he did so in the ordinary respectable way; that is, did not by force compel people to shed their blood, but placed them in a position where they could not live without shedding it.
LYOF N. TOLSTOY: *What Is Religion?,* 1902

Necessity is half a reason. FRENCH PROVERB

Necessity can break iron. GERMAN PROVERB

Necessity teaches art. IBID.

Necessity takes no holidays. (Feriis caret necessitas.) LATIN PROVERB

Necessity overcomes law. (Necessitas vincit legem.) LEGAL MAXIM

Public necessity goes before private. (Necessitas publica major est quam privata.) IBID.

That which necessity compels she excuses. (Quod necessitas cogit, excusat.) IBID.

Necessity breaks all laws. WELSH PROVERB

[*See also* Experience, Man, Need.

Neck

Thy neck is like a tower of David builded for an armory, whereon there hang a thousand bucklers, all shields of mighty men.
SOLOMON'S SONG IV, 4, *c.* 200 B.C.

Thy neck is a tower of ivory.
SOLOMON'S SONG VII, 4

Her neck is like a stately tower
Where Love himself imprison'd lies,
To watch for glances every hour
From her divine and sacred eyes.
THOMAS LODGE: *Rosalynde,* 1590

A lover forsaken
A new love may get;
But a neck, when once broken,
Can never be set.
WILLIAM WALSH: *The Despairing Lover,* 1692

When we say a woman has a handsome neck we reckon into it many of the adjacent parts.
JOSEPH ADDISON: *The Guardian,* July 6, 1713

[*See also* Kiss, Mole (=growth), Pearl, Tears.

Need

O ye gods, grant me this: that I shall have little and need nothing.
APOLLONIUS OF TYANA (*c.* 10 B.C.–80 A.D.)

A friend in need is a friend indeed.
ENGLISH PROVERB, traced by Apperson to the XIII century

Need makes the old wife trot.
ENGLISH PROVERB, traced by Apperson to *c.* 1210

When need is highest, help is nighest.
ENGLISH PROVERB, traced by Smith to *c.* 1250

Who of plenty will take no heed
Shall find default in time of need.
Anon.: *Proverbs of Wisdom, c.* 1450

The needy man can never live happily nor contented, for every least disaster makes him ready to mortgage or sell.
WILLIAM CECIL (LORD BURLEIGH): *Advice to his son, c.* 1555

Need makes greed.
JAMES KELLY: *Complete Collection of Scottish Proverbs,* 1721

Once in ten years one man hath need of another.
THOMAS FULLER: *Gnomologia,* 1732

Think twice before you speak to a friend in need.
AMBROSE BIERCE: *The Devil's Dictionary,* 1906

The needy are always listening.
ARAB PROVERB

[*See also* Charity, Friend, Necessity, Poor.

Needle

A needle in a haystack.
AMERICAN SAYING, based on an English saying, current since the XVI century, in which " a bottle of hay " appears in place of " haystack "

A needle is sharp only at one end.
CHINESE PROVERB

Negative

It is the peculiar and perpetual error of the human intellect to be more moved and excited by affirmatives than by negatives; whereas it ought properly to hold itself indifferently disposed towards both alike. Indeed, in the establishment of any true axiom, the negative instance is the more forcible of the two.
FRANCIS BACON: *Novum Organum,* I, 1620

In the English language two negatives amount to an affirmative.
TOBIAS SMOLLETT: *The Adventures of an Atom,* 1769

Negligence

His noble negligences teach
What others' toils despair to reach.
MATTHEW PRIOR: *Alma,* II, *c.* 1716

Nothing is easy to the negligent.
THOMAS FULLER: *Gnomologia,* 1732

A little neglect may breed mischief: for want of a nail the shoe was lost; for want of a shoe the horse was lost; and for want of a horse the rider was lost.
BENJAMIN FRANKLIN: *Poor Richard's Almanac,* 1757

He trespasses against his duty who sleeps upon his watch, as well as he that goes over to the enemy.
EDMUND BURKE: *Thoughts on the Cause of the Present Discontents,* 1770

Gross negligence is equivalent to intentional wrong. (Culpa lata dolo æquiparatur.)
LEGAL MAXIM

He who loses by his own negligence is not considered to have suffered any damage. (Culpa sua damnum sentiens, non intelligitur damnum pati.)
IBID.

Negotiation

It is generally better to deal by speech than by letter, and by the meditation of a third than by a man's self.
FRANCIS BACON: *Essays,* XLVI, 1625

Negotiators almost always abandon the interest of their principals for that of the success of the negotiation, which gives them credit for having succeeded in their undertaking.
LA ROCHEFOUCAULD: *Maxims,* 1665

[*See also* Bargain.

Negro

Can the Ethiopian change his skin, or the leopard his spots?
JEREMIAH XIII, 23, *c.* 625 B.C.

Black men are pearls in beauteous ladies' eyes.
SHAKESPEARE: *Two Gentlemen of Verona,* V, *c.* 1595

I am apt to suspect the Negroes to be naturally inferior to the whites. There scarcely ever was a civilized nation of that complexion, nor even any individual, eminent either in action or speculation.
DAVID HUME: *Essays, Moral and Political,* II, 1742

Why increase the sons of Africa, by planting them in America, where we have so fair an opportunity, by excluding all blacks and tawnys, of increasing the lovely white and red? But perhaps I am partial to the complexion of my country, for such kind of partiality is natural to mankind.
BENJAMIN FRANKLIN: *Observations Concerning the Increase of Mankind,* 1753

Among the Gentiles in Heaven the Africans are the most beloved, for they receive the goods and truths of Heaven more readily than any others.
EMANUEL SWEDENBORG: *Arcana Cœlestia*, 1756

Am I not a man and a brother?
INSCRIPTION ON THE SEAL OF THE ANTI-SLAVERY SOCIETY OF LONDON, representing a Negro in chains, *c.* 1770

Misery is often the parent of the most affecting touches in poetry. Among the blacks is misery enough, God knows, but no poetry. Love is the peculiar cestrum of the poet. Their love is ardent, but it kindles the senses only, not the imagination.
THOMAS JEFFERSON: *Notes on Virginia*, 1782

I have supposed the black man, in his present state, might not be in body and mind equal to the white man; but it would be hazardous to affirm that, equally cultivated for a few generations, he would not become so.
THOMAS JEFFERSON: *Letter to F. J. de Chastellux*, 1785

There does not exist on earth a population so poor, so wretched, so vile, so loathsome, so utterly destitute of all the comforts, conveniences, and decencies of life, as the unfortunate blacks of Philadelphia, New York and Boston. Liberty has been to them the greatest of calamities, the heaviest of curses.
R. W. HAYNE: Speech in the House of Representatives, Jan. 21, 1830

No tribe of people have ever passed from barbarism to civilization whose middle stage of progress has been more secure from harm, more genial to their character, or better supplied with mild and beneficent guardianship . . . than the Negroes.
J. P. KENNEDY: *Swallow Barn*, XLVI, 1832

The time must come when American slavery shall cease, and when that day shall arrive two races will exist in the same region, whose feelings will be embittered by inextinguishable hatred, and who carry on their faces the respective stamps of their factions. The struggle that will follow will necessarily be a war of extermination.
J. FENIMORE COOPER: *The American Democrat*, XXXVIII, 1838

Eene, meene, meine, mo;
Catch a nigger by the toe;
If he hollers let him go
Eene, meene, meine, mo.
American Children's Rhyme, c. 1840

God has put into every white man's hand a whip to flog the black man.
THOMAS CARLYLE: On meeting Emerson, 1848

A merry-hearted, grinning, dancing, singing, affectionate kind of creature, with a great deal of melody and amenability in his composition.
THOMAS CARLYLE: *The Nigger Question*, 1849 (Fraser's Magazine, Dec.)

Nigger, nigger, never die:
Black face and shiny eye!
American Children's Rhyme, c. 1850

I am for Negro suffrage in every rebel state. If it be just, it should not be denied; if it be necessary, it should be adopted; if it be a punishment to traitors, they deserve it.
THADDEUS STEVENS: Speech in the House of Representatives, June 10, 1850

Some people say that a nigger won't steal:
These bones shall rise again!
I caught one in my corn-fiel':
These bones shall rise again.
American popular song, *c.* 1850

Free them, and make them politically and socially our equals? My own feelings will not admit of this, and if mine would, we well know that those of the great mass of whites will not.
ABRAHAM LINCOLN: Speech at Peoria, Ill., Oct. 16, 1854

The blacks are immeasurably better off here than in Africa, morally, socially and physically. The painful discipline they are undergoing is necessary for their instruction as a race, and I hope will prepare and lead them to better things. How long their subjugation may be necessary is known and ordered by a wise Merciful Providence.
ROBERT E. LEE: *Letter to his wife*, Dec. 27, 1856

For more than a century before the Declaration of Independence the Negroes . . . had no rights which a white man was bound to respect.
CHIEF JUSTICE R. B. TANEY: *Decision in the Dred Scott case*, March 6, 1857

I protest against the counterfeit logic which concludes that, because I do not want a black woman for a slave I must necessarily want her for a wife. I need not have her for either. I can just leave her alone. In some respects she certainly is not my equal; but in her natural right to eat the bread she earns with her own hands without asking leave of any one else, she is my equal, and the equal of all others.
ABRAHAM LINCOLN: Speech on the Dred Scott decision, Springfield, Ill., June 26, 1857

All I ask for the Negro is that if you do not like him, let him alone. If God gave him but little, that little let him enjoy.
ABRAHAM LINCOLN: Speech in Springfield, Ill., July 17, 1858

I do not believe that the Almighty ever intended the Negro to be the equal of the

white man. If He did, He has been a long time demonstrating the fact.
STEPHEN A. DOUGLAS: Debate with Lincoln, Cttawa, Ill., August 21, 1858

I am opposed to Negro citizenship in any and every form. I believe this government was made on the white basis. I believe it was made by white men for the benefit of white men and their posterity for ever; and I am in favor of confining citizenship to white men, men of European birth and descent, instead of conferring it upon Negroes, Indians and other inferior races. IBID.

I have no purpose to introduce political and social equality between the white and the black races. There is a physical difference between the two, which, in my judgment, will probably forever forbid their living together upon the footing of perfect equality; and inasmuch as it becomes a necessity that there must be a difference, I am in favor of the race to which I belong having the superior position.
ABRAHAM LINCOLN: Debate with Douglas, Ottawa, Ill., Aug. 21, 1858

He is of all races the most gentle and kind. The man, the most submissive; the woman, the most affectionate.
A. ROSS: *Slavery Ordained of God,* 1859

The Afrikan may be Our Brother. But the Afrikan isn't our sister & our wife & our uncle. He isn't several of our brothers & all our fust wife's relashuns. He isn't our grandfather and our grate-grandfather & our aunt in the country.
C. F. BROWNE (ARTEMUS WARD): *The Crisis,* 1860

If he knows enough to be hanged, he knows enough to vote.
FREDERICK DOUGLASS: Speech to the American Anti-Slavery Society, Philadelphia, Dec., 1863

Now you are about to have a convention, which, among other things, will probably define the elective franchise. I barely suggest for your private consideration whether some of the colored people may not be let in — as, for instance, the very intelligent, and especially those who have fought gallantly in our ranks.
ABRAHAM LINCOLN: *Letter to Michael Hahn (Governor of Louisiana),* March 13, 1864

There's a nigger in the woodpile.
AMERICAN SAYING, traced by Thornton to 1864, and probably older

It may be quite true that some Negroes are better than some white men; but no rational man, cognizant of the facts, believes that the average Negro is the equal, still less the superior, of the average white man.
T. H. HUXLEY: *Emancipation, Black and White,* 1865

Every family shall have a plot of not more than forty acres of tillable ground.
W. T. SHERMAN: Special Field Order, Savannah, Jan. 16, 1865

The Negro should, of course, be protected in his industry, and encouraged to acquire property, knowledge, trade and every means possible to better his condition, but I think we should all be rather too slow than too fast in extending political rights. These in time will adjust themselves according to the laws of nature and experience. *Festina lente* is a good old maxim.
W. T. SHERMAN: *Letter to Gen. Absalom Baird,* April 3, 1865

Wherever you find the Negro everything is going down around him, and wherever you find the white man you see everything around him improving.
ROBERT E. LEE: To Col. Thomas H. Carter, May, 1865

The Negro is superior to the white race. If the latter do not forget their pride of race and color, and amalgamate with the purer and richer blood of the blacks, they will die out and wither away in unprolific skinniness.
H. W. BEECHER: Speech in New York, 1866

A large portion of the religious life of the Negro is purely emotional, and a large proportion of the Negroes of the United States have never thoroughly associated, either in their theories or their practical life, religion with morality.
J. G. HOLLAND: *Everyday Topics,* 1876

I try to understand all nations and races, but I can never overcome my aversion to Negroes. They appear to me to be a caricature of the white man.
OTTO VON BISMARCK (1815–98)

The Negro pays for what he wants and begs for what he needs.
KELLY MILLER: In the Baltimore Afro-American, *c.* 1924

De nigger is luckier than de white man at night. AMERICAN NEGRO SAYING

Ef yo' say to de white man: " Ain't yo' forget yo' hat? " he say: " Nigger, go get it! "
IBID.

Nigger be nigger, whatever he do. IBID.

Nigger an' white man
Playin' seven-up;
Nigger win de money —
Skeered to pick 'em up.
American Negro song

The Devil of the Negro is white.
BULGARIAN PROVERB

If Negroes were really good their faces would not be black. MOROCCAN PROVERB

Nigger, read and run. If you can't read, run anyhow.

Sign formerly displayed at Sullivan's Hollow, Miss.

[*See also* Abolition, African, Black, Emancipation, Equality, Harvard University, Know-nothingism, Methodist, Mulatto, Slavery, Slave-trade, Suffrage (Negro).

Neighbor

Thou shalt not bear false witness against thy neighbor.

EXODUS XX, 16, *c.* 700 B.C. (Cf. DEUTERONOMY V, 20, *c.* 650 B.C.)

Thou shalt love thy neighbor as thyself.

LEVITICUS XIX, 18, *c.* 700 B.C. (Cf. JAMES II, 8, *c.* 60; MATTHEW XXII, 39, *c.* 75)

He that is void of wisdom despiseth his neighbor; but a man of understanding holdeth his peace. PROVERBS XI, 12, *c.* 350 B.C.

Better is a neighbor that is near than a brother far off. PROVERBS XXVII, 10

When your neighbor's house is afire your own property is at stake.

HORACE: *Epistles*, I, *c.* 5 B.C.

The crop always seems better in our neighbor's field, and our neighbor's cow gives more milk. OVID: *Ars amatoria*, I, *c.* 2 B.C.

The love of our neighbor hath its bounds in each man's love of himself.

ST. AUGUSTINE: *On Lying*, *c.* 395

The love towards our neighbor must be like the pure and chaste love between bride and bridegroom, where all faults are connived at and borne with, and only the virtues regarded.

MARTIN LUTHER: *Table-Talk*, CCCXIV, 1569

All is well with him who is beloved of his neighbors.

GEORGE HERBERT: *Outlandish Proverbs*, 1640

Better learn by your neighbor's skaith nor by your own.

DAVID FERGUSSON: *Scottish Proverbs*, 1641 (*Skaith*=injury)

Here is a talk of the Turk and the pope, but my next neighbor doth me more harm than either of them both.

GEORGE HERBERT: *Jacula Prudentum*, 1651

Love your neighbor, yet pull not down your hedge. IBID.

Every man's neighbor is his looking-glass.

ENGLISH PROVERB, traced by Apperson to 1659

Lock your door and keep your neighbors honest.

THOMAS FULLER: *Gnomologia*, 1732

Nobody can live longer in peace than his neighbor pleases. IBID.

We can live without our friends but not without our neighbors. IBID.

You may love your neighbor and yet not hold his stirrup. IBID.

Not one will change his neighbor with himself.

ALEXANDER POPE: *An Essay on Man*, II, 1732

We are made for one another, and each is to be a supply to his neighbor.

BENJAMIN WHICHCOTE: *Moral and Religious Aphorisms*, 1753

Good neighbors and true friends are two things.

H. G. BOHN: *Handbook of Proverbs*, 1855

No one can love his neighbor on an empty stomach.

WOODROW WILSON: Speech in New York, May 23, 1912

I do not love my neighbor as myself, and apologize to no one. I treat my neighbor as fairly and politely as I hope to be treated, but there is no law in nature or common sense ordering me to go beyond that.

E. W. HOWE: *Success Easier Than Failure*, 1917

In the field of world policy I would dedicate this nation to the policy of the good neighbor.

F. D. ROOSEVELT: Inaugural address, March 4, 1933

It is discouraging to try to be a good neighbor in a bad neighborhood.

WILLIAM R. CASTLE: *Dragon's Teeth in South America*, 1939

If your neighbor gets up early so will you.

ALBANIAN PROVERB

Every neighbor is a teacher. ARAB PROVERB

Keep confidence in thy neighbor by keeping thy door shut. IBID.

These three make bad neighbors: great river, powerful lords, and wide roads.

DANISH PROVERB

A good neighbor doubles the value of a house.

GERMAN PROVERB

If you want to hear the whole truth about yourself, anger your neighbor. IBID.

He who prays for his neighbor will be heard for himself. HEBREW PROVERB

He who wins honor through his neighbor's shame will never reach Paradise. IBID.

The honor of a neighbor should be held as sacred as one's own. IBID.

Once in every ten years every man needs his neighbor. ITALIAN PROVERB

Your neighbor's right is God's right. TURKISH PROVERB

Ask about the neighbors before you buy the house. YIDDISH PROVERB

[*See also* Borrowing, Conformity, Envy, Frenchmen, Golden Rule, House, Injury, Lawyer, Lending, Piety, Wealth.

Neighborhood

[*See* Manners.

Nephew

He to whom God gave no sons the Devil gives nephews. SPANISH PROVERB

[*See also* Gratitude, Son, Stranger.

Nepotism

The field of public office will not be perverted by me into a family property.
THOMAS JEFFERSON: *Letter to Dr. Horatio Turpin,* 1807

Nero (37–68)

Most of what history says about Nero is probably false.
NAPOLEON I: To Gaspard Gourgaud at St. Helena, 1815–1818

Nest

It's an ill bird that fouls its own nest.
ENGLISH PROVERB, borrowed from the Latin and traced to the XIII century

The fearful bird his little house now builds
In trees and walls, in cities and in fields,
The outside strong, the inside warm and neat,
A natural artificer complete.
ANNE BRADSTREET: *Four Elements, Constitutions, Ages of Man, and Seasons of the Year,* 1650

[*See also* Bird, Home.

Net

Anything reticulated or decussated at equal distances, with interstices between the intersections.
SAMUEL JOHNSON: *Dictionary,* 1755

Netherlands

The Netherlands have been for many years the very cockpit of Christendom, the school of arms, and rendezvous of all adventurous spirits.
JAMES HOWELL: *Instructions for Foreign Travel,* 1642

[*See also* Holland.

Nettle

He which toucheth the nettle tenderly is soonest stung. JOHN LYLY: *Euphues,* 1579

Neutrality

A plague o' both your houses.
SHAKESPEARE: *Romeo and Juliet,* III, *c.* 1596

God will have all, or none; serve Him, or fall
Down before Baal, Bel, or Belial:
Either be hot, or cold: God doth despise,
Abhor, and spew out all neutralities.
ROBERT HERRICK: *Noble Numbers,* 1647

There are some opinions in which a man should stand neuter, without engaging his assent to one side or the other.
JOSEPH ADDISON: *The Spectator,* July 14, 1711

I can pray for opposite parties, and for opposite religions, with great sincerity.
ALEXANDER POPE: *Letter to William Trumbull,* Dec. 16, 1715

I have always given it as my decided opinion that no nation had a right to intermeddle in the internal concerns of another; that every one had a right to form and adopt whatever government they liked best to live under themselves; and that, if this country could, consistently with its engagements, maintain a strict neutrality and thereby preserve peace, it was bound to do so by motives of policy, interest, and every other consideration.
GEORGE WASHINGTON: *Letter to James Monroe,* Aug. 25, 1796

The United States must be neutral in fact as well as in name during these days that are to try men's souls. We must be impartial in thought as well as in action, must put a curb upon our sentiments as well as upon every transaction that might be construed as a preference of one party to the struggle before another.
WOODROW WILSON: *Neutrality Proclamation,* Aug. 18, 1914

Neutrals never dominate events. They always sink. Blood alone moves the wheels of history.
BENITO MUSSOLINI: Speech in Parma, Dec. 13, 1914

In the judgment of this government loans by American bankers to any foreign nation at war are inconsistent with the true spirit of neutrality.
W. J. BRYAN (Secretary of State): Statement to the press, Aug. 15, 1914

The basis of neutrality is not indifference; it is not self-interest. The basis of neutrality is sympathy for mankind. It is fairness, it is good will, at bottom. It is impartiality of spirit and of judgment.
WOODROW WILSON: Speech in New York, April 20, 1915

Armed neutrality.
WOODROW WILSON: Address to Congress, Feb. 26, 1917

Neutrals are doused from above and singed from below. GERMAN PROVERB

[*See also* Foreign Relations, Navy, Paper, Treaty.

Never

Never is a long day.
ENGLISH PROVERB, familiar since the XIV century

Quoth the raven, "Nevermore."
E. A. POE: *The Raven,* 1845 (New York Evening Mirror, Jan. 29)

What, never? Hardly ever.
W. S. GILBERT: *H.M.S. Pinafore,* I, 1878

St. Never's Day. (Sanct-Nimmerstag.)
GERMAN PHRASE

Never's a lang word. SCOTTISH PROVERB

[*See also* Late, Now, Once.

New

There is no new thing under the sun.
ECCLESIASTES I, 9, *c.* 200 B.C.

Is there any thing whereof it may be said, See, this is new? it hath been already of old time, which was before us. ECCLESIASTES I, 10

Men love . . . newfangledness.
GEOFFREY CHAUCER: *The Canterbury Tales* (*The Squire's Tale*), *c.* 1386

Newer is truer.
JOHN HEYWOOD: *Proverbs,* 1546

The green new broom sweepeth clean. IBID.

Everything's pretty when 'tis new.
JOHN CLARKE: *Parœmiologia Anglo-Latina,* 1639

Everything new is fine.
GEORGE HERBERT: *Outlandish Proverbs,* 1640

Everything that is new or uncommon raises a pleasure in the imagination, because it fills the soul with an agreeable surprise, gratifies its curiosity, and gives it an idea of which it was not before possessed.
JOSEPH ADDISON: *The Spectator,* June 23, 1712

New things are most looked at.
THOMAS FULLER: *Gnomologia,* 1732

There is nothing new save that which has been forgotten.
Ascribed to MME. BERTIN, milliner to Marie Antoinette, *c.* 1785

[*See also* Bottle, Broom, New and Old, Nothing, Novelty, Opinion.

New and Old

Forsake not an old friend, for the new is not comparable unto him. A new friend is as new wine: when it is old thou shalt drink it with pleasure.
ECCLESIASTICUS IX, 10, *c.* 180 B.C.

No man having drunk old wine straightway desireth new; for he saith, The old is better.
LUKE V, 39, *c.* 75

Man's memory, with new, forgets the old,
One tale is good until another's told.
JOHN WEEVER: *The Mirror of Martyrs,* 1601

Old chains gall less than new.
ENGLISH PROVERB, not recorded before the XIX century

Nothing is new but what has grown old.
MOTTO OF THE REVUE RÉTROSPECTIVE (Paris), 1833

They love the old who do not know the new.
GERMAN PROVERB

Men are better when they are old; things when they are new. KOREAN PROVERB

[*See also* New, Old.

New England

I have lived in a country seven years, and all that time I never heard one profane oath, and all that time I never did see a man drunk in that land. Where was that country? It was New England.
GILES FIRMIN: Sermon to the Lords and Commons, *c.* 1675

If any are scandalized that New England, a place of as serious piety as any I can hear of under Heaven, should be troubled with so much witches, I think 'tis no wonder: where will the Devil show most malice but where he is hated, and hated most?
RICHARD BAXTER: Pref. to the second ed. of COTTON MATHER: *Memorable Providences,* 1691

The New Englanders are a people of God, settled in those which were once the Devil's territories.
COTTON MATHER: *Wonders of the Invisible World,* I, 1693

When England grew very corrupt, God brought over a number of pious persons, and planted them in New England, and this land was planted with a noble vine. But how is the gold become dim! How greatly have we forsaken the pious examples of our fathers!
JONATHAN EDWARDS: *The Great Christian Doctrine of Original Sin Defended,* 1758

The sway of the clergy in New England is indeed formidable. No mind beyond mediocrity dares there to develop itself. If it does, they excite against it the public opinion which they command, and by little, but incessant and tearing persecutions, drive it from among them.
THOMAS JEFFERSON: *Letter to Horatio Gates Spafford,* 1816

I saw but one drunken man through all New England, and he was very respectable.
ANTHONY TROLLOPE: *North America*, I, 1862

If any one will take up the early colonial records of New England, he will be surprised and shocked at the amount of gross immorality which he will find recorded there. Rigidity of doctrine, the fulmination of the most terrific punishments in the future life, the passage and the execution of the most searching and definitive laws against every form of social vice, go hand in hand with every form of vice. There was adultery in high places and adultery in low.
J. G. HOLLAND: *Everyday Topics*, 1876

[*See also* Boston, Clergy, Sunday.

New Hampshire

The God who made New Hampshire
Taunted the lofty land
With little men.
R. W. EMERSON: *Ode Inscribed to W. H. Channing*, 1846

News

How beautiful upon the mountains are the feet of him that bringeth good tidings.
ISAIAH LII, 7, *c.* 700 B.C.

Tell it not in Gath, publish it not in the streets of Askelon; lest the daughters of the Philistines rejoice, lest the daughters of the uncircumcised triumph.
II SAMUEL I, 20, *c.* 500 B.C.

It is the greatest pleasure of the Athenians to wander through the streets asking, What is the news?
DEMOSTHENES: *First Philippic*, 351 B.C.

As cold waters to a thirsty soul, so is good news from a far country.
PROVERBS XXV, 25, *c.* 350 B.C.

Those who wish to tell us good news usually make some fictitious addition, that their news may give us the more joy.
CICERO: *Orationes Philippicæ*, I, *c.* 60 B.C.

Evil news never comes too late.
EDWARD HELLOWES: Tr. of ANTONIO DE GUEVARA: *Familiar Letters*, 1574

Evil news fly faster than good.
THOMAS KYD: *The Spanish Tragedy*, I, 1592

Master, master! news, old news, and such news as you never heard of!
SHAKESPEARE: *The Taming of the Shrew*, III, 1594

News fitting to the night,
Black, fearful, comfortless and horrible.
SHAKESPEARE: *King John*, V, *c.* 1596

There's villainous news abroad.
SHAKESPEARE: *I Henry IV*, II, *c.* 1598

Tidings do I bring, and lucky joys,
And golden times, and happy news of price.
SHAKESPEARE: *II Henry IV*, V, *c.* 1598

No news is good news.
ENGLISH PROVERB, borrowed from the Italian and familiar since the XVII century

With his mouth full of news
Which he will put on us, as pigeons feed their young.
SHAKESPEARE: *As You Like It*, I, *c.* 1600

What's the news?
SHAKESPEARE: *Hamlet*, II, *c.* 1601

Ill news hath wings, and with the wind doth go.
MICHAEL DRAYTON: *The Barons' Wars*, II, 1603

The nature of bad news infects the teller.
SHAKESPEARE: *Antony and Cleopatra*, I, *c.* 1606

Though it be honest, it is never good
To bring bad news; give to a gracious message
An host of tongues; but let ill tidings tell
Themselves.
SHAKESPEARE: *Antony and Cleopatra*, II

Pour out the pack of matter to mine ear,
The good and bad together. IBID.

This news which is called true is so like an old tale that the verity of it is in strong suspicion.
SHAKESPEARE: *The Winter's Tale*, V, *c.* 1611

He knocks boldly at the gate that brings good news.
JOHN WOODROEPHE: *Spared Hours*, 1623

News of doubtful credit, as barbers' news,
And tailors' news, porters', and watermen's news.
BEN JONSON: *The Staple of News*, 1625

Ill news
Are swallow-winged, but what's good
Walks on crutches.
PHILIP MASSINGER: *The Picture*, II, 1630

Good news may be told at any time, but ill in the morning.
GEORGE HERBERT: *Outlandish Proverbs*, 1640

Let the greatest part of the news thou hearest be the least part of what thou believest, lest the greater part of what thou believest be the least part of what is true.
FRANCIS QUARLES: *Enchyridion*, II, 1640

Queen Anne [or Queen Elizabeth] is dead.
Reply to an inquiry for news, signifying that there is none not stale; both forms appear to date from *c.* 1720 (There are various American cognates, e.g., "Bryan has carried Texas")

He was scarce of news that told his father was hanged.
JAMES KELLY: *Complete Collection of Scottish Proverbs,* 1721

Or to some coffee-house I stray
For news — the manna of the day.
MATTHEW GREEN: *The Spleen,* 1737

In a time of war the nation is always of one mind, eager to hear something good of themselves, and ill of the enemy. At this time the task of news-writers is easy; they have nothing to do but to tell that the battle is expected, and afterwards that a battle has been fought, in which we and our friends, whether conquering or conquered, did all, and our enemies did nothing.
SAMUEL JOHNSON: *The Idler,* Nov. 11, 1758

When we hear news we should always wait for the sacrament of confirmation.
VOLTAIRE: *Letter to the Count d'Argental,* Aug. 28, 1760

Whate'er the busy bustling world employs
Our wants and wishes, pleasure, cares, and joys,
These the historians of our times display,
And call it news — the hodge-podge of a day.
BONNELL THORNTON: *The Battle of the Whigs,* 1767

What news? what news? your tidings tell;
Tell me you must and shall —
Say why bareheaded you are come,
Or why you come at all?
WILLIAM COWPER: *John Gilpin,* 1783

I sing of news, and all those vapid sheets
The rattling hawker vends through gaping streets.
GEORGE CRABBE: *The Newspaper,* 1785

The times are big with tidings.
ROBERT SOUTHEY: *Roderick,* xx, 1814

It is not an event, it is only a piece of news.
C. M. TALLEYRAND: On hearing of the death of Napoleon I, 1821

The news, indeed! Pray do you call it news
When shallow noddles publish shallow views?
J. G. SAXE: *The Press,* 1855

We rarely meet a man who can tell us any news which he has not read in a newspaper, or been told by his neighbor; and, for the most part, the only difference between us and our fellow is that he has seen the newspaper, or been out to tea, and we have not.
H. D. THOREAU: *Cape Cod,* 1865

What, what, what,
What's the news from Swat?
Sad news,
Bad news,
Comes by the cable; led
Through the Indian Ocean's bed,
Through the Persian Gulf, the Red
Sea, and the Med-
Iterranean — he's dead;
The Akhoond is dead.
G. T. LANIGAN: *A Threnody,* 1878

If a man bites a dog, that is news.
Ascribed to JOHN BOGART, city editor of the New York Sun, *c.* 1880 (Sometimes the saying appears as "If a dog bites a man it's a story; if a man bites a dog it's a good story." In this form it is commonly ascribed to CHARLES A. DANA, editor of the Sun from 1868 to 1897)

All the news that's fit to print.
MOTTO OF THE NEW YORK TIMES, first printed Oct. 25, 1896

Bad news comes upon the back of worse.
SCOTTISH PROVERB

[*See also* Bird, Bulletin, Journalism, Late, Literature, Newspaper.

Newspaper

A newspaper makes the multitude too familiar with the actions and councils of their superiors and gives them not only an itch but a kind of colorable right and license to be meddling with the government.
ROGER L'ESTRANGE: On taking office as Licenser of the Press, London, May, 1680

Every newspaper editor pays tribute to the Devil.
JEAN DE LA FONTAINE: *Letter to Simon de Troyes,* 1686

It is designed that the country shall be furnished once a month (or, if any glut of occurrences happen, oftener) with an account of such considerable things as have arrived unto our notice.
BENJAMIN HARRIS: *Salutatory of Publick Occurances,* Boston, Sept. 25, 1690

A newspaper consists of just the same number of words, whether there be any news in it or not. HENRY FIELDING: *Tom Jones,* II, 1749

However little some may think of common newspapers, to a wise man they appear the ark of God for the safety of the people.
Anon.: *In the Pennsylvania Gazette,* Jan. 7, 1768

The mass of every people must be barbarous where there is no printing, and consequently knowledge is not generally diffused. Knowledge is diffused among our people by the newspapers.
SAMUEL JOHNSON: *Boswell's Life,* March 31, 1772

The newspapers! Sir, they are the most villainous — licentious — abominable — infernal — not that I ever read them — no — I make it a rule never to look into a newspaper.
R. B. SHERIDAN: *The Critic,* I, 1779

The more of these instructors a man reads, the less he will infallibly understand.

GEORGE CRABBE: *The Newspaper*, pref., 1785

Like baneful herbs the gazer's eye they seize,
Rush to the head, and poison where they please:
Like idle flies, a busy, buzzing train,
They drop their maggots in the trifler's brain:
That genial soil receives the fruitful store,
And there they grow, and breed a thousand more.

IBID.

A newspaper, conducted on the true and natural principles of such a publication, ought to be the register of the times, and faithful recorder of every species of intelligence. It ought not to be engrossed by any particular object, but, like a well-covered table, it should contain something suited to every palate.

JOHN WALKER: *Salutatory of the London Daily Universal Register*, Jan. 1, 1785 (It became the Times Jan. 1, 1788)

There are morning papers for breakfast; there are evening papers for supper, — I beg pardon, I mean dinner; and, lest, during the interval, wind should get into the stomach, there is a paper published, by way of luncheon, about noon.

GEORGE HORNE (BISHOP OF NORWICH): *Pamphlet*, 1787

Were it left to me to decide whether we should have a government without newspapers or newspapers without government, I should not hesitate a moment to prefer the latter.

THOMAS JEFFERSON: *Letter to Edward Carrington*, Jan. 16, 1787

At a very early period of my life, I determined never to put a sentence into any newspaper. I have religiously adhered to the resolution through my life, and have great reason to be contented with it.

THOMAS JEFFERSON: *Letter to Samuel Smith*, 1798

The printers can never leave us in a state of perfect rest and union of opinion. They would be no longer useful and would have to go to the plow.

THOMAS JEFFERSON: *Letter to Elbridge Gerry*, March, 1801

The design of this paper is to diffuse among the people correct information on all interesting subjects, to inculcate just principles in religion, morals and politics, and to cultivate a taste for sound literature.

Anon.: *Salutatory of the New York Evening Post*, Nov. 15, 1801

Newspapers serve to carry off noxious vapors and smoke.

THOMAS JEFFERSON: *Letter to Tadeusz Kosciusko*, April, 1802

Here shall the press the people's right maintain,
Unawed by influence and unbribed by gain;
Here patriot truth her glorious precepts draw,
Pledged to religion, liberty, and law.

JOSEPH STORY: *Motto of the Salem (Mass.) Register*, 1802

The man who never looks into a newspaper is better informed than he who reads them, inasmuch as he who knows nothing is nearer to truth than he whose mind is filled with falsehoods and errors.

THOMAS JEFFERSON: *Letter to John Norvell*, 1807

Nothing can now be believed which is seen in a newspaper.

IBID.

I read but one newspaper and that . . . more for its advertisements than its news.

THOMAS JEFFERSON: *Letter to Charles Pinckney*, 1820

Newspapers always excite curiosity. No one ever lays one down without a feeling of disappointment.

CHARLES LAMB: *Detached Thoughts on Books and Reading*, 1822 (London Magazine, July)

Think how the joys of reading a gazette
Are purchased by all agonies and crimes;
Or if these do not move you, don't forget
Such doom may be your own in after-times.

BYRON: *The Vision of Judgment*, 1823

What is to prevent a daily newspaper from being made the greatest organ of social life? Books have had their day — the theatres have had their day — the temple of religion has had its day. A newspaper can be made to take the lead of all these in the great movements of human thought and of human civilization.

JAMES GORDON BENNETT: *Editorial in the New York Herald*, Aug. 19, 1836

Of the British newspaper press, perhaps the most important of all, and wonderful enough in its secret constitution and procedure, a valuable, descriptive history already exists under the title of "Satan's Invisible World Displayed."

THOMAS CARLYLE: *Sartor Resartus*, I, 1836

Light for all.

MOTTO OF THE BALTIMORE SUN, May 17, 1837

Discreet and observing men have questioned whether, after excluding the notices of deaths and marriages, one half of the circumstances that are related in the newspapers of America as facts are true in their essential features; and, in cases connected with party politics, it may be questioned if even so large a proportion can be set down as accurate.

J. FENIMORE COOPER: *The American Democrat*, XXVII, 1838

I hate to be defended in a newspaper. As long as all that is said, is said against me, I feel a certain assurance of success. But as soon as honeyed words of praise are spoken for me, I feel as one that lies unprotected before his enemies.
R. W. EMERSON: *Compensation,* 1841

There she is — the great engine — she never sleeps. She has her ambassadors in every quarter of the world — her courtiers upon every road. Her officers march along with armies, and her envoys walk into statesmen's cabinets.
W. M. THACKERAY: *Pendennis,* I, 1849

We do not interfere with the duties of statesmen; our vocation is, in one respect, inferior to theirs, for we are unable to wield the power or represent the collective dignity of the country, but in another point of view it is superior, for unlike them, we are able to speak the whole truth without fear or favor.
ROBERT LOWE: *Editorial in the London Times,* Feb. 7, 1852

A newspaper untrammeled by sinister influence from any quarter — the advocate of the right and denouncer of the wrong — an independent vehicle for the free expression of opinions of all candid, honest and intelligent minds — a medium for free discussion, moral, religious, social and scientific.
THOMAS GIBSON: *Salutatory of the Rocky Mountain Herald (Denver, Colo.),* May 1, 1860

I know nothing but what is in the papers.
JOHN BRIGHT: *Letter to Charles Sumner,* Dec., 1861 (Cf. ROGERS, *post, c.* 1928)

Can it be maintained that a person of any education can learn anything worth knowing from a penny paper? It may be said that people may learn what is said in Parliament. Well, will that contribute to their education?
THE MARQUIS OF SALISBURY: Speech in the House of Commons, 1861

It is a newspaper's duty to print the news, and raise hell.
WILBUR F. STOREY: Statement of the aims of the Chicago Times, of which he was editor, 1861

Our papers don't purtend to print o'ny wut guv'ment choose,
An' thet insures us all to git the very best o' noose.
J. R. LOWELL: *The Biglow Papers,* II, 1862

The average consumption of newspapers by an American must amount to about three a day.
ANTHONY TROLLOPE: *North America,* I, 1862

If a man makes money by publishing a newspaper, by poisoning the wells of information, by feeding the people a daily spiritual death, he is the greatest criminal I can conceive.
FERDINAND LASSALLE: Speech in Düsseldorf, Sept. 28, 1863

Not more than two newspapers will be published in Savannah; their editors and proprietors will be held to the strictest accountability, and will be punished severely, in person and property, for any libelous publication, mischievous matter, premature news, exaggerated statements, or any comments whatever upon the acts of the constituted authorities.
W. T. SHERMAN: Special Field Order on occupying Savannah, Dec. 26, 1864

I do not know but it is too much to read one newspaper a week. I have tried it recently, and for so long it seems to me that I have not dwelt in my native region.
H. D. THOREAU: *Cape Cod,* 1865

An institution that should always fight for progress and reform, never tolerate injustice or corruption, always fight demagogues of all parties, never belong to any party, always oppose privileged classes and public plunderers, never lack sympathy with the poor, always remain devoted to the public welfare, never be satisfied with merely printing news, always be drastically independent, never be afraid to attack wrong, whether by predatory plutocracy or predatory poverty.
JOSEPH PULITZER: *Salutatory of the New York World,* May 10, 1883

When "we" come out and praise or blame, I do not care a bit for "we"; for I have seen the "we's" and found them much the same as myself.
CHARLES G. GORDON: *Journal,* Sept. 19, 1884

Newspapers have degenerated. They may now be absolutely relied upon.
OSCAR WILDE: *The Decay of Lying,* 1889

It will be my earnest aim that the New York Times give the news, all the news, in concise and attractive form, in language that is permissible in good society, and give it early, if not earlier, than it can be learned through any other medium. To give the news impartially, without fear or favor, regardless of party, sect, or interest involved; to make the columns of the New York Times a forum for the consideration of all public questions of public importance, and, to that end, to invite intelligent discussion from all shades of opinion.
ADOLPH S. OCHS: *Salutatory on assuming control of the New York Times,* Aug. 18, 1896

There are only two forces that can carry light to all corners of the globe — the sun in the heavens and the Associated Press.
S. L. CLEMENS (MARK TWAIN): Speech in New York, Sept. 19, 1906

I know that my retirement will make no difference in its cardinal principles; that it will always fight for progress and reform; never tolerate injustice or corruption; always fight demagogues of all parties; never belong to any party; always oppose privileged classes and public plunderers; never lack sympathy with the poor; always remain devoted to the public welfare; never be satisfied with merely printing news; always be drastically independent; never be afraid to attack wrong whether by predatory plutocracy or predatory poverty.

JOSEPH PULITZER: On his retirement as publisher of the St. Louis Dispatch, April 10, 1907 (In March, 1932, the St. Louis Post-Dispatch applied for the registration of this statement as a trade-mark, but the application was refused by the Patent Office, July 28, 1932. Cf. PULITZER, *ante*, 1883)

Newspapers are read at the breakfast and dinner tables. God's great gift to man is appetite. Put nothing in the paper that will destroy it.

W. R. NELSON, publisher of the Kansas City Star (1841–1915)

A newspaper is a private enterprise, owing nothing to the public, which grants it no franchise. It is therefore affected with no public interest. It is emphatically the property of its owner, who is selling a manufactured product at his own risk.

Anon.: Editorial in the Wall Street Journal, Jan. 20, 1925

The newspaper is of necessity something of a monopoly, and its first duty is to shun the temptations of monopoly. Its primary office is the gathering of news. At the peril of its soul it must see that the supply is not tainted. Neither in what it gives, nor in what it does not give, nor in the mode of presentation, must the unclouded face of truth suffer wrong. Comment is free but facts are sacred.

C. P. SCOTT: In the Manchester Guardian, May 6, 1926

All I know is what I see in the papers.

WILL ROGERS: Often repeated in his speeches and newspaper articles, *c.* 1928 (Cf. BRIGHT, *ante*, 1861)

The probabilities are all against what one reads in the newspapers. If it is a subject you happen to know something about yourself you always find the papers are wrong.

LORD JUSTICE OF APPEAL GREER: *Obiter dictum*, 1932

The American newspaper today is one of the chief enemies of the Kingdom of God.

Resolution of the Northwest Conference of the Methodist Episcopal Church, Lafayette, Ind., June 24, 1933

There has never lived, and there never will be born, a man wise enough and good enough to be entrusted with the irresponsible power over human thought, and the action which follows thought, which ownership of many newspapers conveys in the modern world, and the freedom to exercise it in the service of his own interests. To say that his interests might also be those of the community is to say something which might periodically be true, but cannot be generally true. It is to forget human pride and human weakness, and to break with history.

WILMOTT LEWIS: Speech in New York, April 20, 1936

The duty of a newspaper is to comfort the afflicted and afflict the comfortable.

Author unidentified

The function of a newspaper is to make the ignorant more ignorant and the crazy crazier.

IBID.

[*See also* Duty, Editor, Journalism, Journalist, London Times, News, Press.

Newton, Isaac (1642–1727)

I do not know what I may appear to the world; but to myself I seem to have been only like a boy playing on the seashore, and diverting myself in now and then finding a smoother pebble or a prettier shell than ordinary, whilst the great ocean of truth lay all undiscovered before me.

ISAAC NEWTON: Quoted in DAVID BREWSTER: *Memoirs of the Life, Writings & Discoveries of Sir Isaac Newton*, II, 1828, *c.* 1725

Nature and nature's laws lay hid in night:
God said, Let Newton be! and all was light.

ALEXANDER POPE: Epitaph for Newton in Westminster Abbey, 1730

And Newton, something more than man,
Div'd into nature's hidden springs,
Laid bare the principles of things,
Above the earth our spirits bore,
And gave us worlds unknown before.

CHARLES CHURCHILL: *The Ghost*, II, 1763

I am persuaded that, had Sir Isaac Newton applied to poetry, he would have made a very fine epic poem.

SAMUEL JOHNSON: *Boswell's Tour to the Hebrides*, Aug. 15, 1773

Patient of contradiction as a child,
Affable, humble, diffident, and mild,
Such was Sir Isaac.

WILLIAM COWPER: *The Progress of Error*, 1782

I should like to know if any man could have laughed if he had seen Sir Isaac Newton rolling in the mud?

SYDNEY SMITH: *Lectures on Wit and Humor*, I, 1805

The statue stood
Of Newton, with his prism and silent face,
The marble index of a mind forever
Voyaging through strange seas of thought alone.

WILLIAM WORDSWORTH: *The Prelude*, III, 1805

Newton was a great man, but you must excuse me if I think that it would take many Newtons to make one Milton.
S. T. COLERIDGE: *Table-Talk,* July 4, 1833

[*See also* Absence, Dryden (John), Greatness, Intelligence, Kepler (Johann).

New Year

No one ever regarded the first of January with indifference. It is the nativity of our common Adam.
CHARLES LAMB: *New Year's Eve,* 1821 (London Magazine, Jan.)

Ring out the old, ring in the new,
Ring, happy bells, across the snow;
The year is going, let him go;
Ring out the false, ring in the true.
ALFRED TENNYSON: *In Memoriam,* CVI, 1850

The roads are very dirty, my boots are very thin,
I have a little pocket to put a penny in.
God send you happy, God send you happy,
Pray God send you a happy New-Year!
Old English carol

New York

The inhabitants are in general brisk and lively, kind to strangers, dress very gay; the fair sex are in general handsome, and said to be very obliging.
PATRICK M'ROBERTS: *Tour Through Part of the North Provinces of America,* I, 1775

The renowned and ancient city of Gotham.
WASHINGTON IRVING: *Salmagundi,* Nov. 11, 1807

New York, like London, seems to be a cloacina of all the depravities of human nature.
THOMAS JEFFERSON: *Letter to William Short,* 1823

Speaking of New York as a traveler, I have two faults to find with it. In the first place, there is nothing to see; and, in the second place, there is no mode of getting about to see anything.
ANTHONY TROLLOPE: *North America,* I, 1862

You cannot imagine what an infatuation church-going has become in New York. Youths and young misses, young gentlemen and ladies, the middle-aged and the old, all swarm to church, morning, noon and night, every Sunday.
S. L. CLEMENS (MARK TWAIN): *Letter from New York to the Alta Californian* (San Francisco), Feb. 18, 1867

The posthumous revenge of the Merchant of Venice.
ELBERT HUBBARD: *Roycroft Dictionary and Book of Epigrams,* 1923

I like to visit New York, but I wouldn't live there if you gave it to me.
AMERICAN SAYING

[*See also* America, City.

Ney, Michel (1769–1815)

Ney was a hero, but he had a weak head.
NAPOLEON I: *Diary of Pulteney Malcolm at St. Helena,* Jan. 11, 1817

Niagara

You can descend a staircase a hundred and fifty feet down, and stand at the edge of the water. After you have done it you will wonder why you did it; but you will then be too late.
S. L. CLEMENS (MARK TWAIN): *Niagara,* 1875

Talk about your Vesuve! Niag'll put her out in three minutes.
Ascribed to an unnamed American by S. S. COX: *Why We Laugh,* IV, 1876

When I first saw the falls I was disappointed in the outline. Every American bride is taken there, and the sight must be one of the earliest, if not the keenest, disappointments in American married life.
OSCAR WILDE: Press interview in New York, 1882

[*See also* Change, Swapping.

Nice

As nice as a nun's hen.
JOHN HEYWOOD: *Proverbs,* 1546

More nice than wise.
BARNABE RICH: *Rich His Farewell,* 1581

A nice man is a man of nasty ideas.
JONATHAN SWIFT: *Thoughts on Various Subjects,* 1706

Nicety

The niceties of the law are not the law. (Apices juris non sunt jura.)
LEGAL MAXIM

Nickname

Excellent Beaumont, in the foremost rank
Of the rarest wits, was never more than Frank.
Mellifluous Shakespeare, whose enchanting quill
Commanded mirth or passion, was but Will,
And famous Jonson, though his learned pen
Be dipped in Castaly, is still but Ben.
THOMAS HEYWOOD: *The Hierarchie of the Blessed Angels,* 1635 (*Castaly*=a spring on Mt. Parnassus)

A nickname is the hardest stone that the Devil can throw at a man.
WILLIAM HAZLITT: *On Nicknames,* 1821

Nicknames and whippings, when they are once laid on, no one has discovered how to take off.
W. S. LANDOR: *Imaginary Conversations,* I, 1824

To the last he called me Charley. I have none to call me Charley now.
CHARLES LAMB: On the death of Randall Norris, Jan., 1826

It is not a good thing to be Tom'd or Bob'd, Jack'd or Jim'd, Sam'd or Ben'd, Neddy'd or Teddy'd, Will'd or Bill'd, Dick'd or Nick'd, Joe'd or Jerry'd as you go through the world.
ROBERT SOUTHEY: *The Doctor,* 1834

Of all eloquence a nickname is the most concise and irresistible. It is a terse, pointed, shorthand mode of reasoning, condensing a volume of meaning into an epithet.
WILLIAM MATHEWS: *Words: Their Use and Abuse,* XII, 1876

The propensity to approach a meaning not directly and squarely, but by circuitous styles of expression, seems a born quality of the common people everywhere, evidenced by nicknames.
WALT WHITMAN: *Slang in America,* 1885

If a man has no nickname he never grows rich.
CHINESE PROVERB

[*See also* Friend, Title.

Nietzsche, F. W. (1844–1900)

I read constantly my crazy friend Nietzsche. I squeeze him, I turn him inside out, press him and turn him upside down, I knead him this way and that, so he now gets one face, now another. I am fond of Nietzsche. Here is this one great man that Germany has, and nobody values him in Germany, hardly anybody knows him.
GEORG BRANDES: *Note, c.* 1872

I am the Anti-Donkey *par excellence,* a monster in the history of the world. I am, in Greek, and not only in Greek, the Antichrist.
F. W. NIETZSCHE: *Ecce Homo,* 1888

An agile but unintelligent and abnormal German, possessed of the mania of grandeur.
LYOF N. TOLSTOY: *What Is Religion?,* 1902

The greatest European event since Goethe.
A. R. ORAGE: *Friedrich Nietzsche,* 1905

Night

Now the night comes — and it is wise to obey the night.
HOMER: *Iliad,* VII, *c.* 800 B.C.

Watchman, what of the night?
ISAIAH XXI, 11, *c.* 700 B.C.

Never greet a stranger in the night, for he may be a demon.
THE TALMUD (*Sanhedrin*), *c.* 200 B.C.

The night cometh, when no man can work.
JOHN IX, 4, *c.* 115

Is not the night mournful, sad and melancholy?
RABELAIS: *Gargantua,* I, 1535

Night is the mother of thoughts.
JOHN FLORIO: *First Frutes,* 1578

O comfort-killing night, image of Hell;
Dim register and notary of shame;
Black stage for tragedies and murders fell;
Vast sin-concealing chaos, nurse of blame.
SHAKESPEARE: *The Rape of Lucrece,* 1594

Come, gentle night, come, loving, black-brow'd night.
SHAKESPEARE: *Romeo and Juliet,* III, *c.* 1596

Now the hungry lion roars
And the wolf howls the moon.
SHAKESPEARE: *A Midsummer Night's Dream,* V, *c.* 1596

Come, come, dear night, love's mart of kisses,
Sweet close of his ambitious line,
The fruitful Summer of his blisses;
Love's glory doth in darkness shine.
CHRISTOPHER MARLOWE and GEORGE CHAPMAN: *Hero and Leander,* 1598

In the dead vast and middle of the night.
SHAKESPEARE: *Hamlet,* I, *c.* 1601

Come, seeling night,
Scarf up the tender eye of pitiful day;
And with thy bloody and invisible hand,
Cancel and tear to pieces that great bond
Which keeps me pale.
SHAKESPEARE: *Macbeth,* III, *c.* 1605
(*Seel*=to close the eyes)

Stay, gentle night, and with thy darkness cover
The kisses of her lover;
Stay, and confound her tears and her shrill cryings,
Her weak denials, vows, and often-dyings;
Stay, and hide all;
But help not, though she call.
BEAUMONT and FLETCHER: *The Maid's Tragedy,* I, 1611

When night
Darkens the streets, then wander forth the sons
Of Belial, flown with insolence and wine.
JOHN MILTON: *Paradise Lost,* I, 1667

The night has a more melancholy air than the day; the stars seem to march more silently than the sun, and our thoughts wander freely because we fancy all the world at rest but ourselves.
BERNARD DE FONTENELLE: *Entretiens sur la pluralité des mondes,* I, 1686

Ralph to Cynthia howls
And makes night hideous.
ALEXANDER POPE: *The Dunciad,* III, 1728

The night look'd black, and boding darkness fell
Precipitate and heavy o'er the world.
DAVID MALLET: *Mustapha,* 1739

Night, sable goddess! from her ebon throne,
In rayless majesty, now stretches forth
Her leaden sceptre o'er a slumbering world.
EDWARD YOUNG: *Night Thoughts,* I, 1742

The curfew tolls the knell of parting day,
The lowing herd winds slowly o'er the lea,

The ploughman homeward plods his weary way,
And leaves the world to darkness and to me.
THOMAS GRAY: *Elegy Written in a Country Churchyard,* 1750

When the sheep are in the fauld, and a' the kye at hame,
And all the weary world to sleep are gane.
ANNE LINDSAY: *Auld Robin Gray,* 1771

Night is the half of life, and the better half.
J. W. GOETHE: *Wilhelm Meisters Lehrjahre,* v, 1795

How beautiful the night!
A dewy freshness fills the silent air;
No mist obscures, nor cloud, nor speck, nor stain,
Breaks the serene of Heaven:
In full-orb'd glory, yonder moon divine
Rolls through the dark-blue depths;
Beneath her steady ray
The desert circle spreads,
Like the round ocean, girdled with the sky.
How beautiful the night!
ROBERT SOUTHEY: *Thalaba,* 1801

Heaven's ebon vault,
Studded with stars unutterably bright,
Through which the moon's unclouded grandeur rolls,
Seems like a canopy which love had spread
To curtain her sleeping world.
P. B. SHELLEY: *Queen Mab,* III, 1813

How beautiful this night! the balmiest sigh
Which vernal zephyrs breathe in evening's ear
Were discord to the speaking quietude
That wraps this moveless scene.
P. B. SHELLEY: *Queen Mab,* IV

Oft, in the stilly night,
Ere slumber's chain has bound me,
Fond memory brings the light
Of other days around me.
THOMAS MOORE: *Oft in the Stilly Night,* c. 1815

Most glorious night!
Thou wert not sent for slumber!
BYRON: *Childe Harold,* III, 1816

O night
And storm and darkness, ye are wondrous strong,
Yet lovely in your strength, as is the light
Of a dark eye in woman. IBID.

Night makes a weird sound of its own stillness.
P. B. SHELLEY: *Alastor,* 1816

The night
Hath been to me a more familiar face
Than that of man; and in her starry shade
Of dim and solitary loveliness
I learn'd the languages of another world.
BYRON: *Manfred,* III, 1817

The night
Shows stars and women in a better light.
BYRON: *Don Juan,* II, 1819

When the sun sinks hissing in the sea, and the night rises with her great passionate eyes, oh! then true pleasure first thrills through me, the breezes lie like flattering maidens on my wild heart, and the stars wink to me, and I rise and sweep over the little earth and the little thoughts of men.
HEINRICH HEINE: *Reisebilder,* II, 1826

Night is the time to weep,
To wet with unseen tears
Those graves of memory where sleep
The joys of other years.
JAMES MONTGOMERY: *The Issues of Life and Death,* c. 1830

The night is dark, and I am far from home.
J. H. NEWMAN: *Lead, Kindly Light,* 1833

I heard the trailing garments of the night
Sweep through her marble halls.
H. W. LONGFELLOW: *Hymn to the Night,* 1841

O holy night! from thee I learn to bear
What man has borne before!
Thou layest thy fingers on the lips of care,
And they complain no more. IBID.

Night slid down one long stream of sighing wind,
And in her bosom bore the baby, sleep.
ALFRED TENNYSON: *The Gardener's Daughter,* 1842

The day is done, and the darkness
Falls from the wings of night,
As a feather is wafted downward
From an eagle in his flight.
H. W. LONGFELLOW: *The Day Is Done,* 1845

And the night shall be filled with music,
And the cares that infest the day
Shall fold their tents like the Arabs,
And as silently steal away. IBID.

Press close, bare-bosom'd night — press close, magnetic nourishing night —
Night of South winds — night of the large few stars.
WALT WHITMAN: *Song of Myself,* 1855

The nearer the dawn the darker the night.
H. W. LONGFELLOW: *Tales of a Wayside Inn,* 1863

The huge and thoughtful night.
WALT WHITMAN: *When Lilacs Last in the Dooryard Bloom'd,* 1865

A murmuring, soft, immeasurable night.
ELIZABETH CHASE (AKERS ALLEN): *The Dream,* 1866

Those long, dreary hours in the twenty-four when the shadow of death is darkest, when despondency is strongest, and when hope is weakest.
CHARLES DICKENS: Speech in London, Feb. 14, 1866

The multitudinous menace of the night.
GEORGE CABOT LODGE: *The Soul's Inheritance,* 1910

The night is no man's friend.
GERMAN PROVERB

In the night there is counsel. (In nocte consilium.)
LATIN PROVERB

[*See also* Dark, Dawn, Day, Day and Night, Evening, Fear, Garden, Memory, Midnight, Morning, Ship, Star, Sunset, Twilight.

Nightingale

What bird so sings, yet so does wail?
Oh, 'tis the ravish'd nightingale.
JOHN LYLY: *Spring's Welcome,* 1584

The nightingale, if she should sing by day,
When every goose is cackling, would be thought
No better a musician than the wren.
SHAKESPEARE: *The Merchant of Venice,* V, *c.* 1597

A nightingale dies for shame if another bird sings better.
ROBERT BURTON: *The Anatomy of Melancholy,* I, 1621

I have heard the nightingale in all its perfection, and I do not hesitate to pronounce that in America it would be deemed a bird of the third rank only, our mocking-bird, and fox-colored thrush being unquestionably superior to it.
THOMAS JEFFERSON: *Letter to Mrs. John Adams,* 1785

I have heard friendly sounds from many a tongue
Which was not human — the lone nightingale
Has answered me with her most soothing song
Out of her ivy bower, when I sate pale
With grief, and sighed beneath.
P. B. SHELLEY: *The Revolt of Islam,* X, 1818

Thou wast not born for death, immortal bird!
No hungry generations tread thee down;
The voice I hear this passing night was heard
In ancient days by emperor and clown:
Perhaps the self-same song that found a path
Through the sad heart of Ruth, when, sick for home,
She stood in tears amid the alien corn;
The same that oft-times hath
Charm'd magic casements, opening on the foam
Of perilous seas, in faery lands forlorn.
JOHN KEATS: *Ode to a Nightingale,* 1819

[*See also* Imitation.

Night-life

A gay night-life [Nachtleben] has the effect on looks and complexion of a long spell of sickness.
JEAN PAUL RICHTER: *Hesperus,* XVI, 1795

Nightmare

Her lips were red, her looks were free,
Her locks were yellow as gold,
Her skin was as white as leprosy,
The nightmare Life-in-Death was she,
Who thicks man's blood with cold.
S. T. COLERIDGE: *The Ancient Mariner,* 1798

I confess an occasional nightmare; but I do not, as in early youth, keep a stud of them.
CHARLES LAMB: *Witches and Other Night-Fears,* 1821 (London Magazine, Oct.)

Nihilism

Our first work must be the annihilation of everything as it now exists. The old world must be destroyed and replaced by a new one. When you have freed your mind from the fear of God, and that childish respect for the fiction of right, then all the remaining chains that bind you — property, marriage, morality, and justice — will snap asunder like threads.
MIKHAIL BAKUNIN: *Dieu et l'état,* 1871

Oh, that is all one! (Ach, das ist ja alles eins!)
JOSEF SKODA, *c.* 1850 (This was Skoda's reply when, after establishing a diagnosis, he was asked about the treatment of the patient. F. H. GARRISON: *History of Medicine,* says that he "was the leading clinician of the New Vienna School and the exponent of its therapeutic nihilism")

A nihilist is a man who bows down to no authority, and takes no principle on faith.
I. S. TURGENEV: *Fathers and Sons,* V, 1862

The nihilist, that strange martyr who has no faith, who goes to the stake without enthusiasm, and dies for what he does not believe in, is a purely literary product. He was invented by Turgenev, and completed by Dostoyevsky.
OSCAR WILDE: *The Decay of Lying,* 1891

[*See also* Anarchist, Socialist.

Nile

We rejoiced when the Nile began to rise; it rose, and we were drowned.
ARAB PROVERB

Nimbleness

Jack be nimble,
Jack be quick,
Jack jump over
The candlestick.
Anon.: *Nursery rhyme, c.* 1750

No

Say nay, and take it.
JOHN HEYWOOD: *Two Hundred Epigrams,* 1555

No is no negative in a woman's mouth.
PHILIP SIDNEY: *Arcadia,* III, 1590

Maids, in modesty, say no to that
Which they would have the profferer construe aye.

SHAKESPEARE: *Two Gentlemen of Verona,* I, *c.* 1595

Have you not heard it said full oft,
A woman's nay doth stand for nought?

SHAKESPEARE (?): *The Passionate Pilgrim,* 1599

A gilded no is more satisfactory than a harsh yes.

BALTASAR GRACIÁN: *The Art of Worldly Wisdom,* LXX, 1647

Say aye no, and you'll never be married.

JAMES KELLY: *Complete Collection of Scottish Proverbs,* 1721

There is something wanting in the man who does not hate himself whenever he is constrained to say no.

R. L. STEVENSON: *Familiar Studies of Men and Books,* IV, 1882

Ten noes are better than one lie.

DANISH PROVERB

" No, thank you " has lost many a good butter-cake.

LANCASHIRE PROVERB

Between a woman's yea and no
There is not room for a pin to go.

OLD ENGLISH RHYME

[*See also* Asking, Coquetry, Lady.

Noah

(The story of Noah and his ark runs from GENESIS VI, 7 to IX, 29, *c.* 700 B.C.)

[*See also* Vineyard.

Nobility

True nobility is exempt from fear.

SHAKESPEARE: *II Henry VI,* IV, *c.* 1591

That which in mean men we entitle patience,
Is pale cold cowardice in noble breasts.

SHAKESPEARE: *Richard II,* I, *c.* 1596

This was the noblest Roman of them all.

SHAKESPEARE: *Julius Cæsar,* V, 1599

Sure my blood gives me I am noble, sure I am of noble kind; for I find myself possessed with all their qualities: love dogs, dice, and drabs, scorn wit in stuff-clothes; have beat my shoemaker, knock'd my seamstress, cuckold' my 'pothecary, and undone my tailor.

JOHN MARSTON: *The Malcontent,* III, 1604

It becomes noblemen to do nothing well.

GEORGE CHAPMAN: *The Gentleman Usher,* I, 1606

Nobility of birth commonly abateth industry.

FRANCIS BACON: *Essays,* XIV, 1612

Nobility is nothing but ancient riches.

JOHN RAY: *English Proverbs,* 1670

Her name was Margaret Lucas, youngest sister to the Lord Lucas of Colchester, a noble family: for all the brothers were valiant and all the sisters virtuous.

Epitaph on Margaret, Duchess of Newcastle, in Westminster Abbey, 1674

Send your noble blood to market and see what it will bring.

THOMAS FULLER: *Gnomologia,* 1732

What can ennoble sots, or slaves, or cowards?
Alas, not all the blood of all the Howards.

ALEXANDER POPE: *An Essay on Man,* IV, 1734

Noble blood is an accident of fortune; noble actions are the chief mark of greatness.

CARLO GOLDONI: *Pamela Nubile,* I, 1757

Those who think nobly are noble.

ISAAC BICKERSTAFF: *The Maid of the Mill,* II, 1765

Nobility is a graceful ornament to the civil order. It is the Corinthian capital of polished society.

EDMUND BURKE: *Reflections on the Revolution in France,* 1790

Nobility obliges. (Noblesse oblige.)

Author unidentified; not recorded before the XIX century

There is
One great society alone on earth:
The noble living and the noble dead.

WILLIAM WORDSWORTH: *The Prelude,* VI, 1805

We always think of a very noble character with a touch of quiet sadness.

ARTHUR SCHOPENHAUER: *The World as Will and Idea,* IV, 1819

Nobility is a dignity based on the presumption that we shall do well because our fathers did well.

JOSEPH JOUBERT: *Pensées,* 1842

Howe'er it be, it seems to me
'Tis only noble to be good.

ALFRED TENNYSON: *Lady Clara Vere de Vere,* 1842

All nobility in its beginnings was somebody's natural superiority.

R. W. EMERSON: *English Traits,* XI, 1856

It was not nobility that gave land, but the possession of land that gave nobility.

HENRY GEORGE: *Progress and Poverty,* VII, 1879

The noble soul has reverence for itself.

F. W. NIETZSCHE: *Beyond Good and Evil,* 1886

[*See also* Accident, Ancestry, Aristocracy, Birth (High), Blood, Gentleman, Heredity, Idleness, Motive, Peerage, Pole, Rank, Title.

Nod

[*See* Lord.

Noise

A noisy man is always in the right.
WILLIAM COWPER: *Conversation*, 1782

A little noiseless noise among the leaves,
Born of the very sigh that silence heaves.
JOHN KEATS: *I Stood Tiptoe Upon a Little Hill*, 1816

What is odious but noise, and people who scream and bewail?
R. W. EMERSON: *The Conduct of Life*, IV, 1860

A stench in the ear.
AMBROSE BIERCE: *The Devil's Dictionary*, 1906

Noise is any undesired sound. Noise is sound at the wrong time and in the wrong place.
N. W. MCLACHLAN: *Noise*, I, 1935

I do not like noise unless I make it myself.
FRENCH PROVERB

[*See also* Empty, Government, Happiness, Passé, Singing.

Non-Conformist

Whoso would be a man must be a nonconformist.
R. W. EMERSON: *Self-Reliance*, 1841

[*See also* Independence.

Nondescript

She is neither fish, nor flesh, nor good red herring. JOHN HEYWOOD: *Proverbs*, 1546

Nonentity

Is it not the chief disgrace in the world, not to be an unit; — not to be reckoned one character; — not to yield that peculiar fruit which each man was created to bear, but to be reckoned in the gross, in the hundred, or the thousand, of the party, the section, to which we belong; and our opinion predicated geographically, as the north, or the south?
R. W. EMERSON: *The American Scholar*, 1837

Better not be at all than be nothing.
CHINESE PROVERB

Non-resistance

He giveth his cheek to him that smiteth him.
LAMENTATIONS III, 30, *c.* 585 B.C.

Resist not evil; but whosoever shall smite thee on thy right cheek, turn to him the other also.
MATTHEW V, 39, *c.* 75 (Cf. LUKE VI, 29, *c.* 75)

Wisdom has taught us to be calm and meek,
To take one blow, and turn the other cheek;
It is not written what a man shall do,
If the rude caitiff smite the other too!
O. W. HOLMES: *Non-Resistance*, *c.* 1855

"Resist not evil" means "Do not resist the evil man," which means "Do no violence to another," which means "Commit no act that is contrary to love."
LYOF N. TOLSTOY: *What I Believe*, 1884
(The first quotation is from MATTHEW V, 39, *ante*, *c.* 75)

Nonsense

Mix a little folly with your wisdom; a little nonsense is pleasant now and then.
HORACE: *Carmina*, IV, *c.* 13 B.C.

No one escapes talking nonsense; the misfortune is to do it seriously.
MICHEL DE MONTAIGNE: *Essays*, III, 1588

As charms are nonsense, nonsense is a charm.
BENJAMIN FRANKLIN: *Poor Richard's Almanac*, 1734

A little nonsense now and then
Is relished by the wisest [or best of] men.
Author unidentified

[*See also* Credulity, Freedom, Poetry, Song, Speech (Free).

Noon

Childe Harold bask'd him in the noontide sun,
Disporting there like any other fly.
BYRON: *Childe Harold*, I, 1812

Now the noonday quiet holds the hill;
The grasshopper is silent in the grass;
The lizard, with his shadow on the stone,
Rests like a shadow, and the cicala sleeps.
ALFRED TENNYSON: *Oenone*, 1840

All at once,
With twelve great shocks of sound, the shameless noon
Was clash'd and hammer'd from a hundred towers. ALFRED TENNYSON: *Godiva*, 1842

Dinner-time for some folks, but just twelve o'clock for me. AMERICAN NEGRO SAYING

Normalcy

America's present need is not heroics but healing; not nostrums but normalcy.
W. G. HARDING: Speech at Boston, May 10, 1920

Norman

[*See* English, Englishman.

North

All evils come out of the North.
ENGLISH PROVERB, traced by Smith to 1598, and then described as "an old saying"

Three ills come from the North: a cold wind, a shrinking cloth, and a dissembling man.
JAMES HOWELL: *Proverbs*, 1659

Cold weather and knaves come out of the North. JOHN RAY: *English Proverbs,* 1670

Ask where's the North. At York it's on the Tweed;
In Scotland at the Orcades; and there
At Greenland, Zembia, or the Lord knows where.
ALEXANDER POPE: *An Essay on Man,* II, 1732

[*See also* Climate, Star, Weather.

North and South

Disguise the fact as you will, there is an enmity between the Northern and Southern people that is deep and enduring, and you never can eradicate it — never!
ALFRED IVERSON: Speech in the Senate, Dec. 5, 1860

[*See also* Union (American).

North Carolina

A strip of land lying between two states.
Ascribed to one STEWART, a Charleston, S. C., journalist, *c.* 1861

A valley of humiliation between two mountains of conceit. Author unidentified

First at Bethel, furthest at Gettysburg, and last at Appomattox. IBID.

Northcliffe, Lord (Alfred Harmsworth) (1865–1922)

If one could find in you some ultimate purpose, even some wholesome and honest hate, you would present a less pitiful spectacle to the world. You would at least be a reality. But you are nothing. In all this great and moving drama of humanity you represent no idea, no passion, no policy, no disinterested enthusiasm. . . . The democracy knows you as the poisoner of the streams of human intercourse, the fermenter of war, the preacher of hate, the unscrupulous enemy of human society.
A. G. GARDNER: *Open letter to Northcliffe,* Dec., 1914

Northwester

A strong nor'wester's blowing, Bill!
Hark! don't ye hear it roar now?
Lord help 'em, how I pities them
Unhappy folks on shore now!
Anon.: *The Sailor's Consolation, c.* 1800

Norwegian

[*See* Scandinavian.

Nose

The wringing of the nose bringeth forth blood.
PROVERBS XXX, 33, *c.* 350 B.C.

Thy nose is as the tower of Lebanon which looketh toward Damascus.
SOLOMON'S SONG VII, 4, *c.* 200 B.C.

Nose, nose, jolly red nose,
And who gave thee that jolly red nose?
Nutmegs and ginger, cinnamon and cloves;
And they gave me this jolly red nose.
BEAUMONT and FLETCHER: *The Knight of the Burning Pestle,* I, 1609

Better a snotty child than his nose wiped off.
GEORGE HERBERT: *Outlandish Proverbs,* 1640

If the nose of Cleopatra had been a little shorter the whole face of the world would have been changed.
BLAISE PASCAL: *Pensées,* VI, 1670

In cleaning the nose, the rules of cleanliness and decency should be exactly followed, always turning a little to one side, and making use of a handkerchief.
ST. JOHN BAPTIST DE LA SALLE: *The Rules of Christian Manners and Civility,* I, 1695

He that has a mickle nose thinks everybody is speaking of it.
JAMES KELLY: *Complete Collection of Scottish Proverbs,* 1721 (*Mickle*= large)

My nose itched, and I knew I should drink wine or kiss a fool.
JONATHAN SWIFT: *Polite Conversation,* 1738

His face, alas, has lost its red,
His cheeks their burning hue,
Ragged and warty is his nose,
But ah, that nose, how blue.
MASON L. WEEMS: *The Drunkard's Looking-Glass, c.* 1800

A gentleman with a pug nose is a contradiction in terms. E. A. POE: *Marginalia,* 1844–49

An inch in a man's nose is much.
H. G. BOHN: *Handbook of Proverbs,* 1855

Lightly was her slender nose
Tip-tilted like the petal of a flower.
ALFRED TENNYSON: *Gareth and Lynette,* 1872

A big nose never spoils a pretty face.
FRENCH PROVERB

If you have a vein across the nose
You'll never live to wear your wedding clothes.
OXFORDSHIRE RHYME

Scanty cheeks mak a lang nose.
SCOTTISH PROVERB

[*See also* Cold, Grindstone, Liszt (Franz), Mayhem, Snuff, Ugliness.

Nostalgia

From the lone shieling on the misty island
Mountains divide us and the waste of seas;
Yet still the blood is strong, the heart is Highland,
And we in dreams behold the Hebrides.
Anon.: *Canadian Boat Song,* 1829 (*Shieling*=a hut)

Oft, when the wine in his glass was red,
He longed for the wayside well instead,
And closed his eyes on his garnished rooms
To dream of meadows and clover-blooms.

J. G. WHITTIER: *Maud Muller,* 1854

[*See also* Homesickness.

Note

When found, make a note of.

CHARLES DICKENS: *Dombey and Son,* XV, 1848

Nothing

Having nothing and yet possessing all things.

II CORINTHIANS VI, 10, *c.* 55

From nothing nothing, and to nothing nothing. (De nihilo nihil, in nihilum nil.)

PERSIUS: *Satires,* I, *c.* 60

Where every something, being blent together
Turns to a wild of nothing.

SHAKESPEARE: *The Merchant of Venice,* III, *c.* 1597

All the ciphers of arithmetic are no better than a single nothing.

JOSEPH GLANVILL: *The Vanity of Dogmatizing,* XV, 1661

Blessed be he who expects nothing, for he shall never be disappointed.

ALEXANDER POPE: *Letter to John Gay,* Oct. 6, 1727 (Described as "a ninth beatitude")

That there should absolutely be nothing at all is utterly impossible. The mind, let it stretch its conceptions ever so far, can never so much as bring itself to conceive of a state of perfect nothing.

JONATHAN EDWARDS: *Notes on Natural Science, c.* 1718

An old nought
Will never be ought.

THOMAS FULLER: *Gnomologia,* 1732

Naught is never in danger. IBID.

A variety of nothing is better than a monotony of something.

JEAN PAUL RICHTER: *Levana,* V, 1807

I am of nothing and to nothing tend,
On earth I nothing have and nothing claim,
Man's noblest works must have one common end,
And nothing crown the tablet of his name.

THOMAS MOORE: *Ode Upon Nothing,* 1835

The little end of nothing whittled down to a point. AMERICAN PHRASE, *c.* 1850

Nothing to do but work,
Nothing to eat but food,
Nothing to wear but clothes,
To keep one from going nude.

BEN KING: *The Pessimist, c.* 1875

Nobody don't never get nothing for nothing, nowhere, no time, nohow.

AMERICAN PROVERB

A bunghole without a barrel around it.

Author unidentified

Nothing's new, and nothing's true, and nothing matters. IBID.

Nothing is good for the eye but bad for the stomach. DANISH PROVERB

Nothing can come from nothing. (Ex nihilo nihil fit.) LATIN PROVERB

I never seen nothin', I don't know nothin', I ain't got nothin', and I don't want nothin'.

Motto attributed (satirically) to Arkansas

[*See also* Ado, Nonentity.

Notoriety

As for being known much by sight, and pointed at, I can not comprehend the honor that lies in that. Whatsoever it be, every mountebank has it more than the best orator, and the hangman more than the Lord Chief Justice of a city.

ABRAHAM COWLEY: *Of Myself,* 1665

Out with you, liars that you are, tell the truth; say you would sell the souls you don't believe in, or do believe in, for notoriety.

GEORGE MOORE: *Confessions of a Young Man,* XII, 1888

[*See also* Fame.

Noun

What is a noun substantive? That that may be seen, felt, heard, or understood.

JOHN HARINGTON: *The Metamorphosis of Ajax,* 1596

[*See also* Adjective.

Novel

Novels are receipts to make a whore.

MATTHEW GREEN: *The Spleen,* 1737

The novel gives a familiar relation of such things as pass every day before our eyes, such as may happen to our friend or to ourselves; and the perfection of it is to represent every scene in so easy and natural a manner and to make them appear so probable as to deceive us into a persuasion (at least while we are reading) that all is real, until we are affected by the joys or distresses of the persons in the story as if they were our own.

CLARA REEVE: *The Progress of Romance,* 1785

Novels not regulated on the chaste principles of friendship, rational love, and connubial duty appear to me totally unfit to form the minds of women, of friends, of wives.

SARAH WENTWORTH MORTON (PHILENIA): *The Power of Sympathy,* pref., 1789 (This was the first American novel)

In writing novels and plays the cardinal rule is to treat one's characters as if they were

chessmen, and not try to win the game by altering the rules — for example, by moving the knight as if he were a pawn.
G. C. LICHTENBERG: *Reflections,* 1799

Novels are to love as fairy-tales to dreams.
S. T. COLERIDGE: *Cervantes,* 1813

A work in which the greatest powers of the mind are displayed, in which the most thorough knowledge of human nature, the happiest delineation of its varieties, the liveliest effusions of wit and humor are conveyed to the world in the best chosen language.
JANE AUSTEN: *Northanger Abbey,* v, 1818

Between the Bible and novels there is a gulf fixed which few novel readers are willing to pass. The consciousness of virtue, the dignified pleasure of having performed one's duty, the serene remembrance of a useful life, the hopes of an interest in the Redeemer, and the promise of a glorious inheritance in the favor of God are never found in novels.
TIMOTHY DWIGHT: *Travels in New England and New York,* I, 1823

The literature of the people begins with fables and ends with novels.
JOSEPH JOUBERT: *Pensées,* 1842

Every novel is a debtor to Homer.
R. W. EMERSON: *Representative Men,* I, 1850

Novels are sweets. All people with healthy literary appetites love them — almost all women; a vast number of clever, hardheaded men.
W. M. THACKERAY: *Roundabout Papers,* 1860

How far off from life and manners and motives the novel still is! Life lies about us dumb; the day, as we know it, has not yet found a tongue.
R. W. EMERSON: *Society and Solitude,* 1870

The phantasmagorical world of novels and of opium.
MATTHEW ARNOLD: *Literature and Dogma,* II, 1873

The great majority of novels are not works of art in anything but a very secondary signification. The purely critical spirit is paramount.
R. L. STEVENSON: *Familiar Studies of Men and Books,* I, 1882

A species of composition bearing the same relation to literature that the panorama bears to art.
AMBROSE BIERCE: *The Devil's Dictionary,* 1906

[*See also* Fiction.

Novelist

Novelists are generally great liars.
ST. JOHN BAPTIST DE LA SALLE: *The Rules of Christian Manners and Civility,* II, 1695

The business of the novelist is not to relate great events, but to make small ones interesting.
ARTHUR SCHOPENHAUER: *On Some Forms of Literature,* 1851

The trade of a novelist is very much that of describing the softness, sweetness, and loving dispositions of women.
ANTHONY TROLLOPE: *North America,* I, 1862

My task which I am trying to achieve is, by the power of the written word to make you hear, to make you feel — it is, before all, to make you *see.* That — and no more, and it is everything.
JOSEPH CONRAD: In the New Review, Dec., 1897

Novelty

Man is by nature fond of novelty.
PLINY THE ELDER: *Natural History,* XII, *c.* 79

I must have novelty — even if there is none left in the world.
JEAN DE LA FONTAINE: *Contes,* 1671

There are three things which the public will always clamor for, sooner or later, namely, novelty, novelty, novelty.
THOMAS HOOD: *Comic Annual,* 1836

Novelty always appears handsome.
H. G. BOHN: *Handbook of Proverbs,* 1855

[*See also* New.

November

The gloomy month of November, when the people of England hang and drown themselves.
JOSEPH ADDISON: *The Spectator,* May 23, 1712 (Ascribed to "a celebrated French novelist")

Short, thick and blustrous, like a day in November.
S. T. COLERIDGE: *Talleyrand to Lord Grenville,* 1800 (London Morning Post, Jan. 10)

November's sky is chill and drear,
November's leaf is red and sear.
WALTER SCOTT: *Marmion,* I, 1808

Red o'er the forest peers the setting sun,
  The line of yellow light dies fast away
That crown'd the eastern copse: and chill and dun
  Falls on the moor the brief November day.
JOHN KEBLE: *The Christian Year,* 1827

Dull November brings the blast,
Then the leaves are whirling fast.
SARA COLERIDGE: *Pretty Lessons in Verse,* 1834

No warmth, no cheerfulness, no healthful ease —
No comfortable feel in any member —

No shade, no shine, no butterflies, no bees,
No fruits, no flowers, no leaves, no birds,
No-vember!

THOMAS HOOD: *No!*, 1844

The eleventh twelfth of a weariness.

AMBROSE BIERCE: *The Devil's Dictionary*, 1906

Who first comes to this world below
With drear November's fog and snow
Should prize the topaz's amber hue —
Emblem of friends and lovers true.

Author unidentified

[*See also* Months.

Now

Now or never.

JOHN DAY: *Humor Out of Breath*, IV, 1608 (Borrowed from a Latin proverb "Nunc aut nunquam")

Better now than never.

SAMUEL PEPYS: *Diary*, March 17, 1667

One of our poets — which is it? — speaks of an everlasting now. If such a condition of existence were offered to us in this world, and if it were put to the vote whether we should accept the offer and fix all things immutably as they are, who are they whose votes would be given in the affirmative?

ROBERT SOUTHEY: *The Doctor*, 1834

[*See also* Present.

Nudity

[*See* Nakedness.

Numbers, Odd

God delights in odd numbers.

VIRGIL: *Eclogues*, VIII, 37 B.C.

Why do we all believe that odd numbers are best?

PLINY THE ELDER: *Natural History*, XXVIII, *c.* 79

They say there is divinity in odd numbers, either in nativity, chance or death.

SHAKESPEARE: *The Merry Wives of Windsor*, V, *c.* 1600

There's luck in odd numbers.

SAMUEL LOVER: *Rory O'More*, 1836

Nun

If a priestess or a nun open a wineshop or enter a wineshop for a drink, they shall burn that woman.

THE CODE OF HAMMURABI, *c.* 2250 B.C.

There was also a nun, a prioress,
That of her smiling was full simple and coy.

GEOFFREY CHAUCER: *The Canterbury Tales*, prologue, *c.* 1386

I hope you are a better Christian than to think of living a nun.

WILLIAM CONGREVE: *The Double Dealer*, IV, 1694

I am not surprised that nuns have so often inspired violent passions; the pity one naturally feels for them, when they seem worthy of another destiny, making an easy way for yet more tender sentiments.

MARY WORTLEY MONTAGU: *Letter to an unidentified correspondent*, Oct. 1, 1716

How happy is the blameless vestal's lot
The world forgetting, by the world forgot.

ALEXANDER POPE: *Eloisa to Abelard*, 1717

Nuns fret not at their convent's narrow room,
And hermits are contented with their cells.

WILLIAM WORDSWORTH: *Nuns Fret Not*, 1807

A nun hath no nation.
Whenever man suffers or woman may soothe,
There her land, there her kindred.

E. R. BULWER-LYTTON (OWEN MEREDITH): *Lucile*, II, 1860

Every libertine in Roman Catholic countries is obsessed with the attraction of nuns. That attractiveness is the result of the tabu laid on nuns.

ROBERT BRIFFAULT: *Sin and Sex*, VII, 1931

[*See also* Convent, Face, Nunnery.

Nunc Dimittis, The

Lord, now lettest thou thy servant depart in peace, according to thy word.

LUKE II, 29, *c.* 75 (The text runs to v. 32)

Nunnery

Get thee to a nunnery: why wouldst thou be a breeder of sinners?

SHAKESPEARE: *Hamlet*, III, *c.* 1601

I assert that nunneries are prisons, and I have seen them so used. They have ever been either prisons or brothels.

HENRY DRUMMOND: Speech in the House of Commons, 1851

I do not believe in keeping penitentiaries for God.

R. G. INGERSOLL: Speech in Chicago, Sept. 20, 1880

[*See also* Nun.

Nurse

It is better to be sick than to attend the sick. The one is a simple ill; the other combines pain of mind and toil of body.

EURIPIDES: *Hippolytus*, 428 B.C.

When your head did but ache,
I knit my handkerchief about your brows,
The best I had, a princess wrought it me,
And I did never ask it you again;
And with my hand at midnight held your head,
And, like the watchful minutes to the hour,
Still and anon cheer'd up the heavy time,
Saying, "What lack you?" and, "Where lies your grief?"

SHAKESPEARE: *King John*, IV, *c.* 1596

Nurses put one bit in the child's mouth and two in their own.
JOHN CLARKE: *Parœmiologia Anglo-Latina,* 1639

One year a nurse, and seven years the worse.
JOHN RAY: *English Proverbs,* 1670 (Ray explains: " because feeding well and doing little she becomes liquorish and gets a habit of idleness ")

The nurse's tongue is privileged to talk.
IBID.

The nurse sleeps sweetly, hir'd to watch the sick,
Whom, snoring, she disturbs.
WILLIAM COWPER: *The Task,* I, 1785

When men-folk are watching them nurse-maids kiss and rock children very vigorously, but when only women are looking on they handle them very quietly.
G. C. LICHTENBERG: *Reflections,* 1799

Let us now remember many honorable women,
Such as bade us turn again when we were like to die.
RUDYARD KIPLING: *Dirge of Dead Sisters,* 1902

[*See also* Child, Childbirth, Husband and Wife, Infant.

Nurture

[*See* Nature *vs.* Nurture.

Nut

An apple, an egg and a nut
You may eat after a slut.
JOHN RAY: *English Proverbs,* 1670

He that would eat the kernel must crack the nut.
LATIN PROVERB

The harder the shell of a nut, the less is there in its center.
WELSH PROVERB

[*See also* Voice.

Nutmeg

If you carry a nutmeg in your pocket you'll be married to an old man.
JONATHAN SWIFT: *Polite Conversation,* 1738

Nuts

Lord Keeper and Treasurer teased me for a week. It was nuts to them.
JONATHAN SWIFT: *Journal to Stella,* Jan. 8, 1712

O

Oak

Howl, O ye oaks of Bashan.
ZECHARIAH XI, 2, *c.* 520 B.C.

The oak, struck by lightning, sprouts anew.
OVID: *Tristia,* IV, *c.* 10

Much safer stands the bowing reed than doth the stubborn oak.
THOMAS TUSSER: *Five Hundred Points of Good Husbandry,* 1580

Great oaks from little acorns grow.
ENGLISH PROVERB, traced by Apperson to *c.* 1635

Oaks are in all respects the perfect image of the manly character.
WILLIAM SHENSTONE: *Unconnected Thoughts on Gardening,* 1764

Those green-robed senators of mighty woods,
Tall oaks, branch-charmed by the earnest stars,
Dream, and so dream all night without a stir.
JOHN KEATS: *Hyperion,* I, 1819

A song to the oak, the brave old oak,
Who hath ruled in the greenwood long;
Here's health and renown to his broad green crown,
And his fifty arms so strong.
H. F. CHORLEY: *The Brave Old Oak,* *c.* 1850

There is in trees no perfect form which can be fixed upon or reasoned out as ideal; but that is always an ideal oak which, however poverty-stricken, or hunger-pinched, or tempest-tortured, is yet seen to have done, under its appointed circumstances, all that could be expected of oak.
JOHN RUSKIN: *Modern Painters,* III, 1856

[*See also* Heart, Lightning, Tree.

Oath

The abolishing of oaths is more useful than any fasting; it is more profitable than any austerity.
ST. JOHN CHRYSOSTOM: *Homilies,* IV, *c.* 388

What fool is not so wise
To lose an oath to win a paradise?
SHAKESPEARE: *Love's Labor's Lost,* IV, *c.* 1595

A good mouth-filling oath.
SHAKESPEARE: *I Henry IV,* III, *c.* 1598

Oaths are straws, men's faiths are water-cakes,
And hold-fast is the only dog.
SHAKESPEARE: *Henry V,* II, *c.* 1599

A terrible oath, with a swaggering accent sharply twanged off, gives manhood more approbation than ever proof itself would have earned him.
SHAKESPEARE: *Twelfth Night,* III, *c.* 1601

If a lie, after it is molded, be not smooth enough, there is no instrument to burnish it but an oath: swearing gives it color, and a bright complexion.
THOMAS DEKKER: *The Seven Deadly Sins of London,* II, 1606

When thou dost tell another's jest, therein
Omit the oath, which true wit cannot need.
GEORGE HERBERT: *The Temple,* 1633

A liar is always prodigal with oaths.
PIERRE CORNEILLE: *Le Menteur,* III, 1642

Oaths are but words, and words but wind.
SAMUEL BUTLER: *Hudibras,* II, 1664

"He shall not die, by ——!" cried my Uncle Toby. The accusing spirit which flew up to Heaven's chancery with the oath, blushed as he gave it in, and the recording angel, as he wrote it down, dropped a tear upon the word, and blotted it out forever.
LAURENCE STERNE: *Tristram Shandy,* II, 1760

I do solemnly swear (or affirm) that I will faithfully execute the office of President of the United States, and will, to the best of my ability, preserve, protect and defend the Constitution of the United States.
CONSTITUTION OF THE UNITED STATES, II, 1789 (Oath prescribed for the President)

In itself an oath is no more sacred than a lie is contemptible.
MAX STIRNER: *The Ego and His Own,* 1845

I take the official oath today with no mental reservations.
ABRAHAM LINCOLN: Inaugural Address, March 5, 1861

In law, a solemn appeal to the Deity, made binding upon the conscience by a penalty for perjury.
AMBROSE BIERCE: *The Devil's Dictionary,* 1906

By Heaven above you, Hell beneath you, by your part of Paradise, by all that God made in six days and seven nights, and by God Himself!
OATH OF SCOTCH BORDERERS

[*See also* Absolution, Agnostic Chinese, Liar, Love, Lover, Reservation (Mental), Swearing, Trust, Vow.

Oats

To sow wild oats.
ENGLISH PHRASE, traced by the New English Dictionary to 1576

A grain which in England is generally given to horses, but in Scotland supports the people.
SAMUEL JOHNSON: *Dictionary,* 1755 (The reply of Lord Elibank is almost as famous: "Very true, and where will you find such horses, and such men?")

Obedience

Obey me, for ye are younger than I.
HOMER: *Iliad,* I, *c.* 800 B.C.

He who obeys with modesty will be worthy some day of being allowed to command.
CICERO: *De legibus,* III, *c.* 50 B.C.

We ought to obey God rather than men.
ACTS V, 29, *c.* 75

God does not listen to the prayer of him who does not obey his parents.
POPE XYSTUS I: *The Ring, c.* 150

Obedience is in a way the mother of all virtues.
ST. AUGUSTINE: *On the Good of Marriage, c.* 401

Let them obey that know not how to rule.
SHAKESPEARE: *II Henry VI,* V, *c.* 1591

It fits thee not to ask the reason why,
Because we bid it.
SHAKESPEARE: *Pericles,* I, *c.* 1608

Those who know the least obey the best.
GEORGE FARQUHAR: *The Recruiting Officer,* IV, 1706

Obedience is much more seen in little things than in great.
THOMAS FULLER: *Gnomologia,* 1732

Let men obey the laws and women their husbands.
NATHANIEL AMES: *Almanac,* 1734

Let thy child's first lesson be obedience, and the second will be what thou wilt.
BENJAMIN FRANKLIN: *Poor Richard's Almanac,* 1739

I do not like the mere servile merit of obedience.
HORACE WALPOLE: *Letter to Hannah More,* June 15, 1787

Come when you're called,
And do as you're bid;
Shut the door after you,
And you'll never be chid.
MARIA EDGEWORTH: *Early Lessons,* 1801

Obedience,
Bane of all genius, virtue, freedom, truth,
Makes slaves of men, and, of the human frame,
A mechanized automaton.
P. B. SHELLEY: *Queen Mab,* III, 1813

Woe to him that claims obedience when it is not due; woe to him that refuses when it is!
THOMAS CARLYLE: *Heroes and Hero-Worship,* VI, 1840 (Lecture in London, May 22)

The ox toils through the furrow,
Obedient to the goad;
The patient ass up flinty paths
Plods with his weary load;
With whine and bound the spaniel
His master's whistle hears;
And the sheep yields her patiently
To the loud clashing shears.
T. B. MACAULAY: *Lays of Ancient Rome,* 1842

Theirs not to make reply,
Theirs not to reason why,
Theirs but to do and die.
ALFRED TENNYSON: *The Charge of the Light Brigade,* 1854

To The States, or any one of them, or any city of The States,
Resist much, obey little;

Once unquestioning obedience, once fully enslaved;
Once fully enslaved, no nation, state, city, of this earth, ever afterward resumes its liberty.
WALT WHITMAN: *Caution*, 1860

You cannot be a true man until you learn to obey.
ROBERT E. LEE: To the students at Washington College, 1867

Obedience is not servitude of man to man, but submission to the will of God, who governs through the medium of men.
POPE LEO XIII: *Immortale Dei*, Nov. 1, 1885

Learn to obey. (Lerne gehorchen.)
GERMAN PROVERB

At your orders, colonel! (Zu Befehl, Herr Oberst!) GERMAN SAYING

The woman who obeys her husband rules him.
SPANISH PROVERB

[*See also* Army, Classes, Command, Discipline, Husband and Wife, Order, Regimentation, Soldier, Vice.

Objector, Conscientious

The conscientious objector . . . has no place in a republic like ours, and should be expelled from it, for no man who won't pull his weight in the boat has a right in the boat.
THEODORE ROOSEVELT: Speech in Baltimore, Sept. 28, 1918

Obligation

There is no kind of life, whether public or private, at home or abroad, – that is free of obligations. In their due discharge is all of life. CICERO: *De officiis*, I, *c.* 80 B.C.

Moral obligation is like all other obligations, and all obligation is nothing more than an inducement of sufficient strength, and resulting, in some way, from the command of another.
WILLIAM PALEY: *The Principles of Moral and Political Philosophy*, II, 1785

[*See also* Duty, Friend, Irishman, Nobility.

Oblivion

What's past and what's to come is strew'd with husks
And formless ruin of oblivion.
SHAKESPEARE: *Troilus and Cressida*, IV, *c.* 1601

Our revels now are ended. These, our actors,
As I foretold you, were all spirits, and
Are melted into air, into thin air;
And, like the baseless fabric of this vision,
The cloud-capped towers, the gorgeous palaces,
The solemn temples, the great globe itself,
Yea, all which it inherit, shall dissolve,
And, like this insubstantial pageant faded,
Leave not a rack behind.
SHAKESPEARE: *The Tempest*, IV, 1611

The iniquity of oblivion blindly scattereth her poppy, and deals with the memory of men without distinction to merit of perpetuity.
THOMAS BROWNE: *Urn Burial*, V, 1658

Man passes away; his name perishes from record and recollection; his history is as a tale that is told, and his very monument becomes a ruin.
WASHINGTON IRVING: *The Sketch-Book*, 1820

Oboe

An ill wood-wind that nobody blows good.
Author unidentified

Obscenity

There is a deep in Gehenna for the user of obscenity, and for the man who hears it willingly. THE TALMUD (*Sabbath*), *c.* 200

I know that the wiser sort of men will consider, and I wish that the ignorant sort would learn, how it is not the baseness or homeliness, either of words or matters, that makes them foul and obscene, but their base minds, filthy conceits, or lewd intents that handle them.
JOHN HARINGTON: *The Metamorphosis of Ajax*, 1596

Wanton jests make fools laugh and wise men frown. Seeing we are civilized Englishmen, let us not be naked savages in our talk. Such rotten speeches are worst in withered age, when men run after that sin in their words which flieth from them in the deed.
THOMAS FULLER: *The Holy State and the Profane State*, 1642

Obscenity in any company is a rustic, uncreditable talent.
JEREMY COLLIER: *A Short View of the Immorality and Profaneness of the English Stage*, intro., 1698

It is the grossness of the spectator that discovers nothing but grossness in the subject.
WILLIAM HAZLITT: *The Pleasure of Painting*, 1821

The test of obscenity is this: whether the tendency of the matter charged as obscenity is to deprave and corrupt those whose minds are open to such immoral influences, and into whose hands a publication of this sort may fall.
MR. CHIEF JUSTICE COCKBURN: *Judgment in Regina* vs. *Hicklin*, 1868

A book is said to be obscene when it is offensive to decency or chastity, which is immodest, which is indelicate, impure, causing lewd thoughts of an immoral tendency.
JUDGE CLARKE of the Federal District Court at Boston: *Charge to the jury in United States* vs. *Heywood*, 1877

A taste for dirty stories may be said to be inherent in the human animal.
GEORGE MOORE: *Confessions of a Young Man*, IX, 1888

Books which professedly treat of, narrate, or teach lewd or obscene subjects are prohibited. Care must be taken not only of faith but also of morals, which are easily corrupted by the reading of such books.

POPE LEO XIII: *General Decrees Concerning the Prohibition and Censorship of Books*, Jan. 25, 1897

Every obscene, lewd or lascivious, and every filthy book, pamphlet, picture, paper, letter, writing, print or other publication of an indecent character . . . is hereby declared to be nonmailable matter, and shall not be conveyed in the mails or delivered from any postoffice by any letter carried.

UNITED STATES CRIMINAL CODE, March 4, 1909

Obscenity in word, gesture, reference, song, joke or by suggestion is forbidden.

A CODE TO GOVERN THE MAKING OF MOTION AND TALKING PICTURES BY THE MOTION PICTURE PRODUCERS AND DISTRIBUTORS OF AMERICA, INC., March 31, 1930

All persons are prohibited from importing into the United States from any foreign country . . . any obscene book, pamphlet, paper, writing, advertisement, circular, print, picture, drawing, or other representation, figure or image on or of paper or other material.

UNITED STATES TARIFF ACT, June 17, 1930

[*See also* Innuendo.

Obscurity

I envy the man who passes through life safely, to the world and fame unknown.

EURIPIDES: *Iphigenia in Tauris, c.* 413 B.C.

How oft the highest talent lurks in obscurity!

PLAUTUS: *Captivi*, I, *c.* 200 B.C.

He has lived not ill who has lived and died unnoticed by the world.

HORACE: *Epistles*, I, *c.* 5 B.C.

If you would be well known of God, be unknown of men.

POPE XYSTUS I: *The Ring, c.* 150

Obscurity is dishonorable.

THOMAS HOBBES: *Leviathan*, I, 1651

The greater part must be content to be as though they had not been, to be found in the register of God, not in the record of man.

THOMAS BROWNE: *Urn Burial*, 1658

The pleasantest condition of life is in *incognito*. What a brave privilege is it to be free from all contentions, from all envying, or being envied, from receiving or paying all kind of ceremonies!

ABRAHAM COWLEY: *Of Myself*, 1665

Thus let me live, unseen, unknown;
Thus unlamented let me die,
Steal from the world, and not a stone
Tell where I lie.

ALEXANDER POPE: *Ode on Solitude*, *c.* 1700

Content thyself to be obscurely good.

JOSEPH ADDISON: *Cato*, IV, 1713

Full many a gem of purest ray serene
The dark unfathom'd caves of ocean bear:
Full many a flower is born to blush unseen,
And waste its sweetness on the desert air.

THOMAS GRAY: *Elegy Written in a Country Churchyard*, 1750

Some village Hampden that with dauntless breast
The little tyrant of his fields withstood;
Some mute inglorious Milton here may rest,
Some Cromwell guiltless of his country's blood.

IBID.

Ah! who can tell how many a soul sublime
Hath felt the influence of malignant star,
And waged with fortune an eternal war;
Check'd by the scoff of pride, by envy's frown,
And poverty's unconquerable bar,
In life's low vale remote hath pined alone
Then dropt into the grave, unpitied and unknown.

JAMES BEATTIE: *The Minstrel*, I, 1771

He is happiest of whom the world says least, good or bad.

THOMAS JEFFERSON: *Letter to John Adams*, 1786

How many a rustic Milton has passed by,
Stifling the speechless longings of his heart,
In unremitting drudgery and care!
How many a vulgar Cato has compelled
His energies, no longer tameless then,
To mold a pin, or fabricate a nail!

P. B. SHELLEY: *Queen Mab*, V, 1813

The illustrious obscure.

P. B. SHELLEY: *Adonais*, pref., 1821 (The phrase was used by Leigh Hunt in a footnote to an article in the Examiner, Sept. 26, 1819. Hunt used it again in the Examiner for June 9, 1822)

I give the fight up: let there be an end,
A privacy, an obscure nook for me.
I want to be forgotten even by God.

ROBERT BROWNING: *Paracelsus*, V, 1835

[*See also* Fame.

Observed

The observed of all observers.

SHAKESPEARE: *Hamlet*, III, *c.* 1601

Obstinacy

Obstinacy is the surest trial of folly and self-conceit. Is there anything so assured, so resolute, so disdainful, so contemplative, so serious and so grave as the ass?

MICHEL DE MONTAIGNE: *Essays*, III, 1588

Obstinacy's ne'er so stiff
As when 'tis in a wrong belief.

SAMUEL BUTLER: *Hudibras*, III, 1678

A fool is better than an obstinate man.
THOMAS FULLER: *Gnomologia*, 1732

He can never be good that is not obstinate.
THOMAS WILSON: *Maxims of Piety and of Christianity*, c. 1755

Obstinacy is incurable. SANSKRIT PROVERB

[*See also* Jew.

Ocean

Is this the mighty ocean? is this all?
W. S. LANDOR: *Gebir*, II, 1798

Calm as a slumbering babe,
Tremendous ocean lay.
P. B. SHELLEY: *The Daemon of the World*, I, 1815

Roll on, thou deep and dark blue ocean — roll!
Ten thousand fleets sweep over thee in vain;
Man marks the earth with ruin — his control
Stops with the shore.
BYRON: *Childe Harold*, IV, 1818

The ocean is a fluid world.
C. C. COLTON: *Lacon*, 1820

Old ocean's grey and melancholy waste.
W. C. BRYANT: *Thanatopsis*, 1821

A life on the ocean wave,
A home on the rolling deep,
Where the scattered waters rave,
And the winds their revels keep!
EPES SARGENT: *A Life on the Ocean Wave*, 1847

But his little daughter whispered
As she took his icy hand,
"Isn't God upon the ocean,
Just the same as on the land?"
JAMES T. FIELDS: *The Ballad of the Tempest*, 1849

A body of water occupying about two-thirds of a world made for man — who has no gills.
AMBROSE BIERCE: *The Devil's Dictionary*, 1906

[*See also* Fate, Land, Pacific Ocean, Sea, Wave.

October

Fresh October brings the pheasant,
Then to gather nuts is pleasant.
SARA COLERIDGE: *Pretty Lessons in Verse*, 1834

The sweet calm sunshine of October, now
Warms the low spot; upon its grassy mold
The purple oak-leaf falls; the birchen bough
Drops its bright spoil like arrow-heads of gold.
W. C. BRYANT: *October*, 1866

October is nature's funeral month. Nature glories in death more than in life. The month of departure is more beautiful than the month of coming, — October than May. Every green thing loves to die in bright colors.
H. W. BEECHER: *Proverbs from Plymouth Pulpit*, 1870

October's child is born for woe,
And life's vicissitudes must know;
But lay an opal on her breast,
And hope will lull those woes to rest.
Author unidentified

[*See also* Months.

Odds

One butcher does not fear many sheep.
Ascribed to ALEXANDER THE GREAT (365–323 B.C.)

It's a good rule never to send a mouse to catch a skunk or a pollywog to tackle a whale.
ABRAHAM LINCOLN: To D. D. Porter, *c.* 1861

Odessa

He who has never been to Odessa has never seen dust. RUSSIAN PROVERB

Odious

[*See* Comparison.

Odor

Odors have an altogether peculiar force, in affecting us through association; a force differing essentially from that of objects addressing the touch, the taste, the sight, or the hearing.
E. A. POE: *Marginalia*, 1844–49

[*See also* Boarding-house, Perfume, Smell.

Odyssey

The surge and thunder of the Odyssey.
ANDREW LANG: *The Odyssey*, *c.* 1880

[*See also* Homer.

Off

[*See* Gone.

Offender

The offender never pardons.
GEORGE HERBERT: *Outlandish Proverbs*, 1640

And love the offender, yet detest the offense.
ALEXANDER POPE: *Eloisa to Abelard*, 1717

Offense

Men are more ready to offend one who desires to be beloved than one who wishes to be feared.
NICCOLÒ MACHIAVELLI: *The Prince*, XVII, 1513

Remember not, Lord, our offenses, nor the offenses of our forefathers; neither take thou vengeance of our sins. Spare us, good Lord.
THE BOOK OF COMMON PRAYER (*The Litany*), 1662

Take care how thou offendest men raised from low condition.
THOMAS FULLER: *Introductio ad Prudentiam*, I, 1731

Men are never more offended than when we depreciate their ceremonies and usages. Seek to oppress them, and it is sometimes a proof of the esteem with which you regard them; depreciate their customs, it is always a mark of contempt.

C. L. DE MONTESQUIEU: *La grandeur et la décadence des Romains,* 1734

[*See also* Law, Offender.

Office

Oh, that estates, degrees, and offices
Were not deriv'd corruptly, and that clear honor
Were purchased by the merit of the wearer!

SHAKESPEARE: *The Merchant of Venice,* II, *c.* 1597

The insolence of office.

SHAKESPEARE: *Hamlet,* III, *c.* 1601

I had rather be shut up in a very modest cottage, with my books, my family and a few old friends, dining on simple bacon, and letting the world roll on as it liked, than to occupy the most splendid post which any human power can give.

THOMAS JEFFERSON: *Letter to A. Donald,* 1788

I shall never ask, never refuse, nor ever resign an office.

BENJAMIN FRANKLIN: *Autobiography,* 1798

The very essence of a free government consists in considering offices as public trusts, bestowed for the good of the country, and not for the benefit of an individual or a party.

JOHN C. CALHOUN: Speech in the Senate, July 13, 1835

The ideally perfect constitution of a public office is that in which the interest of the functionary is entirely coincident with his duty. No mere system will make it so, but still less can it be made so without a system, aptly devised for the purpose.

J. S. MILL: *Representative Government,* II, 1861

Your every voter, as surely as your Chief Magistrate, under the same high sanction, though in a different sphere, exercises a public trust.

GROVER CLEVELAND: Inaugural Address, March 4, 1885

Public office is a public trust.

Democratic National Program, 1892 (Cf. CALHOUN, *ante,* 1835)

By virtue of his office. (Ex officio.)

LATIN PHRASE

The office makes the man. (Magistratus facit hominem.) LATIN PROVERB

[*See also* Impeachment, Jew, Spoils, Trust (Public).

Officeholder

A man who aspires to any high office should have three qualifications: first, he should be prepared to support the constitution of his country; second, he should have a special aptitude for the office he desires; and third, he should have virtue and justice as they are understood by his fellow-citizens.

ARISTOTLE: *Politics,* V, *c.* 322 B.C.

Thou hast seen a farmer's dog bark at a beggar? And the creature run from the cur? There thou might'st behold the great image of authority: a dog's obeyed in office.

SHAKESPEARE: *King Lear,* IV, 1606

Fortune often makes up for the eminence of office by the inferiority of the officeholder.

BALTASAR GRACIÁN: *The Art of Worldly Wisdom,* CLXXXII, 1647

He that puts on a public gown must put off a private person.

THOMAS FULLER: *Gnomologia,* 1732

Jack in an office is a great man. IBID.

They that buy an office must sell something.

IBID.

Every public man pays tribute to malignity, but he is paid in honors and gold.

VOLTAIRE: *Philosophical Dictionary,* 1764

He has erected a multitude of new offices, and sent hither swarms of officers to harass our people and eat out their substance.

THOMAS JEFFERSON: *The Declaration of Independence,* July 4, 1776 (Count in the indictment of George III)

All persons possessing any portion of power ought to be strongly and awfully impressed with an idea that they act in trust, and that they are to account for their conduct in that trust to the one great Master, Author, and Founder of society.

EDMUND BURKE: *Reflections on the Revolution in France,* I, 1790

If a due participation of office is a matter of right, how are vacancies to be obtained? Those by death are few: by resignation, none.

THOMAS JEFFERSON: *Letter to Elias Shipman,* July 12, 1801 (In common usage this has been reduced to " Few die, and none resign ")

Government is a trust and the officers of the government are trustees; and both the trust and the trustees are created for the benefit of the people.

HENRY CLAY: Speech in Ashland, Ky., March, 1829

The very existence of government at all infers inequality. The citizen who is preferred to office becomes the superior of those who are not, so long as he is the repository of power.

J. FENIMORE COOPER: *The American Democrat,* VII, 1838

Are those really congressmen? are those the great judges? is that the President?
Then I will sleep awhile yet — for I see that These States sleep.

WALT WHITMAN: *To the States,* 1860

In politics we must choose between the strong man whose real interests are elsewhere and who will leave office the moment bigger opportunity beckons, and the weakling who will cling because he can't hold a job anywhere else. Public office is the last refuge of the incompetent.

Ascribed to BOISE PENROSE in Collier's Weekly, Feb. 14, 1931

One of the principal qualifications for a political job is that the applicant know nothing much about what he is expected to do.

TERRY M. TOWNSEND: *The Doctor Looks at the Citizen,* 1940 (Address in New York, Jan. 30)

When God gives a man an office, He gives him brains enough to fill it. GERMAN PROVERB

[*See also* Office, Officeseeker.

Officer

An officer is much more respected than any other man who has as little money.

SAMUEL JOHNSON: *Boswell's Life,* April 3, 1776

Our army would be invincible if it could be properly organized and officered. There never were such men in an army before. They will go anywhere and do anything if properly led. But there is the difficulty — proper commanders — and where can they be obtained?

R. E. LEE: *Letter to Gen. J. B. Hood,* May 21, 1863

The officers get all the steak,
And all we get is the bellyache.

Anon.: *Mademoiselle from Armenteers, c.* 1914

[*See also* General, Pastor, Prussia.

Officeseeker

Every time I fill a vacant place I make a hundred malcontents and one ingrate.

Ascribed to LOUIS XIV of France (1638–1715)

Whenever a man has cast a longing eye on offices, a rottenness begins in his conduct.

THOMAS JEFFERSON: *Letter to Tench Coxe,* 1820

This struggle and scramble for office, for a way to live without work, will finally test the strength of our institutions.

ABRAHAM LINCOLN: To W. H. Herndon, 1861

[*See also* Officeholder.

Often

Oftentimes one day is better than sometimes in a whole year.

WILLIAM CAXTON: Tr. of *Reynard the Fox,* 1481

Oil

[*See* Old.

Ointment

Dead flies cause the ointment of the apothecary to send forth a stinking savor.

ECCLESIASTES X, 1, *c.* 200 B.C.

[*See also* Perfume.

Old

As old wood is best to burn, an old horse to ride, old books to read, and old wine to drink, so are old friends always most trusty to use.

LEONARD WRIGHT: *The Display of Duty,* 1589 (The saying is repeated in substance in ANTHONY COPLEY: *Wits, Fits and Fancies,* 1594. It is often ascribed to a mysterious, and probably mythical, ALONSO of Aragon)

Is not old wine wholesomest, old pippins toothsomest, old wood burns brightest, old linen washes whitest? Old soldiers, sweethearts, are surest, and old lovers are soundest.

JOHN WEBSTER and THOMAS DEKKER: *Westward Ho,* II, 1605

Old wine and an old friend are good provisions.

GEORGE HERBERT: *Outlandish Proverbs,* 1640

There's no catching old birds with chaff.

THOMAS SHADWELL: *The Sullen Lovers,* V, 1668

Old bees yield no honey.

JOHN RAY: *English Proverbs,* 1670

Old fish, old oil and an old friend are best.

IBID.

Old pottage is sooner heated than new made.

IBID.

Old friends are best. King James used to call for his old shoes; they were easiest for his feet. JOHN SELDEN: *Table-Talk,* 1689

Old foxes want no tutors.

THOMAS FULLER: *Gnomologia,* 1732

Old porridge is sooner warmed than new made.

IBID.

Old sacks want much patching. IBID.

Old sores are hardly cured. IBID.

Old vessels must leak. IBID.

I'm as old as my tongue, and a little older than my teeth.
JONATHAN SWIFT: *Polite Conversation*, I, 1738

I love everything that's old – old friends, old times, old manners, old books, old wine.
OLIVER GOLDSMITH: *She Stoops to Conquer*, I, 1773

All the mischief in the world may be put down very plausibly to old laws, old customs, and old religions.
G. C. LICHTENBERG: *Reflections*, 1799

The room where I was born, the furniture which has been before my eyes all my life, a book-case which has followed me about like a faithful dog (only exceeding him in knowledge) wherever I have moved, old chairs, old tables, streets, squares, where I have sunned myself, my old school, – these are my mistresses.
CHARLES LAMB: *Letter to William Wordsworth*, Jan. 30, 1801

Nature abhors the old.
R. W. EMERSON: *Circles*, 1841

I am as old as Egypt to myself.
O. W. HOLMES: *Wind-Clouds and Star-Drifts* (In *The Poet at the Breakfast-Table*), 1872

Old birds are hard to pluck.
GERMAN PROVERB

Old pigs have hard snouts. IBID.

One should keep to old roads and old friends.
IBID.

The older first. (Seniores priores.)
LATIN PHRASE

Old truths, old laws, old boots, old books and old friends are the best. POLISH PROVERB

It is as old as the Borcks and the devils.
POMERANIAN PROVERB

One has to be neither strong nor bold to win a victory over the old. WELSH PROVERB

[*See also* Age (Old), Ages, Ancient, Antique, Antiquity, Books, Cat, Dog, Man and Woman, Man (Old), New and Old, Physician, Woman (Old), Young and Old.

Old and New

[*See* New and Old.

Old and Young

[*See* Young and Old.

Oligarchy

Oligarchy is that form of government in which there is a property qualification for suffrage or for officeholding.
ARISTOTLE: *Rhetoric*, I, *c.* 322 B.C.

A worse, a more despotic or unforgiving government than an oligarchy never existed.
NAPOLEON I: To Barry O'Meara at St. Helena, Sept. 7, 1817

[*See also* Centralization, Government.

Olive

The olive tree is assuredly the richest gift of Heaven. I can scarcely except bread.
THOMAS JEFFERSON: *Letter to George Wythe*, 1787

Omnipotence

[*See* God.

Once

The finished man of the world must eat of every apple once.
R. W. EMERSON: *The Conduct of Life*, IV, 1860

Enough.
AMBROSE BIERCE: *The Devil's Dictionary*, 1906

I am willing to try anything once.
AMERICAN SAYING

One time does not make a custom.
FRENCH PROVERB

Once is never. (Einmal ist keinmal.)
GERMAN PROVERB

One

One is no number.
CHRISTOPHER MARLOWE and GEORGE CHAPMAN: *Hero and Leander*, 1598

One is more than a multitude.
BEN JONSON: *Cynthia's Revels*, V, 1601

One and none is all one.
JOHN RAY: *English Proverbs*, 1670

One cloud is enough to eclipse all the sun.
THOMAS FULLER: *Gnomologia*, 1732

One crow does not make a Winter.
GERMAN PROVERB

One man is no man. (Unus vir nullus vir.)
LATIN PROVERB

[*See also* Minority, Swallow, Two, Union.

Onion

If thou hast not a capon feed on an onion.
JOHN RAY: *English Proverbs*, 1670

Onions can make ev'n heirs and widows weep.
BENJAMIN FRANKLIN: *Poor Richard's Almanac*, 1734

How beautiful and strong those buttered onions come to my nose!
CHARLES LAMB: *Letter to Thomas Manning*, Aug. 22, 1800

Let onion atoms lurk within the bowl,
And, half-suspected, animate the whole.
Ascribed to SYDNEY SMITH in *A Memoir of the Rev. Sydney Smith* by his daughter, Lady Holland, 1855

Onion skin very thin,
Mild Winter coming in;
Onion skin thick and tough,
Coming Winter cold and rough.

OLD ENGLISH RHYME

[*See also* Bald, Laughter and Tears.

Opal

[*See* October.

Openmindedness

Examine each opinion: if it seems true, embrace it; if false, gird up thy mind to withstand it.

LUCRETIUS: *De rerum natura,* II, 57 B.C.

I shall adopt new views as fast as they shall appear to be true views.

ABRAHAM LINCOLN: *Letter to Horace Greeley,* Aug. 22, 1862

His mind kept open house.

Author unidentified

Opera

As for operas, they are essentially too absurd and extravagant to mention; I look upon them as a magic scene contrived to please the eyes and the ears at the expense of the understanding.

LORD CHESTERFIELD: *Letter to his son,* Jan. 23, 1752

The Romans cared only for *panem et circenses.* We have omitted *panem,* we care only for *circenses* – that is to say, for comic opera.

VOLTAIRE: *Letter to Mme. Necker,* 1770

In opera the text must be the obedient daughter of the music.

W. A. MOZART: *Letter to his father,* Oct. 13, 1781

I am a person that shuns
All ostentation,
And seldom go to operas
But in formâ pauperis!

CHARLES LAMB: *Letter to William Ayrton,* May 17, 1817

I have sat through an Italian opera till, for sheer pain, and inexplicable anguish, I have rushed out into the noisiest places of the crowded streets, to solace myself with sounds which I was not obliged to follow, and get rid of the distracting torment of endless, fruitless, barren attention.

CHARLES LAMB: *A Chapter on Ears,* 1821 (London Magazine, March)

We went to Mannheim and attended a shivaree – otherwise an opera – the one called "Lohengrin." The banging and slamming and booming and crashing were something beyond belief.

S. C. CLEMENS (MARK TWAIN): *A Tramp Abroad,* IX, 1879

I have never encountered anything more false and foolish than the effort to get truth into opera. In opera everything is based upon the not-true.

P. I. TSCHAIKOVSKY: *Diary,* July 13, 1888

The actor apes a man – at least in shape;
The opera performer apes an ape.

AMBROSE BIERCE: *The Devil's Dictionary,* 1906

Comic operas do not lie.

ISAAC GOLDBERG: *Major Noah,* IV, 1936

[*See also* Nature.

Opinion

If all men defined "honorable" and "wise" alike there would be no debate on earth. As it is, each man defines these words for himself, and only the names remain unchanged.

EURIPIDES: *The Phoenissæ, c.* 410 B.C.

Between knowledge of what really exists and ignorance of what does not exist lies the domain of opinion. It is more obscure than knowledge, but clearer than ignorance.

PLATO: *The Republic,* V, *c.* 370 B.C.

So many men, so many opinions. (Quot homines, tot sententiæ.)

TERENCE: *Phormio,* II, *c.* 160 B.C.

Every man values himself more than all the rest of men, but he always values others' opinion of himself more than his own.

MARCUS AURELIUS: *Meditations,* XII, *c.* 170

As though there were a metempsychosis, and the soul of one man passed into another, opinions do find, after certain revolutions, men and minds like those that first begat them.

THOMAS BROWNE: *Religio Medici,* I, 1642

Where there is much desire to learn, there of necessity will be much arguing, much writing, many opinions; for opinion in good men is but knowledge in the making.

JOHN MILTON: *Areopagitica,* 1644

Congruity of opinions, whether true or false, to our natural constitution is one great incentive to their belief and reception.

JOSEPH GLANVILL: *The Vanity of Dogmatizing,* XIII, 1661

Climates of opinion.

JOSEPH GLANVILL: *The Vanity of Dogmatizing,* XXIII

Opinionative confidence is the effect of ignorance. IBID.

The opinion of the strongest is always the best.

JEAN DE LA FONTAINE: *Fables,* I, 1668

It is force, not opinion, that queens it over the world, but it is opinion that looses the force.

BLAISE PASCAL: *Pensées,* XXIV, 1670

Opinion is something wherein I go about to give reasons why all the world should think as I think.
JOHN SELDEN: *Table-Talk*, 1689

New opinions are always suspected and usually opposed, for no other reason than because they are not already common.
JOHN LOCKE: *Essay Concerning Human Understanding*, dedication, 1690

When any opinion leads to absurdity, it is certainly false; but it is not certain that an opinion is false because it is of dangerous consequence.
DAVID HUME: *An Enquiry Concerning Human Understanding*, III, 1748

Singularity in right hath ruined many: happy those who are convinced of the general opinion.
BENJAMIN FRANKLIN: *Poor Richard's Almanac*, 1757

Opinion has caused more trouble on this little earth than plagues or earthquakes.
VOLTAIRE: *Letter to an unknown correspondent*, Jan. 5, 1759

In two opposite opinions, if one be perfectly reasonable the other can't be perfectly right.
OLIVER GOLDSMITH: *The Good Natur'd Man*, IV, 1768

Every society has a right to preserve public peace and order, and therefore has a good right to prohibit the propagation of opinions which have a dangerous tendency.
SAMUEL JOHNSON: *Boswell's Life*, May 7, 1773

We never are satisfied with our opinions, whatever we may pretend, till they are ratified and confirmed by the suffrages of the rest of mankind. We dispute and wrangle for ever; we endeavor to get men to come to us when we do not go to them.
JOSHUA REYNOLDS: *Discourses*, VII, 1774 (Lecture at the Royal Academy, London, Dec. 10, 1776)

The opinions of men are not the object of civil government, nor under its jurisdiction.
THOMAS JEFFERSON: *Virginia Statute of Religious Freedom*, 1779

His opinions were as pliant as his bows.
FRANCES BURNEY: *Cecilia*, I, 1782

Is uniformity of opinion desirable? No more than that of face and stature.
THOMAS JEFFERSON: *Notes on Virginia*, 1782

No man ought to be molested on account of his opinions, not even on account of his religious opinions, provided his avowal of them does not disturb the public order established by the law.
Declaration of the Rights of Man by The French National Assembly, x, 1789

In proportion as opinions are open they are innocent and harmless. Opinions become dangerous to a state only when persecution makes it necessary for the people to communicate their ideas under the bond of secrecy.
C. J. FOX: Speech in the House of Commons, 1797

It is a golden rule that one should never judge men by their opinions, but rather by what their opinions make of them.
G. C. LICHTENBERG: *Reflections*, 1799

We always formulate opinions at a time when our judgment is at its weakest. IBID.

Opinion is a species of property; and though I am always desirous to share with my friend to a certain extent, I shall ever like to keep some tenets, and some property, properly my own.
CHARLES LAMB: *Letter to Thomas Manning*, 1800

Error of opinion may be tolerated where reason is left free to combat it.
THOMAS JEFFERSON: Inaugural Address, March 4, 1801

Men are never so good or so bad as their opinions.
JAMES MACKINTOSH: *Progress of Ethical Philosophy*, 1830

The world is governed much more by opinion than by laws. It is not the judgment of courts, but the moral judgment of individuals and masses of men, which is the chief wall of defense round property and life.
W. E. CHANNING: *Letter to Jonathan Phillips*, 1839

Every new opinion, at its starting, is precisely in a minority of one. In one man's head alone, there it dwells as yet. One man alone of the whole world believes it; there is one man against all men.
THOMAS CARLYLE: *Heroes and Hero-Worship*, II, 1840 (Lecture in London, May 8)

If the cultivation of the understanding consists in one thing more than in another, it is surely in learning the grounds of one's own opinions.
J. S. MILL: *On Liberty*, II, 1859

We can never be sure that the opinion we are endeavoring to stifle is a false opinion; and even if we were sure, stifling it would be an evil still. IBID.

The only sin which we never forgive in each other is difference of opinion.
R. W. EMERSON: *Clubs*, 1877

So long as there are earnest believers in the world, they will always wish to punish opinions, even if their judgment tells them it is unwise, and their conscience that it is wrong.
WALTER BAGEHOT: *Literary Studies*, 1879

It were not best that we should all think alike; it is difference of opinion that makes horse-races.

S. L. CLEMENS (MARK TWAIN): *Pudd'nhead Wilson*, XIX, 1894

Circumstances are the creators of most men's opinions.

A. V. DICEY: *The Relation Between Law and Public Opinion in England During the Nineteenth Century*, 1905

With effervescing opinions, as with champagne, the quickest way to let them get flat is to let them get exposed to the air.

O. W. HOLMES II: *Letter to the Harvard Liberal Club*, Jan. 12, 1920

[*See also* Age (Old), Argument, Busy, Certainty, Conscience, Duress, Error, Falsehood, Force, History, Honor, Inconsistency, Intolerance, Law, Minority, Novelty, Openmindedness, Party, Press (Free), Principle, Skeptic, Speech (Free), Toleration.

Opinion, Public

The consensus of opinion among all nations, on whatever matter, may be taken for the law of nature.

CICERO: *Tusculanæ disputationes*, I, 45 B.C.

What the multitude says is so, or soon will be so.

BALTASAR GRACIÁN: *The Art of Worldly Wisdom*, CCLXX, 1647

If the major vote may cast it, wisdom and folly must exchange names.

JOSEPH GLANVILL: *The Vanity of Dogmatizing*, XVI, 1661

Who can be secure of private right,
If sovereign sway may be dissolved by might?
Nor is the people's judgment always true:
The more may err as grossly as the few.

JOHN DRYDEN: *Absalom and Achitophel*, I, 1682

The multitude is always in the wrong.

WENTWORTH DILLON (EARL OF ROSCOMMON): *Essay on Translated Verse*, 1684

As force is always on the side of the governed, the governors have nothing to support them but opinion. It is, therefore, on opinion only that government is founded; and this maxim extends to the most despotic and most military governments, as well as to the most free and the most popular.

DAVID HUME: *Essays Moral and Political*, I, 1741

The general will is always just, but the judgment which guides it is not always enlightened.

J.-J. ROUSSEAU: *Du contrat social*, I, 1761

About things on which the public thinks long it commonly attains to think right.

SAMUEL JOHNSON: *Lives of the Poets* (*Addison*), 1778

The individual is foolish; the multitude, for the moment is foolish, when they act without deliberation; but the species is wise, and, when time is given to it, as a species it always acts right.

EDMUND BURKE: Speech in the House of Commons, May 7, 1782

There are times when the belief of the people, though it may be without ground, is as significant as the truth.

J. C. F. SCHILLER: *Don Carlos*, III, 1787

In every age there has been a stream of popular opinion that has carried all before it, and given a family character, as it were, to the century.

MARY WOLLSTONECRAFT: *A Vindication of the Rights of Woman*, II, 1792

It is rare that the public sentiment decides immorally or unwisely, and the individual who differs from it ought to distrust and examine well his own opinion.

THOMAS JEFFERSON: *Letter to William Findley*, March, 1801

Where an opinion is general, it is usually correct.

JANE AUSTEN: *Mansfield Park*, XI, 1814

When public opinion changes, it is with the rapidity of thought.

THOMAS JEFFERSON: *Letter to Charles Yancey*, 1816

There is more wisdom in public opinion than is to be found in Napoleon, Voltaire, or all the ministers of state, present or to come.

C. M. TALLEYRAND: Speech in the French Chamber of Peers, 1821

When the people have no other tyrant, their own public opinion becomes one.

E. G. BULWER-LYTTON: *Ernest Maltravers*, VI, 1837

I am astonished that the ministers neglect the common precaution of a foolometer, with which no public man should be unprovided; I mean, the acquaintance and society of three or four regular British fools as a test of public opinion.

SYDNEY SMITH: *Letter to Archdeacon Singleton*, 1837

The constant appeals to public opinion in a democracy, though excellent as a corrective of public vices, induce private hypocrisy, causing men to conceal their own convictions when opposed to those of the mass, the latter being seldom wholly right, or wholly wrong.

J. FENIMORE COOPER: *The American Democrat*, XIV, 1838

Public opinion is a compound of folly, weakness, prejudice, wrong feeling, right feeling, obstinacy, and newspaper paragraphs.

ROBERT PEEL (1788–1850)

Public opinion is a weak tyrant compared with our own private opinion. What a man thinks

of himself, that it is which determines, or rather indicates, his fate.
H. D. THOREAU: *Walden*, 1854

Popular opinions, on subjects not palpable to sense, are often true, but seldom or never the whole truth.
J. S. MILL: *On Liberty*, II, 1859

Public opinion is stronger than the Legislature, and nearly as strong as the Ten Commandments.
C. D. WARNER: *My Summer in a Garden*, XVI, 1870

Real political issues cannot be manufactured by the leaders of political parties. The real political issues of the day declare themselves, and come out of the depths of that deep which we call public opinion.
JAMES A. GARFIELD: Speech in Boston, Sept. 10, 1878

Any human conclusion that is arrived at with adequate knowledge and with sufficient thought is entitled to respect, and the public opinion of a great nation under such conditions is irresistible, and ought to be so. But what we call public opinion is generally public sentiment.
BENJAMIN DISRAELI: Speech in the House of Commons, Aug. 3, 1880

There is, and always has been, one tremendous ruler of the human race — and that ruler is that combination of the opinions of all, the leveling up of universal sense which is called public sentiment. That is the ever-present regulator and police of humanity.
THOMAS B. REED: Speech in Waterville, Maine, July 30, 1885

Public opinion is no more than this:
What people think that other people think.
ALFRED AUSTIN: *Prince Lucifer*, VI, 1887

The public buys its opinions as it buys its meat, or takes in its milk, on the principle that it is cheaper to do this than to keep a cow. So it is, but the milk is more likely to be watered.
SAMUEL BUTLER: *Note-Books*, *c.* 1890

Public opinion does not need hundreds and thousands of years to formulate itself and spread. It works by contagion, and swiftly seizes a great number of men.
LYOF N. TOLSTOY: *The Kingdom of God Is Within You*, 1893

One should respect public opinion in so far as is necessary to avoid starvation and to keep out of prison, but anything that goes beyond this is voluntary submission to an unnecessary tyranny, and is likely to interfere with happiness in all kinds of ways.
BERTRAND RUSSELL: *The Conquest of Happiness*, IX, 1930

It is the absolute right of the state to supervise the formation of public opinion.
PAUL JOSEPH GOEBBELS: Address to Berlin journalists, Oct., 1933

What is called public opinion in France is the opinion of some 3000 persons; the rest of France is an inarticulate mob.
Author unidentified

Everybody knows better than anybody.
FRENCH PROVERB

[*See also* Majority and Minority, People, Press.

Opium

Opium is pleasing to Turks on account of the agreeable delirium it produces.
EDMUND BURKE: *The Sublime and Beautiful*, intro., 1756

They have adopted these many years the Asiatic custom of taking a dose of opium every morning; and so deeply rooted is it that they would be at a loss how to live without this indulgence; they would rather be deprived of any necessary than forego their favorite luxury.
ST. JOHN DE CRÈVECOEUR: *Letters from an American Farmer*, VIII, 1782 (Said of the Quaker women of Nantucket)

Thou hast the keys of Paradise, O just, subtle, and mighty opium!
THOMAS DE QUINCEY: *Confessions of an English Opium Eater*, II, 1822

[*See also* Novel, Untrustworthy.

Opponent

[*See* Antagonist.

Opportunity

Opportunity has power over all things.
SOPHOCLES: *Philoctetes*, 408 B.C.

Observe the opportunity.
ECCLESIASTICUS IV, 20, *c.* 180 B.C.

Opportunity is lost by deliberation.
PUBLILIUS SYRUS: *Sententiæ*, *c.* 50 B.C.

Opportunity has hair in front but is bald behind. PHAEDRUS: *Fabulæ Æsopiæ*, *c.* 40

Opportunity makes the man.
ENGLISH PROVERB (In this form it seems to be recent. With *thief* instead of *man* it has been traced by Apperson to *c.* 1220)

Make hay while the sun shines.
ENGLISH PROVERB, traced by Smith to 1509

Opportunity hath all her hair on her forehead; when she is past, you may not recall her. She hath no tuft whereby you can lay hold on her, for she is bald on the hinder part of her head, and never returneth again.
RABELAIS: *Gargantua*, I, 1535 (Cf. PHAEDRUS, *ante*, *c.* 40)

When the iron is hot, strike.
JOHN HEYWOOD: *Proverbs*, 1546

O opportunity, thy guilt is great!
'Tis thou that execut'st the traitor's treason:

Thou set'st the wolf where he the lamb may get;
Whoever plots the sin, thou point'st the season.
SHAKESPEARE: *The Rape of Lucrece,* 1594

There is a tide in the affairs of men,
Which, taken at the flood, leads on to fortune;
Omitted, all the voyage of their life
Is bound in shallows and in miseries.
SHAKESPEARE: *Julius Cæsar,* IV, 1599

Opportunity is whoredom's bawd.
WILLIAM CAMDEN: *Remains Concerning Britain,* 1605

He that will not when he may,
When he will he shall have nay.
ROBERT BURTON: *The Anatomy of Melancholy,* III, 1621 (Quoted as a popular rhyme)

There is an hour in each man's life appointed
To make his happiness, if then he seize it.
JOHN FLETCHER: *The Custom of the Country,* II, 1647

The right man is the one who seizes the moment. J. W. GOETHE: *I Faust,* IV, 1808

Master of human destinies am I!
Fame, love and fortune on my footsteps wait.
Cities and fields I walk, I penetrate
Deserts and seas remote, and passing by
Hovel and mart and palace, soon or late
I knock unbidden once at every gate.
J. J. INGALLS: *Opportunity,* 1902

Opportunities come every twelve years.
HINDU PROVERB

He loses all who loses the right moment.
SPANISH PROVERB

[*See also* Fortune, Hell, Optimist and Pessimist, Thief.

Opposites

The morose dislike the gay, and the witty abominate the grave.
HORACE: *Epistles,* I, *c.* 5 B.C.

Sweetest nut hath sourest rind.
SHAKESPEARE: *As You Like It,* III, *c.* 1600

The shortest ladies love the longest men.
BEAUMONT and FLETCHER: *Love's Cure,* III, *c.* 1610

Every white will have its black
And every sweet its sour.
Anon.: *Sir Cauline, c.* 1750

[*See also* Black.

Opposition

The spirit of resistance to government is so valuable on certain occasions that I wish it to be always kept alive. It will often be exercised when wrong, but better so than not to be exercised at all.
THOMAS JEFFERSON: *Letter to Mrs. John Adams,* 1787

Men often oppose a thing merely because they have had no agency in planning it, or because it may have been planned by those whom they dislike.
ALEXANDER HAMILTON: *The Federalist,* LXX, 1788

No government can be long secure without a formidable opposition.
BENJAMIN DISRAELI: *Coningsby,* III, 1844

Oppression

What mean ye that ye beat my people to pieces, and grind the faces of the poor? saith the Lord God of hosts.
ISAIAH III, 15, *c.* 700 B.C.

Government that oppresses is more terrible than tigers.
CONFUCIUS: *The Book of Rites,* II, *c.* 500 B.C.

In a democracy the public has no power that is not expressly conceded by the institutions, and this power, moreover, is only to be used under the forms prescribed by the constitution. All beyond this is oppression.
J. FENIMORE COOPER: *The American Democrat,* XXX, 1838

[*See also* Imperialism, Injustice, Justice, Refugee, Violence.

Optimism

One truth is clear: whatever is, is right.
ALEXANDER POPE: *An Essay on Man,* I, 1732

I am satisfied with, and stand firm as a rock on, the belief that all that happens in God's world is for the best, but what is merely germ, what blossom and what fruit I do not know. J. G. FICHTE: *Die Bestimmung des Menschen,* XVIII, 1800

To look up and not down,
To look forward and not back,
To look out and not in, and
To lend a hand.
E. E. HALE: *Ten Times One Is Ten,* 1870

God is, and all is well.
J. G. WHITTIER: *My Birthday,* 1871

Live obedient to the law, in trust
That what will come, and must come, shall come well.
EDWIN ARNOLD: *The Light of Asia,* VI, 1879

The reason we all like to think so well of others is that we are all afraid of ourselves. The basis of optimism is sheer terror.
OSCAR WILDE: *The Picture of Dorian Gray,* 1891

The doctrine or belief that everything is beautiful, including what is ugly, everything good,

especially the bad, and everything right that is wrong.
AMBROSE BIERCE: *The Devil's Dictionary*, 1906

[*See also* Best.

Optimist

Many of the optimists in the world don't own a hundred dollars, and because of their optimism never will.
E. W. HOWE: *The Blessing of Business*, 1918

A neurotic person with gooseflesh and teeth a-chatter, trying hard to be brave.
ELBERT HUBBARD: *Roycroft Dictionary and Book of Epigrams*, 1923

An optimist is a man who says the bottle is half full when it's half empty.
Author unidentified

An optimist is one who buys from Jews and sells to Scotsmen. IBID.

Optimist and Pessimist

There is one postulate on which pessimists and optimists agree. Both their arguments assume it to be self-evident that life is good or bad according as it does or does not bring a surplus of agreeable feeling.
HERBERT SPENCER: *The Data of Ethics*, III, 1879

A pessimist is a man who thinks all women are bad. An optimist is one who hopes they are.
Ascribed to CHAUNCEY M. DEPEW (1834–1928)

An optimist sees an opportunity in every calamity; a pessimist sees a calamity in every opportunity. Author unidentified

A pessimist is a man who happens to live with an optimist. IBID.

[*See also* Pessimist.

Oracle

I am Sir Oracle,
And when I ope my lips let no dog bark!
SHAKESPEARE: *The Merchant of Venice*, I, *c.* 1597

The oracles are dumb.
JOHN MILTON: *On the Morning of Christ's Nativity*, 1629

Orangutan

[*See* Husband.

Orator

A man skilled in moving to tears.
PLINY THE YOUNGER: *Letters*, *c.* 110

A man . . . that hath a mint of phrases in his brain.
SHAKESPEARE: *Love's Labor's Lost*, I, *c.* 1595

I come not, friends, to steal away your hearts;
I am no orator, as Brutus is.
SHAKESPEARE: *Julius Cæsar*, III, 1599

When he speaks,
The air, a charter'd libertine, is still,
And the mute wonder lurketh in men's ears,
To steal his sweet and honey'd sentences.
SHAKESPEARE: *Henry V*, I, *c.* 1599

There is only one perfect orator in a century.
BALTASAR GRACIÁN: *The Art of Worldly Wisdom*, CCIII, 1647

There are those who speak well, and do not write well. It is because the place, the audience, warms them, and elicits from their mind more than they find in it without this warmth.
BLAISE PASCAL: *Pensées*, IX, 1670

Where judgment has wit to express it there's the best orator.
WILLIAM PENN: *Fruits of Solitude*, 1693

The wisdom of our ancestors being highly sensible, has, to encourage all aspiring adventurers, thought fit to erect three wooden machines for the use of those orators who desire to talk much without interruption. These are, the pulpit, the [hangman's] ladder, and the stage itinerant.
JONATHAN SWIFT: *A Tale of a Tub*, I, 1704

Here comes the orator, with his flood of words, and his drop of reason.
BENJAMIN FRANKLIN: *Poor Richard's Almanac*, 1735

It would be as idle in an orator to waste deep meditation and long research on his speeches as it would be in the manager of a theatre to adorn all the crowd of courtiers and ladies who cross over the stage in a procession with real pearls and diamonds. It is not by accuracy or profundity that men become the masters of great assemblies.
T. B. MACAULAY: *Gladstone on Church and State*, 1839 (Edinburgh Review, April)

He is a good orator who convinces himself.
H. G. BOHN: *Handbook of Proverbs*, 1855

Love, knavery, and necessity make men good orators. IBID.

A course of mobs is good practise for orators.
R. W. EMERSON: *The Conduct of Life*, II, 1860

He who has no hands
Perforce must use his tongue;
Foxes are so cunning
Because they are not strong.
R. W. EMERSON: *The Orator*, 1860 (Dial, March)

An orator wishing to move a crowd must make use of violent affirmations, stated in abusive terms. His methods are to exaggerate, to re-

peat, to avoid any attempt to produce reasonable proof.
GUSTAVE LEBON: *Psychologie des foules*, II, 1895

The best orator is one who can make men see with their ears. ARAB PROVERB

Whoever can speak well can also lie well.
JAPANESE PROVERB

Orators are made; poets are born. (Orator fit; poeta nascitur.) LATIN PROVERB

The better the orator the worse the man. (Bonus orator, pessimus vir.) IBID.

[*See also* Demagogue, Democracy, Douglas (Stephen A.), July Fourth, Oratory.

Oratorio

Nothing can be more disgusting than an oratorio. How absurd to see five hundred people fiddling like madmen about the Israelites in the Red Sea!
SYDNEY SMITH: *Letter to Lady Holland*, 1823

Oratory

Oh, that my tongue were in the thunder's mouth!
Then with a passion would I shake the world.
SHAKESPEARE: *King John*, III, 1596

Oratory is the same in all languages, the same rules being observed, the same method, the same arguments and arts of persuasion.
JOHN EACHARD: *The Grounds and Occasions of the Contempt of the Clergy and Religion*, 1670

Oratory is the power of beating down your adversary's arguments, and putting better in their place.
SAMUEL JOHNSON: *Boswell's Life*, May 8, 1781

Oratory is the huffing and blustering spoiled child of a semi-barbarous age.
C. C. COLTON: *Lacon*, 1820

The object of oratory is not truth, but persuasion.
T. B. MACAULAY: *The Athenian Orators*, 1824

Oratory may be symbolized by a warrior's eye, flashing from under a philosopher's brow. But why a warrior's eye rather than a poet's? Because in oratory the will must predominate.
J. C. and A. W. HARE: *Guesses at Truth*, 1827

I thank God that, if I am gifted with little of the spirit which is able to raise mortals to the skies, I have yet none, as I trust, of that other spirit which would drag angels down.
DANIEL WEBSTER: Speech in the Senate, Jan. 26, 1830

Condense some daily experience into a glowing symbol, and an audience is electrified.
R. W. EMERSON: *Eloquence*, 1877

[*See also* History.

Orchard

In an orchard there should be enough to eat, enough to lay up, enough to be stolen, and enough to rot upon the ground.
Ascribed by JAMES BOSWELL, in his *Life of Johnson*, 1783, to " my friend, Dr. Madden, of Ireland "

It will beggar a doctor to live where orchards thrive. SPANISH PROVERB

Ordeal

[*See* Trial.

Order

Set thine house in order.
ISAIAH XXXVIII, 1, *c.* 700 B.C.

Let all things be done decently and in order.
I CORINTHIANS XIV, 40, *c.* 55

There is no course of life so weak and sottish as that which is managed by order, method, and discipline.
MICHEL DE MONTAIGNE: *Essays*, III, 1588

The heavens themselves, the planets, and this centre
Observe degrees, priority and place,
Insisture, course, proportion, season, form,
Office and custom, in all line of order.
SHAKESPEARE: *Troilus and Cressida*, I, *c.* 1601

The human understanding is of its nature prone to suppose the existence of more order and regularity in the world than it finds.
FRANCIS BACON: *Novum Organum*, I, 1620

At his second bidding darkness fled,
Light shone, and order from disorder sprung.
JOHN MILTON: *Paradise Lost*, III, 1667

We are rational creatures: our virtue and perfection is to love reason, or rather to love order.
NICOLAS MALEBRANCHE: *Traité de moral*, I, 1684

Order is Heaven's first law.
ALEXANDER POPE: *An Essay on Man*, IV, 1734

A great part of that order which reigns among mankind is not the effect of government. It had its origin in the principles of society, and the natural constitution of men. It existed prior to government, and would exist if the formality of government was abolished.
THOMAS PAINE: *The Rights of Man*, I, 1791

Let all your things have their places; let each part of your business have its time.
BENJAMIN FRANKLIN: *Autobiography,* 1798

Have a place for everything and have everything in its place.
H. G. BOHN: *Handbook of Proverbs,* 1855

In its narrowest acceptation, order means obedience. A government is said to preserve order if it succeeds in getting itself obeyed.
J. S. MILL: *Representative Government,* II, 1861

Nothing is orderly till man takes hold of it. Everything in creation lies around loose.
H. W. BEECHER: *Eyes and Ears,* 1862

Law, order, duty an' restraint, obedience, discipline!
RUDYARD KIPLING: *M'Andrew's Hymn,* 1893

[*See also* Cleanliness, Discipline, Mind.

Organ

The organ, to my eyes and ears, is the king of instruments.
W. A. MOZART: *Letter to his father,* Oct. 17, 1777

Seated one day at the organ,
I was weary and ill at ease,
And my fingers wandered idly
Over the noisy keys.
ADELAIDE A. PROCTOR: *A Lost Chord,* 1861

[*See also* Harp.

Origin

Never search for the origin of a saint, a river, or a woman. HINDU PROVERB

From the origin. (Ab origine.)
LATIN PHRASE

Original

[*See* Copy.

Originality

All good things which exist are the fruits of originality.
J. S. MILL: *On Liberty,* III, 1859

Originality is the one thing which unoriginal minds cannot feel the use of. IBID.

Human nature has a much greater genius for sameness than for originality.
J. R. LOWELL: *On a Certain Condescension in Foreigners,* 1869

Originality does not consist in saying what no one has ever said before, but in saying exactly what you think yourself.
JAMES FITZ-JAMES STEPHEN (1829–94)

Originality is imitation that has not been detected. Author unidentified

[*See also* Greatness, Intelligence.

Ornament

The especial condition of true ornament is, that it be beautiful in its place, and nowhere else.
JOHN RUSKIN: *Stones of Venice,* I, 1851

[*See also* Adornment, Decoration, Dress, Finery, Loveliness.

Orphan

Late children, early orphans.
BENJAMIN FRANKLIN: *Poor Richard's Almanac,* 1742

Little bird out in the rain.
ELIZABETH CHASE (AKERS ALLEN): *Gertrudie,* 1866

[*See also* Children, Chivalry, Fatherless, Happiness, Soldier.

Orthodoxy

Orthodox is a hard word, and Greek for claret.
WILLIAM CONGREVE: *The Way of the World,* IV, 1700

If we were all before the gates of Heaven and the question were put, "Which of you is orthodox," the Jew, the Turk and the Christian would answer in unison, "I am."
IMMANUEL KANT: *Lecture at Königsberg,* 1775

Orthodoxy is my doxy; heterodoxy is another man's doxy.
Ascribed to WILLIAM WARBURTON (BISHOP OF GLOUCESTER) (1698–1779)

Ostentation

All their works they do for to be seen of men: they make broad their phylacteries, and enlarge the borders of their garments, and love the uppermost rooms at feasts, and the chief seats in the synagogues.
MATTHEW XXIII, 5–6, *c.* 75

[*See also* Pedant.

Osteopathy

Osteopathy shall be defined as a complete system of therapeutics embracing all scientific subjects pertaining to the healing art except materia medica. Instead it places emphasis on structural integrity as a major essential to health and that [*sic*] any derangement of structural integrity is a fundamental cause of disease, by interfering with the natural function of immunity and nutrition. Practice consists principally in the correction of all structural derangement by manipulative measures including physio and electro therapy, minor surgery, diet, hygiene and obstetrics.
ACTS OF THE LEGISLATURE OF SOUTH CAROLINA, 1938

Outdoors

I am enamour'd of growing outdoors,
Of men that live among cattle, or taste of the ocean or woods.

WALT WHITMAN: *Walt Whitman,* 1855

Outlaw

I am one, my liege,
Whom the vile blows and buffets of the world
Have so incensed that I am reckless what
I do to spite the world.

SHAKESPEARE: *Macbeth,* III, *c.* 1605

A fig for those by law protected!
Liberty's a glorious feast!
Courts for cowards were erected;
Churches built to please the priest.

ROBERT BURNS: *The Jolly Beggars,* 1785

An enemy of the human race. (Hostis humani generis.) LATIN PHRASE

[*See also* Criminal.

Outside

It's only the fellow on the outside who can tell a snail how his shell looks.

ELBERT HUBBARD: *Roycroft Dictionary and Book of Epigrams,* 1923

Over

[*See* Done.

Ovid (43 B.C.–18 A.D.)

Venus' clerk, Ovid,
That hath sown wonder wide,
The great god of love's name.

GEOFFREY CHAUCER: *The House of Fame,* III, *c.* 1384

Owl

Nightly sings the staring owl,
Tu-whit, tu-who.

SHAKESPEARE: *Love's Labor's Lost,* V, *c.* 1595

He's in great want of a bird that will give a groat for an owl.

JOHN RAY: *English Proverbs,* 1670

The gravest bird's an owl.

ALLAN RAMSAY: *Scots Proverbs,* 1737

Do you think I was born in a wood, to be afraid of an owl?

JONATHAN SWIFT: *Polite Conversation,* III, 1738

When cats run home and light is come,
And dew is cold upon the ground,
And the far-off stream is dumb,
And the whirring sail goes round,
And the whirring sail goes round;
Alone and warming his five wits,
The white owl in the belfry sits.

ALFRED TENNYSON: *The Owl,* 1830

A wise old owl sat on an oak,
The more he saw the less he spoke;
The less he spoke the more he heard;
Why aren't we like that wise old bird?

EDWARD HERSEY RICHARDS

[*See also* Cat.

Ownership

[*See* Property.

Ox

The ox is the slave of the poor.

ARISTOTLE: *Politics,* I, *c.* 322 B.C.

Whither shall the ox go where he shall not labor?

GEORGE HERBERT: *Outlandish Proverbs,* 1640

The ox never thanks the pasture.

HAITIAN PROVERB

[*See also* Easy, Muzzle.

Oxford University

Mark the chronicles aright:
When Oxford scholars fall to fight,
Before many months expired
England will with war be fired.

THOMAS FULLER: *Worthies of England,* 1662; a paraphrase of a medieval Latin couplet:

Chronica si penses, cum pugnant Oxonienses
Post paucos menses volet ira Angligenenses.

To the university of Oxford I acknowledge no obligation; and she will as cheerfully renounce me for a son as I am willing to disclaim her for a mother. I spent fourteen months at Magdalen College; they proved the fourteen months the most idle and unprofitable of my whole life.

EDWARD GIBBON: *Outlines of the History of the World,* 1758

The scheme of Revelation, we think, is closed, and we expect no new light on earth to break in upon us. Oxford must guard that sacred citadel.

EDWARD COPLESTON: *A Reply to the Calumnies of the Edinburgh Review Against Oxford,* 1810

You will hear more good things on the outside of a stagecoach from London to Oxford than if you were to pass a twelvemonth with the undergraduates, or heads of colleges, of that famous university.

WILLIAM HAZLITT: *The Ignorance of the Learned,* 1821

Home of lost causes, and forsaken beliefs, and unpopular names, and impossible loyalties.

MATTHEW ARNOLD: *I Essays in Criticism,* pref., 1865

They say that Oxford is half way to Rome.

WILLIAM BLACK: *The Strange Adventures of a Phaeton,* VI, 1872

I wonder anyone does anything here but dream and remember; the place is so beautiful one

expects the people to sing instead of speaking.
W. B. YEATS: *Letter to Katherine Tynan Hinkson, c.* 1925

Oyster

The oyster is unseasonable and unwholesome in all months that have not the letter *R* in their name.
RICHARD BUTTES: *Diet's Dry Dinner,* 1599

The world's mine oyster,
Which I with sword will open.
SHAKESPEARE: *The Merry Wives of Windsor,* II, *c.* 1600

Oysters . . . are ungodly, because they are eaten without grace; uncharitable, because they leave naught but shells; and unprofitable, because they must swim in wine.
Anon.: *Tarlton's Jests,* 1611

He was a very valiant man who first adventured on eating of oysters.
THOMAS FULLER: *Worthies of England,* 1662 (Ascribed to JAMES I)

The gravest fish is an oyster.
ALLAN RAMSAY: *Scots Proverbs,* 1737

Oysters are a cruel meat because we eat them alive; then they are an uncharitable meat, for we leave nothing to the poor.
JONATHAN SWIFT: *Polite Conversation,* 1738 (Cf. Anon., *ante,* 1611)

An oyster may be crossed in love.
R. B. SHERIDAN: *The Critic,* III, 1779

The oyster loves the dredging song
For they come of a gentle kind.
WALTER SCOTT: *The Antiquary,* XL, 1816

Oysters are amatory food.
BYRON: *Don Juan,* II, 1819

Secret, and self-contained, and solitary as an oyster.
CHARLES DICKENS: *A Christmas Carol,* 1843

The oyster with much pain produces its pearl.
I take the pearl.
ALEXANDER SMITH: *Dreamthorp,* XI, 1863

He [Bismarck] also confesses a weakness for fried oysters; this, in my opinion, is treason to gastronomy.
JULES HOCHE: *Bismarck at Home,* 1888

An oyster is a fish built like a nut.
Author unidentified

The great object in the life of an oyster is to convert the whole earth into oysters.
IBID.

Than an oyster
There's nothing moister.
IBID.

[*See also* Envy.

P

Pace

The pace that kills.
ENGLISH PHRASE, not recorded before the XIX century

Pacific Coast

[*See* Twilight.

Pacific Ocean

There is one knows not what sweet mystery about this sea, whose gentle awful stirrings seem to speak of some hidden soul beneath; like those faded undulations of the Ephesian sod over the buried evangelist, St. John.
HERMAN MELVILLE: *Moby Dick,* CX, 1851

Pacifism

The professional pacifist is merely the tool of the sensual materialist who has no ideals, whose shrivelled soul is wholly absorbed in automobiles, and the movies, and money making, and in the policies of the cash register and the stock ticker, and the life of fatted ease.
THEODORE ROOSEVELT: Speech in Kansas City, May 30, 1916

We are not pacifists. We are against imperialist wars, but it is absurd for the proletariat to oppose revolutionary wars that are indispensable for the victory of Socialism.
NIKOLAI LENIN: *Farewell letter to the Swiss workers,* April 8, 1917

The pacifist is as surely a traitor to his country and to humanity as is the most brutal wrongdoer.
THEODORE ROOSEVELT: Speech in Pittsburgh, July 27, 1917

The parlor pacifist, the white-handed or sissy type of pacifist, represents decadence, represents the rotting out of the virile virtues among people who typify the unlovely, senile side of civilization. The rough-neck pacifist, on the contrary, is a mere belated savage who has not been educated to the virtues of national patriotism.
THEODORE ROOSEVELT: Speech in Minneapolis, Sept. 28, 1917

Pacifism is simply undisguised cowardice.
ADOLF HITLER: Speech at Nürnberg, Aug. 21, 1926

Pagan

A pagan suckled in a creed outworn.
WILLIAM WORDSWORTH: *The World Is Too Much With Us,* 1807

I too love the great pagan world, its bloodshed, its slaves, its injustices, its loathing of all that is feeble.
GEORGE MOORE: *Confessions of a Young Man,* X, 1888

[*See also* Christian.

Paganini, Niccolò (1782–1840)

Everybody is talking of Paganini and his violin. The man seems to be a miracle. The newspapers say that long streamy flakes of music fall from his string, interspersed with luminous points of sound which ascend the air and appear like stars. This eloquence is quite beyond me.
T. B. MACAULAY: *Letter to his sister,* May 27, 1831

Pain

When pain is unbearable it destroys us; when it does not it is bearable.
MARCUS AURELIUS: *Meditations,* VII, *c.* 170

The greatest evil is physical pain.
ST. AUGUSTINE: *Soliloquies,* I, *c.* 387

They breathe truth that breathe their words in pain.
SHAKESPEARE: *Richard II,* II, *c.* 1596

One pain is lessen'd by another's anguish.
SHAKESPEARE: *Romeo and Juliet,* I, *c.* 1596

Great pains quickly find ease.
GEORGE HERBERT: *Outlandish Proverbs,* 1640

There is no real ill in life except severe bodily pain; everything else is the child of the imagination; all other ills find a remedy, either from time, or moderation, or strength of mind.
MARIE DE SÉVIGNÉ: *Letters, c.* 1680

Resolved, When I feel pain, to think of the pains of martyrdom, and of Hell.
JONATHAN EDWARDS: *Resolutions,* 1722

Those who do not feel pain seldom think that it is felt.
SAMUEL JOHNSON: *The Rambler,* Sept. 1, 1750

The heart can ne'er a transport know,
That never feels a pain.
GEORGE LYTTELTON: *Song,* 1753

The mind is seldom quickened to very vigorous operations but by pain, or the dread of pain. We do not disturb ourselves with the detection of fallacies which do us no harm.
SAMUEL JOHNSON: *The Idler,* Aug. 12, 1758

Pain is in itself an evil, and, indeed without exception, the only evil.
JEREMY BENTHAM: *Principles of Morals and Legislation,* x, 1789

Real pain can alone cure us of imaginary ills. We feel a thousand miseries till we are lucky enough to feel misery.
S. T. COLERIDGE: *Notebooks,* 1797

Pain, whose unheeded and familiar speech
Is howling, and keen shrieks, day after day.
P. B. SHELLEY: *Prometheus Unbound,* II, 1820

Pain is life — the sharper, the more evidence of life.
CHARLES LAMB: *Letter to Bernard Barton,* Jan. 9, 1824

He preaches patience that never knew pain.
H. G. BOHN: *Handbook of Proverbs,* 1855

Pain is the correlative of some species of wrong — some kind of divergence from that course of action which perfectly fills our requirements.
HERBERT SPENCER: *The Data of Ethics,* xv, 1879

Man endures pain as an undeserved punishment; woman accepts it as a natural heritage.
Author unidentified

Pain is gain. GREEK PROVERB

[*See also* Civilization, Death, Existence, Good and Evil, Happiness, Intelligence, Labor, Life, Mind and Body, Pleasure, Pleasure and Pain, Progress, Thinking, Wisdom.

Paine, Thomas (1737–1809)

This writer has a better hand in pulling down than in building.
JOHN ADAMS: *Letter to Abigail Adams,* March 19, 1776

My countrymen, I know, from their form of government, and steady attachment heretofore to royalty, will come reluctantly to the idea of independence, but time and persecution bring many wonderful things to pass; and by private letters, which I have lately received from Virginia, I find [Paine's] "Common Sense" is working a powerful change there in the minds of many men.
GEORGE WASHINGTON: *Letter to Joseph Reed,* April 1, 1776

Resolved, That the early and continued labors of Thomas Paine and his timely publications merit the approbation of this Congress.
Resolution of Congress, Aug. 26, 1785

In digging up your bones, Tom Paine,
Will Cobbett has done well:
You visit him on earth again,
He'll visit you in Hell.
BYRON: *Letter to Thomas Moore,* Jan. 2, 1820

That filthy little atheist.
THEODORE ROOSEVELT: *Gouverneur Morris,* 1888

Painstaking

No pains, no gains.
ENGLISH PROVERB, traced by Apperson to 1577

Particular pains particular thanks do ask.
BEN JONSON: *Cynthia's Revels,* v, 1601

Pains is the price that God putteth upon all things. JAMES HOWELL: *Proverbs,* 1659

[*See also* Laziness.

Painter

The painter who draws by practise and judgment of the eye without the use of reason is like the mirror which reproduces within itself all the objects which are set opposite to it without knowledge of the same.
LEONARDO DA VINCI: *Notebooks, c.* 1500

I, too, am a painter. (Anch' io sono pittore!)
ANTONIO CORREGGIO: On seeing Raphael's St. Cecilia at Bologna, *c.* 1525

Zeuxis was so excellent in painting that it was easier for any man to view his pictures than to imitate them; who, to make an excellent table, had five Agrigentine virgins naked by him. He painted grapes so lively that birds did fly to eat them.
FRANCIS MERES: *Pallidas Tamia,* 1598 (*Table*=picture)

Painters are subject to tremblings of the joints, blackness of the teeth, discolored complexion, melancholy, and loss of the sense of smell.
BERNARDINO RAMAZZINI: *De morbis artificium diatriba,* 1700

Only God Almighty makes painters.
GODFREY KNELLER: Reply to his tailor, who asked Kneller to take his son as a pupil, *c.* 1710

It was once confessed to me by a painter that no professor of his art ever loved another.
SAMUEL JOHNSON: *The Rambler,* Oct. 27, 1750

A flattering painter, who made it his care
To draw men as they ought to be, not as they are.
OLIVER GOLDSMITH: *Retaliation,* 1774

The most sensible men I know, taken as a class, are painters; that is, they are the most lively observers of what passes in the world about them, and the closest observers of what passes in their own heads.
WILLIAM HAZLITT: *The Pleasure of Painting,* 1821

To be a first-rate painter you mustn't be pious, but rather a little wicked and entirely a man of the world.
JOHN RUSKIN: To C. E. Norton, Oct. 24, 1858

The reason why the old painters were so greatly superior to the modern is that a greatly superior class of men applied themselves to the art.
J. S. MILL: *The Subjection of Women,* III, 1869

[*See also* Actor, Astronomer, Bologna, Master, Painting, Poet.

Painting

What vanity is painting, which attracts admiration by its resemblance to things which in the original we do not admire.
BLAISE PASCAL: *Pensées,* IX, 1670

There are three things I have always loved and never understood — painting, music and women.
BERNARD DE FONTENELLE: *Dialogues des morts,* 1683

Who is the better man for beholding the most beautiful Venus, the best wrought Bacchanal, the images of sleeping Cupids, languishing nymphs, or any of the representations of gods, goddesses, demi-gods, satyrs, Polyphemes, sphinxes, or fawns?
RICHARD STEELE: *The Spectator,* Nov. 19, 1711

There is craft in daubing.
THOMAS FULLER: *Gnomologia,* 1732

I have generally found that persons who had studied painting least were the best judges of it.
WILLIAM HOGARTH: To Horace Walpole, 1761

Painting can illustrate, but cannot inform.
SAMUEL JOHNSON: *Boswell's Life,* 1784

One is never tired of painting, because you have to set down, not what you knew already, but what you have just discovered. There is a continual creation out of nothing going on.
WILLIAM HAZLITT: *The Pleasure of Painting,* 1821

Painting is the intermediate somewhat between a thought and a thing.
S. T. COLERIDGE: *Table-Talk,* Aug. 30, 1827

How weak is painting to describe a man!
CHARLES LAMB: *Letter to William Wordsworth,* Jan. 22, 1830

The power of enjoying music, being common to brutes, must be considered inferior to the capability of appreciating painting, which is peculiar to him who was made after the image of God.
JOHN RUSKIN: *Essay on the Relative Dignity of the Studies of Painting and Music,* 1838

Painting, or art generally, as such, with all its technicalities, difficulties, and particular ends, is nothing but a noble and expressive language, invaluable as the vehicle of thought, but by itself, nothing.
JOHN RUSKIN: *Modern Painters,* I, 1843

Religious paintings are the catechism of the ignorant.
JAMES CARDINAL GIBBONS: *The Faith of Our Fathers,* XV, 1876

A painting has no more spiritual message or meaning than an exquisite fragment of Venetian glass or a blue tile from the wall of Damascus: it is a beautifully colored surface, nothing more.
OSCAR WILDE: *The English Renaissance of Art,* 1882 (Lecture in New York, Jan. 9)

It does not matter how badly you paint, so long as you don't paint badly like other people.
GEORGE MOORE: *Confessions of a Young Man*, VII, 1888

I do not greatly care for the reproduction of landscapes which, in effect, I see whenever I ride or walk. I wish "the light that never was on land or sea" in the pictures that I am to live with.
THEODORE ROOSEVELT: *Letter to P. M. Simons*, March 19, 1904

The art of protecting flat surfaces from the weather and exposing them to the critic.
AMBROSE BIERCE: *The Devil's Dictionary*, 1906

You may weep over a book or on hearing music, but you never weep before a picture or a piece of sculpture.
ALFRED STEVENS (1828–1906)

[*See also* Art, English, Mediocrity, Painter, Perspective, Picture, Poetry, Portrait.

Pale

A pale man is envious.
SCOTTISH PROVERB, traced by Fergusson to 1598

At a pale man draw thy knife. IBID.

Why so pale and wan, fond lover?
  Prithee, why so pale?
Will, when looking well can't move her,
  Looking ill prevail?
  Prithee, why so pale?
JOHN SUCKLING: *Encouragements to a Lover*, 1638

A pale face is worse than the itch.
FRENCH PROVERB

Palestine

[*See* Jew.

Palm

An itching palm.
SHAKESPEARE: *Julius Cæsar*, IV, 1599

Pamphlet

From pamphlets may be learned the genius of the age, the debates of the learned, the *bévues* of government, and mistakes of the courtiers. Pamphlets furnish beaus with their airs; coquettes with their charms. Pamphlets are as modish ornaments to gentlewomen's toilets, as to gentlemen's pockets: they carry reputation of wit and learning to all that make them their companions.
MYLES DAVIES: *Icon libellorum*, 1715
(*Bévue*=blunder)

[*See also* Press (Free).

Pan

And that dismal cry rose slowly
  And sank slowly through the air,
Full of spirit's melancholy
  And eternity's despair!
And they heard the words it said —
Pan is dead! great Pan is dead!
  Pan, Pan is dead!
E. B. BROWNING: *The Dead Pan*, 1844

Panama Canal

It is absolutely indispensable for the United States to effect a passage from the Mexican Gulf to the Pacific Ocean; and I am certain that they will do it.
J. W. GOETHE: *Conversations with Eckermann*, Feb. 21, 1827

I confidently maintain that the recognition of the Republic of Panama was an act justified by the interests of collective civilization. If ever a government could be said to have received a mandate from civilization to effect an object the accomplishment of which was demanded in the interest of mankind, the United States holds that position with regard to the interoceanic canal.
THEODORE ROOSEVELT: Message to Congress, Jan. 4, 1904

I took the Canal Zone and let Congress debate, and while the debate goes on the canal does too.
THEODORE ROOSEVELT: Speech in Berkeley, Calif., March 23, 1911

Pancake

As flat as a pancake.
ENGLISH PHRASE, traced by the New English Dictionary to *c.* 1430

There is a thing called wheaten flour, which the sulphury necromantic cooks do mingle with water, eggs, spice and other tragical magical enchantments, and then they put it little by little into a frying-pan of boiling suet, where it is transformed into the form of a flapjack, which in our translation is called a pancake.
JOHN TAYLOR: *Jack-a-Lent*, 1630

Panegyric

All panegyrics are mingled with an infusion of poppy.
JONATHAN SWIFT: *Thoughts on Various Subjects*, 1706

Panic

There is no fence against a panic fright.
THOMAS FULLER: *Gnomologia*, 1732

Pansy

There is pansies, that's for thoughts.
SHAKESPEARE: *Hamlet*, IV, *c.* 1601

Pantaloons

Why does the President wear red-white-and-blue suspenders? To hold up his pantaloons.
AMERICAN MINSTREL RIDDLE, *c.* 1880

[*See also* Age (Old), Ant, Breeches.

Pantheism

I am everything that is, and that is to be, and that has been.

INSCRIPTION ON THE TEMPLE OF NEITH AT SAÏS (SA EL-HAGAR), EGYPT, *c.* 600 B.C.

God is the universal substance in existing things. He comprises all things. He is the fountain of all being. In Him exists everything that is.

GIORDANO BRUNO: *Summa terminorum metaphysicorum,* 1590

I do account it, not the meanest, but an impiety monstrous to confound God and nature, be it but in terms.

WALTER RALEIGH: *Historie of the World,* pref., 1614

All are but parts of one stupendous whole,
Whose body nature is, and God the soul.

ALEXANDER POPE: *An Essay on Man,* I, 1732

The simplest person, who in his integrity worships God, becomes God.

R. W. EMERSON: *The Over-Soul,* 1841

The chief objection I have to pantheism is that it says nothing. To call the world God is not to explain it; it is only to enrich our language with a superfluous synonym for the word world.

ARTHUR SCHOPENHAUER: *A Few Words on Pantheism,* 1851

They reckon ill who leave me out;
When me they fly, I am the wings;
I am the doubter and the doubt
And I the hymn the Brahmin sings.

R. W. EMERSON: *Brahma,* 1857 (Atlantic Monthly, Nov.)

I am the batsman and the bat,
I am the bowler and the ball,
The umpire, the pavilion cat,
The roller, pitch, and stumps, and all.

ANDREW LANG: *Parody of Emerson: Brahma, c.* 1880 (Cf. EMERSON, *ante,* 1857)

[*See also* God.

Panther

That creature on whose back abound
Black spots upon a yellow ground
A panther is — the fairest beast
That haunteth in the spacious East:
He underneath a fair outside
Does cruelty and treachery hide.

MARY LAMB: *The Beasts in the Tower,* 1809

Panting

As the hart panteth after the water brooks, so panteth my soul after thee, O God.

PSALMS XLII, 1, *c.* 150 B.C.

Pantomime

All foreigners excel
The serious Angles in the eloquence
Of pantomime.

BYRON: *Don Juan,* XIV, 1823

Papa

The word Papa gives a pretty form to the lips. Papa, potatoes, poultry, prunes and prism are all very good words for the lips.

CHARLES DICKENS: *Dombey and Son,* II, 1848

Papacy

The primacy is given to Peter that it may be shown that the Church is one and the See of Christ is one.

ST. CYPRIAN OF CARTHAGE: *The Unity of the Catholic Church, c.* 255

Whenever the papacy has waged war, its power has diminished.

JOHN HUSS: *Simony,* 1442

The papacy is no other than the ghost of the deceased Roman Empire, sitting crowned upon the grave thereof.

THOMAS HOBBES: *Leviathan,* I, 1651

The states of the pope are, I suppose, the worst governed in the civilized world; and the imbecility of the police, the venality of the public servants, the desolation of the country, and the wretchedness of the people, force themselves on the observation of the most heedless traveler.

T. B. MACAULAY: *Letter from Rome,* Dec., 1838

The raree-show of Peter's successor.

ROBERT BROWNING: *Christmas Eve,* XXII, 1850

The hope of Italy and of the whole world lies in the power of the papacy.

POPE LEO XIII: *Inscrutabili,* April 21, 1878

The chair of Peter, that sacred repository of all truth.

POPE PIUS XI: *Quadragesimo anno,* May 15, 1931

[*See also* Pope, Rome, Vatican.

Paper

Paper will tolerate anything.

FRENCH PROVERB

Paperhanger

[*See* Busy.

Papist

[*See* Catholic (Roman).

Parable

The legs of the lame are not equal: so is a parable in the mouth of fools.

PROVERBS XXVI, 7, *c.* 350 B.C.

I will open my mouth in a parable: I will utter dark sayings of old.

PSALMS LXXVIII, 2, *c.* 150 B.C.

He spake many things unto them in parables.

MATTHEW XIII, 3, *c.* 75

Parade

Parading is a fundamental right, not of grace.
Decision of the Superior Court of Los Angeles in the case of the American Peace Mobilization, Dec. 1, 1940

Paradise

Those who believe and do that which is right, we will bring into gardens watered by rivers; therein shall they remain forever, and there shall they enjoy wives free from all impurity; and we will lead them into perpetual shades.
THE KORAN, IV, *c.* 625

For he on honey-dew hath fed,
And drunk the milk of Paradise.
S. T. COLERIDGE: *Kubla Khan,* 1816

[*See also* Heaven.

Paradox

Old fond paradoxes to make fools laugh i' the alehouse. SHAKESPEARE: *Othello,* II, 1604

The paradox is a cheat: it gains attention at first by its novelty, but later it is discredited, when its emptiness becomes apparent.
BALTASAR GRACIÁN: *The Art of Worldly Wisdom,* CXLIII, 1647

Parasite

The wide world is little else, in nature,
But parasites or sub-parasites.
BEN JONSON: *Volpone,* III, 1605

We humans are the greatest of the earth's parasites.
MARTIN H. FISCHER (1879–)

[*See also* Flea.

Pardon

I pardon him, as God shall pardon me.
SHAKESPEARE: *Richard II,* V, *c.* 1596

Oh, show your charity,
And with your pardon, like a cool soft gale,
Fan my poor sweating soul, that wanders through
Unhabitable climes and parched deserts.
JAMES SHIRLEY: *The Cardinal,* V, 1641

Those ends in war the best contentment bring
Whose peace is made up with a pardoning.
ROBERT HERRICK: *Hesperides,* 1648

Upon caution of the future time, a man ought to pardon the offenses past of them that, repenting, desire it. For pardon is nothing but granting of peace.
THOMAS HOBBES: *Leviathan,* XV, 1651

Pardoning the bad is injuring the good.
THOMAS FULLER: *Gnomologia,* 1732

In all supremacy of power there is inherent a prerogative to pardon.
BENJAMIN WHICHCOTE: *Moral and Religious Aphorisms,* 1753

God will pardon me. It is His trade.
HEINRICH HEINE: On his deathbed, 1856

Pardon is the best fruit of victory.
ARAB PROVERB

[*See also* Anathema, Forgiveness, Injury, Mercy, Offender.

Parent

There are three degrees of filial piety. The highest is being a credit to our parents, the next is not disgracing them; the lowest is being able simply to support them.
CONFUCIUS: *The Book of Rites,* XXI, *c.* 500 B.C.

The toil undertaken for a parent should not be remembered.
SOPHOCLES: *Œdipus Coloneus, c.* 450 B.C.

The foolish cockering of some parents, and the overstern carriage of others, causeth more men and women to take ill courses than their own natural instincts.
WILLIAM CECIL (LORD BURLEIGH): *Advice to his son, c.* 1555

The hen who, from the chilly air,
With pious wing protects her care,
And ev'ry fowl that flies at large,
Instructs me in a parent's charge.
JOHN GAY: *Fables,* intro., 1727

The parent's moral right can arise only from his kindness, and his civil right only from his money.
SAMUEL JOHNSON: To Hester Thrale, May 17, 1773

He is unworthy of life that gives no life to another. (Nascitur indigne per quem non nascitur alter.) LATIN PROVERB

In the place of a parent. (In loco parentis.)
LEGAL PHRASE, commonly applied to guardians, schoolmasters, etc.

[*See also* Child, Children, Education, Father, Mother, Obedience, Parricide.

Paris

Here nobody ever sleeps; it is not the way.
THOMAS GRAY: *Letter to Richard West,* April 12, 1739 (Writing from Paris)

The newspapers have given the rage of going to Paris a good name; they call it the French disease.
HORACE WALPOLE: *Letter to Horace Mann,* Oct. 17, 1763

The tendency to dissipation at Paris seems to be irresistible. There is a moral incapacity for industry and application, a *mollesse,* against which I am as ill guarded as I was at the age of twenty.
JOHN QUINCY ADAMS: *Diary,* Feb. 12, 1815 (*Mollesse*=laxity)

" Earth has no such folks — no folks such a city,
So great, or so grand, or so fine, or so pretty,"
Said Louis Quatorze,
" As this Paris of ours! "

R. H. BARHAM: *The Ingoldsby Legends*, II, 1842

Paris is nothing but an immense hospitality.

VICTOR HUGO: Speech at Paris, 1870

France is *l'homme sensuel moyen*, the average sensual man; Paris is the city of *l'homme sensuel moyen*. This has an attraction for all of us.

MATTHEW ARNOLD: *Literature and Dogma*, XI, 1873

A sinister Chicago.

J. K. HUYSMANS: *À rebours*, 1884

How ya gonna keep 'em down on the farm after they've seen Paree?

Title and first line of an American popular song, 1917

In Paris life passes like a dream.

FRENCH PROVERB

[*See also* American, If, London.

Parisian

I admire the Parisians prodigiously. They are the happiest people in the world, I believe, and have the best disposition to make others so.

JOHN ADAMS: *Letter to his wife*, Feb. 13, 1779

Park

The parks are the lungs of London.

Ascribed to WILLIAM PITT (1708–78)

Parley

A city that parleys is half taken.

ENGLISH PROVERB, familiar in one form or another since the XVI century; sometimes *castle* or *woman* is substituted for *city*

Valor that parleys is near yielding.

GEORGE HERBERT: *Jacula Prudentum*, 1651

Parliament

What's the thing call'd a parliament, but a mock? compos'd of a people that are only suffer'd to sit there because they are known to have no virtue, after the exclusion of all others that were not suspected to have any? What are they but pimps of tyranny, who are only employed to draw in the people to prostitute their liberty?

EDWARD SOXBY: *Killing No Murder*, 1657

The freedom of speech, and debates or proceedings in Parliament, ought not to be impeached or questioned in any court or place out of Parliament.

THE ENGLISH BILL OF RIGHTS, IX, Dec., 1689

Parliament is a large council to the king, and the advantage of such a council is, having a great number of men of property concerned in the legislature, who, for their own interest, will not consent to bad laws.

SAMUEL JOHNSON: *Boswell's Life*, April 14, 1775

Parliament can do anything but turn a boy into a girl.

ENGLISH PROVERB, not recorded before the XIX century

A parliament speaking through reporters to Buncombe and the twenty-seven millions, mostly fools.

THOMAS CARLYLE: *Latter-Day Pamphlets*, VI, 1850

England is the mother of parliaments.

JOHN BRIGHT: Speech in Birmingham, Jan. 18, 1865

A parliament is nothing less than a big meeting of more or less idle people.

WALTER BAGEHOT: *The English Constitution*, 1867

Parliamentarism is nauseating to anyone who has ever seen it at close range.

P. A. KROPOTKIN: *Paroles d'un révolté*, 1884

A parliament is only a means to an end, and when it fails to achieve that end other means must be employed.

COUNT CARL STÜRGKH: On proroguing the Austrian Parliament, March 16, 1914

[*See also* Assembly, England, Law, Legislature, Speaker.

Parricide

If a person confess to us that he is going to commit a parricide, we commit it along with him, if, being able, we do not slay him before he can do the deed, when we cannot in some other way prevent or thwart him.

ST. AUGUSTINE: *On Lying*, c. 395

[*See also* Suicide.

Parrot

A parrot next, but dead and stuff'd with art;
(For Poll, when living, lost the lady's heart,
And then his life; for he was heard to speak
Such frightful words as tinged his lady's cheek:)
Unhappy bird! who had no power to prove,
Save by such speech, his gratitude and love.

GEORGE CRABBE: *The Parish Register*, III, 1807

Parsimony

Penny wise and pound foolish.

EDWARD TOPSELL: *History of Fourfooted Beasts*, 1607

Parsimony is the best revenue.

JAMES HOWELL: *Proverbs*, 1659

[*See also* Capital, Miser, Thrift.

Parsley

Parsley must be sown nine times, for the Devil takes all but the last.

SHROPSHIRE PROVERB

Parson

A parson much bemused in beer.

ALEXANDER POPE: *An Epistle to Dr. Arbuthnot,* 1735

[*See also* Absolution, Clergy, Clergyman, Diet, Pastor, Vicar.

Part

Part for the whole. (Pars pro toto.)

LATIN PHRASE

Parting

The Lord watch between me and thee, when we are absent one from another.

GENESIS XXXI, 49, *c.* 700 B.C.

The king of Babylon stood at the parting of the way.

EZEKIEL XXI, 21, *c.* 600 B.C.

Since there's no help, come let us kiss and part, —
Nay I have done, you get no more of me.

MICHAEL DRAYTON: *Love's Farewell,* 1594

Parting is such sweet sorrow.

SHAKESPEARE: *Romeo and Juliet,* II, *c.* 1596

Let us not be dainty of leave-taking,
But shift away.

SHAKESPEARE: *Macbeth,* II, *c.* 1605

If we must part forever,
Give me but one kind word to think upon,
And please myself with, while my heart's breaking.

THOMAS OTWAY: *The Orphan,* III, 1680

Farewell and be hanged; friends must part.

THOMAS FULLER: *Gnomologia,* 1732

And must we part?
Well — if we must, we must — and in that case
The less said the better.

R. B. SHERIDAN: *The Critic,* II, 1779

Since now the hour is come at last,
When you must quit your anxious lover,
Since now our dream of bliss is past,
One pang, my girl, and all is over.

BYRON: *To Emma,* 1805

Maid of Athens, ere we part,
Give, oh give me back my heart!

BYRON: *Maid of Athens,* 1810

It may be for years, and it may be forever.

JULIA CRAWFORD: *Kathleen Mavourneen, c.* 1840

Every parting gives a foretaste of death; every coming together again a foretaste of the resurrection. This is why even people who were indifferent to each other rejoice so much if they come together again after twenty or thirty years' separation.

ARTHUR SCHOPENHAUER: *Further Psychological Observations,* 1851

The best company must part at last, as King Dagobert said to his dogs.

FRENCH PROVERB

[*See also* Absent, Farewell, Goodbye, Goodnight, Guest.

Partnership

Partnership is a synallagmatic and commutative participation in profits.

CIVIL CODE OF LOUISIANA, 1808

The only good partnership is between man and wife.

HINDU PROVERB

The partner of my partner is not my partner. (Socii mei socius, meus socius non est.)

LEGAL MAXIM

Partridge

If the partridge had the woodcock's thigh,
It would be the best bird that ever did fly.

JOHN RAY: *English Proverbs,* 1670

Party

If there are two parties a man ought to adhere to that which he disliketh least, though in the whole he doth not approve it; for whilst he doth not list himself in one or the other party, he is looked upon as such a straggler that he is fallen upon by both.

GEORGE SAVILE (MARQUESS OF HALIFAX): *Political, Moral and Miscellaneous Reflections, c.* 1690

England has this own fate peculiar to her:
Never to want a party to undo her.

DANIEL DEFOE: *The History of the Kentish Petition,* 1701

There can not a greater judgment befall a country than such a dreadful spirit of division as rends a government into two distinct people, and makes them greater strangers and more averse to one another than if they were actually two different nations.

JOSEPH ADDISON: *The Spectator,* July 24, 1711

Party-spirit at best is but the madness of many for the gain of a few.

ALEXANDER POPE: *Letter to Martha Blount,* Aug. 27, 1714

A nation without parties is soon a nation without curiosity.

HORACE WALPOLE: *Letter to Horace Mann,* Oct. 28, 1760

The extinction of party is the origin of faction.

HORACE WALPOLE: *Letter to George Montague,* Dec. 11, 1760

Party divisions, whether on the whole operating for good or evil, are things inseparable from free government.

EDMUND BURKE: *Observations on a Late State of the Nation,* 1769

If I could not go to Heaven but with a party I would not go there at all.
THOMAS JEFFERSON: *Letter to Francis Hopkinson*, March 13, 1789

Recollect that you were not made for the party, but the party for you.
H. H. BRACKENRIDGE: *Modern Chivalry*, 1792

The spirit of party serves always to distract the public councils, and enfeeble the public administration. It agitates the community with ill-founded jealousies and false alarms; kindles the animosity of one part against another; foments occasional riot and insurrection.
GEORGE WASHINGTON: Farewell Address, Sept. 17, 1796

Where there is no liberty they may be exempt from party. It will seem strange, but it scarcely admits a doubt, that there are fewer malcontents in Turkey than in any free state in the world. Where the people have no power they enter into no contests.
FISHER AMES: Oration in Boston, Feb. 8, 1800

No sooner has one party discovered or invented an amelioration of the condition of man, or the order of society, than the opposing party belies it, misconstrues it, misrepresents it, ridicules it, insults it and persecutes it.
JOHN ADAMS: *Letter to Thomas Jefferson*, July 9, 1813

Every political sect has its esoteric and its exoteric school, its abstract doctrines for the initiated, its visible symbols, its imposing forms, its mythological fables for the vulgar. It has its altars and its deified heroes, its relics and pilgrimages, its canonized martyrs and confessors, its festivals and its legendary miracles.
T. B. MACAULAY: *Hallam*, 1828 (Edinburgh Review, Sept.)

Party leads to vicious, corrupt and unprofitable legislation, for the sole purpose of defeating party.
J. FENIMORE COOPER: *The American Democrat*, XLI, 1838

We must suffer men to learn as they have done for six millenniums, a word at a time, to pair off into insane parties, and learn the amount of truth each knows by the denial of an equal amount of truth.
R. W. EMERSON: *The Conservative*, 1841

A party is perpetually corrupted by personality.
R. W. EMERSON: *Politics*, 1841

All parties without exception, when they seek for power, are varieties of absolutism.
P. J. PROUDHON: *Confessions d'un révolutionnaire*, 1849

What should we do with a party, that is, with a collection of asses, who swear by us because they take us for asses like themselves?
FRIEDRICH ENGELS: *Letter to Karl Marx*, Feb. 13, 1851

Party is organized opinion.
BENJAMIN DISRAELI: Speech at Oxford, Nov. 25, 1864

He serves his party best who serves the country best.
R. B. HAYES: Inaugural Address, March 5, 1877

All free governments are party-governments.
JAMES A. GARFIELD: Speech in the House of Representatives, Jan. 18, 1878

I always voted at my party's call,
And I never thought of thinking for myself at all.
W. S. GILBERT: *H.M.S. Pinafore*, I, 1878

The best system is to have one party govern and the other party watch.
THOMAS B. REED: Speech in the House of Representatives, April 22, 1880

Now is the time for all good men to come to the aid of their party.
Practise sentence of novices at the typewriter, *c.* 1885

Party honesty is party expediency.
GROVER CLEVELAND: To an interviewer in New York, Sept. 19, 1889

Parties seldom follow their best men. They follow their average sense.
THOMAS B. REED: Speech in Portland, Maine, July 29, 1896

The old parties are husks, with no real soul within either, divided on artificial lines, boss-ridden and privilege-controlled, each a jumble of incongruous elements, and neither daring to speak out wisely and fearlessly what should be said on the vital issues of the day.
THEODORE ROOSEVELT: Speech before the National Convention of the Progressive party, Chicago, Aug. 6, 1912

I know no more parties; I know only Germans.
EMPEROR WILHELM I: Speech from the throne, Aug. 4, 1914

Party is the historical organ by means of which a class becomes class conscious.
LEON TROTSKY: *What Next?*, II, 1932

[*See also* Faction, Individualism, Insanity, Politics.

Parvenu

There is little doubt that parvenus as often owe their advancement in society to their perseverance as to their pelf.
BENJAMIN DISRAELI: *The Young Duke*, I, 1831

Pass

They shall not pass. (Ils ne passeront pas.)
HENRI PÉTAIN: To General de Castenau, Feb., 1916, on being asked if Verdun should be abandoned to the Germans

Ships that pass in the night, and speak each other in passing,
Only a signal shown and a distant voice in the darkness;
So on the ocean of life, we pass and speak one another,
Only a look and a voice, then darkness again and a silence.

H. W. LONGFELLOW: *Tales of a Wayside Inn,* 1863

Passé

Pharaoh king of Egypt is but a noise; he hath passed the time appointed.

JEREMIAH XLVI, 17, *c.* 625 B.C.

Passion

We also are men of like passions with you.

ACTS XIV, 15, *c.* 75

Chastise your passions, that they may not chastise you.

EPICTETUS: *Encheiridion, c.* 110

All passions that suffer themselves to be relished and digested are but moderate.

MICHEL DE MONTAIGNE: *Essays,* I, 1580

Give me that man
That is not passion's slave.

SHAKESPEARE: *Hamlet,* III, *c.* 1601

One passion doth expel another.

GEORGE CHAPMAN: *Monsieur d'Olive,* V, 1606

The end of passion is the beginning of repentance.

OWEN FELLTHAM: *Resolves,* VIII, *c.* 1620

There is no passion in the mind of man so weak but it mates and masters the fear of death.

FRANCIS BACON: *Essays,* II, 1625

We are ne'er like angels till our passion dies.

THOMAS DEKKER: *II The Honest Whore,* I, 1630

The principal effect of the passions is that they incite and persuade the mind to will the events for which they prepare the body.

RENÉ DESCARTES: *Les passions de l'âme,* 1649

There are six simple and primary passions, to wit, wonder, love, hatred, desire, joy and sorrow. IBID.

Passions unguided are for the most part mere madness.

THOMAS HOBBES: *Leviathan,* VIII, 1651

If we resist our passions it is more from their weakness than from our strength.

LA ROCHEFOUCAULD: *Maxims,* 1665

The duration of our passion is no more dependent upon us than the duration of our life. IBID.

The passions are the only advocates which always persuade. The simplest man with passion will be more persuasive than the most eloquent without. IBID.

Whatever care we take to conceal our passions under the appearance of piety and honor, they are always to be seen through these veils. IBID.

Any sudden gust of passion, as an ecstasy of love in an unexpected meeting, cannot better be expressed than in a word and a sigh, breaking one another. Nature is dumb on such occasions; and to make her speak would be to represent her unlike herself.

JOHN DRYDEN: *Of Dramatic Poesy,* 1668

Passion makes us cowards grow,
What made us brave before.

JOHN DRYDEN: *An Evening's Love,* II, 1671

It is the passions which do and undo everything. If reason ruled, nothing would get on. . . . The passions in men are the winds necessary to put everything in motion, though they often cause storms.

BERNARD DE FONTENELLE: *Dialogues des morts,* I, 1683

Passion is a sort of fever in the mind, which ever leaves us weaker than it found us. It, more than anything, deprives us the use of our judgment; for it raises a dust very hard to see through. It may not unfitly be termed the mob of the man, that commits a riot upon his reason.

WILLIAM PENN: *Fruits of Solitude,* 1693

Passion, joined with power, produceth thunder and ruin.

THOMAS FULLER: *Gnomologia,* 1732

What reason weaves, by passion is undone.

ALEXANDER POPE: *An Essay on Man,* II, 1732

And you, brave Cobham! to the latest breath,
Shall feel your ruling passion strong in death.

ALEXANDER POPE: *Moral Essays,* I (Of the Knowledge and Characters of Men), 1733

Search then the ruling passion; there alone,
The wild are constant, and the cunning known;
The fool consistent, and the false sincere;
Priests, princes, women, no dissemblers here.

IBID.

The impetuous nerve of passion urges on
The native weight and energy of things.

MARK AKENSIDE: *The Pleasures of Imagination,* II, 1744

A man in a passion rides a wild horse.

BENJAMIN FRANKLIN: *Poor Richard's Almanac,* 1749

The end of passion is the beginning of repentance. IBID.

Mankind suffers more by the conflict of contrary passions than by that of passion and reason: yet perhaps the truest way to quench one passion is to kindle up another.
WILLIAM SHENSTONE: *Of Men and Manners,* 1764

Men are often false to their country and their honor, false to duty and even to their interest, but multitudes of men are never long false or deaf to their passions.
FISHER AMES: Oration in Boston, Feb. 8, 1800

Strong as our passions are, they may be starved into submission, and conquered without being killed.
C. C. COLTON: *Lacon,* 1820

The duration of passion runs in proportion to the original resistance of the woman.
BALZAC: *The Physiology of Marriage,* 1830

Knowledge of mankind is a knowledge of their passions.
BENJAMIN DISRAELI: *The Young Duke,* II, 1831

It is not only in the figurative sense that passion knocks at the gates of the heart. Its first effect is always some interference with the circulation of the blood.
ERNST VON FEUCHTERSLEBEN: *Zur Diätetik der Seele,* VI, 1838

No man can guess in cold blood what he may do in a passion.
H. G. BOHN: *Handbook of Proverbs,* 1855

A woman tropical, intense
In thought and act, in soul and sense,
She blended in a like degree
The vixen and the devotee.
J. G. WHITTIER: *Snow-Bound,* 1866

The church combats passion by excision; its remedy is castration. It never inquires how desire can be spiritualized, beautified, deified.
F. W. NIETZSCHE: *The Twilight of the Idols,* 1889

There is always something ridiculous about the passions of people whom one has ceased to love.
OSCAR WILDE: *The Picture of Dorian Gray,* 1891

Passions are like the trout in a pond: one devours the others until only one fat old trout is left. OTTO VON BISMARCK (1815–98)

The natural man has only two primal passions, to get and to beget.
WILLIAM OSLER: *Science and Immortality,* II, 1904

Scenes of passion should not be introduced when not essential to the plot. In general, passion should be so treated that these scenes do not stimulate the lower and baser element.
A CODE TO GOVERN THE MAKING OF MOTION AND TALKING PICTURES BY THE MOTION PICTURE PRODUCERS AND DISTRIBUTORS OF AMERICA, INC., March 31, 1930

The moralist tells us that women display their charms in order to excite men's passions. Very well. What are their charms for?
Author unidentified

Conquer your passions and you conquer the whole world. HINDU PROVERB

[*See also* Absence, Actor, Adultery, Age (Old), Animal, Cause and Effect, Crowd, History, Labor, Marriage, Music, Self-command, Sin, Tragedy.

Passport

Let letters be given me to the governors beyond the river.
NEHEMIAH II, 7, *c.* 300 B.C.

Past

Of one power even God is deprived, and that is the power of making what is past never to have been.
Ascribed to AGATHON (447 B.C.(?)–401 B.C.) in ARISTOTLE: *The Nicomachean Ethics,* VI, *c.* 340 B.C.

Say not thou, What is the cause that the former days were better than these? for thou dost not inquire wisely concerning this.
ECCLESIASTES VII, 10, *c.* 200 B.C.

The dark backward and abysm of time.
SHAKESPEARE: *The Tempest,* I, 1611

What's past is prologue.
SHAKESPEARE: *The Tempest,* II

That which is past is gone and irrevocable, and wise men have enough to do with things present and to come; therefore they do but trifle with themselves that labor in past matters.
FRANCIS BACON: *Essays,* IV, 1625

The water that is past cannot make the mill go.
THOMAS DRAXE: *Bibliotheca scholastica instructissima,* 1633

The misty black and bottomless pit of time.
THOMAS DUFFETT: *The Mock-Tempest,* I, 1675

Old, unhappy, far-off things,
And battles long ago.
WILLIAM WORDSWORTH: *The Solitary Reaper,* 1807

The secrets of the immeasurable past,
In the unfailing consciences of men.
P. B. SHELLEY: *Queen Mab,* II, 1813

I wandered through the wrecks of days departed.
P. B. SHELLEY: *The Revolt of Islam,* II, 1818

The past at least is secure.
DANIEL WEBSTER: Speech in the Senate, Jan. 26, 1830

Let the dead past bury its dead.
H. W. LONGFELLOW: *A Psalm of Life,* 1839

Is the acorn better than the oak which is its fullness and completion? Is the parent better than the child into whom he has cast his ripened being? Whence, then, this worship of the past?
R. W. EMERSON: *Self-Reliance,* 1841

Break, break, break,
At the foot of thy crags, O sea!
But the tender grace of a day that is dead
Will never come back to me.
ALFRED TENNYSON: *Break, Break, Break,* 1842

Tell me the tales that to me were so dear,
Long, long ago – long, long ago.
T. H. BAYLY: *Long, Long Ago,* 1844

Fresh as the first beam glittering on a sail,
That brings our friends up from the underworld,
Sad as the last which reddens over one
That sinks with all we love below the verge;
So sad, so fresh, the days that are no more.
ALFRED TENNYSON: *The Princess,* IV, 1847

No man who is correctly informed as to the past will be disposed to take a morose or desponding view of the present.
T. B. MACAULAY: *History of England,* I, 1848

I respect Assyria, China, Teutonia, and the Hebrews;
I adopt each theory, myth, god and demi-god;
I see that the old accounts, bibles, genealogies, are true, without exception;
I assert that all past days were what they should have been.
WALT WHITMAN: *With Antecedents,* 1860

Is it worth a tear, is it worth an hour,
To think of things that are well outworn?
A. C. SWINBURNE: *The Triumph of Time,* 1866

The past! the dark, unfathom'd retrospect!
The teeming gulf! the sleepers and the shadows!
The past! the infinite greatness of the past!
For what is the present, after all, but a growth out of the past?
WALT WHITMAN: *Passage to India,* 1868

The past is like a funeral gone by.
EDMUND GOSSE: *May-Day,* 1873

The best prophet of the future is the past.
JOHN SHERMAN: Speech in the Senate, June 5, 1890

One's past is what one is. It is the only thing by which people should be judged.
OSCAR WILDE: *An Ideal Husband,* II, 1895

The past is a bucket of ashes.
Author unidentified

[*See also* Antiquity, Change, Happiness, Present.

Pasteur, Louis (1822–95)

It is because of having reflected and studied that I have the faith of a Breton. If I had reflected and studied more, I would have attained to the faith of a Bretoness.
LOUIS PASTEUR: Reply to a student who asked him how, as a scientific man, he could remain a Roman Catholic, *c.* 1890

Pastime

Pastime, like wine, is poison in the morning.
THOMAS FULLER: *The Holy State and the Profane State,* 1642

Pastor

The pastors are become brutish.
JEREMIAH X, 21, *c.* 625 B.C.

The wind shall eat up all thy pastors.
JEREMIAH XXII, 22

A pastor is the deputy of Christ for the reduction of man to the obedience of God.
GEORGE HERBERT: *A Priest to the Temple,* I, 1632

Pastors come for your wine, and officers for your daughters. DUTCH PROVERB

[*See also* Clergyman.

Pasture

Tomorrow to fresh woods, and pastures new.
JOHN MILTON: *Lycidas,* 1638

Paternalism

Were we directed from Washington when to sow, and when to reap, we should soon want bread.
THOMAS JEFFERSON: *Autobiographical note,* 1821

Nothing is so galling to a people, not broken in from the birth, as a paternal, or, in other words a meddling government, a government which tells them what to read, and say, and eat, and drink, and wear.
T. B. MACAULAY: *Southey's Colloquies,* 1830

I hold it for indisputable that the first duty of a state is to see that every child born therein shall be well housed, clothed, fed, and educated, till it attain years of discretion. But in order to the effecting this the government must have an authority over the people of which we now do not so much as dream.
JOHN RUSKIN: *Stones of Venice,* III, 1853

Though the people support the government the government should not support the people.
GROVER CLEVELAND: Message to Congress, Feb. 16, 1887

[*See also* Individualism.

Paternity

It is a wise child that knows its own father.
JOHN RAY: *English Proverbs*, 1670

Inquiry into paternity is forbidden.
THE CODE NAPOLEON, CCCXC, 1804

Paternoster

[*See* Lord's Prayer.

Path

The beaten path is the safest. (Via trita est tutissima.) LATIN PROVERB

Pathos

And pathos, cantering through the minor keys,
Waves all her onions to the trembling breeze.
O. W. HOLMES: *An After-Dinner Poem*, 1843 (Read at a dinner of Phi Beta Kappa, Cambridge, Mass., Aug. 24)

[*See also* Distance, Humor.

Patience

Be patient, my soul: thou hath suffered worse than this.
HOMER: *Odyssey*, XX, *c.* 800 B.C.

Patience provoked often turns to fury.
PUBLILIUS SYRUS: *Sententiæ*, *c.* 50 B.C.

Be patient toward all men.
I THESSALONIANS V, 14, *c.* 51

Let us run with patience the race that is set before us. HEBREWS XII, 1, *c.* 65

In your patience possess ye your souls.
LUKE XXI, 19, *c.* 75

Patience is the companion of wisdom.
ST. AUGUSTINE: *On Patience*, *c.* 425

The man who lacks patience also lacks philosophy. SADI: *The Gulistan*, 1258

Dame Patience sitting there I found,
With face pale, upon a hill of sand.
GEOFFREY CHAUCER: *The Parlement of Foules*, *c.* 1380

All men commend patience, although few be willing to practise it.
THOMAS À KEMPIS: *Imitation of Christ*, III, *c.* 1420

Patience is the best remedy that is for a sick man, the most precious plaster that is for any wound.
JOHN FLORIO: *First Frutes*, 1578

A man must learn to endure that patiently which he cannot avoid conveniently.
MICHEL DE MONTAIGNE: *Essays*, III, 1588

I do oppose
My patience to his fury, and am arm'd
To suffer, with a quietness of spirit,
The very tyranny and rage of his.
SHAKESPEARE: *The Merchant of Venice*, IV, *c.* 1597

Though patience be a tired mare, yet she will plod. SHAKESPEARE: *Henry V*, II, *c.* 1599

She sits like patience on a monument,
Smiling at grief.
SHAKESPEARE: *Twelfth Night*, II, *c.* 1601

Patience, my lord! why 't is the soul of peace;
Of all the virtues, 't is near'st kin to Heaven.
It makes men look like gods.
THOMAS DEKKER: *I The Honest Whore*, V, 1604

How poor are they that have not patience.
What wound did ever heal but by degrees?
SHAKESPEARE: *Othello*, II, 1604

Patience, thou young and rose-lipp'd cherubin.
SHAKESPEARE: *Othello*, IV

Patience is a plaster for all sores.
CERVANTES: *Don Quixote*, II, 1615

He invites a new injury who bears the old patiently. FYNES MORYSON: *Itinerary*, 1617

Patience, the beggar's virtue.
PHILIP MASSINGER: *A New Way to Pay Old Debts*, V, 1633

Though God takes the sun out of the Heaven, yet we must have patience.
GEORGE HERBERT: *Outlandish Proverbs*, 1640

Have patience with all things, but chiefly have patience with yourself. Do not lose courage in considering your own imperfections, but instantly set about remedying them — every day begin the task anew.
Ascribed to ST. FRANCIS DE SALES (1567–1622) in J. P. CAMUS: *L'ésprit de Saint François de Sales*, 1641

Patience is a flower that grows not in everyone's garden.
JAMES HOWELL: *Familiar Letters*, 1644 (Dec. 1)

Patience and delay achieve more than force and rage.
JEAN DE LA FONTAINE: *Fables*, II, 1668

Beware the fury of a patient man.
JOHN DRYDEN: *Marriage à la Mode*, I, 1672

Patience is a flatterer, sir — and an ass, sir.
APHRA BEHN: *The Feigned Courtezans*, III, 1679

Possess your soul with patience.
JOHN DRYDEN: *The Hind and the Panther*, III, 1687

If God has taken away all means of seeking remedy, there is nothing left but patience.
JOHN LOCKE: *Treatises on Government*, II, 1690

Patience is the virtue of an ass,
That trots beneath his burden, and is quiet.
GEORGE GRANVILLE (LORD LANSDOWNE): *Heroic Love*, I, 1698

In doubtful matters courage may do much; in desperate, patience.
THOMAS FULLER: *Gnomologia,* 1732

Job was not so miserable in his sufferings as happy in his patience. IBID.

Patience is a plaister for all sores. IBID.

Patience is the art of hoping.
LUC DE VAUVENARGUES: *Réflexions,* 1746

He that can have patience can have what he will.
BENJAMIN FRANKLIN: *Poor Richard's Almanac,* 1757

Patience is bitter, but its fruits are sweet.
J.-J. ROUSSEAU: *Émile,* III, 1762

Patience is sorrow's salve.
CHARLES CHURCHILL: *The Prophecy of Famine,* 1763

Patience is a good nag, but she'll bolt.
ENGLISH PROVERB, not recorded before the XIX century

Time, that aged nurse,
Rocked me to patience.
JOHN KEATS: *Endymion,* I, 1818

Patience is a necessary ingredient of genius.
BENJAMIN DISRAELI: *Contarini Fleming,* IV, 1832

He preacheth patience that never knew pain.
H. G. BOHN: *Handbook of Proverbs,* 1855

Patience is invincible.
P. J. PROUDHON: *De la justice dans la révolution,* I, 1858

Faith waiting for a nibble.
H. W. SHAW (JOSH BILLINGS): *Josh Billings' Comical Lexicon,* 1877

A handful of patience is worth more than a bushel of brains. DUTCH PROVERB

Patience is bitter, but its fruit is sweet.
FRENCH PROVERB

Patience conquers the Devil.
GERMAN PROVERB

Patience for a moment; comfort for ten years.
GREEK PROVERB

He that has no patience has nothing at all.
ITALIAN PROVERB

The world belongs to the patient man. IBID.

The patient conquer. (Vincit qui patitur.)
LATIN PROVERB

Patience is a gift that God gives only to those He loves. MOROCCAN PROVERB

Patience is the key to Paradise.
TURKISH PROVERB

[*See also* Adversity, Belgian, Fury, Genius, Kingly, Laziness, Medicine, Nobility, Physician, Waiting.

Patient

The art of medicine consists in three things: the disease, the patient and the physician. The patient must combat the disease along with the physician.
HIPPOCRATES: *Aphorisms, c.* 400 B.C.

A bad patient makes a cruel physician.
PUBLILIUS SYRUS: *Sententiæ, c.* 50 B.C.

Keep up the spirits of your patient with the music of the viol and the psaltery, or by forging letters telling of the death of his enemies, or (if he be a cleric) by informing him that he has been made a bishop.
HENRI DE MONDEVILLE: *Treatise on Surgery,* 1316

Whilst others meanly asked whole months to slay,
I oft dispatched the patient in a day.
SAMUEL GARTH: *The Dispensary,* IV, 1699

The condition of the patient is only an accident in the history of the disease.
J. M. CHARCOT: *De l'expectation en médecine,* 1857

What I call a good patient is one who, having found a good physician, sticks to him till he dies.
O. W. HOLMES: *The Young Practitioner,* 1871 (Lecture in New York, March 2)

The best patient is a millionaire with a positive Wassermann. Author unidentified

In the presence of the patient, Latin is the language. (Ante patientum Latina lingua est.) MEDIEVAL MEDICAL MAXIM

[*See also* Disease, Doctor, Physician, Sickness.

Patrick, St. (389(?)–461)

St. Patrick was a gentleman
Who came of decent people;
He built a church in Dublin town,
And on it put a steeple.
HENRY BENNETT: *St. Patrick Was a Gentleman, c.* 1840

Patriot

Such is the patriot's boast, where'er we roam, —
His first, best country ever is at home.
OLIVER GOLDSMITH: *The Traveler,* 1764

From dunghills deep of blackest hue
Your dirt-bred patriots spring to view.
JOHN TRUMBULL: *McFingal,* III, 1782

True patriots we; for be it understood,
We left our country for your country's good.
GEORGE BARRINGTON: Prologue for the opening of the Playhouse, Sydney, New South Wales, Jan. 16, 1796 (The company was composed of convicts. The "your" in the second line is commonly changed to "our")

In time of war the loudest patriots are the greatest profiteers.

AUGUST BEBEL: Speech in the Reichstag, Nov., 1870

Patriots need no ancestors.

FRENCH PROVERB

[*See also* Country, Coward, Cowardice, Patriotism.

Patriotism

It is sweet to serve one's country by deeds, and it is not absurd to serve her by words.

SALLUST: *Catiline, c.* 40 B.C.

Patriotism is nothing more than a feeling of welfare, and the dread of seeing it disturbed.

STANISLAUS LESZCZYNSKI (KING OF POLAND): *Œuvres du philosophe bienfaisant,* 1763

Patriotism is the last refuge of a scoundrel.

SAMUEL JOHNSON: *Boswell's Life,* April 7, 1775

The highest bliss of the human soul is love, and the noblest love is devotion to our fatherland.

FRIEDRICH VON SCHLEGEL: *On the Limits of the Beautiful,* 1794

I would give something to know for whose sake precisely those deeds were really done which report says were done for the fatherland.

G. C. LICHTENBERG: *Reflections,* 1799

Next to the love of God, the love of country is the best preventive of crime. He who is proud of his country will be particularly cautious not to do anything which is calculated to disgrace it.

GEORGE BORROW: *The Bible in Spain,* IV, 1843

Any relation to the land, the habit of tilling it, or mining it, or even hunting on it, generates the feeling of patriotism.

R. W. EMERSON: *The Young American,* 1844

Whatever insults my state insults me.

PRESTON S. BROOKS: Speech in the House of Representatives, July 14, 1856

What scoundrels we would be if we did for ourselves what we are ready to do for Italy.

CAMILLO DI CAVOUR (1810–61)

Treason is in the air around us everywhere. It goes by the name of patriotism.

THOMAS CORWIN: *Letter from Washington, D. C.,* Jan. 16, 1861

I have alreddy given two cousins to the war, & I stand reddy to sacrifiss my wife's brother ruther'n not see the rebelyin krusht.

C. F. BROWNE (ARTEMUS WARD): *Artemus Ward: His Book,* 1862

Patriotism depends as much on mutual suffering as on mutual success, and it is by that experience of all fortunes and all feelings that a great national character is created.

BENJAMIN DISRAELI: Speech in the House of Commons, March 18, 1862

As religion is imitated and mocked by hypocrisy, so public duty is parodied by patriotism.

J. E. THOROLD ROGERS: *Six Centuries of Work and Wages,* 1885

Patriotism takes the place of religion in France. In the service of *la patrie* the doing of one's duty is elevated into the sphere of exalted emotion. More than any other people, the French make patriotism the source and subject of their profoundest emotional life.

W. C. BROWNELL: *French Traits,* 1889

My patriotism stops short of my stomach.

OTTO VON BISMARCK: To William II, on being offered a glass of German champagne, *c.* 1890

No man can be a patriot on an empty stomach.

W. C. BRANN: *Old Glory,* 1893 (Brann's Iconoclast, July 4)

Patriotism is . . . , to most men, a moral necessity. It meets and satisfies that desire for a strong, disinterested enthusiasm in life which is deeply implanted in our nature.

W. E. H. LECKY: *Democracy and Liberty,* II, 1896

Standing as I do in view of God and eternity, I realize that patriotism is not enough. I must have no hatred or bitterness toward anyone. They have all been very kind to me here.

EDITH CAVELL: To the English chaplain at Brussels the night before her execution, Oct. 11, 1915

You'll never have a quiet world till you knock the patriotism out of the human race.

GEORGE BERNARD SHAW: *O'Flaherty, V. C.,* 1915

Patriotism may be defined as a sense of partisan solidarity in respect of prestige.

THORSTEIN VEBLEN: *The Nature of Peace,* 1919

Patriotism is easy to understand in America. It means looking out for yourself by looking out for your country.

CALVIN COOLIDGE: Speech in Northampton, Mass., May 30, 1923

[*See also* Country, Hell, Individualism.

Patron

Is not a patron, my lord, one who looks with unconcern on a man struggling for life in the water, and, when he has reached ground, encumbers him with help?

SAMUEL JOHNSON: *Letter to the Earl of Chesterfield,* Feb. 7, 1755

A wretch who supports with insolence and is repaid with flattery.

SAMUEL JOHNSON: *Dictionary*, 1755

Patronage

The notice you have been pleased to take of my labors, had it been early, had been kind; but it has been delayed till I am indifferent, and cannot enjoy it; till I am solitary, and cannot impart it; till I am known, and do not want it.

SAMUEL JOHNSON: *Letter to the Earl of Chesterfield*, Feb. 7, 1755

Getting patronage is the whole art of life. A man cannot have a career without it.

GEORGE BERNARD SHAW: *Captain Brassbound's Conversion*, II, 1899

Paul, St. (c. 1–65)

Circumcised the eighth day, of the stock of Israel, of the tribe of Benjamin, a Hebrew of the Hebrews.

PHILIPPIANS III, 3, *c.* 60 (Paul's description of himself)

He saw Paul coming, a man of little stature, thin-haired upon the head, crooked in the legs, of good state of body, with eyebrows joining, and nose somewhat hooked, full of grace: for sometimes he appeared like a man, and sometimes he had the face of an angel.

THE ACTS OF PAUL II, 3, *c.* 160

St. Paul, a Catholic of Rome,
For love of Christ he bear,
Did lose his life, but yet his fame
Is spread both far and near.

JOHN THEWLIS: *True Christian Hearts*, 1616

Calm as great Paul at Ephesus was seen
To rend his robes in agonies serene.

W. E. AYTOUN: *Montgomery*, 1855

No sooner had Jesus knocked over the dragon of superstition than Paul boldly set it on its legs again in the name of Jesus.

GEORGE BERNARD SHAW: *Androcles and the Lion*, pref., 1912

[*See also* Hell, Luther (Martin), Peter (St.).

Pauperism

Pauperism, pauper, poor man, are expressions of pity, but pity alloyed with contempt.

CHARLES LAMB: *A Complaint of the Decay of Beggars in the Metropolis*, 1822 (London Magazine, June)

Pauperism is the hospital of the labor army.

KARL MARX: *Das Kapital*, I, 1867

Paupers will raise paupers, even if the children be not their own, just as familiar contact with criminals will make criminals of the children of virtuous parents.

HENRY GEORGE: *Progress and Poverty*, X, 1879

[*See also* Labor, Poor, Poverty.

Pawnbroker

It is not generally known that the three blue balls at the pawnbroker's shops are the ancient arms of Lombardy. The Lombards were the first money-brokers in Europe.

CHARLES LAMB: *Newspapers 35 Years Ago*, 1831 (The Englishman's Magazine, Oct.; cited as a paragraph printed by Bob Allen, a journalist, "when wit failed, or topics ran low")

Pay

To pay him in his own coin.

ENGLISH PHRASE, traced by Apperson to 1589

He that payeth aforehand hath never his work well done.

JOHN FLORIO: *Second Frutes*, 1591

He is well paid that is well satisfied.

SHAKESPEARE: *The Merchant of Venice*, IV, *c.* 1597

He that cannot pay let him pray.

RANDLE COTGRAVE: *French-English Dictionary*, 1611

Those that dance must pay the music.

JOHN TAYLOR: *Taylor's Feast*, 1638 (Usually *piper* appears in place of *music*)

A good payer is master of another man's purse.

GEORGE HERBERT: *Jacula Prudentum*, 1651

He that pays last payeth but once.

JAMES HOWELL: *Proverbs*, 1659

Sweet appears sour when we pay. IBID.

He who pays the piper can call the tune.

JOHN RAY: *English Proverbs*, 1670

As to pay, I beg leave to assure the Congress that as no pecuniary consideration could have tempted me to accept this arduous employment at the expense of my domestic ease and happiness, I do not wish to make any profit from it.

GEORGE WASHINGTON: To Congress on his appointment as commander-in-chief, June 16, 1775

Pass the hat for your credit's sake, and pay — pay — pay!

RUDYARD KIPLING: *The Absent-Minded Beggar*, 1899

Peace

Let there be no strife, I pray thee, between thee and me. GENESIS XIII, 8, *c.* 700 B.C.

Peace be to you. (Pax vobiscum.)

GENESIS XLIII, 23 (The Latin is from the Vulgate)

Go in peace. (Vade in pace.)

EXODUS IV, 18, *c.* 700 B.C. (The Latin is from the Vulgate)

The wolf shall dwell with the lamb, and the leopard shall lie down with the kid.

ISAIAH XI, 6, *c.* 700 B.C.

Peace is a nursing-mother to the land.
HESIOD: *Works and Days, c.* 700 B.C.

They have healed also the hurt of the daughter of my people slightly, saying, Peace, peace; when there is no peace.
JEREMIAH VI, 14, *c.* 625 B.C.

Her ways are ways of pleasantness, and all her paths are peace.
PROVERBS III, 17, *c.* 350 B.C.

Peace becomes mankind; fury is for beasts.
OVID: *Ars amatoria,* III, *c.* 2 B.C.

If it be possible, as much as lieth in you, live peaceably with all men.
ROMANS XII, 18, *c.* 55

The peace of God, which passeth all understanding. PHILIPPIANS IV, 7, *c.* 60

Glory to God in the highest, and on earth peace, good will toward men.
LUKE II, 14, *c.* 75

Peace be to this house. (Pax huic domui.)
LUKE X, 5 (The Latin is from the Vulgate)

Think not that I am come to send peace on earth: I came not to send peace, but a sword.
MATTHEW X, 34, *c.* 75

They make a solitude and call it peace.
Ascribed to CALGACUS, a Caledonian chief defeated by the Romans under Julius Agricola, *c.* 85 (Cf. BYRON, *post,* 1813)

Peace is our final good.
ST. AUGUSTINE: *The City of God,* XV, 427

Peace with honor.
Ascribed to THEOBOLD OF CHAMPAGNE, *c.* 1135

Peace maketh plenty, plenty maketh pride, pride maketh plee, plee maketh poverty, poverty maketh peace.
ENGLISH PROVERB, traced by Apperson to the XV century (*Plee*=extravagance)

A peace is of the nature of a conquest.
For then both parties nobly are subdued,
And neither party loses.
SHAKESPEARE: *II Henry IV,* IV, *c.* 1598

The slave, a member of the country's peace,
Enjoys it; but in gross brain little wots
What watch the king keeps to maintain the peace,
Whose hours the peasant best advantages.
SHAKESPEARE: *Henry V,* IV, *c.* 1599

Peace,
Dear nurse of arts, plenties and joyful births.
SHAKESPEARE: *Henry V,* V

Farewell the neighing steed, and the shrill trump,
The spirit-stirring drum, the ear-piercing fife.
SHAKESPEARE: *Othello,* III, 1604

Plenty and peace breed cowards.
SHAKESPEARE: *Cymbeline,* III, *c.* 1609

The nurse of drones and cowards.
PHILIP MASSINGER: *The Maid of Honor,* I, 1632

The first and fundamental law of nature . . . is to seek peace and follow it.
THOMAS HOBBES: *Leviathan,* I, 1651

It is interest that keeps peace.
OLIVER CROMWELL: Speech in the House of Commons, Sept. 4, 1654

That it may please thee to give to all nations unity, peace, and concord, we beseech thee to hear us, good Lord.
THE BOOK OF COMMON PRAYER (*The Litany*), 1662

'Tis safest making peace with sword in hand.
GEORGE FARQUHAR: *Love and a Bottle,* V, 1699

It is madness for a sheep to treat of peace with a wolf.
THOMAS FULLER: *Gnomologia,* 1732

My instinctive desire is for the accomplishment of this hope of peace; but it remains to be seen whether, all things considered, it is a benefit for the sad human race to prevent it from self-destruction.
JEAN LE ROND D'ALEMBERT: *Letter to Frederick the Great,* Aug. 17, 1771

Peace implies reconciliation.
EDMUND BURKE: Speech on Conciliation with America, March 22, 1775

It is mutual cowardice that keeps us in peace. Were one half of mankind brave and one half cowards the brave would be always beating the cowards. Were all brave we would lead a very uneasy life: all would be continually fighting. But being all cowards, we go on very well.
SAMUEL JOHNSON: *Boswell's Life,* April 28, 1778

When will the world know that peace and propagation are the two most delightful things in it?
HORACE WALPOLE: *Letter to Horace Mann,* July 7, 1778

The peace of a cemetery. (Die Ruhe eines Kirchhofs.)
J. C. F. SCHILLER: *Don Carlos,* III, 1787

The peace of Britain. (Pax Britannica.)
ENGLISH PHRASE, not recorded before the XIX century; derived from " Pax Romana " – The peace of Rome

Peace is seldom denied to the peaceful.
J. C. F. SCHILLER: *Wilhelm Tell,* I, 1804

He makes a solitude, and calls it – peace.
BYRON: *The Bride of Abydos,* II, 1813 (Cf. CALGACUS, *ante, c.* 85)

Peace at any price. (La paix à tout prix.)
ALPHONSE DE LAMARTINE: *Méditations poétiques,* 1820

The empire is peace. (L'empire, c'est la paix.)
NAPOLEON III: Speech at Bordeaux, Oct. 9, 1852

If peace cannot be maintained with honor, it is no longer peace.
LORD JOHN RUSSELL: Speech in Greenoch, Sept. 14, 1853

No nation ever yet enjoyed a protracted and triumphant peace without receiving in its own bosom ineradicable seeds of future decline.
JOHN RUSKIN: *Modern Painters,* IV, 1856

Peace at any price; peace and union.
Slogan of the Know-Nothing party in the Buchanan-Fillmore campaign, 1856

You may either win your peace or buy it—win it, by resistance to evil; buy it, by compromise with evil.
JOHN RUSKIN: *The Two Paths,* V, 1859

The peaceful are the strong.
O. W. HOLMES: *A Voice of the Loyal North,* 1861

No more shall the war cry sever,
Or the winding rivers be red;
They banish our anger forever
When they laurel the graves of our dead.
Under the sod and the dew,
Waiting the judgment day;
Love and tears for the blue,
Tears and love for the gray.
FRANCIS M. FINCH: *The Blue and the Gray,* 1867

Let us have peace.
U. S. GRANT: Speech of acceptance, May 29, 1868

In the tragedy of man peace is but an entr'acte.
REMY DE GOURMONT (1858–1915)

The bloody capitalists cannot conclude an honorable peace. They can conclude only a dishonorable peace, based upon a division of spoils.
NIKOLAI LENIN: *Letters from Afar,* IV, 1917

Peace is better than a place in history.
JUSTO PASTOR BENITEZ (FOREIGN MINISTER OF PARAGUAY): *Speech in Asunción,* 1935

The peace of God. (Rahmat Allah.)
ARABIC PHRASE

A cake eaten in peace is better than two in trouble. DANISH PROVERB

Better keep peace than make peace.
DUTCH PROVERB

One peace is better than ten victories.
GERMAN PROVERB

Depart in peace, ye messengers of peace.
JEWISH PRAYER FOR THE EVE OF SABBATH

May he rest in peace. (Requiescat in pace.)
LATIN PHRASE

Go hence in peace. (Abi in pace.)
LATIN SAYING

[*See also* Ambassador, Arms, Charity, Covenant, Desire, Empire, Foreign Relations, Happiness, Humility, Nunc Dimittis, Pardon, Preparedness, Science, Sleep, Sword, Trade (=commerce), Truce, Victory, War and Peace.

Peace, International

They shall beat their swords into ploughshares, and their spears into pruninghooks: nation shall not lift up a sword against nation, neither shall they learn war any more.
MICAH IV, 3, *c.* 700 B.C.

No war, or battle's sound
Was heard the world around:
The idle spear and shield were high up hung.
JOHN MILTON: *On the Morning of Christ's Nativity,* 1629

Since reason condemns war and makes peace an absolute duty; and since peace cannot be effected or guaranteed without a compact among nations, they must form an alliance of a peculiar kind, which may be called a pacific alliance (*foedus pacificum*), different from a treaty of peace (*pactum pacis*) inasmuch as it would for ever terminate all wars, whereas the latter ends only one.
IMMANUEL KANT: *Perpetual Peace,* II, 1795

What a beautiful fix we are in now: peace has been declared!
NAPOLEON I: After the Treaty of Amiens (March 27), 1802

If they want peace, nations should avoid the pin-pricks that precede cannon-shots.
NAPOLEON I: To the Czar Alexander at Tilsit, June 22, 1807

The war-drum throbb'd no longer, and the battle-flags were furl'd
In the parliament of man, the federation of the world.
ALFRED TENNYSON: *Locksley Hall,* 1842

Buried was the bloody hatchet;
Buried was the dreadful war-club;
Buried were all warlike weapons,
And the war-cry was forgotten,
Then was peace among the nations.
H. W. LONGFELLOW: *Hiawatha,* XIII, 1855

Everlasting peace is a dream, and not even a beautiful one.
HELMUTH VON MOLTKE: *Letter to J. K. Bluntschli,* Dec. 11, 1880

It must be a peace without victory. Only a peace between equals can last: only a peace,

the very principle of which is equality, and a common participation in a common benefit.
WOODROW WILSON: Address to the Senate, Jan. 22, 1917

A steadfast concert for peace can never be maintained except by a partnership of democratic nations. No autocratic government could be trusted to keep faith within it or observe its covenants.
WOODROW WILSON: Message to Congress, April 2, 1917

The high contracting parties solemnly declare in the names of their respective peoples that they condemn recourse to war for the solution of international controversies, and renounce it as an instrument of national policy in their relations with one another. The high contracting parties agree that the settlement or solution of all disputes or conflicts of whatever nature or of whatever origin they may be, which may rise among them, shall never be sought except by pacific means.
THE KELLOGG PEACE PACT, signed at Paris, Aug. 27, 1928

To kill its enemies and cheat its friends,
Each nation its prerogative defends;
Yet some their efforts for goodwill maintain,
In hope, in faith, in patience, and in vain.
COLIN ELLIS: *Mournful Numbers,* 1932

[*See also* Peace, Preparedness, War, War and Peace.

Peacemaker

Blessed are the peacemakers: for they shall be called the children of God.
MATTHEW V, 9, *c.* 75

Those who in quarrels interpose
Must often wipe a bloody nose.
JOHN GAY: *Fables,* I, 1727

The best peacemaker is a stout stick.
FRENCH PROVERB

[*See also* If.

Peace-of-mind

Lovely, lasting peace of mind,
Sweet delight of human kind.
THOMAS PARNELL: *Hymn to Contentment,* 1721

Peacock

[*See* Ape, God.

Pear

Eating pears cleans the teeth.
KOREAN PROVERB

A pear must be eaten to the day;
If you don't eat it then, throw it away.
OLD ENGLISH RHYME

[*See also* Voice.

Pearl

Neither cast ye your pearls before swine.
MATTHEW VII, 6, *c.* 75

[A] pearl of great price. MATTHEW XIII, 46

At the distance of half the globe, a Hindu gains his support by groping at the bottom of the sea for the morbid concretion of a shell-fish, to decorate the throat of a London alderman's wife.
SYDNEY SMITH: In the Edinburgh Review, 1803

Are there not, dear Michal,
Two points in the adventure of the diver,
One — when, a beggar, he prepares the plunge,
One — when, a prince, he rises with his pearl?
ROBERT BROWNING: *Paracelsus,* I, 1835

On a wrinkled neck a pearl weeps.
GERMAN PROVERB

[*See also* February.

Peasant

The peasant speaks, moves, dresses, eats, and drinks as much as a man of the first fashion, but does them all quite differently.
LORD CHESTERFIELD: *Letter to his son,* Nov. 12, 1750

Princes and lords may flourish or may fade
A breath can make them, as a breath has made;
But a bold peasantry, their country's pride,
When once destroyed can never be supplied.
OLIVER GOLDSMITH: *The Deserted Village,* 1770

Or will you praise that homely, healthy fare,
Plenteous and plain, that happy peasants share?
Oh! trifle not with wants you cannot feel,
Nor mock the misery of a stinted meal —
Homely, not wholesome; plain, not plenteous; such
As you who praise would never deign to touch.
GEORGE CRABBE: *The Village,* I, 1783

I have never heard of a peer with an ancient lineage. The real old families of this country are to be found among the peasantry.
BENJAMIN DISRAELI: *Coningsby,* XI, 1844

With the peasant general custom holds the place of individual feeling.
W. H. RIEHL: *Die bürgerliche Gesellschaft,* 1858

A good, honest, well-to-do peasant, who knows nothing of politics, must be very nearly happy.
GEORGE MOORE: *Confessions of a Young Man,* VII, 1888

Bowed by the weight of centuries he leans
Upon his hoe and gazes on the ground,
The emptiness of ages in his face,
And on his back the burden of the world.
EDWIN MARKHAM: *The Man With the Hoe,* 1899

He who would beat a peasant must bring a peasant with him. DUTCH PROVERB

The stupidest peasants have the biggest potatoes. GERMAN PROVERB

When the peasant has money, so has the whole world. IBID.

Call a peasant " brother," and he will demand to be called " father." RUSSIAN PROVERB

[*See also* Farmer, Happiness, Lord, Monastery, Piety, Poet, Poland.

Pedagogue

All those instances to be found in history, whether real or fabulous, of a doubtful public spirit, at which morality is perplexed, reason is staggered, and from which affrighted nature recoils, are their chosen and almost sole examples for the instruction of their youth.
EDMUND BURKE: *Letters on a Regicide Peace,* III, 1797

'Twas a jolly old pedagogue, long ago,
Tall and slender, and sallow and dry;
His form was bent, and his gait was slow,
His long thin hair was white as snow,
But a wonderful twinkle shone in his eye.
And he sang every night as he went to bed,
" Let us be happy down here below;
The living should live, though the dead be dead,"
Said the jolly old pedagogue long ago.
GEORGE ARNOLD: *The Jolly Old Pedagogue,* 1867

One who casts false pearls before real swine.
Author unidentified

[*See also* Teacher, Teaching, Webster (Noah).

Pedant

How fiery and forward our pedant is.
SHAKESPEARE: *The Taming of the Shrew,* III, 1594

His impudence will overrule his ignorance to talk of learned principles, which come from him like a treble part in a bass voice too big for it.
THOMAS ADAMS: *Diseases of the Soul,* 1616

The pedant can hear nothing but in favor of the conceits he is amorous of, and cannot see but out of the grates of his prison.
JOSEPH GLANVILL: *The Vanity of Dogmatizing,* XXIII, 1661

A man who has been brought up among books, and is able to talk of nothing else, is a very indifferent companion, and what we call a pedant.
JOSEPH ADDISON: *The Spectator,* June 30, 1711

The boastful blockhead ignorantly read,
With loads of learned lumber in his head.
ALEXANDER POPE: *An Essay on Criticism,* III, 1711

A pedant is always throwing his system in your face, and applies it equally to all things, times, and places, just like a tailor who would make a coat out of his own head, without any regard to the bulk or figure of the person that must wear it.
MARY WORTLEY MONTAGU: *Letter to Lady D.,* Jan. 13, 1716

Learn'd without sense, and venerably dull.
CHARLES CHURCHILL: *The Rosciad,* 1761

The vacant skull of a pedant generally furnishes out a throne and temple for vanity.
WILLIAM SHENSTONE: *Of Men and Manners,* 1764

He who is not in some measure a pedant, though he may be a wise, cannot be a very happy man.
WILLIAM HAZLITT: *The Round Table,* II, 1817

[*See also* Hell, Man, Museum, Pedantry.

Pedantry

Pedantry is the unseasonable ostentation of learning.
SAMUEL JOHNSON: *The Rambler,* Nov. 12, 1751

Pedantry consists in the use of words unsuitable to the time, place, and company.
S. T. COLERIDGE: *Biographia Literaria,* X, 1817

There is nothing so pedantic as pretending not to be pedantic.
WILLIAM HAZLITT: *The Plain Speaker,* 1826

Pedantry [is] only the scholarship of *le cuistre.* (We have no English equivalent.)
WALTER PATER: *Style,* 1888

[*See also* Pedant.

Pedestrian

A man who has a car and a grown-up daughter.
Author unidentified

Pedigree

If there is any good in philosophy it is this: that it never inspects pedigrees.
SENECA: *Epistulæ morales ad Lucilium,* c. 63

As long as a Welsh pedigree.
ENGLISH PHRASE, in common use since the XVII century

Who asks after the pedigree of a hog he is about to kill? BOHEMIAN PROVERB

John Carnegie lies here,
Descended from Adam and Eve,

If any can boast of a pedigree higher,
He will willingly give them leave.
Epitaph in an Edinburgh churchyard

Nobody asks about the pedigree of a good man.
SPANISH PROVERB

[*See also* Ancestry.

Pedlar

[*See* Ancestry, Little.

Peel, Robert (1788–1850)

[*See* Austerity.

Peer

By the lawful judgment of their peers. (Per legale judicium parum suorum.)
MAGNA CHARTA, 1215

[*See also* Police.

Peerage

French cooks, Scotch pedlars and Italian whores
Were all made lords, or lords' progenitors.
DANIEL DEFOE: *The True-Born Englishman,* I, 1701

Burke's Peerage is the Englishman's Bible.
ENGLISH SAYING (The first edition of JOHN BURKE: *A Genealogical and Heraldic Dictionary of the Peerage and Baronetage of the United Kingdom* was issued in 1826)

[*See also* Nobility.

Peg and Hole

[*See* Vocation.

Pembroke, Mary Sidney, Countess of (c. 1561–1621)

[*See* Epitaph.

Pen

The pen of a ready writer.
PSALMS XLV, 1, *c.* 150 B.C.

Pens may blot but they cannot blush.
JOHN HARINGTON: *The Metamorphosis of Ajax,* 1596 (Quoted as an " old saying ")

Many wearing rapiers are afraid of goose-quills. SHAKESPEARE: *Hamlet,* II, *c.* 1601

How much more cruel the pen may be than the sword.
ROBERT BURTON: *The Anatomy of Melancholy,* I, 1621

Pen and ink is wit's plow.
JOHN CLARKE: *Parœmiologia Anglo-Latina,* 1639

More danger comes by th' quill than by the sword.
MARTIN PARKER: *The Poet's Blind Man's Bough,* 1641

Scholars are men of peace. They carry no arms, but their tongues are sharper than Actus his razors; their pens carry further and make a louder report than thunder. I had rather stand the shock of a basilisco than the fury of a merciless pen.
THOMAS BROWNE: *Religio Medici,* II, 1642 (*Basilisco*=a brass cannon throwing a shot of about 200 pounds)

Cæsar had perished from the world of men
Had not his sword been rescued by his pen.
HENRY VAUGHAN: *Sir Thomas Bodley's Library, c.* 1650

That mighty instrument of little men.
BYRON: *English Bards and Scotch Reviewers,* 1809

The pen is mightier than the sword.
E. G. BULWER-LYTTON: *Richelieu,* II, 1838 (Cf. SHAKESPEARE, *ante, c.* 1601

The world is ruled by the calf, the bee and the goose.
LATIN PROVERB (meaning by parchment, wax and the pen)

[*See also* Author, Writer.

Penalty

If human society cannot be carried on without lawsuits, it cannot be carried on without penalties.
ARISTOTLE: *Politics,* VI, *c.* 322 B.C.

[*See also* Crime and Punishment.

Penance

Penance is a recognition and reëstablishment of the moral order in the world, which is founded on the eternal law, that is, on the living God.
POPE PIUS XI: *Caritate Christi compulsi,* May 3, 1932

[*See also* Absolution, Asceticism, Confession.

Penmanship

[*See* Handwriting.

Pennsylvania

After many waitings, watchings, solicitings, and disputes in Council, this day my country was confirmed to me under the great seal of England, with large powers and privileges, by the name of Pennsylvania, a name the king would give it in honor of my father.
WILLIAM PENN: *Letter to Robert Turner,* March 14, 1681

Pennsylvania is the keystone of the democratic arch.
Address of the Pennsylvania Democratic Committee, 1803

The cradle of toleration and freedom of religion.
THOMAS JEFFERSON: *Letter to Thomas Cooper,* 1822

Pennsylvania has produced but two great men: Benjamin Franklin, of Massachusetts, and Albert Gallatin, of Switzerland.

J. J. INGALLS: Speech in the Senate, *c.* 1885

Penny

A penny for your thoughts.

ENGLISH SAYING, first recorded in 1546

In for a penny, in for a pound.

EDWARD RAVENSCROFT: *The Cautious Guests,* V, 1695

A penny in the purse is the best friend John can have.

JOHN ARBUTHNOT: *John Bull,* II, 1712

A penny in the purse is better than a crown awa. SCOTTISH PROVERB

Nae friend like the penny. IBID.

[*See also* Saving, Thrift.

Pension

I have known men that have come from serving against the Turk, for three or four months they have had pension to buy them new wooden legs and fresh plasters; but, after, 'twas not to be had.

JOHN WEBSTER: *The White Devil,* V, *c.* 1608

An allowance made to anyone without an equivalent. In England it is generally understood to mean pay given to a state hireling for treason to his country.

SAMUEL JOHNSON: *Dictionary,* 1755

Everyone who takes a pension from government goes into the workhouse on a grand scale.

JOHN RUSKIN: *Sesame and Lilies,* I, 1865

I have considered the pension list of the republic a roll of honor.

GROVER CLEVELAND: Veto message to Congress, July 5, 1888

Pentecost

(The events of the day of Pentecost are described in ACTS II, *c.* 75.)

Penury

Chill penury repress'd their noble rage,
And froze the genial current of the soul.

THOMAS GRAY: *Elegy Written in a Country Churchyard,* 1750

Fools live poor to die rich.

H. G. BOHN: *Handbook of Proverbs,* 1855

People

No doubt but ye are the people, and wisdom shall die with you. JOB XII, 2, *c.* 325 B.C.

In the common people there is no wisdom, no penetration, no power of judgment.

CICERO: *Pro Planchio,* 54 B.C.

The common people suffer when the powerful disagree.

PHAEDRUS: *Fabulæ Aesopiæ, c.* 40

The voice of the people is the voice of God. (Vox populi, vox Dei.)

ALCUIN: *Epistles, c.* 800 (Quoted as a familiar saying)

This Bible is for the government of the people, by the people, and of the people.

JOHN WYCLIF: Tr. of the Bible, pref., 1382

The masses of the people resemble a wild beast, which, naturally fierce, and accustomed to live in the woods, has been brought up, as it were, in a prison, and having by accident got its liberty, not being accustomed to search for its good, and not knowing where to conceal itself, easily becomes the prey of the first who seeks to incarcerate it again.

NICCOLÒ MACHIAVELLI: *The Prince,* IV, 1513

He who speaks of the people, speaks of a madman; for the people is a monster full of confusion and mistakes; and the opinions of the people are as far removed from the truth as, according to Ptolemy, the Indies are from Spain.

FRANCESCO GUICCIARDINI: *Storia d'Italia,* 1564

Look, as I blow this feather from my face,
And as the air blows it to me again,
Obeying with my wind when I do blow,
And yielding to another when it blows,
Commanded always by the greater gust;
Such is the lightness of you common men.

SHAKESPEARE: *III Henry VI,* III, *c.* 1591

Do not wonder if the common people speak more truly than those above them: they speak more safely.

FRANCIS BACON: *De augmentis scientiarum,* I, 1623

The people cannot see, but they can feel.

JAMES HARRINGTON: *The Commonwealth of Oceana,* 1658

If by the people you understand the multitude, the *hoi polloi,* 'tis no matter what they think; they are sometimes in the right, sometimes in the wrong; their judgment is a mere lottery.

JOHN DRYDEN: *Of Dramatic Poesy,* 1668

And what the people but a herd confus'd,
A miscellaneous rabble, who extol
Things vulgar?

JOHN MILTON: *Paradise Regained,* III, 1671

Nor is the people's judgment always true:
The most may err as grossly as the few.

JOHN DRYDEN: *Absalom and Achitophel,* I, 1682

Let the people think they govern, and they will be governed.

WILLIAM PENN: *Fruits of Solitude,* 1693

The first humane subject and original of civil power is the people.
JOHN WISE: *A Vindication of the Government of New England Churches,* II, 1717

I know the people: they change in a day. They bestow prodigally their hatred and their love.
VOLTAIRE: *La mort de César,* I, 1725

The people are a many-headed beast.
ALEXANDER POPE: *The First Epistle of the First Book of Horace,* 1735

Men who are rogues in detail are very honest taken together: they love morality.
C. L. DE MONTESQUIEU: *The Spirit of the Laws,* XXV, 1748

It shall be the duty of the legislatures and magistrates . . . to countenance and inculcate the principles of humanity and general benevolence, public and private charity, industry and frugality, honesty and punctuality in their dealings; sincerity, good humor, and all social affections and generous sentiments among the people.
CONSTITUTION OF MASSACHUSETTS, 1780

The animosities of sovereigns are temporary and may be allayed; but those which seize the whole body of a people, and of a people, too, who dictate their own measures, produce calamities of long duration.
THOMAS JEFFERSON: *Letter to C. W. F. Dumas,* 1786

The voice of the people has been said to be the voice of God; and, however generally this maxim has been quoted and believed, it is not true to fact. The people are turbulent and changing; they seldom judge or determine right.
ALEXANDER HAMILTON: Speech in the Federal Convention, June 18, 1787

Do not be too severe upon the errors of the people, but reclaim them by enlightening them.
THOMAS JEFFERSON: *Letter to Edward Carrington,* 1787

The people are the only sure reliance for the preservation of our liberty.
THOMAS JEFFERSON: *Letter to James Madison,* 1787

It is an unquestionable truth that the body of the people in every country desire sincerely its prosperity; but it is equally unquestionable that they do not possess the discernment and stability necessary for systematic government.
ALEXANDER HAMILTON: Speech in the New York Convention, June 24, 1788

The government is of the people and for the people.
THOMAS COOPER: *Some Information Regarding America,* 1795

A pity about the people! They are honest brothers, but they think like soapboilers.
J. C. F. SCHILLER: *Wallenstein's Camp,* XI, 1799

Vain as the leaf upon the stream,
And fickle as a changeful dream;
Fantastic as a woman's mood,
And fierce as frenzy's fevered blood.
Thou many-headed monster-thing,
Oh, who would wish to be thy king?
WALTER SCOTT: *The Lady of the Lake,* V, 1810

I am not among those who fear the people. They, and not the rich, are our dependence for continued freedom.
THOMAS JEFFERSON: *Letter to Samuel Kerchival,* 1816

The people are that part of the state which does not know what it wants.
G. W. F. HEGEL: *Grundlinien der Philosophie des Rechts,* 1821

The welfare of the people is the supreme law. (Salus populi suprema lex.)
MOTTO OF MISSOURI, adopted Jan. 11, 1822

All power is inherent in the people.
THOMAS JEFFERSON: *Letter to John Cartwright,* 1824

The people's government [is] made for the people, made by the people, and answerable to the people.
DANIEL WEBSTER: Speech in the Senate, Jan. 26, 1830

A people is but the attempt of many
To rise to the completer life of one —
And those who live as models for the mass
Are singly of more value than they all.
ROBERT BROWNING: *Luria,* V, 1846

The American idea . . . demands, as the proximate organization thereof, a democracy, — that is, a government of all the people, by all the people, for all the people.
THEODORE PARKER: Speech in Boston, May 29, 1850

Leave this hypocritical prating about the masses. Masses are rude, lame, unmade, pernicious in their demands and influence, and need not to be flattered but to be schooled. I wish not to concede anything to them, but to tame, drill, divide, and break them up, and draw individuals out of them.
R. W. EMERSON: *The Conduct of Life,* VII, 1860

Why should there not be a patient confidence in the ultimate justice of the people? Is there any better or equal hope in the world?
ABRAHAM LINCOLN: Inaugural Address, March 4, 1861

You can fool some of the people all of the time, and all of the people some of the time, but you cannot fool all of the people all the time.
Ascribed, but probably erroneously, to ABRAHAM LINCOLN, *c.* 1862

The voice of the people is the voice of humbug. (Vox populi, vox humbug.)
W. T. SHERMAN: *Letter to his wife,* June 2, 1863 (Sherman used the dog Latin)

We here highly resolve that the dead shall not have died in vain; that this nation, under God, shall have a new birth of freedom, and that government of the people, by the people, and for the people, shall not perish from the earth.
ABRAHAM LINCOLN: *Gettysburg Address,* Nov. 19, 1863

The people rule. (Regnant populi.)
MOTTO OF ARKANSAS, adopted May 3, 1864

The people are to be taken in very small doses.
R. W. EMERSON: *Society and Solitude,* 1870

You cannot keep the people out of government and progress. If their intelligence does not rule, their ignorance will.
THOMAS B. REED: Speech in Waterville, Maine, July 30, 1885

One secret has been kept many centuries: the terrible worthlessness of the people collectively.
E. W. HOWE: *Country Town Sayings,* 1911

He who trusts to the people hangs from a tree.
GERMAN PROVERB

The many. (Hoi polloi.) GREEK PHRASE

The voice of the people is the kettle-drum of God. HINDU PROVERB

He that builds upon the people builds upon the sand. ITALIAN PROVERB

[*See also* Crowd, Democracy, Despot, Foresight, Indictment, Legislation, Mob, Multitude, Opinion (Public), Politician, Populace, Popularity, Priest, Prince, Proletariat, Public, Pun, Rabble, Sovereignty.

Pepper

Peter Piper pick'd a peck of pickled peppers.
Where is the peck of pickled peppers Peter Piper pick'd?
J. K. PAULDING: *Königsmarke,* II, 1823

[*See also* Borrowing and Lending.

Perfection

Be ye therefore perfect, even as your Father which is in Heaven is perfect.
MATTHEW V, 48, *c.* 75

It be a good horse that never stumbles.
JOHN HEYWOOD: *Proverbs,* 1546

Use maketh perfectness.
WILLIAM BULLEIN: *Dialogue Against the Fever Pestilence,* 1564

No perfection is so absolute
That some impurity doth not pollute.
SHAKESPEARE: *The Rape of Lucrece,* 1594

Our erected wit maketh us know what perfection is, and yet our infected will keepeth us from reaching unto it.
PHILIP SIDNEY: *Apologie for Poetrie,* 1595

How many things by season seasoned are
To their right praise and true perfection?
SHAKESPEARE: *The Merchant of Venice,* V, *c.* 1597

Julia, if I chance to die
Ere I print my poetry;
I most humbly thee desire
To commit it to the fire:
Better 'twere my book were dead,
Than to live not perfected.
ROBERT HERRICK: *Hesperides,* 1648

Whoever thinks a faultless piece to see
Thinks what ne'er was, nor is, nor e'er shall be.
ALEXANDER POPE: *Essay on Criticism,* II, 1711

Once in a thousand years
A perfect character appears.
CHARLES CHURCHILL: *The Ghost,* III, 1763

The very pink of perfection.
OLIVER GOLDSMITH: *She Stoops to Conquer,* I, 1773

The desire of perfection is the worst disease that ever afflicted the human mind.
LOUIS FONTANES: To Napoleon I, 1804

What's come to perfection perishes.
ROBERT BROWNING: *Old Pictures in Florence,* 1842

In this broad earth of ours,
Amid the measureless grossness and the slag,
Enclosed and safe within its central heart,
Nestles the seed perfection.
WALT WHITMAN: *Song of the Universal,* 1881

[*See also* Culture, Faultless, Practise, Trifle.

Performance

[*See* Precept.

Perfume

I have perfumed my bed with myrrh, aloes, and cinnamon. Come, let us take our fill of love until the morning.
PROVERBS VII, 17–18, *c.* 350 B.C.

Ointment and perfume rejoice the heart.
PROVERBS XXVII, 9

The smell of thy garments is like the smell of Lebanon.
SOLOMON'S SONG IV, 11, *c.* 200 B.C.

He smells not well whose smell is perfume.
MARTIAL: *Epigrams,* II, 86

Old women should not use perfumes.
PLUTARCH: *Lives, c.* 100

So perfumed that
The winds were love-sick.

SHAKESPEARE: *Antony and Cleopatra,* II, *c.* 1606

The rose looks fair, but fairer we it deem,
For that sweet odor which doth in it live.

SHAKESPEARE: *Sonnets,* LIV, 1609

A woman smells best when she hath no perfume at all.

ROBERT BURTON: *The Anatomy of Melancholy,* III, 1621

Sabean odors from the spicy shore
Of Araby the blest.

JOHN MILTON: *Paradise Lost,* IV, 1667

An amber scent of odorous perfume.

JOHN MILTON: *Samson Agonistes,* 1671

Foreign smells are less intolerable than foreign perfumes.

WILLIAM HAZLITT: *Traveling Abroad,* 1828 (New Monthly Magazine, June)

[*See also* Odor, Smell, Violet.

Perjury

To swear falsely is not at all times perjury, but not to perform that which you have sworn according to the intentions of your mind — *ex animi tui sententiâ,* as our law books have it — that is perjury.

CICERO: *De officiis,* III, 78 B.C.

Perjury in a court of justice is more often committed by women than by men. It may, indeed, be generally questioned whether women ought to be sworn at all.

ARTHUR SCHOPENHAUER: *On Women,* 1851

[*See also* Lover.

Permanence

I am for permanence in all things, at the earliest possible moment, and to the latest possible. Blessed is he that continueth where he is. Here let us rest, and lay out seedfields; here let us learn to dwell.

THOMAS CARLYLE: *Past and Present,* IV, 1843

Perpetuity

In perpetuity. (In perpetuum.)

LATIN PHRASE

Perplexity

In all perplexity there is a portion of fear, which predisposes the mind to anger.

S. T. COLERIDGE: *Biographia Literaria,* IV, 1817

Persecution

He fell to the earth, and heard a voice saying unto him, Saul, Saul, why persecutest thou me?

ACTS IX, 4, *c.* 75 (Cf. XXVI, 14)

Whoever is right, the persecutor must be wrong.

WILLIAM PENN: *Fruits of Solitude,* 1693

To punish a man because he has committed a crime, or because he is believed, though unjustly, to have committed a crime, is not persecution. To punish a man because we infer from the nature of some doctrine which he holds, or from the conduct of other persons who hold the same doctrines with him, that he will commit a crime, is persecution, and is, in every case, foolish and wicked.

T. B. MACAULAY: *Hallam,* 1828 (Edinburgh Review, Sept.)

The history of persecution is a history of endeavors to cheat nature, to make water run up hill, to twist a rope of sand.

R. W. EMERSON: *Compensation,* 1841

Persecution is a very easy form of virtue.

LORD COLERIDGE: *Judgment in Regina* vs. *Ramsey,* 1883

[*See also* Church, Fanaticism, Jew, Martyr, Opinion, Toleration.

Perseverance

God helps those who persevere.

THE KORAN, VIII, *c.* 625

I will spit on my hands and take better hold.

JOHN HEYWOOD: *Proverbs,* 1546

Perseverance deserves neither blame nor praise, inasmuch as it is merely the duration of tastes and opinions which we can neither give nor take away from ourselves.

LA ROCHEFOUCAULD: *Maxims,* 1665

Great works are performed not by strength but by perseverance.

SAMUEL JOHNSON: *Rasselas,* 1759

Neither to change, nor falter, nor repent . . .
This is alone life, joy, empire and victory.

P. B. SHELLEY: *Prometheus Unbound,* IV, 1820

If at first you don't succeed,
Try, try, try again.

WILLIAM E. HICKSON: *Try and Try Again,* *c.* 1850

I purpose to fight it out on this line if it takes all Summer.

U. S. GRANT: Dispatch to H. W. Halleck, near Spottsylvania C. H., May 11, 1864

By perseverance the snail reached the Ark.

C. H. SPURGEON: *Salt Cellars,* 1889

Every day a thread makes a skein in a year.

DUTCH PROVERB

Who hangs on, wins.

PENNSYLVANIA GERMAN PROVERB

Pray to God, but keep rowing to the shore.

RUSSIAN PROVERB

Without perseverance talent is a barren bed.

WELSH PROVERB

[*See also* Doggedness, Kingly, Parvenu, Resolution.

Persian

[*See* Drinking, Heaven.

Persian Language

Adam and Eve made love in Persian, but the angel who drove them out of Paradise spoke Turkish. PERSIAN PROVERB

[*See also* Language.

Person

There is no respect of persons with God.
ROMANS II, 11, *c.* 55

One hates not the person, but the vice.
GIOVANNI TORRIANO: *Italian Proverbs,* 1666

A personal action dies with the person. (Actio personalis moritur cum persona.)
LEGAL MAXIM

[*See* Principle, Respect.

Perspective

Perspective is the bridle and rudder of painting.
LEONARDO DA VINCI: *Notebooks, c.* 1500

Perspicuity

[*See* Style.

Perspiration

[*See* Sweat.

Persuasion

Anything pleasant easily persuades, and while it gives pleasure it fixes itself in the heart.
LACTANTIUS: *Divinæ institutiones,* VI, *c.* 310

We are more easily persuaded, in general, by the reasons we ourselves discover than by those which are given to us by others.
BLAISE PASCAL: *Pensées,* 1670

By winning words to conquer willing hearts,
And make persuasion do the work of fear.
JOHN MILTON: *Paradise Regained,* I, 1671

There is a danger in being persuaded before one understands.
THOMAS WILSON: *Maxims of Piety and of Christianity, c.* 1755

Sudden and irresistible conviction is chiefly the offspring of living speech.
WILLIAM GODWIN: *Thoughts on Man,* 1831

No one can give faith unless he has faith. It is the persuaded who persuade.
JOSEPH JOUBERT: *Pensées,* I, 1842

If you can't make a man think as you do, make him do as you think. Author unidentified

[*See also* Law, Oratory, Passion.

Pertinacity

[*See* Resolution.

Perversity

The perversity of inanimate objects.
Author unidentified (There is a similar phrase in German: "die Tücke des Objekts." It is first found in F. T. VISCHER: *Auch Einer,* 1879)

Pessimism

[*See* Optimist and Pessimist, Pessimist.

Pessimist

Young gentlemen with private means look down from a pinnacle of doleful experience on all the grown and hearty men who have dared to say a good word for life since the beginning of the world.
R. L. STEVENSON: *Familiar Studies of Men and Books,* III, 1882

A pessimist is a man who thinks everybody as nasty as himself, and hates them for it.
GEORGE BERNARD SHAW: *An Unsocial Socialist,* IV, 1883

A pessimist is one who feels bad when he feels good for fear he'll feel worse when he feels better. Author unidentified

A pessimist is one who, when he has the choice of two evils, chooses both. IBID.

[*See also* Optimist and Pessimist.

Petard

'Tis sport to have the engineer hoist with his own petard.
SHAKESPEARE: *Hamlet,* III, *c.* 1601

Peter, St. (?–64?)

When he had turned about and looked on his disciples, he rebuked Peter, saying, Get thee behind me, Satan: for thou savorest not the things that be of God, but the things that be of men.
MARK VIII, 33, *c.* 70 (Cf. MATTHEW XVI, 23, *c.* 75)

Thou art Peter, and upon this rock I will build my church.
MATTHEW XVI, 18, *c.* 75 (Gr. *petros*=a stone)

Robbing Peter to pay Paul.
ENGLISH PHRASE, borrowed from the Latin and familiar since the XIV century

Petition

It is the right of the subjects to petition the king, and all commitments and prosecutions for such petitioning are illegal.
THE ENGLISH BILL OF RIGHTS, V, Dec., 1689

Congress shall make no law . . . abridging . . . the right of the people . . . to petition the government for redress of grievances.
CONSTITUTION OF THE UNITED STATES, Amendment I, Dec. 15, 1791

The people have a right to petition, but not to use that right to cover calumniating insinuations.

THOMAS JEFFERSON: *Letter to James Madison,* 1808

Pettifogger

[*See* Lawyer.

Pettiness

Those who apply themselves too closely to little things become incapable of great things.

LA ROCHEFOUCAULD: *Maxims,* 1665

Small and creeping things are the product of petty souls.

THOMAS BROWNE: *Christian Morals,* I, *c.* 1680

Phantom

She was a phantom of delight
When first she gleamed upon my sight,
A lovely apparition, sent
To be a moment's ornament.

WILLIAM WORDSWORTH: *She Was a Phantom of Delight,* 1807

Pharisee

[*See* Good, Hypocrisy.

Ph. D.

[*See* Quack.

Pheasant

See! from the brake the whirring pheasant springs,
And mounts exulting on triumphant wings:
Short is his joy; he feels the fiery wound,
Flutters in blood, and panting beats the ground.

ALEXANDER POPE: *Windsor Forest,* 1713

If there is a pure and elevated pleasure in this world, it is that of roast pheasant and bread sauce; — barn-door fowls for dissenters, but for the real churchman, the thirty-nine times articled clerk — the pheasant, the pheasant!

SYDNEY SMITH: *Letter to R. H. Barham,* *c.* 1842

Philadelphia

It would (to use a Yankee phrase) puzzle a dozen Philadelphia lawyers.

Anon.: *The Balance,* Nov. 15, 1803

The New England folks have a saying that three Philadelphia lawyers are a match for the very Devil himself.

Anon.: The Salem (Mass.) Observer, March 13, 1824

As fat as a Philadelphia applewoman (or pie-woman). AMERICAN PHRASE

[*See also* London.

Philadelphian

As to the Philadelphians, damnation seize them, body and soul!

WILLIAM COBBETT: *Letter to William Thornton,* 1800

Philanthropist

The friend of all humanity is not to my taste.

J. B. MOLIÈRE: *Le misanthrope,* I, 1666

He is one of those wise philanthropists who in a time of famine would vote for nothing but a supply of toothpicks.

DOUGLAS JERROLD: *Men of Character,* 1838

I go to a convention of philanthropists. Do what I can, I cannot keep my eyes off the clock.

R. W. EMERSON: *Representative Men,* I, 1850

Here, boys, am I; and I have come clear down from that altitude in which I live; take great care of me, and respect and revere me, for I have come to teach you.

H. W. BEECHER: *Royal Truths,* 1862

The philanthropist is the Nero of modern times.

GEORGE MOORE: *Confessions of a Young Man,* VII, 1888

A rich (and usually bald) old gentleman who has trained himself to grin while his conscience is picking his pocket.

AMBROSE BIERCE: *The Devil's Dictionary,* 1906

Philanthropy

A good part of [philanthropy] arises in general from mere vanity and love of distinction, gilded over to others and to themselves with some show of benevolent sentiment.

WALTER SCOTT: *Journal,* Feb. 20, 1828

There is a spirit which, like the father of evil, is constantly "walking to and fro about the earth, seeking whom it may devour": it is the spirit of false philanthropy.

R. W. HAYNE: Speech in the Senate, Jan. 21, 1830

I tell thee, thou foolish philanthropist, that I grudge the dollar, the dime, the cent I give to such men as do not belong to me and to whom I do not belong.

R. W. EMERSON: *Self-Reliance,* 1841

Philanthropies and charities have a certain air of quackery.

R. W. EMERSON: *The Transcendentalist,* 1842

Whenever A and B put their heads together and decide what A, B and C must do for D, there is never any pressure on A and B. They consent to it and like it. There is rarely any pressure on D because he does not like it and contrives to evade it. The pressure all comes on C. He is the Forgotten Man.

W. G. SUMNER: *The Forgotten Man,* 1883

Justice and honesty have got themselves melted away into a miowling and watery philanthropy.

EDWARD CARPENTER: *England's Ideal,* 1887

Philanthropy [has become] simply the refuge of people who wish to annoy their fellow-creatures.
OSCAR WILDE: *An Ideal Husband*, I, 1895

[*See also* Alms, Altruism, Benevolence, Charity, Humanitarianism.

Philip of Macedon

[*See* Gold.

Philippines

We favor an immediate declaration of the nation's purpose to recognize the independence of the Philippine Islands as soon as a stable government can be established, such independence to be guaranteed by us as we guarantee the independence of Cuba.
Democratic National Platform, 1908

We accepted the responsibility of the islands as a duty to civilization and the Filipino people. To leave with our task half done would break our pledges, injure our prestige among nations, and imperil what has already been accomplished. We condemn the Democratic administration for its attempt to abandon the Philippines.
Republican National Platform, 1916

[*See also* Filipino.

Philistia

Moab is my washpot; over Edom will I cast out my shoe; over Philistia will I triumph.
PSALMS CVIII, 9, *c.* 150 B.C.

Philistine

A bastard shall dwell in Ashdod, and I will cut off the pride of the Philistines.
ZECHARIAH IX, 6, *c.* 520 B.C.

The Philistines be upon thee, Samson.
ZECHARIAH XVI, 9 (Cf. 12, 14, 20. At Jena, in 1693, one Pastor Götze preached a sermon from this text at the funeral of a student killed in a battle between town and gown. *Philister* thus came to signify, in German, an uncultured person. The English equivalent was popularized by Matthew Arnold, though, as the quotations show, it had been introduced before his time)

Knowest thou not that the Philistines are rulers over us? JUDGES XV, 11, *c.* 500 B.C.

So the Philistines were subdued, and they came no more. I SAMUEL VII, 13, *c.* 500 B.C.

When the Philistines saw their champion was dead, they fled. I SAMUEL XVII, 51

When they talk'd of their Raphaels, Correggios, and stuff,
He shifted his trumpet, and only took snuff.
OLIVER GOLDSMITH: *Retaliation*, 1774

What is a Philistine?
A hollow gut
Filled with fear and hope —
God have mercy on him!
J. W. GOETHE: *Letter to K. F. Zelter*, Sept. 4, 1831

Philistine: what we call bores, dullards, children of darkness.
THOMAS CARLYLE: *Life of John Stirling*, I, 1851

A man without sentiment, who cares naught for moonlight and music. A low, practical man, who pays his debts. I hate him.
C. F. BROWNE (ARTEMUS WARD): *Marion, a Romance of the French School*, 1860

The people who believe most that our greatness and welfare are proved by our being very rich, and who most give their lives and thoughts to becoming rich, are just the very people whom we call the Philistines.
MATTHEW ARNOLD: *Culture and Anarchy*, 1869

A term of contempt applied by prigs to the rest of their species.
LESLIE STEPHEN: *Hours in a Library*, 1879

[*See also* Art.

Philologist

Philologists chase
A panting syllable through time and space
Start it at home, and hunt it in the dark,
To Gaul, to Greece, and into Noah's Ark.
WILLIAM COWPER: *Retirement*, 1782

A philologist is a man who, horsed upon Grimm's law, chases the evasive syllable over umlauts and ablauts into the faintly echoing recesses of the Himalayas.
R. G. WHITE: *Words and Their Uses;* pref. to 2nd ed., 1876

Philology

The love of much babbling.
HENRY COCKERAM: *English Dictionary*, 1623

Philoprogenitiveness

Gideon had three score and ten sons of his body begotten.
JUDGES VIII, 30, *c.* 500 B.C.

[Jair] had thirty sons that rode on thirty ass colts. JUDGES X, 4

[Abdon] had forty sons and thirty nephews, that rode on three score and ten ass colts.
JUDGES XII, 14

Abijah waxed mighty, and married fourteen wives, and begat twenty and two sons, and sixteen daughters.
II CHRONICLES XIII, 21, *c.* 300 B.C.

Philosopher

Socrates acted wickedly, and is criminally curious in searching into things under the earth, and in the heavens, and in making the worse

appear the better cause, and in teaching these same things to others.
Charge against Socrates as stated in his Apology, 399 B.C.

A philosopher is one who desires to discern the truth. PLATO: *The Republic,* V, *c.* 370 B.C.

Until philosophers are kings, or the kings and princes of this world have the spirit and power of philosophy, and political greatness and wisdom meet in one, and those commoner natures who pursue either to the exclusion of the other are compelled to stand aside, cities will never have rest from their evils. IBID.

The soul of a philosopher runs away from his body and desires to be alone and by herself.
PLATO: *Phaedo, c.* 360 B.C.

There is no statement so absurd that no philosopher will make it.
CICERO: *De divinatione,* II, *c.* 78 B.C.

Then certain philosophers of the Epicureans, and of the Stoics, encountered him. And some said, What will this babbler say?
ACTS XVII, 18, *c.* 75

The first business of the philosopher is to part with conceit, for it is impossible for a man to learn what he thinks he already knows.
EPICTETUS: *Discourses,* II, *c.* 110

Man existed before the philosopher.
TERTULLIAN: *The Testimony of the Christian Soul, c.* 210

He who regardeth another's wife as his mother, another's goods as clods of earth, and all mankind as himself, is a philosopher.
The Hitopadesa, IV, *c.* 500

A philosopher is one who doubts.
MICHEL DE MONTAIGNE: *Essays,* II, 1580

There was never yet philosopher
That could endure the toothache patiently.
SHAKESPEARE: *Much Ado About Nothing,* V, *c.* 1599

Philosophers make imaginary laws for imaginary commonwealths, and their discourses are as the stars, which give little light because they are so high.
FRANCIS BACON: *The Advancement of Learning,* I, 1605

The deepest philosopher that ever was (saving the reverence of the schools) is but an ignorant sot to the simplest Christian.
JOSEPH HALL: *Meditations and Vows,* I, 1606

Philosophers dwell in the moon.
JOHN FORD: *The Lover's Melancholy,* III, 1628

O foolishness of men, that lend their ears
To those budge doctors of the Stoic fur.
JOHN MILTON: *Comus,* 1637

There is only one true philosopher in a century.
BALTASAR GRACIÁN: *The Art of Worldly Wisdom,* CCIII, 1647

No living creature is subject to the privilege of absurdity, but man only. And of men, those are of all most subject to it that profess philosophy.
THOMAS HOBBES: *Leviathan,* I, 1651

A deep, occult philosopher,
As learned as the wild Irish are.
SAMUEL BUTLER: *Hudibras,* I, 1663

Others apart sat on a hill retir'd,
In thoughts more elevate, and reasoned high
Of Providence, foreknowledge, will and fate,
Fixed fate, free will, foreknowledge absolute;
And found no end, in wand'ring mazes lost.
JOHN MILTON: *Paradise Lost,* II, 1667

To ridicule philosophy: that is to be a real philosopher.
BLAISE PASCAL: *Pensées,* VII, 1670

He knows the universe, but not himself.
JEAN DE LA FONTAINE: *Fables,* VIII, 1671

Your philosopher will not believe what he sees, and is always speculating about what he sees not — which is a life, I think, not much to be envied.
BERNARD DE FONTENELLE: *Entretiens sur la pluralité des mondes,* I, 1686

The far greater part, if not all, of those difficulties which have hitherto amused philosophers, and blocked up the way to knowledge, are entirely owing to ourselves. We have first raised a dust, and then complained we cannot see.
GEORGE BERKELEY: *The Principles of Human Knowledge,* intro., 1710

Do you think, if your old philosophers were alive, anyone would speak to them, anyone would pay their bills?
HENRY FIELDING: *The Temple Beau,* I, 1730

Many talk like philosophers and live like fools.
THOMAS FULLER: *Gnomologia,* 1732

Oh, wondrous creature! mount where science guides,
Go measure earth, weigh air, and state the tides;
Instruct the planets in what orbs to run,
Correct old Time, and regulate the sun;
Go teach eternal wisdom how to rule,
Then drop into thyself, and be a fool!
ALEXANDER POPE: *An Essay on Man,* II, 1732

The public would suffer less present inconvenience from the banishment of philosophers than from the extinction of any common trade.
SAMUEL JOHNSON: *The Rambler,* Aug. 6, 1751

A philosopher is a fool who torments himself while he is alive, to be talked about after he is dead.

JEAN LE ROND D'ALEMBERT: *Éléments de philosophie,* 1759

A fanatic philosopher is the greatest of all possible monsters.

FREDERICK THE GREAT: *Letter to Jean le Rond d'Alembert,* March 13, 1771

We philosophers may exist a little longer on our old literary reputation, but such a precarious life cannot last long, and we shall end by becoming the fable of Europe.

JEAN LE ROND L'ALEMBERT: *Letter to Frederick the Great,* Nov. 20, 1772

No monarch will henceforth begin a war before he has obtained the plenary indulgence of the philosophers. These gentlemen will govern Europe.

FREDERICK THE GREAT: *Letter to Voltaire,* Nov. 21, 1773

By nature a philosopher is not in genius and disposition half so different from a street porter as a mastiff is from a greyhound, or a greyhound from a spaniel.

ADAM SMITH: *The Wealth of Nations,* I, 1776

There is nothing so unfortunate as to be a philosopher and a wise man and a reasoner, and to know what can and cannot be done.

HORACE WALPOLE: *Letter to William Mason,* Oct. 5, 1777

I have tried in my time to be a philosopher, but cheerfulness was always breaking in.

OLIVER EDWARDS: To Samuel Johnson, quoted in *Boswell's Life,* April 17, 1778

That kings should become philosophers, or philosophers kings, can scarce be expected; nor is it to be wished, since the enjoyment of power inevitably corrupts the judgment of reason, and perverts its liberty.

IMMANUEL KANT: *Perpetual Peace,* Supplement II, 1795

Philosophers quarreled with one another like drunken men in dark rooms who hate peace without knowing why they fight, or seeing how to take aim.

SYDNEY SMITH: *Lectures on Moral Philosophy,* 1804

I am weary of philosophers, theologians, politicians and historians. They are immense masses of absurdities, vices and lies.

JOHN ADAMS: *Letter to Thomas Jefferson,* June 28, 1812

It is neither possible nor necessary for all men, nor for many, to be philosophers.

S. T. COLERIDGE: *Biographia Literaria,* 1817

What must the English and French think of the language of our philosophers, when we Germans do not understand them ourselves?

G. W. GOETHE: *Conversations with Eckermann,* March 28, 1827

The true philosophical temperament may, we think, be described in four words, much hope, little faith; a disposition to believe that anything, however extraordinary, may be done; an indisposition to believe that anything extraordinary has been done.

T. B. MACAULAY: *Lord Bacon,* 1837

There is no philosopher who is a philosopher at all times.

R. W. EMERSON: *The Conservative,* 1841

To be a philosopher is not merely to have subtle thoughts, nor even to found a school, but so to love wisdom as to live according to its dictates, a life of simplicity, independence, magnanimity, and trust.

H. D. THOREAU: *Walden,* 1854

Fools and philosophers were made out of the same metal.

H. G. BOHN: *Handbook of Proverbs,* 1855

[Philosophers] are given to think that . . . they pursue truth for its own sake, out of pure love for the chase (perhaps mingled with a little human weakness to be thought good shots).

T. H. HUXLEY: *Hume,* VIII, 1878

The lack of an historical sense is the peculiar fault of philosophers. Many of them mistake the latest variety of man, which has arisen under the influence of certain religions, certain political events, as a permanent form. They refuse to learn that man has developed, and that his faculty of knowledge has developed with him.

F. W. NIETZSCHE: *Human All-too-Human,* I, 1878

It is not given to the children of men to be philosophers without envy. Lookers-on can hardly bear the spectacle of the great world.

WALTER BAGEHOT: *Literary Studies,* II, 1879

I put aside a few skeptics, the types of decency in the history of philosophy: the rest haven't the slightest conception of intellectual integrity.

F. W. NIETZSCHE: *The Antichrist,* XII, 1888

Can a donkey be tragic? Is it tragedy to perish under a load one can neither bear nor throw off? This is the case of the philosopher.

F. W. NIETZSCHE: *The Twilight of the Idols,* 1889

The greater the philosopher, the harder it is for him to answer the questions of common people.

HENRYK SIENKIEWICZ: *Quo Vadis?,* XIX, 1895

All are lunatics, but he who can analyze his delusion is called a philosopher.

AMBROSE BIERCE: *Collected Works,* VIII, 1911

One who knows less and less about more and more. Author unidentified

" We two have much to think of," said the louse to the head of the philosopher.
GERMAN SAYING

[*See also* Clearness, Dress, Evolution, Faith, Familiarity, Government, Happiness, Hippocrates, Language, Marriage, Metaphysician, Mind, Misfortune, Music, Philosophy, Poet, Science, Toothache.

Philosopher's Stone

[*See* Contentment.

Philosophy

To have real freedom you must be the slave of philosophy.
EPICURUS: *Aphorisms, c.* 300 B.C.

To say that the time for philosophy has not yet come or that it is passed and gone is like saying that the time for happiness has not yet come or that it is passed and gone.
EPICURUS: *Letter to Menoeceus, c.* 300 B.C.

Philosophy is the cultivation of the mental faculties; it roots out vices and prepares the mind to receive proper seed.
CICERO: *Tusculanæ disputationes*, II, 45 B.C.

Beware lest any man spoil you through philosophy. COLOSSIANS II, 8, *c.* 60

The beginning of philosophy is the recognition of the conflict between opinions.
EPICTETUS: *Discourses*, II, *c.* 110

Philosophy is the art of arts and science of sciences (scientia scientiarum).
JOHN OF DAMASCUS: *Dialectica*, III, *c.* 730

Adversity's sweet milk — philosophy.
SHAKESPEARE: *Romeo and Juliet*, III, *c.* 1596

A little philosophy inclineth man's mind to atheism, but depth in philosophy bringeth men's minds about to religion.
FRANCIS BACON: *Essays*, 1597

There are more things in Heaven and earth, Horatio,
Than are dreamt of in your philosophy.
SHAKESPEARE: *Hamlet*, I, *c.* 1601

How charming is divine philosophy!
Not harsh and crabbed as dull fools suppose,
But musical as is Apollo's lute,
And a perpetual feast of nectared sweets
Where no crude surfeit reigns.
JOHN MILTON: *Comus*, 1637

Philosophy is such knowledge of effects or appearances as we acquire by true ratiocination from the knowledge we have first of their causes or generation: and again, of such causes or generations as may be from knowing first their effects.
THOMAS HOBBES: *Elements of Philosophy*, I, 1656

Discreet apprehenders will not think the better of that philosophy which hath the common cry to vouch it.
JOSEPH GLANVILL: *The Vanity of Dogmatizing*, XVI, 1661

That's absurd in one philosophy which is worthy truth in another.
JOSEPH GLANVILL: *The Vanity of Dogmatizing*, XX

Philosophy triumphs easily over past, and over future evils, but present evils triumph over philosophy.
LA ROCHEFOUCAULD: *Maxims*, 1665

Books bear him up a while, and make him try
To swim with bladders of philosophy.
JOHN WILMOT (EARL OF ROCHESTER): *A Satire Against Mankind*, 1675

Philosophy is such an impertinently litigious lady that a man had as good be engaged in lawsuits as to have to do with her.
ISAAC NEWTON: *Letter to Edmund Halley*, June 20, 1687

Philosophy is nothing but discretion.
JOHN SELDEN: *Table-Talk*, 1689

In the proportion that credulity is a more peaceful possession of the mind than curiosity, so far preferable is that wisdom which converses about the surface to that pretended philosophy which enters into the depth of things, and then comes gravely back with informations and discoveries, that in the inside they are good for nothing.
JONATHAN SWIFT: *A Tale of a Tub*, 1704

Philosophy doth open and enlarge the mind by the general views to which men are habituated in that study, and by the contemplation of more numerous and distant objects than fall within the sphere of mankind in the ordinary pursuits of life.
GEORGE BERKELEY: *The Guardian*, June 1, 1713

Philosophical decisions are nothing but the reflections of common life, methodized and corrected.
DAVID HUME: *An Enquiry Concerning the Human Understanding*, I, 1748

I despise philosophy, and renounce its guidance — let my soul dwell with common sense.
THOMAS REID: *Inquiry Into the Human Mind*, I, 1764

Philosophy is a good horse in the stable, but an arrant jade on a journey.
OLIVER GOLDSMITH: *The Good-Natur'd Man*, I, 1768

The greatest and perhaps the sole use of all philosophy of pure reason is, after all, merelnegative, since it serves, not as an organon for the enlargement [of knowledge], but as a discipline for its delimitation; and instead of discovering truth, has only the modest merit of preventing error.

IMMANUEL KANT: *The Critique of Pure Reason*, II, 1781

The first step towards philosophy is incredulity.

DENNIS DIDEROT: In conversation, 1784

A little philosophy causes men to despise learning, but much philosophy makes them esteem it.

NICOLAS CHAMFORT: *Maximes et pensées*, *c.* 1785 (Cf. BACON, *ante*, 1597)

The flour is the important thing, not the mill; the fruits of philosophy, not the philosophy itself. When we ask what time it is we don't want to know how watches are constructed.

G. C. LICHTENBERG: *Reflections*, 1799

What am I? What ought I to do? What may I hope and believe? All philosophy may be reduced to this. IBID.

Do not all charms fly
At the mere touch of cold philosophy?

JOHN KEATS: *Lamia*, II, 1820

Philosophy will clip an angel's wings. IBID.

In philosophy equally as in poetry, it is the highest and most useful prerogative of genius to produce the strongest impressions of novelty, while it rescues admitted truths from the neglect caused by the very circumstance of their universal admission.

S. T. COLERIDGE: *Aids to Reflection*, 1825

Every man is born an Aristotelian or a Platonist. I do not think it possible that any one born an Aristotelian can become a Platonist; and I am sure no born Platonist can ever change into an Aristotelian. They are the two classes of men, beside which it is next to impossible to conceive a third.

S. T. COLERIDGE: *Table-Talk*, July 20, 1830

Philosophy is the middle state between science, or knowledge, and sophia, or wisdom.

IBID.

Philosophy is utterly useless and fruitless, and, for this very reason is the sublimest of all pursuits, the most deserving attention, and the most worthy of our zeal.

G. W. F. HEGEL: *The Philosophy of History*, 1832

What is philosophy but a continual battle against custom; an ever-renewed effort to transcend the sphere of blind custom, and so become transcendental?

THOMAS CARLYLE: *Sartor Resartus*, III, 1836

Whenever philosophy has taken into its plan religion, it has ended in skepticism; and whenever religion excludes philosophy, or the spirit of free inquiry, it leads to wilful blindness and superstition.

S. T. COLERIDGE: *Allsop's Letters, Conversations, and Recollections of S. T. Coleridge*, 1836

The ancient philosophy was a treadmill, not a path. It was made up of revolving questions, of controversies which were always beginning again. It was a contrivance for having much exertion and no progress.

T. B. MACAULAY: *Lord Bacon*, 1837

Philosophy is the account which the human mind gives to itself of the constitution of the world.

R. W. EMERSON: *Representative Men*, II, 1850

What has philosophy taught men but to promise without practising, and to aspire without attaining? What has the deep and lofty thought of its disciples ended in but eloquent words?

J. H. NEWMAN: *On the Scope and Nature of University Education*, IV, 1852

Knowledge of the lowest kind is un-unified knowledge; science is partially-unified; philosophy is completely-unified knowledge.

HERBERT SPENCER: *First Principles*, I, 1862

Philosophy must be dealt with independent of supernatural revelation.

Proposition condemned by POPE PIUS IX: *Syllabus of Errors*, XIV, Dec. 8, 1864

In the history of philosophy no great thought has ever been brought to light by laborious, conscious trial and induction; it has always been apprehended by the glance of genius, and then elaborated by the understanding.

EDUARD VON HARTMANN: *The Philosophy of the Unconscious*, I, 1869

The philosophical spirit of inquiry may be traced to brute curiosity, and that to the habit of examining all things in search of food.

W. WINWOOD READE: *The Martyrdom of Man*, III, 1872

Philosophy goes no further than probabilities, and in every assertion keeps a doubt in reserve. J. A. FROUDE: *Calvinism*, 1877

Philosophy does not seek to overthrow revelation; it seeks rather to defend it against assailants.

POPE LEO XIII: *Inscrutabili*, April 21, 1878

Philosophy may teach us to bear with equanimity the misfortunes of our neighbors.

OSCAR WILDE: *The English Renaissance of Art*, 1882 (Lecture in New York, Jan. 9)

Every great philosophy is the confession of its originator, and a species of involuntary and unconscious autobiography.

F. W. NIETZSCHE: *Beyond Good and Evil*, 1886

The Protestant pastor is the grandfather of German philosophy.
F. W. NIETZSCHE: *The Antichrist*, X, 1888

All philosophies, if you ride them home, are nonsense.
SAMUEL BUTLER: *Note-Books, c.* 1890

Philosophy, like religion, is the outcome of the belief in the supernatural held by man in his more or less primitive state.
PAUL TOPINARD: *Science et foi*, VII, 1900

A route of many roads leading from nowhere to nothing.
AMBROSE BIERCE: *The Devil's Dictionary*, 1906

Philosophy is a history of falsehood.
AUGUST STRINDBERG: *Zones of the Spirit*, 1913

Most propositions and questions that have been written about philosophical matters are not false, but senseless.
LUDWIG WITTGENSTEIN: *Tractatus logico-philosophicus*, 1921

A philosophy requiring a large volume is too much; a hundred pages is enough.
E. W. HOWE: *Preaching from the Audience*, 1926

The term philosophy signifies that which philosophers are doing. . . . The meaning of the term is a function of two variables — time and clime.
CASSIUS J. KEYSER: *The Pastures of Wonder*, II, 1929

A filter turned upside down, where what goes in clear comes out cloudy.
Author unidentified

Good health or bad makes our philosophy.
FRENCH PROVERB

[*See also* Atheism, Business, Death, Faith, Fanaticism, Friar, Metaphysics, Philosopher, Poetry, Proverb, Skepticism, Theology.

Phlebotomy

[*See* Bleeding.

Phoenician

[*See* Books.

Phonograph

An irritating toy that restores life to dead noises.
AMBROSE BIERCE: *The Devil's Dictionary*, 1906

Phosphorus

Without phosphorus no thought. (Ohne Phosphor kein Gedanke.)
JACOB MOLESCHOTT: *Lehre der Nahrungsmittel*, II, 1858

Phrenology

I have never been able to prevail on myself to think of phrenology as a serious speculation. I have classed it with alchemy, with judicial astrology, with augury.
JOHN QUINCY ADAMS: *Letter to Thomas Sewall*, April 5, 1839

Physic

Throw physic to the dogs; I'll none of it.
SHAKESPEARE: *Macbeth*, V, *c.* 1605

If physic do not work prepare for the kirk.
JOHN RAY: *English Proverbs*, 1670

I was well. I took physic. I am here.
H. J. LOARING: *Epitaphs Quaint, Curious and Elegant*, 1872

[*See also* Diet, Medicine, Physician.

Physician

Into whatever houses I may enter I will go for the benefit of the sick and will abstain from every voluntary act of mischief and corruption, and further from the seduction of females or males, bond or free. Whatever in connection with my professional practice or not in connection with it I may see or hear I will not divulge, for I hold that all such things should be kept secret.
THE HIPPOCRATIC OATH, taken by medical students on receiving their degrees, and supposed to have been drawn up by Hippocrates, *c.* 400 B.C.

I will follow that method of treatment which, according to my judgment, I consider best for my patients, and abstain from whatever is injurious. I will give no deadly medicine to anyone if asked, nor suggest any such counsel. I will not give to a woman any instrument to produce abortion. IBID.

I die by the help of too many physicians.
ALEXANDER THE GREAT: On his deathbed, 323 B.C.

Asa . . . was diseased in his feet, until his disease was exceeding great: yet in his disease he sought not to the Lord, but to the physicians. And Asa slept with his fathers.
II CHRONICLES XVI, 12–13, *c.* 300 B.C.

Honor a physician with the honor due unto him.
ECCLESIASTICUS XXXVIII, 1, *c.* 180 B.C.

The competent physician, before he attempts to give medicine to his patient, makes himself acquainted not only with the disease which he wishes to cure, but also with the habits and constitution of the sick man.
CICERO: *De oratore*, II, *c.* 80 B.C.

That sick man does badly who makes his physician his heir.
PUBLILIUS SYRUS: *Sententiæ*, *c.* 50 B.C.

Other things being equal, a friend makes a better physician than a stranger.
AULUS CORNELIUS CELSUS: *De re medicina,* I, *c.* 10

A physician is only a consoler of the mind.
PETRONIUS ARBITER: *Satyricon, c.* 50

Luke, the beloved physician.
COLOSSIANS IV, 14, *c.* 60

A certain woman, which had an issue of blood twelve years, had suffered many things of many physicians, and had spent all that she had, and was nothing bettered, but rather grew worse. MARK V, 25–26, *c.* 70

They that be whole need not a physician.
MATTHEW IX, 12, *c.* 75

Physician, heal thyself.
LUKE IV, 23, *c.* 75 (Cited by Jesus as " this proverb ")

The physician is only nature's assistant.
GALEN: *De humoribus, c.* 175

A physician who demands no fee is worth none.
THE TALMUD (*Baba Kamma*), *c.* 200

Strive to preserve your health; and in this you will the better succeed in proportion as you keep clear of the physicians, for their drugs are a kind of alchemy concerning which there are no fewer books than there are medicines.
LEONARDO DA VINCI: *Notebooks, c.* 1500

A physician should be the servant of nature, not her enemy.
THEOPHRATUS BOMBAST VON HOHENHEIM (PARACELSUS): *Die grosse Wunderartzney,* 1530

A physician gets no pleasure out of the health of his friends.
MICHEL DE MONTAIGNE: *Essays,* I, 1580

Physicians are the cobblers, rather the botchers, of men's bodies; as the one patches our tattered clothes, so the other solders our diseased flesh.
JOHN FORD: *The Lover's Melancholy,* I, 1628

Physicians, of all men, are most happy: whatever good success soever they have, the world proclaimeth, and what faults they commit, the earth covereth.
FRANCIS QUARLES: *Hieroglyphics of the Life of Man,* 1638

God heals, and the physician hath the thanks.
GEORGE HERBERT: *Outlandish Proverbs,* 1640

I can cure vices by physic when they remain incurable by divinity, and they shall obey my pills when they contemn their precepts. I boast nothing, but plainly say, we all labor against our own cure; for death is the cure of all diseases.
THOMAS BROWNE: *Religio Medici,* II, 1642

Commonly, physicians, like beer, are best when they are old.
THOMAS FULLER: *The Holy State and the Profane State,* 1642

Everyone is a fool or a physician to himself after thirty.
JAMES HOWELL: *Proverbs,* 1659 (Sometimes *forty* is substituted for *thirty*)

Physicians ought not to give their judgment of religion, for the same reason that butchers are not admitted to be jurors upon life and death.
JONATHAN SWIFT: *Thoughts on Various Subjects,* 1706 (Butchers were formerly excluded from juries in capital cases)

The kind physician grants the husband's pray'rs,
Or gives relief to long-expecting heirs.
JONATHAN SWIFT: *On Dreams,* 1724

He's the best physician that knows the worthlessness of the most medicines.
BENJAMIN FRANKLIN: *Poor Richard's Almanac,* 1733

Every physician, almost, hath his favorite disease.
HENRY FIELDING: *Tom Jones,* II, 1749

No man is more worthy of esteem than a physician who, having studied nature from his youth, knows the properties of the human body, the diseases which assail it, and the remedies which will benefit it, who exercises his art with caution, and who gives equal attention to the rich and the poor.
VOLTAIRE: *Philosophical Dictionary,* 1764

When people's ills, they comes to I,
I physics, bleeds, and sweats 'em;
Sometimes they live, sometimes they die.
What's that to I? I lets 'em.
Anon.: *The Physician, c.* 1780

A physician in a great city seems to be the mere plaything of fortune; his degree of reputation is, for the most part, totally casual: they that employ him know not his excellence; they that reject him know not his deficience.
SAMUEL JOHNSON: *Lives of the Poets* (*Mark Akenside*), 1780

You medical people will have more lives to answer for in the other world than even we generals.
NAPOLEON I: To Barry E. O'Meara at St. Helena, Sept. 29, 1817

A physician and a priest ought not to belong to any particular nation, and should be divested of all political opinions.
NAPOLEON I: To Barry E. O'Meara at St. Helena, Oct. 16, 1817

The human body is like a watch, and is designed to run for a certain time. The watchmaker cannot open it, and must work upon it by trial and error. For one time that he

helps it with his instruments, he injures it ten times, and in the end he always destroys it.
NAPOLEON I: To Dr. Antommarchi at St. Helena, Oct. 14, 1820

This is the way physicians mend or end us,
Secundum artem; but although we sneer
In health — when ill, we call them to attend us,
Without the least propensity to jeer.
BYRON: *Don Juan,* X, 1823

Nature, time, and patience are the three great physicians.
H. G. BOHN: *Handbook of Proverbs,* 1855

Forth then issued Hiawatha,
Wandered eastward, wandered westward,
Teaching men the use of simples
And the antidotes for poisons,
And the cure of all diseases.
H. W. LONGFELLOW: *Hiawatha,* XV, 1855

The most dangerous physicians are those who, being born actors, imitate born physicians with perfect imposture.
F. W. NIETZSCHE: *Human All-too-Human,* I, 1878

You doctors have a serious responsibility. You call a man from the gates of death, you give health and strength once more to use or abuse. But for your kindness and skill, this would have been my last book, and now I am in hopes that it will be neither my last nor my best.
ROBERT LOUIS STEVENSON: Inscription in a copy of *Travels with a Donkey* sent to his physician, Dr. William Bambord, 1879

The pleasure of a physician is little, the gratitude of patients is rare, and even rarer is material reward, but these things will never deter the student who feels the call within him. THEODOR BILLROTH (1829–94)

Physicians are the natural attorneys of the poor. RUDOLF VIRCHOW (1821–1902)

One upon whom we set our hopes when ill, and our dogs when well.
AMBROSE BIERCE: *The Devil's Dictionary,* 1906

No man can be a good physician who has never been sick. ARAB PROVERB

My friend was ill: I attended him. He died: I dissected him.
Ascribed to various celebrated physicians; apparently of French origin

A physician is one who pours drugs of which he knows little into a body of which he knows less. Author unidentified

A single doctor like a sculler plies,
And all his art and all his physic tries;
But two physicians, like a pair of oars,
Conduct you soonest to the Stygian shores.
IBID.

An angel when he comes to cure, a devil when he asks for pay.
ENGLISH SAYING, borrowed from the Latin

Two great physicians first
My loving husband tried,
To cure my pain —
In vain,
At last he got a third,
And then I died.
Epitaph in Cheltenham churchyard, England

A lucky physician is better than a good one.
GERMAN PROVERB

All physicians, even good ones, will go to Hell.
HEBREW PROVERB

Better pay honor to thy physician before thou hast need of him. IBID.

Never live in a city where the governor is a physician. IBID.

Unhappy the province whose physician suffers from gout and whose chancellor of the exchequer is one-eyed. IBID.

No physician is really good before he has killed one or two patients. HINDU PROVERB

No really good physician has ever taken physic.
ITALIAN PROVERB

All idiots, priests, Jews, actors, monks, barbers and old women think they are physicians.
MEDIEVAL LATIN PROVERB

Where there are three physicians there are two atheists. (Ubi tres medici, duo athei.)
IBID.

Auld wives and bairns mak fools o' physicians.
SCOTTISH PROVERB

God works the cure and the physician takes the money. SPANISH PROVERB

[*See* also Body-snatcher, Clergyman, Diet, Doctor, Embalming, Forty, Gout, Hippocrates, Lawyer, Magic, Medicine, Patient, Profession, Quack, Skeptic, Thirty.

Physiognomy

Physiognomy as a rule doesn't enable us to judge of the character of men — but it does enable us to make conjectures.
JEAN DE LA BRUYÈRE: *Caractères,* XII, 1688

Physiology

[*See* Experiment.

Pianist

The great pianists have nothing to show save technique and affectation.
LUDWIG VAN BEETHOVEN: To Marie Pachler-Koschak, 1817

The clear cool note of the cuckoo, which has ousted the legitimate nest holder,

The whistle of the railway guard, dispatching the train to the inevitable collision,
The maiden's monosyllabic reply to a polysyllabic proposal,
The fundamental note of the last trump, which is presumably D natural;
All these are sounds to rejoice in, yes, to let your very ribs re-echo with,
But better than all is the absolutely last chord of the apparently inexhaustible pianoforte player.

J. K. STEPHENS: *Parody of Walt Whitman*, c. 1880

Please do not shoot the pianist. He is doing his best.

OSCAR WILDE: *Impressions of America*, 1883 (Usually ascribed to MARK TWAIN)

Don't be ashamed if you can't play the piano; be proud of it.

E. W. HOWE: *Country Town Sayings*, 1911

I never see a latter-day pianist on his travels but I am reminded of a comedian with his rouge-pot, grease-paints, wigs, arms and costumes.

JAMES HUNEKER: *Old Fogy*, xv, 1913

He who plays the piano keeps sane.

ITALIAN PROVERB

Pianoforte

A pianoforte is a harp in a box.

LEIGH HUNT: *The Seer*, XLV, 1840

'Tis wonderful how soon a piano gets into a log-hut on the frontier.

R. W. EMERSON: *Civilization*, 1870

[*See also* Typewriter.

Picketing

There is and can be no such thing as peaceful picketing, any more than there can be chaste vulgarity, or peaceful mobbing, or lawful lynching.

JUDGE SMITH MCPHERSON: *Decision in Atchison* vs. *T. S. F. Rwy. Co.*, 1905

Peaceful picketing can be done. There can be some angels come down from Heaven who can peacefully picket.

JUSTICE G. V. MULLAN OF THE NEW YORK SUPREME COURT: *Decision in Leeds* vs. *Lewis*, 1925

Picketing without a strike is no more unlawful than a strike without picketing.

NEW YORK COURT OF APPEALS: *Decision in Exchange Bakery* vs. *Rifkin*, 1927

Picking

It will never get well if you pick it.

AMERICAN PROVERB

Pickpocket

Pickpockets are sure traders, for they take ready money.

THOMAS FULLER: *Gnomologia*, 1732

Pict

[*See* English.

Picture

Pictures are the books of the ignorant.

ENGLISH PROVERB, familiar since the XVII century

The pictures that are most valued are for the most part those by masters of established renown, which are highly or neatly finished, and of a size small enough to admit of their being placed in galleries or salons, so as to be made subjects of ostentation.

JOHN RUSKIN: *The Political Economy of Art*, 1857

Pictures must not be too picturesque. Nothing astonishes men so much as common sense and plain dealing. All great actions have been simple, and all great pictures are.

R. W. EMERSON: *Art*, 1841

A picture is a mute poem. (Mutum est pictura poema.)

LATIN PROVERB

[*See also* Drawing, Painting, Portrait.

Picturesqueness

What fast friends picturesqueness and typhus often are.

CHARLES DICKENS: Speech in London, Feb. 9, 1858

Pie

Sing a song of sixpence,
  A pocket full of rye;
Four and twenty blackbirds,
  Baked in a pie.

Anon.: *Nursery rhyme*, c. 1750

[*See also* Heart, Heaven, Plum.

Piety

I had rather be a door-keeper in the house of my God than to dwell in the tents of wickedness.

PSALMS LXXXIV, 10, *c.* 150 B.C.

Let them learn first to show piety at home.

I TIMOTHY V, 4, *c.* 60

She was a widow of about fourscore and four years, which departed not from the temple, but served God with fastings and prayers day and night.

LUKE II, 37, *c.* 75

Continence is the foundation of genuine piety.

POPE XYSTUS I: *The Ring*, *c.* 150

All his mind is bent to holiness,
To number Ave-Marias on his beads;
His champions are the prophets and apostles,
His weapons holy saws of sacred writ,
His study is his tilt-yard, and his loves
Are brazen images of canonized saints.

SHAKESPEARE: *II Henry VI*, I, *c.* 1591

Thou villain, thou art full of piety.

SHAKESPEARE: *Much Ado About Nothing*, IV, *c.* 1599

I shall employ it all in pious uses,
Founding of colleges and grammar schools,
Marrying young virgins, building hospitals,
And, now and then, a church.
BEN JONSON: *The Alchemist*, II, 1612

Ah! though I am a pious Christian, the feelings of a man do not the less burn in my breast.
J. B. MOLIÈRE: *Le Tartuffe*, III, 1664

Young Obadias,
David, Josias,
All were pious.
The New England Primer, c. 1688

Mrs. D. is resolved to marry the old greasy curate. She was always High Church to an excessive degree.
MARY WORTLEY MONTAGU: *Letter to Lady* ——, Jan. 13, 1716

Piety requires us to renounce no ways of life where we can act reasonably, and offer what we do to the glory of God.
WILLIAM LAW: *A Serious Call to a Devout and Holy Life*, XI, 1728

At church, with meek and unaffected grace,
His looks adorn'd the venerable place;
Truth from his lips prevailed with double sway,
And fools, who came to scoff, remain'd to pray.
OLIVER GOLDSMITH: *The Deserted Village*, 1770

There is no trusting to . . . crazy piety.
SAMUEL JOHNSON: *Boswell's Life*, March 25, 1776

Piety is sweet to infant minds.
WILLIAM WORDSWORTH: *The Excursion*, IV, 1814

I lie, I cheat, do anything for pelf,
But who on earth can say I am not pious?
THOMAS HOOD: *Blanca's Dream*, 1827

He grew less pious and more polite.
R. H. BARHAM: *The Ingoldsby Legends*, I, 1840

Strange, but true, that those who have loved God most have loved men least.
R. G. INGERSOLL: Speech in New York, April 25, 1881

If your neighbor has made one pilgrimage to Mecca, watch him; if two, avoid him; if three, move to another street.
ARAB PROVERB

Beware of them whose ignorance is joined with piety. HEBREW PROVERB

If the thunder is not loud the peasant forgets to cross himself. RUSSIAN PROVERB

Never leave your corn to dry before the door of a pious man. SPANISH PROVERB

[*See also* Justice, Society, Wrinkle.

Pig

Pigs are a race unjustly calumniated. Pig has, it seems, not been wanting to man, but man to pig. We do not allow him time for his education; we kill him at a year old.
SAMUEL JOHNSON: *Boswell's Life*, 1784

Feed a pig, and you'll have a hog.
H. G. BOHN: *Handbook of Proverbs*, 1855

Pigs are pigs.
CHARLES LAMB: *Letter to S. T. Coleridge*, March 9, 1822 (Cf. BUTLER, *post*, 1906)

Pigs is pigs.
ELLIS PARKER BUTLER: Title of a story, 1906 (Cf. LAMB, *ante*, 1822)

The life of a pig is short and sweet.
FRENCH PROVERB

A calf that associates with a pig will eat garbage. HINDU PROVERB

Even fat pigs give much lean meat.
PORTUGUESE PROVERB

[*See also* Child, Credit, Edible, Hog, Old, Poet, Pork.

Pigeon

[*See* Priest.

Pilgrim

The men told them that they were pilgrims and strangers in the world, and that they were going to their own country, which was the heavenly Jerusalem.
JOHN BUNYAN: *Pilgrim's Progress*, I, 1678

The High Dutch pilgrims, when they beg, sing; the French pilgrims whine and cry; the Spanish curse and blaspheme; the Irish and English steal. SPANISH PROVERB

Pilgrim Fathers

Not as the conqueror comes,
They, the true-hearted, came;
Not with the roll of the stirring drums,
And the trumpet that sings of fame.
FELICIA HEMANS: *The Landing of the Pilgrim Fathers*, 1826

How much better it would have been if Plymouth Rock had landed on the Pilgrims.
Author unidentified

The Pilgrim Fathers landed on the shores of America, and fell upon their knees. Then they fell upon the aborigines. IBID.

[*See also* Freedom (Religious), Puritan, War (American Civil).

Pillow

[*See* Fatigue.

Pilot

O pilot! 'tis a fearful night,
There's danger on the deep.

T. H. BAYLY: *The Pilot,* 1844

The best pilots are ashore. DUTCH PROVERB

Pin

See a pin and pick it up;
All the day you'll have good luck.

OLD ENGLISH RHYME

The man who does not pick up a pin does not love his wife. SPANISH PROVERB

[*See also* Silence.

Pine

The whispering pine.

THEOCRITUS: *Idylls,* I, *c.* 270 B.C.

The pine wishes herself a shrub when the ax is at her root.

THOMAS FULLER: *Gnomologia,* 1732

The pine boughs are singing
Old songs with new gladness.

P. B. SHELLEY: *Prometheus Unbound,* IV, 1820

Who leaves the pine-tree, leaves his friend,
Unnerves his strength, invites his end.

R. W. EMERSON: *Woodnotes,* II, 1841

When the sun rises behind a ridge crested with pine, provided the ridge be at a distance of about two miles, and seen clear, all the trees, for about three or four degrees on each side of the sun, become trees of light, seen in clear flame against the darker sky, and dazzling as the sun itself.

JOHN RUSKIN: *Modern Painters,* V, 1860

A pine cut down, a dead pine, is no more a pine than a dead human carcass is a man.

H. D. THOREAU: *The Maine Woods,* II, 1864

[*See also* Tree, Wind.

Pioneer

It is the poorer sort of people that commonly begin to improve remote deserts: with a small stock they have houses to build, lands to clear and fence, corn to raise, clothes to provide, and children to educate.

JOHN WOOLMAN: *Journal,* II, 1774

They were driven there by misfortunes, necessity of beginnings, desire of acquiring large tracts of land, idleness, frequent want of economy, ancient debts.

ST. JOHN DE CRÈVECOEUR: *Letters from an American Farmer,* III, 1782

The first settler in the woods is generally a man who has outlived his credit or fortune in the cultivated parts.

BENJAMIN RUSH: *Essays,* 1798

For we cannot tarry here,
We must march, my darlings, we must bear the brunt of danger,
We, the youthful sinewy races, all the rest on us depend,
Pioneers! O Pioneers!

WALT WHITMAN: *Pioneers! O Pioneers!,* 1865

Hurrah for Greer county! The land of the free,
The land of the bedbug, grasshopper and flea;
I'll sing of its praises, I'll tell of its fame
While starving to death on my government claim.

Anon.: Song of the Nebraska pioneers, *c.* 1870

We must make allowances for whoever does a thing first. GREEK PROVERB

Pipe

[*See* Tobacco.

Piper

The people piped with pipes, and rejoiced with great joy. I KINGS I, 40, *c.* 500 B.C.

Tom, Tom, the piper's son,
Learnt to play when he was young;
But all the tune that he could play
Was "Over the hills and far away."

Nursery Rhyme, traced to *c.* 1650

Give the piper a penny to play, and two pence to leave off.

THOMAS FULLER: *Gnomologia,* 1732

[*See also* Musician, Pay.

Pirate

No man is a pirate, unless his contemporaries agree to call him so.

S. T. COLERIDGE: *Table-Talk,* March 17, 1832

Pirates, when they chance to cross each other's crossbones, the first hail is—"How many skulls?"

HERMAN MELVILLE: *Moby Dick,* LII, 1851

If I were to advertise in my paper tomorrow for fifty young men to go on a pirate ship and for five men to work on my farm, there would be five hundred applications for the situation on the pirate ship and not one for the farm.

HORACE GREELEY: To an applicant for a post on the New York Tribune, *c.* 1855

A pirate is an enemy to all humanity. (Pirata est hostis humani generis.) LEGAL MAXIM

[*See also* Emperor.

Pistol

Fighting with pistols is dishonorable.

NAPOLEON I: To Gaspard Gourgaud at St. Helena, 1815–1818

Pit

[*See* Hell.

Pitch

[*See* Defilement, Hell.

Pity

It is hard to have pity and be wise.
Ascribed to AGESILAUS (438–361 B.C.)

He that hath pity upon the poor lendeth unto the Lord; and that which he hath given will he pay him again.
PROVERBS XIX, 17, *c.* 350 B.C.

To him that is afflicted pity should be showed from his friend. JOB VI, 14, *c.* 325 B.C.

Youth feels pity out of human kindness; old age out of its infirmity.
ARISTOTLE: *Rhetoric,* II, *c.* 322 B.C.

All feel pity for those like themselves.
CLAUDIUS CLAUDIANUS: *In Eutropium,* I, *c.* 400

My pity hath been balm to heal their wounds,
My mildness hath allay'd their swelling griefs.
SHAKESPEARE: *III Henry VI,* IV, *c.* 1591

Tear-falling pity dwells not in his eye.
SHAKESPEARE: *Richard III,* IV, *c.* 1596

Is there no pity sitting in the clouds,
That sees into the bottom of my grief?
SHAKESPEARE: *Romeo and Juliet,* III, *c.* 1596

But yet the pity of it, Iago! O Iago, the pity of it, Iago! SHAKESPEARE: *Othello,* IV, 1604

Pity is the virtue of the law,
And none but tyrants use it cruelly.
SHAKESPEARE: *Timon of Athens,* III, *c.* 1607

Of all the paths that lead to a woman's love
Pity's the straightest.
BEAUMONT and FLETCHER: *The Knight of Malta,* I, *c.* 1619

He that pities another remembers himself.
GEORGE HERBERT: *Outlandish Proverbs,* 1640

Pity is imagination or fiction of future calamity to ourselves, proceeding from the sense of another man's calamity. But when it lighteth on such as we think have not deserved the same, the compassion is greater, because there then appeareth more probability that the same may happen to us; for the evil that happeneth to an innocent man may happen to every man.
THOMAS HOBBES: *On Human Nature,* IX, 1650

I am not very sensible of pity; and I should wish not to be so at all. Notwithstanding, I would do everything in my power to comfort a person in distress, for miserable people are such fools that it is this which does them the greatest good in the world.
LA ROCHEFOUCAULD: *Self-portrait,* 1658

Pity is a perception of our own misfortunes in those of others; it is a clever foresight of the evils into which we may fall. We succor others in order to engage them to succor us in similar circumstances.
LA ROCHEFOUCAULD: *Maxims,* 1665

To pity the unhappy is not contrary to selfish desire; on the other hand, we are glad of the occasion to thus testify friendship, and attract to ourselves the reputation of tenderness, without giving anything.
BLAISE PASCAL: *Pensées,* VIII, 1670

Pity's akin to love.
THOMAS SOUTHERNE: *Oroonoko,* II, 1696
(The idea is traceable to CHAUCER: *The Legend of Good Women, c.* 1380, but Southerne is responsible for the familiar form)

Pity, though it is the most gentle and the least mischievous of all our passions, is yet as much a frailty of our nature as anger, pride or fear. The weakest minds have generally the greatest share of it.
BERNARD DE MANDEVILLE: *An Inquiry Into the Origin of Moral Virtue,* 1723

If you pity rogues you are no great friend to honest men.
THOMAS FULLER: *Gnomologia,* 1732

We pity in others only those evils that we have ourselves experienced.
J.-J. ROUSSEAU: *Émile,* IV, 1762

Pity is not natural to man. Children are always cruel. Savages are always cruel. Pity is acquired and improved by the cultivation of reason.
SAMUEL JOHNSON: *Boswell's Life,* July 20, 1763

There isn't in the whole creation so savage an animal as a human creature without pity.
RICHARD CUMBERLAND: *The West Indian,* II, 1771

If a madman were to come into this room with a stick in his hand no doubt we should pity the state of his mind, but our primary consideration would be to take care of ourselves. We should knock him down first, and pity him afterward.
SAMUEL JOHNSON: *Boswell's Life,* April 3, 1776

More helpful than all wisdom is one draught of simple human pity that will not forsake us.
MARIAN EVANS (GEORGE ELIOT): *The Mill on the Floss,* VII, 1860

Pity makes the world
Soft to the weak and noble for the strong.
EDWIN ARNOLD: *The Light of Asia,* 1879

Pity stands in opposition to all the tonic passions that augment the energy of the feeling of aliveness: it is a depressant. A man loses power when he pities.
F. W. NIETZSCHE: *The Antichrist,* VII, 1888

True pity consists not so much in fearing suffering as in desiring it. The desire is a faint one and we should hardly wish to see it realized, yet we form it in spite of ourselves, as if nature were committing some great injustice and it were necessary to get rid of all suspicion of complicity with her.
HENRI BERGSON: *Time and Free Will*, I, 1889

A book or poem which has no pity in it had better not be written.
OSCAR WILDE: To Frank Harris, *c.* 1892

Only man helps man. Only man pities; only man tries to save.
ROBERT BLATCHFORD: *God and My Neighbor*, 1903

[*See also* Charity, Childhood, Curiosity, Envy, Fear, Friend, Jest, Judge, Tragedy.

Plagiarism

I am against the prophets, saith the Lord, that steal my words every one from his neighbor.
JEREMIAH XXIII, 30, *c.* 625 B.C.

They lard their lean books with the fat of others' works.
ROBERT BURTON: *The Anatomy of Melancholy*, 1621

I am but a gatherer and disposer of other men's stuff.
HENRY WOTTON: *Elements of Architecture*, pref., 1624

To copy beauties, forfeits all pretence
To fame — to copy faults, is want of sense.
CHARLES CHURCHILL: *The Rosciad*, 1761

Steal! to be sure they may, and egad, serve your best thoughts as gipsies do stolen children, — disfigure them to make 'em pass for their own.
R. B. SHERIDAN: *The Critic*, I, 1779

I did not consider it as any part of my charge to invent new ideas altogether and to offer no sentiment which had ever been expressed before.
THOMAS JEFFERSON: On being accused of plagiarism in the Declaration of Independence, *c.* 1800

Most writers steal a good thing when they can,
And when 'tis safely got 'tis worth the winning.
The worst of 't is we now and then detect 'em.
Before they ever dream that we suspect 'em.
B. W. PROCTOR (BARRY CORNWALL): *Dramatic Scenes*, 1819

If we steal thoughts from the moderns, it will be cried down as plagiarism; if from the ancients, it will be cried up as erudition.
C. C. COLTON: *Lacon*, 1820

Plagiarists are always suspicious of being stolen from — as pickpockets are observed commonly to walk with their hands in their breeches' pockets.
S. T. COLERIDGE: *Table-Talk*, Jan. 4, 1823

To disguise his stolen horse, the uneducated thief cuts off the tail; but the educated thief prefers tying on a new tail at the end of the old one, and painting them both sky blue.
E. A. POE: *Marginalia*, 1844–49

It has come to be practically a sort of rule in literature that a man, having once shown himself capable of original writing, is entitled thenceforth to steal from the writings of others at discretion.
R. W. EMERSON: *Representative Men*, V, 1850

You will, Oscar, you will.
J. MCN. WHISTLER: On hearing Oscar Wilde say "I wish I had said that" during an exchange of witticisms, *c.* 1880

If I take an old plot from a play that has been a dead failure and redress it, put living words into the mouths of its characters, give it the proper technique and action that it lacks, making it an actable play and so a successful one, I claim that play is mine, for I have made from the dead a living thing.
DION BOUCICAULT (1822–90)

[*See also* Jonson (Ben).

Plague

Lord! how sad a sight it is to see the streets empty of people, and very few upon the 'Change. Jealous of every door that one sees shut up, lest it should be the plague; and about us two shops in three, if not more, generally shut up.
SAMUEL PEPYS: *Diary*, Aug. 16, 1665

'Tis the Destroyer, or the Devil, that scatters plagues about the world. . . . [He] impregnates the air with such malignant salts as, meeting with the salt of our microcosm, shall immediately cast us into that fermentation and putrefaction which will utterly dissolve all the vital ties within us.
COTTON MATHER: *The Wonders of the Invisible World*, 1692

[*See also* Haste.

Plain

[*See* Hill.

Plainspeaking

The Macedonians . . . had not the wit to call a spade by any other name than a spade.
NICHOLAS UDALL: Tr. of DESIDERIUS ERASMUS: *Apothegms*, 1542

Christ Himself, speaking of unsavory traditions, scruples not to name the dunghill and the jakes.
JOHN MILTON: *An Apology for Smectymnuus*, 1642

This sublime age reduces everything to its quintessence; all periphrases and expletives

are so much in disuse, that I suppose soon the only way to making love will be to say "Lie down."
HORACE WALPOLE: *Letter to H. S. Conway,* Oct. 23, 1778

As the world is, an honest and wise man should have a rough tongue.
GEORGE GISSING: *The Private Papers of Henry Ryecroft,* 1903

We call figs figs, and a hoe a hoe. (Ficus ficus, ligonem ligonem vocat.) LATIN PROVERB

He that says what he likes will hear what he doesna like. SCOTTISH PROVERB

[*See also* Candor, Frankness, Truth.

Plaintiff

[*See* Lawsuit, Proof.

Planet

[*See* Earth.

Plant

Plants are so many animals which eat and drink; and there are gradations up to man, who is only the most perfect of them all.
NAPOLEON I: To Barry E. O'Meara at St. Helena, Nov. 9, 1816

The maples and ferns are still uncorrupt; yet no doubt, when they come to consciousness, they too will curse and swear.
R. W. EMERSON: *Nature,* 1836

Platitude

The decision of the man who judges that exquisite beauty is preferable to the grossest deformity, or that twice two are equal to four, must certainly be approved of by all the world, but will not, surely, be much admired.
ADAM SMITH: *The Theory of Moral Sentiments,* I, 1759

In modern life nothing produces such an effect as a good platitude. It makes the whole world kin.
OSCAR WILDE: *An Ideal Husband,* II, 1895

Plato (428–347 B.C.)

I would rather be wrong with Plato than right with such men as these [the Pythagoreans].
CICERO: *Tusculanæ disputationes,* 45 B.C.

Plato is dead, and dead is his devise,
Which some thought witty, none thought ever wise.
JOSEPH HALL (BISHOP OF NORWICH): *Virgidemarium,* V, 1598

Plato, in the book of his laws, which no city ever yet received, fed his fancy with making many edicts to his airy burgomasters, which they who otherwise admire him, wish had been rather buried and excused in the genial cups of an academic night.
JOHN MILTON: *Areopagitica,* 1644

Plato and Aristotle were well-bred men, and, like others, laughing with their friends: and when they diverted themselves in making their laws and politics they did it playfully. It was the least philosophic and least serious part of their lives. The most philosophic was living simply and tranquilly.
BLAISE PASCAL: *Pensées,* VIII, 1670

The sum of Plato's wondrous wisdom is,
This is not that, and therefore, that not this.
ROBERT DODSLEY: *Modern Reasoning,* 1748

The sunny mist, the luminous gloom of Plato.
S. T. COLERIDGE: *Notebooks,* 1799

Fashion and authority apart, and bringing Plato to the test of reason, take from him his sophisms, futilities and incomprehensibilities and what remains? His foggy mind is forever presenting the semblances of objects which, half seen through a mist, can be defined neither in form nor dimensions.
THOMAS JEFFERSON: *Letter to John Adams,* 1814

Plato's works are logical exercises for the mind. Little that is positive is advanced in them. Socrates may be fairly represented by Plato in the more moral parts; but in all the metaphysical disquisitions it is Pythagoras.
S. T. COLERIDGE: *Table-Talk,* May 8, 1824

There are not in the world at any one time more than a dozen persons who read and understand Plato.
R. W. EMERSON: *Spiritual Laws,* 1841

He can put light into our eyes.
JOSEPH JOUBERT: *Pensées,* I, 1842

Out of Plato come all things that are still written and debated among men of thought.
R. W. EMERSON: *Representative Men,* II, 1850

Plato is a bore.
F. W. NIETZSCHE: *The Twilight of the Idols,* 1889

[*See also* Greatness, Truth.

Play (=drama)

Where is our usual manager of mirth?
What revels are in hand? Is there no play,
To ease the anguish of a torturing hour?
SHAKESPEARE: *A Midsummer Night's Dream,* V, *c.* 1596

The play's the thing
Wherein I'll catch the conscience of the king.
SHAKESPEARE: *Hamlet,* II, *c.* 1601

Happily some plays may be worthy the keeping; but hardly one in forty.
THOMAS BODLEY: *Letter to Thomas James,* first librarian of the Bodleian Library, 1612

John Marston bade his friends unto a play,
But having come they bade themselves away.
Anon.: MS. in the South Kensington Museum, *c.* 1625

A play ought to be a just and lively image of human nature, representing its passions and humors, and the changes of fortune to which it is subject, for the delight and instruction of mankind.
JOHN DRYDEN: *Of Dramatic Poesy,* 1668

The business of plays is to recommend virtue, and discountenance vice; to show the uncertainty of human greatness, the sudden turns of fate, and the unhappy conclusions of violence and injustice; 'tis to expose the singularities of pride and fancy, to make folly and falsehood contemptible, and to bring everything that is ill under infamy and neglect.
JEREMY COLLIER: *A Short View of the Immorality and Profaneness of the English Stage,* intro., 1698

Athens herself learned virtue at a play.
RICHARD STEELE: *The Funeral,* epilogue, 1701

The value of a theatrical piece can less be determined by an analysis of its conduct than by the ascendant which it gains over the heart, and by the strokes of nature which are interspersed through it.
DAVID HUME: *Letter to the Comtesse de Boufflers,* July 14, 1764

The play is done; the curtain drops,
Slow failing to the prompter's bell:
A moment yet the actor stops,
And looks around, to say farewell.
W. M. THACKERAY: *The End of the Play,* 1848

A farce or a comedy is best played; a tragedy is best read at home.
ABRAHAM LINCOLN: To John Hay, after seeing Edwin Booth in The Merchant of Venice, 1863

I get more help in my work from a good play than from any other kind of thoughtful rest.
JOHN RUSKIN: *Letter to Squire Bancroft,* March 16, 1871

[*See also* Drama, Theatre.

Play (=recreation)

The people sat down to eat and drink, and rose up to play.
EXODUS XXXII, 6, *c.* 700 B.C.

The streets of the city shall be full of boys and girls playing in the streets thereof.
ZECHARIAH VIII, 5, *c.* 520 B.C.

All the beasts of the field play.
JOB XL, 20, *c.* 325 B.C.

As good play for naught as work for naught.
JOHN HEYWOOD: *Proverbs,* 1546

Play with thy peer.
ALEXANDER MONTGOMERIE: *Flyting,* 1629

There is no play without a fool.
JOHN CLARKE: *Parœmiologia Anglo-Latina,* 1639

All work and no play makes Jack a dull boy.
JOHN RAY: *English Proverbs,* 1670

Leave off while the play is good.
JAMES KELLY: *Complete Collection of Scottish Proverbs,* 1721

Play with the hands is the play for boors.
SPANISH PROVERB

Player

[*See* Actor.

Playgoer

Many can tarry at a play two or three hours, whenas they will not abide scarce one hour at a sermon.
JOHN NORTHBROOKE: *Against Dicing,* 1577

There are a multitude of people who are truly and only spectators of a play without any use of their understanding; and these carry it sometimes by the strength of their numbers.
ABRAHAM COWLEY: *Cutter of Coleman Street,* pref., 1663

Playwright

[*See* Dramatist.

Pleasant

Her ways are ways of pleasantness.
PROVERBS III, 17, *c.* 350 B.C.

Pleasant words are as a honeycomb, sweet to the soul, and health to the bones.
PROVERBS XVI, 24

How good and pleasant it is for brethren to dwell together in unity.
PSALMS CXXXIII, 1, *c.* 150 B.C.

The three most pleasant things in the world are a cat's kittens, a goat's kid, and a young woman.
IRISH PROVERB

Pleasing

In men for the sake of women, just as in women for the sake of men, there is implanted, by a defect of nature, the desire to please.
TERTULLIAN: *Women's Dress, c.* 220

They must rise betimes that please all.
JOHN CLARKE: *Parœmiologia Anglo-Latina,* 1639

Pleasing ware is half sold.
GEORGE HERBERT: *Outlandish Proverbs,* 1640

The excessive desire of pleasing goes along almost always with the apprehension of not being liked.
THOMAS FULLER: *Introductio ad Prudentiam,* II, 1731

He who endeavors to please must appear pleased.
SAMUEL JOHNSON: *The Rambler*, Aug. 31, 1751

He that can please nobody is not so much to be pitied as he that nobody can please.
C. C. COLTON: *Lacon*, 1820

Please your eye and plague your heart.
ENGLISH PROVERB, first recorded in the XVIII century, but described by WILLIAM COBBETT: *Advice to Young Men*, III, 1829, as "more than a thousand years old"

Who would please all, and himself too,
Attempts what none could ever do.
ENGLISH RHYME

[*See also* Politeness.

Pleasure

To be a slave to pleasure is the life of a harlot, not of a man.
ANAXANDRIDES: *Fragment*, c. 376 B.C.

He that loveth pleasure shall be a poor man.
PROVERBS XXI, 17, c. 350 B.C.

When pleasure is on her trial we are not impartial judges.
ARISTOTLE: *The Nicomachean Ethics*, II, c. 340 B.C.

Pleasure is the first good. It is the beginning of every choice and every aversion. It is the absence of pain in the body and of trouble in the soul.
EPICURUS: *Letter to Menoeceus*, c. 300 B.C.

The Lord taketh pleasure in them that fear Him.
PSALMS CXLVII, 11, c. 150 B.C.

The most noble and excellent gift of Heaven to man is reason; and of all the enemies that reason has to engage with pleasure is the chief.
CICERO: *De senectute*, c. 78 B.C.

No pleasure ever lasts long enough.
PROPERTIUS: *Elegies*, I, c. 25 B.C.

The pleasure that is safest is the least pleasant.
OVID: *Ars amatoria*, c. 2

There is no such thing as pure pleasure; some anxiety always goes with it.
OVID: *Metamorphoses*, VII, c. 5

She that liveth in pleasure is dead while she liveth.
I TIMOTHY V, 6, c. 60

The pleasures of sin.
HEBREWS XI, 25, c. 65

It is the rare pleasures that especially delight us.
EPICTETUS: *Encheiridion*, c. 110

The Epicureans had the liberty to state the notion, and determine the object of pleasure. Why can't we Christians have the same privilege? What offense is it if we differ from you in the idea of satisfaction? If we won't brighten our humor, and live pleasantly, where's the harm? If anybody has the worst of it, it is only ourselves.
TERTULLIAN: *Apologeticus*, 197

Love of pleasure is the disease which makes men most despicable.
LONGINUS: *On the Sublime*, XLIV, c. 250

An influx of riches, and constant health; a wife who is dear and is of kind and gentle speech; a child who is obedient, and useful knowledge, are the six pleasures of life.
The Hitopadesa, intro., c. 500

Follow pleasure, and then will pleasure flee,
Flee pleasure, and pleasure will follow thee.
JOHN HEYWOOD: *Proverbs*, 1546

Who will in time present pleasure refrain
Shall in time to come the more pleasure obtain.
IBID.

Pleasure is one of the chiefest kinds of profit.
MICHEL DE MONTAIGNE: *Essays*, III, 1588

No pleasure is fully delightful without communication, and no delight absolute except imparted.
IBID.

I hold it as commendable to be wealthy in pleasure
As others do in rotten sheep and pasture.
JOHN FLETCHER: *The Wild-Goose Chase*, II, 1621

All the instances of pleasure have a sting in the tail.
JEREMY TAYLOR: *The Rule and Exercises of Holy Living*, II, 1650

Say to pleasure, Gentle Eve, I will none of your apple.
GEORGE HERBERT: *Jacula Prudentum*, 1651

We must always skim over pleasures. They are like marshy lands that we must travel nimbly, hardly daring to put down our feet.
BERNARD DE FONTENELLE: *Dialogues des morts*, 1683

Pleasures are all alike, simply considered in themselves. He that takes pleasure to hear sermons enjoys himself as much as he that hears plays.
JOHN SELDEN: *Table-Talk*, 1689

Stolen pleasures are the sweetest.
ENGLISH PROVERB, derived from PROVERBS IX, 17: "Stolen waters are sweet"; until the XVIII century *waters* usually appeared instead of *pleasures*

Pleasure is the most real good in this life.
FREDERICK THE GREAT: *Letter to Voltaire*, Sept. 9, 1739

I am advising you as a friend, as a man of the world, as one who would not have you old while you are young, but would have you to

take all the pleasures that reason points out, and that decency warrants.
LORD CHESTERFIELD: *Letter to his son,* May 15, 1749

The public pleasures of far the greater part of mankind are counterfeit.
SAMUEL JOHNSON: *The Idler,* Aug. 12, 1758

The liberty of using harmless pleasure will not be disputed; but it is still to be examined what pleasures are harmless.
SAMUEL JOHNSON: *Rasselas,* 1759

There are but two pleasures permitted to mortal man, love and vengeance; both which are, in a peculiar manner, forbidden to us wretches who are condemned to petticoats.
MARY WORTLEY MONTAGU: *Letter to James Steuart,* July 19, 1759

The best pleasures of this world are not quite pure. J. W. GOETHE: *Clavigo,* IV, 1774

When we talk of pleasure we mean sensual pleasure. When a man says he had pleasure with a woman he does not mean conversation.
SAMUEL JOHNSON: *Boswell's Life,* April 7, 1778

Pleasure is labor too, and tires as much.
WILLIAM COWPER: *Hope,* 1782

Some pleasures live a month and some a year,
But short the date of all we gather here.
WILLIAM COWPER: *Retirement,* 1782

No man is a hypocrite in his pleasures.
SAMUEL JOHNSON: *Boswell's Life,* 1784

I omit much usual declamation upon the dignity and capacity of our nature, the superiority of the soul to the body, of the rational to the animal part of our constitutions; upon the worthiness, refinement, and delicacy of some satisfactions; and the meanness, grossness, and sensuality of others: because I hold pleasures differ in nothing but in continuance and intensity.
WILLIAM PALEY: *The Principles of Moral and Political Philosophy,* I, 1785

Do not bite at the bait of pleasure till you know there is no hook beneath it.
THOMAS JEFFERSON: *Letter to Mrs. Cosway,* 1786

Pleasure is in itself a good; nay, even setting aside immunity from pain, the only good.
JEREMY BENTHAM: *The Principles of Morals and Legislation,* X, 1789

Pleasures are like poppies spread:
You seize the flower, its bloom is shed;
Or like the snowfall in the river:
A moment white, then melts forever.
ROBERT BURNS: *Tam O'Shanter,* 1790

All men feel an habitual gratitude, and something of an honorable bigotry, for the objects which have long continued to please them: we not only wish to be pleased, but to be pleased in that particular way in which we have been accustomed to be pleased.
WILLIAM WORDSWORTH: *Lyrical Ballads,* pref., 1798

When anyone takes great pleasure in doing a thing it is almost always from some motive other than the ostensible one.
G. C. LICHTENBERG: *Reflections,* 1799

Pleasure is to women what the sun is to the flower: if moderately enjoyed, it beautifies, it refreshes, and it improves; if immoderately, it withers, deteriorates, and destroys.
C. C. COLTON: *Lacon,* 1820

Pleasure consists in the harmony between the specific excitability of a living creature and the exciting causes correspondent thereto.
S. T. COLERIDGE: *Aids to Reflection,* 1825

Pleasure is produced by the union of excitement and affection. Hence we can hardly pretend that pleasures are wholly material.
BALZAC: *The Physiology of Marriage,* 1830

The ugliest of trades have their moments of pleasure. If I were a grave-digger, or even a hangman, there are some people I could work for with a good deal of enjoyment.
DOUGLAS JERROLD: *Men of Character,* 1838

There are only three pleasures in life pure and lasting, and all derived from inanimate things — books, pictures, and the face of nature.
WILLIAM HAZLITT: *Criticisms on Art,* I, 1843

Consider not pleasures as they come, but as they go.
H. G. BOHN: *Handbook of Proverbs,* 1855

The great pleasure in life is doing what people say you cannot do.
WALTER BAGEHOT: *Literary Studies,* I, 1879

[*See also* Age (Old), Avarice, English, Enjoyment, Fashion, Gentleman, Good and Evil, Happiness, Hunting, Imagination, Labor, Life, Motive, Persuasion, Pleasure and Pain, Poetry, Poetry and Prose, Sin, Variety.

Pleasure and Pain

I take pleasure in infirmities, in reproaches, in necessities, in persecutions, in distresses for Christ's sake. II CORINTHIANS XII, 10, *c.* 55

Pleasure must be purchased with the price of pain.
GEORGE PETTIE: *Petite Palace of Pettie His Pleasure,* 1576

Pain pays the income of each precious thing.
SHAKESPEARE: *The Rape of Lucrece,* 1594

Fly the pleasure that bites tomorrow.
GEORGE HERBERT: *Outlandish Proverbs*, 1640

Short pleasure, long lament.
JOHN RAY: *English Proverbs*, 1670

Pleasure is nothing else but the intermission of pain, the enjoying of something I am in great trouble for till I have it.
JOHN SELDEN: *Table-Talk*, 1689

Sweet is pleasure after pain.
JOHN DRYDEN: *Alexander's Feast*, I, 1697

All fits of pleasure are balanced by an equal degree of pain or languor; it is like spending this year part of the next year's revenue.
JONATHAN SWIFT: *Thoughts on Various Subjects*, 1706

An hour of pain is as long as a day of pleasure.
THOMAS FULLER: *Gnomologia*, 1732

Pain past is pleasure. IBID.

Self-love and reason to one end aspire:
Pain their aversion, pleasure their desire.
ALEXANDER POPE: *An Essay on Man*, II, 1732

Pain wastes the body; pleasures the understanding.
BENJAMIN FRANKLIN: *Poor Richard's Almanac*, 1735

A man of pleasure is a man of pains.
EDWARD YOUNG: *Night Thoughts*, VIII, 1744

The honest man takes pains, and then enjoys pleasures; the knave takes pleasure, and then suffers pain.
BENJAMIN FRANKLIN: *Poor Richard's Almanac*, 1755

The torments which we may be made to suffer are much greater in their effect on the body and mind than any pleasures which the most learned voluptuary could suggest, or than the liveliest imagination, and the most sound and exquisitely sensible body, could enjoy.
EDMUND BURKE: *The Sublime and Beautiful*, I, 1756

My chief study all my life has been to lighten misfortunes and multiply pleasures, as far as human nature can.
MARY WORTLEY MONTAGU: *Letter to James Steuart*, Oct. 13, 1759

Pleasure and pain are the only springs of action in man, and always will be.
C. A. HÉLVETIUS: *De l'homme*, X, 1773

I do not agree that an age of pleasure is no compensation for a moment of pain.
THOMAS JEFFERSON: *Letter to John Adams*, 1816

Pleasure is oft a visitant; but pain
Clings cruelly to us.
JOHN KEATS: *Endymion*, I, 1818

We are told that the pleasure in this world outweighs the pain, or, at all events, that they balance. If you wish to discover whether this is true, consider the case of two animals, one of which is eating the other.
ARTHUR SCHOPENHAUER: *Parerga und Paralipomena*, 1851

There is a pleasure which is born of pain.
E. R. BULWER-LYTTON (OWEN MEREDITH): *The Wanderer*, I, 1858

Foams round the feet of pleasure
The blood-red must of pain.
A. C. SWINBURNE: *Rococo*, 1866

In calling good the conduct which subserves life, and bad the conduct which hinders or destroys it, and in so implying that life is a blessing and not a curse, we are inevitably asserting that conduct is good or bad according as its total effects are pleasurable or painful.
HERBERT SPENCER: *The Data of Ethics*, III, 1879

The preponderance of pain over pleasure is the cause of our fictitious morality and religion.
F. W. NIETZSCHE: *The Antichrist*, XV, 1888

The most intolerable pain is produced by prolonging the keenest pleasure.
GEORGE BERNARD SHAW: *Maxims for Revolutionists*, 1903

From a short pleasure comes a long repentance.
FRENCH PROVERB

[*See also* Happiness, Morality, Necessity, Utilitarianism, Vice.

Plebeian

[*See* Demagogue.

Pledge

For the support of this Declaration, with a firm reliance on the protection of Divine Providence, we mutually pledge to each other our lives, our fortunes and our sacred honor.
THOMAS JEFFERSON: *The Declaration of Independence*, July 4, 1776

Pleiades

Canst thou bind the sweet influences of Pleiades, or loose the bands of Orion?
JOB XXXVIII, 31, *c.* 325 B.C.

Many a night I saw the Pleiades, rising thro' the mellow shade,
Glitter like a swarm of fire-flies tangled in a silver braid.
ALFRED TENNYSON: *Locksley Hall*, 1842

[*See also* Astrology.

Plenty

The pastures are clothed with flocks; the valleys also are covered over with corn; they shout for joy, they also sing.
PSALMS LXV, 13, *c.* 150 B.C.

Plenty ever breeds contempt.
TERTULLIAN: *Women's Dress, c.* 220

Plenty made him poor.
EDMUND SPENSER: *The Fairie Queene,* I, *c.* 1589

Plenty makes dainty.
JAMES KELLY: *Complete Collection of Scottish Proverbs,* 1721

A shave aff a new-cut loaf's never missed.
SCOTTISH PROVERB

[*See also* Peace.

Pliancy

It is a good blade that bends well.
THOMAS FULLER: *Gnomologia,* 1732

Plow

Speed the plow.
Anon.: Title of a play, *c.* 1500 (*Speed*=prosper)

[*See also* Farmer.

Plowing

Thou shalt not plow with an ox and an ass together. DEUTERONOMY XXII, 10, *c.* 650 B.C.

[*See also* Action.

Plowman

[*See* First, Ignorance.

Plowshare

[*See* Blacksmith, War and Peace.

Plum

Little Jack Horner
Sat in a corner,
Eating his Christmas pie;
He put in his thumb
And pulled out a plum,
And said, " What a good boy am I."
Anon.: *Nursery rhyme, c.* 1750

Plumber

[*See* Author.

Plume

[*See* Blaine (James G.).

Plump

[*See* Health.

Plunder

[*See* Mercenary.

Plymouth Rock

The rock underlies all America: it only crops out here.
WENDELL PHILLIPS: Speech at Plymouth, Mass., Dec. 21, 1855

A doorstep
Into a world unknown, the corner-stone of a nation.
H. W. LONGFELLOW: *The Courtship of Miles Standish,* V, 1858

[*See also* Pilgrim Fathers.

Poaching

A salmon from the pool, a wand from the wood, and a deer from the hills, are thefts which no man was ever ashamed to own.
SCOTTISH PROVERB

Poe, E. A. (1809–49)

This young fellow is highly imaginative, and a little given to the terrific. He is at work upon a tragedy, but I have turned him to drudging upon whatever may make money.
J. P. KENNEDY: To —— White, editor of the Southern Literary Messenger, April 13, 1835

There comes Poe with his raven like Barnaby Rudge,
Three-fifths of him genius, and two-fifths sheer fudge.
J. R. LOWELL: *A Fable for Critics,* 1848

Whenever a book is abused, people take it for granted that it is I who have been abusing it.
E. A. POE: *Marginalia,* 1844–49

He had, to a morbid excess, that desire to rise which is vulgarly called ambition, but no wish for the esteem or the love of his species; only the hard wish to succeed — not shine, nor serve — succeed, that he might have the right to despise a world which galled his self-conceit.
R. W. GRISWOLD: Obituary notice in the New York Tribune, Oct. 9, 1849

Poe is a kind of Hawthorne and delirium tremens.
LESLIE STEPHEN: *Hours in a Library,* I, 1879

I have a distinct and pleasing remembrance of his looks, voice, manner and matter; very kindly and human, but subdued, perhaps a little jaded.
WALT WHITMAN: *Specimen Days,* 1882

There is no more effective way of realizing the distinction of Poe's genius than by imagining American literature without him.
W. C. BROWNELL: *American Prose Masters,* 1909

Poet

Poets are worthy the honor and respect of all men. HOMER: *Odyssey,* VIII, *c.* 800 B.C.

Poets do not effect their object by wisdom, but by a certain natural inspiration and under the influence of enthusiasm like prophets and seers; for these also say many fine things, but they understand nothing that they say. Poets are affected in a similar manner: and at the same time they consider themselves, on account of their poetry, to be the wisest of men in other things, in which they are not.

SOCRATES: *In Plato's Apology of Socrates*, 399 B.C.

Every man is a poet when he is in love.

PLATO: *Symposium*, *c.* 360 B.C.

The poet should prefer probable impossibilities to improbable possibilities.

ARISTOTLE: *The Poetics*, XXIV, *c.* 322 B.C.

Democritus maintains that there can be no great poet without a spice of madness.

CICERO: *De divinatione*, I, *c.* 78 B.C.

I have never known a poet who did not set a very high value on himself.

CICERO: *Tusculanæ disputationes*, V, 45 B.C.

The man is either crazy, or he is a poet.

HORACE: *Satires*, II, *c.* 25 B.C.

I have sung of pastures, of fields, of chieftains. (Cecini pascua, rura, duces.)

VIRGIL: Epitaph for himself, *c.* 15 B.C.

Many brave men lived before Agamemnon, but all upwept and unknown they sleep in endless night, for they had no poets to sound their praises.

HORACE: *Carmina*, IV, *c.* 13 B.C.

Poets were the first teachers of mankind.

HORACE: *De arte poetica*, *c.* 8 B.C.

Physicians practise only what belongs to their art; mechanics work only at their trade; but, learned and unlearned, we all write verse.

HORACE: *Epistles*, II, *c.* 5 B.C.

Great poets do not require an indulgent reader; they charm anyone, however much against his will, and however difficult to please.

OVID: *Epistulæ ex Ponto*, III, *c.* 5

He does not write whose verses no one reads.

MARTIAL: *Epigrams*, I, 86

There is no more self-assured man than a bad poet. MARTIAL: *Epigrams*, II

Poets have a license to lie.

PLINY THE YOUNGER: *Letters*, VI, *c.* 110

A poet is born, not made. (Poeta nascitur non fit.) FLORUS: *De qualitate vitæ*, *c.* 120

The more rhetoric, the more mischief; and the best poets are the worst citizens.

LACTANTIUS: *Divinæ institutiones*, VI, *c.* 310

If anything is certain, it is that women are not composed of moon substance, that their eyes are not twin lotuses, and that their skin is not made of gold. Why do poets try to fool us in these matters?

BHARTRIHARI: *The Sringa Sataka*, *c.* 625

Horses and poets are to be fed, not fattened.

Ascribed to CHARLES IX of France (1550–74)

He is a fool that cannot make a ballad, and more a fool that doth make a ballad.

ANTHONY COPLEY: Tr. of MELCHOR DE SANTA CRUZ: *Floresta Española*, 1574

Astronomers, painters and poets may lie by authority.

JOHN HARINGTON: *Apologie for Poetrie*, 1591 (Cf. PLINY, *ante*, *c.* 110)

Never durst poet touch a pen to write
Until his ink were temper'd with love's sighs.

SHAKESPEARE: *Love's Labor's Lost*, IV, *c.* 1595

The poet's eye, in a fine frenzy rolling,
Doth glance from heaven to earth, from earth to heaven;
And as imagination bodies forth
The forms of things unknown, the poet's pen
Turns them to shapes and gives to airy nothing
A local habitation and a name.

SHAKESPEARE: *A Midsummer Night's Dream*, V, *c.* 1596

As that ship is endangered where all lean to one side; but is in safety, one leaning one way and another another way: so the dissensions of poets among themselves doth make them that they less infect their readers.

FRANCIS MERES: *Pallidas Tamia*, 1598

The poet never maketh any circles about your imagination to conjure you to believe for true what he writes. . . . Of all the writers under the sun, the poet is the least liar.

PHILIP SIDNEY: *Apologie for Poetrie*, 1598

If men will impartially, and not asquint, look toward the offices and function of a poet, they will easily conclude to themselves the impossibility of any man's being a good poet without first being a good man.

BEN JONSON: *Volpone*, II, 1605

Modesty is a virtue not often found in poets, for almost every one of them thinks himself the greatest in the world.

CERVANTES: *Don Quixote*, II, 1615

All poets are mad.

ROBERT BURTON: *The Anatomy of Melancholy*, 1621

A poet has two heads as a drum has: one for making, the other repeating.

BEN JONSON: *The Staple of News*, intro., 1625

A poet is that which, by the Greeks, is called a maker, or a fainer; his art, an art of imitation, of faining, expressing the life of man in fit measure, numbers, and harmony.

BEN JONSON: *Discoveries*, *c.* 1635

Poets and kings are not born every day.

JASPER MAYNE: *Jonsonus Virbius*, 1638

Gold, music, wine, tobacco and good cheer
Make poets soar aloft and sing out clear.

JOHN DAY: *The Parliament of Bees,* v, 1641

A poet soaring in the high reason of his fancies, with his garland and singing robes about him.

JOHN MILTON: *The Reason of Church Government,* II, 1641

He who would not be frustrate of his hope to write well hereafter in laudable things ought himself to be a true poem.

JOHN MILTON: *An Apology for Smectymnuus,* 1642

At Mansfield . . . I was moved to go and speak to one of the wickedest men in the country, one who was a common drunkard, a noted whoremaster, and a rhyme-maker; and I reproved him in the dread of the mighty God for his evil courses.

GEORGE FOX: *Journal,* I, 1694 (*c.* 1649)

Every man would be a poet gladly.

JOHN TAYLOR: *The Certain Travails of an Uncertain Journey,* 1653

I slipt into Bedlam, where I saw several poor miserable creatures in chains; one of them was mad with making verses.

JOHN EVELYN: *Diary,* April 21, 1657

If we do well, but few men find it out, and fewer entertain it kindly. If we commit errors, there is no pardon; if we could do wonders, there would be but little thanks, and that too extorted from unwilling givers.

ABRAHAM COWLEY: *Cutter of Coleman Street,* pref., 1663

Imagination in a poet is a faculty so wild and lawless that, like a high ranging spaniel, it must have clogs tied to it, lest it outrun the judgment. The great easiness of blank verse renders the poet too luxuriant. He is tempted to say many things which might better be omitted, or, at least, shut up in fewer words.

JOHN DRYDEN: *The Rival Ladies,* dedication, 1664

The first happiness of the poet's imagination is properly invention, or finding of the thought; the second is fancy, or the variation, deriving or molding of that thought as the judgment represents it proper to the subject; the third is elocution, or the art of clothing and adorning that thought so found and varied, in apt, significant and sounding words.

JOHN DRYDEN: *Annus Mirabilis,* 1667

The employment of a poet is like that of a curious gunsmith or watchmaker: the iron or silver is not his own, but they are the least part of that which gives the value; the price lies wholly in the workmanship.

JOHN DRYDEN: *An Evening's Love,* pref., 1671

Poets, like whores, are only hated by each other.

WILLIAM WYCHERLEY: *The Country Wife,* III, *c.* 1673

While Butler, needy wretch, was yet alive,
No gen'rous patron would a dinner give.
See him, when starved to death, and turn'd to dust,
Presented with a monumental bust.
The poet's fate is here in emblem shown;
He ask'd for bread, and he received a stone.

SAMUEL WESLEY: Epigram on the erection of a monument to Samuel Butler in Westminster Abbey, *c.* 1680

True poets are the guardians of the state.

WENTWORTH DILLON (EARL OF ROSCOMMON): *Essay on Translated Verse,* 1684

Whenever a poet praises the verses of another poet you may be sure that they are stupid and of no real value.

JEAN DE LA BRUYÈRE: *Caractères,* XII, 1688

Turn pimp, flatterer, quack, lawyer, parson, be chaplain to an atheist, or stallion to an old woman, anything but poet; for a poet is worse, more servile, timorous and fawning, than any I have named.

WILLIAM CONGREVE: *Love for Love,* III, 1695

Ye gods, what crime had my poor father done
That you should make a poet of his son?

JOHN VANBRUGH: *The Confederacy,* prologue, 1705

A poet's success at first, like a gamester's fortune at first, is like to make him a loser at last, and to be undone by his good fortune and merit.

WILLIAM WYCHERLEY: *Letter to Alexander Pope,* May 17, 1709

[Envy] reigns more among bad poets than among any other set of men.

JOSEPH ADDISON: *The Spectator,* Dec. 20, 1711

Poets, like painters, thus unskill'd to trace
The naked nature and the living grace,
With gold and jewels cover every part,
And hide with ornaments their want of art.

ALEXANDER POPE: *An Essay on Criticism,* II, 1711

If on Parnassus' top we sit,
You rarely bite, are always bit;
Each poet of inferior size
On you shall rail and criticize,
And strive to tear you limb from limb;
While others do as much for him.

JONATHAN SWIFT: *On Poetry,* 1712

Q. Pray be so kind as to let me know what you esteem to be the chief qualities of a good poet, especially of one who writes plays.
A. To be a very well-bred man.

RICHARD STEELE: *The Spectator,* Feb. 29, 1712

Poets are the only poor fellows in the world whom anybody will flatter.
ALEXANDER POPE: *Letter to William Trumbull,* March 12, 1713

Yes, every poet is a fool:
By demonstration Ned can show it:
Happy, could Ned's inverted rule
Prove every fool to be a poet.
MATTHEW PRIOR: *Epigram,* 1718

Poets, being liars by profession, ought to have good memories.
JONATHAN SWIFT: *A Letter of Advice to a Young Poet,* Dec. 1, 1720

I hate all boets and bainters.
Ascribed to GEORGE I of England (1660–1727)

Pensive poets painful vigils keep,
Sleepless themselves to give their readers sleep.
ALEXANDER POPE: *The Dunciad,* I, 1728

What poet would not grieve to see
His brother write as well as he?
But rather than they should excel,
Would wish his rivals all in Hell?
JONATHAN SWIFT: *On the Death of Dr. Swift,* 1731

He that lives with the muses shall die in the straw.
THOMAS FULLER: *Gnomologia,* 1732

The poet, of all artificers, is fondest of his works. IBID.

We poets are (upon a poet's word)
Of all mankind the creatures most absurd;
The season when to come, and when to go,
To sing, or cease to sing, we never know.
ALEXANDER POPE: *The First Epistle of the Second Book of Horace,* 1737

Any man of common understanding may, by proper culture, care, attention, and labor, make himself whatever he pleases, except a good poet.
LORD CHESTERFIELD: *Letter to his son,* Oct. 9, 1746

I do not find that God has made you a poet; and I am very glad that he has not.
LORD CHESTERFIELD: *Letter to his son,* Nov. 24, 1749

Could a man live by it, it were not unpleasant enjoyment to be a poet.
OLIVER GOLDSMITH: *Letter to Henry Goldsmith,* Feb., 1759

Poets alone are permitted to tell the real truth. Though an historian should, with as many asseverations as Bishop Burnet, inform mankind that the lustre of the British arms under George II was singly and entirely owing to the charms of Lady Mary Coke, it would not be believed, but the slightest hint of it in a stanza of Gray would carry conviction to the end of time.
HORACE WALPOLE: *Letter to Mary Coke,* Feb. 12, 1761

A poetical genius seems the most elegant of youthful accomplishments; but it is entirely a youthful one.
WILLIAM SHENSTONE: *On Writing and Books,* 1764

The metaphysical poets were men of learning, and to show their learning was their whole endeavor: but, unluckily resolving to show it in rhyme, instead of writing poetry they only wrote verses.
SAMUEL JOHNSON: *Lives of the Poets (Cowley),* 1780

The poets have so many tricks that they remind me of trumpet-players. If we musicians were so bound by rules we'd make music as bad as their books.
W. A. MOZART: *Letter to his father,* Oct. 13, 1781

I never had the least thought or inclination of turning poet till I got once heartily in love.
ROBERT BURNS: *Commonplace-Book,* Aug., 1783

Can poets soothe you when you pine for bread?
GEORGE CRABBE: *The Village,* I, 1783

There are two periods favorable to poets: a rude age, when a genius may hazard anything, and when nothing has been forestalled: the other is, when, after ages of barbarism and incorrection, a master or two produces models formed by purity and taste.
HORACE WALPOLE: *Letter to John Pinkerton,* Oct. 6, 1784

There is a pleasure in poetic pains
Which only poets know.
WILLIAM COWPER: *The Task,* II, 1785

In my infant and boyish days I owe much to an old woman who resided in the family, remarkable for her ignorance, credulity, and superstition. She had, I suppose, the largest collection in the country of tales and songs concerning devils, ghosts, fairies, brownies, witches, warlocks, spunkies, kelpies, elf-candles, dead-lights, wraiths, apparitions, cantraips, giants, enchanted towers, dragons, and other trumpery. This cultivated the latent seeds of poetry.
ROBERT BURNS: *Letter to John Moore,* Aug. 2, 1787

It is lordly to perform great deeds, but it is lordly too to transmit their grandeur to posterity in worthy song.
J. W. GOETHE: *Torquato Tasso,* II, 1790

A poet is a man speaking to men, endowed with more lively sensibility, more enthusiasm and tenderness, who has a greater knowledge of human nature, and a more comprehensive soul than are supposed to be common among mankind; a man pleased with his own passions and volitions, and who rejoices more than other men in the spirit of life that is in him.

WILLIAM WORDSWORTH: *Lyrical Ballads*, pref., 1798

Ne'er
Was flattery lost on poet's ear.

WALTER SCOTT: *The Lay of the Last Minstrel*, v, 1805

A great poet is the most precious jewel of a nation.

LUDWIG VAN BEETHOVEN: *Letter to Bettina von Arnim*, Feb. 10, 1811

Poets and painters, as all artists know,
May shoot a little with a lengthen'd bow.

BYRON: *Hints From Horace*, 1811

The poet is one who, in the excursions of his fancy between Heaven and earth, lights upon a kind of fairyland, in which he places a creation of his own, where he embodies shapes, and gives action and adventure to his ideal offspring: taking captive the imagination of his readers, he elevates them above the grossness of actual being, into the soothing and pleasant atmosphere of supramundane existence.

GEORGE CRABBE: *Tales*, pref., 1812

Did any of my sons show poetical talent, of which, to my great satisfaction, there are no appearances, the first thing I should do would be to inculcate upon him the duty of cultivating some honorable profession, and qualifying himself to play a more respectable part in society than the mere poet.

WALTER SCOTT: *Letter to George Crabbe*, June 1, 1812

He was a poet, sure a lover too.

JOHN KEATS: *I Stood Tiptoe Upon a Little Hill*, 1816

No man was ever yet a great poet, without at the same time being a profound philosopher.

S. T. COLERIDGE: *Biographia Literaria*, xv, 1817

The man that hath not music in his soul can never be a genuine poet. IBID.

A poet is the most unpoetical of anything in existence, because he has no identity; he is continually filling some other body.

JOHN KEATS: *Letter to Richard Woodhouse*, Oct. 27, 1818

A poet is the combined product of such internal powers as modify the nature of others; and of such external influences as excite and sustain these powers; he is not one, but both.

P. B. SHELLEY: *Prometheus Unbound*, pref., 1820

Through the old paths he loved to tread
He glides amid the living throng,
And the past age that mourned him, dead,
Lives only in his deathless song.

LUDWIG UHLAND: *The Poet's Return*, c. 1820

The most envious man I ever heard of is a poet, and a high one.

BYRON: *Letter to John Murray*, Feb. 7, 1821

A poet is a nightingale who sits in darkness and sings to cheer its own solitude with sweet sounds.

P. B. SHELLEY: *The Defence of Poetry*, 1821

In the infancy of society every author is necessarily a poet. IBID.

Poets are the hierophants of an unapprehended inspiration; the mirrors of the gigantic shadows which futurity casts upon the present.

IBID.

It is a lie that poets are envious. I have known the best of them, and can speak to it, that they give each other their merits, and are the kindest critics as well as best authors.

CHARLES LAMB: *Letter to Bernard Barton*, March 6, 1823

Poets often avoid political transactions; they often affect to despise them. But, whether they perceive it or not, they must be influenced by them. As long as their minds have any point of contact with those of their fellowmen, the electric impulse, at whatever distance it may originate, will be circuitously communicated to them.

T. B. MACAULAY: *Dante*, 1824 (Knight's Quarterly Magazine, Jan.)

Why should not one poet write like another? The situations of life are alike; why, then, should those of poems be unlike?

J. W. GOETHE: *Conversations with Eckermann*, Jan. 18, 1825

Perhaps no person can be a poet, or can even enjoy poetry, without a certain unsoundness of mind.

T. B. MACAULAY: *Milton*, 1825 (Edinburgh Review, Aug.)

When I first saw that a literary profession was to be my fate, I endeavored by all efforts of stoicism to divest myself of that irritable degree of sensibility — or, to speak plainly, of vanity — which makes the poetical race miserable and ridiculous. The anxiety of a poet for praise and for compliments I have endeavored to keep down.

WALTER SCOTT: *Journal*, Dec. 28, 1825

I dreamed that I was God Himself,
Great Lord of Universes,
With angels crowding round my throne,
All whooping up my verses.

HEINRICH HEINE: *Mir träumt' ich bin der liebe Gott*, 1827

A poet without love were a physical and metaphysical impossibility.

THOMAS CARLYLE: *Burns*, 1828 (Edinburgh Review, Dec.)

Vex not then the poet's mind
  With thy shallow wit;
Vex not thou the poet's mind,
  For thou canst not fathom it.
Clear and bright it should be ever,
Flowing like a crystal river,
Bright as light, and clear as wind.

ALFRED TENNYSON: *The Poet's Mind*, I, 1830

Every poet, be his outward lot what it may, finds himself born in the midst of prose; he has to struggle from the littleness and obstruction of an actual world into the freedom and infinitude of an ideal.

THOMAS CARLYLE: *Schiller*, 1831 (Fraser's Magazine, March)

As fire is kindled by fire, so is a poet's mind kindled by contact with a brother poet.

JOHN KEBLE: *Lectures on Poetry*, XVI, 1832

A poet who has not produced a good poem before he is twenty-five we may conclude cannot and never will do so.

WILLIAM WORDSWORTH: To E. J. Trelawney, *c.* 1835

It is very singular that no true poet should have arisen from the lower classes, when it is considered that every peasant who can read knows more of books than did Æschylus, Sophocles, or Homer; yet if we except Burns, none such have been.

S. T. COLERIDGE: *Allsop's Letters, Conversations and Recollections of S. T. Coleridge* (*c.* 1820), 1836

All men are poets at heart. They serve nature for bread, but her loveliness overcomes them sometimes.

R. W. EMERSON: *Literary Ethics*, 1838

To the poet all things are friendly and sacred, all events profitable, all days holy, all men divine. R. W. EMERSON: *History*, 1841

In ocean sport the scaly herds,
Wedge-like cleave the air the birds,
To northern lakes fly wind-borne ducks,
Browse the mountain sheep in flocks,
Men consort in camp and town,
But the poet dwells alone.

R. W. EMERSON: *Saadi*, 1842 (Dial, Oct.)

Words become luminous when the poet's finger has passed its phosphorescence over them.

JOSEPH JOUBERT: *Pensées*, 1842

A poet is a person who puts things together, not as a watchmaker steel, or a shoemaker leather, but who puts life into action.

JOHN RUSKIN: *Modern Painters*, I, 1843

The birth of a poet is the principal event in chronology.

R. W. EMERSON: *The Poet*, 1844

Read from some humbler poet,
  Whose songs gushed from his heart,
As showers from the clouds of Summer,
  Or tears from the eyelids start.

H. W. LONGFELLOW: *The Day Is Done*, 1845

To speak of a poet without genius is merely to put forth a flat contradiction in terms.

E. A. POE: *Marginalia*, 1844–49

All that is best in the great poets of all countries is not what is national in them, but what is universal.

H. W. LONGFELLOW: *Kavanagh*, XX, 1849

I do but sing because I must,
And pipe but as the linnets sing.

ALFRED TENNYSON: *In Memoriam*, XXI, 1850

A man is a poet who lives . . . by watching his moods. An old poet comes at last to watching his moods as narrowly as a cat does a mouse.

H. D. THOREAU: *Journal*, Aug. 28, 1851

It is idle nonsense to speak, as some critics speak, of the "present" as alone having claims upon the poet. Whatever is great, or good, or pathetic, or terrible, in any age past or present, belongs to him, and is within his proper province.

J. A. FROUDE: *Arnold's Poems*, 1854 (Westminster Review)

His brain is the ultimate brain. He is no arguer; . . . he is judgment. He judges not as the judge judges but as the sun falling around a helpless thing.

WALT WHITMAN: *Leaves of Grass*, pref., 1855

He bestows on every object or quality its fit
  proportion, neither more nor less,
He is arbiter of the diverse, he is the key,
He is the equalizer of his age and land,
He supplies what wants supplying — he checks
  what wants checking.

WALT WHITMAN: *As I Sat Alone*, 1856

Of all races and eras, These States, with veins
  full of poetical stuff, most need poets, and
  are to have the greatest, and use them the
  greatest;
Their Presidents shall not be their common ref-
  eree so much as their poets shall. IBID.

O silly poets! Love is your hobby-horse;
O silly poets! Love is your hobby-horse.
  O silly poets! Silly poets!
  Love is your hobby-horse, silly poets.

W. S. LANDOR: *Letter to Robert Browning*, 1860

Sunshine cannot bleach the snow,
Nor time unmake what poets know.

R. W. EMERSON: *The Test*, 1861 (Atlantic Monthly, Jan.)

A few first-class poets, philosophs, and authors, have substantially settled and given status to the entire religion, education, law, sociology, &c., of the hitherto civilized world.

WALT WHITMAN: *Democratic Vistas*, 1870

The office of the poet is not that of the moralist.
WALTER PATER: *Wordsworth*, 1874

The poet gives us the eminent experiences only, — a god stepping from peak to peak, nor planting his foot but on a mountain.
R. W. EMERSON: *Poetry and Imagination*, 1876

Poets have morals and manners of their own, and custom is no argument with them.
THOMAS HARDY: *The Hand of Ethelberta*, II, 1876

A mighty good sausage-stuffer was spoiled when the man became a poet. He would look well standing under a descending piledriver.
EUGENE FIELD: *The Tribune Primer*, 1882

If the poet is to speak efficaciously, he must say what is already in his hearer's mind.
R. L. STEVENSON: *Familiar Studies of Men and Books*, III, 1882

The poet is the spectator of all time and of all existence. For him no form is obsolete, no subject out of date.
OSCAR WILDE: *The English Renaissance of Art*, 1882 (Lecture in New York, Jan. 9)

Moon talk by a poet who has not been in the moon is likely to be dull.
S. L. CLEMENS (MARK TWAIN): *Life on the Mississippi*, XLV, 1883

It pleased me to read "Queen Mab" and "Cain," amidst the priests and ignorance of a hateful Roman Catholic college. And there my poets saved me from intellectual savagery.
GEORGE MOORE: *Confessions of a Young Man*, I, 1888

Now comes the public and demands that we tell it what the poet desires to say. The answer to that is: If we knew, he wouldn't be one.
HERMANN BAHR: *Studien zur Kritik der Moderne*, 1890

When man acts he is a puppet. When he describes he is a poet.
OSCAR WILDE: *The Critic as Artist*, 1891

Poets are prophets whose prophesying never comes true.
E. W. HOWE: *Country Town Sayings*, 1911

Nobody loves a poet.
IRVING BABBITT: *Rousseau and Romanticism*, 1919

It is the function of the poet to remove the objects and events of this world out of their practical, empirical and natural reality.
KARL VOSSLER: *Geist und Kultur in der Sprache*, IX, 1925

Verse, that was once an art of general interest, is now, like archery, the concern of a very small minority; and in these days a poet has no more reason than an archer for expecting that many people will care to hear him talk of his craft.
CLIFFORD BAX: *Farewell to My Muse*, 1932

If I had my way, I would give every poet a punch in the *kishgis*.
Author unidentified (Yid. *kishgis*=belly)

The poet can reach where the sun cannot.
HINDU PROVERB

Poets and pigs are not appreciated until they are dead.
ITALIAN PROVERB

[*See also* Astronomer, Author, Bard, Concrete, Critic, Dilletante, Dress, Husband, Imagination, Imitation, Love, Lunatic, Mediocrity, Orator, Poetry, Poetry and Prose, Profession, Prose, Spring, Translator, Verse (Blank), Wine (Claret).

Poetess

A maudlin poetess.
ALEXANDER POPE: *An Epistle to Dr. Arbuthnot*, 1735

Poetry

In the Book of Poetry there are three hundred poems, but the meaning of all of them may be put in a single sentence: Have no debasing thoughts.
CONFUCIUS: *Analects*, II, *c.* 500 B.C.

Poetry is vocal painting, as painting is silent poetry.
Ascribed to SIMONIDES OF CEOS (*c.* 556–468 B.C.)

Epic, tragic, comic and dithyrambic poetry are all in their general conception modes of imitation. They differ from one another in these three respects: the medium, the objects, and the manner of imitation.
ARISTOTLE: *Poetics*, I, *c.* 322 B.C.

Poetry is finer and more philosophical than history; for poetry expresses the universal, and history only the particular.
ARISTOTLE: *Poetics*, IX

Poetry is as charming to our ear as sleep to the weary.
VIRGIL: *Eclogues*, V, 37 B.C.

It has long been a question whether a poem be the result of nature or of art. For my part, I do not see what art could do without the aid of nature, nor nature without art; they require the assistance of each other, and ought always to be closely united.
HORACE: *De arte poetica*, *c.* 8 B.C.

O divine and mighty power of poetry, thou rescuest all things from the grasp of death, and biddest the mortal hero live to all time.
LUCAN: *Pharsalia*, IX, 65

It is indignation that leads to the writing of poetry.
JUVENAL: *Satires*, I, *c.* 110

There is nothing so likely to hand down your name as a poem: all other monuments are frail and fading.
PLINY THE YOUNGER: *Letters*, II, *c.* 110

A well-made poem is a powerful piece of imposture. It masters the fancy, and hurries it nobody knows whither.

LACTANTIUS: *Divinæ institutiones,* VI, *c.* 310

Poetry is the Devil's wine.

ST. AUGUSTINE: *Contra academicos, c.* 387

Many lewd lays (ah, woe is me the more)
In praise of that mad fit which fools call love
I have in th' heat of youth made heretofore.

EDMUND SPENSER: *An Hymn of Heavenly Beauty, c.* 1575

It is easier to write an indifferent poem than to understand a good one.

MICHEL DE MONTAIGNE: *Essays,* I, 1580

The elegancy, facility, and golden cadence of poesy.

SHAKESPEARE: *Love's Labor's Lost,* IV, *c.* 1595

I had rather hear a brazen canstick turn'd,
Or a dry wheel grate on the axle-tree;
And that would set my teeth nothing on edge,
Nothing so much as mincing poetry;
'Tis like the forc'd gait of a shuffling nag.

SHAKESPEARE: *I Henry IV,* III, *c.* 1598

Poesy was ever thought to have some participation of divineness, because it doth raise and erect the mind by submitting the shews of things to the desires of the mind.

FRANCIS BACON: *The Advancement of Learning,* I, 1605

Poetry holdeth so sovereign a power over the mind she can turn brutishness into civility, make the lewd honest, turn hatred to love, cowardice into valor, and in brief, like a queen command overall affection.

HENRY PEACHAM: *The Compleat Gentleman,* 1622

Lap me in soft Lydian airs,
Married to immortal verse,
Such as the meeting soul may pierce,
In notes, with many a winding bout
Of linkéd sweetness long drawn out.

JOHN MILTON: *L'Allegro,* 1632

A verse may find him who a sermon flies.

GEORGE HERBERT: *The Temple,* 1633

Even one verse alone sometimes makes a perfect poem.

BEN JONSON: *Discoveries, c.* 1635

May not a woman be a poet? Yes;
And learn the art with far more easiness
Than any man can do; for poesie
Is but a feigning, feigning is to lie,
And women study that art more than men.

JOHN DAY: *The Parliament of Bees,* V, 1641

Poetry's a gift wherein but few excel;
He doth very ill that doth not passing well.

NATHANIEL WARD: *The Simple Cobbler of Aggawam,* 1646

In sober mornings, do not thou rehearse
The holy incantation of a verse;
But when that men have both well drunk, and fed,
Let my enchantments then be sung, or read.

ROBERT HERRICK: *Hesperides,* 1648

Old-fashioned poetry, but choicely good.

IZAAK WALTON: *The Compleat Angler,* IV, 1653

Oh, what a deal of blasphemy
And heathenish impiety,
In Christian poets may be found,
Where heathen gods with praise are crowned.

MICHAEL WIGGLESWORTH: *The Day of Doom,* 1662

She that with poetry is won
Is but a desk to write upon.

SAMUEL BUTLER: *Hudibras,* I, 1663

A poem, being a premeditated form of thoughts, upon designed occasions, ought not to be unfurnished of any harmony in words or sound.

ROBERT HOWARD: *Four New Plays,* pref., 1665

A kind of ingenious nonsense.

ISAAC BARROW: *Sermons,* 1678

Poetry is a damned weed, and will let nothing good or profitable grow by it; 'tis the language of the Devil.

THOMAS SHADWELL: *A True Widow,* I, 1679

O gracious God! how far have we
Profaned thy heav'nly gift of poesy!
Made prostitute and profligate the muse,
Debased to each obscene and impious use,
Whose harmony was first ordained above
For tongues of angels and for hymns of love!

JOHN DRYDEN: *To the Memory of Mrs. Anne Killigrew,* 1686

Poetry is the daughter of love.

BERNARD DE FONTENELLE: *Entretins sur la pluralité des mondes,* I, 1686

Delight is the chief if not the only end of poesy: instruction can be admitted but in the second place, for poetry only instructs as it delights.

JOHN DRYDEN: *An Essay of Dramatic Poesy,* 1688

It is very seldom seen that any one discovers mines of gold or silver in Parnassus. 'Tis a pleasant air but a barren soil.

JOHN LOCKE: *Some Thoughts of Education,* 1693

A copy of verses kept in the cabinet, and only shown to a few friends, is like a virgin, much sought after and admired; but when printed and published, is like a common whore, whom anybody may purchase for half a crown.

JONATHAN SWIFT: *Thoughts on Various Subjects,* 1706

'Tis not enough no harshness gives offense;
The sound must seem an echo to the sense.

ALEXANDER POPE: *An Essay on Criticism,* II, 1711

Love was the mother of poetry. It makes a footman talk like Oroondates.

JOSEPH ADDISON: *The Spectator,* May 13, 1712

I would advise no man to attempt the writing of verse except he cannot help it, and if he cannot it is in vain to dissuade him from it.

MATTHEW PRIOR: *An Essay on Learning,* c. 1715

Addict not thyself to poetry. Reputation is much oftener lost than gained by verse.

THOMAS FULLER: *Introductio ad Prudentiam,* I, 1731

The language of the age is never the language of poetry, except among the French, whose verse, where the thought or image does not support it, differs in nothing from prose. Our poetry, on the contrary, has a language peculiar to itself, to which almost every one that has written has added something by enriching it with foreign idioms and derivatives, nay, sometimes words of their own composition or invention.

THOMAS GRAY: *Letter to —— West,* 1742

O'er her warm cheek, and rising bosom, move
The bloom of young desire and purple light of love.

THOMAS GRAY: *The Progress of Poesy,* 1757

Poetry and consumptions are the most flattering of diseases.

WILLIAM SHENSTONE: *On Writing and Books,* 1764

What is poetry? Why, Sir, it is much easier to say what it is not. We all *know* what light is, but it is not easy to *tell* what it is.

SAMUEL JOHNSON: *Boswell's Life,* April 11, 1776

Poetry cannot be translated; and, therefore, it is the poets that preserve the languages; for we would not be at the trouble to learn a language if we could have all that is written in it just as well in a translation.

SAMUEL JOHNSON: *Boswell's Life,* 1776

Leeze me on rhyme! it's aye a treasure,
My chief, amaist my only pleasure,
At hame, a-fiel', at wark, or leisure;
The muse, poor hizzie!
Though rough and raploch be her measure,
She's seldom lazy.

ROBERT BURNS: *Second Epistle to Davie,* 1785 (*Leeze me on*=an expression of pleasure; *raploch*=a coarse woolen cloth)

Quantity of pleasure being equal, pushpin is as good as poetry.

JEREMY BENTHAM: *The Principles of Morals and Legislation,* IX, 1789

The man deaf to the voice of poetry is a barbarian, let him be who he may.

J. W. GOETHE: *Torquato Tasso,* V, 1790

The music of poesy may charm for a while the importunate teasing cares of life; but the teased and troubled man is not in a disposition to make that music.

CHARLES LAMB: *Letter to S. T. Coleridge,* Dec. 10, 1796

A child scolding a flower in the words in which he had been himself scolded and whipped, is poetry — passion past with pleasure.

S. T. COLERIDGE: *Notebooks,* 1797

Poetry gives most pleasure when only generally and not perfectly understood. IBID.

Poetry takes its origin from emotion recollected in tranquility.

WILLIAM WORDSWORTH: *Lyrical Ballads,* pref., 1798

The effect of poetry should be to lift the mind from the painful realities of actual existence, from its everyday concerns, and its perpetually-occurring vexations, and give it repose by substituting objects in their place which it may contemplate with some degree of interest and satisfaction.

GEORGE CRABBE: *Tales,* pref., 1812

A poem is not necessarily obscure because it does not aim to be popular. It is enough if a work be perspicuous to those for whom it is written.

S. T. COLERIDGE: *Biographia Literaria,* XXII, 1817

The great end
Of poesy, that it should be a friend
To soothe the cares, and lift the thoughts of men.

JOHN KEATS: *Sleep and Poetry,* 1817

Poetry should surprise by a fine excess and not by singularity; it should strike the reader as a wording of his own highest thoughts, and appear almost as a remembrance.

JOHN KEATS: *Letter to John Taylor,* Feb. 27, 1818

Most wretched men
Are cradled into poetry by wrong;
They learn in suffering what they teach in song.

P. B. SHELLEY: *Julian and Maddalo,* 1818

If one's years can't be better employed than in sweating poesy, a man had better be a ditcher.

BYRON: *Letter to John Murray,* April 6, 1819

In poetry there is always fallacy, and sometimes fiction.

WALTER SCOTT: *The Bride of Lammermoor,* XXI, 1819

I consider poetry very subordinate to moral and political science, and if I were well, certainly I would aspire to the latter.

P. B. SHELLEY: *Letter to T. L. Peacock,* Jan. 24, 1819

Poetry is a mimetic art. It creates, but it creates by combination and representation.
P. B. SHELLEY: *Prometheus Unbound*, pref., 1820

Poetry is the record of the best and happiest moments of the happiest and best minds.
P. B. SHELLEY: *The Defence of Poetry*, 1821

Poetry is that art which selects and arranges the symbols of thought in such a manner as to excite the imagination the most powerfully and delightfully.
W. C. BRYANT: *Lectures on Poetry*, I, 1825

As civilization advances, poetry almost necessarily declines.
T. B. MACAULAY: *Milton*, 1825 (Edinburgh Review, Aug.)

Truth is essential to poetry, but it is the truth of madness. The reasonings are just, but the premises are false. IBID.

Poetry is to philosophy what the Sabbath is to the rest of the week.
J. C. and A. W. HARE: *Guesses at Truth*, 1827

Poetry requires not an examining but a believing frame of mind.
T. B. MACAULAY: *John Dryden*, 1828 (Edinburgh Review, Jan.)

Poetry is certainly something more than good sense, but it must be good sense, at all events; just as a palace is more than a house, but it must be a house, at least.
S. T. COLERIDGE: *Table-Talk*, May 9, 1830

Poetry and truth. (Dichtung und Wahrheit.)
J. W. GOETHE: Title of his autobiography, 1831

To please me, a poem must be either music or sense; if it is neither, I confess I cannot interest myself in it.
S. T. COLERIDGE: *Table-Talk*, April 5, 1833

Would you have your songs endure?
Build them on the human heart.
ROBERT BROWNING: *Sordello*, II, 1840

Poetry we will call musical thought.
THOMAS CARLYLE: *Heroes and Hero-Worship*, III, 1840 (Lecture in London, May 12)

Unless it enraptures it is not poetry.
JOSEPH JOUBERT: *Pensées*, I, 1842

Poems that shuffle with superfluous legs
A blindfold minuet over addled eggs.
O. W. HOLMES: *An After-Dinner Poem*, 1843 (Read at a dinner of Phi Beta Kappa, Cambridge, Mass., Aug. 24)

With me poetry has not been a purpose, but a passion. E. A. POE: *Poems*, pref., 1845

I would define the poetry of words as the rhythmical creation of beauty. Its sole arbiter is taste. With the intellect or with the conscience it has only collateral relations. Unless incidentally, it has no concern whatever either with duty or with truth.
E. A. POE: *The Poetic Principle*, 1845

I hold that a long poem does not exist. I maintain that the phrase, "a long poem" is simply a flat contradiction in terms. IBID.

The more prosaic a poetical style is, the better.
E. A. POE: *Marginalia*, 1844–49

True poetry is truer than science, because it is synthetic, and seizes at once what the combination of all the sciences is able, at most, to attain as a final result.
H. F. AMIEL: *Journal*, Oct. 31, 1852

Young men of talent experience often certain musical sensations which are related to poetry as the fancy of a boy for a pretty face is related to love; and the counterfeit, while it lasts, is so like the reality as to deceive not only themselves but even experienced lookers-on who are not on their guard against the phenomenon.
J. A. FROUDE: *Arnold's Poems*, 1854 (Westminster Review)

In the beauty of poems are the tuft and final applause of science.
WALT WHITMAN: *Leaves of Grass*, pref., 1855

Poetry is "the suggestion, by the imagination of noble grounds for the noble emotions."
JOHN RUSKIN: *Modern Painters*, IV, 1856

Poetry is simply the most beautiful, impressive, and widely effective mode of saying things.
MATTHEW ARNOLD: *Heinrich Heine*, 1865

All good poetry has a latency of meaning beyond the simple statement of facts.
E. S. DALLAS: *The Gay Science*, 1866

All poetry is difficult to read.
ROBERT BROWNING: *The Ring and the Book*, I, 1868

That may be very good Dutch Flat poetry, but it won't do in the metropolis. It is too smooth and blubbery; it reads like buttermilk gurgling from a jug.
S. L. CLEMENS (MARK TWAIN): *Answers to Correspondents*, 1875

Poetry is the endeavor to express the spirit of the thing, to pass the brute body and search the life and reason which causes it to exist; — to see that the object is always flowing away, whilst the spirit or necessity which causes it subsists.
R. W. EMERSON: *Poetry and Imagination*, 1876

One should never talk of a moral or an immoral poem — poems are either well written or badly written, that is all.
OSCAR WILDE: *The English Renaissance of Art*, 1882 (Lecture in New York, Jan. 9)

There should always be an enigma in poetry.
JULES HURET: *Enquête sur l'évolution littéraire,* 1885

I believe poetry to be a great benefit to humanity, but only on condition that it be not the dupe of its own symbols and do not erect its intentions into dogmas.
M. J. GUYAU: *L'irréligion de l'avenir,* intro., 1887

You must have rules in poetry, if it is only for the pleasure of breaking them, just as you must have women dressed, if it is only for the pleasure of imagining them as Venuses.
GEORGE MOORE: *Confessions of a Young Man,* VII, 1888

All bad poetry springs from genuine feeling. To be natural is to be obvious, and to be obvious is to be inartistic.
OSCAR WILDE: *The Critic as Artist,* 1891

Poetry is the language of a state of crisis.
STÉPHANE MALLARMÉ (1842–98)

An actual poem is the succession of experiences — sounds, images, thoughts, emotions — through which we pass when we are reading as poetically as we can.
ANDREW BRADLEY: Inaugural lecture as professor of poetry at Oxford, 1901

A poem is no place for an idea.
E. W. HOWE: *Country Town Sayings,* 1911

It is not the function of poetry to further any moral or social cause, any more than it is the function of bridge-building to further the cause of Esperanto.
J. E. SPINGARN: *Creative Criticism,* 1917

Poetry atrophies when it gets too far from music.
EZRA POUND: *How to Read,* 1931

Poetry represents a bygone phase in the history of the human kind.
CLIFFORD BAX: *Farewell to My Muse,* 1932

Poetry is saying something that cannot be said.
Author unidentified

[*See also* History, Literature, Mediocrity, Music, Rhyme, Slang.

Poetry and Prose

I court others in verse, but I love thee in prose;
And they have my whimsies, but thou hast my heart.
MATTHEW PRIOR: *A Better Answer to Chloe Jealous, c.* 1715

Is not the poet's chiming close
Censur'd by all the sons of prose?
While bards of quick imagination
Despise the sleepy prose narration.
JOHN GAY: *Fables,* I, 1727

It is not poetry, but prose run mad.
ALEXANDER POPE: *An Epistle to Dr. Arbuthnot,* 1735

There is in poesy a decent pride,
Which well becomes her when she speaks to prose,
Her younger sister.
EDWARD YOUNG: *Night Thoughts,* V, 1742

A poet hurts himself by writing prose, as a racehorse hurts his motions by condescending to draw in a team.
WILLIAM SHENSTONE: *On Writing and Books,* 1764

Poetry is not the proper antithesis to prose, but to science. Poetry is opposed to science, and prose to metre. The proper and immediate object of science is the acquirement, or communication, of truth; the proper and immediate object of poetry is the communication of immediate pleasure.
S. T. COLERIDGE: *Lectures on Shakespeare Milton,* I, 1812

All that is not prose passes for poetry.
GEORGE CRABBE: *Tales,* pref., 1812

Didactic poetry is my abhorrence; nothing can be equally well expressed in prose that is not tedious and supererogatory in verse.
P. B. SHELLEY: *Prometheus Unbound,* pref., 1820

Prose — words in their best order; — poetry — the best words in their best order.
S. T. COLERLDGE: *Table-Talk,* July 12, 1827

Why do you write poetry? Why do you not write prose? Prose is so much more difficult.
WALTER PATER: To Oscar Wilde, *c.* 1878

A greater command of language is required to write in prose than in verse.
GEORGE MOORE: *Confessions of a Young Man,* IX, 1888

[*See also* Frenchman, Simile.

Poison

What is food to one man may be poison to another.
LUCRETIUS: *De rerum natura,* IV, 57 B.C.

Learning to the inexperienced is a poison; eating upon a full stomach is a poison; the society of the vulgar is a poison; a young wife to an old man is a poison.
The Hitopadesa, intro., *c.* 500

One poison doth another heal.
JOHN HARINGTON: Tr. of LUDOVICO ARIOSTO: *Orlando Furioso* (1532), 1591

One man's meat is another's poison.
ENGLISH PROVERB, borrowed from the Latin and familiar since the XVII century (Cf. LUCRETIUS, *ante,* 57 B.C.)

In golden pots are hidden the most deadly poisons.
THOMAS DRAXE: *Bibliotheca scholastica instructissima,* 1633

It is only cold-blooded animals whose bite is poisonous.
ARTHUR SCHOPENHAUER: *Our Relation to Others,* 1851

[*See also* Antidote, Tobacco.

Poland

The end of Poland. (Finis Poloniæ.)
TADEUSZ KOSCIUSKO: At the Battle of Maciejowice, Oct. 10, 1794

Poland is not yet lost! (Jeszcze Polska nie zginela!)
JOSEPH WYBICKI: *Dombrowski-March,* 1797

Those who consented to the union of Poland with Russia will be the execration of posterity.
NAPOLEON I: To Barry E. O'Meara at St. Helena, March 3, 1817

An independent Polish state should be erected which should include the territories inhabited by indisputably Polish populations, which should be assured a free and secure access to the sea, and whose political and economic independence and territorial integrity should be guaranteed by international convenant.
WOODROW WILSON: Speech to Congress, Jan. 8, 1918 (One of the Fourteen Points)

Eat in Poland, drink in Hungary, sleep in Germany, and make love in Italy.
POLISH PROVERB

Poland is the hell of peasants and the paradise of Jews.
IBID.

[*See also* Indifference.

Pole

They are a brave nation, and make good soldiers. In the cold which prevails in the northern countries the Pole is better than the Frenchman.
NAPOLEON I: To Barry E. O'Meara at St. Helena, Nov. 5, 1816

Any Pole who can read and write is a nobleman.
Author unidentified

Poles lie even when they are old.
RUSSIAN PROVERB

When God created the world He gave the Poles a little sense and small feet, but a woman took both away.
IBID.

[*See also* Character (National), Cheating.

Police

2nd Watchman. How if a' will not stand?
Dogberry. Why, then, take no note of him, but let him go; and presently call the rest of the watch together, and thank God you are rid of a knave.
SHAKESPEARE: *Much Ado About Nothing,* III, *c.* 1599

The parish makes the constable, and when the constable is made he governs the parish.
JOHN SELDEN: *Table-Talk,* 1689

Policemen are soldiers who act alone; soldiers are policemen who act in unison.
HERBERT SPENCER: *Social Statics,* III, 1851

A policeman's lot is not a happy one.
W. S. GILBERT: *The Pirates of Penzance,* II, 1880

Peers and policemen are the people most utterly devoid of humor on the stage.
JEROME K. JEROME: *Stage-Land,* 1889

If you happen to want a policeman, there's never one within miles.
AMERICAN PROVERB, apparently first recorded by GELETT BURGESS: *Are You a Bromide?,* 1907

Every policeman knows that though governments may change, the police remain.
LEON TROTSKY: *What Next?,* I, 1932

[*See also* Anarchist, Crime and Punishment, Detective, Providence.

Policy

Men ought either to be indulged or utterly destroyed, for if you merely offend them they take vengeance, but if you injure them greatly they are unable to retaliate, so that the injury done to a man ought to be such that vengeance cannot be feared.
NICCOLÒ MACHIAVELLI: *The Prince,* III, 1513

Severities should be dealt out all at once, so that their suddenness may give less offence; benefits ought to be handed out drop by drop, so that they may be relished the more.
NICCOLÒ MACHIAVELLI: *The Prince,* VIII, 1532

Have more than thou showest,
Speak less than thou knowest,
Lend less than thou owest,
Ride more than thou goest,
Learn more than thou trowest,
Set less than thou throwest.
SHAKESPEARE: *King Lear,* I, 1606

Never battle with a man who has nothing to lose, for then the conflict is unequal.
BALTASAR GRACIÁN: *The Art of Worldly Wisdom,* CLXXII, 1647

Do pleasant things yourself, but unpleasant things do through others.
BALTASAR GRACIÁN: *The Art of Worldly Wisdom,* CLXXXVII

It is easier to catch flies with honey than with vinegar.
ENGLISH PROVERB, not recorded before the XVIII century

Grant graciously what you cannot refuse safely, and conciliate those you cannot conquer.
C. C. COLTON: *Lacon,* 1820

It is safest to be moderately base — to be flexible in shame, and to be always ready for what is generous, good, and just, when anything is to be gained by virtue.
SYDNEY SMITH: *Letter to the Electors on the Catholic Question,* 1826

When the sands are all dry he is gay as a lark,
And will talk in contemptuous tones of the shark,
But when the tide rises and sharks are around
His voice has a timid and tremulous sound.
C. L. DODGSON (LEWIS CARROLL): *Alice's Adventures in Wonderland,* x, 1865

I never refuse. I never contradict. I sometimes forget.
BENJAMIN DISRAELI: In explanation of his success with Queen Victoria, 1877

Never vote for a tax bill nor against an appropriation bill.
AMERICAN POLITICAL MAXIM

Deny it — but do it. AMERICAN PROVERB

Molasses catches more flies than vinegar.
IBID.

Better bend the neck than bruise the forehead.
DANISH PROVERB

Whose bread I eat, his song I sing.
GERMAN PROVERB

Keep a bad man on your side.
IRISH PROVERB

[*See also* Discretion, Prudence.

Polish

[*See* Elbow-grease.

Politeness

The superior man is polite but not cringing; the common man is cringing but not polite.
CONFUCIUS: *Analects,* XIII, *c.* 500 B.C.

Fair words brake never bone.
Anon.: *How the Good Wife, c.* 1450

Politeness is the chief sign of culture.
BALTASAR GRACIÁN: *The Art of Worldly Wisdom,* CXVIII, 1647

As in smooth oil the razor best is whet,
So wit is by politeness sharpest set.
EDWARD YOUNG: *Love of Fame,* II, 1728

Gentlemen of the French Guard, fire first.
Ascribed to LORD CHARLES HAY at the Battle of Fontenoy, May 11, 1745

Politeness is a desire to so contrive it, by word and manner, that others will be pleased with us and with themselves.
C. L. DE MONTESQUIEU: *Pensées, c.* 1750

Inferiors, when they come into the company of a superior or speak to him, shall show their respect by pulling their hats.
College rules, Princeton College, 1756

Politeness has been defined as artificial good nature; with much greater propriety it may be said that good nature is natural politeness.
STANISLAUS LESZCZYNSKI (KING OF POLAND): *Œuvres du philosophe bienfaisant,* 1763

Politeness is fictitious benevolence.
SAMUEL JOHNSON: *Boswell's Tour to the Hebrides,* Aug. 21, 1773

He is the very pineapple of politeness.
R. B. SHERIDAN: *The Rivals,* III, 1775

Perhaps if we could examine the manners of different nations with impartiality, we should find no people so rude as to be without any rules of politeness; nor any so polite as not to have some remains of rudeness.
BENJAMIN FRANKLIN: *Remarks Concerning the Savages of North America,* 1784

French politeness consists in officiousness and complaisance; they are quick in seeing what will please, and ready to oblige when the way is pointed out to them; they do not idly torment themselves, nor knowingly persist in giving pain to others.
WILLIAM HAZLITT: *Traveling Abroad,* 1828 (New Monthly Magazine, June)

Politeness has been well defined as benevolence in small things.
T. B. MACAULAY: *Samuel Johnson,* 1831 (Edinburgh Review, Sept.)

Politeness is a tacit agreement that peoples' miserable defects, whether moral or intellectual, shall on either side be ignored and not be made the subject of reproach.
ARTHUR SCHOPENHAUER: *Our Relation to Others,* 1851

That roguish and cheerful vice, politeness.
F. W. NIETZSCHE: *Beyond Good and Evil,* 1886

Be polite. Write diplomatically. Even in a declaration of war one observes the rules of politeness.
OTTO VON BISMARCK (1815–98)

If you bow at all, bow low.
CHINESE PROVERB

A man's hat in his hand never did him any harm. ITALIAN PROVERB

All I ask of you, captain, is common politeness — and damned little of that.
New England story (The demand is that of a whaler mate upon an irascible master)

When you say good-morning to the rabbi, say good-morning also to the rabbi's wife.
YIDDISH PROVERB

[*See also* Character (National), Civility, Courtesy, Manners, Punctuality.

Political Economy

The dismal science.

THOMAS CARLYLE: *Latter-Day Pamphlets*, I, 1850

Politician

A politician . . . one that would circumvent God. SHAKESPEARE: *Hamlet*, V, *c.* 1601

It is as hard and severe a thing to be a true politician as to be truly moral.

FRANCIS BACON: *The Advancement of Learning*, II, 1605

Get thee glass eyes;
And, like a scurvy politician, seem
To see the thing thou dost not.

SHAKESPEARE: *King Lear*, IV, 1606

A politician imitates the Devil, as the Devil imitates a cannon: wheresoever he comes to do mischief, he comes with his backside towards you.

JOHN WEBSTER: *The White Devil*, III, *c.* 1608

In friendship false, implacable in hate,
Resolved to ruin or to rule the state.

JOHN DRYDEN: *Absalom and Achitophel*, I, 1682

Is there not some chosen curse,
Some hidden thunder in the stores of Heaven,
Red with uncommon wrath, to blast the man,
Who owes his greatness to his country's ruin?

JOSEPH ADDISON: *Cato*, I, 1713

He gave it for his opinion, " that whoever could make two ears of corn, or two blades of grass, to grow upon a spot of ground where only one grew before, would deserve better of mankind, and do more essential service to his country, than the whole race of politicians put together."

JONATHAN SWIFT: *Gulliver's Travels*, II, 1726

That politician tops his part,
Who readily can lie with art:
The man's proficient in his trade;
His pow'r is strong, his fortune's made.

JOHN GAY: *Fables*, II, 1738

Among politicians the esteem of religion is profitable; the principles of it are troublesome.

BENJAMIN WHICHCOTE: *Moral and Religious Aphorisms*, 1753

I do not admire politicians; but when they are excellent in their way, one cannot help allowing them their due.

HORACE WALPOLE: *Letter to the Earl of Hertford*, Nov. 17, 1763

The deepest politician toils but for a momentary rattle.

HORACE WALPOLE: *Letter to Horace Mann*, May 14, 1777

A cool blooded and crafty politician, when he would be thoroughly revenged on his enemy, makes the injuries which have been inflicted, not on himself, but on others, the pretext of his attack. C. C. COLTON: *Lacon*, 1820

A politician, where factions run high, is interested not for the whole people, but for his own section of it. The rest are, in his view, strangers, enemies, or rather pirates.

T. B. MACAULAY: *Hallam*, 1828 (Edinburgh Review, Sept.)

A politician must often talk and act before he has thought and read. He may be very ill-informed respecting a question; all his notions about it may be vague and inaccurate; but speak he must; and if he is a man of talents, of tact, and of intrepidity, he soon finds that, even under such circumstances, it is possible to speak successfully.

T. B. MACAULAY: *Gladstone on Church and State*, 1839 (Edinburgh Review, April)

Timid and interested politicians think much more about the security of their seats than about the security of their country.

T. B. MACAULAY: Speech in the House of Commons, May, 1842

A statesman makes the occasion, but the occasion makes the politician.

GEORGE S. HILLARD: *Eulogy on Daniel Webster*, Nov. 30, 1852

Politicians are like the bones of a horse's fore-shoulder — not a straight one in it.

WENDELL PHILLIPS: Speech, July, 1864

Great politicians owe their reputation, if not to pure chance, then to circumstances at least which they themselves could not foresee.

OTTO VON BISMARCK: To M. de Blowitz, Paris correspondent of the London Times, *c.* 1875

To scholars who become politicians the comic rôle is usually assigned; they have to be the good conscience of a state policy.

F. W. NIETZSCHE: *Human All-too-Human*, I, 1878

The members who composed it [a typical Democratic National Convention of the pre-Civil War era] were, seven-eighths of them, the meanest kind of bawling and blowing office-holders, office-seekers, pimps, malignants, conspirators, murderers, fancy-men, custom-house clerks, contractors, kept-editors, spaniels well-train'd to carry and fetch, jobbers, infidels, disunionists, terrorists, mail-riflers, slave-catchers, pushers of slavery, creatures of the President, creatures of would-be Presidents, spies, bribers, compromisers, lobbyers, sponges, ruin'd sports, expell'd gamblers, policy-backers, monte-dealers, duellists, carriers of conceal'd weapons, deaf men, pimpled men, scarr'd inside with vile disease, gaudy outside with gold chains made from the people's money and harlots' money

twisted together; crawling, serpentine men, the lousy combinings and born freedom-sellers of the earth.
WALT WHITMAN: *Origins of Attempted Secession, c.* 1880

When I want to buy up any politicians I always find the anti-monopolists the most purchasable. They don't come so high.
W. H. VANDERBILT: To two newspaper reporters, aboard his special train, approaching Chicago, Oct. 8, 1882 (Chicago Daily News, Oct. 9)

A politician thinks of the next election; a statesman, of the next generation.
JAMES FREEMAN CLARKE (1810–88)

Those who are in Albany escaped Sing Sing, and those who are in Sing Sing were on their way to Albany.
ELBERT HUBBARD: *Roycroft Dictionary and Book of Epigrams,* 1923

In politics it is difficult sometimes to decide whether the politicians are humorless hypocrites or hypocritical humorists; whether in fooling the people they also fool themselves, which means that both the politicians and the people are stupid, or whether the politicians are smarter than the people and know exactly what they are doing. Probably the truth is the politicians are smarter, but not much smarter, and that both are without any humor whatever.
FRANK R. KENT: In the Baltimore Sun, July 24, 1932

There is but one way for a newspaper man to look at a politician, and that is down.
FRANK H. SIMONDS (1878–1936)

A politician is an animal who can sit on a fence and yet keep both ears to the ground.
Author unidentified

[*See also* Democracy, Despotism, English Language, Farmer, Officeholder, Philosophy, Spoils, Statesman.

Politics

If I had engaged in politics, O men of Athens, I should have perished long ago, and done no good either to you or to myself.
SOCRATES: *In Plato's Apology of Socrates,* 399 B.C.

The good of man must be the end of the science of politics.
ARISTOTLE: *The Nicomachean Ethics,* I, *c.* 340 B.C.

Nothing is more foreign to us Christians than politics.
TERTULLIAN: *The Christian's Defence, c.* 215

If the chief party, whether it be people, or army, or nobility, which you think most useful and of most consequence to you for the conservation of your dignity, be corrupt, you must follow their humor and indulge them, and in that case honesty and virtue are pernicious.
NICCOLÒ MACHIAVELLI: *The Prince,* XIX, 1513

We starve our conscience when we thrive in state.
JAMES SHIRLEY: *The Cardinal,* v, 1641

Politics, as the word is commonly understood, are nothing but corruptions.
JONATHAN SWIFT: *Thoughts on Various Subjects,* 1706

When vice prevails and impious men bear sway,
The post of honor is a private station.
JOSEPH ADDISON: *Cato,* IV, 1713

That he was born it cannot be denied,
He ate, drank, slept, talk'd politics, and died.
JOHN CUNNINGHAM: *On Alderman W——, c.* 1750

The first mistake in public business is the going into it.
BENJAMIN FRANKLIN: *Poor Richard's Almanac,* 1758

Politics are now nothing more than means of rising in the world.
SAMUEL JOHNSON: *Boswell's Life,* April 11, 1775

I must not write a word to you about politics, because you are a woman.
JOHN ADAMS: *Letter to his wife,* Feb. 13, 1779

A time like this, a busy, bustling time,
Suits ill with writers, very ill with rhyme:
Unheard we sing, when party-rage runs strong,
And mightier madness checks the flowing song.
GEORGE CRABBE: *The Newspaper,* 1785

Politics is such a torment that I would advise every one I love not to mix with it.
THOMAS JEFFERSON: *Letter to Martha Jefferson Randolph,* 1800

In politics experiments mean revolutions.
BENJAMIN DISRAELI: *Popanilla,* IV, 1827

In politics, what begins in fear usually ends in folly.
S. T. COLERIDGE: *Table-Talk,* Oct. 5, 1830

Vain hope, to make people happy by politics!
THOMAS CARLYLE: *Journal,* Oct. 10, 1831

I hold them [politics] to be subject to laws as fixed as matter itself, and to be as fit a subject for the application of the highest intellectual power.
JOHN C. CALHOUN: Speech in the Senate, Feb. 15, 1833

Government has come to be a trade, and is managed solely on commercial principles. A man plunges into politics to make his fortune, and only cares that the world shall last his days.
R. W. EMERSON: *Letter to Thomas Carlyle,* Oct. 7, 1835

In politics, as in religion, there are devotees who show their reverence for a departed saint by converting his tomb into a sanctuary for crime.

T. B. MACAULAY: *Sir James Mackintosh,* 1835 (Edinburgh Review, July)

That a man before whom the two paths of literature and politics lie open, and who might hope for eminence in either, should choose politics, and quit literature, seems to me madness.

T. B. MACAULAY: *Letter to T. F. Ellis,* Dec. 30, 1835

Contact with the affairs of state is one of the most corrupting of the influences to which men are exposed.

J. FENIMORE COOPER: *The American Democrat,* VIII, 1838

There is a certain satisfaction in coming down to the lowest ground of politics, for we get rid of cant and hypocrisy.

R. W. EMERSON: *Representative Men,* VI, 1850

Concealment, evasion, factious combinations, the surrender of convictions to party objects, and the systematic pursuit of expediency are things of daily occurrence among men of the highest character, once embarked in the contentions of political life.

ROBERT LOWE: Editorial in the London Times, Feb. 7, 1852

Politics is but the common pulse-beat, of which revolution is the fever-spasm.

WENDELL PHILLIPS: Speech before the Massachusetts Anti-Slavery Society, Boston, Jan. 27, 1853

Politics is a deleterious profession, like some poisonous handicrafts. Men in power have no opinions, but may be had cheap for any opinion, for any purpose.

R. W. EMERSON: *The Conduct of Life,* II, 1860

Politics is not an exact science.

OTTO VON BISMARCK: Speech in the Prussian Upper House, Dec. 18, 1863

Politics is the gizzard of society, full of grit and gravel, and the two political parties are its two opposite halves — sometimes split into quarters — which grind on each other. Not only individuals, but states, have thus a confirmed dyspepsia.

H. D. THOREAU: *Life Without Principle,* 1863

Do not preach politics. You have no commission to preach politics. The divinity of the Church is never more strikingly displayed than when it holds on its ever straightforward way in the midst of worldly commotions.

BISHOPS JAMES O. ANDREW, ROBERT PAINE and GEORGE F. PIERCE: Pastoral address to the clergy of the Methodist Episcopal Church South, Columbus, Ga., Aug. 17, 1865

Politics makes strange bedfellows.

C. E. WARNER: *My Summer in a Garden,* XV, 1870

All political questions, all matters of right, are at bottom only questions of might.

AUGUST BEBEL: Speech in the Reichstag, July 3, 1871

A civil ruler dabbling in religion is as reprehensible as a clergyman dabbling in politics. Both render themselves odious as well as ridiculous.

JAMES CARDINAL GIBBONS: *The Faith of Our Fathers,* XII, 1876

I always admired Mrs. Grote's saying that politics and theology were the only two really great subjects.

W. E. GLADSTONE: *Letter to Lord Rosebery,* Sept. 16, 1880

Politics is perhaps the only profession for which no preparation is thought necessary.

R. L. STEVENSON: *Familiar Studies of Men and Books,* V, 1882

We should all be glad if we could step aside and say: "Now let us have a day of rest. Politics are over and the millennium is begun." But we live in a world of sin and sorrow.

THOMAS B. REED: Speech in Philadelphia, Feb. 15, 1884

The results of political changes are hardly ever those which their friends hope or their foes fear.

T. H. HUXLEY: *Government,* 1890

Politics is mostly pill-taking.

THOMAS B. REED: *Letter to John Dalzell,* Aug. 1, 1896

Politics is the doctrine of the possible, the attainable.

OTTO VON BISMARCK (1815–98)

The Decalogue and the Golden Rule have no place in a political campaign, and purity in politics is an iridescent dream.

JOHN J. INGALLS (1883–1900)

The field of politics always presents the same struggle. There are the Right and the Left, and in the middle is the Swamp. The Swamp is made up of the know-nothings, of them who are without ideas, of them who are always with the majority.

AUGUST BEBEL: Speech before the Dresden Congress of the Social-Democratic party, 1903

In politics you can't be true to all of your friends all of the time.

Ascribed to PERRY S. HEATH (1857–1927), secretary to the Republican National Committee, 1900–04

The conduct of public affairs for private advantage.
AMBROSE BIERCE: *The Devil's Dictionary,* 1906

Politics I conceive to be nothing more than the science of the ordered progress of society along the lines of greatest usefulness and convenience to itself.
WOODROW WILSON: Speech in Washington, Jan. 6, 1916

We forbid any priest, secular or religious, to discuss in public any question dealing with legislation of a political nature or affecting candidates for political office. If, in relation to such a topic, there seems to be any matter involving a religious or moral problem which a clergyman thinks should be discussed in public, he must first obtain the permission of the Ordinary of this archdiocese after setting forth his view of the question and the treatment it deserves.
JOHN G. MURRAY (ROMAN CATHOLIC ARCHBISHOP OF ST. PAUL): *Letter to his clergy,* March 8, 1933

[*See also* Business, Conscience, Election, Electioneering, Gallantry, Imponderable, Magnanimity, Moderation, Officeholder, Office-seeking, Opinion (Public), Principle, Spoils.

Pollution

If you want to clear the stream get the hog out of the spring. AMERICAN PROVERB

[*See also* Light.

Polycarp (c. 69–155)

This man is the teacher of Asia. This is the father of the Christians. This is the destroyer of our gods. This is the man who has taught thousands to pray and sacrifice to them no longer.
Bill of charges against Polycarp, 155 (He was burned at Smyrna, Feb. 23)

Polygamy

[Solomon] had seven hundred wives, princesses, and three hundred concubines.
I KINGS XI, 3, *c.* 500 B.C.

Marriages with more than one wife is like a man who is attached to more churches than one, whereby his faith is so distracted that it becomes no faith.
EMANUEL SWEDENBORG: *Heaven and Hell,* 1758

Of all that lead a lawless life,
Of all that love their lawless lives,
In city or in village small,
He was the wildest far of all; —
He had a dozen wedded wives.
WILLIAM WORDSWORTH: *Peter Bell,* 1819

Polygamy may well be held in dread,
Not only as a sin, but as a bore.
BYRON: *Don Juan,* VI, 1823

We demand the extermination of polygamy within the jurisdiction of the United States.
Democratic National Platform, 1904

The following classes of aliens shall be excluded from admission into the United States: . . . polygamists, or persons who admit their belief in the practice of polygamy.
Act of Congress, approved Feb. 20, 1907

An endeavor to get more out of life than there is in it.
ELBERT HUBBARD: *Roycroft Dictionary and Book of Epigrams,* 1923

Uninhibited civilized people, whether men or women, are generally polygamous in their instincts.
BERTRAND RUSSELL: *Marriage and Morals,* X, 1929

[*See also* Man and Woman, Mormonism, Philoprogenitiveness.

Pomp

Pomp and circumstance.
SHAKESPEARE: *Othello,* III, 1604

Take physic, pomp;
Expose thyself to feel what wretches feel.
SHAKESPEARE: *King Lear,* III, 1606

Pretend not thou to scorn the pomp of the world before thou knowest it.
THOMAS FULLER: *Introductio ad Prudentiam,* I, 1731

Lo, all our pomp of yesterday
Is one with Nineveh and Tyre!
RUDYARD KIPLING: *Recessional,* 1897 (London Times, July 17)

[*See also* Death.

Pompey

[*See* Hero.

Pomposity

A vile conceit in pompous words express'd,
Is like a clown in regal purple dress'd.
ALEXANDER POPE: *An Essay on Criticism,* II, 1711

Poniard

[*See* Danger.

Poor

What mean ye that ye beat my people to pieces, and grind the faces of the poor? saith the Lord God of Hosts.
ISAIAH III, 15, *c.* 700 B.C.

The poor man is happy: he expects no change for the worse.
DEMETRIUS: *Fragment, c.* 415 B.C.

All the brethren of the poor do hate him: how much more do his friends go far from him? he pursueth them with words, yet they are wanting to him.
PROVERBS XIX, 7, *c.* 350 B.C.

A poor man is full of fears, and imagines himself despised by all mankind.
MENANDER: *Adelphoi, c.* 300 B.C.

The poor man's wisdom is despised, and his words are not heard.
ECCLESIASTES IX, 16, *c.* 200 B.C.

The needy shall not always be forgotten: the expectation of the poor shall not perish for ever. PSALMS IX, 18, *c.* 150 B.C.

No man lives so poor as he was born.
PUBLILIUS SYRUS: *Sententiæ, c.* 50 B.C.

The poor man, when he tries to ape the powerful, comes to ruin.
PHAEDRUS: *Fabulæ Æsopiæ, c.* 40

It is not the man who has little, but he who desires more, that is poor.
SENECA: *Epistulæ morales ad Lucilium, c.* 63

Blessed be ye poor: for yours is the kingdom of God. LUKE VI, 20, *c.* 75

The poor always ye have with you.
JOHN XII, 8, *c.* 115

As poor as Job.
JOHN GOWER: *Confessio Amantis,* V, *c.* 1390

Poor men have no souls.
JOHN HEYWOOD: *Proverbs,* 1546

As poor as a church mouse.
ENGLISH PHRASE, familiar since the XVII century

How apt the poor are to be proud!
SHAKESPEARE: *Twelfth Night,* III, *c.* 1601

My friends were poor but honest.
SHAKESPEARE: *All's Well that Ends Well,* I, *c.* 1602

Poor and content is rich and rich enough.
SHAKESPEARE: *Othello,* III, 1604

There are God's poor and the Devil's poor.
THOMAS ADAMS: *Sermons,* II, 1629

Man is God's image, but a poor man is
Christ's stamp to boot.
GEORGE HERBERT: *The Temple,* 1633

Poor and proud, fie, fie!
WILLIAM CAMDEN: *Remains Concerning Britain* (4th ed.), 1636

A poor beauty finds more lovers than husbands.
GEORGE HERBERT: *Outlandish Proverbs,* 1640

He is not poor that hath little, but he that desireth much. IBID.

There's none poor but such as God hates.
JAMES HOWELL: *Proverbs,* 1659

The labor of the body frees us from the pains of the mind; that is why the poor are happy.
LA ROCHEFOUCAULD: *Maxims,* 1665

Poor people are apt to think everybody flouts them. THOMAS FULLER: *Gnomologia,* 1732

Wisdom in a poor man is a diamond set in lead.
IBID.

The slaving poor are incapable of any principles.
DAVID HUME: *Essays, Moral and Political,* II, 1742

Let not ambition mock their useful toil,
Their homely joys, and destiny obscure;
Nor grandeur hear with a disdainful smile
The short and simple annals of the poor.
THOMAS GRAY: *Elegy Written in a Country Churchyard,* 1750

A poor man has no honor.
SAMUEL JOHNSON: *Boswell's Life,* Sept. 22, 1777

The public is poor.
EDMUND BURKE: Speech in the House of Commons, Feb. 11, 1780

God has always been hard on the poor, and He always will be.
JEAN PAUL MARAT: *Letter to Camille Desmoulins,* June 24, 1790

It is a truth which admits not a doubt that the comforts and well-being of the poor cannot be permanently secured without some regard on their part, or some effort on the part of the legislature, to regulate the increase of their numbers, and to render less frequent among them early and improvident marriages.
DAVID RICARDO: *Principles of Political Economy,* V, 1817

It was never good times in England since the poor began to speculate upon their condition. Formerly they jogged on with as little reflection as horses.
CHARLES LAMB: *Letter to George Dyer,* Dec. 20, 1830

We should surely consider a little whether among the various forms of the oppression of the poor we may not rank as one of the first and likeliest — the oppression of expecting too much from them.
JOHN RUSKIN: *The Two Paths,* V, 1859

When the miseries of the poor are dilated upon they are thought of as the miseries of the deserving poor instead of being thought of as the miseries of the undeserving, which in large measure they should be.
HERBERT SPENCER: *The Coming Slavery,* 1884

He who knows how to be poor knows everything.
JULES MICHELET: *Mon journal,* 1888

I don't care how the poor live; my only regret is that they live at all.
GEORGE MOORE: *Confessions of a Young Man,* XII, 1888

There is only one class in the community that thinks more about money than the rich, and that is the poor. The poor can think of nothing else. That is the misery of being poor.
OSCAR WILDE: *The Soul of Man Under Socialism,* 1891

Only the poor are wasteful.
E. H. HARRIMAN (1848–1909)

No one ever believes a poor man.
DUTCH PROVERB

When a poor man makes a mistake in figures they call him a thief. MOROCCAN PROVERB

The Devil wipes his tail with the poor man's pride. SPANISH PROVERB

[*See also* Air, Alms, Bologna, Charity, Children, Classes, Contentment, Curse, Damnation, England, Enough, Fortune, Government, King, Mercy, Mockery, Money, Ox, Pauperism, Pity, Poverty, Rich and Poor, Seduction, Summer.

Poorhouse

Parents, who know no children's love, dwell there;
Heart-broken matrons on their joyless bed,
Forsaken wives, and mothers never wed;
Dejected widows with unheeded tears,
And crippled age with more than childhood fears;
The lame, the blind, and, far the happiest they —
The moping idiot, and the madman gay.
GEORGE CRABBE: *The Village,* I, 1783

You may have some pleasant, thrilling, glorious hours, even in a poorhouse.
H. D. THOREAU: *Walden,* 1854

Over the hill to the poorhouse I'm trudgin' my weary way.
WILL CARLETON: *Over the Hill to the Poorhouse,* 1871 (Harper's Weekly, May 27)

Pope

That the Roman pontiff alone can with right be called universal.
That of him alone all princes shall kiss the feet.
That it is permitted him to depose emperors.
That a sentence passed by him may be retracted by no one save himself.
POPE GREGORY VII: Propositions promulgated, *c.* 1080

We declare, we say, we defend and pronounce that to every human creature it is absolutely necessary to salvation to be subject to the Roman pontiff.
POPE BONIFACE VIII: *Unam sanctam,* 1302

We define that the Roman pontiff is the successor of the Blessed Peter, Prince of the Apostles, and the true Vicar of Christ, the head of the whole church, the father and doctor of all Christians, and we declare that to him, in the person of Blessed Peter, was given, by Jesus Christ our Saviour, full power to feed, rule, and govern the universal church.
Decree of the Council of Florence, 1439

The pope derives his institution neither from divine nor from human right, but is a self-chosen human creature and intruder.
MARTIN LUTHER: *Table-Talk,* CCCCXV, 1569

A pope's bull, a dead man's skull, and an old trull are not all worth a pound of wool.
BARNABE RICH: *My Lady's Looking-Glass,* 1616

Ye may not sit in Rome and strive with the pope.
DAVID FERGUSSON: *Scottish Proverbs,* 1641

The pope is the head of the Christians — an ancient idol, kept venerable by custom.
C. L. DE MONTESQUIEU: *Persian Letters,* XXIX, 1721

Though I am not naturally ambitious, I would not have refused the nomination for pope, had the choice of the conclave fallen on me. It is, at all events, a very respectable office, and has a good income attached to it.
HEINRICH HEINE: *Confessions,* 1854

The pope may and must reconcile himself with, and adapt himself to, progress, liberalism, and modern civilization.
Proposition condemned by POPE PIUS IX: *Syllabus of Errors,* LXXX, Dec. 8, 1864

All true followers of Christ, lettered or unlettered, suffer themselves to be guided and led in all things that touch upon faith or morals by the Holy Church of God through its Supreme Pastor, the Roman pontiff, who is himself guided by Jesus Christ our Lord.
POPE PIUS XI: *Casti connubii,* Dec. 31, 1930

Who injures the pope dies.
POPE PIUS XI: Address to missionary students at Castel Gandolfo, July 29, 1938

He who eats what comes from the pope dies of it. FRENCH PROVERB

The nearer the pope, the worse the Christian.
GERMAN PROVERB

Where the pope is, Rome is.
ITALIAN PROVERB

[*See also* Antichrist, Bologna, Cause and Effect, Certainty, Church (Roman Catholic), Curse, Death, Despot, Hard, Heaven and Hell, Infallibility (Papal), Infamy, Italy, Judgment Day, Knowledge, Papacy, Popery.

Pope, Alexander (1688–1744)

Egad, that young fellow will either be a madman or make a very great poet.
RAY SMITH: On Pope at fourteen, 1681

In Pope I cannot read a line,
But with a sigh I wish it mine;
When he can in one couplet fix
More sense than I can do in six,
It gives me such a jealous fit,
I cry, "Pox take him and his wit!"

JONATHAN SWIFT: *On the Death of Dr. Swift,* 1731

Yes, I am proud! I must be proud to see
Men, not afraid of God, afraid of me.

ALEXANDER POPE: *Epilogue to the Satires,* II, 1738

With the unwearied application of a plodding Flemish painter, who draws a shrimp with the most minute exactness, he had all the genius of one of the first masters. Never, I believe, were such talents and such drudgery united.

WILLIAM COWPER: *Letter to William Unwin,* Jan. 5, 1782

He is the moral poet of all civilization; and as such, let us hope that he will one day be the national poet of mankind. He is the only poet that never shocks; the only poet whose faultlessness has been made his reproach.

BYRON: *Letter to John Murray,* Feb. 7, 1821

Pope and his school wrote poetry fit to put round frosted cake.

R. W. EMERSON: *English Traits,* VIII, 1856

One whom it was easy to hate, but still easier to quote.

AUGUSTINE BIRRELL: *Obiter Dicta,* II, 1887

Popery

Tolerated popery, as it extirpates all religions and civil supremacies, so itself should be extirpated, provided first that all charitable and compassionate means be used to win and regain the weak and the misled.

JOHN MILTON: *Areopagitica,* 1644

I like popery as I like chivalry and romance. They all furnish one with ideas and visions, which Presbyterianism does not.

HORACE WALPOLE: *Letter to William Cole,* July 12, 1778

[*See also* Papacy, Pope, Protestant.

Poppy

In Flanders fields the poppies grow
Between the crosses, row on row.

JOHN MCCREA: *In Flanders Fields,* 1915 (Punch, Dec. 8)

Populace

Herds and flocks of people that follow anybody that whistles to them, or drives them to pasture.

JEREMY TAYLOR: *Twenty-seven Sermons,* I, 1651

If we look into the bulk of our species, they are such as are not likely to be remembered a moment after their disappearance: they leave behind them no traces of their existence, but are forgotten as though they had never been.

JOSEPH ADDISON: *The Spectator,* March 4, 1712

The lower classes of men, though they do not think it worth while to record what they perceive, nevertheless perceive everything that is worth noting. The difference between them and a man of learning often consists in nothing more than the latter's facility for expression.

G. C. LICHTENBERG: *Reflections,* 1799

The passions of the populace are as brutal as they are hideous, even during those short and rare intervals when the populace is in the right.

F. P. G. GUIZOT: *Études biographiques sur la révolution d'Angleterre,* 1851

Very few of our race can be said to be yet finished men. We still carry sticking to us some remains of the preceding inferior quadruped organization. We call these millions men; but they are not yet men.

R. W. EMERSON: *The Conduct of Life,* IV, 1860

All the higher circles of human intelligence are, to those beneath, only momentarily and partially open.

JOHN RUSKIN: *Sesame and Lilies,* I, 1865

Earth, crowded, cries, "Too many men!"
My counsel is, kill nine in ten,
And bestow the shares of all
On the remnant decimal.

R. W. EMERSON: *Alphonso of Castile,* 1867

Science finds out ingenious way to kill
Strong men, and keep alive the weak and ill,
That these a sickly progeny may breed:
Too poor to tax, too numerous to feed.

COLIN ELLIS: *Mournful Numbers,* 1932

[*See also* Bread, Crowd, Majority, Masses, Mob, Multitude, People, Popularity, Proletariat, Proverb, Public, Rabble.

Popularity

Woe unto you, when all men shall speak well of you! LUKE VI, 26, *c.* 75

The ladies call him sweet;
The stairs, as he treads on them, kiss his feet.

SHAKESPEARE: *Love's Labor's Lost,* V, *c.* 1595

An habitation giddy and unsure
Hath he that buildeth on the vulgar heart.

SHAKESPEARE: *II Henry IV,* I, *c.* 1598

Ability wins us the esteem of the true men; luck, that of the people.

LA ROCHEFOUCAULD: *Maxims,* 1665

Popularity is a crime from the moment it is sought; it is only a virtue where men have it whether they will or not.

GEORGE SAVILE (MARQUESS OF HALIFAX): *Political, Moral and Miscellaneous Reflections, c.* 1690

I cannot see why people are ashamed to acknowledge their passion for popularity. The love of popularity is the love of being beloved.

WILLIAM SHENSTONE: *Of Men and Manners,* 1764

I would jump down Ætna for any great public good, but I hate a mawkish popularity.

JOHN KEATS: *Letter to J. H. Reynolds,* April 9, 1818

That great baby, the world, however it may cry up and pretend to admire its idols, is just like the little girl who, after dressing up her doll in all its finery, and caressing it till she is tired, is not easy till she has pulled it to pieces again and reduced it to its original rags and wool.

WILLIAM HAZLITT: *The Ruling Passion,* 1829 (The Atlas, Jan. 18)

I don't care a fig for popularity for myself; but, if I believe that my writings contain that which is capable of doing their readers good, I cannot but grieve if it has been my own fault — as in the present instance it has — that I have not had more readers.

COVENTRY PATMORE: *Letter to H. S. Sutton,* April 14, 1847

Popularity is exhausting. The life of the party almost always winds up in a corner with an overcoat over him.

WILSON MIZNER (1876–1933)

Popularity is the small change of glory.

FRENCH PROVERB

[*See also* Author, Lafayette (Marquis de).

Population

Men, thinly scattered, make a shift, but a bad shift, without many things. A smith is ten miles off: they'll do without a nail or a staple. A tailor is far from them: they'll botch their own clothes. It is being concentrated which produces high convenience.

SAMUEL JOHNSON: *Boswell's Tour to the Hebrides,* Aug. 15, 1773

Men, like all other animals, naturally multiply in proportion to the means of their subsistence.

ADAM SMITH: *The Wealth of Nations,* I, 1776

The extreme fertility of the ground always indicates the extreme misery of the inhabitants.

ST. JOHN DE CRÈVECOEUR: *Letters From an American Farmer,* IX, 1782

Population, when unchecked, increases in a geometrical ratio. Subsistence only increases in an arithmetical ratio.

T. R. MALTHUS: *The Principle of Population,* I, 1798

Well-established calculations in political arithmetic enable us to say that the aggregate population of the nation, . . . in the year 1950, will be 200,000,000.

W. H. SEWARD: Speech in the Senate, March 11, 1850

Man tends to increase at a greater rate than his means of subsistence; consequently he is occasionally subjected to a severe struggle for existence.

CHARLES DARWIN: *The Descent of Man,* XXI, 1871

It is not the increase of food that has caused this increase of men; but the increase of men that has brought about the increase of food. There is more food simply because there are more men.

HENRY GEORGE: *Progress and Poverty,* II, 1879

The political problem of problems is how to deal with overpopulation, and it faces us on all sides.

T. H. HUXLEY: *Government,* 1890

[*See also* Land, Struggle for Existence.

Porcupine

Anastasio having heard all this, his hair stood upright like a porcupine's quills.

GIOVANNI BOCCACCIO: *The Decameron,* V, *c.* 1350

Like quills upon the fretful porpentine.

SHAKESPEARE: *Hamlet,* I, *c.* 1601 (*Porpentine*=porcupine)

Pork

There was lately a man that, if pork, or anything made of swine's flesh, were brought into the room, he would fall into a convulsive, sardonic laughter; nor can he for his heart leave as long as that object is before him, so that, if it should not be removed, he would certainly laugh himself to death.

INCREASE MATHER: *Remarkable Providences,* IV, 1684

Kill a pig and eat a year; kill an ox and eat a week.

ITALIAN PROVERB

Fresh pork and new wine bring an early death.

SPANISH PROVERB

[*See also* Hog, Pig, Worst.

Porpoise

A porpoise . . . is always the messenger of tempests.

GEORGE CHAPMAN, BEN JONSON and JOHN MARSTON: *Eastward Ho,* III, 1605

Porpoise is fine eating. The meat is made into balls about the size of billiard balls, and being well seasoned and spiced might be taken for turtle balls or veal balls. The old monks of Dunfermline were very fond of them.

HERMAN MELVILLE: *Moby Dick,* LXIV, 1851

Porter

The sons of Jeduthun were porters.
I CHRONICLES XVI, 42, *c.* 300 B.C.

Portrait

Painted pictures are dead speakers.
NICHOLAS BRETON: *Crossing of Proverbs,* 1616

I desire you will use all your skill to paint my picture truly like me, and not to flatter me at all; but remark all those roughnesses, pimples, warts, and everything as you see me: otherwise I will never pay one farthing for it.
OLIVER CROMWELL: To Peter Lely, 1650

It is pleasant to look on the picture of any face where the resemblance is hit: but the pleasure increases if it be the picture of a face that is beautiful, and is still greater if the beauty be softened with an air of melancholy or sorrow.
JOSEPH ADDISON: *The Spectator,* June 30, 1712

A history-painter paints man in general; a portrait-painter, a particular man, and consequently a defective model.
JOSHUA REYNOLDS: *Discourses,* IV, 1771 (Lecture at the Royal Academy, London, Dec. 10)

I am so hackneyed to the touches of the painter's pencils that I am now altogether at their beck. . . . At first I was as impatient and as restive under the operation as a colt is of the saddle. The next time I submitted very reluctantly, but with less flouncing. Now no dray horse moves more readily to his thill than I do to the painter's chair.
GEORGE WASHINGTON: *Letter to Francis Hopkinson,* 1785

One is never satisfied with the portrait of a person one knows.
J. W. GOETHE: *Elective Affinities,* II, 1808

To sit for one's portrait is like being present at one's own creation.
ALEXANDER SMITH: *Dreamthorp,* XII, 1863

I lately watched an able artist painting a portrait, and endeavored to estimate the number of strokes with his brush, every one of which was thoughtfully and firmly given. During fifteen sittings of three working hours each he worked at the average rate of ten strokes per minute. There were, therefore, 24,000 separate traits in the completed portrait.
FRANCIS GALTON: *Inquiries Into Human Faculty,* 1883

[*See also* Painting, Picture.

Portuguese

Three Moors to a Portugal; three Portugals to an Englishman.
SAMUEL PURCHAS: *Purchas His Pilgrimage,* 1612

The Portuguese ladies . . . would think their charms insulted if, when left alone with a man, he did not at least attempt to be grossly familiar with their persons.
MARY WOLLSTONECRAFT: *A Vindication of the Rights of Woman,* VII, 1792

I have known several drunkards amongst the Portuguese, but, without one exception, they have been individuals who, having traveled abroad, have returned with a contempt for their own country, and polluted with the worst vices of the lands which they have visited.
GEORGE BORROW: *The Bible in Spain,* IV, 1843

A bad Spaniard makes a good Portuguese.
SPANISH PROVERB

[*See also* Character (National).

Port (Wine)

[*See* Wine (Port).

Pose

Though of all poses a moral pose is the most offensive, still to have a pose at all is something. It is a form of recognition of the importance of treating life from a definite and reasoned standpoint.
OSCAR WILDE: *The Critic as Artist,* 1891

Possession

He that hath, to him shall be given; and he that hath not, from him shall be taken even that which he hath.
MARK IV, 25, *c.* 70 (Cf. MATTHEW XXV, 29, *c.* 75)

A bird in the hand is worth two in the bush.
ENGLISH PROVERB, familiar in various forms since the XV century

What we have we prize not to the worth
Whiles we enjoy it; but being lacked and lost,
Why, then we rack the value, then we find
The virtue that possession would not show us
Whiles it was ours.
SHAKESPEARE: *Much Ado About Nothing,* IV, *c.* 1599

Possession is nine points of the law.
ENGLISH PROVERB, familiar since the XVII century (Sometimes *eleven* instead of *nine*)

Possession hinders enjoyment. It merely gives you the right to keep things for or from others, and thus you gain more enemies than friends.
BALTASAR GRACIÁN: *The Art of Worldly Wisdom,* CCLXIII, 1647

The pleasure of possessing
Surpasses all expressing;
But 'tis too short a blessing,
And love too long a pain.
JOHN DRYDEN: *Farewell, Ungrateful Traitor,* 1681

A sparrow in hand is worth more than a pheasant that flieth by.
THOMAS FULLER: *Gnomologia,* 1732

The simple plan
That they should take who have the power,
And they should keep who can.
WILLIAM WORDSWORTH: *Rob Roy's Grave,* 1807

Possession's beef and ale —
Soft bed, fair wife, gay horse, good steel.—
Are they naught?
Possession means to sit astride of the world,
Instead of having it astride of you.
CHARLES KINGSLEY: *The Saint's Tragedy,* I, 1848

Them as has, gits. AMERICAN PROVERB

A sparrow in the hand is worth more than a goose in the air. FRENCH PROVERB

One "take this" is better than two "thou shalt haves." IBID.

A bird on the fire is worth many in the air.
FRISIAN PROVERB

A cucumber in hand is better than the hope of a pumpkin in the future.
HEBREW PROVERB

Possession is stronger than ownership.
HINDU PROVERB

Better one bird in the cage than four in the tree.
ITALIAN PROVERB

Where the rights are equal, the condition of the possessor is best. (In æquali jure melior est conditio possidentis.) LEGAL MAXIM

[*See also* Covetousness, Today and Tomorrow.

Possession, Demoniacal

1. If the party concerned shall reveal secret things, either past or future, which without supernatural assistance could not be known, it argueth possession.
2. If he does speak with strange languages, or discover skill in arts and sciences never learned by him.
3. If he can bear burthens and do things which are beyond human strength.
4. Uttering words without making use of the organs of speech. . . .
5. When the body is become inflexible.
6. When the belly is on a sudden puft up, and instantly flat again.

INCREASE MATHER: *Remarkable Providences,* VI, 1684

Possibility

Everything is possible, including the impossible and absurd.
BENITO MUSSOLINI: Speech in Trieste, Sept. 20, 1920

[*See also* Faith.

Post

[*See* Postoffice.

Post-chaise

If I had no duties, and no reference to futurity, I would spend my life in driving briskly in a post-chaise with a pretty woman.
SAMUEL JOHNSON: *Boswell's Life,* Sept. 19, 1777

Whatever purity found abode,
'Twas certainly *not* on a posting road.
AUSTIN DOBSON: *The Ballad of Beau Brocade,* 1892

Posterity

Believe it, posterity! (Credite, posteri.)
HORACE: *Carmina,* II, *c.* 20 B.C.

A coming age will admire. (Sequens mirabitur ætas.) OVID: *Epistulæ ex Ponto,* II, *c.* 5

Posterity gives every man his true value.
TACITUS: *Annals,* IV, *c.* 110

We are always doing, says he, something for posterity, but I would fain see posterity do something for us.
JOSEPH ADDISON: *The Spectator,* Aug. 20, 1712 (Ascribed to "an old fellow of a college")

Posterity is always the author's favorite.
SAMUEL JOHNSON: To Hester Thrale, Oct. 27, 1777

Here you would know, and enjoy, what posterity will say of Washington. For a thousand leagues have nearly the same effect with a thousand years.
BENJAMIN FRANKLIN: *Letter to George Washington from Paris,* March 5, 1780

What has posterity done for us?
JOHN TRUMBULL: *McFingal,* II, 1782 (Cf. ADDISON, *ante,* 1712)

People will not look forward to posterity who never look backward to their ancestors.
EDMUND BURKE: *Reflections on the Revolution in France,* III, 1790

Contemporaries appreciate the man rather than the merit; but posterity will regard the merit rather than the man.
C. C. COLTON: *Lacon,* 1820

Few can be induced to labor exclusively for posterity, and none will do it enthusiastically. Posterity has done nothing for us; and, theorize on it as we may, practically we shall do very little for it unless we are made to think we are, at the same time, doing something for ourselves.
ABRAHAM LINCOLN: Speech in Springfield, Ill., Feb. 22, 1842

Posterity is a most limited assembly. Those gentlemen who reach posterity are not much more numerous than the planets.
BENJAMIN DISRAELI: Speech in the House of Commons, Jan. 22, 1836

[*See also* Ancestry, Epitaph.

Posthumous

The works of authors departed are generally received with some favor, partly as they are old acquaintances, and in part because there can be no more of them.
GEORGE CRABBE: *Letter to his son*, Oct. 24, 1831

Postoffice

Neither snow nor rain nor heat nor gloom of night stays these couriers from the swift accomplishment of their appointed routes.
HERODOTUS: *Histories*, VI, *c.* 430 B.C. (The reference is to the Persian post-riders)

The post passed from city to city, through the country of Ephriam and Manasseh, even unto Zebulun.
II CHRONICLES XXX, 10, *c.* 300 B.C.

He . . . sent letters by posts on horseback, and riders on mules, camels, and young dromedaries. ESTHER VIII, 10, *c.* 125 B.C.

Carrier of news and knowledge,
Instrument of trade and industry,
Promoter of mutual acquaintance,
Of peace and good-will
Among men and nations.
CHARLES W. ELIOT: Inscription on Post-office Building, Washington, *c.* 1905

The United States may give up the postoffice when it sees fit, but while it carries it on, the use of the mails is almost as much a part of free speech as the right to use our tongues.
MR. JUSTICE O. W. HOLMES: *Dissenting opinion in Milwaukee Social Dem. Pub. Co.* vs. *Burleson*, 1920

Postscript

Jove and my stars be praised! Here is yet a postscript.
SHAKESPEARE: *Twelfth Night*, II, *c.* 1601

A woman seldom writes her mind but in her postscript.
RICHARD STEELE: *The Spectator*, May 31, 1711

Pot

[*See* Recrimination.

Potato

The best part of a potato is underground.
ENGLISH SAYING, not recorded before the XIX century

A hot potato is hard to cool.
AMERICAN PROVERB, apparently of Southern origin

Potomac

All quiet along the Potomac tonight.
ETHEL L. BEERS: *The Picket Guard*, 1861 (Harper's Weekly, Sept. 30)

Pottage

[*See* Birthright.

Potter's Field

And they took counsel, and bought . . . the potter's field, to bury strangers in.
MATTHEW XXVII, 7, *c.* 75

Poverty

Poverty has this defect: it prompts a man to evil deeds. EURIPIDES: *Electra*, *c.* 415 B.C.

To admit poverty is no disgrace to a man, but to make no effort to escape it is indeed disgraceful.
THUCYDIDES: *History*, II, *c.* 410 B.C.

Poverty is a teacher of all the arts.
PLAUTUS: *Stichus*, II, *c.* 200 B.C.

A generous and noble spirit cannot be expected to dwell in the breasts of men who are struggling for their daily bread.
DIONYSIUS OF HALICARNASSUS: *Antiquities of Rome*, IV, *c.* 20 B.C.

Poverty urges us to do and suffer anything that we may escape from it, and so leads us away from virtue.
HORACE: *Carmina*, III, *c.* 20 B.C.

The worst unhappiness of poverty is that it makes men ridiculous.
JUVENAL: *Satires*, III, *c.* 110

It is rare for a thief to visit a garret.
JUVENAL: *Satires*, X, *c.* 125

No one should commend poverty save the poor. ST. BERNARD: *Sermon*, *c.* 1150

Poverty is an odious blessing.
VINCENT OF BEAUVAIS: *Speculum historiale*, *c.* 1250

Poverty is the mother of health.
WILLIAM LANGLAND: *Piers Plowman*, 1377

There is no virtue but poverty will mar it.
JOHN FLORIO: *First Frutes*, 1578

When poverty comes in at the door, love flies out of the window.
ENGLISH PROVERB, current since the XVII century

I am no such pil'd cynic to believe
That beggary is the only happiness,
Or, with a number of these patient fools,
To sing, "My mind to me a kingdom is,"
When the lank hungry belly barks for food.
BEN JONSON: *Every Man Out of His Humor*, I, 1600

Poverty is no sin.
GEORGE HERBERT: *Outlandish Proverbs*, 1640

Bear wealth; poverty will bear itself.
DAVID FERGUSSON: *Scottish Proverbs*, 1641

Everything that poverty touches becomes frightful.
NICHOLAS BOILEAU: *Satires du Sieur D*, VIII, 1666

There's no scandal like rags, nor any crime so shameful as poverty.
GEORGE FARQUHAR: *The Beaux' Stratagem,* I, 1707

Poverty is a pain, but no disgrace.
JAMES KELLY: *Scottish Proverbs,* 1721

Poverty is not a shame, but the being ashamed of it is.
THOMAS FULLER: *Gnomologia,* 1732

The worst part of poverty is to bear it impatiently. IBID.

This mournful truth is everywhere confess'd,
Slow rises worth by poverty depress'd.
SAMUEL JOHNSON: *London,* 1738

To shun poverty and distress, and to ally himself as close as possible to power and riches.
HENRY FIELDING: *Jonathan Wild,* IV, 1743
(Maxim of Wild for the attainment of greatness)

In the prospect of poverty there is nothing but gloom and melancholy; the mind and body suffer together; its miseries bring no alleviations; it is a state in which every virtue is obscured, and in which no conduct can avoid reproach; a state in which cheerfulness is insensibility, and dejection sullenness, of which the hardships are without honor, and the labors without reward.
SAMUEL JOHNSON: *The Rambler,* Sept. 18, 1750

Poverty is certainly and invariably despised.
SAMUEL JOHNSON: *The Rambler,* Oct. 26, 1751

Poverty often deprives a man of all spirit and virtue.
BENJAMIN FRANKLIN: *Poor Richard's Almanac,* 1757

Poverty seduces and withdraws men from Heaven as much as wealth. Great numbers among the poor are as ready as the wicked among the rich to defraud others, and to live in sordid pleasures when they have the opportunity.
EMANUEL SWEDENBORG: *Heaven and Hell,* 1758

There is a degree of poverty that has no disgrace belonging to it; that degree of it, I mean, in which a man enjoys clean linen and good company; and if I never sink below this degree of it, I care not if I never rise above it.
WILLIAM COWPER: *Letter to Clotworthy Rowley,* Sept. 2, 1762

All the arguments which are brought to represent poverty as no evil show it to be evidently a great evil. You never find people laboring to convince you that you may live very happily with a plentiful fortune.
SAMUEL JOHNSON: *Boswell's Life,* July 20, 1763

Have the courage to own that you are poor, and you disarm poverty of its sharpest sting.
STANISLAUS LESZCYNSKI (KING OF POLAND): *Œuvres du philosophe bienfaisant,* 1763

No society can surely be flourishing and happy of which the far greater part of the members are poor and miserable.
ADAM SMITH: *The Wealth of Nations,* I, 1776

Poverty is a great enemy to human happiness; it certainly destroys liberty, and it makes some virtues impracticable, and others extremely difficult.
SAMUEL JOHNSON: *Boswell's Life,* Dec. 7, 1782

We have lived to witness one of the most extraordinary paradoxes that have ever puzzled the world: general poverty produced by universal plenty! The earth has been sick of a plethora, and her bowels have burst with their abundance, and yet distress and want were never so universal.
HANNAH MORE: *Village Politics,* 1793

Hard as it may appear in individual cases, dependent poverty ought to be held disgraceful.
T. R. MALTHUS: *The Principle of Population,* V, 1798

The rude inelegance of poverty.
ROBERT BLOOMFIELD: *The Farmer's Boy,* 1800

Poverty, of course, is no disgrace, but it is damned annoying.
WILLIAM PITT (1759–1806)

There hungry dogs from hungry children steal;
There pigs and chickens quarrel for a meal;
These dropsied infants wail without redress,
And all is want and woe and wretchedness.
GEORGE CRABBE: *The Parish Register,* I, 1807

Thousands upon thousands are yearly brought into a state of real poverty by their great anxiety not to be thought poor.
WILLIAM COBBETT: *Advice to Young Men,* II, 1829

Poverty makes some humble, but more malignant.
E. G. BULWER-LYTTON: *Eugene Aram,* I, 1832

Poverty makes strange bedfellows.
ENGLISH PROVERB, first recorded in 1849

It is life near the bone, where it is sweetest.
H. D. THOREAU: *Walden,* 1854

Among the various characteristics of the age in which we live, as compared with other ages of this not yet *very* experienced world, one of the most notable appears to me the just

and wholesome contempt in which we hold poverty.
JOHN RUSKIN: *The Political Economy of Art*, I, 1857

Poverty is not a misfortune to the poor only who suffer it, but it is more or less a misfortune to all with whom he deals.
H. W. BEECHER: Address at Liverpool, Oct. 16, 1863

All ought to refrain from marriage who cannot avoid abject poverty for their children; for poverty is not only a great evil, but tends to its own increase by leading to recklessness in marriage.
CHARLES DARWIN: *The Descent of Man*, XXI, 1871

Poverty is one ov them kind ov misfortunes that we all ov us dread but none ov us pitty.
H. W. SHAW (JOSH BILLINGS): *Josh Billings' Encyclopedia of Wit and Wisdom*, 1874

Poverty is an anomaly to rich people. It is very difficult to make out why people who want dinner do not ring the bell.
WALTER BAGEHOT: *Literary Studies*, II, 1879

That amid our highest civilization men faint and die with want is not due to the niggardliness of nature, but to the injustice of man.
HENRY GEORGE: *Progress and Poverty*, I, 1879

Poverty is the open-mouthed, relentless hell which yawns beneath civilized society. And it is hell enough.
HENRY GEORGE: *Progress and Poverty*, IX

I am a little impatient of being told that property . . . bears all the burden of the state. It bears those, indeed, which can most easily be borne, but poverty pays with its person the chief expenses of war, pestilence, and famine.
J. R. LOWELL: *Democracy*, 1884 (Address in Birmingham, England, Oct. 6)

Poverty is the strenuous life, — without brass bands, or uniforms, or hysteric popular applause, or lies, or circumlocutions.
WILLIAM JAMES: *The Varieties of Religious Experience*, XIV, 1902

The poor should not be ashamed of their poverty, nor disdain the charity of the rich; for they should have especially in view Jesus the Redeemer, who, though He might have been born in riches, made Himself poor in order that He might ennoble poverty and enrich it with incomparable merits for Heaven.
POPE PIUS X: *Apostolic Letter to the Bishops of Italy on Catholic Social Action*, Dec. 18, 1903

A file provided for the teeth of the rats of reform.
AMBROSE BIERCE: *The Devil's Dictionary*, 1906

Poverty is a shirt of fire.
ARMENIAN PROVERB

Poverty is not a sin, but it is better to hide it.
FRENCH PROVERB

Poverty makes no happiness, and wealth is no disgrace.
GERMAN PROVERB

Poverty makes handsome women ugly.
HEBREW PROVERB

Poverty has no relatives.
ITALIAN PROVERB

Poverty is a blessing hated by all men.
IBID.

Poverty is a bad guard for chastity.
IBID.

To be healthy but poor is to be half sick.
IBID.

Even the street-dog knows the house of a poor man.
JAPANESE PROVERB

Poverty is half laziness.
JUGO-SLAVIC PROVERB

Poverty is not a vice. (Paupertas non est vitium.)
LATIN PROVERB

Poverty may not be a sin, but it is twice as bad.
RUSSIAN PROVERB

Poverty has no shame.
SPANISH PROVERB

The poor man risks nothing when he meets a thief.
IBID.

Poverty is an orphan.
WEST AFRICAN PROVERB

[*See also* Avarice, Beautiful, Bird, Building, Capitalism, Crime, Democracy, Dirt, Fear, Government, Laziness, Love, Money, Pauperism, Peace, Penury, Poor, Rich and Poor, Sleep, Vice, War and Peace, Wealth.

Powder

Put your trust in God, but mind to keep your powder dry.
OLIVER CROMWELL: To his troops at the battle of Edgehill, Oct. 23, 1642

Power

Power is precarious.
HERODOTUS: *Histories*, III, *c.* 430 B.C.

To be able to endure odium is the first art to be learned by those who aspire to power.
SENECA: *Hercules Furens*, *c.* 50

There is no power but from God.
ROMANS XIII, 1, *c.* 55

Power is never stable when it is boundless.
TACITUS: *History*, II, *c.* 100

The power that makes men terrible is a terror first to its possessors; it smiles and frowns; it flatters and deceives; it lifts up and casts down.
ST. CYPRIAN OF CARTHAGE: *The World and its Vanities*, *c.* 250

As soon as the subject of a state becomes too powerful, though he has done no crime, he ceases to be innocent. We do not wait until he dares to act: to be able to act is itself a crime against the state.
PIERRE CORNEILLE: *Nicomède*, II, 1651

The power of a man is his present means to obtain some future apparent good.
THOMAS HOBBES: *Leviathan*, X, 1651

Better to reign in Hell than serve in Heaven.
JOHN MILTON: *Paradise Lost*, I, 1667

They who possess the prince possess the laws.
JOHN DRYDEN: *Absalom and Achitophel*, I, 1682

The great question which, in all ages, has disturbed mankind, and brought on them the greatest part of those mischiefs which have ruined cities, depopulated countries, and disordered the peace of the world, has been, not whether there be power in the world, nor whence it came, but who should have it.
JOHN LOCKE: *Treatises on Government*, I, 1690

Arbitrary power is the natural object of temptation to a prince, as wine or women to a young fellow, or a bribe to a judge, or avarice to old age, or vanity to a woman.
JONATHAN SWIFT: *Thoughts on Various Subjects*, 1706

Let not thy will roar when thy power can but whisper.
THOMAS FULLER: *Introductio ad Prudentiam*, I, 1731

Yes, I am proud; I must be proud to see
Men, not afraid of God, afraid of me.
ALEXANDER POPE: *Epilogue to the Satires*, II, 1738

Right and truth are greater than any power, and all power is limited by right.
BENJAMIN WHICHCOTE: *Moral and Religious Aphorisms*, 1753

What a dreadful thing it is for such a wicked little imp as man to have absolute power!
HORACE WALPOLE: *Letter to William Mason*, July 4, 1778

The mind of man is fond of power; increase his prospects and you enlarge his desires.
GOUVERNEUR MORRIS: Speech in the Constitutional Convention, 1787

In the general course of human nature, a power over a man's subsistence amounts to a power over his will.
ALEXANDER HAMILTON: *The Federalist*, 1788

Power is not happiness. Security and peace are more to be desired than a name at which nations tremble.
WILLIAM GODWIN: *An Enquiry Concerning Political Justice*, 1793

The power behind the throne.
ENGLISH PHRASE, not recorded before the XIX century

I have never been able to conceive how any rational being could propose happiness to himself from the exercise of power over others.
THOMAS JEFFERSON: *Letter to Destutt Tracy*, 1811

Power, like a desolating pestilence,
Pollutes whate'er it touches.
P. B. SHELLEY: *Queen Mab*, III, 1813

Man is a toad-eating animal. The admiration of power in others is as common to man as the love of it in himself; the one makes him a tyrant, the other a slave.
WILLIAM HAZLITT: *Political Essays*, 1819

A power above all human responsibility ought to be above all human attainment.
C. C. COLTON: *Lacon*, 1820

The worst thing that can be said of the most powerful is, that they can take your life; but the same thing can be said of the most weak.
IBID.

To do anything, to dig a hole in the ground, to plant a cabbage, to hit a mark, to move a shuttle, to work a pattern — in a word, to attempt to produce any effect, and to succeed, has something in it that gratifies the lover of power.
WILLIAM HAZLITT: *The Pleasure of Painting*, 1821

Power is not revealed by striking hard or often, but by striking true.
BALZAC: *The Physiology of Marriage*, 1830

Men, such as they are, very naturally seek money or power; and power because it is as good as money.
R. W. EMERSON: *The American Scholar*, 1837

Power always has most to apprehend from its own illusions. Monarchs have incurred more hazards from the follies of their own that have grown up under the adulation of parasites, than from the machinations of their enemies.
J. FENIMORE COOPER: *The American Democrat*, intro., 1838

The highest proof of virtue is to possess boundless power without abusing it.
T. B. MACAULAY: *The Life and Writings of Addison*, 1843 (Edinburgh Review, July)

Political power is merely the organized power of one class to oppress another.
KARL MARX and FRIEDRICH ENGELS: *The Communist Manifesto*, 1848

The imbecility of men is always inviting the impudence of power.
R. W. EMERSON: *Representative Men*, I, 1850

It is wholesomer for the moral nature to be restrained, even by arbitrary power, than to be allowed to exercise arbitrary power without restraint.
J. S. MILL: *The Subjection of Women*, III, 1869

Power is the first good.
R. W. EMERSON: *Inspiration*, 1876

The way to have power is to take it.
Ascribed to W. M. TWEED (1823–78)

All public power proceeds from God.
POPE LEO XIII: *Immortale Dei*, Nov. 1, 1885

Wherever I found a living creature, there I found the will to power.
F. W. NIETZSCHE: *Thus Spake Zarathustra*, XXXIV, 1885

A living being seeks, above all, to discharge its strength. Life is will to power. Self-preservation is only one of the indirect results of that will to power, though it is the most frequent.
F. W. NIETZSCHE: *Beyond Good and Evil*, 1886

In order to obtain and hold power a man must love it. Thus the effort to get it is not likely to be coupled with goodness, but with the opposite qualities of pride, craft and cruelty. Without hypocrisy, lying, punishments, prisons, fortresses and murders, no new power can arise and no existing one hold its own.
LYOF N. TOLSTOY: *The Kingdom of God is Within You*, 1893

Power feeds on its spoils, and dies when its victims refuse to be despoiled. They can't persuade it to death; they can't vote it to death; they can't shoot it to death; but they can always starve it to death.
BENJAMIN R. TUCKER: *Instead of a Book*, 1893

Economic power is headstrong and vehement, and if it is to prove beneficial to mankind it must be securely curbed and regulated with prudence.
POPE PIUS XI: *Quadragesimo anno*, May 15, 1931

Use power to curb power.
CHINESE PROVERB

Power weakens the wicked.
WELSH PROVERB

[*See also* Ambition, Army, Atheism, Democracy, Force, Freedom, Good, Government, Greatness, Happiness, Honorable, Household, Imperialism, Independence, King, Knowledge, Land, Laughter, Law, Life, Oppression, Pardon, Passion, Philosopher, Precedent, Silence, Sovereignty, State, Struggle for Existence, Truth, Tyranny, Union, Wealth.

Power, Balance of

Now Europe's balanc'd, neither side prevails;
For nothing's left in either of the scales.
ALEXANDER POPE: *The Balance of Europe*, 1715

Power, Military

The people at large are governed much by custom. To acts of legislation or civil authority they have ever been taught to yield a willing obedience, without reasoning about their propriety; on those of military power, whether immediate or derived originally from another source, they have ever looked with a jealous and suspicious eye.
GEORGE WASHINGTON: *Letter to the President of the Continental Congress*, Dec. 14, 1777

[*See also* Militarism.

Powers, Reserved

The powers not delegated to the United States by the Constitution, nor prohibited by it to the States, are reserved to the States respectively, or to the people.
CONSTITUTION OF THE UNITED STATES, Amendment X, Dec. 15, 1791

Practise

Practise is everything.
Attributed to PERIANDER OF CORINTH, *c.* 600 B.C.

Practise makes perfect.
ENGLISH PROVERB (In its present form it is first recorded in 1560, but Apperson traces it in the form of "Use makes mastery" to 1340)

Oft bend the bow, and thou with ease shalt do,
What others can't with all their strength put to.
ROBERT HERRICK: *Hesperides*, 1648

Practise is nine-tenths.
R. W. EMERSON: *The Conduct of Life*, II, 1860

Practise is the best master. (Exercitatio optimus est magister.)
LATIN PROVERB

[*See also* Principle.

Pragmatism

Whatever satisfies the soul is truth.
WALT WHITMAN: *Leaves of Grass*, pref., 1855

All truths change, says pragmatism; that assertion is true, pragmatism also says; then that assertion will change, implying some truths do not change, which is the contradictory of the fundamental assertion of pragmatism.
H. H. HORNE: *Free Will and Human Responsibiltiy*, 1912

Pragmatism has failed us because it has attempted to fill the place that only a national poetry can adequately fill.
VAN WYCK BROOKS: *Letters and Leadership*, 1918

Prague

If you throw a stone in Prague, you throw a bit of history.
CZECH PROVERB

Prairie

Th' illimitable plain
Depastured by erratic buffaloes.

JOHN D. MCKINNON: *Descriptive Poems,* 1802

Oh, bury me not on the lone prairie,
Where the wild coyotes will howl over me,
Where the buffalo roams and the wind roars free;
Oh, bury me not on the lone prairie!

Anon.: Cowboy song, *c.* 1875

Praise

The sweetest of all sounds is praise.

ZENOPHON: *Hiero,* I, *c.* 373 B.C.

Praise ye the Lord: for it is good to sing praises unto our God; for it is pleasant; and praise is comely. PSALMS CXLVII, 1, *c.* 150 B.C.

We are all excited by the love of praise, and it is the noblest spirits that feel it most.

CICERO: *Pro archia poeta,* 62 B.C.

Falsely praising a person is lying.

ST. AUGUSTINE: *On Lying, c.* 395

Thou, O God, we praise. (Te Deum laudamus.)

Title and first line of a Latin hymn in the Roman Breviary, often ascribed to ST. AMBROSE (*c.* 340–397), but more probably written by ST. CÆSARIUS, and first recorded in his Rule for monks, *c.* 500

He who praises you for what you have not wishes to take from you what you have.

DON JUAN MANUEL: *El Conde Lucanor, c.* 1325

He is not praised whose praiser deserveth not praise.

GABRIEL HARVEY: *The Trimming of Thomas Nashe,* 1597

Our praises are our wages.

SHAKESPEARE: *The Winter's Tale,* I, *c.* 1611

[If] some infamous bawd or whore
Should praise a matron, what could hurt her more?

BEN JONSON: *To the Memory of My Beloved, the Author Mr. William Shakespeare* (in the First Folio Shakespeare), 1623

Old praise dies unless you feed it.

GEORGE HERBERT: *Outlandish Proverbs,* 1640

True praise roots and spreads. IBID.

He who refuses praise only wants to be praised again. LA ROCHEFOUCAULD: *Maxims,* 1665

In whatever terms people may praise us, they never teach us anything new. IBID.

The praise we give newcomers into the world arises from the envy we bear to those who are established. IBID.

We do not like to praise, and we never praise without a motive. Praise is flattery, artful, hidden, delicate, which gratifies differently him who praises and him who is praised. The one takes it as the reward of merit, the other bestows it to show his impartiality and discernment. IBID.

We praise heartily only those who admire us.

IBID.

I would have praised you more if you had praised me less.

LOUIS XIV OF FRANCE: To Nicholas Boileau, on receiving from him a complimentary poem, 1670

Simple praise does not put a man at his ease; there must be something solid mixed with it; and the best way of praising is to praise with the hands.

J. B. MOLIÈRE: *Le bourgeois gentilhomme,* I, 1670

With faint praises one another damn.

WILLIAM WYCHERLEY: *The Plain Dealer, c.* 1674

Praise is a debt we owe unto the virtue of others, and due unto our own from all whom malice hath not made mutes, or envy struck dumb.

THOMAS BROWNE: *Christian Morals,* I, *c.* 1680

It would be a kind of ferocity to reject indifferently all sorts of praise. One should be glad to have that which comes from good men who praise in sincerity things that are really praiseworthy.

JEAN DE LA BRUYÈRE: *Caractères,* IV, 1688

Spite of all modesty, a man must own a pleasure in the hearing of his praise.

GEORGE FARQUHAR: *The Twin Rivals,* III, 1702

Praise is the daughter of present power.

JONATHAN SWIFT: *Thoughts on Various Subjects,* 1706

Be thou the first true merit to befriend,
His praise is lost who stays till all commend.

ALEXANDER POPE: *An Essay on Criticism,* II, 1711

To what base ends, and by what abject ways
Are mortals urged through sacred lust of praise.

IBID.

There can hardly be imagined a more desirable pleasure than that of praise unmixed with any possibility of flattery.

RICHARD STEELE: *The Spectator,* Dec. 3, 1711

The love of praise, howe'er conceal'd by art,
Reigns more or less, and glows in ev'ry heart.

EDWARD YOUNG: *Love of Fame,* I, 1728

Be not extravagantly high in expression of thy commendations of men thou likest; it may make the hearer's stomach rise.

THOMAS FULLER: *Introductio ad Prudentiam,* I, 1731

Praise makes good men better and bad men worse.
THOMAS FULLER: *Gnomologia,* 1732

They that value not praise will never do anything worthy of praise. IBID.

Praise undeserv'd is scandal in disguise.
ALEXANDER POPE: *An Essay on Man,* I, 1733 (Sometimes *satire* displaces *scandal*)

Praise, tho' it may be our due, is not like a bank-bill, to be paid upon demand; to be valuable, it must be voluntary. When we are dun'd for it, we have a right and privilege to refuse it.
COLLEY CIBBER: *Apology For His Life,* II, 1740

He who loves praise, loves temptation.
THOMAS WILSON: *Maxims of Piety and of Christianity, c.* 1755

Of praise a mere glutton, he swallowed what came,
And the puff of a dunce, he mistook it for fame.
OLIVER GOLDSMITH: *Retaliation,* 1774

Praise [and] money are the two powerful corrupters of mankind.
SAMUEL JOHNSON: To Hester Thrale, Oct. 27, 1783

I praise loudly; I blame softly.
CATHERINE II OF RUSSIA (1729–96)

Approbation from Sir Hubert Stanley is praise indeed.
THOMAS MORTON: *A Cure for the Heartache,* V, 1797

Praise to the face is open disgrace.
ENGLISH PROVERB, not recorded before the XIX century

It is perhaps almost as difficult at once with judgment and feeling to praise great actions as to perform them.
FISHER AMES: Oration in Boston, 1800 (Feb. 8)

Among the smaller duties of life I hardly know any one more important than that of not praising where praise is not due.
SYDNEY SMITH: *Lectures on Moral Philosophy,* 1804

Praises of the unworthy are robberies of the deserving.
S. T. COLERIDGE: *Biographia Literaria,* III, 1817

Only the praise of one who has been praised can give pleasure.
LUDWIG VAN BEETHOVEN: *Conversation-book,* 1825 (Cf. HARVEY, *ante,* 1597)

The praise of a fool is incense to the wisest of us.
BENJAMIN DISRAELI: *Vivian Grey,* VII, 1827

I did some excellent things indifferently,
Some bad things excellently. Both were praised,
The latter loudest.
E. B. BROWNING: *Aurora Leigh,* III, 1857

It is only the young who can receive much reward from men's praise: the old, when they are great, get too far beyond and above you to care what you think of them.
JOHN RUSKIN: *The Political Economy of Art,* I, 1857

There is no weapon that slays
Its victim so surely (if well aimed) as praise.
E. R. BULWER-LYTTON (OWEN MEREDITH): *Lucile,* II, 1860

Beware of the man who is praised by everybody. ARAB PROVERB

If one man praises you a thousand will repeat the praise. JAPANESE PROVERB

Praise is the beginning of blame. IBID.

Never believe those who praise you. (Ne credas laudatoribus tuis.) LATIN PROVERB

Praise the wise man behind his back, but a woman to her face. WELSH PROVERB

[*See also* Admonition, Ambition, Approbation, Blame, Censure, Child, Damn, Fame, Modesty, Self-praise.

Prayer

Pray, for all men need the aid of the gods.
HOMER: *Odyssey,* III, *c.* 800 B.C.

Pray without ceasing.
I THESSALONIANS V, 17, *c.* 51

Pray for us. (Orate pro nobis.)
II THESSALONIANS III, I, *c.* 51 (The Latin is from the Vulgate)

The effectual fervent prayer of a righteous man availeth much. JAMES V, 16, *c.* 60

Nothing is so expensive as what is acquired by prayer. SENECA: *De beneficiis,* II, *c.* 63

What things soever ye desire, when ye pray, believe that ye receive them, and ye shall have them. MARK XI, 24, *c.* 70

Watch and pray. (Vigilate et orate.)
MARK XIII, 33 (The Latin is from the Vulgate)

When thou prayest, thou shalt not be as the hypocrites are: for they love to pray standing in the synagogues and in the corners of the streets, that they may be seen of men. But thou, when thou prayest, enter into thy closet, and when thou hast shut thy door, pray to thy Father which is in secret; and thy Father which seeth in secret shall reward thee openly. MATTHEW VI, 5–6, *c.* 75

Ask, and it shall be given you; seek, and ye shall find; knock, and it shall be opened unto you. MATTHEW VII, 7

Men ought always to pray, and not to faint.
LUKE XVIII, 1, *c.* 75

The only prayer which a well-meaning man can pray is, O ye gods, give me whatever is fitting unto me!
APOLLONIUS OF TYANA (*c.* 10 B.C.–80 A.D.)

God does not listen to the prayer of the lazy.
POPE XYSTUS I: *The Ring, c.* 150

Pray to God only for those things which you cannot obtain from man. IBID.

Prayer is conversation with God.
CLEMENT OF ALEXANDRIA: *Stromateis*, VII, *c.* 193

Prayers for rain should not be offered just before the season for rain.
THE TALMUD (*Ta'anit*), *c.* 200

Pray to God for mercy until the last shovelful of earth is cast upon thy grave. IBID.

Prayer altogether blots out very little and daily sins.
ST. AUGUSTINE: *On Faith, Hope, and Charity, c.* 421

In a single day I have prayed as many as a hundred times, and in the night almost as often. ST. PATRICK: *Confessio, c.* 450

Praying at work. (Orando laborando.)
MOTTO OF RUGBY SCHOOL, England, *c.* 1575

His worst fault is, he's given to prayer; he is something peevish that way.
SHAKESPEARE: *The Merry Wives of Windsor*, I, *c.* 1600

My words fly up, my thoughts remain below.
SHAKESPEARE: *Hamlet*, III, *c.* 1601

We, ignorant of ourselves,
Beg often our own harms, which the wise powers
Deny us for our good; so find we profit
By losing of our prayers.
SHAKESPEARE: *Antony and Cleopatra*, II, *c.* 1606

Prayer should be the key of the morning and the lock of the night.
OWEN FELLTHAM: *Resolves, c.* 1620

Resort to sermons, but to prayers most:
Praying's the end of preaching.
GEORGE HERBERT: *The Temple*, 1633

Who goes to bed and doth not pray
Maketh two nights to ev'ry day. IBID.

She's now at her devotions,
Busy with Heaven, and wearing out the earth
With her stiff knees.
JAMES SHIRLEY: *The Cardinal*, IV, 1641

A good prayer, though often used, is still fresh and fair in the ears and eyes of Heaven.
THOMAS FULLER: *Good Thoughts in Bad Times*, 1645

In prayer the lips ne'er act the winning part,
Without the sweet concurrence of the heart.
ROBERT HERRICK: *Noble Numbers*, 1647

If by prayer
Incessant I could hope to change the will
Of Him who all things can, I would not cease
To weary Him with my assiduous cries.
JOHN MILTON: *Paradise Lost*, XI, 1667

Prayer should be short, without giving God Almighty reasons why He should grant this, or that; He knows best what is good for us. If your boy should ask you a suit of clothes, and give your reasons, would you endure it? You know it better than he; let him ask a suit of clothes.
JOHN SELDEN: *Table-Talk*, 1689

None can pray well but he that lives well.
THOMAS FULLER: *Gnomologia*, 1732

O God, help our side, and if you can't, then at least don't help those scoundrels.
PRINCE LEOPOLD OF ANHALT-DESSAU: Prayer before the battle of Kesseldorf, Dec. 14, 1745

Work as if you were to live 100 years; pray as if you were to die tomorrow.
BENJAMIN FRANKLIN: *Poor Richard's Almanac*, 1757

A single grateful thought toward Heaven is the most perfect prayer.
G. E. LESSING: *Minna von Barnhelm*, II, 1767

I have never made but one prayer to God, a very short one: "O Lord, make my enemies ridiculous." And God granted it.
VOLTAIRE: *Letter to M. Damiliville*, May 16, 1767

At church, with meek and unaffected grace,
His looks adorn'd the venerable place;
Truth from his lips prevailed with double sway,
And fools, who came to scoff, remain'd to pray.
OLIVER GOLDSMITH: *The Deserted Village*, 1770

The wish to talk to God is absurd. We cannot talk to one we cannot comprehend — and we cannot comprehend God; we can only believe in Him. The uses of prayer are thus only subjective.
IMMANUEL KANT: Lecture at Königsberg, 1775

Now I lay me down to sleep;
I pray the Lord my soul to keep.
If I should die before I wake,
I pray the Lord my soul to take.
Author unknown (First printed in a late edition of the *New England Primer*, 1781)

I was alarmed, and prayed God that, however He might afflict my body, He would spare my understanding. This prayer, that I might try

the integrity of my faculties, I made in Latin verse. The lines were not very good.
SAMUEL JOHNSON: *Letter to Hester Thrale,* June 19, 1783

I know of no good prayers but those in the Book of Common Prayer.
SAMUEL JOHNSON: *Boswell's Life,* June 11, 1784

He prayeth best who loveth best
All things both great and small;
For the dear God who loveth us,
He made and loveth all.
S. T. COLERIDGE: *The Ancient Mariner,* VII, 1798

Oh, sweeter than the marriage-feast,
'Tis sweeter far to me,
To walk together to the kirk
With a goodly company:
To walk together to the kirk,
And all together pray. IBID.

To pray together, in whatever tongue or ritual, is the most tender brotherhood of hope and sympathy that men can contract in this life.
ANNA LOUISE DE STAËL: *Corinne,* X, 1807

I used my prayers as gunners use their swivels, turning them every way as the various cases required.
WILLIAM HUNTINGTON: *God the Guardian of the Poor,* 1820

The prayers of an old man are the only contributions left in his power.
THOMAS JEFFERSON: *Letter to Mrs. K. D. Morgan,* 1822

He pray'd by quantity,
And with his repetitions, long and loud,
All knees were weary.
ROBERT POLLOK: *The Course of Time,* VIII, 1827

No man ever prayed heartily without learning something. R. W. EMERSON: *Nature,* 1836

More things are wrought by prayer
Than this world dreams of.
ALFRED TENNYSON: *Morte d'Arthur,* 1842

The man sprang to his feet,
Stood erect, caught at God's skirts, and prayed.
ROBERT BROWNING: *Instans Tyrannus,* 1846

Do not usually pray, extempore, above eight or ten minutes (at most) without intermission.
The Doctrines and Discipline of the Methodist Episcopal Church South, I, 1846

Kneel undisturbed, fair saint!
Pour out your praise or plaint
Meekly and duly;
I will not enter there,
To sully your pure prayer
With thoughts unruly.
W. M. THACKERAY: *The Church Porch,* 1849

Now, boys, remember one thing: do not make long prayers; always remember that the Lord knows something.
Ascribed by JOSEPH H. CHOATE to a speaker addressing a graduating class at a theological seminary in Tennessee, *c.* 1850

The dull pray; the geniuses are light mockers.
R. W. EMERSON: *Representative Men,* IV, 1850

He offered a prayer so deeply devout that he seemed kneeling and praying at the bottom of the sea.
HERMAN MELVILLE: *Moby Dick,* IX, 1851

And that inverted bowl they call the sky,
Whereunder crawling coop'd we live and die,
Lift not your hands to it for help — for it
As impotently moves as you or I.
EDWARD FITZGERALD: Tr. of OMAR KHAYYÁM: *Rubáiyát* (*c.* 1100), 1857

We, on our side, are praying Him to give us victory, because we believe we are right; but those on the other side pray Him, too, for victory, believing they are right. What must He think of us?
ABRAHAM LINCOLN: To the Rev. Byron Sunderland, chaplain of the Senate, 1862

Both read the same Bible, and pray to the same God; and each invokes His aid against the other.
ABRAHAM LINCOLN: Inaugural address, March 4, 1865

I bow my forehead to the dust,
I veil mine eyes for shame,
And urge, in trembling self-distrust,
A prayer without a claim.
J. G. WHITTIER: *The Eternal Goodness,* 1867

Prayer is and remains always a native and deepest impulse of the soul of man.
THOMAS CARLYLE: *Letter to George A. Duncan,* June 9, 1870

The feeling which prompts prayer . . . I should like to see guided, not extinguished — devoted to practicable objects instead of wasted upon air.
JOHN TYNDALL: *Fragments of Science for Unscientific People,* II, 1871

Whenever a man lives by prayer you will find that he eats considerable besides.
R. G. INGERSOLL: Speech in Chicago, Nov. 26, 1882

Man obtains by prayer whatever he wills.
POPE LEO XIII: *Exeunte jam anno,* Dec. 25, 1888

When the gods wish to punish us they answer our prayers.
OSCAR WILDE: *An Ideal Husband,* II, 1895

Plenty well, no pray; big bellyache, heap God.
Ascribed by AMBROSE BIERCE to " the simple Red Man of the Western Wild," 1906

Prayer is not to be used as a confessional, to cancel sin. Such an error would impede true religion. Sin is forgiven only as it is destroyed by Christ — Truth and Light.
MARY BAKER G. EDDY: *Science and Health*, I, 1908

I like long prayers,
The kind that stretch
Like elastic bands.
I always sit around,
Holding my breath,
Hoping they'll snap back
And hit the preacher
On the nose.
R. C. BROWN: *My Marjonary*, 1915

Prayer will remove the fundamental cause of present day difficulties.
POPE PIUS XI: *Caritate Christi compulsi*, May 3, 1932

You may talk about me just as much as you please,
I'm goin' to talk about you when I git on my knees.
American Negro song

Prayer is the pillow of religion.
ARAB PROVERB

I pray like a beggar asking alms at the door of a farmhouse he longs to set afire.
Author unidentified

Pray for the soul of Gabriel John,
Who died in the year eighteen-hundred and one
You may if you please, or let it alone,
For it's all one
To Gabriel John,
Who died in the year eighteen-hundred and one.
IBID.

Hail to the jewel in the lotus. (Om, mani padme hom.)
Buddhist formula of prayer

Come to prayer! Come to prayer!
For prayer is better than sleep!
(Haya ala salat! Haya ala salat!
Inna al salat khair minn ill naum!)
Call of the Moslem muezzin at the five daily hours of prayer

Prayer is a cry of hope.
FRENCH PROVERB

The fewer the words, the better the prayer.
GERMAN PROVERB

God does not listen to the prayers of the proud.
HEBREW PROVERB

Pray and toil. (Ora et labora.)
LATIN PHRASE (Cf. MOTTO OF RUGBY, *ante*, 1575)

To have prayed well is to have endeavored well. (Bene orasse est bene studuisse.)
LATIN PROVERB

Prayer at the right time is better than the whole world and everything in it.
MOROCCAN PROVERB

Pray to God, but row for the shore.
RUSSIAN PROVERB

Whenever you pray, you pray for a miracle.
IBID.

God does not hear silent prayer.
SPANISH PROVERB

Pray to God, but hammer away.
IBID.

[*See also* Blessing, Creed, Curse, Ejaculation, Exegesis, Fasting, Fighting, Hypocrite, Justice, Labor, Marriage, Meal, Piety, Prudence, Sea.

Prayer, Lord's

[*See* Lord's Prayer.

Preacher

A good preacher should have these qualities and virtues: first, to teach systematically; second, he should have a ready wit; third, he should be eloquent; fourth, he should have a good voice; fifth, a good memory; sixth, he should know when to make an end; seventh, he should be sure of his doctrine; eighth, he should venture and engage body and blood, wealth and honor, in the world; ninth, he should suffer himself to be mocked and jeered of everyone.
MARTIN LUTHER: *Table-Talk*, CCCC, 1569

A preacher must be both soldier and shepherd. He must nourish, defend, and teach; he must have teeth in his mouth, and be able to bite and to fight.
MARTIN LUTHER: *Table-Talk*, CCCCIII

An upright, godly, and true preacher should direct his preaching to the poor, simple sort of people, like a mother that stills her child, dandles and plays with it, presenting it with milk from her own breast, and needing neither malmsey nor muscadin for it.
MARTIN LUTHER: *Table-Talk*, CCCCXXVII

No one should be allowed to preach who is not a pastor of some congregation; and he ought to preach to his own flock exclusively, and nowhere else.
EDWIN SANDYS (BISHOP OF LONDON): *Letter to Henry Bullinger of Zürich*, setting forth the principles of the Puritans, 1573

When Attila entered even into the bowels of Europe all the preachers of Christendom did nothing else but bewail the wretchedness of that time.
PHILIP MORNAY: *De la vérité de la religion chrétienne*, 1581

The test of a preacher is that his congregation goes away saying, not What a lovely sermon, but, I will do something!
ST. FRANCIS DE SALES: *Introduction to the Devout Life*, 1609

He preaches well that lives well.
CERVANTES: *Don Quixote*, II, 1615

The worst speak something good. If all want sense,
God takes a text, and preaches patience.
GEORGE HERBERT: *The Temple*, 1633

His preaching much, but more his practise wrought;
A living sermon of the truths he taught.
JOHN DRYDEN: *The Character of a Good Parson*, 1680

Our new curate preached, a pretty hopeful young man, yet somewhat raw, newly come from college, full of Latin sentences, which in time will wear off.
JOHN EVELYN: *Diary*, May 20, 1681

I preach forever, but I preach in vain.
GEORGE CRABBE: *The Parish Register*, II, 1807

See yonder preacher to his people pass,
Borne up and swelled by tabernacle-gas.
GEORGE CRABBE: *The Borough*, IV, 1810

First, the preacher speaks through his nose:
Second, his gesture is too emphatic:
Thirdly, to waive what's pedagogic,
The subject-matter itself lacks logic:
Fourthly, the English is ungrammatic.
ROBERT BROWNING: *Christmas Eve*, 1850

The pig-of-lead-like pressure
Of the preaching man's immense stupidity.
IBID.

A powerful preacher is open to the same sense of enjoyment — an awful, tremulous, goose-flesh sort of state, but still enjoyment — that a great tragedian feels when he curdles the blood of his audience.
O. W. HOLMES: *The Guardian Angel*, XIII, 1867

Every preacher who preaches ably has two doors to his church; one where he attracts people in and the other through which he preaches them out.
ELBERT HUBBARD: *Roycroft Dictionary and Book of Epigrams*, 1923

The preacher for this day must have the heart of a lion, the skin of a hippopotamus, the agility of a greyhound, the patience of a donkey, the wisdom of an elephant, the industry of an ant, and as many lives as a cat.
EDGAR DEWITT JONES: Address at Transylvania College, Lexington, Ky., June 4, 1934

When de preacher comes in, de chickens cry.
AMERICAN NEGRO SAYING

The unruliest students make the most pious preachers.
GERMAN PROVERB

[*See also* Clergy, Clergyman, Gallows, Hell, Monday, Preaching, Priest, Pulpit, Sermon.

Preaching

It pleased God by the foolishness of preaching to save them that believe.
I CORINTHIANS I, 21, *c.* 55

Preach the word; be instant in season, out of season; reprove, rebuke, exhort with all long-suffering and doctrine.
II TIMOTHY IV, 2, *c.* 65

Paul preached . . . until midnight.
ACTS XX, 7, *c.* 75

As Paul was long preaching, [Eutychus] sunk down with sleep, and fell down from the third loft, and was taken up dead.
IBID.

The preaching of the word of God unto the people . . . the Scripture calleth meat; not strawberries, that come but once a year, and tarry not long, but are soon gone; but it is meat, it is no dainties.
HUGH LATIMER: *Sermon of the Ploughers*, Jan. 18, 1548

To preach plain and simply is a great art: Christ Himself talks of tilling ground, of mustard seed, &c.; He used altogether homely and simple similitudes.
MARTIN LUTHER: *Table-Talk*, CCCCX, 1569

The finical goosery of your neat sermon actor.
JOHN MILTON: *An Apology for Smectymnuus*, 1642

Amongst the first things that seem to be useless may be reckoned the high tossing and swaggering preaching, either mountingly eloquent, or profoundly learned.
JOHN EACHARD: *The Grounds and Occasions of the Contempt of the Clergy and Religion*, 1670

The preaching of divines helps to preserve well-inclined men in the course of virtue, but seldom or never reclaims the vicious.
JONATHAN SWIFT: *Thoughts on Various Subjects*, 1706

The frightful engines of ecclesiastical councils, of diabolical malice, and Calvinistical good-nature never failed to terrify me exceedingly whenever I thought of preaching.
JOHN ADAMS: *Letter to Richard Cranch*, Aug. 29, 1756

A woman's preaching is like a dog's walking on its hind legs. It is not done well, and you are surprised to find it done at all.
SAMUEL JOHNSON: *Boswell's Life*, July 30, 1763

A man who preaches in the stocks will always have hearers enough.
SAMUEL JOHNSON: *Boswell's Life*, May 7, 1773

The clergy are allowed about twenty-six hours every year for the instruction of their fellow-creatures.
SYDNEY SMITH: *Six Sermons*, pref., 1800

The object of preaching is constantly to remind mankind of what mankind are constantly forgetting; not to supply the defects of human intelligence, but to fortify the feebleness of human resolutions. IBID.

When we preach unworthily it is not always quite in vain. There is poetic truth concealed in all the commonplaces of prayer and of sermons, and though foolishly spoken, they may be wisely heard.
R. W. EMERSON: Address at the Divinity College, Cambridge, Mass., July 15, 1838

I like the silent church before the service begins, better than any preaching.
R. W. EMERSON: *Self-Reliance*, 1841

We recommend morning preaching at five o'clock in the Summer, and six in the Winter, wherever it is practicable.
The Doctrines and Discipline of the Methodist Episcopal Church South, I, 1846

It is our duty to bark in the house of the Lord.
Saying of medieval preachers

[*See also* Clergyman, Devil, Politics, Preacher, Sermon.

Precedence

An two men ride of a horse, one must ride behind.
SHAKESPEARE: *Much Ado About Nothing*, III, *c.* 1599

We reverence gray-headed doctrines, though feeble, decrepit and within a step of dust; and on this account maintain opinions which have nothing but our charity to uphold them.
JOSEPH GLANVILL: *The Vanity of Dogmatizing*, XV, 1661

They who are in dignity, or in office, have precedence in all places: but whilst they are young they ought to respect them who are their equals in birth or other qualities, although they have not any public charge, if they be much more aged, principally if they have the degree of doctorship: nay, when they give to them the chiefest place, they ought notwithstanding at the first to refuse it, afterwards to take it civilly with thanksgiving.
FRANCIS HAWKINS: *Youth's Behavior*, II, 1663

There is no settling the point of precedency between a louse and a flea.
SAMUEL JOHNSON: *Boswell's Life*, 1783

Some ne'er advance a judgment of their own,
But catch the spreading notion of the town;
They reason and conclude by precedent,
And own stale nonsense which they ne'er invent.
ALEXANDER POPE: *An Essay on Criticism*, II, 1711

Precedent, though it be evidence of law, is not law in itself.
LORD MANSFIELD: *Judgment in Jones* vs. *Randall*, 1774

One precedent in favor of power is stronger than an hundred against it.
THOMAS JEFFERSON: *Notes on Virginia*, 1782

It is better for the subject that even faulty precedents should not be shaken than that the law should be uncertain.
MR. JUSTICE GROSE: *Judgment in Heathcote* vs. *Crookshanks*, 1787

A precedent embalms a principle.
WILLIAM SCOTT (BARON STOWELL): Opinion as Attorney-General of England, 1788

Adhere to precedents and do not unsettle things established. (Stare decisis, et non quieta movere.)
LEGAL MAXIM (Commonly called the doctrine of *stare decisis*)

[*See also* Judgment, Law.

Precept

Precept must be upon precept, precept upon precept; line upon line, line upon line, here a little, and there a little.
ISAIAH XXVIII, 10, *c.* 700 B.C.

Precept has generally been posterior to performance.
SAMUEL JOHNSON: *The Rambler*, Aug. 31, 1751

[*See also* Age (Old), Example.

Precocity

There cannot be sound sap in that which has too quickly acquired maturity.
CICERO: *De oratore*, II, *c.* 80 B.C.

It is seldom that a premature shoot of genius arrives at maturity.
QUINTILIAN: *De institutione oratoria*, I, *c.* 90

It early pricks that will be a thorn.
ENGLISH PROVERB, traced to the XIV century

A man of five may be a fool of fifteen.
JAMES KELLY: *Complete Collection of Scottish Proverbs*, 1721

A man at sixteen will prove a child at sixty.
THOMAS FULLER: *Gnomologia*, 1732

Early ripe, early rotten. IBID.

As yet a child, nor yet a fool to fame,
I lisp'd in numbers, for the numbers came.
ALEXANDER POPE: *An Epistle to Dr. Arbuthnot*, 1735

Nature wishes children to be children before they are men. If we pervert this order we shall produce precocious fruits — fruits which have neither maturity nor savor, and are soon corrupted. We shall have young sages and old children.

J.-J. ROUSSEAU: *Émile,* I, 1762

At ten years a wonder-child; at fifteen a talented youth; at twenty a common man.

JAPANESE PROVERB

He who is precociously wise dies before he is old. LATIN PROVERB

[*See also* Prodigy.

Predestination

No man can hasten my doom. The fate of the coward and the brave has been alike determined from their birth.

HOMER: *Iliad,* VI, *c.* 800 B.C.

Has any good fortune befallen thee? If so, it has been predestined since the beginning of the world.

MARCUS AURELIUS: *Meditations,* IV, *c.* 170

The age, the actions, the wealth, the knowledge, and even the death, of every one is determined in his mother's womb.

The Hitopadesa, intro., *c.* 500

Predestination we call the eternal decree of God whereby He has determined what He would have to become of every individual of mankind. Eternal life is ordained for some, and eternal damnation for others.

JOHN CALVIN: *Institutes of the Christian Religion,* III, 1536

Before a child comes into the world, it has its lot assigned already, and it is ordained and determined what and how much it shall have.

MARTIN LUTHER: *Table-Talk,* CXXIII, 1569

That God has foreordained everything is self-evident.

RENÉ DESCARTES: *Principles of Philosophy,* I, 1644

By the decree of God for the manifestation of His glory, some men and angels are predestinated unto everlasting life, and others foreordained to everlasting death.

THE SAVOY DECLARATION, 1658

O Thou, wha in the heavens dost dwell,
Wha, as it pleases best thysel',
Sends ane to Heaven, and ten to Hell,
A' for thy glory,
And no for ony guid or ill
They've done afore thee!

ROBERT BURNS: *Holy Willie's Prayer,* 1785

I am a predestinarian, as much so as the Turks are. I have always been so. When destiny wills, it must be obeyed.

NAPOLEON I: To Barry E. O'Meara at St. Helena, Nov. 9, 1816

The recognition of God's absolute sovereignty in the natural and moral worlds, and especially the absolute sovereignty of His free grace as the only ground of human salvation.

J. G. SCHOLTEN: *Abschiedsrede,* 1881

From coupler-flange to spindle-guide I see
Thy Hand, O God —
Predestination in the stride o' yon connecting-rod.

RUDYARD KIPLING: *M'Andrew's Hymn,* 1893

Interdependence absolute, foreseen, ordained, decreed. IBID.

There was a young man who said " Damn!
It is borne upon me that I am
An engine which moves
In predestinate grooves;
I'm not even a bus: I'm a tram."

Author unidentified

The pestilence lasted seven years, but not a man died before his year.

HEBREW PROVERB

[*See also* Determinism, Eternal Recurrence, Fate.

Preface

Presumption or meanness are both too often the only articles to be discovered in a preface. Whilst one author haughtily affects to despise the public attention, another timidly courts it.

GEORGE CRABBE: *Inebriety,* pref., 1775

In the preface the author usually gives a summary of what has been written on the same subject before; he acknowledges the assistance he has received from different sources, and the reasons of his dissent from former writers; he confesses that certain parts have been less attentively considered than others, and that information has come to his hands too late to be made use of; he points out many things in the composition of his work which he thinks may provoke animadversion, and endeavors to defend or palliate his own practice.

EDWARD COPLESTON (BISHOP OF LLANDAFF): *Advice to a Young Reviewer,* 1807

A preface is written to the public — a thing I cannot help looking upon as an enemy, and which I cannot address without feelings of hostility.

JOHN KEATS: *Letter to J. H. Reynolds,* April 9, 1818

The essays want no preface: they are all preface. A preface is nothing but a talk with the reader; and they do nothing else.

CHARLES LAMB: *Essays of Elia,* dedication, 1823

It is very seldom that the preface of a work is read.

GEORGE BORROW: *The Bible in Spain,* pref., 1843

Three great prefaces challenge the admiration of scholars — Calvin's to his Institutes, De Thou's to his History, and Casaubon's to his Polybius.

O. W. HOLMES: *Scholastic and Bedside Teaching,* 1867 (Lecture at Harvard, Nov. 6)

Prefaces are like speeches before the curtain; they make even the most self-forgetful performers self-conscious.

W. A. NEILSON: In the Saturday Review (New York), March 9, 1940

Pregnancy

It is a sad burden to carry a dead man's child.

THOMAS FULLER: *Church History,* II, 1655 (Cited as a proverb)

A ship under sail and a big-bellied woman are the handsomest two things that can be seen common.

BENJAMIN FRANKLIN: *Poor Richard's Almanac,* 1735

As women wish to be who love their lords.

JOHN HOME: *Douglas,* I, 1756

Next at our altar stood a luckless pair,
Brought by strong passions and a warrant there;
By long rent cloak, hung loosely, strove the bride,
From every eye, what all perceived, to hide.

GEORGE CRABBE: *The Parish Register,* II, 1807

[*See also* Ferry, Hysteria.

Prejudice

A fox should not be of the jury at a goose's trial. THOMAS FULLER: *Gnomologia,* 1732

Our prejudices are our mistresses; reason is at best our wife, very often needed, but seldom minded.

LORD CHESTERFIELD: *Letter to his son,* April 13, 1752

He who never leaves his country is full of prejudices.

CARLO GOLDONI: *Pamela Nubile,* I, 1757

Chase prejudices out of the door and they return through the window.

FREDERICK THE GREAT: *Letter to Voltaire,* March 19, 1771

To be prejudiced is always to be weak; yet there are prejudices so near to laudable that they have been often praised, and are always pardoned.

SAMUEL JOHNSON: *Taxation No Tyranny,* 1775

He finds his fellow guilty of a skin
Not colored like his own.

WILLIAM COWPER: *The Task,* 1785

An oration proving that the religion of Mahomet is false would fatigue us, because we are already convinced; so, if it attempted to show that it is true, because we can never be persuaded that it is true.

T. J. HOGG: *Letter to P. B. Shelley,* Feb., 1820

No wise man can have a contempt for the prejudices of others; and he should even stand in a certain awe of his own, as if they were aged parents and monitors. They may in the end prove wiser than he.

WILLIAM HAZLITT: *Characteristics,* LV, 1823

America owes most of its social prejudices to the exaggerated religious opinions of the different sects which were so instrumental in establishing the colonies.

J. FENIMORE COOPER: *The American Democrat,* XV, 1838

Without the aid of prejudice and custom, I should not be able to find my way across the room.

WILLIAM HAZLITT: *Sketches and Essays,* 1839

In the last analysis, we see only what we are ready to see, what we have been taught to see. We eliminate and ignore everything that is not a part of our prejudices.

J. M. CHARCOT: *De l'expectation en médecine,* 1857

My corns ache, I get gouty, and my prejudices swell like varicose veins.

JAMES HUNEKER: *Old Fogy,* I, 1913

I try not to be prejudiced, but do not make much headway against it.

E. W. HOWE: *Sinner Sermons,* 1926

[*See also* Animal, Error, Judge.

Prelate

Who is the most diligent bishop and prelate in all England, and passeth all the rest in doing his office? I will tell you: it is the Devil.

HUGH LATIMER: *Sermons,* I, 1549

Pope, cardinals, bishops, are a pack of guzzling, stuffing wretches, rich, wallowing in wealth and laziness, resting secure in their power, and never, for a moment, thinking of accomplishing God's will.

MARTIN LUTHER: *Table-Talk,* CCCCXXXII, 1569

Discretion, gentle manners, common sense, and good nature are, in men of high ecclesiastical station, of far greater importance than the greatest skill in discriminating between sublapsarian and supralapsarian doctrines.

SYDNEY SMITH: In the Edinburgh Review, 1822

[*See also* Abbot, Bishop.

Premiss

[*See* Fact.

Preparedness

Keep the munition, watch the way, make thy loins strong, fortify thy power mightily.
NAHUM II, 1, *c.* 625 B.C.

Draw thee waters for the siege, fortify thy strong holds: go into clay, and tread the mortar, making strong the brickkiln.
NAHUM III, 14

To lead an untrained people to war is to throw them away.
CONFUCIUS: *Analects*, XIII, *c.* 500 B.C.

It is from their enemies, not their friends, that cities are taught to build walls and ships of war. This lesson saves their children, their homes and their goods.
ARISTOPHANES: *The Birds*, 414 B.C.

We should lay up in peace what we shall need in war.
PUBLILIUS SYRUS: *Sententiæ*, *c.* 50 B.C.

Let your loins be girded about, and your lights burning. LUKE XII, 35, *c.* 75

Preparation gives more to hope than it brings with it. A man doth often strip himself into his doublet, to leap shorter than he did in his gown.
MICHEL DE MONTAIGNE: *Essays*, III, 1588

The sword drawn to prevent the drawing of swords.
SAMUEL PURCHAS: *Purchas His Pilgrimage*, 1612

The commonwealth of Venice in their armory have this inscription: "Happy is that city which in time of peace thinks of war."
ROBERT BURTON: *The Anatomy of Melancholy*, II, 1621

They that are booted are not always ready.
GEORGE HERBERT: *Outlandish Proverbs*, 1640

In fair weather prepare for foul.
THOMAS FULLER: *Gnomologia*, 1732

There is nothing so likely to produce peace as to be well prepared to meet an enemy.
GEORGE WASHINGTON: *Letter to Elbridge Gerry*, Jan. 29, 1780

If we are wise, let us prepare for the worst.
GEORGE WASHINGTON: *Letter to James McHenry*, 1782

To be prepared for war is one of the most effectual means of preserving peace.
GEORGE WASHINGTON: Address to Congress, Jan. 8, 1790

A free people ought not only to be armed, but disciplined. IBID.

If we desire to avoid insult we must be able to repel it; if we desire to secure peace, one of the powerful instruments of our rising prosperity, it must be known that we are at all times ready for war.
GEORGE WASHINGTON: Address to Congress, Dec. 3, 1793

Sound principles will not justify our taxing the industry of our fellow citizens to accumulate treasure for wars to happen we know not when, and which might not perhaps happen but from the temptations offered by that treasure.
THOMAS JEFFERSON: Message to Congress, 1801

No wolf will leave a sheep to dine upon a porcupine. C. C. COLTON: *Lacon*, 1820

Pride, arrogance and the lust of conquest are the natural and bitter fruits of military preparation — fruits fatal to national peace and happiness.
JOHN JAY: *A Review of the Causes and Consequences of the Mexican War*, XXXVII, 1849

Let us set Germany, so to speak, in the saddle. It will soon know how to ride.
OTTO VON BISMARCK: Speech in the North-German Reichstag, March 11, 1867

We are more than ready; there is not a gaiter button wanting.
EDMOND LE BŒUF (MINISTER OF WAR): To the French Legislative Assembly on the outbreak of the Franco-Prussian War, 1870

We don't want to fight, but by jingo if we do
We've got the ships, we've got the men, we've got the money too.
G. W. HUNT: Music-hall song, 1878

Again and again we have owed peace to the fact that we were prepared for war.
THEODORE ROOSEVELT: Speech at the Naval War College, June, 1897

The voice of the weakling or the craven counts for nothing when he clamors for peace; but the voice of the just man armed is potent. We need to keep in a condition of preparedness, especially as regards our navy, not because we want war, but because we desire to stand with those whose plea for peace is listened to with respectful attention.
THEODORE ROOSEVELT: Speech in New York, Nov. 11, 1902

Who carries a sword, carries peace.
FRENCH PROVERB

One sword keeps another in the scabbard.
GERMAN PROVERB

In time of peace prepare for war.
GREEK PROVERB

If you want peace be prepared for war. (Si vis pacem, para bellum.) LATIN PROVERB

Always prepared. (Semper paratus.)
LATIN SAYING

Preposition

A preposition is a very bad word to end a sentence with.
Ascribed to an unnamed English school-inspector

Presbyterian

Presbytery is no religion for a gentleman.
CHARLES II OF ENGLAND: To the Earl of Lauderdale, *c.* 1660

A Presbyterian? Sour.
ALEXANDER POPE: *Moral Essays*, I (Of the Knowledge and Characters of Men), 1733

The dog is a Scotchman, and a Presbyterian, and everything he should not be.
SAMUEL JOHNSON: *Boswell's Life*, April 20, 1781

The Presbyterian clergy are the loudest, the most intolerant of all sects; the most tyrannical and ambitious, ready at the word of the law-giver, if such a word could now be obtained, to put their torch to the pile, and to rekindle in this virgin hemisphere the flame in which their oracle, Calvin, consumed poor Servetus.
THOMAS JEFFERSON: *Letter to William Short*, April 13, 1820

The religion of the Scotch Protestants is simply pork-eating Judaism.
HEINRICH HEINE: *Confessions*, 1854

[*See also* Blue.

Present

Enjoy the present. (Carpe diem.)
HORACE: *Carmina*, I, *c.* 20 B.C.

Past and to come seem best; things present worst.
SHAKESPEARE: *II Henry IV*, I, *c.* 1598

Praise they that will times past, I joy to see
Myself now live: this age best pleaseth me.
ROBERT HERRICK: *Hesperides*, 1648

Present joys are more to flesh and blood
Than a dull prospect of a distant good.
JOHN DRYDEN: *The Hind and the Panther*, III, 1687

Many witty authors compare the present time to an isthmus or narrow neck of land that rises in the midst of an ocean, immeasurably diffused on either side of it.
JOSEPH ADDISON: *The Spectator*, Sept. 6, 1714

The present hour alone is man's.
SAMUEL JOHNSON: *Irene*, III, 1749

There is no time like the present time.
TOBIAS SMOLLETT: *Humphrey Clinker*, 1771

The present is a mighty goddess.
J. W. GOETHE: *Torquato Tasso*, IV, 1790

A narrow isthmus 'twixt two boundless seas,
The past, the future, two eternities.
THOMAS MOORE: *Lalla Rookh*, 1817 (Cf. ADDISON, *ante*, 1714)

The present is our own; but while we speak,
We cease from its possession, and resign
The stage we tread on to another race,
As vain, and gay, and mortal as ourselves.
THOMAS LOVE PEACOCK: *Time*, 1837

Of all the ages, the present hour and circumstance is the cumulative result; this is the best throw of the dice of nature that has yet been, or that is yet possible.
R. W. EMERSON: *The Conservative*, 1841

The past belongs to God: the present only is ours. And short as it is, there is more in it, and of it, than we can well manage. That man who can grapple it, and measure it, and fill it with his purpose, is doing a man's work; none can do more: but there are thousands who do less.
DONALD G. MITCHELL: *Reveries of a Bachelor*, IV, 1850

He is blessed over all mortals who loses no moment of the passing life in remembering the past.
H. D. THOREAU: *Excursions*, 1863

He that praises the past blames the present.
FINNISH PROVERB

[*See also* Action, Change, Golden Age, Happiness, Past.

Presidency

The perpetual reëligibility of the President, I fear, will make an office for life, and then hereditary.
THOMAS JEFFERSON: *Letter to George Washington*, 1788

I most heartily wish the choice to which you allude [election to the Presidency] may not fall on me. . . . If I should conceive myself in a manner constrained to accept, I call Heaven to witness that this very act would be the greatest sacrifice of my personal feelings and wishes that I ever have been called upon to make.
GEORGE WASHINGTON: *Letter to Benjamin Lincoln*, Oct. 26, 1788

My movements to the chair of government will be accompanied by feelings not unlike those of a culprit who is going to the place of his execution. . . . Integrity and firmness are all I can promise.
GEORGE WASHINGTON: *Letter to Benjamin Harrison*, March 9, 1789

No man will ever bring out of the Presidency the reputation which carries him into it.
THOMAS JEFFERSON: *Letter to Edward Rutledge*, 1796

The second office of the government is honorable and easy; the first is but a splendid misery.

THOMAS JEFFERSON: *Letter to Elbridge Gerry*, 1797

I am tired of an office where I can do no more good than many others who would be glad to be employed in it. To myself, personally, it brings nothing but unceasing drudgery and daily loss of friends.

THOMAS JEFFERSON: *Letter to John Dickinson*, 1807

I would take no one step to advance or promote pretensions to the Presidency. If that office was to be the prize of cabal and intrigue, of purchasing newspapers, bribing by appointments, or bargaining for foreign missions, I had no ticket in that lottery. Whether I had the qualifications necessary for a President of the United States, was, to say the least, very doubtful to myself. But that I had no talents for obtaining the office by such means was perfectly clear.

JOHN QUINCY ADAMS: *Diary*, Feb. 25, 1821

No man who ever held the office of President would congratulate a friend on obtaining it. He will make one man ungrateful, and a hundred men his enemies, for every office he can bestow.

JOHN ADAMS: On hearing of the election of his son, John Quincy Adams, 1824

The President has paid dear for his White House. It has commonly cost him all his peace and the best of his manly attributes. To preserve for a short time so conspicuous an appearance before the world, he is content to eat dust before the real masters who stand erect behind the throne.

R. W. EMERSON: *Compensation*, 1841

I have been selected to fill an important office for a brief period, and am now, in your eyes, invested with an influence which will soon pass away; but should my administration prove to be a very wicked one, or what is more probable, a very foolish one, if you, the people, are true to yourselves and the Constitution, there is but little harm I can do, thank God.

ABRAHAM LINCOLN: Speech at Lawrenceburg, Ind., Feb. 28, 1861

If you are as happy, my dear sir, on entering this house as I am in leaving it and returning home, you are the happiest man in this country.

JAMES BUCHANAN: To Abraham Lincoln at the White House, March 4, 1861

I would rather that the people should wonder why I wasn't President than why I am.

SALMON P. CHASE: To the editor of the Indianapolis Independent, July, 1864

If forced to choose between the penitentiary and the White House for four years, I would say the penitentiary, thank you.

W. T. SHERMAN: *Letter to H. W. Halleck*, Sept., 1864

I will not accept if nominated, and will not serve if elected.

W. T. SHERMAN: Telegram to John B. Henderson, chairman of the Republican National Convention at Chicago, declining the presidential nomination, June 5, 1884

I am convinced that the office of the President is not such a very difficult one to fill, his duties being mainly to execute the laws of Congress.

GEORGE DEWEY: Announcement of his candidacy for the Democratic nomination, April 3, 1900

Congress is very generous to the President. . . . I have been able to save from my four years about $100,000.

WILLIAM H. TAFT: *Letter to Woodrow Wilson*, Nov. 15, 1912

[*See also* Choose, President, Statesman.

President

An executive is less dangerous to the liberties of the people when in office during life, than for seven years.

ALEXANDER HAMILTON: Speech in the Federal Convention, June 18, 1787

You are apprehensive of monarchy; I, of aristocracy. I would therefore have given more power to the President and less to the Senate.

JOHN ADAMS: *Letter to Thomas Jefferson*, Nov. 16, 1787

The executive power shall be vested in a President of the United States of America. He shall hold his office during the term of four years.

CONSTITUTION OF THE UNITED STATES, Art. II, 1789

We declare it to be the unwritten law of this Republic, established by custom and usage of one hundred years, and sanctioned by the examples of the greatest and wisest of those who founded and have maintained our government, that no man should be eligible for a third term of the Presidential office.

Democratic National Platform, 1896

We favor a single presidential term, and to that end urge the adoption of an amendment to the Constitution making the President of the United States ineligible for reëlection, and we pledge the candidate of this convention to this principle.

Democratic National Platform, 1912

The duty of the President to see that the laws be executed is a duty that does not go beyond the laws or require him to achieve more than Congress sees fit to leave within his power.

MR. JUSTICE O. W. HOLMES: *Dissenting opinion in Meyers* vs. *United States*, 1926

[*See also* Impeachment, Officeholder, Pantaloons, Presidency, Treaty, Vice-President.

Press

The press is like the air, a chartered libertine.

WILLIAM PITT: To Lord Grenville, *c.* 1757

The press is the best instrument for enlightening the mind of man, and improving him as a rational, moral, and social being.

THOMAS JEFFERSON: *Letter to M. Coray*, 1823

There have been three silent revolutions in England: first, when the professions fell off from the church; secondly, when literature fell off from the professions; and, thirdly, when the press fell off from literature.

S. T. COLERIDGE: *Table-Talk*, April 21, 1832

The press, like fire, is an excellent servant, but a terrible master.

J. FENIMORE COOPER: *The American Democrat*, XXV, 1838

The press is not public opinion.

OTTO VON BISMARCK: Speech in the Prussian Lower House, Sept. 30, 1862

The capitalist press is the worst enemy of the people. . . . It holds the publisher's capital the most sacred thing in the world.

FERDINAND LASSALLE: Speech in Düsseldorf, Sept. 28, 1863

In order to guarantee to all workers real freedom of opinion, the Russian Socialist Federated Soviet Republic abolishes the dependence of the press on capitalism and places at the disposal of the working class and the peasantry all the technical and material means for the publication of newspapers, pamphlets, books, and all other productions of the press, and guarantees free circulation for them throughout the country.

CONSTITUTION OF THE U.S.S.R., Jan. 31, 1924

[*See also* Journalism, Journalist, Newspaper, Press (Free).

Press, Free

If we think we regulate printing, thereby to rectify manners, we must regulate all recreations and pastimes, all that is delightful to man. No music must be heard, no song be set or sung, but what is grave and doric.

JOHN MILTON: *Areopagitica*, 1644

It is unreasonable what some assert, "that printers ought not to print anything but what they approve"; since if all of that business should make such a resolution, and abide by it, an end would thereby be put to free writing, and the world would afterwards have nothing to read but what happen'd to be the opinions of printers.

BENJAMIN FRANKLIN: *An Apology for Printers*, June 10, 1731

Newspapers, if they are to be interesting, must not be molested.

FREDERICK THE GREAT: Dispatch to the Prussian minister at St. Petersburg, June 5, 1740 (The Russian Foreign Office had complained of certain anti-Russian articles in Berlin newspapers. The dispatch was signed by Count Podewits, a member of the Prussian Cabinet, but it is commonly ascribed to Frederick himself)

The liberty of the press is indeed essential to the nature of a free state, but this consists in laying no previous restraints upon publications, and not in freedom from censure for criminal matter when published.

WILLIAM BLACKSTONE: *Commentaries on the Laws of England*, IV, 1765

The liberty of the press is the palladium of all the civil, political, and religious rights of an Englishman.

Letters of Junius, dedication, 1772

As for the freedom of the press, I will tell you what it is: the liberty of the press is that a man may print what he pleases without license. As long as it remains so, the liberty of the press is not restrained.

LORD CHIEF JUSTICE MANSFIELD: Charge to the jury in the trial of H. W. Woodfall, 1772

The freedom of the press is one of the great bulwarks of liberty and can never be restrained but by despotic governments.

GEORGE MASON: *The Virginia Declaration of Rights*, XII, June 15, 1776

Liberty of the press is essential to freedom in the state. It ought not to be restricted in this commonwealth.

CONSTITUTION OF MASSACHUSETTS, 1780

The press shall be free to every citizen who undertakes to examine the official conduct of men acting in a public capacity, and any citizen may print freely on any subject, being responsible for the abuse of that liberty.

CONSTITUTION OF DELAWARE, 1782

Our liberty depends on the freedom of the press, and that cannot be limited without being lost.

THOMAS JEFFERSON: *Letter to James Currie*, 1786

The legislature of the United States shall pass no law on the subject of religion nor touching or abridging the liberty of the press.

CHARLES PINCKNEY: Resolution offered in the Constitutional Convention, 1787

What is the liberty of the press? Who can give it any definition which does not leave the utmost latitude for evasion? I hold it to be impracticable, and from this I infer that its security, whatever fine declarations may be inserted in any constitution respecting it, must altogether depend on public opinion, and on the general spirit of the people and of the government.

ALEXANDER HAMILTON: *The Federalist*, LXXXIV, 1788

The liberty of the press on general subjects comprehends and implies as much strict observance of positive law as is consistent with perfect purity of intention, and equal and useful society; and what the latitude is cannot be promulgated in the abstract, but must be judged of in the particular instance.

THOMAS ERSKINE: Speech to the jury on the trial of John Stockdale, 1789

Congress shall make no law abridging the freedom of speech or of the press.

CONSTITUTION OF THE UNITED STATES, Amendment I, Dec. 15, 1791

No government ought to be without censors; and, where the press is free, no one ever will.

THOMAS JEFFERSON: *Letter to George Washington*, 1792

A man may publish anything which twelve of his countrymen think not blamable.

LORD KENYON: *Judgment in Cuthell's Case*, 1799

The liberty of the press consists, in my idea, in publishing the truth, from good motives and for justifiable ends, though it reflect on the government, on magistrates, or individuals. If it be not allowed, it excludes the privilege of canvassing men, and our rulers. It is vain to say, you may canvass measures. This is impossible without the right of looking to men.

ALEXANDER HAMILTON: Speech in New York, 1804

Give me but the liberty of the press, and I will give to the minister a venal House of Peers — I will give him a corrupt and servile House of Commons — I will give him the full sway of the patronage of office — . . . and yet . . . I will go forth to meet him undismayed — I will attack the mighty fabric he has reared with that mightier engine — I will shake down from its height corruption, and bury it amidst the ruins of the abuses it was meant to shelter.

R. B. SHERIDAN: Speech in the House of Commons, 1810

Where the press is free and every man able to read, all is safe.

THOMAS JEFFERSON: *Letter to Charles Yancey*, 1816

Despotism can no more exist in a nation until the liberty of the press be destroyed, than the night can happen before the sun is set.

C. C. COLTON: *Lacon*, 1820

Without the knowledge of what is done by their representatives, in the use of the powers entrusted to them, the people cannot profit by the power of choosing them, and the advantages of good government are unattainable. It will not surely cost many words to satisfy all classes of readers that, without the free and unrestrained use of the press, the requisite knowledge cannot be obtained.

JAMES MILL: *On Liberty of the Press*, 1821

The only security of all is in a free press. The force of public opinion cannot be resisted when permitted freely to be expressed. The agitation it produces must be submitted to. It is necessary to keep the waters pure.

THOMAS JEFFERSON: *Letter to Lafayette*, 1823

The liberty of thinking and of publishing whatever one likes . . . is the fountain-head of many evils.

POPE LEO XIII: *Immortale Dei*, Nov. 1, 1885

If unbridled license of speech and of writing be granted to all, nothing will remain sacred and inviolate; even the highest and truest mandates of nature, justly held to be the common and noblest heritage of the human race, will not be spared.

POPE LEO XIII: *Libertas praestantissimum*, June 20, 1888

Why should freedom of speech and freedom of the press be allowed? Why should a government which is doing what it believes to be right allow itself to be criticized? It would not allow opposition by lethal weapons. Ideas are much more fatal things than guns. Why should any man be allowed to buy a printing press and disseminate pernicious opinions calculated to embarrass the government?

NIKOLAI LENIN: Speech in Moscow, 1920

A free press stands as one of the great interpreters between the government and the people. To allow it to be fettered is to fetter ourselves.

Decision of the Supreme Court of the United States in Grosjean vs. *the American Press Co.*, 1936

Freedom of discussion cannot be curtailed without affecting the right of the people to be informed through sources independent of the government concerning matters of public interest. There must be an untrammeled publication of news and opinion.

MR. JUSTICE L. A. CANNON, of the Supreme Court of Canada: *Decision in the Alberta Press Act case*, March 4, 1938

The liberty of the press is not confined to newspapers and periodicals. It necessarily embraces pamphlets and leaflets. These indeed have been historic weapons in the defense of liberty, as the pamphlets of Thomas Paine and others in our own history abundantly attest.

Decision of the Supreme Court of the United States in Lovell vs. *City of Griffin*, 1938

The right to distribute literature and pamphlets does not imply the right to force acceptance by placing them on another person's premises without his permission.

JUDGE L. R. YANKWICH: *Decision in Buxbom* vs. *City of Riverside, Calif.*, 1939

Freedom of conscience, of education, of speech, of assembly are among the very fundamentals of democracy and all of them would be nullified should freedom of the press ever be successfully challenged.

F. D. ROOSEVELT: *Letter to W. N. Hardy*, Sept. 4, 1940

Freedom of the press is the staff of life for any vital democracy.

WENDELL L. WILLKIE: *Letter to W. N. Hardy*, Sept. 18, 1940

[*See also* American, Books, Censorship, Journalist, Liberty, Newspaper, Opinion, Speech (Free), Violence.

Pretense

[*See* Affectation.

Prettiness

Prettiness dies first.

GEORGE HERBERT: *Outlandish Proverbs*, 1640

She is pretty to walk with,
And witty to talk with,
And pleasant too, to think on.

JOHN SUCKLING: *Brennoralt*, II, 1646

A pretty woman, if she has a mind to be wicked, can find a readier way than another.

SAMUEL JOHNSON: *Boswell's Life*, June 5, 1781

[*See also* Beauty.

Prevention

Prevention is better than cure.

DESIDERIUS ERASMUS: *Adagia*, 1508

Prevention is the daughter of intelligence.

WALTER RALEIGH: *Letter to Robert Cecil*, May 10, 1593

An ounce of prevention is worth a pound of cure.

ENGLISH PROVERB, not recorded before the XVIII century (Cf. ERASMUS, *ante*, 1508)

[*See also* Punishment.

Price

As in other things, so in men, not the seller but the buyer determines the price. For let a man (as most men do) rate themselves at the highest value they can; yet their true value is no more than it is esteemed by others.

THOMAS HOBBES: *Leviathan*, I, 1651

All those men have their price.

Ascribed to ROBERT WALPOLE, *c.* 1740, in WILLIAM COXE: *Memoirs of the Life and Administration of Robert Walpole*, IV, 1798 (The usual form, when cited, is "Every man has his price")

The real price of everything, what everything really costs to the man who wants to acquire it, is the toil and trouble of acquiring it. What everything is really worth to the man who has acquired it, and who wants to dispose of it, or exchange it for something else, is the toil and trouble which it can save to himself, and which it can impose upon other people.

ADAM SMITH: *The Wealth of Nations*, I, 1776

No price is too low for a bear or too high for a bull.

STOCK EXCHANGE PROVERB, not recorded before the XIX century

[*See also* Buying and Selling, Cheating, Cynic, Value.

Pride

When pride cometh, then cometh shame.

PROVERBS XI, 2, *c.* 350 B.C.

The Lord will destroy the house of the proud.

PROVERBS XV, 25

Pride goeth before destruction, and a haughty spirit before a fall. PROVERBS XVI, 18

A man's pride shall bring him low: but honor shall uphold the humble in spirit.

PROVERBS XXIX, 23

Pride is hateful before God and man.

ECCLESIASTICUS X, 7, *c.* 180 B.C.

Consider what men are when they are eating, sleeping, generating, easing themselves, and so forth. Then what kind of men they are when they are imperious and arrogant, or angry and scolding from their elevated place.

MARCUS AURELIUS: *Meditations*, X, *c.* 170

Three sparks kindle in all hearts — pride, envy, and avarice. DANTE: *Inferno*, VI, *c.* 1320

Pride will have a fall.

ENGLISH PROVERB, traced by Apperson to 1509 (Cf. PROVERBS XVI, 18, *ante*, *c.* 350 B.C. A variant is "Pride goeth before a fall")

Pride goeth before and shame cometh after.

RICHARD HILLES: *Commonplace book*, *c.* 1535 (Cf. PROVERBS XI, 2, *ante*, *c.* 350 B.C.)

My pride fell with my fortunes.

SHAKESPEARE: *As You Like It*, I, *c.* 1600

He that is proud eats himself up; pride is his own glass, his own trumpet, his own chronicle.

SHAKESPEARE: *Troilus and Cressida*, II, *c.* 1601

I do hate a proud man as I hate the engendering of toads.

IBID.

A falcon, tow'ring in her pride of place,
Was by a mousing owl hawk'd at and kill'd.

SHAKESPEARE: *Macbeth*, II, *c.* 1605

Prouder than rustling in unpaid-for silk.

SHAKESPEARE: *Cymbeline*, III, *c.* 1609

I have ventured,
Like little wanton boys that swim on bladders,
This many Summers in a sea of glory;
But far beyond my depth: my high-blown pride
At length broke under me; and now has left me,
Weary and old with service, to the mercy
Of a rude stream that must for ever hide me.

SHAKESPEARE and JOHN FLETCHER: *Henry VIII*, III, 1613

The pride of the rich makes the labor of the poor.

NICHOLAS BRETON: *Crossing of Proverbs*, 1616

They are proud in humility; proud in that they are not proud.

ROBERT BURTON: *The Anatomy of Melancholy*, I, 1621

Pride feels no pain.

BEN JONSON: *The New Inn*, II, 1629

It is good beating proud folks, for they will not complain.

JOHN CLARKE: *Parœmiologia Anglo-Latina*, 1639

I thank God, amongst those millions of vices I do inherit and hold from Adam, I have escaped one, and that a mortal enemy to charity, — the first and father sin, not only of man, but of the Devil, — pride.

THOMAS BROWNE: *Religio Medici*, II, 1642

Two, of a thousand things, are disallow'd,
A lying rich man, and a poor man proud.

ROBERT HERRICK: *Hesperides*, 1648

From pride, vain-glory, and hypocrisy; from envy, hatred, and malice, and all uncharitableness, good Lord, deliver us.

THE BOOK OF COMMON PRAYER (*The Litany*), 1662

If we had no pride we should not complain of that of others.

LA ROCHEFOUCAULD: *Maxims*, 1665

It would seem that nature, which has so wisely ordered the organs of our body for our happiness, has also given us pride to spare us the mortification of knowing our imperfections.

IBID.

Pride has a larger part than goodness in our remonstrances with those who commit faults, and we reprove them not so much to correct them as to persuade them that we ourselves are free from their faults.

IBID.

Pride counterbalances all miseries. Either it conceals its miseries; or, if it discover them, it glorifies itself for knowing them.

BLAISE PASCAL: *Pensées*, III, 1670

Pride feels no cold.

JOHN RAY: *English Proverbs*, 1670

Pride is a kind of pleasure produced by a man thinking too well of himself.

BARUCH SPINOZA: *Ethica*, III, 1677

Pride is a sin that sticks close to nature, and is one of the first follies wherein it shows itself to be polluted. For even in childhood, even in little children, pride will first of all show itself; it is a hasty, an early appearance of the sin of the soul.

JOHN BUNYAN: *The Life and Death of Mr. Badman*, 1680

Pride (of all others the most dang'rous fault)
Proceeds from want of sense, or want of thought.

WENTWORTH DILLON (EARL OF ROSCOMMON): *Essay on Translated Verse*, 1684

Pride may be allowed to this or that degree, else a man cannot keep up his dignity. In gluttony there must be eating, in drunkenness there must be drinking; 'tis not the eating, nor 'tis not the drinking that is to be blamed, but the excess. So in pride.

JOHN SELDEN: *Table-Talk*, 1689

The first peer and president of Hell.

DANIEL DEFOE: *The True-Born Englishman*, I, 1701

Of all the causes which conspire to blind
Man's erring judgment, and misguide the mind,
What the weak head with strongest bias rules
Is pride, the never failing vice of fools.

ALEXANDER POPE: *An Essay on Criticism*, II, 1711

Pride, when wit fails, steps in to our defense,
And fills up all the mighty void of sense.

IBID.

'T's pride, rank pride, and haughtiness of soul;
I think the Romans call it stoicism.

JOSEPH ADDISON: *Cato*, I, 1713

Thus unlamented pass the proud away,
The gaze of fools and pageant of a day;
So perish all, whose breast ne'er learn'd to glow
For others' good, or melt at others' woe.

ALEXANDER POPE: *Elegy to the Memory of an Unfortunate Lady*, 1717

Pride and grace dwelt never in one place.

JAMES KELLY: *Complete Collection of Scottish Proverbs*, 1721

Every good thought that we have, every good action that we do, lays us open to pride, and exposes us to the assaults of vanity and self-satisfaction.

WILLIAM LAW: *A Serious Call to a Devout and Holy Life*, XVI, 1728

Likeness begets love, yet proud men hate one another.

THOMAS FULLER: *Gnomologia*, 1732

Nothing more thankful than pride when complied with. IBID.

Pride had rather go out of the way than go behind. IBID.

Pride is as loud a beggar as want, and a great deal more saucy. IBID.

Pride will spit in pride's face. IBID.

Ask for what end the heav'nly bodies shine,
Earth for whose use — pride answers " 'Tis for mine."

ALEXANDER POPE: *An Essay on Man*, I, 1732

Lauk! what a monstrous tail our cat has got!

HENRY CAREY: *The Dragons of Wantley*, II, 1737

How low, how little are the proud.

THOMAS GRAY: *Ode to Spring*, 1748

The proud hate pride — in others.

BENJAMIN FRANKLIN: *Poor Richard's Almanac*, 1751

Nobody has occasion for pride but the poor; everywhere else it is a sign of folly.

THOMAS GRAY: *Letter to Thomas Wharton*, Oct. 18, 1753

A proud man hath no God.

BENJAMIN WHICHCOTE: *Moral and Religious Aphorisms*, 1753

Pride breakfasted with plenty, dined with poverty, and supped with infamy.

BENJAMIN FRANKLIN: *The Way to Wealth*, 1758

Pride is seldom delicate: it will please itself with very mean advantages.

SAMUEL JOHNSON: *Rasselas*, IX, 1759

He was so proud that should he meet
The Twelve Apostles in the street
He'd turn his nose up at them all
And shove his Saviour from the wall.

CHARLES CHURCHILL: *Independence*, 1764 (The reference is to William Warburton, Bishop of Gloucester)

Pride in their port, defiance in their eye,
I see the lords of humankind pass by.

OLIVER GOLDSMITH: *The Traveler*, 1764

Men are sometimes accused of pride merely because their accusers would be proud themselves if they were in their places.

WILLIAM SHENSTONE: *Of Men and Manners*, 1764

Men of fine parts, they say, are often proud; I answer, dull people are seldom so, and both act upon an appearance of reason. IBID.

The Devil did grin, for his darling sin
Is pride that apes humility.

S. T. COLERIDGE: *The Devil's Thoughts*, 1799 (London Morning Post, Sept. 6)

There is a certain noble pride through which merits shine brighter than through modesty.

JEAN PAUL RICHTER: *Titan*, XXXIV, 1803

Of all the marvellous works of the Deity perhaps there is nothing that angels behold with such supreme astonishment as a proud man.

C. C. COLTON: *Lacon*, 1820

There is a paradox in pride — it makes some men ridiculous, but prevents others from becoming so. IBID.

Oh, why should the spirit of mortal be proud?
Like a fast-flitting meteor, a fast-flying cloud,
A flash of the lightning, a break of the wave,
He passes from life to his rest in the grave.

WILLIAM KNOX: *Mortality*, 1824

A pride there is of rank — a pride of birth,
A pride of learning, and a pride of purse,
A London pride — in short, there be on earth
A host of prides, some better and some worse;
But of all prides, since Lucifer's attaint,
The proudest swells a self-elected saint.

THOMAS HOOD: *Blanca's Dream*, 1827

Pride ruined the angels.

R. W. EMERSON: *The Sphinx*, 1841 (Dial, Jan.)

Pride loves no man, and is beloved of no man.

H. G. BOHN: *Handbook of Proverbs*, 1855

Pride is at the bottom of all great mistakes.

JOHN RUSKIN: *Modern Painters*, IV, 1856

The prouder a man is, the more he thinks he deserves; and the more he thinks he deserves, the less he really does deserve.

H. W. BEECHER: *Royal Truths*, 1862

There is such a thing as a man being too proud to fight.

WOODROW WILSON: Speech at Philadelphia, May 10, 1915 (OSWALD GARRISON VILLARD: *Fighting Years*, 1939, says that he was the author of the phrase)

There was one who thought he was above me, and he was above me until he had that thought.

ELBERT HUBBARD: *Roycroft Dictionary and Book of Epigrams*, 1923

A little dog, a cow without horns, and a short man are generally proud.

DANISH PROVERB

The nobler the blood, the less the pride.

IBID.

Even the dog of a great man is proud.

JAPANESE PROVERB

A man on horseback doesn't recognize his father. RUSSIAN PROVERB

When pride's in the van, begging's in the rear. SCOTTISH PROVERB

God hates the proud. TURKISH PROVERB

When pride is highest, catastrophe is nearest. WELSH PROVERB

[*See also* Abomination, Adam (Old), Age (Old), Anarchy, Anger, Character (National), Charity, Chastity, Comfort, Curiosity, Debauchery, Devil, Discouragement, Egoism, Evil, Greatness, Hatred, Humility, Idleness, Ingratitude, Jealousy, Knowledge, Love, Mortality, Peace, Poor, Prosperity, Sin, Vanity, Virtue.

Pride and Shame

No virtue male or female can we name
But what will grow on pride or grow on shame.

ALEXANDER POPE: *An Essay on Man,* II, 1732

Pride, Local

What you say in commendation of a whole town is received with pleasure by all the inhabitants.

BERNARD DE MANDEVILLE: *An Inquiry Into the Origin of Moral Virtue,* 1723

Pride, National

The cheapest sort of pride is national pride; for if a man is proud of his own nation, it argues that he has no qualities of his own of which he can be proud; otherwise, he would not have recourse to those which he shares with so many millions of his fellow-men.

ARTHUR SCHOPENHAUER: *Position,* 1851

Priest

Like people, like priest.

HOSEA IV, 9, *c.* 740 B.C.

Whosoever he be of thy seed in their generations that hath any blemish, let him not approach to offer the bread of his God. For whatsoever man he be that hath a blemish, he shall not approach: a blind man, or a lame, or he that hath a flat nose, or anything superfluous, or a man that is brokenfooted, or brokenhanded, or crookbackt, or a dwarf, or that hath a blemish in his eye, or be scurvy, or scabbed, or hath his stones broken.

LEVITICUS XXI, 17–20, *c.* 700 B.C.

He made a house of high places, and made priests of the lowest of the people.

I KINGS XII, 31, *c.* 500 B.C.

Every priest standeth daily ministering and offering oftentimes the same sacrifices, which can never take away sins.

HEBREWS X, 11, *c.* 65

Why should any honest man need a priest? The gods need no mediator to make them kind to him.

APOLLONIUS OF TYANA (*c.* 10 B.C.–80 A.D.)

Hell is paved with priests' skulls.

ST. JOHN CHRYSOSTOM: *De sacerdotio,* *c.* 390

A priest should never be put at the head of affairs. Even when the object for which he was engaged hath been completed, he refuseth to resign. *The Hitopadesa,* II, *c.* 500

The sons of rustics may not be ordained without the consent of the lord on whose land they are known to have been born.

CONSTITUTION OF CLARENDON, 1164

You robbers of the poor, you assassins, you brigands, you sacrilegious scoundrels!

JOHN HUSS: *Simony,* 1442

If a man nowadays have two sons, the one impotent, weak, sickly, lisping, stuttering and stammering, or have any misshape in his body, what doth the father of such one commonly say? This boy is fit for nothing else but to set to learning and make a priest of.

ROGER ASHAM: *Toxiphilus,* 1545

There's no mischief, as they say commonly, but a priest at one end.

Anon.: *Misogonus,* 1577

He that in a neat house will dwell
Must priest and pigeon thence expel.

RANDLE COTGRAVE: *French-English Dictionary,* 1611

The smiles of courtiers and the harlot's tears,
The tradesman's oaths, and mourning of an heir
Are truths to what priests tell.

JOHN DRYDEN and NATHANIEL LEE: *Œdipus,* I, 1679

For priests of all religions are the same:
Of whatsoe'er descent their Godhead be,
Stock, stone, or other homely pedigree,
In his defence his servants are as bold,
As if he had been born of beaten gold.

JOHN DRYDEN: *Absalom and Achitophel,* I, 1682

God's word they had not, but the priest's they had. JOHN DRYDEN: *Religio Laici,* 1682

In the duchy of Gulic a popish curate, having ineffectually tried many charms to eject the Devil out of a damsel possessed, passionately bid the Devil come out of her into himself, but the Devil answered him, What need I meddle with one whom I am sure to have and hold at the Last Day as my own forever?

COTTON MATHER: *The Wonders of the Invisible World,* I, 1693

The priesthood is the profession of a gentleman.

JEREMY COLLIER: *A Short View of the Immorality and Profaneness of the English Stage,* III, 1698

To expose a priest, much more to burlesque his function, is an affront to the Deity. IBID.

The scandal that is given by particular priests reflects not on the sacred function. A satirical poet is the check of the layman on bad priests. When a clergyman is whipped, his gown is first taken off, by which the dignity of his office is secured.

JOHN DRYDEN: *Fables, Ancient and Modern*, intro., 1699

Whores and priest will never want excuse.

DANIEL DEFOE: *The True-Born Englishman*, II, 1701

By priests I understand only the pretenders to power and dominion, and to a superior sanctity of character, distinct from virtue and good morals. These are very different from clergymen, who are set apart to the care of sacred matters, and the conducting our public devotions with greater decency and order. There is no rank of men more to be respected than the latter.

DAVID HUME: *Essays, Moral and Political*, I, 1741

Cries Sylvia to a reverend dean,
What reason can be given,
Since marriage is a holy thing,
That there is none in Heaven?
There are no women, he replied.
She quick returns the jest: —
Women there are, but I'm afraid
They cannot find a priest.

ROBERT DODSLEY: *Song*, 1746

Priests are extremely like other men, and neither the better nor the worse for wearing a gown or a surplice: but if they are different from other people, probably it is rather on the side of religion and morality, or, at least, decency, from their education and manners of life.

LORD CHESTERFIELD: *Letter to his son*, May 10, 1748

People have no security against being priest-ridden but by keeping all imperious bishops and other clergymen who love to "lord it over God's heritage" from getting their foot into the stirrup at all. Let them be once fairly mounted, and their "beasts, the laity," may prance and flounce about to no purpose; and they will at length be so jaded and hacked by these reverend jockeys that they will not even have spirits enough to complain that their backs are galled.

JONATHAN MAYHEW: *A Discourse Concerning Unlimited Submission and Non-Resistance to the Higher Powers*, 1750

Priests and conjurors are of the same trade.

THOMAS PAINE: *The Age of Reason*, 1794

Every man is a priest in his own house.

ENGLISH PROVERB, not recorded before the XIX century

It is too late in the day for men of sincerity to pretend they believe in the Platonic mysticisms that three are one, and one is three; and yet that the one is not three, and that the three are not one; to divide mankind by a single letter into Homoiousians and Homoousians. But this constitutes the craft, the power and the profit of priests. Sweep away their gossamer fabrics of factitious religion, and they would catch no more flies.

THOMAS JEFFERSON: *Letter to John Adams*, 1813

How ludicrous the priest's dogmatic roar!
The weight of his exterminating curse,
How light! and his affected charity,
To suit the pressure of the changing times,
What palpable deceit!

P. B. SHELLEY: *Queen Mab*, VI, 1813

Priests dare babble of a God of peace,
Even whilst their hands are red with guiltless blood,
Murdering the while, uprooting every germ
Of truth, exterminating, spoiling all,
Making the earth a slaughter-house.

P. B. SHELLEY: *Queen Mab*, VII

In every country and in every age the priest has been hostile to liberty. He is always in alliance with the despot, abetting his abuses in return for protection to his own.

THOMAS JEFFERSON: *Letter to Horatio Gates Spafford*, 1814

You judge truly that I am not afraid of the priests. They have tried upon me all their various batteries, of pious whining, hypocritical canting, lying and slandering, without being able to give me one moment of pain.

THOMAS JEFFERSON: *Letter to Horatio Gates Spafford*, 1816

Oh, that the wise from their bright minds would kindle
Such lamps within the dome of this dim world
That the pale name of priest might shrink and dwindle
Into the Hell from which it first was hurled.

P. B. SHELLEY: *Ode to Liberty*, 1820

I took the repeal of the Corn Laws as light amusement compared with the difficult task of inducing the priests of all denominations to agree to suffer the people to be educated.

WILLIAM COBDEN: *Letter to a friend*, 1846

It is the old story again: once we had wooden chalices and golden priests, now we have golden chalices and wooden priests.

R. W. EMERSON: *The Preacher*, 1867

Mothers, wives, and maids,
These be the tools wherewith priests manage men.

ROBERT BROWNING: *The Ring and the Book*, IV, 1869

The influence of priests over women is attacked by Protestant and Liberal writers less for being bad in itself than because it is a rival authority to the husband, and raises up a revolt against his infallibility.

J. S. MILL: *The Subjection of Women*, IV, 1869

To the carnal eye the priest looks like other men, but to the eye of faith he is exalted above the angels, because he exercises powers not given even to angels.

JAMES CARDINAL GIBBONS: *The Faith of Our Fathers*, XXVIII, 1876

The Catholic priest, from the moment he becomes a priest, is a sworn officer of the pope.

OTTO VON BISMARCK: Speech in the Prussian Upper House, April 12, 1886

So long as the priest, that professional denier, calumniator and poisoner of life, is accepted as a higher variety of man, there can be no answer to the question, What is Truth?

F. W. NIETZSCHE: *The Antichrist*, VIII, 1888

These turkey-cocks of God.

F. W. NIETZSCHE: *The Antichrist*, XIII

The priest is still, and will, we think, remain, one of the necessary types of humanity. . . . It is his triumph to achieve as much faith as possible in an age of negation.

WALTER PATER: *Review of Robert Elsmere*, 1888 (London Guardian, March 28)

The priests will always be too many for you.

BENJAMIN JOWETT (1817–93)

The man who has no mind of his own lends it to the priests.

GEORGE MEREDITH: To Edward Clodd, *c.* 1900 (Fortnightly Review, July, 1909)

A powerful god has fat priests.

CHINESE PROVERB

For one son who becomes a priest, nine generations go to Heaven.

IBID.

A priest's pocket can never be filled.

DANISH PROVERB

An ape, a priest, and a louse are three devils in one house.

DUTCH PROVERB

Priests and women forget nothing.

GERMAN PROVERB

The friend of God is the enemy of the priest.

IBID.

The bite of a priest, like that of a wolf, is hard to heal.

IBID.

The priest's pig gets the most porridge.

IRISH PROVERB

Three things I have never seen — the eye of an ant, the foot of a snake, and the charity of a priest.

PERSIAN PROVERB

It is foolish to ask for change from a priest.

RUSSIAN PROVERB

The eyes of a priest and the mouth of a wolf are never satisfied.

IBID.

The poor should never show a priest to the kitchen.

IBID.

Such priest, such offering.

SCOTTISH PROVERB

[*See also* Absolution, Beer, Blasphemy, Brave, Bravery, Cause and Effect, Celibacy, Charity, Children, Clergy, Clergyman, Collar, Devil, Freedom, Hanging, Happiness, Hell, King, Lawyer, Living, Malta, Mass, Mother, Physician, Poet, Poetry and Prose, Preacher, Profession, Relic, Sin, Theocracy, War.

Priestcraft

[*See* Agnostic.

Priestess

[*See* Nun.

Prig

We must have a weak spot or two in a character before we can love it much. People that do not laugh or cry, or take more of anything than is good for them, or use anything but dictionary-words, are admirable subjects for biographies. But we don't care most for those flat pattern flowers that press best in the herbarium.

O. W. HOLMES: *The Professor at the Breakfast-Table*, III, 1859

[*See also* Character, Hell.

Prima-Donna

The prima-donna, though a little old,
And haggard with a dissipated life,
And subject, when the house is thin, by cold,
Has some good notes.

BYRON: *Don Juan*, IV, 1821

[*See also* Singer.

Primrose

A primrose by a river's brim,
A yellow primrose was to him,
And it was nothing more.

WILLIAM WORDSWORTH: *Peter Bell*, I, 1819

Primrose Way

[*See* Dalliance, Damnation.

Prince

If a prince does wrong, let him make atonement with his head.

TELIPINUS (KING OF THE HITTITES): *Proclamation*, *c.* 1650 B.C.

Who made thee a prince and a judge over us?

EXODUS II, 14, *c.* 700 B.C.

Princes drink in calumny with greedy ears.

HERODOTUS: *Histories*, III, *c.* 430 B.C.

Put not your trust in princes.

PSALMS CXLVI, 3, *c.* 150 B.C.

A prince is to have no other design, nor thought, nor study but war and the arts and disciplines of it; for indeed, that is the only profession worthy of a prince.

NICCOLÒ MACHIAVELLI: *The Prince*, XIV, 1513

So oblique is human judgment that we nearly always praise the lavish habits of princes, though they be joined with rapacity; more so, in fact, than we praise their parsimony, which is usually attended by a sacred regard for the property of others.

FRANCIS GUICCIARDINI: *Storia d'Italia*, 1564

The judicial laws of Moses are binding upon Christian princes, and they ought not in the slightest degree to depart from them.

EDWIN SANDYS (BISHOP OF LONDON): *Letter to Henry Bullinger of Zürich*, setting forth the principles of the Puritans, 1573

Princes give me sufficiently, if they take nothing from me; and do me much good if they do me no hurt.

MICHEL DE MONTAIGNE: *Essays*, III, 1588

When beggars die, there are no comets seen;
The heavens themselves blaze forth the death of princes.

SHAKESPEARE: *Julius Cæsar*, II, 1599

Princes give rewards with their own hands,
But death or punishment by the hands of others.

JOHN WEBSTER: *The White Devil*, V, *c.* 1608

Princes are like to heavenly bodies, which cause good or evil times; and which have much veneration, but no rest.

FRANCIS BACON: *Essays*, XIX, 1612

How wretched
Is that poor man that hangs on princes' favors!
There is, betwixt that smile we would aspire to,
That sweet aspect of princes, and their ruin,
More pangs and fears than wars and women have;
And when he falls, he falls like Lucifer,
Never to hope again.

SHAKESPEARE and JOHN FLETCHER: *Henry VIII*, III, 1613

When a prince shares a secret with an inferior, he does not grant a favor; he is only relieving himself.

BALTASAR GRACIÁN: *The Art of Worldly Wisdom*, CCXXXVII, 1647

Princes are venison in Heaven.

GEORGE HERBERT: *Jacula Prudentum*, 1651

To praise princes for virtues they do not possess is to speak evil of them with impunity.

LA ROCHEFOUCAULD: *Maxims*, 1665

They who possess the prince, possess the laws.

JOHN DRYDEN: *Absalom and Achitophel*, I, 1682

When one must take the truth into the presence of princes it becomes a heavy burden.

C. L. DE MONTESQUIEU: *Persian Letters*, CXL, 1721

Princes, like beauties, from their youth
Are strangers to the voice of truth.

JOHN GAY: *Fables*, I, 1727

A prince who writes against flattery is something as strange as a pope writing against infallibility.

VOLTAIRE: *Letter to Frederick the Great*, Jan. 26, 1740

The penetration of princes seldom goes deeper than the surface. It is the exterior that always engages their hearts; and I would never advise you to give yourself much trouble about their understanding.

LORD CHESTERFIELD: *Letter to his son*, Nov. 3, 1749

A prince is the first servant and the first magistrate of the state.

FREDERICK THE GREAT: *Mémoirs de Brandebourg*, 1750 (The same thought appears in many other places in Frederick's writings. Büchman traces the idea back to Suetonius, *c.* 150)

Many princes sin with David, but few repent with him.

BENJAMIN FRANKLIN: *Poor Richard's Almanac*, 1754

The advice given to princes is usually of service only to those who give it.

STANISLAUS LESZCYNSKI (KING OF POLAND): *Œuvres du philosophe bienfaisant*, 1763

Princes and asses must always be urged.

GERMAN PROVERB

Princes have long hands and many ears.

IBID.

Like prince, like people. (Qualis rex, talis grex.)

LATIN PROVERB

It is safe to eat with a prince, but not to play with him.

WELSH PROVERB

[*See also* Courtier, Favor, Fear, Foresight, Grace (=clemency), Heaven and Hell, King, Monarchy, Peasant, Power, Ruler, Tragedy.

Principal

[*See* Accessory.

Principle

Men of principle are always bold, but those who are bold are not always men of principle.

CONFUCIUS: *Analects*, XIV, *c.* 500 B.C.

The principle is more than half of the whole question.

ARISTOTLE: *The Nicomachean Ethics*, I, *c.* 340 B.C.

What are our natural principles except our accustomed principles? And in children, those that they have received from the custom of their fathers, as the chase in animals. A different custom will give other natural principles. BLAISE PASCAL: *Pensées,* IV, 1670

Manners with fortunes, humors turn with climes,
Tenets with books, and principles with times.
ALEXANDER POPE: *Moral Essays,* I (Of the Knowledge and Characters of Men), 1733

He who governs himself according to what he calls his principles may be punished either by one party or the other for those very principles. He who proceeds without principle, as chance, timidity, or self-preservation directs, will not perhaps fare better; but he will be less blamed.
ST. JOHN DE CRÈVECOEUR: *Letters from an American Farmer,* XII, 1782

Every honest man will suppose honest acts to flow from honest principles, and the rogues may rail without intermission.
THOMAS JEFFERSON: *Letter to Benjamin Rush,* 1801

Principles become modified in practise by facts.
J. FENIMORE COOPER: *The American Democrat,* XXIX, 1838

A marciful Providence fashioned us holler
O' purpose thet we might our principles swaller.
J. R. LOWELL: *The Biglow Papers,* I, 1848

The principles which men profess on any controverted subject are usually a very incomplete exponent of the opinions they really hold.
J. S. MILL: *Representative Government,* I, 1861

Important principles may and must be flexible.
ABRAHAM LINCOLN: Speech in Washington, April 11, 1865

The value of a principle is the number of things it will explain.
R. W. EMERSON: *The Preacher,* 1867

It is personalities not principles that move the age.
OSCAR WILDE: *The Picture of Dorian Gray,* 1891

I have never lived on principles. When I have had to act, I never first asked myself on what principles I was going to act, but I went at it and did what I thought fit. I have often reproached myself for my want of principle.
OTTO VON BISMARCK (1815–98)

It isn't the money I am thinking of; it's the principle of the thing.
AMERICAN PROVERB, apparently first recorded by GELETT BURGESS: *Are You a Bromide?,* 1907

In politics a man must learn to rise above principle. AMERICAN POLITICAL PROVERB

Principles are not proved; they prove. (Principia probant, non probantur.)
LEGAL MAXIM

[*See also* Character, Government, Precedent.

Printer

Printers are educated in the belief that when men differ in opinion both sides ought equally to have the advantage of being heard by the public; and that when truth and error have fair play, the former is always an overmatch for the latter: hence they cheerfully serve all contending writers that pay them well, without regarding on which side they are of the question in dispute.
BENJAMIN FRANKLIN: *An Apology for Printers,* June 10, 1731

When you consider with how little mental power and corporeal labor a printer can get a guinea a week, it is a very desirable occupation.
SAMUEL JOHNSON: *Boswell's Life,* March 27, 1775

Printers and booksellers are born to be the most dilatory and tedious of all creatures.
WILLIAM COWPER: To William Unwin May 23, 1781

The body of
Benjamin Franklin, printer,
(Like the cover of an old book,
Its contents worn out,
And stript of its lettering and gilding)
Lies here, food for worms!
Yet the work itself shall not be lost,
For it will, as he believed, appear once more
In a new
And more beautiful edition,
Corrected and amended
By its Author!
BENJAMIN FRANKLIN: Epitaph for himself, April 19, 1790

The jour printer with gray head and gaunt jaws works at his case,
He turns his quid of tobacco, while his eyes blur with the manuscript.
WALT WHITMAN: *Leaves of Grass,* 1855

The printer has a hard time. He has to set type all night, and play Pedro for the beer all day. We would like to be a printer if it were not for the night work.
EUGENE FIELD: *The Tribune Primer,* 1882

[*See also* Books, Press (Free).

Printing

The art preservative of all arts. (Ars artium omnium conservatrix.)
Inscription on a house at Haarlem, Holland, once occupied by Lourens Janszoon Coster (*d.* 1441), who was formerly thought by some to have been the real inventor of printing; the inscription, which is in the Latin form, dates from *c.* 1550

The invention of printing, though ingenious, compared with the invention of letters is no great matter.
THOMAS HOBBES: *Leviathan*, IV, 1651

I thank God there are no free schools nor printing, and I hope we shall not have these hundred years; for learning has brought disobedience and heresy and sects into the world, and printing has divulged them, and libels against the best government. God keep us from both!
WILLIAM BERKELEY (Governor of Virginia): Report to the English Committee for the Colonies, 1671

Providence . . . permitted the invention of printing as a scourge for the sins of the learned.
ALEXANDER POPE: *The Dunciad*, proem, 1728

He who first shortened the labor of copyists by the device of movable types was disbanding hired armies, and cashiering most kings and senates, and creating a whole new democratic world: he had invented the art of printing.
THOMAS CARLYLE: *Sartor Resartus*, I, 1836

Print never blushes. ITALIAN PROVERB

[*See also* Books, Handwriting, Press, Printer.

Printing-office

[*See* College.

Prioress

[*See* Nun.

Prison

There was never fair prison.
JOHN DAVIES: *The Scourge of Folly*, 1611

A bean in liberty is better than a comfit in prison.
GEORGE HERBERT: *Outlandish Proverbs*, 1640

Stone walls do not a prison make,
Nor iron bars a cage,
Minds innocent and quiet take
That for an hermitage.
RICHARD LOVELACE: *To Althea, from Prison*, 1642

Prisons are built with stones of law, brothels with bricks of religion.
WILLIAM BLAKE: *The Marriage of Heaven and Hell*, 1790

Under a government which imprisons any unjustly, the true place for a just man is also a prison.
H. D. THOREAU: *An Essay on Civil Disobedience*, 1849

I know not whether laws be right,
Or whether laws be wrong;
All that we know who be in gaol
Is that the wall is strong;
And that each day is like a year,
A year whose days are long.
OSCAR WILDE: *The Ballad of Reading Gaol*, V, 1898

The vilest deeds like poison weeds
Bloom well in prison-air:
It is only what is good in man
That wastes and withers there:
Pale anguish keeps the heavy gate,
And the warder is despair. IBID.

While we have prisons it matters little which of us occupy the cells.
GEORGE BERNARD SHAW: *Maxims for Revolutionists*, 1903

Better in prison with a wise man than in Paradise with a fool. RUSSIAN PROVERB

[*See also* Brave, Liberty, Ship.

Prisoner

I was in prison, and ye came unto me.
MATTHEW XXV, 36, *c.* 75

That it may please thee to show thy pity upon all prisoners and captives; We beseech thee to hear us, good Lord.
THE BOOK OF COMMON PRAYER (*The Litany*), 1662

And make each prisoner pent
Unwillingly represent
A source of innocent merriment,
Of innocent merriment.
W. S. GILBERT: *The Mikado*, I, 1885

Privacy

He who thought it not good for man to be alone, preserve me from the more prodigious monstrosity of being never by myself!
CHARLES LAMB: *Letter to Mrs. Wordsworth*, Feb. 18, 1818

The private life of a citizen ought to be within walls.
C. M. TALLEYRAND: *Letter to M. Colomb*, Oct. 31, 1823

No rights can be dearer to a man of cultivation than exemptions from unseasonable invasions on his time by the coarse-minded and ignorant.
J. FENIMORE COOPER: *The American Democrat*, XX, 1838

Friends will be much apart. They will respect more each other's privacy than their communion.
H. D. THOREAU: *Journal*, Feb. 22, 1841

A man has a right to pass through this world, if he wills, without having his pictures published, his business enterprises discussed, his successful experiments written up for the benefit of others, or his eccentricities com-

mented upon, whether in handbills, circulars, catalogues, newspapers or periodicals.
CHIEF JUSTICE ALTON B. PARKER (New York Court of Appeals): *Decision in Roberson* vs. *Rochater Folding Box Co.*, 1901

The right to be alone — the most comprehensive of rights, and the right most valued by civilized men.
MR. JUSTICE LOUIS D. BRANDEIS: *Opinion in Olmstead* vs. *United States,* 1928

No more privacy than a goldfish.
Ascribed to HECTOR H. MUNRO (SAKI)

Public laws favor domestic privacy. (Jura publica favent privata domus.)
LEGAL MAXIM

[*See also* Alone, American, Fish, House.

Privilege

The common ambition strains for elevations, to become some privileged exclusive.
WALT WHITMAN: *Democratic Vistas,* 1870

What men prize most is a privilege, even if it be that of chief mourner at a funeral.
J. R. LOWELL: Address at Birmingham, Eng., Oct. 6, 1884

When a privilege has been enjoyed for a hundred years or from time immemorial it is to be assumed that it was obtained lawfully.
THE CODE OF CANON LAW, V, May 19, 1918

[*See also* Equality, Liberalism.

Probabilism

If any opinion is supported by authority, it is lawful to follow it, even if the opposite opinion is supported by better authority.
BARTHOLOMEO DE MEDINA: *Commentaria in primam secundæ,* 1577

A person may do what he considers allowable according to a probable opinion, though the contrary opinion may appear the safer one. The opinion of a single grave doctor is enough.
MANOEL DE SA: *Aphorismi confessariorum,* 1595

The authority of a learned and pious man is entitled to very great consideration. If the testimony of such a man has influence in convincing us that such and such an event occurred, say at Rome, why should it not have the same weight in a question in morals?
TOMAS SANCHEZ: *Consilia moralia, c.* 1600

A doctor, on being consulted, may give an advice, not only probable according to his own opinion, but contrary to his opinion, provided this judgment happens to be more favorable or more agreeable to the person that consults him. Nay, I go further, and say, that there would be nothing unreasonable in his giving those who consult him a judgment held to be probable by some learned person, even though he should be satisfied in his own mind that it is absolutely false.
PAUL LAYMANN: *Theologia moralis,* 1625

An opinion is called probable when it is founded upon reasons of some consideration. Hence it may sometimes happen that a single very grave doctor may render an opinion probable. For a man particularly given to study would not adhere to an opinion unless he was drawn to it by a good and sufficient reason.
ANTONIO ESCOBAR: *Summula casuum conscientiæ,* I, 1627

Beyond dispute, a monk who has a probable opinion of his own is not bound to obey his superior, though the opinion of the latter is the more probable. For the monk is at liberty to adopt the opinion which is more agreeable to himself. And though the order of his superior be just, that does not oblige him to obey, for it is not just at all points or in every respect, but only probably so; and consequently he is only probably bound to obey and probably not bound.
FERNANDO DE CASTRO PALAO: *Opus morale,* 1631

Probability

Probability must atone for the want of truth.
MATTHEW PRIOR: *Solomon on the Vanity of the World,* pref., 1718

Lest men suspect your tale untrue
Keep probability in view.
JOHN GAY: *Fables,* I, 1727

He who has heard the same thing told by 12,000 eye-witnesses has only 12,000 probabilities, which are equal to one strong probability, which is far from certainty.
VOLTAIRE: *Philosophical Dictionary,* 1764

Fate laughs at probabilities.
E. G. BULWER-LYTTON: *Eugene Aram,* I, 1832

A reasonable probability is the only certainty.
E. W. HOWE: *Sinner Sermons,* 1926

It is probable that many things will happen contrary to probability.
Author unidentified

A thousand probabilities do not make one fact.
ITALIAN PROVERB

[*See also* Faith, Knowledge, Poet, Probabilism, Truth, Truth and Falsehood.

Procrastination

Procrastination is the thief of time.
EDWARD YOUNG: *Night Thoughts,* I, 1742

Never put off till tomorrow what you can do today.
LORD CHESTERFIELD: *Letter to his son,* Dec. 26, 1749

By and bye is easily said.
H. G. BOHN: *Handbook of Proverbs,* 1855

One of these days is none of these days.
IBID.

At once is two hours and a half.
SCOTTISH PROVERB

By the street of By-and-bye one reaches the house of Never. SPANISH PROVERB

[*See also* Industry.

Procreation

The procreation of mankind is a great marvel and mystery. Had God consulted me in the matter, I should have advised him to continue the generation of the species by fashioning them of clay, in the way Adam was fashioned.
MARTIN LUTHER: *Table-Talk,* DCCLII, 1569

I could be content that we might procreate like trees, without conjunction, or that there were any way to perpetuate the world without this trivial and vulgar way of coition: it is the foolishest act a wise man commits in all his life.
THOMAS BROWNE: *Religio Medici,* II, 1642

Urge, and urge, and urge;
Always the procreant urge of the world.
WALT WHITMAN: *Walt Whitman,* 1855

[*See also* Intercourse, Philoprogenitiveness.

Prodigality

We commonly say of a prodigal man that he is no man's foe but his own.
JOHN KING: *Sermon,* 1594

A fat housekeeper makes lean executors.
JOHN RAY: *English Proverbs,* 1670

No man distributes his money to others, but every one his life and time. We are not so prodigal of anything as of those whereof to be covetous would be both commendable and profitable to us.
MICHEL DE MONTAIGNE: *Essays,* III, 1588

Prodigy

Nothing can be done without a cause, nor has anything been done which cannot be done again. If that has been done which could be done, it ought not to be regarded as a prodigy. There are, therefore, no prodigies.
CICERO: *De divinatione,* II, *c.* 78 B.C.

Hey, diddle, diddle,
The cat and the fiddle,
The cow jumped over the moon;
The little dog laughed
To see such sport,
And the dish ran away with the spoon.
Anon.: *Nursery rhyme, c.* 1750

None could run so fast as he could,
None could dive so deep as he could,
None could swim so far as he could;
None had made so many journeys,
None had seen so many wonders.
H. W. LONGFELLOW: *Hiawatha,* XI, 1855

[*See also* Miracle, Precosity.

Profanity

[*See* Swearing.

Profession

Let a man practise the profession which he best knows.
CICERO: *Tusculanæ disputationes,* I, 45 B.C.

Husbandmen, seamen, soldiers, artisans and merchants are the very pillars of any commonwealth: all the other great professions do rise out of the infirmities and miscarriages of these.
WILLIAM PETTY: *Political Arithmetic,* I, *c.* 1677

Every profession does imply a trust for the service of the public. The artist's skill ought to be the buyer's security.
BENJAMIN WHICHCOTE: *Moral and Religious Aphorisms,* 1753

Of the professions, it may be said that soldiers are becoming too popular, parsons too lazy, physicians too mercenary, and lawyers too powerful. C. C. COLTON: *Lacon,* 1820

Every true science bears necessarily within itself the germ of a cognate profession, and the more you can elevate trades into professions the better.
S. T. COLERIDGE: *Table-Talk,* March 14, 1833

The bourgeoisie has stripped of its halo every occupation hitherto honored and looked up to with reverent awe. It has converted the physician, the lawyer, the priest, the poet, the man of science, into its paid wage-laborers.
KARL MARX and FRIEDRICH ENGELS: *The Communist Manifesto,* 1848

The best augury of a man's success in his profession is that he thinks it the finest in the world.
MARIAN EVANS (GEORGE ELIOT): *Daniel Deronda,* II, 1876

[*See also* Ethics (Professional), Expert, Trade (=craft), Vocation.

Professor

The professors were in a rage, all pleading for sin and imperfection, and could not endure to hear talk of perfection, and of a holy and sinless life.
GEORGE FOX: *Journal,* I (*c.* 1647), 1694
(*Professor*=one professing Christianity)

This world and life itself are only fragments; I'll go to a German professor and ask him to put them together; sitting in his dressing-gown and nightcap he'll make a neat system of them, and chink all the gaps in the universe.

HEINRICH HEINE: *Zu fragmentarisch ist Welt und Leben*, 1827

Whenever the cause of the people is entrusted to professors it is lost.

NIKOLAI LENIN: *Political Parties and the Proletariat*, 1917

" Red " professors are frequently distinguished from the old reactionary professors, not by a firmer backbone, but by a profounder illiteracy.

LEON TROTSKY: *The Permanent Revolution*, III, 1930

A professor of Greek is one who knows little Greek, and nothing else.

Author unidentified

[*See also* Pedagogue, Teaching.

Profit

Honor and profit lie not in one sack.

GEORGE HERBERT: *Outlandish Proverbs*, 1640

In the state of nature profit is the measure of right.

THOMAS HOBBES: *Philosophical Rudiments Concerning Government and Society*, I, 1651

Small profits and quick returns.

ENGLISH PHRASE, not recorded before the XIX century

Nothing contributes so much to the prosperity and happiness of a country as high profits.

DAVID RICARDO: *On Protection to Agriculture*, 1820

To put pressure upon the destitute for the sake of gain and to make a profit out of the need of another is condemned by all laws, human or divine.

POPE LEO XIII: *Rerum novarum*, May 15, 1891

We have learned the lesson that when opportunities for profit diminish, opportunities for jobs likewise disappear.

Resolution of the Executive Council of the American Federation of Labor, Jan. 31, 1940

Profit is better than fame. DANISH PROVERB

[*See also* Capital, Capital and Labor, Civilization, Honor, Nihilism, Partnership, Usury.

Profit and Loss

No great loss but some small profit.

JOHN RAY: *English Proverbs*, 1670

What I make on d' peanut I lose on d' damn banan'.

An Italian fruit-vendor in New York: To Theodore Roosevelt, *c.* 1890

You never lost money by taking a profit.

AMERICAN SAYING

Where profit is, loss is hidden near by.

JAPANESE PROVERB

Profiteer

At the conclusion of a ten years' war, how are we recompensed for the death of multitudes and the expense of millions but by contemplating the sudden glories of paymasters and agents, contractors and commissaries, whose equipages shine like meteors, and whose palaces rise like exhalations?

SAMUEL JOHNSON: *Thoughts Respecting Falkland's Islands*, 1771

[*See also* Patriot.

Profligate

[*See* Lady.

Profundity

It is better to be profound in clear terms than in obscure terms.

JOSEPH JOUBERT: *Pensées*, I, 1842

Prognosis

Those who swoon often, and without apparent cause, will die suddenly. A brusque answer from a courteous patient is a bad sign. Labored sleep in any disease is a bad sign.

HIPPOCRATES: *Aphorisms*, *c.* 400 B.C.

Progress

Alas, how faint,
How slow, the dawn of beauty and of truth,
Breaks the reluctant shades of gothic night
Which yet involve the nations!

MARK AKENSIDE: *The Pleasures of Imagination*, II, 1744

The ferocity of our ancestors, as of other nations, produced not fraud, but rapine. They had not yet learned to cheat, and attempted only to rob.

SAMUEL JOHNSON: *Memorandum prepared for James Boswell*, 1772

The march of the human mind is slow.

EDMUND BURKE: Speech on Conciliation with America, March 22, 1775

Laws and institutions must go hand in hand with the progress of the human mind. As that becomes more developed, more enlightened, as new discoveries are made, new truths disclosed, and manners and opinions change with the change of circumstances, institutions must advance also, and keep pace with the times.

THOMAS JEFFERSON: *Letter to Samuel Kercheval*, July 12, 1816

Man does not move in cycles, though nature does. Man's course is like that of an arrow.

S. T. COLERIDGE: *Table-Talk*, May 18, 1833

Progress is
The law of life; man is not man as yet.

ROBERT BROWNING: *Paracelsus*, V, 1835

The civilized man has built a coach, but has lost the use of his feet. He is supported on crutches, but lacks so much support of muscle. He has got a fine Geneva watch, but he has lost the skill to tell the hour by the sun.
R. W. EMERSON: *Self-Reliance,* 1841

Yet I doubt not thro' the ages one increasing purpose runs,
And the thoughts of men are widen'd with the process of the suns.
ALFRED TENNYSON: *Locksley Hall,* 1842

Every line of history inspires a confidence that we shall not go far wrong; that things mend.
R. W. EMERSON: *The Young American,* 1844

Oh, yet we trust that somehow good
Will be the final goal of ill,
To pangs of nature, sins of will,
Defects of doubt, and taints of blood.
ALFRED TENNYSON: *In Memoriam,* LIV, 1850

As natural selection works solely by and for the good of each being, all corporeal and mental endowments will tend to progress toward perfection.
CHARLES DARWIN: *The Origin of Species,* XV, 1859

Thoughtful men, once escaped from the blinding influences of traditional prejudice, will find in the lowly stock whence man has sprung the best evidence of the splendor of his capacities; and will discern in his long progress through the past a reasonable ground of faith in his attainment of the future.
T. H. HUXLEY: *Evidence as to Man's Place in Nature,* II, 1863

No one whose opinion deserves a moment's consideration can doubt that most of the great positive evils of the world are in themselves removable, and will, if human affairs continue to improve, be in the end reduced within narrow limits.
J. S. MILL: *Utilitarianism,* II, 1863

Progress, man's distinctive mark alone,
Not God's, and not the beast's.
ROBERT BROWNING: *A Death in the Desert,* 1864

Progress is only possible in those happy cases where the force of legality has gone far enough to bind the nation together, but not far enough to kill out all varieties and destroy nature's perpetual tendency to change.
WALTER BAGEHOT: *Physics and Politics,* 1869

The causes which most disturbed or accelerated the normal progress of society in antiquity were the appearance of great men; in modern times they have been the appearance of great inventions.
W. E. H. LECKY: *History of European Morals,* I, 1869

The history of progress is written in the lives of infidels.
R. G. INGERSOLL: Speech in New York, May 1, 1881

Not a change for the better in our human housekeeping has ever taken place that wise and good men have not opposed it — have not prophesied that the world would wake up to find its throat cut in consequence.
J. R. LOWELL: *Democracy,* 1884 (Address in Birmingham, Eng., Oct. 6)

The reason why the race of man moves slowly is because it must move all together.
THOMAS B. REED: Speech in Waterville, Maine, July 30, 1885

Every step forward is made at the cost of mental and physical pain to someone.
F. W. NIETZSCHE: *The Genealogy of Morals,* III, 1887

The pig that is being slaughtered as I write this line will leave the world better than it found it.
GEORGE MOORE: *Confessions of a Young Man,* XII, 1888

All progress is based upon a universal innate desire on the part of every organism to live beyond its income.
SAMUEL BUTLER: *Note-Books, c.* 1890

Great historical movements are never begun for the attainment of remote and imperfectly comprehended ends. They demand something concrete to work for; they need clearly defined, particular aims.
J. L. JAURÈS: *Études socialistes,* XII, 1902

Progress needs the brakeman, but the brakeman should not spend all his time putting on the brakes.
ELBERT HUBBARD: *Roycroft Dictionary and Book of Epigrams,* 1923

No progress is going back. LATIN PROVERB

[*See also* Change, Disobedience, Evolution, Laughter, Leadership, Liberalism.

Prohibition

There is a crying for wine in the streets; all joy is darkened, the mirth of the land is gone.
ISAIAH XXIV, 11, *c.* 700 B.C.

If you say, "Would there were no wine" because of the drunkards, then you must say, going on by degrees, "Would there were no steel," because of the murderers, "Would there were no night," because of the thieves, "Would there were no light," because of the informers, and "Would there were no women," because of adultery.
ST. JOHN CHRYSOSTOM: *Homilies, c.* 388

To forbid us anything is to make us have a mind for it.
MICHEL DE MONTAIGNE: *Essays,* II, 1580

I rejoice, as a moralist, at the prospect of a reduction of the duties on wine. It is an error to view a tax on that liquor as merely a tax on the rich. Prohibition of its use to the middling class is condemnation of them to poison whiskey.

THOMAS JEFFERSON: *Letter to M. de Neuville*, Dec. 12, 1818

Prohibition will work great injury to the cause of temperance. It is a species of intemperance within itself, for it goes beyond the bounds of reason in that it attempts to control a man's appetite by legislation, and makes a crime out of things that are not crimes. A Prohibition law strikes a blow at the very principles upon which our government was founded.

ABRAHAM LINCOLN: Speech in the Illinois House of Representatives, Dec. 18, 1840

Prohibition only drives drunkenness behind doors and into dark places, and does not cure it or even diminish it.

S. L. CLEMENS (MARK TWAIN): *Letter from New York to the Alta Californian* (San Francisco), May 28, 1867

I'd rather that England should be free than that England should be compulsorily sober. With freedom we might in the end attain sobriety, but in the other alternative we should eventually lose both freedom and sobriety.

W. C. MAGEE (ARCHBISHOP OF YORK): Sermon at Peterborough, 1868

To pass prohibitory laws to govern localities where the sentiment does not sustain them is simply equivalent to allowing free liquor, plus lawlessness.

THEODORE ROOSEVELT: *Letter to W. H. Taft*, July 16, 1908

After one year from the ratification of this article the manufacture, sale or transportation of intoxicating liquors within, the importation thereof into, or the exportation thereof from the United States and all territory subject to the jurisdiction thereof for beverage purposes is hereby prohibited.

CONSTITUTION OF THE UNITED STATES, Amendment XVIII, Jan. 29, 1919 (In force Jan. 16, 1920; repealed Dec. 5, 1933)

There aint gonna be no whiskey; there aint gonna be no gin;
There aint gonna be no highball to put the whiskey in;
There aint gonna be no cigarettes to make folks pale and thin;
But you can't take away that tendency to sin, sin, sin.

VAUGHN MILLER: *There Aint Gonna Be No Whiskey*, 1919 (Mr. Miller's copyright is dated July 30, 1919. The ditty was popular during the years of Prohibition, and developed many variants. In one of the most familiar the last line became " There aint gonna be no women to make you sin, sin, sin ")

The Republican administration has failed to enforce the Prohibition law; is guilty of trafficking in liquor permits, and has become the protector of violators of this law. The Democratic party pledges itself to respect and enforce the Constitution and all laws.

Democratic National Platform, 1924

A great social and economic experiment, noble in motive and far-reaching in purpose.

HERBERT C. HOOVER: *Letter to William E. Borah*, Feb. 28, 1928

We advocate the repeal of the Eighteenth Amendment. We urge the enactment of such measures by the several states as will actually promote temperance, effectively prevent the return of the saloon and bring the liquor traffic into the open under complete supervision and control by the states.

Democratic National Platform, 1932

We regard voluntary total abstinence from all intoxicants as the obligation of the citizen, and the complete legal prohibition of the traffic in alcoholic drinks as the duty of civil government.

The Doctrines and Discipline of the Methodist Episcopal Church, II, 1932

Proletariat

The hungry and wretched proletarians suck dry the public treasury.

CICERO: *Ad Atticum*, I, c. 50 B.C.

In dirt and darkness hundreds stink content.

ALEXANDER POPE: *The First Epistle of the First Book of Horace*, 1735

I am one of " the sons of little men."

ROBERT BURNS: *Letter to Mrs. Dunlop*, Jan. 15, 1787

Nature, in forming some men, intended that they should always remain in a subaltern situation.

NAPOLEON I: To Barry E. O'Meara at St. Helena, Feb. 28, 1817

The German proletariat is the theorist of the European proletariat; the English proletariat is its political economist; and the French is its politician.

KARL MARX: *On the King of Prussia and Social Reform*, 1845

Look at the Paris Commune. That was the dictatorship of the proletariat.

FRIEDRICH ENGELS: Introduction to KARL MARX: *Civil War in France*, 1871

The rights of man are incomplete and mutilated in the proletarian, for he cannot perform a single act in his life without alienating a part of his individuality. . . . He cannot eat, work, clothe, or shelter himself without paying a ransom of one sort or another to the capitalist class.

JEAN JAURÈS: *Études socialistes,* I, 1902

What the proletariat needs is a bath of blood.

BENITO MUSSOLINI: Speech in Milan, July 22, 1919

The dictatorship of the proletariat means the rule of the proletariat over the bourgeoisie. It is a rule unhampered by law, and it is based upon force.

JOSEPH STALIN: Speech at Sverdloff University, April, 1924

The Academy thinks. The bourgeoisie believes. The proletariat feels. FRENCH PROVERB

[*See also* Classes, Communism, Culture (Proletarian), Demagogue, Mob, Multitude, People, Populace, Rabble.

Prologue

It is a foolish thing to make a long prologue, and be short in the story itself.

II MACCABEES II, 32, *c.* 75 B.C.

Promise

Promise is most given when the least is said.

CHRISTOPHER MARLOWE and GEORGE CHAPMAN: *Hero and Leander,* 1598

He was ever precise in promise-keeping.

SHAKESPEARE: *Measure for Measure,* I, 1604

His promises were, as he then was, mighty;
But his performance, as he is now, nothing.

SHAKESPEARE and JOHN FLETCHER: *Henry VIII,* IV, 1613

Great men,
Till they have gained their ends, are giants in
Their promises, but, those obtained, weak pigmies
In their performance.

PHILIP MASSINGER: *The Great Duke of Florence,* II, 1636

Promises are the pitfalls of fools.

BALTASAR GRACIÁN: *The Art of Worldly Wisdom,* CXCI, 1647

We promise according to our hopes, and perform according to our fears.

LA ROCHEFOUCAULD: *Maxims,* 1665

A man apt to promise is apt to forget.

THOMAS FULLER: *Gnomologia,* 1732

I defy the boldest liar among travelers to say that he has ever encountered a country or tribe where it is laudable to break one's word.

VOLTAIRE: *Letter to Frederick the Great,* Oct., 1737

Promises and pie-crust are made to be broken.

JONATHAN SWIFT: *Polite Conversation,* 1738

Undertake not what you cannot perform but be careful to keep your promise.

GEORGE WASHINGTON: *Early copy-book,* before 1748

No promise binds, although it has been accepted by the other party, if it afterward becomes impossible, or very harmful, or unlawful, or inexpedient, or, generally speaking, if any notable change of circumstances takes place, so that, if it had been foreseen, no promise would have been made.

ALPHONSO MARIA DI LIGOURI: *Theologia moralis,* IV, 1753

If you want to get on in this world, make many promises, but don't keep them.

NAPOLEON I: To Gaspard Gourgaud at St. Helena, 1815–1818

It is hard to promise, but easy to perform.

MOTTO OF COUNT ANDRASSY (1823–1890)

Oh, promise me.

HARRY B. SMITH: Title of a song in *Robin Hood,* I, 1890 (Music by REGINALD DE KOVEN)

A Christian cannot promise to do or not to do a given thing at a given moment, for he cannot know what the law of love, which is the rule of his life, may require of him at that moment.

LYOF N. TOLSTOY: *The Kingdom of God is Within You,* 1893

The more you promise, the less you will have to deliver. AMERICAN POLITICAL MAXIM

We make large promises to avoid making small presents. FRENCH PROVERB

A promise is a kind of debt.

MOROCCAN PROVERB

[*See also* Man, Oath.

Pronoun

A pronoun is used instead of a noun,
As: " James was tired, and he sat down."

OLD ENGLISH RHYME

Pronunciation

Write with the learned, pronounce with the vulgar.

BENJAMIN FRANKLIN: *Poor Richard's Almanac,* 1738

Proof

In the eyes of a wise judge, proofs by reasoning are of more value than witnesses.

CICERO: *De republica,* I, *c.* 50 B.C.

The proof of the pudding is in the eating.

ENGLISH PROVERB, derived from the Latin and current since the XIV century

Be sure of it; give me the ocular proof.

SHAKESPEARE: *Othello,* III, 1604

When one's proofs are aptly chosen four are as valid as four dozen.

MATTHEW PRIOR: *Alma,* I, *c.* 1716

That which proves too much, proves nothing.
THOMAS FULLER: *Gnomologia,* 1732

The proof of gold is fire; the proof of a woman, gold; the proof of a man, a woman.
BENJAMIN FRANKLIN: *Poor Richard's Almanac,* 1757

Nothing in this world is provable.
JOHN KEATS: *Letter to Benjamin Bailey,* March 13, 1818

The burden of proof lies on the plaintiff. (Actori incumbit onus probandi.)
LEGAL MAXIM

The proof lies upon him who affirms, not upon him who denies. (Affirmanti, non neganti, incumbit probatio.) IBID.

That which is asserted without proof may also be denied without proof. (Quod gratis asseritur, gratis negatur.) IBID.

Which was to be proved. (Quod erat demonstrandum.)
LATIN PHRASE, generally contracted to Q.E.D.

Thus I prove. (Sic probo.)
Medieval scholastic formula

[*See also* Evidence.

Propaganda

Each government accuses the other of perfidy, intrigue and ambition, as a means of heating the imagination of their respective nations, and incensing them to hostilities.
THOMAS PAINE: *The Rights of Man,* I, 1791

Talk much about a thing, and you will put it into the people's heads.
H. H. BRACKENRIDGE: *Modern Chivalry,* 1792

Government, as government, can bring nothing but the influence of hopes and fears to support its doctrines. It carries on controversy, not with reasons, but with threats and bribes.
T. B. MACAULAY: *Southey's Colloquies,* 1830

There is no need for propaganda to be rich in intellectual content.
P. J. GOEBBELS: Speech at Nürnberg, Aug. 20, 1926

Propagation

[*See* Peace, Procreation, Reproduction.

Property

The property of the lazy and shiftless belongs to those who are willing to face labor and danger.
DEMOSTHENES: *First Philippic,* 351 B.C.

Is it not lawful for me to do what I will with mine own? MATTHEW XX, 15, *c.* 75

Property was at first a creature of the human will, but once it was established one man was prohibited by the law of nature from seizing the property of another against his will.
HUGO GROTIUS: *De jure belli ac pacis,* I, 1625

It is good and just that each should be given his own, and the use and possession thereof should be granted him without annoyance.
HENRY MORE: *Enchiridion ethicum,* IV, 1667

That dog is mine, said those poor children; that place in the sun is mine. Such is the beginning of usurpation throughout the earth.
BLAISE PASCAL: *Pensées,* VII, 1670

The reason why men enter into society is the preservation of their property.
JOHN LOCKE: *Treatises on Government,* II, 1690

Few enjoyments are given us from the open and liberal hand of nature; but by art, labor and industry we can extract them in great abundance. Hence the ideas of property become necessary in all civil society.
DAVID HUME: *An Enquiry Concerning the Principles of Morals,* III, 1751

Mine is better than ours.
BENJAMIN FRANKLIN: *Poor Richard's Almanac,* 1756

The great end for which men entered into society was to preserve their property. That right is preserved sacred and incommunicable in all instances where it has not been taken away or abridged by some public law for the good of the whole.
LORD CAMDEN: *Judgment in Entick* vs. *Carrington,* 1765 (Cf. LOCKE, *ante,* 1690)

[It is an] essential, unalterable right in nature, engrafted into the British constitution as a fundamental law, and ever held sacred and irrevocable by the subjects within the realm, that what a man has honestly acquired is absolutely his own, which he may freely give, but cannot be taken from him without his consent.
SAMUEL ADAMS: *The Massachusetts Circular Letter,* Feb. 11, 1768

In nature, exclusive property is theft.
J. P. BRISSOT DE WARVILLE: *Théorie des lois criminelles,* 1780 (Cf. PROUDHON, *post,* 1840)

Whenever there is, in any country, uncultivated land and unemployed poor, it is clear that the laws of property have been so far extended as to violate natural right.
THOMAS JEFFERSON: *Letter to James Madison,* 1785

In as far as a man is in a way to derive either happiness or security from any object which belongs to the class of things, such thing is said to be his property.

JEREMY BENTHAM: *The Principles of Morals and Legislation*, XVI, 1789

The right to property being inviolable and sacred, no one ought to be deprived of it except in cases of evident public necessity legally ascertained, and on condition of a previous just indemnity.

Declaration of the Rights of Man by the French National Assembly, XVII, 1789

The power of perpetuating our property in our families is one of the most valuable and interesting circumstances belonging to it, and that which tends the most to the perpetuation of society itself. It makes our weakness subservient to our virtue; it grafts benevolence even upon avarice.

EDMUND BURKE: *Reflections on the Revolution in France*, III, 1790

From the respect paid to property flow, as from a poisoned fountain, most of the evils and vices which render this world such a dreary scene to the contemplative mind.

MARY WOLLSTONECRAFT: *A Vindication of the Rights of Woman*, IX, 1792

Kill a man's family, and he may brook it,
But keep your hands out of his breeches' pocket.

BYRON: *Don Juan*, X, 1823

The natural tendency of every society in which property enjoys tolerable security is to increase in wealth.

T. B. MACAULAY: *Sir James Mackintosh*, 1835 (Edinburgh Review, July)

Property has been well compared to snow — "if it fall level today, it will be blown into drifts tomorrow."

R. W. EMERSON: *Nature*, 1836

It is the right of the possessor of property to be placed on an equal footing with all his fellow-citizens, in every respect. If he is not to be exalted on account of his wealth, neither is he to be denounced.

J. FENIMORE COOPER: *The American Democrat*, XXVIII, 1838

Property is desirable as the ground work of moral independence, as a means of improving the faculties, and of doing good to others, and as the agent in all that distinguishes the civilized man from the savage. IBID.

Every human being, be he idolater, Mahometan, Jew, papist, Socinian, Deist, or atheist, naturally loves life, shrinks from pain, and desires comforts which can be enjoyed only in communities where property is secure.

T. B. MACAULAY: *Gladstone on Church and State*, 1839 (Edinburgh Review, April)

Property is theft. (La propriété c'est le vol.)

P. J. PROUDHON: *Qu'est-ce que la propriété?*, 1840 (Cf. BRISSOT, *ante*, 1780)

I laid my bones to, and drudged for the good I possess; it was not got by fraud, nor by luck, but by work, and you must show me a warrant like these stubborn facts in your own fidelity and labor before I suffer you, on the faith of a few fine words, to ride into my estate, and claim to scatter it as your own.

R. W. EMERSON: *The Conservative*, 1841

The law may in a mad freak say that all shall have power except the owners of property; they shall have no vote. Nevertheless, by a higher law, the property will, year after year, write every statute that respects property.

R. W. EMERSON: *Politics*, 1841

Property is the right to use and abuse. It is the absolute, irresponsible dominion of man over his person and his goods. If it ceased to be the right to abuse it would cease to be property.

P. J. PROUDHON: *Système des contradictions économiques*, I, 1845

Property exists by grace of the law. It is not a fact, but a legal fiction.

MAX STIRNER: *The Ego and His Own*, 1845

To what property am I entitled? To any property that I can get hold of. IBID.

You reproach us with planning to do away with your property. Precisely; that is just what we propose.

KARL MARX and FRIEDRICH ENGELS: *The Communist Manifesto*, 1848

No man acquires property without acquiring with it a little arithmetic also.

R. W. EMERSON: *Representative Men*, IV, 1850

The only true foundation of any right to property is man's labor. That is property, and that alone, which labor of man has made such.

GALUSHA A. GROW: Speech in the House of Representatives, 1852

The highest law gives a thing to him who can use it.

H. D. THOREAU: *Journal*, Nov. 9, 1852

Property is desirable, is a positive good in the world. Let not him who is houseless pull down the house of another, but let him work diligently and build one for himself, thus by example assuring that his own shall be safe from violence when built.

ABRAHAM LINCOLN: Reply to a committee, March 21, 1864

By right or wrong,
Lands and goods go to the strong.
Property will brutely draw
Still to the proprietor;
Silver to silver creep and wind,
And kind to kind.

R. W. EMERSON: *Initial Dæmonic and Celestial Love*, III, 1867

No state shall . . . deprive any person of life, liberty, or property without due process of law.
CONSTITUTION OF THE UNITED STATES, Amendment XIV, July 28, 1868

Private property is at once the consequence and the basis of the state.
M. A. BAKUNIN: *Dieu et l'état,* 1871

The church . . . enjoins that the right of property and of its disposal, which are derived from nature, should in every case remain inviolate.
POPE LEO XIII: *Quod apostolici muneris,* Dec. 28, 1878

There can be to the ownership of anything no rightful title which is not derived from the title of the producer and does not rest upon the natural right of the man to himself.
HENRY GEORGE: *Progress and Poverty,* VII, 1879

A vested right of action is property in the same sense in which tangible things are property, and is equally protected against arbitrary interference. Whether it springs from contract or the principles of the Common Law, it is not competent for the legislature to take it away.
MR. JUSTICE STANLEY MATTHEWS: *Decision in the Supreme Court of the United States in Pritchard* vs. *Morton,* 1882

The last thing we need to be anxious about is property. It always has friends or the means of making them.
J. R. LOWELL: *Democracy,* 1884 (Address in Birmingham, Eng., Oct. 6)

Property is the most fundamental and complex of social facts, and the most important of human interests; it is, therefore, the hardest to understand, the most delicate to meddle with, and the easiest to dogmatize about.
W. G. SUMNER: *The Family and Property,* 1888

Every man has by nature the right to possess property of his own. This is one of the chief points of distinction between man and the lower animals.
POPE LEO XIII: *Rerum novarum,* May 15, 1891

Equal liberty, in the property sphere, is such a balance between the liberty to take and the liberty to keep that the two liberties may coexist without conflict or invasion.
BENJAMIN R. TUCKER: *Instead of a Book,* 1893

Property is based on violence and slaying and the threat thereof.
LYOF N. TOLSTOY: *The Kingdom of God is Within You,* 1893

Few rich men own their own property. The property owns them.
R. G. INGERSOLL: Speech in New York, Oct. 29, 1896

Property is a legal relation by virtue of which some one has, within a certain group of men, the exclusive privilege of ultimately disposing of a thing.
PAUL ELTZBACHER: *Anarchism,* 1900

The instinct of ownership is fundamental in man's nature.
WILLIAM JAMES: *The Varieties of Religious Experience,* XI, 1902

Of the goods of the earth man has not merely the use, like the brutes, but he also has the right of permanent proprietorship; and not merely of those things which are consumed by use, but also of those not consumed by use.
POPE PIUS X: *Apostolic Letter to the Bishops of Italy on Catholic Social Action,* Dec. 18, 1903

The right of private property, the fruit of labor or industry, or of concession or donation by others, is an incontrovertible natural right; and everybody can dispose reasonably of such property as he thinks fit. IBID.

The great body of property is socially administered now, and the function of private ownership is to divine in advance the equilibrium of social desires.
O. W. HOLMES II: Speech in New York, Feb. 15, 1913

The right to hold property is a natural right. It is the safeguard of family life, the stimulus and the reward of work.
Pastoral Letter of the French Roman Catholic Hierarchy, Spring, 1919

Things have come to a hell of a pass
When a man can't wallop his own jackass.
Author unidentified (Often quoted by HENRY WATTERSON, *c.* 1900)

The state does not recognize ownership as the absolute dominion of the person over the thing, but it considers it the most useful of social functions. No property can be reserved exclusively by a person as if it were a very part of him; nor is it lawful for a slothful proprietor to allow it to remain idle or to dispose of it unwisely, to the exclusion of others.
GABRIELLE D'ANNUNZIO: *Constitution of the Free State of Fiume,* Aug. 27, 1920

The immense numbers of propertyless wage-earners on the one hand, and the superabundant wealth of the propertied few on the other, offers unanswerable proof that, in this age of industrialism, the earthly goods that are so abundantly produced are distributed among and shared by the various classes of men in a far from equitable manner.
POPE PIUS XI: *Quadragesimo anno,* May 15, 1931

The natural law, which is God's will made manifest, demands that proper order be observed in the utilization of natural resources for human need, and it is essential to that right order that everything have its proper owner. IBID.

The riches and goods of Christians are not common, as touching the right, title and possession of the same, as some do falsely boast. The Doctrines and Discipline of the Methodist Episcopal Church, I, 1932

He who feeds the hen ought to have the egg. DANISH PROVERB

As long as I live I'll spit in my own parlor. IRISH PROVERB

Who has, is. (Chi ha, è.) ITALIAN PROVERB

He who owns the surface owns also up to the sky above it, and the center of the earth beneath it. (Cujus est solum ejus est usque ad coelum et ad inferos.) LEGAL MAXIM

It is for the public good that no one use his property badly. (Expedit rei publicæ ne sua re quis male utatur.) IBID.

Whoever owns the river bank owns the fish. RUSSIAN PROVERB

[*See also* Bequest, Capital, Capitalism, Classes, Communism, Covetousness, Democracy, Divine Right, Government, Inheritance, Land, Mine and Thine, Possession, Slavery, State, Suffrage (Universal), Taxes, Wealth.

Prophecy

Despise not prophesying. I THESSALONIANS V, 20, *c.* 51

In my letters from England I learned that the Bishop of Worcester was of opinion that in the year 1715 the city of Rome would be burnt to the ground, that before the year 1745 the popish religion would be rooted out of the world, that before the year 1790 the Jews and Gentiles would be converted to Christianity and then would begin the millennium. WILLIAM BYRD: *Diary*, March 31, 1710

Wise men may well be mistaken in futures. THOMAS FULLER: *Gnomologia*, 1732

The obscurity or unintelligibleness of one part of a prophecy does not, in any degree, invalidate the proof of foresight arising from the appearing completion of those other parts which are understood. JOSEPH BUTLER: *The Analogy of Religion*, II, 1736

Don't never prophesy — onless ye know. J. R. LOWELL: *The Biglow Papers*, II, 1862

To deal in prophecies is to deal in lies. WELSH PROVERB

[*See also* Dream, Prophet.

Prophet

If the prophet be deceived when he hath spoken a thing, I the Lord have deceived that prophet, and I will stretch out my hand upon him, and will destroy him. EZEKIEL XIV, 9, *c.* 600 B.C.

Is Saul also among the prophets? I SAMUEL X, 11, *c.* 500 B.C.

A prophet is not without honor, but in his own country, and among his own kin, and in his own house. MARK VI, 4, *c.* 70 (Cf. MATTHEW XIII, 57; JOHN IV, 44, *c.* 115)

Beware of false prophets, which come to you in sheep's clothing, but inwardly they are ravening wolves. MATTHEW VII, 15, *c.* 75

Many false prophets shall rise, and shall deceive many. MATTHEW XXIV, 11

I am the voice of one crying in the wilderness. JOHN I, 23, *c.* 115

The wisest prophets make sure of the event first. HORACE WALPOLE: *Letter to Thomas Walpole*, Feb. 9, 1785

The revelations of devout and learn'd
Who rose before us, and as prophets burn'd,
Are all but stories, which, awoke from sleep
They told their comrades, and to sleep return'd.
EDWARD FITZGERALD: Tr. of OMAR KHAYYÁM: *Rubáiyát* (*c.* 1100), 1857

It is the sad destiny of a prophet that when, after working twenty years, he convinces his contemporaries, his adversaries also succeed, and he is no longer convinced himself. F. W. NIETZSCHE: *Human All-too-Human*, II, 1878

God has given to every people a prophet in its own tongue. ARAB PROVERB

The best prophets are children and fools. FRENCH PROVERB

The best guesser is the best prophet. GREEK PROVERB

Whoever dies without recognizing the prophet of his time dies a pagan. MOHAMMEDAN PROVERB

[*See also* Arms, Historian, Jester, Marx (Karl), Poet, Prophecy, Theocracy, Water.

Proposal

To represent in a novel a girl proposing marriage to a man would be deemed unnatural, but nothing is more common; there are few young men who have not received at least a dozen offers, nay, more. GEORGE MOORE: *Confessions of a Young Man*, XI, 1888

Propriety

If it were not for the rules of propriety father and son might have the same mate. CONFUCIUS: *The Book of Rites*, I, *c.* 500 B.C.

The laws of propriety have the least force behind them but they are the best obeyed.
LA ROCHEFOUCAULD: *Maxims,* 1665

. . . not proper to be related by a female pen.
SARAH KEMBLE KNIGHT: *Diary,* 1704

The perfect hostess will see to it that the works of male and female authors be properly separated on her book shelves. Their proximity, unless they happen to be married, should not be tolerated.
LADY GOUGH: *Etiquette,* 1863

[*See also* Fashion.

Prose

For more than forty years I have been speaking prose without knowing it.
J. B. MOLIÈRE: *Le bourgeois gentilhomme,* II, 1670

I might have been a poet if I had given up my mind to it. In prose I found more room.
W. S. LANDOR: *Letter to Robert Browning,* Nov. 12, 1845

When the brain gets as dry as an empty nut,
When the reason stands on its squarest toes,
When the mind (like a beard) has a formal cut, —
There is place and enough for the pains of prose.
AUSTIN DOBSON: *The Ballad of Prose and Rhyme,* 1873

Order, precision, directness are the radical merits of prose thought, and it is more than merely legitimate that they should form the criterion of prose style.
WALTER PATER: *English Literature,* 1886 (London Guardian, Feb. 17)

A perfect prose is the last word in literature, since it contains every kind of rhythm to be found in verse, and other rhythms as well, and all in such a rich variety and seeming irregularity that while no rhythm is insistent every rhythm is heard.
A. R. ORAGE: *Selected Essays,* 1935

[*See also* Metaphor, Poetry and Prose.

Proselyte

A man is glad to gain numbers on his side, as they serve to strengthen him in his private opinions. Every proselyte is like a new argument for the establishment of the faith.
JOSEPH ADDISON: *The Spectator,* Oct. 2, 1711

[*See also* Convert.

Prosperity

The Lord was with Joseph, and he was a prosperous man. GENESIS XXXIX, 2, *c.* 700 B.C.

A state that is prosperous always honors the gods.
ÆSCHYLUS: *The Seven Against Thebes,* *c.* 490 B.C.

In prosperity there is never any dearth of friends. EURIPIDES: *Hecuba, c.* 426 B.C.

In prosperity let us particularly avoid pride, disdain, and arrogance.
CICERO: *De officiis,* I, 78 B.C.

So long as a man enjoys prosperity, he cares not whether he is beloved.
LUCAN: *Pharsalia,* VII, 65

The remembrance of past wants makes present prosperity more pleasant.
ST. JOHN CHRYSOSTOM: *Homilies,* XIII, *c.* 388

Prosperity doth bewitch men, seeming clear;
As seas do laugh, show white, when rocks are near.
JOHN WEBSTER: *The White Devil,* V, *c.* 1608

Prosperity's the very bond of love.
SHAKESPEARE: *The Winter's Tale,* IV, *c.* 1611

Prosperity lets go the bridle.
GEORGE HERBERT: *Outlandish Proverbs,* 1640

Prosperity makes very few friends.
LUC DE VAUVENARGUES: *Réflexions,* 1746

The prosperity of any commercial nation is regulated by the prosperity of the rest. If they are poor, she cannot be rich; and her condition, be it what it may, is an index of the height of the commercial tide in other nations.
THOMAS PAINE: *The Rights of Man,* II, 1791

Prosperity is the surest breeder of insolence I know.
S. L. CLEMENS (MARK TWAIN): *Letter from New York to the Alta Californian* (San Francisco), Feb. 23, 1867

There are those who believe that, if you will only legislate to make the well-to-do prosperous, their prosperity will leak through to those below. The Democratic idea, however, has been that if you legislate to make the masses prosperous, their prosperity will find its way up through every class which rests upon them.
W. J. BRYAN: Speech at the Democratic National Convention, Chicago, July 8, 1896

If we are brought face to face with the naked issue of either keeping or totally destroying a prosperity in which the majority share, but in which some share improperly, why, as sensible men, we must decide that it is a great deal better that some people should prosper too much than that no one should prosper enough.
THEODORE ROOSEVELT: Speech in Fitchburg, Mass., Sept. 2, 1902

The slogan of progress is changing from the full dinner pail to the full garage.
HERBERT HOOVER: Speech in New York, Oct. 22, 1928

Man can bear all things except good days.
DUTCH PROVERB

Good times make bad people.
GERMAN PROVERB

The prosperity of this world is like writing on water.
HINDU PROVERB

In prosperous times no altars smoke.
ITALIAN PROVERB

In prosperity be cautious; in adversity, patient.
PORTUGUESE PROVERB

[*See also* Adversity, Chicken, Friend, Friendship, Greatness, Happiness, Profit, Soap.

Prostitute

A prostitute is a furnace of love, burning youth and money.
BHARTRIHARI: *The Sringa Sataka, c.* 625

No woman is worth money that will take money.
JOHN VANBRUGH: *The Relapse,* II, 1696

Nor are the nymphs that breathe the rural air
So fair as Cynthia, nor so chaste as fair:
These to the town afford each fresher face,
And the clown's trull receives the peer's embrace;
From whom, should chance again convey her down,
The peer's disease in turn attacks the clown.
GEORGE CRABBE: *The Village,* II, 1783

Prostitutes . . . trample on virgin bashfulness with a sort of bravado, and, glorifying in their shame, become more audaciously lewd than men, however depraved.
MARY WOLLSTONECRAFT: *A Vindication of the Rights of Woman,* VII, 1792

A devoted part of the sex — devoted for the salvation of the rest.
MARY WOLLSTONECRAFT: *A Vindication of the Rights of Woman,* VIII

Prostitutes are a necessity. Without them, men would attack respectable women in the streets.
NAPOLEON I: To Gaspard Gourgaud at St. Helena, Jan. 9, 1817

The life of a *fille de joie* is as bare of joy as it is of honor.
ARTHUR SCHOPENHAUER: *Parerga und Paralipomena,* 1851

The prostitute draggles her shawl, her bonnet bobs on her tipsy and pimpled neck;
The crowd laugh at her blackguard oaths, the men jeer and wink to each other;
(Miserable! I do not laugh at your oaths, nor jeer you).
WALT WHITMAN: *Walt Whitman,* 1855

Be composed — be at ease with me — I am Walt Whitman, liberal and lusty as nature,
Not till the sun excludes you do I exclude you,
Not till the waters refuse to glisten for you and the leaves to rustle for you do my words refuse to glisten and rustle for you.
WALT WHITMAN: *To a Common Prostitute,* 1860

Herself the supreme type of vice, she is ultimately the most efficient guardian of virtue. But for her, the unchallenged purity of countless happy homes would be polluted, and not a few who, in the pride of their untempted chastity, think of her with an indignant shudder, would have known the agony of remorse and of despair. In that one degraded and ignoble form are concentrated the passions that might have filled the world with shame. She remains, while creeds and civilizations rise and fall, the eternal priestess of humanity, blasted for the sins of the people.
W. E. H. LECKY: *History of European Morals,* v, 1869

The white slave.
BARTLEY CAMPBELL: Title of a play, 1882

Prostitution, as it exists in Christian countries, is an extraordinarily undesirable career.
BERTRAND RUSSELL: *Marriage and Morals,* XI, 1929

He who marries his daughter to an old man makes a prostitute of her.
HEBREW PROVERB

[*See also* Bawdy-house, Brothel, Harlot, Slang, Whore.

Protestant

We seek our pardons from our heavenly hope,
And not by works, or favor from the pope;
To saints we make no prayer, or intercession,
And unto God alone we make confession.
JOHN TAYLOR: *Mad Fashions,* 1642

I die not only a Protestant, but with a heart full of hatred of popery, prelacy, and all superstition whatsoever.
ARCHIBALD, EARL OF ARGYLE: Last words on the scaffold, 1661

A real Protestant is a person who has examined the evidences of religion for himself, and who accepts them because, after examination, he is satisfied of their genuineness and sufficiency.
P. G. HAMERTON: *French and English,* 1889

[*See also* Arms, Bible, Christian, Irish.

Protestantism

At the Reformation the English rejected Purgatory and kept Hell.
Ascribed to J. HORNE TOOKE (1736–1812) in G. H. POWELL: *Reminiscences and Table-Talk of Samuel Rogers,* 1903

If Protestantism always keeps the same name, though its belief is perpetually shifting, it is because that name is purely negative, and means only the denial of Catholicism, so that the less it believes, and the more it protests, the more consistently Protestant it becomes. Since, then, its name becomes continually truer, it must subsist until it perishes, just as an ulcer disappears with the last atom of the flesh which it has been eating away.
JOSEPH DE MAISTRE: *Du pape*, II, 1819

No Christian nation, which did not adopt the principles of the Reformation before the end of the Sixteenth Century, should ever have adopted them. Catholic communities have, since that time, become infidel and become Catholic again; but none has become Protestant.
T. B. MACAULAY: *Von Ranke*, 1840 (Edinburgh Review, Oct.)

England is the head of Protestantism, the center of its movements, and the stronghold of its power. Weakened in England, it is paralyzed everywhere; conquered in England, it is conquered throughout the world.
HENRY CARDINAL MANNING: Speech at the Third Provincial Council of Westminster, 1859

Definition of Protestantism: hemiplegic paralysis of Christianity — and of reason.
F. W. NIETZSCHE: *The Antichrist*, X, 1888

The uncleanest variety of Christianity that exists, and the most incurable and indestructible.
F. W. NIETZSCHE: *The Antichrist*, LXI

From Wyclif to Socinus, or even to Münzer, Rothmann and John of Leyden, I fail to find a trace of any desire to set reason free. The most that can be discovered is a proposal to change masters. From being the slave of the papacy the intellect was to become the serf of the Bible.
T. H. HUXLEY: *Controverted Questions*, 1892

What we call Protestantism was really a free thought movement; a revolt against religion.
E. W. HOWE: *Preaching From the Audience*, 1926

[*See also* Bible, Calvinism, Convert, King.

Protestation

The lady doth protest too much methinks.
SHAKESPEARE: *Hamlet*, III, *c.* 1601

Proverb

A proverb and a byword.
I KINGS IX, 7, *c.* 500 B.C.

Despise not the discoveries of the wise, but acquaint thyself with their proverbs, for of them thou shalt learn instruction.
ECCLESIASTICUS VIII, 8, *c.* 180 B.C.

I am proverb'd with a grandsire phrase.
SHAKESPEARE: *Romeo and Juliet*, I, *c.* 1596

Proverbs are old-said sooth.
HENRY PORTER: *Two Angry Women of Abington*, I, 1599

Patch grief with proverbs.
SHAKESPEARE: *Much Ado About Nothing*, V, *c.* 1599

The proverb is something justy.
SHAKESPEARE: *Hamlet*, III, *c.* 1601

I do not say a proverb is amiss when aptly and seasonably applied; but to be forever discharging them, right or wrong, hit or miss, renders conversation insipid and vulgar.
CERVANTES: *Don Quixote*, II, 1615

Proverbs may not improperly be called the philosophy of the common people.
JAMES HOWELL: *Proverbs*, 1659

A proverb is much matter decocted into few words.
THOMAS FULLER: *Worthies of England*, II, 1662

Proverbs . . . receive their chief value from the stamp and esteem of ages through which they have passed.
WILLIAM TEMPLE: *Of Ancient and Modern Learning*, 1692

Wise men make proverbs, but fools repeat 'em.
SAMUEL PALMER: *Moral Essays on Proverbs*, pref., 1710

Constant popping off of proverbs will make thee a by-word thyself.
THOMAS FULLER: *Introductio ad Prudentiam*, I, 1731

Proverbial expressions and trite sayings are the flowers of the rhetoric of a vulgar man.
LORD CHESTERFIELD: *Letter to his son*, Sept. 27, 1749

The proverbial wisdom of the populace in the streets, on the roads, and in the markets instructs the ear of him who studies man more fully than a thousand rules ostentatiously arranged.
Anon.: *Proverbs, or the Manual of Wisdom*, 1804

Proverbs consist usually of a natural fact selected as a picture or parable of a moral truth. Thus: A rolling stone gathers no moss; A bird in the hand is worth two in the bush. In their primary sense these are trivial facts, but we repeat them for the value of their analogical import.
R. W. EMERSON: *Nature*, 1836

Proverbs are the sanctuary of the intuitions.
R. W. EMERSON: *Compensation*, 1841

The ready money of human experience.
J. R. LOWELL: *My Study Windows*, 1871

The use of proverbs is characteristic of an unlettered people. They are invaluable treasures to dunces with good memories.
JOHN HAY: *Castilian Days*, XII, 1872

A proverb is one man's wit and all men's wisdom.
Ascribed to LORD JOHN RUSSELL (1792–1878)

The old sayings we quote from day to day represent the wisdom of thousands of years. The old books in your house are mainly rubbish: some one has squeezed the good out of them, and is repeating it on the highways. E. W. HOWE: *Sinner Sermons*, 1926

A proverb is a racial aphorism which has been, or still is, in common use, conveying advice or counsel, invariably camouflaged figuratively, disguised in metaphor or allegory.
S. G. CHAMPION: *Racial Proverbs*, intro., 1938

A proverb is to speech what salt is to food.
ARAB PROVERB

Proverbs in talk are torches in the dark.
BOSNIAN PROVERB

Judge a man by his favorite proverbs.
FRENCH PROVERB

A man's life is often built upon a proverb.
GERMAN PROVERB

Judge a country by the quality of its proverbs.
IBID.

He who knows proverbs well can get out of almost any difficulty. HINDU PROVERB

Nothing can beat a proverb. IRISH PROVERB

There is no proverb without its grain of truth.
RUSSIAN PROVERB

A proverb is a little gospel. SPANISH PROVERB

[*See also* Adage, Ages, Aphorism, Books, Maxim.

Providence

The Lord killeth, and maketh alive, he bringeth down to the grave, and bringeth up. The Lord maketh poor, and maketh rich: he bringeth low, and lifteth up. He raiseth up the poor out of the dust, and lifteth up the beggar from the dunghill, to set them among princes, and to make them inherit the throne of glory. I SAMUEL II, 6–8, *c.* 500 B.C.

Man proposes, God disposes.
PLAUTUS: *Bacchides*, I, *c.* 200 B.C.

God never sendeth mouth but he sendeth meat.
JOHN HEYWOOD: *Proverbs*, 1546

He that doth the ravens feed,
Yea, providently caters for the sparrow,
Be comfort to my age!
SHAKESPEARE: *As You Like It*, II, *c.* 1600

There's a special providence in the fall of a sparrow. If it be now, 'tis not to come; if it be not to come, it will be now; if it be not now, yet it will come.
SHAKESPEARE: *Hamlet*, V, *c.* 1601

What in me is dark,
Illumine; what is low, raise and support;
That to the height of this great argument
I may assert eternal Providence,
And justify the ways of God to men.
JOHN MILTON: *Paradise Lost*, I, 1667

If you leap into a well Providence is not bound to fetch you out.
THOMAS FULLER: *Gnomologia*, 1732

God tempers the wind to the shorn lamb.
LAURENCE STERNE: *A Sentimental Journey*, II, 1768 (Quoted as a proverb; for its earlier history see under Lamb)

God has made the back to the burthen.
WILLIAM COBBETT: *Rural Rides*, 1822

However benevolent may be the intentions of Providence, they do not always advance the happiness of the individual.
WILHELM VON HUMBOLDT: *Letter*, Sept. 10, 1826

Providence has a wild, rough, incalculable road to its end, and it is of no use to try to whitewash its huge, mixed instrumentalities, or to dress up that terrific benefactor in a clean shirt and white neckcloth of a student in divinity.
R. W. EMERSON: *The Conduct of Life*, I, 1860

Heaven protects children, sailors and drunken men.
THOMAS HUGHES: *Tom Brown at Oxford*, XII, 1861

Heaven, on the stage, is always on the side of the hero and heroine, and against the police.
JEROME K. JEROME: *Stage-Land*, 1889

I firmly believe in Divine Providence. Without belief in Providence I think I should go crazy. Without God the world would be a maze without a clue.
WOODROW WILSON: Speech in London, 1919

What God sends is better than what men ask for. CROATIAN PROVERB

When God gives a man a pebble to chew He first softens it. RUSSIAN PROVERB

God who gives the wound gives the salve.
SPANISH PROVERB

God builds the nest of the blind bird.
TURKISH PROVERB

[*See also* Blind, Chance.

Provincialism

The frog in the well knows nothing of the ocean. JAPANESE PROVERB

Prudence

How unutterably blessed is prudence in a good disposition.
DEMETRIUS: *Fragment, c.* 415 B.C.

He who flees will fight again. (Qui fugiebat, rursus proeliabitur.)
TERTULLIAN: *De fuga in persecutione, c.* 200

He that fights and runs away
Will live to fight another day.
OLD ENGLISH RHYME, traced by Apperson, in various forms, to *c.* 1320

Love all, trust a few, do wrong to none.
SHAKESPEARE: *All's Well that Ends Well,* II, *c.* 1602

People who live in glass houses should not throw stones.
ENGLISH PROVERB, traced by Apperson to 1640

Prudence is a presumption of the future, contracted from the experience of time past.
THOMAS HOBBES: *Leviathan,* III, 1651

Prudence and love were not made for each other: as love increases, prudence diminishes. LA ROCHEFOUCAULD: *Maxims,* 1665

A serious apprehension that Christianity may be true lays persons under the strictest obligations of a serious regard to it.
JOSEPH BUTLER: *The Analogy of Religion,* 1736

Distrust yourself, and sleep before you fight,
'Tis not too late tomorrow to be brave.
JOHN ARMSTRONG: *The Art of Preserving Health,* IV, 1744

One virtue he had in perfection, which was prudence – often the only one that is left us at seventy-two.
OLIVER GOLDSMITH: *The Vicar of Wakefield,* II, 1766

Prudence, like experience, must be paid for.
R. B. SHERIDAN: *The School for Scandal,* IV, 1777

Prudence is a rich, ugly old maid courted by Incapacity.
WILLIAM BLAKE: *The Marriage of Heaven and Hell,* 1790

Put all your eggs in one basket – and watch that basket.
S. L. CLEMENS (MARK TWAIN): *Pudd'nhead Wilson,* XV, 1894

When the water reaches the upper deck, follow the rats. AMERICAN POLITICAL PROVERB

Don't whistle until you're out of the woods.
AMERICAN PROVERB

I'd rather have them say " There he goes " than " Here he lies." IBID.

A prudent man never makes his goat his gardener. HUNGARIAN PROVERB

The best armor is to keep out of gunshot.
ITALIAN PROVERB

No call alligator long mouth till you pass him.
JAMAICAN PROVERB

If there be but prudence. (Si sit prudentia.)
LATIN PHRASE

If you are afraid of wolves don't go into the forest. RUSSIAN PROVERB

Pray to God, but do not offend the Devil.
IBID.

Be ever the last to go over a deep river.
SPANISH PROVERB

Three things a prudent man never shows: the bottom of his purse, the bottom of his knowledge, and the bottom of his heart.
WELSH PROVERB

[*See also* Caution, Courage, Destiny, Failure, Foresight, Fortune, General, Haste, Love, Luck, Policy, Success, Virtue, Virtue and Vice.

Prudery

Each one avoideth to see a man born, but all run hastily to see him die. To destroy him we seek a spacious field and a full light; but to construct him we hide ourselves in some dark corner, and work as close as we may.
MICHEL DE MONTAIGNE: *Essays,* III, 1588

A prude is one who blushes modestly at the indelicacy of her thoughts and virtuously flies from the temptation of her desires.
AMBROSE BIERCE: *Collected Works,* VIII, 1911

[*See also* Grundy.

Pruning-hook

[*See* War and Peace.

Prussia

War is the national industry of Prussia.
G. H. R. DE MIRABEAU: *De la monarchie prussienne,* 1788

Prussia, though a despotism in theory, is governed as mildly, and, apart from political justice, as equitably and legally, as any other country. The will of the sovereign is never made to interfere, arbitrarily, with the administration of law, and the law itself proceeds from the principles that properly influence all legislation, though it can only receive its authority from the will of the king.
J. FENIMORE COOPER: *The American Democrat,* I, 1838

The national spirit of Prussia is monarchical through and through.
OTTO VON BISMARCK: Speech in the Prussian Lower House, Jan. 22, 1864

Psalm

The twenty-third psalm is the nightingale of the psalms. It is small, of a homely feather, singing shyly out of obscurity; but it has filled the air of the whole world with melodious joy, greater than the heart can conceive.
H. W. BEECHER: *Life Thoughts,* 1858

[*See also* Age (Old).

Psychiatry

Canst thou not minister to a mind diseas'd,
Pluck from the memory a rooted sorrow,
Raze out the written troubles of the brain,
And with some sweet oblivious antidote
Cleanse the stuff'd bosom of that perilous stuff
Which weighs upon the heart?
SHAKESPEARE: *Macbeth,* v, *c.* 1605

Psychoanalysis

Psychoanalysis is the disease it purports to cure.
KARL KRAUS: In *Die Fackel* (Vienna), June, 1913

Psychology

Hardly any medical practitioner is a psychologist. Respecting the mental characteristics of women their observations are of no more worth than those of common men.
J. S. MILL: *The Subjection of Women,* I, 1869

Public

He that does anything for the public is accounted to do it for nobody.
THOMAS FULLER: *Gnomologia,* 1732

The public is a fool.
ALEXANDER POPE: *The First Epistle of the Second Book of Horace,* 1737

The public is a ferocious beast: one must either chain it up or flee from it.
VOLTAIRE: *Letter to Mlle. Quinault,* Aug. 16, 1738

The public! The public! How many fools are needed to make a public!
NICOLAS CHAMFORT: *Maximes et pensées,* *c.* 1785

Better than an individual should suffer an injury than that the public should suffer an inconvenience.
MR. JUSTICE ASHURST: *Judgment in Russell* vs. *the Mayor of Devon,* 1788

The public is pusillanimous and cowardly because it is weak. It knows itself to be a great dunce, and that it has no opinions but upon suggestion.
WILLIAM HAZLITT: *On Living to One's Self,* 1821

The public is an old woman. Let her maunder and mumble.
THOMAS CARLYLE: *Journal,* 1835

He who serves the public hath but a scurvy master.
H. G. BOHN: *Handbook of Proverbs,* 1855

The public is just a great baby.
JOHN RUSKIN: *Sesame and Lilies,* I, 1865

The public be damned.
W. H. VANDERBILT: To two newspaper reporters, aboard his special train, approaching Chicago, Oct. 8, 1882 (Chicago Daily News, Oct. 9)

To disagree with three-fourths of the British public on all points is one of the first elements of sanity, one of the deepest consolations in all moments of spiritual doubt.
OSCAR WILDE: *The English Renaissance of Art,* 1882 (Lecture in New York, Jan. 9)

The public have an insatiable curiosity to know everything, except what is worth knowing.
OSCAR WILDE: *The Soul of Man Under Socialism,* 1891

[*See also* Artist, Mob, Opinion (Public), People, Populace, Rabble.

Public Domain

[*See* Land.

Publicity

Without publicity there can be no public spirit, and without public spirit every nation must decay.
BENJAMIN DISRAELI: Speech in the House of Commons, Aug. 8, 1871

Pitiless publicity.
Phrase popularized by Woodrow Wilson, *c.* 1912 (It occurs in R. W. EMERSON: *The Conduct of Life,* VI, 1860)

Public-school

[*See* Education.

Public Spirit

We Athenians believe that a man who takes no part in public affairs is not merely lazy, but good for nothing.
THUCYDIDES: *History,* II, *c.* 410 B.C.

No man can conceive, until he come to try it, how great a pain it is to be a public-spirited person.
JONATHAN SWIFT: *The Tatler,* Sept. 13, 1709

Public spirit must be nurtured by private virtue, or it will resemble the factitious sentiment which makes women careful to preserve their reputation and men their honor.
MARY WOLLSTONECRAFT: *A Vindication of the Rights of Woman,* VIII, 1792

Publisher

K——, the publisher, trying to be critical, talks about books pretty much as a washerwoman would about Niagara Falls or a poulterer about a phœnix.

E. A. POE: *Fifty Suggestions,* 1845 (Graham's Magazine, June)

Barabbas was a publisher.

Usually ascribed, though without ground, to BYRON, who is said to have had John Murray in mind; the probable author was Thomas Campbell, 1777–1844 (A parody on JOHN XVIII, 40: "Now Barabbas was a robber")

[*See also* Author, Books, Bookseller.

Pudding

A smell like an eating-house and a pastrycook's next door to each other, with a laundress's next door to that. That was the pudding.

CHARLES DICKENS: *A Christmas Carol,* III, 1843

[*See also* Beef, Proof.

Pull

A long pull, a strong pull, and a pull all together.

FREDERICK MARRYAT: *Jacob Faithful,* XII, 1834

Pulpit

Every pulpit is a pillory in which stands a convict; every member of the church stands over him with a club, called a creed. He is an intellectual slave, and dare not preach his honest thought.

R. G. INGERSOLL: Speech in New York, April 16, 1882

When Wall Street yells war, you may rest assured every pulpit in the land will yell war.

EUGENE V. DEBS: Speech in Canton, O., June 16, 1918

[*See also* Clergyman, Orator, Preacher, Preaching, Sermon.

Pulse

My pulse, as yours, doth temp'rately keep time,
And makes as healthful music.

SHAKESPEARE: *Hamlet,* III, *c.* 1601

There are worse occupations in this world than feeling a woman's pulse.

LAURENCE STERNE: *A Sentimental Journey,* I, 1768

Pumpkin

If fresh meat be wanting to fill up our dish
We have carrots and pumpkins and turnips and fish;
We have pumpkins at morning and pumpkins at noon;
If it was not for pumpkins we should be undone.

Anon.: *New England Annoyances,* 1630

Peter, Peter, pumpkin-eater,
Had a wife and couldn't keep her;
He put her in a pumpkin-shell,
And there he kept her very well.

Nursery rhyme

Pun

The seeds of punning are in the minds of all men, and though they may be subdued by reason, reflection, and good sense, they will be very apt to shoot up in the greatest genius.

JOSEPH ADDISON: *The Spectator,* LXI, May 10, 1711

He that would pun would pick a pocket.

ALEXANDER POPE: *The Dunciad,* note, 1728 (Ascribed to "a great critic")

Riddle, and Rebus, Riddle's dearest son,
And false Conundrum, and insidious Pun.

R. O. CAMBRIDGE: *The Scribbleriad,* 1751

A good pun may be admitted among the smaller excellencies of lively conversation.

JAMES BOSWELL: *Life of Samuel Johnson,* 1791

Where the common people like puns, and make them, the nation is on a high level of culture.

G. C. LICHTENBERG: *Reflections,* 1799

A pun is a noble thing *per se.* It fills the mind; it is as perfect as a sonnet; better.

CHARLES LAMB: *Letter to S. T. Coleridge, c.* 1810

I never knew an enemy to puns who was not an ill-natured man.

CHARLES LAMB: *Letter to J. B. Dibdin,* June, 1826

My little dears, who learn to read,
Pray early learn to shun
That very foolish thing indeed
The people call a pun.

THEODORE HOOK: *Cautionary Verses to Youth, c.* 1830

Of puns it has been said that those most dislike who are least able to utter them.

E. A. POE: *Marginalia,* 1844–49

People that make puns are like wanton boys that put coppers on the railroad tracks.

O. W. HOLMES: *The Autocrat of the Breakfast-Table,* I, 1858

Punctilious

As punctilious as the husband of George Eliot, who never ventured to address her as George, even in the privacy of their chamber, but always called her Mr. Eliot.

Author unidentified

Punctuality

Punctuality is the politeness of kings. (L'exactitude est la politesse des rois.)

Ascribed to LOUIS XVIII of France (1755–1824)

Your people of quality
Pique themselves justly on strict punctuality.

R. H. BARHAM: *The Ingoldsby Legends,* III, 1842

Punctuality is the soul of business.
H. G. BOHN: *Handbook of Proverbs,* 1855

Punctuality is the thief of time.
OSCAR WILDE: *The Picture of Dorian Gray,* 1891

Punctuation

Even where the sense is perfectly clear, a sentence may be deprived of half its force — its spirit — its point — by improper punctuation. For the want of merely a comma, it often occurs that an axiom appears a paradox, or that a sarcasm is converted into a sermonoid.
E. A. POE: *Marginalia,* 1844–49

Punishment

If a man destroy the eye of another man, they shall destroy his eye.
THE CODE OF HAMMURABI, *c.* 2250 B.C.

If a man strike his father, they shall cut off his hand. IBID.

Branding is the punishment for 1000 crimes. Cutting off the nose is the punishment for another 1000. Cutting off the foot is the punishment for 500, castration for 300, and death for 200.
CHINESE CODE OF THE TENTH CENTURY B.C.

Cain said unto the Lord, My punishment is greater than I can bear.
GENESIS IV, 13, *c.* 700 B.C.

Eye for eye, tooth for tooth, hand for hand, foot for foot. Burning for burning, wound for wound, stripe for stripe.
EXODUS XXI, 24–25, *c.* 700 B.C.

Breach for breach, eye for eye, tooth for tooth: as he hath caused a blemish in a man, so shall it be done to him.
LEVITICUS XXIV, 20, *c.* 700 B.C.

Life shall go for life, eye for eye, tooth for tooth, hand for hand, foot for foot.
DEUTERONOMY XIX, 21, *c.* 650 B.C.

The fathers shall not be put to death for the children, neither shall the children be put to death for the fathers: every man shall be put to death for his own sin.
DEUTERONOMY XXIV, 16

It is for the general good of all that the wicked should be punished.
EURIPIDES: *Hecuba, c.* 426 B.C.

Punishment brings wisdom; it is the healing art of wickedness.
PLATO: *Georgias, c.* 360 B.C.

He who desires to inflict rational punishment does not retaliate for a past wrong which cannot be undone; he has regard to the future, and is desirous that the man who is punished, and he who sees him punished, may be deterred from doing wrong again.
PLATO: *Protagoras, c.* 360 B.C.

Punishment is a sort of medicine.
ARISTOTLE: *The Nicomachean Ethics,* II, *c.* 340 B.C.

We withdraw our wrath from the man who admits that he is justly punished.
ARISTOTLE: *Rhetoric,* II, *c.* 322 B.C.

Whosoever will not do the law of thy God, and the law of the king, let judgment be executed speedily upon him, whether it be unto death, or to banishment, or to confiscation of goods, or to imprisonment.
EZRA VII, 26, *c.* 300 B.C.

We must take care that crimes are not more severely punished than they deserve, and that one be not punished for an act for which another is not called to account.
CICERO: *De officiis,* I, 78 B.C.

Let the punishment match the offense. (Noxiæ pœna par esto.)
CICERO: *De legibus, c.* 50 B.C.

He hurts the good who spares the bad.
PUBLILIUS SYRUS: *Sententiæ, c.* 50 B.C.

It is less to suffer punishment than to have deserved it.
OVID: *Epistulæ ex Ponto,* I, *c.* 5

Before the king metes out punishment to an offender, he shall consider the time and place of the offense and the offender's education and capacity. THE CODE OF MANU, *c.* 100

Human punishment is execrable even when just. POPE XYSTUS I: *The Ring, c.* 150

Sin is a suppurating wound; punishment is the surgeon's knife.
ST. JOHN CHRYSOSTOM: *Homilies,* VI, *c.* 388

When the bad are punished, others become better.
ST. JOHN CHRYSOSTOM: *Homilies,* XIII

Ah, God, punish, we pray thee, with pestilence and famine, and with what evil and sickness may be else on earth; but be not silent, Lord, towards us!
MARTIN LUTHER: *Table-Talk,* LXXXIII, 1569

Thou shalt be whipp'd with wire, and stew'd in brine,
Smarting in ling'ring pickle.
SHAKESPEARE: *Antony and Cleopatra,* II, *c.* 1606

The gods
Grow angry with your patience. 'Tis their care,
And must be yours, that guilty men escape not.
BEN JONSON: *Catiline,* III, 1611

Punishment is lame, but it comes.
GEORGE HERBERT: *Outlandish Proverbs,* 1640

Excessive bail ought not to be required, nor excessive fines imposed, nor cruel and unusual punishments inflicted.
THE ENGLISH BILL OF RIGHTS, X, Dec., 1689

Man punishes the action, but God the intention.
THOMAS FULLER: *Gnomologia,* 1732

To punish and not prevent is to labor at the pump and leave open the leak. IBID.

In all, or nearly all, the states of Europe punishment for crimes has diminished or increased in proportion as they have approached nearer or removed farther from liberty.
C. L. DE MONTESQUIEU: *The Spirit of the Laws,* VI, 1748

Punishment has in it the notion of a remedy, and has the place of a mean, not of an end.
BENJAMIN WHICHCOTE: *Moral and Religious Aphorisms,* 1753

Frequency of punishment is always a sign of weakness or supineness in a government. There is no knave that may not be made good for something. No one ought to be put to death, even for the sake of example, except the man who cannot be preserved without danger.
J.-J. ROUSSEAU: *Du contrat social,* II, 1761

The aim of punishment is to make sure that the guilty man does not repeat his crime, and to deter others, by his punishment, from committing it.
C. B. BECCARIA: *Trattato dei delitti e delle pene,* 1764 (Cf. PLATO, *ante, c.* 360 B.C.)

Punishment should be public, prompt, in proportion to the crime, determined by law, and the least severe that is possible under the circumstances. IBID.

All punishments the world can render
Serve only to provide th' offender;
The will gains strength from treatment horrid,
As hides grow harder when they're curried.
JOHN TRUMBULL: *M'Fingal,* 1782

It is essential to the idea of a law that it be attended with a sanction; or, in other words, a penalty or punishment for disobedience.
ALEXANDER HAMILTON: *The Federalist,* 1788

It is more dangerous that even a guilty person should be punished without the forms of law than that he should escape.
THOMAS JEFFERSON: *Letter to William Carmichael,* 1788

Punishment is an artificial consequence annexed by political authority to an offensive act.
JEREMY BENTHAM: *The Principles of Morals and Legislation,* XII, 1789

The value of the punishment must not be less in any case than what is sufficient to outweigh the profit of the offense.
JEREMY BENTHAM: *The Principles of Morals and Legislation,* XIV

The law ought to impose no other penalties than such as are absolutely and evidently necessary; and no one ought to be punished, but in virtue of a law promulgated before the offense and legally applied.
Declaration of the Rights of Man by the French National Assembly, VIII, 1789

Excessive bail shall not be required, nor excessive fines imposed, nor cruel and unusual punishments inflicted.
CONSTITUTION OF THE UNITED STATES, Amendment VIII, Dec. 15, 1791 (Cf. the English Bill of Rights, *ante,* 1689)

It is the perfection of the administration of criminal justice to take care that the punishment should come to few and the example to many.
LORD KENYON: *Judgment in Eaton's case,* 1793

Nothing can be clearer than that, if you punish at all, you ought to punish enough. The pain caused by punishment is pure unmixed evil, and never ought to be inflicted except for the sake of some good. It is mere foolish cruelty to provide penalties which torment the criminal without preventing the crime.
T. B. MACAULAY: *Gladstone on Church and State,* 1839 (Edinburgh Review, April)

The object of punishment is prevention from evil; it never can be made impulsive to good.
HORACE MANN: *Lectures on Education,* I, 1840

The seeking for rewards and punishments out of this life leads men to a ruinous ignorance of the fact that their inevitable rewards and punishments are here.
T. H. HUXLEY: *Letter to Charles Kingsley,* Sept. 23, 1860

Every unpunished delinquency has a family of delinquencies.
HERBERT SPENCER: *The Study of Sociology,* postscript, 1873

Let no guilty man escape.
U. S. GRANT: Indorsement on a letter charging his secretary, O. E. Babcock, with complicity in the Whiskey Ring, July 29, 1875

The punishment of the criminal is measured by the degree of astonishment of the judge who finds his crime incomprehensible.
F. W. NIETZSCHE: *Human All-too-Human,* II, 1878

My object all sublime
I shall achieve in time —
To let the punishment fit the crime —
The punishment fit the crime.
W. S. GILBERT: *The Mikado,* II, 1885

A community is infinitely more brutalized by the habitual employment of punishment than it is by the occasional occurrence of crime.
OSCAR WILDE: *The Soul of Man Under Socialism,* 1891

The iron gin that waits for sin
Had caught us in its snare.
OSCAR WILDE: *The Ballad of Reading Gaol,* 1898

God punish England! (Gott strafe England!)
Apparently first used by Alfred Funke in a novel called *Swords and Myrtle* (*Schwert und Myrte*), which was published serially in a German popular magazine, the Sonntagszeitung für das deutsche Haus, 1914

No one is punishable for another person's crime. (Nemo punitur pro alieno delicto.)
LEGAL MAXIM

No one should be twice punished for one crime. (Nemo debet bis puniri pro uno delicto.)
IBID.

I chastise thee, not because I hate thee, but because I love thee. (Castigo te non quod odio habeam, sed quod amem.)
MEDIEVAL LATIN SAYING of schoolmasters flogging their pupils

He reads his sin in his punishment.
SCOTTISH PROVERB

[*See also* Child, Crime and Punishment, Hanging, Intention, Jeopardy, Judgment Day, Law, Murder, Murderer, Persecution, Populace, Punishment (Capital), Son, Theft.

Punishment, Capital

Death is to be expiated only by death.
OVID: *Metamorphoses,* VIII, *c.* 5

They therefore brought him out, to do with him according to their law; and first they scourged him, then they buffeted him, then they lanced his flesh with knives; after that they stoned him with stones, then pricked him with their swords; and, last of all, they burned him to ashes at the stake.
JOHN BUNYAN: *Pilgrim's Progress,* I, 1678

The execution of malefactors is not more for the credit of governors than the death of patients is for the credit of physicians.
BENJAMIN WHICHCOTE: *Moral and Religious Aphorisms,* 1753

Let the punishments of criminals be useful. A hanged man is good for nothing, but a man condemned to public works still serves the country, and is a living person.
VOLTAIRE: *Philosophical Dictionary,* 1764

When we execute a murderer it may be that we fall into the same mistake as the child that strikes a chair it has collided with.
G. C. LICHTENBERG: *Reflections,* 1799

When men are taught that a crime of a certain character is connected inseparably with death, the moral habits of a population become altered, and you may in the next age remit the punishment which in this it has been necessary to inflict with stern severity.
WALTER SCOTT: *Journal,* Feb. 20, 1828

A people who are revolted by an execution but not shocked at an assassination require that the public authorities should be armed with much sterner powers of repression than elsewhere, since the first indispensable requisites of civilized life have nothing else to rest on.
J. S. MILL: *Representative Government,* I, 1861

The society which inflicts capital punishment does not commit murder. Murder is an offensive act. The term cannot be applied legitimately to any defensive act.
BENJAMIN R. TUCKER: *Instead of a Book,* 1893

It is no sin to kill a killer. HINDU PROVERB

[*See also* Execution, Guillotine, Hanging, Murderer, Punishment.

Pupil

Poor is the pupil who does not surpass his master.
LEONARDO DA VINCI: *Notebooks, c.* 1500

In the position of a pupil. (In statu pupillari.)
LEGAL PHRASE

[*See also* Student, Teacher.

Purgatory

The Catholic Church, instructed by the Holy Ghost, has from the sacred Scriptures and the ancient tradition of the Fathers, taught that there is a Purgatory, and that the souls detained therein are helped by the suffrages of the faithful, but principally by the sacrifice of the mass.
Decree of the Council of Trent, xxv, 1564

Readers, we entreat ye pray
For the soul of Lucia;
That in little time she be
From her Purgatory free:
In th' interim she desires
That your tears may cool her fires.
ROBERT HERRICK: *Hesperides,* 1648

The very notion of a state of probation has darkness in it. The All-knower has no need of satisfying His eyes by seeing what we will do, when He knows before what we will do.
CHARLES LAMB: *Letter to Bernard Barton,* July 2, 1825

Penniless souls maun pine in Purgatory.
SCOTTISH PROVERB (*Maun*=must)

[*See also* Cause and Effect, Limbo, Protestantism.

Puritan

Pure in show, an upright holy man,
Corrupt within — and called a Puritan.
Anon.: *A Song of the Puritan, c.* 1605

One Puritan amongst them sings psalms to hornpipes.
SHAKESPEARE: *The Winter's Tale,* IV, *c.* 1611

To Banbury came I, O profane one!
Where I saw a Puritan once
Hanging of his cat on Monday,
For killing of a mouse on Sunday.

RICHARD BRATHWAITE: *Itinerarium,* 1638

We have been reputed a colluvies of wild opinionists, swarmed into a remote wilderness to find elbow-room for our fanatic doctrines and practises.

NATHANIEL WARD: *The Simple Cobbler of Aggawam,* 1646 (*Colluvies*=a collection of filth)

These Puritan preachers, if they have anything good, they have it out of popish books, although they will not acknowledge it for fear of displeasing the people.

JOHN SELDEN: *Table-Talk,* 1689

Bear-baiting was esteemed heathenish and unchristian; the sport of it, not the inhumanity, gave offense.

DAVID HUME: *The History of Great Britain,* I, 1754

A formal Puritan,
A solemn and unsexual man.

P. B. SHELLEY: *Peter Bell the Third,* VI, 1819

The Puritan was made up of two different men, the one all self-abasement, penitence, gratitude, passion, the other proud, calm, inflexible, sagacious. He prostrated himself in the dust before his Maker; but he set his foot on the neck of his king.

T. B. MACAULAY: *Milton,* 1825 (Edinburgh Review, Aug.)

The Puritan hated bear-baiting, not because it gave pain to the bear, but because it gave pleasure to the spectators.

T. B. MACAULAY: *History of England,* I, 1848 (Cf. HUME, *ante,* 1754)

What the Puritans gave the world was not thought but action.

WENDELL PHILLIPS: Speech in Plymouth, Mass., Dec. 21, 1855

Is it not strange that the descendants of those Pilgrim Fathers who crossed the Atlantic to preserve their own freedom of opinion have always proved themselves intolerant of the spiritual liberty of others?

ROBERT E. LEE: *Letter to his wife,* Dec. 27, 1856

The Puritans of Boston are simple in their habits and simple in their expenses. Champagne and canvas-back ducks I found to be the provisions most in vogue among those who desired to adhere closely to the manner of their forefathers.

ANTHONY TROLLOPE: *North America,* 1862

The Puritans nobly fled from a land of despotism to a land of freedim, where they could not only enjoy their own religion, but prevent everybody else from enjoyin *his.*

C. F. BROWNE (ARTEMUS WARD): *The London Punch Letters,* V, 1866

They were a very wonderful people. . . . If they were narrow it was not a blighting and destructive narrowness, but a vital and productive narrowness.

CALVIN COOLIDGE: Speech in Watertown, Mass., 1930

The zeal for superior morality of the Puritans was, like the zeal for superior morality of the ancient Jews, the refuge for humiliated self-esteem. It was the natural reaction of frustrated ambition against the contempt of arrogant aristocratic rulers.

ROBERT BRIFFAULT: *Sin and Sex,* III, 1931

The Puritan always thinks below the belt.

Author unidentified

[*See also* Baptism, Christian, Home, Puritanism.

Puritanism

The Church of Christ admits of no other government than that by presbyteries; viz., by the minister, elders and deacons.

EDWIN SANDYS (BISHOP OF LONDON): *Letter to Henry Bullinger of Zürich* setting forth the principles of the Puritans, 1573

Puritanism, believing itself quick with the seed of religious liberty, laid, without knowing it, the egg of democracy.

J. R. LOWELL: *Among My Books,* I, 1870

The whole history of English progress since the Restoration, on its moral and spiritual sides, has been the history of Puritanism.

J. R. GREEN: *A Short History of the English People,* VIII, 1874

Puritanism does not regard ascetic self-torture as a virtue, but regards enjoyment as sin. It is therefore not concerned with practising the former, but with suppressing the latter.

ROBERT BRIFFAULT: *Sin and Sex,* III, 1931

[*See also* Instinct.

Purity

Unto the pure all things are pure. (Omnia munda mundis.)

TITUS I, 15, *c.* 60 (The Latin is from the Vulgate)

Blessed are the pure in heart: for they shall see God.

MATTHEW V, 8, *c.* 75

The mouth of a woman, the breasts of a maiden, the prayer of a child and the smoke of sacrifice are always pure.

THE CODE OF MANU, *c.* 100

The body is the soul's image; therefore keep it pure.

POPE XYSTUS I: *The Ring, c.* 150

Purity of soul cannot be lost without consent.

ST. AUGUSTINE: *On Lying, c.* 395

The purest gold is most ductile.

THOMAS FULLER: *Gnomologia,* 1732

Oh! she was good as she was fair.
None — none on earth above her!
As pure in thought as angels are;
To know her was to love her.
SAMUEL ROGERS: *Jacqueline,* I, 1814

How like a lovely flower,
So fair, so pure thou art;
I watch thee and a prayer
Comes stealing through my heart;
I lay my hands upon thee
And ask God to adjure
That thou shalt be forever
So sweet, so fair — so pure.
HEINRICH HEINE: *Du bist wie eine Blume,* 1827

My good blade carves the casques of men,
My tough lance thrusteth sure,
My strength is as the strength of ten,
Because my heart is pure.
ALFRED TENNYSON: *Sir Galahad,* 1842

There's a woman like a dew-drop,
She's so purer than the purest.
ROBERT BROWNING: *A Blot on the 'Scutcheon,* I, 1843

She was a pure and innocent girl until you came here with your slick city ways and oily tongue. Old melodrama line

The pure are not fortune's favorites.
WELSH PROVERB

[*See also* Chastity, Gold, Monasticism, Temptation.

Purpose

Infirm of purpose.
SHAKESPEARE: *Macbeth,* II, *c.* 1605

Life, to be worthy of a rational being, must be always in progression; we must always purpose to do more or better than in time past. The mind is enlarged and elevated by mere purposes, though they end as they begin by airy contemplation.
SAMUEL JOHNSON: To Hester Thrale, Nov. 29, 1783

I doubt not thro' the ages one increasing purpose runs.
ALFRED TENNYSON: *Locksley Hall,* 1842

The cant (implied or direct) about the amelioration of society, etc., is but a very usual trick among authors, whereby they hope to add such a tone of dignity or utilitarianism to their pages as shall gild the pill of their licentiousness.
E. A. POE: *Marginalia,* 1844–49

There is no action so slight, nor so mean, but it may be done to a great purpose, and ennobled therefore; nor is any purpose so great but that slight actions may help it, and may be so done as to help it much.
JOHN RUSKIN: *The Seven Lamps of Architecture,* 1849

The secret of success is constancy to purpose.
BENJAMIN DISRAELI: Speech in London, June 24, 1872

[*See also* Success.

Purse

Let us all have one purse.
PROVERBS I, 14, *c.* 350 B.C.

Do thou better, do thou worse;
Do after him that beareth the purse.
ENGLISH RHYME, traced by Smith to *c.* 1350

When purse is heavy ofttime the heart is light.
ALEXANDER BARCLAY: *Eclogues,* 1515

Light gains make heavy purses.
JOHN HEYWOOD: *Proverbs,* 1546

He that shows his purse longs to be rid of it.
JOHN CLARKE: *Parœmiologia Anglo-Latina,* 1639

Little, not often, fills the purse.
GIOVANNI TORRIANO: *Italian Proverbs,* 1666

He that has a full purse never wanted a friend.
JAMES KELLY: *Complete Collection of Scottish Proverbs,* 1721

He that shows his purse bribes the thief.
IBID.

The master-organ, soul's-seat, and true pineal gland of the body social.
THOMAS CARLYLE: *Sartor Resartus,* I, 1836

[*See also* Money.

Pylorus

[*See* Soul.

Pyramid

The pyramids themselves, doting with age, have forgotten the names of their founders.
THOMAS FULLER: *The Holy State and the Profane State,* 1642

The tap'ring pyramid, the Egyptian's pride,
And wonder of the world, whose spiky top
Has wounded the thick cloud.
ROBERT BLAIR: *The Grave,* 1743

Soldiers, twenty centuries look down upon you from these pyramids.
NAPOLEON I: To his troops before the Battle of the Pyramids, July 2, 1797

Nile shall pursue his changeless way:
Those pyramids shall fall;
Yea! not a stone shall stand to tell
The spot whereon they stood.
Their very site shall be forgotten,
As is their builder's name.
P. B. SHELLEY: *Queen Mab,* II, 1813

As for the pyramids, there is nothing to wonder at in them so much as the fact that so many men could be found degraded enough to spend their lives constructing a tomb for some ambitious booby, whom it would have been wiser and manlier to have drowned in the Nile, and then given his body to the dogs. H. D. THOREAU: *Walden,* 1854

Who shall doubt " the secret hid
Under Egypt's pyramid "
Was that the contractor did
Cheops out of several millions?
RUDYARD KIPLING: *A General Summary,* 1886

Every nation has a prominent citizen who builds a pyramid.
E. W. HOWE: *Sinner Sermons,* 1926

Q

Quackery

In all times, in the opinion of the multitude, witches and old women and impostors have had a competition with physicians.
FRANCIS BACON: *The Advancement of Learning,* II, 1605

Out, you impostors!
Quack salving, cheating mountebanks! your skill
Is to make sound men sick, and sick men kill.
PHILIP MASSINGER and THOMAS DEKKER: *The Virgin Martyr,* IV, 1622

Mountebanks, empirics, quack-salvers, mineralists, wizards, alchemists, cast-apothecaries, old wives and barbers are all suppositors to the right worshipful doctor.
JOHN FORD: *The Lover's Melancholy,* I, 1628 (*Suppositor*=supporter)

We have no longer faith in miracles and relics, and therefore with the same fury run after recipes and physicians. The same money which three hundred years ago was given for the health of the soul is now given for the health of the body, and by the same sort of people — women and half-witted men.
MARY WORTLEY MONTAGU: *Letter to Wortley Montagu,* April 24, 1748

Quacks are gamesters, and they play
With craft and skill to ruin and betray;
With monstrous promise they delude the mind,
And thrive on all that tortures humankind.
GEORGE CRABBE: *The Borough,* VII, 1810

It is better to have recourse to a quack, if he can cure our disorder, although he cannot explain it, than to a physician, if he can explain our disease, but cannot cure it.
C. C. COLTON: *Lacon,* 1820

A Cagliostro, many Cagliostros, prominent world-leaders do prosper by their quackery, for a day. It is like a forged banknote; they get it passed out of their worthless hands; others, not they, have to smart for it. Nature bursts-up in fire-flames, French Revolutions and such-like, proclaiming with terrible veracity that forged notes are forged.
THOMAS CARLYLE: *Heroes and Hero-Worship,* I, 1840 (Lecture in London, May 5)

Quackery and idolatry are all but immortal.
O. W. HOLMES: *The Medical Profession in Massachusetts,* 1869 (Lecture in Boston, Jan. 29)

Quacks sent to prison are always replaced by other quacks.
RUDOLF VIRCHOW (1821–1902)

Quaker

Quakers are under the strong delusion of Satan.
INCREASE MATHER: *Remarkable Providences,* XI, 1684

Why should the papist with his seven sacraments be worse than the Quaker with no sacraments at all?
DANIEL DEFOE: *The Shortest Way With the Dissenters,* 1702

A Quaker? Sly.
ALEXANDER POPE: *Moral Essays,* I (Of the Knowledge and Characters of Men), 1733

Every Quakeress is a lily.
CHARLES LAMB: *A Quaker's Meeting,* 1821 (London Magazine, April)

Thousands would go to see a Quaker hanged that would be indifferent to the fate of a Presbyterian or an Anabaptist.
CHARLES LAMB: *Letter to Bernard Barton,* Dec. 1, 1824

A Quaker is made up of ice and flame. He has no composition, no mean temperature. Hence he is rarely interested about any public measure but he becomes a fanatic, and oversteps, in his irrespective zeal, every decency and every right opposed to his course.
S. T. COLERIDGE: *Table-Talk,* Aug. 14, 1833

The sect of the Quakers in their best representatives appear to me to have come nearer to the sublime history and genius of Christ than any other of the sects.
R. W. EMERSON: Lecture on Natural Religion, Boston, April 4, 1869

[*See also* Face, Institution.

Quality

Quality, without quantity, is little thought of.
JAMES KELLY: *Complete Collection of Scottish Proverbs,* 1721

Good things cost less than bad ones.
ITALIAN PROVERB

Quantum

[*See* Causality.

Quarrel

In quarreling the truth is always lost.
PUBLILIUS SYRUS: *Sententiæ, c.* 50 B.C.

Thou wilt quarrel with a man that hath a hair more, or a hair less, in his beard than thou hast: thou wilt quarrel with a man for cracking nuts, having no other reason but because thou hast hazel eyes.
SHAKESPEARE: *Romeo and Juliet,* III, *c.* 1596

Beware
Of entrance to a quarrel; but being in,
Bear 't that the opposed may beware of thee.
SHAKESPEARE: *Hamlet,* I, *c.* 1601

A quarrel between friends, when made up, adds a new tie to friendship, as experience shows that the callosity formed round a broken bone makes it stronger than before.
Ascribed to ST. FRANCIS DE SALES (1567–1622) in J. P. CAMUS: *L'esprit de Saint François de Sales,* 1641

In the nature of man we find three principal causes of quarrel. First, competition; second, diffidence; thirdly, glory. The first maketh men invade for gain; the second for safety; and the third for reputation.
THOMAS HOBBES: *Leviathan,* XIII, 1651

Quarrels would not last long if the fault was only on one side.
LA ROCHEFOUCAULD: *Maxims,* 1665

'Tis by our quarrels that we spoil our prayers.
COTTON MATHER: *The Wonders of the Invisible World,* I, 1693

Quarreling dogs come halting home.
THOMAS FULLER: *Gnomologia,* 1732

There must be two at least to a quarrel. IBID.

The quarrels of friends in the latter part of life are never truly reconciled.
WILLIAM SHENSTONE: *Egotisms From My Own Sensations,* 1764

The quarrel is a very pretty quarrel as it stands; we should only spoil it by trying to explain it.
T. B. SHERIDAN: *The Rivals,* IV, 1775

An association of men who will not quarrel with one another is a thing which never yet existed, from the greatest confederacy of nations down to a town meeting or a vestry.
THOMAS JEFFERSON: *Letter to John Taylor,* 1798

Scolding and quarreling have something of familiarity, and a community of interest; they imply acquaintance; they are of resentment, which is of the family of dearness.
CHARLES LAMB: *Letter to Bernard Barton,* July 3, 1829

There is no such test of a man's superiority of character as in the well-conducting of an unavoidable quarrel.
HENRY TAYLOR: *The Statesman,* 1836

There are quarrels in which even Satan, bringing help, were not unwelcome.
THOMAS CARLYLE: *The French Revolution,* III, 1837

Quarrelsome dogs get dirty coats.
SAMUEL LOVER: *Handy Andy,* XLVI, 1842 (Cited as an old saying)

None but cats and dogs are allowed to quarrel in my house.
H. G. BOHN: *Handbook of Proverbs,* 1855

Dog-snap and cat-claw, curse and counterblast.
ROBERT BROWNING: *The Ring and the Book,* II, 1868

From one quarrel come a hundred sins.
ARAB PROVERB

When two quarrel, both are to blame.
DUTCH PROVERB

Quarreling is the weapon of the weak.
HEBREW PROVERB

An old quarrel can be easily revived.
ITALIAN PROVERB

The second word makes the quarrel.
JAPANESE PROVERB

The morning is the best time for settling a quarrel. WEST AFRICAN PROVERB

[*See also* Brother, Contention, Fire, Haste, Hungarian, Just, Lawyer, Lover, Man and Woman.

Quartette

When I am in the country I know no more charming delight than listening to quartette music.
LUDWIG VAN BEETHOVEN: *Letter to the Archduke Rudolph of Austria,* July 24, 1813

Queen

A woman by whom the realm is ruled when there is a king, and through whom it is ruled when there is not.
AMBROSE BIERCE: *The Devil's Dictionary,* 1906

When a woman reigns the Devil governs.
ITALIAN PROVERB

A king's wife is a widow for life.
WELSH PROVERB

[*See also* Happiness.

Queer

All the world is queer but me and thee, dear; and sometimes I think thee is a little queer.
Ascribed to an anonymous Quaker, speaking to his wife

Question

It is not every question that deserves an answer.
PUBLILIUS SYRUS: *Sententiæ, c.* 50 B.C.

A fool may ask more questions in an hour than a wise man can answer in seven years.
JOHN RAY: *English Proverbs,* 1670

Ask me no questions, and I'll tell you no fibs.
OLIVER GOLDSMITH: *She Stoops to Conquer,* III, 1773 (Usually, *lies*)

Questioning is not the mode of conversation among gentlemen.
SAMUEL JOHNSON: *Boswell's Life,* 1776

Hasty questions require slow answers.
DUTCH PROVERB

[*See also* Examination, Lying.

Quickness

The desire to have things done quickly prevents their being done thoroughly.
CONFUCIUS: *Analects,* XIII, *c.* 500 B.C.

Quick at meat and quick at work.
JOHN CLARKE: *Parœmiologia Anglo-Latina,* 1639

Quicker than greased lightning.
AMERICAN PHRASE, traced by Thornton to 1833

Quick ripe, quick rotten. ITALIAN PROVERB

It is done quickly enough if it is done well. (Sat cito si sat bene.) LATIN PROVERB

Quickly enough if safe enough. (Sat cito si sat tuto.) IBID.

What is quickly done is quickly undone. (Quod cito fit, cito perit.) IBID.

[*See also* Decision, Eating, Haste, Hurry.

Quid pro quo

No checkee; no shirtee.
Ascribed to the Chinese laundrymen in America, *c.* 1875

Quiet

The good and the wise lead quiet lives.
EURIPIDES: *Ion, c.* 420 B.C.

Better is an handful with quietness, than both the hands full with travail and vexation of spirit. ECCLESIASTES IV, 6, *c.* 200 B.C.

Study to be quiet.
I THESSALONIANS IV, 11, *c.* 51

When all is done and said, in the end thus shall you find,
He most of all doth bathe in bliss that hath a quiet mind.
THOMAS VAUX: *Content, c.* 1550

No wealth is like the quiet mind.
Anon.: *The Quiet Mind, c.* 1588

Anything for a quiet life.
THOMAS MIDDLETON: Title of a play, *c.* 1620

Quiet persons are welcome everywhere.
THOMAS FULLER: *Gnomologia,* 1732

Quiet, to quick bosoms, is a hell.
BYRON: *Childe Harold,* III, 1816

It is difficult to keep quiet if you have nothing to do.
ARTHUR SCHOPENHAUER: *Our Relation to Ourselves,* 1851

All quiet along the Potomac tonight.
GEORGE B. MCCLELLAN: Phrase often used in his dispatches from the Army of the Potomac, 1861–62 (Cf. BEERS, *ante,* under Potomac. A similar phrase, "Im Westen nichts neues" (Nothing new in the West) occurred in the communiqués of German GHQ, 1914–18; Erich Remarque used it as the title of a novel, 1929. It was sometimes mistranslated as "All quiet on the Western front")

I like a quiet life . . . and I don't like seeing people cry or die.
JOHN RUSKIN: *Time and Tide,* XIX, 1867

[*See also* Doctor.

Quinine

Quinine is made of the sweat of ships' carpenters. SAILORS' SAYING

Quotation

In quoting of books, quote such authors as are usually read; others you may read for your own satisfaction, but not name them.
JOHN SELDEN: *Table-Talk,* 1689

He that has but ever so little examined the citations of writers cannot doubt how little credit the quotations deserve, where the originals are wanting; and, consequently, how much less quotations of quotations can be relied on.
JOHN LOCKE: *Essay Concerning the Human Understanding,* IV, 1690

Some, for renown, on scraps of learning dote,
And think they grow immortal as they quote.
EDMUND YOUNG: *Love of Fame,* I, 1728

Every quotation contributes something to the stability or enlargement of the language.
SAMUEL JOHNSON: *Dictionary,* pref., 1755

Nothing gives an author so much pleasure as to find his works respectfully quoted by other learned authors.
BENJAMIN FRANKLIN: *Poor Richard's Almanac,* 1758

Classical quotation is the parole of literary men all over the world.
SAMUEL JOHNSON: *Boswell's Life,* May 8, 1781

Quotation, like much better things, has its abuses. One may quote till one compiles.
ISAAC D'ISRAELI: *Curiosities of Literature,* 1791

Those who never quote, in return are seldom quoted.
IBID.

Every book is a quotation, and every house is a quotation out of all forests and mines and stone-quarries, and every man is a quotation from all his ancestors.
R. W. EMERSON: *Representative Men,* II, 1850

To be occasionally quoted is the only fame I care for.
ALEXANDER SMITH: *Dreamthorp,* VII, 1863

Next to the originator of a good sentence is the first quoter of it.
R. W. EMERSON: *Letters and Social Aims,* III, 1875

One must be a wise reader to quote wisely and well.
A. BRONSON ALCOTT: *Table-Talk,* I, 1877

Books are published with an expectation, if not a desire, that they will be criticized in reviews, and if deemed valuable that parts of them will be used as affording illustrations by way of quotation, or the like, and if the quantity taken be neither substantial nor material, if, as it has been expressed by some judges, "a fair use" only be made of the publication, no wrong is done and no action can be brought.
LORD HATHERLEY: *Judgment in Chatterton* vs. *Cave,* 1877

[*See also* Learning, Reference.

R

R

The dog's letter.
PERSIUS: *Satires, c.* 60 (The epithet seems to have come into English before 1500. The sound of the letter is supposed to suggest a snarl)

Rabbit

[*See* Hunting.

Rabble

The dregs of the people. (Faex populi.)
CICERO: *Ad fratrem,* II, *c.* 60 B.C.

The venal herd. (Venale pecus.)
JUVENAL: *Satires,* VIII, 118

Tag and rag, cut and longtail — everyone that can eat an egg.
JOHN CLARKE: *Parœmiologia Anglo-Latina,* 1639 ("Rag, tag and bobtail" was a contemporary variant, still surviving)

The great unwashed.
Author unidentified; not recorded before the XIX century

The rabble is nothing. It can do nothing on its own.
NAPOLEON I: To Gaspard Gourgaud at St. Helena, Feb. 24, 1817

[*See also* Masses, Mob, Multitude, People, Populace, Proletariat.

Rabelais, François (1494?–1553)

Rabelais, at his best, is the greatest of all buffoons.
VOLTAIRE: *Letter to Mme. du Deffand,* April 12, 1760

I think with some interest upon the fact that Rabelais and Luther were born in the same year. Glorious spirits! glorious spirits!
S. T. COLERIDGE: *Table-Talk,* May 1, 1833

[*See also* Swift (Jonathan).

Race

God hath made of one blood all nations of men.
ACTS XVII, 26, *c.* 75

What I would most desire would be the separation of the white and black races.
ABRAHAM LINCOLN: Speech in Springfield, Ill., July 17, 1858

The race is great, but the men whiffling and unsure.
R. W. EMERSON: *The Conduct of Life,* VII, 1860

Race is precisely of as much consequence in man as it is in any other animal.
JOHN RUSKIN: *Modern Painters,* V, 1860

No man will treat with indifference the principle of race. It is the key of history, and why history is so often confused is that it has been written by men who were ignorant of this principle and all the knowledge it involves.
BENJAMIN DISRAELI: *Endymion,* II, 1880

The instincts and faculties of different men and races differ in a variety of ways almost as profoundly as those of animals in different cages of the zoölogical gardens.
FRANCIS GALTON: *Inquiries Into Human Faculty,* 1883

Little Indian, Sioux or Crow,
Little Frosty Eskimo,
Little Turk or Japanee,
Oh, don't you wish that you were me?
R. L. STEVENSON: *Foreign Children,* 1885

The race to which we belong is the most arrogant and rapacious, the most exclusive and indomitable in history. It is the conquering and the unconquerable race, through which alone man has taken possession of the physical and moral world. All other races have been its enemies or its victims.
J. J. INGALLS: Speech in the Senate, Jan. 23, 1890

[*See also* Aryan, Chance, Extinction, Gambling, Indian, Mongolian, Nationality, Negro, War.

Race-suicide

[*See* Birth-control.

Racine, Jean (1639–99)

The fashion for Racine will pass off like that for coffee.
Ascribed to MARIE DE SÉVIGNÉ (1626–96)

Racing

[*See* Horse-racing, Sports.

Rack

The rack is a kind of syllogism which has been used with good effect, and has made multitudes of converts.
JOSEPH ADDISON: *The Spectator*, Dec. 4, 1711

[*See also* Death.

Radical

A radical is a man with both feet firmly planted — in the air.
F. D. ROOSEVELT: Radio Speech, Oct. 26, 1939

Radicalism

Hide-bound radicalism — a to me well nigh insupportable thing.
THOMAS CARLYLE: *Letter to R. W. Emerson*, Nov. 5, 1836

The spirit of our American radicalism is destructive and aimless; it is not loving; it has no ulterior and divine ends; but is destructive only out of hatred and selfishness.
R. W. EMERSON: *Politics*, 1841

Radio

To converse at the distance of the Indies by sympathetic contrivances may be as natural to future times as to us is a literary correspondence.
JOSEPH GLANVILL: *The Vanity of Dogmatizing*, 1661

Around the world thoughts shall fly
In the twinkling of an eye.
Anon.: *The Prophecie of Mother Shipton*, 1862

Government supervision must secure to all the people the advantage of radio communication and likewise guarantee the right of free speech. Official control in contravention of this guarantee should not be tolerated.
Democratic National Platform, 1928

We stand for the administration of the radio facilities of the United States under wise and expert government supervision, which will, first, secure to every home in the nation, whether city or country, the great educational and inspirational values of broadcast programmes, adequate in number and varied in character; and second, assign the radio communication channels — regional, continental, and transoceanic — in the best interest of the American business man, the American farmer, and the American public generally.
Republican National Platform, 1928

The radio is of unique usefulness for bringing peoples together. Until it was invented they saw each other only in the distorting mirror of the newspapers. But the radio shows them as they are, and reveals their most attractive side.
ALBERT EINSTEIN: Address at the opening of the German Radio Exhibition, 1930

Rage

Rage strengthens the hands, however feeble they may be. OVID: *Amores*, I, *c.* 10

Rage is a vulgar passion with vulgar ends.
ERNST VON FEUCHTERSLEBEN: *Zur Diätetik der Seele*, I, 1838

[*See also* Charity.

Rags

Rags are royal raiment when worn for virtue's sake.
BARTLEY CAMPBELL: *The White Slave*, III, 1882

Raillery

Raillery is a form of speaking in favor of one's wit against one's good nature.
C. L. DE MONTESQUIEU: *Pensées*, *c.* 1750

Railroad

The time will come when people will travel in stages moved by steam engines, from one city to another, almost as fast as birds fly, fifteen or twenty miles an hour.
OLIVER EVANS: *Patent Right Oppression Exposed*, 1813

Railway aids traveling by getting rid of all avoidable obstructions of the road, and leaving nothing to be conquered but pure space.
R. W. EMERSON: *Manners*, 1844

Going by railroad I do not consider as traveling at all; it is merely being sent to a place, and very little different from becoming a parcel.
JOHN RUSKIN: *Modern Painters*, III, 1856

Your railroad, when you come to understand it, is only a device for making the world smaller. IBID.

The railroads are not run for the benefit of the dear public. That cry is all nonsense. They are built for men who invest their money and expect to get a fair percentage on the same.
W. H. VANDERBILT: To two newspaper reporters, aboard his special train, approaching Chicago, Oct. 8, 1882 (Chicago Daily News, Oct. 9)

What would the Crusaders have done with railroads?
THOMAS B. REED: Speech in the House of Representatives, Nov. 1, 1894

[*See also* Government Ownership, Land.

Rain

The rain was upon the earth forty days and forty nights. GENESIS VII, 12, *c.* 700 B.C.

The rain cometh down, and the snow from heaven, and returneth not thither, but watereth the earth, and maketh it bring forth and bud, that it may give seed to the sower, and bread to the eater.
ISAIAH LV, 10, *c.* 700 B.C.

Hath the rain a father? or who hath begotten the drops of dew?
JOB XXXVIII, 28, *c.* 325 B.C.

God sendeth down water from Heaven, and causeth the earth to revive after it hath been dead. Verily, herein is a sign of the resurrection unto people who hearken.
THE KORAN, XVI, *c.* 625

A little rain stops a big wind.
ENGLISH PROVERB, traced by Apperson to before 1225

I have something laid by for a rainy day.
ENGLISH SAYING, traced by Smith to *c.* 1580

The rain it raineth every day.
SHAKESPEARE: *Twelfth Night,* V, *c.* 1601

When God will, no wind but brings rain.
GEORGE HERBERT: *Outlandish Proverbs,* 1640

Send us, we beseech thee, in this our necessity, such moderate rain and showers that we may receive the fruits of the earth to our comfort, and to thy honor; through Jesus Christ our Lord, Amen.
THE BOOK OF COMMON PRAYER (*Prayers and Thanksgivings upon Several Occasions*), 1662

It never rains but it pours.
ENGLISH PROVERB, apparently not current before the early XVIII century

Neither coat nor cloak will hold out against rain upon rain.
THOMAS FULLER: *Gnomologia,* 1732

Rain is good for vegetables, and for the animals who eat those vegetables, and for the animals who eat those animals.
SAMUEL JOHNSON: *Boswell's Life,* July 6, 1763

The big rain comes dancing to the earth.
BYRON: *Childe Harold,* III, 1816

O rain! with your dull two-fold sound,
The clash hard by, and the murmur all round!
S. T. COLERIDGE: *An Ode to the Rain,* 1817

As the drops beat against the window they give me the same sensation as a quart of cold water offered to revive a half-drowned devil — no feel of the clouds dropping fatness, but as if the roots of the earth were rotten cold and drenched.
JOHN KEATS: *Letter to J. H. Reynolds,* April 9, 1818

Rain from the East;
Rain three days at least.
AMERICAN RHYME, *c.* 1830

How beautiful is the rain!
After the dust and heat,
In the broad and fiery street,
In the narrow lane,
How beautiful is the rain!
H. W. LONGFELLOW: *Rain in Summer,* 1846

And a thousand recollections
Weave their bright hues into woof
As I listen to the patter
Of the soft rain on the roof.
COATES KINNEY: *Rain on the Roof,* 1849

This rain is warm as tears.
CINCINNATUS HEINE (JOAQUIN MILLER): *Ida,* V, 1871

Evening gray and morning red
Send the shepherd wet to his bed.
EAST ANGLIAN RHYME

When the sun shines through rain the Devil is beating his wife. FRENCH PROVERB

Heavy rain does not last long.
ITALIAN PROVERB

Rain after the wedding is a sign of a fruitful marriage. JUGO-SLAVIC PROVERB

A fly on your nose;
You slap and it goes;
If it comes back again
It will bring a good rain.
OLD ENGLISH RHYME

When the grass is dry at morning light
Look for rain before the night. IBID.

When God wills, it rains with any wind.
SPANISH PROVERB

Rain is an orphan. WEST AFRICAN PROVERB

[*See also* Excess, February, Flea, Fly, Fog, Guest, July, Moon, Prayer, Umbrella, Woods.

Rainbow

I do set my bow in the cloud, and it shall be for a token of a covenant between me and the earth. GENESIS IX, 13, *c.* 700 B.C.

Look upon the rainbow, and praise him that made it.
ECCLESIASTICUS XLIII, 11, *c.* 180 B.C.

Rainbow at night: sailors' delight;
Rainbow in morning: sailors take warning.
ENGLISH RHYME, apparently not recorded before the XIX century

My heart leaps up when I behold
A rainbow in the sky.
WILLIAM WORDSWORTH: *My Heart Leaps Up,* 1807

Rainbow, stay,
Gleam upon gloom,
Bright as my dream,
 Rainbow, stay!

ALFRED TENNYSON: *Becket*, III, 1884

Rainbow to windward, foul fall the day;
Rainbow to leeward, damp runs away.

SAILORS' RHYME

Rake

[*See* Woman, Steel (Richard).

Raleigh, Walter (1552–1618)

I will prove you the notoriousest traitor that ever came to the bar. . . . Nay, I will prove all: thou art a monster; thou hast an English face, but a Spanish heart.

EDWARD COKE: At Raleigh's trial, Nov. 17, 1603

Rank

The very same acts, according as they proceed from a person of high or low rank, are either much extolled or left unnoticed.

PLINY THE YOUNGER: *Letters*, VI, *c.* 110

Dost thou wish to enjoy the first rank? First concede that place to another.

ST. JOHN CHRYSOSTOM: *Homilies*, XIII, *c.* 388

Rank is to merit what dress is to a pretty woman.

LA ROCHEFOUCAULD: *Maxims*, 1665

Better be the head of the yeomanry than the tail of the gentry.

JOHN RAY: *English Proverbs*, 1670

It is a maxim that those to whom everybody allows the second place have an undoubted title to the first.

JONATHAN SWIFT: *A Tale of a Tub*, 1704

He who is eclipsed in the first rank shines in the second.

VOLTAIRE: *La Henriade*, I, 1723

Two persons may have equal merit, and on that account may have an equal claim to attention; but one of them may have also fortune and rank, and so may have a double claim.

SAMUEL JOHNSON: *Boswell's Life*, April, 1776

The rank is but the guinea's stamp,
The man's the gowd for a' that.

ROBERT BURNS: *For a' That and a' That*, 1795 (*Gowd*=gold)

Rank is a great beautifier.

E. G. BULWER-LYTTON: *The Lady of Lyons*, II, 1838

Social station, in the main, is a consequence of property. So long as there is civilization there must be the rights of property, and so long as there are the rights of property, their obvious consequences must follow.

J. FENIMORE COOPER: *The American Democrat*, XVI, 1838

He who takes his rank lightly raises his own dignity.

HEBREW PROVERB

[*See also* Ancestry, Aristocracy, Birth (High), Heredity, Nobility.

Rape

History, sacred and profane, and the common experience of mankind teach that women of the character shown in this case are prone to make false accusations both of rape and of insult upon the slightest provocation or without even provocation, for ulterior purposes.

JUDGE JAMES E. HORTON: Memorandum granting a new trial in the Scottsboro case, June 22, 1933

Rarity

Rarity gives charm. Thus early fruits are most esteemed; thus Winter roses obtain a higher price: thus coyness sets off a mistress.

MARTIAL: *Epigrams*, IV, *c.* 95

[*See also* Bird, June, Pleasure.

Rascal

Put in every honest hand a whip
To lash the rascals naked through the world.

SHAKESPEARE: *Othello*, IV, 1604

Every man of any education would rather be called a rascal than accused of deficiency in the graces.

SAMUEL JOHNSON: *Boswell's Life*, April 29, 1776

A rascal who would make dominoes out of his father's bones.

BALZAC: *Père Goriot*, III, 1834

Rascals are always sociable.

ARTHUR SCHOPENHAUER: *Our Relation to Ourselves*, 1851

Turn the rascals out!

CHARLES A. DANA: In the New York Sun, *c.* 1871 (Referring to the Tweed ring)

[*See also* Atheist, Bald, Hypocrisy, Mass, Song.

Rashness

Rashness often makes a man immortal; even if he falls he is praised in song.

J. W. GOETHE: *Iphigenie auf Tauris*, V, 1787

[*See also* Courage, Valor.

Raspberry

There is something in the red of a raspberry pie that looks as good to a man as the red in a sheep looks to a wolf.

E. W. HOWE: *Sinner Sermons*, 1926

Rat

The rats always leave a sinking ship (or falling house).

ENGLISH PROVERB, familiar in various forms since the XVI century

Do you not smell a rat?
BEN JONSON: *A Tale of a Tub*, IV, 1633

Mr. Speaker, I smell a rat. I see him floating in the air. But mark me, sir, I will nip him in the bud.
BOYLE ROCHE: Speech in the Irish Parliament, *c.* 1790

Rats are the most despised and contemptible parts of God's earth.
CHARLES LAMB: *Letter to Robert Southey*, March 20, 1799

Anything like the sound of a rat
Makes my heart go pit-a-pat!
ROBERT BROWNING: *The Pied Piper*, IV, 1842

The rat's head is worth more than the lion's tail.
SPANISH PROVERB

[*See also* Cat, Death, Indiscretion.

Rationalism

Rationalism may be defined as the mental attitude which unreservedly accepts the supremacy of reason and aims at establishing a system of philosophy and ethics verifiable by experience and independent of all arbitrary assumptions of authority.
Memorandum of the Aims and Objects of the Rationalist Press Association, London, *c.* 1895

[*See also* Catholicism (Roman).

Rationalist

Rationalists as such are not philosophers. They are not pantheists nor speculative materialists. They ignore, if they do not despise, metaphysics, and in practise eschew the search for first principles.
A. J. BALFOUR: *The Foundations of Belief*, II, 1895

Reaction

Reaction is the consequence of a nation waking from its illusions.
BENJAMIN DISRAELI: Speech in the House of Commons, Feb. 3, 1848

[*See also* Cell.

Reactionary

A reactionary is a somnambulist walking backward.
F. D. ROOSEVELT: Radio Speech, Oct. 26, 1939

[*See also* Judge.

Reader

Who reads
Incessantly, and to his reading brings not
A spirit and judgment equal or superior,
(And what he brings what need he elsewhere seek?)
Uncertain and unsettled still remains,
Deep versed in books and shallow in himself.
JOHN MILTON: *Paradise Regained*, IV, 1671

A reader seldom peruses a book with pleasure until he knows whether the writer of it be a black man or a fair man, of a mild or choleric disposition, married or a bachelor.
JOSEPH ADDISON: *The Spectator*, March 1, 1711

A man must have virtue in him before he will enter upon the reading of a Seneca or an Epictetus.
JOSEPH ADDISON: *The Spectator*, Sept. 25, 1711

I knew a gentleman who was so good a manager of his time that he would not even lose that small portion of it which the calls of nature obliged him to pass in the necessary-house; but gradually went through all the Latin poets in those moments.
LORD CHESTERFIELD: *Letter to his son*, Dec. 11, 1747

A well-read fool is the most pestilent of blockheads: his learning is a flail which he knows not how to handle, and with which he breaks his neighbor's shins as well as his own.
STANISLAUS LESZCYNSKI (KING OF POLAND): *Œuvres du philosophe bienfaisant*, 1763

Busy readers are seldom good readers. He who would read with pleasure and profit should have nothing else to do or to think of.
C. M. WIELAND: *Die Abderiten*, I, 1774

Some read to think, these are rare; some to write, these are common; and some read to talk, and these form the great majority.
C. C. COLTON: *Lacon*, 1820

The indefatigable readers of books are like the everlasting copiers of pictures; who, when they attempt to do anything of their own, find they want an eye quick enough, a hand steady enough, and colors bright enough, to trace the living forms of nature.
WILLIAM HAZLITT: *The Ignorance of the Learned*, 1821

To the friendly and judicious reader who will take these papers as they were meant; not understanding everything perversely in the absolute and literal sense, but giving fair construction, as to an after-dinner conversation.
CHARLES LAMB: *Essays of Elia*, dedication, 1822

A reading-machine, always wound up and going,
He mastered whatever was not worth the knowing.
J. R. LOWELL: *A Fable for Critics*, 1848

The plain reader be damned.
EUGENE JOLAS: *The Language of Night*, 1932

[*See also* Books, Literature, Poet, Reading.

Reading

If thou wouldst profit by thy reading, read humbly, simply, honestly, and not desiring to win a character for learning.

THOMAS À KEMPIS: *Imitation of Christ*, I, *c.* 1420

Reading maketh a full man, conference a ready, and writing an exact man.

FRANCIS BACON: *Essays*, II, 1597

To what use serves my reading?
You should have taught me what belongs to horses,
Dogs, dice, hawks, banquets, masques, free and fair meetings,
To have studied gowns and dressings.

JOHN FLETCHER: *The Wild-Goose Chase*, III, 1621

Read, mark, learn, and inwardly digest.

THE BOOK OF COMMON PRAYER (*Collect for the Second Sunday in Advent*), 1662

When I am reading a book, whether wise or silly, it seems to me to be alive and talking to me.

JONATHAN SWIFT: *Thoughts on Various Subjects*, 1706

Read much, but not too many books.

BENJAMIN FRANKLIN: *Poor Richard's Almanac*, 1738

Let blockheads read what blockheads wrote.

LORD CHESTERFIELD: *Letter to his son*, Nov. 1, 1750

I have been a rake at reading.

MARY WORTLEY MONTAGU: *Letter to the Countess of Bute*, April 11, 1759

A man ought to read just as inclination leads him; for what he reads as a task will do him little good. A young man should read five hours in a day, and so may acquire a great deal of knowledge.

SAMUEL JOHNSON: *Boswell's Life*, July 14, 1763

History, poetry and philosophy I commonly read on horseback, having other employment at other times.

JOHN WESLEY: *Journal*, March 19, 1770

The greatest part of a writer's time is spent in reading, in order to write; a man will turn over half a library to make one book.

SAMUEL JOHNSON: *Boswell's Life*, 1775

The progress which the understanding makes through a book has more pain than pleasure in it.

SAMUEL JOHNSON: *Boswell's Life*, May 1, 1783

He that runs may read.

WILLIAM COWPER: *Tirocinium*, 1785 (A misquotation of HABAKKUK II, 2, *c.* 590 B.C.: "he may run that readeth")

I forget the greater part of what I read, but all the same it nourishes my mind.

G. C. LICHTENBERG: *Reflections*, 1799

Lessing's belief that he had read almost too much for his good sense shows how good his sense really was. IBID.

Reading means borrowing. IBID.

Some of the greatest geniuses who ever lived never read half so much as our mediocre scholars of today. Not a few of those mediocrities might have become greater men if they had not read so much. IBID.

It is no more necessary that a man should remember the different dinners and suppers which have made him healthy than the different books which have made him wise. Let us see the result of good food in a strong body, and the result of great reading in a full and powerful mind.

SYDNEY SMITH: Lecture on the Conduct of the Understanding, I, 1806

For a person to read his own works over with any great delight, he ought first to forget that he ever wrote them.

WILLIAM HAZLITT: *The Pleasure of Painting*, 1821

We read to say that we have read.

CHARLES LAMB: In the New Times, Jan. 13, 1825

How dare I read Washington's campaigns, when I have not answered the letters of my own correspondents? Is not that a just objection to much of our reading? It is a pusillanimous desertion of our work to gaze after our neighbors. It is peeping.

R. W. EMERSON: *Spiritual Laws*, 1841

In science, read by preference the newest works; in literature, the oldest. The classic literature is always modern.

E. G. BULWER-LYTTON: *The Caxtons*, 1849

Read the best books first, or you may not have a chance to read them at all.

H. D. THOREAU: *A Week on the Concord and Merrimack Rivers*, 1849

What books shall I read? is a question constantly put by the student to the teacher. My reply usually is, "None; write your notes out carefully and fully; strive to understand them thoroughly; come to me for the explanation of anything you cannot understand, and I would rather you did not distract your mind by reading."

T. H. HUXLEY: *A Lobster, or The Study of Zoölogy*, 1861

Be sure to read no mean books. Shun the spawn of the press on the gossip of the hour. Do not read what you shall learn, without asking, in the street and the train.

R. W. EMERSON: *Books*, 1877

All that wearies profoundly is to be condemned for reading. The mind profits little by what is termed heavy reading.
LAFCADIO HEARN: *Reading*, 1881 (New Orleans Item, April 22)

If you cannot enjoy reading a book over and over again, there is no use reading it at all.
OSCAR WILDE: *The Decay of Lying*, 1889

Boys read one thing, men another, old men yet another. (Aliud legunt pueri, aliud viri, aliud senes.)
LATIN PROVERB

Read all of it if you wish to understand the whole. (Lege totum si vis scire totum.)
IBID.

Reading rots the brain.
NEW ENGLAND PROVERB

[*See also* Books, Experience, Literature.

Ready

Always ready. (Semper paratus.)
LATIN PHRASE

Realism

A mere picture of imbecility is revolting simply; we cannot conceive ourselves acting in the same way under the same circumstances, and we can therefore feel neither sympathy with the actor nor interest in his fate.
J. A. FROUDE: *Arnold's Poems*, 1854 (Westminster Review)

All bad art comes from returning to life and nature, and elevating them into ideals.
OSCAR WILDE: *The Decay of Lying*, 1889

It is essential to preserve the veracity of the document, the precision of detail, the fibrous and nervous language of realism, but it is equally essential to become the well-digger of the soul, and not to attempt to explain what is mysterious by mental maladies.
J. K. HUYSMANS: *Certains*, 1889

Realism is nothing more and nothing less than the truthful treatment of material.
W. D. HOWELLS: *Criticism and Fiction*, 1892

Reality

There is nothing in words; believe what is before your eyes.
OVID: *Fasti*, II, *c.* 5

Whatsoever accidents or qualities our senses make us think there be in the world, they be not there, but are seeming and apparitions only: the things that really are in the world without us are those motions by which these seemings are caused.
THOMAS HOBBES: *Leviathan*, I, 1651

We are but shadows: we are not endowed with real life, and all that seems most real about us is but the thinnest substance of a dream, — till the heart be touched. That touch creates us — then we begin to be — thereby we are beings of reality and inheritors of eternity.
NATHANIEL HAWTHORNE: *American Note-Books*, Oct. 4, 1840

[*See also* Travel.

Reason

Come now, and let us reason together.
ISAIAH I, 18, *c.* 700 B.C.

The law of things is a law of universal reason, but most men live as if they had a wisdom of their own.
HERACLITUS: *Fragment*, *c.* 500 B.C.

I desire to reason with God.
JOB XIII, 3, *c.* 325 B.C.

Reason is the mistress and queen of all things. (Domina omnium et regina ratio.)
CICERO: *Tusculanæ disputationes*, II, 45 B.C.

Reason is the greatest enemy that faith has: it never comes to the aid of spiritual things, but — more frequently than not — struggles against the divine Word, treating with contempt all that emanates from God.
MARTIN LUTHER: *Table-Talk*, CCCLIII, 1569

Every why hath a wherefore.
SHAKESPEARE: *The Comedy of Errors*, II, 1593

Neither rhyme nor reason.
IBID.

I have no other but a woman's reason:
I think him so, because I think him so.
SHAKESPEARE: *Two Gentlemen of Verona*, I, *c.* 1595

The will of man is by his reason sway'd.
SHAKESPEARE: *A Midsummer Night's Dream*, II, *c.* 1596

His reasons are as two grains of wheat hid in two bushels of chaff; you shall seek all day ere you find them, and when you have them, they are not worth the search.
SHAKESPEARE: *The Merchant of Venice*, I, *c.* 1597

I have a woman's reason: I will not dance because I will not dance.
THOMAS MIDDLETON: *Blurt, Master Constable*, I, 1601 (Cf. SHAKESPEARE, *ante*, *c.* 1595)

There are and can be only two ways of searching into and discovering truth. The one flies from the senses and particulars to the most general axioms, and from these principles, the truth of which it takes for settled and immovable, proceeds to judgment and to the discovery of middle axioms. This way is now in fashion. The other derives axioms from the senses and particulars, rising by a gradual and unbroken ascent, so that it arrives at the most general axioms last of all. This is the true way, but as yet untried.
FRANCIS BACON: *Novum Organum*, I, 1620

Everything by reason. (Tout par raison.)
ARMAND CARDINAL RICHELIEU: *Mirame*, *c.* 1625

Reason is the life of the law; nay, the Common Law itself is nothing else but reason.
EDWARD COKE: *Institutes*, I, 1628

Reason lies between the spur and the bridle.
GEORGE HERBERT: *Outlandish Proverbs*, 1640

Reason is but choosing.
JOHN MILTON: *Areopagitica*, 1644

When a man reasoneth he does nothing else but conceive a sum total from addition of parcels, or conceives a remainder from subtraction of one sum from another.
THOMAS HOBBES: *Leviathan*, I, 1651

Reason rules all things.
JAMES HOWELL: *Proverbs*, 1659

Men never wish ardently for what they only wish for from reason.
LA ROCHEFOUCAULD: *Maxims*, 1665

His tongue
Dropt manna, and could make the worse appear
The better reason.
JOHN MILTON: *Paradise Lost*, II, 1667

The reasoning of the strongest is always the best.
JEAN DE LA FONTAINE: *Fables*, I, 1668

A man without reason is a beast in season.
JOHN RAY: *English Proverbs*, 1670

Dim as the borrowed beams of moon and stars
To lonely, weary, wand'ring travelers,
Is reason to the soul.
JOHN DRYDEN: *Religio Laici*, 1682

Reason, thou vain impertinence,
Deluding hypocrite, begone!
And go and plague your men of sense,
But let my love and me alone.
Anon.: *Miscellany of Poems and Translations by Oxford Hands*, 1685

Reason, the power
To guess at right and wrong, the twinkling lamp
Of wand'ring life, that wings and wakes by turns
Fooling the follower 'twixt shade and shining.
WILLIAM CONGREVE: *The Mourning Bride*, III, 1697

We love without reason, and without reason we hate.
J. F. REGNARD: *Les folies amoureuses*, 1704

Let any man but look back upon his own life, and see what use he has made of his reason, how little he has consulted it, and how less he has followed it.
WILLIAM LAW: *A Serious Call to a Devout and Holy Life*, XVI, 1728

Logicians have but ill defin'd,
As rational, the human kind;
Reason, they say, belongs to man;
But let them prove it if they can.
JONATHAN SWIFT: *The Logicians Refuted*, 1731

Who reasons wisely is not therefore wise;
His pride in reasoning, not in acting, lies.
ALEXANDER POPE: *Moral Essays*, I (Of the Knowledge and Characters of Men), 1733

Reason is the only faculty we have wherewith to judge concerning anything, even revelation itself.
JOSEPH BUTLER: *The Analogy of Religion*, II, 1736

Reason is, and ought only to be, the slave of the passions.
DAVID HUME: *A Treatise of Human Nature*, I, 1739

Swift instinct leaps; slow reason feebly climbs.
EDWARD YOUNG: *Night Thoughts*, VII, 1744

If there be a God, He is the Author of nature as well as of revelation. He gave us the one to explain the other, and reason to make them agree.
J. O. DE LA METTRIE: *L'Homme machine*, 1748

Plain right reason is, nine times in ten, the fettered and shackled attendant of the triumph of the heart and the passions.
LORD CHESTERFIELD: *Letter to his son*, March 16, 1752

He that gives reason for what he saith has done what is fit to be done, and the most that can be done; he that gives not reason speaks nothing, though he saith never so much.
BENJAMIN WHICHCOTE: *Moral and Religious Aphorisms*, 1753

Those that differ upon reason may come together by reason. IBID.

If you will not hear reason, she will surely rap your knuckles.
BENJAMIN FRANKLIN: *Poor Richard's Almanac*, 1757

Within the brain's most secret cells
A certain lord chief justice dwells
Of sovereign power, whom one and all,
With common voice, we reason call.
CHARLES CHURCHILL: *The Ghost*, IV, 1763

Passion and prejudice govern the world; only under the name of reason.
JOHN WESLEY: *Letter to Joseph Benson*, Oct. 5, 1770

Hercules vanquished the Nemean lion, and a strong athlete named Voltaire has crushed the hydra of fanaticism under his feet. Reason becomes stronger every day in our Europe.
FREDERICK THE GREAT: *Letter to Voltaire*, June 18, 1776

I look upon human reason as I do on the parts of a promising child — it surprises, may improve or stop short, but is not come to maturity.

HORACE WALPOLE: *Letter to the Countess of Upper Ossory,* Jan. 19, 1777

No work that bears the stamp of reason, and has been undertaken to extend her power, can ever be wholly lost in the onward progress of the ages. The sacrifices which the irregular violence of nature extorts from reason must at least exhaust, satiate, and appease that violence.

F. G. FICHTE: *Die Bestimmung des Menschen,* II, 1800

The sole end of reason is pure activity, absolutely by itself alone, having no need of any instrument out of itself, — independence of everything which is not reason — absolute freedom. IBID.

Error of opinion may be tolerated where reason is left free to combat it.

THOMAS JEFFERSON: Inaugural Address, March 4, 1801

It is reason that produces everything: virtue, genius, wit, talent, and taste. What is virtue? Reason in practise. Talent? Reason enveloped in glory. Wit? Reason which is chastely expressed. Taste is nothing else than reason delicately put in force, and genius is reason in its most sublime form.

M. J. DE CHÉNIER: *Épître à Voltaire,* 1806

Every man's own reason must be his oracle.

THOMAS JEFFERSON: *Letter to Dr. Benjamin Rush,* 1813

Reason is founded on the evidence of our senses.

P. B. SHELLEY: *Queen Mab,* notes, 1813

Reason is nothing but the analysis of belief.

FRANZ SCHUBERT: *Diary,* March 27, 1824

You know, my friends, with what a brave carouse
I made a second marriage in my house;
Divorced old barren reason from my bed,
And took the daughter of the vine to spouse.

EDWARD FITZGERALD: Tr. of OMAR KHAYYÁM: *Rubáiyát* (*c.* 1100), 1857

If there is no higher reason — and there is not —, then my own reason must be the supreme judge of my life.

LYOF N. TOLSTOY: *My Confession,* 1879

Reason is only a tool.

F. W. NIETZSCHE: *Beyond Good and Evil,* 1886

I can stand brute force, but brute reason is quite unbearable. There is something unfair about its use. It is hitting below the intellect.

OSCAR WILDE: *The Picture of Dorian Gray,* 1891

Reason unites us, not only with our contemporaries, but with men who lived two thousand years before us, and with those who will live after us.

LYOF N. TOLSTOY: *Of Reason, Faith and Prayer,* 1901

The life of reason is no fair reproduction of the universe, but the expression of man alone.

GEORGE SANTAYANA: *The Life of Reason,* II, 1905

Reason is justified of her children, not of her caricaturists.

W. C. BROWNELL: *Criticism,* 1914

If we would guide by the light of reason, we must let our minds be bold.

MR. JUSTICE LOUIS D. BRANDEIS: *Opinion in Jay Burns Baking Co.* vs. *Bryan,* 1924

When a man begins to reason he ceases to feel.

FRENCH PROVERB

The reason which persuades. (Ratio suasoria.)

LATIN PHRASE

The reason which justifies. (Ratio justifica.)

IBID.

What is inconsistent with and contrary to reason is not permitted in law. (Quod est inconveniens et contra rationem non est permissum in lege.) LEGAL MAXIM

Reason is the wise man's guide, example the fool's. WELSH PROVERB

[*See also* Beast, Cause and Effect, Energy, Error, Faith, Genius, God, Golden Rule, Instinct, Judgment, Man, Might, Passion, Pleasure, Prejudice, Religion, Shibboleth, Skeptic, Talent, Taste, Temperance, Truth, Virtue, Wit.

Rebellion

Rebellion is as the sin of witchcraft.

I SAMUEL XV, 23, *c.* 500 B.C.

An evil man seeketh only rebellion.

PROVERBS XVII, 11, *c.* 350 B.C.

The rebellions of the belly are the worst.

FRANCIS BACON: *Essays,* XV, 1625

Who draws his sword against his prince must throw away the scabbard.

JAMES HOWELL: *Proverbs,* 1659

Rebellion to tyrants is obedience to God.

Motto on Thomas Jefferson's seal, *c.* 1770

Patriotism is not necessarily included in rebellion. A man may hate his king, yet not love his country.

SAMUEL JOHNSON: Address to the Electors of Great Britain, 1774

A little rebellion now and then . . . is a medicine necessary for the sound health of government.

THOMAS JEFFERSON: *Letter to James Madison,* 1787

My call is the call of battle — I nourish active rebellion;
He going with me must go well arm'd.

WALT WHITMAN: *Song of the Open Road,* 1856

Among freemen there can be no successful appeal from the ballot to the bullet.

ABRAHAM LINCOLN: *Letter to J. C. Conkling,* Aug. 26, 1863

The only justification of rebellion is success.

THOMAS B. REED: Speech in the House of Representatives, April 12, 1878

[*See also* Assassination, Disobedience, Election, Insurrection, Jesuit, King, Revolution.

Rebirth

Ye must be born again. JOHN III, 7, *c.* 115

Rebuke

Rebukes ought not to have a grain of salt more than of sugar.

THOMAS FULLER: *Gnomologia,* 1732

Receiver

No receiver, no thief.

ENGLISH PROVERB, traced by Smith to the XIV century

The receiver is as bad as the thief.

THOMAS FULLER: *Worthies of England,* 1662

Reciprocity

One good turn deserves another.

ENGLISH PROVERB, traced by Smith to *c.* 1400

Claw my back, and I will claw thy toe.

JOHN PALSGRAVE: *L'éclaircissement de la langue française,* 1530

For one good turn another doth itch,
Claw my elbow and I'll claw thy breech.

JOHN RAY: *English Proverbs,* 1670

You tickle me, and I'll tickle you.

AMERICAN PROVERB

Hand me the cinnamon, and I'll hand you the senna. RUSSIAN PROVERB

Reckoning

So comes a reck'ning when the banquet's o'er,
The dreadful reck'ning, and men smile no more.

JOHN GAY: *What D'ye Call It?,* II, 1715

Recollection

[*See* Autobiography, Memory.

Reconciliation

Reconciliation with our enemies is only a desire of bettering our condition, a weariness of contest, and the fear of some disaster.

LA ROCHEFOUCAULD: *Maxims,* 1665

As thro' the land at eve we went,
And pluck's the ripen'd ears,
We fell out, my wife and I,
Oh, we fell out, I know not why,
And kiss'd again with tears.

ALFRED TENNYSON: *The Princess,* I, 1847

[*See also* Friend, Peace.

Reconstruction

I am one of those who believe the war ended too soon. We have whipped the South, but not enough. The loyal masses constitute an overwhelming majority of the people of this country, and they intend to march again on the South and intend that the " second war " shall be no child's play. The " second army " will, as they ought to, make the entire South as God found the earth, without form, and void.

W. P. (PARSON) BROWNLOW: Speech in Philadelphia, May, 1865

I know it means something like barbarian conquest, I will allow, but I do not believe there will be any peace until 347,000 men of the South are either hanged or exiled.

WENDELL PHILLIPS: Speech in Boston, 1865

Unless the law of nations is a dead letter, the late war between two acknowledged belligerents severed their original compacts, and broke all the ties that bound them together. The future condition of the conquered power depends on the will of the conqueror.

THADDEUS STEVENS: Speech in the House of Representatives, Dec. 18, 1865

If I had the power I would arm every wolf, panther, catamount and bear in the mountains of America, every crocodile in the swamps of Florida, every Negro in the South, every devil in Hell, clothe him in the uniform of the Federal Army, and then turn them loose on the rebels of the South and exterminate every man, woman and child south of Mason and Dixon's line.

W. P. (PARSON) BROWNLOW: Speech in New York, 1866

The old issues are dead; the corpse of the war-feeling cannot be galvanized into life again; and the political issues of the present are cold, hard questions of commercial ambition.

LAFCADIO HEARN: *More Biography,* 1880 (New Orleans Item, March 4)

Recreation

There be delights, there be recreations and jolly pastimes that will fetch the day about from sun to sun, and rock the tedious year as in a delightful dream.

JOHN MILTON: *Areopagitica,* 1644

God, who knows the weakness of our nature, authorizes us to take that rest and refreshment which are necessary to keeping up the strength of mind and body. In the brightest days of the church, the faithful, though still animated by pristine fervor, devoted certain days to rest and to rejoicing.

ST. JOHN BAPTIST DE LA SALLE: *The Rules of Christian Manners and Civility*, II, 1695

[*See also* Amusement, Entertainment, Game (=recreation).

Recrimination

The pot calls the kettle black.

ENGLISH PROVERB, not recorded in its present form before APHRA BEHN: *The Feign'd Courtezans*, v, 1679

Experience informs us that the first defence of weak minds is to recriminate.

S. T. COLERIDGE: *Biographia Literaria*, II, 1817

Recruit

Experience proves that recruits can be taught the drill without beating them. Any officer to whom this appears impossible is one who lacks the necessary ability to teach.

G. J. D. VON SCHARNHORST: Order to the Prussian Army on military punishments, 1812

The men that fought at Minden, they was rookies in their time —
So was them that fought at Waterloo.
All the 'ole command, yuss, from Minden to Maiwand,
They was once dam' sweeps like you.

RUDYARD KIPLING: *The Men That Fought at Minden*, 1892

[*See also* Soldier.

Rectitude

A mind conscious of its own rectitude. (Mens sibi conscia recti.)

VIRGIL: *Æneid*, I, 19 B.C.

Red

The flaming red denotes a callous mind,
Too harsh for love, or sentiment refined.

CHARLES STEARNS: *The Ladies' Philosophy of Love*, 1797

Red is the color of England; I cannot bear the sight of it.

NAPOLEON I: To Gaspard Gourgaud at St. Helena, 1815–1818

The bugle-cry of red.

J. K. HUYSMANS: *À rebours*, 1884

Any color, so long as it's red,
Is the color that suits me best.

EUGENE FIELD: *Red*, 1885

[*See also* Bull, Color, Milk, Mirth, Sky.

Redemption

[*See* Salvation.

Red-head

[*See* Hair (Red).

Red-tape

Whatever was required to be done, the Circumlocution Office was beforehand with all the public departments in the art of perceiving how not to do it.

CHARLES DICKENS: *Little Dorrit*, III, 1857

Reference

You will find it a very good practise always to verify your references.

M. J. ROUTH (president of Magdalen College, Oxford): To J. W. Burgon, 1847 (The ascription first appears in an article by Burgon in the Quarterly Review, London, July, 1878. *Quotations* is often substituted for *references*)

Reform

To make a crooked stick straight, we bend it the contrary way.

MICHEL DE MONTAIGNE: *Essays*, III, 1588

I'll purge, and leave sack, and live cleanly.

SHAKESPEARE: *I Henry IV*, v, *c.* 1598

Never came reformation in a flood.

SHAKESPEARE: *Henry V*, I, *c.* 1599

Man may at first transgress, but next do well:
Vice doth in some but lodge a while, not dwell.

ROBERT HERRICK: *Hesperides*, 1648

Repentance for past crimes is just and easy; but sin no more's a task too hard for mortals.

JOHN VANBRUGH: *The Relapse*, v, 1696

It is easier to bear what's amiss than go about to reform it.

THOMAS FULLER: *Gnomologia*, 1732

Truths would you teach, or save a sinking land?
All fear, none aid you, and few understand.

ALEXANDER POPE: *An Essay on Man*, IV, 1734

This season I have never been, nor do I intend again to be, a guest in the mansions of gross sensuality.

JAMES BOSWELL: *Letter to William Temple*, May 1, 1761

All zeal for a reform, that gives offence
To peace and charity, is mere pretence.

WILLIAM COWPER: *Charity*, 1782

The hole and the patch should be commensurate.

THOMAS JEFFERSON: *Letter to James Madison*, 1787

The man who has at heart the regeneration of his species should always bear in mind two principles: to regard hourly progress in the discovery and dissemination of truth as essential, and calmly to let years pass before he urges the carrying into effect of his teaching.

WILLIAM GODWIN: *An Enquiry Concerning Political Justice*, 1793

Every reform, however necessary, will by weak minds be carried to an excess which will itself need reforming.
S. T. COLERIDGE: *Biographia Literaria*, I, 1817

Reform is a good replete with paradox; it is a cathartic which our political quacks recommend to others, but will not take themselves; it is admired by all who cannot effect it, and abused by all who can.
C. C. COLTON: *Lacon*, 1820

Reform has no gratitude, no prudence, no husbandry.
R. W. EMERSON: *The Conservative*, 1841

Whenever A and B put their heads together and decide what A, B and C must do for D, there is never any pressure on A and B. They consent to it and like it. There is rarely any pressure on D because he does not like it and contrives to evade it. The pressure all comes on C. Now, who is C? He is always the man who, if let alone, would make a reasonable use of his liberty without abusing it. He would not constitute any social problem at all and would not need any regulation. He is the Forgotten Man.
W. G. SUMNER: *The Forgotten Man*, 1883

The only way a woman can ever reform a man is by boring him so completely that he loses all possible interest in life.
OSCAR WILDE: *The Picture of Dorian Gray*, 1891

An indefinable something is to be done, in a way nobody knows how, at a time nobody knows when, that will accomplish nobody knows what.
THOMAS B. REED: *Letter to Sereno E. Payne*, Dec. 2, 1902

Healing the sick and reforming the sinner are one and the same thing in Christian Science. Both cures require the same method, and are inseparable in Truth.
MARY BAKER G. EDDY: *Science and Health*, XII, 1908

Reform must come from within, not from without. You cannot legislate for virtue.
JAMES CARDINAL GIBBONS: Address in Baltimore, Sept. 13, 1909

We have had all the reform that we want in this city for some time to come.
JOHN F. HYLAN (MAYOR OF NEW YORK): Speech to the Civil Service Reform Association, Jan. 10, 1918

There is no historical spectacle more tragic and at the same time more repulsive than the fetid disintegration of reformism amid the wreckage of all its conquests and hopes.
LEON TROTSKY: *What Next?*, intro., 1932

A man who reforms himself has contributed his full share toward the reformation of his neighbor.
Author unidentified

Reforms should begin at home and stay there.
IBID.

You never hear of a man marrying a woman to reform her.
IBID.

Ye may end him, but ye'll ne'er mend him.
SCOTTISH PROVERB

[*See also* Liberalism, Remorse, Repentence.

Reformation

If Luther had been born in the Tenth Century he would have effected no Reformation. If he had never been born at all it is evident that the Sixteenth Century could not have elapsed without a great schism in the church.
T. B. MACAULAY: *John Dryden*, 1828 (Edinburgh Review, Jan.)

A king whose character may be best described by saying that he was despotism itself personified, unprincipled ministers, a rapacious aristocracy, a servile Parliament: such were the instruments by which England was delivered from the yoke of Rome.
T. B. MACAULAY: *Hallam*, 1828 (Edinburgh Review, Sept.)

It cannot be denied that corruption of morals prevailed in the Sixteenth Century to such an extent as to call for a sweeping reformation, and that laxity of discipline invaded even the sanctuary.
JAMES CARDINAL GIBBONS: *The Faith of Our Fathers*, III, 1876

[*See also* Erasmus (Desiderius), Luther (Martin), Protestantism.

Reformer

The Thurians ordained that whosoever would go about to abolish an old law, or establish a new one, should present himself with a halter around his neck, to the end that, if his proposal were not approved, he might be hanged at once.
MICHEL DE MONTAIGNE: *Essays*, I, 1580 (*Thurians*=a people of Southern Italy)

I have a greater windmill in my brain than a new politician with a head full of reformation.
THOMAS SHADWELL: *The Sullen Lovers*, I, 1668

Wild enthusiasts, projectors, politicians, inamoratos, castle-builders, chymists, and poets.
ALEXANDER POPE: *The Dunciad*, III, 1728

Tyrants have no consciences, and reformers no feeling; and the world suffers both by the plague and by the cure.
HORACE WALPOLE: *Letter to the Earl of Strafford*, June 26, 1790

Ye sage reformers of this vicious age,
Like wanton mountebanks, who skip the stage,
All you devise — a rare reform indeed,

Makes vice triumphant, and scorn'd virtue bleed.

DAVID BENEDICT: Poem read before the Philandrian Society, Taunton, Mass., 1807

My prospects for this year are squally, and unless I can make something by other people's gambling and drink I shall be strongly tempted myself.

MASON L. WEEMS: *Letter to Matthew Carey*, 1812

Does Mr. Wilberforce care a farthing for the slaves in the West Indies, or if they were all at the Devil, so that *his* soul were saved?

S. T. COLERIDGE: To Thomas Allsop, *c.* 1820

I thank my God the sun and moon
Are both stuck up so high,
That no presumptuous hand can stretch
And pluck them from the sky.
If they were not, I do believe
That some reforming ass
Would recommend to take them down
And light the world by gas.

Anon.: *Popular rhyme, c.* 1832

With most men reform is a trade — with some a swindling trade — with others an honest but yet a lucrative trade. Reform for its own sake seldom thrives.

JOHN QUINCY ADAMS: *Letter,* April 21, 1837

Nay I may ask, is not every true reformer, by the nature of him, a priest first of all? He appeals to Heaven's invisible justice against earth's visible force; knows that it, the invisible, is strong and alone strong. He is a believer in the divine truth of things; a seer, seeing through the shows of things; a worshipper, in one way or the other, of the divine truth of things; a priest, that is.

THOMAS CARLYLE: *Heroes and Hero-Worship,* IV, 1840 (Lecture in London, May 15)

Madmen, madwomen, men with beards, Dunkers, Muggletonians, Come-outers, Agrarians, Seventh-day Baptists, Quakers, Abolitionists, Calvinists, Unitarians, and philosophers.

R. W. EMERSON: Description of the Chardon Street Convention in Boston, 1840

We are reformers in Spring and Summer; in Autumn and Winter we stand by the old; reformers in the morning, conservers at night.

R. W. EMERSON: *The Conservative,* 1841

In efforts to soar above our nature we invariably fall below it. Your reformist demigods are merely devils turned inside out.

E. A. POE: *Marginalia,* 1844–49

The people who think it a shame when anything goes wrong — who rush to the conclusion that the evil could and ought to have been prevented, are those who, in the long run, do most to make the world better.

J. S. MILL: *Representative Government,* III, 1861

The eager and often inconsiderate appeals of reformers and revolutionists are indispensable to counterbalance the inertness and fossilism making so large a part of human institutions.

WALT WHITMAN: *Democratic Vistas,* 1870

Nothing is more unpleasant than a virtuous person with a mean mind.

WALTER BAGEHOT: *Literary Studies,* 1879

A creature effeminate without being either masculine or feminine; unable to beget or bear; possessing neither fecundity nor virility; endowed with the contempt of men and the derision of women; and doomed to sterility, isolation and extinction.

J. J. INGALLS: Speech in the Senate, *c.* 1885

The fact that every sort of reform movement teems with neuropaths is to be explained by the transference of interest from censored egoistic (erotic or violent) tendencies of the unconscious to fields where they can work themselves out without any self-reproach.

S. FERENCZI: *Introjection and Transference,* 1909

A reformer is a guy who rides through a sewer in a glass-bottomed boat.

JAMES J. WALKER (MAYOR OF NEW YORK): Speech in New York, 1928

The politicians of reformism, those dexterous wire-pullers, artful intriguers and careerists, expert parliamentary and ministerial machinators, are no sooner thrown out of their habitual sphere by the course of events and set face to face with momentous contingencies, than they reveal themselves to be inept boobies.

LEON TROTSKY: *What Next?,* I, 1932

At twenty a man is full of fight and hope. He wants to reform the world. When he's seventy he still wants to reform the world, but he knows he can't.

CLARENCE DARROW: To a newspaper interviewer, April 18, 1936

[*See also* Comstockery.

Refugee

This country has always been the refuge of the oppressed from every land — exiles for conscience's sake.

Democratic National Platform, 1892

Refusal

The great refusal. (Il gran rifiuto.)

Applied to the action of Pope Celestine V, who resigned the papacy in 1294, five months after his election

Better a friendly refusal than an unwilling promise. GERMAN PROVERB

Regicide

States decree the most illustrious rewards, not to him who catches a thief, but to him who kills a tyrant.

ARISTOTLE: *Politics,* II, *c.* 322 B.C.

It is a stern business killing of a king. But if you once go to war with him, it lies there; this and all else lies there. Once at war, you have made wager of battle with him: it is he to die, or else you.

THOMAS CARLYLE: *Heroes and Hero-Worship*, VI, 1840 (Lecture in London, May 22)

[*See also* Assassination.

Regimentation

Men will submit to any rule by which they may be exempted from the tyranny of caprice and of chance. They are glad to supply by external authority their own want of constancy and resolution, and court the government of others when long experience has convinced them of their own inability to govern themselves.

SAMUEL JOHNSON: *Letter to Joseph Baretti*, June 10, 1761

Regret

I regret nothing in the past but the dead and the failure.

ROBERT TOOMBS: On returning from Europe, 1867 (Alluding to the American Civil War)

Reincarnation

[*See* Eternal Recurrence.

Rejection

Mr. Dodsley presents his compliments to the gentleman who favored him with the enclosed poem, which he has returned, as he apprehends the sale of it would probably not enable him to give any consideration. He does not mean by this to insinuate a want of merit in the poem, but rather a want of attention in the public.

JAMES DODSLEY: Form used in rejecting MSS., 1780 (Quoted in GEORGE CRABBE: *The Poet's Journal*, April 28)

Rejoicing

Let the heavens be glad, and let the earth rejoice: and let men say among the nations, The Lord reigneth.

I CHRONICLES XVII, 31, *c.* 300 B.C.

Relative

Dreadful indeed are the feuds of relatives, and difficult the reconciliation.

EURIPIDES: *The Phoenissæ*, *c.* 410 B.C.

It is hard to find the relatives of a poor man.

MENANDER: *Adelphoi*, *c.* 300 B.C.

No man will be respected by others who is despised by his own relatives.

PLAUTUS: *Trinummus*, III, *c.* 190 B.C.

Nature ordains friendship with relatives, but it is never very stable.

CICERO: *De amicitia*, *c.* 50 B.C.

The worst hatred is that of relatives.

TACITUS: *Annals*, XLII, *c.* 110

A medley of kindred, that 'twould puzzle a convocation of casuists to resolve their degree of consanguinity.

CERVANTES: *Don Quixote*, I, 1605

A man cannot bear all his kin on his back.

JAMES KELLY: *Complete Collection of Scottish Proverbs*, 1721

I advise thee to visit thy relations and friends; but I advise thee not to live too near them.

THOMAS FULLER: *Introductio ad Prudentiam*, I, 1731

Visit your aunt, but not every day; and call at your brother's, but not every night.

BENJAMIN FRANKLIN: *Poor Richard's Almanac*, 1742

Fate gives us our relatives, but we choose our friends. JACQUES DELILLE: *La pitié*, 1803

A poor relation is an odious approximation, — a preposterous shadow, lengthening in the noontide of your prosperity, — an unwelcome remembrancer, — a rebuke to your rising, — a stain in your blood, a blot on your 'scutcheon, — a rent in your garment, — a death's head at your banquet, — a lion in your path, — a frog in your chamber, — a fly in your ointment, — a mote in your eye, — a triumph to your enemy, — an apology to your friends, — the one thing not needful, — the hail in harvest, — the ounce of sour in a pound of sweet.

CHARLES LAMB: *Poor Relations*, 1823 (London Magazine, May)

A man is reputed to have thought and eloquence; he cannot, for all that, say a word to his cousin or his uncle.

R. W. EMERSON: *Friendship*, 1841

And so do his sisters and his cousins and his aunts
His sisters and his cousins
Whom he reckons up by dozens,
And his aunts.

W. S. GILBERT: *H.M.S. Pinafore*, I, 1878

I can't help detesting my relations. I suppose it comes from the fact that we can't stand other people having the same fault as ourselves.

OSCAR WILDE: *The Picture of Dorian Gray*, 1891

Relations are simply a tedious pack of people who haven't got the remotest knowledge of how to live, nor the smallest instinct about when to die.

OSCAR WILDE: *The Importance of Being Earnest*, III, 1895

Relatives are persons who live too near and die too seldom. Author unidentified

Relatives are the worst friends, said the fox as the dogs took after him. DANISH PROVERB

The best use of bad wine is to drive away poor relations. FRENCH PROVERB

The more relatives, the more trouble. IBID.

One friend is worth a hundred relatives. IBID.

The rich never lack relatives. ITALIAN PROVERB

The unfortunate have no relatives. (Infelicium nulli sunt affines.) ITALIAN PROVERB

He who refuses to die does not love his relatives. WEST AFRICAN PROVERB

[*See also* Cousin, Dead, Monkey.

Relative-in-law

I beg to be remembered to and by Mrs. Crowfoot, Sen., my — what shall I call the relationship? We are the father and mother of our son and daughter, but in what legal affinity I cannot determine.
GEORGE CRABBE: *Letter to Henchman Crowfoot,* Jan. 19, 1831

Marry an island woman, and you marry the whole island.
IRISH PROVERB (Sometimes *mountain* or *glen* appears in place of *island*)

Better quarrel with your in-laws than with your neighbors. HINDU PROVERB

[*See also* Daughter-in-law, Mother-in-law, Son-in-law.

Relativity

When we see an effect always taking place in the same manner, we conclude that there is a natural necessity for it, as, that the sun will rise tomorrow, etc.; but nature often deceives us, and does not bow to her own laws.
BLAISE PASCAL: *Pensées,* IV, 1670

Elephants are always drawn smaller than life, but a flea always larger.
JONATHAN SWIFT: *Thoughts on Various Subjects,* 1706

Everything is twice as large, measured on a three-year-old's three-foot scale as on a thirty-year-old's six-foot scale.
O. W. HOLMES: *The Poet at the Breakfast-Table,* I, 1872

To a mouse, a cat is a lion. ALBANIAN PROVERB

The smaller the woods the larger seems the hare. DUTCH PROVERB

To a dwarf all other men are giants. GERMAN PROVERB

To the ant a few drops of rain is a flood. JAPANESE PROVERB

Reliability

They all had trust in his cussedness
And knowed he would keep his word.
JOHN HAY: *Jim Bludso,* 1871

Relic

Every priest praises his own relics.
ENGLISH PROVERB, traced to the XIV century, and probably borrowed from the Latin

Relief

For this relief, much thanks.
SHAKESPEARE: *Hamlet,* I, *c.* 1601

Relief, Public

When money failed in the land of Egypt, and in the land of Canaan, all the Egyptians came unto Joseph, and said, Give us bread.
GENESIS XLVII, 15, *c.* 700 B.C.

The Federal government must and shall quit this business of relief.
F. D. ROOSEVELT: Message to Congress, Jan. 4, 1935

Religion

Religion is a disease, but it is a noble disease.
HERACLITUS: *Fragment, c.* 500 B.C.

Since the masses of the people are inconstant, full of unruly desires, passionate, and reckless of consequence, they must be filled with fears to keep them in order. The ancients did well, therefore, to invent gods, and the belief in punishment after death. It is rather the moderns, who seek to extirpate such beliefs, who are to be accused of folly.
POLYBIUS: *Histories,* VI, *c.* 125 B.C.

Religion is not removed by removing superstition. CICERO: *De divinatione,* II, *c.* 78 B.C.

How many evils have flowed from religion!
LUCRETIUS: *De rerum natura,* I, 57 B.C.

Either take away religion in every case, or preserve it in every case.
CICERO: *Second Oration Against Mark Antony,* 44 B.C.

It is for the good of states that men should be deluded by religion.
VARRO: *Antiquitatum rerum humanarum et divinarum, c.* 40 B.C.

The myths about Hades and the gods, though they are pure invention, help to make men virtuous.
DIODORUS SICULUS: *Bibliotheca historica, c.* 20 B.C.

It was fear that first brought gods into the world.
PETRONIUS ARBITER: *Satyricon, c.* 50

Pure religion, and undefiled before God and the Father, is this, To visit the fatherless and widows in their affliction, and to keep himself unspotted from the world.
JAMES I, 27, *c.* 60

It is when we are in misery that we revere the gods; the prosperous seldom approach the altar. SILIUS ITALICUS: *Punica*, VII, *c.* 75

Count religion but a childish toy,
And hold there is no sin but ignorance.
CHRISTOPHER MARLOWE: *The Jew of Malta*, I, *c.* 1590

In religion,
What damnèd error, but some sober brow
Will bless it and approve it with a text,
Hiding the grossness with fair ornament?
SHAKESPEARE: *The Merchant of Venice*, III, *c.* 1597

What excellent fools
Religion makes of men.
BEN JONSON: *Sejanus*, V, 1603

Religion, oh, how it is commeddled with policy! The first bloodshed in the world happened about religion.
JOHN WEBSTER: *The White Devil*, III, *c.* 1608

One religion is as true as another.
ROBERT BURTON: *The Anatomy of Melancholy*, 1621

Jest not with the eye, or with religion.
GEORGE HERBERT: *Outlandish Proverbs*, 1640

Religion is a stalking horse to shoot other fowl.
IBID.

There is not any burden that some would not gladlier post off to another than the charge and care of their religion.
JOHN MILTON: *Areopagitica*, 1644

God requireth not any uniformity of religion to be enacted and enforced in any civil state; which enforced uniformity (sooner or later) is the greatest occasion of civil war, ravishment of conscience, persecution of Jesus Christ in His servants, and of the hypocrisy and destruction of millions of souls.
ROGER WILLIAMS: *The Bloudy Tenent of Persecution*, 1644

Fear of power invisible, feigned by the mind or imagined from tales publicly allowed, [is] religion; not allowed, superstition.
THOMAS HOBBES: *Leviathan*, I, 1651

The truth of religion lies in its very obscurity, in the little light we have on it, and in our indifference to that light.
BLAISE PASCAL: *Pensées*, VIII, 1670

If we submit every thing to reason, our religion will have nothing in it mysterious or supernatural. If we violate the principles of reason, our religion will be absurd and ridiculous. BLAISE PASCAL: *Pensées*, XIV

Men have contempt for religion, and fear that it is true. To cure this it is necessary to commence by showing that religion is not contrary to reason; then that it is venerable, and worthy of respect; next to make it amiable, and make the good wish that it were true; and finally to show that it is true.
BLAISE PASCAL: *Pensées*, XXIV

You must also own religion in his rags, as well as when in his silver slippers; and stand by him, too, when bound in irons, as well as when he walketh the streets with applause.
JOHN BUNYAN: *Pilgrim's Progress*, I, 1678

Religion is like the fashion: one man wears his doublet slashed, another laced, another plain; but every man has a doublet; so every man has a religion. We differ about the trimming.
JOHN SELDEN: *Table-Talk*, 1689

Religion is nothing else but love to God and man.
WILLIAM PENN: *Fruits of Solitude*, 1693

That religion cannot be right that a man is the worse for having. IBID.

In matters of religion, it is very easy to deceive a man, and very hard to undeceive him.
PIERRE BAYLE: *Dictionary*, 1697

We have just enough religion to make us hate, but not enough to make us love, one another.
JONATHAN SWIFT: *Thoughts on Various Subjects*, 1706

Religion may be considered under two general heads. The first comprehends what we are to believe, the other what we are to practise.
JOSEPH ADDISON: *The Spectator*, Aug. 16, 1712

A man is quickly convinced of the truth of religion, who finds it is not against his interest that it should be true.
JOSEPH ADDISON: *The Spectator*, Aug. 23, 1712

Men of sense are really all of one religion. But men of sense never tell what it is.
ANTHONY A. COOPER (EARL OF SHAFTSBURY): *Characteristics of Men, Manners, Opinions, Times*, *c.* 1713

Religion supposes Heaven and Hell, the word of God, and sacraments, and twenty other circumstances which, taken seriously, are a wonderful check to wit and humor.
JONATHAN SWIFT: *A Letter of Advice to a Young Poet*, Dec. 1, 1720

Resolved, Never to allow any pleasure or grief, joy or sorrow, nor any affection at all, nor any degree of affection, nor any circumstance relating to it, but what helps religion.
JONATHAN EDWARDS: *Resolutions*, 1722

A good life is the only religion.
THOMAS FULLER: *Gnomologia*, 1732

One is of Martin's religion, another of Luther's.
IBID.

Religion is the best armor in the world, but the worst cloak. IBID.

A proof, even a demonstrative one, of a future life would not be a proof of religion. . . . But as religion implies a future state, any presumption against such a state is a presumption against religion.

JOSEPH BUTLER: *The Analogy of Religion,* I, 1736

Religion is the idol of the mob; it adores everything it does not understand.

FREDERICK THE GREAT: *Letter to Voltaire,* July 6, 1737

What religion is he of? Why, he is an Anythingarian.

JONATHAN SWIFT: *Polite Conversation,* I, 1738

By these two things religion is recommended to us above all other things whatsoever: first, by the satisfaction we thereby enjoy in life; second, by the expectation we have thereby at death.

BENJAMIN WHICHCOTE: *Moral and Religious Aphorisms,* 1753

The writers against religion, whilst they oppose every system, are wisely careful never to set up any of their own.

EDMUND BURKE: *A Vindication of Natural Society,* I, 1756

I believe all that I can understand of religion, and respect the rest without rejecting it.

J.-J. ROUSSEAU: *La nouvelle Héloïse,* V, 1761

Where religion speaks, reason has only a right to hear.

STANISLAUS LESZCYNSKI (KING OF POLAND): *Œuvres du philosophe bienfaisant,* 1763

The truths of religion are never so well understood as by those who have lost the power of reasoning.

VOLTAIRE: *Philosophical Dictionary,* 1764

Religion and morality put a brake on nature's strength, but they cannot destroy it. The drunkard in a cloister, reduced to a half-sétier of cider at each meal, will no longer get drunk, but he will always like wine.

IBID.

Religion is too important a matter to its devotees to be a subject of ridicule. If they indulge in absurdities they are to be pitied rather than ridiculed.

IMMANUEL KANT: Lecture at Königsberg, 1775

Compulsion in religion is distinguished peculiarly from compulsion in every other thing. I may grow rich by an art I am compelled to follow; I may recover health by medicines I am compelled to take against my own judgment; but I cannot be saved by a worship I disbelieve and abhor.

THOMAS JEFFERSON: *Notes on Religion,* 1776

Our religion is in a book; we have an order of men whose duty it is to teach it; we have one day in the week set apart for it, and this is in general pretty well observed: yet ask the first ten gross men you meet, and hear what they have to tell of their religion.

SAMUEL JOHNSON: *Boswell's Life,* April 26, 1776

To be of no church is dangerous. Religion, of which the rewards are distant, and which is animated only by faith and hope, will glide by degrees out of the mind unless it be invigorated and reimpressed by external ordinances, by stated calls to worship, and the salutary influence of example.

SAMUEL JOHNSON: *Lives of the Poets* (Milton), 1778

The first ideas of religion arose, not from a contemplation of the works of nature, but from a concern with regard to the events of life, and from the incessant hopes and fears which actuate the human mind.

DAVID HUME: *Dialogues Concerning Natural Religion,* I, 1779

The various modes of worship which prevailed in the Roman world were all considered by the people as equally true; by the philosopher as equally false; and by the magistrate as equally useful.

EDWARD GIBBON: *The Decline and Fall of the Roman Empire,* II, 1781

Religion! What treasure untold
Resides in that heavenly word!
More precious than silver and gold,
Or all that this earth can afford.

WILLIAM COWPER: *Verses Supposed to be Written by Alexander Selkirk,* 1782

A man who has never had religion before, no more grows religious when he is sick, than a man who has never learnt figures can count, when he has need of calculation.

SAMUEL JOHNSON: *Boswell's Life,* April 28, 1783

Prisons are built with stones of law, brothels with bricks of religion.

WILLIAM BLAKE: *The Marriage of Heaven and Hell,* 1790

The body of all true religion consists in obedience to the will of the Sovereign of the world, in a confidence in His declarations, and an imitation of His perfections.

EDMUND BURKE: *Reflections on the Revolution in France,* III, 1790

Man is by his constitution a religious animal.

IBID.

Religion is the basis of civil society, and the source of all good and of all comfort. IBID.

Persecution is not an original feature in any religion; but is always the strongly-marked feature of all law-religions, or religions established by law. Take away the law-establishment, and every religion re-assumes its original benignity.

THOMAS PAINE: *The Rights of Man,* I, 1791

The world is my country, all mankind are my brethren, and to do good is my religion.

THOMAS PAINE: *The Age of Reason,* III, 1794

I sometimes wish to introduce a religious turn of mind; but habits are strong things, and my religious fervors are confined, alas! to some fleeting moments of occasional solitary devotion.

CHARLES LAMB: *Letter to S. T. Coleridge,* June 10, 1796

Of all the dispositions and habits which lead to political prosperity, religion and morality are indispensable supports. In vain would that man claim the tribute of patriotism who should labor to subvert these great pillars of human happiness, these firmest props of the duties of men and citizens.

GEORGE WASHINGTON: Farewell Address, Sept. 17, 1796

All the different religions are only so many religious dialects.

G. C. LICHTENBERG: *Reflections,* 1799

May it not be that good men venerate religion, instead of religion making men good?

IBID.

The time will come when our present religious ideas will seem as singular as the spirit of chivalry does today. IBID.

To make man as religion would have him is only another degree of the impossible.

IBID.

The cry of a child, the fall of a book, the most trifling occurrence is sufficient to dissipate religious thought, and to introduce a more willing train of ideas: a sparrow fluttering about the church is an antagonist which the most profound theologian in Europe is wholly unable to overcome.

SYDNEY SMITH: *Six Sermons,* pref., 1800

A nation must have a religion, and that religion must be under the control of the government.

NAPOLEON I: To Count Antoine Thibaudeau, June, 1801

If thinking men would have the courage to think for themselves, and to speak what they think, it would be found they do not differ in religious opinions as much as is supposed.

THOMAS JEFFERSON: *Letter to John Adams,* 1813

Prolific fiend,
Who peoplest earth with demons, Hell with men,
And Heaven with slaves.

P. B. SHELLEY: *Queen Mab,* VI, 1813

I would believe in a religion if it existed ever since the beginning of time, but when I consider Socrates, Plato, Mahomet, I no longer believe. All religions have been made by men.

NAPOLEON I: To Gaspard Gourgaud at St. Helena, Jan. 28, 1817

All religions united with government are more or less inimical to liberty. All, separated from government, are compatible with liberty.

HENRY CLAY: Speech in the House of Representatives, March 24, 1818

There's naught so much the spirit calms as rum and true religion.

BYRON: *Don Juan,* II, 1819

Religion and thoroughbass are settled things. There should be no disputing about them.

LUDWIG VAN BEETHOVEN: To Anton Schindler, *c.* 1820

Men will wrangle for religion; write for it; fight for it; die for it, anything but — live for it.

C. C. COLTON: *Lacon,* 1820

I am no enemy to religion, but the contrary. As a proof, I am educating my natural daughter a strict Catholic; for I think people can never have enough of religion, if they are to have any.

BYRON: *Letter to Thomas Moore,* March 4, 1822

Every sect is a moral check on its neighbor. Competition is as wholesome in religion as in commerce.

W. S. LANDOR: *Imaginary Conversations,* I, 1824

Religion is, in its essence, the most gentlemanly thing in the world. It will alone gentilize, if unmixed with cant; and I know nothing else that will, alone.

S. T. COLERIDGE: *Table-Talk,* May 5, 1830

A man who should act, for one day, on the supposition that all the people about him were influenced by the religion which they professed, would find himself ruined before night.

T. B. MACAULAY: *Civil Disabilities of the Jews,* 1831 (Edinburgh Review, Jan.)

The first and last lesson of religion is, "The things that are seen are temporal; the things that are unseen are eternal." It puts an affront upon nature.

R. W. EMERSON: *Nature,* 1836

Religion is neither a theology nor a theosophy; it is more than that, it is a discipline, a law, a yoke, an indissoluble engagement.

JOSEPH JOUBERT: *Pensées,* 1838

A man's religion is the chief fact with regard to him.

THOMAS CARLYLE: *Heroes and Hero-Worship,* I, 1840 (Lecture in London, May 5)

Religion among the low becomes low.

R. W. EMERSON: *The Conservative,* 1841

Religion is the opium of the people.
KARL MARX: *A Criticism of the Hegelian Philosophy of Law,* 1844 (The slogan of the Russian Bolsheviks, *c.* 1919; in Russian, " Religia opium dlia naroda ")

What we all love is good touched up with evil —
Religion's self must have a spice of devil.
A. H. CLOUGH: *Dipsychus,* 1850

Religion is the *chef d'œuvre* of the art of animal training, for it trains people in the way they shall think.
ARTHUR SCHOPENHAUER: *Parerga und Paralipomena,* 1851

Anything which makes religion its second object, makes religion *no* object. . . . He who makes religion his first object, makes it his whole object.
JOHN RUSKIN: *Lectures on Architecture and Painting,* IV, 1853

No people, at the present day, can be explained by their national religion. They do not feel responsible for it; it lies far outside of them.
R. W. EMERSON: *English Traits,* XIII, 1856

I say that the real and permanent grandeur of These States must be their religion;
Otherwise there is no real and permanent grandeur:
(Nor character, nor life worthy the name, without religion;
Nor land, nor man or woman, without religion).
WALT WHITMAN: *Starting from Paumanok,* 1860

I am for religion against religions.
VICTOR HUGO: *Les misérables,* 1862

Every established fact which is too bad to admit of any other defense is always presented to us as an injunction of religion.
J. S. MILL: *The Subjection of Women,* II, 1869

Even in religious fervor there is a touch of animal heat.
WALT WHITMAN: *Democratic Vistas,* 1870

All religions, with their gods, demigods, prophets, messiahs and saints, are the product of the fancy and credulity of men who have not yet reached the full development and complete possession of their intellectual powers.
M. A. BAKUNIN: *Dieu et l'état,* 1871

No state is ever without religion, or can be without it. Consider the freest states in the world — the United States and the Swiss Confederacy — and note how Divine Providence figures in all their public utterances. IBID.

Where it is a duty to worship the sun it is pretty sure to be a crime to examine the laws of heat. JOHN MORLEY: *Voltaire,* 1872

The true meaning of religion is not simply morality, but morality touched by emotion.
MATTHEW ARNOLD: *Literature and Dogma,* I, 1873

Religion and poetry address themselves, at least in one of their aspects, to the same part of the human constitution: they both supply the same want, that of ideal conceptions grander and more beautiful than we see realized in the prose of human life.
J. S. MILL: *Three Essays on Religion,* III, 1874

A civil ruler dabbling in religion is as reprehensible as a clergyman dabbling in politics. Both render themselves odious as well as ridiculous.
JAMES CARDINAL GIBBONS: *The Faith of Our Fathers,* XII, 1876

That venerable and holy glory, the shining gift of religion.
POPE LEO XIII: *In scrutabili,* April 21, 1878

There is not enough religion in the world even to destroy the world's religions.
F. W. NIETZSCHE: *Human All-too-Human,* I, 1878

When two do not agree about religion, it is nearly always futile to hope for agreement in other things.
POPE LEO XIII: *Arcanum divinæ sapientiæ,* Feb. 10, 1880

The country that has got the least religion is the most prosperous, and the country that has got the most religion is in the worst condition.
R. G. INGERSOLL: Speech in Boston, April 23, 1880

Religion embraces all knowledge and all power that are not scientific.
JAMES DARMESTETER: *Essais orientaux,* 1883

Religion is a functional weakness.
MAX NORDAU: *Conventional Lies of Our Civilization,* 1884

A religion without myth, without dogma, without cult, without rites is no more than that bastard thing, natural religion, and is easily resolvable into a system of metaphysical hypotheses.
M. J. GUYAU: *L'irréligion de l'avenir,* intro., 1887

Religion is a sociology conceived as a physical, metaphysical and moral explanation of all things; it is the reduction of all natural, and even supernatural forces to a human type, and the reduction of their relations to social relations. IBID.

Religion is full of difficulties, but if we are often puzzled what to think, we need seldom be in doubt what to do.
JOHN LUBBOCK (LORD AVEBURY): *The Pleasures of Life,* II, 1887

Women have never invented a religion; they are untainted with that madness, and they are not moralists.
GEORGE MOORE: *Confessions of a Young Man,* XII, 1888

A religious man thinks only of himself.
F. W. NIETZSCHE: *The Antichrist*, LXI, 1888

A propitiation or conciliation of powers superior to man which are believed to control the course of nature or of human life.
J. G. FRAZER: *The Golden Bough*, I, 1890

Truth, in matters of religion, is simply the opinion that has survived.
OSCAR WILDE: *The Critic as Artist*, 1891

Religions die when they are proved to be true. Science is the record of dead religions.
OSCAR WILDE: *Phrases and Philosophies for the Use of the Young*, 1894

The metaphysical proof of a religious system is, like those from prophecy and miracles, merely a part of its apologetics and not of its appeal.
W. C. BROWNELL: *Victorian Prose Masters*, 1901

Religion is a monumental chapter in the history of human egotism.
WILLIAM JAMES: *The Varieties of Religious Experience*, XX, 1902

True religion is the establishment by man of such a relation to the Infinite Life around him, as, while connecting his life with this Infinitude and directing his conduct, is also in agreement with his reason and with human knowledge.
LYOF N. TOLSTOY: *What Is Religion?*, 1902

Religions are not revealed: they are evolved. If a religion were revealed by God, that religion would be perfect in whole and in part, and would be as perfect at the first moment of its revelation as after ten thousand years of practise. There has never been a religion which fulfils those conditions.
ROBERT BLATCHFORD: *God and My Neighbor*, 1903

I regard religion itself as quite unnecessary for a nation's life; science is far above superstition; and what is religion, Buddhism or Christianity, but superstition, and therefore a possible source of weakness to a nation?
HIROBUMI ITO (1841–1909): Quoted in S. L. GULICK: *The Evolution of the Japanese*, 1903

Religion is a species of mental disease. It has always had a pathological reaction on mankind.
BENITO MUSSOLINI: Speech in Lausanne, July, 1904

Religion is a sum of scruples which impede the free exercise of our faculties.
SALOMON REINACH: *Cultes, mythes, et religions*, I, 1904

A daughter of Hope and Fear, explaining to Ignorance the nature of the Unknowable.
AMBROSE BIERCE: *The Devil's Dictionary*, 1906

When religion is banished, human authority totters to its fall.
POPE BENEDICT XV: *Ad beatissimi*, Nov. 1, 1914

To know but one religion is not to know that one.
ELBERT HUBBARD: *Roycroft Dictionary and Book of Epigrams*, 1923

Religion is not an intelligence test, but a faith.
E. W. HOWE: *Sinner Sermons*, 1926

There are two branches of religion — high and low, mystical sleep-walkers and practical idealists.
J. M. KEYNES: *A Short View of Russia*, I, 1926

We guarantee the right of every citizen to combat by argument, propaganda, and agitation any and all religion. The Communist party cannot be neutral toward religion. It stands for science, and all religion is opposed to science.
JOSEPH STALIN: Interview with the first American labor delegation to Russia, Sept. 9, 1927

No film or episode may throw ridicule on any religious faith. Ministers of religion, in their character as such, should not be used as comic characters or as villains. Ceremonies of any definite religion should be carefully and respectfully handled.
A CODE TO GOVERN THE MAKING OF MOTION AND TALKING PICTURES BY THE MOTION PICTURE PRODUCERS AND DISTRIBUTORS OF AMERICA, INC., March 31, 1930

Religion belongs to that realm that is inviolable before the law of causation and therefore closed to science.
MAX PLANCK: *Where is Science Going?*, V, 1932

Get religion like a Methodist.
Experience it like a Baptist.
Be sure of it like a Disciple.
Stick to it like a Lutheran.
Conciliate it like a Congregationalist.
Be proud of it like an Episcopalian.
Simplify it like a Quaker.
Glorify it like a Jew.
Pay for it like a Presbyterian.
Practise it like a Christian Scientist.
Work at it like the Salvation Army.
Propagate it like a Roman Catholic.
Enjoy it like a Negro.
EDGAR DEWITT JONES: Address in Washington, Sept. 26, 1934 (The joint composition of Dr. Jones and Frederick W. Burnham, of Richmond, Va.)

I am suspicious of all who agree with my religion. MARTIN H. FISCHER (1879–)

No man has ever sat down calmly unbiased to reason out his religion, and not ended by rejecting it. Author unidentified

Religion is a man using a divining rod. Philosophy is a man using a pick and shovel.
IBID.

Religion is an infectious disease, the rapid spread of which is due to the social instincts of mankind. IBID.

Religion takes refuge in the unknowable from the terrors of the unknown. IBID.

All religions start in Asia. JAPANESE PROVERB

A man who is without religion is like a horse without bridle. (Homo sine religione, sicut equus sine fræno.) LATIN PROVERB

[*See also* Art, Asceticism, Buddhism, Business, Children, Chinese, Christian, Church, Church and State, Communism, Country, Credo, Death, Education, England, Evildoing, Fanaticism, Freedom (Religious), Friendship, Gentlemen, Happiness, Hypocrisy, Intolerance, Irishman, Japanese, Jest, Jew, Martyrdom, Monotheism, Morality, Morality (National), Mystery, Patriotism, Philosophy, Physician, Pleasure, Politician, Politics, Prayer, Self-interest, Skepticism, Slovenliness, State, Sun, Superstition, Toleration.

Rembrandt van Rhyn, Paul (1607–69)

I have seen an old head by Rembrandt at Burleigh House, and if I could produce a head at all like Rembrandt in a year, in my lifetime, it would be glory and felicity, and wealth and fame enough for me.
WILLIAM HAZLITT: *Table-Talk*, 1821

Remedy

For extreme diseases, extreme remedies.
HIPPOCRATES: *Aphorisms*, c. 400 B.C.

To do nothing is sometimes a good remedy.
IBID.

There are remedies worse than the disease.
PUBLILIUS SYRUS: *Sententiæ*, c. 50 B.C.

At the beginning no one tries extreme remedies.
SENECA: *Agamemnon*, c. 60

Desperate diseases require desperate remedies.
ENGLISH PROVERB, traced to the XVII century, and apparently borrowed from the Hippocratic apothegm (cf. *ante*, c. 400 B.C.)

For every ill beneath the sun
There is some remedy or none;
If there be one, resolve to find it;
If not, submit, and never mind it.
Anon.: *Maxims, Morals*, etc., 1843

A doubtful remedy is better than none at all.
LATIN PROVERB

Where there is a right there is a remedy. (Ubi jus, ibi remedium.) LEGAL MAXIM

[*See also* Cure, Law, Medicine, Patience.

Remembrance

Praising what is lost
Makes the remembrance dear.
SHAKESPEARE: *All's Well that Ends Well*, v, c. 1602

When to the sessions of sweet silent thought
I summon up remembrance of things past,
I sigh the lack of many a thing I sought,
And with old woes new wail my dear time's waste. SHAKESPEARE: *Sonnets*, 1609

How sharp the point of this remembrance is.
SHAKESPEARE: *The Tempest*, v, 1611

Th' hypdroptic drunkard and night-scouting thief,
The itchy lecher and self-tickling proud
Have the remembrance of past joys for relief
Of coming ills.
JOHN DONNE: *Holy Sonnets*, III, c. 1617

Remembrance wakes with all her busy train,
Swells at my breast, and turns the past to pain.
OLIVER GOLDSMITH: *The Deserted Village*, 1770

I remember, I remember
The house where I was born;
The little window where the sun
Came creeping in at morn.
THOMAS HOOD: *I Remember*, 1826

When other lips and other hearts
Their tales of love shall tell
In language whose excess imparts
The power they feel so well,
There may perhaps in such a scene
Some recollection be,
Of days that have as happy been
And you'll remember me.
ALFRED BUNN: *The Bohemian Girl*, I, 1843 (Drury Lane, Nov. 27)

Where is the heart that doth not keep,
Within its inmost core,
Some fond remembrance hidden deep,
Of days that are no more?
ELLEN CLEMENTINE HOWARTH: *'Tis But a Little Faded Flower*, 1864

In eternal remembrance. (Memoria in æterna.)
LATIN PHRASE

[*See also* Absence, Ages, Memory, Rosemary.

Remorse

Farewell, remorse: all good to me is lost;
Evil, be thou my good.
JOHN MILTON: *Paradise Lost*, IV, 1667

Remorse goes to sleep when we are in the enjoyment of prosperity, but makes itself felt in adversity.
J.-J. ROUSSEAU: *Confessions*, III, 1766

Remorse is nothing save the anticipation of the pain to which our offense has exposed us.
C. A. HÉLVETIUS: *De l'homme*, VII, 1773

Remorse begets reform.
WILLIAM COWPER: *The Task*, 1785

Oh, pah! how sick I am of that lie, a mean one I once told! — I stink in the midst of respect.
CHARLES LAMB: *Letter to Bernard Barton*, Feb. 25, 1824

Remorse is a sign that it wasn't quite as pleasant as one expected it to be.
Author unidentified

In young, pleasure; in old age, remorse. (Jung gefreut, alt gereut.) GERMAN PROVERB

[*See also* Repentance.

Renaissance

The revival of letters was not owing to any free government, but to the encouragement and protection of Leo X and Francis I; the one as absolute a pope, and the other as despotic a prince, as ever reigned.
LORD CHESTERFIELD: *Letter to his son*, Feb. 7, 1739

The mind of the Renaissance was not a pilgrim mind, but a sedentary city mind, like that of the ancients.
GEORGE SANTAYANA: *The Genteel Tradition at Bay*, I, 1931

Renegade

There is no malice like the malice of a renegade.
T. B. MACAULAY: *Hallam*, 1828 (Edinburgh Review, Sept.)

Renown

[*See* Fame.

Rent

Rent is always the difference between the produce obtained by the employment of two equal quantities of capital and labor.
DAVID RICARDO: *Principles of Political Economy*, II, 1817

[*See also* Land, Progress, Usury.

Repairs

A ship and a woman are ever repairing.
GEORGE HERBERT: *Outlandish Proverbs*, 1640

If you do not repair your gutter, you will have your whole house to repair.
SPANISH PROVERB

Repentance

I abhor myself, and repent in dust and ashes.
JOB XLII, 6, *c.* 325 B.C.

Joy shall be in heaven over one sinner that repenteth, more than over ninety and nine just persons, which need no repentance.
LUKE XV, 7, *c.* 75

If my wind were but long enough to say my prayers, I would repent.
SHAKESPEARE: *The Merry Wives of Windsor*, IV, *c.* 1600

He repents on thorns that sleeps in beds of roses.
FRANCIS QUARLES: *Emblems*, I, 1635

Who after his transgression doth repent,
Is half, or altogether, innocent.
ROBERT HERRICK: *Hesperides*, 1648

That it may please thee to give us true repentance; to forgive us all our sins, negligences, and ignorances; and to endue us with the grace of thy Holy Spirit to amend our lives according to thy holy Word; We beseech thee to hear us, good Lord.
THE BOOK OF COMMON PRAYER (*The Litany*): 1662

Repentance is the virtue of weak minds.
JOHN DRYDEN: *The Indian Emperor*, II, 1665

Our repentance is not so much regret for the ill we have done as fear of the ill that may happen to us in consequence.
LA ROCHEFOUCAULD: *Maxims*, 1665

I view my crime, but kindle at the view,
Repent old pleasures, and solicit new.
ALEXANDER POPE: *Eloisa to Abelard*, 1717

Then turns repentant, and his God adores
With the same spirit that he drinks and whores.
ALEXANDER POPE: *Moral Essays*, I (Of the Knowledge and Characters of Men), 1733

He that repents is angry with himself; I need not be angry with him.
BENJAMIN WHICHCOTE: *Moral and Religious Aphorisms*, 1753

With the morning cool repentance came.
WALTER SCOTT: *Rob Roy*, XII, 1817

The seeds of repentance are sown in youth by pleasure, but the harvest is reaped in age by pain. C. C. COLTON: *Lacon*, 1820

Repentance is quite out of date, and beside, if a woman really repents, she has to go to a bad dressmaker, otherwise no one believes in her.
OSCAR WILDE: *Lady Windermere's Fan*, III, 1892

The best part of repentance is the sinning.
ARAB PROVERB

Few women repent while the sun is shining brightly. Author unidentified

If only one man repents for his sins, the whole world is pardoned. HEBREW PROVERB

Late repentance is seldom true. (Pœnitentia sera raro vera.)
MEDIEVAL LATIN PROVERB

[*See also* Acquaintance, Anger, Confession, Passion, Pleasure, Reform, Sin.

Repetition

Nothing is ever said that has not been said before.
TERENCE: *Eunuchus*, prologue, *c.* 160 B.C.

No sweetness in a cabbage twice boiled, nor in a tale twice told.

THOMAS FULLER: *Gnomologia,* 1732

[*See also* Education, New.

Report

Of money, wit and virtue, believe one-fourth of what you hear.

H. G. BOHN: *Handbook of Proverbs,* 1855

Reporter

[*See* Journalism, Journalist, Methodist.

Repose

Our foster-nurse of nature is repose,
The which he lacks; that to provoke in him,
Are many simples operative, whose power
Will close the eye of anguish.

SHAKESPEARE: *King Lear,* IV, 1606

Representation

That the subject is not bound by acts when he is not represented is a sound maxim of the law, and not peculiar to the British Constitution, but a maxim of the ancient Roman law: "What concerns all shall be judged of by all."

JOHN ADAMS: *On Behalf of the People of Boston,* Dec. 20, 1765

[*See also* Taxes.

Representative

Your representative owes you, not his industry only, but his judgment, and he betrays instead of serving you if he sacrifices it to your opinion.

EDMUND BURKE: To his constituents at Bristol, 1774

[*See also* Legislature.

Reproof

Reprove not a scorner, lest he hate thee: rebuke a wise man, and he will love thee.

PROVERBS IX, 8, *c.* 350 B.C.

The reproof of a father is an agreeable medicine; for the profit is greater than the pain.

EPICTETUS: *Encheiridion, c.* 110

Reproofs from authority ought to be grave, and not taunting.

FRANCIS BACON: *Essays,* XI, 1625

Fear not the anger of the wise to raise;
Those best can bear reproof who merit praise.

ALEXANDER POPE: *An Essay on Criticism,* III, 1711

Only the upright may reprove the lame.

DANISH PROVERB

A reproof is nae poison.

SCOTTISH PROVERB

Republic

Republics in which high birth gives no right to the government of the state are in that respect the most happy; for the people have less reason to envy an authority which they confer on whom they will, and which they can again take away when they choose.

C. L. DE MONTESQUIEU: *La grandeur et la décadence des Romains,* 1734

The tyranny of a prince does not bring a state into greater danger than indifference to the public good places a republic. IBID.

Republics are brought to their ends by luxury; monarchies by poverty.

C. L. DE MONTESQUIEU: *The Spirit of the Laws,* VII, 1748

Ladies . . . ever have more influence in republics than in a monarchy. . . . Votes are easily acquired by the fair, and she who has the most beauty or art has a great sway in the senate.

MARY WORTLEY MONTAGU: *Letter to the Countess of Bute,* Oct. 31, 1758

There are few positions more demonstrable than that there should be in every republic some permanent body to correct the prejudices, check the intemperate passions, and regulate the fluctuations of a popular assembly.

ALEXANDER HAMILTON: Speech in the Convention of New York, June 24, 1788

It is of great importance in a republic not only to guard against the oppression of its rulers, but to guard one part of society against the injustice of the other part.

ALEXANDER HAMILTON: *The Federalist,* 1788

The United States shall guarantee to every state in this Union a republican form of government.

CONSTITUTION OF THE UNITED STATES, Art. IV, 1789

Government in a well constituted republic requires no belief from man beyond what his reason authorizes. He sees the *rationale* of the whole system, its origin, and its operation; and as it is best supported when best understood, the human faculties act with boldness, and acquire, under this form of government, a gigantic manliness.

THOMAS PAINE: *The Rights of Man,* I, 1791

The republic has no use for scientists.

The president of the French Revolutionary Tribunal: To Lavoisier, 1794

A monarchy is a merchantman which sails well, but will sometimes strike on a rock, and go to the bottom; a republic is a raft which will never sink, but then your feet are always in water.

FISHER AMES: Speech in the House of Representatives, 1795

A republican government is slow to move, yet when once in motion, its momentum becomes irresistible.

THOMAS JEFFERSON: *Letter to F. C. Gray,* 1815

In a republic, all are masters, and each tyrannizes over the others.
MAX STIRNER: *The Ego and His Own*, 1845

A republic may be called the climate of civilization.
VICTOR HUGO: Speech in the French Constituent Assembly, 1851

Republics exist only on tenure of being agitated.
WENDELL PHILLIPS: Speech in Boston, Jan. 28, 1852

We assert that no nation can long endure half republic and half empire.
Democratic National Platform, 1900

The early history of most of the world's republics is the best part of their history.
JULIUS KAHN: Speech in the House of Representatives, 1917

Republics have risen and fallen, and a transition from party to personal government has preceded every failure since the world began.
W. G. HARDING: Speech of acceptance, July 22, 1920

Republics are ungrateful.
Author unidentified

It is all over with the republic. (Actum est de republica.) LATIN SAYING

[*See also* Democracy, Despotism, Government (Representative), Imperialism, Majority, Monarchy.

Republican Party

It is a party of one idea; but that is a noble one — an idea that fills and expands all generous souls; the idea of equality — the equality of all men before human tribunals and human laws, as they all are equal before the divine tribunal and divine laws.
WILLIAM H. SEWARD: Speech in Rochester, N. Y., Oct. 25, 1858

Republicans are for both the man and the dollar, but in case of conflict the man before the dollar.
ABRAHAM LINCOLN: *Letter to H. L. Pierce*, April 6, 1859

The Republican party is the first party that was not founded on some compromise with the Devil. It is the first party of pure, square, honest principles; the first one.
R. G. INGERSOLL: Speech in Indianapolis, Sept. 21, 1876

Republicans are not ungrateful.
Republican National Platform, 1920

[*See also* Democratic Party, Party, Socialism.

Reputation

Men are generally more pleased with a widespread than with a great reputation.
PLINY THE YOUNGER: *Letters*, IV, *c.* 110

The purest treasure mortal times afford
Is spotless reputation; that away,
Men are but gilded loam or painted clay.
SHAKESPEARE: *Richard II*, I, *c.* 1596

Reputation is an idle and most false imposition; oft got without merit, and lost without deserving. SHAKESPEARE: *Othello*, II, 1604

Oh, I have lost my reputation! I have lost the immortal part of myself, and what remains is bestial. IBID.

The reputation of a woman may also be compared to a mirror of crystal, shining and bright, but liable to be sullied by every breath that comes near it.
CERVANTES: *Don Quixote*, I, 1605

I am now past the craggy paths of study, and come to the flowery plains of honor and reputation. BEN JONSON: *Volpone*, II, 1605

Work is the price which is paid for reputation.
BALTASAR GRACIÁN: *The Art of Worldly Wisdom*, XVIII, 1647

Some people resemble ballads, which are only sung for a certain time.
LA ROCHEFOUCAULD: *Maxims*, 1665

Whoever robs a woman of her reputation despoils a poor defenseless creature of all that makes her valuable, turns her beauty into loathsomeness, and leaves her friendless, abandoned and undone.
RICHARD STEELE: *The Guardian*, June 3, 1713

The blaze of a reputation cannot be blown out, but it often dies in the socket.
SAMUEL JOHNSON: *Letter to Hester Thrale*, May 1, 1780

The worst of me is known, and I can say that I am better than my reputation.
J. C. F. SCHILLER: *Maria Stuart*, III, 1800

It is one of the greatest privileges that belong to the nature of man that he possesses a sensibility to fame and a love of glory, and that the individual, by the combination of opinion and force of character, begets in his own reputation a property more valuable than the mere materials to which the crude notions of property are first applied.
MR. CHIEF JUSTICE ABBOTT: *Judgment in Rex* vs. *Francis Burdette*, 1820

I am accounted by some people a good man. How cheap that character is acquired! Pay your debts, don't borrow money, nor twist your kitten's neck off, nor disturb a congregation, etc., your business is done. I know things (thoughts or things, thoughts *are* things) of myself, which would make every friend I have fly me as a plague patient.
CHARLES LAMB: *Letter to Bernard Barton*, Feb. 25, 1824

Achievements which serve no materially useful end . . . will vary in regard to the chances they have of meeting with timely recognition and due appreciation; and their order of precedence, beginning with those who have the greatest chance, will be somewhat as follows: acrobats, circus-riders, ballet-dancers, jugglers, actors, singers, musicians, composers, poets, architects, painters, sculptors, philosophers.

ARTHUR SCHOPENHAUER: *On Reputation,* 1851

How many people live on the reputation of the reputation they might have made!

O. W. HOLMES: *The Autocrat of the Breakfast-Table,* III, 1858

What people say behind your back is your standing in the community in which you live.

E. W. HOWE: *Sinner Sermons,* 1926

Some say she do and some say she don't.

AMERICAN NEGRO SAYING

A man's good deeds are known only at home; his bad deeds far away.

CHINESE PROVERB

A good reputation is like the cypress; once cut, it never puts forth leaf again.

ITALIAN PROVERB

To have a bad reputation is to be half hanged.

IBID.

The reputation of a thousand years may be determined by the conduct of one hour.

JAPANESE PROVERB

When I did well, I heard it never;
When I did ill, I heard it ever.

OLD ENGLISH RHYME

Better be ill spoken of by one before all than by all before one. SCOTTISH PROVERB

He who has lost his reputation is a walking corpse. SPANISH PROVERB

[*See also* Lying, Name, Presidency, Soldier, Success.

Research

I do not know what I may appear to the world, but to myself I seem to have been only like a boy playing on the seashore, and diverting myself in now and then finding a smoother pebble or a prettier shell than ordinary, whilst the great ocean of truth lay all undiscovered before me.

ISAAC NEWTON: *David Brewster's Memoirs,* I, 1855 (The date of the saying was probably *c.* 1725)

Speak ye the pure delight whose favored steps
The lamp of science through the jealous maze
Of nature guides, when haply you reveal
Her secret honors.

MARK AKENSIDE: *The Pleasures of Imagination,* II, 1744

Lost in a gloom of uninspired research.

WILLIAM WORDSWORTH: *The Excursion,* IV, 1814

The mysterious and unsolved problem of how things came to be does not enter the empirical province of objective research, which is confined to a description of things as they are.

ALEXANDER VON HUMBOLDT: *Kosmos,* I, 1845 (Originally in a lecture in Berlin, 1828)

To discover and teach are distinct functions; they are also distinct gifts, and are not commonly found united in the same person.

J. H. NEWMAN: *On the Scope and Nature of University Education,* 1852

It is a matter of primary importance in the cultivation of those sciences in which truth is discoverable by the human intellect that the investigator should be free, independent, unshackled in his movement; that he should be allowed and enabled to fix his mind intently, nay, exclusively, on his special object, without the risk of being distracted every other minute in the process and progress of his inquiry by charges of temerariousness, or by warnings against extravagance or scandal.

J. H. NEWMAN: *Christianity and Scientific Investigation,* 1855

The investigator should have a robust faith — and yet not believe.

CLAUDE BERNARD: *Introduction à la médecine expérimentale,* 1865

I pay the captain of the Cunard steamship to carry me quickly and safely to Liverpool, not to make a chart of the Atlantic for after voyagers.

O. W. HOLMES: *Scholastic and Bedside Teaching,* 1867 (Lecture at the Harvard Medical School, Nov. 6)

The investigation of nature is an infinite pasture-ground, where all may graze, and where the more bite, the longer the grass grows, the sweeter is its flavor, and the more it nourishes.

T. H. HUXLEY: *Administrative Nihilism,* 1871

Truth is the aim of all research, no matter how sharply this truth may conflict with our social, ethical and political conditions. This is the unifying bond of the modern university.

THEODOR BILLROTH: *Medical Sciences in the German University,* 1876

Research, though toilsome, is easy; imagination, though delightful, is difficult.

A. C. BRADLEY: *Oxford Lectures on Poetry,* 1909

A man may do research for the fun of doing it, but he cannot expect to be supported for the fun of doing it.

J. HOWARD BROWN: Presidential address before the Society of American Bacteriologists, Dec. 28, 1931

[*See also* Freedom (Academic), Scientist.

Reservation, Mental

My tongue hath sworn, but not my mind.
EURIPIDES: *Hippolytus*, 428 B.C.

[*See also* Oath.

Resignation

The Lord gave, and the Lord hath taken away; blessed be the name of the Lord.
JOB I, 21, *c.* 325 B.C.

Not what I will, but what thou wilt.
MARK XIV, 36, *c.* 70 (Cf. MATTHEW XXVI, 39, *c.* 75; LUKE XXII, 42, *c.* 75)

A wise man cares not for what he cannot have.
GEORGE HERBERT: *Outlandish Proverbs*, 1640

Let God be magnified,
Whose everlasting strength
Upholds me under sufferings
Of more than ten years' length.
MICHAEL WIGGLESWORTH: *The Day of Doom*, prologue, 1662

Job feels the rod,
Yet blesses God.
The New England Primer, *c.* 1688

Welcome death, quoth the rat, when the trap fell. THOMAS FULLER: *Gnomologia*, 1732

Thou shalt do without! (Entbehren sollst! Du sollst entbehren!)
J. W. GOETHE: *I Faust*, I, 1808

What is called resignation is confirmed desperation. H. D. THOREAU: *Walden*, 1854

New measures, other feet anon!
My dance is finished.
ROBERT BROWNING: *A Grammarian's Funeral*, 1855

Let the long contention cease!
Geese are swans, and swans are geese,
Let them have it how they will!
Thou art tired; best be still.
MATTHEW ARNOLD: *The Last Word*, 1867

Not our will, but His, be done.
WILLIAM MCKINLEY: On his deathbed, Sept. 11, 1901

If I have no feather-bed I'll sleep on straw.
GERMAN SAYING

Resistance

The spirit of resistance to government is so valuable on certain occasions that I wish it to be always kept alive. It will often be exercised when wrong, but better so than not to be exercised at all.
THOMAS JEFFERSON: To Abigail Adams, 1787

[*See also* Liberty.

Resistance, Passive

Passive resistance is the most potent weapon ever wielded by man against oppression.
BENJAMIN R. TUCKER: *Instead of a Book*, 1893

Resolution

It is the character of a brave and resolute man not to be ruffled by adversity and not to desert his post.
CICERO: *De officiis*, I, 78 B.C.

The resolved mind hath no cares.
GEORGE HERBERT: *Outlandish Proverbs*, 1640

I will hold New Orleans in spite of Urop and all Hell.
Ascribed to ANDREW JACKSON, 1812

I am in earnest — I will not equivocate — I will not excuse — I will not retreat a single inch and I will be heard.
WILLIAM LLOYD GARRISON: In the first issue of the Liberator, Jan. 1, 1831

I have begun several times many things, and I have often succeeded at last. I will sit down, but the time will come when you will hear me.
BENJAMIN DISRAELI: Maiden speech in the House of Commons, Dec. 7, 1837

Having chosen our course, without guile and with pure purpose, let us renew our trust in God, and go forward without fear and with manly hearts.
ABRAHAM LINCOLN: Message to Congress, July 4, 1861

I purpose to fight it out on this line if it takes all Summer.
U. S. GRANT: Despatch to H. M. Halleck, near Spottsylvania C. H., May 11, 1864

I'll hold her nozzle agin the bank
Till the last galoot's ashore.
JOHN HAY: *Jim Bludso*, 1871

The fatality of good resolutions is that they are always too late.
OSCAR WILDE: *The Picture of Dorian Gray*, 1891

The way to Hell is plastered with good resolutions. GERMAN PROVERB

[*See also* Ability.

Respect

Thou shalt not respect the person of the poor.
LEVITICUS XIX, 15, *c.* 700 B.C.

Ye shall not respect persons in judgment; but ye shall hear the small as well as the great.
DEUTERONOMY I, 17, *c.* 650 B.C.

To feed men and not to love them is to treat them as if they were barnyard cattle. To love them and not to respect them is to treat them as if they were household pets.
MENCIUS: *Discourses*, *c.* 300 B.C.

Is there no respect of place, persons, nor time in you?
SHAKESPEARE: *Twelfth Night*, II, *c.* 1601

He that respects not is not respected.
GEORGE HERBERT: *Outlandish Proverbs,* 1640

Respect a man, he will do the more.
JAMES HOWELL: *Proverbs,* 1659

[*See also* Clothes, Person.

Respectability

To be respectable implies a multitude of little observances, from the strict keeping of Sunday down to the careful tying of a cravat.
VICTOR HUGO: *Toilers of the Sea,* I, 1866

The respectable are not led so much by any desire of applause as by a positive need for countenance. The weaker and the tamer the man, the more will he require this support.
R. L. STEVENSON: *Familiar Studies of Men and Books,* VIII, 1882

Respectability! — a suburban villa, a piano in the drawing room, and going home to dinner. Such things are no doubt very excellent, but they do not promote intensity of feeling, fervor of mind.
GEORGE MOORE: *Confessions of a Young Man,* IX, 1888

The more things a man is ashamed of, the more respectable he is.
GEORGE BERNARD SHAW: *Man and Superman,* I, 1903

[*See also* Hat.

Responsibility

He who weighs his responsibilities can bear them. MARTIAL: *Epigrams,* XII, *c.* 100

The vast majority of persons of our race have a natural tendency to shrink from the responsibility of standing and acting alone.
FRANCIS GALTON: *Inquiries Into Human Faculty,* 1883

[*See also* Liberty.

Rest

Too much rest becomes a pain.
HOMER: *Odyssey,* XV, *c.* 800 B.C.

On the seventh day God ended his work which he had made; and he rested on the seventh day. GENESIS II, 2, *c.* 700 B.C.

Six days may work be done; but in the seventh is the sabbath of rest.
EXODUS XXXI, 15, *c.* 700 B.C.

The seventh year shall be a sabbath of rest unto the land, a sabbath for the Lord: thou shalt neither sow thy field, nor prune thy vineyard. LEVITICUS XXV, 4, *c.* 700 B.C.

Thus saith the Lord, Stand ye in the ways, and see, and ask for the old paths, where is the good way, and walk therein, and ye shall find rest for your souls.
JEREMIAH VI, 16, *c.* 625 B.C.

There the wicked cease from troubling; and there the weary be at rest.
JOB III, 17, *c.* 325 B.C.

Come unto me, all ye that labor and are heavy laden, and I will give you rest.
MATTHEW XI, 28, *c.* 75

I like to rest, whether sitting or lying down, with my heels as high as my head, or higher.
MICHEL DE MONTAIGNE: *Essays,* III, 1588

Sleep after toil, port after stormy seas,
Ease after war, death after life.
EDMUND SPENSER: *The Faerie Queene,* I, *c.* 1589

Labor is held up by the hope of rest.
ROBERT HERRICK: *Hesperides,* 1648

He that can take rest is greater than he that can take cities.
BENJAMIN FRANKLIN: *Poor Richard's Almanac,* 1737

O rest! thou soft word! autumnal flower of Eden! moonlight of the spirit!
JEAN PAUL RICHTER: *Hesperus,* XXXVIII, 1795

Rest is for the dead.
THOMAS CARLYLE: *Journal,* June 22, 1830

All things have rest, and ripen toward the grave
In silence; ripen, fall and cease:
Give us long rest or death.
ALFRED TENNYSON: *The Lotos-Eaters,* 1833

Here we rest.
MOTTO OF ALABAMA, adopted Dec. 29, 1868

Rest in bed will do more for more diseases than any other single procedure.
LOGAN CLENDENING: *Modern Methods of Treatment,* I, 1924

[*See also* Death, Exercise, Fame, Idleness, Inn.

Restlessness

He was as restless as a hyena.
THOMAS DE QUINCEY: *On Murder Considered as One of the Fine Arts,* 1827

Restlessness is the hallmark of existence.
ARTHUR SCHOPENHAUER: *Parerga und Paralipomena,* 1851

Restraint

No restraint, be it ever so little, but is imprisonment. EDWARD COKE: *Institutes,* I, 1628

The mind of man naturally hates everything that looks like a restraint upon it.
JOSEPH ADDISON: *The Spectator,* June 23, 1712

All that makes existence valuable to anyone depends on the enforcement of restraints upon the actions of other people.
J. S. MILL: *On Liberty,* I, 1859

Resurrection

Many of them that sleep in the dust of the earth shall awake, some to everlasting life, and some to shame and everlasting contempt.
DANIEL XII, 2, *c.* 165 B.C.

For as in Adam all die, even so in Christ shall all be made alive.
I CORINTHIANS XV, 22, *c.* 55

When they heard of the resurrection of the dead, some mocked: and others said, We will hear thee again of this matter.
ACTS XVII, 32, *c.* 75

Why should it be thought a thing incredible with you, that God should raise the dead?
ACTS XXVI, 8

The sea gave up the dead which were in it; and death and hell delivered up the dead which were in them: and they were judged every man according to his works.
REVELATION XX, 13, *c.* 95

The hour is coming in which all that are in the grave shall hear his voice, and shall come forth; they that have done good, unto the resurrection of life; and they that have done evil, unto the resurrection of damnation.
JOHN V, 28–29, *c.* 115

Let none of you say that this flesh is not judged and does not rise again . . . , for as you were called in the flesh, you shall also come in the flesh.
ST. CLEMENT: *Second Epistle to the Corinthians, c.* 150

The elders came unto Pilate, saying, Give us soldiers to watch his sepulchre for three days, lest his disciples come and steal the body away, and the people suppose that he is risen from the dead.
THE GOSPEL OF PETER VIII, *c.* 150

This visible flesh, which is properly called so, we must without doubting believe will rise again.
ST. AUGUSTINE: *Of the Faith and of the Creed, c.* 393

At the resurrection the substance of our bodies, however disintegrated, will be reunited. We must not fear that the omnipotence of God cannot recall all the particles that have been consumed by fire or by beasts, or dissolved into dust and ashes, or decomposed into water, or evaporated into air.
ST. AUGUSTINE: *The City of God,* XXII, *c.* 427

In the resurrection everyone will receive that bodily stature which he had in his prime, even though he has died an old man.
IBID.

Some say that women shall not rise again in the female sex, but all in the male; but they seem to me wiser who have no hesitation in affirming that all shall rise again in their own sex.
IBID.

We could not call it resurrection unless the soul returned to the same body, for resurrection means a second rising.
THOMAS AQUINAS: *Summa theologicæ,* III, *c.* 1265

God knows in what part of the world every grain of every man's dust lies; and *sibilat populum suum* (as his Prophet speaks in another case), He whispers, He hisses, He beckons for the bodies of His saints, and in the twinkling of an eye, that body that was scattered over all the elements is sate down at the right hand of God, in a glorious resurrection.
JOHN DONNE: *LXXX Sermons,* 1640

I believe that our estranged and divided ashes shall unite again; that our separated dust, after so many pilgrimages and transformations into the parts of minerals, plants, animals, elements, shall, at the voice of God, return to their primitive shapes, and join again to make up their primary and predestinate forms.
THOMAS BROWNE: *Religio Medici,* I, 1642

I do believe, that die I must,
And be return'd from out my dust:
I do believe, that when I rise,
Christ I shall see, with these same eyes.
ROBERT HERRICK: *Noble Numbers,* 1647

Earth to earth, ashes to ashes, dust to dust, in sure and certain hope of the resurrection.
THE BOOK OF COMMON PRAYER (*Burial of the Dead*), 1662

What reason have atheists for saying that we cannot rise again? Which is the more difficult, to be born, or to rise again? That what has never been, should be, or that what has been, should be again? Is it more difficult to come into being than to return to it?
BLAISE PASCAL: *Pensées,* XXIV, 1670

Some Negroes who believe the resurrection think that they shall rise white.
THOMAS BROWNE: *Christian Morals,* II, *c.* 1680

This mortal does not put on immortality, this corruption does not put on incorruption, until after the coming of Christ. . . . The resurrection is not yet.
THE BOOK OF MORMON (*Alma XL,* 2–3), 1830

Lord, he thought He'd make a man;
Dese bones shill rise again!
Made him out o' mud an' a handful o' san';
Dese bones shill rise again!
Negro spiritual, *c.* 1840

In the hereafter angels may
Roll the stone from its grave away.
J. G. WHITTIER: *Maud Muller,* 1854

I looks into the East,
I looks into the West,

Lord, I sees dead a-risin'
From every graveyard.
American Negro song, quoted by HOWARD W. ODUM: *Wings On My Feet*, VIII, 1929

I shall rise again. (Resurgam.)
LATIN PHRASE

[*See also* Alchemy, Cremation, Daughter, Heaven, Hell, Immortality.

Retaliation

O true believers, the law of retaliation is ordained you for the slain: the free shall die for the free, and the servant for the servant, and a woman for a woman.
THE KORAN, II, *c.* 625

An eye for an eye, and a tooth for a tooth. That does not mean that if I put out another man's eye, therefore I must lose one of my own (for what is he the better for that?), though this be commonly received; but it means, I shall give him what satisfaction an eye shall be judged to be worth.
JOHN SELDEN: *Table-Talk*, 1689

[*See also* Punishment.

Reticence

[*See* Taciturnity.

Retirement

Oh, that I had in the wilderness a lodging place of wayfaring men; that I might leave my people, and go from them.
JEREMIAH IX, 2, *c.* 625 B.C.

And this our life, exempt from public haunt,
Finds tongues in trees, books in the running brooks,
Sermons in stones, and good in everything.
SHAKESPEARE: *As You Like It*, II, *c.* 1600

Happy is the man who, ignored by the world, lives contented with himself in some retired nook.
NICHOLAS BOILEAU: *Épîtres*, VI, 1670

Thus let me live, unseen, unknown,
Thus unlamented let me die,
Steal from the world, and not a stone
Tell where I lie.
ALEXANDER POPE: *Ode on Solitude*, *c.* 1700 (Pope says in a letter to Henry Cromwell, July 17, 1709, that it was written when he was " not twelve years old ")

Walk sober off before the sprightlier age
Comes titt'ring on, and shoves you from the stage.
ALEXANDER POPE: *Second Epistle of the Second Book of Horace*, 1738

Far from the madding crowd's ignoble strife
Their sober wishes never learn'd to stray;
Along the cool sequester'd vale of life
They kept the noiseless tenor of their way.
THOMAS GRAY: *Elegy Written in a Country Churchyard*, 1750

The love of retirement has, in all ages, adhered closely to those minds which have been most enlarged by knowledge, or elevated by genius.
SAMUEL JOHNSON: *The Rambler*, April 10, 1750

O blest retirement! friend to life's decline —
Retreats from care, that never must be mine,
How blest is he who crowns, in shades like these,
A youth of labor with an age of ease!
OLIVER GOLDSMITH: *The Deserted Village*, 1770

Oh, that the desert were my dwelling-place,
With one fair spirit for my minister,
That I might all forget the human race,
And, hating no one, love but only her.
BYRON: *Childe Harold*, IV, 1818

And when I'm stretched beneath the pines,
Where the evening star so holy shines,
I laugh at the lore and the pride of man,
At the sophist schools, and the learned clan.
R. W. EMERSON: *Good-Bye*, 1839

[*See also* Age (Old), Happiness, Hermit, Obscurity, Office, Superannuation.

Retort

The retort courteous.
SHAKESPEARE: *As You Like It*, V, *c.* 1600

[*See also* Argument.

Retreat

A fine retreat is as good as a gallant attack.
BALTASAR GRACIÁN: *The Art of Worldly Wisdom*, XXXVIII, 1647

In all the trade of war no feat
Is nobler than a brave retreat.
SAMUEL BUTLER: *Hudibras*, I, 1663

[*See also* Lame, Moreau (J. V.).

Retribution

They have sown the wind, and they shall reap the whirlwind.
HOSEA VIII, 7, *c.* 740 B.C.

The way of transgressors is hard.
PROVERBS XIII, 15, *c.* 350 B.C.

Whoso diggeth a pit shall fall therein.
PROVERBS XXVI, 27 (Cf. ECCLESIASTES X, 8, *c.* 200 B.C.)

They that plough iniquity, and sow wickedness, reap the same.
JOB IV, 8, *c.* 325 B.C.

Whatsoever a man soweth, that shall he also reap.
GALATIANS VI, 7, *c.* 50

He that leadeth into captivity shall go into captivity; he that killeth with the sword must be killed with the sword.
REVELATION XIII, 10, *c.* 95

Most men employ their first years so as to make their last miserable.
THOMAS FULLER: *Gnomologia*, 1732

The thorns which I have reap'd are of the tree
I planted – they have torn me – and I bleed!
I should have known what fruit would spring
from such a seed.
BYRON: *Childe Harold*, IV, 1818

Opinions alter, manners change, creeds rise and fall, but the moral law is written on the tablets of eternity. For every false word or unrighteous deed, for cruelty and oppression, for lust or vanity, the price has to be paid at last, not always by the chief offenders, but paid by some one.
J. A. FROUDE: *The Science of History*, 1864 (Lecture in London, Feb. 5)

The mills of the gods grind slowly, but they grind exceedingly fine.
ENGLISH PROVERB, with both Greek and Latin prototypes, and common in various forms in England for centuries; it appears in Longfellow's translation of one of FRIEDRICH VON LOGAU'S *Sinngedichte*, 1654, as "Though the mills of God grind slowly, yet they grind exceedingly small"

If you scatter thorns, don't go barefoot.
ITALIAN PROVERB

Reunion

Oh, that 't were possible
After long grief and pain
To find the arms of my true love
Round me once again!
ALFRED TENNYSON: *Maud*, II, 1855

Revelation

Revelation . . . explains all mysteries except her own.
WILLIAM COWPER: *The Task*, 1785

The most detestable wickedness, the most horrid cruelties, and the greatest miseries, that have afflicted the human race, have had their origin in this thing called revelation, or revealed religion. It has been the most dishonorable belief against the character of the Divinity, the most destructive to morality, and the peace and happiness of man, that ever was propagated since man began to exist.
THOMAS PAINE: *The Age of Reason*, III, 1794

If God has spoken, why is the universe not convinced?
P. B. SHELLEY: *Queen Mab*, notes, 1813

The authority of the Deity [is] the sole ground of duty, and His communicated will the only ultimate standard of right and wrong.
JONATHAN DYMOND: *Essays on the Principles of Morality*, II, 1831

The vast bulk of the population believe that morality depends entirely on revelation; and if a doubt could be raised among them that the Ten Commandments were given by God from Mount Sinai, men would think they were at liberty to steal, and women would consider themselves absolved from the restraints of chastity.
JOHN CAMPBELL (BARON CAMPBELL): *Argument for the prosecution in Rex* vs. *H. Hetherington*, 1835

A revelation is not made for the purpose of showing to indolent men that which, by faculties already given to them, they may show to themselves; no: but for the purpose of showing that which the moral darkness of man will not, without supernatural light, allow him to perceive.
THOMAS DE QUINCEY: *The True Relations of the Bible to Merely Human Science*, *c.* 1845

It will all come out in the wash.
AMERICAN PROVERB

[*See also* Faith, Miracle, Oxford University, Philosophy.

Revelation, Book of

The Apocalypse of St. John is the majestic image of a high and stately tragedy, shutting up and intermingling her solemn scenes and acts with a sevenfold chorus of hallelujahs and harping symphonies.
JOHN MILTON: *The Reason of Church Government*, 1641

Revelry

When night
Darkens the streets, then wander forth the sons
Of Belial, flown with insolence and wine.
JOHN MILTON: *Paradise Lost*, I, 1667

There was a sound of revelry by night,
And Belgium's capital had gather'd then
Her beauty and her chivalry, and bright
The lamps shone o'er fair women and brave
men.
BYRON: *Childe Harold*, III, 1816

Let us have wine and woman, mirth and laughter,
Sermons and soda-water the day after.
BYRON: *Don Juan*, II, 1819

We won't go home till morning.
J. B. BUCKSTONE: *Billy Taylor*, I, 1850

I am for those who believe in loose delights –
I share the midnight orgies of young men;
I dance with the dancers, and drink with the
drinkers.
WALT WHITMAN: *Native Moments*, 1860

[*See also* Merriment.

Revenge

Thou shalt not avenge.
LEVITICUS XIX, 18, *c.* 700 B.C.

The revenger of blood himself shall slay the murderer; when he meeteth him, he shall slay him.
NUMBERS XXXV, 19, *c.* 700 B.C.

The Lord revengeth and is furious; the Lord will take vengeance on his adversaries.
NAHUM I, 2, *c.* 625 B.C.

Revenge is just.
ARISTOTLE: *Rhetoric,* I, *c.* 322 B.C.

Revenge is an inhuman word.
SENECA: *De Ira,* II, *c.* 43

Vengeance is mine; I will repay, saith the Lord.
ROMANS XII, 19, *c.* 55 (Cf. HEBREWS X, 30, *c.* 65)

Revenge is the poor delight of little minds.
JUVENAL: *Satires,* XIII, 128

It is better to avenge a friend than mourn him.
Anon.: *Beowulf,* VII, *c.* 750

Men ought either to be indulged or utterly destroyed, for if you merely offend them they take vengeance, but if you injure them greatly they are unable to retaliate, so that the injury done to a man ought to be such that vengeance cannot be feared.
NICCOLÒ MACHIAVELLI: *The Prince,* III, 1513

Vengeance is sweet.
WILLIAM PAINTER: *The Palace of Pleasure,* II, 1567 (A proverb; another form is "Revenge is sweet")

Blood and revenge are hammering in my head.
SHAKESPEARE: *Titus Andronicus,* II, 1594

A man that studieth revenge keeps his own wounds green.
FRANCIS BACON: *Essays,* IV, 1597

Revenge is a kind of wild justice, which, the more man's nature runs to, the more ought law to weed it out; for as for the first wrong, it doth but offend the law, but the revenge of that wrong putteth the law out of office.
IBID.

The whirligig of time brings in his revenges.
SHAKESPEARE: *Twelfth Night,* V, *c.* 1601

Had all his hairs been lives, my great revenge
Had stomach for them all.
SHAKESPEARE: *Othello,* V, 1604

Since all dream, let us dream of revenge.
Anon.: *Humor Out of Breath,* I, 1608

Neglect will kill an injury sooner than revenge.
OWEN FELLTHAM: *Resolves, c.* 1620

Delay in vengeance gives a heavier blow.
JOHN FORD: *'Tis Pity She's a Whore,* IV, 1633

Revenge, that thirsty dropsy of our souls,
Which makes us covet that which hurts us most,
Is not alone sweet, but partakes of tartness.
PHILIP MASSINGER and JOHN FLETCHER: *A Very Woman,* IV, 1634

Living well is the best revenge.
GEORGE HERBERT: *Outlandish Proverbs,* 1640

In revenges men look not at the greatness of the evil past, but the greatness of the good to follow.
THOMAS HOBBES: *Leviathan,* I, 1651

What though the field be lost?
All is not lost — th' unconquerable ill,
And study of revenge, immortal hate,
And courage never to submit or yield.
JOHN MILTON: *Paradise Lost,* I, 1667

Women do most delight in revenge.
THOMAS BROWNE: *Christian Morals,* III, *c.* 1680

Who'll sleep in safety that has done me wrong?
THOMAS OTWAY: *The Orphan,* IV, 1680

Women will do more for revenge than they'll do for the Gospel.
JOHN VANBRUGH: *The Provok'd Wife,* II, 1697

In taking revenge a man is but even with his enemy; but in passing it over, he is superior.
THOMAS FULLER: *Gnomologia,* 1732

The revenge of an idiot is without mercy.
IBID.

There's small revenge in words, but words may be greatly revenged.
BENJAMIN FRANKLIN: *Poor Richard's Almanac,* 1757

The only kind of revenge which a man of sense need take upon a scoundrel is, by a series of worthy behavior, to force him to admire and esteem his enemy and yet irritate his animosity by declining a reconciliation.
WILLIAM SHENSTONE: *Of Men and Manners,* 1764

Vengeance is a dish that should be eaten cold.
ENGLISH PROVERB, not recorded before the XIX century

Revenge is barren. It feeds on its own dreadful self; its delight is murder; and its satiety is despair.
J. C. F. SCHILLER: *Wilhelm Tell,* V, 1804

Vengance to God alone belongs;
But when I think of all my wrongs,
My blood is liquid flame.
WALTER SCOTT: *Marmion,* VI, 1808

All men enjoy revenge; and most exult
Over the tortures they can never feel —
Flattering their secret peace with others' pain.
P. B. SHELLEY: *The Cenci,* I, 1819

I will not be revenged, and this I owe to my enemy; but I will remember, and this I owe to myself.
C. C. COLTON: *Lacon,* 1820

Revenge is a debt in the paying of which the greatest knave is honest and sincere, and, so far as he is able, punctual.
IBID.

Revenge and wrong bring forth their kind;
The foul cubs like their parents are.
P. B. SHELLEY: *Hellas,* 1822

To come upon your wife in the arms of her lover, and kill them both — this is not revenge; it is the kindest service you can render them.
BALZAC: *The Physiology of Marriage,* 1830

Revenge! (Revanche!)
Slogan of the French after the loss of Alsace and Lorraine, 1871

Revenge does not long remain unrevenged.
GERMAN PROVERB

Revenge is a morsel reserved for God.
ITALIAN PROVERB

[*See also* Crime, Enmity, Forgiveness, Man and Woman, Pleasure, Policy, Politician.

Revenue

All bills for raising revenue shall originate in the House of Representatives.
CONSTITUTION OF THE UNITED STATES, Art. I, 1789

Reverence

Always and in everything let there be reverence.
CONFUCIUS: *The Book of Rites*, I, *c.* 500 B.C.

But yesterday the word of Cæsar might
Have stood against the world; now lies he there,
And none so poor to do him reverence.
SHAKESPEARE: *Julius Cæsar*, III, 1599

Let thy speeches be seriously reverent when thou speakest of God or His attributes; for to jest or utter thyself lightly in matters divine is an unhappy impiety, provoking Heaven to justice, and urging all men to suspect thy belief.
FRANCIS HAWKINS: *Youth's Behavior*, VII, 1663

To yield reverence to another, to hold ourselves and our lives at his disposal, is not slavery; often, it is the noblest state in which a man can live in this world.
JOHN RUSKIN: *Stones of Venice*, II, 1853

All real joy and power of progress in humanity depend on finding something to reverence, and all the baseness and misery of humanity begin in a habit of disdain.
JOHN RUSKIN: *The Crown of Wild Olive*, IV, 1866

The spiritual attitude of a man to a god and a dog to a man.
AMBROSE BIERCE: *The Devil's Dictionary*, 1906

Review

I look upon reviews as a sort of infant disease to which new-born books are subject.
G. C. LICHTENBERG: *Reflections*, 1799

I never read a book before reviewing it. It prejudices one so!
Ascribed to SYDNEY SMITH in *A Memoir of the Rev. Sydney Smith* by his daughter, LADY HOLLAND, 1855

[*See also* Criticism.

Reviewer

Reviewers are like sextons, who, in a charnel-house, can tell you to what John Thompson or to what Tom Matthews such a skull or such belonged — but who wishes to know?
HORACE WALPOLE: *Letter to William Cole*, Aug. 22, 1778

[*See also* Critic.

Revolution

Revolutions in democracies are mainly the work of demagogues. Partly by persecuting men of property and partly by arousing the masses against them, they induce them to unite, for a common fear brings even enemies together.
ARISTOTLE: *Politics*, V, *c.* 322 B.C.

Revolutions are not about trifles, but they are produced by trifles.
ARISTOTLE: *Politics*, VII

Governments are not overthrown by the poor, who have no power, but by the rich — when they are insulted by their inferiors, and cannot obtain justice.
DIONYSIUS OF HALICARNASSUS: *Antiquities of Rome*, V, *c.* 20 B.C.

Those who give the first shock to a state are the first overwhelmed in its ruin; the fruits of public commotion are seldom enjoyed by him who was the first mover; he only beats the water for another's net.
MICHEL DE MONTAIGNE: *Essays*, I, 1580

The blow by which kings fall causes a long bleeding.
PIERRE CORNEILLE: *Cinna*, III, 1639

There is a kind of revolution of so general a character that it changes the tastes as well as the fortunes of the world.
LA ROCHEFOUCAULD: *Maxims*, 1665

The art of revolutionizing and overturning states is to undermine established customs, by going back to their origin, in order to mark their want of justice.
BLAISE PASCAL: *Pensées*, IV, 1670

Whenever the legislators endeavor to take away and destroy the property of the people, or to reduce them to slavery under arbitrary power, they put themselves into a state of war with the people, who are thereupon absolved from any further obedience, and are left to the common refuge which God hath provided for all men against force and violence.
JOHN LOCKE: *Treatises on Government*, II, 1690

I would not be at the trouble of composing a distich to achieve a revolution. 'Tis equal to me what names are on the scene.
HORACE WALPOLE: *Letter to George Montague*, Dec. 30, 1761

Everything I see about me is sowing the seeds of a revolution that is inevitable, though I shall not have the pleasure of seeing it. The lightning is so close at hand that it will strike at the first chance, and then there will be a pretty uproar. The young are fortunate, for they will see fine things.

VOLTAIRE: *Leter to M. de Chauvelin,* April 2, 1764 (Voltaire was then 70)

The most sensible and jealous people are so little attentive to government that there are no instances of resistance until repeated, multiplied oppressions have placed it beyond a doubt that their rulers had formed settled plans to deprive them of their liberties; not to oppress an individual or a few, but to break down the fences of a free constitution, and deprive the people at large of all share in the government, and all the checks by which it is limited.

JOHN ADAMS: *Novanglus,* 1774

Whenever any government becomes destructive of these ends [life, liberty and the pursuit of happiness] it is the right of the people to alter or abolish it, and to institute a new government, laying its foundations on such principles, and organizing its powers in such form, as to them shall seem most likely to effect their safety and happiness.

THOMAS JEFFERSON: *The Declaration of Independence,* July 4, 1776

The community hath an indubitable, inalienable, and indefeasible right to reform, alter or abolish government, in such manner as shall be by that community judged most conducive to the public weal.

The Pennsylvania Declaration of Rights, 1776

It is an observation of one of the profoundest inquirers into human affairs that a revolution of government is the strongest proof that can be given by a people of their virtue and good sense. JOHN ADAMS: *Diary,* 1786

What country can preserve its liberties if their rulers are not warned from time to time that their people preserve the spirit of resistance? Let them take arms.

THOMAS JEFFERSON: *Letter to W. S. Smith,* Nov. 13, 1787

Sire, it is not a revolt; it is a revolution.

THE DUC DE ROCHEFOUCAULD-LIANCOURT: To Louis XVI, on the storming of the Bastille, July 14, 1789

To dare: that is the whole secret of revolutions.

ANTOINE SAINT-JUST: Speech to the French National Convention, 1793

In revolutions power always remains in the hands of nobodies.

GEORGES DANTON: On being sentenced to death, 1794

In revolutions everything is forgotten. The benefits you confer today are forgotten tomorrow. The side once changed, gratitude, friendship, parentage, every tie vanishes, and all that is sought for is self-interest.

NAPOLEON I: To Barry E. O'Meara at St. Helena, July 25, 1816

An oppressed people are authorized whenever they can to rise and break their fetters.

HENRY CLAY: Speech in the House of Representatives, March 4, 1818

Wherever a man comes, there comes revolution. The old is for slaves.

R. W. EMERSON: Address at the Divinity College, Cambridge, Mass., July 15, 1838

Any people anywhere, being inclined and having the power, have the right to rise up and shake off the existing government and form a new one that suits them better.

ABRAHAM LINCOLN: Speech in the House of Representatives, 1848

Let the ruling classes tremble at a Communist revolution. The proletarians have nothing to lose but their chains. They have a world to win. Working men of all countries, unite!

KARL MARX and FRIEDRICH ENGELS: *The Communist Manifesto,* 1848

All men recognize the right of revolution: that is, the right to refuse allegiance to, and to resist, the government when its tyranny or its inefficiency are great and unendurable.

H. D. THOREAU: *An Essay on Civil Disobedience,* 1849

Insurgents are like conquerors: they must go forward. The moment they are stopped they are lost.

Ascribed to the DUKE OF WELLINGTON, *c.* 1849

A revolution is a natural phenomenon governed by physical laws different from the rules which govern the development of society in normal times.

FRIEDRICH ENGELS: *Letter to Karl Marx,* Feb. 13, 1851

Revolutions begin with infatuation and end with incredulity. In their origin proud assurance is dominant; the ruling opinion disdains doubt, and will not endure contradiction. At their completion skepticism takes the place of disdain, and there is no longer any care for individual convictions, or any belief in truth.

F. P. G. GUIZOT: *Études biographiques sur la révolution d'Angleterre,* 1851

Revolutions are not made: they come. A revolution is as natural a growth as an oak. It comes out of the past. Its foundations are laid far back.

WENDELL PHILLIPS: Speech in Boston, Jan. 28, 1852

Revolutions never go backwards.

W. H. SEWARD: Speech in Rochester, N. Y., Oct. 25, 1858

This country, with its institutions, belongs to the people who inhabit it. Whenever they shall grow weary of the existing government they can exercise their constitutional right of amending it, or their revolutionary right to dismember or overthrow it.

ABRAHAM LINCOLN: Inaugural Address, March 4, 1861

Great revolutions, whatever may be their causes, are not lightly commenced, and are not concluded with precipitation.

BENJAMIN DISRAELI: Speech in the House of Commons, Feb. 5, 1863

In revolutions men fall and rise. Long before this war is over, much as you hear me praised now, you may hear me cursed and insulted.

W. T. SHERMAN: *Letter to his wife,* 1864

A reform is a correction of abuses; a revolution is a transfer of power.

E. G. BULWER-LYTTON: Speech in the House of Commons, 1866

Whenever the ends of government are perverted, and public liberty manifestly endangered, and all other means of redress are ineffectual, the people may, and of a right ought to reform the old, or establish a new government; the doctrine of non-resistance against arbitrary power and oppression is absurd, slavish and destructive of the good and happiness of mankind.

Declaration of Rights of Maryland, 1867

A hundred revolutionists, firmly bound together, would be enough for the international organization of all Europe.

M. A. BAKUNIN: *Statuts secrets de l'alliance,* c. 1870

There are but three ways for the populace to escape its wretched lot. The first two are by the routes of the wine-shop or the church; the third is by that of the social revolution.

M. A. BAKUNIN: *Dieu et l'état,* 1871

Revolutions are not made by men in spectacles.

O. W. HOLMES: *The Young Practitioner,* 1871 (Lecture in New York, March 2)

All mental revolutions are attended by catastrophe.

W. WINWOOD READE: *The Martyrdom of Man,* III, 1872

Revolutions are not made with rose-water.

E. G. BULWER-LYTTON: *The Parisians,* V, 1873

It is not the insurrections of ignorance that are dangerous, but the revolts of intelligence.

J. R. LOWELL: Speech at Birmingham, Eng., Oct. 6, 1884

The right of revolution is an inherent one. When people are oppressed by their government, it is a natural right they enjoy to relieve themselves of the oppression, if they are strong enough, either by withdrawal from it, or by overthrowing it and substituting a government more acceptable.

U. S. GRANT: *Personal Memoirs,* I, 1885

Inciting to revolution is treason, not only against man, but also against God.

POPE LEO XIII: *Immortalie Dei,* Nov. 1, 1885

Every revolution by force only puts more violent means of enslavement into the hands of the persons in power.

LYOF N. TOLSTOY: *The Kingdom of God is Within You,* 1893

How will it be with kingdoms and with kings —
With those who shaped him to the thing he is —
When this dumb terror shall rise to judge the world,
After the silence of the centuries?

EDWIN MARKHAM: *The Man With the Hoe,* 1899

Arise, ye prisoners of starvation,
Arise, ye wretched of the earth,
For justice thunders condemnation,
A better world's in birth.
No more tradition's chain shall bind us
Arise, ye slaves! no more in thrall!
The earth shall rise on new foundations,
We have been naught; we shall be all.

EUGENE POTTIER: *The Internationale,* c. 1900

Revolutions can no longer be achieved by minorities. No matter how energetic and intelligent a minority may be, it is not enough, in modern times at least, to make a revolution. The coöperation of a majority, and a large majority too, is needed.

JEAN JAURÈS: *Études socialistes,* VI, 1905

A violent revolution falls into the hands of narrow-minded fanatics and of tyrannical hypocrites at first. Afterward comes the turn of all the pretentious intellectual failures of the time. Such are the chiefs and the leaders. The scrupulous and the just, the noble, humane and devoted natures; the unselfish and the intelligent may begin a movement — but it passes away from them. They are not the leaders of a revolution. They are its victims.

JOSEPH CONRAD: *Under Western Eyes,* 1911

One of the chief symptoms of every revolution is the sharp and sudden increase in the number of ordinary people who take an active, independent, and forceful interest in politics.

NIKOLAI LENIN: *The Tasks of the Proletariat in Our Revolution,* 1917

It is impossible to predict the time and progress of revolution. It is governed by its own more or less mysterious laws. But when it comes it moves irresistibly.

NIKOLAI LENIN: Address in the Polytechnic Museum, Moscow, Aug. 23, 1918

A single revolutionary spark may kindle a fire that, smouldering for a time, may burst into a sweeping and destructive conflagration. It cannot be said that the state is acting arbitrarily or unreasonably when, in the exercise of its judgment as to the measures necessary to protect the public peace and safety, it seeks to extinguish the spark without waiting until it has kindled the flame or blazed into the conflagration.

MR. JUSTICE E. T. SANFORD: *Majority opinion of the Supreme Court of the United States in Gitlow* vs. *the People of New York*, 1924

The history of mankind is one long record of giving revolution another trial, and limping back at last to sanity, safety, and work.

E. W. HOWE: *Preaching From the Audience*, 1926

The Socialist revolution begins on national grounds, but it cannot be completed on these grounds. Its maintenance within a national framework can only be a provisional state of affairs, even though, as the experience of the Soviet Union shows, one of long duration.

LEON TROTSKY: *The Permanent Revolution*, intro., 1930

There have been more revolutions which succeeded at the first assault than revolutions which were intercepted and brought to a halt.

ADOLF HITLER: Speech before the governors of the former Federal States of Germany, Berlin, July 6, 1933

We must enter and take possession of the consciences of the children, of the consciences of the young, because they do belong and should belong to the revolution.

PLUTARCO CALLES: Speech at Guadalajara, July 19, 1934

The revolutionary way out of the crisis begins with the fight for unemployment insurance, against wage-cuts, for wage increases, for relief to the farmers — through demonstrations, strikes, general strikes, leading up to the seizure of power, to the destruction of capitalism by a revolutionary workers' government.

Manifesto of the American Communist party, April, 1934

Those who are inclined to compromise can never make a revolution.

KEMAL ATATÜRK (1881–1938)

A successful effort to get rid of a bad government and set up a worse.

Author unidentified

[*See also* Atheist, Imperialism, Insurrection, Politics, Rebellion, Secession, Taste, War.

Revolution, American

He that accepts protection, stipulates obedience. We have always protected the Americans; we may therefore subject them to government.

SAMUEL JOHNSON: Address to the Electors of Great Britain, 1774

If there was ever a just war since the world began, it is this in which America is now engaged.

THOMAS PAINE: *The Crisis*, 1776

If every nerve is not strained to recruit the new army with all possible expedience I think the game is pretty near up.

GEORGE WASHINGTON: *Letter to his brother*, Dec. 18, 1776

I desired as many as could to join together in fasting and prayer, that God would restore the spirit of love and of a sound mind to the poor deluded rebels in America.

JOHN WESLEY: *Journal*, Aug. 1, 1777

If I were an American, as I am an Englishman, while a foreign troop was landed in my country I never would lay down my arms, — never! never! never!

WILLIAM PITT: Speech in the House of Commons, Nov. 18, 1777

If ever there was a holy war, it was that which saved our liberties and gave us independence.

THOMAS JEFFERSON: *Letter to J. W. Eppes*, 1813

[The American Revolution] was a vindication of liberties inherited and possessed. It was a conservative revolution.

W. E. GLADSTONE: *Kin Beyond Sea*, 1878 (North American Review, Sept.–Oct.)

Revolution, French

The French revolution was a machine invented and constructed for the purpose of manufacturing liberty; but it had neither lever-cogs, nor adjusting powers, and the consequences were that it worked so rapidly that it destroyed its own inventors, and set itself on fire.

C. C. COLTON: *Lacon*, 1820

That which distinguishes the French Revolution from other political movements is that it was directed by men who had adopted certain speculative *à priori* conceptions of political right, with the fanaticism and proselytizing fervor of a religious belief, and the Bible of their creed was the "Contrat Social" of Rousseau.

W. E. H. LECKY: *History of England in the Eighteenth Century*, v, 1885

[*See also* Rich and Poor.

Reward

Still to our gains our chief respect is had;
Reward it is that makes us good or bad.

ROBERT HERRICK: *Hesperides*, 1648

Blessings ever wait on virtuous deeds,
And though a late, a sure reward succeeds.

WILLIAM CONGREVE: *The Mourning Bride*, v, 1697

Never to reward any one equal to his merit; but always to insinuate that the reward was above it.

HENRY FIELDING: *Jonathan Wild*, IV, 1743 (Maxim of Wild for the attainment of greatness)

[*See also* Labor.

Rhetoric

Rhetoric is the power of determining in a particular case what are the available means of persuasion.

ARISTOTLE: *Rhetoric*, I, *c.* 322 B.C.

I know them that think rhetoric to stand wholly upon dark words, and he that can catch an inkhorn term by the tail, him they count to be a fine Englishman and a good rhetorician.

THOMAS WILSON: *The Arte of Rhetorique*, 1553

For rhetoric, he could not ope
His mouth, but out there flew a trope.

SAMUEL BUTLER: *Hudibras*, I, 1663

Rhetoric is either very good, or stark naught; there is no medium in rhetoric. If I am not fully persuaded, I laugh at the orator.

JOHN SELDEN: *Table-Talk*, 1689

Rhetoric without logic is like a tree with leaves and blossoms, but no root; yet more are taken with rhetoric than logic, because they are caught with fine expressions when they understand not reason. IBID.

His speech was a fine sample, on the whole,
Of rhetoric, which the learn'd call rigmarole.

BYRON: *Don Juan*, I, 1819

That pestilent cosmetic, rhetoric.

T. H. HUXLEY: *Science and Morals*, 1886

[*See also* Poet.

Rheumatism

Some men ('gainst rain) do carry in their backs
Prognosticating aching almanacs;
Some by a painful elbow, hip or knee
Will shrewdly guess what weather's like to be.

JOHN TAYLOR: *Drink and Welcome*, 1637

[*See also* Ages, Gout, Law (Natural).

Rhine

Who first called thee Rhine meant to say, I think, wine.

FRIEDRICH VON LOGAU: *Erstes Hundert Teutscher Reimensprüche*, 1638

The river nobly foams and flows,
The charm of this enchanted ground,
And all its thousand turns disclose
Some fresher beauty varying round.

BYRON: *Childe Harold*, III, 1816

Fast stands and true the watch — the watch on the Rhine. (Fest steht und treu die Wacht — die Wacht am Rhein.)

MAX SCHNECKENBURGER: *Die Wacht am Rhein*, 1840 (The familiar musical setting was made by Karl Wilhelm, 1854)

The beautifulest river in the earth, I do believe — and my first idea of a world-river.

THOMAS CARLYLE: *Letter to R. W. Emerson*, May 13, 1853

When you think about the defense of England you no longer think of the chalk cliffs of Dover. You think of the Rhine. That is where our frontier lies today.

STANLEY BALDWIN: Speech in the House of Commons, July 30, 1934

Rhineland is wineland. (Rheinland ist Weinland.) GERMAN PROVERB

[*See also* Belgium, Cologne, River.

Rhyme

It is not rhyming and versing that maketh poesy. One may be a poet without versing, and a versifier without poetry.

PHILIP SIDNEY: *Apologie for Poesie*, 1598

Not marble, nor the gilded monuments
Of princes, shall outlive this powerful rhyme.

SHAKESPEARE: *Sonnets*, LV, 1609

Love will make a dog howl in rhyme.

JOHN FLETCHER and PHILIP MASSINGER: *The Queen of Corinth*, IV, *c.* 1616

Rhyme the rudder is of verses,
With which, like ships, they steer their courses.

SAMUEL BUTLER: *Hudibras*, I, 1663

The great easiness of blank verse renders the poet too luxuriant; he is tempted to say many things which might better be omitted, or at least shut up in fewer words. But when the difficulty of artful rhyming is interposed, where the poet commonly confines his sense to his couplet, and must contrive that sense into such words that the rhyme shall naturally follow them, not they the rhyme, the fancy then gives leisure to the judgment to come in, which, seeing so heavy a tax imposed, is ready to cut off all unnecessary expenses.

JOHN DRYDEN: *The Rival Ladies*, pref., 1664

Rhyme often makes mysterical nonsense pass with the critics for wit.

WILLIAM WYCHERLEY: *The Plain Dealer*, II, *c.* 1674

Verse without rhyme is a body without a soul.

JONATHAN SWIFT: *A Letter of Advice to a Young Poet*, Dec. 1, 1720

Grove,	Heart,	Kiss,
Night,	Prove,	Blest,
Rove,	Impart,	Bliss,
Delight.	Love.	Rest.

LEIGH HUNT: Outline for a love-song, 1822

It is for most part a very melancholy, not to say an unsupportable business, that of reading rhyme. Rhyme that had no inward necessity to be rhymed: — it ought to have told us

plainly, without any jingle, what it was aiming at.
THOMAS CARLYLE: *Heroes and Hero-Worship,* III, 1840 (Lecture in London, May 12)

Whenever the May-blood stirs and glows,
And the young year draws to the "golden prime,"
And Sir Romeo sticks in his ear a rose, —
Then hey! for the ripple of laughing rhyme!
AUSTIN DOBSON: *The Ballad of Prose and Rhyme,* 1873

Notice the beautiful rhythm; how nicely these words chime and gink together.
JAMES A. REED of Missouri: Speech in the Senate, July 16, 1917

[*See also* Poetry, Reason, Verse.

Riband

[*See* Traitor.

Rice

Rice is the best food for the soldier.
NAPOLEON I: To Gaspard Gourgaud at St. Helena, 1815–1818

Rich

The rich have many consolations.
PLATO: *The Republic,* I, *c.* 370 B.C.

No just man ever became rich suddenly.
MENANDER: *Adsentator, c.* 300 B.C.

They that will be rich fall into temptation and a snare, and into many foolish and hurtful lusts, which drown men in destruction and perdition.
I TIMOTHY VI, 9, *c.* 60

Go to now, ye rich men, weep and howl for your miseries that shall come upon you.
JAMES V, 1, *c.* 60

It is easier for a camel to go through the eye of a needle, than for a rich man to enter into the kingdom of God.
MARK X, 25, *c.* 70 (Cf. MATTHEW XIX, 24, *c.* 75; LUKE XVIII, 25, *c.* 75)

Thou sayest, I am rich, and increased with goods, and have need of nothing; and knowest not that thou art wretched, and miserable, and poor, and blind, and naked.
REVELATION III, 17, *c.* 95

It is difficult for a rich person to be modest, or a modest person rich.
EPICTETUS: *Encheiridion, c.* 110

He who wishes to become rich wishes to become so speedily.
JUVENAL: *Satires,* XIV, 128

The rich man is not one who is in possession of much, but one who gives much.
ST. JOHN CHRYSOSTOM: *Homilies,* II, *c.* 388

We ask not what he is but what he has.
ENGLISH PROVERB, traced to the XVI century

He is wise that is rich.
NICHOLAS BRETON: *Crossing of Proverbs,* 1616

The rich knows not who is his friend.
GEORGE HERBERT: *Outlandish Proverbs,* 1640

It is a vain enterprise to try to turn a rich and silly man to ridicule: the laughers are all on his side.
JEAN DE LA BRUYÈRE: *Caractères,* VI, 1688

'Tis a sort of duty to be rich, that it may be in one's power to do good.
MARY WORTLEY MONTAGU: *Letter to Wortley Montagu,* Sept. 24, 1714

Perhaps you will say a man is not young; I answer, he is rich; he is not gentle, handsome, witty, brave, good-humored, but he is rich, rich, rich, rich, rich, — that one word contradicts everything you can say against him.
HENRY FIELDING: *The Miser,* III, 1733

Rich men without wisdom and learning are called
Sheep with golden fleeces.
NATHANIEL AMES: *Almanac,* 1734

I am rich beyond the dreams of avarice.
EDWARD MOORE: *The Gamester,* II, 1753

Their vices are probably more favorable to the prosperity of the state than those of the indigent, and partake less of moral depravity.
ALEXANDER HAMILTON: Speech on the Compromises of the Constitution, June 21, 1788

I am indeed rich, since my income is superior to my expense, and my expense is equal to my wishes.
EDWARD GIBBON: *Memoirs,* 1795

A man is rich in proportion to the number of things which he can afford to let alone.
H. D. THOREAU: *Walden,* 1854

To be thought rich is as good as to be rich.
W. M. THACKERAY: *The Virginians,* II, 1859

The rich should tremble at the threatenings of Jesus Christ.
POPE LEO XIII: *Rerum novarum,* May 15, 1891

Them as has, gits. AMERICAN PROVERB

Deceive the rich and powerful if you will, but don't insult them. JAPANESE PROVERB

The rich do all things magnificently. (A divitibus omnia magnifice fiunt.)
LATIN PROVERB

Whoever is rich is my brother.
RUSSIAN PROVERB

Get what you can, and keep what you hae: that's the way to get rich.
SCOTTISH PROVERB

A rich man is either a scoundrel or the heir of one. SPANISH PROVERB

The foolish sayings of a rich man pass for wise ones. IBID.

[*See also* Classes, Contentment, Enough, Envy, Gentleman, Giving, Grave, Husband, Money, Property, Rich and Poor, Riches, Wealth.

Rich and Poor

Vice is concealed by wealth, and virtue by poverty. THEOGNIS: *Elegies, c.* 550 B.C.

The rich have a cloak for their ills, but poverty is transparent and abject.
ANTIPHANES: *Fragment, c.* 350 B.C.

The rich man's wealth is his strong city: the destruction of the poor is their poverty.
PROVERBS X, 15, *c.* 350 B.C.

The poor is hated even of his own neighbor, but the rich hath many friends.
PROVERBS XIV, 20

It is the nature of the poor to hate and envy men of property.
PLAUTUS: *Captivi,* III, *c.* 200 B.C.

A rich man beginning to fall is held up by his friends: but a poor man being down is thrust also away by his friends.
ECCLESIASTICUS XIII, 21, *c.* 180 B.C.

Riches bring oft harm, and ever fear, where poverty passeth without grudge or grief.
JOHN HEYWOOD: *Proverbs,* 1546

Plate sin with gold,
And the strong lance of justice hurtling breaks;
Arm it in rags, a pigmy's straw doth pierce it.
SHAKESPEARE: *King Lear,* IV, 1606

Rich men are stewards for the poor.
NICHOLAS BRETON: *Crossing of Proverbs,* 1616

The pride of the rich makes the labor of the poor. IBID.

A poor man's cow dies, a rich man's child.
GEORGE HERBERT: *Outlandish Proverbs,* 1640

Poor and liberal, rich and covetous. IBID.

God help the rich; the poor can beg.
JAMES HOWELL: *Proverbs,* 1659

There is nothing between a poor man and a rich man but a piece of an ill year.
JAMES KELLY: *Complete Collection of Scottish Proverbs,* 1721

The pleasures of the rich are bought with the tears of the poor.
THOMAS FULLER: *Gnomologia,* 1732

The poor man must walk to get meat for his stomach, the rich man to get a stomach to his meat.
BENJAMIN FRANKLIN: *Poor Richard's Almanac,* 1735

The leaders of the French Revolution, from the beginning, excited the poor against the rich: this has made the rich poor, but it will never make the poor rich.
FISHER AMES: Oration in Boston, 1800 (Feb. 8)

If rich, it is easy enough to conceal our wealth; but if poor, it is not quite so easy to conceal our poverty. It is less difficult to hide a thousand guineas than one hole in our coat.
C. C. COLTON: *Lacon,* 1820

The greatest and the most amiable privilege which the rich enjoy over the poor is that which they exercise the least—the privilege of making them happy. IBID.

I see the rich man's garden shine,
The golden harvests glow;
Alas, the barren road is mine,
Where toil and sorrow go.
LUDWIG UHLAND: *Poor Man's Song, c.* 1820

As far as the palaces of the rich stretch through Mayfair and Belgravia and South Kensington, so far (and farther) must the hovels of the poor inevitably stretch in the opposite direction.
EDWARD CARPENTER: *England's Ideal,* 1887

We all get about the same amount of ice. The rich get it in Summer and the poor in Winter.
Ascribed to BAT MASTERSON, *c.* 1900

It's the same the whole world over:
It's the poor that gets the blame;
It's the rich that has the pleasure—
Ain't it all a bloody shame!
Anon.: *She Was Poor But She Was Honest* (Sung by British soldiers, 1914–18)

One poor man and one rich man are equal to one rich man. Author unidentified

It is harder to be poor without complaining than to be rich without boasting.
CHINESE PROVERB

A poor man is a healthy man; a healthy man is a rich man. GERMAN PROVERB

The poor must dance as the rich pipe. IBID.

None is poorer than the dog and none richer than the pig. HEBREW PROVERB

The poor man is despised even by his own wife and children; the rich man is praised even by folk in other countries. JAPANESE PROVERB

As long as I am rich reputed
With solemn voice I am saluted,
But wealth away once worn,
Not one will say good morn.
OLD ENGLISH RHYME

[*See also* Boasting, Charity, Health, Imperialism, Justice, Law, Poor, Poverty, Pride, Rich Stomach, Virtue, Youth.

Richard I of England (1157–99)

Cœur-de-Lion was not a theatrical popinjay with greaves and steel-cap on it, but a man living upon victuals.
THOMAS CARLYLE: *Past and Present,* 1843

Richardson, Samuel (1689–1761)

If you were to read Richardson for the story, your impatience would be so much fretted that you would hang yourself. You must read him for the sentiment.
SAMUEL JOHNSON: *Boswell's Life,* April 6, 1772

[*See also* Fielding (Henry).

Richelieu, Arman Cardinal (1585–1642)

The first man in Europe, but only the second in his own country.
Author unidentified (Richelieu was prime minister to Louis XIII of France, 1624–42)

Riches

The advantage of riches is that they enable a man to indulge his passions, and help him to bear up against whatever harm befalls him.
HERODOTUS: *Histories,* I, *c.* 430 B.C.

The quest for riches darkens the sense of right and wrong.
ANTIPHANES: *Fragment, c.* 350 B.C.

Riches certainly make themselves wings; they fly away as an eagle toward heaven.
PROVERBS XXIII, 5, *c.* 350 B.C.

He heapeth up riches, and knoweth not who shall gather them.
PSALMS XXXIX, 6, *c.* 150 B.C.

Virtue, glory, honor, all things human and divine, are slaves to riches.
HORACE: *Satires,* II, *c.* 25 B.C.

The shortest road to riches is by way of contempt for riches.
SENECA: *Epistulæ morales ad Lucilium, c.* 63

How hardly shall they that have riches enter into the kingdom of God. MARK X, 23. *c.* 70

Riches are not forbidden, but the pride of them is.
ST. JOHN CHRYSOSTOM: *Homilies,* II, *c.* 388

A little house well filled, a little land well tilled, and a little wife well willed, are great riches.
Author unidentified; traced to the XVI century

If thou art rich, thou art poor;
For, like an ass whose back with ingots bows,
Thou bear'st thy heavy riches but a journey,
And death unloads thee.
SHAKESPEARE: *Measure for Measure,* III, 1604

How rich a man is, all desire to know;
But none inquires if good he be, or no.
ROBERT HERRICK: *Hesperides,* 1648

Riches are like muck which stinks in a heap, but spread abroad makes the earth fruitful.
JOHN RAY: *English Proverbs,* 1670

It takes a kind of genius to make a fortune, and especially a large fortune. It is neither goodness, nor wit, nor talent, nor strength, nor delicacy. I don't know precisely what it is: I am waiting for some one to tell me.
JEAN DE LA BRUYÈRE: *Caractères,* VI, 1688

Nothing lasts longer than a moderate fortune, and nothing comes to an end sooner than a large one. IBID.

It is not a sin to have riches, but it is a sin to fix our hearts upon them.
ST. JOHN BAPTIST DE LA SALLE: *Les devoirs du chrétien,* XIV, 1703

Riches are gotten with pain, kept with care, and lost with grief.
THOMAS FULLER: *Gnomologia,* 1732

Riches have made more covetous men than covetousness hath made men rich. IBID.

To whom can riches give repute or trust,
Content or pleasure, but the good and just?
ALEXANDER POPE: *An Essay on Man,* IV, 1734

Sudden fortunes of every kind are the least substantial, because it is seldom that they are the fruit of merit. The mature, but laborious, fruits of prudence are always slowly produced.
LUC DE VAUVENARGUES: *Réflexions,* 1746

Riches ennoble a man's circumstances, but not himself.
IMMANUEL KANT: Lecture at Königsberg, 1775

I have not observed men's honesty to increase with their riches.
THOMAS JEFFERSON: *Letter to Jeremiah Moor,* 1800

Many speak the truth when they say that they despise riches, but they mean the riches possessed by other men.
C. C. COLTON: *Lacon,* 1820

Riches are chiefly good because they give us time.
CHARLES LAMB: *Letter to Bernard Barton.* Oct. 9, 1822

The possessions of new families are commonly exaggerated in the public mind, while those of long established families are as commonly diminished.
J. FENIMORE COOPER: *The American Democrat,* XXVIII, 1838

A man is rich in proportion to the number of things which he can afford to let alone.
H. D. THOREAU: *Walden,* 1854

Virtue is of noble birth, but riches take the wall of her.
H. G. BOHN: *Handbook of Proverbs,* 1855

Riches do not bring freedom from sorrow and are of no avail for eternal happiness, but rather are obstacles.
POPE LEO XIII: *Rerum novarum,* May 15, 1891

In an ugly and unhappy world the richest man can purchase nothing but ugliness and unhappiness.
GEORGE BERNARD SHAW: *Maxims for Revolutionists,* 1903

Riches are often abused, never refused.
DANISH PROVERB

A fu' purse never lacks friends.
SCOTTISH PROVERB

[*See also* Avarice, Boasting, Brewery, Children, Classes, Devil, Fortune, Gentility, God, Inheritance, Money, Nobility, Rich, Upright, Wealth.

Rider

[*See* Cause and Effect, Fall, Horse, Riding.

Ridicule

Man learns more readily and remembers more willingly what excites his ridicule than what deserves his esteem and respect.
HORACE: *Epistles,* II, *c.* 5 B.C.

Ridicule dishonors more than dishonor.
LA ROCHEFOUCAULD: *Maxims,* 1665

He corrects morals by ridicule. (Castigat ridendo mores.)
Motto of the Italian harlequin, JOSEPH BIANCOLELLI (1640–88)

Truth, 'tis supposed, may bear all lights; and one of those principal lights or natural mediums by which things are to be viewed in order to a thorough recognition is ridicule.
ANTHONY A. COOPER (EARL OF SHAFTESBURY): *Essay on the Freedom of Wit and Humor,* I, 1709

The talent of turning men into ridicule, and exposing to laughter those one converses with, is the qualification of little ungenerous tempers.
JOSEPH ADDISON: *The Spectator,* Dec. 15, 1711

All fools have still an itching to deride,
And fain would be upon the laughing side.
ALEXANDER POPE: *An Essay on Criticism,* I, 1711

How comes it to pass that we appear such cowards in reasoning, and are so afraid to stand the test of ridicule?
ANTHONY A. COOPER (EARL OF SHAFTESBURY): *Characteristics of Men, Manners, Opinions, Times,* I, *c.* 1713

Yes, I am proud; I must be proud to see
Men, not afraid of God, afraid of me;
Safe from the bar, the pulpit, and the throne,
Yet touch'd and shamed by ridicule alone.
ALEXANDER POPE: *Epilogue to the Satires,* II, 1738

Ridicule is more deadly than all the arguments in the world. Few men can reason, but all fear ridicule.
FREDERICK THE GREAT: *Letter to Voltaire,* Oct. 31, 1760

Resort is had to ridicule only when reason is against us.
THOMAS JEFFERSON: *Letter to James Madison,* 1813

We grow tired of everything but turning others into ridicule, and congratulating ourselves on their defects.
WILLIAM HAZLITT: *The Plain Speaker,* I, 1826

The natural and proper object of ridicule is those smaller improprieties in character and manners which do not rouse our feelings of moral indignation, or impress us with a melancholy sense of human depravity.
DUGALD STEWART: *Philosophy of the Active and Moral Powers of Man,* I, 1828

No kind of power is more formidable than the power of making men ridiculous.
T. B. MACAULAY: *The Life and Writings of Addison,* 1843 (Edinburgh Review, July)

I have endured a great deal of ridicule without much malice, and have received a great deal of kindness not quite free from ridicule.
ABRAHAM LINCOLN: *Letter to J. H. Hackett,* Nov. 2, 1863

Because I make use of ridicule it does not follow that I am writing merely for amusement.
W. WINWOOD READE: *The Martyrdom of Man,* III, 1872

Ridiculous

A man is a fool who holds anything to be ridiculous save that which is bad.
PLATO: *The Republic,* V, *c.* 370 B.C.

The ridiculous is produced by any defect that does not involve pain or death; an ugly face causes laughter if it is not caused by pain.
ARISTOTLE: *Poetics,* V, *c.* 322 B.C.

The descent from the terrible to the ridiculous is little by little.
LONGINUS: *On the Sublime,* III, *c.* 250

There is an infinity of modes of conduct which appear ridiculous, the secret reasons of which are wise and sound.
LA ROCHEFOUCAULD: *Maxims,* 1665

The magnificent and the ridiculous are so close that they touch.
BERTRAND DE FONTENELLE: *Dialogues des morts,* I, 1683

One step above the sublime makes the ridiculous, and one step above the ridiculous makes the sublime again.
THOMAS PAINE: *The Age of Reason*, II, 1794

[*See also* Sublime.

Riding

Riding a horse makes gentlemen of some and grooms of others.
CERVANTES: *Don Quixote*, II, 1615

If you ride a horse, sit close and tight;
If you ride a man, sit easy and light.
BENJAMIN FRANKLIN: *Poor Richard's Almanac*, 1734

There's nothing so good for the inside of a man as the outside of a horse.
Ascribed to LORD PALMERSTON (1784–1865)

[*See also* Education.

Rift

[*See* Lute.

Right

I will follow the right even to the fire — but avoiding the fire if possible.
MICHEL DE MONTAIGNE: *Essays*, II, 1580

Whatever is, is right.
ALEXANDER POPE: *An Essay on Man*, I, 1732

For modes of faith let graceless zealots fight;
His can't be wrong whose life is in the right.
ALEXANDER POPE: *An Essay on Man*, III, 1733

The ultimate notion of right is that which tends to the universal good; and when one's acting in a certain manner has this tendency he has a right thus to act.
FRANCIS HUTCHESON: *A System of Moral Philosophy*, II, 1755

Nature in an absolute manner wills that right should at length obtain the victory.
IMMANUEL KANT: *Perpetual Peace*, Supplement I, 1795

Be sure you are right; then go ahead.
DAVID CROCKETT: His motto in the War of 1812

Whether I shall persuade others that I have acted right I know not. It is enough for me as an Englishman to be myself satisfied that I have done so.
MR. JUSTICE BEST: *Judgment in the case of Sir F. Burdett*, 1820

If mankind had wished for what is right, they might have had it long ago.
WILLIAM HAZLITT: *The Plain Speaker*, I, 1826

No man in the world acts up to his own standard of right.
T. B. MACAULAY: *Hallam*, 1828 (Edinburgh Review, Sept.)

If it be right to me, it is right.
MAX STIRNER: *The Ego and His Own*, 1845

Right is a delusion, created by a ghost. IBID.

Sir, I would rather be right than be President.
HENRY CLAY: Speech in the Senate, 1850

One man in the right will finally get to be a majority.
R. G. INGERSOLL: Speech in New York, Oct. 23, 1880

Right is only right by a very small majority that has got to be kept up every day.
THOMAS B. REED: Speech in Philadelphia, Feb. 15, 1884

Those who want to do right have little difficulty in finding out the right.
CALVIN COOLIDGE: Speech in Washington, 1926

Right's right, and fair's fair.
ENGLISH SAYING

By what right? (Quo jure?) LATIN PHRASE

[*See also* Force, Law, Mercy, Might, Power, Remedy, Right and Might.

Right and Might

May right, and might, and Zeus all help me.
ÆSCHYLUS: *Choephori*, *c.* 490 B.C.

Might is right, and justice is the interest of the stronger.
PLATO: *The Republic*, I, *c.* 370 B.C.

The more might, the more right.
PLAUTUS: *Truculentus*, *c.* 190 B.C.

Might makes right.
ENGLISH PROVERB, traced by Apperson to *c.* 1311

It is right and might that govern everything in this world — might waiting on right.
JOSEPH JOUBERT: *Pensées*, 1842

Whatever you have the might to be you have the right to be.
MAX STIRNER: *The Ego and His Own*, 1845

Let us have faith that right makes might, and in that faith let us to the end dare to do our duty as we understand it.
ABRAHAM LINCOLN: Speech in New York, Feb. 21, 1859

Right is more than right, and justice more than mail.
J. G. WHITTIER: *Brown of Ossawatomie*, 1859

Any man, be his name Bill Sykes or Alexander Romanoff, and any set of men, whether the Chinese highbinders or the Congress of the

United States, have the right, if they have the power, to kill or coerce other men and to make the entire world subservient to their ends.
BENJAMIN R. TUCKER: *Instead of a Book*, 1893

Might overcomes right. (Force passe droit.)
FRENCH PROVERB

A handful of might is better than a sackful of right.
GERMAN PROVERB

Right goes before might. (Recht geht vor Macht.)
IBID.

[*See also* Faith, Force, Politics.

Right and Wrong

It is possible to go wrong in many ways, but right in only one. The former is thus easy and the latter difficult.
ARISTOTLE: *The Nicomachean Ethics*, II, *c.* 340 B.C.

Extremity of right is wrong.
JOHN CLARKE: *Parœmiologia Anglo-Latina*, 1639

He that hath right, fears; he that hath wrong, hopes.
GEORGE HERBERT: *Outlandish Proverbs*, 1640

Little between right and wrong.
JOHN RAY: *English Proverbs*, 1670

When all the world is wrong, all the world is right.
P. C. NIVELLE DE LA CHAUSSÉE: *La gouvernante*, I, *c.* 1725

Our ideas of right and wrong are simple ideas, and must therefore be ascribed to some power of immediate perception in the human mind. He that doubts this need only try to give definitions of them which shall amount to more than synonymous expressions.
RICHARD PRICE: *The Principal Questions in Morals*, I, 1758

Right and wrong are the same for all in the same circumstances.
THOMAS REID: *Essay on the Active Powers*, V, 1788

Two wrongs can never make a right.
ENGLISH PROVERB, not recorded before the XIX century

Everything we do has a result. But that which is right and prudent does not always lead to good, nor the contrary to what is bad; frequently the reverse takes place.
J. W. GOETHE: *Conversations with Eckermann*, June 11, 1825

We are not satisfied to be right unless we can prove others to be quite wrong.
WILLIAM HAZLITT: *Conversations of James Northcote*, 1830

The only right is what is after my constitution, the only wrong what is against it.
R. W. EMERSON: *Self-Reliance*, 1841

I trust in God, — the right shall be the right
And other than the wrong, while He endures.
ROBERT BROWNING: *A Soul's Tragedy*, I, 1846

Wrong never comes right.
R. C. TRENCH (ARCHBISHOP OF DUBLIN): *Lessons in Proverbs*, 1853

Actions are right in proportion as they tend to promote happiness; wrong as they tend to produce the reverse of happiness. By happiness is intended pleasure, and the absence of pain; by unhappiness, pain, and the privation of pleasure.
J. S. MILL: *Utilitarianism*, II, 1863

As happiness is an essential part of the general good, the greatest happiness principle indirectly serves as a nearly safe standard of right and wrong.
CHARLES DARWIN: *The Descent of Man*, XXI, 1871

It is absurd to speak of right and wrong *per se.* Injury, violation, exploitation, annihilation cannot be wrong in themselves, for life in its essence presupposes injury, violation, exploitation and annihilation.
F. W. NIETZSCHE: *The Genealogy of Morals*, II, 1887

There is always a right and a wrong way, and the wrong way always seems the more reasonable.
GEORGE MOORE: *The Bending of the Bough*, IV, 1900

Right is the opposite of wrong; and wrong consists in inflicting injuries on other people.
ROBERT BRIFFAULT: *Sin and Sex*, XIII, 1931

To determine what is to be done, what not to be done; in other words, to determine right and wrong, is an insistent problem for all organisms; it is not something that begins with man. With all organisms life is a continuous process of selecting one line of action and rejecting another; the determining whether certain actions are right or wrong.
H. S. JENNINGS: *The Universe and Life*, 1933

It is easy to know and do right. When in doubt, simply do whatever you least want to do.
Author unidentified

A hundred years of wrong do not make a single year of right.
GERMAN PROVERB

Right wrongs no man.
SCOTTISH PROVERB

[*See also* Bible, Child, Ethics, Good and Evil, Law, Lawyer, Majority, Morality, Virtue.

Right, Divine

[*See* Divine Right.

Righteousness

He put on righteousness as a breastplate.
ISAIAH XLIX, 17, *c.* 700 B.C.

The righteous perisheth and no man layeth it to heart.
ISAIAH LVII, 1

All our righteousnesses are as filthy rags.
ISAIAH LXIV, 6

Righteousness exalteth a nation.
PROVERBS XIV, 34, *c.* 350 B.C.

Be not righteous overmuch.
ECCLESIASTES VII, 16, *c.* 200 B.C.

I have been young, and now am old; yet have I not seen the righteous forsaken, nor his seed begging bread.
PSALMS XXXVII, 25, *c.* 150 B.C.

Verily there is a reward for the righteous.
PSALMS LVIII, 11

The righteous shall flourish like the palm-tree: he shall grow like a cedar in Lebanon.
PSALMS XCII, 12

Unclean in the sight of God is everyone who is unrighteous; clean therefore is everyone who is righteous; if not in the sight of men, yet in the sight of God, who judges without error.
ST. AUGUSTINE: *On Lying, c.* 395

[*See also* Golden Rule, Virtue.

Rights

A right is a moral quality annexed to the person, justly entitling him to possess some particular privilege, or to perform some particular act.
HUGO GROTIUS: *De jure belli ac pacis,* I, 1625

The right of nature, which writers commonly call *jus naturale,* is the liberty each man hath to use his own power as he will himself for the preservation of his own nature; that is to say, of his own life; and consequently, of doing anything which, in his own judgment and reason, he shall conceive to be the aptest means thereunto.
THOMAS HOBBES: *Leviathan,* XIV, 1651

If the plaintiff has a right, he must of necessity have a means to vindicate and maintain it; and, indeed, it is a vain thing to imagine a right without a remedy; for want of right and want of remedy are reciprocal. It is no objection to say that it will occasion multiplicity of actions; for if men will multiply injuries, actions must be multiplied too; for every man that is injured ought to have his recompense.
JOHN HOLT (LORD HOLT): *Judgment in Ashby* vs. *Aylesbury,* 1702

The public good is in nothing more essentially interested than in the protection of every individual's private rights.
WILLIAM BLACKSTONE: *Commentaries on the Laws of England,* I, 1765

Among the natural rights of the colonists are these: first, a right to life; secondly, to liberty; thirdly, to property; together with the right to defend them in the best manner they can.
SAMUEL ADAMS: *The Rights of the Colonists,* 1772

Everyone is bound to assert his rights and resist their invasion by others.
IMMANUEL KANT: Lecture at Königsberg, 1775

Political right and public happiness are different words for the same idea. They who wander into metaphysical labyrinths, or have recourse to original contracts, to determine the rights of men, either impose on themselves or mean to delude others.
SAMUEL ADAMS: Speech on American Independence, July 4, 1776

We hold these truths to be self-evident — that all men are created equal; that they are endowed by their Creator with certain inalienable rights; that among these are life, liberty and the pursuit of happiness.
THOMAS JEFFERSON: *The Declaration of Independence,* July 4, 1776

Men who their duties know,
But know their rights, and, knowing, dare maintain.
WILLIAM JONES: *An Ode in Imitation of Alcæus,* 1781

In a free government the security for civil rights must be the same as that for religious rights. It consists in the one case in the multiplicity of interests, and in the other in the multiplicity of sects.
ALEXANDER HAMILTON: *The Federalist,* 1788

The end of all political associations is the preservation of the natural and imprescriptible rights of man; and these rights are liberty, property, security, and resistance of oppression.
Declaration of the Rights of Man by the French National Assembly, II, 1789

If we cannot secure all our rights, let us secure what we can.
THOMAS JEFFERSON: *Letter to James Madison,* March, 1789

The moment you abate anything from the full rights of men to each govern himself, and suffer any artificial positive limitation upon those rights, from that moment the whole organization of government becomes a consideration of convenience.
EDMUND BURKE: *Reflections on the Revolution in France,* 1790

The enumeration in the Constitution of certain rights shall not be construed to deny or disparage others retained by the people.
CONSTITUTION OF THE UNITED STATES, Amendment IX, Dec. 15, 1791

I think that men are entitled to equal rights, but to equal rights to unequal things.
Ascribed to CHARLES JAMES FOX (1749–1806)

No man has a natural right to commit aggression on the equal rights of another; and this is all from which the laws ought to restrain him.
THOMAS JEFFERSON: *Letter to F. W. Gilmer*, 1816

The great right of all, without which there is, in fact, no right, is the right of taking a part in the making of the laws by which we are governed.
WILLIAM COBBETT: *Advice to Young Men*, VI, 1829

The right of the laborer to wages, the right of every innocent man to his own person, the right of all to equity before the laws, — these are no longer abstractions of speculative visionaries, no longer innovations, but the established rights of humanity.
W. E. CHANNING: *Letter to Jonathan Phillips*, 1839

The word *right* should be excluded from political language, as the word *cause* from the language of philosophy. Both are theological and metaphysical conceptions; and the former is as immoral and subversive as the latter is unmeaning and sophistical.
AUGUSTE COMTE: *Catéchisme positiviste*, 1852

The provisions of the Constitution of the United States and of this state apply as well in time of war as in time of peace, and any departure therefrom or violation thereof, under the plea of necessity or any other plea, is subversive of good government, and tends to anarchy and despotism.
Declaration of Rights of Maryland, XLIV, 1867

The right to unite freely and to separate freely is the first and most important of all political rights.
M. A. BAKUNIN: *Proposition motivée*, 1868

The equal right of all men to the use of land is as clear as their equal right to breathe the air — it is a right proclaimed by the fact of their existence. For we cannot suppose that some men have a right to be in this world, and others no right.
HENRY GEORGE: *Progress and Poverty*, VII, 1879

Freedom of the press, freedom of association, the inviolability of the domicile, and all the rest of the rights of man are respected only so long as no one tries to use them against the privileged classes. On the day they are launched against privilege they are thrown overboard.
P. A. KROPOTKIN: *Paroles d'un révolté*, 1884

A right is a privilege.
F. W. NIETZSCHE: *The Antichrist*, LVII, 1888

Every human being has a right to the full development of his physical and moral potentialities. Therefore he has the right to demand of mankind whatever he needs to supplement his own effort.
JEAN JAURÈS: *Études socialistes*, II, 1902

Anyone who possesses a natural right may make use of all legitimate means to protect it, and to safeguard it from violation.
WILLIAM CARDINAL O'CONNELL: *Pastoral Letter on the Laborer's Rights*, Nov. 23, 1912

The constitution of Soviet Russia must ensure equal rights for all citizens regardless of sex, creed, race, or nationality.
NIKOLAI LENIN: *Materials Relating to the Revision of the Party Programme*, 1917

We must not be so insistent upon demanding our rights as in discharging our obligations.
POPE BENEDICT XV: *Letter to the Bishop of Bergamo*, March 11, 1920

Men speak of natural rights, but I challenge any one to show where in nature any rights existed or were recognized until there was established for their declaration and protection a duly promulgated body of corresponding laws.
CALVIN COOLIDGE: Speech of acceptance, July 27, 1920

A double right (jus duplicatum); a feudal lord's right to deflower a vassal's bride (jus primæ noctis); a right not enforceable (jus precarium); a legal right (jus legitimum); a wife's right to her dower (jus relictæ); common rights (jura communia); marital right (jus conjugialia); the common right (jus publicum); the right of a husband to his wife's property (jus mariti); the right of nature (jus naturale); the right of possession (jus possessionis); the right to abuse, i.e., complete ownership (jus abutendi); the right to a thing (jus ad rem); the right to citizenship (jus civitatis); the right to dispose of property (jus disponendi); the right to hold public office (jus honorum); the right to keep (jus retentionis); the right to property (jus proprietatis); the right to put to death (jus gladii).
LATIN PHRASES

A right sometimes sleeps, but it never dies. (Dormit aliquando jus, moritur nunquam.)
LEGAL MAXIM

He who exercises his own right injures no one. (Qui jure suo utitur neminem lædit.)
IBID.

Rights are lost by disuse. (Ex desuetudine amittuntur privilegia.)
IBID.

[*See also* Alien, Capital and Labor, Equality, Family, Freedom, Inequality, Land, Law,

Minority, Negro, Press (Free), Property, Taxes, War.

Rights, Bill of

A Bill of Rights is what the people are entitled to against every government on earth, general or particular; and what no just government should refuse, or rest on inferences.
THOMAS JEFFERSON: *Letter to James Madison,* Dec., 1787

[*See also* Magna Charta.

Rights, Women's

In the new code of laws which I suppose it will be necessary for you to make I desire you would remember the ladies and be more generous and favorable to them than your ancestors.
ABIGAIL ADAMS: *Letter to John Adams,* March 31, 1776

The best right a woman has is the right to a husband.
ANTHONY TROLLOPE: *North America,* I, 1862

Riot

Our Sovereign Lord the King chargeth and commandeth all persons being assembled immediately to disperse themselves, and peaceably to depart to their habitations or to their lawful business, upon the pains contained in the act made in the first year of King George for preventing tumultuous and riotous assemblies. God save the King.
English Riot Act, 1714

A popular entertainment given to the military by innocent bystanders.
AMBROSE BIERCE: *The Devil's Dictionary,* 1906

[*See also* Fat.

Ripe

Soon ripe, soon rotten.
ENGLISH PROVERB, first recorded by WILLIAM LANGLAND: *Piers Plowman,* 1377

Rising

If thou art sluggish on arising, let this thought occur: I am rising to a man's work.
MARCUS AURELIUS: *Meditations,* IV, *c.* 170

Rising, Early

Getting up before daybreak makes for health, wealth and wisdom.
ARISTOTLE: *Economics,* I, *c.* 320 B.C.

Up rose the sun, and up rose Emily.
GEOFFREY CHAUCER: *The Canterbury Tales* (*The Knight's Tale*), *c.* 1386

Early rising maketh a man whole in body, wholer in soul, and richer in goods.
JOHN FITZHERBERT: *Book of Husbandry,* 1523

Rise with the lark, and go to bed with the lamb.
ENGLISH PROVERB, traced by Apperson to *c.* 1555

We go to bed with the lamb and rise with the lark, which makes us healthful as the Spring.
Anon.: *A Deep Snow,* 1615

Early to bed and early to rise
Makes a man healthy, wealthy and wise.
JOHN CLARKE: *Parœmiologia Anglo-Latina,* 1639

He that will thrive must rise at five;
He that hath thriven may lie till seven.
IBID.

Who hath once the fame to be an early riser may sleep till noon.
JAMES HOWELL: *Proverbs,* 1659

Defiers of sleep seem not to remember that though it must be granted them that they are crawling about before the break of day, it can seldom be said that they are perfectly awake.
SAMUEL JOHNSON: *The Adventurer,* March 20, 1753

Cheerful at morn, he wakes from short repose,
Breathes the keen air, and carols as he goes.
OLIVER GOLDSMITH: *The Traveler,* 1764

I have, all my life long, been lying till noon; yet I tell all young men, and tell them with great sincerity, that nobody who does not rise early will ever do any good.
SAMUEL JOHNSON: *Boswell's Tour to the Hebrides,* Sept. 15, 1773

The worm was punished for early rising.
J. G. SAXE: *Early Rising,* 1860

The next mornin I 'rose with the lark. (N.B.— I don't sleep with the lark, tho'. A goak.)
C. F. BROWNE (ARTEMUS WARD): *Artemus Ward: His Book,* 1862

God helps those who rise early.
BULGARIAN PROVERB

Daybreak comes no sooner for your early rising.
SPANISH PROVERB

[*See also* Luck.

Rising, Late

Midday slumbers are golden: they make the body fat, the skin fair, the flesh plump, delicate and tender; they set a russet color on the cheeks of young women, and make lusty courage to rise up in men.
THOMAS DEKKER: *The Gull's Hornbook,* II, 1609

He that riseth late must trot all day, and shall scarce overtake his business at night.
BENJAMIN FRANKLIN: *Poor Richard's Almanac,* 1742

Lying late in the morning is never found in company with longevity. It also tends to make people corpulent.
LEIGH HUNT: *The Indicator*, XXI, 1821

A birdie with a yellow bill,
Hopped upon the window-sill,
Cocked his shining eye and said:
" Ain't you 'shamed, you sleepy-head? "
R. L. STEVENSON: *A Child's Garden of Verses*, 1885

[*See also* Late, Rising (Early).

Ritual

Rituals, liturgies, credos, Sinai thunder: I know more or less the history of these; the rise, progress, decline and fall of these. Can thunder from all the thirty-two azimuths, repeated daily for centuries of years, make God's laws more godlike to me? Brother, no.
THOMAS CARLYLE: *Past and Present*, III, 1843

Every particular church may ordain, change, or abolish rites and ceremonies, so that all things may be done to edification.
The Doctrines and Discipline of the Methodist Episcopal Church, I, 1932

Rivalry

In ev'ry age and clime we see
Two of a trade can never agree.
JOHN GAY: *Fables*, I, 1727

And each upon his rival glared,
With foot advanced, and blade half bared.
WALTER SCOTT: *The Lady of the Lake*, II, 1810

One is never wholly just toward a rival.
FRENCH PROVERB

Your worst enemy is always a man of your own trade. SPANISH PROVERB

River

He who had never seen a river mistook the first he saw for the sea.
MICHEL DE MONTAIGNE: *Essays*, I, 1580

He makes sweet music with the enamell'd stones,
Giving a gentle kiss to every sedge
He overtaketh in his pilgrimage.
SHAKESPEARE: *Two Gentlemen of Verona*, II, *c.* 1595

By shallow rivers, to whose falls
Melodious birds sing madrigals.
CHRISTOPHER MARLOWE: *The Passionate Shepherd to His Love*, 1599

There is not any one town or city which hath a navigable river at it that is poor, nor scarce any that are rich which want a river with the benefit of boats.
JOHN TAYLOR: *A New Discovery by Sea*, 1623

Rivers are roads that move.
BLAISE PASCAL: *Pensées*, VII, 1670

And see the rivers how they run
Through wood and mead, in shade and sun,
Sometimes swift, sometimes slow,
Wave succeeding wave, they go
A various journey to the deep
Like human life to endless sleep.
JOHN DYER: *Grongar Hill*, 1726

All rivers do what they can for the sea.
THOMAS FULLER: *Gnomologia*, 1732

Alph, the sacred river, ran
Through caverns measureless to man
Down to a sunless sea.
S. T. COLERIDGE: *Kubla Khan*, 1816

What are the Tibers and Scamanders, measured by the Missouri and the Amazon? Or what the loveliness of Ilissus or Avon, by the Connecticut or the Potomac? The waters of these American rivers are as pure and sweet, and their names would be as poetical, were they familiar to us in song, as the others, which have been immortalized for ages.
S. L. KNAPP: *Lectures on American Literature*, 1829

The majestic river floated on,
Out of the mist and hum of that low land,
Into the frosty starlight.
MATTHEW ARNOLD: *Sohrab and Rustum*, 1853

If you can't see the bottom, don't try to cross the river. ITALIAN PROVERB

[*See also* Mountain, Property, Prudence.

Road

Good roads and postchaises, if they have abridged the king's dominions, have at least tamed his subjects.
HORACE WALPOLE: *Letter to George Montague*, March 25, 1761

What a delightful thing's a turnpike road!
So smooth, so level, such a mode of shaving
The earth, as scarce the eagle in the broad
Air can accomplish, with his wide wings waving. BYRON: *Don Juan*, X, 1823

Afoot and light-hearted, I take to the open road,
Healthy, free, the world before me,
The long brown path before me, leading wherever I choose.
WALT WHITMAN: *Song of the Open Road*, 1856

The grand road from the mountain goes shining to the sea,
And there is traffic on it and many a horse and cart,
But the little roads of Cloonagh are dearer far to me,
And the little roads of Cloonagh go rambling through my heart.
EVA GORE-BOOTH: *The Roads of Cloonagh*, *c.* 1900

[*See also* Change, Old, Travel.

Roaming

A woman or hen that's given to roam
One of these nights will not come home.
JOHN HAY: *Castilian Days*, XII, 1872
(Cited as a Spanish proverb)

Roar

I will aggravate my voice so that I will roar you as gently as any sucking dove.
SHAKESPEARE: *A Midsummer Night's Dream*, I, *c.* 1596

Oh, that I were
Upon the hill of Bashan, to outroar
The hornéd herd.
SHAKESPEARE: *Antony and Cleopatra*, III, *c.* 1606

Roast

It is a poor roast that gives no dripping.
DANISH PROVERB

[*See also* Cook, Cookery.

Robbery

He that is robb'd, not wanting what is stol'n,
Let him not know't, and he's not robb'd at all.
SHAKESPEARE: *Othello*, III, 1604

To rob a fellow man is worse than robbing God.
HEBREW PROVERB

Robespierre, Maximilien (1758–94)

Robespierre was a fanatic, a monster, but he was incorruptible, and incapable of robbing, or of causing the deaths of others, either from personal enmity, or a desire of enriching himself. He was an enthusiast, but one who really believed that he was acting right, and he died not worth a sou.
NAPOLEON I: To Barry E. O'Meara at St. Helena, Aug. 25, 1817

O sea-green incorruptible.
THOMAS CARLYLE: *The French Revolution*, II, 1837

Robespierre came out of the pages of Rousseau as surely as the People's Palace rose out of the debris of a novel.
OSCAR WILDE: *The Decay of Lying*, 1889

Robin

[*See* Wind (North).

Rockefeller, John D. (1839–1937)

I believe the most useful man who has ever lived is John D. Rockefeller.
E. W. HOWE: *The Blessing of Business*, 1918

Rod

[*See* Child, Son.

Rogue

Rogues are always found out in some way. Whoever is a wolf will act as a wolf; that is the most certain of all things.
JEAN DE LA FONTAINE: *Fables*, III, 1668

No rogue like to the godly rogue.
THOMAS FULLER: *Gnomologia*, 1732

Not one in a thousand is capable of being a complete rogue.
HENRY FIELDING: *Jonathan Wild*, IV, 1743

A rogue is a roundabout fool; a fool *in circumbendibus*.
S. T. COLERIDGE: *Table-Talk*, Jan. 4, 1823

When you are kissed by a rogue, count your teeth immediately. HEBREW PROVERB

Rogues are rarely poor. ITALIAN PROVERB

The biggest rogue cries loudest out.
SCOTTISH PROVERB

[*See also* Actor, Greatness, Hypocrisy, Like, Luck, Wedding.

Rolling

The rolling stone gathers no moss.
ENGLISH PROVERB, first recorded in its present form by JOHN HEYWOOD: *Proverbs*, 1546

Roman

Wherever the Roman conquers, there he settles down.
SENECA: *Ad Helviam de consolatione*, 42

I had rather be a dog, and bay the moon,
Than such a Roman.
SHAKESPEARE: *Julius Cæsar*, IV, 1599

This was the noblest Roman of them all.
SHAKESPEARE: *Julius Cæsar*, V

Never were there any people more distinguished by their keen enjoyment of natural pleasures, or their excess in every intellectual and mental indulgence, than the Romans; never were any people more mighty in strength, more lawless, intemperate, and cruel than that nation.
FRIEDRICH VON SCHLEGEL: *On the Limits of the Beautiful*, 1794

The Romans were a blunt, flat people.
W. S. LANDOR: *Letter to Robert Southey*, Nov. 30, 1809

The Roman nature was fierce, rugged, almost brutal.
J. A. FROUDE: *The Lives of the Saints*, 1852
(Eclectic Review)

However truly the Roman might say of himself that he was born of Mars, and suckled by the wolf, he was nevertheless, at heart, more of a farmer than a soldier.
JOHN RUSKIN: *The Crown of Wild Olive*, III, 1866

Would that the Roman people had but one neck!
Ascribed variously to NERO, CALIGULA, HELIOGABALUS and others

Last of the Romans. (Ultimus romanorum.)
LATIN PHRASE

I am a Roman citizen. (Civis sum romanus.)
LATIN SAYING

[*See also* Brave, Citizen, Conformity, English, Fashion, Nobility, Utopia.

Roman Catholic

[*See* Catholic (Roman).

Roman Catholicism

[*See* Catholicism (Roman).

Romance

I call the classic healthy, the romantic sickly.
J. W. GOETHE: *Conversations with Eckermann,* April 2, 1829

The worst of having a romance is that it leaves one so unromantic.
OSCAR WILDE: *The Picture of Dorian Gray,* 1891

When one is in love one begins by deceiving oneself, one ends by deceiving others. That is what the world calls romance. IBID.

There is no such thing as romance in our day, women have become too brilliant; nothing spoils a romance so much as a sense of humor in the woman.
OSCAR WILDE: *A Woman of No Importance,* II, 1893

Twenty years of romance make a woman look like a ruin, but twenty years of marriage make her something like a public building.
IBID.

Confound romance! . . . And all unseen
Romance brought up the nine-fifteen.
RUDYARD KIPLING: *The King,* 1894

And that's the end. He passes away under a cloud, inscrutable at heart, forgotten, unforgiven, and excessively romantic.
JOSEPH CONRAD: *Lord Jim,* XLV, 1909

Rome

Everything is for sale at Rome. (Omnia venalia Romæ.)
SALLUST: *The Jugurthine War, c.* 40 B.C.

I found Rome brick and I leave it marble.
AUGUSTUS: On his deathbed, Aug. 18, 14

First among cities, home of the gods, golden Rome. (Prima urbes inter, divum domus, aurea Roma.)
AUSONIUS: *Epigrams, c.* 360

Rome is the capital of the world.
POPE INNOCENT II: To the Second Lateran Council, 1139

All roads lead to Rome.
LATIN PROVERB, familiar in English since the XIV century

When at Rome, do as the Romans do.
[*See* under Conformity.

Rome was not built in a day.
P. A. MANZOLLI: *Zodiacus vitæ,* 1543

There's no place here on earth that the heavens have embraced with such influence of favors and grace, and with such constancy. Even her ruin is glorious with renown and swollen with glory.
MICHEL DE MONTAIGNE: *Essays,* III, 1588

A traveler to Rome must have the back of an ass, the belly of a hog, and a conscience as broad as the king's highway.
FYNES MORYSON: *Itinerary,* III, 1617

See the wild waste of all-devouring years,
How Rome her own sad sepulchre appears,
With nodding arches, broken temples spread,
The very tombs now vanish'd like their dead.
ALEXANDER POPE: *Moral Essays,* V (To Mr. Addison), 1720

I know not why any one but a school-boy in his declamation should whine over the Commonwealth of Rome, which grew great only by the misery of the rest of mankind.
SAMUEL JOHNSON: *Boswell's Life,* 1756

After a diligent inquiry, I can discern four principal causes of the ruin of Rome, which continued to operate in a period of more than a thousand years. I. The injuries of time and nature. II. The hostile attacks of the barbarians and Christians. III. The use and abuse of the materials. And IV. The domestic quarrels of the Romans.
EDWARD GIBBON: *The Decline and Fall of the Roman Empire,* last chapter, 1788

As I sat musing amidst the ruins of the Capitol, while the barefooted friars were singing vespers in the Temple of Jupiter, . . . the idea of writing the decline and fall of the city first started to my mind.
EDWARD GIBBON: *Memoirs,* 1795 (The date was April 15, 1764)

Where Cicero and Antoninus lived,
A cowled and hypocritical monk
Prays, curses and deceives.
P. B. SHELLEY: *Queen Mab,* II, 1813

When falls the Coliseum, Rome shall fall;
And when Rome falls — the world.
BYRON: *Childe Harold,* IV, 1818

The history of Rome is pretty much the history of the world.
NAPOLEON I: To Gaspard Gourgaud at St. Helena, 1815–1818

Only in Rome have I felt what it really is to be a man.
J. W. GOETHE: *Conversations with Eckermann,* Oct. 9, 1828

The true key to the declension of the Roman Empire — which is not to be found in all Gibbon's immense work — may be stated in two words: the imperial character overlaying, and finally destroying, the national char-

acter. Rome under Trajan was an empire without a nation.
S. T. COLERIDGE: *Table-Talk*, Aug. 15, 1833

The grandeur that was Rome.
E. A. POE: *To Helen*, 1836 (Southern Literary Messenger, March)

The barbarians who broke up the Roman empire did not arrive a day too soon.
R. W. EMERSON: *The Conduct of Life*, VII, 1860

Every one soon or late comes round by Rome.
ROBERT BROWNING: *The Ring and the Book*, IV, 1869

If you live in Rome, don't quarrel with the pope. FRENCH PROVERB

He who goes to Rome a beast returns a beast.
ITALIAN PROVERB

Rome, the mother of men. (Roma virum genitrix.) LATIN PHRASE

The nearer Rome, the worse Christian. (Quo Romanæ propiores, tanto christiani tepidiores.) MEDIEVAL LATIN PROVERB

Rome has spoken; the case is concluded. (Roma locuta est, causa finita est.)
MEDIEVAL LATIN SAYING, apparently suggested by a passage in one of St. Augustine's sermons

[*See also* Conformity, Jesuit, Oxford, Pope, Roman.

Roosevelt, Theodore (1858–1919)

A combination of St. Paul and St. Vitus.
Ascribed to JOHN MORLEY, *c.* 1900

Rooster

[*See* Cock.

Rope

One should not mention a rope in one's house that was hanged.
THOMAS SHELTON: Tr. of CERVANTES: *Don Quixote*, II (1615), 1620

Rose

Let us crown ourselves with rosebuds before they be withered.
WISDOM OF SOLOMON II, 8, *c.* 100 B.C.

No rose without a thorn.
ENGLISH PROVERB, traced by Smith to the XV century

A rose is sweeter in the bud than full blown.
JOHN LYLY: *Euphues*, 1579

I'll say she looks as clear
As morning roses newly wash'd with dew
SHAKESPEARE: *The Taming of the Shrew*, II, 1594

The rose by any other name would smell as sweet.
SHAKESPEARE: *Romeo and Juliet*, II, *c.* 1596

Best jewel that the earth doth wear.
JOHN DAVIES: *Hymns of Astraea*, 1599

And I will make thee beds of roses
And a thousand fragrant posies.
CHRISTOPHER MARLOWE: *The Passionate Shepherd to His Love*, 1599

The rose looks fair, but fairer we it deem
For that sweet odor which doth in it live.
SHAKESPEARE: *Sonnets*, LIV, 1609

Go, lovely rose!
Tell her that wastes her time and me
That now she knows,
When I resemble her to thee,
How sweet and fair she seems to be.
EDMUND WALLER: *Go, Lovely Rose*, *c.* 1635

While we taste the fragrance of the rose,
Glows not her blush the fairer?
MARK AKENSIDE: *The Pleasures of Imagination*, II, 1744

Oh, my love's like a red, red rose
That's newly sprung in June.
ROBERT BURNS: *A Red, Red Rose*, 1794

You may break, you may shatter the vase if you will,
But the scent of the roses will hang round it still. THOMAS MOORE: *Farewell*, *c.* 1800

'Tis the last rose of Summer,
Left blooming alone;
All her lovely companions
Are faded and flown.
THOMAS MOORE: *The Last Rose of Summer*, 1812

Each morn a thousand roses brings, you say;
Yes, but where leaves the rose of yesterday?
EDWARD FITZGERALD: Tr. of OMAR KHAYYÁM: *Rubáiyát* (*c.* 1100), 1857

I sometimes think that never blows so red
The rose as where some buried Cæsar bled.
IBID.

Perhaps few people have ever asked themselves why they admire a rose so much more than all other flowers. If they consider, they will find, first, that red is, in a delicately graduated state, the loveliest of all pure colors; and secondly, that in the rose there is *no shadow*, except which is composed of color. All its shadows are fuller in color than its lights, owing to the translucency and reflective power of its leaves.
JOHN RUSKIN: *Modern Painters*, V, 1860

A rose, but one, none other rose had I,
A rose, one rose, and this was wondrous fair,
One rose, a rose that gladden'd earth and sky,
One rose, my rose, that sweeten'd all mine air—

I cared not for the thorns; the thorns were there.
ALFRED TENNYSON: *Pelleas and Ettarre,* 1869

Time brings roses. PORTUGUESE PROVERB

[*See also* June, Oxford University, Perfume, Spring, Thorn.

Rosemary

There's rosemary, that's for remembrance: pray you, love, remember.
SHAKESPEARE: *Hamlet,* IV, *c.* 1601

Rossini, Giachino (1792–1868)

Rossini would have been a great composer if his teacher had given him enough blows *ad posteriora.*
LUDWIG VAN BEETHOVEN: To Anton Schindler, 1824

Rotten

One rotten apple in a barrel spoils all the rest.
ENGLISH PROVERB, borrowed from the Latin and traced to the XIV century

There's small choice in rotten apples.
SHAKESPEARE: *The Taming of the Shrew,* I, 1594

Something is rotten in the state of Denmark.
SHAKESPEARE: *Hamlet,* I, *c.* 1601

You can't spoil a rotten egg. IRISH PROVERB

[*See also* Ripe.

Roulette

[*See* Gambling.

Rousseau, Jean-Jacques (1712–78)

Of all men of letters in Europe, since the death of Montesquieu, you are the person whom I most revere, both for the force of your genius and the greatness of your mind.
DAVID HUME: *Letter to Rousseau,* July 2, 1762 (Cf. HUME, *post,* 1766)

Rousseau is a very bad man. I would sooner sign a sentence for his transportation than that of any felon who has gone from the Old Bailey these many years.
SAMUEL JOHNSON: *Boswell's Life,* Feb. 15, 1766

He is surely the blackest and most atrocious villain, beyond comparison, that now exists in the world; and I am heartily ashamed of anything I ever wrote in his favor.
DAVID HUME: *Letter to Hugh Blair,* July 1, 1766 (Cf. HUME, *ante,* 1762)

Rousseau knows he is talking nonsense, and laughs at the world for staring at him.
SAMUEL JOHNSON: *Boswell's Life,* Sept. 30, 1769

The self-torturing sophist, wild Rousseau,
The apostle of affliction, he who threw
Enchantment over passion, and from woe
Wrung overwhelming eloquence.
BYRON: *Childe Harold,* III, 1816

Rousseau in his own person slandered human nature, but he was true to it in respect to our primitive weakness for wishing to appear in the eyes of the world as something different from what we really are. His self-portraiture is a lie, admirably executed, but still only a brilliant lie.
HEINRICH HEINE: *Confessions,* 1854

[He] clothed passion in the garb of philosophy, and preached the sweeping away of injustice by the perpetration of further injustice.
T. H. HUXLEY: *On the Natural Inequality of Man,* 1890

[*See also* Idiot.

Royalty

We have explored the temple of royalty, and found that the idol we have bowed down to has eyes which see not, ears that hear not our prayers, and a heart like the nether millstone.
SAMUEL ADAMS: Speech in Philadelphia, Aug. 1, 1776

[*See also* King, Monarchy, Prince.

Rub

Ay, there's the rub.
SHAKESPEARE: *Hamlet,* III, *c.* 1601

Ruby

[*See* July.

Rudeness

Rudeness is better than any argument; it totally eclipses intellect.
ARTHUR SCHOPENHAUER: *Position,* 1851

Ruin

When fortune is determined upon the ruin of a people, she can so blind them as to be insensible to all danger.
LIVY: *History of Rome,* V, *c.* 10

Ruin is like an usurer; the greater the sum of dignity and office, the greater is the interest in penalties which a man has to pay.
ST. CYPRIAN OF CARTHAGE: *The World and its Vanities, c.* 250

Resolv'd to ruin or to rule the state.
JOHN DRYDEN: *Absalom and Achitophel,* I, 1682

All men that are ruined are ruined on the side of their natural propensities.
EDMUND BURKE: *Letters on a Regicide Peace,* I, 1797

The road to ruin is always kept in good repair.
Author unidentified

[*See also* Gold.

Ruins

The next Augustan age will dawn on the other side of the Atlantic. There will, perhaps, be a Thucydides at Boston, a Xenophon at New York, in time a Virgil at Mexico, and a Newton at Peru. At last some curious traveler from Lima will visit England, and give a description of the ruins of St. Paul's, like the editions of Balbec and Palmyra.

HORACE WALPOLE: *Letter to Horace Mann,* Nov. 24, 1774

Thinkest thou the thousand eyes that shine with rapture on a ruin,
Would have looked with half their wonder on the perfect pile?

M. F. TUPPER: *Proverbial Philosophy,* I, 1837

[*See also* Church (Roman Catholic).

Rule

[*See* Exception, Majority.

Rule of Three

[*See* Arithmetic.

Ruler

The ruler over a country of a thousand chariots must give diligent attention to business; he must be sincere; he must be economical; he must love his people; and he must provide employment for them at the proper seasons.

CONFUCIUS: *Analects,* I, *c.* 500 B.C.

He who rules will ever be impatient of a partner. LUCAN: *Pharsalia,* I, 65

He shall rule them with a rod of iron.

REVELATION II, 27, *c.* 95

Nothing is more becoming a ruler than to despise no one, nor be insolent, but to preside over all impartially.

EPICTETUS: *Encheiridion, c.* 110

Ill can he rule the great that cannot reach the small.

EDMUND SPENSER: *The Faerie Queene,* V, *c.* 1589

That it may please thee to bless and preserve all Christian rulers and magistrates, giving them grace to execute justice, and to maintain truth; we beseech thee to hear us, good Lord.

THE BOOK OF COMMON PRAYER (*The Litany*), 1662

Rulers are men before God and gods before men. NATHANIEL AMES: *Almanac,* 1734

One still strong man in a blatant land,
Whatever they call him, what care I,
Aristocrat, democrat, autocrat — one
Who can rule and dare not lie.

ALFRED TENNYSON: *Maud,* I, 1855

A man who has tastes like mine, but in greater power, will rule me any day, and make me love my ruler.

R. W. EMERSON: *Eloquence,* 1877

The first duty of the rulers of a state should be to see that the laws and institutions, the general constitution and administration of the commonwealth, shall be such as to produce of themselves the public well-being and private prosperity.

POPE LEO XIII: *Rerum novarum,* May 15, 1891

If the people rule, then how can I rule?

Ascribed to CHIANG KAI-SHEK in ANNA LOUISE STRONG: *Inside China,* 1941

As the bird feels about the net that entangles it so do men feel about those who rule them.

CHINESE PROVERB

[*See also* Government, Iron, King, President, Prince.

Rum

There's nought, no doubt, so much the spirit calms
As rum and true religion.

BYRON: *Don Juan,* II, 1819

Fifteen men on a dead man's chest —
Yo-ho-ho and a bottle of rum.
Drink and the Devil had done for the rest —
Yo-ho-ho and a bottle of rum.

R. L. STEVENSON: *Treasure Island,* 1883

[*See also* Teetotaler.

Rumor

Rumor is not always wrong.

TACITUS: *Life of Agricola, c.* 98

Even when it brings some truth with it, rumor is not free from the flaw of falsehood, for it ever takes away from, adds to, and alters the truth.

TERTULLIAN: *The Christian's Defence, c.* 215

Rumor is a pipe
Blown by surmises, jealousies, conjectures,
And of so easy and so plain a stop
That the blunt monster with uncounted heads,
The still-discordant wavering multitude,
Can play upon it.

SHAKESPEARE: *II Henry IV,* I, *c.* 1598

Rumor doth double, like the voice and echo,
The numbers of the fear'd.

SHAKESPEARE: *II Henry IV,* III

The flying rumors gather'd as they roll'd,
Scarce any tale was sooner heard than told;
And all who told it added something new,
And all who heard it made enlargements too.

ALEXANDER POPE: *The Temple of Fame,* 1714

When rumors increase, and when there is abundance of noise and clamor, believe the second report.
ALEXANDER POPE: *Letter to William Trumbull,* Dec. 16, 1715

" They say so " is half a lie.
THOMAS FULLER: *Gnomologia,* 1732

Thy friend is dead: believe it. Thy friend has become rich: believe it not.
HEBREW PROVERB

[*See also* Gossip, Report.

Runaway

[*See* Monk.

Ruskin, John (1819–1900)

A bottle of beautiful soda-water.
THOMAS CARLYLE: *Letter to John Carlyle,* Nov. 27, 1855

[*See also* Disciple.

Russia

The joy of Russia is getting drunk.
Ascribed to VLADIMAR THE SAINT, the first Christian sovereign of Russia (?–1015)

A colossus of brass on a pedestal of clay.
JOSEPH II OF AUSTRIA (1741–90)

Russia is the land of possibilities.
Quoted as an old saying in J. G. SEUME: *Life and Character of the Empress Catherine II,* 1797

Despotism tempered by assassination: that is our Magna Charta.
An anonymous Russian nobleman: To Count Münster, Hanoverian minister to St. Petersburg, on the assassination of the Czar Paul I, 1801

Within the space of a decade a small group of Russian intellectuals has changed a multitude of world views and split itself into fifty hostile groups, and all the while the vast Russian nation has preserved its monotonous and stubborn faith in God.
ALEXANDER BLOK: *Letter to his mother,* Nov. 27, 1907

Here is a fit partner for a League of Honor.
WOODROW WILSON: Address to Congress, April 2, 1917

If you don't like the United States why don't you go back to Russia?
Challenge to Communists, *c.* 1919

Our government offers no objection to the carrying on of commerce by our citizens with the people of Russia. Our government does not propose, however, to enter into relations with another régime which refuses to recognize the sanctity of international obligations. I do not propose to barter away for the privilege of trade any of the cherished rights of humanity. I do not propose to make merchandise of any American principles.
CALVIN COOLIDGE: Message to Congress, Dec. 6, 1923

In the law of capitalist development Russia is just the antipode of England.
LEON TROTSKY: *A Necessary Discussion with Our Syndicalist Comrades,* 1923

Russia's cholera is the cold.
ESTONIAN PROVERB

[*See also* Czar, Poland.

Russian

Scratch a Russian, and you will wound a Tartar.
JOSEPH DE MAISTRE: *Soirées de Saint-Petersbourg,* 1821

Do scoundrels have no songs? Then how is it that the Russians have them?
F. W. NIETZSCHE: *The Twilight of the Idols,* 1889

The Russian will never be able to dispense with the German.
OTTO VON BISMARCK (1815–98)

Make ye no truce with Adam-zad — the Bear that walks like a man.
RUDYARD KIPLING: *The Truce of the Bear,* 1898

When the Russian is not singing songs, saturated with vodka or melancholy, he is spinning stories shot through with the fantastic, or grim with the pain and noise of life.
JAMES HUNEKER: *Mezzotints in Modern Music,* 1899

A person with a Caucasian body and a Mongolian soul.
AMBROSE BIERCE: *The Devil's Dictionary,* 1906

No Russian is any good unless he is first beaten.
GERMAN PROVERB

If you beat a Russian enough he can do anything, even make a watch.
RUSSIAN PROVERB

The Russian is clever, but always too late.
IBID.

[*See also* Anti-Semitism, Cheating, Jew, Thief.

Russian Language

Russian is nothing but sneezing.
E. R. BULWER-LYTTON (OWEN MEREDITH): *Lucile,* I, 1860

Rust

If I rest, I rust. (Rast' ich, so rost' ich.)
Ascribed to MARTIN LUTHER (1483–1546)

Rye

Gin a body meet a body
Comin' through the rye,

Gin a body kiss a body
Need a body cry?

ROBERT BURNS: *Comin' Through the Rye*, c. 1792 (An adaptation of an old Scots song)

S

Sabbath

God blessed the seventh day, and sanctified it: because that in it he had rested from all his work which God created and made.

GENESIS II, 3, *c.* 700 B.C.

Remember the sabbath day, to keep it holy. Six days shalt thou labor, and do all thy work: but the seventh day is the sabbath of the Lord thy God: in it thou shalt not do any work, thou, nor thy son, nor thy daughter, thy manservant, nor thy maidservant, nor thy cattle, nor thy stranger that is within thy gates: for in six days the Lord made heaven and earth, the sea, and all that in them is, and rested the seventh day: wherefore the Lord blessed the sabbath day, and hallowed it.

EXODUS XX, 8–11, *c.* 700 B.C. (Cf. DEUTERONOMY V, 12–14, *c.* 650 B.C.)

Ye shall kindle no fire throughout your habitations upon the sabbath day.

EXODUS XXXV, 3

In those days I saw in Judah some treading winepresses on the sabbath, and bringing in sheaves, and lading asses; as also wine, grapes, and figs, and all manner of burdens, which they brought into Jerusalem on the sabbath day. JOB XIII, 15, *c.* 325 B.C.

The sabbath was made for man, and not man for the sabbath. MARK II, 27, *c.* 70

Rabbi Meir says that a one-legged man may wear his wooden leg on the Sabbath, but Rabbi Jossi prohibits it.

THE TALMUD (*Sabbath*, VI), *c.* 200

Ye know what befel those of your nation who transgressed on the Sabbath day. We said unto them, Be ye changed into apes.

THE KORAN, II, *c.* 625

Ned will not keep the Jewish Sabbath, he,
Because the church hath otherwise ordain'd;
Nor yet the Christian, for he does not see
How alt'ring of the day can be maintain'd.
Thus seeming for to doubt of keeping either,
He halts 'twixt them both, and so keeps neither.

JOHN HEATH: *Two Centuries of Epigrams*, 1610

When Christians dare God's Sabbath to abuse
They make themselves a scorn to Turks and Jews.

JOHN TAYLOR: *Observations and Travel from London to Hamburg*, 1617

To the end that the Sabbath may be celebrated in a religious manner we appoint that all may surcease their labor every Saturday throughout the year at three o'clock in the afternoon, and that they spend the rest of the day in catechizing and preparations for the Sabbath as the ministers shall direct.

Instructions to John Endicott by the Massachusetts Company, 1628

So sang they, and the empyrean rung
With hallelujahs. Thus was Sabbath kept.

JOHN MILTON: *Paradise Lost*, VII, 1667

And never broke the Sabbath, but for gain.

JOHN DRYDEN: *Absalom and Achitophel*, I, 1682

When very young I went astray from God, and my mind was altogether taken with vanities and follies. Of the manifold sins which then I was guilty of, none so sticks upon me as that, being very young, I was whittling on the Sabbath-day; and for fear of being seen, I did it behind the door. A specimen of that atheism that I brought into the world with me. NATHANIEL MATHER: *Diary*, 1685

O children, don't profane God's Sabbath by idleness, playing, by needless speaking about worldly matters; much less by any thing in itself sinful; but employ the Sabbath in praying, reading the Holy Bible and good books, learning your catechism, receiving the good instructions of parents and masters; in going to the house of God, and there diligently and reverently attending on His holy worship.

BENJAMIN WADSWORTH: *A Course of Sermons on Early Piety*, 1721

Resolved, Never to utter any thing that is sportive, or matter of laughter, on a Lord's day.

JONATHAN EDWARDS: *Resolutions*, 1722

See Christians, Jews, one heavy Sabbath keep,
And all the western world believe and sleep.

ALEXANDER POPE: *The Dunciad*, III, 1728

One of the miseries of war is that there is no Sabbath, and the current of work and strife has no cessation. How can we be pardoned for all our offenses?

R. E. LEE: *Letter to his daughter Annie*, Dec. 8, 1861

[*See also* Rest, Sunday.

Sacrament

An outward and visible sign of an inward and spiritual grace.

THE BOOK OF COMMON PRAYER (*The Catechism*), 1662

Q. How many sacraments hath Christ ordained in His church? *A.* Two only, as generally necessary to salvation, that is to say, baptism and the supper of the Lord. IBID.

Embodied acts, such as the sacramental act, are beneath acts purely mental and spiritual, such as prayer is.

BENJAMIN WHICHCOTE: *Moral and Religious Aphorisms*, 1753

There are two sacraments ordained of Christ our Lord in the Gospel; that is to say, Baptism and the Supper of the Lord.
The Doctrines and Discipline of the Methodist Episcopal Church I, 1932

[*See also* Absolution, Actor, Eucharist.

Sacrifice

Solomon offered a sacrifice of peace offerings, which he offered unto the Lord, two and twenty thousand oxen and a hundred and twenty thousand sheep.
I KINGS VIII, 63, *c.* 500 B.C.

The sacrifices of God are a broken spirit: a broken and a contrite heart, O God, thou wilt not despise.
PSALMS LI, 17, *c.* 150 B.C.

The same god who is propitiated by the blood of a hundred bulls is also propitiated by the smallest offering of incense.
OVID: *Tristia,* II, *c.* 10

It is not possible that the blood of bulls and of goats should take away sins.
HEBREWS X, 4, *c.* 65

It has been the custom, when a man dies, for his people to sacrifice themselves by strangling, or to strangle others as a sacrifice, or to sacrifice the dead man's horse, or to bury valuable things in his grave, or to cut off their hair, or to stab themselves in the thigh. Let all such old customs be abolished.
THE LAWS OF KOTOKU (Japan), *c.* 650

To make large sacrifices in big things is easy, but to make sacrifices in little things is what we are seldom capable of.
J. W. GOETHE: *Elective Affinities,* I, 1808

A woman who loves sacrifices her honor; a god who loved became a Jew.
F. W. NIETZSCHE: *The Twilight of the Idols,* 1889

[*See also* Condolence, Lamb, Morality.

Sacrilege

Sacred things should not only not be touched with the hands, but may not be violated even in thought.
CICERO: *Oration Against Verres, c.* 60 B.C.

[*See also* Historian.

Sadness

Sickness is better than sadness.
THOMAS FULLER: *Gnomologia,* 1732

A sadder and a wiser man,
He rose the morrow morn.
S. T. COLERIDGE: *The Ancient Mariner,* VII, 1798

'Twas far too strange and wonderful for sadness.
JOHN KEATS: *Endymion,* II, 1818

A feeling of sadness and longing,
That is not akin to pain,
And resembles sorrow only
As the mist resembles the rain.
H. W. LONGFELLOW: *The Day is Done,* 1845

[*See also* Grief, Laughter, Melancholy, Merriment.

Safety

The desire for safety stands against every great and noble enterprise.
TACITUS: *Annals,* XV, *c.* 110

Best safety lies in fear.
SHAKESPEARE: *Hamlet,* I, *c.* 1601

It's safe riding with two anchors.
EDWARD WARD: *Female Policy,* 1716

The way to be safe is never to feel secure.
H. G. BOHN: *Handbook of Proverbs,* 1855

Safety first.
MOTTO OF THE NATIONAL COUNCIL FOR INDUSTRIAL SAFETY, 1915

It is better to be safe than sorry.
AMERICAN PROVERB

The trodden path is the safest. (Via trita est tutissima.)
LEGAL MAXIM

[*See also* Ale, Honorable, July Fourth, Liberty, Middle, Path, Pleasure.

Safety, Public

The safety of the people is the supreme law.
CICERO: *De legibus,* III, *c.* 50 B.C.

Nothing will ruin the country if the people themselves will undertake its safety; and nothing can save it if they leave that safety in any hands but their own.
DANIEL WEBSTER: Speech in the Senate, March 18, 1834

[*See also* Strike.

Said

The least said the soonest mended.
ENGLISH PROVERB, traced by Apperson to *c.* 1555

He himself has said it. (Ipse dixit.)
LATIN PHRASE

The more said, the less done.
SCOTTISH PROVERB

Sailing

A wet sheet and a flowing sea,
A wind that follows fast
And fills the white and rustling sails,
And bends the gallant mast;
And bends the gallant mast, my boys,
While, like the eagle free,
Away the good ship flies, and leaves
Old England on the lee.
ALLAN CUNNINGHAM: *A Wet Sheet and a Flowing Sea,* 1825

[*See also* Ship.

Sailor

They that go down to the sea in ships, that do business in great waters; these see the works of the Lord, and his wonders in the deep.
PSALMS CVII, 23–24, *c.* 150 B.C.

A fair complexion is unbecoming a sailor: he ought to be swarthy from the waters of the sea and the rays of the sun.
OVID: *Ars amatoria,* I, *c.* 2 B.C.

Carnal seamen, in a storm,
Turn pious converts, and reform.
SAMUEL BUTLER: *Hudibras,* III, 1678

Seamen are the nearest to death and the farthest from God.
THOMAS FULLER: *Gnomologia,* 1732

Sailors get money like horses and spend it like asses.
TOBIAS SMOLLETT: *Peregrine Pickle,* II, 1751 (Quoted as "an old saying")

No man will be a sailor who has contrivance enough to get himself into a jail; for being in a ship is being in a jail, with the chance of being drowned. . . . A man in a jail has more room, better food, and commonly better company.
SAMUEL JOHNSON: *Boswell's Life,* 1759

How impure are the channels through which trade hath a conveyance! How great is that danger to which poor lads are now exposed, when placed on shipboard to learn the art of sailing!
JOHN WOOLMAN: *Journal,* X, 1774

And what do you think they got for their dinner?
'Twas water soup, but slightly thinner.
And what do you think they got for their suppers?
Belaying pin soup and a roll in the scuppers.
Anon.: *Blow, Boys, Blow* (sailors' chanty), *c.* 1812

O'er the glad waters of the dark blue sea,
Our thoughts as boundless, and our souls as free,
Far as the breeze can bear, the billows foam,
Survey our empire, and behold our home.
BYRON: *The Corsair,* I, 1814

The sole business of a seaman on shore, who has to go to sea again, is to take as much pleasure as he can.
LEIGH HUNT: *The Indicator,* XXIX, 1821

Of winds and dashing waves the sport,
By perils, while at sea, beset,
The sailor found himself, in port,
Exposed to greater perils yet.
JOHN PIERPONT: *Hymn Written for the Opening of the Mariners' House in Ann Street, Boston,* May, 1837

When I go to sea, I go as a simple sailor, right before the mast, plumb down into the forecastle, aloft there to the royal masthead.
HERMAN MELVILLE: *Moby Dick,* I, 1851

Seafaring men range from one end of the earth to the other; but the multiplicity of external objects which they have encountered forms no symmetrical and consistent picture upon their imagination; they see the tapestry of human life as if it were on the wrong side, and it tells no story.
J. H. NEWMAN: *On the Scope and Nature of University Education,* V, 1852

The wonder is always new that any sane man can be a sailor.
R. W. EMERSON: *English Traits,* II, 1856

The power which the sea requires in a sailor makes a man of him very fast, and the change of shores and population clears his head of much nonsense of his wigwam.
R. W. EMERSON: *Civilization,* 1870

A British tar is a soaring soul,
As free as a mountain bird,
His energetic fist should be ready to resist
A dictatorial word.
W. S. GILBERT: *H.M.S. Pinafore,* I, 1878

The life of a sailor is very unhealthy.
FRANCIS GALTON: *Inquiries Into Human Faculty,* 1883

And there were men of all the ports
From Mississip to Clyde,
And regally they spat and smoked,
And fearsomely they lied.
RUDYARD KIPLING: *The Ballad of Fisher's Boarding-House,* 1892

The wind that blows, the ship that goes
And the lass that loves a sailor.
OLD ENGLISH TOAST

[*See also* Children, Marine, Profession, Sea, Ship, Soldier, Vocation.

Saint

The Lord . . . forsaketh not his saints.
PSALMS XXXVII, 28, *c.* 150 B.C.

From a private gentlewoman you have made me first a marchioness, then a queen; and, as you can raise me no higher in this world, you are now sending me to be a saint in Heaven.
ANNE BOLEYN: *Last Message to Henry VIII,* 1536

The invocation of saints is a most abominable blindness and heresy; yet the papists will not give it up. The pope's greatest profit arises from the dead; for the calling on dead saints brings him infinite sums of money and riches, far more than he gets from the living.
MARTIN LUTHER: *Table-Talk,* CLXXVIII, 1569

The tears of saints more sweet by far,
Than all the songs of sinners are.
ROBERT HERRICK: *Noble Numbers,* 1647

Those saints which God loves best,
The Devil tempts not least.
IBID.

A saint's of th' heav'nly realm a peer.
SAMUEL BUTLER: *Hudibras*, II, 1664

To make a man a saint, it must indeed be by grace; and whoever doubts this does not know what a saint is, or a man.
BLAISE PASCAL: *Pensées*, XXIV, 1670

All are not saints that go to church.
Anon.: *Poor Robin's Almanac*, 1687

A young whore, an old saint.
THOMAS FULLER: *Gnomologia*, 1732

The worst of madmen is a saint run mad.
ALEXANDER POPE: *The First Epistle of the First Book of Horace*, 1735

The sight of hell-torments will exalt the happiness of the saints for ever.
JONATHAN EDWARDS: *The Eternity of Hell-Torments*, 1739

Some of . . . the disciplinarians, such as [John] Penry, the author of Martin Marprelate, instead of saints, styled some of the Apostles and the Virgin Mary, in derision, Sirs; as, Sir Peter, Sir Paul, Sir Mary.
ZACHARY GREY: *Note to* SAMUEL BUTLER: *Hudibras*, II (1664), 1744 (PENRY'S *Marprelate Tracts* were published in 1588)

With regard to the Christians, assuredly their greatest and most venerable saints were those whose brains had sustained the severest shock.
VOLTAIRE: *Philosophical Dictionary*, 1764

And Satan trembles when he sees
The weakest saint upon his knees.
WILLIAM COWPER and JOHN NEWTON: *Olney Hymns*, 1779

Saints in stone have done more in the world than living ones.
G. C. LICHTENBERG: *Reflections*, 1799

Saints will aid if men will call,
For the blue sky bends over all.
S. T. COLERIDGE: *Christabel*, 1816

Some reputed saints that have been canonized ought to have been cannonaded.
C. C. COLTON: *Lacon*, 1820

One should be fearful of being wrong in religion when one thinks differently from the saints.
JOSEPH JOUBERT: *Pensées*, I, 1842

I hope those old water-logged saints that died soaking in damp stone cells were taken to Heaven. They had Hell enough on earth.
H. W. BEECHER: *Royal Truths*, 1862

A heart tenderly attached to the saints will give vent to its feelings in the language of hyperbole, just as an enthusiastic lover will call his future bride his adorable queen, without any intention of worshipping her as a goddess.
JAMES CARDINAL GIBBONS: *The Faith of Our Fathers*, XIII, 1876

The only difference between a saint and a sinner is that every saint has a past, and every sinner has a future.
OSCAR WILDE: *A Woman of No Importance*, III, 1893

The history of the saints is mainly the history of insane people.
BENITO MUSSOLINI: Speech in Lausanne, July, 1904

A sinner who kept on trying.
Author unidentified

In honor of the Holy and Undivided Trinity, for the exaltation of the Catholic faith and the growth of the Christian religion, by the authority of our Lord Jesus Christ, of the blessed Apostles Peter and Paul, and by our own, after mature deliberation, after offering many prayers to God, after having conferred with our venerable brethren, the Cardinals of the Holy Roman Church, and with the Patriarchs and Bishops present in Rome, we declare that the Blessed —— is a Saint and we inscribe his/her name in the list of Saints, in the name of the Father, and of the Son and of the Holy Ghost. Amen.
Formula used by the popes in proclaiming the canonization of a saint

The greater the saint, the sweeter the incense.
FRENCH PROVERB

When the saint's day is over goodbye to the saint.
IBID.

When God doesn't help, neither do the saints.
GERMAN PROVERB

Young saint, old devil.
ITALIAN PROVERB

They're no a' saints that get the name o't.
SCOTTISH PROVERB

[*See also* Admiration, Blush, Doctor, God, Hell, Image, Judgment Day, Logician, Origin, Pride, Sin, Speech.

Saint Swithin's Day

St. Swithin's day, if thou dost rain,
For forty days it will remain;
St. Swithin's day, if thou be fair,
For forty days 'twill rain na mair.
OLD SCOTTISH RHYME

Salad

In a good salad there should be more oil than vinegar or salt.
Ascribed to ST. FRANCIS DE SALES (1567–1622) in J. P. CAMUS: *L'esprit de Saint François de Sales*, 1641

Oh, herbaceous treat!
'Twould tempt the dying anchorite to eat;
Back to the world he'd turn his fleeting soul,
And plunge his fingers in the salad bowl;
Serenely full the epicure would say,
"Fate cannot harm me, — I have dined today."
SYDNEY SMITH: *A Receipt for a Salad*, c. 1810

According to the Spanish proverb, four persons are wanted to make a good salad: a spendthrift for oil, a miser for vinegar, a counsellor for salt, and a madman to stir all up.
ABRAHAM HAYWARD: *The Art of Dining*, 1852

The better the salad, the worse the dinner.
ITALIAN PROVERB

Salad-days

My salad days;
When I was green in judgment.
SHAKESPEARE: *Antony and Cleopatra*, I, *c.* 1606

Salamander

[*See* Chastity.

Sales, St. Francis de (1567–1622)

A gentleman-saint.
LEIGH HUNT: Title of an essay on de Sales, 1840 (*The Seer*, XLI)

Salesmanship

To things of sale a seller's praise belongs.
SHAKESPEARE: *Love's Labor's Lost*, IV, *c.* 1595

The salesman knows nothing of what he is selling save that he is charging a great deal too much for it.
OSCAR WILDE: *House Decoration*, 1882 (Lecture in New York, May 11)

Salic Law

[*See* Law (Salic).

Salmon

Of all God's creatures, the salmon is the cleanest.
WELSH PROVERB

Salon

I'll have
My house the academy of wits, who shall
Exalt with rich sack and sturgeon,
Write panegyrics of my feasts, and praise
The method of my witty superfluities.
JAMES SHIRLEY: *The Lady of Pleasure*, I, 1637

She tried to found a salon, but only succeeded in opening a restaurant.
OSCAR WILDE: *The Picture of Dorian Gray*, 1891

Saloon

The saloon must go.
Slogan of the Anti-Saloon League, organized Dec. 18, 1895

The saloon is the poor man's club.
BISHOP CHARLES D. WILLIAMS, of Michigan, *c.* 1900

I will never advocate nor approve any law which directly or indirectly permits the return of the saloon.
ALFRED E. SMITH: Speech of acceptance, July, 1928

I ask especially that no state shall, by law or otherwise, authorize the return of the saloon, either in its old form or in some modern guise.
F. D. ROOSEVELT: Proclamation on the repeal of the Eighteenth Amendment, Dec. 5, 1933

Saloonkeeper

[*See* Democrat.

Salt

Salt is white and pure, — there is something holy in salt.
NATHANIEL HAWTHORNE: *American Note-Books*, Oct. 4, 1840

Salt is what makes things taste bad when it isn't in them.
Author unidentified

Meat without salt is fit only for dogs.
HEBREW PROVERB

With a grain of salt. (Cum grano salis.)
LATIN PHRASE

Nothing more useful than the sun and salt. (Nil sole et sale utilius.)
LATIN PROVERB

There are six flavors, and of them all salt is the chief.
SANSKRIT PROVERB

[*See also* Acquaintance, Best, Borrowing and Lending, Bread, Salad, Trust.

Salt Lake City

A 2nd Soddum & Germorrer.
C. F. BROWNE (ARTEMUS WARD): *Artemus Ward: His Travels*, 1865

Salutation

Hail, Emperor; we salute you. (Ave Imperator, te salutamus.)
Salutation of Roman gladiators on entering the arena, *c.* 100

Salvation

Strait is the gate, and narrow is the way, which leadeth unto life, and few there be that find it.
MATTHEW VII, 14, *c.* 75

Outside the church there is no salvation. (Extra ecclesiam nulla salus.)
MAXIM OF THE ROMAN CATHOLIC CHURCH, based upon the first article of the Athanasian Creed, *c.* 400

If a man born among infidels and barbarians does what lies in his power God will reveal to him what is necessary for salvation, either by inward inspiration or by sending him a preacher of the faith.
THOMAS AQUINAS: *Summa theologicæ*, II, *c.* 1265

Salvation by the cross. (In cruce salus.)
THOMAS À KEMPIS: *Imitation of Christ*, II, *c.* 1420

I may compare the state of a Christian to a goose, tied up over a wolf's pit to catch wolves. About the pit stand many ravening wolves, that would willingly devour the goose, but she is preserved alive, while they, leaping at her, fall into the pit, are taken and destroyed. Even so, we that are Christians are preserved by the sweet loving angels, so that the devils, those ravening wolves, the tyrants and persecutors, cannot destroy us.

MARTIN LUTHER: *Table-Talk*, DCLXXXVIII, 1569

Despair of ever being saved, " except thou be born again," or of seeing God " without holiness," or of having part in Christ except thou " love Him above father, mother, or thy own life." This kind of despair is one of the first steps to Heaven.

RICHARD BAXTER: *The Saint's Everlasting Rest*, VI, 1650

All that is necessary to salvation is contained in two virtues: faith in Christ, and obedience to laws.

THOMAS HOBBES: *Leviathan*, XLIII, 1651

'Twas to save thee, child, from dying,
Save my dear from burning flame,
Bitter groans and endless crying,
That thy blest Redeemer came.

ISAAC WATTS: *Divine Songs for Children*, 1715

Jesus, Lover of my soul,
Let me to Thy bosom fly,
While the nearer waters roll,
While the tempest still is high.
Hide me, O my Saviour, hide,
Till the storm of life is past:
Safe into the haven guide;
O, receive my soul at last.

CHARLES WESLEY: *In Temptation*, 1740

No man has the right to abandon the care of his salvation to another.

THOMAS JEFFERSON: *Notes on Religion*, 1776

It takes a rubber ball to bounce,
It takes a baseball to roll,
But it takes a dam' good preacher
To send salvation to my soul.

American Negro song, quoted by HOWARD W. ODUM: *Wings On My Feet*, VII, 1929

Salvation through Christ the Redeemer. (Salus per Christum redemptorem.)

MEDIEVAL LATIN PHRASE

Salvation comes from God alone. (Solo Deo salus.)

MEDIEVAL LATIN PROVERB

[*See also* Atonement, Augustine (St.), Blood, Faith, Grace, Hair, Infidel, Jew, Redemption, Sin.

Salvation Army

The Salvation Army reaches a class of people that churches never do.

AMERICAN PROVERB, apparently first recorded by GELETT BURGESS: *Are You a Bromide?*, 1907

Salzburg

In his first year a newcomer to Salzburg becomes stupid, in his second year he becomes crazy, in his third year he becomes a Salzburger.

SALZBURG PROVERB

Samaritan

(The story of the Good Samaritan is in LUKE X, 30–37, *c.* 75.)

Same

No like is the same.

WILLIAM ROWLEY: *The Shoemaker a Gentleman*, II, 1638

Always the same. (Semper idem.)

LATIN PHRASE

[*See also* Like.

Sanctimonious

A solemn, unsmiling, sanctimonious old iceberg that looked like he was waiting for a vacancy in the Trinity.

S. L. CLEMENS (MARK TWAIN): *Letter from New York to the Alta Californian* (San Francisco), June 6, 1867

Sandal

If anything in the way of shoeing is required, sandals are the cleanest wear; they leave the feet more exposed and are certainly more manly than shoes.

TERTULLIAN: *The Cloak Versus the Toga*, *c.* 222

Sanity

Who then is sane? (Quisnam igitur sanus?)

HORACE: *Satires*, II, *c.* 25 B.C.

Sanskrit Language

A comparative philologist without a knowledge of Sanskrit is like an astronomer without a knowledge of mathematics.

F. MAX MÜLLER: Inaugural address at Oxford, 1868

Santa Claus

No sane local official who has hung up an empty stocking over the municipal fireplace is going to shoot Santa Claus just before a hard Christmas.

ALFRED E. SMITH: Press interview in New York, Nov. 30, 1933 (On the New Deal; first mention of shooting Santa Claus)

Sapphire

[*See* September.

Sappho

Who knows Sappho smiles at other whores.

ALEXANDER POPE: *Satires of Dr. John Donne Versified*, II, 1735

[*See also* Hero.

Sarcasm

Keep a store of sarcasms, and know how to use them.

BALTASAR GRACIÁN: *The Art of Worldly Wisdom*, XXXVII, 1647

Sarcasm [is] the language of the Devil.
THOMAS CARLYLE: *Sartor Resartus*, II, 1836

This is rote sarcastikul.
C. F. BROWNE (ARTEMUS WARD): *A Visit to Brigham Young*, 1866

An undertaker in tears.
H. W. SHAW (JOSH BILLINGS): *Josh Billings' Comical Lexicon*, 1877

Sardonyx

[*See* August.

Satan

[*See* Devil.

Satiety

Satiety runs closest on the greatest pleasures.
CICERO: *De oratore*, III, *c.* 80 B.C.

To the glutted blackbird all cherries are bitter.
GERMAN PROVERB

Satin

[*See* Luxury.

Satire

It has been my constant aim in all my writings to lash vice, but to spare persons.
MARTIAL: *Epigrams*, X, *c.* 95

In the present state of the world it is difficult not to write satire.
JUVENAL: *Satires*, I, *c.* 110

I first adventure, follow me who list
And be the second English satirist.
JOSEPH HALL (BISHOP OF NORWICH): *Virgidemiae*, prologue, 1597

The satire should be like the porcupine,
That shoots sharp quills out in every angry line,
And wounds the blushing cheek and fiery eye
Of him that hears and readeth guiltily.
JOSEPH HALL (BISHOP OF NORWICH): *Virgidemiae*, v, 1598

He that hath a satirical vein, as he maketh others afraid of his wit, so he had need be afraid of others' memory.
FRANCIS BACON: *Essays*, XXXII, 1612

Satires . . . must lance wide
The wounds of men's corruption; ope the side
Of vice; search deep for dead flesh and rank cores.
JOHN DAY: *The Parliament of Bees*, v, 1641

Men are satirical more from vanity than from malice.
LA ROCHEFOUCAULD: *Maxims*, 1665

Satire will always be unpleasant to those that deserve it.
THOMAS SHADWELL: *A True Widow*, pref., 1679

The boldest way, if not the best,
To tell men freely of their foulest faults,
To laugh at their vain deeds and vainer thoughts.
JOHN SHEFFIELD (DUKE OF BUCKINGHAM): *An Essay on Satire*, *c.* 1679

How easy it is to call rogue and villain, and that wittily, but how hard to make a man appear a fool, a blockhead, or a knave, without using any of those opprobrious terms. To spare the grossness of the names, and to do the thing yet more severely, is to draw a full face and to make the nose and cheeks stand out, and yet not employ any depth of shadowing. This is the mystery of that noble trade, which yet no master can teach to his apprentice.
JOHN DRYDEN: *Discourse Concerning the Original and Progress of Satire*, 1693

Satire is a sort of glass wherein beholders do generally discover everybody's face but their own, which is the chief reason for that kind reception it meets with in the world.
JONATHAN SWIFT: *The Battle of the Books*, pref., 1704

If any fool is by our satire bit,
Let him hiss loud, to show you all he's hit.
ALEXANDER POPE: *Prologue for Three Hours After Marriage*, 1717 (The play has been ascribed to John Gay, John Arbuthnot and Pope himself)

Satire should, like a polished razor keen,
Wound with a touch that's scarcely felt or seen.
MARY WORTLEY MONTAGU: *Verses Addressed to an Imitator of Horace*, *c.* 1720

Heroes and gods make other poems fine;
Plain satire calls for sense in every line.
EDWARD YOUNG: *Love of Fame*, II, 1728

On me, when dunces are satiric,
I take it for a panegyric.
JONATHAN SWIFT: *To Dr. Delany*, 1729

Satire's my weapon, but I'm too discreet
To run amuck, and tilt at all I meet.
ALEXANDER POPE: *The First Satire of the Second Book of Horace*, 1733

How terrible a weapon is satire in the hand of a great genius!
COLLEY CIBBER: *Apology For His Life*, II, 1740

I love not the satiric Muse:
No man on earth would I abuse;
Nor with empoison'd verses grieve
The most offending son of Eve.
It hardens man to see his name
Exposed to public mirth or shame;
And rouses, as it spoils his rest,
The baser passions of his breast.
GEORGE CRABBE: *Satire*, *c.* 1785

The finest satire is the one in which ridicule is combined with so little malice and so much conviction that it forces a laugh even from those it hits.
G. C. LICHTENBERG: *Reflections*, 1799

Fools are my theme, let satire be my song.
BYRON: *English Bards and Scotch Reviewers*, 1809

He who satire loves to sing
On himself will satire bring.
GEORGE BORROW: Tr. of GRUFFYDD HIRAETHOG: *Couplet* (*c.* 1550), 1862

Satire [is] always as sterile as it is shameful and as impotent as it is insolent.
OSCAR WILDE: *The English Renaissance of Art*, 1882 (Lecture in New York, Jan. 9)

The satirist holds a place half-way between the preacher and the wit. He has the purpose of the first and uses the weapons of the second. He must both hate and love.
HUMBERT WOLFE: *Notes on English Verse Satire*, I, 1929

[*See also* Fool, Voltaire.

Saturday

If you want a neat wife, choose her on a Saturday.
BENJAMIN FRANKLIN: *Poor Richard's Almanac*, 1737

[*See also* Days, Demon, Nail, Sneezing, Wedding-day.

Sauce

Sauce for the goose is sauce for the gander.
ENGLISH PROVERB (JOHN RAY: *English Proverbs*, 1670, says that it is " a woman's proverb ")

Though the sauce be good, yet you need not forsake the meat for it.
THOMAS FULLER: *Gnomologia*, 1732

[*See also* Appetite, England, Fish, Hunger, Mayonnaise.

Sauerkraut

Rain forty days, rain forty nights;
Sauerkraut sticking out the smokestack.
American popular song, *c.* 1875

Sauerkraut is good for a cold.
GERMAN PROVERB

Sauerkraut and bacon drive all care away.
PENNSYLVANIA GERMAN PROVERB

Sausage

Let them make sausages of me and serve them up to the students.
ARISTOPHANES: *The Clouds*, 423 B.C.

Everything has an end, except a sausage, which has two.
DANISH PROVERB

[*See also* Bologna.

Savage

I am as free as nature first made man,
Ere the base laws of servitude began,
When wild in the woods the noble savage ran.
JOHN DRYDEN: *The Conquest of Granada*, I, 1670

In the lands lately discovered the inhabitants are scarcely to be called men: they are rather animals in human shape.
BERNARD DE FONTENELLE: *Entretiens sur la pluralité des mondes*, II, 1686

The savage is to ages what the child is to years.
P. B. SHELLEY: *The Defence of Poetry*, 1821

A savage is a man of one story, and that one story a cellar. When a man begins to be civilized, he raises another story. When you Christianize and civilize the man, you put story upon story, for you develop faculty after faculty; and you have to supply every story with your productions. The savage is a man one story deep; the civilized man is thirty stories deep.
H. W. BEECHER: Address in Liverpool, Oct 16, 1863

[*See also* Conservatism, Freedom.

Saving

[*See* Thrift, Wealth.

Saviour

[*See* Jesus Christ.

Saw

Full of wise saws and modern instances.
SHAKESPEARE: *As You Like It*, II, *c.* 1600

Saxony

Saxony is the schoolmaster of Germany.
GERMAN PROVERB

Scaffold

Every step of progress the world has made has been from scaffold to scaffold, and from stake to stake.
WENDELL PHILLIPS: Speech in Worcester, Mass., Oct. 15, 1851

Frankie walked up to the scaffold, as calm as a girl could be,
She turned her eyes to Heaven and said " Good Lord, I'm coming to Thee;
He was my man, but I done him wrong."
Anon.: *Frankie and Johnnie*, *c.* 1875

[*See also* Gallows, Hanging.

Scale

[*See* Weights and Measures.

Scandal

Greatest scandal waits on greatest state.
SHAKESPEARE: *The Rape of Lucrece*, 1594

At every word a reputation dies.
ALEXANDER POPE: *The Rape of the Lock*, III, 1712

Of unknown duchesses lewd tales we tell.
ALEXANDER POPE: *The Temple of Fame,* 1714

Scandal is but amusing ourselves with the faults, foibles, follies and reputations of our friends.
ROYALL TYLER: *The Contrast,* II, 1790

Dead scandals form good subjects for dissection. BYRON: *Don Juan,* I, 1819

You write that in some book I am said to be the natural son of the King of Prussia. I heard this long ago, but I have made it a rule never either to write anything about myself or to answer anything written about me by others.
LUDWIG VAN BEETHOVEN: *Letter to Dr. Wegler,* Oct. 7, 1826

It must be that scandals come, but woe to him by whom the scandal cometh.
Author unidentified: quoted by JAMES CARDINAL GIBBONS: *The Faith of Our Fathers,* III, 1876

One should never make one's début with a scandal; one should reserve that to give interest to one's old age.
OSCAR WILDE: *The Picture of Dorian Gray,* 1891

There is so much good in the worst of us,
And so much bad in the best of us,
That it hardly becomes any one of us
To talk about the rest of us.
Author unidentified

The most shy woman has courage enough to talk scandal. DUTCH PROVERB

[*See also* Chastity, Gossip, Praise, Sin, Slander, Tea.

Scandinavian

The Irish and the Dutch,
They don't amount to much,
But hooroo for the Scandinoovian!
AMERICAN FOLK RHYME, *c.* 1885 (*Dutch*= Germans)

[*See also* Dane, Norwegian, Swede.

Scapegoat

[*See* Goat.

Scar

He jests at scars that never felt a wound.
SHAKESPEARE: *Romeo and Juliet,* II, *c.* 1595

A scar nobly got, or a noble scar, is a good livery of honor.
SHAKESPEARE: *All's Well That Ends Well,* IV, *c.* 1602

Scratch a scar, and you are wounded twice.
RUSSIAN PROVERB

Scarecrow

The scarecrow does not uncover, even to the emperor.
DANSUI HOJO: *The Scarecrow, c.* 1700

It will remain to be examined in how far the scarecrow, as a clothed person, is not entitled to benefit of clergy, and trial by jury: nay, perhaps considering his high function (for is not he too a defender of property, and sovereign armed with the terrors of the law?), to a certain royal immunity and inviolability.
THOMAS CARLYLE: *Sartor Resartus,* I, 1836

Scenery

Scenery is fine, but human nature is finer.
JOHN KEATS: *Letter to Benjamin Bailey,* March 13, 1818

On a fair prospect some have looked,
And felt, as I have heard them say,
As if the moving time had been
A thing as steadfast as the scene
On which they gazed themselves away.
WILLIAM WORDSWORTH: *Peter Bell,* I, 1819

[*See also* Landscape, Travel.

Sceptre

[*See* Abdication.

Scheme

The best-laid schemes o' mice and men,
Gang aft a-gley,
And lea'e us nought but grief and pain,
For promised joy.
ROBERT BURNS: *To a Mouse,* 1785

Schiller, J. C. F. (1759–1805)

Schiller's blank verse is bad. He moves in it as a fly in a glue bottle. His thoughts have their connection and variety, it is true, but there is no sufficiently corresponding movement in the verse.
S. T. COLERIDGE: *Table-Talk,* June 2, 1834

Has nobody found Schiller out yet?
F. W. NIETZSCHE: *The Twilight of the Idols,* 1889

[*See also* Advice, Generosity.

Schism

[*See* Heresy.

Scholar

The scholar who loves comfort is not fit to be a scholar. CONFUCIUS: *Analects, c.* 500 B.C.

The scholar must keep himself free from stain. He does not go among the low to make himself seem high. He does not seek out the foolish to make himself seem wise. He does not praise those who think as he does, or condemn those who differ.
CONFUCIUS: *The Book of Rites,* XXXVIII, *c.* 500 B.C.

A scholar, possessing nothing of this world's goods, is like unto God.
POPE XYSTUS I: *The Ring, c.* 150

'Twere heavenly sport to see a train of scholars
Like old trained soldiers skirmish in the schools,
Traverse their ergos and discharge their jests
Like pearls of small-shot.
ANON.: *Humor Out of Breath,* I, 1608

An excellent scholar! One that hath a head filled with calves' brains without any sage in it.
JOHN WEBSTER: *The White Devil,* I, *c.* 1608

He was a scholar, and a ripe and good one;
Exceeding wise, fair-spoken, and persuading.
SHAKESPEARE and JOHN FLETCHER: *Henry VIII,* IV, 1613

A mere scholar, a mere ass.
ROBERT BURTON: *The Anatomy of Melancholy,* I, 1621

He that robs a scholar robs twenty men.
JOHN CLARKE: *Parœmiologia Anglo-Latina,* 1639

To talk in public, to think in solitude, to read and to hear, to inquire and answer inquiries, is the business of a scholar.
SAMUEL JOHNSON: *Rasselas,* VIII, 1759

A scholar knows nothing of boredom.
JEAN PAUL RICHTER: *Hesperus,* 1795

A mere scholar, who knows nothing but books, must be ignorant even of them.
WILLIAM HAZLITT: *The Ignorance of the Learned,* 1821

The office of the scholar is to cheer, to raise, and to guide men by showing them facts amidst appearances.
R. W. EMERSON: *The American Scholar,* 1837

A scholar is the favorite of Heaven and earth, the excellency of his country, the happiest of men.
R. W. EMERSON: *Literary Ethics,* 1838

The " thousand profound scholars " may have failed, first, because they were scholars, secondly, because they were profound, and thirdly, because they were a thousand.
E. A. POE: *The Rationale of Verse,* 1843 (The Pioneer, March)

Scholars are wont to sell their birthright for a mess of learning.
H. D. THOREAU: *A Week on the Concord and Merrimack Rivers,* 1849

The world's great men have not commonly been great scholars, nor its great scholars great men.
O. W. HOLMES: *The Autocrat of the Breakfast-Table,* VI, 1858

A man of learning, of habits, of whims and crotchets, such as are hardly to be found, except in old, unmarried students, — the double flowers of college culture, their stamina all turned to petals, their stock in the life of the race all funded in the individual.
O.W. HOLMES: *The Guardian Angel,* I, 1867

Every scholar is surrounded by wiser men than he.
R. W. EMERSON: *Clubs,* 1877

[*See also* Classes, Eminence, Learning, Pen, Politician, Schoolmaster, Steele (Richard).

Scholarship

When a woman turns to scholarship there is usually something wrong with her sexual apparatus.
F. W. NIETZSCHE: *Beyond Good and Evil,* 1886

The history of scholarship is a record of disagreements.
CHARLES E. HUGHES: Speech in Washington, May 7, 1936

[*See also* Learning, Scholar.

School

Thou hast most traitorously corrupted the youth of the realm in erecting a grammar school: and whereas, before, our forefathers had no other books but the score and the tally, thou hast caused printing to be used.
SHAKESPEARE: *II Henry VI,* IV, *c.* 1591

To go to school in a Summer morn,
Oh, it drives all joy away!
Under a cruel eye outworn,
The little ones spend the day —
In sighing and dismay.
WILLIAM BLAKE: *The Schoolboy, c.* 1790

At boarding-schools . . . the relaxation of the junior boys is mischief; and of the senior, vice.
MARY WOLLSTONECRAFT: *A Vindication of the Rights of Woman,* XII, 1792

The public school system of the several states is the bulwark of the American republic, and with a view to its security and permanence we recommend an amendment to the Constitution of the United States forbidding the application of any public funds or property for the benefit of any schools or institutions under sectarian control.
Republican National Platform, 1876

The free school is the promoter of that intelligence which is to preserve us a free nation; therefore the state or nation, or both combined, should support free institutions of learning sufficient to afford to every child growing up in the land the opportunity of a good common school education.
Republican National Platform, 1888

The frequenting of non-Catholic schools, whether neutral or mixed, those, namely, which are open to Catholics and non-Catholics alike, is forbidden for Catholic children, and can be at most tolerated on the approval of the ordinary alone.

POPE PIUS XI: *Divini illius magistri,* Dec. 31, 1929

[*See also* Boarding-school, Education.

Schoolboy

And then the whining schoolboy, with his satchel
And shining morning face, creeping like snail
Unwillingly to school.

SHAKESPEARE: *As You Like It,* II, *c.* 1600

'Twas in the prime of Summer time
An evening calm and cool,
And four-and-twenty happy boys
Came bounding out of school.

THOMAS HOOD: *Eugene Aram,* 1829

What money is better bestowed than that of a schoolboy's tip?

W. M. THACKERAY: *The Newcomes,* I, 1854

[*See also* Friendship, Vacation.

Schoolgirl

[*See* Maiden.

Schoolmaster

It is repetition, like cabbage served at every meal, that wears out the schoolmaster's life.

JUVENAL: *Satires,* VII, 118

A pure pedantic schoolmaster, sweeping his living from the posteriors of little children.

BEN JONSON: To William Drummond of Hawthornden, 1618

One father is more than a hundred schoolmasters.

GEORGE HERBERT: *Outlandish Proverbs,* 1640

It is boasted sometimes of a schoolmaster that such a brave man had his education under him, but it is never said how many who might have been brave men have been ruined by him.

COTTON MATHER: *Essays To Do Good,* 1710

There, in his noisy mansion, skill'd to rule,
The village master taught his little school;
A man severe he was, and stern to view, —
I knew him well, and every truant knew;
Well had the boding tremblers learn'd to trace
The day's disasters in his morning face;
Full well they laugh'd with counterfeited glee
At all his jokes, for many a joke had he;
Full well the busy whisper circling round
Convey'd the dismal tidings when he frown'd.

OLIVER GOLDSMITH: *The Deserted Village,* 1770

We are not quite at our ease in the presence of a schoolmaster because we are conscious that he is not quite at his ease in ours. He is awkward, and out of place, in the society of his equals. He comes like Gulliver from among his little people, and he cannot fit the stature of his understanding to yours. He is so used to teaching that he wants to be teaching *you.*

CHARLES LAMB: *The Old and the New Schoolmaster,* 1821 (London Magazine, May)

The schoolmaster is abroad, and I trust more to him, armed with his primer, against the soldier in full military array, for upholding and extending the liberties of his country.

HENRY BROUGHAM (LORD BROUGHAM and VAUX): Speech in the House of Commons, Jan. 29, 1828

Every good scholar is not a good schoolmaster.

H. G. BOHN: *Handbook of Proverbs,* 1855

When the Prussians beat the Austrians it is a victory of the Prussian schoolmaster over the Austrian schoolmaster.

OSKAR PESCHEL: *Die Lehren der jüngsten Kriegsgeschichte,* 1866 (Peschel's essay was published in a magazine on July 17, two weeks after the Battle of Sadowa. The common form of the saying is " The Prussian schoolmaster won the Battle of Sadowa." It was so used by Helmuth von Moltke in a speech in the Reichstag, Feb. 16, 1874)

A schoolmaster should have an atmosphere of awe, and walk wonderingly, as if he was amazed at being himself.

WALTER BAGEHOT: *Literary Studies,* I, 1879

One good schoolmaster is worth a thousand priests.

R. G. INGERSOLL: Speech in New York, May 1, 1881

Boys are given the impression that the masters know everything.

JOHN LUBBOCK (LORD AVEBURY): *The Pleasures of Life,* X, 1887

A schoolmaster spends his life telling the same people the same things about the same things.

GREEK PROVERB

[*See also* Education, Father, Fear, Pedagogue, Teacher, Teaching.

School, Public

[*See* Education.

Schopenhauer, Arthur (1788–1860)

A Schopenhauer, with logic and learning and wit, teaching pessimism, — teaching that this is the worst of all possible worlds, and inferring that sleep is better than waking, and death than sleep, — all the talent in the world cannot save him from being odious.

R. W. EMERSON: *Resources,* 1876

Schopenhauer is the last German to be really reckoned with. He is not a mere local or national phenomenon, but a European event like Goethe, Hegel and Heine.

F. W. NIETZSCHE: *The Twilight of the Idols,* 1889

Schubert, Franz (1797–1828)

My compositions spring from my sorrows. Those that give the world the greatest delight were born of my deepest griefs.

FRANZ SCHUBERT: *Diary,* March 27, 1824

Music has here entombed a rich possession, but still more beautiful hopes. (Die Tonkunst begrub hier einen reichen Besitz aber noch viel schoenere Hoffnungen.)

INSCRIPTION ON THE MONUMENT TO SCHUBERT IN VIENNA, 1872

Schubert, though he was inferior as an artist to other great musicians, had nevertheless the largest store of musical wealth. In his works are endless unused inventions: the greatness of his successors will consist in making use of them.

F. W. NIETZSCHE: *Human All-too-Human,* II, 1878

Schumann, Robert (1810–56)

A pathological case, a literary man turned composer.

JAMES HUNEKER: *Old Fogy,* XI, 1913

Science

To be acceptable as scientific knowledge a truth must be a deduction from other truths.

ARISTOTLE: *The Nicomachean Ethics,* VI, *c.* 340 B.C.

Keep that which is committed to thy trust, avoiding profane and vain babblings, and oppositions of science falsely so called.

I TIMOTHY VI, 20, *c.* 60

The skill of proceeding upon general and infallible rules.

THOMAS HOBBES: *Leviathan,* I, 1651

Science is the knowledge of consequences, and dependence of one fact upon another.

THOMAS HOBBES: *Leviathan,* V

Science [is] knowledge of the truth of propositions, and how things are called.

THOMAS HOBBES: *Human Nature,* VI, 1651

Is it not evident, in these last hundred years, that more errors of the school have been detected, more useful experiments in philosophy have been made, more noble secrets in optics, medicine, anatomy, astronomy, discovered, than in all those credulous and doting ages, from Aristotle to us? So true it is, than nothing spreads more fast than science, when rightly and generally cultivated.

JOHN DRYDEN: *Of Dramatic Poesy,* 1668

Science! thou fair effusive ray
From the great source of mental day,
Free, generous, and refin'd!

MARK AKENSIDE: *Hymn to Science,* 1739

There prevails among men of letters an opinion that all appearance of science is particularly hateful to women.

SAMUEL JOHNSON: *The Rambler,* Nov. 12, 1751

Science is nothing but good sense and sound reason.

STANISLAUS LESZCZYNSKI (KING OF POLAND): *Œuvres du philosophe bienfaisant,* 1763

Is it not true that the doctrine of attraction and gravity has done nothing but astonish our imagination? Is it not true that all the chemical discoveries have done only the same?

FREDERICK THE GREAT: *Letter to Jean le Rond D'Alembert,* Jan. 7, 1768

It is a fraud of the Christian system to call the sciences human invention; it is only the application of them that is human. Every science has for its basis a system of principles as fixed and unalterable as those by which the universe is regulated and governed. Man cannot make principles; he can only discover them.

THOMAS PAINE: *The Age of Reason,* I, 1794

Science has succeeded to poetry, no less in the little walks of children than with men. Is there no possibility of averting this sore evil?

CHARLES LAMB: *Letter to S. T. Coleridge,* Oct. 23, 1802

If science produces no better fruits than tyranny, murder, rapine and destitution of national morality, I would rather wish our country to be ignorant, honest and estimable, as our neighboring savages are.

THOMAS JEFFERSON: *Letter to John Adams,* 1812

Science [is]
But an exchange of ignorance for that
Which is another kind of ignorance.

BYRON: *Manfred,* II, 1817

Man is born not to solve the problems of the universe, but to find out where the problem begins, and then to restrain himself within the limits of the comprehensible.

J. W. GOETHE: *Conversations with Eckermann,* June 11, 1825

Without my attempts in natural science, I should never have learned to know mankind such as it is. In nothing else can we so closely approach pure contemplation and thought, so closely observe the errors of the senses and of the understanding.

J. W. GOETHE: *Conversations with Eckermann,* Feb. 13, 1829

The origin of all science is in the desire to know causes; and the origin of all false science and imposture is in the desire to accept false causes rather than none; or, which is the same thing, in the unwillingness to acknowledge our own ignorance.

WILLIAM HAZLITT: *Burke and the Edinburgh Phrenologists,* 1829 (The Atlas, Feb. 15)

Go on, fair science; soon to thee
Shall nature yield her idle boast;
Her vulgar fingers formed a tree,
But thou hast trained it to a post.

O. W. HOLMES: *The Meeting of the Dryads,* 1830

Can we unlearn the arts that pretend to civilize, and then burn the world? There is a march of science; but who shall beat the drums for its retreat?

CHARLES LAMB: *Letter to George Dyer,* Dec. 20, 1830

Science moves, but slowly, slowly, creeping on from point to point.

ALFRED TENNYSON: *Locksley Hall,* 1842

The work of science is to substitute facts for appearances, and demonstrations for impressions.

JOHN RUSKIN: *Stones of Venice,* III, 1853

Science is nothing but trained and organized common sense, differing from the latter only as a veteran may differ from a raw recruit: and its methods differ from those of common sense only as far as the guardsman's cut and thrust differ from the manner in which a savage wields his club.

T. H. HUXLEY: *On the Educational Value of the Natural History Sciences,* 1854 (Lecture in London)

Experience is the mother of science.

H. G. BOHN: *Handbook of Proverbs,* 1855

The task of science is to stake out the limits of the knowable, and to center consciousness within them.

RUDOLF VIRCHOW: *Cellular-Pathologie,* 1858

It is always observable that the physical and exact sciences are the last to suffer under despotisms.

R. H. DANA: *To Cuba and Back,* XIX, 1859

The generalizations of science sweep on in ever-widening circles, and more aspiring flights, through a limitless creation.

T. H. HUXLEY: *Letter to the London Times,* Dec. 26, 1859

The mortmain of theorists extinct in science clings as close as that of ecclesiastics defunct in law.

O. W. HOLMES: Address to the Massachusetts Medical Society, Boston, May 30, 1860

Science is organized knowledge.

HERBERT SPENCER: *Education,* II, 1861

Science concerns itself with the coexistence and sequences among phenomena; groups these at first into generalizations of a simple or low order, and rising gradually to higher and more extended generalizations.

HERBERT SPENCER: *First Principles,* I, 1862

Science has fulfilled her function when she has ascertained and enunciated truth.

T. H. HUXLEY: *Evidence as to Man's Place in Nature,* II, 1863

In science the important thing is to modify and change one's ideas as science advances.

CLAUDE BERNARD: *Introduction à la médecine expérimentale,* 1865

Science increases our power in proportion as it lowers our pride. IBID.

The growth [of science] consists in a continual analysis of facts of rough and general observation into groups of facts more precise and minute.

WALTER PATER: *Coleridge,* 1865

Science is a first-rate piece of furniture for a man's upper chamber, if he has common sense on the ground floor.

O. W. HOLMES: *The Poet at the Breakfast-Table,* V, 1872

The love of science, and the energy and honesty in the pursuit of science, in the best of the Aryan races, seem to correspond in a remarkable way to the love of conduct, and the energy and honesty in the pursuit of conduct, in the best of the Semitic.

MATTHEW ARNOLD: *Literature and Dogma,* XIII, 1873

My kingdom is as wide as the world, and my desire has no limit. I go forward always, freeing spirits and weighing worlds, without fear, without compassion, without love, and without God. Men call me science.

GUSTAVE FLAUBERT: *La tentation de Saint-Antoine,* 1874

Science arises from the discovery of identity amidst diversity.

W. J. JEVONS: *The Principles of Science,* 1874

Every science begins by accumulating observations, and presently generalizes these empirically; but only when it reaches the stage at which its empirical generalizations are included in a rational generalization does it become developed science.

HERBERT SPENCER: *The Data of Ethics,* IV, 1879

Scientific truths, of whatever order, are reached by eliminating perturbing or conflicting factors, and recognizing only fundamental factors.

HERBERT SPENCER: *The Data of Ethics,* XV

All human science is but the increment of the power of the eye.

JOHN FISKE: *The Destiny of Man,* VI, 1884

Science preceded the theory of science, and is independent of it. Science preceded naturalism, and will survive it.
A. J. BALFOUR: *The Foundations of Belief,* II, 1895

Science has promised us truth — an understanding of such relationships as our minds can grasp; it has never promised us either peace or happiness.
GUSTAVE LEBON: *Psychologie des foules,* intro., 1895

What is called science today consists of a haphazard heap of information, united by nothing, often utterly unnecessary, and not only failing to present one unquestionable truth, but as often as not containing the grossest errors, today put forward as truths, and tomorrow overthrown.
LYOF N. TOLSTOY: *What Is Religion?,* 1902

I hate and fear science because of my conviction that, for long to come if not for ever, it will be the remorseless enemy of mankind. I see it destroying all simplicity and gentleness of life, all the beauty of the world; I see it restoring barbarism under a mask of civilization: I see it darkening men's minds and hardening their hearts.
GEORGE GISSING: *The Private Papers of Henry Ryecroft,* 1903

Fed on the dry husks of facts, the human heart has a hidden want which science cannot supply.
WILLIAM OSLER: *Science and Immortality,* 1904

Science is nothing but developed perception, interpreted intent, common sense rounded out and minutely articulated.
GEORGE SANTAYANA: *The Life of Reason,* V, 1905

The extraordinary development of modern science may be her undoing. Specialism, now a necessity, has fragmented the specialities themselves in a way that makes the outlook hazardous. The workers lose all sense of proportion in a maze of minutiæ.
WILLIAM OSLER: Address before the Classical Association at Oxford, May 16, 1919

Science is an allegory that asserts that the relations between the parts of reality are similar to the relations between terms of discourse.
SCOTT BUCHANAN: *Poetry and Mathematics,* IV, 1929

Every great advance in science has issued from a new audacity of imagination.
JOHN DEWEY: *The Quest For Certainty,* XI, 1929

Science? Pooh! Whatever good has science done the world? Damned bosh!
GEORGE MOORE: To Philip Gosse, 1932

Scientific discovery and scientific knowledge have been achieved only by those who have gone in pursuit of them without any practical purpose whatsoever in view.
MAX PLANCK: *Where is Science Going?,* IV, 1932

Science has its being in a perpetual mental restlessness.
WILLIAM TEMPLE (ARCHBISHOP OF YORK): *Essays and Studies by Members of the English Association,* XVII, 1932

Science will fulfill what is demanded of it only on condition that it retain its freedom and independence in its work. In spite of all necessary limitations, liberty remains an essential characteristic of science, and spiritual and intellectual freedom is a necessity for scientists. Every true scientist desires to serve his nation. His work, however, cannot be complete if it is merely a service to his nation.
FERDINAND SAUERBRUCH: Speech at Dresden, Sept. 22, 1936

[*See also* Art, Constructive, Controversy, Criticism, Culture, Discovery, Fact, Faith, Falsehood, Freedom, Knowledge, Language, Mind, Philosopher, Philosophy, Poetry, Poetry and Prose, Research, Scientist, Superstition.

Science and Religion

Science is the great antidote to the poison of enthusiasm and superstition.
ADAM SMITH: *The Wealth of Nations,* V, 1776

Geology, ethnology, what not? —
(Greek endings, each the little passing bell
That signifies some faith's about to die.)
ROBERT BROWNING: *Bishop Blougram's Apology,* 1855

Religion has been compelled by science to give up one after another of its dogmas, of those assumed cognitions which it could not substantiate. In the meantime, science substituted for the personalities to which religion ascribed phenomena, certain metaphysical entities: and in doing this it trespassed on the province of religion; since it classed among the things which it comprehended certain forms of the incomprehensible.
HERBERT SPENCER: *First Principles,* I, 1862

Science, testing absolutely all thoughts, all works, has already burst well upon the world — a sun, mounting, most illuminating, most glorious — surely never again to set. But against it, deeply entrench'd, holding possession, yet remains, (not only through the churches and schools, but by imaginative literature, and unregenerate poetry,) the fossil theology of the mythic-materialistic, superstitious, untaught and credulous fable-loving, primitive ages of humanity.
WALT WHITMAN: *Democratic Vistas,* 1870

The church in no way forbids that each branch of learning have its own principles and methods, but, having recognized this freedom, she watches that they do not fall into error by opposing divine doctrine or overstepping their own bounds to usurp the field of faith.
Decree of the Vatican Council, April 24, 1870

The history of science is not a mere record of isolated discoveries; it is a narrative of the conflict of two contending powers, the expansive force of the human intellect on one side, and the compression arising from traditionary faith and human interest on the other.
J. W. DRAPER: *History of the Conflict Between Religion and Science*, pref., 1874

It is all up with priests and gods when man becomes scientific.
F. W. NIETZSCHE: *The Antichrist*, XLVIII, 1888

We should endow neither; we should treat them as we treat conservatism and liberalism, encouraging both, so that they may keep watch upon one another, and letting them go in and out of power with the popular vote concerning them.
SAMUEL BUTLER: *Note-Books*, *c.* 1890

Science is the record of dead religions.
OSCAR WILDE: *Phrases and Philosophies for the Use of the Young*, 1894

The church saves sinners, but science seeks to stop their manufacture.
ELBERT HUBBARD: *Roycroft Dictionary and Book of Epigrams*, 1923

Scientist

All scientific men were formerly accused of practising magic. And no wonder, for each said to himself: "I have carried human intelligence as far as it will go, and yet So-and-so has gone further than I. *Ergo*, he has taken to sorcery."
C. L. DE MONTESQUIEU: *Persian Letters*, CXLV, 1721

The republic has no use for scientists.
Slogan of the Jacobins at the trial of A. L. Lavoisier before the Revolutionary Tribunal at Paris, 1794

I traveled the highroad of science in the manner of dogs taken out for exercise by their masters. That is, I turned backward and forward a hundred times, and when I arrived I was very tired.
G. C. LICHTENBERG: *Reflections*, 1799

Professors in every branch of the sciences prefer their own theories to truth: the reason is that their theories are private property, but the truth is common stock.
C. C. COLTON: *Lacon*, 1820

He has something demoniacal about him who can discern a law or couple two facts.
H. D. THOREAU: *Excursions*, 1863

It is in the darker areas of science that great men win recognition; they are distinguished by ideas which light up phenomena hitherto obscure, and so carry science forward.
CLAUDE BERNARD: *Introduction à la médecine expérimentale*, 1865

Their business is not with the possible, but the actual — not with a world which might be, but with a world that is. They have but one desire — to know the truth. They have but one fear — to believe a lie.
JOHN TYNDALL: Address in Liverpool, Sept. 16, 1870

What men of science want is only a fair day's wages for more than a fair day's work.
T. H. HUXLEY: *Administrative Nihilism*, 1871

Up to the age of thirty or beyond it, poetry such as Milton, Byron, Wordsworth, etc. gave me great delight. But now for many years I cannot endure to read a line of poetry. I have lost my taste for pictures and music. My mind seems to have become a kind of machine for grinding general laws out of large collections of facts.
CHARLES DARWIN: Autobiographical note, *c.* 1875

I suppose that the first chemists seemed to be very hard-hearted and unpoetical persons when they scouted the glorious dream of the alchemists that there must be some process for turning base metals into gold. I suppose that the men who first said, in plain, cold assertion, there is no fountain of eternal youth, seemed to be the most cruel and cold-hearted adversaries of human happiness.
W. G. SUMNER: *The Forgotten Man*, 1883

Bourgeois scientists make sure that their theories are not dangerous to God or to capital.
GEORGE PLECHANOFF: *Karl Marx*, 1903

The scientist does not study nature because it is useful; he studies it because he delights in it, and he delights in it because it is beautiful.
HENRI POINCARÉ (1854–1912)

All the conditions of happiness are realized in the life of the man of science.
BERTRAND RUSSELL: *The Conquest of Happiness*, X, 1930

It is not the *possession* of knowledge, of irrefutable truths, that constitutes the man of science, but the disinterested, incessant *search* for truth.
KARL POPPER: *Logik der Forschung*, 1935

There is no possibility of telling whether the issue of scientists' work will prove them to be fiends, or dreamers, or angels.
LORD RAYLEIGH: Address to the British Association, Cambridge, 1939

[*See also* Artist, Laboratory, Research, Science, Truth.

Scoffing

[*See* Piety.

Scold

A frank scold is a devil of the feminine gender; a serpent perpetually hissing, and spitting of venom; a composition of ill-nature and clamor. You may call her animated gunpowder, a walking Mount Etna that is always belching forth flames of sulphur, or a real Purgatory, more to be dreaded in this world than the pope's imaginary hothouse in the next.

Anon.: *Poor Robin's True Character of a Scold,* 1678

He fasts enough whose wife scolds all dinner-time.

H. G. BOHN: *Handbook of Proverbs,* 1855

Scorn

The scorner is an abomination to men.

PROVERBS XXIV, 9, *c.* 350 B.C.

Oh, what a deal of scorn looks beautiful
In the contempt and anger of his lip!

SHAKESPEARE: *Twelfth Night,* III, *c.* 1601

We shall find no fiend in Hell can match the fury of a disappointed woman, — scorned, slighted, dismissed without a parting pang.

COLLEY CIBBER: *Love's Last Shift,* IV, 1696

Heaven has no rage like love to hatred turned,
Nor Hell a fury like a woman scorned.

WILLIAM CONGREVE: *The Mourning Bride,* III, 1697

Never was a scornful person well received.

THOMAS FULLER: *Gnomologia,* 1732

[*See also* Jest.

Scotch

Scots are like witches: do but whet your pen,
Scratch till the blood come, they'll not hurt
you then.

JOHN CLEVELAND: *The Rebel Scot,* 1647

A dark, carnal people.

GEORGE FOX: *Journal,* XI, 1694 (*c.* 1657)

A nation famed for song, and beauty's charms;
Zealous, yet modest; innocent, though free;
Patient of toil; serene amidst alarms;
Inflexible in faith; invincible in arms.

JAMES BEATTIE: *The Minstrel,* I, 1771

They are a nation just rising from barbarity; long contented with necessaries, now somewhat studious of convenience, but not yet arrived at delicate discrimination.

SAMUEL JOHNSON: *Letter to Hester Thrale,* Sept. 30, 1773

The whole nation hitherto has been void of wit and humor, and even incapable of relishing it.

HORACE WALPOLE: *Letter to Horace Mann,* 1778

What is the reason that the Scots are in general more religious, more faithful, more honest, and industrious than the Irish? I do not mean to insinuate national reflections, God forbid!

ST. JOHN DE CRÈVECOEUR: *Letters From an American Farmer,* III, 1782

Scots, wha hae wi' Wallace bled,
Scots, wham Bruce has aften led,
Welcome to your gory bed,
Or to victory!

ROBERT BURNS: *Bruce to His Men at Bannockburn,* 1793

[*See also* Ballad, Irish, Scotsman.

Scotched

We have scotch'd the snake, not killed it.

SHAKESPEARE: *Macbeth,* III, *c.* 1605

Scotland

This realme of Scotland is our inheritance as a porcione of the warld allowit to our natione and antecessouris, quhame we succeid. Than quhair may thir be bettir weir than to meanteine this our naturall inheritaunce?

JOHN STEWART (DUKE OF ALBANY and REGENT OF SCOTLAND): *Proclamation,* 1522

He that will England win,
Must with Scotland first begin.

ENGLISH PROVERB, traced to the early XVI century

Whoso will France win
Must with Scotland first begin.

RAPHAEL HOLINSHED: *Chronicles,* 1577

Had Cain been Scot, God would have changed
his doom,
Nor forced him wander, but confined him
home.

JOHN CLEVELAND: *The Rebel Scot,* 1647

There none are swept by sudden fate away,
But all whom hunger spares with age decay.

SAMUEL JOHNSON: *London,* 1738

Seeing Scotland is only seeing a worse England.

SAMUEL JOHNSON: *Boswell's Life,* April 7, 1778

If one man in Scotland gets possession of two thousand pounds what remains for the rest of the nation?

SAMUEL JOHNSON: *Boswell's Life,* May 8, 1781

Itchland, Scratchland, Scotland.

FRANCIS GROSE: *A Classical Dictionary of the Vulgar Tongue,* 1785

O Caledonia! stern and wild,
Meet nurse for a poetic child!
Land of brown heath and shaggy wood,
Land of the mountain and the flood,
Land of my sires! what mortal hand
Can e'er untie the filial band,
That knits me to thy rugged strand!

WALTER SCOTT: *The Lay of the Last Minstrel,* VI, 1805

My birth-land is always as the cave of Trophonius to me; I return from it with a haste to which the speed of steam is slow.
THOMAS CARLYLE: *Letter to R. W. Emerson,* May 8, 1841

Scotland, that knuckle-end of England, that land of Calvin, oatcakes and sulphur.
Ascribed to SYDNEY SMITH in *A Memoir of the Rev. Sydney Smith* by his daughter, Lady Holland, 1855

In Scotland, there is a rapid loss of all grandeur of mien and manners; a provincial eagerness and acuteness appear; the poverty of the country makes itself remarked, and a coarseness of manners; and, among the intellectual, is the insanity of dialectics.
R. W. EMERSON: *English Traits,* IV, 1856

I wonder'd not when I was told
The venal Scot his country sold:
I rather very much admire
How he could ever find a buyer.
Author unidentified

[*See also* Oats, Scotch, Scotsman, Switzerland.

Scotsman

In every quarter of the world you will find a Scot, a rat and a Newcastle grindstone.
ENGLISH PROVERB, first recorded in 1662

As false as a Scot.
JOHN RAY: *English Proverbs,* 1670

The noblest prospect which a Scotchman ever sees is the high road that leads him to England.
SAMUEL JOHNSON: *Boswell's Life,* July 6, 1763

Much may be made of a Scotchman, if he be caught young.
SAMUEL JOHNSON: *Boswell's Life,* April 19, 1772

Three failures and a fire make a Scotsman's fortune.
ENGLISH PROVERB, not recorded before the XIX century

I have been trying all my life to like Scotchmen, and am obliged to desist from the experiment in despair. . . . Is he orthodox — he has no doubts. Is he an infidel — he has none either. Between the affirmative and the negative there is no borderland with him. His taste never fluctuates. His morality never abates. He cannot compromise, or understand middle actions. There can be but a right and a wrong.
CHARLES LAMB: *Imperfect Sympathies,* 1821 (London Magazine, Aug.)

The Scot will not fight until he sees his own blood.
WALTER SCOTT: *The Fortunes of Nigel,* I, 1822 (Cited as a proverb)

Mackintosh came up from Scotland with a metaphysical head, a cold heart, and open hands.
SAMUEL PARR (1747–1825): Said of Sir James Mackintosh (1765–1832)

I have generally found a Scotchman with a little literature very disagreeable. He is a superficial German or a dull Frenchman.
S. T. COLERIDGE: *Table-Talk,* Aug. 6, 1832

It requires a surgical operation to get a joke well into a Scotch understanding.
Ascribed to SYDNEY SMITH in *A Memoir of the Rev. Sydney Smith* by his daughter, Lady Holland, 1855

It has been my lot to have found myself in many distant lands. I have never been in one without finding a Scotchman, and I never found a Scotchman who was not at the head of the poll — he was prosperous; he was thriving; often the confidential adviser of persons of the highest position, even of rulers of states.
BENJAMIN DISRAELI: Speech in Glasgow, Nov. 19, 1873

They tell me it takes a surgical operation to get a joke into a Scotsman's head, but I don't see how you could get a joke into anyone's head by a surgical operation.
Ascribed to an anonymous Scotsman; author unidentified

Propinquity: in close and intimate association, as a Scotchman and a louse.
Author unidentified

[*See also* Character (National), Lawyer, Presbyterian, Scotch, Scotland, Soldier.

Scott, Walter (1771–1832)

The Ariosto of the North.
BYRON: *Childe Harold,* IV, 1818

The big bow-wow strain I can do like anyone going, but the exquisite touch which renders ordinary commonplace things and characters interesting, from the truth of the description and the sentiment, is denied to me.
WALTER SCOTT: *Diary,* March, 1826

When I am very ill indeed, I can read Scott's novels, and they are almost the only books I can then read. I cannot at such times read the Bible; my mind reflects on it, but I can't bear the open page.
S. T. COLERIDGE: *Table-Talk,* Nov. 1, 1833

Of all the habits of life, none clung longer to him than his extreme repugnance to being helped in anything.
J. G. LOCKHART: *Life of Scott,* II, 1838

Scoundrel

He who slanders an absent friend, he who does not defend him when he is attacked, he who seeks eagerly to raise the senseless laugh and acquire the fame of wit, he who cannot keep

a friend's secret; that man is a scoundrel. Mark him and avoid him.
HORACE: *Satires*, I, *c.* 25 B.C.

[*See also* Gambling, Liberal, May, Patriotism.

Scrap of Paper

[*See* Treaty.

Scratching

Scratching is bad, because it begins with pleasure and ends with pain.
THOMAS FULLER: *Gnomologia*, 1732

[*See also* Scotland.

Scribe

Beware of the scribes, which love to go in long clothing, and love salutations in the marketplaces, and the chief seats in the synagogues, and the uppermost rooms at feasts: which devour widows' houses, and for a pretence make long prayers: these shall receive greater damnation. MARK XII, 38–40, *c.* 70

Scripture

[*See* Bible.

Scruple

He could raise scruples dark and nice,
And after solve 'em in a trice:
As if divinity had catch'd
The itch, of purpose to be scratch'd.
SAMUEL BUTLER: *Hudibras*, I, 1663

Too much scruple is only concealed pride.
J. W. GOETHE: *Iphigenie auf Tauris*, IV, 1787

In times like these in which we live, it will not do to be overscrupulous.
ALEXANDER HAMILTON: *Letter to John Jay*, 1800

Sculpture

A fellow will hack half a year at a block of marble to make something in stone that hardly resembles a man. The value of statuary is owing to its difficulty. You would not value the finest head cut upon a carrot.
SAMUEL JOHNSON: *Boswell's Life*, March 19, 1776

The cold marble leapt to life a god.
H. H. MILMAN: *The Belvedere Apollo*, *c.* 1820

It is the great scope of the sculptor to heighten nature into heroic beauty; i.e., in plain English, to surpass his model.
BYRON: *Letter to John Murray*, Feb. 7, 1821

Upon all forms of sculptural ornament the effect of time is such, that if the design be poor, it will enrich it; if overcharged, simplify it; if harsh and violent, soften it; if smooth and obscure, exhibit it.
JOHN RUSKIN: *Modern Painters*, II, 1846

Sculpture is not the mere cutting of the *form* of any thing in stone; it is the cutting of the *effect* of it.
JOHN RUSKIN: *Lectures on Architecture and Painting*, II, 1853

[*See also* Painting.

Scythian

[*See* Drinking, Wine.

Sea

All the rivers run into the sea, yet the sea is not full. ECCLESIASTES I, 7, *c.* 200 B.C.

The sea is his, and he made it.
PSALMS XCV, 5, *c.* 150 B.C.

Praise the sea; on shore remain.
JOHN FLORIO: *Second Frutes*, 1591

Unpathed waters, undreamed shores.
SHAKESPEARE: *The Winter's Tale*, IV, *c.* 1611

He that will learn to pray, let him go to sea.
GEORGE HERBERT: *Jacula Prudentum*, 1651

He goes a great voyage that goes to the bottom of the sea.
THOMAS FULLER: *Gnomologia*, 1732

The sea refuses no river. IBID.

Day after day, day after day the same —
A weary waste of waters!
ROBERT SOUTHEY: *Madoc in Wales*, IV, 1805

There is a pleasure in the pathless woods,
There is a rapture on the lonely shore;
There is society, where none intrudes,
By the deep sea, and music in its roar.
BYRON: *Childe Harold*, IV, 1818

The sea I found
Calm as a cradled child in dreamless slumber bound.
P. B. SHELLEY: *The Revolt of Islam*, I, 1818

Perilous seas, in faery lands forlorn.
JOHN KEATS: *To a Nightingale*, 1819

I never saw the use of the sea. Many a sad heart it has caused, and many a sick stomach has it occasioned. The boldest sailor climbs on board with a heavy soul, and leaps on land with a light spirit.
BENJAMIN DISRAELI: *Vivian Grey*, 1837

Salt water cures love sooner than anything else.
FREDERICK MARRYAT: *Poor Jack*, 1840

It was the schooner Hesperus,
That sailed the wintry sea.
H. W. LONGFELLOW: *The Wreck of the Hesperus*, 1841

Break, break, break,
On thy cold gray stones, O sea!
And I would that my tongue could utter
The thoughts that arise in me.
ALFRED TENNYSON: *Break, Break, Break*, 1842

And to our age's drowsy blood
Still shouts the inspiring sea.
J. R. LOWELL: *The Vision of Sir Launfal*, I, 1848

I am in the habit of going to sea whenever I begin to grow hazy about the eyes, and to be overconscious of my lungs.
HERMAN MELVILLE: *Moby Dick*, I, 1851

Sea of stretch'd ground-swells!
Sea breathing broad and convulsive breaths!
Sea of the brine of life! sea of unshovell'd yet always-ready graves!
Howler and scooper of storms! capricious and dainty sea!
I am integral with you — I too am of one phase, and of all phases.
WALT WHITMAN: *Walt Whitman*, 1855

I find the sea-life an acquired taste, like that for tomatoes and olives. The confinement, cold, motion, noise, and odor are not to be dispensed with.
R. W. EMERSON: *English Traits*, II, 1856

The sea drowns out humanity and time: it has no sympathy with either, for it belongs to eternity, and of that it sings its monotonous song for ever and ever.
O. W. HOLMES: *The Autocrat of the Breakfast-Table*, XI, 1858

The sea is feline. It licks your feet — its huge flanks purr very pleasant for you; but it will crack your bones and eat you, for all that, and wipe the crimsoned foam from its jaws as if nothing had happened. IBID.

There are certain things — as, a spider, a ghost,
The income-tax, gout, an umbrella for three —
That I hate, but the thing that I hate the most
Is a thing they call the sea.
C. L. DODGSON (LEWIS CARROLL): *A Sea Dirge*, 1869

The sea hath no king but God alone.
D. G. ROSSETTI: *The White Ship*, 1881

Take back your golden fiddles, and we'll beat to open sea.
RUDYARD KIPLING: *The Last Chantey*, 1892

Who hath desired the sea? — the immense and contemptuous surges?
The shudder, the stumble, the swerve, as the star-stabbing bowsprit emerges?
RUDYARD KIPLING: *The Sea and the Hills*, 1902

There does be a power of young men floating round in the sea.
J. M. SYNGE: *Riders to the Sea*, 1904

Faithful to no race after the manner of the kindly earth, receiving no impress from valor and toil and self-sacrifice, recognizing no finality of dominion, the sea has never adopted the cause of its masters like the land.
JOSEPH CONRAD: *The Mirror of the Sea*, XII, 1906

Absolute freedom of navigation upon the seas, outside territorial waters, alike in peace and in war, except as the seas may be closed in whole or in part by international action for the enforcement of international covenants.
WOODROW WILSON: Address to Congress, Jan. 8, 1918 (One of the Fourteen Points)

One penny is better on land than ten on the sea.
DANISH PROVERB

If you were born at sea, you will die on it.
JAPANESE PROVERB

God has given the earth to the faithful, and the sea to the infidels. TURKISH PROVERB

[*See also* Black Sea, Churchyard, Diary, Evil, Fish, Land, Navy (British), Ocean, Sailor, Seasickness, Ship, Untameable.

Sea-change

[*See* Change.

Seaman

[*See* Sailor.

Seaport

All seaports are harlots. Author unidentified

Sea-power

The trident of Neptune is the sceptre of the world.
A. M. LEMIERRE: *Commerce*, *c.* 1775

[*See also* Admiralty, Gun, Shipping.

Search

The right of the people to be secure in their persons, houses, papers, and effects, against unreasonable searches and seizures, shall not be violated, and no warrants shall issue but upon probable cause, supported by oath or affirmation, and particularly describing the place to be searched, and the persons or things to be seized.
CONSTITUTION OF THE UNITED STATES, Amendment IV, Dec. 15, 1791

Seasickness

The best of remedies is a beefsteak,
Against seasickness; try it, sir, before
You sneer. BYRON: *Don Juan*, II, 1819

The only cure for seasickness is to sit on the shady side of an old brick church in the country. ENGLISH SAILORS' PROVERB

[*See also* Black Sea, Travel.

Season

To every thing there is a season, and a time to every purpose under the heaven.
ECCLESIASTES III, 1, *c.* 200 B.C.

Out of season, out of price.
ROBERT SOUTHWELL: *Loss in Delay*, *c.* 1595

War, Holy

When ye encounter the unbelievers, strike off their heads, until ye have made a great slaughter among them. Verily, if God pleased, He could take vengeance on them without your assistance, but He commandeth you to fight His battles.

THE KORAN, XLVII, *c.* 625

War-horse

He saith among the trumpets, Ha, Ha! and he smelleth the battle afar off, the thunder of the captains, and the shouting.

JOB XXIX, 25, *c.* 325 B.C.

Wariness

Cautelous suspense, for want of assurance, is better than confident presumption, upon pregnancy of imagination.

BENJAMIN WHICHCOTE: *Moral and Religious Aphorisms,* 1753 (*Cautelous*= wary)

Warlike

In military affairs, and all others of like nature, the study of the sciences does more soften and enervate the courage of men than fortify and incite it. . . . Rome was more valiant before she grew so learned; and the most warlike nations of our time are the most ignorant.

MICHEL DE MONTAIGNE: *Essays,* I, 1580

[*See also* Army.

War, Mexican

We come to overthrow the tyrants who have destroyed your liberties, but we come to make no war upon the people of Mexico.

ZACHARY TAYLOR: Proclamation to the people of Mexico, July 9, 1846

Base in object, atrocious in beginning, immoral in all its influence, vainly prodigal of treasure and life, it is a war of infamy, which must blot the pages of our history.

CHARLES SUMNER: Speech in Boston, Nov. 5, 1846

The war has not been waged with a view to conquest.

JAMES POLK: Message to Congress, Dec. 8, 1846

I believe it to be a war of pretexts, a war in which the true motive is not distinctly avowed, but in which pretenses, afterthoughts, evasions and other methods are employed to put a case before the community which is not the true case.

DANIEL WEBSTER: Speech in Springfield, Mass., Sept. 29, 1847

To this day [I] regard the war as one of the most unjust ever waged by a stronger against a weaker nation. It was an instance of a republic following the bad example of European monarchies, in not considering justice in their desire to acquire additional territory.

U. S. GRANT: *Personal Memoirs,* III, 1885

Warning

No man provokes me with impunity. (Nemo me impune lacessit.)

MOTTO OF THE ORDER OF THE THISTLE, 1540

Don't take any wooden nickels.

AMERICAN SAYING

[*See also* Advice, Thanks, Touch.

War of 1812

A war not of defense, but of conquest, of aggrandizement, of ambition — a war foreign to the interests of this country; to the interests of humanity itself.

JOHN RANDOLPH: Speech in the House of Representatives, Dec. 10, 1811

In such a cause, with the aid of Providence, we must come out crowned with success; but, if we fail, let us fail like men, lash ourselves to our gallant tars, and expire together in one common struggle, fighting for free trade and seamen's rights.

HENRY CLAY: Speech in the House of Representatives, Jan. 8, 1813

The last American war was to us only something to talk or read about; but to the Americans it was the cause of misery in their own homes.

S. T. COLERIDGE: *Table-Talk,* May 21, 1830

Warrior

The free man is a warrior. He tramples ruthlessly upon that contemptible kind of comfort that grocers, Christians, cows, women, Englishmen and other democrats worship.

F. W. NIETZSCHE: *The Twilight of the Idols,* 1889

[*See also* Soldier.

Warship

[*See* Liner, Navy.

Wart

[*See* Portrait.

War, World

The lamps are going out all over Europe; we shall not see them lit again in our lifetime.

EDWARD GREY: To a caller at the Foreign Office, Aug. 3, 1914

They shall not pass. (Ils ne passeront pas.)

HENRI PÉTAIN: To General de Castelnau at Verdun, Feb., 1916

The plain truth is that the war is imperialistic on both sides.

NIKOLAI LENIN: *Letters from Afar,* I, March 20, 1917

The man who does not think it was America's duty to fight for her own sake in view of the infamous conduct of Germany toward us stands on a level with a man who wouldn't think it necessary to fight in a private quarrel because his wife's face was slapped.

THEODORE ROOSEVELT: Speech in Oyster Bay, L. I., April, 1917

We are fighting in the quarrel of civilization against barbarism, of liberty against tyranny. Germany has become a menace to the whole world. She is the most dangerous enemy of liberty now existing. She has shown herself utterly ruthless, treacherous, and brutal. When I use these words, I use them with scientific precision. IBID.

The right is more precious than peace, and we shall fight for the things which we have always carried nearest our hearts, — for democracy, for the right of those who submit to authority to have a voice in their own governments, for the rights and liberties of small nations, for a universal dominion of right by such a concert of free peoples as shall bring peace and safety to all nations and make the world itself at last free.

WOODROW WILSON: Address to Congress, April 2, 1917

Lafayette, we are here.

COL. C. E. STANTON: Speech in Paris, July 4, 1917

This war, like the next war, is a war to end war.

Ascribed to DAVID LLOYD GEORGE, *c.* 1917

They say it is a terrible war, parley-voo
They say it is a terrible war,
But what the hell are we fighting it for?
Hinkey Dinkey, parley-voo!

Anon.: British soldiers' song, 1914–18

This is the culminating and final war for human liberty.

WOODROW WILSON: Message to Congress, Jan. 8, 1918

The allied and associated governments affirm and Germany accepts the responsibility of Germany and her allies for causing all the loss and damage to which the allied and associated governments and their nationals have been subjected as a consequence of the war imposed upon them by the aggression of Germany and her allies.

TREATY OF VERSAILLES, CCXXXI, 1919

Washday

Home, and, being washing-day, dined upon cold meat.

SAMUEL PEPYS: *Diary*, April 4, 1666

They that wash Monday got all the week to dry,
They that wash Tuesday are pretty near by,
They that wash Wednesday make a good housewife,
They that wash Thursday must wash for their life,
They that wash Friday must wash in need,
They that wash Saturday are sluts indeed.

OLD ENGLISH RHYME

Washing

Wash your hands often, your feet seldom, and your head never.

JOHN RAY: *English Proverbs*, 1670

It belongs to decency to wash the hands before sitting down to table, and it is even considered indispensably necessary.

ST. JOHN BAPTIST DE LA SALLE: *The Rules of Christian Manners and Civility*, II, 1695

[*See also* Hygiene.

Washington, George (1732–99)

A gentleman of one of the first fortunes upon the continent . . . sacrificing his ease, and hazarding all in the cause of his country.

JOHN ADAMS: *Letter to Elbridge Gerry*, June 18, 1775

The father of his country.

FRANCIS BAILEY: *Lancaster Almanack*, 1779

His memory will be adored while liberty shall have votaries, his name will triumph over time and will in future ages assume its just station among the most celebrated worthies of the world.

THOMAS JEFFERSON: *Notes on Virginia*, 1782

O Washington, how do I love thy name! How have I often adored and blessed thy God for creating and forming thee the great ornament of human kind.

EZRA STILES: *The United States Elevated to Glory and Honor*, 1783

The character and service of this gentleman are sufficient to put all those men called kings to shame. While they are receiving from the sweat and labors of mankind a prodigality of pay to which neither their abilities nor their services can entitle them, he is rendering every service in his power, and refusing every pecuniary reward. He accepted no pay as commander-in-chief; he accepts none as President of the United States.

THOMAS PAINE: *The Rights of Man*, II, 1791

He errs as other men do, but errs with integrity.

THOMAS JEFFERSON: *Letter to W. B. Giles*, 1795

As to you, sir, treacherous to private friendship (for so you have been to me, and that in the day of danger) and a hypocrite in public life, the world will be puzzled to decide whether you are an apostate or an impostor, whether you have abandoned good principles or whether you ever had any.

THOMAS PAINE: *Letter to Washington*, July 30, 1796 (Cf. PAINE, *ante*, 1791)

There are features in his face totally different from what I ever observed in that of any other human being; the sockets of the eyes, for instance, are larger, and the upper part of the nose broader. All his features are indicative of the strongest passions; yet his judgment and great self-command make him appear a man of a different cast in the eyes of the world.

GILBERT STUART: To Isaac Weld, *c.* 1797

First in war, first in peace, and first in the hearts of his countrymen.

HENRY (LIGHT-HORSE HARRY) LEE: *Eulogy on Washington*, Dec. 26, 1799

There has scarcely appeared a really great man whose character has been more admired in his lifetime, or less correctly understood by his admirers. . . . His talents . . . were adapted to lead without dazzling mankind, and to draw forth and employ the talents of others without being misled by them.

FISHER AMES: Oration in Boston, Feb. 8, 1800

I can't tell a lie, Pa; you know I can't tell a lie. I did cut it with my hatchet.

MASON L. WEEMS: *The Life of George Washington*, I, 1800 (This was the first appearance of the cherry-tree story)

His mind was great and powerful, without being of the very first order; his penetration strong, though not so acute as that of a Newton, Bacon, or Locke; and as far as he saw, no judgment was ever sounder. It was slow in operation, being little aided by invention or imagination, but sure in conclusion.

THOMAS JEFFERSON: *Letter to Walter Jones*, Jan., 1814

Washington . . . sold the very charger who had taken him through all his battles.

JOHN KEATS: *Letter to Georgiana Keats*, Oct. 14–31, 1818

America has furnished to the world the character of Washington. And if our American institutions have done nothing else that alone would have entitled them to the respect of mankind.

DANIEL WEBSTER: Address on laying the cornerstone of the Bunker Hill Monument, June 17, 1825

Washington's face was as cut and dry as a diagram.

LEIGH HUNT: *The Companion*, XIII, 1828

Surely Washington was the greatest man that ever lived in this world uninspired by divine wisdom and unsustained by supernatural virtue.

HENRY BROUGHAM (LORD BROUGHAM AND VAUX): *Statesmen in the Time of George III*, III, 1839

Washington is the mightiest name on earth — long since mightiest in the cause of civil liberty; still mightiest in moral reformation. On that name an eulogy is expected. Let none attempt it. In solemn awe pronounce the name and in its naked, deathless splendor leave it shining on.

ABRAHAM LINCOLN: Speech in Springfield, Ill., Feb. 22, 1842

Old George Washington's forte was not to hev eny public man of the present day resemble him to eny alarmin extent.

C. F. BROWNE (ARTEMUS WARD): *Artemus Ward: His Book*, 1862

George Washington, as a boy, was ignorant of of the commonest accomplishments of youth. He could not even lie.

S. L. CLEMENS (MARK TWAIN): *Brief Biographical Sketch of George Washington*, 1867

In Washington, America found a leader who could be induced by no earthly motive to tell a falsehood, or to break an engagement, or to commit any dishonorable act.

W. E. H. LECKY: *History of England in the Eighteenth Century*, I, 1878

[*See also* Dignity, Greatness, Pay, Posterity, Presidency.

Wasp

Of all the plagues that Heaven has sent,
A wasp is most impertinent.

JOHN GAY: *Fables*, I, 1727

See the wasp. He has pretty yellow stripes around his body, and a darning needle in his tail. If you will pat the wasp upon the tail we will give you a nice picture book.

EUGENE FIELD: *The Tribune Primer*, 1882

Waste

Wilful waste brings woeful want.

THOMAS FULLER: *Gnomologia*, 1732

The nakedness of the indigent world may be clothed from the trimmings of the vain.

OLIVER GOLDSMITH: *The Vicar of Wakefield*, IV, 1766

Waste is not grandeur.

WILLIAM MASON: *The English Garden*, II, 1772

Waste not; want not.

ENGLISH PROVERB, not recorded in its present form before the XIX century

It is the elimination and utilization of waste, waste effort, waste time and material, the minimizing of destruction and damage, wear and tear that produce the great results in the industrial world. There is no magic in these accomplishments. The leaders in action or thought are not magicians, but steady persistent workers.

THEODORE N. VAIL (1845–1920)

He is as wasteful as one who salts the sea.

WELSH PROVERB

[*See also* Haste, Son (Younger).

Sect

The union of a sect within itself is a pitiful charity; it's no concord of Christians, but a conspiracy against Christ; and they that love one another for their opinionative concurrences love for their own sakes, not their Lord's.
JOSEPH GLANVILL: *The Vanity of Dogmatizing*, XXIII, 1661

Petulant capricious sects,
The maggots of corrupted texts.
SAMUEL BUTLER: *Hudibras*, III, 1678

A thousand daily sects rise up and die;
A thousand more the perished race supply.
JOHN DRYDEN: *Religio Laici*, 1682

With respect to what are called denominations of religion, if everyone is left to judge of his own religion, there is no such thing as a religion that is wrong; but if they are to judge of each other's religion, there is no such thing as a religion that is right; and therefore all the world is right, or all the world is wrong.
THOMAS PAINE: *The Rights of Man*, I, 1791

In America the taint of sectarianism lies broad upon the land. The nation is sectarian, rather than Christian.
J. FENIMORE COOPER: *The American Democrat*, XLV, 1838

Sect-founders are a class I do not like. No truly great man, from Jesus Christ downwards, ever founded a sect — I mean wilfully intended founding one.
THOMAS CARLYLE: *Letter to R. W. Emerson*, Nov. 17, 1842

[*See also* Religion, Theology.

Secularism

A form of opinion which concerns itself only with questions, the issues of which can be tested by the experience of this life.
G. J. HOLYOAKE: *The Origin and Nature of Secularism*, 1896

These are the blighters who want to rob us of our bloody religion!
Exclamation of a drunken woman who rushed out of a pub in East London to protest against a street meeting of secularists

Security

[*See* Property, Uncertainty.

Sedition

These filthy dreamers . . . despise dominion, and speak evil of dignities. JUDE 8, *c.* 50

Them that . . . despise government, presumptuous are they, selfwilled, they are not afraid to speak evil of dignities.
II PETER II, 10 *c.* 60

Libels and licentious discourses against the state, when they are frequent and open; and in like sort, false news often running up and down, to the disadvantage of the state, and hastily embraced, are amongst the signs of troubles.
FRANCIS BACON: *Essays*, XV, 1625

If men should not be called to account for possessing the people with an ill opinion of the government, no government can subsist; for it is very necessary for every government that the people should have a good opinion of it.
LORD HOLT: *Judgment in Tuchin's case*, 1704

The question in every case is whether the words used are used in such circumstances and are of such a nature as to create a clear and present danger that they will bring about the substantive evils that Congress has a right to prevent. It is a question of proximity and degree. When a nation is at war many things that might be said in time of peace are such a hindrance to its effort that their utterance will not be endured so long as men fight, and no court could regard them as protected by any constitutional right.
MR. JUSTICE O. W. HOLMES: *Opinion in Schenck* vs. *the United States*, 1919

[*See also* Flesh, Sin, Treason.

Seducer

None are more struck with the charms of virtue in the fair sex than those who, by their very admiration of it, are carried to a desire of ruining it.
JOSEPH ADDISON: *The Spectator*, Dec. 8, 1711

Seduction

If a man entice a maid that is not betrothed, and lie with her, he shall surely endow her to be his wife. EXODUS XXII, 16, *c.* 700 B.C.

In part to blame is she
Which hath without consent been only tried:
He comes too near that comes to be denied.
THOMAS OVERBURY: *Characters*, 1614

I'll rifle first her darling chastity;
It will be after time enough to poison her.
JAMES SHIRLEY: *The Cardinal*, V, 1641

A maid that laughs is half taken.
JOHN RAY: *English Proverbs*, 1670

Let him who wantonly sports away the peace of a poor lady consider what discord he sows in families; how often he wrings the heart of a hoary parent; how often he rouses the fury of a jealous husband; how he extorts from the abused woman curses poured out in the bitterness of her soul.
RICHARD STEELE: *The Guardian*, June 3, 1713

He vows, he swears, he'll give me a green gown:
Oh dear! I fall adown, adown, adown!
JOHN GAY: *The Shepherd's Week*, 1714

If a man has seduced a maiden on a promise of marriage, is he bound to keep his promise if he is much superior to the maiden in birth, and she was aware of that disparity? I think he is not the least bound.

ST. ALPHONSUS DI LIGOURI: *Theologia moralis*, IV, 1753

There is nothing more shameful than to seduce an honest girl.

W. A. MOZART: *Letter to his father*, July 18, 1778

The man who, under pretensions of marriage, can plant thorns in the bosom of an innocent, unsuspecting girl is more detestable than a common robber, in the same proportion as private violence is more despicable than open force, and money of less value than happiness.

ROYALL TYLER: *The Contrast*, III, 1790

Compose yourself, Antonia. Resistance is unavailing, and I need disavow my passion for you no longer. I possess you here alone; you are absolutely in my power, and I burn with desires which I must either gratify or die. My lovely girl! My adorable Antonia! let me instruct you in joys to which you are still a stranger, and teach you to feel those pleasures in my arms, which I must soon enjoy in yours.

M. G. (MONK) LEWIS: *Ambrosio, or The Monk*, 1795

Be cautious in listening to the addresses of men. Art thou pleased with smiles and flattering words? Remember that man often smiles and flatters most when he would betray thee.

NOAH WEBSTER: *The American Spelling Book*, rev. ed., 1804

A man (I do not say a gentleman) in the West sought the destruction of an innocent ——, and to accomplish his designs "wished that Heaven might never receive his soul nor earth his body if he did not perform his contract" — and afterwards boasted of his worse than diabolical act; but God took him at his word, for he was shot by an Indian, and rotted above ground.

LORENZO DOW: *Reflections on Matrimony*, 1833 (The blank is in the original)

It is one of the misfortunes of the professional Don Juan that his honor forbids him to refuse battle; he is in life like the Roman soldier upon duty, or like the sworn physician who must attend on all diseases.

R. L. STEVENSON: *Familiar Studies of Men and Books*, II, 1882

She was poor but she was honest
And her parents was the same
Till she met a city feller
And she lost her honest name.

Anon.: *She Was Poor But She Was Honest* (Sung by British soldiers, 1914–18)

Seduction or rape. (a) They should never be more than suggested, and only when essential for the plot, and even then never shown by explicit method. (b) They are never the proper subject for comedy.

A CODE TO GOVERN THE MAKING OF MOTION AND TALKING PICTURES BY THE MOTION PICTURE PRODUCERS AND DISTRIBUTORS OF AMERICA, INC., March 31, 1930

[*See also* Bishop, Might, Name, Physician.

Seeing

We are less convinced by what we hear than by what we see.

HERODOTUS: *Histories*, I, *c.* 430 B.C.

Seeing is believing.

ENGLISH PROVERB, borrowed from the Latin and familiar since the XVII century

There's a lot of difference between say-so and take-a-look. AMERICAN PROVERB

When the eye does not see the heart does not grieve. ARAB PROVERB

[*See also* Belief, Eye, Flesh, Glass, Sight.

Seeking

Seek, and ye shall find.

MATTHEW VII, 7, *c.* 75

Seer

Innumerable men had passed by, across this universe, with a dumb vague wonder, such as the very animals may feel; or with a painful, fruitlessly inquiring wonder, such as men only feel; — till the great thinker came, the *original* man, the seer; whose shaped spoken thought awakes the slumbering capability of all into thought.

THOMAS CARLYLE: *Heroes and Hero-Worship*, I, 1840 (Lecture in London, May 5)

Self

Man can never escape from himself.

J. W. GOETHE: *Torquato Tasso*, I, 1790

Why don't you speak for yourself, John?

H. W. LONGFELLOW: *The Courtship of Miles Standish*, 1858

Self-accusation

Tho' there may be art in a man's accusing himself, even then it will be more pardonable than self-commendation.

COLLEY CIBBER: *Apology For His Life*, XVI, 1740

No person . . . shall be compelled in any criminal case to be a witness against himself.

CONSTITUTION OF THE UNITED STATES, Amendment V, Dec. 15, 1791

The thorns which I have reap'd are of the tree
I planted; they have torn me, and I bleed.

BYRON: *Childe Harold*, III, 1816

No one is obliged to accuse himself. (Nemo tenetur se ipsum accusare.)
LEGAL MAXIM

[*See also* Self-deprecation.

Self-approval

One self-approving hour whole years outweighs
Of stupid starers and of loud huzzas.
ALEXANDER POPE: *An Essay on Man,* IV, 1734

Self-assurance

[*See* Poet.

Self-betrayal

Out of thine own mouth will I judge thee.
LUKE XIX, 22, *c.* 75

Self-censure

All censure of a man's self is oblique praise. It is in order to show how much he can spare. It has all the invidiousness of self-praise, and all the reproach of falsehood.
SAMUEL JOHNSON: *Boswell's Life,* April 25, 1778

[*See also* Self-reproach.

Self-command

I am my own emperor.
PLAUTUS: *Mercator,* V, *c.* 200 B.C.

No one is free who commands not himself.
EPICTETUS: *Encheiridion, c.* 110

In vain he seeketh others to suppress
Who hath not learned himself first to subdue.
EDMUND SPENSER: *The Faerie Queene,* VI, *c.* 1589

To keep my passions regular
I've full command within;
I'm pleased without impertinence
And angry without sin.
DANIEL DEFOE: *A Review of the Affairs of France and of All Europe,* VIII, 1712

If you can command yourself, you can command the world.
CHINESE PROVERB

[*See also* Self-conquest, Self-mastery.

Self-confidence

Some men are just as firmly convinced of what they think as others are of what they know.
ARISTOTLE: *The Nicomachean Ethics,* VII, *c.* 340 B.C.

'Tis with our judgments as our watches, none
Go just alike, yet each believes his own.
ALEXANDER POPE: *An Essay on Criticism,* I, 1711

[*See also* Fool.

Self-conquest

He conquers who conquers himself. (Vincit qui se vincit.)
LATIN PROVERB

[*See also* Self-command.

Self-conscious

[*See* Nose.

Self-contempt

Self-contempt, bitterer to drink than blood.
P. B. SHELLEY: *Prometheus Unbound,* II, 1820

[*See also* Contempt.

Self-contradiction

Every individual character is in the right that is in strict consistence with itself. Self-contradiction is the only wrong.
J. C. F. SCHILLER: *Wallenstein's Death,* I, 1799

Self-deception

Nothing is so easy as to deceive one's self.
DEMOSTHENES: *Third Olynthiac,* 348 B.C.

It is as easy to deceive oneself without perceiving it as it is difficult to deceive others without their perceiving it.
LA ROCHEFOUCAULD: *Maxims,* 1665

When a mouse falls into a meal sack, he thinks he is the miller himself.
DUTCH PROVERB

Self-defense

No man is supposed, at the making of a commonwealth, to have abandoned the defense of his life or limbs, where the law cannot arrive time enough to his assistance.
THOMAS HOBBES: *Leviathan,* II, 1651

Self-defense is nature's eldest law.
JOHN DRYDEN: *Absalom and Achitophel,* I, 1682

No man was ever yet so void of sense
As to debate the right of self-defense.
DANIEL DEFOE: *The True-Born Englishman,* II, 1701

The life of a state is like that of a man. A man has the right to kill in self-defense, and a state has the right to make war for self-preservation.
C. L. DE MONTESQUIEU: *The Spirit of the Laws,* X, 1748

That animal is very vicious: when it is attacked it defends itself.
FRENCH PROVERB

In self-defense. (Se defendendo.)
LATIN PHRASE

[*See also* Self-preservation.

Self-denial

The more we deny to ourselves, the more the gods supply our wants.
HORACE: *Carmina,* III, *c.* 20 B.C.

If any man will come after me, let him deny himself, and take up his cross, and follow me.
MATTHEW XVI, 24, *c.* 75

'Tis much the doctrine of the times that men should not please themselves, but deny themselves everything they take delight in; not look upon beauty, wear no good clothes, eat no good meat, &c. which seems the greatest accusation that can be upon the Maker of all good things. If they be not to be used, why did God make them? The truth is, they that preach against them cannot make use of them theirselves, and then again, they get esteem by seeming to condemn them.

JOHN SELDEN: *Table-Talk*, 1689

The worst education which teaches self-denial is better than the best which teaches everything else and not that.

JOHN STERLING: *Essays and Tales*, 1840

There is a great deal of self-denial and manliness in poor and middle-class houses, in town and country, that has not got into literature, and never will, but that keeps the earth sweet.

R. W. EMERSON: *The Conduct of Life*, IV, 1860

Self-denial is not a virtue; it is only the effect of prudence on rascality.

GEORGE BERNARD SHAW: *Maxims for Revolutionists*, 1903

Self-denial is indulgence of a propensity to forego.

AMBROSE BIERCE: *Collected Works*, VIII, 1911

Self-deprecation

He who blames himself takes a by-road to praise; and, like the rower, turns his back to the place whither he desires to go.

Ascribed to ST. FRANCIS DE SALES (1567–1622) in J. P. CAMUS: *L'esprit de Saint François de Sales*, 1641

Self-determination

Every nation, every province and every commune has an unlimited right to complete self-determination, provided only its constitution does not threaten the independence and liberty of its neighbors.

M. A. BAKUNIN: *Fédéralisme, socialisme et antithéologisme*, c. 1875

Self-determination is not a mere phrase. It is an imperative principle of action, which statesmen will henceforth ignore at their peril.

WOODROW WILSON: Address to Congress, Feb. 11, 1918

[*See also* Self-government.

Self-dispraise

A man should be careful never to tell tales of himself to his own disadvantage. People may be amused and laugh at the time, but they will be remembered and brought against him upon some subsequent occasion.

SAMUEL JOHNSON: *Boswell's Life*, March 25, 1776

There is a luxury in self-dispraise;
And inward self-disparagement affords
To meditative spleen a grateful feast.

WILLIAM WORDSWORTH: *The Excursion*, IV, 1814

[*See also* Self-accusation, Self-censure, Self-deprecation.

Self-education

A clever self-educated man often sees what men trained in routine do not see, but falls into errors for want of knowing things which have long been known. He has acquired much of the preëxisting knowledge, or he could not have got on at all; but what he knows of it he has picked up in fragments and at random.

J. S. MILL: *The Subjection of Women*, III, 1869

Self-esteem

Every animal esteems itself.

CICERO: *De finibus*, c. 50 B.C.

Ofttimes nothing profits more
Than self-esteem, grounded on just and right
Well manag'd.

JOHN MILTON: *Paradise Lost*, VIII, 1667

A man is little the better for liking himself if nobody else like him.

THOMAS FULLER: *Gnomologia*, 1732

It is easy for every man, whatever be his character with others, to find reasons for esteeming himself.

SAMUEL JOHNSON: *The Rambler*, Dec. 18, 1750

Few men survey themselves with so much severity as not to admit prejudices in their own favor.

SAMUEL JOHNSON: *The Rambler*, Jan. 7, 1752

I am very willing to admit that I have some poetical abilities.

ROBERT BURNS: *Letter to Dr. J. Moore*, Jan. 23, 1787

$$\text{Self-esteem} = \frac{\text{Success}}{\text{Pretensions}}$$

WILLIAM JAMES: *Psychology, Briefer Course*, XII, 1892

[*See also* Self-love.

Self-examination

Go to your bosom;
Knock there, and ask your heart what it doth know.

SHAKESPEARE: *Measure for Measure*, II, 1604

Self-flattery

The arch-flatterer, with whom all the petty flatterers have intelligence, is a man's self.

FRANCIS BACON: *Essays*, X, 1597

Without self-flattery there would be little pleasure in life. FRENCH PROVERB

Self-government

There are very few so foolish that they had not rather govern themselves than be governed by others.

THOMAS HOBBES: *Leviathan,* I, 1651

He that has no government of himself has no enjoyment of himself.

BENJAMIN WHICHCOTE: *Moral and Religious Aphorisms,* 1753

The larger the society, provided it lie within a practical sphere, the more duly capable it will be of self-government.

ALEXANDER HAMILTON: *The Federalist,* 1788

Self-government is the natural government of man.

HENRY CLAY: Speech in the House of Representatives, March 24, 1818

I have done with this mighty argument of self-government. Go, sacred thing! Go in peace.

ABRAHAM LINCOLN: Speech in Peoria, Ill., Oct. 16, 1854

Civilization consists in teaching men to govern themselves by letting them do it.

BENJAMIN R. TUCKER: *Instead of a Book,* 1893

Every people has a right to choose the sovereignty under which they shall live.

WOODROW WILSON: Address in Washington, May 27, 1916

[*See also* Abolition, Anglo-Saxon, Democracy, Despotism, Education, Government, Republic, Self-determination.

Self-help

God lends a helping hand to the man who tries hard.

ÆSCHYLUS: *The Persians, c.* 490 B.C.

The gods help him who helps himself.

EURIPIDES: *Fragment, c.* 425 B.C. (Apparently a proverb)

No man who is not willing to help himself has any right to apply to his friends, or to the gods.

DEMOSTHENES: *Second Olynthiac,* 349 B.C.

Every man for himself, and God for us all.

JOHN HEYWOOD: *Proverbs,* 1546

Self do, self have. IBID.

God helps them that help themselves.

ENGLISH PROVERB, borrowed from the Greek, and traced by Apperson to 1580

Fortune helps them who help themselves.

ENGLISH PROVERB, familiar since the XVII century

Do not lie in a ditch and say, God help me; use the lawful tools He hath lent thee.

GEORGE CHAPMAN: *May-Day,* I, 1611

He whipped his horses withal, and put his shoulder to the wheel.

ROBERT BURTON: *The Anatomy of Melancholy,* II, 1621

Put your trust in God, but mind to keep your powder dry.

OLIVER CROMWELL: To his troops at the Battle of Edgehill, Oct. 23, 1642

God reaches us good things by our own hands.

THOMAS FULLER: *Gnomologia,* 1732

Robinson had a servant even better than Friday: his name was Crusoe.

F. W. NIETZSCHE: *Human All-too-Human,* II, 1878

We are told what fine things would happen if every one of us would go and do something for the welfare of somebody else; but why not contemplate also the immense gain which would ensue if everybody would do something for himself?

W. G. SUMNER: *An Examination of a Noble Sentiment,* 1889

God is a hard worker, but He likes to be helped.

BASQUE PROVERB

God gives the nuts, but he does not crack them.

GERMAN PROVERB

[*See also* Help, Independence.

Self-interest

Even wisdom has to yield to self-interest.

PINDAR: *Pythian Odes,* III, *c.* 475 B.C.

Every man is a friend to him that giveth gifts.

PROVERBS XIX, 6, *c.* 350 B.C.

As far as the stars are from the earth, and as different as fire is from water, so much do self-interest and integrity differ.

LUCAN: *Pharsalia,* VIII, 65

Self-interest is the enemy of all true affection.

TACITUS: *History,* I, *c.* 100

Nothing is to thy interest that ever forces thee to break thy promise, to surrender thine honor, to play the hypocrite, to hate, suspect or curse anyone, to lust after anything behind walls and curtains.

MARCUS AURELIUS: *Meditations,* III, *c.* 170

I know on which side my bread is buttered.

JOHN HEYWOOD: *Proverbs,* 1546

A man is a lion in his own cause.

DAVID FERGUSSON: *Scottish Proverbs,* 1641

I conceive that when a man deliberates whether he shall do a thing or not do it, he does nothing else but consider whether it be better for himself to do it or not to do it.

THOMAS HOBBES: *Questions Concerning Liberty,* 1656

We are all mortals, and each is for himself.

J. B. MOLIÈRE: *L'école des femmes,* II, 1662

The virtues are lost in interest, as rivers are lost in the sea.
LA ROCHEFOUCAULD: *Maxims*, 1665

A man is quickly convinced of the truth of religion who finds it not against his interest that it should be true.
JOSEPH ADDISON: *The Spectator*, Aug. 23, 1712

Let me gain by you, and no matter whether you love me or not.
THOMAS FULLER: *Gnomologia*, 1732

'Tis not contrary to reason to prefer the destruction of the whole world to the scratching of my finger.
DAVID HUME: *A Treatise of Human Nature*, I, 1739

To know no distinction of men from affection; but to sacrifice all with equal readiness to his interest.
HENRY FIELDING: *Jonathan Wild*, IV, 1743
(Maxim of Wild for the attainment of greatness)

If the physical universe be subject to the laws of motion, the moral universe is equally so to those of interest.
C. A. HELVÉTIUS: *De l'esprit*, II, 1758

I ne'er could any lustre see
In eyes that would not look on me;
I ne'er saw nectar on a lip
But where my own did hope to sip.
R. B. SHERIDAN: *The Duenna*, 1775

It is not from the benevolence of the butcher, the brewer, or the baker that we expect our dinner, but from their regard to their own interest.
ADAM SMITH: *The Wealth of Nations*, II, 1776

The world is governed by self-interest only.
J. C. F. SCHILLER: *Wallenstein's Death*, I, 1799

The only persons I really care for are those who are of use to me.
NAPOLEON I: To Gaspard Gourgaud at St. Helena, 1815–1818

Take care of number one, says the worldling, and the Christian says so too; for he has taken the best care of number one who takes care that number one shall go to Heaven.
C. C. COLTON: *Lacon*, 1820

In all the outward relations of this life, in all our outward conduct and actions, both in what we should do and in what we should abstain from, the dictates of virtue are the very same with those of self-interest; tending to, though they do not proceed from, the same point.
S. T. COLERIDGE: *Aids to Reflection*, 1825

Man seeks his own good at the whole world's cost.
ROBERT BROWNING: *Luria*, I, 1846

I scent what pays the best, an' then
Go into it baldheaded.
J. R. LOWELL: *The Biglow Papers*, I, 1848

I declare my belief that it is not your duty to do anything that is not to your own interest. Whenever it is unquestionably your duty to do a thing, then it will benefit you to perform that duty.
E. W. HOWE: *Country Town Sayings*, 1911

No good rat will injure the grain near its hole.
CHINESE PROVERB

My teeth are nearer to me than my relatives.
SPANISH PROVERB

Hear all, see all, say nowt.
Eat all, drink all, pay nowt.
And if tha does owt for nowt
Do it for theysen.
YORKSHIRE RHYME

[*See also* Fawning, Flattery, Giving, Morality.

Selfishness

The wretch concentred all in self,
Living, shall forfeit fair renown,
And, doubly dying, shall go down
To the vile dust from whence he sprung,
Unwept, unhonor'd and unsung.
WALTER SCOTT: *The Lay of the Last Minstrel*, VI, 1805

Selfishness is not living as one wishes to live. It is asking others to live as one wishes to live.
OSCAR WILDE: *The Soul of Man Under Socialism*, 1891

Self, self, has half filled Hell.
SCOTTISH PROVERB

He that eats his fowl alone must saddle his horse alone.
SPANISH PROVERB

[*See also* Caution.

Self-judgment

We judge ourselves by what we feel capable of doing, while others judge us by what we have already done.
H. W. LONGFELLOW: *Kavanagh*, I, 1849

He who will have no judge but himself condemns himself.
H. G. BOHN: *Handbook of Proverbs*, 1855

No one should be a judge in his own case. (In propria causa nemo judex sit.)
LEGAL MAXIM

Self-knowledge

Know thyself.
INSCRIPTION ON THE TEMPLE TO APOLLO AT DELPHI; ascribed to SOLON (*c.* 600 B.C.)

Thales was asked what was most difficult to man; he answered: "To know one's self."
DIOGENES LAERTIUS: *Lives of the Philosophers* (Thales), *c.* 150 B.C.

A man is least known to himself.

CICERO: *De oratore,* III, *c.* 80 B.C.

Retire into thyself, and thou wilt blush to find how little is there.

PERSIUS: *Satires,* IV, *c.* 60

We that acquaint ourselves with every zone
And pass both tropics and behold the poles,
When we come home are to ourselves unknown,
And unacquainted still with our own souls.

JOHN DAVIES: *Nosce Teipsum,* 1599

We know what we are, but know not what we may be.

SHAKESPEARE: *Hamlet,* IV, *c.* 1601

Oh, that you could turn your eyes towards the napes of your necks, and make but an interior survey of your good selves.

SHAKESPEARE: *Coriolanus,* II, *c.* 1607

Every man is best known to himself.

JOHN CLARKE: *Parœmiologia Anglo-Latina,* 1639

We know ourselves so little that many think they are going to die when they are well, and many think they are well when they are near dying.

BLAISE PASCAL: *Pensées,* XXV, 1670

Although men are accused for not knowing their own weakness, yet, perhaps, as few know their own strength. It is in men as in soils, where sometimes there is a vein of gold which the owner knows not of.

JONATHAN SWIFT: *Thoughts on Various Subjects,* 1706

All our knowledge is ourselves to know.

ALEXANDER POPE: *An Essay on Man,* IV, 1734

Oh, wad some power the giftie gie us
To see oursels as others see us!
It wad frae mony a blunder free us,
And foolish notion.

ROBERT BURNS: *To a Louse,* 1785

If self-knowledge is the road to virtue, so is virtue still more the road to self-knowledge.

JEAN PAUL RICHTER: *Hesperus,* XII, 1795

The first step to self-knowledge is self-distrust.

J. C. and A. W. HARE: *Guesses at Truth,* 1827

Man is a darkened being; he knows not whence he comes, nor whither he goes; he knows little of the world, and least of himself. I know not myself, and God forbid I should!

J. W. GOETHE: *Conversations with Eckermann,* April 10, 1829

He who knows himself best esteems himself least.

H. G. BOHN: *Handbook of Proverbs,* 1855

No man is the worse for knowing the worst of himself. IBID.

The only thing a man knows is himself. The world outside he can know only by hearsay.

ALEXANDER SMITH: *Dreamthorp,* VIII, 1863

Self-love

All men love themselves.

PLAUTUS: *Captivi,* III, *c.* 200 B.C.

I to myself am dearer than a friend.

SHAKESPEARE: *Two Gentlemen of Verona,* II, *c.* 1595

Self-love is not so vile a sin
As self-neglecting.

SHAKESPEARE: *Henry V,* II, *c.* 1599

Why should I be angry with a man for loving himself better than me?

FRANCIS BACON: *Essays,* IV, 1625

Every man is naturally a Narcissus, and each passion in us no other but self-love sweetened by milder epithets.

JOSEPH GLANVILL: *The Vanity of Dogmatizing,* XIII, 1661

Our self-love endures more impatiently the condemnation of our tastes than of our opinions.

LA ROCHEFOUCAULD: *Maxims,* 1665

Self-love is more cunning than the most cunning man in the world. IBID.

Whatever discoveries may have been made in the territory of self-love, there still remain in it many unknown tracts. IBID.

Self-love, in nature rooted fast,
Attends us first, and leaves us last.

JONATHAN SWIFT: *Cadenus and Vanessa,* 1713

None loves himself too little.

BENJAMIN WHICHCOTE: *Moral and Religious Aphorisms,* 1753

Self-love is the instrument of our preservation; it resembles the provision for the reproduction of mankind: it is necessary, it gives us pleasure, and we must conceal it.

VOLTAIRE: *Philosophical Dictionary,* 1764

Man has almost constant occasion for the help of his brethren, and it is in vain for him to expect it from their benevolence only. He will be more likely to prevail if he can interest their self-love in his favor, and show them that it is for their own advantage to do for him what he requires of them.

ADAM SMITH: *The Wealth of Nations,* II, 1776

Nature is incorrigible — there is no crevice so small or intricate at which our self-love will not contrive to creep in.

WILLIAM HAZLITT: *Traveling Abroad,* 1828 (New Monthly Magazine, June)

To love one's self is the beginning of a life-long romance.

OSCAR WILDE: *Phrases and Philosophies for the Use of the Young,* 1894

Self-love makes the eyes dim.
GERMAN PROVERB

Many will hate you if you love yourself. (Multi te oderint si teipsum ames.)
LATIN PROVERB

[*See also* Debauchery, Egoism, Friendship, Injustice, Jealousy, Self-esteem, Virginity.

Self-made

Just as poets always like their own poems and parents love their own children, so those who have made their own fortunes are delighted with their wealth, as the work of their own hands.
PLATO: *The Republic,* I, *c.* 370 B.C.

Every man is the architect of his own fortune.
ENGLISH PROVERB, borrowed from the Greek and familiar since the XVI century (Sometimes *artificer* appears in the place of *architect*)

What I am I have made myself: I say this without vanity, and in pure simplicity of heart.
Ascribed to HUMPHRY DAVY (1778–1829)

Our self-made men are the glory of our institutions.
WENDELL PHILLIPS: Speech in Boston, Dec. 21, 1860

He is a self-made man, and worships his creator.
JOHN BRIGHT: Said of Benjamin Disraeli, *c.* 1868

A new man. (Novus homo.)
Latin term for a self-made man

[*See also* Greeley (Horace).

Self-mastery

It matters not how strait the gate,
How charged with punishments the scroll,
I am the master of my fate:
I am the captain of my soul.
W. E. HENLEY: *Invictus,* 1888

The most intelligent men, like the strongest, find their happiness where others would find only disaster: in the labyrinth, in being hard with themselves and with others, in effort; their delight is in self-mastery; in them asceticism becomes second nature, a necessity, an instinct.
F. W. NIETZSCHE: *The Antichrist,* LVII, 1888

[*See also* Self-command.

Self-medication

It is ill jesting with the joiner's tools, worse with the doctor's.
BENJAMIN FRANKLIN: *Poor Richard's Almanac,* 1752

Self-pity

[*See* Invalid.

Self-praise

Let another man praise thee, and not thine own mouth.
PROVERBS XXVII, 2, *c.* 350 B.C.

He who praises himself will soon find someone to deride him.
PUBLILIUS SYRUS: *Sententiæ, c.* 50 B.C.

God hates those who praise themselves.
ST. CLEMENT: *First Epistle to the Corinthians, c.* 125

Self-praise stinks.
ENGLISH PROVERB, borrowed from the Latin and familiar since the XVII century

He that praiseth himself spattereth himself.
GEORGE HERBERT: *Outlandish Proverbs,* 1640

Fondly we think we honor merit then,
When we but praise ourselves in other men.
ALEXANDER POPE: *An Essay on Criticism,* II, 1711

When you die your trumpeter will be buried.
THOMAS FULLER: *Gnomologia,* 1732

If you wish in this world to advance
Your merits you're bound to enhance;
You must stir it and stump it,
And blow your own trumpet,
Or, trust me, you haven't a chance.
W. S. GILBERT: *Ruddigore,* II, 1887

[*See also* Self-Censure.

Self-preservation

Every man for himself, and the Devil take the hindmost.
ENGLISH PROVERB, familiar since the XIV century

Every man for himself, and God for us all.
JOHN HEYWOOD: *Proverbs,* 1546

No law can oblige a man to abandon his own preservation.
THOMAS HOBBES: *Leviathan,* II, 1651

Self-preservation is the first law of nature.
ENGLISH PROVERB, traced by Smith and Apperson to *c.* 1678

In a narrow pass there is no brother and no friend.
ARAB PROVERB

[*See also* Self-defense, Self-love.

Self-reliance

Let every vat stand upon its own bottom.
WILLIAM BULLEIN: *Dialogue Against the Fever Pestilence,* 1564 (*Tub* usually appears in place of *vat*)

No bird soars too high if he soars with his own wings.
WILLIAM BLAKE: *The Marriage of Heaven and Hell,* 1790

He who would gather immortal palms must not be hindered by the name of goodness, but must explore if it be goodness. Nothing is at last sacred but the integrity of our own mind.
R. W. EMERSON: *Self-Reliance,* 1841

His brow is wet with honest sweat,
He earns whate'er he can,
And looks the whole world in the face,
For he owes not any man.
H. W. LONGFELLOW: *The Village Blacksmith,* 1841

Whate'er your lot may be,
Paddle your own canoe.
EDWARD P. PHILPOTS: *Paddle Your Own Canoe,* 1854

Every man must scratch his head with his own nails. ARAB PROVERB

[*See also* Conformity, Independence.

Self-reproach

There is luxury in self-reproach. When we blame ourselves we feel no one else has a right to blame us.
OSCAR WILDE: *The Picture of Dorian Gray,* 1891

[*See also* Self-censure.

Self-respect

Self-respect — that cornerstone of all virtue.
JOHN HERSCHEL: Address in London, Jan. 29, 1833

There is no calamity which a great nation can invite which equals that which follows from a supine submission to wrong and injustice, and the consequent loss of national self-respect and honor, beneath which are shielded and defended a people's safety and greatness.
GROVER CLEVELAND: Message to Congress on the Venezuelan question, Dec. 17, 1895

Most of all reverence thyself. (Maxime omnium teipsum reverere.) LATIN PROVERB

[*See also* Self-esteem.

Self-revelation

Give me six lines written by the most honest man in the world, and I shall find enough evidence in them to hang him.
ARMAND CARDINAL RICHELIEU: *Mirame,* c. 1625

When a man is attempting to describe another person's character, he may be right or he may be wrong; but in one thing he will always succeed, that is, in describing himself.
S. T. COLERIDGE: *Omniana,* CX, 1812

All life, all creation, is tell-tale and betraying. A man reveals himself in every glance and step and movement and rest.
R. W. EMERSON: *Demonology,* 1877

[*See also* Character.

Self-righteous

O ye wha are sae guid yoursel',
Sae pious and sae holy,
Ye've nought to do but mark and tell
Your neebour's fauts and folly.
ROBERT BURNS: *An Address to the Unco Guid,* 1785

Self-sacrifice

Greater love hath no man than this, that a man lay down his life for his friends.
JOHN XV, 13, *c.* 115

Then out spake brave Horatius,
The captain of the gate:
"To every man upon this earth
Death cometh soon or late.
And how can man die better
Than facing fearful odds,
For the ashes of his fathers
And the temples of his gods?"
T. B. MACAULAY: *Lays of Ancient Rome,* 1842

Whether on the scaffold high,
Or in the battle's van,
The fittest place where man can die
Is where he dies for man.
M. J. BARRY: *The Place to Die,* 1844 (Dublin Nation, Sept. 28)

Self-sacrifice is the real miracle out of which all the reported miracles grew.
R. W. EMERSON: *Courage,* 1877

Self-sacrifice is a thing that should be put down by law. It is so demoralizing to the people for whom one sacrifices oneself.
OSCAR WILDE: *An Ideal Husband,* III, 1895

Self-sacrifice enables us to sacrifice other people without blushing.
GEORGE BERNARD SHAW: *Maxims for Revolutionists,* 1903

[*See also* Capitalist.

Self-satisfaction

The punishment for self-satisfaction is general contempt.
BALTASAR GRACIÁN: *The Art of Worldly Wisdom,* CXLI, 1647

While all complain of our ignorance and error, everyone exempts himself.
JOSEPH GLANVILL: *The Vanity of Dogmatizing,* VII, 1661

Fortunate people never correct themselves. They always fancy they are in the right as long as fortune supports their ill conduct.
LA ROCHEFOUCAULD: *Maxims,* 1665

No one is ever satisfied with his fortune or dissatisfied with his understanding.
ANTOINETTE DESHOULIÈRES: *Réflexion sur le jeu,* c. 1675

Only madmen and fools are pleased with themselves; no wise man is good enough for his own satisfaction.
BENJAMIN WHICHCOTE: *Moral and Religious Aphorisms,* 1753

Making myself known is not what is uppermost in my mind — it is something that can satisfy only the most mediocre vanity. I am aiming at something better: to please myself.
GUSTAVE FLAUBERT: *Letter to Maxime du Camp,* June 26, 1852

[*See also* Laughter, Self-esteem.

Self-taught

He that was only taught by himself had a fool to his master.
BEN JONSON: *Discoveries, c.* 1635

[*See also* Education, Self-education.

Selling

Did you ever hear a fishwife cry stinking mackerel? JOHN WILSON: *The Cheats,* IV, 1664

A man trying to sell a blind horse always praises its feet. GERMAN PROVERB

[*See also* Buying and Selling, Measure, Salesmanship, Trade (=commerce).

Senate

The Senate of the United States shall be composed of two senators from each state, chosen by the Legislature thereof, for six years; and each senator shall have one vote.
CONSTITUTION OF THE UNITED STATES, Art. I, 1789 (The direct election of senators was substituted by Amendment XVII, May 31, 1913)

This is a Senate of equals, of men of individual honor and personal character, and of absolute independence. We know no masters, we acknowledge no dictators. This is a hall for mutual consultation and discussion; not an arena for the exhibition of champions.
DANIEL WEBSTER: Speech in the Senate, Jan. 26, 1830

A body of elderly gentlemen charged with high duties and misdemeanors.
AMBROSE BIERCE: *The Devil's Dictionary,* 1906

The great object for us to seek here, for the Constitution identifies the Vice-Presidency with the Senate, is to continue to make this chamber, as it was intended by the fathers, the citadel of liberty.
CALVIN COOLIDGE: Inaugural address as Vice-President, March 4, 1921

[*See also* Congress, Treaty, Vice-President.

Senator

No person shall be a senator who shall not have attained to the age of thirty years, and been nine years a citizen of the United States, and who shall not, when elected, be an inhabitant of that state for which he shall be chosen.
CONSTITUTION OF THE UNITED STATES, Art. I, 1789

We favor an amendment to the Federal Constitution providing for election of United States senators by the direct vote of the people.
Democratic National Platform, 1900

[*See also* Senate, Treaty.

Seneca (c. 10–65)

You may get a motto for every sect in religion, or line of thought in morals or philosophy, from Seneca; but nothing is ever thought out by him.
S. T. COLERIDGE: *Table-Talk,* June 26, 1830

The toreador of virtue.
F. W. NIETZSCHE: *The Twilight of the Idols,* 1889

Senility

Last scene of all,
That ends this strange eventful history,
Is second childishness and mere oblivion,
Sans teeth, sans eyes, sans taste, sans everything.
SHAKESPEARE: *As You Like It,* II, *c.* 1600

Bodily decay is gloomy in prospect, but of all human contemplations the most abhorrent is body without mind.
THOMAS JEFFERSON: *Letter to John Adams,* 1816

[*See also* Age (Old).

Sensation

As it is impossible for me to see or feel anything without an actual sensation of that thing, so is it impossible for me to conceive in my thoughts any sensible thing or object distinct from the sensation or perception of it. In truth, the object and the sensation are the same thing, and cannot therefore be abstracted from each other.
GEORGE BERKELEY: *The Principles of Human Knowledge,* I, 1710

Oh, for a life of sensations rather than of thoughts!
JOHN KEATS: *Letter to Benjamin Bailey,* Nov. 22, 1817

Nerves have no more sensation, apart from what belief bestows upon them, than the fibres of a plant.
MARY BAKER G. EDDY: *Science and Health,* XIV, 1908

[*See also* Senses.

Sense

He is a man of sense who does not grieve for what he has not, but rejoices in what he has.
EPICTETUS: *Encheiridion, c.* 110

Some will grant you precedence in good luck or good temper, but none in good sense.
BALTASAR GRACIÁN: *The Art of Worldly Wisdom,* VII, 1647

There are times when sense may be unseasonable, as well as truth.
WILLIAM CONGREVE: *The Double Dealer,* I, 1694

Who would die a martyr to sense in a country where the religion is folly?

WILLIAM CONGREVE: *Love for Love*, I, 1695

Where sense is wanting, everything is wanting.

BENJAMIN FRANKLIN: *Poor Richard's Almanac*, 1754

It is a dangerous thing for a man to have more sense than his fellow-citizens.

C. M. WIELAND: *Die Abderiten*, I, 1774

Good sense is at the bottom of everything: virtue, genius, wit, talent and taste.

M. J. DE CHÉNIER: *Épître à Voltaire*, 1806

There is never much chance for a sensible man.

LUDWIG TIECK: *Fortunat*, 1812

In the world a man will often be reputed to be a man of sense, only because he is not a man of talent.

HENRY TAYLOR: *The Statesman*, 1836

[*See also* Fortune, Poetry, Sense (Common), Taste, Wisdom, Wise.

Sense, Common

The worst kind of pedants among learned men are such as are naturally endowed with a very small share of common sense.

JOSEPH ADDISON: *The Spectator*, June 30, 1711

Common sense (which, in truth, is very uncommon) is the best sense I know of: abide by it, it will counsel you best.

LORD CHESTERFIELD: *Letter to his son*, Sept. 27, 1748

Common sense holds nothing of philosophy, nor needs her aid. But, on the other hand, philosophy (if I may be permitted to change the metaphor) has no other root but the principles of common sense; it grows out of them, and draws its nourishment from them.

THOMAS REID: *Inquiry Into the Human Mind*, II, 1764

Nothing astonishes men so much as common sense and plain dealing.

R. W. EMERSON: *Art*, 1841

Common sense is the measure of the possible: it is composed of experience and prevision: it is calculation applied to life.

H. F. AMIEL: *Journal*, Nov. 12, 1852

Common sense is compelled to make its way without the enthusiasm of anyone; all admit it grudgingly.

E. W. HOWE: *The Indignations of E. W. Howe*, 1933

[*See also* Credulity, King, Lunacy, Philosophy, Sense.

Senses

What can give us surer knowledge than our senses? With what else can we better distinguish the true from the false?

LUCRETIUS: *De rerum natura*, I, 57 B.C.

There is no conception in a man's mind which hath not at first, totally or by parts, been begotten upon the organs of sense. The rest are derived from that original.

THOMAS HOBBES: *Leviathan*, I, 1651

The knowledge we have comes from our senses, and the dogmatist can go no higher for the original of his certainty.

JOSEPH GLANVILL: *The Vanity of Dogmatizing*, XXII, 1661

We feel neither extreme heat nor extreme cold. Excessive qualities are inimical to us, and not discernible; we no longer feel them, we suffer them.

BLAISE PASCAL: *Pensées*, II, 1670

What thin partitions sense from thought divide!

ALEXANDER POPE: *An Essay on Man*, I, 1732

The senses have that advantage over conscience which things necessary must always have over things chosen.

SAMUEL JOHNSON: *The Rambler*, April 10, 1750

People earnestly seek what they do not want, while they neglect the real blessings in their possession — I mean the innocent gratification of their senses, which is all we can properly call our own.

MARY WORTLEY MONTAGU: *Letter to James Steuart*, Jan. 13, 1761

I have my sight, hearing, taste, pretty perfect; and can read the Lord's Prayer in common type, by the help of a candle, without making many mistakes.

CHARLES LAMB: *Letter to Mr. and Mrs. Bruton*, Jan. 6, 1823

We can, at any time, double the true beauty of an actual landscape by half closing our eyes as we look at it. The naked senses sometimes see too little — but then always they see too much.

E. A. POE: *Marginalia*, 1844–49

From the senses come all trustworthiness, all good conscience, all evidence of truth.

F. W. NIETZSCHE: *Beyond Good and Evil*, 1886

[*See also* Brain, Hearing, Hero, Landscape, Sensation, Sight.

Sensibility

I would not enter on my list of friends
(Though graced with polish'd manners and fine sense,
Yet wanting sensibility) the man
Who needlessly sets foot upon a worm.

WILLIAM COWPER: *The Task*, VI, 1785

Sensuality

Sensuality is the vice of young men and of old nations.

W. E. H. LECKY: *History of European Morals*, I, 1869

The success of the wicked is a temptation to many others.
PHAEDRUS: *Fabulæ Æsopiæ*, c. 40

The sun also shines on the wicked.
SENECA: *De beneficiis*, III, c. 63

No one is so wicked that he wants to seem wicked.
QUINTILIAN: *De institutione oratoria*, III, c. 90

God bears with the wicked, but not forever.
CERVANTES: *Don Quixote*, II, 1615

There are wicked people who would be much less dangerous if they were wholly without goodness.
LA ROCHEFOUCAULD: *Maxims*, 1665

Keep the wicked always at enmity with one another; the safety of the world depends on that. Sow among them dissension, or you will never have any peace.
JEAN DE LA FONTAINE: *Fables*, VII, 1671

The happiness of the wicked passes away like a torrent. JEAN RACINE: *Athalie*, II, 1690

A wicked man is his own Hell.
THOMAS FULLER: *Gnomologia*, 1732

The wicked are always surprised to find ability in the good.
LUC DE VAUVENARGUES: *Réflexions*, 1746

If it be true, that men are miserable because they are wicked, it is likewise true, that many are wicked because they are miserable.
S. T. COLERIDGE: *Aids to Reflection*, 1825

I's wicked, I is.
HARRIET BEECHER STOWE: *Uncle Tom's Cabin*, xx, 1852

The wicked flee when no man pursueth, but they make better time when someone is after them.
Ascribed to CHARLES H. PARKHURST (1842–1933)

[*See also* Death, Sinner.

Wickedness

Ye have plowed wickedness, ye have reaped iniquity. HOSEA X, 13, *c.* 740 B.C.

Though wickedness be sweet in his mouth, though he hide it under his tongue; though he spare it, and forsake it not, but keep it still within his mouth; yet his meat in his bowels is turned; it is the gall of asps within him. JOB XX, 12–14, *c.* 325 B.C.

Wickedness lies in hesitating about an act, even though it be not perpetrated.
CICERO: *De officiis*, III, 78 B.C.

No man ever became very wicked all at once.
JUVENAL: *Satires*, II, *c.* 110

What rein can hold licentious wickedness
When down the hill he holds his fierce career?
SHAKESPEARE: *Henry V*, III, *c.* 1599

There is a method in man's wickedness —
It grows up by degrees.
BEAUMONT and FLETCHER: *A King and No King*, v, 1611

Wickedness is weakness.
JOHN MILTON: *Samson Agonistes*, 1671

Wickedness, like a flood, is like to drown our English world. It begins already to be above the tops of the mountains; it has almost swallowed up all; our youth, middle age, old age, and all, are almost carried away of this flood.
JOHN BUNYAN: *The Life and Death of Mr. Badman*, 1680

Your wickedness makes you, as it were, heavy as lead, and to tend downwards with great weight and pressure towards Hell; and if God should let you go, you would immediately sink and swiftly descend and plunge into the bottomless gulf, and your healthy constitution, and your own care and prudence, and best contrivance, and all your righteousness, would have no more influence to uphold you and keep you out of Hell than a spider's web would have to stop a falling rock.
JONATHAN EDWARDS: *Sinners in the Hands of an Angry God*, 1741 (Sermon, July 8)

The world loves a spice of wickedness.
H. W. LONGFELLOW: *Hyperion*, VII, 1839

Wickedness is a myth invented by good people to account for the curious attraction of others.
OSCAR WILDE: *Phrases and Philosophies for the Use of the Young*, 1894

The more wicked a man is the less fault he finds with himself. WELSH PROVERB

[*See also* Sin.

Wide

[*See* Narrow.

Widow

Ye shall not afflict any widow, or fatherless child. EXODUS XXII, 22, *c.* 700 B.C.

When thou gatherest the grapes of thy vineyard, thou shalt not glean it afterward: it shall be for the stranger, for the fatherless, and for the widow.
DEUTERONOMY XXIV, 21, *c.* 700 B.C.

I caused the widow's heart to sing for joy.
JOB XXIX, 13, *c.* 325 B.C.

Honor widows that are widows indeed.
I TIMOTHY V, 3, *c.* 60

The younger widows . . . have begun to wax wanton against Christ, they will marry.
I TIMOTHY V, 11

There came a certain poor widow, and she threw in two mites, which make a farthing.
MARK XII, 42, *c.* 70 (Cf. LUKE XXI, 2, *c.* 75)

Woe unto you, scribes and Pharisees, hypocrites! for ye devour widows' houses.
MATTHEW XXIII, 14, *c.* 75 (Cf. LUKE XX, 46–7, *c.* 75)

She was a widow of about fourscore and four years.
LUKE II, 37, *c.* 75

On the tombs of her seven husbands Chloe put the inscription: "The work of Chloe." How could she have said it more plainly?
MARTIAL: *Epigrams*, IX, *c.* 95

Second marriages are lawful, but holy widowhood is better.
ST. AUGUSTINE: *On the Good of Widowhood, c.* 413

Such of you as shall die and leave wives ought to bequeath their wives a year's maintenance, without putting them out of their houses.
THE KORAN, II, *c.* 625

He'll have a lusty widow now
That shall be wooed and wedded in a day.
SHAKESPEARE: *The Taming of the Shrew*, IV, 1594

What's a widow but an axle broke,
Whose one part failing, neither part can move?
JOHN DAVIES: *A Contention Betwixt a Wife, a Widow, and a Maid*, 1602

She that hath had a husband had to bury,
And is therefore, in heart not sad but merry,
Yet if in show, good manners she would keep,
Onions and mustard seed will make her weep.
JOHN HARINGTON: *The Englishman's Doctor*, 1608

The devout widow never desires to be esteemed either beautiful or comely, contenting herself with being such as God desires her to be, that is to say, humble and abject in her own eyes.
ST. FRANCIS DE SALES: *Introduction to the Devout Life*, XL, 1609

He first deceased; she for a little tried
To live without him, liked it not, and died.
HENRY WOTTON: *Upon the Death of Sir Morton's Wife, c.* 1610

There be things called widows, dead men's wills,
I never lov'd to prove those; nor never long'd yet
To be buried alive in another man's cold monument.
JOHN FLETCHER: *The Wild-Goose Chase*, I, 1621

Marry a widow before she leaves mourning.
GEORGE HERBERT: *Outlandish Proverbs*, 1640

I think with them who, both in prudence and elegance of spirit, would choose a virgin of mean fortunes, honestly bred, before the wealthiest widow.
JOHN MILTON: *An Apology for Smectymnuus*, 1642

Widowhood is pitiable in its solitariness and loss, but amiable and comely when it is adorned with gravity and purity, and not sullied with remembrances of the passed license, nor with present desires of returning to a second bed.
JEREMY TAYLOR: *The Rule and Exercises of Holy Living*, II, 1650

Take heed of . . . a widow thrice married.
GEORGE HERBERT: *Jacula Prudentum*, 1651

Who marries a widow and two daughters marries three thieves.
IBID.

It is a sad burden to carry a dead man's child.
THOMAS FULLER: *Church History*, II, 1655 (Cited as a proverb)

Here I see what creatures widows are in weeping for their husbands and then presently leaving off.
SAMUEL PEPYS: *Diary*, Oct. 17, 1667

He that woos a maid must seldom come in her sight,
But he that woos a widow must woo her day and night.
JOHN RAY: *English Proverbs*, 1670

Long a widow weds with shame.
IBID.

He that has a pretension to a widow must never give over for a little ill usage.
WILLIAM WYCHERLEY: *The Plain Dealer*, II, *c.* 1674

I am a relict and executrix of known plentiful assets and parts, who understand myself and the law.
IBID.

It's a delicious thing to be a young widow.
JOHN VANBRUGH: *The Relapse*, I, 1696

I never yet could meet with a sorrowful relict but was herself enough to make a hard bargain with me.
RICHARD STEELE: *The Funeral*, I, 1701 (Said by Sable the undertaker)

No crafty widows shall approach my bed:
Those are too wise for bachelors to wed.
ALEXANDER POPE: *January and May*, 1709

Widows are the most perverse creatures in the world.
JOSEPH ADDISON: *The Spectator*, March 25, 1711

[In Vienna] it is indecent for a widow ever to wear green or rose color, but all the other gayest colors at her own discretion.
MARY WORTLEY MONTAGU: *Letter to an unidentified correspondent*, Oct. 1, 1716

Never marry a widow unless her first husband was hanged.
JAMES KELLY: *Complete Collection of Scottish Proverbs*, 1721

Why are those tears? Why droops your head?
Is, then, your other husband dead?

Or does a worse disgrace betide?
Hath no one since his death applied?
JOHN GAY: *Fables,* I, 1727

The comfortable estate of widowhood is the only hope that keeps up a wife's spirits.
JOHN GAY: *The Beggar's Opera,* II, 1728

A good season for courtship is when the widow returns from the funeral.
THOMAS FULLER: *Gnomologia,* 1732

The rich widow cries with one eye and laughs with the other. IBID.

The new-made widow too I've sometimes spied,
Sad sight! slow moving o'er the prostrate dead:
Listless she crawls along in doleful black,
While bursts of sorrow gush from either eye,
Fast falling down her now untasted cheek.
ROBERT BLAIR: *The Grave,* 1743

When widows exclaim loudly against second marriages, I would always lay a wager that the man, if not the wedding-day, is absolutely fixed on.
HENRY FIELDING: *Amelia,* VI, 1752

A wanton widow Leezie was,
As canty as a kittlin;
But, och! that night, amang the shaws,
She got a fearfu' settlin'!
ROBERT BURNS: *Halloween,* 1785 (*Canty*=lively; *shaws*=the leaves and stalks of root-vegetables)

Twelve months her sables she in sorrow wore,
And mourn'd so long that she could mourn no more.
GEORGE CRABBE: *Tales,* VI (The Frank Courtship), 1812

Beware of widders.
CHARLES DICKENS: *The Pickwick Papers,* XXIV, 1837

Widders are 'ceptions to ev'ry rule. I have heerd how many ord'nary women one widder's equal to, in pint o' comin' over you. I think it's five-and-twenty, but I don't rightly know vether it ain't more. IBID.

I am a lone lorn creetur.
CHARLES DICKENS: *David Copperfield,* III, 1849

A widow of doubtful age will marry almost any sort of a white man.
Ascribed to HORACE GREELEY (1811–72)

Now, if you must marry, take care she is old —
A troop-sergeant's widow's the nicest, I'm told.
RUDYARD KIPLING: *The Young British Soldier,* 1891

A pathetic figure that the Christian world has agreed to take humorously, although Christ's tenderness towards widows was one of the most marked features of His character.
AMBROSE BIERCE: *The Devil's Dictionary,* 1906

A virtuous widow is the most loyal of mortals; she is faithful to that which is neither pleased nor profited by her fidelity.
AMBROSE BIERCE: *Collected Works,* VIII, 1911

So far as is known, no widow ever eloped.
E. W. HOWE: *Country Town Sayings,* 1911

A widow who marries the second time doesn't deserve to be one.
ELBERT HUBBARD: *Roycroft Dictionary and Book of Epigrams,* 1923

A widow is a rudderless boat.
CHINESE PROVERB

A maid marries to please her parents; a widow to please herself. IBID.

Few women turn gray because their husbands die. DANISH PROVERB

The rich widow's tears soon dry. IBID.

This turf has drunk a widow's tear,
Three of her husbands slumber here.
Epitaph in a Staffordshire churchyard, England

The three most pleasant things are: a cat's kitten, a goat's kid, and a young widow woman. IRISH PROVERB

In the widow's house there is no fat mouse.
JAPANESE PROVERB

A man does with a maiden as he wills; with a widow as she wills. POLISH PROVERB

He who has not married a young widow doesn't know what misfortune is.
RUSSIAN PROVERB

He that marries a widow and twa dochters has three back doors to his house.
SCOTTISH PROVERB (*Dochter*=daughter)

A comely widow should either re-marry, be killed, or be shut up in a convent.
SPANISH PROVERB

He who marries a widow will often have a dead man's head thrown in his dish. IBID.

He who marries a widow with three children marries four thieves. SWEDISH PROVERB

[*See also* Charity, Chastity, Chivalry, Danger, Epitaph, Funeral, Marriage, Merriment, Onion, Orphan, Piety, Soldier, Vineyard, Virgin, Wife.

Widower

The death of the first wife makes such a hole in the heart that all the rest slip through.
JAMES KELLY: *Complete Collection of Scottish Proverbs,* 1721

My wife was in my mind: she would have been pleased. Having now nobody to please, I am little pleased.
SAMUEL JOHNSON: *Diary in France,* Oct. 17, 1775

Houses she kept for widowers lately made;
For now she said, "They'll miss th' endearing friend,
And I'll be there the soften'd heart to mend."

GEORGE CRABBE: *The Borough*, xv, 1810

Oh, 'tis a precious thing, when wives are dead,
To find such numbers who will serve instead;
And in whatever state a man be thrown
'Tis that precisely they would wish their own.

GEORGE CRABBE: *Tales of the Hall*, 1819

I will not blaze cambric and crape in the public eye like a disconsolate widower, that most affected of all characters.

WALTER SCOTT: *Journal*, May 16, 1826 (Lady Scott died May 15)

After such years of dissension and strife,
Some wonder that Peter should weep for his wife;
But his tears on her grave are nothing surprising, —
He's laying her dust, for fear of its rising.

THOMAS HOOD: *Peter and His Wife*, c. 1830

By the calamity of April last, I lost my little all in this world; and have no soul left who can make any corner of this world into a *home* for me any more. Bright, heroic, tender, true and noble was that lost treasure of my heart, who faithfully accompanied me in all the rocky ways and climbings; and I am forever poor without her.

THOMAS CARLYLE: *Letter to R. W. Emerson*, Jan. 27, 1867

Cried Ned to his neighbors, as onward they pressed,
Conveying his wife to the place of long rest,
"Take, friends, I beseech you, a little more leisure;
For why should we thus make a toil of a pleasure?"

Author unidentified

Wife

Every wise man loves the wife he has chosen.

HOMER: *Iliad*, IX, *c.* 800 B.C.

Though you love your wife, do not tell her all you know; tell her some trifle, and conceal the rest. HOMER: *Odyssey*, XI, *c.* 800 B.C.

The Lord God said, It is not good that the man should be alone; I will make him a help meet for him. GENESIS II, 18, *c.* 700 B.C.

And Adam said, This is now bone of my bones, and flesh of my flesh. GENESIS II, 23

A man [shall] leave his father and his mother, and shall cleave unto his wife: and they shall be one flesh.

GENESIS II, 24 (Cf. EPHESIANS V, 31, *c.* 60; MARK X, 7–8, *c.* 70; MATTHEW XIX, 5, *c.* 75)

It came to pass, when men began to multiply on the face of the earth, and daughters were born unto them, that the sons of God saw the daughters of men that they were fair; and they took them wives of all which they chose. GENESIS VI, 1–2

They shall not take a wife that is a whore, or profane; neither shall they take a woman put away from her husband.

LEVITICUS XXI, 7, *c.* 700 B.C.

The wife of thy bosom.

DEUTERONOMY XIII, 6, *c.* 650 B.C.

When a woman, in her husband's absence, seeks to display her beauty, mark her as a wanton.

EURIPIDES: *Electra*, *c.* 415 B.C.

Let thy fountain be blessed: and rejoice with the wife of thy youth. Let her be as the loving hind and pleasant roe; let her breasts satisfy thee at all times; and be thou ravished always with her love.

PROVERBS V, 18–19, *c.* 350 B.C.

A virtuous woman is a crown to her husband: but she that maketh ashamed is as rottenness in his bones. PROVERBS XII, 4

Whoso findeth a wife findeth a good thing, and obtaineth favor of the Lord.

PROVERBS XVIII, 22

The contentions of a wife are a continual dropping. PROVERBS XIX, 13

A prudent wife is from the Lord.

PROVERBS XIX, 14

Depart not from a wise and good wife, whom thou hast gotten in the fear of the Lord: for the grace of her modesty is above gold.

ECCLESIASTICUS VII, 21, *c.* 180 B.C.

Blessed is the man that hath a virtuous wife, for the number of his days shall be double.

ECCLESIASTICUS XXVI, 1

The obedience of a wife is a kind of command.

PUBLILIUS SYRUS: *Sententiæ*, *c.* 50 B.C.

Strife is the dowry of a wife.

OVID: *Remedia amoris*, *c.* 10

There is difference also between a wife and a virgin. The unmarried woman careth for the things of the Lord, that she may be holy both in body and in spirit; but she that is married careth for the things of the world, how she may please her husband.

I CORINTHIANS VII, 34, *c.* 55

He that loveth his wife loveth himself.

EPHESIANS V, 28, *c.* 60

The weaker vessel. I PETER III, 7, *c.* 60

Give me a wife not too learned.

MARTIAL: *Epigrams*, II, 86

Lyeoris has buried all the female friends she had, Fabianus: would she were the friend of my wife! MARTIAL: *Epigrams*, IV, *c.* 95

Your seventh wife, Phileros, is now being buried in your field. No man's field brings him greater profit than yours, Phileros.

MARTIAL: *Epigrams*, X, *c.* 95

tum, is, in his own conceit, the only Shake-scene in a country.
ROBERT GREENE: *A Groatsworth of Wit,* 1592

Shakespeare thou, whose honey-flowing vein
(Pleasing the world) thy praises doth obtain;
Whose "Venus" and whose "Lucrece" (sweet and chaste)
Thy name in fame's immortal book have pace't.
RICHARD BARNFIELD: *Poems in Divers Humors,* 1598

As Plautus and Seneca are accounted the best for comedy and tragedy among the Latins, so Shakespeare among the English is the most excellent in both kinds for the stage.
FRANCIS MERES: *Pallidas Tamia,* 1598

As the soul of Euphorbus was thought to live in Pythagoras, so the sweet, witty soul of Ovid lives in mellifluous and honey-tongued Shakespeare. IBID.

The English tongue is mightily enriched, and gorgeously invested in rare ornaments and resplendent habiliments by Sir Philip Sidney, Spenser . . . Shakespeare. . . . IBID.

Honey-tongued Shakespeare, when I saw thine issue,
I swore Apollo got them and none other,
Their rosy-tainted features cloth'd in tissue,
Some heaven-born goddess said to be their mother.
JOHN WEEVER: *Epigrams in the Oldest Cut,* IV, 1599

Upon a time when Burbage played Richard III there was a citizen grew so far in liking with him that before she went from the play she appointed him to come that night unto her by the name of Richard III. Shakespeare, overhearing their conclusion, went before, was entertained, and at his game ere Burbage came. Then message being brought that Richard III was at the door, Shakespeare caused return to be made that William the Conqueror was before Richard III.
JOHN MANNINGHAM: *Diary,* 1602–3 (Burbage was the most celebrated actor of the time, and Shakespeare's partner in various theatrical enterprises)

I have ever truly cherish'd my good opinion of other men's worthy labors, especially of that full and height'ned style of Master Chapman; the labor'd and understanding works of Master Jonson; . . . and lastly, without wrong last to be named, the right happy and copious industry of M. Shakespeare.
JOHN WEBSTER: *The White Devil,* dedication, *c.* 1608

Alas! 'tis true I have gone here and there,
And made myself a motley to the view,
Gored mine own thoughts, sold cheap what is most dear.
SHAKESPEARE: *Sonnets,* CX, 1609

The last . . . authors I have seen on the subject of love . . . are Sir William Alexander and Shakespeare, who have lately published their works.
WILLIAM DRUMMOND OF HAWTHORNDEN: *Works,* 1711 (Probably written in 1615)

His censure of the English poets was . . . that Shakespeare wanted art.
WILLIAM DRUMMOND OF HAWTHORNDEN: *Informations and Manners of Ben Jonson,* 1618

His mind and hand went together. What he thought he uttered with that earnestness that we have scarce received from him a blot in his papers.
JOHN HEMING and HENRY CONDELL: Pref. to the First Folio Shakespeare, 1623

Soul of the age!
Th' applause! delight! the wonder of our stage!
My Shakespeare rise! I will not lodge thee by
Chaucer, or Spenser, or bid Beaumont lie
A little further, to make thee a room;
Thou art a monument without a tomb,
And art alive still, while thy book doth live,
And we have wits to read, and praise to give.
BEN JONSON: *To the Memory of My Beloved, the Author, Wm. Shakespeare* (in the First Folio Shakespeare), 1623

He was not of an age, but for all time. IBID.

My gentle Shakespeare. . . . Sweet swan of Avon. IBID.

Thou hadst small Latin and less Greek. IBID.

What need my Shakespeare for his honored bones
The labor of an age in piléd stones,
Or that his hallowed relics should be hid
Under a starry-pointing pyramid? . . .
Thou in our wonder and astonishment
Hast built thyself a lasting monument.
JOHN MILTON: *An Epitaph on the Admirable Dramatic Poet, W. Shakespeare* (in the Second Folio Shakespeare), 1632

I remember the players have often mentioned it as an honor to Shakespeare, that in his writing (whatsoever he penned) he never blotted out a line. My answer hath been, would he had blotted a thousand, which they thought a malevolent speech. I had not told posterity this but for their ignorance, who chose that circumstance to commend their friend by, whereby he most faulted.
BEN JONSON: *Discoveries, c.* 1635

He redeemed his vices with his virtues. There was ever more in him to be praised than to be pardoned. IBID.

I loved the man, and do honor his memory, on this side idolatry, as much as any. IBID.

Some second Shakespeare must of Shakespeare write.
LEONARD DIGGES: *Upon Master William Shakespeare* (in Shakespeare's Poems), 1640

Or sweetest Shakespeare, fancy's child,
Warble his native wood-notes wild.

JOHN MILTON: *L'Allegro*, 1645

I saw "Hamlet, Prince of Denmark" played, but now the old plays begin to disgust this refined age.

JOHN EVELYN: *Diary*, Nov. 26, 1661

Many were the wit combats betwixt him and Ben Jonson, which two I behold like a Spanish great galleon and an English man-of-war. Master Jonson, like the former, was built far higher in learning — solid, but slow in his performances; Shakespeare, with the English man-of-war, lesser in bulk but lighter in sailing, could turn with all tides, tack about, and take advantage of all winds by the quickness of his wit and invention.

THOMAS FULLER: *Worthies of England*, 1662

Shakespeare, Drayton and Ben Jonson had a merry meeting, and it seems drank too hard, for Shakespeare died of a fever there contracted.

JOHN WARD: *Diary*, c. 1662

To the King's theater, where we saw "Midsummer Night's Dream," which I had never seen before, nor shall ever again, for it is the most insipid, ridiculous play that ever I saw in my life.

SAMUEL PEPYS: *Diary*, Sept. 29, 1662

Shakespeare (with some errors, not to be avoided in that age) had, undoubtedly, a larger soul of poesy than ever any of our nation.

JOHN DRYDEN: *The Rival Ladies*, dedication, 1664

When he describes anything you more than see it; you feel it.

JOHN DRYDEN: *Of Dramatic Poesy*, 1668

The immortal Shakespeare.

NATHANIEL LEE: *Mithridates*, dedication, 1678

The divine Shakespeare.

JOHN CROWNE: *The Misery of Civil War*, prologue, 1680

Though some others may pretend to a more exact decorum and economy, especially in tragedy, never any expressed a more lofty and tragic height, never any represented nature more purely to the life, and where the polishments of art are most wanting (for his learning was not extraordinary) he pleased with a certain wild and native elegance.

WILLIAM WINSTANLEY: *England's Worthies*, 1684

The godlike Shakespeare.

THOMAS BETTERTON: Epilogue for the operatic form of BEAUMONT and FLETCHER: *The Prophetess*, 1690

The pride of nature and the shame of schools,
Born to create and not to learn from rules.

CHARLES SEDLEY: Prologue to HENRY HIGDEN: *The Wary Widow*, 1693

If he had had the advantage of art and learning, he would have surpassed the very best and strongest of the ancients.

JOHN DENNIS: *An Essay on the Genius and Writings of Shakespeare*, 1712

Shakespeare was a great copier of nature.

RICHARD STEELE: *The Guardian*, Aug. 26, 1713

Shakespeare (whom you, and every playhouse bill
Style the divine, the matchless, what you will)
For gain, not glory, wing'd his roving flight,
And grew immortal in his own despite.

ALEXANDER POPE: *The First Epistle of the Second Book of Horace*, 1737

When learning's triumph o'er her barb'rous foes
First rear'd the stage, immortal Shakespeare rose;
Each change of many-colored life he drew,
Exhausted worlds, and then imagin'd new.

SAMUEL JOHNSON: Prologue for the opening of Drury Lane, 1747

Shikspur? Shikspur? Who wrote it? No, I never read Shikspur.

JAMES TOWNLEY: *High Life Below Stairs*, II, 1759

I said a long while ago that if Shakespeare had lived in Addison's time, he would have reinforced his genius with Addison's elegance and purity. His genius was his own; his faults were those of the age he lived in.

VOLTAIRE: *Letter to Horace Walpole*, July 15, 1768

Shakespeare never had six lines together without a fault. Perhaps you may find seven, but this does not refute my general assertion.

SAMUEL JOHNSON: *Boswell's Life*, Oct. 19, 1769

It was most injudicious in Johnson to select Shakespeare as one of his principal authorities [for his Dictionary]. Play-writers, in describing low scenes and vulgar characters, use low language, language unfit for decent company; and their ribaldry has corrupted our speech, as well as the public morals.

NOAH WEBSTER: *Letter to Thomas Dawes*, Aug. 5, 1809

The greatest genius that perhaps human nature has yet produced.

S. T. COLERIDGE: *Biographia Literaria*, XV, 1817

I acknowledge Shakespeare to be the world's greatest dramatic poet, but regret that no parent could place the uncorrected book in the hands of his daughter, and therefore I have prepared the Family Shakespeare.

THOMAS BOWDLER: *The Family Shakespeare*, pref., 1818

Thomas Moore knew Sheridan. Sheridan knew Johnson, who was the friend of Savage, who knew Steele, who knew Pope. Pope was intimate with Congreve, and Congreve with Dryden. Dryden [knew] Davenant, with whom he was intimate. Davenant knew Hobbes, who knew Bacon, who knew Ben Jonson, who was intimate with Beaumont and Fletcher, Chapman, Donne, Drayton, Camden, Selden, Clarendon, Sydney, Raleigh, and . . . Shakespeare.

LEIGH HUNT: *The Indicator,* x, 1821

If we wish to know the force of human genius we should read Shakespeare. If we wish to see the insignificance of human learning we may study his commentators.

WILLIAM HAZLITT: *Table-Talk,* I, 1824

The greatest poet that ever lived.

T. B. MACAULAY: *John Dryden,* 1828 (Edinburgh Review, Jan.)

Shakespeare, Madam, is obscene, and thank God, we are sufficiently advanced to have found it out!

An unnamed American: To Frances Trollope (quoted in her *Domestic Manners of the Americans,* IX, 1832), *c.* 1830

I believe Shakespeare was not a whit more intelligible in his own day than he is now to an educated man, except for a few local allusions of no consequence. He is of no age — nor of any religion, or party, or profession. The body and substance of his works came out of the unfathomable depths of his own oceanic mind: his observation and reading, which was considerable, supplied him with the drapery of his figures.

S. T. COLERIDGE: *Table-Talk,* March 15, 1834

Shakespeare is the chief of all poets hitherto; the greatest intellect who, in our recorded world, has left record of himself in the way of literature.

THOMAS CARLYLE: *Heroes and Hero-Worship,* III, 1840 (Lecture in London, May 12)

Could Shakespeare give a theory of Shakespeare?

R. W. EMERSON: *Spiritual Laws,* 1841

What point of morals, of manners, of economy, of philosophy, of religion, of taste, of the conduct of life, has he not settled? What mystery has he not signified his knowledge of? What office, or function, or district of man's work, has he not remembered? What maiden has not found him finer than her delicacy? What lover has he not outloved? What sage has he not outseen?

R. W. EMERSON: *Representative Men,* v, 1850

I should like to have been Shakespeare's shoeblack — just to have lived in his house, just to have worshipped him — to have run on his errands, and seen that sweet serene face.

W. M. THACKERAY: *The English Humorists,* 1853

Shakespeare was forbidden of Heaven to have any plans. To *do* any good or *get* any good, in the common sense of good, was not to be within his permitted range of work. Not, for him, the founding of institutions, the preaching of doctrines, or the repression of abuses.

JOHN RUSKIN: *Modern Painters,* v, 1860

The poet paramount.

H. W. LONGFELLOW: *Shakespeare,* 1875

I know no more heart-rending reading than Shakespeare. How a man must have suffered in order to find it necessary to make such a clown of himself!

F. W. NIETZSCHE: *Ecce Homo,* 1888

The works of Shakespeare, borrowed as they are, and externally, like mosaics, artificially fitted together piecemeal from bits invented for the occasion, have nothing whatever in common with art and poetry.

LYOF N. TOLSTOY: *On Shakespeare,* 1906

[*See also* Boston, Burke (Edmund), Dante Alighieri, Epitaph, Greatness, Jonson (Ben), Metaphysics, Milton (John), Nickname.

Shame

Shame is the mark of a base man, and belongs to a character capable of shameful acts.

ARISTOTLE: *The Nicomachean Ethics,* IV, *c.* 340 B.C.

It is natural to feel no shame before those whom one holds in contempt.

ARISTOTLE: *Rhetoric,* II, *c.* 322 B.C.

When a woman once begins to be ashamed of what she ought not to be ashamed of, she will not be ashamed of what she ought.

CATO THE CENSOR: *In Support of the Oppian Law,* 215 B.C.

Of all kinds of shame, the worst, surely, is being ashamed of frugality or poverty.

LIVY: *History of Rome,* XXXIV, *c.* 10

Life is easy to a man who has no shame.

The Dhammapada, XVIII, *c.* 100

When we sin, we are all ashamed at the presence of our inferiors.

ST. JOHN CHRYSOSTOM: *Homilies,* XIII, *c.* 388

In shame there is no comfort, but to be beyond all bounds of shame.

PHILIP SYDNEY: *Arcadia,* II, 1590

Shame leaves us by degrees.

SAMUEL DANIEL: *The Complaynt of Rosamond,* 1592

O shame! Where is thy blush?

SHAKESPEARE: *Hamlet,* III, *c.* 1601

A nightingale dies for shame if another bird sings better.

ROBERT BURTON: *The Anatomy of Melancholy,* 1621

Love taught him shame; and shame, with love at strife,
Soon taught the sweet civilities of life.

JOHN DRYDEN: *Cymon and Iphigenia,* 1699

I never wonder to see men wicked, but I often wonder to see them not ashamed.

JONATHAN SWIFT: *Thoughts on Various Subjects,* 1706

He is without the sense of shame or glory, as some men are without the sense of smelling.

JONATHAN SWIFT: *The Character of Lord Wharton,* 1710

Men the most infamous are fond of fame,
And those who fear not guilt, yet start at shame.

CHARLES CHURCHILL: *The Author,* 1763

Whilst shame keeps its watch, virtue is not wholly extinguished in the heart.

EDMUND BURKE: *Reflections on the Revolution in France,* I, 1790

Every woe a tear can claim,
Except an erring sister's shame.

BYRON: *The Giaour,* 1813

Be not ashamed of anything but to be ashamed.

Author unidentified

Shame has a longer life than poverty.

DUTCH PROVERB

So long as there is shame there is hope for virtue. GERMAN PROVERB

He who puts a friend to public shame is as guilty as a murderer. HEBREW PROVERB

When the heart's past hope the face is past shame. SCOTTISH PROVERB

[*See also* Age (Old), Anarchy, Blush, Crowd, Fame, Fool, Love, Nature, Poverty, Pride, Sin.

Shaving

The first man to be shaved every day was Scipio Africanus.

PLINY THE ELDER: *Natural History,* VII, 77 (Apparently Scipio Africanus Minor, *c.* 185–129 B.C.)

Well lathered is half shaven.

THOMAS FULLER: *Gnomologia,* 1732

I could never discover more than two reasons for shaving: the one is to get a beard, the other is to get rid of one.

HENRY FIELDING: *Tom Jones,* VIII, 1749

Of a thousand shavers, two do not shave so much alike as not to be distinguished.

SAMUEL JOHNSON: *Boswell's Life,* Sept. 19, 1777

It is easier to bear a child once a year than to shave every day. RUSSIAN PROVERB

Shaving destroys the image of God. IBID.

[*See also* Barber, Beard, Handsaw.

She

Whoe'er she be –
That not impossible she
That shall command my heart and me.

RICHARD CRASHAW: *Wishes to His Supposed Mistress,* 1646

Sheep

Baa, baa, black sheep,
  Have you any wool?
Yes, marry, have I
  Three bags full:
One for the master,
  And one for my dame,
And one for the little boy
  Who lives in the lane.

Anon.: *Nursery rhyme, c.* 1750

Little Bo-peep has lost her sheep
  And can't tell where to find them;
Leave them alone and they'll come home,
  And bring their tails behind them. IBID.

The mountain sheep are sweeter,
But the valley sheep are fatter;
We therefore deemed it meeter
To carry off the latter.

T. L. PEACOCK: *The Misfortunes of Elphin,* II, 1829

One sheep follows another. (Ovis ovem sequitur.) LATIN PROVERB

[*See also* Crowd, Devil, Foolishness, Goat, Man, Peace.

Shelley, P. B. (1792–1821)

Percy Bysshe Shelley, the unearthly brightness
  And wild expression of thy fearful eye
Prove thou hast forfeited thy bosom's whiteness,
  And leagued thy soul to shame and perfidy.

J. W. DALBY: Untitled stanzas, 1821 (Literary Chronicle, June 9)

He had a fire in his eye, a fever in his blood, a maggot in his brain, a hectic flutter in his speech, which mark out the philosophic fanatic.

WILLIAM HAZLITT: *Table-Talk,* 1821

Shelley . . . is, to my knowledge, the least selfish and the mildest of men – a man who has made more sacrifices of his fortune and feelings for others than any I ever heard of. With his speculative opinions I have nothing in common, nor desire to have.

BYRON: *Letter to Thomas Moore,* March 4, 1822

Shelley I saw once. His voice was the most obnoxious squeak I ever was tormented with.

CHARLES LAMB: *Letter to Bernard Barton,* Oct. 9, 1822

No one was ever the wiser or better for reading Shelley.

CHARLES LAMB: *Letter to Bernard Barton,* Aug. 17, 1824 (Quoting Hazlitt)

With all his genius (and I think *most* highly of it), he was a base, bad man.
ROBERT SOUTHEY: *Letter to Henry Taylor,* Feb. 28, 1830

He was a liar and a cheat; he paid no regard to truth, nor to any kind of moral obligation. It was mortifying to discover this, for I never saw a youth of whom I could have hoped better things.
ROBERT SOUTHEY: *Letter to Henry Taylor,* Feb. 29, 1830

The qualities that struck any one newly introduced to Shelley were, first, a gentle and cordial goodness that animated his intercourse with warm affection and helpful sympathy; the other, the eagerness and ardor with which he was attached to the cause of human happiness and improvement; and the fervent eloquence with which he discussed such subjects.
MARY GODWIN SHELLEY: Pref. to the first Collected Edition of Shelley, 1839

And did you once see Shelley plain,
And did he stop and speak to you,
And did you speak to him again?
How strange it seems and new.
ROBERT BROWNING: *Memorabilia,* 1842

If ever mortal " wreaked his thoughts upon expression," it was Shelley. If ever poet sang — as a bird sings — earnestly — impulsively — with utter abandonment — to himself solely — and for the mere joy of his own song — that poet was the author of " The Sensitive Plant." Of art — beyond that which is instinctive with genius — he either had little or disdained all.
E. A. POE: *Marginalia,* 1844–49

Shelley, who fired my youth with passion, and purified and upbore it for so long, is now to me as nothing; not a dead or faded thing, but a thing out of which I personally have drawn all the sustenance I may draw from him; and, therefore, it (that part which I did not absorb) concerns me no more.
GEORGE MOORE: *Confessions of a Young Man,* II, 1888

He would have died a Tory had he lived to be fifty — and president of the Bible Society.
AUGUSTINE BIRRELL: Written in the margin of his copy of GEORG BRANDES: *Main Currents in Nineteenth Century Literature,* 1918

Shepherd

The Lord is my shepherd; I shall not want.
PSALMS XXIII, 1, *c.* 150 B.C.

The first holy men were shepherds.
ST. AUGUSTINE: *The City of God,* XV, 427

My name is Norval; on the Grampian hill
My father feeds his flocks.
JOHN HOME: *Douglas,* III, 1756

Trust a shepherd to be a fool.
HINDU PROVERB

[*See also* Goat.

Sheridan, Philip H. (1831–88)

And Sheridan twenty miles away.
T. B. READ: *Sheridan's Ride,* 1864

The death of General Sheridan was a national affliction. The army then lost the grandest of its chiefs.
GROVER CLEVELAND: Message to Congress, Dec. 3, 1888

Sheridan, R. B. (1751–1816)

Why, Sir, Sherry is dull, naturally dull; but it must have taken him a great deal of pains to become what we now see him. Such an excess of stupidity, sir, is not nature.
SAMUEL JOHNSON: *Boswell's Life,* 1763 (Meaning Sheridan's father, Thomas, 1719–88)

I never saw Sheridan but in large parties. He had a Bardolph countenance with heavy features, but his eye possessed the most distinguished brilliancy.
WALTER SCOTT: *Journal,* Jan. 13, 1826

Sherman, W. T. (1820–91)

Sherman was comfortable when in the field, but at home suffered from allergic attacks: he was sensitive to house dust.
Anon.: In the Journal of the American Medical Association, Sept. 21, 1940

[*See also* Brotherhood.

Sherry

[*See* Wine (Sherry).

Shibboleth

The Gileadites took the passages of Jordan before the Ephraimites: and it was so, that when those Ephraimites which were escaped said, Let me go over, that the men of Gilead said unto him, Art thou an Ephraimite? If he said, Nay; then said they unto him, Say now Shibboleth: and he said Sibboleth: for he could not frame to pronounce it right. Then they took him, and slew him at the passages of Jordan.
JUDGES XII, 5–6, *c.* 500 B.C.

Reason and argument are incapable of combating certain words and formulas. They are uttered with solemnity in the presence of crowds, and as soon as they have been pronounced an expression of respect is visible on every countenance, and all heads are bowed.
GUSTAVE LEBON: *Psychologie des foules,* 1895

Shin

[*See* Dark.

Ship

Ships are but boards, sailors but men.
SHAKESPEARE: *The Merchant of Venice,* I, *c.* 1597

What is a ship but a prison?
ROBERT BURTON: *The Anatomy of Melancholy,* II, 1621

A ship and a woman are ever repairing.
GEORGE HERBERT: *Outlandish Proverbs,* 1640

Ships fear fire more than water. IBID.

To a crazy ship all winds are contrary. IBID.

I saw a ship a-sailing,
A-sailing on the sea,
And oh, it was all laden
With pretty things for thee.
Anon.: *Nursery rhyme, c.* 1750

A ship is worse than a jail. There is, in jail, better air, better company, better conveniency of every kind; and a ship has the additional disadvantage of being in danger.
SAMUEL JOHNSON: *Boswell's Life,* March 18, 1776

Don't give up the ship!
Ascribed variously to JAMES MUGFORD, commander of the schooner Franklin, during a fight with the British in Boston harbor, May 19, 1776; to JAMES LAWRENCE, commander of the frigate Chesapeake, during a fight with the British frigate Shannon, June 1, 1813; and to OLIVER HAZARD PERRY, commodore of the American flotilla at the Battle of Lake Erie, Sept. 10, 1813 (Only Perry's use of the phrase seems to be authenticated)

She walks the waters like a thing of life.
BYRON: *The Corsair,* I, 1814

Why is a ship under sail more poetical than a hog in a high wind? The hog is all nature, the ship is all art.
BYRON: *Letter to John Murray,* Feb. 7, 1821

Ships that pass in the night.
H. W. LONGFELLOW: *Tales of a Wayside Inn,* 1863 (BEATRICE HARRADEN: Title of a novel, 1893)

Of all the living creatures upon land and sea, it is ships alone that cannot be taken in by barren pretenses, that will not put up with bad art from their masters.
JOSEPH CONRAD: *The Mirror of the Sea,* III, 1906

Better in an old carriage than in a new ship.
DANISH PROVERB

All ships leak. ITALIAN PROVERB

[*See also* Adornment, Enigma, Mystery, Pregnancy, Rat, Sailor, Sea.

Shipping

In all the ancient states and empires those who had the shipping had the wealth.
WILLIAM PETTY: *Poetical Arithmetic,* I, *c.* 1677

I believe a communication from one part of the world to some other parts of it, by sea, is, at times, consistent with the will of our Heavenly Father; and to educate some youth in the practise of sailing, I believe, may be right.
JOHN WOOLMAN: *Journal,* X, 1774

[*See also* Sea-power.

Shipwreck

Then rose from sea to sky the wild farewell —
Then some leap'd overboard with fearful yell.
BYRON: *Don Juan,* II, 1819

Shirt

It's a lonesome washing that there's not a man's shirt in. IRISH PROVERB

When Bryan O'Lynn had no shirt to put on,
He took him a sheepskin to make him a' one.
"With the skinny side out, and the woolly side in,
'Twill be warm and convanient," said Bryan O'Lynn. IRISH RHYME

[*See also* Skin.

Shirt-button

[*See* Misery.

Shirtsleeves

No gentleman can be permitted to come to the public table without his coat.
R. W. EMERSON: *The Conduct of Life,* IV, 1860 (Described as a sign displayed "in the hotels on the banks of the Mississippi")

There are but three generations from shirtsleeves to shirtsleeves.
AMERICAN PROVERB

Shoe

Every shoe fits not every foot.
SCOTTISH PROVERB

[*See also* Old.

Shoemaker

Shoemaker, stick to your last.
ENGLISH SAYING, borrowed from the Latin and familiar since the XVI century

I am a surgeon to old shoes.
SHAKESPEARE: *Julius Cæsar,* I, 1599

[*See also* Cobbler, Shoemaking, Vocation.

Shoemaking

The gentle craft.
THOMAS DEKKER: *The Shoemaker's Holiday,* I, 1599

Shopkeeping

Keep thy shop, and thy shop will keep thee.
GEORGE CHAPMAN, BEN JONSON and JOHN MARSTON: *Eastward Ho,* I, 1605

A man who finds it painful to smile should not open a shop. CHINESE PROVERB

These three are not to be trusted even when asleep: a crow, a dog, and a shopkeeper.
HINDU PROVERB

[*See also* English, Untrustworthy, Vocation.

Shopping

Shopping alone, and shopping together,
At all hours of the day and in all sorts of weather,
For all manner of things that a woman can put
On the crown of her head or the sole of her foot,
Or wrap round her shoulders, or fit round her waist,
Or that can be sewed on, or pinned on, or laced,
Or tied on with a string, or stitched on with a bow,
In front or behind, above or below.

WILLIAM ALLEN BUTLER: *Nothing to Wear*, 1857

Short

Good things are twice as good when they are short.

BALTASAR GRACIÁN: *The Art of Worldly Wisdom*, CV, 1647

Short folk are soon angry.

JAMES KELLY: *Complete Collection of Scottish Proverbs*, 1721

Short men eat more than tall ones.

FRENCH PROVERB

Short hair is soon brushed.

PENNSYLVANIA GERMAN PROVERB

[*See also* Horse, Long, Marriage, Tall.

Shot

By the rude bridge that arched the flood,
Their flag to April's breeze unfurled,
Here once the embattled farmers stood
And fired the shot heard round the world.

R. W. EMERSON: Hymn sung at the completion of Concord monument, April 19, 1836

Shout

The universal host up sent
A shout that tore Hell's conclave, and beyond,
Frighted the reign of Chaos and old Night.

JOHN MILTON: *Paradise Lost*, I, 1667

Shrew

Every man can rule a shrew save he that hath her.

JOHN HEYWOOD: *Proverbs*, 1546

It is better to marry a shrew than a sheep.

JAMES HOWELL: *Familiar Letters*, I, 1645

Shyness

In society I am like a fish on the sand, which writhes and writhes, but cannot get away until some benevolent Galatea casts it back into the sea.

LUDWIG VAN BEETHOVEN: *Letter to Bettina Brentano*, Aug. 11, 1810

Shy and proud men are more liable than any others to fall into the hands of parasites and creatures of low character. For in the intimacies which are formed by shy men, they do not choose, but are chosen.

HENRY TAYLOR: *The Statesman*, 1836

[*See also* Bashfulness.

Sicilian

It is interesting to pass from Malta to Sicily — from the highest specimen of an inferior race, the Saracenic, to the most degraded class of a superior race, the European.

S. T. COLERIDGE: *Table-Talk*, April 16, 1834

Sick

Be not slow to visit the sick.

ECCLESIASTICUS VII, 35, *c.* 180 B.C.

Is any sick among you? let him call for the elders of the church; and let them pray over him, anointing him with oil in the name of the Lord.

JAMES V, 14, *c.* 60

Before all, and above all, attention shall be paid to the care of the sick, so that they shall be served as if they were Christ Himself.

THE RULE OF ST. BENEDICT, *c.* 529

Visiting any sick body, do not play suddenly the doctor of physic's part, if thou therein understand nothing.

FRANCIS HAWKINS: *Youth's Behavior*, II, 1663

How few of his friends' houses would a man choose to be at when sick.

SAMUEL JOHNSON: *Boswell's Life*, 1783

Hazlitt, who boldly says all he feels, avows that not only he does not pity sick people, but he hates them.

CHARLES LAMB: *Letter to Bernard Barton*, April, 1824

[*See also* Advice, Doctor, Illness, Patience, Patient, Sickness.

Sickly

Sickly body, sickly mind.

GERMAN PROVERB

Sickness

Who can help sickness? quoth the drunken wife when she fell in the gutter.

JAMES KELLY: *Complete Collection of Scottish Proverbs*, 1721

He who was never sick dies the first fit.

THOMAS FULLER: *Gnomologia*, 1732

How sickness enlarges the dimension of a man's self to himself! He is his own exclusive object. He has nothing to think of but how to get well.

CHARLES LAMB: *The Convalescent*, 1825 (London Magazine, July)

I am always sick; I am sicker and worse in body and mind, a little, for the present; but it has no deep significance.

THOMAS CARLYLE: *Letter to R. W. Emerson*, Nov. 5, 1836

Be lang sick, that ye may be soon hale.
SCOTTISH PROVERB

Sickness arrives on horseback and departs on foot.
WALLOON PROVERB

[*See also* Health, Illness, Mind, Mind and Body, Modesty, Solitude, Ventilation.

Side-show

I have always looked upon it as a high point of indiscretion in monster-mongers, and other retailers of strange sights, to hang out a fair large picture over the door, drawn after the life, with a most eloquent description underneath. This hath saved me many a threepence; for my curiosity was fully satisfied, and I never offered to go in, though often invited by the urging and attending orator.
JONATHAN SWIFT: *A Tale of a Tub*, v, 1704

Sidney, Philip (1554–86)

[*See* Epitaph.

Siege

Thou shalt eat the fruit of thine own body, the flesh of thy sons and of thy daughters, which the Lord thy God hath given thee, in the siege.
DEUTERONOMY XXVIII, 53, *c.* 650 B.C.

The city sinks to quietude and peace,
Sleeping, like Saturn, in a ring of fire.
ELIZABETH CHASE (AKERS ALLEN): *In the Defences*, 1864

Siesta

Long sleep in afternoons, by stirring fumes,
Breeds sloth and agues, aching heads and rheums.
JOHN HARINGTON: *The Englishman's Doctor*, 1608

There is perhaps no solitary sensation so exquisite as that of slumbering on the grass or hay, shaded from the hot sun by a tree, with the consciousness of a fresh but light air running through the wide atmosphere, and the sky stretching far overhead upon all sides.
LEIGH HUNT: *The Indicator*, XXI, 1821

[*See also* Nap, Sleep.

Sigh

A plague of sighing and grief! It blows a man up like a bladder.
SHAKESPEARE: *I King Henry IV*, II, *c.* 1598

The passing tribute of a sigh.
THOMAS GRAY: *Elegy Written in a Country Churchyard*, 1750

Sighing is no medicine.
ITALIAN PROVERB

With every sigh goes a tear.
WELSH PROVERB

[*See also* Love.

Sight

The sense of sight is the keenest of all our senses.
CICERO: *De oratore*, *c.* 80 B.C.

Our sight is the most perfect and most delightful of all our senses. It fills the mind with the largest variety of ideas, converses with its objects at the greatest distance, and continues the longest in action without being tired or satiated with its proper enjoyments.
JOSEPH ADDISON: *The Spectator*, June 21, 1712

[*See also* Eye, Faculty, Seeing, Senses.

Sign

By this sign thou wilt conquer. (In hoc signo vinces.)
In his successful battle against the rival Emperor Maxentius, near Rome, Oct. 27, 312, Constantine I saw a luminous cross in the sky with the Greek words, En touto nika (Latin: Hoc vince; English: By this conquer). This omen is said to have made a Christian of him. The more familiar form dates from after Constantine's death in 337

If he be not in love with some woman, there is no believing old signs: a' brushes his hat o' mornings; what should that bode?
SHAKESPEARE: *Much Ado About Nothing*, III, *c.* 1599

Silence

He that keepeth his mouth keepeth his life; but he that openeth wide his lips shall have destruction.
PROVERBS XIII, 3, *c.* 350 B.C.

Even a fool, when he holdeth his peace, is counted wise: and he that shutteth his lips is esteemed a man of understanding.
PROVERBS XVII, 28

I regret often that I have spoken; never that I have been silent.
PUBLILIUS SYRUS: *Sententiæ*, *c.* 50 B.C.

God has given to man a cloak whereby he can conceal his ignorance, and in this cloak he can enwrap himself at any moment, for it always lies near his hand. This cloak is silence.
BHARTRIHARI: *The Niti Sataka*, *c.* 625

Silence gives consent.
ENGLISH PROVERB, traced to the XIV century, and probably derived from POPE BONIFACE VIII: *Liber sextus*, v, 1298: "Qui tacet consentire videtur" — He who is silent is understood to consent

Still waters run deep.
ENGLISH PROVERB, traced by Smith to *c.* 1435 (*Smooth* sometimes appears in place of *still*)

Hear and see, and be still.
Anon.: *The Proverbs of Wisdom*, *c.* 1450

Listen, look, and be silent, if you wish to live in peace. (Audi, vide, tace, si vis vivere in pace.)
THE GESTA ROMANORUM, *c.* 1472

He speaks best that hath the skill when for to hold his peace.
THOMAS VAUX: *Content*, *c.* 1550

The heart hath treble wrong
When it is barr'd the aidance of the tongue.
SHAKESPEARE: *Venus and Adonis,* 1593

Silence is only commendable
In a neat's tongue dried and a maid not vendible.
SHAKESPEARE: *The Merchant of Venice,* I, *c.* 1597

Silence is the perfectest herald of joy: I were but little happy if I could say how much.
SHAKESPEARE: *Much Ado About Nothing,* II, *c.* 1599

The rest is silence.
SHAKESPEARE: *Hamlet,* V, *c.* 1601

More have repented speech than silence.
GEORGE HERBERT: *Outlandish Proverbs,* 1640

Nature suffers extreme violence when a woman is moved to be silent.
PIERRE CORNEILLE: *Le Menteur,* I, 1642

Still-born silence! thou that art
Flood-gate of the deeper heart!
Offspring of a heavenly kind!
Frost o' the mouth, and thaw o' the mind!
Secrecy's confident, and he
Who makes religion mystery!
RICHARD FLECKNOE: *Lover's Kingdom,* 1644

Cautious silence is the holy of holies of worldly wisdom.
BALTASAR GRACIÁN: *The Art of Worldly Wisdom,* III, 1647

Silence is the best resolve for him who distrusts himself.
LA ROCHEFOUCAULD: *Maxims,* 1665

He that hears much and speaks not at all shall be welcome both in bower and hall.
JOHN RAY: *English Proverbs,* 1670

Silence is the greatest persecution.
BLAISE PASCAL: *Pensées,* XXIV, 1670

Silent people are dangerous.
JEAN DE LA FONTAINE: *Fables,* VIII, 1671

The world would be happier if men had the same capacity to be silent that they have to speak. BARUCH SPINOZA: *Ethica,* II, 1677

Think not silence the wisdom of fools; but, if rightly timed, the honor of wise men, who have not the infirmity, but the virtue of taciturnity.
THOMAS BROWNE: *Christian Morals,* III, *c.* 1680

Keep your mouth shut and your eyes open.
SAMUEL PALMER: *Moral Essays on Proverbs,* 1710

The parson's cant, the lawyer's sophistry,
Lord's quibble, critic's jest, all end in thee;
All rest in peace at last, and sleep eternally.
ALEXANDER POPE: *Silence,* 1712 (Imitation of the Earl of Rochester)

Silence catches a mouse.
THOMAS FULLER: *Gnomologia,* 1732

I know enough to hold my tongue, but not to speak. IBID.

Silence seldom hurts. IBID.

Silence is become his mother-tongue.
OLIVER GOLDSMITH: *The Good-Natur'd Man,* II, 1768

The people, doubtless, have the right to murmur, but they have also the right to be silent, and their silence is the lesson of kings.
JEAN DE BEAUVAIS: Sermon at the funeral of Louis XV, July 27, 1774

Great souls endure silently.
J. C. F. SCHILLER: *Don Carlos,* I, 1787

It is an immense advantage never to have said anything.
ANTOINE DE RIVAROL: *Petit almanac,* 1788

You might have heard a pin drop.
ENGLISH PHRASE, not recorded before the XIX century

Silent upon a peak in Darien.
JOHN KEATS: *On First Looking Into Chapman's Homer,* 1819 (The Examiner, Dec.)

The most silent people are generally those who think most highly of themselves. They fancy themselves superior to every one else; and not being sure of making good their secret pretensions, decline entering the lists altogether.
WILLIAM HAZLITT: *Characteristics,* 1823

Thought works in silence, so does virtue. One might erect statues to silence.
THOMAS CARLYLE: *Diary,* Sept., 1830

Silence is deep as eternity, speech is shallow as time.
THOMAS CARLYLE: *Sir Walter Scott,* 1838 (Westminster Review, Jan.)

Silence is more eloquent than words.
THOMAS CARLYLE: *Heroes and Hero-Worship,* II, 1840 (Lecture in London, May 8)

Silence is the mother of truth.
BENJAMIN DISRAELI: *Tancred,* IV, 1847

Silence reigned in the streets; from the church no angelus sounded,
Rose no smoke from the roofs, and gleamed no lights from the windows.
H. W. LONGFELLOW: *Evangeline,* I, 1847

As the truest society approaches always nearer to solitude, so the most excellent speech finally falls into silence. Silence is audible to all men, at all times, and in all places.
H. D. THOREAU: *A Week on the Concord and Merrimack Rivers,* 1849

Beware of a silent dog and still water.
H. G. BOHN: *Handbook of Proverbs,* 1855

Silent in all the tongues of Europe.
CINCINNATUS HEINE (JOAQUIN MILLER): *Ina*, v, 1871

Silence is a still noise.
H. W. SHAW (JOSH BILLINGS): *Josh Billings' Encyclopedia of Wit and Wisdom*, 1874

Blessed is the man who having nothing to say, abstains from giving us wordy evidence of the fact.
MARIAN EVANS (GEORGE ELIOT): *The Impressions of Theophratus Such*, IV, 1879

The still sow gets the swill.
AMERICAN PROVERB (In the form of "The still sow eats up all the draff" Apperson traces the proverb to 1546, but he does not report any instance of its use in England in its American form)

Most of us know how to say nothing; few of us know when. Author unidentified

The words of a silent man are never brought to court. DANISH PROVERB

Silence makes no mistakes. FRENCH PROVERB

We must have reasons for speech, but we need none for silence. IBID.

Speech is silver; silence is golden.
GERMAN PROVERB

The art of silence is as great as that of speech.
IBID.

The god of the lucky is silence. IBID.

Let me be silent, for so are the gods.
GREEK SAYING

If a word be worth one shekel, silence is worth two. HEBREW PROVERB

Silence is a healing for all ailments. IBID.

Silence is the fence round wisdom. IBID.

Silence never loses; speech always regrets.
IBID.

God rewards the silent. HINDU PROVERB

If you don't know how to be silent, hang yourself. IBID.

He who knows nothing else knows enough if he knows when to be silent.
ITALIAN PROVERB

Silence cannot be put on paper. IBID.

The silent man is the best to listen to.
JAPANESE PROVERB

In silence. (Sub silentio.) LATIN PHRASE

Obsequious silence. (Silentium obsequiosum.)
IBID.

Keep quiet and people will think you a philosopher. LATIN PROVERB

God protects the silent man.
PERSIAN PROVERB

Speech sows, silence reaps. IBID.

Silence is often mistaken for saintliness.
PORTUGUESE PROVERB

Silence is the ornament of the illiterate.
SANSKRIT PROVERB

Silence and thought hurt nae man.
SCOTTISH PROVERB

Beware of the silent man and the dog that does not bark. SPANISH PROVERB

It is bad luck to live near the home of a silent person. IBID.

Silence is the fool's wisdom. IBID.

Silence is power. WEST AFRICAN PROVERB

[*See also* Anger, Criticism, Joy, Life, Lying, Mouth, Speaking, Taciturnity, Talk, Tongue, Woman.

Silk

The fairest silk is soonest soiled.
JOHN LYLY: *Euphues*, 1579

Whenas in silks my Julia goes,
Then, then (methinks) how sweetly flows
That liquefaction of her clothes.
ROBERT HERRICK: *Hesperides*, 1648

We are all Adam's children, but silk makes the difference.
THOMAS FULLER: *Gnomologia*, 1732

If I kept a seraglio the ladies would all wear linen gowns, or cotton — I mean stuffs made of vegetable substances. I would have no silk: you cannot tell when it is clean.
SAMUEL JOHNSON: *Boswell's Tour of the Hebrides*, Sept. 17, 1773

[*See also* Linen, Luxury.

Silly

It is a silly goose that comes to a fox's sermon.
H. G. BOHN: *Handbook of Proverbs*, 1855

[*See also* Laughter.

Silver

[*See* Bimetallism, Cloud, God.

Silver, Free

[*See* Bimetallism, Gold Standard, Money.

Simile

Similes should be sparingly used in prose, for they are at bottom poetical.
ARISTOTLE: *Rhetoric*, III, *c.* 322 B.C.

Similitudes carry with them but very small force of argument, unless there be an exact agreement with that which is compared, of

which there is very seldom any sufficient care taken.
JOHN EACHARD: *The Grounds and Occasions of the Contempt of the Clergy and Religion,* 1670

A simile, to be perfect, must both illustrate and ennoble the subject; must show it to the understanding in a clearer view, and display it to the fancy with greater dignity; but either of these qualities may be sufficient to recommend it.
SAMUEL JOHNSON: *Lives of the Poets* (*Alexander Pope*), 1780

It is not easy to make a simile go on all-fours.
T. B. MACAULAY: *John Bunyan,* 1830 (Edinburgh Review, Dec.)

Simony

[*See* Cause and Effect.

Simplicity

Dress not thy thoughts in too fine a raiment. And be not a man of superfluous words or superfluous deeds.
MARCUS AURELIUS: *Meditations,* III, *c.* 170

Affected simplicity is refined imposture.
LA ROCHEFOUCAULD: *Maxims,* 1665

There is a certain majesty in simplicity which is far above all the quaintness of wit.
ALEXANDER POPE: *Letter to George Walsh,* 1706

A refined simplicity is the characteristic of all high bred deportment, in every country.
J. FENIMORE COOPER: *The American Democrat,* XXXII, 1838

Nothing is more simple than greatness; indeed, to be simple is to be great.
R. W. EMERSON: *Literary Ethics,* 1838

The art of art, the glory of expression and the sunshine of the light of letters, is simplicity.
WALT WHITMAN: *Leaves of Grass,* pref., 1855

[*See also* Beauty, Jeffersonian, Style.

Sin

Sin is disease, deformity, weakness.
PLATO: *The Republic,* IV, *c.* 370 B.C.

Sin maketh nations miserable.
PROVERBS XIV, 34, *c.* 350 B.C.

There is no man which sinneth not.
II CHRONICLES VI, 36, *c.* 300 B.C. (Cf. ECCLESIASTES VII, 20, *c.* 200 B.C.)

If Jupiter were to hurl a thunderbolt as often as men sin, he would soon have no thunderbolts left to hurl.
OVID: *Tristia,* II, *c.* 10

Most people are angry with the sinner, not with the sin.
SENECA: *De Ira,* II, *c.* 43

Other men's sins are before our eyes; our own are behind our back.
IBID.

The works of the flesh are manifest, which are these: adultery, fornication, uncleanness, lasciviousness, idolatry, witchcraft, hatred, variance, emulations, wrath, strife, seditions, heresies, envyings, murders, drunkenness, revellings, and such like: of the which I tell you before, as I have also told you in times past, that they who do such things shall not inherit the kingdom of God.
GALATIANS V, 19–21, *c.* 50

Sin is not imputed when there is no law.
ROMANS V, 13, *c.* 55

The wages of sin is death.
ROMANS VI, 23

He that is without sin among you, let him cast the first stone.
JOHN VIII, 7, *c.* 115

Neither do I condemn thee: go, and sin no more.
JOHN VIII, 11

Sins that are easiest to amend bring the greatest punishment.
ST. JOHN CHRYSOSTOM: *Homilies,* X, *c.* 388

No one sins by an act he cannot avoid.
ST. AUGUSTINE: *De libero arbitrio,* III, *c.* 390

All sin is a kind of lying.
ST. AUGUSTINE: *To Consentius, Against Lying, c.* 400

We may not sin in order to prevent another's sinning.
IBID.

Every sin is more injury to him who does than to him who suffers it.
ST. AUGUSTINE: *On Faith, Hope, and Charity, c.* 421

We sin from two causes: either from not seeing what we ought to do, or from not doing what we see ought to be done.
IBID.

Old sin, new shame.
JOHN GOWER: *Confessio amantis, c.* 1390

My sin, my sin, my grievous sin. (Mea culpa, mea culpa, mea maxima culpa.)
The Confiteor of the Roman Mass, probably not older than the XIV century

God, who is perfect righteousness, cannot love the iniquity which He sees in all. All of us, therefore, have that within us which deserves the hatred of God.
JOHN CALVIN: *Institutes of the Christian Religion,* II, 1536

Indeed, sometimes I do repent
And pardon do obtain,
But yet, alas, incontinent,
I fall to sin again.
JOHN CARELESSE: *A Godly and Virtuous Song,* 1556

More and greater sins are committed when people are alone than when they are in society. In solitary places the Devil has opportunity to mislead people. But whosoever is in honest company is ashamed to sin, or at least has no occasion for it.

MARTIN LUTHER: *Table-Talk*, DCLXIII, 1569

Commit
The oldest sins the newest kind of ways.

SHAKESPEARE: *II Henry IV*, IV, *c.* 1598

Sin is a coward, madam.

GEORGE CHAPMAN: *Bussy d'Ambois*, III, 1604

Some rise by sin, and some by virtue fall.

SHAKESPEARE: *Measure for Measure*, II, 1604

Plate sin with gold,
And the strong lance of justice hurtless breaks;
Arm it in rags, a pigmy's straw doth pierce it.

SHAKESPEARE: *King Lear*, IV, 1606

Few love to hear the sins they love to act.

SHAKESPEARE: *Pericles*, I, *c.* 1608

Since Christ from sin us to release
Hath suffered all this pain,
Why do we not from sin then cease,
But still in sin remain?

Anon.: *Behold Our Saviour Crucified*, *c.* 1610

In order to sin and become culpable in the sight of God, it is necessary to know that the thing we wish to do is not good, or at least to doubt that it is; to fear or to judge that God takes no pleasure in the action which we contemplate, but forbids it; and in spite of this, to commit the deed, leap the fence, and transgress.

ÉTIENNE BAUMY: *The Summary of Sins*, 1633

The cheapest sins most dearly punished are.

GEORGE HERBERT: *The Temple*, 1633

Every sin, the oftener it is committed, the more it acquireth in the quality of evil; as it succeeds in time, so it proceeds in degrees of badness; for as they proceed they ever multiply, and, like figures in arithmetic, the last stands for more than all that went before it.

THOMAS BROWNE: *Religio Medici*, I, 1642

He that falls into sin is a man; that grieves at it, is a saint; that boasteth of it, is a devil.

THOMAS FULLER: *The Holy State and the Profane State*, 1642

Three fatal sisters wait upon each sin;
First, fear and shame without, then guilt within.

ROBERT HERRICK: *Noble Numbers*, 1647

The desires and other passions of men are in themselves no sin. No more are the actions that proceed from those passions, till they know a law that forbids them: which till laws be made they cannot know: nor can any law be made till they have agreed upon the person that shall make it.

THOMAS HOBBES: *Leviathan*, XIII, 1651

A soul, in God's account, is valued at the price of the blood, and shame, and tortures of the Son of God; and yet we throw it away for the exchange of sins that a man is naturally ashamed to own; we lose it for the pleasure, the sottish, beastly pleasure of a night.

JEREMY TAYLOR: *Twenty-seven Sermons*, 1651

Q. What kind of sins are the greatest? *A.* Adultery, fornication, murder, theft, swearing, lying, covetousness, witchcraft, sedition, heresies, or any the like.

JOHN BUNYAN: *Instruction for the Ignorant*, 1675

He that lies in sin, and looks for happiness hereafter, is like him that soweth cockle, and thinks to fill his barn with wheat or barley.

JOHN BUNYAN: *Pilgrim's Progress*, II, 1678

Sin pulled angels out of Heaven, pulls men down to Hell, and overthroweth kingdoms.

JOHN BUNYAN: *The Life and Death of Mr. Badman*, 1680

The sin lieth in the scandal.

APHRA BEHN: *The Roundheads*, III, 1682

Among us lewd mortals the deeper the sin the sweeter.

WILLIAM CONGREVE: *The Old Bachelor*, I, 1693

The sin against the Holy Ghost
Has least of honor, and of guilt the most;
Distinguished from all other crimes by this,
That 'tis a crime which no man will confess.

DANIEL DEFOE: *The True-Born Englishman*, II, 1701

There is no man, by human wit,
Can keep his sin conceal'd,
When He that made him thinks it fit
The same should be reveal'd.

Anon.: *The Wages of Sin*, 1732

It is sin not to be angry with sin.

THOMAS FULLER: *Gnomologia*, 1732

God's permitting sin was as high an exercise of holiness as any we can think of.

SAMUEL HOPKINS: *Sin, Through Divine Interposition, an Advantage to the Universe*, *c.* 1750

It is a great deal easier to commit a second sin than it was to commit the first, and a great deal harder to repent of a second than it was to repent of the first.

BENJAMIN WHICHCOTE: *Moral and Religious Aphorisms*, 1753

Sin is a reflection upon God. IBID.

He that swims in sin will sink in sorrow.

Anon.: *Goody Two-Shoes*, 1766

The sin forgiven by Christ in Heaven
By man is cursed alway.

N. P. WILLIS: *Unseen Spirits*, 1843

The church holds that it were better for sun and moon to drop from Heaven, for the earth to fail, and for all the many millions who are upon it to die of starvation in extremest agony, so far as temporal affliction goes, than that one soul, I will not say should be lost, but should commit one single venial sin, should tell one wilful untruth, though it harmed no one, or steal one poor farthing without excuse.

J. H. NEWMAN: *Difficulties of Anglicans,* I, 1850

Sin is not in the act, but in the choice.

JOHN RUSKIN: *Stones of Venice,* II, 1853

O thou, who didst with pitfall and with gin
Beset the road I was to wander in,
Thou wilt not with predestin'd evil round
Enmesh, and then impute my fall to sin.

EDWARD FITZGERALD: Tr. of OMAR KHAYYÁM: *Rubáiyát* (*c.* 1100), 1857

Soldiers! we have sinned against Almighty God. We have forgotten His signal mercies, and have cultivated a revengeful, haughty, and boastful spirit. We have not remembered that the defenders of a just cause should be pure in His eyes.

R. E. LEE: General orders to the Army of Northern Virginia, Aug. 13, 1863

Presuming on God's mercy, despair, resisting the known truth, envy of another's spiritual good, obstinacy in sin, and final impenitence, are the six sins against the Holy Ghost.

JOHN MCCAFFREY: *A Catechism of Christian Doctrine for General Use,* 1866

Pride, covetousness, lust, anger, gluttony, envy, and sloth, are the seven capital sins. IBID.

Wilful murder, sodomy, oppression of the poor, and defrauding laborers of their wages are the four sins that cry to Heaven for vengeance. IBID.

Sin sweet beyond forgiving
And brief beyond regret.

A. C. SWINBURNE: *Before Dawn,* 1866

"Sins" are indispensable to every society organized on an ecclesiastical basis; they are the only reliable weapons of power; the priest lives upon sins; it is necessary to him that there be "sinning."

F. W. NIETZSCHE: *The Antichrist,* XXVI, 1888

Sin is man's self-desecration *par excellence.* It was invented in order to make science, culture, and every elevation and ennobling of man impossible.

F. W. NIETZSCHE: *The Antichrist,* XLIX

The sin they do by two and two they must pay for one by one.

RUDYARD KIPLING: *Tomlinson,* 1891

Sin in some shape or other is the great staple of history, and the sole object of law.

F. W. MAITLAND: *History of English Law,* I, 1895

He said he was against it.

CALVIN COOLIDGE: On being asked what had been said by a clergyman who preached on sin, *c.* 1925

The essence of Jewish-Christianity is sin and absolution. The essence of Nordic Paganism is blood and honor. Everlasting consciousness of sin is a symptom of racial crossbreeding and degeneration. Worried consciousness of sin is at the opposite pole from proud consciousness of race, and the two can never meet.

BUSSO LOEWE: *Creed of the German Pagan Movement,* 1936

A sin concealed is half forgiven.

FRENCH PROVERB

Not to be ashamed of sin is to sin double.

GERMAN PROVERB

Better to be called a fool all one's days than to sin for one hour. HEBREW PROVERB

Sin is insanity. IBID.

There is no purging of sins that are denied. (Non purgat peccata qui negat.)

LATIN PROVERB

Of these four we all have more than we know: sins, debts, foes, and years.

PERSIAN PROVERB

Even a saint sins at least seven times a day.

POLISH PROVERB

No sin; no salvation. UKRAINIAN PROVERB

Though the sin be stale, the shame is fresh and frequent. WELSH PROVERB

[*See also* Absolution, Accessory, Age (Old), Alms, Baptism, Boredom, Charity, Church (Roman Catholic), Daughter, Dead, Debauchery, Devil, End, Flesh, Forgiveness, Good and Evil, Grief, Hell, Idiot, Kiss, Laughter, Law, Love, Lying, Man and Woman, Mercy, Punishment, Sacrifice, Sinner, Slavery, Sorrow, Twenty.

Sincerity

There is no greater delight than to be conscious of sincerity.

MENCIUS: *Discourses,* VII, *c.* 300 B.C.

The sincerity which is not charitable proceeds from a charity which is not sincere.

Ascribed to ST. FRANCIS DE SALES (1567–1622) in J. P. CAMUS: *L'esprit de Saint François de Sales,* 1641

Sincerity is an openness of heart; we find it in very few people. What we usually see is only an artful dissimulation to win the confidence of others.

LA ROCHEFOUCAULD: *Maxims,* 1665

I have sometimes known saints really religious, blusterers really brave, reformers of manners

really honest, and prudes really chaste.
LORD CHESTERFIELD: *Letter to his son,* Dec. 19, 1749

Use no hurtful deceit; think innocently and justly and, if you speak, speak accordingly.
BENJAMIN FRANKLIN: *Autobiography,* 1788

A little sincerity is a dangerous thing, and a great deal of it is absolutely fatal.
OSCAR WILDE: *The Critic as Artist,* 1891

The value of an idea has nothing whatever to do with the sincerity of the man who expresses it.
OSCAR WILDE: *The Picture of Dorian Gray,* 1891

It is dangerous to be sincere unless you are also stupid.
GEORGE BERNARD SHAW: *Maxims for Revolutionists,* 1903

It is a dangerous man who believes everything he says. Author unidentified

To be sincere is to be nude. IBID.

[*See also* Style, Virtue.

Singer

The noise of them that sing do I hear.
EXODUS XXXII, 18, *c.* 700 B.C.

The singers sang loud.
NEHEMIAH XII, 42, *c.* 300 B.C.

I would rather hear thee sing, O Daphnis, than suck the honeycomb.
THEOCRITUS: *Idylls,* VIII, *c.* 270 B.C.

And who can sing so merry a note
As may he who cannot change a groat?
JOHN HEYWOOD: *Proverbs,* 1546

Singers are merry and free from sorrow and care.
MARTIN LUTHER: *Table-Talk,* DCCCXXXIX, 1569

Yes, I can sing, fool, if you'll bear the burden; and I can play upon instruments, scurvily, as gentlemen do. Oh, that I had been gelded!
JOHN MARSTON: *The Malcontent,* I, 1604

She will sing the savageness out of a bear.
SHAKESPEARE: *Othello,* IV, 1604

Come, sing now, sing; for I know you sing well;
I see you have a singing face.
JOHN FLETCHER: *The Wild Goose Chase,* II, 1621

When a musician hath forgot his note,
He makes as though a crumb stuck in his throat.
JOHN CLARK: *Parœmiologia Anglo-Latina,* 1639

Thou singest like a bird called a swine.
JOHN RAY: *English Proverbs,* 1670

I see you have a singing face — a heavy, dull, sonata face.
GEORGE FARQUHAR: *The Inconstant,* II, 1702 (Cf. FLETCHER, *ante,* 1621)

The singing man keeps his shop in his throat.
THOMAS FULLER: *Gnomologia,* 1732

Let the singing singers
With vocal voices most vociferous,
In sweet vociferation out-vociferize
Even sound itself.
HENRY CAREY: *Chrononhotonthologos,* I, 1734

Swans sing before they die — 'twere no bad thing
Should certain persons die before they sing.
S. T. COLERIDGE: *On a Bad Singer,* 1800

He that can charm a whole company by singing, and at the age of thirty, has no cause to regret so dangerous a gift, is a very extraordinary, and I may add, a very fortunate man.
C. C. COLTON: *Lacon,* 1820

When he sang, the village listened;
All the warriors gathered round him,
All the women came to hear him.
H. W. LONGFELLOW: *Hiawatha,* VI, 1855

A singer able to sing so much as sixteen measures of good music in a natural, well-poised and sympathetic voice, without effort, without affectation, without tricks, without exaggeration, without hiatuses, without hiccuping, without barking, without baa-ing — such a singer is a rare, a very rare, an excessively rare bird.
HECTOR BERLIOZ: *À travers chants,* IV, 1862

The German imagines even God as a singer.
F. W. NIETZSCHE: *The Twilight of the Idols,* 1889

Let him who sings worst begin the singing. (Qui pessime canit, primus incipit.)
LATIN PROVERB

[*See also* Actor, Baritone, Choir, Concert, Conductor, Contralto, Eminence, Prima-donna, Singing, Song, Soprano, Untrustworthy.

Singing

The morning stars sang together, and all the sons of God shouted for joy.
JOB XXXVIII, 7, *c.* 325 B.C.

O come, let us sing unto the Lord; let us make a joyful noise to the rock of our salvation.
PSALMS XCV, 1, *c.* 150 B.C.

The exercises of singing is delightful to nature, and good to preserve the health of man. It doth strengthen all parts of the breast, and doth open the pipes.
WILLIAM BYRD: *Psalms, Sonnets and Songs,* pref., 1588

The lewd trebles squeak nothing but bawdy, and the basses roar blasphemy.
WILLIAM CONGREVE: *The Way of the World,* V, 1700

Singing . . . is as natural and common to all men as it is to speak high when they threaten in anger, or to speak low when they are dejected and ask for a pardon.
WILLIAM LAW: *A Serious Call to a Devout and Holy Life*, xv, 1728

Man was never meant to sing;
And all his mimic organs e'er expressed
Was but an imitative howl at best.
JOHN LANGHORNE: *The Country Justice*, II, 1766

That which isn't worth the trouble of speaking they sing.
CARON DE BEAUMARCHAIS: *Le barbier de Séville*, I, 1775

Where the people sing, no man is ever robbed.
J. G. SEUME: *Die Gesänge*, *c.* 1800

Singin' wid a sword in ma han', Lawd,
Singin' wid a sword in ma han'.
Negro spiritual, *c.* 1830

Do not suffer the people to sing too slow. This naturally tends to formality, and is brought in by those who have either very strong or very weak voices.
The Doctrines and Discipline of the Methodist Episcopal Church South, I, 1846

Then they began to sing,
That extremely lovely thing,
"Scherzando! ma non troppo, ppp."
W. S. GILBERT: *The Bab Ballads*, 1869

[*See also* Bird, Choir, Drinking, Music, Singer, Song.

Sink or Swim

[*See* Indomitable.

Sinner

My son, if sinners entice thee, consent thou not.
PROVERBS I, 10, *c.* 350 B.C.

The way of sinners is made plain with stones, but at the end thereof is the pit of hell.
ECCLESIASTICUS XXI, 10, *c.* 180 B.C.

God be merciful to me a sinner.
LUKE XVIII, 13, *c.* 75

Every one of us is a sinner. We are men, not gods.
PETRONIUS ARBITER: *Satyricon*, *c.* 50

Prosperous sinners fare worst of all in the end.
ST. JOHN CHRYSOSTOM: *Homilies*, VI, *c.* 388

I am a man
More sinn'd against than sinning.
SHAKESPEARE: *King Lear*, III, 1606

She that knows sin knows best how to hate sin.
THOMAS MIDDLETON: *A Trick to Catch the Old One*, V, 1608

Have mercy upon us miserable sinners.
THE BOOK OF COMMON PRAYER (*The Litany*), 1662

There are only two sorts of men: the one the just, who believe themselves sinners; the other sinners, who believe themselves just.
BLAISE PASCAL: *Pensées*, XXV, 1670

And while the lamp holds out to burn
The vilest sinner may return.
ISAAC WATTS: *Hymns and Spiritual Songs*, I, 1707

Resolved, To act, in all respects, both speaking and doing, as if nobody had been so vile as I, and as if I had committed the same sins, or had the same infirmities or failings as others; and that I will let the knowledge of their failings promote nothing but shame in myself, and prove only an occasion of my confessing my own sins and misery to God.
JONATHAN EDWARDS: *Resolutions*, 1722

Some men spend their whole lives, from their infancy to their dying day, in going down the broad way to destruction. They not only draw nearer to Hell as to time, but they every day grow more ripe for destruction; they are more assimilated to the inhabitants of the infernal world.
JONATHAN EDWARDS: *The Christian Pilgrim*, *c.* 1745

A sinner is a person of violent practise, and one who doth unnatural acts.
BENJAMIN WHICHCOTE: *Moral and Religious Aphorisms*, 1753

We let them perish rather than lose their love; we let them go quietly to Hell, lest we should offend them.
The Doctrines and Discipline of the Methodist Episcopal Church South, I, 1846

When a man gets any pleasure out of the notion that he has been saved from sin, it is not necessary for him to be actually sinful, but merely to feel sinful.
F. W. NIETZSCHE: *The Antichrist*, XXIII, 1888

Better to be known as a sinner than a hypocrite.
DANISH PROVERB

I have sinned. (Peccavi.)
LATIN PHRASE

[*See also* Hypocrisy, Judgment Day, Sin.

Sin, Original

The whole clay of humanity is a condemned clay.
ST. AUGUSTINE: *The City of God*, XXI, 427

Original sin, after regeneration, is like a wound that begins to heal; though it be a wound, yet it is in course of healing, though it still runs and is sore. So original sin remains in Christians until they die, yet itself is mortified and continually dying. Its head is crushed in pieces, so that it cannot condemn us.
MARTIN LUTHER: *Table-Talk*, CCLVI, 1569

But Adam's guilt our souls hath spilt,
His fault is charged on us;

And that alone hath overthrown,
  And utterly undone us.
MICHAEL WIGGLESWORTH: *The Day of Doom*, 1662

Of man's first disobedience, and the fruit
Of that forbidden tree whose mortal taste
Brought death into the world and all our woe.
JOHN MILTON: *Paradise Lost*, I, 1667

The world was early bad, and the first sin the most deplorable of any.
THOMAS BROWNE: *Christian Morals*, III, *c.* 1680

In Adam's Fall
We sinned all.
The New England Primer, *c.* 1688

Q. How came we to be born in sin? A. We are born in sin owing to the disobedience of our first parents in eating the forbidden fruit.
JOHN MCCAFFREY: *A Catechism of Christian Doctrine for General Use*, 1866

Original sin. (Peccatum originale.)
LATIN PHRASE

[*See also* Adam (Old).

Siren

What song the sirens sang, or what name Achilles assumed when he hid himself among women.
THOMAS BROWNE: *Urn Burial*, V, 1658

Sister

A ministering angel shall my sister be.
SHAKESPEARE: *Hamlet*, V, *c.* 1601

The brother had rather see his sister rich than make her so.
THOMAS FULLER: *Gnomologia*, 1732

Reproof a parent's province is;
A sister's discipline is this:
By studied kindness to effect
A little brother's young respect.
MARY LAMB: *The Broken Doll*, 1809

My sister! my sweet sister! if a name
Dearer and purer were, it should be thine.
BYRON: *Epistle to Augusta*, 1816

There is no friend like a sister
In calm or stormy weather;
To cheer one on the tedious way,
To fetch one if one goes astray,
To lift one if one totters down,
To strengthen whilst one stands.
CHRISTINA ROSSETTI: *Goblin Market*, 1862

[*See also* Brother, Kiss.

Sitting

It's as cheap sitting as standing.
GIOVANNI TORRIANO: *Italian Proverbs*, 1666

It is the mind, and not the limbs, that taints by long sitting. Think of the patience of tailors! Think how long the Lord Chancellor sits! Think of the brooding hen!
CHARLES LAMB: *Letter to Bernard Barton*, Nov. 22, 1823

Sixty

Threescore, I think, is pretty high;
'Twas time in conscience he should die.
JONATHAN SWIFT: *A Satirical Elegy on the Death of a Late Famous General*, 1722

What tutor shall we find for a child of sixty years old?
THOMAS FULLER: *Gnomologia*, 1732

At sixty, labor ought to be over, at least from direct necessity. It is painful to see old age working itself to death, in what are called civilized countries, for its daily bread.
THOMAS PAINE: *The Rights of Man*, II, 1791

Every year sees a man less easy to save. At sixty all missionary effort is hopeless; it takes burning at the stake.
JEAN PAUL RICHTER: *Levana*, I, 1807

No general should be retained in the service after the age of sixty.
NAPOLEON I: To Gaspard Gourgaud at St. Helena, 1815–1818

Spring still makes Spring in the mind,
  When sixty years are told;
Love wakes anew this throbbing heart,
  And we are never old.
Over the Winter glaciers,
  I see the Summer glow,
And, through the wild-piled snowdrift,
  The warm rosebuds below.
R. W. EMERSON: *The World-Soul*, 1847

At sixty man learns how to value home.
E. G. BULWER-LYTTON: *Walpole*, II, 1869

Chaucer, at Woodstock with the nightingales,
At sixty wrote the Canterbury Tales.
H. W. LONGFELLOW: *Morituri Salutamus*, 1875

After a man passes sixty, his mischief is mainly in his head.
E. W. HOWE: *Sinner Sermons*, 1926

[*See also* Age (Old), Ages, Dancing, Death, Labor, Precocity, Superannuation.

Size

It doesn't depend on size, or a cow would catch a rabbit.
PENNSYLVANIA GERMAN PROVERB

Skeleton

The skeleton at the feast.
ENGLISH PHRASE, current since the XVII century

They have a skeleton in their closet.
W. M. THACKERAY: *The Newcomes*, LV, 1854

Skeptic

The skeptics affected an indifferent aequipondious neutrality as the only means to their ataraxia and freedom from passionate disturbances.

JOSEPH GLANVILL: *The Vanity of Dogmatizing*, XXIII, 1661 (*Aequipondious*=balanced; *ataraxia*=stoical calm)

A skeptic has no notion of conscience, no relish for virtue, nor is under any moral restraints from hope or fear. Such a one has nothing to do but to consult his ease, and gratify his vanity, and fill his pocket.

JEREMY COLLIER: *A Short View of the Immorality and Profaneness of the English Stage*, intro., 1698

I am ready to reject all belief and reasoning, and can look upon no opinion even as more probable or likely than another.

DAVID HUME: *A Treatise of Human Nature*, I, 1739

What danger can ever come from ingenious reasoning and inquiry? The worst speculative skeptic ever I knew was a much better man than the best superstitious devotee and bigot.

DAVID HUME: *Letter to Gilbert Elliot*, March 10, 1751

Hume, and other skeptical innovators, are vain men, and will gratify themselves at any expense. Truth will not afford sufficient food for their vanity, so they have betaken themselves to error. Truth is a cow which will yield such people no more milk, and so they are gone to milk the bull.

SAMUEL JOHNSON: *Boswell's Life*, July 21, 1763

"Wherefore a God?", cries the skeptic. "The world itself suffices for itself." And the piety of no Christian praises God more than does this skeptic's blasphemy.

J. C. F. SCHILLER: *Don Carlos*, III, 1787

No person who shall deny the being of God, or the truth of the Christian religion, shall be capable of holding any office or place of trust or profit.

CONSTITUTION OF NORTH CAROLINA, 1836

It is only badly educated physicians who are skeptics.

ERNST VON FEUCHTERSLEBEN: *Zur Diätetik der Seele*, XII, 1838

He wears his skepticism as a coquette wears her ribbons, — to annoy if he cannot subdue, — and when his purpose is served, he puts his skepticism aside — as the coquette puts her ribbons.

ALEXANDER SMITH: *Dreamthorp*, XI, 1863

To one who finds no sense in the universe,
And doubts survival, my advice would be —
Set your affairs in order, hire a hearse,
Choose some snug cemetery, and wait and see.

BRENDON MOORE: *Such Things Happen*, 1936

Skeptics are never deceived.

FRENCH PROVERB

[*See also* Agnostic, Antichrist, Atheist, Doubter, Heathen, Infidel, Missouri, Philosopher, Skepticism.

Skepticism

What do I know? What does it matter? (Que sais-je? Qu'importe?)

MOTTO OF MICHEL DE MONTAIGNE (1533–92)

Skepticism is less reprehensible in inquiring years, and no crime in a juvenile exercitation.

JOSEPH GLANVILL: *The Vanity of Dogmatizing*, dedication, 1661

With most people, doubt about one thing is simply blind belief in another.

G. C. LICHTENBERG: *Reflections*, 1799

I am the spirit that always denies. (Ich bin der Geist der stets verneint.)

J. W. GOETHE: *I Faust*, I, 1808

We owe the great writers of the Golden Age of our literature to that fervid awakening of the public mind which shook to dust the oldest and most oppressive form of the Christian religion.

P. B. SHELLEY: *Prometheus Unbound*, pref., 1820

Whenever philosophy has taken into its plan religion it has ended in skepticism.

S. T. COLERIDGE: To Thomas Allsop, *c.* 1831

Skepticism means, not intellectual doubt alone, but moral doubt.

THOMAS CARLYLE: *Heroes and Hero-Worship*, V, 1840 (Lecture in London, May 19)

While it is the summit of human wisdom to learn the limit of our faculties, it may be wise to recollect that we have no more right to make denials than to put forth affirmatives about what lies beyond that limit.

T. H. HUXLEY: *Hume*, 1878

Great intellects are skeptical.

F. W. NIETZSCHE: *The Antichrist*, LIV, 1888

Believe nothing and be on your guard against everything. (Nil credam et omnia cavebo.)

LATIN PROVERB

[*See also* Absolute, Agnosticism, Atheism, Credulity, Critic, Disillusion, Doubt, Faith, Skeptic.

Skill

Skill and confidence are an unconquered army.

GEORGE HERBERT: *Outlandish Proverbs*, 1640

[*See also* Ability, Capacity, Talent.

Skin

Can the Ethiopian change his skin?
JEREMIAH XIII, 23, *c.* 625 B.C.

Skin and bone.
ENGLISH PHRASE, traced by Smith to *c.* 1430

My shirt is near me, but my skin is nearest.
THOMAS LODGE: *A Margarite of America,* 1596

I'll not shed her blood;
Nor scar that whiter skin of hers than snow,
And smooth as monumental alabaster.
SHAKESPEARE: *Othello* V, 1604

[*See also* Complexion, Dermatologist, Heat.

Sky

The sky . . . is . . . as a molten looking-glass.
JOB XXXVII, 18, *c.* 325 B.C.

When it is evening, ye say, It will be fair weather: for the sky is red.
MATTHEW XVI, 2, *c.* 75

The spacious firmament on high
And all the blue ethereal sky
And spangled heavens, a shining frame,
Their great Original proclaim.
JOSEPH ADDISON: *The Spectator,* Aug. 23, 1712

Deep sky is, of all visual impressions, the nearest akin to a feeling.
S. T. COLERIDGE: *Notebooks,* 1805

The soft blue sky did never melt
Into his heart; he never felt
The witchery of the soft blue sky.
WILLIAM WORDSWORTH: *Peter Bell,* I, 1819

And that inverted bowl they call the sky,
Whereunder crawling coop'd we live and die,
Lift not your hands to it for help — for it
As impotently rolls as you or I.
EDWARD FITZGERALD: Tr. of OMAR KHAYYÁM: *Rubáiyát* (*c.* 1100), 1857

It is remarkable how few people seem to derive any pleasure from the beauty of the sky.
JOHN LUBBOCK (LORD AVEBURY): *The Pleasures of Life,* VIII, 1887

[*See also* Firmament, Property, Star, Weather.

Skylark

Hail to thee, blithe spirit!
Bird thou never wert,
That from heaven, or near it,
Pourest thy full heart
In profuse strains of unpremeditated art.
P. B. SHELLEY: *To a Skylark,* 1819

[*See also* Lark.

Slander

Slander injures three: the slanderer, the person who hears the slander, and the person slandered.
THE TALMUD (*Arachin*), *c.* 200

Slander is worse than cannibalism.
ST. JOHN CHRYSOSTOM: *Homilies,* III, *c.* 388

Those who cast imputations upon chaste women, and do not bring four witnesses to prove their charges, shall be scourged with fourscore stripes, and their testimony shall never be received afterward.
THE KORAN, XXIV, *c.* 625

It may be a slander, but it is no lie.
JOHN HEYWOOD: *Proverbs,* 1546

I had better slander them truly, which is no slander indeed, than flatter them falsely.
BRIAN MELBANCKE: *Philotinus,* 1583

Slander lives upon succession,
Forever housed where it gets possession.
SHAKESPEARE: *The Comedy of Errors,* III, 1593

Done to death by slanderous tongues.
SHAKESPEARE: *Much Ado About Nothing,* V, *c.* 1599

Slander,
Whose edge is sharper than the sword, whose tongue
Out venoms all the worms of Nile, whose breath
Rides on the posting winds and doth belie
All corners of the world.
SHAKESPEARE: *Cymbeline,* III, *c.* 1609

Where may a maiden live securely free,
Keeping her honor fair? Not with the living.
They feed upon opinions, errors, dreams,
And make 'em truths; they draw a nourishment
Out of defamings, grow upon disgraces,
And, when they see a virtue fortified
Strongly above the batt'ry of their tongues,
Oh, how they case to sink it! and, defeated,
Soul-sick with poison, strike the monuments
Where noble names lie sleeping, till they sweat,
And the cold marble melt.
BEAUMONT and FLETCHER: *Philaster,* III, 1611

Who's angry at a slander makes it true.
BEN JONSON: *Catiline,* III, 1611

If I am traduced by tongues which neither know
My faculties nor person, yet will be
The chronicles of my doing, let me say
'Tis but the fate of place.
SHAKESPEARE and JOHN FLETCHER: *Henry VIII,* I, 1613

Slander is a shipwreck by a dry tempest.
GEORGE HERBERT: *Outlandish Proverbs,* 1640

Thou vermin slander, bred in abject minds,
Of thoughts impure, by vile tongues animate.
JOHN SUCKLING: *Detraction Execrated,* 1646

Slander rends in pieces the very heart and vital parts of charity: it makes an evil man party, and witness, and judge, and executioner of the innocent.
JEREMY TAYLOR: *Twenty-seven Sermons,* XXVII, 1651

A slanderer cannot succeed unless he has a reputation for hating slander.
BLAISE PASCAL: *Provincial Letters*, XVI, 1657

Whoever robs a woman of her reputation despoils a poor defenseless creature of all that makes her valuable, turns her beauty into loathsomeness, and leaves her friendless, abandoned and undone.
RICHARD STEELE: *The Guardian*, June 3, 1713

Soft-buzzing slander; silly moths that eat
An honest name.
JAMES THOMSON: *Liberty*, IV, 1736

There never was a man of mark who was not slandered, nor any blackguard who never slandered such a man.
G. C. LICHTENBERG: *Reflections*, 1799

My rule of life has been never to harass the public with fendings and provings of personal slanders. . . . I have ever trusted to the justice and consideration of my fellow citizens, and have no reason to repent it, or to change my course.
THOMAS JEFFERSON: *Letter to Martin Van Buren*, 1824

The mouth of a cannon is safer than the mouth of a slanderer. ARAB PROVERB

There is no cure for slander.
DANISH PROVERB

No listeners, no slanderers.
FRENCH PROVERB

He who slanders a fellow man denies God.
HEBREW PROVERB

The slanderer soon becomes the victim of slander. HINDU PROVERB

To do good and have evil said of you is a kingly thing. (Bene facere et male audire regium est.)
MOTTO ON THE TOWNHALL OF ZITTAU, GERMANY

[*See also* Calumny, Forgiveness, Gossip, Journalism, Libel, Scandal, Treachery.

Slang

In poetry slang of every kind is to be avoided.
CHARLES LAMB: *Letter to John Clare*, Aug. 31, 1822

The language of the street is always strong. What can describe the folly and emptiness of scolding like the word *jawing?*
R. W. EMERSON: *Journals*, 1840

Many of the slang words among fighting men, gamblers, thieves, prostitutes, are powerful words. These words ought to be collected — the bad words as well as the good. Many of these bad words are fine.
WALT WHITMAN: *An American Primer*, *c.* 1856

Slang is the language of street humor, of fast, high and low life.
Anon.: *A Dictionary of Modern Slang, Cant, and Vulgar Words*, 1860

Correct English is the slang of prigs who write history and essays. And the strongest slang of all is the slang of poets.
MARIAN EVANS (GEORGE ELIOT): *Middlemarch*, XI, 1872

Phrases of slang . . . fix into portable shape the nebulous ideas of the vulgar.
JOHN HAY: *Castilian Days*, XII, 1872

Slang, profoundly consider'd, is the lawless germinal element, below all words and sentences, and behind all poetry, and proves a certain perennial rankness and protestantism in speech.
WALT WHITMAN: *Slang in America*, 1885

Slang is a conventional tongue with many dialects, which are as a rule unintelligible to outsiders.
ALBERT BARRÈRE: *A Dictionary of Slang, Jargon and Cant*, pref., 1889

Slang is the speech of him who robs the literary garbage carts on their way to the dumps.
AMBROSE BIERCE: *Collected Works*, VIII, 1911

A people who are prosperous and happy, optimistic and progressive, will produce much slang; it is a case of play; they amuse themselves with the language.
W. G. SUMNER, A. G. KELLER and M. R. DAVIE: *The Science of Society*, IV, 1927

[*See also* American language.

Slave

If a slave says to his master, Thou are not my master, his master shall cut off his ear.
THE CODE OF HAMMURABI, *c.* 2250 B.C.

Zeus takes away half the worth of a man when he makes him a slave.
HOMER: *Odyssey*, XVII, *c.* 800 B.C.

Of the children of the strangers that do sojourn among you, of them ye shall buy, and of their families that are with you, which they begat in your land: and they shall be your possession. LEVITICUS XXV, 45, *c.* 700 B.C.

Only one thing shames the slave — the name. In everything else he is no worse off than the free-born. EURIPIDES: *Ion*, *c.* 420 B.C.

Some men are born free, others slaves. For the latter slavery is both expedient and right.
ARISTOTLE: *Politics*, *c.* 322 B.C.

Corrupted freemen are the worst of slaves.
DAVID GARRICK: Prologue to EDWARD MOORE: *The Gamester*, 1753

The air of England has long been too pure for a slave, and every man is free who breathes it.
LORD MANSFIELD: *Judgment in the case of James Somersett*, a Negro, June 22, 1772

I would not have a slave to till my ground,
To carry me, to fan me while I sleep,
And tremble when I wake, for all the wealth
That sinews bought and sold have ever earn'd.

WILLIAM COWPER: *The Task*, II, 1785

Slaves cannot breathe in England, if their lungs
Receive our air, that moment they are free;
They touch our country, and their shackles fall.

IBID. (Cf. MANSFIELD, *ante*, 1772)

Nothing can be conceived more inert than a slave; his unwilling labor is discovered in every step that he takes; he moves not if he can avoid it; if the eyes of the overseer be off him he sleeps; the ox and the horse, driven by the slave, appear to sleep also; all is listless inactivity.

WILLIAM STRICKLAND: *Observations on the Agriculture of the United States*, 1801

No refuge could save the hireling and slave
From the terror of flight, or the gloom of the grave.

F. S. KEY: *The Star-Spangled Banner*, 1814 (Baltimore American, Sept. 16)

Slaves frequently are well fed and well clad, but slaves dare not speak, they dare not be suspected to think differently from their masters.

WILLIAM COBBETT: *Advice to Young Men*, I, 1829

Born slaves, bred slaves,
Branded in the blood and bone slaves.

ROBERT BROWNING: *A Soul's Tragedy*, I, 1846

I would as soon return my own brother or sister into bondage as I would return a fugitive slave. Before God, and Christ, and all Christian men, they are my brothers and sisters.

HORACE MANN: Speech in Boston, Feb. 15, 1850

If slavery is as disagreeable to Negroes as we think it is, why don't they all march over the border, where they would be received with open arms? It all amazes me. I am always studying these creatures. They are to me inscrutable in their way and past finding out.

MARY BOYKIN CHESNUT: *Diary*, Richmond, Va., July 27, 1861

In giving freedom to the slave we assure freedom to the free, — honorable alike in what we give and what we preserve.

ABRAHAM LINCOLN: Message to Congress, Dec. 1, 1862

Of the ten measures of sleep that came down into the world, slaves received nine and the rest of the world only one.

HEBREW PROVERB

Better to be a slave to a rich man than the wife of a poor one. HINDU PROVERB

[*See also* Abolition, Emancipation, Fool, Freedom, Good and Evil, King, Master and Servant, Negro, Obedience, Prostitute, Slavery, Soldier, Work.

Slaveholder

[*See* Slavery.

Slavery

Too much liberty leads both men and nations to slavery.

CICERO: *De republica*, *c.* 50 B.C.

O men, made for slavery! (O homines, ad servitutem paratos!)

Ascribed to the EMPEROR TIBERIUS (42 B.C.–37 A.D.)

Slavery is a prison for the soul, a public dungeon.

LONGINUS: *On the Sublime*, XLIV, *c.* 250

The prime cause of servitude is sin.

ST. AUGUSTINE: *The City of God*, XIX, 427

No Indian may be reduced to slavery, whether for making war, for rebellion or for any other reason, and no one shall work an Indian as a servant or in any other capacity against his will.

CHARLES V OF SPAIN: *Ordinance*, 1542

Slavery is as ancient as war, and war as human nature.

VOLTAIRE: *Philosophical Dictionary*, 1764

There is not a man living who wishes more sincerely than I do to see a plan adopted for the abolition of slavery. But there is only one proper way and effectual mode by which it can be accomplished, and that is by legislative authority.

GEORGE WASHINGTON: *Letter to Robert Morris*, April 12, 1786

I never mean, unless some particular circumstance should compel me to it, to possess another slave by purchase, it being among my first wishes to see some plan adopted by which slavery in this country may be abolished by law.

GEORGE WASHINGTON: *Letter to John Francis Mercer*, Sept. 9, 1786

Man is easily accustomed to slavery, and learns quickly to be obedient when his freedom is taken from him.

J. W. GOETHE: *Iphigenie auf Tauris*, V, 1787

This abomination must have an end. And there is a superior bench reserved in Heaven for those who hasten it.

THOMAS JEFFERSON: *Letter to Edward Rutledge*, 1787

No person held to service or labor in one state, under the laws thereof, escaping into another, shall, in consequence of any law or regulation therein, be discharged from such service of labor, but shall be delivered up, on claim of the party to whom such service or labor is due.

CONSTITUTION OF THE UNITED STATES, IV, 1789 (Vitiated by Amendment XIII, *post*, Dec. 18, 1865)

O thou chief curse, since curses here began;
First guilt, first woe, first infamy of man!

TIMOTHY DWIGHT: *Greenfield Hill*, II, 1794

The Constitution admits that slavery and a republican form of government are not incongruous.

WILLIAM PINKNEY: Speech in the Senate, Feb. 15, 1820

Slavery is the great and foul stain upon the North American Union, and it is a contemplation worthy of the most exalted soul whether its total abolition is or is not practicable: if practicable, by what it may be effected, and if a choice of means be within the scope of the object, what means would accomplish it at the smallest cost of human suffering. A dissolution, at least temporary, of the Union, as now constituted, would be certainly necessary.

JOHN QUINCY ADAMS: *Diary*, Feb. 24, 1820

Whatever difference of opinion may exist as to the effect of slavery on national wealth and prosperity, if we may trust to experience, there can be no doubt that it has never yet produced any injurious effect on individual or national character.

R. W. HAYNE: Speech in the Senate, Jan. 21, 1830

All organized slavery is inevitably but a temporary phase of human condition. Interest, necessity and instinct all work to give progression to the relations of mankind, and finally to elevate each tribe or race to its maximum of refinement and power.

J. P. KENNEDY: *Swallow Barn*, XLVI, 1832

The delegates of the annual conference are decidedly opposed to modern Abolitionism, and wholly disclaim any right, wish, or intention to interfere in the civil and political relation between master and slave as it exists in the slave-holding states of the Union.

Resolution of the General Conference of the Methodist Episcopal Church, Cincinnati, May, 1836

They believe that the institution of slavery is founded on both injustice and bad policy, but that the promulgation of Abolition doctrines tends rather to increase than abate its evils. They believe that the Congress of the United States has no power under the Constitution to interfere with the institution of slavery in the different states.

Resolutions adopted at Springfield, Ill., March 3, 1837, and signed by Abraham Lincoln

Slavery is no more sinful, by the Christian code, than it is sinful to wear a whole coat, while another is in tatters, to eat a better meal than a neighbor, or otherwise to enjoy ease and plenty, while our fellow creatures are suffering and in want.

J. FENIMORE COOPER: *The American Democrat*, XXXVIII, 1838

If you put a chain around the neck of a slave, the other end fastens itself around your own.

R. W. EMERSON: *Compensation*, 1841

I hold it to be a paramount duty of us in the free states, due to the union of the states, and perhaps to liberty itself (paradox though it may seem), to let the slavery of the other states alone; while, on the other hand, I hold it to be equally clear that we should never knowingly lend ourselves, directly or indirectly, to prevent that slavery from dying a natural death — to find new places for it to live in, when it can no longer exist in the old.

ABRAHAM LINCOLN: *Letter to Williamson Durley*, Oct. 3, 1845

We declare that we are as much as ever convinced of the great evil of slavery: therefore, no slaveholder shall be eligible to any official station in our church hereafter, where the laws of the state in which he lives will admit of emancipation, and permit the liberated slave to enjoy freedom.

The Doctrines and Discipline of the Methodist Episcopal Church South, II, 1846

Shall I tell you which is the one intolerable sort of slavery; the slavery over which the very gods weep? It is the slavery of the strong to the weak; of the great and noble-minded to the small and mean.

THOMAS CARLYLE: *The Nigger Question*, 1849 (Fraser's Magazine, Dec.)

Poets, with voices of melody, sing for freedom. Who could tune for slavery?

CHARLES SUMNER: Speech in the Senate, Aug. 26, 1852

If the Negro is a man, why then my ancient faith teaches me that "all men are created equal," and that there can be no moral right in connection with one man's making a slave of another.

ABRAHAM LINCOLN: Speech at Peoria, Ill., Oct. 16, 1854

Slavery, south of Mason and Dixon's line, will cease to exist so soon as it ceases to be the interest of the landowners to hold, and work their fields with, slaves.

JOHN H. B. LATROBE: *The History of the Mason and Dixon's Line*, 1854 (Address before the Historical Society of Pennsylvania, Philadelphia, Nov. 8)

In this enlightened age there are few, I believe, but what will acknowledge that slavery as an institution is a moral and political evil in any country. It is useless to expatiate on its disadvantages. I think it, however, a greater evil to the white than to the black race, and while my feelings are strongly enlisted in behalf of the latter, my sympathies are more strong for the former.

R. E. LEE: *Letter to his wife*, Dec. 27, 1856

We must get rid of slavery or we must get rid of freedom.

R. W. EMERSON: *The Assault upon Mr. Sumner's Speech*, May 26, 1856

Congress has no power under the Constitution to interfere with or control the domestic institutions of the several states, and such states are the sole and proper judges of everything appertaining to their own affairs not prohibited by the Constitution; all efforts of the Abolitionists, or others, made to induce Congress to interfere with questions of slavery, or to take incipient steps in relation thereto, are calculated to lead to the most alarming and dangerous consequences.

Democratic National Platform, 1856

Slavery destroys, or vitiates, or pollutes, whatever it touches. No interest of society escapes the influence of its clinging curse. It makes Southern religion a stench in the nostrils of Christendom: it makes Southern politics a libel upon all the principles of republicanism; it makes Southern literature a travesty upon the honorable profession of letters.

H. R. HELPER: *The Impending Crisis*, 1857

The right of property in a slave is distinctly and expressly affirmed in the Constitution. No word can be found in the Constitution which gives Congress a greater power over slave property or which entitles property of that kind to less protection than property of any other description.

ROGER B. TANEY: *Decision in the Dred Scott case*, March 6, 1857

The right of property is before and higher than any constitutional sanction, and the right of the owner of a slave to such slave and its increase is the same, and as inviolable as the right of the owner of any property whatever.

Proposed CONSTITUTION FOR KANSAS, VII, adopted at Lecompton, Nov. 7, 1857

Slaves, if you please, are not property like other property in this: that you can easily rob us of them; but as to the *right* in them, that man has to overthrow the whole history of the world, he has to overthrow every treatise on jurisprudence, he has to ignore the common sentiment of mankind, . . . ere he can reach the conclusion that the person who owns a slave . . . has no other property in that slave than the mere title which is given by the statute law of the land where it is found.

JUDAH P. BENJAMIN: Speech in the Senate, March 11, 1858

I believe this government can not endure permanently half slave and half free. I do not expect the Union to be dissolved; I do not expect the house to fall; but I do expect that it will cease to be divided. It will become all one thing, or all the other.

ABRAHAM LINCOLN: Speech in Springfield, Ill., June 16, 1858

I have no purpose, either directly or indirectly, to interfere with the institution of slavery in the states where it exists. I believe I have no lawful right to do so, and I have no inclination to do so.

ABRAHAM LINCOLN: First debate with Douglas, Ottawa, Ill., Aug. 21, 1858

I do not now, or ever did, stand pledged against the admission of any more slave states into the union. I do not stand pledged to the prohibition of the slave-trade between the states.

ABRAHAM LINCOLN: First debate with Douglas, Freeport, Ill., Aug. 27, 1858

It is an irrepressible conflict between opposing and enduring forces, and it means that the United States must and will, sooner or later, become either entirely a slave-holding nation, or entirely a free-labor nation.

WILLIAM H. SEWARD: Speech in Rochester, N. Y., Oct. 25, 1858

This is a world of compensations, and he who would be no slave must consent to have no slave. Those who deny freedom to others deserve it not for themselves, and, under a just God, they cannot long retain it.

ABRAHAM LINCOLN: *Letter to H. L. Pierce*, April 6, 1859

By the law of slavery, man, created in the image of God, is divested of the human character, and declared to be a mere chattel.

CHARLES SUMNER: Speech in New York, May 9, 1859

No bill . . . denying or impairing the right of property in Negro slaves shall be passed.

CONSTITUTION OF THE CONFEDERATE STATES, IX, March 11, 1861

Our new government's foundations are laid, its cornerstone rests, upon the great truth that the Negro is not equal to the white man, that slavery — subordination to the superior race — is his natural and normal condition.

ALEXANDER H. STEPHENS: Speech in Savannah, Ga., March 21, 1861

If I could save the Union without freeing any slave, I would do it; if I could save it by freeing all the slaves, I would do it; and if I could save it by freeing some and leaving others alone, I would also do that.

ABRAHAM LINCOLN: *Letter to Horace Greeley*, Aug. 22, 1862

I never knew a man who wished himself to be a slave. Consider if you know any *good* thing that no man desires for himself.

ABRAHAM LINCOLN: Written in an album sold at a Sanitary Commission fair, 1864

I am naturally anti-slavery. If slavery is not wrong, nothing is wrong.
ABRAHAM LINCOLN: *Letter to A. C. Hodges*, April 4, 1864

Where slavery is, there liberty cannot be; and where liberty is, there slavery cannot be.
CHARLES SUMNER: Speech in New York, Nov. 5, 1864

Looking upon African slavery from the same standpoint held by the noble framers of our Constitution, I have ever considered it one of the greatest blessings (both for themselves and us) that God ever bestowed upon a favorite nation.
JOHN WILKES BOOTH: Letter left with his sister Asia before his assassination of Abraham Lincoln, 1865

If the people of the South had stood by the Constitution, I for one would have fought for the protection of the slave property just as much as for any other kind of property, because the Constitution was a contract, signed, sealed and delivered, and we had no right to go behind it. But when the people and states of the South undertook to save their slave property by themselves, breaking the Constitution, they themselves released us of our honorary and legal obligation, and we are free to deal with slavery as we please.
W. T. SHERMAN: *Letter to General Absalom Baird*, from Goldsboro, N. C., April 3, 1865

Neither slavery nor involuntary servitude, except as a punishment for crime whereof the party shall have been duly convicted, shall exist within the United States, or any place subject to their jurisdiction.
CONSTITUTION OF THE UNITED STATES, Amendment XIII, Dec. 18, 1865

Every enslavement of another man is a limitation on my own freedom. It is a negation of my human existence by his bestial existence.
M. A. BAKUNIN: *Dieu et l'état*, 1871

Slavery was a vice instituted and fostered in the American colonies by aristocratic and monarchical England. Efforts made by various colonies to check the slave trade were rebuked by the English government.
CHARLES BRADLAUGH: *Five Dead Men Whom I Knew When Living*, 1876

Without slavery there would have been no Grecian state, no Grecian art and science, and no Roman Empire . . . no modern Europe . . . no modern Socialism.
FRIEDRICH ENGELS: *Anti-Dühring*, 1877

When, amid the slave multitude whom she has numbered among her children, some, led astray by some hope of liberty, have had recourse to violence and sedition, the church has always condemned these unlawful efforts, and through her ministers has applied the remedy of patience.
POPE LEO XIII: *Letter to the bishops of Brazil*, 1888

The essence of all slavery consists in taking the produce of another's labor by force. It is immaterial whether this force be founded upon ownership of the slave or ownership of the money that he must get to live.
LYOF N. TOLSTOY: *What Shall We Do?*, 1891

Up from slavery.
BOOKER T. WASHINGTON: Title of a book, 1901

[*See also* Abolition, Abolitionist, Church (Roman Catholic), Emancipation, Liberty, Money, Negro, Secession, Slave, Socialism, Union.

Slave-trade

About the last of August came in a Dutch man of warre that sold us twenty Negars.
JOHN ROLFE: *Diary*, 1619

It is to be hoped that by expressing a national disapprobation of this trade we may destroy it, and make ourselves free from reproaches, and our posterity from the imbecility ever attendant on a country filled with slaves.
JAMES MADISON: Speech in the House of Representatives, May 13, 1789

The abolition of the slave trade has been rejected by the House of Commons, though Mr. Pitt and Mr. Fox united earnestly to carry it: but commerce chinked its purse, and that sound is generally prevalent with the majority.
HORACE WALPOLE: *Letter to Mary Berry*, April 23, 1791

That execrable sum of all villainies.
JOHN WESLEY: *Journal*, Feb. 12, 1792

The importation of Negroes of the African race, from any other than the slave-holding states or territories of the United States of America, is hereby forbidden; and Congress is required to pass such laws as shall effectually prevent the same.
CONSTITUTION OF THE CONFEDERATE STATES, IX, March 11, 1861

Sleep

Sleep [is] the twin of death.
HOMER: *The Iliad*, XIV, *c.* 800 B.C.

O precious balm of sleep, thou that soothest disease, how pleasant that thou camest to me in the time of need! O divine oblivion of my sufferings, how wise thou art, and a goddess to be invited by all in distress!
EURIPIDES: *Orestes*, 408 B.C.

When thou liest down, thou shalt not be afraid: yea, thou shalt lie down, and thy sleep shall be sweet. PROVERBS III, 24, *c.* 350 B.C.

How long wilt thou sleep, O sluggard? when wilt thou arise out of thy sleep?
PROVERBS VI, 9

Yet a little sleep, a little slumber, a little folding of the hands to sleep.
PROVERBS VI, 10

Love not sleep, lest thou come to poverty.
PROVERBS XX, 13

When they are asleep you cannot tell a good man from a bad one.
ARISTOTLE: *The Nicomachean Ethics,* I, *c.* 340 B.C.

The sleep of a laboring man is sweet, whether he eat little or much, but the abundance of the rich will not suffer him to sleep.
ECCLESIASTES V, 12, *c.* 200 B.C.

Sound sleep cometh of moderate eating.
ECCLESIASTICUS XXI, 20, *c.* 180 B.C.

I will lay me down in peace, and sleep.
PSALMS IV, 8, *c.* 150 B.C.

He giveth his beloved sleep.
PSALMS CXXVII, 2

What is sleep but the image of cold death?
OVID: *Amores,* II, *c.* 10

Six hours sleep is enough.
REGIMEN SALERNITANUM, *c.* 1275

I never sleep in comfort save when I am hearing a sermon or praying to God.
RABELAIS: *Gargantua,* I, 1535

Scarcely any minor annoyance angers me more than being suddenly awakened out of a pleasant sleep.
MARTIN LUTHER: *Table-Talk,* DCCLXXXII, 1569

When we sleep too much all the moistures and humors of the body, with the natural heat, retire to the extreme parts thereof, nowhere purging or evacuating whatsoever is redundant.
JOHN NORTHBROOKE: *Against Dicing,* 1577

Come, sleep; O sleep! the certain knot of peace,
The baiting-place of wit, the balm of woe,
The poor man's wealth, the prisoner's release,
Th' indifferent judge between the high and low.
PHILIP SIDNEY: *Astrophel and Stella,* XXXI, 1591

Her eyes, like marigolds, had sheath'd their light;
And, canopied in darkness, sweetly lay,
Till they might open to adorn the day.
SHAKESPEARE: *The Rape of Lucrece,* 1594

Care-charmer sleep, sweet ease in restless misery,
The captive's liberty, and his freedom's song,
Balm of the bruised heart, man's chief felicity,
Brother of quiet death, when life is too, too long!
BARTHOLOMEW GRIFFIN: *Fidessa More Chaste Than Kind,* 1596

I pray you let none of your people stir me: I have an exposition of sleep come upon me.
SHAKESPEARE: *A Midsummer Night's Dream,* IV, *c.* 1596

O sleep, O gentle sleep,
Nature's soft nurse.
SHAKESPEARE: *II Henry IV,* III, *c.* 1598

Why rather, sleep, liest thou in smoky cribs,
Upon uneasy pallets stretching thee,
And hush'd with buzzing night-flies to thy slumber,
Than in the perfum'd chambers of the great?
IBID.

The honey-heavy dew of slumber.
SHAKESPEARE: *Julius Cæsar,* II, 1599

Sleep is a reconciling,
A rest that peace begets.
Anon.: *Weep You No More, Sad Fountains,* 1603

Not poppy, nor mandragora,
Nor all the drowsy syrups of the world
Shall ever medicine thee to that sweet sleep
Which thou ow'dst yesterday.
SHAKESPEARE: *Othello,* III, 1604

Sleep that knits up the ravell'd sleave of care,
The death of each day's life, sore labor's bath,
Balm of hurt minds, great nature's second course,
Chief nourisher in life's feast.
SHAKESPEARE: *Macbeth,* II, *c.* 1605

Methought I heard a voice cry, "Sleep no more!
Macbeth does murder sleep," the innocent sleep.
IBID.

Sleep . . . is so inestimable a jewel that if a tyrant would give his crown for an hour's slumber it cannot be bought; of so beautiful a shape is it that though a man lie with an empress his heart cannot be quiet till he leaves her embracements to be at rest with the other.
THOMAS DEKKER: *The Gull's Hornbook,* II, 1609

Sleep is the golden chain that ties health and our bodies together.
IBID.

O sleep, thou ape of death!
SHAKESPEARE: *Cymbeline,* II, *c.* 1609

Weariness
Can snore upon the flint, when resty sloth
Finds the down pillow hard.
SHAKESPEARE: *Cymbeline,* III

Immoderate sleep is rust to the soul.
THOMAS OVERBURY: *Characters,* 1614

May blessings light upon him who first invented sleep! It is food for the hungry, drink for the thirsty, heat for the cold, and cold for the hot. It is the coin that buys all things, and the balance that makes the king even with the shepherd, and the fool with the wise.
CERVANTES: *Don Quixote,* II, 1615

Sleep's but a short death; death's but a longer sleep.
PHINEAS FLETCHER: *The Locusts,* I, 1627

One hour's sleep before midnight is worth three after.
GEORGE HERBERT: *Outlandish Proverbs*, 1640

Sleep is a death. Oh, make me try,
By sleeping, what it is to die.
THOMAS BROWNE: *Religio Medici*, II, 1642

We are somewhat more than ourselves in our sleeps; and the slumber of the body seems to be but the waking of the soul. It is the ligation of sense, but the liberty of reason; and our waking conceptions do not match the fancies of our sleeps. IBID.

The cool and silent shades of sleep.
ROBERT HERRICK: *Hesperides*, 1648

His sleep
Was aery light, from pure digestion bred.
JOHN MILTON: *Paradise Lost*, v, 1667

Six hours for a man, seven for a woman, and eight for a fool.
ENGLISH PROVERB, not recorded before the XVIII century

Sleep is such a dull, stupid state of existence that even amongst mere animals we despise them most which are most drowsy.
WILLIAM LAW: *A Serious Call to a Devout and Holy Life*, XIV, 1728

He hath slept well that remembers not that he hath slept ill.
THOMAS FULLER: *Gnomologia*, 1732

If you sleep till noon you have no right to complain that the days are short. IBID.

Sleeping all the morning makes it night till noon. IBID.

I am going to the land of Nod.
JONATHAN SWIFT: *Polite Conversation*, 1738 (*Land of Nod*=land of nodding, or sleep — a pun on the Biblical place-name, GENESIS IV, 16)

Up, sluggard, and waste not life; in the grave will be sleeping enough.
BENJAMIN FRANKLIN: *Poor Richard's Almanac*, 1741

Tired nature's sweet restorer, balmy sleep.
EDWARD YOUNG: *Night Thoughts*, I, 1742

Come, gentle sleep! attend thy votary's prayer,
And, though death's image, to my couch repair;
How sweet, though lifeless, yet with life to lie,
And, without dying, oh, how sweet to die!
JOHN WOLCOT: Tr. of a Latin epigram by THOMAS WARTON, *c.* 1785

The wild winds weep,
And the night is a-cold;
Come hither, sleep,
And my griefs unfold.
WILLIAM BLAKE: *Mad Song*, 1789

The long sleep of death cures our scars and the short sleep of life our wounds.
JEAN PAUL RICHTER: *Hesperus*, XX, 1795

Oh, sleep, it is a gentle thing,
Beloved from pole to pole.
To Mary Queen the praise be given:
She sent the gentle sleep from Heaven
That slid into my soul.
S. T. COLERIDGE: *The Ancient Mariner*, v, 1798

Visit her, gentle sleep! with wings of healing.
S. T. COLERIDGE: *Dejection*, VIII, 1802 (London Morning Post, Oct. 4)

Thou hast been called, O sleep! the friend of woe;
But 'tis the happy who have called thee so.
ROBERT SOUTHEY: *The Curse of Kehama*, XV, 1810

How wonderful is death, death and his brother sleep! P. B. SHELLEY: *Queen Mab*, I, 1813

Some say that gleams of a remoter world
Visit the soul in sleep.
P. B. SHELLEY: *Mont Blanc*, 1816

Soft closer of our eyes!
Low murmurer of tender lullabies!
Light hoverer around our happy pillows!
Wreather of poppy buds, and weeping willows!
JOHN KEATS: *Sleep and Poetry*, 1817

O magic sleep! O comfortable bird,
That broodest o'er the troubled sea of the mind
Till it is hush'd and smooth!
JOHN KEATS: *Endymion*, I, 1818

And still she slept an azure-lidded sleep,
In blanched linen, smooth, and lavender'd.
JOHN KEATS: *The Eve of St. Agnes*, 1820

Blinded alike from sunshine and from rain,
As though a rose should shut, and be a bud again. IBID.

Strange state of being! (for 'tis still to be)
Senseless to feel, and with seal'd eyes to see.
BYRON: *Don Juan*, IV, 1821

Sleep, the fresh dew of languid love, the rain
Whose drops quench kisses till they burn again.
P. B. SHELLEY: *Epipsychidion*, 1821

Gentle sleep!
Scatter thy drowsiest poppies from above;
And in new dreams not soon to vanish, bless
My senses with the sight of her I love.
HORACE SMITH: *Poppies and Sleep*, 1826

Sleep sweetly, tender heart, in peace;
Sleep, holy spirit, blessed soul,
While the stars burn, the moons increase,
And the great ages onward roll.
ALFRED TENNYSON: *To J. S.*, 1833

Sleep! to the homeless thou art home.
EBENEZER ELLIOTT: *Sleep*, 1840

The native strength of [the Marquesans'] constitution is no way shown more emphatically than in the quantity of sleep they can endure. To many of them life is little else than an often interrupted and luxurious nap.
HERMAN MELVILLE: *Typee*, XIX, 1846

Sleep, my little one, sleep, my pretty one, sleep.
ALFRED TENNYSON: *The Princess*, III, 1847

Slowly Sir Launfal's eyes grew dim,
Slumber fell like a cloud on him.
J. R. LOWELL: *The Vision of Sir Launfal*, 1848

If thou wilt ease thine heart
Of love and all its smart,
Then sleep, dear, sleep!
T. L. BEDDOES: *Death's Jest-Book*, 1850

Sleep, kinsman thou to death and trance
And madness.
ALFRED TENNYSON: *In Memoriam*, LXX, 1850

Sleep is the interest we have to pay on the capital which is called in at death; and the higher the rate of interest and the more regularly it is paid, the further the date of redemption is postponed.
ARTHUR SCHOPENHAUER: *Our Relation to Ourselves*, 1851

To sleep is to strain and purify our emotions, to deposit the mud of life, to calm the fever of the soul, to return into the bosom of maternal nature, thence to re-issue, healed and strong. Sleep is a sort of innocence and purification.
H. F. AMIEL: *Journal*, March 20, 1853

In sleep, what difference is there between Solomon and a fool?
H. G. BOHN: *Handbook of Proverbs*, 1855

Over my slumber your loving watch keep —
Rock me to sleep, mother; rock me to sleep.
ELIZABETH CHASE (AKERS ALLEN): *Rock Me to Sleep*, 1860 (Saturday Evening Post, June 9)

I am weary of days and hours,
Blown buds of barren flowers,
Desires and dreams and powers
And everything but sleep.
A. C. SWINBURNE: *The Garden of Proserpine*, 1866

It is no small art to sleep: to achieve it one must keep awake all day.
F. W. NIETZSCHE: *Thus Spake Zarathustra*, I, 1885

There is only one thing people like that is good for them: a good night's sleep.
E. W. HOWE: *Country Town Sayings*, 1911

Sleep upstairs and live long.
FRENCH PROVERB

The beginning of health is sleep.
IRISH PROVERB

Sleep makes all men pashas.
MOORISH PROVERB

Nature requires five [hours],
Custom takes seven,
Idleness takes nine
And wickedness eleven.
OLD ENGLISH RHYME

In sleep we are all equal.
SPANISH PROVERB

Disease and sleep keep far apart.
WELSH PROVERB

The wiser the man, the less he sleeps in the morning.
IBID.

[*See also* Advice, Bed, Care, Day, Death, Dream, Drinking, Eating, Eating and Drinking, Eight-hour Day, Fasting, Fatigue, Gluttony, Graceful, Husband, Insomnia, Interruption, Jealousy, Labor, Man, Medicine, Midnight, Nap, Night, Rising (Early), Rising (Late), Siesta, Sloth, Soul.

Sleigh-bells

Hear the sledges with the bells —
Silver bells!
What a world of merriment their melody foretells!
How they tinkle, tinkle, tinkle,
In the icy air of night!
E. A. POE: *The Bells*, 1849 (Sartain's Union Magazine, Nov.)

Slip

There's many a slip 'twixt the cup and the lip.
R. B. BARHAM: *The Ingoldsby Legends*, 1840 (Apperson traces early forms to 1539)

A slip of the tongue. (Lapsus linguae.)
LATIN PHRASE

Sloth

The slothful man saith, There is a lion in the way; a lion is in the streets.
PROVERBS XXVI, 13, *c.* 350 B.C. (Cf. XXII, 13)

As the door turneth upon its hinges, so doth the slothful upon his bed.
PROVERBS XXVI, 14

We make a pretext of difficulty to excuse our sloth.
QUINTILIAN: *De institutione oratoria*, I, *c.* 90

The slothful man is the beggar's brother.
JAMES KELLY: *Complete Collection of Scottish Proverbs*, 1721

Sloth, like rust, consumes faster than labor wears, while the used key is always bright, as Poor Richard says. But dost thou love life, then do not squander time, for that is the stuff life is made of, as Poor Richard says.
BENJAMIN FRANKLIN: *Poor Richard's Almanac*, 1757

[*See also* Classes, Fault, Idleness, Laziness, Moderation, Sin, Weariness.

Slough

[*See* Despond.

Slovenliness

Women were made to give our eyes delight;
A female sloven is an odious sight.
EDWARD YOUNG: *Love of Fame*, VI, 1728

Slovenliness is no part of religion.
JOHN WESLEY: *Sermons*, LXXXVIII, *c.* 1791

We become slovenly in proportion as personal decay requires the contrary.
THOMAS JEFFERSON: *Letter to Mary Jefferson Eppes*, 1798

[*See also* Dress, Manly.

Slow

The help of the gods comes slowly, but it is not weak. EURIPIDES: *Ion*, *c.* 420 B.C.

Slow but sure.
ENGLISH PHRASE, familiar since the XVII century

Slow at meat, slow at work.
JAMES KELLY: *Complete Collection of Scottish Proverbs*, 1721

Great bodies move slowly.
H. G. BOHN: *Handbook of Proverbs*, 1855

Go slow, because I am in a hurry.
ITALIAN SAYING

A slow hand makes a sober fortune.
SCOTTISH PROVERB

[*See also* Haste, Hurry, Retribution, Swift.

Sluggard

Go to the ant, thou sluggard; consider her ways, and be wise. PROVERBS VI, 6, *c.* 150 B.C.

As vinegar to the teeth, and as smoke to the eyes, so is the sluggard to them that send him. PROVERBS X, 26

The soul of the sluggard desireth, and hath nothing. PROVERBS XIII, 4

The sluggard is wiser in his own conceit than seven wise men that can render a reason.
PROVERBS XXVI, 16

The rewards of the sluggard are three: shame, disease and misery. WELSH PROVERB

[*See also* Sleep.

Slum

[*See* Labor.

Slut

Of all tame beasts I hate sluts.
JOHN RAY: *English Proverbs*, 1670

She is a bold and impudent slut; she will talk with any man.
JOHN BUNYAN: *Pilgrim's Progress*, II, 1678

[*See also* Nut.

Small

Who hath despised the day of small things?
ZECHARIAH IV, 10, *c.* 520 B.C.

He that contemneth small things shall fall by little and little.
ECCLESIASTICUS XIX, 1, *c.* 180 B.C.

A small leak will sink a great ship.
THOMAS FULLER: *Gnomologia*, 1732

He who can take no interest in what is small will take false interest in what is great.
JOHN RUSKIN: *Modern Painters*, II, 1846

All of nature is to be found in the smallest things. (Tota in minimis existit natura.)
LATIN PROVERB

Small, but my own. (Klein, aber mein.)
GERMAN SAYING

[*See also* Little.

Smallpox

Smallpox, in its ordinary form, is simply an effort of the blood to rid itself of impurities. It is invariably followed by more vigorous health.
VOLTAIRE: *Letter to Baron de Bretuil*, Dec., 1723

[*See also* Measles, Vaccination.

Smell

A woman smells well when she smells of nothing. PLAUTUS: *Mostellaria*, *c.* 200 B.C.

Where all stink, one is not smelt.
ST. BERNARD: *Meditationes piissimae*, *c.* 1140

The rankest compound of villainous smell that ever offended nostril.
SHAKESPEARE: *The Merry Wives of Windsor*, III, *c.* 1600

A very ancient and fish-like smell.
SHAKESPEARE: *The Tempest*, II, 1611

A dunghill at a distance sometimes smells like musk, and a dead dog like elder-flowers.
S. T. COLERIDGE: *Table-Talk*, Jan. 4, 1823

The sense of smell is especially effective in arousing memories.
ARTHUR SCHOPENHAUER: *Parerga und Paralipomena*, 1851

[*See also* Bread, Dog, Flower, Odor, Perfume.

Smile

Seldom he smiles, and smiles in such a sort
As if he mock'd himself, and scorn'd his spirit
That could be mov'd to smile at anything.
SHAKESPEARE: *Julius Cæsar*, I, *c.* 1599

One may smile, and smile, and be a villain.
SHAKESPEARE: *Hamlet*, I, *c.* 1601

There's daggers in men's smiles.
SHAKESPEARE: *Macbeth*, II, *c.* 1605

Eternal smiles his emptiness betray,
As shallow streams run dimpling all the way.
ALEXANDER POPE: *An Epistle to Dr. Arbuthnot*, 1735

Without the smile from partial beauty won,
Oh, what were man? – a world without a sun.
THOMAS CAMPBELL: *The Pleasures of Hope*, II, 1799

And then their features started into smiles,
Sweet as blue heavens o'er enchanted isles.

JOHN KEATS: *Calidore,* 1817

In came Mrs. Fezziwig, one vast substantial smile.

CHARLES DICKENS: *A Christmas Carol,* II, 1843

Her voice lives on the breeze,
And her spirit comes at will;
In the midnight on the seas
Her bright smile haunts me still.

J. E. CARPENTER: *Her Bright Smile Haunts Me Still,* c. 1870 (A popular song throughout the 70's and 80's)

Smile, damn you; smile!

AMERICAN SAYING, *c.* 1910

[*See also* Dead, Hypocrisy, Laughter, Shopkeeping, Villain.

Smith

There was no smith found throughout all the land of Israel.

I SAMUEL XIII, 19, *c.* 500 B.C.

Fate tried to conceal him by naming him Smith.

O. W. HOLMES: *The Boys,* 1859

Smoke

There is no smoke without fire.

PLAUTUS: *Curculio,* I, *c.* 200 B.C.

Three things drive a man out of his house; that is to say, smoke, dropping of rain, and wicked wives.

GEOFFREY CHAUCER: *The Canterbury Tales (The Tale of Melibeus), c.* 1386

There is no fire without some smoke.

JOHN HEYWOOD: *Proverbs,* 1546

Smoke at home is brighter than fire elsewhere.

LATIN PROVERB

[*See also* Fire, House.

Smoking

A custom loathsome to the eye, harmful to the brain, dangerous to the lungs, and in the black stinking fume thereof, nearest resembling the horrible Stygian smoke of the pit that is bottomless.

JAMES I OF ENGLAND: *Counterblaste to Tobacco,* 1604

Surely smoke becomes a kitchen far better than a dining chamber; and yet it makes a kitchen oftentimes in the inward parts of men, soiling and infecting with an unctuous and oily kind of soot, as hath been found in some great tobacco takers, that after death were opened.

IBID.

Smoking is a shocking thing — blowing smoke out of our mouths into other people's mouths, eyes and noses, and having the same thing done to us.

SAMUEL JOHNSON: *Boswell's Tour to the Hebrides,* Aug. 19, 1773

He who doth not smoke hath either known no great griefs, or refuseth himself the softest consolation, next to that which comes from Heaven.

E. G. BULWER-LYTTON: *What Will He Do With It?,* I, 1858

Do not smoke in the street until after dark, and then remove your cigar from your mouth if you meet a lady.

C. B. HARTLEY: *The Gentleman's Book of Etiquette,* IV, 1873

One must never smoke, without consent, in the presence of a clergyman, and one must never offer a cigar to any ecclesiastic.

IBID.

[*See also* Cigar, Cigarette, Pipe, Teetotaler, Tobacco.

Smooth

Smooth as monumental alabaster.

SHAKESPEARE: *Othello,* V, 1604

A rugged stone grows smooth from hand to hand.

GEORGE HERBERT: *Outlandish Proverbs,* 1640

[*See also* Still.

Snail

How ingenious an animal is a snail. When it encounters a bad neighbor it takes up its house and moves away.

PHILEMON: *Fragment, c.* 300 B.C.

A snail's pace.

ENGLISH PHRASE, current since the XV century

Tramp on a snail, and she'll shoot out her horns.

JAMES KELLY: *Complete Collection of Scottish Proverbs,* 1721

The snail slides up the tower at last.

THOMAS FULLER: *Gnomologia,* 1732

When black snails on the road you see,
Then on the morrow rain will be.

OLD ENGLISH RHYME

[*See also* Perseverance.

Snake

A snake lurks in the grass. (Latet anguis in herba.)

VIRGIL: *Eclogues,* III, 37 B.C.

No will-o'-the-wisp mislight thee,
Nor snake or slow-worm bite thee.

ROBERT HERRICK: *Night-Piece to Julia,* 1648

Put a snake in your bosom, and it will sting when it is warm.

JAMES KELLY: *Complete Collection of Scottish Proverbs,* 1721

There are no snakes to be met with throughout the whole island.

Ascribed by SAMUEL JOHNSON to "The Natural History of Iceland, from the Danish Horrebow" (*Boswell's Life*, April 13, 1778. He said that the sentence constituted "a complete chapter" of the book. It is frequently ascribed to an imaginary volume on Ireland)

She was a gordian shape of dazzling hue,
Vermilion-spotted, golden, green, and blue;
Striped like a zebra, freckled like a pard,
Eyed like a peacock, and all crimson barr'd.

JOHN KEATS: *Lamia*, I, 1820

The monkey may have a horror at the sight of a snake, and a repugnance to its ways, but a snake is just as perfect an animal as a monkey.

FRANCIS GALTON: *Inquiries Into Human Faculty*, 1883

Snakes change even milk to poison.

SANSKRIT PROVERB

[*See also* Company, Edible, Horsehair, Serpent.

Snare

In vain the net is spread in the sight of any bird. PROVERBS I, 17, *c.* 350 B.C.

And why, it is asked, are there so many snares? That we may not fly low, but seek the things that are above.

ST. JOHN CHRYSOSTOM: *Homilies*, XV, *c.* 388

A delusion, a mockery, and a snare.

LORD DENMAN: *Judgment in Regina* vs. *O'Connell*, 1844 (Usually quoted as "a snare and a delusion")

Sneer

Who can refute a sneer?

WILLIAM PALEY: *The Principles of Moral and Political Philosophy*, V, 1785

There was a laughing devil in his sneer.

BYRON: *The Corsair*, I, 1814

[He] shaped his weapon with an edge severe,
Sapping a solemn creed with solemn sneer.

BYRON: *Childe Harold*, III, 1816

It is just as hard to do your duty when men are sneering at you as when they are shooting at you.

WOODROW WILSON: Speech in Brooklyn, May 11, 1914

[*See also* Damn.

Sneezing

Whence comes the custom of blessing and saying "God help" to those that sneeze? We produce three sorts of wind: that issuing from below is too indecent; that from the mouth implieth some reproach of gourmandize; the third is sneezing: and because it cometh from the head, and is without imputation, we thus kindly entertain it.

MICHEL DE MONTAIGNE: *Essays*, III, 1588

Sneezing absorbs all the faculties of the soul.

BLAISE PASCAL: *Pensées*, XXV, 1670

Sudden, with starting tears each eye o'erflows,
And the high dome reëchoes to his nose.

ALEXANDER POPE: *The Rape of the Lock*, V, 1712

You must not sneeze. If you have a vehement cold you must take no notice of it; if your nose membranes feel a great irritation you must hold your breath; if a sneeze still insists upon making its way you must oppose it by keeping your teeth grinding together; if the violence of the pulse breaks some blood-vessel you must break the blood-vessel — but not sneeze.

FRANCES BURNEY: *Letter to Esther Burney*, Dec. 17, 1785 (Directions for Coughing, Sneezing or Moving before the King and Queen)

Sneeze on Monday, sneeze for danger;
Sneeze on Tuesday, kiss a stranger;
Sneeze on Wednesday, sneeze for a letter;
Sneeze on Thursday, something better;
Sneeze on Friday, sneeze for sorrow;
Sneeze on Saturday, joy tomorrow;
Sneeze on Sunday, company coming.

ENGLISH FOLK-RHYME; date undetermined

Sneeze on a Saturday, your sweetheart tomorrow;
Sneeze on a Sunday, your safety seek:
The Devil will have you the whole of the week.

Another version

Man sneezes as God pleases.

SPANISH PROVERB

[*See also* Hiccup.

Snob

He drinks to none beneath the salt, and it is his grammar rule without exception not to confer with an inferior in public.

THOMAS ADAMS: *Diseases of the Soul*, 1616

He who meanly admires a mean thing is a snob.

W. M. THACKERAY: *The Book of Snobs*, II, 1847

The snob is now the ark that floats triumphant over the democratic wave; the faith of the old world reposes in his breast, and he shall proclaim it when the waters have subsided.

GEORGE MOORE: *Confessions of a Young Man*, IX, 1888

Snoring

Here snores Tophas,
That amorous ass.

JOHN LYLY: *Endymion*, III, 1591

He snored so loud that we thought he was driving his hogs to market.

JONATHAN SWIFT: *Polite Conversation*, 1738

Laugh, and the world laughs with you. Snore, and you sleep alone. Author unidentified

Snoring is sleeping out loud. IBID.

All who snore are not asleep.

DANISH PROVERB

[*See also* Midnight, Sleep.

Snout

[*See* Durable.

Snow

But where are the snows of yester year? (Mais où sont les neiges d'antan?)

FRANÇOIS VILLON: *Ballade des dames du temps jadis, c.* 1462

A snow year, a rich year.

GEORGE HERBERT: *Outlandish Proverbs,* 1640

Under water, famine; under snow, bread.

IBID.

The frolic architecture of the snow.

R. W. EMERSON: *The Snow-Storm,* 1841

In the range of inorganic nature, I doubt if any object can be found more perfectly beautiful than a fresh, deep, snowdrift, seen under warm light. Its curves are of inconceivable perfection and changefulness, its surface and transparency alike exquisite, its light and shade of inexhaustible variety and inimitable finish, the shadows sharp, pale, and of heavenly color, the reflected lights intense and multitudinous, and mingled with the sweet occurrences of transmitted light.

JOHN RUSKIN: *Modern Painters,* II, 1846

Beautiful snow! It can do nothing wrong.

J. W. WATSON: *Beautiful Snow,* 1858

The drowned and desolate world
Lies dumb and white in a trance of snow.

ELIZABETH CHASE (AKERS ALLEN): *Snow,* 1866

No cloud above, no earth below —
A universe of sky and snow.

J. G. WHITTIER: *Snow-Bound,* 1866

Wherever snow falls there is usually civil freedom.

R. W. EMERSON: *Society and Solitude,* 1870

Deep snow in Winter; tall grain in Summer.

ESTONIAN PROVERB

Year of snow
Fruit will grow.

OLD ENGLISH RHYME

[*See also* January, Wind (North), Winter.

Snowball

[*See* Chance.

Snuff

You abuse snuff! Perhaps it is the final cause of the human nose.

S. T. COLERIDGE: *Table-Talk,* Jan. 14, 1823

Snug

Here Skugg
Lies snug
As a bug
In a rug.

BENJAMIN FRANKLIN: Epitaph for the pet squirrel of Miss Georgiana Shipley, sent to her in a letter, Sept. 26, 1772

[*See also* England.

Soap

Soap is a measure of the prosperity and culture of a nation.

JUSTUS VON LIEBIG: *Chemische Briefe,* 1844

Sobriety

The gods love the sober-minded.

SOPHOCLES: *Ajax, c.* 450 B.C.

I am as sober as a judge.

HENRY FIELDING: *Don Quixote in England,* III, 1733

[*See also* Drinking, Drunk, Drunkenness.

Sociability

A fifth law of nature is complaisance; that is, that every man strive to accommodate himself to the rest. . . . The observers of this law may be called sociable; the Latins call them *commodi.*

THOMAS HOBBES: *Leviathan,* I, 1651

A man's sociability stands very nearly in inverse ratio to his intellectual value: to say that so-and-so is very unsociable is almost tantamount to saying that he is a man of capacity.

ARTHUR SCHOPENHAUER: *Our Relation to Ourselves,* 1851

[*See also* Society.

Socialism

Socialism will bring in an efflorescence of morality, civilization, and science such as has never before been seen in the history of the world.

FERDINAND LASSALLE: *Arbeiter-Programm,* 1862

Slavery comes to life again: the state an assemblage of slaves without personal liberty — that is Socialism.

WILLIAM E. VON KETTELER: *Can a Workingman Be a Socialist?,* 1877

These monstrous views, . . . these venomous teachings.

POPE LEO XIII: *Quod apostolici muneris,* Dec. 28, 1878

The ideal of Socialism is grand and noble; and it is, I am convinced, possible of realization; but such a state of society cannot be manufactured — it must grow. Society is an organism, not a machine.

HENRY GEORGE: *Progress and Poverty,* VI, 1879

Socialism is not at all the enemy of civilization. It only wants to extend civilization to all hu-

manity; under capitalism, civilization is the monopoly of a privileged minority.
WILHELM LIEBKNECHT: *How Shall Socialism Be Put into Practise?*, 1881

All Socialism involves slavery.
HERBERT SPENCER: *The Coming Slavery*, 1884

The main tenet of Socialism, namely, the community of goods, must be rejected without qualification, for it would injure those it pretends to benefit, it would be contrary to the natural rights of man, and it would introduce confusion and disorder into the commonwealth.
POPE LEO XIII: *Rerum novarum*, May 15, 1891

Socialism is the legitimate heir of Liberalism, not only chronologically, but also spiritually.
EDWARD BERNSTEIN: *Evolutionary Socialism*, III, 1899

There is only one sovereign method for the achievement of Socialism — the winning of a legal majority.
JEAN JAURÈS: *Études socialistes*, XII, 1902

The trend of Democracy is toward Socialism, while the Republican party stands for a wise and regulated individualism. Socialism would destroy wealth; Republicanism would prevent its abuse. Socialism would give to each an equal right to take; Republicanism would give to each an equal right to earn. Socialism would offer an equality of position which would soon leave no one anything to possess; Republicanism would give equality to each.
Republican National Platform, 1908

The adoption of a logical and extreme Socialistic system would spell sheer destruction; it would produce grosser wrong and outrage, fouler immorality than any existing system. But this does not mean that we may not with great advantage adopt certain of the principles proposed by some given set of men who happen to call themselves Socialists.
THEODORE ROOSEVELT: Speech at the Sorbonne, April 23, 1910

Socialism is a fake, a comedy, a phantom, and a blackmail.
BENITO MUSSOLINI: Speech in Milan, July 22, 1919

Socialism changes its color according to its environment. For the street-corner and the club-room it wears the flaming scarlet of class-war; for the intellectuals its red is shot with tawny; for the sentimentalists it becomes a delicate rose-pink; and in clerical circles it assumes a virgin-white, just touched with a faint flush of generous aspiration.
RAMSAY MUIR: *The Socialist Class Explained*, I, 1925

Socialism is a stage in social development from a society guided by the dictatorship of the proletariat to a society wherein the state will have ceased to exist.
JOSEPH STALIN: Speech to the students of the University of the Peoples of the East, May 18, 1925

The temporary victory of Socialism in one country alone is possible, but its lasting victory in one country alone is impossible: that demands the victory of the revolution in other lands as well.
JOSEPH STALIN: *Leninism*, I, 1926

The combination of religious sentimentality, industrial insanity, and moral obliquity.
F. J. C. HEARNSHAW: *A Survey of Socialism*, II, 1928

Socialism appears to be afraid of its own principles, and of the conclusions drawn from them by the Communists. In consequence, it is drifting toward truths which the Christian tradition has always supported. Indeed, it cannot be denied that its programme often comes close to the just demands of Christian reformers.
POPE PIUS XI: *Quadragesimo anno*, May 15, 1931

[*See also* Church (Roman Catholic), Communism, Imperialism, Individualism.

Socialist

Socialists, Communists, and Nihilists . . . strive to uproot the foundations of civilized society.
POPE LEO XIII: *Quod apostolici muneris*, Dec. 28, 1878

The curse of our time is that many . . . share care with the high and obscurity with the low, but wealth and comfort with neither. This state of things is the origin of loafers, tramps, corner-boys, roughs, Socialists and other pests of society.
GERARD MANLEY HOPKINS: *Letter to Robert Bridges*, Feb., 1888

Whom do I hate most heartily among the rabbles of today? The rabble of Socialists, the apostles to the Chandala, who undermine the workingman's instincts, his pleasure, his feeling of contentment with his petty existence — who make him envious and teach him revenge.
F. W. NIETZSCHE: *The Antichrist*, LVII, 1888

We are all Socialists now-a-days.
THE PRINCE OF WALES (afterward Edward VII): Speech at the Mansion House, London, 1895

The word Socialist may mean anything.
V. G. SIMKHOVITCH: *Marxism* vs. *Socialism*, I, 1913

No one can be, at the same time, a sincere Catholic and a true Socialist.
POPE PIUS XI: *Quadragesimo anno*, May 15, 1931

[*See also* Capitalism, Communist.

Society

We were born to unite with our fellow-men, and to join in community with the human race. CICERO: *De finibus,* IV, *c.* 50 B.C.

The intelligence of the universe is social. It made the lower for the benefit of the higher, and it fitted the higher to one another.
MARCUS AURELIUS: *Meditations,* V, *c.* 170

What is not good for the swarm is not good for the bee.
MARCUS AURELIUS: *Meditations,* VI

Civil society doth more content the nature of man than any private kind of solitary living.
RICHARD HOOKER: *The Laws of Ecclesiastical Polity,* I, 1594

Two foundations there are which bear upon public societies: the one a natural inclination whereby all men desire sociable life and fellowship; the other an order, expressly or secretly agreed upon, touching the manner of their union in living together. IBID.

Man seeketh in society comfort, use, and protection.
FRANCIS BACON: *The Advancement of Learning,* II, 1605

Society is no comfort to one not sociable.
SHAKESPEARE: *Cymbeline,* IV, *c.* 1609

Two things do make society to stand;
The first commerce is, and the next command.
ROBERT HERRICK: *Hesperides,* 1648

The original of all great and lasting societies consisted not in the mutual good will men had towards each other, but in the mutual fear they had of each other.
THOMAS HOBBES: *Philosophical Rudiments Concerning Government and Society,* I, 1651

We do not by nature seek society for its own sake, but that we may receive some honor or profit from it; these we desire primarily, that secondarily. IBID.

Men would not live long in society were they not the dupes of one another.
LA ROCHEFOUCAULD: *Maxims,* 1665

In society the man of sense always yields first. Thus the wisest are led by the most foolish and bizarre. We study their foibles, their humors and their caprices. We adapt ourselves to them, and avoid knocking our heads against them.
JEAN DE LA BRUYÈRE: *Caractères,* V, 1688

Justice and truth are the common ties of society.
JOHN LOCKE: *Essay Concerning Human Understanding,* I, 1690

It is as manifest that we were made for society, and to promote the happiness of it, as that we were intended to take care of our own life, and health, and private good.
JOSEPH BUTLER: *Sermons Upon Human Nature,* I, 1726

Society was invented for a remedy against injustice.
WILLIAM WARBURTON (BISHOP OF GLOUCESTER): *The Divine Legation of Moses,* I, 1737

Society is the union of men, but not men themselves; the citizen may perish, but man remains.
C. L. DE MONTESQUIEU: *The Spirit of the Laws,* X, 1748

Man was formed for society, and is neither capable of living alone, nor has the courage to do it.
WILLIAM BLACKSTONE: *Commentaries on the Laws of England,* I, 1765

Life is of no value but as it brings us gratifications. Among the most valuable of these is rational society. It informs the mind, sweetens the temper, cheers our spirits, and promotes health.
THOMAS JEFFERSON: *Letter to James Madison,* 1784

Society is a partnership in all science; a partnership in all art; a partnership in every virtue, and in all perfection. As the ends of such a partnership cannot be obtained in many generations, it becomes a partnership not only between those who are living, but between those who are living, those who are dead, and those who are to be born.
EDMUND BURKE: *Reflections on the Revolution in France,* 1790

Society performs for itself almost everything which is ascribed to government.
THOMAS PAINE: *The Rights of Man,* I, 1791

No one man is capable, without the aid of society, of supplying his own wants; and those wants acting upon every individual, impel the whole of them into society, as naturally as gravitation acts to a centre.
THOMAS PAINE: *The Rights of Man,* II

There is
One great society alone on earth:
The noble living and the noble dead.
WILLIAM WORDSWORTH: *The Prelude,* XI, 1805

We submit to the society of those that can inform us, but we seek the society of those whom we can inform.
C. C. COLTON: *Lacon,* 1820

All men seek the society of those who think and act somewhat like themselves.
WILLIAM COBBETT: *Advice to Young Men,* I, 1829

Narrow the circle as we will, there must still be some society left — someone to act with us, someone to confide our villainies to, someone to approve them.

WILLIAM HAZLITT: *The Late Murders*, 1829 (The Atlas, Jan. 18)

That is the most excellent state of society in which the patriotism of the citizen ennobles, but does not merge, the individual energy of the man.

S. T. COLERIDGE: *Table-Talk*, Aug. 19, 1832

Society is divided into two classes: the shearers and the shorn. We should always be with the former against the latter.

Ascribed to C. M. DE TALLEYRAND (1754–1838)

Society is a joint stock company in which the members agree, for the better securing of his bread to each shareholder, to surrender the liberty and culture of the eater.

R. W. EMERSON: *Self-Reliance*, 1841

Though the world contains many things which are thoroughly bad, the worst thing in it is society.

ARTHUR SCHOPENHAUER: *Our Relation to Ourselves*, 1851

As man masters nature in modern society he becomes enslaved to other men or to his own ignominy.

KARL MARX: Speech in London, April 14, 1856

Society is always diseased, and the best is the most so. H. D. THOREAU: *Excursions*, 1863

When a man meets his fitting mate society begins.

R. W. EMERSON: *Lecture on Social Aims*, Boston, Dec. 4, 1864

Man was made of social earth.

R. W. EMERSON: *Initial, Daemonic and Celestial Love*, II, 1867

If society had not been invented man would have remained a wild beast forever, or, what amounts to the same thing, a saint.

M. A. BAKUNIN: *Dieu et l'état*, 1871

The law of society is, each for all, as well as all for each. No one can keep to himself the good he may do, any more than he can keep the bad.

HENRY GEORGE: *Progress and Poverty*, IX, 1879

It is not from top to bottom that societies die; it is from bottom to top.

HENRY GEORGE: *Progress and Poverty*, X

The most complex and difficult subject which we now have to study is the constitution of human society, the forces which operate in it, and the laws by which they act, and we know less about these things than about any others which demand our attention.

W. G. SUMNER: *The Forgotten Man*, 1883

Society differs from nature in having a definite moral object.

T. H. HUXLEY: *The Struggle for Existence in Human Society*, 1888

Society has come to be man's dearest possession. Pure air is good, but no one wants to breathe it alone. Independence is good, but isolation is too heavy a price to pay for it.

BENJAMIN R. TUCKER: *Instead of a Book*, 1893

Human society, as established by God, is composed of unequal elements, just as parts of the human body are unequal; to make them all equal is impossible, and would mean the destruction of human society itself.

POPE PIUS X: *Apostolic Letter to the Bishops of Italy on Catholic Social Action*, Dec. 18, 1903

Society is a madhouse whose wardens are the officials and police.

AUGUST STRINDBERG: *Zones of the Spirit*, 1913

These are the three pillars of society — education, charity, and piety.

HEBREW PROVERB

[*See also* Agreeable, Company, Government, Law, Property, Sociability, Socialism, Solitude.

Society (fashionable)

Society at court is like a house built of marble: it is made up of very hard and very polished people.

JEAN DE LA BRUYÈRE: *Caractères*, VIII, 1688

She was born under Gemini, which may incline her to society.

WILLIAM CONGREVE: *Love for Love*, II, 1695

Pray, madam, who were the company? Why, there was all the world and his wife.

JONATHAN SWIFT: *Polite Conversation*, III, 1738

Good company is that company which all the people of the place call, and acknowledge to be, good company, notwithstanding some objections which they may form to some of the individuals who compose it.

LORD CHESTERFIELD: *Letter to his son*, Oct. 12, 1748

Society is now one polish'd horde,
Form'd of two mighty tribes, the bores and bored. BYRON: *Don Juan*, XIII, 1823

The glare, and heat, and noise, this congeries of individuals without sympathy, and dishes without flavor; this is society.

BENJAMIN DISRAELI: *The Young Duke*, 1831

I decline all invitations of society that are declinable: a London rout is one of the mad-

dest things under the moon; a London dinner makes me sicker for a week.
THOMAS CARLYLE: *Letter to R. W. Emerson,* March 16, 1838

There are only about four hundred people in New York society.
WARD MCALLISTER: Interview with Charles H. Crandall in the New York Tribune, 1888

I suppose society is wonderfully delightful. To be in it is merely a bore. But to be out of it is simply a tragedy.
OSCAR WILDE: *A Woman of No Importance,* III, 1893

To get into the best society nowadays, one has either to feed people, amuse people, or shock people. IBID.

Other people are quite dreadful. The only possible society is oneself.
OSCAR WILDE: *An Ideal Husband,* III, 1895

Society has gone to the dogs: a lot of nobodies talking about nothing. IBID.

Never speak disrespectfully of society. Only people who can't get into it do that.
OSCAR WILDE: *The Importance of Being Earnest,* II, 1895

High society is for those who have stopped working and no longer have anything important to do.
WOODROW WILSON: Speech in Washington, Feb. 24, 1915

Socrates (469–399 B.C.)

Socrates is guilty of rejecting the gods of Athens and introducing new ones. He is also guilty of corrupting the youth of the city.
Indictment of Socrates, laid before the Court of the Archon in Athens by Meletus, Anytus and Lycon, 399 B.C.

Socrates acted wickedly, and is criminally curious in searching into things under the earth, and in the heavens, and in making the worse appear the better cause, and in teaching these same things to others.
Charge against Socrates as stated in his Apology, 399 B.C.

Socrates was the first who brought down philosophy from Heaven, introducing it into the abodes of men, and compelling them to study the science of life, of human morals, and the effects of things good and bad.
CICERO: *Tusculanæ disputationes,* V, 45 B.C.

The character of Socrates does not rise upon me. The more I read about him, the less I wonder that they poisoned him.
T. B. MACAULAY: *Letter to T. F. Ellis,* May 29, 1835

Socrates belonged to the lowest of the low: he was the mob. You can still see for yourself how ugly he was.
F. W. NIETZSCHE: *The Twilight of the Idols,* 1889

[*See also* Argument, Honor, Philosopher, Truth.

Sofa

Necessity invented stools,
Convenience next suggested elbow-chairs,
And luxury the accomplish'd sofa last.
WILLIAM COWPER: *The Task,* I, 1785

Softness

Fair and softly goes far.
ENGLISH PROVERB, traced to the XIV century

Not with the softness of the answer which turneth away wrath, but with that of the pillow which smothered Desdemona.
T. H. HUXLEY: *Letter to James Knowles,* May 4, 1889 (The reference is to a proposed reply to the Bishop of Peterborough)

Soldier

When soldiers run away in war they never blame themselves: they blame their general or their fellow-soldiers.
DEMOSTHENES: *Third Olynthiac,* 348 B.C.

War, as the saying goes, is full of false alarms, a fact which professional soldiers have had the best chance to learn; thus they appear brave because of other men's ignorance of the true situation.
ARISTOTLE: *The Nicomachean Ethics,* III, *c.* 340 B.C.

Soldiers fight and die to advance the wealth and luxury of the great, and they are called masters of the world without having a sod to call their own.
TIBERIUS SEMPRONIUS GRACCHUS: Speech in Rome, 133 B.C.

Let the soldier yield to the civilian. (Cedant arma togæ.)
CICERO: *Orationes Philippicæ,* II, *c.* 60 B.C.

A soldiery dull and lazy, and corrupted by the circus and the theatres.
TACITUS: *History,* V, *c.* 100

It is easier to find false witnesses against the civilian than anyone willing to speak the truth against the interest and honor of the soldier. JUVENAL: *Satires,* XVI, 128

Soldiers in peace are like chimneys in Summer.
WILLIAM CECIL (LORD BURLEIGH): *Advice to His Son, c.* 1555

The hardiest soldiers be either slain or maimed, [or], if they escape all hazards, and return home again, if they be without relief of their friends they will surely desperately rob and steal, and either shortly be hanged or miserably die in prison.
THOMAS HARMAN: *A Caveat or Warning for Common Cursetors,* I, 1566

There were three lusty soldiers
Went through a town of late;

The one loved Bess, the other Sis,
The third loved bouncing Kate.
Anon.: *Choice of Inventions*, II, *c.* 1575

I am a soldier and unapt to weep
Or to exclaim on fortune's fickleness.
SHAKESPEARE: *I Henry VI*, V, 1592

Because such as are to become men of war are to be of a perfect age most apt for all manner of services and best able to support and endure the infinite toils and continual hazards of the wars, I have chosen all between the age of eighteen and fifty to become trained soldiers.
HENRY KNYVETT: *The Defence of the Realme*, 1596

There's no love lost between soldiers and sailors.
ENGLISH PROVERB, traced by Smith to 1599

Give them great meals of beef and iron and steel, they will eat like wolves and fight like devils.
SHAKESPEARE: *Henry V*, III, *c.* 1599

Then a soldier,
Full of strange oaths and bearded like the pard,
Jealous in honor, sudden and quick in quarrel,
Seeking the bubble reputation
Even in the cannon's mouth.
SHAKESPEARE: *As You Like It*, II, *c.* 1600

I love them [soldiers] for their virtues' sake, and for their greatness of mind. . . . If we may have peace, they have purchased it; and if we must have war, they must manage it.
ROBERT DEVEREAUX (EARL OF ESSEX): *Change*, *c.* 1600

A soldier's but a man;
A life's but a span;
Why, then, let a soldier drink.
SHAKESPEARE: *Othello*, II, 1604

He is a soldier fit to stand by Cæsar. IBID.

Fie, my lord, fie! a soldier and afear'd?
SHAKESPEARE: *Macbeth*, V, *c.* 1605

He that gives a soldier the lie looks to receive the stab.
THOMAS DEKKER: *The Seven Deadly Sins of London*, II, 1606

They say soldiers and lawyers could never thrive both together in one shire.
BARNABE RICH: *The Anothomy of Ireland*, 1615

I hate that heady and adventurous crew . . .
That by death only seek to get a living,
Make scars their beauty and count loss of limbs
The commendation of a proper man.
Anon.: *Nero*, I, 1624

I know not how, but martial men are given to love. I think it is, but as they are given to wine; for perils commonly ask to be paid in pleasures.
FRANCIS BACON: *Essays*, X, 1625

To take a soldier without ambition is to pull off his spurs. FRANCIS BACON: *Essays*, XXXVI

Some undone widow sits upon mine arm,
And takes away the use of it, and my sword,
Glued to my scabbard with wronged orphan's tears,
Will not be drawn.
PHILIP MASSINGER: *A New Way to Pay Old Debts*, V, 1633

Our God and soldiers we alike adore
Ev'n at the brink of danger; not before:
After deliverance, both alike requited,
Our God's forgotten, and our soldiers slighted.
FRANCIS QUARLES: *Emblems*, 1635

Water, fire and soldiers quickly make room.
GEORGE HERBERT: *Outlandish Proverbs*, 1640

He that enrolleth himself a soldier taketh away the excuse of a timorous nature, and is obliged not only to go to the battle but also not to run from it, without his captain's leave.
THOMAS HOBBES: *Leviathan* XXI, 1651

Soldiers and travelers may lie by authority.
JAMES HOWELL: *Proverbs*, 1659

Ay me! what perils do environ
The man that meddles with cold iron!
SAMUEL BUTLER: *Hudibras*, I, 1663

Women adore a martial man.
WILLIAM WYCHERLEY: *The Plain Dealer*, II, *c.* 1674

You stink of brandy and tobacco, most soldier-like.
WILLIAM CONGREVE: *The Old Bachelor*, III, 1693

He shall turn soldier, and rather depend upon the outside of his head than the lining.
WILLIAM CONGREVE: *Love For Love*, I, 1695

Drinking is the soldier's pleasure.
JOHN DRYDEN: *Alexander's Feast*, 1697

The military pedant . . . always talks in a camp, and is storming towns, making lodgments and fighting battles from one end of the year to the other. Everything he speaks smells of gunpowder; if you take away his artillery from him he has not a word to say for himself.
JOSEPH ADDISON: *The Spectator*, June 30, 1711

The soldier smiling hears the widow's cries,
And stabs the son before the mother's eyes.
With like remorse his brother of the trade,
The butcher, fells the lamb beneath his blade.
JONATHAN SWIFT: *On Dreams*, 1724

Of boasting more than bomb afraid,
A soldier should be modest as a maid.
EDWARD YOUNG: *Love of Fame*, IV, 1728

The wise old soldier is never in haste to strike a blow.
PIETRO METASTASIO: *Adriano*, II, 1735

How sleep the brave, who sink to rest,
By all their country's wishes blest!
WILLIAM COLLINS: *Ode Written in the Year 1746*

A soldier worthy of the name he bears,
As brave and senseless as the sword he wears.
MARY WORTLEY MONTAGU: *Letter to James Steuart,* July 19, 1759

French officers will always lead, if the soldiers will follow: and English soldiers will always follow, if their officers will lead.
SAMUEL JOHNSON: *On the Bravery of the English Common Soldiers, c.* 1760

The broken soldier, kindly bade to stay,
Sat by his fire, and talk'd the night away;
Wept o'er his wounds, or, tales of sorrow done,
Shoulder'd his crutch, and show'd how fields were won.
OLIVER GOLDSMITH: *The Deserted Village,* I, 1770

Every man thinks meanly of himself for not having been a soldier.
SAMUEL JOHNSON: *Boswell's Life,* April 10, 1778

Oh, why the deuce should I repine,
And be an ill foreboder?
I'm twenty-three, and five feet nine —
I'll go and be a sodger.
ROBERT BURNS: *Extempore,* 1784

If my soldiers were to begin to think, not one would remain in the ranks.
Ascribed to FREDERICK THE GREAT (1712–86)

No soldier shall, in time of peace, be quartered in any house without the consent of the owner, nor in time of war but in a manner to be prescribed by law.
CONSTITUTION OF THE UNITED STATES, Amendment III, Dec. 15, 1791

A soldier is a man whose business it is to kill those who never offended him, and who are the innocent martyrs of other men's iniquities. Whatever may become of the abstract question of the justifiableness of war, it seems impossible that the soldier should not be a depraved and unnatural thing.
WILLIAM GODWIN: *The Enquirer,* V, 1797

Dead on the field of honor. (Mort au champ d'honneur.)
Théophile de la Tour d'Auvergne, called the First Grenadier of France, was killed at Oberhausen, June 27, 1800. Thereafter, as the roll of his regiment was called each morning, the first sergeant answered to his name with these words. The same custom was later instituted in other French regiments in memory of other gallant soldiers.

When soldiers brave death, they drive him into the enemy's ranks.
NAPOLEON I: To a regiment of chasseurs, before Jena, Oct. 12, 1806

I don't know what effect these men will have on the enemy, but, by God, they frighten *me.*
THE DUKE OF WELLINGTON: On a draft of troops sent to him in Spain, 1809

Soldier, rest! thy warfare o'er,
Dream of fighting fields no more:
Sleep the sleep that knows not breaking,
Morn of toil, nor night of waking.
WALTER SCOTT: *The Lady of the Lake,* I, 1810

Every citizen [should] be a soldier. This was the case with the Greeks and Romans, and must be that of every free state.
THOMAS JEFFERSON: *Letter to James Monroe,* 1813

I love a brave soldier who has undergone the baptism of fire, whatever nation he may belong to.
NAPOLEON I: To Barry E. O'Meara at St. Helena, Aug. 30, 1816

In order to have good soldiers, a nation must always be at war.
NAPOLEON I: To Barry E. O'Meara at St. Helena, Oct. 26, 1816

He lay like a warrior taking his rest.
CHARLES WOLFE: *The Burial of Sir John Moore,* 1817

Soldiers are made on purpose to be killed.
NAPOLEON I: To Gaspard Gourgaud at St. Helena, 1815–1818

A modern general has said that the best troops would be as follows: an Irishman half drunk, a Scotchman half starved, and an Englishman with his belly full.
C. C. COLTON: *Lacon,* 1820

Ben Battle was a soldier bold,
And used to war's alarms;
But a cannon-ball took off his legs,
So he laid down his arms.
THOMAS HOOD: *Faithless Nellie Gray,* 1840

He fell on the field:
His country mourned him,
And his father is resigned.
E. G. BULWER-LYTTON: *The Caxtons,* XVIII, 1849

Were not here the real priests and martyrs of that loud-babbling rotten generation?
THOMAS CARLISLE: *Letter to R. W. Emerson,* June 25, 1852 (On " the Prussian soldiery " of Frederick the Great's time)

Theirs not to make reply,
Theirs not to reason why,
Theirs but to do and die.
ALFRED TENNYSON: *The Charge of the Light Brigade,* 1854

Only the defeated and deserters go to the war.
H. D. THOREAU: *Walden,* 1854

The blood of the soldier makes the glory of the general.
H. G. BOHN: *Handbook of Proverbs,* 1855

A soldier has a hard life, and but little consideration.
ROBERT E. LEE: *Letter to his wife,* Nov. 5, 1855

A clergyman, or a doctor, or a lawyer feels himself no whit disgraced if he reaches the end of his worldly labors without special note or honor. But to a soldier or a sailor such indifference to his merit is wormwood. It is the bane of the profession. Nine men out of ten who go into it must live discontented, and die disappointed.
ANTHONY TROLLOPE: *The Three Clerks,* 1858

The soldier's trade is not slaying, but being slain. This, without well knowing its own meaning, the world honors it for.
JOHN RUSKIN: *Unto This Last,* I, 1862

I know that there must be soldiers; but as to every separate soldier I regret that he should be one of them.
ANTHONY TROLLOPE: *North America,* I, 1862

Uncover your head and hold your breath:
This boon not every lifetime hath —
To look on men who have walked with death,
And have not been afraid.
ELIZABETH CHASE (AKERS ALLEN): *The Return of the Regiment,* 1865

A soldier's vow to his country is that he will die for the guardianship of her domestic virtue, of her righteous laws, and of her anyway challenged or endangered honor. A state without virtue, without laws, and without honor, he is bound not to defend.
JOHN RUSKIN: *The Crown of Wild Olive,* III, 1866

So 'ere's to you, Fuzzy-Wuzzy, at your 'ome in the Sudan;
You're a pore benighted 'eathen but a first-class fightin' man.
RUDYARD KIPLING: *Fuzzy-Wuzzy,* 1890

A soldier is Christ's warrior. As such he should regard himself, and so he should behave. Consider your corps as your family; your commander as your father; your comrade as your brother; your inferior as a young relative. Then all will be happy and friendly and easy. Don't think of yourself, think of your comrades; they will think of you. Perish yourself, but save your comrade.
M. I. DRAGOMIROFF: *Notes for Soldiers, c.* 1890

Love ain't enough for a soldier.
RUDYARD KIPLING: *The Young British Soldier,* 1891

Oh, it's Tommy this, an' Tommy that, an' "Tommy, wait outside";
But it's "Special train for Atkins" when the trooper's on the tide.
RUDYARD KIPLING: *Tommy,* 1892

Single men in barricks don't grow into plaster saints.
IBID.

A soldier is an anachronism of which we must get rid.
GEORGE BERNARD SHAW: *The Devil's Disciple,* III, 1897

Old soldiers never die;
They simply fade away.
Anon.: British soldiers' song, popular in 1914–18

A soldier is a slave — he does what he is told to do — everything is provided for him — his head is a superfluity. He is only a stick used by men to strike other men.
ELBERT HUBBARD: *Roycroft Dictionary and Book of Epigrams,* 1923

Done give myself to Uncle Sam,
Now I ain't worth a good goddam,
I don't want no mo' camp,
Lawd, I want to go home.
American Negro song, quoted by HOWARD W. ODUM: *Wings On My Feet,* IV, 1929

The functions of a citizen and a soldier are inseparable.
BENITO MUSSOLINI: *Decree,* Sept. 18, 1934

Soldiers ought to fear their general more than their enemy. Author unidentified

The first qualification of a soldier is fortitude under fatigue and privation. Courage is only the second. Hardships, poverty, and actual want are the soldier's best school.
Author unidentified; often ascribed to NAPOLEON I or to GEORGE WASHINGTON

Good iron is not for nails, nor good men for soldiers. CHINESE PROVERB

It is better to have no son than one who is a soldier. IBID.

The best soldiers are not warlike. IBID.

Old soldier, old idiot. FRENCH PROVERB

The soup makes the soldier. IBID.

Soldiers deserve to be well paid and well hanged. GERMAN PROVERB

Young soldiers, old beggars. IBID.

Soldiers fight, and kings are heroes.
HEBREW PROVERB

Among flowers, the best is the cherry blossom; among men, the best is the soldier.
JAPANESE PROVERB

The first duty of a soldier is obedience.
MILITARY PROVERB

Flog two to death, and train one.
RUSSIAN PROVERB

The best soldier comes from the plow.
SPANISH PROVERB

[*See also* Adams (John), Army, Art, Baton, Blasphemy, Brandy, Brave, Captain, Citizen, Conscription, Continental, Coward, Cowardice, Dead, Death, Democrat, Devotion, Drinking, General, Gun, King, Love, Marine, Mercenary, Obedience, Police, Profession, Recruit, Uniform, Veteran, War, War and Peace, Warrior, Water.

Solemnity

I regard solemnity as a disease. I had rather a thousand times to be feverish and feeble, as I now am, than to think lugubriously.

VOLTAIRE: *Letter to Frederick the Great,* July, 1737

If you would succeed in life, you must be solemn, solemn as an ass. All the great monuments of earth have been built over solemn asses.

Ascribed to THOMAS CORWIN (1794–1865) in DONN PIATT: *Memoirs of the Men Who Saved the Union,* 1879

Solemnity is a condition precedent to believing anything without evidence.

R. G. INGERSOLL: Speech in Chicago, Nov. 26, 1882

[*See also* Ability.

Solitary

God has created mankind for fellowship, and not for solitariness, which is clearly proved by this strong argument: God, in the creation of the world, created man and woman, to the end that the man in the woman should have a fellow.

MARTIN LUTHER: *Table-Talk,* DCLXIII, 1569

A solitary man is either a brute or an angel.

H. G. BOHN: *Handbook of Proverbs,* 1855

[*See also* Alone, Solitude.

Solitude

Little do men perceive what solitude is, and how far it extendeth. For a crowd is not company; and faces are but a gallery of pictures; and talk but a tinkling cymbal where there is no love.

FRANCIS BACON: *Essays,* XXVII, 1625

There is no such thing as solitude, nor anything that can be said to be alone and by itself, save God.

THOMAS BROWNE: *Religio Medici,* II, 1642

If a man be a coxcomb solitude is his best school, and if he be a fool it is his best sanctuary.

ALEXANDER POPE: *Letter to William Wycherley,* Oct. 26, 1705

O sacred solitude, divine retreat,
Choice of the prudent, envy of the great;
By thy pure stream, or in thy waving shade,
We court fair wisdom, that celestial maid.

EDWARD YOUNG: *Love of Fame,* V, 1728

Far from the madding crowd's ignoble strife.

THOMAS GRAY: *Elegy Written in a Country Churchyard,* 1750

The happiest of all lives is a busy solitude.

VOLTAIRE: *Letter to Frederick the Great,* Aug., 1751

Solitude begets whimsies.

MARY WORTLEY MONTAGU: *Letter to James Steuart,* July 19, 1759

Solitude excludes pleasure, and does not always secure peace.

SAMUEL JOHNSON: *Letter to Mrs. Aston,* Nov. 17, 1767

Solitude holds a cup sparkling with bliss in her right hand, a raging dagger in her left; to the blest she offers her goblet, but stretches toward the wretch the ruthless steel.

F. B. KLOPSTOCK: *Messias,* IV, 1773

I praise the Frenchman; his remark was shrewd,—
"How sweet, how passing sweet is solitude."
But grant me still a friend in my retreat,
Whom I may whisper "Solitude is sweet."

WILLIAM COWPER: *Retirement,* 1782

I am monarch of all I survey
My right there is none to dispute.

WILLIAM COWPER: *Verses Supposed to Have Been Written by Alexander Selkirk,* 1782

O solitude! where are the charms
That sages have seen in thy face?
Better dwell in the midst of alarms,
Than reign in this horrible place. IBID.

I could bear sickness better if I were relieved from solitude.

SAMUEL JOHNSON: *Letter to James Boswell,* Dec. 24, 1783

Oh, for a lodge in some vast wilderness,
Some boundless contiguity of shade,
Where rumor of oppression and deceit,
Of unsuccessful or successful war,
Might never reach me more!

WILLIAM COWPER: *The Task,* II, 1785

How blest the solitary's lot,
Who, all-forgetting, all-forgot,
Within his humble cell,
The cavern wild with tangling roots,
Sits o'er his newly-gathered fruits,
Beside his crystal well.

ROBERT BURNS: *Despondency,* 1786

Talent is best nurtured in solitude.

J. W. GOETHE: *Torquato Tasso,* I, 1790

That inward eye
Which is the bliss of solitude.

WILLIAM WORDSWORTH: *I Wandered Lonely as a Cloud,* 1807

In solitude, where we are least alone.

BYRON: *Childe Harold,* III, 1816

Solitude should teach us how to die.

BYRON: *Childe Harold,* IV, 1818

Solitude, though it may be silent as light, is, like light, the mightiest of agencies; for solitude is essential to man. All men come into this world alone; all leave it alone.
THOMAS DE QUINCEY: *Confessions of an English Opium-Eater,* 1822

I never found the companion that was so companionable as solitude.
H. D. THOREAU: *Walden,* 1854

I would rather sit on a pumpkin and have it all to myself than be crowded on a velvet cushion. IBID.

The thoughtful soul to solitude retires.
EDWARD FITZGERALD: Tr. of OMAR KHAYYÁM: *Rubáiyát* (*c.* 1100), 1857

Solitude, the safeguard of mediocrity, is to genius the stern friend, the cold, obscure shelter where molt the wings which will bear it farther than suns and stars.
R. W. EMERSON: *The Conduct of Life,* IV, 1860

Solitude makes us love ourselves.
A. BRONSON ALCOTT: *Tablets,* I, 1868

A good place to visit but a poor place to stay.
H. W. SHAW (JOSH BILLINGS): *Josh Billings' Comical Lexicon,* 1877

Solitude is better than bad company.
ARAB PROVERB

Solitude is intolerable, even in Paradise.
ITALIAN PROVERB

Solitude is terrible even when drowning.
RUSSIAN PROVERB

[*See also* Alone, City, Hermit, Isolation, Loneliness, Peace, Retirement, Talent.

Solomon

[*See* Age (Old), Concubine, Polygamy.

Sometimes

[*See* Often.

Son

The king was much moved, and went up in the chamber over the gate, and wept: and as he went, thus he said, O my son Absalom, my son, my son Absalom! would God I had died for thee, O Absalom, my son, my son!
II SAMUEL XVIII, 33, *c.* 500 B.C.

He that spareth his rod hateth his son: but he that loveth him chasteneth him betimes.
PROVERBS XIII, 24, *c.* 350 B.C.

Chasten thy son while there is hope, and let not thy soul spare for his crying.
PROVERBS XIX, 18

The younger son . . . wasted his substance with riotous living. LUKE XV, 13, *c.* 75

Son, thou art ever with me, and all that I have is thine. LUKE XV, 31

A son can bear with complacency the loss of his father, but the loss of his patrimony may reduce him to despair.
NICCOLÒ MACHIAVELLI: *The Prince,* XVII, 1513

Great men's sons seldom do well.
ENGLISH PROVERB, borrowed from the Greek and traced by Smith to 1539

O lord! my boy, my Arthur, my fair son!
My life, my joy, my food, my all the world!
My widow-comfort, and my sorrow's cure!
SHAKESPEARE: *King John,* III, *c.* 1596

He that hath one hog makes him fat, and he that hath one son makes him a fool.
GEORGE HERBERT: *Outlandish Proverbs,* 1640

That unfeather'd two-legged thing, a son.
JOHN DRYDEN: *Absalom and Achitophel,* I, 1682

He dies only half who leaves an image of himself in his sons.
CARLO GOLDONI: *Pamela nubile,* II, 1757

How pleasant it is to be lulled into the sleep of death by a son's prayer – that is the true requiem.
J. C. F. SCHILLER: *The Robbers,* II, 1781

Preachers' sons always turn out badly.
AMERICAN PROVERB

A stupid son is better than a crafty daughter.
CHINESE PROVERB

He who has sons cannot long remain poor; he who has none cannot long remain rich.
IBID.

One unfilial son involves nine others in ruin.
IBID.

The ungrateful son is a wart on his father's face; to leave it is a blemish, to cut it off is painful. IBID.

The son who does not look like his father shames his mother. FRENCH PROVERB

Sons are the props of a house.
GREEK PROVERB

One son is no son, as one eye is no eye.
HINDU PROVERB

The owl always believes his son is a hawk.
HUNGARIAN PROVERB

A virtuous son is the sun of his family.
SANSKRIT PROVERB

[*See also* Achievement, Chastisement, Children, Clergyman, Daughter, Father, Father and Mother, Father and Son, Heredity, Man and Woman, Miser, Misfortune, Philoprogenitiveness, Punishment, Sorrow.

Song

Every man, when at work, even alone, has a song, however rude, to soften his labor.
QUINTILIAN: *De institutione oratoria,* I, *c.* 90

I never heard the old song of Percy and Douglas that I found not my heart moved more than with a trumpet.
PHILIP SIDNEY: *Apologie for Poetrie*, 1598

I can suck melancholy out of a song.
SHAKESPEARE: *As You Like It*, II, *c.* 1600

That old and antique song we heard last night;
Methought it did relieve my passion much,
More than light airs and recollected terms
Of these most brisk and giddy-paced times.
SHAKESPEARE: *Twelfth Night*, II, *c.* 1601

Soft words, with nothing in them, make a song.
EDMUND WALLER: *To Mr. Creech*, *c.* 1635

Let me make the songs of a nation, and I care not who makes its laws.
ANDREW FLETCHER: *An Account of a Conversation Concerning the Right to Regulation of Governments*, 1703

Odds life! must one swear to the truth of a song?
MATTHEW PRIOR: *A Better Answer to Chloe Jealous*, *c.* 1715

What will a child learn sooner than a song?
ALEXANDER POPE: *The First Epistle of the Second Book of Horace*, 1737

A careless song, with a little nonsense in it now and then, does not misbecome a monarch.
HORACE WALPOLE: *Letter to Horace Mann*, 1774

Rascals have no songs.
J. G. SEUME: *Die Gesänge*, *c.* 1800

Our sweetest songs are those that tell of saddest thought.
P. B. SHELLEY: *To a Skylark*, 1819

On the wings of song. (Auf Flügeln des Gesanges.)
HEINRICH HEINE: *Lyrische Intermezzo*, IX, 1823

Why should the Devil have all the good tunes?
Ascribed to ROWLAND HILL (1744–1833)

All deep things are song. It seems somehow the very central essence of us, song; as if all the rest were but wrappages and hulls.
THOMAS CARLYLE: *Heroes and Hero-Worship*, III, 1840 (Lecture in London, May 12)

I cannot sing the old songs I sang long years ago,
For heart and voice would fail me, and foolish tears would flow.
CHARLOTTE A. BARNARD: *I Cannot Sing the Old Songs*, *c.* 1855

And so make life, death and that vast forever
One grand, sweet song.
CHARLES KINGSLEY: *A Farewell*, 1858

I would rather be remembered by a song than by a victory.
ALEXANDER SMITH: *Dreamthorp*, I, 1863

The art of song had its origin in flattery.
W. WINWOOD READE: *The Martyrdom of Man*, III, 1872

There are German songs which can make a stranger to the language cry.
S. L. CLEMENS (MARK TWAIN): *A Tramp Abroad*, Appendix D, 1879

I have a song to sing, O!
Sing me your song, O!
W. S. GILBERT: *The Yeoman of the Guard*, 1888

[*See also* Ages, Ballad, Concert, Folk-song, Heart, Melancholy, Music, Singer, Singing, Speech.

Son-in-law

He who is fortunate in a son-in-law finds a son; he who is unfortunate loses a daughter.
EPICTETUS: *Encheiridion*, *c.* 110

The love of a son-in-law and the sun in Winter have the same amount of warmth.
GERMAN PROVERB

When you die your son-in-law will have crape on his hat and joy in his heart.
SPANISH PROVERB

[*See also* Gratitude, Mother-in-law, Stranger.

Sonnet

Scorn not the sonnet. Critic, you have frowned,
Mindless of its just honors; with this key
Shakespeare unlocked his heart.
WILLIAM WORDSWORTH: *Scorn Not the Sonnet*, 1827

A sonnet is a moment's monument.
D. G. ROSSETTI: *Sonnets*, 1881

Soothing

[*See* Music.

Soothsayer

[*See* Magician.

Sophistry

The scholiast's learning, sophist's cant,
The visionary bigot's rant,
The monk's philosophy.
MARK AKENSIDE: *Hymn to Science*, 1739

Hence! ye, who snare and stupefy the mind,
Sophists, of beauty, virtue, joy, the bane!
Greedy and fell, though impotent and blind,
Who spread your filthy nets in truth's fair fane.
JAMES BEATTIE: *The Minstrel*, I, 1771

Sophocles (495–406 B.C.)

When I was a boy, I was fondest of Æschylus; in youth and middle age I preferred Euripides; now in my declining years I admire Sophocles. I can now at length see that Sophocles is the most perfect. Yet he never rises to the sublime simplicity of Æschylus — a

simplicity of design, I mean — nor diffuses himself in the passionate outpourings of Euripides.
S. T. COLERIDGE: *Table-Talk*, July 1, 1833

Soprano

If she can strike a low *G* or *F* like a death-rattle and a high *F* like the shriek of a little dog when you step on its tail, the house will resound with acclamations.
HECTOR BERLIOZ: *À travers chants*, IV, 1862

Sorcery

The offense of sorcery is so vast and so comprehensive that it includes in itself almost every other crime.
PAUL LAYMANN: *Processus juridicus contra sagas et veneficos*, 1629

[*See also* Witchcraft.

Sordidness

Sordid and dunghill minds, composed of earth,
In that gross element fix all their happiness.
JOHN FLETCHER and PHILIP MASSINGER: *The Elder Brother*, I, 1635

Sorrow

It is wrong to sorrow without ceasing.
HOMER: *Odyssey*, XVIII, *c.* 800 B.C.

It is good to grow wise by sorrow.
ÆSCHYLUS: *Eumenides*, *c.* 490 B.C.

A clamorous sorrow spends itself in sound.
SOPHOCLES: *Antigone*, *c.* 450 B.C.

By sorrow of the heart the spirit is broken.
PROVERBS XV, 13, *c.* 350 B.C.

Sorrow is better than laughter: for by the sadness of the countenance the heart is made better. ECCLESIASTES VII, 3, *c.* 200 B.C.

It is folly to tear one's hair in sorrow, as if grief could be assuaged by baldness.
CICERO: *Tusculanæ disputationes*, III, 45 B.C.

There is no day without its sorrow.
SENECA: *Troades*, *c.* 60

Sorrow is given us on purpose to cure us of sin.
ST. JOHN CHRYSOSTOM: *Homilies*, V, *c.* 388

Sorrow need not be hastened on,
For he will come without calling anon.
EDMUND SPENSER: *The Shepheard's Calender*, 1579

Sorrow breaks seasons and reposing hours,
Makes the night morning, and the noon-tide night.
SHAKESPEARE: *Richard III*, I, *c.* 1592

If sorrow can admit society,
Tell o'er your woes again by viewing mine.
SHAKESPEARE: *Richard III*, IV

I will instruct my sorrows to be proud.
SHAKESPEARE: *King John*, III, *c.* 1596

Sorrow ends not when it seemeth done.
SHAKESPEARE: *Richard II*, I, *c.* 1596

Hang sorrow, care 'll kill a cat.
BEN JONSON: *Every Man in His Humor*, I, 1601

More in sorrow than in anger.
SHAKESPEARE: *Hamlet*, I, *c.* 1601

When sorrows come, they come not single spies,
But in battalions. SHAKESPEARE: *Hamlet*, IV

Past sorrows, let us moderately lament them;
For those to come, seek wisely to prevent them.
JOHN WEBSTER: *The Duchess of Malfi*, III, *c.* 1614

God send you joy, for sorrow will come fast enough.
JOHN CLARKE: *Parœmiologia Anglo-Latina*, 1639

When sorrow is asleep wake it not.
JAMES HOWELL: *Proverbs*, 1659

Sorrow is a disease in which every patient must treat himself.
VOLTAIRE: *Letter to an unknown woman*, 1728

Sorrow never comes too late.
THOMAS GRAY: *Ode on a Distant Prospect of Eton College*, 1747

Our joys as winged dreams do fly,
Why then should sorrow last?
THOMAS PERCY: *Reliques of Ancient English Poetry* (*The Friar of Orders Gray*), 1765

Some drops of comfort on the favor'd fall,
But showers of sorrow are the lot of all.
GEORGE CRABBE: *The Library*, 1781

There is no wisdom in useless and hopeless sorrow; but there is something in it so like virtue that he who is wholly without it cannot be loved, nor will by me at least be thought worthy of esteem.
SAMUEL JOHNSON: *Letter to Hester Thrale*, April 12, 1781

Sorrows are like thunder-clouds: in the distance they look black, but overhead they are hardly gray.
JEAN PAUL RICHTER: *Hesperus*, XIV, 1795

Sorrow is brief.
J. C. F. SCHILLER: *Die Jungfrau von Orleans*, V, 1801

Come then, sorrow!
Sweetest sorrow!
Like an own babe I nurse thee on my breast:
I thought to leave thee
And deceive thee,
But now of all the world I love thee best.
JOHN KEATS: *Endymion*, IV, 1818

Sorrow is wisdom.
JOHN KEATS: *Letter to J. H. Reynolds*, May 3, 1818

How beautiful, if sorrow had not made
Sorrow more beautiful than beauty's self.
JOHN KEATS: *Hyperion*, I, 1819

The sorrow for the dead is the only sorrow from which we refuse to be divorced. Every other wound we seek to heal, every other affliction to forget; but this wound we consider it a duty to keep open, this affliction we cherish and brood over in solitude.
WASHINGTON IRVING: *The Sketch-Book*, 1820

Every man has his secret sorrows which the world knows not; and oftentimes we call a man cold when he is only sad.
H. W. LONGFELLOW: *Hyperion*, III, 1839

A sorrow's crown of sorrow is remembering happier things.
ALFRED TENNYSON: *Locksley Hall*, 1842

O sorrow, wilt thou live with me
No casual mistress, but a wife,
My bosom-friend and half of life?
ALFRED TENNYSON: *In Memoriam*, LIX, 1850

Sorrow makes us wise.
ALFRED TENNYSON: *In Memoriam*, CVIII

Two in distress makes sorrow less.
H. G. BOHN: *Handbook of Proverbs*, 1855

Each time we love,
We turn a nearer and a broader mark
To that keen archer, sorrow, and he strikes.
ALEXANDER SMITH: *City Poems*, 1857

Great sorrows are silent. ITALIAN PROVERB

Sorrow for the death of a father lasts six months; sorrow for a mother, a year; sorrow for a wife, until another wife; sorrow for a son, for ever. SANSKRIT PROVERB

Sorrow an' ill weather come unca'd.
SCOTTISH PROVERB

There's aye sorrow at somebody's door.
IBID.

[*See also* Care, Contentment, Despair, Fat, Fire, Friend, Grief, Joy and Sorrow, Knowledge, Laughter, Learning, Memory, Mirth, Parting, Sin, Tears, Woe.

Soul

Man became a living soul.
GENESIS II, 7, *c.* 700 B.C.

The human soul develops up to death.
HIPPOCRATES: *Aphorisms*, *c.* 400 B.C.

Our soul is escaped as a bird out of the snare of the fowlers.
PSALMS CXXIV, 7, *c.* 150 B.C.

The soul in sleep gives proofs of its divine nature; for when free and disengaged from the service of the body, it has a foresight of things to come, whence we may conceive what will be its state when entirely freed from this bodily prison.
CICERO: *De senectute*, *c.* 78 B.C.

Whatever that principle is which feels, conceives, lives, and exists, it is heavenly and divine, and therefore must be eternal.
CICERO: *Tusculanæ disputationes*, I, 45 B.C.

There is a god within each human breast.
OVID: *Epistulæ ex Ponto*, III, *c.* 5

What shall it profit a man, if he shall gain the whole world, and lose his own soul?
MARK VIII, 36, *c.* 70 (Cf. MATTHEW XVI, 26, *c.* 75)

The soul is not a boon to Romans and Greeks alone.
TERTULLIAN: *The Testimony of the Christian Soul*, *c.* 210

There are souls in all living things, even in those which live in the waters.
ORIGEN: *De principiis*, II, *c.* 254

The life whereby we are joined unto the body is called the soul.
ST. AUGUSTINE: *Of the Faith and of the Creed*, *c.* 393

Mount, mount, my soul! thy seat is up on high;
Whilst my gross flesh sinks downward, here to die. SHAKESPEARE: *Richard II*, V, *c.* 1596

Think'st thou I'll endanger my soul gratis?
SHAKESPEARE: *The Merry Wives of Windsor*, II, *c.* 1600

There is something in us that can be without us and will be after us; though it is strange that it has no history what it was before us, nor cannot tell how it entered us.
THOMAS BROWNE: *Religio Medici*, I, 1642

The seat of the soul is the pylorus.
J. B. VAN HELMONT: *Ortus medicinæ*, 1648

The part of the body in which the soul functions is neither the heart nor the brain, but a certain very small gland in the middle of the brain.
RENÉ DESCARTES: *Treatise on the Passions of the Soul*, XXXI, 1649 (The pineal gland)

Large was his soul: as large a soul as e'er
Submitted to inform a body here;
High as the place 't was shortly in Heaven to have,
But low and humble as his grave.
ABRAHAM COWLEY: *On the Death of Mr. William Hervey*, 1656

If we do but observe how our wit grows up by degrees, flourishes for a time, and at last decays, keeping the same pace with the changes that age and years bring into our body, which observes the same laws that flowers and plants do; what can we suspect, but that the soul of man, which is so magnificently spoken of amongst the learned, is nothing else but a temperature of body, and that it grows and spreads with it, both in bigness and virtues, and withers and dies as the body does, or at least that it does wholly depend on the body in its operations, and that therefore there is no sense nor perception of anything after death?

HENRY MORE: *The Immortality of the Soul,* 1659

The soul, considered abstractedly from its passions, is of a remiss and sedentary nature, slow in its resolves, and languishing in its executions.

JOSEPH ADDISON: *The Spectator,* Dec. 22, 1711

The soul is the mirror of an indestructible universe.

G. W. LEIBNIZ: *The Monadology,* LXXVII, 1714

The soul is not where it lives but where it loves.

THOMAS FULLER: *Gnomologia,* 1732

The soul appears to me to discover herself most in the mouth and eyes; with this difference, that the mouth seems the more expressive of the temper, and the eye of the understanding.

WILLIAM SHENSTONE: *On Taste,* 1764

A great soul in a small destiny. (Une âme grande dans un petit destin.)

NICOLAS GILBERT (1751–80): On Luc de Vauvenargues (1715–47)

Throughout this varied and eternal world
Soul is the only element.

P. B. SHELLEY: *Queen Mab,* III, 1813

The soul wears out the breast.

BYRON: *We'll Go No More A-Roving,* 1817

If I have a soul, then pigs and dogs also have souls.

NAPOLEON I: To Gaspard Gourgaud at St. Helena, Dec. 17, 1817

A soul? Give my watch to a savage, and he will think it has a soul. IBID.

Either we have an immortal soul, or we have not. If we have not, we are beasts; the first and wisest of beasts, it may be; but still true beasts. We shall only differ in degree, and not in kind; just as the elephant differs from the slug. But by the concession of all the materialists of all the schools, or almost all, we are not of the same kind as beasts — and this also we say from our own consciousness. Therefore, it must be the possession of a soul within us that makes the difference.

S. T. COLERIDGE: *Table-Talk,* Jan. 3, 1823

Everywhere the human soul stands between a hemisphere of light and another of darkness; on the confines of two everlasting hostile empires, necessity and free will.

THOMAS CARLYLE: *Goethe,* 1828 (Foreign Review, July)

Dust thou art, to dust returnest,
Was not spoken of the soul.

H. W. LONGFELLOW: *A Psalm of Life,* 1839

Not a single one of the many sciences in which we surpass the Blackfoot Indians throws the smallest light on the state of the soul after the animal life is extinct.

T. B. MACAULAY: *Von Ranke,* 1840 (Edinburgh Review, Oct.)

Full eighteen years around did roll
Before I thought of my poor soul;
Which makes me shudder when I think
How near I stood upon the brink.

Anon.: *Miss Hathaway's Experience,* *c.* 1840

I sent my soul through the invisible,
Some letter of that after-life to spell;
And by and by my soul return'd to me,
And answer'd "I myself am Heav'n and Hell."

EDWARD FITZGERALD: Tr. of OMAR KHAYYÁM: *Rubáiyát* (*c.* 1100), 1857

Build thee more stately mansions, O my soul,
As the swift seasons roll!
Leave thy low-vaulted past!
Let each new temple, nobler than the last,
Shut thee from Heaven with a dome more vast,
Till thou at length are free,
Leaving thine outgrown shell by life's unresting sea!

O. W. HOLMES: *The Chambered Nautilus,* 1858 (Atlantic Monthly, Feb.)

The windows of my soul I throw
Wide open to the sun.

J. G. WHITTIER: *My Psalm,* 1859

The soul sits on a throne of nucleated cells.

O. W. HOLMES: *Border Lines of Knowledge in Some Provinces of Medical Science,* 1861 (Lecture at the Harvard Medical School, Nov. 6)

Does not a subtle criticism lead us to make, even on the good looks and politeness of our aristocratic class, and of even the most fascinating half of that class, the feminine half, the one qualifying remark, that in these charming gifts there should perhaps be, for ideal perfection, a shade more *soul?*

MATTHEW ARNOLD: *Culture and Anarchy,* I, 1869

Out of the night that covers me,
Black as the pit from pole to pole,
I thank whatever gods may be
For my unconquerable soul.

W. E. HENLEY: *Invictus,* 1888

A man may lose his money, and yet die rich. He may lose his health, and yet die of old age. But once he loses his immortal soul it's good-bye, John!

EDGAR W. (BILL) NYE (1850–96)

[*See also* Adult, Body and Soul, Church (Roman Catholic), Confession, Crisis, Immortality, Worship.

Sound

Hark! from the tombs a doleful sound.
ISAAC WATTS: *Hymns and Spiritual Songs,* II, 1707

A sound so fine, there's nothing lives
'Twixt it and silence.
J. S. KNOWLES: *Virginius,* v, 1820

[*See also* Noise.

Soup

In taking soup, it is necessary to avoid lifting too much in the spoon, or filling the mouth so full as almost to stop the breath.
ST. JOHN BAPTIST DE LA SALLE: *The Rules of Christian Manners and Civility,* II, 1695

Of soup and love, the first is the best.
THOMAS FULLER: *Gnomologia,* 1732

Whoever tells a lie cannot be pure in heart – and only the pure in heart can make a good soup. LUDWIG VAN BEETHOVEN: To Mme. Streicher, 1817

Beautiful soup! Who cares for fish
Game, or any other dish?
Who would not give all else for two p
ennyworth only of beautiful soup?
C. L. DODGSON (LEWIS CARROLL): *Alice's Adventures in Wonderland,* x, 1865

Never blow your soup if it is too hot, but wait until it cools. Never raise your plate to your lips, but eat with your spoon.
C. B. HARTLEY: *The Gentlemen's Book of Etiquette,* III, 1873

[*See also* Age (Old), Liar, Meat, Soldier.

Sour

[*See* Grape, Sweet.

Source

The stream is always purest at its source.
BLAISE PASCAL: *Provincial Letters,* 1657

A stream can never rise above its source.
ENGLISH PROVERB, not recorded before the early XVIII century

South

The South! The South! God knows what will become of her!
JOHN C. CALHOUN: On his deathbed, March 31, 1850

The South is one great brothel, where half a million of women are flogged to prostitution, or, worse still, are degraded to believe it honorable.
WENDELL PHILLIPS: Speech before the Massachusetts Anti-Slavery Society, Boston, Jan. 27, 1853

O magnet-South. O glistening, perfumed South! My South!
O quick mettle, rich blood, impulse, and love! Good and evil!
O all dear to me!
WALT WHITMAN: *Longings for Home,* 1860

The solid South.
AMERICAN PHRASE, apparently first used in the national campaign of 1876 (Thornton's first example is dated 1878)

Alas for the South: her books have grown fewer –
She never was much given to literature.
J. GORDON COOGLER: *Purely Original Verse,* 1897

[*See also* Climate, Dixie, North and South.

South America

[*See* America (South).

South Carolina

South Carolina is too small for a republic and too large for a lunatic asylum.
J. L. PETIGRU: On being asked if he were in favor of Secession, 1860

[*See also* Secession.

Southey, Robert (1774–1843)

I likened him to one of those huge sandstone grinding cylinders which I had seen at Manchester, turning with inconceivable velocity. For many years these stones grind so, at such a rate; till at last (in some cases) comes a moment when the stone's cohesion is quite worn out, overcome by the stupendous velocity long continued; and while grinding its fastest, it flies off altogether, and settles some yards from you, a grinding-stone no longer, but a cartload of quiet sand.
THOMAS CARLYLE: *Reminiscences of Sundry,* 1867

Souvenir

Who hath not saved some trifling thing
More prized than jewels rare,
A faded flower, a broken ring,
A tress of golden hair?
ALLEN CLEMENTINE HOWARTH: *'Tis But a Little Faded Flower,* 1864

Sovereign

The rajah should, like a father, protect his subjects from robbers, from the officers of government, from the common enemy, from the royal favorites, and from his own avarice.
The Hitopadesa, II, *c.* 500

A subject and a sovereign are clean different things.
CHARLES I OF ENGLAND: On the scaffold, Jan. 30, 1649

A sovereign's ear ill brooks a subject's questioning. S. T. COLERIDGE: *Zapolya,* I, 1817

[*See also* King, Prince, Ruler, Sovereignty, Subject.

Sovereignty

An original, supreme, absolute, and uncontrollable earthly power must exist in and preside over every society, from whose final decisions there can be no appeal but directly to

Heaven. It is, therefore, originally and ultimately in the people; . . . and [they] never did in fact freely, nor can they rightfully, make an absolute, unlimited renunciation of this divine right. It is ever in the nature of the thing given in trust, and on a condition the performance of which no mortal can dispense with, namely, that the person or persons on whom the sovereignty is conferred by the people, shall incessantly consult their good.

JAMES OTIS: *The Rights of the British Colonies Asserted and Proved,* 1764

Sovereignty lies in me alone. The legislative power is mine unconditionally and indivisibly. The public order emanates from me, and I am its supreme guardian. My people is one with me.

LOUIS XV OF FRANCE: To the Paris Parliament, March 3, 1766

In sovereignty there are no gradations. There may be limited royalty, there may be limited consulship; but there can be no limited government. There must in every society be some power or other from which there is no appeal.

SAMUEL JOHNSON: *Taxation No Tyranny,* 1775

Necessities which dissolve a government do not convey its authority to an oligarchy or a monarchy. They throw back into the hands of the people the powers they had delegated, and leave them as individuals to shift for themselves.

THOMAS JEFFERSON: *Notes on Virginia,* 1782

It is inherent in the nature of sovereignty not to be amenable to the suit of an individual without its consent.

ALEXANDER HAMILTON: *The Federalist,* 1788

A government that relies on thirteen independent sovereignties for the means of its existence is a solecism in theory, and a mere nullity in practise.

JAMES MADISON: Speech before the Convention of Virginia, June 16, 1788

The nation is essentially the source of all sovereignty: nor can any individual or any body of men be entitled to any authority which is not expressly derived from it.

Declaration of the Rights of Man by the French National Assembly, III, 1789

This corporeal globe, and everything upon it, belong to its present corporeal inhabitants, during their generation. They alone have a right to direct what is the concern of themselves alone, and to declare the law of that direction.

THOMAS JEFFERSON: *Letter to Samuel Kercheval,* July 12, 1816

In spite of all that has been said, I maintain that sovereignty is in its nature indivisible. It is the supreme power in a state, and we might just as well speak of half a square, or half a triangle, as of half a sovereignty. It is a gross error to confound the exercise of sovereign powers with sovereignty itself, or the delegation of such powers with the surrender of them.

JOHN C. CALHOUN: Speech in the Senate, Feb. 15, 1833

The people of this state have the sole and exclusive right of regulating the internal government and police thereof, as a free sovereign and independent state.

Declaration of Rights of Maryland, IV, 1867

[*See also* Conquest, Government, Sovereign.

Sow

[*See* Error, Fat, Silence.

Space and Time

Space and time, and with them all phenomena, are not things by themselves, but representations, and cannot exist outside the mind.

IMMANUEL KANT: *The Critique of Pure Reason,* I, 1781

Spade

[*See* Plainspeaking.

Spain

Pride, the first peer, and president of Hell,
To his share Spain, the largest province, fell.

DANIEL DEFOE: *The True-Born Englishman,* I, 1701

All the causes of the decay of Spain resolve themselves into one cause, bad government.

T. B. MACAULAY: *The War of the Succession in Spain,* 1833 (Edinburgh Review, Jan.)

Whoever wishes to be well acquainted with the morbid anatomy of governments, whoever wishes to know how great states may be made feeble and wretched, should study the history of Spain. IBID.

It requires, men say, a good constitution to travel in Spain.

R. W. EMERSON: *English Traits,* VI, 1856

There has never been any discussion in Spain. (Nunca se disputó España.)

Ascribed to "an eminent Spanish writer" in JOHN HAY: *Castilian Days,* X, 1872

There is nothing bad in Spain but that which speaks. SPANISH PROVERB

[*See also* Ballad, Christianity, Italy, Spaniard.

Spaniard

Impatience is the failing of the Spaniard.

BALTASAR GRACIÁN: *The Art of Worldly Wisdom,* CCXLII, 1647

A feeble, imbecile, and superstitious race.
NAPOLEON I: To Barry E. O'Meara at St. Helena, Nov. 9, 1816

The nationality of the Spaniards was not founded on any just ground of good government or wise laws, but was, in fact, very little more than a rooted antipathy to all strangers as such.
S. T. COLERIDGE: *Table-Talk,* June 26, 1831

Gravity and sedateness are the leading characteristics of the Spaniards.
GEORGE BORROW: *The Bible in Spain,* XL, 1843

We Spaniards have no morals. One cannot live without morality! But we *do* live without it.
PÍO BAROJA: *La Feria de los Discretos,* 1908

[*See also* Character (National), Cheating, Complexion, Freedom, Pilgrim, Portuguese, Spain.

Spaniel

[*See* Beating.

Spanish Language

[*See* Language.

Sparrow

[*See* Providence.

Spartan

[*See* Enemy, Epitaph.

Speaker

The *praeses* of the lower house of Parliament is called *speaker* because he is not allowed to speak. W. M. PRAED: *Nicknames, c.* 1821

[*See also* Eloquence.

Speaking

When a wise man chooses a fit subject he always speaks well.
EURIPIDES: *The Bacchae, c.* 410 B.C.

Let your speech be always with grace, seasoned with salt. COLOSSIANS IV, 6, *c.* 60

Things are well spoken if they be well taken.
HENRY PORTER: *Two Angry Women of Abingdon,* I, 1599

She speaks poniards, and every word stabs.
SHAKESPEARE: *Much Ado About Nothing,* II, *c.* 1599

Speak low if you speak love. IBID.

Speak fair, and think what you will.
WILLIAM CAMDEN: *Remains Concerning Britain,* 1605

Hear much, speak little.
RICHARD BURTON: *The Anatomy of Melancholy,* II, 1621

Never speak to a fasting man.
JOHN CLARKE: *Parœmiologia Anglo-Latina,* 1639

Speak fitly, or be silent wisely.
GEORGE HERBERT: *Outlandish Proverbs,* 1640

Speak when you are spoken to; come when you are called.
JOHN RAY: *English Proverbs,* 1670

When all men speak no man hears.
JAMES KELLY: *Complete Collection of Scottish Proverbs,* 1721

He cannot speak well that cannot hold his tongue.
THOMAS FULLER: *Gnomologia,* 1732

He mouths a sentence as curs mouth a bone.
CHARLES CHURCHILL: *The Rosciad,* 1761

If wisdom's ways you wisely seek,
Five things observe with care:
Of whom you speak – to whom you speak,
And how – and when – and where.
Anon.: *Favorite Album Verses, c.* 1845

An itch for speaking. (Cacoethes loquendi.)
LATIN PRASE

He spoke as if every word would lift a dish.
SCOTTISH SAYING

[*See also* Mouth, Silence, Speech, Taciturnity, Talk, Tongue.

Speaking, Public

The practice of public speaking flourishes in every peaceful and free state.
CICERO: *De oratore,* II, *c.* 80 B.C.

You'd scarce expect one of my age
To speak in public on the stage;
And if I chance to fall below
Demosthenes or Cicero,
Don't view me with a critic's eye,
But pass my imperfections by.
Large streams from little fountains flow,
Tall oaks from little acorns grow.
DAVID EVERETT: *Lines Written for Declamation, c.* 1800

One may discover a new side to his most intimate friend when for the first time he hears him speak in public. The longest intimacy could not foretell how he would behave then.
H. D. THOREAU: *Journal,* Feb. 6, 1841

These dinner speeches tire me; they are tedious, flat and stale;
From a hundred thousand tables comes a melancholy wail,
As a hundred thousand banqueters sit up in evening dress
And salute each moldy chestnut with a signal of distress.
I. H. BROMLEY: *Our Chauncey,* 1891

[*See also* **Orator.**

Spear

[*See* War and Peace.

Specialist

A due balance and equilibrium of the mind is best preserved by a large and multiform knowledge: but knowledge itself is best served by an exclusive (or at least paramount) dedication of one mind to one science.

THOMAS DE QUINCEY: *Superficial Knowledge, c.* 1847

No man can be a pure specialist without being in the strict sense an idiot.

GEORGE BERNARD SHAW: *Maxims for Revolutionists,* 1903

[*See also* Dermatologist.

Species

This law the Omniscient Power was pleased to give,
That every kind should by succession live:
That individuals die, His will ordains;
The propagated species still remains.

JOHN DRYDEN: *Palamon and Arcite,* III, *c.* 1698

There are as many different species of animals and plants as there were different forms created by God in the beginning.

CAROLUS LINNÆUS: *Systema naturæ,* 1735

No one definition has satisfied all naturalists; yet every naturalist knows vaguely what he means when he speaks of a species.

CHARLES DARWIN: *The Origin of Species,* II, 1859

[*See also* Natural Selection.

Spectacle

We are made a spectacle unto the world, and to angels, and to men.

I CORINTHIANS IV, 9, *c.* 55

Spectator

The spectator ofttimes sees more than the gamester.

JAMES HOWELL: *Familiar Letters,* I, 1645 (May 1, 1635)

The spectator is not the arbiter of the work of art. He is one who is admitted to contemplate the work of art, and if the work be fine, to forget in its contemplation all the egotism that mars him — the egotism of his ignorance, or the egotism of his information.

OSCAR WILDE: *The Soul of Man Under Socialism,* 1891

[*See also* Kibitzer, Looker-on.

Speculation

The wealth acquired by speculation and plunder is fugacious in its nature, and fills society with the spirit of gambling.

THOMAS JEFFERSON: *Letter to George Washington,* 1787

October. This is one of the peculiarly dangerous months to speculate in stocks in. The others are July, January, September, April, November, May, March, June, December, August and February.

S. L. CLEMENS (MARK TWAIN): *Pudd'nhead Wilson,* XIII, 1894

Speech

In the sixth place he imparted them understanding, and in the seventh speech, an interpreter of the cogitations thereof.

ECCLESIASTICUS XVII, 5, *c.* 180 B.C.

It is reason and speech that unite men to one another; there is nothing else in which we differ so entirely from the brute creation.

CICERO: *De officiis,* I, 78 B.C.

Speech is the mirror of the soul; as a man speaks, so he is.

PUBLILIUS SYRUS: *Sententiæ, c.* 50 B.C.

Out of the abundance of the heart the mouth speaketh.

MATTHEW XII, 34, *c.* 75

Speech shows what a man is.

JOHN CLARKE: *Parœmiologia Anglo-Latina,* 1639

Speech is the picture of the mind.

JOHN RAY: *English Proverbs,* 1670

Speech was given to the ordinary sort of men whereby to communicate their mind, but to wise men whereby to conceal it.

ROBERT SOUTH: Sermon Preached in Westminster Abbey, April 30, 1676

The common fluency of speech in many men, and most women, is owing to a scarcity of matter, and a scarcity of words; for whoever is a master of language, and has a mind full of ideas, will be apt, in speaking, to hesitate upon the choice of both; whereas common speakers have only one set of ideas and one set of words to clothe them in; and these are always ready at the mouth: so people come faster out of a church when it is almost empty, than when a crowd is at the door.

JONATHAN SWIFT: *Thoughts on Various Subjects,* 1706

Write with the learned, but speak with the vulgar.

THOMAS FULLER: *Gnomologia,* 1732

Every man is born with the faculty of reason and the faculty of speech, but why should he be able to speak before he has anything to say?

BENJAMIN WHICHCOTE: *Moral and Religious Aphorisms,* 1753

The speech of angels consists of distinct words like human speech, and is equally sonorous; for angels have a mouth, a tongue, and ears; also an atmosphere in which the sound of their speech is articulated.

EMANUEL SWEDENBORG: *Heaven and Hell,* 1758

The true use of speech is not so much to express our wants as to conceal them.
OLIVER GOLDSMITH: *The Bee*, Oct. 20, 1759 (Cf. SOUTH, *ante*, 1676)

I pay attention only to what people say. I have little interest in what they think.
NAPOLEON I: To Gaspard Gourgaud at St. Helena, Jan. 20, 1818

Speech that leads not to action, still more that hinders it, is a nuisance on the earth.
THOMAS CARLYLE: *Letter to Jane Welsh*, Nov. 4, 1825

Speech is reason's brother, and a kingly prerogative of man,
That likeneth him to his Maker, who spake, and it was done.
M. F. TUPPER: *Proverbial Philosophy*, I, 1837

Silence is deep as eternity, speech is shallow as time.
THOMAS CARLYLE: *Sir Walter Scott*, 1838 (Westminster Review, Jan.)

All speech, even the commonest speech, has something of song in it: not a parish in the world but has its parish-accent; — the rhythm or tune to which the people there sing what they have to say.
THOMAS CARLYLE: *Heroes and Hero-Worship*, III, 1840 (Lecture in London, May 12)

Spartans, stoics, heroes, saints and gods use a short and positive speech.
R. W. EMERSON: *The Superlative*, 1847

Who hath given man speech? or who hath set therein
A thorn for peril and a snare for sin?
A. C. SWINBURNE: *Atalanta in Calydon*, 1865

The specific moving power to the working out of speech was not the monkeyish tendency to imitation, but the human tendency to sociability.
W. D. WHITNEY: *Oriental and Linguistic Studies*, I, 1873

In a continuous discourse there is no separation between the words except where we pause to take breath, or for emphasis: the words of a sentence are run together exactly in the same way as the syllables of a word are.
HENRY SWEET: *A New English Grammar*, intro., 1891

Speech is the index of the mind. (Index animi sermo.)
LEGAL MAXIM

[*See also* Accent, Grammar, Language, Orator, Silence, Speaking.

Speech, Free

In a free state there must be free speech. (In libera civitate oportet etiam linguas esse liberas.)
Ascribed to DOMITIAN (EMPEROR OF ROME), *c.* 90

It is the felicity of the times that you may think as you wish, and speak as you think.
TACITUS: *Annals*, I, *c.* 110

There is nothing so necessary for the preservation of the prince and the state as free speech, and without this it is a scorn and a mockery to call it a Parliament house; for in truth it is none, but a very school of flattery and dissimulation, and so a fit place to serve the Devil and his angels in.
PETER WENTWORTH: Speech in the House of Commons, 1575

Liberty of speech inviteth and provoketh liberty to be used again, and so bringeth much to a man's knowledge.
FRANCIS BACON: *The Advancement of Learning*, II, 1605

Give me the liberty to know, to utter, and to argue freely according to conscience, above all liberties.
JOHN MILTON: *Areopagitica*, 1644

The freedom of speech, and debates or proceedings in Parliament, ought not to be impeached or questioned in any court or place out of Parliament.
THE ENGLISH BILL OF RIGHTS, IX, Dec., 1689

Nations cramped by restrain, when permitted to be drawn out and examined, may, by the reduction of their obliquities, and the correction of their virulency, at length acquire strength and proportion.
WILLIAM WARBURTON (BISHOP OF GLOUCESTER): *The Divine Legation of Moses*, dedication, 1737

The enjoyment of liberty, and even its support and preservation, consists in every man's being allowed to speak his thoughts, and lay open his sentiment.
C. L. DE MONTESQUIEU: *The Spirit of the Laws*, 1748

A good cause demands but a distinct exposition, and a fair hearing, and we may say, with great propriety, it will speak for itself.
GEORGE CAMPBELL: *Dissertation on Miracles*, 1762

The world always lets a man tell what he thinks, his own way.
SAMUEL JOHNSON: *Boswell's Tour to the Hebrides*, Aug. 19, 1773

Freedom of speech and debate in Congress shall not be impeached or questioned in any court, or place out of Congress, and the members of Congress shall be protected in their persons from arrests and imprisonments, during the time of their going to and from, and attendance on Congress, except for treason, felony, or breach of the peace.
ARTICLES OF CONFEDERATION, V, Nov., 1777

Every citizen may freely speak, write and publish his sentiments on all subjects, being responsible for the abuse of that right; and no law shall be passed to restrain or abridge the liberty of speech or of the press.

CONSTITUTION OF THE STATE OF NEW YORK, 1777

Every man has a right to utter what he thinks truth, and every other man has a right to knock him down for it.

SAMUEL JOHNSON: *Boswell's Life*, 1780

I don't see why a man is not to speak his mind to a lady as well as to a gentleman, providing he does it in a complaisant fashion.

FRANCES BURNEY: *Cecilia*, x, 1782

The freedom of thought and speech arising from and privileged by our constitution gives a force and poignancy to the expressions of our common people not to be found under arbitrary governments, where the ebullitions of vulgar wit are checked by the fear of the bastinado, or of a lodging during pleasure in some jail or castle.

FRANCIS GROSE: *A Classical Dictionary of the Vulgar Tongue*, pref., 1785

My people and I have come to an agreement which satisfies us both. They are to say what they please, and I am to do what I please.

Ascribed to FREDERICK THE GREAT (1712–86)

The unrestrained communication of thoughts and opinions being one of the most precious rights of man, every citizen may speak, write, and publish freely, provided he is responsible for the abuse of this liberty in cases determined by the law.

Declaration of the Rights of Man by the French National Assembly, xi, 1789

Congress shall make no law . . . abridging the freedom of speech or of the press.

CONSTITUTION OF THE UNITED STATES, Amendment I, Dec. 15, 1791

When men can freely communicate their thought and their sufferings, real or imaginary, their passions spend themselves in air, like gunpowder scattered upon the surface — but pent up by terrors, they work unseen, burst forth in a moment, and destroy everything in their course. Let reason be opposed to reason, and argument to argument, and every good government will be safe.

THOMAS ERSKINE: *In defense of Thomas Paine*, 1792

As men are seldom disposed to complain until they at least imagine themselves injured, so there is no injury which they will remember so long, or resent so deeply, as that of being threatened into silence.

ROBERT HALL: *Apology for the Freedom of the Press*, 1793

The power of communication of thoughts and opinions is the gift of God, and the freedom of it is the source of all science, the first fruits and the ultimate happiness of society; and therefore it seems to follow that human laws ought not to interpose, nay, cannot interpose, to prevent the communication of sentiments and opinions in voluntary assemblies of men.

MR. CHIEF JUSTICE EYRE: *Judgment in Hardy's Case*, 1794

Nor wealth, nor power, can compensate for the loss of that luxury which he has who can speak his mind, at all times and in all places.

Ascribed to J. HORNE TOOKE (1736–1812) in G. H. POWELL: *Reminiscences and Table-Talk of Samuel Rogers*, 1903

For God's sake, let us freely hear both sides!

THOMAS JEFFERSON: *Letter to M. Dufief*, April 19, 1814

When people talk of the freedom of writing, speaking or thinking I cannot choose but laugh. No such thing ever existed. No such thing now exists; but I hope it will exist. But it must be hundreds of years after you and I shall write and speak no more.

JOHN ADAMS: *Letter to Thomas Jefferson*, July 15, 1818

It ought not to be permitted to speak well of public functionaries without an equal liberty of speaking ill.

JAMES MILL: *On Liberty of the Press*, 1821

Men are never so likely to settle a question rightly as when they discuss it freely.

T. B. MACAULAY: *Southey's Colloquies*, 1830

I honor the man who is willing to sink
Half his present repute for the freedom to think,
And when he has thought, be his cause strong or weak,
Will risk t'other half for the freedom to speak.

J. R. LOWELL: *A Fable for Critics*, 1848

Free speech is to a great people what winds are to oceans and malarial regions, which waft away the elements of disease, and bring new elements of health. Where free speech is stopped miasma is bred, and death comes fast.

H. W. BEECHER: *Royal Truths*, 1862

Men have no right to make themselves bores and nuisances; and the common sense of mankind inflicts wholesome inconveniences on those who carry their "right of private judgment" to any such extremities.

J. A. FROUDE: *A Plea for the Free Discussion of Theological Difficulties*, 1863 (Fraser's Magazine)

Every man who says frankly and fully what he thinks is so far doing a public service. We should be grateful to him for attacking most unsparingly our most cherished opinions.

LESLIE STEPHEN: *The Suppression of Poisonous Opinions*, 1883

If any appreciable number of persons are inclined to advocate murder on principle, I should wish them to state their opinions openly and fearlessly, because I should think that the shortest way of exploding the principle and of ascertaining the true causes of such a perversion of moral sentiment.

IBID.

Freedom of discussion is in England little else than the right to write or say anything which a jury consisting of twelve shopkeepers think it expedient should be said or written.

A. V. DICEY: *Introduction to the Study of the Law of the Constitution,* 1885

The great literary battle of our day is not to be fought for either realism or romanticism, but for freedom of speech.

GEORGE MOORE: Preface to ÉMILE ZOLA: *Pot-Bouille,* 1885

Men have a right freely and prudently to propagate throughout the state what things soever are true and honorable, so that as many as possible may possess them; but lying opinions, than which no mental plague is greater, and vices which corrupt the heart and moral life, should be diligently repressed by public authority, lest they insidiously work the ruin of the state.

POPE LEO XIII: *Libertas præstantissimum,* June 20, 1888

Let them say just what they like. Let them propose to cut every throat and burn every house — if so they like it. We have nothing to do with a man's words or a man's thoughts except to put against them better words and better thoughts, and so to win in the great moral and intellectual duel that is always going on, and on which all progress depends.

AUBERON HERBERT: In the Westminster Gazette, Nov. 22, 1893

I maintain that Congress has the right and the duty to declare the objects of the war, and the people have the right and the obligation to discuss it.

ROBERT M. LAFOLLETTE, SR.: Speech in the Senate, Oct. 6, 1917

I realize that there are certain limitations placed upon the right of free speech. I may not be able to say all I think, but I am not going to say anything I do not think.

EUGENE V. DEBS: Speech in Canton, O., June, 1918

The most stringent protection of free speech would not protect a man in falsely shouting fire in a theater and causing a panic.

MR. JUSTICE O. W. HOLMES: *Decision of the Supreme Court in Schenck* vs. *the United States,* 1919

I have always been among those who believed that the greatest freedom of speech was the greatest safety, because if a man is a fool the best thing to do is to encourage him to advertise the fact by speaking.

WOODROW WILSON: Address at the Institute of France, Paris, May 10, 1919

Sworn to no party,
Of no sect am I;
I won't keep quiet
And I will not lie.

ADMIRAL LORD FISHER (1841–1920)

We reaffirm our respect for the great principles of free speech and a free press, but assert as an indisputable proposition that they afford no toleration of enemy propaganda or the advocacy of the overthrow of the government of the state or nation by force or violence.

Democratic National Platform, 1920

Freedom of speech and press does not protect disturbances to the public peace or the attempt to subvert the government. It does not protect publications or teachings which tend to subvert or imperil the government, or to impede or hinder it in the performance of its governmental duties. It does not protect publications prompting the overthrow of government by force.

MR. JUSTICE E. T. SANFORD: *Decision of the Supreme Court in Gitlow* vs. *the People of New York,* 1924

Freedom of speech and of the press — which are protected by the First Amendment from abridgement by Congress — are among the fundamental personal rights and liberties protected by the due process clause of the Fourteenth Amendment from impairment by the states.

IBID.

I express many absurd opinions. But I am not the first man to do it; American freedom consists largely in talking nonsense.

E. W. HOWE: *Preaching from the Audience,* 1926

Free speech does not live many hours after free industry and free commerce die.

HERBERT HOOVER: Speech in New York City, Oct. 22, 1928

It is no longer open to doubt that the liberty of the press and of speech is within the liberty safeguarded from invasion by state action.

MR. CHIEF JUSTICE C. E. HUGHES: *Decision of the Supreme Court in Near* vs. *Minnesota,* 1931

You often hear that this is a free country, and that a man is at liberty to express his opinions. It is not true.

E. W. HOWE: *The Indignations of E. W. Howe,* 1933

The right to comment freely and criticize the action, opinions, and judgment of courts is of primary importance to the public generally. Not only is it good for the public, but it has a salutary effect on courts and judges as well.

MR. CHIEF JUSTICE JAMES P. HUGHES of the Indiana Supreme Court: *Decision in the State* vs. *Don Nixon,* Jan. 9, 1935

[*See also* American, Freedom, Liberty, Opinion, Parliament, Press (Free), Violence.

Speed

Sober speed is wisdom's leisure.
ROBERT SOUTHWELL: *Loss in Delay,* c. 1595

I'll put a girdle round about the earth in forty minutes.
SHAKESPEARE: *A Midsummer Night's Dream,* II, c. 1596

All the speed is in the spurs.
DAVID FERGUSSON: *Scottish Proverbs,* 1641

[*See also* Haste, Morning.

Spelling

It is possible to spell a word correctly by chance, or because someone prompts you, but you are a scholar only if you spell it correctly because you know how.
ARISTOTLE: *The Nicomachean Ethics,* II, c. 340 B.C.

Let all the foreign tongues alone
Till you can spell and read your own.
ISAAC WATTS: *The Art of Reading and Writing English,* 1721

Orthography is so absolutely necessary for a man of letters, or a gentleman, that one false spelling may fix a ridicule upon him for the rest of his life; and I know a man of quality who never recovered the ridicule of having spelled *wholesome* without the *w.*
LORD CHESTERFIELD: *Letter to his son,* Nov. 19, 1750

Take care that you never spell a word wrong. Always before you write a word, consider how it is spelled, and, if you do not remember it, turn to a dictionary. It produces great praise to a lady to spell well.
THOMAS JEFFERSON: *Letter to Martha Jefferson,* 1783

As our alphabet now stands, the bad spelling, or what is called so, is generally the best, as conforming to the sound of the letters and of the words.
BENJAMIN FRANKLIN: *Letter to Mrs. Jane Mecom,* July 4, 1786

Spell well, if you can.
THE COUNTESS DOWAGER OF CARLISLE: *Thoughts in the Form of Maxims,* 1790

A pretty deer is dear to me,
A hare with downy hair,
A hart I love with all my heart,
But barely bear a bear.
Anon.: *The Beauties of English Orthography,* c. 1850

The spelling of words is subordinate. Morbidness for nice spelling and tenacity for or against some one letter or so means dandyism and impotence in literature.
WALT WHITMAN: *An American Primer,* c. 1856

I don't see any use in spelling a word right, and never did. I mean I don't see any use in having a uniform and arbitrary way of spelling words. We might as well make all our clothes alike and cook all dishes alike.
S. L. CLEMENS (MARK TWAIN): Speech in Hartford, Conn., May, 1875

Who cares about spelling? Milton spelt *dog* with two *g's.* The American Milton, when he comes, may spell it with three, while all the world wonders, if he is so minded.
AUGUSTINE BIRRELL: *Men, Women and Books,* 1894

When the English tongue we speak
Why is *break* not rhymed with *freak?*
Will you tell me why it's true
We say *sew* but likewise *Jew?*
EVELYN BARING (EARL CROMER): In the London Spectator, Aug. 9, 1902

Spending

Spend, and God will send.
ENGLISH PROVERB, traced by Smith to c. 1350

Soon gotten, soon spent.
JOHN HEYWOOD: *Proverbs,* 1546

Spend as you get.
JOHN CLARKE: *Parœmiologia Anglo-Latina,* 1639

He that gains well and spends well needs no account book.
GEORGE HERBERT: *Outlandish Proverbs,* 1640

To gain teacheth how to spend. IBID.

Small shots, paid often, waste a vast estate.
ROBERT HERRICK: *Hesperides,* 1648

Spend and be free, but make no waste.
JOHN RAY: *English Proverbs,* 1670

Who more than he is worth doth spend,
He makes a rope his life to end. IBID.

[*See also* Character (National), Magnificent.

Spenser, Edmund (1552?–99)

Discouraged, scorned, his writings vilified,
Poorly — poor man — he lived; poorly — poor man — he died.
PHINEAS FLETCHER: *The Purple Island,* IV, 1633

[*See also* Allegory.

Sphinx

The Sphinx is drowsy,
Her wings are furled;
His ear is heavy,
She broods on the world.
R. W. EMERSON: *The Sphinx,* 1841 (Dial, Jan.)

Spice

If you beat spice it will smell the sweeter.
THOMAS FULLER: *Gnomologia,* 1732

Spider

Why doth the spider spin her artificial web thick in one place and thin in another? And now useth one, and then another knot, except she had an imaginary kind of deliberation, forethought and conclusion?
MICHEL DE MONTAIGNE: *Essays*, II, 1580

Everything belonging to the spider is admirable.
JONATHAN EDWARDS: *The Spider*, *c.* 1715

Spiders that kill a man cure an ape.
THOMAS FULLER: *Gnomologia*, 1732

Who made the spider parallels design
Such as Demoivre, without rule or line?
ALEXANDER POPE: *An Essay on Man*, III, 1732 (*Demoivre*=a French mathematician, 1667–1754)

Little Miss Muffet
Sat on a tuffet,
Eating of curds and whey;
Along came a spider
And sat down beside her,
And frightened Miss Muffet away.
Anon.: *Nursery rhyme*, *c.* 1750 (*Tuffet*= a footstool)

"Will you walk into my parlor?" said a spider to a fly,
"'Tis the prettiest little parlor that ever you did spy."
MARY HOWITT: *The Forest Minstrels*, 1821

But for the robin and the wren
A spider would overcome a man.
ENGLISH RHYME

He who would wish to thrive
Must let spiders run alive. IBID.

A spider seen in the morning brings bad luck; seen at noon, it brings good luck.
FRENCH PROVERB

[*See also* Amber, Bed, Bee.

Spinach

Spinach is the broom of the stomach.
FRENCH PROVERB

Spine

Your head sits on one end and you sit on the other. Author unidentified

Spinoza, Baruch (1632–77)

A God-drunk man. (Ein Gottbetrunkener Mensch.)
FRIEDRICH VON HARDENBERG (NOVALIS): *Fragments*, 1799

Spinster

'Tis an old proverb, and you know it well,
That women dying maids lead apes in Hell.
Anon.: *The London Prodigal*, I, 1605

My soul abhors the tasteless dry embrace
Of a stale virgin with a Winter face.
ALEXANDER POPE: *January and May*, 1709

The sweetest woman ever fate
Perverse denied a household mate.
J. G. WHITTIER: *Snow-Bound*, 1866

Quite young and all alive,
Like an old maid of forty-five.
W. C. HAZLITT: *English Proverbs*, 1869

An old maid is an unposted letter.
HUNGARIAN PROVERB

[*See also* Celibacy, Maiden.

Spirit

The letter killeth, but the spirit giveth life.
II CORINTHIANS III, 6, *c.* 55

The spirit indeed is willing, but the flesh is weak. MATTHEW XXVI, 41, *c.* 75

Nor stony tower, nor walls of beaten brass,
Nor airless dungeon, nor strong links of iron,
Can be retentive to the strength of spirit.
SHAKESPEARE: *Julius Cæsar*, I, 1599

[*See also* God, Soul.

Spirits

Millions of spiritual creatures walk the earth
Unseen, both when we wake, and when we sleep.
JOHN MILTON: *Paradise Lost*, IV, 1667

Spirits when they please
Can either sex assume, or both; so soft
And uncompounded is their essence pure,
Not tied or manacled with joint or limb,
Nor founded on the brittle strength of bones.
IBID.

There are many intellectual beings in the world beside ourselves, and several species of spirits, who are subject to different laws and economics from those of mankind.
JOSEPH ADDISON: *The Spectator*, July 1, 1712

Unnumbered spirits round thee fly,
The light militia of the lower sky.
ALEXANDER POPE: *The Rape of the Lock*, I, 1712

To my mind the doctrine of empty space and that of spirits which exist without organs are the height of human folly.
FREDERICK THE GREAT: *Letter to Voltaire*, Jan. 25, 1778

Spite

He cut off his nose to spite his face.
ENGLISH SAYING, traced by Apperson, by way of the French, to the Latin of Publilius Syrus, *c.* 50 B.C.

Spitting

I will spit in my hands, and take better hold.
JOHN HEYWOOD: *Proverbs*, 1546

It is not decent to spit upon the fire.
FRANCIS HAWKINS: *Youth's Behavior*, I, 1663

When in a holy place, in the presence of superiors, or in clean apartments, one should always spit into a handkerchief. Children are guilty of unpardonable rudeness when they spit in the face of a companion; neither are they excusable who spit from windows, or on the walls or furniture.

ST. JOHN BAPTIST DE LA SALLE: *The Rules of Christian Manners and Civility*, I, 1695

Spit not against Heaven; 'twill fall back into thy own face.

THOMAS FULLER: *Gnomologia*, 1732

If you spit on the floor at home, spit here; we want to make you feel at home.

Sign hung in country hotels, filling-station rest-rooms, etc., probably originating before 1850

Don't spit; remember the Johnstown flood.

AMERICAN PROVERB

Who spits against the wind spits in his own face.

ITALIAN PROVERB

A good sailor spits to leeward.

NAUTICAL PROVERB

[*See also* French, Independence.

Spoils

Ye shall spoil the Egyptians.

EXODUS III, 22, *c.* 700 B.C.

But the women, and the little ones, and the cattle, and all that is in the city, even all the spoil thereof, shalt thou take unto thyself.

DEUTERONOMY XX, 14, *c.* 650 B.C.

To the victor belongs the spoils of the enemy.

WILLIAM L. MARCY: Speech in the Senate, Jan. 21, 1832

You may say for me that offices will be held by politicians.

RICHARD CROKER: Press interview, Jan. 4, 1893 (After the election of Hugh Gilroy as mayor of New York)

The spoils system, that practice which turns public offices, high and low, from public trusts into objects of prey and booty for the victorious party, may without extravagance of language be called one of the greatest criminals in our history, if not the greatest. In the whole catalogue of our ills there is none more dangerous to the vitality of our free institutions.

CARL SCHURZ: Address in Chicago, Ill., Dec. 12, 1894

The man who pulls the plow gets the plunder in politics.

HUEY P. LONG: Speech in the Senate, Jan. 30, 1934

[*See also* Office (Public).

Sport

There is no sport where there is neither old folk nor bairns.

JAMES KELLY: *Complete Collection of Scottish Proverbs*, 1721

There are some pleasures that degrade a gentleman as much as some trades could do. Sottish drinking, indiscriminate gluttony, driving coaches, rustic sports, such as fox-chases, horse-races, etc., are, in my opinion, infinitely below the honest and industrious profession of a tailor and a shoemaker, which are said to *déroger*.

LORD CHESTERFIELD: *Letter to his son*, April 19, 1749

Three things are thrown away on a bowling green, namely, time, money and oaths.

WALTER SCOTT: *The Fortunes of Nigel*, XII, 1822

I have never been able to understand why pigeon-shooting at Hurlingham should be refined and polite, while a rat-killing match in Whitechapel is low.

T. H. HUXLEY: *Administrative Nihilism*, 1871

When a man wants to murder a tiger he calls it sport: when the tiger wants to murder him he calls it ferocity.

GEORGE BERNARD SHAW: *Maxims for Revolutionists*, 1903

As I emphatically disbelieve in seeing Harvard or any other college turn out mollycoddles instead of vigorous men, I may add that I do not in the least object to a sport because it is rough.

THEODORE ROOSEVELT: Speech in Cambridge, Mass., Feb. 23, 1907

Growth, development, posture, like health, depends to a large extent on the freedom for the individual to join in any play, game or sport, to exert himself according to his powers, and to know when he has had enough. Food, fun and frolic are of more importance than drill and discipline.

H. A. HARRIS: *The Anatomical and Physiological Basis of Physical Training*, 1939 (British Medical Journal, Nov. 11)

[*See also* Amusement, Game (=recreation).

Sportsmanship

When the rules of the game prove unsuitable for victory, the gentlemen of England change the rules of the game.

HAROLD LASKI: Address before the Communist Academy, Moscow, July, 1934

Spring

It is Spring everywhere, and everywhere in the pastures the udders are swelling with milk, and the lambkins are suckling.

THEOCRITUS: *Idylls*, VIII, *c.* 270 B.C.

The flowers appear on the earth; the time of the singing of birds is come, and the voice of the turtle is heard in our land.
SOLOMON'S SONG II, 12, *c.* 200 B.C.

Now every field is clothed with grass, and every tree with leaves; now the woods put forth their blossoms, and the year assumes its gay attire. VIRGIL: *Eclogues,* III, 37 B.C.

When lovers are far apart they are made even sadder by the loveliness of Spring.
BHARTRIHARI: *The Sringa Sataka, c.* 625

The fields breathe sweet, the daisies kiss our feet,
Young lovers meet, old wives a-sunning sit,
In every street these tunes our ears do greet,
Cuckoo, jug-jug, pu-we, to-witta-woo!
Spring! the sweet Spring!
THOMAS NASHE: *Spring, c.* 1590

It was a lover, and his lass,
With a hey, and a ho, and a hey nonino,
That o'er the green cornfield did pass,
In Springtime, the only pretty ring time,
When birds do sing, hey ding a ding, ding;
Sweet lovers love the Spring.
SHAKESPEARE: *As You Like It,* V, *c.* 1600

For now the fragrant flowers do spring and sprout in seemly sort,
The little birds do sit and sing, the lambs do make fine sport;
The lords and ladies now abroad, for their disport and play,
Do kiss sometimes upon the grass, and sometimes in the hay.
BEAUMONT and FLETCHER: *The Knight of the Burning Pestle,* 1609

In those vernal seasons of the year, when the air is calm and pleasant, it were an injury and sullenness against nature not to go out and see her riches, and partake in her rejoicing.
JOHN MILTON: *Tractate on Education,* 1644

The cuckoo tells aloud her painful love;
The turtle's voice is heard in ev'ry grove;
The pastures change; in warbling linnets sing:
Prepare to welcome in the gaudy Spring.
AMBROSE PHILIPS: *Pastorals,* VI, 1709

Come, gentle Spring, ethereal mildness, come!
JAMES THOMSON: *The Seasons,* II, 1727

When a poet mentions the Spring we know that the zephyrs are about to whisper, that the groves are to recover their verdure, the linnets to warble forth their notes of love, and the flocks and herds to frisk over vales painted with flowers.
SAMUEL JOHNSON: *The Adventurer,* Nov. 13, 1753

Spring makes everything young again, save man.
JEAN PAUL RICHTER: *Hesperus,* XIV, 1795

The course of the seasons is a piece of clockwork, with a cuckoo to call when it is Spring.
G. C. LICHTENBERG: *Reflections,* 1799

The Spring comes slowly up this way.
S. T. COLERIDGE: *Christabel,* I, 1816

Behold! Spring sweeps over the world again,
Shedding soft dews from her ethereal wings;
Flowers on the mountains, fruits over the plain,
And music on the waves and woods, she flings,
And love on all that lives, and calm on lifeless things.
P. B. SHELLEY: *The Revolt of Islam,* IX, 1818

From all the blasts of Heaven thou hast descended:
Yes, like a spirit, like a thought, which makes
Unwonted tears throng to the horny eyes,
And beatings haunt the desolated heart,
Which should have learnt repose: thou has descended
Cradled in tempests; thou dost wake, O Spring!
P. B. SHELLEY: *Prometheus Unbound,* II, 1820

Buttercups and daisies —
Oh, the pretty flowers!
Coming ere the Springtime,
To tell of sunny hours.
When the trees are leafless;
When the fields are bare;
Buttercups and daisies
Spring up here and there.
MARY HOWITT: *Buttercups and Daisies,* 1823

In the Spring a livelier iris changes on the burnish'd dove;
In the Spring a young man's fancy lightly turns to thoughts of love.
ALFRED TENNYSON: *Locksley Hall,* 1842

Alas, that Spring should vanish with the rose!
EDWARD FITZGERALD: Tr. of OMAR KHAYYÁM: *Rubáiyát* (*c.* 1100), 1857

Turn swiftlier round, O tardy ball!
And sun this frozen side,
Bring hither back the robin's call,
Bring back the tulip's pride.
R. W. EMERSON: *May-Day,* 1867

Spring at last, and all Hell's afire!
Author unidentified

Spring has come when you can put your foot on three daisies at once. IBID.

Spring is sooner recognized by plants than by men. CHINESE PROVERB

[*See also* Seasons, Swallow, Thunder.

Spy

A prince should have a spy to observe what is necessary, and what is unnecessary, in his own as well as in his enemy's country. He is the king's eye; and he who hath him not is blind. *The Hitopadesa,* III, *c.* 500

The life of spies is to know, not to be known.
GEORGE HERBERT: *Outlandish Proverbs,* 1640

A man who is capable of so infamous a calling as that of a spy . . . will be more industrious to carry that which is grateful than that which is true.
JOSEPH ADDISON: *The Spectator,* July 24, 1712

He that spies is the one that kills.
IRISH PROVERB

Square Deal

If elected, I shall see to it that every man has a square deal, no less and no more.
THEODORE ROOSEVELT: Campaign speech, Nov. 4, 1904

When I say I believe in a square deal I do not mean, and nobody who speaks the truth can mean, that he believes it possible to give every man the best hand. If the cards do not come to any man, or if they do come, and he has not got the power to play them, that is his affair. All I mean is that there shall not be any crookedness in the dealing.
THEODORE ROOSEVELT: Speech in Dallas, Tex., April 5, 1905

Squinting

How is it that animals do not squint? Is this another prerogative of the human species?
G. C. LICHTENBERG: *Reflections,* 1799

[*See also* Character.

Stable-door

[*See* Late.

Staël, Anna Louise de (1766–1817)

I by no means intend to insinuate that Madame de Staël was ugly — but beauty is something else. HEINRICH HEINE: *Confessions,* 1854

Stag

The stag at eve had drunk his fill.
WALTER SCOTT: *The Lady of the Lake,* I, 1810

Stage

The mimes are our instructors in infamy, and each spectator delights to see repeated on the stage what he has done at home, or to hear what he may do on his return. Adultery is learnt while it is seen.
ST. CYPRIAN OF CARTHAGE: *The World and Its Vanities, c.* 250

The stage being the representation of the world and the actions in it, how can it be imagined that the picture of human life can be more exact than life itself is?
JOHN DRYDEN: *The Rival Ladies,* dedication, 1664

We might as soon attempt to reform the gambler, by teaching him fair game, or the thief, by teaching him concealment, as attempt to reform the stage; its reform, from its very nature, is impossible.
TIMOTHY DWIGHT: *An Essay on the Stage,* 1824

His daughter, she married the prompter,
Grew bulky and quitted the stage.
W. S. GILBERT: *The Bab Ballads,* 1869

[*See also* Actor, Drama, Evidence, Orator, Play, Theatre.

Stage-coach

[*See* Change.

Stalin, Joseph (1879–

The master of ignorance and disloyalty.
LEON TROTSKY: *The Permanent Revolution,* IV, 1930

Stammering

A stammering man is never a worthless one. Physiology can tell you why. It is an excess of delicacy, excess of sensibility to the presence of his fellow-creature, that makes him stammer.
THOMAS CARLYLE: *Letter to R. W. Emerson,* Nov. 17, 1843

Standard

There is an element of change in art; criticism must never for a moment forget that "the artist is the child of his time." But besides these conditions of time and place, and independent of them, there is also an element of permanence, a standard of taste, which genius confesses.
WALTER PATER: *Studies in the History of the Renaissance,* 1873

The cause of letters, the cause of art, is not that of its practitioners — hardly that of its practise — but of its constituting standards.
W. C. BROWNELL: *Standards,* VII, 1917

[*See also* Criticism.

Star

The stars in their courses fought against Sisera.
JUDGES V, 20, *c.* 500 B.C.

The morning stars sang together, and all the sons of God shouted for joy.
JOB XXXVIII, 7, *c.* 325 B.C.

He telleth the number of the stars; he calleth them all by their names.
PSALMS CXLVII, 4, *c.* 150 B.C.

There is one glory of the sun, and another glory of the moon, and another glory of the stars, for one star differeth from another star in glory. I CORINTHIANS XV, 41, *c.* 55

The bright and morning star.
REVELATION XXII, 16, *c.* 95 (Applied by Jesus to Himself)

There's not the smallest orb which thou behold'st
But in his motion like an angel sings.
SHAKESPEARE: *The Merchant of Venice,* v, *c.* 1597

There was a star danced, and under that I was born.
SHAKESPEARE: *Much Ado About Nothing,* II, *c.* 1599

There's husbandry in Heaven;
Their candles are all out.
SHAKESPEARE: *Macbeth,* II, *c.* 1605

The stars, with deep amaze,
Stand fix'd in steadfast gaze.
JOHN MILTON: *On the Morning of Christ's Nativity,* 1629

Let not the dark thee cumber:
What though the moon does slumber?
The stars of the night
Will lend thee their light
Like tapers clear without number.
ROBERT HERRICK: *Night-Piece to Julia,* 1648

Twinkle, twinkle, little star!
How I wonder what you are,
Up above the world so high,
Like a diamond in the sky.
ANN and JANE TAYLOR: *Rhymes for the Nursery,* 1806

Heaven's ebon vault,
Studded with stars unutterably bright,
Through which the moon's unclouded grandeur rolls,
Seems like a canopy which love has spread
To curtain her sleeping world.
P. B. SHELLEY: *Queen Mab,* IV, 1813

Point me out the way
To any one particular beauteous star,
And I will flit into it with my lyre,
And make its silvery splendor pant with bliss.
JOHN KEATS: *Hyperion,* III, 1819

Silently, one by one, in the infinite meadows of Heaven,
Blossomed the lovely stars, the forget-me-nots of the angels.
H. W. LONGFELLOW: *Evangeline,* I, 1847

While the stars that oversprinkle
All the heavens, seem to twinkle
With a crystalline delight.
E. A. POE: *The Bells,* 1849 (Sartain's Union Magazine, Nov.)

The star of the North. (Étoile du Nord.)
MOTTO OF MINNESOTA, adopted 1858

The stars are golden fruit upon a tree
All out of reach.
MARIAN EVANS (GEORGE ELIOT): *The Spanish Gypsy,* II, 1868

Hitch your wagon to a star.
R. W. EMERSON: *Society and Solitude,* 1870

The tawny, solemn night, child of the East,
Behold, how in her gorgeous flow of hair
Glitter a million mellow yellow gems.
CINCINNATUS HEINE (JOAQUIN MILLER): *Ida,* II, 1871

By night those soft, lasceevious stars leered from those velvet skies.
RUDYARD KIPLING: *McAndrew's Hymn,* 1893

A star, however willing, cannot help the moon.
CHINESE PROVERB

A thousand stars are not equal to one moon.
HINDU PROVERB

The stars make no noise. IRISH PROVERB

The stars rule men but God rules the stars. (Astra regunt homines, sed regit astra Deus.) MEDIEVAL LATIN PROVERB

[*See also* Ambition, Aspiration, Night, Pleiades, Sun.

Stare Decisis

[*See* Precedent.

Star of Bethlehem

Lo, the star which they saw in the east went before them, till it came and stood over where the young child was. MATTHEW II, 9, *c.* 75

State

A prosperous state is an honor to the gods.
ÆSCHYLUS: *The Seven Against Thebes,* *c.* 490 B.C.

States are as the men are; they grow out of human characters.
PLATO: *The Republic,* VIII, *c.* 370 B.C.

In the body politic, as in the natural, those disorders are most dangerous that flow from the head.
PLINY THE YOUNGER: *Letters,* IV, *c.* 110

I have done the state some service, and they know't. SHAKESPEARE: *Othello,* v, 1604

States are great engines moving slowly.
FRANCIS BACON: *The Advancement of Learning,* II, 1605

In the youth of a state arms do flourish; in the middle age of a state learning; and then both of them together for a time; in the declining age of a state mechanical arts and merchandise.
FRANCIS BACON: *Essays,* LVIII, 1625

A state is a perfect body of free men, united together to enjoy common rights and advantages.
HUGO GROTIUS: *De jure belli ac pacis,* I, 1625

States have their conversions and periods as well as natural bodies.
GEORGE HERBERT: *Jacula Prudentum,* 1651

I am the state. (L'état, c'est moi.)

Commonly credited, probably apocryphally, to LOUIS XIV OF FRANCE: Speech to the Parliament of Paris, 1655

In the birth of societies it is the chiefs of a state who give it its special character; and afterward it is this special character that forms the chiefs of state.

C. L. DE MONTESQUIEU: *La grandeur et décadence des Romains,* 1734

Honest mediocrity is the most suitable condition for states; riches lead to softness and corruption.

FREDERICK THE GREAT: *Letter to Voltaire,* Dec. 28, 1774

What constitutes a state?
Not high-raised battlement or labored mound,
Thick wall or moated gate;
Not cities proud with spires and turrets crowned;
Not bays and broad-armed ports,
Where, laughing at the storm, rich navies ride.

WILLIAM JONES: *An Ode in Imitation of Alcaeus,* 1781

New states may be admitted by the Congress into this Union; but no new state shall be formed or erected within the jurisdiction of any other state, nor any state be formed by the junction of two or more states, or parts of states, without the consent of the Legislatures of the states concerned as well as of the Congress.

CONSTITUTION OF THE UNITED STATES, Art. IV, 1789

A state is not, like the soil upon which it is situated, a patrimony. It consists of a society of men, over whom the state alone has a right to command and dispose. It is a trunk which has its own roots.

IMMANUEL KANT: *Perpetual Peace,* I, 1795

A thousand years scarce serve to form a state;
An hour may lay it in the dust.

BYRON: *Childe Harold,* II, 1812

If 50,000 men were to perish for the welfare of the state, I would mourn them, but reasons of state must come before everything else.

NAPOLEON I: To Gaspard Gourgaud at St. Helena, Feb. 8, 1816

In dealing with the state we ought to remember that its institutions are not aboriginal, though they existed before we were born: that they are not superior to the citizen: that every one of them was once the act of a single man: every law and usage was a man's expedient to meet a particular case: that they all are imitable, all alterable; we may make as good; we may make better.

R. W. EMERSON: *Politics,* 1841

The state calls its own violence law, but that of the individual crime.

MAX STIRNER: *The Ego and His Own,* 1845

The state always has the sole purpose to limit, tame, subordinate, the individual – to make him subject to some generality or other.

IBID.

For the bourgeoisie the sole duty of the state is to protect the personal liberty and property of the individual. It looks upon the state as the image of the policeman, whose sole duty is, theoretically, to prevent theft and burglary.

FERDINAND LASSALLE: *Arbeiter-Programm,* 1862

I saw that the state was half-witted, that it was timid as a lone woman with her silver spoons, and that it did not know its friends from its foes, and I lost all my remaining respect for it, and pitied it.

H. D. THOREAU: *Cape Cod,* 1865

Powerful states can maintain themselves only by crime. Little states are virtuous only because they are weak.

M. A. BAKUNIN: *Proposition motivée,* 1868

The state is an historically temporary arrangement, a transitory form of society.

M. A. BAKUNIN: *Dieu et l'état,* 1871

The state is force incarnate. Worse, it is the silly parading of force. It never seeks to prevail by persuasion. Whenever it thrusts its finger into anything it does so in the most unfriendly way. Its essence is command and compulsion.

IBID.

The state is no more than a machine for the oppression of one class by another; this is true of a democracy as well as of a monarchy.

FRIEDRICH ENGELS: Introduction to the German edition of KARL MARX: *The Civil War in France,* 1871

States are made up of a considerable number of the ignorant and foolish, a small proportion of genuine knaves, and a sprinkling of capable and honest men, by whose efforts the former are kept in a reasonable state of guidance and the latter of repression.

T. H. HUXLEY: *Administrative Nihilism,* 1871

When it becomes possible to speak of freedom, the state, as such, will cease to exist.

FRIEDRICH ENGELS: *Letter to August Bebel,* March 18, 1875

When all the fine phrases are stripped away, it appears that the state is only a group of men with human interests, passions, and desires, or, worse yet, the state is only an obscure clerk hidden in some corner of a governmental bureau. In either case the assumption of superhuman wisdom and virtue is proved false.

W. G. SUMNER: *Commercial Crises,* 1879

The origin of the state, and its reason for existence, lie in the fact that it works in favor of the propertied minority and against the propertyless.

P. A. KROPOTKIN: *Paroles d'un révolté*, 1884

The word *state* is identical with the word *war.* Each state tries to weaken and ruin another in order to force upon that other its laws, its policies and its commerce, and to enrich itself thereby. IBID.

A state from which religion is banished can never be well governed.

POPE LEO XIII: *Immortale Dei,* Nov. 1, 1885

To force a man to pay for the violation of his own liberty is indeed an addition of insult to injury. But that is exactly what the state is doing.

BENJAMIN R. TUCKER: *Instead of a Book,* 1893

The state is no longer necessary for me.

LYOF N. TOLSTOY: *The Kingdom of God Is Within You,* 1893

The state is a legal relation by virtue of which a supreme authority exists in a certain territory.

PAUL ELTZBACHER: *Anarchism,* 1900

Wherever there is a force in human society the problem is to use it and regulate it; to get the use and prevent the abuse of it. The state is no exception; on the contrary, it is the chief illustration.

W. G. SUMNER: *Bequests of the Nineteenth Century to the Twentieth,* 1901

The ancients understood the regulation of power better than the regulation of liberty. They concentrated so many prerogatives in the state as to leave no footing from which a man could deny its jurisdiction or assign bounds to its authority.

J. E. E. DALBERG (LORD ACTON): *The History of Liberty,* 1907

The function of the civil authority in the state is to protect and to foster, but by no means to absorb, the family and the individual, or to substitute itself for them.

POPE PIUS XI: *Divini illius magistri,* Dec. 31, 1929

The National Socialist [Nazi] party is the state.

ADOLF HITLER: Speech before the assembled governors of the former Federal States of Germany, Berlin, July 6, 1933

[*See also* Christianity, Family, Father, Godless, Government, Law, Paternalism, Patriotism, Self-defense, Union (American).

Statesman

A statesman who is ignorant of the way in which events originate is like a physician who does not know the causes of the diseases he undertakes to cure.

POLYBIUS: *Histories,* III, *c.* 125 B.C.

He was a kind of statesman that would sooner have reckon'd how many cannon bullets he had discharged against a town, to count his expense that way, than how many of his valiant and deserving subjects he lost before it.

JOHN WEBSTER: *The White Devil,* V, *c.* 1608

With grave
Aspect he rose, and in his rising seem'd
A pillar of state; deep on his front engraven
Deliberation sat, and public care;
And princely counsel in his face yet shone
Majestic, though in ruin.

JOHN MILTON: *Paradise Lost,* II, 1667

Had I a son I would sooner breed him a cobbler than courtier, and a hangman than statesman.

THE EARL OF SHREWSBURY: *Letter to Baron Somers,* 1701

The first and essential quality towards being a statesman is to have a public spirit.

RICHARD STEELE: *The Tatler,* July 8, 1710

Statesman, yet friend to truth; of soul sincere,
In action faithful, and in honor clear;
Who broke no promise, serv'd no private end,
Who gain'd no title, and who lost no friend.

ALEXANDER POPE: *On James Craggs,* 1720

A disposition to preserve, and an ability to improve, taken together, would be my standard of a statesman.

EDMUND BURKE: *Reflections on the Revolution in France,* II, 1790

Almost all ministers are liars. Talleyrand is their corporal; next come Castlereagh, Metternich, Hardenberg.

NAPOLEON I: To Barry E. O'Meara at St. Helena, June 6, 1817

The three ends which a statesman ought to propose to himself in the government of a nation, are — 1. Security to possessors; 2. Facility to acquirers; and 3. Hope to all.

S. T. COLERIDGE: *Table-Talk,* June 25, 1831

The mode of flattery which, being at once safe and efficacious, is the best adapted to the purposes of a statesman is the flattery of listening. He that can wear the appearance of drinking in every word that is said with thirsty ears possesses such a faculty for conciliating mankind as a siren might envy.

HENRY TAYLOR: *The Statesman,* 1836

You can always get the truth from an American statesman after he has turned seventy, or given up all hope of the Presidency.

WENDELL PHILLIPS: Speech in Boston, Nov. 7, 1860

A ginooine statesman should be on his guard,
Ef he must hev beliefs, not to b'lieve 'em tu hard.

J. R. LOWELL: *The Biglow Papers,* II, 1862

A constitutional statesman is in general a man of common opinions and uncommon abilities.
WALTER BAGEHOT: *Biographical Studies,* 1880

Woe to the statesman who does not find a reason for war that will hold water when the war is over. OTTO VON BISMARCK (1815–98)

The first duty of a statesman is to the poorest of the people.
EDWARD CLARKE: Speech in the House of Commons, 1906

The politician says: "I will give you what you want." The statesman says: "What you think you want is this. What it is possible for you to get is that. What you really want, therefore, is the following."
WALTER LIPPMANN: *A Preface to Morals,* XIII, 1929

A dead politician. Author unidentified.

[*See also* Burke (Edmund), Democracy, Dishonesty, Fool, Government (English), Orator, Politician, Ruler.

States' Rights

Each state retains its sovereignty, freedom and independence, and every power, jurisdiction and right which is not by this confederation expressly delegated to the United States, in Congress assembled.
ARTICLES OF CONFEDERATION, II, Nov. 15, 1777

The states should be left to do whatever acts they can do as well as the general government.
THOMAS JEFFERSON: *Letter to John Harvie,* 1790

The powers not delegated to the United States in the Constitution, nor prohibited by it to the states, are reserved to the states, respectively, or to the people.
CONSTITUTION OF THE UNITED STATES, Amendment X, Dec. 15, 1791

What an augmentation of the field for jobbing, speculating, plundering, office-building and office-hunting would be produced by an assumption of all the state powers into the hand of the general government! The true theory of our Constitution is surely the wisest and best, that the states are independent as to everything within themselves and united as to everything respecting foreign nations. Let the general government be reduced to foreign concerns only.
THOMAS JEFFERSON: *Letter to Gideon Granger,* 1800

If the Federal government, in all, or any, of its departments, is to prescribe the limits of its own authority, and the states are bound to submit to the decision, and are not to be allowed to examine and decide for themselves when the barriers of the Constitution shall be overleaped, this is practically "a government without limitation of powers." The states are at once reduced to mere petty corporations.
ROBERT Y. HAYNE: Speech in the Senate, Jan. 21, 1830

The maintenance inviolate of the rights of the states, and especially the right of each state to order and control its own domestic institutions, according to its own judgment exclusively, is essential to the balance of powers on which the perfection and endurance of our political fabric depend.
ABRAHAM LINCOLN: *Letter to Duff Green,* Dec. 28, 1860

Each state is a sovereign, and thus may reclaim the grants which it has made to any agent whomsoever.
JEFFERSON DAVIS: Speech in the Senate, Jan. 21, 1861

States' rights should be preserved when they mean the people's rights, but not when they mean the people's wrongs; not, for instance, when they are invoked to prevent the abolition of child labor, or to break the force of the laws which prohibit the importation of contract labor to this country.
THEODORE ROOSEVELT: Address before the Harvard Union, Cambridge, Mass., Feb. 23, 1907

We demand that the states of the Union shall be preserved in all their vigor and power. They constitute a bulwark against the centralizing and destructive tendencies of the Republican party. We condemn the efforts of the Republican administration to nationalize the functions and duties of the states.
Democratic National Platform, 1924

To bring about government by oligarchy, masquerading as democracy, it is fundamentally essential that practically all authority and control be centralized in our Federal government. . . . The individual sovereignty of our states must first be destroyed.
F. D. ROOSEVELT: Radio speech, March 2, 1930

[*See also* Centralization, Slavery, Union (American).

States, United

[*See* United States

Stationer

A stationer, on obvious accounts, will excuse us for thinking his a very dull and bald-headed business.
LEIGH HUNT: *The Indicator,* XXXIX, 1821

Statistics

Statistics is a science which ought to be honorable, the basis of many most important sciences; but it is not to be carried on by steam, this science, any more than others are; a wise head is requisite for carrying it on. Conclusive facts are inseparable from inconclusive except by a head that already understands and knows.

THOMAS CARLYLE: *Chartism*, II, 1839

The object of statistical science is to discover methods of condensing information concerning large groups of allied facts into brief and compendious expressions suitable for discussion. The possibility of doing this is based on the constancy and continuity with which objects of the same species are found to vary.

FRANCIS GALTON: *Inquiries Into Human Faculty*, 1883

There are three kinds of lies: lies, damned lies, and statistics. Author unidentified

[*See also* Figures.

Statue

[*See* Monument.

Stature

Which of you by taking thought can add one cubit unto his stature?

MATTHEW VI, 27, *c.* 75

The other beauties belong to women: the beauty of stature is the only beauty of men. Where there is a contemptible stature, neither the largeness and roundness of the forehead, nor the delicacy and sweetness of the eyes, nor the moderate proportion of the nose, nor the littleness of the ears and mouth, nor the evenness and whiteness of the teeth, nor the thickness of a wellset brown beard, shining like the husk of a chestnut, nor curled hair, nor the just proportion of the head, nor a fresh complexion, nor a pleasant air of the face, nor a body without any offensive scent, nor the just proportion of limbs, can make a handsome man.

MICHEL DE MONTAIGNE: *Essays*, II, 1580

Statute

According to the form of the statute. (Secundum formam statuti.) LEGAL PHRASE

Steadfastness

This is the mark of a really admirable man: steadfastness in the face of trouble.

LUDWIG VAN BEETHOVEN: *Diary*, 1816

Here I am, here I stay. (J'y suis, j'y reste.)

MAURICE DE MACMAHON: After taking the Malakoff at Sebastopol, Sept. 8, 1855

[*See also* Resolution.

Stealing

[*See* Theft.

Steam

Steam is a tyrant.

JOHN WILSON: *Noctes Ambrosianæ*, XXXVI, 1822

Steam is almost an Englishman. I do not know but they will send him to Parliament, next, to make laws.

R. W. EMERSON: *English Traits*, V, 1856

Lord, send a man like Robbie Burns to sing the song o' steam!

RUDYARD KIPLING: *McAndrew's Hymn*, 1893

Steele, Richard (1672–1729)

His writings have set all our wits and men of letters on a new way of thinking, of which they had little or no notion before.

JOHN GAY: *The Present State of Wit*, 1711

A rake among scholars, and a scholar among rakes.

T. B. MACAULAY: *The Life and Writings of Addison*, 1843 (Edinburgh Review, July)

Step

[*See* Watchfulness.

Stepchild

[*See* Stepmother.

Stepfather

[*See* Stepmother.

Stepmother

Stepmothers hate their stepchildren.

EURIPIDES: *Ion*, *c.* 420 B.C. (Cited as a proverb)

Her mother died when she was young,
Which gave her cause to make great moan;
Her father married the warst woman
That ever lived in Christendom.

Anon.: *Kemp Owyne*, *c.* 1600

Take heed of a stepmother: the very name of her sufficeth.

GEORGE HERBERT: *Jacula Prudentum*, 1651

A good stepmother is as rare as a white raven.

GERMAN PROVERB

A stepmother at home is as a bear in the woods.

IBID.

With a stepmother a child also gets a stepfather. GREEK PROVERB

Sterilization

If you boil the water first the ink will not so soon mold.

WILLIAM MATHER: *The Young Man's Companion*, 1681

Public magistrates have no direct power over the bodies of their subjects; therefore, where no crime has been committed and there is no cause present for grave punishment they can never directly harm, or tamper with, the integrity of the body, either for the reasons of eugenics or for any other reason.

POPE PIUS XI: *Casti connubii*, Dec. 31, 1930

Any person suffering from a hereditary disease may be rendered incapable of procreation by means of a surgical operation if the experience of medical science shows that it is highly probable that his descendants would suffer from some serious physical or mental hereditary defect.
German Law for the Prevention of Hereditarily Diseased Offspring (Gesetz zur Verhütung erbkranken Nachwuchses), I, July 14, 1933

Stern

[*See* Just.

Sterne, Laurence (1713–68)

I'm afraid — God help him — a falser and wickeder man it's difficult to read of.
W. M. THACKERAY: *Letter to T. W. Gibbs,* Sept. 12, 1851

Stevenson, R. L. (1850–94)

I think of Mr. Stevenson as a consumptive youth weaving garlands of sad flowers with pale, weak hands, or leaning to a large plate-glass window, and scratching thereon exquisite profiles with a diamond pencil.
GEORGE MOORE: *Confessions of a Young Man,* x, 1888

A careless, slovenly style like Scott's will outlive that of R. L. S.
AUGUSTINE BIRRELL: Written in the margin of his copy of GEORG BRANDES: *Main Currents in Nineteenth Century Literature,* 1918

[*See also* Ape, Epitaph.

Stick

Speak softly and carry a big stick — you will go far.
THEODORE ROOSEVELT: Speech at the Minnesota State Fair, Sept. 2, 1901 (Quoted; apparently Roosevelt's first use of the maxim)

A stick in the hand is better than a tongue in the mouth.
YIDDISH PROVERB

[*See also* Club, Peacemaker.

Still

Still (or smooth) waters run deep.
ENGLISH PROVERB, traced by Smith to *c.* 1430

The stillest humors are always the worst.
JOHN RAY: *English Proverbs,* 1670

[*See also* Night.

Stingy

He is as free of his gift as a poor man is of his eye.
JAMES HOWELL: *Proverbs,* 1659

The stingy are always poor.
FRENCH PROVERB

St. Louis

The first time I ever saw St. Louis I could have bought it for six million dollars, and it was the mistake of my life that I did not do it.
S. L. CLEMENS (MARK TWAIN): *Life on the Mississippi,* XXII, 1883

Stockbroker

Is it not odd that the only generous person I ever knew, who had money to be generous with, should be a stockbroker?
P. B. SHELLEY: *Letter to Leigh Hunt, c.* 1820 (Referring to Horace Smith)

With an evening coat and a white tie, even a stockbroker can gain a reputation for being civilized.
OSCAR WILDE: *The Picture of Dorian Gray,* 1891

[*See also* Financier.

Stock-market

There is no moral difference between gambling at cards or in lotteries or on the race track and gambling in the stock-market. One method is just as pernicious to the body politic as the other kind, and in degree the evil worked is far greater.
THEODORE ROOSEVELT: Message to Congress, Jan. 31, 1908

The purchase and quick resale of stocks is not any more gambling than the purchase and quick resale of lots, and the length of time a man may hold stocks or lots depends largely upon the temperament and ability of the man.
BISHOP JAMES CANNON, JR.: *Unspotted From the World,* Aug. 3, 1929

[*See also* Gambling.

Stoic

Till the Stoics became coxcombs they were a very sensible sect.
WILLIAM COWPER: *Letter to Clotworthy Rowley,* Sept. 2, 1762

[*See also* Artist, Christian, Speech.

Stoicism

'Tis pride, rank pride, and haughtiness of soul;
I think the Romans call it stoicism.
JOSEPH ADDISON: *Cato,* I, 1713

[*See also* Desire.

Stolen

Stolen waters are sweet, and bread eaten in secret is pleasant.
PROVERBS IX, 17, *c.* 350 B.C.

Stolen pleasures are the sweetest.
ENGLISH PROVERB, probably borrowed from PROVERBS IX, 17, *ante*

Stolen sweets are best.
COLLEY CIBBER: *The Rivals Fools,* I, 1709

Stomach

A stomach that is seldom empty despises common food. HORACE: *Satires*, II, *c.* 25 B.C.

He was a man
Of an unbounded stomach.
SHAKESPEARE and JOHN FLETCHER: *Henry VIII*, IV, 1613

So, if unprejudiced you scan
The going of this clock-work, man,
You find a hundred movements made
By fine devices in his head;
But 'tis the stomach's solid stroke
That tells his being what's o'clock.
MATTHEW PRIOR: *Alma*, III, *c.* 1716

The way to a man's heart is through his stomach.
ENGLISH PROVERB, not recorded before the XIX century

When the stomach speaks wisdom is silent.
ARAB PROVERB

It is easier to fill the stomach than the eye.
GERMAN PROVERB

Poor folk seek meat for their stamacks, and rich folk stamacks for their meat.
SCOTTISH PROVERB

There is no caste system among stomachs.
WEST AFRICAN PROVERB

[*See also* Appetite, Belly, Eating, Happiness, Patriotism, Spinach.

Stone

[*See* Blood.

Storm

He maketh the deep to boil like a pot.
JOB XLI, 31, *c.* 325 B.C.

Blow wind, swell billow, and swim bark!
The storm is up, and all is on the hazard.
SHAKESPEARE: *Julius Cæsar*, V, 1599

Blow winds and crack your cheeks! rage! blow!
You cataracts and hurricanes, spout
Till you have drenched our steeples.
SHAKESPEARE: *King Lear*, III, 1606

I have bedimm'd
The noontide sun, call'd forth the mutinous winds,
And 'twixt the green sea and the azur'd vault
Set roaring war.
SHAKESPEARE: *The Tempest*, V, 1611

A strong nor'wester's blowing, Bill!
Hark! don't ye hear it roar now?
Lord help 'em, how I pities them
Unhappy folks on shore now!
Anon.: *The Sailor's Consolation*, *c.* 1780

Any port in a storm.
ENGLISH PROVERB, not recorded before the XIX century

The storm is master; wind and waves play ball with men.
J. C. F. SCHILLER: *Wilhelm Tell*, IV, 1804

The breaking waves dash'd high
On a stern and rock-bound coast,
And the woods, against a stormy sky,
Their giant branches tosst.
FELICIA HEMANS: *The Landing of the Pilgrim Fathers*, 1826

The terrors of the storm are chiefly confined to the parlor and the cabin.
R. W. EMERSON: *Prudence*, 1841

" Oh dear, oh dear!
Sir, will it clear? "
Loud wailed a dame on deck.
As they heaved the lead
The skipper said,
" It allus has, by heck! "
Author unidentified

[*See also* Calm, Whirlwind.

Story

A story is either to be considered as a story, or as a treatise, which, besides that, addeth many things for profit and ornament. As a story, he is nothing but a narration of things done, with the beginnings, causes, and appendices thereof.
PHILIP SIDNEY: *Letter to Robert Sidney*, Oct. 18, 1580

That's another story.
LAURENCE STERNE: *Tristram Shandy*, II, 1760

It is no easy thing to tell a story plainly and distinctly by mouth; but to tell one on paper is difficult indeed, so many snares lie in the way. People are afraid to put down what is common on paper, they seek to embellish their narratives, as they think, by philosophic speculations and reflections; they are anxious to shine, and people who are anxious to shine can never tell a plain story.
GEORGE BORROW: *Lavengro*, XXXVI, 1851

But that is another story.
RUDYARD KIPLING: *Plain Tales from the Hills*, 1888 (Cf. STERNE, *ante*, 1760)

[*See also* Fiction, Prologue, Tale.

Stradivarius, Antonio (1644–1737)

[*See* Violin.

Strange

'Twas strange, 'twas passing strange.
SHAKESPEARE: *Othello*, I, 1604

Stranger

A stranger in a strange land.
EXODUS II, 22, *c.* 700 B.C.

Thou shalt neither vex a stranger, nor oppress him: for ye were strangers in the land of Egypt. EXODUS XXII, 21 (Cf. XXIII, 9)

Ye shall not eat of any thing that dieth of itself: thou shalt give it unto the stranger that is in thy gates, that he may eat it.
DEUTERONOMY XIV, 21, *c.* 650 B.C.

Unto a stranger thou mayest lend upon usury.
DEUTERONOMY XXIII, 20

Everyone is ready to speak evil of a stranger.
ÆSCHYLUS: *The Suppliants, c.* 490 B.C.

I was a stranger, and ye took me in.
MATTHEW XXV, 35, *c.* 75

I was a stranger, and ye took me not in.
MATTHEW XXV, 43

I do desire we may be better strangers.
SHAKESPEARE: *As You Like It,* III, *c.* 1600

A stranger's eyes sees clearest.
CHARLES READE: *The Cloister and the Hearth,* LVIII, 1861

Ships that pass in the night, and speak each other in passing,
Only a signal shown and a distant voice in the darkness,
So on the ocean of life, we pass and speak one another,
Only a look and a voice, then darkness again and a silence.
H. W. LONGFELLOW: *Tales of a Wayside Inn,* 1863

These three are always strangers: death, a son-in-law, and a nephew. HINDU PROVERB

Strangers should not whisper.
WEST AFRICAN PROVERB

[*See also* Alien, Angel, Charity, Guest, Hospitality, Law, Night, Usury, Vineyard.

Strategy

Strategy is a system of makeshifts.
HELMUTH VON MOLTKE: *Essay on Strategy,* 1871

You can't beat something with nothing.
AMERICAN POLITICAL MAXIM

The man who makes the first bad move always loses the game. JAPANESE PROVERB

Strauss, Johann (1825–99)

[*See* Strauss (Richard).

Strauss, Richard (1864–

Such an astounding lack of talent was never before united to such pretentiousness.
P. I. TSCHAIKOVSKY: *Letter to Modeste Tschaikovsky,* Jan., 1888

If it must be Richard, I prefer Wagner: if it must be Strauss, I prefer Johann.
Author unidentified

Straw

Straws show which way the wind blows.
ENGLISH PROVERB, traced by Smith to 1689

[*See also* Last.

Strawberry

Doubtless God could have made a better berry, but doubtless God never did.
Ascribed to WILLIAM BUTLER, or BOTELER (?–1621) in IZAAK WALTON: *The Compleat Angler,* I, 1653

For my part, I confess I fairly swill
And stuff myself with strawberries; and abuse
The doctors all the while, draught, powder, and pill,
And wonder how any sane head can choose
To have their nauseous jalaps, and their bill,
All which, like so much poison, I refuse,
Give me a glut of strawberries; and lo!
Sweet through my blood, and very bones, they go.
LEIGH HUNT: Tr. from an unidentified Italian poet, 1840

Stream

[*See* Swapping.

Street

The street which is called Straight.
ACTS IX, 11, *c.* 75

The man in the street.
ENGLISH PHRASE, not recorded before the XIX century

Strength

His strength is in his loins.
JOB XL, 16, *c.* 325 B.C.

The gods always favor the strong.
TACITUS: *Annals,* IV, *c.* 110

It is excellent
To have a giant's strength, but it is tyrannous
To use it like a giant.
SHAKESPEARE: *Measure for Measure,* II, 1604

We confide in our strength, without boasting of it; we respect that of others, without fearing it.
THOMAS JEFFERSON: *Letter to Carmichael and Short,* 1793

A man is not strong who takes convulsion-fits; though six men cannot hold him then. He that can walk under the heaviest weight without staggering, he is the strong man.
THOMAS CARLYLE: *Heroes and Hero-Worship,* V, 1840 (Lecture in London, May 19)

A strong being is the proof of the race, and of the ability of the universe;
When he or she appears, materials are overaw'd.
WALT WHITMAN: *Song of the Broad-Ax,* 1856

That cause is strong which has, not a multitude, but one strong man behind it.
J. R. LOWELL: Speech in Chelsea, Mass., Dec. 22, 1885

To require of strength that it should not be strength, that it should not show itself as a

wish to overpower, a wish to overthrow, a wish to be master, a thirst for enemies and antagonisms and triumphs, is just as absurd as to demand of weakness that it should express itself as strength.
F. W. NIETZSCHE: *The Genealogy of Morals*, I, 1887

These three things deplete man's strength: fear, travel, and sin. HEBREW PROVERB

It is hard to be strong and not rash.
JAPANESE PROVERB

Three things give hardy strength: sleeping on hairy mattresses, breathing cold air, and eating dry food. WELSH PROVERB

[*See also* Force, Union, Weakness.

Strenuous

I wish to preach, not the doctrine of ignoble ease, but the doctrine of the strenuous life.
THEODORE ROOSEVELT: Speech in Chicago, April 10, 1899

[*See also* Poverty.

Strike

Back to the mines, slaves! There will be no strike tonight. Melodrama line, *c.* 1875

The worker has the right to refuse to work, that is, to strike, and to induce by peaceful and lawful methods others to strike with him.
WILLIAM CARDINAL O'CONNELL: Pastoral letter on the Laborer's Rights, Nov. 23, 1912

There is no right to strike against the public safety by anyone, anywhere, any time.
CALVIN COOLIDGE: Telegram to Samuel Gompers, Sept. 14, 1919 (The occasion was the Boston police strike)

With respect to government service, we hold distinctly that the rights of the people are paramount to the right to strike.
Democratic National Platform, 1920

We deny the right to strike against the government.
Republican National Platform, 1920

Neither the common law nor the Fourteenth Amendment confers the absolute right to strike.
MR. JUSTICE L. D. BRANDEIS: *Opinion in Dorchy* vs. *Kansas*, 1926

Strong

[*See* Strength, Victory.

Struggle for Existence

The wolf eats the sheep, the great fish the small.
ALEXANDER BARCLAY: *The Ship of Fools*, 1509

Fishes live in the sea . . . as men do a-land: the great ones eat up the little ones.
SHAKESPEARE: *Pericles*, II, *c.* 1608

The life of the wolf is the death of the lamb.
JOHN CLARKE: *Parœmiologia Anglo-Latina*, 1639

The little cannot be great unless he devour many.
GEORGE HERBERT: *Outlandish Proverbs*, 1640

Innumerable artifices and stratagems are acted in the howling wilderness and in the great deep that can never come to our knowledge.
JOSEPH ADDISON: *The Spectator*, July 19, 1711

Hobbes clearly proves that every creature
Lives in a state of war by nature.
JONATHAN SWIFT: *On Poetry*, 1712

Nothing exists but what has its enemy; one species pursue and live upon the other.
ST. JOHN DE CRÈVECOEUR: *Letters from an American Farmer*, II, 1782

The perpetual struggle for room and food.
T. R. MALTHUS: *An Essay on the Principle of Population*, III, 1798

The vices of mankind are active and able ministers of depopulation. Should they fail in this war of extermination, sickly seasons, epidemics, pestilence and plague advance in terrific array, and sweep off their thousands and ten thousands. Should success be still incomplete, gigantic inevitable famine stalks in the rear, and with one mighty blow levels the population with the food of the world.
T. R. MALTHUS: *An Essay on the Principle of Population*, VII

The beautiful battle of ten dogs for one bone.
EBENEZER ELLIOTT: *The Village Patriarch*, pref., 1840

Nature red in tooth and claw.
ALFRED TENNYSON: *In Memoriam*, LVI, 1850

Oh, horrible vulturism of earth! from which not the mightiest whale is free.
HERMAN MELVILLE: *Moby Dick*, LXVIII, 1851

Nature is one with rapine, a harm no preacher can heal;
The mayfly is torn by the swallow, the sparrow speared by the shrike,
And the whole little wood where I sit is a world of plunder and prey.
ALFRED TENNYSON: *Maud*, I, 1855

Through it the lion has gained its strength, the deer its speed, the dog its sagacity. The suffering which the conflict involves may indicate that God has made even animals for some higher end than happiness — that He cares for animals' perfection as well as for animals' enjoyment. The ends are eminently worthy of a Divine Intelligence.
ROBERT FLINT: *Theism*, 1877

Lizard fed on ant, and snake on him,
And kite on both; and the fish-hawk robbed

The fish-tiger of that which it had seized;
The shrike chasing the bulbul, which did hunt
The jeweled butterflies; till everywhere
Each slew a slayer, and in turn was slain,
Life living upon death.

EDWIN ARNOLD: *The Light of Asia*, I, 1879

The famous struggle for existence seems to me to be more of an assumption than a fact. It does occur, but only as an exception. The general condition of life is not one of want or famine, but rather one of riches, of lavish luxuriance, and even of absurd prodigality. Where there is a struggle, it is a struggle for power.

F. W. NIETZSCHE: *The Twilight of the Idols*, 1889

[*See also* Classes, Darwinism, Evolution, Fish, Majority, Natural Selection, Nature, Population, Treaty.

Stubbornness

Stubbornness is as iniquity and idolatry.

I SAMUEL XV, 23, *c.* 500 B.C.

A stubborn and rebellious generation.

PSALMS LXXVIII, 8, *c.* 150 B.C.

Fate leads the willing but drives the stubborn.

SENECA: *Epistulæ morales ad Lucilium*, *c.* 63

Stuck-up

Up was he stuck
And in the very upness
Of his stuckitude
He fell.

EUGENE WARE: Epitaph on Robert G. Ingersoll, 1899

Student

When a student, upon a fair trial of two years, is found, from mental inability, incapable to learn or improve, such pupils shall, at the request of the trustees, be removed from the institution, and others selected to fill the vacancy.

Law of the Choctaw Nation, Nov., 1842

Study

It is hard to find a man who has studied for three years without making some progress in virtue.

CONFUCIUS: *Analects*, VIII, *c.* 500 B.C.

Much study is a weariness of the flesh.

ECCLESIASTES XII, 12, *c.* 200 B.C.

Study as if you were to live forever. Live as if you were to die tomorrow.

ISIDORE OF SEVILLE (*c.* 560–636)

As plants are suffocated and drowned with too much moisture, and lamps with too much oil, so is the active part of the understanding with too much study.

MICHEL DE MONTAIGNE: *Essays*, I, 1580

Study is like the Heaven's glorious sun
That will not be deep-searched with saucy looks;
Small have continual plodders ever won,
Save base authority from others' books.

SHAKESPEARE: *Love's Labor's Lost*, I, *c.* 1595

Studies serve for delight, for ornament, and for ability.

FRANCIS BACON: *Essays*, L, 1625

Study is nothing else but a possession of the mind, that is to say, a vehement motion made by some one object in the organs of sense, which are stupid to all other motions as long as this lasteth.

THOMAS HOBBES: *Leviathan*, I, 1651

The noblest exercise of the mind within doors, and most befitting a person of quality, is study.

WILLIAM RAMESY: *The Gentleman's Companion*, 1672

In my early years I read very hard. It is a sad reflection, but a true one, that I knew almost as much at eighteen as I do now.

SAMUEL JOHNSON: *Boswell's Life*, July 20, 1763

Business and action strengthen the brain, but too much study weakens it.

H. G. BOHN: *Handbook of Proverbs*, 1855

Those who do not study are only cattle dressed up in men's clothes.

CHINESE PROVERB

Study is more meritorious than sacrifice.

HEBREW PROVERB

A full belly does not study willingly. (Plenus venter non studet libenter.)

LATIN PROVERB

[*See also* Drinking, Gluttony, Learning, Virtue.

Stupidity

He thinks the moon is made of green cheese.

ENGLISH SAYING, traced by Smith to *c.* 1529

Would you wipe with the water and wash with the towel?

THOMAS FULLER: *Gnomologia*, 1732

You are so cunning you know not what weather it is when it rains.

IBID.

Against stupidity the gods themselves fight in vain.

J. C. F. SCHILLER: *Die Jungfrau von Orleans*, III, 1801

On account of the stupidity of some people, or (if talent be a more respectable word) on account of their talent for misconception. . . .

E. A. POE: *The Rationale of Verse*, 1843 (The Pioneer, March)

[In stupidity] there is an opulence of murky stagnancy, an inexhaustibility, a calm infinitude, which will baffle even the gods,—which will say calmly, "Yes, try all your lightnings here; see whether my dark belly cannot hold them!"

THOMAS CARLYLE: *Oliver Cromwell's Letters and Speeches,* 1845

What we opprobriously call stupidity, though not an enlivening quality in common society, is nature's favorite resource for preserving steadiness of conduct and consistency of opinion.

WALTER BAGEHOT: *Letter to the London Inquirer,* 1851

A stupid person's notions and feelings may confidently be inferred from those which prevail in the circle by which the person is surrounded.

J. S. MILL: *The Subjection of Women,* I, 1869

The stupid have always hated me. (Die Dummer haben mich immer gehast.)

RICHARD WAGNER: A favorite saying in his later life, *c.* 1855–83

[*See also* Dutch, Liberty, Motive, Propaganda, Sincerity, Wisdom.

Style

A good style must, first of all, be clear. It must not be mean or above the dignity of the subject. It must be appropriate.

ARISTOTLE: *Rhetoric,* III, *c.* 322 B.C.

A good style must have an air of novelty, at the same time concealing its art. IBID.

Care should be taken, not that the reader *may* understand, but that he *must* understand.

QUINTILIAN: *De institutione oratoria, c.* 90

He that will write well in any tongue must follow this counsel of Aristotle, to speak as the common people do, to think as wise men do. ROGER ASCHAM: *Toxophilus,* 1545

Among all other lessons this should be learned, that we never affect any strange inkhorn terms, but to speak as is commonly received, neither seeking to be over fine nor yet living over careless.

THOMAS WILSON: *The Arte of Rhetorique,* 1553

The way of speaking that I love is natural and plain, as well in writing as speaking, and a sinewy and significant way of expressing one's self, short and pithy, and not so elegant and artificial as prompt and vehement. Rather hard than harsh, free from affectation; irregular, incontinuous, and bold, where every piece makes up an entire body: not like a pedant, a preacher, or a pleader, but rather a soldier-like style, as Suetonius calls that of Cæsar; and yet I see no reason why he should call it so.

MICHEL DE MONTAIGNE: *Essays,* I, 1580

Style is a constant and continual phrase or tenor of speaking and writing, extending to the whole tale or process of the poem or history, and not properly to any piece or member of a tale; but is of words, speeches, and sentences together, a certain contrived form and quality.

GEORGE PUTTENHAM: *The Art of English Poesie,* 1589

Taffeta phrases, silken terms precise,
Three-piled hyperboles, spruce affectation,
Figures pedantical.

SHAKESPEARE: *Love's Labor's Lost,* V, *c.* 1595

You must not hunt for wild, outlandish terms
To stuff out a peculiar dialect:
But let your matter run before your words.

BEN JONSON: *Cynthia's Revels,* I, 1601

It is most true, *stylus virum arguit,* — our style bewrays us.

ROBERT BURTON: *The Anatomy of Melancholy,* 1621

Let your style be furnished with solid matter, and compact of the best, choice and most familiar words.

HENRY PEACHAM: *The Compleat Gentleman,* 1622

Hold your tongue. Your wretched style only makes me hate them.

FRANÇOISE DE MALHERBE: On his deathbed, 1628, to his confessor, who was describing the joys of Heaven in bad French

For a man to write well, there are required three necessaries: to read the best authors, observe the best speakers, and much exercise of his own style.

BEN JONSON: *Discoveries, c.* 1635

The chief virtue of style is perspicuity, and nothing so vicious in it, as to need an interpreter. BEN JONSON: *Grammar,* 1640

I could have stepped into a style much higher than this in which I have here discoursed, and could have adorned all things more than here I have seemed to do, but I dare not. . . . I may not play in my relating of them, but be plain and simple, and lay down the thing as it was.

JOHN BUNYAN: *Grace Abounding to the Chief of Sinners,* 1666

The Royal Society . . . have exacted from all their members a close, naked, natural way of speaking, positive expressions, clear senses, a native eas'ness, bringing all things as near the mathematical plainness as they can, and preferring the language of artisans, countrymen and merchants before that of wits and scholars.

THOMAS SPRAT: *History of the Royal Society,* 1667

When we encounter a natural style we are always astonished and delighted, for we expected to see an author, and found a man.

BLAISE PASCAL: *Pensées,* VII, 1670

Whatever is well conceived is expressed clearly, and the words flow easily.
NICOLAS BOILEAU: *L'Art poétique,* I, 1674

Abstruse and mystic thoughts you must express
With painful care, but seeming easiness;
For truth shines brightest thro' the plainest dress.
WENTWORTH DILLON (EARL OF ROSCOMMON): *Essay on Translated Verse,* 1684

The noblest deeds can be adequately stated in simple language; they are spoiled by emphasis. It is insignificant matters that stand in need of high-flown words, because it is the expression, the tone, and the manner that alone give them effect.
JEAN DE LA BRUYÈRES: *Caractères,* v, 1688

A vile conceit in pompous words expressed
Is like a clown in regal purple dressed.
ALEXANDER POPE: *An Essay on Criticism,* II, 1711

Soft is the strain when zephyr gently blows,
And the smooth stream in smoother numbers flows;
But when loud surges lash the sounding shore
The hoarse, rough verse should like the torrent roar.
IBID.

When Ajax strives some rock's vast weight to throw,
The line too labors, and the words move slow.
IBID.

A man's style is as much a part of him as his face, his figure, or the rhythm of his pulse.
FRANÇOIS FÉNELON: *Dialogues des morts,* 1712

All styles are good save the boresome kind.
VOLTAIRE: *L'Enfant prodigue,* 1736

When a language abounds with original writers in every kind, the more a person is endowed with abilities, the more difficult he thinks it will be to surpass them. He therefore tries a new road. But as every style analogous to the character of the language and to his own has been already used by preceding writers, he has nothing left but to deviate from analogy. Thus in order to be an original, he is obliged to contribute to the ruin of a language, which, a century sooner, he would have helped to improve.
E. B. DE CONDILLAC: *Essai sur l'origine des connaissances humaines,* II, 1746

A man who writes well writes not as others write, but as he himself writes: it is often in speaking badly that he speaks well.
C. L. DE MONTESQUIEU: *Pensées,* c. 1750

It is natural to depart from familiarity of language upon occasions not familiar. Whatever elevates the sentiments will consequently raise the expression; whatever fills us with hope or terror, will produce some perturbation of images and some figurative distortions of phrase.
SAMUEL JOHNSON: *The Rambler,* Aug. 31, 1751

The style is the man himself. (Le style est l'homme même.)
GEORGE DE BUFFON: Address on his reception into the French Academy, Aug. 25, 1753 (The saying is commonly reduced to "Le style c'est l'homme")

The true lyric style, with all its flights of fancy, ornaments, and heightening of expression, and harmony of sound, is in its nature superior to every other style; which is just the cause why it could not be borne in a work of great length, no more than the eye could bear to see all this scene that we constantly gaze upon — the verdure of the fields and woods, the azure of the sea and skies — turned into one dazzling expanse of gems.
THOMAS GRAY: *Letter to William Mason,* 1756

Whatever is clearly expressed is well wrote.
MARY WORTLEY MONTAGU: *Letter to James Steuart,* July 19, 1759

I hate a style, as I do a garden, that is wholly flat and regular; that slides along like an eel, and never rises to what one can call an inequality.
WILLIAM SHENSTONE: *On Writing and Books,* 1764

Language is the dress of thought: and as the noblest mien, or most graceful action, would be degraded and obscured by a garb appropriated to the gross employments of rustics or mechanics; so the most heroic sentiments will lose their efficacy, and the most splendid ideas drop their magnificence, if they are conveyed by words used commonly upon low and trivial occasions, debased by vulgar mouths, and contaminated by inelegant applications.
SAMUEL JOHNSON: *Lives of the Poets* (Cowley), 1778

Style, in writing or speaking, is formed very early in life, while the imagination is warm, and impressions are permanent.
THOMAS JEFFERSON: *Letter to J. Bannister,* 1785

The turgid style of Johnson, the purple glare of Gibbon, and even the studied and thick-set metaphors of Junius are all equally unnatural, and should not be admitted into our company.
BENJAMIN RUSH: *A Plan of a Federal University,* 1788

The style of an author should be the image of his mind, but the choice and command of language is the fruit of exercise.
EDWARD GIBBON: *Miscellaneous Works,* I, 1796

Many intelligent people, when they set about writing books, force their minds to fit some notion that they have about style, just as they screw up their faces when they sit for their portraits.

G. C. LICHTENBERG: *Reflections,* 1799

Purists would destroy all strength and beauty of style by subjecting it to a rigorous compliance with their rules. Fill up all the ellipses and syllepses of Tacitus, Sallust, Livy, &c. and the elegance and force of their sententious brevity are extinguished.

THOMAS JEFFERSON: *Letter to John Waldo,* 1813

Whatever is translatable in other and simpler words of the same language, without loss of sense or dignity, is bad.

S. T. COLERIDGE: *Biographia Literaria,* I, 1817

No style is good that is not fit to be spoken or read aloud with effect.

WILLIAM HAZLITT: *The Conversation of Authors,* 1821

I confess to you I love a nobility and amplitude of style, provided it never sweeps beyond the subject. There are people who cut short the tails of their dogs; and such dogs are proper for such masters; but the generous breeds, coursers of the lordly stag, and such as accompanied the steps of Hippolytus and Adonis, were unmutilated.

W. S. LANDOR: *Imaginary Conversations,* I, 1824

Obscurity and affectation are the two greatest faults of style. Obscurity of expression generally springs from confusion of ideas; and the same wish to dazzle at any cost which produces affectation in the manner of a writer is likely to produce sophistry in his reasonings.

T. B. MACAULAY: *Machiavelli,* 1827

Works of imagination should be written in very plain language; the more purely imaginative they are the more necessary it is to be plain.

S. T. COLERIDGE: *Table-Talk,* May 31, 1830

The two capital secrets in the art of prose composition are these: first, the philosophy of transition and connection; or the art by which one step in an evolution of thought is made to arise out of another: all fluent and effective composition depends on the connections; secondly, the way in which sentences are made to modify each other; for the most powerful effects in written eloquence arise out of this reverberation, as it were, from each other in a rapid succession of sentences.

THOMAS DE QUINCEY: *Sketches of Life and Manners,* 1835

The first rule of all writing — that rule to which every other is subordinate — is that the words used by the writer shall be such as most fully and precisely convey his meaning to the great body of his readers. All considerations about the purity and dignity of style ought to bend to this consideration.

T. B. MACAULAY: *Letter to Macvey Napier,* April 18, 1842

It is by the use of familiar words that style affects the reader. People feel that using them is the mark of a man who knows life and its daily concerns, and maintains contact with them.

JOSEPH JOUBERT: *Pensées,* I, 1842

Uncommon things must be said in common words, if you would have them to be received in less than a century.

COVENTRY PATMORE: *Letter to H. S. Sutton,* March 25, 1847

I know not anywhere the book that seems less written. It is the language of conversation transferred to a book. Cut these words, and they would bleed; they are vascular and alive.

R. W. EMERSON: *Representative Men,* IV, 1850 (Said of Montaigne's Essays)

Style is the physiognomy of the mind.

ARTHUR SCHOPENHAUER: *Parerga und Paralipomena,* II, 1851

Books themselves have their peculiar words, — namely, those that are never used in living speech in the real world, but only used in the world of books. Nobody ever actually talks as books and plays talk.

WALT WHITMAN: *An American Primer,* *c.* 1856

There is no way of writing well and also of writing easily.

ANTHONY TROLLOPE: *Barchester Towers,* 1857

Style went out with the men who wore knee-breeches and buckles in their shoes. We write more easily now.

ALEXANDER SMITH: *Dreamthorp,* II, 1863

I would never use a long word where a short one would answer the purpose. I know there are professors in this country who "ligate" arteries. Other surgeons only tie them, and it stops the bleeding just as well.

O. W. HOLMES: *Scholastic and Bedside Teaching,* 1867 (Lecture at Harvard, Nov. 6)

The secret of the style of the great Greek and Roman authors is that it is the perfection of good sense.

J. S. MILL: Inaugural address as Lord Rector of St. Andrew's University, 1867

If a writer who assumes a style for the sake of a style ever acquires a place in literature, it is in so far as he assumes the style of those whose style is not assumed.

IBID.

Style that is not the outgrowth of a man's individuality is without significance or value. It is never thoroughly formed until character is formed, and until the expression of thought has become habitual.

J. G. HOLLAND: *Everyday Topics,* 1876

A perfect style must be of its age.

GERARD MANLEY HOPKINS: *Letter to Canon Dixon,* Dec., 1881

The unique word, phrase, sentence, paragraph, essay or song, absolutely proper to the single mental presentation or vision within.

WALTER PATER: *Style,* 1888

In all unimportant matters, style, not sincerity, is the essential. In all important matters, style, not sincerity, is the essential.

OSCAR WILDE: *Phrases and Philosophies for the Use of the Young,* 1894

The virtues of good style are more negative than positive. The man who knows what to avoid is already the owner of style.

H. W. FOWLER: *Matter and Manners,* 1902

A severe, unadorned style like Merimée's survives the works written in the florid style as surely as the bronze statue survives the blossoming tree.

AUGUSTINE BIRRELL: Written in the margin of his copy of GEORG BRANDES: *Main Currents in Nineteenth Century Literature,* 1918

The style proclaims the man. (Stilus virum arguit.)

LATIN PROVERB

[*See also* Addison (Joseph), Bible, Expression, Grammar, Idiom, Johnson (Samuel), Language, Metaphor, Milton (John), Speech, Words, Writing.

Subject

Every subject's duty is the king's; but every subject's soul is his own.

SHAKESPEARE: *Henry V,* IV, *c.* 1599

The obligation of subjects to the sovereign is understood to last as long, and no longer, than the power lasteth by which he is able to protect them.

THOMAS HOBBES: *Leviathan,* II, 1651

I think that we should be men first, and subjects afterward.

H. D. THOREAU: *An Essay on Civil Disobedience,* 1849

[*See also* Sovereign.

Sublime

The sublime, introduced at the right moment, carries all before it with the rapidity of lightning, and reveals at a glance the mighty power of genius.

LONGINUS: *On the Sublime,* I, *c.* 250

Whatever is fitted in any sort to excite the ideas of pain and danger, that is to say, whatever is in any sort terrible or is conversant about terrible objects, or operates in a manner analogous to terror, is a source of the sublime.

EDMUND BURKE: *The Sublime and Beautiful,* I, 1756

One step above the sublime makes the ridiculous, and one step above the ridiculous makes the sublime again.

THOMAS PAINE: *The Age of Reason,* II, 1794

Young people, like nations, always appreciate the sublime more readily than the beautiful.

JEAN PAUL RICHTER: *Titan,* 1803

It is but one step from the sublime to the ridiculous.

HEINRICH HEINE: *Reisebilder,* II, 1826

Sublimity is Hebrew by birth.

S. T. COLERIDGE: *Table-Talk,* July 25, 1832

Submarine

It is automa, runs under water
With a snug nose, and has a nimble tail,
Made like an auger, with which tail she wriggles
Betwixt the coats of a ship and sinks it straight.

BEN JONSON: *The Staple of News,* III, 1625

Under water men shall walk,
Shall ride, shall sleep, and talk.

Anon.: *The Prophecie of Mother Shipton,* 1862

"Ship" shall include any description of boat, vessel, or other craft or battery, made to move either on the surface or under water, or sometimes on the surface and sometimes under water.

ACT OF PARLIAMENT, 1879 (33 & 34 Victoria, 90)

To the end that prohibition of the use of submarines as commerce destroyers shall be accepted universally as part of the law of nations, the signatory powers herewith accept that prohibition as binding between themselves, and invite all other nations to adhere thereto.

The Washington Naval Conference, Feb. 6, 1922

Submission

Submit, and thou conquerest; serve, and thou'lt command.

OVID: *Ars amatoria,* II, *c.* 2 B.C.

Subservience

[*See* Regimentation.

Substitute

So doth the greater glory dim the less:
A substitute shines brightly as a king,
Until a king be by.

SHAKESPEARE: *The Merchant of Venice,* V, *c.* 1597

Success

The superior man makes the difficulty to be overcome his first interest; success comes only later.
CONFUCIUS: *Analects*, XII, *c.* 500 B.C.

Along with success comes a reputation for wisdom. EURIPIDES: *Hippolytus*, 428 B.C.

More worship the rising than the setting sun.
PLUTARCH: *Lives*, *c.* 100

Success hath made me wanton.
BEN JONSON: *Volpone*, III, 1605

Success rarely brings satisfaction.
BALTASAR GRACIÁN: *The Art of Worldly Wisdom*, CLXXXV, 1647

Success, the mark no mortal wit,
Or surest hand, can always hit:
For whatsoe'er we perpetrate,
We do but row, we're steer'd by fate.
SAMUEL BUTLER: *Hudibras*, I, 1663

In this world there are only two ways of getting on — either by one's own industry or by the imbecility of others.
JEAN DE LA BRUYÈRE: *Caractères*, VI, 1688

'Tis not in mortals to command success,
But we'll do more, Sempronius, —
We'll deserve it.
JOSEPH ADDISON: *Cato*, I, 1713

Success is never blamed.
THOMAS FULLER: *Gnomologia*, 1732

Success generally depends upon knowing how long it takes to succeed.
C. L. DE MONTESQUIEU: *Pensées*, *c.* 1750

To succeed in the world we must look foolish but be wise. IBID.

Success has ruin'd many a man.
BENJAMIN FRANKLIN: *Poor Richard's Almanac*, 1752

An earnest desire to succeed is almost always prognostic of success.
STANISLAUS LESZCZYNSKI (KING OF POLAND): *Œuvres du philosophe bienfaisant*, 1763

Be commonplace and creeping, and you will be a success.
CARON DE BEAUMARCHAIS: *Le barbier de Séville*, III, 1775

I knew very well what I was undertaking, and very well how to do it, and have done it very well.
SAMUEL JOHNSON: *Boswell's Life*, Oct. 10, 1779 (Speaking of his Dictionary)

He owed his success neither to distinguished abilities, nor to skill-supplying industry, but to the art of uniting suppleness to others with confidence in himself.
FRANCES BURNEY: *Cecilia*, I, 1782

Nothing succeeds like success.
ENGLISH PROVERB, apparently borrowed from the French; not recorded before the XIX century

'Tis an old lesson; time approves it true,
And those who know it best, deplore it most;
When all is won that all desire to woo,
The paltry prize is hardly worth the cost.
BYRON: *Childe Harold*, II, 1812

Success, as I see it, is a result, not a goal.
GUSTAVE FLAUBERT: *Letter to Maxime du Camp*, June 26, 1852

Success makes a fool seem wise.
H. G. BOHN: *Handbook of Proverbs*, 1855 (Cf. MONTESQUIEU, *ante*, *c.* 1750)

Success is the necessary misfortune of life, but it is only to the very unfortunate that it comes early.
ANTHONY TROLLOPE: *Orley Farm*, 1862

The secret of success is constancy to purpose.
BENJAMIN DISRAELI: Speech in the House of Commons, June 24, 1870

If I have talent and intelligence I shall get on; if not, it isn't worth pulling me out of the mud. M. P. MUSSORGSKY: *Letter to M. A. Balakirev*, March 11, 1872

Often a certain abdication of prudence and foresight is an element of success.
R. W. EMERSON: *Demonology*, 1877

Have success, and there will always be fools to say that you have talent.
EDOUARD PAILLERON: *Le monde où l'on s'ennuie*, 1881

Success has always been a great liar.
F. W. NIETZSCHE: *Beyond Good and Evil*, 1886

The higher the type of man, the greater the improbability that he will succeed. IBID.

All you need in this life is ignorance and confidence, and then success is sure.
S. L. CLEMENS (MARK TWAIN): *Letter to Mrs. Foote*, Dec. 2, 1887

If I die prematurely, at any rate I shall be saved from being bored by my own success.
SAMUEL BUTLER: *Note-Books*, *c.* 1890

The secret of success in life is known only to those who have not succeeded.
J. CHURTON COLLINS: *Maxims and Reflections*, 1890

When a man succeeds, he does it in spite of everybody, and not with the assistance of everybody.
E. W. HOWE: *Country Town Sayings*, 1911

The end of hope. Author unidentified

If you would succeed, you must not be too good. ITALIAN PROVERB

If you wish to be a success in the world, acquire a knowledge of Latin, a horse, and money.
SPANISH PROVERB

[*See also* Adams (John Quincy), Audacity, Bold, Determinism, England, Happiness, Luck, Poet, Purpose.

Sucker

A sucker is born every minute.
AMERICAN PROVERB, commonly ascribed to P. T. BARNUM (1810–91)

Never give a sucker an even break.
AMERICAN PROVERB, popularized by Texas Guinan, *c.* 1925

Suckling

Suck, baby! suck! mother's love grows by giving:
Drain the sweet founts that only thrive by wasting.
CHARLES LAMB: *Sonnet in a letter to Mrs. Bryan W. Procter,* Jan. 29, 1829

Suffering

I reckon that the sufferings of this present time are not worthy to be compared with the glory which shall be revealed in us.
ROMANS VIII, 18, *c.* 55

Our suffering is not worthy the name of suffering. When I consider my crosses, tribulations, and temptations, I shame myself almost to death, thinking what are they in comparison of the sufferings of my blessed Saviour Christ Jesus.
MARTIN LUTHER: *Table-Talk,* CXCVI, 1569

He's truly valiant that can suffer wisely
The worst that man can breathe and make his wrongs
His outsides, to wear them like his raiment, carelessly.
SHAKESPEARE: *Timon of Athens,* III, *c.* 1607

No pain, no palm; no thorns, no throne; no gall, no glory; no cross, no crown.
WILLIAM PENN: *No Cross, No Crown,* 1669

To each his suff'rings: all are men,
Condemn'd alike to groan;
The tender for another's pain,
Th' unfeeling for his own.
THOMAS GRAY: *Ode on a Distant Prospect of Eton College,* 1747

It requires more courage to suffer than to die.
NAPOLEON I: To Gaspard Gourgaud at St. Helena, April 16, 1816

There are deeds
Which have no form, sufferings which have no tongue.
P. B. SHELLEY: *The Cenci,* III, 1819

I have learned at my own cost what a human heart can endure without breaking, and what power God has deposited under the left nipple of man.
ESAIAS TEGNÉR: *Letter to F. M. Franzén,* Nov. 13, 1825

Know how sublime a thing it is
To suffer and be strong.
H. W. LONGFELLOW: *The Reaper and the Flowers,* 1839

Man, the bravest of the animals and the one most inured to suffering, does not repudiate suffering in itself: he wills it, he even seeks it out, provided he can find a meaning in it, a purpose for it.
F. W. NIETZSCHE: *The Genealogy of Morals,* III, 1887

To suffer and to endure is the lot of humanity.
POPE LEO XIII: *Quadragesimo anno,* May 15, 1931

We must die young or suffer much.
PORTUGUESE PROVERB

[*See also* Experience, Fortitude, Golden Rule, Misery, Pity.

Sufficiency

As much as is sufficient. (Quantum sufficit.)
LATIN PHRASE employed in physicians' prescriptions, and generally abbreviated to *q.s.*

Suffrage

[*See* Vote.

Suffrage, Negro

[*See* Negro.

Suffragette

One who has ceased to be a lady and not yet become a gentleman.
Author unidentified, *c.* 1906

Suffrage, Universal

Universal suffrage could not long exist in a community where there was great inequality of property. The holders of estates would be obliged in such case either in some way to restrain the right of suffrage, or else such right of suffrage would ere long divide the property.
DANIEL WEBSTER: Speech in Boston, 1820

Universal suffrage, furloughs and whiskey have ruined us.
GENERAL BRAXTON BRAGG, C.S.A.: After Shiloh, April, 1862

Let any competently instructed person turn over in his mind the great epochs of scientific invention and social change during the past two centuries, and consider what would have occurred if universal suffrage had been established at any one of them. Universal suffrage would certainly have prohibited the spinning-jenny and the power-loom. It would certainly have forbidden the threshing-machine. It would have prevented the adoption of the Gregorian Calendar; and it would have restored the Stuarts. It would have proscribed the Roman Catholics, with the mob which burned Lord Mansfield's house and library in

1780; and it would have proscribed the Dissenters, with the mob which burned Dr. Priestley's house and library in 1791.

HENRY MAINE: *Popular Government*, 1885

Universal suffrage, to justify itself, must be based on universal service. It is only you and your kind who have the absolutely clear title to the management of the Republic.

THEODORE ROOSEVELT: Speech to the soldiers at Camp Upton, Nov. 18, 1917

Suffrage, Woman

I go for all sharing the privileges of the government who assist in bearing its burdens. Consequently I go for admitting all whites to the right of suffrage who pay taxes or bear arms, by no means excluding females.

ABRAHAM LINCOLN: Announcement of his candidacy for the Illinois Legislature, July 13, 1836

We recommend the extension of the franchise to the women of the country by the states upon the same terms as to men.

Democratic National Platform, 1916

The Republican party, reaffirming its faith in government of the people, by the people, for the people, as a measure of justice to one-half the adult people of the country, favors the extension of the suffrage to women, but recognizes the right of each state to settle this question for itself.

Republican National Platform, 1916

The right of citizens of the United States to vote shall not be denied or abridged by the United States or by any state on account of sex.

CONSTITUTION OF THE UNITED STATES, Amendment XIX, Aug. 26, 1920

I welcome it as a great instrument of mercy and a mighty agency of peace.

CALVIN COOLIDGE: Speech of acceptance, Aug. 14, 1924

Suffrance

Suffrance is not quittance.

JOHN HEYWOOD: *Proverbs*, 1546

[*See also* Jew.

Suggestion

They'll take suggestion as a cat laps milk.

SHAKESPEARE: *The Tempest*, II, 1611

Sometimes man acts only under the influence of feeling, and strives to attain his desires. Sometimes he acts under the influence of reason alone, which indicates to him his duties. Sometimes, and most often, man acts because he himself or other men have suggested to him a certain activity and he unconsciously submits to the suggestion.

LYOF N. TOLSTOY: *What Is Religion?*, 1902

Suicide

When Ahithophel saw that his counsel was not followed, he saddled his ass, and arose, and gat him home to his house, to his city, and put his household in order, and hanged himself, and died.

II SAMUEL XVII, 23, *c.* 500 B.C.

[Judas] cast down the pieces of silver in the temple, and departed, and went and hanged himself.

MATTHEW XXVII, 5, *c.* 75

Amid the miseries of our life on earth, suicide is God's best gift to man.

PLINY THE ELDER: *Natural History*, II, 77

Parricide is more wicked than homicide, but suicide is the most wicked of all.

ST. AUGUSTINE: *On Patience*, *c.* 425

It is very certain that, as to all persons who have killed themselves, the Devil put the cord round their necks, or the knife to their throats.

MARTIN LUTHER: *Table-Talk*, DLXXXIX, 1569

Life, being weary of these worldly bars,
Never lacks power to dismiss itself.

SHAKESPEARE: *Julius Cæsar*, I, 1599

Thus, weary of my life, at length
I yielded up my vital strength
Within a ditch of loathsome scent
Where carrion dogs did much frequent.

Anon.: *Jane Shore*, *c.* 1600

Who would bear the whips and scorns of time,
The oppressor's wrong, the proud man's contumely,
The pangs of dispriz'd love, the law's delay,
The insolence of office, and the spurns
That patient merit of the unworthy takes,
When he himself might his quietus make
With a bare bodkin?

SHAKESPEARE: *Hamlet*, III, *c.* 1601

It is silliness to live when to live is torment.

SHAKESPEARE: *Othello*, I, 1604

He
That kills himself to avoid misery, fears it,
And, at the best, shows but a bastard valor.

PHILIP MASSINGER: *The Maid of Honor*, IV, 1632

If you like not hanging, drown yourself.

PHILIP MASSINGER: *A New Way to Pay Old Debts*, II, 1633

We hold in our hands the power to end our sorrows, and he who is willing to die may brave any calamity.

PIERRE CORNEILLE: *Horace*, III, 1639

A man that lived at Brafield, by Northampton, named John Cox, took his razor, and cut up a great hole in his side, out of which he pulled and cut off some of his guts, and threw them, with the blood, up and down the chamber. But this not speeding of him so soon as he desired, he took the same razor and therewith cut his throat.

JOHN BUNYAN: *The Life and Death of Mr. Badman*, 1680

If suicide be supposed a crime, it is only cowardice can impel us to it. If it be no crime, both prudence and courage should engage us to rid ourselves at once of existence when it becomes a burden.
DAVID HUME: *Essays Moral and Political*, I, 1741

When one has lost everything, when one has no more hope, life is a disgrace, and death is a duty.
VOLTAIRE: *Mérope*, II, 1743

Nine men in ten are suicides.
BENJAMIN FRANKLIN: *Poor Richard's Almanac*, 1749

There are said to be occasions when a wise man kills himself, but generally speaking it is not an excess of reason that makes people take their own lives.
VOLTAIRE: *Letter to James Marriott*, Feb. 26, 1767

Suicide is not abominable because God forbids it; God forbids it because it is abominable.
IMMANUEL KANT: Lecture at Königsberg, 1775

I have a hundred times wished that one could resign life as an officer resigns a commission.
ROBERT BURNS: *Letter to Mrs. Dunlop*, Jan. 21, 1788

If suicides gave their reasons for the act in set terms not much light would be thrown on the matter. But this is precisely what everyone who hears of a suicide tries to do. All he really accomplishes is to reduce the case to his own language, thus making it something different from the reality.
G. C. LICHTENBERG: *Reflections*, 1799

I would have committed suicide long ago had I not read somewhere that it is a sin to part from life voluntarily so long as one can still do a good deed. Life is so beautiful, but for me it is forever poisoned.
LUDWIG VAN BEETHOVEN: *Letter to Franz Wegeler*, May 2, 1810

It is cowardice to commit suicide.
NAPOLEON I: To Gaspard Gourgard at St. Helena, March 17, 1817

Before shooting one's self one should deliver a soliloquy. Most men, on such occasions, use Hamlet's " To be, or not to be."
HEINRICH HEINE: *Reisebilder*, II, 1826

There is no refuge from confession but suicide; and suicide is confession.
DANIEL WEBSTER: Argument in the trial of Capt. White, April 6, 1830

One more unfortunate
Weary of breath,
Rashly importunate,
Gone to her death.
THOMAS HOOD: *The Bridge of Sighs*, 1846

If you must commit suicide, always contrive to do it as decorously as possible; the decencies, whether of life or of death, should never be lost sight of.
GEORGE BORROW: *Lavengro*, XXIII, 1851

There is nothing in the world to which every man has a more unassailable title than to his own life and person.
ARTHUR SCHOPENHAUER: *On Suicide*, 1851

The relatives of a suicide always take it in bad part that he did not remain alive out of consideration for the family dignity.
F. W. NIETZSCHE: *Human All-too-Human*, I, 1878

Suicide is not a remedy.
JAMES A. GARFIELD: Inaugural Address, March 4, 1881

It is always consoling to think of suicide: in that way one gets through many a bad night.
F. W. NIETZSCHE: *Beyond Good and Evil*, IV, 1886

Out of the very love one bears to life one should wish death to be free, deliberate, and a matter neither of chance or of surprise.
F. W. NIETZSCHE: *The Twilight of the Idols*, 1889

There are cases in which it is indecent to go on living. . . . One should die proudly when it is no longer possible to live proudly.
IBID.

Those books are prohibited which defend suicide as lawful.
POPE LEO XIII: General Decrees Concerning the Prohibition and Censorship of Books, Jan. 25, 1897

I think that the possibility of killing oneself is a safety-valve. Having it, man has no right to say that life is unbearable. If it were impossible to live, then one would kill oneself; and consequently one cannot speak of life as being unbearable.
LYOF N. TOLSTOY: *Letter to a friend*, 1898

Statistical evidence shows that the greater the intellectual freedom, and the higher the general average of intelligence in a community, the greater is also the number of suicides.
SVEND RANULF: *The Jealousy of the Gods and Criminal Law at Athens*, II, 1934

Felony upon himself. (Felo de se.)
LEGAL PHRASE

[*See also* Confession, Drunkenness.

Sulphur

[*See* Hell.

Summer

Sumer is icumen in,
Lhude sing cuccu.
Groweth sed, and bloweth med,
And springth the wude nu,
Sing cuccu!
Anon.: *Sumer Is Icumen In*, *c.* 1250

Go not yet away, bright soul of the sad year;
The earth is hell when thou leavest to appear.
THOMAS NASHE: *Waning Summer,* 1592

Summer is a seemly time.
JAMES KELLY: *Complete Collection of Scottish Proverbs,* 1721

Summer is the mother of the poor.
ITALIAN PROVERB

[*See also* February, One, Seasons, Swallow.

Sumner, Charles (1811–74)

He identifies himself so completely with the universe that he is not at all certain whether he is a part of the universe or the universe is a part of him.
S. S. COX: *Why We Laugh,* 1876

Sun

And thou, O sun, thou seest all things and hearest all things in thy daily round.
HOMER: *Iliad,* III, *c.* 800 B.C.

God made two great lights: the greater light to rule the day, and the lesser light to rule the night.
GENESIS I, 16, *c.* 700 B.C.

The sun stood still. JOSHUA X, 13, *c.* 500 B.C.

Truly the light is sweet, and a pleasant thing it is for the eyes to behold the sun.
ECCLESIASTES XI, 7, *c.* 200 B.C.

The sun shines into cesspools but is not corrupted.
DIOGENES LAERTIUS: *Lives of the Philosophers,* VI, *c.* 150 B.C.

The sun shines even on the wicked.
SENECA: *De beneficiis,* III, *c.* 63

The sun is very beautiful, but it is too imbecile and weak to be a god.
ST. JOHN CHRYSOSTOM: *Homilies,* X, *c.* 388

The sun is no worse for shining on a dunghill.
ENGLISH PROVERB, traced by Smith to 1303 (Cf. DIOGENES LAERTIUS, *ante, c.* 150 B.C.)

Up rose the sun, and up rose Emily.
GEOFFREY CHAUCER: *The Canterbury Tales* (The Knight's Tale), *c.* 1386

I gin to be aweary of the sun.
SHAKESPEARE: *Macbeth,* V, *c.* 1605

Let us not concede that the sun is moved by the earth, which is absurd. We must concede that the sun is immoveable, and that the earth moves.
JOHN KEPLER: *Astronomia nova,* 1609

A morning sun, a wine-bred child and a Latin-bred woman seldom end well.
GEORGE HERBERT: *Outlandish Proverbs,* 1640

Anaxagoras, long agone,
Saw hills, as well as you, i' th' moon,
And held the sun was but a piece
Of red-hot iron as big as Greece.
SAMUEL BUTLER: *Hudibras,* II, 1664

They were come unto the Land of Beulah, where the sun shineth night and day.
JOHN BUNYAN: *Pilgrim's Progress,* II, 1678

Sun, how I hate thy beams!
SAMUEL JOHNSON: *Boswell's Life,* June 11, 1784

The sun, — my almighty physician.
THOMAS JEFFERSON: *Letter to James Monroe,* 1785

The sun came up upon the left,
Out of the sea came he!
And he shone bright, and on the right
Went down into the sea.
S. T. COLERIDGE: *The Ancient Mariner,* 1798

Free as the sun, and lonely as the sun.
WILLIAM WORDSWORTH: *The Excursion,* III, 1814

Were I to choose a religion, I would probably become a worshiper of the sun. It gives life and fertility to all things. It is the true God of the earth.
NAPOLEON I: To Gaspard Gourgaud at St. Helena, 1815–1818

The sun is but a morning star.
H. D. THOREAU: *Walden,* 1854

The sun was shining on the sea,
Shining with all his might!
He did his very best to make
The billows smooth and bright —
And this was odd, because it was
The middle of the night.
C. L. DODGSON (LEWIS CARROLL): *Through the Looking-Glass,* 1871

The night has a thousand eyes,
And the day but one;
Yet the light of the bright world dies
With the dying sun.
F. W. BOURDILLON: *The Night Has a Thousand Eyes,* 1873

Friend sun!
SIDNEY LANIER: *Florida: Its Scenery, Climate and History,* 1875

The sun *do* move.
Ascribed to a Negro preacher of Richmond, Va., Jasper by name, *c.* 1885

We don't want to cast anyone in the shade, but we also demand our own place in the sun (Platz an der Sonne).
BERNHARD VON BÜLOW: Speech in the Reichstag, Dec. 6, 1897

With open mouth he drank the sun
As though it had been wine.
OSCAR WILDE: *The Ballad of Reading Gaol,* 1898

No one can dispute with us the place in the sun that is our due.
WILLIAM II OF GERMANY: Speech in Hamburg, Aug. 27, 1911 (Cf. BÜLOW, *ante,* 1897)

Mr. Darrow – The Bible says Joshua commanded the sun to stand still for the purpose of lengthening the day, doesn't it, and you believe it?
Mr. Bryan – I do.
From the record of the Scopes trial, Dayton, Tenn., July 21, 1925 (Cf. JOSHUA X, 13, *ante, c.* 500 B.C.)

Mr. Darrow – Do you think the sun was made on the fourth day?
Mr. Bryan – Yes.
IBID. (Cf. GENESIS I, 16, *ante, c.* 700 B.C.)

In every country the sun rises in the morning.
GERMAN PROVERB

The sun will set without thy assistance.
HEBREW PROVERB

All cannot live on the piazza, but everyone may enjoy the sun. ITALIAN PROVERB

[*See also* Bride, Caution, Cosmology, December, Star.

Sunday

Sunday clears away the rust of the whole week.
JOSEPH ADDISON: *The Spectator,* July 9, 1711

Of all the days that's in the week,
I dearly love but one day,
And that's the day that comes betwixt
A Saturday and Monday.
HENRY CAREY: *Sally in Our Alley,* 1729

If you have done no ill the six days, you may play the seventh.
THOMAS FULLER: *Gnomologia,* 1732

I always love to begin a journey on Sundays, because I shall have the prayers of the church to preserve all that travel by land or by water.
JONATHAN SWIFT: *Polite Conversation,* 1738

Sunday should be different from another day. People may walk, but not throw stones at birds.
SAMUEL JOHNSON: *Boswell's Tour to the Hebrides,* Aug. 20, 1773

Whenever I miss church on a Sunday I resolve to go another day. But I do not always do it.
SAMUEL JOHNSON: *Boswell's Life,* Oct. 10, 1779

The Sunday is the core of our civilization, dedicated to thought and reverence.
R. W. EMERSON: *Character,* 1844

I do not think there can be the smallest doubt that to sit judicially on Sunday on any business would be indecent and improper, and ought never to be done if it can be helped.
MR. JUSTICE BLACKBURN: *Judgment in Winsor* vs. *Regina,* 1866

The one great poem of New England is her Sunday.
H. W. BEECHER: *Proverbs from Plymouth Pulpit,* 1870

It was a masterstroke of the English to make Sunday so solemn and gloomy that the workman unconsciously longs for his work to begin again.
F. W. NIETZSCHE: *Beyond Good and Evil,* 1886

A child born on Sunday never dies of the plague. FRENCH PROVERB

Sunday is not a judicial day. (Dies dominicus non est juridicus.) LEGAL MAXIM

Sunday shaven, Sunday shorn:
Better had'st thou ne'er been born.
OLD ENGLISH RHYME

Come day, go day, God send Sunday.
SCOTCH PROVERB

What a child is taught on Sunday it will remember on Monday. WELSH PROVERB

[*See also* Boredom, Days, Friday, Nail, Sabbath, Sunlight, Sunrise, Sunset.

Sunday-school

Why drag this dead weight of a Sunday-school over the whole Christendom? It is natural and beautiful that childhood should inquire, and maturity should teach; but it is time enough to answer questions when they are asked.
R. W. EMERSON: *Spiritual Laws,* 1841

Sunlight

Sunlight is painting.
NATHANIEL HAWTHORNE: *American Note-Books,* 1838

Where there is sunshine the doctor starves.
FLEMISH PROVERB

[*See also* Afternoon.

Sunrise

Like a lobster boil'd, the morn
From black to red began to turn.
SAMUEL BUTLER: *Hudibras,* II, 1664

The heav'n is streak'd with dappled fires,
And fleck'd with blushes like a rifled maid.
JOHN DRYDEN and NATHANIEL LEE: *The Duke of Guise,* 1682

O'er night's brim, day boils at last.
ROBERT BROWNING: *Pippa Passes,* I, 1841

Wake! For the sun who scatter'd into flight
The stars before him from the field of night,
Drives night along with them from heav'n, and strikes
The sultan's turret with a shaft of light.
EDWARD FITZGERALD: Tr. of OMAR KHAYYÁM: *Rubáiyát* (*c.* 1100), 1857

[*See also* Color, Dawn, Morning.

Sunset

The gaudy, blabby, and remorseful day
Is crept into the bosom of the sea.
SHAKESPEARE: *II Henry VI,* IV, *c.* 1591

The weary sun hath made a golden set,
And, by the bright track of his fiery car,
Gives signal of a goodly day tomorrow.
SHAKESPEARE: *Richard III*, V, *c.* 1592

Men shut their doors against a setting sun.
SHAKESPEARE: *Timon of Athens*, I, *c.* 1607

Parting day
Dies like the dolphin, whom each pang imbues
With a new color as it gasps away,
The last still loveliest, till — 'tis gone — and all
is gray. BYRON: *Childe Harold*, IV, 1818

The sun was down,
And all the west was paved with sullen fire,
I cried, " Behold! the barren beach of Hell
At ebb of tide."
ALEXANDER SMITH: *A Life Drama*, 1853

Nobody of any real culture ever talks nowadays about the beauty of the sunset. Sunsets are quite old-fashioned.
OSCAR WILDE: *The Decay of Lying*, 1889

[*See also* Color, Evening, Night, Twilight.

Superannuation

From the age of fifty years they shall cease waiting upon the service [of the tabernacle], and shall serve no more.
NUMBERS VIII, 25, *c.* 700 B.C.

I have made noise enough in the world already, perhaps too much, and am now getting old, and want retirement.
NAPOLEON I: To Barry E. O'Meara at St. Helena, Oct. 1, 1816

My second fixed idea is the uselessness of men above 60 years of age, and the incalculable benefit it would be in commercial, political and professional life if, as a matter of course, men stopped work at this age.
WILLIAM OSLER: Speech in Baltimore, Feb. 22, 1905

Supererogation

[*See* Excess.

Superfluity

Everything that is superfluous will flow out of the mind, like liquid out of a full vessel.
HORACE: *De arte poetica*, *c.* 8 B.C.

The superfluous is very necessary.
VOLTAIRE: *Le mondaine*, 1736

[*See also* Excess.

Superiority

There are three marks of a superior man: being virtuous, he is free from anxiety; being wise, he is free from perplexity; being brave, he is free from fear.
CONFUCIUS: *Analects*, XIV, *c.* 500 B.C.

What the superior man seeks is in him; what the common man seeks is in others.
CONFUCIUS: *Analects*, XV

Superiority is always detested.
BALTASAR GRACIÁN: *The Art of Worldly Wisdom*, VII, 1647

The poorest mechanic, nay, the man who lives upon common alms, gets him his set of admirers, and delights in that superiority which he enjoys over those who are in some respects beneath him.
JOSEPH ADDISON: *The Spectator*, Nov. 10, 1711

Such is the delight of mental superiority that none on whom nature or study have conferred it would purchase the gifts of fortune by its loss.
SAMUEL JOHNSON: *The Rambler*, Aug. 24, 1751

To be loved we must merit but little esteem; all superiority attracts awe and aversion.
C. A. HELVÉTIUS: *De l'esprit*, 1758

Those who think must govern those that toil.
OLIVER GOLDSMITH: *The Traveler*, 1764

There must always be some advantage on one side or the other, and it is better that advantage should be had by talents than by chance.
SAMUEL JOHNSON: *Boswell's Tour to the Hebrides*, Aug. 15, 1773

No two men can be half an hour together but one shall acquire an evident superiority over the other.
SAMUEL JOHNSON: *Boswell's Life*, 1776

I caught sight of a haze upon his face — of that mist which arises invariably from the blissful feeling that one is superior to others.
G. C. LICHTENBERG: *Reflections*, 1799

He who surpasses or subdues mankind,
Must look down on the hate of those below.
BYRON: *Childe Harold*, III, 1816

He alone deserves to have any weight or influence with posterity who has shown himself superior to the particular and predominant error of his own times.
C. C. COLTON: *Lacon*, 1820

Nothing costs us so much as an acknowledgement of superiority, which is always forced from us; and nothing is such relief as any pretense or opportunity afforded us for shaking off the uneasy obligation.
WILLIAM HAZLITT: *The Ruling Passion*, 1829 (The Atlas, Jan. 18)

We can all perceive the difference between ourselves and our inferiors, but when it comes to a question of the difference between us and our superiors we fail to appreciate merits of which we have no proper conceptions.
J. FENIMORE COOPER: *The American Democrat*, XX, 1838

A people is but the attempt of many
To rise to the completer life of one;

And those who live as models for the mass
Are singly of more value than they all.
ROBERT BROWNING: *Luria*, V, 1846

My continual aim has been to show the eternal superiority of some men to others, sometimes even of one man to all others; and to show also the advisability of appointing such persons or person to guide, to lead, or on occasion even to compel and subdue, their inferiors, according to their own better knowledge and wiser will.
JOHN RUSKIN: *Unto This Last*, III, 1862

There are men too superior to be seen except by the few, as there are notes too high for the scale of most ears.
R. W. EMERSON: Lecture on Table-Talk, Boston, Dec. 18, 1864

The one eternal and immutable delight of life is to think, for one reason or another, that we are better than our neighbors. This is why I wrote this book, and this is why it is affording you so much pleasure.
GEORGE MOORE: *Confessions of a Young Man*, XI, 1888

[*See also* Breeding, Civilization, Classes, Comfort, Death, Mediocrity, Monopoly, Nobility, Politeness, Tyranny.

Superman

I teach you the superman. Man is something to be surpassed.
F. W. NIETZSCHE: *Thus Spake Zarathustra*, prologue, 1885

Superstition

When superstition goes religion remains.
CICERO: *De divinatione*, *c.* 78 B.C.

Superstition is a senseless fear of God.
CICERO: *De natura deorum*, I, 45 B.C.

Superstition brings the gods into even the smallest matters.
LIVY: *History of Rome*, XXVII, *c.* 10

Such is the way of all superstition, whether in astrology, dreams, omens, divine judgments, or the like; wherein men, having a delight in such vanities, mark the events where they are fulfilled, but where they fail, though this happen much oftener, neglect and pass them by.
FRANCIS BACON: *Novum Organum*, I, 1620

The greatest burden in the world is superstition, not only of ceremonies in the church, but of imaginary and scarecrow sins at home.
JOHN MILTON: *Doctrine and Discipline of Divorce*, 1633

Superstition is the weakness of the human mind; it is inherent in that mind; it has always been, and always will be.
FREDERICK THE GREAT: *Letter to Voltaire*, Sept. 13, 1766

Superstition is the religion of feeble minds.
EDMUND BURKE: *Reflections on the Revolution in France*, 1790

Superstition is the poetry of life; thus it does not hurt a poet to be superstitious.
J. W. GOETHE: *Maxims*, III, 1790

Most men of education are more superstitious than they admit — nay, than they think.
G. C. LICHTENBERG: *Reflections*, 1799

Superstition is the only religion of which base souls are capable.
JOSEPH JOUBERT: *Pensées*, 1842

The superstition of science scoffs at the superstition of faith.
J. A. FROUDE: *The Lives of the Saints*, 1852 (Eclectic Review)

A superstition is something that has been left to stand over, like unfinished business, from one session of the world's witenagemot to the next.
J. R. LOWELL: *Among My Books*, I, 1870

Superstition is . . . religion which has grown incongruous with intelligence.
JOHN TYNDALL: *Fragments of Science for Unscientific People*, II, 1871

[*See also* Agnostic, Atheism, Atheist, Cause and Effect, Infamy, Paul (St.), Religion.

Supper

Great and late suppers are very offensive to the whole body, especially to the head and eyes, by reason of the multitude of vapors that ascend from the meats that have been plentifully received.
TOBIAS VENNER: *Via Recta*, 1620

If ever I ate a good supper at night,
I dreamed of the Devil, and waked in a fright.
CHRISTOPHER ANSTEY: *The New Bath Guide*, 1766

Who goes to bed supperless tosses all night.
ITALIAN PROVERB

[*See also* Dinner, Exercise, Fasting.

Supply and Demand

Supply-and-demand, — alas! For what noble work was there ever yet any audible demand in that poor sense? The man of Macedonia, speaking in vision to an Apostle Paul, "Come over and help us," did not specify what rate of wages he would give.
THOMAS CARLYLE: *Past and Present*, III, 1843

An object of art creates a public capable of finding pleasure in its beauty. Production, therefore, not only produces an object for the subject, but also a subject for the object.
KARL MARX: *A Critique of Political Economy*, 1859

[*See also* Laissez-faire.

Supreme Court

It is a very dangerous doctrine to consider the judges as the ultimate arbiters of all constitutional questions. It is one which would place us under the despotism of an oligarchy.
THOMAS JEFFERSON: *Letter to W. C. Jarvis,* 1820

I do not think the United States would come to an end if we lost our power to declare an act of Congress void.
O. W. HOLMES II: Speech in New York, Feb. 15, 1913

[*See also* Judiciary.

Sure

It is not sure. (Non constat.) LEGAL MAXIM

Surety

He that is surety for a stranger shall smart for it, and he that hateth suretyship is sure.
PROVERBS XI, 15, *c.* 350 B.C.

He who is surety is never sure.
C. H. SPURGEON: *John Ploughman's Talks,* 1869

Surfeit

They are as sick that surfeit with too much as they that starve with nothing.
SHAKESPEARE: *The Merchant of Venice,* I, *c.* 1597

Surgeon

If a surgeon make a deep incision upon a man with his bronze lancet and cause the man's death, or operate on the eye socket of a man and destroy the man's eye, they shall cut off his hand.
THE CODE OF HAMMURABI, *c.* 2250 B.C.

War is the only proper school of the surgeon.
HIPPOCRATES: *Wounds of the Head, c.* 415 B.C.

A surgeon must have hands well-shaped, with long, small fingers. He must have a body that does not shake, and be of subtle wit.
LANFRANC: *Chirurgia magna,* 1296

Many more surgeons know how to cause supperation than to heal a wound.
HENRI DE MONDEVILLE: *Treatise on Surgery,* 1316

A pitiful surgeon makes a dangerous sore.
JOHN MARSTON: *The Malcontent,* IV, 1604

'Tis the chirurgeon's praise, and height of art,
Not to cut off, but cure the vicious part.
ROBERT HERRICK: *Hesperides,* 1648

A good surgeon must have an eagle's eye, a lion's heart, a lady's hand.
JOHN RAY: *English Proverbs,* 1670

If a man had a sore leg, and he should go to an honest judicious chirurgeon, and he should only bid him keep it warm, and anoint with such an oil (an oil well known) that would do the cure, haply he would not much regard him, because he knows the medicine beforehand an ordinary medicine. But if he should go to a surgeon that should tell him, your leg will gangrene within three days, and it must be cut off, and you will die unless you do something that I could tell you, what listening there would be to this man!
JOHN SELDEN: *Table-Talk,* 1689

The best surgeon is he that has been well hacked himself.
THOMAS FULLER: *Gnomologia,* 1732

A surgeon does not undertake that he will perform a cure, nor does he undertake the highest possible degree of skill: there may be persons who have higher education and greater advantages than he has. But he undertakes to bring a fair, reasonable and competent degree of skill.
LORD CHIEF JUSTICE TINDAL: *Judgment in Lanphier and wife* vs. *Phipos,* 1838

A good surgeon is a good medical man who can cut. Most of the surgeons have forgotten their medicine but go right on cutting.
MARTIN H. FISCHER (1879–)

The surgeon practices on the head of an orphan. MEDIEVAL LATIN PROVERB

[*See also* Cure, Medicine, Physician, Surgery.

Surgery

What drugs cannot heal, the knife can heal; what the knife cannot heal the cautery can heal; what the cautery cannot heal is incurable.
HIPPOCRATES: *Aphorisms, c.* 400 B.C.

All practice is theory; all surgery is practise; ergo, all surgery is theory.
LANFRANC: *Chirurgia magna,* 1296

Th' incurable cut off, the rest reform.
BEN JONSON: *Cynthia's Revels,* V, 1601

Surgery does the ideal thing — it separates the patient from his disease. It puts the patient back to bed and the disease in a bottle.
LOGAN CLENDENING: *Modern Methods of Treatment,* I, 1924

It is not surgery that kills people; it is *delayed* surgery.
Ascribed to W. J. MAYO (1861–1939)

The practice of medicine is a thinker's art, the practice of surgery a plumber's.
MARTIN H. FISCHER (1879–)

Surgery is the cry of defeat in medicine.
IBID.

[*See also* Cure.

Surgery, Plastic

Do you know Doctor Plaster-face? He is the most exquisite in forging of veins, sprightning of eyes, dyeing of hair, sleeking of

skins, blushing of cheeks, surphling of breasts, blanching and bleaching of teeth, that ever made an old lady gracious by torch-light.
JOHN MARSTON: *The Malcontent,* II, 1604
(*Surphle*=a cosmetic)

Surname

[*See* Name.

Surplus

[*See* Wealth.

Surplus Value

[*See* Capitalism.

Surprise

The fool of nature stood with stupid eyes
And gaping mouth, that testified surprise.
JOHN DRYDEN: *Cymon and Iphigenia,* 1699

A wise man is never surprised.
SAMUEL JOHNSON: *The Rambler,* June 26, 1750

You might have knocked me down with a feather.
ENGLISH SAYING, not recorded before the XIX century

[*See also* Laughter.

Surrender

The Guard dies, but never surrenders. (Le garde meurt et ne se rend pas.)
Ascribed to COUNT PIERRE DE CAMBRONNE, commander of a division of the French Old Guard, at Waterloo, June 18, 1815 (The saying is apochryphal and was probably invented by a contemporary war correspondent)

Don't shoot; I'll come down.
Ascribed by David Crockett (1786–1836) to a raccoon treed by a famous Kentucky rifleman

No terms except an unconditional and immediate surrender can be accepted. I propose to move immediately upon your works.
U. S. GRANT: Message to General Simon B. Buckner, C.S.A., at Fort Donelson, Feb. 16, 1862

Survival of the Fittest

[*See* Natural Selection, Struggle for Existence.

Suspense

It is a miserable thing to live in suspense; it is the life of a spider.
JONATHAN SWIFT: *Thoughts on Various Subjects,* 1706

Suspicion

Cæsar's wife should be above suspicion.
JULIUS CÆSAR: On divorcing Pompeia, 62 B.C.

The losing side is always full of suspicion.
PUBLILIUS SYRUS: *Sententiæ, c.* 50 B.C.

Suspicion always haunts the guilty mind.
SHAKESPEARE: *III Henry VI,* V, *c.* 1591

Suspicions amongst thoughts are like bats amongst birds: they ever fly by twilight.
FRANCIS BACON: *Essays,* XXXI, 1612

There is nothing makes a man suspect much more than to know little. IBID.

The virtue of a coward is suspicion.
GEORGE HERBERT: *Jacula Prudentum,* 1651

Suspicion may be no fault, but showing it may be a great one.
THOMAS FULLER: *Gnomologia,* 1732

The less we know the more we suspect.
H. W. SHAW (JOSH BILLINGS): *Josh Billings' Encyclopedia of Wit and Wisdom,* 1874

If you would avoid suspicion do not lace your shoes in a melon field. CHINESE PROVERB

[*See also* Ambition, Husband, Judge.

Swabian

[*See* Liar.

Swallow

One swallow does not make a Spring.
ARISTOTLE: *The Nicomachean Ethics,* I, *c.* 340 B.C.

One swallow does not make a Summer.
ENGLISH PROVERB, familiar since the XVI century (Cf. ARISTOTLE, *ante, c.* 340 B.C.)

When the swallows homeward fly. (Wenn die Schwalben heimwärts ziehn.)
CARL HERLOSSOHN: *Wenn die Schwalben heimwärts ziehn,* 1830

Swallow, my sister, O sister swallow,
How can thine heart be full of the Spring?
A thousand Summers are over and dead,
What hast thou found in the Spring to follow?
What has thou found in thine heart to sing?
A. C. SWINBURNE: *Itylus,* 1866

[*See also* Cat.

Swallowing

It is not easy to blow and to swallow at the same time.
PLAUTUS: *Mostellaria,* II, *c.* 200 B.C.

Swan

He makes a swan-like end,
Fading in music.
SHAKESPEARE: *The Merchant of Venice,* III, *c.* 1597

The dying swan, when years her temples pierce,
In music-strains breathes out her life and verse,
And, chanting her own dirge, tides on her wat'ry hearse.
PHINEAS FLETCHER: *The Purple Island,* I, 1633

The swan, with arched neck
Between her white wings mantling proudly, rows
Her state with oary feet.

JOHN MILTON: *Paradise Lost*, VII, 1667

[*See also* Goose.

Swapping

I do not allow myself to suppose that either the convention or the League have concluded to decide that I am either the greatest or best man in America, but rather they have concluded that it is not best to swap horses crossing the river.

ABRAHAM LINCOLN: Address to a delegation from the National Union League, June 9, 1864

Don't swap barrels going over Niagara.

Slogan ascribed ironically to the Republicans during the Hoover-Roosevelt campaign of 1932

Swearing

Swearing is worse than theft.

ST. JOHN CHRYSOSTOM: *Homilies*, x, *c.* 388

A terrible oath, with a swaggering accent sharply twanged off, gives manhood more approbation than ever proof itself would have earned him.

SHAKESPEARE: *Twelfth Night*, III, *c.* 1601

If at any time, or times, after the end of this present session of Parliament, any person or persons do, or shall, in any stageplay, interlude, show, etc., jestingly or profanely speak or use the Holy Name of God, or of Christ Jesus, or of the Holy Ghost, or of the Trinity, which are not to be spoken but with fear and reverence, he or they shall forfeit for every such offense, by him or them committed, ten pounds.

ACT OF PARLIAMENT, 1606

When a gentleman is disposed to swear, it is not for any standers-by to curtail his oaths.

SHAKESPEARE: *Cymbeline*, II, *c.* 1609

From a child I had but few equals, especially considering my years, which were tender, both for cursing, swearing, lying and blaspheming the holy name of God.

JOHN BUNYAN: *Grace Abounding to the Chief of Sinners*, 1666

Some swear by idols, as by the mass, by our lady, by saints, beasts, birds, and other creatures; but the usual way of our profane ones in England is to swear by God, Christ, faith, and the like.

JOHN BUNYAN: *The Life and Death of Mr. Badman*, 1680

"Our armies swore terribly in Flanders," cried my Uncle Toby, "but nothing to this."

LAURENCE STERNE: *Tristram Shandy*, II, 1760

If any shall be heard to swear, curse, or blaspheme the name of God, the commander is strictly enjoined to punish them for every offense by causing them to wear a wooden collar or some shameful badge, for so long a time as he shall judge proper.

JOHN ADAMS: *Rules for the Regulation of the Navy of the United Colonies*, adopted by the Continental Congress, Nov. 28, 1775

The general is sorry to be informed that the foolish and wicked practice of profane cursing and swearing, a vice heretofore little known in an American army, is growing into fashion. He hopes the officers will, by example as well as influence, endeavor to check it, and that both they and the men will reflect that we can have little hope of the blessing of Heaven on our arms if we insult it by our impiety and folly.

GEORGE WASHINGTON: General Order to the Continental Army, July, 1776

When massa curse, he break no bone.

Quoted as a NEGRO PROVERB by JOHN DAVIS: *Travels of Four Years and a Half in the United States of America*, 1802

As he knew not what to say, he swore.

BYRON: *The Island*, III, 1823

I confess to some pleasure from the stinging rhetoric of a rattling oath in the mouth of truckmen and teamsters. How laconic and brisk it is by the side of a page of the North American Review.

R. W. EMERSON: *Journal*, June 24, 1840

"Now thunder and turf!" Pope Gregory said,
And his hair raised his triple crown right off his head.

R. H. BARHAM: *The Ingoldsby Legends*, II, 1842

Although I didn't shed no tear
Perhaps I cussed a few.

ANON: *Stray Subjects*, 1848

He'd be a much nicer fellow if he had a good swear now and then.

JOHN TYNDALL: Said of Herbert Spencer, *c.* 1870

Though "Bother it" I may
Occasionally say,
I never never use a big, big *D*.

W. S. GILBERT: *H.M.S. Pinafore*, I, 1878

Pointed profanity (this includes the words *God, Lord, Jesus, Christ* — unless used reverently — *hell, s.o.b., damn, Gawd*), or every other profane or vulgar expression, however used is forbidden.

A CODE TO GOVERN THE MAKING OF MOTION AND TALKING PICTURES BY THE MOTION PICTURE PRODUCERS AND DISTRIBUTORS OF AMERICA, INC., V, March 31, 1930

[*See also* Abbot, Blasphemy, Fish, Oath, Sin.

Sweat

In the sweat of thy face shalt thou eat bread.
GENESIS III, 19, *c.* 700 B.C.

They shall not gird themselves with anything that causes sweat.
EZEKIEL XLIV, 18, *c.* 600 B.C.

It is not manly to fear sweat.
SENECA: *Epistulæ morales ad Lucilium*, *c.* 63

His sweat was as it were great drops of blood falling down to the ground.
LUKE XXII, 44, *c.* 75

Falstaff sweats to death
And lards the lean earth as he walks along.
SHAKESPEARE: *I Henry IV*, II, *c.* 1598

Sweats hot as sulphur
Boil through my pores! Affliction hath in store
No torture like to this.
JOHN FORD: *The Broken Heart*, IV, 1633

I see no virtues where I smell no sweat.
FRANCIS QUARLES: *Emblems*, 1635

When excessive perspiration makes it needful to wipe the face, it ought to be done with a handkerchief, and not with the hand, except in the case of extreme necessity; by attending to this, serious inconvenience may be avoided, for the rubbing of the hand on the face may give rise to ringworm, pimples, etc.
ST. JOHN BAPTIST DE LA SALLE: *The Rules of Christian Manners and Civility*, I, 1695

Sweat of the brow; and up from that to sweat of the brain, sweat of the heart; which includes all Kepler calculations, Newton meditations, all sciences, all spoken epics, all acted heroisms, martyrdoms, — up to that "agony of bloody sweat" which all men have called divine.
THOMAS CARLYLE: *Past and Present*, III, 1843

Without sweat and labor no work is brought to perfection. (Absque sudore et labore nullum opus perfectum est.) LATIN PROVERB

[*See also* Labor.

Sweatshop

[*See* Labor.

Swede

[*See* Scandinavian.

Swedenborg, Emanuel (1688–1772)

He is one of the most ingenious, lively, entertaining madmen that ever set pen to paper. But his waking dreams are so wild, so far remote both from Scripture and common sense, that one might as easily swallow the stories of Tom Thumb or Jack the Giant-killer.
JOHN WESLEY: *Journal*, March 19, 1770

One of the missouriums and mastadons of literature, he is not to be measured by whole colleges of ordinary scholars. His stalwart presence would flutter the gowns of an university.
R. W. EMERSON: *Representative Men*, III, 1850

Swedenborgian

The Swedenborgians inform me that they have discovered all that I said in a magazine article, entitled "Mesmeric Revelation," to be absolutely true, although at first they were very strongly inclined to doubt my veracity — a thing which, in that particular instance, I never dreamed of not doubting myself. The story is a pure fiction from beginning to end.
E. A. POE: *Marginalia*, 1844–49

Sweet

I am glad that my Adonis hath a sweet tooth in his head.
JOHN LYLY: *Euphues and His England*, 1580

A surfeit of the sweetest things.
The deepest loathing to the stomach brings.
SHAKESPEARE: *A Midsummer Night's Dream*, II, *c.* 1596

Sweetest nut hath sourest rind.
SHAKESPEARE: *As You Like It*, III, *c.* 1600

Sweets to the sweet.
SHAKESPEARE: *Hamlet*, V, *c.* 1601

He hath not deserved the sweet which hath not tasted the sour.
RICHARD TAVERNER: Tr. of DESIDERIUS ERASMUS: *Adagia* (1508), 1539

Sweet appears sour when we pay.
JAMES HOWELL: *Proverbs*, 1659

Sweet in the on taking, but sour in the off putting.
JAMES KELLY: *Complete Collection of Scottish Proverbs*, 1721

Sweet things are bad for the teeth.
JONATHAN SWIFT: *Polite Conversation*, II, 1738

The rose is red;
  The violet blue;
Sugar is sweet,
  And so are you.
Favorite stanza for autograph albums, *c.* 1875

Sweets stay long in the stomach.
JAPANESE PROVERB

[*See also* Honey, Stolen.

Sweetness

[*See* Culture.

Swift

Too swift arrives as tardy as too slow.
SHAKESPEARE: *Romeo and Juliet*, II, *c.* 1596

Swifter than arrow from the Tartar's bow.
SHAKESPEARE: *A Midsummer Night's Dream*, III, *c.* 1596

[*See also* Chance, Victory.

Swift, Jonathan (1667–1745)

Good God! What a genius I had when I wrote that book.
JONATHAN SWIFT, in his old age, *c.* 1740, on *A Tale of a Tub*, 1704

Dean Swift was so intoxicated with the love of flattery that he sought it amongst the lowest of people, and the silliest of women; and was never so well pleased with any companions as those that worshipped him, while he insulted them.
MARY WORTLEY MONTAGU: *Letter to the Countess of Bute*, 1752

Swift has a higher reputation than he deserves. His excellence is strong sense; his humor, though very well, is not remarkably good.
SAMUEL JOHNSON: *Boswell's Life*, July 28, 1763

He had a countenance sour and severe, which he seldom softened by any appearance of gaiety. He stubbornly resisted any tendency to laughter.
SAMUEL JOHNSON: *Lives of the Poets* (Swift), 1778

Swift was *anima Rabelaisii habitans in sicco* — the soul of Rabelais dwelling in a dry place.
S. T. COLERIDGE: *Table-Talk*, June 15, 1830

Swimming

I can swim like a duck.
SHAKESPEARE: *The Tempest*, II, 1611

Good swimmers are oftenest drowned.
THOMAS FULLER: *Gnomologia*, 1732

Mother, may I go out to swim?
Yes, my darling daughter;
Hang your clothes on a hickory limb,
But don't go near the water.
Author unidentified

Swinburne, A. C. (1837–1909)

Having read Mr. Swinburne's defence of his prurient poetics, Punch hereby gives him his royal license to change his name to what is evidently its true form — Swine-born.
Anon.: *Review of Poems and Ballads in Punch*, 1866

The fleshly school.
ROBERT BUCHANAN: In the Contemporary Review, Oct., 1871 (Applied to Swinburne, William Morris, D. G. Rossetti and others)

I attempt to describe Mr. Swinburne; and lo! the Bacchanal screams, the sterile Dolores sweats, serpents dance, men and women wrench, wriggle, and form in an endless alliteration of heated and meaningless words, the veriest garbage of Baudelaire flowered over with the epithets of the Della Cruscans.
IBID.

Words in his hands are like the ivory balls of a juggler, and all words seem to be in his hands.
E. C. STEDMAN: *The Victorian Poets*, 1875

[*See also* Baudelaire (Charles).

Swine

[*See* Hog, Pearl, Pig.

Swiss

The Swiss are more martial than their neighbors, and in consequence more free.
NICCOLÒ MACHIAVELLI: *The Prince*, XII, 1513

No money, no Swiss.
JEAN RACINE: *Les plaideurs*, I, 1668

The Swiss are offended at being called gentlemen.
BLAISE PASCAL: *Pensées*, V, 1670

The Swiss are a grave people.
VOLTAIRE: *Letter to M. Bertrand*, Jan. 8, 1764

[*See also* Law.

Switzerland

Half of Switzerland is Hell, but the other half is Paradise.
VOLTAIRE: *Letter to James Marriott*, Feb. 26, 1767

I look upon Switzerland as an inferior sort of Scotland.
SYDNEY SMITH: *Letter to Lord Holland*, 1815

Switzerland is a curst, selfish, swinish country of brutes, placed in the most romantic region of the world.
BYRON: *Letter to Thomas Moore*, Sept. 19, 1821

In Switzerland what a pale historic coloring; what a penury of relics and monuments! I pined for a cathedral or a gallery.
HENRY JAMES: *At Isella*, 1871 (Galaxy, Aug.)

Sword

The sword is the protector of all. (Omnis in ferro est salus.)
SENECA: *Hercules Furens*, *c.* 50

I came not to send peace, but a sword.
MATTHEW X, 34, *c.* 75

All they that take the sword shall perish with the sword.
MATTHEW XXVI, 52

He that striketh with the sword shall be stricken with the scabbard.
JOHN HEYWOOD: *Proverbs*, 1546

Cowards and faint-hearted runaways
Look for oration when the foe is near;

Our swords shall play the orator for us.
CHRISTOPHER MARLOWE: *I Tamburlaine*, I, *c.* 1588

A valiant man's look is more than a coward's sword.
GEORGE HERBERT: *Outlandish Proverbs*, 1640

In choosing a wife and buying a sword we ought not to trust to another. IBID.

One sword keeps another in its sheath. IBID.

The sword is the weapon of the brave.
NAPOLEON I: To Gaspard Gourgaud at St. Helena, 1815–1818

King Arthur's sword, Excalibur,
Wrought by the lonely maiden of the lake.
Nine years she wrought it, sitting in the deeps
Upon the hidden bases of the hills.
ALFRED TENNYSON: *Mort d'Arthur*, 1842

[*See also* Peace, Pen, Preparedness, War and Peace.

Sycophant

Whosoever is king, thou shalt be his man.
THOMAS FULLER: *Gnomologia*, 1732

The beadle always agrees with the rector.
FRENCH PROVERB

Syllable

Syllables govern the world.
EDWARD COKE: *Institutes*, I, 1628

The ponderous syllables, like sullen waves
In the half-glutted hollows of reef-rocks
Came booming thus.
JOHN KEATS: *Hyperion*, II, 1819

[*See also* Philologist.

Symbol

[*See* Thinking.

Symmetry

The beauty of a face is not known by the eye or nose; it consists in a symmetry, and 'tis the comparative faculty which votes it.
JOSEPH GLANVILL: *The Vanity of Dogmatizing*, VII, 1661

Sympathy

As man laughs with those that laugh, so he weeps with those that weep; if thou wish me to weep, thou must first shed tears thyself; then thy sorrows will touch me.
HORACE: *De arte poetica*, *c.* 8 B.C.

Rejoice with them that do rejoice, and weep with them that weep.
ROMANS XII, 15, *c.* 55

Remember them that are in bonds, as bound with them; and them which suffer adversity, as being yourselves also in the body.
HEBREWS XIII, 3, *c.* 65

We are so fond of each other because our ailments are the same.
JONATHAN SWIFT: *Journal to Stella*, Feb. 1, 1710

When we read of torments, wounds, death, and the like dismal accidents, our pleasure does not flow so properly from the grief which such melancholy descriptions give us, as from the secret comparison which we make between ourselves and the person who suffers.
JOSEPH ADDISON: *The Spectator*, June 30, 1712

Dear honest Ned is in the gout,
Lies rack'd with pain, and you without:
How patiently you hear him groan!
How glad the case is not your own!
JONATHAN SWIFT: *On the Death of Dr. Swift*, 1731

Teach me to feel another's woe,
To hide the fault I see:
That mercy I to others show,
That mercy show to me.
ALEXANDER POPE: *The Universal Prayer*, 1738

Large was his bounty, and his soul sincere,
Heav'n did a recompense as largely send:
He gave to mis'ry all he had, a tear,
He gain'd from Heav'n ('twas all he wish'd) a friend.
THOMAS GRAY: *Elegy Written in a Country Churchyard*, 1750

When we see a stroke aimed and just ready to fall upon the leg or arm of another person we naturally shrink and draw back our own leg or our own arm, and when it does fall we feel it in some measure, and are hurt by it as well as the sufferer.
ADAM SMITH: *The Theory of Moral Sentiments*, I, 1759

A man may sympathize with a woman in childbed, though it is impossible he should conceive himself suffering her pains in his own proper person and character.
ADAM SMITH: *The Theory of Moral Sentiments*, VII

Our sympathy is cold to the relation of distant misery.
EDWARD GIBBON: *The Decline and Fall of the Roman Empire*, III, 1781

But why should I for others groan,
When none will sigh for me?
BYRON: *Childe Harold*, I, 1812

For compassion a human heart suffices; but for full, adequate sympathy with joy, an angel's.
S. T. COLERIDGE: *Notebooks*, 1817

No one really understands the grief or joy of another. We always imagine that we are approaching some other, but our lines of travel are actually parallel.
FRANZ SCHUBERT: *Diary*, March 27, 1824

I am sitting opposite a person who is making strange distortions with the gout, which is not unpleasant — to me at least. What is the reason we do not sympathize with pain, short of some terrible surgical operation?
CHARLES LAMB: *Letter to Bernard Barton*, April, 1824

What is more harmful than any vice? Practical sympathy for the botched and the weak — Christianity.
F. W. NIETZSCHE: *The Antichrist*, II, 1888

[*See also* Crowd, Laughter.

Symptom

[*See* Disease.

Synagogue

He who spits at the synagogue spits into the pupil of his own eye. HEBREW PROVERB

[*See also* Churches.

Synonym

Many words in every language are generally thought to be synonymous; but those who study the language attentively will find that there is no such thing; they will discover some little difference, some distinction between all those words that are vulgarly called synonymous; one hath always more energy, extent, or delicacy, than another.
LORD CHESTERFIELD: *Letter to his son*, March 16, 1752

Syrian

[*See* Cheating.

T

Taciturnity

He that hath knowledge spareth his words.
PROVERBS XVII, 27, *c.* 350 B.C.

Let thy words be few.
ECCLESIASTES V, 2, *c.* 200 B.C.

Men of few words are the best men.
SHAKESPEARE: *Henry V*, III, *c.* 1599

Give every man thine ear, but few thy voice.
SHAKESPEARE: *Hamlet*, I, *c.* 1601

Suffer thy legs, but not thy tongue to walk:
God, the most wise, is sparing of His talk.
ROBERT HERRICK: *Noble Numbers*, 1647

Who knows most speaks least.
GIOVANNI TORRIANO: *Italian Proverbs*, 1666

Speak little, do much.
BENJAMIN FRANKLIN: *Poor Richard's Almanac*, 1755

In case of doubt, it is better to say too little than too much.
THOMAS JEFFERSON: *Letter to George Washington*, 1791

One learns taciturnity best among people who have none, and loquacity among the taciturn.
JEAN PAUL RICHTER: *Hesperus*, XII, 1795

[*See also* Mouth, Silence, Talk, Tongue.

Tacitus (c. 55–120)

Tacitus seems to me rather to have made notes for an historical work than to have written a history. SAMUEL JOHNSON: *Boswell's Life*, April 15, 1772

Tact

'Tis ill talking of halters in the house of a man that was hanged.
CERVANTES: *Don Quixote*, I, 1605

Without tact you can learn nothing. Tact teaches you when to be silent. Inquirers who are always inquiring never learn anything.
BENJAMIN DISRAELI: *Endymion*, LXI, 1880

To have the reputation of possessing the most perfect social tact, talk to every woman as if you loved her, and to every man as if he bored you.
OSCAR WILDE: *A Woman of No Importance*, III, 1893

Women and foxes, being weak, are distinguished by superior tact.
AMBROSE BIERCE: *Collected Works*, VIII, 1911

Everything is pardoned save want of tact.
FRENCH PROVERB

Tail

The *os coccyx* in man, though functionless as a tail, plainly represents this part in other vertebrate animals. At an early embryonic period it is free and projects beyond the lower extremities.
CHARLES DARWIN: *The Descent of Man*, I, 1871

Nothing is so hard to skin as the tail.
FRENCH PROVERB

[*See also* Cat, Devil, Fox, Head.

Tailor

It takes nine tailors to make a man.
ENGLISH PROVERB, apparently borrowed from the French, *c.* 1600 (Apperson shows that, until the end of the century, there was some uncertainty about the number. In JOHN WEBSTER and THOMAS DEKKER: *Westward Ho*, II, 1605, it appeared as three)

Never trust a tailor that does not sing at his work.
BEAUMONT and FLETCHER: *The Knight of the Burning Pestle*, II, 1609

The tailor makes the man.
BEN JONSON: *The Staple of News*, I, 1625

There's knavery in all trades, but most in tailors.
ROGER L'ESTRANGE: Tr. of ÆSOP: *Fables*, 1692

[*See also* Cheating, Sitting, Thief.

Tale

An honest tale speeds best, being plainly told.
SHAKESPEARE: *Richard III*, IV, *c.* 1592

A tale which holdeth children from play, and old men from the chimney corner.
PHILIP SIDNEY: *Apologie for Poetrie*, 1598

And thereby hangs a tale.
SHAKESPEARE: *As You Like It*, II, *c.* 1600

I could a tale unfold whose lightest word
Would harrow up thy soul, freeze thy young blood,
Make thy two eyes, like stars, start from their spheres,
Thy knotted and combined locks to part
And each particular hair to stand on end,
Like quills upon the fretful portentine.
SHAKESPEARE: *Hamlet*, I, *c.* 1601
(*Portentine*=porcupine)

Tush! These are trifles, and mere old wives' tales.
CHRISTOPHER MARLOWE: *Dr. Faustus*, V, 1604

I will a round unvarnish'd tale deliver.
SHAKESPEARE: *Othello*, I, 1604

Every shepherd tells his tale
Under the hawthorn in the vale.
JOHN MILTON: *L'Allegro*, 1632

A tale never loses in the telling.
JAMES KELLY: *Complete Collection of Scottish Proverbs*, 1721

What so tedious as a twice-told tale?
ALEXANDER POPE: Tr. of HOMER: *Odyssey*, XII, 1726

I cannot tell how the truth may be;
I say the tale as 'twas said to me.
WALTER SCOTT: *The Lay of the Last Minstrel*, II, 1805

A schoolboy's tale, the wonder of an hour.
BYRON: *Childe Harold*, II, 1812

Half a tale is enough for a wise man.
SCOTTISH PROVERB

It's a dry tale that doesna end in a drink.
IBID.

[*See also* Fiction, Story.

Talebearer

Thou shalt not go up and down as a talebearer among thy people.
LEVITICUS XIX, 16, *c.* 700 B.C.

Where no wood is, there the fire goeth out: so where there is no talebearer, the strife ceaseth.
PROVERBS XXVI, 20, *c.* 350 B.C.

The words of a talebearer are as wounds, and they go down into the innermost parts of the belly.
PROVERBS XXVI, 22

Beware of him that telleth tales.
Anon.: *The Proverbs of Wisdom*, *c.* 1450

Talebearers are just as bad as talemakers.
R. B. SHERIDAN: *The School for Scandal*, I, 1777

[*See also* Gossip.

Talent

Every man hath his proper gift of God, one after this manner, and another after that.
I CORINTHIANS V, 7, *c.* 55

No one respects a talent that is concealed.
DESIDERIUS ERASMUS: *Adagia*, 1508

There are some bad qualities which make great talents.
LA ROCHEFOUCAULD: *Maxims*, 1665

Let us not overstrain our talents, for if we do we shall do nothing with grace; a clown, whatever he may do, will never pass for a gentleman.
JEAN DE LA FONTAINE: *Fables*, IV, 1668

Talent is a gift which God has given us secretly, and which we reveal without perceiving it.
C. L. DE MONTESQUIEU: *Pensées*, *c.* 1750

By different methods different men excel,
But where is he who can do all things well?
CHARLES CHURCHILL: *Epistle to William Hogarth*, 1763

Talents are best nurtured in solitude; but character is best formed in the stormy billows of the world.
J. W. GOETHE: *Torquato Tasso*, I, 1790

If every man stuck to his talent the cows would be well tended.
J. P. DE FLORIAN: *Fables*, 1792

What is talent? Reason manifested gloriously.
M. J. DE CHÉNIER: *Épître à Voltaire*, 1806

The talent sucks the substance of the man.
R. W. EMERSON: *The Superlative*, 1847

Every natural power exhilarates; a true talent delights the possessor first.
R. W. EMERSON: *The Scholar*, 1876

Talent is commonly developed at the expense of character, and the greater it grows, the more is the mischief and misleading.
IBID.

The tools to him who has the ability to handle them.
FRENCH PROVERB

Talent without sense is a torch in folly's hand.
WELSH PROVERB

[*See also* Ability, Actor, Aristocracy, Capacity, Democracy, Industry, Obscurity, Solitude, Success, Superiority, Talent and Genius.

Talent and Genius

Between genius and talent there is the proportion of the whole to its part.
JEAN DE LA BRUYÈRE: *Caractères*, XII, 1688

Genius must have talent as its complement and implement, just as in like manner imagination must have fancy. In short, the higher intellectual powers can only act through a corresponding energy of the lower.
S. T. COLERIDGE: *Table-Talk*, Aug. 20, 1833

Talent finds its models, methods, and ends in society, exists for exhibition, and goes to the soul only for power to work. Genius is its own end, and draws its means and the style of its architecture from within.
R. W. EMERSON: *The Method of Nature*, 1841 (Address at Waterville College, Maine, Aug. 11)

To do what is impossible to talent is the mark of genius.
H. F. AMIEL: *Journal*, Oct. 27, 1856

Genius does what it must, and talent does what it can.
E. R. BULWER-LYTTON (OWEN MEREDITH): *Last Words*, 1860 (Cornhill Magazine, Nov.)

Talent is that which is in a man's power; genius is that in whose power a man is.
J. R. LOWELL: *Among My Books*, I, 1870

How many young geniuses we have known, and none but ourselves will ever hear of them for want in them of a little talent!
R. W. EMERSON: *The Scholar*, 1876

Genius knows better than talent how to hide its barrel-organ. Yet it too can only play its seven old pieces over and over again.
F. W. NIETZSCHE: *Human All-too-Human*, II, 1878

Genius is the talent of dead men.
Author unidentified

Talent is an infinite capacity for imitating genius. IBID.

[*See also* Genius, Talent.

Talk

Should a wise man utter vain knowledge, and fill his belly with the east wind?
JOB XV, 2, *c.* 325 B.C.

Let your speech be alway with grace, seasoned with salt, that ye may know how ye ought to answer every man.
COLOSSIANS VI, 6, *c.* 60

He who talks too much commits a sin.
THE TALMUD (*Pirké Aboth*), *c.* 200

Talkers are no good doers.
SHAKESPEARE: *Richard III*, I, *c.* 1592

Every time the sheep bleats it loses a mouthful.
ENGLISH PROVERB, apparently borrowed from the Italian and familiar since the XVII century

If I chance to talk a little wild, forgive me;
I had it from my father.
SHAKESPEARE and JOHN FLETCHER: *Henry VIII*, I, 1613

The red wine first must rise
In their fair cheeks, my lord; then we shall have 'em
Talk us to silence. IBID.

He that talketh what he knoweth will also talk what he knoweth not.
FRANCIS BACON: *Essays*, VI, 1625

Whom the disease of talking once possesseth, he can never hold his peace. Rather than he will not discourse, he will hire men to hear him. BEN JONSON: *Discoveries*, *c.* 1635

When talking, be as brief as if you were making your will; the fewer the words the less litigation.
BALTASAR GRACIÁN: *The Art of Worldly Wisdom*, CLX, 1647

Then he will talk — good gods, how he will talk!
NATHANIEL LEE: *The Rival Queens*, I, 1677

I will talk of things heavenly, or things earthly; things moral, or things evangelical: things sacred, or things profane; things past, or things to come; things foreign, or things at home; things more essential, or things circumstantial.
JOHN BUNYAN: *Pilgrim's Progress*, I, 1678

But far more numerous was the herd of such
Who think too little and who talk too much.
JOHN DRYDEN: *Absalom and Achitophel*, I, 1682

Who talks much must talk in vain.
JOHN GAY: *Fables*, intro., 1727

Men like to talk of what they love.
THOMAS FULLER: *Gnomologia*, 1732

People who have little to do are great talkers. The less we think the more we talk; thus women talk more than men; from laziness they are not inclined to think. A nation where women set the fashion is a nation of talkers.
C. L. DE MONTESQUIEU: *Pensées*, *c.* 1750

They would talk of nothing but high life, and high-lived company, and other fashionable topics, such as pictures, taste, Shakespeare, and the musical glasses.
OLIVER GOLDSMITH: *The Vicar of Wakefield*, 1766

Women cure all their sorrows by talking.
JEAN PAUL RICHTER: *Hesperus*, XVI, 1795

Talk is cheap.
ENGLISH PROVERB, apparently not current before the XIX century

Both Americans and English are subject to loquacious imbecility. Their subjects only differ. The American talks of his government, the Englishman of himself.
JOHN DAVIS: *Travels of Four Years and a Half in the United States of America*, II, 1802

Where all are talkers, and where none can teach.
GEORGE CRABBE: *The Parish Register*, I, 1807

Talking is like playing on the harp; there is as much in laying the hands on the strings to stop their vibrations as in twanging them to bring out their music.
O. W. HOLMES: *The Autocrat of the Breakfast-Table*, I, 1858

Better things are said, more incisive, more wit and insight are dropped in talk and forgotten by the speaker, than get into books.
R. W. EMERSON: Lecture on Table-Talk, Boston, Dec. 18, 1864

Talk that does not end in any kind of action is better suppressed altogether.
THOMAS CARLYLE: Inaugural address in Edinburgh, 1866

" The time has come," the Walrus said,
" To talk of many things:
Of shoes — and ships — and sealing-wax —
Of cabbages — and kings —
And why the sea is boiling hot —
And whether pigs have wings."
C. L. DODGSON (LEWIS CARROLL): *Through the Looking-Glass*, III, 1871

Big talk won't boil de pot.
AMERICAN NEGRO SAYING

Great talker, great liar. (Grand parleur, grand menteur.)
FRENCH PROVERB

It's no use talking. (Es gibt gar kein Use dass Man talken tut.)
PENNSYLVANIA DUTCH SAYING

Women are nine times more talkative than men.
YIDDISH PROVERB

[*See also* Accent, Marriage, Meat, Speaking, Taciturnity.

Tall

God is proud of those who are tall.
THE TALMUD (*Bechoroth*), *c.* 200

Long be thy legs, and short be thy life.
JOHN HEYWOOD: *Proverbs*, 1546

If long, she is lazy; if little, she is loud.
JOHN FLORIO: *Second Frutes*, 1591

While the tall maid is stooping the little one sweeps the house.
ENGLISH PROVERB, current since the XVII century

My Lord St. Albans said that wise nature did never put her precious jewels into a garret four stories high; and therefore that exceeding tall men had ever very empty heads.
FRANCIS BACON: *Apothegms*, 1624

A daughter of the gods, divinely tall,
And most divinely fair.
ALFRED TENNYSON: *A Dream of Fair Women*, 1833

[*See also* Hero, Short.

Talleyrand, C. M. de (1754–1838)

Talleyrand was the vilest of the jobbers; a corrupt man without opinion, but a man of genius.
NAPOLEON I: To Barry E. O'Meara at St. Helena, Aug. 25, 1817

[*See also* Statesman.

Tammany Hall

Tammany Hall bears the same relation to a penitentiary as a Sunday-school to the church.
R. G. INGERSOLL: Speech in Indianapolis, Sept. 21, 1876

Tar-and-feathers

A robber convicted of theft shall be shorn like a hired fighter, and boiling tar shall be poured over his head, and feathers from a pillow shall be shaken out over his head.
Laws of Richard Couer de Lion for the crusaders of the Third Crusade, 1189

Tarred and feathered and carried on a cart
By the women of Marblehead.
J. G. WHITTIER: *Skipper Ireson's Ride*, 1857 (Atlantic Monthly, Dec.)

[*See also* Boston.

Tariff

I hope a crusade will be kept up against the duty on books until those in power shall become sensible of this stain on our legislation, and shall wipe it from their code, and from the remembrance of man, if possible.
THOMAS JEFFERSON: *Letter to Jared Sparks*, 1824

We demand that all custom-house taxation shall be only for revenue.
Democratic National Platform, 1876

The tariff is a local issue.
W. S. HANCOCK: Speech during his campaign for the Presidency, 1880

It is beyond the sphere of true governmental power to tax one man to help the business of another. It is taking money from one to give it to another. This is robbery, nothing more nor less.
FRANK H. HURD: Speech in the House of Representatives, Feb. 18, 1881

We demand that the imposition of duties on foreign imports shall be made, not "for revenue only," but so to afford security to our

diversified industries and protection to the rights and wages of the laborer.
Republican National Platform, 1884

Tariff regulation by treaty diminishes that independent control over its own revenues which is essential for the safety and welfare of any government.
GROVER CLEVELAND: Message to Congress, Dec. 8, 1885

The protective system must be maintained. Its abandonment has always been followed by general disaster to all interests, except those of the usurer and the sheriff.
Republican National Platform, 1888

The Federal government has no constitutional power to impose and collect tariff duties, except for the purposes of revenue only.
Democratic National Platform, 1892

We believe that on all imports coming into competition with the products of American labor there should be levied duties equal to the difference between wages abroad and at home.
Republican National Platform, 1892

Tariff laws should be amended by putting the products of trusts upon the free list, to prevent monopoly under the plea of protection.
Democratic National Platform, 1900

I believe in the protective tariff policy, and know we will be calling for its saving Americanism again.
WARREN G. HARDING: Speech of acceptance, July 22, 1920

We advocate a competitive tariff for revenue, with a fact-finding tariff commission free from executive interference, reciprocal tariff agreements with other nations, and an international economic conference designed to restore international trade and facilitate exchange.
Democratic National Platform, 1932

The American farmer is entitled not only to tariff schedules on his products but to protection from substitutes therefor.
Republican National Platform, 1932

Tartar

A Tartar does not eat pig, because he is a pig himself.
RUSSIAN PROVERB

[*See also* Russian.

Taste

Every man as he loveth, quoth the good man when he kissed the cow.
JOHN HEYWOOD: *Proverbs*, 1546

At table, I prefer the witty before the grave; in bed, beauty before goodness; and in common discourse, eloquence, whether or no there be sincerity.
MICHEL DE MONTAIGNE: *Essays*, I, 1580

The fairest ladies like the blackest men.
BEAUMONT and FLETCHER: *Love's Cure*, III, *c.* 1610

There's scarce a man amongst a thousand found
But hath his imperfection: one distastes
The scent of roses, which to infinites
Most pleasing is and odoriferous.
THOMAS MIDDLETON and WILLIAM ROWLEY: *The Changeling*, I, *c.* 1623

He who would deny that honey is sweet, because it appears not so to men of a distempered taste, would be wrong.
HUGO GROTIUS: *De jure belli ac pacis*, I, 1625

It is the special privilege of good taste to enjoy everything at its ripest.
BALTASAR GRACIÁN: *The Art of Worldly Wisdom*, XXXIX, 1647

Many men, many tastes.
BALTASAR GRACIÁN: *The Art of Worldly Wisdom*, CI

Bad taste springs from lack of knowledge.
BALTASAR GRACIÁN: *The Art of Worldly Wisdom*, CCLXX

There is such a thing as a general revolution which changes the taste of men as it changes the fortunes of the world.
LA ROCHEFOUCAULD: *Maxims*, 1665

Some love the meat, some love to pick a bone.
JOHN BUNYAN: *Pilgrim's Progress*, I, 1678

Between good sense and good taste there is the difference between cause and effect.
JEAN DE LA BRUYÈRE: *Caractères*, XII, 1688

To him that has a bad taste sweet is bitter.
THOMAS FULLER: *Gnomologia*, 1732

What, then is taste? A discerning sense
Of decent and sublime, with quick disgust
From things deformed, or disarranged, or gross
In species.
MARK AKENSIDE: *The Pleasures of Imagination*, III, 1744

Some like it hot,
Some like it cold,
Some like it in the pot,
Nine days old.
Anon.: *Nursery rhyme*, *c.* 1750

The cause of a wrong taste is a defect of judgment.
EDMUND BURKE: *The Sublime and Beautiful*, intro., 1756

There is rather less difference upon matters of taste among mankind than upon most of those which depend upon the naked reason; and men are far better agreed on the excellence of a description in Virgil than on the truth or falsehood of a theory of Aristotle.
IBID.

Could we teach taste or genius by rules, they would be no longer taste and genius.
JOSHUA REYNOLDS: *Discourses*, III, 1770 (Lecture at the Royal Academy, London, Dec. 14)

Taste cannot be controlled by law.
THOMAS JEFFERSON: *Notes on a Money Unit*, 1784

No one ever thinks of how much pain every man of taste has had to suffer before he gives any.
ANTOINE RIVAROL: *Petit almanac*, 1788

Genius creates, and taste preserves. Taste is the good sense of genius; without taste, genius is only sublime folly.
F. A. R. DE CHATEAUBRIAND: *Le génie du Christianisme*, 1802

Taste is nothing but a delicate good sense.
M. J. DE CHÉNIER: *Épître à Voltaire*, 1806

His taste was gorgeous, but it still was taste.
GEORGE CRABBE: *Tales*, II (The Gentleman Farmer), 1812

A man's palate can, in time, become accustomed to anything.
NAPOLEON I: To Gaspard Gourgaud at St. Helena, 1815–1818

Those who seem to lead the public taste are, in general, merely outrunning it in the direction which it is spontaneously pursuing.
T. B. MACAULAY: *John Dryden*, 1828 (Edinburgh Review, Jan.)

Taste is the instinctive and instant preferring of one material object to another without any obvious reason, except that it is proper to human nature in its perfection so to do.
JOHN RUSKIN: *Modern Painters*, I, 1843

All liquors are not for every one's liking.
H. G. BOHN: *Handbook of Proverbs*, 1855

Our purity of taste is best tested by its universality, for if we can only admire this thing or that, we may be sure that our cause for liking is of a finite and false nature.
JOHN RUSKIN: *Modern Painters*, III, 1856

What France admires is good enough for France. J. G. SAXE: *The Money-King*, 1860

I have never heard any of your lectures, but from what I can learn I should say that for people who like the kind of lectures you deliver, they are just the kind of lectures such people like.
C. F. BROWNE (ARTEMUS WARD): Letter of recommendation ascribed (humorously) to ABRAHAM LINCOLN, *c.* 1863

Now, who shall arbitrate?
Ten men love what I hate,
Shun what I follow, slight what I receive.
ROBERT BROWNING: *Rabbi Ben Ezra*, 1864

Taste is not only a part and an index of morality – it is the only morality. The first, and last, and closest trial questions to any living creature is, "What do you like?" Tell me what you like, and I'll tell you what you are.
JOHN RUSKIN: *The Crown of Wild Olive*, II, 1866

It is only an auctioneer who can equally and impartially admire all schools of art.
OSCAR WILDE: *The Critic as Artist*, 1891

To enjoy is, as it were, to create; to understand is a form of equality, and the full use of taste is an act of genius.
JOHN LA FARGE: *Considerations on Painting*, 1895

Taste . . . is essentially a matter of tradition. No one originates his own. Of the many instances in which mankind is wiser than any man it is one of the chief.
W. C. BROWNELL: *Standards*, I, 1916

Every man to his own poison.
AMERICAN PROVERB

Everyone to his taste. (Chacun à son gout.)
FRENCH PROVERB

There is no disputing about taste. (De gustibus non disputandum.) LATIN PROVERB

[*See also* Ages, Criticism, Dress, Faculty, Genius, Golden Rule, Greatness, Hunger, Imagination, Poetry, Standard.

Tavern

The next places that are filled, after the playhouses be emptied, are, or ought to be, taverns.
THOMAS DEKKER: *The Gull's Hornbook*, VI, 1609

What things have we seen
Done at the Mermaid! Heard words that have been
So nimble, and so full of subtle flame
As if that every one from whence they came
Had meant to put his whole wit in a jest,
And had resolved to live a fool the rest
Of his dull life.
FRANCIS BEAUMONT: *To Ben Jonson*, *c.* 1610

A tavern is a little Sodom, where as many vices are daily practised as ever were known in the great one.
THOMAS BROWNE: *Talks Round London*, *c.* 1700

There is no private house in which people can enjoy themselves so well as at a capital tavern.
SAMUEL JOHNSON: *Boswell's Life*, March 21, 1776

Souls of poets dead and gone,
What Elysium have ye known,
Happy field or mossy cavern,
Choicer than the Mermaid tavern?
JOHN KEATS: *Lines on the Mermaid Tavern*, 1819

The tavern will compare favorably with the church. H. D. THOREAU: *Excursions,* 1863

[*See also* Ale-house, Inn.

Taxes

Joseph made it a law over the land of Egypt unto this day, that Pharaoh should have the fifth part. GENESIS XLVII, 26, *c.* 700 B.C.

He exacted the silver and the gold of the people of the land, of everyone according to his taxation, to give it unto Pharaoh-nechoh. II KINGS XXIII, 35, *c.* 500 B.C.

There went out a decree from Cæsar Augustus that all the world should be taxed. LUKE II, 1, *c.* 75

It is against the franchises of the land for freemen to be taxed but by their consent in Parliament. EDWARD COKE: *Institutes,* II, 1642

What reason is there that he which laboreth much, and, sparing the fruits of his labor, consumeth little, should be more charged than he that, living idly, getteth little and spendeth all he gets, seeing the one hath no more protection from the commonwealth than the other? THOMAS HOBBES: *Leviathan,* II, 1651

The art of taxation consists in so plucking the goose as to obtain the largest amount of feathers with the least possible amount of hissing. Ascribed to J. B. COLBERT (1619–83), *c.* 1665

Levying money for or to the use of the Crown, by pretense of prerogative, without grant of Parliament, for longer time or in other manner than the same is or shall be granted, is illegal. THE ENGLISH BILL OF RIGHTS, IV, Dec., 1689

In constitutional states liberty is compensation for the heavy taxation; in despotic states the equivalent of liberty is light taxes. C. L. DE MONTESQUIEU: *The Spirit of the Laws,* XIII, 1748

When plunder bears the name of impost fortitude is intimidated and wisdom confounded: resistance shrinks from an alliance with rebellion, and the villain remains secure in the robes of the magistrate. SAMUEL JOHNSON: *The Rambler,* Aug. 17, 1751

What is't to us if taxes rise or fall?
Thanks to our fortune, we pay none at all. CHARLES CHURCHILL: *Night,* 1762

Taxation and representation are inseparably united. God hath joined them; no British Parliament can put them asunder. CHARLES PRATT (LORD CAMDEN): Speech in the House of Lords, 1765

That it is inseparably essential to the freedom of a people and the undoubted right of Englishmen that no taxes be imposed on them but with their own consent, given personally, or by their representatives. Resolution of delegates from nine American Colonies, New York, 1765

We cannot be happy without being free; we cannot be free without being secure in our property; we cannot be secure in our property if, without our consent, others may, as by right, take it away; taxes imposed on us by Parliament do thus take it away. JOHN DICKINSON: *Letter from a Farmer in Pennsylvania to the Inhabitants of the British Colonies,* 1767

To tax and to please, no more than to love and to be wise, is not given to men. EDMUND BURKE: *On American Taxation,* 1774

The less is included in the greater. That power which can take away life, may seize upon property. SAMUEL JOHNSON: Address to the Electors of Great Britain, 1774

A tax is a payment exacted by authority from part of the community for the benefit of the whole. SAMUEL JOHNSON: *Taxation No Tyranny,* 1775

The subjects of every state ought to contribute towards the support of the government, as nearly as possible, in proportion to their respective abilities; that is, in proportion to the revenue which they respectively enjoy under the protection of the state. ADAM SMITH: *The Wealth of Nations,* II, 1776

A common contribution being necessary for the support of the public force, and for defraying the other expenses of government, it ought to be divided equally among the members of the community, according to their abilities. Declaration of the Rights of Man, by the French National Assembly, XIII, 1789

In this world nothing is certain but death and taxes. BENJAMIN FRANKLIN: *Letter to M. Leroy,* 1789

The tendency of taxation is to create a class of persons who do not labor, to take from those who do labor the produce of that labor, and to give it to those who do not labor. WILLIAM COBBETT: *Paper Against Gold,* 1811

Taxes should be continued by annual or biennial reënactments, because a constant hold, by the nation, of the strings of the public purse is a salutary restraint from which an honest government ought not to wish, nor a corrupt one to be permitted to be free. THOMAS JEFFERSON: *Letter to J. W. Eppes,* Sept., 1813

Taxation under every form presents but a choice of evils; if it does not act on profit, or other sources of income, it must act on expenditures.

DAVID RICARDO: *Principles of Political Economy*, IX, 1817

The power to tax involves the power to destroy.

MR. CHIEF JUSTICE JOHN MARSHALL: *Decision in McCulloch* vs. *Maryland*, March 6, 1819

The schoolboy whips his taxed top, the beardless youth manages his taxed horse with a taxed bridle, on a taxed road; and the dying Englishman, pouring his medicine, which has paid seven per cent., flings himself back on his chintz bed, which has paid twenty-two per cent., and expires in the arms of an apothecary who has paid a license of a hundred pounds for the privilege of putting him to death.

SYDNEY SMITH: *Review of Seybert's Annals*, 1830 (Edinburgh Review)

Of all debts, men are least willing to pay taxes. What a satire is this on government!

R. W. EMERSON: *Politics*, 1841

The thing generally raised on city land is taxes.

C. D. WARNER: *My Summer in a Garden*, XVI, 1870

The state and municipality go to great expense to support policemen and sheriffs and judicial officers, to protect people against themselves, that is, against the results of their own folly, vice, and recklessness. Who pays for it? Undoubtedly the people who have not been guilty of folly, vice, or recklessness.

W. G. SUMNER: *The Forgotten Man*, 1883

Unnecessary taxation is unjust taxation.

Democratic National Platform, 1884

The immense and ever increasing sums which the state wrings from the people are never enough for it; it mortgages the income of future generations, and steers resolutely toward bankruptcy.

P. A. KROPOTKIN: *Paroles d'un révolté*, 1884

The power to tax carries with it the power to embarrass and destroy.

SUPREME COURT OF THE UNITED STATES: *Decision in Evans* vs. *Gore*, 1920 (Cf. MARSHALL, *ante*, 1819)

We oppose the so-called nuisance taxes, sales taxes, and all other forms of taxation that unfairly shift to the consumer the burdens of taxation.

Democratic National Platform, 1924

The power to tax is not the power to destroy while this court sits.

MR. JUSTICE O. W. HOLMES: *Dissenting opinion in Panhandle Oil Co.* vs. *Mississippi*, 1930 (Cf. MARSHALL, *ante*, 1819)

Taxes are paid in the sweat of every man who labors. If those taxes are excessive, they are reflected in idle factories, in tax-sold farms, and in hordes of hungry people, tramping the streets and seeking jobs in vain. Our workers may never see a tax bill, but they pay. They pay in deductions from wages, in increased cost of what they buy, or in unemployment throughout the land.

F. D. ROOSEVELT: Speech in Pittsburgh, Oct. 19, 1932

Taxation is not a method by which the community corporately provides itself with essential services, but a fund to be divided between different interests with political claims upon the state.

NEVILLE CHAMBERLAIN: Budget speech in the House of Commons, 1934

His horse went dead, and his mule went lame,
And he lost six cows in a poker game;
Then a hurricane came on a Summer day,
And blew the house where he lived away;
An earthquake came when that was gone,
And swallowed the land the house stood on.
And then the tax collector came around,
And charged him up with the hole in the ground.

Author unidentified

Work and earn; pay taxes and die.

GERMAN PROVERB

[*See also* Highlander, Liberty.

Taxpayer

The poor taxpaying masses. (Misera contribuens plebs.)

Decree of Maria Theresa of Austria-Hungary, 1751

Tax, Single

The tax upon land values is the most just and equal of all taxes. It falls only upon those who receive from society a peculiar and valuable benefit, and upon them in proportion to the benefit they receive. It is the taking by the community, for the use of the community, of that value which is the creation of the community.

HENRY GEORGE: *Progress and Poverty*, VIII, 1879

Tea

Tea! thou soft, thou sober, sage, and venerable liquid, thou female tongue-running, smile-soothing, heart-opening, wink-tippling cordial, to whose glorious insipidity I owe the happiest moments of my life, let me fall prostrate.

COLLEY CIBBER: *The Lady's Last Stake*, I, 1708

Love and scandal are the best sweeteners of tea.

HENRY FIELDING: *Love in Several Masques*, IV, 1728

Polly, put the kettle on,
And let's drink tea.

Anon.: *Nursery rhyme*, *c.* 1750

The cups that cheer but not inebriate.
WILLIAM COWPER: *The Task*, IV, 1785
(Usually quoted in the singular)

Tea possesses an acrid astringent quality, peculiar to most leaves and exterior bark of trees, and corrodes and paralyzes the nerves.
JESSEY TORREY: *The Moral Instructor*, 1819

Don't pour out tea before putting sugar in the cup, or some one will be drowned.
AMERICAN NEGRO PROVERB

[*See also* Tobacco.

Teacher

What nobler employment, or more valuable to the state, than that of the man who instructs the rising generation?
CICERO: *De divinatione*, II, *c.* 78 B.C.

An instructor of the foolish, a teacher of babes.
ROMANS II, 20, *c.* 55

Teachers are greater benefactors than parents.
POPE XYSTUS I: *The Ring*, *c.* 150

He teacheth ill who teacheth all.
JOHN RAY: *English Proverbs*, 1670

A teacher should be sparing of his smile.
WILLIAM COWPER: *Charity*, 1782

Not any profane man, not any sensual, not any liar, not any slave can teach, but only he can give who has.
R. W. EMERSON: Address at the Divinity College, Cambridge, Mass., July 15, 1838

The true teacher defends his pupils against his own personal influence.
A. BRONSON ALCOTT: *Orphic Sayings*, 1841 (The Dial)

He who can does. He who cannot, teaches.
GEORGE BERNARD SHAW: *Maxims for Revolutionists*, 1903

The teacher's life should have three periods — study until 25, investigation until 40, profession until 60, at which age I would have him retired on a double allowance.
WILLIAM OSLER: Speech in Baltimore, Feb. 22, 1905

The teacher of youth, whether in a public or a private school, has no absolute rights of his own. All that he exercises have been given to him by others. Every Christian child has an inalienable right to instruction that is in harmony with the teachings of the church, the pillar and foundation of all truth.
POPE PIUS XI: *Divini illius magistri*, Dec. 31, 1929

More is to be got from one teacher than from two books.
GERMAN PROVERB

[*See also* Education, Pedagogue, Poet, Schoolmaster, Teaching.

Teaching

I can easier teach twenty what were good to be done, than be one of the twenty to follow my own teaching.
SHAKESPEARE: *The Merchant of Venice*, I, *c.* 1597

Men must be taught as if you taught them not,
And things unknown proposed as things forgot.
ALEXANDER POPE: *An Essay on Criticism*, III, 1711

Delightful task! to rear the tender thought,
To teach the young idea how to shoot.
JAMES THOMSON: *The Seasons* (Spring), 1728

Teaching of others teacheth the teacher.
THOMAS FULLER: *Gnomologia*, 1732

Go teach your grannam to suck eggs.
JONATHAN SWIFT: *Polite Conversation*, 1738 (The saying, with *to spin* or *to grope ducks* in place of *to suck eggs* goes back to the XVI century)

To know how to suggest is the great art of teaching. To attain it we must be able to guess what will interest; we must learn to read the childish soul as we might a piece of music.
H. F. AMIEL: *Journal*, Oct. 27, 1864

Everybody who is incapable of learning has taken to teaching.
OSCAR WILDE: *The Decay of Lying*, 1889

The right to impart instruction, harmless in itself or beneficial to those who receive it, is a substantial right of property.
MR. JUSTICE JOHN M. HARLAN: *Decision in Berea College* vs. *Kentucky*, 1908

A college professor is in the business of teaching. His business is not to give information.
BRONSON CUTTING: Speech in the Senate, June 14, 1934

The secret of teaching is to appear to have known all your life what you learned this afternoon.
Author unidentified

[*See also* Authority, Learning, Pedagogue, Schoolmaster, Teacher.

Tearing down

[*See* Destruction.

Tears

He fell upon his brother Benjamin's neck, and wept; and Benjamin wept upon his neck.
GENESIS XLV, 14, *c.* 700 B.C.

A time to weep and a time to laugh.
ECCLESIASTES III, 4, *c.* 200 B.C.

I am weary with my groaning; all the night make I my bed to swim; I water my couch with my tears.
PSALMS VI, 6, *c.* 150 B.C.

Weeping may endure for a night, but joy cometh in the morning. PSALMS XXX, 5

They that sow in tears shall reap in joy. PSALMS CXXVI, 5

Women have learned to shed tears in order that they may lie the better.
PUBLILIUS SYRUS: *Sententiæ*, c. 50 B.C.

Hence these tears. (Hinc illæ lacrymæ.)
HORACE: *Epistles*, I, c. 5 B.C.

Tears sometimes weigh as much as words.
OVID: *Epistulæ ex Ponto*, III, c. 5

It is a relief to weep; grief is satisfied and carried off by tears. OVID: *Tristia*, IV, c. 10

There shall be weeping and gnashing of teeth.
MATTHEW VIII, 12, c. 75 (The saying often appears as "There shall be weeping and wailing and gnashing of teeth," apparently by assimilation with MATTHEW XIII, 42: "There shall be wailing and gnashing of teeth"; cf. MATTHEW XIII, 50; XXII, 13; XXIV, 51; XXV, 30; LUKE XIII, 28)

Jesus wept.
JOHN XI, 35, c. 115 (The shortest verse in the Bible)

Weep no more, lady! weep no more;
Thy sorrow is in vain;
For violets plucked, the sweetest showers
Will ne'er make grow again.
Anon.: *The Friar of Orders Gray*, c. 1550

I cannot weep; for all my body's moisture
Scarce serves to quench my furnace-burning heart.
SHAKESPEARE: *III Henry VI*, II, c. 1591

Then fresh tears
Stood on her cheeks, as doth the honey-dew
Upon a gather'd lily almost wither'd.
SHAKESPEARE: *Titus Andronicus*, III, 1594

Why, man, if the river were dry, I am able to fill it with my tears; if the wind were down, I could drive the boat with my sighs.
SHAKESPEARE: *Two Gentlemen of Verona*, II, c. 1595

If you have tears, prepare to shed them now.
SHAKESPEARE: *Julius Cæsar*, III, 1599

The big round tears
Coursed one another down his innocent nose
In piteous chase.
SHAKESPEARE: *As You Like It*, II, c. 1600

'Tis the best brine a maiden can season her praise in.
SHAKESPEARE: *All's Well that Ends Well*, I, c. 1602

Trust not a woman when she cries,
For she'll pump water from her eyes
With a wet finger, and in faster showers
Than April when he rains down flowers.
THOMAS DEKKER: *I The Honest Whore*, V, 1604

If that the earth could teem with woman's tears,
Each drop she falls would prove a crocodile.
SHAKESPEARE: *Othello*, IV, 1604

Tears live in an onion.
SHAKESPEARE: *Antony and Cleopatra*, I, c. 1606

I, an ass, am onion-ey'd.
SHAKESPEARE: *Antony and Cleopatra*, IV

Let not woman's weapons, water drops,
Stain my man's cheeks.
SHAKESPEARE: *King Lear*, II, 1606

She shook
The holy water from her heavenly eyes.
SHAKESPEARE: *King Lear*, IV

There's nothing sooner dries than women's tears.
JOHN WEBSTER: *The White Devil*, V, c. 1608

Tears, though they are here below the sinner's brine,
Above they are the angels' spiced wine.
ROBERT HERRICK: *Hesperides*, 1648

One weeps to achieve a reputation for tenderness, weeps to be pitied, weeps to be bewept; in fact, one weeps to avoid the disgrace of not weeping.
LA ROCHEFOUCAULD: *Maxims*, 1665

Thrice he assay'd, and thrice in spite of scorn
Tears, such as angels weep, burst forth.
JOHN MILTON: *Paradise Lost*, I, 1667

Now and then a sigh he stole,
And tears began to flow.
JOHN DRYDEN: *Alexander's Feast*, IV, 1697

It is as much intemperance to weep too much as to laugh too much.
THOMAS FULLER: *Gnomologia*, 1732

Tears are for lighter woes.
GEORGE LILLO: *Fatal Curiosity*, I, 1736

Woe awaits a country when
She sees the tears of bearded men.
WALTER SCOTT: *Marmion*, V, 1808

The rose is sweetest wash'd with morning dew,
And love is loveliest when embalm'd in tears.
WALTER SCOTT: *The Lady of the Lake*, IV, 1810

The homage of a tear.
BYRON: *Childe Harold*, II, 1812

There are tears o' pity, an' tears o' wae,
An' tears for excess o' joy will fa',
Yet the tears o' luve are sweeter than a'!
ALFRED TENNYSON: *Scotch Song*, 1827

Tears, idle tears, I know not what they mean,
Tears from the depth of some divine despair
Rise in the heart, and gather to the eyes,
In looking on the happy Autumn-fields,
And thinking of the days that are no more.
ALFRED TENNYSON: *The Princess*, IV, 1847

Tears are Summer showers to the soul.
ALFRED AUSTIN: *Savonarola*, IV, 1881

Crying is the refuge of plain women, but the ruin of pretty ones.
OSCAR WILDE: *Lady Windermere's Fan*, III, 1892

When I consider life and its few years —
A wisp of fog betwixt us and the sun;
A call to battle, and the battle done
Ere the last echo dies within our ears;
A rose choked in the grass; an hour of fears;
The gusts that past a darkening shore do beat;
The burst of music down an unlistening street —
I wonder at the idleness of tears.
LIZETTE WOODWORTH REESE: *Tears*, 1899 (Scribner's Nov.)

The world's greatest water power is woman's tears.
J. KENFIELD MORLEY: *Some Things I Believe*, 1937

Shed blood and men believe; shed tears and they doubt.
FRENCH PROVERB

Men should be wary of making women weep, for God counts their tears.
HEBREW PROVERB

Tears are good for the complexion.
HINDU PROVERB

Tears before a judge are wasted.
ITALIAN PROVERB

Excuse these tears. (Da veniam lacrymis.)
LATIN SAYING

Red eyes will never set the fields afire.
LOUISIANA CREOLE PROVERB

Where there are tears there is conscience.
RUSSIAN PROVERB

[*See also* Art, Beauty, Bride, Busy, Death, Incredible, Laughter, Man, Man and Woman, Trust.

Teasing

Those that tease each other, love each other.
GERMAN PROVERB

Tedious

So tedious is this day,
As in the night before some festival
To an impatient child that hath new robes,
And may not wear them.
SHAKESPEARE: *Romeo and Juliet*, III, *c.* 1596

Be not tedious in discourse or in reading unless you find the company pleased therewith.
GEORGE WASHINGTON: Early copy-book before 1748

Teeth

Tooth for tooth.
EXODUS XXI, 24, *c.* 700 B.C. (Cf. LEVITICUS XXIV, 20, *c.* 700 B.C.; DEUTERONOMY XIX, 21, *c.* 650 B.C.; MATTHEW V, 38, *c.* 75)

Thy teeth are like a flock of sheep that are even shorn, which came up from the washing.
SOLOMON'S SONG IV, 2, *c.* 200 B.C.

Every tooth in a man's head is more valuable to him than a diamond.
CERVANTES: *Don Quixote*, I, 1605

It is necessary to clean the teeth frequently, more especially after meals, but not on any account with a pin, or the point of a penknife, and it must never be done at table.
ST. JOHN BAPTIST DE LA SALLE: *The Rules of Christian Manners and Civility*, I, 1695

My teeth are nearer to me than my kindred is.
THOMAS FULLER: *Gnomologia*, 1732

Hot things, sharp things, sweet things, cold things, all rot the teeth.
BENJAMIN FRANKLIN: *Poor Richard's Almanac*, 1734

The fine lady, or the gentleman, who show me their teeth, show me bones.
CHARLES LAMB: *The Praise of Chimney-Sweeps*, 1822 (London Magazine, May)

Ne'er shaw your teeth unless ye can bite.
SCOTTISH PROVERB

[*See also* Age (Old), Bread, Sweet.

Teething

[*See* Adam and Eve.

Teetotaler

Your Turks are infidels, and believe not in the grape. Your Mahometan, your Musselman, is a dry stinkard.
WILLIAM CONGREVE: *The Way of the World*, IV, 1700

What man can pretend to be a believer in love who is an abjurer of wine?
R. B. SHERIDAN: *The School for Scandal*, III, 1777

Dip him in the river who loves water.
WILLIAM BLAKE: *The Marriage of Heaven and Hell*, 1790

We, cold water girls and boys,
Freely renounce the treacherous joys
Of brandy, whiskey, rum, and gin;
The serpent's lure to death and sin.
Anon.: Song of the Cold Water Army of Connecticut, *c.* 1840

Whiskey and rum he tasted not —
He thought it was a sin —
I thought so much o' Deacon Bedott
I never got married agin.
FRANCES M. WHITCHER: *The Widow Bedott Papers*, 1855

Take that liquor away; I never touch strong drink. I like it too well to fool with it.
T. J. (STONEWALL) JACKSON: In Richmond, 1862, on being offered a mint julep (The incident is described in a letter from George E. Pickett to his wife, June 3, 1864)

My experience through life has convinced me that, while moderation and temperance in all things are commendable and beneficial, abstinence from spirituous liquors is the best safeguard of morals and health.
ROBERT E. LEE: *Letter to S. G. M. Miller and others,* Dec. 9, 1869

No woman should marry a teetotaler, or a man who does not smoke.
R. L. STEVENSON: *Virginibus Puerisque,* I, 1881

I promise never to drink, buy, or give
Alcoholic liquors while I live;
From all tobacco I'll abstain
And never take God's name in vain.
Author unidentified

Beware of the man who does not drink.
ITALIAN PROVERB

[*See also* Abstinence, Prohibition, Temperance.

Telegraph

Attention, the universe! By kingdoms, right wheel!
Message sent by telegraph at the time of Samuel Morse's first demonstration of it in New York, Sept., 1837

What hath God wrought!
First long-distance message by the Morse telegraph sent by Alfred Vail from the courtroom of the Supreme Court in Washington to Baltimore, May 24, 1844; said to have been suggested by Anne Ellsworth, daughter of Henry L. Ellsworth, commissioner of patents. It is from NUMBERS XXIII, 23

We are in great haste to construct a magnetic telegraph from Maine to Texas; but Maine and Texas, it may be, have nothing important to communicate.
H. D. THOREAU: *Walden,* 1854

Telling

Women are apt to tell before the intrigue, as men after it.
WILLIAM WYCHERLEY: *The Country Wife,* III, *c.* 1673

[*See also* Kiss.

Temper

A perverse temper and fretful disposition will make any state of life whatsoever unhappy.
CICERO: *De senectute, c.* 78 B.C.

The brain may devise laws for the blood, but a hot temper leaps o'er a cold decree.
SHAKESPEARE: *The Merchant of Venice, c.* 1597

Good temper is an estate for life.
WILLIAM HAZLITT: *The Plain Speaker,* II, 1826

An ill-tempered woman is the Devil's door-nail.
DANISH PROVERB

He who restrains his temper will have all his sins forgiven.
HEBREW PROVERB

Temperament

The four temperaments are: 1. The melancholic or earthy; 2. The phlegmatic or aqueous; 3. The choleric or fiery; 4. The sanguine or ethereal.
JACOB BOEHME: *Von der Geburt und Bezeichnung aller Wesen, c.* 1620

Temperament is a fate from whose jurisdiction its victims hardly escape, but do its bidding herein, be it murder or martyrdom.
A. BRONSON ALCOTT: *Tablets,* II, 1868

[*See also* Hair (Dark).

Temperance

Temperance is the noblest gift of the gods.
EURIPIDES: *Medea,* 431 B.C.

We become temperate by abstaining from indulgence, and we are the better able to abstain from indulgence after we have become temperate.
ARISTOTLE: *The Nicomachean Ethics,* II, *c.* 340 B.C.

Temperance is the moderating of one's desires in obedience to reason.
CICERO: *De finibus,* II, *c.* 50 B.C.

Meekness, temperance: against such there is no law.
GALATIANS V, 23, *c.* 50

Temperate in all things.
I CORINTHIANS IX, 25, *c.* 55

Temperance is the greatest of all the virtues.
PLUTARCH: *Moralia, c.* 75

Temperance is simply a disposition of the mind which sets bounds to the passions.
THOMAS AQUINAS: *Summa theologiæ,* LVII, *c.* 1265

Do not charge most innocent nature,
As if she would her children should be riotous
With her abundance; she, good cateress,
Means her provision only to the good,
That live according to her sober laws,
And holy dictate of spare temperance.
JOHN MILTON: *Comus,* 1637

By temperance I understand a measurable abstinence from all hot or heightening meats or drinks, as also from all venerous and tactual delights of the body, from all softness and effeminacy, a constant and peremptory adhesion to the perfectest degree of chastity in the single life and that of continency in wedlock that can be attained to.
HENRY MORE: *Enthusiasmus triumphatus,* LII, 1656

The smaller the drink, the clearer the head, and the cooler the blood.
WILLIAM PENN: *Fruits of Solitude,* 1693

Temperance has those advantages over all other means of health that it may be practised by all ranks and conditions, at any season, or in any place. It is a kind of regimen into which

every man may put himself, without interruption to business, expense of money, or loss of time.
JOSEPH ADDISON: *The Spectator*, Oct. 13, 1711

Eat not to dullness; drink not to elevation.
BENJAMIN FRANKLIN: *Rules for his own conduct*, c. 1730

Temperance and labor are the two best physicians of man. Labor sharpens his appetite and temperance prevents him abusing it.
J.-J. ROUSSEAU: *Émile*, I, 1762

Damn temperance and he that first invented it!
CHARLES LAMB: *Letter to Dorothy Wordsworth*, Aug., 1810

Temperate men drink the most, because they drink the longest.
C. C. COLTON: *Lacon*, 1820

Is not temperance a virtue? Aye, assuredly it is. But wherefore? Because by restraining enjoyment for a time, it afterwards elevates it to that very pitch which leaves, on the whole, the largest addition to the stock of happiness.
JEREMY BENTHAM: *Deontology*, 1834

Temperance is the best physic.
H. G. BOHN: *Handbook of Proverbs*, 1855

The Republican party cordially sympathizes with all wise and well-directed efforts for the promotion of temperance and morality.
Republican National Platform, 1888

He that eats but ae dish seldom needs the doctor.
SCOTTISH PROVERB (*Ae*=one)

[*See also* Abstemiousness, Adversity, Breakfast, Chastity, Eating and Drinking, Kingly, Medicine, Moderation, Prohibition, Too Much, Virtue.

Temperature

Very high and very low temperature extinguishes all human sympathy and relations. It is impossible to feel affection beyond 78°, or below 20° of Fahrenheit; human nature is too solid or too liquid beyond these limits.
SYDNEY SMITH: *Letter to an unidentified woman*, July, 1836

Tempest

A tempest in a teapot.
ENGLISH PHRASE, borrowed from the Latin (Until the XVII century *cream-bowl* appeared in place of *teapot*. In later times *teacup* has been substituted)

Temple, William (1628–99)

Sir William Temple was the first writer who gave cadence to English prose.
SAMUEL JOHNSON: *Boswell's Life*, April 9, 1778

He was a man of the world among men of letters, a man of letters among men of the world.
T. B. MACAULAY: *Sir William Temple*, 1838

Temptation

The woman whom thou gavest to be with me, she gave me of the tree, and I did eat.
GENESIS III, 12, *c.* 700 B.C.

If sinners entice thee, consent thou not.
PROVERBS I, 10, *c.* 350 B.C.

The lips of a strange woman drop as a honeycomb, and her mouth is smoother than oil.
PROVERBS V, 3

I have perfumed my bed with myrrh, aloes, and cinnamon. Come, let us take our fill of love.
PROVERBS VII, 17–18

The mouth of a strange woman is a deep pit: he that is abhorred of the Lord shall fall therein.
PROVERBS XXII, 14

Count it all joy when you fall into divers temptations; knowing this, that the trying of your faith worketh patience.
JAMES I, 1–2, *c.* 60

Blessed is the man that endureth temptation; for when he is tried, he shall receive the crown of life.
JAMES I, 12

Watch ye and pray, lest ye enter into temptation. The spirit truly is ready, but the flesh is weak.
MARK XIV, 38, *c.* 70

Lead us not into temptation.
MATTHEW VI, 13, *c.* 75 (Cf. LUKE XI, 4, *c.* 75)

God delights in our temptations, and yet hates them; He delights in them when they drive us to prayer: He hates them when they drive us to despair.
MARTIN LUTHER: *Table-Talk*, XC, 1569

Ah me, how many perils do enfold
The righteous man, to make him daily fall.
EDMUND SPENSER: *The Faerie Queene*, I, *c.* 1589

How oft the sight of means to do ill deeds
Makes ill deeds done!
SHAKESPEARE: *King John*, IV, *c.* 1596

Most dangerous
Is that temptation that doth goad us on
To sin in loving virtue.
SHAKESPEARE: *Measure for Measure*, II, 1604

Temptations hurt not, though they have access;
Satan o'ercomes none but by willingness.
ROBERT HERRICK: *Hesperides*, 1648

(1) They make me abhor myself. (2) They keep me from trusting my heart. (3) They convince me of the insufficiency of all inherent righteousness. (4) They show me the necessity of flying to Jesus. (5) They press me to pray unto God. (6) They show me the need I have to watch and be sober. (7) And provoke me to look to God, through Christ,

to help me, and carry me through this world. Amen.
JOHN BUNYAN: *Grace Abounding to the Chief of Sinners,* 1666

An open door may tempt a saint.
THOMAS FULLER: *Gnomologia,* 1732

Satan now is wiser than of yore,
And tempts by making rich, not making poor.
ALEXANDER POPE: *Moral Essays,* III (Of the Use of Riches), 1732

Whoever stands to parley with temptation
Parleys to be o'ercome.
GEORGE LILLO: *Fatal Curiosity,* III, 1736

Few can review the days of their youth without recollecting temptations which shame rather than virtue enabled them to resist.
SAMUEL JOHNSON: *The Rambler,* Sept. 24, 1751

Ye high, exalted, virtuous dames,
Tied up in godly laces,
Before ye gie poor frailty names,
Suppose a change o' cases;
A dear-loved lad, convenience snug,
A treacherous inclination –
But, let me whisper i' your lug,
Ye're aiblins nae temptation.
ROBERT BURNS: An Address to the Unco Guid, 1785 (*Aiblins*=perhaps)

While discretion points out the impropriety of my conduct, inclination urges me on to ruin.
SUSANNA ROWSON: *Charlotte Temple,* XI, 1790

More pure as tempted more.
WILLIAM WORDSWORTH: *Character of the Happy Warrior,* 1807

Greater is he who is above temptation than he who, being tempted, overcomes.
A. BRONSON ALCOTT: *Orphic Sayings,* 1841 (The Dial)

It is good to be without vices, but it is not good to be without temptations.
WALTER BAGEHOT: *Biographical Studies,* 1880

I can resist everything except temptation.
OSCAR WILDE: *Lady Windermere's Fan,* II, 1892

Never resist temptation: prove all things: hold fast that which is good.
GEORGE BERNARD SHAW: *Maxims for Revolutionists,* 1903

Everything is a temptation to the man who fears temptation.
FRENCH PROVERB

The cold teaches everyone to steal charcoal.
MOROCCAN PROVERB

He that shows his purse tempts the thief.
SCOTTISH PROVERB

A strong box with the door open will tempt even a bishop.
SLOVENIAN PROVERB

[*See also* Beautiful, Enticement, Idleness, Praise, Seduction, Virtue.

Tenderness

O Douglas, O Douglas!
Tendir and trewe.
RICHARD HOLLAND: *The Buke of the Howlat, c.* 1450

It is as tender as a parson's leman.
JOHN HEYWOOD: *Proverbs,* 1546

You are so tender you dare not be hanged for fear of galling your neck.
THOMAS FULLER: *Gnomologia,* 1732

An infinitude of tenderness is the chief gift and inheritance of all the truly great men.
JOHN RUSKIN: *The Two Paths,* I, 1859

The bravest are the tenderest, –
The loving are the daring.
BAYARD TAYLOR: *The Song of the Camp,* 1864

[*See also* Art.

Tennessee

[*See* Evolution.

Tennis

[*See* Gentleman.

Tennyson, Alfred (1809–92)

Tennyson is a beautiful half of a poet.
R. W. EMERSON: *Journal,* Sept. 21, 1838

Tennyson I regard as the noblest poet that ever lived. I call him, and think him the noblest of poets – not because the impressions he produces are, at all times, the most profound – not because the poetical excitement which he induces is, at all times, the most intense – but because it is, at all times, the most ethereal – in other words, the most elevating and the most pure.
E. A. POE: *The Poetic Principle,* 1845

Baron Alfred T. de T.
Are we at last in sweet accord?
I learn – excuse the girlish glee –
That you've become a noble lord;
So now that time to think you've had
Of what it is makes charming girls,
Perhaps you find they're not so bad –
Those daughters of a hundred earls.
Anon.: *The Vere de Vere to Tennyson* (on his acceptance of a peerage), 1884

Tenor

The tenor's voice is spoilt by affectation.
BYRON: *Don Juan,* IV, 1821

His voice was like the distressing noise which a nail makes when you screech it across a window pane.
S. L. CLEMENS (MARK TWAIN): *A Tramp Abroad,* X, 1879

There are three sexes: men, women and tenors.
Author unidentified

[*See also* Choir.

Terror

The terror of God.
GENESIS XXXV, 5, *c.* 700 B.C.

Terrible as an army with banners.
SOLOMON'S SONG VI, 4, *c.* 200 B.C.

Things which are terrible are always great.
EDMUND BURKE: *The Sublime and Beautiful,* II, 1756

And the silken, sad, uncertain rustling of each purple curtain
Thrilled me, — filled me with fantastic terrors never felt before.
E. A. POE: *The Raven,* 1845 (New York Evening Mirror, Jan. 29)

Terror at any object is quickly taught if it is taught consistently, whether the terror be reasonable or not.
FRANCIS GALTON: *Inquiries Into Human Faculty,* 1883

[*See also* Sublime.

Testament

I owe much; I have nothing; I give the rest to the poor. RABELAIS: Last will, 1553

Let's choose executors and talk of wills.
SHAKESPEARE: *Richard II,* III, *c.* 1596

My sword I give to him that shall succeed me in my pilgrimage, and my courage and skill to him that can get it. My marks and scars I carry with me, to be a witness for me, that I have fought His battles who now will be my reward.
JOHN BUNYAN: *Pilgrim's Progress,* II, 1674

The only points of stage law on which we are all clear are as follows: That if a man dies without leaving a will, then all his property goes to the nearest villain, but if he leaves a will, then all his property goes to whoever can get possession of that will.
JEROME K. JEROME: *Stage-Land,* 1889

More people have died because they made their wills than because they were sick.
SPANISH PROVERB

Testament, New

It would be a poor story to be prejudiced against the Life of Christ because the book has been edited by Christians.
H. D. THOREAU: *A Week on the Concord and Merrimack Rivers,* 1849

One had better put on gloves before reading the New Testament. The presence of so much filth makes it very advisable.
F. W. NIETZSCHE: *The Antichrist,* XLVI, 1888

[*See also* Bible.

Testimonial

Nobody ever acted on a testimonial who had not afterward cause to regret it.
BENJAMIN DISRAELI: Speech in the House of Commons, March 22, 1867

Testy

[*See* Age (Old).

Texas

New states, of convenient size, not exceeding four in number, in addition to the said state of Texas, and having sufficient population, may hereafter, by the consent of said state, be formed out of the territory thereof, which shall be entitled to admission under the provisions of the Federal Constitution.
Joint Resolution of Congress for the annexation of Texas, March 1, 1845

If I owned Hell and Texas I'd rent out Texas and live in Hell.
P. H. SHERIDAN: Speech at Fort Clark, Texas, 1855

Texas is one great, windy lunatic.
SOCRATES HYACINTH: In the Overland Monthly, Aug., 1869

The place where there are the most cows and the least milk and the most rivers and the least water in them, and where you can look the furthest and see the least.
Author unidentified

Thackeray, W. M. (1811–63)

A big, fierce, weeping, hungry man; not a strong one.
THOMAS CARLYLE: *Letter to R. W. Emerson,* Sept. 9, 1853

There is a want of heart in all he writes, which is not to be balanced by the most brilliant sarcasm and the most perfect knowledge of the workings of the human heart.
EDMUND YATES: *Portrait of Thackeray,* 1858 (Town Talk, June 12)

No one has so light a touch and no one can stir us so deeply, leaving the nerves unassailed.
W. C. BROWNELL: *Victorian Prose Masters,* 1901

Thankless

[*See* Child.

Thanks

No duty is more urgent than that of returning thanks.
ST. AMBROSE: *On Bereavement, c.* 380

Evermore thanks, the exchequer of the poor.
SHAKESPEARE: *Richard II,* I, *c.* 1596

Thank me no thanks.
SHAKESPEARE: *Romeo and Juliet,* III, *c.* 1596

Beggar that I am, I am even poor in thanks.
SHAKESPEARE: *Hamlet,* II, *c.* 1601

He loseth his thanks who promiseth and delayeth.
JOHN RAY: *English Proverbs,* 1670

I'll thank you for the next, for this I am sure of.
IBID.

Words are but empty thanks.
COLLEY CIBBER: *Woman's Wit,* V, 1697

Though my mouth be dumb my heart shall thank you.
NICHOLAS ROWE: *Jane Shore,* II, 1714

My dame fed her hens with mere thanks, and they laid no eggs.
THOMAS FULLER: *Gnomologia,* 1732

Tak your thanks to feed your cat.
SCOTTISH PROVERB

Three things for which thanks are due: an invitation, a gift, and a warning.
WELSH PROVERB

[*See also* Duty, Gratitude.

Thanksgiving

It is a good thing to give thanks unto the Lord.
PSALMS XCII, 1, *c.* 150 B.C.

O give thanks unto the Lord, for he is good: for his mercy endureth forever.
PSALMS CVII, 1

In every thing give thanks.
I THESSALONIANS V, 18, *c.* 51

Let never day nor night unhallow'd pass,
But still remember what the Lord hath done.
SHAKESPEARE: *II Henry VI,* II, *c.* 1591

Thanksgiving for a former, doth invite
God to bestow a second benefit.
ROBERT HERRICK: *Noble Numbers,* 1647

Now thank we all our God,
With heart and hand and voices
Who wondrous things hath done,
In whom His world rejoices.
CATHERINE WINKWORTH: Tr. of JOHANN CRÜGER: *Nun danket alle Gott,* 1648

Almighty God, Father of all mercies, we, thine unworthy servants, do give thee most humble and hearty thanks for all thy goodness and loving-kindness to us, and to all men.
THE BOOK OF COMMON PRAYER (*The Litany*), 1662

Some people always sigh in thanking God.
E. B. BROWNING: *Aurora Leigh,* I, 1857

[*See also* Grace (=thanksgiving), Thanks.

Theatre

A certain woman went to the theatre and brought the Devil home with her. And when the unclean spirit was pressed in the exorcism, and asked how he durst attack a Christian, "I have done nothing," says he, "but what I can justify, for I seized her upon my own ground."
TERTULLIAN: *De spectaculis, c.* 200

Spending time in the theatres produces fornication, intemperance, and every kind of impurity.
ST. JOHN CHRYSOSTOM: *Homilies,* XV, *c.* 388

All ages, all places have constantly suspected the chastity, yea branded the honesty of those females who have been so immodest as to resort to theatres, to stage-plays, which either find or make them harlots.
WILLIAM PRYNNE: *Histriomastix,* 1632

Whereas, the distressed state of Ireland, steeped in her own blood, the distracted state of England, threatened with a cloud of blood by a civil war, call for all possible means to appease and avert the wrath of God appearing in these judgments, . . . it is therefore thought fit, and ordered by the Lords and Commons in this Parliament assembled, that while these sad causes and set-times of humiliation do continue, public stage-plays shall cease and be forborne.
Ordinance of Parliament, Sept. 2, 1642

Every person or persons which shall be present and a spectator at any stage-play or interlude shall for every time he shall be so present forfeit and pay the sum of five shillings to the use of the poor of the parish.
Ordinance of Parliament, Feb. 9, 1647

In the theatre the demon of impurity displays his pomp with so many charms and seductive graces that the most solid virtue can hardly withstand it.
ST. JOHN BAPTIST DE LA SALLE: *Les devoirs du chrétien,* VII, 1703

Whoever condemns the theatre is an enemy to his country.
VOLTAIRE: *Letter to the commissioner of police of Paris,* June 20, 1733

Is it a stale remark to say that I have constantly found the interest excited at a playhouse to bear an exact inverse proportion to the price paid for admission?
CHARLES LAMB: In the Examiner, Dec. 19, 1813

One half the pleasure experienced at a theatre arises from the spectator's sympathy with the rest of the audience, and, especially, from his belief in their sympathy with him.
E. A. POE: *Marginalia,* 1844–49

Not to go to the theatre is like making one's toilet without a mirror.
ARTHUR SCHOPENHAUER: *Parerga und Paralipomena,* 1851

To my mind there is no sadder spectacle of artistic debauchery than a London theatre; the overfed inhabitants of the villa in the stalls hoping for gross excitement to assist them through their hesitating digestions; an ignorant mob in the pit and gallery forgetting the miseries of life in imbecile stories reeking of the sentimentality of the back-stairs.

GEORGE MOORE: *Confessions of a Young Man*, IX, 1888

One should never take one's daughter to a theatre. Not only are plays immoral; the house itself is immoral.

ALEXANDRE DUMAS *fils* (1824–95)

[*See also* Drama, Evidence, Play (=drama), Speech (Free), Stage, Tragedy.

Theft

Thou shalt not steal.

EXODUS XX, 15, *c.* 700 B.C. (Cf. LEVITICUS XIX, 11, *c.* 700 B.C.; DEUTERONOMY V, 19, *c.* 650 B.C.; ROMANS XIII, 9, *c.* 55; MARK X, 19, *c.* 70; MATTHEW XIX, 18, *c.* 75; LUKE XVIII, 20, *c.* 75)

If a man shall steal an ox, or a sheep, and kill it, or sell it: he shall restore five oxen for an ox, and four sheep for a sheep.

EXODUS XXII, 1

If a man or woman steal, cut off their hands.

THE KORAN, V, *c.* 625

It is rascally to steal a purse, daring to steal a million, and a proof of greatness to steal a crown. The blame diminishes as the guilt increases.

J. C. F. SCHILLER: *The Fiesco*, III, 1784

If a man steal enough, he may be sure that his punishment will practically amount but to the loss of a part of the proceeds of his theft; and if he steal enough to get off with a fortune, he will be greeted by his acquaintances as a viking might have been greeted after a successful cruise.

HENRY GEORGE: *Progress and Poverty*, X, 1879

Suppose that picking a man's pocket excited in him joyful emotions, by brightening his prospects: would theft be counted among crimes?

HERBERT SPENCER: *The Data of Ethics*, III, 1879

In a society where certain kinds of theft are the common rule, the utility of abstinence from such theft on the part of a single individual becomes exceedingly doubtful, even though the common rule is a bad one.

G. E. MOORE: *Principia Ethica*, V, 1903

No people is wholly civilized where a distinction is drawn between stealing an office and stealing a purse.

THEODORE ROOSEVELT: Speech in Chicago, June 22, 1912

First a turnip, then a sheep, then a cow, and then the gallows.

DUTCH PROVERB

He who steals from a thief is as guilty as the thief.

HEBREW PROVERB

He who steals a handful of gold is put in jail; he who steals a whole country is made king.

JAPANESE PROVERB

[*See also* Lying, Plagiarism, Property, Sin, Thief.

Theocracy

Theocracy, government of God, is precisely the thing to be struggled for. All prophets, zealots, priests, are there for that purpose. Hildebrand wished a theocracy; Cromwell wished it, fought for it; Mahomet attained it. Nay, is it not what all zealous men, whether called priests, prophets, or whatsoever else called, do essentially wish, and must wish?

THOMAS CARLYLE: *Heroes and Hero-Worship*, IV, 1840 (Lecture in London, May 15)

[*See also* Government.

Theologian

Theologians are all alike, of whatever religion or country they may be; their aim is always to wield despotic authority over men's consciences; they therefore persecute all of us who have the temerity to unveil the truth.

FREDERICK THE GREAT: *Letter to Voltaire*, Nov. 4, 1736

Dull though impatient, peevish though devout,
With wit disgusting, and despised without;
Saints in design, in execution men,
Peace in their looks, and vengeance in their pen.

GEORGE CRABBE: *The Library*, 1781

Controversial divines have changed the rule of life into a standard of disputation. They have employed the temple of the Most High as a fencing-school, where gymnastic exercises are daily exhibited, and where victory serves only to excite new contests.

DAVID DALRYMPLE (LORD HAILES): *An Inquiry Into the Secondary Causes Which Mr. Gibbon Has Assigned to the Rapid Growth of Christianity*, 1786

Whatever a theologian regards as true must be false: there you have almost a criterion of truth.

F. W. NIETZSCHE: *The Antichrist*, IX, 1888

When people talk to me of a great theologian I say, what waste of time and energy, if he were really a great man, potentially.

GEORGE MEREDITH: To Edward Clodd (Fortnightly Review, July, 1909), *c.* 1900

The God of the theologians is the creation of their empty heads.

BENITO MUSSOLINI: Speech in Lausanne, July, 1904

The heart makes the theologian. (Pectus facit theologum.)

MEDIEVAL LATIN PROVERB

[*See also* Bench, Evolution, Laughter, Philosopher, Theology

Theology

It is taught by demons, it teaches about demons, and it leads to demons.
ALBERTUS MAGNUS: *Summa theologiæ*, 1280

Theology should be empress, and philosophy and the other arts merely her servants.
MARTIN LUTHER: *Table-Talk*, CLXXVIII, 1569

In theology we must consider the predominance of authority; in philosophy the predominance of reason.
JOHN KEPLER: *Astronomia nova*, 1609

As for those wingy mysteries in divinity, and airy subtleties in religion, which have unhinged the brains of better heads, they never stretched the *pia mater* of mine.
THOMAS BROWNE: *Religio Medici*, I, 1642

To be still searching what we know not by what we know, still closing up truth to truth as we find it (for all her body is homogeneal and proportional), this is the golden rule in theology as well as in arithmetic, and makes up the best harmony in a church.
JOHN MILTON: *Areopagitica*, 1644

What makes all doctrines plain and clear? —
About two hundred pounds a year.
And that which was prov'd true before
Prove false again? Two hundred more.
SAMUEL BUTLER: *Hudibras*, III, 1678

Many a long dispute among divines may be thus abridg'd: It is so; It is not so, It is so; It is not so.
BENJAMIN FRANKLIN: *Poor Richard's Almanac*, 1743

The study of theology, as it stands in Christian churches, is the study of nothing; it is founded on nothing; it rests on no principles; it proceeds by no authorities; it has no data; it can demonstrate nothing; and it admits of no conclusion.
THOMAS PAINE: *The Age of Reason*, 1794

A professorship of theology should have no place in our institution.
THOMAS JEFFERSON: *Letter to Thomas Cooper*, 1814 (The University of Virginia)

The post-obits of theology.
BYRON: *Don Juan*, I, 1819

Divinity is essentially the first of the professions, because it is necessary for all at all times; law and physic are only necessary for some at some times.
S. T. COLERIDGE: *Table-Talk*, March 14, 1833

Pantheism, pottheism, mydoxy, thydoxy, are nothing at all to me; a weariness the whole jargon, which I avoid speaking of, decline listening to: *live*, for God's sake, with what faith thou couldst get; leave off *speaking* about faith!
THOMAS CARLYLE: *Letter to R. W. Emerson*, Nov. 7, 1838

The theological problems of original sin, origin of evil, predestination, and the like are the soul's mumps, and measles, and whooping-coughs.
R. W. EMERSON: *Spiritual Laws*, 1841

Theology is anthropology.
L. A. FEUERBACH: *Das Wesen des Christenthums*, 1841

University education without theology is simply unphilosophical. Theology has at least as good a right to claim a place there as astronomy.
J. H. NEWMAN: *On the Scope and Nature of University Education*, I, 1852

Theological propositions [are] held to be absolute, universal, admitting of no exceptions, and explaining every phenomenon.
J. A. FROUDE: *The Book of Job*, 1853 (Westminster Review)

Theology . . . is the most noble of studies.
POPE LEO XIII: *Æterni patris*, Aug. 4, 1879

Whoever has theological blood in his veins is shifty and dishonorable in all things.
F. W. NIETZSCHE: *The Antichrist*, IX, 1888

A blind man in a dark room searching for a black cat which isn't there — and finding it.
Author unidentified

The rancor of theology. (Odium theologicum.)
LATIN PHRASE

[*See also* Demonology, Dogma, Knowledge, Politics, Theologian.

Theory

The supreme misfortune is when theory outstrips performance.
LEONARDO DA VINCI: *Notebooks*, *c.* 1500

The moment a person forms a theory, his imagination sees, in every object, only the traits which favor that theory.
THOMAS JEFFERSON: *Letter to Charles Thomson*, 1787

A favorite theory is a possession for life.
WILLIAM HAZLITT: *Characteristics*, 1823

What is a theory but an imperfect generalization caught up by a predisposition?
J. A. FROUDE: *The Lives of the Saints*, 1852 (Eclectic Review)

[*See also* Fact.

Theresa, St.

[*See* Knox (John).

Thermopylae, Battle of

[*See* Epitaph.

Thief

Men do not despise a thief, if he steal to satisfy his soul when he is hungry.
PROVERBS VI, 30, *c.* 350 B.C.

When thieves fall out, honest men come by their own.
ENGLISH PROVERB, traced to 1546

Save a thief from the gallows and he will be the first shall do thee a mischief.
BRIAN MELBANCKE: *Philotimus,* 1583

He that fears the gallows shall never be a good thief.
ROBERT GREEN: *A Dispute between a He Cony-Catcher and a She Cony-Catcher,* 1592

A plague upon it when thieves cannot be true one to another.
SHAKESPEARE: *I Henry IV,* II, *c.* 1598

The sun's a thief, and with his great attraction
Robs the vast sea; the moon's an arrant thief,
And her pale fire she snatches from the sun:
The sea's a thief, whose liquid surge resolves
The moon into salt tears: the earth's a thief,
That feeds and breeds by a composture stolen
From general excrement.
SHAKESPEARE: *Timon of Athens,* I, *c.* 1607

He that will steal an egg will steal an ox.
JOHN CLARKE: *Parœmiologia Anglo-Latina,* 1639

Put a miller, a tailor and a weaver in a bag and shake them: the first who cometh out will be a thief.
JAMES HOWELL: *Proverbs,* 1659

Set a thief to catch a thief.
RICHARD HOWARD: *The Committee,* I, 1665
(Quoted as "an old saying")

War makes thieves, and peace hangs them.
JOHN RAY: *English Proverbs,* 1670

The little thieves hang for't, while the great ones sit upon the bench.
ROGER L'ESTRANGE: Tr. of ÆSOP: *Fables,* 1692

There is honor among thieves.
ENGLISH PROVERB, borrowed from the Latin, and familiar in English since the early XVIII century

The thief is sorry he is to be hanged, but not that he is a thief.
THOMAS FULLER: *Gnomologia,* 1732

The fiends laugh, they say, when one thief robs another.
WALTER SCOTT: *Ivanhoe,* XXI, 1819

The Russian steals in order to relieve his immediate wants; but when the German steals, he thinks of the future, of provision for his wife and children, and robs with an *énergie teutonique.*
OTTO VON BISMARCK (1813–98)

The thief who understands his business never steals in his own neighborhood.
ARAB PROVERB

The thief thinks everybody steals.
DANISH PROVERB

Little thieves are hanged by the neck, great thieves by the purse.
DUTCH PROVERB

When two thieves quarrel the farmer gets back his cow.
FINNISH PROVERB

When thieves quarrel, robberies are discovered.
FRENCH PROVERB

All valets are thieves, and all barons swindlers.
GERMAN PROVERB

There are more thieves than gallows.
IBID.

The thief who has no chance to steal considers himself an honest man.
HEBREW PROVERB

Thunder makes the thief honest.
ITALIAN PROVERB

The thief who begins by stealing an egg will end by stealing a camel.
PERSIAN PROVERB

Not caught, not a thief.
RUSSIAN PROVERB

When the thief prays, the Devil listens.
IBID.

Hang a thief when he's young, and he'll not steal when he's auld.
SCOTTISH PROVERB

People who live on the seacoast are all thieves.
SPANISH PROVERB

The best way to make a thief honest is to trust him.
IBID.

[*See also* Adulterer, Butcher, Crime and Punishment, Criminal, Dog, Gallows, Gentleman, Hanging, Hunger, Jailer, Judge, Jury, Liar, Opportunity, Theft, War and Peace.

Thigh

The joints of thy thighs are like jewels.
SOLOMON'S SONG VII, 1, *c.* 200 B.C.

[*See also* Breeches, Eye, Hip, Leg.

Thin

As thin as the homeopathic soup that was made by boiling the shadow of a pigeon that had starved to death.
ABRAHAM LINCOLN: Speech in Quincy, Ill., Oct. 13, 1858

There was a young lady of Lynn
Who was so excessively thin
That when she essayed
To drink lemonade
She looked down the straw and fell in.
Author unidentified

Death upon wires.
IRISH SAYING

Thin women live long. WELSH PROVERB

[*See also* Lean.

Thinker

In every epoch of the world, the great event, parent of all others, is it not the arrival of a thinker in the world?

THOMAS CARLYLE: *Heroes and Hero-Worship,* 1840 (Lecture in London, May 5)

Beware when the great God lets loose a thinker on this planet.

R. W. EMERSON: *Circles,* 1841

[*See also* Seer.

Thinking

As he thinketh in his heart, so is he.

PROVERBS XXIII, 7, *c.* 350 B.C.

To think is to live. (Vivere est cogitare.)

CICERO: *Tusculanæ disputationes,* V, 45 B.C.

Which of you by taking thought can add one cubit unto his stature?

MATTHEW VI, 27, *c.* 75 (Cf. LUKE XII, 25, *c.* 75)

Men have the power of thinking that they may avoid sin.

ST. JOHN CHRYSOSTOM: *Homilies,* XV, *c.* 388

Oh, who can hold a fire in his hand,
By thinking on the frosty Caucasus?
Or cloy the hungry edge of appetite
By bare imagination of a feast?
Or wallow naked in December snow
By thinking on fantastic Summer's heat?

SHAKESPEARE: *Richard II,* I, *c.* 1596

Yond Cassius has a lean and hungry look;
He thinks too much: such men are dangerous.

SHAKESPEARE: *Julius Cæsar,* I, 1599

There is nothing either good or bad, but thinking makes it so.

SHAKESPEARE: *Hamlet,* II, *c.* 1601

I think; therefore I am. (Cogito, ergo sum.)

RENÉ DESCARTES: *Discourse on Method,* 1636

Man is but a reed, the most feeble thing in nature, but he is a thinking reed.

BLAISE PASCAL: *Pensées,* II, 1670

A waking man, being under the necessity of having some ideas constantly in his mind, is not at liberty to think or not to think.

JOHN LOCKE: *Essay Concerning Human Understanding,* II, 1690

Why should I disparage my parts by thinking what to say? None but dull rogues think.

WILLIAM CONGREVE: *The Double Dealer,* IV, 1694

The hermit's solace in his cell,
The fire that warms the poet's brain,
The lover's heaven, or his hell,
The madman's sport, the wise man's pain.

AMBROSE PHILIPS: *Pastorals,* 1709

If the power of reflecting on the past, and darting the keen eye of contemplation into futurity, be the grand privilege of man, it must be granted that some people enjoy this prerogative in a very limited degree.

MARY WOLLSTONECRAFT: *A Vindication of the Rights of Woman,* IX, 1792

Impressions arrive at the brain and make it enter into activity just as food falling into the stomach excites it to secretion.

PIERRE CABANIS: *Rapports du physique et du moral de l'homme,* 1796

All motion in this world has its origin in something that is not motion. Why, then, shouldn't the universal force be the cause of my thoughts just as it is the cause of fermentation?

G. C. LICHTENBERG: *Reflections,* 1799

I never could find any man who could think for two minutes together.

SYDNEY SMITH: *Lectures on Moral Philosophy,* XIX, 1804

What exile from himself can flee?
To zones, though more and more remote,
Still, still pursues, where'er I be,
The blight of life – the demon thought.

BYRON: *Childe Harold,* I, 1812

Thinking is but an ideal waste of thought,
And naught is everything, and everything is naught.

JAMES and HORACE SMITH: *Rejected Addresses,* 1812

The power of thought, – the magic of the mind.

BYRON: *The Corsair,* I, 1814

Though the proportion of those who think be extremely small, yet every individual flatters himself that he is one of the number.

C. C. COLTON: *Lacon,* pref., 1820

As the development of the mind proceeds, symbols, instead of being employed to convey images, are substituted for them. Civilized men think as they trade, not in kind, but by means of a circulating medium.

T. B. MACAULAY: *John Dryden,* 1828 (Edinburgh Review, Jan.)

Thought, true labor of any kind, highest virtue itself, is it not the daughter of pain? Born as out of the black whirlwind; – true effort, in fact, as of a captive struggling to free himself: that is thought.

THOMAS CARLYLE: *Heroes and Hero-Worship,* III, 1840 (Lecture in London, May 5)

Thought once awakened does not again slumber.

IBID.

What is the hardest task in the world? To think.

R. W. EMERSON: *Intellect,* 1841

Northern thought is slow and durable.
ROBERT BROWNING: *Luria,* v, 1846

The brain secretes thought as the stomach secretes gastric juice, the liver bile, and the kidneys urine.
KARL VOGT: *Köhlerglaube und Wissenschaft,* 1854 (Cf. CABANIS, *ante,* 1796)

Thinking is very far from knowing.
H. G. BOHN: *Handbook of Proverbs,* 1855

One of the worst diseases to which the human creature is liable is its disease of thinking. If it would only just *look* at a thing instead of thinking what it must be like, or *do* a thing, instead of thinking it cannot be done, we should all get on far better.
JOHN RUSKIN: *The Political Economy of Art,* 1857

To think is to speak low. To speak is to think aloud.
F. MAX MÜLLER: *Lectures on the Science of Language,* I, 1861

A thought comes when it wishes, not when I wish.
F. W. NIETZSCHE: *Beyond Good and Evil,* 1886

The excesses of an unbridled intellect, which unfailingly end in the oppression of the untutored multitude, are no less rightly controlled by the authority of the law than the injuries inflicted by violence upon the weak.
POPE LEO XIII: *Libertas praestantissimum,* June 20, 1888

Thinking is the most unhealthy thing in the world, and people die of it just as they die of any other disease. Fortunately, in England at any rate, thought is not catching.
OSCAR WILDE: *The Decay of Lying,* 1889

All thought is immoral. Its very essence is destruction. If you think of anything you kill it. Nothing survives being thought of.
OSCAR WILDE: *A Woman of No Importance,* II, 1893

Every act of thinking is identical with the molecular activity of the brain-cortex that coincides with it.
AUGUSTE FOREL: *Die psychischen Fähigkeiten der Ameisen,* 1901

We think so because all other people think so;
Or because – or because – after all, we do think so;
Or because we were told so, and think we must think so;
Or because we once thought so, and think we still think so;
Or because, having thought so, we think we will think so.
Ascribed to HENRY SIDGWICK (1838–1901)

It takes longer to think clearly than it takes to learn rifle-shooting, round-arm bowling, or piano-playing. The great mass of the people (of all classes) cannot think at all. That is why the majority never rule. They are led like sheep by the few who know that they cannot think.
ROBERT BLATCHFORD: *God and My Neighbor,* 1903

I think that I think; therefore, I think I am. (Cogito cogito, ergo cogito sum.)
AMBROSE BIERCE: *The Devil's Dictionary,* 1906 (Cf. DESCARTES, *ante,* 1636)

The stream of thinking is only a careless name for what, when scrutinized, reveals itself to consist chiefly of the stream of my breathing.
WILLIAM JAMES: *Essays in Radical Empiricism,* I, 1912

Thought is only a flash between two long nights, but this flash is everything.
HENRI POINCARÉ (1854–1912)

Most people think dramatically, not quantitatively.
O. W. HOLMES II: Speech in New York, Feb. 15, 1913

To think is to differ.
CLARENCE DARROW: From the court records of the Scopes trial, Dayton, Tenn., July 13, 1925

No one can be hanged for thinking.
PENNSYLVANIA GERMAN PROVERB

[*See also* Books, Character, Clarity, Memory, Phosphorus, Soldier, Thought (Free), Thoughts.

Thirst

In that day shall the fair virgins and young men faint for thirst. AMOS VIII, 13, *c.* 750 B.C.

It is a miserable job to dig a well while you are thirsty.
PLAUTUS: *Mostellaria,* II, *c.* 200 B.C.

I was thirsty, and ye gave me drink.
MATTHEW XXV, 35, *c.* 75

Thirst comes by drinking.
RABELAIS: *Gargantua,* I, 1535

He that goes to bed thirsty rises healthy.
ENGLISH PROVERB, traced by Apperson to 1640

How dry I am! How dry I am!
Nobody knows how dry I am!
American popular song, date uncertain

Whoever is master of his thirst is master of his health. FRENCH PROVERB

Those who are really thirsty drink in silence.
GREEK PROVERB

A pathological thirst. (Polydipsia.)
MEDICAL TERM

[*See also* Charity, Drinking, Eating and Drinking.

Thirty

Tiberius was wont to mock at the arts of physicians, and at those who, after thirty years of age, needed counsel as to what was good or bad for their bodies.
TACITUS: *Annals, c.* 100

Better than old beef is the tender veal:
I want no woman thirty years of age.
GEOFFREY CHAUCER: *The Canterbury Tales* (The Merchant's Tale), *c.* 1386

Of all the great human actions I ever heard or read of, of what sort soever, I have observed, both in former ages and our own, more performed before thirty than after; and ofttimes in the lives of the same men.
MICHEL DE MONTAIGNE: *Essays,* I, 1580

Every one is a fool or a physician to himself after thirty.
JAMES HOWELL: *Proverbs,* 1659 (Sometimes the age is stated to be forty. Cf. TACITUS, *ante, c.* 100)

I swear she's no chicken; she's on the wrong side of thirty, if she be a day.
JONATHAN SWIFT: *Polite Conversation,* 1738

I think, till thirty, or with some a little longer, people should dress in a way that is most likely to procure the love of the opposite sex.
WILLIAM SHENSTONE: *On Dress,* 1764

No man,
Till thirty, should perceive there's a plain woman.
BYRON: *Don Juan,* XIII, 1823

Men and women at thirty years, and even earlier, have lost all spring and vivacity, and if they fail in their first enterprises, they throw up the game.
R. W. EMERSON: *The Tragic,* 1844

The man who has reached thirty feels at times as if he had come out of a great battle. Comrade after comrade has fallen; his own life seems to have been charmed.
ALEXANDER SMITH: *Dreamthorp,* III, 1863

The knell of my thirtieth year has sounded; in three or four years my youth will be as a faint haze on the sea, an illusive recollection.
GEORGE MOORE: *Confessions of a Young Man,* XII, 1888

[*See also* Ages, Duchess, Mind and Body, Senator.

Thirty-eight

One's thirty-eighth year is an evil and dangerous year, bringing many heavy and great sicknesses; naturally, by reason perhaps of the comets and conjunctions of Saturn and of Mars, but spiritually, by reason of the innumerable sins of the people.
MARTIN LUTHER: *Table-Talk,* DCCLXXXVII, 1569

Thirty-five

Ladies, stock and tend your hive,
Trifle not at thirty-five;
For, howe'er we boast and strive,
Life declines from thirty-five;
He that ever hopes to thrive
Must begin by thirty-five.
SAMUEL JOHNSON: To Hester Thrale on her thirty-fifth birthday, 1776

Too old for youth, — too young, at thirty-five,
To herd with boys, or hoard with good threescore, —
I wonder people should be left alive;
But since they are, that epoch is a bore.
BYRON: *Don Juan,* XIII, 1823

One backward look — the last — the last!
One silent tear — for youth is past!
N. P. WILLIS: *Thirty-Five,* 1835

The intellectual powers are most capable of enduring great and sustained efforts in youth, up to the age of thirty-five at the latest; from which period their strength begins to decline, though very gradually.
ARTHUR SCHOPENHAUER: *The Ages of Life,* 1851

[*See also* Mind and Body.

Thirty-seven

[*See* Marriage.

Thirty-six

It is high time, Excellency, if they want any more work out of me. I am already thirty-six.
FRIEDRICH WILHELM, FREIHERR VON SEYDLITZ: To Gen. von Zieten, on being given the Ordre Pour le Mérite, June 20, 1757

My days are in the yellow leaf;
The flowers and fruits of love are gone;
The work, the canker and the grief
Are mine alone.
BYRON: *On My Thirty-Sixth Year,* 1824

Thirty-three

Through life's road, so dim and dirty,
I have dragged to three and thirty:
What have these years left to me?
Nothing, except thirty-three.
BYRON: *Diary,* Jan. 22, 1821

Thoreau, H. D. (1817–62)

He thought everything a discovery of his own, from moonlight to the planting of acorns and nuts by squirrels. This is a defect in his character, but one of his chief charms as a writer.
J. R. LOWELL: *Thoreau,* 1865 (North American Review, Oct.)

Thoreau's thin, penetrating, big-nosed face, even in a bad woodcut, conveys some hint of the limitations of his mind and character. With his almost acid sharpness of insight, with his almost animal dexterity in act, there went none of that large, unconscious geniality of the world's heroes. He was not easy, not ample, not urbane, not even kind.

R. L. STEVENSON: *Familiar Studies of Men and Books*, IV, 1882

Thorn

[*See* Crown of Thorns.

Thoroughness

Whatever is worth doing at all is worth doing well.

LORD CHESTERFIELD: *Letter to his son*, Oct. 9, 1746

Thought

[*See* Thinking, Thoughts.

Thought, Free

Thought is free.

JOHN GOWER: *Confessio Amantis, c.* 1390

This is the gradation of thinking, preaching, and acting: if a man thinks erroneously he may keep his thoughts to himself, and nobody will trouble him; if he preaches erroneous doctrine society may expel him; if he acts in consequence of it, the law takes place, and he is hanged.

SAMUEL JOHNSON: *Boswell's Life*, May 7, 1773

I will war, at least in words (and should
My chance so happen — deeds) with all who war
With thought. BYRON: *Don Juan*, IX, 1823

To be able to think freely, a man must be certain that no consequences will follow whatever he writes.

ERNEST RENAN: *L'Église chrétienne*, 1879

If there is any principle of the Constitution that more imperatively calls for attachment than any other it is the principle of free thought — not free thought for those who agree with us but freedom for the thought that we hate.

MR. JUSTICE O. W. HOLMES: *Dissenting opinion in the United States* vs. *Rozsika Schwimmer*, 1928

Thoughts are toll-free, but not Hell-free.

GERMAN PROVERB

[*See also* Freedom (Religious), Liberty, Opinion, Press (Free), Speech (Free), Violence.

Thoughts

The Lord knoweth the thoughts of men, that they are vanity.

PSALMS XCIV, 11, *c.* 150 B.C.

A penny for your thoughts.

JOHN HEYWOOD: *Proverbs*, 1546

Heavy thoughts bring on physical maladies; when the soul is oppressed, so is the body.

MARTIN LUTHER: *Table-Talk*, DCXLV, 1569

They are never alone that are accompanied with noble thoughts.

PHILIP SIDNEY: *Arcadia*, I, 1590

My thoughts are whirled like a potter's wheel.

SHAKESPEARE: *I Henry VI*, I, 1592

Thoughts are but dreams till their effects be tried.

SHAKESPEARE: *The Rape of Lucrece*, 1594

As angels in some brighter dreams,
Call to the soul when man doth sleep,
So some strange thoughts transcend our wonted themes,
And into glory peep.

HENRY VAUGHAN: *They Are All Gone*, 1646

The secret thoughts of a man run over all things, holy, profane, clean, obscene, grave, and light, without shame or blame.

THOMAS HOBBES: *Leviathan*, VIII, 1651

I can easily conceive of a man without hands, feet, head, for it is only experience that teaches us that the head is more necessary than the feet. But I cannot conceive of a man without thoughts, — it would be a stone or a brute. BLAISE PASCAL: *Pensées*, II, 1670

It is mere chance that suggests thoughts; it is mere chance that obliterates them from the world; there is no particular method by which they may be preserved or acquired.

IBID.

The thoughts that come often unsought, and, as it were, drop into the mind, are the most valuable of any we have, and therefore should be secured, because they seldom return again.

JOHN LOCKE: *Letter to Samuel Bold*, May 16, 1699

Perish that thought!

COLLEY CIBBER: *Adaptation of* SHAKESPEARE: *Richard III*, V, 1700

Thoughts shut up want air
And spoil, like bales unopened to the sun.

EDWARD YOUNG: *Night Thoughts*, II, 1742

When a thought is too weak to be simply expressed, it is a proof that it should be rejected.

LUC DE VAUVENARGUES: *Réflexions*, 1746

He that will not command his thoughts . . . will soon lose the command of his actions.

THOMAS WILSON: *Sacra Privata, c.* 1755

One thought fills immensity.

WILLIAM BLAKE: *The Marriage of Heaven and Hell*, 1790

There are two distinct classes of what are called thoughts: those that we produce in ourselves by reflection and the act of thinking, and those that bolt into the mind of their own accord.

THOMAS PAINE: *The Age of Reason*, I, 1794

Every thought is something in itself — the false as well as the true. The false are simply weeds that we can't use in our housekeeping.

G. C. LICHTENBERG: *Reflections*, 1799

Sudden a thought came like a full-blown rose,
Flushing his brow.
JOHN KEATS: *The Eve of St. Agnes,* 1820

A thought by thought is piled, till some great truth
Is loosened, and the nations echo round,
Shaken to their roots.
P. B. SHELLEY: *Prometheus Unbound,* II, 1820

Thought precedes action as lightning does thunder.
HEINRICH HEINE: *History of Religion and Philosophy in Germany,* 1834

Our thoughts are often worse than we are.
MARIAN EVANS (GEORGE ELIOT): *Mr. Gilfil's Love Story,* 1857

The highest possible stage in moral culture is when we recognize that we ought to control our thoughts.
CHARLES DARWIN: *The Descent of Man,* IV, 1871

Thoughts may be bandits. Thoughts may be raiders. Thoughts may be invaders. Thoughts may be disturbers of the international peace.
WOODROW WILSON: Speech, May 16, 1916

Don't let your hat know the thoughts it covers.
FRENCH PROVERB

Sinful thoughts are even more dangerous than sin itself. HEBREW PROVERB

No one suffers punishment for his thoughts. (Cogitationis poenam nemo patitur.)
LEGAL MAXIM

Thoughts beguile maidens.
SCOTTISH PROVERB

[*See also* Action, Ethics, Forehead, Idea, Language, Mind, Night, Phosphorus, Thinking, Thought (Free).

Thought, Second

Second thoughts are the wisest.
EURIPIDES: *Hippolytus,* 428 B.C.

Had I wist comes too late.
JOHN CLARKE: *Parœmiologia Anglo-Latina,* 1639

Second thoughts are best.
JOHN DRYDEN: *The Spanish Friar,* II, 1681
(Quoted as a proverb)

Second thoughts oftentimes are the very worst of all thoughts. First and third very often coincide. Indeed, second thoughts are too frequently formed by the love of novelty, of showing penetration, of distinguishing ourselves from the mob, and have consequently less of simplicity, and more of affectation.
WILLIAM SHENSTONE: *Of Men and Manners,* 1764

Threat

It is prudent for a man to abstain from threats or contemptuous expressions, for neither weaken the enemy: threats make him more cautious, and contemptuous remarks excite his hatred and a desire to revenge himself.
NICCOLÒ MACHIAVELLI: *Discorsi,* II, 1531

If you cannot bite never show your teeth.
JOHN RAY: *English Proverbs,* 1670

A threatened man lives seven years.
DUTCH PROVERB

Three

Three are too many to keep a secret, and too few to be merry.
THOMAS FULLER: *Gnomologia,* 1732

All good things are three. (Alle guten Dinge sind drei.) GERMAN PROVERB

The third time's lucky. SCOTTISH PROVERB

Thrift

I shall cut my coat after my cloth.
JOHN HEYWOOD: *Proverbs,* 1546

Sparing is good getting.
JOHN LYLY: *Euphues and His England,* 1580

A penny saved is a penny earned.
ENGLISH PROVERB, familiar since the XVII century

He that will not stoop for a pin will never be worth a pound.
ENGLISH PROVERB, quoted by SAMUEL PEPYS: *Diary,* Jan. 3, 1668

It is better to have a hen tomorrow than an egg today.
THOMAS FULLER: *Gnomologia,* 1732

Penny and penny,
Laid up, will be many. IBID.

The most substantial people are the most frugal, and make the least show, and live at the least expense.
FRANCIS MOORE: *A Voyage to Georgia, Begun in the Year 1735,* 1744

I knew once a very covetous, sordid fellow who used to say, "Take care of the pence, for the pounds will take care of themselves."
LORD CHESTERFIELD: *Letter to his son,* Nov. 6, 1747

Thrift is care and scruple in the spending of one's means. It is not a virtue, and it requires neither skill nor talent.
IMMANUEL KANT: Lecture at Königsberg, 1775

A man who both spends and saves money is the happiest man, because he has both enjoyments.
SAMUEL JOHNSON: *Boswell's Life,* April 25, 1778

Spare when you are young, and spend when you are old.
H. G. BOHN: *Handbook of Proverbs,* 1855

Thrift is good revenue. IBID.

Oh, why don't you save
All the money you earn?
If I didn't have to eat
I'd have money to burn.
Anon.: *Hallelujah, I'm a Bum*, *c.* 1907

Though you live near a forest, do not waste fire-wood. CHINESE PROVERB

He who really wants to save should begin with his mouth. DANISH PROVERB

Saving is greater than earning. GERMAN PROVERB

Frae saving comes having. SCOTTISH PROVERB

[*See also* Economy, Frugality.

Throne

The throne is only a bit of gilded wood trimmed with velvet.
NAPOLEON I: To the French Senate, 1814

That fierce light which beats upon a throne
And blackens every blot.
ALFRED TENNYSON: *Idylls of the King*, dedication, 1842

[*See also* Abdication, Altar, King, Power.

Thrush

[*See* Nightingale.

Thucydides (c. 471–390 B.C.)

This day I finished Thucydides, after reading him with inexpressible interest and admiration. He is the greatest historian that ever lived.
T. B. MACAULAY: Written in a copy of THUCYDIDES: *History*, Feb. 27, 1835

Thunder

The Lord thundered from heaven, and the Most High uttered his voice.
II SAMUEL XXII, 14, *c.* 500 B.C.

He thundereth with the voice of his excellency.
JOB XXXVII, 4, *c.* 325 B.C.

The thunder of the captains. JOB XXXIX, 25

He surnamed them Boanerges, which is, The sons of thunder. MARK III, 17, *c.* 70

The deep, dread-bolted thunder.
SHAKESPEARE: *King Lear*, IV, 1606

That deep and dreadful organ-pipe.
SHAKESPEARE: *The Tempest*, III, 1611

Thunderstorms are often caused by Satan, and sometimes by good angels. Thunder is the voice of God, and, therefore, to be dreaded. All places in the habitable world are subject to it more or less. No amulets can preserve men from being hurt thereby.
INCREASE MATHER: *Remarkable Providences*, 1684

Thunders are observed oftener to break upon churches than upon any other buildings.
COTTON MATHER: *The Wonders of the Invisible World*, 1692

That great artillery of God Almighty.
WILLIAM TEMPLE: *Of Ancient and Modern Learning*, 1692

From peak to peak the rattling crags among
Leaps the live thunder.
BYRON: *Childe Harold*, III, 1816

If it thunders in March one may well say "alas" (hélas). FRENCH PROVERB

While the thunder lasted two bad men were friends. HINDU PROVERB

Harmless thunderbolt. (Brutum fulmen.)
LATIN PHRASE

Thunder in Spring
Cold will bring. OLD ENGLISH RHYME

[*See also* Thief.

Thursday

Thursday come, and the week is gone.
GEORGE HERBERT: *Outlandish Proverbs*, 1640

On Thursday at three
Look out and you'll see
What Friday will be. OLD ENGLISH RHYME

[*See also* Days, Nail, Sneezing, Wedding-Day.

Thyme

I know a bank where the wild thyme blows.
SHAKESPEARE: *A Midsummer Night's Dream*, II, *c.* 1596

Tibet

The roof of the world.
T. E. GORDON: Title of a book, 1876

The forbidden land.
W. S. LANDOR: Part of the title of a book, 1898

[*See also* Buddhism.

Tickling

A momentary pain and apprehension of pain with an immediately succeeding removal of these, and their alternate recurrency.
DAVID HARTLEY: *Observations on Man*, I, 1749

[*See also* Tit for Tat, Trout.

Tide

[*See* Time.

Tidings

[*See* News.

Tiger

Tiger, tiger, burning bright
In the forests of the night,
What immortal hand or eye

Could frame thy fearful symmetry?
WILLIAM BLAKE: *The Tiger*, 1794

How strong his muscles! He with ease
Upon the tallest man could seize;
In his large mouth away could bear him,
And into thousand pieces tear him.
MARY LAMB: *The Beasts in the Tower*, 1809

A tiger has a natural right to eat a man; but if he may eat one man he may eat another, so that a tiger has a right of property in all men, as potential tiger-meat.
T. H. HUXLEY: *Natural Rights and Political Rights*, 1890

There was a young lady of Niger
Who smiled as she rode on a tiger;
They came back from the ride
With the lady inside
And the smile on the face of the tiger.
Author unidentified

[*See also* Butcher, Sport.

Time

Take time by the forelock.
ENGLISH PROVERB, borrowed from the Greek, and traced to Pittacus of Mitylene, *c.* 600 B.C.

Time will reveal everything. It is a babbler, and speaks even when not asked.
EURIPIDES: *Fragment*, *c.* 425 B.C.

Time makes all things worse.
DEMETRIUS: *Fragment*, *c.* 415 B.C.

To everything there is a season, and a time to every purpose under heaven.
ECCLESIASTES III, 1, *c.* 200 B.C. (The seven verses following list some of these times, e.g., to be born, to love, to kill, to die)

A thousand years in thy sight are but as yesterday when it is past, and as a watch in the night. PSALMS XC, 4, *c.* 150 B.C.

Our time is a very shadow that passeth away.
WISDOM OF SOLOMON II, 5, *c.* 100 B.C.

Do you not see even stones yield to the power of time, lofty towers fall to decay, and rocks molder away? Temples and statues of the gods go to ruin, nor can the gods themselves prolong their date or get reprieve from fate.
LUCRETIUS: *De rerum natura*, V, 57 B.C.

There is nothing done by the hands of man which sometime or other time does not destroy. CICERO: *Pro Marcello*, 46 B.C.

The hours fly around in a circle. (Volat hora per orbem.)
MARCUS MANILIUS: *Astronomica*, I, *c.* 40 B.C.

When time flies it cannot be recalled. (Fugit irreparabile tempus.)
VIRGIL: *Georgics*, III, 30 B.C.

What the gods dared not promise to thy prayers, lo time, as it rolls on, has bestowed.
VIRGIL: *Æneid*, IX, 19 B.C.

Time will bring to light whatever is hidden, and it will conceal and cover up what is now shining with the greatest splendor.
HORACE: *Epistles*, I, *c.* 5 B.C.

Time flies. (Tempora labuntur.)
OVID: *Fasti*, VI, *c.* 5 (More commonly, "Tempus fugit")

Time discovers the truth. (Veritatem dies aperit.) SENECA: *De Ira*, II, *c.* 43

Time heals what reason cannot.
SENECA: *Agamemnon*, *c.* 60

The speed of time is infinite.
SENECA: *Epistulæ morales ad Lucilium*, XLIV, *c.* 63

Trust to time: it is the wisest of all counsellors.
PLUTARCH: *Lives*, *c.* 100

The happier the time, the faster it goes.
PLINY THE YOUNGER: *Letters*, VII, *c.* 110

My time is not yet come. JOHN VII, 6, *c.* 115

Time is like a river. As soon as a thing is seen it is carried away and another takes its place, and then that other is carried away also.
MARCUS AURELIUS: *Meditations*, IV, *c.* 170

All hail the power of time! The pleasures of the town, the glories of the king with his court of fawners, his ministers who stand respectfully before him, his women with faces as lovely as the shining moon, his crowds of haughty noblemen, his poets and writers — all go down the stream of time to nothingness.
BHARTRIHARI: *The Vairagya Sataka*, *c.* 625

Time and tide wait for no man.
ENGLISH PROVERB, traced by Apperson to Chaucer, *c.* 1386, though the form here given appears to be recent

There is a time for all things.
ENGLISH PROVERB, traced by Apperson to 1399 (Cf. ECCLESIASTES, *ante*, *c.* 200 B.C.)

Time is, time was, time is past.
ENGLISH PROVERB, traced to the XVI century

Time discloseth all things.
RICHARD TAVERNER: *Proverbs*, 1539 (Cf. HORACE, *ante*, *c.* 5 B.C.)

The nick of time.
ENGLISH PHRASE, traced by Smith to 1577

Time is the father of truth.
JOHN FLORIO: *First Frutes*, 1578 (Cf. SENECA, *ante*, *c.* 43)

Who hath time hath life. IBID.

Time wasteth years, and months, and hours,
  Time doth consume fame, honor, wit and strength,
Time kills the greenest herbs and sweetest flowers,
  Time wears out youth and beauty's looks at length,
    Time doth convey to ground both foe and friend,
    And each thing else but love, which hath no end.

THOMAS WATSON: *Ecatompathia,* 1582

O time too swift! O swiftness never ceasing!

GEORGE PEELE: *Polyhymnia,* 1590

Time is the nurse and breeder of all good.

SHAKESPEARE: *Two Gentlemen of Verona,* III, *c.* 1595

Time wears all his locks before,
  Take thy hold upon his forehead;
When he flies he turns no more,
  And behind his scalp is naked.

ROBERT SOUTHWELL: *Loss in Delay,* *c.* 1595

Time travels in divers paces with divers persons. I'll tell you who time ambles withal, who time trots withal, who time gallops withal, and who he stands still withal.

SHAKESPEARE: *As You Like It,* III, *c.* 1600

Beauty, wit
High birth, vigor of bone, desert in service,
Love, friendship, charity, are subjects all
To envious and calumniating time.

SHAKESPEARE: *Troilus and Cressida,* III, *c.* 1601

Time hath, my lord, a wallet at his back,
Wherein he puts alms for oblivion. IBID.

Time is like a fashionable host
That slightly shakes his parting guest by the hand;
And with his arms outstretch'd, as he would fly,
Grasps in the comer: welcome ever smiles,
And farewell goes out sighing. IBID.

The end crowns all,
And that old common arbitrator, time,
Will one day end it.

SHAKESPEARE: *Troilus and Cressida,* IV

The whirligig of time brings in his revenges.

SHAKESPEARE: *Twelfth Night,* V, *c.* 1601

That old bald cheater, time.

BEN JONSON: *The Poetaster,* I, 1602

Let's take the instant by the forward top;
For we are old, and on our quick'st decrees
The inaudible and noiseless foot of time
Steals ere we can effect them.

SHAKESPEARE: *All's Well that Ends Well,* V, *c.* 1602

He that hath time, and looks for time, loseth time.

WILLIAM CAMDEN: *Remains Concerning Britain,* 1605

Time shall unfold what plaited cunning hides.

SHAKESPEARE: *King Lear,* I, 1606

Time's the king of men,
He's both their parent, and he is their grave,
And gives them what he will, not what they crave.

SHAKESPEARE: *Pericles,* II, *c.* 1608

The dark backward and abysm of time.

SHAKESPEARE: *The Tempest,* I, 1611

To choose time is to save time.

FRANCIS BACON: *Essays,* XXV, 1612

E'en such is time, which takes in trust
  Our youth, our joys, and all we have;
And pays us naught but age and dust,
  Which, in the dark and silent grave,
When we have wandered all our ways,
Shuts up the story of our days.

WALTER RALEIGH: Written in his Bible, *c.* 1617

All that really belongs to us is time; even he who has nothing else has that.

BALTASAR GRACIÁN: *The Art of Worldly Wisdom,* CCXLVII, 1647

Gather ye rose-buds while ye may,
  Old time is still a flying:
And this same flower that smiles today,
  Tomorrow will be dying.

ROBERT HERRICK: *Hesperides,* 1648

Time and I. (Le temps et moi.)

MOTTO OF JULES CARDINAL MAZARIN (1602–61)

Time is a great manager: it arranges things well.

PIERRE CORNEILLE: *Sertorius,* II, 1662

Time flies, and drags us with it. The moment in which I speak is already gone.

NICOLAS BOILEAU: *Épîtres,* III, 1670

Time cures sorrows and squabbles because we all change, and are no longer the same persons. Neither the offender nor the offended is the same.

BLAISE PASCAL: *Pensées,* VI, 1670

Time tries the truth.

JOHN RAY: *English Proverbs,* 1670

Time cuts down all,
Both great and small.

The New England Primer, c. 1688

No preacher is listened to but time, which gives us the same train and turn of thought that elder people have in vain tried to put into our heads before.

JONATHAN SWIFT: *Thoughts on Various Subjects,* 1706

Whenever I attempt to frame a simple idea of time, abstracted from the succession of ideas in my mind, which flows uniformly, and is participated by all beings, I am lost and embrangled in inextricable difficulties.

GEORGE BERKELEY: *The Principles of Human Knowledge,* 1710

We travel through time as through a country filled with many wild and empty wastes, which we would fain hurry over, that we may arrive at those several little settlements or imaginary points of rest which are dispersed up and down in it.
JOSEPH ADDISON: *The Spectator,* June 16, 1711

Let time, that makes you homely, make you sage.
THOMAS PARNELL: *To an Old Beauty,* 1722

Time is the slave of error.
WILLIAM WARBURTON (BISHOP OF GLOUCESTER): *The Causes of Prodigies and Miracles,* I, 1727

Nought treads so silent as the foot of time.
EDWARD YOUNG: *Love of Fame,* V, 1728

A stitch in time saves nine.
ENGLISH PROVERB, borrowed from the Latin, but not recorded before 1732

Take time while time is, for time will away.
THOMAS FULLER: *Gnomologia,* 1732

The sun has stood still, but time never did.
IBID.

Those that make the best use of their time have none to spare.
IBID.

We take no note of time
But from its loss.
EDWARD YOUNG: *Night Thoughts,* I, 1742

Take care of the minutes, for the hours will take care of themselves.
LORD CHESTERFIELD: *Letter to his son,* Oct. 4, 1746

Time is money.
BENJAMIN FRANKLIN: *Advice to a Young Tradesman,* 1748

Know the true value of time; snatch, seize, and enjoy every moment of it. No idleness, no laziness, no procrastination.
LORD CHESTERFIELD: *Letter to his son,* Dec. 26, 1749

The angels in Heaven do not know what time is, for in Heaven there are no days and years, but only changes of state.
EMANUEL SWEDENBORG: *Arcana Coelestia,* 1756

Time shall every grief remove,
With life, with memory, and with love.
THOMAS GRAY: Epitaph on Mrs. Jane Clarke, 1757

Lost time is never found again, and what we call time enough always proves little enough.
BENJAMIN FRANKLIN: *Poor Richard's Almanac,* 1757

Do not squander time, for that is the stuff life is made of.
BENJAMIN FRANKLIN: *The Way to Wealth,* 1758

How insignificant this will appear a twelvemonth hence.
SAMUEL JOHNSON: *Boswell's Life,* July 6, 1763

Time whereof the memory of man runneth not to the contrary.
WILLIAM BLACKSTONE: *Commentaries on the Laws of England,* I, 1765 (A Latin legal phrase)

There's scarce a point whereon mankind agree
So well as in their boast of killing me;
I boast of nothing, but, when I've a mind,
I think I can be even with mankind.
Anon.: *On Killing Time,* 1797

The slow, the silent power of time.
J. C. F. SCHILLER: *Wallenstein's Death,* I, 1799

You may ask me for anything you like except time.
NAPOLEON I: To one of his officers, 1803

Time, stern huntsman! who can baulk?
Staunch as hound, and fleet as a hawk.
WALTER SCOTT: *Hunting Song,* 1808

Time is our consciousness of the succession of ideas in our mind.
P. B. SHELLEY: *Queen Mab,* notes, 1813

O time! the beautifier of the dead,
Adorner of the ruin, comforter
And only healer when the heart hath bled —
Time! the corrector where our judgments err,
The test of truth, love, sole philosopher.
BYRON: *Childe Harold,* IV, 1818

Time, the avenger.
IBID.

Touch us gently, time!
Let us glide adown thy stream
Gently, — as we sometimes glide
Through a quiet dream.
B. W. PROCTOR (BARRY CORNWALL): *A Petition to Time,* 1820

How like death-worms the wingless moments crawl!
P. B. SHELLEY: *Prometheus Unbound,* II, 1820

Time! what an empty vapor 'tis!
And days, how swift they are:
Swift as an Indian arrow —
Fly on like a shooting star;
The present moment just is here,
Then slides away in haste,
That we can never say they're ours,
But only say they're past.
ABRAHAM LINCOLN: Unnamed poem, *c.* 1828

One always has time enough, if only one applies it well.
J. W. GOETHE: *Dichtung und Wahrheit,* II, 1831

Lives of great men all remind us
We can make our lives sublime,

And, departing, leave behind us
Footprints on the sands of time.
H. W. LONGFELLOW: *A Psalm of Life*, 1839

The illimitable, silent, never-resting thing called time, rolling, rushing on, swift, silent, like an all-embracing ocean tide, on which we and all the universe swim like exhalations, like apparitions which *are*, and then *are not*: this is forever very literally a miracle; a thing to strike us dumb.
THOMAS CARLYLE: *Heroes and Hero-Worship*, I, 1840 (Lecture in London, May 5)

The years teach much which the days never know. R. W. EMERSON: *Experience*, 1841

Time dissipates to shining ether the solid angularity of facts.
R. W. EMERSON: *History*, 1841

My stern chase after time is, to borrow a simile from Tom Paine, like the race of a man with a wooden leg after a horse.
JOHN QUINCY ADAMS: *Diary*, March 25, 1844

Time was made for slaves.
J. B. BUCKSTONE: *Billy Taylor*, I, 1850

She saw
Time, like a pulse, shake fierce
Through all the worlds.
D. G. ROSSETTI: *The Blessed Damozel*, 1850

Time, a maniac scattering dust.
ALFRED TENNYSON: *In Memoriam*, L, 1850

Time is that in which all things pass away; it is the form under which the will to live has revealed to it that its efforts are in vain; it is the agent by which at every moment all things in our hands become as nothing, and lose all value.
ARTHUR SCHOPENHAUER: *The Vanity of Existence*, 1851

Time is wiser than we.
J. A. FROUDE: *Arnold's Poems*, 1854 (Westminster Review)

Time is but the stream I go fishing in.
H. D. THOREAU: *Walden*, 1854

Time is a file that wears and makes no noise.
H. G. BOHN: *Handbook of Proverbs*, 1855

What's time? Leave Now for dogs and apes:
Man has Forever.
ROBERT BROWNING: *A Grammarian's Funeral*, 1855

The bird of time has but a little way
To flutter – and the bird is on the wing.
EDWARD FITZGERALD: Tr. of OMAR KHAYYÁM: *Rubáiyát* (*c.* 1100), 1857

Those who have most to do, and are willing to work, will find the most time.
SAMUEL SMILES: *Self-Help*, I, 1859

A time for labor and thought,
A time to serve and to sin.
A. C. SWINBURNE: *Atalanta in Calydon*, 1865

Time is on our side.
W. E. GLADSTONE: Speech in the House of Commons, 1866

We are not sure of sorrow,
And joy was never sure;
To-day will die to-morrow;
Time stoops to no man's lure.
A. C. SWINBURNE: *The Garden of Proserpine*, 1866

Damsels of time, the hypocritic days,
Muffled and dumb like barefoot dervishes,
And marching single in an endless file,
Bring diadems and faggots in their hands.
R. W. EMERSON: *Days*, 1867

Old time, in whose banks we deposit our notes,
Is a miser who always wants guineas for groats;
He keeps all his customers still in arrears
By lending them minutes and charging them years.
O. W. HOLMES: *Our Banker*, 1874

Time is the only true purgatory.
SAMUEL BUTLER: *Note-Books*, *c.* 1890

A time filled with varied and interesting experiences seems short in passing, but long as we look back. On the other hand, a tract of time empty of experience seems long in passing, but in retrospect short.
WILLIAM JAMES: *Psychology, Briefer Course*, XVII, 1892

Time is waste of money.
OSCAR WILDE: *Phrases and Philosophies for the Use of the Young*, 1894

Time has upset many fighting faiths.
MR. JUSTICE O. W. HOLMES: *Dissenting Opinion in Abrams* et al vs. *the United States*, 1919

Time is a tyranny to be abolished.
EUGENE JOLAS: *The Language of Night*, 1932

Time is something that we ain't got nothing but. AMERICAN SAYING

Those who try to kill time will discover that time can stand the racket longer than they can. Author unidentified

Time is a great legaliser. IBID.

There is no mortar that time will not loose.
FRENCH PROVERB

Time brings roses. GERMAN PROVERB

Time covers and uncovers. (Zeit verdeckt und entdeckt.) IBID.

Time heals all. (Zeit heilt alles.) IBID.

Time is the best medicine for anger. IBID.

Who waits for time, loses time.
ITALIAN PROVERB

Know your time. (Nosce tempus.)
LATIN PROVERB

Time is the devourer of all things. (Tempus edax rerum.)
IBID.

Time is sometimes a mother and sometimes a stepmother.
MONTENEGRIN PROVERB

These three will be effaced by time: a debt, a sore, and a stain.
SANSKRIT PROVERB

A day to come seems langer than a year that's gane.
SCOTTISH PROVERB

It is time, not medicine, that cures the sick.
SPANISH PROVERB

Time and I against any two.
IBID.

[*See also* Afternoon, Days, End, Eternity, Friend, Grief, Love, Man and Woman, Medicine, Nation, Patience, Physician, Procrastination, Punctuality, Rose, Truth.

Time and Space

Nothing puzzles me more than time and space; and yet nothing puzzles me less, for I never think about them.
CHARLES LAMB: *Letter to Thomas Manning,* Jan. 2, 1810

Times

Oh, the times! Oh, the manners! (O tempora, O mores!)
CICERO: *Oration in Catilinam,* 50 B.C.

He who yields to his times acts wisely.
PUBLILIUS SYRUS: *Sententiæ, c.* 50 B.C.

Can ye not discern the signs of the times?
MATTHEW XVI, 3, *c.* 75

The time is out of joint.
SHAKESPEARE: *Hamlet,* I, *c.* 1601 (Usually quoted in the plural)

These most brisk and giddy-paced times.
SHAKESPEARE: *Twelfth Night,* II, *c.* 1601

Accusing the times is but excusing ourselves.
THOMAS FULLER: *Gnomologia,* 1732

These are the times that try men's souls.
THOMAS PAINE: *The Crisis,* I, 1776 (Pennsylvania Journal, Dec. 19)

These feeble and fastidious times.
WILLIAM WORDSWORTH: *Letter to Alexander Dyce,* 1830

These times of ours are serious and full of calamity, but all times are essentially alike.
R. W. EMERSON: Lecture on Public and Private Education, Boston, Nov. 27, 1864

A sign of better times. (Auspicium melioris ævi.)
LATIN PHRASE

Timidity

Where heart has failed
There shall no castle be assailed.
JOHN GOWER: *Confessio Amantis, c.* 1390

Faint hearts fair ladies never win.
WILLIAM ELDERTON: *Britain's Ida,* 1569 (The more usual form, "Faint heart never won fair lady," dates from the following century)

He is not able to say boo to a goose.
Anon.: *The Martin Marprelate Tracts,* 1588

Timidity is a fault for which it is dangerous to reprove persons whom we wish to correct of it.
LA ROCHEFOUCAULD: *Maxims,* 1665

He either fears his fate too much,
Or his deserts are small,
That dares not put it to the touch,
To gain or lose it all.
JAMES GRAHAM (MARQUESS OF MONTROSE): *My Dear and Only Love,* 1711

Man is timid and apologetic; he is no longer upright; he dares not say "I think," "I am," but he quotes some saint or sage.
R. W. EMERSON: *Self-Reliance,* 1841

We are afraid of truth, afraid of fortune, afraid of death, and afraid of each other.
IBID.

He wasna the inventor o' gunpowder.
SCOTTISH SAYING

[*See also* Coward, Cowardice, Fear.

Tinfoil

I have never yet met anyone who did not think it was an agreeable sensation to cut tinfoil with scissors.
G. C. LICHTENBERG: *Reflections,* 1799

Tipperary

It's a long way to Tipperary, it's a long way to go.
HARRY WILLIAMS and JACK JUDGE: *It's a Long Way to Tipperary;* adopted as a marching song by the British army, 1914

Tipping

I like to pay postilions and waiters rather more liberally than perhaps is right. I hate grumbling and sour faces; and the whole saving will not exceed a guinea or two for being cursed and damned from Dan to Beersheba.
WALTER SCOTT: *Journal,* April 9, 1828

Tired

I have no time to be tired. (Ich habe keine Zeit, müde zu sein.)
WILLIAM I OF GERMANY: On his deathbed, 1888

Tiresome

[*See* Boredom.

Tit-for-tat

One good turn deserves another.
ENGLISH PROVERB, traced by Smith to *c.* 1400

Claw me, and I'll claw thee.

ENGLISH SAYING, traced by Smith to 1531

Ka me, ka thee; one good turn asketh another.

JOHN HEYWOOD: *Proverbs,* 1546 (*Ka*= help)

Tit-for-tat.

ENGLISH PHRASE, not recorded before *c.* 1550 and apparently derived from an earlier " tip-for-tap "

One complimentary letter asketh another.

THOMAS NASHE: *Have With You to Saffron Walden,* 1596

Tit for tat,
If you kill my dog
I'll kill your cat.

Anon.: *Nursery rhyme, c.* 1750

You scratch my back and I'll scratch yours.

Ascribed to SIMON CAMERON, *c.* 1850

You tickle me, and I'll tickle you.

AMERICAN POLITICAL SAYING

[*See also* Turn.

Title

Let me not . . . give flattering titles unto man.

JOB XXXII, 21, *c.* 325 B.C.

It is not titles that honor men, but men that honor titles.

NICCOLÒ MACHIAVELLI: *Discorsi,* III, 1531

Writing letters, or speaking to any person of honor and quality, thou shalt give to each one the title which belongs to him, answerable to his degree, and the custom of the country.

FRANCIS HAWKINS: *Youth's Behavior,* II, 1663

I weigh the man, not his title: 'tis not the king's inscription can make the metal better or heavier.

WILLIAM WYCHERLEY: *The Plain Dealer, c.* 1674

The deathbed shows the emptiness of titles in a true light. A poor dispirited sinner lies trembling under the apprehension of the state he is entering on; and is asked by a grave attendant, how his holiness does?

JOSEPH ADDISON: *The Spectator,* Nov. 10, 1711

To be proud of an hereditary title is to rant it in a dead man's clothes.

THOMAS FULLER: *Gnomologia,* 1732

No state shall . . . grant any title of nobility.

CONSTITUTION OF THE UNITED STATES, Art. I, 1789

The new government has shown genuine dignity, in my opinion, in exploding adulatory titles. They are the offerings of abject baseness, and nourish that degrading vice in the people.

THOMAS JEFFERSON: *Letter to James Madison,* 1789

Titles are but nicknames, and every nickname is a title. The thing is perfectly harmless in itself, but it marks a sort of foppery in the human character which degrades it. It renders man diminutive in things which are great, and the counterfeit of woman in things which are little.

THOMAS PAINE: *The Rights of Man,* I, 1791

Titles are abolished; and the American Republic swarms with men claiming and bearing them.

W. M. THACKERAY: *Roundabout Papers,* 1860

Empty heads are very fond of long titles.

GERMAN PROVERB

[*See also* Abdication, Honors, King.

Toad

Experience has proved the toad to be endowed with valuable qualities. If you run a stick through three toads, and, after having dried them in the sun, apply them to any pestilent tumor, they draw out all the poison, and the malady will disappear.

MARTIN LUTHER: *Table-Talk,* DCCLXXX, 1569

[*See also* Ugliness.

Toast

Drink to all healths, but drink not to thine own.

JOSEPH HALL (BISHOP OF NORWICH): *Virgidemarium,* III, 1597

I drink to the general joy o' the whole table.

SHAKESPEARE: *Macbeth,* III, *c.* 1605

Here's to the maiden of bashful fifteen;
  Here's to the widow of fifty;
Here's to the flaunting, extravagant quean;
  And here's to the housewife that's thrifty.

R. B. SHERIDAN: *The School for Scandal,* III, 1777

But the standing toast that pleased the most
Was, " The wind that blows, the ship that goes,
And the lass that loves a sailor! "

CHARLES DIBDIN: *The Round Robin,* 1811

Here's a sigh to those who love me,
  And a smile to those who hate;
And whatever sky's above me,
  Here's a heart for every fate.

BYRON: *Letter to Thomas Moore,* July 10, 1817

I fill this cup to one made up
  Of loveliness alone,
A woman, of her gentle sex,
  The seeming paragon.

E. C. PINKNEY: *A Health,* 1825

May they have sugar to their strawberries!

LEIGH HUNT: Tr. from an unidentified Italian poet, 1840

Here's to your good health, and your family's good health, and may you all live long and prosper.

DION BOUCICAULT: *Rip Van Winkle*, II, 1866

Here's a health to all those that we love,
Here's a health to all those that love us,
Here's a health to all those that love them that love those
That love them that love those that love us.

Author unidentified

Here's to our wives and sweethearts: may they never meet. IBID.

Here's to the whole world, lest some damn fool take offense. IBID.

May you be in Heaven half an hour before the Devil knows you're dead. IRISH TOAST

Here's to us. Who's like us? Damned few.

IBID.

Here's to you, as good as you are,
And here's to me, as bad as I am;
But as good as you are and as bad as I am,
I'm as good as you are, as bad as I am. IBID.

May all your troubles be little ones.

IBID. (Toast to a bridal couple)

I drink to you. (Propino tibi.)

LATIN TOAST

Tobacco

The leaves being dried and brought into powder, they used to take the fume or smoke thereof by sucking it through pipes made of clay into their stomach and head, from whence it purgeth superfluous phlegm and other gross humors, and openeth all the pores and passages of the body.

THOMAS HARRIOT: *A Briefe and True Reporte of the New Found Land of Virginia*, 1584

Ods me, I marvel what pleasure or felicity they have in taking their roguish tobacco. It is good for nothing but to choke a man, and fill him full of smoke and embers.

BEN JONSON: *Every Man in His Humor*, III, 1601

Herein is not only a great vanity, but a great contempt of God's good gifts, that the sweetness of man's breath, being a good gift of God, should be wilfully corrupted by this stinking smoke.

JAMES I OF ENGLAND: *Counterblaste to Tobacco*, 1604

Much victuals serve for gluttony,
  To fatten men like swine,
But he's a frugal man indeed,
  That with a leaf can dine,
And needs no napkin for his hands,
  His fingers' ends to wipe,
But keeps his kitchen in a box
  And roast meat in a pipe.

SAMUEL ROWLANDS: *The Knave of Clubs*, 1609

Tobacco is a fantastical attracter, and glutton-feeder of the appetite, rather taken of many for wantonness when they have nothing else to do than of any absolute or necessary use.

EDMUND GARDINER: *The Trial of Tobacco*, 1610

Neither do thou lust after that tawney weed tobacco.

BEN JONSON: *Bartholomew Fair*, II, 1614

Earth ne'er did breed
Such a jovial weed.

BARTEN HOLYDAY: *Technogamia*, I, 1618

Tobacco drieth the brain, dimmeth the sight, vitiateth the smell, hurteth the stomach, destroyeth the concoction, disturbeth the humors and spirits, corrupteth the breath, induceth a trembling of the limbs, exsiccateth the windpipe, lungs, and liver, annoyeth the milt, scorcheth the heart, and causeth the blood to be adusted.

TOBIAS VENNER: *Via recta*, 1620

Divine, rare, super-excellent tobacco . . . goes far beyond all the panaceas, potable gold and philosopher's stones, [and] is a sovereign remedy to all diseases.

ROBERT BURTON: *The Anatomy of Melancholy*, II, 1621

Tobacco is the delight of Dutchmen, as it diffuses a torpor and pleasing stupefaction.

EDMUND BURKE: *The Sublime and Beautiful*, intro., 1756

Tobacco was not known in the Golden Age. So much the worse for the Golden Age.

WILLIAM COWPER: *Letter to William Bull*, June 3, 1783

Tobacco surely was designed
To poison and destroy mankind.

PHILIP FRENEAU: *Tobacco*, 1786

We shall not refuse tobacco the credit of being sometimes medical, when used temperately, though an acknowledged poison.

JESSE TORREY: *The Moral Instructor*, 1819

Sublime tobacco! which from east to west,
Cheers the tar's labor or the Turkman's rest;
Which on the Moslem's ottoman divides
His hours, and rivals opium and his brides;
Magnificent in Stamboul, but less grand,
Though not less loved, in Wapping or the Strand.

BYRON: *The Island*, II, 1823

For thy sake, tobacco, I
Would do anything but die.

CHARLES LAMB: *A Farewell to Tobacco*, c. 1830

A lone man's companion, a bachelor's friend, a hungry man's food, a sad man's cordial, a wakeful man's sleep, and a chilly man's fire.

CHARLES KINGSLEY: *Westward Ho*, VII, 1855

We record our solemn judgment that the habitual use of tobacco is a practise out of harmony with the best Christian life.
The Doctrines and Discipline of the Methodist Episcopal Church, II, 1932

Tobacco is an evil weed,
It was the Devil sowed the seed;
It stains your fingers, burns your clothes
And makes a chimney of your nose.
Author unidentified

After a meal a pipe of tobacco – and that is in the Bible (un dos schteht in der Biwel).
PENNSYLVANIA GERMAN PROVERB

Coffee without tobacco is meat without salt.
PERSIAN PROVERB

Vodka is cursed, tea is twice cursed, coffee and tobacco are thrice cursed.
RUSSIAN PROVERB

[*See also* Cigar, Cigarette, Pipe, Poet, Smoking, Soldier.

Tobacco-chewing

I did in Drury lane see two or three houses marked with a red cross upon the doors, and "Lord have mercy upon us" writ there. . . . It put me into an ill conception of myself and my smell, so that I was forced to buy some roll tobacco to smell and to chaw, which took away the apprehension.
SAMUEL PEPYS: *Diary*, June 7, 1665

In comes a tall country fellow with his alfogeos full of tobacco; for they seldom lose their cud, but keep chewing and spitting as long as their eyes are open.
SARAH KEMBLE KNIGHT: *The Private Journal on a Journey from Boston to New York*, Oct. 7, 1704 (*Alfogeos*=cheek)

Should an American gentleman, during a visit to England, be seen chewing tobacco, it matters not what may be his dress, or his letters of introduction; he will immediately be set down as a low-bred mechanic, or, at best, as the master of a merchant vessel.
JOHN GRIGG: *The American Chesterfield*, 1827

Chewing is particularly obnoxious to me. Go out and remove that quid, and never appear before me again chewing tobacco.
ROBERT E. LEE: To a student at Washington College, 1867

How well I remember my grandmother's asking me not to use tobacco, good old soul! She said: "You're at it again, are you, you whelp! Now don't ever let me catch you chewing tobacco before breakfast again, or I lay I'll blacksnake you within an inch of your life."
S. L. CLEMENS (MARK TWAIN): *History Repeats Itself*, 1870 (Galaxy, Dec.)

I larnt him to chaw terbacker
To keep his milk-teeth white.
JOHN HAY: *Little Breeches*, 1871

Henrik Ibsen's old housekeeper declared that she had never seen her master smoke. He chewed tobacco, and furthermore, the housekeeper said, it wasn't even respectable tobacco, but the cheapest brand of American twist, imported to Norway for Ibsen's particular use.
London cablegram to the New York Herald-Tribune, June 7, 1926

[*See also* Tobacco.

Today

Today is the pupil of yesterday.
PUBLILIUS SYRUS: *Sententiæ*, *c.* 50 B.C.

[*See also* Here, Today and Tomorrow.

Today and Tomorrow

Tomorrow's life is too late; live today.
MARTIAL: *Epigrams*, I, 86

The goodness that thou mayest do this day, do it; and . . . delay it not till tomorrow.
GEOFFREY CHAUCER: *The Canterbury Tales* (The Tale of Melibeus), *c.* 1386 (Cited as "an old proverb")

Never put off until tomorrow what you can do today.
ENGLISH PROVERB, traced by Smith to the XVII century

He that falls today may rise tomorrow.
THOMAS SHELTON: Tr. of CERVANTES: *Don Quixote*, II (1615), 1620

One today is worth two tomorrows.
FRANCIS QUARLES: *Enchyridion*, 1640

It is better to have an egg today than tomorrow a hen.
GIOVANNI TORRIANO: *Italian Proverbs*, 1666

Happy the man, and happy he alone,
He who can call today his own;
He who, secure within, can say,
Tomorrow, do thy worst, for I have liv'd today.
JOHN DRYDEN: *Imitations of Horace*, III, 1693

We are here today and gone tomorrow.
Anon.: *Poor Robin's Almanac*, 1731

If today will not, tomorrow may.
THOMAS FULLER: *Gnomologia*, 1732

One hour today is worth two tomorrow.
IBID. (Cf. QUARLES, *ante*, 1640)

Today me, tomorrow thee. IBID.

Tomorrow, tomorrow, only not today! (Morgen, morgen, nur nicht heute!)
C. F. WEISSE: *Der Aufschub*, *c.* 1790

The present is Hell, and the coming tomorrow
But brings, with new torture, the curses of today.
BYRON: *To Caroline*, 1805

Never do today what you can do as well tomorrow.
Ascribed to AARON BURR in JAMES PARTON: *Life and Times of Aaron Burr*, 1858 (*c.* 1835)

Oh, to be wafted away,
From this black Aceldama of sorrow,
Where the dust of an earthy today
Is the earth of a dusty tomorrow!
W. S. GILBERT: *Patience*, II, 1881

It may be a fire today, but tomorrow it will be only ashes. ARAB PROVERB

Today gold, tomorrow dust.
DANISH PROVERB

Give me today, and take tomorrow.
GREEK PROVERB

Today, not tomorrow. (Hodie, non cras.)
LATIN PHRASE

Tomorrow will have the same sun and the same moon as today. WEST AFRICAN PROVERB

[*See also* Caution, Today, Tomorrow, Turn.

Toddy

The cordial drop, the morning dram, I sing,
The midday toddy, and the evening sling.
Anon.: In the Baltimore Weekly Magazine, Aug. 30, 1800

Toil

[*See* Work.

Toilet

Cats, flies and women are ever at their toilets.
FRENCH PROVERB

Toleration

It is forbidden to decry other sects; the true believer gives honor to whatever in them is worthy of honor.
Decree of Asoka, Buddhist emperor of India (264–228 B.C.)

One believeth that he may eat all things: another, who is weak, eateth herbs. Let not him that eateth despise him that eateth not; and let not him which eateth not judge him that eateth. ROMANS XIV, 2–3, *c.* 55

Pray you use your freedom,
And, so far as you please, allow me mine.
To hear you only; not to be compelled
To take your moral potions.
PHILIP MASSINGER: *The Duke of Milan*, IV, 1623

Live and let live.
DAVID FERGUSSON: *Scottish Proverbs*, 1641

I am of a constitution so general that it consorts and sympathiseth with all things. I have no antipathy, or rather idiosyncrasy, in diet, humor, air, anything.
THOMAS BROWNE: *Religio Medici*, II, 1642

It is the will and command of God that . . . a permission of the paganish, Jewish, Turkish, or anti-Christian consciences and worships be granted to all men in all nations and countries; and they are only to be fought against with that sword which is only (in soul matters) able to conquer, to wit, the sword of God's spirit, the Word of God.
ROGER WILLIAMS: *The Bloudy Tenent of Persecution*, 1644

He that is willing to tolerate any religion, or discrepant way of religion, besides his own, unless it be in matters merely indifferent, either doubts of his own, or is not sincere in it.
NATHANIEL WARD: *The Simple Cobbler of Aggawam*, 1646

No person or persons whatsoever within this province, or the islands, ports, harbors, creeks or havens thereunto belonging, professing to believe in Jesus Christ shall from henceforth be any ways troubled, molested or discountenanced for or in respect of his religion nor in the free exercise thereof.
The Maryland Toleration Act, April 2, 1649

Whatsoever is against the foundation of faith, or contrary to good life, or the laws of obedience, or destructive to human society and the public and just interests of bodies politic, is out of the limits of my question and does not pretend to compliance or toleration.
JEREMY TAYLOR: *A Discourse on the Liberty of Prophesying*, 1649

Never force your subjects to change their religion. Violence can never persuade men; it serves only to make hypocrites. Grant civil liberty to all, not in approving everything as indifferent, but in tolerating with patience whatever Almighty God tolerates, and endeavoring to convert men by mild persuasion.
FRANÇOIS DE FENELON: *Letter to the Old Pretender, son of James II of England*, *c.* 1715

All religions must be tolerated, and the sole concern of the authorities should be to see that one does not molest another, for here every man must be saved in his own way.
FREDERICK THE GREAT: Cabinet Order, June 22, 1740

Toleration is good for all, or it is good for none.
EDMUND BURKE: Speech in the House of Commons, 1773

It is the right as well as the duty of all men in society publicly and at stated seasons to worship the Supreme Being, the Great Creator and Preserver of the universe. Every denomination of Christians, demeaning themselves peaceably and as good subjects of the commonwealth, shall be equally under the protection of the law.
CONSTITUTION OF MASSACHUSETTS, 1780

It is now no more that toleration is spoken of as if it was by the indulgence of one class of the people that another enjoyed the exercise of their inherent natural rights. Happily, the government of the United States, which gives to bigotry no sanction, to persecution no assistance, requires only that those who live under its protection should demean themselves as good citizens in giving it on all occasions their effectual support.

GEORGE WASHINGTON: *Letter to the Jewish congregation of Newport, R. I.,* Aug. 1790

Toleration is not the opposite of intoleration, but is the counterfeit of it. Both are despotisms. The one assumes to itself the right of withholding liberty of conscience, and the other of granting it. The one is the pope, armed with fire and fagot, and the other is the pope selling or granting indulgences.

THOMAS PAINE: *The Rights of Man,* I, 1791

Every individual has a natural and unalienable right to worship God according to the dictates of his own conscience and reason. Every denomination of Christians, demeaning themselves quietly and as good citizens of the state, shall be equally under the protection of the law.

CONSTITUTION OF NEW HAMPSHIRE, 1792

I tolerate with the utmost latitude the right of others to differ from me in opinion without imputing to them criminality. I know too well the weakness and uncertainty of human reason to wonder at its different results.

THOMAS JEFFERSON: *Letter to Mrs. John Adams,* 1804

We are none of us tolerant in what concerns us deeply and entirely.

S. T. COLERIDGE: *Allsop's Letters, Conversations, and Recollections of S. T. Coleridge,* 1836

We are not altogether here to tolerate. We are here to resist, to control and vanquish withal.

THOMAS CARLYLE: *Heroes and Hero-Worship,* IV, 1840 (Lecture in London, May 15)

The United States, knowing no distinction of her own citizens on account of religion or nativity, naturally believes in a civilization the world over which will secure the same universal views.

U. S. GRANT: *Letter appointing Benjamin F. Peixotto consul at Bucharest,* Dec. 8, 1870

The equal toleration of all religions . . . is the same thing as atheism.

POPE LEO XIII: *Immortale Dei,* Nov. 1, 1885

In a republic we must learn to combine intensity of conviction with a broad tolerance of difference of conviction. Wide differences of opinion in matters of religious, political and social belief must exist if conscience and intellect alike are not to be stunted.

THEODORE ROOSEVELT: Speech at the Sorbonne, April 23, 1910

Nothing is more logical than persecution. Religious tolerance is a kind of infidelity.

AMBROSE BIERCE: *Collected Works,* VIII, 1911

If tolerance is tolerant of intolerance it fears being destroyed by intolerance. If it is intolerant of intolerance, then it destroys itself.

ARTHUR E. MORGAN: In Antioch News (Antioch College), Jan., 1934

[*See also* Freedom (Religious), Intolerance, Pennsylvania, Travel.

Tolstoy, Lyof N.

[*See* Disciple.

Tomb

The fairer tomb, the fouler is thy name,
The greater pomp procuring greater shame;
Thy monument make thou thy living deeds;
No other tomb than that true virtue needs.

JOSEPH HALL (BISHOP OF NORWICH): *Virgidemarium,* III, 1597

If a man do not erect in this age his own tomb ere he dies, he shall live no longer in monument than the bell rings, and the widow weeps.

SHAKESPEARE: *Much Ado About Nothing,* V, *c.* 1599

And so sepulchred in such pomp dost lie
That kings for such a tomb would wish to die.

JOHN MILTON: *An Epitaphy on the Admirable Dramatic Poet, W. Shakespeare,* 1630

Tombs are the clothes of the dead. A grave is but a plain suit, and a rich monument is one embroidered.

THOMAS FULLER: *The Holy State and the Profane State,* 1642

Hark! from the tomb a doleful sound.

ISAAC WATTS: *Hymns and Spiritual Songs,* II, 1707

The Sabbath of the tomb.

ALEXANDER POPE: *To Mrs. M. B. on Her Birthday,* 1723

Yet ev'n these bones from insult to protect
Some frail memorial still erected nigh,
With uncouth rhymes and shapeless sculpture deck'd,
Implores the passing tribute of a sigh.

THOMAS GRAY: *Elegy Written in a Country Churchyard,* 1750

Falsehoods upon a tomb or monument may be entitled to some excuse in the affection, the gratitude, and piety of surviving friends. Grief disposes us to magnify the virtues of a relation, as visible objects also appear larger through tears.

WILLIAM SHENSTONE: *On Vanity,* 1764

Respect for the dead is not really shown by laying great stones on them to tell us where

they are laid; but by remembering where they are laid, without a stone to help us.
JOHN RUSKIN: *The Political Economy of Art,* II, 1857

The grander the tomb, the greater hypocrite was the corpse in life. HINDU PROVERB

[*See also* Epitaph, Fame, Grave, Monument, Sound.

Tomorrow

Boast not thyself of tomorrow; for thou knowest not what a day may bring forth.
PROVERBS XXVII, 1, *c.* 150 B.C.

Tomorrow will give us something to think about. CICERO: *Ad Atticum,* XV, *c.* 50 B.C.

Take therefore no thought for the morrow: for the morrow shall take thought for the things of itself. Sufficient unto the day is the evil thereof. MATTHEW VI, 34, *c.* 75

Tomorrow, and tomorrow, and tomorrow,
Creeps in this petty pace from day to day
To the last syllable of recorded time,
And all our yesterdays have lighted fools
The way to dusty death.
SHAKESPEARE: *Macbeth,* V, *c.* 1605

Tomorrow I found a horseshoe.
THOMAS SHELTON: Tr. of CERVANTES: *Don Quixote,* II (1615), 1620

Tomorrow to fresh woods, and pastures new.
JOHN MILTON: *Lycidas,* 1638

When I consider life, 'tis all a cheat,
Yet fool'd with hope, men favor the deceit;
Trust on, and think tomorrow will repay;
Tomorrow's falser than the former day.
JOHN DRYDEN: *Aurengzebe,* IV, 1676

Last night is certainly gone, and tomorrow may never arrive.
RICHARD STEELE: *The Spectator,* May 9, 1712

A man he seems of cheerful yesterdays
And confident tomorrows.
WILLIAM WORDSWORTH: *The Excursion,* VII, 1814

Tomorrow! — Why, tomorrow I may be
Myself with yesterday's sev'n thousand years.
EDWARD FITZGERALD: Tr. of OMAR KHAYYÁM: *Rubáiyát* (*c.* 1100), 1857

Tomorrow comes! Tomorrow, where art thou?
R. H. NEWELL (ORPHEUS C. KERR): *The Dying Year,* 1864

Yes, tomorrow. (Ishi naga.)
ETHIOPIAN SAYING

Leave tomorrow till tomorrow.
GERMAN PROVERB

Tomorrow is endless. RUSSIAN PROVERB

Tomorrow. (Mañana.) SPANISH SAYING

[*See also* Here, Hope, Prudence, Today and Tomorrow, Yesterday.

Tom-tit

On a tree by a river a little tom-tit
Sang " Willow, tit-willow, tit-willow."
W. S. GILBERT: *The Mikado,* II, 1885

Tongue

An unbridled tongue is the worst of diseases.
EURIPIDES: *Orestes,* 408 B.C.

A soft tongue breaketh the bone.
PROVERBS XXV, 15, *c.* 350 B.C.

My tongue is the pen of a ready writer.
PSALMS XIV, 1, *c.* 150 B.C.

Keep thy tongue from evil, and thy lips from speaking guile. PSALMS XXXIV, 13

Many have fallen by the edge of the sword; but not so many as have fallen by the tongue.
ECCLESIASTICUS XXVIII, 18, *c.* 180 B.C.

The tongue is a fire, a world of iniquity.
JAMES III, 6, *c.* 60

The tongue can no man tame; it is an unruly evil, full of deadly poison. JAMES III, 8

The tongue is the vile slave's vilest part.
JUVENAL: *Satires,* IX, 118

Nature hath barried and hedged nothing in so strongly as the tongue, with two rows of teeth, and therewith two kips; besides she hath placed it far from the heart, that it should not utter that which the heart conceived.
JOHN LYLY: *Euphues,* 1579 (*Kip*= a beak)

We may knit that knot with our tongues that we shall never undo with our teeth.
JOHN LYLY: *Euphues and His England,* 1580

That man that hath a tongue, I say, is no man,
If with his tongue he cannot win a woman.
SHAKESPEARE: *Two Gentlemen of Verona,* III, *c.* 1595

He hath a heart as sound as a bell, and his tongue is the clapper; for what his heart thinks his tongue speaks.
SHAKESPEARE: *Much Ado About Nothing,* III, *c.* 1599

Many a man's tongue shakes out his master's undoing.
SHAKESPEARE: *All's Well that Ends Well,* II, *c.* 1602

He that strikes with his tongue must ward with his head.
GEORGE HERBERT: *Outlandish Proverbs,* 1640

Better the feet slip than the tongue.
GEORGE HERBERT: *Jacula Prudentum,* 1651

Our tongues belie our hearts more than our pocket-glasses do our faces.
WILLIAM WYCHERLEY: *The Plain Dealer,* II, *c.* 1674

A fool's tongue is always long enough to cut his own throat.
ENGLISH PROVERB, traced by Apperson to 1732

Birds are entangled by their feet and men by their tongues.
THOMAS FULLER: *Gnomologia,* 1732

The tongue is the rudder of our ship. IBID.

A sharp tongue is the only edge tool that grows keener with constant use.
WASHINGTON IRVING: *Rip Van Winkle,* 1820

The magic of the tongue is the most dangerous of all spells.
E. G. BULWER-LYTTON: *Eugene Aram,* I, 1832

One tongue is enough for two women.
H. G. BOHN: *Handbook of Proverbs,* 1855

The tongue runs fastest when the brain is in neutral. Author unidentified

The tongue is one half of man; the other half is the heart. HINDU PROVERB

The tongue is the noblest of all the organs of the body. IBID.

Thistles and thorns prick sore,
But evil tongues prick more.
OLD ENGLISH RHYME

A long tongue shortens life.
PERSIAN PROVERB

Gie your tongue mair holidays than your head.
SCOTTISH PROVERB

Keep your tongue a prisoner, and your body will gang free. IBID.

The longer the tongue the shorter the hand.
SPANISH PROVERB

Though the tongue is boneless, it can break bones. TURKISH PROVERB

[*See also* Heart, Mischief, Mouth, Silence, Taciturnity.

Tool

It is ill jesting with edged tools.
ROBERT GREENE: *Pandosto,* IV, 1588

An ill workman quarrels with his tools.
JOHN RAY: *English Proverbs,* 1670

Man is a tool-using animal. Nowhere do you find him without tools; without tools he is nothing, with tools he is all.
THOMAS CARLYLE: *Sartor Resartus,* I, 1836

The tools to him that can handle them.
ENGLISH PROVERB, apparently borrowed from the French

[*See also* Body, Machine, Man.

Too Much

Too much of a good thing is worse than none at all.
ENGLISH PROVERB, current since Chaucer's time, *c.* 1385

Can one desire too much of a good thing?
SHAKESPEARE: *As You Like It,* IV, *c.* 1600

The rule of Not too much, by temperance taught.
JOHN MILTON: *Paradise Lost,* XI, 1667

Too much noise deafens us; too much light dazzles us; too much distance or too much proximity impedes vision; too much length or too much brevity of discourse obscures it; too much truth astonishes us.
BLAISE PASCAL: *Pensées,* II, 1670

Our nature hardly allows us to have enough of anything without having too much.
GEORGE SAVILE (MARQUESS OF HALIFAX): *Character of Gilbert Burnet, Bishop of Salisbury, c.* 1690

Nothing too much. (Rien de superflu.)
J.-J. ROUSSEAU: *Émile,* II, 1762

[*See also* Excess.

Toothache

There was never yet philosopher
That could endure the toothache patiently.
SHAKESPEARE: *Much Ado About Nothing,* V, *c.* 1599

For the toothache I have found the following medicine very available: brimstone and gunpowder compounded with butter; rub the mandible with it, the outside being first warmed.
JOHN JOSSELYN: *An Account of Two Voyages,* 1663

The tongue is ever turning to the aching tooth.
THOMAS FULLER: *Gnomologia,* 1732

My curse upon thy venomed stang,
That shoots my tortured gums alang;
And through my lugs gies monie a twang,
Wi' gnawing vengeance,
Tearing my nerves wi' bitter pang,
Like racking engines!
ROBERT BURNS: *Address to the Toothache,* 1789

The man with toothache thinks everyone happy whose teeth are sound.
GEORGE BERNARD SHAW: *Maxims for Revolutionists,* 1903

If you have a toothache, cut off your tongue; if you have a sore eye, cut off your hand.
HINDU PROVERB

[*See also* Music.

Top

There is always room at the top.
Ascribed to DANIEL WEBSTER (1782–1852)

[*See also* Bold.

Topaz

[*See* November.

Torment

Their torment was as the torment of a scorpion, when he striketh a man.
REVELATION IX, 5, *c.* 95

Toronto

Every other city in Canada despises Toronto, and yet wants to be like it.
Ascribed to RUPERT BROOKE (1887–1915)

Torpedo

Damn the torpedoes! Captain Drayton, go ahead! Jouett, full speed!
DAVID G. FARRAGUT: At Mobile Bay, Aug. 5, 1864

Tortoise

[*See* Contempt.

Tory

A cant term, derived, I suppose, from an Irish word, signifying a savage.
SAMUEL JOHNSON: *Dictionary,* 1755

A Whig may be a fool, a Tory must be so.
HORACE WALPOLE: *Letter to William Mason,* July 4, 1778

Though a Tory may now be very like what a Whig was a hundred and twenty years ago, the Whig is as much in advance of the Tory as ever.
T. B. MACAULAY: *The War of the Succession in Spain,* 1833 (Edinburgh Review, Jan.)

[*See also* Conservative, Whig.

Touch

Touch not; taste not; handle not.
COLOSSIANS II, 21, *c.* 60

Touch me not. (Noli me tangere.)
JOHN XX, 17, *c.* 115 (The Latin is from the Vulgate)

Touchstone

[*See* Gold.

Town

God made the country, and man made the town.
WILLIAM COWPER: *The Task,* I, 1785 (Borrowed from VARRO: *Rerum rusticarum,* 26 B.C.)

The axis of the earth sticks out visibly through the centre of each and every town or city.
O. W. HOLMES: *The Autocrat of the Breakfast-Table,* VI, 1858

The country in town. (Rus in urbe.)
LATIN PHRASE

[*See also* City, Countryside.

Trade (=commerce)

Trade is most vigorously carried on in every state and government by the heterodox part of the same; and such as profess opinions different from what are publicly established.
WILLIAM PETTY: *Political Arithmetic,* I, *c.* 1677

It is no sin to sell dear, but a sin to give ill measure.
JAMES KELLY: *Complete Collection of Scottish Proverbs,* 1721

A merchant may, perhaps, be a man of an enlarged mind, but there is nothing in trade connected with an enlarged mind.
SAMUEL JOHNSON: *Boswell's Tour to the Hebrides,* Oct. 18, 1773

Nobody ever saw a dog make a fair and deliberate exchange of one bone for another with another dog. Nobody ever saw one animal by its gestures and natural cries signify to another, this is mine, that yours; I am willing to give this for that.
ADAM SMITH: *The Wealth of Nations,* I, 1776

Trade could not be managed by those who manage it if it had much difficulty.
SAMUEL JOHNSON: To Hester Thrale, Nov. 16, 1779

Trade is a plant which grows wherever there is peace, as soon as there is peace, and as long as there is peace.
R. W. EMERSON: *The Young American,* 1844

Trade is a social act.
J. S. MILL: *On Liberty,* 1859

All trade is and must be in a sense selfish; trade not being infinite, nay, the trade of a particular place or district being possibly very limited, what one man gains another loses. In the hand-to-hand war of commerce men fight on without much thought of others, except a desire to excel or to defeat them.
LORD COLERIDGE: *Judgment in Mogul* vs. *McGregor,* 1888

[*See also* Business, Buying and Selling, Clergy, Commerce, East, Trade (Free).

Trade (=craft)

Every man to his trade.
ENGLISH PROVERB, traced by Smith to 1539

He that changes his trade makes soup in a basket.
SAMUEL PALMER: *Moral Essays on Proverbs,* 1710

He that hath a trade hath an estate, and he that hath a calling hath an office of profit and honor.
BENJAMIN FRANKLIN: *Poor Richard's Almanac,* 1757

Jack of all trades and master of none.
MARIA EDGEWORTH: *Popular Tales,* 1800

There are foolish people, but no foolish trades.
FRENCH PROVERB

A man at work at his trade is the equal of the most learned doctor. HEBREW PROVERB

He who does not teach his son a trade teaches him to be a robber. IBID.

The man who has a trade may go anywhere.
SPANISH PROVERB

A skilful trade is better than an inherited fortune. WELSH PROVERB

[*See also* Ethics (Professional), Expert, Profession, Vocation.

Trade, Free

I am for free commerce with all nations.
THOMAS JEFFERSON: *Letter to Elbridge Gerry,* 1799

The merchants will manage commerce the better, the more they are left free to manage for themselves.
THOMAS JEFFERSON: *Letter to Gideon Granger,* 1800

Free trade, one of the greatest blessings which a government can confer on a people, is in almost every country unpopular.
T. B. MACAULAY: *On Mitford's History of Greece,* 1824 (Knight's Quarterly, Nov.)

The call for free trade is as unavailing as the cry of a spoiled child for the moon. It never has existed; it never will exist.
HENRY CLAY: Speech in the Senate, Feb. 2, 1832

Free trade is not a principle; it is an expedient.
BENJAMIN DISRAELI: Speech in the House of Commons, April 25, 1843

The time has come for the people of the United States to declare themselves in favor of free seas and progressive free trade throughout the world, and, by solemn manifestations, to place their moral influence at the side of their successful example.
Democratic National Platform, 1856

Congress shall have the power to lay and collect taxes, duties, imposts and excises for revenue necessary to pay the debts, provide for the common defense and carry on the government of the Confederate States; but no bounties shall be granted from the treasury, nor shall any duties or taxes on importations from foreign nations be laid to promote or foster any branch of industry.
CONSTITUTION OF THE CONFEDERATE STATES, Art. I, 1861

Trade should be free, even in Hell.
DUTCH SAYING

[*See also* Tariff, Trade (=commerce), War of 1812.

Tradesman

[*See* Lying.

Trades Union

[*See* Labor Union.

Tradition

Hold the traditions which ye have been taught.
II THESSALONIANS II, 15, *c.* 51

The tradition of the elders. MARK VII, 3, *c.* 70

The tradition of all past generations weighs like an Alp upon the brain of the living.
KARL MARX: *18th Brumaire,* 1852

The effigies and splendors of tradition are not meant to cramp the energies or the development of a vigorous and various nation. They are not meant to hold in mortmain the proper territory of human intelligence and righteous aspiration. They live and teach their lessons in our annals, they have their own worshippers and their own shrines, but the earth is not theirs nor the fulness thereof.
LORD ROSEBERY: Address at Aberdeen, Nov. 5, 1880

Tradition is a great retarding force, the *vis inertiæ* of history.
FRIEDRICH ENGELS: *Socialism, Utopian and Scientific,* 1891

Tradition is the fence of the law.
HEBREW PROVERB

[*See also* Heredity, Taste.

Tragedy

Tragedy is an imitation of an action that is serious, complete, and of a certain magnitude, effecting through pity and fear the proper katharsis, or purgation, of emotions.
ARISTOTLE: *Poetics,* I, *c.* 322 B.C.

The aim of tragedy is, by plausible speeches and actions, to move and astonish the audience, but only temporarily.
POLYBIUS: *Histories,* II, *c.* 125 B.C.

Tragedy represents the life of princes; comedy serves to depict the actions of the people.
FRANÇOIS D'AUBIGNAC: *La pratique de théâtre, c.* 1660

There is no theatre in the world has anything so absurd as the English tragi-comedy. Here, a course of mirth; there, another of sadness and passion; a third of honor; and the fourth a duel. Thus, in two hours and a half we run through all the fits of Bedlam.
JOHN DRYDEN: *Of Dramatic Poesy,* 1668

Every tragedy ought to be a very solemn lecture, inculcating a particular Providence and showing it plainly protecting the good, and chastising the bad, or at least the violent. . . . If it is otherwise, it is either an empty amusement, or a scandalous and pernicious libel upon the government of the world.

JOHN DENNIS: *The Advancement and Reformation of Modern Poetry,* 1701

Tragedy must be something bigger than life, or it would not affect us. In nature the most violent passions are silent; in tragedy they must speak, and speak with dignity too.

LORD CHESTERFIELD: *Letter to his son,* Jan. 23, 1752

The delight of tragedy proceeds from our consciousness of fiction; if we thought murders and treasons real they would please no more.

SAMUEL JOHNSON: Preface to his edition of Shakespeare, 1765

There can be no tragedy without a struggle; nor can there be genuine emotion for the spectator unless something other and greater than life is at stake.

FERDINAND BRUNETIÈRE: *Questions de critique,* I, 1888

There is something infinitely mean about other people's tragedies.

OSCAR WILDE: *The Picture of Dorian Gray,* 1891

In this world there are only two tragedies. One is not getting what one wants, and the other is getting it. The last is much the worst; the last is a real tragedy!

OSCAR WILDE: *Lady Windermere's Fan,* III, 1892

One can play comedy; two are required for melodrama; but a tragedy demands three.

ELBERT HUBBARD: *Roycroft Dictionary and Book of Epigrams,* 1923

[*See also* Comedy, Drama, Hero, Life.

Trail

There's a long, long trail a-winding into the land of my dreams.

STODDARD KING: Title of a popular song, 1913 (Music by Zo Elliott)

Training

Train up a child in the way he should go, and when he is old he will not depart from it.

PROVERBS XXII, 6, *c.* 350 B.C.

I feel myself free only because I went through the mill of a complete schooling. If I can go beyond the fugue it is because I know how to write it.

CLAUDE DEBUSSY: To Ernest Guiraud, *c.* 1890

[*See also* Education.

Traitor

Traitors are disliked even by those they favor.

TACITUS: *History,* I, *c.* 100

Though those that are betray'd
Do feel the treason sharply, yet the traitor
Stands in worse case of woe.

SHAKESPEARE: *Cymbeline,* III, *c.* 1609

A traitor never sees his danger until his ruin is at hand.

PIETRO METASTASIO: *Temistocle,* III, 1735

Show me the man who makes war on the government, and fires on its vessels, and I will show you a traitor. If I were President of the United States, I would have all such arrested, and when tried and convicted, by the Eternal God I would hang them.

ANDREW JOHNSON: Public statement, March 2, 1861

Traitors' words ne'er yet hurt honest cause.

SCOTTISH PROVERB

[*See also* Criminal, Treason.

Tramp

[*See* Vagabond.

Tranquility

Along the cool sequestered vale of life,
They kept the noiseless tenor of their way.

THOMAS GRAY: *Elegy Written in a Country Churchyard,* 1750

If old folks would be satisfied with tranquility they would find more of it attainable than any former objects of their pursuits.

HORACE WALPOLE: *Letter to the Countess of Upper Ossory,* Nov. 10, 1793

Tranquility is the old man's milk. I go to enjoy it in a few days, and to exchange the roar and tumult of bulls and bears for the prattle of my grandchildren and senile rest.

THOMAS JEFFERSON: *Letter to Edward Rutledge,* 1797

[*See also* Age (Old), Christianity, Happiness.

Transcendentalist

[Transcendentalists] are not good citizens, not good members of society; unwillingly they bear their part in the public and private burdens; they do not willingly share in the public charities, in the public religious rites, in the enterprises of education, of missions foreign or domestic.

R. W. EMERSON: *The Transcendentalist,* 1842

A transcendentalist is one who has keen sight but little warmth of heart; who has fine conceits but is destitute of the rich glow of love. He is all nerve and no blood — colorless.

ISAAC T. HECKER: *Diary,* June 14, 1844

Transfiguration

After six days Jesus taketh Peter, James, and John his brother, and bringeth them up into a high mountain apart, and was transfigured

before them: and his face did shine as the sun, and his raiment was white as the light.
MATTHEW XVII, 1–2, *c.* 75 (Cf. MARK IX, 1–2, *c.* 70)

All that sat in the council, looking steadfastly on him, saw his face as it had been the face of an angel. ACTS VI, 15, *c.* 75

Transgressor

The way of transgressors is hard.
PROVERBS XIII, 15, *c.* 350 B.C.

Translation

Not versions but perversions. (Non versiones sed eversiones.)
ST. JEROME: Said of the Latin translations of the Bible before the Vulgate, *c.* 400

No literal translation can be just to an excellent original in a superior language; but it is a great mistake to imagine (as many have done) that a rash paraphrase can make amends for this general defect.
ALEXANDER POPE: Tr. of HOMER: *Iliad,* pref., 1715

It is impossible to translate poetry. Can you translate music?
VOLTAIRE: *Letter to Mme. du Deffand,* May 19, 1754

When a book is not of such character that even a bad translation can't spoil it for an intelligent reader, then it is certainly not a book written for posterity.
G. C. LICHTENBERG: *Reflections,* 1799

With what a charm, the moon, serene and bright,
Lends on the bank its soft reflected light!
Sit we, I pray; and let us sweetly hear
The strains melodious with a raptured ear;
For soft retreats, and night's impressive hour,
To harmony impart divinest power.
LEIGH HUNT: *The Indicator,* II, 1821 (Offered as what "a foreign translator, of the ordinary kind," would make of the speech beginning "How sweet the moonlight sleeps upon this bank" in SHAKESPEARE: *The Merchant of Venice,* v, *c.* 1597)

Translations ought never to be written in a verse which requires much command of rhyme. The stanza becomes a bed of Procrustes; and the thoughts of the unfortunate author are alternately racked and curtailed to fit their new receptacle.
T. B. MACAULAY: *Dante,* 1824 (Knight's Quarterly Magazine, Jan.)

We should so render the original that the version should impress the people for whom it is intended just as the original impresses the people for whom it (the original) is intended. E. A. POE: *Marginalia,* 1844–49

Translation is at best an echo.
GEORGE BORROW: *Lavengro,* XXV, 1851

I do not hesitate to read good books in translations. What is really best in any book is translatable — any real insight or broad human sentiment.
R. W. EMERSON: *Books,* 1877

There is no translation except a word-for-word translation.
GEORGE MOORE: *Confessions of a Young Man,* VII, 1888

[*See also* Bishop, Poetry, Translator.

Translator

Interpreters and translators should not work alone; for good *et propria verba* do not always occur to one mind.
MARTIN LUTHER: *Table-Talk,* III, 1569

A distinction must be made amongst translators, betwixt cobblers and workmen.
THOMAS FULLER: *Worthies of England,* 1662

Translators: sellers of old mended shoes and boots, between cobblers and shoemakers.
FRANCIS GROSE: *A Classical Dictionary of the Vulgar Tongue,* 1785

A translator, like a witness on the stand, should hold up his right hand and swear to "tell the truth, the whole truth, and nothing but the truth."
H. W. LONGFELLOW: *Letter to John Neal,* Aug. 2, 1867

If the translator is a good poet, he substitutes his verse for that of the original; — I don't want his verse, I want the original; if he is a bad poet, he gives us bad verse, which is intolerable.
GEORGE MOORE: *Confessions of a Young Man,* VII, 1888

Translators, traitors. (Traduttore, traditore.)
ITALIAN PROVERB

[*See also* Admiration.

Transubstantiation

The substance of the bread and wine is changed interiorly into the flesh and blood of Christ.
RADBERTUS PASCHASIUS: *De corpore et sanguine Domini, c.* 840

Priests who claim that they can create the body of Christ whenever they want to are blasphemers. JOHN HUSS: *Simony,* 1442

If any shall say that in the holy sacrament of the eucharist there remains the substance of the bread and wine, and shall deny the wonderful and singular conversion of the whole substance of the bread into the body of our Lord Jesus Christ and of the wine into His blood, the species only of the bread and wine remaining, then let him be anathema.
Decrees of the Council of Trent, XIII, 1563

When we reflect that Sir Thomas More was ready to die for the doctrine of transubstantiation, we cannot but feel some doubt whether the doctrine of transubstantiation may not triumph over all opposition.

T. B. MACAULAY: *Von Ranke*, 1840 (Edinburgh Review, Oct.)

[*See also* Catholicism (Roman), Eucharist, Mohammedan.

Travel

There is nothing worse for mortals than a wandering life.

HOMER: *Odyssey*, XV, *c.* 800 B.C.

Many shall run to and fro, and knowledge shall be increased. DANIEL XII, 4, *c.* 165 B.C.

A pleasant companion reduces the length of the journey.

PUBLILIUS SYRUS: *Sententiæ*, *c.* 50 B.C.

Thrice I suffered shipwreck, a night and a day I have been in the deep; in journeyings often, in perils of waters, in perils of robbers, in perils by mine own countrymen, in perils by the heathen, in perils in the city, in perils in the wilderness, in perils in the sea, in perils among false brethren; in weariness and painfulness, in watchings often, in hunger and thirst, in fastings often, in cold and nakedness.

II CORINTHIANS XI, 25–27, *c.* 55 (Paul's account of his missionary journeys)

Every change of scene is a delight.

SENECA: *Epistulæ moralis ad Lucilium*, *c.* 63

Travel only with thy equals or thy betters; if there are none, travel alone.

The Dhammapada, V, *c.* 100

Three things are weakening: fear, sin and travel. THE TALMUD (*Gittin*), *c.* 200

The fool that far is sent, some wisdom to attain,
Returns an idiot as he went, and brings the fool again. GEORGE WHITNET: *Emblems*, 1586

He that traveleth into a country before he hath some entrance into the language, goeth to school, and not to travel.

FRANCIS BACON: *Essays*, IX, 1597

A traveler must have a falcon's eye, an ass's ears, an ape's face, a merchant's words, a camel's back, a hog's mouth, and a stag's legs.

ENGLISH PROVERB, current in various forms since the late XVI century

When I was at home, I was in a better place.

SHAKESPEARE: *As You Like It*, II, *c.* 1600

See one promontory (said Socrates of old), one mountain, one sea, one river, and see all.

ROBERT BURTON: *The Anatomy of Melancholy*, I, 1621

Travelers, poets and liars are three words all of one significance.

RICHARD BRATHWAITE: *The English Gentleman*, 1631

He that wants legs, feet, and brains, and wit
To be a traveler is most unfit.

JOHN TAYLOR: *A Short Relation of a Long Journey*, 1652

A class of men who are exceedingly tiresome are those who, having traveled, talk of nothing but their adventures, the countries which they have seen or traversed, the dangers, whether real or fictitious, which they have encountered, repeating the same things an hundred times over.

ST. JOHN BAPTIST DE LA SALLE: *The Rules of Christian Manners and Civility*, II, 1695

The young fellows of this age profit no more by their going abroad than they do by their going to church.

JOHN VANBRUGH: *The Relapse*, I, 1696

A gentleman ought to travel abroad but dwell at home.

THOMAS FULLER: *Gnomologia*, 1732

If an ass goes traveling he'll not come home a horse. IBID.

Travel makes a wise man better, but a fool worse. IBID.

Led by my hand, he saunter'd Europe round,
And gather'd ev'ry vice on Christian ground.

ALEXANDER POPE: *The Dunciad*, IV, 1741

Those who travel heedlessly from place to place, observing only their distance from each other, and attending only to their accommodation at the inn at night, set out fools, and will certainly return so.

LORD CHESTERFIELD: *Letter to his son*, Oct. 30, 1747

Let observations with extensive view,
Survey mankind from China to Peru;
Remark each anxious toil, each eager strife,
And watch the busy scenes of crowded life.

SAMUEL JOHNSON: *The Vanity of Human Wishes*, 1749

A wise traveler never despises his own country.

CARLO GOLDONI: *Pamela nubile*, I, 1757

Traveling is one way of lengthening life, at least in appearance.

BENJAMIN FRANKLIN: *Letter to Mary Stevenson*, Sept. 14, 1767

Travelers . . . seem to have no other purpose by taking long journeys but to procure themselves the pleasure of railing at everything they have seen or heard.

JOSEPH BARETTI: *An Account of the Manners and Customs of Italy*, II, 1768

Traveling is the ruin of all happiness. There's no looking at a building here after seeing Italy. FRANCES BURNEY: *Cecilia*, II, 1782

How much a dunce that has been sent to roam
Excels a dunce that has been kept at home.

WILLIAM COWPER: *The Progress of Error*, 1782

I am much pleased that you are going on a very long journey, which may by proper conduct restore your health and prolong your life. Observe these rules:
1. Turn all care out of your head as soon as you mount the chaise.
2. Do not think about frugality; your health is worth more than it can cost.
3. Do not continue any day's journey to fatigue.
4. Take now and then a day's rest.
5. Get a smart sea-sickness, if you can.
6. Cast away all anxiety, and keep your mind easy.

SAMUEL JOHNSON: *Letter to Henry Perkins,* July 28, 1782

The use of traveling is to regulate imagination by reality, and, instead of thinking how things may be, to see them as they are.

SAMUEL JOHNSON: *Mrs. Piozzi's Anecdotes,* 1786

Traveling makes men wiser, but less happy. When men of sober age travel, they gather knowledge which they may apply usefully for their country; but they are subject ever after to recollections mixed with regret; their affections are weakened by being extended over more objects; and they learn new habits which cannot be gratified when they return home.

THOMAS JEFFERSON: *Letter to Peter Carr,* 1787

That man travels to no purpose who sits down alone to his meals.

JOHN DAVIS: *Travels of Four Years and a Half in the United States of America,* II, 1802

The more I see of other countries the more I love my own.

ANNA LOUISE DE STAËL: *Corinne,* 1807

Without a sigh he left, to cross the brine,
And traverse Paynim shores, and pass earth's central line.

BYRON: *Childe Harold,* I, 1812

I have been a wanderer among distant fields. I have sailed down mighty rivers.

P. B. SHELLEY: *The Revolt of Islam,* pref., 1818

He traveled here, he traveled there; —
But not the value of a hair
Was head or heart the better.

WILLIAM WORDSWORTH: *Peter Bell,* 1819

Traveling in the company of those we love is home in motion.

LEIGH HUNT: *The Indicator,* XLIX, 1821

The soul of a journey is liberty, perfect liberty, to think, feel, do just as one pleases. We go a journey chiefly to be free of all impediments and of all inconveniences; to leave ourselves behind, much more to get rid of others.

WILLIAM HAZLITT: *On Going a Journey,* 1822

I should like to spend the whole of my life traveling, if I could anywhere borrow another life to spend at home.

WILLIAM HAZLITT: *Table-Talk,* 1824

Travel teaches toleration.

BENJAMIN DISRAELI: *Contarini Fleming,* V, 1832

The least change in our point of view gives the whole world a pictorial air. A man who seldom rides needs only to get into a coach and traverse his own town, to turn the street into a puppet-show.

R. W. EMERSON: *Nature,* 1836

It is for want of self-culture that the superstition of traveling, whose idols are Italy, England, Egypt, retains its fascination for all educated Americans.

R. W. EMERSON: *Self-Reliance,* 1841

What people travel for is a mystery.

T. B. MACAULAY: *Letter to Lady Trevelyan,* Aug. 21, 1843

I love to sail forbidden seas, and land on barbarous coasts.

HERMAN MELVILLE: *Moby Dick,* I, 1851

The man who goes alone can start today, but he who travels with another must wait till that other is ready.

H. D. THOREAU: *Walden,* 1854

Afoot and light-hearted I take to the open road,
Healthy, free, the world before me,
The long brown path before me leading wherever I choose.

WALT WHITMAN: *Song of the Open Road,* 1856

Men run away to other countries because they are not good in their own, and run back to their own because they pass for nothing in the new places. For the most part, only the light characters travel.

R. W. EMERSON: *The Conduct of Life,* IV, 1860

I travel not to go anywhere, but to go. I travel for travel's sake. The great affair is to move.

R. L. STEVENSON: *Travels with a Donkey,* 1879

Age is a bad traveling companion.

DANISH PROVERB

No man ever came home better from a long voyage. FLEMISH PROVERB

The heaviest baggage for a traveler is an empty purse. GERMAN PROVERB

Long voyages — great lies.

ITALIAN PROVERB

[*See also* Amusement, Company, Inn, Strength, Sunday, Wanderer, Wants.

Treachery

There is treachery, O Ahaziah.

II KINGS IX, 23, *c.* 500 B.C.

You too, Brutus! (Et tu, Brute!)
SHAKESPEARE: *Julius Cæsar,* III, 1599 (The Latin is in the text)

Treachery and slander have long lives.
DANISH PROVERB

[*See also* Calumny, Cunning, Happiness.

Treason

Athaliah rent her clothes, and cried, Treason, treason.
II KINGS XI, 14, *c.* 500 B.C. (Cf. II CHRONICLES XXIII, 13, *c.* 300 B.C.)

Treason is but trusted like the fox
Who, ne'er so tame, so cherish'd and locked up,
Will have a wild trick of his ancestors.
SHAKESPEARE: *I Henry IV,* V, *c.* 1598

Treason doth never prosper: what's the reason?
Why if it prosper, none dare call it treason.
JOHN HARINGTON: *Alcilia,* 1613

The seeds of treason choke up as they spring,
He acts the crime that gives it cherishing.
ROBERT HERRICK: *Hesperides,* 1648

Cæsar had his Brutus, Charles the First his Cromwell, and George the Third ["Treason!" cried the Speaker] — may profit by their example. If this be treason, make the most of it.
PATRICK HENRY: Speech in the Virginia House of Burgesses, May 29, 1765

Treason against the United States shall consist only in levying war against them, or in adhering to their enemies, giving them aid and comfort. No person shall be convicted of treason unless on the testimony of two witnesses to the same overt act, or on confession in open court. The Congress shall have power to declare the punishment of treason; but no attainder of treason shall work corruption of blood, or forfeiture except during the life of the person attainted.
CONSTITUTION OF THE UNITED STATES, Art. III, 1789

Fellowship in treason is a bad ground of confidence.
EDMUND BURKE: *Remarks on the Policy of the Allies,* 1793

[*See also* Assassination, Impeachment, Laughter, Patriotism, Pension, Traitor, Treaty, Trust.

Treasure

Lay not up for yourselves treasures upon earth, where moth and rust doth corrupt, and where thieves break through and steal.
MATTHEW VI, 19, *c.* 75

Treaty

It is a vain attempt
To bind th' ambitious and unjust by treaties:
These they elude a thousand specious ways;
Or, if they cannot find a fair pretext,
They blush not in the face of Heaven to break them.
JAMES THOMSON: *Coriolanus,* 1749

No state shall enter into any treaty, alliance or confederation.
CONSTITUTION OF THE UNITED STATES, Art. I, 1789

The President shall have power, by and with the advice and consent of the Senate, to make treaties, provided two-thirds of the Senators present concur.
CONSTITUTION OF THE UNITED STATES, Art. II

Treaties at best are but complied with so long as interest requires their fulfilment. Consequently, they are virtually binding on the weaker party only; or, in plain truth, they are not binding at all.
WASHINGTON IRVING: *Knickerbocker's History of New York,* 1809

A treaty must be made in conformity with the Constitution, and where a provision in either a treaty or a law is found to contravene the principles of the Constitution, such provision must give way to the superior force of the Constitution.
JAMES G. BLAINE: (as Secretary of State): *Note to Chen Lae Pin,* March 25, 1881

All treaties between great states cease to be binding when they come into conflict with the struggle for existence.
OTTO VON BISMARCK (1815–98)

Just for a word — neutrality, a word which in war-time has so often been disregarded — just for a scrap of paper Great Britain is going to make war.
THEOBALD VON BETHMANN-HOLLWEG: *Note to Sir Edward Goschen,* Aug. 4, 1914

Tree

The tree of life.
GENESIS II, 9, *c.* 700 B.C.

The tree of knowledge of good and evil.
IBID.

I will plant in the wilderness the cedar, the shittah tree, and the myrtle, and the oil tree; I will set in the desert the fir tree, and the pine, and the box tree together.
ISAIAH XLI, 19, *c.* 700 B.C.

If the tree fall toward the south, or toward the north, in the place where the tree falleth, there it shall be.
ECCLESIASTES XI, 3, *c.* 200 B.C.

A good tree cannot bring forth evil fruit.
MATTHEW VII, 18, *c.* 75

The tree is known by his fruit.
MATTHEW XII, 33 (Cf. LUKE VI, 44, *c.* 75)

Under the greenwood tree
Who loves to lie with me,
And tune his merry note
Unto the sweet bird's throat?
SHAKESPEARE: *As You Like It,* II, *c.* 1600

Great trees are good for nothing but shade.
GEORGE HERBERT: *Outlandish Proverbs,* 1640

Generations pass while some trees stand, and old families last not three oaks.
THOMAS BROWNE: *Urn Burial,* v, 1658

He that plants trees loves others beside himself.
THOMAS FULLER: *Gnomologia,* 1732

I felt a sense of pain when I beheld the silent trees.
WILLIAM WORDSWORTH: *Nutting,* 1800

Woodman, spare that tree!
  Touch not a single bough!
In youth it sheltered me,
  And I'll protect it now.
G. P. MORRIS: *Woodman, Spare That Tree,* 1830

The trees are imperfect men, and seem to bemoan their imprisonment, rooted in the ground.
R. W. EMERSON: *Nature,* 1836

Beneath some patriarchal tree
  I lay upon the ground;
His hoary arms uplifted he
And all the broad leaves over me
Clapped their little hands in glee,
  With one continuous sound.
H. W. LONGFELLOW: *Voices of the Night,* 1839

A man does not plant a tree for himself; he plants it for posterity.
ALEXANDER SMITH: *Dreamthorp,* XI, 1863
(Cf. FULLER, *ante,* 1732)

Of all man's works of art, a cathedral is greatest. A vast and majestic tree is greater than that.
H. W. BEECHER: *Proverbs from Plymouth Pulpit,* 1870

How strong, vital, enduring! how dumbly eloquent! What suggestions of imperturbability and being, as against the human trait of mere seeming. Then the qualities, almost emotional, palpably artistic, heroic, of a tree; so innocent and harmless, yet so savage.
WALT WHITMAN: *Specimen Days,* Sept. 1, 1877

Except during the nine months before he draws his first breath, no man manages his affairs as well as a tree does.
GEORGE BERNARD SHAW: *Maxims for Revolutionists,* 1903

A great tree attracts much wind.
CHINESE PROVERB

The finer the tree the more pliant the twig.
DUTCH PROVERB

It is a bad tree that falls at the first stroke of the ax.
GERMAN PROVERB

Do not judge a tree by its bark.
ITALIAN PROVERB

The tree casts its shade upon all, even upon the wood-cutter.
SANSKRIT PROVERB

[*See also* Forest, Fruit, Husbandman, Malta, Ugliness, Vine, Woods.

Trembling

With fear and trembling.
II CORINTHIANS VII, 15, *c.* 55

Trespass

By the laws of England, every invasion of private property, be it ever so minute, is a trespass. No man can set his foot upon my ground without my license, but he is liable to an action, though the damage be nothing.
LORD CHIEF JUSTICE CAMDEN: *Judgment in Entick* vs. *Carrington,* 1765

[*See also* Forgiveness.

Trial

He who flies from trial confesses his crime.
PUBLILIUS SYRUS: *Sententiæ, c.* 50 B.C.

A fox should not be of the jury at a goose's trial.
THOMAS FULLER: *Gnomologia,* 1732

If they are condemned unheard, it is because there is no need of a trial. The crime is manifest and notorious. All trial is the investigation of something doubtful.
SAMUEL JOHNSON: *Taxation No Tyranny,* 1775

These are the times that try men's souls.
THOMAS PAINE: *The Crisis,* I, 1776 (Pennsylvania Journal, Dec. 19)

Consider how you would like, though conscious of your innocence, to be tried before a jury for a capital crime once a week.
SAMUEL JOHNSON: *Boswell's Life,* April 3, 1776

[*See also* Criminal, Defense, Evidence, Peer, Treason.

Trial by Jury

In all criminal prosecutions, the accused shall enjoy the right to a speedy and public trial, by an impartial jury of the state and district wherein the crime shall have been committed, which districts shall have been previously ascertain by law, and to be informed of the nature and cause of the accusation; to be confronted with the witnesses against him; to have compulsory process for obtaining witnesses in his favor, and to have the assistance of counsel for his defense.
CONSTITUTION OF THE UNITED STATES, Amendment VI, Dec. 15, 1791

Triangle

A triangle is the poorest in its effect of almost any figure that can be presented to the eye.
EDMUND BURKE: *The Sublime and Beautiful,* II, 1756

[*See also* God.

Triangle, Eternal

The eternal triangle.
The phrase came into English late in the XVIII century, and was apparently suggested by the Italian *triangolo equilatero,* used in the same sense

The husband, the wife and the lover. (Le mari, la femme et l'amant.) FRENCH PHRASE

Tribulation

In the world ye shall have tribulation.
JOHN XVI, 33, *c.* 115

If there were no tribulation, there would be no rest; if there were no Winter, there would be no Summer.
ST. JOHN CHRYSOSTOM: *Homilies,* IV, *c.* 388

[*See also* Cross.

Tribute

Tribute to whom tribute is due.
ROMANS XIII, 7, *c.* 55

We prefer war in all cases to tribute under any form, and to any people whatever.
THOMAS JEFFERSON: *Letter to Thomas Barclay,* 1791

[*See also* Defense (National).

Trick

I know a trick worth two of that.
SHAKESPEARE: *I Henry IV,* II, *c.* 1598

[*See also* Dog.

Trifle

A trifle is often pregnant with high importance; the prudent man neglects no circumstance.
SOPHOCLES: *Œdipus Coloneus, c.* 450 B.C.

Trifles make perfection — and perfection is no trifle.
Ascribed to MICHELANGELO BUONARROTI (1475–1564)

Trifles light as air.
SHAKESPEARE: *Othello,* III, 1604

A snapper-up of unconsidered trifles.
SHAKESPEARE: *The Winter's Tale,* IV, *c.* 1611

What mighty contests rise from trivial things.
ALEXANDER POPE: *The Rape of the Lock,* I, 1712

Think naught a trifle, though it small appear;
Small sands the mountain, moments make the year,
And trifles life.
EDWARD YOUNG: *Love of Fame,* VI, 1728

The trivial round, the common task.
JOHN KEBLE: *The Christian Year,* 1827

Trifles make up the happiness or the misery of mortal life. The majority of men slip into their graves without having encountered on their way thither any signal catastrophe or exaltation of fortune or feeling.
ALEXANDER SMITH: *Dreamthorp,* VII, 1863

The law does not concern itself about trifles. (De minimis non curat lex.)
LEGAL MAXIM

[*See also* Character, France, Jealousy.

Trifling

There must be a time in which every man trifles; and the only choice that nature offers us is to trifle in company or alone.
SAMUEL JOHNSON: *The Rambler,* Jan. 22, 1751

Trinity

There are three that bear record in Heaven, the Father, the Word, and the Holy Ghost, and these three are one. I JOHN V, 7, *c.* 115

The Trinity is One God, not so that the Father be the same Person, who is also the Son and the Holy Ghost; but that the Father be the Father, and the Son be the Son, and the Holy Ghost be the Holy Ghost, and this Trinity One God.
ST. AUGUSTINE: *Of the Faith and of the Creed, c.* 393

Holy Trinity, superadmirable Trinity, and superinenarrable, and superinscrutable, and superinaccessible, superincomprehensible, superintelligible, superessential, superessentially surpassing all sense, all reason, all intellect, all intelligence, all essence of supercelestial minds; which can neither be said, nor thought, nor understood, nor known, even by the eyes of angels.
Anon.: *Book of Soliliquies, c.* 420 (This work is often ascribed to St. Augustine, but most scholars reject it)

The three persons in the Godhead are three in one sense and one in another. We cannot tell how — and that is the mystery.
SAMUEL JOHNSON: *Boswell's Tour to the Hebrides,* Aug. 22, 1773

I devoutly wish the three were four,
On purpose to believe so much the more.
BYRON: *Don Juan,* X, 1823

I believe in the Father, the Son, and the Holy Ghost, as three distinct Persons; but I believe that above our knowledge there is a point of coincidence and unity between them. What it is I do not know. That is the unrevealed part. H. W. BEECHER: *Royal Truths,* 1862

The three Persons of the Blessed Trinity are one and the same God, having one and the same divine nature, or substance.
JOHN MCCAFFREY: *A Catechism of Christian Doctrine for General Use,* 1866

The Catholic Church teaches that there is but one God, who is infinite in knowledge, in power, in goodness, and in every other perfection; who created all things by His omnipotence, and governs them by his Providence. In this one God there are three distinct Persons, — the Father, the Son, and the Holy Ghost, who are perfectly equal to each other.

JAMES CARDINAL GIBBONS: *The Faith of Our Fathers,* I, 1876

One may say with one's lips: "I believe that God is one, and also three"; — but no one can believe it, because the words have no sense.

LYOF N. TOLSTOY: *What Is Religion?,* 1902

There is but one living and true God, everlasting, without body or parts, of infinite power, wisdom and goodness; the maker and preserver of all things, visible and invisible. And in unity of this Godhead there are three persons, of one substance, power, and eternity — the Father, the Son, and the Holy Ghost.

The Doctrines and Discipline of the Methodist Episcopal Church, I, 1932

[*See also* Sanctimonious.

Tripe

How say you to a fat tripe finely broil'd?

SHAKESPEARE: *The Taming of the Shrew,* IV, 1594

Tripe's good meat if it be well wiped.

JOHN RAY: *English Proverbs,* 1670

Tripe broth is better than no porridge.

H. G. BOHN: *Handbook of Proverbs,* 1855

Triumph

The daughters of the uncircumcised triumph.

II SAMUEL I, 20, *c.* 500 B.C.

Hail to the chief who in triumph advances!

WALTER SCOTT: *The Lady of the Lake,* II, 1810

If it had not been for these thing I might have live out my life talking at street-corners to scorning men. I might have die, unmarked, unknown, a failure. Now we are not a failure. This is our career and our triumph. Never in our full life could we hope to do such work for tolerance, for justice, for man's understanding of man as now we do by accident. Our words — our lives — our pains — nothing! The taking of our lives — lives of a good shoemaker and a poor fish-peddler — all! That last moment belongs to us — that agony is our triumph.

BARTOLOMEO VANZETTI: Statement after being sentenced to death at Dedham, Mass., April 9, 1927

[*See also* Conquest, Victory.

Tropics

Droops the heavy-blossom'd bower, hangs the heavy-fruited tree —
Summer isles of Eden lying in dark-purple spheres of sea.

ALFRED TENNYSON: *Locksley Hall,* 1842

I'd seen the tropics first that run — new fruit, new smells, new air —
How could I tell — blind-fou wi' sun — the Deil was lurkin' there?

RUDYARD KIPLING: *McAndrew's Hymn,* 1893

[*See also* Climate, Coal.

Trouble

Man is born unto trouble, as the sparks fly upward.

JOB V, 7, *c.* 325 B.C.

Man that is born of woman is of few days, and full of trouble.

JOB XIV, 1

It is pleasant to recall past troubles.

CICERO: *De finibus,* II, *c.* 50 B.C.

He that seeks trouble always finds it.

ENGLISH PROVERB, current in various forms since the XV century (In its earlier forms *sorrow* or *danger* commonly appears in place of *trouble*)

A sea of troubles.

SHAKESPEARE: *Hamlet,* III, *c.* 1601

Double, double toil and trouble;
Fire burn, and cauldron bubble.

SHAKESPEARE: *Macbeth,* IV, *c.* 1605

Nobody knows de trouble I've seen,
Nobody knows but Jesus.

American Negro spiritual, *c.* 1845

It takes just as long to get out of any trouble as it took to get into it, and sometimes longer.

J. KENFIELD MORLEY: *Some Things I Believe,* 1937

Never trouble trouble till trouble troubles you.

AMERICAN PROVERB

He who would have no trouble in this world must not be born in it.

ITALIAN PROVERB

[*See also* Laughter, Man.

Trousers

[*See* Breeches.

Trout

The trout must be caught with tickling.

SHAKESPEARE: *Twelfth Night,* II, *c.* 1601

No taking of trout with dry breeches.

CERVANTES: *Don Quixote,* II, 1615

You must lose a fly to catch a trout.

GEORGE HERBERT: *Jacula Prudentum,* 1651

Trowel

Well said: that was laid on with a trowel.

SHAKESPEARE: *As You Like It,* I, *c.* 1600

Truce

The cat and the rat make peace over a carcass.
HEBREW PROVERB

Truculence

His nose should pant and his lip should curl,
His cheeks should flame and his brow should furl,
His bosom should heave and his heart should glow,
And his fist be ever ready for a knock-down blow.
W. S. GILBERT: *H.M.S. Pinafore*, I, 1878

True

To thine own self be true,
And it must follow, as the night the day,
Thou canst not then be false to any man.
SHAKESPEARE: *Hamlet*, I, *c.* 1601

The true, the good and the beautiful. (*Ger.* Das Wahre, das Gute, das Schöne. *Fr.* Le vrai, le bon, le beau.)
Author unidentified

Trumpet

If ye go to war . . . ye shall blow an alarm with the trumpets.
NUMBERS X, 9, *c.* 700 B.C.

Make all our trumpets speak; give them all breath,
Those clamorous harbingers of blood and death.
SHAKESPEARE: *Macbeth*, V, *c.* 1605

The trumpet's loud clangor
Excites us to arms,
With shrill notes of anger,
And mortal alarms.
JOHN DRYDEN: *A Song for St. Cecilia's Day*, 1687

Let the loud trumpet sound
Till the roofs all around
The shrill echoes rebound.
ALEXANDER POPE: *Ode for Music on St. Cecilia's Day*, 1708

The silver, snarling trumpets 'gan to chide.
JOHN KEATS: *The Eve of St. Agnes*, 1820

[*See also* Battle, Cornet, Heart, War.

Trust

Though he slay me, yet will I trust in him.
JOB XIII, 15, *c.* 325 B.C.

In God have I put my trust: I will not be afraid what man can do unto me.
PSALMS LVI, 11, *c.* 150 B.C.

Trust, like the soul, never returns, once it is gone.
PUBLILIUS SYRUS: *Sententiæ*, *c.* 50 B.C.

In trust is treason.
ENGLISH PROVERB, traced by Smith to the XV century

Little love, little trust.
ENGLISH PROVERB, traced by Apperson to before 1500

Trust no man unless thou hast first eaten a bushel of salt with him.
RICHARD TAVERNER: *Proverbs*, 1539

Trust none;
For oaths are straws, men's faiths are wafer-cakes,
And hold-fast is the only dog.
SHAKESPEARE: *Henry V*, II, *c.* 1599

Immortal gods, I crave no pelf;
I pray for no man but myself;
Grant I may never prove so fond,
To trust man on his oath or bond.
SHAKESPEARE: *Timon of Athens*, I, *c.* 1607

God provides for him that trusteth.
GEORGE HERBERT: *Outlandish Proverbs*, 1640

The trust that we put in ourselves makes us feel trust in others.
LA ROCHEFOUCAULD: *Maxims*, 1665

Poor Trust is dead; Bad Pay killed him.
ENGLISH PROVERB, traced by Apperson to 1666

If we are bound to forgive an enemy we are not bound to trust him.
THOMAS FULLER: *Gnomologia*, 1732

Trust him no further than you can throw him.
IBID.

Not to trust him who hath deceived you, nor who knows he hath been deceived by you.
HENRY FIELDING: *Jonathan Wild*, IV, 1743
(Maxim of Wild for the attainment of greatness)

I would rather trust my money to a man who has no hands, and so a physical impossibility to steal, than to a man of the most honest principles.
SAMUEL JOHNSON: *Boswell's Life*, May 26, 1783

We generally most covet that particular trust which we are least likely to keep. He that thoroughly knows his friends, might perhaps, with safety, confide his wife to the care of one, his purse to another, and his secrets to a third; when to permit them to make their own choice would be his ruin.
C. C. COLTON: *Lacon*, 1820

The man who trusts other men will make fewer mistakes than he who distrusts them.
Ascribed to CAMILLO DI CAVOUR (1810–61)

Trust everybody, but yourself most of all.
DANISH PROVERB

God save me from him I trust.
FRENCH PROVERB

Do not trust the man who tells you all his troubles but keeps from you his joys.
HEBREW PROVERB

Trust was a good man, but Trust-not was a better. ITALIAN PROVERB

Trust only yourself and your own horse. JUGO-SLAVIC PROVERB

Never trust a sleeping dog, a swearing Jew, a praying drunkard, or a weeping woman. POLISH PROVERB

[*See also* Confidence, Mistrust, Office, Prince.

Trust, Breach of

If a man hire a man to oversee his farm and hand over to him implements and intrust him with oxen and contract with him for the cultivation of the field; if that man steal either the seed grain or the fodder and it be found in his hand, they shall cut off his hand. THE CODE OF HAMMURABI, *c.* 2250 B.C.

Trust, Public

When a man assumes a public trust, he should consider himself as public property. THOMAS JEFFERSON: *Letter to Baron von Humboldt*, 1807

[*See also* Office (Public).

Trusts

The trusts and combinations — the communism of pelf. GROVER CLEVELAND: *Letter to Representative T. C. Catchings of Mississippi*, Aug., 1894

The great corporations which we have grown to speak of rather loosely as trusts are the creatures of the state, and the state not only has the right to control them, but it is in duty bound to control them whenever the need of such control is shown. THEODORE ROOSEVELT: Speech at Providence, R. I., Aug. 23, 1902

[*See also* Monopoly.

Truth

Those who know the truth are not equal to those who love it. CONFUCIUS: *Analects*, VI, *c.* 500 B.C.

The aim of the superior man is truth. CONFUCIUS: *Analects*, XV

Nature has buried truth at the bottom of the sea. Ascribed to DEMOCRITUS, *c.* 400 B.C.

If you will be persuaded by me, pay little attention to Socrates, but much more to the truth, and if I appear to you to say anything true, assent to it, but if not, oppose me with all your might, taking good care that in my zeal I do not deceive both myself and you, and like a bee depart, leaving my sting behind. SOCRATES: *In* PLATO: *Phaedo*, 360 B.C.

Truth is the beginning of every good thing, both in Heaven and on earth; and he who would be blessed and happy should be from the first a partaker of the truth, for then he can be trusted. PLATO: *Laws*, IV, *c.* 360 B.C.

Buy the truth, and sell it not. PROVERBS XXIII, 23, *c.* 350 B.C.

The high-minded man must care more for the truth than for what people think. ARISTOTLE: *The Nicomachean Ethics*, IV, *c.* 340 B.C.

Plato is dear to me, but dearer still is truth. (Amicus Plato, sed magis amica veritas.) Ascribed to ARISTOTLE (384–322 B.C.)

The way of truth is like a great highway. It is not hard to find. MENCIUS: *Discourses*, VI, *c.* 300 B.C.

Truth lies at the bottom of a well. DIOGENES LAERTIUS: *Lives of the Philosophers*, *c.* 150 B.C. (Cf. DEMOCRITUS, *ante*, *c.* 400 B.C.)

Nature has given our minds an insatiable appetite for the truth. CICERO: *Tusculanæ disputationes*, I, 45 B.C.

Truth is often eclipsed, but never extinguished. LIVY: *History of Rome*, XXII, *c.* 10

Am I therefore become your enemy, because I tell you the truth? GALATIANS IV, 16, *c.* 50

The language of truth is simple. SENECA: *Epistulæ morales ad Lucilium*, *c.* 63

Truth is open to all men. IBID.

Truth is the same in every part. IBID.

Ye shall know the truth, and the truth shall make you free. JOHN VIII, 32, *c.* 115

Pilate saith unto him, What is truth? (*Lat.* Quid est veritas? *Fr.* Qu'est-ce que la vérité? *Ger.* Was ist Wahrheit?) JOHN XVIII, 38

Truth, from her first appearance, is an enemy. TERTULLIAN: *The Christian's Defence*, *c.* 215

In the end the truth will conquer. JOHN WYCLIF: To the Duke of Lancaster, 1381

Truth is the highest thing that man may keep. GEOFFREY CHAUCER: *The Canterbury Tales* (The Franklin's Tale), *c.* 1386

Truth did never his master shame. Anon.: Coventry mystery play, *c.* 1450

If it is not true, it is well invented. (Se non è vero, è ben trovato.) Ascribed to HIPPOLITO CARDINAL D'ESTE (1479–1520)

Time trieth truth. JOHN HEYWOOD: *Proverbs*, 1546

There is a common saying amongst us: Say the truth and shame the Devil.
HUGH LATIMER: Sermon, 1552 (This appears as "Tell truth and shame the Devil" in SHAKESPEARE: *I Henry IV*, III, *c.* 1597)

Superstition, idolatry, and hypocrisy have ample wages, but truth goes a begging.
MARTIN LUTHER: *Table-Talk*, LIII, 1569

It is a common saying: Veritas odium parit: Truth purchaseth hatred.
THOMAS WILSON: *Discourse Upon Usury*, 1572

Truth itself hath not the privilege to be employed at all times and in every kind: be her use never so noble, it hath its circumscriptions and limits.
MICHEL DE MONTAIGNE: *Essays*, III, 1588

Children and fools speak true.
JOHN LYLY: *Endymion*, II, 1591

Truth hath a quiet breast.
SHAKESPEARE: *Richard II*, I, *c.* 1596

'Tis true, 'tis true, 'tis pity;
And pity 'tis 'tis true.
SHAKESPEARE: *Hamlet*, II, *c.* 1601

Truth is truth
To the end of reckoning.
SHAKESPEARE: *Measure for Measure*, V, 1604

Truth goes, when she goes best, stark naked.
THOMAS DEKKER: *The Gull's Hornbook*, II, 1609

Although it may not be always advisable to say all that is true, yet it is never allowable to speak against the truth.
ST. FRANCIS DE SALES: *Introduction to the Devout Life*, XXX, 1609

The inquiry of truth, which is the love-making or wooing of it; the knowledge of truth, which is the presence of it; and the belief of truth, which is the enjoying of it, is the sovereign good of human nature.
FRANCIS BACON: *Essays*, I, 1625

"What is truth?" said jesting Pilate, and would not stay for an answer. IBID.

Truth is as impossible to be soiled by any outward touch as the sunbeam.
JOHN MILTON: *Doctrine and Discipline of Divorce*, 1633

Truth hast always a good face, though often but bad clothes.
THOMAS FULLER: *Historie of the Holy Warre*, III, 1639

Truth needs not many words. IBID.

Truth never grows old. IBID.

Every man is not a proper champion for truth, nor fit to take up the gauntlet in the cause of verity. A man may be in as just possession of truth as of a city, and yet be forced to surrender; 'tis therefore far better to enjoy her with peace than to hazard her on a battle.
THOMAS BROWNE: *Religio Medici*, I, 1642

There may be a sanctified bitterness against the enemies of truth.
JOHN MILTON: *An Apology for Smectymnuus*, 1642

Truth is strong, next to the Almighty; she needs no policies, nor stratagems, nor licensings to make her victorious; those are the shifts and the defenses that error uses against her power: give her but room, and do not bind her when she sleeps, for then she speaks not true. JOHN MILTON: *Aeropagitica*, 1644

[Truth's] first appearance to our eyes, bleared and dimmed with prejudice and custom, is more unsightly and unplausible than many errors; even as the person is of many a great man slight and contemptible to see to.
IBID.

Who ever knew truth put to the worse in a free and open encounter? IBID.

Truth is for the minority.
BALTASAR GRACIÁN: *The Art of Worldly Wisdom*, XLIII, 1647

Truth always lags behind, limping along on the arm of time.
BALTASAR GRACIÁN: *The Art of Worldly Wisdom*, CXLVI

It is as hard to tell the truth as to hide it.
BALTASAR GRACIÁN: *The Art of Worldly Wisdom*, CLXXXI

All truths are not to be told.
GEORGE HERBERT: *Jacula Prudentum*, 1651

Follow not truth too near the heels, lest it dash out thy teeth. IBID.

The truth, the whole truth, and nothing but the truth.
LEGAL PHRASE, traced by Smith to 1659

Truth is never alone; to know one will require the knowledge of many. They hang together in a chain of mutual dependence; you cannot draw one link without many others.
JOSEPH GLANVILL: *The Vanity of Dogmatizing*, VII, 1661

Truth, like a point or line, requires an acuteness and intention to its discovery. IBID.

The beauty of truth, as of a picture, is not acknowledg'd but at a distance.
JOSEPH GLANVILL: *The Vanity of Dogmatizing*, XV

Truth is precious and divine;
Too rich a pearl for carnal swine.
SAMUEL BUTLER: *Hudibras*, II, 1664

Truth does not do so much good in the world as its appearances do evil.
LA ROCHEFOUCAULD: *Maxims*, 1665

We arrive at the truth, not by the reason only, but also by the heart.
BLAISE PASCAL: *Pensées*, x, 1670

Truth is God's daughter.
JOHN RAY: *English Proverbs*, 1670

The truth does not act impetuously.
NICOLAS BOILEAU: *L'Art poétique*, I, 1674

There are times when truth hardly seems probable.
NICOLAS BOILEAU: *L'Art poétique*, III

Truth has such a face and such a mien,
As to be lov'd needs only to be seen.
JOHN DRYDEN: *The Hind and the Panther*, I, 1687

The exact contrary of what is generally believed is often the truth.
JEAN DE LA BRUYÈRE: *Caractères*, XII, 1688

My efforts are ever striving toward no other end than, as far as in me lieth, to set the truth before my eyes, to embrace it, and to lay out to good account the small talent that I've received: in order to draw the world away from its old heathenish superstition, to go over to the truth, and to cleave unto it.
ANTONY VAN LEEUWENHOEK: *Letter to George Garden*, 1694

Truth will out.
ENGLISH PROVERB, not recorded before the XVIII century

To love truth for truth's sake is the principal part of human perfection in this world, and the seed-plot of all other virtues.
JOHN LOCKE: *Letter to Anthony Collins*, Oct. 29, 1703

There are certain times when most people are in a disposition of being informed, and 'tis incredible what a vast good a little truth might do, spoken in such seasons.
ALEXANDER POPE: *Letter to William Wycherley*, June 23, 1705

Truth enters the mind so easily that when we hear it for the first time it seems as if we were simply recalling it to memory.
BERNARD DE FONTENELLE: *Histoire du renouvellement de l'Académie des Sciences*, pref., 1708

There are two kinds of truths: those of reasoning and those of fact. The truths of reasoning are necessary and their opposite is impossible; the truths of fact are contingent and their opposite is possible.
G. W. LEIBNIZ: *The Monadology*, XXXIII, 1714

Truth . . . raises no emotion, or but that of the lowest kind, which we call approbation.
WILLIAM WARBURTON (BISHOP OF GLOUCESTER): *The Causes of Prodigies and Miracles*, I, 1727

Beware of telling an improbable truth.
THOMAS FULLER: *Introductio ad Prudentiam*, II, 1731

Face to face, the truth comes out.
THOMAS FULLER: *Gnomologia*, 1732

Truth makes the Devil blush. IBID.

There are not many certain truths in this world.
ALEXANDER POPE: *An Essay on Man*, pref., 1732

Truth and good are one.
MARK AKENSIDE: *The Pleasures of Imagination*, I, 1744

Remember, as long as you live, that nothing but strict truth can carry you through the world, with either your conscience or your honor unwounded.
LORD CHESTERFIELD: *Letter to his son*, Sept. 21, 1747

Deal ingenuously with truth, and love it for itself.
BENJAMIN WHICHCOTE: *Moral and Religious Aphorisms*, 1753

I know mankind too well to think they are capable of receiving the truth, much less of applauding it.
MARY WORTLEY MONTAGU: *Letter to the Countess of Bute*, Oct. 1, 1758

There are truths which are not for all men, nor for all occasions.
VOLTAIRE: *Letter to François Cardinal de Bernis*, April 23, 1761 (Cf. MONTAIGNE, *ante*, 1588)

Truth is a fruit which should not be plucked until it is quite ripe.
VOLTAIRE: *Letter to the Countess de Barcewitz*, Dec. 24, 1761

When fiction rises pleasing to the eye,
Men will believe, because they love the lie;
But truth herself, if clouded with a frown,
Must have some solemn proof to pass her down.
CHARLES CHURCHILL: *Epistle to William Hogarth*, 1763

Plain truth needs no flowers of speech.
LORD MANSFIELD: *Judgment in Wilkes* vs. *Wood*, 1763

Truth from his lips prevailed with double sway,
And fools who came to scoff remained to pray.
OLIVER GOLDSMITH: *The Deserted Village*, 1770

He who made all men hath made the truths necessary to human happiness obvious to all.
SAMUEL ADAMS: Speech in Philadelphia, Aug. 1, 1776

It is the characteristic of truth to need no proof but truth.
JEREMY BENTHAM: *Fragment on Government*, 1776

You have no business with consequences; you are to tell the truth.
SAMUEL JOHNSON: *Boswell's Life*, 1784

Everything possible to be believ'd is an image of truth.
WILLIAM BLAKE: *The Marriage of Heaven and Hell*, 1790

The mind, in discovering truths, acts in the same manner as it acts through the eye in discovering an object; when once any object has been seen, it is impossible to put the mind back to the same condition it was in before it saw it.
THOMAS PAINE: *The Rights of Man*, I, 1791

Such is the irresistible nature of truth that all it asks, and all it wants, is the liberty of appearing. The sun needs no inscription to distinguish him from darkness.
THOMAS PAINE: *The Rights of Man*, II

There's nane ever feared that the truth should be heard,
But they wham the truth wad indite.
ROBERT BURNS: *A Health to Them That's Awa'*, 1792

To hate truth as truth . . . is the same as to hate goodness for its own sake.
ETHAN ALLEN: *Reason the Only Oracle of Man*, I, 1794

Truth ever lovely — since the world began,
The foe of tyrants, and the friend of man.
THOMAS CAMPBELL: *The Pleasures of Hope*, II, 1799

A truth that's told with bad intent
Beats all the lies you can invent.
WILLIAM BLAKE: *Auguries of Innocence*, *c.* 1802

I cannot tell how the truth may be;
I say the tale as 'twas said to me.
WALTER SCOTT: *The Lay of the Last Minstrel*, II, 1805

To all new truths, or renovation of old truths, it must be as in the ark between the destroyed and the about-to-be renovated world. The raven must be sent out before the dove, and ominous controversy must precede peace and the olive-wreath.
S. T. COLERIDGE: *Omniana*, 1812

I can never feel certain of any truth, but from a clear perception of its beauty.
JOHN KEATS: *Letter to George Keats*, 1818

Whatever is reasonable is true, and whatever is true is reasonable.
G. W. F. HEGEL: *Grundlinien der Philosophie des Rechts*, pref., 1821

Truth is always strange — stranger than fiction.
BYRON: *Don Juan*, XIV, 1823

There is small chance of truth at the goal where there is not a child-like humility at the starting-post.
S. T. COLERIDGE: *Aids to Reflection*, 1825

It is one thing to wish to have truth on our side, and another to wish sincerely to be on the side of truth.
RICHARD WHATELY: *On the Love of Truth*, 1825

There is not a truth existing which I fear, or would wish unknown to the whole world.
THOMAS JEFFERSON: *Letter to Henry Lee*, 1826

Man passes away; generations are but shadows; there is nothing stable but truth.
JOSIAH QUINCY, JR.: Speech in Boston, Sept. 17, 1830

I will be as harsh as truth and as uncompromising as justice.
WILLIAM LLOYD GARRISON: *Salutatory of the Liberator*, Jan. 1, 1831

I have known many, especially women, love the good for the good's sake; but very few indeed, and scarcely one woman, love the truth for the truth's sake.
S. T. COLERIDGE: *Table-Talk*, Aug. 6, 1831

Truth travels down from the heights of philosophy to the humblest walks of life, and up from the simplest perceptions of an awakened intellect to the discoveries which almost change the face of the world. At every stage of its progress it is genial, luminous, creative.
EDWARD EVERETT: Address at Amherst College, Aug. 25, 1835

I tell the honest truth in my paper, and I leave the consequence to God.
JAMES GORDON BENNETT THE ELDER: In the New York Herald, May 10, 1836

Truth! though the Heavens crush me for following her.
THOMAS CARLYLE: *Sartor Resartus*, II, 1836

Truth is such a fly-away, such a sly-boots, so untransportable and unbarrelable a commodity, that it is as bad to catch as light.
R. W. EMERSON: *Literary Ethics*, 1838

A new truth is looked upon with as much jealousy as a " new man " in an aristocracy, and has often to pass through two or three generations ere its nobility is entirely accredited.
Anon.: In the Lancet, Sept. 8, 1838

God offers to every mind its choice between truth and repose. Take which you please — you can never have both.
R. W. EMERSON: *Intellect*, 1841

It is the nature of truth in general, as of some ores in particular, to be richest when most superficial.
E. A. POE: *The Rationale of Verse*, 1843 (The Pioneer, March)

The demands of truth are severe. She has no sympathy with the myrtles. All that which is so indispensable in song, is precisely all that with which she has nothing whatever to do.

It is but making her a flaunting paradox, to wreathe her in gems and flowers.
E. A. POE: *The Poetic Principle,* 1845

So long as you believe in some truth you do not believe in yourself. You are a servant, a man of faith.
MAX STIRNER: *The Ego and His Own,* 1845

Truths are phrases, ways of speaking, words.
IBID.

Truth, like all other good things, may be loved unwisely — may be pursued too keenly — may cost too much.
VICE-CHANCELLOR KNIGHT-BRUCE: *Judgment in Pearse* vs. *Pearse,* 1846

Men of the world value truth . . . not by its sacredness, but for its convenience.
R. W. EMERSON: *The Superlative,* 1847

A truth that we pick up from others is ours only in the sense that a false tooth is ours.
ARTHUR SCHOPENHAUER: *Parerga und Paralipomena,* I, 1851

Ethical truth is as exact and peremptory as physical truth.
HERBERT SPENCER: *Social Statics,* II, 1851

Truth means facts and their relations, which stand towards each other pretty much as subjects and predicates in logic.
J. H. NEWMAN: *On the Scope and Nature of University Education,* II, 1852

Nothing from man's hands, nor law, nor constitution, can be final. Truth alone is final.
CHARLES SUMNER: Speech in the Senate, Aug. 26, 1852

Who never sold the truth to serve the hour.
ALFRED TENNYSON: *Ode on the Death of the Duke of Wellington,* 1852

Rather than love, than money, than fame, give me truth. H. D. THOREAU: *Walden,* 1854

Truth is truth to the end of the reckoning.
H. G. BOHN: *Handbook of Proverbs,* 1855

Truths and roses have thorns about them.
IBID.

The simplest and most necessary truths are always the last believed.
JOHN RUSKIN: *Modern Painters,* IV, 1856

Truth is tough.
O. W. HOLMES: *The Professor at the Breakfast-Table,* V, 1859

Time is precious, but truth is more precious than time.
BENJAMIN DISRAELI: Speech at Aylesbury, Sept. 21, 1865

Truth is scattered far and wide in small portions among mankind, mingled in every system with the dross of error, grasped perfectly by no one, and only in some degree discovered by the careful comparison and collation of opposing systems.
W. E. H. LECKY: *History of Rationalism,* 1865

All truth is safe, and nothing else is safe.
MAX MÜLLER: *Chips from a German Workshop,* 1867

Time, whose tooth gnaws away everything else, is powerless against truth.
T. H. HUXLEY: *Administrative Nihilism,* 1871

The deepest truths are best read between the lines, and, for the most part, refuse to be written.
A. BRONSON ALCOTT: *Concord Days,* 1872

What I tell you three times is true.
C. L. DODGSON (LEWIS CARROLL): *The Hunting of the Snark,* I, 1876

Every truth leads in another.
R. W. EMERSON: *The Sovereignty of Ethics,* 1878

Nobody dies nowadays of fatal truths: there are too many antidotes to them.
F. W. NIETZSCHE: *Human All-too-Human,* I, 1878

One's belief in truth begins with a doubt of all the truths one has believed hitherto.
F. W. NIETZSCHE: *Human All-too-Human,* II

It is the quest after truth, not its possession, that falls to our human lot, that gladdens us, that fills our lives — nay, that hallows them.
AUGUST WEISMANN: *Dauer des Lebens,* 1881

Man discovers truth by reason only, not by faith. LYOF N. TOLSTOY: *On Life,* 1887

Reason teaches that the truths of divine revelation and those of nature cannot really be opposed to one another, and that whatever is at variance with them must necessarily be false.
POPE LEO XIII: *Libertas praestantissimum,* June 20, 1888

Truth is not something that one man has and another man has not.
F. W. NIETZSCHE: *The Antichrist,* LIII, 1888

If we would only stop lying, if we would only testify to the truth as we see it, it would turn out at once that there are hundreds, thousands, even millions of men just as we are, who see the truth as we do, are afraid as we are of seeming to be singular by confessing it, and are only waiting, again as we are, for some one to proclaim it.
LYOF N. TOLSTOY: *The Kingdom of God Is Within You,* 1893

A truth ceases to be true when more than one person believes in it.
OSCAR WILDE: *Phrases and Philosophies for the Use of the Young,* 1894

When you want to fool the world, tell the truth.
OTTO VON BISMARCK (1815–98)

Truth is given the eternal years of God because she needs them every one.
THOMAS B. REED: Speech at Bowdoin College, Maine, July 25, 1902

My way of joking is to tell the truth.
GEORGE BERNARD SHAW: *John Bull's Other Island*, II, 1904

If more men accept a doctrine than reject it, and those who accept it are more intelligent than its opponents, it is as near the truth as we can get at present.
E. W. HOWE: *Country Town Sayings*, 1911

Nothing is true except a few simple fundamentals every man has demonstrated for himself. When there is doubt, continue to doubt.
IBID.

There is a constant protest from unreliable sources because the truth is true, but at the bottom of every heart is the knowledge that it is, and every man not a fool steps off the railroad track when he sees a train approaching.
IBID.

The truth has always been dangerous to the rule of the rogue, the exploiter, the robber. So the truth must be suppressed.
EUGENE V. DEBS: Speech in Canton, O., June, 1918

The best test of truth is the power of the thought to get itself accepted in the competition of the market.
MR. JUSTICE O. W. HOLMES: *Dissenting opinion in Abrams* vs. *United States*, 1919

The "truths" that come down the ages are like a long string of grasshoppers standing in single file who jump over one another's backs. They continue without pause, always "moving ahead," until they arrive over and over again at the point where they began. And where was that?
BENJAMIN DE CASSERES: *Fantasia Impromptu*, 1933

The truth is everywhere the same.
ROBERT M. HUTCHINS: *The Higher Learning in America*, I, 1936

He who has the truth is in the majority, even though he be one.
ARAB PROVERB

The truth is virtuous, but indiscreet.
Author unidentified

Truth angers those whom it does not convince.
IBID.

Truth is not necessarily comforting; if some have found it so, the luckier they are.
IBID.

Truth is stranger than fiction, but not so popular.
IBID.

To withhold truth is to bury gold.
DANISH PROVERB

Truth without fear. (Vérité sans peur.)
FRENCH PHRASE

Truth does not always seem truthful. (Le vrai n'est toujours vraisemblable.)
FRENCH PROVERB

What is true is possible.
IBID.

It takes a great many shovelfuls to bury the truth.
GERMAN PROVERB

The grave of one who dies for the truth is holy ground.
IBID.

The truth is brought by a limping messenger.
IBID.

Truth does not lurk in rat-holes.
IBID.

Truth is an orphan.
IBID.

Truth is to the ears what smoke is to the eyes and vinegar to the teeth.
IBID.

Truth hardens itself under the hammer.
GREEK PROVERB

Truth is its own witness.
HEBREW PROVERB

The name of God is Truth.
HINDU PROVERB

Truth is sweeter than sugar.
IBID.

A thousand probabilities do not make one truth.
ITALIAN PROVERB

The naked truth. (Nuda veritas.)
LATIN PHRASE

The suppression of the truth. (Suppressio veri.)
IBID.

Truth conquers all things. (Vincit omnia veritas.)
LATIN PROVERB

Truth fears nothing save being hidden. (Veritas nihil veretur nisi abscondi.)
IBID.

Whatever is true is safe. (Quod verum tutum.)
IBID.

Suppression of the truth is a false representation. (Suppressio veri, expressio falsi.)
LEGAL MAXIM

Truth is a lion.
MOROCCAN PROVERB

Truth is the most horrible joke of all.
PORTUGUESE PROVERB

Truth will out, even if buried in a golden coffin.
RUSSIAN PROVERB

Nowadays truth's news.
SCOTTISH PROVERB

The truth is always green.
SPANISH PROVERB

The truth is usually discreditable to all concerned, including God.
IBID.

Truth stretches but does not break.
IBID.

Truth shines in the dark. WELSH PROVERB

[*See also* Algebra, Art, Beauty, Candor, Children, Christian, Civilization, Clarity, Counsel, Critic, Criticism, Dead, Discussion, Doubt, Error, Extremes, Fact, Falsehood, Fear, Fighting, Fool, Frankness, God, Half, History, Ignorance, Institution, Jest, Just, Justice, King, Laughter, Liar, Libel, Lying, Man, Martyrdom, Minority, Money, Mystery, Opinion (Public), Philosophy, Plainspeaking, Poetry, Power, Pragmatism, Press (Free), Prince, Proverb, Science, Scientist, Silence, Skeptic, Society, Style, Theologian, Time, Truth and Error, Truth and Falsehood, Truth-telling.

Truth and Error

Truth on one side of the Pyrenees; error on the other. BLAISE PASCAL: *Pensées,* III, 1670

Each truth is convictive of some error, and each truth helps on the discovery of another.
BENJAMIN WHICHCOTE: *Moral and Religious Aphorisms,* 1753

It is error alone which needs the support of government. Truth can stand by itself.
THOMAS JEFFERSON: *Notes on Virginia,* 1782

Truth is one, but error multifarious, since there may be a thousand opinions on any subject, but usually one that is right.
C. C. COLTON: *Lacon,* 1820

The thing is not only to avoid error, but to attain immense masses of truth.
THOMAS CARLYLE: *Journal,* Oct. 28, 1833

Truth crushed to earth shall rise again:
Th' eternal years of God are hers;
But error, wounded, writhes in pain,
And dies among his worshippers.
W. C. BRYANT: *The Battlefield,* 1839

It was Henrik Ibsen who said that the value of a truth lasted about fifteen years; then it rotted into error.
JAMES HUNEKER: *Old Fogy,* I, 1913

Truth is an imaginary line dividing error into two parts.
ELBERT HUBBARD: *Roycroft Dictionary and Book of Epigrams,* 1923

[*See also* Error, Truth.

Truth and Falsehood

The lip of truth shall be established for ever: but a lying tongue is but for a moment.
PROVERBS XII, 19, *c.* 350 B.C.

Falsehood is so vile that though it should praise the great works of God it offends against His divinity; truth is of such excellence that if it praise the meanest things they become ennobled.
LEONARDO DA VINCI: *Notebooks, c.* 1500

The truth . . . shall always prevail above lies, as the oil above the water.
THOMAS SHELTON: Tr. of CERVANTES: *Don Quixote,* II (1615), 1620

Truth is only falsehood well disguised.
GEORGE FARQUHAR: *The Constant Couple,* III, 1699

Blunt truths more mischief than nice falsehoods do.
ALEXANDER POPE: *An Essay on Criticism,* III, 1711

The most candid and enlightened must give their assent to a probable falsehood rather than to an improbable truth.
C. C. COLTON: *Lacon,* 1820

The ability to discriminate between that which is true and that which is false is one of the last attainments of the human mind.
J. FENIMORE COOPER: *The American Democrat,* XLIV, 1838

Truth, fact, is the life of all things; falsity, "fiction," or whatever it may call itself, is certain to be the death.
THOMAS CARLYLE: *Latter-Day Pamphlets,* VIII, 1850

A hair perhaps divides the false and true.
EDWARD FITZGERALD: Tr. of OMAR KHAYYÁM: *Rubáiyát* (*c.* 1100), 1857

Truth has many faces, and any one of them alone is a lie. Author unidentified

Truth's cloak is often lined with lies.
DANISH PROVERB

Between truth and falsehood there is a distance of only four fingers. HINDU PROVERB

A little truth helps the lie to go down.
ITALIAN PROVERB

Truth stings; falsehood heals. IBID.

Truth will not feed you, and a lie will not choke you. POLISH PROVERB

[*See also* Falsehood, Truth, Truth and Error.

Truth-seeking

There is nothing of permanent value (putting aside a few human affections), nothing that satisfies quiet reflection, except the sense of having worked according to one's capacity and light to make things clear and get rid of cant and shams of all sorts.
T. H. HUXLEY: *Letter to W. Platt Ball,* Oct. 27, 1890

[*See also* Philosopher, Research, Truth.

Truth-telling

Speak ye every man the truth to his neighbor.
ZECHARIAH VIII, 16, *c.* 520 B.C.

What hinders one from smiling when speaking the truth? HORACE: *Satires,* I, *c.* 25 B.C.

All truths are not to be told.
ENGLISH PROVERB, traced by Smith to *c.* 1350

I tell the truth, not as much as I would but as much as I dare — and I dare more and more as I grow older.
MICHEL DE MONTAIGNE: *Essays,* III, 1588

Tell truth and shame the Devil.
SHAKESPEARE: *I Henry IV,* III, *c.* 1598

I never speak falsehood, but I do not tell the truth to everyone.
PAOLO SARPI: *History of the Council of Trent,* I, 1619

Fools and madmen commonly tell truth.
ROBERT BURTON: *The Anatomy of Melancholy,* II, 1621

Better speak truth rudely than lie correctly.
GEORGE HERBERT: *Outlandish Proverbs,* 1640

It is better to remain silent than speak the truth ill-humoredly, and so spoil an excellent dish by covering it with bad sauce.
Ascribed to ST. FRANCIS DE SALES (1567–1622) in J. P. CAMUS: *L'esprit de Saint François de Sales,* 1641

Children and fools speak truth.
JOHN RAY: *English Proverbs,* 1670 (Cf. BURTON, *ante,* 1621)

Would you have a man speak truth to his ruin?
WILLIAM WYCHERLEY: *The Plain Dealer,* I, *c.* 1674

My talent is chiefly that of speaking truth, which I don't expect should ever recommend me to people of quality.
WILLIAM CONGREVE: *The Old Bachelor,* I, 1693

I deny the lawfulness of telling a lie to a sick man, for fear of alarming him. You have no business with consequences; you are to tell the truth.
SAMUEL JOHNSON: *Boswell's Life,* June 13, 1784

By soothsaying it is quite possible to make a good living in the world, but not by truth-saying.
G. C. LICHTENBERG: *Reflections,* 1799

Veracity does not consist in saying, but in the intention of communicating, truth.
S. T. COLERIDGE: *Biographia Literaria,* IX, 1817

He that speaks the truth executes no private function of an individual will, but the world utters a sound by his lips.
R. W. EMERSON: *Character,* 1844

Who knows the truth and does not tell it is indeed a miserable wretch. (Wer die Wahrheit kennet und saget sie nicht, der ist fürwahr ein erbärmlicher Wicht.)
Anon.: Song of the Jena students, *c.* 1848 (The Berlin students had a parody: " Who knows the truth and tells it free, lands in the Berlin city jail " — Wer die Wahrheit kennet und saget sie frei, der kommt in Berlin auf die Stadtvogtei)

Speaking truth is like writing fair, and only comes by practise.
JOHN RUSKIN: *The Seven Lamps of Architecture,* II, 1849

Truth never hurts the teller.
ROBERT BROWNING: *Fifine at the Fair,* XXXII, 1872

When in doubt, tell the truth.
S. L. CLEMENS (MARK TWAIN): *Notebook,* Feb. 2, 1894

If one tells the truth, one is sure, sooner or later, to be found out.
OSCAR WILDE: *Phrases and Philosophies for the Use of the Young,* 1894

When you shoot an arrow of truth dip its point in honey.
ARAB PROVERB

It is hard to believe that a man is telling the truth when you know that you would lie if you were in his place.
Author unidentified

Speak the truth and run.
JUGO-SLAVIC PROVERB

He that would speak truth must first have one foot in the stirrup.
TURKISH PROVERB

He who tells the truth must expect to be turned out of nine cities.
IBID.

[*See also* Hell, Truth, Wine.

Tschaikovsky, P. I. (1840–93)

Tschaikovsky studied Liszt with one eye; the other he kept on Bellini and the Italians. What might have happened if he had been one-eyed I cannot pretend to say.
JAMES HUNEKER: *Old Fogy,* I, 1913

His " Manfred " is a libel on Byron, who was a libel on God.
JAMES HUNEKER: *Old Fogy,* XVI

Tub

[*See* Independence, Self-reliance.

Tuberculosis

The captain of all the men of death that came against him to take him away was the consumption, for it was that that brought him down to the grave.
JOHN BUNYAN: *The Life and Death of Mr. Badman,* 1680

Tuberose

The sweet tuberose,
The sweetest flower for scent that blows.
P. B. SHELLEY: *The Sensitive Plant,* 1820

Tuesday

[*See* Days, Nail, Sneezing, Wedding-day.

Tumult

Debates, envyings, wraths, strifes, backbitings, whisperings, swellings, tumults.
II CORINTHIANS XII, 20, *c.* 55

The tumult and the shouting dies;
The captains and the kings depart.
RUDYARD KIPLING: *Recessional*, 1897 (London Times, July 17)

Tune

The tune the old cow died of (or on).
ENGLISH PHRASE, not recorded before the XVIII century

[*See also* Devil, Melody, Music, Song.

Turgenev, I. S. (1818–83)

[*See* Howells, W. D.

Turk

The Turks are the people of the wrath of God.
MARTIN LUTHER: *Table-Talk*, DCCCLXXV, 1569

God suffereth the wicked and cursed seed of Ismael to be a scourge and whip for our sins.
RICHARD KNOLLES: *The General History of the Turks*, 1603

Where the Turk's horse sets his foot the grass never grows.
ENGLISH PROVERB, described as old by THOMAS FULLER: *Historie of the Holy Warre*, V, 1639

Turk: A cruel, hard-hearted man; Turkish treatment: barbarous usage.
FRANCIS GROSE: *A Classical Dictionary of the Vulgar Tongue*, 1785

I see not much difference between ourselves and the Turks save that we have foreskins and they have none – and that we talk much, and they little.
BYRON: *Letter to Henry Drury*, May 3, 1810

He was a Turk, the color of mahogany.
BYRON: *Beppo*, 1818

The Turks have no church; religion and state are one; hence there is no counterpoise, no mutual support. This is the very essence of their unitarianism. They have no past; they are not an historical people; they exist only in the present.
S. T. COLERIDGE: *Table-Talk*, Jan. 1, 1823

The unspeakable Turk.
Apparently first used by W. E. GLADSTONE in an article in the Contemporary Review (London), 1876

[*See also* Antichrist, Arab, Character (National), Chesterfield (Earl of), Criminal, Drinking, Jew, Judgment Day, Koran, Predestination, Teetotaler.

Turkey (=country)

The sick man of Europe.
Author unidentified (Ascribed to various persons, including Nicholas I of Russia, and Gladstone. Edward Latham, in *Famous Sayings and Their Authors*, says that it was first used by Thomas Roe (*c.* 1567–1644), English ambassador at Constantinople. On Jan. 11, 1844, Nicholas I said to Sir George Hamilton Seymour, British chargé d'affaires at St. Petersburg: "We have on our hands a sick man, a very sick man. It would be a great misfortune if one of these days he should happen to die before the necessary arrangements are made")

Turkey (=fowl)

Job's turkey.
AMERICAN PHRASE, usually "as poor as Job's turkey," but sometimes "as patient as Job's turkey"; origin unknown, traced by Thornton to 1824

[*See also* Hops.

Turkish Language

[*See* Language, Persian Language.

Turn

One good turn deserves another.
JOHN FLETCHER and PHILIP MASSINGER: *The Little French Lawyer*, III, *c.* 1620

Turn about is fair play.
ENGLISH PROVERB, not recorded before the XIX century

My turn today, yours tomorrow.
LATIN SAYING

[*See also* Tit-for-tat.

Turner, J. M. W. (1775–1851)

This man, this Turner, will one day take his place beside Shakespeare and Verulam in the annals of the light of England.
JOHN RUSKIN: *Lectures on Architecture and Painting*, II, 1853

Turnip

[*See* Blood, Hard.

Turquoise

[*See* December.

Tweedledum and Tweedledee

Some say, compar'd to Bononcini,
That Meyheer Handel's but a ninny;
Others aver that he to Handel
Is scarcely fit to hold a candle:
Strange all this difference should be,
Twixt tweedledum and tweedledee!
JOHN BYROM: *Miscellaneous Poems*, I, 1773

Tweedledum and Tweedledee
Agreed to have a battle;
For Tweedledum said Tweedledee
Had spoiled his nice new rattle.

Just then flew down a monstrous crow,
  As black as a tar barrel,
Which frightened both the heroes so,
  They quite forgot their quarrel.

C. L. DODGSON (LEWIS CARROLL): *Through the Looking-Glass,* 1871

Twenty

She that tastes not sin before twenty, twenty to one that she'll taste it after.

THOMAS MIDDLETON: *A Trick to Catch the Old One,* v, 1608

[*See also* Adult, Ages, Precocity, Prodigy.

Twenty-five

She had her useful arts, and could contrive,
In time's despite, to stay at twenty-five.

GEORGE CRABBE: *The Borough,* xv, 1810

Ah, what shall I be at fifty
Should nature keep me alive,
If I find the world so bitter
When I am but twenty-five?

ALFRED TENNYSON: *Maud,* I, 1855

The first twenty-five years of one's life are worth all the rest of the longest life of man.

GEORGE BORROW: *The Romany Rye,* xxx, 1857

After a man's children reach twenty-five, he has none. No parent was ever very comfortable with a child after it had reached twenty-five.

E. W. HOWE: *Sinner Sermons,* 1926

[*See also* Husband, Mind, Poet.

Twenty-one

I do feel
The powers of one and twenty, like a tide,
Flow in upon me.

BEN JONSON: *The Staple of News,* I, 1625

Wherein have I injured you? Did I bring a physician to your father when he lay expiring, and endeavor to prolong his life, and you one-and-twenty?

WILLIAM CONGREVE: *The Old Bachelor,* v, 1693

Long as the year's dull cycle seems to run
When the brisk minor pants for twenty-one.

ALEXANDER POPE: *The First Epistle of the First Book of Horace,* 1735

Towering in the confidence of twenty-one.

SAMUEL JOHNSON: *Letter to Bennet Langton,* Jan. 9, 1758

In the brave days when I was twenty-one.

W. M. THACKERAY: *The Garret,* 1845

Twilight

The crow makes wing to the rooky wood,
Good things of day begin to droop and drowse,
And night's black agents to their preys do rouse.

SHAKESPEARE: *Macbeth,* II, *c.* 1605

Now came still evening on; and twilight gray
Had in her sober livery all things clad:
Silence accompanied for beast and bird,
They to their grassy couch, these to their nests,
Were slunk, all but the wakeful nightingale.

JOHN MILTON: *Paradise Lost,* IV, 1667

Now fades the glimmering landscape on the sight,
  And all the air a solemn stillness holds,
Save where the beetle wheels his droning flight,
  And drowsy tinklings lull the distant folds.

THOMAS GRAY: *Elegy Written in a Country Churchyard,* 1750

It is the hour when from the boughs
  The nightingale's high note is heard;
It is the hour when lovers' vows
  Seem sweet in every whisper'd word.

BYRON: *Parisina,* I, 1816

Twilight, ascending slowly from the east,
Entwined in duskier wreaths her braided locks
O'er the fair front and radiant eyes of day.

P. B. SHELLEY: *Alastor,* 1816

'Twas twilight, and the sunless day went down
  Over the waste of waters like a veil.

BYRON: *Don Juan,* II, 1819

When day is done, and clouds are low,
  And flowers are honey-dew,
And Hesper's lamp begins to glow
  Along the western blue;
And homeward wing the turtle-doves,
Then comes the hour the poet loves.

GEORGE CROLY: *The Poet's Hour, c.* 1820

One by one the flowers close,
Lily and dewy rose
Shutting their tender petals from the moon.

CHRISTINA ROSSETTI: *Twilight Calm,* 1862

They forget to put in the twilight when they made the Pacific Coast.

S. L. CLEMENS (MARK TWAIN): *Letter from New York to the Alta Californian* (San Francisco), April 16, 1867

At twilight nature becomes a wonderfully suggestive effect, and is not without loveliness, though perhaps its chief use is to illustrate quotations from the poets.

OSCAR WILDE: *The Decay of Lying,* 1891

[*See also* Adulterer, Evening, Gloaming, Night, Sunset.

Twins

A lusty brace of twins
May weed her of her folly.

ALFRED TENNYSON: *The Princess,* v, 1847

One of us was born a twin;
And not a soul knew which.

H. S. LEIGH: *The Twins,* 1869

2 mutch.

H. W. SHAW (JOSH BILLINGS): *Josh Billings' Comical Lexicon,* 1877

No man has ever become famous who had a twin brother. Author unidentified

Two

Two are better than one.
ECCLESIASTES IV, 9, *c.* 200 B.C.

Two of a trade seldom agree.
ENGLISH PROVERB, familiar since the XVII century

God hates the dual number; being known
The luckless number of division:
And when He blest each sev'ral day, whereon
He did His curious operation;
'Tis never read there (as the Fathers say)
God blest His work done on the second day:
Wherefore two prayers ought not to be said,
Or by ourselves, or from the pulpit read.
ROBERT HERRICK: *Noble Numbers,* 1647

It is good to have two strings to one's bow.
H. G. BOHN: *Handbook of Proverbs,* 1855

Two are an army to one. GERMAN PROVERB

When two do the same thing it is not the same thing. (Duo cum faciunt idem, non est idem.) MEDIEVAL LATIN PROVERB

Tycoon

[*See* Lincoln (Abraham).

Tyler, John (1790–1862)

Tyler is a political sectarian, of the slave-driving, Virginian, Jeffersonian school, principled against all improvement, with all the interests and passions and vices of slavery rooted in his moral and political constitution — with talents not above mediocrity, and a spirit incapable of expansion to the dimensions of the station upon which he has been cast by the hand of Providence, unseen through the apparent agency of chance.
JOHN QUINCY ADAMS: *Diary,* April 4, 1841

Typewriter

The typewriting machine, when played with expression, is not more annoying than the piano when played by a sister or near relation.
OSCAR WILDE: *Letter to Robert Ross,* May, 1897

Tyrannicide

It is lawful and hath been held so through all ages for any one who have the power to call to account a tyrant or wicked king, and after due conviction to depose and put him to death.
JOHN MILTON: *The Tenure of Kings and Magistrates,* 1649

If a sovereign oppresses his people to a degree they will rise and cut off his head. There is a remedy in human nature against tyranny that will keep us safe under every form of government.
SAMUEL JOHNSON: *Boswell's Life,* March 31, 1772

Thus be it ever with tyrants. (Sic semper tyrannis.)
MOTTO OF VIRGINIA, adopted Oct., 1779 (Cry of John Wilkes Booth on assassinating Abraham Lincoln, April 14, 1865)

Tyranny

Bleed, bleed, poor country!
Great tyranny! lay thou thy basis sure,
For goodness dares not check thee.
SHAKESPEARE: *Macbeth,* IV, *c.* 1605

Tyranny brings ignorance and brutality with it. It degrades men from their just rank into the class of brutes; it damps their spirits; it suppresses arts; it extinguishes every spark of noble ardor and generosity in the breasts of those who are enslaved by it; it makes naturally strong and great minds feeble and little, and triumphs over the ruins of virtue and humanity.
JONATHAN MAYHEW: *A Discourse Concerning Unlimited Submission and Non-Resistance to the Higher Powers,* 1750

Where law ends, tyranny begins.
WILLIAM PITT: Speech in the case of Wilkes, Jan. 9, 1770

No government power can be abused long. Mankind will not bear it.
SAMUEL JOHNSON: *Boswell's Life,* March 31, 1772

Some boast of being friends to government; I am a friend to righteous government, to a government founded upon the principles of reason and justice; but I glory in publicly avowing my eternal enmity to tyranny.
JOHN HANCOCK: Speech on the Boston Massacre, Boston, 1774

'T is a strange species of generosity which requires a return infinitely more valuable than anything it could have bestowed; that demands as a reward for a defence of our property, a surrender of those inestimable privileges to the arbitrary will of vindictive tyrants, which alone give value to that very property.
SAMUEL ADAMS: Speech in Philadelphia, Aug. 1, 1776

Tyranny, like Hell, is not easily conquered.
THOMAS PAINE: *The Crisis,* 1776

There are few minds to which tyranny is not delightful; power is nothing but as it is felt, and the delight of superiority is proportionate to the resistance overcome.
SAMUEL JOHNSON: *Letter to Hester Thrale,* Oct. 21, 1779

The tyranny of a multitude is a multiplied tyranny.
EDMUND BURKE: *Letter to Thomas Mercer,* Feb. 26, 1790

I have sworn upon the altar of God eternal hostility against every form of tyranny over the mind of man.
THOMAS JEFFERSON: *Letter to Benjamin Rush,* 1800

The evils of tyranny are rarely seen but by him who resists it.

JOHN HAY: *Castilian Days*, II, 1872

The history of woman is the history of the worst form of tyranny the world has ever known: the tyranny of the weak over the strong. It is the only tyranny that lasts.

OSCAR WILDE: *A Woman of No Importance*, III, 1893

[*See also* Democracy, Freedom, Government, Law, Opinion (Public), Tyrannicide, Tyrant.

Tyrant

Tyrants surround themselves with bad men, for they like to be flattered. No man of high and generous spirit will flatter them.

ARISTOTLE: *Politics*, V, *c.* 322 B.C.

We must not marvel if the Lord lets loose the bridle to tyrants, and suffereth them still to exercise their cruelty against His church, for the consolation is ready, to wit: having used them as His vassals to correct His people, He will visit their pride and arrogance.

JOHN CALVIN: *A Commentary Upon the Prophecy of Isaiah*, 1551

The highest step of their greatness is tied to a halter, and they be but God's scourges which He will cast into the fire when He hath done with them.

PHILIP MORNAY: *De la vérité de la religion chrétienne*, 1581

A bloody tyrant, and a homicide:
One rais'd in blood, and one in blood establish'd;
One that made means to come by what he hath,
And slaughter'd those that were the means to help him.

SHAKESPEARE: *Richard III*, V, *c.* 1592

'Tis time to fear when tyrants seem to kiss.

SHAKESPEARE: *Pericles*, I, *c.* 1608

Men would be tyrants, tyrants would be gods;
Thus they become our scourges, we their rods.

FULKE GREVILLE (LORD BROOKE): *A Treatie of Warre*, *c.* 1625

'Twixt kings and tyrants there's this difference known;
Kings seek their subjects' good: tyrants their own.

ROBERT HERRICK: *Hesperides*, 1648

Nature has left this tincture in the blood,
That all men would be tyrants if they could.

DANIEL DEFOE: *The History of the Kentish Petition*, 1701

Smart tyrants never come to grief.

VOLTAIRE: *Mérope*, V, 1743

The thought, he'll soon be food for worms,
From all his pleasures torn,
Blasts ev'ry op'ning bud of joy,
And makes the tyrant mourn.

Anon.: *The Excellency of the Female Character Vindicated*, IV, 1828

[*See also* Certainty, King, Liberty, Mob, Tyrannicide, Tyranny.

U

Ugliness

Thersites was the ugliest man that came beneath the walls of Troy. He was bandy-legged and lame in one foot, his shoulders were crooked and drawn together toward his breast, his head was pointed, and the hair on it was woolly.

HOMER: *Iliad*, II, *c.* 800 B.C.

I cannot tell by what logic we call a toad, a bear, or an elephant ugly; they being created in those outward shapes and figures which best express the actions of their inward forms; and having passed that general visitation of God, who saw that all that He had made was good.

THOMAS BROWNE: *Religio Medici*, I, 1642

She is most splendidly, gallantly ugly.

WILLIAM WYCHERLEY: *The Plain Dealer*, II, *c.* 1674

Such a red, spongy, warty nose! Such a squint! In short, he is ugly beyond expression.

MARY WORTLEY MONTAGU: *Letter to Lady* ——, Jan. 13, 1716

The fault lies with the gods, who have made her so ugly.

J. B. L. GRESSET: *Le méchant*, II, 1747

Though ugliness be the opposite to beauty, it is not the opposite to proportion and fitness. For it is possible that a thing may be very ugly with any proportions, and with a perfect fitness to any uses.

EDMUND BURKE: *The Sublime and Beautiful*, II, 1756

She has an ee — she has but ane,
The cat has twa the very color;
Five rusty teeth, forbye a stump,
A clapper-tongue wad deave a miller:
A whiskin' beard about her mou',
Her nose and chin they threaten ither —
Sic a wife as Willie had,
I wadna gie a button for her.

ROBERT BURNS: *Willie Wastle*, 1792
(*Deave*=to deafen)

How happy for us mortals 'twere
Had Eve been such a woman!
The Devil ne'er had tempted her
And she had tempted no man.

S. T. COLERIDGE: *On a Very Ugly Woman*, 1800

She is as ugly as sin.

MARIA EDGEWORTH: *Popular Tales*, 1800

I hold that place among men which stubnosed brunettes with meeting eyebrows do among women.

JOHN KEATS: *Letter to Fanny Brawne*, July 25, 1819

If for silver, or for gold,
You could melt ten thousand pimples
Into half a dozen dimples,

Then your face we might behold,
  Looking, doubtless, much more smugly,
  Yet ev'n then 'twould be d——d ugly.

BYRON: *Letter to John Murray*, Aug. 12, 1819

Prickly, and pulpous, and blistering, and blue,
Livid, and starred with a lurid dew.

P. B. SHELLEY: *The Sensitive Plant*, 1820

A square leaf on any tree would be ugly, being a violation of the laws of growth in trees, and we ought to feel it so.

JOHN RUSKIN: *Lectures on Architecture and Painting*, 1853

The secret of ugliness consists not in irregularity, but in being uninteresting.

R. W. EMERSON: *The Conduct of Life*, VIII, 1860

The pathos exquisite of lovely minds
Hid in harsh forms.

MARIAN EVANS (GEORGE ELIOT): *A Minor Prophet*, 1865

No object is so ugly that, under certain conditions of light and shade, or proximity to other things, it will not look beautiful; no object is so beautiful that, under certain conditions, it will not look ugly.

OSCAR WILDE: Lecture to art students, Royal Academy, London, June 30, 1883

An emetic for the eyes.

JORIS-KARL HUYSMANS: *À rebours*, 1884

Everything ugly weakens and depresses man. It reminds him of decay, danger, impotence.

F. W. NIETZSCHE: *The Twilight of the Idols*, 1889

[*See also* Beautiful, Good, Industry, Ludicrous, Money, Useful, Vice.

Ukulele

A so-called musical instrument which, when listened to, you can't tell whether one is playing on it, or just monkeying with it.

Ascribed to WILL ROGERS, *c.* 1925

Umbrella

If you leave your umbrella at home, it is sure to rain.

AMERICAN PROVERB, apparently first recorded by GELETT BURGESS: *Are You a Bromide?*, 1907

Rainy days will surely come
Take your friend's umbrella home.

Author unidentified

Unanimity

They all said the same. (Vox omnibus una.)

VIRGIL: *Æneid*, V, 19 B.C.

Unanimity is the best fortress.

DANISH PROVERB

Unbecoming

Proposing a measure for party purposes, which I do not think it would become me to adopt.

JOHN JAY: Notation on a letter from Alexander Hamilton, 1800

Unbelief

[*See* Belief, Cause and Effect, Skepticism.

Unbeliever

[*See* Hell.

Uncertainty

Uncertainty and expectation are the joys of life. Security is an insipid thing, and the overtaking and possessing of a wish discovers the folly of the chase.

WILLIAM CONGREVE: *Love for Love*, IV, 1695

The uncertain is counted as nothing. (Incerta pro nullis habentur.)

LEGAL MAXIM

Unchastity

If unchastity in a woman, whom St. Paul terms the glory of man, be such a scandal and dishonor, then certainly in a man, who is both the image and glory of God, it must, though commonly not so thought, be much more deflowering and dishonorable.

JOHN MILTON: *An Apology for Smectymnuus*, 1642

One false step entirely damns her fame,
In vain with tears the loss she may deplore,
In vain look back on what she was before;
She sets like stars that fall, to rise no more.

NICHOLAS ROWE: *Jane Shore*, I, 1714

Girls in this way fall every day,
And have been falling for ages.
Who is to blame? You know his name:
It's the boss that pays starvation wages.

JOE HILL: *The White Slave*, *c.* 1907

[*See also* Adultery, Fornication.

Uncle

Old fox-brained and ox-browed uncles.

THOMAS MIDDLETON: *A Trick to Catch the Old One*, I, 1608

To talk like a Dutch uncle.

ENGLISH PHRASE, not recorded before the XIX century

Unclean

If any beast, of which ye may eat, die; he that toucheth the carcass thereof shall be unclean until the even.

LEVITICUS XI, 39, *c.* 700 B.C.

If a woman have conceived seed, and born a man child: then she shall be unclean seven days.

LEVITICUS XII, 2

If she bear a maid child, then she shall be unclean two weeks.

LEVITICUS XII, 5

Whosoever toucheth one that is slain with a sword in the open fields, or a dead body, or a bone of a man, or a grave, shall be unclean seven days. NUMBERS XIX, 16, *c.* 700 B.C.

[*See also* Grave.

Unconscious

The uttered part of a man's life bears to the unuttered, unconscious part a small unknown proportion. He himself never knows it, much less do others.
THOMAS CARLYLE: *Sir Walter Scott,* 1838 (Westminster Review, Jan.)

Unction

Lay not that flattering unction to your soul.
SHAKESPEARE: *Hamlet,* III, *c.* 1601

Underling

The fault, dear Brutus, is not in our stars,
But in ourselves, that we are underlings.
SHAKESPEARE: *Julius Cæsar,* I, 1599

Understanding

If you would judge, understand.
SENECA: *Medea, c.* 60

I shall light a candle of understanding in thine heart, which shall not be put out.
II ESDRAS, XIV, 25, *c.* 100

I have tried sedulously not to laugh at the acts of man, nor to lament them, nor to detest them, but to understand them.
BARUCH SPINOZA: *Tractatus theologico-politicus,* 1677

That which we understand we can't blame.
J. W. GOETHE: *Torquato Tasso,* II, 1790

To understand all makes one very indulgent. (Tout comprendre rend très indulgent.)
ANNA LOUISE DE STAËL: *Corinne,* XVIII, 1807 (The saying is commonly changed to "Tout comprendre c'est tout pardonner" — To understand all is to pardon all)

The first condition under which we can know a man at all is, that he be in essentials something like ourselves.
J. A. FROUDE: *The Dissolution of the Monasteries,* 1857 (Fraser's Magazine)

[*See also* Brain, Controversy.

Undertaker

Diaulus, who was once a doctor, is now an undertaker; what he does as an undertaker is exactly what he used to do as a doctor.
MARTIAL: *Epigrams,* I, 86

The houses that he makes last till doomsday.
SHAKESPEARE: *Hamlet,* V, *c.* 1601

An undertaker walking merrily drunk by the side of a hearse is a horrid object; but an undertaker singing and hammering in his shop is only rapping death himself on the knuckles.
LEIGH HUNT: *The Indicator,* XLI, 1821

[*See also* Doctor, Funeral, Grave.

Uneducable

It is enough to make one despair of the future that Demos and the Bourbons seem to be much alike in their want of capacity for either learning or forgetting.
T. H. HUXLEY: *On the Natural Inequality of Man,* 1890

[*See also* Bourbon.

Unemployment

In order to mitigate unemployment attending business depression, we urge the enactment of legislation authorizing that construction and repair of public works be initiated in periods of acute unemployment.
Democratic National Platform, 1924

[*See also* Capitalism, Work, Worker.

Unexpected

The more unexpected events are, the more do they frighten and terrorize mankind.
FRANCESCO GUICCIARDINI: *Storia d'Italia,* 1564

It is the unexpected that always happens.
ENGLISH PROVERB, not recorded before the XIX century

Unfaithfulness

Were she to be unfaithful to me she ought to be pierced with a Corsican poignard.
JAMES BOSWELL: *Letter to William Temple,* Feb. 1, 1767

Wise married women don't trouble themselves about infidelity in their husbands.
SAMUEL JOHNSON: *Boswell's Life,* Oct. 10, 1779

Unforeseen

There is nothing certain but the unforeseen.
J. A. FROUDE: *Oceana,* VII, 1886 (Cited as "a proverb")

Unhappiness

Oh, that was a good time, when I was unhappy.
Ascribed to SOPHIE ARNOULD (1744–1802)

We are so curiously made that one atom put in the wrong place in our original structure will often make us unhappy for life.
WILLIAM GODWIN: *Letter to Mary Godwin Shelley,* 1827

Men who are unhappy, like men who sleep badly, are always proud of the fact.
BERTRAND RUSSELL: *The Conquest of Happiness,* I, 1930

[*See also* Family, Greatness, Happiness, Misery.

Unhonored

[*See* Unwept.

Uniform

A soldier must learn to love his profession, must look to it to satisfy all his tastes and his sense

of honor. That is why handsome uniforms are useful.
NAPOLEON I: To Gaspard Gourgaud at St. Helena, 1815–1818

A good uniform must work its way with the women.
CHARLES DICKENS: *The Pickwick Papers,* XXXVII, 1837

I was without a sword, as I usually was when on horseback in the field, and wore a soldier's blouse for a coat, with the shoulder straps of my rank to indicate to the army who I was.
U. S. GRANT: *Personal Memoirs,* LXVI, 1885 (He is describing his uniform at the surrender of Lee, April 9, 1865)

The uniform 'e wore
Was nothin' much before,
An' rather less than 'arf o' that be'ind.
RUDYARD KIPLING: *Gunga Din,* 1890

[*See also* Soldier.

Uniformity

[*See* Opinion.

Unintelligible

It was Greek to me.
SHAKESPEARE: *Julius Cæsar,* I, 1599

It is Hebrew to me.
J. B. MOLIÈRE: *L'Étourdi,* III, 1653

Union

Union gives strength and firmness to the humblest.
PUBLILIUS SYRUS: *Sententiæ, c.* 50 B.C.

We two form a multitude.
OVID: *Metamorphoses,* I, *c.* 5

There are three unions in this world: Christ and the Church, husband and wife, spirit and flesh.
ST. AUGUSTINE: *Of Continence, c.* 425

Be united – united – united. (Seid einig – einig – einig.)
J. C. F. SCHILLER: *Wilhelm Tell,* IV, 1804

All for one; one for all.
ALEXANDRE DUMAS *père: The Three Musketeers,* IX, 1844

Three united against a town will ruin it.
ARAB PROVERB

Union makes power. (L'Union fait la force.)
FRENCH PROVERB

Union makes strength. (Einigkeit macht stark.)
GERMAN PROVERB

[*See also* Liberty, Society, Unity.

Union, American

Then join hand and hand, brave Americans all –
By uniting we stand, by dividing we fall.
JOHN DICKINSON: *The Patriot's Appeal,* 1776

From many, one. (E pluribus unum.)
MOTTO OF THE UNITED STATES, adopted 1777 (It is first found on the title page of the Gentleman's Miscellany, Jan., 1692)

The said colonies unite themselves so as never to be divided by any act whatever, and hereby severally enter into a firm league of friendship with each other, for their common defence, the security of their liberties, and their mutual and general welfare.
ARTICLES OF CONFEDERATION, II, Nov. 15, 1777

My idea is that we should be made one nation in every case concerning foreign affairs, and separate ones in whatever is merely domestic.
THOMAS JEFFERSON: *Letter to J. Blair,* 1787

The local interests of a state ought in every case to give way to the interests of the Union; for when a sacrifice of one or the other is necessary, the former becomes only an apparent, partial interest, and should yield, on the principle that the small good ought never to oppose the great one.
ALEXANDER HAMILTON: Speech in New York, June 24, 1788

United we stand; divided we fall.
MOTTO OF KENTUCKY, adopted 1792 (Cf. DICKINSON, *ante,* 1776)

Who are the true friends of the Union? Those who would confine the Federal government strictly within the limits prescribed by the Constitution; who would preserve to the states and the people all powers not expressly delegated; who would make this a federal and not a national Union.
ROBERT Y. HAYNE: Speech in the Senate, Jan. 21, 1830

Liberty and Union, now and forever, one and inseparable!
DANIEL WEBSTER: Speech in the Senate, Jan. 26, 1830

Can there ever be any thorough national fusion of the Northern and Southern states? I think not. In fact, the Union will be shaken almost to dislocation whenever a very serious question between the states arises. The American Union has no centre, and it is impossible now to make one.
S. T. COLERIDGE: *Table-Talk,* Jan. 4, 1833

My hopes of the long continuance of this Union are extinct. The people must go the way of all the world, and split up into an uncertain number of rival communities, enemies in war, in peace friends.
JOHN QUINCY ADAMS: *Diary,* July 30, 1834

What were the states before the Union? The hope of their enemies, the fear of their

friends, and arrested only by the Constitution from becoming the shame of the world.
HORACE BINNEY: *The Life and Character of Chief Justice Marshall,* 1835

I never use the word "nation" in speaking of the United States. I always use the word "union" or "confederacy." We are not a nation, but a *union,* a confederacy of equal and sovereign states.
JOHN C. CALHOUN: *Letter to Oliver Dyer,* Jan. 1, 1849

Every state that then came into the Union, and every state that has since come into the Union, came into it binding itself by indissoluble bands to remain within the Union itself, and to remain within it by its posterity forever. It is a marriage which no human authority can dissolve or divorce the parties from.
HENRY CLAY: Speech in the Senate, Feb. 6, 1850

Sail on, O Union, strong and great!
Humanity with all its fears,
With all the hopes of future years,
Is hanging breathless on thy fate.
H. W. LONGFELLOW: *The Building of the Ship,* 1850

I owe a paramount allegiance to the whole Union — a subordinate one to my own state.
HENRY CLAY: Speech in the Senate, July 22, 1850

We join ourselves to no party that does not carry the flag and keep step to the music of the Union.
RUFUS CHOATE: *Letter to the Whig National Convention,* 1855

The Union is necessarily perpetual. No state can lawfully withdraw or be expelled from it. The Federal Constitution is as much a part of the constitution of every state as if it had been textually inserted therein.
JEREMIAH S. BLACK: *Opinion as Secretary of State,* Dec. 17, 1860

I can anticipate no greater calamity for the country than a dissolution of the Union. It would be an accumulation of all the evils we complain of, and I am willing to sacrifice anything but honor for its preservation.
ROBERT E. LEE: *Letter,* Jan. 23, 1861

I hold that in contemplation of universal law, and of the Constitution, the Union of these states is perpetual. Perpetuity is implied, if not expressed, in the fundamental law of all national governments.
ABRAHAM LINCOLN: Inaugural Address, March 4, 1861

The states have their status in the Union, and they have no other legal status. The Union is older than any of the states, and, in fact, it created them as states.
ABRAHAM LINCOLN: Message to Congress, July 4, 1861

Gentlemen talk about the Union as if it was an end instead of a means. They talk about it as if it was the Union of these states which alone had brought into life the principles of public and of personal liberty. Sir, they existed before, and they may survive it.
JOHN C. BRECKENRIDGE: Speech in the Senate, Aug. 1, 1861

My paramount object in this struggle is to save the Union, and is not either to save or to destroy slavery.
ABRAHAM LINCOLN: *Letter to Horace Greeley,* Aug. 22, 1862

Let's have the Union restored as it was, if we can; but if we can't I'm in favor of the Union as it wasn't.
C. F. BROWNE (ARTEMUS WARD): *Artemus Ward: His Travels,* 1865

[*See also* Constitution (American), Secession, Slavery, United States, War (American Civil).

Union, Labor

[*See* Labor Union.

Unique

Are you seeking Alcides's equal? No one is, except himself.
SENECA: *Hercules Furens, c.* 50

Nature made him, and then broke the mold.
LUDOVICO ARIOSTO: *Orlando Furioso,* x, 1532

Unitarianism

Unitarianism is, in effect, the worst of one kind of atheism joined to the worst of one kind of Calvinism, like two asses tied tail to tail.
S. T. COLERIDGE: *Table-Talk,* April 4, 1832

Unitarianism is a mattress for ex-Christians to fall on. Author unknown

United States

Within our own borders we possess all the means of sustenance, defence, and commerce; at the same time, these advantages are so distributed among the different states of this continent as if nature had in view to proclaim to us — be united among yourselves, and you will want nothing from the rest of the world.
SAMUEL ADAMS: Speech on American Independence, July 4, 1776

The stile of this confederacy shall be "The United States of America."
ARTICLES OF CONFEDERATION, I, Nov. 15, 1777

I tremble for my country when I reflect that God is just.
THOMAS JEFFERSON: *Notes on Virginia,* 1782

His Britannic Majesty acknowledges the said United States, viz., New-Hampshire, Massachusetts-Bay, Rhode-Island and Providence

Plantations, Connecticut, New-York, New-Jersey, Pennsylvania, Delaware, Maryland, Virginia, North-Carolina, South-Carolina, and Georgia, to be free, sovereign and independent states; that he treats with them as such; and for himself, his heirs and successors, relinquishes all claims to the government, property and territorial rights of the same, and every part thereof.

TREATY OF PARIS, I, Sept. 3, 1783

I do believe we shall continue to grow, to multiply, and prosper until we exhibit an association powerful, wise, and happy beyond what has yet been seen by men.

THOMAS JEFFERSON: *Letter to John Adams,* 1812

The possible destiny of the United States of America — as a nation of a hundred millions of freemen — stretching from the Atlantic to the Pacific, living under the laws of Alfred, and speaking the language of Shakespeare and Milton, is an august conception. Why should we not wish to see it realized? America would then be England viewed through a solar microscope; Great Britain in a state of glorious magnification.

S. T. COLERIDGE: *Table-Talk,* April 10, 1833

If destruction be our lot we must ourselves be its author and finisher. As a nation of freemen we must live through all time, or die by suicide.

ABRAHAM LINCOLN: Speech in Springfield, Ill., Jan. 27, 1837

There is in the United States more taxation, poverty and general oppression as ever known in any other country.

THOMAS BROTHERS: *The United States as They Are,* 1840

'Tis a wild democracy, the riot of mediocrities. . . . Our few fine persons are apt to die.

R. W. EMERSON: *Letter to Thomas Carlyle,* April 19, 1853

The United States themselves are essentially the greatest poem.

WALT WHITMAN: *Leaves of Grass,* pref., 1855

Either some Cæsar or Napoleon will seize the reigns of government with a strong hand, or your republic will be as fearfully plundered and laid waste by barbarians in the Twentieth Century as the Roman Empire was in the Fifth; with this difference, that the Huns and Vandals who ravaged the Roman Empire came from without, and that your Huns and Vandals will have engendered within your own country by your own institutions.

T. B. MACAULAY: *Letter to H. S. Randall,* May 23, 1857

Gigantic daughter of the West
We drink to thee across the flood . . .
For art not thou of English blood?

ALFRED TENNYSON: *Hands All Round,* 1862

Who is the United States? Not the judiciary; not the President; but the sovereign power of the people, exercised through their representatives in Congress, with the concurrence of the executive.

THADDEUS STEVENS: Speech in the House of Representatives, Dec. 18, 1865

The true nationality of the states, the genuine union, when we come to a mortal crisis, is, and is to be, after all, neither the written law, nor, (as is generally supposed,) either self-interest, or common pecuniary or material objects — but the fervid and tremendous Idea, melting everything else with resistless heat, and solving all lesser and definite distinctions in vast, indefinite, spiritual, emotional power.

WALT WHITMAN: *Democratic Vistas,* 1870

To me, the wonder is that a poor man ever consents to live out of America, or a rich man to live in it.

R. F. BURTON: Tr. of *The Arabian Nights,* appendix, 1888

It is a noble land that God has given us: a land that can feed and clothe the world; a land whose coastlines would enclose half the countries of Europe; a land set like a sentinel between the two imperial oceans of the globe, a greater England with a nobler destiny.

A. J. BEVERIDGE: Speech in Indianapolis, Sept. 16, 1898

I hope we shall never forget that we created this nation, not to serve ourselves, but to serve mankind.

WOODROW WILSON: Address to the G.A.R. at Washington, Sept. 28, 1915

You are right in your impression that a number of persons are urging me to come to the United States. But why on earth do you call them my friends?

GEORGE BERNARD SHAW: *Letter to O. G. Villard,* Aug. 4, 1921

[*See also* America, American, Billion, England, Imperialism, Union (American).

Unity

Behold how good and how pleasant it is for brethren to dwell together in unity.

PSALMS CXXXIII, *c.* 150 B.C.

Unity of feelings and affections makes the strongest relationship.

PUBLILIUS SYRUS: *Sententiæ, c.* 50 B.C.

One Lord, one faith, one baptism.

EPHESIANS IV, 5, *c.* 60

We must all hang together or assuredly we shall all hang separately.

BENJAMIN FRANKLIN: To John Hancock, on signing the Declaration of Independence, July 4, 1776

Unity is the goal toward which mankind moves ceaselessly.

M. A. BAKUNIN: *Proposition motivée,* 1868

There is but one way in which the unity of Christians may be fostered, and that is by furthering the return to the one true Church of Christ of those who are separated from it.
POPE PIUS XI: *Mortalium animos*, Jan. 6, 1928

One people, one country, one leader. (Ein Volk, ein Reich, ein Führer.)
Slogan of the German Nazis, *c.* 1933

[*See also* Charity, Union.

Universality

At all times, everywhere and by all. (Quod semper et ubique et ab omnibus.)
ST. VINCENT OF LÉRINS: *Commonitorium*, 434 (Vincent used the phrase in his argument that whatever has been universally believed must be true)

Universe

There is nothing uncultivated, nothing sterile, nothing dead in the universe; there is no chaos, no confusion except in appearance.
G. W. LEIBNIZ: *The Monadology*, LXIX, 1714

It is not impossible that to some infinitely superior being the whole universe may be as one plain, the distance between planet and planet being only as the pores in a grain of sand, and the spaces between system and system no greater than the intervals between one grain and the grain adjacent.
S. T. COLERIDGE: *Omniana*, 1812

There is no chance, and no anarchy, in the universe. All is system and gradation. Every god is there sitting in his sphere.
R. W. EMERSON: *The Conduct of Life*, IX, 1860

The universe is anonymous.
W. WINWOOD READE: *The Martyrdom of Man*, III, 1872

Taken as a whole, the universe is absurd.
WALTER BAGEHOT: *Literary Studies*, I, 1879

The universe is not run by the God of the churches. It is the manifestation of eternal and indestructible matter, and nothing more.
BENITO MUSSOLINI: Speech in Lausanne, July, 1904

[*See also* Change, Nature.

University

I well know there are whole universities that won't believe there are living creatures in the male seed, but such things don't worry me: I know I am right.
ANTONY VAN LEEUWENHOEK: *Sendbrieven*, XLI, *c.* 1700

Universities are fit for nothing but to debauch the principles of young men, to poison their minds with romantic notions of knowledge and virtue.
HENRY FIELDING: *The Temple Beau*, I, 1730

A girl out of a village or a nursery [is] more capable of receiving instruction than a lad just set free from the university. It is not difficult to write on blank paper, but 'tis a tedious if not an impossible task to scrape out nonsense already written.
MARY WORTLEY MONTAGU: *Letter to James Steuart*, April 7, 1760

O Granta! sweet Granta! where studious of ease,
I slumbered seven years, and then lost my degrees.
CHRISTOPHER ANSTEY: *The New Bath Guide*, 1766

Whene'er with haggard eyes I view
This dungeon that I'm rotting in,
I think of those companions true
Who studied with me at the U-
Niversity of Gottingen.
GEORGE CANNING: *The Anti-Jacobin*, XXX, June 4, 1798

The true university of these days is a collection of books.
THOMAS CARLYLE: *Heroes and Hero-Worship*, V, 1840 (Lecture in London, May 19)

A university is a place of instruction where universal knowledge is professed.
J. H. NEWMAN: *On the Scope and Nature of University Education*, 1852

Universities are of course hostile to geniuses, which, seeing and using ways of their own, discredit the routine: as churches and monasteries persecute youthful saints. Yet we all send our sons to college, and though he be a genius, the youth must take his chance.
R. W. EMERSON: *English Traits*, XII, 1856

If the pupil be of a texture to bear it, the best university that can be recommended to a man of ideas is the gauntlet of the mob.
R. W. EMERSON: *Society and Solitude*, 1870

A university should be a place of light, of liberty, and of learning.
BENJAMIN DISRAELI: Speech in the House of Commons, March 8, 1873

The medieval university looked backwards; it professed to be a storehouse of old knowledge. . . . The modern university looks forward, and is a factory of new knowledge.
T. H. HUXLEY: *Letter to E. Ray Lankester*, April 11, 1892

I asked W.: "What would you say of the university and modern life?" "I wouldn't say anything: I'd rather be excused."
HORACE TRAUBEL: *With Walt Whitman in Camden*, IV, 1914

The use of a university is to make young gentlemen as unlike their fathers as possible.
WOODROW WILSON: Address in Pittsburgh, Oct. 24, 1914

A university studies politics, but it will not advocate Fascism or Communism. A university studies military tactics, but it will not promote war. A university studies peace, but it will not organize crusades of pacifism. It will study every question that affects human welfare, but it will not carry a banner in a crusade for anything except freedom of learning.
L. D. COFFMAN (president of the University of Minnesota): In the Journal of the American Association of University Women, Jan., 1936

An American university is an athletic institution in which a few classes are held for the feebleminded.
Ascribed to a Chinese student

Harvard offers education à la carte, Yale a substantial table d'hôte, Columbia a quick lunch, and Princeton a picnic.
Author unidentified

[*See also* Books, College, Freedom (Academic), Knowledge, Library, Pedagogue, Professor.

University, German

The most intensely cultivated and the most productive intellectual corporations the world has ever seen.
T. H. HUXLEY: *A Liberal Education, and Where to Find It,* 1868 (Address in London)

Unkindness

This was the most unkindest cut of all.
SHAKESPEARE: *Julius Cæsar,* III, 1599

In nature there's no blemish but the mind;
None can be call'd deform'd but the unkind.
SHAKESPEARE: *Twelfth Night,* III, *c.* 1601

[*See also* Drinking.

Unknowable

[*See* God.

Unknown

Everything unknown is taken to be magnificent.
TACITUS: *Life of Agricola,* XXX, *c.* 98

Not to know me argues yourselves unknown.
JOHN MILTON: *Paradise Lost,* IV, 1667

An unknown land. (Terra incognita.)
LATIN PHRASE

[*See also* Magnificent.

Unlawful

It is not lawful. (Non licet.) LATIN PHRASE

Unlucky

Unlucky in love; lucky at cards.
ENGLISH PROVERB, not recorded before the XVIII century

If an unlucky man went into business selling shrouds no one would die. ARAB PROVERB

If the unlucky man became a barber, men would begin to be born without heads.
GERMAN PROVERB

If my father had brought me up a hatter men would have stopped wearing hats.
IRISH PROVERB

The unlucky man feels the rain on his backside even when he is sitting down.
ITALIAN PROVERB

[*See also* May.

Unnatural

Nothing is unnatural that is not physically impossible.
R. B. SHERIDAN: *The Critic,* II, 1779

Unnecessary

Forget not on every occasion to ask thyself, Is this not one of the unnecessary things?
MARCUS AURELIUS: *Meditations,* IV, *c.* 170

Unrest

We are like a man running downhill, who cannot keep on his legs unless he runs on, and will inevitably fall if he stops; or, again, like a pole balanced on the tip of one's finger; or like a planet, which would fall into its sun the moment it ceased to hurry forward on its way. Unrest is the mark of existence.
ARTHUR SCHOPENHAUER: *The Vanity of Existence,* 1851

Unrighteousness

[*See* Mammon, Man.

Unseen

Unseen, unrued. SCOTTISH PROVERB

Untamable

Three things are untamable: idiots, women, and the salt sea. WELSH PROVERB

Untrustworthy

These three are not to be trusted: a singer, a shopkeeper, and an opium eater.
HINDU PROVERB

Unwept

Unwept, unhonored, uninterred he lies.
ALEXANDER POPE: Tr. of HOMER: *Iliad,* XXII (*c.* 800 B.C.), 1720

Unwept, unnoted, and for ever dead.
ALEXANDER POPE: Tr. of HOMER: *Odyssey,* V (*c.* 800 B.C.), 1726

Unwept, unhonored, and unsung.
WALTER SCOTT: *The Lay of the Last Minstrel,* VI, 1805

Unwept, unshrouded, and unsepulchred.
ROBERT SOUTHEY: *A Tale of Paraguay,* I, 1825

Unworthy

I would that I were low laid in my grave:
I am not worth this coil that's made for me,
SHAKESPEARE: *King John,* II, *c.* 1596

Not worthy to carry guts after a bear.
JOHN RAY: *English Proverbs,* 1670

Uplift

I maintain that there is a moral interference with our fellow-creatures at home and abroad, not only to be asserted as a right, but binding as a duty.
W. E. CHANNING: *Letter to Jonathan Phillips,* 1839

If I cannot retain my moral influence over a man except by occasionally knocking him down, if that is the only basis upon which he will respect me, then for the sake of his soul I have got occasionally to knock him down.
WOODROW WILSON: Speech, May 16, 1916

The object of the uplift is to give the uplifter a lift. Author unidentified

Upright

Lord, who shall abide in thy tabernacle? who shall dwell in thy holy hill? He that walketh uprightly, and worketh righteousness, and speaketh the truth in his heart.
PSALMS XV, 1–2, *c.* 150 B.C.

Mark the perfect man, and behold the upright: for the end of that man is peace.
PSALMS XXXVII, 37

An upright man ought to be like a strong-smelling goat, so that a stranger, coming near him, will perceive him, whether he wills it or not.
MARCUS AURELIUS: *Meditations,* XI, *c.* 170

The upright never grow rich in a hurry.
DANISH PROVERB

Uproar

The Jews . . . took unto them certain lewd fellows of the baser sort, and set all the city on an uproar. ACTS XVII, 5, *c.* 75

Use

Use almost can change the stamp of nature.
SHAKESPEARE: *Hamlet,* III, *c.* 1601

The used key is always bright.
BENJAMIN FRANKLIN: *Poor Richard's Almanac,* 1758

Oh, to what uses shall we put
The wildweed-flower that simply blows?
And is there any moral shut
Within the bosom of the rose?
ALFRED TENNYSON: *The Day-Dream,* 1842

Keep a thing seven years, and ye'll find a use for't. SCOTTISH PROVERB

Useful

What praise is implied in the simple epithet useful! What reproach in the contrary!
DAVID HUME: *An Enquiry Concerning the Principles of Morals,* II, 1751

Whatever is useful is common and ugly. The most useful part of a house is the privy.
THÉOPHILE GAUTIER: *Caprices et zigzags,* 1845

Useless

There is nothing useless to men of sense.
JEAN DE LA FONTAINE: *Fables,* V, 1668

A useless life is only an earlier death.
J. W. GOETHE: *Iphigenie auf Tauris,* I, 1787

Wood in a wilderness, moss on a mountain, and wit in a poor man's pow, are little thought o'.
SCOTTISH PROVERB

Usury

Thou shalt not lend upon usury to thy brother; usury of money, usury of victuals, usury of anything that is lent upon usury: unto a stranger thou mayest lend upon usury, but unto thy brother thou shalt not lend upon usury.
DEUTERONOMY XXIII, 19–20, *c.* 650 B.C.

The usurer is as deaf as a door-nail.
THOMAS WILSON: *A Discourse upon Usury,* 1572

A legal thief, a bloodless murderer,
A fiend incarnate, a false usurer.
JOSEPH HALL (BISHOP OF NORWICH): *Virgidemarium,* IV, 1598

There are three forms of usury: interest on money, rent of land and houses, and profit in exchange. Whoever is in receipt of any of these is a usurer.
BENJAMIN R. TUCKER: *Instead of a Book,* 1893

Here lies old thirty-three-and-a-third per cent,
The more he got the more he lent,
The more he lent the more he craved —
Good Lord, can such a man be saved?
Author unidentified

Usury is murder. HEBREW PROVERB

[*See also* Clergyman.

Utilitarianism

By the principle of utility is meant that principle which approves or disapproves of every action whatsoever according to the tendency which it appears to have to augment or diminish the happiness of the party whose interest is in question.
JEREMY BENTHAM: *The Principles of Morals and Legislation,* I, 1789

Actions are right in proportion as they tend to promote happiness; wrong as they tend to produce the reverse of happiness. By happiness is intended pleasure, and the absence of pain; by unhappiness, pain, and the privation of pleasure.
J. S. MILL: *Utilitarianism,* II, 1863

[*See also* Golden Rule, Morality, Virtue.

Utility

The stomach, the lungs, the liver, as well as other parts, are incomparably well adapted to their purposes; yet they are far from having any beauty.
EDMUND BURKE: *The Sublime and Beautiful*, II, 1756

[*See also* Art, Morality.

Utopia

Utopia.
THOMAS MORE: Title of a book, 1516

There shall be in England seven half-penny loaves sold for a penny: the three-hooped pot shall have ten hoops; and I will make it felony to drink small beer.
SHAKESPEARE: *II Henry VI*, IV, *c.* 1591

Philosophers make imaginary laws for imaginary commonwealths, and their discourses are as the stars which give little light because they are so high.
FRANCIS BACON: *The Advancement of Learning*, I, 1605

We must reform and have a new creation
Of state and government, and on our chaos
Will I sit brooding up another world.
GEORGE CHAPMAN: *The Conspiracy of Byron*, I, 1608

The idea of a perfect and immortal commonwealth will always be found as chimerical as that of a perfect and immortal man.
DAVID HUME: *The History of Great Britain*, VII, 1761

There's a good time coming, boys,
A good time coming;
The pen shall supersede the sword,
And right, not might, shall be the lord
In the good time coming.
Worth, not birth, shall rule mankind
And be acknowledged stronger;
The proper impulse has been given; —
Wait a little longer.
CHARLES MACKAY: *The Good Time Coming*, 1834

An acre in Middlesex is better than a principality in Utopia.
T. B. MACAULAY: *Lord Bacon*, 1837

All shall have a good house to live in, with a garden back or front, just as the occupier likes; good clothing to keep him warm and to make him look respectable, and plenty of good food and drink to make him look and feel happy.
G. J. HARNEY: In the London Democrat, April 27, 1839

Then none was for a party;
Then all were for the state;
Then the great man helped the poor,
And the poor man loved the great:
Then lands were fairly portioned;
Then spoils were fairly sold:
The Romans were like brothers
In the brave days of old.
T. B. MACAULAY: *Lays of Ancient Rome*, 1842

If the wisest man were at the top of society, and the next-wisest next, and so on till we reached the Demerara nigger (from whom downwards, through the horse, &c., there is no question hitherto), then were this a perfect world.
THOMAS CARLYLE: *The Nigger Question*, 1849 (Fraser's Magazine, Dec.)

Lands undiscoverable in the unheard-of-West,
Round which the strong stream of a sacred sea
Rolls without wind forever, and the sun
There shows not her white wings and windy feet,
Nor thunder, nor swift rain saith anything,
Nor the sun burns, — but all things rest and thrive.
A. C. SWINBURNE: *Atalanta in Calydon*, 1865

Whenever great intellectual cultivation has been combined with that suffering which is inseparable from extensive changes in the condition of the people, men of speculative or imaginative genius have sought in the contemplation of an ideal society a remedy, or at least a consolation, for evils which they were practically unable to remove.
J. E. E. DALBERG (LORD ACTON): *The History of Freedom in Antiquity*, 1877

The future is lighted for us with the radiant colors of hope. Strife and sorrow shall disappear. Peace and love shall reign supreme. The dream of poets, the lesson of priest and prophet, the inspiration of the great musician, is confirmed in the light of modern knowledge.
JOHN FISKE: *The Destiny of Man*, XVI, 1884

In the Big Rock Candy Mountains,
The jails are made of tin,
And you can bust right out again
As soon as they put you in.
Anon.: Hoboes' song, *c.* 1885

[*See also* Leadership.

V

Vacation

No more lessons, no more books,
No more teacher's sassy looks,
No more Latin, no more French,
No more sitting on a hard board bench.
Schoolboys' song, *c.* 1850

Vaccination

I am patriot enough to take pains to bring this useful invention into fashion in England; and I should not fail to write to some of our doctors very particularly about it if I knew any one of them that I thought had virtue enough to destroy such a considerable branch of their revenue for the good of mankind.

MARY WORTLEY MONTAGU: *Letter to Sarah Chiswell*, April 1, 1717 (Written at Adrianople)

If my next-door neighbor is allowed to let his children go unvaccinated, he might as well be allowed to leave strychnine lozenges about in the way of mine.

T. H. HUXLEY: *Administrative Nihilism*, 1871

Vacillation

Vacillation is the prominent feature of genius. Alternately inspired and depressed, its inequalities of mood are stamped upon its labors. E. A. POE: *Marginalia*, 1844–49

Vacuum

A vacuum is repugnant to reason.

RENÉ DESCARTES: *Principles of Philosophy*, II, 1644

The American people abhor a vacuum.

THEODORE ROOSEVELT: Speech in Cairo, Ill., Oct. 3, 1907

Nature abhors a vacuum. (Natura abhorret vacuum.) LATIN PROVERB

Vagabond

A vagabond who straggles his way through the world without hope, without habitation, without sustenance, without faith. (Vagadonus qui errat per mundum sine spe, sine sede, sine re, sine fide.)

MEDIEVAL LEGAL DEFINITION

[*See also* Actor, Barroom, Jew.

Valentine's Day

Tomorrow is Saint Valentine's Day,
All in the morning betime
And I a maid at your window,
To be your Valentine.

SHAKESPEARE: *Hamlet*, IV, *c.* 1601

Valet

[*See* Hero, Thief.

Valetudinarian

I do not know a more disagreeable character than a valetudinarian, who thinks he may do anything that is for his ease, and indulges himself in the grossest freedoms. Sir, he brings himself to the state of a hog in a sty.

SAMUEL JOHNSON: *Boswell's Life*, Sept. 15, 1777

Valor

The better part of valor is discretion.

SHAKESPEARE: *I Henry IV*, V, *c.* 1598

That's a valiant flea that dare eat his breakfast on the lip of a lion.

SHAKESPEARE: *Henry V*, III, *c.* 1599

True valor lies in the middle, between cowardice and rashness.

CERVANTES: *Don Quixote*, II, 1615

A valiant man
Ought not to undergo, or tempt a danger,
But worthily, and by selected ways,
He undertakes with reason, not by chance.
His valor is the salt t' his other virtues,
They're all unseason'd without it.

BEN JONSON: *The New Inn*, IV, 1629

Valor that parleys is near yielding.

GEORGE HERBERT: *Outlandish Proverbs*, 1640

Perfect valor is to do without witnesses what one would do before all the world.

LA ROCHEFOUCAULD: *Maxims*, 1665

My valor is certainly going! — it is sneaking off! — I feel it oozing out, as it were, at the palms of my hands.

R. B. SHERIDAN: *The Rivals*, V, 1775

For valor.

Inscription on the badge of the Victoria Cross, instituted Jan. 29, 1856

Valor and boastfulness never buckle on the same sword. JAPANESE PROVERB

[*See also* Bravery, Courage, Virtue.

Value

A thing is worth whatever the buyer will pay for it.

PUBLILIUS SYRUS: *Sententiæ*, *c.* 50 B.C.

A piece of a kid is worth two of a cat.

JOHN HEYWOOD: *Proverbs*, 1546

What is worth in anything
But so much money as 'twill bring?

SAMUEL BUTLER: *Hudibras*, I, 1663

The sovereign ability consists in knowing thoroughly the value of things.

LA ROCHEFOUCAULD: *Maxims*, 1665

Necessaries of life, that are not food, and all other conveniences, have their values estimated by the proportion of food consumed while we are employed in procuring them.

BENJAMIN FRANKLIN: *Positions to be Examined Concerning National Wealth*, April 4, 1769

All good things are cheap; all bad are very dear.

H. D. THOREAU: *Journal*, March 3, 1841

The value of a thing is the amount of laboring or work that its possession will save the possessor.

HENRY GEORGE: *The Science of Political Economy*, 1898

According to the value. (Ad valorem.)

LATIN PHRASE

[*See also* Capitalism, Cynic, Labor, Price.

Vanbrugh, John (1664–1726)

[*See* Architect.

Van Buren, Martin (1782–1862)

Van Buren is a demagogue with a tincture of aristocracy — an amalgamated metal of lead and copper.
JOHN QUINCY ADAMS: *Diary*, Oct. 9, 1834

Vanity

Vanity of vanities, all is vanity. (Vanitas vanitatum, et omnia vanitas.)
ECCLESIASTES I, 2, *c.* 200 B.C. (The Latin is from the Vulgate. Cf. XII, 8)

I have seen all the works that are done under the sun; and behold, all is vanity and vexation of spirit. ECCLESIASTES I, 14

Every man at his best state is altogether vanity.
PSALMS XXXIX, 5, *c.* 150 B.C.

Surely men of low degree are vanity, and men of high degree are a lie: to be laid in the balance they are altogether lighter than vanity. PSALMS LXII, 9

There was never yet fair woman but she made mouths in a glass.
SHAKESPEARE: *King Lear*, III, 1606

You shall easily know a vainglorious man: his own commendation rumbles within him till he hath bulked it out, and the air of it is unsavory.
THOMAS ADAMS: *Diseases of the Soul*, 1616

All our geese are swans.
ROBERT BURTON: *The Anatomy of Melancholy*, I, 1621

If vanity does not entirely overthrow the virtues, at least it makes them all totter.
LA ROCHEFOUCAULD: *Maxims*, 1665

Virtue would not travel so far if vanity did not keep her company. IBID.

What renders the vanity of others insupportable is that it wounds our own. IBID.

Those who write against vanity wish to have the glory of having written well, and those who read them wish to have the glory of reading well, and I who write this have the same desire, and maybe also those who read this.
BLAISE PASCAL: *Pensées*, II, 1670

The greatest magnifying glasses in the world are a man's own eyes when they look upon his own person.
ALEXANDER POPE: *Letter to William Wycherley*, June 23, 1705

To be vain is rather a mark of humility than pride. Vain men delight in telling what honors have been done them, what great company they have kept, and the like, by which they plainly confess that these honors were more than their due, and such as their friends would not believe, if they had not been told; whereas a man truly proud thinks the greatest honors below his merit, and consequently scorns to boast. I therefore deliver it as a maxim, that whoever desires the character of a proud man, ought to conceal his vanity.
JONATHAN SWIFT: *Thoughts on Various Subjects*, 1706

What a dust have I raised! quoth the fly upon the coach.
THOMAS FULLER: *Gnomologia*, 1732 (Apperson traces the story to 1586, and it is probably much older)

If a man has a mind to be thought wiser, and a woman handsomer than they really are, their error is a comfortable one to themselves, and an innocent one with regard to other people.
LORD CHESTERFIELD: *Letter to his son*, Oct. 16, 1747

Vanity is a sin against the Holy Ghost, not to be forgiven in this world or the next.
MARY WORTLEY MONTAGU: *Letter to James Steuart*, July 19, 1759

Nothing can exceed the vanity of our existence but the folly of our pursuits.
OLIVER GOLDSMITH: *The Good Natur'd Man*, I, 1768

He who denies his own vanity usually has it in so brutal a form that he must shut his eyes in order to avoid despising himself.
F. W. NIETZSCHE: *Human All-too-Human*, II, 1878

Nothing makes one so vain as being told that one is a sinner.
OSCAR WILDE: *The Picture of Dorian Gray*, 1891

An ounce of vanity spoils a hundred-weight of merit. FRENCH PROVERB

God made us, but we admire ourselves.
SPANISH PROVERB

[*See also* Author, Benevolence, Character (National), Coward, Cowardice, Education, Flattery, Mirror, Motive, Pedant, Philanthropy, Poet, Pride, Virtue.

Vanity Fair

When they were got out of the wilderness, they presently saw a town before them, and the name of that town is Vanity; and at the town there is a fair kept, called Vanity Fair. At this fair are all such merchandise sold, as houses, lands, trades, places, honors, preferments, titles, countries, kingdoms, lusts, pleasures, and delights of all sorts, as whores, bawds, wives, husbands, children, masters, servants, lives, blood, bodies, souls, silver, gold, pearls, precious stones, and what not.
JOHN BUNYAN: *Pilgrim's Progress*, I, 1678

Vanity Fair.
W. M. THACKERAY: Title of a novel, 1848

Vanquished

Woe to the vanquished! (Vae victis!)
BRENNUS, chief of the Senones, *c.* 390 B.C. (The saying is to be found in PLAUTUS: *Pseudolus,* v, *c.* 200 B.C.)

Brave men do not make war on the vanquished.
VIRGIL: *Æneid,* XI, 19 B.C.

Vantage

A dwarf on a giant's shoulder sees farther of the two.
GEORGE HERBERT: *Jacula Prudentum,* 1651

Variety

No pleasure lasts long unless there is variety in it.
PUBLILIUS SYRUS: *Sententiæ, c.* 50 B.C.

Age cannot wither her, nor custom stale
Her infinite variety.
SHAKESPEARE: *Antony and Cleopatra,* II, *c.* 1606

It takes all sorts to make a world.
ENGLISH PROVERB, traced by Smith to 1620

Variety: that is my motto.
JEAN DE LA FONTAINE: *Contes,* 1671

Variety is the soul of pleasure.
APHRA BEHN: *II The Rover,* II, 1681

Variety's the very spice of life.
WILLIAM COWPER: *The Task,* II, 1785

The moral and intellectual wealth of a nation largely consists in the multifarious variety of the gifts of the men who compose it, and it would be the very reverse of improvement to make all its members assimilate to a common type.
FRANCIS GALTON: *Inquiry Into Human Faculty,* 1883

[*See also* Ages.

Vatican

The pope's shop. (La bottega del papa.)
ITALIAN SAYING

[*See also* Papacy, Rome.

Vegetarianism

In the latter times some shall depart from the faith, giving heed to seducing spirits, and doctrines of devils; . . . commanding to abstain from meats, which God hath created to be received with thanksgiving of them which believe and know the truth.
I TIMOTHY IV, 1–3, *c.* 60

Persons living entirely on vegetables are seldom of a plump and succulent habit.
WILLIAM CULLEN: *First Lines of the Practice of Physic,* III, 1774

There is no disease, bodily or mental, which adoption of vegetable diet and pure water has not infallibly mitigated, wherever the experiment has been fairly tried.
P. B. SHELLEY: *Queen Mab,* notes, 1813

I have no doubt that it is a part of the destiny of the human race, in its gradual improvement, to leave off eating animals, as surely as the savage tribes have left off eating each other when they came in contact with the more civilized.
H. D. THOREAU: *Walden,* 1854

I have a friend, a vegetarian seer,
By name Elias Baptist Butterworth,
A harmless, bland, disinterested man.
MARIAN EVANS (GEORGE ELIOT): *A Minor Prophet,* 1865

Veil

It is God's order that you should be veiled.
TERTULLIAN: *Women's Dress, c.* 220

Velvet

[*See* Luxury.

Vengeance

[*See* Revenge.

Venice

Be thou perpetual! (Esto perpetua!)
PAOLO SARPI: Last words (an apostrophe to his native Venice), 1623

The sight of a town whose towers and mosques rise out of the water, and of a multitude of people where one would expect to find only fish, will always excite astonishment.
C. L. DE MONTESQUIEU: *Persian Letters,* XXXI, 1721

I stood in Venice, on the Bridge of Sighs;
A palace and a prison on each hand;
I saw from out the wave her structure rise
As from the stroke of the enchanter's wand.
A thousand years their cloudy wings expand
Around me, and a dying glory smiles
O'er the far times, when many a subject land
Look'd to the winged Lion's marble piles,
Where Venice sate in state, throned on her hundred isles.
BYRON: *Childe Harold,* IV, 1818

The Venice of modern fiction and drama is a thing of yesterday, a mere efflorescence of decay, a stage dream which the first ray of daylight must dissipate into dust.
JOHN RUSKIN: *Stones of Venice,* II, 1853

Venice would be a fine city if it were only drained.
Ascribed to U. S. GRANT during his visit to Venice, 1879

[*See also* King.

Venison

[*See* Meat.

Ventilation

Sickness is caused by bad ventilation.
OVID: *Ars amatoria,* II, *c.* 2 B.C.

The first care in building of cities is to make them airy and well perflated; infectious

distempers must necessarily be propagated amongst mankind living close together.
JOHN ARBUTHNOT: *The Effect of Air on Human Bodies,* 1733

Venture

Nothing venture, nothing gain.
ENGLISH PROVERB, borrowed from the Latin and current since the XIV century

Things out of hope are compassed oft with venturing.
SHAKESPEARE: *Venus and Adonis,* 1593

First weigh; then venture. (Erst wägen; dann wagen.)
GERMAN PROVERB

Verb

A verb is a word which signifies to be, to do, or to suffer.
SAMUEL KIRKHAM: *English Grammar in Familiar Lectures,* II, 1829

Verbosity

He draweth out the thread of his verbosity finer than the staple of his argument.
SHAKESPEARE: *Love's Labor's Lost,* V, *c.* 1595

As it is the mark of great minds to say many things in a few words, so it is that of little minds to use many words to say nothing.
LA ROCHEFOUCAULD: *Maxims,* 1665

[*See also* Gladstone (W. E.).

Vermont

I love Vermont because of her hills and valleys, her scenery and invigorating climate, but most of all because of her indomitable people.
CALVIN COOLIDGE: Speech in Bennington, Vt., Sept. 21, 1928

[*See also* Maine.

Versatility

A man so various, that he seem'd to be
Not one, but all mankind's epitome;
Stiff in opinions, always in the wrong,
Was everything by starts, and nothing long;
But in the course of one revolving moon,
Was chemist, fiddler, statesman, and buffoon.
JOHN DRYDEN: *Absalom and Achitophel,* I, 1682

Verse

A verse may find him who a sermon flies,
And turn delight into a sacrifice.
GEORGE HERBERT: *The Temple,* 1633

'Tis a fine thing for children to learn to make verse; but when they come to be men, they must speak like other men, or else they will be laughed at.
JOHN SELDEN: *Table-Talk,* 1689

I chose verse, and even rhyme, for two reasons. The one will appear obvious: that principles, maxims or precepts, so written, both strike the reader more strongly at first and are more easily retained by him afterward. The other may seem odd, but it is true: I found I could express them more shortly this way than in prose.
ALEXANDER POPE: *An Essay on Man,* pref., 1732

To be able to write good verse a man must formulate his metre before he chooses his words. The form of the thought must appear to him before the thought itself.
G. C. LICHTENBERG: *Reflections,* 1799

[*See also* Lyric, Monosyllable, Poet, Poetry, Translation.

Verse, Blank

Imagination in a poet is a faculty so wild and lawless that, like an high-ranging spaniel, it must have clogs tied to it lest it outrun the judgment. The great easiness of blank verse renders the poet too luxuriant.
JOHN DRYDEN: *The Rival Ladies,* pref., 1664

[*See also* Poet.

Vespers

Vespers is the opera for servant girls.
Ascribed to CLAUDE BERNARD (1813–1878) by Sir Michael Foster (1836–1907)

And when the evening bell peals low,
Then, Lord, I speak with Thee.
LUDWIG UHLAND: *Poor Man's Song, c.* 1820

Vestal

How happy is the blameless vestal's lot,
The world forgetting, by the world forgot.
ALEXANDER POPE: *Eloisa to Abelard,* 1717

[*See also* Nun.

Vestment

(The vestments of Jewish priests are described in EXODUS XXVIII, 4–39, *c.* 700 B.C.)

Veteran

And when they're worn,
Hacked, hewn with constant service, thrown aside,
To rust in peace, and rot in hospitals.
THOMAS SOUTHERN: *The Loyal Brother,* 1682

Superfluous lags the vet'ran on the stage.
SAMUEL JOHNSON: *The Vanity of Human Wishes,* 1749

The nation which forgets its defenders will be itself forgotten.
CALVIN COOLIDGE: Speech of acceptance, July 27, 1920

The Federal government should treat with the utmost consideration every disabled soldier, sailor and marine of the World War, whether his disability be due to wounds received in line of action or to health impaired in service; and for the dependents of the brave men who died in line of duty the government's tenderest concern and richest bounty should be their requital.

Democratic National Platform, 1920

Veto

I don't permit. (Nie pozwalam.)

Veto of Polish nobles in their Diet, 1572–1697 (One adverse vote was sufficient to reject a proposed measure)

Every bill which shall have passed the House of Representatives and the Senate shall, before it become a law, be presented to the President of the United States; if he approve, he shall sign it; but if not he shall return it, with his objections, to that House in which it shall have originated, who shall enter the objections at large on their journal, and proceed to reconsider it. If after such reconsideration two-thirds of that House shall agree to pass the bill, it shall be sent, together with the objections, to the other House, by which it shall likewise be reconsidered; and if approved by two-thirds of that House it shall become law.

CONSTITUTION OF THE UNITED STATES, Art. I, 1789

The qualified veto of the President destroys nothing; it only delays the passage of a law, and refers it to the people for their consideration and decision. It is the reference of a law, not to a committee of the House, or of the whole House, but to the committee of the whole Union.

THOMAS H. BENTON: Speech in the Senate, Jan. 12, 1837

Vicar

By the skirts of the vicar the Devil climbs up to the steeple.

JAMES HOWELL: *Proverbs,* 1659

[*See also* Clergyman, Parson, Priest.

Vice

There will be vices as long as there are men.

TACITUS: *History,* IV, *c.* 100

No one ever reached the worst of a vice at one leap.

JUVENAL: *Satires,* II, *c.* 110

There is no vice so completely contrary to nature that it obliterates all trace of nature.

ST. AUGUSTINE: *The City of God,* XIX, 427

As one virtue bringeth in another, so one vice nourisheth another: pride engendereth envy, and idleness is an entrance into lust.

JOHN NORTHBROOKE: *Against Dicing,* 1577

Vice
Is like a fury to the vicious mind,
And turns delight itself to punishment.

BEN JONSON: *Cynthia's Revels,* V, 1601

The gods are just, and of our pleasant vices
Make instruments to plague us.

SHAKESPEARE: *King Lear,* V, 1606

When our vices leave us we flatter ourselves with the idea that we have left them.

LA ROCHEFOUCAULD: *Maxims,* 1665

Vice may be had at all prices.

THOMAS BROWNE: *Christian Morals,* II, *c.* 1680

The same vices that are gross and insupportable in others we do not notice in ourselves.

JEAN DE LA BRUYÈRE: *Caractères,* 1688

No vices are so incurable as those which men are apt to glory in.

JOSEPH ADDISON: *The Spectator,* July 19, 1714

Vices are learned without a master.

THOMAS FULLER: *Gnomologia,* 1732

Vice would be frightful if it did not wear a mask.

IBID.

Vice is a monster of so frightful mien
As to be hated needs but to be seen;
Yet seen too oft, familiar with her face,
We first endure, then pity, then embrace.

ALEXANDER POPE: *An Essay on Man,* II, 1732

What maintains one vice would bring up two children.

BENJAMIN FRANKLIN: *Poor Richard's Almanac,* 1747

The greatest part of human gratifications approach nearly to vice.

SAMUEL JOHNSON: *The Rambler,* Sept. 28, 1751

If vice itself could be excused, there is yet a certain display of it, a certain outrage to decency, and violation of public decorum, which, for the benefit of society, should never be forgiven.

Letters of Junius, June 22, 1769

Vice itself lost half its evil by losing all its grossness.

EDMUND BURKE: *Reflections on the Revolution in France,* 1790

Vice may be defined to be a miscalculation of chances, a mistake in estimating the value of pleasures and pains. It is false moral arithmetic.

JEREMY BENTHAM: *Deontology,* I, 1834

Vice is grown aweary of her gauds, and donneth russet garments,
Loving for change to walk as a nun, beneath a modest veil.

M. F. TUPPER: *Proverbial Philosophy,* I, 1837

As crabs, goats, scorpions, the balance and the waterpot lose all their meanness when hung as signs in the zodiac, so I can see my own

vices without heat in the distant persons of Solomon, Alcibiades, and Catiline.
R. W. EMERSON: *History*, 1841

There is a great deal of vice which really is sheer inadvertence.
BENJAMIN DISRAELI: Speech in London, July 13, 1879

Vice is waste of life. Poverty, obedience and celibacy are the canonical vices.
GEORGE BERNARD SHAW: *Maxims for Revolutionists*, 1903

Vice offends more from its ugliness than from its sinfulness.
J. A. HOBSON: The Moncure D. Conway lecture, 1933

Cultivate vices when you are young, and when you are old they will not forsake you.
Author unidentified

He who wants to lead a life of vice needs no schoolmaster. DANISH PROVERB

We may change our skins before we change our vices. ITALIAN PROVERB

[*See also* Age (Old), Avarice, Children, Climate, Curiosity, Idleness, Man and Woman, Manners, Sin, Virtue and Vice.

Vice-President

The Vice-President of the United States shall also be president of the Senate, but shall have no vote unless they be equally divided.
CONSTITUTION OF THE UNITED STATES, Art. I, 1789

In case of the removal of the President from office, or of his death, resignation, or inability to discharge the powers and duties of the said office, the same shall devolve on the Vice-President.
CONSTITUTION OF THE UNITED STATES, Art. II

I paid a visit this morning to Mr. Tyler, who styles himself President of the United States, and not Vice-President acting as President, which would be the correct style. It is a construction in direct violation both of the grammar and context of the Constitution, which confers upon the Vice-President, on the decease of the President, not the office, but the powers and duties of the said office.
JOHN QUINCY ADAMS: *Diary*, April 16, 1841

The Vice-President of the United States is like a man in a cataleptic state: he cannot speak; he cannot move; he suffers no pain; and yet he is perfectly conscious of everything that is going on about him.
THOMAS R. MARSHALL: Statement to the press, *c.* 1920

A spare tire on the automobile of government.
JOHN N. GARNER: Statement to the press, June 19, 1934

[*See also* Impeachment, Treaty.

Vicissitude

There are vicissitudes in all things. (Omnium rerum vicissitudo est.)
TERENCE: *Eunuchus*, *c.* 160 B.C.

A man used to vicissitudes is not easily dejected. SAMUEL JOHNSON: *Rasselas*, 1759

Victory

Victory often changes her side.
HOMER: *Iliad*, VI, *c.* 800 B.C.

One more such victory and we are undone.
PYRRHUS (KING OF EPIRUS): On his victory over the Romans at Asculum, 279 B.C.

The race is not to the swift, nor the battle to the strong.
ECCLESIASTES IX, 11, *c.* 200 B.C.

His enemies shall lick the dust.
PSALMS LXXII, 9, *c.* 150 B.C.

It is no doubt a good thing to conquer on the field of battle, but it needs greater wisdom and greater skill to make use of victory.
POLYBIUS: *Histories*, X, *c.* 125 B.C.

Victory is by nature insolent and haughty.
CICERO: *Pro Marcello*, 46 B.C.

Who asks whether bravery or cunning beat the enemy? VIRGIL: *Æneid*, II, 19 B.C.

Hannibal knew how to gain a victory, but not how to use it. PLUTARCH: *Lives*, *c.* 100

The object of a good general is not to fight, but to win. He has fought enough if he gains a victory. THE DUKE OF ALVA, *c.* 1560

The more hard the fight is, the more haughty is the conquest; and the more doubtful the battle, the more doughty the victory.
GEORGE PETTIE: *Petite Palace of Pettie His Pleasure*, 1576

Nothing can seem foul to those that win.
SHAKESPEARE: *I Henry IV*, V, *c.* 1598

A victory is twice itself when the achiever brings home full numbers.
SHAKESPEARE: *Much Ado About Nothing*, I, *c.* 1599

All victories breed hate.
BALTASAR GRACIÁN: *The Art of Worldly Wisdom*, VII, 1647

The enemy came. He was beaten. I am tired. Goodnight.
VICOMTE TURENNE: After the battle of Dünen, June 14, 1658

Then was the Scots army all in disorder and running, both right wing and left, and main battle, and the general made a halt and sung the hundred and seventeenth psalm.
JOHN HODGSON: *Memoirs*, *c.* 1660 (Describing Oliver Cromwell's victory over the Scots under David Leslie at the Race of Dunbar, Sept. 3, 1650)

Save and deliver us, we humbly beseech thee, from the hands of our enemies; that we, being armed with thy defence, may be preserved evermore from all perils, to glorify thee, who are the only giver of all victory; through the merits of thy Son, Jesus Christ our Lord. Amen.
THE BOOK OF COMMON PRAYER (*Prayers and Thanksgivings Upon Several Occasions*), 1662

Westminster Abbey, or victory!
HORATIO NELSON: On giving orders for boarding the San Josef at the battle of Cape St. Vincent, Feb. 14, 1797

But what good came of it at last?
Quoth little Peterkin.
Why, that I cannot tell, said he,
But 'twas a famous victory.
ROBERT SOUTHEY: *The Battle of Blenheim*, 1800

We have met the enemy and they are ours — two ships, two brigs, one schooner and one sloop.
O. H. PERRY: Dispatch to W. H. Harrison announcing his victory at the battle of Lake Erie, Sept. 10, 1813, dated from the brig Niagara, "off the Western Sisters, Sept. 19, 4 p.m."

There is nothing so dreadful as a great victory — except a great defeat.
Ascribed to M. R. D'ARGENSON, *c.* 1830

Even the final decision of a war is not to be regarded as absolute. The conquered nation often sees it as only a passing evil, to be repaired in after times by political combinations.
CARL VON CLAUSEWITZ: *Vom Kriege*, I, 1832

I have just received your dispatch announcing the capture of Atlanta. In honor of your great victory I have ordered a salute to be fired with *shotted* guns from every battery bearing on the enemy. The salute will be fired within an hour, amid great rejoicing.
U. S. GRANT: Telegram to W. T. Sherman, 9 p.m., Sept. 4, 1864

It must be a peace without victory.
WOODROW WILSON: Address to the Senate, Jan. 22, 1917

This solemn moment of triumph, one of the greatest moments in the history of the world . . . is going to lift up humanity to a higher plane of existence for all the ages of the future.
DAVID LLOYD GEORGE: Speech in London, Nov. 11, 1918

On the day of victory no one is tired.
ARAB PROVERB

After a victory tighten your helmet-strap.
JAPANESE PROVERB

The conquered mourns, the conqueror is undone. (Flet victus, victor interiit.)
LATIN PROVERB

Victory loves trouble. (Amat victoria curam.)
IBID.

[*See also* Conquest, Fighting, General, Monument, Pardon, Peace, Prayer, Spoils.

Vienna

There's only one imperial city,
There's only one Vienna.
('s gibt nur a Kaiserstadt,
's gibt nur a Wien.)
KARL VON HOLTEI: *Die Wiener in Berlin*, 1825 (Holtei borrowed the couplet from ADOLF BÄUERLE: *Aline*, 1822, translating it into the Viennese dialect. Buchman says that the second half was a common phrase in Vienna as early as 1781)

Once there was a waltz; once there was a Vienna. (Es war einmal ein Walzer; es war einmal ein Wien.)
Viennese popular song, *c.* 1920

Viennese

The Viennese, speaking generally, dislike and misunderstand anything serious and sensible; they care only for trash — burlesques, harlequinades, magical tricks, farces, and antics.
LEOPOLD MOZART: *Letter to Lorenz Hagenauer*, Feb. 3, 1768

Vigilance

The laws aid the vigilant, not those who sleep. (Leges vigilantibus, non dormientibus subveniunt.)
LEGAL MAXIM

[*See also* Liberty.

Village

[*See* City, Town.

Villain

My conscience hath a thousand several tongues,
And every tongue brings in a several tale,
And every tale condemns me for a villain.
SHAKESPEARE: *Richard III*, V, *c.* 1592

He is deformed, crooked, old, and sere,
Ill-faced, worse-bodied, shapeless everywhere;
Vicious, ungentle, foolish, blunt, unkind,
Stigmatical in making, worse in mind.
SHAKESPEARE: *The Comedy of Errors*, IV, 1593

O villain, villain, smiling damned villain!
My tables! Meet it is I set it down,
That one may smile, and smile, and be a villain.
SHAKESPEARE: *Hamlet*, I, *c.* 1601

Bloody, bawdy villain!
Remorseless, treacherous, lecherous, kindless villain!
SHAKESPEARE: *Hamlet*, II

[*See also* Hypocrisy.

Villification

To villify a great man is the readiest way in which a little man can himself attain greatness. The Crab might never have become a Constellation but for the courage it evinced in nibbling Hercules on the heel.
E. A. POE: *Marginalia*, 1844–49

Vinci, Leonardo da (1452–1519)

I can make nobles at will, and even very great lords; God alone can make such a man as we are about to lose.
FRANCIS I OF FRANCE: To his courtiers at the deathbed of Leonardo, 1519

Vine

They shall sit every man under his vine and under his fig tree. MICAH IV, 4, *c.* 700 B.C.

Then said the trees unto the vine, Come thou, and reign over us. And the vine said unto them, Should I leave my wine, which cheereth God and man, and go to be promoted over the trees?
JUDGES IX, 12–13, *c.* 500 B.C.

Vinegar

The sweetest wine turneth to the sharpest vinegar. JOHN LYLY: *Euphues*, 1579

[*See also* Cajolery, Fly, Policy.

Vineyard

Noah began to be a husbandman, and he planted a vineyard.
GENESIS IX, 20, *c.* 700 B.C.

When thou gatherest the grapes of thy vineyard, thou shalt not glean it afterward: it shall be for the stranger, for the fatherless, and for the widow.
DEUTERONOMY XXIV, 21, *c.* 650 B.C.

The very best of vineyards is the cellar.
BYRON: *Don Juan*, XIII, 1823

Vintner

[*See* Wine, Wineseller.

Violence

Violence is just when kindness is vain.
PIERRE CORNEILLE: *Héraclius*, I, 1647

Violence is never permanent.
GIOVANNI SAGREDO: Report to the Venetian Senate, *c.* 1656

It is far more convenient to commit an act of violence, and afterwards excuse it, than laboriously to consider convincing arguments, and lose time in listening to objections. This very boldness itself indicates a sort of conviction of the legitimacy of the action, and the God of success (*bonus eventus*) is afterward the best advocate.
IMMANUEL KANT: *Perpetual Peace*, Appendix I, 1795

Nine-tenths of mankind are more afraid of violence than of anything else.
WALTER BAGEHOT: *Biographical Studies*, 1880

The right to resist oppression by violence is beyond doubt. But its exerciser would be unwise unless the suppression of free thought, free speech, and a free press were enforced so stringently that all other means of throwing it off had become hopeless.
BENJAMIN R. TUCKER: *Instead of a Book*, 1893

We Fascisti are violent when it is necessary to be so, but this necessary violence of ours must have a character and style of its own; it must be aristocratic, it must be surgical.
BENITO MUSSOLINI: Speech in Bologna, April 3, 1921

There is a violence that liberates, and there is a violence that enslaves; there is moral violence and stupid, immoral violence.
BENITO MUSSOLINI: Speech in Udine, Sept. 20, 1922

Violence in a house is like a worm on vegetables. HEBREW PROVERB

The violent by violence fall.
WELSH PROVERB

[*See also* Communism, Property, State.

Violet

That which above all others yields the sweetest smell in the air is the violet.
FRANCIS BACON: *Essays*, XLVI, 1625

Welcome, maids of honor!
You do bring
In the Spring,
And wait upon her.
ROBERT HERRICK: *Hesperides*, 1648

A violet by a mossy stone
Half hidden from the eye!
Fair as a star when only one
Is shining in the sky.
WILLIAM WORDSWORTH: *She Dwelt Among the Untrodden Ways*, 1800

The violet is a nun.
THOMAS HOOD: *Flowers*, 1827

The blue eyes of Springtime.
HEINRICH HEINE: *Die Blauen Frühlingsaugen*, 1831

Surely as cometh the Winter, I know
There are Spring violets under the snow.
R. H. NEWELL (ORPHEUS C. KERR): *Spring Violets Under the Snow*, 1864

Violin

Sharp violins proclaim
Their jealous pangs, and desperation,
Fury, frantic indignation,
Depth of pain, and height of passion.
JOHN DRYDEN: *A Song for St. Cecilia's Day*, 1687

The tongues of violins!
(I think, O tongues, ye tell this heart, that cannot tell itself;
This brooding, yearning heart, that cannot tell itself.)

WALT WHITMAN: *Proud Music of the Storm,* 1870

A squeak's heard in the orchestra,
The leader draws across
The intestines of the agile cat
The tail of the noble hoss.

G. T. LANIGAN: *The Amateur Orlando,* 1875

'Tis God gives skill,
But not without men's hands: He could not make
Antonio Stradivari's violins
Without Antonio.

MARIAN EVANS (GEORGE ELIOT): *Stradivarius,* 1876

[*See also* Dancing, Fiddling, Husband, Paganini (Niccolò).

Violinist

I heard that stupendous violinist, Signor Nicholao, whom I never heard mortal man exceed on that instrument. He has a stroke so sweet, and made it speak like the voice of a man, and, when he pleased, like a concert of several instruments.

JOHN EVELYN: *Diary,* Oct. 19, 1674

Virgil (70–19 B.C.)

None one author serveth to so divers wits as doth Virgil.

THOMAS ELYOT: *The Governour,* 1531

You rarely meet with anything in Virgil but truth.

JOHN DRYDEN: *A Defense of "An Essay of Dramatic Poesy,"* 1668

Virgil is a thousand books to a thousand persons. Take the book into your two hands, and read your eyes out; you will never find what I find.

R. W. EMERSON: *Spiritual Laws,* 1841

[*See also* Greatness.

Virgin

A virgin intact. (Virgo intacta.)

CATULLUS: *Carmina, c.* 60 B.C.

If a virgin marry, she hath not sinned.

I CORINTHIANS VII, 28, *c.* 55

If any man think that he behaveth uncomely toward his virgin, if she pass the flower of her age, and need so require, let him do what he will.

I CORINTHIANS VII, 36

I will say it boldly, though God can do all things, He cannot raise a virgin up after she has fallen.

ST. JEROME: *The Virgin's Profession, c.* 420

There is nothing our Lord delighteth more in than virgins, nor wherein angels more gladly abide, and play with, and talk with.

LEWES VIVES: *The Instruction of a Christian Woman,* 1541

Happy is love's sugared thrall,
But unhappy maidens all,
Who esteem your virgin blisses
Sweeter than a wife's sweet kisses.

ROBERT GREENE: *Philomela's Ode in Her Arbor, c.* 1592

A fair-built steeple without bells.

HENRY PORTER: *Two Angry Women of Abington,* III, 1599

If I know more of any man alive
Than that which maiden modesty doth warrant,
Let all my sins lack mercy.

SHAKESPEARE: *Much Ado About Nothing,* IV, *c.* 1599

On all true virgins at their birth
Nature hath set a crown of excellence,
That all the wives and widows of the earth
Should give them place and do them reverence.

JOHN DAVIES: *A Contention Betwixt a Wife, a Widow, and a Maid,* 1602

There was never virgin got till virginity was first lost.

SHAKESPEARE: *All's Well that Ends Well,* I, *c.* 1602

An artificial maid, a doctored virgin.

THOMAS MIDDLETON: *The Phoenix,* II, 1607

Virgins have need of a chastity extremely sincere, nice, and tender, to banish from their hearts all sorts of curious thoughts.

ST. FRANCIS DE SALES: *Introduction to the Devout Life,* XII, 1609

A virgin should be tender of her honor,
Close, and secure.

JOHN FLETCHER: *The Wild-Goose Chase,* I, 1621

Virgins should be seen more than they're heard.

THOMAS MIDDLETON: *More Dissemblers Besides Women,* I, *c.* 1625

A maid and a virgin is not all one.

JOHN CLARKE: *Parœmiologia Anglo-Latina,* 1639

The virgin sends prayers to God; but she carries but one soul to him.

JEREMY TAYLOR: *Twenty-seven Sermons,* XVII, 1651

The modest fan was lifted up no more,
And virgins smiled at what they blushed before.

ALEXANDER POPE: *An Essay on Criticism,* II, 1711

I am not as cold as a virgin in lead.

MARY WORTLEY MONTAGU: *The Lover,* 1748

[*See also* Chastity, Girl, Maiden, Marriage, Seduction, Spinster, Virginity.

Virgin Birth

Behold, a virgin shall conceive and bear a son and shall call his name Immanuel.
ISAIAH VII, 14, *c.* 700 B.C.

Behold, a virgin shall be with child, and shall bring forth a son, and they shall call his name Emmanuel, which being interpreted is, God with us.
MATTHEW I, 23, *c.* 75 (Cf. ISAIAH, *ante*, *c.* 700 B.C.)

When we say that the Logos, the first-begotten of God, our master Jesus Christ, was born of a virgin, without any human mixture, we say no more than the authors most in vogue among you say of the sons of Jove.
JUSTIN MARTYR: *I Apology*, XX, *c.* 150

I believe that Christ was born of a Virgin because I have read it in the Gospel.
ST. AUGUSTINE: *On the Christian Conflict*, *c.* 397

A Virgin conceived, a Virgin bore, and after the birth was a Virgin still.
ST. AUGUSTINE: *On the Creed*, *c.* 401

It beseemeth not the majesty of Allah that he should beget a son.
THE KORAN, XIX, *c.* 625

The angel of the Lord declared unto Mary, and she conceived of the holy Ghost. (Angelus Domini nuntiavit Mariæ, et concepit de Spiritu Sancto.) *The Angelus*, *c.* 1250

The Turks are of opinion that 'tis no uncommon thing for a virgin to bear a child. I would by no means introduce this belief into my family.
MARTIN LUTHER: *Table-Talk*, DCCXXIII, 1569

Why cannot a virgin bear a child? Does not a hen lay eggs without a cock?
BLAISE PASCAL: *Pensées*, 1670

[*See also* Faith, Virgin Mary.

Virginia

If Virginia had but horses and kine in some reasonable proportion, I dare assure myself, being inhabited with English, no realm in Christendom were comparable to it.
RALPH LANE: *Letter to Richard Hakluyt*, Sept. 3, 1585

This country wants nothing but to be peopled with a well-born race to make it one of the best colonies in the world; but for want of a governor we are ruled by a council, some of whom have been perhaps transported criminals, who, having acquired great estates, are now become Your Honor and Right Worshipful, and possess all places of authority.
APHRA BEHN: *The Widow Ranter, or The History of Bacon in Virginia*, I, 1690

Breathes there a man with soul so dead
Who never to himself hath said,
This is District No. 1?
Parody current in Virginia during Reconstruction days, when the state was Military District No. 1, *c.* 1868

You can work for Virginia, to build her up again, to make her great again. You can teach your children to love and cherish her.
ROBERT E. LEE: To the young daughter of Dr. Prosser Tabb, at White Marsh, Gloucester county, Va., May, 1870

Virginian

The Virginians have little money and great pride, contempt of Northern men, and great fondness for a dissipated life. They do not understand grammar.
NOAH WEBSTER: *Letter from Williamsburg, Va.*, 1785

The higher Virginians seem to venerate themselves as men.
JOHN DAVIS: *Travels of Four Years and a Half in the United States of America*, IX, 1802

Patriotism with a Virginian is a noun personal. It is the Virginian himself and something over. He loves Virginia *per se* and *propter se:* he loves her for herself and for himself — because she is Virginia and — everything else beside. He loves to talk about her.
J. G. BALDWIN: *Flush Times in Alabama and Mississippi*, 1853

Save in the defense of my native state, I never desire again to draw my sword.
ROBERT E. LEE: *Letter to Winfield Scott*, April 20, 1861 (Same in a letter to his brother, Sydney Smith Lee, same date)

Never ask people where they are from. If they are from Virginia they will tell you so; if not, it will embarrass them to have to confess that they aren't. Author unidentified

[*See also* American.

Virginity

Virginity stands as far above marriage as the heavens above the earth.
ST. JOHN CHRYSOSTOM: *De virginitate*, IX, *c.* 390

Virginity has a special reward hereafter.
ST. AUGUSTINE: *On Holy Virginity*, *c.* 402

Virginity is not commanded; it is a free offering to the Lord. IBID.

The gift of virginity has been poured most abundantly upon women, seeing that it was from a woman it began.
ST. JEROME: *The Virgin's Profession*, *c.* 420

Virginity can be lost even by a thought.
IBID.

Virginity is natural and marriage came after the Fall. IBID.

What [is] virginity but sweet self-love?
JOHN DAVIES: *A Contention Betwixt a Wife, a Widow, and a Maid,* 1602

Virginity is peevish, proud, idle, made of self-love, which is the most inhibited sin in the canon.
SHAKESPEARE: *All's Well that Ends Well,* I, *c.* 1602

No evil thing that walks by night
In fog or fire, by lake or moorish fen,
Blue meager hag, or stubborn unlaid ghost
That breaks his magic chains at curfew time,
No goblin, or swart faery of the mine,
Hath hurtful power o'er true virginity.
JOHN MILTON: *Comus,* 1637

Here lie the remains of Schultz's Charlotte
Who died a highly respected harlot;
For fourteen years she kept her virginity—
A long, long while for this vicinity.
Epitaph reported (probably apocryphally) from York county, Pa.

[*See also* Celibacy, Chastity, Children, Marriage, Spinster, Virgin.

Virgin Mary

As the saffron-bag that hath been full of saffron, or hath had saffron in it, doth ever after savor and smell of the sweet saffron that it contained, so our Blessed Lady, which conceived and bare Christ in her womb, did ever after resemble the manners and virtues of that precious babe that she bare.
HUGH LATIMER: *Sermon of the Ploughers,* Jan. 18, 1548

True Thomas, he pu'd aff his cap,
And louted low down on his knee:
"Hail to thee, Mary, Queen of Heaven!
For thy peer on earth could never be.
Anon.: *Thomas the Rhymer, c.* 1550

Ordered: that all such pictures as have the representation of the Virgin Mary upon them shall be forthwith burnt.
Order of the House of Commons, 1645

To work a wonder, God would have her shown,
At once, a bud, and yet a rose full-blown.
ROBERT HERRICK: *Noble Numbers,* 1647

Mother and maiden
Was never none but she!
Well might such a lady
God's mother be.
OLD ENGLISH CAROL

[*See also* Annunciation, Hail Mary, Immaculate Conception, Immortality.

Virtue

The superior man thinks always of virtue; the common man thinks of comfort.
CONFUCIUS: *Analects,* IV, *c.* 500 B.C.

Those who are firm, enduring, simple and unpretentious are the nearest to virtue.
CONFUCIUS: *Analects,* XIII

Virtue is never left to stand alone. He who has it will have neighbors.
CONFUCIUS: *Analects,* XVI

Five things constitute perfect virtue: gravity, magnanimity, earnestness, sincerity, kindness.
CONFUCIUS: *Analects,* XVII

Virtue proceeds through effort.
EURIPIDES: *Heraclidæ, c.* 425 B.C.

Virtue is a kind of health, beauty and good habit of the soul.
PLATO: *The Republic,* IV, *c.* 370 B.C.

Virtue, like art, constantly deals with what is hard to do, and the harder the task the better the success.
ARISTOTLE: *The Nicomachean Ethics,* II, *c.* 340 B.C.

The greatest virtues are those which are most useful to other persons.
ARISTOTLE: *Rhetoric,* I, *c.* 322 B.C.

The virtues of a naturally higher class are more noble than those of a naturally lower class; thus the virtues of men are nobler than those of women.
IBID.

He who dies for virtue's sake does not perish.
PLAUTUS: *Captivi,* III, *c.* 200 B.C.

The more virtuous any man is, the less easily does he suspect others to be vicious.
CICERO: *Ad fratrem,* I, *c.* 60 B.C.

Virtue is its own reward.
CICERO: *De finibus,* III, *c.* 50 B.C.

Silver yields to gold, gold to virtue.
HORACE: *Epistles,* I, *c.* 5 B.C.

The fruit of the Spirit is love, joy, peace, long-suffering, gentleness, goodness, faith, meekness, temperance: against such there is no law.
GALATIANS V, 22–23, *c.* 50

Nature does not bestow virtue; to be good is an art.
SENECA: *Epistulæ morales ad Lucilium,* XC, *c.* 63

Virtue, though she gets her beginning from nature, yet receives her finishing touches from learning.
QUINTILIAN: *De institutione oratoria,* XII, *c.* 90

Sweeter than the perfume of sandalwood or of the lotus-flower is the perfume of virtue.
The Dhammapada, IV, *c.* 100

When virtue is praised it freezes.
JUVENAL: *Satires,* VIII, 118

Let your every act and word and thought be those of a man ready to depart from life this moment.
MARCUS AURELIUS: *Meditations,* II, *c.* 170

Where virtue is, there are many snares.
ST. JOHN CHRYSOSTOM: *Homilies,* I, *c.* 388

So good a thing is virtue that even its enemies applaud and admire it.
ST. JOHN CHRYSOSTOM: *Homilies,* VI

It is not enough to serve God in the hope of future reward; a man must do right and avoid wrong because he is a man, and owes it to his manhood to seek perfection.
MAIMONIDES: *The Siraj,* 1168

Virtue lives after the funeral. (Vivit post funera virtus.)
Epitaph of Thomas Linacre in St. Paul's Cathedral, London, *c.* 1555

God does not ask the impossible, but instructs you to do what you are able, and to pray for aid in doing what you are not able to do yourself, that He may help you.
Decrees of the Council of Trent, VI, 1564

Of all the benefits that virtue confers upon us, the contempt of death is one of the greatest.
MICHEL DE MONTAIGNE: *Essays,* I, 1580

Virtue is like a rich stone, — best plain set.
FRANCIS BACON: *Essays,* III, 1597

Virtue is like precious odors, — most fragrant when they are crushed. IBID.

Dost thou think, because thou art virtuous, there shall be no more cakes and ale?
SHAKESPEARE: *Twelfth Night,* II, *c.* 1601

Virtue is bold, and goodness never fearful.
SHAKESPEARE: *Measure for Measure,* III, 1604

Virtue is not malicious.
GEORGE CHAPMAN: *Monsieur D'Olive,* I, 1606

I do profess to be no less than I seem; to serve him truly that will put me in trust; to love him that is honest; to converse with him that is wise, and says little; to fear judgment; to fight when I cannot choose; and to eat no fish. SHAKESPEARE: *King Lear,* I, 1606

Men's evil manners live in brass; their virtues
We write in water.
SHAKESPEARE and JOHN FLETCHER: *Henry VIII,* IV, 1613

Virtue could see to do what virtue would
By her own radiant light, though sun and moon
Were in the flat sea sunk.
JOHN MILTON: *Comus,* 1637

There is no road or ready way to virtue.
THOMAS BROWNE: *Religio Medici,* I, 1642

I cannot praise a fugitive and cloistered virtue unexercised, and unbreathed, that never sallies out and seeks her adversary, but slinks out of the race, where that immortal garland is to be run for, not without dust and heat.
JOHN MILTON: *Areopagitica,* 1644

Most virtuous women are like hidden treasures — safe only because they are not sought for.
LA ROCHEFOUCAULD: *Maxims,* 1665

There are few virtuous women who are not weary of their profession. IBID.

The virtue of women is often love of their reputation and of their quiet. IBID.

What we take for virtue is often nothing but an assemblage of different actions, and of different interests, that fortune or our industry knows how to arrange; and it is not always from valor and from chastity that men are valiant, and that women are chaste.
IBID.

Virtue is an intellectual force of the soul which so rules over animal suggestions or bodily passions that it easily attains that which is absolutely and simply the best.
HENRY MORE: *Enchiridion ethicum,* III, 1667

The power of a man's virtue should not be measured by his special efforts, but by his ordinary doing.
BLAISE PASCAL: *Pensées,* VIII, 1670

Most men admire
Virtue, who follow not her lore.
JOHN MILTON: *Paradise Regained,* I, 1671

Virtue is everywhere that which is thought praiseworthy; and nothing else but that which has the allowance of public esteem is called virtue.
JOHN LOCKE: *Essay Concerning Human Understanding,* II, 1690

Virtue, though in rags, will keep me warm.
JOHN DRYDEN: *Imitations of Horace,* III, 1693

Virtue's an ass.
JOHN VANBRUGH: *The Provok'd Wife,* I, 1697

There is no charm in the female sex that can supply the place of virtue. Without innocence, beauty is unlovely, and quality contemptible, good-breeding degenerates into wantonness, and wit into impudence.
EUSTACE BUDGELL: *The Spectator,* June 2, 1712

Oh, let us still the secret joy partake,
To follow virtue even for virtue's sake.
ALEXANDER POPE: *The Temple of Fame,* I, 1714

I believe long habits of virtue have a sensible effect on the countenance.
BENJAMIN FRANKLIN: *The Busy-Body,* Feb. 18, 1729

Virtue and happiness are mother and daughter.
THOMAS FULLER: *Gnomologia,* 1732

Know then this truth (enough for man to know):
Virtue alone is happiness below.
ALEXANDER POPE: *An Essay on Man,* IV, 1734

Virtue, as such, naturally procures considerable advantages to the virtuous.
JOSEPH BUTLER: *The Analogy of Religion,* 1736

Virtue, study, and gaiety are three sisters who should not be separated.
VOLTAIRE: *Letter to Frederick the Great,* 1737

His crimes forgive; forgive his virtues too.
EDWARD YOUNG: *Night Thoughts,* IX, 1745

The utility of virtue is so manifest that even the wicked practise it in self-interest.
LUC DE VAUVENARGUES: *Réflexions,* 1746

Virtue should have limits.
C. L. DE MONTESQUIEU: *The Spirit of the Laws,* XI, 1748

Every quality of the mind which is useful or agreeable to the person himself or to others communicates a pleasure to the spectator, engages his esteem, and is admitted under the honorable denomination of virtue or merit.
DAVID HUME: *An Enquiry Concerning the Principles of Morals,* IX, 1751

To be proud of virtue is to poison yourself with the antidote.
BENJAMIN FRANKLIN: *Poor Richard's Almanac,* 1756

He who will warrant his virtue in every possible situation is either an impostor or a fool.
C. A. HELVÉTIUS: *De l'esprit,* II, 1758

Virtue is an errant strumpet, and loves diamonds as well as my Lady Harrington, and is as fond of a coronet as my Lord Melcombe. Worse! worse! She will set men to cutting throats, and pick their pockets at the same time.
HORACE WALPOLE: *Letter to the Countess of Ailesbury,* Oct. 10, 1761

Virtues, like essences, lose their fragrance when exposed. They are sensitive plants, which will not bear too familiar approaches.
WILLIAM SHENSTONE: *On Reserve,* 1764

The virtue which requires to be ever guarded is scarcely worth the sentinel.
OLIVER GOLDSMITH: *The Vicar of Wakefield,* V, 1766

We seldom speak of the virtue which we have, but much oftener of that which we lack.
G. E. LESSING: *Minna von Barnhelm,* II, 1767

No virtue is ever so strong that it is beyond temptation.
IMMANUEL KANT: Lecture at Königsberg, 1775

Tell me, ye divines, which is the most virtuous man, he that begets twenty bastards, or he that sacrifices an hundred thousand lives?
HORACE WALPOLE: *Letter to Horace Mann,* July 7, 1778

We love to talk of virtue and to admire its beauty, while in the shade of solitude and retirement; but when we step forth into active life, if it happen to be in competition with any passion or desire, do we observe it to prevail?
ST. JOHN DE CRÈVECOEUR: *Letters from an American Farmer,* IX, 1782

The only amaranthine flower on earth
Is virtue.
WILLIAM COWPER: *The Task,* 1785

Virtue is the doing good to mankind, in obedience to the will of God, and for the sake of everlasting happiness.
WILLIAM PALEY: *The Principles of Moral and Political Philosophy,* I, 1785

Virtue is the compensation to the poor for the want of riches.
HORACE WALPOLE: *Letter to Hannah More,* Sept. 22, 1788

Virtue and pleasure are not, in fact, so nearly allied in this life as some eloquent writers have labored to prove.
MARY WOLLSTONECRAFT: *A Vindication of the Rights of Woman,* IV, 1792

Virtue is a desire to promote the benefit of intelligent beings in general, the quantity of virtue being as the quantity of desire.
WILLIAM GODWIN: *An Enquiry Concerning Political Justice,* 1793

The ordeal of virtue is to resist all temptation to evil.
T. R. MALTHUS: *The Principle of Population,* I, 1798

A man has virtues enough if he deserves pardon for his faults on account of them.
G. C. LICHTENBERG: *Reflections,* 1799

Deliberate virtue is never worth much: the virtue of feeling or habit is the thing. IBID.

To many people virtue consists mainly in repenting faults, not in avoiding them. IBID.

Gentlemen ought to explain their virtues upon a first acquaintance, to prevent mistakes.
CHARLES LAMB: *Letter to Thomas Manning,* 1800

What is virtue? Reason in practise.
M. J. DE CHÉNIER: *Épître à Voltaire,* 1806

Virtue is no more to be learned than genius.
ARTHUR SCHOPENHAUER: *The World as Will and Idea,* I, 1819

Let those who would affect singularity with success, first determine to be very virtuous, and they will be sure to be very singular.
C. C. COLTON: *Lacon,* 1820

Innocence is beautiful in itself, but adult virtue is only a plaster, the scar of a surgical operation.
RAHEL VARNHAGEN VON ENSE: *Letter to David Veit,* 1820

Virtue is not hereditary.
THOMAS JEFFERSON: *Letter to William Johnson*, 1823

I dislike the frequent use of the word *virtue*, instead of *righteousness*, in the pulpit: in prayer or preaching before a Christian community it sounds too much like pagan philosophy.
S. T. COLERIDGE: *Aids to Reflection*, 1825

A virtuous woman has in her heart one fibre more or one fibre less than other women. Either she is stupid or she is sublime.
BALZAC: *The Physiology of Marriage*, 1830

Virtue is like health: the harmony of the whole man.
THOMAS CARLYLE: *Journal*, Nov. 1, 1833

The only reward of virtue is virtue.
R. W. EMERSON: *Friendship*, 1841

The less a man thinks or knows about his virtues, the better we like him.
R. W. EMERSON: *Spiritual Laws*, 1841

What is called virtue in the common sense of the word [has] nothing to do with this or that man's prosperity, or even happiness.
J. A. FROUDE: *The Book of Job*, 1853 (Westminster Review)

The wicked are wicked, no doubt, and they go astray and they fall, and they come by their deserts; but who can tell the mischief which the very virtuous do?
W. M. THACKERAY: *The Newcomes*, I, 1854

He hath no mean portion of virtue that loveth it in another.
H. G. BOHN: *Handbook of Proverbs*, 1855

Virtue which parleys is near a surrender.
IBID.

Humility, liberality, chastity, meekness, temperance, brotherly love, and diligence, are the virtues contrary to the Seven Capital Sins.
JOHN MCCAFFREY: *A Catechism of Christian Doctrine for General Use*, 1866

Prudence, justice, fortitude, and temperance, are the Four Cardinal Virtues. IBID.

Every virtue has its privileges — for example, that of contributing its own little faggot to the pyre of the condemned.
F. W. NIETZSCHE: *Human All-too-Human*, I, 1878

When virtue has slept, it will arise again all the fresher. IBID.

The sons of the divvel
In alcohol are swimmin'
But the straight and narrow path for me;
It's all very well
Bookin' certs and chasin' women,
But the straight and narrow path for me.
English popular song, *c.* 1900 (*Cert*= a sure thing at the racetrack)

Our vocabulary is defective; we give the same name to woman's lack of temptation and man's lack of opportunity.
AMBROSE BIERCE: *Collected Works*, VIII, 1911

We do not stop being virtuous when we violate virtue, but when we stop believing in it.
Author unidentified

Never trust a woman who mentions her virtue.
FRENCH PROVERB

Virtue carries a lean purse.
JAPANESE PROVERB

By virtue and industry. (Virtute et opera.)
LATIN PHRASE

By virtue and toil. (Virtute ac labore.) IBID.

The love of virtue. (Virtutis amor.) IBID.

Virtue (or valor) in difficulties. (Virtus in arduis.) IBID.

Virtue is always green. LATIN PROVERB

Virtue is worth a thousand shields. IBID.

Virtue rejoices in trial. IBID.

Virtue smells sweet after death. IBID.

Virtue is more persecuted by the wicked than loved by the good. SPANISH PROVERB

[*See also* Ascetic, Blush, Calamity, Charity, Chastity, Climate, Despotism, Fame, Friendship, Good, Happiness, Honor, Hypocrisy, Law, Liberty, Marriage, Money, Sin, Vanity, Virtue and Vice, Wife, Wisdom.

Virtue and Vice

There are poets who, though they praise virtue, represent it, nevertheless, as difficult and laborious, and much inferior to vice in administering delight.
PLATO: *The Republic*, II, *c.* 370 B.C.

Virtue is a mean state between two vices, the one of excess and the other of deficiency.
ARISTOTLE: *The Nicomachean Ethics*, II, *c.* 340 B.C.

Virtue consists in fleeing vice.
HORACE: *Epistles*, I, *c.* 5 B.C.

The best virtue that I have has in it some flavor of vice.
MICHEL DE MONTAIGNE: *Essays*, II, 1580

Virtue itself turns vice, being misapplied.
SHAKESPEARE: *Romeo and Juliet*, II, *c.* 1596

There is no vice so simple but assumes
Some mark of virtue on his outward parts.
SHAKESPEARE: *The Merchant of Venice*, III, *c.* 1597

Vice hath golden cheeks, oh pity, pity!
She in every land doth monarchize.

Virtue is exiled from every city,
 Virtue is a fool, vice only wise.
THOMAS DEKKER: *Old Fortunatus*, I, 1600

In the fatness of these pursy times
Virtue itself of vice must pardon beg.
SHAKESPEARE: *Hamlet*, II, *c.* 1601

That virtue which is but a youngling in the contemplation of evil, and knows not the utmost that vice promises to her followers, and rejects it, is but a blank virtue, not a pure; her whiteness is but an excremental whiteness.
JOHN MILTON: *Areopagitica*, 1644

The vices enter into the composition of the virtues, as poisons into that of medicines. Prudence collects and arranges them, and uses them beneficially against the ills of life.
LA ROCHEFOUCAULD: *Maxims*, 1665

We do not despise all those who have vices, but we despise those who have not a single virtue. IBID.

I prefer an accommodating vice to an obstinate virtue.
J. B. MOLIÈRE: *Amphitryon*, I, 1668

We do not maintain ourselves in virtue by our own strength, but by the counterpoise of two opposing vices, as we remain standing between two contrary winds: remove one of these vices, we fall into the other.
BLAISE PASCAL: *Pensées*, XXV, 1670 (Cf. ARISTOTLE, *ante*, *c.* 340 B.C.)

Virtue and vice divide the world, but vice has got the greater share.
THOMAS FULLER: *Gnomologia*, 1732

 The diff'rence is too nice
Where ends the virtue or begins the vice.
ALEXANDER POPE: *An Essay on Man*, II, 1732

Virtuous and vicious ev'ry man must be,
Few in th' extreme, but all in the degree.
IBID.

But sometimes virtue starves while vice is fed.
What then? Is the reward of virtue bread?
ALEXANDER POPE: *An Essay on Man*, IV, 1734

Virtue can stand without assistance, and considers herself as very little obliged by countenance and approbation; but vice, spiritless and timorous, seeks the shelter of crowds and support of confederacy.
SAMUEL JOHNSON: *The Rambler*, Nov. 9, 1751

If [he] does really think that there is no distinction between virtue and vice, why, sir, when he leaves our houses let us count our spoons.
SAMUEL JOHNSON: *Boswell's Life*, July 6, 1763

Extraordinary vices and extraordinary virtues are equally the produce of a vigorous mind: little souls are alike incapable of the one and the other.
THOMAS GRAY: *Letter to Horace Walpole*, Feb. 25, 1768

My dear sir, never accustom yourself to mingle virtue and vice. The woman's a whore, and there's an end on't.
SAMUEL JOHNSON: *Boswell's Life*, May 7, 1773

 Vice
Is discord, war, and misery; virtue
Is peace, and happiness and harmony.
P. B. SHELLEY: *Queen Mab*, III, 1813

Virtue fills our heads, but vice our hearts.
C. C. COLTON: *Lacon*, 1820

Virtue consists, not in abstaining from vice, but in not desiring it.
GEORGE BERNARD SHAW: *Maxims for Revolutionists*, 1903

[*See also* Ambition, Good and Evil, Hypocrisy, Martyrdom, Play (=drama), Vice, Virtue, Weakness.

Vision

Where there is no vision, the people perish.
PROVERBS XXIX, 18, *c.* 350 B.C.

Your old men shall dream dreams, your young men shall see visions.
JOEL II, 28, *c.* 350 B.C.

Vision is the art of seeing things invisible.
JONATHAN SWIFT: *Thoughts on Various Subjects*, 1706

Visionary

The visionary lies to himself; the liar only to others.
F. W. NIETZSCHE: *Human All-too-Human*, II, 1878

Visiting

Friendship increases in visiting friends, but in visiting them seldom.
THOMAS FULLER: *Gnomologia*, 1732

Visits should be short, like a Winter's day.
BENJAMIN FRANKLIN: *Poor Richard's Almanac*, 1733

Fish and visitors smell in three days.
BENJAMIN FRANKLIN: *Poor Richard's Almanac*, 1736

A man who stays a week with another, makes him a slave for a week.
SAMUEL JOHNSON: *Boswell's Life*, May 15, 1783

They made no fuss with us, which I was heartily glad to see, for where I give trouble I am sure that I cannot be welcome.
WILLIAM COWPER: *Letter to Lady Hesketh*, June 4, 1786

The best moments of a visit are those which again and again postpone its close.
JEAN PAUL RICHTER: *Hesperus*, XVI, 1795

Visits always give pleasure — if not the coming, then the going. PORTUGUESE PROVERB

[*See also* Guest, Hospitality, Stranger.

Vocabulary

[*See* Language.

Vocation

More will be accomplished, and better, and with more ease, if every man does what he is best fitted to do, and nothing else.
PLATO: *The Republic*, II, *c.* 370 B.C.

It is impossible for men engaged in low and groveling pursuits to have noble and generous sentiments. A man's thought must always follow his employment.
DEMOSTHENES: *Third Olynthiac*, 348 B.C.

Every man is worth just so much as the things he busies himself with.
MARCUS AURELIUS: *Meditations*, VII, *c.* 170

Why, Hal, 'tis my vocation. 'Tis no sin for a man to labor in his vocation.
SHAKESPEARE: *I Henry IV*, I, *c.* 1598

Some live by the water as herrings do; such are brewers, vintners, dyers, mariners, fishermen and scullers; and many, like moles, live by the earth, as griping usurers, racking landlords, toiling plowmen, moiling laborers, painful gardeners, and others.
JOHN TAYLOR: *The Great Eater of Kent*, 1630

If you choose to represent the various parts in life by holes upon a table, of different shapes — some circular, some triangular, some square, some oblong — and the persons acting these parts by bits of wood of similar shapes, we shall generally find that the triangular person has got into the square hole, the oblong into the triangular, and a square person has squeezed himself into the round hole.
SYDNEY SMITH: *Lecture on the Conduct of the Understanding*, I, 1806

There is no trade or employment but the young man following it may become a hero.
WALT WHITMAN: *Song of Myself*, 1855

If there is anything vitally important to the happiness of human beings it is that they should relish their habitual pursuit. This requisite of any enjoyable life is very imperfectly granted, or altogether denied, to a large part of mankind.
J. S. MILL: *The Subjection of Women*, IV, 1869

The young man drawn to medical studies, or to botany, can no more account for his profoundest aspirations than the beetle attracted by the smell of a dead animal or the butterfly by a flower.
ÉDOUARD CLAPARÈDE: *Les animaux sont-ils conscients?*, 1901

When a German family has a son who is a brute, it makes him a doctor; when it has one who is a thief, it makes him a lawyer; when it has one who is an idiot, it makes him a clergyman. GERMAN SAYING

Let not a man teach his son to be an ass-driver, nor a camel-driver, nor a barber, nor a sailor, nor a shepherd, nor a shopkeeper, for their trades are those of thieves.
HEBREW PROVERB

[*See also* Happiness, Profession, Shoemaker, Trade (=craft).

Vodka

Vodka is the aunt of wine.
RUSSIAN PROVERB

[*See also* Tobacco.

Voice

The voice is Jacob's voice, but the hands are the hands of Esau.
GENESIS XXVII, 22, *c.* 700 B.C.

The voice of him that crieth in the wilderness.
ISAIAH XL, 3, *c.* 700 B.C.

Lift up thy voice like a trumpet.
ISAIAH LVIII, 1

A still, small voice.
I KINGS XIX, 12, *c.* 500 B.C.

The voice of one crying in the wilderness.
MARK I, 3, *c.* 70 (Cf. MATTHEW III, 3, *c.* 75; LUKE III, 4, *c.* 75, and JOHN I, 23, *c.* 115. A quotation from ISAIAH XL, 3, *ante*, *c.* 700 B.C.)

The human voice is nothing but flogged air.
SENECA: *Naturales quæstiones*, *c.* 63

I'll speak in a monstrous little voice.
SHAKESPEARE: *A Midsummer Night's Dream*, I, *c.* 1596

I will aggravate my voice so that I will roar you as gently as any sucking dove. IBID.

What plea so tainted and corrupt,
But, being season'd with a gracious voice,
Obscures the show of evil?
SHAKESPEARE: *The Merchant of Venice*, III, *c.* 1597

Her voice was ever soft,
Gentle and low, an excellent thing in woman.
SHAKESPEARE: *King Lear*, V, 1606

How sweetly sounds the voice of a good woman!
It is so seldom heard, that, when it speaks,
It ravishes all senses.
THOMAS MIDDLETON, PHILIP MASSINGER and WILLIAM ROWLEY: *The Old Law*, IV, 1656

His voice no touch of harmony admits,
Irregularly deep, and shrill by fits.

The two extremes appear like man and wife
Coupled together for the sake of strife.
CHARLES CHURCHILL: *The Rosciad,* 1761

When the beloved has gone from the earth and even from fantasy, the beloved voice still comes back.
JEAN PAUL RICHTER: *Hesperus,* XXIII, 1795

A voice so thrilling ne'er was heard
In Springtime from the cuckoo-bird.
WILLIAM WORDSWORTH: *The Solitary Reaper,* 1807

There be none of beauty's daughters
With a magic like thee;
And like music on the waters
Is thy sweet voice to me.
BYRON: *Stanzas for Music,* 1815

The Devil hath not, in all his quiver's choice,
An arrow for the heart like a sweet voice.
BYRON: *Don Juan,* XV, 1824

There is no index of character so sure as the voice.
BENJAMIN DISRAELI: *Tancred,* II, 1847

Many voices are not human, but more or less bovine, porcine, canine, and one's soul dies away in sorrow in the sound of them.
THOMAS CARLYLE: *Letter to R. W. Emerson,* May 13, 1855

A call in the midst of the crowd;
My own voice, orotund, sweeping, and final.
WALT WHITMAN: *Walt Whitman,* 1855

Never trust a woman with a man's voice.
FRENCH PROVERB

Apples, pears, and nuts spoil the voice.
ITALIAN PROVERB

An ugly voice can be heard farther than a beautiful one. JUGO-SLAVIC PROVERB

All voice and nothing else. (Vox et preterea nihil.) LATIN SAYING

[*See also* Baritone, Italian, Prophet, Singer, Soprano, Tenor.

Void

What peaceful hours I once enjoyed!
How sweet their memory still!
But they have left an aching void,
The world can never fill.
WILLIAM COWPER: *Olney Hymns,* I, 1779

Volcano

We are dancing on a volcano.
N. A. DE SALVANDY: To the Duke of Orleans at a fête to the King of Naples, May 31, 1830

A volcano is a sick mountain.
Author unidentified

Volition

The feeling we call volition is not the cause of a voluntary act, but the symbol of that state of the brain which is the immediate cause of that act.
T. H. HUXLEY: *On the Hypothesis that Animals are Automata,* 1874

[*See also* Will (Free).

Voltaire (François Marie Arouet) (1694–1778)

I know this author cannot be depended on with regard to facts; but his general views are sometimes sound and always entertaining.
DAVID HUME: *Letter to Lord Minto,* May 1, 1760

The godless arch-scoundrel Voltaire is dead – dead like a dog, like a beast.
W. A. MOZART: *Letter to his father,* July 3, 1778

Voltaire ought to have pretended to die after "Alzire," "Mahomet," and "Semiramis," and not have produced his wretched last pieces.
HORACE WALPOLE: *Letter to Lady Craven,* Dec. 11, 1788

I have just been reading Voltaire's correspondence – one of those heroes who liked better to excite martyrs than to be one.
HORACE WALPOLE: *Letter to Mary Berry,* July 9, 1789

His forte lay in exposing and ridiculing the superstitions which priestcraft, united with statecraft, had interwoven with governments. It was not from the purity of his principles, or his love of mankind (for satire and philanthropy are not naturally concordant), but from his strong capacity of seeing folly in its true shape, and his irresistible propensity to expose it, that he made those attacks. He merits the thanks rather than the esteem of mankind.
THOMAS PAINE: *The Rights of Man,* I, 1791

Voltaire, in the days of Louis IV, would probably have been, like most of the literary men of that time, a zealous Jansenist, eminent among the defenders of efficacious grace, a bitter assailant of the lax morality of the Jesuits and the unreasonable decisions of the Sorbonne.
T. B. MACAULAY: *John Dryden,* 1828 (Edinburgh Review, Jan.)

Voltaire is the prince of buffoons. His merriment is without disguise or restraint. He gambols; he grins; he shakes the sides; he points the finger; he turns up the nose; he shoots out the tongue.
T. B. MACAULAY: *The Life and Writings of Addison,* 1843 (Edinburgh Review, July)

Voltaire was an apostle of Christian ideas; only the names were hostile to him.
R. W. EMERSON: *Character,* 1844

Voltaire did more for human liberty than any other man who ever lived or died.
R. G. INGERSOLL: Speech in New York, May 1, 1881

[*See also* Europe, Imitation.

Vomiting

[*See* Emesis.

Vote

I do solemnly bind myself in the sight of God that when I shall be called to give my voice touching any such matter of this state in which freemen are to deal, I will give my vote and suffrage as I shall judge in my own conscience may best conduce and tend to the public weal of the body, without respect of persons, or favor of any man.
STEPHEN DAYE: *The Oath of a Free Man,* 1639

Sink or swim, live or die, survive or perish, I give my hand and my heart to this vote.
DANIEL WEBSTER: *Eulogy on Adams and Jefferson,* Aug. 2, 1826

The man who can right himself by a vote will seldom resort to a musket.
J. FENIMORE COOPER: *The American Democrat,* x, 1838

Voting for the right is doing nothing for it.
H. D. THOREAU: *An Essay on Civil Disobedience,* 1849

As long as I count the votes, what are you going to do about it?
WILLIAM M. TWEED, *c.* 1872

Your every voter, as surely as your chief magistrate, under the same high sanction, though in a different sphere, exercises a public trust.
GROVER CLEVELAND: Inaugural Address, March 4, 1885

[*See also* Ballot, Negro.

Vow

Better is it that thou shouldest not vow, than that thou shouldest vow and not pay.
ECCLESIASTES V, 5, *c.* 200 B.C.

Vows begin when hope dies.
LEONARDO DA VINCI: *Notebooks, c.* 1500

A vow not only makes the good works done in consequence of it more acceptable to God, but also encourages us to put them in execution; it gives to God not only the good works, which are the fruits of our good will, but dedicates likewise to Him the will itself, which is the tree of all our actions.
ST. FRANCIS DE SALES: *Introduction to the Devout Life,* XL, 1609

They that vow anything contrary to any law of nature, vow in vain; as being a thing unjust to pay such vow. And if it be a thing commanded by the law of nature, it is not the vow, but the law that binds them.
THOMAS HOBBES: *Leviathan,* XIV, 1651

Vows made in storms are forgot in calms.
THOMAS FULLER: *Gnomologia,* 1732

[*See also* Chastity, Friendship, Marriage.

Vowel

Spenserian vowels that elope with ease,
And float along like birds o'er Summer seas.
JOHN KEATS: *Epistle to Charles Cowden Clarke,* 1816

I discovered the color of the vowels: *A* black, *E* white, *I* red, *O* blue, *U* green.
ARTHUR RIMBAUD: *Une saison en enfer,* 1873

[*See also* Language.

Voyage

[*See* Travel.

Vulgarity

The vulgar are found in all ranks, and are not to be distinguished by the dress they wear.
SENECA: *De vita beata,* II, *c.* 58

All men are as the vulgar in what they do not understand.
EDMUND BURKE: *The Sublime and Beautiful,* II, 1756

The vain ramblings of a vulgar taste.
GEORGE CRABBE: *The Parish Register,* II, 1807

Disorder in a drawing-room is vulgar, in an antiquary's study, not; the black battle-stain on a soldier's face is not vulgar, but the dirty face of a housemaid is.
JOHN RUSKIN: *Modern Painters,* V, 1860

Simple and innocent vulgarity is merely an untrained and undeveloped bluntness of body and mind: but in true, inbred vulgarity there is a dreadful callousness which in extremity becomes capable of every sort of bestial habit and crime, without fear, without pleasure, without horror, and without pity.
JOHN RUSKIN: *Sesame and Lilies,* 1865

No crime is vulgar, but all vulgarity is crime.
OSCAR WILDE: *Phrases and Philosophies for the Use of the Young,* 1894

Vulgarity is simply the conduct of other people, just as falsehoods are the truths of other people.
OSCAR WILDE: *An Ideal Husband,* III, 1895

[*See also* Fashion, Haste, Jeffersonian.

Vulnerability

People who live in glass houses should not throw stones.
ENGLISH PROVERB, traced by Apperson to 1640 (At earlier periods *have glass heads* appeared in place of *live in glass houses*)

He that hath a head of wax must not walk in the sun.
GEORGE HERBERT: *Outlandish Proverbs,* 1640

He who has a head of butter must not come near the oven.
DUTCH PROVERB

[*See also* Prudence.

W

Wag

I never yet knew a wag who was not a dunce.
JONATHAN SWIFT: *Thoughts on Various Subjects,* 1706

[*See also* Jest, Joke, Wit.

Wage-earner

[*See* Wages, Worker.

Wager

[*See* Betting.

Wages

Be content with your wages.
MARK III, 14, *c.* 70

By means of the wars which our king had with other countries . . . the clothiers had most of their cloth lying on their hands, and that which they sold was at so low a rate that the money scantly paid for the wool and workmanship. Whereupon they sought to ease themselves by abating the poor workmen's wages.
THOMAS DELONEY: *Jack of Newbury,* VI, 1597

The value or worth of a man is . . . his price — that is to say, so much as would be given for the use of his power.
THOMAS HOBBES: *Leviathan,* I, 1651

The iron law of wages. (La loi d'airain du salaire.)
A. R. J. TURGOT: *Réflexions sur la formation et la distribution des richesses,* 1766

Wages should be left to the fair and free competition of the market, and should never be controlled by the interference of the legislature.
DAVID RICARDO: *Principles of Political Economy,* V, 1817

A fair day's wages for a fair day's work: it is as just a demand as governed men ever made of governing.
THOMAS CARLYLE: *Past and Present,* I, 1843

The bad workmen who form the majority of the operatives in many branches of industry are decidedly of opinion that bad workmen ought to receive the same wages as good.
J. S. MILL: *On Liberty,* IV, 1859

It is but a truism that labor is most productive where its wages are largest. Poorly paid labor is inefficient labor, the world over.
HENRY GEORGE: *Progress and Poverty,* IX, 1879

Wages ought not to be insufficient to support a frugal and well-behaved wage-earner.
POPE LEO XIII: *Rerum novarum,* May 15, 1891

Large consumption is at the basis of saving in manufacture, and hence high wages contribute their share to progress.
THOMAS B. REED: Speech in the House of Representatives, Nov. 1, 1894

Instead of the conservative motto, "A fair day's wages for a fair day's work," we must inscribe on our banner the revolutionary watchword, "Abolition of the wage system."
Preamble to the platform of the I.W.W., adopted at Chicago, June, 1905

The maintenance of a home is the minimum wage dictated by the law of nature, and prompted by the highest public policy. It is the clear right of the wage-earner, and to protect this right he may make use of all legitimate means.
WILLIAM CARDINAL O'CONNELL: *Pastoral Letter on the Laborer's Rights,* Nov. 23, 1912

A living wage includes not merely decent maintenance for the present but also a reasonable provision for such future needs as sickness, invalidity, and old age.
Pastoral Letter of the Roman Catholic Archbishops and Bishops of the United States, Feb. 22, 1920

If a business be unprofitable on account of bad management, want of enterprise, or out-worn methods, that is not a just reason for reducing the wages of its workers.
POPE PIUS XI: *Quadragesimo anno,* May 15, 1931

Whenever possible the wage-contract should be modified by a partnership-contract, whereby the wage-earner is made to share in the ownership, the management or the profits.
IBID.

No business which depends for existence on paying less than living wages to its workers has any right to continue in this country. By business I mean the whole of commerce as well as the whole of industry; by workers I mean all workers — the white-collar class as well as the man in overalls; and by living wages I mean more than a bare subsistence level — I mean the wages of decent living.
F. D. ROOSEVELT: Public statement, June 16, 1933

[*See also* Capital and Labor, Classes, Labor, Laborer, Unchastity, Work.

Wagner, Richard (1813–83)

When one would become free from an unbearable yoke, one needs hasheesh. Well, I needed Wagner. Wagner is the counter-poison against all that is German. He is poison — that I do not dispute.
F. W. NIETZSCHE: *Ecce Homo,* 1888

Is Wagner actually a man? Is he not rather a disease? Everything he touches falls ill: he has made music sick.
F. W. NIETZSCHE: *The Twilight of the Idols,* 1889

I like Wagner's music better than any other music. It is so loud that one can talk the whole time without people hearing what one says. That is a great advantage.
OSCAR WILDE: *The Picture of Dorian Gray,* 1891

Wagner told them that his music required brains — Aha! said the German, he means me; that his music was not cheap, pretty, and sensual, but spiritual, lofty, ideal — Oho! cried the German, he means me again.
JAMES HUNEKER: *Old Fogy,* III, 1913

Wagner, thank the fates, is no hypocrite. He says out what he means, and he usually means something nasty.
JAMES HUNEKER: *Old Fogy,* XVI

Wagner's music is better than it sounds.
Author unidentified; ascribed to S. L. Clemens (Mark Twain), E. W. (Bill) Nye, and others

[*See also* Strauss (Richard).

Wagon

Creaking wagons last the longest.
DUTCH PROVERB

[*See also* Empty.

Waist

A woman and a greyhound should be small in the waist. SPANISH PROVERB

Waiter

[*See* Tipping.

Waiting

They also serve who only stand and wait.
JOHN MILTON: *Sonnet on His Blindness,* *c.* 1650

Waitings which ripen hopes are not delays.
EDWARD BENLOWES: *Theophila,* 1652

Everything comes to him who waits.
ENGLISH PROVERB, not recorded before the XIX century

Learn to labor and to wait.
H. W. LONGFELLOW: *A Psalm of Life,* 1839

All wisdom may be reduced to two words — wait and hope.
ALEXANDRE DUMAS *père: The Count of Monte Cristo,* CXVII, 1844

She only said, "My life is dreary,
He cometh not," she said;
She said, "I am aweary, aweary;
I would that I were dead!"
ALFRED TENNYSON: *Mariana,* 1845

We shall not, I believe, be obliged to alter our policy of watchful waiting.
WOODROW WILSON: Message to Congress, Dec. 2, 1913 (In the course of a discussion of Mexico. The first appearance of the phrase)

For a good dinner and a gentle wife you can afford to wait. DANISH PROVERB

People count up the faults of those who keep them waiting. FRENCH PROVERB

The future belongs to him who knows how to wait. RUSSIAN PROVERB

[*See also* Patience.

Wales

Wales is so little different from England that it offers nothing to the speculation of the traveler.
SAMUEL JOHNSON: *Letter to James Boswell,* Oct. 1, 1774

Walking

A hurried walk is unbecoming in a clergyman, except when danger demands it, or a real necessity.
ST. AMBROSE: *A Clergyman's Duties,* I, *c.* 390

Move not to and fro in walking, go not like a ninny, nor hang thy hands downwards, shake not thine arms, kick not the earth with thy feet, throw not thy legs across here and there, and walking trail not thy feet after thee, truss not up thy breeches at every hand, go not upon the top of thy toes, nor in a dancing fashion, nor in a stooping, nor in a capering, nor in a tripping manner with thy heels.
FRANCIS HAWKINS: *Youth's Behavior,* V, 1663

I nauseate walking; 'tis a country diversion; I loathe the country.
WILLIAM CONGREVE: *The Way of the World,* IV, 1700

Of all exercises walking is the best.
THOMAS JEFFERSON: *Letter to T. M. Randolph, Jr.,* 1786

The walking of man and all animals is a falling forward.
R. W. EMERSON: *Spiritual Laws,* 1841

There was a young girl of Majorca
Whose aunt was a very fast walker;
She walked sixty miles
And leaped fifteen stiles,
Which astonished that girl of Majorca.
EDWARD LEAR: *The Book of Nonsense,* 1846

I have two doctors — my left leg and my right.
Author unidentified

Walking makes for a long life.
HINDU PROVERB

Walk till the blood appears on the cheek, but not the sweat on the brow.
SPANISH PROVERB

[*See also* Bird.

Wall

Walls have eyes to see.
JOHN HARINGTON: Tr. of LUDOVICO ARIOSTO: *Orlando Furioso* (1532), 1591

Walls have ears.
JAMES SHIRLEY: *A Bird in a Cage*, I, 1633

Over the garden wall,
The sweetest girl of all;
  There never were yet
  Such eyes of jet,
  And you may bet
  I'll never forget
  The night our lips in kisses met
Over the garden wall.
HARRY HUNTER: *Over the Garden Wall*, *c.* 1875

One family builds a wall and two families get the benefit of it. CHINESE PROVERB

White walls are fools' writing paper.
DUTCH PROVERB

Wall Street

A thoroughfare that begins in a graveyard and ends in a river. Author unidentified

Walnut

He who plants a walnut-tree expects not to eat of the fruit.
THOMAS FULLER: *Gnomologia*, 1732

[*See also* Beating.

Walpole, Robert (Earl of Oxford) (1676–1745)

Sir Robert Walpole said he always talked bawdy at his table, because in that all could join.
SAMUEL JOHNSON: *Boswell's Life*, April, 1776

The conformation of his mind was such that whatever was little seemed to him great, and whatever was great seemed to him little.
T. B. MACAULAY: *Horace Walpole*, 1833 (Edinburgh Review, June)

Walton, Isaak (1593–1683)

The quaint old cruel coxcomb, in his gullet
Should have a hook, and a small trout to pull it.
BYRON: *Don Juan*, XIII, 1823

[*See also* Fishing.

Waltz

Imperial waltz; imported from the Rhine
(Famed for the growth of pedigrees and wine),
Long be thine import from all duty free,
And hock itself be less esteem'd than thee.
BYRON: *The Waltz*, 1815

Wanderer

As a bird that wandereth from her nest, so is a man that wandereth from his place.
PROVERBS XXVII, 8, *c.* 350 B.C.

For to admire an' for to see,
  For to be'old this world so wide —
It never done no good to me,
  But I can't drop it if I tried.
RUDYARD KIPLING: *For to Admire*, 1892

[*See also* Travel.

Want

[*See* Need, Poverty, Waste.

Wanting

Thou art weighed in the balances, and art found wanting. DANIEL V, 27, *c.* 165 B.C.

[*See also* Judgment.

Wants

All our wants, beyond those which a very moderate income will supply, are purely imaginary.
HENRY ST. JOHN (VISCOUNT BOLINGBROKE): *Letter to Jonathan Swift*, March 17, 1719

Man wants but little nor that little long.
EDWARD YOUNG: *Night Thoughts*, IV, 1742 (Cf. GOLDSMITH, *post*, 1764)

Such is the diligence with which, in countries completely civilized, one part of mankind labors for another, that wants are supplied faster than they can be formed, and the idle and luxurious find life stagnate for want of some desire to keep it in motion. This species of distress furnishes a new set of occupations; and multitudes are busied from day to day in finding the rich and the fortunate something to do.
SAMUEL JOHNSON: *The Idler*, Nov. 11, 1758

Man wants but little here below,
Nor wants that little long.
OLIVER GOLDSMITH: *The Hermit*, 1764 (In *The Vicar of Wakefield*, 1766. Cf. YOUNG, *ante*, 1742)

Whoever has less than he wants must know that he has more than he deserves.
G. C. LICHTENBERG: *Reflections*, 1799

There are three wants which can never be satisfied: that of the rich, who wants something more; that of the sick, who wants something different; and that of the traveler, who says, "Anywhere but here."
R. W. EMERSON: *The Conduct of Life*, VII, 1860

[*See also* Buddhism, Money, Prosperity, Society, Speech.

War

Men would rather have their fill of sleep, love, singing and dancing than of war.
HOMER: *Iliad*, XIII, *c.* 800 B.C.

Thou hast heard, O my soul, the sound of the trumpet, the alarm of war.
JEREMIAH IV, 19, *c.* 625 B.C.

The god of war hates those who hesitate.
EURIPIDES: *Heraclidæ*, *c.* 425 B.C.

In war there is never any chance for a second mistake.
Ascribed to LAMACHUS (*c.* 465–414 B.C.)

In war we must always leave room for strokes of fortune, and accidents that cannot be foreseen. POLYBIUS: *Histories*, II, *c.* 125 B.C.

It is not the object of war to annihilate those who have given provocation for it, but to cause them to mend their ways; not to ruin the innocent and guilty alike, but to save both. POLYBIUS: *Histories*, V

The sinews of war are infinite money.
CICERO: *Orationes Philippicæ*, V, *c.* 60 B.C.

In war trivial causes produce momentous events.
JULIUS CÆSAR: *The Gallic War*, I, 51 B.C.

The laws are silent in the midst of arms. (Silent leges inter arma.)
CICERO: *Pro Milano*, *c.* 50 B.C.

Wars are the dread of mothers. (Bella detestata matribus.)
HORACE: *Carmina*, I, *c.* 20 B.C.

The event corresponds less to expectations in war than in any other case whatever.
LIVY: *History of Rome*, XXX, *c.* 10

The fear of war is worse than war itself.
SENECA: *Hercules Furens*, *c.* 50

The fortunes of war are always doubtful.
SENECA: *Phoenissæ*, *c.* 60

Ye shall hear of wars and rumors of war.
MATTHEW XXIV, 6, *c.* 75

In war we must be speedy.
SILIUS ITALICUS: *Punica*, I, *c.* 75

To carry on war three things are necessary: money, money, and yet more money.
GIAN JACOPO TRIVULZIO: To King Louis XII of France, 1499 (Cf. CICERO, *ante*, *c.* 60 B.C.)

War is sweet to those who don't know it.
DESIDERIUS ERASMUS: *Adagia*, 1508

The war is just which is necessary.
NICCOLÒ MACHIAVELLI: *The Prince*, XXVI, 1513

Though fraud in other activities be detestable, in the management of war it is laudable and glorious, and he who overcomes an enemy by fraud is as much to be praised as he who does so by force.
NICCOLÒ MACHIAVELLI: *Discorsi*, III, 1531

War is the greatest plague that can afflict humanity; it destroys religion, it destroys states, it destroys families. Any scourge is preferable to it.
MARTIN LUTHER: *Table-Talk*, DCCCXXI, 1569

The same reasons that make us quarrel with a neighbor cause war between two princes.
MICHEL DE MONTAIGNE: *Essays*, II, 1580

We'll lead you to the stately tent of war,
Where you shall hear the Scythian Tamburlaine
Threatening the world with high astounding terms
And scourging kingdoms with his conquering sword.
CHRISTOPHER MARLOWE: *I Tamburlaine*, prologue, *c.* 1588

O war! thou son of Hell!
SHAKESPEARE: *II Henry VI*, V, *c.* 1591

Oh! now doth death line his dead chaps with steel;
The swords of soldiers are his teeth, his fangs;
And now he feasts, mousing the flesh of men,
In undetermin'd differences of kings.
SHAKESPEARE: *King John*, II, *c.* 1596

Let slip the dogs of war.
SHAKESPEARE: *Julius Cæsar*, III, 1599

The pride, pomp and circumstance of glorious war. SHAKESPEARE: *Othello*, III, 1604

Religious canons, civil laws are cruel;
Then what should war be?
SHAKESPEARE: *Timon of Athens*, IV, *c.* 1607

O great corrector of enormous times,
Shaker of o'er-rank states, thou grand decider
Of dusty and old titles, that healest with blood
The earth when it is sick, and curest the world
O' the pleurisy of people.
SHAKESPEARE and JOHN FLETCHER: *The Two Noble Kinsmen*, V, 1613

A civil war is like the heat of a fever; but a foreign war is like the heat of exercise, and serveth to keep the body in health.
FRANCIS BACON: *Essays*, XXIX, 1625

The perfect type of Hell.
FULKE GREVILLE (LORD BROOKE): *A Treatie of Warre*, *c.* 1625

No war without a woman.
JOHN CLARKE: *Paræmiologia Anglo-Latina*, 1639

In war, hunting and love, men for one pleasure a thousand griefs prove.
GEORGE HERBERT: *Outlandish Proverbs*, 1640

War is death's feast. IBID.

The war of all against all. (Bellum omnium contra omnes.)
THOMAS HOBBES: *De Cive*, pref., 1642

Few wage honorable war.
BALTASAR GRACIÁN: *The Art of Worldly Wisdom*, CXIV, 1647

Those possessions short-liv'd are,
Into the which we come by war.
ROBERT HERRICK: *Hesperides*, 1648

The beginning of all war may be discerned not only by the first act of hostility, but by the counsels and preparations foregoing.
JOHN MILTON: *Eikonoklastes*, x, 1649

A wolf will not make war against another wolf.
GEORGE HERBERT: *Jacula Prudentum*, 1651

When war begins, then Hell openeth.
IBID.

Force and fraud are in war the two cardinal virtues.
THOMAS HOBBES: *Leviathan*, I, 1651 (Cf. MACHIAVELLI, *ante*, 1531)

In the nature of man we find three principal causes of quarrel. First, competition; secondly, diffidence; thirdly, glory. The first maketh men invade for gain; the second, for safety; the third, for reputation. IBID.

War consisteth not in battle only, or the act of fighting; but in a tract of time, wherein the will to contend by battle is sufficiently known. IBID.

The brazen throat of war.
JOHN MILTON: *Paradise Lost*, IX, 1667

To overcome in battle, and subdue
Nations, and bring home spoils with infinite
Manslaughter, shall be held the highest pitch
Of human glory.
JOHN MILTON: *Paradise Lost*, XI

All delays are dangerous in war.
JOHN DRYDEN: *Tyrannic Love*, I, 1669 (Cf. SILIUS ITALICUS, *ante*, *c.* 75)

Can any thing be more ridiculous than that a man has a right to kill me because he dwells the other side of the water, and because his prince has a quarrel with mine, although I have none with him?
BLAISE PASCAL: *Pensées*, IV, 1670

When war begins, the Devil makes Hell bigger.
JOHN RAY: *English Proverbs*, 1670

God is ordinarily for the big battalions against the little ones.
ROGER, COUNT BUSSY-RABUTIN: *Letter*, Oct. 18, 1677

War is the trade of kings.
JOHN DRYDEN: *King Arthur*, II, 1691

One minute gives invention to destroy
What to rebuild will a whole age employ.
WILLIAM CONGREVE: *The Double Dealer*, I, 1694

War is quite changed from what it was in the days of our forefathers; when in a hasty expedition and a pitch'd field, the matter was decided by courage; but now the whole art of war is in a manner reduced to money; and nowadays that prince who can best find money to feed, clothe and pay his army, not he that hath the most valiant troops, is surest of success and conquest.
CHARLES D'AVENANT: *Essay on Ways and Means of Supplying the War*, 1695

War, he sung, is toil and trouble;
Honor but an empty bubble.
JOHN DRYDEN: *Alexander's Feast*, 1697

'Tis hard for a poor woman to lose nine husbands in a war, and no notice taken; nay, three of 'em, alas, in the same campaign.
RICHARD STEELE: *The Funeral*, III, 1701

My voice is still for war.
Gods! can a Roman senate long debate
Which of the two to choose, slavery or death?
JOSEPH ADDISON: *Cato*, II, 1713

I have loved war too well.
LOUIS XIV OF FRANCE: On his deathbed, 1715

One to destroy is murder by the law,
And gibbets keep the lifted hand in awe;
To murder thousands takes a specious name,
War's glorious art, and gives immortal fame.
EDWARD YOUNG: *Love of Fame*, VII, 1728

The true strength of a prince does not consist so much in his ability to conquer his neighbors as in the difficulty they find in attacking him.
C. L. DE MONTESQUIEU: *The Spirit of the Laws*, IX, 1748

Even war is pusillanimously carried on in this degenerate age; quarter is given; towns are taken, and the people spared; even in a storm, a woman can hardly hope for the benefit of a rape.
LORD CHESTERFIELD: *Letter to his son*, Jan. 12, 1757

Among the calamities of war may be justly numbered the diminution of the love of truth by the falsehoods which interest dictates and credulity encourages. A peace will equally leave the warrior and the relater of wars destitute of employment; and I know not whether more is to be dreaded from streets filled with soldiers accustomed to plunder, or from garrets filled with scribblers accustomed to lie.
SAMUEL JOHNSON: *The Idler*, Nov. 11, 1758

God is always on the side of the heaviest battalions.
VOLTAIRE: *Letter to M. de Riche*, Feb. 6, 1770 (Cf. BUSSY-RABUTIN, *ante*, 1677)

It is wonderful with what coolness and indifference the greater part of mankind see war commenced.
SAMUEL JOHNSON: *Thoughts Respecting Falkland's Islands*, 1771

The most unjust war, if supported by the greatest force, always succeeds; hence the most just ones, when supported only by their justice, as often fail.
ST. JOHN DE CRÈVECOEUR: *Letters from an American Farmer*, IX, 1782

The fortunes of war flow this way and that, and no prudent fighter holds his enemy in contempt.
J. W. GOETHE: *Iphigenie auf Tauris*, v, 1787

War is not the most favorable moment for divesting the monarchy of power. On the contrary, it is the moment when the energy of a single hand shows itself in the most seducing form.
THOMAS JEFFERSON: *Letter to St. John de Crèvecoeur*, 1788

War is a game, but unfortunately the cards, counters, and fishes suffer by an ill run more than the gamesters.
HORACE WALPOLE: *Letter to Viscount Beauchamp*, July 13, 1788

War to the castles; peace to the cottages. (Guerre aux châteaux; paix aux chaumières.)
NICOLAS CHAMFORT: Motto for the French Revolution, 1790

Each government accuses the other of perfidy, intrigue and ambition, as a means of heating the imagination of their respective nations, and incensing them to hostilities. Man is not the enemy of man, but through the medium of a false system of government.
THOMAS PAINE: *The Rights of Man*, I, 1791

A war, or any wild-goose chase, is, as the vulgar use the phrase, a lucky turn-up of patronage for the minister, whose chief merit is the art of keeping himself in place.
MARY WOLLSTONECRAFT: *A Vindication of the Rights of Woman*, IX, 1792

It would puzzle a keen casuist to prove the reasonableness of the greater number of wars that have dubbed heroes. IBID.

I have seen enough of one war never to wish to see another.
THOMAS JEFFERSON: *Letter to John Adams*, 1794

War is as much a punishment to the punisher as to the sufferer.
THOMAS JEFFERSON: *Letter to Tench Coxe*, May, 1794

To make war with those who trade with us is like setting a bulldog upon a customer at the shop-door.
THOMAS PAINE: *The Age of Reason*, 1794

A state shall not, during war, admit of hostilities of a nature that would render reciprocal confidence in a succeeding peace impossible: such as employing assassins (*percussores*), poisoners (*venefici*), violation of capitulations, secret instigation to rebellion (*perduellio*), etc.
IMMANUEL KANT: *Perpetual Peace*, I, 1795

With men, the state of nature (*status naturalis*) is not a state of peace, but of war; if not of open war, then at least ever ready to break out.
IMMANUEL KANT: *Perpetual Peace*, II

War requires no particular motive; it appears ingrafted on human nature; it passes even for an act of greatness, to which the love of glory alone, without any other motive, impels.
IMMANUEL KANT: *Perpetual Peace*, Supplement I

The best amusement of our morning meal.
S. T. COLERIDGE: *Fears in Solitude*, 1798

What millions died — that Cæsar might be great!
THOMAS CAMPBELL: *The Pleasures of Hope*, II, 1799

And is not war a youthful king,
A stately hero clad in mail?
Beneath his footsteps laurels spring;
Him earth's majestic monarchs hail
Their friend, their playmate! and his bold bright eye
Compels the maiden's love-confessing sigh.
S. T. COLERIDGE: *A Christmas Carol*, 1799 (London Morning Post, Dec. 25)

War is a rough, violent trade. (Es ist der Krieg ein roh gewaltsam Handwerk.)
J. C. F. SCHILLER: *The Piccolomini*, I, 1799

War nourishes war. IBID.

Now tell us all about the war,
And what they fought each other for.
ROBERT SOUTHEY: *The Battle of Blenheim*, 1800

All is fair in love and war.
ENGLISH PROVERB, apparently unrecorded in its present form before the XIX century (In BEAUMONT and FLETCHER: *The Lovers' Progress*, v, 1623, it appears as "All stratagems in love, and that the sharpest war, are lawful")

War is the sport of kings.
ENGLISH PROVERB, apparently not recorded before the XIX century (Cf. DRYDEN, *ante*, 1691)

We wage no war with women nor with priests.
ROBERT SOUTHEY: *Madoc in Wales*, XV, 1805

How easy it is to shed human blood; how easy it is to persuade ourselves that it is our duty to do so — and that the decision has cost us a severe struggle; how much in all ages have wounds and shrieks and tears been the cheap and vulgar resources of the rulers of mankind.
SYDNEY SMITH: *Peter Plymley's Letters*, 1808

The hunting tribes of earth and air,
Respect the brethren of their birth;
Nature, who loves the claim of kind,
Less cruel chase to each assigned;

The falcon, poised on soaring wing,
Watches the wild duck by the spring,
The slow hound wakes the fox's lair,
The greyhound presses on the hare;
The eagle pounces on the lamb,
The wolf devours the fleecy dam;
Even tiger fell, and sullen bear,
Their likeness and their lineage spare,
Man, only, mars kind nature's plan,
And turns the fierce pursuit on man.

WALTER SCOTT: *Rokeby*, III, 1813

The ruin, the disgrace, the woe of war.

P. B. SHELLEY: *Queen Mab*, IV, 1813

War is the statesman's game, the priest's delight,
The lawyer's jest, the hired assassin's trade.

IBID.

There is more of misery inflicted upon mankind by one year of war than by all the civil peculations and oppressions in a century. Yet it is a state into which the mass of mankind rush with a greatest avidity, hailing official murderers, in scarlet, gold, and cock's feathers, as the greatest and most glorious of human creatures.

SYDNEY SMITH: In the Edinburgh Review, 1813

A great country can have no such thing as a little war.

THE DUKE OF WELLINGTON, *c.* 1815

Kubla heard from far
Ancestral voices prophesying war.

S. T. COLERIDGE: *Kubla Khan*, 1816

Leave untended the herd,
The flock without shelter;
Leave the corpse uninterred,
The bride at the altar;
Leave the deer, leave the steer,
Leave nets and barges:
Come with your fighting gear,
Broadswords and targes.

WALTER SCOTT: *Pibroch of Donald Dhu*, 1816

War is a singular art. I assure you that I have fought sixty battles, and I learned nothing but what I knew when I fought the first.

NAPOLEON I: To Gaspard Gourgaud at St. Helena, 1815–1818

If there had never been war there could never have been tyranny in the world.

P. B. SHELLEY: *A Philosophical View of Reform*, 1819

Wars are to the body politic what drams are to the individual. There are times when they may prevent a sudden death, but if frequently resorted to, or long persisted in, they heighten the energies, only to hasten the dissolution.

C. C. COLTON: *Lacon*, 1820

Wars of opinion, as they have been the most destructive, are also the most disgraceful of conflicts; being appeals from right to might, and from argument to artillery.

IBID.

I detest war. It spoils armies.

GRAND DUKE CONSTANTINE OF RUSSIA, *c.* 1820

Cockneys of London! Muscadins of Paris!
Just ponder what a pious pastime war is.

BYRON: *The Vision of Judgment*, 1823
(*Muscadin*=a dandy)

No war ought ever to be undertaken but under circumstances which render all intercourse of courtesy between the combatants impossible. It is a bad thing that men should hate each other; but it is far worse that they should contract the habit of cutting one another's throats without hatred. War is never lenient but where it is wanton; when men are compelled to fight in self-defence, they must hate and avenge: this may be bad; but it is human nature.

T. B. MACAULAY: *Milford's History of Greece*, 1824

Strike — till the last armed foe expires;
Strike — for your altars and your fires;
Strike — for the green graves of your sires;
God — and your native land!

FITZ-GREENE HALLECK: *Marco Bozzaris*, 1825

A war between the governments of two nations is a war between all the individuals of the one and all the individuals of . . . the other.

JAMES KENT: *Commentaries on American Law*, I, 1826

To carry the spirit of peace into war is a weak and cruel policy. When an extreme case calls for that remedy which is in its own nature most violent, and which, in such cases, is a remedy only because it is violent, it is idle to think of mitigating and diluting. Languid war can do nothing which negotiation or submission will not do better: and to act on any other principle is, not to save blood and money, but to squander them.

T. B. MACAULAY: *Hallam*, 1828 (Edinburgh Review, Sept.)

War is an act of violence whose object is to constrain the enemy, to accomplish our will.

KARL VON CLAUSEWITZ: *Vom Kriege*, I, 1832

War is nothing but a duel on a large scale.

IBID.

War is not merely a political act, but also a political instrument, a continuation of political relations, a carrying out of the same by other means.

IBID.

The lower people everywhere desire war. Not so unwisely; there is then a demand for lower people — to be shot!

THOMAS CARLYLE: *Sartor Resartus*, III, 1836

And ever since historian writ,
And ever since a bard could sing,

Doth each exalt with all his wit
The noble art of murdering.

W. M. THACKERAY: *The Chronicle of the Drum,* 1840

I understand well the respect of mankind for war, because war breaks up the Chinese stagnation of society, and demonstrates the personal merits of all men.

R. W. EMERSON: *The Conservative,* 1841

Under the sky is no uglier spectacle than two men with clenched teeth, and hellfire eyes, hacking one another's flesh; converting precious living bodies, and priceless living souls, into nameless masses of putrescence, useful only for turnip-manure.

THOMAS CARLYLE: *Past and Present,* III, 1843

The whole art of war consists in getting at what is on the other side of the hill, or, in other words, in learning what we do not know from what we do.

THE DUKE OF WELLINGTON: To J. W. Croker, *c.* 1845

The Bible nowhere prohibits war. In the Old Testament we find war and even conquest positively commanded, and although war was raging in the world in the time of Christ and His Apostles, still they said not a word of its unlawfulness and immorality.

H. W. HALLECK: *Elements of Military Art and Science,* intro., 1846

Ez fer war, I call it murder, —
Ther you hev it plain and flat;
I don't want to go no furder
Than my Testyment fer that.

J. R. LOWELL: *The Biglow Papers,* I, 1848

The difference of race is one of the reasons why I fear war may always exist; because race implies difference, difference implies superiority, and superiority leads to predominance.

BENJAMIN DISRAELI: Speech in the House of Commons, Feb. 1, 1849

War is on its last legs; and a universal peace is as sure as is the prevalence of civilization over barbarism, of liberal governments over feudal forms. The question for us is only How soon?

R. W. EMERSON: *War,* 1849

It is magnificent, but it is not war.

PIERRE BOSQUET: At the Battle of Balaklava, on seeing the charge of the Light Brigade, Oct. 25, 1854

I believe that war is at present productive of good more than of evil.

JOHN RUSKIN: *Modern Painters,* IV, 1856

Suppose you go to war, you cannot fight always; and when, after much loss on both sides, and no gain on either, you cease fighting, the identical old questions as to terms of intercourse are again upon you.

ABRAHAM LINCOLN: Inaugural Address, March 4, 1861

" All quiet along the Potomac," they said,
" Except, now and then a stray picket
Is shot as he walks on his beat to and fro
By a rifleman hid in the thicket."

ETHEL L. BEERS: *The Picket Guard,* 1861 (Harper's Weekly, Sept. 30)

It is well that war is so terrible — we would grow too fond of it.

ROBERT E. LEE: To James Longstreet at Fredericksburg, Dec. 13, 1862 (Cf. LOUIS XIV, *ante,* 1715)

What a cruel thing is war: to separate and destroy families and friends, and mar the purest joys and happiness God has granted us in this world; to fill our hearts with hatred instead of love for our neighbors, and to devastate the fair face of this beautiful world.

ROBERT E. LEE: *Letter to his wife,* Dec. 25, 1862

Think ye I made this ball
A field of havoc and war,
Where tyrants great and tyrants small
Might harry the weak and poor?

R. W. EMERSON: *Boston Hymn,* 1863 (Read in Music Hall, Boston, Jan. 1)

War and its horrors, and yet I sing and whistle.

GEORGE E. PICKETT: *Letter to his wife,* May, 1864

A nation is not worthy to be saved if, in the hour of its fate, it will not gather up all its jewels of manhood and life, and go down into the conflict, however bloody and doubtful, resolved on measureless ruin or complete success.

JAMES A. GARFIELD: Speech in the House of Representatives, June 25, 1864

When this cruel war is over.

C. C. SAWYER: Title of a popular song, 1864

I begin to regard the death and mangling of a couple thousand men as a small affair, a kind of morning dash — and it may be well that we become so hardened.

W. T. SHERMAN: *Letter to his wife,* July, 1864

You cannot qualify war in harsher terms than I will. War is cruelty, and you cannot refine it.

W. T. SHERMAN: *Letter to James M. Calhoun and others,* Atlanta, Sept. 12, 1864

I shall always respect war hereafter. The cost of life, the dreary havoc of comfort and time, are overpaid by the vistas it opens of eternal life, eternal law, reconstructing and uplifting society, — breaks up the old horizon, and we see through the rifts a wider vista.

R. W. EMERSON: *Letter to Thomas Carlyle,* Sept. 26, 1864

Know'st thou not, there is but one theme for ever-enduring bards?
And that is the theme of war, the fortune of battles,
The making of perfect soldiers?

WALT WHITMAN: *As I Ponder'd in Silence,* 1870

It is not probable that war will ever absolutely cease until science discovers some destroying force so simple in its administration, so horrible in its effects, that all art, all gallantry, will be at an end, and battles will be massacres which the feelings of mankind will be unable to endure.

W. WINWOOD READE: *The Martyrdom of Man,* III, 1872

War makes the victor stupid and the vanquished vengeful.

F. W. NIETZSCHE: *Human All-too-Human,* I, 1878

The success of a war is gauged by the amount of damage it does.

VICTOR HUGO: *Ninety-Three,* 1879

War is hell.

Ascribed to W. T. SHERMAN (The words, as commonly quoted, are not to be found in any of his writings or speeches. Apparently they have been derived from a sentence in a speech he made at Columbus, O., Aug. 11, 1880: "There is many a boy here today who looks on war as all glory, but, boys, it is all hell")

Eternal peace is a dream, and not even a beautiful one. War is a part of God's world order. In it are developed the noblest virtues of man: courage and abnegation, dutifulness and self-sacrifice. Without war the world would sink into materialism.

HELMUTH VON MOLTKE: *Letter to J. K. Bluntschli,* Dec. 11, 1880

War is a perpetual struggle with embarrassments.

COLMAR VON DER GOLTZ: *Das Volk in Waffen,* II, 1883

War is the usual condition of Europe. A thirty years' supply of causes of war is always on hand.

P. A. KROPOTKIN: *Paroles d'un révolté,* 1884

Ye say, a good cause will hallow even war? I say unto you: a good war halloweth every cause.

F. W. NIETZSCHE: *Thus Spake Zarathustra,* III, 1885

The man who has renounced war has renounced a grand life.

F. W. NIETZSCHE: *The Twilight of the Idols,* 1889

In war a soldier must expect short commons, short sleep, and sore feet. Even an old soldier finds it difficult, and for a green one it is hard. But if it's hard for you it isn't easier for the enemy; maybe harder still. Only you see your own hardships, but don't see the enemy's.

M. I. DRAGOMIROFF: *Notes for Soldiers,* *c.* 1890

As long as war is regarded as wicked it will always have its fascinations. When it is looked upon as vulgar, it will cease to be popular.

OSCAR WILDE: *Intentions,* 1891

Then it's Tommy this, an' Tommy that, an'
"Tommy, go away";
But it's "Thank you, Mister Atkins," when the
band begins to play.

RUDYARD KIPLING: *Tommy,* 1892

War is kind.

STEPHEN CRANE: Title of a poem, 1895

God will see to it that war shall always recur, as a drastic medicine for ailing humanity.

HEINRICH VON TREITSCHKE: *Politik,* I, 1897

You furnish the pictures and I'll furnish the war.

W. R. HEARST: Cablegram to Frederic Remington, then in Cuba for the Hearst newspapers, March, 1898

What we now need to discover in the social realm is the moral equivalent of war: something heroic that will speak to men as universally as war does, and yet will be as compatible with their spiritual selves as war has proved itself to be incompatible.

WILLIAM JAMES: *The Varieties of Religious Experience,* XIV, 1902

War and revolution never produce what is wanted, but only some mixture of the old evils with new ones.

W. G. SUMNER: *War,* 1903

War is the contention between two or more states through their armed forces for the purpose of overpowering each other and imposing such conditions of peace as the victor pleases.

L. F. L. OPPENHEIM: *International Law,* II, 1906

War is a dreadful thing, and unjust war is a crime against humanity. But it is such a crime because it is unjust, not because it is war.

THEODORE ROOSEVELT: Speech at the Sorbonne, April 23, 1910

War is a biological necessity of the first importance.

FRIEDRICH VON BERNHARDI: *Germany and the Next War,* 1911

Till the world comes to an end the ultimate decision will rest with the sword.

WILHELM II OF GERMANY: Speech in Berlin, 1913

War is only a sort of dramatic representation, a sort of dramatic symbol of a thousand forms of duty.

WOODROW WILSON: Speech at Brooklyn, May 11, 1914

The appalling thing about war is that it kills all love of truth.

GEORG BRANDES: *Letter to Georges Clemenceau,* March, 1915 (Cf. JOHNSON, *ante,* 1758)

War is a phase in the life-effort of the state towards completer self-realization, a phase of the eternal *nisus,* the perpetual omnipresent strife of all being towards self-fulfilment.

J. A. CRAMB: *The Origins and Destiny of Imperial Britain,* II, 1915

I have seen war, and faced modern artillery, and I know what an outrage it is against simple men.

T. M. KETTLE: *The Ways of War,* 1915

When a war is waged by two opposing groups of robbers for the sake of deciding who shall have a freer hand to oppress more people, then the question of the origin of the war is of no real economic or political significance.

NIKOLAI LENIN: Article in Pravda, April 26, 1917

War means an ugly mob-madness, crucifying the truth-tellers, choking the artists, sidetracking reforms, revolutions, and the working of social forces.

JOHN REED: *Whose War?,* April, 1917

There mustn't be any more war. It disturbs too many people.

An old French peasant woman: To Aristide Briand, *c.* 1917

Sooner or later every war of trade becomes a war of blood.

EUGENE V. DEBS: Speech in Canton, O., June 16, 1918

The first hundred years are the hardest.

Saying of American soldiers during the World War, 1917–18

Is there any man here or any woman – let me say, is there any child – who does not know that the seed of war in the modern world is industrial and commercial rivalry?

WOODROW WILSON: Speech in St. Louis, Sept. 5, 1919

War hath no fury like a non-combatant.

C. E. MONTAGUE: *Disenchantment,* XV, 1922

Our government should secure a joint agreement with all nations for world disarmament and also for a referendum on war, except in case of actual or threatened attack. Those who must furnish the blood and bear the burdens imposed by war should, whenever possible, be consulted before this supreme sacrifice is required of them.

Democratic National Platform, 1924

In the event of war in which the man power of the nation is drafted, all other resources should likewise be drafted. This will tend to discourage war by depriving it of its profits.

IBID.

I'd prefer to eat a little dirt rather than have another war.

Ascribed to THOMAS R. MARSHALL (1854–1925)

The power to wage war is the power to wage war successfully.

CHARLES E. HUGHES: *The Supreme Court of the United States,* 1927

The high contracting parties solemnly declare in the names of their respective peoples that they condemn recourse to war for the solution of international controversies, and renounce it as an instrument of national policy in their relations with one another.

The Kellogg Peace Pact, signed at Paris, Aug. 27, 1928 (First proposed to the United States June 20, 1927 by Aristide Briand; signed by Great Britain, Germany, Italy, France, Belgium, Japan, Poland and Czechoslovakia)

I do not think that a philosophic view of the world would regard war as absurd.

MR. JUSTICE O. W. HOLMES: *Dissenting opinion in United States* vs. *Schwimmer,* 1928

The only war I ever approved of was the Trojan war; it was fought over a woman and the men knew what they were fighting for.

WILLIAM LYON PHELPS: Sermon in Riverside Church, New York, June 25, 1933

Life brings three great things: battle, labor and love. All are by nature holy. We love battle. If battle should at length die out of the world, then all joy would die out of life.

BUSSO LOEWE: *Creed of the German Pagan Movement,* 1936

I have seen war. I have seen war on land and sea. I have seen blood running from the wounded. I have seen men coughing out their gassed lungs. I have seen the dead in the mud. I have seen cities destroyed. I have seen 200 limping, exhausted men come out of the line – the survivors of a regiment of 1,000 that went forward 48 hours before. I have seen children starving. I have seen the agony of mothers and wives. I hate war.

F. D. ROOSEVELT: Speech at Chautauqua, N. Y., Aug. 14, 1936

In war, whichever side may call itself the victor, there are no winners, but all are losers.

NEVILLE CHAMBERLAIN: Speech at Kettering, England, July 2, 1938

A great war always creates more scoundrels than it kills. Author unidentified

War is a business that ruins those who succeed in it. IBID.

Most wars are caused by either priests or women. CZECH PROVERB

When elephants fight it is the country that suffers. EAST AFRICAN PROVERB

War to extremity. (Guerre à outrance.)
FRENCH PHRASE

War to the death. (Guerre à mort.) IBID.

It is war. (C'est la guerre.)
FRENCH SAYING

A great war leaves a country with three armies — an army of cripples, an army of mourners, and an army of thieves.
GERMAN PROVERB

War is war. (Krieg ist Krieg.)
GERMAN SAYING

He who has land has war. ITALIAN PROVERB

Many return from the war who can't give an account of the battle. IBID.

The fear of war is worse than war. IBID.

A cause of war. (Casus belli.)
LATIN PHRASE

The greatest wars have the most trivial causes. (Maxima bella ex levissimis causis.)
LATIN PROVERB

All are not soldiers that go to war.
SPANISH PROVERB

War to the knife. (Guerra al cuchillo.)
SPANISH PHRASE

War is blind. WEST AFRICAN PROVERB

[*See also* Advice, Army, Artillery, Attack, Battle, Bayonet, Cannon, Cavalry, Childbirth, Compensation, Conquest, Council, Defeat, Democracy, Doctrine, Enemy, Extermination, Fairplay, Fasting, Fighting, Fortune, General, Gun, Haste, Infantry, King, Land, Love, Militarism, Militia, Monarchy, Money, Music, Papacy, Patriot, Peace, Peace (International), Philosopher, Prayer, Preparedness, Prince, Profiteer, Prussia, Pulpit, Self-defense, Slavery, Soldier, State, Statesman, Traitor, Treason, Trumpet, Victory, War and Peace, War (Civil).

War, Aerial

[*See* Aviation, Balloon.

War, American Civil

The war against the Confederate States is unconstitutional and repugnant to civilization, and will result in a bloody and shameful overthrow of our Constitution, and while recognizing the obligations of Maryland to the Union, we sympathize with the South in the struggle for their rights; for the sake of humanity we are for peace and reconciliation, and solemnly protest against this war, and will take no part in it.
Resolution of the Maryland Legislature, May 10, 1861

A reckless and unprincipled tyrant has invaded your soil. Abraham Lincoln, regardless of all moral, legal and constitutional restraints, has thrown his Abolition hosts among you, who are murdering and imprisoning your citizens, confiscating and destroying your property, and committing other acts of violence and outrage too shocking and revolting to humanity to be enumerated.
P. G. T. BEAUREGARD: Proclamation to the people of Virginia, June 1, 1861

This war was really never contemplated in earnest. I believe if either the North or the South had expected that their differences would result in this obstinate struggle, the cold-blooded Puritan and the cock-hatted Huguenot and Cavalier would have made a compromise.
GEORGE E. PICKETT: *Letter to his fiancée,* June 27, 1862

Our strife pertains to ourselves — to the passing generations of men; and it can without convulsion be hushed forever with the passing of one generation.
ABRAHAM LINCOLN: Message to Congress, Dec. 1, 1862

Any order of the President, or under his authority, made at any time during the existence of the present rebellion, shall be a defense in all courts for any seizure, arrest or imprisonment, made, done or committed, or acts omitted to be done under and by virtue of such order.
Act of Congress, March 3, 1863

A rich man's war and a poor man's fight.
Slogan of the draft rioters in New York, July, 1863 (The draft exempted anyone able to pay $300 for a substitute)

Only two things stand in the way of an amicable settlement of the whole difficulty: the Landing of the Pilgrims and Original Sin.
HOWELL COBB: On the effort to terminate the Civil War by compromise, 1863

I worked night and day for twelve years to prevent the war, but I could not. The North was mad and blind, would not let us govern ourselves, and so the war came. Now it must go on until the last man of this generation falls in his tracks and his children seize his musket and fight our battles.
JEFFERSON DAVIS: To J. F. Jaquess and J. R. Gilmore, July 17, 1864

If the people [of Georgia] raise a howl against my barbarity and cruelty, I will answer that war is war, and not popularity-seeking. If they want peace, they and their relatives must stop the war.
W. T. SHERMAN: *Letter to H. W. Halleck,* Sept. 4, 1864

I give full credit to your statements of the distress that will be occasioned by it and yet shall not revoke my order, because my orders

are not designed to meet the humanities of the case.
W. T. SHERMAN: Reply to a protest of the Mayor of Atlanta against his order requiring all civilians to leave the city within five days, Sept. 12, 1864

The rapier had been tried for three long years, and Lee, that great swordsman, had parried every lunge. What was his Federal adversary of the huge bulk and muscle to do now, in those last days? One course alone was left him — to take the sledge hammer and smash the rapier in pieces, blow by blow.
JOHN ESTEN COOKE: *Hammer and Rapier*, 1871 (The reference is to the Wilderness campaign)

[The Civil War] was a fearful lesson, and should teach us the necessity of avoiding wars in the future.
U. S. GRANT: *Personal Memoirs*, conclusion, 1885

[*See also* Appomattox, Chasm.

War, American Revolutionary

[*See* Revolution (American).

War and Peace

They shall beat their swords into ploughshares, and their spears into pruning-hooks; nation shall not lift up sword against nation; neither shall they learn war any more.
ISAIAH II, 4, *c.* 700 B.C. (Also in MICAH IV, 3, *c.* 700 B.C.)

The aim of war is to be able to live unhurt in peace. CICERO: *De officiis*, I, 78 B.C.

The cruelty of war makes for peace.
STATIUS: *Thebaid*, VII, *c.* 90

A bad peace is even worse than war.
TACITUS: *Annals*, III, *c.* 110

The purpose of all war is peace.
ST. AUGUSTINE: *The City of God*, XV, 427

The most disadvantageous peace is better than the most just war.
DESIDERIUS ERASMUS: *Adagia*, 1508

To reap the harvest of perpetual peace,
By this one bloody trial of sharp war.
SHAKESPEARE: *Richard III*, V, *c.* 1592

He is a fool who preaches peace in a country that is in the midst of war.
TORQUATO TASSO: *Gerusalemme*, V, 1592

In peace, there's nothing so becomes a man
As modest stillness and humility;
But when the blast of war blows in our ears,
Then imitate the action of the tiger.
SHAKESPEARE: *Henry V*, III, *c.* 1599

Peace is tranquil freedom, and is contrary to war, of which it is the end and the destruction.
HUGO GROTIUS: *De jure belli et pacis*, I, 1625

Peace hath her victories
No less renowned than war.
JOHN MILTON: *To the Lord General Cromwell*, 1630

He that makes a good war makes a good peace.
GEORGE HERBERT: *Outlandish Proverbs*, 1640

He that will not have peace, God gives him war. IBID.

War makes thieves, and peace hangs them.
IBID.

Every man is bound by nature, as much as in him lieth, to protect in war the authority by which he is himself protected in time of peace.
THOMAS HOBBES: *Leviathan*, conclusion, 1651

War ends in peace, and morning light
Mounts upon midnight's wing.
MICHAEL WIGGLESWORTH: *Meat Out of the Eater*, 1669

Peace itself is war in masquerade.
JOHN DRYDEN: *Absalom and Achitophel*, I, 1682

There never was a good war or a bad peace.
BENJAMIN FRANKLIN: *Letter to Josiah Quincy*, Sept. 11, 1773 (Cf. TACITUS, *ante*, *c.* 110)

No treaty of peace shall be esteemed valid in which is tacitly reserved matter for future war.
IMMANUEL KANT: *Perpetual Peace*, I, 1795

In times of peace the people look most to their representatives; but in war, to the executive solely.
THOMAS JEFFERSON: *Letter to Cæsar A. Rodney*, 1810

An honorable peace is attainable only by an efficient war.
HENRY CLAY: Speech in the House of Representatives, Jan. 8, 1813

War is undertaken for the sake of peace, which is its only lawful end and purpose.
JAMES KENT: *Commentaries on American Law*, I, 1826 (Cf. CICERO, *ante*, 78 B.C.; ST. AUGUSTINE, *ante*, 427)

War crushes with bloody heel all justice, all happiness, all that is God-like in man. In our age there can be no peace that is not honorable; there can be no war that is not dishonorable.
CHARLES SUMNER: *The True Grandeur of Nations*, 1845 (Speech in Boston, July 4)

Better a lean peace than a fat victory.
H. G. BOHN: *Handbook of Proverbs*, 1855

Better an egg in peace than an ox in war.
IBID.

Both peace and war are noble or ignoble according to their kind and occasion.
JOHN RUSKIN: *The Two Paths*, v, 1859

All great nations learned their truth of word, and strength of thought, in war; they were nourished in war, and wasted by peace; taught by war, and deceived by peace; trained by war, and betrayed by peace; — in a word, they were born in war and expired in peace.
JOHN RUSKIN: *The Crown of Wild Olive*, III, 1866

War appears to be as old as mankind, but peace is a modern invention.
HENRY MAINE: *Early History of Institutions*, 1875

Ye shall love peace only as a means to new wars — and the short peace more than the long.
F. W. NIETZSCHE: *Thus Spake Zarathustra*, x, 1885

Two contrary laws seem to be wrestling with each other nowadays; the one, a law of blood and of death, ever imagining new means of destruction and forcing nations to be constantly ready for the battlefield — the other, a law of peace, work and health, ever evolving new means of delivering man from the scourges which beset him.
LOUIS PASTEUR: Address at the opening of the Pasteur Institute, Paris, Nov. 14, 1888

We shall never make war except for peace.
WILLIAM MCKINLEY: Speech at El Paso, Texas, May 6, 1901

A boy who hears a lesson in history ended by the beauty of peace, and how Napoleon brought ruin upon the world and that he should be forever cursed, will not long have much confidence in his teacher. He wants to hear more about the fighting and less about the peace negotiations.
WILLIAM LEE HOWARD: *Peace, Dolls and Pugnacity*, 1903

War begets poverty, poverty peace.
Ascribed to J. HORNE TOOKE (1736–1812) in G. H. POWELL: *Reminiscences and Table-Talk of Samuel Rogers*, 1903

War makes rattling good history, but peace is poor reading.
THOMAS HARDY: *The Dynasts*, II, 1906

War is not merely justifiable, but imperative, upon honorable men, upon an honorable nation, where peace can only be obtained by the sacrifice of conscientious conviction or of national welfare.
THEODORE ROOSEVELT: Message to Congress, Dec. 3, 1906

It takes at least two to make a peace, but one can make a war.
NEVILLE CHAMBERLAIN: Speech in Birmingham, Jan. 28, 1939

When after many battles past,
Both, tired with blows, make peace at last,
What is it, after all, the people get?
Why, taxes, widows, wooden legs, and debt.
Author unidentified

Better a dog in time of peace than a man in time of war.
CHINESE PROVERB

Peace is the daughter of war.
FRENCH PROVERB

Peace is produced by war. (Paritur pax bello.)
LATIN PROVERB

Eternal peace lasts only until the next year.
RUSSIAN PROVERB

[*See also* Money, Pardon, Peace, Preparedness, Thief, War, Washington (George).

War, Boer

You entered into these two republics for philanthropic purposes and remained to commit burglary.
DAVID LLOYD GEORGE: Speech in the House of Commons, July 25, 1900

War, Civil

There is nothing unhappier than a civil war, for the conquered are destroyed by, and the conquerors destroy, their friends.
DIONYSIUS OF HALICARNASSUS: *Antiquities of Rome*, VI, *c.* 20 B.C.

Make us enemies of every people on earth, but save us from civil war.
LUCAN: *Pharsalia*, 65

The civil wars of France made a million atheists and thirty thousand witches.
GEORGE HERBERT: *Jacula Prudentum*, 1651

Civil wars strike deepest of all into the manners of the people. They vitiate their politics; they corrupt their morals; they pervert even the natural taste and relish of equity and justice. By teaching us to consider our fellow-citizens in a hostile light, the whole body of our nation becomes gradually less dear to us.
EDMUND BURKE: *Letter to the sheriffs of Bristol*, April 3, 1777

The proudest capitals of Western Europe have streamed with civil blood.
T. B. MACAULAY: *History of England*, II, 1848

A foreign war is a scratch on the arm; a civil war is an ulcer which devours the vitals of a nation.
VICTOR HUGO: *Ninety-Three*, 1879

War, Declaration of

Hostilities must not be begun without previous and explicit warning in the form of a reasoned declaration of war, or of an ultimate embracing a conditional declaration.
THE HAGUE CONVENTION, 1907

War, Holy

When ye encounter the unbelievers, strike off their heads, until ye have made a great slaughter among them. Verily, if God pleased, He could take vengeance on them without your assistance, but He commandeth you to fight His battles.

THE KORAN, XLVII, *c.* 625

War-horse

He saith among the trumpets, Ha, Ha! and he smelleth the battle afar off, the thunder of the captains, and the shouting.

JOB XXIX, 25, *c.* 325 B.C.

Wariness

Cautelous suspense, for want of assurance, is better than confident presumption, upon pregnancy of imagination.

BENJAMIN WHICHCOTE: *Moral and Religious Aphorisms,* 1753 (*Cautelous*= wary)

Warlike

In military affairs, and all others of like nature, the study of the sciences does more soften and enervate the courage of men than fortify and incite it. . . . Rome was more valiant before she grew so learned; and the most warlike nations of our time are the most ignorant.

MICHEL DE MONTAIGNE: *Essays,* I, 1580

[*See also* Army.

War, Mexican

We come to overthrow the tyrants who have destroyed your liberties, but we come to make no war upon the people of Mexico.

ZACHARY TAYLOR: Proclamation to the people of Mexico, July 9, 1846

Base in object, atrocious in beginning, immoral in all its influence, vainly prodigal of treasure and life, it is a war of infamy, which must blot the pages of our history.

CHARLES SUMNER: Speech in Boston, Nov. 5, 1846

The war has not been waged with a view to conquest.

JAMES POLK: Message to Congress, Dec. 8, 1846

I believe it to be a war of pretexts, a war in which the true motive is not distinctly avowed, but in which pretenses, afterthoughts, evasions and other methods are employed to put a case before the community which is not the true case.

DANIEL WEBSTER: Speech in Springfield, Mass., Sept. 29, 1847

To this day [I] regard the war as one of the most unjust ever waged by a stronger against a weaker nation. It was an instance of a republic following the bad example of European monarchies, in not considering justice in their desire to acquire additional territory.

U. S. GRANT: *Personal Memoirs,* III, 1885

Warning

No man provokes me with impunity. (Nemo me impune lacessit.)

MOTTO OF THE ORDER OF THE THISTLE, 1540

Don't take any wooden nickels.

AMERICAN SAYING

[*See also* Advice, Thanks, Touch.

War of 1812

A war not of defense, but of conquest, of aggrandizement, of ambition – a war foreign to the interests of this country; to the interests of humanity itself.

JOHN RANDOLPH: Speech in the House of Representatives, Dec. 10, 1811

In such a cause, with the aid of Providence, we must come out crowned with success; but, if we fail, let us fail like men, lash ourselves to our gallant tars, and expire together in one common struggle, fighting for free trade and seamen's rights.

HENRY CLAY: Speech in the House of Representatives, Jan. 8, 1813

The last American war was to us only something to talk or read about; but to the Americans it was the cause of misery in their own homes.

S. T. COLERIDGE: *Table-Talk,* May 21, 1830

Warrior

The free man is a warrior. He tramples ruthlessly upon that contemptible kind of comfort that grocers, Christians, cows, women, Englishmen and other democrats worship.

F. W. NIETZSCHE: *The Twilight of the Idols,* 1889

[*See also* Soldier.

Warship

[*See* Liner, Navy.

Wart

[*See* Portrait.

War, World

The lamps are going out all over Europe; we shall not see them lit again in our lifetime.

EDWARD GREY: To a caller at the Foreign Office, Aug. 3, 1914

They shall not pass. (Ils ne passeront pas.)

HENRI PÉTAIN: To General de Castelnau at Verdun, Feb., 1916

The plain truth is that the war is imperialistic on both sides.

NIKOLAI LENIN: *Letters from Afar,* I, March 20, 1917

The man who does not think it was America's duty to fight for her own sake in view of the infamous conduct of Germany toward us stands on a level with a man who wouldn't think it necessary to fight in a private quarrel because his wife's face was slapped.

THEODORE ROOSEVELT: Speech in Oyster Bay, L. I., April, 1917

We are fighting in the quarrel of civilization against barbarism, of liberty against tyranny. Germany has become a menace to the whole world. She is the most dangerous enemy of liberty now existing. She has shown herself utterly ruthless, treacherous, and brutal. When I use these words, I use them with scientific precision. IBID.

The right is more precious than peace, and we shall fight for the things which we have always carried nearest our hearts, — for democracy, for the right of those who submit to authority to have a voice in their own governments, for the rights and liberties of small nations, for a universal dominion of right by such a concert of free peoples as shall bring peace and safety to all nations and make the world itself at last free.

WOODROW WILSON: Address to Congress, April 2, 1917

Lafayette, we are here.

COL. C. E. STANTON: Speech in Paris, July 4, 1917

This war, like the next war, is a war to end war.

Ascribed to DAVID LLOYD GEORGE, *c.* 1917

They say it is a terrible war, parley-voo
They say it is a terrible war,
But what the hell are we fighting it for?
Hinkey Dinkey, parley-voo!

Anon.: British soldiers' song, 1914–18

This is the culminating and final war for human liberty.

WOODROW WILSON: Message to Congress, Jan. 8, 1918

The allied and associated governments affirm and Germany accepts the responsibility of Germany and her allies for causing all the loss and damage to which the allied and associated governments and their nationals have been subjected as a consequence of the war imposed upon them by the aggression of Germany and her allies.

TREATY OF VERSAILLES, CCXXXI, 1919

Washday

Home, and, being washing-day, dined upon cold meat.

SAMUEL PEPYS: *Diary,* April 4, 1666

They that wash Monday got all the week to dry,
They that wash Tuesday are pretty near by,
They that wash Wednesday make a good housewife,
They that wash Thursday must wash for their life,
They that wash Friday must wash in need,
They that wash Saturday are sluts indeed.

OLD ENGLISH RHYME

Washing

Wash your hands often, your feet seldom, and your head never.

JOHN RAY: *English Proverbs,* 1670

It belongs to decency to wash the hands before sitting down to table, and it is even considered indispensably necessary.

ST. JOHN BAPTIST DE LA SALLE: *The Rules of Christian Manners and Civility,* II, 1695

[*See also* Hygiene.

Washington, George (1732–99)

A gentleman of one of the first fortunes upon the continent . . . sacrificing his ease, and hazarding all in the cause of his country.

JOHN ADAMS: *Letter to Elbridge Gerry,* June 18, 1775

The father of his country.

FRANCIS BAILEY: *Lancaster Almanack,* 1779

His memory will be adored while liberty shall have votaries, his name will triumph over time and will in future ages assume its just station among the most celebrated worthies of the world.

THOMAS JEFFERSON: *Notes on Virginia,* 1782

O Washington, how do I love thy name! How have I often adored and blessed thy God for creating and forming thee the great ornament of human kind.

EZRA STILES: *The United States Elevated to Glory and Honor,* 1783

The character and service of this gentleman are sufficient to put all those men called kings to shame. While they are receiving from the sweat and labors of mankind a prodigality of pay to which neither their abilities nor their services can entitle them, he is rendering every service in his power, and refusing every pecuniary reward. He accepted no pay as commander-in-chief; he accepts none as President of the United States.

THOMAS PAINE: *The Rights of Man,* II, 1791

He errs as other men do, but errs with integrity.

THOMAS JEFFERSON: *Letter to W. B. Giles,* 1795

As to you, sir, treacherous to private friendship (for so you have been to me, and that in the day of danger) and a hypocrite in public life, the world will be puzzled to decide whether you are an apostate or an impostor, whether you have abandoned good principles or whether you ever had any.

THOMAS PAINE: *Letter to Washington,* July 30, 1796 (Cf. PAINE, *ante,* 1791)

There are features in his face totally different from what I ever observed in that of any other human being; the sockets of the eyes, for instance, are larger, and the upper part of the nose broader. All his features are indicative of the strongest passions; yet his judgment and great self-command make him appear a man of a different cast in the eyes of the world.

GILBERT STUART: To Isaac Weld, *c.* 1797

First in war, first in peace, and first in the hearts of his countrymen.

HENRY (LIGHT-HORSE HARRY) LEE: *Eulogy on Washington,* Dec. 26, 1799

There has scarcely appeared a really great man whose character has been more admired in his lifetime, or less correctly understood by his admirers. . . . His talents . . . were adapted to lead without dazzling mankind, and to draw forth and employ the talents of others without being misled by them.

FISHER AMES: Oration in Boston, Feb. 8, 1800

I can't tell a lie, Pa; you know I can't tell a lie. I did cut it with my hatchet.

MASON L. WEEMS: *The Life of George Washington,* I, 1800 (This was the first appearance of the cherry-tree story)

His mind was great and powerful, without being of the very first order; his penetration strong, though not so acute as that of a Newton, Bacon, or Locke; and as far as he saw, no judgment was ever sounder. It was slow in operation, being little aided by invention or imagination, but sure in conclusion.

THOMAS JEFFERSON: *Letter to Walter Jones,* Jan., 1814

Washington . . . sold the very charger who had taken him through all his battles.

JOHN KEATS: *Letter to Georgiana Keats,* Oct. 14–31, 1818

America has furnished to the world the character of Washington. And if our American institutions have done nothing else that alone would have entitled them to the respect of mankind.

DANIEL WEBSTER: Address on laying the cornerstone of the Bunker Hill Monument, June 17, 1825

Washington's face was as cut and dry as a diagram.

LEIGH HUNT: *The Companion,* XIII, 1828

Surely Washington was the greatest man that ever lived in this world uninspired by divine wisdom and unsustained by supernatural virtue.

HENRY BROUGHAM (LORD BROUGHAM AND VAUX): *Statesmen in the Time of George III,* III, 1839

Washington is the mightiest name on earth — long since mightiest in the cause of civil liberty; still mightiest in moral reformation. On that name an eulogy is expected. Let none attempt it. In solemn awe pronounce the name and in its naked, deathless splendor leave it shining on.

ABRAHAM LINCOLN: Speech in Springfield, Ill., Feb. 22, 1842

Old George Washington's forte was not to hev eny public man of the present day resemble him to eny alarmin extent.

C. F. BROWNE (ARTEMUS WARD): *Artemus Ward: His Book,* 1862

George Washington, as a boy, was ignorant of of the commonest accomplishments of youth. He could not even lie.

S. L. CLEMENS (MARK TWAIN): *Brief Biographical Sketch of George Washington,* 1867

In Washington, America found a leader who could be induced by no earthly motive to tell a falsehood, or to break an engagement, or to commit any dishonorable act.

W. E. H. LECKY: *History of England in the Eighteenth Century,* I, 1878

[*See also* Dignity, Greatness, Pay, Posterity, Presidency.

Wasp

Of all the plagues that Heaven has sent,
A wasp is most impertinent.

JOHN GAY: *Fables,* I, 1727

See the wasp. He has pretty yellow stripes around his body, and a darning needle in his tail. If you will pat the wasp upon the tail we will give you a nice picture book.

EUGENE FIELD: *The Tribune Primer,* 1882

Waste

Wilful waste brings woeful want.

THOMAS FULLER: *Gnomologia,* 1732

The nakedness of the indigent world may be clothed from the trimmings of the vain.

OLIVER GOLDSMITH: *The Vicar of Wakefield,* IV, 1766

Waste is not grandeur.

WILLIAM MASON: *The English Garden,* II, 1772

Waste not; want not.

ENGLISH PROVERB, not recorded in its present form before the XIX century

It is the elimination and utilization of waste, waste effort, waste time and material, the minimizing of destruction and damage, wear and tear that produce the great results in the industrial world. There is no magic in these accomplishments. The leaders in action or thought are not magicians, but steady persistent workers.

THEODORE N. VAIL (1845–1920)

He is as wasteful as one who salts the sea.

WELSH PROVERB

[*See also* Haste, Son (Younger).

Watchfulness

Always on the watch. (Toujours en vedette.)
MOTTO OF FREDERICK THE GREAT (1712–86)

A watched pot never boils.
ENGLISH PROVERB, not recorded in its present form before the XIX century

Watch your step. AMERICAN SAYING

Watchman

Watchman, what of the night?
ISAIAH XXI, 11, *c.* 700 B.C.

Water

Water is the best of all things.
PINDAR: *Olympian Odes*, I, *c.* 475 B.C.

The natural, temperate and necessary beverage for the thirsty is water.
CLEMENT OF ALEXANDRIA: *Paedagogus*, II, *c.* 190

The people of England drink no water save at certain times for penance.
JOHN FORTESCUE: *De laudibus legum Angliæ*, *c.* 1462

Much water goeth by the mill that the miller knoweth not of.
JOHN HEYWOOD: *Proverbs*, 1546

Water is a very good servant, but it is a cruel master.
JOHN BULLEIN: *The Bulwarke Against all Sickness*, 1562

Honest water ne'er left man in the mire.
SHAKESPEARE: *Timon of Athens*, I, *c.* 1607

Water . . . doth very greatly deject the appetite, destroy the natural heat, and overthrow the strength of the stomach, and consequently, confounding the concoction, it is the cause of crudities, fluctuations, and windiness in the body.
TOBIAS VENNER: *Via recta*, 1620

Water is insipid, inodorous, colorless, and smooth; it is found, when not cold, to be a great resolver of spasms, and lubricator of the fibres; this power it probably owes to its smoothness.
EDMUND BURKE: *The Sublime and Beautiful*, IV, 1756

Water, water, everywhere,
Nor any drop to drink.
S. T. COLERIDGE: *The Ancient Mariner*, II, 1798

The greatest necessity of the soldier is water.
NAPOLEON I: To Barry E. O'Meara at St. Helena, Feb. 17, 1817

While this cold water fills my cup,
Duns dare not assail me;
Sheriffs shall not lock me up,
Nor my neighbors bail me.
JOHN PIERPONT: *Airs of Palestine*, 1840

Water is the only drink for a wise man.
H. D. THOREAU: *Walden*, 1854

Drinking water neither makes a man sick, nor in debt, nor his wife a widow.
H. G. BOHN: *Handbook of Proverbs*, 1855

You never miss the water till the well runs dry.
ROWLAND HOWARD: *You Never Miss the Water*, 1876

But if it comes to slaughter
You will do your work on water,
An' you'll lick the bloomin' boots of 'im that's got it.
RUDYARD KIPLING: *Gunga Din*, 1890

And if from man's vile arts I flee
And drink pure water from the pump,
I gulp down infusoria
And quarts of raw bacteria,
And hideous rotatoræ,
And wriggling polygastricæ,
And slimy diatomacæ,
And various animalculæ
Of middle, high and low degree.
WILLIAM JUNIPER: *The True Drunkard's Delight*, 1933

Any water in the desert. ARAB PROVERB

Water is feared less than fire, yet fewer suffer by fire than by water. CHINESE PROVERB

Water is the prophet's drink.
DUTCH PROVERB

[*See also* Cleanliness, Cosmetics, Drinking, Drunkenness, Feasting, Fire and Water, Wine.

Water, Holy

[*See* Devil.

Waterloo, Battle of (June 18, 1815)

Those English who are lovers of liberty will one day lament with tears having gained the battle of Waterloo. It was as fatal to the liberties of Europe in its effects as that of Philippi was to those of Rome.
NAPOLEON I: To Barry E. O'Meara at St. Helena, Feb. 18, 1818

The battle of Waterloo was won here.
THE DUKE OF WELLINGTON: While watching a cricket match at Eton, *c.* 1825 (Usually, " The battle of Waterloo was won on the playing fields of Eton ")

[*See also* Napoleon I.

Wave

Old ocean rolls a lengthened wave to the shore,
Down whose green back the short-lived foam, all hoar,
Bursts gradual, with a wayward indolence.
JOHN KEATS: *Endymion*, II, 1818

What are the wild waves saying?
CHARLES DICKENS: *Dombey and Son*, 1848

Way

Her ways are ways of pleasantness, and all her paths are peace.
PROVERBS III, 17, *c.* 350 B.C.

I am the way, the truth, and the life: no man cometh unto the Father, but by me.
JOHN XIV, 6, *c.* 115

The longest way round is the shortest way home.
ENGLISH PROVERB, traced by Apperson to 1635

Weakness

Even the feeble can push over what already totters. OVID: *Tristia,* III, *c.* 10

The weakest goes to the wall.
SHAKESPEARE: *Romeo and Juliet,* I, *c.* 1596

Virtue has a greater enemy in weakness than in vice. LA ROCHEFOUCAULD: *Maxims,* 1665

To be weak is miserable.
JOHN MILTON: *Paradise Lost,* I, 1667

The concessions of the weak are the concessions of fear.
EDMUND BURKE: Speech on Conciliation with America, March 22, 1775

An amiable weakness.
R. B. SHERIDAN: *The School for Scandal,* V, 1777

The more weakness, the more falsehood; strength goes straight; every cannon-ball that has in it hollows and holes goes crooked. Weaklings must lie.
JEAN PAUL RICHTER: *Hesperus,* IV, 1795

The highest wisdom that a weak man can attain is a facility in finding out the weaknesses of better men.
G. C. LICHTENBERG: *Reflections,* 1799

Weak men are always timorous and suspicious.
NAPOLEON I: To Barry E. O'Meara at St. Helena, July 13, 1816

What 'twas weak to do
'Tis weaker to lament, once being done.
P. B. SHELLEY: *The Cenci,* V, 1819

The weak and the botched shall perish: first principle of our charity. And one should help them to it.
F. W. NIETZSCHE: *The Antichrist,* II, 1888

Pull gently at a weak rope. DUTCH PROVERB

The greatest weakness is the fear of appearing weak. FRENCH PROVERB

Whether the knife fall on the melon, or the melon on the knife, the melon suffers.
HINDU PROVERB

Whether the pitcher knocks the stone or the stone knocks the pitcher, it is equally bad for the pitcher. SPANISH PROVERB

[*See also* Evil, Evolution, Law, Mind, Passion, Strength.

Wealth

When wealth is centralized the people are dispersed; when wealth is distributed the people are brought together.
CONFUCIUS: *Analects,* X, *c.* 500 B.C.

Wealth is the thing most honored among men, and the source of the greatest power.
EURIPIDES: *The Phoenissæ, c.* 410 B.C. (Cited as a proverb)

The character which results from wealth is that of a prosperous fool.
ARISTOTLE: *Rhetoric,* II, *c.* 322 B.C.

The fool and the brutish person perish, and leave their wealth to others.
PSALMS XLIX, 10, *c.* 150 B.C.

High descent and meritorious deeds, unless united to wealth, are as useless as sea-weed.
HORACE: *Satires,* II, *c.* 25 B.C.

Nothing is more intolerable than a wealthy woman. JUVENAL: *Satires,* V, *c.* 110

He does not see, poor wretch, that his life is but a gilded torture, that he is bound fast by his wealth, and that his money owns him rather than he owns it.
ST. CYPRIAN OF CARTHAGE: *The World and Its Vanities, c.* 250

The bread that you store up belongs to the hungry; the cloak that lies in your chest belongs to the naked; and the gold that you have hidden in the ground belongs to the poor. ST. BASIL: *Homilies, c.* 375

Nothing is more fallacious than wealth. Today it is for thee, tomorrow it is against thee. It arms the eyes of the envious everywhere. It is a hostile comrade, a domestic enemy.
ST. JOHN CHRYSOSTOM: *Homilies,* II, *c.* 388

Great wealth cannot still hunger, but rather occasions more dearth; for where rich people are, there things are always dear. Moreover, money makes no man merry, but much rather pensive and full of sorrow.
MARTIN LUTHER: *Table-Talk,* LXXXII, 1569

Wealth is the smallest thing on earth, the least gift that God has bestowed on mankind.
MARTIN LUTHER: *Table-Talk,* CLXVII

Excess of wealth is cause of covetousness.
CHRISTOPHER MARLOWE: *The Jew of Malta,* I, *c.* 1590

What is got over the Devil's back will be spent under his belly.
ENGLISH PROVERB, traced by Smith to 1607

Wealth is the conjuror's devil,
Whom, when he thinks he hath, the Devil hath him.
GEORGE HERBERT: *The Temple,* 1633

I bless God I do find that I am worth more than ever I yet was, which is £6,200, for which the Holy Name of God be praised.
SAMUEL PEPYS: *Diary,* Oct. 31, 1666

It is good for a man to have that wherewith he may live well and happily.
HENRY MORE: *Enchiridion ethicum,* IV, 1667

Wealth is wisdom. He that's rich is wise.
DANIEL DEFOE: *The True-Born Englishman,* II, 1701

In all well-instituted commonwealths, care has been taken to limit men's possessions; which is done for many reasons, and, among the rest, for one which, perhaps, is not often considered, that when bounds are set to men's desires, after they have acquired as much as the laws will permit them, their private interest is at an end, and they have nothing to do but to take care of the public.
JONATHAN SWIFT: *Thoughts on Various Subjects,* 1706

Many a man would have been worse if his estate had been better.
BENJAMIN FRANKLIN: *Poor Richard's Almanac,* 1751

Wealth is the general centre of inclination, the point to which all minds persevere an invariable tendency.
SAMUEL JOHNSON: *The Rambler,* June 18, 1751

Ill fares the land, to hastening ills a prey,
Where wealth accumulates and men decay.
OLIVER GOLDSMITH: *The Deserted Village,* 1770

I saw that a humble man, with the blessing of the Lord, might live on a little; and that where the heart was set on greatness success in business did not satisfy the craving; but that commonly, with an increase of wealth, the desire of wealth increased.
JOHN WOOLMAN: *Journal,* II, 1774

The insolence of wealth will creep out.
SAMUEL JOHNSON: *Boswell's Life,* April 14, 1778

As wealth is power, so all power will infallibly draw wealth to itself by some means or other.
EDMUND BURKE: Speech in the House of Commons, Feb. 11, 1780

Wealth *per se* I never too much valued, and my acquaintance with its possessors has by no means increased my veneration for it.
FRANCES BURNEY: *Diary,* Dec. 8, 1782

Wealth is a power usurped by the few, to compel the many to labor for their benefit.
P. B. SHELLEY: *Queen Mab,* notes, 1813

Wealth is a great means of refinement; and it is a security for gentleness, since it removes disturbing anxieties; and it is a pretty promoter of intelligence, since it multiplies the avenues for its reception; and it is a good basis for a generous habit of life; it even equips beauty, neither hardening its hand with toil, nor tempting the wrinkles to come early.
DONALD G. MITCHELL (IK MARVEL): *Reveries of a Bachelor,* III, 1850

Superfluous wealth can buy superfluities only.
H. D. THOREAU: *Walden,* 1854

The lawful basis of wealth is, that a man who works should be paid the fair value of his work, and that if he does not choose to spend it today, he should have free leave to keep it, and spend it tomorrow.
JOHN RUSKIN: *The Crown of Wild Olive,* I, 1866

No man is any the worse off because another acquires wealth by trade, or by the exercise of a profession; on the contrary, he cannot have acquired his wealth except by benefiting others to the full extent of what they considered to be its value.
T. H. HUXLEY: *Administrative Nihilism,* 1871

Wealth can be accumulated but to a slight degree, and communities really live, as the vast majority of individuals live, from hand to mouth. Wealth will not bear much accumulation; except in a few unimportant forms it will not keep.
HENRY GEORGE: *Progress and Poverty,* II, 1879

The vast wealth which Stephen Girard had was itself alone evidence of greatness.
THOMAS B. REED: Speech in Philadelphia, 1898

Surplus wealth is a sacred trust which its possessor is bound to administer in his lifetime for the good of the community.
ANDREW CARNEGIE: *The Gospel of Wealth,* I, 1900

Probably the greatest harm done by vast wealth is the harm that we of moderate means do ourselves when we let the vices of envy and hatred enter deep into our own natures.
THEODORE ROOSEVELT: Speech in Providence, R. I., Aug. 23, 1902

Inherited wealth is a big handicap to happiness. It is as certain death to ambition as cocaine is to morality.
W. K. VANDERBILT: Press interview, 1905

The men of greatest usefulness are those who have a surplus; those who have only good will and love for their fellows cannot equal in well-doing those who have money and success to their credit.
E. W. HOWE: *The Blessing of Business,* 1918

The savings of many in the hands of one.
EUGENE V. DEBS (1855–1926)

A man seldom gets rich without ill-got gain; as a horse does not fatten without feeding in the night. CHINESE PROVERB

More wealth, less health. FRENCH PROVERB

Wealth breeds a pleurisy, ambition a fever, liberty a vertigo, and poverty a palsy.
IRISH PROVERB

Few have too much and fewer too little.
NORWEGIAN PROVERB

A little among neighbors is worth more than riches in a wilderness. WELSH PROVERB

[*See also* Agriculture, Atheism, Avarice, Capital, Character, Envy, Equality, Gold, Government, Health, Interruption, Landlord, Little, Malefactor, Marriage, Money, Money-getting, Monopoly, Poverty, Property, Rich and Poor, Riches, Shipping, Speculation.

Weapon

There is no weapon too short for a brave man.
RICHARD STEELE: *The Guardian,* Aug. 25, 1713 (Ascribed to "a king of Arabia")

Wear

Everything is the worse for the wearing.
THOMAS WILSON: *The Arte of Rhetorique,* 1553

Weariness

There the wicked cease from troubling; and there the weary be at rest.
JOB III, 17, *c.* 325 B.C. (A paraphrase, perhaps more familiar than the original, forms a couplet in GERALD MASSEY: *Jerusalem the Golden, c.* 1869: "Where the wicked cease from troubling, and the weary are at rest")

Weariness
Can snore upon the flint, when resty sloth
Finds the down pillow hard.
SHAKESPEARE: *Cymbeline,* III, *c.* 1609

Methinks I have outlived myself, and begin to be weary of the sun.
THOMAS BROWNE: *Religio Medici,* 1642

I am tired of keeping myself up in the water without corks, and without strength to swim. I should like to go to sleep, and be born again.
MARGARET FULLER OSSOLI: *Letter to R. W. Emerson,* Dec. 20, 1847

I have grown weary of dust and decay,
Weary of flinging my heart's wealth away —
Weary of sowing for others to reap;
Rock me to sleep, mother, rock me to sleep.
ELIZABETH CHASE (AKERS ALLEN): *Rock Me to Sleep,* 1860 (Saturday Evening Post, June 9)

To a weary horse even his own tail is a burden.
CZECH PROVERB

Weariness of life. (Tædium vitæ.)
LATIN PHRASE

[*See also* Death, Heaven.

Weasel

[*See* Word.

Weather

Fair weather cometh out of the north.
JOB XXXVII, 22, *c.* 325 B.C.

When it is evening, ye say, It will be fair weather: for the sky is red. And in the morning, It will be foul weather today: for the sky is red and lowring.
MATTHEW XVI, 2–3, *c.* 75

By my troth, here's a weather is able to make a man call his father whoreson.
ROBERT GREENE: *Friar Bacon and Friar Bungay,* I, 1594

Almighty and most merciful Father, we pray thee to send us such seasonable weather that the earth may, in due time, yield her increase for our use and benefit.
THE BOOK OF COMMON PRAYER, 1662

A cloudy day, or a little sunshine, have as great an influence on many constitutions as the most real blessings or misfortunes.
JOSEPH ADDISON: *The Spectator,* Sept. 5, 1711

Change of weather is the discourse of fools.
THOMAS FULLER: *Gnomologia,* 1732

When two Englishmen meet, their first talk is of the weather.
SAMUEL JOHNSON: *The Idler,* June 24, 1758

There is nothing more universally commended than a fine day; the reason is, that people can commend it without envy.
WILLIAM SHENSTONE: *Of Men and Manners,* 1764

'Tis the hard gray weather
Breeds hard English men.
CHARLES KINGSLEY: *Ode to the Northeast Wind,* 1854

Oh, what a blamed uncertain thing
This pesky weather is;
It blew and snew and then it thew,
And now, by jing, it's friz.
PHILANDER JOHNSON, *c.* 1895

Everybody talks about the weather but nobody does anything about it.
Author unidentified; commonly ascribed to S. L. CLEMENS (MARK TWAIN), but not found in his published works

Weather varies every hundred miles.
CHINESE PROVERB

Whoever wants to lie need only begin to talk about the weather. HAUSSA PROVERB

[*See also* Advice, Child, Sky.

Weaver

[*See* Thief.

Webster, Daniel (1782–1852)

Such is human nature in the gigantic intellect, the envious temper, the ravenous ambition, and the rotten heart of Daniel Webster. His treatment of me has been, is, and will be an improved edition of Andrew Jackson's gratitude.
JOHN QUINCY ADAMS: *Diary,* Sept. 17, 1841

Daniel Webster struck me much like a steam-engine in trousers.
Ascribed to SYDNEY SMITH in *A Memoir of the Rev. Sydney Smith,* by his daughter, Lady Holland, 1855

Webster, Noah (1758–1843)

I view Webster as a mere pedagogue, of very limited understanding.
THOMAS JEFFERSON: *Letter to James Madison,* Aug. 12, 1801

I have made many mistakes, but I love my country, and have labored for the youth of my country, and I trust no precept of mine has taught any dear youth to sin.
NOAH WEBSTER: On his deathbed, 1843

He taught millions how to spell, but none how to sin. Author unidentified

Wedding

Behold thou art consecrated to me with this ring according to the laws of Moses and Israel. (Harei ath m'kidusheth li b'tabaath su kh'dath Moshe v'Yisroael.)
Jewish marriage ritual, *c.* 1200

A man may weep upon his wedding day.
SHAKESPEARE and JOHN FLETCHER: *Henry VIII,* prologue, 1613

To church in the morning, and there saw a wedding in the church, which I have not seen many a day; and the young people so merry one with another! and strange to see what delight we married people have to see those poor fools decoyed into our condition, every man and woman gazing and smiling at them.
SAMUEL PEPYS: *Diary,* Dec. 25, 1665

The time approached; to church the parties went,
At once with carnal and devout intent.
ALEXANDER POPE: *January and May,* 1709

One wedding begets another.
JOHN GAY: *The Wife of Bath,* 1713

The last wedding is that of Peg Pelham, and I think I have never seen so comfortable a prospect of happiness; according to all appearance she cannot fail of being a widow in six weeks at farthest, and accordingly she has been so good a housewife to line her wedding-clothes with black.
MARY WORTLEY MONTAGU: *Letter to the Countess of Mar,* March, 1727

The fate of the house hangs on the wedding night.
BALZAC: *The Physiology of Marriage,* 1830

Hear the mellow wedding-bells,
Golden bells!
What a world of happiness their harmony foretells!
E. A. POE: *The Bells,* 1849 (Sartain's Universal Magazine, Nov.)

Do not be downcast! Tomorrow is our wedding-day, and as I live, here come the villagers! Old operetta line, *c.* 1850

Brightly dawns our wedding day;
Joyous hour, we give thee greeting!
Whither, whither art thou fleeting?
Fickle moment, prithee stay!
W. S. GILBERT: *The Mikado,* II, 1885

Cheer for the sergeant's weddin' —
Give 'em one cheer more!
Gray gun-'orses in the lando,
An' a rogue is married to a whore.
RUDYARD KIPLING: *The Sergeant's Wedding,* 1892

A wedding takes only a day or two, but the misery goes on forever. CZECH PROVERB

Monday for wealth,
Tuesday for health,
Wednesday the best day of all;
Thursday for crosses,
Friday for losses,
Saturday no luck at all.
OLD ENGLISH RHYME

Something old, something new,
Something borrowed, something blue.
IBID. (The wedding dress)

They that marry in green,
Their sorrow is soon seen.
OLD SCOTCH RHYME

The woman cries before the wedding; the man afterward. POLISH PROVERB

It is a sin to go to a wedding and not get drunk.
RUSSIAN PROVERB

Wedding and ill wintering tame baith man and best. SCOTTISH PROVERB

[*See also* Bride, Marriage, Miser.

Wednesday

[*See* Days, Demon, Nail, Sneezing, Wedding.

Weed

Sweet flowers are slow and weeds make haste.
SHAKESPEARE: *Richard III,* II, *c.* 1592

Many things grow in the garden that were never sowed there.
THOMAS FULLER: *Gnomologia*, 1732

The frost hurts not weeds.
IBID.

There poppies, nodding, mock the hope of toil;
There the blue bugloss paints the sterile soil;
Hardy and high, above the slender sheaf,
The slimy mallow waves her silky leaf.
GEORGE CRABBE: *The Village*, I, 1783

A weed is no more than a flower in disguise.
J. R. LOWELL: *A Fable for Critics*, 1848

Weeds never die.
DANISH PROVERB

[*See also* Garden.

Weeping

[*See* Tears.

Weighed

Thou art weighed in the balances and art found wanting.
DANIEL V, 27, *c.* 165 B.C.

Weight

A good man, weighing two hundred and fifty pounds.
WILLIAM O. BARTLETT: Said of W. S. Hancock, Democratic candidate for the Presidency, in an article in the New York Sun, Oct. 19, 1880

No gentleman ever weighs over two hundred pounds.
THOMAS B. REED: To David B. Henderson, in the House lobby, *c.* 1895

[*See also* Measure, Weights and Measures.

Weights and Measures

A false balance is an abomination to the Lord: but a just weight is his delight.
PROVERBS XI, 1, *c.* 350 B.C.

Divers weights are an abomination unto the Lord; and a false balance is not good.
PROVERBS XX, 23

Weight and measure take away strife.
GEORGE HERBERT: *Outlandish Proverbs*, 1640

Our present weights and measures come down to us from a remote antiquity, and some of them correspond to the earliest forms as closely as one-tenth of a gram.
RUDOLF VIRCHOW: Address to the German Association for Anthropology, Ethnology and Pre-History, Vienna, Aug. 5, 1889

Weird

Saw you the weird sisters?
SHAKESPEARE: *Macbeth*, IV, *c.* 1605

Welcome

His worth is warrant for his welcome.
SHAKESPEARE: *Two Gentlemen of Verona*, II, *c.* 1595

Sir, you are very welcome to our house:
It must appear in other ways than words,
Therefore I scant this breathing courtesy.
SHAKESPEARE: *The Merchant of Venice*, V, *c.* 1597

A hundred thousand welcomes: I could weep
And I could laugh; I am light and heavy;
Welcome!
SHAKESPEARE, *Coriolanus*, II, *c.* 1607

You are as welcome as the flowers in May.
CHARLES MACKLIN: *Love à la Mode*, I, 1759

'Tis sweet to hear the watch-dog's honest bark
Bay deep-mouth'd welcome as we draw near home;
'Tis sweet to know there is an eye will mark
Our coming, and look brighter when we come.
BYRON: *Don Juan*, I, 1819

Welcome her, thunders of fort and of fleet!
Welcome her, thundering cheer of the street!
Welcome her, all things youthful and sweet,
Scatter the blossoms under her feet!
ALFRED TENNYSON: *A Welcome to Alexandria*, 1863

Come in the evening, come in the morning,
Come when expected, come without warning;
Thousands of welcomes you'll find here before you,
And the oftener you come, the more we'll adore you.
OLD IRISH RHYME

Welcome's the best dish in the kitchen.
SCOTTISH PROVERB

[*See also* Feasting, Guest, Hospitality, Inn.

Welfare

The Congress shall have power to . . . provide for the general welfare of the United States.
CONSTITUTION OF THE UNITED STATES, Art. I, 1789

The general welfare is not my welfare. The general welfare may exult aloud while I lie like a whipped dog. The state may go on in splendor while I starve.
MAX STIRNER: *The Ego and His Own*, 1845

[*See also* People.

Well

[*See* Thirst, Water.

Well-bred

A well-bred youth neither speaks of himself, nor, being spoken to, is silent.
GEORGE HERBERT: *Outlandish Proverbs*, 1640

Everyone thinks himself well-bred.
ANTHONY A. COOPER (EARL OF SHAFTESBURY): *Characteristics of Men, Manners, Opinions, Times*, I, *c.* 1713

Let tenderness, compassion and good nature be all the fine breeding that you show in any place.

WILLIAM LAW: *A Serious Call to a Devout and Holy Life,* XIX, 1728

The characteristic of a well-bred man is to converse with his inferiors without insolence, and with his superiors with respect and ease.

LORD CHESTERFIELD: *Letter to his son,* May 17, 1748

He is not well-bred that cannot bear ill-breeding in others.

BENJAMIN FRANKLIN: *Poor Richard's Almanac,* 1748

A moral, sensible, and well-bred man
Will not affront me, and no other can.

WILLIAM COWPER: *Conversation,* 1782

Good breeding differs, if at all, from high breeding only as it gracefully remembers the rights of others, rather than gracefully insists on its own rights.

THOMAS CARLYLE: *Sartor Resartus,* III, 1836

Bachelors' wives and auld maids' bairns are aye well-bred. SCOTTISH PROVERB

[*See also* Breeding, Classes, Manners.

Well-doing

Let us not be weary in well-doing; for in due season we shall reap, if we faint not.

GALATIANS VI, 9, *c.* 50

Were I the chooser, a dram of well-doing should be preferred before many times as much the forcible hindrance of evil-doing. For God sure esteems the growth and completing of one virtuous person more than the restraint of ten vicious.

JOHN MILTON: *Areopagitica,* 1644

Whatever is worth doing at all is worth doing well.

LORD CHESTERFIELD: *Letter to his son,* March 10, 1746

If you want a thing well done, do it yourself.

ENGLISH PROVERB, not recorded before the XIX century

Wellington, Duke of (1769–1852)

Judging from Wellington's actions, from his despatches, and above all from his conduct towards Ney, I should pronounce him to be a man of little genius, without generosity, and without greatness of soul.

NAPOLEON I: To Barry E. O'Meara at St. Helena, Sept. 20, 1817

This man has the bad fortune to meet with good fortune wherever the greatest men in the world were unfortunate, and that angers us, and makes him hateful. We see in him only the victory of stupidity over genius.

HEINRICH HEINE: *English Fragments,* 1828

Welsh

[*See* English.

Welshman

The older the Welshman the more madman.

JAMES HOWELL: *Proverbs,* 1659

A Welshman is a man who prays on his knees on Sunday and preys on his friends the rest of the week. Author unidentified

[*See also* Character (National).

Wesley, John (1703–91)

[*See* Calvin (John).

West

Westward, ho!

GEORGE PEELE: *The Chronicle of Edward I,* 1593 (CHARLES KINGSLEY: Title of a novel, 1855)

Westward the course of empire takes its way;
The four first acts already past,
A fifth shall close the drama with the day;
Time's noblest offspring is the last.

GEORGE BERKELEY: *On the Prospect of Planting Arts and Learning in America,* 1735 – (Sometimes *course* is changed to *star*)

Oh, young Lochinvar came out of the West,
Through all the wide border his steed was the best. WALTER SCOTT: *Marmion,* V, 1808

Go West, young man, and grow up with the country.

HORACE GREELEY: *Hints Toward Reforms,* 1850

The land of the heart is the land of the West.

G. P. MORRIS: *The West,* 1851

Go West, young man, go West.

J. L. B. SOULE: Editorial in the Terre Haute (Ind.) Express, 1851 (Cf. GREELEY, *ante,* 1850)

I think it was Jekyll who used to say that the further he went West, the more convinced he felt that the wise men came from the East.

Ascribed to SYDNEY SMITH in *A Memoir of the Rev. Sydney Smith,* by his daughter, Lady Holland, 1855

Out where the handclasp's a little stronger,
Out where the smile dwells a little longer,
That's where the West begins.

ARTHUR CHAPMAN: *Out Where the West Begins,* 1917

Whale

The Lord had prepared a great fish to swallow up Jonah. And Jonah was in the belly of the fish three days and three nights.

JONAH I, 17, *c.* 400 B.C.

Whales in the sea
God's voice obey.

New England Primer, c. 1688

Ye whales that stir the boiling deep
Or in its dark recesses sleep,
Remote from human eye,
Praise Him by whom ye all are fed,
Praise Him without whose heavenly aid
Ye languish, faint and die.

CHRISTOPHER SMART: *The Benedicite Paraphrased,* 1746

Mr. Darrow — But when you read that Jonah swallowed the whale — or that the whale swallowed Jonah, how do you interpret that? Mr. Bryan — When I read that a big fish swallowed Jonah — it does not say whale — I believe it; and I believe in a God who can make a whale and can make a man, and make both do what He pleases.

From the records of the Scopes trial, Dayton, Tenn., July 21, 1925

[*See also* Fish, Miracle.

What

What is what? (Quid est quid?)

MEDIEVAL LATIN PHRASE

Wheel

Wheels within wheels.

ENGLISH PHRASE, familiar since the XVII century; probably derived from EZEKIEL I, 16: " A wheel in the middle of a wheel," *c.* 600 B.C. (Cf. EZEKIEL X, 10)

He . . . put his shoulder to the wheel.

ROBERT BURTON: *The Anatomy of Melancholy,* II, 1621

He who greases his wheels helps his oxen.

THOMAS FULLER: *Gnomologia,* 1732

[*See also* Worst.

Wheelbarrow

The greatest of human inventions is the wheelbarrow. It taught the Irish to walk upon their hind legs. AMERICAN SAYING, *c.* 1850

Where

Ye immortal gods, where in the world are we?

CICERO: *Oration in Catilinam,* I, *c.* 50 B.C.

Mr. Speaker, where are we at?

Ascribed to various American Congressmen of the era 1875–85

Whifflebat

A whifflebat is a queer kind of bird that flies backward, knows very little about where it came from and nothing about where it's going.

Ascribed to JAMES LEE KEY, mayor of Atlanta (Ga.), 1919–22, 1931–36

Whig

The first Whig was the Devil.

SAMUEL JOHNSON: *Boswell's Life,* April 28, 1778

The difference between the Whig and Tory of England is, that the Whig deduces his rights from the Anglo-Saxon source, and the Tory from the Norman.

THOMAS JEFFERSON: *Letter to John Cartwright,* 1824

[*See also* Democrat, Liberal, Tory.

Whip

My father hath chastised you with whips, but I will chastise you with scorpions.

I KINGS XII, 11, *c.* 500 B.C.

Oil of whip [is] the proper plaster for the cramp of laziness.

THOMAS FULLER: *Worthies of England,* 1662

A whip for a fool and a rod for a school is always in good season.

JOHN RAY: *English Proverbs,* 1670

Whirlwind

They have sown wind, and they shall reap the whirlwind. HOSEA VIII, 7, *c.* 740 B.C.

A great whirlwind shall be raised up from the coasts of the earth.

JEREMIAH XXV, 32, *c.* 625 B.C.

Out of the south cometh the whirlwind.

JOB XXXVII, 9, *c.* 325 B.C.

Rides in the whirlwind, and directs the storm.

JOSEPH ADDISON: *The Campaign,* 1704 (Addison's reference was to the Duke of Marlborough, the victor of Blenheim, Aug. 13, 1704. The line was borrowed by ALEXANDER POPE in *The Dunciad,* III, 1728, and applied ironically to John Rich, manager of Covent Garden Theatre)

There were some who were carried away in the whirlwind; and whither they went no man knoweth, save that they know they were carried away.

THE BOOK OF MORMON (*III Nephi VIII,* 16), 1830

Whiskers

As to whiskers, having never worn any, do you not think people would call it a piece of silly affectation if I were to begin it now?

ABRAHAM LINCOLN: *Letter to Grace Bedell,* Oct. 19, 1860

And the wind blew through his whiskers.

AMERICAN COUNTER-PHRASE, *c.* 1885

Whiskey

O whiskey! soul o' plays and pranks!
Accept a bardie's gratefu' thanks!
When wanting thee, what tuneless cranks
Are my poor verses!

ROBERT BURNS: *Scotch Drink,* 1785

Freedom and whiskey gang thegither.

ROBERT BURNS: *The Author's Earnest Cry and Prayer, c.* 1785

Wi' usquabae, we'll face the Devil.

ROBERT BURNS: *Tam o' Shanter,* 1790

I like it: I always did, and that is the reason I never use it.
ROBERT E. LEE: On being ordered whiskey by his physician, *c.* 1850

Ever see a bear cat hug a lion?
No, good God, no.
Well, whiskey make rabbit hug lion,
Yes, good God, yes.
American Negro song, quoted by HOWARD W. ODUM: *Rainbow Round My Shoulder,* IX, 1928

He'd go to mass every mornin' if holy water were whiskey. IRISH PROVERB

What butter or whiskey'll not cure, there's no cure for. IBID.

[*See also* Beer, Cocktail, Drinker, Drugs, Irishman, Teetotaler, Wine Women and Song.

Whisper

A whisperer separateth chief friends.
PROVERBS XVI, 28, *c.* 350 B.C.

All that hate me whisper together against me.
PSALMS XLI, 7, *c.* 150 B.C.

Where there is whispering there is lying.
ENGLISH PROVERB, familiar since the XVII century

Foul whisperings are abroad.
SHAKESPEARE: *Macbeth,* V, 1605

What is whispered is heard all over town.
DANISH PROVERB

[*See also* Credit, Gossip, Scandal, Stranger.

Whistler, James A. McN. (1834–1903)

I have seen, and heard, much of cockney impudence before now; but never expected to hear a coxcomb ask two hundred guineas for flinging a pot of paint in the public's face.
JOHN RUSKIN: *On Whistler,* 1877

I regard Mr. Whistler's famous peacock room as the finest thing in color and decoration which the world has known since Correggio painted that wonderful room in Italy where the little children are dancing on the walls.
OSCAR WILDE: *House Decoration,* 1882 (Lecture in New York, May 11)

Mr. Whistler has always spelt art with a capital I.
OSCAR WILDE: Lecture in London, 1885

Whistling

Whistling to keep myself from being afraid.
JOHN DRYDEN: *Amphitryon,* III, 1690

He whistled as he went, for want of thought.
JOHN DRYDEN: *Cymon and Iphigenia,* 1699

A whistling woman and a crowing hen
Are neither fit for God nor men.
ENGLISH PROVERB, not recorded before the XVIII century

The schoolboy, with his satchel in his hand,
Whistling aloud to keep his courage up.
ROBERT BLAIR: *The Grave,* I, 1743 (Cf. DRYDEN, *ante,* 1690)

Though father and mother and a' should gae mad,
Oh, whistle and I'll come to you, my lad.
ROBERT BURNS: *Whistle and I'll Come to You,* 1793

He felt the cheering power of Spring, —
It made him whistle, it made him sing.
ROBERT SOUTHEY: *The Inchcape Rock,* 1801

[*See also* Luck.

White

The limpid confidence of white.
J. K. HUYSMANS: *À rebours,* 1884

White things [are] ever an afterthought — the doubles, or seconds, of real things, and themselves but half-real, half-material — the white queen, the white witch, the white mass, which, as the black mass is a travesty of the true mass turned to evil by horrible old witches, is celebrated by young candidates for the priesthood with an unconsecrated host, by way of rehearsal.
WALTER PATER: *Marius the Epicurean,* II, 1885 (Quotation from an unnamed "quaint German mystic")

[*See also* Black, Color, Elephant.

White House

[*See* Presidency.

Whither

Whither goest thou? (Quo vadis?)
JOHN XIII, 36, *c.* 115 (The Latin is from the Vulgate)

White Supremacy

[*See* Negro.

Whitman, Walt (1819–92)

I greet you at the beginning of a great career, which must yet have had a long foreground somewhere, for such a start. I rubbed my eyes a little to see if this sunbeam were no illusion; but the solid sense of the book is a sober certainty. It has the best merits, namely, of fortifying and encouraging.
R. W. EMERSON: *Letter to Whitman,* July 21, 1855 (On the appearance of *Leaves of Grass*)

Mr. Whitman is an American writer who some years back attracted attention by a volume of so-called poems which were chiefly remarkable for their absurd extravagances and shameless obscenity, and who has since, we are glad to say, been little heard of among decent people.
Anon.: In the London Saturday Review, 1876

Mr. Emerson once did the world great mischief by praising him.
J. G. HOLLAND: *Everyday Topics*, 1876

Whitman does not in any measure deserve the great attention we are giving him. He has not enriched American literature with any such congruous material as will enter into it and become a portion of the common stock appropriated by the public taste or the public need. You might strike out of existence all he has written, and the world would not be consciously poorer.
J. G. HOLLAND: *Letter to R. W. Gilder*, Sept. 19, 1880

Mr. Whitman's muse is at once indecent and ugly, lascivious and gawky, lubricious and coarse.
LAFCADIO HEARN: *Leaves of Grass*, 1882 (New Orleans Times-Democrat, July 30)

A large shaggy dog, just unchained, scouring the beaches of the world and baying at the moon.
R. L. STEVENSON: *Familiar Studies of Men and Books*, III, 1882

Some of our English cousins have undertaken to hold Walt Whitman up as the herald of the coming literature of American democracy, merely because he departed from all received forms, and indulged in barbarous eccentricities. They mistake difference for originality.
H. C. LODGE: *Colonialism in the United States*, 1884

I had my choice when I commenced. I bid neither for soft eulogies, big money returns, nor the approbation of existing schools and conventions. . . . I have had my say entirely my own way, and put it unerringly on record – the value thereof to be decided by time.
WALT WHITMAN: *A Backward Glance O'er Travel'd Roads*, 1888 (Pref. to *November Boughs*)

Two things are incompossible when the world of being has scope enough for one of them, but not enough for both – as Walt Whitman's poetry and God's mercy to man.
AMBROSE BIERCE: *The Devil's Dictionary*, 1906

A Balaam come to judgment.
ALEISTER CROWLEY: *Art in America*, 1922

Whittier, J. G. (1807–92)

In Whittier lives the zeal, the moral energy, that founded New England.
WALT WHITMAN: *Specimen Days*, April 16, 1881

Whole

[*See* Half.

Whore

By means of a whorish woman a man is brought to a piece of bread.
PROVERBS VI, 26, *c.* 350 B.C.

The whore and the whoremonger shall be scourged with a hundred stripes.
THE KORAN, XXIV, *c.* 625

He that hath a fool to his wife,
Her neighbors oft will flout her;
But he that hath a whore to his wife
Were better be without her.
Anon.: *Choice of Inventions*, II, *c.* 1575

Once a whore, always a whore.
ENGLISH PROVERB, familiar since the XVII century

Who drives an ass and leads a whore
Hath toil and sorrow evermore.
FYNES MORYSON: *Itinerary*, III, 1617 (Quoted as an Italian proverb)

An old whore's curse is a blessing.
JOHN RAY: *English Proverbs*, 1670

A young whore, an old saint. IBID.

She plays the whore for apples, and then bestows them upon the sick.
ENGLISH PROVERB, traced by Smith to 1678

I loathe a whore, and startle at the name.
ALEXANDER POPE: *January and May*, 1709

The whore is proud her beauties are the dread
Of peevish virtue and the marriage-bed.
EDWARD YOUNG: *Love of Fame*, I, 1728

[*See also* Harlot, Novel, Poet, Priest, Virtue and Vice, Wedding.

Whoremonger

[*See* Adulterer.

Why

Every why hath a wherefore.
SHAKESPEARE: *The Comedy of Errors*, II, 1593

Wicked

There is no peace unto the wicked.
ISAIAH XLVIII, 22, *c.* 700 B.C.

Wickedness proceedeth from the wicked.
I SAMUEL XXIV, 13, *c.* 500 B.C. (Cited as "the proverb of the ancients")

The wicked flee when no man pursueth.
PROVERBS XXVIII, 1, *c.* 350 B.C.

How oft is the candle of the wicked put out! and how oft comes their destruction upon them! JOB XXI, 17, *c.* 325 B.C.

The wicked bend their bow, they make ready their arrow upon the string, that they may privily shoot at the upright in heart.
PSALMS XI, 2, *c.* 150 B.C.

I have seen the wicked in great power, and spreading himself like a green bay tree. Yet he passed away, and, lo, he was not: yea, I sought him, but he could not be found.
PSALMS XXXVII, 35–36

The success of the wicked is a temptation to many others.
PHAEDRUS: *Fabulæ Æsopiæ, c.* 40

The sun also shines on the wicked.
SENECA: *De beneficiis,* III, *c.* 63

No one is so wicked that he wants to seem wicked.
QUINTILIAN: *De institutione oratoria,* III, *c.* 90

God bears with the wicked, but not forever.
CERVANTES: *Don Quixote,* II, 1615

There are wicked people who would be much less dangerous if they were wholly without goodness.
LA ROCHEFOUCAULD: *Maxims,* 1665

Keep the wicked always at enmity with one another; the safety of the world depends on that. Sow among them dissension, or you will never have any peace.
JEAN DE LA FONTAINE: *Fables,* VII, 1671

The happiness of the wicked passes away like a torrent. JEAN RACINE: *Athalie,* II, 1690

A wicked man is his own Hell.
THOMAS FULLER: *Gnomologia,* 1732

The wicked are always surprised to find ability in the good.
LUC DE VAUVENARGUES: *Réflexions,* 1746

If it be true, that men are miserable because they are wicked, it is likewise true, that many are wicked because they are miserable.
S. T. COLERIDGE: *Aids to Reflection,* 1825

I's wicked, I is.
HARRIET BEECHER STOWE: *Uncle Tom's Cabin,* XX, 1852

The wicked flee when no man pursueth, but they make better time when someone is after them.
Ascribed to CHARLES H. PARKHURST (1842–1933)

[*See also* Death, Sinner.

Wickedness

Ye have plowed wickedness, ye have reaped iniquity. HOSEA X, 13, *c.* 740 B.C.

Though wickedness be sweet in his mouth, though he hide it under his tongue; though he spare it, and forsake it not, but keep it still within his mouth; yet his meat in his bowels is turned; it is the gall of asps within him. JOB XX, 12–14, *c.* 325 B.C.

Wickedness lies in hesitating about an act, even though it be not perpetrated.
CICERO: *De officiis,* III, 78 B.C.

No man ever became very wicked all at once.
JUVENAL: *Satires,* II, *c.* 110

What rein can hold licentious wickedness
When down the hill he holds his fierce career?
SHAKESPEARE: *Henry V,* III, *c.* 1599

There is a method in man's wickedness —
It grows up by degrees.
BEAUMONT and FLETCHER: *A King and No King,* V, 1611

Wickedness is weakness.
JOHN MILTON: *Samson Agonistes,* 1671

Wickedness, like a flood, is like to drown our English world. It begins already to be above the tops of the mountains; it has almost swallowed up all; our youth, middle age, old age, and all, are almost carried away of this flood.
JOHN BUNYAN: *The Life and Death of Mr. Badman,* 1680

Your wickedness makes you, as it were, heavy as lead, and to tend downwards with great weight and pressure towards Hell; and if God should let you go, you would immediately sink and swiftly descend and plunge into the bottomless gulf, and your healthy constitution, and your own care and prudence, and best contrivance, and all your righteousness, would have no more influence to uphold you and keep you out of Hell than a spider's web would have to stop a falling rock.
JONATHAN EDWARDS: *Sinners in the Hands of an Angry God,* 1741 (Sermon, July 8)

The world loves a spice of wickedness.
H. W. LONGFELLOW: *Hyperion,* VII, 1839

Wickedness is a myth invented by good people to account for the curious attraction of others.
OSCAR WILDE: *Phrases and Philosophies for the Use of the Young,* 1894

The more wicked a man is the less fault he finds with himself. WELSH PROVERB

[*See also* Sin.

Wide

[*See* Narrow.

Widow

Ye shall not afflict any widow, or fatherless child. EXODUS XXII, 22, *c.* 700 B.C.

When thou gatherest the grapes of thy vineyard, thou shalt not glean it afterward: it shall be for the stranger, for the fatherless, and for the widow.
DEUTERONOMY XXIV, 21, *c.* 700 B.C.

I caused the widow's heart to sing for joy.
JOB XXIX, 13, *c.* 325 B.C.

Honor widows that are widows indeed.
I TIMOTHY V, 3, *c.* 60

The younger widows . . . have begun to wax wanton against Christ, they will marry.
I TIMOTHY V, 11

There came a certain poor widow, and she threw in two mites, which make a farthing.
MARK XII, 42, *c.* 70 (Cf. LUKE XXI, 2, *c.* 75)

Woe unto you, scribes and Pharisees, hypocrites! for ye devour widows' houses.
MATTHEW XXIII, 14, *c.* 75 (Cf. LUKE XX, 46–7, *c.* 75)

She was a widow of about fourscore and four years. LUKE II, 37, *c.* 75

On the tombs of her seven husbands Chloe put the inscription: "The work of Chloe." How could she have said it more plainly?
MARTIAL: *Epigrams*, IX, *c.* 95

Second marriages are lawful, but holy widowhood is better.
ST. AUGUSTINE: *On the Good of Widowhood*, *c.* 413

Such of you as shall die and leave wives ought to bequeath their wives a year's maintenance, without putting them out of their houses.
THE KORAN, II, *c.* 625

He'll have a lusty widow now
That shall be wooed and wedded in a day.
SHAKESPEARE: *The Taming of the Shrew*, IV, 1594

What's a widow but an axle broke,
Whose one part failing, neither part can move?
JOHN DAVIES: *A Contention Betwixt a Wife, a Widow, and a Maid*, 1602

She that hath had a husband had to bury,
And is therefore, in heart not sad but merry,
Yet if in show, good manners she would keep,
Onions and mustard seed will make her weep.
JOHN HARINGTON: *The Englishman's Doctor*, 1608

The devout widow never desires to be esteemed either beautiful or comely, contenting herself with being such as God desires her to be, that is to say, humble and abject in her own eyes.
ST. FRANCIS DE SALES: *Introduction to the Devout Life*, XL, 1609

He first deceased; she for a little tried
To live without him, liked it not, and died.
HENRY WOTTON: *Upon the Death of Sir Morton's Wife*, *c.* 1610

There be things called widows, dead men's wills,
I never lov'd to prove those; nor never long'd yet
To be buried alive in another man's cold monument.
JOHN FLETCHER: *The Wild-Goose Chase*, I, 1621

Marry a widow before she leaves mourning.
GEORGE HERBERT: *Outlandish Proverbs*, 1640

I think with them who, both in prudence and elegance of spirit, would choose a virgin of mean fortunes, honestly bred, before the wealthiest widow.
JOHN MILTON: *An Apology for Smectymnuus*, 1642

Widowhood is pitiable in its solitariness and loss, but amiable and comely when it is adorned with gravity and purity, and not sullied with remembrances of the passed license, nor with present desires of returning to a second bed.
JEREMY TAYLOR: *The Rule and Exercises of Holy Living*, II, 1650

Take heed of . . . a widow thrice married.
GEORGE HERBERT: *Jacula Prudentum*, 1651

Who marries a widow and two daughters marries three thieves. IBID.

It is a sad burden to carry a dead man's child.
THOMAS FULLER: *Church History*, II, 1655
(Cited as a proverb)

Here I see what creatures widows are in weeping for their husbands and then presently leaving off.
SAMUEL PEPYS: *Diary*, Oct. 17, 1667

He that woos a maid must seldom come in her sight,
But he that woos a widow must woo her day and night.
JOHN RAY: *English Proverbs*, 1670

Long a widow weds with shame. IBID.

He that has a pretension to a widow must never give over for a little ill usage.
WILLIAM WYCHERLEY: *The Plain Dealer*, II, *c.* 1674

I am a relict and executrix of known plentiful assets and parts, who understand myself and the law. IBID.

It's a delicious thing to be a young widow.
JOHN VANBRUGH: *The Relapse*, I, 1696

I never yet could meet with a sorrowful relict but was herself enough to make a hard bargain with me.
RICHARD STEELE: *The Funeral*, I, 1701
(Said by Sable the undertaker)

No crafty widows shall approach my bed:
Those are too wise for bachelors to wed.
ALEXANDER POPE: *January and May*, 1709

Widows are the most perverse creatures in the world.
JOSEPH ADDISON: *The Spectator*, March 25, 1711

[In Vienna] it is indecent for a widow ever to wear green or rose color, but all the other gayest colors at her own discretion.
MARY WORTLEY MONTAGU: *Letter to an unidentified correspondent*, Oct. 1, 1716

Never marry a widow unless her first husband was hanged.
JAMES KELLY: *Complete Collection of Scottish Proverbs*, 1721

Why are those tears? Why droops your head?
Is, then, your other husband dead?

Or does a worse disgrace betide?
Hath no one since his death applied?
JOHN GAY: *Fables*, I, 1727

The comfortable estate of widowhood is the only hope that keeps up a wife's spirits.
JOHN GAY: *The Beggar's Opera*, II, 1728

A good season for courtship is when the widow returns from the funeral.
THOMAS FULLER: *Gnomologia*, 1732

The rich widow cries with one eye and laughs with the other. IBID.

The new-made widow too I've sometimes spied,
Sad sight! slow moving o'er the prostrate dead:
Listless she crawls along in doleful black,
While bursts of sorrow gush from either eye,
Fast falling down her now untasted cheek.
ROBERT BLAIR: *The Grave*, 1743

When widows exclaim loudly against second marriages, I would always lay a wager that the man, if not the wedding-day, is absolutely fixed on.
HENRY FIELDING: *Amelia*, VI, 1752

A wanton widow Leezie was,
As canty as a kittlin;
But, och! that night, amang the shaws,
She got a fearfu' settlin'!
ROBERT BURNS: *Halloween*, 1785 (*Canty*=lively; *shaws*=the leaves and stalks of root-vegetables)

Twelve months her sables she in sorrow wore,
And mourn'd so long that she could mourn no more.
GEORGE CRABBE: *Tales*, VI (The Frank Courtship), 1812

Beware of widders.
CHARLES DICKENS: *The Pickwick Papers*, XXIV, 1837

Widders are 'ceptions to ev'ry rule. I have heerd how many ord'nary women one widder's equal to, in pint o' comin' over you. I think it's five-and-twenty, but I don't rightly know vether it ain't more. IBID.

I am a lone lorn creetur.
CHARLES DICKENS: *David Copperfield*, III, 1849

A widow of doubtful age will marry almost any sort of a white man.
Ascribed to HORACE GREELEY (1811–72)

Now, if you must marry, take care she is old —
A troop-sergeant's widow's the nicest, I'm told.
RUDYARD KIPLING: *The Young British Soldier*, 1891

A pathetic figure that the Christian world has agreed to take humorously, although Christ's tenderness towards widows was one of the most marked features of His character.
AMBROSE BIERCE: *The Devil's Dictionary*, 1906

A virtuous widow is the most loyal of mortals; she is faithful to that which is neither pleased nor profited by her fidelity.
AMBROSE BIERCE: *Collected Works*, VIII, 1911

So far as is known, no widow ever eloped.
E. W. HOWE: *Country Town Sayings*, 1911

A widow who marries the second time doesn't deserve to be one.
ELBERT HUBBARD: *Roycroft Dictionary and Book of Epigrams*, 1923

A widow is a rudderless boat.
CHINESE PROVERB

A maid marries to please her parents; a widow to please herself. IBID.

Few women turn gray because their husbands die. DANISH PROVERB

The rich widow's tears soon dry. IBID.

This turf has drunk a widow's tear,
Three of her husbands slumber here.
Epitaph in a Staffordshire churchyard, England

The three most pleasant things are: a cat's kitten, a goat's kid, and a young widow woman. IRISH PROVERB

In the widow's house there is no fat mouse.
JAPANESE PROVERB

A man does with a maiden as he wills; with a widow as she wills. POLISH PROVERB

He who has not married a young widow doesn't know what misfortune is.
RUSSIAN PROVERB

He that marries a widow and twa dochters has three back doors to his house.
SCOTTISH PROVERB (*Dochter*=daughter)

A comely widow should either re-marry, be killed, or be shut up in a convent.
SPANISH PROVERB

He who marries a widow will often have a dead man's head thrown in his dish. IBID.

He who marries a widow with three children marries four thieves. SWEDISH PROVERB

[*See also* Charity, Chastity, Chivalry, Danger, Epitaph, Funeral, Marriage, Merriment, Onion, Orphan, Piety, Soldier, Vineyard, Virgin, Wife.

Widower

The death of the first wife makes such a hole in the heart that all the rest slip through.
JAMES KELLY: *Complete Collection of Scottish Proverbs*, 1721

My wife was in my mind: she would have been pleased. Having now nobody to please, I am little pleased.
SAMUEL JOHNSON: *Diary in France*, Oct. 17, 1775

Houses she kept for widowers lately made;
For now she said, "They'll miss th' endearing friend,
And I'll be there the soften'd heart to mend."
GEORGE CRABBE: *The Borough,* XV, 1810

Oh, 'tis a precious thing, when wives are dead,
To find such numbers who will serve instead;
And in whatever state a man be thrown
'Tis that precisely they would wish their own.
GEORGE CRABBE: *Tales of the Hall,* 1819

I will not blaze cambric and crape in the public eye like a disconsolate widower, that most affected of all characters.
WALTER SCOTT: *Journal,* May 16, 1826 (Lady Scott died May 15)

After such years of dissension and strife,
Some wonder that Peter should weep for his wife;
But his tears on her grave are nothing surprising, —
He's laying her dust, for fear of its rising.
THOMAS HOOD: *Peter and His Wife, c.* 1830

By the calamity of April last, I lost my little all in this world; and have no soul left who can make any corner of this world into a *home* for me any more. Bright, heroic, tender, true and noble was that lost treasure of my heart, who faithfully accompanied me in all the rocky ways and climbings; and I am forever poor without her.
THOMAS CARLYLE: *Letter to R. W. Emerson,* Jan. 27, 1867

Cried Ned to his neighbors, as onward they pressed,
Conveying his wife to the place of long rest,
"Take, friends, I beseech you, a little more leisure;
For why should we thus make a toil of a pleasure?"
Author unidentified

Wife

Every wise man loves the wife he has chosen.
HOMER: *Iliad,* IX, *c.* 800 B.C.

Though you love your wife, do not tell her all you know; tell her some trifle, and conceal the rest. HOMER: *Odyssey,* XI, *c.* 800 B.C.

The Lord God said, It is not good that the man should be alone; I will make him a help meet for him. GENESIS II, 18, *c.* 700 B.C.

And Adam said, This is now bone of my bones, and flesh of my flesh. GENESIS II, 23

A man [shall] leave his father and his mother, and shall cleave unto his wife: and they shall be one flesh.
GENESIS II, 24 (Cf. EPHESIANS V, 31, *c.* 60; MARK X, 7–8, *c.* 70; MATTHEW XIX, 5, *c.* 75)

It came to pass, when men began to multiply on the face of the earth, and daughters were born unto them, that the sons of God saw the daughters of men that they were fair; and they took them wives of all which they chose. GENESIS VI, 1–2

They shall not take a wife that is a whore, or profane; neither shall they take a woman put away from her husband.
LEVITICUS XXI, 7, *c.* 700 B.C.

The wife of thy bosom.
DEUTERONOMY XIII, 6, *c.* 650 B.C.

When a woman, in her husband's absence, seeks to display her beauty, mark her as a wanton.
EURIPIDES: *Electra, c.* 415 B.C.

Let thy fountain be blessed: and rejoice with the wife of thy youth. Let her be as the loving hind and pleasant roe; let her breasts satisfy thee at all times; and be thou ravished always with her love.
PROVERBS V, 18–19, *c.* 350 B.C.

A virtuous woman is a crown to her husband: but she that maketh ashamed is as rottenness in his bones. PROVERBS XII, 4

Whoso findeth a wife findeth a good thing, and obtaineth favor of the Lord.
PROVERBS XVIII, 22

The contentions of a wife are a continual dropping. PROVERBS XIX, 13

A prudent wife is from the Lord.
PROVERBS XIX, 14

Depart not from a wise and good wife, whom thou hast gotten in the fear of the Lord: for the grace of her modesty is above gold.
ECCLESIASTICUS VII, 21, *c.* 180 B.C.

Blessed is the man that hath a virtuous wife, for the number of his days shall be double.
ECCLESIASTICUS XXVI, 1

The obedience of a wife is a kind of command.
PUBLILIUS SYRUS: *Sententiæ, c.* 50 B.C.

Strife is the dowry of a wife.
OVID: *Remedia amoris, c.* 10

There is difference also between a wife and a virgin. The unmarried woman careth for the things of the Lord, that she may be holy both in body and in spirit; but she that is married careth for the things of the world, how she may please her husband.
I CORINTHIANS VII, 34, *c.* 55

He that loveth his wife loveth himself.
EPHESIANS V, 28, *c.* 60

The weaker vessel. I PETER III, 7, *c.* 60

Give me a wife not too learned.
MARTIAL: *Epigrams,* II, 86

Lycoris has buried all the female friends she had, Fabianus: would she were the friend of my wife! MARTIAL: *Epigrams,* IV, *c.* 95

Your seventh wife, Phileros, is now being buried in your field. No man's field brings him greater profit than yours, Phileros.
MARTIAL: *Epigrams,* X, *c.* 95

In choosing a wife look down; in choosing a friend look up.
THE TALMUD (*Jebamoth*), c. 200

Have no fear, blessed sisters; no wife is ugly to her own husband.
TERTULLIAN: *Women's Dress*, c. 220

Who is the best beloved creature on earth? The faithful wife.
BHARTRIHARI: *The Niti Sataka*, c. 625

Your wives are your tillage.
THE KORAN, II, c. 625

It's no lack to lack a wife.
ENGLISH PROVERB, current since the XVI century

No beauty recommends a wife so much to her husband as the probity of her life, and her obedience. THOMAS MORE: *Utopia*, 1516

He that will thrive must ask leave of his wife.
JOHN HEYWOOD: *Proverbs*, 1546

The best or worst thing for man in this life
Is good or ill choosing his good or ill wife.
IBID.

A preacher of the gospel, if he is able with a good conscience to remain unmarried, let him so remain; but if he cannot abstain, living chastely, then let him take a wife; God has made that plaster for that sore.
MARTIN LUTHER: *Table-Talk*, DCCXV, 1569

He who has an old, spiteful, quarrelsome, sickly wife, may fairly reckon himself in Purgatory.
MARTIN LUTHER: *Table-Talk*, DCCXL

He that hath a drunken wife
That spends all at the alehouse,
Were better take a cord in hand
And hang him at the gallows.
Anon.: *Choice of Inventions*, I, c. 1575

My dear, my better half.
PHILIP SIDNEY: *Arcadia*, III, 1590

If long, she is lazy;
If little, she is loud;
If fair, she is sluttish;
If foul, she is proud.
JOHN FLORIO: *Second Frutes*, 1591

I will attend my husband, be his nurse,
Diet his sickness, for it is my office.
SHAKESPEARE: *The Comedy of Errors*, V, 1593

I will be master of what is mine own;
She is my goods, my chattels; she is my house,
My household stuff, my field, my barn,
My horse, my ox, my ass, my anything.
SHAKESPEARE: *The Taming of the Shrew*, III, 1594

She is mine own,
And I as rich in having such a jewel
As twenty seas, if all their sand were pearl,
The water nectar and the rocks pure gold.
SHAKESPEARE: *Two Gentlemen of Verona*, II, c. 1595

Two things doth prolong thy life:
A quiet heart and a loving wife.
THOMAS DELONEY: *Strange Histories*, c. 1595

His wife wore the breeches.
JOHN HARINGTON: *The Metamorphosis of Ajax*, 1596

She is not well married that lives married long:
But she's best married that dies married young.
SHAKESPEARE: *Romeo and Juliet*, IV, c. 1596

You are my true and honorable wife,
As dear to me as are the ruddy drops
That visit my sad heart.
SHAKESPEARE: *Julius Cæsar*, II, 1599

O ye gods,
Render me worthy of this noble wife! IBID.

Maids are May when they are maids, but the sky changes when they are wives.
SHAKESPEARE: *As You Like It*, IV, c. 1600

Wives may be merry and yet honest too.
SHAKESPEARE: *The Merry Wives of Windsor*, IV, c. 1600

Every true wife hath an indented heart,
Wherein the covenants of love are writ,
Whereof her husband keeps the counterpart,
And reads his comforts and his joys in it.
JOHN DAVIES: *A Contention Betwixt a Wife, a Widow, and a Maid*, 1602

There never was a wife that liked her lot.
IBID.

I am wanton and lascivious,
And cannot live without a wife.
CHRISTOPHER MARLOWE: *Dr. Faustus*, II, 1604

Let husbands know,
Their wives have sense like them: they see, and smell,
And have their palates both for sweet and sour,
As husbands have.
SHAKESPEARE: *Othello*, IV, 1604

To " Get out of my house " and " What do you want with my wife? " there is no answer.
CERVANTES: *Don Quixote*, I, 1605

Who hath a loving wife and loves her not,
He is not better than a witless sot.
J. M.: *The New Metamorphosis*, c. 1611

Should all despair
That have revolted wives, the tenth of mankind
Would hang themselves.
SHAKESPEARE: *The Winter's Tale*, I, c. 1611

A wife with a strawberry breath, cherry lips, apricot cheeks, and a soft velvet head, like a melicotton.
BEN JONSON: *Bartholomew Fair*, I, 1614
(*Melicotton*=a peach grafted on a quince)

He makes a false wife that suspects a true.
NATHANIEL FIELD: *Amends for Ladies*, I, 1618

In the election of a wife, as in
A project of war, to err but once is
To be undone forever.
THOMAS MIDDLETON: *Anything for a Quiet Life*, I, *c.* 1620

Man's best possession is a loving wife.
ROBERT BURTON: *The Anatomy of Melancholy*, III, 1621

Why should I be at charge to keep a wife of mine own,
When other honest married men will ease me,
And thank me too, and be beholding to me?
JOHN FLETCHER: *The Wild-Goose Chase*, II, 1621

Wives are young men's mistresses, companions for middle age, and old men's nurses.
FRANCIS BACON: *Essays*, VIII, 1625

Those that marry fools live ladies' lives.
THOMAS MIDDLETON: *Women Beware Women*, I, *c.* 1625

My own lawfully begotten wife.
BEN JONSON: *The New Inn*, IV, 1629

If you give your wife a yard she'll take an ell.
THOMAS DEKKER: *II The Honest Whore*, II, 1630

The sum of all that makes a just man happy
Consists in the well choosing of his wife.
PHILIP MASSINGER: *A New Way to Pay Old Debts*, IV, 1633

He that tells his wife news is but newly married.
GEORGE HERBERT: *Outlandish Proverbs*, 1640

He knows little who will tell his wife all he knows.
THOMAS FULLER: *The Holy State and the Profane State*, I, 1642 (Cf. HOMER, *ante*, *c.* 800 B.C.)

Next to no wife, a good wife is best.
THOMAS FULLER: *The Holy State and the Profane State*, III (Ascribed to "a bachelor")

Suspicion, discontent, and strife,
Come in for dowry with a wife.
ROBERT HERRICK: *Hesperides*, 1648

When a man dwells in love, then the breasts of his wife are pleasant as the droppings upon the hill of Hermon, her eyes are fair as the light of Heaven, she is a fountain sealed, and he can quench his thirst, and ease his cares, and lay his sorrow down upon her lap, and can retire home as to his sanctuary and refectory, and his garden of sweetness and chaste refreshment.
JEREMY TAYLOR: *The Mysteriousness of Marriage*, 1651

A woman . . . hath no sanctuary to retire to from an evil husband; she must dwell upon her sorrow, and hatch the eggs which her own folly or infelicity hath produced.
IBID.

Who will have a handsome wife, let him choose her upon Saturday, and not upon Sunday, viz: when she is in her fine clothes.
JAMES HOWELL: *Proverbs*, 1659

Who is the fool who does not wish his wife were dumb?
J. B. MOLIÈRE: *Le médecin malgré lui*, II, 1666

Heaven's last best gift, my ever new delight.
JOHN MILTON: *Paradise Lost*, V, 1667

Thy perfect gift, so good,
So fit, so acceptable, so divine.
JOHN MILTON: *Paradise Lost*, X

A cheerful wife is the joy of life.
JOHN RAY: *English Proverbs*, 1670

A good wife and health are man's best wealth.
IBID.

A little house well filled,
A little land well tilled,
A little wife well willed.
IBID.

A wife that expects to have a good name
Is always at home, as if she were lame.
IBID.

He that loseth his wife and a sixpence hath lost a tester.
IBID. (*Tester*=a sixpence)

It's a good horse that never stumbles,
And a good wife that never grumbles.
IBID.

There is one good wife in the country, and every man thinks he hath her.
IBID.

Good wives and private soldiers should be ignorant.
WILLIAM WYCHERLEY: *The Country Wife*, I, *c.* 1673

Here lies my wife! here let her lie!
Now she's at rest, and so am I.
Ascribed to JOHN DRYDEN, *c.* 1680

'Tis reason a man that will have a wife should be at the charge of her trinkets, and pay all the scores she sets on him. He that will keep a monkey 'tis fit he should pay for the glasses he breaks.
JOHN SELDEN: *Table-Talk*, 1689

That very name of wife and marriage
Is poison to the dearest sweets of love.
JOHN DRYDEN: *Amphitryon*, I, 1690

She is too proud, too inconstant, too affected, too witty and too handsome for a wife.
WILLIAM CONGREVE: *The Old Bachelor*, I, 1693

What rugged ways attend the noon of life!
Our sun declines, and with what anxious strife,
What pain we tug that galling load, a wife!
WILLIAM CONGREVE: *The Old Bachelor*, V

Thy wife is a constellation of virtue; she's the moon, and thou art the man in the moon.
WILLIAM CONGREVE: *Love for Love*, II, 1695

Two years of marriage has debauched my senses. Everything I see, everything I hear, everything I feel, everything I smell, and everything I taste — methinks has wife in't.
JOHN VANBRUGH: *The Provok'd Wife*, I, 1697

The partner of my soul,
My wife, the kindest, dearest, and the truest,
That ever wore the name.
NICHOLAS ROWE: *The Royal Convert*, II, 1707

All other goods by fortune's hand are given:
A wife is the peculiar gift of Heav'n.
ALEXANDER POPE: *January and May*, 1709

To please a wife, when her occasions call,
Would busy the most vigorous of us all.
And trust me, sir, the chastest you can choose,
Will ask observance, and exact her dues.
IBID.

Horses (thou sayst) and asses men may try,
And ring suspected vessels ere they buy;
But wives, a random choice, untried they take;
They dream in courtship, but in wedlock wake.
ALEXANDER POPE: *The Wife of Bath*, 1714

All are good lasses, but where come the ill wives?
JAMES KELLY: *Complete Collection of Scottish Proverbs*, 1721

Many one blames their wife for their own unthrift.
IBID. (Kelly says: "I never saw a Scottish wife who had not this at her fingers' ends")

The man to Jove his suit preferr'd;
He begg'd a wife. His prayer was heard.
Jove wonder'd at his bold addressing:
For how precarious is the blessing!
JOHN GAY: *Fables*, I, 1727

Why is a handsome wife adored
By every coxcomb but her lord?
JONATHAN SWIFT: *Strephon and Chloe*, 1731

A fair wife without a fortune is a fine house without furniture.
THOMAS FULLER: *Gnomologia*, 1732

Choose a wife rather by your ear than your eye. IBID.

He has great need of a wife that marries Mamma's darling. IBID.

He that speaks ill of his wife dishonors himself.
IBID.

The good or ill hap of a good or ill life
Is the good or ill choice of a good or ill wife.
IBID.

The wife is the key of the house. IBID.

You may beat the Devil into your wife, but you'll never bang him out again. IBID.

He that takes a wife takes care.
BENJAMIN FRANKLIN: *Poor Richard's Almanac*, 1736

Three things are men most likely to be cheated in, a horse, a wig, and a wife. IBID.

The world's great Author did create
The sex to fit the nuptial state,
And meant a blessing in a wife
To solace the fatigues of life.
MATTHEW GREEN: *The Spleen*, 1737

A dead wife under the table is the best goods in a man's house.
JONATHAN SWIFT: *Polite Conversation*, I, 1738

Wife, from thy spouse each blemish hide,
More than from all the world beside.
BENJAMIN FRANKLIN: *Poor Richard's Almanac*, 1741

A wife? That is none of the indispensable requisites of life.
DAVID HUME: *Letter to John Clephane*, Jan. 5, 1753

Here lies my wife,
Here lies she;
Hallelujah!
Hallelujee!
Anon.: In Norfolk's Epitaphs, 1761

Nobody knows how to manage a wife but a bachelor.
GEORGE COLMAN THE ELDER: *The Jealous Wife*, IV, 1761

It is not enough that a wife should be faithful: her husband, along with his friends and neighbors, must believe in her fidelity.
J.-J. ROUSSEAU: *Émile*, V, 1762

Have the courage to listen to your wife when you should and not to listen when you should not.
STANISLAUS LESZCYNSKI (KING OF POLAND): *Œuvres du philosophe bienfaisant*, 1763

A wife ought in reality to love her husband above all the world; but this preference I think should, in point of politeness, be concealed. The reason is, that it is disgusting to see an amiable woman monopolized; and it is easy by proper management to waive (all I contend for) the appearance.
WILLIAM SHENSTONE: *Of Men and Manners*, 1764

To take a wife merely as an agreeable and rational companion will commonly be found to be a grand mistake.
LORD CHESTERFIELD: *Letter to his son*, Oct. 12, 1765

Happy the man who has a good wife; he lives twice as long.

J. W. GOETHE: *Goetz von Berlichingen*, I, 1771

The wives of great men are generally excellent wives, and attached to their glory.

HORACE WALPOLE: *Letter to George Hardinge*, July 9, 1777

We poor common people must take wives whom we love and who love us.

W. A. MOZART: *Letter to his father*, Feb. 7, 1778

I want (who does not want?) a wife
Affectionate and fair,
To solace all the woes of life
And all its days to share;
Of temper sweet, of yielding will,
Of firm yet placid mind,
With all my faults to love me still,
With sentiments refined.

JOHN QUINCY ADAMS: *The Wants of Man*, *c.* 1787

I hae a wife o' my ain,
I'll partake wi' naebody;
I'll tak cuckold frae nane,
I'll gie cuckold to naebody.

ROBERT BURNS: *Verses in a letter to James Johnson*, Nov. 15, 1788

Distant praise, from whatever quarter, is not so delightful as that of a wife whom a man loves and esteems.

SAMUEL JOHNSON: *Boswell's Life*, 1791

The scale of good wifeship I divide into ten parts: good nature, four; good sense, two; wit, one; personal charms — namely, a sweet face, eloquent eyes, fine limbs, graceful carriage (I would add a fine waist too, but that is soon spoiled, you know), all these, one; as for the other qualities belonging to or attending on a wife, such as fortune, connections, education, family blood, etc., divide the two remaining degrees among them as you please.

ROBERT BURNS: *Letter to Alexander Cunningham*, Sept. 10, 1792

She is a winsome wee thing,
She is a handsome wee thing,
She is a bonnie wee thing,
This sweet wee wife o' mine.

ROBERT BURNS: *My Wife's a Winsome Wee Thing*, 1792

The rainbow in the storms of life,
The evening beam that smiles the clouds away.

BYRON: *The Bride of Abydos*, I, 1813

He knew whose gentle hand was at the latch
Before the door had given her to his eyes.

JOHN KEATS: *Isabella*, 1820

Think you, if Laura had been Petrarch's wife,
He would have written sonnets all his life?

BYRON: *Don Juan*, III, 1821

Please your taste, my children; and so that you get an honest woman, and a pleasing one, take no care for the remainder.

JOHN GRIGG: *The American Chesterfield*, 1827

The things which you ought to desire in a wife are, 1. chastity; 2. sobriety; 3. industry; 4. frugality; 5. cleanliness; 6. knowledge of domestic affairs; 7. good temper; 8. beauty.

WILLIAM COBBETT: *Advice to Young Men*, III, 1829

A married woman is a slave who demands to be set on a throne.

BALZAC: *The Physiology of Marriage*, 1830

When a man beats his mistress he inflicts a wound; when he beats his wife he commits suicide.

IBID.

Every one wishes a Desdemona or Ophelia for a wife — creatures who, though they may not always understand you, do always feel you, and feel with you.

S. T. COLERIDGE: *Table-Talk*, Sept. 27, 1830

Wives never tolerate an intimacy between their husbands and any old friends, except in two cases: the one, when the old friend was, before the marriage, a friend of both wife and husband; the other, when the friendship is of later date than the marriage.

T. B. MACAULAY: *Letter to T. F. Ellis*, Sept. 15, 1838

He will hold thee, when his passion shall have spent its novel force,
Something better than his dog, a little dearer than his horse.

ALFRED TENNYSON: *Locksley Hall*, 1842

The world well tried — the sweetest thing in life
Is the unclouded welcome of a wife.

N. P. WILLIS: *Lady Jane*, II, 1844

As thro' the land at eve we went,
And pluck'd the ripen'd ears,
We fell out, my wife and I,
Oh, we fell out, I know not why,
And kiss'd again with tears.

ALFRED TENNYSON: *The Princess*, II, 1847

The bourgeois sees in his wife a mere instrument of production.

KARL MARX and FRIEDRICH ENGELS: *The Communist Manifesto*, 1848

Men, dying, make their wills, but wives
Escape a work so sad;
Why should they make what all their lives
The gentle dames have had?

J. G. SAXE: *Woman's Will*, 1849

The first wife is matrimony, the second company, the third heresy.

H. G. BOHN: *Handbook of Proverbs*, 1855

A sweetheart is a bottle of wine; a wife is a wine bottle.

CHARLES BAUDELAIRE (1821–67)

One can, to an almost laughable degree, infer what a man's wife is like from his opinions about women in general.

J. S. MILL: *The Subjection of Women*, I, 1869

Here lies my dear wife, a sad slattern and shrew;
If I said I regretted her, I should lie too.

H. J. LOARING: *Epitaphs Quaint, Curious and Elegant,* 1872

If a man stay away from his wife for seven years, the law presumes the separation to have killed him; yet, according to our daily experience, it might well prolong his life.

C. J. DARLING: *Scintillæ Juris,* 1877

She will tend him, nurse him, mend him,
Air his linen, dry his tears;
Bless the thoughtful fates that send him
Such a wife to soothe his years.

W. S. GILBERT: *The Sorcerer,* I, 1877

Teacher, tender comrade, wife,
A fellow-farer true through life.

R. L. STEVENSON: *My Wife,* 1887

We've been together now for forty years,
An' it don't seem a day too much;
There ain't a lady livin' in the land
As I'd swop for my dear old Dutch.

ALBERT CHEVALIER: *My Old Dutch,* c. 1895

Of all the expensive hobbies the collection of wives is among the most expensive.

JUSTICE HENRY G. WENZEL, JR., of the Supreme Court of New York: *Decision in Boyce* vs. *Boyce,* 1932

If you want peace in the house, do what your wife wants. AFRICAN PROVERB

She sift de meal and gimme de husk,
She bake de bread and gimme de crust,
She fry de meat and gimme de skin,
And den she kick me on de shin.

AMERICAN NEGRO JINGLE

A quiet wife is mighty pretty.

AMERICAN NEGRO SAYING

A wife is one who stands by a man in all the troubles he wouldn't have had if he hadn't married her. Author unidentified

The difference between the wife and the mistress is that the wife makes a better bargain.

IBID.

Other people's wives are always the best.

CHINESE PROVERB

Take a wife for her virtue and a concubine for her beauty. IBID.

When a man's vessel is upset and its masts broken he is poor for a time; but when he marries a bad wife he is poor for life.

IBID.

Choose your wife, not at a dance, but in the harvest-field. CZECH PROVERB

When an old man marries a young wife death laughs. GERMAN PROVERB

A bad wife is like Winter in a house.

GREEK PROVERB

All the blessings of a household come through the wife. HEBREW PROVERB

If thy wife is small, bend down to her and whisper in her ear. IBID.

The wife of a righteous man is righteous herself; the wife of a murderer is as he is.

IBID.

Joking spoils a wife. HINDU PROVERB

Never strike your wife, even with a flower.

IBID.

A mill and a wife are always wanting something. ITALIAN PROVERB

Grief for a dead wife lasts as far as the door.

IBID.

He who lets his wife go to every feast, and his horse drink at every water, shall neither have good wife nor good horse. IBID.

In buying a horse and taking a wife, shut your eyes and throw yourself on the mercy of God.

IBID.

When the wife sins, the husband is not innocent. IBID.

Wise is the young man who is always thinking of taking a wife and never takes one.

IBID.

All married women are not wives.

JAPANESE PROVERB

A wife is never to be trusted, even if she has borne her husband seven children. IBID.

A young wife, in her own house, should be only a shadow and an echo. IBID.

Beat your wife on the wedding day, and your married life will be happy. IBID.

A man is happy only two times in his life: when he marries his wife and when he buries her.

JUGO-SLAVIC PROVERB

A third wife is a glass of poison. IBID.

He who loves his wife should watch her.

MOROCCAN PROVERB

He that goes a great way for a wife is either cheated or means to cheat.

NORWEGIAN PROVERB

A good wife and health
Is man's best wealth. OLD ENGLISH RHYME

The reputation of a man with an ugly wife is always safe. PORTUGUESE PROVERB

Wives and sheep should be brought home before dark. IBID.

When a man takes a wife, he ceases to dread Hell. RUMANIAN PROVERB

A drunken wife is better than an obstinate one.
RUSSIAN PROVERB

A wife is not an instrument that can be hung against the wall when you have played on it.
IBID.

A wife may love a husband who never beats her, but she does not respect him. IBID.

Beat your wife before dinner, and again before supper. IBID.

The third wife is picked by the Devil.
IBID.

The young wife of an old man is neither girl, wife, nor widow. IBID.

Every man can guide an ill wife weel but him that has her. SCOTTISH PROVERB

He that has a wife has a maister. IBID.

He who has a bonny wife needs mair than twa een. IBID. (*Een*=eyes)

He who has a handsome wife, a castle on the frontier, or a vineyard by the roadside, is never without war. SPANISH PROVERB

Seed wheat and wives should not be chosen by candlelight. IBID.

Who hath a wife hath also an enemy. IBID.

A man without a wife is like a man without hands. UKRAINIAN PROVERB

A wife is perfect only twice: when she enters the house after the wedding, and when she is carried out. IBID.

Never praise your wife until you have been married seven years. IBID.

A silent wife is as rare as dry water or wet fire.
WELSH PROVERB

No woman is a wife who is not a mother too.
IBID.

The advice of a wife is worthless, but woe to the man who does not take it. IBID.

The nearer her father's house, the worse the wife. IBID.

Trust your wife with your life, but never with your secret. IBID.

[*See also* Adams (Abigail), Adultery, Bachelor, Best, Blind, Bride, Careless, Family, Flesh, Fruitfulness, Husband, Husband and Wife, Jealousy, Leg, Letter, Little, Maiden, Man and Woman, Marriage, Misfortune, Shrew, Slave, Sorrow, Trust, Virgin, Waiting, Whore.

Wife and Children

He that hath wife and children hath given hostages to fortune, for they are impediments to great enterprises, either of virtue or mischief. FRANCIS BACON: *Essays,* XIV, 1625

He that loves not his wife and children, feeds a lioness at home, and breeds a nest of sorrow.
JEREMY TAYLOR: *Twenty-five Sermons,* 1653

Whoever has a wife and children has given hostages to Mrs. Grundy.
J. S. MILL: *The Subjection of Women,* IV, 1869

The day you marry your wife you marry your children. IRISH PROVERB

[*See also* Children, Wife.

Wife and Mother

Her children arise up and call her blessed; her husband also, and he praiseth her.
PROVERBS XXXI, 28, *c.* 350 B.C.

Helmer — Before all else you are a wife and mother.
Nora — I don't believe that any longer. I think that before all else I am a human being, just as much as you are.
HENRIK IBSEN: *A Doll's House,* III, 1879

[*See also* Mother, Wife.

Wilderness

Oh, for a lodge in some vast wilderness,
Some boundless contiguity of shade,
Where rumor of oppression and deceit,
Of unsuccessful or successful war,
Might never reach me more!
WILLIAM COWPER: *The Task,* 1785

[*See also* Prophet, Retirement, Voice.

Will

Not my will, but thine, be done.
LUKE XXII, 42, *c.* 75

Where there's a will there's a way.
ENGLISH PROVERB, traced to the XVII century

Where the will is ready the feet are light.
GEORGE HERBERT: *Jacula Prudentum,* 1651

There is no power in man greater to effect anything than a will determined to exert its utmost force.
RICHARD CUMBERLAND: *De legibus naturæ,* I, 1672

Let not thy will roar when thy power can but whisper.
THOMAS FULLER: *Introductio ad Prudentiam,* I, 1731

You must take the will for the deed.
JONATHAN SWIFT: *Polite Conversation,* II, 1738

Will without power is like children playing at soldiers. Anon.: *The Rovers,* IV, 1798

The will to do, the soul to dare.
WALTER SCOTT: *The Lady of the Lake,* I, 1810

Will is the master of the world. Those who want something, those who know what they want, even those who want nothing, but want it badly, govern the world.
FERDINAND BRUNETIÈRE: *Questions de critique,* I, 1888

The king wills it. (Le roi le veut.)
Form of assent of the English kings

An act done against my will is not my act. (Actus me invito factus non est meus actus.)
LEGAL MAXIM

The will is taken for the deed. (Voluntas habetur pro facto.) IBID.

[*See also* End, Majority, Majority and Minority, Will (Free).

Will, Free

No one can rob us of our free choice.
EPICTETUS: *Encheiridion,* III, *c.* 110

Not only in works, but also in faith, God has given man freedom of the will.
IRENÆUS: *Adversus hæreses,* IV, *c.* 180

The power of choosing good and evil is within the reach of all.
ORIGEN: *De principiis,* II, *c.* 254

Man is not possessed of free will for good works unless it be assisted by grace, and that special grace which is bestowed on the elect alone.
JOHN CALVIN: *Institutes of the Christian Religion,* II, 1536

Mankind has free will, but it is only to milk kine, to build houses, &c. So long as a man is at ease and in safety, so long he thinks he has free will; but when want and need appear, so that there is neither meat, drink, nor money, where is then free will?
MARTIN LUTHER: *Table-Talk,* CCLXII, 1569

For what I will, I will, and there an end.
SHAKESPEARE: *Two Gentlemen of Verona,* I, *c.* 1595

That our will is free is self-evident.
RENÉ DESCARTES: *Principles of Philosophy,* I, 1644

If a man should talk to me of a round quadrangle, or accidents of bread in cheese, or immaterial substances, or of a free subject, a free will, or any free, but free from being hindered by opposition, I should not say he were in an error, but that his words were without meaning — that is to say, absurd.
THOMAS HOBBES: *Leviathan,* I, 1651

The liberty of man, though subordinate to God's decree, freely willeth the very same thing and no other than that which it would have willed if (upon a supposition of impossibility) there had been no decree.
JOHN NORTON: *The Orthodox Evangelist,* 1654

Will is one of the principal organs of belief, not that it forms belief, but because things are true or false according to the side on which we look at them.
BLAISE PASCAL: *Pensées,* IV, 1670

There is no such thing as free will. The mind is induced to wish this or that by some cause, and that cause is determined by another cause, and so on back to infinity.
BARUCH DE SPINOZA: *Ethica,* II, 1677

Man is a free agent. In respect to truth he is capable of searching after it notwithstanding the difficulty he finds in meditation; and in respect to order, he is able to follow it in spite of all the efforts of concupiscence.
NICOLAS MALEBRANCHE: *Traité de morale,* I, 1684

It is as insignificant to ask whether man's will be free as to ask whether his sleep be swift or his virtue square: liberty is as little applicable to the will as swiftness of motion is to sleep or squareness to virtue.
JOHN LOCKE: *Essay Concerning Human Understanding,* II, 1690

A man on the rack is not at liberty to lay by the idea of pain, and divert himself with other contemplations.
JOHN LOCKE: *Essay Concerning Human Understanding,* XXI

The will is that by which the mind chooses anything.
JONATHAN EDWARDS: *The Freedom of the Will,* I, 1754

We are no more free agents than the queen of clubs when she takes the knave of hearts.
MARY WORTLEY MONTAGU: *Letter to James Steuart,* Jan. 13, 1761

Man is a free agent; were it otherwise, the priests could not damn him.
VOLTAIRE: *Philosophical Dictionary,* 1764

We know our will is free, and there's an end on't.
SAMUEL JOHNSON: *Boswell's Life,* Oct. 10, 1769

All theory is against the freedom of the will; all experience for it.
SAMUEL JOHNSON: *Boswell's Life,* April 15, 1778

The will of a rational being can be his own only if he acts on the idea that it is free, and therefore this idea must, as a practical matter, be ascribed to all rational beings.
IMMANUEL KANT: *Grundlegung zur Metaphysik der Sitten,* III, 1785

In my immediate consciousness I seem to myself to be free, but by meditation upon the whole of nature I discover that freedom is impossible. The former idea must be subordinated to the latter, for it is to be explained only through it.
J. G. FICHTE: *Die Bestimmung des Menschen,* II, 1800

Freedom is a fundamental character of will, as weight is of matter. . . . That which is free is the will. Will without freedom is an empty word.

G. W. F. HEGEL: *Grundlinien der Philosophie des Rechts,* intro., 1820

If we grant freedom to man, there is an end to the omniscience of God; for if the Divinity knows how I shall act, I must act so perforce.

J. W. GOETHE: *Conversations with Eckermann,* June 11, 1825

Everywhere the human soul stands between a hemisphere of light and another of darkness; on the confines of two everlasting hostile empires, necessity and free will.

THOMAS CARLYLE: *Goethe,* 1828 (Foreign Review, July)

Our wills are ours, we know not how.

ALFRED TENNYSON: *In Memoriam,* intro., 1850

It may be true that we can act as we choose, but can we *choose?* Is not our choice determined for us?

J. A. FROUDE: *Spinoza,* 1855 (Westminster Review)

To hazard the contradiction — freedom is necessary.

R. W. EMERSON: *The Conduct of Life,* I, 1860

What is called freedom of the will is essentially the feeling of supremacy over him who must obey. I am free. He must obey. This consciousness is inherent in every exercise of will.

F. W. NIETZSCHE: *Beyond Good and Evil,* 1886

The abrupt intervention of the will is a kind of *coup d'état* which our mind foresees and which it tries to legitimate beforehand by a formal deliberation.

HENRY BERGSON: *Time and Free Will,* III, 1889

Free will is an egregious theological trick for making mankind "responsible" in the theological sense — which is to say, responsible to theologians.

F. W. NIETZSCHE: *The Twilight of the Idols,* 1889

The question of free will is insoluble on strictly psychologic grounds.

WILLIAM JAMES: *Psychology, Briefer Course,* XXVI, 1892

The human will has no more freedom than that of the higher animals, from which it differs only in degree, not in kind.

ERNST HAECKEL: *The Riddle of the Universe,* VII, 1899

The belief in the freedom of the will is inconsistent with the truth of evolution. Modern physiology shows clearly that the will is never really free in man or animal, but determined by the organization of the brain; and that this in turn acquires its individual character by the laws of heredity and the influence of environment.

ERNST HAECKEL: *Der Kampf um den Entwickelungsgedanken,* III, 1905

"There's no free will," says the philosopher; "to hang is most unjust."
"There is no free will," assents the officer; "we hang because we must."

AMBROSE BIERCE: *Collected Works,* VIII, 1911

The freedom of the ego here and now, and its independence of the causal chain, is a truth that comes from the immediate dictate of the human consciousness.

MAX PLANCK: *Where Is Science Going?,* V, 1932

The will cannot be compelled. (Voluntas non potest cogi.)

LATIN PROVERB

[*See also* Cause and Effect, Determinism, Evolution, Insanity, Volition.

Will, Good

[*See* Good-will.

William the Conqueror (1027–87)

[*See* Gentleman.

Willing

Barkis is willin'.

CHARLES DICKENS: *David Copperfield,* I, 1849

The willing ewe is sucked by every lamb.

FRENCH PROVERB

Whatever is borne willingly is borne easily. (Portatur leviter quod portat quisque libenter.)

LATIN PROVERB

No injury can be done to one who is willing. (Volenti non fit injuria.)

LEGAL MAXIM

A willing mind maks a light foot.

SCOTTISH PROVERB

Will, Last

[*See* Testament.

Willow

We hanged our harps upon the willows.

PSALMS CXXXVII, 2, *c.* 150 B.C.

The willow does not need a brush to paint the wind.

SARYU: *The Willow, c.* 1700

Like a sorrowful woman, standing there
With dropping garments and drifting hair.

ELIZABETH CHASE (AKERS ALLEN): *Rothermel's Widow,* 1866

Will to Power

[*See* Power.

Wilson, Woodrow (1856–1924)

Wilson is a very adroit and able (but not forceful) hypocrite.
THEODORE ROOSEVELT: *Letter to Anna Roosevelt Cowles,* Feb. 3, 1916

He has made our statesmanship a thing of empty elocution. He has covered his fear of standing for the right behind a veil of rhetorical phrases. He has wrapped the true heart of the nation in a spangled shroud of rhetoric.
THEODORE ROOSEVELT: Speech in Cooper Union, New York, Nov. 2, 1916

He is the most perfect example we have produced of the culture which has failed and is dying out.
LINCOLN STEFFENS: *Letter to Allen H. Suggett,* June 28, 1919

It was harder to de-bamboozle this old Presbyterian than it had been to bamboozle him, for the former involved his belief in and respect for himself.
JOHN MAYNARD KEYNES: *The Economic Consequences of the Peace,* III, 1920

Wind

The wind goeth toward the south, and turneth about unto the north; it whirleth about continually, and the wind returneth again according to the circuits.
ECCLESIASTES I, 6, *c.* 200 B.C.

The wings of the wind.
PSALMS XVIII, 10, *c.* 150 B.C.

The wind passeth over it, and it is gone; and the place thereof shall know it no more.
PSALMS CIII, 16

The wind bloweth where it listeth.
JOHN III, 8, *c.* 115

It's an ill wind that blows nobody good.
ENGLISH PROVERB, traced by Apperson to *c.* 1540

After wind cometh rain.
EDWARD HALLE: *The Union of the Families of Lancaster and York,* 1542 (Cited as " the old proverb ")

Blow, wind, and crack your cheeks! Rage! Blow!
SHAKESPEARE: *King Lear,* III, 1606

A little wind kindles, much puts out the fire.
GEORGE HERBERT: *Jacula Prudentum,* 1651

The learned Æolists maintain the original cause of all things to be wind, from which principle this whole universe was at first produced, and into which it must at last be resolved; that the same breath which had kindled, and blown up the flame of nature, should one day blow it out.
JONATHAN SWIFT: *A Tale of a Tub,* VIII, 1704

No weather's ill,
If the wind be still.
THOMAS FULLER: *Gnomologia,* 1732

Sail, quoth the king; Hold, saith the wind.
IBID.

If wind blows on you through a hole,
Make your will and take care of your soul.
BENJAMIN FRANKLIN: *Poor Richard's Almanac,* 1736

The stormy winds do blow.
THOMAS CAMPBELL: *Ye Mariners of England,* 1801

The wind which turns our mills, and even the heat of the sun, work for us; but happily no one has yet been able to say, the " wind and the sun are mine, and the service which they render must be paid for."
J. B. SAY: *Traité d'économique politique,* II, 1803

A wind arose among the pines; it shook
The clinging music from their boughs, and then
Low, sweet, faint sounds, like the farewell of ghosts,
Were heard: Oh, follow, follow, follow me.
P. B. SHELLEY: *Prometheus Unbound,* II, 1820

A wet sheet and a flowing sea,
  A wind that follows fast,
And fills the white and rustling sail,
  And bends the gallant mast.
ALLAN CUNNINGHAM: *A Wet Sheet and a Flowing Sea,* 1825

Through woods and mountain passes
The winds like anthems roll.
H. W. LONGFELLOW: *Midnight Mass for the Dying Year,* 1839

When descends on the Atlantic
  The gigantic
Storm-wind of the equinox,
Landward in his wrath he scourges
  The toiling surges,
Laden with seaweed from the rocks.
H. W. LONGFELLOW: *Seaweed,* 1844

And wind, that grand old harper, smote
His thunder harp of pines.
ALEXANDER SMITH: *A Life Drama,* 1853

O wind, a-blowing all day long,
O wind, that sings so loud a song!
R. L. STEVENSON: *The Wind,* 1885

The Devil sends the wicked wind
  To blow our skirts knee-high,
But God is just and sends the dust
  To blind the bad man's eye.
Author unidentified, *c.* 1895

A gale of wind makes the sea look old.
JOSEPH CONRAD: *The Mirror of the Sea,* VIII, 1906

Wind in the face makes a man wise.
FRENCH PROVERB

Blow, wind, blow! and go, mill, go!
  That the miller may grind his corn;

That the baker may take it and into rolls make it,
And send us some hot in the morn.
OLD ENGLISH RHYME

If the wind were always Southwest by West women might take ships to sea.
SAILORS' PROVERB

If it were not for the wind spider-webs would cover the sky. SERBIAN PROVERB

[*See also* Change, Danger, King, Lamb, Moon, Ship, Storm, Straw, Tree, Whirlwind.

Wind, East

When the wind is in the East,
It's good for neither man nor beast.
THOMAS FULLER: *Gnomologia,* 1732

I am always conscious of an uncomfortable sensation when the wind is blowing in the East.
CHARLES DICKENS: *Bleak House,* VI, 1853

The only argument available with an East wind is to put on your overcoat.
J. R. LOWELL: *Democracy,* 1884 (Address in Birmingham, England, Oct. 6)

Wind, North

When the wind is in the North,
The skilful fisher goes not forth.
THOMAS FULLER: *Gnomologia,* 1732

The North wind doth blow
And we shall have snow,
And what will the robin do then, poor thing?
Anon.: *Nursery rhyme, c.* 1750

[*See also* Fire, Fireplace.

Window

Storied windows richly dight,
Casting a dim religious light.
JOHN MILTON: *Il Penseroso,* 1632

A woman at a window is as grapes on the highway.
GIOVANNI TORRIANO: *Italian Proverbs,* 1666

Windpipe

[*See* Eating.

Wind, South

I am but mad North-north-west; when the wind is southerly, I know a hawk from a handsaw.
SHAKESPEARE: *Hamlet,* II, *c.* 1601

When the wind is in the South
It's in the rain's mouth.
THOMAS FULLER: *Gnomologia,* 1732

When the wind's in the South,
It blows the bait into the fishes' mouth.
OLD ENGLISH RHYME

Wind, West

When the wind's in the West
The weather's at the best.
THOMAS FULLER: *Gnomologia,* 1732

O wild West wind, thou breath of Autumn's being,
Thou, from whose unseen presence the leaves dead
Are driven like ghosts from an enchanter fleeing,
Yellow, and black, and pale, and hectic red.
P. B. SHELLEY: *Ode to the West Wind,* 1819

Sweet and low, sweet and low,
Wind of the western sea,
Low, low, breathe and blow,
Wind of the western sea!
ALFRED TENNYSON: *The Princess,* II, 1847

Wind, Winter

The Winter wind tosses women's hair from side to side, makes them close their eyes, blows their garments hither and thither, thrills their bodies, embraces them, makes them utter low sounds of fear and delight, and kisses their lips; and in doing all this it acts with the charm of a lover.
BHARTRIHARI: *The Sringa Sataka, c.* 625

Blow, blow, thou Winter wind!
Thou art not so unkind
As man's ingratitude.
SHAKESPEARE: *As You Like It,* II, *c.* 1600

Perhaps the wind
Wails so in Winter for the Summer's dead,
And all sad sounds are nature's funeral cries
For what has been and is not.
MARIAN EVANS (GEORGE ELIOT): *The Spanish Gypsy,* I, 1868

Wine

Wine gives strength to weary men.
HOMER: *Iliad,* VI, *c.* 800 B.C.

Wine leads to folly. It makes even the wisest laugh too much. It makes him dance. It makes him say what should have been left unsaid. HOMER: *Odyssey,* XIV, *c.* 800 B.C.

Noah began to be an husbandman, and he planted a vineyard: and he drank of the wine, and was drunken.
GENESIS IX, 20–21, *c.* 700 B.C.

The blood of grapes.
GENESIS XLIX, 11 (Cf. DEUTERONOMY XXXII, 14, *c.* 650 B.C.)

There is a crying for wine in the streets; all joy is darkened, the mirth of the land is gone.
ISAIAH XXIV, 11, *c.* 700 B.C.

Ho, every one that thirsteth, come ye to the waters, and he that hath no money; come ye, buy, and eat; yea, come, buy wine and milk without money and without price.
ISAIAH LV, 1

Do not drink wine nor strong drink, thou, nor thy sons with thee, when ye go into the tabernacle of the congregation, lest ye die.
LEVITICUS X, 9, *c.* 700 B.C.

In the holy place shalt thou cause the strong wine to be poured unto the Lord for a drink offering. NUMBERS XXVIII, 7, *c.* 700 B.C.

I set before the sons of the house of the Rechabites pots full of wine, and cups; and I said unto them, Drink ye wine.
JEREMIAH XXXV, 5, *c.* 625 B.C.

All the Jews returned out of all places whither they were driven, and came to the land of Judah, to Gedaliah, unto Mizpah, and gathered wine and summer fruits very much.
JEREMIAH XLIX, 12

Corn shall make the young men cheerful, and new wine the maids.
ZECHARIAH IX, 17, *c.* 520 B.C.

When I take wine my cares go to rest.
ANACREON: *Fragment, c.* 500 B.C.

Wine . . . cheereth God and man.
JUDGES IX, 13, *c.* 500 B.C.

The asses be for the king's household to ride on; and the bread and summer fruit for the young men to eat; and the wine, that such as be faint in the wilderness may drink.
II SAMUEL XVI, 2, *c.* 500 B.C.

When men drink wine they are rich, they are busy, they push lawsuits, they are happy, they help their friends.
ARISTOPHANES: *The Knights,* 424 B.C.

Where there is no wine, love perishes, and everything else that is pleasant to man.
EURIPIDES: *The Bacchæ, c.* 410

I like best the wine drunk at the cost of others.
Ascribed to DIOGENES THE CYNIC, *c.* 380 B.C.

Boys should abstain from all use of wine until their eighteenth year, for it is wrong to add fire to fire. PLATO: *Laws,* II, *c.* 360 B.C.

Wine is a remedy for the moroseness of old age.
IBID.

Wine is a mocker, strong drink is raging: and whosoever is deceived thereby is not wise.
PROVERBS XX, 1, *c.* 350 B.C.

Who hath woe? who hath sorrow? who hath contentions? who hath babbling? who hath wounds without cause? who hath redness of eyes? They that tarry long at the wine; they that go to seek mixed wine.
PROVERBS XXIII, 29–30

Look not upon the wine when it is red, when it giveth his color in the cup, when it moveth itself aright. At the last it biteth like a serpent, and stingeth like an adder. Thine eyes shall behold strange women, and thine heart shall utter perverse things.
PROVERBS XXIII, 31–33

Give strong drink unto him that is ready to perish, and wine unto those that be of heavy hearts. Let him drink, and forget his poverty, and remember his misery no more.
PROVERBS XXXI, 6–7

Howl, all ye drinkers of wine.
JOEL I, 5, *c.* 350 B.C.

Wine maketh merry.
ECCLESIASTES X, 19, *c.* 200 B.C.

I have drunk my wine with my milk; eat, O friends; drink, yes, drink abundantly O beloved. SOLOMON'S SONG V, 1, *c.* 200 B.C.

The best wine . . . goeth down sweetly, causing the lips of those that are asleep to speak.
SOLOMON'S SONG VII, 9

The great evil in wine is that it first seizes the feet; it is a crafty wrestler.
PLAUTUS: *Pseudolus,* V, *c.* 190 B.C.

Wine drunken with moderation is the joy of the soul and the heart.
ECCLESIASTICUS XXXI, 36, *c.* 180 B.C.

Wine . . . maketh glad the heart of men.
PSALMS CIV, 15, *c.* 150 B.C.

Who prates of war or want after taking wine?
HORACE: *Carmina,* I, *c.* 20 B.C.

Wine is mighty to inspire new hopes and wash away the bitters of care.
HORACE: *Carmina,* IV, *c.* 13 B.C.

Wine brings to light the hidden secrets of the soul, gives being to our hopes, bids the coward fight, drives dull care away, and teaches new means for the accomplishment of our wishes. HORACE: *Epistles,* I, *c.* 5 B.C.

Wine kindles wrath. (Vinum incendit iram.)
SENECA: *De Ira, c.* 43

It is good neither to eat flesh, nor to drink wine, nor anything whereby thy brother stumbleth, or is offended, or is made weak.
ROMANS XIV, 21, *c.* 55

Drink no longer water, but use a little wine for thy stomach's sake and thine often infirmities. I TIMOTHY V, 23, *c.* 60

Nothing gathers foreign smells to itself quicker than wine.
COLUMELLA: *De re rustica, c.* 70

No man having drunk old wine straightway desireth new: for he saith, The old is better.
LUKE V, 39, *c.* 75

In wine there is truth. (In vino veritas.)
PLINY THE ELDER: *Natural History,* XIV, *c.* 79 (Cited as "a common proverb")

A person warmed with wine will never either teach, or be convinced by, one who is sober.
EPICTETUS: *Encheiridion, c.* 110

Every man at the beginning doth set forth good wine; and when men have well drunk, then that which is worse. JOHN II, 10 *c.* 115

Toward evening, about supper-time, when the serious studies of the day are over, is the time to take wine.
CLEMENT OF ALEXANDRIA: *Paedagogus*, II, *c.* 190

When the wine goes in the murder comes out.
THE TALMUD (*Erubin*), *c.* 200

The Scythians are the only people who drink wine without mixing any water with it.
CLAUDIUS AELIANUS: *Varia historia*, *c.* 220

Wine was given us of God, not that we might be drunken, but that we might be sober; that we might be glad, not that we get ourselves pain.
ST. JOHN CHRYSOSTOM: *Homilies*, I, *c.* 388

I hear many cry when deplorable excesses happen, " Would there were no wine! " Oh, folly! oh, madness! Is it the wine that causes this abuse? No. It is the intemperance of those who take an evil delight in it. Cry rather: " Would to God there were no drunkenness, no luxury." If you say, " Would there were no wine " because of the drunkards, then you must say, going on by degrees, " Would there were no steel," because of the murderers, " Would there were no night," because of the thieves, " Would there were no light," because of the informers, and " Would there were no women," because of adultery.
ST. JOHN CHRYSOSTOM: *Homilies*, I

Wine is the first weapon that devils use in attacking the young.
ST. JEROME: *The Virgin's Profession*, *c.* 420

There is not a corner nor burrow in all my body where this wine doth not ferret out my thirst.
RABELAIS: *Gargantua*, I, 1535

Drink wine, and have the gout;
Drink none, and have the gout.
JOHN COGAN: *The Haven of Health*, 1584

Water and wine is good against the heat of the liver.
ROBERT GREENE: *A Quip for an Upstart Courtier*, 1592

Give me a bowl of wine:
I have not that alacrity of spirit,
Nor cheer of mind, that I was wont to have.
SHAKESPEARE: *Richard III*, V, *c.* 1592

Let my liver rather heat with wine
Than my heart cool with mortifying groans.
SHAKESPEARE: *The Merchant of Venice*, I, *c.* 1597

Give me a bowl of wine;
In this I bury all unkindness.
SHAKESPEARE: *Julius Cæsar*, IV, 1599

Good wine needs no bush.
SHAKESPEARE: *As You Like It*, epilogue, *c.* 1600 (A proverb borrowed from the Latin and first recorded in an English form in 1539)

Good wine is a good familiar creature, if it be well used; exclaim no more against it.
SHAKESPEARE: *Othello*, II, 1604

O thou invisible spirit of wine, if thou hast no name to be known by, let us call thee Devil!
IBID.

Five qualities there are wine's praise advancing:
Strong, beautiful, fragrant, cool, and dancing.
JOHN HARINGTON: *The Englishman's Doctor*, 1608

I'll arm and fortify with lusty wine,
'Gainst shame and blushing.
JOHN WEBSTER: *The White Devil*, I, *c.* 1608

Wine works the heart up, wakes the wit;
There is no cure 'gainst age but it;
It helps the headache, cough and phthisic,
And is for all diseases physic.
JOHN FLETCHER and BEN JONSON: *The Bloody Brother*, *c.* 1616

Wine . . . is a great increaser of the vital spirits: it very greatly comforteth a weak stomack, helpeth concoction, distribution and nutrition, mightily strengtheneth the natural heat, openeth obstruction, discusseth windiness, taketh away sadness, and other hurt of melancholy.
TOBIAS VENNER: *Via recta*, 1620

Wine, the cheerer of the heart
And lively refresher of the countenance.
THOMAS MIDDLETON and WILLIAM ROWLEY: *The Changeling*, I, *c.* 1623

If God forbade drinking would He have made wine so good?
ARMAND CARDINAL RICHELIEU: *Mirame*, *c.* 1625

The modest nymph [i.e., water] saw its God and blushed. (Nympha pudica Deum vidit, et erubuit.)
RICHARD CRASHAW: *Epigrammatum Sacrorum*, 1634 (On the miracle at Cana)

The sweet poison of misused wine.
JOHN MILTON: *Comus*, 1637

Wine makes old wives wenches.
JOHN CLARKE: *Parœmiologia Anglo-Latina*, 1639

When thirsty grief in wine we steep,
When healths and draughts go free,
Fishes that tipple in the deep
Know no such liberty.
RICHARD LOVELACE: *To Althea from Prison*, 1642

Wine fills the veins, and healths are understood
To give our friends a title to our blood;
Who, naming me, doth warm his courage so,
Shows for my sake what his bold hand would do.
EDMUND WALLER: *For Drinking of Healths*, 1645

O thou the drink of gods, and angels! Wine!
ROBERT HERRICK: *Hesperides,* 1648

Finding my head grow weak now-a-days, if I come to drink wine, and therefore hope that I shall leave it off of myself which I pray God I could do.
SAMUEL PEPYS: *Diary,* May 14, 1661

A friend and a bottle is all my design;
He has no room for treason that's top-full of wine.
JOHN OLDHAM: *The Careless Good Fellow,* 1683

Wine whets the wit, improves its native force,
And gives a pleasant flavor to discourse.
JOHN POMFRET: *The Choice,* I, 1700

Aristotle, that master of arts,
Had been but a dunce without wine,
And what we ascribe to his parts
Is but due to the juice of the vine.
Anon.: *Wine and Wisdom,* 1710

By wine we are generous made;
It furnishes fancy with wings;
Without it we ne'er should have had
Philosophers, poets or kings. IBID.

Generous wines do every day prevail, and that in great points, where ten thousand times their value would have been rejected with indignation.
RICHARD STEELE: *The Spectator,* June 2, 1712

Wine lets no lover unrewarded go.
ALEXANDER POPE: *The Wife of Bath,* 1714

Inflaming wine, pernicious to mankind,
Unnerves the limbs, and dulls the noble mind.
ALEXANDER POPE: Tr. of HOMER: *Iliad,* VI (*c.* 800 B.C.), 1717

Wine can of their wits the wise beguile,
Make the sage frolic, and the serious smile.
ALEXANDER POPE: Tr. of HOMER: *Odyssey,* XIV, 1726 (Cf. HOMER, *ante, c.* 800 B.C.)

Wine can clear
The vapors of despair,
And make us light as air.
JOHN GAY: *The Beggar's Opera,* III, 1728

When the wine is in the wit is out.
THOMAS FULLER: *Gnomologia,* 1732

Wine hath drowned more men than the sea. IBID.

Wine is a turn-coat; first a friend, and then an enemy. IBID.

Wine turns a man inside outwards. IBID.

Take counsel in wine, but resolve afterwards in water.
BENJAMIN FRANKLIN: *Poor Richard's Almanac,* 1733

From wine what sudden friendship springs!
JOHN GAY: *Fables,* II, 1738

Wine rejoices the heart of man, and joy is the mother of all virtue.
J. W. GOETHE: *Goetz von Berlichingen,* I, 1771

Wine . . . is one of the noblest cordials in nature.
JOHN WESLEY: *Journal,* Sept. 9, 1771

What man can pretend to be a believer in love, who is an abjurer of wine?
R. B. SHERIDAN: *The School for Scandal,* III, 1777

Wine gives great pleasure, and every pleasure is of itself a good.
SAMUEL JOHNSON: *Boswell's Life,* April 28, 1778

Wine gives a man nothing. It neither gives him knowledge nor wit; it only animates a man, and enables him to bring out what a dread of the company has repressed. This is one of the disadvantages of wine: it makes a man mistake words for thoughts. IBID.

In certain studies there is no harm in doing one's thinking and writing while slightly drunk, and then revising one's work in cold blood. The stimulus of wine is favorable to the play of invention, and to fluency of expression.
G. C. LICHTENBERG: *Reflections,* 1799

Wine invents nothing; it only tattles.
J. C. F. SCHILLER: *The Piccolomini,* IV, 1799

Wine, like the rising sun, possession gains,
And drives the mist of dullness from the brains;
The gloomy vapor from the spirit flies,
And views of gaiety and gladness rise.
GEORGE CRABBE: *The Borough,* X, 1810

No nation is drunken where wine is cheap; and none sober where the dearness of wine substitutes ardent spirits as the common beverage. It is, in truth, the only antidote to the bane of whiskey.
THOMAS JEFFERSON: *Letter to M. de Neuville,* Dec. 12, 1818

Oh, for a beaker full of the warm South,
Full of the true, the blushful Hippocrene,
With beaded bubbles winking at the brim.
JOHN KEATS: *Ode to a Nightingale,* 1819

Fan the sinking flame of hilarity with the wing of friendship; and pass the rosy wine.
CHARLES DICKENS: *The Old Curiosity Shop,* VII, 1841

A man will be eloquent if you give him good wine.
R. W. EMERSON: *Representative Men,* IV, 1850

Give me wine to wash me clean
Of the weather-stains of cares.
R. W. EMERSON: *From the Persian of Hafiz,* 1851

Drink wine in Winter for cold, and in Summer for heat.
H. G. BOHN: *Handbook of Proverbs,* 1855

I wonder often what the vintners buy
One-half so precious as the stuff they sell.
EDWARD FITZGERALD: Tr. of OMAR KHAYYÁM: *Rubáiyát* (*c.* 1100), 1857

The grape that can with logic absolute
The two-and-seventy jarring sects confute;
The sovereign alchemist that in a trice
Life's leaden metal into gold transmute.
IBID.

You know, my friends, with what a brave carouse
I made a second marriage in my house;
Divorced old barren reason from my bed,
And took the daughter of the vine to spouse.
IBID.

Here, clad in burning robes, are laid
Life's blossomed joys, untimely shed,
And here those cherished forms have strayed
We miss awhile, and call them dead.
What wizard fills the wondrous glass?
What soil the enchanted clusters grew?
That buried passions wake and pass
In beaded drops of fiery dew?
O. W. HOLMES: *Mare Rubrum,* 1858

Wine . . . is a food.
O. W. HOLMES: Address to the Massachusetts Medical Society, Boston, May 30, 1860

In the judgment of the House of Bishops the use of the unfermented juice of the grape, as the lawful and proper wine of the Holy Eucharist, is unwarranted by the example of our Lord, and an unauthorized departure from the custom of the Catholic Church.
Resolution of the House of Bishops of the Protestant Episcopal Church, Chicago, Oct. 26, 1886

Wine is the most healthful and most hygienic of beverages. LOUIS PASTEUR (1822–95)

God made man, frail as a bubble;
Man made love — love made trouble.
God made the vine —
Then is it a sin
That man made wine
To drown trouble in? Author unidentified

Nothing can match the joy of the wine-drinker save the joy of the wine in being drunk.
IBID.

Burgundy for kings, champagne for duchesses, and claret for gentlemen.
FRENCH PROVERB

Wine on milk is good; milk on wine is poison.
IBID.

Wine wears no breeches. IBID.

If the housewife is beautiful, the wine is good.
GERMAN PROVERB

After melon, wine is a felon.
ITALIAN PROVERB

One barrel of wine can work more miracles than a church full of saints. IBID.

The sword kills many, but wine more. IBID.

Wine and youth are fire upon fire. IBID.

At the first cup man drinks wine, at the second wine drinks wine, at the third wine drinks man. JAPANESE PROVERB

Metal is tested by fire; men by wine. IBID.

Nothing is more unhealthful than too much wine. (Nihil est sanitati multo vino nocentius.) LATIN PROVERB

Drink wine, and you will sleep well. Sleep, and you will not sin. Avoid sin, and you will be saved. *Ergo,* drink wine and be saved.
MEDIEVAL GERMAN SAYING

Old men's milk. (Lac senum.)
MEDIEVAL LATIN PHRASE

Drink a glass of wine after your soup, and you steal a rouble from the doctor.
RUSSIAN PROVERB

When wine sinks, words soom.
SCOTTISH PROVERB (*Soom*=swim)

Wine softens a hard bed. SPANISH PROVERB

Wine has two defects: if you add water to it, you ruin it; if you do not add water, it ruins you. IBID.

[*See also* Abbot, Ale, Beer, Best, Bottle, Brandy, Champagne, Cocktail, Drinking, Drunkard, Drunkenness, Fish, French, Honey, Meat, Milk, Old and New, Poet, Pork, Prohibition, Relatives, Soldier, Sun, Talk, Vinegar, Vodka.

Winebibber

Be not among winebibbers; among riotous eaters of flesh.
PROVERBS XXIII, 20, *c.* 350 B.C.

The Son of Man came eating and drinking, and they say, Behold, a man gluttonous, and a winebibber, a friend of publicans and sinners.
MATTHEW XI, 19, *c.* 75 (Cf. LUKE VII, 34, *c.* 75)

There are more old wine-drinkers than old doctors. GERMAN PROVERB

Wine, Burgundy

The milk of Burgundy.
SHAKESPEARE: *King Lear,* I, 1606

Burgundy tastes of cooked grapes.
BORDELAIS PROVERB

Wine, Champagne

[*See* Champagne.

Wine, Claret

Give poets claret, they grow idle soon.
GEORGE CRABBE: *The Newspaper*, 1785

[*See also* Brandy.

Wine, Port

Port speaks the sentences of wisdom.
GEORGE MEREDITH: *The Egoist*, XX, 1879

In a village in the country,
There her parents now do live,
Drinking port wine that she sends them,
But they never can forgive.
Anon.: *She Was Poor But She Was Honest* (Sung by British soldiers, 1914–18)

All wine would be Port if it could.
PORTUGUESE PROVERB

[*See also* Blackstone (William), Brandy.

Wine, Rhine

In Spain, that land of monks and apes,
The thing called wine doth come from grapes;
But on the noble river Rhine
The thing called gripes doth come from wine.
S. T. COLERIDGE: *Impromptu*, *c.* 1825 (In J. C. YOUNG: *A Memoir of Charles Mayne Young*, 1871)

The Rhine's breastmilk, gushing cold and bright,
Pale as the moon, and maddening as her light.
Author unidentified

Rhine wine, fine wine. GERMAN PROVERB

[*See also* Rhine.

Wine-seller

If outlaws hatch a conspiracy in the house of a wine-seller, and she do not arrest them and bring them to the palace, she shall be put to death.
THE CODE OF HAMMURABI, *c.* 2250 B.C.

[*See also* Wine.

Wine, Sherry

If I had a thousand sons the first human principle I would teach them should be to forswear thin potations and to addict themselves to sack.
SHAKESPEARE: *II Henry IV*, IV, *c.* 1598 (*Sack*=sherry)

Old sack is our money; old sack is our wealth.
THOMAS RANDOLPH: *Poems*, 1638

Wine, Women (and Song)

Whoredom and wine and new wine take away the heart. HOSEA IV, 11, *c.* 740 B.C.

Wine and women will make men of understanding to fall away.
ECCLESIASTICUS XIX, 2, *c.* 180 B.C.

Women, wine and dice
Will bring a man to lice.
JOHN FLORIO: *Second Frutes*, 1591

Those two main plagues and common dotages of human kind, wine and women, have infatuated and besotted myriads of people. They go commonly together.
ROBERT BURTON: *The Anatomy of Melancholy*, I, 1621

Gaming, women and wine,
While they laugh they make men pine.
GEORGE HERBERT: *Outlandish Proverbs*, 1640

Play, women and wine undo men laughing.
JOHN RAY: *English Proverbs*, 1670

Wine and wenches empty men's purses.
IBID.

Women and wine, game and deceit
Make the wealth small and the wants great.
THOMAS FULLER: *Gnomologia*, 1732

Who loves not wine, women and song,
Remains a fool his whole life long.
(Wer nicht liebt Wein, Weib und Gesang
Bleibt ein Narr sein Lebenlang.)
Commonly ascribed to MARTIN LUTHER (1483–1546), but not to be found in his writings (Büchmann says that its probable author was J. H. VOSS (1751–1826), who printed it in the Musenalmanack, Hamburg, in 1777, under the title of "Gesundheit" and with the signature, "Dr. M. Luther")

Did you ever hear of Captain Wattle?
He was all for love and a little for the bottle.
CHARLES DIBDIN: *Captain Wattle and Miss Roe*, *c.* 1790

Plenty moee-moee (sleep) — plenty ki-ki (eat) — plenty whihenee (young girls).
HERMAN MELVILLE: *Typee*, XXXII, 1846

I believe in women, wine, whiskey, and war.
J. A. MCDOUGALL: Speech in the Senate, Feb., 1861

Play, wine and women consume a man laughing. ITALIAN PROVERB

[*See also* Katzenjammer, King Cole.

Wing

[*See* Bird.

Wink

He that winketh with the eye causeth sorrow.
PROVERBS X, 10, *c.* 350 B.C.

He winketh with the one eye and looketh with the other:
I will not trust him though he were my brother.
JOHN HEYWOOD: *Proverbs*, 1546

When most I wink, then do my eyes best see.
SHAKESPEARE: *Sonnets*, XLIII, 1609

He sees most that seems to wink.
WILLIAM WYCHERLEY: *The Gentleman Dancing Master*, V, 1671

There's a time to wink as well as to see.
BENJAMIN FRANKLIN: *Poor Richard's Almanac*, 1747

Winner

[*See* Victory.

Winter

From Winter, plague, and pestilence, good Lord, deliver us!
THOMAS NASHE: *Autumn*, c. 1590

Winter tames man, woman and beast.
SHAKESPEARE: *The Taming of the Shrew*, IV, 1594

The rawish dank of clumsy Winter ramps
The fluent Summer's vein; and drizzling sleet
Chilleth the wan bleak cheek of the numb'd earth,
While snarling gusts nibble the juiceless leaves
From the nak'd shuddering branch.
JOHN MARSTON: *Antonio's Revenge*, prologue, 1602

A sad tale's best for Winter.
SHAKESPEARE: *The Winter's Tale*, III, c. 1611

Every mile is two in Winter.
GEORGE HERBERT: *Outlandish Proverbs*, 1640

He that passeth a Winter's day escapes an enemy.
IBID.

A green Winter makes a fat churchyard.
JOHN RAY: *English Proverbs*, 1670

Cruel as death, and hungry as the grave.
JAMES THOMSON: *The Seasons*, I, 1726

The nakedness and asperity of the wintry world always fill the beholder with pensive and profound astonishment.
SAMUEL JOHNSON: *The Rambler*, Dec. 22, 1750

Winter lingering chills the lap of May.
OLIVER GOLDSMITH: *The Traveler*, 1764

I crown thee king of intimate delights,
Fireside enjoyments, home-born happiness,
And all the comforts that the lowly roof
Of undisturb'd retirement, and the hours
Of long uninterrupted evening know.
WILLIAM COWPER: *The Task*, IV, 1785

Come, Winter, with thine angry howl,
And raging bend the naked tree:
Thy gloom will soothe my cheerless soul,
When nature all is sad like me.
ROBERT BURNS: *Song*, 1786

If Winter comes, can Spring be far behind?
P. B. SHELLEY: *Ode to the West Wind*, 1819

Pictures of Winter scenery are nearly as common as moonlights, and are usually executed by the same order of artists, that is to say, the most incapable.
JOHN RUSKIN: *Modern Painters*, II, 1846

Every Winter,
When the great sun has turned his face away,
The earth goes down into a vale of grief,
And fasts, and weeps, and shrouds herself in sables.
CHARLES KINGSLEY: *The Saint's Tragedy*, III, 1848

In Winter, when the dismal rain
Came down in slanting lines,
And wind, that grand old harper, smote
His thunder-harp of pines.
ALEXANDER SMITH: *A Life Drama*, 1853

Oh, the long and dreary Winter!
Oh, the cold and cruel Winter!
H. W. LONGFELLOW: *Hiawatha*, XX, 1855

Winter either bites with its teeth or lashes with its tail.
MONTENEGRIN PROVERB

[*See also* One, Seasons, Snow.

Wisdom

Happy is the man that findeth wisdom, and the man that getteth understanding.
PROVERBS III, 13, c. 350 B.C.

Her ways are ways of pleasantness, and all her paths are peace.
PROVERBS III, 17

Wisdom is the principal thing; therefore get wisdom; and with all thy getting get understanding.
PROVERBS IV, 7

The price of wisdom is above rubies.
JOB XXVIII, 18, c. 325 B.C.

In much wisdom is much grief.
ECCLESIASTES I, 18, c. 200 B.C.

Wisdom giveth life to them that have it.
ECCLESIASTES VII, 12

He is happy in his wisdom who learned at another's expense.
PLAUTUS: *Mercator*, IV, c. 200 B.C.

The fear of the Lord is the beginning of wisdom.
PSALMS CXI, 10, c. 150 B.C.

The wisdom of this world is foolishness with God.
I CORINTHIANS III, 19, c. 55

Wisdom is justified of her children.
MATTHEW XI, 19, c. 75 (Cf. LUKE VII, 35, c. 75)

The chief aim of wisdom is to enable one to bear with the stupidity of the ignorant.
POPE XYSTUS I: *The Ring*, c. 120

The greatest good is wisdom.
ST. AUGUSTINE: *Soliloquies*, I, c. 387

If all the sky were paper, and all the trees pens, and all the waters of the earth ink, they would not suffice to record my wisdom.
Ascribed to SACCAI, a medieval Jewish sage, c. 1350

He hath wisdom at his will
That can with angry heart be still.
Anon.: *Proverbs of Good Counsel, c.* 1460

The most certain sign of wisdom is a continual cheerfulness; her state is like that of things in the regions above the moon, always clear and serene.
MICHEL DE MONTAIGNE: *Essays,* I, 1580

Wisdom is not an art that may be learned; wisdom comes from the stars.
PAUL FLEMMING: *Weisheit, c.* 1635

'Tis wisdom sometimes to seem a fool.
THOMAS FULLER: *The Holy State and the Profane State,* 1642

The world looks upon solitary wisdom as folly.
BALTASAR GRACIÁN: *The Art of Worldly Wisdom,* CXXXIII, 1647

Almost all men think they have [wisdom] in a greater degree than the vulgar — that is, than all men but themselves, and a few others, whom by fate, or for concurring with themselves, they approve.
THOMAS HOBBES: *Leviathan,* I, 1651

Our wisdom is not less at the mercy of fortune than our property.
LA ROCHEFOUCAULD: *Maxims,* 1665

To know
That which before us lies in daily life,
Is the prime wisdom.
JOHN MILTON: *Paradise Lost,* VIII, 1667

Wisdom's nothing but a pretending to know and believe more than we really do. You read of but one wise man, and all he knew was that he knew nothing.
WILLIAM CONGREVE: *The Old Bachelor,* I, 1693

Wisdom denotes the pursuing of the best ends by the best means.
FRANCES HUTCHESON: *An Inquiry Into the Original of Our Ideas of Beauty and Virtue,* II, 1725

Wisdom in a poor man is a diamond set in lead.
THOMAS FULLER: *Gnomologia,* 1732

Wisdom is a good purchase, though we pay dear for it. IBID.

Wisdom is neither inheritance nor legacy.
IBID.

The clouds may drop down titles and estates;
Wealth may seek us; but wisdom must be sought.
EDWARD YOUNG: *Night Thoughts,* VIII, 1744

The doors of wisdom are never shut.
BENJAMIN FRANKLIN: *Poor Richard's Almanac,* 1755

Our wisest reflections (if the word wise may be given to humanity) are tainted by our hopes and fears.
MARY WORTLEY MONTAGU: *Letter to James Steuart,* April 12, 1762

Wisdom makes but a slow defence against trouble, though at last a sure one.
OLIVER GOLDSMITH: *The Vicar of Wakefield,* XXI, 1766

Wisdom is humble that he knows no more.
WILLIAM COWPER: *The Task,* VI, 1785

Wisdom is ofttimes nearer when we stoop
Than when we soar.
WILLIAM WORDSWORTH: *The Excursion,* III, 1814

Wisdom is folly.
JOHN KEATS: *Letter to J. H. Reynolds,* May 3, 1818

I love wisdom more than she loves me.
BYRON: *Don Juan,* VI, 1823

Wisdom is a skeleton without flesh or blood.
FRANZ SCHUBERT: *Diary,* March 29, 1824

Much of the wisdom of the world is not wisdom, and the most illuminating class of men are no doubt superior to literary fame, and are not writers.
R. W. EMERSON: *The Over-Soul,* 1841

Great is wisdom; infinite is the value of wisdom. It cannot be exaggerated; it is the highest achievement of man.
THOMAS CARLYLE: Address at Edinburgh, April 2, 1866

Wisdom consists in rising superior both to madness and to common sense, and in lending one's self to the universal delusion without becoming its dupe.
H. F. AMIEL: *Journal,* Dec. 11, 1872

The growth of wisdom may be gauged accurately by the decline of ill-temper.
F. W. NIETZSCHE: *Human All-too-Human,* II, 1878

Wisdom is a special knowledge in excess of all that is known.
AMBROSE BIERCE: *Collected Works,* VIII, 1911

Nine-tenths of wisdom consists in being wise in time.
THEODORE ROOSEVELT: Speech in Lincoln, Neb., June 14, 1917

Wisdom is divided into two parts: (*a*) having a great deal to say, and (*b*) not saying it.
Author unidentified

He who thinks wisdom is greater than virtue will lose his wisdom. HEBREW PROVERB

Wisdom is stronger than fate. (Fato prudentia major.) LATIN PROVERB

All wisdom must be paid for with pain.
WELSH PROVERB

[*See also* Age (Old), Beauty, Books, Chance, Cheerfulness, Danger, Experience, Folly, Fool, Force, Husband and Wife, Ignorance, Instinct, Knowledge *vs.* Wisdom, Law,

Learning, Leisure, Liberty, Love, Memory, Nature, Opinion (Public), Patience, Philosophy, Piety, Proverb, Silence, Sorrow, Wealth, Wise, Wit.

Wisdom, Worldly

Be wisely worldly, but not worldly wise.
FRANCIS QUARLES: *Emblems,* II, 1635

Let the great book of the world be your serious study; read it over and over, get it by heart, adopt its style, and make it your own.
LORD CHESTERFIELD: *Letter to his son,* July 9, 1750

As Christian was walking solitarily by himself, he espied one afar off, come crossing over the field to meet him; and their hap was to meet just as they were crossing the way of each other. The gentleman's name that met him was Mr. Worldly Wiseman: he dwelt in the town of Carnal Policy, a very great town.
JOHN BUNYAN: *Pilgrim's Progress,* I, 1678

[*See also* Silence, Wit.

Wise

After the event even a fool is wise.
HOMER: *Iliad,* XVII, *c.* 800 B.C.

It is a high advantage for a wise man not to seem wise.
ÆSCHYLUS: *Prometheus Bound, c.* 490 B.C.

I am wiser than this man, for neither of us appears to know anything great and good: but he fancies he knows something, although he knows nothing, whereas I, as I do not know anything, so I do not fancy I do.
SOCRATES: *In Plato's Apology of Socrates,* 399 B.C.

No man alone is wise enough.
PLAUTUS: *Miles Glorioso,* III, 205 B.C.

God hath chosen the foolish things of the world, to confound the wise.
I CORINTHIANS I, 27, *c.* 55

No man ever became wise by chance.
SENECA: *Epistulæ morales ad Lucilium,* XCIV, *c.* 63

No one is wise at all times.
PLINY THE ELDER: *Natural History,* VII, 77

He is not wise who is not wise for himself.
ENGLISH PROVERB, borrowed from the Latin, and traced by Apperson to 1478

A wise man will see to it that his acts always seem voluntary and not done by compulsion, however much he may be compelled by necessity.
NICCOLÒ MACHIAVELLI: *Discorsi,* I, 1531

Ye are wise enough if ye keep ye warm.
JOHN HEYWOOD: *Proverbs,* 1546

A wise man sees as much as he ought, not as much as he can.
MICHEL DE MONTAIGNE: *Essays,* II, 1580

A wise man is not wise in everything.
MICHEL DE MONTAIGNE: *Essays,* III, 1588

A word to the wise is sufficient.
ENGLISH PROVERB, borrowed from the Latin, and traced by Apperson to *c.* 1598

I am a wise fellow; and, which is more, an officer; and, which is more, a house-holder; and, which is more, as pretty a piece of flesh as any in Messina; and one that knows the law, go to; and a rich fellow enough, go to; and a fellow that hath had losses; and one that hath two gowns, and everything handsome about him.
SHAKESPEARE: *Much Ado About Nothing,* IV, *c.* 1599

It is easy to be wise after the event.
ENGLISH PROVERB, borrowed from the Greek, and traced by Smith to 1609

The wise man must carry the fool on his shoulders.
JOHN WODROEPHE: *Spared Houres,* 1623

The wise man, even when he holds his tongue, says more than the fool when he speaks.
THOMAS FULLER: *The Holy State and the Profane State,* 1642

Nature and fame are favorable to the wise, but luck is generally jealous of them.
BALTASAR GRACIÁN: *The Art of Worldly Wisdom,* CLXXI, 1647

If the wise erred not it would go hard with fools.
GEORGE HERBERT: *Jacula Prudentum,* 1651

Such is the nature of men that however they may acknowledge many others to be more witty, or more eloquent, or more learned, yet they will hardly believe there be many so wise as themselves.
THOMAS HOBBES: *Leviathan,* XIII, 1651

Even the wisest show their wisdom only in indifferent matters, never in really important matters.
LA ROCHEFOUCAULD: *Maxims,* 1665

It is a great folly to wish only to be wise.
IBID.

The wisest man is he who does not believe that he is.
NICOLAS BOILEAU: *Satires du Sieur D.,* I, 1666

You may be a wise man though you can't make a watch.
JOHN RAY: *English Proverbs,* 1670

The first and wisest of them all professed
To know this one: that he nothing knew.
JOHN MILTON: *Paradise Regained,* IV, 1671

It is not wise to be wiser than is necessary.
PHILIPPE QUINAULT: *Armide,* 1686

The latter part of a wise man's life is taken up in curing the follies, prejudices, and false opinions he contracted in the former.
JONATHAN SWIFT: *Thoughts on Various Subjects,* 1706

The hours of a wise man are lengthened by his ideas.
JOSEPH ADDISON: *The Spectator,* June 18, 1711

We think our fathers fools, so wise we grow;
Our wiser sons, no doubt, will think us so.
ALEXANDER POPE: *An Essay on Criticism,* II, 1711

A wise man will make tools of what comes to hand.
THOMAS FULLER: *Gnomologia,* 1732

What is it to be wise?
'Tis but to know how little can be known;
To see all others' faults, and feel our own.
ALEXANDER POPE: *An Essay on Man,* IV, 1734

He who is only wise lives a sad life.
VOLTAIRE: *Letter to Frederick the Great,* 1740

Be wiser than other people if you can; but do not tell them so.
LORD CHESTERFIELD: *Letter to his son,* Nov. 19, 1745

The wisest man sometimes acts weakly, and the weakest sometimes wisely.
LORD CHESTERFIELD: *Letter to his son,* April 26, 1748

Some folks are wise, and some are otherwise.
TOBIAS SMOLLETT: *Roderick Random,* VI, 1748

There was a man in our town
And he was wondrous wise:
He jumped into a bramble-bush
And scratched out both his eyes;
And when he saw his eyes were out,
With all his might and main
He jumped into another bush
And scratched them in again.
Anon.: *Nursery rhyme, c.* 1750

A wise man will not communicate his differing thoughts to unprepared minds, or in a disorderly manner.
BENJAMIN WHICHCOTE: *Moral and Religious Aphorisms,* 1753

I was tired of being always wise.
OLIVER GOLDSMITH: *The Vicar of Wakefield,* X, 1766

A sadder and a wiser man
He rose the morrow morn.
S. T. COLERIDGE: *The Ancient Mariner,* VII, 1798

A wise good man contented to be poor.
GEORGE CRABBE: *The Parish Register,* III, 1807

They only are wise who know that they know nothing.
THOMAS CARLYLE: *Sartor Resartus,* I, 1836

YY U R, YY U B,
I C U R YY for me.
Anon.: *Favorite Album Verses, c.* 1845

There needs but one wise man in a company and all are wise, so rapid is the contagion.
R. W. EMERSON: *Representative Men,* I, 1850

He is wise that follows the wise.
EDWARD FITZGERALD: *Polonius,* 1852

In Cocaigne we are all wise, for that is our religion.
JAMES BRANCH CABELL: *Jurgen,* XX, 1919

A wise man's day is worth a fool's whole life.
ARAB PROVERB

A wise man understands with half a word.
FRENCH PROVERB

Wisest is he who knows not he is wise. IBID.

An empty purse and a new house make a man wise, but too late. PORTUGUESE PROVERB

One is wiser at dawn than at night.
RUSSIAN PROVERB

A wise man gets learning frae them that hae none. SCOTTISH PROVERB

A wise man wavers; a fool is fixed. IBID.

[*See also* Books, Character (National), Egoism, Experience, Folly, Fool, Happiness, Heart, Honesty, Idea, Ignorance, Inheritance, Laughter, Learning, Least, Leisure, Love, Luck, Madness, Marriage (Early), Merriment, Misfortune, Opinion, Philosopher, Pity, Proverb, Sorrow, Surprise, Travel, Wealth, Wisdom, Word.

Wishing

Thy wish was father, Harry, to that thought.
SHAKESPEARE: *II Henry IV,* IV, *c.* 1598

Wishers were ever fools.
SHAKESPEARE: *Antony and Cleopatra,* IV, *c.* 1606

Always leave something to wish for; otherwise you will be miserable from your very happiness.
BALTASAR GRACIÁN: *The Art of Worldly Wisdom,* CC, 1647

If wishes were horses beggars might ride.
JOHN RAY: *English Proverbs,* 1670

Our wishes lengthen as our sun declines.
EDWARD YOUNG: *Night Thoughts,* V, 1742

Wistfulness

I never saw a man who looked
With such a wistful eye
Upon that little tent of blue
Which prisoners call the sky,
And at every drifting cloud that went
With sails of silver by.

OSCAR WILDE: *The Ballad of Reading Gaol,* 1898

Wit

Those who jest with good taste are called witty.

ARISTOTLE: *The Nicomachean Ethics,* II, *c.* 340 B.C.

Wit is educated insolence.

ARISTOTLE: *Rhetoric,* II, *c.* 322 B.C.

At their wit's end.

PSALMS CVII, 27, *c.* 150 B.C.

The distinction between a witticism and a low, rude joke is that the former may be indulged in, if it be seasonable, and in hours of relaxation, by a virtuous man; the latter is unworthy of any human being.

CICERO: *De officiis,* I, 78 B.C.

Thy wit is a very bitter sweeting: it is most sharp sauce.

SHAKESPEARE: *Romeo and Juliet,* II, *c.* 1596

I am not only witty in myself, but the cause that wit is in other men.

SHAKESPEARE: *II Henry IV,* I, *c.* 1598

When the age is in, the wit is out.

SHAKESPEARE: *Much Ado About Nothing,* III, *c.* 1599

Sir, your wit ambles well; it goes easily.

SHAKESPEARE: *Much Ado About Nothing,* V

I shall ne'er be ware of mine own wit till I break my shins against it.

SHAKESPEARE: *As You Like It,* II, *c.* 1600

They have a plentiful lack of wit.

SHAKESPEARE: *Hamlet,* II, *c.* 1601

Methinks sometimes I have no more wit than a Christian or an ordinary man has.

SHAKESPEARE: *Twelfth Night,* I, *c.* 1601

He's winding up the watch of his wit; by and by it will strike.

SHAKESPEARE: *The Tempest,* II, 1611

Wit's an unruly engine, wildly striking
Sometimes a friend, sometimes the engineer.

GEORGE HERBERT: *The Temple,* 1633

Natural wit consisteth principally of two things: celerity of imagining (that is, swift succession of one thought to another), and steady direction to some approved end.

THOMAS HOBBES: *Leviathan,* I, 1651

The true touchstone of wit is the impromptu.

J. B. MOLIÈRE: *Les précieuses ridicules,* IX, 1659

Although he had much wit,
He was very shy of using it.

SAMUEL BUTLER: *Hudibras,* I, 1663

If it were not for the company of fools, a witty man would often be greatly at a loss.

LA ROCHEFOUCAULD: *Maxims,* 1665

Wit enables us to act rudely with impunity.

IBID.

Sayer of *bons mots:* bad character.

BLAISE PASCAL: *Pensées,* VI, 1670

Weak men had need to be witty.

JOHN RAY: *English Proverbs,* 1670

Wit is folly unless a wise man hath the keeping of it.

IBID.

Wit is more necessary than beauty; and I think no young woman ugly who has it, and no handsome woman agreeable without it.

WILLIAM WYCHERLEY: *The Country Wife,* I, *c.* 1673

There is a powerful faction against wit.

THOMAS SHADWELL: *A True Widow,* I, 1679

Great wits are sure to madness near allied,
And thin partitions do their bounds divide.

JOHN DRYDEN: *Absalom and Achitophel,* I, 1682

Wit and wisdom are born with a man.

JOHN SELDEN: *Table-Talk,* 1689

Wit must be foiled by wit: cut a diamond with a diamond.

WILLIAM CONGREVE: *The Double Dealer,* I, 1694

Who cares for anybody that has more wit than himself?

WILLIAM CONGREVE: *Love for Love,* 1695

Wit's as slow in growth as grace.

JOHN VANBRUGH: *The Relapse,* pref., 1696

A wit should be no more sincere than a woman constant; one argues a decay of the parts, as t'other of beauty.

WILLIAM CONGREVE: *The Way of the World,* I, 1700

Wit may be defined a justness of thought and a facility of expression, or (in the midwives' phrase) a perfect conception with an easy delivery.

ALEXANDER POPE: *Letter to William Wycherley,* Dec. 26, 1704

It is with wits as with razors, which are never so pat to cut those they are employed on as when they have lost their edges.

JONATHAN SWIFT: *A Tale of a Tub,* pref., 1704

It is grown almost into a maxim that good-natured men are not always men of the most wit. This observation, in my opinion, has no foundation in nature. The greatest wits I have conversed with are men eminent for their humanity.

JOSEPH ADDISON: *The Spectator*, Sept. 13, 1711

True wit is nature to advantage dress'd,
What oft was thought, but ne'er so well expressed.

ALEXANDER POPE: *An Essay on Criticism*, II, 1711

Fools are only laugh'd at; wits are hated.

ALEXANDER POPE: Prologue for *Three Hours After Marriage*, 1717 (The play has been ascribed to John Gay, John Arbuthnot and Pope himself)

There is not, perhaps, any harder task than to tame the natural wildness of wit.

THOMAS TICKNELL: Preface to *The Works of Joseph Addison*, 1721

Wit, as the chief of virtue's friends,
Disdains to serve ignoble ends.

JONATHAN SWIFT: *To Dr. Delany*, 1729

Much wit, much froth.

THOMAS FULLER: *Gnomologia*, 1732

Wit helps us to play the fool with more confidence. IBID.

There's many witty men whose brains can't fill their bellies.

BENJAMIN FRANKLIN: *Poor Richard's Almanac*, 1735

A wit is a very unpopular denomination, as it carries terror along with it; and people in general are as much afraid of a live wit, in company, as a woman is of a gun.

LORD CHESTERFIELD: *Letter to his son*, Oct. 12, 1748

The hapless wit has his labors always to begin, the call for novelty is never satisfied, and one jest only raises expectation of another.

SAMUEL JOHNSON: *The Rambler*, July 23, 1751

Wit raises human nature above its level; humor acts a contrary part, and equally depresses it.

OLIVER GOLDSMITH: *Polite Learning in Europe*, XI, 1759

Why should we despise those who have no wit? It is not a voluntary evil.

STANISLAUS LESZCYNSKI (KING OF POLAND): *Œuvres du philosophe bienfaisant*, 1763

Wits uniformly exclaim against fools, yet fools are their proper foil, and it is from them alone they can learn what figure themselves make.

WILLIAM SHENSTONE: *Of Men and Manners*, 1764

What brutes all wits are!

CARON DE BEAUMARCHAIS: *Le barbier de Séville*, I, 1775

There's no possibility of being witty without a little ill-nature; the malice of a good thing is the barb that makes it stick.

R. B. SHERIDAN: *The School for Scandal*, I, 1777

Wit is that which is at once natural and new; that which, though not obvious, is, upon its first production, acknowledged to be just; that which he that never found it wonders how he missed.

SAMUEL JOHNSON: *Lives of the Poets* (Cowley), 1780

Wit may be considered a combination of dissimilar images, or discovery of occult resemblances in things apparently unlike.

IBID.

His wit invites you by his looks to come
But when you knock it never is at home.

WILLIAM COWPER: *Conversation*, 1782

Professed wits, though they are generally courted for the amusement they afford, are seldom respected for the qualities they possess.

SYDNEY SMITH: *Lectures on Wit and Humor*, I, 1805

What is wit? Reason expressed artfully.

M. J. DE CHÉNIER: *Épître à Voltaire*, 1806

Wit is the best sense in the world.

RICHARD PORSON (1759–1808)

Wit consists in discerning the resemblance between things that differ, and the difference between things that are alike.

ANNA LOUISE DE STAËL: *De l'Allemagne*, III, 1810

Those who cannot miss an opportunity of saying a good thing . . . are not to be trusted with the management of any great question.

WILLIAM HAZLITT: *Characteristics*, 1823

A grain of wit is more penetrating than the lightning of the night-storm, which no curtains or shutters will keep out.

R. W. EMERSON: *Carlyle's Past and Present*, 1843

Wit is the clash and reconcilement of incongruities, the meeting of extremes round a corner. LEIGH HUNT: *Table-Talk*, 1851

Nothing more smooth than glass, yet nothing more brittle; nothing more fine than wit, yet nothing more fickle.

H. G. BOHN: *Handbook of Proverbs*, 1855

The less wit a man has, the less he knows that he wants it. IBID.

A little wit had pleased me more by half;
I didn't come to learn, I came to laugh.

J. G. SAXE: *The Press*, 1855

Wit throws a single ray, separated from the rest, — red, yellow, blue, or any intermediate

shade, — upon an object; never white light; that is the province of wisdom.
O. W. HOLMES: *The Autocrat of the Breakfast-Table,* III, 1858

Wit is not worldly wisdom.
ALEXANDER SMITH: *Dreamthorp,* VII, 1863

Humor is the electric atmosphere; wit is the flash.
H. R. HAWEIS: *Music and Morals,* I, 1871

Wit makes its own welcome, and levels all distinctions. No dignity, no learning, no force of character, can make any stand against good wit.
R. W. EMERSON: *The Comic,* 1876

There must be more malice than love in the hearts of all wits.
R. B. HAYDON: *Table-Talk,* 1876

Wit is the epitaph of an emotion.
F. W. NIETZSCHE: *Human All-too-Human,* II, 1878

I would not trust a saturnine man, but I would trust a wit.
WOODROW WILSON: Speech in Chicago, Feb. 12, 1909

To be comic is merely to be playful, but wit is a serious matter. To laugh at it is to confess that you do not understand.
AMBROSE BIERCE: *Collected Works,* VIII, 1911

His foe was folly and his weapon wit.
ANTHONY HOPE HAWKINS: Inscription on the tablet to W. S. Gilbert, Victoria Embankment, London, 1915

Wit that is kindly is not very witty.
E. W. HOWE: *Sinner Sermons,* 1926

Wit is the sudden marriage of ideas which before their union were not perceived to have any relation. Author unidentified

Big heads have little wit. FRENCH PROVERB

An ounce of mother-wit is worth a pound of school-wit. GERMAN PROVERB

Attic salt. (Sal Atticum.) LATIN PHRASE

Where there is much laughter there is little wit. PORTUGUESE PROVERB

Gude wit jumps. SCOTTISH PROVERB

[*See also* Age (Old), Blasphemy, Brevity, Chance, Child, Epigram, Fashion, Fool, Frenchman, German, Head, Humor, Imagination, Jest, Laughter, Madness, Malice, Man, Mirth, Proverb.

Witchcraft

Thou shalt not suffer a witch to live.
EXODUS XXII, 18, *c.* 700 B.C.

There shall not be found among you anyone that maketh his son or daughter to pass through the fire, or that useth divination, or an observer of times, or an enchanter, or a witch, or a charmer, or a consulter with familiar spirits, or a wizard, or a necromancer.
DEUTERONOMY XVIII, 10–11, *c.* 650 B.C.

Then said Saul unto his servants, Seek me a woman that hath a familiar spirit, that I may go to her, and inquire of her. And his servants said to him, Behold, there is a woman that hath a familiar spirit at En-dor.
I SAMUEL XVIII, 7, *c.* 500 B.C.

[Manasseh] observed times, and used enchantments, and used witchcraft, and dealt with a familiar spirit, and with wizards.
II CHRONICLES XXXIII, 6, *c.* 300 B.C.

When I was a child there were many witches, and they bewitched both cattle and men, especially children. But now such things are less heard of, for the gospels have thrust the Devil out of his seat.
MARTIN LUTHER: *Commentary on Galatians,* 1519

Saw you the weird sisters?
SHAKESPEARE: *Macbeth,* IV, *c.* 1605

I have ever believed, and do now know, that there are witches. They that doubt of these do not only deny them, but spirits: and are obliquely and upon consequence, a sort, not of infidels, but atheists.
THOMAS BROWNE: *Religio Medici,* I, 1642

Our witches are justly hanged because they think themselves so, and suffer deservedly for believeing they did mischief, because they meant it.
JOHN DRYDEN: *Of Dramatic Poesy,* 1668

This woman is a witch, and it is by virtue of her sorceries that this ground is enchanted. Whoever doth lay their head down in her lap had as good lay it down upon that block over which the ax doth hang; and whoever lay their eyes upon her beauty are counted the enemies of God.
JOHN BUNYAN: *Pilgrim's Progress,* II, 1678

Whereas some pretend that the bodies of witches are possessed with the Devil, and are on that account incapable of sinking under water . . . , witness the Gadarene hogs, which were no sooner possessed with the Devil but they ran into the water and there perished.
INCREASE MATHER: *Remarkable Providences,* VIII, 1684

The law against witches does not prove there be any; but it punishes the malice of those people that use such means to take away men's lives. If one should profess that by turning his hat thrice, and crying buz, he could take away a man's life, though in truth he could do no such thing, yet this were a just law made by the state, that whosoever should turn his hat thrice, and cry buz, with an intention to take away a man's life, shall be put to death.

JOHN SELDEN: *Table-Talk*, 1689

Witchcraft . . . has driven many poor people to despair, and persecuted their minds with such buzzes of atheism and blasphemy as has made them even run distracted with terror.

COTTON MATHER: *The Wonders of the Invisible World*, 1692

I believe in general that there is and has been such a thing as witchcraft, but at the same time can give no credit to any particular instance of it.

JOSEPH ADDISON: *The Spectator*, July 14, 1711

Midnight hags,
By force of potent spells, of bloody characters,
And conjurations horrible to hear,
Call fiends and spectres from the yawning deep,
And set the ministers of Hell at work.

NICHOLAS ROWE: *Jane Shore*, IV, 1714

That there are such angels as witches it is without question.

MATTHEW HALE: *History of the Pleas of the Crown*, 1736

To deny the possibility, nay, actual existence, of witchcraft and sorcery is flatly to contradict the revealed word of God.

WILLIAM BLACKSTONE: *Commentaries on the Laws of England*, IV, 1765

Any person or persons who shall kill another for a witch or wizard shall suffer death. And any person who shall publicly state that he himself or she herself is a witch or wizard, or shall say that such a person or persons are witches or wizards, and he or she knows it to be so, shall receive sixty lashes on the bare back.

Law of the Choctaw Nation, Nov. 8, 1834

Witchcraft, and all manner of spectre-work, and demonology, we have now named madness, and diseases of the nerves, seldom reflecting that still the new question comes upon us: What is madness, what are nerves?

THOMAS CARLYLE: *Sartor Resartus*, III, 1836

She who is kinder than a mother is a witch.

HINDU PROVERB

[*See also* Flesh, New England, Sin, Sorcery, Wizard.

Withers

[*See* Jade.

Witness

God is my witness. ROMANS I, 9, *c.* 55

A cloud of witnesses. HEBREWS XII, 1, *c.* 65

Witnesses, like watches, go
Just as they're set, too fast or slow.

SAMUEL BUTLER: *Hudibras*, II, 1664

Do we ever hear the most recent fact related exactly in the same way, by the several people who were at the same time eyewitnesses of it? No. One mistakes, another misrepresents, and others warp it a little to their own turn of mind, or private views.

LORD CHESTERFIELD: *Letter to his son*, April 26, 1748

I have always told a jury that if a fact is fully proved by two witnesses it is as good as if proved by a hundred.

MR. JUSTICE BULLER: *Judgment in Calliand vs. Vaughan*, 1798

A witness has no business to concern himself with the merits of the case in which he is called on to give evidence, or whether, when given, it will be material to the cause.

LORD LANGDALE: *Judgment in Langley vs. Fisher*, 1843

One witness is no witness. (Testis unus, testis nullus.) LEGAL MAXIM

Witnesses are weighed, not numbered. (Testes ponderantur non numerantur.) IBID.

If you have nothing else to do go to court and be a witness. SERBIAN PROVERB

[*See also* Evidence, Lawsuit, Trial by Jury.

Wits

The very brutish and savage beasts have wit: oxen and asses by their wit choose out the best pastures to feed in.

GABRIEL HARVEY: *The Trimming of Thomas Nashe*, 1597

Wizard

Regard not them that have familiar spirits, neither seek after wizards, to be defiled by them: I am the Lord your God.

LEVITICUS XIX, 31, *c.* 700 B.C.

Seek unto them that have familiar spirits, and unto wizards that peep.

ISAIAH VIII, 19, *c.* 700 B.C.

Out of a hundred words all these scoundrels who pretend to be wizards do not speak two that are true, and go on deceiving these poor people to get things from them, as do many others in this world who resemble these gentry.

SAMUEL DE CHAMPLAIN: *Les voyages*, II, 1613

[*See also* Witchcraft.

Woe

Woe brings woe upon woe.

SOPHOCLES: *Ajax*, *c.* 450 B.C.

An Iliad of woes.

CICERO: *Ad Atticum*, VIII, *c.* 50 B.C.

I have suffered as many woes as there are stars in Heaven, or atoms in the dust.

OVID: *Tristia*, I, *c.* 10

All these woes shall serve
For sweet discourses in our time to come.
SHAKESPEARE: *Romeo and Juliet*, III, *c.* 1596

One woe doth tread upon another's heel
So fast they follow.
SHAKESPEARE: *Hamlet*, IV, *c.* 1601

Woes cluster; rare are solitary woes;
They love a train, they tread each other's heel.
EDWARD YOUNG: *Night Thoughts*, III, 1742 (Cf. SHAKESPEARE, *ante*, *c.* 1601)

A man of woe.
WALTER SCOTT: *The Lay of the Last Minstrel*, I, 1805

If all the oceans were of ink,
And paper all the skies,
Should I attempt to write my woes,
They never would suffice.
JOHN CAM HOBHOUSE: Tr. of a Greek folk-song, 1813

No scene of mortal life but teems with mortal woe.
WALTER SCOTT: *The Lord of the Isles*, II, 1815

The luxury of woe.
THOMAS MOORE: *Anacreontic*, *c.* 1820

We are all the same – the fools of our own woes!
MATTHEW ARNOLD: *Empedocles on Etna*, 1852

[*See also* Haste, Hope, Laughter, Misery, Misfortune, Sorrow.

Wolf

Any man who says he has been et by a wolf is a liar.
SAM MARTIN, a celebrated Canadian trapper (*c.* 1900)

Talk of the wolf and his tail appears.
DUTCH PROVERB

Better to be devoured by the wolf than the fleas.
GERMAN PROVERB

The wolf may lose his teeth, but ne'er his nature.
SCOTTISH PROVERB

[*See also* Character, Foolishness, Peace, Struggle for Existence, War.

Woman

No trust is to be placed in women.
HOMER: *Odyssey*, XI, *c.* 800 B.C.

There is no fouler fiend than a woman when her mind is bent to evil.
IBID.

The Lord God caused a deep sleep to fall upon Adam, and he slept: and he took one of his ribs, and closed up the flesh instead thereof; and the rib, which the Lord God had taken from man, made he a woman, and brought her unto the man. And Adam said, This is now bone of my bones, and flesh of my flesh: she shall be called Woman, because she was taken out of man.
GENESIS II, 21–23, *c.* 700 B.C.

Nature has given horns to bulls, hoofs to horses, swiftness to hares, the power of swimming to fishes, of flying to birds, understanding to men. She had nothing more for women.
ANACREON: *Fragment*, *c.* 500 B.C.

It is thy place, woman, to hold thy peace, and keep within doors.
ÆSCHYLUS: *The Seven Against Thebes*, *c.* 490 B.C.

Silence gives the proper grace to women.
SOPHOCLES: *Ajax*, *c.* 450 B.C.

The gods have sent medicines for the venom of serpents, but there is no medicine for a bad woman. She is more noxious than the viper, or than fire itself.
EURIPIDES: *Andromache*, *c.* 427 B.C.

There's nothing in the world worse than woman – save some other woman.
ARISTOPHANES: *Thesmophoriazusae*, *c.* 425 B.C.

The best ornaments of a woman are silence and modesty.
EURIPIDES: *Heracles*, *c.* 420 B.C.

Woman's wit is to scheme quickly.
EURIPIDES: *Iphigenia in Tauris*, *c.* 413 B.C.

I trust only one thing in a woman: that she will not come to life again after she is dead. In all other things I distrust her.
ANTIPHANES: *Fragment*, *c.* 350 B.C.

The lips of a strange woman drop as an honeycomb, and her mouth is smoother than oil.
PROVERBS V, 3, *c.* 350 B.C.

It is better to dwell in a corner of the housetop than with a brawling woman in a wide house.
PROVERBS XXI, 9 (Cf. XXV, 24)

Who can find a virtuous woman? for her price is far above rubies.
PROVERBS XXXI, 10 (There follows a roster of a woman's virtues, 11–31)

How can he be clean that is born of a woman?
JOB XXV, 4, *c.* 325 B.C.

Woman may be said to be an inferior man.
ARISTOTLE: *Poetics*, XV, *c.* 322 B.C.

Of all the wild beasts on land or sea, the wildest is woman.
MENANDER: *Supposititio*, *c.* 300 B.C.

Suffer women once to arrive at an equality with you, and they will from that moment become your superiors.
CATO THE CENSOR: *In Support of the Oppian Law*, 215 B.C.

Two women are worse than one.
PLAUTUS: *Curculio, c.* 200 B.C.

A woman finds it much easier to do ill than well. PLAUTUS: *Truculentus, c.* 190 B.C.

All wickedness is but little to the wickedness of a woman.
ECCLESIASTICUS XXV, 19, *c.* 180 B.C.

I know the ways of women: they won't when thou wilt, and when thou won't they are passionately fond.
TERENCE: *Eunuchus,* IV, *c.* 160 B.C.

The vows that a woman makes to her lover are only fit to be written on air.
CATULLUS: *Carmina,* LXX, *c.* 60 B.C.

A woman either loves or hates; she knows no medium.
PUBLILIUS SYRUS: *Sententiæ, c.* 50 B.C.

In evil counsel women always beat men.
IBID.

You should make a woman angry if you wish her to love. IBID.

Woman is always fickle and changeful. (Varium et mutabile semper femina.)
VIRGIL: *Æneid,* IV, 19 B.C.

A woman is always buying something.
OVID: *Ars amatoria,* I, *c.* 2 B.C.

Whether they yield or refuse, it delights women to have been asked. IBID.

A woman's mind is swayed by the meanest gifts.
LIVY: *History of Rome,* VI, *c.* 10

Let your women keep silence in the churches: for it is not permitted unto them to speak; but they are commanded to be under obedience, as also saith the law.
I CORINTHIANS XIV, 33, *c.* 55

Let the women learn in silence with all subjection. I TIMOTHY II, 11, *c.* 60

I suffer not a woman to teach, nor to usurp authority over the man, but to be in silence.
I TIMOTHY II, 12

The weaker vessel. I PETER III, 7, *c.* 60

Wherever women are honored, there the gods are pleased.
THE CODE OF MANU, III, *c.* 100

In childhood a woman must be subject to her father; in youth, to her husband; when her husband is dead, to her sons. A woman must never be free of subjugation.
THE CODE OF MANU, V

Though a woman may be burning herself, she delights in her lover's torment.
JUVENAL: *Satires,* III, *c.* 110

A woman should be covered with shame by the thought that she is a woman.
CLEMENT OF ALEXANDRIA: *Paedagogus,* II, *c.* 190

The judgment of God upon your sex endures even today; and with it inevitably endures your position of criminal at the bar of justice. You are the gateway of the Devil.
TERTULLIAN: *Women's Dress, c.* 220

Nothing so much casts down the mind of man from its citadel as do the blandishments of women, and that physical contact without which a wife cannot be possessed.
ST. AUGUSTINE: *Soliloquies,* I, *c.* 387

The beauty of woman is the greatest snare. Or rather, not the beauty of woman, but unchastened gazing.
ST. JOHN CHRYSOSTOM: *Homilies,* XV, *c.* 388

Despise not yourselves, ye women; the Son of God was born of a woman.
ST. AUGUSTINE: *On the Christian Conflict, c.* 397

I believed that one woman was devoted to me, but she is now attracted by another man, and another man takes pleasure in her, while a second woman interests herself in me. Curses on them both, and on the god of love, and on the other woman, and on myself!
BHARTRIHARI: *The Nita Sataka, c.* 625

A woman talks to one man, looks at a second, and thinks of a third.
BHARTRIHARI: *The Sringa Sataka, c.* 625

Woman is the chain by which man is attached to the chariot of folly. IBID.

The intelligence of woman equals that of 70 weavers; that of a weaver equals that of 70 schoolmasters. IBN AL-JANZI, *c.* 1200

A woman hath nine lives like a cat.
JOHN HEYWOOD: *Proverbs,* 1546

To promote a woman to bear rule, superiority, dominion, or empire above any realm, nation, or city, is repugnant to nature; contumely to God, a thing most contrarious to His revealed will and approved ordinances; and finally, it is the subversion of good order, of all equity and justice.
JOHN KNOX: *The First Blast of the Trumpet Against the Monstrous Regiment of Women,* 1558

The years that a woman subtracts from her age are not lost. They are added to the ages of other women.
COUNTESS DIANE OF POITIERS (1499–1566)

What defects women have, we must check them for in private, gently by word of mouth, for woman is a frail vessel.
MARTIN LUTHER: *Table-Talk,* DCCXXXVII, 1569

Woman is the very root of wickedness, the cause of the bitterest pain, a mine of suffering. TULSĪ DĀS: *Rāmāyan,* 1574

He waters, plows, and soweth in the sand,
And hopes the flick'ring wind with net to hold,
Who hath his hopes laid upon woman's hand.
PHILIP SIDNEY: *Arcadia*, II, 1590

Ten teams of oxen draw much less
Than one hair of Helen's tress.
JOHN FLORIO: *Second Frutes*, 1591

'Tis beauty that doth oft make women proud;
'Tis virtue that doth make them most admired;
'Tis government that makes them seem divine.
SHAKESPEARE: *III Henry VI*, I, *c.* 1591

She's beautiful and therefore to be woo'd:
She is a woman, therefore to be won.
SHAKESPEARE: *I Henry VI*, V, 1592

In woman's speech is death, in her smile is Hell.
TORQUATO TASSO: *Gerusalemme*, XIX, 1592

A woman mov'd is like a fountain troubled,
Muddy, ill-seeming, thick, bereft of beauty.
SHAKESPEARE: *The Taming of the Shrew*, V, 1594

Why are our bodies soft and weak and smooth,
Unapt to toil and trouble in the world,
But that our soft conditions and our hearts
Should well agree with our external parts?
IBID.

A child of our grandmother Eve, a female; or, for thy more sweet understanding, a woman.
SHAKESPEARE: *Love's Labor's Lost*, I, *c.* 1595

Dumb jewels often in their silent kind
More than quick words do move a woman's mind.
SHAKESPEARE: *Two Gentlemen of Verona*, III, *c.* 1595

If she do frown, 'tis not in hate of you,
But rather to beget more love in you;
If she do chide, 'tis not to have you gone,
For why, the fools are mad if left alone.
IBID.

To be slow in words is a woman's only virtue.
IBID.

We cannot fight for love, as men may do;
We should be woo'd and were not made to woo.
SHAKESPEARE: *A Midsummer Night's Dream*, II, *c.* 1596

All women are ambitious naturally.
CHRISTOPHER MARLOWE and GEORGE CHAPMAN: *Hero and Leander*, I, 1598

A poor lone woman.
SHAKESPEARE: *II Henry IV*, II, *c.* 1598

Ah me, how weak a thing
The heart of woman is!
SHAKESPEARE: *Julius Cæsar*, II, 1599

I grant I am a woman, but withal,
A woman that Lord Brutus took to wife:
I grant I am a woman; but withal
A woman well-reputed; Cato's daughter.
IBID.

If ladies be but young and fair,
They have the gift to know it.
SHAKESPEARE: *As You Like It*, II, *c.* 1600

Do you not know I am a woman? When I think, I must speak.
SHAKESPEARE: *As You Like It*, III

I thank God I am not a woman, to be touched with so many giddy offences as He hath generally taxed their whole sex withal. IBID.

Frailty, thy name is woman.
SHAKESPEARE: *Hamlet*, I, *c.* 1601

Women are as roses, whose fair flower
Being once display'd, doth fall that very hour.
SHAKESPEARE: *Twelfth Night*, II, *c.* 1601

Fair and foolish, little and loud,
Long and lazy, black and proud;
Fat and merry, lean and sad,
Pale and pettish, red and bad.
THOMAS WRIGHT: *The Passions of the Mind in General*, 1601

Were there no women, man might live like gods.
THOMAS DEKKER: *I The Honest Whore*, I, 1604

Women, at best, are bad.
THOMAS DEKKER: *I The Honest Whore*, III

Sing of the nature of women; and then the song shall be surely full of variety, old crotchets, and most sweet closes; it shall be humorous, grave, fantastic, amorous, melancholy, sprightly, one in all, and all in one.
JOHN MARSTON: *The Malcontent*, III, 1604

You are pictures out of doors,
Bells in your parlors, wild-cats in your kitchens,
Saints in your injuries, devils being offended,
Players in your housewifery, and housewives in your beds.
SHAKESPEARE: *Othello*, II, 1604

It never displeases a woman to make love to her. CERVANTES: *Don Quixote*, I, 1605

Let no man value at a little price
A virtuous woman's counsel; her wing'd spirit
Is feather'd oftentimes with heavenly words.
GEORGE CHAPMAN: *The Gentleman Usher*, IV, 1606

Man was made when nature was but an apprentice, but woman when she was a skillful mistress of her art.
Anon.: *Cupid's Whirligig*, 1607

Were 't not for gold and women, there would be no damnation.
CYRIL TOURNEUR: *The Revenger's Tragedy*, II, 1607

Silver is the king's stamp; man God's stamp, and a woman is man's stamp; we are not current till we pass from one man to another.
JOHN WEBSTER and THOMAS DEKKER: *Northward Ho*, I, 1607

Women are in churches, saints; abroad, angels; at home, devils.
GEORGE WILKINS: *The Miseries of Enforced Marriage,* I, 1607

Women are like curst dogs: civility keeps them tied all daytime, but they are let loose at midnight; then they do most good, or most mischief.
JOHN WEBSTER: *The White Devil,* I, *c.* 1608

Woman to man
Is either a god or a wolf.
JOHN WEBSTER: *The White Devil,* IV

Who is't can read a woman?
SHAKESPEARE: *Cymbeline,* V, *c.* 1609

He that holds a woman has an eel by the tail.
BEAUMONT and FLETCHER: *The Scornful Lady,* II, 1610

When I trust a wild fool, and a woman,
May I lend gratis, and build hospitals.
BEAUMONT and FLETCHER: *The Scornful Lady,* III

That foolish man
That reads the story of a woman's face
And dies believing it, is lost for ever.
BEAUMONT and FLETCHER: *Philaster,* III, 1611

All the creatures,
Made for Heaven's honors, have their ends, and good ones,
All but the cozening crocodiles, false women.
They reign here like those plagues, those killing sores,
Men pray against; and when they die, like tales
Ill told and unbeliev'd, they pass away,
And go to dust forgotten.
BEAUMONT and FLETCHER: *The Maid's Tragedy,* IV, 1611

For several virtues
Have I lik'd several women; never any
With so full soul, but some defect in her
Did quarrel with the noblest grace she ow'd,
And put it to the foil.
SHAKESPEARE: *The Tempest,* III, 1611

O woman, woman, woman, woman, woman!
Torturous as Hell, insatiate as the grave.
NATHANIEL FIELD: *A Woman Is a Weathercock,* III, 1612

Two women plac'd together makes cold weather.
SHAKESPEARE and JOHN FLETCHER: *Henry VIII,* I, 1613

Wit and woman are two frail things.
THOMAS OVERBURY: *Characters,* 1614

What cannot a neat knave with a smooth tale
Make a woman believe?
JOHN WEBSTER: *The Duchess of Malfi,* I, *c.* 1614

In the time of peace women do allure and corrupt the manners of men by their pride and vanity, and many times, by their enticing provocations, the course of justice is checked and perverted and most injurious wrongs committed, and in the time of war they do hinder the service by their temerity and fear.
BARNABE RICH: *The Anothomy of Ireland,* 1615

Every woman, no matter how ill-favored, delights in being called beautiful.
CERVANTES: *Don Quixote,* II, 1615

Have you felt the wool of beaver,
Or swan's down ever?
Or have smelt o' the bud o' the brier,
Or the nard in the fire?
Or have tasted the bag of the bee?
O so white, O so soft, O so sweet is she!
BEN JONSON: *The Devil Is an Ass,* 1616

Shall I, wasting in despair,
Die because a woman's fair?
Or make pale my cheeks with care
Cause another's rosy are?
Be she fairer than the day,
Or the flow'ry meads in May;
If she be not so to me,
What care I how fair she be?
GEORGE WITHER: Song, 1619

Is there ne'er a land
That you have read or heard of (for I care not how far it be,
Nor under what pestiferous star it lies),
A happy kingdom, where there are no women,
Nor have been ever, nor no mention
Of any such lewd things with lewder qualities?
JOHN FLETCHER: *The Wild-Goose Chase,* V, 1621

One woman reads another's character
Without the tedious trouble of deciphering.
BEN JONSON: *The New Inn,* IV, 1629

Women are like medlars, — no sooner ripe but rotten. A woman last was made, but is spent first.
THOMAS DEKKER: *II The Honest Whore,* I, 1630

There's no music when a woman is in the concert.
THOMAS DEKKER: *II The Honest Whore,* II

Whoever trusts women plows the winds, sows the deserts of the sea, and writes his memoirs in the snow.
PAUL FLEMMING: *Der beste Rath, c.* 1635

O woman!
How far thy tongue and heart do live asunder!
JAMES SHIRLEY: *Hyde Park,* III, 1637

A woman and a glass are ever in danger.
GEORGE HERBERT: *Outlandish Proverbs,* 1640

A ship and a woman are ever repairing.
IBID.

Women laugh when they can and weep when they will. IBID.

Women enjoyed, whate'er before they've been,
Are like romances read, or sights once seen.
JOHN SUCKLING: *Against Fruition, c.* 1640

Women are the baggage of life: they are
Troublesome, and hinder us in the great march,
And yet we cannot be without 'em.
JOHN SUCKLING: *Brennoralt*, I, 1646

She is pretty to walk with,
And witty to talk with,
And pleasant, too, to think on.
JOHN SUCKLING: *Brennoralt*, II

The world is full of care, much like unto a bubble,
Women and care, and care and women, and women and care and trouble.
NATHANIEL WARD: *The Simple Cobbler of Aggawam*, 1646

The very gizzard of a trifle, the product of a quarter of a cipher, the epitome of nothing, fitter to be kicked if she were of a kickable substance, than either honor'd or humor'd.
IBID.

O Jupiter, sho'd I speak ill
Of woman-kind, first die I will;
Since that I know, 'mong all the rest
Of creatures, woman is the best.
ROBERT HERRICK: *Hesperides*, 1648

Let Greeks be Greeks, and women what they are. ANNE BRADSTREET: *Several Poems*, prologue, 1650

One hair of a woman can draw more than a hundred pair of oxen.
JAMES HOWELL: *Familiar Letters*, III, 1650

Take heed of a young wench, a prophetess, and a Latin-bred woman.
GEORGE HERBERT: *Jacula Prudentum*, 1651

There is no mischief but a woman is at one end of it. Anon.: *Wit Restored*, 1658

A woman is like ivy, which grows beautifully so long as it twines round a tree, but is of no use when it is separated.
J. B. MOLIÈRE: *Sganarelle*, I, 1660

A good woman is a hidden treasure; he who discovers her will do well not to boast about it. LA ROCHEFOUCAULD: *Maxims*, 1665

It is of no advantage to a woman to be young without being pretty, or to be pretty without being young. IBID.

Of all the violent passions the one that is most becoming to woman is love. IBID.

The intellect of the generality of women serves more to fortify their folly than their reason.
IBID.

There are few women whose charm survives their beauty. IBID.

The smallest fault of women who give themselves up to love is to love. IBID.

He that does not love a woman sucked a sow.
ROGER L'ESTRANGE: Tr. of FRANCISCO DE QUEVEDO: *Sueños* (1627), 1667

Oh, why did God,
Creator wise, that peopled highest Heaven
With spirits masculine, create at last
This novelty on earth, this fair defect
Of nature, and not fill the world at once
With men as angels without feminine,
Or find some other way to generate
Mankind? This mischief had not then befallen.
JOHN MILTON: *Paradise Lost*, IX, 1667

A bevy of fair women.
JOHN MILTON: *Paradise Lost*, XI

Woman's work is never done.
ENGLISH PROVERB, traced by Smith to 1670

A woman's mind and the Winter wind change oft. JOHN RAY: *English Proverbs*, 1670

If a woman were little as she is good,
A peascod would make her a gown and a hood.
IBID.

Joan's as good as my lady, in the dark. IBID.

What worse than asps upon the earth can be?
The tiger far exceeds in cruelty.
Than cruel tiger what is found more fell?
The Devil. But what worser can we tell?
A woman him exceeds in wickedness,
But worser than a woman nothing is.
Anon.: Written in a copy of Juvenal's Satires, *c.* 1670

Women serve but to keep a man from better company.
WILLIAM WYCHERLEY: *The Country Wife*, I, *c.* 1673

Women do most delight in revenge.
THOMAS BROWNE: *Christian Morals*, III, *c.* 1680

One wise woman is two fools.
ROGER L'ESTRANGE: Tr. of ERASMUS: *Colloquia* (1524), 1680

What mighty ills have not been done by woman!
Who was't betray'd the Capitol? A woman;
Who lost Mark Antony the world? A woman;
Who was the cause of a long ten years' war,
And laid at last old Troy in ashes? Woman;
Destructive, damnable, deceitful woman!
THOMAS OTWAY: *The Orphan*, III, 1680

O woman! lovely woman! Nature made thee
To temper man: we had been brutes without you;
Angels are painted fair, to look like you:
There's in you all that we believe of Heaven,
Amazing brightness, purity, and truth,
Eternal joy, and everlasting love.
THOMAS OTWAY: *Venice Preserved*, I, 1682

When a beautiful woman approves the beauty of another woman, you may be sure that she has more of the same kind herself.
JEAN DE LA BRUYÈRE: *Caractères*, XII, 1688

I met with a sort of people that held women have no souls, adding, in a light manner, no more than a goose. But I reproved them, and told them that was not right; for Mary said, "My soul doth magnify the Lord, and my spirit hath rejoiced in God my Saviour."
GEORGE FOX: *Journal*, I (*c.* 1647), 1694 (The quotation is from LUKE I, 46–47, *c.* 75)

Providence, that formed the fair
In such a charming skin,
Their outside made His only care,
And never look'd within.
THOMAS D'URFEY: *Song*, *c.* 1695

We shall find no fiend in Hell can match the fury of a disappointed woman, — scorn'd! slighted! dismiss'd without a parting pang.
COLLEY CIBBER: *Love's Last Shift*, IV, 1696 (Cf. CONGREVE, *post*, 1697)

Once a woman has given you her heart you can never get rid of the rest of her.
JOHN VANBRUGH: *The Relapse*, II, 1606

Heaven has no rage like love to hatred turned,
Nor Hell a fury like a woman scorned.
WILLIAM CONGREVE: *The Mourning Bride*, III, 1697 (Cf. CIBBER, *ante*, 1696)

A woman of sense and manners is the finest and most delicate part of God's creation, the glory of her Maker, and the great instance of His singular regard to man.
DANIEL DEFOE: *An Essay Upon Projects*, 1697

I'll sooner undertake to teach sincerity to a courtier, generosity to an usurer, honesty to a lawyer, nay, humility to a divine, than discretion to a woman I see has once set her heart upon playing the fool.
JOHN VANBRUGH: *The Provok'd Wife*, II, 1697

Whilst there is a world 'tis woman that will govern it.
JOHN VANBRUGH: *The Provok'd Wife*, III

The woman was made of a rib out of the side of Adam; not out of his feet to be trampled upon by him, but out of his side to be equal with him, under his arm to be protected, and near his heart to be loved.
MATTHEW HENRY: *Exposition of Genesis II*, 1704

Last week I saw a woman flayed, and you will hardly believe how much it altered her person for the worse.
JONATHAN SWIFT: *A Tale of a Tub*, 1704

A very little wit is valued in a woman, as we are pleased with a few words spoken plain by a parrot.
JONATHAN SWIFT: *Thoughts on Various Subjects*, 1706

How a little love and conversation improve a woman!
GEORGE FARQUHAR: *The Beaux' Stratagem*, IV, 1707

Woman, the last, the best reserv'd of God.
ALEXANDER POPE: *January and May*, 1709

To be well dressed, in good humor, and cheerful in the command of her family, are the arts and sciences of female life.
RICHARD STEELE: *The Tatler*, Oct. 1, 1709

An animal that delights in finery.
JOSEPH ADDISON: *The Spectator*, Jan. 3, 1712 (Credited to " one of the fathers ")

The woman that deliberates is lost.
JOSEPH ADDISON: *Cato*, IV, 1713

I have never had any great esteem for the generality of the fair sex, and my only consolation for being of that gender has been the assurance it gave me of never being married to any one among them.
MARY WORTLEY MONTAGU: *Letter to the Hon. Miss Calthorpe*, Dec., 1723

Nothing hinders women from playing the fool, but not having it in their power. IBID.

Not ev'n the soldier's fury, rais'd in war,
The rage of tyrants, when defiance stings 'em!
The pride of priests, so bloody when in power,
Are half so dreadful as a woman's vengeance.
RICHARD SAVAGE: *Sir Thomas Overbury*, 1724

Such, Polly, are your sex — part truth, part fiction;
Some thought, much whim, and all a contradiction.
RICHARD SAVAGE: To a Young Lady, *c.* 1725

We men have many faults;
Poor women have but two —
There's nothing good they say,
There's nothing good they do.
Anon.: *On Women's Faults*, 1727

'Tis woman that seduces all mankind;
By her we first were taught the wheedling arts;
Her very eyes can cheat; when most she's kind,
She tricks us of our money with our hearts.
JOHN GAY: *The Beggar's Opera*, I, 1728

I must have women — there is nothing unbends the mind like them.
JOHN GAY: *The Beggar's Opera*, II

Man may escape from rope and gun,
Nay, some have outlived the doctor's pill;
Who takes a woman must be undone,
That basilisk is sure to kill. IBID.

To cheat a man is nothing; but the woman must have fine parts, indeed, who cheats a woman.
IBID.

Authorities, both old and recent,
Direct that women must be decent.
JONATHAN SWIFT: *Strephon and Chloe*, 1731

A cat has nine lives and a woman has nine cats' lives.
THOMAS FULLER: *Gnomologia*, 1732

All women are good; viz., good for something, or good for nothing. IBID.

A woman, a spaniel, and a walnut tree,
The more they're beaten the better they be.
IBID.

When an ass climbeth a ladder you may find wisdom in women. IBID.

Ev'ry woman is at heart a rake.
ALEXANDER POPE: *Moral Essays*, II (Of the Characters of Women), 1735

Heaven, when it strives to polish all it can
Its last best work, but forms a softer man.
IBID.

In men we various ruling passions find;
In women two almost divide the kind;
Those only fixed, they first or last obey,
The love of pleasure, and the love of sway.
IBID.

Most women have no characters at all. IBID.

Women always have some afterthought (arrière-pensée).
P. N. DESTOUCHES: *Le dissipateur*, V, 1736

First, then, a woman will or won't, depend on't;
If she will do't, she will; and there's an end on't.
AARON HILL: *Zara*, epilogue, 1736

Women are only children of a larger growth; they have an entertaining tattle, and sometimes wit; but for solid reasoning, good sense, I never knew in my life one that had it, or who reasoned or acted consequentially for four-and-twenty hours together.
LORD CHESTERFIELD: *Letter to his son*, Sept. 5, 1748

Women are to be talked to as below men, and above children.
LORD CHESTERFIELD: *Letter to his son*, Sept. 20, 1748

Women are much more like each other than men.
LORD CHESTERFIELD: *Letter to his son*, Dec. 19, 1749

Women prefer being amused without being loved to being loved without being amused.
Ascribed to MME. DE RIEUX, *c.* 1750

He seldom errs
Who thinks the worst he can of womankind.
JOHN HOME: *Douglas*, II, 1756

Women, like princes, find few real friends:
All who approach them their own ends pursue.
GEORGE, BARON LYTTELTON: *Advice to a Lady*, *c.* 1760

Her dignity consists in being unknown to the world; her glory is in the esteem of her husband; her pleasures in the happiness of her family. J.-J. ROUSSEAU: *Émile*, I, 1762

There is nothing that so much seduces reason from vigilance as the thought of passing life with an amiable woman.
SAMUEL JOHNSON: *Letter to Joseph Baretti*, Dec. 21, 1762

Sir, a woman preaching is like a dog's walking on his hind legs. It is not done well; but you are surprised to find it done at all.
SAMUEL JOHNSON: *Boswell's Life*, July 31, 1763

When lovely woman stoops to folly,
And finds too late that men betray,
What charm can soothe her melancholy?
What art can wash her guilt away?
OLIVER GOLDSMITH: *The Hermit*, 1764 (Inserted in *The Vicar of Wakefield*, 1766)

Woman, I tell you, is a microcosm: and rightly to rule her requires as great talents as to govern a state.
SAMUEL FOOTE: *The Devil Upon Two Sticks*, I, 1768

Nature meant woman to be her masterpiece.
G. E. LESSING: *Emilia Galotti*, V, 1772

The profession of woman is very hard.
LOUISE D'EPINAY: *Les conversations d'Emilie*, 1774

A woman of fortune, being used to the handling of money, spends it judiciously; but a woman who gets the command of money for the first time upon her marriage has such a gust in spending it that she throws it away with great profusion.
SAMUEL JOHNSON: *Boswell's Life*, March 28, 1776

Women have a great advantage that they may take up with little things, without disgracing themselves; a man cannot, except with fiddling.
SAMUEL JOHNSON: *Boswell's Life*, April 7, 1778

What is woman? Only one of nature's agreeable blunders.
HANNAH COWLEY: *Who's the Dupe?*, II, 1779

Women, destined to be obedient, ought to be disciplined early to bear wrongs without murmuring.
H. H. KAMES: *Loose Hints Upon Education*, 1781

What signifies the life o' man,
And 'twere na for the lasses?
ROBERT BURNS: *Green Grow the Rashes*, 1784

Women have a perpetual envy of our vices; they are less vicious than we, not from choice, but because we restrict them.
SAMUEL JOHNSON: *Boswell's Life*, June 10, 1784

There are two things I have always loved madly: they are women and celibacy.
NICOLAS DE CHAMFORT: *Maximes et pensées*, *c.* 1785

I look on the sex with something like the admiration with which I regard the starry sky in a frosty December night. I admire the beauty of the Creator's workmanship; I am charmed with the wild but graceful eccentricity of their motions; and — wish them good-night.

ROBERT BURNS: *Letter to Miss Chalmers*, Sept. 23, 1787

The thoughts of women ever hover round their persons.

MARY WOLLSTONECRAFT: *A Vindication of the Rights of Woman*, IV, 1792

I am glad that I am not a man, for then I should have to marry a woman.

ANNA LOUISE DE STAËL: *De l'influence des passions*, 1796 (Cf. MONTAGU, *ante*, 1723)

Without the smile from partial beauty won,
Oh! what were man? — a world without a sun.

THOMAS CAMPBELL: *The Pleasures of Hope*, II, 1799

Among women all ideas are converted into persons.

JEAN PAUL RICHTER: *Titan*, CIV, 1803

I am no great physiognomist, nor have I much confidence in a science which pretends to discover the inside from the out; but where I have seen fine eyes, a beautiful complexion, grace and symmetry in women, I have generally thought them amazingly well-informed and extremely philosophical. In contrary instances, seldom or never.

SYDNEY SMITH: *Letter to Francis Jeffrey*, 1804

The appointment of a woman to office is an innovation for which the public is not prepared, nor am I.

THOMAS JEFFERSON: *Letter to Albert Gallatin*, Jan., 1807

The reason firm, the temperate will,
Endurance, foresight, strength, and skill;
A perfect woman, nobly planned,
To warn, to comfort, and command.

WILLIAM WORDSWORTH: *She Was a Phantom of Delight*, 1807

Where there are no women there are no good manners.

J. W. GOETHE: *Elective Affinities*, II, 1808

O woman! in our hours of ease,
Uncertain, coy, and hard to please,
And variable as the shade
By the light quivering aspen made, —
When pain and anguish wring the brow,
A ministering angel thou!

WALTER SCOTT: *Marmion*, VI, 1808

Believe a woman or an epitaph.

BYRON: *English Bards and Scotch Reviewers*, 1809

Women hazard everything upon one cast of the die; — when youth is gone all is gone.

SYDNEY SMITH: In the Edinburgh Review, 1810

I treat the charwomen like duchesses, and the duchesses like charwomen.

G. B. (BEAU) BRUMMELL: On being asked the secret of his success with women, *c.* 1815

Women are nothing but machines for producing children.

NAPOLEON I: To Gaspard Gourgaud at St. Helena, Jan. 9, 1817

Women, when they are bad, are worse than men, and more ready to commit crimes. The soft sex, when degraded, falls lower than the other. Women are always much better or much worse than men.

NAPOLEON I: To Barry E. O'Meara at St. Helena, May 16, 1817

The generality of women appear to me as children whom I would rather give a sugar plum than my time.

JOHN KEATS: *Letter to George and Georgiana Keats*, Oct. 21, 1818

There was a woman, beautiful as morning.

P. B. SHELLEY: *The Revolt of Islam*, I, 1818

If any woman were to hang a man for stealing her picture, although it were set in gold, it would be a new case in law.

C. C. COLTON: *Lacon*, 1820

My only books
Were woman's looks,
And folly's all they've taught me.

THOMAS MOORE: *The Time I've Lost in Wooing*, *c.* 1820

In her first passion woman loves her lover;
In all the others, all she loves is love.

BYRON: *Don Juan*, III, 1821

A tigress robb'd of young, a lioness,
Or any interesting beast of prey,
Are similes at hand for the distress
Of ladies who cannot have their own way.

BYRON: *Don Juan*, V

Women have often more of what is called good sense than men. They have fewer pretensions; are less implicated in theories; and judge of objects more from their immediate and involuntary impression on the mind, and, therefore, more truly and naturally. They cannot reason wrong; for they do not reason at all.

WILLIAM HAZLITT: *The Ignorance of the Learned*, 1821

Without woman the beginning of our life would be helpless, the middle without pleasure, and the end void of consolation.

VICTOR DE JOUY: *Sylla*, II, 1821

I've seen your stormy seas and stormy women,
And pity lovers rather more than seamen.

BYRON: *Don Juan*, VI, 1823

What a strange thing is man! and what a stranger
Is woman! What a whirlwind is her head,

And what a whirlpool full of depth and danger
Is all the rest about her.

BYRON: *Don Juan*, IX

The dignity of womanhood.

THOMAS CAMPBELL: *Theodric*, 1824

From a woman in love we may expect anything — and to her we may safely impute anything.

BALZAC: *The Physiology of Marriage*, 1830

The eternal feminine draws us upward. (Das Ewig-Weibliche zieht uns hinan.)

J. W. GOETHE: *II Faust*, II, 1832

A beautiful woman is a picture which drives all beholders nobly mad.

R. W. EMERSON: *Art*, 1841

Woman's love is writ in water,
Woman's faith is traced in sand.

W. E. AYTOUN: *Lays of the Scottish Cavaliers*, 1848

Woman is as variable as a feather in the wind.
(La donna è mobile
Qual piuma al vento.)

F. M. PIAVE: *Rigoletto*, I, 1851 (Set to music by Giuseppe Verdi)

A woman represents a sort of intermediate stage between a child and a man.

ARTHUR SCHOPENHAUER: *Parerga und Paralipomena*, 1851

Woman pays her debt to life, not by what she does, but by what she suffers. IBID.

Dissimulation is innate in woman, and almost as much a quality of the stupid as of the clever. It is as natural for them to make use of it on every occasion as it is for animals to employ their means of defence when they are attacked. A woman who is perfectly truthful is perhaps an impossibility.

ARTHUR SCHOPENHAUER: *On Women*, 1851

It is only the man whose intellect is clouded by his sexual impulse that could give the name of the fair sex to that undersized, narrow-shouldered, broad-hipped, and short-legged race. IBID.

The fundamental fault of the female character is that it has no sense of justice. IBID.

The natural feeling between men is mere indifference, but between women it is actual enmity. The reason for this is that trade-jealousy — *odium figulinum* — which, in the case of men does not go beyond the confines of their own particular pursuit; but, with women, embraces the whole sex; since they have only one kind of business. Even when they meet in the street, women look at one another like Guelphs and Ghibellines. IBID.

Oh, the women! we must forgive them much, for they love much — and many. Their hate is, in fact, only love turned inside out.

HEINRICH HEINE: *Confessions*, 1854

When women write they always have one eye on the paper and the other on a man.

HEINRICH HEINE: *Lutezia*, 1854

Be not ashamed, woman — your privilege encloses the rest, and is the exit of the rest;
You are the gates of the body, and you are the gates of the soul.

WALT WHITMAN: *I Sing the Body Electric*, 1855

Woman will be the last thing civilized by man.

GEORGE MEREDITH: *The Ordeal of Richard Feverel*, I, 1859

The happiest women, like the happiest nations, have no history.

MARIAN EVANS (GEORGE ELIOT): *The Mill on the Floss*, VI, 1860

Strong-minded, able-bodied women are my aversion, and I run out of the road of one as I would from a mad cow.

JANE WELSH CARLYLE: *Letter to Mrs. Russell*, Aug. 30, 1861

Look for the woman. (Cherchez la femme.)

ALEXANDRE DUMAS, *père: Les Mohicans de Paris*, II, 1864

Women rather take to terrible people; prize-fighters, pirates, highwaymen, rebel generals, Grand Turks, and Bluebeards generally have a fascination for the sex; your virgin has a natural instinct to saddle your lion.

O. W. HOLMES: *The Guardian Angel*, XIII, 1867

Women wish to be loved without a why or a wherefore; not because they are pretty, or good, or well-bred, or graceful, or intelligent, but because they are themselves.

H. F. AMIEL: *Journal*, March 17, 1868

To understand one woman is not necessarily to understand any other woman.

J. S. MILL: *The Subjection of Women*, I, 1869

There is no sea-wave without salt;
There is no woman without fault.

JOHN HAY: *Castilian Days*, XII, 1872 (Translation of a Spanish proverb)

A woman doth the mischief brew
In nineteen cases out of twenty.

W. S. GILBERT: *Engaged*, I, 1877

Stupidity in a woman is unfeminine.

F. W. NIETZSCHE: *Human All-too-Human*, II, 1878

Woman is capricious and coy, and has less straightforwardness than man.

FRANCIS GALTON: *Inquiries Into Human Faculty*, 1883

Thou goest to women? Don't forget thy whip.

F. W. NIETZSCHE: *Thus Spake Zarathustra*, XVIII, 1885

Seek not for the favor of women. So shall you find it indeed.

Does not the boar break cover just when you're lighting a weed?

RUDYARD KIPLING: *Certain Maxims of Hafiz,* 1886

Did any woman ever acknowledge profundity in another woman's mind, or justice in another woman's heart?

F. W. NIETZSCHE: *Beyond Good and Evil,* 1886

Man wishes woman to be peaceable, but in fact she is essentially warlike, like the cat.

IBID.

When a woman inclines to learning there is usually something wrong with her sex apparatus.

IBID.

Whenever the stake of the game is neither love nor hatred women play badly. IBID.

Woman learns how to hate in proportion as she forgets how to charm. IBID.

Nature intended woman for the warrior's relaxation, to succeed as actresses, queens, and courtesans — yes, and as saints.

GEORGE MOORE: *Confessions of a Young Man,* x, 1888

God created woman. In the act he brought boredom to an end — and also many other things. Woman was the second mistake of God.

F. W. NIETZSCHE: *The Antichrist,* XLVIII, 1888

Among women: Truth? Is it not an outrage upon all our *pudeurs?*

F. W. NIETZSCHE: *The Twilight of the Idols,* 1889

These anthropomorphs, these half apes, this horde of half-developed animals, these women whose intellects are of the Age of Bronze.

AUGUST STRINDBERG: *Comrades,* 1890

No one but a woman and an Indian ever scalps the dead.

JOHN J. INGALLS: Said after his unsuccessful campaign for the Senate in 1891, in which Mary Elizabeth Lease opposed him violently

Never trust a woman who wears mauve, or a woman over thirty-five who is fond of pink ribbons. It means they have a history.

OSCAR WILDE: *The Picture of Dorian Gray,* 1891

No woman is a genius: women are a decorative sex. They never have anything to say, but they say it charmingly. They represent the triumph of matter over mind, just as men represent the triumph of mind over morals.

IBID.

The charm of the past is that it is past, but women never know when the curtain has fallen. They always want a sixth act. IBID.

An' I learned about women from 'er.

RUDYARD KIPLING: *The Ladies,* 1892

The colonel's lady and Judy O'Grady
Are sisters under their skins. IBID.

The world is packed with good women. To know them is a middle-class education.

OSCAR WILDE: *Lady Windermere's Fan,* II, 1892

Women are pictures, men are problems: if you want to know what a woman really means, look at her, don't listen to her.

OSCAR WILDE: *A Woman of No Importance,* I, 1893

Women have always been picturesque protests against the mere existence of common sense.

IBID.

The Bible says that woman was the last thing God made. Evidently he made her on Saturday night. She reveals His fatigue.

ALEXANDRE DUMAS *fils* (1825–95)

Woman inspires us to great things — and prevents us accomplishing them. IBID.

The way to behave to a woman is to make love to her if she is pretty, and to some one else if she is plain.

OSCAR WILDE: *The Importance of Being Earnest,* II, 1895

A rag and a bone and a hank of hair.

RUDYARD KIPLING: *The Vampire,* 1897

For study of the good and the bad in woman two women are a needless expense.

AMBROSE BIERCE: *Collected Works,* VIII, 1911

He gets on best with women who best knows how to get on without them. IBID.

Woman would be more charming if one could fall into her arms without falling into her hands. IBID.

The female of the species is more deadly than the male.

RUDYARD KIPLING: *The Female of the Species,* 1911

The body of woman is a temple and not a tavern. VANCE THOMPSON: *Woman,* 1917

It is reputed that quite a number of women have had consciences.

JAMES BRANCH CABELL: *Jurgen,* XXXVI, 1919

Ashes to ashes, dust to dust,
Never seen a woman a man could trust.

American Negro song, quoted by HOWARD W. ODUM: *Wings On My Feet,* IX, 1929

Can you recall a woman who ever showed you with pride her library?

BENJAMIN DECASSERES: *Fantasia Impromptu,* 1933

Some women are like Pompeii; some are like Verdun; some are like Kokomo, Ind., on a Sunday afternoon. IBID.

A squaw's tongue runs faster than the wind's legs. AMERICAN INDIAN PROVERB

I am not one of those who say, "It is nothing; it is a woman drowning." LA FONTAINE

It is hard to forget a woman with whom one has been happy. Author unidentified

It is less difficult for a woman to become celebrated for genius than to be forgiven for it. IBID.

It's a weary world and full of women. IBID.

Many men have many minds,
But women have but two:
Everything would they have,
And nothing would they do. IBID.

My son, I've traveled round the world
And many maids I've met:
There are two kinds you should avoid —
The blonde and the brunette. IBID.

No wonder Ithaca is celebrated: one woman was faithful there! IBID.

Oh, the gladness of their gladness when they're glad,
And the sadness of their sadness when they're sad;
But the gladness of their gladness, and the sadness of their sadness,
Are as nothing to their badness when they're bad. IBID.

Not she with trait'rous kiss her Saviour stung,
Nor she denied Him with unholy tongue;
She, while apostles shrank, could danger brave,
Last at His cross, and earliest at His grave. IBID.

Virtue, with some women, is but the precaution of locking the door. IBID.

Women are demons that make us enter Hell through the door of Paradise. IBID.

Women are the wild life of a country. Morality corresponds to game laws. IBID.

Never trust a woman, even though she has given you ten sons. CHINESE PROVERB

There is no such poison in the green snake's mouth or the hornet's sting as in a woman's heart. IBID.

All keys hang not at one woman's girdle. DANISH PROVERB

All women are Lutherans at heart. IBID.

No woman is too bashful to talk scandal. DUTCH PROVERB

Virtue is fairer when it appears in a handsome woman. FINNISH PROVERB

A man of straw is worth a woman of gold. FRENCH PROVERB

No mirror ever reflected an ugly woman. IBID.

The woman most praised is the one never spoken of at all. IBID.

Women are often different. (Souvent femme varie.) IBID.

Woman is stronger by reason of her feelings than man by reason of his strength. IBID.

Woman, like good wine, is a sweet poison. IBID.

Woman's wishes are God's wishes. IBID.

A woman has the form of an angel, the heart of a serpent, and the mind of an ass. GERMAN PROVERB

A woman's advice is good only every seven years. IBID.

A woman without religion is as a flower without scent. IBID.

Hares are caught with dogs, fools with flattery, and women with money. IBID.

It is easier to keep watch over a bag of fleas than over a woman. IBID.

Never believe a woman, not even a dead one. IBID.

The first advice of a woman is always the best. IBID.

Whatever a beautiful woman says is right. IBID.

When a woman has no answer, the sea is empty of water. IBID.

Whenever a woman dies there is one quarrel less on earth. IBID.

Women are like death: they pursue those who flee from them, and flee from those who pursue them. IBID.

Women, like the moon, shine with borrowed light.

Women must be praised, whether it is true or false. IBID.

Take away the light, and all women are alike. GREEK PROVERB

The cause of a woman's envy is always to be found in another woman. HEBREW PROVERB

Ugliness is the one effective guardian of woman. IBID.

Where there are many women there is much superstition. IBID.

A thousand men can easily live together in peace, but two women, even if they be sisters, can never do so. HINDU PROVERB

The word of a woman is like a bundle of water. IBID.

There are three without rule: a mule, a pig and a woman. IRISH PROVERB

Women are shy, and shame prevents them from refusing a man. IBID.

A fair woman and a slashed gown always find some nail in the way. ITALIAN PROVERB

A learned woman is twice a fool. IBID.

No woman ever told the whole truth. IBID.

These three need strong hands to break them: women, asses and nuts. IBID.

When a beautiful woman smiles, somebody's purse weeps. IBID.

Women are wise on a sudden, but fools upon premeditation. IBID.

Women know a shade more than the Devil. IBID.

Women resist in order to be conquered. IBID.

A woman's tongue is only three inches long, but it can kill a man six feet high. JAPANESE PROVERB

Woman's thoughts are always afterthoughts. JAPANESE PROVERB (Cf. DESTOUCHES, *ante*, 1736)

Woman's tongue is a sword which never rusts. IBID.

The only secrets women keep are those they don't know. JUGO-SLAVIC PROVERB

What is lighter than a feather? Dust. Than dust? The wind. Than the wind? Woman. Than woman? Nothing. (Quid pluma levius? Pulvis. Quid pulvere? Ventus. Quid vento? Mulier. Quid muliere? Nihil.) LATIN PROVERB

Women are implacable when injured. (Implacabiles plerumque læsæ mulieres.) IBID.

Woman is an evil, but a necessary evil. (Malum est mulier, sed necessarium malum.) IBID.

The man is the head but the woman is the neck, and the neck turns the head. OXFORDSHIRE PROVERB

Woman is a calamity, but every house must have its curse. PERSIAN PROVERB

Do not trust a good woman, and keep away from a bad one. PORTUGUESE PROVERB

These three things are bad when lean: a goose, a woman, and a goat. IBID.

A woman has more tricks than a wheel has turns. RUSSIAN PROVERB

A woman's hair is long, but her tongue is longer. IBID.

A woman's sense is always shorter than her hair. IBID.

When the Devil fails himself he sends a woman as his agent. IBID.

A woman's advice is of little value, but he who does not take it is a fool. SPANISH PROVERB

A woman's tears, like a dog's limping, are seldom real. IBID.

Beware of women who tell fortunes or who know Latin. IBID.

Judge a woman by the manner of her walking and drinking. IBID.

Tell a woman she's a beauty, and the Devil will make her believe it. IBID.

There are many good women, but they are all dead. IBID.

When listening to a woman, believe only one word in forty. TURKISH PROVERB

Three things are useless: whispering to the deaf, grieving for the dead, and advising a woman against her will. WELSH PROVERB

Women are sisters nowhere. WEST AFRICAN PROVERB

Woman has long hair but the sense of a cat. YIDDISH PROVERB

[*See also* Adornment, Advice, Age, Ages, Anger, Arms, Asceticism, Beard, Beating, Beauty, Bluestocking, Brave, Bravery, Bride, Caution, Celibacy, Change, Chastity, Convert, Cook, Cookery, Corset, Cosmetics, Damage, Damnation, Darkness, Deceit, Desire, Dog, Drama, Dress, Drinking, Drunk, England, Evil, Fair, Faith, Female, Feminine, Flattery, Flirtation, Folly, Fool, Forgiveness, Frailty, Friend, Friendship, Girl, God, Greyhound, Hair, Handsome, Happiness, Hatred, Honor, Husband and Wife, Inconstancy, Indecency, Indelicate, Indiscretion, Intrigue, Jealousy, Jewelry, Kindness, Lady, Language, Lean, Love, Lover, Man and Woman, Market, Marriage, Marriage (Second), Memory, Mirror, Misogyny, Monk, Mourning, Music, Naturalization, No, Perfume, Pleasure, Poetry, Postscript, Preaching, Pretty, Priest, Reason, Scholarship, Shopping, Silence, Slander, Slovenliness, Smell, Soldier, Sun, Talk, Tears, Temper, Temptation, Thirty, Toilet, Tongue, Truth, Tyranny, Uniform, Untameable, Virago, Virgin, Virginity, Virtue, Voice, War, Whistling, Widow, Wife.

Woman, American

The typical American woman is not, and never has been, a beer-drinking or a wine-drinking woman; and to this fact mainly we attribute her wealth of loveliness.
J. G. HOLLAND: *Everyday Topics,* 1876

An American woman seems to have no other object in life than to fill her house with other people, even when she does the cooking herself.
GEORGE BERNARD SHAW: Address in New York, April 11, 1933

Woman, Old

When the old crone frolics, she flirts with death.
PUBLILIUS SYRUS: *Sententiæ, c.* 50 B.C.

An old wife is dowisome.
JAMES KELLY: *Complete Collection of Scottish Proverbs,* 1721 (*Dowisome*= melancholy)

A pretty pig makes an ugly old sow.
THOMAS FULLER: *Gnomologia,* 1732

In your amours you should prefer old women to young ones. This you call a paradox, and demand my reasons. They are: . . . 8th and lastly: they are so grateful.
BENJAMIN FRANKLIN: *Letter to a young man,* June 25, 1745

There is hardly such a thing to be found as an old woman who is not a good woman.
IBID.

Time has the same effect on the mind as on the face. The predominant passion, the strongest feature, become more conspicuous from the others retiring; the various views of life are abandoned, from want of ability to pursue them, as the fine complexion is lost in wrinkles; but, as surely as a large nose grows larger, and a wide mouth wider, the tender child in your nursery will be a tender old woman.
MARY WORTLEY MONTAGU: *Letter to the Countess of Bute,* Sept. 5, 1758

Who are the most despicable creatures? Certainly old women. What pleasure can an old woman take? Only witchcraft. I think this argument as clear as any of the devout Bishop of Cloyne's metaphysics.
MARY WORTLEY MONTAGU: *Letter to James Steuart,* Nov. 14, 1758 (The Bishop of Cloyne was George Berkeley, *d.* 1753)

There are three classes into which all the women past seventy that ever I knew were to be divided: (1) that dear old soul; (2) that old woman; (3) that old witch.
S. T. COLERIDGE: *Table-Talk,* July 7, 1831

Women sit, or move to and fro – some old, some young;
The young are beautiful – but the old are more beautiful than the young.
WALT WHITMAN: *Beautiful Women,* 1860

Silvered is the raven hair –
Spreading is the parting straight,
Mottled the complexion fair,
Halting is the youthful gait.
Hollow is the laughter free,
Spectacled the limped eye,
Little will be left of me,
In the coming by-and-by.
W. S. GILBERT: *Patience,* II, 1881

An old woman will be soon tired with anything she will do.
J. M. SYNGE: *Riders to the Sea,* 1904

Leave him with his grief – he has married an old woman. ARAB PROVERB

What it takes the Devil a year to do, an old woman does in an hour. IBID.

When young, women are grapes; when old, raisins. GERMAN PROVERB

Where the Devil can't go he sends an old woman. IBID.

A woman of sixty, like a girl of six, runs at the sound of wedding music.
HEBREW PROVERB

It is safer to anger a dog than an old woman.
ITALIAN PROVERB

When a woman grows old there is nothing left in her but poison. MOROCCAN PROVERB

[*See also* Age (Old), Good, Man (Old), Perfume, Physician.

Woman Suffrage

[*See* Suffrage (Woman).

Woman, Young

Nothing enchants the soul so much as young women. They alone are the cause of evil, and there is no other.
BHARTRIHARI: *The Sringa Sataka, c.* 625

[*See also* Marriage (Early).

Wonder

Wonder implies the desire to learn; the wonderful is therefore the desirable.
ARISTOTLE: *Rhetoric,* I, *c.* 322 B.C.

This wonder (as wonders last) lasted nine days.
JOHN HEYWOOD: *Proverbs,* 1546

Wonder is the daughter of ignorance.
THOMAS FULLER: *Gnomologia,* 1732

And still they gazed, and still the wonder grew,
That one small head should carry all it knew.
OLIVER GOLDSMITH: *The Deserted Village,* 1770

Worth seeing? Yes; but not worth going to see.
SAMUEL JOHNSON: *Boswell's Life,* Oct. 12, 1779 (He was speaking of the Giant's Causeway)

A schoolboy's tale, the wonder of an hour.
BYRON: *Childe Harold,* II, 1812

The man who cannot wonder, who does not habitually wonder (and worship), were he president of innumerable Royal Societies and carried . . . the epitome of all laboratories and observatories, with their results, in his single head, — is but a pair of spectacles behind which there is no eye.
THOMAS CARLYLE: *Sartor Resartus,* I, 1836

No wonder can last more than three days.
ITALIAN PROVERB

[*See also* God, Ignorance, Worship.

Wonderful

There be three things which are too wonderful for me, yes, four which I know not: the way of an eagle in the air; the way of a serpent upon a rock; the way of a ship in the midst of the sea; and the way of a man with a maid. PROVERBS XXX, 18–19, *c.* 350 B.C.

O wonderful, wonderful, and most wonderful wonderful! and yet again wonderful.
SHAKESPEARE: *As You Like It,* III, *c.* 1600

A wonderful year. (Annus mirabilis.)
LATIN PHRASE

Wonderful to relate. (Mirabile dictu.) IBID.

Wonderful to the sight. (Mirabile visu.)
IBID.

[*See also* Fearfully.

Wood

[*See* Old.

Woodchuck

How much wood would a woodchuck chuck
If a woodchuck could chuck wood?
AMERICAN FOLK-RHYME; date undetermined

Woodcock

[*See* Partridge.

Woodman

[*See* Tree.

Woods

Some boundless contiguity of shade.
WILLIAM COWPER: *The Task,* II, 1785

The woods are full of them.
ALEXANDER WILSON: *American Ornithology,* I, 1808

In the woods a man casts off his years, as the snake his slough, and at what period soever of life, is always a child.
R. W. EMERSON: *Nature,* 1836

In the woods it rains twice.
GERMAN PROVERB

You can't see the woods for the trees.
GERMAN SAYING

[*See also* Forest, Gods, Landscape, Tree.

Wooing

His left hand should be under my head, and his right hand should embrace me.
SOLOMON'S SONG VIII, 3, *c.* 200 B.C.

Was ever woman in this humor woo'd?
Was ever woman in this humor won?
SHAKESPEARE: *Richard III,* I, *c.* 1592

That man that hath a tongue, I say, is no man,
If with his tongue he cannot win a woman.
SHAKESPEARE: *Two Gentlemen of Verona,* III, *c.* 1595

O gentle Romeo,
If thou dost love, pronounce it faithfully.
Or if thou think'st I am too quickly won,
I'll frown and be perverse and say thee nay,
So thou wilt woo.
SHAKESPEARE: *Romeo and Juliet,* II, *c.* 1596

Men are April when they woo, December when they wed.
SHAKESPEARE: *As You Like It,* IV, *c.* 1600

Feed thou on me, and I will feed on thee,
And love shall feed us both.
THOMAS HEYWOOD: *The Fair Maid of the Exchange,* 1607

Blessed is the wooing
That is not long a-doing.
ROBERT BURTON: *The Anatomy of Melancholy,* III, 1621

Women are won when they begin to threaten.
Anon.: *Nero,* II, 1624

He that will win his dame, must do
As love does, when he bends his bow;
With one hand thrust the lady from,
And with the other pull her home.
SAMUEL BUTLER: *Hudibras,* I, 1663

He that would the daughter win
Must with the mother first begin.
JOHN RAY: *English Proverbs,* 1670

'Tis fit men should be coy when women woo.
WILLIAM CONGREVE: *The Old Bachelor,* IV, 1693

A queen, if she had to do with a groom, would expect a mark of his kindness from him, though it were but his curry-comb.
ALEXANDER POPE: *Letter to William Wycherley,* Feb. 5, 1706 (Ascribed to "a Spanish lady")

I'll woo her as the lion woos his brides.
JOHN HOME: *Douglas,* I, 1756

Not much he kens, I ween, of woman's breast,
Who thinks that wanton thing is won by sighs.
BYRON: *Childe Harold,* II, 1812

Our troth had been plighted,
Not by moonbeam, or starbeam, or fountain or grove,
But in a front parlor most brilliantly lighted,
Beneath the gas-fixtures we whispered our love;
Without any romance, or raptures, or sighs,
Without any tears in Miss Flora's blue eyes,
Or blushes or transports, or such silly actions,
It was one of the quietest business transactions.

WILLIAM ALLEN BUTLER: *Nothing to Wear,* 1857

Why don't you speak for yourself, John?

H. W. LONGFELLOW: *The Courtship of Miles Standish,* III, 1858

Perhaps if you address the lady
Most politely, most politely,
Flatter and impress the lady
Most politely, most politely,
Humbly beg and humbly sue,
She may deign to look on you.

W. S. GILBERT: *The Princess Ida,* I, 1884

Bitin' and scratchin' is Scots folk's wooing.

SCOTTISH PROVERB

[*See also* Courtship, Male and Female, Man and Woman, Proposal, Tongue, Widow.

Word

For one word a man is often set down as wise, and for one word he is as often set down as a fool.

CONFUCIUS: *Analects,* XIX, *c.* 500 B.C.

A flaw in a piece of white jade may be ground away, but a word spoken amiss may not be called back.

CONFUCIUS: *The Book of Poetry, c.* 500 B.C.

Words are the physicians of a distempered mind.

ÆSCHYLUS: *Prometheus Bound, c.* 490 B.C.

A word fitly spoken is like apples of gold in pictures of silver.

PROVERBS XXV, 11, *c.* 350 B.C.

How forcible are right words!

JOB VI, 25, *c.* 325 B.C.

Let no man deceive you with vain words.

EPHESIANS V, 6, *c.* 60

Heaven and earth shall pass away, but my words shall not pass away.

MATTHEW XXIV, 35, *c.* 75

He was clothed with a vesture dipped in blood: and his name is called The Word of God.

REVELATION XIX, 13, *c.* 95

In the beginning was the Word, and the Word was with God, and the Word was God.

JOHN I, 1, *c.* 115

The Word was made flesh, and dwelt among us.

JOHN I, 14

Better throw a stone at random than a word.

POPE XYSTUS I: *The Ring, c.* 150

Fair words break no bones.

ENGLISH PROVERB, traced by Apperson to 1460

Beware as long as thou livest of strange words, as thou wouldst take heed and eschew great rocks in the sea.

THOMAS WILSON: *The Arte of Rhetorique,* 1553

There are no colors so contrary as white and black, nor elements so disagreeing as fire and water, nor anything so opposite as men's thoughts and their words.

JOHN LYLY: *Endymion,* IV, 1591

These words are razors to my wounded heart.

SHAKESPEARE: *Titus Andronicus,* I, 1594

A fine volley of words, gentlemen, and quickly shot off.

SHAKESPEARE: *Two Gentlemen of Verona,* II, *c.* 1595

Here are a few of the unpleasant'st words
That ever blotted paper.

SHAKESPEARE: *The Merchant of Venice,* III, *c.* 1597

His very words are a fantastical banquet, just so many strange dishes.

SHAKESPEARE: *Much Ado About Nothing,* II, *c.* 1599

Fine words butter no parsnips.

ENGLISH PROVERB, borrowed from the Latin and familiar since the XVII century

A word to the wise is sufficient.

ENGLISH PROVERB, traced by Apperson to *c.* 1600 and apparently borrowed from TERENCE: *Phormio,* III, *c.* 160 B.C.: "Dictum sapienti sat est"; the latter seems to have given rise to a Latin proverb: "Verbum sapienti satis est," commonly abbreviated to "Verbum sap"

Words pay no debts.

SHAKESPEARE: *Troilus and Cressida,* III, *c.* 1601

Words are the tokens current and accepted for conceits, as moneys are for values.

FRANCIS BACON: *The Advancement of Learning,* II, 1605

Men believe that their reason governs words; but it is also true that words react on the understanding; and this it is that has rendered philosophy and the sciences sophistical and inactive.

FRANCIS BACON: *Novum Organum,* I, 1620

A blow with a word strikes deeper than a blow with a sword.

ROBERT BURTON: *The Anatomy of Melancholy,* I, 1621

Evening words are not like to morning.
GEORGE HERBERT: *Outlandish Proverbs*, 1640

Fair words make me look to my purse. IBID.

Words are feminine; deeds are masculine.
BALTASAR GRACIÁN: *The Art of Worldly Wisdom*, CCII, 1647

Words are the shadows of deeds. IBID.

Manly deeds and womanly words. (Fatti maschii, parole femine.)
MOTTO OF MARYLAND, adopted 1648 (Cf. GRACIÁN, *ante*, 1647)

Words have not their import from the natural power of particular combinations of character, or from the real efficacy of certain sounds, but from the consent of those that use them, and arbitrarily annex certain ideas to them, which might have been signified with equal propriety by any other.
OLIVER CROMWELL: *Reply to the Humble Petition and Advice of Parliament* (asking him to take the title of king), 1657

The world is satisfied with words; few care to dive beneath the surface.
BLAISE PASCAL: *Provincial Letters*, 1657

Man ever had, and ever will have, leave
To coin new words well suited to the age.
Words are like leaves, some wither every year,
And every year a younger race succeeds.
WENTWORTH DILLON (EARL OF ROSCOMMON): Tr. of HORACE: *De arte poetica* (*c.* 8 B.C.), 1680

We should have a great many fewer disputes in the world if words were taken for what they are, the signs of our ideas only, and not for things themselves.
JOHN LOCKE: *Essay Concerning Human Understanding*, III, 1690

A barren superfluity of words.
SAMUEL GARTH: *The Dispensary*, II, 1699

Harsh words, though pertinent, uncouth appear;
None please the fancy who offend the ear.
SAMUEL GARTH: *The Dispensary*, IV

In words, as fashions, the same rule will hold:
Alike fantastic, if too new, or old:
Be not the first by whom the new are tried,
Nor yet the last to lay the old aside.
ALEXANDER POPE: *An Essay on Criticism*, II, 1711

Words, when well chosen, have so great a force in them that a description often gives us more lively ideas than the sight of things themselves.
JOSEPH ADDISON: *The Spectator*, June 27, 1712

Fair words cost nothing.
JOHN GAY: *The Mohocks*, II, 1712

As fire is kindled by bellows, so is anger by words.
THOMAS FULLER: *Gnomologia*, 1732

High words break no bones.
HENRY FIELDING: *Don Quixote in England*, II, 1733

Fair words will not make the pot boil.
NATHANIEL BAILEY: *Etymological Dictionary*, 1736

I am not yet so lost in lexicography as to forget that words are the daughters of earth, and that things are the sons of Heaven.
SAMUEL JOHNSON: *Dictionary*, pref., 1755

Most of the disputes in the world arise from words.
LORD MANSFIELD: *Judgment in Morgan* vs. *Jones*, 1773

Words are always bolder than deeds.
J. C. F. SCHILLER: *The Piccolomini*, I, 1799

All words are no more to be taken in a literal sense at all times than a promise given to a tailor.
CHARLES LAMB: *Letter to Thomas Manning*, 1801

When ideas fail, words come in very handy.
J. W. GOETHE: *I Faust*, I, 1808

Religion — freedom — vengeance — what you will,
A word's enough to raise mankind to kill.
BYRON: *Lara*, II, 1814

Oh! many a shaft, at random sent,
Finds mark the archer little meant,
And many a word, at random spoken,
May soothe or wound a heart that's broken.
WALTER SCOTT: *The Lord of the Isles*, V, 1815

Words which were weapons.
P. B. SHELLEY: *The Revolt of Islam*, II, 1818

With words we govern men.
BENJAMIN DISRAELI: *Contarini Fleming*, I, 1832

What are the voices of birds,
Ay, and of beasts — but words, our words,
Only so much more sweet?
ROBERT BROWNING: *Pippa Passes*, I, 1841

Words as hard as cannon-balls.
R. W. EMERSON: *Self-Reliance*, 1841

Articulate words are a harsh clamor and dissonance. When man arrives at his highest perfection, he will again be dumb. For I suppose he was dumb at the Creation, and must go around an entire circle in order to return to that blessed state.
NATHANIEL HAWTHORNE: *American Note-Books*, April, 1841

Every word was once a poem. Every new relation is a new word.
R. W. EMERSON: *The Poet*, 1844

By ringing small changes on the words *leg-of-mutton* and *turnip* (changes so gradual as to escape detection), I could "demonstrate" that a turnip was, is, and of right ought to be, a leg-of-mutton.

E. A. POE: *Marginalia,* 1844–49

How very commonly we hear it remarked that such and such thoughts are beyond the compass of words. I do not believe that any thought, properly so called, is out of the reach of language. For my own part, I have never had a thought which I could not set down in words, with ever more distinctness than that with which I conceived it. IBID.

I sometimes hold it half a sin
To put in words the grief I feel;
For words, like nature, half reveal
And half conceal the soul within.

ALFRED TENNYSON: *In Memoriam,* v, 1850

Deliver your words not by number but by weight.

H. G. BOHN: *Handbook of Proverbs,* 1855

He who gives fair words feeds you with an empty spoon. IBID.

What so wild as words are?

ROBERT BROWNING: *A Woman's Last Word,* 1855

When we talk about ourselves we almost invariably use Latin words, and when we talk about our neighbors we use Saxon words.

H. W. BEECHER: *Royal Truths,* 1862

It is not of so much consequence what you say, as how you say it. Memorable sentences are memorable on account of some single irradiating word.

ALEXANDER SMITH: *Dreamthorp,* II, 1863

Our words have wings, but fly not where we would.

MARIAN EVANS (GEORGE ELIOT): *The Spanish Gypsy,* III, 1868

Every word is a preconceived judgment.

F. W. NIETZSCHE: *Human All-too-Human,* II, 1878

Words are less needful to sorrow than to joy.

HELEN HUNT JACKSON: *Ramona,* 1884

An average English word is four letters and a half. By hard, honest labor I've dug all the large words out of my vocabulary and shaved it down till the average is three and a half. . . . I never write *metropolis* for seven cents, because I can get the same price for *city.* I never write *policeman,* because I can get the same money for *cop.*

S. L. CLEMENS (MARK TWAIN): Speech in New York, Sept. 19, 1906

One of our defects as a nation is a tendency to use what have been called weasel words. When a weasel sucks eggs the meat is sucked out of the egg. If you use a weasel word after another there is nothing left of the other.

THEODORE ROOSEVELT: Speech in St. Louis, May 31, 1916

Words are the most powerful drug used by mankind.

RUDYARD KIPLING: Speech in London, Feb. 14, 1923

A word travels further than a man.

GERMAN PROVERB

Burning words. (Ardentia verba.)

LATIN PHRASE

The spoken word flies away; the written one remains. (Vox emissa volat; litera scripta manet.) LEGAL MAXIM

Words are to be understood with reference to the subject-matter. (Verba accipienda sunt secundum subjectam materiam.) IBID.

Words ought to be made subservient to the intent. (Verba intentioni debent inservire.) IBID.

Sticks and stones may break my bones,
But words can never harm me.

OLD ENGLISH RHYME

Evil words cut mair than swords.

SCOTTISH PROVERB

Fair words are nae cause o' feuds. IBID.

Stabs heal, but bad words never.

SPANISH PROVERB

Many words, little honesty.

TURKISH PROVERB

[*See also* Abbot, Anger, Meaning, Music, Poetry and Prose, Silence, Slang, Speaking, Speech, Style, Synonym, Taciturnity.

Wordsworth, William (1770–1852)

Friend of the wise, and teacher of the good.

S. T. COLERIDGE: *To William Wordsworth,* 1805

Who both by precept and example shows
That prose is verse, and verse is merely prose.

BYRON: *English Bards and Scotch Reviewers,* 1809

Wordsworth has left a bad impression wherever he visited in town by his egotism, vanity and bigotry. Yet he is a great poet if not a philosopher.

JOHN KEATS: *Letter to his brother,* 1818

His muse invites us to the treasures of his retirement in beautiful, noble, and inexhaustible language; but she does it, after all, rather like a teacher than a persuader, and fails in impressing upon us the last and best argument, that she herself is happy.

LEIGH HUNT: *The Seer,* XXIV, 1840

Just for a handful of silver he left us,
Just for a riband to stick in his coat.

ROBERT BROWNING: *The Lost Leader,* 1845
(Browning admitted, in a letter to A. B.

Grosart, Feb. 24, 1875, that he had Wordsworth in mind when he wrote this poem, but hinted that the indignation of his "hasty youth" had cooled)

He made the impression of a narrow and very English mind; of one who paid for his rare elevation by general tameness and conformity. Off his own beat, his opinions were of no value.
R. W. EMERSON: *English Traits*, I, 1856

A right good old steel-grey figure, with rustic simplicity and dignity about him, and a vivacious strength looking through him which might have suited one of those old steel-grey markgrafs whom Henry the Fowler set up to ward the marches and do battle with the intrusive heathen in a stalwart and judicious manner.
THOMAS CARLYLE: *Reminiscences of Sundry*, 1867

Nowhere is there so perplexed a mixture as in Wordsworth's poetry of work touched with intense and individual power with work of almost no character at all.
WALTER PATER: *Wordsworth*, 1874

[*See also* Ape.

Work

Never work when hungry.
HIPPOCRATES: *Aphorisms, c.* 400 B.C.

Where our work is, there let our joy be.
TERTULLIAN: *Women's Dress, c.* 220

To live well is to work well, to show a good activity.
THOMAS AQUINAS: *Summa theologicæ*, LVII, *c.* 1265

They must hunger in frost that will not work in heat. JOHN HEYWOOD: *Proverbs*, 1546

All work and no play makes Jack a dull boy.
JAMES HOWELL: *Proverbs*, 1659

It's all in the day's work.
ENGLISH SAYING, not recorded before the XVIII century

Let us work without protest; it is the only way to make life endurable.
VOLTAIRE: *Candide*, XXX, 1759

Work keeps at bay three great evils: boredom, vice, and need. IBID.

Writing music is my one and only passion and joy. W. A. MOZART: *Letter to his father*, Oct. 10, 1777

What is the use of health, or of life, if not to do some work therewith?
THOMAS CARLYLE: *Sartor Resartus*, I, 1836

All work, even cotton-spinning, is noble; work is alone noble.
THOMAS CARLYLE: *Past and Present*, III, 1843

All work of man is as the swimmer's; a waste ocean threatens to devour him; if he front it not bravely, it will keep its word. IBID.

Blessed is he who has found his work; let him ask no other blessedness. He has a work, a life-purpose; he has found it, and will follow it. IBID.

Work! God wills it. That, it seems to me, is clear.
GUSTAVE FLAUBERT: *Letter to Louise Colet*, 1845

Work — work — work,
Till the brain begins to swim:
Work — work — work,
Till the eyes are heavy and dim.
THOMAS HOOD: *The Song of the Shirt*, 1846

The provisional government of the French Republic undertakes to guarantee the existence of the workmen by work. It undertakes to guarantee work for every citizen.
Decree of the French Provisional Government, Feb. 25, 1848

It is far better to give work which is above the men than to educate the men to be above their work.
JOHN RUSKIN: *The Seven Lamps of Architecture*, 1849

It's all in the day's work, as the huntsman said when the lion ate him.
CHARLES KINGSLEY: *Westward Ho*, IV, 1855

When God wanted sponges and oysters, He made them, and put one on a rock, and the other in the mud. When He made man, He did not make him to be a sponge or an oyster; He made him with feet, and hands, and head, and heart, and vital blood, and a place to use them, and said to him, "Go, work!"
H. W. BEECHER: *Royal Truths*, 1862

My destiny is solitude, and my life is work.
RICHARD WAGNER: *Letter to Nathalie Planer*, June 20, 1863

Most men would feel insulted if it were proposed to employ them in throwing stones over a wall, and then in throwing them back, merely that they might earn their wages. But many are no more worthily employed now.
H. D. THOREAU: *Life Without Principle*, 1863 (Atlantic Monthly, Oct.)

The moment a man can really do his work he becomes speechless about it. All words become idle to him, all theories.
JOHN RUSKIN: *Sesame and Lilies*, 1865

Work is the grand cure for all the maladies and miseries that ever beset mankind, — honest work, which you intend getting done.
THOMAS CARLYLE: Address in Edinburgh, April 2, 1866

Eight hours for work,
Eight hours for sleep,
Eight hours for what you will.
Slogan of the National Labor Union of the United States, 1866

Work, still work, and always work. (Du travail, encore du travail, et toujours du travail!)
LÉON GAMBETTA: Speech in Versailles, June 24, 1872

A man is not a slave in being compelled to work against his will, but in being compelled to work without hope and without reward.
W. WINWOOD READE: *The Martyrdom of Man*, III, 1872

I find I must let things take their time. I am constant to my schemes; but I must work at them fitfully as the humor moves.
R. L. STEVENSON: *Letter to Sidney Colvin*, June, 1874

The sum of wisdom is, that the time is never lost that is devoted to work.
R. W. EMERSON: *Success*, 1877

I like work; it fascinates me. I can sit and look at it for hours. I love to keep it by me: the idea of getting rid of it nearly breaks my heart.
JEROME K. JEROME: *Three Men in a Boat*, XV, 1889

I ha' lived and I ha' worked: be thanks to Thee, Most High.
RUDYARD KIPLING: *McAndrew's Hymn*, 1893

I don't pity any man who does hard work worth doing. I admire him. I pity the creature who doesn't work, at whichever end of the social scale he may regard himself as being.
THEODORE ROOSEVELT: Speech in Chattanooga, Tenn., Sept. 8, 1902

Oh, why don't you work
Like other men do?
How the hell can I work
When there's no work to do?
Anon.: *Hallelujah, I'm a Bum*, *c.* 1907

Tenacità! Disciplina! Coraggio!
And *work!*
Definition of Fascism by BENITO MUSSOLINI, written for Robert H. Davis, of the New York Sun, Sept. 13, 1926 (The last two words were in English)

Work in all its forms — intellectual, technical and manual —, both organizing or executive, is a social duty. On this score, and only on this score, it is protected by the state.
THE GRAND COUNCIL OF FASCISM: *The Labor Charter*, I, April 21, 1927

I never did anything worth doing by accident, nor did any of my inventions come by accident; they came by work.
THOMAS A. EDISON (1847–1931)

Good work makes beautiful things, and good work lasts.
LORD DUNSANY: *My Ireland*, VI, 1938

It is my belief that every man has the divine right to work. If he cannot find work in private industry, it is the duty of the government to create work.
ERNEST LUNDEEN: Speech in the Senate, April 8, 1939

Work is a necessity for man. Man invented the alarm-clock.
PABLO RUIZ Y PICASSO: Quoted by Janet Flanner in the New Yorker, Dec. 9, 1939

Work only tires a woman, but it ruins a man.
AFRICAN PROVERB

Only horses work, and they turn their backs on it.
AMERICAN HOBO PROVERB

Work is the curse of the drinking classes.
Author unidentified

Working at your calling is half praying.
ITALIAN PROVERB

The work proves the workman. (Opus opificem probat.)
LATIN PROVERB

[*See also* Burden, Busy, Eight-hour Day, Happiness, Labor, Man and Woman, Money-getting, Night, Nothing, Play (=recreation), Property, Quick, Value, Wages, Worker.

Worker

The sleep of a laboring man is sweet.
ECCLESIASTES V, 12, *c.* 200 B.C.

The laborer is worthy of his reward.
I TIMOTHY V, 18, *c.* 60

The laborer is worthy of his hire.
LUKE X, 7, *c.* 75

The workman is worthy of his meat.
MATTHEW X, 10, *c.* 75

The good workman receives the bread of his labor with boldness; the lazy and careless cannot look his employer in the face.
ST. CLEMENT: *First Epistle to the Corinthians*, *c.* 125

Mechanic slaves
With greasy aprons, rules and hammers.
SHAKESPEARE: *Antony and Cleopatra*, V, *c.* 1606

A bad workman quarrels with his tools.
ENGLISH PROVERB, traced by Apperson to 1611 and probably much older

Laboring men count the clock oftenest.
JOHN WEBSTER: *The Duchess of Malfi*, III, *c.* 1614

It is the fate of those who toil at the lower employments of life to be rather driven by the fear of evil than attracted by the prospect of good; to be exposed to censure without hope of praise; to be disgraced by miscarriage, or punished for neglect, where success would have been without applause, and diligence without reward.

SAMUEL JOHNSON: *Dictionary*, pref., 1755

At the workingman's house hunger looks in but dares not enter.

BENJAMIN FRANKLIN: *Poor Richard's Almanac*, 1757

Hardened to hope, insensible to fear,
Scarce living pulleys of a dead machine,
Mere wheels of work and articles of trade.

P. B. SHELLEY: *Queen Mab*, IV, 1813

Workingmen have no country.

KARL MARX and FRIEDRICH ENGELS: *The Communist Manifesto*, 1848

The glory of a workman, still more of a master-workman, that he does his work well, ought to be his most precious possession; like the honor of a soldier, dearer to him than life.

THOMAS CARLYLE: *Shooting Niagara*, VII, 1867

The working class includes all those who live exclusively or primarily by their own labor and who do not grow rich through the labor of others. Beside wage-earners it includes the small farmers and small shopkeepers.

WILHELM LIEBKNECHT: *How Shall Socialism Be Put Into Practice?*, 1881

The workman begins to realize the incapacity of the ruling classes. He sees how incompetent they are either to understand his own situation or to manage the production and distribution of goods.

P. A. KROPOTKIN: *Paroles d'un révolté*, 1884

It is a shameful and inhuman thing to treat men as mere chattels for profit, or to regard them as simply so much muscle power.

POPE LEO XIII: *Rerum novarum*, May 15, 1891

The wage earner relies for work upon the ventures of confident and contented capital. This failing him, his condition is without alleviation, for he can neither prey on the misfortune of others nor hoard his labor.

GROVER CLEVELAND: Message to Congress, Aug. 8, 1893

The workers are the saviors of society, the redeemers of the race.

EUGENE V. DEBS: Speech in New York, Dec. 10, 1905

Spain is a republic of workers of all kinds.

CONSTITUTION OF THE SPANISH REPUBLIC, I, 1931

It is by working that we become workmen. (Fabricando fabri fimus.)

LATIN PROVERB

[*See also* Bricklayer, Capital and Labor, Carpenter, Classes, Environment, Exploitation, Labor, Socialist, Strike, Tool, Wages.

Works

Let us not be weary in well-doing: for in due season we shall reap, if we faint not.

GALATIANS VI, 9, *c.* 50

Let your light so shine before men, that they may see your good works, and glorify your Father which is in heaven.

MATTHEW V, 16, *c.* 75

There was at Joppa a certain disciple named Tabitha, which by interpretation is called Dorcas: this woman was full of good works and almsdeeds which she did.

ACTS IX, 36, *c.* 75

Men's works have an age, like themselves; and though they outlive their authors, yet have they a stint and period to their duration.

THOMAS BROWNE: *Religio Medici*, I, 1642

Almsgiving, prayer, and fasting are the Three Eminent Good Works.

JOHN MCCAFFREY: *A Catechism of Christian Doctrine for General Use*, 1866

[*See also* Faith, Grace and Works.

World

World without end.

ISAIAH XLV, 17, *c.* 700 B.C.

The friendship of the world is enmity with God; whosoever therefore will be a friend of the world, is the enemy of God.

JAMES IV, 4, *c.* 60

Lo, I am with you alway, even unto the end of the world. MATTHEW XXVIII, 20, *c.* 75

The world passeth away, and the lust thereof.

I JOHN II, 17, *c.* 115

The world that is and the world to come are enemies. . . . We cannot be the friends of both; but must bid farewell to this world to consort with that to come.

ST. CLEMENT: *Second Epistle to the Corinthians*, *c.* 150

Come, follow me, and leave the world to its gabble. DANTE: *Purgatorio*, V, *c.* 1320

This world is but a thoroughfare full of woe,
And we be pilgrims passing to and fro.

GEOFFREY CHAUCER: *The Canterbury Tales* (The Knight's Tale), *c.* 1386

Let the world wag.

JOHN SKELTON: *The Spanish Parrot*, *c.* 1530

The world has always been the same; and there is always as much good fortune as bad in it.

NICCOLÒ MACHIAVELLI: *Discorsi*, intro., 1531

Half the world does not know how the other half lives. RABELAIS: *Pantagruel*, 1533

The world is nothing but a reversed Decalogue, or the Ten Commandments backwards, a mask and picture of the Devil.

MARTIN LUTHER: *Table-Talk*, CLV, 1569

The world is nothing but an endless seesaw.
MICHEL DE MONTAIGNE: *Essays*, III, 1588

What is in this world but grief and woe?
SHAKESPEARE: *III Henry VI*, II, *c.* 1591

Mad world. Mad kings. Mad composition.
SHAKESPEARE: *King John*, II, *c.* 1596

A stage where every man must play a part;
And mine a sad one.
SHAKESPEARE: *The Merchant of Venice*, I, *c.* 1597

It takes all sorts to make a world.
ENGLISH PROVERB, traced to the XVII century

Oh, how full of briers is this working-day world!
SHAKESPEARE: *As You Like It*, I, *c.* 1600

All the world's a stage,
And all the men and women merely players:
They have their exits and their entrances,
And one man in his time plays many parts,
His acts being seven ages.
SHAKESPEARE: *As You Like It*, II

How the world wags! IBID.

The world's mine oyster,
Which I with sword will open.
SHAKESPEARE: *The Merry Wives of Windsor*, II, *c.* 1600

The world is but a play.
Anon.: Song, 1601

How weary, stale, flat and unprofitable
Seem to me all the uses of this world.
SHAKESPEARE: *Hamlet*, I, *c.* 1601

So runs the world away.
SHAKESPEARE: *Hamlet*, III

A mad world, my masters.
NICHOLAS BRETON: Title of a dialogue, 1603 (The phrase is probably much older. It was used as the title of a play by Thomas Middleton, 1608)

In this earthly world . . . to do harm
Is often laudable, to do good sometime
Accounted dangerous folly.
SHAKESPEARE: *Macbeth*, IV, *c.* 1605

The world, as in the ark of Noah, rests,
Compos'd as then: few men and many beasts.
LORD HERBERT OF CHERBURY: *The State Progress of Ill*, 1608

O brave new world.
SHAKESPEARE: *The Tempest*, V, 1611

The world is a long journey.
NICHOLAS BRETON: *Crossing of Proverbs*, 1616

The world is all a carcass and vanity,
The shadow of a shadow, a play
And in one word, just nothing.
OWEN FELLTHAM: *Resolves*, *c.* 1620

What a world's this!
Nothing but craft and cozenage!
JOHN FLETCHER: *The Wild-Goose Chase*, V, 1621

Oh, what a crocodilian world is this!
FRANCIS QUARLES: *Emblems*, I, 1635

The world to me is but a dream or mock show, and we all therein but pantaloons and antics.
THOMAS BROWNE: *Religio Medici*, I, 1642

For the world I count it not an inn, but an hospital, and a place not to live, but to die in.
THOMAS BROWNE: *Religio Medici*, II

The world in itself has no value, it is merely zero; but with Heaven before it, it means much.
BALTASAR GRACIÁN: *The Art of Worldly Wisdom*, CCXI, 1647

The world is like a ladder: one goeth up, the other down.
JAMES HOWELL: *Proverbs*, 1659

The pomp and vanity of this wicked world.
THE BOOK OF COMMON PRAYER (*The Catechism*), 1662

The world, the flesh and the Devil.
THE BOOK OF COMMON PRAYER (*The Litany*)

Open, ye heavens, your living doors; let in
The great Creator from His work return'd
Magnificent, His six days' work, a world!
JOHN MILTON: *Paradise Lost*, VII, 1667

The world do not grow old at all, but is in as good condition in all respects as ever it was.
SAMUEL PEPYS: *Diary*, Feb. 3, 1667

All this visible world is but an imperceptible point in the ample bosom of nature.
BLAISE PASCAL: *Pensées*, II, 1670

The world is as you take it.
JOHN RAY: *English Proverbs*, 1670

The created world is but a small parenthesis in eternity, and a short interposition, for a time, between such a state of duration as was before it and may be after it.
THOMAS BROWNE: *Christian Morals*, III, *c.* 1680

It is a very good world to live in,
To lend, or to spend, or to give in,
But to beg or to borrow, or to get a man's own,
'Tis the very worst world that ever was known.
JOHN WILMOT (EARL OF ROCHESTER): *Poems of Several Occasions*, 1680

The world in all doth but two nations bear,
The good, the bad, and these mixed everywhere.
ANDREW MARVELL: *The Loyal Scot*, 1681

A brave world, sir, full of religion, knavery and change! We shall shortly see better days.
APHRA BEHN: *The Roundheads*, I, 1682

He that will live in this world must be endued with the three rare qualities of dissimulation, equivocation, and mental reservation.

IBID.

There was never a merry world since the fairies left dancing, and the parson left conjuring.

JOHN SELDEN: *Table-Talk,* 1689

It is the fools and the knaves that make the wheels of the world turn. They are the world; those few who have sense or honesty sneak up and down single, but never go in herds.

GEORGE SAVILE (MARQUESS OF HALIFAX): *Political, Moral and Miscellaneous Reflections, c.* 1690

Like pilgrims to the appointed place we tend;
The world's an inn, and death the journey's end.

JOHN DRYDEN: *Palamon and Arcite,* III, *c.* 1698

When the world has once begun to use us ill, it afterwards continues the same treatment with less scruple or ceremony, as men do to a whore.

JONATHAN SWIFT: *Thoughts on Various Subjects,* 1706

Once kick the world, and the world and you will live together at a reasonably good understanding.

JONATHAN SWIFT: *A Letter of Advice to a Young Poet,* Dec. 1, 1720

It is a good world, but they are ill that are on't.

JAMES KELLY: *Complete Collection of Scottish Proverbs,* 1721

The world is a great cheat.

THOMAS FULLER: *Introductio ad Prudentiam,* I, 1731

It is the ordinary way of the world to keep folly at the helm, and wisdom under the hatches.

THOMAS FULLER: *Gnomologia,* 1732

'Tis a wicked world, and we make part of it.

IBID.

What is this world?
What but a spacious burial-field unwalled,
Strewed with death's spoils, the spoils of animals
Savage and tame, and full of dead men's bones!

ROBERT BLAIR: *The Grave,* 1743

Let not the cooings of the world allure thee:
Which of her lovers ever found her true?

EDWARD YOUNG: *Night Thoughts,* VIII, 1744

Courts and camps are the only places to learn the world in.

LORD CHESTERFIELD: *Letter to his son,* Oct. 2, 1747

The world is a country which nobody ever yet knew by description; one must travel through it one's self to be acquainted with it. IBID.

The world, in its best state, is nothing more than a larger assembly of beings, combining to counterfeit happiness which they do not feel, employing every art and contrivance to embellish life, and to hide their real condition from the eyes of one another.

SAMUEL JOHNSON: *The Adventurer,* Dec. 29, 1753

It is one of the most difficult things in life to know when one has enough of the world.

THOMAS WILSON: *Maxims of Piety and of Christianity, c.* 1755

The world is a beautiful book, but of little use to him who cannot read it.

CARLO GOLDONI: *Pamela nubile,* I, 1757

All is for the best in the best of possible worlds.

VOLTAIRE: *Candide,* XXX, 1759

The world is mine.

OLIVER GOLDSMITH: *The Traveller,* 1764

The world is a comedy to those who think, a tragedy to those who feel.

HORACE WALPOLE: *Letter to Horace Mann,* Dec. 31, 1769

I am leaving at last a world where the heart must either break or turn to bronze.

NICOLAS CHAMFORT: Before his suicide, 1794

The natural world, which is in such continual labor . . . will doubtless come to an end. These revolutions are not for nothing. There is some great event and issue of things, some grand period aimed at.

JONATHAN EDWARDS: *Remarks on Important Theological Controversies,* 1796

This unintelligible world.

WILLIAM WORDSWORTH: *Tintern Abbey,* 1798

The world is ruled by interest alone.

J. C. F. SCHILLER: *Wallenstein's Death,* I, 1799

It is a wild and miserable world!
Thorny, and full of care,
Which every fiend can make his prey at will.

P. B. SHELLEY: *Queen Mab,* VI, 1813

This world is all a fleeting show,
For man's illusion given.

THOMAS MOORE: *This World Is All a Fleeting Show,* 1815

I have not loved the world, nor the world me.

BYRON: *Childe Harold,* III, 1816

I do not live in this world alone, but in a thousand worlds.

JOHN KEATS: *Letter to George and Georgiana Keats,* Oct. 21, 1818

Well, well, the world must turn upon its axis,
And all mankind turn with it, heads or tails,
And live and die, make love and pay our taxes,
And as the veering winds shift, shift our sails.

BYRON: *Don Juan,* II, 1819

There are many that despise half the world; but if there be any that despise the whole of it, it is because the other half despises them.

C. C. COLTON: *Lacon,* 1820

The world itself is a volume larger than all the libraries in it.
WILLIAM HAZLITT: *The Conversation of Authors,* 1821

O world! O life! O time!
P. B. SHELLEY: *A Lament,* 1821

If the world were good for nothing else, it is a fine subject for speculation.
WILLIAM HAZLITT: *Characteristics,* 1823

This is the way of the world — all they want is someone (no matter who) to turn the laugh from themselves.
WILLIAM HAZLITT: *The Ruling Passion,* 1829 (The Atlas, Jan. 18)

The world is a thing that a man must learn to despise, and even to neglect, before he can learn to reverence it, and work in it and for it.
THOMAS CARLYLE: *Letter to John Carlyle,* July 2, 1832

The world is a singularly stupendous fool.
J. W. GOETHE: *II Faust,* II, 1832

The world is an old woman, and mistakes any gilt farthing for a gold coin.
THOMAS CARLYLE: *Sartor Resartus,* II, 1836

The world will commonly end by making men what it thinks them.
HENRY TAYLOR: *The Statesman,* 1836

The world is his who can see through its pretension.
R. W. EMERSON: *The American Scholar,* 1837

Oime! what a foolish goose of a world this is!
THOMAS CARLYLE: *Letter to R. W. Emerson,* Nov. 7, 1838

The world is a league of rogues against the true people, of the vile against the generous.
GIACOMO LEOPARDI: *Pensieri,* 1838

Good-by, proud world! I'm going home:
Thou art not my friend, and I'm not thine.
R. W. EMERSON: *Good-By,* 1839

One half of the world must sweat and groan that the other half may dream.
H. W. LONGFELLOW: *Hyperion,* I, 1839

This world, after all our science and sciences, is still a miracle; wonderful, inscrutable, magical and more, to whosoever will think of it.
THOMAS CARLYLE: *Heroes and Hero-Worship,* I, 1840 (Lecture in London, May 5)

The year's at the Spring
And day's at the morn;
Morning's at seven;
The hillside's dew-pearled;
The lark's on the wing;
The snail's on the thorn:
God's in his Heaven —
All's right with the world!
ROBERT BROWNING: *Pippa Passes,* 1841

The world is all outside; it has no inside.
R. W. EMERSON: *Experience,* 1841

The great soul of this world is just.
THOMAS CARLYLE: *Letter to Thomas Erskine,* June 12, 1847

There are two worlds; the world that we can measure with line and rule, and the world that we feel with our hearts and imaginations.
LEIGH HUNT: *Men, Women, and Books,* 1847

This fine old world of ours is but a child
Yet in the go-cart. Patience! Give it time
To learn its limbs: there is a hand that guides.
ALFRED TENNYSON: *The Princess,* 1847

The world is a looking-glass, and gives back to every man the reflection of his own face.
W. M. THACKERAY: *Vanity Fair,* I, 1848

The world is something that had better not have been.
ARTHUR SCHOPENHAUER: *Parerga und Paralipomena,* 1851

This world's no blot for us,
Nor blank; it means intensely, and means good.
ROBERT BROWNING: *Fra Lippo Lippi,* 1855

You've seen the world —
The beauty and the wonder and the power,
The shapes of things, their colors, lights and shades,
Changes, surprises — and God made it all.
IBID.

When you and I behind the veil are past,
Oh, but the long, long while the world shall last!
EDWARD FITZGERALD: Tr. of OMAR KHAYYÁM: *Rubáiyát* (*c.* 1100), 1857

The history of the world is all suffering.
H. W. BEECHER: *Life Thoughts,* 1858

The world is a nettle; disturb it, it stings;
Grasp it firmly, it stings not.
E. R. BULWER-LYTTON (OWEN MEREDITH): *Lucile,* I, 1860

What a glorious world Almighty God has given us! How thankless and ungrateful we are, and how we labor to mar His gifts.
ROBERT E. LEE: *Letter to his wife,* Aug. 4, 1861

It is a very good world for the purposes for which it was built; and that is all anything is good for.
H. W. BEECHER: *Royal Truths,* 1862

I say the world is lovely,
And that loveliness is enough.
ROBERT W. BUCHANAN: *London Poems,* 1866

Roll on, thou ball, roll on!
Through pathless realms of space roll on!
What, though I'm in a sorry case?

What, though I cannot meet my bills?
What, though I suffer toothache's ills?
What, though I swallow countless pills?
Never *you* mind!
Roll on! [*It rolls on*].

W. S. GILBERT: *The Bab Ballads*, 1869

The world, as a world, barely makes a living.

Ascribed to HORACE GREELEY (1811–72)

You can make me live in your world, O Creator, but you cannot make me admire it.

W. WINWOOD READE: *The Martyrdom of Man*, III, 1872

The world is so full of a number of things,
I'm sure we should all be as happy as kings.

R. L. STEVENSON: *A Child's Garden of Verse*, 1885

This may not be the best of all possible worlds, but to say that it is the worst is mere petulant nonsense.

T. H. HUXLEY: *The Struggle for Existence in Human Society*, 1888

The world will, in the end, follow only those who have despised as well as served it.

SAMUEL BUTLER: *Note-Books, c.* 1890

This is a world that goes slowly, because it has an eternity to go in.

THOMAS B. REED: Speech in Philadelphia, April 9, 1890

God has not created us for the transitory and perishable things of this earth: He has given us this world only as a place of exile, and not as our true country.

POPE LEO XIII: *Rerum novarum*, May 15, 1891

Gawd bless this world! Whatever she 'ath done —
Excep' when awful long — I've found it good.
So write, before I die, " 'E liked it all! "

RUDYARD KIPLING: *Sestina of the Tramp-Royal*, 1896

The world is everything that is the case. (Der Welt ist alles, was der Fall ist.)

LUDWIG WITTGENSTEIN: *Tractatus logico-philosophicus*, 1921

This is a good world. We need not approve of all the items in it, nor of all the individuals in it; but the world itself, which is more than its parts or individuals, which has a soul, a spirit, a fundamental relation to each of us deeper than all other relations — is a friendly world.

JAN C. SMUTS: Address at St. Andrews University, Oct. 17, 1934

The world is a corpse, and they who seek it are dogs. ARAB PROVERB

The world is divided into people who think they are right. Author unidentified

The world always ends by condemning those whom it accuses. FRENCH PROVERB

The world grows wiser. IBID.

Fall, and the whole world will run over you.

GERMAN PROVERB

Take the world as it is, not as it ought to be.

IBID.

The world stands on three pillars: law, worship, and charity. HEBREW PROVERB

[*See also* Books, Eternity, History, Life, Living, Man, Right and Wrong, Wisdom (Worldly).

World Court

We believe in the pacific settlement of international disputes, and favor the establishment of a world court for that purpose.

Republican National Platform, 1916

[*See also* League of Nations.

Worm

The heart is a triumphant and mighty emperor that ends as the breakfast of a silly little worm.

MICHEL DE MONTAIGNE: *Essays*, II, 1580

The smallest worm will turn, being trodden on.

SHAKESPEARE: *III Henry VI*, II, *c.* 1591 (A proverb, commonly reduced to " The worm will turn ")

The spirit of the worm beneath the sod
In love and worship blinds itself with God.

P. B. SHELLEY: *Epipsychidion*, 1821

[*See also* Cruelty, Death, Early, Edible, Epitaph, Fishing, Grave, Greatness, Hell, Man, Measure, Metempsychosis.

Worry

A hundred load of worry will not pay an ounce of debt.

GEORGE HERBERT: *Jacula Prudentum*, 1651

It is not work that kills, but worry.

ENGLISH PROVERB, not recorded before the XIX century

[*See also* Anxiety, Hygiene.

Worse

[*See* Bad, Good and Bad, Worst.

Worship

God is to be worshipped by faith, hope, and love.

ST. AUGUSTINE: *On Faith, Hope, and Charity, c.* 421

Among the papists they do almost everywhere think that they have fully worshipped God when they have long and much sung and piped.

JOHN NORTHBROOKE: *Against Dicing*, 1577

Our fathers worshipp'd stocks and stones.

JOHN MILTON: *On the Late Massacre in Piedmont, c.* 1650

I imagine it great vanity in me to suppose that the Supremely Perfect does in the least regard such an inconsiderable nothing as man. More especially, since it is impossible for me to have any positive clear idea of that which is infinite and incomprehensible, I cannot conceive otherwise than that He, the Infinite Father, expects or requires no worship or praise from us, but that He is even infinitely above it.

BENJAMIN FRANKLIN: *Articles of Belief and Acts of Religion,* Nov. 20, 1728

There is not one command in all the Gospel for public worship. . . . The frequent attendance at it is never so much as mentioned in all the New Testament.

WILLIAM LAW: *A Serious Call to a Devout and Holy Life,* I, 1728

The soul does not contemplate and worship God when it is not disturbed by the body, or disaffected through vice.

BENJAMIN WHICHCOTE: *Moral and Religious Aphorisms,* 1753

Wonder is the basis of worship.

THOMAS CARLYLE: *Journal,* June 8, 1830

It is only when men begin to worship that they begin to grow.

CALVIN COOLIDGE: Speech in Fredericksburg, Va., July 6, 1922

[*See also* Idolatry, Toleration.

Worst

When remedies are past, the griefs are ended
By seeing the worst, which late on hopes depended.

SHAKESPEARE: *Othello,* I, 1604

Let the worst come to the worst.

JOHN MARSTON: *The Dutch Courtezan,* III, 1605

The worst is not
So long as we can say " This is the worst."

SHAKESPEARE: *King Lear,* IV, 1606

No man is the worse for knowing the worst of himself.

THOMAS FULLER: *Gnomologia,* 1732

The worst wheel of the cart makes the most noise.

BENJAMIN FRANKLIN: *Poor Richard's Almanac,* 1737

Cheer up! The worst is yet to come.

PHILANDER JOHNSON, *c.* 1900

The worst people are a poor boaster and a rich thief.

FRENCH PROVERB

Three worst things: a poor Jew, lean pork and a drunken woman.

HUNGARIAN PROVERB

[*See also* Bad, Fear, Hope.

Worth

Worth makes the man, and want of it the fellow;
The rest is all but leather and prunella.

ALEXANDER POPE: *An Essay on Man,* IV, 1734

This mournful truth is everywhere confess'd,
Slow rises worth, by poverty depress'd.

SAMUEL JOHNSON: *London,* 1738

The worth of a thing is what it will bring.

H. G. BOHN: *Handbook of Proverbs,* 1855

Worth may be blamed, but ne'er be shamed.

SCOTTISH PROVERB

[*See also* Possession, Price, Value.

Worthless

Three things are nought worth: fair face in a whore, great strength in a porter, fine wit in the poor.

JOHN FLORIO: *Second Frutes,* 1591

The worthless generally live long.

BALTASAR GRACIÁN: *The Art of Worldly Wisdom,* CXC, 1647

The worthless and offensive members of society, whose existence is a social pest, invariably think themselves the most ill-used people alive, and never get over their astonishment at the ingratitude and selfishness of their contemporaries.

R. W. EMERSON: *Representative Men,* I, 1850

Wound

One shall say unto him, What are these wounds in thine hands? Then he shall answer, Those with which I was wounded in the house of my friends.

ZECHARIAH XIII, 6, *c.* 520 B.C.

The blueness of a wound cleanseth away evil.

PROVERBS XX, 30, *c.* 350 B.C.

The secret wound lives on within the breast.

VIRGIL: *Aeneid,* IV, 19 B.C.

A certain Samaritan . . . bound up his wounds, pouring in oil and wine.

LUKE X, 33–34, *c.* 75

The wound that bleedeth inwardly is most dangerous.

JOHN LYLY: *Euphues,* 1579

He jests at scars that never felt a wound.

SHAKESPEARE: *Romeo and Juliet,* II, *c.* 1596

What wound did ever heal but by degrees?

SHAKESPEARE: *Othello,* II, 1604

My wound is great because it is so small.

JOHN DRYDEN: *All for Love,* I, 1678

What deep wounds ever closed without a scar?

BYRON: *Childe Harold,* III, 1816

[*See also* Patience.

Wrath

Wrath killeth the foolish man.

JOB V, 2, *c.* 325 B.C.

Let not the sun go down upon your wrath.
EPHESIANS IV, 26, *c.* 60

I heard a great voice out of the temple saying to the seven angels, Go your ways, and pour out the vials of the wrath of God upon the earth. REVELATION XVI, 1, *c.* 95

I am Wrath. I had neither father nor mother: I leap'd out of a lion's mouth when I was scarce half an hour old; and ever since I have run up and down the world with this case of rapiers, wounding myself when I had nobody to fight withal.
CHRISTOPHER MARLOWE: *Dr. Faustus,* II, 1604

Nursing her wrath to keep it warm.
ROBERT BURNS: *Tam o' Shanter,* 1790

The tigers of wrath are wiser than the horses of instruction.
WILLIAM BLAKE: *The Marriage of Heaven and Hell,* 1790

He chewed
The thrice-turned cud of wrath, and cooked his spleen.
ALFRED TENNYSON: *The Princess,* I, 1847

Mine eyes have seen the coming of the glory of the Lord:
He is tramping out the vintage where the grapes of wrath are stored.
JULIA WARD HOWE: *Battle Hymn of the Republic,* 1862 (Atlantic Monthly, Feb.)

He who curbs his wrath merits forgiveness for his sins. HEBREW PROVERB

[*See also* Anger, Envy, Flesh, God, Judgment Day.

Wreck

Such was the wreck of the Hesperus
In the midnight and the snow,
Christ save us all from a death like this
On the reef of Norman's Woe.
H. W. LONGFELLOW: *The Wreck of the Hesperus,* 1841

Wren, Christopher

[*See* Epitaph.

Wrestler

Wrestlers are a sluggish set, and of dubious health. They sleep out their lives, and whenever they depart ever so little from their regular diet they fall seriously ill.
PLATO: *The Republic,* III, *c.* 370 B.C.

Wretch

A needy, hollow-eyed, sharp-looking wretch,
A living-dead man.
SHAKESPEARE: *The Comedy of Errors,* V, 1593

Wretched

The wretched hasten to embrace their miseries.
SENECA: *Hercules Oetaeus, c.* 60

That man is wretched whom none can please.
MARTIAL: *Epigrams,* V, *c.* 95

[*See also* Death.

Wrinkle

Thou hast filled me with wrinkles, which is a witness against me. JOB XVI, 8, *c.* 325 B.C.

No piety can delay the wrinkles.
HORACE: *Carmina,* II, *c.* 20 B.C.

The wrinkles on his forehead were graven by his deeds.
PIERRE CORNEILLE: *The Cid,* I, 1636

An old wrinkle never wears out.
THOMAS FULLER: *Gnomologia,* 1732

Wrinkles (the damned democrats) won't flatter. BYRON: *Don Juan,* X, 1823

Time heals our scars, but our wrinkles are more stubborn. Author unidentified

[*See also* Age (Old), Dalliance, Labor, Laughter, Pearl.

Writer

He writes nothing whose writings are not read.
MARTIAL: *Epigrams,* III, *c.* 95

If you wish to be a writer, write.
EPICTETUS: *Discourses,* II, *c.* 110

Would a writer know how to behave himself with relation to posterity, let him consider in old books what he finds that he is glad to know, and what omissions he most laments.
JONATHAN SWIFT: *Thoughts on Various Subjects,* 1706

I have seen some Roman Catholic authors who tell us that vicious writers continue in Purgatory so long as the influence of their writings continues upon posterity: for Purgatory (say they) is nothing else but a cleansing us of our sins, which cannot be said to be done away so long as they continue to operate and corrupt mankind.
JOSEPH ADDISON: *The Spectator,* Sept. 10, 1711

Tailors and writers must mind the fashion.
THOMAS FULLER: *Gnomologia,* 1732

One of the amusements of idleness is reading without the fatigue of close attention; and the world, therefore, swarms with writers whose wish is not to be studied, but to be read.
SAMUEL JOHNSON: *The Idler,* Nov. 11, 1758

The greatest part of a writer's time is spent in reading, in order to write; a man will turn over half a library to make one book.
SAMUEL JOHNSON: *Boswell's Life,* April 6, 1775

The language of any country is in no hazard of being corrupted by bad writers. The hazard is only when a writer of considerable talents hath not a perfect chastity of taste.

GEORGE CAMPBELL: *The Philosophy of Rhetoric*, III, 1776

No man but a blockhead ever wrote except for money.

SAMUEL JOHNSON: *Boswell's Life*, April 5, 1776

Writers, especially when they act in a body, and in one direction, have great influence on the public mind.

EDMUND BURKE: *Reflections on the Revolution in France*, 1790

Bad writers are those who try to express their own feeble ideas in the language of good ones.

G. C. LICHTENBERG: *Reflections*, 1799

The mark of a really great writer is that he gives expression to what the masses of mankind think or feel without knowing it. The mediocre writer simply writes what everyone would have said. IBID.

I am convinced more and more every day that (excepting the human friend philosopher) a fine writer is the most genuine being in the world. . . . I look upon fine phrases like a lover.

JOHN KEATS: *Letter to Benjamin Bailey*, Aug. 15, 1819

Of all priesthoods, aristocracies, governing classes at present extant in the world, there is no class comparable for importance to that priesthood of the writers of books.

THOMAS CARLYLE: *Heroes and Hero-Worship*, V, 1840 (Lecture in London, May 19)

Whomsoever a thought however complex, a vision however apocalyptic, surprises without words to convey it, is not a writer.

THÉOPHILE GAUTIER: *Caprices et zigzags*, 1845

What a writer asks of his reader is not so much to *like* as to *listen*.

H. W. LONGFELLOW: *Letter to J. S. Dwight*, Dec. 10, 1847

Talent alone cannot make a writer. There must be a man behind the book.

R. W. EMERSON: *Representative Men*, VII, 1850

Of human notabilities men of letters are the most interesting, and this arises mainly from their outspokenness as a class. The writer makes himself known in a way that no other man makes himself known.

ALEXANDER SMITH: *Dreamthorp*, VII, 1863

Who can tell how many of the most original thoughts put forth by male writers belong to a woman by suggestion, to themselves only by verifying and working out? If I may judge by my own case, a very large proportion indeed.

J. S. MILL: *The Subjection of Women*, III, 1869

The writer, like the priest, must be exempted from secular labor. His work needs a frolic health; he must be at the top of his condition.

R. W. EMERSON: *Poetry and Imagination*, 1876

Good writers have two things in common: they prefer being understood to being admired, and they do not write for the over-critical and too shrewd reader.

F. W. NIETZSCHE: *Human All-too-Human*, II, 1878

The reason why so few good books are written is that so few people who can write know anything.

WALTER BAGEHOT: *Literary Studies*, I, 1879

Writers, like teeth, are divided into incisors and grinders. IBID.

I have a very high regard for the writer's calling. If he is not truth's ordained priest, then he is fit only for the scrapheap.

GEORG BRANDES: *Letter to Georges Clemenceau*, March, 1915

Writers seldom write the things they think. They simply write the things they think other folks think they think.

ELBERT HUBBARD: *Roycroft Dictionary and Book of Epigrams*, 1923

Great writers are not the only interesting writers.

J. C. SQUIRE: In the London Mercury, Sept., 1933

It is not necessary for a writer to be crazy, but it is useful. Author unidentified

[*See also* Author, Authorship, Literature, Pen, Writing.

Writing

The writing on the wall.

ENGLISH PHRASE, based on DANIEL V, 25, *c.* 165 B.C.: "This is the writing that was written, MENE, MENE, TEKEL, UPHARSIN"

If you want to be read more than once, do not hesitate to blot often.

HORACE: *Satires*, I, *c.* 25 B.C.

I do not write so much from the impulse of genius as to soothe the cares of love, and to bewail life's unabating woe.

PROPERTIUS: *Elegies*, I, *c.* 25 B.C.

He who has hit upon a subject suited to his powers will never fail to find eloquent words and lucid arrangement.

HORACE: *De arte poetica*, *c.* 8 B.C.

The knowledge of men and manners is the first principle and fountainhead of good writing.
IBID.

What I have written I have written.
JOHN XIX, 22, *c.* 115

The desire to write grows with writing. (Crescit scribendo scribendi studium.)
DESIDERIUS ERASMUS: *Adagia,* 1508

He that will write well in any tongue must follow this counsel of Aristotle: to speak as the common people do, to think as wise men do.
ROGER ASCHAM: *Toxiphilus,* 1545

Scribbling seemeth to be symptom or passion of an irregular and licentious age. When filled the Romans so many volumes as in the times of their ruin?
MICHEL DE MONTAIGNE: *Essays,* III, 1588

Is not this a lamentable thing, that of the skin of an innocent lamb should be made parchment? that parchment, being scribbled o'er, should undo a man?
SHAKESPEARE: *II Henry VI,* IV, *c.* 1591

Devise, wit; write, pen; for I am for whole volumes in folio.
SHAKESPEARE: *Love's Labor's Lost,* I, *c.* 1595

Ask how to live? Write, write, write, anything.
JOHN FLETCHER: *Wit Without Money,* II, *c.* 1614

Give me six lines written by the most honorable of men, and I will find an excuse in them to hang him.
ARMAND CARDINAL RICHELIEU: *Mirame,* *c.* 1625

Ready writing makes not good writing, but good writing brings on ready writing; yet when we think we have got the faculty it is even then good to resist it.
BEN JONSON: *Discoveries, c.* 1635

Eagerness of imagination, by over pleasing fanciful men, flatters them into the danger of writing.
JOHN DRYDEN: *The Rival Ladies,* dedication, 1664

Think much, speak little, and write less.
GIOVANNI TORRIANO: *Italian Proverbs,* 1666

Whatever we conceive well we express clearly.
NICOLAS BOILEAU: *L'Art poétique,* 1674

Of all those arts in which the wise excel
Nature's chief masterpiece is writing well.
JOHN SHEFFIELD (DUKE OF BUCKINGHAM): *An Essay on Poetry,* 1682

It is the glory and merit of some men to write well, and of others not to write at all.
JEAN DE LA BRUYÈRE: *Caractères,* 1688

Truth is the best guide to make a man write forcibly, naturally, and delicately. IBID.

I am now trying an experiment, very frequent among modern authors; which is, to write upon nothing.
JONATHAN SWIFT: *A Table of a Tub,* conclusion, 1704

True ease in writing comes from art, not chance,
As those move easiest who have learn'd to dance.
ALEXANDER POPE: *An Essay on Criticism,* II, 1711 (Cf. *The Second Epistle of the Second Book of Horace,* 1738)

Blot out, correct, insert, refine,
Enlarge, diminish, interline;
Be mindful, when invention fails,
To scratch your head, and bite your nails.
JONATHAN SWIFT: *On Poetry,* 1712

Those write because all write, and so have still
Excuse for writing, and for writing ill.
ALEXANDER POPE: *Satires of Dr. John Donne Versified,* II, 1735

Every kind of writing is good save that which bores.
VOLTAIRE: *L'Enfant prodigue,* pref., 1736

Next to doing things that deserve to be written, there is nothing that gets a man more credit, or gives him more pleasure, than to write things that deserve to be read.
LORD CHESTERFIELD: *Letter to his son,* 1739

The things that I have written fastest have always pleased the most. IBID.

What a devil of a profession! But it has its charms.
VOLTAIRE: *Letter to Frederick the Great,* Aug., 1751

To write well is to think well, to feel well, and to appear well; it is to possess at once intellect, soul, and taste.
GEORGE DE BUFFON: *Discours sur le style,* 1753

Writing, when properly managed, is but a different name for conversation.
LAURENCE STERNE: *Tristram Shandy,* II, 1760

Fine writing is generally the effect of spontaneous thoughts and a labored style.
WILLIAM SHENSTONE: *On Writing and Books,* 1764

I will be candid and avow to you, that till four-score-and-ten, whenever the humor takes me, I will write, because I like it; and because I like myself better when I do so. If I do not write much, it is because I cannot.
THOMAS GRAY: *Letter to Horace Walpole,* Feb. 25, 1768

A man may write at any time, if he will set himself doggedly to it.
SAMUEL JOHNSON: *Boswell's Tour to the Hebrides,* Aug. 16, 1773

It has been said there is pleasure in writing, particularly in writing verses. I allow you may have pleasure from writing, after it is over, if you have written well; but you don't go willingly to it again. I know when I have been writing verses I have run my finger down the margin, to see how many I had made, and how few I had to make.

SAMUEL JOHNSON: *Boswell's Life,* May 1, 1783

No instance exists of a person's writing two languages perfectly. That will always appear to be his native language which was most familiar to him in his youth.

THOMAS JEFFERSON: *Letter to J. Bannister,* 1785

A man may write himself out of reputation when nobody else can do it.

THOMAS PAINE: *The Rights of Man,* II, 1791

Until I am master of a tune, in my own singing (such as it is), I can never compose for it. My way is: I consider the poetic sentiment correspondent to my idea of the music expression; then choose my theme; begin one stanza; when that is composed, which is generally the most difficult part of the business, I walk out, sit down now and then, look out for objects in nature round me that are in unison or harmony with the cogitations of my fancy and workings of my bosom, humming every now and then the air, with the verses I have framed. When I feel my muse beginning to jade, I retire to the solitary fireside of my study, and there commit my effusions to paper, swinging at intervals on the hind legs of my elbow chair, by way of calling forth my own critical strictures, as my pen goes on.

ROBERT BURNS: *Letter to James Thomson,* 1793

The ancients wrote at a time when the great art of writing badly had not yet been invented. In those days to write at all meant to write well.

G. C. LICHTENBERG: *Reflections,* 1799

Easy writing's curst hard reading.

R. B. SHERIDAN: *Clio's Protest, c.* 1800

Write what will sell! To this Golden Rule every minor canon must be subordinate; and must be either immediately deducible from it, or at least be made consistent with it.

EDWARD COPLESTON (BISHOP OF LLANDOFF): *Advice to a Young Reviewer,* 1807

I am convinced more and more every day that fine writing is, next to fine doing, the top thing in the world.

JOHN KEATS: *Letter to J. H. Reynolds,* Aug. 23, 1819

Whenever I find myself growing vaporish, I rouse myself, wash and put on a clean shirt, brush my hair and clothes, tie my shoe-strings neatly, and in fact adonize as I were going out — then, all clean and comfortable, I sit down to write.

JOHN KEATS: *Letter to George and Georgiana Keats,* Sept. 17, 1819

The secret of writing well is to know thoroughly what one writes about, and not to be affected.

Ascribed to ALEXANDER POPE in JOSEPH SPENCE: *Anecdotes,* 1820 (*c.* 1740)

My writing-desk is to me a place of punishment, and, as my penmanship sufficiently testifies, I always bend over it with some degree of impatience.

WILLIAM WORDSWORTH: *Letter to Archdeacon Wrangham,* 1820

The very greatest writers write best when calm, and exerting themselves upon subjects unconnected with party.

S. T. COLERIDGE: *Table-Talk,* Jan. 4, 1823

Never think of mending what you write. Let it go. No patching; no after-pointing. As your pen moves, bear constantly in mind that it is making strokes which are to remain for ever.

WILLIAM COBBETT: *Grammar of the English Language,* 1823

With the exception of an epilogue for a private theatrical, I have written nothing now for near six months. It is in vain to spur me on. I must wait. I cannot write without a genial impulse, and I have none.

CHARLES LAMB: *Letter to Bernard Barton,* May 15, 1824

Write — and all your friends will hate you — all will suspect you.

CHARLES LAMB: In the New Times, Jan. 31, 1825

The misfortune of writing fast is that one cannot at the same time write concisely.

WALTER SCOTT: *Journal,* April 28, 1829

Incessant scribbling is death to thought.

THOMAS CARLYLE: *Letter to John Carlyle,* March 28, 1831

The first law of writing, that law to which all other laws are subordinate, is this: that the words employed shall be such as convey to the reader the meaning of the writer.

T. B. MACAULAY: *The War of the Succession in Spain,* 1833 (Edinburgh Review, Jan.)

With the art of writing the true reign of miracles for mankind commenced. It related, with a wondrous new contiguity and perpetual closeness, the past and distant with the present in time and place; all times and all places with this are actual here and now. All things were altered for men.

THOMAS CARLYLE: *Heroes and Hero-Worship,* v, 1840 (Lecture in London, May 19)

All writing comes by the grace of God.
R. W. EMERSON: *Experience,* 1841

I am irritated by my writing. I am like a violinist whose ear is true, but whose fingers refuse to reproduce precisely the sounds he hears within.
GUSTAVE FLAUBERT: *Letter to Louise Colet,* 1845

Whenever, on account of its vagueness, I am dissatisfied with a conception of the brain, I resort forthwith to the pen, for the purpose of obtaining, through its aid, the necessary form, consequence and precision.
E. A. POE: *Marginalia,* 1844–49

"It is only an afternoon, it is only an evening" people say to me over and over again; but they don't know that it is impossible to command one's self sometimes to any stipulated and set disposal of five minutes, or that the mere consciousness of an engagement will sometimes worry a whole day. These are the penalties paid for writing books.
CHARLES DICKENS: *Letter to Maria Winter,* April 3, 1855

I have sat here in my garret, wriggling and wrestling on the worst terms with a task that I cannot do, that generally seems to me not worth doing, and yet must be done.
THOMAS CARLYLE: *Letter to R. W. Emerson,* May 13, 1855 (While at work on his *Frederick the Great*)

The business of writing has altogether become contemptible to me; and I am become confirmed in the notion that nobody ought to write, — unless sheer fate force him to do it; — and then he ought (if not of the mountebank genus) to beg to be shot rather.
THOMAS CARLYLE: *Letter to R. W. Emerson,* June 2, 1858

Writing is more and more a terror to old scribes. R. W. EMERSON: *Journal,* 1864

Write without pay until somebody offers pay. If nobody offers within three years the candidate may look upon this circumstance with the most implicit confidence as the sign that sawing wood is what he was intended for.
S. L. CLEMENS (MARK TWAIN): *A General Reply,* 1870 (Galaxy, Nov.)

Three hours a day will produce as much as a man ought to write.
ANTHONY TROLLOPE (1815–82)

There ain't nothing more to write about, and I am rotten glad of it, because if I'd a knowed what a trouble it was to make a book I wouldn't a tackled it, and ain't agoing to no more.
S. L. CLEMENS (MARK TWAIN): *Huckleberry Finn,* XLIII, 1885

Of all that has been written, I love only that which was written in blood.
F. W. NIETZSCHE: *Thus Spake Zarathustra,* VII, 1885

I have great love and respect for my native tongue, and take great pains to use it properly. Sometimes I write essays half a dozen times before I get them into the proper shape; and I believe I become more fastidious as I grow older.
T. H. HUXLEY: *Letter to H. de Varigny,* May 17, 1891

This writing is an unnatural business. It makes your head hot and your feet cold, and it stops the digesting of your food.
JOHN BURROUGHS (1837–1931)

An itch for writing. (Cacoëthes scribendi.)
LATIN PHRASE

A mania for writing. (Furor scribendi.)
IBID.

By writing you learn to write. (Scribendo disces scribere.) LATIN PROVERB

The spoken word perishes; the written word remains. (Vox audita perit; litera scripta manet.) IBID.

[*See also* Advice, Authorship, Criticism, Drawing, Feeling, Grammar, Literature, Punctuation, Spelling, Style, Writer.

Wrong

The cowardice of doing wrong.
JOHN MILTON: *Tractate on Education,* 1644

Brother, brother; we are both in the wrong.
JOHN GAY: *The Beggar's Opera,* II, 1728

It is better to suffer wrong than to do it, and happier to be sometimes cheated than not to trust.
SAMUEL JOHNSON: *The Rambler,* Dec. 18, 1750

Two wrongs do not make a right.
ENGLISH PROVERB, not recorded before the XIX century

Envenom'd with irrevocable wrong.
BYRON: *Childe Harold,* IV, 1818

It is not a man's duty, as a matter of course, to devote himself to the eradication of any, even the most enormous wrong; he may still properly have other concerns to engage him; but it is his duty, at least, to wash his hands of it, and, if he gives it no thought longer, not to give it practically his support.
H. D. THOREAU: *An Essay on Civil Disobedience,* 1849

He was her man, but he done her wrong.
Anon.: *Frankie and Johnny, c.* 1850

Popular wrongs are but popular rights in embryo.
C. J. DARLING: *Scintillæ Juris,* 1877

One wrong does not justify another. (Inuria non excusat injuriam.) LEGAL MAXIM

[*See also* King, Punishment, Revenge, Right and Wrong, Rights.

Wyclif, John (c. 1320–84)

Though they digged up his body, burned his bones, and drowned his ashes, yet the word of God and truth of his doctrine, with the fruit and success thereof, they could not burn.
JOHN FOXE: *The Book of Martyrs,* I, 1563

X

Xenophilia

Two circumstances will operate against me. I am not a foreigner; I am a New Englandman. A foreigner ushered in with titles and letters, with half my abilities, would have the whole city in his train.
NOAH WEBSTER: *Letter to John Pickering,* 1786

Xenophobia

I never read books of travels, at least not farther than Paris or Rome. I can just endure Moors, because of their connection as foes with Christians; but Abyssinians, Ethiops, Esquimaux, dervishes, and all that tribe, I hate.
CHARLES LAMB: *Letter to Robert Southey,* May 6, 1815

Y

Yale University

[*See* Education.

Yankee

In acuteness, cautiousness, industry and perseverance he resembles the Scotch; in habits of frugal neatness he resembles the Dutch; in love of lucre he doth greatly resemble the sons of Abraham.
FRANCES TROLLOPE: *Domestic Manners of the Americans,* XIV, 1832

Jews . . . cannot flourish among Yankees, who are said to out-jew them in trading.
LORENZO DOW: *Dealings of God, c.* 1834

The Hottentots and Kickapoos are very well in their way. The Yankees alone are preposterous.
E. A. POE: *The Philosophy of Furniture,* 1840 (Burton's Gentleman's Magazine, May)

[*See also* American, Character (National), New England, Puritan.

Yawning

In yawning howl not, and thou shouldst abstain as much as thou canst to yawn, especially when thou speakest.
FRANCIS HAWKINS: *Youth's Behavior,* I, 1663

One yawn makes two yawners.
FRENCH PROVERB

Yawp

I sound my barbaric yawp over the roofs of the world.
WALT WHITMAN: *Song of Myself,* 1855

Year

A thousand years in thy sight are but as yesterday.
PSALMS XC, 4, *c.* 150 B.C.

We spend our years as a tale that is told.
PSALMS XC, 9

Each passing year takes something from us.
HORACE: *Epistles,* II, *c.* 5 B.C.

Nothing goes swifter than the years. (Nihil est annis velocius.)
OVID: *Metamorphoses,* XX, *c.* 5

Say no ill of the year till it be past.
GEORGE HERBERT: *Outlandish Proverbs,* 1640

The year doth nothing else but open and shut.
IBID.

Years know more than books.
GEORGE HERBERT: *Jacula Prudentum,* 1651

The years teach much which the days never know.
R. W. EMERSON: *Experience,* 1841

A year begun is to be reckoned as one finished. (Annus inceptus habetur pro completo.)
LEGAL MAXIM

Yellow

He will come to her in yellow stockings, and 'tis a color she abhors.
SHAKESPEARE: *Twelfth Night,* II, *c.* 1601

The sear, the yellow leaf.
SHAKESPEARE: *Macbeth,* V, *c.* 1605

All looks yellow to the jaundiced eye.
ALEXANDER POPE: *An Essay on Criticism,* II, 1711

The hallelujahs of yellow.
J. K. HUYSMANS: *À rebours,* 1884

[*See also* Color, Jaundice, Journalism.

Yes

[*See* Coquetry, Lady, No.

Yesterday

We are but of yesterday, and know nothing, because our days upon earth are a shadow.
JOHN VIII, 9, *c.* 325 B.C.

A thousand years in thy sight are but as yesterday when it is past.
PSALMS XC, 4, *c.* 150 B.C.

Oh, call back yesterday; bid time return.
SHAKESPEARE: *Richard II,* III, *c.* 1596

And all our yesterdays have lighted fools
The way to dusty death.
SHAKESPEARE: *Macbeth,* V, *c.* 1605

Tomorrow I will live, the fool does say;
Today itself's too late; the wise lived yesterday.
ABRAHAM COWLEY: Tr. of MARTIAL: *Epigrams,* V (*c.* 95), 1643

I was not born yesterday.
ENGLISH SAYING, not recorded before the XIX century

A man he seems of cheerful yesterdays.
WILLIAM WORDSWORTH: *The Excursion,* VII, 1814

[*See also* Past, Today.

Yew

Careless, unsocial plant! that loves to dwell
'Midst skulls and coffins, epitaphs and worms.
ROBERT BLAIR: *The Grave,* 1743

Yielding

Yielded with coy submission, modest pride,
And sweet reluctant amorous delay.
JOHN MILTON: *Paradise Lost,* IV, 1667

Y.M.C.A.

You can test a modern community by the degree of its interest in its Young Men's Christian Association. . . . I know of no test that can be more conclusively put to a community than that.
WOODROW WILSON: Address at the Y.M.C.A., Pittsburgh, Oct. 24, 1914

Yoke

My yoke is easy, and my burden is light.
MATTHEW XI, 30, *c.* 75

Wherever there is a neck there is a yoke.
RUSSIAN PROVERB

Young

[*See* Youth.

Young and Old

[*See* Youth and Age.

Youth

Youth is quick in temper but weak in judgment. HOMER: *Iliad,* XXIII, *c.* 800 B.C.

Youth passes as quickly as thought.
THEOGNIS: *Elegies, c.* 550 B.C.

Youth feeds on flowery pastures.
SOPHOCLES: *Trachiniæ, c.* 450 B.C.

Youth is the best time to be rich, and the best time to be poor.
EURIPIDES: *Heracles, c.* 420 B.C.

The glory of young men is their strength.
PROVERBS XX, 29, *c.* 350 B.C.

Youth is easily deceived, because it is quick to hope.
ARISTOTLE: *Rhetoric,* II, *c.* 322 B.C.

Youth loves honor and victory more than money. It really cares next to nothing about money, for it has not yet learned what the lack of it means. IBID.

Beautiful is the bloom of youth, but it does not last.
THEOCRITUS: *Idylls,* XXIII, *c.* 270 B.C.

Rejoice, O young man, in thy youth; and let thy heart cheer thee in the days of thy youth, and walk in the ways of thine heart.
ECCLESIASTES XI, 9, *c.* 200 B.C.

Remember now thy Creator in the days of thy youth, while the evil days come not, nor the years draw nigh when thou shalt say, I have no pleasure in them. ECCLESIASTES XII, 1

Thy youth is renewed like an eagle's.
PSALMS CIII, 5, *c.* 150 B.C.

The desires of youth show the future virtues of the man. CICERO: *Ad Caelium, c.* 50 B.C.

Youth flies. (Fugit juventus.)
HORACE: *Epodes, c.* 20 B.C.

While thy blood is warm, and thou art without wrinkles, enjoy thyself.
PROPERTIUS: *Elegies,* IV, *c.* 15 B.C.

The flower of youth. (Flos juventutis.)
LIVY: *History of Rome,* XXXVII, *c.* 10

Fortunate indeed is that man who was able to maintain control of his carnal senses in the time of his youth.
BHARTRIHARI: *The Sringa Sataka, c.* 625

Youth will have his course.
JOHN LYLY: *Euphues,* 1579 (Cited as "an old proverb")

Young blood doth not obey an old decree.
SHAKESPEARE: *Love's Labor's Lost,* IV, *c.* 1595

Young men are fitter to invent than to judge, fitter for execution than for counsel, and fitter for new projects than for settled business. FRANCIS BACON: *Essays,* VIII, 1597

Why should a man whose blood is warm within
Sit like his grandsire cut in alabaster?
SHAKESPEARE: *The Merchant of Venice,* I, *c.* 1597

We have some salt of our youth in us.
SHAKESPEARE: *The Merry Wives of Windsor,* II, *c.* 1600

The morn and liquid dew of youth.
SHAKESPEARE: *Hamlet,* I, *c.* 1601

Youth's a stuff will not endure.
SHAKESPEARE: *Twelfth Night,* II, *c.* 1601

My salad days;
When I was green in judgment.
SHAKESPEARE: *Antony and Cleopatra*, I, *c.* 1606

He wears the rose
Of youth upon him.
SHAKESPEARE: *Antony and Cleopatra*, III

Beauty like a shadow flies,
And our youth before us dies.
EDMUND WALLER: *To Phyllis*, 1645

The age is best which is the first,
When youth and blood are warmer.
ROBERT HERRICK: *Hesperides*, 1648

Youth is a perpetual intoxication; it is the fever of reason.
LA ROCHEFOUCAULD: *Maxims*, 1665

Youth and white paper take any impression.
JOHN RAY: *English Proverbs*, 1670

Youth should watch joys and shoot them as they fly.
JOHN DRYDEN: *Aurengzebe*, III, 1676

My youth may wear and waste, but it shall never rust.
WILLIAM CONGREVE: *The Way of the World*, II, 1700

No wise man ever wished to be younger.
JONATHAN SWIFT: *Thoughts on Various Subjects*, 1706

My Peggy is a young thing,
Just entered in her teens,
Fair as the day, and sweet as May,
Fair as the day, and always gay;
My Peggy is a young thing,
And I'm not very auld.
ALLAN RAMSAY: *The Gentle Shepherd*, 1725

The atrocious crime of being a young man, which the honorable gentleman has with such spirit and decency charged upon me, I shall neither attempt to palliate nor deny; but content myself with wishing that I may be one of those whose follies may cease with their youth, and not of that number who are ignorant in spite of experience.
WILLIAM PITT: Speech in the House of Commons, March 6, 1741

The young leading the young is like the blind leading the blind.
LORD CHESTERFIELD: *Letter to his son*, Nov. 6, 1747

It is very natural for young men to be vehement, acrimonious and severe.
SAMUEL JOHNSON: *The Rambler*, May 14, 1751

Young fellows will be young fellows.
ISAAC BICKERSTAFF: *Love in a Village*, II, 1762

Would a sensible man become young again on the same conditions he once was so?
STANISLAUS LESZCYNSKI (KING OF POLAND): *Œuvres du philosophe bienfaisant*, 1763

Young heads are giddy, and young hearts are warm,
And make mistakes for manhood to reform.
WILLIAM COWPER: *Tirocinium*, 1785

Youth will be served.
ENGLISH PROVERB, not recorded before the XIX century (Cf. LYLY, *ante*, 1579)

You'd scarce expect one of my age
To speak in public on the stage.
DAVID EVERETT: *Lines Written for Declamation*, *c.* 1800

Bliss was it in that dawn to be alive,
But to be young was very Heaven.
WILLIAM WORDSWORTH: *The Prelude*, XI, 1805

How lovely the intrepid front of youth!
How sweet the smiles of taintless infancy!
P. B. SHELLEY: *The Dæmon of the World*, II, 1815

Both were young, and one was beautiful.
BYRON: *The Dream*, 1816

What would youth be without love?
BYRON: *Beppo*, 1818

What a young man has written is always best enjoyed by young people. Even if the world progresses generally, youth will always begin at the beginning.
J. W. GOETHE: *Conversations with Eckermann*, Jan. 15, 1827

Remember, sinful youth, you must die! you must die!
Remember, sinful youth, you must die!
Remember, sinful youth, who hate the way of truth,
And in your pleasures boast, you must die!
Anon.: *Pious Songs*, 1836

When we are young, we think not only ourselves, but that all about us, are immortal.
BENJAMIN DISRAELI: *Venetia*, IV, 1837

In the lexicon of youth, which fate reserves
For a bright manhood, there is no such word
As fail.
E. G. BULWER-LYTTON: *Richelieu*, II, 1838

Bear through sorrow, wrong and ruth,
In thy heart the dew of youth.
H. W. LONGFELLOW: *Maidenhood*, 1841

Almost everything that is great has been done by youth.
BENJAMIN DISRAELI: *Coningsby*, III, 1844

Take her up tenderly,
Lift her with care;
Fashioned so slenderly,
Young, and so fair.
THOMAS HOOD: *The Bridge of Sighs*, 1846

Youth will be served, every dog hath his day, and mine has been a fine one.
GEORGE BORROW: *Lavengro*, XCII, 1851

The fewer his years the fewer his tears.
H. G. BOHN: *Handbook of Proverbs,* 1855

The thoughts of youth are long, long thoughts.
H. W. LONGFELLOW: *My Lost Youth,* 1855
(Credited to "a Lapland song")

Youth is somewhat reckless in assertion, and when one is juvenile and curly one takes a pride in sarcasm and invective.
BENJAMIN DISRAELI: Speech in the House of Commons, June 7, 1859

When all the world is young lad,
And all the trees are green;
And every goose a swan, lad,
And every lass a queen;
Then hey, for boot and horse, lad,
And round the world away;
Young blood must have its course, lad
And every dog his day.
CHARLES KINGSLEY: *The Water Babies,* 1863

Youth means love.
ROBERT BROWNING: *The Ring and the Book,* I, 1868

How beautiful is youth! how bright it gleams
With its illusions, aspirations, dreams!
Book of beginnings, story without end,
Each maid a heroine, and each man a friend!
H. W. LONGFELLOW: *Morituri Salutamus,* 1875

Let us live then, and be glad
While young life's before us
After youthful pastime had,
After old age hard and sad,
Earth will slumber over us.
J. A. SYMONDS: Tr. of *Gaudeamus Igitur* (*c.* 1400), 1875

Youth is the time to go flashing from one end of the world to the other both in mind and body; to try the manners of different nations; to hear the chimes at midnight.
R. L. STEVENSON: *Virginibus Puerisque,* 1881

If youth be a defect, it is one that we outgrow only too soon.
J. R. LOWELL: Address in Cambridge, Mass., Nov. 8, 1886

I remember my youth and the feeling that will never come back any more — the feeling that I could last forever, outlast the sea, the earth, and all men.
JOSEPH CONRAD: *Youth,* 1903

I would make land by myself. I would beat the other boats. Youth! All youth! The silly, charming, beautiful youth. IBID.

They are generally thought to be arch radicals. As a matter of fact, they are the most conservative people I have ever dealt with.
WOODROW WILSON: Address at the Y.M.C.A., Pittsburgh, Oct. 24, 1914

Youth, youth, Springtime of beauty! (Giovinezza giovinezza, primavera di belleza!)
Official song of the Italian Fascists, *c.* 1921

From tavern to tavern youth dances along
With an arm full of girl and a heart full of song.
Author unidentified

Youth is a fire, and the years are a pack of wolves who grow bolder as the fire dies down. IBID.

Ask the young; they know everything.
FRENCH PROVERB

Youth is a lunatic. HINDU PROVERB

Youth is useless to a poor man.
SANSRIT PROVERB

[*See also* Adolescence, Affront, Ages, Appetite, Boy, Childhood, Colt, Day, Death, Devil, Education, Folly, Girl, Happiness, Health, Hyperbole, Learning, Piracy, Twenty-One, Youth and Age.

Youth and Age

I shall go out with the chariots to counsel and command, for that is the privilege of the old; the young must fight in the ranks.
HOMER: *Iliad,* IV, *c.* 800 B.C.

It is shameful for the young to question their elders. HOMER: *Odyssey,* III, *c.* 800 B.C.

He has an old mind in a young body.
ÆSCHYLUS: *The Seven Against Thebes,* *c.* 490 B.C.

If we could be twice young and twice old we could correct all our mistakes.
EURIPIDES: *The Suppliant Women,* *c.* 421 B.C.

The young shall be silent before their elders, and give them place, and rise up before them.
PLATO: *The Republic,* IV, *c.* 370 B.C.

Your young men shall dream dreams; your old men shall see visions.
JOEL II, 28, *c.* 350 B.C.

I am young, and ye are very old; wherefore I was afraid, and durst not show you mine opinion. JOB XXXII, 6, *c.* 325 B.C.

Rashness attends youth, as prudence does old age. CICERO: *De senectute, c.* 78 B.C.

It is natural for a young man to love, but a crime for an old one.
PUBLILIUS SYRUS: *Sententiæ, c.* 50 B.C.

Youth must store up; age must use.
SENECA: *Epistulæ morales ad Lucilium,* *c.* 63

Young saint; old devil.
ENGLISH PROVERB, traced by Smith to *c.* 1470, and probably much older.

Reckless youth makes gowsty age.
SCOTTISH PROVERB, traced by Smith to *c.* 1520 (*Gowsty*=dreary)

Youth witless is, and frail; age, sickly and forlorn;

Then best it is to die betime, or never to be born. Anon.: A Ballad, *c.* 1550

Youth riotously led breedeth a loathsome old age.
THOMAS COGAN: *The Haven of Health,* 1588

Young in limbs, in judgment old.
SHAKESPEARE: *The Merchant of Venice,* II, *c.* 1597

A man can not more separate age and covetousness than he can part young limbs and lechery.
SHAKESPEARE: *II Henry IV,* I, *c.* 1598

Crabbed age and youth cannot live together;
Youth is full of pleasure, age is full of care;
Youth like Summer morn, age like Winter weather;
Youth like Summer brave, age like Winter bare.
Youth is full of sport, age's breath is short;
Youth is nimble, age is lame;
Youth is holt and hold, age is weak and cold;
Youth is wild, and age is tame.
Age, I do abhor thee; youth I do adore thee.
SHAKESPEARE (?): *The Passionate Pilgrim,* XII, 1599

Youth no less becomes
The light and careless livery that it wears
Than settled age his sables and his weeds.
SHAKESPEARE: *Hamlet,* IV, *c.* 1601

Young men think old men are fools, but old men know young men are fools.
GEORGE CHAPMAN: *All Fools,* V, 1605

Rule youth well, and age will rule itself.
DAVID FERGUSSON: *Scottish Proverbs,* 1641

An idle youth, a needy age.
GEORGE HERBERT: *Jacula Prudentum,* 1651

Youth lives on hope, old age on remembrance.
IBID.

Youth changes its tastes by the warmth of its blood, age retains its tastes by habit.
LA ROCHEFOUCAULD: *Maxims,* 1665

If youth knew what age would crave,
It would both get and save.
JOHN RAY: *English Proverbs,* 1670

They who would be young when they are old, must be old when they are young. IBID.

The majority of men employ the first part of life in making the rest miserable.
JEAN DE LA BRUYÈRE: *Caractères,* 1688

It is as absurd in an old man to wish for the strength of a youth as it would be in a young man to wish for the strength of a bull or a horse.
RICHARD STEELE: *The Spectator,* Aug. 25, 1711

Young men soon give, and soon forget, affronts;
Old age is slow in both.
JOSEPH ADDISON: *Cato,* II, 1713

Youth only lays up sighs for age.
EDWARD YOUNG: *Love of Fame,* I, 1728

Nothing's more playful than a young cat, nor more grave than the old one.
THOMAS FULLER: *Gnomologia,* 1732

Beware of the young doctor and the old barber.
BENJAMIN FRANKLIN: *Poor Richard's Almanac,* 1733

The conversation of the old and young ends generally with contempt or pity on either side.
SAMUEL JOHNSON: *The Rambler,* Nov. 17, 1750

Young men have more virtue than old men; they have more generous sentiments in every respect.
SAMUEL JOHNSON: *Boswell's Life,* July 21, 1763

In the life of man, as in books, there are blank leaves at the two ends — childhood and old age.
JEAN PAUL RICHTER: *Hesperus,* XX, 1795

The excesses of our youth are drafts upon our old age, payable with interest, about thirty years after date.
C. C. COLTON: *Lacon,* 1820

The disappointment of manhood succeeds to the delusion of youth; let us hope that the heritage of old age is not despair.
BENJAMIN DISRAELI: *Vivian Gray,* VIII, 1827

Gone are the games of childhood,
And gone forever is youth,
And gone is the world that was kind to us,
And love, and faith, and truth.
HEINRICH HEINE: *Mein Kind, wir waren Kinder,* 1827

When two men shake hands and part, mark which of the two takes the sunny side [of the street]: he will be the younger man of the two.
E. G. BULWER-LYTTON: *What Will He Do With It?,* II, 1858

In youth, we clothe ourselves with rainbows, and go as brave as the zodiac. In age, we put out another sort of perspiration, — gout, fever, rheumatism, caprice, doubt, fretting, avarice.
R. W. EMERSON: *The Conduct of Life,* I, 1860

All sorts of allowances are made for the illusions of youth; and none, or almost none, for the disenchantments of age.
R. L. STEVENSON: *Virginibus Puerisque,* 1881

What youth deemed crystal, age finds out was dew.
ROBERT BROWNING: *Jocahanan Hakkodosh,* 1883

Young men want to be faithful and are not; old men want to be faithless and cannot.
OSCAR WILDE: *The Picture of Dorian Gray,* 1891

Forty is the old age of youth; fifty is the youth of old age. FRENCH PROVERB

In youth we believe many things that are not true; in old age we doubt many truths.
GERMAN PROVERB

The old age of an eagle is better than the youth of a sparrow. GREEK PROVERB

In old men there is no taste; in young no insight. HEBREW PROVERB

The young do not know what age is, and the aged forget what youth was.
IRISH PROVERB

The sins of youth are paid for in old age. (Quæ peccamus juvenes ea luimus senes.)
LATIN PROVERB

The old man shows what the young man was.
SWEDISH PROVERB

Youth supposes; age knows.
WELSH PROVERB

[*See also* Affront, Age (Old), Ages, Ague, Appetite, Brother, Death, Dream, Faithful, Judge, Judgment, Laziness, Praise, Precedence, Precocity, Youth.

Z

Z

Thou whoreson Zed! thou unnecessary letter!
SHAKESPEARE: *King Lear,* III, 1606

Zeal

He . . . was clad with zeal as a cloak.
ISAIAH XLIX, 17, *c.* 700 B.C.

My zeal hath consumed me.
PSALMS CXIX, 139, *c.* 150 B.C.

It is good to be zealously affected always in a good thing. GALATIANS IV, 18, *c.* 50

Zeal without knowledge is sister of folly.
JOHN DAVIES: *The Scourge of Folly,* 1611

Zeal's a dreadful termagant
That teaches saints to tear and cant.
SAMUEL BUTLER: *Hudibras,* III, 1678

Violent zeal for truth hath an hundred to one odds to be either petulancy, ambition, or pride.
JONATHAN SWIFT: *Thoughts on Religion,* 1728

Zeal is fit only for wise men, but is found mostly in fools.
THOMAS FULLER: *Gnomologia,* 1732

Zeal without knowledge is fire without light.
IBID.

Nothing spoils human nature more than false zeal. The good nature of an heathen is more God-like than the furious zeal of a Christian.
BENJAMIN WHICHCOTE: *Moral and Religious Aphorisms,* 1753

The zeal of friends it is that knocks me down, and not the hate of enemies.
J. C. F. SCHILLER: *Wallenstein's Death,* III, 1799

Above all, no zeal! (Surtout, pas du zèle!)
Ascribed to C. M. TALLEYRAND (1754–1838)

The greatest dangers to liberty lurk in insidious encroachment by men of zeal, well-meaning but without understanding.
MR. JUSTICE LOUIS D. BRANDEIS: *Opinion in Olmstead* vs. *United States,* 1928

[*See also* Moderation.

Zeus

[*See* God, Gods.

Zionism

The aim of Zionism is to create for the Jewish people a home in Palestine secured by public law and, for the attainment of this end, it is necessary to promote the colonization of Palestine by Jewish agricultural and industrial workers, organize Jewry through local and general associations, strengthen Jewish national sentiment and consciousness, and take preparatory steps towards obtaining the government consent necessary to the achievement of the aim of Zionism.
Resolution of the First Zionist Congress, Basle, Aug. 29, 1897

[*See also* Jew.

Zola, Émile (1840–1902)

He flung into the air with one kick all the toilet-articles of literature, and washed with a dish-cloth the bedizened face of truth.
EDMONDO DE AMICIS: *On Zola's L'Assommoir,* 1880

His work is evil, and he is one of those unhappy beings of whom one can say that it would be better had he never been born.
JACQUES THIBAULT (ANATOLE FRANCE): *Review of La Terre,* 1888

The delight to stink. (Die Freude zu stinken.)
F. W. NIETZSCHE: *The Twilight of the Idols,* 1889

Zoo

This place, methinks, resembleth well
The world itself in which we dwell:
Perils and snares on every ground,
Like these wild beasts, beset us round.
MARY LAMB: *The Beasts in the Tower,* 1809

A NOTE ON THE TYPE

The text of this book is set in Caledonia, a Linotype face designed by W. A. Dwiggins. Caledonia belongs to the family of printing types called " modern face " by printers — a term used to mark the change in style of type-letters that occurred about 1800. Caledonia is in the general neighborhood of Scotch Modern in design, but is more freely drawn than that letter.

Mr. Dwiggins contrived the typographic scheme and designed the binding and jacket. The book was composed, printed, and bound by The Plimpton Press, Norwood, Massachusetts.